MATTHEW AND Q BIBLIOGRAPHY 1950-1995

BIBLIOTHECA EPHEMERIDUM THEOLOGICARUM LOVANIENSIUM

CXL-A

# THE GOSPEL OF MATTHEW
# AND THE SAYINGS SOURCE Q

## A CUMULATIVE BIBLIOGRAPHY
## 1950-1995

COMPILED BY

F. NEIRYNCK – J. VERHEYDEN
R. CORSTJENS

VOLUME ONE

LEUVEN
UNIVERSITY PRESS

UITGEVERIJ PEETERS
LEUVEN

1998

ISBN 90 6186 933 1 (Leuven University Press)
D/1998/1869/73
ISBN 90-429-0715-0 (Uitgeverij Peeters)
D/1999/0602/4
ISBN 2-87723-418-5 (Editions Peeters)

Leuven University Press / Presses Universitaires de Louvain
Universitaire Pers Leuven
Blijde-Inkomststraat 5, B-3000 Leuven-Louvain (Belgium)

© Uitgeverij Peeters, Bondgenotenlaan 153, B-3000 Leuven (Belgium)

# PREFACE

This bibliographical tool on Matthew and Q was conceived after the model of "The Gospel of Mark 1950-1990" which was published in 1992 in the same series[1]. Likewise beginning in 1950, it covers a longer period, up to 1995. Information about more recent publications is restricted to supplements to earlier works on Matthew or Q (new parts of the same studies, as well as new editions, translations, and reviews).

In Part I, Alphabetical List, the works are listed alphabetically by author. Publications by the same author are given in chronological order. For each item the date of publication is also noted in the margin. This marginal number will be used as a reference system in the Indexes.

Reprints, revised or enlarged editions, and translations are listed under one entry (in small print). Occasionally, thoroughly revised works are treated as new entries.

Collective works with more than two contributions on Matthew or Q are given under the name of the (first) editor and signaled by an asterisk in the margin.

References to dissertations include the date, the name of the University, and the name of the director. For unpublished dissertations, reference is made to *Dissertation Abstracts* and *Studia Biblica et Theologica*.

Additional information is given in small print: references to *New Testament Abstracts* (NTA); specifications of the topics treated (introduced by Esp.); cross-references (→); and a selection of reviews.

Part II, Indexes, is printed in a separate volume (BETL, 140-B). It contains two sections, Matthew and Q, and each has an Index of Gospel Passages and a Subject Index. References are given by name of author, year of publication, and occasionally page numbers. Bold print is used for specific monographs on the topic and more notable contributions.

---

1. F. NEIRYNCK – J. VERHEYDEN – F. VAN SEGBROECK – G. VAN OYEN – R. CORSTJENS, *The Gospel of Mark. A Cumulative Bibliography 1950-1990* (BETL, 102), Leuven, University Press – Peeters, 1992, XII-717 p.

PART ONE

# ALPHABETICAL LIST

1947<sup>R</sup>   Reprint (or revised edition) of a work published before 1950
1974*   Collective work (under the editor's name)

→ name (date)   Cross-reference
→ date          Publication by the same author

# A

**AAGAARD, A.M.**

1988 Doing God's Will. Matthew 26:36-46. — *International Review of Mission* (Genève) 77 (1988) 221-228. [NTA 32, 1121]

**AALEN, Sverre**

1958 Lysets begrep i de synoptiske evangelier. [The notion of light in the synoptic gospels] — *SEÅ* 22-23 (1957-58) 17-31. Esp. 17-21.26-31 [5,13-14]; 21-23 [6,22-23]. [NTA 3, 580]

1962 'Reign' and 'House' in the Kingdom of God in the Gospels. — *NTS* 8 (1961-62) 215-240. Esp. 222-223 [6,13]; 227 [25,34]; 229-230 [12,25-26]; 231-232 [11,12]. [NTA 7, 88]

1963 Das Abendmahl als Opfermahl im Neuen Testament. — *NT* 6 (1963) 128-152. Esp. 147-152.

1965 Guds kungavälde eller Guds rike? [God's kingdom or God's reign?] — *SEÅ* 30 (1965) 37-69. Esp. 40-42 [5,20; 6,10.33]; 63-68 [8,16; 9,29.34; 12,28]. [NTA 12, 1025]; = ID., *Gud i Kristus*, 1986, 7-39. Esp. 10-12.33-38.

1968 *Jesu forkynnelse om Guds rike. Etter de synoptiske evangelier* [Jesus' knowledge of the kingdom of God]. Oslo: Universitetsforlaget, 1968, 98 p.

1971a *Matteus-evangeliet. Forelesningsreferat ved T. Raddum, G. Salomonsen, O. Skjevesland* [The gospel of Matthew. Lectures]. Oslo: Universitetsforlaget, 1971, 289 p.

1971b Jesu kristologiske selvbevissthet. Et utkast til "jahvistisk kristologi". [Jesus' christological selfconsciousness. An outline to a "Jahwistic christology"] — *TidsTeolKirk* 42 (1971) 81-98; = ID., *Gud i Kristus*, 1986, 41-58. Esp. 43-53 [10,18.22.37].

1973 Visdomsforestillingen og Jesu kristologiske selvbevissthet. [The concept of wisdom and Jesus' christological selfconsciousness] — *SEÅ* 37-38 (1972-73) 35-46. Esp. 39, 44 [11,19; 23,37-39. [NTA 18, 799]; = ID., *Gud i Kristus*, 1986, 59-70. Esp. 63, 68.

1984 Versuch einer Analyse des Diakonia-Begriffes im Neuen Testament. — WEINRICH, W.C. (ed.), *The New Testament Age*. FS B. Reicke, 1984, I, 1-13. Esp. 2-5 [25,35-45].

1986 *Gud i Kristus. Nytestamentlige studier* [God and Christ. New Testament studies]. Oslo: Universitetsforlaget, 1986, 128 p. → 1965, 1971b, 1973

**ABEGG, Martin G., Jr.**

1995 The Messiah at Qumran: Are We Still Seeing Double? — *Dead Sea Discoveries* (Leiden) 2 (1995) 125-144. Esp. 142-144 [Q 7,18-23].

**ABEL, Ernest L.**

1969a Jesus and the Cause of Jewish National Independence. [22,15-22] — *RevÉtudJuiv* 128 (1969) 247-252.

1969b The Virgin Birth. Was it a Christian Apologetic? — *Ibid.*, 395-399.

1971 Who Wrote Matthew? — *NTS* 17 (1970-71) 138-152. Esp. 138-141 [Papias]; 139-142 [Q]; 143-147 [Judaism]; 147-148 [date]; 148-151 [anti-Judaism]. [NTA 15, 836]

1974 The Genealogies of Jesus ὁ Χριστός. — *NTS* 20 (1973-74) 203-210. [NTA 18, 849]

**ABESAMIS, Carlos H.**

1987 The Mission of Jesus and Good News to the Poor. Exegetico-pastoral Considerations for a Church in the Third World. — *AsiaJT* 1 (1987) 429-460. Esp. 434-437: "The sayings source ('Q')"; 440-443; 456-457.

1988    La buena noticia para los pobres. [11,4-5] — *Concilium* (Madrid) 24 (1988) 41-51.

**ABOGUNRIN, Samuel Oyinloye**

1985    The Three Variant Accounts of Peter's Call: A Critical and Theological Examination
of the Texts. — *NTS* 31 (1985) 587-602. Esp. 588-590: "The Marcan tradition (Mk 1.16-20 cf.
Mt 4.18-22)". [NTA 30, 595]

1987    The Synoptic Gospel Debate: A Re-Examination in the African Context. — *African
Journal of Biblical Studies* (Ibadan, Nigeria) 2 (1987) 25-51. [NTA 34, 592]
The Synoptic Gospel Debate. A Re-Examination from an African Point of View. — DUNGAN, D.L. (ed.),
*The Interrelations of the Gospels*, 1990, 381-407. Esp. 388-395: "Patristic traditions of the sequential order
of the gospels".

**ABOU-CHAAR, K.**

1982    The Two Builders. A Study of the Parable in Luke 6:47-49. — *NESTR* 5 (1982) 44-58.
[NTA 26, 888]

**ABRAHAMS, Israel**

1917[R]    *Studies in Pharisaism and the Gospels. First and Second Series* [Cambridge: University Press,
1917/1924] (Library of Biblical Studies). New York: Ktav, 1967, XXXIV-178 p.; X-226
p. Esp. I, 18-29: "The greatest commandment"; 30-35: "John the Baptist"; 36-46: "Pharisaic baptism"; 47-
50: "The dove and the voice"; 51-53: "Leaven"; 54-61: "Publicans and sinners"; 62-65: "Give unto Caesar";
66-78: "Jewish divorce in the first century"; 82-89: "The cleansing of the temple"; 90-107: "The parables";
108-112: "Disease and miracle"; 113-117: "Poverty and wealth"; 121-128: "Fasting"; 129-135: "The
sabbath"; 136-138: "The personal use of the term 'Messiah'"; 139-149: "God's forgiveness"; 150-167:
"Man's forgiveness"; II, 4-14 [11,28-30]; 15-16 [5,14]; 29-32 [23,27-28]; 47-49 [10,28]; 62-63 [10,16-23];
94-108: "The Lord's Prayer"; 129-137: "The tannaite tradition and the trial narratives"; 183-184 [8,22]; 184-
185 [26,28]; 187-188 [8,12]; 191-192 [6,30]; 192-193 [10,32-33]; 193-194 [27,10]; 195-196 [7,6]; 196-197
[24,43]; 201-202 [27,16-17]; 203-205 [23,5]; 205-206 [5,28]; 206-207 [5,43]; 208 [19,24]; 208-210 [6,34].

**ABRAMOWSKI, Luise**

1984    Die Entstehung der dreigliedrigen Taufformel – ein Versuch. Mit einem Exkurs: Jesus
der Naziräer. — *ZTK* 81 (1984) 417-446. Esp. 422-428 [28,19]; 441-446 [2,23]. [NTA 29, 535];
= ID., *Formula and Context: Studies in Early Christian Thought (Variorum Reprints)*,
Hampshire: Variorum, 1992, 417-446. → Hubbard 1974

**ACERBI, Antonio**

1989    *L'Ascensione di Isaia. Cristologia e profetismo in Siria nei primi decenni del II. secolo*
(Studia patristica mediolanensia, 17). Milano: Vita e Pensiero, 1989, XII-327 p. Esp. 128-
137 [ἀγαπητός]; 149-153 [1,18-25/AscIs]; 210-217 [27,62-66; 28,2-4.11-15/AscIs].

**ACHTEMEIER, Paul John**

1972    The Origin and Function of the Pre-Marcan Miracle Catenae. — *JBL* 91 (1972) 198-
221. Esp. 219-221 [14,17.19; 15,34.36]. [NTA 17, 142]

1975    Miracles and the Historical Jesus: A Study of Mark 9:14-29. — *CBQ* 37 (1975) 471-
491. Esp. 473-478 [17,14-21/Mk]. [NTA 20, 802]

1980    "He taught them many things": Reflections on Marcan Christology. — *CBQ* 42 (1980)
465-481. Esp. 472-473; 474-476 [διδάσκαλος; διδαχή]. [NTA 25, 484]

1983a   An Apocalyptic Shift in Early Christian Tradition: Reflections on Some Canonical
Evidence. — *CBQ* 45 (1983) 231-248. Esp. 241-244. [NTA 28, 290]

1983b   It's the Little Things that Count (Mark 14:17-21; Luke 4:1-13; Matthew 18:10-14). —
*BibArch* 46 (1983) 30-31. Esp. 31. [NTA 27, 952]

1990    *Omne verbum sonat*: The New Testament and the Oral Environment of Late Western
Antiquity. — *JBL* 109 (1990) 3-27. Esp. 21-22 [5,3-12.21-48]. [NTA 34, 1012]
M. SLUSSER, *JBL* 111 (1992) 499; F.D. GILLIARD, *JBL* 112 (1993) 689-694.

**ACHTEMEIER, P. Mark**
1990    Matthew 13:1-23. — *Interpr* 44 (1990) 61-65.

**ACKERMAN, James S.** → Juel 1978

**ACKROYD, Peter B.**
1964    Threefoldness in the Teaching of Jesus. — *ExpT* 75 (1963-64) 316. [NTA 9, 116] → Mitton 1964

**ACOCELLA, Nicola**
1954    *La Traslazione di san Matteo. Documenti e Testimonianze*. Salerno: Di Giacomo, 1954, 64 p.
        R. GROSJEAN, *AnBoll* 74 (1956) 271-273.

**ADAM, Andrew K.M.**
1990    The Sign of Jonah: A Fish-Eye View. — *Semeia* 51 (1990) 177-191. [NTA 35, 1134]
1994    Matthew's Readers, Ideology, and Power. — *SBL 1994 Seminar Papers*, 435-449.

**ADAMS, David L.**
1974    Serendipity (Mt 6:33). — *Asbury Seminarian* (Wilmore, KY) 29/3 (1974) 13-17.

**ADAMS, W.W.**
1962    Jesus and his Church. — *RExp* 59 (1962) 464-480. [NTA 7, 470]

**ADASZEK, Marek**
1983    *"Ecce prandium meum paravi, venite ad nuptias"* (Mt 22,1-14). I temi teologici spirituali e catechetici del Convito escatologico (Domenica 28ª "per annum" - Ciclo A) (Collectio Urbaniana, 3249). Roma: Pont. Univ. Urbaniana, 1983, 77 p.

**ADDLEY, W.P.**
1976    Matthew 18 and the Church as the Body of Christ. — *BibTheol* 26 (1976) 12-18. [NTA 21, 83]

**ADDUCE, Giuseppe**
1985    *Peccato e perdono nella comunità di Matteo*. Diss. Napoli, 1985, 163 p. (V. Fusco).

**ADINOLFI, Marco**
1959    Preistoria di una vocazione (Matt. 9,9). — *BibOr* 1 (1959) 133-134. [NTA 4, 77]
1960    La condanna a tre città orgogliose (Matt. 11,20-24). — *BibOr* 2 (1960) 58-62. [NTA 5, 79]
1961a   L'insegnamento escatologico nelle parabole. — *Ant* 36 (1961) 137-172. Esp. 154-170 [24,45-51; 25,14-30]. [NTA 6, 78]
1961b   L'interpretazione delle parabole. — *RivBib* 9 (1961) 97-111, 243-258. Esp. 98-104: "Le parabole dei sinottici". [NTA 6, 420/750]
1962a   *Il Vangelo. Commento*. Bologna: Nuova Abes, 1962, XVI-635 p.
1962b   Le parabole della rete e del lievito nel Vangelo di Tommaso. — *SBF/LA* 13 (1962-63) 33-52. Esp. 43-48 [13,47-48/Th 8]; 48-51 [13,33/Th 96]. [NTA 8, 1162]
1971    Il celibato di Gesù. — *BibOr* 13 (1971) 145-158. Esp. 145-147 [19,12]; = ID., *Il Verbo*, 1992, 9-21. Esp. 9-11.
1972    Gesù e il matrimonio. Riflessioni sui testi evangelici. [5,32; 19,9] — *BibOr* 14 (1972) 13-29, 118.
1973    Il desiderio della donna in Matteo 5,28. — CANFORA, G. (ed.), *Fondamenti biblici*, 1973, 273-281.

1981    *Il femminismo della bibbia* (Spicilegium Pontificii Athenaei Antoniani, 22). Roma: Pont.
        Athenaeum Antonianum, 1981, 343 p. Esp. 99-115: "Il matrimonio nell'insegnamento di Gesù"
        [19,10]; 117-145: "La donna nella dottrina di Gesù"; 147-172: "La donna nella vita di Gesù"; 173-192: "Le
        discepole di Gesù".

1983    La preghiera del Signore: il Padre Nostro (Mt 6,9-13). — DE GENNARO, G. (ed.), *La
        preghiera nella Bibbia*, Napoli: Dehoniane, 1983, 283-291; = ID., *Il Verbo*, 1992, 23-
        35.

1985    *L'apostolato dei Dodici nella vita di Gesù* (La Parola di Dio, NS 3). Milano – Cinisello
        Balsamo: Paoline, 1985, 220 p.

1990    → C. Bottini 1990

1992    *Il Verbo uscito dal silenzio. Temi di cristologia biblica* (Collana biblica, 5). Roma:
        Dehoniane, 1992, 190 p. → 1971, 1983

        **ADLER, Nikolaus**
1951*   (ed.), *Vom Wort des Lebens. Festschrift für Max Meinertz zur Vollendung des 70.*
        *Lebensjahres 19. Dezember 1950. Dargeboten von seinen Freunden, Kollegen und*
        *Schülern* (NTAbh, 1. Ergänzungsband). Münster: Aschendorff, 1951, 167 p. → P. Benoit,
        Crehan, J. Schmid, H.J. Vogels

        **ADNÈS, Pierre**
1983    Le sacrement de pénitence. Chapitre II: Ses fondements néotestamentaires; Chapitre IV:
        Le "blasphème contre l'esprit saint" dans les synoptiques. — *EVie* 93 (1983) 385-392,
        503-508. Esp. 387-389 [16,17-19; 18,15-18]; 503-504 [12,31-32]. [NTA 28, 291/685].

        **AEJMELAEUS, Anneli**
1986    Vanhan testamentin käyttö Matteuksen evankeliumissa Mt 21:4-5 valossa. [The use of
        the OT in the Gospel of Mt exemplified by Mt 21:4-5] — *TAik* 91 (1986) 98-102.

        **AEJMELAEUS, Lars**
1985    *Wachen vor dem Ende. Die traditionsgeschichtlichen Wurzeln von 1. Thess 5:1-11 und*
        *Luk 21:34-36* (Schriften der Finnischen Exegetischen Gesellschaft, 44). Helsinki:
        Finnische Exegetische Gesellschaft, 1985, IV-157 p. Esp. 61-79 [24,36-51]; 80-86 [24,30-31].

1994    *Jeesuksen Ylösnousemus.* II: *Synoptiset evankeliumit ja apostolen text (Die Auferstehung*
        *Jesu.* II. *Teil: Die synoptischen Evangelien und die Apostelgeschichte)* (Schriften der
        Finnischen Exegetischen Gesellschaft, 59). Helsinki: Finnische Exegetische
        Gesellschaft, 1994, 355 p. Esp. 99-128 [27,51-53]; 129-161 [27,62-66; 28,2-4.11-15]; 162-171 [28,9-
        10]; 172-216 [28,16-20].

        **AERTS, Lode**
1990    *Gottesherrschaft als Gleichnis? Eine Untersuchung zur Auslegung der Gleichnisse Jesu*
        *nach Eberhard Jüngel* (EHS, XXIII/403). Frankfurt/M: Lang, 1990, 346 p. Esp. 141-170
        [13,44]; 171-190 [13,45-46]; 219-221 [13,47-48]; 225-226 [20,1-15]; 228-229 [22,1-14]. — Diss. Pont. Univ.
        Greg., Roma, 1989 (F. Lentzen-Deis).

        **AERTS, Theo**
1965    En zij "volgden" hem in de boot (Mt 8,23). — *Ons Geestelijk Leven* 42 (1965) 220-
        231.

1966    Suivre Jésus. Évolution d'un thème biblique dans les Évangiles synoptiques. — *ETL* 42
        (1966) 476-512. Esp. 495-496 [8,19-22]; 504-508. [NTA 11, 1022] — Diss. Pont. Univ. S. Thomae,
        Roma, 1962 (C. Kearns).

        **AGBANOU, Victor Kossi**
1983    *Le discours eschatologique de Matthieu 24-25. Tradition et rédaction* (Études bibliques,

NS 2). Paris: Gabalda, 1983, 228 p. Esp. 17-35: "Le contexte du discours eschatologique dans l'Évangile de Matthieu"; 37-44: "La structure de Mt 24–25"; 47-60 [24,1-3]; 61-80 [24,4-14]; 81-92 [24,15-22]; 93-102 [24,23-28]; 103-119 [24,29-36]; 123-131 [24,37-44]; 133-142 [24,45-51]; 143-153 [25,1-13]; 155-169 [25,14-30]; 173-198 [25,31-46]; 199-207 [tradition; redaction]. [NTA 29, p. 86]. — Diss. München, 1982 (J. Gnilka).

E. COTHENET, EVie 94 (1984) 412-413; J. GUILLET, RSR 74 (1986) 242-243; V. MORA, RB 95 (1988) 280-284.

1993   La parole de Dieu. Les paroles de Jésus. [11,25-27] — *Revue de l'Institut Catholique de l'Afrique de l'Ouest* (Abidjan) 4 (1993) 31-38.

**AGNEW, Francis**

1968   Vocatio primorum discipulorum in traditione synoptica. — *VD* 46 (1968) 129-147. Esp. 131-133.143-145 [4,18-22/Mk 1,16-20]. [NTA 13, 581]

**AGNEW, F.H.**

1995   Almsgiving, Prayer, and Fasting. [6,1-18] — *BiTod* 33 (1995) 239-244. [NTA 40, 166]

**AGNEW, Peter W.**

1983   The Two-Gospel Hypothesis and a Biographical Genre for the Gospels. — FARMER, W.R. (ed.), *New Synoptic Studies*, 1983, 481-499. Esp. 492-494 [genre].

**AGOURIDES, Sabbas**

1966   The Beatitudes. [Greek] — ID., *Biblika Meletemata* 1, Thessaloniki, 1966, 111-209.

1967   *The Character of the Birth and Infancy Narratives in Matthew and Luke* [Greek]. Athens, 1967, 27 p.

1970   La tradition des Béatitudes chez Matthieu et Luc. — DESCAMPS, A.L. – DE HALLEUX, A. (eds.), *Mélanges bibliques*. FS B. Rigaux, 1970, 9-27. Esp. 12-22: "L'idée directrice des sermons"; 22-26: "Structure et caractère des deux textes".

1974   The Sermon on the Mount (Introduction). [Greek] — *DeltBM* 2 (1974) 183-217, 271-328; 3 (1975) 47-60. [NTA 19, 529/946; 20, 437]; sep. Athens: Artos Zoes, 1975, 110 p.

1981   Young People, Young Missionaries in the Following of Jesus according to the Gospel of Matthew. [Greek] [18,1-14] — *DeltBM* 10 (1981) 5-14. [NTA 27, 903]

1984   "Little Ones" in Matthew. — *BTrans* 35 (1984) 329-334. Esp. 329-332 [18,1-4]; 332-334 [10,40-42]. [NTA 29, 78]

1992   The Birth of Jesus and the Herodian Dynasty: An Understanding of Matthew, Chapter 2. — *Greek Orthodox Theological Review* (Brookline, MA) 37 (1992) 135-146. [NTA 38, 1359]

1993   Matthew as Theologian of the Church of his Time (Tradition and Renewal). [Greek] — *DeltBM* 22 (1993) 5-17. [NTA 39, 785]

**AGRELL, Göran**

1976   *Work, Toil and Sustenance. An Examination of the View of Work in the New Testament, Taking into Consideration Views Found in Old Testament, Intertestamental, and Early Rabbinic Writings.* Lund: Verbum-Ohlsson, 1976, X-261 p. Esp. 68-94 [6,25-34; Q 12,22-32]. — Diss. Lund, 1976.

**AGTERBERG, Marinus**

1958   Saint Augustin, exégète de l'"Ecclesia–Virgo". — *Augustiniana* (Leuven) 8 (1958) 237-266. Esp. 241-247 [25,1-13].

**AGUIRRE MONASTERIO, Rafael**

1972   Mateo 27,51b-53. Historia de la tradición y redacción de un texto difícil. — *ScriptVict* 19 (1972) 241-272; 20 (1973) 121-154. → 1980

1975 Evangelios sinópticos. Repercusiones pastorales de una exégesis científica. — *SalT* 63 (1975) 83-96. Esp. 85-86, 93-96.

1979 El Reino de Dios y la muerte de Jesús en el evangelio de Mateo. — *EstE* 54 (1979) 363-382. Esp. 364-370: "Indicaciones previas"; 370-374: "Sentido de 27,51b-53"; 374-382: "La muerte de Jesús". [NTA 24, 431]
Cross and Kingdom in Matthew's Theology. — *TDig* 29 (1981) 149-153.

1980 *Exégesis de Mateo, 27,51b-53. Para una teología de la muerte de Jesús en el evangelio de Mateo* (Institución San Jeronimo, 9). Vitoria: ESET, 1980, 257 p. Esp. 29-56: "Estudio del vocabulario y del trasfondo bíblico de Mt. 27,51b-53"; 57-97: "Construcción literaria de Mt. 27,51b-53"; 98-108: "Conclusiones sobre Mt 27,51b-53 como texto preexistente a Mateo y consecuencias para su interpretación"; 109-152: "El origen y la tradición de Mt. 27,51b-53 en la exégesis reciente"; 153-171: "Mt. 27,51b-53 y el descenso de Jesús a los infiernos"; 172-251: "Interpretación de Mt. 27,51b-53 en el contexto del evangelio de Mateo". [NTA 26, p. 79] — Diss. Salamanca, 1977 (X. Pikaza). → 1972; → Senior 1976a.c, 1987b
M. ARIAS R., *TVida* 22 (1981) 70; G. BARBAGLIO, *CrnStor* 6 (1985) 603-604; M.-É. BOISMARD, *RB* 90 (1983) 621-622; J. GALOT, *Greg* 62 (1981) 637-638; J. GUILLET, *RSR* 74 (1986) 245-246; S.B. MARROW, *JBL* 102 (1983) 500-501; F. MONTAGNINI, *RivBib* 30 (1982) 234-235; F.F. SEGOVIA, *CBQ* 43 (1981) 637-638.

1981* & GARCÍA LÓPEZ, F. (eds.), *Escritos de Biblia y Oriente. Miscelánea conmemorativa del 25.° aniversario del Instituto Español Bíblico y Arqueológico (Casa de Santiago) de Jerusalén* (Bibliotheca Salmanticensis, Estudios 38). Salamanca: Universidad Pontificia; Jerusalem: Instituto español bíblico y arqueológico, 1981, 412 p.; = *Salmanticensis* 28 (1981) 1-409. → Aguirre Monasterio, Boismard

1981 Jesús y la multitud a la luz de los Sinópticos. — *Salmanticensis* 28 (1981) 259-282. Esp. 268-272. [NTA 26, 454]

1982 Los poderes del Sanedrín y notas de crítica histórica sobre la muerte de Jesús. [26,57-68] — *Estudios de Deusto* (Bilbao) 30 (1982) 241-270. [NTA 27, 888]

1989 Pedro en el evangelio de Mateo. — *EstBíb* 47 (1989) 343-361. Esp. 344-346: "Mateo y los textos petrinos de Marcos"; 346-348: "Textos propios de Mateo"; 348-352: "Mateo 16,16-19"; 352-357: "Tipo del discípulo y 'escriba supremo' de la Iglesia"; 357-361: "El evangelio de Mateo en la 'trayectoria petrina'". [NTA 34, 1120]

1991 (ed.), *Pedro en la Iglesia Primitiva* (Institución San Jerónimo, 23). Estella: Verbo Divino, 1991, 258 p.

1992 & RODRÍGUEZ CARMONA, A., *Evangelios sinópticos y Hechos de los Apóstoles* (Introducción al Estudio de la Bibbia, 6). Estella: Verbo Divino, 1992, 404 p.
*Vangeli sinottici e Atti degli Apostoli* (Introduzione allo studio della Bibbia, 6). Brescia: Paideia, 1995, 339 p.

1993 La comunidad de Mateo y el judaísmo. — *EstBíb* 51 (1993) 233-249. Esp. 236-238 [gentile]; 238-249 [Jewish-Christian]. [NTA 38, 136]

1994a Composición y trama del evangelio de Mateo. — *Reseña Bíblica* (Estella) 2 (1994) 5 – 13.

1994b El Judaismo y la Iglesia en el evangelio de Mateo. — *Ibid.*, 44-52.

**AGULLES ESTRADA, Juan**

1965 *Bienaventurados los puros de corazón. Mt. 5,8 en la teología greco-cristiana hasta Orígenes.* Valencia: Pont. Institutum Orientalium Studiorum, 1965, 129 p. Esp. 11-12 [Hermas]; 13-16 [apologists]; 17-24 [Irenaeus]; 25-45.46-62 [Clement of Alexandria]; 63-88.89-106.107-117 [Origen].

1988 Mt 5,8 en la tradición patrística. — *Communio* (Madrid) 10/6 (1988) 540-550.

**AHIRIKA, Edwin A.**

1990 The Theology of Matthew in the Light of the Nativity Story. — *Bible Bhashyam* 16 (1990) 5-19. Esp. 5-10 [1,17-25]; 11-14 [2,1-12]; 14-17 [2,13-23]. [NTA 35, 130]

1992 The Theology of Matthean Baptism Narrative. [3,13-17] — *Bible Bhashyam* 18 (1992) 131-139. [NTA 37, 1248]

**AICHELE, George**
1989 Literary Fantasy and the Composition of the Gospels. — *Forum* 5/3 (1989) 42-60. Esp. 47-49 [Th/Q]; 54-56 [Mt]. [NTA 35, 101]
1990 The Fantastic in the Parabolic Language of Jesus. — *Neotestamentica* 24 (1990) 93-105. Esp. 94-100 [Th/Mt 13]. [NTA 35, 604]
1992 The Fantastic in the Discourse of Jesus. — *Semeia* 60 (1992) 53-66. Esp. 56 [15,17-20]; 57-58 [12,22-30]; 59-60 [16,13-23]. [NTA 38, 87]
    Response: J. DEWEY, *ibid.*, 83-86.

**AICHINGER, Hermann**
1976 Quellenkritische Untersuchung der Perikope vom Ährenraufen am Sabbat. Mk 2,23-28 par Mt 12,1-8 par Lk 6,1-5. — *SNTU* 1 (1976) 110-153. Esp. 112-120: "Sprachliche Gemeinsamkeiten"; 120-141: "Die Unterschiede"; 141-147: "Gemeinsamkeiten zwischen Mt und Lk gegen Mk". → Neirynck 1980b
1978 Zur Traditionsgeschichte der Epileptiker-Perikope Mk 9,14-29 par Mt 17,14-21 par Lk 9,37-43a. — *SNTU* 3 (1978) 114-143. Esp. 117-129: "Redaktion des Dmk"; 129-137: "Redaktion des Mt". → Neirynck 1980b

**AILLET, Marc**
1993 *Lire la Bible avec S. Thomas. Le passage de la littera à la res dans la Somme théologique* (Studia Friburgensia, NS 80). Freiburg/Schw: Éd. universitaires, 1993, XI-355 p. Esp. 197-208: "Le commentaire du Sermon sur la montagne: I-II Q.108, A.3"; 221-235: "Le commentaire du Pater: II-II Q.83, A.9".

**AJURIA, J.**
1971 *Marcos, Mateo, Lucas y Juan: palabras basicas del evangelio* (Collección "Humanitas"). Madrid: EPESA, 1971, 500 p.

**AKANDE, Samuel T. Ola**
1973 *The Concept of Eschatological Suddenness in the Synoptic Tradition.* Diss. Southern Baptist Theol. Sem., Louisville, KY, 1973, 279 p. (W.E. Hull). — *DissAbstr* 34 (1973-74) 7874.

**AKANO, Yoshiyuki**
1992 The Ethical Teaching of Matthew 25:31-46. [Japanese] — *Katorikku Kenkyu* (Tokyo) 31 (1992) 141-165. [NTA 37, 1273]

**AKERBOOM, Dick**
1994* et al. (eds.), *Broeder Jehosjoea. Opstellen voor Ben Hemelsoet bij zijn afscheid als hoogleraar in de exegese van het Nieuwe Testament van de Katholieke Theologische Universiteit te Utrecht.* Kampen: Kok, 1994, 335 p. → Hendriks, van Ogtrop, Weren

**AKIN, Daniel L.**
1987 A Discourse Analysis of the Temptation of Jesus Christ as Recorded in Matthew 4:1-11. — *OPTAT* 1 (1987) 78-86. [NTA 31, 1059]

**ALAND, Barbara**
→ K. Aland [Nestle-Aland 1979, 1993; Bauer-Aland 1988]
1981 Die Philoxenianisch-Harklensische Übersetzungstradition. Ergebnisse einer Untersuchung der neutestamentlichen Zitate in der syrischen Literatur. — *Muséon* 92 (1981) 321-383. Esp. 366-368 [1,22-23; 3,15; 7,15-16; 14,35-36; 28,11-15]. [NTA 27, 35]

1982a   Monophysitismus und Schriftauslegung. Der Kommentar zum Matthäus- und Lukasevangelium des Philoxenus von Mabbug. — HAUPTMANN, P. (ed.), *Unser ganzes Leben Christus unserm Gott überantworten*. *Studien zur ostkirchlichen Spiritualität*. *Fairy von Lilienfeld zum 65. Geburtstag* (Kirche im Osten, 17), Göttingen: Vandenhoeck & Ruprecht, 1982, 142-166.

1982b   → K. Aland 1982

1989   Die Rezeption des neutestamentlichen Textes in den ersten Jahrhunderten. — SEVRIN, J.-M. (ed.), *The New Testament in Early Christianity*, 1989, 1-38. Esp. 6-12 [Ptolemaeus].

1992   Das Zeugnis der frühen Papyri für den Text der Evangelien. Diskutiert am Matthäusevangelium. — VAN SEGBROECK, F., et al. (eds.), *The Four Gospels 1992*. FS F. Neirynck, 1992, I, 325-335.

**ALAND, Kurt**

1957   Neue neutestamentliche Papyri. — *NTS* 3 (1956-57) 261-286. Esp. 265 [6,33-34]. [NTA 2, 235]; 9 (1962-63) 303-316. Esp. 309 [P$^{64/67}$]. [NTA 8, 40]; 22 (1975-76) 375-396. Esp. 383. [NTA 21, 16] → 1967b
Neue neutestamentliche Papyri: P$^7$, P$^{68}$, P$^{11}$ ("ergänzt und berichtigt"). — ID., *Studien*, 1967, 137-154 (= 1957, 262-278). Esp. 139-140.

1963   *Kurzgefaßte Liste der griechischen Handschriften des Neuen Testaments* (Arbeiten zur neutestamentlichen Textforschung, 1). Berlin: de Gruyter, 1963, 431 p.; (Arbeiten, 1bis), $^2$1994, XIX-507 p. ("neubearbeitete und ergänzte Auflage"). → 1969

1967a   *Studien zur Überlieferung des Neuen Testaments und seines Textes* (Arbeiten zur neutestamentlichen Textforschung, 2). Berlin: de Gruyter, 1967, IX-229 p. → 1957, 1967b

1967b   Das Neue Testament auf Papyrus. — *Ibid.*, 91-136. Esp. 107 [P$^1$]; 110 [P$^7$]; 113 [P$^{19.21}$]; 115 [P$^{25}$]; 118-119 [P$^{35}$]; 119 [P$^{37}$]; 123 [P$^{44}$]; 123-124 [P$^{45}$]; 126-127 [P$^{53}$]; 130 [P$^{62}$]; 131 [P$^{64/67}$]; 133 [P$^{70}$]; 134 [P$^{71}$]; 134 [P$^{73}$]. → 1957

1967c   *Die Stellung der Kinder in den frühen christlichen Gemeinden – und ihre Taufe* (Theologische Existenz heute, NF 138). München: Kaiser, 1967, 36 p. Esp. 7-13 [18,1-5; 21,15-16]; = ID., *Neutestamentliche Entwürfe*, 1979, 198-232. Esp. 202-208.

1969*   (ed.), *Materialien zur neutestamentlichen Handschriftenkunde*. I (Arbeiten zur neutestamentlichen Textforschung, 3). Berlin: de Gruyter, 1969, VII-292 p. → K. Aland, Ferreira, Junack, Peppermüller

1969   Die griechischen Handschriften des Neuen Testaments. Ergänzungen zur "Kurzgefaßten Liste" (Fortsetzungsliste VII). — *Ibid.*, 1-53. → 1963

1972a   Zur Vorgeschichte der christlichen Taufe. — BALTENSWEILER, H. – REICKE, B. (eds.), *Neues Testament und Geschichte*. FS O. Cullmann, 1972, 1-14. Esp. 3 [28,19]; 3-4 [3,11-12.14-15]; = ID., *Neutestamentliche Entwürfe*, 1979, 183-197. Esp. 185-187.

1972b   → Jülicher 1938

1976   *Repertorium der Griechischen Christlichen Papyri*. I: *Biblische Papyri. Altes Testament, Neues Testament, Varia, Apokryphen* (Patristische Texte und Studien, 18). Berlin – New York: de Gruyter, 1976, XIV-473 p. Esp. 36-39; 44; 215-216 [P$^1$]; 239 [P$^{19}$]; 241 [P$^{21}$]; 246 [P$^{25}$]; 257 [P$^{35}$]; 259 [P$^{37}$]; 268 [P$^{44}$]; 269-272 [P$^{45}$]; 283 [P$^{53}$]; 291 [P$^{62}$]; 293-294 [P$^{64.67}$]; 301 [P$^{70}$]; 302 [P$^{71}$]; 305 [P$^{73}$]; 313 [P$^{77}$]; 320 [P$^{86}$]; 331 [27,35]; 350-356 [1,1; 4,23; 6,9-13]. → 1995

1979a   *Neutestamentliche Entwürfe* (Theologische Bücherei. Neues Testament, 63). München: Kaiser, 1979, 413 p. → 1967c, 1972a, 1979b

1979b   Das Verhältnis von Kirche und Staat nach dem Neuen Testament und den Aussagen des 2. Jahrhunderts. — *Ibid.*, 26-123. Esp. 30-38: "Die Evangelien".
Das Verhältnis von Kirche und Staat in der Frühzeit. — *ANRW* II.23.1 (1979) 60-246 (163-246 = 1979b). Esp. 167-174.

1981    Der neue 'Standard-Text' in seinem Verhältnis zu den frühen Papyri und Majuskeln.
        — EPP, E.J. – FEE, G.D. (eds.), *New Testament Textual Criticism*. FS B.M. Metzger,
        1981, 257-275. Esp. 265-267.

1982    & B. ALAND, *Der Text des Neuen Testaments. Einführung in die wissenschaftlichen
        Ausgaben sowie in Theorie und Praxis der modernen Textkritik*. Stuttgart: Deutsche
        Bibelgesellschaft, 1982, 342 p.; [2]1989, 374 p. Esp. 233-243.258-259.314-318[21,28-32]; 284-318
        [illustrations].
        *The Text of the New Testament. An Introduction to the Critical Editions and to the Theory and Practice of
        Modern Textual Criticism*, trans. E.F. Rhodes. Grand Rapids, MI: Eerdmans; Leiden: Brill, 1987, XVIII-338
        p.; [2]1989, XVIII-366 p.; paperback 1995.
        *Il Testo del Nuovo Testamento*, trans. S. Timpanaro. Genova: Marietti, 1987, XII-372 p.

1987    Alter und Entstehung des D-Textes im Neuen Testament. Betrachtungen zu $P^{69}$ und
        0171. — JANERAS, S. (ed.), *Miscellània papirològica Ramon Roca-Puig en el seu
        vuitantè aniversari*, Barcelona: Fundacio Salvador Vives Casajuana, 1987, 37-61. Esp.
        45-48 [0171]; = ID., *Supplementa zu den neutestamentlichen und den
        kirchengeschichtlichen Entwürfen*, ed. B. Köster, U. Rosenbaum, M. Welte, Berlin –
        New York: de Gruyter, 1990, 72-96. Esp. 80-83.

1995    & ROSENBAUM, H.-U., *Repertorium der Griechischen Christlichen Papyri*. II:
        *Kirchenväter – Papyri*. Teil 1: *Beschreibungen* (Patristische Texte und Studien, 42).
        Berlin – New York: de Gruyter, 1995, CXXVIII-580 p. Esp. 431-433 [Origen: Mt 24,4ff]. →
        1976

NESTLE-ALAND

1956    *Novum Testamentum Graece cum apparatu critico curavit D. Eberhard Nestle, novis
        curis elaboravit D. Erwin Nestle adiuvante D. Kurt Aland*. Stuttgart: Württembergische
        Bibelanstalt, [22]1956; *elaboraverunt Erwin Nestle et Kurt Aland*, [23]1957, [24]1960, [25]1963,
        110*-671 p. (Nachdruck: [1]1965, [2]1968, [3]1970, [4]1972, [5]1973, [6]1975, [7]1977, [8]1978). Esp.
        1-83: "Κατὰ Μαθθαῖον". → Nestle 1950

1979    *Novum Testamentum Graece. Post Eberhard Nestle et Erwin Nestle communiter
        ediderunt Kurt Aland, Matthew Black, Carlo M. Martini, Bruce M. Metzger, Allen
        Wikgren. Apparatum criticum recensuerunt et editionem novis curis elaboraverunt Kurt
        Aland et Barbara Aland una cum Instituto studiorum textus Novi Testamenti
        Monasteriensi (Westphalia)*. Stuttgart: Deutsche Bibelstiftung, [26]1979, [IX]-78*-779 p.
        ([2]1980, [3]1980, [4]1981: "4. revidierter Druck", [5]1982, [6]1983, [7]1983: "7. revidierter
        Druck", [8]1986, [9]1987, [10]1988, [11]1990, [12]1991). Esp. 1-87: "Κατὰ Μαθθαῖον". → Baarda 1980,
        H.-W. Bartsch 1981, Borger 1987, H.J. de Jonge 1980, J.K. Elliott 1981
        F. NEIRYNCK, *ETL* 57 (1981) 359-360.

1993    *Novum Testamentum Graece. Post Eberhard et Erwin Nestle editione vicesima septima
        revisa communiter ediderunt Barbara et Kurt Aland, Johannes Karavidopoulos, Carlo
        M. Martini, Bruce M. Metzger. Apparatum criticum novis curis elaboraverunt Barbara
        et Kurt Aland una cum Instituto studiorum textus Novi Testamenti Monasterii
        Westphaliae*. Stuttgart: Deutsche Bibelgesellschaft, [27]1993, VIII-89*-810 p. (Nachdruck,
        [2]1994). Esp. 1-87: "Κατὰ Μαθθαῖον". → J.K. Elliott 1994b-c, 1996
        F. NEIRYNCK, *ETL* 70 (1994) 154-157.

        *Novum Testamentum Graece et Latine*. Stuttgart, [17]1956, [18]1957, [19]1958, [20]1959, [21]1960,
        [22]1963 (Nachdruck: [1]1969, [2]1970, [3]1974, [4]1976, [5]1978). → R. Weber 1969
        1984 ($N^{26}$, 7. Druck; Nova Vulgata 1979) ([2]1985, [3]1987, [4]1990), [2]1991, 44*-779 (1-680
        double) p. → Vulgata 1979
        F. NEIRYNCK, *ETL* 60 (1984) 398-399.
        [3]1994 ($N^{27}$ 1993, Nova Vulgata [2]1986), XVII-46*-810 (1-680 double) p.

*Das Neue Testament Griechisch und Deutsch.* Stuttgart, [16]1957, [17]1960, [18]1968 (Nach-druck: [1]1973, [2]1974, [3]1976, [4]1978).
1986 (N[26], 7. Druck; Lutherbibel 1984, EÜ 1979), [2]1987, [3]1990, 44*-779 (1-680 double) p.
[4]1995 (N[27] 1993; Luther 1984, EÜ 1979).

*Greek-English New Testament.* Stuttgart, 1981 (N[26], 4. Druck; RSV [2]1971), [2]1985 (revised), [3]1986, [4]1988, [5]1990, [6]1992, [7]1993, 40*-779 (1-680 double) p.
[8]1994 (N[27] 1993; RSV [2]1971), x-46*-810 (1-680 double) p.

GNT

1966    & BLACK, M. – METZGER, B.M. – WIKGREN, A., *The Greek New Testament.* Stuttgart
– London – New York: United Bible Societies, 1966, LV-920 p. Esp. 1-117: "Κατὰ
Μαθθαῖον"; [2]1968 [+ C.M. MARTINI and in cooperation with the Institute for New
Testament Textual Research], LV-934 p.

1975    [3]1975, LXII-918 p.; Corrected, 1983, LXII-926 p. Esp. 1-117: "Κατὰ Μαθθαῖον". → J.K. Elliott
1978b, Neirynck 1976d, Ross 1976
J.K. ELLIOTT, *NT* 26 (1984) 377-379; G.D. KILPATRICK, *TLZ* 104 (1979) 260-270; *TRev* 80 (1984) 458-
459.

1993    [4]1993 (2nd print 1994), XIII-61*-918 p. Esp. 1-117: "Κατὰ Μαθθαῖον". → Baarda 1994c, J.K.
Elliott 1994a.c, 1996
J.K. ELLIOTT, *JTS* 45 (1994) 280-282; F. NEIRYNCK, *ETL* 69 (1993) 421-424.

SYNOPSIS

1963    *Synopsis Quattuor Evangeliorum. Locis parallelis evangeliorum apocryphorum et
patrum adhibitis.* Stuttgart, 1963, XXX-590 p.; [2]1964, [3]1966, [4]1967 ("revisa"), [5]1968,
[6]1969, [7]1971, [8]1973. → Léon-Dufour 1972c

1976    [9]1976 (N[26] = GNT[3]), XXXII-590 p.; [10]1978, [11]1980, [12]1982. → Neirynck 1976c, 1976d

1985    [13]1985 (Apparatus revised) ([2]1986, [3]1988, [4]1990) → J.K. Elliott 1986, 1991, Neirynck 1986c

1995    [14]1995 (*Bericht*, 1995, 18).

*Synopsis of the Four Gospels. Greek-English Edition of the Synopsis Quattuor Evange-
liorum with the Text of the Revised Standard Version.* London–Stuttgart: United Bible
Societies, 1972 (N[25]; RSV [2]1971), XXX-361 (1-338 double) p.; [2]1975 (revised), [3]1979,
[4/5]1982, [6]1983 (revised), [7]1984, [8]1987, [10]1993 (N[26]).

*Synopse der vier Evangelien. Griechisch-Deutsche Ausgabe der Synopsis Quattuor
Evangeliorum. Auf der Grundlage des Novum Testamentum Graece von Nestle-Aland,
26. Auflage, und des Greek New Testament, 3rd Edition, sowie der Lutherbibel,
revidierter Text 1984, und der Einheitsübersetzung 1979.* Stuttgart: Deutsche Bibelgesellschaft, 1989, XXIX-361 (1-338 double) p.

CONCORDANCE

*Vollständige Konkordanz zum Griechischen Neuen Testament. Unter Zugrundelegung
aller modernen kritischen Textausgaben und des Textus Receptus in Verbindung mit H.
Riesenfeld, H.-U. Rosenbaum, Chr. Hannick, B. Bonsack neu zusammengestellt unter
der Leitung von K. ALAND.*

1983    Band I (Arbeiten zur neutestamentlichen Textforschung, 4/1). Berlin – New York: de
Gruyter, 2 vols., 1983, XIX-752 and 753-1352 p.

1978    Band II: *Spezialübersichten* (Arbeiten zur neutestamentlichen Textforschung, 4/2). 1978,
VII-557 p. → Neirynck 1976a, 1983a, 1984a

**BAUER-ALAND**

1988 *Griechisch-deutsches Wörterbuch zu den Schriften des Neuen Testaments und der frühchristlichen Literatur von Walter Bauer*, 6. völlig neu bearbeitete Auflage, unter Mitwirkung von V. Reichmann herausgegeben von K. Aland und B. Aland. Berlin – New York: de Gruyter, 1988, XXIV-1796 col. → W. Bauer 1952; → Borger 1989, Neirynck 1988e, Rehkopf 1991, Strecker 1991
J.G. VAN DER WATT, *Neotestamentica* 25 (1991) 438-440.

**ALBERS, Robert H.**

1984 Perspectives on the Parables. Glimpses of the Kingdom of God. — *WWorld* 4 (1984) 437-454. Esp. 441-442 [18,21-35]; 442-444 [20,1-16]; 444-445 [21,28-32]; 448-450 [21,33-43]; 450-453 [22,1-14]. [NTA 29, 509]

**ALBERTI, Angelo**

1957 Il divorzio nel Vangelo di Matteo. — *DivThom* 60 (1957) 398-410. [NTA 3, 72]

1962 *Matrimonio e divorzio nella Bibbia* (Collana "Il nostro tempo"). Milano: Massimo, 1962, 191 p. → Vaccari 1962

**ALBERTZ, Heinrich**

1981 Was meine ich, wenn ich das Vaterunser bitte? — *IZT/Concilium* (Mainz) 17 (1981) 264-265.

**ALBERTZ, Martin**

1922R Zur Formengeschichte der Auferstehungsberichte. [1922] — HOFFMANN, P. (ed.), *Zur neutestamentlichen Überlieferung von der Auferstehung Jesu*, 1988, 259-270.

1947R *Die Botschaft des Neuen Testamentes*. I: *Die Entstehung der Botschaft*; II: *Die Entfaltung der Botschaft*. Zürich: Evangelischer Verlag, I/1, 1947, 301 p. Esp. 173-179 [Q]; 210-224 [Mt]; I/2, 1952, 502 p.; II/1, 1954, 315 p.; II/2, 1957, 357 p.

**ALBL, Martin C.**

1993* & EDDY, P.R. – MIRKES, R. (eds.), *Directions in New Testament Methods* (Marquette Studies in Theology, 2). Milwaukee, WI: Marquette University Press, 1993, VIII-129 p. → Garry, Mirkes, Rossol

**ALBRECHT, Evelin**

1977 *Zeugnis durch Wort und Verhalten untersucht an ausgewählten Texten des Neuen Testaments* (Theologische Dissertationen, 13). Basel: Reinhardt, 1977, 236 p. Esp. 15-24 [11,2-6]; 31-38 [8,5-13]; 51-67: "Die Zusammengehörigkeit von Wort und Tat Jesu nach Matthäus" [4,23; 9,35]; 95-133: "Der Zeugnischarakter des Verhaltens bei den Jüngern nach Matthäus" [5,13-16; 6,1-2.5.16]. — Diss. Basel, 1976 (B. Reicke).

**ALBRIGHT, William Foxwell**

1971 & MANN, C.S., *Matthew. Introduction, Translation, and Notes* (The Anchor Bible, 26). Garden City, NY: Doubleday, 1971, CXCVIII-366 p. [NTA 16, p. 234] → Sabourin 1973, Scroggs 1972, Ziesler 1985
F.H. BORSCH, *Interpr* 26 (1972) 359-360; B. CELADA, *CuBíb* 32 (1975) 293-296; D.J. CLARK, *BTrans* 25 (1974) 358-360; T.C. DE KRUIJF, *Bijdragen* 34 (1973) 323-324; D. FLUSSER, *IsrExplJourn* 26 (1976) 147-148; R.H. FULLER, *TS* 33 (1972) 580-582; *WestTJ* 35 (1972-73) 83-84; H.B. GREEN, *JTS* 23 (1972) 480-483; T. HOLTZ, *TLZ* 97 (1972) 593-596; X. JACQUES, *NRT* 94 (1972) 1096-1097; B.M. METZGER, *PrincSemB* 65 (1972-73) 89-90; J. MURPHY-O'CONNOR, *RB* 80 (1973) 306-307; G. RINALDI, *BibOr* 15 (1973) 267; W.G. THOMPSON, *CBQ* 34 (1972) 481-485; M ZERWICK, *Bib* 56 (1975) 142-148.

**ALEGRE, Xavier**

1988 La tempesta apaivagada (Mc 4,35-41; Mt 8,18-27; Lc 8,22-25). — *Butlletí de l'Associació Bíblica de Catalunya* (Barcelona) 34 (1988) 13-32.

**ALEIXANDRE, Dolores**

1987a En torno a la cuarta petición del Padrenuestro. — *EstBíb* 45 (1987) 325-336. [NTA 33, 119]

1987b Volver al Padrenuestro. — *SalT* 75 (1987) 437-446.

**ALEIXO DINIZ, Edwin A.**

1991 *Joy in the Presence of Jesus Christ according to the Synoptics* (Studia Theologica - Teresianum, 8). Roma: Teresianum, 1991, 243 p. Esp. 17-20; 70-75 [μακάριος]; 56-58 [5,12]; 58-67 [11,5]; 75-86 [1,21]; 86-93 [2,10]; 102-120 [9,14-15]; 120-130 [13,44-46]; 131-150 [5,3-12]; 150-161 [6,25-30]; 162-178 [12,1-8].

**ALEMANY (BRIZ), José J.**

1976 Mesianismo sufriente de Jesús en el evangelio de Mateo. — *CuBíb* 33 (1976) 3-19.

**ALEPUZ, M.** → Mateos 1977b, Urbán Fernandez 1977a

**ALETTI, Jean-Noël**

1972 Problème synoptique et théorie des permutations. — *RSR* 60 (1972) 575-594. [NTA 17, 881] → Frey 1972

1985 Mort de Jésus et théorie du récit. — *RSR* 73 (1985) 147-160. Esp. 148-152, 153-154, 158-160 [passion narrative]. [NTA 30, 84]

1993 Matthieu et Paul: deux évangiles divergents? — DORÉ, J. - THEOBALD, C. (eds.), *Penser la foi*. FS J. Moingt, 1993, 95-106.

1994 *Jésus-Christ fait-il l'unité du Nouveau Testament?* ("Jésus et Jésus-Christ", 61). Paris: Desclée, 1994, 296 p. Esp. 119-166: "Tradition synoptique et Actes"; 183-185; 189-191; 195-209: "Matthieu: Justice par la Loi?".

1995 La sagesse dans le Nouveau Testament. État de la question. — TRUBLET, J. (ed.), *La sagesse biblique. De l'Ancien au Nouveau Testament. Actes du XV^e Congrès de l'ACFEB (Paris, 1993)* (LD, 160), Paris: Cerf, 1995, 265-278. Esp. 272-276: "Jésus et la figure de la Sagesse".

**ALEU, José**

1971 La resurrección de Jesús en los evangelios. — *EstBíb* 30 (1971) 47-75. Esp. 59-60 [28,7-8]; 65-66.70-72 [28,16-20]. [NTA 16, 507]

**ALEXANDER, Joseph Addison**

1860^R *The Gospel according to Matthew* [1860] (Thornapple Commentaries). Grand Rapids, MI: Baker, 1980, 456 p.

**ALEXANDER, James S.**

1973 A Note on the Interpretation of the Parable of the Threshing Floor at the Conference at Carthage of A.D. 411. [3,12] — *JTS* 24 (1973) 512-519.

**ALEXANDER, Philip S.**

1984 Midrash and the Gospels. — TUCKETT, C.M. (ed.), *Synoptic Studies*, 1984, 1-18. Esp. 13-15. → Goulder 1974

**ALEXANDER, William Menzies**

1902^R *Demonic Possession in the New Testament. Its Historical, Medical, and Theological Aspects* [1902]. Grand Rapids, MI: Baker, 1980, XII-291 p. Esp. 174-193 [12,22-30]; 194-215 [8,28-34].

**ALFECHE, Mamerto**

1986 The Basis of Hope in the Resurrection of the Body according to Augustine. — *Augustiniana* (Leuven) 36 (1986) 240-296. Esp. 241-263: "An attempt to harmonize the resurrection narratives" [28,1-10].

**ALFORD, Henry**

1849[R] *The Greek Testament: With a Critically Revised Text, a Digest of Various Readings, Marginal References to Verbal and Idiomatic Usage, Prolegomena, and a Critical and Exegetical Commentary* [1849]. I: *The Four Gospels*, revised by E.F. Harrison, Chicago, IL: Moody, 1958; 1968, [155]-930 p. Esp. 1-308: "Κατὰ Ματθαῖον" (925-927).

**ALGISI, Leone**

1962 Il Vangelo di S. Matteo. — MORALDI, L. - LYONNET, S. (eds.), *Introduzione alla Bibbia*, 1962, 157-220; [3]1973, 157-216. Esp. 160-171 [structure]; 177-183 [author]; 184-187 [sources]; 203-214 [theology]; 215-216 [date].

1963 *Gesù e le sue parole*. Torino: Marietti, 1963, 395 p.

**ALIQUÒ, Salvatore**

1969 (trans.), *Girolamo. Commento al vangelo di Matteo*. Roma: Città Nuova, 1969, 327 p.
   G. BOZIO, *Sal* 32 (1970) 497-498.

**ALLAN, Graeme**

1983 He shall be called – a Nazirite? [2,23; 26,71] — *ExpT* 95 (1983-84) 81-82. [NTA 28, 489]
   → D.B. Taylor 1981

**ALLEN, Charles L.**

1963 *The Lord's Prayer. An Interpretation*. Westwood, NJ: Revell, 1963, 64 p.

1966 *The Sermon on the Mount*. Westwood, NJ: Revell, 1966, 187 p.

**ALLEN, E.L.**

1954 On this Rock. [16,17-19] — *JTS* 5 (1954) 59-62.

**ALLEN, R.E.**

1974 *Divine Dividends. An Inspirational Reading of the Sermon on the Mount*. Nashville, TN: Nelson, 1974, 160 p.

**ALLEN, Ronald J.**

1982 *Our Eyes Can be Opened. Preaching the Miracle Stories of the Synoptic Gospels Today*. Washington, DC: University Press of America, 1982, XVI-129 p.

**ALLEN, William Loyd**

1992a The Sermon on the Mount in the History of the Church. — *RExp* 89 (1992) 245-262. [NTA 37, 715]

1992b Matthew 4:1-11 – The Devil at the Crossroads. — *Ibid.*, 529-533.

**ALLIATA, Eugenio**

1984 La *krypte* di Lc 11,33 e le grotte ripostiglio della antiche case palestinesi. — *SBF/LA* 34 (1984) 53-66. Esp. 58-63 [Q 11,33]. [NTA 30, 155]

**ALLISON, Dale C., Jr.**

1982 The Pauline Epistles and the Synoptic Gospels: The Pattern of the Parallels. — *NTS* 28 (1982) 1-32. Esp. 2-5; 10-11 [5-7]; 12-13 [10,1-16]; 16-17 [22,15-22.34-40]; 19-21 [Q]; 21 [23,43-44]. [NTA 26, 940] → Neirynck 1986f, Tuckett 1984b, N. Walter 1985

1983 Matt. 23:39 = Luke 13:35b as a Conditional Prophecy. — *JSNT* 18 (1983) 75-84. [NTA 28, 101]; = EVANS, C.A. - PORTER, S.E. (eds.), *The Historical Jesus*, 1995, 262-270. → 1997j, 192-201 ("corrected and enlarged edition")

1984 Eunuchs because of the Kingdom of Heaven (Matt. 19:12). — *TSF Bulletin* (Madison, WI) 8/2 (1984) 2-5.

1985a   *The End of the Ages Has Come. An Early Interpretation of the Passion and Resurrection of Jesus.* Philadelphia, PA: Fortress, 1985; Edinburgh: Clark, 1987, XIII-194 p. Esp. 40-50 [27,51-54; 28,2-4.16-20]; 118-123 [10,34-36; 11,11-12]; 133-135 [10,32-33]; 140-141 [6,9-13]. — Diss. Duke Univ., Durham, NC, 1982 (W.D. Davies).

1985b   Paul and the Missionary Discourse. — *ETL* 61 (1985) 369-375. [NTA 30, 1165] → Tuckett 1984b; → 1997e, 105-111 ("revised")

1987a   The Eye Is the Lamp of the Body (Matthew 6.22-23 = Luke 11.34-36). — *NTS* 33 (1987) 61-83. Esp. 69-71: "The eye as a lamp"; 71-73: "The reconstruction of Q"; 73-79: "Interpretation"; 79: "Luke 11.36 again"; 80-81: "An origin with Jesus?". [NTA 31, 1073] → 1997g ("thoroughly revised and much expanded")

1987b   Jesus and the Covenant: A Response to E.P. Sanders. [*Paul and Palestinian Judaism*, 1977] — *JSNT* 29 (1987) 57-78. Esp. 58-61 [3,7-12]; 64 [5,17-18; 8,22]; 66-67 [10,32-33]; 67 [5,3-6]; 71 [11,16-19]. [NTA 31, 1006]; = EVANS, C.A. - PORTER, S.E. (eds.), *The Historical Jesus*, 1995, 61-82. Esp. 63-66; 68-71; 72-74; 74; 78.

1987c   Jesus and Moses (Mt 5:1-2). — *ExpT* 98 (1986-87) 203-205. [NTA 31, 1067]

1987d   The Son of God in Israel: A Note on Matthean Christology. [2,15; 3,17; 4,1-11] — *IBS* 9 (1987) 74-81. [NTA 32, 104] → D. Hill 1980, 1984a, 1986b, Kingsbury 1984

1987e   The Structure of the Sermon on the Mount. — *JBL* 106 (1987) 423-445. Esp. 424-429 [Bornkamm]; 429-438 [structure]; 438-441 [triads; hermeneutics]; 442-445 [setting]. [NTA 32, 583]

1988a   DAVIES, W.D. - ALLISON, D.C., Jr., *A Critical and Exegetical Commentary on The Gospel According to Saint Matthew.* Volume I: *Introduction and Commentary on Matthew I-VII* (The International Critical Commentary). Edinburgh: Clark, 1988, XLVII-731 p. Esp. 1-148: "Introduction"; 149-731: "Commentary"; excursions: 190-195: "The sources of Mt 1.18–2.23"; 431-442: "The beatitudes (Mt 5.3-12; Lk 6.20-3)"; 505-509: "The interpretation of Mt 5.21-48"; 590-599: "The Lord's Prayer (Mt 6.9-13 = Lk 11.2-4)". [NTA 33, p. 384] → G. Claudel 1993
    D.R. BAUER, *Asbury Theological Journal* (Wilmore, KY) 44/2 (1989) 96-98; M. BORG, *BibReview* 6/6 (1990) 10-11; J.A. BURNS, *Criswell Theological Review* (Dallas, TX) 4 (1989-90) 192-194; E. CUVILLIER, *ETR* 64 (1989) 288-289; D.S. DOCKERY, *RExp* 89 (1992) 113-114; A. FUCHS, *SNTU* 15 (1990) 158-161; A.E. GARDNER, *AusBR* 39 (1991) 73-73; I.H. JONES, *JTS* 43 (1992) 162-166; J.D. KINGSBURY, *JBL* 110 (1991) 344-346; S. MCKNIGHT, *CBQ* 53 (1991)697-699; P.M. MEAGHER, *Vidyajyoti* 53 (1989) 629-631; M. MÜLLER, *DanskTeolTids* 53 (1990) 75; M.A. POWELL, *Interpr* 45 (1991) 294-296; C.S. RODD, *ExpT* 100 (1988-89) 228-230; R. SCHNACKENBURG, *BZ* 35 (1991) 131-133; M.G. STEINHAUSER, *TorontoJT* 6 (1990) 129-131; C.M. TUCKETT, *ScotJT* 42 (1989) 574-575; A. VARGAS-MACHUCA, *EstE* 65 (1990) 93-94; N. WATSON, *Pacifica* 3 (1990) 112-114; T.R. WOLTHUIS, *CalvTJ* 26 (1991) 423-424.
    Volume II: *Commentary on Matthew VIII–XVIII,* 1991, XVII-807 p. Esp. 1-5: "Matthew 8–9"; 43-52: "The son of man"; 160-162: "The structure of the missionary discourse"; 233-234: "The structure of Matthew 11–12"; 370-372: "The structure of Matthew 13"; 378-382: "The parables"; 594-601: "Jesus as Messiah"; 647-652: "Peter in Matthew"; 750-751: "The structure of chapter 18". [NTA 36, p. 420]
    E. CUVILLIER, *ETR* 67 (1992) 455-457; R.A. DÍEZ ARAGÓN, *EstAgust* 27 (1992) 203-204; A. FUCHS, *TPQ* 141 (1993) 201-202; I.H. JONES, *JTS* 45 (1994) 212-215; M. KNOWLES, *TorontoJT* 9 (1993) 258-259; R.K. MCIVER, *AndrUnS* 31 (1993) 62-64; M. MÜLLER, *DanskTeolTids* 55 (1992) 150-151; C.S. RODD, *ExpT* 104 (1992-93) 149-150; D.P. SCAER, *ConcTQ* 58 (1994) 188-190; É. TROCMÉ, *RHPR* 73 (1993) 194; C.M. TUCKETT, *ScotJT* 45 (1992) 408-409; N. WATSON, *Pacifica* 6 (1993) 104-106.
    Volume III: *Commentary on Matthew XIX–XXVIII,* 1997, XVIII-789 p. Esp. 1-3: "The arrangement of Mt 19.1-23.39"; 257-263: "Preface to chapter 23"; 573-577: "The formula quotations". → 1997a; → Horbury 1997
    D.J. HARRINGTON, *Bib* 78 (1997) 582-586; F. NEIRYNCK, *ETL* 73 (1997) 448-450.

1988b   Matthew 10:26-31 and the Problem of Evil. — *St. Vladimir's Theological Quarterly* (Tuckahoe, NY) 32 (1988) 293-308. [NTA 33, 608]

1988c   A New Approach to the Sermon on the Mount. — *ETL* 64 (1988) 405-414. Esp. 406-411: "A pre-Matthean source?"; 411-413: "A dialogue with hellenistic philosophy?"; 413-414: "No theological interest in the passion and resurrection?". [NTA 33, 1118r] → H.D. Betz 1985a; → 1997c, 67-95 ("mostly new")

1988d   Two Notes on a Key Text: Matthew 11:25-30. — *JTS* 39 (1988) 477-485. Esp. 478-483 [OT]; 483-485 [Par. Jer]. [NTA 33, 610]

1989a   Gnilka on Matthew. — *Bib* 70 (1989) 526-538. Esp. 527-532 [Moses]; 532-536 [structure]; 536-537 [Israel]. [NTA 34, 600r] → Gnilka 1986-88

1989b   Who Will Come from East and West? Observations on Matt 8.11-12 – Luke 13.28-29. — *IBS* 11 (1989) 158-170. [NTA 34, 625] → 1997i ("much expanded edition")

1990   'The hairs of your head are all numbered'. [Q 12,7] — *ExpT* 101 (1989-90) 334-336. [NTA 35, 142] → 1997h ("new edition")

1991a   → 1988a

1991b   → W.D. Davies 1991b

1992a   The Baptism of Jesus and a New Dead Sea Scroll. [3,16] — *BibArchRev* 18/2 (1992) 58-60. [NTA 36, 1572]

1992b   Eschatology. — *DJG*, 1992, 206-209. Esp. 208.

1992c   Matthew: Structure, Biographical Impulse, and the *Imitatio Christi*. — VAN SEGBROECK, F., et al. (eds.), *The Four Gospels 1992*. FS F. Neirynck, 1992, II, 1203-1221. Esp. 1203-1208 [structure]; 1208-1220 [biography].

1992d   → W.D. Davies 1992b

1993a   *The New Moses. A Matthean Typology*. Minneapolis, MN: Augsburg/Fortress; Edinburgh: Clark, 1993, XVI-396 p. Esp. 135-290: "The new Moses in Matthew"; 298-306 [W.D. Davies 1963]; 311-319 [Kingsbury 1975a]; 320-323 [Mohrlang 1984]; 324-325 [T.L. Donaldson 1985]; 325-328 [O. Betz 1987b]. [NTA 38, p. 455]
    K.A. BARTA, *CBQ* 58 (1996) 145-146; E. CUVILLIER, *ETR* 71 (1996) 86-87; S.A. HUNT, *JSNT* 59 (1995) 123; J.D. KINGSBURY, *JBL* 115 (1996) 356-358; A.J. LEVINE, *JRel* 75 (1995) 406-408; J. ROLOFF, *Bib* 76 (1995) 574-578; C. TUCKETT, *ExpT* 106 (1994-95) 55; W.J. VAN BEKKUM, *JSJ* 25 (1994) 314-315; B.T. VIVIANO, *RB* 103 (1996) 137-138.

1993b   Divorce, Celibacy and Joseph (Matthew 1.18-25 and 19.1-12). — *JSNT* 49 (1993) 3-10. [NTA 38, 152]

1993c   What Was the Star that Guided the Magi? — *BibReview* 9/6 (1993) 20-24, 63. [NTA 38, 750]

1994a   Anticipating the Passion: The Literary Reach of Matthew 26:47-27:56. — *CBQ* 56 (1994) 701-714. Esp. 703-705 [5,38-42]; 705-707 [10,17-23]; 707-710 [17,1-8]; 710-711 [20,20-28]. [NTA 40, 178]

1994b   A Plea for Thoroughgoing Eschatology. — *JBL* 113 (1994) 651-668. Esp. 661-664 [Q]; 666-667 [Q 17,23-24]. [NTA 39, 1396]

1997a   *The Jesus Tradition in Q*. Harrisburg, PA: Trinity Press International, 1997, XII-243 p. → 1988a/91/97
    F. NEIRYNCK, U. Luz and D.C. Allison's Retrospect on Q. — *ETL* 74 (1998) 121-125.

1997b   The Compositional History of Q. — *Ibid.*, 1-66. Esp. 3-8: "An early sapiential recension of Q?"; 8-11 [Q 3,7 – 7,35]; 11-15 [Q 9,57 – 11,13]; 16-21 [Q 11,14-52]; 21-25 [Q 12,2-32]; 26-30 [Q 12,33 – 22,30]; 30-36: "A theory of Q's compositional history"; 36-40: "Parallels to the proposed compositional theory"; 41-42: "The implications for Q's genre"; 43-46: "The implications for Q's place within early christianity"; 47-49: "The question of original language"; 49-54: "Q's date and place of composition"; 54-60: "Paul and Q"; 60-62: "Jesus and Q"; 62-66: "Papias once again".

1997c   The Sermon on the Plain, Q 6:20-49. Its Plan and Its Sources. — *Ibid.*, 67-95. Esp. 67-77: "The theory of Hans Dieter Betz"; 77-79: "The Sermon on the Plain in Q"; 79-95: "The sources of the Sermon in the Plain". → 1988c; → H.D. Betz 1985a

1997d   Four Beatitudes, Q 6:20-23. A Unified Composition. — *Ibid.*, 96-103.

1997e   The Missionary Discourse, Q 10:2-16. Its Use by Paul. — *Ibid.*, 104-119. Esp. 105-111:
        "Paul and the missionary discourse" (→ 1985b); 111-119: "Paul's allusions to the Jesus tradition" [Q 16,17].

1997f   The Returning Spirit, Q 11:24-26. Multiple Meanings. — *Ibid.*, 120-132.

1997g   The Eye as a Lamp, Q 11:34-36. Finding the Sense. — *Ibid.*, 133-167. Esp. 135-143:
        "Ancient theories of vision"; 144-148: "Jewish sources"; 148-149: "The eye as a lamp"; 150-152: "The
        reconstruction of Q"; 153-161: "Interpretation"; 161-162: "A parallel in Testament of Benjamin 4:2"; 162-
        163: "Luke 11:36 again"; 163-165: "The origin of Q 11:34-35"; 165-167: "11:34-36 and Q". → 1987a

1997h   The hairs of your head are numbered, Q 12:7a. Evil and Ignorance. — *Ibid.*, 168-175.
        Esp. 172-175: "The composition of Q 12,4-7". → 1990

1997i   From East and West, Q 13:28-29. Salvation for the Diaspora. — *Ibid.*, 176-191. Esp.
        177-178: "Q 13:28-29 as an isolated saying"; 178-182: "East and west and north and south"; 182-185: "The
        gentiles"; 185-186: "The eschatological ingathering of the dispersion"; 186-188: "Q 13:28-29 and Jesus";
        189-191: "The literary interpretations". → 1989b

1997j   The Forsaken House, Q 13:34-35. Jerusalem's Repentance. — *Ibid.*, 192-204. Esp. 192-
        195: "Two different interpretations"; 196-201: "Q 13,35b as a conditional sentence"; 201-203: "The location
        and function of Q 13:35b in Q" (supplement). → 1983

1997k   → 1988a

**ALLMEN, Jean-Jacques VON**

1977    *La primauté de l'Église de Pierre et de Paul. Remarques d'un protestant* (Cahiers
        œcuméniques, 10). Freiburg/Schw: Éd. universitaires; Paris: Cerf, 1977, 125 p. Esp.
        62-79.

**ALONSO, Joaquín María**

1972    *Die Mutter Jesu im Neuen Testament.* Una síntesis de Marialogía bíblica
        neotestamentaria. — *EphMar* 22 (1972) 77-112. Esp. 80-83, 100-104. → Räisänen 1969

1973    "… y sin haberla conocido" (Mt. 1,25). — *EphMar* 23 (1973) 437-441. → Tavares 1972

**ALONSO DÍAZ, José**

1954    *Padre Nuestro. Estudio exegético.* Santander: Sal Terrae, 1954, 112 p.

1959    El problema literario del Padre Nuestro. — *EstBíb* 18 (1959) 63-75. Esp. 64-65:
        "Comparación de las formas de Mateo y Lucas y de la 'Didajé'"; 65-75: "Explicación de los hechos". [NTA
        4, 386]

1960    El Padre Nuestro dentro del problema general de la Escatología. — *MiscCom* 34-35
        (1960) 297-308. Esp. 297-305.

1962    El bautismo de fuego anunciado por el Bautista y su relación con la profecía de
        Malaquías. [3,11; 11,10] — *MiscCom* 38 (1962) 121-133. [NTA 8, 125]; = *EstBíb* 23 (1964)
        319-331. [NTA 10, 901]

1963a   Pasaje de la calma de la tormenta en el Evangelio, según Mateo. [8,18-27] — *CuBíb* 20
        (1963) 149-157. [NTA 8, 577]

1963b   Cuestión sinóptica y universalidad del mensaje cristiano en el pasaje evangélico de la
        mujer cananea (Mc 7,24-30; Mt 15,21-28). — *Ibid.*, 274-279. [NTA 8, 963]

1963c   Los elementos de la tradición eucarística en relación con Jesucristo. [26,26-29] —
        *RevistEspTeol* 23 (1963) 47-60. [NTA 8, 656]

1965    Padrenuestro. — *Enciclopédia de la Bíblia* (Barcelona) 5 (1965; ²1969) 762-765.

1967    La anunciación a S. José o un santo bíblico ante un caso de conciencia. [1,18-25] — *SalT*
        55 (1967) 659-666.

1969    Cómo explicar las tentaciones de Jesús en el desierto. [4,1-11] — *SalT* 57 (1969)
        819-828.

1970    Nomismo e antinomismo através da Bíblia. — *Theologica* 5 (1970) 11-41. Esp. 28-34.

1973 ¿El evangelio de Mateo, evangelista para ricos? Dificultades de la Iglesia primitiva en marcha para integrar a los ricos dentro del Evangelio. — *SalT* 61 (1973) 3-22.

1975a La indisolubilidad del matrimonio o el divorcio hoy, visto por escrituristas y teólogos. — *StOvet* 3 (1975) 203-226. [NTA 20, 935]
La indisolubilidad del matrimonio hoy, vista por escrituristas y teólogos. — *SalT* 63 (1975) 609-616; = *RazFe* 195 (1977) 20-27. [NTA 21, 902]

1975b El Padre Nuestro como oración actual. — *SalT* 63 (1975) 196-202.

1977 Sentido del "Juicio Final" de Yahvé en la Apocalíptica y en Mt 25. — *StOvet* 5 (1977) 77-98. [NTA 23, 106]

1978 Matrimonio y divorcio. Praxis de la Iglesia. [5,32; 19,9] — *BibFe* 4 (1978) 59-74.

1983 ¡Felices, los perseguidos por la justicia! [5,10] — *BibFe* 9 (1983) 200-207.

1987 De una interpretación maximalista de la Biblia como Palabra de Dios a una interpretación minimalista. — CAZELLES, H. (ed.), *La vie de la Parole*. FS P. Grelot, 1987, 305-317. Esp. 308-309 [Augustine: 27,3-10].

**ALONSO SCHÖKEL, Luis**
1976 → J. Mateos 1976

1978 → Proulx 1978

1992 Notas de Antiguo Testamento a los Evangelios de la Infancia. — *EstBíb* 50 (1992) 13-18. Esp. 15-16: "El relato de los magos"; 18 [11,28-30].

**ALSOP, John R.**
1972 *An Index to the Bauer–Arndt–Gingrich Greek Lexicon*. Grand Rapids, MI: Zondervan, 1972, XIII-489 p. Esp. 1-67. → W. Bauer 1952/69

**ALSUP, John E.**
1975 *The Post-Resurrection Appearance Stories of the Gospel Tradition. A History-of-Tradition Analysis With Text-Synopsis* (Calwer theologische Monographien, 5). Stuttgart: Calwer, 1975, 307 p. Esp. 86-95: "Synoptic tradition"; 108-114 [28,1-10]; 116-117 [27,62-66; 28,2-4.11-15]; 144.147 [28,16-20]; 153-154.160-161 [28,16-18]; 177-181 [28,18-20]. — Diss. München, 1973 (L. Goppelt).

**ALT, Franz**
1983 *Frieden ist möglich. Die Politik der Bergpredigt* (Serie Piper, 284). München: Piper, 1983, 119 p.
B. HANEKE, *MüTZ* 35 (1984) 316.
*L'arme absolue, les béatitudes; la politique selon le discours sur la Montagne*, trans. J. Toulat. Paris: OEIL, 1983, 158 p.
J. PINTARD, *EVie* 97 (1987) 607-608.
*Vrede is mogelijk. De politiek van de Bergrede*. Baarn: Ten Have, 1984, 112 p.
R. HOET, *Collationes* 16 (1986) 244.
*Peace is Possible. The Politics of the Sermon on the Mount*, trans. J. Neugroschel. New York: Schocken, 1985, 117 p.

1985 *Liebe ist möglich. Die Bergpredigt im Atomzeitalter* (Serie Piper, 429). München: Piper, ²1985, 220 p.
A. FUCHS, *SNTU* 13 (1988) 218-219.

**ALTENDORF, Hans-Dietrich**
1966 *Wiederkunft und Kreuz. Zur Auslegung von Mt 24,30 in der Alten Kirche und zur Deutung einiger Kreuzdarstellungen in der frühchristlichen Kunst*. Diss. Tübingen, 1966.

**ALTHAUS, Paul**

1956    Luther und die Bergpredigt. — *Luther* 27 (1956) 1-16.

1961    (ed.), *M. Luther, Auslegung der Bergpredigt.* Göttingen: Vandenhoeck & Ruprecht, 1961, 278 p.

**ALTHOFF, K.F.**

1978    *Das Vaterunser. Die Wortgestalt des Menschheitsgebetes auf ihrem Weg durch die Kulturen der Völker.* Stuttgart: Urachhaus, 1978, 280 p.

**ALTMANN, Walter**

1979    Libertação e justificação. [25,31-46] — *Perspectiva Theologica* (São Leopoldo) 11 (1979) 5-15.

**ÁLVAREZ, Carlos G.**

1979    El ministerio de sanación en el evangelio de san Mateo. — *Vida Espiritual* (Bogotá) 62 (1979) 17-24.

**ÁLVAREZ, César G.**

1967    "Soy luz" (Jn 8,12); "sois luz" (Mt 5,14). — *CiudDios* 180 (1967) 257-263. [NTA 12, 230]

**ALVES, Herculano**

1988    Parábola da ovelha perdida (Mt. 18,10-14; Lc. 15,1-7; EvTom 107). (Estudo histórico-literário). — *Humanística e Teologia* (Porto) 9 (1988) 299-327.

**AMBROZIC, Aloysius M.**

1972    Indissolubility of Marriage in the New Testament: Law or Ideal? — *Studia Canonica* 6 (1972) 269-288.

1974    Die Zeichenforderung und der christliche Dialog mit der Welt. — MERKLEIN, H. - LANGE, J. (eds.), *Biblische Randbemerkungen.* FS R. Schnackenburg, 1974, 273-282. Esp. 273-276 [12,38].

1990    Reflections on the First Beatitude. — *Communio* (Notre Dame, IN) 17 (1990) 95-104. [NTA 34, 1133]

**AMMASSARI, Antonio**

1973    Gesù ha veramente insegnato la risurrezione! [22,23-33] — *BibOr* 15 (1973) 65-73. [NTA 18, 496]

1975    *La resurrezione.* Vol. I: *Nell'insegnamento nella profezia nelle apparizioni di Gesù.* Vol. II: *La gloria del Risorto nelle testimonianze ricevute dalla prima Chiesa.* Roma: Città Nuova, I, 1975, 232 p.; ²1976, 280 p.; II, 1976, 125 p. Esp. I, 23-57 [22,23-33]; 71-84 [26,61]; 105-119 [28,1-10]; 139-155 [27,62-66]; 157-184 [28,16-20]; 185-196 [28,19]; II, 14-19 [17,1-9].

1977    La famiglia del Messia. Note sugli Evangeli dell'infanzia di Gesù. — *BibOr* 19 (1977) 195-203. Esp. 197-198.201-202 [1,18-25]. [NTA 22, 755]

1982    *I Dodici. Note esegetiche sulla vocazione degli apostoli* (Collana scritturistica). Roma: Città Nuova, 1982, 148 p.

**AMOS, Thomas L.**

1990    The *Catechesis Cracoviensis* and Hiberno-Latin Exegesis on the *Pater Noster.* — *ProcIrBibAss* 13 (1990) 77-107.

**AMPHOUX, Christian-Bernard**

1987    La révision marcionite du "Notre Père" de Luc (11,2-4) et sa place dans l'histoire du texte. — GRYSON, R. - BOGAERT, P.-M. (eds.), *Recherches sur l'histoire de la Bible latine. Colloque organisé à Louvain-la-Neuve pour la promotion de H.J. Frede au doctorat* honoris causa *en théologie le 18 avril 1986* (Cahiers de la RTL, 19), Louvain-la-Neuve: Faculté de Théologie, 1987, 105-121. Esp. 105-109: "La tradition manuscrite"; 109-117: "La révision marcionite". → Baarda 1990, Delobel 1989b

1988   La parabole matthéenne du Fils prodigue. La version du Codex Bezae (D05 du NT). [21,28-32] — *Langues orientales anciennes, philologie et linguistique* (Louvain) 1 (1988) 167-171.

1990   Étude synoptique: La purification du lépreux (Mt 8,2-4 / Mc 1,40-45 / Lc 5,12-16 (14bis) / Egerton 2). — *BLOS* 4 (1990) 3-12. → Hermant 1990b, Rolland 1990b

1993   *La parole qui devient Évangile. L'Évangile – ses rédacteurs – son auteur.* Paris: Seuil, 1993, 208 p. Esp. 23-26: "Matthieu"; 114-120 [TC recension]; 123; 137-139.

1995   La composition de *Matthieu* inscrite dans dix prophéties de la Bible grecque. — DORIVAL, G. – MUNNICH, O. (eds.), *Κατὰ τοὺς O' – Selon les Septante. Trente études sur la Bible grecque des Septante. En hommage à Marguerite Harl*, Paris: Cerf, 1995, 333-369. Esp. 334-340: "Dix prophéties de la Bible grecque"; 340-344: "La formule introductive"; 344-353: "Les ensembles narratifs de Mt"; 353-356: "Les paroles de Jésus"; 356-364: "La composition matthéenne".

**AMSTUTZ, Joseph**

1968   *Ἁπλότης. Eine begriffsgeschichtliche Studie zum jüdisch-christlichen Griechisch* (Theophaneia, 19). Bonn: Hanstein, 1968, 160 p. Esp. 96-102 [6,22-23].

**ANDERSEN, Francis I.**

1961   The Diet of John the Baptist. [3,4] — *Abr-Nahrain* (Leiden) 3 (1961-62) 60-74.

**ANDERSEN, Øivind**

1976   *Bergprekenen* [Sermon on the Mount] (Biblia, 8). Oslo: Lunde, 1976, 58 p.; [2]1977, 61 p.

**ANDERSON, Ana Flora**

1973   & DA SILVA GORGULHO, G., *Evangelho de Mateus* (Deus Fala Hoje, 1). São Paulo: Paulinas, 1973, 81 p.
       S. VOIGT, *REB* 34 (1974) 727-728.

**ANDERSON, Charles C.**

1969   *Critical Quests of Jesus.* Grand Rapids, MI: Eerdmans, 1969, 208 p. Esp. 91-93 [historical Jesus/Q].

1972   *The Historical Jesus: A Continuing Quest.* Grand Rapids, MI: Eerdmans, 1972, 271 p.

**ANDERSON, Hugh**

1962   Existential Hermeneutics. Features of the New Quest. — *Interpr* 16 (1962) 131-155. Esp. 142-143 [11,27]. [NTA 7, 13]

1964   *Jesus and Christian Origins. A Commentary on Modern Viewpoints.* New York: Oxford University Press, 1964, XIV-368 p. Esp. 222-226: "Matthew's easter witness"; 247-253 [fulfilment quotations].

1965   The Easter Witness of the Evangelists. — ID. – BARCLAY, W. (eds.), *The New Testament in Historical and Contemporary Perspective. Essays in Memory of G.H.C. Macgregor*, Oxford: Blackwell, 1965, 35-55. Esp. 44-47 [28,16-20].

**ANDERSON, Janice Capel**

1983   Matthew: Gender and Reading. — *Semeia* 28 (1983) 3-27. Esp. 6-21: "Gender in Matthew" [1,1-17; 9,18-31; 15,21-28; 26,6-13; 27,55-56]; 21-26: "Gender and the implied reader" [22,41-46]. [NTA 28, 907]

1985   Double and Triple Stories, the Implied Reader, and Redundancy in Matthew. — *Semeia* 31 (1985) 71-89. Esp. 72-76 [doublets]; 76-79 [triads: 9,27-31; 15,21-28; 20,29-34]; 79-80 [12,38-42; 16,1-4]; 80-82 [14,13-21; 15,30-38]; 84-85 [implied reader]. [NTA 30, 99]

1987 Mary's Difference: Gender and Patriarchy in the Birth Narratives. — *JRel* 67 (1987) 183-202. Esp. 186-190. [NTA 31, 1056]

1988 Matthew: Sermon and Story. — *SBL 1988 Seminar Papers*, 496-507. Esp. 498-500 [5,31-32]; 500-505 [7,15-20]; = BAUER, D.R. - POWELL, M.A. (eds.), *Treasures New and Old*, 1996, 233-250. Esp. 237-239; 239-246; 249-250: "Epilogue 1995".

1994 *Matthew's Narrative Web. Over, and Over, and Over Again* (JSNT SS, 91). Sheffield: JSOT, 1994, 261 p. Esp. 11-45: "Introduction and method"; 46-77: "Narrative rhetoric: narrator and narratee, direct commentary, and point of view"; 78-132: "Character"; 133-191: "Plot"; 192-225: "Literary analysis of repetition in narrative, reader-response and aurality"; 226-242: "Extended verbal repetition in the gospel of Matthew". [NTA 39, p. 133] — Diss. Divinity School, Chicago, IL, 1985 (J.Z. Smith). J.T. CARROLL, *JBL* 115 (1996) 351-353; N. CLARK, *ExpT* 106 (1994-95) 87; S. MCKNIGHT, *JBL* 115 (1996) 141-143; E.M. WAINWRIGHT, *CBQ* 58 (1996) 146-147.

1995 Life on the Mississippi: New Currents in Matthaean Scholarship 1983-1993. — *Currents in Research: Biblical Studies* (Sheffield) 3 (1995) 169-218. Esp. 173-184: "Social scientific criticism"; 184-189: "Literary criticism"; 189-194: "Reader-response criticism"; 194-196: "Postmodern/poststructuralist criticism"; 196-200: "Feminist criticism"; 202-218: "Bibliography". [NTA 40, 1448]

**ANDERSON, Paul N.**

1996 *The Christology of the Fourth Gospel. Its Unity and Disunity in the Light of John 6* (WUNT, II/78). Tübingen: Mohr, 1996, XV-329 p. Esp. 232-250 [16,17-19/Jn 6,67-71]. — Diss. Glasgow, 1988.

**ANDREW, C.R.**

1962 Doorkeeper in the House of the Lord. [24,42-44] — *Foundations* (Rochester, NY) 5 (1962) 265-269.

**ANGELINI, Cesare**

1970 Portrait de saint Matthieu. — *ÉtFranc* 20 (1970) 81-84. [NTA 15, 125]

1982 *Il Gesù di Matteo*, ed. R. Colla. Vicenza: Locusta, 1982, 88 p. M. BALDINI, *Città di vita* (Firenze) 38 (1983) 93-94.

**ANGÉNIEUX, J.**

1970 Les différents types de structure du "Pater" dans l'histoire de son exégèse. — *ETL* 46 (1970) 40-77, 325-359. Esp. 40-77: "De Tertullien aux grands scolastiques"; 325-344: "De saint Thomas d'Aquin aux exégètes récents"; 344-359: "Essai de synthèse". [NTA 15, 140/847]

**ANHEIM, Jean-Claude**

1980 *Le "dit" de Jonas dans la tradition évangélique* [12,38-39; 16,1-4; Q 11,16.29; Q 12,54-56]. Diss. Strasbourg, 1980, XI-308 p. (J. Schmitt).

**ANNAND, Rupert**

1956 Papias and the Four Gospels. — *ScotJT* 9 (1956) 46-62. Esp. 55-57.

**ANNEN, Franz**

1976a *Heil für die Heiden. Zur Bedeutung und Geschichte der Tradition vom besessenen Gerasener (Mk 5,1-20 parr.)* (Frankfurter theologische Studien, 20). Frankfurt/M: Knecht, 1976, VII-253 p. Esp. 29-38: "Vergleich Mk-Mt"; 207-209: "Redaktion des Mt". — Diss. Pont. Inst. Bibl., Roma, 1974 (I. de la Potterie).

1976b Die Dämonenaustreibungen Jesu in den synoptischen Evangelien. — *Theologische Berichte* (Zürich) 5 (1976) 107-146. Esp. 108-112: "Der synoptische Befund"; 112-117: "Die Tatsachen im Leben Jesu"; = *TJb*, 1981, 94-123.

**ANNO, Yoshito**
1984   *The Mission to Israel in Matthew. The Intention of Matthew 10:5b-6 Considered in the Light of the Religio-Political Background.* Diss. Lutheran School of Theology, Chicago, IL, 1984, V-367 p. (W. Linss).

**ANSALDI, Jean**
1987   Le Sermon sur la montagne ou les tribulations d'un théologien protestant. — *LumièreV* 183 (1987) 67-84. [NTA 32, 584] → Duquoc 1987

**ANTOLIN, Teofilo**
1962   Las parábolas del Evangelio ¿contienen una sola y no varias lecciones doctrinales? — *Concepto de la Iglesia en el Nuevo Testamento. Otros estudios* (XIX Semana Biblica Española), Madrid: Consejo Superior de Investigaciones Científicas, 1962, 305-318.

**ANTONA, Giannino**
1985   I miracoli di guarigione di Gesù. Un'ipotesi esplicativa. — *Studia Patavina* 32 (1985) 23-41. [NTA 30, 65]

**ANTWI, Daniel J.**
1991   Did Jesus Consider His Death to Be an Atoning Sacrifice? — *Interpr* 45 (1991) 17-28. Esp. 19-20 [8,4]; 20-21 [5,23-24]; 21-23 [12,1-8]; 24-25 [9,5-6]; 25-26 [26,7-13]; 26-27 [18,23-35]. [NTA 35, 587]

**APARICIO, Miguel**
1990   El Espíritu de Jesús Mesías y la novedad de la historia. Perfil de cristología sinóptica del Espíritu. — *Mayéutica* 16 (1990) 325-481. [NTA 36, 115]

**APARICIO RODRÍGUEZ, Angel**
1993   La madre del pueblo en el anti-éxodo y en el nuevo exodo (Mat 2,13-23). — *EphMar* 43 (1993) 61-78. [NTA 38, 155]

**APECECHEA PERURENA, Juan**
1983   Comentario del Padrenuestro de Joaquín Lizarraga, el Vicario de Elcano. — *ScriptVict* 30 (1983) 65-89; 31 (1984) 182-202; 32 (1985) 414-432; 34 (1987) 102-119; 35 (1988) 413-432; 38 (1991) 387-411.

**APREA, Mariano**
1987a  Tre visioni profetiche dell'Antico Testamento nel frontespizio al Vangelo di San Matteo, nel codice Parisinus graecus 74. — *Studi e Ricerche dell'Oriente Cristiano* (Roma) 10 (1987) 65-78.
1987b  Il frontespizio del Vangelo di San Matteo dell'Evangeliario di Ottone III. — *Ibid.*, 79 – 92.

**ARAI, Sasagu**
1976   Das Gleichnis vom verlorenen Schaf – Eine traditionsgeschichtliche Untersuchung. — *AJBI* 2 (1976) 111-137. Esp. 117-119 [18,14]; 119-122 [18,12-14/Th 107]; 122-126: "Das Jesusbild der Q-Gemeinde"; 126-132: "Das Jesusbild der Q-Gruppe". [NTA 21, 425]

**ARANDA PÉREZ, Gonzalo**
1978   Los Evangelios de la infancia de Jesús. — *ScriptTheol* 10 (1978) 793-848 (English summary, 847-848). Esp. 795-800: "Características del Evangelio de la infancia según s. Mateo"; 813-842: "La veracidad historica del Evangelio de la infancia"; 843-846: "La concepción virginal". [NTA 23, 813]
1982   La concepción virginal de Jesús. — *ScriptTheol* 14 (1982) 831-846. Esp. 832-835.837-838 [1,18-25]. [NTA 27, 880r] → de Freitas Ferreira 1980

1984 *El Evangelio de San Mateo en Copto Sahídico (Texto del M 569, estudio preliminar y aparato crítico)* (Textos y estudios "Cardenal Cisneros", 35). Madrid: Consejo Superior de Investigaciones Científicas, 1984, 296 p. [NTA 29, p. 321] → 1988a
M.J. BLANCHARD, *RelStR* 12 (1986) 293; F. BRÄNDLE, *EstJos* 42 (1988) 255; M. GUERRA, *ScriptTheol* 18 (1986) 276-277; Y. JANSSENS, *Muséon* 99 (1986) 187; D. JOHNSON, *CBQ* 48 (1986) 550-551; G.D. KILPATRICK, *NT* 28 (1986) 284; H.-M. SCHENKE, *Archiv für Papyrusforschung* (Leipzig) 34 (1988) 62-65; R. TREVIJANO, *Salmanticensis* 32 (1985) 230-231.

1988a *El Evangelio de San Mateo en Copto Sahídico. Texto del M 569 y aparato crítico* (Textos y estudios "Cardenal Cisneros", 45). Madrid: Consejo Superior de Investigaciones Científicas, 1988, 150 p. → 1984
J.A. CARRASCO, *EstJos* 46 (1992) 96.

1988b La versión sahídica de San Mateo en Bodmer XIX y Morgan 569. — *EstBíb* 46 (1988) 217-230. Esp. 220-226: "Variantes propias de Bodmer XIX"; 226-230: "Características textuales de Morgan 569(M)". [NTA 33, 1105]

1989 El apostol Pedro en la literatura gnóstica. — *EstBíb* 47 (1989) 65-92. Esp. 70-75 [Acta Petri]; 76-81 [Apoc. Petri]. [NTA 34, 997]

1992 Los relatos evangélicos de la concepción y nacimiento de Jesús en los escritos de Nag Hammadi. — *EstBíb* 50 (1992) 19-34. Esp. 21-31: "Concepción y nacimiento de Jesús".

1994* & BASEVI, C. – CHAPA, J. (eds.), *Biblia, Exegesis y Cultura. Estudios en honor del Prof. D. José María Casciaro* (Facultad de Teologia. Universidad de Navarra. Colección teologica, 83). Pamplona: Universidad de Navarra, 1994, 763 p. → García-Cordero, Luzarraga, Muñoz Iglesias, O'Callaghan, Pérez Rodríguez

1995 María en los evangelios: ¿Mito, símbolo o realidad? — *EphMar* 45 (1995) 43-68. Esp. 50-54 [1-2]. [NTA 40, 108]

**ARBANITIS, Konstantinos A.**

1966 Matthew. [Greek] — Θρησκευτικη και Ηθικη Εγκυκλοπαιδεια (Athens) 8 (1966) 819-828.

**ARCHER, Gleason L.**

1983 & CHIRICHIGNO, G., *Old Testament Quotations in the New Testament*. Chicago, IL: Moody, 1983, XXXII-167 p.

**ARCHIBALD, P.**

1987 Interpretation of the Parable of the Dragnet (Matthew 13:47-50). — *Vox Reformata* (Geelong, Australia) 48 (1987) 3-14. [NTA 32, 125]

**ARDIZZONI, Anthos**

1985 I disoccupati dell'ultima ora (Riflessioni su Matteo 20,1-16). — *Giornale italiano di filologia* (Napoli) 37 (1985) 3-14.

**ARENS, Edmund**

1981 Gleichnisse als kommunikative Handlungen Jesu. Überlegungen zu einer pragmatischen Gleichnistheorie. — *TheolPhil* 56 (1981) 47-69. [NTA 25, 837]

1982 *Kommunikative Handlungen. Die paradigmatische Bedeutung der Gleichnisse Jesu für eine Handlungstheorie*. Düsseldorf: Patmos, 1982, 424 p. Esp. 19-108: "Gleichnisse als Metaphern – Gleichnisse als Sprachhandlungen Jesu"; 109-169: "Theologische Gleichnistheorien"; 323-385: "Gleichnisse als innovatorische Sprachhandlungen Jesu". — Diss. Münster, 1982 (J.B. Metz).

1988 Metaphorische Erzählungen und kommunikative Handlungen Jesu. Zum Ansatz einer Gleichnistheorie. — *BZ* 32 (1988) 52-71. Esp. 69-70. [NTA 32, 1090]

**ARENS, Eduardo**

1976 *The ἠλθον-Sayings in the Synoptic Tradition. A Historico-Critical Investigation* (Orbis

Biblicus et Orientalis, 10). Freiburg/Schw: Universitätsverlag; Göttingen: Vandenhoeck
& Ruprecht, 1976, 370 p. Esp. 28-63 [9,10-13]; 63-90 [10,34-36]; 91-116 [5,17-20]; 117-161 [20,25-
28]; 191-193 [18,11]; 212-215 [8,29]; 221-243 [11,16-19]; 243-248 [17,10-13]; 288-294 [3,11; 11,3; 21,9;
23,39]; 300-302 [8,7]; 311 [10,40]; 315-320 [15,24]; 322-323 [3,1]; 328-333 [5,17; 10,34; 20,28]; 340-341.
— Diss. Freiburg/Schw, 1975 (G. Schelbert).

### ARGES, Michael

1987   New Evidence Concerning the Date of Thomas Aquinas' *Lectura* on Matthew. —
*Mediaeval Studies* (Toronto, Ont.) 49 (1987) 517-523.

### ARGYLE, A.W.

1950   The Evidence for the Belief that Our Lord Himself Claimed to Be Divine. — *ExpT* 61
(1949-50) 228-232. Esp. 228 [10,38-39; 16,24-25]; 229 [10,32-33; 11,27]; 230 [10,40; 18,20]; 230-231
[25,31-46]. → Lattey 1950

1951   Paul and Q. [Q 10,3] — *ExpT* 62 (1950-51) 157.

1953   The Accounts of the Temptations of Jesus in Relation to the Q Hypothesis. — *ExpT* 64
(1952-53) 382. → B.M. Metzger 1954

1954   Scriptural Quotations in Q Material. — *ExpT* 65 (1953-54) 285-286. → B.M. Metzger 1954

1955   Did Jesus Speak Greek? [5,39-40] — *ExpT* 67 (1955-56) 92-93, 383. [NTA 1, 63/180] →
H.M. Draper 1956, R.McL. Wilson 1957a

1961   Agreements Between Matthew and Luke. — *ExpT* 73 (1961-62) 19-22. Esp. 20-21 [minor
agreements]; 21-22 [Q]. [NTA 6, 445] → Cherry 1962

1963   *The Gospel According to Matthew* (The Cambridge Bible Commentary). Cambridge:
University Press, 1963, IX-228 p. [NTA 8, p. 288]
    M.-É. BOISMARD, *RB* 71 (1964) 447; M. D'ALMEIDA, *Brotéria* (Rio de Janeiro) 78 (1964) 765; H.B.
GREEN, *JTS* 16 (1965) 160-161; G. HAUFE, *TLZ* 90 (1965) 683; S.E. JOHNSON, *ATR* 46 (1964) 448-449;
J. KAHMANN, *TijdTheol* 5 (1964) 460; F.W. KOESTER, *TheolPhil* 42 (1967) 306; J. LEDWIDGE, *RevistBíb*
28 (1966) 184-185; X. LÉON-DUFOUR, *RSR* 59 (1971) 600-601; I.H. MARSHALL, *EvQ* 36 (1964) 118-
119; H.K. MOULTON, *BTrans* 16 (1965) 51-52; J.R. PERKIN, *ScotJT* 19 (1966) 234-236; J. REUMANN,
*JBL* 83 (1964) 224-225; V. TAYLOR, *ExpT* 75 (1963-64) 203; M. ZERWICK, *VD* 42 (1964) 307.

1964a   Evidence for the View that St. Luke Used St. Matthew's Gospel. — *JBL* 83 (1964) 390-
396. Esp. 390-392 [3,5.7-10; 4,1; 9,7.17; 13,55]; 393 [5,3.6.48]; 394 [5,17-20; 6,16-18; 7,24-27; 8,28-34];
394-395 [9,18-26]; 395 [9,37-38; 10,10]; 396 [14,13-14.20; 16,21; 17,14-21]. [NTA 9, 854]; =
BELLINZONI, A.J., Jr. (ed.), *The Two-Source Hypothesis*, 1985, 371-379.

1964b   'Hypocrites' and the Aramaic Theory. [6,2] — *ExpT* 75 (1963-64) 113-114. [NTA 8, 885]

1964c   The Methods of the Evangelists and the Q Hypothesis. — *Theology* 67 (1964) 156-157.
[NTA 8, 886]

1970   M and the Pauline Epistles. — *ExpT* 81 (1969-70) 340-342. [NTA 15, 486]

1975   Wedding Customs at the Time of Jesus. [25,1-13] — *ExpT* 86 (1974-75) 214-215. [NTA
20, 91]

1976   Notes on the New Testament Vulgate. — *NTS* 22 (1975-76) 223-228. Esp. 224-225 [παῖς];
225 [δοξάζειν]; 227 [2,4; 10,16; 28,8]. [NTA 20, 715]

### ARIAS, Mortimer

1991   Rethinking the Great Commission. [28,16-20] — *TTod* 47 (1990-91) 410-418.

1992   & JOHNSON, A., *The Great Commission. Biblical Models for Evangelism* [28,16-20].
Nashville, TN: Abingdon, 1992, 142 p.

### ARICHEA, Daniel C., Jr.

1978   "Faith" in the Gospels of Matthew, Mark, and Luke. — *BTrans* 29 (1978) 420-424.
[NTA 23, 403]

1980   Translating the Lord's Prayer (Matthew 6.9-13). — *BTrans* 31 (1980) 219-223. [NTA 25, 73]

1981   Matthew 2.13-15, 19-23: Some Pronoun Problems. — *BTrans* 32 (1981) 243-244. [NTA 26, 86]

**ARMBRUSTER, Carl J.**

1964   The Messianic Significance of the Agony in the Garden. — *Scripture* 16 (1964) 111-119. [NTA 9, 550]

**ARMSTRONG, Edward A.**

1967   *The Gospel Parables*. London: Hodder & Stoughton, 1967; New York: Sheed & Ward, 1969, 220 p. Esp. 33-38 [13,3-9]; 40-44 [13,24-30]; 44-46 [13,47-50]; 52-55 [13,31-32]; 55-58 [13,33]; 59-61 [24,32-33]; 64-66 [6,28-30]; 71-72 [24,43-44]; 75-76 [12,43-45]; 82-83 [7,9-11]; 93-95 [11,16-19]; 98-101 [25,1-13]; 103-106 [22,1-10]; 106-108 [22,11-14]; 120-122 [24,45-51]; 125-128 [20,1-16]; 128-130 [25,14-30]; 131-132 [5,14-16]; 133 [5,22-23]; 133-135 [5,13]; 135-136 [13,52]; 138-139 [5,25-26]; 139-143 [18,23-35]; 146-149 [21,33-41]; 149-151 [7,24-27]; 154-157 [13,44-46]; 177-178 [21,28-32]; 182-185 [18,12-14]; 190-191 [9,12]; 191-195 [25,31-46].

**ARNAL, William E.**

1995a   Redactional Fabrication and Group Legitimation. The Baptist's Preaching in Q 3:7-9,16-17. — KLOPPENBORG, J.S. (ed.), *Conflict and Invention*, 1995, 165-180. Esp. 167-174 [reconstruction].

1995b   The Rhetoric of Marginality: Apocalypticism, Gnosticism, and Sayings Gospels. — *HTR* 88 (1995) 471-494. Esp. 480-492: "Sayings gospels: social history and marginality"; 492-494: "Later developments: apocalypticism and gnosticism". [NTA 41, 178]

**ARNALDICH, Luis**

1962   Influencias de Qumran en la primitiva comunidad judío-cristiana de Jerusalén. — *Concepto de la Iglesia en el Nuevo Testamento. Otros estudios* (XIX Semana Biblica Española), Madrid: Consejo Superior de Investigaciones Científicas, 1962, 135-196. Esp. 186-195: "Qumran y el Nuevo Testamento" [3,13-17].

**ARNÉRA, G.**

1984   Du rocher d'Esaïe aux douze montagnes d'Hermas. [16,18] — *ETR* 59 (1984) 215-220. [NTA 29, 107] → Chevallier 1982

**ARNOTT, Arthur G.**

1984   "The first day of unleavened...": Mt 26.17, Mk 14.12, Lk 22.7. — *BTrans* 35 (1984) 235-238. Esp. 236 [26,17]. [NTA 28, 920]

**ARON, Robert**

1966   Les origines juives du Pater. — *La Maison-Dieu* (Paris) 85 (1966) 36-40. [NTA 11, 204]

**ARTHUR, Richard L.**

1976   *The Gospel of Thomas and the Coptic New Testament*. Diss. Graduate Theological Union, California, CA, 1976.

**ARVEDSON, Tomas**

1951   Phil. 2,6 und Mt. 10,39. — *StudTheol* 5 (1951) 49-51.

1956   Några notiser till två nytestamentliga perikoper. [Some notes on two New Testament pericopes]. — *SEÅ* 21 (1956) 27-29. Esp. 27-28 [20,1-16]. [NTA 3, 77]

1964   Lärjungaskapets "demoni". Några reflexioner till Mk 8,33 par. [The disciples and satan. Reflections on Mk 8,33 par.] [16,23] — *SEÅ* 28-29 (1963-64) 54-63. Esp. 58-59 [4,10]. [NTA 10, 137]

1967   Lärjungakretsen kring Jesus. [The disciples around Jesus] — *Religion och Bibel* (Uppsala) 26 (1967) 21-36. Esp. 23-24 [11,25-30]; 26 [16,18].

1968 En nytestamentlig nyckeltext. Mt 11,25-30. [A key pericope in the New Testament] — *Religion och Bibel* 27 (1968) 35-54.

> *Das Mysterium Christi. Eine Studie zu Mt 11.25-30* (Arbeiten und Mitteilungen aus dem neutestamentlichen Seminar zu Uppsala, 7). Leipzig: Lorentz; Uppsala: Lundequistska Bokhandeln, 1937, XVI-254 p.

**ASENSIO, Félix**

1958 *Las Bienaventuranzas.* Bilbao: Mensajero del S. Corazón de Jesús, 1958, 208 p.

> S. DEL PÁRAMO, *EstE* 34 (1960) 118.

1968a Formación apostólica de los "Doce" y misión histórico-simbólica de ensayo. — *Greg* 49 (1968) 58-74. [NTA 12, 826]

1968b Trasfondo profético-evangélico del πᾶσα ἐξουσία de la "Gran Misión". — *EstBíb* 27 (1968) 27-48. Esp. 28-38: "'Poder' universal y absoluto" [28,18-20]; 38-44: "'Poder' doctrinal"; 44-46: "'Poder' judicial"; 46-48: "'Poder' en diversos campos". [NTA 14, 150]

1970 *Le Beatitudini: Preludio di Luce nel Vetero Testamento e Luce piena nel Nuovo.* Roma: Libreria editrice dell'Univ. Gregoriana, 1970, 120 p.

> P. BARBAGLI, *EphCarm* 21 (1970) 428; S. CARTECHINI, *Doctor Communis* (Roma) 23 (1970) 83-84; D. GRASSO, *CC* 121/3 (1970) 319.

1970 Los pasajes bíblicos de la "Gran Misión" y el Vaticano II. — *EstBíb* 29 (1970) 213-226. [NTA 15, 863]

**ASGEIRSSON, Jon Ma.** → IQP

**ASHBECK, David**

1971 The Literary Genre of Matthew 1-2. — *BiTod* 57 (1971) 572-578. [NTA 16, 531]

**ASHBY, Eric**

1961 The Coming of the Son of Man. — *ExpT* 72 (1960-61) 360-363. Esp. 360-361 [11,19]; 361 [18,11]; 361-362 [20,28]. [NTA 6, 455]

**ASHBY, Godfrey**

1975 The Parable of the Ten Virgins. [25,1-13] — *JTSouthAfr* 10 (1975) 62-64. [NTA 20, 92]

**ASHLEY, Benedict M.**

1979 What Do We Pray in the Lord's Prayer? — *Spirituality Today* (Chicago, IL) 31 (1979) 121-136. [NTA 24, 88]

**ASHTON, John**

1977 Le Notre Père. — *Christus* 24 (1977) 459-470. [NTA 22, 395]

> Our Father. — *Way* 18 (1978) 83-91. [NTA 23, 434]

1991 *Understanding the Fourth Gospel.* Oxford: Clarendon, 1991, XVII-599 p. Esp. 326-328 [11,25-27/Jn].

**ATENOLFI, Talamo**

1958 *I testi medioevali degli atti di S. Matteo evangelista.* Roma: Bestetti, 1958, 133 p. → de Gaiffier 1962a

**ATTAL, Francesco Salvatore**

1962 L'orazione domenicale. — *MiscFranc* 62 (1962) 135-154.

**ATTRIDGE, Harold W.**

1992 Reflections on Research into Q. — *Semeia* 55 (1992) 223-234. Esp. 224-227: "The stratigraphic model"; 227-230: "Rhetoric, reality, and Jesus"; 231-233 [Q-Thomas]. → Catchpole 1992c, R.A. Horsley 1992b, Mack 1992b

**ATWOOD, Richard**

1993    *Mary Magdalene in the New Testament. Gospels and Early Tradition* (EHS, XXIII/457).
Bern–Berlin: Lang, 1993, 235 p. Esp. 43-46 [27,55-56]; 67-95 [27,57-61]; 100-104 [28,1-8]; 127-129 [28,9-10]. — Diss. Basel, 1990 (B. Reicke – E. Stegemann).

**AUBERT, Marcel**

1953    L'adoration des Mages dans l'art du Haut Moyen Âge. — *BibVieChrét* 4 (1953) 34-39.

**AUBINEAU, Michel**

1961    Exégèse patristique de Mt. 24,12: *Quoniam abundavit iniquitas, refrigescet charitas multorum.* — *Studia Patristica* 4 (1961) 3-19; = ID., *Recherches patristiques. Enquêtes sur des manuscrits. Textes inédits. Études,* Amsterdam: Hakkert, 1974, 333-349.

1993    & LEROY, F.-J., Une homélie grecque inédite attribuée à Éphrem, "Lorsque les mages se présentèrent à Jérusalem" (BHG 1912m, CPG 4107). — *Orpheus* (Catania) 14 (1993) 40-75.

**AUDET, Jean-Paul**

1958a   *La Didachè. Instructions des Apôtres* (Études bibliques). Paris: Gabalda, 1958, XVII-498 p. Esp. 62-67.420-423 [21,9.15]; 166-186: "La *Didachè* et les évangiles" [6,5.9-13.16; 7,6.12; 10,10; 12,31; 18,15-17; 24,10-12.24.30-31.42-44].

1958b   Esquisse historique du genre littéraire de la "bénédiction" juive et de l'"eucharistie" chrétienne. — *RB* 65 (1958) 371-399. Esp. 384-390 [εὐχαριστέω]. [NTA 4, 571]
Literary Forms and Contents of a Normal Εὐχαριστία in the First Century. — *Studia Evangelica* 1 (1959) 643-662. Esp. 648-654.

**AUER, Wilhelm**

1959    Iota unum aut unus apex non praeteribit a lege... (Mt 5,18). — *BK* 14 (1959) 97-103.
[NTA 4, 646]

**AUGSBURGER, Myron S.**

1972    *The Expanded Life. The Sermon on the Mount for Today.* Nashville, TN: Abingdon, 1972, 128 p.

1982    *Matthew* (The Communicator's Commentary, 1). Waco, TX: Word, 1982, 336 p.
A. FASOL, *SWJT* 25 (1982-83) 94; G.F. SNYDER, *ChrCent* 100 (1983) 505-506.

**AUGUSTIJN, Cornelis**

1971    De Bergrede in 1523. De visie van Luther, van de radikalen en van Zwingli. [The Sermon on the Mount in 1523. The opinion of Luther, the radicals, and Zwingli] — *Rondom het Woord* (Haarlem) 13 (1971) 321-336. Esp. 321-325 [Luther]; 325-329 [radicals]; 329-332 [Zwingli].

**AUKRUST, Tor**

1979    Bergpredigt II. Ethisch. — *TRE* 5 (1979) 618-626. → G. Barth 1979

**AUNE, David Edward**

1972*   (ed.), *Studies in New Testament and Early Christian Literature. Essays in Honor of Allen P. Wikgren* (SupplNT, 33). Leiden: Brill, 1972, VIII-274 p. → Beardslee, Filson, Linton, B.M. Metzger, Reicke, Suggs

1975a   Christian Prophecy and the Sayings of Jesus: An Index to Synoptic Pericopae Ostensibly Influenced by Early Christian Prophets. — *SBL 1975 Seminar Papers,* II, 131-142. Esp. 131-135.

1975b   The Significance of the Delay of the Parousia for Early Christianity. — HAWTHORNE, G.F. (ed.), *Current Issues in Biblical and Patristic Interpretation.* FS M.C. Tenney, 1975, 87-109. Esp. 97-99 [Q].

1980a  *Jesus and the Synoptic Gospels* (TSF-IBR Bibliographic Studies Guides). Madison, WI: Theological Students Fellowship, 1980, VI-93 p.

1980b  Magic in Early Christianity. — *ANRW* II.23.2 (1980) 1507-1557. Esp. 1523-1535; 1541-1543.

1981  The Problem of the Genre of the Gospels: A Critique of C.H. Talbert's What Is a Gospel? — FRANCE, R.T. - WENHAM, D. (eds.), *Studies of History and Tradition*, 1981, 9-60. Esp. 44-48. → C.H. Talbert 1977

1983  *Prophecy in Early Christianity and the Ancient Mediterranean World*. Grand Rapids, MI: Eerdmans, 1983, XII-522 p. Esp. 157-159 [5,11-12; 23,34-36.37-39]; 168-169 [12,39]; 213 [Q: prophecy]; 222-224 [7,15-23]; 231.

1987  *The New Testament in Its Literary Environment* (Library of Early Christianity, 8). Philadelphia, PA: Westminster, 1987, 260 p. Esp. 17-45: "The genre of the gospels"; 46-76: "The gospel as ancient biography"; 238-240: "Early christian apocalypticism" [John; Q].

1991  Oral Tradition and the Aphorisms of Jesus. — WANSBROUGH, H. (ed.), *Jesus and the Oral Gospel Tradition*, 1991, 211-265. Esp. 227-236: "Types and forms of aphorisms"; 236-240: "Compositional tendencies"; 242-258: "Inventory".

1992a  Christian Prophecy and the Messianic Status of Jesus. — CHARLESWORTH, J.H., et al. (eds.), *The Messiah*, 1992, 404-422. Esp. 413-414 [3,17].

1992b  Eschatology (Early Christian). — *ABD* 2 (1992) 594-609. Esp. 604 [Mt; Q].

**AURELIO, Tullio**

1977  *Disclosures in den Gleichnissen Jesu. Eine Anwendung der disclosure-Theorie von I.T. Ramsey, der modernen Metaphorik und der Theorie der Sprechakte auf die Gleichnisse Jesu* (Regensburger Studien zur Theologie, 8). Frankfurt/M: Lang, 1977, 361 p. Esp. 116-137; 145-154 [13,44-46]; 166-177 [20,1-16]; 178-190 [25,1-13]; 191-200 [21,33-46]; 229-258 [disclosure].

**AUS, Roger D.**

1987  The Magi at the Birth of Cyrus, and the Magi at Jesus' Birth in Matt 2:1-12. — NEUSNER, J., et al. (eds.), *New Perspectives on Ancient Judaism*, Lanham, MD: University Press of America, 1987, 99-114; = ID., *Barabbas and Esther*, 1992, 95-111.

1988  *Weihnachtsgeschichte – Barmherziger Samariter – Verlorener Sohn. Studien zu ihrem jüdischen Hintergrund* (Arbeiten zur neutestamentlichen Theologie und Zeitgeschichte, 2). Berlin: Inst. Kirche und Judentum, 1988, 189 p. Esp. 11-58: "Die Weihnachtsgeschichte im Lichte jüdischer Traditionen vom Mose-Kind und Hirten-Messias (Lukas 2,1-20)".

1992a  *Barabbas and Esther and Other Studies in the Judaic Illumination of Earliest Christianity* (South Florida Studies in the History of Judaism, 54). Atlanta, GA: Scholars, 1992, XI-205 p. → 1987, 1992b

1992b  Excursus on Pilate's Wife in Matt 27:19. — *Ibid.*, 22.

1994  *Samuel, Saul and Jesus. Three Early Palestinian Jewish Christian Gospel Haggadoth* (South Florida Studies in the History of Judaism, 105). Atlanta, GA: Scholars, 1994, XVI-202 p. Esp. 129-133: "The origin, historicity, date and original language of Matt 27:51b-53".

**AVANZO, Martín**

1973  El compromiso con el necesitado en el judaísmo y en el Evangelio. — *RevistBíb* 35 (1973) 23-41. Esp. 38-41 [25,31-46/rabbinism]. [NTA 18, 476]

1974  El sentido del bautismo en el judaísmo y en el Evangelio. — *RevistBíb* 36 (1974) 309-321. [NTA 19, 1075]

1976  María en las primeras tradiciones evangélicas. — *RevistBíb* 38 (1976) 49-57. [NTA 21, 37]

**AVEMARIE, Friedrich**

1996 *Tora und Leben. Untersuchungen zur Heilsbedeutung der Tora in der frühen rabbinischen Literatur* (Texte und Studien zum Antiken Judentum, 55). Tübingen: Mohr, 1996, XIV-664 p. Esp. 589-594: "Christus, Gesetz und Leben im Neuen Testament" [Mt]. — Diss. Tübingen, 1994 (M. Hengel).

**AVILA, Mariano**

1979 *The Fall of Jerusalem and the Parousia of the Son of Man. An Interpretation of Crucial Verses in Matthew 24*. Diss. Calvin College, Grand Rapids, MI, 1979, v-129 p. (B. Van Elderen).

**AYNARD, Laure**

1990 *La Bible au féminin. De l'ancienne tradition à un christianisme hellénisé* (LD, 138). Paris: Cerf, 1990, 326 p. Esp. 195-212: "Attitude de Jésus envers les femmes".

**AYO, Nicholas**

1992 *The Lord's Prayer. A Survey Theological and Literary*. Notre Dame, IN – London: University Press, 1992, XIV-258 p. Esp. 21-52: "The Thou-petitions"; 55-107: "The We-petitions"; 111-190: "Other commentary". [NTA 37, p. 111]

**AZNAR GIL, Federico R.**

1983 Fundamentos bíblicos de la indisolubilidad matrimonial. Nota a propósito de dos libros recientes. — *Revista Española de Derecho Canonico* (Madrid) 39 (1983) 349-355. → Baltensweiler 1967a/81, Marucci 1982

# B

**BAADER, Franz Hinrich**

1987   *Die Auferstehung Jesu in der theologischen Diskussion seit dem 19. Jahrhundert.* Diss.
Erlangen–Nürnberg, 1987, XII-339 p. (J. Track). Esp. 223-242: "Themen der gegenwärtigen
neutestamentlichen Theologie im Blick auf die Auferstehung Jesu".

**BAARDA, Tjitze J.**

1960a   The Gospel Text in the Biography of Rabbula. — *VigChr* 14 (1960) 102-127. Esp. 107-
114 [1,23; 4,1; 5,45; 6,10.11.13; 11,29; 13,22-23.45-46; 17,5]. [NTA 5, 345]; = ID., *Early
Transmission of Words of Jesus*, 1983, 11-36. Esp. 16-23.

1960b   Thomas en Tatianus. — SCHIPPERS, R. - BAARDA, T., *Het Evangelie van Thomas*,
1960, 135-155.
Thomas and Tatian. — ID., *Early Transmission of Words of Jesus*, 1983, 37-50.

1967   *De betrouwbaarheid van de Evangeliën* (Cahiers voor de gemeente, 2). Kampen: Kok,
1967, ³1969, 92 p. Esp. 34-40 [sayings]; 25-34 [narratives].

1969a   *Vier = één. Enkele bladzijden uit de geschiedenis van de harmonistiek der Evangeliën.*
Kampen: Kok, 1969, 64 p. Esp. 49-64 [Diatessaron: 28,1-10].
The Resurrection Narrative in Tatian's Diatessaron according to Three Syrian Patristic
Witnesses. — ID., *Early Transmission of Words of Jesus*, 1983, 103-115.

1969b   Gadarenes, Gerasenes, Gergesenes and the "Diatessaron" Traditions. [8,28] — ELLIS,
E.E. - WILCOX, M. (eds.), *Neotestamentica et Semitica.* FS M. Black, 1969, 181-197;
= ID., *Early Transmission of Words of Jesus*, 1983, 85-101.

1973   Markus 14,11: ἐπηγγείλαντο. 'Bron' of 'Redaktie'? — *GTT* 73 (1973) 65-75. Esp. 68-72
[26,14-16]. [NTA 19, 115]

1980   Op weg naar een standaardtekst van het Nieuwe Testament? Enkele opmerkingen bij de
verschijning van de 26ste druk van 'Nestle'. — *GTT* 80 (1980) 83-137. → K. Aland [Nestle-
Aland 1979]

1983   *Early Transmission of Words of Jesus: Thomas, Tatian and the Text of the New
Testament. A Collection of Studies Selected and Edited by J. Helderman and S.J.
Noorda.* Amsterdam: V.U. Boekhandel, 1983, 333 p. → 1960a-b, 1969a-b

1986   To the Roots of the Syriac Diatessaron Tradition (T^A 25:1-3). — *NT* 28 (1986) 1-25.
Esp. 4-5 [17,24]; 5-10 [18,1]. [NTA 30, 1078]; = ID., *Essays*, 1994, 111-132. Esp. 113-114; 115-
118.

1987   The Sabbath in the Parable of the Shepherd (*Evangelium Veritatis 32,18-34*) — *NTT* 41
(1987) 17-28. Esp. 19-20 [18,10-14]; 25 [12,11-12]. [NTA 31, 1416]; = ID., *Essays*, 1994, 133-
145. Esp. 135-136; 142.

1988*   et al. (eds.), *Text and Testimony. Essays on New Testament and Apocryphal Literature
in Honour of A.F.J. Klijn.* Kampen: Kok, 1988, 286 p. → Drijvers, Hilhorst, Mussies

1988a   Geven als vreemdeling. Over de herkomst van een merkwaardige variant van Ms. 713
in Mattheus 17,26. — *NTT* 42 (1988) 99-113. [NTA 32, 1113]

1988b   "If you do not sabbatize the Sabbath...". The Sabbath as God or World in Gnostic
Understanding (Ev. Thom., Log. 27). — VAN DEN BROEK, R. - BAARDA, T. -
MANSFELD, J. (eds.), *Knowledge of God in the Graeco-Roman World* (Études
préliminaires aux religions orientales dans l'Empire romain, 112), Leiden: Brill, 1988,
178-201. Esp. 190-192 [12,11]; = ID., *Essays*, 1994, 147-171. Esp. 159-161.

1989a    Διαφωνία – συμφωνία: Factors in the Harmonization of the Gospels, Especially in the
         Diatessaron of Tatian. — PETERSEN, W.L. (ed.), *Gospel Traditions*, 1989, 133-154.
         Esp. 153-154 [Celsus]; = ID., *Essays*, 1994, 29-47. Esp. 45-46.

1989b    "A staff only, not a stick". Disharmony of the Gospels and the Harmony of Tatian
         (Matthew 10,9f.; Mark 6,8f.; Luke 9,3 and 10,4). — SEVRIN, J.-M. (ed.), *The New
         Testament in Early Christianity*, 1989, 311-333. Esp. 316-326 [Ephrem]; = ID., *Essays*,
         1994, 173-196. Esp. 178-189.

1990     De korte tekst van het Onze Vader in Lucas 11:2-4: een Marcionitische corruptie? —
         *NTT* 44 (1990) 273-287. [NTA 35, 676] → Amphoux 1987

1991*    & DE JONGE, H.J. — MENKEN, M.J.J. (eds.), *Jodendom en vroeg christendom:
         continuïteit en discontinuïteit. Opstellen van leden van de Studiosorum Novi Testamenti
         Conventus*. Kampen: Kok, 1991, 191 p. → M. de Jonge, Luttikhuizen, Noorda, van Henten

1991     "Chose" or "Collected": Concerning an Aramaism in Logion 8 of the *Gospel of
         Thomas* and the Question of Independence. [13,47-50] — *HTR* 84 (1991) 373-397. Esp.
         375-379: "*Gos. Thom.* 8 and Matt 13:47-50"; 380-386: "Thomas and Tatian"; 390-396: "Thomas and
         Matthew". [NTA 37, 1095]; = ID., *Essays*, 1994, 241-262. Esp. 242-246; 246-250; 256-261.

1992a    'He holds the fan in his hand...' (Mt 3:12, Lk 3:17) and Philoxenus. Or, How to
         Reconstruct the Original Diatessaron Text of the Saying of John the Baptist? — *Muséon*
         105 (1992) 63-86. [NTA 37, 130]; = ID., *Essays*, 1994, 197-218.

1992b    The Parable of the Fisherman in the Heliand. The Old Saxon Version of Matthew
         13:47-50. — *Amsterdamer Beiträge zur älteren Germanistik* 36 (1992) 39-58; = ID.,
         *Essays*, 1994, 263-281.

1992c    Philoxenus and the Parable of the Fisherman. Concerning the Diatessaron Text of Mt
         13,47-50. — VAN SEGBROECK, F., et al. (eds.), *The Four Gospels 1992*. FS F.
         Neirynck, 1992, II, 1403-1423. Esp. 1404: "The setting of the quotation"; 1405-1407: "The first part
         of the quotation"; 1407-1408: "The second part of the quotation"; 1408-1409: "The fisherman who cast his
         net"; 1410-1415: "A Tatianic reading?"; 1415-1422: "The other readings: Philoxenus and the Diatessaron";
         = ID., *Essays*, 1994, 219-239. Esp. 220-221; 221-223; 223-225; 225-226; 226-231; 231-238. →
         1993a

1993a    Clement of Alexandria and the Parable of the Fisherman. Mt 13,47-48 or Independent
         Tradition? — FOCANT, C. (ed.), *The Synoptic Gospels*, 1993, 582-598. Esp. 583-584: "The
         fisher of men"; 584-590: "The unique pearl and the beauty-fish"; 591-597: "The parable of the fisherman";
         = ID., *Essays*, 1994, 283-298. Esp. 284-285; 285-291; 291-297. → 1992c

1993b    Van "stof" tot "zout". Een motief in de Verhandelingen van Afrahat. [5,13] — *KerkT*
         44 (1993) 211-218.

1994a    *Essays on the Diatessaron* (Contributions to Biblical Exegesis and Theology, 12).
         Kampen: Kok Pharos, 1994, 320 p. → 1986, 1987, 1988b, 1989a-b, 1991, 1992a-c, 1993a

1994b    Matthew 18:14c. An "Extra-Canonical" Addition in the Arabic Diatessaron? — *Muséon*
         107 (1994) 135-149. [NTA 39, 155]

1994c    The Textual Apparatus in the Fourth Edition. [GNT⁴] — *BTrans* 45 (1994) 353-356. [NTA
         39, 682] → K. Aland [GNT 1993]

1995     "The Cornerstone". An Aramaism in the Diatessaron and the Gospel of Thomas? — *NT*
         37 (1995) 285-300. Esp. 286-293 [Diatessaron]; 293-300 [Th]. [NTA 40, 754]

**BAARLINK, Heinrich**

1978     De wonderen van de knecht des Heren. Traditie en interpretatie van Mat. 8:16v. en
         12:15-21. — GROSHEIDE, H.H., et al. (eds.), *De knechtsgestalte van Christus*. FS H.N.
         Ridderbos, 1978, 23-33. Esp. 24-27: "De marcinische traditie en haar verwerking"; 27-30: "De citaten
         uit Deutero-Jesaja en hun verwerking".

1984 Vervulling en voleinding volgens de synoptische evangeliën. — ID. - DUVEKOT, W.S. - GEENSE, A. (eds.), *Vervulling en voleinding. De toekomstverwachting in het Nieuwe Testament*, Kampen: Kok, 1984, 95-220. Esp. 125-169.

*Die Eschatologie der synoptischen Evangelien* (BWANT, 120). Stuttgart: Kohlhammer, 1986, VI-200 p. Esp. 67-121: "Das Matthäusevangelium" [structure, fulfilment, Israel/Gentiles, judgment].

1990 Blijvende aandacht voor het koninkrijk van God. — *GTT* 90 (1990) 65-83. [NTA 35, 321]

1992* & BAARDA, T. - DEN HEYER, C.J., et al., *Christologische perspectieven. Exegetische en hermeneutische studies. Artikelen van en voor prof. dr. Heinrich Baarlink, uitgegeven ter gelegenheid van zijn afscheid als hoogleraar in de nieuwtestamentische vakken aan de Theologische Universiteit van de Gereformeerde Kerken in Nederland te Kampen.* Kampen: Kok, 1992, 330 p. → Baarlink 1992a-c, den Heyer, Klijn

1992a "Want zie, het Koninkrijk van God is bij u." (Lucas 17,22). De tegenwoordigheid van het Rijk en de christelijke ethiek. — *Ibid.*, 28-88. Esp. 56-69: "De tegenwoordigeid van het Koninkrijk en de ethiek bij Matteüs".

1992b "En wat zal het teken zijn, wanneer al deze dingen in vervulling zullen gaan?" De vraag naar de tekenen der tijden. — *Ibid.*, 140-152. Esp. 141-144 [16,1-4]; 144-146 [12,38-40]; 146-151 [24].

1992c "Gelijk de Vader Mij gezonden heeft, zo zend Ik ook u." (Johannes 20,21). De zending in bijbels perspectief. — *Ibid.*, 153-170. Esp. 162-166 [10,1.10.14].

**BAASLAND, Ernst**

1982 Der Jakobusbrief als neutestamentliche Weisheitsschrift. — *StudTheol* 36 (1982) 119-139. Esp. 125-127 [Q/Jac], 130. [NTA 27, 1076]

1983 Jesu minste bud? Eksegetiske bemerkninger til Matteus 5,19(f). [The least of Jesus' commandments? Exegetical remarks on Mt 5,19f.] — *TidsTeolKirk* 54 (1983) 1-12. [NTA 27, 914]

**BACCHIOCCHI, Samuele**

1977 *From Sabbath to Sunday. A Historical Investigation of the Rise of Sunday Observance in Early Christianity.* Roma: Pont. Univ. Greg., 1977, 372 p.; [6]1980. Esp. 17-73: "Christ and the Lord's Day" [12,1-8.9-21; 24,20]. — Diss. Pont. Univ. Greg., Roma, 1974 (V. Monachino). *Du Sabbat au Dimanche. Une recherche historique sur les origines du Dimanche chrétien*, trans. D. Sébire. Berrien Springs, MI: Biblical Perspectives, 1977, 304 p.; (Bible et Vie Chrétienne), Paris: Lethielleux, 1984.

1984 Matthew 11:28-30. Jesus' Rest and the Sabbath. — *AndrUnS* 22 (1984) 289-316. [NTA 29, 528]

**BACHMAN, Danel W.**

1980 Joseph Smith and the Parables of Matthew 13. — *A Symposium on the New Testament. August 14, 15, 16, 1980, Brigham Young University, Provo, Utah*, Salt Lake City: Church of Jesus Christ of Latter-Day Saints, 1980, 34-38.

**BACHMANN, Michael**

1980 Johannes der Täufer bei Lukas: Nachzügler oder Vorläufer? — HAUBECK, W. - BACHMANN, M. (eds.), *Wort in der Zeit. FS K.H. Rengstorf*, 1980, 123-155. Esp. 127-129 [Q 7,27]; 146 [Q 16,16].

**BACKHAUS, Knut**

1991 *Die "Jüngerkreise" des Täufers Johannes. Eine Studie zu den religionsgeschichtlichen Ursprüngen des Christentums* (Paderborner theologische Studien, 19). Paderborn: Schöningh, 1991, XVIII-405 p. Esp. 47-112: "Das religionsgeschichtliche Verhältnis Jesu zum Täuferkreis" [11,7-11.12-13.16-19; 21,23-27.31-32; 14,1-2]; 116-137 [11,2-6]; 155-158 [9,14-17]; 170 [14,1-12]; 340-341 [3,14-15]. — Diss. Paderborn, 1989 (J. Ernst).

1995 Kirchenkrise und Auferstehungschristologie. Zum ekklesiologischen Ansatz des
Matthäusevangeliums. — ERNST, J. - LEIMGRUBER, S. (eds.), *Surrexit Dominus vere.*
FS J.J. Degenhardt, 1995, 127-139. Esp. 128-129.134-135 [28,16-20]; 131-133 [22,1-14].

**BACKHERMS, Robert E.**

1963 *Religious Joy in General in the New Testament and its Sources in Particular.*
Freiburg/Schw: St. Paul, 1963, 184 p. Esp. 53-54 [2,1-10]. — Diss. Freiburg, 1958 (C. Spicq).

**BACKUS, Iréna**

1980 *The Reformed Roots of the English New Testament. The Influence of Theodore Beza on
the English New Testament* (The Pittsburgh Theological Monograph Series, 28).
Pittsburgh, PA: Pickwick, 1980, XXII-216 p. Esp. 44-65: "Influence of Beza on the English
synoptic gospels" [1,11; 2,6.11.16; 3,8-9; 4,10.12; 5,18.21.29.47; 6,2.7.34; 7,3.14.23; 8,18.32; 9,16;
10,9.18; 11,28; 12,18; 13,11; 14,2; 15,5-6; 18,19.26; 19,28; 20,23; 21,37; 23,2; 24,31; 26,26].

1990 Deux cas d'évolution théologique dans les Paraphrases d'Érasme. La version inédite du
fragment de la Paraphrase sur Matthieu (1521) et de l'Épître de Ferdinand (1522). —
CHOMARAT, J. - GODIN, A. (eds.), *Érasme. Actes du colloque international (Tours
1986)* (Travaux d'Humanisme et Renaissance, 239), Genève: Droz, 1990, 141-151.

**BACON, Benjamin W.**

1918[R] Die "fünf Bücher" des Matthäus gegen die Juden. [English, 1918] — LANGE, J. (ed.), *Das
Matthäus-Evangelium*, 1980, 41-51.

**BACQ, Philippe**

1983 & RIBADEAU DUMAS, O., Lire une parabole: Le bon grain et l'ivraie (Mt 13). —
*LumVit* 38 (1983) 417-429.
Reading a Parable. The Good Wheat and the Tares (Mt 13). — *LumVit* 39 (1984) 181-194. [NTA 29, 103]

**BADER, Erwin**

1983 Bergpredigt – Sozialphilosophische Aspekte. — *BLtg* 56 (1983) 144-149.

**BADKE, William B.**

1990 Was Jesus a Disciple of John? — *EvQ* 62 (1990) 195-204. Esp. 195-200 [3,7-17]. [NTA 35,
104]

**BAECHER, C.**

1994 & UMMEL, M., De quelques "crucifixions" du Sermon sur la montagne. Vers une
approche christoséquente de Mt 5-7. — *Hokhma* 55 (1994) 27-50. [NTA 38, 1360]

**BAGATTI, Bellarmino**

1952 Espressioni bibliche nelle antiche iscrizioni cristiane della Palestina. — *SBF/LA* 3 (1952-
53) 111-148.

1979 La fuga in Egitto: prova per la S. Famiglia. [NT apocrypha] — *Sacra Doctrina* (Bologna)
24 (1979) 131-141. [NTA 24, 79]

**BAHR, Gordon J.**

1965 The Use of the Lord's Prayer in the Primitive Church. — *JBL* 84 (1965) 153-159. [NTA
10, 115]; = BROCKE, M. - PETUCHOWSKI, J.J. (eds.), *The Lord's Prayer*, 1978, 149-
155.

**BAILEY, James L.**

1987 & SAUNDERS, S.P., God's Merciful Community. — *CurrTMiss* 14 (1987) 325-333. Esp.
329-333 [5-7]. [NTA 32, 336]

1993 Sermon on the Mount: Model for Community. — *CurrTMiss* 20 (1993) 85-94. [NTA 37,
1250]

**BAILY, M.**

1959 Our Lord in the Scriptures, St. Matthew's Gospel. — *DoctLife* 9 (1959) 5-12. [NTA 4, 69]

**BAIRD, J. Arthur**

1963 *The Justice of God in the Teaching of Jesus* (The New Testament Library). London: SCM, 1963, 283 p. Esp. 52-53 [God as father]; 64-67 [18,23-35]; 91-92 [10,32-33]; 110-112 [Q 17,22-37: Lk]; 126-128 [21,28-32]; 129-133 [25,1-13]; 134-135 [13,24-30]; 135-137 [13,36-43]; 137-139 [13,47-50]; 139-141 [7,24-27; 18,23-35; 20,1-16]; 180-181 [6,22-23]; 181-183 [5,13-16]; 199-227 [τέλος]; 239-242 [Q 12,49-53: Lk]; 242-243 [Q 12,54-56: Lk]; 244-246 [5,25].

1969 *Audience Criticism and the Historical Jesus*. Philadelphia, PA: Westminster, 1969, 208 p. Esp. 32-53: "The identification of Jesus' audience"; 174-188: "Total listing of logia". → J.J. Herzog 1972

1971 & FREEDMAN, D.N., *A Critical Concordance to the Synoptic Gospels* (Computer Bible, 1). Wooster, OH: Biblical Research Associates, 1971, 344 p.

1982 *Rediscovering the Power of the Gospels. Jesus' Theology of the Kingdom*. Wooster, OH: Iona Press, 1982, XI-237 p.

1991 *Comparative Analysis of the Gospel Genre: The Synoptic Mode and Its Uniqueness* (Studies in the Bible and Early Christianity, 24). Lewiston, NY – Queenston, Ont. – Lampeter, UK: Mellen, 1991, IV-166 p.

**BAIRD, Michael Warren**

1982 *Jesus' Use of the Decalogue in the Synoptics: An Exegetical Study*. Diss. Southwestern Baptist Theol. Sem., Fort Worth, TX, 1982. — *DissAbstr* 42 (1981-82) 1583; *SBT* 13 (1983) 92.

**BAIRD, William**

1987 Luke's Use of Matthew: Griesbach Revisited. — *PerkJourn* 40/3 (1987) 35-38. [NTA 32, 149] → W.R. Farmer 1987b

1988 Abraham in the New Testament. Tradition and the New Identity. — *Interpr* 42 (1988) 367-379. Esp. 370 [3,9]. [NTA 33, 340]

**BAJŠIĆ, Alois**

1967 Pilatus, Jesus und Barabbas. — *Bib* 48 (1967) 7-28. Esp. 10 [27,26]; 22-23 [27,19]. [NTA 12, 97] → Soltero 1967

**BAKER, Aelred**

1964 Pseudo-Macarius and the Gospel of Thomas. — *VigChr* 18 (1964) 215-225. Esp. 217-218 [11,11/Th 46]; 219-220 [8,20/Th 86]. [NTA 10, 348] → Klijn 1965b

1965 "Fasting to the World". — *JBL* 84 (1965) 291-294. Esp. 294 [10,38/Th 55]. [NTA 10, 728]

1966 Pseudo-Macarius and Gregory of Nyssa. [7,14; 11,12; 16,24] — *VigChr* 20 (1966) 227-234. → Klijn 1965b

1968 Justin's Agraphon in the Dialogue with Trypho. — *JBL* 98 (1968) 277-287. Esp. 286 [Justin/7,22-23; 24,40-41]. [NTA 13, 712]

1969 Syriac and the Scriptural Quotations of Pseudo-Macarius. — *JTS* 20 (1969) 133-149. Esp. 139-141 [5,39-40; 7,14; 24,2; 25,40; 28,20].

1971 Lead Us Not into Temptation. — *NBlackfr* 52 (1971) 64-69. [NTA 15, 848]

1973 What Sort of Bread Did Jesus Want Us to Pray For? [6,11] — *NBlackfr* 54 (1973) 125-129. [NTA 17, 908]

**BAKER, Gordon Pratt**

1953 The Constant Meek. Blessed are the meek: for they shall inherit the earth. – Matthew 5:5. — *Interpr* 7 (1953) 34-41.

**BAKKEN, Norman K.**

1985 Teologia em Matteus. — *Estudos Teologicos* (São Leopoldo) 25 (1985) 101-108.

**BAKKER, Jean Taeke**

1989  Wereldse heiligheid. Luther over de bergrede. — GÄBLER, K.U., et al. (eds.), *Geloof dat te denken geeft. Opstellen aangeboden aan Prof. dr. H.M. Kuitert*, Baarn: Ten Have, 1989, 9-29.

**BALABANSKI, Vicky**

1997  *Eschatology in the Making. Mark, Matthew and the Didache* (SNTS MS, 97). Cambridge: University Press, 1997, XVII-241 p. Esp. 24-54: "Matthew 25:1-13 as a window on eschatological change"; 135-179: "Matthew 24: eschatological expectation after the Jewish war"; 180-205: "Didache 16 as a development in Christian eschatology". — Diss. Melbourne, 1993 (F. Moloney — G. Jenkins).

**BALAGUÉ, Miguel**

1967  La Transfiguración. [17,1-9] — *CuBíb* 24 (1967) 356-365; = *RevistBíb* 29 (1967) 51-57.58. [NTA 12, 133]

**BALCH, David L.**

1972  Backgrounds of I Cor. vii: Sayings of the Lord in Q; Moses as an Ascetic θεῖος ἀνήρ in II Cor. iii. — *NTS* 18 (1971-72) 351-364. Esp. 352-358: "Ascetic words of the Lord in Q". [NTA 17, 213]

1991*  (ed.), *Social History of the Matthean Community. Cross-Disciplinary Approaches*. Minneapolis, MN: Fortress, 1991, XXIII-286 p. [NTA 36, p. 260] → Balch, Gundry, Kingsbury, Meier, Perkins, A.J. Saldarini, Schoedel, Segal, Stark, L.M. White, Wire
A. BATTEN, *TorontoJT* 9 (1993) 117-118; R.A. BOISCLAIR, *JEcuSt* 31 (1994) 383-384; E. CUVILLIER, *ETR* 68 (1993) 577-579; M. DE BURGOS, *Communio* (Sevilla) 26 (1993) 96-97; F. LANGLAMET, *RB* 99 (1992) 765-766; W.G. MOORE, *ExpT* 103 (1991-92) 282; W.G. MORRICE, *ExpT* 103 (1991-92) 282; R.E. OLSON, *LuthQ* 7 (1993) 354-356; C. OSIEK, *CBQ* 55 (1993) 833-835; M.A. POWELL, *Interpr* 47 (1993) 311-312; G. STANTON, *ScotJT* 48 (1995) 394-396.

1991  The Greek Political Topos περὶ νόμων and Matthew 5:17, 19, and 16:19. — *Ibid.*, 68-84.

**BALDI, Donato**

1955  Nazaret ed i suoi santuari. — *SBF/LA* 5 (1954-55) 213-260. Esp. 213-215.

1960  Il problema del sito di Bethsaida e delle moltiplicazioni dei pani. — *SBF/LA* 10 (1959-60) 120-146. Esp. 131-136 [14,13-22]; 141-143 [15,32-39].

**BALDUCELLI, Roger**

1975  The Decision for Celibacy. — *TS* 36 (1975) 219-242. Esp. 223-226 [19,12].

**BALDUCCI, Ernesto**

1991  Beati i miti perché erediteranno la terra. — BALLIS, G. (ed.), *Il mondo dell'uomo nascosto*, 1991, 63-90.

**BALLANTYNE, Adrian**

1989  A Reassessment of the Exposition on the Gospel according to St Matthew in Manuscript "Alençon 26". — *RTAM* 56 (1989) 19-57.

**BALLARD, Paul H.**

1972  Reasons for Refusing the Great Supper. — *JTS* 23 (1972) 341-350. [NTA 17, 561]

**BALLESTEROS, F.**

1983  La valeur historique des récits de l'enfance. — *CahRenan* 31 (1983) 11-19. [NTA 27, 910]

**BALLIS, Giovanni**

1991*  (ed.), *Il mondo dell'uomo nascosto. Le Beatitudine*. Roma: Borla, 1991, 167 p. → Balducci, D'Agostino, Galot, Molari, Rossi de Gasperis

**BALOGH, Vince**

1959 *"Selig die Barmherzigen". Die christliche Barmherzigkeit bei Matthäus im allgemeinen und in der fünften Seligpreisung im besonderen im Lichte des Alten Testamentes.* Diss. Pont. Univ. Greg., Roma, 1959, 280 p. Esp. 1-57: "Die christliche Barmherzigkeit nach der Exegese von Mt 5,7 bei den modernen Erklärern" (= Eisenstadt: Graphisch, 1984, 67 p.); 261-280: "Die Barmherzigkeit bei Matthäus" [9,13; 12,7; 18,23-35; 23,23].

**BALTENSWEILER, Heinrich**

1959a *Die Verklärung Jesu. Historisches Ereignis und synoptische Berichte* (ATANT, 33). Zürich: Zwingli, 1959, 150 p. Esp. 125-133: "Die Verklärungsgeschichte in den Evangelien von Matthäus und Lukas". – Diss. Basel, 1958 (O. Cullmann).

1959b Die Ehebruchsklauseln bei Matthäus. Zu Matth. 5,32; 19,9. — *TZ* 15 (1959) 340-356. [NTA 4, 647]

1967a *Die Ehe im Neuen Testament. Exegetische Untersuchungen über Ehe, Ehelosigkeit und Ehescheidung* (ATANT, 52). Zürich–Stuttgart: Zwingli, 1967, 288 p. Esp. 82-119: "Das Matthäusevangelium (Kap. 19,1-12; 5,27-32)". – Diss. Basel, 1965 (B. Reicke – O. Cullmann). *Il matrimonio nel Nuovo Testamento. Ricerche esegetiche su matrimonio, celibato e divorzio* (Biblioteca di cultura religiosa, 38). Brescia: Paideia, 1981, 327 p. → Aznar Gil 1983

1967b Wunder und Glaube im Neuen Testament. — *TZ* 23 (1967) 241-256. [NTA 12, 688]

1972* & REICKE, B. (eds.), *Neues Testament und Geschichte. Historisches Geschehen und Deutung im Neuen Testament. Oscar Cullmann zum 70. Geburtstag.* Zürich: Theologischer Verlag; Tübingen: Mohr, 1972, VIII-344 p. → K. Aland, Gerhardsson 1971a, G. Klein, O. Michel, S. Schulz

**BALTHASAR, Hans Urs VON**

1981 Die "Seligkeiten" und die Menschenrechte. — *IKZ/Communio* (Rodenkirchen) 10 (1981) 526-537.

**BALZ, Horst Robert**

1967 *Methodische Probleme der neutestamentlichen Christologie* (WMANT, 25). Neukirchen-Vluyn: Neukirchener, 1967, 310 p. Esp. 164-174: "Synoptische Tradition und Paulustradition" [Q 10,2-12]. – Diss. Erlangen–Nürnberg, 1965-66 (G. Friedrich).

**BAMMEL, Ernst**

1958 Is Luke 16.16-18 of Baptist's Provenience? — *HTR* 51 (1958) 101-106.

1961a Matthäus 10,23. — *StudTheol* 15 (1961) 79-92. [NTA 7, 507] Weichet von Ort zu Ort (Matthäus 10,23). — ID., *Judaica et Paulina. Kleine Schriften*, II (WUNT, 91), Tübingen: Mohr, 1997, 140-153.

1961b A New Text of the Lord's Prayer. [6,9-13] — *ExpT* 73 (1961-62) 54. [NTA 6, 452] Ein neuer Vater-Unser-Text. — *ZNW* 52 (1961) 280-281. [NTA 6, 770]

1964 Erwägungen zur Eschatologie Jesu. — *Studia Evangelica* 3 (1964) 3-32. Esp. 6-19 [kingdom]; 19-28 [Son of Man].

1970 Das Ende von Q. — BÖCHER, O. – HAACKER, K. (eds.), *Verborum Veritas*. FS G. Stählin, 1970, 39-50.

1971 The Baptist in Early Christian Tradition. — *NTS* 18 (1971-72) 95-128. Esp. 99-101 [11,2-6]; 102-104 [21,23-46]. [NTA 16, 453]

1973 P64(67) and the Last Supper. — *JTS* 24 (1973) 189. [NTA 18, 112]

1984* & MOULE, C.F.D. (eds.), *Jesus and the Politics of His Day.* Cambridge: University Press, 1984, XI-511 p. → Bammel 1984a-b, M. Black 1970b, F.F. Bruce, Catchpole, H.St.J. Hart, Horbury, Merkel, Styler, Sweet; → Brandon 1951, 1967

1984a The Feeding of the Multitude. [14,13-21] — *Ibid.*, 211-240.

1984b    The *titulus*. [27,37] — *Ibid.*, 353-364.

1986    Die Versuchung Jesu nach einer jüdischen Quelle. — ID., *Judaica: Kleine Schriften*, I (WUNT, 37), Tübingen: Mohr, 1986, 253-256.

1988    *Jesu Nachfolger. Nachfolgeüberlieferungen in der Zeit des frühen Christentums* (Studia Delitzschiana, III/1). Heidelberg: L. Schneider, 1988, 96 p. Esp. 53-54.58-59 [16,16-19]; 74-83 [Q 22,28-30].

1993    Der Anfang des Spruchbuchs. — FOCANT, C. (ed.), *The Synoptic Gospels*, 1993, 467-475.

1995    Der Prozess Jesu in der Erklärung des Origenes. [26,57-68] — DORIVAL, G. - LE BOULLUEC, A. (eds.), *Origeniana Sexta*, 1995, 551-558.

**BAMMERSBERGER, A.**
1978    On the Gloss to Mt 26,8 in the Lindisfarne Gospels. — JAZAYERY, M.A. - POLOME, E.C. (eds.), *Linguistic and Literary Studies in Honor of Archibald A. Hill*, III (Trends in Linguistics, 9), Den Haag: Mouton, 1978, 9-12.

**BANASZEK, A.**
1993    *Kierunki rozwoju relacji o wydarzeniu w Betanii (Mt 26,6-13; Mk 14,2-9; J 12,1-11; Lk 7,36-50)* (Les directions du développement de la péricope sur l'événement de Béthanie). Diss. Warszawa, 1993, 319 p. (M. Czajkowski).

**BANDSTRA, Andrew J.**
1981    The Original Form of the Lord's Prayer. — *CalvTJ* 16 (1981) 15-37. Esp. 15-30: "The original text of the Lord's prayer"; 30-37: "The origin of the two forms of the Lord's prayer". [NTA 25, 855] → van Bruggen 1982

1982    The Lord's Prayer and Textual Criticism: A Response. — *CalvTJ* 17 (1982) 88-97. → van Bruggen 1979, 1982

**BANESCU, Marcu**
1985    The Function of Metapher in the "Sermon on the Mount". [Rumenian] — *Mitropolia Banatului* (Timisoara) 35 (1985) 15-23.

**BANG, Erik**
1992    *Matthaeusevangeliet* (Bibelvaerk for menigheden, 12). Fredericia: Lohse, 1992, 191 p.

**BANKS, Robert**
1973    Jesus and Custom. — *ExpT* 84 (1972-73) 265-269. Esp. 265-266 [17,24-27]; 267-268 [8,21-22]. [NTA 18, 63]

1974    Matthew's Understanding of the Law: Authenticity and Interpretation in Matthew 5:17-20. — *JBL* 93 (1974) 226-242. [NTA 19, 85]; = ID., *Jesus and the Law*, 1975, 203-226. → D. Wenham 1979a

1975    *Jesus and the Law in the Synoptic Tradition* (SNTS MS, 28). Cambridge: University Press, 1975, X-310 p. Esp. 90-107: "Incidental sayings and actions"; 107-173: "Debates and controversies" [9,9-13; 12,1-8]; 173-236: "Extended teaching" [5,17-20.21-48; 23,1-36]. — Diss. Cambridge, 1969 (G.W.H. Lampe). → 1974

**BANNACH, Horst**
1969    et al., *Ich aber sage euch. Sechs Bibelarbeiten über die Bergpredigt (Matthäus 5-7) beim 14. Deutschen Evangelischen Kirchentag Stuttgart 1969*. Stuttgart-Berlin: Kreuz, 1969, 160 p. [NTA 14, p. 242] → Demmer 1969

**BANTERLE, Gabriele**

1990  (trans.), *San Cromazio di Aquileia, Commento a Matteo* (Scriptores circa Ambrosium, 3/2). Milano: Biblioteca Ambrosiana; Roma: Città Nuova, 1990, 438 p.

**BARBAGLI, Pietro**

1966  Il regno di Dio come preparazione della Chiesa nei Sinottici. [4,17] — *EphCarm* 17 (1966) 31-87. [NTA 11, 1023]

1967  "Joseph, fili David, noli timere accipere Mariam coniugem tuam" (Mt. 1,20). — *De Beata Virgine Maria in Evangeliis Synopticis* (Maria in Sacra Scriptura. Acta congressus mariologici-mariani in Republica Dominicana anno 1965 celebrati, IV/4), Roma: Pont. Acad. Mariana Int., 1967, 445-463.

1968  La promessa fatta a Pietro in Mat. XVI,16-18. — *EphCarm* 19 (1968) 323-353. [NTA 14, 144]

**BARBAGLIO, Giuseppe**

1972  L'attesa della venuta del Signore (Mt 24–25). — *ParVi* 17 (1972) 353-364.

1975  Il Vangelo di Matteo. — ID. - FABRIS, R. - MAGGIONI, B., *I Vangeli*, Assisi: Cittadella, 1975, 41-618.

1978a  La parabola del banchetto di nozze nella versione di Matteo. — DUPONT, J., et al. (eds.), *La parabola degli invitati al banchetto*, 1978, 63-101. Esp. 64-75: "La parabola nel suo contesto letterario"; 75-87: "La redazione matteana della parabola"; 87-101: "Significato della parabola matteana".

1978b  I peccati nel Vangelo di Matteo. — *ScuolC* 106 (1978) 213-226. Esp. 214-217 [18]. [NTA 23, 420]

1986  L'uomo non separi ciò che Dio ha unito. — *ParSpirV* 14 (1986) 121-141. Esp. 133-138: "La prospettiva del vangelo di Matteo".

1989  Paolo e Matteo. Due termini di confronto. — PENNA, R. (ed.), *Antipaolinismo. Reazioni a Paolo tra il I e il II secolo. Atti del II convegno nazionale di studi neotestamentari (Bressanone, 10-12.XI.1987)* — *Ricerche storico-bibliche* (Bologna) 1 (1989) 5-22.

1991a  *Dio violento? Lettura delle Scritture ebraiche e cristiane.* Assisi: Cittadella, 1991. *Dieu est-il violent? Une lecture des Écritures juives et chrétiennes*, trans. D. Caldizoli & R. Arrighi (Parole de Dieu, 33). Paris: Seuil, 1994, 340 p. Esp. 172-230.

1991b  L'atteggiamento vero i beni e la Regola d'oro. [7,12] — *Credere oggi* 11 (1991) 67-79.

1992  Le genti nella genealogia di Mt 1. — *ParSpirV* 26 (1992) 101-110. Esp. 101-106 [Son of Abraham]; 106-110 [1,1-17].

**BARBI, Augusto**

1991  La giustizia di fronte a Dio e la preghiera del Padre Nostro (Mt 6,1-18). — *Credere oggi* 11 (1991) 42-66.

**BARBOUR, Robin S.**

1970  Gethsemane in the Tradition of the Passion. — *NTS* 16 (1969-70) 231-251. Esp. 238 [26,36-46]. [NTA 15, 174]

1971  Uncomfortable Words. VIII. Status and Titles. [23,8-9] — *ExpT* 82 (1970-71) 137-142. [NTA 15, 855]

**BARCLAY, William**

1956  *The Gospel of Matthew. I. Chapters I to X. II. Chapters XI to XXVIII* (The Daily Study Bible). Edinburgh: St. Andrew, 1956; Philadelphia, PA: Westminster, 1958, XXVI-412 and XII-417 p. [NTA 5, p. 110]
J. DUPONT, *LumièreV* 46 (1959) 30; W.E. HULL, *RExp* 56 (1959) 419-420; B. MCGRATH, *CBQ* 21 (1959) 534-535.

*The Gospel of Matthew. Translation with an Introduction and Interpretation*, rev. ed., 1975, XII-401 and
379 p. [NTA 21, p. 323]
*Matthäusevangelium*, trans. E. Leseberg (Auslegung des Neuen Testaments). Wuppertal: Aussaat, 1971,
352 p.
Trans. Chinese 1969.

1959    Great Themes of the New Testament. VI. Matthew xxiv. — *ExpT* 70 (1958-59) 326-
330, 376-379. [NTA 4, 391]

1960    *The Promise of the Spirit.* London: Epworth, 1960, 120 p. Esp. 21-29.

1963    *Many Witnesses, One Lord.* London: SCM, 1963, 128 p. Esp. 12-19: "The synoptic gospels".
*Viele Zeugen, ein Herr. Vielfalt des Evangelien-Zeugnisses,* trans. M. Quer (Kleine Kasseler Bibelhilfe).
Kassel: Oncken, 1968, 132 p.

1966    *The First Three Gospels.* London: SCM; Philadelphia, PA: Westminster, 1966, 317 p.
→ 1976

1970    *And Jesus Said. A Handbook on the Parables of Jesus.* Philadelphia, PA: Westminster,
1970, 224 p.

1975    New Wine in Old Wine-Skins: Xb. Law in the New Testament. — *ExpT* 86 (1974-75)
100-103. [NTA 19, 1076]

1976    *The Gospels and Acts.* Vol. I: *The First Three Gospels.* London: SCM, 1976, 303 p.
Esp. 93-102: "The hypothesis of Q"; 103-110: "The special material of Matthew and Luke"; 148-185: "The
gospel of Matthew"; 225-249: "The development of gospel criticism"; 250-278: "Redaction criticism". →
Ziesler 1985
*Introduction to the First Three Gospels. A Revised Edition of* The First Three Gospels. Philadelphia, PA:
Westminster, 1976, x-303 p. → 1966

**BAREFOOT, H.**
1962    The Ethics of Jesus. — *RExp* 59 (1962) 481-491. [NTA 7, 471]

**BARILIER, Roger**
1991    Le divorce. Étude biblique et pastorale. — *RRéf* 42 (1991) 5-43. Esp. 18-24 [5,32; 19,9].
[NTA 36, 920]

**BARIŠIC, Marin**
1979    *La Galilea e Gerusalemme negli studi recenti. I problemi nei racconti pasquali.* Diss.
Pont. Univ. Greg., Roma, 1979, VII-436 p. (É. Dhanis).

**BARKER, K.L.**
1994    & KOHLENBERGER, J.R. (eds.), *Zondervan NIV Bible Commentary.* Vol. 2: *New
Testament.* Grand Rapids, MI: Zondervan, 1994, x-1243 p.

**BARKER, William P.**
1964    *As Matthew Saw the Master.* Westwood, NJ: Fleming H. Revell, 1964, 154 p. [NTA 10,
p. 134]
S.R., *BibOr* 9 (1967) 218.

**BARKEY WOLF, Aert Gerard**
1950    *De Evangelisten en hun geschriften.* Kampen: Kok, 1950, 115 p. Esp. 19-35 [theology].

**BARKHUIZEN, J.H.**
1993    Romanos Melodos, "On the Ten Virgins" (48 Oxf. = 51sc). — *Acta Classica* 31
(1993) 39-54.

1995    John Chrysostom, *Homily 50* on Matthew 14:23-36 (*PG* 58,503-510): A Perspective on
His Homiletic Art. — *Acta Classica* 38 (1995) 43-56.

**BARNARD, Leslie W.**
1957    Matt. III.11 // Luke III.16. — *JTS* 8 (1957) 107. [NTA 2, 267]

**BARNARD, Will J.**

1986 & VAN 'T RIET, P., *Zonder Tora leest niemand wel. Bouwstenen voor een leeswijze van de evangeliën gebaseerd op Tenach en Joodse traditie*. Kampen: Kok, 1986, 188 p. Esp. 30-31 [11,28-30]; 33-36 [5,38-39]; 36-40 [23,35]; 80-110: "De evangeliën als midrasj"; 123-132 [4,1-11].

**BARNETT, Paul W.**

1977 Who Were the "Biastai" (Matthew 11:12-13)? — *RTR* 36/3 (1977) 65-70. [NTA 22, 400]

**BARNETTE, Henlee H.**

1956 The Ethic of the Sermon on the Mount. — *RExp* 53 (1956) 23-33.

**BARNI, Lorenzo**

1987 Il recente dibattito sul "logion" degli eunuchi (Mt 19,10-12). — *Studia Patavina* 34 (1987) 129-151. [NTA 32, 127]

**BARNS, John W.B.**

1960 & ZILLIAENS, H., *The Antinoopolis Papyri*, II. London: Egypt Exploration Society, 1960, XI-133 p. Esp. 6-7 [6,10-13].

**BARR, David Lawrence**

1976 The Drama of Matthew's Gospel: A Reconsideration of Its Structure and Purpose. — *TDig* 24 (1976) 349-359. [NTA 21, 715]

1987 *New Testament Story. An Introduction*. Belmont, CA: Wadsworth, 1987, XIX-379 p.

**BARR, James**

1990 The Hebrew/Aramaic Background of 'Hypocrisy' in the Gospels. — DAVIES, P.R. – WHITE, R.T. (eds.), *A Tribute to Geza Vermes*, 1990, 307-326. Esp. 308 [6,2]; 317-319 [22,18].

**BARRÉ, Michael L.**

1984 Blessed Are the Pure of Heart. [5,8] — *BiTod* 22 (1984) 236-242. [NTA 29, 94]

1986 The Workers in the Vineyard. [20,1-16] — *BiTod* 24 (1986) 173-180. [NTA 30, 1062]

**BARRERA, P.**

1993 The Indigenous Kairos and the Pagan Faith in Saint Matthew. — *International Review of Mission* (Genève) 82 (1993) 39-49. [NTA 37, 1236]

**BARRETO CÉSAR, Ely Eser**

1992 The Historical Radicality of the Reign of God: A Paradigm for Our Missionary Efforts. — *TorontoJT* 8 (1992) 148-160. Esp. 149-157: "The historical project of Jesus in Matthew's gospel". [NTA 37, 124]

**BARRETT, Charles Kingsley**

1943[R] Q: A Reexamination. [1943] — BELLINZONI, A.J., Jr., et al. (eds.), *The Two-Source Hypothesis*, 1985, 259-268.

1947[R] *The Holy Spirit and the Gospel Tradition* [1947] (SPCK Paperbacks). London: SPCK, 1966, VIII-176 p. Esp. 5-8 [1,18-25]; 25-45 [3,13-17]; 46-53 [4,1-11]; 59-63 [12,22-32]; 102-103 [28,19]; 103-107 [12,31-32]; 107-112 [22,43]; 127-132 [10,1-42].
*El Espíritu Santo en la tradición sinóptica*, trans. J.L. Aurrecoechea (Koinonia, 8). Salamanca: Secr. Trinitario, 1978, 175 p.

1954 New Testament Commentaries. II. Gospels and Acts. — *ExpT* 65 (1953-54) 143-146. Esp. 144.

1955 *The Gospel according to St John: An Introduction with Commentary and Notes on the Greek Text*. London: SPCK, 1955, XII-531 p. Esp. 14-16: "Sources: the synoptic gospels"; 34-45:

"The synoptic tradition"; [2]1978, XV-638 p. Esp. 15-17.42-54.

*Das Evangelium nach Johannes* (KEK NT). Göttingen: Vandenhoeck & Ruprecht, 1990, 608 p. Esp. 33-35.59-71.

1967 *Jesus and the Gospel Tradition.* London: SPCK, 1967; Phildadelphia, PA: Fortress, 1968, XI-116 p. Esp. 21 [16,16]; 21-22 [22,41-45]; 22 [26,63-64]; 23 [21,11]; 26 [11,27]; 80 [19,28].

1968 I Am Not Ashamed of the Gospel. — *Foi et Salut selon S. Paul (Épître aux Romains 1,16). Colloque œcuménique à l'abbaye de S. Paul hors les murs, 16-21 avril 1968* (AnBib, 42), Roma: Institut biblique pontifical, 1970, 19-41 (41-50: Discussion). Esp. 23-28 [10,32-33]; = ID., *New Testament Essays*, London: SPCK, 1972, 116-143. Esp. 121-124.

1970 Ψευδαπόστολοι (2 Cor 11.13). — DESCAMPS, A.L. - DE HALLEUX, A. (eds.), *Mélanges bibliques.* FS B. Rigaux, 1970, 377-396. Esp. 381-382 [7,15]; = ID., *Essays on Paul*, London: SPCK, 1982, 87-107. Esp. 91.

1985 Sayings of Jesus in the Acts of the Apostles. — GANTOY, R. (ed.), *À cause de l'Évangile.* FS J. Dupont, 1985, 681-708. Esp. 688 [Act 1,11/Mt 24,30; 26,64]; 690 [Act 7,52/Mt 5,12; 13,57; 23,29-32.34-36.37-39]; 693 [Act 13,51/Mt 10,14]; 696 [Act 28,26/Mt 13,13]; 700 [Act 8,19-20/Mt 10,8]; 702 [Act 15,10/Mt 11,29-30]; 703 [Act 20,29/Mt 7,15; 10,16]; 705 [Act 26,20/Mt 3,8].

**BARRETT, J. Edward**

1988 Can Scholars Take the Virgin Birth Seriously? — *BibReview* 4/5 (1988) 10-15, 29. [NTA 33, 86]

**BARRICK, W. Boyd**

1977 The Rich Man from Arimathea (Matt 27:57-60) and 1QIsaᵃ. — *JBL* 96 (1977) 235-239. [NTA 22, 93]

**BARROSSE, Thomas**

1958 Christianity: Mystery of Love. An Essay in Biblical Theology. — *CBQ* 20 (1958) 137-172. Esp. 141; 152-153; 159-160; 163-164. [NTA 3, 183]

1959 The Seven Days of the New Creation in St. John's Gospel. — *CBQ* 21 (1959) 507-516. Esp. 511-512 [Mt 16,15-19/Jn]. [NTA 4, 423]

**BARSI, Istvan Balazs**

1982 *La péricope du jeune homme riche dans la littérature paléochrétienne* [19,16-22]. Diss. Strasbourg, 1982, 2 vols., VI-486 and 145 p. (C. Munier).

**BARTA, Karen Ann**

1979 *Mission and Discipleship in Matthew. A Redaction-critical Study of Mt 10,34.* Diss. Marquette Univ., Milwaukee, WI, 1979, 180 p. — *DissAbstr* 40 (1979-80) 5477.

1988 Mission in Matthew: The Second Discourse as Narrative. — *SBL 1988 Seminar Papers*, 527-535. Esp. 528-529: "The narrative frame of Matt 9:35–11,1"; 529-533: "The story within the discourse"; 533-535: "The mission story within the gospel".

**BARTELINK, Gerhardus Johannes Marinus**

1973 Φυλακτήριον – phylacterium. — *Mélanges Christine Mohrmann. Nouveau recueil offert par ses anciens élèves*, Utrecht: Spectrum, 1973, 25-60. Esp. 29-32.47-48 [23,5].

**BARTELS, Ch.** → Ben-Chorin 1975

**BARTH, Eugene Howard**

1972* & COCROFT, R.E. (eds.), *Festschrift to Honor F. Wilbur Gingrich. Lexicographer, Scholar, Teacher, and Committed Christian Layman.* Leiden: Brill, 1972, 226 p. → K.W. Clark, Enslin, Fitzmyer, Holtzclaw

**BARTH, Gerhard**

1959 Das Gesetzesverständnis des Evangelisten Matthäus. — BORNKAMM, G., et al.,
*Überlieferung und Auslegung*, 1959, 54-154. Esp. 54-58: "Gerichtserwartung und Mahnung zum
Tun des Willens Gottes"; 58-70: "Die bleibende Gültigkeit des Gesetzes"; 70-98: "Die Auslegung des
Gesetzes"; 98-117: "Vom Wesen des Jüngerseins"; 117-149: "Gesetz und Christologie"; 149-154: "Die
Antinomisten bei Matthäus". — Diss. Heidelberg, 1955 (G. Bornkamm).
Matthew's Understanding of the Law. — BORNKAMM, G., et al., *Tradition and Interpretation*, 1963, 58-164.
Esp. 58-62; 62-75; 75-105; 105-125; 125-159; 159-164.

1965 Jüngerschaft und Kirche im Matthäus-Evangelium. — *Estudos Teologicos* (São
Leopoldo) 5 (1965) 1-15.

1975 Glaube und Zweifel in den synoptischen Evangelien. — *ZTK* 72 (1975) 269-292. Esp.
272-277 [17,20; 21,21]; 284-286 [28,17]; 287-290 [14,22-33]. [NTA 20, 419]

1978 Auseinandersetzungen um die Kirchenzucht im Umkreis des Matthäusevangeliums. —
*ZNW* 69 (1978) 158-177. Esp. 159-161 [13,24-30]; 162-165 [13,36-43]; 166-176 [18,15-17]. [NTA
23, 806]
*SelT* 19 (1980) 165-172.

1979 Bergpredigt I. Im Neuen Testament. — *TRE* 5 (1979) 603-618. Esp. 603-604: "Das
Überlieferungsgut"; 604-605: "Der Aufbau"; 605-607: "Der Inhalt"; 608-611: "Die Bergpredigt im Rahmen
des Matthäusevangeliums"; 611-615: "Auslegung- und Wirkungsgeschichte". → Aukrust 1979

1981 *Die Taufe in frühchristlicher Zeit* (Biblisch-Theologische Studien, 4). Neukirchen-
Vluyn: Neukirchener, 1981, 151 p. Esp. 13-17 [28,19]; 23-28 [3,11-12].

1992 *Der Tod Jesu im Verständnis des Neuen Testaments*. Neukirchen-Vluyn: Neukirchener,
1992, VIII-176 p.
*Il significato della morte di Gesù. L'interpretazione del Nuovo Testamento* (Piccola biblioteca teologica, 38).
Torino: Claudiana, 1995, 259 p.

**BARTH, Hans-Martin**

1990 Das Vaterunser als ökumenisches Gebet. — *Una Sancta* 45 (1990) 99-109, 113. [NTA
35, 132]

**BARTH, Karl**

1905R Der Hauptmann zu Kapernaum. [1905] — ID., *Gesamtausgabe III. Vorträge und kleinere
Arbeiten 1905-1909*, eds. H.A. Drewes – H. Stoevesandt, Zürich: Theologischer
Verlag, 1992, 46-60. Esp. 47-51.

1906R Der ursprüngliche Gestalt des Unser Vaters. [1906] — *Ibid.*, 126-147.

1908R Die Vorstellung vom *Descensus Christi ad inferos* in der kirchlichen Literatur bis
Origenes. [1908] — *Ibid.*, 244-312. Esp. 257-258.274-281 [27,51-54].

1961 An Exegetical Study of Matthew 28:16-20. — ANDERSON, G.H. (ed.), *The Theology
of the Christian Mission*, New York: McGraw-Hill, 1961, 55-71.

1965 *Das Vaterunser nach den Katechismen der Reformation*. Zürich: Evangelischer Verlag,
1965, 116 p. → McKim 1982

**BARTHÉLEMY, Dominique**

1974 Qui est Symmaque? — *CBQ* 36 (1974) 451-465. Esp. 458-460; = ID., *Études d'histoire
du texte de l'Ancien Testament* (Orbis Biblicus et Orientalis, 21), Freiburg/Schw: Éd.
universitaires; Göttingen: Vandenhoeck & Ruprecht, 1978, 307-321. Esp. 314-316.

**BARTINA, Sebastián**

1955 El milenario salernitano de San Mateo y la XIII Semana Bíblica Italiana. — *EstBíb* 14
(1955) 81-108. Esp. 102-108.

1958 Another New Testament Papyrus (P67). — *CBQ* 20 (1958) 290-291. [3,9.15; 5,20-22.25-28].
[NTA 3, 20]

1959 Jesús, el Cristo, ben David ben Abrahán (Mt 1,1). Los apellidos de la Biblia y su traducción al castellano. — *EstBíb* 18 (1959) 375-393. Esp. 383-388. [NTA 5, 74]

1960a Los macarismos del Nuevo Testamento. Estudio de la forma. — *EstE* 34 (1960) 57-88. Esp. 74-81: "Vida de Jesús"; = *Concepto de la Iglesia en el Nuevo Testamento. Otros estudios* (XIX Semana Bíblica Española), Madrid: Consejo Superior de Investigaciones Científicas, 1962, 319-349. Esp. 336-342.

1960b La red esparavel del Evangelio (Mt 4,18; Mc 1,16). — *EstBíb* 19 (1960) 215-227. [NTA 5, 709]

1962a Jesús y los saduceos. "El Dios de Abraham, de Isaac y de Jacob es 'El que hace existir'" (Mt 22,23-33; Mc 12,18-27; Lc 20,27-40; Hebr 11,13-16). — *EstBíb* 21 (1962) 151-160. [NTA 8, 951]

1962b San José y el libelo de repudio (Mt 1,18-19). — *EstJos* 16 (1962) 192-194.

1965 Reconstrucción del evangelio por las parábolas. — *EstE* 40 (1965) 319-336. Esp. 323-329 [kingdom]; 329-331 [Messiah]; 331-336 [Judaism].

1966 ¿Casa o caserío? Los magos en Belén (Mt 2,11; 10,12-14). — *EstBíb* 25 (1966) 355-357. [NTA 12, 552]

1970 Y desde Egipto lo he proclamado hijo mío (Mt 2,15; Os 11,1). — *EstBíb* 29 (1970) 157-160. [NTA 15, 842]

1971 San José en los vaticinios del Antiguo Testamento. — *EstJos* 25 = *CahJos* 19 (1971) 31-52. Esp. 45-52 [1-2/OT].

1973 Jesús y el divorcio. La solución de Tarcisio Stramare. — *EstBíb* 32 (1973) 385-388. [NTA 19, 531] → Stramare 1971b

1974 Las mujeres en la genealogía de Jesús. — *Lumen* (Vitoria) 23 (1974) 397-412.

1978 Pedro, voz de Dios el Padre. Nota a Mt 16,17. — *EstBíb* 37 (1978) 291-293. [NTA 25, 77]

1981 Pedro de Morales, s.j. (1538-1614) y su tratado "In caput primum Matthaei". — *EstJos* 35 = *CahJos* 29 (1981) 85-92.

1988 Sentido de la palabra justo (*díkaios*) en Mateo 1,19. — *EstJos* 42 (1988) 197-204.

1991 Los sueños o éxtasis de San José (Mt 1,20-24; 2,13-14.19-22). — *EstJos* 45 = *CahJos* 39 (1991) 43-53. [NTA 36, 1257]

1993 *El Padrenuestro comentado según su trasfondo semítico.* Barcelona: Balmes, 1993, 109 p.

**BARTLETT, David Lyon**

1978 Jeremiah 31:15-20. — *Interpr* 32 (1978) 73-78. Esp. 77 [2,18].

1993 *Ministry in the New Testament* (Overtures to Biblical Theology). Minneapolis, MN: Fortress, 1993, XIII-210 p. Esp. 58-88: "Ministry in Matthew".

**BARTNICKI, Roman**

1972 Prorok z Nazaretu w Galilei (Mt 21,11) (Le prophète de Nazareth en Galilée). — *RuBi* 25 (1972) 213-218.

1973 Mesjański charakter perykopy Marka o wjeździe Jezusa do Jerozolimy (Mk 11,1-10). — *RoczTK* 20/1 (1973) 5-16. [NTA 19, 113]
Il carattere messianico delle pericopi di Marco e Matteo sull'ingresso di Gesù in Gerusalemme (*Mc.* 11,1-10; *Mt.* 21,1-9). — *RivBib* 25 (1977) 5-27. [NTA 23, 853]

1976a Tekst Za 9,9-10 w perykopach Mt 21,1-11 i J 12,12-19 (Le texte de Za 9,9-10 dans les péricopes Mt 21,1-11 et Jn 12,12-19). — *StudTheolVars* 14/2 (1976) 47-66. [NTA 21, 728] → 1976b

1976b Das Zitat von Zach ix,9-10 und die Tiere im Bericht von Matthäus über dem Einzug Jesu in Jerusalem (Mt xxi,1-11). — *NT* 18 (1976) 161-166. [NTA 21, 729] → 1976a

1977 Teologia ewangelistów w perykopach o wjeździe Jezusa do Jerozolimy (Die Theologie der Evangelisten in den Berichten über den Einzug Jesu in Jerusalem). — *StudTheolVars* 15/2 (1977) 55-76. [NTA 22, 412]

1980 Ewangelia dziecięctwa Jezusa w aspekcie kerygmatycznym. [The gospels of the infancy of Jesus in their kerygmatic aspect]. — *Śląskie studia historyczno-teologiczne* (Katowice) 13 (1980) 203-231. Esp. 219-223.

1981 Ewangeliczne zapowiedzi męki, śmierci i zmartwychwstania w świetle kryteriów autentyczności logiów Jezusa (The evangelical announcements of the passion, death and resurrection in the light of the criteria for distinguishing the authentic words of Jesus). — *CollTheol* 51/2 (1981) 53-64. Esp. 57-61 [passion predictions]; 61-64 [12,38-42; 16,1-4]. [NTA 26, 445]

1984 Współczesne rozwiązania problemu synoptycznego i ich konfrontacja z badaniami nad Mt 10 (Recherches sur Matthieu 10). — *StudTheolVars* 22/1 (1984) 179-194. Esp. 179-182 [synoptic problem]; 182-189 [10]. [NTA 30, 573]

1985a *Uczeń Jezusa jako głosiciel Ewangelii. Tradycja i redakcja Mt 9,35-11,1* [The disciples of Jesus as mouthpiece of the gospel]. Warszawa: Akademia Teologii Katolickiej, 1985, 283 p. [NTA 30, p. 348] — Diss. Warszawa, 1984. → 1988
   S. Grzybek, *RuBi* 39 (1986) 174-175; J. Łach, *CollTheol* 56/4 (1986) 175-178.

1985b Tekst Mt 10,17-18 jako wyraz polemiki z judaizmem i uniwersalizmu redaktora Ewangelii Mateusza (Le texte de l'Évangile selon Matthieu [Mat. 10,17-18] comme expression d'une polémique du rédacteur de l'Évangile selon Matthieu avec le judaïsme). — *StudTheolVars* 23/2 (1985) 143-149. [NTA 31, 121]

1987a Der Bereich der Tätigkeit der Jünger nach Mt 10,5b-6. — *BZ* 31 (1987) 250-256. [NTA 32, 122]

1987b Redakcyjna praca Mateusza w Mt 9,35-11,1. [Redactional work of Matthew in Mt 9,35-11,1] — *RuBi* 40 (1987) 280-288.

1987c Das Trostwort an die Jünger in Mt 10,23. — *TZ* 43 (1987) 311-319. Esp. 310-314: "Überblick über die Meinungen der Ausleger"; 314-319: "Sinn des Logions". [NTA 32, 602]

1988 Die Jünger Jesu in Mt 9,35-11,1. — *CollTheol* 58 (special issue, 1988) 39-56. Esp. 45-48.51-53 [10,5-6; 28,19]; 50-51 [10,23]; 53-55 [10]. [NTA 34, 122] → 1985a

1989a Najnowsze rozwiązania problemu synoptycznego. [Latest solutions to the synoptic problem] — *RuBi* 42 (1989) 28-41.

1989b Powstanie Ewangelii synoptycznych według hipotezy dwóch Ewangelii w ujęciu Bernarda Orcharda. [The formation of the synoptic gospels according to the Two-Gospel Hypothesis of Bernard Orchard]. — *CollTheol* 59/3 (1989) 5-25. [NTA 35, 1115] → Orchard

1989c Problem synoptyczny dawniej i dzisiaj (Das synoptische Problem ehemals und heute). — *StudTheolVars* 27/1 (1989) 15-73. Esp. 24-35 [Two-Source hypothesis]; 35-71 [other solutions]. [NTA 34, 95]

1992 Pochodzenie Ewangelii synoptycznych w świetle tradycji starożytngo Kościoła (The origin of the synoptic gospels in the light of the statements of the Church Fathers). — *CollTheol* 62/4 (1992) 25-43. [NTA 38, 130]

**BARTNIK, Czesław**

1988 Judasz Iskariota - Historia i teologia. — *CollTheol* 58/2 (1988) 5-17. [NTA 33, 1071]
   Judas l'Iscariote, histoire et théologie. — *CollTheol* 58 (special issue, 1988) 57-69. Esp. 57-58 [10,1-4]; 59-60 [26,47-56]; 60-61.65 [26,20-25]; 62 [26,6-13]; 62-64 [27,3-10].

**BARTOLOMÉ, Juan José**

1991 Los pájaros y los lirios. Una aproximación a la cuestión ecológica desde Mt 6,25-34. — *EstBíb* 49 (1991) 165-190. Esp. 170-190: "Mt 6,25-34: un texto 'ecológico' de Jesús". [NTA 36, 1268]

1992a *La resurrección de Jesús. Experiencia y testimonios neotestamentarios* (Colección Folletos Bíblicos, 3). Caracas: Asociación Bíblica Salesiana, 1992, 48 p.

1992b O Dios o Mammona (Mt 6,24; Lc 16,13). Para un discernimiento evangélico sobre la primacía social del capital. — *Proyecto Centro Salesiano de Estudios* (Buenos Aires) 4 (1992) 333-345.

**BARTON, Stephen C.**

1992a Child, Children. — *DJG*, 1992, 100-104. Esp. 102.

1992b Family. — *Ibid.*, 226-229. Esp. 227.

1994* & STANTON, G.N. (eds.), *Resurrection. Essays in Honour of Leslie Houlden*. London: SPCK, 1994, XIII-233 p. → Barton, Stanton, F. Watson

1994a The Hermeneutics of the Gospel Resurrection Narratives. — *Ibid.*, 45-57. Esp. 51-53.

1994b *Discipleship and Family Ties in Mark and Matthew* (SNTS MS, 80). Cambridge: University Press, 1994, XIII-261 p. Esp. 125-219: "Discipleship and family ties in Matthew" [4,18-22; 8,18-22; 10,16-23.34-36.37-38; 12,46-50; 13,53-58; 19,10-12.27-30]. [NTA 39, p. 500] — Diss. London, 1991 (G.N. Stanton).
D.L. BALCH, *CBQ* 58 (1996) 532-534; C.L. BLOMBERG, *CRBR* 8 (1995) 165-167; E.L. BODE, *BTB* 25 (1995) 194-195; E. CUVILLIER, *ETR* 71 (1996) 88-89; S. GUIJARRO, *RB* 103 (1996) 100-103; F. NEIRYNCK, *ETL* 72 (1996) 238-239.

**BARTSCH, C.**

1994 Translating the Lord's Prayer: Are We Telling God What to Do? — *Notes on Translation* (Dallas, TX) 8/1 (1994) 1-3. [NTA 39, 1449]

**BARTSCH, Hans-Werner**

1947[R] Parusieerwartung und Osterbotschaft. [1947] — ID., *Entmythologisierende Auslegung*, 1962, 61-69. Esp. 64-67 [28,16-20].

1959a Die Passions- und Ostergeschichten bei Matthäus. Ein Beitrag zur Redaktionsgeschichte des Evangeliums. — HERMELINK, J. - MARGULL, H.J. (eds.), *Basileia. Walter Freytag zum 60. Geburtstag*, Stuttgart: Evang. Missionsverlag, 1959; Darmstadt: Wissenschaftliche Buchgesellschaft, [2]1961, 27-41. Esp. 30-38 [27,3-10.19.24-25.51-54.62-66; 28,2-4.9.11-15.16-20]; = ID., *Entmythologisierende Auslegung*, 1962, 80-92. Esp. 83-89.

1959b Zum Problem der Parusieverzögerung bei den Synoptikern. — *EvT* 19 (1959) 116-131. Esp. 127-129 [28,18-20]; = ID., *Entmythologisierende Auslegung*, 1962, 69-80. Esp. 77-79.

1960a Der Ansatz evangelischer Ethik im Neuen Testament. — *Kirche in der Zeit* 15 (1960) 222-224; = ID., *Entmythologisierende Auslegung*, 1962, 95-104.

1960b Feldrede und Bergpredigt. Redaktionsarbeit in Luk. 6. — *TZ* 16 (1960) 5-18. [NTA 5, 96]; = ID., *Entmythologisierende Auslegung*, 1962, 116-124.

1960c Das Thomas-Evangelium und die synoptischen Evangelien. Zu G. Quispels Bemerkungen zum Thomas-Evangelium. — *NTS* 6 (1959-60) 249-261. Esp. 251-252 [6,24/Th 47]; 253-255 [7,16-21/Th 45]; 256-257 [10,37/Th 55]; 259-260 [13,47-48/Th 8]; 260-261 [12,29/Th 21]. [NTA 5, 224] → Quispel 1959b

1962a *Entmythologisierende Auslegung. Aufsätze aus den Jahren 1940 bis 1960* (Theologische Forschung, 26). Hamburg–Bergstedt: Reich, 1962, 209 p. → 1947, 1959a-b, 1960a-b

1962b Die "Verfluchung" des Feigenbaums. [17,20] — *ZNW* 53 (1962) 256-260. [NTA 7, 791]

1963 *Wachet aber zu jeder Zeit! Entwurf einer Auslegung des Lukasevangeliums.* Hamburg–Bergstedt: Reich, 1963, 123 p. Esp. 66-76 [Q 6,20-49 (Lk)]; 109-111 [Q 19,11-27 (Lk)]; 111-112 [Q 12,22-34 (Lk)]; 114-117 [Q 17,22-37 (Lk)].

1965a *Das Auferstehungszeugnis. Sein historisches und sein theologisches Problem* (Theologische Forschung, 41). Hamburg–Bergstedt: Reich, 1965, 31 p. Esp. 11-12.15 [28,2-4].

1965b Early Christian Eschatology in the Synoptic Gospels (A Contribution to Form-critical Research). — *NTS* 11 (1964-65) 387-397. Esp. 391-392 [24,4-14]. [NTA 10, 499]

1975 Der Ursprung des Osterglaubens. — *TZ* 31 (1975) 16-31. Esp. 17-18 [Sondergut Mt]. [NTA 20, 65]

1981 Ein neuer Textus Receptus für das griechische Neue Testament? — *NTS* 27 (1980-81) 585-592. → K. Aland [Nestle-Aland 1979]

1982 Inhalt und Funktion des urchristlichen Osterglaubens. — *ANRW* II.25.1 (1982) 794-890. Esp. 812-813 [17,4].

1983 Über den Umgang der frühen Christenheit mit dem Text der Evangelien. Das Beispiel des Codex Bezae Cantabrigiensis. — *NTS* 29 (1983) 167-182. Esp. 168 [10,25]; 172-173 [20,28]. [NTA 27, 876]

1984 Traditionsgeschichtliches zur "goldenen Regel" und zum Aposteldekret. [7,12] — *ZNW* 75 (1984) 128-132. [NTA 29, 97]

**BARUCQ, André**
1961* et al. (eds.), *À la rencontre de Dieu. Mémorial Albert Gelin* (Bibliothèque de la Faculté catholique de théologie de Lyon, 8). Le Puy: Mappus, 1961, 445 p. → Duplacy, Dupont 1959b, George, J. Guillet, Perrot

**BASSARAK, Gerhard**
1981 Zur Problematik des päpstlichen Primats im Lichte des Neuen Testaments. — *ComViat* 24 (1981) 241-255. Esp. 249-253 [Peter].

1983 Es geht um den Frieden. Versuch zur Jahreslosung Matth 5,9. — *ComViat* 26 (1983) 129-141. [NTA 28, 492]

**BASSER, Herbert W.**
1985a The Meaning of 'Shtuth', Gen. R. 11 in Reference to Mt 5.29-30 and 18.8-9. — *NTS* 31 (1985) 148-151. [NTA 29, 930]

1985b Derrett's "Binding" Reopened. [16,19; 18,18] — *JBL* 104 (1985) 297-300. [NTA 30, 121] → Derrett 1983a

1990 Marcus's "Gates": A Response. [16,18-19] — *CBQ* 52 (1990) 307-308. [NTA 35, 143] → J. Marcus 1988b

**BASSET, Jean-Claude**
1982 Dernières paroles du ressuscité et mission de l'Église aujourd'hui (À propos de Mt 28,18-20 et parallèles). — *RTP* 32 (1982) 349-367. Esp. 350-359. [NTA 27, 933]

**BASSLER, Jouette M.**
1986 A Man for All Seasons. David in Rabbinic and New Testament Literature. — *Interpr* 40 (1986) 156-169. Esp. 164-165. [NTA 30, 1249]

1991 *God & Mammon. Asking for Money in the New Testament.* Nashville, TN: Abingdon, 1991, 144 p. Esp. 37-62: "Perspectives from the gospels: Radical poverty" [6,25-33; 10,5-16].

**BASTIAENS, Jean C.**
1986 Oog voor oog, tand voor tand. Over ver-geld-ing en verzoening (Mt 5,38-39). — WEREN, W. – POULSEN, N. (eds.), *Bij de put van Jakob. Exegetische opstellen* [FS M.

Rijkhoff] (Theologische Faculteit Tilburg – Studies, 5), Tilburg: University Press, 1986, 72-97. Esp. 73-76 [5,38-39/OT]; 83-86: "Mt 5,38 in het licht van Mt 5,17-20"; 86-92: "Mt 5,38-39 en 40-42"; 92-93: "Mt 5,38-39 en 43-47".

1992   Mannelijk en vrouwelijk schiep hij hen. De interpretatie van Genesis 1,27; 2,24 en Deuteronomium 24,1 in Matteüs 19,3-12. — VERDEGAAL, C. - WEREN, W. (eds.), *Stromen uit Eden. Genesis 1–11 in bijbel, joodse exegese en moderne literatuur. Aangeboden aan Prof. Dr. N.R.M. Poulssen, bij gelegenheid van zijn afscheid als hoogleraar in de exegese van het Oude Testament en het Hebreeuws aan de Theologische Faculteit Tilburg op 22 mei 1992*, Boxtel: Katholieke Bijbelstichting; Brugge: Tabor, 1992, 111-125. Esp. 111-113 [19,3-12]; 113-115 [19,4-6/Gen 1,27; 2,4]; 115-118 [19,7-8/Dt 24,1]; 118-119 [19,9]; 119-120 [19,10-12].

**BASTIAENSEN, Antoon**

1988   Le 'praeceptum aureum' dans la tradition épigraphique et littéraire. [7,12] — *RBén* 98 (1988) 251-257.

**BASTIÁN, Jean Pierre**

1980   De los pobres es el reino. — *Cristianismo y Sociedad* 18 (1980) 129-133.

**BASTIN, Marcel**

1976a  *Jésus devant sa passion* (LD, 92). Paris: Cerf, 1976, 188 p. Esp. 71-75 [Q 11,47-51]; 75-76 [17,12]; 76-77 [23,37-39]; 114-115 [8,11-12]; 159-160 [20,22-23].

1976b  L'annonce de la passion et les critères de l'historicité. — *RevSR* 50 (1976) 289-329; 51 (1977) 187-213. [NTA 21, 422/765]

1983   Jésus a fait des miracles. Textes de Mt 8. — *LumVit* 38 (1983) 370-378.
       Jesus Worked Miracles. Texts from Mt 8. — *LumVit* 39 (1984) 131-139. [NTA 29, 98]

**BASTIT, Agnes**

1995a  Conception du commentaire et tradition exégétique dans les *In Matthaeum* d'Origène et d'Hilaire de Poitiers. — DORIVAL, G. - LE BOULLUEC, A. (eds.), *Origeniana Sexta*, 1995, 675-692.

1995b  L'interprétation de l'évangile comme récit dans l'*In Matthaeum* d'Origène. — *La narrativa cristiana antica: codici narrativi, strutture formali, schemi retorici* (Studia ephemeridis Augustinianum, 50), Roma: Institutum patristicum Augustinianum, 1995, 267-282.

**BATAILLON, Louis-Jacques**

1974   Un sermon de S. Thomas d'Aquin sur la parabole du festin. [22,1-14] — *RSPT* 58 (1974) 451-456.

1983   Le sermon inédit de saint Thomas, *Homo quidam fecit cenam magnam*. Introduction et édition. [22,1-14] — *RSPT* 67 (1983) 353-369. Esp. 360-368 [edition].

**BATDORF, Irvin Wesley**

1950   *The Spirit of God in the Synoptic Gospels: An Historical Comparison and a Re-Appraisal*. Diss. Theol. Sem., Princeton, NJ, 1950, 524 p. — *DissAbstr* 38 (1977-78) 2858-2859.

1959   How Shall We Interpret the Sermon on the Mount? — *JBR* 27 (1959) 211-217. [NTA 4, 75]

1966   *Interpreting the Beatitudes*. Philadelphia, PA: Westminster, 1966, 160 p. Esp. 21-36: "The Beatitudes in Matthew"; 49-63: "The raw materials from the Christian tradition" [Q]; 85-124: "The Beatitudes in the teaching of Jesus".
       B. MCGRATH, *CBQ* 28 (1966) 337-338; J.T. MILLER, *RelLife* 36 (1967) 145-147.

**BATES, William R.**

1951 *The Relation of the Messianic Kingdom to the Kingdom of God in Matthew.* Diss. Southern Baptist Theol. Sem., Louisville, KY, 1951.

**BATEY, Richard A.**

1970* (ed.), *New Testament Issues* (Harper Forum Books). New York – Evanston, IL: Harper & Row; London: SCM, 1970, 241 p. → Beare 1968a, Hunter 1960, J. Jeremias 1960

1971 *New Testament Nuptial Imagery.* Leiden: Brill, 1971, X-82 p. Esp. 41-44 [22,1-14]; 45-47 [25,1-13]; 59-62 [9,14-15]. — Diss. Vanderbilt Univ., Nashville, TN, 1961 (L.E. Keck).

**BATTAGLIA, Oscar**

1985 *Le parabole del Regno. Ricerca esegetica e pastorale sulle sette parabole del cap. 13 di Matteo* (Ricerche teologiche). Assisi: Cittadella, 1985, 219 p.
E. RASCO, *CC* 138/2 (1987) 513; A. ROLLA, *Asprenas* 33 (1986) 336-337.

**BATTEN, Alicia**

1994 More Queries for Q: Women and Christian Origins. — *BTB* 24 (1994) 44-51. [NTA 39, 1435]

**BATTO, Bernard F.**

1987 The Sleeping God: An Ancient Near Eastern Motif of Divine Sovereignty. — *Bib* 68 (1987) 153-177. Esp. 172-176 [8,23-27; 14,22-33].

**BAUCKHAM, Richard J.**

1977 Synoptic Parousia Parables and the Apocalypse. — *NTS* 23 (1976-77) 162-176. Esp. 163-165 [10,32]; 165-169 [24,42-51]. [NTA 21, 528]; = ID., *The Climax of Prophecy*, 1993, 92-112. Esp. 94-96; 96-103. → 1983b

1978 The Sonship of the Historical Jesus in Christology. — *ScotJT* 31 (1978) 245-260. Esp. 251-257 [11,27]. [NTA 23, 232]

1983a The Liber Antiquitatum Biblicarum of Pseudo-Philo and the Gospels as 'Midrash'. — FRANCE, R.T. – WENHAM, D. (eds.), *Studies in Midrash and Historiography*, 1983, 33-76. Esp. 62-68: "LAB and the gospels".

1983b Synoptic Parousia Parables Again. — *NTS* 29 (1983) 129-134. Esp. 132-133 [24,42-51; 25,1-13]. [NTA 27, 681]; = ID., *The Climax of Prophecy*, 1993, 112-117. Esp. 115-116. → 1977

1985a The Son of Man: 'A Man in My Position' or 'Someone'? — *JSNT* 23 (1985) 23-33; 26 (1986) 118. Esp. 25 [8,20; 9,6; 11,19; 12,32]; 26.30 [10,32-33]; 31 [26,64]. [NTA 29, 1090r]; = EVANS, C.A. – PORTER, S.E. (eds.), *The Historical Jesus*, 1995, 245-255. Esp. 247-248; 249.254; 254. → P.M. Casey 1987, Lindars 1983, 1985

1985b The Study of Gospel Traditions Outside the Canonical Gospels: Problems and Prospects. — WENHAM, D. (ed.), *The Jesus Tradition Outside the Gospels*, 1985, 369-403. Esp. 377-383: "The sources of the canonical gospels" [pre-synoptic tradition, Q, Matthew's special source, Ur-Gospel]; 386-398: "The problems of establishing dependence: Ignatius and Matthew as a paradigm case".

1985c The Two Fig Tree Parables in the Apocalypse of Peter. — *JBL* 104 (1985) 269-287. Esp. 271-278 [24/ApocPeter 1-2]; 278-280 [24,32-36]; 283-287 [Mt/ApocPeter]. [NTA 30, 454] → 1988a

1986 The Coin in the Fish's Mouth. — WENHAM, D. – BLOMBERG, C. (eds.), *The Miracles of Jesus*, 1986, 219-252. Esp. 219-225: "Preliminary exegesis"; 225-228: "Place in Matthew's gospel"; 228-230: "Matthew's source"; 230-233: "Verses 25-26 as an authentic saying of Jesus"; 233-237: "Verse 27 and the historical Jesus"; 237-244: "Parallels in folklore and rabbinic literature".

1987 The Parable of the Vine: Rediscovering a Lost Parable of Jesus. — *NTS* 33 (1987) 84-101. Esp. 92-94 [13,31-32; 15,13]. [NTA 31, 1403]

1988a The Apocalypse of Peter: An Account of Research. — *ANRW* II.25.6 (1988) 4712-4750. Esp. 4723-4724. → 1985c

1988b  Jesus' Demonstration in the Temple. — LINDARS, B. (ed.), *Law and Religion. Essays on the Place of the Law in Israel and Early Christianity by Members of the Ehrhardt Seminar of Manchester University*, Cambridge: Clarke, 1988, 72-89.

1990  *Jude and the Relatives of Jesus in the Early Church.* Edinburgh: Clark, 1990, IX-459 p. Esp. 6-19; 49-50 [12,46-50].

1993  *The Climax of Prophecy. Studies on the Book of Revelation.* Edinburgh: Clark, 1993, XVIII-550 p. → 1977, 1983b

1994  The Brothers and Sisters of Jesus: An Epiphanian Response to John P. Meier. — *CBQ* 56 (1994) 686-700. Esp. 694-695 [12,46; 13,55]. [NTA 40, 115] → Meier 1991a

1995a  The Messianic Interpretation of Isa. 10:34 in the Dead Sea Scrolls, 2 Baruch and the Preaching of John the Baptist. — *Dead Sea Discoveries* (Leiden) 2 (1995) 202-216. Esp. 210-216 [3,10]. [NTA 40, 1154]

1995b  Tamar's Ancestry and Rahab's Marriage: Two Problems in the Matthean Genealogy. — *NT* 37 (1995) 313-329. Esp. 314-320 [1,3]; 320-328 [1,5]. [NTA 40, 814]

**BAUDLER, Georg**

1986  *Jesus im Spiegel seiner Gleichnisse. Das erzählerische Lebenswerk Jesu – ein Zugang zum Glauben.* Stuttgart: Calwer; München: Kösel, 1986, 330 p. Esp. 60-61.238-241.288-289 [25,31-46]; 79-88 [13,31-32]; 88-103.184-186.282-284 [18,23-35]; 124-125.165-167 [22,2-10]; 124-125.161-162.278-279 [25,1-13]; 158-159 [13,45-46]; 182-184.280-281 [20,1-15]; 187-190 [25,14-30]; 207-208 [12,43-45]; 236-237 [13,47-48]; 266-267 [13,33]; 284-285 [11,16-19].

**BAUDOZ, Jean-François**

1995  *Les miettes de la table. Étude synoptique et socio-religieuse de Mt 15,21-28 et de Mc 7,24-30* (Études bibliques, NS 27). Paris: Gabalda, 1995, 451 p. Esp. 25-55: "Dépendance ou indépendance littéraire des deux péricopes?"; 56-341: "La syro-phénicienne de Marc et la cananéenne de Matthieu: lecture comparée des deux textes"; 342-400: "L'histoire des traditions et la diversité des pratiques ecclésiales à l'endroit des païens". [NTA 40, p. 138] — Diss. Paris, 1993 (C. Perrot).
    D.J. GRAHAM, *CRBR* 9 (1996) 178-180; C. MANGAN, *CBQ* 58 (1996) 534-535; F. NEIRYNCK, *ETL* 71 (1995) 457-459.

**BAUER, Bruno**

1850R  *Kritik der Evangelien und Geschichte ihres Ursprungs* [1850-51, 3 vols.]. Esp. II, 160-198: "Die Compilation des Matthäus"; III, 310-316: "Das Matthäusevangelium". Aalen: Scientia, 1983, 2 vols., XVI-366+295; 340+148 p.

**BAUER, David R.**

1988a  *The Structure of Matthew's Gospel. A Study in Literary Design* (JSNT SS, 31; Bible and Literature Series, 15). Sheffield: Almond, 1988, 182 p. Esp. 21-55.150-154: "Survey of investigations into Matthew's structure"; 57-63.154-155: "The structure of Matthew: repetition of comparison" [disciples]; 65-71.155-156: "The structure of Matthew: repetition of contrast" [opponents]; 73-108.156-158: "The structure of Matthew: repetition of particularization and climax with preparation and causation" [Messiah]; 109-128.158-161: "Climax with inclusio" [28,16-20]; 129-134.161: "The structure of Matthew: relationship between great discourses and narrative framework". [NTA 33, p. 242] — Diss. Union Theol. Sem., Richmond, VA, 1985 (J.D. Kingsbury). → Neirynck 1988c
    E. CUVILLIER, *ETR* 64 (1989) 289-290; D.E. GARLAND, *Interpr* 44 (1990) 89.92; D.E. GREEN, *JTS* 41 (1990) 175-178; R.H. GUNDRY, *Bib* 71 (1990) 126-129; E. KRENTZ, *CurrTMiss* 19 (1992) 56-57; A. LINCOLN, *JSNT* 41 (1991) 120; F. NEIRYNCK, *ETL* 65 (1989) 163-164; M.A. POWELL, *CBQ* 52 (1990) 338-339; J.-M. ROUSÉE, *RB* 96 (1989) 317; W. SCHENK, *TLZ* 114 (1989) 812-813; J.S. SIKER, *JBL* 109 (1990) 536-538; S.H. TRAVIS, *ExpT* 100 (1988-89) 471-472; B.T. VIVIANO, *RB* 97 (1990) 616-617.

1988b  The Interpretation of Matthew's Gospel in the Twentieth Century. — *Summary of the Proceedings of the American Theological Library Association* (St. Meinrad, IN) 42 (1988) 119-145. [NTA 33, 1106]

1990    The Literary Function of the Genealogy in Matthew's Gospel. — *SBL 1990 Seminar Papers*, 451-468. Esp. 453-464: "The structure of the genealogy"; 464-468: "The genealogy as introduction to the gospel".
The Literary and Theological Function... — ID. - POWELL, M.A. (eds.), *Treasures New and Old*, 1996, 129-159. Esp. 133-152; 152-159.

1992a   The Major Characters of Matthew's Story. Their Function and Significance. — *Interpr* 46 (1992) 357-367. Esp. 357-361: "Jesus"; 361-363: "Disciples"; 363-366: "Israel". [NTA 37, 698]

1992b   Matthew. — CARPENTER, E.E. - McCOWN, W. (eds.), *Asbury Bible Commentary*, Grand Rapids, MI: Zondervan, 1992.

1992c   Son of David. — *DJG*, 1992, 766-769. Esp. 768-769.

1992d   Son of God. — *Ibid.*, 769-775. Esp. 773-774.

1995    The Kingship of Jesus in the Matthean Infancy Narrative: A Literary Analysis. — *CBQ* 57 (1995) 306-323. [NTA 40, 815]

1996*   & POWELL, M.A. (eds.), *Treasures New and Old. Recent Contributions to Matthean Studies* (SBL Symposium Series, 1). Atlanta, GA: Scholars, 1996, XIV-454 p. [NTA 40, p. 518] → J.C. Anderson 1988, D.R. Bauer 1990, 1996, Garland 1987a, Hagner 1985c, A.-J. Levine, Luz, M.A. Powell 1991, Pregeant 1990, Schnackenburg 1989b, B.B. Scott 1993b, Snodgras 1988, D.J. Weaver 1992b
R. DORAN, *CBQ* 59 (1996) 600-602; F. LANGLAMET, *RB* 104 (1997) 135-136; F. NEIRYNCK, *ETL* 72 (1996) 446-447.

1996    Introduction. — *Ibid.*, 1-25.

**BAUER, Erika**

1966    (ed.), *Paternoster-Auslegung. Zugeschrieben Jakob von Jüterborg. Verdeutscht von Heinrich Haller* (Lunder germanistische Forschungen, 39). Lund: Gleerup; København: Munksgaard, 1966, 299 p. → Guyot 1969

**BAUER, Johannes Baptist**

1951    "Quod si sal infatuatum fuerit". (Mt 5,13; Mc 9,50; Lc 14,34). — *VD* 29 (1951) 228-230.

1953a   Num beatitudinis accidentalis varii gradus Scripturarum testimoniis probari queant? — *VD* 31 (1953) 274-281.

1953b   "Ostiarii inferorum". [16,18] — *Bib* 34 (1953) 430-431. → Eppel 1950

1956a   Libera nos a malo (Mt 6,13). — *VD* 34 (1956) 12-15. [NTA 1, 40]

1956b   Salvator nihil medium amat (cf. Apc 3,15. Mt 25,29 par. Hb 4,12). — *Ibid.*, 352-355.

1957a   Ehescheidung wegen Ehebruch? Die Ehebruchsklauseln Mt. 5,32 und 19,9. — *BLtg* 24 (1956-57) 118-121. → 1965a, 1966

1957b   Nova et Vetera, Mt. 13,52. — *Oberrheinisches Pastoralblatt* (Sankt Peter, Schwarzw.) 58 (1957) 163-166.

1957c   Πῶς in der griechischen Bibel. — *NT* 2 (1957-58) 81-91. Esp. 82-84. [NTA 3, 317]; = ID., *Scholia Biblica et Patristica*, 1972, 29-39. Esp. 30-32.

1959    De agraphis genuinis evangelii secundum Thomam coptici. — *VD* 37 (1959) 129-146. Esp. 139-140 [23,13/Th 40]; 141-142 [5,10-12/Th 59]; 144. [NTA 4, 530]

1960    Sermo Peccati. Hieronymus und das Nazaräerevangelium. — *BZ* 4 (1960) 122-128. [NTA 5, 82]; = ID., *Scholia Biblica et Patristica*, 1972, 226-232.

1961a   Gnadenlohn oder Tageslohn (Mt 20,8-16)? — *Bib* 42 (1961) 224-228. [NTA 6, 458]; = ID., *Scholia Biblica et Patristica*, 1972, 62-66.

1961b   Das milde Joch und die Ruhe, Matth. 11,28-30. — *TZ* 17 (1961) 99-106. [NTA 6, 127]; = ID., *Scholia Biblica et Patristica*, 1972, 53-60.

1961c   Variantes de traduction sur l'Hébreu? [10,16] — *Muséon* 74 (1961) 435-439. [NTA 7, 54];
        = ID., *Scholia Biblica et Patristica*, 1972, 111-115.

1962    De "labore" Salvatoris. Evang. Thom. Log. 28. 98. 107. — *VD* 40 (1962) 123-130.
        Esp. 128-130 [22,1-10/Th 64]. [NTA 7, 641] → Hunzinger 1960

1965a   Die matthäische Ehescheidungsklausel (Mt 5,32 und 19,9). — *BLtg* 38 (1964-65) 101-
        106. [NTA 9, 906]; = ID., *Evangelienforschung*, 1968, 147-158. → 1957a, 1966

1965b   De veste nuptiali (Matth. 22,11-13). — *VD* 43 (1965) 15-18. [NTA 10, 121]; = ID.,
        *Scholia Biblica et Patristica*, 1972, 69-72.

1966    De coniugali foedere quid dixerit Matthaeus? (Mt 5,31s; 19,3-9). — *VD* 44 (1966) 74-
        78. [NTA 11, 201] → 1957a, 1965a

1968*   (ed.), *Evangelienforschung. Ausgewählte Aufsätze deutscher Exegeten*. Graz: Styria,
        1968, 315 p. → J.B. Bauer 1965a, W. Pesch 1963, J. Schmid 1951, 1953, 1959, Schnackenburg 1964a,
        Trilling 1960b

1972    *Scholia Biblica et Patristica*. Graz: Akademische Druck- und Verlagsanstalt, 1972, VII-
        293 p. → 1957c, 1960, 1961a-c, 1965b

1974    Einige christliche Stücke aus der Wiener Papyrussammlung. [26,26-27] — *Archiv für
        Papyrusforschung* (Leipzig) 22-23 (1974) 216-217.

1980    Bemerkungen zu den mattäischen Unzuchtsklauseln (Mt 5,32; 19,9). — ZMIJEWSKI, J.
        — NELLESSEN, E. (eds.), *Begegnung mit dem Wort*. FS H. Zimmermann, 1980, 23-33.

1987    Le texte biblique et son interprétation chez le Pseudo-Hilaire (*Libellus*). — MARAVAL,
        P., et al., *Lectures anciennes de la Bible* [FS André Benoît] (Cahiers de Biblia
        Patristica, 1), Strasbourg: Centre d'analyse et de documentation patristiques, 1987, 261-
        281.
        Der Bibeltext und seine Interpretation bei Pseudo-Hilarius (*Libellus*). — ID., *Studien*, 1997, 73-93.

1989a   Christus sidereus. Die Tempelaustreibung, Hieronymus und das Nazaräerevangelium.
        — KERTELGE, K., et al. (eds.), *Christus bezeugen*. FS W. Trilling, 1989, 257-266. Esp.
        263-266; = ID., *Studien*, 1997, 226-241.

1989b   Vidisti fratrem, vidisti dominum tuum (Agraphon 144 Resch und 126 Resch). [25,40] —
        *Zeitschrift für Kirchengeschichte* (Stuttgart) 100 (1989) 71-76; = ID., *Studien*, 1997,
        37-44.

1992    "Josef gedachte Maria heimlich zu verlassen" (Mt 1,19; AscIs 11,3). — *TZ* 48 (1992)
        218-220. [NTA 37, 531]; = ID., *Studien*, 1997, 205-208.

1997    *Studien zu Bibeltext und Väterexegese*, ed. A. Felber (Stuttgarter Biblische
        Aufsatzbände, 23). Stuttgart: Katholisches Bibelwerk, 1997, 288 p. → 1987, 1989a-b, 1992

        **BAUER, Rudolf**

1959    Ihre Engel schauen immerfort? [18,10] — *TPQ* 107 (1959) 321-323.

        **BAUER, Ulrich**

1988    *"Rechtssätze" im Neuen Testament?* Eine form- und gattungsgeschichtliche
        *Untersuchung zu den Synoptikern*. Diss. Bamberg, 1988 (P. Hoffmann).

        **BAUER, Walter**

1914R   Matth. 19,12 und die alten Christen. [1914] — ID., *Aufsätze und kleine Schriften*, 1967,
        253-263.

1917R   Das Gebot der Feindesliebe und die alten Christen. [1917] — ID., *Aufsätze und kleine
        Schriften*, 1967, 225-252.

1952 *Griechisch-deutsches Wörterbuch zu den Schriften des Neuen Testaments und der übrigen urchristlichen Literatur* [²1928; ³1937]. Berlin: Töpelmann, ⁴1952, XVI-1634 col.; ⁵1958, XV-1780 col. → K. Aland [Bauer-Aland 1988]
*A Greek-English Lexicon of the New Testament and Other Early Christian Literature*, trans. and adapted by W.F. Arndt & F.W. Gingrich. Cambridge: University Press; Chicago, IL: University Press, 1957 [German ⁴1952], 1969, XXXVII-909 p.; revised by F.W. Gingrich & F.W. Danker, ²1979 [German ⁵1958], XL-900 p. → Alsop 1972

1959 → A. Meyer 1959

1967 *Aufsätze und kleine Schriften*, ed. G. Strecker. Tübingen: Mohr, 1967, XI-341 p. → 1914, 1917

**BAUERNFEIND, Otto**

1956 *Eid und Frieden. Fragen zur Anwendung und zum Wesen des Eides* (Forschungen zur Kirchen- und Geistesgeschichte, 2). Stuttgart: Kohlhammer, 1956, 187 p. Esp. 94-100 [5,33-37; 23,16-22].

1965 Der Eid in der Sicht des Neuen Testaments. [5,33-37] — BETHKE, H. (ed.), *Eid, Gewissen, Treuepflicht*, Frankfurt/M: Stimme, 1965, 79-112.

**BAUM, Gregory**

1961 *The Jews and the Gospel. A Re-examination of the New Testament*. Westminster, MD: Newman, 1961, VIII-288 p.; London: Bloomsbury, 1961, 290 p.
*Is the New Testament Anti-Semitic? A Re-Examination of the New Testament*. New York: Paulist, 1965, 350 p. Esp. 100-108: "The Gospel of saint Matthew: Matthew 27:25".
*Die Juden und das Evangelium. Eine Überprüfung des Neuen Testaments*, trans. V.E. Strakosch. Einsiedeln–Köln: Benziger, 1963, 381 p.
*Les juifs et l'évangile*, trans. J. Mignon (LD, 41). Paris: Cerf, 1965, 330 p. Esp. 51-91: "L'évangile de saint Matthieu".
*Los judíos y el evangelio*, trans. J. Álvarez del Carmen. Madrid: Aguilar, 1965, XXVII-384 p.

**BAUMAN, Clarence**

1985 *The Sermon on the Mount. The Modern Quest for Its Meaning*. Macon, GA: Mercer, 1985, X-440 p. Esp. 11-35 [L. Tolstoy]; 37-51 [W. Herrmann]; 53-73 [L. Ragaz]; 75-93 [F. Naumann]; 95-110 [J. Weiß]; 111-128 [A. Schweitzer]; 129-138 [J. Müller]; 139-152 [O. Baumgarten]; 153-161 [K. Bornhäuser]; 163-175 [G. Wünsch]; 177-185 [C. Stange]; 187-196 [G. Kittel]; 197-207 [R. Bultmann]; 209-228 [H. Windisch]; 229-248 [M. Dibelius]; 249-274 [D. Bonhoeffer]; 275-289 [E. Thurneysen]; 291-298 [J. Jeremias]; 299-304 [W. Städeli]; 331-340 [G. Eichholz; U. Luck; H.-T. Wrege; P. Pokorný]; 383-396: "Jesus and the law". [NTA 30, p. 349]
C. MERCER, *RelStR* 18 (1992) 141.

**BAUMANN, Maurice**

1993 *Les paraboles et le langage de changement*. — *ETR* 68 (1993) 185-202. Esp. 192-194 [20,1-16]. [NTA 38, 131]

**BAUMANN, Richard**

1950 *Des Petrus Bekenntnis und Schlüssel*. Stuttgart: Schwabenverlag, 1950, 232 p. Esp. 106-114: "Matthäus 16 – Eigentum der römischen Kirche". → Cipriani 1953

1956 *Der Fels der Welt. Kirche des Evangeliums und Papsttum*. Tübingen: Katzmann, 1956, 458 p. Esp. 156-167: "Welche Kirche hat die Verheißung von Matthäus 16?".

1988 *Was Christus dem Petrus verheißt. Eine Entdeckung im Urtext von Matthäus 16* (Via, Veritas, Vita). Stein am Rhein: Christiana, 1988, 112 p. [NTA 35, p. 99]

**BAUMANN, Rolf**

1964 *Heil euch, ihr Armen!* Die ursprüngliche Botschaft der Seligpreisungen. — *BK* 19 (1964) 79-85. [NTA 9, 524]

1966 Evangelium an Allerheiligen (Mt 5,3-12). Das Heil und die Armen. — *Am Tisch des Wortes* (Stuttgart) 13 (1966) 33-43.

1973    Der Raum der Freiheit. Zum Wandel von Bedingungen der Nachfolge. — FELD, H. -
NOLTE, J. (eds.), *Wort Gottes in der Zeit.* FS K.H. Schelkle, 1973, 436-450. Esp. 438-
439 [19,10-12]; 440-442 [10,37; 19,27-30]; 442-444 [10,38; 16,24]; 444-445 [10,39; 16,25].

1986    Bergpredigt und Weltfrieden. — *Orientierung* 50 (1986) 5-9, 20-23, 89-93.

1994    Die produktive Spannung von "Liebe" und "Gerechtigkeit". Annäherungen an ein
ungelöstes Problem. — SCHOENBORN, U. - PFÜRTNER, S. (eds.), *Der bezwingende
Vorsprung des Guten. Exegetische und theologische Werkstattberichte. FS Wolfgang
Harnisch* (Theologie, 1), Münster–Hamburg: LIT, 1994, 79-93. Esp. 87-89 [5,43-44; 7,12];
90-93 [7,21].

**BAUMBACH, Günther**

1963    *Das Verständnis des Bösen in den synoptischen Evangelien* (Theologische Arbeiten, 19).
Berlin: Evangelische Verlagsanstalt, 1963, 236 p. Esp. 53-121: "Das Verständnis des Bösen im
Matthäus-Evangelium". — Diss. Berlin, 1961.

1967    Die Mission im Matthäus-Evangelium. — *TLZ* 92 (1967) 889-893. [NTA 13, 145]

1968    Jesus und die Pharisäer. Ein Beitrag zur Frage nach dem historischen Jesus. — *BLtg*
41 (1968) 112-131. [NTA 13, 107]
Jesus and the Pharisees. — *TDig* 17 (1969) 233-240.

1971    Das Sadduzäerverständnis bei Josephus Flavius und im Neuen Testament. — *Kairos* 13
(1971) 17-37. Esp. 28-35.

1973    Die Stellung Jesu im Judentum seiner Zeit. — *FZPT* 20 (1973) 285-305. Esp. 292-294
[18,23-35]. [NTA 19, 66]

1975    Das Verständnis von *eirēnē* im Neuen Testament. — *TVers* 5 (1975) 33-52. Esp. 34-35
[10,34].

1982    Zum gegenwärtigen Stand der Interpretation neutestamentlicher Abendmahlstexte. —
*Die Zeichen der Zeit* (Berlin) 36 (1982) 169-175.

1983    Antijudaismus im Neuen Testament – Fragestellung und Lösungsmöglichkeit. — *Kairos*
25 (1983) 68-85. Esp. 72-73. [NTA 28, 687]

1989    Randbemerkungen zu Jesu Judaizität. — KERTELGE, K., et al. (eds.), *Christus
bezeugen.* FS W. Trilling, 1989, 74-83. Esp. 75-79.

**BAUM-BODENBENDER, Rosel**

1984    *Hoheit in Niedrigkeit. Johanneische Christologie im Prozeß Jesu vor Pilatus (Joh
18,27–19,16a)* (FzB, 49). Würzburg: Echter, 1984, XI-394 p. Esp. 176-218: "Vergleich der
johanneischen Erzählung mit den entsprechenden synoptischen Parallelen" [27,1-2.11-27/Jn 18,28–19,16].
— Diss. Mainz, 1982 (L. Schenke). → Sabbe 1991c

**BAUMEISTER, Theofried**

1980    *Die Anfänge der Theologie des Martyriums* (Münsterische Beiträge zur Theologie, 45).
Münster: Aschendorff, 1980, XI-356 p. Esp. 66-76: "Jesus und seine Jünger"; 76-81: "Abweisung
und Verfolgung der Boten Jesu nach der Logienquelle" [Q 10,2-12; 11,47-51]; 90-107: "Prophetengeschick
und Leidensnachfolge im Mattäusevangelium" [5,10-12; 10,17-20.26-33; 16,24-27; 21,28–22,14; 23,29-39].
— Diss. Münster, 1976 (B. Kötting).

**BAUMERT, Norbert**

1984    *Ehelosigkeit und Ehe im Herrn. Eine Neuinterpretation von 1 Kor 7* (FzB, 47).
Würzburg: Echter, 1984, 576 p. Esp. 489-490 [10,19]; 490-498 [6,25-34].

1992    *Antifeminismus bei Paulus? Einzelstudien* (FzB, 68). Würzburg: Echter, 1992, 484 p.
Esp. 207-260: "Die Freiheit der/des unschuldig Geschiedenen: 1 Kor 7,10f" [5,28.32; 19,9]. → Neirynck
1986f, 1996a.c

**BAUMGARDT, David**

1991 Kaddish and the Lord's Prayer. — *Jewish Bible Quarterly (Dor LeDor)* (Jerusalem) 19 (1991) 164-169. [NTA 35, 1128]

**BAUMSTARK, Anton**

1956 Die Zitate des Mt.-Evangeliums aus dem Zwölfprophetenbuch. [2,6.15; 21,5; 26,31; 27,9-10] — *Bib* 37 (1956) 296-313. [NTA 1, 37]

**BAYER, Hans F.**

1986 *Jesus' Predictions of Vindication and Resurrection. The Provenance, Meaning and Correlation of the Synoptic Predictions* (WUNT, II/20). Tübingen: Mohr, 1986, XI-289 p. Esp. 110-145: "The sign of Jonah" [12,38-40]; 182-190: "Matthew's passion and resurrection predictions"; 211-213: "The problem of Q and the phrase 'Son of Man'"; 244-247 [10,23]. — Diss. Aberdeen, 1984 (R.S. Barbour – I.H. Marshall).

**BAYER, Oswald**

1975 Sprachbewegung und Weltveränderung. Ein systematischer Versuch als Auslegung von Mt 5,43-48. — *EvT* 35 (1975) 309-321. [NTA 20, 86]

**BEA, Augustin**

1964a La storicità dei vangeli sinottici. — *CC* 115/2 (1964) 417-436. [NTA 9, 105] → 1964c
A historicidade dos Evangelhos. — *RevistCuBíb* 7 (1963) 1-44. [NTA 9, 838]
La historicidad de los evangelios sinópticos. — *RevistBíb* 25 (1963) 159-172. [NTA 9, 106]; = *RazFe* 170 (1964) 9-28.

1964b Il carattere storico dei vangeli sinottici come opere ispirate. — *Ibid.*, 526-545. [NTA 9, 33] → 1964c
El carácter de los evangelios sinópticos como obras inspiradas y palabra de Dios. — *RevistBíb* 26 (1964) 16-30. [NTA 9, 34]

1964c *La storicità dei Vangeli*. Brescia: Morcelliana, 1964. → 1964a + 1964b
*La historicidad de los evangelios sinópticos* (Biblioteca "Razon y Fe" de cuestiones actuales, 57). Madrid: Fax, 1965, 141 p.
*The Study of the Synoptic Gospels. New Approaches and Outlooks*, ed. J.A. Fitzmyer. London: Chapman; New York: Harper & Row, 1965, 95 p.
*Die Geschichtlichkeit der Evangelien*, trans. J. Hosse. Paderborn: Schöningh, 1966, 101 p.
*De historiciteit van de synoptische evangeliën*, trans. P. van Antwerpen. Bilthoven: Nelissen, 1967, 111 p.

**BEAGLEY, Alan James**

1987 *The 'Sitz im Leben' of the Apocalypse with Particular Reference to the Role of the Church's Enemies* (BZNW, 50). Berlin: de Gruyter, 1987, XIV-207 p. Esp. 158-162 [Jerusalem in Mt]. — Diss. Fuller Theol. Sem., Pasadena, CA, 1983 (R.P. Martin – D.A. Hagner).

**BEALE, Timothy Kandler**

1991 Bringing Out the New and the Old: An Interactive Approach to Reading the Parable Instanced in Matthew 13:51-52. — MORGAN, J.H. (ed.), *Church Divinity 1989/90*, Bristol, IN: Graduate Theological Foundation, 1991, 106-122.

**BEARDSLEE, William Armitage**

1967 The Wisdom Tradition and the Synoptic Gospels. — *JAAR* 35 (1967) 231-240. Esp. 234-234 [Mt]; 236-238 [Q]. [NTA 12, 536]

1968 The Motif of Fulfillment in the Eschatology of the Synoptic Gospels. — RYLAARSDAM, J.C. (ed.), *Transitions in Biblical Scholarship* (Essays in Divinity, 6), Chicago, IL: University Press, 1968, 171-191. Esp. 173-180 [Q].

1970a *Literary Criticism of the New Testament* (Guides to Biblical Scholarship. New Testament Series). Philadelphia, PA: Fortress, 1970, X-86 p. Esp. 36-39 [beatitudes]; 39-41 [proverbs]; 72-74 [Q]; [2]1971.

*Kort overzicht van de literaire kritiek van het Nieuwe Testament*, trans. E. de Vries (Gidsen bij de bijbelwetenschap, 2). Kampen: Kok, 1979, 112 p. Esp. 55-58; 58-61; 96-98. Trans. Japanese 1983.

1970b  Uses of the Proverb in the Synoptic Gospels. [5,44; 7,24-27; 8,19-22] — *Interpr* 24 (1970) 61-73. [NTA 14, 834]; = ID., *Margins of Belonging*, 1991, 13-24.

1972  Proverbs in the Gospel of Thomas. — AUNE, D.E. (ed.), *Studies in New Testament*. FS A.P. Wikgren, 1972, 92-103. Esp. 94 [11,28-31/Th 58]; 97 [7,3-5/Th 26]; 98 [12,29/Th 35; 15,14/Th 34].

1979  Saving One's Life By Losing It. [10,39; 16,25] — *JAAR* 47 (1979) 57-72. [NTA 24, 111]; = ID., *Margins of Belonging*, 1991, 25-42.

1991  *Margins of Belonging. Essays on the New Testament and Theology* (American Academy of Religion. Studies in Religion, 58). Atlanta, GA: Scholars, 1991, IX-246 p. → 1970b, 1979

**BEARE, Francis Wright**

1951  The Parable of the Guests at the Banquet: A Sketch of the History of Its Interpretation. [22,1-14] — JOHNSON, S.E. (ed.), *The Joy of Study. Papers on New Testament and Related Subjects Presented to Honor Frederick Clifton Grant*, New York: Macmillan, 1951, 1-14.

1962  *The Earliest Records of Jesus. A Companion to the* Synopsis of the First Three Gospels by Albert Huck. Oxford: Blackwell; New York – Nashville, TN: Abingdon, 1962, 254 p. Esp. 29-247: "Notes on the text of the first three gospels". → Huck 1936/52

1967  Sayings of the Risen Jesus in the Synoptic Tradition: An Inquiry into their Origin and Significance. — FARMER, W.R., et al. (eds.), *Christian History and Interpretation*. FS J. Knox, 1967, 161-181. Esp. 164-166 [28,9-10.19-20]; 174-177 [7,21; 10,5; 13,37-43; 18,20].

1968a  Concerning Jesus of Nazareth. — *JBL* 87 (1968) 125-135. [NTA 13, 144]; = BATEY, R. (ed.), *New Testament Issues*, 1970, 57-70.

1968b  The Sayings of Jesus in the Gospel according to St. Matthew. — *Studia Evangelica* 4 (1968) 146-157.

1970  The Mission of the Disciples and the Mission Charge: Matthew 10 and Parallels. — *JBL* 89 (1970) 1-13. [NTA 14, 857]

1972  The Synoptic Apocalypse: Matthean Version. — REUMANN, J.H. (ed.), *Understanding the Sacred Text. Essays in Honor of Morton S. Enslin on the Hebrew Bible and Christian Beginnings*, Valley Forge, PA: Judson, 1972, 115-133.

1974  On the Synoptic Problem: A New Documentary Theory. — *ATR* SS 3 (1974) 15-28. [NTA 19, 39r] → Boismard 1972

1981  *The Gospel according to Matthew. A Commentary*. Oxford: Blackwell, 1981, IX-550 p. *The Gospel according to Matthew. Translation, Introduction and Commentary*. San Francisco, CA: Harper & Row; Toronto, Ont: Fitzhenry & Whiteside, 1981, IX-550 p. [NTA 26, p. 317] → Nolland 1983, Ziesler 1985

G. BARBIERO, *Sal* 46 (1984) 133-134; R.A. BARTELS, *WWorld* 3 (1983) 194-197; J.M. COURT, *JTS* 33 (1982) 553-555; W.P. DE BOER, *CalvTJ* 20 (1985) 281-284; P. ELLINGWORTH, *BTrans* 33 (1982) 342-343; D.E. GARLAND, *Interpr* 37 (1983) 405-407; H.B. GREEN, *JSNT* 20 (1984) 114-116; G. GREENFIELD, *SWJT* 25/1 (1982-83) 89-90; D. HILL, *IBS* 4 (1982) 51-55; J.L. HOULDEN, *HeythJ* 24 (1983) 442-443; J.F. JANSEN, *TTod* 39 (1982-83) 456-458; J.D. KINGSBURY, *JBL* 103 (1984) 112-114; G. MAIER, *Bib* 64 (1983) 434-437; D.L. MEALAND, *ScotJT* 37 (1984) 113-115; M. MÜLLER, *DanskTeolTids* 46 (1983) 274-275; J. MURPHY-O'CONNOR, *RB* 90 (1983) 303-304; B.M. NOLAN, *IrTQ* 50 (1983-84) 77-78; R.I. PERVO, *ATR* 67 (1985) 280-281; D.E. SMITH, *JAAR* 52 (1984) 171-172; S.D. TOUSSAINT, *BS* 140 (1983) 288.

*Il Vangelo secondo Matteo. Commento*, trans. B. Maresca. Roma: Dehoniane, 1990, 646 p.
G.C. BOTTINI, *SBF/LA* 44 (1994) 693-695; *RivBib* 44 (1996) 377-379; A.B. DU TOIT, *Skrif en Kerk* (Pretoria) 15 (1994) 328-329; M. LÀCONI, *RivBib* 40 (1992) 242-245; V. PASQUETTO, *Teresianum* 44 (1993) 747-749.

1982  Jesus as Teacher and Thaumaturge: The Matthaean Portrait. — *Studia Evangelica* 7 (1982) 31-39.

**BEASLEY, J.**
1991  et al., *An Introduction to the Bible*. Nashville, TN: Abingdon, 1991, 496 p.

**BEASLEY-MURRAY, George Raymond**
1954  *Jesus and the Future. An Examination of the Criticism of the Eschatological Discourse, Mark 13, with Special Reference to the Little Apocalypse Theory.* London: Macmillan; New York: St. Martin's Press, 1954, XI-287 p. Esp. 227-230: "Matthew 24"; 230-231: "Q". → 1993

1962  *Baptism in the New Testament*. London: Macmillan; New York: St. Martin's Press, 1962, X-424 p. Esp. 31-44: "The baptism of John the Baptist"; 45-67: "The baptism of Jesus"; 77-92: "The missionary commission of the Risen Lord and baptism: Mt 28.18-20".

1970  Jesus and the Spirit. — DESCAMPS, A.L. – DE HALLEUX, A. (eds.), *Mélanges bibliques*. FS B. Rigaux, 1970, 463-478. Esp. 468-470 [12,28].

1986a  *Jesus and the Kingdom of God*. Grand Rapids, MI: Eerdmans; Exeter: Paternoster, 1986, X-446 p. Esp. 71-107.355-366: "Sayings of Jesus on the coming of the kingdom of God in the present" [11,5-6.11-12; 12,28; 13,16-17]; 108-143.366-371: "Parables of Jesus on the coming of the kingdom of God in the present" [12,29/Mk; 13,31-32/Mk; 13,24-30.44-46.47-50; 18,23-35; 20,1-16; 22,1-14]; 147-193.371-382: "Sayings of Jesus on the coming of the kingdom of God in the future" [5,3-12.20; 6,9-13; 7,21; 8,8-9/Mk; 8,11-12; 16,19; 18,3/Mk; 19,23/Mk; 21,31; 23,13]; 194-218.382-387: "Parables of Jesus on the coming of the kingdom of God in the future" [13,1-9.31-32/Mk; 13,24-30.47-56; 24,43-44; 25,1-13.14-30]; 219-312.387-409: "The Son of Man and the kingdom of God" [8,20; 10,23.32; 11,19; 12,39-40; 16,27/Mk; 19,28; 23,37-39; 25,31-46; 26,26-29/Mk]; 313-322.409-412: "The Q apocalypse: Luke 17:22-37". → H.M. Evans 1987

1986b  John 3:3,5: Baptism, Spirit and the Kingdom. — *ExpT* 97 (1985-86) 167-170. Esp. 167 [18,3]. [NTA 31, 185]

1989  Matthew 6:33: The Kingdom of God and the Ethics of Jesus. "Seek first his kingdom and righteousness, and all these things will be added to you." — MERKLEIN, H. (ed.), *Neues Testament und Ethik*. FS R. Schnackenburg, 1989, 84-98.

1992  The Kingdom of God in the Teaching of Jesus. — *JEvTS* 35 (1992) 19-30. Esp. 20-24, 28. [NTA 37, 94]
Response: C.L. BLOMBERG, *ibid.*, 31-36; G.R. BEASLEY-MURRAY, Comments on C.L. Blomberg's Response, *ibid.*, 37-38.

1993  *Jesus and the Last Days: The Interpretation of the Olivet Discourse*. Peabody, MA: Hendrickson, 1993, X-518 p. → 1954

**[Béatitudes]**
1952  Le vocabulaire des béatitudes. [5,4.9] — *LumièreV* 8 (1952) 18-23; 10 (1953) 17-25.

**BEATRICE, Pier Franco**
1978  Il significato di *Ev. Thom.* 64 per la critica letteraria della parabola del banchetto (*Mt.* 22,1-14 / *Lc.* 14,15-24). — DUPONT, J., et al. (eds.), *La parabola degli invitati al banchetto*, 1978, 237-277. Esp. 237-243: "Questioni di metodo"; 243-252: "Il problema della redazione gnostica"; 252-265: "Affinità giudeo-cristiane"; 265-274: "Confronto sinottico".

1989  Une citation de l'Évangile de Matthieu dans l'épître de Barnabé. [22,14/Barn 4,14] — SEVRIN, J.-M. (ed.), *The New Testament in Early Christianity*, 1989, 231-245.

**BEAUCAMP, Évode**

1985   *Israël en prière. Des Psaumes au Notre Père* (Lire la Bible, 69). Paris: Cerf, 1985, 258
p. Esp. 131-203: "Des Psaumes au demandes du Pater".

**BEAUCHAMP, Paul**

1977   Jésus-Christ n'est pas seul. L'accomplissement des Écritures dans la Croix. — *RSR* 65
(1977) 243-278. Esp. 267-269 [11,25-27]; 269-270 [23,37-39]. [NTA 22, 216]

1988   L'Évangile de Matthieu et l'héritage d'Israël. — *RSR* 76 (1988) 5-38. Esp. 6-21: "La
'formule' matthéenne"; 21-30: "Des contradictions à la vie: le foyer central"; 30-37: "Les difficultés de Mt
5,17-20". [NTA 32, 1098]

1991   & VASSE, D., *La violence dans la Bible* (Cahiers Évangile, 76). Paris: Cerf, 1991, 68
p. Esp. 53-58 [5-7].

**BEAUDE, Pierre-Marie**

1984a  Tu es le Messie, le Fils du Dieu vivant. [16,13-20] — ID., et al., *Jésus. Treize textes du
Nouveau Testament* (Cahiers Évangile, 50), Paris: Cerf, 1984, 18-21.

1984b  Allez! De toutes les nations faites des disciples. [28,16-20] — *Ibid.*, 38-41.

**BEAUPÈRE, René**

1955   Dialogue œcuménique autour du "Saint Pierre" de M. Oscar Cullmann. — *Istina* (Paris)
2 (1955) 347-372. Esp. 356-358 [16,17-19]. → Cullmann 1952

**BEAUVERY, Robert**

1974   La sagesse se rend justice... Mt 11,25-30. — *AssSeign* II/45 (1974) 17-24. [NTA 19, 88]

**BEAVIS, Mary Ann**

1990   Parable and Fable. — *CBQ* 52 (1990) 473-498. Esp. 497-498. [NTA 35, 116]

1992   Ancient Slavery as an Interpretive Context for the New Testament Servant Parables
with Special Reference to the Unjust Steward (Luke 16:1-8). — *JBL* 111 (1992) 37-54.
Esp. 39-43 [18,23-35; 24,45-51; 25,14-30]. [NTA 37, 209]

**BECK, B.**

1988   Gethsemane in the Four Gospels. [26,36-46] — *EpworthR* 15 (1988) 57-65. [NTA 32, 562]

**BECK, Brian E.**

1978   *Reading the New Testament Today: An Introduction to New Testament Study*. Atlanta,
GA: Knox, 1978, 164 p.

**BECK, Edmund**

1989   Der syrische Diatessaronkommentar zu der unvergebbaren Sünde wider den Heiligen
Geist übersetzt und erklärt. [12,31-32] — *Oriens Christianus* 73 (1989) (Wiesbaden) 1-37.

1992   Der syrische Diatessaronkommentar zur Perikope vom reichen Jüngling. [19,16-30] —
*Oriens Christianus* 76 (1992) 1-45.

1993   Ephräm und der Diatessaronkommentar im Abschnitt über die Wunder beim Tode Jesu
am Kreuz. [27,51-53] — *Oriens Christianus* 77 (1993) 104-119.

**BECK, E.**

1980   *È nato il Salvatore. I racconti del Natale nei vangeli di Matteo e Luca*. Bologna:
Dehoniane, 1980, 192 p.
      G. GIAVINI, *ScuolC* 109 (1981) 567.

**BECK, Norman A.**

1985   *Mature Christianity. The Recognition and Repudiation of the Anti-Jewish Polemic of the
New Testament*. Selinsgrove: Susquehanna University Press, 1985, 327 p.

*Mature Christianity in the 21st Century. The Recognition and Repudiation of the Anti-Jewish Polemic of the New Testament* (Shared Ground among Jews and Christians. A Series of Explorations, 5). New York: Crossroad, 1994, 372 p. Esp. 168-173 [Q]; 174-198 [Mt].

### BECK, William F.

1959 *The Christ of the Gospels. The Life and Work of Jesus as Told by Matthew, Mark, Luke, and John.* St. Louis, MO: Concordia P.H., 1959, 227 p.

### BECKER, Aimé

1967 *De l'instinct du bonheur à l'extase de la béatitude. Théologie et pédagogie du bonheur dans la prédication de S. Augustin.* Paris: Lethielleux, 1967, 352 p. – Diss. Strasbourg, 1965 (J. Plagnieux).

1977 *L'appel des béatitudes. À l'écoute de saint Augustin.* Paris–Freiburg/Schw: St. Paul, 1977, 262 p. Esp. 19-70.
> R. DESJARDINS, *BullLitEccl* 79 (1978) 159-160; G. FRITZ, *ZKT* 102 (1980) 259-260; M. MARIN, *VetChr* 15 (1978) 173-174; F. SCHNITZLER, *TTZ* 87 (1978) 323-324; G. TRAPÉ, *Augustinianum* 17 (1977) 584-585.

### BECKER, Hans-Jürgen

1990 *Auf der Kathedra des Mose. Rabbinisch-theologisches Denken und antirabbinische Polemik in Matthäus 23,1-12* (Arbeiten zur neutestamentlichen Theologie und Zeitgeschichte, 4). Berlin: Institut Kirche und Judentum, 1990, 267 p. Esp. 52-120: "Die Aufforderung zum Handeln gemäß der Weisung der chakhamim in der rabbinischen Tradition und nach Mt 23,2f"; 121-168: "Die Verbindung von direkter Polemik und indirekter Anklage gegen die chakhamim im Motiv der 'schweren Lasten' (Mt 23,4)"; 169-218: "Das Motiv zum Handeln nach der Tora in der rabbinischen Tradition und nach Mt 23,5-12". [NTA 35, p. 99] – Diss. Berlin, 1988 (P. von der Osten-Sacken).
> I. BROER, *TLZ* 117 (1992) 428-430; E.E. ELLIS, *SWJT* 34/2 (1991-92) 66; A. FUCHS, *SNTU* 16 (1991) 215-216; B.T. VIVIANO, *RB* 98 (1991) 624; *CBQ* 54 (1992) 141-143.

### BECKER, Joachim

1969 Erwägungen zu Fragen der neutestamentlichen Exegese. – *BZ* 13 (1969) 99-102. Esp. 99: "Das Gleichnis vom Schatz des Hausvaters (Mt 13,52)". [NTA 13, 785]

1976 Wurzel und Wurzelsproß. Ein Beitrag zur hebräischen Lexikographie. – *BZ* 20 (1976) 22-44. Esp. 40 [3,10].

### BECKER, Jürgen

1964 *Das Heil Gottes. Heils- und Sündenbegriffe in den Qumrantexten und im Neuen Testament* (SUNT, 3). Göttingen: Vandenhoeck & Ruprecht, 1964, 301 p. Esp. 190-217: "Die Verkündigung Jesu" [11,5-6.19; 12,25-27]. – Diss. Heidelberg, 1961 (K.G. Kuhn).

1972 *Johannes der Täufer und Jesus von Nazareth* (Biblische Studien, 63). Neukirchen-Vluyn: Neukirchener, 1972, 126 p. Esp. 27-37 [3,7-10]; 75-77 [11,11-12]; 90-95 [Q 17,22-37]; 101-103 [Q 12,8-9].

1975 Das Gottesbild Jesu und die älteste Auslegung von Ostern. – STRECKER, G. (ed.), *Jesus Christus in Historie und Theologie.* FS H. Conzelmann, 1975, 105-126. Esp. 112-114 [11,19]; = HOFFMANN, P. (ed.), *Zur neutestamentlichen Überlieferung von der Auferstehung Jesu*, 1988, 203-227. Esp. 211-213; = ID., *Annäherungen*, 1995, 23-47. Esp. 31-32.

1981a Feindesliebe – Nächstenliebe – Bruderliebe. Exegetische Beobachtungen als Anfrage an ein ethisches Problemfeld. – *ZEvEth* 25 (1981) 5-18. Esp. 6-9 [5,38-48]; = ID., *Annäherungen*, 1995, 383-394. Esp. 383-386.

1981b Zukunft und Hoffnung im Neuen Testament. – SCHMIDT, W.H. – BECKER, J., *Zukunft und Hoffnung* (Biblische Konfrontationen. Kohlhammer Taschenbücher, 1014), Stuttgart: Kohlhammer, 1981, 92-184. Esp. 95-117: "Die nahe Gottesherrschaft in der Verkündigung Jesu"; 173-178: "Enderwartung im Matthäusevangelium".

1989 Das Ethos Jesu und die Geltung des Gesetzes. — MERKLEIN, H. (ed.), *Neues Testament und Ethik*. FS R. Schnackenburg, 1989, 31-52. Esp. 37-38 [8,21-22]; = ID., *Annäherungen*, 1995, 1-22. Esp. 7-8.

1995 *Annäherungen: Zur urchristlichen Theologiegeschichte und zum Umgang mit ihren Quellen: Ausgewählte Aufsätze zum 60. Geburtstag mit einer Bibliographie des Verfassers*, ed. U. Mell (BZNW, 76). Berlin – New York: de Gruyter, 1995, VIII-495 p. → 1975, 1981a, 1989

**BECKING, Bob**
1989 "Bedrukte Rachel schort dit waren". Jeremia 31:15-17; Mattheüs 2:18 en Vondels Gysbrecht. — ID. – VAN DORP, J. – VAN DER KOOIJ, A. (eds.), *Door het oog van de Profeten. Exegetische studies aangeboden aan prof. dr. C. van Leeuwen* (Utrechtse theologische reeks, 8), Utrecht: Rijksuniversiteit, 1989, 9-22. Esp. 10-12.19-21. 'A Voice Was Heard in Ramah'. Some Remarks on Structure and Meaning of Jeremiah 31,15-17. — *BZ* 38 (1994) 229-242. Esp. 230-232: "A textual comparison of Mt 2,18 with Jr 31,15"; 240-242: "A comparison between Jr 31,15-17 and Mt 2,18 on the level of meaning". [NTA 39, 797]

**BECKWITH, Roger T.**
1984 The Feast of New Wine and the Question of Fasting. [9,14-17] — *ExpT* 95 (1983-84) 334-335. [NTA 29, 547] → Brooke 1984

**BEDENBAUGH, J.B.**
1955 The Ransom Saying of Our Lord (Mt 20:28; Mk 10:45). — *LuthQ* 7 (1955) 26-31.

**BEDNARZ, Michał**
1971 *Les éléments parénétiques dans la description de la Passion chez les synoptiques*. Diss. Pont. Univ. S. Thomae, Roma, 1971, 109 p.

1976 Warunki osiągnięcia Królestwa Niebieskiego według ewangelii Mateusza. [The conditions of receiving the kingdom according to Mt] — *Rozprawy Wydziału Teologiczno-Kanonicznego* (Lublin) 41 (1976) 143-156.

1977 Znaczenie rodowodu Jezusa w Ewangelii Mateusza. [The meaning of the genealogy of Jesus in the Gospel of Matthew]. — *Tarnowskie Studia Teologiczne* (Tarnów) 6 (1977) 121-133.

**BEHM, Johannes**
1936[R] *Einleitung in das Neue Testament* [P. Feine, 1913]. Heidelberg: Quelle & Meyer [[8]1936], [9]1950, XX-378 p. Esp. 14-46: "Die synoptische Frage"; 46-55: "Das Matthäusevangelium". → Kümmel 1963a

**BEHNISCH, Martin**
1985 The Golden Rule as an Expression of Jesus' Preaching. — *BangalTF* 17/1 (1985) 83-97. [NTA 30, 147]

**BEIJER, Erik**
1960 *Kristologi och etik i Jesu Bergspredikan* [Christology and ethics in the Sermon on the Mount]. Stockholm: Diakonistyrelsen, 1960, 360 p.
E.M. CARLSON, *LuthQ* 14 (1992) 78-80; L.-M. DEWAILLY, *RB* 68 (1961) 269-272; G. LINDESKOG, *SvenskTeolKvart* 37 (1961) 61-65; E. OLSSON, *Lumen* (København) 4 (1960) 134-139.

1992 *Den törnekrönte konungen. Del 1: Passionshistorien enligt Matteus, Markus och Lukas* [The king crowned with thorns. I: The passion narrative according to Matthew, Mark and Luke]. Stockholm: Verbum, 1992, 199 p.

**BEILNER, Wolfgang**

1959   *Christus und die Pharisäer. Exegetische Untersuchung über Grund und Verlauf der Auseinandersetzungen.* Wien: Herder, 1959, XII-271 p. Esp. 1-8 [3,7-12]; 9-25 [9,1-17]; 25-37 [12,1-14]; 50-62 [12,22-37]; 62-64 [12,43-45]; 64-67 [16,1-4]; 67-71 [12,38-42]; 81-86 [15,1-20]; 89-101 [5–7]; 102-109 [18,12-14]; 129-135 [22,15-22]; 174-178 [21,1-17]; 182-185 [21,28-32]; 185-192 [21,33-46]; 192-197 [22,1-14]; 197-200 [22,41-46]; 200-235 [23].

1967   Das offenbarende Wirken Jesu und seine Entfaltung in der Urkirche. — *LebZeug* 22/1 (1967) 22-42. Esp. 23-25 [8,5-13].

1969   Die Kindheitsgeschichten der Evangelien. — *TPQ* 117 (1969) 301-314. Esp. 302-308.

1971   *Der historische Jesus und der Christus der Evangelien* (Reihe X). Graz: Styria, 1971, 68 p.

1988   "Einer ist euer Vater" (Mt 23,9). Neutestamentliches zum Titel Abt. — *Sancta Crux* 49/106 (1988) 20-32.

1991   "Gesetz und Propheten erfüllen". Zum Gesetzesverständnis Jesu. — REITERER, F.V. (ed.), *Ein Gott, eine Offenbarung. Beiträge zur biblischen Exegese, Theologie und Spiritualität. Festschrift für Notker Füglister OSB zum 60. Geburtstag*, Würzburg: Echter, 1991, 439-460. Esp. 440-452 [5,17-19; 11,12-13]; 453-455 [4,23–5,1; 7,28-29]; 455-458 [5,3-12.17-20.21-48].

1994   Ehescheidung im Neuen Testament. — *TPQ* 142 (1994) 338-342. Esp. 339-341 [5,32; 19,3-12].

**BEKER, J. Christiaan**

1990   The New Testament View of Judaism. — CHARLESWORTH, J.H. (ed.), *Jews and Christians. Exploring the Past, Present, and Future* (Shared Ground among Jews and Christians, 1), New York: Crossroad, 1990, 60-69 (discussion, 70-75). Esp. 65-66.

**BÉKÉS, Gerardo J.**

1978   Christ's Progam. Service to Men (Mt 20,20-28; Mk 10,35-45). [Hungarian] — *Szolgálat* (Eisenstadt) 39 (1978) 15-23.

**BELL, James B.**

1983   *The Roots of Jesus. A Genealogical Investigation* [1,1-17], ed. R.I. Abrams. Garden City, NY: Doubleday, 1983, XIII-195 p.

**BELL, T.**

1994   Der Mensch als Esel Christi: Jesu Einzug in Jerusalem nach Mt 21 als Bildrede bei Bernhard von Clairvaux, Wenzeslaus Linck und Martin Luther. — *Luther* 65 (1994) 9-21.

**BELLET, Maurice**

1972   L'irrémissible ou le péché sans pardon. [12,31-32] — *Christus* 19 (1972) 261-268. [NTA 17, 123]

1985   Sur la bonté du Christ. Matthieu 11,2-6 (cf. Luc 7,18-23). — *Christus* 32 (1985) 475-483.

**BELLINI, Enzo**

1978   L'interpretazione origeniana delle parabole nel "Commento a Matteo". — *ScuolC* 106 (1978) 393-413.

**BELLINZONI, Arthur J.**

1967   *The Sayings of Jesus in the Writings of Justin Martyr* (SupplNT, 17). Leiden: Brill, 1967, VII-152 p. Esp. 8-48: "The sayings that occur more than once" [3,10; 4,10; 5,45.48; 6,25-26; 7,15-16.19.22-23; 8,11-12; 10,40; 11,27; 16,21; 19,16-17; 22,37-39; 23,13.16.23-24.27; 24,5; 26,39]; 57-

69: "Sayings that reflect dependence on Matthew only" [5,28.34-37; 6,1.19-20; 7,21; 8,12; 13,42-43.50; 19,11-12]; 70-72 [5,32.39-40]; 76-86: "Sayings showing features of harmonization of Mt/Lk" [5,42-47; 9,13; 22,15-21]; 87-88 [5,29; 18,9/Mk]; 89-95: "Sayings that combine different parts of the same gospel" [5,22.41.46; 6,20.21.33; 16,26]; 100-106: "Dialogue 35:3" [7,15; 24,11.24]; 107-130: "The miscellaneous synoptic sayings" [5;20; 10,28; 11,12-15; 12,39; 13,3-8; 16,4; 17,10-13; 19,26; 21,12-13; 22,30; 23,15; 25,30.41; 27,46]. — Diss. Harvard Univ., Cambridge, MA, 1962-63 (H. Koester).

1976    Approaching the Synoptic Problem from the Second Century: A Prolegomenon. — *SBL 1976 Seminar Papers*, 461-465. Esp. 462-465 [II Clem; Didache]; 463-464 [Thomas].

1985*   & TYSON, J.B. – WALKER, W.O. (eds.), *The Two-Source Hypothesis. A Critical Appraisal*. Macon, GA: Mercer University Press, 1985, X-486 p. Esp. 21-93: "The case for the priority of Mark"; 95-217: "The case against the priority of Mark"; 219-317: "The case for the Q hypothesis"; 319-433: "The case against the Q hypothesis". → Argyle 1964a, C.K. Barrett 1943, Bellinzoni 1985, Bradby 1957, Butler 1951, 1969, Downing 1965, Dungan 1970, W.R. Farmer 1964a/76, 1975a, Farrer 1955, Fitzmyer 1970, Kümmel 1973/75, Neirynck 1976f, N.H. Palmer 1967, P. Parker 1979, Rosché 1960, E.P. Sanders 1969a-b, R.T. Simpson 1966, Streeter 1924, Styler 1962, V. Taylor 1959, Tyson 1985, H.G. Wood 1953; → Fusco 1987
        A. FUCHS, *SNTU* 12 (1987) 199-201; F. NEIRYNCK, *ETL* 61 (1985) 395-397.

1985    Introduction. — *Ibid.*, 3-19. Esp. 17-18: "The case for the Q hypothesis"; 18-19: "The case against the Q hypothesis".

1987    Extra-Canonical Literature and the Synoptic Problem. — SANDERS, E.P. (ed.), *Jesus, the Gospels, and the Church*. FS W.R. Farmer, 1987, 3-15.

1992    The Gospel of Matthew in the Second Century. — *SecCent* 9 (1992) 197-258. Esp. 201-217: "Matthew and the apostolic fathers"; 217-236: "Matthew and other second century writings"; 236-245: "The gospel of Matthew in the mid-second century"; 245-254: "The gospel of Matthew in the last half of the second century". [NTA 37, 699] → Koester 1957a, Massaux 1950/1990; → Everding 1992, Farkasfalvy 1992a, Nardoni 1992

**BENASSI, B.**

1960    Genere letterario delle dispute tra Gesù e i farisei nei Sinottici. — MARINI, O., et al., *I vangeli nella critica moderna*, 1960, 89-104.

**BENASSI, Vincenzo M.**

1956    "Chi è mia madre, chi soni i miei fratelli?" (Mt. 12,48ss). — *Marianum* 18 (1956) 347-354. [NTA 2, 41]

**BEN-CHORIN, Samuel**

1975    & BARTELS, C., Gemeinsame Bibelarbeit über Mt 26,36-46. — *Freiburger Rundbrief* 27 (1975) 57-61.

**BEN-DAVID, A.**

1976    "Gebt dem Kaiser, was des Kaisers ist". Der Zinsgroschen, ein römischer Silberdenar oder eine Bronzemünze des Herodes Philippus II mit dem Bild des römischen Kaisers? Numismatisch-historische Bemerkungen zu Mt 22,15-22 und Parallelen. — *Emuna* (Frankfurt/M) 11/5-6 (1976) 1-11.

**BENDINELLI, Guido**

1993    Un confronto. I commentari a Matteo di Origene e Ilario di Poitiers. — *DivThom* 96/3 (1993) 214-237. Esp. 217-223 [14,13-21]; 223-229 [17,14-20]; 229-233 [21,17-22].

**BENECCI, V.**

1982    Il *"Padre nostro"*. *Programma di vita e di testimonianza per la comunità cristiana* (Piccola collana moderna, teol. 44). Torino: Claudiana, 1982, 62 p.

**BÉNÉTREAU, Samuel**

1981    Baptêmes et ablutions dans le Judaïsme. L'originalité de Jean-Baptiste. — *FoiVie* 80/1 = *Cahiers bibliques* 19 (1981) 96-108. Esp. 97-101 [3,13-17]. [NTA 25, 850]

**BENI, Arraldo**

1953 Variazioni protestantiche sul "Tu es Petrus". — *Città di Vita* (Firenze) 8 (1953) 242-255.

**BENJAMIN, Don C.** → V.H. Matthews 1991

**BENNETT, Thomas J.**

1987 Matthew 7:6 - A New Interpretation. — *WestTJ* 49 (1987) 371-386. Esp. 371-374: "History of interpretation"; 374-378: "Form and redaction critical approaches". [NTA 32, 596]

**BENOIT, Jean-Daniel**

1966 Le Notre Père dans le culte et la prière des Églises protestantes. — *La Maison-Dieu* (Paris) 85 (1966) 101-116. [NTA 11, 204]

**BENOIT, Pierre**

1943ᴿ Jésus devant le Sanhédrin. [1943] — ID., *Exégèse et Théologie*, I, 1961, 290-311. Esp. 290-295: "Le récit de s. Matthieu et de s. Marc"; 302-309: "Comparaison de s. Jean et des Synoptiques". Jesus before the Sanhedrin. — ID., *Jesus and the Gospel*, I, 1973, 147-166. Esp. 147-151; 158-165.

1950 *L'Évangile selon saint Matthieu* (La Sainte Bible). Paris: Cerf, 1950, 173 p.
   J. CAMBIER, *ETL* 27 (1951) 143-144; X. DUCROS, *BullLitEccl* 56 (1955) 162-163; R. LECONTE, *MSR* 8 (1951) 281; A. VIARD, *RSPT* 47 (1953) 225.
   *L'Évangile selon saint Matthieu. Traduction, introduction et notes* (La Sainte Bible en français sous la direction de l'École Biblique de Jérusalem). Paris: Cerf, ³1961, 182 p. [NTA 6, p. 268]; ⁴1973.
   S. DEL PÁRAMO, *EstBíb* 26 (1967) 370; B. MCGRATH, *CBQ* 24 (1962) 322-323. L. SABOURIN, *BTB* 4 (1974) 344-348.

1951 La Septante est-elle inspirée? — ADLER, N. (ed.), *Vom Wort des Lebens*. FS M. Meinertz, 1951, 41-49. Esp. 45-47 [1,23]; = ID., *Exégèse et Théologie*, I, 1961, 3-12. Esp. 7-9.
   The Inspiration of the Septuagint. — ID., *Jesus and the Gospel*, I, 1973, 1-10. Esp. 5-7.

1952 Prétoire, lithostroton et gabbatha. — *RB* 59 (1952) 531-550. Esp. 544 [27,27]; = ID., *Exégèse et Théologie*, I, 1961, 316-339. Esp. 331.
   Praetorium, Lithostroton and Gabbatha. — ID., *Jesus and the Gospel*, I, 1973, 167-188. Esp. 181.

1953a La divinité de Jésus. — *LumièreV* 9 (1953) 43-74. Esp. 51-53 [Messiah]; 53-62 [Son of God]; 62-72 [Son of Man]; = ID., *Exégèse et Théologie*, I, 1961, 117-142. Esp. 124-126; 126-133; 133-140.
   The Divinity of Christ in the Synoptic Gospels. — GELIN, A. (ed.), *Son and Saviour. The Divinity of Jesus Christ in the Scriptures*, London: Chapman, 1960, rev. ed. 1962, 59-92. Esp. 68-71; 71-80; 80-89.
   The Divinity of Jesus in the Synoptic Gospels. — ID., *Jesus and the Gospel*, I, 1973, 47-70. Esp. 53-55; 55-62; 62-69.

1953b La mort de Judas. [27,3-10] — SCHMID, J. - VÖGTLE, A. (eds.), *Synoptische Studien*. FS A. Wikenhauser, 1953, 1-19; = ID., *Exégèse et Théologie*, I, 1961, 340-359.
   The Death of Judas. — ID., *Jesus and the Gospel*, I, 1973, 189-208.

1953c Saint Pierre d'après O. Cullmann. — *RB* 60 (1953) 565-579; = ID., *Exégèse et Théologie*, II, 1961, 285-308. → Cullmann 1952
   St Peter according to Oscar Cullmann. — ID., *Jesus and the Gospel*, II, 1974, 154-175.

1955a La foi dans les évangiles synoptiques. — *LumièreV* 22 (1955) 45-64/469-488; = ID., *Exégèse et Théologie*, I, 1961, 143-159.
   Faith in the Synoptic Gospels. — ID., *Jesus and the Gospel*, I, 1973, 71-86.

1955b La primauté de saint Pierre selon le Nouveau Testament. — *Istina* (Paris) 2 (1955) 305-334. Esp. 319-323; = ID., *Exégèse et Théologie*, II, 1961, 250-284. Esp. 267-271. → Cassianus 1955
   The Primacy of St Peter. — ID., *Jesus and the Gospel*, II, 1974, 121-153. Esp. 135-138.

1960   Marie-Madeleine et les disciples au tombeau selon Joh 20,1-18. — ELTESTER, W. (ed.),
       *Judentum, Urchristentum, Kirche*. FS J. Jeremias, 1960, 141-152. Esp. 145.150-151 [28,9-
       10/Jn]. [NTA 5, 756]; = ID., *Exégèse et Théologie*, III, 1968, 270-282. Esp. 275.280-282.
       Maria Magdalena und die Jünger am Grabe nach Joh 20,1-18. — HOFFMANN, P. (ed.), *Zur
       neutestamentlichen Überlieferung von der Auferstehung Jesu*, 1988, 360-376. Esp. 365-366.375-376.

1961a  *Exégèse et Théologie*. I-II (Cogitatio Fidei, 1-2). Paris: Cerf, 1961, I, XI-416 p. → 1943,
       1951, 1952, 1953a-b; 1955a; II, 453 p. → 1953c, 1955b
       *Jesus and the Gospel*. I-II: *A Translation of Selected Articles from the First Volume of* Exégèse et Théologie,
       trans. B. Weatherhead. London: Darton, Longman & Todd; New York: Seabury/Continuum, I, 1973, 253
       p.; II, 1974, 185 p.
       Trans. Spanish 1974.

1961b  Qumrân et le Nouveau Testament. — *NTS* 7 (1960-61) 276-296. Esp. 279-288: "Influence
       directe". [NTA 6, 314]; = ID., *Exégèse et Théologie*, III, 1968, 361-386. Esp. 365-376.
       Qumran and the New Testament. — *TDig* 11 (1963) 167.

1962   Les outrages à Jésus prophète (Mc xiv 65 par.). [26,67-68] — *Neotestamentica et
       Patristica*. FS O. Cullmann, 1962, 92-110. Esp. 92-96, 100-102, 106-107; = ID., *Exégèse
       et Théologie*, III, 1968, 251-269. Esp. 251-255; 259-261; 265-266. → Neirynck 1987a

1963   Les épis arrachés (Mt 12,1-8 et par.). — *SBF/LA* 13 (1962-63) 76-92. Esp. 77-80:
       "Relations littéraires de Mt et Lc avec Mc"; 80-87: "Accords de Mt et Lc contre Mc"; 87-90: "La marche
       de l'argumentation et les versets propres à Mt 5-7". [NTA 8, 944]; = ID., *Exégèse et Théologie*, III,
       1968, 228-242. Esp. 229-231; 231-238; 238-242.

1965   & BOISMARD, M.-É., *Synopse des quatre Évangiles en français avec parallèles des
       apocryphes et des Pères*. Tome I: *Textes*. Paris: Cerf, 1965; ²1973 (rev. P. Sandevoir),
       XV-374 p. → Boismard 1972, Léon-Dufour 1972c, Neirynck 1979a (pp. 385-387)
       & BOISMARD, M.-É. (– MALILLOS, J.L.), *Sinopsis de los cuatro evangelios*. Tomo I: *Textos*. Bilbao: Desclée
       De Brouwer, 1975, 375 p.

1966   *Passion et Résurrection du Seigneur* (Lire la Bible, 6). Paris: Cerf, 1966, 390 p. Esp.
       22-24 [26,36-46]; 50-53 [26,47-56]; 74-77 [26,69-75]; 93-95 [26,67-68]; 105-108.115-117 [26,57-66]; 160-
       163 [27,11-31]; 175-206 [27,32-44]; 207-235 [27,45-56]; 245-247 [27,57-61]; 263-283 [28,1-15]; 375-382
       [28,16-20].
       *Passione e resurrezione del Signore. Il mistero pasquale nei quattro evangeli*. Torino: Gribaudi, 1967, 492 p.
       *The Passion and Resurrection of Jesus Christ*, trans. B. Weatherhead. New York: Herder & Herder; London:
       Darton, Longman & Todd, 1969, x-342 p. Esp. 13-15; 39-42; 61-64; 79-80; 90-92; 99-101; 139-142; 153-
       180; 181-204; 215-216; 231-261; 332-338.
       *Pasión y resurrección del Señor*, trans. J.M. Bernáldez y Romero (Col. Actualidad Bíblica, 24). Madrid: Fax,
       1971, 382 p.

1968   *Exégèse et Théologie*. III (Cogitatio Fidei, 30). Paris: Cerf, 1968, VIII-446 p. → 1960,
       1961b, 1962, 1963

1975   Jésus et le serviteur de Dieu. — DUPONT, J. (ed.), *Jésus aux origines de la christologie*,
       1975, 111-140; ²1989 (note additionnelle, 419). Esp. 121-123 [12,18-21]; 124 [11,2-6].

1982   Les récits évangéliques de l'enfance de Jésus. — ID., *Exégèse et Théologie*. IV, Paris:
       Cerf, 1982, 63-94. Esp. 65-72: "Critique littéraire"; 73-80: "Critique historique"; 80-93: "Exégèse et
       théologie".

**BENRATH, Gustav Adolf**

1966   *Wyclifs Bibelkommentar* (Arbeiten zur Kirchengeschichte, 36). Berlin: de Gruyter,
       1966, XII-415 p. Esp. 96-242: "Die Evangelienauslegung Wyclifs"; 352-354 [5,13]; 354-362 [11,28]. —
       Diss. Heidelberg, 1964 (H. Bornkamm – H. von Campenhausen).

**BENSON, G.P.**

1987   Virgin Birth, Virgin Conception. — *ExpT* 98 (1986-87) 139-140. → Bostock 1986, 1987

**BENTUÉ, Antoni**

1986 El espíritu mesiánico de Jesús. — *RevistCatTeol* 11 (1986) 255-282. Esp. 260-280: "El espiritu de Jesús". [NTA 32, 554]

**BERDER, Michel**

1996 *"La pierre rejetée par les bâtisseurs": Psaume 118,22-23 et son emploi dans les traditions juives et dans le Nouveau Testament* (Études bibliques, NS 31). Paris: Gabalda, 1996, 473 p. Esp. 249-297: "La citation de Ps 118,22(-23) en Mt 21,42-43 // Mc 12,10-11 // Lc 20,17-18". — Diss. Strasbourg 1995 (J. Schlosser).

**BERECZKY, A.**

1958 *Der Becher fliesst über. Die Seligpreisungen für unsere Zeit ausgelegt.* Berlin: Evangelische Verlagsanstalt, 1958, 94 p.

**BERG, Ludwig**

1974 Das neutestamentliche Liebesgebot – Prinzip der Sittlichkeit. — *TTZ* 83 (1974) 129-145. Esp. 139-143 [7,12]. [NTA 19, 271]

**BERG, Werner**

1979 *Die Rezeption alttestamentlicher Motive im Neuen Testament – dargestellt an den See-wandelerzählungen* [14,22-33] (HochschulSammlung Theologie, Exegese, 1). Freiburg: Hochschul Verlag, 1979, IX-374 p. — Diss. München, 1979 (J. Scharbert).

**BERGAMASCHI, Aldo**

1965 Dieu n'est pas une proie. *Oudeis dunatai.* Mt VI,24. — *ÉtFranc* 15/36 (1965) 36-53.

**BERGANT, Francisco**

1987 Discurso parabólico de Mateo. Estudio de redacción e interpretación teológica. — *Teología* 24 (1987) 5-27.

**BERGE, Paul S.**

1975 An Exposition of Matthew 16:13-20. — *Interpr* 29 (1975) 283-288.

**BERGEMANN, Thomas**

1993 *Q auf dem Prüfstand. Die Zuordnung des Mt/Lk-Stoffes zu Q am Beispiel der Bergpredigt* (FRLANT, 158). Göttingen: Vandenhoeck & Ruprecht, 1993, 319 p. Esp. 14-60: "Die Logienquelle"; 61-306: "Die Grundrede". [NTA 38, p. 456] — Diss. Hamburg, 1992 (C.-H. Hunzinger). → A. Denaux 1995b
     E. BEST, *ExpT* 105 (1993-94) 300; A. FUCHS, *SNTU* 19 (1994) 210-213; J.S. KLOPPENBORG, *JBL* 114 (1995) 325-327.

**BERGER, Klaus**

1968 Vaterunser. — *Sacramentum mundi* (Freiburg) 4 (1969) 1147-1152.
     Lord's Prayer. — *Sacramentum mundi* (London – New York) 3 (1968) 343-346.

1970a *Die Amen-Worte Jesu. Eine Untersuchung zum Problem der Legitimation in apokalyp-tischer Rede* (BZNW, 39). Berlin: de Gruyter, 1970, XII-182 p. Esp. 71-86: "Die matthäischen Amen-Worte" [5,18; 11,11.22; 13,16-17; 18,13.18; 21,21; 25,12.40.45]; 153-163 [Hasler 1969].

1970b Zu den sogenannten Sätzen heiligen Rechts. — *NTS* 17 (1970-71) 10-40. Esp. 14-16 [5,19.22.28.32]; 16-17 [5,31; 15,5; 18,15-17; 23,16.18]; 19-20 [6,14; 10,39; 16,25; 23,11]; 25-26 [12,32]; 32-33 [17,20; 18,18]; 35 [5,21]. [NTA 15, 483] → 1972b; → Käsemann 1955

1972a *Die Gesetzesauslegung Jesu. Ihr historischer Hintergrund im Judentum und im Alten Testament.* Teil I: *Markus und Parallelen* (WMANT, 40). Neukirchen-Vluyn: Neukirchener, 1972, XI-631 p. Esp. 202-232: "Die Schriftauslegung in Mt 22,34-40"; 444-453: "Die Gesetzesauslegung in Mt 19,16-22"; 497-505: "Der Schriftbeweis in Mt 15,1-20"; 570-574: "Die Gesetzesauslegung in Mt 19,3-12".

1972b  Die sog. "Sätze heiligen Rechts" im N.T. Ihre Funktion und ihr Sitz im Leben. — *TZ* 28 (1972) 305-330. Esp. 314-316 [19,28-29]. [NTA 17, 883] → 1970b

1973a  Die königlichen Messiastraditionen des Neuen Testaments. — *NTS* 20 (1973-74) 1-44. Esp. 13-15 [christology in Mt 11–12]; 32 [Son of David; Son of God]; 15-18 [4,1-11]; 28-31 [21,1-9]; 32 [11,29-30]. [NTA 18, 625]

1973b  Materialien zu Form und Überlieferungsgeschichte neutestamentlicher Gleichnisse. — *NT* 15 (1973) 1-37. Esp. 2-9 [TestJob 18 / Mt 13,44-46]; 17-18 [2 Sam 12,1-7 / Mt 18,12-14]; 23 [21,28-31]. [NTA 17, 882]

1976   *Die Auferstehung des Propheten und die Erhöhung des Menschensohnes. Traditionsgeschichtliche Untersuchungen zur Deutung des Geschickes Jesu in frühchristlichen Texte* (SUNT, 13). Göttingen: Vandenhoeck & Ruprecht, 1976, 650 p. Esp. 180-181.185.226-228 [28,16-20].

1977   *Exegese des Neuen Testaments. Neue Wege vom Text zur Auslegung* (Uni-Taschenbücher, 658). Heidelberg: Quelle & Meyer, 1977, ²1984, 288 p.

1980   PREUSS, H.D. – BERGER, K., *Bibelkunde des Alten und Neuen Testaments.* Zweiter Teil: *Neues Testament* (Uni-Taschenbücher, 972). Heidelberg: Quelle & Meyer, 1980, V-239-527 p. Esp. 248-264.

1981   Unfehlbare Offenbarung. Petrus in der gnostischen und apokalyptischen Offenbarungsliteratur. — MÜLLER, P.-G. – STENGER, W. (eds.), *Kontinuität und Einheit. Für Franz Mußner*, Freiburg: Herder, 1981, 261-326. Esp. 280-290: "Zur Rezeption der neutestamentlichen Petrustexte".

1984a  *Formgeschichte des Neuen Testaments.* Heidelberg: Quelle & Meyer, 1984, 400 p. Esp. 40-62 [parables]; 67-80 [discourses]; 80-93 [chreia]; 357-359 [infancy narrative]. → 1984b

1984b  Hellenistische Gattungen im Neuen Testament. — *ANRW* II.25.2 (1984) 1031-1432, 1831-1885. Esp. 1110-1124 [parables]; 1059-1065 [gnome]. → 1984a

1987   & COLPE, C., *Religionsgeschichtliches Textbuch zum Neuen Testament* (Texte zum Neuen Testament, 1). Göttingen-Zürich: Vandenhoeck & Ruprecht, 1987, 328 p. Esp. 96-112: "Texte der Logienquelle". → Boring 1995a
       *Testi religiosi per lo studio del Nuovo Testamento*, ed. G. Firpo (Nuovo Testamento. Supplementi, 9). Brescia: Paideia, 1993, 351 p.

1988   Jesus als Pharisäer und frühe Christen als Pharisäer. — *NT* 30 (1988) 231-262. Esp. 233-237: "Die Evidenz früher Quellen"; 237-248: "Pharisäische Züge in der Überlieferung von Jesus"; 258-259. [NTA 33, 426]

1991   *Historische Psychologie des Neuen Testament* (SBS, 146-147). Stuttgart: Katholisches Bibelwerk, 1991, 303 p. Esp. 97-102 [Q 6,43-45 (Lk)]; 230-234 [Q 17,6 (Lk)]; 238-239 [14,26-33]; 263-273 [Q 14,26-27 (Lk)].

1992   Neutestamentliche Texte im Lichte der Weisheitsschrift aus der Geniza von Alt-Kairo. — *ANRW* II.26.1 (1992) 412-428. Esp. 421-423 [5,43].

1993   Rhetorical Criticism, New Form Criticism, and New Testament Hermeneutics. — PORTER, S.E. – OLBRICHT, T.H. (eds.), *Rhetoric in the New Testament. Essays from the 1992 Heidelberg Conference* (JSNT SS, 90), Sheffield: JSOT, 1993, 390-396. Esp. 393-395: "Matthew 11.25-30 as an example".

1994   *Theologiegeschichte des Urchristentums. Theologie des Neuen Testaments* (Uni-Taschenbücher für Wissenschaft. Große Reihe). Tübingen–Basel: Francke, 1994, XXIII-746 p. Esp. 324-329: "Paulus und die Logienquelle" [Q 6,27-28; 11,49; 13,34-35]; 330-340: "Paulus und Matthäus" [6,1-18; 11,25-27; 16,16-17]; 560-567: "Die Johannes-Apokalypse und synoptische Tradition" [10,32; 16,27; 23,35; 24,30; 26,18]; 629-633: "Gemeinsamkeiten zwischen Markusevangelium und Logienquelle" [Q 9,48.50; 10,25-28; 11,21-23.29-32.33]; 643-657: "Der Standort der Logienquelle" [Q 4,1-13; 10,21-22; 16,16]; 677-685: "Der Standort des Matthäusevangeliums" [25,40.45].

**BERGER, Paul-Richard**

1980 Die Stadt auf dem Berge. Zum kulturhistorischen Hintergrund von Mt 5,14. — HAUBECK, W. — BACHMANN, M. (eds.), *Wort in der Zeit*. FS K.H. Rengstorf, 1980, 82-85.

1986 Zum Aramäischen der Evangelien und der Apostelgeschichte. — *TRev* 82 (1986) 1-18. → M. Black 1946/67

**BERGER, Rupert**

1964 Die Magna Charta der Gottesherrschaft. — SCHMAUS, M. – LÄPPLE, A. (eds.), *Wahrheit und Zeugnis. Aktuelle Themen der Gegenwart in theologischer Sicht*, Düsseldorf: Patmos, 1964, 117-127. Esp. 107-119: "Inhalt und Aufbau der Bergpredigt"; 119-121: "Formgeschichtliche Fragen"; 121-125: "Der Sinn der Bergpredigt"; = *TJb* 1967, 113-123. Esp. 113-115; 115-118; 118-122.

**BERGMAN, Jan**

1977 Zum Zwei-Wege-Motiv. Religionsgeschichtliche und exegetische Bemerkungen. — *SEÅ* 41-42 (1976-77) 27-56. Esp. 40-42 [4,1-11]; 42-43 [7,13-14]. [NTA 23, 653]

**BERGQUIST, James A.**

1962 *The Resurrection of Jesus in the New Testament. An Exegetical Study*. Diss. Univ. of South California, Los Angeles, CA, 1962.

**BERGREN, Theodore A.**

1990 *Fifth Ezra. The Text, Origin and Early History* (SBL Septuagint and Cognate Studies, 25). Atlanta, GA: Scholars, 1990, XVII-479 p. Esp. 265-270.321-328 [24,34-39/5 Ez]. — Diss. Univ. of Pennsylvania, Philadelphia, PA, 1989 (R.A. Kraft).

**BERKEY, Robert F.**

1963 Ἐγγίζειν, φθάνειν, and Realized Eschatology. [4,17; 12,28] — *JBL* 82 (1963) 177-187. [NTA 8, 133]

**BERKLEY, Timothy W.**

1994 OT Exegesis and the Death of Judas. — *Proceedings EGLBS* 14 (1994) 29-45. Esp. 34-38: "Creative composition".

**BERMEJO, Luis M.**

1977 The Alleged Infallibility of Councils. — *Bijdragen* 38 (1977) 128-162. Esp. 134-136 [28,16-20].

**BERNABE UBIETA, Carmen**

1993 La mujer en el Evangelio de Mateo: paradoja subversiva de Dios. — *EphMar* 43 (1993) 101-111. Esp. 107-108 [9,20-22]; 108-109 [15,21-28]. [NTA 38, 137]

**BERNARD, Jacques**

1987 Le saliah: de Moïse à Jésus Christ et de Jésus Christ aux Apôtres. — CAZELLES, H. (ed.), *La vie de la Parole*. FS P. Grelot, 1987, 409-420. Esp. 413-417.

**BERNARDI, Jean**

1991 "Cent, soixante et trente": Matthieu 13,8. — *RB* 98 (1991) 398-402. [NTA 36, 726]

**BERNDT, Rainer**

1985 Marsilius von Inghen als Erklärer des Matthäus-Evangeliums. — DOERR, W. (ed.), *Semper apertus. Sechshundert Jahre Rupert Karls-Universität Heidelberg 1386-1986. Festschrift in sechs Bänden. I: Mittelalter und frühe Neuzeit*, Berlin–Heidelberg: Springer, 1985, 71-84.

**BERNER, Ursula**

1979 *Die Bergpredigt. Rezeption und Auslegung im 20. Jahrhundert* (Göttinger theologische Arbeiten, 12). Göttingen: Vandenhoeck & Ruprecht, 1979, 273 p. Esp. 19-71: "Die theologische Auslegung der Bergpredigt im 20. Jahrhundert"; 72-105: "Die historisch-kritische Erforschung der Bergpredigt im 20. Jahrhundert". [NTA 24, p. 78]; [2]1983; [3]1985, 290 p. — Diss. Göttingen, 1978 (G. Strecker). → Frankemölle 1983c
      A. FUCHS, *SNTU* 5 (1980) 151-152; N.J. MCELENEY, *CBQ* 44 (1982) 140-141; P. POKORNÝ, *TLZ* 106 (1981) 186-188.

**BERNSTEIN, Alan E.**

1993 *The Formation of Hell. Death and Retribution in the Ancient and Early Christian Worlds*. Ithaca, NY: Cornell University Press, 1993, XIII-392 p. Esp. 229-239 [judgment/hell].

**BERROUARD, M.-François**

1952 L'indissolubilité du mariage dans le Nouveau Testament. — *Lumière V* 4 (1952) 21-40. Esp. 21-26 [5,31-32]; 27-30 [19,3-9].

1956 Le mérite dans les Évangiles synoptiques. — *Istina* (Paris) 3 (1956) 191-209. [NTA 2, 31]

**BERTETTO, Domenico**

1976 "Fate penitenza" (Mt 3,2). — *VCons* 12 (1976) 123-127.

**BERTÓN, Norberto**

1984 Tesis evangélicas fundantes para la diaconía de la Iglesia. Notas en base a un estudio de Mateo 20:20-28. — *Vox Evangelii* (Buenos Aires) 1 (1984) 85-96. [NTA 29, 533]

**BERTON, Vittorio**

1983 "I Vangeli dell'infanzia" di René Laurentin. — *Miles Immaculatae* (Roma) 19 (1983) 249-267. → Laurentin 1982a

**BERTRAM, Robert W.**

1980 An Epiphany Crossing – Programming Matthew 2:1-12 for Readers Today. — *CurrTMiss* 7 (1980) 328-336. [NTA 25, 469]

**BERTRAND, Daniel Alain**

1973 *Le baptême de Jésus. Histoire de l'exégèse aux deux premiers siècles* (Beiträge zur Geschichte der biblischen Exegese, 14). Tübingen: Mohr, 1973, XII-161 p. Esp. 10-12 [3,13-17]. — Diss. Strasbourg, 1971.

1980 L'*Évangile des Ébionites*: une harmonie évangélique antérieure au *Diatessaron*. — *NTS* 26 (1979-80) 548-563. [NTA 25, 354]

**BERTRAND, Guy-M.**

1994 Les récits de l'Enfance selon Eugène Drewermann. — *CahJos* 42 (1994) 287-292. [NTA 39, 1444] → Drewermann 1992

**BERTRANGS, Albert**

1959 De acht zaligheden. — *Getuigenis* 3 (1959) 253-267. Esp. 253-254 [genre]; 255-259 [theology]; 259-267 [paraenesis]. → 1962

1962 *Les Béatitudes*. Bruxelles: La Pensée Catholique; Paris: Office général du livre, 1962, 51 p. Esp. 5-22: "Les béatitudes en général"; 23-50: "Les huit béatitudes" [25-43: Mt/Lk; 43-50: Mt] (= 1959).
      J. PONTHOT, *RevDiocTournai* 18 (1963) 190.

1964 Voorschriften uit hoofdstuk 7 van Mattheus. [7,1-14] — *RevEcclLiège* 50 (1964) 286-291.

1965 *Open voor God. Wezen en nieuwtestamentische uitdrukkingsvormen van de spiritualiteit der anawim*. Antwerpen: Patmos, 1965, 116 p. Esp. 31-50 [5,3-10]; 51-63 [6,9-13]; 64-87 [repentance]; 91-93 [6,16-18; 9,14-17].

**BESSA, Kodjo**

1982 *La marche derrière Jésus d'après les évangiles synoptiques.* Diss. Strasbourg, 1982, 344 p. (É. Trocmé).

**BESSIÈRE, Gérard**

1969* (ed.), *Que dites-vous du Christ? De saint Marc à Bonhoeffer.* Paris: Cerf, 1969, 237 p. → Cornillon, J. Guillet, E. Morin

**BEST, Ernest**

1960 Spirit-Baptism. — *NT* 4 (1960) 236-243. Esp. 236-237 [3,11-12]; 239. [NTA 6, 79]

1961 Matthew v.3. — *NTS* 7 (1960-61) 255-258. [NTA 6, 120]

1970a 1 Peter and the Gospel Tradition. — *NTS* 16 (1969-70) 95-113. Esp. 103-108 [Lk/Mt]; 108-111 [5,5.10.11-12.16.44-45.48; 6,25-27; 7,24-27; 10,28; 11,28; 13,16-17; 16,15-16.18; 17,25-27; 18,2-4; 19,14; 20,25.28; 21,42; 22,21; 23,12; 24,42; 26,32-33.40-41]. [NTA 14, 968] → Gundry 1974a, G. Maier 1985

1970b Uncomfortable Words. VII. The Camel and the Needle's Eye (Mk 10,25). — *ExpT* 82 (1970-71) 83-89. Esp. 87-88 [6,19-21.24; 8,19-20; 10,9]. [NTA 15, 875]

1976 An Early Sayings Collection. — *NT* 18 (1976) 1-16. [NTA 20, 786]; = ID., *Disciples and Discipleship. Studies in the Gospel according to Mark,* Edinburgh: Clark, 1986, 64-79.

1979* & WILSON, R.McL. (eds.), *Text and Interpretation. Studies in the New Testament Presented to Matthew Black.* Cambridge: University Press, 1979, XV-268 p. → H.D. Betz, Fitzmyer, Klijn, B.M. Metzger

**BEST, Thomas F.**

1974 *Transfiguration and Discipleship in Matthew.* Diss. Graduate Theol. Union, California, CA, 1974, 198 p. — *DissAbstr* 35 (1974-75) 3098.

**BETHGE, Hans-Gebhard**

1992 Fragmente eines sahidischen Manuskriptes des Matthäus- und Johannes-Evangeliums in der British Library (Ms. Or. 14149 [13-27]). — RASSART-DEBERGH, M. - RIES, J. (eds.), *Actes du IVᵉ Congrès Copte, Louvain-la-Neuve, 5-10 septembre 1988* (Publications de l'Institut Orientaliste de Louvain, 41), Louvain-la-Neuve: Institut Orientaliste, 1992, 245-253.

**BETTE, J.C.**

1989 & VAN DEN BRINK, G. - COURTZ, H., *Het evangelie naar Matteüs* (Studiebijbel, 2). Soest: In de Ruimte, ²1989, XX-797 p. [NTA 37, p. 442]

**BETTENCOURT, Estevâo**

1968 Os Magos, Herodes e Jesus. — *RevistCuBíb* 5 (1968) 30-42. [NTA 14, 473]

1972 Confissão de fé e primado em Mt 16,17-19. — *RevistCuBíb* 9 (1972) 52-65. [NTA 18, 473]

**BETZ, Felicitas**

1969 "Selig die Barmherzigen, denn sie werden Barmherzigkeit erlangen". — MÜSSLE, M. (ed.), *Der "politische" Jesus,* 1969, 65-77.

**BETZ, Hans Dieter**

1967a *Nachfolge und Nachahmung Jesu Christi im Neuen Testament* (Beiträge zur historischen Theologie, 37). Tübingen: Mohr, 1967, VII-237 p. Esp. 5-43: "Zur Vorstellung der Nachfolge Jesu in den Evangelien". — Diss. Mainz, 1965-66 (H. Braun).

1967b The Logion of the Easy Yoke and of Rest (Matt 11,28-30). — *JBL* 86 (1967) 10-24. Esp. 11-20 [OT and Hellenistic parallels]; 20-24 [interpretation]. [NTA 11, 1032]; = ID., *Synoptische Studien,* 1992, 1-17.

1968 Jesus as Divine Man. — TROTTER, F.T. (ed.), *Jesus and the Historian. Written in Honor of Ernest Cadman Colwell*, Philadelphia, PA: Westminster, 1968, 114-133; = ID., *Synoptische Studien*, 1992, 18-34.

Jesus als göttlicher Mensch. — SUHL, A. (ed.), *Der Wunderbegriff im Neuen Testament*, 1980, 416-434.

1975a *Plutarch's Theological Writings and Early Christian Literature* (Studia ad Corpus Hellenisticum Novi Testamenti, 3). Leiden: Brill, 1975, XIV-369 p.

1975b Eine judenchristliche Kult-Didache in Matthäus 6,1-18. Überlegungen und Fragen im Blick auf das Problem des historischen Jesus. — STRECKER, G. (ed.), *Jesus Christus in Historie und Theologie*. FS H. Conzelmann, 1975, 445-457. Esp. 446-451.454-457 [6,1-18]; 451-453 [6,7-15]; = ID., *Studien zur Bergpredigt*, 1985, 49-61. Esp. 50-54.57-61; 55-57; = ID., *Synoptische Studien*, 1992, 127-139.

A Jewish-Christian Cultic *Didache* in Matt. 6:1-18: Reflections and Questions on the Problem of the Historical Jesus. — ID., *Essays*, 1985, 55-69. Esp. 56-62.65-69; 62-64.

1978a *Plutarch's Ethical Writings and Early Christian Literature* (Studia ad Corpus Hellenisticum Novi Testamenti, 4). Leiden: Brill, 1978, XI-584 p.

1978b Die Makarismen der Bergpredigt (Matthäus 5,3-12). Beobachtungen zur literarischen Form und theologischen Bedeutung. — ZTK 75 (1978) 3-19. Esp. 4-7: "Standortbestimmung"; 7-10: "Zum formgeschichtlichen Problem der Seligpreisungen"; 11-17: "Die Form und die Bedeutung des ersten Makarismus". [NTA 22, 762]; = ID., *Studien zur Bergpredigt*, 1985, 17-33. Esp. 18-21; 21-24; 24-31; = ID., *Synoptische Studien*, 1992, 92-110.

The Beatitudes of the Sermon on the Mount (Matt. 5:3-12). Observations on Their Literary Form and Theological Significance. — ID., *Essays*, 1985, 17-36. Esp. 19-22; 22-25; 26-33

1979a Matthew vi.22f and Ancient Greek Theories of Vision. — BEST, E.- WILSON, R.McL. (eds.), *Text and Interpretation*. FS M. Black, 1979, 43-56. Esp. 44-46: "On the form and composition"; 46-54: "The theme"; 54-56: "The concept of vision in Matt. vi.22f"; = ID., *Essays*, 1985, 71-87. Esp. 72-75; 75-84; 84-87; = ID., *Synoptische Studien*, 1992, 140-154.

Matthäus 6,22-23 und die antiken griechischen Sehtheorien. — ID., *Studien zur Bergpredigt*, 1985, 62-77. Esp. 63-65; 65-74; 75-77.

1979b The Sermon on the Mount: Its Literary Genre and Function. — *JRel* 59 (1979) 285-297. [NTA 24, 82]; = ID., *Essays*, 1985, 1-16; = ID., *Synoptische Studien*, 1992, 77-91.

Die Bergpredigt. Ihre literarische Gattung und Funktion. — ID., *Studien zur Bergpredigt*, 1985, 1-16.

1981 Eine Episode im Jüngsten Gericht (Mt 7,21-23). — ZTK 78 (1981) 1-30. Esp. 1-6: "Die literarische Komposition"; 7-24: "Das Quellenproblem"; 24-27: "Das christologische Problem"; 27-30: "Die Funktion der Perikope innerhalb der Bergpredigt". [NTA 25, 856]; = ID., *Studien zur Bergpredigt*, 1985, 111-140. Esp. 111-116; 117-134; 134-137; 137-140; = ID., *Synoptische Studien*, 1992, 188-218.

An Episode in the Last Judgment (Matt. 7:21-23). — ID., *Essays*, 1985, 125-157. Esp. 125-131; 132-151; 151-154; 154-157.

1982 Die hermeneutischen Prinzipien in der Bergpredigt (Mt 5,17-20). — JÜNGEL, E. - WALLMANN, J. - WERBECK, W. (eds.), *Verifikationen. Festschrift für Gerhard Ebeling zum 70. Geburtstag*, Tübingen: Mohr, 1982, 27-41. Esp. 29-32 [5,17]; 32-34 [5,18]; 35-39 [5,19]; 39-41 [5,20]; = ID., *Studien zur Bergpredigt*, 1985, 34-48; = ID., *Synoptische Studien*, 1992, 111-126.

The Hermeneutical Principles of the Sermon on the Mount (Mt. 5:17-20). — JTSouthAfr 42 (1983) 17-28. Esp. 19-21; 21-23; 23-27; 27-28. [NTA 28, 92]; = ID., *Essays*, 1985, 37-53.

1983 Gottmensch II (Griechisch-römische Antike u. Urchristentum). — RAC 12 (1983) 234-311. Esp. 275-303 [Q; Mt].

1984 Kosmogonie und Ethik in der Bergpredigt. — ZTK 81 (1984) 139-171. Esp. 139-145: "Das Problem"; 145-166: "Interpretation von Mt 6,25-34"; 166-171: "Soteriologie und Ethik in der Bergpredigt". [NTA 29, 87]; = ID., *Studien zur Bergpredigt*, 1985, 78-110. Esp. 78-84; 84-105; 105-110; =

ID., *Synoptische Studien*, 1992, 155-187.
Cosmogony and Ethics in the Sermon on the Mount. — ID., *Essays*, 1985, 89-123. Esp. 89-95; 95-118; 118-123.

1985a *Studien zur Bergpredigt*. Tübingen: Mohr, 1985, X-154 p. [NTA 30, p. 93] → 1975b, 1978b, 1979a-b, 1981, 1982, 1984
   L. DEVILLERS, *RThom* 86 (1986) 312-315; J. DUPONT, *RTL* 17 (1986) 88-89; T. FORNBERG, *SEÅ* 53 (1988) 123-124; G. SEGALLA, *Studia Patavina* 34 (1987) 161-164; V. SUBILIA, *Protestantesimo* 43 (1988) 218-219; F. VOUGA, *ETR* 61 (1986) 427-428.
   *Essays on the Sermon on the Mount*, trans. L.L. Welborn. Philadelphia, PA: Fortress, 1985, XVII-170 p. [NTA 29, p. 322] → 1991b; → Allison 1988c, 1997c, Carlston 1985, 1988, Stanton 1987
   C. BURCHARD, *TLZ* 112 (1987) 508-509; B. CHILTON, *ExpT* 97 (1985-86) 22; J.F. CRAGHAN, *BTB* 16 (1986) 120; R.A. EDWARDS, *TTod* 43 (1986-87) 132.134; D.P. EFROYMSON, D.P., *JEcuSt* 25 (1988) 462-463; E.J. EPP, *JBL* 106 (1987) 177-178; B. GERHARDSSON, *SvenskTeolKvart* 65 (1989) 169; J.D. KINGSBURY, *ChrCent* 102 (1985) 775-776; H. KVALBEIN, *TidsTeolKirk* 60 (1989) 142-143; N. MCELENEY, *Horizons* (Villanova, PA) 13 (1986) 420; J.P. MEIER, *Interpr* 41 (1987) 202-203; E.L. MILLER, *TZ* 46 (1990) 81-82; E.P. SANDERS, *JRel* 67 (1987) 87-89; G.N. STANTON, *JTS* 37 (1986) 521-523; B.T. VIVIANO, *RB* 94 (1987) 147-148.

1985b Eschatology in the Sermon on the Mount and the Sermon on the Plain. — *SBL 1985 Seminar Papers*, 343-350. Esp. 343-347; = ID., *Synoptische Studien*, 1992, 219-229. Esp. 219-223.

1990a The Problem of Christology in the Sermon on the Mount. — JENNINGS, T.W. (ed.), *Text and Logos*. FS H.W. Boers, 1990, 191-209. Esp. 194-195 [5,11]; 195-196 [5,17-20]; 196-198 [6,9-13]; 198.205-209 [7,21-23]; = ID., *Synoptische Studien*, 1992, 230-248.

1990b Zum Problem der Auferstehung Jesu im Lichte der griechischen magischen Papyri. — ID., *Hellenismus und Urchristentum. Gesammelte Aufsätze*, I, Tübingen: Mohr, 1990, 230-261. Esp. 250-251 [27,54; 28,18].

1990c The Sermon on the Mount and Q. Some Aspects of the Problem. — GOEHRING, J.E., et al. (eds.), *Gospel Origins*. FS J.M. Robinson, 1990, 19-34. Esp. 20-32: "The history of scholarship"; 32-33: "The present options"; = ID., *Synoptische Studien*, 1992, 249-269.

1991a The Sermon on the Mount in Matthew's Interpretation. — PEARSON, B.A., et al. (eds.), *The Future of Early Christianity*. FS H. Koester, 1991, 258-275. Esp. 258-265: "Presuppositions"; 265-266: "The delimitation of the Sermon on the Mount"; 266-270: "The place of the Sermon on the Mount in Matthew's life of Jesus"; 271-275: "The place of the Sermon on the Mount in Matthew's history of the church"; = ID., *Synoptische Studien*, 1992, 270-289.

1991b The Sermon on the Mount: In Defense of a Hypothesis. — *BR* 36 (1991) 74-80. [NTA 36, 1260] → 1985a; → E.W. Saunders 1991, Snodgrass 1991

1992a *Synoptische Studien. Gesammelte Aufsätze II*. Tübingen: Mohr, 1992, IX-322 p. → 1967b, 1968, 1975b, 1978b, 1979a-b, 1981, 1982, 1984, 1985b, 1990a.c, 1991a

1992b Sermon on the Mount/Plain. — *ABD* 5 (1992) 1106-1112.

1994 Jesus and the Cynics: Survey and Analysis of a Hypothesis. — *JRel* 74 (1994) 453-475. Esp. 453-460, 470-475. [NTA 39, 739] → Downing 1988a, Mack 1988

1995 *The Sermon on the Mount. A Commentary on the Sermon on the Mount, Including the Sermon on the Plain (Matthew 5:3-7:27; Luke 6:20-49)* (Hermeneia). Augsburg, MN: Fortress, 1995, XXXVII-695 p. Esp. 5-88: "The major problems of research in historical perspective"; 91-153 [5,3-12]; 154-165 [5,13-16]; 166-197 [5,17-20]; 198-328 [5,21-48]; 329-422 [6,1-18]; 423-519 [6,17-7,12]; 520-556 [7,13-23]; 557-568 [7,24-27]; 571-640 [Lk 6,20-49]. [NTA 40, p. 333]
   D.C. ALLISON, *JBL* 117 (1998) 136-138; L.R. DONELSON, *Interpr* 51 (1997) 299-302; G.E. PAUL, *ChrCent* 113 (1996) 270-274. [NTA 38, 134r]; J. TOPEL, *CBQ* 59 (1997) 370-372.

**BETZ, Johannes**

1958 Die Gründung der Kirche durch den historischen Jesus. — *TQ* 138 (1958) 152-183. Esp. 152-157.165-176 [16,17-19]; 162-165 [mission]. [NTA 3, 687]; = *TJb*, 1960, 148-170. Esp. 148-151.157-166; 154-157.

1960    Christus – Petra – Petrus. — ID. – FRIES, H. (eds.), *Kirche und Überlieferung. [Joseph Rupert Geiselmann zum 70. Geburtstag am 27. Februar 1960]*, Freiburg: Herder, 1960, 1-21. Esp. 13-21: "Der Apostel Simon Bar-Jona als Fels".

Christus – Petra – Petrus. — ID. – FRIES, H. (eds.), *Église et tradition*, Le Puy–Lyon: Mappus, 1963, 13-34. Esp. 25-34.

1961    *Die Eucharistie in der Zeit der griechischen Väter.* Band II/1: *Die Realpräsenz des Leibes und Blutes Jesu im Abendmahl nach dem Neuen Testament.* Freiburg: Herder, 1961, XXI-223 p. Esp. 10-13; 19-27; 130-143: "Der synoptische Einsetzungsbericht".

**BETZ, Otto**

1957a    Felsenmann und Felsengemeinde (Eine Parallele zu Mt 16,17-19 in den Qumran-psalmen). — *ZNW* 48 (1957) 49-77; = ID., *Jesus. Der Messias Israels*, 1987, 99-126.

1957b    Jesu Heiliger Krieg. — *NT* 2 (1957-58) 116-137. Esp. 125-129 [11,12]; 129-130 [10,34]; 131-133 [12,40]; 133-134 [24,24-25]. [NTA 3, 353]; = ID., *Jesus. Der Messias Israels*, 1987, 77-98. Esp. 86-90; 90-91; 91-94; 94-95.

1958a    Die Proselytentaufe der Qumransekte und die Taufe im Neuen Testament. — *RQum* 1 (1958) 213-234. Esp. 222-224 [John the Baptist]. [NTA 3, 747]; = ID., *Jesus. Der Herr der Kirche*, 1990, 21-48 (additional note, 44-48). Esp. 30-33.

1958b    Das Volk seiner Kraft. Zur Auslegung der Qumran–Hodajah III,1-18. — *NTS* 5 (1958-59) 67-75. Esp. 74-75 [παιδίον]. [NTA 3, 748]; = ID., *Jesus. Der Messias Israels*, 1987, 16-24. Esp. 23-24.

1959    Le ministère cultuel dans la secte de Qumrân et dans le christianisme primitif. — VAN DER PLOEG, J. (ed.), *La secte de Qumrân et les origines du christianisme* (Recherches bibliques, 4), Brugge: Desclée De Brouwer, 1959, 163-202. Esp. 187-193.

Early Christian Cult in the Light of Qumran. — *Religious Studies Bulletin* (Sudbury, Ont.) 2 (1982) 73-85 (abridged).

Der heilige Dienst in der Qumrangemeinde und bei den ersten Christen. — ID., *Jesus. Der Herr der Kirche*, 1990, 4-20 (abridged).

1960    → O. Michel 1960

1963*    & HENGEL, M. – SCHMIDT, P. (eds.), *Abraham unser Vater. Juden und Christen im Gespräch über die Bibel. Festschrift für Otto Michel zum 60. Geburtstag* (Arbeiten zur Geschichte des Spätjudentums und Urchristentums, 5). Leiden-Köln: Brill, 1963, VII-503 p. → Finkel, H. Haag, Hengel, J. Jeremias, Kamlah, Rengstorf

1964    The Dichotomized Servant and the End of Judas Iscariot (Light on the Dark Passages: Matthew 24,51 and Parallel; Acts 1,18). — *RQum* 5 (1964) 43-58. Esp. 43-44.54-58. [NTA 9, 925]; = ID., *Jesus. Der Messias Israels*, 1987, 169-184. Esp. 169-170.180-184.

1967a    The Eschatological Interpretation of the Sinai-Tradition in Qumran and in the New Testament. — *RQum* 6 (1967) 89-107. Esp. 99-105 [11,12]. [NTA 12, 422]; = ID., *Jesus. Der Herr der Kirche*, 1990, 66-87 (additional note, 84-87). Esp. 76-82.

1967b    Manifest des Christen in der Welt. Das Vaterunser heute. — *BK* 22 (1967) 86-92.

1969    Einführung. [Sermon on the Mount] — MÜSSLE, M. (ed.), *Der "politische" Jesus*, 1969, 8-17.

Grund zur Hoffnung. Zum Abschluß der Sendereihe. — *Ibid.*, 117-129.

1973    Neues und Altes im Geschichtshandeln Gottes. Bemerkungen zu Mattäus 13,51f. — FELD, H – NOLTE, J. (eds.), *Wort Gottes in der Zeit. FS K.H.* Schelkle, 1973, 69-84. Esp. 69-72: "Das Problem"; 72-76: "Die alttestamentliche Grundlage: Jesaja 43,18f"; 76-78: "Das Neue"; 78-80: "Das Alte (Mt 13,34f)"; 80-84: "Die Verbindung von Neuem und Altem: der christliche Schriftgelehrte"; = ID., *Jesus. Der Messias Israels*, 1987, 285-300. Esp. 285-287; 288-292; 292-294; 294-296; 296-300.

1976 Rechtfertigung in Qumran. — FRIEDRICH, J. - PÖHLMANN, W. - STUHLMACHER, P. (eds.), *Rechtfertigung. Festschrift für Ernst Käsemann zum 70. Geburtstag*, Tübingen: Mohr; Göttingen: Vandenhoeck & Ruprecht, 1976, 17-36. Esp. 26-29: "Das Tun der Gerechtigkeit und die Gerechtigkeit Gottes nach Matthäus"; = ID., *Jesus. Der Messias Israels*, 1987, 39-58. Esp. 48-51.

1977a *Begegnungen mit Jesus: 7 Abschnitte aus dem Matthäus-Evangelium, zur 40. Bibelwoche 1977/78 (der Arbeitsgemeinschaft Missionarische Dienste)*. Gladbeck i.W.: Schriftenmissions-Verlag, 1977, 120 p.

1977b & GRIMM, W., *Wesen und Wirklichkeit der Wunder Jesu. Heilungen – Rettungen – Zeichen – Aufleuchtungen. Jes. 60,5 "Da wirst du schauen und strahlen, dein Herz wird beben und weit werden"* (Arbeiten zum Neuen Testament und Judentum, 2). Frankfurt/M: Lang, 1977, VII-155 p. Esp. 26-152: "Neutestamentliche Wundergeschichten".

1979 *Das Vaterunser: 7 Abschnitte über Matthäus 6,9-13, zur 42. Bibelwoche 1979/80 (der Arbeitsgemeinschaft Missionarische Dienste)*. Gladbeck i.W.: Schriftenmissions-Verlag, 1979, 84 p.

1982 Göttliche und menschliche Gerechtigkeit in der Gemeinde von Qumran und ihre Bedeutung für das Neue Testament. — GÜNZLER, C. (ed.), *Ethik und Lebenswirklichkeit. Festschrift für Heinz-Horst Schrey*, Darmstadt: Wissenschaftliche Buchgesellschaft, 1982, 1-18. Esp. 6-10 [righteousness]; = ID., *Jesus. Der Herr der Kirche*, 1990, 275-292. Esp. 280-284.

1983 Jesu Evangelium vom Gottesreich. — STUHLMACHER, P. (ed.), *Das Evangelium und die Evangelien*, 1983, 55-77. Esp. 62 [Q 7,22]; 65-69: "Matthäus und das Evangelium vom Gottesreich"; = ID., *Jesus. Der Messias Israels*, 1987, 232-254. Esp. 239; 243-247. Jesus' Gospel of the Kingdom. — STUHLMACHER, P. (ed.), *The Gospel and the Gospels*, 1991, 53-74. Esp. 60; 63-67.

1984 Jesu Lieblingspsalm. Die Bedeutung von Psalm 103 für das Werk Jesu. — *TBei* 15 (1984) 253-269. Esp. 255-259: "Das 'Vater Unser' und Psalm 103"; 259-262: "Psalm 103 und die Vergebungsgleichnisse Jesu" [18,23-35]; 265 [20,1-16]; = ID., *Jesus. Der Messias Israels*, 1987, 185-201. Esp. 187-191; 191-194; 197.

1985a *Jesus und das Danielbuch. II: Die Menschensohnworte Jesu und die Zukunftserwartung des Paulus (Daniel 7,13-14)* (Arbeiten zum Neuen Testament und Judentum, 6/2). Frankfurt/M: Lang, 1985, 176 p. Esp. 69-71 [11,18-19]; 71 [10,39]; 71-72 [Q 12,49]; 75-80.90-95 [10,23]; 101-102 [5,17; 11,3].

1985b Die Bedeutung der Qumranschriften für die Evangelien des Neuen Testaments. — *BK* 40 (1985) 54-64. Esp. 55-56 [John the Baptist]. [NTA 30, 376]; = ID., *Jesus. Der Messias Israels*, 1987, 318-332. Esp. 319-321. *SelT* 27 (1988) 3-10.

1987a *Jesus. Der Messias Israels. Aufsätze zur biblischen Theologie* (WUNT, 42). Tübingen: Mohr, 1987, IX-482 p. → 1957a-b, 1958b, 1964, 1973, 1976, 1983, 1984, 1985b, 1987b

1987b Bergpredigt und Sinaitradition. Zur Gliederung und zum Hintergrund von Matthäus 5-7. — *Ibid.*, 333-384. Esp. 338-345: "Die Gerechtigkeit als Thema der Bergpredigt"; 345-349: "Torastudium und Trachten nach Gottes Gerechtigkeit (6,19-34)"; 349-354: "Die Erwartung von Gottes richtender Gerechtigkeit nach Mt 7,1-27"; 354-375: "Das Proömium der Bergpredigt und die Sinaigesetzgebung". → Allison 1993a

1987c Firmness in Faith: Hebrews 11:1 and Isaiah 28:16. — THOMPSON, B.P. (ed.), *Scripture: Meaning and Method. Essays Presented to Anthony Tyrrell Hanson for His Seventieth Birthday*, Hull: Univ. Press, 1987, 92-113. Esp. 98-100 [Is 28,16/Mt 16,18]; = ID., *Jesus. Der Herr der Kirche*, 1990, 425-446 (additional note, 445-446). Esp. 431-433.

1990 *Jesus. Der Herr der Kirche. Aufsätze zur biblischen Theologie*, II (WUNT, 52). Tübingen: Mohr, 1990, VIII-514 p. → 1958a, 1959, 1967a, 1982, 1987c

1992 Kontakte zwischen Christen und Essenern. — MAYER, B. (ed.), *Christen und Christliches in Qumran?* (Eichstätter Studien, 32), Regensburg: Pustet, 1992, 157-175. Esp. 159-164 [John the baptist]; 164-169.

**BEUMER, Johannes**

1973 Die "törichten Jungfrauen" oder die "einfältigen Mädchen"? Zu Mt 25,1ff. — *Königsteiner Studien* 19 (1973) 147-149.

**BEUTLER, Johannes**

1994 Ihr seid das Salz des Landes (Mt 5,13). — MAYER, C., et al. (eds.), *Nach den Anfängen fragen.* FS G. Dautzenberg, 1994, 85-94.

**BEYER, Klaus**

1962 *Semitische Syntax im Neuen Testament.* Band I: *Satzlehre Teil 1* (SUNT, 1). Göttingen: Vandenhoeck & Ruprecht, 1962, 324 p. Esp. 66-74 [καί-apodosis]; 75-295 [conditional clause]. — Diss. Heidelberg, 1961 (K.G. Kuhn).

**BEYSCHLAG, Karlmann**

1953 Die Bergpredigt bei Franz von Assisi und Luther. — *TLZ* 78 (1953) 688-689.

1955 *Die Bergpredigt und Franz von Assisi* (Beiträge zur Förderung christlicher Theologie, II/57). Gütersloh: Bertelsmann, 1955, 243 p.

1977 Zur Geschichte der Bergpredigt in der Alten Kirche. — *ZTK* 74 (1977) 291-322. Esp. 301-307 [5,8]; 307-313 [7,7]; 313-316 [5,44]. [NTA 22, 83]; = ID., *Evangelium als Schicksal: 5 Studien zur Geschichte der Alten Kirche*, München: Claudius, 1979, 77-92.

**BIANCHI, Enzo**

1989 Gesù alla tavola dei peccatori, amico dei pubblicani e delle prostitute. Mc 2,13ss e par. — *ParSpirV* 20 (1989) 127-149. Esp. 136-142 [9,9-13/Mk 2,13-17]; 142-145 [11,19].

1991 Il Cristo e il sabato nei quattro Vangeli. — *ParSpirV* 23 (1991) 125-143. Esp. 128-140.

**BIARD, Pierre**

1960 *La puissance de Dieu* (Travaux de l'Institut Catholique de Paris, 7). Paris: Bloud et Gay, 1960, 206 p. Esp. 107-122: "L'activité du Christ et le rayonnement de sa puissance d'après les évangiles synoptiques"; 162-190: "L'Esprit Saint et la puissance de l'Église Corps du Christ".

**[Biblia Patristica]**

1975 *Biblia Patristica. Index des citations et allusions bibliques dans la littérature patristique*, ed. Centre d'analyse et de documentation patristiques. Paris: Centre national de la recherche scientifique. I. *Des origines à Clément d'Alexandrie et Tertullien*, 1975, 546 p. Esp. 223-293. II. *Le troisième siècle (Origène excepté)*, 1977, 468 p. Esp. 235-299. III. *Origène*, 1980, 472 p. Esp. 224-281. IV. *Eusèbe de Césarée, Cyrille de Jérusalem, Épiphane de Salamine*, 1987, 330 p. Esp. 209-239. V. *Basile de Césarée, Grégoire de Nazianze, Grégoire de Nysse, Amphiloque d'Iconium*, 1991, 412 p. Esp. 252-285. VI. *Hilaire de Poitiers, Ambroise de Milan, Ambrosiaster*, 1995, 376 p.

**BIBZA, J.**

1985 *A Critical Analysis of the Publications of D.P. Fuller, G.E. Ladd, I.H. Marshall, and M.C. Tenney on the Resurrection of Jesus Christ, with Special Attention to the Problem of the Locale of the Post-Resurrection Appearances.* Diss. Princeton Theol. Sem., Princeton, NJ, 1984-85, IV-239 p.

**BIEBER, Anneliese**

1993   *Johannes Bugenhagen zwischen Reform und Reformation. Die Entwicklung seiner frühen Theologie anhand des Matthäuskommentars und der Passions- und Auferstehungs-harmonie* (Forschungen zur Kirchen- und Dogmengeschichte, 51). Göttingen: Vandenhoeck & Ruprecht, 1993, 330 p. Esp. 119-148 [3,1-12. 16,18-19; 18,18]; 149-185 [5–7]; 199-214 [20,1-16]; 295-305 [9,1-8; 13,31-32; 15,21-28; 17,20]. — Diss. Münster, 1990-91 (W.-D. Hauschild).

**BIEDER, Werner**

1953   Um den Ursprung der christlichen Taufe im Neuen Testament. — *TZ* 9 (1953) 161-173. Esp. 169-170 [28,19].

1959   Die Botschaft des Matthäus-Evangeliums an die Gemeinde. - *KirchRefSchweiz* 114 (1959) 98-101.

1961   *Die Berufung im Neuen Testament* (ATANT, 38). Zürich: Zwingli, 1961, 110 p. Esp. 7-15: "Die Berufungsgeschichten Mrk. 1,16-20; Mtth. 4,18-22"; 26-31: "Synoptische Nachfolgesprüche. Mtth. 8,18-22; Luk. 9,57-60"; 70-73 [22,1-14]; 73-76 [20,1-16].

1965   *Gottes Sendung und der missionarische Auftrag der Kirche nach Matthäus, Lukas, Paulus und Johannes* (Theologische Studien, 82). Zürich: EVZ, 1965, 52 p. Esp. 3-4, 7-18: "Gottes Sendung und unsere Aufgabe nach dem Matthäusevangelium".

1966   *Die Verheißung der Taufe im Neuen Testament.* Zürich: EVZ, 1966, 320 p. Esp. 86-87 [3,13-17]; 107-117 [28,19]; 278-285: "Die Königsherrschaft Gottes in ihrer Diakoniegestalt im Matthäus-Evangelium" [5,19-20; 11,11; 13; 20,1-16; 21,33-43; 22,1-14; 25].

**BIEDERMANN, Hermenegild**

1968   Das Primatswort Mt 16,18 in römischem, orthodoxem und protestantischem Verständnis. — *BK* 23 (1968) 55-58. [NTA 13, 169]

**BIENECK, Joachim**

1951   *Sohn Gottes als Christusbezeichnung der Synoptiker* (ATANT, 21). Zürich: Zwingli, 1951, 90 p. Esp. 35-44: "Die synoptischen Gottessohn-Aussagen; ein Überblick"; 75-87 [11,25-30]. — Diss. Basel, 1951 (K.L. Schmidt – O. Cullmann).

**BIENERT, Wolfgang A.**

1987   Jesu Verwandtschaft. — SCHNEEMELCHER, W. (ed.), *Neutestamentliche Apokryphen*, I, ⁵1987, 373-386. Esp. 384-386. → A. Meyer 1959

**BIERZYCHUDEK, Eduard**

1970   La Iglesia primitiva: Boletín. — *RevistBíb* 32 (1970) 47-53. [NTA 15, 287]

**BIETENHARD, Hans**

1963a   *Die Botschaft vom Reiche Gottes im Neuen Testament.* Bern: Haller, 1963, 29 p.

1963b   Die Dekapolis von Pompeius bis Traian. Ein Kapitel aus der neutestamentlichen Zeitgeschichte. — *ZDPV* 79 (1963) 24-58. Esp. 51-53 [2,1]; 53-54.

1979   Die Handschriftenfunde vom Toten Meer (Hirbet Qumran) und die Essener-Frage. Die Funde in der Wüste Juda. — *ANRW* II.19.1 (1979) 704-778. Esp. 752-760: "Qumran und das Neue Testament" [5,43-47].

1982   "Der Menschensohn" – ὁ υἱὸς τοῦ ἀνθρώπου. Sprachliche und religionsgeschichtliche Untersuchungen zu einem Begriff der synoptischen Evangelien. I. Sprachlicher und religionsgeschichtlicher Teil. — *ANRW* II.25.1 (1982) 265-350. Esp. 272-276.300-302.

**BIGANE, John E.**

1981   *Faith, Christ, or Peter: Matthew 16:18 in Sixteenth Century Roman Catholic Exegesis.* Washington, DC: University Press of America, 1981, IX-237 p. [NTA 26, p. 80] — Diss. Marquette Univ., Milwaukee, WI, 1979.
       S. PARSONS, *Angelicum* 60 (1983) 152-153; P. VALLIN, *RSR* 73 (1985) 411-412.

**BIGG, Howard C.**
1988    The Present State of the Q Hypothesis. — *Vox Evangelica* (London) 18 (1988) 63-73.

**BIGGS, H.**
1981    The Q Debate since 1955. — *Themelios* 6/2 (1981) 18-28. [NTA 25, 838]

**BIGUZZI, Giancarlo**
1979    Mc. 11,23-25 e il Pater. — *RivBib* 27 (1979) 57-68. Esp. 58-60 [6,14/Mk 11,25]; 60-68 [6,9-13/Mk 11,23-25]. [NTA 24, 811]
1987    Ortodossia e ortoprassi nel Vangelo di Matteo. — *EuntDoc* 40 (1987) 167-187. [NTA 32, 105]

**BILLERBECK, Paul**
1922[R]   STRACK, H.L. - BILLERBECK, P., *Das Evangelium nach Matthäus erläutert aus Talmud und Midrasch* [1922] (Kommentar zum Neuen Testament aus Talmud und Midrasch, 1). München: Beck, [2]1965, VIII-1055 p.
1928[R]   STRACK, H.L. - BILLERBECK, P., *Exkurse zu einzelnen Stellen des Neuen Testaments. Abhandlungen zur neutestamentlichen Theologie und Archäologie* [1928] (Kommentar zum Neuen Testament aus Talmud und Midrasch, 4/1-2). München: Beck, [3]1961, VII-610 and 611-1323 p. Esp. 1-22: "Zur Bergpredigt Jesu"; 41-76: "Das Passamahl (zu Mt 26,17ff.)", 77-114: "Vom altjüdischen Fasten (zu Mt 6,16ff.); 115-152: "Das altjüdische Synagogeninstitut (zu Mt 4,23)"; 250-276: "Die T'phillin oder Gebetsriemen (zu Mt 23,5)"; 277-292: "Die Çiçijjoth oder Schaufäden (zu Mt 23,5)"; 334-352: "Die Pharisäer u. Sadduzäer in der altjüdischen Literatur (zu Mt 3,7)"; 452-465: "Der 110. Psalm in der altrabbinischen Literatur (zu Mt 22,43ff. u. Hebr 5,6)"; 484-500: "Das Gleichnis von den Arbeitern im Weinberg Mt 20,1-16 u. die altsynagogale Lohnlehre"; 536-558: "Die altjüdische Privatwohltätigkeit (zu Mt 6,2-4)"; 559-610: "Die altjüdischen Liebeswerke (zu Mt 25,35ff.)"; 640-697: "Die Abgaben von den Bodenerzeugnissen (zu Mt 23,23; Lk 11,42; Hebr 7,5)"; 745-763: "Aussatz und Aussätzige (zu Mt 8,2)"; 764-798: "Der Prophet Elias nach seiner Entrückung aus dem Diesseits (zu Mt 11,14; 17,3; 27,47.49)"; 799-976: "Diese Welt, die Tage des Messias u. die zukünftige Welt (zu Mt 12,32)"; 977-1015: "Vorzeichen u. Berechnung der Tage des Messias (zu Mt 24,3ff.)"; 1199-1212: "Gerichtsgemälde aus der altjüdischen Literatur (zu Mt 25,31ff.)".

**BINDEMANN, Walther**
1985    Das Mahl des Königs. Gründe und Hintergründe der Redaktion von Mt 22,1-14. — *TVers* 15 (1985) 21-29.
1991    Das Brot für morgen gib uns heute. Sozialgeschichtliche Erwägungen zu den Wir-Bitten des Vaterunsers. — *BTZ* 8 (1991) 199-215. Esp. 202-206 [6,11]; 207-212 [6,9-13]. [NTA 36, 718]

**BINDER, Hermann**
1979    Von Markus zu den Grossevangelien. — *TZ* 35 (1979) 283-289. Esp. 283-286 [two-source hypothesis]; 286-288 [Q]. [NTA 24, 763]

**BINGHAM, Dwight Jeffrey**
1995    *Irenaeus's Use of Matthew's Gospel in "Adversus Haereses"*. Diss. Theol. Sem., Dallas, TX, 1995, 474 p. (C.A. Blaising - S.R. Spencer - E.E. Ellis). — *DissAbstr* 56 (1995-96) 1844.

**BINZ, S.**
1989    *The Passion and Resurrection Narratives of Jesus. A Commentary*. Collegeville, MN: Liturgical Press, 1989, 127 p.

**BIRDSALL, J. Neville**
1956    The Text of the Gospels in Photius. — *JTS* 7 (1956) 43-55, 190-198. Esp. 48-53. [NTA 1, 19]
1963    Ἐγρηγορέω. [26,38.40] — *JTS* 14 (1963) 390-391. [NTA 8, 587]

1971 Khanmeti Fragments of the Synoptic Gospels from Ms. Vind. Georg. 2. — *Oriens Christianus* (Wiesbaden) 55 (1971) 62-89. Esp. 63-66 [26,38-47].

1976 The Sources of the Pepysian Harmony and Its Links with the Diatessaron. — *NTS* 22 (1975-76) 215-223. Esp. 218-219 [26,48]; 220-221 [8,8]. [NTA 20, 737] → van den Broek 1974

1980 The Dialogue of Timothy and Aquila and the Early Harmonistic Traditions. — *NT* 22 (1980) 66-77. Esp. 76-77 [21,33-41]. [NTA 24, 1040]

1989 The Western Text of the Second Century. — PETERSEN, W.L. (ed.), *Gospel Traditions*, 1989, 3-17. Esp. 6-7 [10,17-32]; 10-11 [3,16-17]; 15 [5,32]

1992 A Note on the Textual Evidence for the Omission of Matthew 9.34. — DUNN, J.D.G. (ed.), *Jews and Christians*, 1992, 117-122. → Stanton 1992g

**BISCHOFF, Bernhard**

1954 Wendepunkte in der Geschichte der lateinischen Exegese im Frühmittelalter. — *Sacris Erudiri* (Steenbrugge) 6 (1954) 189-281. Esp. 236-241: "Die vier Evangelien"; 241-257: "Matthaeus"; = ID., *Mittelalterliche Studien. Ausgewählte Aufsätze zur Schriftkunde und Literaturgeschichte*, I, Stuttgart: Hiersemann, 1966, 205-273. Esp. 240-244; 244-257. Turning-Points in the History of Latin Exegesis in the Early Middle Ages. — MCNAMARA, M. (ed.), *Biblical Studies. The Medieval Irish Contribution* (Proceedings of the Irish Biblical Association, 1), Dublin: Dominican Publications, 1976, 74-160. Esp. 113-129; 145-149.

1994 & LAPIDGE, M. (eds.), *Biblical Commentaries from the Canterbury School of Theodore and Hadrian* (Cambridge Studies in Anglo-Saxon England, 10). Cambridge: University Press, 1994, XIV-612 p. Esp. 392-395; 396-406 [edition].

**BISER, Eugen**

1965 *Die Gleichnisse Jesu. Versuch einer Deutung*. München: Kösel, 1965, 188 p. Esp. 62-63 [12,43-45]; 63-64 [13,44/Th 109; 13,45-46/Th 76]; 65-69 [25,14-30]; 71-72 [7,24-27]; 83-86 [20,1-16]; 87-91 [22,2-14]; 100-103 [18,23-35]; 137-138 [21,33-46]; 145-151 [25,31-46].

1973 Sprache und Person. Zur Signatur des antipersonalen Sprachtyps. — EBELING, G., et al. (eds.), *Festschrift für Ernst Fuchs*, 1973, 67-89. Esp. 73-81: "Das Modell der christologischen Selbstaussagen" [Q 11,20; 12,49; Mt 5,21-22; 10,34; 11,21-22].

1993 *Glaubensbekenntnis und Vaterunser. Eine Neuauslegung*. Düsseldorf: Patmos, 1993, 190 p. Esp. 135-186: "Das Vaterunser"; ²1994.
E.A. THEODOROU, Θεολογία (Athens) 65 (1994) 981-984.

**BISHOP, Eric F.F.**

1951 Jesus and the Lake. — *CBQ* 13 (1951) 398-414. Esp. 405-407 [4,18-22]; 408-410 [8,23-27]; 410-414 [14,22-33].

1953a "Church" in the New Testament. — *PEQ* 85 (1953) 66-68.

1953b Jesus and Capernaum. — *CBQ* 15 (1953) 427-437. Esp. 427-429.

1954 Θησαυρῷ κεκρυμμένῳ ἐν τῷ ἀγρῷ (Mt xiii.44) - σκάψω περὶ (συνῆν) (Lk xiii.8). — *ExpT* 65 (1953-54) 287.

1962 The Parable of the Lost or Wandering Sheep. Matthew 18.10-14; Luke 15.3-7. — *ATR* 44 (1962) 44-57. Esp. 45 [18,10-14/Th]; 46-53 [18,12]. [NTA 6, 779] → Bussby 1963

1965 "Scripture Says". [4,1-11] — *EvQ* 37 (1965) 218-220. [NTA 10, 507]

1967 Some Reflections on Justin Martyr and the Nativity Narratives. — *EvQ* 39 (1967) 30-39. [NTA 11, 1028]

**BISSOLI, Cesare**

1972a Le parole "forti" di Gesù: i miracoli. Per una lettura esegetico-pastorale di Mt 8-9. — *ParVi* 17 (1972) 187-202.

1972b Vita e strutture della Chiesa alla luce di Mt 16-18. Note di catechesi. — *Ibid.*, 283-292.

**BISSOLI, Giovanni**

1994    *Il tempio nella letteratura giudaica e neotestamentaria: Studio sulla corrispondenza fra tempio celeste e tempio terrestre* (Studium Biblicum Franciscanum. Analecta, 37). Jerusalem: Franciscan Printing Press, 1994, XIV-239 p. — Diss. Pont. Inst. Bibl., Roma, 1993 (R. Le Déaut).

**BITTENCOURT, B.P.**

1969    *A forma dos evangelhos e a problemática dos Sinóticos*. São Paulo: Imprensa metodista, 1969, 172 p.

**BITTNER, Wolfgang J.**

1993    "Lasset beides miteinander wachsen bis zur Ernte...". Jesu Gleichnis vom Unkraut unter dem Weizen (Mt 13,24-30.36-43). — DÜRR, H. – RAMSTEIN, C. (eds.), *Basileia. FS Eduard Buess*, Basel: Mitenand, 1993, 15-35.

**BIVIN, David**

1983    & BLIZZARD, R., Jr., *Understanding the Difficult Words of Jesus. New Insights from a Hebraic Perspective*. Austin, TX: Center for Judaic-Christian Studies, 1983, 172 p. Esp. 119-120 [5,3]; 123-125 [11,12]; 143-149 [16,19]; 150-155 [5,17-20].

1991a   A New Solution to the Synoptic Problem. [Lindsey] — *Jerusalem Perspective* 4 (1991) 3-5. [NTA 36, 684]

1991b   A Measure of Humility. [7,2] — *Ibid.*, 13-14. [NTA 36, 1270]

1992    Prayers for Emergencies. — *Jerusalem Perspective* 5 (1992) 16-17. [NTA 37, 142]

1993    *Jerusalem Synoptic Commentary* Preview. The Rich Young Ruler Story. [19,16-30] — *Jerusalem Perspective* 38-39 (1993) 3-31. [NTA 38, 166]

1994a   Counting the Cost of Discipleship: Lindsey's Reconstruction of the Rich Young Ruler Complex. [19,16-30] — *Jerusalem Perspective* 42-44 (1994) 23-35. [NTA 38, 1369]

1994b   Jesus' Attitude Toward Pacifism. [5,39] — *Jerusalem Perspective* 45 (1994) 3-6. [NTA 39, 145]

1994c   Jesus' Attitude Towards Riches. [6,19-20; 8,20] — *Ibid.*, 12-13. [NTA 39, 98]

1994d   King Parables. [25,1-12] — *Ibid.*, 14-15. [NTA 39, 123]

1994e   Matthew 16:18. The *Petros-petra* Wordplay – Greek, Aramaic, or Hebrew? — *Jerusalem Perspective* 46-47 (1994) 32-38. [NTA 39, 1455]

**BJERKELUND, Carl J.**

1968    En tradisjons- og redaksjonshistorisk analyse av perikopene om tempelrenselsen. [A tradition-historical and redaction-historical analysis of the pericope on the Cleansing of the Temple] — *NorskTeolTids* 69 (1968) 206-218. [NTA 14, 168]

**BLACK, C. Clifton, III**

1989    Depth of Characterization and Degrees of Faith in Matthew. — *SBL 1989 Seminar Papers*, 604-623. Esp. 605-607 [Kingsbury]; 607-621 [characterization].

**BLACK, David Alan**

1987    The Translation of Matthew 5.2. — *BTrans* 38 (1987) 241-243. [NTA 32, 118]

1988a   Jesus on Anger: The Text of Matthew 5:22a Revisited. — *NT* 30 (1988) 1-8. [NTA 32, 590]

1988b   Some Dissenting Notes on R. Stein's *The Synoptic Problem* and Markan "Errors". — *FilolNT* 1 (1988) 95-101. Esp. 95-98 [minor agreements: Mk 1,12; 2,4; 4,41; 10,20; 16,6]. [NTA 33, 585] → R.H. Stein 1987

1989a   Remarks on the Translation of Matthew 7:14. — *FilolNT* 2 (1989) 193-195. [NTA 34, 1138] → G.H.R. Horsley 1990

1989b Conjectural Emendations in the Gospel of Matthew. — *NT* 31 (1989) 1-15. Esp. 1-3 [5,3]; 3-4 [6,28]; 4-5 [7,6]; 5-6 [8,22]; 6-7 [21,41]; 7-8 [17,22; 25,21.23; 26,32]; 10 [1,1]; 10-11 [6,5]; 11 [6,28]; 11-12 [12,31-32]; 12 [12,44; 14,29; 18,20]; 12-13 [21,9]; 13 [19,4; 24,26]. [NTA 34, 104] → Sahlin 1982

1992 Dreams. — *DJG*, 1992, 199-200.

**BLACK, Mark Cothran**

1990 *The Rejected and Slain Messiah who Is Coming with His Angels: The Messianic Exegesis of Zechariah 9-14 in the Passion Narratives.* Diss. Emory Univ., Atlanta, GA, 1990, 281 p. (C.R. Holladay). — *DissAbstr* 51 (1990-91) 3433.

**BLACK, Matthew**

1946[R] *An Aramaic Approach to the Gospels and Acts* [1946]. Oxford: Clarendon, [2]1954, VIII-304 p.; 3rd rev. ed., 1967, 359 p., with an Appendix on *The Son of Man* by Geza Vermes (310-330). Esp. 186-196 [Q]; 197-208: "Mistranslation and interpretation of Aramaic: Matthew and Q" [2,23; 6,11; 7,6; 8,22; 12,33]; 244-270: "Aramaic as a cause of textual variants" [9,16; 10,42; 11,5.20; 12,19; 16,16; 20,21; 23,13.16; 24,51]. → P.-R. Berger 1986, Le Déaut 1968
*Die Muttersprache Jesu. Das Aramäische der Evangelien und der Apostelgeschichte*, trans. G. Schwarz (BWANT, 115). Stuttgart: Kohlhammer, 1982, VIII-358 p. Esp. 186-196; 197-208; 244-270.

1950a Let the Dead Bury Their Dead. [8,22] — *ExpT* 61 (1949-50) 219-220. → Donn 1950

1950b The New Testament Peshitta and Its Predecessors. — *Bulletin of the SNTS* 1 (1950; [2]1963) 51-62. Esp. 58-60 [3,17; 11,28; 12,32].

1953a The Beatitudes. — *ExpT* 64 (1952-53) 125-126. → J.J. Collins 1954

1953b The Text of the Peshitta Tetraevangelium. — *Studia Paulina in honorem Johannis de Zwaan septuagenarii*, Haarlem: Bohn, 1953, 20-27. Esp. 22, 24.

1959 The Arrest and Trial of Jesus and the Date of the Last Supper. — HIGGINS, A.J.B. (ed.), *New Testament Essays*. FS T.W. Manson, 1959, 19-33. Esp. 22-23 [26,64]. → Jaubert 1957

1960 The Parables as Allegory. — *BJRL* 42 (1959-60) 273-287. Esp. 279-283 [21,33-46/Mk]. [NTA 5, 53]
Die Gleichnisse als Allegorien. — HARNISCH, W. (ed.), *Gleichnisse Jesu*, 1982, 262-280. Esp. 270-275.

1966 → K. Aland [GNT 1966]

1969 The "Son of Man" Passion Sayings in the Gospel Tradition. — *ZNW* 60 (1969) 1-8. Esp. 1-2 [Q]. [NTA 14, 425]

1970a Ἐφφαθά (Mk 7.34), [τὰ] πάσχα (Mt 26.18 W), [τὰ] σάββατα (passim), [τὰ] δίδραχμα (Mt 17.24 bis). — DESCAMPS, A. - DE HALLEUX, A. (eds.), *Mélanges bibliques*. FS B. Rigaux, 1970, 57-62. Esp. 60-62.

1970b Uncomfortable Words. III. The Violent Word. — *ExpT* 81 (1969-70) 115-118. [NTA 14, 858]
"Not Peace but a Sword": Matt 10:34ff; Luke 12:51ff. — BAMMEL, E. - MOULE, C.F.D. (eds.), *Jesus and the Politics of His Day*, 1984, 287-294.

1972 The Syriac Versional Tradition. — ALAND, K. (ed.), *Die alten Übersetzungen des Neuen Testaments, die Kirchenväterzitate und Lektionare. Der gegenwärtige Stand ihrer Erforschung und ihre Bedeutung für die griechische Textgeschichte* (Arbeiten zur neutestamentlichen Textforschung, 5), Berlin: de Gruyter, 1972, 120-159. Esp. 123-128; 143-150 [1,18-20].

1976 Some Greek Words with "Hebrew" Meanings in the Epistles and Apocalypse. [ἀδικέω: 20,23] — MCKAY, J.R. - MILLER, J.F. (eds.), *Biblical Studies*. FS W. Barclay, 1976, 145-146, 214-218.

1978 Jesus and the Son of Man. — *JSNT* 1 (1978) 4-18. Esp. 7-8.16 [Q 12,8-9]; 8 [Q 7,35]. [NTA 23, 621]

1984    Aramaic Barnāshā and the 'Son of Man'. — *ExpT* 95 (1983-84) 200-206. Esp. 200 [8,20];
        203 [10,32-33]; 203-204 [12,40-41]. [NTA 28, 1106r] → Lindars 1983

1989    The Use of Rhetorical Terminology in Papias on Mark and Matthew. — *JSNT* 37
        (1989) 31-41. [NTA 34, 976]

1990a   The Aramaic Dimension in Q with Notes on Luke 17.22 Matthew 24.26 (Luke 17.23).
        — *JSNT* 40 (1990) 33-41. [NTA 35, 1116]; = EVANS, C.A. – PORTER, S.E. (eds.), *The
        Historical Jesus*, 1995, 237-244. → Kloppenborg 1987a

1990b   The Doxology to the *Pater Noster* with a Note on Matthew 6.13b. — DAVIES, P.R. –
        WHITE, R.T. (eds.), *A Tribute to Geza Vermes*, 1990, 327-338. Esp. 333-336.

**BLACKBURN, Barry L.**

1992    Miracles and Miracle. — *DJG*, 1992, 549-560. Esp. 553-554.

1994    The Miracles of Jesus. — CHILTON, B. – EVANS, C.A. (eds.), *Studying the Historical
        Jesus*, 1994, 353-394. Esp. 354-362: "Jesus as exorcist"; 386-389.

**BLACKMAN, E. Cyril**

1969    New Methods of Parable Interpretation. — *CanJournTheol* 15 (1969) 3-13. [NTA 14, 462]

**BLÄSER, Peter**

1955a   La vocacion de los discipulos (Mt 5,13-16). — *RevistBíb* 16 (1955) 119-121.

1955b   Actitud de Jesús frente al matrimonio (Mt. 5,27-32). — *RevistBíb* 17 (1955) 39−41,
        78−80.

1956    Las bienaventuranzas. — *RevistBíb* 18 (1956) 20-24, 91-97.

1987    Las promesas del primado (Mt 16,13-20). — *RevistBíb* 49 (1987) 129-153.

**BLAIR, Edward P.**

1959    Recent Study of the Sources of Matthew. — *JBR* 27 (1959) 206-210. [NTA 4, 70] → 1960;
        → Butler 1951, Vaganay 1954a

1960    *Jesus in the Gospel of Matthew. A Reappraisal of the Distinctive Elements in Matthew's
        Christology.* New York – Nashville, TN: Abingdon, 1960, 176 p. [NTA 5, p. 243] → 1959
        W.D. DAVIES, *JBL* 80 (1961) 92; D.T. ROWLINGSON, *JBR* 29 (1961) 141-142; R.T. SIEBENECK, *CBQ*
        23 (1961) 345-347; K. STENDAHL, *Interpr* 16 (1962) 461-464.

1967    Jesus and Salvation in the Gospel of Matthew. — *McCormick Quarterly* (Chicago, IL)
        20 (1967) 301-308. [NTA 12, 142]

**BLAIR, H.A.**

1964    Matthew 1,16 and the Matthaean Genealogy. — *Studia Evangelica* 2 (1964) 149-154.

**BLAKE, Robert P.**

1933[R]  *The Old Georgian Version of the Gospel of Matthew from the Adysh Gospels with the
        Variants of the Opiza and Tbet' Gospels. Edited with a Latin Translation* [1933]
        (Patrologia orientalis, 24/1). Turnhout: Brepols, 1976, 167 p.

**BLANCHARD, Yves-Marie**

1993a   *Aux sources du canon, le témoignage d'Irénée* (Cogitatio fidei, 175). Paris: Cerf, 1993,
        363 p. Esp. 207-229: "Les paroles du Seigneur".

1993b   et al., *Évangile et Règne de Dieu* (Cahiers Évangile, 84). Paris: Cerf, 1993, 68 p.
        *Evangelio y reino de Dios* (Cuadernos Bíblicos, 84). Estella: Verbo Divino, 1995, 68 p.

**BLANCO PACHECO, Severiano**

1983    Más sobre los Evangelios de la Infancia. — *EphMar* 33 (1983) 325-334. [NTA 28, 87r]
        → Laurentin 1982a

1993 Las mujeres en la genealogía mateana de Jesús (Mt 1,1-17). — *EphMar* 43 (1993) 9-28. [NTA 38, 151]

**BLANCHARD, M.**

1959 Davidic Descent and the Virgin Birth. — *IndianJT* 8 (1959) 98-102.

**BLANK, Josef**

1969 *Schriftauslegung in Theorie und Praxis* (Biblische Handbibliothek, 5). München: Kösel, 1969, 260 p. Esp. 109-128: "Wunderberichte und Wunderdeutung in der Logienquelle Q" [Q 4,1-13; 7,1-10.18-23; 11,14.19-20].

1973 Neutestamentliche Petrus-Typologie und Petrusamt. — *IZT/Concilium* (Mainz) 9 (1973) 173-179.

1974 Die Sendung des Sohnes. Zur christologischen Bedeutung des Gleichnisses von den bösen Winzern Mk 12,1-12. — GNILKA, J. (ed.), *Neues Testament und Kirche*. FS R. Schnackenburg, 1974, 11-41. Esp. 22-23 [Q 11,49-51]; 23-24 [Q 13,34-35]; 27 [Q 12,8-9]; 27-28 [Q 4,1-13]; 28-33 [Q 10,21-22]; = ID., *Jesus*, 1981, 117-156. Esp. 131-132; 132-134; 137-138; 139-145.

1975 Das Jesus-Bild in der christlichen Exegese von heute. — FALATURI, A. – STROLZ, W. (eds.), *Glaube an den Einen Gott. Menschliche Gotteserfahrung im Christentum und im Islam*, Freiburg: Herder, 1975, 22-44; = ID., *Jesus*, 1981, 75-94. Esp. 80-83 [Q]; 88-89.

1978 Lernprozesse im Jüngerkreis Jesu. — *TQ* 158 (1978) 163-177. Esp. 171-172; = ID., *Jesus*, 1981, 95-116. Esp. 108-110.

1979 Petrus und Petrus-Amt im Neuen Testament. — *Papsttum als ökumenischer Frage*, München: Kaiser; Mainz: Matthias-Grünewald, 1979, 59-103. Esp. 74-89: "Matthäus: Petrus ald Felsenfundament der Kirche" [14,28-31; 16,17-19; 17,24-27]; = ID., *Vom Urchristentum zur Kirche. Kirchenstrukturen im Rückblick auf den biblischen Ursprung*, München: Kösel, 1982, 89-147. Esp. 109-129.

1981 *Der Jesus des Evangeliums. Entwürfe zur biblischen Christologie*. München: Kösel, 1981, 270 p. → 1974, 1975, 1978

1982 Die Seligpreisungen. — HOCHGREBE, V. (ed.), *Provokation Bergpredigt*, 1982, 19-31.

1983 Frauen in den Jesusüberlieferungen. — DAUTZENBERG, G., et al. (eds.), *Die Frau im Urchristentum*, 1983, 9-91. Esp. 29-39: "Aus der Matthäusüberlieferung" [13,33; 21,28-32; 25,1-13].

1986 Liebe und Glaube. Die Bergpredigt nach dem Verständnis des Matthäus. — DOHNA, L. – MOKROSCH, R. (eds.), *Werden und Wirkung der Reformation*, 1986, 147-152.

1989a Das Gleichnis von den Arbeitern im Weinberg oder vom gütigen Hausherrn. Mt 20,1-15 als Beitrag zum Gottesverständnis Jesu. — LANGER, M. – BILGRI, A. (eds.), *Weite des Herzens. Weite des Lebens. Beiträge zum Christsein in moderner Gesellschaft. Festschrift zum 25jährigen Abtsjubiläum des Abts von St. Bonifaz München/Andechs Dr. Odilo Lechner OSB*, Regensburg: Pustet, 1989, I, 567-573.

1989b Schwört überhaupt nicht. — *Orientierung* 53 (1989) 97-99. [NTA 33, 1124] *SelT* 29 (1990) 196-198.

**BLANK, Reiner**

1981 *Analyse und Kritik der formgeschichtlichen Arbeiten von Martin Dibelius und Rudolf Bultmann* (Theologische Dissertationen, 16). Basel: Reinhardt, 1981, 221 p. Esp. 42 [infancy narrative]; 60-64 [Q]; 164-165 [MtR]; 202-207: "Die Hypothese von der Markuspriorität und der Quelle Q". — Diss. Basel, 1978 (B. Reicke). F. NEIRYNCK, *ETL* 59 (1983) 370.

**BLASI, Anthony J.**

1986   Role Structures in the Early Hellenistic Church. — *Sociological Analysis* 47 (1986) 226-248. [NTA 31, 557]

Evidence of Role Structures in "Q". — ID., *Early Christianity*, 1988, 103-148.

1988   *Early Christianity as a Social Movement* (Toronto Studies in Religion, 5). New York – Bern: Lang, 1988, V-240 p. Esp. 19-50: "A social hermeneutic of the earlier christian sayings"; 103-148 (→ 1986); 149-175: "Matthew and the christian organisation" [Mt/Mk; Mt/Paul].

**BLASS, Friedrich** → Debrunner 1913

**BLATZ, Beate**

1987   Das Koptische Thomasevangelium. — SCHNEEMELCHER, W. (ed.), *Neutestamentliche Apokryphen*, I, ⁵1987, 93-113. Esp. 96. → H.-C. Puech 1959

**BLENKINSOPP, Joseph**

1961   The Oracle of Judah and the Messianic Entry. — *JBL* 80 (1961) 55-64. Esp. 58 [21,40-42]. [NTA 6, 130]

1962   Apropos of the Lord's Prayer. — *HeythJ* 3 (1962) 51-60. [NTA 6, 768]

**BLESSING, Kamila**

1990   Call not Unclean: The Pigs in the Story of the Legion of Demons. [8,30] — *Proceedings EGLBS* 10 (1990) 92-106.

**BLIGH, John**

1964   C.H. Dodd on John and the Synoptics. — *HeythJ* 5 (1964) 276-296. Esp. 285-286, 288-293. [NTA 9, 745r] → Dodd 1963

1968a  *The Infancy Narratives* (Scripture for Meditation, 1). London: St. Paul, 1968, 110 p. [NTA 13, p. 266]; Staten Island, NY: Alba, 1975.

      M. DAVIES, *NBlackfr* 50 (1968-69) 661-662; R. GAUTHIER, *CahJos* 20 (1972) 296-297; B. MCGRATH, *CBQ* 31 (1969) 244; M. ZERWICK, *VD* 47 (1969) 50-52.
      *I racconti dell'infanzia di Gesù*, trans. M. Petrozzi. Pescara-Francavilla: Paoline, 1969, 148 p.
      V. FUSCO, *RasT* 11 (1970) 427.

1968b  Matching Passages in the Gospels. — *Way* 8 (1968) 306-317. [NTA 13, 520]
      Matching Passages, 2. St Matthew's Passion Narrative. [26-27]; 3. The Resurrection Narratives. [28]; 4. The Sermon on the Mount. I; 5. The Sermon on the Mount II. — *Way* 9 (1969) 59-73, 148-161, 234-242, 321-330. [NTA 14, 148/149/138/483]

1969   The Gerasene Demoniac and the Resurrection of Christ. [8,1-32; 27,50-63; 28,1-15] — *CBQ* 31 (1969) 383-390. [NTA 14, 505]

1975   *The Sermon on the Mount. A Discussion on Mt 5-7*. Slough: St Paul Publications, 1975, 164 p. [NTA 20, p. 234]

**BLIGH, Philip H.**

1971   Eternal Fire, Eternal Punishment, Eternal Life (Mt 25,41.46). — *ExpT* 83 (1971-72) 9-11. [NTA 16, 543]

**BLINZLER, Josef**

1951   *Der Prozess Jesu. Das jüdische und das römische Gerichtsverfahren gegen Jesus Christus auf Grund der ältesten Zeugnisse dargestellt und beurteilt.* Stuttgart: Katholisches Bibelwerk, 1951; Regensburg: Pustet, ²1955, 224 p.; 3rd rev. ed., 1960, 375 p.
      *Der Prozess Jesu*. Regensburg: Pustet, ⁴1969, 520 p. Esp. 73-101 [26,47-56]; 115-117 [26,1-5]; 166-168 [26,3]; 301-317 [27,15-26]; 321-328.337-346 [27,26-31]; 357-374 [27,32-56]; 385-404 [27,57-61]; 404-410 [26,6-13].

*The Trial of Jesus, the Jewish and Roman Proceedings against Jesus Christ Described and Assessed from the Oldest Accounts* [German, ²1955], trans. I. and F. McHugh. Westminster, MD: Newman, 1959, XIV-132 p. *El proceso de Jesús*. Barcelona: Litúrgica, 1959, 398 p. *Le procès de Jésus*, trans. G. Daubié (Lumine in Fidei) [German, ³1960]. Paris: Mame, 1962, 559 p. *Il processo di Gesù*, trans. M.A. Colao Pellizzari (Biblioteca di cultura religiosa, 6) [German, ³1960]. Brescia: Paideia, 1966, 472 p. Trans. Swedish 1962.

1952    Zur Auslegung der Evangelienberichte über Jesu Begräbnis. — *MüTZ* 3 (1952) 403-414. Esp. 405-408 [27,62-66; 28,2-4.11-15].

1954    Jesu Worte an und über seine Mutter. — *Gloria Dei* (Graz) 9 (1954) 168-193.

1957a   Das Jahr der Geburt Christi. — *Klerusblatt* 37 (1957) 402-404. [NTA 2, 507]

1957b   Εἰσὶν εὐνοῦχοι. Zur Auslegung von Mt 19,12. — *ZNW* 48 (1957) 254-270. Esp. 254-255: "Quellenlage"; 255-264: "Der Sinn des Logions"; 264-267: "Die Frage der Zugehörigkeit von v. 11 und v. 12d zum Logion"; 268-270: "Der historische Ort". [NTA 2, 525] "Zur Ehe unfähig...". Auslegung von Mt 19,12. — ID., *Aus der Welt und Umwelt des Neuen Testaments*, 1969, 20-40 (expanded version). Esp. 20; 21-31; 31-34; 35-39.

1958    Zum Problem der Brüder des Herrn. — *TTZ* 67 (1958) 129-145, 224-246. Esp. 137-140 [1,25]. [NTA 3, 49/334]; = *TJb*, 1960, 68-101. Esp. 75-77.

1963*   & KUSS, O. – MUSSNER, F. (eds.), *Neutestamentliche Aufsätze. Festschrift für Prof. Josef Schmid zum 70. Geburtstag*. Regensburg: Pustet, 1963, 340 p. → Dupont, Kilpatrick, Molitor, Schürmann, Trilling

1963    Bereitschaft für das Kommen des Herrn! (Mt 25,1-13). — *BLtg* 37 (1963-64) 89-100.

1964    Gottes schenkende Güte: Mt 20,1-16. — *Ibid.*, 229-247.

1965    *Johannes und die Synoptiker. Ein Forschungsbericht* (SBS, 5). Stuttgart: Katholisches Bibelwerk, 1965, 100 p. Esp. 10-12; 47-48; 58-59. *Juan y los Sinópticos*, trans. J. Alcaraz (Estela, 49). Salamanca: Sígueme, 1968, 147 p. *Giovanni e i Sinottici. Rassegna informativa*, trans. G. Miola (Studi biblici, 5). Brescia: Paideia, 1969, 123 p.

1967a   *Die Brüder und Schwestern Jesu* (SBS, 21). Stuttgart: Katholisches Bibelwerk, 1967, 158 p. Esp. 28-31 [13,55/Mk 6,3]; 50-55 [1,18-25]; 73-82 [27,56.61; 28,1/Mk]; 84-85 [27,56]; 86-87: "Die Brüder Jesu in den einzelnen Evangelien" [Mt]. *I fratelli e le sorelle di Gesù*, trans. G. Cecchi (Studi biblici, 29). Brescia: Paideia, 1974.

1967b   Die Brüder Jesu. — *TGeg* 10 (1967) 8-15. Esp. 12 [1,25]; = ID., *Aus der Welt und Umwelt des Neuen Testaments*, 1969, 54-61. Esp. 58.

1969    *Aus der Welt und Umwelt des Neuen Testaments. Gesammelte Aufsätze I* (SBB). Stuttgart: Katholisches Bibelwerk, 1969, 199 p. → 1957b, 1967b

1970a   Die Heimat Jesu. [4,12-16] — *BK* 25 (1970) 14-20. Esp. 14-16: "Bethlehem"; 16-18: "Nazareth"; 18-20: "Kapharnaum". [NTA 15, 80]

1970b   Justinus Apol. I, 15,4 und Matthäus 19,11-12. — DESCAMPS, A.L. – DE HALLEUX, A. (eds.), *Mélanges bibliques*. FS B. Rigaux, 1970, 45-55.

1974    Die Grablegung Jesu in historischer Sicht. — DHANIS, É. (ed.), *Resurrexit*, 1974, 56-103 (discussion, 103-107). Esp. 68-71 [27,57-61].

**BLIZZARD, Roy, Jr.** → Bivin 1983

**BLOCH, Renée**

1957    "Juda engendra Pharès et Zara de Thamar" (Matth., I,3). — *Mélanges bibliques*. FS A. Robert, 1957, 381-389. Juda Begot Phares and Zara of Thamar (Matt. 1:3). — *TDig* 9 (1961) 21-22.

**BLOCK-HOELL, Nils E.**

1979    Extra ecclesiam nulla salus? [25,31-46] — *NorskTeolTids* 80 (1979) 19-27.

**BLOEM, Henk**

1987 *Die Ostererzählung des Matthäus. Aufbau und Aussage von Mt 27,57–28,20.* Zeist: [no publ.], 1987, 106 p. Esp. 5-10: "Die wörtlichen Reden als Mittel der innerkirchlichen Verkündigung und der Polemik"; 11-22: "Die Zitate: Mt 27,63.64; 28,5-6"; 23-58: "Die Aufträge Mt 28,7.10.13 und 18-20". — Diss. Pont. Inst. Bibl., Roma, 1985 (F. Lentzen-Deis). → P. Hoffmann 1988*
F.J. MOLONEY, *CBQ* 51 (1989) 739-740.

**BLOMBERG, Craig L.**

1984 New Testament Miracles and Higher Criticism: Climbing up the Slippery Slope. — *JEvTS* 27 (1984) 425-438. Esp. 433-434 [17,24-27]. [NTA 30, 66]

1985 Tradition and Redaction in the Parables of the Gospel of Thomas. — WENHAM, D. (ed.), *The Jesus Tradition Outside the Gospels*, 1985, 177-205. Esp. 182-183 [13,24-30/Th 57]; 184-186 [13,3-9/Th 9]; 186-187 [13,31-32/Th 20]; 187-189 [22,2-14/Th 64]; 189-190 [21,33-44/Th 65]; 190-191 [18,12-14/Th 107]; 191-192 [13,47-50/Th 8]; 193 [13,45-46/Th 76]; 193-194 [13,33/Th 96]; 194-195 [13,44/Th 109].

1986 The Miracles as Parables. — WENHAM, D. - BLOMBERG, C. (eds.), *The Miracles of Jesus*, 1986, 327-359. Esp. 330-333 [21,18-22]; 337-340 [14,13-21]; 340-342 [8,23-27]; 342-345 [14,22-33].

1987 *The Historical Reliability of the Gospels.* Leicester - Downers Grove, IL: Inter-Varsity, 1987, xx-268 p. Esp. 12-18: "The synoptic problem"; 113-152: "Contradictions among the Synoptics"; 204-206: "The Didache and Q"; 206-207: "Ignatius and M".

1990a *Interpreting the Parables.* Downers Grove, IL: InterVarsity, 1990, 334 p. Esp. 179-184 [18,12-14]; 186-190 [21,28-32]; 190-193 [24,45-51]; 193-197 [25,1-13]; 197-200 [13,24-30.36-43]; 201-203 [13,47-50]; 208-210 [11,16-19]; 214-221 [25,14-30]; 221-225 [20,1-16]; 233-240 [22,1-14]; 240-243 [18,23-35]; 256-260 [7,24-27]; 277-278 [24,43-44]; 279-281 [13,44-46]; 284-287 [13,31-33].

1990b Marriage, Divorce, Remarriage, and Celibacy: An Exegesis of Matthew 19:3-12. — *TrinJ* NS 11 (1990) 161-196. [NTA 35, 1140]

1991a Interpreting the Parables of Jesus: Where Are We and Where Do We Go from Here? — *CBQ* 53 (1991) 50-78. Esp. 51-62: "The state of the art"; 62-78: "Classification and interpretation". [NTA 35, 1117]

1991b The Liberation of Illegitimacy: Women and Rulers in Matthew 1-2. — *BTB* 21 (1991) 145-150. [NTA 36, 705]

1992a *Matthew* (New American Commentary, 22). Nashville, TN: Broadman, 1992, 464 p. [NTA 37, p. 273]
D. GREENE, *PerspRelSt* 22 (1995) 196-197; D.J. HARRINGTON, *CBQ* 56 (1994) 131-132; A.-J. LEVINE, *CRBR* 7 (1994) 142-144; V.D. VERBRUGGE, *CalvTJ* 29 (1994) 546-548; D. WENHAM, *The European Journal of Theology* (Carlisle) 2 (1993) 177-178.

1992b Healing. — *DJG*, 1992, 299-307. Esp. 302-303.

1992c On Wealth and Worry: Matthew 6:19-34 – Meaning and Significance. — *Criswell Theological Review* (Dallas, TX) 6 (1992) 73-89. [NTA 37, 1260]

1994 Historical Criticism of the New Testament. — DOCKERY, D.S., et al. (eds.), *Foundations for Biblical Interpretation*, Nashville, TN: Broadman & Holman, 1994, 414-433.

**BLOOMFIELD, Morton Wilfred**

1979 et al. (eds.), *Incipits of Latin Works on the Virtues and Vices, 1100-1500 A.D. Including a Section of Incipits of Works on the Pater Noster.* Cambridge, MA: The Mediaeval Academy of America, 1979, XIV-779 p. Esp. 567-686: "Incipits of works on the Pater Noster".

**BLOUNT, Brian K.**

1993 A Socio-Rhetorical Analysis of Simon of Cyrene: Mark 15:21 and Its Parallels. — *Semeia* 64 (1993) 171-198. Esp. 181-187 [27,32]. [NTA 39, 836]

**BLUMENSTEIN, John Max**

1991 *An Exegetical Study of Matthew 27:38-54*. Diss. Union Theol. Sem., Richmond, VA, 1991, 178 p. — *DissAbstr* 53 (1992-93) 1545.

**BOADT, Lawrence**

1989 Understanding the *Mashal* and Its Value for the Jewish-Christian Dialogue in a Narrative Theology. — THOMA, C. — WYSCHOGROD, M. (eds.), *Parable and Story*, 1989, 159-188. Esp. 160-166.166-172. → Milavec 1989, D. Stern 1989

**BOCK, Darrell L.**

1987 → S. Cunningham 1987

1994a *Luke*. I: *1:1-9:50*; II: *9:51-24:53* (Baker Exegetical Commentary on the New Testament, 3). Grand Rapids, MI: Baker, 2 vols., 1994-1996, I, XX-987 p.; II, XV-957(sic)-2148 p. Esp. I, 7-11 [sources]; 914-917: "Sources and synoptic relationships"; 918-923: "The genealogies of Matthew and Luke"; 931-945: "The sermon on the plain in Luke: Its relationship to Matthew".

1994b Current Messianic Activity and OT Davidic Promise: Dispensationalism, Hermeneutics, and NT Fulfillment. — *TrinJ* 15 (1994) 55-87. Esp. 74-75 [3,1-12]; 80-82 [13,51-52]. [NTA 39, 10]

**BOCKMUEHL, K.**

1987 The Great Commandment. [22,34-40] — *Crux* 23/3 (1987) 10-20. [NTA 32, 608]

**BOCKMUEHL, Markus**

1989 Matthew 5.32; 19.9 in the Light of Pre-Rabbinic Halakhah. — *NTS* 35 (1989) 291-295. [NTA 33, 1123]

1994 *This Jesus. Martyr, Lord, Messiah*. Edinburgh: Clark, 1994, XI-242 p. Esp. 24-41 [infancy narratives]; 42-59 [Messiah]; 126-136 [prayer].

1995 The Noachide Commandments and the New Testament Ethics. With Special Reference to Acts 15 and Pauline Halakhah. — *RB* 102 (1995) 72-101. Esp. 92-93. [NTA 39, 1682]

**BODE, Edward Lynn**

1970a *The First Easter Morning. The Gospel Accounts of the Women's Visit to the Tomb of Jesus* (AnBib, 45). Roma: Biblical Institute Press, 1970, XI-217 p. Esp. 5-24: "The gospel texts compared"; 50-58: "The gospel of Matthew"; 105-126: "Resurrection on the third day and the empty tomb". — Diss. Pont. Univ. S. Thomae, Roma, 1969 (C. Kearns).

1970b On the Third Day according to the Scriptures. — *BiTod* 48 (1970) 3297-3303. Esp. 3299 [12,38-42]. [NTA 15, 104]

**BÖCHER, Otto**

1968 Wölfe in Schafspelzen. Zum religionsgeschichtlichen Hintergrund von Matth. 7,15. — *TZ* 24 (1968) 405-426. [NTA 13, 865]

1970* & HAACKER, K. (eds.), *Verborum Veritas. Festschrift für Gustav Stählin zum 70. Geburtstag*. Wuppertal: Brockhaus, 1970, XII-383 p. → Bammel, F. Hahn, Kümmel, Strobel

1970 *Dämonenfurcht und Dämonenabwehr. Ein Beitrag zur Vorgeschichte der christlichen Taufe* (BWANT, 90). Stuttgart: Kohlhammer, 1970, 387 p. — Diss. Mainz (Part I), 1968 (G. Stählin).

1972a *Christus Exorcista. Dämonismus und Taufe im Neuen Testament* (BWANT, 96). Stuttgart: Kohlhammer, 1972, 218 p. Esp. 166-175: "Christus und die Dämonen". — Diss. Mainz (Part II).

1972b *Das Neue Testament und die dämonischen Mächte* (SBS, 58). Stuttgart: Katholisches Bibelwerk, 1972, 92 p. Esp. 13-32: "Dämonenfurcht im Neuen Testament"; 33-52: "Antidämonischer Zauber im Neuen Testament"; 53-59: "Der Sieg über die Dämonen"; 60-72: "Der Sieg über den Dämonismus".

1978   Johannes der Täufer in der neutestamentlichen Überlieferung. — MÜLLER, G. (ed.),
       *Rechtfertigung Realismus Universalismus in Biblischer Sicht*, Darmstadt:
       Wissenschaftliche Buchgesellschaft, 1978, 45-68. Esp. 45-52; = ID., *Kirche in Zeit und
       Endzeit. Aufsätze zur Offenbarung des Johannes*, Neukirchen–Vluyn: Neukirchener,
       1983, 70-89.

1979   Lukas und Johannes der Täufer. — *SNTU* 4 (1979) 27-44. Esp. 30-38 [Q: John the Baptist].
       [NTA 25, 496]

1981a  & JACOBS, M. – HILD, H., *Die Bergpredigt im Leben der Christenheit* (Bensheimer
       Hefte, 56). Göttingen: Vandenhoeck & Ruprecht, 1981, 55 p. [NTA 28, p. 310] → Böcher,
       Hild, Jacobs

1981b  Die Bergpredigt – Lebensgesetz der Urchristenheit. — *Ibid.*, 7-16.

1982   Exorzismus. I. Neues Testament. — *TRE* 10 (1982) 747-750.

1988a  Matthäus und die Magie. — SCHENKE, L. (ed.), *Studien zum Matthäusevangelium*. FS
       W. Pesch, 1988, 11-24. Esp. 14-21 [Mk/Mt].

1988b  Johannes der Täufer. — *TRE* 17 (1988) 172-181.

**BÖCKLE, Franz**

1976   Glaube und Handeln. — FEINER, J. – LÖHRER, M. (eds.), *Mysterium Salutis. Grundriß
       heilsgeschichtlicher Dogmatik*. V: *Zwischenzeit und Vollendung der Heilsgeschichte*,
       Zürich–Einsiedeln–Köln: Benziger, 1976, 21-115. Esp. 63-75: "Die sittliche Botschaft Jesu".

**BÖCKMANN, Aquinata**

1977   What Does the New Testament Say about the Church's Attitude to the Poor? —
       *Concilium* (London) 104 (1977) 36-45. Esp. 37-41.

**BÖHL, Felix**

1976   Die Demut (ה ו נ ע) als höchste der Tugenden. Bemerkungen zu Mt 5,3.5. — *BZ* 20
       (1976) 217-223. [NTA 21, 376]

**BOER, Harry R.**

1982   *The Four Gospels and Acts. A Short Introduction*. Grand Rapids, MI: Eerdmans, 1982,
       V-112 p. Esp. 12-22: "Matthew"; 53-63: "The synoptic problem".

**BOERS, Arthur P.**

1992   *Lord, Teach Us to Pray. A New Look at the Lord's Prayer*. Waterloo, Ont. – Scottdale,
       PA: Herald, 1992, 184 p. [NTA 37, p. 112]

**BOERS, Hendrikus**

1971   *Theology Out of the Ghetto. A New Testament Exegetical Study Concerning Religious
       Exclusiveness*. Leiden: Brill, 1971, XI-125 p. Esp. 45-54: "Jesus and the sect of John the Baptist
       (Mt. 11:4-19)"; 63-73: "Mt. 25:31-46. Christianity as humanism".

1972   Where Christology Is Real. A Survey of Recent Research on New Testament
       Christology. — *Interpr* 26 (1972) 300-327. Esp. 302-315 [Son of Man]. [NTA 17, 254]

1980   Language Usage and the Production of Matthew 1:18-2:23. — SPENCER, R.A. (ed.),
       *Orientation by Disorientation. Studies in Literary Criticism and Biblical Literary
       Criticism. Presented in Honor of William A. Beardslee* (Pittsburgh Theological MS, 35),
       Pittsburgh, PA: Pickwick, 1980, 217-234. Esp. 222-229: "The production of Matthew 1:18-2:23".

1989   *Who Was Jesus? An Interpretation of the Christological Passages in the Synoptic
       Gospels*. San Francisco, CA: Harper & Row, 1989, XIX-143 p.

1991   Die Nuwe-Testamentiese kanon: 'n 'Ruiker' van die vroegste Christelike literatuur.
       [The New Testament canon. A 'bouquet' of the earliest christian literature] — ROBERTS,

J.H., et al. (eds.), *Teologie in Konteks. [Opgedra aan Prof. A.B. du Toit]*, Pretoria: Orion, 1991, 597-612. Esp. 599-603.

**BOERWINKEL, Feitse**

1977 *Meer dan het gewone. Over Jezus en zijn bergrede.* Baarn: Ambo, 1977, 141 p. Esp. 55-99.

**BOFF, Leonardo**

1979 *O pai-nosso. A oração da libertação integral.* Petrópolis: Vozes, 1979.
*Vater unser. Das Gebet umfassender Befreiung*, trans. H. Goldstein. Düsseldorf: Patmos, 1981, 200 p.
*The Lord's Prayer. The Prayer of Integral Liberation*, trans. T. Morrow. Melbourne: Dove Communications, 1983, IV-140 p.
*Onze Vader, gebed van totale bevrijding*, trans. H.S.M. Groenen. Averbode: Altiora, 1984, 159 p.
J. LAMBRECHT, *Collationes* 14 (1984) 472-473.
*Le Notre Père, une prière de libération intégrale*, trans. C. & L. Durban (Théologies). Paris: Cerf; Montréal: Bellarmin, 1988, 168 p.
G.-M. OURY, *EVie* 98 (1988) 351.

**BOGUSLAWSKI, Stephen C.**

1992 Jesus' Mother and the Bestowal of the Spirit. — *IBS* 14 (1992) 106-129. Esp. 109-120 [Mt/Jn 19,16-42]. [NTA 37, 245]

**BOHREN, Rudolf**

1952 *Das Problem der Kirchenzucht im Neuen Testament.* Zollikon–Zürich: Evangelischer Verlag, 1952, 119 p.

1969 *Seligpreisungen der Bibel – heute. 2. Auflage mit einem Anhang: Traktat über das Lesen von Predigten.* Neukirchen-Vluyn: Neukirchener, 1969, 159 p.

**BOICE, James Montgomery**

1972 *The Sermon on the Mount.* Grand Rapids, MI: Zondervan, 1972, 328 p.
R.D. CONGDON, *BS* 130 (1973) 362-363.

**BOISMARD, Marie-Émile**

1955 La Loi et l'Esprit. — *LumièreV* 21 (1955) 65-82. Esp. 65-71.

1956 Élie dans le Nouveau Testament. — *Élie le prophète. I. Selon les Écritures et les traditions chrétiennes* (Les Études Carmélitaines, 35/1), Paris–Brugge: Desclée De Brouwer, 1956, 116-128.

1962 Le lépreux et le serviteur du centurion. [8,1-13] — *AssSeign* I/17 (1962) 29-44.

1965 → P. Benoit 1965

1966a Évangile des Ébionites et problème synoptique (*Mc*, 1,2-6 et par.). — *RB* 73 (1966) 321-352. Esp. 322-327.335-338 [3,1-6]; 327-331 [Gospel of the Ebionites]; 331-332 [11,7-19]; 342-352: "À la recherche d'un Mt-primitif". [NTA 11, 1046] → Neirynck 1968

1966b Satan selon l'Ancien et le Nouveau Testament. — *LumièreV* 78 (1966) 61-76. Esp. 74-76: "Les évangiles synoptiques". [NTA 11, 1170]

1972 *Synopse des quatre Évangiles en français avec parallèles des apocryphes et des Pères.* Tome II: *Commentaire.* Paris: Cerf, 1972, 456 p. Esp. 29-34: "Le Mt-intermédiaire"; 34-40: "L'ultime rédaction matthéenne"; 53-55: "Le document Q"; 61-452 [commentary]. → Beare 1974, P. Benoit 1965, de Solages 1973c, 1975, Léon-Dufour 1972b, McHugh 1973b, Neirynck 1974c, 1979a, O'Connell 1978, Sabourin 1973, Vanhoye 1974
*Sinopsis de los cuatro evangelios.* II. Bilbao: Desclée De Brouwer, 1977, 430 p.

1974 Influences matthéennes sur l'ultime rédaction de l'évangile de Marc. — SABBE, M. (ed.), *L'Évangile selon Marc*, 1974, 93-101; ²1988 (note additionnelle, 102). Esp. 93-96: "Discussion sur les traditions pharisaïques" [15,1-20/Mk]; 96-97: "Le pardon des offenses" [6,14/Mk]; 97-100: "Le sommaire de Mc., iii,7-8" [12,15-16]; 100-101: "Entrée en scène du Baptiste" [3,1-3/Mk]. → Neirynck 1974c

1979   The Two-Source Theory at an Impasse. — *NTS* 26 (1979-80) 1-17. Esp. 5-11 [minor
       agreements: Mt 14,13-14]; 12-14 [19,1-2]. [NTA 24, 764] → 1990b; Neirynck 1984c, 1990d
1981   La guérison du lépreux (Mc 1,40-45 et par.). — *Salmanticensis* 28 (1981) 283-291.
       [NTA 26, 494] → 1990b; Neirynck 1985a, 1990d
1986a  & LAMOUILLE, A., *Synopsis Graeca Quattuor Evangeliorum*. Leuven–Paris: Peeters,
       1986, LXXVIII-418 p. → J.K. Elliott 1991, Neirynck 1987b
1986b  L'hypothèse synoptique de Griesbach. — BELAVAL, Y. - BOUREL, D. (eds.), *Le siècle
       des Lumières et la Bible* (Bible de tous les temps, 7), Paris: Beauchesne, 1986, 129 – 137.
1989   Une tradition para-synoptique attestée par les Pères anciens. — SEVRIN, J.-M. (ed.),
       *The New Testament in Early Christianity*, 1989, 177-195. Esp. 181-186 [5,17]; 186-191 [5,16];
       191-195 [5,37].
1990a  Théorie des niveaux multiples. — DUNGAN, D.L. (ed.), *The Interrelations of the
       Gospels*, 1990, 231-243. Esp. 231-233: "Son principe fondamental"; 233-239: "Justification du principe
       fondamental"; 239-243: "Témoignages extra-synoptiques". → Peabody 1990a
1990b  Introduction au premier récit de la multiplication des pains (Mt 14:13-14; Mc 6:30-34;
       Lc 9:10-11). — *Ibid.*, 244-253 (Appendice: La guérison du lépreux, 254-258). Esp. 245-
       246; 249-251 [14,13-14]; 254-258 [8,2-4]. → 1979, 1981; → Neirynck 1990d
1990c  Réponse aux deux autres hypothèses. I. La Théorie des Deux Sources. II. La "Two-
       Gospel Hypothesis". — *Ibid.*, 259-265, 265-288. Esp. 261.264-265 [4,23-5,2]; 267-274: "Les
       sections communes à Mt/Lc" [24]; 274-283: "Les sections communes aux trois Synoptiques". → McNicol
       1990a, Neirynck 1990d
1991   Le titre de 'fils de Dieu' dans les évangiles. Sa portée salvifique. — *Bib* 72 (1991) 442-
       450. Esp. 447-448. [NTA 36, 900]
1992a  *Le Diatessaron: de Tatien à Justin* (Études bibliques, NS 15). Paris: Gabalda, 1992,
       171 p. Esp. 29-66: "L'harmonie de Pepys"; 67-82: "De Tatien à Justin"; 93-125: "La tradition syriaque";
       127-154: "Le baptême du Christ".
       F. NEIRYNCK, *ETL* 69 (1993) 186-188.
1992b  Étude sur Mc 1,32-34. [8,16] — VAN SEGBROECK, F., et al. (eds.), *The Four Gospels
       1992*. FS F. Neirynck, 1992, II, 987-995.
1992c  Jean 4,46-54 et les parallèles synoptiques. — DENAUX, A. (ed.), *John and the
       Synoptics*, 1992, 239-259. Esp. 240-249 [24,24/Jn 4,48-49]; 250-259 [8,5-13/Jn 4,46-54]. → Neirynck
       1995d
1992d  Two-Source Hypothesis. — *ABD* 6 (1992) 679-682.
1994   *L'Évangile de Marc. Sa préhistoire* (Études bibliques. NS 26). Paris: Gabalda, 1994,
       308 p. Esp. 29-39: "Les influences matthéennes" [Mt 8,28-34; 17,14-18/Mk]. → Neirynck 1995c
1995a  *Faut-il encore parler de "résurrection"? Les données scripturaires* (Théologies). Paris:
       Cerf, 1995, 183 p. Esp. 124-136: "La tradition synoptique".
1995b  "Notre pain quotidien" (Mt 6,11). — *RB* 102 (1995) 371-378. [NTA 40, 823]

**BOISSARD, Edmond**
1952   Note sur l'interprétation du texte: "Multi sunt vocati, pauci vero electi". — *RThom* 52
       (1952) 569-585. Esp. 580-585 [22,14].
       "Many Are Called, Few Are Chosen". — *TDig* 3 (1955) 46-50.

**BOJORGE, Horacio**
1975   *La figura de María a través de los Evangelistas* (Evangelio y Vida). Buenos Aires:
       Paulinas, 1975, 95 p.; (Biblia Vida, 9), Buenos Aires: Paulinas, [2]1982, 86 p.; (Alcance,
       34), Santander: Sal Terrae, [3]1984, 100 p.
       *A figura de Maria através dos evangelistas*. São Paulo: Loyola, 1977, [2]1982, 72 p.
       *The Image of Mary according to the Evangelists*, trans. A. Owen. New York: Alba House, 1978, IX-61 p.

*Maria zoals de evangelisten haar zien*, trans. P. Penning de Vries. Nijmegen: Gottmer; Brugge: Emmaüs, 1978, 64 p.
Trans. Japanese 1981.

**BOLES, H.L.**

1936[R] *A Commentary on the Gospel according to Matthew* [1936] (New Testament Commentaries, 1). Nashville, TN: Gospel Advocate Comp., 1976, XIII-574 p.

**BOLOGNESI, Giancarlo**

1967 La traduzione armena del Vangelo. Problemi di critica testuale. — *Studi sull'Oriente e la Bibbia*. FS G. Rinaldi, 1967, 123-140. Esp. 125, 127, 132, 134, 136-140.

1977 Le glosse anglosassoni di Rushworth al Vangelo di Matteo. — ID. (ed.), *Studi di filologia germanica e di letteratura tedesca in onore di Gil Vitale Accolti*, Firenze: Olschki, 1977, 85-107.

**BOLOGNESI, Pietro**

1979 Rilievi sulla genealogia di Gesù secondo Matteo. [1,1-17] — *Protestantesimo* 37 (1979) 222-230.

1987 Matteo 18,20 e la dottrina della Chiesa. — *BibOr* 29 (1987) 171-177. [NTA 32, 1114]

1988 Matteo 28,16-20 e la sua struttura. — *BibOr* 30 (1988) 129-137. [NTA 33, 619]

1989 Matteo 28,16-20 e il suo contenuto. — *Studi di Teologia dell'Istituto Biblico Evangelico* (Roma) NS 1 (1989) 25-39.

**BOLSINGER, Gustav**

1957 Die Ahnenreihe Christi nach Matthäus und Lukas. — *BK* 12 (1957) 112-117.

**BOLYKI, János**

1998 *Jesu Tischgemeinschaften* (WUNT, II/96). Tübingen: Mohr, 1998, XI-261 p. Esp. 68-74: "Logien aus der Logienquelle (Q)" [Q 7,33-35; 13,28-29]; 75-78 [Q 14,16-24]; 82-84 [9,14-17/Mk]; 84-87 [15,21-28/Mk]; 89-94 [14,13-21/Mk]; 148-150 [26,26-29/Mk]; 166-170. — Diss. Budapest, 1993.

**BOMAN, Thorleif**

1963 Das letzte Wort Jesu. [27,45-50] — *StudTheol* 17 (1963) 103-119. [NTA 8, 958]; = ID., *Die Jesus-Überlieferung*, 1967, 221-236.

1964 Der Gebetskampf Jesu. — *NTS* 10 (1963-64) 261-273. [NTA 8, 956]; = ID., *Die Jesus-Überlieferung*, 1967, 208-221.

1967 *Die Jesus-Überlieferung im Lichte der neueren Volkskunde*. Göttingen: Vandenhoeck & Ruprecht, 1967, 259 p. Esp. 101-123: "Die Logienquelle"; 137-141: "Die Sonderüberlieferungen im Matthäusevangelium"; 148-183: "Der Menschensohn". → 1963, 1964

**BOMBO, Constantino**

1973 As Tentações de Jesus nos Sinóticos. — *RevistCuBíb* 10 (1973) 83-102. [NTA 19, 104]

**BOMMER, Josef**

1974 Das Vaterunser in der Seelsorglichen Praxis. — BROCKE, M., et al. (eds.), *Das Vaterunser*, 1974, 231-243.
The Lord's Prayer in Pastoral Usage. — BROCKE, M. - PETUCHOWSKI, J.J. (eds.), *The Lord's Prayer*, 1978, 157-168.

**BOMPOIS, Léon-Noël**

1965 *Synopse d'après la traduction E. Osty – J. Trinquet*. Paris: Mame, 1965, XLIV-385 p.

**BONAR, C.**

1994 The Spirituality of the Beatitudes. — *Emmanuel* 100 (1994) 299-303; 365-368; 429-431.
[NTA 39, 140/141/799]

**BONHAM, Tal D.**

1967    *The Demands of Discipleship. The Relevance of the Sermon on the Mount.* Pine Bluff,
       AR: Discipleship Book Company, 1967. — Diss. Southwestern Baptist Theol. Sem., Fort Worth,
       TX, 1963.

**BONHOEFFER, Dietrich**

1937[R]  *Nachfolge* [1937], ed. M. Kuske – I. Tödt (Werke, 4). München: Kaiser, 1989, 390 p.
       Esp. 97-149 [5]; 150-175 [6]; 176-192 [7]; 193-211 [9,35–10,42].
       *Le prix de la grâce. Sermon sur la montagne*, trans. R. Revet. Neuchâtel: Delachaux et Niestlé, 1962, 239
       p. Esp. 68-109; 109-131; 131-145; 146-161. [NTA 7, p. 265]
       L.M. DEWAILLY, *RB* 70 (1963) 615; J.T. FORESTELL, *CBQ* 25 (1963) 146; H.H. ROWLEY, *ExpT* 74
       (1962-63) 319; J.M. TISON, *Bijdragen* 24 (1963) 209-210.
       *Navolging*, trans. E.A. Franken-Duparc (Carillon-reeks, S6). Amsterdam: Ten Have, 1964, 303 p. Esp. 84-
       137; 137-165; 165-183; 184-203.

**BONIN, Edmond**

1983    *The Lord's Prayer. A Commentary by St. Cyprian of Carthage.* Westminster, MD:
       Christian Classics, 1983, XVI-112 p.

**BONNARD, Émile**

1977    (ed.), *Saint Jérôme. Commentaire sur S. Matthieu. I: Livres I–II. Texte latin.
       Introduction, traduction et notes*; II: *Livres III–IV* (SC, 242 and 259). Paris: Cerf, 1977
       and 1979, 348 and 345 p. Esp. 9-56: "Introduction"; 59-345 and 9-319: "Texte et traduction".
       H. CROUZEL, *BullLitEccl* 80 (1979) 124-126; 82 (1981) 143-145; I.-H. DALMAIS, *La Maison-Dieu*
       (Paris) 142 (1980) 116; L. DUQUENNE, *NRT* 103 (1981) 429; Y. DUVAL, *EVie* 90 (1980) 324-325; C.
       GRANADO, *EstE* 55 (1980) 387-388; É. JUNOD, *RTP* 30 (1980) 199; C. KANNENGIESSER, *RSR* 70 (1982)
       586-587; J. MAGNIN, *Proche Orient Chrétien* (Jerusalem) 30 (1980) 369-370; C. MARTIN, *NRT* 101
       (1979) 93-94; J. MURPHY-O'CONNOR, *RB* 89 (1982) 303; P. NAUTIN, *RHR* 198 (1981) 85-86; N.
       SILANES, *EstTrin* 14 (1980) 281-282.

**BONNARD, Pierre**

1953a   Le livre d'O. Cullmann sur l'apôtre Pierre et l'Église. — *RTP* 3 (1953) 31-34. →
       Cullmann 1952

1953b   Le Sermon sur la montagne. — *RTP* 3 (1953) 233-246; = ID., *Anamnesis*, 1980, 81-92.
       El sermón del monte. — *CuadTheol* 9 (1954) 40-54.

1963    *L'Évangile selon saint Matthieu* (Commentaire du Nouveau Testament, 1).
       Neuchâtel–Paris: Delachaux & Niestlé, 1963, 424 p. [NTA 9, p. 250]; [2]1970, 466 p. [NTA
       16, p. 236]; [3]1992, 457 p. → C. Masson 1964
       E. BEST, *ScotJT* 18 (1965) 358-361; M. BOUTTIER, *ETR* 39 (1964) 62-64; M. CAMBE, *VSp* 112 (1965)
       97-98; V. HASLER, *TZ* 22 (1966) 215-216; X. LÉON-DUFOUR, *RSR* 53 (1965) 610-616; E. LÖVESTAM,
       *SvenskTeolKvart* 41 (1965) 105-106; E. MOELLER, *Questions liturgiques et paroissiales* (Leuven) 45
       (1964) 288-289; E. RASCO, *Greg* 48 (1967) 358-361; G. RINALDI, *BibOr* 7 (1965) 140-141; L.F.
       RIVERA, *RevistBíb* 29 (1967) 124-125; F. RONCHI, *Protestantesimo* 30 (1966) 234-236; H.H. ROWLEY,
       *ExpT* 76 (1964-65) 358; F.S., *Verbum Caro* (Taizé) 19 (1965) 107-108; C.W.F. SMITH, *JBL* 84 (1965)
       80-84; É. TROCMÉ, *RHPR* 44 (1964) 254-255; J.C. TURRO, *TS* 26 (1965) 436-438; J.I. VICENTINI,
       *Stromata* (San Miguel, Arg.) 21 (1965) 118-121; G.F. WOOD, *CBQ* 26 (1964) 478-479.
       H.-P. BERGERON, *CahJos* 26 (1978) 243-246; J.A. CARRASCO, *EstJos* 26 (1972) 232-233; M. DE
       BURGOS, *Communio* (Sevilla) 5 (1972) 192; M. LÀCONI, *RivBib* 20 (1972) 421-423; C. MATEOS,
       *EstAgust* 6 (1970) 519; J. MURPHY-O'CONNOR, *RB* 81 (1974) 144; O. ROUSSEAU, *Irénikon* 43 (1970)
       292; F. SALVONI, *RicBibRel* 7 (1972) 369.
       É. COTHENET, *EVie* 104 (1994) 43; E. CUVILLIER, *ETR* 68 (1993) 573-574.

1966    → Dupont 1966d

1967    Composition et signification historique de Matthieu XVIII. — DE LA POTTERIE, I. (ed.),
       *De Jésus aux Évangiles.* FS J. Coppens, 1967, 130-140. Esp. 130-137: "Contenu et
       composition de Matthieu XVIII"; 137-140: "Signification historique de Matthieu XVIII". (IT, 1971, 166-178);
       = ID., *Anamnesis*, 1980, 111-120. Esp. 111-117; 117-120.

1968*   & DUPONT, J. – REFOULÉ, F. (eds.), *Notre Père qui es aux cieux. La prière œcuménique* (Cahiers de la Traduction Œcuménique de la Bible, 3). Paris: Cerf/Les Bergers et les Mages, 1968, 118 p. → Dupont 1966d, Refoulé
        S. GONZÁLEZ DE CARREA, *EstBíb* 29 (1970) 186-187; X. JACQUES, *NRT* 93 (1971) 679.

1970a   Matthieu, éducateur du peuple chrétien. — DESCAMPS, A.L. – DE HALLEUX, A. (eds.), *Mélanges bibliques*. FS B. Rigaux, 1970, 1-7; = ID., *Anamnesis*, 1980, 105-110.

1970b   → Delorme 1970

1977    Matthieu 25,31-46. Questions de lecture et d'interprétation. — *FoiVie* 76/5 = *Cahiers bibliques* 16 (1977) 81-87. [NTA 24, 100]

1980    *Anamnesis. Recherches sur le Nouveau Testament* (Cahiers RTP, 3). Genève: RTP, 1980, XIII-230 p. → 1953b, 1967, 1970a

1981    → Zumstein 1981

1991    Qui cherche trouve ... le sens. — RÖMER, T. (ed.), *Lectio difficilior probabilior? L'exégèse comme expérience de décloisonnement. Mélanges offerts à Françoise Smyth-Florentin* (Dielheimer Blätter zum Alten Testament und seiner Rezeption in der Alten Kirche, Beiheft 12), Heidelberg: DBAT, 1991, 271-276. Esp. 272-274 [kingdom]; 275-276 [7,7].

**BONNARD, Pierre-Émile**

1966    *La Sagesse en personne annoncée et venue: Jésus Christ* (LD, 44). Paris: Cerf, 1966, 164 p. Esp. 124-133 [11,19.25-30; 23,34-36].

1979    De la Sagesse personnifiée dans l'Ancien Testament à la Sagesse en personne dans le Nouveau. — GILBERT, M. (ed.), *La Sagesse de l'Ancien Testament* (BETL, 51), Gembloux: Duculot; Leuven: University Press, 1979, 117-149. Esp. 136-139 [23,34-36]; Leuven: University Press / Peeters, ²1990.

**BONNEAU, Normand**

1994    The Synoptic Gospels in the Sunday Lectionary: Ordinary Time. — *Questions Liturgiques* (Leuven) 75 (1994) 154-169. Esp. 158-162. [NTA 39, 777]

**BONO, Luigi**

1971    L'infanzia di Gesù nell'esegesi degli ultimi quarant'anni. — *Ministero Pastorale* (Torino) 46 (1971) 16-23.

**BONSIRVEN, Joseph**

1951    *Théologie du Nouveau Testament* (Théologie, 22). Paris: Aubier, 1951, 470 p. Esp. 35-41 [Son of Man]; 41-54 [Son of God]; 55-107 [kingdom]; 126-147 [ethics]; 148-159 [faith]; 160-173 [ecclesiology].
        *Theology of the New Testament*, trans. S.F.L. Tye. London: Burns & Oates; Westminster, MD: Newman, 1963, XXIV-413 p.

1956    La constitution sociale du Règne de Dieu. I-II. — *Revue d'ascétique et de mystique* (Toulouse) 125 (1956) 3-32; 167 (1956) 257-283. [NTA 1, 233/234]

1957    *Le Règne de Dieu* (Théologie, 37). Paris: Aubier, 1957, 230 p. Esp. 84-96 [5,3.11-12; 6,25-34]; 110-116 [5,21-22.25-26; 7,3-5; 18,6-7]; 117-121 [5,38-42.43-45]; 124-143 [5,8.27-28.32.33-37; 6,22-23; 11,28-30; 19,9.10-12; 23,25-26]; 153-169 [6,9-13]; 192-195 [16,16-19].

**BONY, Paul**

1974    Ministères, mariage et célibat. — DELORME, J. (ed.), *Le ministère et les ministères*, 1974, 495-505. Esp. 496-497 [19,10-12].

**BONZI, M.**

1985    *Analisi della parabola degli operai nella vigna (Mt. 20,1-16)*. Diss. Milano, 1985 (G. Ghiberti).

**BOOBYER, George Henry**

1951    The Interpretation of the Parables of Jesus. — *ExpT* 62 (1950-51) 131-134.

**BOONSTRA, H.**

1980    Satire in Matthew. — *Christianity & Literature* (Grand Rapids, MI) 29 (1980) 32-45.
[NTA 26, 458]

**BOOTH, Charles E.**

1976    An Exegesis of Matthew 25:31-46. — *Foundations* (Rochester, NY) 19 (1976) 214-215.

**BORCHERT, Gerald L.**

1992    Matthew 5:48 – Perfection and the Sermon. — *RExp* 89 (1992) 265-269.

**BORDONI, Marcello**

1982    Istanze pneumatologiche di una cristologia in prospettiva universale. — MARCHESELLI,
C.C. (ed.), *Parole e Spirito*. FS S. Cipriani, 1982, II, 1017-1041. Esp. 1026-1031.

**BORG, Marcus J.**

1973    A New Context for Romans xiii. — *NTS* 19 (1972-73) 205-218. Esp. 206 [5,43-46]. [NTA
17, 1039]

1987a   *Jesus: A New Vision. Spirit, Culture, and the Life of Discipleship*. San Francisco, CA:
Harper & Row, 1987, VIII-216 p.; ²1993.

1987b   The Jesus Seminar and the Passion Sayings. — *Forum* 3/2 (1987) 81-95. [NTA 32, 84]

1992    The Teaching of Jesus Christ. — *ABD* 3 (1992) 804-812.

1994    *Meeting Jesus Again for the First Time. The Historical Jesus & the Heart of
Contemporary Faith*. San Francisco, CA: HarperCollins, 1994, IX-150 p. Esp. 39-95:
"Jesus and wisdom: teacher of alternative wisdom"; 96-118: "Jesus, the wisdom of God: Sophia become
flesh".

**BORGEN, Peder**

1959    John and the Synoptics in the Passion Narrative. — *NTS* 5 (1958-59) 246-259. Esp. 247-
249 [27,57-60]; 249-251 [26,42.51-52]; 251-252 [27,27-29]; 253 [27,33.35-37.56]; 254-255 [27,11.19-23];
255-257 [26,57-58.67.72-74]; 257-259 [28,1-10]. [NTA 4, 359]; = ID., *Logos Was the True Light*,
1983, 67-80. Esp. 68-70; 70-72; 72-73; 74-75; 75-78; 78-80. → Buse 1960

1966    Den såkalte gyldne regel (Matt. 7:12, Luk 6:31), dens forekomst i Det nye testamentes
omverden og dens innhold i evangelienes kontekst. — *NorskTeolTids* 67 (1966) 129-
146. [NTA 11, 699]
Eine allgemein-ethische Maxime. — *Temenos* 5 (1969) 37-53.
The Golden Rule, with Emphasis on Its Usage in the Gospels. — ID., *Paul Preaches
Circumcision*, 1983, 99-114.

1971    En tradisjonhistorisk analyse av materialet om Jesu fødsel hos Ignatius. — *TidsTeolKirk*
42 (1971) 37-44.
Ignatius and Traditions on the Birth of Jesus. — ID., *Paul Preaches Circumcision*,
1983, 155-163.

1979    The Use of Tradition in John 12.44-50. — *NTS* 26 (1979-80) 18-35. Esp. 24 [10,40]; 30-31
[10,34-35]; 31 [7,26]. [NTA 24, 845]; = ID., *Logos Was the True Light*, 1983, 49-66. Esp. 55;
61-62; = ID., *Philo, John and Paul. New Perspectives on Judaism and Early
Christianity* (Brown Judaic Studies, 131), Atlanta, GA: Scholars, 1987, 185-204. Esp.
191-192; 197-198.

1983a   *Paul Preaches Circumcision and Pleases Men and Other Essays on Christian Origins*
("Relieff", 8). Trondheim: Tapir, 1983, 228 p. → 1966, 1971

1983b   *Logos Was the True Light and Other Essays on the Gospel of John* ("Relieff", 9).
Trondheim: Tapir, 1983, 172 p. → 1959, 1979

1987    John and the Synoptics: Can Paul Offer Help? — HAWTHORNE, G.F. – BETZ, O. (eds.), *Tradition and Interpretation*. FS E.E. Ellis, 1987, 80-94. Esp. 89-91 [12,1-8/Jn 5,1-18]. → 1990a-b

1990a   John and the Synoptics. — DUNGAN, D.L. (ed.), *The Interrelations of the Gospels*, 1990, 408-437 (→ 1987, revised and expanded). Esp. 424-432 [12,1-8/Jn 5,1-18]; 432-436 [21,10-12/Jn 2,13-22]; = ID., *Early Christianity*, 1996, 121-157 (additional note, 156-157). Esp. 140-149; 149-155. → 1987; → Neirynck 1990e

1990b   John and the Synoptics: A Reply. — *Ibid.*, 451-458. Esp. 454-456 [12,1-8/Jn 5,1-18]; = ID., *Early Christianity*, 1996, 174-182. Esp. 178-180. → 1987; → Neirynck 1990e

1991    The Sabbath Controversy in John 5:1-18 and Analogous Controversy Reflected in Philo's Writings. — *The Studia Philonica Annual* (Atlanta, GA) 3 (1991) 209-221. Esp. 210-216 [12,1-8/Jn 5,1-18]; = ID., *Early Christianity*, 1996, 105-120. Esp. 106-113.

1992    The Independence of the Gospel of John. Some Observations. — VAN SEGBROECK, F., et al. (eds.), *The Four Gospels 1992*. FS F. Neirynck, 1992, III, 1815-1833. Esp. 1819-1820 [5,32; 19,9/1 Cor]; 1821-1823 [10,40/Jn 13,20]; 1826-1828 [18,3/Jn 3,3.5]; 1829-1830 [16,19; 18,18 /Jn 20,23]; = ID., *Early Christianity*, 1996, 183-204. Esp. 186-189; 190-193; 196-198; 199-201.

1996    *Early Christianity and Hellenistic Judaism*. Edinburgh: Clark, 1996, XI-376 p. → 1990a-b, 1991, 1992, Neirynck 1990e

**BORGER, Rykle**

1987    NA²⁶ und die neutestamentliche Textkritik. — *TR* 52 (1987) 1-58. Esp. 21-25 [10,31; 12,47; 15,5; 20,30]. [NTA 31, 977] → K. Aland [Nestle-Aland 1979]

1989    Zum Stande der neutestamentlichen Lexikographie. Die Neubearbeitung des Wörterbuchs von W. Bauer. — *Göttingische gelehrte Anzeigen* 241 (1989) 103-146. → K. Aland [Bauer-Aland 1988]

**BORGONOVO, G.** → Ghiberti 1993

**BORI, Pier Cesare**

1986    "Date a Cesare quel che è di Cesare..." (Mt 22,21). Linee di storia dell'interpretazione antica. — *CrnStor* 7 (1986) 451-464; = ID., *L'estasi del profeta, ed altri saggi tra ebraismo e cristianesimo dalle origini fino ad "Mosè" di Freud*, Bologna: Il Mulino, 1989, 53-68.

**BORING, M. Eugene**

1972    How May We Identify Oracles of Christian Prophets in the Synoptic Tradition? Mark 3:28-29 as a Test Case. — *JBL* 91 (1972) 501-521. Esp. 505-506: "The synoptics and Acts"; 511-515 [12,31-32]; 519-520. [NTA 17, 532]

1976a   Christian Prophecy and Matt 10:23: A Test Exegesis. — *SBL 1976 Seminar Papers*, 127-133.

1976b   The Unforgivable Sin Logion Mark iii 28-29 / Matt xii 31-32 / Luke xii 10: Formal Analysis and History of the Tradition. — *NT* 18 (1976) 258-279. Esp. 259-265: "Was the Markan form derived from Matthew?"; 265-267: "What was the Q form of the saying?"; 267-270: "Was the Markan form derived from the Q form?"; 270-274: "Is the Markan form older than the Q form?". [NTA 21, 745]

1977    Christian Prophecy and Matthew 23:34-6. A Test Exegesis. — *SBL 1977 Seminar Papers*, 117-126.

1982    *Sayings of the Risen Jesus. Christian Prophecy in the Synoptic Tradition* (SNTS MS, 46). Cambridge: University Press, 1982, XV-327 p. Esp. 43-47.260: "Sources" [Mt]; 137-182.272-281: "Christian prophecy in Q" [Q 6,22-23; 10,2-16.21-22.23-44; 11,29-32.39-52; 12,2-12.22-34.51-56.57-59; 13,23-30.34-35; 16,17; 17,22-37; 22,28-30]; 204-218.286-288: "Christian prophecy in Matthew" [5,3-12.18.19; 6,14-15; 7,2.13-23; 10,5-42; 11,28-30; 12,33-35; 13,35; 16,17-19; 17,20; 18,18.19-20; 19,12.23; 22,3; 23,1-39; 28,18-20]. → 1991

1983 Christian Prophecy and the Sayings of Jesus: The State of the Question. — *NTS* 29 (1983) 104-112. Esp. 106-107. [NTA 27, 492] → J.D.G. Dunn 1978b, D. Hill 1979a

1985 Criteria of Authenticity. The Lucan Beatitudes as a Test Case. — *Forum* 1/4 (1985) 3-38. Esp. 20-31 [Q 6,20-23]. [NTA 31, 1116] → Funk 1986b
The Historical-Critical Method's "Criteria of Authenticity": The Beatitudes in Q and Thomas as a Test Case. — *Semeia* 44 (1988) 9-44. Esp. 24-35. [NTA 33, 648]

1988 A Proposed Reconstruction of Q 10:23-24. — *SBL 1988 Seminar Papers*, 456-471.

1989 A Proposed Reconstruction of Q 13:28-29. — *SBL 1989 Seminar Papers*, 1-22.

1991 *The Continuing Voice of Jesus. Christian Prophecy and the Gospel Tradition.* Louisville, KY: Westminster – Knox, 1991, 303 p. Esp. 191-234: "Prophetic sayings of the risen Jesus in Q". → 1982

1992a Prophecy (Early Christian). — *ABD* 5 (1992) 495-502. Esp. 499.

1992b The Synoptic Problem, "Minor" Agreements, and the Beelzebul Pericope. — VAN SEGBROECK, F., et al. (eds.), *The Four Gospels 1992*. FS F. Neirynck, 1992, I, 587-619. Esp. 587-588: "Introduction: the continuing problem"; 588-595: "Clarifying the issues in the debate"; 596-600: "A proposal on each of the disputed issues"; 600-607: "The Beelzebul pericope as probe and illustration"; 608-618: "The major theories from a redaction-critical perspective applied to this pericope".

1993 Rhetoric, Righteousness and the Sermon on the Mount. — O'DAY, G.R. – LONG, T.G. (eds.), *Listening to the Word* [FS F.B. Craddock], Nashville, TN: Abingdon, 1993, 53-75.

1994 The Convergence of Source Analysis, Social History, and Literary Structure in the Gospel of Matthew. — *SBL 1994 Seminar Papers*, 587-611. Esp. 589-592: "The variety of proposed outlines"; 592-597: "Phenomena of the text"; 598-605: "A new beginning point"; 605-610: "The structure of 1:2–12:21"; 610-611: "The structure of 12:22–28:20".

1995a & BERGER, K. – COLPE, C. (eds.), *Hellenistic Commentary to the New Testament*. Nashville, TN: Abingdon, 1995, 633 p. Esp. 33-168: "The gospel of Matthew (and Parallels)"; 182-237: "The gospel of Luke (and Parallels)". → K. Berger 1987

1995b Theological Reflections on the Gospel of Matthew. — *The New Interpreter's Bible*, 8, Nashville, TN: Abingdon, 1995, 87-505.

**BORLAND, James A.**

1982 Re-examining New Testament Textual-Critical Principles and Practices Used to Negate Inerrancy. — *JEvTS* 25 (1982) 499-506. Esp. 501-503 [1,7-10]. [NTA 28, 38]

**BORMANN, Lukas**

1994* & DEL TREDICI, K. – STANDHARTINGER, A. (eds.), *Religious Propaganda and Missionary Competition in the New Testament World. Essays Honoring Dieter Georgi* (SupplNT, 74). Leiden: Brill, 1994, XIII-570 p. → Bormann, J.M. Robinson, D.E. Smith

1994 Die Verrechtlichung der frühesten christlichen Überlieferung im lukanischen Schrifttum. — *Ibid.*, 283-311. Esp. 288-293 [Q 12,11-12].

**BORNE, Gerhard**

1982a *Bergpredigt und Frieden.* Olten: Walter, 1982, 147 p. → Frankemölle 1983c
J. BOADA, *ActBibl* 20 (1983) 231-233.

1982b *Widerstand und Glück. Betrachtungen zum Vaterunser.* Neukirchen: Neukirchener, 1982, 101 p.

**BORNKAMM, Günther**

1938ᴿ Das Wort Jesu von Bekennen. [1938] — ID., *Geschichte und Glaube*, I, 1968, 25-36. Esp. 27-28 [10,32-33].

1946[R]  Der Lohngedanke im Neuen Testament. [1946] — ID., *Studien zu Antike und Urchristentum. Gesammelte Aufsätze Band II* (BevT, 28), München: Kaiser, 1959; [2]1963, 69-92. Esp. 71-73 [25,14-30]; 81-87 [20,1-16]; = ID., *Studien*, 1985, 72-95. Esp. 74-76; 84-90. → 1961

1948[R]  Die Sturmstillung im Matthäus-Evangelium. [1948] — ID., et al., *Überlieferung und Auslegung*, 1959, 48-53; = LANGE, J. (ed.), *Das Matthäus-Evangelium*, 1980, 112-118.
The Stilling of the Storm in Matthew. — ID., et al., *Tradition and Interpretation*, 1963, 52-57.

1951   Die Verzögerung der Parusie. Exegetische Bemerkungen zu zwei synoptischen Texten. — SCHMAUCH, W. (ed.), *In Memoriam Ernst Lohmeyer*, 1951, 116-126. Esp. 119-126 [25,1-13]; = ID., *Geschichte und Glaube*, I, 1968, 46-55. Esp. 49-55.

1954a  Das Doppelgebot der Liebe. — ELTESTER, W. (ed.), *Neutestamentliche Studien*. FS R. Bultmann, 1954, 85-93. Esp. 92-93 [22,34-40]; = ID., *Geschichte und Glaube*, I, 1968, 37-45. Esp. 44-45.

1954b  Die Gegenwartsbedeutung der Bergpredigt. — *Universitas* 9 (1954) 1283-1285. → 1956a, 201-204

1954c  Matthäus als Interpret der Herrenworte. — *TLZ* 79 (1954) 341-346. → 1956b; → Eltester 1954

1956a  *Jesus von Nazareth* (Urban-Bücher, 19). Stuttgart: Kohlhammer, 1956, 214 p. Esp. 11-23: "Glaube und Geschichte in den Evangelien"; 48-57: "Jesus von Nazareth"; 58-87 [kingdom]; 88-132 [ethics]; 133-140 [discipleship]; 141-154 [passion narrative]; 155-163.204-208 [Messiah]; 165-170 [resurrection]; 170-172 [church]; 197-201: "Die Geschichte und Vorgeschichte der synoptischen Evangelien"; 201-204: "Zur Geschichte der Auslegung der Bergpredigt" (→ 1954b); [2]1957; [3]1959; [10]1975; [15]1995.
*Jesus of Nazareth*, trans. I. & F. McLuskey & J.M. Robinson. London: Hodder & Stoughton; New York: Harper & Row, 1960, 239 p. Esp. 13-26; 53-63; 64-95; 96-143; 144-152; 153-168; 169-178.226-231; 180-186; 186-188; 188-191; 215-220; 221-225; paperback 1995.
Faith and History in the Gospels. — *Ibid.*, 13-26; Jesus of Nazareth. — *Ibid.*, 53-63; = MCARTHUR, H.K. (ed.), *In Search of the Historical Jesus*, 1969, 41-53; 164-173.
*Jezus van Nazareth* (Phoenix Pocket, 90). Zeist: de Haan; Antwerpen: Standaard, 1963, 208 p.
*Qui est Jésus de Nazareth?*, trans. M. Barth & S. de Bussy (Parole de Dieu, 9). Paris: Seuil, 1973, 252 p.
*Jesús de Nazaret* (Biblioteca de estudios bíblicos, 13). Salamanca: Sígueme, 1975, 231 p.
*Gesù di Nazaret. I risultati di quaranta anni di ricerche sul "Gesù della storia"*, trans. E. Paschetto (Nuovi studi teologici, 3). Torino: Claudiana, 1968, 250 p.; [2]1977.
Trans. Afrikaans 1974; Portuguese 1976; Serbo-Croatian 1981.

1956b  Enderwartung und Kirche im Matthäusevangelium. — DAVIES, W.D. – DAUBE, D. (eds.), *The Background of the New Testament*. FS C.H. Dodd, 1956, 222-260. Esp. 223-232: "Die Verbindung von Eschatologie und Ekklesiologie in den Reden des Matth.-Evs."; 232-240: "Die bessere Gerechtigkeit"; 241-247: "Christologie und Gesetz im Matth.-Ev."; 247-260: "Ekklesiologie und Christologie"; = ID., et al., *Überlieferung und Auslegung*, 1959, 13-47 ("überarbeitet"). Esp. 13-21; 21-29; 29-35; 35-47; = LANGE, J. (ed.), *Das Matthäus-Evangelium*, 1980, 223-264. Esp. 223-231; 232-239; 240-245; 245-256. → 1954c; → Dermience 1985
End-Expectation and Church in Matthew. — ID., et al., *Tradition and Interpretation*, 1963, 15-51. Esp. 15-24; 24-32; 32-38; 38-51.

1957   Bergpredigt. I. Biblisch. — *RGG* 1 ([3]1957) 1047-1050.

1958   Evangelien, synoptische. — *RGG* 2 ([3]1958) 753-766. Esp. 758-760: "Spruchquelle"; 762-763 [Mt].

1959a  & BARTH, G. – HELD, H.J., *Überlieferung und Auslegung im Matthäusevangelium* (WMANT, 1). Neukirchen-Vluyn: Neukirchener, 1959; [2]1961, 304 p.; [4]1965; [5]1968; [6]1970, 326 p. → 1948, 1956b, 1964, G. Barth, Held; → Rohde 1965
R. BAUMANN, *BK* 26 (1971) 94; M.-É. BOISMARD, *RB* 68 (1961) 299-300; G. DELLING, *TLZ* 85 (1960) 925-928; J. DUPONT, *LumièreV* 49 (1960) 29-30; X. LÉON-DUFOUR, *RSR* 50 (1962) 91-94; J.

RADERMAKERS, *NRT* 90 (1968) 676-677; E. SCHWEIZER, *EvT* 23 (1963) 611-612; P. STUHLMACHER, *VerkFor* 1958-59/2-3 (1962) 120-124; K. THIEME, *Freiburger Rundbrief* 14 (1962) 73-74; A. VIARD, *RSPT* 45 (1961) 286-287.
*Tradition and Interpretation in Matthew*, trans. P. Scott (The New Testament Library). Philadelphia, PA: Westminster; London: SCM, 1963, 307 p. [NTA 8, p. 150]; 2nd rev. ed., 1982, 345 p. [NTA 28, p. 80] → Fannon 1965, Feiler 1983
   J. BLIGH, *HeythJ* 5 (1964) 525-526; W. BROWNING, *Theology*, 66 (1963) 337-338; F.V. FILSON, *TTod* 21 (1964-65) 237-238; J.C. HINDLEY, *IndianJT* 15 (1966) 32-34; R.A. KRAFT, *JBL* 83 (1964) 193-194; B. LINDARS, *JTS* 15 (1964) 123-126; A.T. MOLLEGEN, *ATR* 46 (1964) 109-110; R.H. MOUNCE, *ChrTod* 8 (1963-64) 756; R.A. NUNZ, *DunRev* 4 (1964) 242-245; A. PATRIQUIN, *JBR* 33 (1965) 69-70; D.W.B. ROBINSON, *RTR* 22 (1963) 92-93; J.S. RUEF, *Interpr* 18 (1964) 222-225; V. TAYLOR, *ExpT* 74 (1962-63) 363.

1959b   Ehescheidung und Wiederverheiratung im Neuen Testament. — SUCKER, W., et al. (eds.), *Die Mischehe. Handbuch für die evangelische Seelsorge*, Göttingen: Vandenhoeck & Ruprecht, 1959, 50-53; = ID., *Geschichte und Glaube*, I, 1968, 56-59.

1961   *Der Lohngedanke im Neuen Testament* (Bensheimer Hefte, 15). Göttingen: Vandenhoeck & Ruprecht, 1961, 30 p. Esp. 14-15 [5,12]; 16-17 [25,31-46]; 17-22 [20,1-16]. → 1946

1964   *Der Auferstandene und der Irdische. Mt 28,16-20.* — DINKLER, E. (ed.), *Zeit und Geschichte*. FS R. Bultmann, 1964, 171-191. Esp. 173-175 [28,18]; 175-178.185-187 [28,19-20]; 180-181 [5,17-20]; 183-184 [16,18]; 188-190 [1-2]; = ID., et al., *Überlieferung und Auslegung*, ⁴1965, 289-310. Esp. 291-293; 293-297; 303-304; 299; 302-303; 307-309.
*The Risen Lord and the Earthly Jesus. Matthew 28.16-20.* — ROBINSON, J.M. (ed.), *The Future of Our Religious Past*. FS R. Bultmann, 1971, 203-229. Esp. 205-208; 208-213.222-223; 215-216; 219-220; 225-228.

1968   *Geschichte und Glaube. Erster Teil: Gesammelte Aufsätze Band III* (BevT, 48). München: Kaiser, 1968, 287 p. → 1938, 1951, 1954a, 1959b

1970*   & RAHNER, K. (eds.), *Die Zeit Jesu. Festschrift für Heinrich Schlier*. Freiburg: Herder, 1970, 336 p. → G. Bornkamm, Kremer, Schnackenburg, H. Zimmermann

1970   *Die Binde- und Lösegewalt in der Kirche des Matthäus. — Ibid.*, 93-107. Esp. 94-99 [18,1-22]; 99-101 [18,15-20]; 101-107 [16,17-19; 18,18]; = ID., *Geschichte und Glaube*, II, 1971, 37-50. Esp. 37-42; 42-44; 45-50; = *TJb* 15 (1972) 277-289. Esp. 277-280; 280-282; 282-289.
*The Authority to "Bind" and "Loose" in the Church in Matthew's Gospel: The Problem of Sources in Matthew's Gospel.* — BUTTRICK, D.G. (ed.), *Jesus and Man's Hope*. I, 1970, 37-50. Esp. 37-42; 42-44; 45-50. [NTA 15, 146]; = STANTON, G. (ed.), *The Interpretation of Matthew*, 1983, 85-97. Esp. 86-89; 89-90; 90-92; 92-95; ²1995, 101-114. Esp. 102-105; 105-107; 107-109; 109-112.

1971a   *Bibel. Das Neue Testament. Eine Einführung in seine Schriften im Rahmen der Geschichte des Urchristentums* (Themen der Theologie, 9). Stuttgart–Berlin: Kreuz, 1971, 175 p. Esp. 35-80: "Die synoptischen Evangelien" [71-76: Mt].
& WOLFF, H.W., *Zugang zur Bibel. Eine Einführung in die Schriften des Alten und Neuen Testaments* (Themen der Theologie, 7 und 9 Studienausgabe). Stuttgart–Berlin: Kreuz, 1980, IV-353 p.
*The New Testament. A Guide to its Writings*, trans. R.H. Fuller & I. Fuller. Philadelphia, PA: Fortress, 1973, VIII-166 p.
*Le Nouveau Testament. Problèmes d'introduction. Ses livres dans le cadre de l'histoire du christianisme des origines*, trans. É. de Peyer. Genève: Labor et Fides, 1973, 207 p.
*Bibbia. Il Nuovo Testamento. Introduzione nel quadro del cristianesimo primitivo*. Brescia: Morcelliana, 1974. Trans. Portuguese 1981.

1971b   *Geschichte und Glaube. Zweiter Teil: Gesammelte Aufsätze Band IV* (BEvT, 53). München: Kaiser, 1971, 276 p. → 1970, 1971c

1971c   *Wandlungen im alt- und neutestamentlichen Gesetzesverständnis. — Ibid.*, 73-119. Esp. 73-80 [5,17-20]; 92-94 [22,34-40]; 94-96 [7,12]; = ID., *Studien*, 1985, 25-71. Esp. 25-32; 44-46; 46-48.

1978 Der Aufbau der Bergpredigt. — *NTS* 24 (1977-78) 419-432. Esp. 419-421 [research]; 421-424; 424-431 [6,19-34; 7,1-5.7-11]. [NTA 23, 429]

1985 *Studien zum Neuen Testament.* München: Kaiser, 1985, 334 p. → 1946, 1971c

**BORNKAMM, Karin**

1988 Umstrittener "spiegel eines Christlichen lebens". Luthers Auslegung der Bergpredigt in seinen Wochenpredigten von 1530 bis 1532. — *ZTK* 85 (1988) 409-454. Esp. 412-430: "Das Verständnis der Bergpredigt im Mittelalter wie im Schwärmertum und Luthers Neuansatz"; 430-450: "Grundzüge der Bergpredigtauslegung Luthers".

**BØRRESEN, Kari Elisabeth**

1982 L'usage patristique de métaphores féminines dans le discours sur Dieu. — *RTL* 13 (1982) 205-220. Ep. 209-210 [23,37]. → Doignon 1983

**BORSCH, Frederick Houk**

1967 *The Son of Man in Myth and History* (The New Testament Library). London: SCM; Philadelphia, PA: Westminster, 1967, 431 p. Esp. 314-401: "The synoptic Son of Man". → Maddox 1971

1970 *The Christian and Gnostic Son of Man* (Studies in Biblical Theology, II/14). London: SCM, 1970, XII-130 p. Esp. 1-28: "The priority of the Son of Man in rival parallel sayings" [5,11; 8,20; 9,8; 10,32-33; 11,19; 12,31-32; 16,4.13-21.28; 19,28; 24,43-44].

1975 Jesus, the Wandering Preacher? — HOOKER, M.D. – HICKLING, C. (eds.), *What about the New Testament?* FS C. Evans, 1975, 45-63. Esp. 48-49 [10,5-23]; 50-52 [8,19-22]; 52 [11,21-23].

1983 *Power in Weakness. New Hearing for Gospel Stories of Healing and Discipleship.* Philadelphia, PA: Fortress, 1983, XVIII-156 p. Esp. 1-8 [12,22]; 9-21 [9,1-8]; 35-50 [8,28-34]; 51-66 [15,21-28]; 67-84 [12,9-14]; 99-109 [20,29-34].

1988 *Many Things in Parables. Extravagant Stories on New Community.* Philadelphia, PA: Fortress, 1988, X-167 p. [NTA 32, p. 240]

1992 Further Reflections on "the Son of Man": The Origins and Development of the Title. — CHARLESWORTH, J.H., et al. (eds.), *The Messiah*, 1992, 130-144. Esp. 143-144 [12,32].

**BORSE, Udo**

1987 Der Evangelist als Verfasser der Emmauserzählung. — *SNTU* 12 (1987) 35-67. Esp. 37-48: "Die Vorgabe des Matthäusevangeliums" [28,8-10]. [NTA 33, 185]; = ID., *Studien zur Entstehung und Auslegung des Neuen Testaments*, ed. R. Börschel, et al. (Stuttgarter Biblische Aufsatzbände, 21), Stuttgart: Katholisches Bibelwerk, 1996, 175-210. Esp. 178-189.

1992 Der Mehrheitstext Mk 15,27f.32c: Die Kreuzigung Jesu zwischen zwei Räubern als Schrifterfüllung. — *SNTU* 17 (1992) 169-194. Esp. 183-191: "Das Kreuzigungsbild in den anderen Evangelien" [27,38.44]. [NTA 37, 1300]; = ID., *Studien*, 1996, 11-38. Esp. 26-34.

**BOSCH, David**

1959 *Die Heidenmission in der Zukunftsschau Jesu. Eine Untersuchung zur Eschatologie der synoptischen Evangelien* (ATANT, 36). Zürich: Zwingli, 1959, 210 p. Esp. 43-131: "Jesus und die Entscheidung für die Heidenmission"; 80-86: "Mt. 10 und der Zwölferkreis"; 184-182: "Der Missionsbefehl des Auferstandenen" [28,16-20]. — Diss. Basel, 1956 (O. Cullmann).

1983 The Structure of Mission: An Exploration of Matthew 28,16-20. — SHENK, W.R. (ed.), *Exploring Church Growth*, Grand Rapids, MI, 1983, 218-248.

1991 *Transforming Mission. Paradigm Shifts in the Theology of Mission* (American Society of Missiology Series, 16). Maryknoll, NY: Orbis, 1991, XIX-587 p. Esp. 56-83: "Matthew: mission as disciple-making".

**BOSLOOPER, Thomas**
1962	*The Virgin Birth*. London: SCM; Philadelphia, PA: Westminster, 1962, 272 p. Esp. 202-204 [1,23/OT]; 212-214 [1,18-25]; 214-216 [1,16].

**BOSOLD, Iris**
1978	*Pazifismus und prophetische Provokation. Das Grußverbot Lk 10,4b und sein historischer Kontext* (SBS, 90). Stuttgart: Katholisches Bibelwerk, 1978, 98 p. Esp. 24-42: "Allgemeiner literarkritischer Überblick über die synoptischen Aussendungsperikopen"; 43-51: "Der ursprüngliche Charakter der Aussendungsperikope in Q: gehörte Lk 10,4b zur Q-Perikope?"; 52-72: "Die zeitgeschichtliche Rahmen"; 73-92: "Das Grußverbot im Rahmen des historischen Wirkens der Jünger". — Diss. Tübingen, 1975 (G. Lohfink).
	A. FUCHS, *SNTU* 4 (1979) 149-150.

**BOSTOCK, Gerald**
1986	Virgin Birth or Human Conception? — *ExpT* 97 (1985-86) 260-263. Esp. 262 [1,23]. [NTA 31, 77] → Benson 1987

1987	Divine Birth, Human Conception. — *ExpT* 98 (1986-87) 331-333. [NTA 32, 73] → Benson 1987

**BOTHA, F.J.**
1967	Recent Research on the Lord's Prayer. — *Neotestamentica* 1 (1967) 42-50. [NTA 18, 106]

**BOTTE, Bernard**
1954	Le problème synoptique. — *BibVieChrét* 7 (1954) 116-122. → Vaganay 1954a

**BOTTINI, Claudio**
1990	& ADINOLFI, M., *Il vangelo secondo Matteo, lettura esegetico-esistenziale* (IV Settimana Biblica Abruzzese, 3-8.VII.1989), ed. R. Corona. L'Aquila: Curia O.F.M., 1990, 183 p.

**BOTTINI, Giovanni Claudio** → Cignelli 1990, 1991, 1993, 1994

**BOTTINO, Adriana**
1992	Rilettura poetica di Mt 2,11 nell'*Inno alla Natività* di Romano il Melode. — SERRA, A. - VALENTINI, A. (eds.), *I Vangeli dell'infanzia*, I, 1992, 111-118.

**BOUCHER, Madeleine I.**
1977	*The Mysterious Parable. A Literary Study* (CBQ MS, 6). Washington, DC: Catholic Biblical Association, 1977, IX-101 p. Esp. 21-22.34-35 [13,24-30]; 34-35.38-40 [13,36-43]; 38-39 [18,12-14]. — Diss. Brown Univ., Providence, RI, 1973 (W.R. Schoedel).

1981	*The Parables* (New Testament Message, 7). Wilmington, DE: Glazier; Dublin: Veritas, 1981, 159 p. Esp. 67-76 [13,31-33/Mk-Q]; 77-81 [13,3-9.18-23/Mk]; 81-86 [13,24-30.36-43.47-50]; 88-91 [20,1-16]; 91-93 [21,28-32]; 96-98 [18,12-14]; 101-104 [22,1-14]; 106-107 [13,44-46]; 116-118 [18,23-35]; 122-124 [7,24-27]; 127-131 [25,1-13]; 136-143 [25,14-30]; 143-146 [24,45-51]; 146-152 [21,33-46].

**BOUGEROL, Jacques Guy**
1991	"In cruce omnia manifestantur". Rilettura di un sermone di Bonaventura. [11,28] — *Doctor Seraphicus* (Bagnoregio) 38 (1991) 115-121.

**BOUHOT, Jean-Paul**
1970	Remarques sur l'histoire du texte de l'Opus Imperfectum in Matthaeum. — *VigChr* 24 (1970) 197-209. → F.W. Schlatter 1985, Stuiber 1973

**BOUHOURS, Jean-François**
1972	Une étude de l'ordonnance de la triple tradition. — *RSR* 60 (1972) 595-614. [NTA 17, 884] → Frey 1972

**BOULEY, Allan**

1981 *From Freedom to Formula. The Evolution of the Eucharistic Prayer from Oral Improvisation to Written Texts* (CUA Studies in Christian Antiquity, 21). Washington, DC: CUA, 1981, XVII-302 p. Esp. 42-52: "The prayer of Jesus"; 69-70 [26,26-29].

**BOULOGNE, Charles-Damian**

1955 La tentation de Jésus au désert. — *VSp* 92 (1955) 364-380.

**BOULTON, P.H.**

1959 Διακονέω and its Cognates in the Four Gospels. — *Studia Evangelica* 1 (1959) 415-422. Esp. 417 [22,1-14]; 420 [25,42-45].

**BOUMA, Hans**

1979 *Het Onze Vader. Mattheüs 6* (Verklaring van een Bijbelgedeelte). Kampen: Kok, [1979], 96 p.

**BOUMIS, Panagiotis J.**

1980 The Rock of the Apostle Peter. Contribution to the Interpretation of Mt 16,18. [Greek] — Θεολογία (Athens) 51 (1980) 146-157 (English summary, 963); = (Archive of Ecclesiastical and Canon Law), Athens, 1981, 15 p.

**BOURGOIN, Henri**

1977 Le pain quotidien. — *CahRenan* 25/101 (1977) 1-17. [NTA 22, 396]

1979 'Επιούσιος expliqué par la notion de préfixe vide. — *Bib* 60 (1979) 91-96. [NTA 24, 89]

**BOURKE, Joseph**

1960 The Wonderful Counsellor. An Aspect of Christian Messianism. — *CBQ* 22 (1960) 123-143. Esp. 124-129: "The Messiah of two worlds". [NTA 5, 184]

**BOURKE, Myles M.**

1960 The Literary Genus of Matthew 1-2. — *CBQ* 22 (1960) 160-175. Esp. 161-166: "The infancy gospel and the life of Moses"; 166-167: "The origin and significance of the star-motif"; 167-173: "The motif Jesus-Israel"; 174-175: "The historicity of the infancy gospel". [NTA 5, 73]
   *TDig* 9 (1961) 20-21.

1967 Infancy Gospel. — *NewCathEnc* 7 (1967) 499-500.

1972 The Miracle Stories of the Gospels. — *DunRev* 12 (1972) 21-34. [NTA 17, 56]

**BOUSSET, Wilhelm**

1913[R] *Kyrios Christos. Geschichte des Christusglaubens von den Anfängen des Christentums bis Irenaeus* [1913, ²1921] (FRLANT, 21). Göttingen: Vandenhoeck & Ruprecht, ⁵1964, ⁶1967, XXIII-394 p. Esp. 44-50 [11,25-30]; 50-51 [7,21-22].
   *Kyrios Christos: A History of the Belief in Christ from the Beginnings of Christianity to Irenaeus*, trans. J.E. Steely. Nashville, TN – New York: Abingdon, 1970, 496 p.

**BOUTERSE, Johannes**

1986 *De boom en zijn vruchten. Bergrede en Bergredechristendom bij Reformatoren, Anabaptisten en Spiritualisten in de zestiende eeuw*. Kampen: Kok, 1986, 460 p. Esp. 15-21.292-295 [John Chrysostom]; 21-32.295-300 [Augustine]; 33-45.301-306 [Middle Ages]; 46-65.307-316 [Erasmus]; 66-103.317-335 [Luther]; 104-125.336-343 [Zwingli]; 126-172.344-361 [Anabaptists]; 173-207.362-378 [Bucer]; 208-222.379-385 [Oecolampadius]; 223-239.386-392 [Bullinger]; 240-255.393-403 [W. Musculus]; 256-278.404-416 [Calvin]. — Diss. Leiden, 1986 (G. Meyjes).
   J. LAMBRECHT, *Bijdragen* 51 (1990) 446; W. NIJENHUIS, *NTT* 42 (1988) 347-349.

**BOUTON, André**

1962    "C'est toi qui lui donneras le nom de Jésus". [1,18-25] — *AssSeign* I/8 (1962) 37-50; cf. II/8 (1972) 17-25. [NTA 17, 511]

**BOUTTIER, Michel**

1973    Les paraboles du maître dans la tradition synoptique. — *ETR* 48 (1973) 175-195. Esp. 178-182; 187-189. [NTA 18, 449]

1976    Commencement, force et fin de l'évangile. — *ETR* 51 (1976) 465-493. Esp. 473-474 [sayings]. [NTA 21, 393]

1978    Hésiode et le Sermon sur la montagne. [5,46] — *NTS* 25 (1978-79) 129-130. [NTA 23, 433]

1985    Le Père manifesté dans les actes et caché à la piété. Contraste et unité des chap. 5 et 6 du Sermon sur la montagne selon Matthieu. — GANTOY, R. (ed.), *À cause de l'Évangile*. FS J. Dupont, 1985, 39-56. Esp. 42-54: "Les trois énoncés de Mt 6,1.2-4.5.6.16-18"; 54-56: "Unité des chapitres 5 et 6 de Matthieu".

1986    Les béatitudes. — *ETR* 61 (1986) 245-246. [NTA 31, 114]

**BOUVAREL-BOURD'HORS, Anne**

1987    *Catalogue des fragments coptes*. I. *Fragments bibliques nouvellement identifiés*. Paris: Bibliothèque nationale, 1987, 126 p.

**BOUWMAN, Gijs**

1961    *De Bijbel over volgen en navolgen* (De Bijbel over..., 8). Roermond–Maaseik: Romen, 1961, 95 p. Esp. 10-18.79-86 [10,37-38; 16,24]; 63-70 [5,48].

1986    *Nieuw en Oud*. Over het evangelie van Matteüs (Cahiers voor levensverdieping, 51). Averbode: Altiora; Kampen: Kok, 1986, 159 p.
          P. BEENTJES, *Streven* 54 (1986-87) 375; W.H. BERFLO, *TijdTheol* 27 (1987) 404; W. VAN SOOM, *Collationes* 17 (1987) 110.

**BOVER, José Maria**

1943[R]  (ed.), *Novi Testamenti Biblia graeca et latina critico apparatu aucta* [1943]. Madrid: Consejo Superior de Investigaciones Científicas, [2]1950, [3]1953, [4]1959, [5]1968, LXXX-772 p. Esp. 1-99: "Κατὰ Μαθθαῖον". → O'Callaghan 1977

1950    El nombre de Simón Pedro. — *EstE* 24 (1950) 479-497. Esp. 480, 489, 491-497.

1951    La parábola del Remiendo (Mt. 9,16; Mc. 2,21; Lc. 5,36). — METZINGER, A. (ed.), *Miscellanea Biblica et Orientalia R.P. Athanasio Miller o.s.b. Secretario Pontificiae Commissionis Biblicae completis LXX annis oblata* (Studia Anselmiana, 27-28), Roma: Orbis Catholicus – Herder, 1951, 327-339. Esp. 328-332: "Valor y sentido de πλήρωμα en Mt.".

1952a   Dos casos de toponimia y de crítica textual. — *Sefarad* 12 (1952) 271-282. Esp. 272-275 [15,8]; 275-280 [8,28]; 280-282 [15,39].

1952b   Problemas inherentes a la interpretación de la parábola del Sembrador. [13,1-9.18-23] — *EstE* 26 (1952) 169-185.

1953a   Si peccaverit in te frater tuus. ... Mt. 18,15. Un caso interesante de crítica textual. — *EstBíb* 12 (1953) 195-198.

1953b   Variantes semíticas del texto antiqueno en san Mateo. — DÍAZ, R.M. (ed.), *Miscellanea Biblica B. Ubach*, 1953, 323-327. [11,23; 12,31-32; 15,6.8; 26,60; 27,43].

1954a   "El Maestro y el Señor" en la historia del rabinismo. [23,7-10] — *Sefarad* 14 (1954) 366–368.

1954b   "Nada hay encubierto que no se descubra". — *EstBíb* 13 (1954) 319-323. Esp. 321-323 [10,26-27].

1955a Diferente género literario de los evangelistas en la narracción de las tentaciones de Jesús en el desierto. [4,1-11] — *En torno al problema de la escatologia individual del Antiguo Testamento. Otros estudios* (XV Semana Biblica Española), Madrid: Consejo Superior de Investigaciones Científicas, 1955, 213-219.

1955b Un caso típico de critica textual. Mt. 27,28. — *Ibid.*, 221-226.

**BOVON, François**

1989a *Das Evangelium nach Lukas*. 1. Teilband: *Lk 1,1-9,50* (EKK NT, III/1). Zürich: Benziger; Neukirchen-Vluyn: Neukirchener, 1989, VIII-524 p. Esp. 166-167 [Q 3,1-9.14-18(Lk)]; 191-204 [Q 4,1-13]; 293-306 [Q 6,20-26]; 306-328 [Q 6,27-38]; 328-343 [Q 6,39-49]; 346-347 [Q 7,1-10]; 367-383 [Q 7,18-35]. → 1996
*L'Évangile selon saint Luc (1,1–9,50)* (Commentaire du Nouveau Testament, IIIa). Genève: Labor et Fides, 1991, 515 p. Esp. 162-163; 187-198; 287-299; 300-321; 324-335; 338-339; 359-374.
*Das Evangelium nach Lukas*. 2. Teilband: *Lk 9,51-14,35* (EKK NT, III/2). Zürich–Düsseldorf: Benziger; Neukirchen-Vluyn: Neukirchener, 1996, VIII-556 p. Esp. 32-34 [Q 9,57-62]; 45-49 [Q 10,2-12.13-15.16]; 67-69 [Q 10,21-24]; 120-122 [Q 11,2-4]; 146-148.153-154 [Q 11,9-13]; 167-168 [Q 11,14-26]; 196-197 [Q 11,29-32]; 207-209 [Q 11,33.34-35]; 220-223 [Q 11,39-52]; 244-246 [Q 12,2-12]; 296-301 [Q 12,22-31.33-34]; 322-325 [Q 12,39-46]; 346-349 [Q 12,49-59]; 410-412 [Q 13,18-21]; 428-430 [Q 13,23-30]; 444-446 [Q 13,34-35]; 476-478 [Q 14,5]; 504-507 [Q 14,16-24]; 527-532 [Q 14,26-27.34-35].

1989b Parabel des Evangeliums – Parabel des Gottesreiches. [12,46-50; 13,1-23] — WEDER, H. (ed.), *Die Sprache der Bilder. Gleichnis und Metapher in Literatur und Theologie* (Gütersloher Taschenbücher Siebenstern, 558), Gütersloh: Gütersloher Verlagshaus, 1989, 11-21.
Paraboles d'Évangile, parabole du Royaume. — *RTP* 40 (1990) 33-41. [NTA 34, 1112]

1991 La funzione della Scritture nella formazione dei raconti evangelici. Le tentazioni di Gesù (Lc 4,1-13 e par.) et la moltiplicazione dei pani (Lc 9,10-17 e par.). — O'COLLINS, G. - MARCONI, G. (eds.), *Luca–Atti*, 1991, 38-45.
The Role of the Scriptures in the Composition of the Gospel Accounts: The Temptations of Jesus (Lk 4:1-13 par.) and the Multiplication of the Loaves (Lk 9:10-17 par.). — O'COLLINS, G. - MARCONI, G. (eds.), *Luke and Acts*, 1993, 26-31. Esp. 28-29 [14,31-21]; 29-31 [4,1-13].
Le rôle des Écritures dans la constitution des récits évangéliques. À propos des tentations de Jésus (Luc 4,1-13 par.) et de la multiplication des pains (Luc 9,10-17 par.). — ID.. *Révélations et écritures*, 1993, 47-54. Esp. 50-51; 51-53.

1993a Le discours missionnaire de Jésus: réception patristique et narration apocryphe. — *ETR* 68 (1993) 481-497. [NTA 38, 765]

1993b Wetterkundliches bei den Synoptikern (Lk 12,54-56 par.). — *BTZ* 10 (1993) 175-186.
Esp. 178-180: "Die Quelle Q 12,54-56"; 180-182: "Der Sinn von Vers 56". [NTA 38, 836]
La pluie et le beau temps (Lc 12,54-56). — ID., *Révélations et écritures*, 1993, 55-63.

1993c *Révélations et écritures. Nouveau Testament et littérature apocryphe chrétienne. Recueil d'articles* (Le monde de la Bible, 26). Genève: Labor et Fides, 1993, 298 p. → 1991, 1993b
*New Testament Traditions and Apocryphal Narratives*, trans. J. Haapiseva-Hunter (Princeton Theological Monograph Series, 36). Allison Park, PA: Pickwick, 1995, X-256 p.

1995 Jesus' Missionary Speech as Interpreted in the Patristic Commentaries and the Apocryphal Narratives. — FORNBERG, T. - HELLHOLM, D. (eds.), *Texts and Contexts*. FS L. Hartman, 1995, 871-886.

1996 → 1989a

**BOWIE, Walter Russell**

1951 The Parables. — BUTTRICK, G.A. (ed.), *The Interpreter's Bible*, VII, 1951, 165-175.

**BOWMAN, John Wick**

1957a & TAPP, R.W., *The Gospel from the Mount, a New Translation and Interpretation of Matthew, Chs. 5 to 7*. Philadelphia, PA: Westminster, 1957, 199 p. [NTA 2, p. 199]
W. BARCLAY, *ExpT* 69 (1957-58) 172; G.R. EDWARDS, *Interpr* 12 (1958) 229; S.M. GILMOUR, *JBL* 77 (1958) 372-374; L. JOHNSTON, *CBQ* 21 (1959) 375-376; J.E. JONES, *RExp* 55 (1958) 435-436; H.C. KEE, *JRel* 38 (1958) 201; M. SMITH, *JBR* 26 (1958) 253.

1957b Traveling the Christian Way. The Beatitudes. — *RExp* 54 (1957) 377-392.

1959a Phylacteries. — *Studia Evangelica* 1 (1959) 523-538. Esp. 523-524 [23,5].

1959b The Term *Gospel* and its Cognates in the Palestinian Syriac. [4,23] — HIGGINS, A.J.B. (ed.), *New Testament Essays*. FS T.W. Manson, 1959, 54-67. Esp. 58.

1974 The Significance of Mt. 27:25. — *Milla wa-Milla* (Victoria, Australia) 14 (1974) 26-31. [NTA 20, 95]

1987 Jonah and Jesus. [12,38-42] — *Abr-Nahrain* (Leiden) 25 (1987) 1-12. [NTA 32, 1110]

1989 David, Jesus Son of David and Son of Man. — *Abr-Nahrain* 27 (1989) 1-22. [NTA 35, 304]

**BOWNE, Dale Russell**

1963 *An Exegesis of Matthew 11,25-30 – Luke 10,21-22*. Diss. Union Theol. Sem., New York, 1963, 455 p. — *DissAbstr* 24 (1963-64) 2146.

**BOYCE, James L.**

1993 Transformed for Disciple Community: Matthew in Pentecost. — *WWorld* 13 (1993) 308-317. [NTA 38, 138]

**BOYD, Gregory A.**

1995 *Cynic Sage or Son of God?* Wheaton, IL: BridgePoint, 1995, 416 p. Esp. 53-55; 65-67; 97-99; 104-105; 136-145: "The 'Q Gospel'"; 151-153; 275-277. → J.D. Crossan 1991a, Mack 1993

**BOYD, W.J. Peter**

1980 Gehenna – According to J. Jeremias. — LIVINGSTONE, E.A. (ed.), *Studia Biblica 1978*, II, 1980, 9-12.

**BOYER, James L.**

1988 Relative Clauses in the Greek New Testament: A Statistical Study. — *GraceTJ* 9 (1988) 233-256. Esp. 252-253 [26,50]. [NTA 33, 1051]

**BOYER, Jean-Paul**

1995 Parler du roi et pour le roi. [21,5] – *RSPT* 79 (1995) 193-248.

**BRAAKSMA, S.**

1982 *Zeg ons, wanneer zal dat geschieden? Christus' rede in Mattheüs 24*. Groningen: Vuurbaak, ²1982, 148 p.

**BRADBY, E.L.**

1957 In Defence of Q. — *ExpT* 68 (1956-57) 315-318. Esp. 316 [12,1-21; 13,1-23]; 317 [10,1-42]; 317-318 [16,13-28]. [NTA 2, 269]; = BELLINZONI, A.J., Jr., et al. (eds.), *The Two-Source Hypothesis*, 1985, 287-293. → Farrer 1955

**BRÄNDLE, Francisco**

1979 San José, el Justo (Mt 1,18ss). — *EstJos* 33 (1979) 27-42.

1980 ¡Bienaventurados los que buscan la paz! — *RevistEspir* 39 (1980) 9-22. [NTA 24, 787]

1981 "La huída a Egipto". Reflexiones bíblico-teológicas. — *EstJos* 35 = *CahJos* 29 (1981) 25-36. Esp. 26-28 [apocryphal literature]; 28-30 [Fathers]; 30-35. [NTA 27, 96]

1983 Bienaventurados, ¿cuándo, dónde, por qué? Aproximación a una letura de las "bienaventuranzas" bíblicas. — *RevistEspir* 42 (1983) 197-218.

1984  Jesucristo, único maestro y sabiduría de Dios en Mateo. — *RevistEspir* 43 (1984) 187-209. [NTA 29, 511]

1986a  Historia Józefa i jej wpływ na teologię świetojózefową według Ewangelii Mateusza (L'histoire de Joseph et son influence sur la théologie de St. Joseph selon l'Évangile de St. Matthieu). — *Ateneum Kaplanskie* (Wroclaw) 107 (1986) 227-238. Esp. 236-238. La historia de José y su influjo en la teología de San José según San Mateo. — *EstJos* 41 (1987) 59-68. Esp. 66-68.

1986b  San José desde el Evangelio. — *EstJos* 40 (1986) 153-162. Esp. 153-156 [1,19]; 156-159 [Son of David].

1990  La oración en San Mateo. Acogida de la voluntad de Dios. [6,1-15; 7,7-11] — *RevistEspir* 49 (1990) 9-25. [NTA 36, 128]

**BRÄNDLE, Max**

1960  Theologie der Versuchung Jesu. — *Der große Entschluß* (Wien) 15 (1960) 292-298.

1963  Neue Diskussion um das Felsenwort. Matthäus 16,18-19. — *Orientierung* 27 (1963) 172-176. [NTA 8, 580]

1964  Die Versuchung Jesu. — *Der große Entschluß* 19 (1963-64) 245-248, 295-297.

1967  Die synoptischen Grabeserzählungen. — *Orientierung* 31 (1967) 179-184. Esp. 183-184 [28,1-10]. [NTA 12, 537]
       Narratives of the Synoptics about the Tomb. — *TDig* 16 (1968) 22-26.

**BRÄNDLE, Rudolf**

1977  Jean Chrysostome – l'importance de Matth. 25,31-46 pour son éthique. — *VigChr* 31 (1977) 47-52.

1979  *Matth. 25,31-46 im Werk des Johannes Chrysostomos. Ein Beitrag zur Auslegungsgeschichte und zur Erforschung der Ethik der griechischen Kirche um die Wende vom 4. zum 5. Jahrhundert* (Beiträge zur Geschichte der biblischen Exegese, 22). Tübingen: Mohr, 1979, VIII-386 p. Esp. 9-74 [text]; 123-283 [spirituality]; 284-342 [theology]. — Diss. Basel, 1978 (O. Cullmann). → 1980
       H. BOJORGE, *Stromata* 38 (1982) 422-425; J. DUPONT, *ComLtg* 61 (1979) 569; M. FORLIN PATRUCCO, *RivStoLR* 16 (1980) 483; É. JUNOD, *RTP* 32 (1982) 184; J. MURPHY-O'CONNOR, *RB* 89 (1982) 305; A. NATALI, *RHPR* 62 (1982) 297-298; A. ORBE, *Greg* 62 (1981) 780-781; O. PASQUATO, *Sal* 43 (1981) 690-691; H.-J. SIEBEN, *TheolPhil* 55 (1980) 590-591; S. ZINCONE, *Studi storico religiosi* (L'Aquila) 5 (1981) 319-321.

1980  Zur Interpretation von Mt 25,31-46 im Matthäuskommentar des Origenes. — *TZ* 36 (1980) 17-25. → 1979

1992  Die fünfte Bitte in der Auslegung Gregors von Nyssa. [6,12] — *TZ* 48 (1992) 70-76.

**BRAGANÇA, Joaquim O.**

1972  A Parábola das Virgens na espiritualidade medieval. [25,1-13] — *Didaskalia* 2 (1972) 113-140.

**BRAKEMEIER, Gottfried**

1966  Exegese e Meditação sôbre Mt 21,33-46. — *Estudos Teologicos* (São Leopoldo) 6 (1966) 32-40.

1981  A parábola dos trabalhadores na vinha: a bondosa justiça de Deus. [20,1-16] — *Tempo e Presença* (Rio de Janeiro) 168 (1981) 38-43.

**BRANDENBURG, Albert**

1960  Umfrage über Mt 16,18 und 28,18. — *Catholica* 14 (1960) 157-159. [NTA 5, 398] → Javierre 1958a

**BRANDENBURGER, Egon**

1973  *Frieden im Neuen Testament. Grundlinien urchristlichen Friedensverständnisses.* Gütersloh: Mohn, 1973, 75 p. Esp. 33-47: "Die synoptische Konzeption vom Frieden stiftenden Messiaskönig Jesus".

1980  *Das Recht des Weltenrichters. Untersuchung zu Matthäus 25,31-46* (SBS, 99). Stuttgart: Katholisches Bibelwerk, 1980, 152 p. Esp. 17-55: "Scheidung von Tradition und Redaktion in Mt 25,31-46"; 56-97: "Untersuchungen zum Traditionsstück Mt 25,32b-46"; 98-138: "Die Aufnahme des Traditionsstücks 25,32b-46 in das Matthäus-Evangelium". [NTA 26, p. 80]
    H. GIESEN, *TRev* 79 (1983) 22-24; N. WALTER, *TLZ* 109 (1984) 887-889.

1990  Taten der Barmherzigkeit als Dienst gegenüber dem königlichen Herrn (Mt 25,31-46). — SCHÄFER, G.K. – STROHM, T. (eds.), *Diakonie – Biblische Grundlagen und Orientierungen*, Heidelberg: Heidelberger Verlagsanstalt, 1990, 297-326. Esp. 297-301: "Aufbau und Erzählstil"; 302-306: "Scheidung von Tradition und Redaktion"; 306-317: "Deutung der vormatthäischen Tradition"; 317-326: "Das Traditionsstück in der Konzeption des Matthäusevangeliums"; = ID., *Studien*, 1993, 95-130. Esp. 95-100; 100-106; 106-119; 119-130.

1991  Gerichtskonzeptionen im Urchristentum und ihre Voraussetzungen. Eine Problemstudie. — *SNTU* 16 (1991) 5-54. Esp. 24; 32-34; 48-51. [NTA 37, 372]; = ID., *Studien*, 1993, 289-338. Esp. 308; 316-318; 332-335.

1993  *Studien zur Geschichte und Theologie des Urchristentums* (Stuttgarter Biblische Aufsatzbände, 15). Stuttgart: Katholisches Bibelwerk, 1993, 381 p. → 1990, 1991

**BRANDON, Samuel George Frederick**

1951  *The Fall of Jerusalem and the Christian Church. A Study of the Effects of the Jewish Overthrow of A.D. 70 on Christianity.* London: SPCK, 1951, ²1957, XX-284 p. Esp. 217-243: "The gospel of Matthew and the origins of Alexandrian christianity"; 244-248: "The bearing of the evidence of textual variants on the problem of the origin of the Matthean gospel" [15,24; 21,44; 24,15.36; 27,4.17.49]. → Bammel 1984*, Sweet 1984

1965  Matthaean Christianity. — *The Modern Churchman* (Oxford) 8 (1965) 152-161. [NTA 9, 1147r] → W.D. Davies 1963a

1967  *Jesus and the Zealots. A Study of the Political Factor in Primitive Christianity.* Manchester: University Press; New York: Scribner, 1967, XVI-413 p. Esp. 283-321: "The concept of the pacific Christ: its origin and development". → Bammel 1984*, Styler 1984, Sweet 1984

1968a  *The Trial of Jesus of Nazareth* (Historic Trials Series). London: Batsford; New York: Stein & Day, 1968, 223 p. Esp. 107-116: "Other versions of the trial of Jesus: the gospel of Matthew".
    *Het proces tegen Jezus van Nazareth*, trans. C.E. van Amerongen-van Straten (Achtergronden, nieuwe reeks). Amsterdam: Arbeiderspers, 1969, 263 p. Esp. 122-132.
    *Il processo a Gesù*, trans. M. Segre. Milano: Comunità, 1974, 312 p.

1968b  Pontius Pilate in History and Legend. — *History Today* (London) 18 (1968) 523-530.

**BRANDSCHEIDT, Renate**

1990  Messias und Tempel. Die alttestamentlichen Zitate in Mt 21,1-17. — *TTZ* 99 (1990) 36-48. Esp. 37-42 [21,5]; 42-44 [21,9]; 44-46 [21,13]; 46-48 [21,16]. [NTA 34, 1140]

**BRANDT, Wilhelm**

1966  *Neutestamentliche Bibelkunde. Eine Einführung in Inhalt und Gestalt der urchristlichen Botschaft.* Gladbeck: Schriftenmissions-Verlag, ⁸1966, 213 p. Esp. 51-69: "Das Matthäus-Evangelium".

**BRANSCOMB, B. Harvie**

1960  *The Message of Jesus. A Survey of the Teaching of Jesus Contained in the Synoptic Gospels*, rev. by E.W. Saunders. New York – Nashville, TN: Abingdon, 1960, 184 p.

**BRATCHER, Robert G.**

1958 A Study of Isaiah 7:14. Its Meaning and Use in the Masoretic Text, the Septuagint and the Gospel of Matthew. — *BTrans* 9 (1958) 98-126. Esp. 116-125: "Isaiah 7:14 in Matthew 1:23". [NTA 3, 69]

1981 *A Translator's Guide to the Gospel of Matthew* (Helps for Translators). London – New York – Stuttgart: United Bible Societies, 1981, VIII-388 p. [NTA 25, p. 194] → B.M. Newman 1988

1989 "Righteousness" in Matthew. — *BTrans* 40 (1989) 228-235. Esp. 231-235. [NTA 34, 105]

1992 That Troublesome καί in Matthew 21:5. — *Notes on Translation* (Dallas, TX) 6/2 (1992) 14-15. [NTA 37, 1269]

**BRAUMANN, Georg**

1960 Zum traditionsgeschichtlichen Problem der Seligpreisungen Mt v 3-12. — *NT* 4 (1960) 253-260. [NTA 6, 765]

1961 "Dem Himmelreich wird Gewalt angetan" (Mt 11,12 par.). — *ZNW* 52 (1961) 104-109. [NTA 6, 454]

1963 Jesu Erbarmen nach Matthäus. — *TZ* 19 (1963) 305-317. [NTA 8, 931]

1965 Mit euch, Matth. 26,29. — *TZ* 21 (1965) 161-169. [NTA 10, 128]

1966 Der sinkende Petrus, Matth. 14,28-31. — *TZ* 22 (1966) 403-414. [NTA 11, 1034]

1968 Die Zweizahl und Verdoppelungen im Matthäusevangelium. — *TZ* 24 (1968) 255-266. [NTA 13, 556]

1973 Wozu (Mark 15,34). — DIETRICH, W., et al. (eds.), *Festgabe für K.H. Rengstorf*, 1973, 155-165. Esp. 163 [27,46].

**BRAUN, François-Marie**

1953 L'Apôtre Pierre devant l'exégèse et l'histoire. — *RThom* 53 (1953) 389-403. Esp. 390-392.395-401. → Cullmann 1952
O. Cullmann, 'Saint Peter', Disciple – Apostle – Martyr. — *TDig* 2 (1954) 178.

1978 Le pain dont nous avons besoin. *Mt 6*,11; *Lc 11*,3. — *NRT* 100 (1978) 559-568. [NTA 23, 98]

**BRAUN, Herbert**

1953 Entscheidende Motive in den Berichten über die Taufe Jesu von Markus bis Justin. [3,16] — *ZTK* 50 (1953) 39-43; = ID., *Gesammelte Studien zum Neuen Testament und seiner Umwelt*, Tübingen: Mohr, 1962, ²1967, 168-172.

1957 *Spätjüdisch-häretischer und frühchristlicher Radikalismus. Jesus von Nazareth und die essenische Qumransekte.* I: *Das Spätjudentum*; II: *Die Synoptiker* (Beiträge zur historischen Theologie, 24). Tübingen: Mohr, 1957, VII-163 p.; V-154 p.

1962 Qumran und das Neue Testament. Ein Bericht über 10 Jahre Forschung (1950-1959). — *TR* 28 (1962) 97-234. Esp. 103-156: "Matthäus". [NTA 7, 654]; 29 (1963) 142-176, 189-266. [NTA 8, 1178]; 30 (1964) 1-38, 89-137. [NTA 9, 375/720]
*Qumran und das Neue Testament.* Tübingen: Mohr, 1966, 2 vols., 326 p. and x-403 p. Esp. I, 7-60.

1969 *Jesus – Der Mann aus Nazareth und seine Zeit* (Themen der Theologie, 1). Stuttgart-Berlin: Kreuz, 1969, 175 p.; (Gütersloher Taschenbücher, 70), Gütersloh: Mohn, 1973, 128 p. → 1984
*Jesús, el hombre de Nazaret y su tiempo.* Salamanca: Sígueme, 1975, 170 p.
*Jesus of Nazareth. The Man and His Time*, trans. E.R. Kalin. Philadelphia, PA: Fortress, 1979, XI-147 p.

1984 *Jesus – Der Mann aus Nazareth und seine Zeit. Um 12 Kapitel erweiterte Studienausgabe.* Stuttgart: Kreuz, 1984, 277 p.; (Gütersloher Taschenbücher/Siebenstern, 1422), Gütersloh: Mohn, rev. ed., 1988, 268 p. → 1969

**BRAUN, Willi**

1991    The Historical Jesus and the Mission Speech in Q 10:2-12. — *Forum* 7 (1991) 279-316. Esp. 279-287: "From the gospels to Q"; 287-302: "The history of the mission speech"; 302-312: "Testing the individual units". [NTA 38, 830]

1995    *Feasting and Social Rhetoric in Luke 14* (SNTS MS, 55). Cambridge: University Press, 1995, XII-221 p. Esp. 68-73 [Q 14,16-24 (Lk)]. — Diss. Toronto, Ont., 1993 (J.S. Kloppenborg).

**BRAVO, Carlos**

1989    Pueblo de las bienaventuranzas. — *Christus* (México) 54 (1989) 33-42. *SelT* 29 (1990) 199-206.

**BRAVO, Ernesto**

1994    Jesus y el sabado. — *RevistBíb* 56 (1994) 149-174, 237-249. Esp. 161-164 [12,1-8].

**BRAWLEY, Robert L.**

1990    Joseph in Matthew's Birth Narrative and the Irony of Good Intentions. — *Cumberland Seminarian* (Memphis, TN) 28 (1990) 69-76. [NTA 35, 618]

1995    Table Fellowship: Bane and Blessing for the Historical Jesus. — *PerspRelSt* 22 (1995) 13-31. Esp. 17-20 [11,18-19]. [NTA 39, 1481]

**BRECKENRIDGE, James**

1983    Evangelical Implications of Matthean Priority. — *JEvTS* 26 (1983) 117-121. [NTA 28, 479]

**BREECH, Earl**

1976    *Crucifixion as Ordeal: Tradition and Interpretation in Matthew 26–28.* Diss. Harvard Univ., Cambridge, MA, 1976.

1978    Kingdom of God and the Parables of Jesus. — *Semeia* 12 (1978) 15-40. Esp. 19-20 [11,12.16-19]; 32-33 [13,44-46]; 35 [20,1-16]. [NTA 23, 405]

**BREECH, James**

1983    *The Silence of Jesus. The Authentic Voice of the Historical Man.* Philadelphia, PA: Fortress, 1983, X-245 p. Esp. 22-31 [John the Baptist]; 51-55 [Lord's prayer]; 66-85 [kingdom-parables]; 114-141 [22,1-14]; 142-157 [20,1-16].

**BRENNAN, Joseph P.**

1964    Virgin and Child in Isaiah 7:14. — *BiTod* 15 (1964) 968-974. [NTA 9, 901]

**BRENNECKE, Hanns Christof**

1992    Ecclesia est in re publica, id est in imperio Romano (Optatus III 3). Das Christentum in der Gesellschaft an der Wende zum 'Konstantinischen Zeitalter'. — *JbBT* 7 (1992) 209-239. Esp. 217-218 [24,14]; 218-226 [28,19-20].

**BRENTANO, Robert**

1983    Francis of Assis's Gloss of Matthew 6:34. — *Miscellanea di studi in onore di Vittore Branca. I: Dal Medioevo al Petrarca*, Firenze: Olschki, 1983, 37-46.

**BRETON, Stanislas**

1994    Ne jugez pas: Réflexions sur un impératif évangélique. [7,1-2] — *Revue de l'Institut catholique de Paris* 49 (1994) 41-50.

**BRETSCHER, Paul G.**

1966    *The Temptation of Jesus in Matthew.* Diss. Concordia Sem., 1966, 196 p.

1967    "Whose Sandals"? (Matt 3,11). — *JBL* 86 (1967) 81-87. [NTA 11, 1029]

1968    Exodus 4,22-23 and the Voice from Heaven. — *JBL* 87 (1968) 301-311. Esp. 301-303 [3,17]; 303-305 [12,18]. [NTA 13, 580]

1972 "The log in your own eye" (Matt. 7:1-5). — *ConcTM* 43 (1972) 645-686.

1995 When Everything was "Q". [oral tradition] — *Proceedings EGLBS* 15 (1995) 53-64. Esp. 61.

**BRETZKE, James Thomas**

1989 *The Notion of Moral Community in the* Analects *of Confucius and Matthew's Sermon on the Mount. A Hermeneutical Approach for the Inculturation of Moral Theology in Korea.* Diss. Pont. Univ. Greg., Roma, 1989, 530 p. (J. Dupuis). Esp. 279-354: "Sons and daughters of the heavenly Father: the notion of moral community in Matthew's Sermon on the Mount".

**BREUKELMAN, Frans H.**

1966 Eine Erklärung des Gleichnisses vom Schalksknecht (Matth. 18,23-35). — BUSCH, E., et al. (eds.), Παρρησία. *Karl Barth zum 80. Geburtstag am 10 Mai 1966*, Zürich: Evang. Verlag, 1966, 261-287.

1983 Als nun Jesus gezeugt war ... Matthäus 2,1-23. — *TK* 20 (1983) 5-30.

1984a *Bijbelse theologie.* Deel III: *De theologie van de evangelist Mattheüs.*
Afl. 1: *De ouverture van het Evangelie naar Mattheüs. Het verhaal over de* γένεσις *van Jezus Christus (Mattheüs 1:1–2:23).* Kampen: Kok, 1984, 236 p. Esp. 18-49 [γένεσις]; 50-82 [1,1-17]; 83-143 [1,18–2,23]; 145-149 [4,12]; 149-151 [12,15]; 151-155 [14,13]; 155-166 [15,21]; 166-174 [προσκυνεῖν]; 174-175 [καλέω]. [NTA 31, p. 360]
        M.H. BOLKESTEIN, *KerkT* 37 (1986) 71.

Afl. 2: *Het evangelie naar Matteüs als "Die Heilsbotschaft vom Königtum".* Kampen: Kok, 1996, 286 p. Esp. 21-61 [εὐαγγέλιον]; 62-78 [26,1-2]; 84-107 [3]; 107-111 [4,1-11]; 112-167 [25,31-46]; 168-193.226-228 [18,23-35]; 194-199.253-255 [6,12]; 243-249 [16,27].

1984b Al deze woorden (Matth. 26:1,2). — DEURLOO, K. - ZUURMOND, R. (eds.), *De Bijbel maakt school: een Amsterdamse weg in de exegese*, Baarn: Ten Have, 1984, 42-50.

1989 De werkwijze van een evangelist (Exegese van Mattheüs 26:1-2). — *Amsterdamse Cahiers* 10 (1989) 103-119 (English summary, 150).

1996 → 1984a

**BREYTENBACH, Cilliers**

1991* & PAULSEN, H. (eds.), *Anfänge der Christologie. Festschrift für Ferdinand Hahn zum 65. Geburtstag.* Göttingen: Vandenhoeck & Ruprecht, 1991, 493 p. → H. Klein, von Lips, Luz, Paulsen

1992 Vormarkinische Logientradition. Parallelen in der urchristlichen Briefliteratur. — VAN SEGBROECK, F., et al. (eds.), *The Four Gospels 1992.* FS F. Neirynck, 1992, II, 725-749. Esp. 733-735 [15,11]; 736-739 [Q 16,18]; 739-740 [11,15]; 743-745 [Q 17,1-2]; 746-747 [Q 6,38].

1993 Das Markusevangelium als traditionsgebundene Erzählung? Anfragen an die Markusforschung der achtziger Jahre. — FOCANT, C. (ed.), *The Synoptic Gospels*, 1993, 77-110. Esp. 94-98 [Mk/Q].

1995 Jesusforschung: 1990-1995. Neuere Gesamtdarstellungen in deutscher Sprache. — *BTZ* 12 (1995) 226-249. Esp. 243-247 [Q]. [NTA 40, 1417]

**BRIÈRE, Jean**

1987 Salomon dans le Nouveau Testament. — *DBS* 11/61 (1987) 480-485. Esp. 481-482 [12,42]; 483-484.

**BRIESKORN, Norbert**

1993 Mt 13,24-30. Eine ideengeschichtliche Untersuchung. — DORÉ, J. - THEOBALD, C. (eds.), *Penser la foi.* FS J. Moingt, 1993, 37-49.

**BRIGGS, R.C.**

1969 *Interpreting the Gospels. An Introduction to Methods and Issues in the Study of the Synoptic Gospels.* Nashville, TN - New York: Abingdon, 1969, 188 p. → 1973

1973    *Interpreting the New Testament Today. An Introduction to Methods and Issues in the
        Study of the New Testament*. Nashville, TN – New York: Abingdon, rev. ed., 1973,
        288 p. Esp. 82-86 [3,11-17]; 104-106 [12,46-50]; 106-107 [8,23-27]; 107-109 [9,1-8]; 134-137 [11,2-6].
        → 1969

**BRIGHT, Laurence**

1971    (ed.), *Scripture Discussion Commentary*. Vol. VII: *Mark and Matthew*. Chicago, IL:
        Adult Catechetical Teaching Aids Foundation, 1971, VIII-245 p.

**BRINDLE, Wayne Allan**

1988    *A Definition of the Title "Son of God" in the Synoptic Gospels*. Diss. Theol. Sem.,
        Dallas, TX, 1988, 356 p. — *DissAbstr* 50 (1989-90) 1337.

**BRINKTRINE, Johannes**

1962    An et quomodo existentia Hierarchiae Ecclesiasticae e Sacris Scripturis erui possit?
        [16,18-19; 28,18-20] — *Divinitas* 6 (1962) 134-137. [NTA 7, 148]

**BRISCOE, Holly L.**

1966    *A Comparison of the Parables in the Gospel according to Thomas and the Synoptic
        Gospels*. Diss. Southwestern Baptist Theol. Sem., Fort Worth, TX, 1965-66, 198 p.

**BRISCOE, Peter**

1989    Faith Confirmed through Conflict – The Matthean Redaction of Mk 2:1–3:6. —
        CATHCART, K.J. – HEALEY, J.F. (eds.), *Back to the Sources. Biblical and Near Eastern
        Studies. In Honour of Dermot Ryan*, Dublin: Glendale, 1989, 104-128.

**BRISEBOIS, Mireille** → P. Guillemette 1987

**BROADHEAD, Edwin Keith**

1989    An Example of Gender Bias in UBS[3]. [21,28-32] — *BTrans* 40 (1989) 336-338. [NTA 34,
        130]

1995    Echoes of an Exorcism in the Fourth Gospel? — *ZNW* 86 (1995) 111-119. Esp. 114
        [12,15-21.22-30]; 115-116 [7,21-27]. [NTA 40, 268]

**BROCK, Sebastian P.**

1969    An Additional Fragment of 0106? [13,32.36] — *JTS* 20 (1969) 226-228. [NTA 14, 50]

1970    The Baptist's Diet in Syriac Sources. [3,4-6] — *Oriens Christianus* (Wiesbaden) 54
        (1970) 113-124.

1992    A Palimpsest Folio of Matt 20:23-31 (Peshitta) in Sinai Ar. 514 ("Codex Arabicus").
        — *Orientalia* (Roma) 61 (1992) 102-105. [NTA 37, 733] → R.G. Jenkins 1993, Pickering 1993a

**BROCKE, Michael**

1974*   & PETUCHOWSKI, J.J. – STROLZ, W. (eds.), *Das Vaterunser. Gemeinsames im Beten
        von Juden und Christen* (Veröffentlichungen der Stiftung Oratio Dominica.
        Schriftenreihe zur großen Ökumene, 1). Freiburg: Herder, 1974, 285 p.; [2]1980 →
        Bommer, Deissler, Rijk, Strolz, Vögtle
            L. KAUFMANN, *Orientierung* 38 (1974) 257; M. PRAGER, *Freiburger Rundbrief* 27 (1975) 134-135; A.
            WEISER, *LebZeug* 30/4 (1975) 68-70.
        PETUCHOWSKI, J.J. – BROCKE, M. (eds.), *The Lord's Prayer and Jewish Liturgy*, trans.
        E.R. Petuchowski (A Crossroad Book). New York: Seabury; London: Burns & Oats,
        1978, X-224 p. [NTA 23, p. 97] → Bahr 1965, Bommer 1974, Carmignac 1969, Deisler 1974, Strolz
        1974, Vögtle 1974
            M.D. AMBROSE, *IndianTS* 25 (1988) 110-111; R. JUDD, *NBlackfr* 60 (1979) 92-93; G. KANIARAKATH,
            *Jeevadhara* 11 (1981) 146-147; C. KLEIN, *CleR* 64 (1979) 458; D. KUCK, *CurrTMiss* 6 (1979) 189; H.
            MACCOBY, *Theology* 82 (1979) 144-145; B.J. MALINA, *BTB* 9 (1979) 89; A. PAUL, *RSR* 68 (1980) 545-
            546; C.S. RODD, *ExpT* 89 (1977-78) 289-290.

**BRODIE, Thomas Louis**

1989 Luke 9:57-62. A Systematic Adaptation of the Divine Challenge to Elijah (1 Kings 19). — *SBL 1989 Seminar Papers*, 237-245. Esp. 245: "The implications for Q".

1992a Fish, Temple Tithe, and Remission: The God-Based Generosity of Deuteronomy 14-15 as One Component of Matt 17:22-18:35. — *RB* 99 (1992) 697-718. Esp. 698-700: "General introduction to Matthew's use of Deuteronomy"; 700-705: "The texts"; 705-715: "A more detailed analysis" [17,24-27; 18,15-35]. [NTA 37, 1266]

1992b Not Q but Elijah: The Saving of the Centurion's Servant (Luke 7:1-10) as an Internalization of the Saving of the Widow and Her Child (1 Kgs 17:1-16). — *IBS* 14 (1992) 54-71. [NTA 37, 198]

1993a *The Quest for the Origin of John's Gospel. A Source-oriented Approach.* New York: Oxford University Press, 1993, X-194 p. Esp. 101-115: "John's systematic use of Matthew".

1993b Vivid, Positive, Practical: The Systematic Use of Romans in Matthew 1-7. — *ProcIrBibAss* 16 (1993) 36-55. [NTA 39, 792]

1997 Intertextuality and Its Use in Tracing Q and Proto-Luke. — TUCKETT, C.M. (ed.), *The Scriptures in the Gospels*, 1997, 469-477. Esp. 475-477.

**BROER, Ingo**

1970 Das Gericht des Menschensohnes über die Völker. Auslegung von Mt 25,31-46. — *BibLeb* 11 (1970) 273-295. Esp. 275-285: "Literarkritische Untersuchung"; 285-288: "Eine jüdische Vorlage?"; 288-289: "Zur Interpretation der Vorlage des Matthäus"; 289-295: "Die Redaktionsarbeit des ersten Evangeliums". [NTA 15, 860]

1971 Die Bedeutung der "Jungfrauengeburt" im Matthäusevangelium. — *BibLeb* 12 (1971) 248-260. Esp. 250-255 [1,18-25]. [NTA 17, 113]

1972 *Die Urgemeinde und das Grab Jesu. Eine Analyse der Grablegungsgeschichte im Neuen Testament* (SANT, 31). München: Kösel, 1972, 348 p. Esp. 69-75 [27,62-66]; 75-78 [28,11-15]. — Diss. Freiburg, 1970 (A. Vögtle).

1975a Die Antithesen und der Evangelist Mattäus. Versuch, eine alte These zu revidieren. — *BZ* 19 (1975) 50-63. Esp. 50-55: "Das Problem von Tradition und Redaktion des Stoffes Mt 5,20-48 in der Literatur"; 55-56: "Methodenprobleme"; 56-62: "Mattäus und die Antithesen"; 62-63: "Warum greift Mattäus zur Form der Antithese?". [NTA 19, 949]

1975b Das Ringen der Gemeinde um Israel. Exegetischer Versuch über Mt 19,28. — PESCH, R., et al. (eds.), *Jesus und der Menschensohn*. FS A. Vögtle, 1975, 148-165. Esp. 149-154: "Die Frage nach der Mt 19,28 zugrunde liegende Tradition"; 155-159: "Die Vorstellungswelt der Mt 19,28 zugrunde liegende Tradition"; 159-164: "Interpretation dieser Tradition"; 164-165: "Die Interpretation der Tradition durch Mattäus".

1977 Die Kindheitsgeschichte im Matthäusevangelium und die neuere Exegese. — *Siegener Pädagogische Studien* 23 (1977-78) 46-55.

1978 Die Gleichnisexegese und die neuere Literaturwissenschaft. Ein Diskussionsbeitrag zur Exegese von Mt 20,1-16. — *BibNot* 5 (1978) 13-27. Esp. 18-21; = KREUZER, H. - BONFIG, K.W. (eds.), *Entwicklungen der siebziger Jahre. Studien aus der Gesamthochschule Siegen*, Gerabronn: Hohenloher, 1978.

1980 *Freiheit vom Gesetz und Radikalisierung des Gesetzes. Ein Beitrag zur Theologie des Evangelisten Matthäus* (SBS, 98). Stuttgart: Katholisches Bibelwerk, 1980, 144 p. Esp. 11-74: "Mt 5,17-20"; 75-113: "Die Antithesen des Matthäusevangeliums"; 114-122: "Das Verhältnis Jesu zum Gesetz in den matthäischen Streitgesprächen - dargestellt an Mt 15,1-20"; 123-130: "Mt 5 und das Gesetzesverständnis des Matthäus". [NTA 25, p. 194]
   H. GIESEN, *TRev* 79 (1983) 283-285; W. SCHENK, *TLZ* 108 (1983) 428-429; R. SCHNACKENBURG, *BZ* 26 (1982) 151; F. ZEITLINGER, *TPQ* 130 (1982) 176.

1981 Jesusflucht und Kindermord – Exegetische Anmerkungen zum zweiten Kapitel des Mattäusevangeliums. — PESCH, R. (ed.), *Zur Theologie der Kindheitsgeschichten*, 1981, 74-96. Esp. 74-79 [patristic exegesis]; 79-83: "Mt 2 und die griechisch-römische Antike"; 83-87 [Moses]; 87-90: "Theologische Motive".

1982 Plädierte Jesus für Gewaltlosigkeit? Eine historische Frage und ihre Bedeutung für die Gegenwart. — *BK* 37 (1982) 61-69. Esp. 62-67 [5,39-42]. [NTA 27, 301]

1984 *Friede durch Gewaltverzicht? Vier Abhandlungen zu Friedensproblematik und Bergpredigt* (Kleine Reihe zur Bibel, 25). Stuttgart: Katholisches Bibelwerk, 1984, 80 p. Esp. 22-39.60-80 [5,39-42].

1985 Die Parabel vom Verzicht auf das Prinzip von Leistung und Gegenleistung (Mt 18,23-35). — GANTOY, R. (ed.), *À cause de l'Évangile*. FS J. Dupont, 1985, 145-164. Esp. 147-157: "Die Gestalt der Parabel Jesu"; 157-160: "Die Aussage der Jesusparabel"; 160-163: "Die Parabel und das 'Judentum' zur Zeit Jesu".

1986a *Die Seligpreisungen der Bergpredigt. Studien zu ihrer Überlieferung und Interpretation* (BBB, 61). Königstein/Ts–Bonn: Hanstein, 1986, 110 p. Esp. 15-38: "Zur Überlieferungsform der Seligpreisungen und Weherufe in der vorlukanischen und vormatthäischen Tradition"; 39-52: "Formgeschichtliches zu den Seligpreisungen"; 53-63: "Zum Problem der matthäischen Sondergut-Makarismen"; 64-67: "Der Zusammenhang der Makarismen mit Jes 61"; 68-98: "Voraussetzungen für eine Interpretation der Seligpreisungen". [NTA 30, p. 350] → Hengel 1987, Neirynck 1997d
R. BAUMANN, *BK* 42 (1987) 84-85; J. BEUTLER, *TheolPhil* 63 (1988) 256-257; C.E. CARLSTON, *CBQ* 49 (1987) 331-332; H. FRANKEMÖLLE, *TRev* 83 (1987) 461-463; A. FUCHS, *SNTU* 11 (1986) 230-232; G. GEIGER, *BLtg* 59 (1986) 143-144; J. LAMBRECHT, *Bijdragen* 48 (1987) 78-79; L. OBERLINNER, *BZ* 31 (1987) 283-285; A. STÖGER, *TPQ* 134 (1986) 402; G. STRECKER, *TLZ* 112 (1987) 187-188.

1986b Anmerkungen zum Gesetzesverständnis des Matthäus. — KERTELGE, K. (ed.), *Das Gesetz im Neuen Testament*, 1986, 128-145. Esp. 130-136: "Die Antithesen des Matthäus und das jüdische Gesetz"; 136-142: "Jesus und das Ritualgesetz nach Matthäus" [12,1-8; 15,1-20]; 142-145: "Das Verhältnis von Gesetz und Evangelium bei Matthäus".

1988a Bemerkungen zur Redaktion der Passionsgeschichte durch Matthäus. — SCHENKE, L. (ed.), *Studien zum Matthäusevangelium*. FS W. Pesch, 1988, 25-46. Esp. 27-29: "Die matthäische Redaktion des Prozesses Jesu"; 29-34: "Mt 26,59-64: Die Logik des Zusammenhangs"; 34-35: "Mt 26,63-65: Die Blasphemie"; 35-46: "Mt 27,3-10: Die Tradition vom Tode des Judas".

1988b Der Prozeß gegen Jesus von Nazareth. — KERTELGE, K. (ed.), *Der Prozeß gegen Jesus. Historische Rückfrage und theologische Deutung* (QDisp, 112), Freiburg: Herder, 1988, ²1989, 84-110. Esp. 84-89: "Einige Anmerkungen zur Methode redaktionsgeschichtlicher Arbeit am Matthäus-Evangelium"; 89-110: "Redaktionsgeschichtliche Auslegung von Mt 26,57-27,25".

1989 Bergpredigt. — GÖRG, M. - LANG, B. (eds.), *Neues Bibel-Lexikon*, I/2, Zürich: Benziger, 1989, 272-274.

1991 Antijudaismus im Neuen Testament? Versuch einer Annäherung anhand von zwei Texten (1 Thess 2,14-16 und Mt 27,24f). — OBERLINNER, L. - FIEDLER, P. (eds.), *Salz der Erde*. FS A. Vögtle, 1991, 321-356. Esp. 332-347 [27,24-25].

1992 Versuch zur Christologie des ersten Evangeliums. — VAN SEGBROECK, F., et al. (eds.), *The Four Gospels 1992*. FS F. Neirynck, 1992, II, 1251-1282. Esp. 1252-1253: "Hoheitstitel erster und zweiter Ordnung?"; 1253-1266: "Jesus als Davidssohn und Messias im Mt-Evangelium"; 1266-1270: "Jesus als Kyrios im Mt-Evangelium"; 1270-1278: "Jesus als Gottessohn im Mt-Evangelium"; 1278-1282: "Der Zusammenhang der Hoheitstitel untereinander".

1993a Die Antithesen der Bergpredigt. Ihre Bedeutung und Funktion für die Gemeinde des Matthäus. [5,17-48] — *BK* 48 (1993) 128-133. [NTA 38, 756]

1993b Redaktionsgeschichtliche Aspekte von Mt. 24:1-28. — *NT* 35 (1993) 209-233. Esp. 211-219: "Das Verständnis der Jüngerfrage"; 219-221: "Mt. 24:3 als Szenenbeginn?"; 221-223: "Der Standort"; 223-231: "Einzelanalyse"; 231-232: "Aussageabsicht". [NTA 38, 168]

1993c  Zur Wirkungsgeschichte des Talio-Verbots in der Alten Kirche. [5,38-39] — *BibNot* 66 (1993) 23-31. [NTA 37, 1257]

1994  Das Ius Talionis im Neuen Testament. — *NTS* 40 (1994) 1-21. Esp. 11-20 [5,38-48]. [NTA 38, 1362]

**BRON, Bernhard**

1975  *Das Wunder: das theologische Wunderverständnis im Horizont des neuzeitlichen Natur- und Geschichtsbegriffs* (Göttinger theologische Arbeiten, 2). Göttingen: Vandenhoeck & Ruprecht, 1975, ²1979, 346 p. Esp. 229-230: "Das Wunderverständnis bei Matthäus".

**BROOKE, George J.**

1980  The Lord's Prayer Interpreted through John and Paul. — *DownR* 98 (1980) 298-311. Esp. 303-306 [Jn]; 306-309 [Paul]. [NTA 25, 473]

1984  The Feast of New Wine and the Question of Fasting. — *ExpT* 95 (1983-84) 175-176. [NTA 28, 933] → Beckwith 1984

1989  The Wisdom of Matthew's Beatitudes (4QBeat and Mt. 5:3-12). — *ScriptB* 19 (1989) 35-41. [NTA 34, 616]

1992  Ezekiel in Some Qumran and New Testament Texts. — TREBOLLE BARRERA, J. – VEGAS MONTANER, L. (eds.), *The Madrid Qumran Congress. Proceedings of the International Congress on the Dead Sea Scrolls. Madrid 18-21 March, 1991* (Studies on the Texts of the Desert of Judah, 11/1), Leiden: Brill, 1992, 317-337. Esp. 332 [27,52].

1995  4Q500 1 and the Use of Scripture in the Parable of the Vineyard. — *Dead Sea Discoveries* (Leiden) 2 (1995) 268-294. Esp. 279-291: "The parable of the vineyard" [21,33-46]. [NTA 40, 1764]

**BROOKS, James A.**

1991  *The New Testament Text of Gregory of Nyssa* (The New Testament in the Greek Fathers, 2). Atlanta, GA: Scholars, 1991, IX-267p. Esp. 29-72: "Gregory's text of Matthew". — Diss. Oxford, 1979 (G.D. Kilpatrick).

1992  The Unity and Structure of the Sermon on the Mount. — *Criswell Theological Review* (Dallas, TX) 6 (1992) 15-28. Esp. 15-24 [Q 6,20-49]; 25-28 [structure]. [NTA 37, 1251]

**BROOKS, Oscar S.**

1981  Matthew xxviii 16-20 and the Design of the First Gospel. — *JSNT* 10 (1981) 2-18. Esp. 3-5: "Authority and teaching in the commissioning paragraph"; 5-14: "Authority and teaching in the gospel". [NTA 26, 100]

1985  *The Sermon on the Mount. Authentic Human Values.* Lanham, MC – London: University Press of America, 1985, XII-111 p. [NTA 30, p. 93]
       K.A. BARTA, *BTB* 17 (1987) 31.

**BROOKS, Stephenson Humphries**

1987  *Matthew's Community. The Evidence of his Special Sayings Material* (JSNT SS, 16). Sheffield: JSOT, 1987, 212 p. Esp. 25-46.130-139 [5,17–6,18]; 47-48.139-144 [10]; 59-71.144-148 [23]; 73-85.148-153: "Analysis of the M sayings"; 87-110.153: "Isolation of further M sayings"; 111-123.156-158: "The history of the Matthean community as reflected in the M sayings traditions". [NTA 32, p. 369] — Diss. Columbia Univ./Union Theol. Sem., NY, 1986 (R.E. Brown – J.L. Martyn).
       L. ALEXANDER, *JSNT* 41 (1991) 120-121; D.R. BAUER, *Interpr* 43 (1989) 424.426: H.B. GREEN, *JTS* 40 (1989) 556-560; J. GUIJARRO, *EstBíb* 47 (1989) 423-424; D.J. HARRINGTON, *CBQ* 51 (1989) 363-364; U. LUZ, *TLZ* 116 (1991) 738-739; M.A. POWELL, *JBL* 108 (1989) 523-524; G. STANTON, *ExpT* 100 (1988-89) 310; B.T. VIVIANO, *RB* 97 (1990) 615-616.

**BROSZIO, G.**

1994 *Genealogia Christi: Die Stammbäume Jesu in der Auslegung der christlichen Schriftsteller der ersten fünf Jahrhunderte* (Bochumer Altertumswissenschaftliches Colloquium, 18). Trier: WVT, 1994, 389 p. [NTA 39, p. 502] — Diss. Bochum, 1993 (W. Geerlings).

**BROWN, Basil S.**

1962 The Great Apostasy in the Teaching of Jesus. — *AusBR* 10 (1962) 14-20. Esp. 15-17 [24,10-12.23-25.26-27]; 18-20 [Q 12,8-9.10]. [NTA 8, 94]

**BROWN, Colin**

1984 *Miracles and the Critical Mind.* Grand Rapids, MI: Eerdmans, 1984, VIII-383 p. Esp. 310-317: "The gospel according to Matthew".

1985 *That You May Believe. Miracles and Faith Then and Now.* Grand Rapids, MI: Eerdmans; Exeter: Paternoster, 1985, XIV-232 p. Esp. 131-140 [12,40].

1986 Synoptic Miracle Stories. A Jewish Religious and Social Setting. — *Forum* 2/4 (1986) 55-76. Esp. 67-72. [NTA 31, 1040]

1987a The Gates of Hell: An Alternative Approach. [16,18] — *SBL 1987 Seminar Papers*, 357-367. Esp. 357-362: "Traditional approaches"; 362-367 : "An alternative approach".

1987b The Gates of Hell and the Church. — BRADLEY, J.E. – MULLER, R.A. (eds.), *Church, Word, and Spirit. Historical and Theological Essays in Honor of Geoffrey W. Bromiley*, Grand Rapids, MI: Eerdmans, 1987, 15-43. Esp. 15-34: "Interpretations of Matt 16:18c"; 34-43: "An alternative interpretation of Matt 16:18c".

**BROWN, Dennis**

1983 Saint Jerome as a Biblical Exegete. — *IBS* 5 (1983) 138-155. Esp. 148-149 [13,44-46].

**BROWN, Herbert**

1957 Das "Stirb und werde" in der Antike und im Neuen Testament. — MATTHIAS, W. – WOLF, E. (eds.), *Libertas christiana. Friedrich Delekat zum 65. Geburtstag* (BEvT, 26), München: Kaiser, 1957, 9-29. Esp. 10-11 [10,39; 16,25].

**BROWN, John Pairman**

1959 An Early Revision of the Gospel of Mark. — *JBL* 78 (1959) 215-227. Esp. 221-227 [8,2-4; 9,17; 13,11.55; 14,20; 17,17; 21,24; 26,64.68; 27,36]. [NTA 4, 374] → Glasson 1966b

1961a The Form of "Q" Known to Matthew. — *NTS* 8 (1961-62) 27-42. Esp. 29 [Marcan supplement, parables]; 29-33 [M-sayings], 33-38 [Q$^{Mt}$]; 38-39 [Thomas]; 39 [Celsus]; 39-40 [1 Clem 13,2]; 40 [Ignatius]; 41-42 [Didache]; 42 [Papias]. [NTA 6, 446]

1961b Mark as Witness to an Edited Form of Q. — *JBL* 80 (1961) 29-44. Esp. 31-34 [10,18.35-36.38-39]; 34 [12,40]; 34-35 [10,40.42]; 35 [9,35-10,16]; 35-36 [12,22-32.38-40; 13,31-33.44-48]; 36-37 [5-6]; 37-38 [5,13.29-30]; 38-39 [17,20; 18,19.35; 19,28; 23,5-7.11]; 39 [24-25]; 40-41 [24,26.39-41]; 41 [5,17-18; 24,11.24]; 42 [5,11-12.18; 6,9-13; 7,2]; 42-43 [11,10.14]. [NTA 6, 135]

1963 Synoptic Parallels in the Epistles and Form-History. — *NTS* 10 (1963-64) 27-48. Esp. 30-31 [5,10-12]; 31 [5,13-16]; 32 [5,29-32.34-37]; 33 [5,38-42]; 34 [5,44.48]; 35 [6,9-13]; 35-36 [6,19-21.25-33]; 36 [7,1-2.16-27]; 37 [9,37-10,16]; 38-39 [10,17-22; 12,22-32]; 39-40 [10,32-39]; 40-41 [10,40-42; 25,31-46]; 41 [18,6-14]; 41-42 [18,15-20]; 42-43 [23,8-12]; 43-44 [23,25-26]; 44 [23,13-36]; 45-46 [24-25]; 46 [24,45-51]. [NTA 8, 887]

1977 The Son of Man: "This Fellow". — *Bib* 58 (1977) 361-387. Esp. 376-377 [11,19]; 379-382 [8,20; 11,12; 24,27.37.44]. [NTA 22, 898]

1993 From Hesiod to Jesus: Laws of Human Nature in the Ancient World. [5,43; 7,1-2] — *NT* 35 (1993) 313-343. [NTA 38, 1031]

**BROWN, Milton P., Jr.**

1967    Matthew as εἰρηνοποίος. — DANIELS, B.L. - SUGGS, M.J. (eds.), *Studies in the History and Text of the New Testament.* FS K.W. Clark, 1967, 39-50. Esp. 40-44 [law]; 44-46 [teacher-disciple]; 46-47 [mission]; = *IBS* 4 (1982) 66-81. Esp. 67-72; 72-76; 76-78. [NTA 27, 91]

**BROWN, R.B.**

1962    The Gospel of Matthew in Recent Research. — *RExp* 59 (1962) 445-456. [NTA 7, 493]

**BROWN, Raymond Edward**

1958    The Semitic Background of the New Testament *mysterion.* — *Bib* 39 (1958) 426-448. Esp. 427-431 [13,10-15]. [NTA 3, 540]; 40 (1959) 70-87. [NTA 4, 131]

1961a   Incidents That Are Units in the Synoptic Gospels but Dispersed in St. John. — *CBQ* 23 (1961) 143-160. Esp. 143-148: "The agony in the garden" [26,36-46]; 148-152: "The Caiphas trial" [26,59-68]; 152-155: "The temptations of Jesus" [4,1-11]; 155-160: "The confession of Peter" [16,13-20]. [NTA 6, 159]
        John and the Synoptic Gospels: A Comparison. — ID., *New Testament Essays*, 1965, 192-213. Esp. 192-198; 198-203; 203-207; 207-212.

1961b   The Pater Noster as an Eschatological Prayer. — *TS* 22 (1961) 175-208; = ID., *New Testament Essays*, 1965, 217-253.
        *TDig* 10 (1962) 3-10; *SelT* 1/3 (1962) 54-62.

1962a   The Gospel Miracles. — McKENZIE, J.L. (ed.), *The Bible in Current Catholic Thought. Memorial M.J. Gruenthaner* (St. Mary's Theology Studies, 1), New York: Herder and Herder, 1962, 184-201. Esp. 186-193: "The synoptic *dunameis*"; = ID., *New Testament Essays*, 1965, 168-191. Esp. 170-180.

1962b   Parable and Allegory Reconsidered. [13,18-23] — *NT* 5 (1962) 36-45. [NTA 7, 91]; = ID., *New Testament Essays*, 1965, 254-264.

1965a   The Beatitudes according to St. Luke. [Q 6,20-22] — *BiTod* 18 (1965) 1176-1180. [NTA 10, 150]; = ID., *New Testament Essays*, 1965, 265-271.
        Le "beatitudini" secondo san Luca. — *BibOr* 7 (1965) 3-8. [NTA 9, 952]

1965b   *New Testament Essays.* Milwaukee, WI: Bruce, 1965, XVI-280 p.; London: Chapman, 1966; (Image, D251), Garden City, NY: Doubleday, 1968, 351 p.; Ramsey, NJ: Paulist, 1982. → 1961a-b, 1962a-b, 1965a

1967a   How Much Did Jesus Know? A Survey of the Biblical Evidence. — *CBQ* 29 (1967) 315-345/9-39. Esp. 322 [12,39-40]; 326 [10,23]; 338 [11,27]. [NTA 12, 126] → 1967b
        *TDig* 17 (1969) 44-50; *RasT* 11 (1970) 269-281.

1967b   *Jesus God and Man. Modern Biblical Reflections* (Impact Books). Milwaukee, WI: Bruce; London: Chapman, 1967, XVI-109 p. Esp. 39-102: "How much did Jesus know?". → 1967a
        *Jesus God en Mens.* Antwerpen: De Nederlandse Boekhandel, 1970, 120 p. Esp. 54-117.
        *Gesù Dio e Uomo,* trans.F. Spaduzzi ("Nuove Frontiere"). Assisi: Citadella, 1970, 126 p.
        *Jesus Dios y Hombre,* trans. J. Alonso Díaz. Santander: Sal Terrae, 1973, 147 p.

1968*   & FITZMYER, J.A. - MURPHY, R.E. (eds.), *The Jerome Biblical Commentary.* Englewood Cliffs, NJ: Prentice Hall, 2 vols. in one, 1968; London: Chapman, 1969, XXXVI-637 and 835 p. → 1990*; → Gast, J.L. McKenzie
        *Grande commentario biblico.* Brescia: Queriniana, 1973, XXXII-1974 p.
        *Comentario Bíblico "San Jeronimo".* Madrid: Cristiandad, 5 vols., 1971-72.

1972    The Problem of the Virginal Conception of Jesus. — *TS* 33 (1972) 3-34. Esp. 28-29. [NTA 16, 787]; = ID., *The Virginal Conception*, 1973, 21-68. → Fitzmyer 1973, Lawler 1972
        *USQR* 27/3 (1972) 131-135 (abridged). [NTA 16, 788]

1973a & DONFRIED, K.P. – REUMANN, J.H. (eds.), *Peter in the New Testament. A Collaborative Assessment by Protestant and Roman Catholic Scholars*. New York – Paramus, NJ – Toronto, Ont.: Paulist; Minneapolis, MN: Augsburg, 1973; London: Chapman, 1974, IX-181 p. Esp. 75-107: "Peter in the gospel of Matthew" [14,28-31; 16,16-19; 17,24-27].
*Saint Pierre dans le Nouveau Testament*, trans. J. Winandy (LD, 79). Paris: Cerf, 1974, 223 p. Esp. 95-134.
*Der Petrus der Bibel. Eine ökumenische Untersuchung*, introd. by F. Hahn & R. Schnackenburg, trans. E. Füssl. Stuttgart: Calwer / Katholisches Bibelwerk, 1976, 255 p. Esp. 68-95.
*Petrus in het geloof van de jonge Kerk. Over theorie en praxis van een mogelijk Petrusambt voor de ene Kerk van de toekomst*, trans. E. de Bekker. Boxtel: Katholieke Bijbelstichting; Brugge: Emmaüs, 1976, 180 p. Esp. 65-90.
*Pedro en el Nuevo Testamento* (Palabra Inspirada, 15). Santander: Sal Terrae, 1976, 166 p.
*Pietro nel Nuovo Testamento. Un'indagine ricognitiva fatta in collaborazione da studiosi protestanti e cattolici*, trans. S. Lugato (Bibbia e rinnovamento). Roma: Borla, 1988, 206 p.
Trans. Japanese 1977.

1973b *The Virginal Conception and Bodily Resurrection of Jesus*. New York: Paulist; London: Chapman, 1973, VIII-136 p. Esp. 21-68 (→ 1972); 96-112: "The gospel narratives and the appearances to the Twelve"; 113-124: "The gospel narratives and the Empty Tomb". → Muñoz Iglesias 1978
*Jezus de Christus, geboren uit een vrouw, opgestaan uit de dood*. Boxtel: Katholieke Bijbelstichting, 1975, 128 p.
*La concezione verginale e la risurrezione corporea di Gesù* (Giornale di Teologia, 99). Brescia: Queriniana, 1977, 178 p.; ²1992.
Trans. Portuguese 1987.

1974 *The Relation of "The Secret Gospel of Mark" to the Fourth Gospel*. — *CBQ* 36 (1974) 466-485. Esp. 471-474: "Chart of close parallels between SGM and the canonical gospels". [NTA 19, 894r]

1975 *The Meaning of the Magi; the Significance of the Star*. — *Worship* 49 (1975) 574-582. [NTA 20, 431]; = ID., *An Adult Christ at Christmas. Essays on the Three Biblical Christmas Stories*, Collegeville, MN: Liturgical, 1978.
Trans. Italian 1988; Portuguese, Spanish 1990.

1977 *The Birth of the Messiah. A Commentary on the Infancy Narratives in Matthew and Luke*. Garden City, NY: Doubleday, 1977; London: Chapman, 1978, 594 p. Esp. 25-41: "Introduction"; 43-232: "The Matthean infancy narrative". [NTA 22, p. 85] → 1993; → Laurentin 1979, McHugh 1978.1980, Medisch 1979, Mejía 1978, Miguéns 1980, F.J. Moloney 1979b, Mulholland 1981, North 1978, Redford 1979, Segalla 1983a, 1985b, Sloyan 1979a
ExpT 90 (1978-79) 65-66; H.-P. BERGERON, *CahJos* 30 (1982) 283-285; M.M. BOURKE, *CBQ* 40 (1978) 120-124; J. COPPENS, *ETL* 54 (1978) 266-269; B.R. DOYLE, *AusBR* 26 (1978) 44; J.D.G. DUNN, *ScotJT* 33 (1980) 85-87; J. DUPONT, *ComLtg* 58 (1977) 545-546; J. FENTON, *Theology* 82 (1979) 58-60; R.H. FULLER, *CBQ* 40 (1978) 116-120; D. HILL, *JSNT* 1 (1978) 61-65; L. JOHNSTON, *HeythJ* 19 (1978) 439-441; J.D. KINGSBURY, *JBL* 98 (1979) 442-444; R. LAURENTIN, *RSPT* 62 (1978) 99-101; L. LEGRAND, *IndianTS* 5 (1978) 291-293; X. LÉON-DUFOUR, *RSR* 66 (1978) 128-131; M.-V. LEROY, *RThom* 85 (1985) 134-137; I.H. MARSHALL, *EvQ* 51 (1979) 105-110; 52 (1980) 112-114; N.J. McELENEY, *TS* 39 (1978) 771-772; F.J. MOLONEY, *Sal* 40 (1978) 684-686; S. MUÑOZ IGLESIAS, *EstBíb* 36 (1977) 132-134; G. O'COLLINS, *Greg* 59 (1978) 756-757; H. RUSCHKE, *ZMiss* 66 (1982) 77; J.A. SANDERS, *USQR* 33 (1977-78) 193-196; L. SWAIN, *ScriptB* 25 (1995) 32-34; C.H. TALBERT, *PerspRelStud* 5 (1978) 212-216; A. VIARD, *EVie* 88 (1978) 686-688; J. VOLCKAERT, *Vidyajyoti* 43 (1979) 42-43.
*La nascita del Messia secondo Matteo e Luca*, trans. G. Natalini. Assisi: Cittadella, 1981, 797 p. → Spadafora 1982
A. BOTTINO, *Marianum* 44 (1982) 645-657; L. DE LORENZI, *Benedictina* 30 (1983) 258-261; V. FUSCO, *RasT* 23 (1982) 272-273; F. MONTAGNINI, *Humanitas* 38 (1983) 307; M. ORSATTI, *ParVi* 30 (1985) 474-476; V. PASQUETTO, *Teresianum*, 34 (1983) 516; A. SALAS, *CiudDios* 195 (1982) 500-501.
*El nacimiento del Mesías. Comentario a los relatos de la infancia*, trans. T. Arriba Urraca (Biblioteca Bíblica). Madrid: Cristiandad, 1982, 622 p.
M. ALCALÁ, *RazFe* 207 (1983) 218; X. ALEGRE, *ActBibl* 19 (1982) 251; J.A. CARRASCO, *EstJos* 37 (1983) 251-252.

1978 & DONFRIED, K.P. – FITZMYER, J.A. – REUMANN, J.H. (eds.), *Mary in the New Testament. A Collaborative Assessment by Protestant and Roman Catholic Scholars*. Philadelphia, PA: Fortress; New York: Paulist, 1978; London: Chapman, 1979, XII-323 p. Esp. 73-103: "Mary in the gospel of Matthew". → McHugh 1980

*Maria im Neuen Testament. Eine Gemeinschaftsstudie von protestantischen und römisch-katholischen Gelehrten*, trans. U. Schierse. Stuttgart: Katholisches Bibelwerk, 1981, 304 p.

Grundlagen und Schlußfolgerungen einer ökumenischen Untersuchung. — *TJb*, 1983, 174-203. Esp. 178-180: "Die Kindheitsgeschichten"; 182-183: "Das Evangelium nach Matthäus".

*María en el Nuevo Testamento*. Salamanca: Sígueme, 1982, 299 p.

*Maria nel Nuovo Testamento*, trans. M. Perale. Assisi: Cittadella, 1985, 337 p.

*Maria no Novo Testamento*. São Paulo: Paulinas, 1985, 336 p.

1982 *Rachab* in Mt 1,5 Probably Is Rahab of Jericho. — *Bib* 63 (1982) 79-80. [NTA 26, 839] → J.D. Quinn 1981

1983 & MEIER, J.P., *Antioch and Rome. New Testament Cradles of Catholic Christianity*. London: Chapman, 1983; New York – Ramsey, NJ: Paulist, XII-242 p. → Meier 1983

*Antioche et Rome. Berceaux du christianisme* (LD, 131). Paris: Cerf, 1988, 324 p.

1984a *The Churches the Apostles Left Behind*. London: Chapman; New York: Paulist, 1984, 156 p. Esp. 124-145: "The heritage of jewish/gentile christianity in Matthew: authority that does not stifle Jesus".

*L'Église héritée des apôtres*. Paris: Cerf, 1987, 269 p. Esp. 205-244.

1984b The Passion according to Matthew. — *Worship* 58 (1984) 98-107. [NTA 28, 921]; = ID., *A Crucified Christ in Holy Week. Essays on the Four Gospel Passion Narratives*, Collegeville, MN: Liturgical Press, 1986.

Trans. Italian 1988; Spanish 1989; Chinese 1992; Catalan 1994.

1985a *Biblical Exegesis and Church Doctrine*. New York – Mahwah, NJ: Paulist; London: Chapman, 1985, 171 p. Esp. 66-85: "Conservative misunderstanding of the interaction between biblical criticism and dogma"; 86-100: "The contribution of critical exegesis to an understanding of Mary and Marian doctrine"; 156-161: "Appended notes on R. Laurentin's exegesis of the infancy narratives". → 1985b; → Laurentin 1982a, McHugh 1975

1985b More Polemical than Instructive: R. Laurentin on the Infancy Narratives. — *Marianum* 47 (1985) 188-207. [NTA 30, 562r] → 1985a; → Laurentin 1982a

1986a Gospel Infancy Narrative Research from 1976 to 1986: Part I (Matthew). — *CBQ* 48 (1986) 468-483. Esp. 468-473: "Bibliography"; 474-478: "The infancy narratives in general"; 478-479: "Matthean infancy narrative"; 479-481: "Matthean genealogy"; 481 [1,18–2,23]; 481-482: "Annunciation to Joseph"; 482-483: "The magi; dating by the star"; 483: "Herod and Bethlehem; Flight to Egypt". [NTA 31, 108]

1986b Matthew's Genealogy of Jesus Christ. A Challenging Advent Homily. — *Worship* 60 (1986) 483-490. [NTA 31, 581]; = ID., *A Coming Christ in Advent*, 1988, 16-26.

1987a The Annunciation to Joseph (Matthew 1:18-25). — *Worship* 61 (1987) 482-492. [NTA 32, 580]; = ID., *A Coming Christ in Advent*, 1988, 27-39.

1987b The *Gospel of Peter* and Canonical Gospel Priority. — *NTS* 33 (1987) 321-343. Esp. 329-332 [27,51-53.54.62-66; 28,11-15]; 333-338: "Relationship between GP and the canonical gospels". [NTA 32, 470] → 1994a; → J.D. Crossan 1985

1988a *A Coming Christ in Advent: Essays on the Gospel Narratives Preparing for the Birth of Jesus. Matthew 1 and Luke 1*. Collegeville, MN: Liturgical Press, 1988, 71 p. [NTA 33, p. 243] → 1986b, 1987a

M. BÉDARD, CahJos 38 (1990) 273-274.

*Avvento: il Cristo che viene. Saggi sui racconti evangelici di preparazione alla nascità di Gesù* (Matteo 1 e Luca 1), trans. E. Gatti (Meditazioni, 83). Brescia: Queriniana, 1989, 114 p.

1988b The Burial of Jesus (Mark 15:42-47). — *CBQ* 50 (1988) 233-245. Esp. 238-245 [27,57-61]. [NTA 32, 1145]

1990*  & FITZMYER, J.A. – MURPHY, R.E. (eds.), *The New Jerome Biblical Commentary*. Englewood Cliffs, NJ: Prentice Hall, 1990, XLVIII-1484 p. → 1968*; → R.E. Brown 1990a-b, A.Y. Collins, Donahue, Meier, Neirynck, Senior, Viviano
  F. NEIRYNCK, *ETL* 68 (1992) 426-428.
  *Nuovo grande commentario biblico*. Brescia: Queriniana, 1997, XLV-1936 p.

1990a  Christology. — *Ibid.*, 1354-1359.
  Cristologia. — ID., et al., *Nuovo grande commentario biblico*, 1997, 1780-1787.

1990b  The Resurrection of Jesus. — *Ibid.*, 1373-1377. Esp. 1377.
  La risurrezione di Gesù. — ID., et al., *Nuovo grande commentario biblico*, 1997, 1805-1810. Esp. 1810.

1990c  Infancy Narratives. — *DBI*, 1990, 311-312.

1990d  The Resurrection in Matthew (27:62-28:20). — *Worship* 64 (1990) 157-170. [NTA 34, 1143]; = ID., *A Risen Christ in EasterTime. Essays on the Gospel Narratives of the Resurrection*, Collegeville, MN: Liturgical Press, 1991, 23-38.
  Trans. Italian 1992; Catalan, Chinese 1994.

1992  Infancy Narratives in the NT Gospels. — *ABD* 3 (1992) 410-415.

1993  *The Birth of the Messiah. A Commentary on the Infancy Narrative in Matthew and Luke* (The Anchor Bible Reference Library). Garden City, NY: Doubleday; London: Chapman, new updated ed., 1993, 752 p. Esp. 25-41; 43-232; 573-583.583-617: "Supplement". [NTA 38, p. 288] → 1977
  E. CUVILLIER, *ETR* 70 (1995) 277.

1994a  *The Death of the Messiah: From Gethsemane to the Grave. A Commentary on the Passion Narratives in the Four Gospels* (The Anchor Bible Reference Library). Garden City, NY: Doubleday; London: Chapman, 2 vols., 1994, XXVII-877 p. and XVIII-879-1608 p. Esp. 26-30: "The passion theology" [Mk/Mt]; 39-39; 40-46: "Interdependence among the synoptic gospels"; 57-63: "The Matthean passion narrative and its special material"; 85-86: "John and Matthew"; 100-101; 110-234 [26,30-46]; 235-310 [26,47-56]; 315-560 [26,57-66]; 563-660 [26,67-27,10]; 665-877 [27,11-31a]; 884-1198 [27,31b-56]; 1201-1313 [27,57-66]; 1321-1336 [Gospel of Peter]; 1385-1388 [26,50]; 1404-1410 [27,3-10; Judas]; 1424-1434 [Jewish leaders]; 1441-1442 [26,36]; 1445-1467 [OT background]; 1469-1482.1484-1489 [passion predictions]. → 1987b; → J.D. Crossan 1995b, McConvery 1995, Neirynck 1994a-b, 1995b, Senior 1994
  R.S. ASCOUGH, *Churchman* 108 (1994) 370-372; D. BOCK, *ChrTod* 38 (1994) 34.37; U. BUSSE, *Bib* 78 (1997) 124-128; J.T. CARROLL, *JBL* 115 (1996) 351-353; K. GRAYSTON, *NBlackfr* 76 (1995) 49-52; L. HOULDEN, *Theology* 97 (1994) 383-384; L.T. JOHNSON, *Commonweal* 121 (1994) 25-27; D.H. JUEL, *TTod* 52 (1995-96) 119-121; F.J. MATERA, *TS* 55 (1994) 739-741; J. MURPHY-O'CONNOR, *RB* 103 (1996) 135-137; P. PERKINS, *America* 170/6 (1994) 19-20; R. SCROGGS, *USQR* 48/1 (1994) 187-190; D. SENIOR, *ChrCent* 111 (1994) 900-904; D.M. SMITH, *PrincSemB* 16 (1995) 360-363; H. WANSBROUGH, *Priests & People* (London) 8 (1994) 443-444.

1994b  *An Introduction to New Testament Christology*. New York – Mahwah, NJ: Paulist; London: Chapman, 1994, XII-226 p. Esp. 32, 54 [10,23], 74-76, 82-84, 88 [11,27], 118-120, 129-130.
  *Introduzione alla cristologia del Nuovo Testamento*, trans. L. de Santis (Biblioteca biblica, 19). Brescia: Queriniana, 1995, 224 p.
  *Jésus dans les quatre évangiles. Introduction à la christologie du Nouveau Testament*, trans. J.-B. Degorce & D. Barrios Delgado (Lire la Bible, 11). Paris: Cerf, 1996, 311 p.
  F. NEIRYNCK, *ETL* 73 (1997) 171-172.

**BROWN, Robert Layton**

1991  *Matthew's Presentation of the Law in Light of Early Christian-Jewish Dialogue*. Diss. Southern Baptist Theol. Sem., Louisville, KY, 1991, 219 p. (D.E. Garland). — *DissAbstr* 52 (1991-92) 3632.

**BROWN, Robert N.**

1982  Jesus and the Child as a Model of Spirituality. — *IBS* 4 (1982) 178-192. Esp. 179-181 [18,1-5]; 183-184 [19,13-15]. [NTA 27, 945]

**BROWN, Schuyler**

1969    *Apostasy and Perseverance in the Theology of Luke* (AnBib, 36). Roma: Pontifical Biblical Institute, 1969, XVI-166 p. Esp. 16-19 [Q 4,1-13]; 62-65 [Q 22,28-30]. — Diss. Münster, 1968 (J. Gnilka).

1977    The Two-fold Representation of the Mission in Matthew's Gospel. [10,5-6; 28,19] — *StudTheol* 31 (1977) 21-32. [NTA 22, 89]

1978    The Mission to Israel in Matthew's Central Section (Mt 9,35–11,1). — *ZNW* 69 (1978) 73-90. Esp. 79-90 [10,5-6.18.23; 23,34]. [NTA 23, 824]

1979    The Matthean Apocalypse. — *JSNT* 4 (1979) 2-27. Esp. 4-6 [23,32-39]; 6-7 [24,1-3]; 7-14 [24,4-31]; 14-18 [24,32–25,30]; 18-19 [25,31-46]. [NTA 24, 97]

1980    The Matthean Community and the Gentile Mission. — *NT* 22 (1980) 193-221. Esp. 193-199.213-219. [NTA 25, 67]

1984    *The Origins of Christianity. A Historical Introduction to the New Testament* (The Oxford Bible Series). Oxford: University Press, 1984, X-169 p. Esp. 107-114: "Matthew's special material"; rev. ed. 1993, X-179 p. Esp. 115-122.

1989a    Jesus, History, and the Kerygma. A Hermeneutical Reflection. — FRANKEMÖLLE, H. – KERTELGE, K. (eds.), *Vom Urchristentum zu Jesus*. FS J. Gnilka, 1989, 487-496. Esp. 490-493 [Q; historical Jesus].

1989b    Universalism and Particularism in Matthew's Gospel: A Jungian Approach. — *SBL 1989 Seminar Papers*, 388-399.

1990    Faith, the Poor and the Gentiles: A Tradition-Historical Reflection on Matthew 25:31-46. — *TorontoJT* 6 (1990) 171-181. Esp. 171-174: "The judgment scene in its Matthean context"; 174-176: "The parable of the sheep and the goats"; 176-178: "Faith, the gentiles and the poor". [NTA 35, 1145]

**BROWN, Scott Kent**

1992    Sayings of Jesus, Oxyrhynchus. — *ABD* 5 (1992) 999-1001.

**BROWN, Virginia**

1987    A New Commentary on Matthew in Beneventan Script at Venosa. — *Mediaeval Studies* (Toronto, Ont.) 49 (1987) 443-465.

**BROWNE, Gerald M.**

1994    *Bibliorum sacrorum versio palaeonubiana* (CSCO, 547). Leuven: Peeters, 1994, IX-131 p. Esp. 1-6.

**BROWNLEE, William Hugh**

1956    Messianic Motifs of Qumran and the New Testament. — *NTS* 3 (1956-57) 12-30, 195-210. Esp. 17-18 [18,15-17]; 197-198 [21,5]. [NTA 2, 156/157]

**BROX, Norbert**

1964    Das messianische Selbstverständnis des historischen Jesus. — SCHUBERT, K. (ed.), *Vom Messias zum Christus*, 1964, 165-201. Esp. 188-190 [law]; 190-191 [kingdom].

1973    Suchen und Finden. Zur Nachgeschichte von Mt 7,7b / Lk 11,9b. — HOFFMANN, P., et al. (eds.), *Orientierung an Jesus*. FS J. Schmid, 1973, 17-36. Esp. 20-25 [gnosis]; 25-29 [Irenaeus, Tertullian]; 29-35 [Clement, Origen, Augustine].

1987*    et al. (eds.), *Anfänge der Theologie. Charisteion Johannes B. Bauer zum Jänner 1987*. Graz–Wien–Köln: Styria, 1987, XVIII-449 p. → Heuberger, Mali, Schwank, Trummer

**BROYLES, Craig C.**

1992    Gospel (Good News). — *DJG*, 1992, 282-286. Esp. 286.

**BROZ, Ludec**

1988   Theology of the First Petition. [6,9] — *ComViat* 31 (1988) 243-251. [NTA 34, 621]

**BRUCE, Frederick Fyvie**

1961   The Book of Zechariah and the Passion Narrative. — *BJRL* 43 (1960-61) 336-353. Esp. 339-341 [21,5]. [NTA 6, 80]

1968   *This is That. The New Testament Development of Some Old Testament Themes.* Exeter: Paternoster, 1968, 122 p. Esp. 106-107 [21,5]; 108-110 [27,9-10].

1969a  *The New Testament History.* London: Nelson, 1969; Garden City, NY: Doubleday, 1972, XIV-462 p. Esp. 152-162: "John the Baptist"; 163-177: "Jesus and the kingdom of God"; 178-194: "Jesus and the kingdom of the world"; 195-204: "Trial and execution of Jesus".

1969b  Jesus and the Gospels in the Light of the Scrolls. — BLACK, M. (ed.), *The Scrolls and Christianity. Historical and Theological Significance* (Theological Collections, 11), London: SPCK, 1969, 70-82.

1970   *St. Matthew.* Grand Rapids, MI: Eerdmans, 1970, 95 p.
       *Das Matthäus-Evangelium,* trans. F. Schwan (Kurzauslegung zum Neuen Testament = Brockhaus-Taschenbücher, 1039). Wuppertal: Brockhaus, 1973, 127 p.

1972   *The Message of the New Testament.* Exeter: Paternoster, 1972; Grand Rapids, MI: Eerdmans, 1973, 120 p. Esp. 62-72: "Jesus Christ the teacher. The message of the gospel of Matthew". *El mensaje del Nuevo Testamento.* Buenos Aires: Certeza, 1975, 157 p.

1974   *Jesus and Christian Origins Outside the New Testament.* London: Hodder & Stoughton, 1974, 216 p. Esp. 99-105 [Gospel of the Hebrews]; 105-109 [Gospel of the Ebionites]; 110-156 [Gospel of Thomas].
       *Außerbiblische Zeugnisse über Jesus und das frühe Christentum,* ed. E. Güting, trans. J. Geitz, et al. Gießen–Basel: Brunnen, 1991, 190 p.

1982   The Background to the Son of Man Sayings. — ROWDON, H.H. (ed.), *Christ the Lord,* FS D. Guthrie, 1982, 50-70. Esp. 51-61.

1983   *The Hard Sayings of Jesus* (The Jesus Library). Downers Grove, IL: Inter-Varsity, 1983, 266 p.

1984   Render to Caesar. [22,15-22] — BAMMEL, E. - MOULE, C.F.D. (eds.), *Jesus and the Politics of His Day,* 1984, 249-263.

**BRUCE, J.A.**

1984   The Flight into Egypt. The Dreams of Fathers. — *St. Luke's Journal of Theology* (Sewanee, TN) 27 (1984) 287-296. [NTA 29, 85]

**BRUCKNER, E.**

1988   The Temptation of Jesus. [Chinese] — *ColcTFu* 75 (1988) 17-26.

**BRUEGGEMANN, Walter**

1972   Weariness, Exile and Chaos (A Motif in Royal Theology). — *CBQ* 34 (1972) 19-38. Esp. 37-38 [11,28-29].

**BRUG, J.F.**

1995   Show Love to Your Neighbor. [5,43-48] — *Wisconsin Lutheran Quarterly* (Mequon, WI) 92 (1995) 294-295. [NTA 40, 822]

**BRUMMEL, Lec**

1984   Tuve hombre. Mateo 25:31-46 en la predicación de Juan Crisóstomo. — *Vox Evangelii* (Buenos Aires) 1 (1984) 97-116.

**BRUNEC, Michael**

1952   Sermo eschatologicus. — *VD* 30 (1952) 214-218 [24,3]; 265-277 [24,5-13]; 321-333 [24,15-

24]; 31 (1953) 13-20 [24,15]; 83-94 [Lk 17,20-37]; 156-163 [24,28; Q 17,37]; 211-220 [24,29-31]; 282-290 [24,32-35]; 344-351 [24,36-51].

1957 De Legatione Ioannis Baptistae (Mt. 11,2-24). — *VD* 35 (1957) 193-203 [11,3-6], 262-270 [11,11], 321-331 [11,12.14]. [NTA 2, 526]

**BRUNER, Frederick D.**

1987 *The Christbook. A Historical/Theological Commentary. Matthew 1-12.* Waco, TX: Word, 1987, XXX-475 p. [NTA 32, p. 99]
    D. FRANCE, *EvQ* 60 (1988) 360-362; F.D. HOLWERDA, *CalvTJ* 24 (1989) 151-154; R.K. MCIVER, *AndrUnS* 26 (1988) 87-88; T.L. WILKINSON, *RTR* 47 (1988) 19-20

1990 *The Churchbook. Matthew 13-28. A Commentary.* Waco, TX: Word, 1990, XX-651 p. [NTA 35, p. 100]
    E. KRENTZ, *CurrTMiss* 19 (1992) 299-300; C.S. RODD, *ExpT* 104 (1992-93) 149-150; P. ROGERS, *IrTQ* 58 (1992) 314-315; J. SINGLETON, *Interpr* 47 (1993) 310-311; D.T. WILLIAMS, *JEvTS* 34 (1991) 125-126.

**BRUNI, Giancarlo**

1973 La comunità nell'Evangelo di Matteo. — *Servitium* 7 (1973) 411-422. [NTA 18, 459]

**BRUNNER, Klaus**

1978 Textkritisches zu Mt 6,28: οὐ ξαίνουσιν statt αὐξάνουσιν vorgeschlagen. — *ZKT* 100 (1978) 251-256. [NTA 23, 100]

**BRUNNER, Robert** → W. Lüthi 1936, 1962

**BRUNS, Bernhard**

1976 *Ehescheidung und Wiederheirat im Fall von Ehebruch. Eine rechts- und dogmengeschichtliche Untersuchung zu Kanon 7 der 24. Sitzung des Konzils von Trient* (Annuarium Historiae Conciliorum, Suppl. 3). München–Paderborn: Schöningh, 1976, 200 p. Esp. 40-44, 59-65, 101-106: "Die exegetische Beweisführung". — Diss. Freiburg, 1974 (C.G. Fürst).

**BRUNS, J. Edgar**

1961 The Magi Episode in Matthew 2. — *CBQ* 23 (1961) 51-54. [NTA 5, 705]

1963 *Hear His Voice Today. A Guide to the Content and Comprehension of the Bible.* New York: Kenedy & Sons, 1963, IX-207 p. Esp. 114-117.

1964 Matthew's Genealogy of Jesus. — *BiTod* 15 (1964) 980-985. [NTA 9, 897]

1967 Genealogy of Jesus. — *NewCathEnc* 6 (1967) 319-321.

1992 The Priestly Lineage of Mary and Jesus Reconsidered. — PILLINGER, R. – RENHART, E. (eds.), *The Divine Life, Light and Love.* FS P.B.T. Bilaniuk, Graz: Schnider, 1992, 57-65.

**BRUPPACHER, Hans**

1965a Ein neues Jesuswort. [5,48] — *KirchRefSchweiz* 121 (1965) 242-244. [NTA 10, 511]

1965b Zur Auslegung der 6. Bitte. Und Führe uns nicht in Versuchung. Matth. 6,13a. — *Ibid.*, 257-258. [NTA 10, 512]

1966 Kleine Beiträge zu einer kommenden Revision der Zürcher Bibel. — *KirchRefSchweiz* 122 (1966) 100-101 [5,9.48], 150-151 [6,13]. [NTA 11, 200/207]

1967 Was sagte Jesus in Matthäus 5,48? — *ZNW* 58 (1967) 145. [NTA 12, 150]

**BUBAR, Wallace W.**

1995 Killing Two Birds with One Stone: The Utter De(con)struction of Matthew and His Church. — *BibInt* 3 (1995) 144-157. Esp. 145-147 [16,13-20]; 147-155 [Peter]. [NTA 40, 173]

**BUBOLZ, Georg**

1987 Die Gleichnisse Jesu. Exegetische, dogmatische und didaktische Erwägungen am Beispiel von Mt 20,1-15. — *Religionsunterricht an höheren Schulen* (Düsseldorf) 30 (1987) 227-235. Esp. 227-230.

**BUCCELLATI, Giorgio**

1972 Le beatitudini sullo sfondo della tradizione sapienziale Mesopotamica. — *BibOr* 14 (1972) 241-264.

**BUCHAN, William M.**

1989 Research on the Lord's Prayer. — *ExpT* 100 (1988-89) 336-339. [NTA 34, 117]

**BUCHANAN, George Wesley**

1964 Jesus and the Upper Class. — *NT* 7 (1964-65) 195-209. Esp. 202-208: "Jesus and the social classes". [NTA 10, 68]

1965 Some Vow and Oath Formulas in the New Testament. — *HTR* 58 (1965) 319-326. Esp. 319-324 [15,5]. [NTA 10, 518] → Falk 1966

1970 *The Consequences of the Covenant* (SupplNT, 20). Leiden: Brill, 1970, XX-342 p. Esp. 272-275: "The sect of St. Matthew"; 306-307.

1971 Reaction to Talbert and McKnight, "Can the Griesbach Hypothesis Be Falsified?" — *SBL 1971 Seminar Papers*, I, 111-138. Esp. 111-115 [28,1-8]; 115-120 [16,13-23]; 120-123 [12,1-8]; 123-124 [3,13-17]; 127-134 [5,39-47; 7,12]; 134-137 [12,38-42]; 137-138 [24,37-39]. → Talbert 1971 Has the Griesbach Hypothesis Been Falsified? — *JBL* 93 (1974) 550-572. Esp. 550-556 [28,1-8]; 556-560 [16,13-23]; 560-562 [12,1-8]; 563-568 [5,39-47; 7,12]; 568-570 [12,38-42]; 570-571 [24,37-39]. [NTA 19, 515]

1977 Current Synoptic Studies. Orchard, the Griesbach Hypothesis, and Other Alternatives. — *RelLife* 46 (1977) 415-425. [NTA 22, 746]

1983 Matthean Beatitudes and Traditional Promises. — FARMER, W.R. (ed.), *New Synoptic Studies*, 1983, 161-184. Esp. 168-180 [5,3-10]; = *Journal from the Radical Reformation* (Morrow, GA) 3 (1993) 45-69. [NTA 38, 754]

1984 *Jesus. The King and His Kingdom.* Macon, GA: Mercer, 1984, XVI-347 p. Esp. 82-91 [8,19-22; 12,36-50]; 97-110 [7,13-14; 9,36-37; 10,37-39; 12,43-45; 13,44-46; 25,31-46]; 120-122 [24,45-51]; 134-137 [15,1-20]; 141-151 [13,24-30.47-48; 20,1-16; 21,28-32]; 157-160 [22,1-14]; 167-168 [12,11-12]; 192-197 [7;7-11; 15,12-13]; 212-214 [13,31-33]; 218-220 [11,2-6]; 226-238 [7,24-27; 11,12-13; 12,31-32.38-39; 13,52; 18,21-22.23-35; 19,3-6]; 291-297: "Matthean deductions"; 298-300 [13,54-57].

1987 *Typology and the Gospel.* Lanham, MD: University Press of America, 1987, X-142 p.

**BUCHANAN, P.** → S.E. Porter 1991

**BUCHER, Anton A.**

1990 *Gleichnisse verstehen lernen. Strukturgenetische Untersuchungen zur Rezeption synoptischer Parabeln* (Praktische Theologie im Dialog, 5). Freiburg/Schw: Universitätsverlag, 1990, X-192 p.

**BUCICHOWSKI, Wacław**

1979 (ed.), *Benedicti Hesse Lectura super Evangelium Matthaei* I: *Capitulum I* (Textus et studia historiam theologiae in Polonia excultae spectantia, 8). Warszawa: Akademia teologii katolickiej, 1979, 342 p.; II: *Capitula II–IV* (Textus, 13). 1982, 280 p.; III: *Capitulum V* (Textus, 16). 1983, 267 p.; IV: *Capitula VI–VIII* (Textus, 18). 1984, 331 p.; V: *Capitula IX–XIII* (Textus, 21). 1986, 424 p.; VI: *Capitula XIV–XVII* (Textus, 24). 1987, 354 p.; VII: *Capitula XVIII–XX* (Textus, 26). 1990, 342 p.
A. SAND, *TRev* 76 (1980) 277-278.

**BUCK, Erwin**

1986   Anti-Judaic Sentiments in the Passion Narrative According to Matthew. —
RICHARDSON, P. — GRANSKOU, D. (eds.), *Anti-Judaism in Early Christianity*. I: *Paul
and the Gospels* (Studies in Christianity and Judaism, 2), Waterloo, Ont.: Laurier,
1986, 165-180.

**BUCKLEY, S.**

1962   The Pater Noster. — *Eucharist & Priest* (Alwaye, Kerala) 68 (1962) 151-161.

**BUCKLEY, Thomas W.**

1981   Preaching Matthew's Gospel. — *BiTod* 19 (1981) 25-29. [NTA 25, 470]

1991   *Seventy Times Seven: Sin, Judgment, and Forgiveness in Matthew* (Zacchaeus Studies:
New Testament). Collegeville, MN: Liturgical Press, 1991, 102 p. [NTA 36, p. 108]
   A.-J. LEVINE, *CRBR* 5 (1992) 184-186; B.T. VIVIANO, *RB* 101 (1994) 454-455.

**BUCKWALTER, H. Douglas**

1995   The Virgin Birth of Jesus Christ: A Union of Theology and History. — *EvJ* 13 (1995)
3-14. [NTA 40, 118]

**BÜCHELE, Herwig**

1981   Bergpredigt und Gewaltfreiheit. — *Stimmen der Zeit* (München) 199 (1981) 632-640;
= *Reformatio* 31 (1982) 14-23.

**BÜCHNER, Dirk L.**

1993   Micah 7:6 in the Ancient Old Testament Versions. [10,35] — *Journal of Northwest
Semitic Languages* (Stellenbosch) 19 (1993) 159-168. [NTA 39, 150]

**BÜHNER, Jan-A.**

1971   Zur Form, Tradition und Bedeutung der ἦλθον-Sprüche. — *Das Institutum Iudaicum
der Universität Tübingen, 1968-1970*, Tübingen: Institutum Iudaicum, 1971, 45-68.

**BÜHRING, Gernot**

1984   *Vaterunser polyglott. Das Gebet des Herrn in 42 Sprachen mit 75 Textfassungen sowie
einer Bibliographie der bekannten Paternoster-Polyglotten*. Hamburg: Buske, 1984,
278 p.
   S. JANERAS, *RevistCatTeol* 12 (1987) 231-233.

**BUETUBELA BALEMBO, Paul**

1986   "Et ne nous soumets pas à la tentation". La difficile actualisation de Mt 6,13. — *RAfrT*
10 (1986) 5-13. [NTA 32, 121]

1988   The Father of Jesus Christ. — *Biblical Pastoral Bulletin* (Nairobi) 1 (1988) 16-24.

1990   Le vêtement de noce: exégèse symbolique de Mt 22,11-14. — *RAfrT* 14 (1990) 33-45.

1993   Le bonheur des simples. Exégèse de Mt 11,25-27 par. — ADESO, P., et al., *5ième
Congrès des biblistes africains. Universalisme et mission dans la Bible, Abidjan 16-
23.VII.1991*, Nairobi: Kath. Jungschar Österreichs – Cath. Biblical Centre for Africa
and Madagascar, 1993, 68-85.

1994   L'universalisme du salut et Mt 2,1-12. — *RAfrT* 18 (1994) 149-159. [NTA 40, 816]

**BUIJS, Ludovicus**

1944[R]  De theologia morali et Sermone Montano. [Dutch, 1944] — *Studia Moralia* (Roma) 2
(1964) 11-41.

**BULCKE, Michel**

1984   The Translator's Theology. A Response to "Taking Theology Seriously in the
Translation Task". [1,24-25; 22,44] — *BTrans* 35 (1984) 134-135. [NTA 28, 912]

**BULCKENS, Jozef**

1980* (ed.), *Parabels meerstemmig* (Verslagboek van de Vliebergh-Sencie-Leergang Catechese en Bijbel, 1979). Antwerpen–Amsterdam: Patmos, 1980, 176 p. → Dupont, Kevers, Lamberigts

**BULMAN, James M.**

1956 Parables of Revelation and Judgment. — *RExp* 53 (1956) 314-325.

**BULTMANN, Rudolf K.**

1913[R] What the Sayings Source Reveals about the Early Church. [German, 1913] — KLOPPENBORG, J.S. (ed.), *The Shape of Q*, 1994, 23-34.

1919[R] Die Frage nach dem messianischen Bewusstsein Jesu und das Petrus-Bekenntnis. [1919] — ID., *Exegetica*, 1967, 1-9 (IT 1971, 13-23). Esp. 5-7 [16,17-19].

1925[R] *Die Erforschung der synoptischen Evangelien* [1925] (Aus der Welt der Religion, NF 1). Berlin: Töpelmann, 3rd rev. ed., 1960, 54 p.; Berlin: de Gruyter, [4]1961; [5]1966; = ID., *Glauben und Verstehen. Gesammelte Aufsätze*, IV, Tübingen: Mohr, 1965, [2]1967, 1-41.
The Study of the Synoptic Gospels. [English, 1934] — GRANT, F.C. (ed.), *Form Criticism. Two Essays on New Testament Research*, repr. New York: Harper, 1962, 11-76.
*Storia dei Vangeli sinottici* [[6]1964], trans. P.A. di Marco (Suppl. di Teologia Biblica, 3). Bologna: Dehoniane, 1969, X-132 p.
La ricerca sui Vangeli sinottici. — ID., *Credere e comprendere*, Brescia: Paideia, 1977, 879-917.

1926[R] Ein neuer Zugang zum synoptischen Problem. [1926] — HAHN, F. (ed.), *Zur Formgeschichte des Evangeliums* (Wege der Forschung, 81), Darmstadt: Wissenschaftliche Buchgesellschaft, 1985, 233-255.
The New Approach to the Synoptic Problem. — ID., *Existence and Faith*, 1960, 35-54.

1931[R] *Die Geschichte der synoptischen Tradition* [1921] (FRLANT, 29). Göttingen: Vandenhoeck & Ruprecht, 2. neubearbeitete Auflage, 1931, 408 p.; [3]1957; [4]1958; [5]1961; [6]1964; [7]1967; [8]1970; [9]1979; [10]1995, X-452 p. Esp. 8-222: "Die Überlieferung der Worte Jesu"; 223-346: "Die Überlieferung des Erzählungsstoffes"; 347-392: "Die Redaktion des Traditionsstoffes" [Mt: 358-359.376-384]. → Cerfaux 1932, Theisohn 1975
*Ergänzungsheft*, 1958, 51 p.; [2]1962, 56 p.; [3]1966; bearbeitet von G. Theißen und P. Vielhauer, [4]1971, 125 p.; [5]1979.
*The History of the Synoptic Tradition*, trans. J. Marsh. Oxford: Blackwell; New York – Evanston, IL: Harper & Row, 1963, VIII-456 p.; [2]1968, VIII-462 p. Esp. 9-205; 207-317; 319-374; 375-455 (supplement [2]1962).
*L'histoire de la tradition synoptique*, trans. A. Malet. Paris: Seuil, 1973, 729 p. Esp. 23-256; 257-387; 389-453; 455-671 (supplement [4]1971).
Die Geschichte der synoptischen Tradition. [1931, 260-261, 282-308; *Ergänzungsheft*, 1958, 38-43] — LIMBECK, M. (ed.), *Redaktion und Theologie des Passionberichtes*, 1981, 21-56.

1936[R] The Sermon on the Mount and the Justice of the State. [German, 1936] — ID., *Existence and Faith*, 1960, 202-205.

1941[R] Die Frage nach der Echtheit von Mt 16,17-19. [1941] — ID., *Exegetica*, 1967, 255-277 (IT 1971, 25-52).

1948[R] *Theologie des Neuen Testaments* (Neue theologische Grundrisse). Tübingen: Mohr, 1948-1953, XII-608 p. Esp. 1-33: "Die Verkündigung Jesu"; 33-64: "Das Kerygma der Urgemeinde"; [2]1954, XII-603 p.; [3]1958; [5]1965, XVI-620 p. (Nachtrag, 612-620); [7]1976; [8]1980, ed. O. Merk (Uni-Taschenbücher, 630), Tübingen: Mohr, XIX-704 p., 622-704: "Nachträge (1965-1979/80)"; [9]1984, XXII-753 p.
*Theology of the New Testament*, trans. K. Grobel. London: SCM, I, 1952, IX-395 p.; II, 1955, VI-278 p.
*Teología del Nuevo Testamento* (Biblioteca de estudios bíblicos, 32). Salamanca: Sígueme, 1981, 749 p.
*Teologia del Nuovo Testamento* (Biblioteca di teologia contemporanea, 46). Brescia: Queriniana, 1985.

1960 *Existence and Faith. Shorter Writings of Rudolf Bultmann.* Selected, translated, and Introduced by Schubert M. Ogden. New York: Living Age Books, 1960; London: Hodder & Stoughton, 1961, 320 p. → 1926, 1936

1967 *Exegetica. Aufsätze zur Erforschung des Neuen Testaments*, ed. E. Dinkler. Tübingen: Mohr, 1967, XXVII-554 p. → 1919, 1941
*Exegetica*, trans. B. Deslex Muff (Le idee e la vita, 60). Torino: Borla, 1971, 197 p.

**BUNDY, David D.**

1983 The Syriac Version of *De Chananaea* Attributed to John Chrysostom (CPG 4529). [15,21-28] — *Muséon* 96 (1983) 97-132.

**BUNDY, Walter E.**

1955 *Jesus and the First Three Gospels. An Introduction to the Synoptic Tradition.* Cambridge, MA: Harvard University Press; London: Cumberledge, 1955, XXIII-598 p.

**BUNN, James C.**

1952 *The Element of Determinism in Prophecy as It Is Reflected in the Gospel of Matthew.* Diss. Southwestern Baptist Theol. Sem., Fort Worth, TX, 1952.

**BUNTE, Wolfgang**

1994 *Rabbinische Traditionen bei Nikolaus von Lyra. Ein Beitrag zur Schriftauslegung des Spätmittelalters* (Judentum und Umwelt, 58). Frankfurt/M: Lang, 1994, 324 p. ["Tractatus contra quendam Judaeum impugnatorem evangelii secundum Matthaeum"].

**BUONO, Anthony**

1993 Praying with the Beatitudes. — *Emmanuel* 99 (1993) 466-470. [NTA 38, 753]

**BURCHARD, Christoph**

1970a Das doppelte Liebesgebot in der frühen christlichen Überlieferung. — LOHSE, E., et al. (eds.), *Der Ruf Jesu.* FS J. Jeremias, 1970, 39-62. Esp. 39-40 [22,34-40]; 42-43.48-49 [Q 10,25-28]; 44-46 [Didache; Justin]; 61 [9,13; 12,7].

1970b Fußnoten zum neutestamentlichen Griechisch. — *ZNW* 61 (1970) 157-171. Esp. 157-158 [26,5]. [NTA 15, 770] → 1978b

1975 Versuch, das Thema der Bergpredigt zu finden. — STRECKER, G. (ed.), *Jesus Christus in Historie und Theologie.* FS H. Conzelmann, 1975, 409-432. The Theme of the Sermon on the Mount. — SCHOTTROFF, L., et al., *Essays on the Love Commandment*, 1978, 57-91.

1976 Kerygma and Martyria in the New Testament. — SOVIK, A. (ed.), *Christian Witness and the Jewish People. The Report of a Consultation Held under the Auspices of the Lutheran World Federation, Department of Studies. Oslo, August 1975*, Genève: Lutheran World Federation, 1976, 10-25. Esp. 22-23. → 1978a

1978a Formen der Vermittlung christlichen Glaubens im Neuen Testament. Beobachtungen anhand von κήρυγμα, μαρτυρία und verwandten Wörtern. — *EvT* 38 (1978) 313-340. Esp. 333-335 [κηρύσσω]. [NTA 23, 633] → 1976

1978b Fußnoten zum neutestamentlichen Griechisch II. — *ZNW* 69 (1978) 143-157. Esp. 143-145 [2,2]. [NTA 23, 764] → 1970b

1980 Jesus für die Welt. Über das Verhältnis von Reich Gottes und Mission. — SUNDERMEIER, T., et al. (eds.), *Fides pro mundi vita. Missiontheologie heute. Hans-Werner Gensichen zum 65. Geburtstag* (Missionswissenschaftliche Forschungen, 14), Gütersloh: Mohn, 1980, 13-27. Esp. 15-18 [Q 11,20].

1985 Bergpredigt. — *EKL* 1 ($^{3}$1985) c. 433-436. → 1987b

1987a Jesus von Nazareth. — BECKER, J., et al. (eds.), *Die Anfänge des Christentums. Alte Welt und neue Hoffnung*, Stuttgart: Kohlhammer, 1987, 12-58. Esp. 20-35 [kingdom]. Jesus of Nazareth. — BECKER, J., et al. (eds.), *Christian Beginnings. Word and Community from Jesus to Post-Apostolic Times*, Louisville, KY: Westminster/Knox, 1993, 15-72.

1987b Le thème du Sermon sur la montagne. — *ETR* 62 (1987) 1-17. [NTA 31, 1061] → 1985

1988 Senfkorn, Sauerteig, Schatz und Perle in Matthäus 13. — *SNTU* 13 (1988) 5-35. Esp. 5-19: "Mt 13 im Überblick"; 19-32: "Schatz, Perle und Fischnetz (Mt 13,44-50)"; 32-35: "Senfkorn und Sauerteig (13,31-33)". [NTA 33, 1134]

1993 Zu Matthäus 8,5-13. — *ZNW* 84 (1993) 278-288. Esp. 278-280 [8,5]; 281-285 [8,9]; 285-287 [8,10-12]. [NTA 38, 764]

**BURCHILL, John Patrick**

1975 *Are There "Evangelical Counsels" of Perpetual Continence and Poverty? A Study of the Tradition, a Reinterpretation of Mt. 19:10-12, 16-22ff. (and par.), and Implications for a Biblical Basis of Religious Life*. Diss. Dominican House of Studies, Washington, DC, 1975, XV-531 p. (T.R. Heath). Esp. 68-134 [19,10-12]; 177-231.416-462 [19,16-30]. — *DissAbstr* 36 (1975-76) 6164.

1977 Biblical Basis of Religious Life. — *RRel* 36 (1977) 900-917. Esp. 903-906 [19,16-22]; 906-909: "Relation of Mt 19 to the Sermon on the Mount"; 909-914 [19,21]. [NTA 22, 404]

1980 Discipleship is Perfection. Discipleship in Matthew. — *RRel* 39 (1980) 36-42. [NTA 24, 777]

**BURGER, Christoph**

1970 *Jesus als Davidssohn. Eine traditionsgeschichtliche Untersuchung* (FRLANT, 98). Göttingen: Vandenhoeck & Ruprecht, 1970, 185 p. Esp. 72-106: "Der Davidssohn bei Matthäus" [1,1-17.18-25; 2,1-18; 9,27-31; 12,22-24; 15,21-28; 20,29-34; 21,1-16; 22,41-46]. — Diss. Tübingen, 1968 (F. Lang).

1973 Jesu Taten nach Matthäus 8 und 9. — *ZTK* 70 (1973) 272-287. [NTA 18, 856]

**BURGERS, Wim**

1960 De instelling van de Twaalf in het evangelie van Marcus. — *ETL* 36 (1960) 625-654. Esp. 628-631: "Een synoptische theorie" [Vaganay]. [NTA 6, 137] — Diss. Leuven, 1959 (A. Descamps).

**BURGESS, Joseph Anders**

1976 *A History of the Exegesis of Matthew 16:17-19 from 1781 to 1965*. Ann Arbor, MI: Edwards Brothers, 1976, VII-269 p. [NTA 21, p. 323] — Diss. Basel, 1966 (O. Cullmann). Y. CONGAR, *RSPT* 64 (1980) 592; R.H. GUNDRY, *JBL* 97 (1978) 142-143; J.P. MEIER, *CBQ* 39 (1977) 586-587; G. STRECKER, *Zeitschrift für Kirchengeschichte* (Stuttgart) 90 (1979) 138-141.

**BURGGRAF, David L.**

1988 Principles of Discipline in Matthew 18:15-17. I: A Contextual Study. II: An Exegetical Study. III: A Practical Study. — *Calvary Baptist Theological Journal* (Lansdale, PA) 4/2 (1988) 1-23; 5/1 (1989) 1-11; 5/2 (1989) 1-29.

**BURGMANN, Hans**

1988 *Die essenischen Gemeinden von Qumrân und Damaskus in der Zeit der Hasmonäer und Herodier (130 ante-68 post)* (Arbeiten zum Neuen Testament und Judentum, 8). Frankfurt/M: Lang, 1988, 541 p. Esp. 451-503 [5-7/Qumran].

**BURKE, Thomas J.M.**

1954 The Our Father. — *AmEcclRev* 130 (1954) 176-182, 250-258.

**BURKETT, Delbert**

1994 The Nontitular Son of Man: A History and Critique. — *NTS* 40 (1994) 504-521. Esp. 511-513.517-519. [NTA 39, 1019]

**BURKHARDT, Helmut**

1984 Die Bergpredigt – eine allgemeine Handlungsanweisung? Kritische Erwägungen zu dem Aufsatz von A. Strobel: Die Bergpredigt als ethische Weisung heute. — *TBeitr* 15 (1984) 137-140. [NTA 29, 88] → Strobel 1984

**BURKILL, T. Alec**

1966 The Syrophoenician Woman: The Congruence of Mark 7,24-31. — *ZNW* 57 (1966) 23-37. Esp. 25-28 [15,21-28]. [NTA 11, 241]
The Congruence of Mark 7:24-31. — ID., *New Light on the Earliest Gospel*, 1972, 71-95. Esp. 74-78.

1967 The Historical Development of the Story of the Syrophoenician Woman (Mark vii:24-31). — *NT* 9 (1967) 161-177. Esp. 177 [15,21-28]. [NTA 12, 565]
The Syrophoenician Woman: Mark 7,24-31. — *Studia Evangelica* 4 (1968) 166-170 (= 1967, 172-177).
The Life History of Mark 7:24-31. — ID., *New Light on the Earliest Gospel*, 1972, 96-120. Esp. 120.

1972 *New Light on the Earliest Gospel. Seven Markan Studies*. Ithaca, NY – London: Cornell University Press, 1972, XIII-275 p. → 1966, 1967

**BURNETT, Charles S.F.**

1985 The 'Expositio orationis dominicae'. "Multorum legimus orationes". Abelard's Exposition of the Lord's Prayer? — *RBén* 95 (1985) 60-72.

**BURNETT, Fred W.**

1981 *The Testament of Jesus-Sophia. A Redaction-Critical Study of the Eschatological Discourse in Matthew*. Washington, DC: University of America Press, 1981, XXIII-467 p. [NTA 26, p. 194] — Diss. Vanderbilt Univ., Nashville, TN, 1979-80 (J.R. Donahue).
K.A. BARTA, *CBQ* 45 (1983) 307-308; J.C. FENTON, *JTS* 35 (1984) 199-200; D.R.A. HARE, *JBL* 102 (1983) 644-646; D. HILL, *ExpT* 93 (1981-82) 310-311; M.D. JOHNSON, *Interpr* 37 (1983) 216-217; C.P. MÄRZ, *TLZ* 109 (1984) 336-337.

1983 Παλιγγενεσία in Matt. 19:28: A Window on the Matthean Community? — *JSNT* 17 (1983) 60-72. [NTA 27, 926]

1985 Prolegomenon to Reading Matthew's Eschatological Discourse: Redundancy and the Education of the Reader in Matthew. — *Semeia* 31 (1985) 91-109. Esp. 93-98 [redundancy]; 98-101 [24,3]. [NTA 30, 124]

1987 Characterization in Matthew. Reader Construction of the Disciple Peter. — *McKendree Pastoral Review* (Lebanon, IL) 4 (1987) 13-43. [NTA 33, 111] → 1993

1989 Characterization and Christology in Matthew: Jesus in the Gospel of Matthew. — *SBL 1989 Seminar Papers*, 588-603. Esp. 591 [1,1-17]; 591-595 [1,21-25]; 595-597 [28,20]; 597-598 [Son of Man]; 598-600 [christology].

1991 The Undecidability of the Proper Name "Jesus" in Matthew. — *Semeia* 54 (1991) 123-144. Esp. 124-126 [Jesus]; 126-127 [1,1-17]; 127-129 [1,21-25]; 130-132 [1,17-25]; 132-134 [28,20]; 134-135 [Son of Man]. [NTA 36, 1249]

1992a Exposing the Anti-Jewish Ideology of Matthew's Implied Author: The Characterization of God As Father. — *Semeia* 59 (1992) 155-191. Esp. 156-164 [narrative criticism]; 164-173 [ὁ πατήρ]. [NTA 38, 140]

1992b "M" Tradition. — *DJG*, 1992, 511-512.

1992c Wisdom. — *Ibid.*, 873-877. Esp. 874-876.

1993 Characterization and Reader Construction of Characters in the Gospels. — *Semeia* 63 (1993) 3-28. Esp. 20-23: "Peter in Matthew". [NTA 38, 1308] → 1987

**BURNHAM, James Leonard** → dos Santos 1985

**BURNS, A.L.**

1953 Two Words for 'Time' in the New Testament. — *AusBR* 3 (1953) 7-22. Esp. 9-11.

**BURNS, Paul C.**

1981    *The Christology in Hilary of Poitiers' Commentary on Matthew* (Studia Ephemeridis "Augustinianum", 16). Roma: Institutum Patristicum Augustinianum, 1981, 149 p.
J.K. COYLE, *ÉglT* 17 (1986) 374-376; H. CROUZEL, *BullLitEccl* 84 (1983) 67-68; G. DE DURAND, *RSPT* 67 (1983) 612-613; A. DE HALLEUX, *ETL* 58 (1982) 174; J. DOIGNON, *RivStoLR* 18 (1982) 465-466; A. ORBE, *Greg* 64 (1983) 159-160; G. PELLAND, *SE* 33 (1981) 411-412; M. SIMONETTI, *Studi storico religiosi* (L'Aquila) 5 (1981) 329-330; B. STUDER, *Augustinianum* 22 (1982) 611-614..

**BURR, D.**

1976    The Date of Petrus Johannis Olivi's Commentary on Matthew. — *Collectanea Franciscana* (Roma) 46 (1976) 131-138.

**BURRIDGE, Richard A.**

1992    *What Are the Gospels? A Comparison with Graeco-Roman Biography* (SNTS MS, 70). Cambridge: University Press, 1992, XIV-292 p. Esp. 191-219: "The synoptic gospels". — Diss. Nottingham, 1989 (P.M. Casey).

1994    *Four Gospels, One Jesus? A Symbolic Reading.* Grand Rapids, MI: Eerdmans, 1994, XVI-191 p. [NTA 39, p. 502]

**BURROWS, Edward W.**

1970    *A Study of the Agreements of Matthew and Luke against Mark.* Diss. Oxford, 1969-70 (G.D. Kilpatrick).

1974    Old Testament Ethics and the Ethics of Jesus. — CRENSHAW, J.L. – WILLIS, J.T. (eds.), *Essays in Old Testament Ethics (J. Philip Hyatt, In Memoriam)*, New York: Ktav, 1974, 225-243.

1976    The Use of Textual Theories to Explain Agreements of Matthew and Luke against Mark. — ELLIOTT, J.K. (ed.), *Studies in New Testament Language and Text.* FS G.D. Kilpatrick, 1976, 87-99.

1977    *Jesus in the First Three Gospels.* Nashville, TN: Abingdon, 1977, 304 p. Esp. 17-22 [1,1-17]; 23-32 [1,18-25; 2,1-23]; 57-86 [5-7].

**BURSEY, Ernest James**

1992    *Exorcism in Matthew* [7,15-23; 9,32-34; 10,1-10.24-27; 12,22-37; 17,14-20]. Diss. Yale University, New Haven, CA, 1992, 242 p. (A.J. Malherbe). — *DissAbstr* 53 (1992-93) 3564.

**BURTNESS, James H.**

1974    Life-Style and Law: Some Reflections on Matthew 5:17. — *Dialog* (Minneapolis, MN) 14 (1974) 13-20. [NTA 19, 948]

1986    Now You See It, Now You Don't: Ethical Reflections on a Textual Variant in Matthew Six. [6,4.6.18] — *WWorld* 6 (1986) 161-169. [NTA 30, 1046]

**BURTON, Ernest Dewitt**

1951    *Study of the Three Earlier Gospels, Matthew, Mark, and Luke.* Chicago, IL: Am. Inst. of Sacred Lit., Univ. of Chicago, 1951.

**BUSCEMI, A. Marcello**

1985    La prolessi nel NT. — *SBF/LA* 35 (1985) 37-68. [NTA 31, 54]

**BUSCH, Jörg W.**

1994    Vom einordnenden Sammeln zur argumentierenden Darstellung. Beobachtungen zum Umgang mit Kirchenrechtssätzen im 11. und frühen 12. Jahrhundert. [16,18] — *Frühmittelalterliche Studien* (Münster) 28 (1994) 243-256.

**BUSE, Ivor**

1958 The Cleansing of the Temple in the Synoptics and in John. — *ExpT* 70 (1958-59) 22-24. [NTA 3, 347]

1959 St. John and "the First Synoptic Pericope". [3,1-6] — *NT* 3 (1959) 57-61. [NTA 4, 360]

1960 St John and the Passion Narratives of St Matthew and St Luke. — *NTS* 7 (1960-61) 65-76. Esp. 66-68: "Similarities with St Matthew" [26,11.23.51.72; 27,29.49-50.57-60]; 68-76 [Mt, Lk, Jn]. [NTA 5, 440] → Borgen 1959

1963 The Gospel Accounts of the Feeding of the Multitudes. — *ExpT* 74 (1962-63) 167-170. Esp. 168 [14,13-21]. [NTA 7, 756]

**BUSS, Martin J.**

1988 Appropriateness in the Form Criticism of the Teaching Source. A Response to James Williams. — *Semeia* 43 (1988) 115-119. → J.G. Williams 1988

**BUSSBY, Frederick**

1950 Mark viii.33: A Mistranslation from the Aramaic? [4,10] — *ExpT* 61 (1949-50) 159.

1954 Is Q an Aramaic Document? — *ExpT* 65 (1953-54) 272-275.

1963 Did a Shepherd Leave Sheep upon the Mountains or in the Desert? A Note on Matthew 18.12 and Luke 15.4. — *ATR* 45 (1963) 93-94. [NTA 7, 786] → Bishop 1962

1964 A Note on ρακα (Matthew v.22) and βαττολογέω (Matthew vi.7) in the Light of Qumran. — *ExpT* 76 (1964-65) 26. [NTA 9, 525]

**BUSSE, Ulrich**

1977 *Die Wunder des Propheten Jesus. Die Rezeption, Komposition und Interpretation der Wundertradition im Evangelium des Lukas* (FzB, 24). Stuttgart: Katholisches Bibelwerk, 1977, 512 p.; [2]1979, IV-547 p. Esp. 141-155 [Q 7,1-10]; 176-180 [Q 7,18-23]; 275-285 [Q 11,14-26]; 307-309 [Q 14,5]— Diss. Münster, 1975-76 (J. Gnilka).

**BUSSMANN, Claus**

1991* & RADL, W. (eds.), *Der Treue Gottes trauen. Beiträge zum Werk des Lukas. Für Gerhard Schneider.* Freiburg: Herder, 1991, 400 p. → J. Ernst, Neirynck, Schnackenburg, Schürmann

**BUTH, Randall**

1990 Matthew's Aramaic Glue. — *Jerusalem Perspective* 3 (1990) 10-12. [NTA 35, 614]

1991 Pursuing Righteousness. [5,10] — *Jerusalem Perspective* 4 (1991) 11-12, 15. [NTA 36, 712]

1993 Singular and Plural Forms of Address in the Sermon on the Mount. — *BTrans* 44 (1993) 446-447. [NTA 38, 752]

**BUTLER, Basil Christopher**

1947[R] The Priority of St Matthew's Gospel. [1947] — ID., *Searchings. Essays and Studies*, ed. V. Rice, London: Chapman, 1974, 76-85.

1951 *The Originality of St. Matthew. A Critique of the Two-Document Hypothesis.* Cambridge: University Press, 1951, VII-179 p. Esp. 1-22: "The Q hypothesis tested"; 23-36: "Arguments for Q"; 37-48: "The great sermon"; 49-61: "Further evidence"; 62-71: "The Lachmann fallacy"; 72-106: "Matthew's great discourses"; 107-122: "Streeter and Burney on Mark's use of Q"; 123-137: "Miscellaneous passages" [4,17; 6,14; 8,28-32; 9,28; 13,55; 15,1-20.21-28; 16,1-4.13-23; 19,16-30; 20,20-28]; 138-146: "Doublets in Matthew"; 147-156: "*Inclusio*, formulae and aramaisms". → E.P. Blair 1959, J.J. Collins 1954, Graf 1952, Meynell 1963, van der Voort 1952

  *Bib* 42 (1961) 111; *ExpT* 63 (1951-52) 43; C.K. BARRETT, *Theology* 55 (1952) 106-107; P. BONNARD, *RTP* 8 (1958) 329-330; P.I. BRATSIOTIS, Θεολογία 25 (1954) 485-487; J.J. CASTELOT, *CBQ* 15 (1953) 388-392; J. DE FRAINE, *Bijdragen* 13 (1952) 320; D. EDWARDS, *ChurchQR* 153 (1952) 491-497; A.

FARRER, *JTS* 3 (1952) 102-106; J.M. GONZÁLEZ RUIZ, *EstBíb* 11 (1952) 244; A. GREEN-ARMITAGE, *DownR* 70 (1951) 75-78; R. HEARD, *ChurchQR* 153 (1952) 117-118; F.-M. LEMOINE, *RB* 59 (1952) 617-619; X. LÉON-DUFOUR, *RSR* 42 (1954) 552-557; J. LEVIE, *NRT* 74 (1952) 983-985; H.J. MCLACHLAN, *HibbJourn* 50 (1951-52) 304-305; J.A. O'FLYNN, *IrTQ* 18 (1951) 390-392; W. REES, *Blackfriars* (Oxford) 33 (1951) 89-91; C. SANT, *MelTheol* 5/2 (1952) 117-121; J. SCHMID, *TRev* 52 (1956) 51; J.N. SEVENSTER, *VigChr* 7 (1953) 188-189; A. WIKGREN, *JRel* 32 (1952) 219-220; E.K. WINTER, *Judaica* 8 (1952) 185-189.

The Lachmann Fallacy. [1951, 62-71] — BELLINZONI, A.J., Jr. (ed.), *The Two-Source Hypothesis*, 1985, 133-142. → H.G. Wood 1953, Styler 1962

1953a    Notes on the Synoptic Problem. — *JTS* 4 (1953) 24-27.

1953b    The Synoptic Problem. — ORCHARD, B. - SUTCLIFFE, E.F. - FULLER, R.C. - RUSSELL, R. (eds.), *A Catholic Commentary on Holy Scripture*, Edinburgh: Nelson, 1953, ²1963, 760-764. → 1969

1955a    M. Vaganay and the 'Community Discourse'. — *NTS* 1 (1954-55) 283-290. Esp. 285-287 [10,42]; 287-290 [18,6-14]. → 1955b, Vaganay 1954a

1955b    The Synoptic Problem Again. — *DownR* 73 (1955) 24-46. Esp. 25-30 [P. Parker 1953]; 30-46 [L. Vaganay 1954a]. → 1955a

1955c    According to Matthew. [Israel in Mt] — *The Bridge* 1 (1955) 75-95.

1958     St. Peter: History and Theology. — *CleR* 43 (1958) 449-461, 513-530. Esp. 513-530 [16,17-19]. [NTA 3, 335] → Cullmann 1952/53

1960     The Literary Relations of Didache, ch. XVI. — *JTS* 11 (1960) 265-283. Esp. 276-283 [24/Did]. [NTA 6, 555]

1961     The "Two Ways" in the Didache. [7,12; 15,19; 24,4/Did] — *JTS* 12 (1961) 27-38.

1964     Spirit and Institution in the New Testament. — *Studia Evangelica* 3 (1964) 138-165. Esp. 150-152; 158-161 [16,18].

1969     The Synoptic Problem. — FULLER, R.C. - JOHNSTON, L. - KEARNS, C. (eds.), *A New Catholic Commentary on Holy Scripture*, London: Nelson, 1969, 815-821; = BELLINZONI, A.J., Jr., et al. (eds.), *The Two-Source Hypothesis*, 1985, 97-118. → 1953b

**BUTTRICK, David G.**

1970*    (ed.), *Jesus and Man's Hope*. I (A Perspective Book). Pittsburgh, PA: Pittsburgh Theological Seminary, 1970, 273 p. → G. Bornkamm, Dungan, Fitzmyer, Léon-Dufour, Talbert

**BUTTRICK, George Arthur**

*1951    (ed.), *The Interpreter's Bible*. VII: *General Articles on the New Testament. The Gospel According to St. Matthew. The Gospel According to St. Mark*. New York - Nashville, TN: Abingdon, 1951, X-917 p. → Bowie, C.T. Craig, S.E. Johnson, B.M. Metzger, A.M. Perry, Strachan, V. Taylor, Wilder

**BUTTS, James R.**

1987a    Probing the Polling. Jesus Seminar Results on the Kingdom Sayings. — *Forum* 3/1 (1987) 98-128. Esp. 102-108.113-127. [NTA 31, 1013]

1987b    & CAMERON, R., Sayings of Jesus. Classification by Source and Authenticity. — *Forum* 3/2 (1987) 96-116. Esp. 97-103.106-107 [sayings in Q and/or Th and another source]; 104-105 [only in Q]; 106 [only in Q and Th]; 107 [Q and Mk and other]; 107-108 [Th and the triple tradition]; 109 [Th and special Mt]; 109-110 [Mk and Mt]; 110-113 [triple tradition]; 113-114 [only in special Mt]; 115 [special Mt and other]. [NTA 32, 93]

1987c    Passion Apologetic, the Chreia, and the Narrative. — *Forum* 3/3 (1987) 96-127. Esp. 96-98 [4,18-22]; 107-111 [passion predictions]; 112 [16,23]; 112-113 [26,2]; 114-115 [Q 17,23-24]; 119-123 [28,16-20]. [NTA 32, 539]

1987d    The Voyage of Discipleship: Narrative, Chreia, and Call Story. — EVANS, C.A. - STINESPRING, W.F. (eds.), *Early Jewish and Christian Exegesis. Studies in Memory of William Hugh Brownlee*, Atlanta, GA: Scholars, 1987, 199-219. → Droge 1983

1988     → Funk 1988

**BUZZETTI, Carlo**

1978 Analisi letteraria del racconto matteano. [22,1-14] — DUPONT, J., et al. (eds.), *La parabola degli invitati al banchetto*, 1978, 11-61.

1983 'You are a Rock, Peter...' in Italy. [16,18] — *BTrans* 34 (1983) 308-311. [NTA 28, 97]

1984 Parallels in the Synoptic Gospels: A Case Study. — *BTrans* 35 (1984) 425-431. [NTA 29, 502]

1990 La folla nei sinottici. — LIBERTI, V. (ed.), *I laici nel popolo di Dio. Esegesi biblica* (Pubblicazioni dello studio biblico-teologico Aquilano, 10), Roma: Dehoniane, 1990, 151-171.

1992 Per l'attualizzazione di una parabola: la guida di due applicazioni precedenti. Un criterio e un esempio. — *RivBib* 40 (1992) 193-212. Esp. 200-212 [22,1-14]. [NTA 37, 119]

1994a Il discorso sul monte (Mt cc. 5–7). Introduzione. — LÀCONI, M. (ed.), *Vangeli sinottici*, 1994, 263-273.

1994b Le beatitudini (Mt 5,3-12). — *Ibid.*, 275-287.

**BYINGTON, Steven T.**

1953 Jesus' Mountain Sides. [21,17] — *ExpT* 65 (1953-54) 94.

**BYRON, Brian**

1963 The Meaning of "Except it be for fornication". — *AustralasCR* 40 (1963) 90-95. [NTA 8, 584] → Considine 1956

**BYRSKOG, Samuel**

1994 *Jesus the Only Teacher. Didactic Authority and Transmission in Ancient Israel, Ancient Judaism and the Matthean Community* (ConBibNT, 24). Stockholm: Almqvist & Wiksell, 1994, 501 p. Esp. 197-398: "Jesus as teacher and transmission in the Matthean community". [NTA 38, p. 457] — Diss. Lund, 1994 (B. Gerhardsson).
R.A. BURRIDGE, *ExpT* 106 (1994-95) 309-310; S. BYRSKOG, *TyndB* 45 (1994) 413-414; J.F. CRAGHAN, *BTB* 25 (1995) 91-92; E. CUVILLIER, *ETR* 71 (1996) 85-86; G. HARVEY, *JJS* 46 (1995) 296-297; H. KVALBEIN, *SvenskTeolKvart* 70 (1994) 185-189; R.K. MCIVER, *JBL* 114 (1995) 734-736; A.J. SALDARINI, *CBQ* 57 (1995) 383-384; J.-L. SKA, *NRT* 117 (1995) 273-275; N.H. TAYLOR, *BibInt* 3 (1995) 380-381; T. VEGGE, *NorskTeolTids* 95 (1994) 252-253; J. VERHEYDEN, *ETL* 70 (1994) 471-475; B.T. VIVIANO, *RB* 102 (1995) 618-619.

# C

**CABA, José**

1971  *De los Evangelios al Jesús histórico. Introducción a la Cristología* (Biblioteca de autores cristianos, 316). Madrid: Católica, 1971, XXXI-434 p. Esp. 122-126 [Papias]; 127-132 [Mt]; 158-173: "Núcleo común en las redacciones de los evangelios"; 174-193: "Diversidad de redacciones en la formulación externa: Evangelio de Mateo"; 252-265: "Diversidad en la estructuración interna del conjunto de cada Evangelio: Mateo"; 325-353: "El problema sinóptico"; 354-371 [form criticism]; 372-403: "Addexo al Jesús histórico".

1973  El poder de la petición comunitaria (Mt. 18,19-20). — *Greg* 54 (1973) 609-654 (English summary, 653-654). Esp. 610-635: "Labor redaccional"; 635-639: "Tradición previa a la redacción de Mt. 18,19-20"; 639-651: "Tradición de Mt. 18,19-20 en contacto con Jesús". [NTA 18, 859]

1974  *La oración de petición. Estudio exegético sobre los Evangelios sinópticos y los escritos joaneos* (AnBib, 62). Roma: Biblical Institute Press, 1974, 389 p. Esp. 63-93 [7,7-11; Q 11,9-13]; 97-146.168-190 [17,20; 21,21; Q 17,6]; 147-156 [21,22]; 193-222 [18,19-20]; 308-316 [common tradition]; 317-323 [historical Jesus]; 326-328 [Mt]. — Diss. Pont. Inst. Bibl., Roma, 1973 (I. de la Potterie).

1975a  Evangelio según san Mateo. — CANTERA BURGOS, F. - IGLESIAS GONZALES, M. (eds.), *Sagrada Biblia. Versión crítica sobre los textos hebreo, arameo y griego* (Biblioteca de autores cristianos. Series maior, 10), Madrid: Católica, 1975, 1076-1122.

1975b  La oración de petición: del Jesús histórico a los Evangelios. — *Manresa* 47 (1975) 311-334. [NTA 20, 738]

1977  *El Jesús de los Evangelios* (Biblioteca de autores cristianos, 392). Madrid: Católica, 1977, XXXII-335 p. Esp. 35-54: "Presentación de la figura de Jesús en el evangelio de Mateo"; 132-153 [Christ/Messiah]; 175-183, 253-268 [Son of Man]; 226-234 [11,2-6]; 300-312 [11,27].

1986  *Resucitó Cristo, mi esperanza. Estudio exegético* (Biblioteca de autores cristianos, 475). Madrid: Católica, 1986, XXXII-407 p. Esp. 139-165: "El mensaje de San Mateo sobre la resurrección de Jesús".
  *Cristo, mia speranza, è risorto. Studio esegetico dei "vangeli" pasquali*, trans. G. Sanguinetti Ferrero (Parola di Dio II/8). Cinisello Balsamo: Paoline, 1988, 436 p.

1991  Dalla parenesi lucana alla cristologia giovannea. Studio comparato di Lc 9,23-24 e Gv 12,25-26. — O'COLLINS, G. - MARCONI, G. (eds.), *Luca–Atti*, 1991, 72-104.
  From Lukan Parenesis to Johannine Christology: Luke 9:23-24 and John 12:25-26. — O'COLLINS, G. - MARCONI, G. (eds.), *Luke and Acts*, 1993, 48-71. Esp. 49-53 [16,24]; 53-55 [10,38]; 55-58 [16,25]; 58-62 [10,39].

**CABALLERO, Jose**

1965  Tentaciones de Jesús. [4,1-11] — *Enciclopédia de la Bíblia* (Barcelona) 6 (1965; ²1969) 926-929.

**CABANISS, Allen**

1962  Christmas Echoes at Paschaltide. — *NTS* 9 (1962-63) 67-69. Esp. 68 [2,11.23]. [NTA 7, 501]

**CABODEVILLA, José María**

1978  *El demonio retórico* [4,1-11]. Salamanca: Sígueme, 1978, 196 p.

1984  *Las formas de felicidad son ocho. Comentario a las bienaventuranzas* (Biblioteca de autores cristianos). Madrid: Católica, 1984, 378 p.

**CABRAJA, Ilija**

1985  *Der Gedanke der Umkehr bei den Synoptikern. Eine exegetisch-religionsgeschichtliche*

*Untersuchung* (Dissertationen Theologische Reihe, 10). St. Ottilien: EOS, 1985, 265 p. Esp. 25-67: "Die Umkehr in der Logienquelle" [Q 3,7-9; 10,12-15; 11,29-32]; 97-113: "Die Umkehr bei Matthäus" [3,2.11; 4,17]. — Diss. München, 1985 (J. Gnilka).

**CACITTI, Remo**

1991 "Ad caelestes thesauros". L'esegesi della pericope del "giovane ricco" nella parenesi di Cipriano di Cartagine. — *Aevum* 65 (1991) 151-169. Esp. 154-156 [19,29]; 67 (1993) 129-171. Esp. 142-147 [19,16-30].

**CADBURY, Henri Joel**

1954 The Single Eye. [6,22-23] — *HTR* 47 (1954) 69-74. → Thienemann 1955

**CADMAN, W.H.**

1951 The Mind of Christ. VI. The Rule of the Father. — *ExpT* 62 (1950-51) 323-326.

**CAEMMERER, Richard R., Sr.**

1969 *Earth with Heaven. An Essay in Sayings of Jesus.* St. Louis, MO: Concordia, 1969, 124 p.

**CAHILL, Lisa Sowle**

1987 The Ethical Implications of the Sermon on the Mount. — *Interpr* 41 (1987) 144-156. [NTA 31, 1062]

**CAI, Raphael**

1951 (ed.), *S. Thomae Aquinatis. Super Evangelium S. Matthaei Lectura, Editio V revisa.* Torino–Roma: Marietti, 1951, IX-429 p.
  J. BONSIRVEN, *Bib* 35 (1954) 244; J. CAMBIER, *ETL* 29 (1953) 675; U. GALLIZIA, *Sal* 15 (1953) 180; R.M. IANNARONE, *Sapienza* (Roma) 6 (1953) 348.

**CAIRD, George B.**

1965 Expounding the Parables: I. The Defendant (Matthew 5,25f.; Luke 12,58f.). — *ExpT* 77 (1965-66) 36-39. [NTA 10, 509]

1969 Uncomfortable Words. II. Shake off the Dust from Your Feet (Mk 6,11). [10,14] — *ExpT* 81 (1969-70) 40-43. [NTA 14, 506]

1976 The Study of the Gospels. I. Source Criticism. II. Form Criticism. III. Redaction Criticism. — *ExpT* 87 (1975-76) 99-104, 137-141, 168-172. Esp. 99-102, 137-141, 169. [NTA 20, 739/740/741]

1994 *New Testament Theology*, completed and edited by L.D. Hurst. Oxford: Clarendon, 1994, XIX-498 p. Esp. 345-408: "The theology of Jesus".

**CALABUIG, Ignacio M.**

1985 Consensi e perplessità à proposito di "Les Évangiles de l'enfance du Christ" di René Laurentin. — *Marianum* 47 (1985) 175-176. → Laurentin 1982a

**CALAMBROGIO, Leone**

1995 Storia di violenza e di salvezza in Mt 1–2. — *Laós* 2/2 (1995) 21-33.

**CALDARELLI, G.**

1983 *S. Gregorio di Nissa, La preghiera del Signore. Omilie sul Padre Nostro.* Roma: Paoline, 1983, 117 p.

**CALKINS, Arthur Burton**

1988 The Justice of Joseph Revisited. [1,18-19] — *HomPastR* 88/9 (1988) 8-19. [NTA 32, 1101]; = Κεχαριτωμένη. FS R. Laurentin, 1990, 165-177.

**CALLAHAN, Johannes F.**

1992 (ed.), *Gregorii Nysseni De oratione dominica. De beatitudinibus* (Gregorii Nysseni Opera, VII/2). Leiden: Brill, 1992, LII-180 p. Esp. 1-74: "De oratione dominica"; 75-170: "De beatitudinibus".

P. MARAVAL, *RHPR* 73 (1993) 326-327.

**CALLOUD, Jean**

1973 *L'analyse structurale du récit: éléments de méthode; tentations de Jésus au désert* [4,1-11] (Publications de la Faculté catholique de Lyon. Faculté de Théologie. Essais et recherches). Lyon: Profac, 1973, 80 p.

*Structural Analysis of Narrative*, trans. D. Patte (SBL Semeia Supplements, 4). Philadelphia, PA: Fortress; Missoula, MT: Scholars, 1976, XV-108 p. Esp. 47-108: "Temptation of Jesus in the wilderness. Structural analysis of a narrative".

1996 → Genuyt 1996

**CALVERT, N.L.**

1992 Abraham. — *DJG*, 1992, 3-7. Esp. 4-5.

**CAMACHO ACOSTA, Fernando**

1981 → J. Mateos 1981

1983 Las bienaventuranzas de Mateo (5,3-10). Análisis semántico y comentario exegético. — *Communio* (Sevilla) 16 (1983) 151-181. Esp. 151-161: "Dos constataciones y una pregunta"; 161-176: "Relectura de las bienaventuranzas como programa del Reino"; 177-180: "Sintesis teologica". [NTA 28, 914]

1986 *La proclama del reino. Análisis semántico y comentario exegético de las bienaventuranzas de Mateo (5,3-10)* (Lectura del Nuevo Testamento. Estudios criticos y exegéticos, 4). Madrid: Cristiandad, 1986, 282 p.

M. ALCALÁ, *RazFe* 216 (1987) 1034-1035; X. ALEGRE, *ActBibl* 26 (1989) 35; E. BARÓN, *Proyección* 34 (1987) 241; D.A. BLACK, *FilolNT* 2 (1989) 99-100; J.M. CABALLERO, *Burgense* 30 (1989) 283-284; J. PELÁEZ, *FilolNT* 1 (1988) 224-225.

1995 → J. Mateos 1995

**CAMBE, Michel**

1963 Le fils de l'homme dans les évangiles synoptiques. — *LumièreV* 62 (1963) 32-64. Esp. 34-36 [26,64/Mk]; 36-40 [24,1-44/Mk]; 40-41 [10,23]; 41-42 [16,27-28/Mk]; 42-43 [19,28]; 44-46 [16,21]; 47-48 [20,28/Mk]; 48-49 [8,20]; 50-51 [11,18-19]; 51 [12,28-30]; 54-61 [25,31-46]. [NTA 8, 95]

1979 & LUCAS, N., Le "Notre Père" (Matthieu 6,9-13). Éléments d'analyse structurale. — *FoiVie* 78/3 = *Cahiers bibliques* 18 (1979) 113-117. [NTA 24, 421]

**CAMBIER, Jules**

1957 Historicité des évangiles synoptiques et Formgeschichte. — HEUSCHEN, J. (ed.), *La formation des évangiles*, 1957, 195-212.

1964 Justice de Dieu, salut de tous les hommes et foi. La doctrine paulinienne du salut d'après *Rom.* — *RB* 71 (1964) 537-583. Esp. 541-542 [1,21/Rom 1,16]. [NTA 10, 209]

**[The Cambridge History]**

1970 *The Cambridge History of the Bible*. Volume 1: *From the Beginnings to Jerome*, ed. P.R. ACKROYD & C.F. EVANS. Cambridge: University Press, 1970, X-649 p.

Volume 2: *The West From the Fathers to the Reformation*, ed. G.W.H. LAMPE, 1969, IX-566 p.

Volume 3: *The West from the Reformation to the Present Day*, ed. S.L. GREENSLADE, 1963, X-590 p.

**CAMELI, Louis John**

1975  *Ministerial Consciousness: A Biblical–Spiritual Study* (AnGreg, 198). Roma: Pont. Univ. Greg., 1975, XX-253 p. Esp. 95-103 [20,20-28]. — Diss. Pont. Univ. Greg., Roma, 1974 (E. Malatesta).

**CAMERON, Peter Scott**

1984  *Violence and the Kingdom. The Interpretation of Matthew 11:12* (Arbeiten zum Neuen Testament und Judentum, 5). Frankfurt/M: Lang, 1984, 310 p. Esp. 4-35: "The fathers"; 36-47: "The Middle Ages"; 48-76: "1521-1832"; 77-134: "1836-1907"; 135-213: "The 20th. century after Harnack"; 214-246 [context; language]. [NTA 30, p. 227]; [2]1988, 215 p.
　　　 K.A. BARTA, *CBQ* 48 (1986) 133-135; B.G. POWLEY, *ExpT* 96 (1984-85) 283.
　　　 R.L. WEBB, *JSNT* 43 (1991) 124.

1990  'Lead us not into temptation'. [6,13] — *ExpT* 101 (1989-90) 299-301. [NTA 35, 135] → W.E. Moore 1991, S.E. Porter 1990

**CAMERON, Ron**

1984  *Sayings Traditions in the Apocryphon of James* (Harvard Theological Studies, 34). Philadelphia, PA: Fortress, 1984, XXI-145 p. Esp. 33-35 [Q 3,7-9/ApJas 9,24–10,6]; 40-41 [Q 11,49/ApJas 10,1]; 66-67 18,3/ApJas 2,29-33]; 76-78 [Q 17,3-4/ApJas 4,25-28]; 78-80 [Q 11,4/ApJas 4,28-31]; 108-112 [Papias]. — Diss. Harvard Univ., Cambridge, MA, 1983 (H. Koester). → 1990

1986  Parable and Interpretation in the Gospel of Thomas. — *Forum* 2/2 (1986) 3-39. Esp. 14 [25,29/Th 8,2]; 14-15 [Q 12,33/Th 76,2]; 16-19 [Q 14,16-24/Th 64,2]; 24-30 [13,45-46/Th 76,1]; 30-31 [Q 13,18-19/Th 20]. [NTA 31, 1417]

1987  → Butts 1987b

1988  → Fallon 1988

1990  "What have you come out to see?". Characterizations of John and Jesus in the Gospels. — *Semeia* 49 (1990) 35-69. Esp. 36-45.50-61 [Q 7,18-35]. [NTA 35, 176] → 1984
　　　 Response: B.L. MACK, *ibid.*, 169-176.

1991  The *Gospel of Thomas* and Christian Origins. — PEARSON, B.A., et al. (eds.), *The Future of Early Christianity*. FS H. Koester, 1991, 381-392. Esp. 385.388-390 [Q/Th].

1992a  Hebrews, Gospel of the. — *ABD* 3 (1992) 105-106.

1992b  Thomas, Gospel of. — *ABD* 6 (1992) 535-540. Esp. 536-538.

1992c  Matthew's Parable of the Two Sons. [21,28-32] — *Forum* 8 (1992) 191-209. [NTA 40, 833]

**CAMPANILE, Enrico**

1970  La traduzione gotica del Vangelo e una congettura del Lachmann a Mt 7,25. — *Studi e saggi linguistici*, 10, Pisa: Istituto di Glossologia, 1970, 190-192.

**CAMPBELL, Cynthia M.**

1992  Matthew 28:16-20. — *Interpr* 46 (1992) 402-405.

**CAMPBELL, Donald K.**

1953  *Interpretation and Exposition of the Sermon on the Mount*. Diss. Theol. Sem., Dallas, TX, 1953.

**CAMPBELL, Ken M.**

1978  The New Jerusalem in Matthew 5.14. — *ScotJT* 31 (1978) 335-363. Esp. 335-336.358-363 [5,14]; 353-354 [Jerusalem]. [NTA 23, 94]

**CAMPENHAUSEN, Hans VON**

1952  *Der Ablauf der Osterereignisse und das leere Grab* (Sitzungsberichte der Heidelberger Akademie der Wissenschaften. Philosophisch-historische Klasse, 4. Abhandlung). Heidelberg: Winter, 1952, 55 p.; [2]1958; [3]1966, 67 p. ("durchgesehen und ergänzt").

Esp. 28-35 [28,1-10]; = ID., *Tradition und Leben. Kräfte der Kirchengeschichte. Aufsätze und Vorträge*, Tübingen: Mohr, 1960, 48-113. Esp. 76-81.
The Events of Easter and the Empty Tomb. — ID., *Tradition and Life in the Early Church*, Philadelphia, PA, 1988, 54ff.

1958 Das Martyrium des Zacharias. Seine früheste Bezeugung im zweiten Jahrhundert. — *Historisches Jahrbuch* 77 (1958) 383-386; = ID., *Aus der Frühzeit des Christentums. Studien zur Kirchengeschichte des ersten und zweiten Jahrhunderts*, Tübingen: Mohr, 1963, 302-307.

1962a *Die Jungfrauengeburt in der Theologie der alten Kirche* (Sitzungsberichte der Heidelberger Akademie der Wissenschaften. Philosophisch-historische Klasse, 3. Abhandlung). Heidelberg: Winter, 1962, 69 p. Esp. 14-16; 19-22; = ID., *Urchristliches und Altkirchliches*, 1979, 63-161. Esp. 79-81; 87-90. → 1962b

1962b Die Jungfrauengeburt in der Theologie der alten Kirche. [1,18-25] — *KerDog* 8 (1962) 1-26. [NTA 7, 319] → 1962a

1968 *Die Entstehung der christlichen Bibel* (Beiträge zur historischen Theologie, 39). Tübingen: Mohr, 1968, VI-393 p. Esp. 16-24: "Jesus und das Gesetz (bei Matthäus)"; 153-160 [Papias].
*La formation de la Bible chrétienne*, trans. D. Appia – M. Dominice (Le monde de la Bible). Neuchâtel: Delachaux et Niestlé, 1971, 309 p.
*The Formation of the Bible*, trans. J.A. Baker. Philadelphia, PA: Fortress, 1972, 393 p.

1977 Gebetserhörung in den überlieferten Jesusworten und in der Reflexion des Johannes. — *KerDog* 23 (1977) 157-171. Esp. 157-164: "Die synoptische Überlieferung"; = ID., *Urchristliches und Altkirchliches*, 1979, 162-181. Esp. 162-170.

1979 *Urchristliches und Altkirchliches. Vorträge und Aufsätze*. Tübingen: Mohr, 1979, VII-360 p. → 1962a, 1977

**CAMPS, Guiu M.**

1963 *Evangeli segons Sant Mateu* (La Biblia, 18. Evangelis Sinòptics, 1). Barcelona: Abbey of Montserrat, 1963, 352 p. [NTA 10, p. 136]
*BibOr* 7 (1965) 88; J. ALONSO DÍAZ, *EstBíb* 24 (1965) 405; F. DREYFUS, *RB* 75 (1968) 619-621; X. LÉON-DUFOUR, *RSR* 53 (1965) 601-604; J. PRADO, *Sefarad* 24 (1964) 138-143; R. REUL, *RBén* 74 (1964) 187-188.

1965 Sinóptica, Cuestión. — *Enciclopédia de la Bíblia* (Barcelona) 6 (1965; ²1969) 736-744.

1974 *Evangeli segons Sant Mateu. Anónimas y colectivas*. Barcelona: Abbey of Montserrat, 1974, 274 p.

**CAMPS I GASET, Montserrat**

1989 La felicitat humana segons Epictet. [6,31-33] — *RevistCatTeol* 14 (1989) 493-498.

**CANAL SÁNCHEZ, José María**

1975 Doctrina sobre San José en los autores latinos de los siglos VIII-XII: desde Beda hasta Pedro Lombardo. — *EstJos* 29 (1975) 15-58.

**CAÑELLAS, Gabriel**

1983a Origen y mensaje del Padrenuestro. — *BibFe* 9 (1983) 5-16.

1983b Las Bienaventuranzas. Origen, estructura y mensaje. — *Ibid.*, 117-125.

**CANFORA, Giovanni**

1967* (ed.), *San Pietro* (Atti della XIX Settimana Biblica). Brescia: Paideia, 1967, 564 p. → Cipriani, da Sortino, da Spinetoli

1968* & Rossano, P. – Zedda, S. (eds.), *Il Messaggio della Salvezza. Corso completo di studi biblici*. IV: *Nuovo Testamento. Vangeli*. Torino-Leumann: Elle Di Ci, 1968, XV-1024 p. → Danieli, Làconi, Martini, Tosatto

1973* (ed.), *Fondamenti biblici della teologia morale* (Atti della XXII Settimana Biblica). Brescia: Paideia, 1973, 424 p. → Adinolfi, Di Pinto, Giavini 1972a

**CANIVET, Pierre**

1972 L'apôtre Pierre dans les écrits de Théodoret de Cyr. — FONTAINE, J. – KANNENGIESSER, C. (eds.), *Epektasis*. FS J. Daniélou, 1972, 29-46. Esp. 30-31: "Le fondement de l'Église: *Matth.*, 16,16-19".

**CANNATA, P.** → Spadafora 1967

**CANNING, Raymond**

1984 "Love Your Neighbour as Yourself" (Matt. 22.39). Saint Augustine on the Lineaments of the Self to Be Loved. — *Augustiniana* (Leuven) 34 (1984) 145-197.

1986 Augustine on the Identity of the Neighbour and the Meaning of True Love for Him "as Ourselves" (Matt. 22.39) and "as Christ Has Loved Us" (Jn. 13.34). — *Augustiniana* 36 (1986) 161-239.

**CANNIZZO, Antonio**

1983 Parole di Gesù sul divorzio. — *CC* 134/4 (1983) 562-566. [NTA 27, 1140r] → Marucci 1982

**CANTELLI, Silvia**

1989 L'esegesi al tempo di Ludovico il Pio e Carlo il Calvo. [Paschasius Radbertus] — *Giovanni Scoto nel suo tempo: l'organizzazzione del sapere in età carolingia. Atti del XXIV Convegno storico internazionale. Todi 11-14 ottobre 1987*, Spoleto: CSAM, 1989, 261-336.

**CANTWELL, Laurence**

1982 The Parentage of Jesus. Mt 1:18-21. — *NT* 24 (1982) 304-315. [NTA 27, 508]

**CAPON, Robert Farrar**

1988 *The Parables of Grace*. Grand Rapids, MI: Eerdmans, 1988, VI-184 p. Esp. 19-30 [17,24-27]; 40-50 [18,23-35].

1989 *The Parables of Judgment*. Grand Rapids, MI: Eerdmans, 1989, VI-181 p. Esp. 51-57 [20,1-16]; 81-85 [25,14-30]; 118-128 [22,1-14]; 154-166 [25,1-13]; 167-178 [25,31-46].

**CAPPS, Donald**

1985 The Beatitudes and Erikson's Life Cycle Theory. — *Pastoral Psychology* (Princeton, NJ) 33 (1985) 226-244. [NTA 30, 110]

**CAPRILE, Giovanni**

1960 La responsabilità del popolo ebreo nella morte di Gesù. [27,25] — *PalCl* 39 (1960) 969-976. [NTA 5, 402] → Vandone 1964

**CARAGOUNIS, Chrys C.**

1986 *The Son of Man. Vision and Interpretation* (WUNT, 38). Tübingen: Mohr, 1986, IX-310 p. Esp. 145-243: "The New Testament Son of Man and the Danielic 'SM'" [8,20; 24; 26,64; Q 12,8-9].

1989 Kingdom of God, Son of Man and Jesus' Self-understanding. [12,25-32] — *TyndB* 40 (1989) 3-23, 223-238. [NTA 34, 125/627]

1990 *Peter and the Rock* (BZNW, 58). Berlin: de Gruyter, 1990, IX-157 p. Esp. 61-68 [16,17-19]; 69-87 [16,13-20]; 88-113 [16,18]. [NTA 34, p. 382] → Passoni dell'Acqua 1993
   F.W. Burnett, *CRBR* 4 (1991) 177-178; G. Claudel, *Bib* 71 (1990) 570-576; C. Grappe, *RHPR* 72

(1992) 201-202; J. GUILLET, *RSR* 79 (1991) 472; D. HILL, *ExpT* 102 (1990-91) 54-55; H. HOET, *Bijdragen* 53 (1992) 88-89; J.D. KARAVIDÓPOULOS, *DeltBM* 19 (1990) 76-78; J.P. MEIER, *CBQ* 53 (1991) 492-493; S. PORTER, *JSNT* 42 (1991) 125; J.-M. ROUSÉE, *RB* 97 (1990) 314-315; A. SAND, *TRev* 88 (1992) 29-30; J.N. SEVENSTER, *NTT* 46 (1992) 63.

1992a  Kingdom of God / Kingdom of Heaven. — *DJG*, 1992, 417-430. Esp. 425-428.

1992b  The Kingdom of God in John and the Synoptics: Realized or Potential Eschatology? — DENAUX, A. (ed.), *John and the Synoptics*, 1992, 473-480. Esp. 473-474 [18,3/Jn 3,3.5]; 475-476 [Q 11,20].

**CARDELLINI, Innocenzo**

1992  Stranieri ed "emigrati-residenti" in una sintesi di teologia storico-biblica. — *RivBib* 40 (1992) 129-181. Esp. 165-167 [23,14-15.23]; 173-174 [22,1-14]; 174 [25,31-46]. [NTA 37, 375]

**CARDELLINO, Lodovico**

1995  Occhio per occhio, guancia per guancia. [5,38] — *BibOr* 37 (1995) 95-126. Esp. 109-110; 117-119; 125-126. [NTA 40, 780]

**CARDENAL, Ernesto**

1978  Jesús ante el sanedrín (Mt 26,57-68). — *Christus* (México) 43 (1978) 42-45.

**CARDMAN, F.**

1975  (trans.), *The Preaching of Augustine, "Our Lord's Sermon on the Mount"* (The Preacher's Paperback Library). Philadelphia, PA: Fortress, 1975.
      A. CANTELMI, *Augustinianum* 15 (1975) 490.

**CARDOSO, Brito**

1969a  *Sinopse dos quatro evangelhos*. Coimbra: Gráfica de Coimbra, ²1969, 302 p.

1969b  A forma literária de Mateus I e II. — *Lumen* (Vitoria) 33 (1969) 405-411.

**CARGAL, Timothy B.**

1991  'His blood be upon us and upon our children': A Matthean Double Entendre? [27,24-25] — *NTS* 37 (1991) 101-112. [NTA 35, 1146]

**CARLI, G.**

1953  Ancora sulla dannazione di Giuda. [27,3-10] — *PalCl* 32 (1953) 390-394.

**CARLISLE, Charles Richard**

1985  Jesus' Walking on the Water: A Note on Matthew 14.22-33. — *NTS* 31 (1985) 151-155. [NTA 29, 936]

**CARLSON, Jeffrey**

1994*  & LUDWIG, R.A. (eds.), *Jesus and Faith. A Conversation on the Work of John Dominic Crossan*. Maryknoll, NY: Orbis, 1994, XI-180 p. → J.D. Crossan 1994b-c, B.B. Scott, van Beeck

**CARLSTON, Charles Edwin**

1962  A *Positive* Criterion of Authenticity? — *BR* 7 (1962) 33-44. Esp. 39-41 [13,24-30]. [NTA 7, 757]

1968  The Things that Defile (Mark vii.14) and the Law in Matthew and Mark. — *NTS* 15 (1968-69) 75-96. Esp. 77-83 [5,17-20]; 83-84 [28,18-20]. [NTA 13, 883]

1971  & NORLIN, D., Once More – Statistics and Q. — *HTR* 64 (1971) 59-78. [NTA 15, 827] → Honoré 1968, Matilla 1994, Rosché 1960

1975a  *The Parables of the Triple Tradition*. Philadelphia, PA: Fortress, 1975, XVIII-249 p. Esp. 3-9: "Matthew's interpretation of the Markan theory of the parables" [13,10-17]; 10-51: "The Markan parables in Matthew" [5,13.15; 9,12-13.14-17; 10,26; 12,22-30.43-45; 13,1-9.10-17.18-23.31-32; 15,1-20.21-28; 21,33-46; 24,32-33].

1975b   Interpreting the Gospel of Matthew. — *Interpr* 29 (1975) 3-12. Esp. 4-8 [Sondergut]; 8-10
[editorial revision]; 11-12: "Changes in wording and order". [NTA 19, 933]; = MAYS, J.L. (ed.),
*Interpreting*, 1981, 55-65.

1978    On Q and the Cross. — GASQUE, W.W. – LASOR, W.S. (eds.), *Scripture, Tradition
and Interpretation. Essays Presented to Everett F. Harrison by his Students and
Colleagues in Honor of his 75th Birthday*, Grand Rapids, MI: Eerdmans, 1978, 27-33.

1980    Proverbs, Maxims, and the Historical Jesus. — *JBL* 99 (1980) 87-105. Esp. 99-102 [NTA
24, 736]

1982    Wisdom and Eschatology in Q. — DELOBEL, J. (ed.), *Logia*, 1982, 101-119. Esp. 99-107:
"Wisdom in narrative". [Q 4,1-13; 6,46-49; 7,31-35; 10,21-22; 11,49-51; 12,8; 13,34-36]; 108-116:
"Maxims".

1985    Recent American Interpretation of the Sermon on the Mount. — *BangalTF* 17/1 (1985)
9-22. [NTA 30, 565] → H.D. Betz 1985a, W.D. Davies 1963a, Guelich 1982

1987    Matthew 6:24-34. — *Interpr* 41 (1987) 179-183.

1988    Betz on the Sermon on the Mount – A Critique. — *CBQ* 50 (1988) 47-57. [NTA 32, 585r]
→ H.D. Betz 1985a

1992    Christology and Church in Matthew. — VAN SEGBROECK, F., et al. (eds.), *The Four
Gospels 1992*. FS F. Neirynck, 1992, II, 1283-1304. Esp. 1283-1290 [christology]; 1290-1291:
"Scribes"; 1291-1294: "Prophets"; 1294-1295: "Disciples"; 1296-1302: "Peter"; 1302-1304 [Church].

**CARMIGNAC, Jean**

1965    "Fais que nous n'entrions pas dans la tentation". La portée d'une négation devant un
verbe au causatif. — *RB* 72 (1965) 218-226. Esp. 224-225 [6,13; 26,41]. [NTA 10, 513]

1969    *Recherches sur le "Notre Père"*. Paris: Letouzey & Ané, 1969, 608 p. Esp. 9-52:
"Questions préliminaires"; 53-333: "Étude analytique"; 335-397: "Étude synthétique". [NTA 14, p. 244] →
1971a; → Swetnam 1971
        A. BAKER, *RQum* 7 (1970) 431-433; P.-M. BOGAERT, *BibVieChrét* 93 (1970) 86; M. BOUTTIER, *ETR*
        45 (1970) 394-397; F. BOVON, *RTP* 13 (1973) 402-403; R.E. BROWN, *CBQ* 32 (1970) 264-266; M.A.
        CHEVALLIER, *RHPR* 51 (1971) 388-389; É. COTHENET, *EVie* 80 (1970) 631-634; J. DECROIX, *BibTS* 121
        (1970) 23-24; M. DELCOR, *BullLitEccl* 71 (1970) 127-130; J. GIBLET, *RTL* 1 (1970) 460; X. JACQUES,
        *NRT* 92 (1970) 318-319; M.-É. LAUZIÈRE, *RThom* 71 (1971) 133-134; L. LELOIR, *RHE* 66 (1971) 553-
        556; J.É. MÉNARD, *RHR* 178 (1970) 193-197; J. MURPHY-O'CONNOR, *RB* 79 (1972) 307-309; B.
        PIEPIÓRKA, *ZKT* 93 (1971) 229-230; N. SILANES, *EstTrin* 8 (1973) 469-470; R. SILVA, *Burgense* 11
        (1970) 437-439; *Compostellanum* 15 (1970) 139-140; *EstBib* 29 (1970) 378-379; M.E. THRALL, *JTS* 21
        (1970) 474-475; H.F. WEISS, *TLZ* 96 (1971) 506-509; S. ZEDDA, *RivBib* 19 (1971) 434-438.
        The Spiritual Wealth of the Lord's Prayer. [1969, 387-395] — BROCKE, M. – PETUCHOWSKI, J.J. (eds.), *The
        Lord's Prayer*, 1978, 137-146.

1970    Studies in the Hebrew Background of the Synoptic Gospels. — *ASTI* 7 (1968-69) [1970]
64-93. Esp. 65-69: "Mistranslations" [8,32; 24,29]; 69-73: "Plays upon words" [6,12-13; 8,4; 9,8.16;
14,11.12; 21,12; 24,7; 26,38]; 73-79: "Visual omissions" [8,25; 9,10; 13,22; 16,13; 17,2.26.57; 21,9;
22,32; 26,6-7.71; 27,12.29]; 79-85: "Synoptic variants" [3,11; 13,23.32; 16,13.21; 17,14-15; 21,2.17.19;
22,19; 27,27.34.54; 28,6.8]. [NTA 16, 130]

1971a   *À l'écoute du Notre Père*. Paris: Éd. de Paris, 1971, 123 p. Esp. 7-91 [commentary: 6,9-13].
[NTA 18, p. 106] → 1969
        É. COTHENET, *EVie* 81 (1971) 368.

1971b   Pourquoi Jérémie est-il mentionné en Matthieu 16,14? — JEREMIAS, G., et al. (eds.),
*Tradition und Glaube*. FS K.G. Kuhn, 1971, 283-298. Esp. 291-298: "Jérémie figure de
Jésus?".

1978a   Le complément d'agent après un verbe passif dans l'hébreu et l'araméen de Qumrân.
— *RQum* 9 (1977-78) 409-427. Esp. 410-414. [NTA 23, 668]

1978b Hebrew Translations of the Lord's Prayer: An Historical Survey. — TUTTLE, G.A. (ed.), *Biblical and Near Eastern Studies. Essays in Honor of William Sanford LaSor*, Grand Rapids, MI: Eerdmans, 1978, 18-79. Esp. 21-59: "Texts" [9th-20th c.]; 59-69: "Analysis". → 1982

1979 *Le mirage de l'eschatologie. Royauté, Règne et Royaume de Dieu ... sans eschatologie.* Paris: Letouzey & Ané, 1979, 250 p. Esp. 19-20; 35-42: "La source commune à Matthieu et Luc" [Q 6,20; 7,28; 9,2; 11,2.19-20.52; 12,29-31; 13,20-21.28-29; 16,16]; 43-55: "Les textes propres à Matthieu" [4,23; 5,19-20; 7,21; 13,24-30.36-43.44-52; 16,17-19; 18,1-4.23-35; 19,12; 20,1-16.20-28; 21,31-32.43; 22,1-14; 24,14; 25,1-13].
J. CARMIGNAC, *NTS* 26 (1979-80) 252-258; F. NEIRYNCK, *ETL* 56 (1980) 414-416.

1982 (ed.), *Traductions hébraïques des Évangiles.* 1. *The Four Gospels Translated into Hebrew by William Greenfield in 1831.* Turnhout: Brepols, 1982, XLII-82 p. Esp. 1-23. 2. *Évangiles de Matthieu et de Marc traduits en hébreu en 1668 par Giovanni Battista Iona retouchés en 1805 par Thomas Yeates.* 1982, XLI-184 p. (double pages). Esp. 2-113.
P.-M. BOGAERT, *RTL* 14 (1983) 239-241; F. FORESTI, *Teresianum* 34 (1983) 513-515; X. JACQUES, *NRT* 105 (1983) 598-599; F. NEIRYNCK, *ETL* 59 (1983) 141-142.
4. *Die vier Evangelien ins Hebräische übersetzt von Franz Delitzsch (1877-1890-1902).* 1984, LIV-206 p. (double pages). Esp. 1-58.
F. NEIRYNCK, *ETL* 60 (1984) 401-402.
5. *The Four Gospels Translated into Hebrew by the London Society for Promoting Christianity amongst the Jews (1838 + 1864).* 1985, XXXVI-212 p. (double pages). Esp. 1-59.
F. NEIRYNCK, *ETL* 62 (1986) 191-192.

1983 La datation des évangiles: État actuel de la recherche. — *RRéf* 34 (1983) 111-121. [NTA 28, 452] → J.A.T. Robinson 1976

1984 *La naissance des Évangiles Synoptiques.* Paris: OEIL, 1984, ²1984, ³1985, 119 p. Esp. 25-50.75-92 [semitisms]; 51-57: "Problème synoptique". → Grelot 1984a, 1986a, Rasco 1986, Rossé 1988, Spadafora 1986, Vrancken 1986
*The Birth of the Synoptic Gospels*, trans. M.J. Wrenn. Chicago, IL: Franciscan Herald, 1987, X-109 p.
*La nascità dei vangeli sinottici* (Problemi e dibattiti, 2). Milano–Cinisello Balsamo: Paoline, 1985, 112 p. → P. Sacchi 1986
F. NEIRYNCK, *ETL* 60 (1984) 404-405.

1985 Scientifique. Oui ou non? — *Marianum* 47 (1985) 177-187. [NTA 30, 562r] → Laurentin 1982a

**CARMODY, Timothy R.**

1989 Matt 18:15-17 in Relation to Three Texts from Qumran Literature (CD 9:2-8, 16-22; 1QS 5:25-6:1). — HORGAN, M.P. - KOBELSKI, P.J. (eds.), *To Touch the Text.* FS J.A. Fitzmyer, 1989, 141-158. Esp. 150-158.

**CARNEIRO DE ALMEIDA, M.**

1957 *Evangelho segundo São Mateus.* Rio de Janeiro: Libraria Agir, 1957, 136 p.

**CARNELUTTI, Francesco**

1950 *Chiose al Vangelo di Matteo.* Roma: Ateneo, 1950, 368 p.
F. SPADAFORA, *CC* 102/1 (1951) 669; *PalCl* 29 (1950) 926-927.

**CARNLEY, Peter**

1987 *The Structure of Resurrection Belief.* Oxford: Clarendon, 1987, XIII-394 p. Esp. 44-61: "The historical evidence: the empty tomb"; 234-249: "The gospel narratives of appearances"; ²1993.

**CARON, Gerard**

1982 Did Jesus Allow Divorce? (Mt. 5:31-32). A Preaching Problem. — *AfEcclR* 24 (1982) 309-316. [NTA 27, 513]

**CAROZZA, Giuseppe**

1986   L'idea della "vigilanza" nella parabola delle dieci vergini (Mt 25,1-13). Diss. Milano, 1986, 318 p. (G. Ghiberti).

**CARR, David MacLain**

1991   From D to Q. A Study of Early Jewish Interpretations of Solomon's Dream at Gibeon (SBL MS, 44). Atlanta, GA: Scholars, 1991, XII-257 p. Esp. 164-172.203-214: "Q 12:22-31". — Diss. Claremont Graduate School, 1988 (J.A. Sanders).

**CARR, Dyanchand**

1981   Jesus, the King of Zion. A Traditio-historical Inquiry into the So-Called "Triumphal Entry" of Jesus [21,1-9]. Diss. London, 1981, 320 p. (G.N. Stanton).

**CARRASCO, José Antonio**

1974   La genealogía de San Mateo (1,1-17) y sus implicaciones teológicas. — EstJos 28 (1974) 139-151.

1978   Orientaciones de los estudios bíblicos modernos sobre Mt 1. — EstJos 32 (1978) 181-200. Esp. 190-195 [1,19]; 195-198 [1,25].

**CARREIRA DAS NEVES, Joaquim**

1974   Quem são os ἐθνικοί do evangelho de Mateus? — Didaskalia 4 (1974) 229-235. Esp. 229-230 [5,47]; 230-233 [6,7]; 233 [18,17]. [NTA 21, 721]

**CARREZ, Maurice**

1977   L'héritage de l'Ancien Testament. — LÉON-DUFOUR, X. (ed.), Les miracles de Jésus, 1977, 45-58. Esp. 46-48 [8,17; 9,13; 12,17-21]; 50-52 [14,13-21].

1992   Quelques aspects christologiques de l'Évangile de Thomas. — VAN SEGBROECK, F., et al. (eds.), The Four Gospels 1992. FS F. Neirynck, 1992, III, 2263-2276. Esp. 2265 [13,12/Th 70; 9,37-38/Th 73]; 2266 [11,29/Th 90; 6,24/Th 47]; 2267 [10,37-38/Th 55]; 2268-2269 [13,47.50/Th 8-9]; 2269-2270: [13,31-32/Th 20-21]; 2270-2271 [5,5-6/Th 56-58]; 2272 [13,45-46/Th 76; 13,33/Th 96].

**CARRIÈRE, Jean-Marie**

1981   L'obéissance à la loi. Matthieu chapitres 5 à 7. — Christus 28 (1981) 422-430.

**CARRILLO-GUELBERT, Francine**

1982   Si vous ne devenez comme les enfants... [18,1-6] — Bulletin du Centre protestant d'études (Genève) 34 (1982) 5-24. [NTA 27, 103]

1993   "Une seule chair": L'imaginaire à l'épreuve du réel. [19,1-12] — Bulletin du Centre protestant d'études 45 (1993) 21-32. [NTA 37, 1267]

**CARROLL, John T.**

1988   Response to the End of History. Eschatology and Situation in Luke–Acts (SBL DS, 92). Atlanta, GA: Scholars, 1988, VII-208 p. Esp. 88-94 [Q 17,22-37 (Lk)]; 97-103 [Q 19,12-27 (Lk)].

1990*  & COSGROVE, C.H. – JOHNSON, E.E. (eds.), Faith and History. Essays in Honor of Paul W. Meyer (Scholars Press homage series). Atlanta, GA: Scholars, 1990, VIII-377 p. → J.T. Carroll, Plank, B.B. Scott, D.M. Smith

1990   Jesus and Early Christian Eschatology. — Ibid., 18-34. Esp. 26-29; 31-32 [12,28].

1995*  & GREEN, J.B. (eds.), The Death of Jesus in Early Christianity. Peabody, MA: Hendrickson, 1995, XVIII-318 p. → J.T. Carroll, J. Marcus, Senior

1995a  & GREEN, J.B., "His Blood on Us and on Our Children": The Death of Jesus in the Gospel according to Matthew. — Ibid., 39-59.

1995b  Sickness and Healing in the New Testament Gospels. — Interpr 49 (1995) 130-142. Esp. 133-134.137-139. [NTA 39, 1388]

**CARROLL, Kenneth L.**

1963 "Thou art Peter". [16,17-19] — *NT* 6 (1963) 268-276. [NTA 9, 155]

**CARRÓN, Julián**

1993 Das zweite Gebot im Neuen Testament. "Euer Ja sei ein Ja, euer Nein ein Nein". [5,33-37] — *IKZ/Communio* (Rodenkirchen) 22 (1993) 36-53. [NTA 37, 1463]
The Second Commandment in the New Testament. Your Yes is Yes, Your No is No. — *Communio* (Washington, DC) 20 (1993) 5-25.

**CARRUTH, Shawn** → IQP

1983 Ears to Hear. [Q/Th] — *BiTod* 21 (1983) 89-95. [NTA 27, 893]

1992 *Persuasion in Q: A Rhetorical Critical Study of Only Q 6:20-49.* Diss. Claremont Graduate School, 1992, 341 p. (J.M. Robinson). — *DissAbstr* 53 (1992-93) 1182-1183.

1995 Strategies of Authority. A Rhetorical Study of the Character of the Speaker in Q 6:20-49. — KLOPPENBORG, J.S. (ed.), *Conflict and Invention*, 1995, 98-115.

**CARSON, Donald A.**

1978 *The Sermon on the Mount. An Evangelical Exposition of Matthew 5-7.* Grand Rapids, MI: Baker, 1978, 157 p. [NTA 25, p. 345]; 1986.
L. CRANFORD, *SWJT* 23 (1980-81) 96; A. PATZIA, *JEvTS* 23 (1980) 144-145; V.D. VERBRUGGE, *CalvTJ* 14 (1979) 88-90.
G. ABBÀ, *Sal* 50 (1988) 225-226.

1982a Christological Ambiguities in the Gospel of Matthew. — ROWDON, H.H. (ed.), *Christ the Lord.* FS D. Guthrie, 1982, 97-114. Esp. 100-103 [Christ]; 103-107 [Son of David]; 107-111 [Lord]; 111-113 [Son of God]; 113-114 [Son of Man].

1982b Gundry on Matthew. A Critical Review. — *TrinJ* NS 3 (1982) 71-91. [NTA 27, 93r] → Gundry 1982

1982c Jesus and the Sabbath in the Four Gospels. — ID. (ed.), *From Sabbath to Lord's Day: A Biblical, Historical, and Theological Investigation* (Contemporary Evangelical Perspectives), Grand Rapids, MI: Zondervan, 1982, 57-97. Esp. 66-68 [12,1-8]; 73-74 [24,20]; 74-76 [11,28-30; 12,1-8]; 77-79 [5,17-20].

1982d The Jewish Leaders in Matthew's Gospel. A Reappraisal. — *JEvTS* 25 (1982) 161-174. Esp. 167-174: "A sampling of Matthean passages" [2,4; 3,7; 8,18-19; 11,26; 12,14; 13,52; 16,1-12; 21,33-46; 27,24]. [NTA 27, 500]

1983 Criticism: On the Legitimacy and Illegitimacy of a Literary Tool. — ID. - WOODBRIDGE, J.D. (eds.), *Scripture and Truth*, Grand Rapids, MI: Zondervan, 1983, 119-142. Esp. 128-130 [5,17-20]; 131-137 [9,16-21].

1984 et al., *Matthew, Mark, Luke* (The Expositor's Bible Commentary, 8). Grand Rapids, MI: Zondervan, 1984, XVI-1059 p. Esp. 1-599: "Matthew" (Carson). → G. Maier 1987
R.T. FRANCE, *TrinJ* 6 (1985) 108-112; R.G. GRUENLER, *JEvTS* 28 (1985) 246-248.

1985 The ὅμοιος Word-Group as Introduction to Some Matthean Parables. — *NTS* 31 (1985) 277-282. [NTA 30, 100]

1987 *When Jesus Confronts the World: An Exposition of Matthew 8-10.* Grand Rapids, MI: Baker, 1987, 154 p. [NTA 32, p. 240]
J.E. JONES, *RExp* 85 (1988) 562; R.P. MENZIES, *EvQ* 61 (1989) 163-164; D.L. TURNER, *Criswell Theological Review* (Dallas, TX) 3 (1988-89) 388-389; M.J. WILKINS, *JEvTS* 32 (1989) 388-389.

1992 & MOO, D.J. - MORRIS, L., *An Introduction to the New Testament.* Grand Rapids, MI: Zondervan; Leicester: Apollos/InterVarsity, 1992, 537 p. Esp. 19-60: "The synoptic gospels"; 61-87: "Matthew".

1994a Do the Prophets and the Law Quit Prophesying before John? A Note on Matthew 11.13. — EVANS, C.A. - STEGNER, W.R. (eds.), *The Gospels and the Scriptures of Israel*, 1994, 179-194.

1994b Matthew 11:19b / Luke 7:35: A Test Case for the Bearing of Q Christology on the Synoptic Problem. — GREEN, J.B. – TURNER, M.B.B. (eds.), *Jesus of Nazareth*. FS I.H. Marshall, 1994, 128-146.

**CARSON, Mary Catherine**

1990 *And They Said Nothing to Anyone: A Redaction-Critical Study of the Role and Status of Women in the Crucifixion, Burial and Resurrection Stories of the Canonical and Apocryphal Gospels* [27,62–28,20]. Diss. University of Newcastle, 1990, 404 p. — *DissAbstr* 53 (1992-93) 842.

**CARTER, Warren C.**

1992 Kernels and Narrative Blocks: The Structure of Matthew's Gospel. — *CBQ* 54 (1992) 463-481. Esp. 466-467: "Matera's discussion of plot"; 468-472: "A critique"; 472-480: "An alternative reading". [NTA 37, 700] → Matera 1987b

1993 The Crowds in Matthew's Gospel. — *CBQ* 55 (1993) 54-67. [NTA 38, 141]

1994a *Households and Discipleship. A Study of Matthew 19–20* (JSNT SS, 103). Sheffield: JSOT, 1994, 249 p. Esp. 15-29: "The coherency of Matthew 19–20 and Matthaean discipleship"; 30-55: "Methods"; 56-89 [19,3-12]; 90-114 [19,13-15]; 115-145 [19,16-30]; 146-160 [20,1-16]; 161-192 [20,17-28]; 193-203 [20,29-34]. [NTA 39, p. 135] — Diss. Princeton Theol. Sem., Princeton, NJ, 1991 (P.W. Meyer – J. Marcus).
   D.L. BALCH, *CBQ* 58 (1996) 540-542; E. CUVILLIER, *ETR* 71 (1996) 89-90); I.H. JONES, *ExpT* 106 (1994-95) 212; D.J. WEAVER, *CRBR* 9 (1996) 185-189; N. WILLERT, *DanskTeolTids* 54 (1991) 241-260.

1994b *What Are They Saying About Matthew's Sermon on the Mount*. New York – Mahwah, NJ: Paulist, 1994, VI-136 p. Esp. 9-34: "The sources of the SM"; 35-55: "The structure"; 56-77: "The function and socio-historical setting of Matthew's Sermon on the Mount"; 78-126: "The content". [NTA 38, p. 458]
   J.A. MINDLING, *NewTheolRev* 8/3 (1995) 95-96; D.J. WEAVER, *CRBR* 9 (1996) 185-189.

1995a Challenging by Conforming, Renewing by Repeating. The Parables of the "Reign of the Heavens" in Matthew 13 as Embedded Narratives. — *SBL 1995 Seminar Papers*, 399-424.

1995b Recalling the Lord's Prayer: The Authorial Audience and Matthew's Prayer as Familiar Liturgical Experience. — *CBQ* 57 (1995) 514-530. [NTA 40, 1459]

**CARTON, Gilles**

1959a Comme des anges dans le ciel. [22,23-33] — *BibVieChrét* 28 (1959) 46-52. [NTA 4, 91]

1959b → Roulin 1959a

**CARUCCI, Arturo**

1953 *L'apostolo Matteo*. Salerno: Privately published, 1953, 90 p.
   *CC* 106/1 (1955) 427.

1955 *L'Etiopia di S. Matteo nella letteratura patristica (3-6 secolo)*. Salerno: Jannone, 1955, 28 p.
   P. NOBER, *VD* 35 (1957) 376.

**CASÁ, Felix**

1974 Figuras de la navidad. [2] — *RevistBíb* 36 (1974) 221-253. [NTA 19, 468]

1976 Parábolas y catequesis (Mt 20,1-16). — *Debarim* (Córdoba) 16 (1976) 3-6.

**CASALEGNO, Alberto**

1978 La parabola del granello di senape (*Mc*. 4,30-32). — *RivBib* 26 (1978) 139-161. Esp. 139-154 [minor agreements: 13,31-32]. [NTA 23, 466]

**CASALINI, Nello**

1987 Una iniziazione alla pratica dell'esegesi evangelica. — *RivBib* 35 (1987) 195-206. [NTA 32, 544r] → Grelot 1986a

1990a *Libro dell'origine di Gesù Cristo. Analisi letteraria e teologica di Matt 1-2* (Studium Biblicum Franciscanum. Analecta, 28). Jerusalem: Franciscan Printing Press, 1990, 173 p. Esp. 19-43: "Unità letteraria e narrativa"; 45-58: "Testo e traduzione"; 59-113: "Analisi letteraria e narrativa"; 115-152: "Uso dell'Antico Testamento in Matt 1-2". [NTA 34, p. 382]
J.J. BARTOLOMÉ, *Sal* 53 (1991) 578; C. BISSOLI, *Sal* 55 (1993) 589; G. DE VIRGILIO, *RivBib* 39 (1991) 56-58; J. GUILLET, *RSR* 79 (1991) 420-421; J.-M. ROUSÉE, *RB* 97 (1990) 314.

1990b *Il Vangelo di Matteo come racconto teologico. Analisi delle sequenze narrative* (Studium Biblicum Franciscanum. Analecta, 30). Jerusalem: Franciscan Printing Press, 1990, 115 p. Esp. 17-22: "Il vangelo di Matteo come racconto"; 23-74: "Analisi delle sequenze narrative"; 75-99: "La trama del racconto"; 101-113: "I problemi della trama". [NTA 34, p. 382]
X. ALEGRE, *EstBíb* 52 (1994) 225-256; J.A. CARRASCO, *EstJos* 46 (1992) 103-104; J.F. CUENCA MOLINA, *Carthaginensia* 8 (1992) 933; G. DE VIRGILIO, *RivBib* 39 (1991) 59-60; J. GUILLET, *RSR* 79 (1991) 419-420; S.B. MARROW, *CBQ* 54 (1992) 144-145; J.-M. ROUSÉE, *RB* 97 (1990) 636.

**CASALIS, Georges**

1969 The Lord's Prayer and the World Situation. — *ComViat* 12 (1969) 125-137. [NTA 14, 889]
*Das Vater Unser und die Weltlage.* — *EvT* 29 (1969) 357-371.

**CASAMASSA, Antonio**

1955 Nota sul "Commentarius in Matthaeum" di S. Ilario di Poitiers. — ID., *Scritti patristici*, I (Lateranum NS, 21), Roma: Pont. Athenaei Lateranensi, 1955, 207-214.

**CASANOVA, J.**

1960 Encore Mt 5,3. — *BBudé* 4 (1960) 106-112. → Delebecque 1959, Vernotte 1960

**CASAS GARCÍA, Victoriano**

1976 Los exorcismos de Jesús: posesos y endemoniados. — *BibFe* 2 (1976) 60-76. [NTA 20, 744]

1978 El matrimonio ¿indisoluble?. La praxis del cristianismo primitivo. — *BibFe* 4 (1978) 47-58. [NTA 22, 917]

1983a ¡Padre, danos nuestro pan! [6,11] — *BibFe* 9 (1983) 44-51.

1983b ¡Felices, los que ansían justicia! [5,6] — *Ibid.*, 159-169.

**CASCIARO RAMIREZ, José María**

1962 Iglesia y pueblo de Dios en el Evangelio de San Mateo. — *Concepto de la Iglesia en el Nuevo Testamento. Otros estudios* (XIX Semana Biblica Española), Madrid: Consejo Superior de Investigaciones Científicas, 1962, 19-99. Esp. 20-26 [ἐκκλησία]; 26-30 [16,18]; 32-37 [18,17]; 51-67: "La nocion de Reino de los cielos en san Mateo"; 67-70: "La nocion de *ecclesia* segun las enseñanzas de las parabolas"; 70-75 [18]; 75-80 [10]; 80-87 [Peter]; 87-92 [28,18-20]; 92-96 [24,22].

1969 El vocabulario técnico de Qumrân en relación con el concepto de comunidad. Estudios preliminares para una eclesiología bíblica. [16,18] — *ScriptTheol* 1 (1969) 7-56, 243-313. Esp. 296-298: "Qumrân y la ἐκκλησία de Mateo"; 303-307: "Relación concreta del logion de Mt 16,18 con los textos de Qumrân". [NTA 14, 343/1031]

1976 *Evangelio según san Mateo. Introducción, traducción castellana y comentarios.* Pamplona: Universidad de Navarra, 1976, 403 p. → 1983
M. GUERRA, *ScriptTheol* 9 (1977) 1171-1176.
*The Navarre Bible. Saint Matthew's Gospel in the Revised Standard Version and New Vulgate with a Commentary by the Faculty of Theology, University of Navarre*, trans. M. Adams. Dublin: Four Courts Press, 1988, 236 p. [NTA 33, p. 110]

1980 El acceso a Jesús y la historicidad de los Evangelius. Balance de veinticinco años de investigación. — *ScriptTheol* 12 (1980) 907-941.

1982a *Estudios sobre Cristología del Nuevo Testamento*. Pamplona: Universidad de Navarra, 1982, 395 p.

1982b Universalidad de la etica cristiana. — *ScripTheol* 14 (1982) 305-327. Esp. 309-322: "Las 'antítesis' del Discurso de la montaña".

1983 et al. (eds.), *Sagrada Biblia traducida y anotada. Santos Evangelios. Introducción, traducción castellana y comentarios*. Pamplona: Universidad de Navarra, 1983, 1524 p. Esp. 1-403 [Mt]; 3rd rev. ed., 1990, 1518 p. → 1976 Trans. Portuguese 1985; Italian 1988

1986 La Encarnacion del Verbo y la corporeidad humana. (Apuntes exegéticos para una teología del cuerpo humano y del sexo). — *ScripTheol* 18 (1986) 751-770 (English summary, 769-770). Esp. 761-769 [1,18-25]. [NTA 32, 642]

1987 La disputa de Jesús con los saduceos (Mt. 22,23-33 y par.). Apuntes exegéticos para una teología bíblica del cuerpo humano y del sexo. — COLLADO BERTOMEU, V. - VILAR HUESO, V. (eds.), *Actas del II Simposio Bíblico Español (Córdoba, 1985)*, Córdoba-Valencia: Fundación Bíblica Española, 1987, 419-428.

1989 Las antítesis de Mt 5,21-48, ¿halakhot de la Torah o algo más? — *RevistCatTeol* 14 (1989) 123-132 (English summary, 132). Esp. 123-128: "La formula de las 'antítesis'"; 128-131: "El valor del verbo 'decir'".

1991a Una búsqueda del alcance de las antítesis de Mt 5,21-48. — CARREIRA DAS NEVES, et al. (eds.), *Actas del III Simposio Bíblico Español (I Luso-Español)*, Valencia-Lisboa: Fundación Bíblica Española, 1991, 409-423.

1991b La oración de Jesús en los Evangelios sinópticos. — *ScriptTheol* 23 (1991) 215-227. Esp. 219-221 [11,25-30]. [NTA 36, 116]

1991c Las parábolas de los Evangelios Sinópticos. — ESPONERA, A. (ed.), *La palabra de Dios y la hermenéutica. Actas del VI Simposio de Teología Histórica*, Valencia: Fac. de Teología, 1991, 263-287.

1992 *Las parábolas de Jesús: transmisión y hermenéutica* (Colección teológica). Pamplona: EUNSA, 1992, 196 p.

**CASEY, P. Maurice**

1976 The Son of Man Problem. — *ZNW* 67 (1976) 147-154. Esp. 150 [12,32]; 151 [10,33; 16,27]. [NTA 21, 880]; = ID., *Son of Man*, 1979, 224-240. Esp. 230-232.

1979 *Son of Man. The Interpretation and Influence of Daniel 7*. London: SPCK, 1979, XVI-272 p. Esp. 157-223: "The gospels and acts"; 224-240 (→ 1976). — Diss. Durham, UK, 1977 (C.K. Barrett). → F.J. Moloney 1980

1985a Aramaic Idiom and Son of Man Sayings. — *ExpT* 96 (1984-85) 233-236. Esp. 235 [8,20; 10,32-33; 11,18-19]. [NTA 30, 784]

1985b The Jackals and the Son of Man (Matt. 8.20 // Luke 9.58). — *JSNT* 23 (1985) 3-22. [NTA 29, 934]

1987 General, Generic and Indefinite: The Use of the Term 'Son of Man' in Aramaic Sources and in the Teaching of Jesus. — *JSNT* 29 (1987) 21-56. Esp. 36-40 [8,20; 11,19; 12,32]; 46-47. [NTA 31, 1256] → Bauckham 1985a, Lindars 1983, 1985

1991a *From Jewish Prophet to Gentile God. The Origin and Development of New Testament Christology* (The Edward Cadbury Lectures 1985-86). Cambridge: J. Clarke; Louisville, KY: Westminster/Knox, 1991, 197 p. Esp. 147-156.

1991b Method in Our Madness, and Madness in Their Methods. Some Approaches to the Son of Man Problem in Recent Scholarship. — *JSNT* 42 (1991) 17-43. Esp. 19-20 [11,18-19; 12,32; 21,38-39]. [NTA 36, 368]

**CASEY, Robert Pierce**

1956 Gnosis, Gnosticism and the New Testament. — DAVIES, W.D. - DAUBE, D. (eds.), *The Background of the New Testament*. FS C.H. Dodd, 1956, 52-80. Esp. 62 [16,17]; 63.74 [11,27]; 65.

**CASONATTO, Odalberto D.**

1987 Jesus e a Lei. — *RevistBíbBras* 4 (1987) 103-109.

**CASSIANUS (Bishop)**

1955 Saint Pierre et l'Église dans le Nouveau Testament (Le problème de la primauté). — *Istina* (Paris) 2 (1955) 261-304. Esp. 276-282 [16,17-19]. → P. Benoit 1955b

1959 The Interrelation of the Gospels: Matthew-Luke-John. — *Studia Evangelica* 1 (1959) 129-147. Esp. 130-132 [Mt]; 132-142 [Mt/Lk].

**CASSIDY, Richard J.**

1979 Matthew 17:24-27 – A Word on Civil Taxes. — *CBQ* 41 (1979) 571-580. [NTA 24, 425]

**CASTELLINI, G.M.**

1954 Struttura letteraria di Mt. 7,6. — *RivBib* 2 (1954) 310-317.

**CASTELLINO, Giorgio R.**

1960 L'abito di nozze nella parabola del convito e una lettera di Mari (Matteo 22,1-14). — *EstE* 34 (1960) 819-824. [NTA 6, 460]; = *Miscelanea Biblica Andres Fernandez*, 1960, 515-520.

**CASTELLO, G.**

1991 *L'interrogatorio di Gesù davanti al Sinedrio. Contributo esegetico-storico alla cristologia neotestamentaria* [26,57-68]. Diss. Pont. Univ. Greg., Roma, 1991, 277 p. (P. Grech).

**CASTILLO, José J.**

1973 Exigencias de fe para el hombre en el evangelio de Mateo. — *Christus* (México) 38 (1973) 17-21.

**CASTRO, Secondino**

1995 La oración de Jesús, experiencia colmante de Dios. [6,9-13] — *RevistEspir* 54 (1995) 265-292. [NTA 40, 761]

**CATCHPOLE, David R.**

1970 The Problem of the Historicity of the Sanhedrin Trial. — BAMMEL, E. (ed.), *The Trial of Jesus. Cambridge Studies in Honour of C.F.D. Moule* (Studies in Biblical Theology, II/13), London: SCM, 1970, 47-65. Esp. 50 [5,17]; 52 [5,39-43]; 53-54 [11,12].

1971a *The Trial of Jesus. A Study in the Gospels and Jewish Historiography from 1770 to the Present Day* (Studia Post-Biblica, 18). Leiden: Brill, 1971, XIV-324 p. Esp. 110-112; 145-147 [11,25-30]; 215-217 [26,63]. — Diss. Cambridge, 1968 (E. Bammel).

1971b The Answer of Jesus to Caiaphas (Matt. xxvi.64). — *NTS* 17 (1970-71) 213-226. Esp. 215-217 [26,25]; 220-223 [26,64]; 223-226 [12,4; 21,10-17; 26,59-64]. [NTA 15, 862]

1974 The Synoptic Divorce Material as a Traditio-Historical Problem. — *BJRL* 57 (1974-75) 92-127. Esp. 93-110 [19,3-12]; 112-113 [Q 16,18]. [NTA 20, 105]

1977a The Son of Man's Search for Faith (Luke xviii 8b). — *NT* 19 (1977) 81-104. Esp. 82-87 [Q 17,24.26-30]; 89-91 [Q 11,9-13]. [NTA 22,125]

1977b Tradition History. — MARSHALL, I.H. (ed.), *New Testament Interpretation*, 1977, 165-180. Esp. 169-171 [11,2-19].

1978a John the Baptist, Jesus and the Parable of the Tares. — *ScotJT* 31 (1978) 557-570. Esp. 558-560 [13,47-50]; 560-563 [13,36-43]; 563-569 [13,24-30]. [NTA 23, 828]

1978b On Doing Violence to the Kingdom (Mt 11,12 / Lc 16,16). — *JTSouthAfr* 25 (1978) 50-61. [NTA 24, 794]; = *IBS* 3 (1981) 77-92. [NTA 26, 93]

1979 The Poor on Earth and the Son of Man in Heaven. A Re-Appraisal of Matthew xxv.31-46. — *BJRL* 61 (1978-79) 355-397. Esp. 356-361 [10,40-42]; 361-373 [Mk 9,33-37.41]; 373-378 [19,28]; 378-395 [25,31-46]. [NTA 24, 101] → Jurgens 1983

1981a The Ravens, the Lilies and the Q Hypothesis. A Form-critical Perspective on the Source-critical Problem. [6,25-33/Q 12,22-31] — *SNTU* 6-7 (1981-82) 77-87. [NTA 28, 917] → 1993b, 31-39

1981b The Sermon on the Mount in Today's World. — *TheolEvang* 14 (1981) 4-11. [NTA 26, 465]

1982 The Angelic Son of Man in Luke 12:8. — *NT* 24 (1982) 255-265. Esp. 255-257 [12,32]; 260 [18,10]. [NTA 27, 139]

1983a Q and 'The Friend at Midnight' (Luke xi. 5-8/9). — *JTS* 34 (1983) 407-424. Esp. 413-419 [Q 11,9-13]; 419-421 [Q 11,2-4]; 421-422 [Q 12,22-31]; 422-423 [6,7-8]. [NTA 28, 536] → 1989; → Tuckett 1989b
Prayer and the Kingdom. — ID., *The Quest for Q*, 1993, 201-228 (adapted). Esp. 211-218 [Q 11,11-13]; 218-223 [Q 11,9-10]; 223-228 [Q 11,5-13].

1983b Reproof and Reconciliation in the Q Community. A Study of the Tradition-History of Mt 18,15-17.21-22 / Lk 17,3-4. — *SNTU* 8 (1983) 79-90. [NTA 30, 1060]
Reproof and Reconciliation. — ID., *The Quest for Q*, 1993, 135-150.

1984 The "Triumphal" Entry. [21,1-10] — BAMMEL, E. – MOULE, C.F.D. (eds.), *Jesus and the Politics of His Day*, 1984, 319-334.

1986 Jesus and the Community of Israel – The Inaugural Discourse in Q. — *BJRL* 68 (1985-86) 296-316. Esp. 298-300 [Q 6,20-23]; 301-302 [Q 6,46]; 303-309 [Q 6,27-35]; 309-312 [Q 6,36-38]; 312-313 [18,15-22]; 314-315 [Q 6,43-45]. [NTA 31, 631]
The Inaugural Discourse. — ID., *The Quest for Q*, 1993, 79-134 (revised). Esp. 81-94 [Q 6,20-23.24-26]; 94-101 [Q 6,46.47-49]; 101-116 [Q 6,27-35]; 116-133 [Q 6,36-45].

1987 The Law and the Prophets in Q. — HAWTHORNE, G.F. – BETZ, O. (eds.), *Tradition and Interpretation*. FS E.E. Ellis, 1987, 95-109. Esp. 95-98 [Q 16,16]; 99-101 [Q 11,16.29-32]; 101-106 [Q 17,23-24.26-30.37].
The Law and the Prophets. — ID., *The Quest for Q*, 1993, 229-255 (revised). Esp. 232-241; 241-247 [Q 11,31-32]; 247-255.

1989 Q, Prayer, and the Kingdom: A Rejoinder. — *JTS* 40 (1989) 377-388. → 1983a; → Tuckett 1989b

1990 Beatitudes. — *DBI*, 1990, 79-82. → 1993b, 16-23

1991a Ein Schaf, eine Drachme und ein Israelit. Die Botschaft Jesu in Q. [Q 15,4-7] — DEGENHARDT, J.J. (ed.), *Die Freude an Gott – unsere Kraft. Festschrift für Otto Bernhard Knoch zum 65. Geburtstag*, Stuttgart: Katholisches Bibelwerk, 1991, 89-101.
The Whole People of God. — ID., *The Quest for Q*, 1993, 189-200.

1991b Temple Traditions in Q. — HORBURY, W. (ed.), *Templum Amicitiae. Essays on the Second Temple Presented to Ernst Bammel* (JSNT SS, 48), Sheffield: JSOT, 1991, 305-329. Esp. 306-307.322-323 [Q 13,34-35]; 308-318 [Q 11,37-52].
Tradition and Temple. — ID., *The Quest for Q*, 1993, 256-279 (revised). Esp. 257-258.271-278; 259-270.

1992a The Beginning of Q: A Proposal. — *NTS* 38 (1992) 205-221. Esp. 207-213 [11,7-11]; 213-221 [Mk 1,1-11/Q]. [NTA 36, 1228] → Neirynck 1996b
The Beginning of Q. — ID., *The Quest for Q*, 1993, 60-78. Esp. 63-70; 70-78.

1992b	The Centurion's Faith and its Function in Q. — VAN SEGBROECK, F., et al. (eds.), *The Four Gospels 1992*. FS F. Neirynck, 1992, I, 517-540. Esp. 522-528: "Help requested and promised: Q 7,2-6"; 528-532: "The intermediaries: Luke 7,3-6a.7a"; 532-537: "The centurion's speech: Q 7,6b.7b-8"; 537-540: "Jesus' pronouncement: Q 7,9".
	Faith. — ID., *The Quest for Q*, 1993, 280-308. Esp. 286-293; 293-298; 298-304; 304-308.

1992c	The Mission Charge in Q. — *Semeia* 55 (1992) 147-174. Esp. 147-152 [Mk/Q]; 152-157 [Q 10,2]; 157-161 [10,5-6]; 162-163 [Q 10,13-15]; 163-164 [Q 10,12]; 164-66 [Q 10,8]; 166-167 [Q 10,16]; 167-172 [Q 10,3-7]. [NTA 36, 1229] → Attridge 1992
	The Mission Charge. — ID., *The Quest for Q*, 1993, 151-188. Esp. 152-158; 158-164; 165-171; 171-174; 174-176; 176-178; 178-179; 179-187.

1992d	The Question of Q. — *Sewanee Theological Review* (Sewanee, TN) 36 (1992) 33-44. [NTA 37, 1226]

1993a	*The Quest for Q*. Edinburgh: Clark, 1993, XV-344 p. [NTA 38, p. 289] → 1983a-b, 1986, 1987, 1991a-b, 1992a-c, 1993b
	S. CARRUTH, *CRBR* 8 (1995) 186-188; B. CHILTON, *Sewanee Theological Review* 38 (1994) 287-288; R.B. EDWARDS, *ExpT* 105 (1993-94) 284; M. GOULDER, *NT* 36 (1994) 204-207; P.J. HARTIN, *Neotestamentica* 28 (1994) 260-263; T. KLUTZ, *JSNT* 58 (1995) 115; F. LANGLAMET, *RB* 101 (1994) 142-143; F. NEIRYNCK, *ETL* 70 (1994) 164-167; W.R. TELFORD, *Theology* 98 (1995) 308-309.

1993b	Did Q Exist? — *Ibid.*, 1-59. Esp. 7-12 [Q 3,7-9.16-17]; 12-16 [Q 4,1-13]; 16-23 [Q 6,20-23]; 23-26 [Q 6,29]; 26-28 [Q 6,27-28.32-36]; 28-31 [Q 11,2-4]; 31-39 [Q 12,22-31]; 39-43 [Q 6,43-45.46; 13,26-27]; 43-45 [Q 7,18-23]; 45-46 [Q 16,16]; 47-48 [Q 7,31-35]; 48-51 [Q 11,14-16]; 51-53 [Q 11,29-32]; 54-55 [Q 10,23-24]; 55-56 [Q 11,44]; 56-59 [Q 12,39-40]. → 1981a, 1990

1993c	The Anointed One in Nazareth. — DE BOER, M.C. (ed.), *From Jesus to John*. FS M. de Jonge, 1993, 231-251. Esp. 235-236 [Q 4,16(Lk)].

## CATHERINET, F.-M.

1950	Note sur un verset de l'Évangile de saint Jean: XX,17. — *Mémorial J. Chaine* (Bibliothèque de la Faculté catholique de théologie de Lyon, 5), Lyon: Fac. catholiques, 1950, 51-59. Esp. 55-58 [28,10].

## CATTANEO, Enrico

1981	*Trois homélies pseudo-chrysostomiennes sur la Pâque comme œuvre d'Apollinaire de Laodicée. Attribution et étude théologique* (Théologie historique, 58). Paris: Beauchesne, 1981, XX-269 p. Esp. 57-104: "L'interprétation des jours de la Pâque" [20,1-16].

1986	Spirito e profezia. Il peccato irremissibile contro lo Spirito Santo (*Mt* 12,31s) in Ireneo di Lione. — LORIZIO, G. - SCIPPA, V. (eds.), *Ecclesiae Sacramentum. Studi in onore di A. Marrancini*, Napoli: d'Auria, 1986, 169-181.

1989	La bestemmia contro lo Spirito Santo (Mt 12,31-32) in S. Atanasio. — *Studia Patristica* 21 (1989) 420-425.

## CAUBET ITURBE, Francisco Javier

1961	Superioridad de la virginidad sobre el matrimonio a la luz de los Evangelios. Renovación de la doctrina del Tridentino. — *CuBíb* 18 (1961) 347-357. Esp. 349-353 [19,10-12]; 353-356 [22,29-30]. [NTA 7, 138]

1965	Una cadena patrística, conservada en árabe, del Evangelio de San Mateo. — *EstBíb* 24 (1965) 135-151. Esp. 143-151. [NTA 11, 187] → 1970

1970	*La cadena árabe del Evangelio de San Mateo*. I: *Texto*. II: *Versión* (Studi e Testi, 254-255). Città del Vaticano: Biblioteca apostolica Vaticana, 1970, LIX-254 and LV-315 p. — Diss. Commissio Biblica, Roma, 1964. → 1965
	M.-É. BOISMARD, *RB* 80 (1973) 612; J.M. CASCIARO, *ScriptTheol* 4 (1972) 266-269; *EstBíb* 32 (1973) 409-412; J.S. COATTO, *RevistBíb* 34 (1972) 228; A. PENNA, *RivBib* 20 (1972) 169-172.

1975   La cadena copto-árabe de los evangelios y Severo de Antioquía. — ALVAREZ VERDES,
       L. – ALONSO HERNÁNDEZ, E.J. (eds.), *Homenaje a Juan Prado. Miscelánea de estudios
       bíblicos y hebraicos*, Madrid: Consejo Superior de Investigaciones Científicas, 1975,
       421-432. Esp. 423-427.

**CAUSSE, Maurice**
1977   Études sur le problème synoptique. — *ETR* 52 (1977) 125-132. [NTA 21, 707] → Frey 1972,
       Neirynck 1974a
1980   Réflexions sur le problème synoptique. — *ETR* 55 (1980) 113-119. Esp. 115-118 [Q]. [NTA
       24, 773r] → Orchard 1978*

**CAVALLARIN, Anna Maria** → Ossola 1985

**CAVALLERI, Guido**
1981   La strage degli Innocenti. [2,16] — *Studi Cattolici* (Milano) 25 (1981) 635-637.

**CAVALLERO, Pablo A.**
1991   Alcance teológico de μή + indicativo: A propósito de Jn 3,18 y otros *loci* neotestamen-
       tarios. — *EstBíb* 49 (1991) 483-495. Esp. 486 [22,24.29]; 487 [25,29]. [NTA 37, 50]

**CAVALLETTI, Sofia**
1960   I sogni di San Giuseppe. [1,18-25] — *BibOr* 2 (1960) 149-151. [NTA 5, 391]
1961   Gesù Messia e Mosè. — *Ant* 36 (1961) 94-101. Esp. 99-101. [NTA 6, 246]

**CAVALLIN, Hans**
1987   Jesus gör de döda levande. [Jesus brings the dead to life] — *SEÅ* 51-52 (1986-87) 40-
       49. Esp. 44-46 [22,23-33]. [NTA 31, 665]

**CAVALLO, Jo Ann**
1992   Agricultural Imagery in the Gospel of Matthew and the Gospel of Truth. — *Religion
       & Literature* (Notre Dame, IN) 24 (1992) 27-38. [NTA 37, 1643]

**CAVE, C.H.**
1963   St Matthew's Infancy Narrative. — *NTS* 9 (1962-63) 382-390. Esp. 384-385 [1,18-25]; 385-
       387 [2,3-8.11]; 387-388 [2,19-23]; 388-389 [2,18]; 389-390 [2,23]. [NTA 8, 121]
1964   The Sermon at Nazareth and the Beatitudes in the Light of the Synagogue Lectionary.
       [Q 6,20-26] — *Studia Evangelica* 3 (1964) 231-235.
1965   The Parables and the Scriptures. — *NTS* 11 (1964-65) 374-387. Esp. 383-385 [13,24-30].
       [NTA 10, 501]

**CAVEDO, Romeo**
1972   Una storia che si fa parabola (Mt 20,1-16; 21,28–22,14). — *ParVi* 17 (1972) 335-351.

**CAVERO, Ignacio**
1963   Tu es Petrus. Notas bíblicas para el enriquecimiento de un texto dogmático. — *EstBíb*
       22 (1963) 351-362. Esp. 354-360 [16,18-19/OT]; 360-362 [16,18-19]. [NTA 9, 914]

**CAWLEY, Martin**
1981   Health of the Eyes – Gift of the Father. In the Gospel Tradition "Q". [11,5] — *Word
       and Spirit* (Still River, MA) 3 (1981) 41-70.

**CAZA, Lorraine**
1989   *"Mon Dieu, mon Dieu, pourquoi m'as-tu abandonné?" Comme bonne nouvelle de Jésus
       Christ, Fils de Dieu, comme bonne nouvelle de Dieu pour la multitude* (Recherches, NS
       24). Montreal: Bellarmin; Paris: Cerf, 1989, 546 p. Esp. 97-98.110 [27,46]; 214-215.218-220
       [27,51]; 236-239.243-245 [27,54]; 259 [27,39-44]; 466-477: "La croix matthéenne et le cri d'abandon"
       [27,51-53]. — Diss. Collège dominicain, Ottawa, 1986. (Y.-B. Trémel).

**CAZEAUX, Jacques**

1989   La parabole attire la parabole, ou le problème des séquences de paraboles. — DELORME, J. (ed.), *Les paraboles évangéliques*, 1989, 403-424. Esp. 406-421: "La séquence parabolique de la *plante* dans Matthieu".

**CAZELLES, Henri**

1954   Mariage (NT). — *DBS* 5/27 (1954) 926-935. Esp. 931-935.

1987*  (ed.), *La vie de la Parole. De l'Ancien au Nouveau Testament. Études d'exégèse et d'herméneutique bibliques offertes à Pierre Grelot professeur à l'Institut Catholique de Paris* (Département des études bibliques de l'Institut Catholique de Paris). Paris: Desclée, 1987, XLV-486 p. → Alonso Díaz, Bernard, Dubarle, Gourgues, J. Guillet, Haudebert

1990   Sur l'histoire de Bethléhem. — Κεχαριτωμένη. FS R. Laurentin, 1990, 145-152.

**CECNI, A.M.**

1995   *La parola di Dio nel vangelo di Matteo.* Casale Monferrato: Piemme, 1995, 316 p.

**CELADA, Benito**

1959   Un texto evangélico que se quería aducir como favorable al divorcio. Notable coincidencia de los autores en una nueva interpretación. [5,32; 19,9] — *CuBíb* 16 (1959) 47.

1962   Las bienaventuranzas. Por los métodos críticos a la más ferviente piedad del Evangelio. [5,3-10] — *CuBíb* 19 (1962) 375-382. → López Melús 1962

1965   El Padre Nuestro. Progresos en la inteligencia de la oración de los cristianos. [6,9-13] — *CuBíb* 22 (1965) 279-283. [NTA 10, 905]

1969a  Más acerca del camello y la aguja (Mt 19,24; Mc 10,25; Lc 18,25). — *CuBíb* 26 (1969) 157-158.

1969b  Textos evangélicos acerca del número de los que se salvan (Mt 7:13-14). — *Ibid.*, 159-160.

1970   Mateo 19:16-30 y la perfección cristiana. — *CuBíb* 27 (1970) 106-109.

**CENTI, Tito S.**

1975   A proposito di riconciliazione: dalla correzione fraterna alla tolleranza. (Riflessioni su un articolo confusionario del P.J. Galot). [18,15-18] — *Rassegna di Ascetica e Mistica* (Firenze) 26 (1975) 177-185. [NTA 20, 443] → Galot 1974

**Centre national de pastorale liturgique**

1966   La traduction commune du "Notre Père". — *Questions Liturgiques et Paroissiales* (Leuven) 47 (1966) 141-145. [NTA 11, 202]

**CERESA-GASTALDO, Aldo**

1988   "Dio mio, Dio mio, perché mi hai abbandonato?" (*Matteo* 27,46 e *Marco* 15,34). — *Renovatio* 23 (1988) 101-106.

**CERETI, Giovanni**

1977   *Divorzio, nuove nozze e penitenza nella Chiesa primitiva* [5,32; 19,9]. Bologna: Dehoniane, 1977, 416 p. → Crouzel 1977

**CERFAUX, Lucien**

1932R  "L'histoire de la tradition synoptique" d'après Rudolf Bultmann. [1932] — ID., *Recueil*, I, 1954, 353-367. → Bultmann 1931

1935R  À propos des sources du troisième Évangile: proto-Luc ou proto-Matthieu? [1935] — ID., *Recueil*, I, 1954, 389-414. Esp. 390-395: "Les théories sur la 'double tradition' dans l'Évangile de Luc"; 395-404: "L'état de la 'double tradition' dans l'Évangile de Luc et les péricopes propres à Luc"; 404-414: "L'hypothèse d'un proto-Matthieu, source de Luc".

1936[R]  Parallèles canoniques et extra-canoniques de "l'Évangile inconnu" (*Pap. Egerton 2*).
[1936] — ID., *Recueil*, I, 1954, 279-299. Esp. 286-288 [8,1-4]; 288-292 [22,15-22]; 292-296 [21,18-22].

1938[R]  Encore la question synoptique. [1938] — ID., *Recueil*, I, 1954, 415-424.

1946[R]  *La voix vivante de l'Évangile au début de l'Église* [1946] (Bible et Vie Chrétienne).
Tournai–Paris: Casterman, [2]1956, 157 p. Esp. 37-54: "L'évangile selon saint Matthieu".
*Die lebendige Stimme des Evangeliums in der Frühzeit der Kirche*, trans. I. Klimmer. Mainz: Matthias-Grünewald, 1953, 152 p.
*De levende stem van het Evangelie in de begintijd van de Kerk*, trans. A.J. Kern. Tielt: Lannoo, 1955, 192 p.;
(Woord en Beleving), Tielt – Den Haag: Lannoo, [2]1959, 194 p. Esp. 47-69.
*La voz viva del Evangelio al comienzo de la Iglesia*, trans. F. Pegenante Rubio (Prisma, 43). San Sebastián: Dinor, 1958, 177 p.
*The Four Gospels. An Historical Introduction*, trans. P. Hepburne-Scott, with an introduction by L. Johnston. Westminster, MD: Newman; London: Darton, Longman & Todd, 1960, XXII-145 p.

1950  *Kyrios*. — DBS 5/27 (1950) 200-227. Esp. 214-222.

1951  La mission de Galilée dans la tradition synoptique. — ETL 27 (1951) 369-389. Esp. 370-372 [proto-Mt]; 374-380 [13,53–14,21/Mk 6,1-44]; 380-389 [10,2-4/Mk 3,13-19]; 28 (1952) 629-647.
Esp. 629-643 [9,35–10,52/Mk 6,7-13]; 643-646 [4,23–5,2/Mk 3,7-19]; = ID., *Recueil*, I, 1954, 425-469. Esp. 426-429; 431-437; 438-448; 449-464; 465-468.

1953a  La section des pains (*Mc* VI,31–VIII,26; *Mt* XIV,13–XVI,12). — SCHMID, J. - VÖGTLE, A. (eds.), *Synoptische Studien*. FS A. Wikenhauser, 1953, 64-77. Esp. 65-68 [14,13–15,28/Mk]; 69-72 [15,29–16,12/Mk]; = ID., *Recueil*, I, 1954, 471-485. Esp. 472-476; 476-480.

1953b  Saint Pierre et sa succession. — RSR 41 (1953) 188-202. Esp. 192-193 [16,17-19]; = ID., *Recueil*, II, 239-251. Esp. 243-244.

1954a  *Recueil Lucien Cerfaux. Études d'exégèse et d'histoire religieuse de Monseigneur Cerfaux, réunies à l'occasion de son soixante-dixième anniversaire* Vol. I-II (BETL, 6-7). Gembloux: Duculot, 1954, XLIII-504 and 558 p. I → 1932, 1935, 1936, 1938, 1951, 1953a; II → 1953b

1954b  Le problème synoptique. À propos d'un livre récent. [Vaganay 1954a] — NRT 76 (1954) 494-505; = ID., *Recueil*, III, 1962, 83-97. → Levie 1954, McCool 1956

1954c  Les sources scripturaires de Mt., XI,25-30. — ETL 30 (1954) 740-746 [11,25/Dan 2,23]; 31 (1955) 331-342. Esp. 331-336 [11,26-27/Is 51]; 336-342 [11,28-30]. [NTA 1, 24]; = ID., *Recueil*, III, 1962, 139-159. Esp. 139-146; 146-152; 153-159.

1956  La connaissance des secrets du Royaume d'après Matt. xiii.11 et parallèles. — NTS 2 (1955-56) 238-249. [NTA 1, 34]; = ID., *Recueil*, III, 1962, 123-138.

1957a  *Discours de mission dans l'Évangile de saint Matthieu* (Spiritualité biblique). Tournai: Desclée, 1957, 147 p. Esp. 19-82: "La mission"; 83-147: "Les promesses de Dieu".
G. BERNINI, Greg 40 (1959) 142; M.-É. BOISMARD, RB 65 (1958) 303; I. DE LA POTTERIE, Bijdragen 19 (1958) 199; P. DELHAYE, MSR 15 (1958) 157; J. DELORME, AmiCler 68 (1958) 670; J. GIBLET, CollMech 42 (1957) 424; M. SABBE, CollBrugGand 4 (1958) 268-269; A. VIARD, RSPT 42 (1958) 342.
*De Zendingsrede in het Evangelie van Mattheüs. Overwegingen over het apostolaat*. Tournai: Desclée, 1959, 156 p.
*Apostle and Apostolate, According to the Gospel of St. Matthew*, trans. D.D. Duggan. New York: Desclée, 1960, VI-184 p. [NTA 5, p. 110] — B. MCGRATH, CBQ 23 (1961) 82-83.
*Il Discorso missionario di Gesù nel Vangelo di San Matteo*. Milano: Pont. Ist. Missioni Estere, 1962, 136 p. — C. LO GIUDICE, CC 114/4 (1963) 50-51.

1957b  En marge de la question synoptique. Les unités littéraires antérieures aux trois premiers évangiles. — HEUSCHEN, J. (ed.), *La formation des évangiles*, 1957, 24-33. Esp. 26-29: "La phase galiléenne"; 29-31: "La phase de la passion"; 31-33: "Vers la construction des évangiles actuels";
= ID., *Recueil*, III, 1962, 99-110. Esp. 101-105; 105-108; 108-109.

1957c  Les Paraboles du Royaume dans l'"Évangile de Thomas". — *Muséon* 70 (1957) 307-327. Esp. 307-310: "Texte et traduction" (G. Garitte); 311-316: "Rapports littéraires avec les évangiles canoniques" [12,29/Th 98; 13,24-30/Th 56; 13,31-32/Th 20; 13,33/Th 96; 13,44-46/Th 77; 13,44/Th 108; 18,12-14/Th 106]; = ID., *Recueil*, III, 1962, 61-80. Esp. 61-64; 65-70.

1958   L'Évangile de Jean et "le logion johannique" des Synoptiques. — BRAUN, F.M. (ed.), *L'Évangile de Jean. Études et problèmes* (Recherches bibliques, 3), Brugge: Desclée De Brouwer, 1958, 147-159. Esp. 148-153 [11,27; 13,11.16-17; 24,36]; = ID., *Recueil*, III, 1962, 161-174. Esp. 162-168.

1961   Le message des Apôtres à toutes les nations. — *Scrinium Lovaniense. Mélanges historiques. Historische opstellen Étienne Van Cauwenbergh*, Leuven: Bibl. Univ., 1961, 99-107. Esp. 102-103 [28,19-20]; = ID., *Recueil*, III, 1962, 7-15. Esp. 10-11.

1962   *Recueil Lucien Cerfaux. Études d'exégèse et d'histoire religieuse*. Vol. III (BETL, 18). Gembloux: Duculot, 1962, 458 p. Nouvelle édition revue et complétée, ed. F. Neirynck (BETL, 71). Leuven: University Press / Peeters, 1985, LXXX-458 p. → 1954b-c, 1956, 1957b-d, 1958, 1961

1964   La mission apostolique des Douze et sa portée eschatologique. — *Mélanges Eugène Tisserant*, 1964, I, 43-66. Esp. 46-47 [11,5]; 51-54 [kingdom]; 54-59 [10,5-41].

1966   *Le trésor des paraboles. Spiritualité biblique*. Tournai: Desclée, 1966, 164 p. Esp. 27-32 [13,1-9]; 33-42 [13,24-30]; 51-60 [13,31-32]; 60-63 [13,33]; 65-73 [13,44-45]; 109-111 [21,28-32]; 111-116 [21,33-46]; 116-120 [22,1-14]; 120-122 [21,43]; 128-132 [20,1-16]; 141-148 [25,14-30]; 148-156 [25,1-13].
*The Treasure of the Parables*, trans. M. Bent. De Pere, WI: St. Norbert Abbey Press, 1968, 143 p.
*Il tesoro delle parabole*, trans. L. Melotti ("Orizzonte biblici"). Torino: Elle Di Ci, 1968, 128 p.
*Er redete in Gleichnissen*, trans. R. Tschady. München: Ars Sacra, 1969, 159 p.
*Mensaje de las parábolas*, trans. A.G. Fraile (Actualidad Bíblica, 11). Madrid: Fax, 1969, 238 p.
*O tesouro das parábolas*, trans. A. Rubim (A Palavra Viva). São Paulo: Paulinas, 1973, 150 p.

1968   *Jésus aux origines de la Tradition. Matériaux pour l'histoire évangélique* (Pour une histoire de Jésus, 3). Brugge: Desclée De Brouwer, 1968, 301 p. Esp. 55-65 [John the Baptist]; 71-72 [11,7-11]; 72-80 [Sermon on the Mount]; 80-91 [10,5-42]; 91-93 [11,21-24; 12,41-42]; 105-108 [13]; 115-118 [11,25-30]; 125-127 [8,11-12; 16,1-4]; 139-140 [12,22-32]; 153-156 [21,1-9]; 162-164 [21,28-22,14]; 223-224 [28,9-10]; 228 [28,16-20]; 251-271: "Les Logia du Seigneur".
*Jezus aan de bronnen van de overlevering*, trans. L. Van den Eynden (De geschiedenis van Jezus, 3). Brugge: Desclée De Brouwer, 1970, 299 p.
*Jesús en los orígines de la tradición. Para una historia de Jesús*, trans. L. de Aguirre Vergara. Bilbao: Desclée De Brouwer, 1970, 268 p.
*Gesù alle origini della tradizione*, trans. C. Benincasa, G. & R. Pagannone (La parola di Dio). Roma: Paoline, 1970, 323 p.; ²1972.
*Jesus nas origens da tradição*, trans. F. Santacatarina (Colleción Bíblica, 16). São Paulo: Paulinas, 1972, 230 p.

1969   En relisant une thèse. [A.-M. Charue, 1929] — TROISFONTAINES, C. (ed.), *Au service de la Parole de Dieu*. FS A.-M. Charue, 1969, 9-20. Esp. 12, 14.

1973   L'utilisation de la Source Q par Luc. Introduction du Séminaire. — NEIRYNCK, F. (ed.), *L'Évangile de Luc*, 1973, 61-69. Esp. 61-63: "La source Q"; 63-66: "Synopse critique de la grande séquence"; 66-68: "La construction littéraire du ch. 7 de Luc"; ²1989, 285-293. Esp. 285-287; 287-290; 290-292.

## CEROKE, Christian P.

1960   Is Mk 2,10 a Saying of Jesus? — *CBQ* 22 (1960) 369-390. Esp. 383-387: "Gospel usage of the title 'Son of Man'" [10,32; 16,13.28]. [NTA 5, 406]

1962   The Divinity of Christ in the Gospels. — *CBQ* 24 (1962) 125-139. Esp. 125-127.136-138. [NTA 7, 103]

**CERUTTI, Agostino**

1957    L'interpretazione del testo di S. Matteo XII,46-50 nei Padri. — *Marianum* 19 (1957) 185-221. [NTA 2, 527]

**CHABROL, Claude**

1974*   & MARIN, L. (eds.), *Le récit évangélique* (Bibliothèque de sciences religieuses). Paris: Aubier Montaigne/Cerf/Desclée De Brouwer, 1974, 254 p. → A.J.-J. Cohen, L. Marin 1971b, Mellon 1973

**CHADWICK, Henry**

1956    The Authorship of the Egerton Papyrus No. 3. — *HTR* 49 (1956) 145-151. [NTA 1, 176] → Leaney 1955

**CHAFER, Lewis Sperry**

1951    The Teachings of Christ Incarnate.— *BS* 108 (1951) 389-413 [Sermon on the Mount]; 109 (1952) 4-36 [24-25]; 103-135.

1952    The Baptism of the Holy Spirit. — *BS* 109 (1952) 199-216. Esp. 201-203 [3,11].

**CHAMBERAS, Peter A.**

1970    The Transfiguration of Christ: A Study in the Patristic Exegesis of Scripture. [17,1-8] — *St. Vladimir's Theological Quarterly* (Tuckahoe, NY) 14 (1970) 48-65.

**CHAMBERLAIN, William D.**

1953    Till the Son of Man Be Come. — *Interpr* 7 (1953) 3-13. Esp. 4.12 [10,23]; 6-8 [11,12].

**CHAMBLIN, J.K.**

1989    Matthew. — ELWELL, W.A. (ed.), *Evangelical Commentary on the Bible*, Grand Rapids, MI: Baker, 1989.

**CHAMBLIN, Knox**

1964a   Gospel and Judgment in the Preaching of John the Baptist. — *Tyndale House Bulletin* 13 (1964) 7-15.

1964b   John the Baptist and the Kingdom of God. — *Tyndale House Bulletin* 15 (1964) 10-16.

**CHAMPLIN, Russell**

1964    *Family II in Matthew* (Studies and Documents, 24). Salt Lake City, UT: Univ. of Utah Press, 1964, VII-170 p. Esp. 45-145: "Text and apparatus of the gospel of Matthew". [NTA 9, p. 270] J. DUPLACY, *Bib* 49 (1966) 537-540; H.H. OLIVER, *JBL* 84 (1965) 204-205.

1966    *Family E and Its Allies in Matthew (with Collation of Codex 903 by Jacob Geerlings)* (Studies and Documents, 28). Salt Lake City, UT: Univ. of Utah Press, 1966, VIII-200 p. Esp. 65-115: "Text and apparatus of the gospel of Matthew"; 156-162 [Codex Y and Family II]; 163-169 [Codex M]; 170-177 [Codex 903: Geerlings]. J. DUPLACY, *Bib* 52 (1971) 92-94; H.H. OLIVER, *JBL* 86 (1967) 354-355.

**CHANG CH'UEN-SHEN, A.B.**

1970    Research on the Mystery of the Temptations. [Chinese] — *ColcTFu* 4 (1970) 195-213.

**CHANG, Hung-Kil**

1995    *Neuere Entwürfe zur Ethik des Neuen Testaments im deutschsprachigen Raum. Ihre Sichtung und kritische Würdigung.* Diss. Erlangen–Nürnberg, 1995, VI-238 p. (O. Merk). Esp. 30-35: "Zur Bergpredigt".

**CHARALAMBAKIS, Christoph**

1974    Vier literarische Papyri der Kölner Sammlung. — *ZPapEp* 14 (1974) 29-40. Esp. 37-40 [P86].

**CHARBEL, Antonio**

1961 O conceito de παλιγγενεσία em Mt 19,28. — *Revista de Cultura Teológica* (São Paulo) 1 (1961) 51-65.

O conceito de "palingenesia" ou regeneraçâo em Mt. 19,28. — *RevistCuBíb* 7 (1963) 13-17. [NTA 8, 949]

1971 Mt 2,1.7: Os Reis Magos eram Nabateus? — *RevistCuBíb* 8 (1971) 96-103. [NTA 17, 513]

*Mt.* 2,1.7: I Magi erano nabatei? — *RivBib* 20 suppl. (1972) 571-583. Esp. 571-578 [2,1-12]. [NTA 19, 83]

I Magi nell'ambiente nabateo. — *Terra Santa* (Jerusalem) 64 (1988) 4-12.

1978 A sepultura de Jesús como resulta dos evangelhos. [27,59-60] — *RevistCuBíb* 2 (1978) 351-362. [NTA 24, 66]

1983 Mt 2,1-12: Os Magos no ambiente do Reino Nabateu. — *RevistCuBíb* 7 (1983) 90-100. [NTA 28, 488]

Mateo 2:1-12: los Magos en el ambiente del Reino Nabateo. — *RevistBíb* 46 (1984) 147-158.

Matteo 2,1-12: i magi nella cornice del regno nabateo. — *Studia Patavina* 32 (1985) 81-88. [NTA 30, 108]

1985 Os evangelhos da infância de Cristo. — *RevistCuBíb* 9 (1985) 156-159. [NTA 30, 109]

**CHARETTE, Blaine**

1990 A Harvest for the People? An Interpretation of Matthew 9.37f. — *JSNT* 38 (1990) 29-35. [NTA 35, 139]

1992a *The Theme of Recompense in Matthew's Gospel* (JSNT SS, 79). Sheffield: JSOT, 1992, 184 p. Esp. 21-62: "The Old Testament covenantal background to the Matthaean teaching on recompense"; 63-118: "The teaching on reward in the gospel of Matthew" [5,5.12.43-48; 6,1-6.16-18.19-24; 10,40-42; 16,24-28; 19,16-20,16]; 119-161: "The teaching on punishment in the gospel of Matthew" [3,7-12; 7,15-23; 8,11-12; 12,33-37; 13,24-30.36-43; 15,13; 21,18-22.33-44; 22,1-14; 24,45-51; 25,14-30.31-46]. [NTA 38, p. 289] — Diss. Sheffield, 1992 (D. Hill – A. Lincoln).

D.C. ALLISON, *Interpr* 48 (1994) 303-304; E. CUVILLIER, *ETR* 68 (1993) 580-581; R.A. EDWARDS, *CBQ* 56 (1994) 585-586; N.N. HINGLE, *EvQ* 67 (1995) 268-270; A.G. HUNTER, *JTS* 45 (1994) 215-216; D. MEALAND, *ExpT* 105 (1993-94) 87; E.M. WAINWRIGHT, *CRBR* 7 (1994) 158-160.

1992b 'To Proclaim Liberty to the Captives'. Matthew 11.28-30 in the Light of OT Prophetic Expectation. — *NTS* 38 (1992) 290-297. [NTA 36, 1274]

1993 "Speaking against the Holy Spirit": The Correlation between Messianic Task and National Fortunes in the Gospel of Matthew. — *Journal of Pentecostal Theology* (Sheffield) 3 (1993) 51-70. [NTA 39, 151]

**CHARITY, A.C.**

1966 *Events and Their Afterlife. The Dialectics of Christian Typology in the Bible and Dante.* Cambridge: University Press, 1966, XI-288 p. Esp. 112-129 [servant, Son of Man]; 130-135 [Israel].

**CHARLES, J. Daryl**

1989 The "Coming One" / "Stronger One" and His Baptism: Matt 3:11-12, Mark 1:8, Luke 3:16-17. — *Pneuma* (Gaithersburg, MD) 11 (1989) 37-50. [NTA 35, 131]

1992 The Greatest or the Least in the Kingdom? The Disciple's Relationship to the Law (Matt 5:17-20). — *TrinJ* NS 13 (1992) 139-162. Esp. 141-143: "Matt 5:17-20 within the gospel"; 143-147: "'Righteousness' in Matthew"; 147-158: "Commentary". [NTA 37, 1254]

**CHARLESWORTH, James Hamilton**

1974 Tatian's Dependence Upon Apocryphal Traditions. — *HeythJ* 15 (1974) 5-17. Esp. 11-16 [3,13-17]. [NTA 18, 789]

1985   *The Old Testament Pseudepigrapha and the New Testament. Prolegomena for the Study of Christian Origins* (SNTS MS, 54). Cambridge: University Press, 1985, XXIV-213 p. Esp. 72 [2,17-18/OT]; 111-113 [χριστός].

1990   Exploring Opportunities for Rethinking Relations among Jews and Christians. — ID. (ed.), *Jews and Christians. Exploring the Past, Present, and Future* (Shared Ground among Jews and Christians, 1), New York: Crossroad, 1990, 35-53 (discussion, 54-59). Esp. 43-47.51-53.

1992*  et al. (eds.), *The Messiah. Developments in Earliest Judaism and Christianity. The First Princeton Symposium on Judaism and Christian Origins.* Minneapolis, MN: Fortress, 1992, XXIX-597 p. → Aune, Borsch, A.Y. Collins, W.D. Davies 1990, Mack, Priest

1992   Has the Name "Peter" Been Found among the Dead Sea Scrolls? — MAYER, B. (ed.), *Christen und Christliches in Qumran?* (Eichstätter Studien, 32), Regensburg: Pustet, 1992, 213-225. Esp. 213-217.

1994a  & HARDING, M. - KILEY, M., *The Lord's Prayer and Other Prayer Texts from the Greco-Roman Era.* Valley Forge, PA: Trinity Press International, 1994, IX-292 p. [NTA 39, p. 135] → Charlesworth, Harding, Kiley

1994b  A Caveat on Textual Transmission and the Meaning of *Abba*: A Study of the Lord's Prayer. — *Ibid.*, 1-14.

1994c  & EVANS, C.A., Jesus in the Agrapha and Apocryphal Gospels. — CHILTON, B. - EVANS, C.A. (eds.), *Studying the Historical Jesus*, 1994, 479-533. Esp. 483-491 [agrapha]; 493-494 [apocryphal gospels]; 496-503 [Gospel of Thomas]; 503-514 [Gospel of Peter]; 522-523 [Gospel of the Nazoreans].

### CHARLET, Jean-Louis

1983   Prudence et la Bible. — *Recherches augustiniennes* (Paris) 18 (1983) 3-149. Esp. 35-38, 59-70.

### CHARLIER, André

1965   L'Église corps du Christ chez saint Hilaire de Poitiers. — *ETL* 41 (1965) 451-477. Esp. 454-456: "Le commentaire de saint Matthieu".

### CHARLIER, Célestin

1954   Les tentations de Jésus au désert. — *BibVieChrét* 5 (1954) 85-92.

1957   L'action de grâces de Jésus (Luc 10,17-24 et Matth. 11,25-30). — *BibVieChrét* 17 (1957) 87-99. [NTA 2, 32]

### CHARLIER, Jean-Pierre

1968   *Les miracles dans l'Évangile* (Cahiers de recyclage théologique, 4). La Sarte–Huy: Couvent des Dominicains, 1968, 85 p. Esp. 33-34 [8,23-27]; 38 [14,22-33]; 59-60 [20,29-34]; 73-74.

1979   Du berceau au tombeau. Préface et postface de l'évangile de Matthieu. — *VSp* 133 (1979) 8-25, 172-191. [NTA 23, 816]

1987   *Signes et prodiges. Les miracles dans l'Évangile* (Lire la Bible, 79). Paris: Cerf, 1987, 189 p. Esp. 50-51 [8,14-15]; 61-63 [20,29-34]; 91-92.96-97 [9,18-26]; 157-159 [8,18-27]; 169-170 [14,22-33].

### CHARPENTIER, Étienne

1967   *Ce Testament toujours Nouveau* (Jalons. Je sais, je crois. Encyclopédie du Catholique au XXᵉ siècle). Paris: Fayard, 1967, 213 p. Esp. 144-152.

1973   *Christ est ressuscité!* (Cahiers Évangile, 3). Paris: Cerf, 1973, 69 p. Esp. 51; 52; 55.
       *Cristo ha resucitado*, trans. N. Darrical (Cuadernos Bíblicos, 5). Estella: Verbo Divino, 1976, 110 p.
       *Cristo è risorto* (Bibbia oggi, 9). Torino: Gribaudi, 1979, 60 p.
       *Cristo ressuscitaou.* São Paulo: Paulinas, 1984, 105 p.

1974a  & DUPUY, B. – DUPREZ, A., *Les miracles de l'Évangile* (Cahiers Évangile, 8). Paris: Cerf, 1974, 69 p. Esp. 21-26.
*I miracoli del vangelo.* Torino: Gribaudi, 1978, 60 p.

1974b  & LE POITTEVIN – LÉGASSE, S., *Lecture de l'évangile selon saint Matthieu* (Cahiers Évangile, 9). Paris: Cerf, 1974, 68 p.
*Lettura del vangelo di Matteo.* Assisi: Cittadella, 1975.
*Evangelio según San Mateo,* trans. N. Darrical (Cuadernos Bíblicos, 2). Estella: Verbo Divino, 1976, 68 p.; ²1978.
　　　J.A. CARRASCO, *EstJos* 33 (1979) 251; L.L. SIMÓN, *BibFe* 3 (1977) 341-342.

1976  *Des évangiles à l'Évangile* ("Croire et Comprendre"). Paris: Centurion, 1976, 168 p.
Esp. 84-94: "Évangile selon saint Matthieu".
*Dos evangelhos ao evangelho.* São Paulo: Paulinas, 1977, 176 p.
*Il vangelo e i vangeli* (La fede oggi). Bologna: Dehoniane, 1978, 243 p.

1979  Le chapitre des paraboles chez Matthieu (Mt 13). — *FoiVie* 78/3 = *Cahiers bibliques* 18 (1979) 101-106. [NTA 24, 423]

1981a  *Évangiles synoptiques et Actes des Apôtres* (Petite Bibliothèque des sciences bibliques. Nouveau Testament, 4). Paris: Desclée, 1981, 294 p.

1981b  *Pour lire le Nouveau Testament.* Paris: Cerf, 1981, 128 p. Esp. 69-80.
*Para leer el Nuevo Testamento.* Estella: Verbo Divino, 1981, 128 p.
*How to Read the New Testament,* trans. J. Bowden. New York: Crossroad; London: SCM, 1982, 128 p.
*Führer durch das Neue Testament: Anleitung zum Selbst- und Gruppenstudium,* trans. F.J. Schierse. Düsseldorf: Patmos, ³1987, 175 p.
*Wegwijs in het Nieuwe Testament.* Baarn: Ten Have, 1987, 128 p.

1981c  Pour une lecture solennelle de la passion. — VANHOYE, A., et al., *La Passion selon les quatre Évangiles* (Lire la Bible, 55), Paris: Cerf, 1981, 109-123. Esp. 109-112: "La passion selon saint Matthieu".

**CHASE, Keith William**
1990  *The Synoptic πειρασμοί of Jesus. Their Christological Significance.* Diss. Baptist Theol. Sem., New Orleans, 1990, 217 p. (B.E. Simmons). — *DissAbstr* 51 (1990-91) 1646-1647.

**CHAVASSE, Claude**
1971  Not the Mountain Appointed. Studies in Texts: Matthew 28:16. — *Theology* 74 (1971) 478. [NTA 16, 544]

**CHENDERLIN, Fritz**
1976  Distributed Observance of the Passover. A Preliminary Test of the Hypothesis. — *Bib* 57 (1976) 1-24. Esp. 10-13 [26,3-5; 27,1.18.20.62; 28,1]. [NTA 21, 353]

**CHENEY, Emily Ramsay**
1994  *Reading Strategies and Gender Dynamics of Biblical Texts: Selected Texts from the Gospel of Matthew as Case Studies.* Diss. Vanderbilt Univ., Nashville, TN, 1994, 297 p. (M.A. Tolbert). — *DissAbstr* 55 (1994-95) 3542.

**CHERIAN, K.K.**
1995  Mission: In the Perspective of the Gospels. — *Bible Bhashyam* 21 (1995) 115-120. Esp. 116-117. [NTA 40, 1410]

**CHERNICK, Michael** → Swidler 1989

**CHERRY, R. Stephen**
1962  Agreements Between Matthew and Luke. — *ExpT* 74 (1962-63) 63. [NTA 7, 494] → Argyle 1961

**CHEVALLIER, Max-Alain**

1958   *L'Esprit et le Messie dans le Bas-judaïsme et le Nouveau Testament* (Études d'histoire et de philosophie religieuses, 49). Paris: PUF, 1958, 154 p. Esp. 54-57 [3,11]; 57-67 [3,16-17]; 67-69 [4,1]; 71-72 [17,6]; 72-74 [12,18-21]; 77-79 [11,2-6]; 79 [5,3-4]; 92-94 [12,28].

1974   Note à propos de l'exégèse de *Mt*. 25,31-46. — *RevSR* 48 (1974) 398-400. [NTA 19, 702]

1978   *Souffle de Dieu. Le Saint-Esprit dans le Nouveau Testament*. I (Le point théologique, 26). Paris: Beauchesne, 1978, 264 p. Esp. 91-53: "Témoignages synoptiques" [1,18-20; 3,11-12.13-17; 4,1; 10,19-20; 12,31-32; 22,43; 26,41]; 154-159: "Textes particuliers à Matthieu" [12,18.28; 28,19]. *Aliento de Dios. El Espíritu Santo en el Nuevo Testamento*. Salamanca: Secretariado Trinitario, 1982, 256 p.

1982   "Tu es Pierre, tu es le nouvel Abraham" (Mt 16/18). — *ETR* 57 (1982) 375-387. [NTA 27, 102] → 1983; → Arnéra 1984

1983   À propos de "Tu es Pierre, tu es le nouvel Abraham". — *ETR* 58 (1983) 354. [NTA 28, 98] → 1982

1986   L'apologie du baptême d'eau à la fin du premier siècle. Introduction secondaire de l'étiologie dans les récits du baptême de Jésus. — *NTS* 32 (1986) 528-543. Esp. 533-534 [3,13-17]. [NTA 31, 110]; = ID., *Souffle de Dieu. Le Saint-Esprit dans le Nouveau Testament*. III (Le point théologique, 55), Paris: Beauchesne, 1991, 43-58. Esp. 48-49.

1990   Jésus a-t-il voulu l'Église? — *ETR* 65 (1990) 489-503. Esp. 498-502 [16,18-19]. [NTA 35, 820]

1992   *Relire le Notre-Père*, ed. M. Chevallier & P. Viallaneix. Paris: Réforme, 1992, 50 p.
       É. COTHENET, *EVie* 102 (1992) 410.

**CHICO, Gabriel**

1989   Jesús y Beelzebul. La presencia del Reino en un cuadro polémico (Mt. 12,22-32; Mc 3,22-30; Lc 11,14-23; 12,10). — *EfMex* 7 (1989) 165-178. Esp. 165-169: "Estructura de la pericopa"; 169-177: "La doctrina que el texto nos sugiere"; = *Communio* (Sevilla) 22 (1989) 41-52. Esp. 41-44; 45-52. [NTA 34, 124]

**CHILDS, Brevard S.**

1984   *The New Testament as Canon: An Introduction*. London: SCM, 1984, XXV-572 p. Esp. 57-78: "Matthew"; 157-209: "A canonical harmony of the gospels" [3,1-17; 16,13-23; 19,16-22; 21,18-22; 26,6-13; 28,1-10]; 531-540; 547-548; Philadelphia, PA: Trinity, 1994, XIII-298 p.

1992   *Biblical Theology of the Old and New Testaments. Theological Reflection on the Christian Bible*. London: SCM, 1992, XXII-745 p. Esp. 251-261: "The formation of the gospels" [genre; Q]; 270-276 [Mt]; 337-347: "Matthew 21.33-46: Parable of the wicked tenants"; 430-432 [covenant]; 689-693 [ethics]; 601-605 [faith]; 636-646 [kingdom].

**CHILTON, Bruce David**

1978   "Amen": An Approach through Syriac Gospels. — *ZNW* 69 (1978) 203-211. Esp. 209. [NTA 23, 765]; = ID., *Targumic Approaches*, 1986, 15-23.

1979   *God in Strength. Jesus' Announcement of the Kingdom* (SNTU, B1). Linz: SNTU; Freistadt: Plöchl, 1979, 347 p. Esp. 97-121 [4,12-17]; 179-201 [8,11-12/Q 13,28-29]; 203-230 [11,12-13/Q 16,16]; 301-310: "The text of Mt 4,16.17"; 311-313 [Ναζαρά]; (The Biblical Seminar), Sheffield: JSOT, 1987, 347 p. — Diss. Cambridge, 1976 (E. Bammel). *God in Strength*. [1979, 277-293] — ID. (ed.), *The Kingdom of God*, 1984, 121-132.

1980a  Targumic Transmission and Dominical Tradition. — FRANCE, R.T. - WENHAM, D. (eds.), *Studies of History and Tradition*, 1980, 21-45. Esp. 30-38 [4,1-11]; = ID., *Targumic Approaches*, 1986.

1980b  The Transfiguration: Dominical Assurance and Apostolic Vision. — *NTS* 27 (1980-81) 115-124. Esp. 121-123 [17,1-9]. [NTA 25, 492]

1982a A Comparative Study of Synoptic Development: The Dispute between Cain and Abel in the Palestinian Targums and the Beelzebul Controversy in the Gospels. — *JBL* 101 (1982) 553-562. Esp. 559-562 [12,24-30]. [NTA 27, 921]; = ID., *Targumic Approaches*, 1986, 137-149.

1982b Jesus *ben David*: Reflections on the *Davidssohnfrage*. [22,41-45] — *JSNT* 14 (1982) 88-112. [NTA 26, 868]; = EVANS, C.A. - PORTER, S.E. (eds.), *The Historical Jesus*, 1995, 192-215.

1984* (ed.), *The Kingdom of God in the Teaching of Jesus* (Issues in Religion and Theology, 5). Philadelphia, PA: Fortress; London: SPCK, 1984, XI-162 p. → 1979, 1984a; → Grässer 1974, Kümmel 1964/71, N. Perrin 1976

1984a Introduction. — *Ibid.*, 1-26.

1984b *A Galilean Rabbi And His Bible. Jesus' Own Interpretation of Isaiah.* London: SPCK, 1984, 216 p. Esp. 57-147: "Jesus and the targum to Isaiah".
*A Galilean Rabbi And His Bible. Jesus' Use of the Interpreted Scripture of his Time* (Good News Studies, 8). Wilmington, DE: Glazier, 1984, 216 p.

1985 The Gospel according to Thomas as a Source of Jesus' Teaching. — WENHAM, D. (ed.), *The Jesus Tradition Outside the Gospels*, 1985, 155-175. Esp. 155-159: "Is Thomas an Eastern 'Q'?".

1986a *Targumic Approaches to the Gospels. Essays in the Mutual Definition of Judaism and Christianity* (Studies in Judaism). Lanham, MD - London: University of America Press, 1986, XII-185 p. → 1978, 1980a, 1982a, 1986b

1986b Shebna, Eliakim, and the Promise to Peter. — *Ibid.*, 63-80; = NEUSNER, J., et al. (eds.), *The Social World of Formative Christianity and Judaism*. FS H. Kee, Philadelphia, PA: Fortress, 1988, 311-326.

1987a & MCDONALD, J.I.H., *Jesus and the Ethics of the Kingdom* (Biblical Foundations in Theology, 2). London: SPCK, 1987, XII-148 p. Esp. 33-34 [25,1-13]; 34-35 [22,1-14]; 41-42.83-87 [18,3; 19,13-15]; 103-104 [5,39-42].

1987b Kingdom Come, Kingdom Sung. Voices in the Gospels. — *Forum* 3/2 (1987) 51-75. Esp. 55-58.62-66 [NTA 32, 67]

1989 *Profiles of a Rabbi. Synoptic Opportunities in Reading About Jesus* (Brown Judaic Studies, 177). Atlanta, GA: Scholars, 1989, IX-225 p. Esp. 3-26: "The modern dilemma of the 'synoptic problem'"; 39-41 [13,24-30.36-43]; 60-65 [5,32; 19,3-12]; 93-65 [10,26-33]; 131-133 [12,22-32]; 141-143 [22,2-14].

1990 A Coin of Three Realms (Matthew 17.24-27). — CLINES, D.A.J., et al. (eds.), *The Bible in Three Dimensions*, 1990, 269-282. Esp. 271-275: "The first realm: the Temple"; 275-279: "The second realm: the Matthaean community"; 279-281: "The third realm: Jesus and his movement".

1991a Forgiving at and Swearing by the Temple. — *Forum* 7 (1991) 45-50. Esp. 46-47 [5,23-24]; 47-49 [23,15-24]. [NTA 38, 156]; = ID., *Judaic Approaches*, 1994.

1991b [ὡς] φραγέλλιον ἐκ σχοινίων (John 2.15). — HORBURY, W. (ed.), *Templum Amicitiae. Essays on the Second Temple Presented to Ernst Bammel* (JSNT SS, 48), Sheffield: JSOT, 1991, 330-344. Esp. 334-335 [21,12]; 339 [17,24-27]; 343 [sacrifice]; = ID., *Judaic Approaches*, 1994.

1992a *The Temple of Jesus. His Sacrificial Program within a Cultural History of Sacrifice.* University Park, PA: Pennsylvania State Univ. Press, 1992, XII-209 p. Esp. 91-112: "Jesus' occupation of the temple" [21,12-16]; 113-136: "The sacrificial program of Jesus" [5,21-48; 8,1-4; 10,11-14; 17,24-27; 18,15-35].

1992b Jesus in the NT. — *ABD* 3 (1992) 845-848. Esp. 845-846.

1992c The Purity of Kingdom as Conveyed in Jesus' Meals. — *SBL 1992 Seminar Papers*, 473-488. Esp. 479-480 [11,18-19]; 480-481 [9,9-13]; 484-485 [15,11]; 486 [10,9-14]; 487-488 [27,34].

1992d The Son of Man: Human and Heavenly. — VAN SEGBROECK, F., et al. (eds.), *The Four Gospels 1992*. FS F. Neirynck, 1992, I, 203-218. Esp. 205-207 [10,29-31]; 209 [8,18-22]; 214-216 [Q 12,8-9]; = ID., *Judaic Approaches*, 1994.

1993a God as "Father" in the Targumim, in Non-Canonical Literatures of Early Judaism and Primitive Christianity, and in Matthew. — CHARLESWORTH, J.H. – EVANS, C.A. (eds.), *The Pseudepigrapha and Early Biblical Interpretation* (Journal for the Study of the Pseudepigrapha, SS 14), Sheffield: JSOT, 1993, 151-169. Esp. 166-169; = ID., *Judaic Approaches*, 1994.

1993b Jesus and the Question of Anti-Semitism. — EVANS, C.A. – HAGNER, D.A. (eds.), *Anti-Semitism and Early Christianity. Issues of Polemic and Faith*, Minneapolis, MN: Fortress, 1993, 39-52.

1994* & EVANS, C.A. (eds.), *Studying the Historical Jesus. Evaluations of the State of Current Research* (NTTS, 19). Leiden: Brill, 1994, XVI-611 p. → Blackburn, Charlesworth, Chilton 1994a-b, J.D.G. Dunn, C.A. Evans, S.E. Porter, Webb

1994a The Kingdom of God in Recent Discussion. — *Ibid.*, 255-280. Esp. 267-239.

1994b & EVANS, C.A. Jesus and Israel's Scriptures. — *Ibid.*, 281-335. Esp. 320-321 [Q 3,7-9]; 321-325 [OT/Q 7,22].

1994c *A Feast of Meanings. Eucharistic Theologies from Jesus through Johannine Circles* (SupplNT, 72). Leiden: Brill, 1994, XI-210 p. Esp. 13-45: "The purity of the kingdom" [26,29]; 46-74: "The surrogate of sacrifice" [5,23-24; 8,1-4; 16,17-19; 17,24-27; 21,12-16]; 93-108: "The Passover"; 109-130: "Pauline and synoptic symposia" [26,26-29]; 169-171 [26,29]; 172-176 [17,24-27].

1994d *Judaic Approaches to the Gospels* (University of Florida International Studies in Formative Christianity and Judaism, 2). Atlanta, GA: Scholars, 1994, XII-321 p. → 1991a-b, 1992d, 1993a

1995 & NEUSNER, J., *Judaism in the New Testament. Practices and Beliefs*. London–New York: Routledge, 1995, XIX-203 p. Esp. 115-118; 124-126 [Q 10,2-12].

**CHIRICHIGNO, Gregory** → Archer 1983

**CHO, Byoung-Soo**

1994 *"Mehr als ein Prophet". Studien zum Bild Johannes des Täufers im Neuen Testament auf dem Hintergrund der Prophetenvorstellungen im Zeitgenössischen Judentum*. Diss. Münster, 1994, 229 p. (M. Rese). Esp. 123-150: "Johannes der Täufer im Matthäusevangelium".

**CHO, Tae Yeon**

1992 *The Son of Man Came Eating and Drinking (Matt 11:19): A Study of the Table Fellowship in Qumran and Q*. Diss. Drew Univ., Madison, NJ, 1992, 257 p. (L.K.K. Dey). — *DissAbstr* 53 (1992-93) 1958.

**CHOPINEAU, Jacques**

1978 Un notarikon en Matthieu 1/1. Note sur la généalogie de l'Évangile de Matthieu. — *ETR* 53 (1978) 269-270. [NTA 23, 89] → W. Hammer 1980

**CHORUS, Alfons**

1959 *De vier evangelisten als menselijke typen. Een psychologische kijk op de evangeliën*. Haarlem: De Toorts, 1959, 103 p. Esp. 41-49.
*Die Evangelisten als Menschen. Eine psychologische Betrachtung der Evangelien*, trans. M. de Weijer. Essen: Ludgerus-Verlag, 1961, 104 p.

**CHOUINARD, Larry E.**

1988 *A Literary Study of Christology in Matthew*. Diss. Fuller Theol. Sem., Pasadena, CA, 1988, 476 p. (D.A. Hagner). — *DissAbstr* 51 (1990-91) 898.

**CHOURAQUI, André**

1990 *Les Évangiles. Matthieu – Marc – Luc – Jean.* Turnhout: Brepols, 1990, 425 p.

**CHOW, Daniel T.W.**

1984 A Study of the Sermon on the Mount. With Special Reference to Matthew 5:21-48. — *East Asia Journal of Theology* (Tokyo) 2 (1984) 312-314.

**CHOW, Simon**

1993 The Sign of Jonah Reconsidered: Matthew 12:38-42 and Luke 11:29-32. — *Theology & Life* (Hong Kong) 15-16 (1993) 53-60. [NTA 41, 209]

1995 *The Sign of Jonah Reconsidered. A Study of Its Meaning in the Gospel Traditions* (ConBibNT, 27). Stockholm: Almqvist & Wiksell, 1995, 244 p. Esp. 45-93 [12,15-50]; 147-174 [Q 11,14-35]. — Diss. Uppsala, 1995.

**CHRIST, Felix**

1970a *Jesus Sophia. Die Sophia-Christologie bei den Synoptikern* (ATANT, 57). Zürich: Zwingli, 1970, 196 p. Esp. 63-80 [11,16-19; Q 7,31-35]; 81-99 [11,25-27; Q 10,21-22]; 100-119 [11,28-30]; 120-135 [23,34-36; Q 11,49-51]; 136-152 [23,37-39; Q 13,34-35]. — Diss. Basel, 1969 (O. Cullmann).
F. MUSSNER, *BZ* 16 (1972) 133-134.

1970b Das Petrusamt im Neuen Testament. — DENZLER, G., et al., *Zum Thema Petrusamt*, 1970, 36-50. Esp. 46-49 [16,17-19].

**CHRISTE, Yves**

1973 *La vision de Matthieu (Matth. XXIV–XXV). Origines et développement d'une image de la seconde parousie* (Bibliothèque des Cahiers Archéologiques, 10). Paris: Klincksieck, 1973, 93 p. [NTA 18, p. 381]

**CHRISTENSEN, Jens**

1956 Menneskesønnen gaar bort, som der staar skrevet om ham (Mc 14,21). — *DanskTeolTids* 19 (1956) 83-92.
Le fils de l'homme s'en va, ainsi qu'il est écrit de lui. [26,24.31] — *StudTheol* 10 (1956) 28-39. [NTA 2, 535]

1988 Opstanden på den tredje dag efter skrifterne. — *DanskTeolTids* 51 (1988) 91-103. Esp. 92 [16,21; 17,23; 20,19; 26,24]; 94 [12,40].
"And that He Rose on the Third Day according to the Scriptures". — *Scandinavian Journal of the Old Testament* (Aarhus) 2 (1990) 101-113. Esp. 102; 104. [NTA 35, 762]

**CHRISTIAENS, Marc**

1983 Pastoraal van de echtscheiding volgens Matteüs. Vragen rond de "ontuchtclausule". — *TijdTheol* 23 (1983) 3-23 (English summary, 23). Esp. 3-16 [5,32]; 16-23 [19,3-9]. [NTA 27, 915]

**CHRISTIAN, Paul**

1975 *Jesus und seine geringsten Brüder. Mt 25,31-46 redaktionsgeschichtlich untersucht* (Erfurter theologische Schriften, 12). Leipzig: St. Benno, 1975, XXIX-108 p. Esp. 11-36.77-94: "Mt 25,31-46 – Gerichtsmaßstab für Heiden oder für alle Völker?"; 37-47.94-101: "Die Identifizierung des Königs mit den Geringsten"; 48-56.101-103: "Die Identifizierung des Königs mit den Geringsten im Kontext des Matthäusevangeliums". [NTA 21, p. 84] — Diss. Erfurt, 1971 (H. Schürmann).
H. BOJORGE, *RevistBíb* 42 (1980) 179; J.D. KINGSBURY, *CBQ* 39 (1977) 429-430; O. MERK, *TLZ* 105 (1980) 111-112; J. MURPHY-O'CONNOR, *RB* 84 (1977) 469; L. SABOURIN, *Bib* 58 (1977) 455-457.

1977 Was heisst für Mattäus: "In meinem Namen versammelt" (Mt 18,20)? — ERNST, W., et al. (eds.), *Dienst der Vermittlung*, 1977, 97-105.

**[Chromatius Episcopus]**

1989 *Chromatius Episcopus: 388-1988. Giornate di studio per il 16. Centenario dell'elevazione all'episcopato di San Cromazio Vescovo di Aquileia, Aquileia 23-25 settembre 1988* (Antichità altoadriatiche, 34). Udine: Arti Grafiche Friulane, 1989, 231 p. → di Nicola, Lemarié, Nauroy

**CHROSTOWSKI, Waldemar**

1988a Blasphemy against the Holy Spirit (Mt 12,31 and par.) [Polish] — *Przegląd Powszechny* (Warszawa) 798 (1988) 208-221.

1988b "You are Peter" (Mt 16,17-19). The Biblical Foundations of Papal Primacy in the Church. [Polish] — *Przegląd Powszechny* 806 (1988) 7-23.

**CHRUPCAŁA, Leslaw D.**

1994 Il dito di Dio (Lc 11,20) nell'esegesi moderna e patristica. — *SBF/LA* 44 (1994) 83-110. Esp. 91-95 [12,28]. [NTA 40, 1503]

**CHUNG, Hoon Taik**

1989 *Aan hun vruchten zult gij hen kennen. Een onderzoek naar het inwendig verband tussen geloven en handelen in het evangelie naar Mattheus.* Kampen: Kok, 1989, X-431 p. Esp. 21-37 [structure]; 37-50 [time conception]; 51-102 [Jesus; christology]; 102-112 [kingdom]; 113-163 [law: 5,17-20.21-48; 11,28-29; 16,19; 18,18; 22,34-40]; 165-228 [faith: 13,58; 16,13-28; 21,25-32; 27,42]; 229-282 [works: 3,15; 5,6.10.20; 6,1.33; 7,16-20; 12,33-34; 13; 21,32]; 282-344 [relation works-faith: 5,3-16.17-20; 7,21]; 345-349 [English summary]. — Diss. Kampen, 1989 (H. Baarlink).

**CHWOLSON, Daniel**

1892ᴿ *Das letzte Passamahl Christi und der Tag seines Todes nach den in Übereinstimmung gebrachten Berichten der Synoptiker und des Evangelium Johannis nebst Anhang über das Verhältnis der Juden, Pharisäer und Sadducäer zu Christus, nach rabbinischen Quellen erläutert* [1892; ²1908]. Amsterdam: APA-Philo, 1979, XI-190 p. Esp. 3-4; 114-118: "Parallelen aus der alten rabbinischen Literatur zu Matth. XXIII"; 133-145: "Über das Datum im Evangelium Matthäi XXVI,17: τῇ δὲ πρώτῃ τῶν ἀζύμων".

**CIACCIO, Virgílio**

1985 A vivência das bem-aventuranças como caminho da espiritualidade. — *Convergência* (Rio de Janeiro) 20 (1985) 154-164.

**CIGNELLI, Lino**

1984 Il tema *Logos–Dynamis* in Origene. — *SBF/LA* 34 (1984) 239-272. Esp. 262-266 [CommMt].

1990 & BOTTINI, G.C., La concordanza del pronome relativo nel greco biblico. — *SBF/LA* 40 (1990) 47-69. [NTA 36, 619]

1991 & BOTTINI, G.C., L'articolo nel greco biblico. — *SBF/LA* 41 (1991) 159-199. [NTA 37, 1153]

1993 & BOTTINI, G.C., Le diatesi del verbo nel greco biblico. — *SBF/LA* 43 (1993) 115-139; 44 (1994) 215-252. [NTA 40, 69/1367]

**CIPOLLA, Maria Adele**

1988 Matteo XXVI,70–XXVII,1: Interpretazione ed edizione di un frammento della Bibbia gotica. — *Annali dell'Istituto Universitario Orientale di Napoli* 30-31 (1987-88) 215-236.

**CIPRIANI, Settimio**

1953 "Tu es Petrus". I protestanti e il primato. — *Humanitas* 8 (1953) 1085-1099. → Rich. Baumann 1950, Cullmann 1952

1955   La dottrina della Chiesa in S. Matteo. Alcuni aspetti del problema. — *RivBib* 3 (1955) 1-31; = ID., *Volto e anima della Chiesa*, 1970, 9-33.

1961   Il "gaudio" delle Beatitudini e l'angoscia dell'esistenzialismo moderno. — *Tabor* (Roma) 29 (1961) 340-352.

1967   La confessione di Pietro in Giov. 6,69-71 e suoi rapporti con quella dei sinottici (Mc. 8,27-33 e paralleli). — CANFORA, G. (ed.), *San Pietro*, 1967, 93-111. Esp. 101-102 [16,17-19].

1970a  *Volto e anima della Chiesa. Saggi biblico-teologici sul "mistero" della Chiesa*. Napoli: D'Auria, 1970. → 1955, 1970b

1970b  Pietro nei Sinottici. — *Ibid.*, 35-69; = *MiscFranc* 74 (1974) 318-345. Esp. 330-338 [16,17-19]; = *Pietro nella Santa Scrittura*, Firenze: Città di Vita, 1975, 71-98.

1979   Significato cristologico o anche ecclesiologico nella citazione del Salmo 118,22-23 al termine della parabola dei vignaioli omicidi? — *Asprenas* 26 (1979) 235-249. Esp. 237-240 [21,42]; 244-247 [21,43-44].

1984   Un controverso testo di Matteo (27,9-10) a proposito del tradimento di Giuda. — *Asprenas* 31 (1984) 383-396. Esp. 384-385 [26,15]; 385-395 [27,9-10].

**CIRILLO, Luigi**

1986   Un recente volume su Papia. — *CrnStor* 7 (1986) 553-563. Esp. 555-558, 561-563. [NTA 31, 1089r] → Kürzinger 1983a

1993   I vangeli giudeocristiani. — NORELLI, E. (ed.), *La Bibbia nell'antichità cristiana*. I: *Da Gesù a Origene* (La Bibbia nella storia, 15), Bologna: Dehoniane, 1993, 275-318. Esp. 276-278 [Papias].

**CITRINI, Tullio**

1983   La ricerca su Simon Pietro. Traguardi e itinerari a trent'anni dal libro di Cullmann. — *ScuolC* 111 (1983) 512-556. Esp. 524-528. [NTA 28, 1119] → Cullmann 1952

**CITRON, Bernhard**

1954   The Multitude in the Synoptic Gospels. — *ScotJT* 7 (1954) 408-418.

**CIUBA, Edward J.**

1974   *Who Do You Say That I Am? An Adult Inquiry into the First Three Gospels*. New York: Alba House, 1974, XVII-155 p.; ²1993.

**CLARK, Carl A.**

1960   The Neglected Commandment I (Matthew 22:34-40). — *SWJT* 3 (1960) 61-73. → R. Douglas 1960

**CLARK, David J.**

1979a  Our Father in Heaven. — *BTrans* 30 (1979) 210-213. [NTA 24, 399]
       Notre Père qui es aux cieux. — *Cahiers de traduction biblique* (Pierrefitte) 2 (1984) 16-21.

1979b  After Three Days. — *Ibid.*, 340-343. [NTA 24, 30]

1982   & DE WAARD, J., Discourse Structure in Matthew's Gospel. — *Scriptura* special issue 1 (1982) 1-97. [NTA 27, 501]

**CLARK, K.S.L.**

1974   *The Gospel according to Saint Matthew* (The Student's Jerusalem Bible). London: Darton, Longman & Todd, 1974, 239 p. [NTA 19, p. 264]

**CLARK, Kenneth Willis**

1940R  "Realized Eschatology". [12,28] [1940] —ID., *The Gentile Bias*, 1980, 48-64.

1947[R] The Gentile Bias in Matthew. [1947] — ID., *The Gentile Bias*, 1980, 1-8. Esp. 6 [23,5]. Die heidenchristliche Tendenz im Matthäusevangelium. — LANGE, J. (ed.), *Das Matthäus-Evangelium*, 1980, 103-111.

1966 The Theological Relevance of Textual Variation in Current Criticism of the Greek New Testament. — *JBL* 85 (1966) 1-16. Esp. 8-11 [1,19; 5,47; 12,46; 13,44; 16,19; 17,26; 18,28; 19,9.11-12; 21,44; 27,24]. [NTA 10, 829]; = ID., *The Gentile Bias*, 1980, 104-119. Esp. 111-114.

1972 The Meaning of ἄρα. — BARTH, E.H. - COCROFT, R.E. (eds.), *Festschrift to Honor F. Wilbur Gingrich*, 1972, 70-84. Esp. 74-75; = ID., *The Gentile Bias*, 1980, 192-206. Esp. 196-197.

1980 *The Gentile Bias and Other Essays*, ed. J.L. Sharpe III (SupplNT, 54). Leiden: Brill, 1980, XIV-229 p. → 1940, 1947, 1966, 1972

**CLARK, Neville**

1956 *An Approach to the Theology of the Sacraments* (Studies in Biblical Theology, 17). London: SCM, 1956, 96 p. Esp. 9-18: "The baptism of Jesus".

**CLARK, R.**

1963 Eschatology and Matthew 10:23 (Part I). — *RestQ* 7 (1963) 73-81. [NTA 8, 941] Matthew 10:23 and Eschatology (II). — *RestQ* 8 (1965) 53-68. [NTA 9, 908]

**CLARK, S.**

1963 Matthew. — *A Survey of the Bible*, London: Robinson, 1963, 3-40.

**CLAUDEL, Gérard**

1988 *La confession de Pierre. Trajectoire d'une péricope évangélique* (Études bibliques, NS 10). Paris: Gabalda, 1988, 544 p. Esp. 7-45: "État de la question" [16,17-19]; 54-57 [27,62–28,20]; 63-78 [28,1-8/Mk 16,1-8]; 94-106 [14,28-31]; 106-109 [14,28-31/Jn 21,7-8]; 177-180 [16,13-20]; 186-195.208-227 [16,13-14/Mk 8,27-28]; 196-208 [14,1-2/Mk 6,14-16]; 231-244 [16,15-16/Mk 8,29]; 248-255 [16,20/Mk 8,30]; 255-259.267-275 [16,21-22/Mk 8,31-32]; 288-303 [16,23/Mk 8,33]; 309-388: "Le Sondergut matthéen" [16,17-19]. [NTA 33, p. 383] — Diss. Strasbourg, 1986 (J. Schlosser). → Feuillet 1991 J. GUILLET, *RSR* 79 (1991) 426-427; J. GUTIÉRREZ, *CiudDios* 207 (1994) 196-197; F. REFOULÉ, *RB* 99 (1992) 261-287; J.-M. ROUSÉE, *RB* 96 (1989) 318.

1993 Davies–Allison et le retour de Matthieu. — *Bib* 74 (1993) 97-111. [NTA 38, 142r] → (Davies–)Allison 1988a

1995 Jean 20,23 et ses parallèles matthéens. — *RevSR* 69 (1995) 71-86. Esp. 72-77 [16,17; 18,18]. [NTA 39, 1545]

**CLAUDEL, Pierre**

1968 La formation des synoptiques. Le fond traditionnel et l'apport des rédacteurs. — WEBER, J.J., et al., *Où en sont les études bibliques? Les grands problèmes actuels de l'exégèse* (L'église en son temps, 14), Paris: Centurion, 1968, 135-165. Esp. 137-146.

**CLAVIER, Henri**

1954 Πέτρος καὶ πέτρα. — ELTESTER, W. (ed.), *Neutestamentliche Studien*. FS R. Bultmann, 1954, 94-109. Esp. 94-100: "Aperçu schématique des interprétations"; 101-109: "Le problème linguistique".

1956 L'ironie dans l'enseignement de Jésus. — *NT* 1 (1956) 3-20. Esp. 13; 15-16 [25,14-30]; 17 [11,16-19]. [NTA 1, 24]

1957a Brèves remarques sur les Commentaires Patristiques de Matth. XVI,18a. — *Studia Patristica* 1 (1957) 253-261.

1957b Matthieu 5,39 et la non-résistance. — *RHPR* 37 (1957) 44-57. Esp. 44-49: "Bref aperçu des interprétations anciennes"; 49-56: "Analyse et critique du texte". [NTA 2, 42]

1959a Jésus résistant. [5,39] — *Studia Evangelica* 1 (1959) 435-440.

1959b La multiplication des pains dans le ministère de Jésus. — *Ibid.*, 441-457. Esp. 442-445 [Mk/Mt].

1976 *Les variétés de la pensée biblique et le problème de son unité. Esquisse d'une Théologie de la Bible sur les textes originaux et dans leur contexte historique* (SupplNT, 43). Leiden: Brill, 1976, XVI-424 p. Esp. 158-168: "Le prophétisme dans le Nouveau Testament"; 172-174; 190-192 [5,3].

**CLEARY, Michael**
1988 The Baptist of History and Kerygma. — *IrTQ* 54 (1988) 211-227. [NTA 33, 1075]

**CLÉMENT, Olivier**
1984 Église et vie quotidienne (Commentaire ébauché du "Notre Père"). — *Contacts* 36 (1984) 82-111.

**CLERICI, Agostini**
1994 *Il Padre Nostro commentato dai Padri della Chiesa* (La Parola e le parole, 33). Milano: Paoline, 1994, 154 p.

**CLINES, David J.A.**
1990* & FOWL, S.E. - PORTER, S.E. (eds.), *The Bible in Three Dimensions. Essays in Celebration of Forty Years of Biblical Studies in the University of Sheffield* (JSOT SS, 87). Sheffield: JSOT, 1990, 408 p. → Chilton, Hickling, Lincoln

1995 Ethics as Deconstruction, and, the Ethics of Deconstruction. — ROGERSON, J.W. et al. (eds.), *The Bible in Ethics. The Second Sheffield Colloquium* (JSOT SS, 207), Sheffield: JSOT, 1995, 77-106. Esp. 89-97 [22,16-21].

**CLOER, Ernst**
1967 Theologische Überlegungen zur "Kindheitsgeschichte Jesu" (Mt 1–2; Lk 1–2). — *Katholischer Erzieher* (Bochum) 20 (1967) 388-392, 412-418.

**CLOETE, Daan**
1985 In the Meantime, Trouble for the Peacemakers: Matthew 5:10-12. — *JTSouthAfr* 52 (1985) 42-48. [NTA 30, 567]

**CLOGG, F. Bertram**
1950 Abiding Standards. — *Interpr* 4 (1950) 416-426. Esp. 421-422.

**COASSOLO, Grazia Pia**
1959 "Panem nostrum quotidianum da nobis hodie" in S. Agostino. — RAPISARDA, E. (ed.), *Convivium Dominicum*, 1959, 45-66.

**CÓBRECES, Ignacio R.**
1990 "Los obreros de la viña". Elementos midráshicos en la parábola de Mt 20,1-16. — *Studium* (Madrid) 30 (1990) 485-505. Esp. 489-502: "Interpretación midráshica". [NTA 35, 1142]

**COCCHINI, Francesca**
1982 Un discorso sulla Scrittura per greci, giudeii, gnostici e cristiani; Mt 13,44. — *Studi storico-religiosi* (Roma) 6 (1982) 105-134.

**COEBERGH, Carolus**
1966 Les péricopes d'évangile de la fête de Noël à Rome. — *RBén* 76 (1966) 128-133. → Ruth 1994

**COGGAN, Donald**

1967 *The Prayers of the New Testament*. Washington, CD – Cleveland, OH: Corpus Books, 1967, XI-190 p. Esp. 18-41 [6,9-13]; 41-44 [11,25-26]; 44-46 [26,39.42]; 46-47 [27,46].

1993 Lord's Prayer. — METZGER, B.M. – COOGAN, M.D. (eds.), *The Oxford Companion to the Bible*, 1993, 464-465.

**COGGINS, R.J.**

1990* & HOULDEN, J.L. (eds.), *A Dictionary of Biblical Interpretation*. London: SCM; Philadelphia, PA: Trinity Press International, 1990, XVI-751 p. → R.E. Brown, Catchpole, Stanton 1990a-b, Stevenson

**COHEN, Alain J.-J.**

1974 Réflexions sur le spectacle du sens dans le récit parabolique chez Matthieu. — CHABROL, C. – MARIN, L. (eds.), *Le récit évangélique*, 1974, 137-146.

**COHEN, Jonathan**

1993 *The Origins and Evolution of the Moses Nativity Story* (Studies in the History of Religions, 58). Leiden: Brill, 1993, VII-205 p. Esp. 157-171: "The gospel according to Matthew" [2].

**COHEN, Matty**

1977 La controverse de Jésus et des Pharisiens à propos de la cueillette des épis, selon l'Évangile de saint Matthieu. — *MSR* 34 (1977) 3-12. [NTA 21, 725]
The Controversy over Plucking Ears of Grain: Matthew 12:1-8. — *TDig* 26 (1978) 46-49.

**COHN, Haim**

1968 *The Trial and Death of Jesus* [Hebrew original, 1968]. New York: Harper & Row, 1971; New York: Ktav, ²1977, XXIV-421 p. Esp. 142-145; 163-165; 170-179; 197-197; 217-218; 222-223; 227-230; 261-264; 271-273.

**COHN-SHERBOK, Dan M.**

1979 An Analysis of Jesus' Arguments Concerning the Plucking of Grain on the Sabbath. [12,1-8] — *JSNT* 2 (1979) 31-41. [NTA 23, 826]; = EVANS, C.A. – PORTER, S.E. (eds.), *The Historical Jesus*, 1995, 131-139.

1981a Jesus' Defence of the Resurrection of the Dead. [22,31-32] — *JSNT* 11 (1981) 64-73. [NTA 26, 97]; = EVANS, C.A. – PORTER, S.E. (eds.), *The Historical Jesus*, 1995, 157-166.

1981b A Jewish Note on τὸ ποτήριον τῆς εὐλογίας. [26,30] — *NTS* 27 (1980-81) 704-709. [NTA 26, 451]

1982 Jesus' Cry on the Cross: An Alternative View. [27,46] — *ExpT* 93 (1981-82) 215-217. [NTA 26, 875]

**COHON, B.D.**

1956 *Jacob's Well. Some Jewish Sources and Parallels to the Sermon on the Mount*. New York: Bookman, 1956, 112 p.
R.E. WOLFE, *JBR* 25 (1957) 85-86.

**COINER, H.G.**

1963 Divorce and Remarriage. Toward Pastoral Practice. [5,32] — *ConcTM* 34 (1963) 541-554. [NTA 8, 129]

1968 Those "Divorce and Remarriage" Passages (Matt. 5,32; 19,9; 1 Cor. 7,10-16). With Brief Reference to the Mark and Luke Passages. — *ConcTM* 39 (1968) 367-384. [NTA 13, 160]

**COLE, Charles E.**

1987 To the End of Time: Preaching from Matthew in Pentecost. [21,28-32.33-43; 22,1-14.15-22.34-46; 23,1-12; 25,1-13.14-30] — *QuartRev* 7/3 (1987) 54-73.

**COLE, D.I.**

1964 The Star of Bethlehem. — *Monthly Notes of the Astronomical Society of Southern Africa* (Cape Town) 23 (1964) 152-172.

**COLELLA, Pasquale**

1971a De mamona iniquitatis. [6,24] — *RivBib* 19 (1971) 427-428. [NTA 17, 164]

1971b Cambiamonete. [21,12] — *Ibid.*, 429-430. [NTA 17, 126]

1973 Trenta denari. [26,15; 27,3.5.9] — *RivBib* 21 (1973) 325-327. [NTA 19, 544]

**COLEMAN, Robert E.**

1991 The Promise of the Great Commission. [28,19-20] — *EvJ* 9 (1991) 75-85. [NTA 36, 924]

**COLEMAN, Robert O.**

1962 Matthew's Use of the Old Testament. — *SWJT* 5 (1962) 29-39.

**COLEMAN, R.S.**

1992 The Promise of the Spirit for the Great Commission. — *Evangelical Review of Theology* (Exeter) 16 (1992) 271-283. [NTA 36, 924]

**COLEMAN-NORTON, P.R.**

1950 An Amusing *Agraphon*. [24,51] — *CBQ* 12 (1950) 439-449. → Stuiber 1973

**COLES ROBREDILLO, Lope**

1992 *Jesuological Foundations for a Theology of the Transformation of Society*. Diss. Pont. Univ. S. Thomae, 1992, XXI-272 p. (A. Paretsky). Esp. 27-31 [5,3-9; Q 6,20-21]; 41-44 [11,19; Q 7,34]; 71-74 [8,22; Q 9,60]; 129-134 [12,28; Q 11,20]; 134-136 [11,5; Q 7,22]; 142-146 [15,24]; 146-151 [6,9; Q 11,2]; 161-168 [23,9]; 168-173 [6,25-34]; 174-182 [5,14-16]; 182-189 [5,39-41].

**COLLANGE, Jean-François**

1980 *De Jésus à Paul. L'éthique du Nouveau Testament* (Le champ éthique, 3). Genève: Labor et Fides, 1980, XIII-313 p. Esp. 50-53 [5,21-48].

**COLLIER, Gary D.**

1995 Rethinking Jesus on Divorce. — *RestQ* 37 (1995) 80-86. [NTA 40, 200]

**COLLIN, Matthieu**

1990 & LENHARDT, P., *Évangile et tradition d'Israël* (Cahiers Évangile, 73). Paris: Cerf, 1990, 68 p. Esp. 17-18 [7,12]; 32-35 [11,27-30].

**COLLINS, Adela YARBRO**

1987 The Origin of the Designation of Jesus as "Son of Man". — *HTR* 80 (1987) 391-407. Esp. 401-403. [NTA 32, 326]; = ID., *Cosmology and Eschatology*, 1996, 139-158. Esp. 151-153.

1988 Narrative, History, and Gospel. — *Semeia* 43 (1988) 145-153. Esp. 151-153. → J.G. Williams 1988

1989 The Son of Man Sayings in the Sayings Source. — HORGAN, M.P. - KOBELSKI, P.J. (eds.), *To Touch the Text*. FS J.A. Fitzmyer, 1989, 369-389. Esp. 370-373: "The sayings source and wisdom"; 373-382: "The Son of Man sayings in the history of the tradition of Q"; 382-389: "Q and the Gospel of Thomas".

1990 Eschatology and Apocalypticism. — BROWN, R.E., et al. (eds.), *The New Jerome Biblical Commentary*, 1990, 1359-1364. Esp. 1363.

Escatologia e apocalittica. — BROWN, R.E., et al., *Nuovo grande commentario biblico*, 1997, 1787-1793. Esp. 1792.

1992a  Apocalypses and Apocalypticism (Early Christian). — *ABD* 1 (1992) 288-292. Esp. 289-290.

1992b  The "Son of Man" Tradition and the Book of Revelation. — CHARLESWORTH, J.H., et al. (eds.), *The Messiah*, 1992, 536-568. Esp. 543-547 [24,30/Rev 1,7]; 559-562 [10,32-33/Rev 3,5]; 564-567 [13,36-43/Rev 14,14-20]; = ID., *Cosmology and Eschatology*, 1996, 159-197. Esp. 167-172; 187-189; 192-194.

1993  The Influence of Daniel on the New Testament. — COLLINS, J.J., *Daniel* (Hermeneia – A Critical and Historical Commentary on the Bible), Minneapolis, MN: Fortress, 1993, 90-112. Esp. 96-97: "The Son of Man in the synoptic sayings source"; 98-99: "Matthew"; 110-111.

1996  *Cosmology and Eschatology in Jewish and Christian Apocalypticism* (Supplements to the Journal for the Study of Judaism, 50). Leiden: Brill, 1996, XII-261 p. → 1987, 1992b

**COLLINS, John J.**

1952  Bulletin of the New Testament. — *TS* 13 (1952) 205-219. Esp. 217-219 [19,9].

1954  Bulletin of the New Testament. — *TS* 15 (1954) 389-415. Esp. 392-398 [5,3-10; 16,18; 24,16; 27,57]. → M. Black 1953a, Butler 1951

**COLLINS, John J.**

1994  The Works of the Messiah. — *Dead Sea Discoveries* (Leiden) 1 (1994) 98-112. Esp. 106-112 [Q 7,18-23].

**COLLINS, L.L., Jr.**

1973  *The Significance of the Use of Isaiah in the Gospel of Matthew*. Diss. Southwestern Baptist Theol. Sem., Fort Worth, TX, 1973.

**COLLINS, Oral**

1964  Divorce in the New Testament. — *Gordon Review* 7 (1964) 158-169.

**COLLINS, Raymond Francis**

1964  "Thy Will Be Done on Earth As It Is in Heaven" – Matthew 6:10. — *BiTod* 14 (1964) 911-917. [NTA 9, 529]

1969  Christian Personalism and the Sermon on the Mount. — *ANQ* 10 (1969) 19-30. [NTA 14, 476]; = ID., *Christian Morality*, 1986, 223-237.

1971  The Ten Commandments and the Christian Response. — *LouvSt* 3 (1970-71) 308-322. Esp. 314-315 [19,16-30]; 315-317 [5,17-48]; = ID., *Christian Morality*, 1986, 64-81. Esp. 69-70; 71-73.

1974  The Temptation of Jesus. — *MelTheol* 26 (1974) 32-45. Esp. 35-45. [NTA 19, 962]

1978  The Bible and Sexuality II. The New Testament. — *BTB* 8 (1978) 3-18. Esp. 7-11. [NTA 22, 553]
Human Sexuality in the Christian Scriptures. — ID., *Christian Morality*, 1986, 183-207. Esp. 186-192.

1983  *Introduction to the New Testament*. Garden City, NY: Doubleday; London: SCM, 1983, XXIX-449 p.; paperback 1987; [2]1992. Esp. 128-130: "The synoptic problem"; 130-133: "The sayings source"; 211-213: "Redaction criticism: Mt".

1984  Jesus' Ministry to the Deaf and Dumb. — *MelTheol* 35 (1984) 12-36. Esp. 14-16 [9,32-34]; 16-20 [12,22-30]; 20-23 [11,2-6]; 23-26 [15,29-31]. [NTA 29, 72]

1986  *Christian Morality: Biblical Foundations*. Notre Dame, IN: University Press, 1986, VI-258 p. → 1969, 1971, 1978

1992a  *Divorce in the New Testament* (Good News Studies, 38). Collegeville, MN: Liturgical Press, 1992, XV-389 p. Esp. 104-145.279-297: "The debate reconsidered" [19,3-12]; 146-183.297-309:

"An old saying" [5,32; Q 16,18]; 184-213.309-323: "An exception" [5,32; 19,9]; 214-231.323-327: "The development of a tradition".

1992b   Beatitudes. — *ABD* 1 (1992) 629-631. Esp. 630-631.

1992c   Binding and Loosing. — *Ibid.*, 743-745. Esp. 744.

1992d   Keys of the Kingdom. [16,19] — *ABD* 4 (1992) 31.

1992e   Marriage (NT). — *Ibid.*, 569-572. Esp. 569-570.

1992f   Matthew's ἐντολαί. Towards an Understanding of the Commandments in the First Gospel. — VAN SEGBROECK, F., et al. (eds.), *The Four Gospels 1992*. FS F. Neirynck, 1992, II, 1325-1348. Esp. 1326-1331 [19,16-22]; 1331-1336 [15,1-20]; 1336-1343 [22,34-40]; 1344-1347 [5,17-20].

1993    The Transformation of a Motif. "They Entered the House of Simon and Andrew (Mark 1,29)". — *SNTU* 18 (1993) 5-40. Esp. 19-40: "Matthew" [7,24-27; 10,5-6; 15,21-28; Q 6,47-49]. [NTA 39, 161]

1995    Is the "Our Father" Jesus' Own Prayer? — *Living Light* (Washington, DC) 31 (1995) 24-30. [NTA 40, 167]

**COLLISON, J.G.F.**

1979    The Church in the Synoptics. The Gospel of Matthew. — *IndianJT* 28 (1979) 158-168. [NTA 25, 68]

**COLPE, Carsten**

1969    Der Begriff "Menschensohn" und die Methode der Erforschung messianischer Prototypen. — *Kairos* 11 (1969) 241-263; 12 (1970) 81-112; 13 (1971) 1-17; 14 (1972) 241-257. Esp. 1-17.241-251: "Neuanfang in der Verkündigung Jesu". [NTA 15, 86/798; 16, 492; 17, 1087] → Maddox 1971

1970    Der Spruch von der Lästerung des Geistes. — LOHSE, E., et al. (eds.), *Der Ruf Jesu*. FS J. Jeremias, 1970, 63-79. Esp. 65 [Q 12,10]; 76-77 [12,31-32]; 77-78 [Gospel of Bartholomew].

1971    Traditionsüberschreitende Argumentationen zu Aussagen Jesu über sich selbst. — JEREMIAS, G., et al. (eds.), *Tradition und Glaube*. FS K.G. Kuhn, 1971, 230-245. Esp. 237-238 [11,2-19]; 238-239 [8,20].

1981    Neue Untersuchungen zum Menschensohn-Problem. — *TRev* 77 (1981) 353-371. [NTA 26, 650]

1987    → K. Berger 1987

**COLQUHOUN, Frank**

1984    *Four Portraits of Jesus. Christ in the Gospels*. Downers Grove, IL: Inter-Varsity, 1984, VIII-84 p.

**COLSON, Jean**

1962    Les noces du Christ (Nouveau Testament). — WIÉNER, C. - COLSON, J., *Un roi fit des noces à son fils*, Brugge: Desclée De Brouwer, 1962, 81-165. Esp. 86-95 [22,1-14; 25,1-13].

**COLTON, C.E.**

1960    *The Sermon on the Mount*. Grand Rapids, MI: Zondervan, 1960, 158 p.
        C.A. NASH, *BS* 118 (1961) 176-177.

**COLUNGA, Alberto**

1953    "A nadie llaméis padre sobre la tierra, porque uno sólo es vuestro Padre, el que está en los cielos" (Mt., 23,9). — DÍAZ, R.M. (ed.), *Miscellanea Biblica B. Ubach*, 1953, 333-347. Esp. 340-341: "La paternidad divina en los Sinópticos".

1960    La abominación de la desolación (Mat. 24,15). — *CuBíb* 17 (1960) 183-185. [NTA 5, 401]

1962 Bienaventurados los mansos porque ellos poseerân la tierra. — *Salmanticensis* 9 (1962) 589-597. [NTA 8, 127]

**COMBER, Joseph Augustine**

1975 *Jesus and the Jews in Matthew 11 and 12.* Diss. Univ. of Chicago, 1975.

1977 The Composition and Literary Characteristics of Matt 11:20-24. — *CBQ* 39 (1977) 497-504. Esp. 497-501: "Composition"; 501-502: "Literary characteristics". [NTA 22, 402]

1978 The Verb *therapeuō* in Matthew's Gospel. — *JBL* 97 (1978) 431-434. [NTA 23, 421]

**COMBET-GALLAND, Corina**

1979 Petit tableau des approches structurales de Matthieu. — *FoiVie* 78/3 = *Cahiers bibliques* 18 (1979) 118-122. [NTA 24, 400]

1982 Du champ des moissonneurs au chant des serviteurs. Matthieu 9,35–11,1. — *FoiVie* 81/4 = *Cahiers bibliques* 21 (1982) 31-39. [NTA 27, 518]

**COMBI, E.**

1991 Il discorso della montagna nella catechesi. — *Credere oggi* 11 (1991) 109-121.

**COMBLIN, Joseph**

1960 *Théologie de la paix.* I. *Principes*; II. *Applications.* Paris: Éd. universitaires, 1960, 325 and 419 p. Esp. I, 181-201: "La paix dans l'Évangile de Galilée".

**COMBRINK, Hans Jacob Bernardus**

1968 *Die diens van Jesus. 'n Eksegetiese beskouing oor Markus 10:45.* Groningen: VRB, 1968, 201 p. Esp. 77-83 [4,11]; 97-104 [25,44]. — Diss. Amsterdam, 1968 (R. Schippers).

1977 Structural Analysis of Mt 9:35–11:1. — *Neotestamentica* 11 (1977) 98-114 (addendum, 24-28).

1979 Die vervulling van die Ou Testament in die Matteusevangelie. [The fulfillment of the Old Testament in the gospel of Matthew] — ODENDAAL, D.H., et al. (eds.), *Die Ou Testament vandag*, Kaapstad: N.G. Kerk-uitgewers, 1979, 51-63.

1982 The Macrostructure of the Gospel of Matthew. — *Neotestamentica* 16 (1982) 1-20.

1983a et al., *Guide to the New Testament.* Volume IV: *The Synoptic Gospels and Acts. Introduction and Theology*, trans. D.R. Briggs. Pretoria: N.G. Kerkboekhandel, 1983, XVI-281 p. Esp. 40-45.
et al., *Handleiding by die Nuwe Testament.* Band IV: *Die Sinoptiese Evangelies en Handelinge. Inleiding en Teologie.* Pretoria: N.G. Kerkboekhandel, 1988, XIV-293 p. Esp. 41-45.

1983b Enkele aspekte van Calvyn se uitleg van die Matteusevangelie. [Some aspects of Calvin's interpretation of the gospel of Matthew] — BROWN, E. (ed.), *Calvyn Aktueel? 'n Bundel opstelle*, Kaapstad: N.G. Kerk-uitgewers, 1983, 43-51.

1983c The Structure of the Gospel of Matthew as Narrative. — *TyndB* 34 (1983) 61-90. Esp. 63-69: "The gospel of Matthew as narrative"; 69-73: "'Textual means' of narration and the structure of Matthew"; 73-87: "'Textual message': the structure of the narrative". [NTA 28, 85]

1985 Nuwe-Testamentiese uitsprake oor die (on)ontbindbaarheid van die huwelik. [New Testament statements concerning the (in)dissolubility of marriage] — *NduitseGT* 26 (1985) 131-151. [NTA 30, 335]

1988 Die funksie van die saligsprekinge in die Bergrede. [The function of the Beatitudes in the Sermon on the Mount] — COETZEE, J.C. (ed.), *Koninkryk, Gees en Woord: Huldigingsbundel aangebied aan prof dr Lambertus Floor*, Pretoria: N.G. Kerkboekhandel, 1988, 180-198.

1989 Die evangelie volgens Matteus. [The gospel according to Matthew] — VAN ZYL, A.H. (ed.), *Verklarende Bybel (1983-vertaling)*, Kaapstad: Lux Verbi, 1989, 1-41.

1991a    Dissipelskap as die doen van God se wil in die wêreld. [Discipleship as doing God's will in the world] — ROBERTS, J.H., et al. (eds.), *Teologie in Konteks. [Opgedra aan Prof. A.B. du Toit]*, Pretoria: Orion, 1991, 1-31. Esp. 2-4 [structure]; 4-6 [God]; 6-8 [OT]; 8-20 [christology]; 20-22 [salvation history]; 22-23 [Kingdom of God]; 23-24 [church]; 25-27 [discipleship]; 27-28 [mission].

1991b    The Gospel of Matthew in an African Context - in Dialogue with Chris Manus. — *Scriptura* 39 (1991) 81-90. → Manus 1991b

1992a    Reference and Rhetoric in the Gospel of Matthew. — *Scriptura* 40 (1992) 1-17. [NTA 37, 701]

1992b    Die eise van die regter volgens Matteus. [The requirements of the judge according to the gospel of Matthew]. — *Scriptura* S9a (1992) 1-23.

1992c    Die geboorteverhaal in die evangelie van Matteus. [The birth narrative in the gospel of Matthew] — SWANEPOEL, F.A. (ed.), *Kersfees: Gister, vandag en môre*, Pretoria: C.B. Powell-Bybelsentrum, 1992, 21-32.

1994a    Resente Matteusnavorsing in Suid-Afrika. [Recent research on the gospel of Matthew in South Africa] — *HervTS* 50 (1994) 169-193. [NTA 39, 786]

1994b    The Use of Matthew in the South African Context During the Last Few Decades. — *Neotestamentica* 28 (1994) 339-358. [NTA 40, 149]

### COMFORT, Philip W.

1990     *Early Manuscripts and Modern Translations of the New Testament*. Wheaton, IL: Tyndale House, 1990, XX-235 p. Esp. 31-73: "A description of early New Testament manuscripts"; 78-82 [Mt].

1995     Exploring the Common Identification of Three New Testament Manuscripts: $P^4$, $P^{64}$ and $P^{67}$. — *TyndB* 46 (1995) 43-54.
         C.P. THIEDE, Notes on $P^4$ = Bibliothèque Nationale Paris, Supplementum Graece 1120/5. — *Ibid.*, 55-57.

### COMISKEY, John P.

1972     Begone, Satan! [4,1-11] — *BiTod* 58 (1972) 620-626. [NTA 16, 873]

### CONARD, Audrey

1991     The Fate of Judas in Matthew 27:3-10. — *TorontoJT* 7 (1991) 158-168. [NTA 36, 1283]

### CONDON, Kevin

1980     Apropos of the Divorce Sayings. — *IBS* 2 (1980) 40-51. Esp. 44-46 [5,32; 19,9]. [NTA 24, 962]

### CONGAR, Yves-Marie

1964     Konzil als Versammlung und grundsätzliche Konziliarität der Kirche. — METZ, J.B., et al. (eds.), *Gott in Welt*. FS K. Rahner, 1964, II, 135-165. Esp. 157-165: "Eine Zusammenstellung von Texten, die sich auf Mt 18,20 beziehen".

1972     Die Wesenseigenschaften der Kirche. — FEINER, J. - LÖHRER, M. (eds.), *Mysterium Salutis. Grundriß heilsgeschichtlicher Dogmatik*. IV/1: *Das Heilsgeschehen in der Gemeinde*, Zürich-Einsiedeln-Köln: Benziger, 1972, 357-599. Esp. 571-585: "Die Vorrechte des Petrus nach dem NT" [16,13-19].

1974     Blasphemy against the Holy Spirit. — *Concilium* (London) 10/9-10 (1974) 47-57. [NTA 21, 548]
         Le blasphème contre le Saint Esprit (*Mt* 9,32-34; 12,22-32; *Mc* 3,20-30; *Lc* 11,14-23; 12,8-10). — *L'expérience et l'Esprit. Mélanges E. Schillebeeckx* (Le point théologique, 18), Paris: Beauchesne, 1976, 17-29.

**CONGDON, Roger D.**

1978   Did Jesus Sustain the Law in Matthew 5? — *BS* 135 (1978) 117-125. [NTA 22, 764]

**CONNICK, C. Milo**

1972   *The New Testament. An Introduction to Its History, Literature, and Thought.* Encino-Belmont, CA: Dickenson, 1972, XIV-444 p. Esp. 71-103: "The records"; 104-136: "Jesus and his mission"; 137-169: "The message and the messenger"; 169-198: "The mission resumed".

**CONNOLLY, Dermot**

1957   Matthew and his Gospel. — *Catholic Digest* (Saint Paul, MN) 21 (1957) 43-46.

1967   Ad miracula sanationum apud Matthaeum. — *VD* 45 (1967) 306-325. Esp. 308-314 [11,2-6]; 316-318 [8,17]; 318-319 [8,2-4]; 320-323 [8,5-13]; 323-325 [8,14-15]. [NTA 13, 146]

**CONRAD, Edgar W.**

1985   The Annunciation of Birth and the Birth of the Messiah. — *CBQ* 47 (1985) 656-663. Esp. 659-662: "'Fear not' in the New Testament texts" [1,21]. [NTA 30, 561]

**CONSIDINE, T.**

1956   Except It Be for Fornication. — *AustralasCR* 33 (1956) 214-223. Esp. 214-218 [5,32; 19,9]. [NTA 1, 390] → Byron 1963

**CONTE, Nunzio**

1984   *"La 'ora' in cui il Signore verrà" (Mt 24,44b). I Divini Misteri e l'Escatologia. Domenica I di Avvento – Ciclo A).* Roma: Pont. Univ. Urbaniana, 1984, 687 p. (T. Federici). Esp. 326-364 [24,37-44].

**CONTI, Franco**

1993   Un'analisi di tipo logico-matematico su Mt 12,30 e Mc 9,40. — *RivBib* 41 (1993) 73-74. [NTA 37, 1264]

**CONTI, Martino**

1971   Fondamenti biblici della povertà nel ministero apostolico (*Mt.* 10,9-10). — *Ant* 46 (1971) 393-426. Esp. 395-405. [NTA 16, 861] → 1972

1972   Il mandato di Cristo alla Chiesa (*Mt.* 10,7-8.11-15). — *Ant* 47 (1972) 17-68. Esp. 19-26: "Tematica del discorso missionario"; 26-55: "Il ministero apostolico"; 55-65: "Il dono della pace". [NTA 17, 121] → 1971

1986   La via della beatitudine e della rovina secondo il Salmo I. — *Ant* 61 (1986) 3-39. Esp. 34-36: "Risonanza in Mt 7,13-14". [NTA 31, 346]

**CONTRERAS MOLINA, Francisco**

1988   Las cartas a las siete Iglesias. — *EstBíb* 46 (1988) 141-172. Esp. 163-168: "Concreción de la situación apocalíptica sinóptica" [24,9-13]. [NTA 33, 1317]

**CONZELMANN, Hans**

1957   Gegenwart und Zukunft in der synoptischen Tradition. — *ZTK* 54 (1957) 277-296. Esp. 284-286; = ID., *Theologie als Schriftauslegung*, 1974, 42-61. Esp. 48-53.
Present and Future in the Synoptic Tradition. — *Journal for Theology and the Church* (New York) 5 (1968) 26-44. [NTA 13, 551]

1967   Historie und Theologie in den synoptischen Passionsberichten. — ID., et al., *Zur Bedeutung des Todes Jesu. Exegetische Beiträge* (Schriftenreihe des theologischen Ausschusses der Evangelischen Kirche der Union), Gütersloh: Mohn, 1967, 35-53. Esp. 48-51; = ID., *Theologie als Schriftauslegung*, 1974, 74-90. Esp. 85-88.
History and Theology in the Passion Narratives of the Synoptic Gospels. — *Interpr* 24 (1970) 178-197. Esp. 191-195. [NTA 15, 117]

1968    *Grundriß der Theologie des Neuen Testaments* (Einführung in die evangelische
        Theologie, 2). München: Kaiser, 1968, 407 p. Esp. 115-172: "Das synoptische Kerygma" [164-
        169: Mt]; ³1976, 411 p.
        *An Outline of the Theology of the New Testament*, trans. J. Bowden (The New Testament Library).
        London: SCM; New York – Evanston, IL: Harper & Row, 1969, XVIII-373 p. Esp. 97-152 [144-149: Mt].
        *Théologie du Nouveau Testament*, trans. É. de Peyer. Paris: Centurion; Genève: Labor et Fides, 1969, 390
        p. Esp. 111-164 [157-161: Mt].

1972    Literaturbericht zu den Synoptischen Evangelien. — *TR* 37 (1972) 220-272. Esp. 237-239:
        "Die synoptische Frage"; 239-243: "Die Quelle Q"; 257-263: "Das Matthäusevangelium". [NTA 17, 885]

1974    *Theologie als Schriftauslegung. Aufsätze zum Neuen Testament* (BEvT, 65). München:
        Kaiser, 1974, 243 p. → 1957, 1967

1975    & LINDEMANN, A., *Arbeitsbuch zum Neuen Testament* (Uni-Taschenbücher, 52).
        Tübingen: Mohr, 1975, XVI-440 p. Esp. 51-60: "Literarkritik der synoptischen Evangelien"; 60-67:
        "Die Logienquelle (Q)"; 250-259: "Das Matthäusevangelium"; ²1976; ³1977, 441 p.; ⁵1980, XVI-
        456 p. ("überarbeitet"); ⁶1982; ⁷1983; ⁸1985; ⁹1988, XVIII-477 p. ("überarbeitet und
        erweitert"). Esp. 61-70; 71-77; 276-285; ¹¹1995, XIX-565 p.
        *Guida allo studio del Nuovo Testamento* [⁷1983], trans. M. Pesce (Commentario storico-esegetico dell'Antico
        e del Nuovo Testamento. "Strumenti", 1). Casale Monferrato: Marietti, 1986, XVI-454 p.
        *Interpreting the New Testament. An Introduction to the Principles and Methods of NT Exegesis* [⁸1985], trans.
        S.S. Schatzmann. Peabody, MA: Hendrickson, 1988, XV-389 p. Esp. 45-53; 53-59; 221-229.

1978    Literaturbericht zu den Synoptischen Evangelien. — *TR* 43 (1978) 3-51, 321-327. Esp.
        16-18: "Die Quelle Q"; 35-43: "Das Matthäusevangelium". [NTA 23, 76/406] → Lindemann 1984

**COOK, Donald E.**

1987    A Gospel Portrait of the Pharisees. — *RExp* 84 (1987) 221-233. Esp. 223-226. [NTA 31,
        1042]

**COOK, Johann**

1993    The Dead Sea Scrolls and the New Testament. — *Old Testament Essays* (Pretoria) 6
        (1993) 233-247. Esp. 237-238 [John the Baptist]; 239-240 [Sermon on the Mount].

**COOK, John G.**

1988    The Sparrow's Fall in Mt 10,29b. — *ZNW* 79 (1988) 138-144. [NTA 33, 121]

1993    Some Hellenistic Responses to the Gospels and Gospel Traditions. — *ZNW* 84 (1993)
        233-254. Esp. 242.247-248. [NTA 38, 1150]

**COOK, Michael Joseph**

1978    *Mark's Treatment of the Jewish Leaders* (SupplNT, 51). Leiden: Brill, 1978, XII-104
        p. Esp. 18-28: "The implications of Matthew's and Luke's dependence on Mark for their portrayal of certain
        Jewish leadership groups". — Diss. Hebrew Union College, Cincinnati, OH, 1975 (S. Sandmel).

1983    Interpreting "Pro-Jewish" Passages in Matthew. [5,17-20; 10,5-6; 15,24; 23,2] — *HUCA* 54
        (1983) 135-146. [NTA 29, 79]

**COOLS, P.J.**

1957    De synoptische evangeliën. — *De Wereld van de Bijbel. Inleiding tot het lezen van de
        Heilige Schrift*, Utrecht–Antwerpen: Spectrum, 1957, 750-779. Esp. 750-757 [synoptic
        problem]; 757-760 [Mt]; 765-768 [kingdom]; 771-775 [Sermon on the Mount]; ³1964, 725-768. Esp 725-
        735 [synoptic problem]; 738-742 [Mt]; 755-758 [kingdom].

**COOPER, Eugene J.**

1967    Understanding Sin in the New Testament. — *LouvSt* 1 (1966-67) 298-311. Esp. 301-303
        [12,28; 22,39-40]. [NTA 12, 684]

**COOPER, John C.**

1986 Q (Quelle). — GENTZ, W.H. (ed.), *The Dictionary of Bible and Religion*, Nashville, TN: Abingdon, 1986, 862.

**COOPER, R.M.**

1968 Prayer. A Study in Matthew and James. — *Encounter* 29 (1968) 268-277. [NTA 13, 325]

**COOPER, Thomas** → Navone 1986

**COPE, O. Lamar**

1969 Matthew xxv: 31-46. "The Sheep and the Goats" Reinterpreted. — *NT* 11 (1969) 32-44. Esp. 33-34: "The pericope in its context"; 34-36: "The form of the pericope"; 36-41: "The imagery and language"; 41-43; "The source of the judgment picture". [NTA 14, 146] → Jurgens 1983

1971 The Beelzebul Controversy, Mk. 3:19-30 and Parallels: A Model Problem in Source Analysis. [12,22-32] — *SBL 1971 Seminar Papers*, I, 251-256.

1973 Matthew 12:40 and the Synoptic Source Question. — *JBL* 92 (1973) 115. [NTA 17, 912] → Talbert 1971

1976a *Matthew. A Scribe Trained for the Kingdom of Heaven* (CBQ MS, 5). Washington, DC: Catholic Biblical Association, 1976, IX-142 p. Esp. 11-83: "Mid-point texts in Matthew" [9,10-34; 10,34-39; 11,7-15; 12; 13,1-52; 15,1-20]; 84-94: "The function of other Old Testament texts in Matthew" [1,18–2,23; 4,15-16; 8,17; 11,5; 21,5.41-45; 27,3-10]; 95-120: "Pericopes modeled on Old Testament Passages" [8,23-27; 17,1-9; 19,16-22; 27,26-46]. [NTA 21, p. 84] — Diss. Union Theological Sem., New York, 1971 (J.L. Martyn).

H. BOJORGE, *RevistBíb* 42 (1980) 119-121; J. COPPENS, *ETL* 52 (1976) 391-392; J.-D. DUBOIS, *ETR* 62 (1987) 433-434; R.H. GUNDRY, *JBL* 96 (1977) 605-606; C.J.A. HICKLING, *JTS* 29 (1978) 192-194; M.-É. LAUZIÈRE, *RThom* 77 (1977) 477; R. MORGAN, *ScriptB* 11 (1980) 37; J. MURPHY-O'CONNOR, *RB* 84 (1977) 467-469; J.O. RUSTAD, *CurrTMiss* 4 (1977) 122; L. SABOURIN, *Bib* 58 (1977) 294-295; A. SUHL, *TLZ* 104 (1979) 47-49; W.G. THOMPSON, *CBQ* 39 (1977) 145-147.

1976b The Death of John the Baptist in the Gospel of Matthew; or, the Case of the Confusing Conjunction. [14,13] — *CBQ* 38 (1976) 515-519. [NTA 21, 381]

1983 The Argument Revolves: The Pivotal Evidence for Markan Priority Is Reversing Itself. — FARMER, W.R. (ed.), *New Synoptic Studies*, 1983, 143-159. Esp. 144-148 [13,11/Mk]; 148-150 [14,12-13/Mk]; 150-153 [19,17/Mk]; 153-156 [15,11/Mk].

1989 'To the Close of the Age': The Role of Apocalyptic Thought in the Gospel of Matthew. — MARCUS, J. – SOARDS, M.L. (eds.), *Apocalyptic and the New Testament. FS J.L. Martyn*, 1989, 113-124.

1992 → W.R. Farmer 1992a/93/94/95

**COPELAND, E.L.**

1967 The Great Commission and Missions. — *SWJT* 9 (1967) 79-89.

**COPPENS, Joseph**

1959* & DESCAMPS, A. - MASSAUX, É. (eds.), *Sacra Pagina. Miscellanea Biblica Congressus Internationalis Catholici de Re Biblica* (BETL, 12-13). Gembloux: Duculot; Paris: Gabalda, 2 vols., 1959, 579 and 486 p. II: → Dupont, George, Muñoz Iglesias 1958, Vögtle

1961 Le Fils d'homme daniélique et les relectures de Dan., VII,13, dans les apocryphes et les écrits du Nouveau Testament. — *ETL* 37 (1961) 5-51. Esp. 35-40: "Le Fils de l'homme dans les évangiles"; 43-46: "Textes néo-testamentaires"; 46-50 (Tödt 1959). [NTA 6, 114]

1968 Le messianisme royal. VI. Jésus et l'accomplissement de l'attente royale messianique. — *NRT* 90 (1968) 936-975. Esp. 946-972: "La conscience messianique de Jésus ne réclame pas un accomplissement littéral du messianisme royal". [NTA 13, 836]; = ID., *Le messianisme royal. Ses origines. Son développement. Son accomplissement* (LD, 54), Paris: Cerf, 1968, 159-198. Esp. 169-195.

1974a  *Le messianisme et sa relève prophétique. Les anticipations vétérotestamentaires. Leur accomplissement en Jésus* (BETL, 38). Gembloux: Duculot, 1974; Leuven: Peeters / University Press, rev. ed., 1989, XIII-265 p. Esp. 163-171: "Jésus prophète"; 172-174: "Jésus prophète eschatologique et nouveau Moïse. Les évangiles"; 181-194: "Jésus le serviteur de Dieu" [3,17; 8,16-17; 11,5; 12,18-21; 17,5].

1974b  Les béatitudes. — *ETL* 50 (1974) 256-260. → Dupont 1969a

1974c  Le Fils de l'homme dans la tradition évangélique. — *Ibid.*, 260-263. → J. Lange 1973

1979  *La relève apocalyptique du messianisme royal. I. La Royauté – le Règne. Le Royaume de Dieu cadre de la relève apocalyptique* (BETL, 50), Leuven: Peeters / University Press, 1979, 325 p. Esp. 275-302: "La relecture néotestamentaire de la croyance en la Royauté divine. Sa problématique".

1980  Où en est le problème de Jésus "Fils de l'homme". — *ETL* 56 (1980) 282-302. Esp. 294-297 [Q]. [NTA 25, 1032]; = ID., *La rélève apocalyptique*, III, 1981, 1-21. Esp. 13-16.

1981  *La relève apocalyptique du messianisme royal. III. Le Fils de l'homme néotestamentaire*, ed. F. Neirynck (BETL, 55). Leuven: University Press / Peeters, 1981, XIV-192 p. Esp. 1-21 (→ 1980); 105-107 [Q]; 157-186: "Le Fils de l'homme dans la Quelle" [Q 6,22; 7,34; 9,58; 11,30; 12,8-9.10.39-40; 17,22-37]. → Schürmann 1975b

1983  *La relève apocalyptique du messianisme royal. II. Le Fils d'homme vétéro- et intertestamentaire*, ed. J. Lust (BETL, 61). Leuven: University Press / Peeters, 1983, XVII-269 p. Esp. 139-147: "Les analogies chrétiennes du Livre des Paraboles" [1 Enoch/Mt 13,40-43; 19,28; 24,31; 25,31].

**CORBIN, Michel**

1969  Nature et signification de la Loi évangélique. — *RSR* 57 (1969) 5-48. Esp. 8-9; 13-20: "Le Sermon sur la montagne est une parénèse"; 20-31: "Kérygme et Didachè" [5-7/Paul]. [NTA 14, 136] *SelT* 9 (1970) 340-350.

1981  "Votre récompense est grande dans les cieux". Matthieu 5,12. — *Christus* 28 (1981) 65-77. Esp. 66-71 [5,12]; 71-72 [5,43-47]; 75 [7,12]. [NTA 25, 854]

**CORELL, J.**

1972  La parábola de la cizaña y su explicación. [13,36-43] — *Escritos del Vedat* (Valencia) 2 (1972) 3-51. [NTA 17, 914]

**CORLEY, Bruce**

1992  Trial of Jesus. — *DJG*, 1992, 841-854.

**CORLEY, Kathleen E.**

1989  Were the Women around Jesus Really Prostitutes? Women in the Context of Greco-Roman Meals. — *SBL 1989 Seminar Papers*, 487-521. Esp. 519-521 [21,31].

1993a  *Private Women, Public Meals. Social Conflict in the Synoptic Tradition* [1,1-17; 9,9-13; 11,18-19; 21,31-32]. Peabody, MA: Hendrickson, 1993, XXI-217 p. — Diss. Claremont Graduate School, 1992 (B.L. Mack).

1993b  Jesus' Table Practice: Dining with "Tax Collectors and Sinners", Including Women. — *SBL 1993 Seminar Papers*, 444-459. Esp. 449-450 [21,31-32].

**CORNELIUS, Friedrich**

1969  *Die Glaubwürdigkeit der Evangelien. Philologische Untersuchungen*. München–Basel: Reinhardt, 1969, 96 p. Esp. 21-28: "Der aramäische Matthäus"; 45-59: "Das Thomas-Evangelium und seine Bedeutung für die Neutestamentliche Quellenscheidung, besonders die Quelle Q"; 60-68: "Das Sondergut des Matthäus".

**CORNILLON, Michel**

1969 Les évangiles de l'enfance. — BESSIÈRE, G. (ed.), *Que dites-vous du Christ?*, 1969, 213-222.

**CORRENS, Dietrich**

1963 Die Verzehntung der Raute. Luk xi 42 und M Schebi ix 1. [23,23] — *NT* 6 (1963) 110-112. [NTA 8, 983]

1980 Jona und Salomo. [12,41-42] — HAUBECK, W. — BACHMANN, M. (eds.), *Wort in der Zeit*. FS K.H. Rengstorf, 1980, 86-94.

**CORSANI, Bruno**

1964 Linee di ricerca per lo studio della composizione del Vangelo di Matteo. — *Protestantesimo* 19 (1964) 6-22.

1968 La posizione di Gesù di fronte alla legge secondo il Vangelo di Matteo e l'interpretazione di Matteo 5,17-20. — *RicBibRel* 3 (1968) 193-230. Esp. 199-204 [12,1-8]; 204-206 [12,9-14]; 206-214 [22,34-40]; 214-217 [5,31-32; 19,1-9]; 217-219 [5,21-48]; 219-230 [5,17-20].

1970 → G. Miegge 1970

1972 *Introduzione al Nuovo Testamento*. I. *Vangeli e Atti*. Torino: Claudiana, 1972, 333 p. Esp. 127-169 [Q; synoptic problem]; [2]1991.

1973 → Cuminetti 1973

1975 L'uomo nelle parabole di Gesù. — *L'uomo nella Bibbia e nelle culture ad essa contemporanee. Atti del Simposio per il XXV dell'A.B.I.*, Brescia: Paideia, 1975, 163-170.

1977 "... e su di te come su una pietra..." (Mt. 16:18). — *ParVi* 22 (1977) 73-76.

1982 *Testimoni della verità: Marco, Matteo, Luca. Guida alla lettura della Bibbia*. Torino: Claudiana/Scuola Domenicale, 1982, 345 p.

1987 Il Discorso della montagna nella Bibbia wycleffita e nel N.T. di W. Tyndale. — BARISONE, E. (ed.), *John Wyclif e la tradizione degli studi biblici in Inghilterra. [FS Mary Corsani]*, Genova: Il Melangolo, 1987, 103-142.

**CORTÉS, Juan B.**

1968 & GATTI, F.M., The Son of Man or the Son of Adam. — *Bib* 49 (1968) 457-502. Esp. 462-477. [NTA 13, 837]
    *TDig* 17 (1969) 121-127.

**CORTI, G.**

1956 Pietro, fondamento e pastore perenne della Chiesa. — *ScuolC* 84 (1956) 321-335, 427-450; 85 (1957) 25-58. Esp. 435-440 [19,28]. → Cullmann 1952

**COSTA, Juan Francisco**

1977 *Los evangelios y el sermón del monte*. Montevideo: Banda Oriental, 1977, 96 p.

**COSTANZA, Salvatore**

1959 La quarta petizione in Venanzio Fortunato (Rapporti con Agostino, Tertulliano, Cipriano). — RAPISARDA, E. (ed.), *Convivium Dominicum*, 1959, 87-97.

**COSTE, René**

1985 *Le grand secret des Béatitudes. Une théologie et une spiritualité pour aujourd'hui*. Paris: S.O.S., 1985, 300 p.

1989 *La charte du Royaume* [Sermon on the Mount]. Paris: S.O.S., 1989, 220 p.

**CÔTÉ, Pierre-René**

1986    Les eunuques pour le Royaume (Mt 19,12). — *ÉglT* 17 (1986) 321-334. [NTA 31, 1080]

**COTHENET, Édouard**

1954    La II⁰ Épître aux Thessaloniciens et l'Apocalypse synoptique. [24,1-44] — *RSR* 42 (1954) 5-39.

1972a   Les prophètes chrétiens dans l'Évangile selon saint Matthieu. — DIDIER, M. (ed.), *L'Évangile selon Matthieu*, 1972, 281-308. Esp. 285-290: "Une interprétation: les prophètes comme chefs des premières communautés chrétiennes"; 290-305: "Jalons pour une recherche sur le prophétisme chrétien dans Mt".

1972b   Prophétisme dans le Nouveau Testament. — *DBS* 8/47 (1972) 1222-1337. Esp. 1251-1254, 1258-1260 [John the Baptist]; 1267-1275: "Les données de l'évangile selon s. Matthieu".

1974    Sainteté de l'Église et péchés des chrétiens. Comment le Nouveau Testament envisage-t-il leur pardon? — *NRT* 96 (1974) 449-470. Esp. 465-469 [18,15-18]. [NTA 19, 275] = ID., *Exégèse et liturgie*, 1988, 143-169. Esp. 163-168.

1975    Pureté et impureté, III: Nouveau Testament. — *DBS* 9/50 (1975) 508-554. Esp. 530-540: "Les Synoptiques".

1979    Matthieu (Saint). 1. L'Évangile selon s. Matthieu. — *Catholicisme* 8/36 (1979) 902-929. Esp. 905-907 [structure]; 907-913 [sources]; 913-917 [style]; 917-920 [audience-date]; 920-928 [theology].

1984a   Le baptême selon s. Matthieu. — *SNTU* 9 (1984) 79-94. Esp. 81-86 [3,11-17]; 86-93 [28,18-20]. [NTA 30, 1044]; = ID., *Exégèse et liturgie*, 1988, 23-40. Esp. 23-25; 26-31.

1984b   Béatitudes. — POUPARD, P. (ed.), *Dictionnaire des Religions*, Paris: PUF, 1984, 154; ²1985, ³1993, 191-192.

1984c   La formule trinitaire baptismale de Matthieu 28,19. — TRIACCA, A.M. – PISTOIA, A. (eds.), *Trinité et liturgie: Conférences Saint-Serge, XXX⁰ Seminaire d'études liturgiques, Paris, 28 juin – 1er juillet 1983* (Bibliotheca "Ephemerides Liturgicae". Subsidia, 32), Roma: Ed. liturgiche, 1984, 59-77.

1984d   → Perrot 1984

1988    *Exégèse et liturgie* (LD, 133). Paris: Cerf, 1988, 356 p. → 1974, 1984a

**COTTER, Wendy J.**

1986    "For it was not the season for figs". — *CBQ* 48 (1986) 62-66. Esp. 63-64 [γάρ]. [NTA 30, 1082]

1987    The Parable of the Children in the Market-Place, Q (Lk) 7:31-35: An Examination of the Parable's Image and Significance. — *NT* 29 (1987) 289-304. Esp. 289-293: "The reconstruction of the Q text" [11,16-19]; 293-295: "Interpretations of the parable in recent scholarship"; 295-304: "A new look at an old parable" [significance-application]. [NTA 32, 649]

1989    Children Sitting in the Agora. Q (Luke) 7:31-35. — *Forum* 5/2 (1989) 63-82. Esp. 63-66: "The reconstruction of Q 7:31-35"; 66-80: "Q 7:31-35 as a composite unit". [NTA 34, 164]

1992    The Parables of the Mustard Seed and the Leaven: Their Function in the Earliest Stratum of Q. — *TorontoJT* 8 (1992) 38-51. Esp. 38-41: "The distinctive features of the Q parables"; 41-43: "The character of the images in Q 13,18-21"; 43-48: "The significance of the mustard seed and leaven parables in the context of Q". [NTA 37, 204]

1995a   Prestige, Protection and Promise: A Proposal for the Apologetics of Q². — PIPER, R.A. (ed.), *The Gospel Behind the Gospels*, 1995, 117-138. Esp. 118-124 [Q¹]; 124-129 [Q²]; 129-137 [Q: apologetics].

1995b   "Yes, I tell you, and more than a prophet". The Function of John in Q. — KLOPPENBORG, J.S. (ed.), *Conflict and Invention*, 1995, 135-150. Esp. 136-140 [Q 3,7-9.16-17]; 140-148 [Q 7,18-35].

**COTTIAUX, Jean**

1982 *La sacralisation du mariage de la Genèse aux incises matthéennes: contribution à une théologie du développement dogmatique, à l'histoire de la discipline des mœurs, et aux problèmes posés par l'absolue indissolubilité du mariage chrétien.* Paris: Cerf, 1982, 793 p. Esp. 662-691: "Les précisions matthéennes". [NTA 28, p. 95] → Crouzel 1988

**COUFFIGNAL, Robert**

1989 Le conte merveilleux des mages et du cruel Hérode. — *RThom* 89 (1989) 97-117. Esp. 99-104: "Analyse fonctionnelle"; 105-107: "Le modèle actantiel"; 108-112: "Les structures discursives"; 112-116: "L'interprétation psychologique". [NTA 33, 1115]

**COULOT, Claude**

1979 *Matériaux pour une étude de la relation "maître et disciple" dans l'Ancien et le Nouveau Testament.* Diss. Strasbourg, 1979, 2 vols., 300 and 135 p. (J. Schmitt). → 1987

1982 La structuration de la péricope de l'homme riche et ses différentes lectures (Mc 10,17-31; Mt 19,16-30; Lc 18,18-30). — *RevSR* 56 (1982) 240-252. Esp. 248-251 [19,16-30]. [NTA 27, 949]

1987 *Jésus et le disciple. Étude sur l'autorité messianique de Jésus* (Études bibliques, NS 8). Paris: Gabalda, 1987, 479 p. Esp. 18-40 [8,18-22/Q 9,57-62]; 42-44.59-65 [10,37/Q 14,26]; 68-69.73-75 [10,38/Q 14,27]; 86-88.91-94 [10,39/Q 17,33]; 101-103.109-112.124-126 [19,16-30]; 142-144.152-159 [4,18-22]. — Diss. Strasbourg, 1985 (J. Schlosser). → 1979

1995 "Il vous baptisera d'Esprit Saint". Le logion de Jean-Baptiste sur les deux baptêmes (Mc 1,7-8; Mt 3,11; Lc 3,16; Jn 1,26-27.33). — KUNTZMANN, R. (ed.), *Ce Dieu qui vient. Études sur l'Ancien et le Nouveau Testament offertes au Professeur Bernard Renaud à l'occasion de son soixante-cinquième anniversaire* (LD, 159), Paris: Cerf, 1995, 291-305. Esp. 292-294.297-299 [3,11].

**COUNE, Michel**

1969 Baptême, transfiguration et passion. — *FoiVie* 68/3 = *Cahiers bibliques* 7 (1969) 38-55. Esp. 42-45 [3,13-17]; 47-52 [17,1-9]; = *NRT* 92 (1970) 165-179. Esp. 168-171; 172-173. [NTA 14, 835] → Sabbe 1958, 1962a

1973 Radieuse transfiguration. Mt 17,1-9; Mc 9,2-10; Lc 9,28-36. — *AssSeign* II/15 (1973) 44-84. Esp. 56-63. [NTA 17, 948]

**COURCELLE, Pierre**

1954 Fragments non identifiés de Fleury-sur-Loire. Vulgate, Matth. VIII 28–IX 7. — *Revue des études latines* (Paris) 32 (1954) 93-94.

**COURCIER, J.**

1974 L'analyse ordinale des évangiles synoptiques. — *RSPT* 58 (1974) 619-630. [NTA 19, 925r] → de Solages 1959, Frey 1972, Gaboury 1970

**COUROYER, Bernard**

1970 "De la mesure dont vous mesurez il vous sera mesuré". [7,2] — *RB* 77 (1970) 366-370. [NTA 15, 849]

**COURT, John M.**

1981 The Didache and St. Matthew's Gospel. — *ScotJT* 34 (1981) 109-120. [NTA 26, 358]

1985 Right and Left: The Implications for Matthew 25.31-46. — *NTS* 31 (1985) 223-233. [NTA 30, 126]

**COURTENAY, William J.**

1980 The Lost Matthew Commentary of Robert Holcot O.P. — *Archivum fratrum praedicatorum* (Roma) 50 (1980) 103-112.

COURTZ, H. → Bette 1989

**COUSIN, Hugues**

1971    Le figuier desséché. Un exemple de l'actualisation de la geste évangélique: Marc 11,12-14.20-25; Matthieu 21,18-22. — *Reconnaissance à Suzanne de Diétrich*, 1971, 82-93.

1974a   Les récits de pâques. [28,1-8] — *LumièreV* 119 (1974) 18-34. [NTA 19, 915]

1974b   Une autre exégèse de la conception virginale est-elle possible? — *Ibid.*, 106-111. [NTA 19, 941] → Laurentin 1974

1974c   Sépulture criminelle et sépulture prophétique. — *RB* 81 (1974) 375-393. Esp. 380-381 [27,3-10]; 389-393 [23,29-31]. [NTA 19, 911]

1976    *Le prophète assassiné. Histoire des textes évangéliques de la Passion.* Paris: Delarge / Éd. universitaires, 1976, 247 p.

   *Il profeta assassinato. Storia dei testi evangelici sulla passione*, trans. L. Bacchiarello. Roma: Borla, 1976, 210 p.

   *O profeta assassinado. História dos textos evangélicos da paixão.* São Paulo: Paulinas, 1978, 213 p.

   *El profeta asesinado. Los textos evangélicos de la pasión.* Estella: Verbo Divino, 1981, 262 p.

1988a   *Récits de miracles en milieux juif et païen* (Cahiers Évangile, Supplément 66). Paris: Cerf, 1988, 83 p.

   *Relatos de milagros en los textos judíos y paganos*, trans. N. Darrical (Documentos en torno a la Bibia, 17). Estella: Verbo Divino, 1989, 83 p.

1988b   Marie dans le Nouveau Testament. — *LumièreV* 189 (1988) 5-17. Esp. 8-11. [NTA 33, 850]

1992    "Les yeux levés sur ses disciples, Jésus disait...". — *VSp* 147 (1992) 5-18. Esp. 13-18 [5,3-12]. [NTA 36, 1327]

**COVA, Gian Domenico**

1993    Il profeta e la grande città. Prolegomeni a una lettura biblica dall'annuncio a Ninive al segno di Giona. — MANICARDI, E. (ed.), *Teologia ed evangelizzazione. Saggi in onore di mons. Serafino Zardoni* (Studi e saggi della Sezione Seminario regionale dello Studio teologico accademico bolognese), Bologna: Dehoniane, 1993, 63-80. Esp. 72-77 [12,38-42; 16,1-4].

**COWLEY, Roger W.**

1988    *Ethiopian Biblical Interpretation. A Study in Exegetical Tradition and Hermeneutics* (Univ. of Cambridge. Oriental Publications, 38). Cambridge: University Press, 1988, XVI-490 p. Esp. 46-54 [2,1-12]; 55-62 [26,6-13].

1989    The "Blood of Zechariah" (Mt 23:35) in Ethiopian Exegetical Tradition. — *Studia Patristica* 18/1 (1989) 293-302.

**COX, Dermot**

1976    New Testament Sources and the Religious Life. — *Ant* 51 (1976) 377-393. Esp. 377-379; 383-386 [10,6-10]; 386-388 [10,37-39]. [NTA 21, 905]

**COX, G.E.P.**

1932[R]  St. Matthew. — DAVIES, G.H. - RICHARDSON, A. (eds.), *The Teacher's Commentary* [1932], London: SCM, [6]1952, [7]1955 (rev. ed.), 381-402.

1952    *The Gospel according to St Matthew* (The Torch Bible Commentaries). New York: Macmillan, 1952, 168 p.; London: SCM, 1953; repr. 1956. Esp. 17-27: "Introduction"; 28-168: "Commentary".

   A.C. KING, *ExpT* 64 (1952-53) 171; H. ROLSTON, *Interpr* 7 (1953) 369-370.

**COX, J.J.C.**

1971    "Bearers of *Heavy* Burdens". A Significant Textual Variant. [11,28] — *AndrUnS* 9 (1971) 1-15. [NTA 15, 851]

**CRADDOCK, Fred B.**

1981 *The Gospels* [3,13-17; 7,21-23; 14,22-33; 25,1-13] (Interpreting Biblical Texts). Nashville, TN: Abingdon, 1981, 159 p. [NTA 25, 301]

**CRAGHAN, John F.**

1967 A Redactional Study of Lk 7,21 in the Light of Dt 19,15. — *CBQ* 29 (1967) 353-367 (47-61). Esp. 354-358: "The two accounts and their setting" [11,2-6]. [NTA 12, 196]

1970 Mary's "Ante Partum" Virginity. The Biblical View. — *AmEcclRev* 162 (1970) 361-372. Esp. 363-365. [NTA 15, 130]

**CRAIG, Clarence Tucker**

1951 The Proclamation of the Kingdom. — BUTTRICK, G.A. (ed.), *The Interpreter's Bible*, VII, 1951, 145-154.

**CRAIG, William Lane**

1981 *The Son Rises.* Chicago, IL: Moody, 1981, 156 p.
*Knowing the Truth about the Resurrection. Our Response to the Empty Tomb.* Ann Arbor, MI: Servant, 1988, XIV-153 p.

1984 The Guard at the Tomb. [27,62-66; 28,4.11-15] — *NTS* 30 (1984) 273-281. [NTA 28, 922]

1985 The Historicity of the Empty Tomb of Jesus. — *NTS* 31 (1985) 39-67. Esp. 59-60 [27,62-66; 28,11-15]. [NTA 29, 911]

1989 *Assessing the New Testament Evidence for the Historicity of the Resurrection of Jesus* (Studies in the Bible and Early Christianity, 16). Lewiston, Ont. - Lampeter, UK: Mellen, 1989, XIX-442 p.

**CRAMER, John Anthony**

1840ᴿ (ed.), *Catenae Graecorum Patrum in Novum Testamentum. I. In Evangelia S. Matthaei et S. Marci* [1840]. Repr. Hildesheim, 1967, XXX-499 p. Esp. 1-257.

**CRAMER, Winfrid**

1975 Mt 18,10b in frühsyrischer Deutung. — *Oriens Christianus* (Wiesbaden) 59 (1975) 130-146.

1984 Zur Rezeption der Bergpredigt bei Afrahat. — *Jahres- und Tagungsbericht der Görres-Gesellschaft*, Köln, 1984, 132-133.

1990 Die Seligpreisung der Friedenstifter. Zur Rezeption der Bergpredigt bei Afrahat. — SCHULZ, R. - GÖRG, M. (eds), *Lingua restituta orientalis. Festgabe für Julius Assfalg* (Ägypten und Altes Testament, 20), Wiesbaden: Harrassowitz, 1990, 68-79.

**CRAMPSEY, James A.**

1989 The Lord's Prayer. A Prayer of the Ageing. — *The Month* (London) 250 (1989) 4-9. [NTA 33, 603]

**CRANE, Thomas E.**

1982 *The Synoptics. Mark, Matthew and Luke Interpret the Gospel.* London: Sheed and Ward, 1982, VI-231 p.

**CRANFIELD, Charles Ernest Burland**

1961 Diakonia. Matthew 25,31-46. — *LondQuartHolRev* 30 (1961) 275-281. [NTA 6, 781]

1988 Some Reflections on the Subject of the Virgin Birth. — *ScotJT* 41 (1988) 177-189. [NTA 33, 88]

1990 The Resurrection of Jesus Christ. — *ExpT* 101 (1989-90) 167-172. Esp. 171 [27,62-66; 28,11-15]. [NTA 34, 1103] → Eddy 1990

1994 Who Are Christ's Brothers (Matthew 25.40)? — *Metanoia* (Praha) 4 (1994) 31-39. [NTA 39, 812] → S.W. Gray 1989

**CRANFORD, Lorin L.**

1992   Bibliography for the Sermon on the Mount. — *SWJT* 35 (1992) 34-38. [NTA 37, 132]

**CRANMER, David J.**

1984   Digressions Introduced by "For...". [8,8-9; 23,5; 26,10-11.31] — *BTrans* 35 (1984) 240-241. [NTA 28, 866]

**CRAWFORD, Barry S.**

1978   *Near Expectation in the Sayings of Jesus*. Diss. Vanderbilt Univ., Nashville, TN, 1978, 290 p. (P.W. Meyer). — *DissAbstr* 39 (1978-89) 6180.

1982   Near Expectation in the Sayings of Jesus. — *JBL* 101 (1982) 225-244. Esp. 228-229.232-235.238-243 [5,18.26; 10,23; 23,39; 26,29.34]. [NTA 27, 61]

**CRAWFORD, L.**

1985   Tu es Pierre, et sur cette pierre... — *CahRenan* 33 (1985) 13-16. [NTA 30, 1058]

**CREHAN, Joseph**

1951   Peter the Dispenser. — ADLER, N. (ed.), *Vom Wort des Lebens*. FS M. Meinertz, 1951, 60-67. Esp. 60.64 [16,18].

**CREMER, Franz Gerhard**

1965   *Die Fastenansage Jesu. Mk 2,20 und Parallelen in der Sicht der patristischen und scholastischen Exegese* (BBB, 23). Bonn: Hanstein, 1965, XXX-185 p. Esp. 64-67.89-93.112-115.119-121.128-136.149-151.164-167.171-173 [9,14-17]. — Diss. Bonn, 1963 (K.T. Schäfer).

1967a  Das Fastenstreitgespräch (Mk 2,18-22 parr) bei Beda Venerabilis und Hrabanus Maurus. Zur Charakteristik mittelalterlicher Florilegien. [9,14-17] — *RBén* 77 (1967) 157-174. [NTA 12, 177]

1967b  Christian von Stablo als Exeget. Beobachtungen zur Auslegung von Mt 9,14-17. — *Ibid.*, 328-341. [NTA 12, 870]

1967c  "Die Söhne des Brautgemachs" (Mk 2,19 parr) in der griechischen und lateinischen Schrifterklärung. [9,14-17] — *BZ* 11 (1967) 246-253. [NTA 12, 563]

1970   Zum Problem der verschiedenen Sprecher im Fastenstreitgespräch (Mk 2,18 parr). Ein Blick in die Kommentare der Patristik und Scholastik. — GRANFIELD, P. - JUNGMANN, J.A. (eds.), *Kyriakon*. FS J. Quasten, 1970, I, 162-181. Esp. 163-164.168-173.175-181 [9,14].

**CRESPY, Georges**

1968   Maladie et guérison dans le Nouveau Testament. — *LumièreV* 86 (1968) 45-69. Esp. 46-61: "Maladie et guérison dans les évangiles". [NTA 13, 387]

**CRIPPS, K.R.J.**

1957   A Note on Matthew xxii.12. — *ExpT* 69 (1957-58) 30. [NTA 2, 278]

1964   'Love your neighbour as yourself'. Matthew xxii.39 et par. — *ExpT* 76 (1964-65) 26. [NTA 9, 544] → J.H. Watson 1964

1979   *A Critical Examination of the Sayings of Jesus in the Synoptic Gospels on Reward and Punishment*. Diss. Newcastle, 1979.

**CRISCI, Edoardo**

1988   Un frammento palinsesto del "Commento al Vangelo di S. Matteo" di Origene nel codice Criptense *G.b.* VI. [13,18-19.25-26] — *Jahrbuch der Österreichischen Byzantinistik* (Wien) 38 (1988) 95-112.

**CRISSEY, C.M.**

1981   *Matthew* (Layman's Bible Book Commentary, 15). Nashville, TN: Broadman, 1981, 152 p. [NTA 26, p. 81]

**CRISWELL, W.A.**

1961 *Expository Notes on the Gospel of Matthew*. Grand Rapids, MI: Zondervan, 1961, 168 p. [NTA 7, p. 135]

**CROATTO, J. Severino**

1970 El mesías liberador de los pobres. — *RevistBíb* 32 (1970) 233-240. [NTA 15, 474]

1979 Los oprimidos poseerán la tierra (Recontextualización de um tema bíblico). [5,5] — *RevistBíb* 41 (1979) 245-248. [NTA 24, 785]

**CROCKER, P.T.**

1991 Nets, Styli and Ophthalmology – A Mystery Solved. [7,5] — *Buried History* (Melbourne) 27 (1991) 59-63. [NTA 36, 721]

**CROCKETT, Benny R., Jr.**

1986 *The Missionary Experience of the Matthean Community: A Redactional Analysis of Matthew 10*. Diss. Baptist Theol. Sem., New Orleans, LA, 1986, 232 p. (R.E. Glaze).
— *DissAbstr* 47 (1986-87) 4421-4422; *SBT* 15 (1987) 270-271.

**CROSBY, Michael H.**

1981 *Spirituality of the Beatitudes. Matthew's Challenge for First World Christians*. Maryknoll, NY: Orbis, 1981, IX-244 p. Esp. 1-24: "The relevance of Matthew's gospel"; 25-48: "Whose is the Reign of God?"; 49-73 [5,3]; 74-95 [5,4]; 96-117 [5,5]; 118-139 [5,6]; 140-158 [5,7]; 159-177 [5,8]; 178-198 [5,9]; 199-217 [5,10]. [NTA 26, p. 81]
   J.M. KOLANSKI, *RRel* 41 (1982) 638-639.

1988 *House of Disciples. Church, Economics, and Justice in Matthew*. Maryknoll, NY: Orbis, 1988; Grand Rapids, MI: Eerdmans; Exeter: Paternoster, 1989, XII-345 p. Esp. 21-48.274-283: "The environment of Matthew's gospel"; 49-75.283-290: "*Oikía* in the structure of Matthew's gospel"; 76-98.290-294: "*Exousía* in Matthew's gospel"; 99-125.294-300: "The household churches: rightly-ordered relationships and resources"; 126-146.300-302: "Ethos/ethics: Jesus/Church"; 147-170.303-306: "The beatitudes: building blocks for a house of wisdom"; 171-195.306-310: "The Sermon on the Mount: building a house on the rock of justice"; 196-215: "The call to conversion in a society resisting change"; 216-228.313-315: "A sign of the kingdom in the house church"; 229-267.315-324: "Matthew's message for the third millennium". [NTA 33, p. 105] — Diss. Graduate Theol. Union, Berkeley, CA, 1987 (W.J. Short).
   J.S. KLOPPENBORG, *RelStR* 16 (1990) 333; R.L. ROHRBAUGH, *CBQ* 52 (1990) 552-553; J.G. WILLIAMS, *CRBR* 3 (1990) 193-195.

**CROSSAN, John Dominic**

1968 Structure & Theology of Mt. 1.18–2.23. — *CahJos* 16 (1968) 119-135. Esp. 119-120: "The messianic theme"; 120-131: "The Mosaic theme"; 131-135: "The theology". [NTA 13, 158]

1969 The Presence of God's Love in the Power of Jesus' Works. — *Concilium* (New York) 50 (1969) 65-79. Esp. 67-71 [miracles]; 71-76 [4,1-11].

1971 The Parable of the Wicked Husbandmen. — *JBL* 90 (1971) 451-465. Esp. 451-455: "The synoptic tradition: Allegory"; 456-461: "The gospel of Thomas: Parable". [NTA 16, 887]
   Parables of Action: The Wicked Husbandmen. — ID., *In Parables*, 1973, 86-96.

1972 Parable and Example in the Teaching of Jesus. — *NTS* 18 (1971-72) 285-307. Esp. 287-288 [Lk 10,25-28(Q)]; 302-303 [22,1-10]. [NTA 17, 102]
   Parables of Reversal. — ID., *In Parables*, 1983, 53-78. Esp. 58-59; 69-75.
   Gleichnisse der Verkehrung. — HARNISCH, W. (ed.), *Die neutestamentliche Gleichnisforschung*, 1982, 127-158. Esp. 134-135; 148-152.

1973a Mark and the Relatives of Jesus. — *NT* 15 (1973) 81-113. Esp. 82-98 [Mk 3,20-35/Mt]; 98-105 [Mk 6,1-6/Mt]; 105-110 [Mk 15,40.47; 16,1/Mt]. [NTA 18, 121] → Lambrecht 1974b

1973b Parable as Religious and Poetic Experience. — *JRel* 53 (1973) 330-358. Esp. 352-358. [NTA 18, 90]
   Parables and the Temporality of the Kingdom. — ID., *In Parables*, 1973, 4-36. Esp. 32-36.

1973c  The Seed Parables of Jesus. — *JBL* 92 (1973) 244-266. Esp. 244-261: "The history of tradition" [13,3-8.19-23.24-30.31-32.36-43]; 261-266: "The meaning for Jesus". [NTA 18, 91]
Parables of Advent. — ID., *In Parables*, 1973, 37-52. Esp. 38-44 [13,3-9]; 45-51 [13,31-32].

1973d  The Servant Parables of Jesus. — *SBL 1973 Seminar Papers*, II, 94-118. Esp. 96 [24,45-51]; 96-98 [25,14-30]; 99-100 [18,23-35]; 102-103 [21,33-39]; 103-104 [20,1-13]; = *Semeia* 1 (1974) 17-62. Esp. 22, 22-24, 27-28, 33-34, 34-37. [NTA 19, 920]
Parables of Action: The Servant Parables. — ID., *In Parables*, 1973, 96-120.

1973e  *In Parables. The Challenge of the Historical Jesus*. New York – Evanston, IL: Harper & Row, 1973, XVIII-141 p. → 1971, 1972, 1973b-d

1974a  Parable and Example in the Teaching of Jesus. — *Semeia* 1 (1974) 63-104. Esp. 66-69 [22,34-40/Lk].
Responses: D.O. VIA, *ibid.*, 105-133.222-234; N.R. PETERSEN, 134-181; R.W. FUNK, 182-191; J.D. CROSSAN, 192-221.

1974b  A Basic Bibliography for Parables Research. — *Ibid.*, 236-274. Esp. 236-256: "Traditiocritical"; 256-273: "Structuralist bibliography". [NTA 19, 919]

1975a  *The Dark Interval. Towards a Theology of Story*. Niles, IL: Argus Communications, 1975, 134 p. Esp. 109-119 [22,1-14].

1975b  Jesus and Pacifism. [5,39] — FLANAGAN, J.W. – WEISBROD ROBINSON, A. (eds.), *No Famine in the Land. Studies in Honor of John L. McKenzie*, Missoula, MT: Scholars, 1975, 195-208. Esp. 196-205: "The meaning of the aphorism"; 205-207: "The origin of the aphorism".

1976  Hidden Treasure Parables in Late Antiquity. — *SBL 1976 Seminar Papers*, 359-379. Esp. 370-372 [13,44].

1979  *Finding is the First Act. Trove Folktales and Jesus' Treasure Parable* (SBL Semeia Supplements). Philadelphia, PA: Fortress; Missoula, MT: Scholars, 1979, VIII-141 p. Esp. 73-122: "Loss: Jesus' treasure parable" [13,44-46].
J. GUILLET, *RSR* 68 (1980) 584-585; C.J.A. HICKLING, *ExpT* 92 (1980-81) 88-89; H.-J. KLAUCK, *TRev* 77 (1981) 288-289; J. LAMBRECHT, *ETL* 56 (1980) 446-447; D. NORMAN, *RelLife* 49 (1980) 243-244; R. PENNA, *Greg* 62 (1981) 768-769; P. PERKINS, *CBQ* 42 (1980) 558-559; G.A. PHILLIPS, *JBL* 100 (1981) 646-648.

1980  *Cliffs of Fall. Paradox and Polyvalence in the Parables of Jesus* (A Crossroad Book). New York: Seabury, 1980, VIII-120 p.

1982  Kingdom and Children. A Study in Aphoristic Tradition. — *SBL 1982 Seminar Papers*, 63-80. Esp; 70-71 [18,1-4]. → Patte 1982

1983a  *In Fragments. The Aphorisms of Jesus*. San Francisco, CA: Harper & Row, 1983, X-389 p. Esp. 29-34 [23,13; Q 11,52/Th 39a; 102]; 42-47 [19,30; 20,16; Q 13,30/Th 4b]; 47-50 [12,30; Q 11,23/POxy 1224]; 50-54 [7,12; Q 6,31/Th 6b]; 54-56 [4,17]; 57-66 [24,43-44; Q 12,39-40/Th 21b; 103]; 68-73 [11,15; 13,9.43/Th 8; 21; 24; 63; 65; 96]; 79-80 [12,8]; 85-88 [10,24-25; Q 6,40]; 89-94 [10,39; 16,25; Q 17,33]; 95-104 [7,7-8; 21,22; Q 11,9-10/Th 94]; 104-119 [10,40; 18,5; Q 10,16]; 121-127 [9,16-17/Th 47b]; 128-131 [6,19-20; Q 12,33/Th 76b]; 131-137 [10,37-38; 16,24; Q 14,26-27/Th 55ab]; 137-145 [8,11-12; Q 13,28-29]; 145-152 [18,6-7; Q 17,1-2]; 158-160 [7,16-20; 12,33-35; Q 6,43-45/Th 43b; 45]; 168-171 [5,3-12; Q 6,20-23/Th]; 172-174 [23; Q 11,39-52]; 175-179 [24,27.37-39; Q 17,24.26-30]; 179-181 [7,1-2; Q 6,37-38]; 184-191 [12,22-30; Q 11,14-23/Th 35]; 191-197 [11,25-27; Q 10,21-22]; 197-202 [13,12; 25,29; Q 19,26/Th 41]; 202-204 [19,28; Q 22,28-30]; 205-213 [5,32; 19,9; Q 16,18]; 220-221 [19,24]; 238-243 [8,19-22; Q 9,57-62/Th 86]; 246-250 [16,1-3; Q 12,54-56/Th 91]; 250-255 [15,11/Th 14c]; 257-260 [11,28-30/Th 90]; 261 [22,41-46]; 268-272 [10,16.28; Q 10,3; Q 12,4-5]; 272-276 [18,15.21-22; Q 17,3-4]; 281-285 [13,57/Th 31]; 287-288 [23,11]; 295-302 [18,19; 21,21/Th 48; 106]; 318-327 [18,1-4/Th 22]; 330-341: "Corpus of aphorisms"; 342-345: "Appendix 2: Sequence of Q presumed in this book".
W.H. KELBER, *Forum* 1/1 (1985) 23-30; S.M. PRAEDER, *CBQ* 46 (1987) 784-785; V.K. ROBBINS, *Forum* 1/2 (1985) 31-64; B.B. SCOTT, *Forum* 1/1 (1985) 15-21.

1983b  The Hermeneutical Jesus. [22,1-14] — *Michigan Quarterly Review* (Ann Arbor, MI) 22 (1983) 237-249.

1983c Kingdom and Children: A Study in the Aphoristic Tradition. — *Semeia* 29 (1983) 75-95. Esp. 87-88 [18,1-5]; 89-90 [18,3/Jn 3,3.5]. [NTA 28, 938] → Silberman 1983
Response: R.P. TANNEHILL, *ibid.*, 103-107.

1984 Parable as History and Literature. — *Listening* 19 (1984) 5-18. Esp. 8-15 [21,33-46]. [NTA 28, 899]

1985 *Four Other Gospels. Shadows on the Contours of Canon.* Minneapolis, MN – Chicago, IL – New York: Winston, 1985, 208 p. Esp. 39-52 [22,1-14/Th 64]; 53-62 [21,33-43/Th 65-66]; 77-87 [22,15-22/PapEg 2]; 149-164 [27,57-60.62-66; 28,1-8/Gospel of Peter]; 165-181 [28,1-10.11-15/Gospel of Peter]. → R.E. Brown 1987b
A.J. DEWEY, *Forum* 5/3 (1989) 103-111. [NTA 35, 482]

1986a *Sayings Parallels. A Workbook for the Jesus Tradition* (Foundations and Facets). Philadelphia, PA: Fortress, 1986, XX-233 p. → Duling 1990

1986b Jesus and Gospel. — COLLINS, J.J. – CROSSAN, J.D. (eds.), *The Biblical Heritage in Modern Catholic Scholarship* [FS B. Vawter], Wilmington, DE: Glazier, 1986, 106-130. Esp. 115-118 [18,3].

1987 The Cross that Spoke. The Earliest Narrative of the Passion and Resurrection. — *Forum* 3/2 (1987) 3-22. Esp. 7-11. [NTA 32, 471] → 1988a

1988a *The Cross that Spoke. The Origins of the Passion Narrative.* San Francisco, CA: Harper & Row, 1988, XV-425 p. Esp. 146-147 [26,67-68]; 154-155 [27,27-31]; 155-156 [27,49]; 166-167 [27,38]; 213-214 [27,34.46-49]; 239 [27,57-60]; 267-272 [27,62-66]; 351-358 [28,2-4]; 388-393 [27,51-54]; 397-399 [28,11-15]. → 1987
A.J. DEWEY, *Semeia* 49 (1990) 101-127. [NTA 35, 483]

1988b Aphorism in Discourse and Narrative. — *Semeia* 43 (1988) 121-140. Esp. 123-125 [21,22/Mk 11,24]; 125-129 [Q 11,9-10]. [NTA 33, 563] → Tannehill 1988

1988c Divine Immediacy and Human Immediacy. Towards a New First Principle in Historical Jesus Research. — *Semeia* 44 (1988) 121-140. Esp. 127-136: "Transmissional analysis of an aphoristic cluster" [5,39-42]. [NTA 33, 576] → Funk 1986b

1988d Materials and Methods in Historical Jesus Research. — *Forum* 4/4 (1988) 3-24. Esp. 12-23 [sayings: classification]. [NTA 33, 1079]

1991a *The Historical Jesus. The Life of a Mediterranean Jewish Peasant.* San Francisco, CA: HarperCollins, 1991, XXXIV-507 p. Esp. 427-450: "An inventory of the Jesus tradition". → G.A. Boyd 1995, Fredriksen 1995, Neirynck 1994a
*Jesús. Vida de un campesino judío*, trans. T. de Lozoya. Barcelona: Crítica, 1994, 566 p. → Espinel Marcos 1995
*Jesus. A Revolutionary Biography.* San Francisco, CA: Harper Collins, 1994, XIV-209 p.

1991b Open Healing and Open Eating. Jesus as a Jewish Cynic? — *BR* 36 (1991) 6-18. Esp. 6-7 [22,1-14/Th 64]; 7-8.12-13 [10,1.7.10-14/Th 14]. [NTA 36, 1205]

1992a Lists in Early Christianity: A Response to *Early Christianity, Q and Jesus.* — *Semeia* 55 (1992) 235-243. → Kloppenborg 1992a

1992b Parable. — *ABD* 5 (1992) 146-152.

1993 → Gaventa 1993

1994a *The Essential Jesus. What Jesus Really Taught.* San Francisco, CA: HarperCollins, 1994, VII-199 p. Esp. 145-170: "Notes on texts" [sayings].

1994b The Historical Jesus in Earliest Christianity. — CARLSON, J. – LUDWIG, R.A. (eds.), *Jesus and Faith*, 1994, 1-21. Esp. 11-15: "Q christianity".

1994c Responses and Reflections. — *Ibid.*, 142-164. Esp. 147-149, 156-158.

1995a *Who Killed Jesus? Exposing the Roots of Anti-Semitism in the Gospel Story of the Death of Jesus.* San Francisco, CA: HarperCollins, 1995, XII-238 p. Esp. 177-181 [Gospel of Peter].
F. NEIRYNCK, *ETL* 71 (1995) 455-457.

1995b Commentary and History. — *JRel* 75 (1995) 247-253. [NTA 40, 131r] → R.E. Brown 1994a

CROSSAN, Robert D.

1984  Matthew 26,47-56 – Jesus Arrested. — FRANCIS, F.O. – WALLACE, R.P. (eds.), *Tradition as Openness to the Future: Essays in Honor of Willis W. Fisher*, Lanham, MD – New York – London: Univ. Press of America, 1984, 175-190.

CROUCH, James E.

1991  How Early Christians Viewed the Birth of Jesus. — *BibReview* 7/5 (1991) 34-38. [NTA 36, 706]

CROUZEL, Henry

1963a  *Virginité et mariage selon Origène* (Museum Lessianum. Section théologique, 58). Paris–Brugge: Desclée De Brouwer, 1963, 217 p. Esp. 86-90 [19,12]; 148-152 [5,32; 19,9].

1963b  La parabole des invités aux noces commentée par Origène. [22,1-14] — *AssSeign* I/74 (1963) 67-83.

1966  Séparation et remariage selon les Pères anciens. [5,32; 19,9] — *Greg* 47 (1966) 472-494. Separazione o nuove nozze secondo gli antichi Padri. — *CC* 117/3 (1966) 137-157.

1968  Le divorce pour motif d'impudicité (Matthieu 5,32; 19,9). — *RSR* 56 (1968) 337-384. [NTA 13, 567]

1969  Les Pères de l'Église ont-ils permis le remariage après séparation? — *BullLitEccl* 70 (1969) 3-43. Esp. 6-7 [Augustine]; 18-20 [Chrysostom]; 26-31 [Origen]; = ID., *Mariage et divorce*, 1982, 3-43. Esp. 6-7, 18-20, 26-31. → Moingt 1968

1971a  *L'Église primitive face au divorce. Du premier au cinquième siècle* (Théologie historique, 13). Paris: Beauchesne, 1971, 140 p. Esp. 74-89 [Origen]; 151-156 [Gregory of Nazianze]; 180-187 [John Chrysostom]; 287-291 [Jerome]; 297-303 [Opus imperf. in Mt]; 317-322.340-343 [Augustine]. → Marucci 1990a, Pelland 1972

1971b  Remarriage after Divorce in the Primitive Church: A Propos of a Recent Book. [V.J. Pospishil 1967] — *IrTQ* 28 (1971) 21-41. Esp. 29-39; = ID., *Mariage et divorce*, 1982, 67-87. Esp. 75-85.
Nuove nozze dopo il divorzio nella Chiesa primitiva? A proposito di un libro recente. — *CC* 121/4 (1970) 455-463, 550-561.

1972  Le texte patristique de Matthieu v.32 et xix.9. — *NTS* 19 (1972-73) 98-119. Esp. 100-103: "Les Anténicéens"; 104-111: "Orientaux des IVᵉ et Vᵉ siècles"; 111-117: "Occidentaux". [NTA 17, 906]; = ID., *Mariage et divorce*, 1982, 92-113. Esp. 94-97; 98-105; 105-111. → 1981; → Marucci 1990a

1973  Das Gebet Jesu. — *IKZ/Communio* (Rodenkirchen) 2 (1973) 1-15. Esp. 1-8: "Das Gebet Christi nach den synoptischen Evangelien".

1974a  À propos du concile d'Arles. Faut-il mettre *non* avant *prohibentur nubere* dans le canon 11 (ou 10) du concile d'Arles de 314 sur le remariage après divorce? — *BullLitEccl* 75 (1974) 25-40. Esp. 28-30, 36-39; = ID., *Mariage et divorce*, 1982, 127-142. Esp. 130-132, 138-141. → Nautin 1973

1974b  Le remariage après séparation pour adultère selon les Pères latins. — *Ibid.*, 189-204. Esp. 190-194, 199-203; = ID., *Mariage et divorce*, 1982, 143-158. Esp. 144-148, 153-157. → Nautin 1974

1976  Divorce et remariage dans l'Église primitive. Quelques réflexions de méthodologie historique. [5,32; 19,9]. — *NRT* 98 (1976) 891-917. Esp. 897, 901, 903-904, 912-913; = ID., *Mariage et divorce*, 1982, 165-191. Esp. 171, 175, 177-178, 186-187.

1977  Un nouvel essai pour prouver l'acceptation des secondes noces après divorce dans l'Église primitive. [5,32; 19,9] — *Augustinianum* 17 (1977) 555-566; = ID., *Mariage et divorce*, 1982, 193-203. → Cereti 1977

1978 La indisolubilidad del matrimonio en los Padres de la Iglesia. — GARCÍA BARBERENA, T. (ed.), *El vínculo matrimonial. ¿Divorcio o indisolubilidad?* (Biblioteca de autores cristianos, 395), Madrid: BAC, 1978, 61-116.

1980* & QUACQUARELLI, A. (eds.), *Origeniana Secunda. Second colloque international des études origéniennes (Bari, 20-23 septembre 1977)* (Quaderni di "Vetera Christianorum", 15). Roma: Ateneo, 1980, 403 p. → Gögler, Lies, M. Marin, Sgherri, H.J. Vogt

1981 Quelques remarques concernant le texte patristique de Mt 19,9. — *BullLitEccl* 82 (1981) 83-92. [NTA 26, 96]; = ID., *Mariage et divorce*, 1982, 233-242. → 1972

1982 *Mariage et divorce, célibat et caractère sacerdotaux dans l'Église ancienne. Études diverses* (Études d'histoire du culte et des institutions chrétiennes, 2). Torino: Bottega d'Erasmo, 1982, VII-265 p. → 1969, 1971b, 1972, 1974a-b, 1976, 1977, 1981

1984 Encore sur divorce et remariage selon Épiphane. — *VigChr* 38 (1984) 271-280. → Nautin 1983

1988 Le sens de "porneia" dans les incises matthéennes. — *NRT* 110 (1988) 903-910. [NTA 33, 849r] → Cottiaux 1982

**CRUMP, David Michael**
1992a *Jesus the Intercessor. Prayer and Christology in Luke-Acts* (WUNT, II/49). Tübingen: Mohr, 1992, XIV-295 p. Esp. 49-75: "Jesus rejoices and thanks God for hearing his prayers (Luke 10:21-24)".

1992b Applying the Sermon on the Mount: Once You Have Read It What Do You Do With It? — *Criswell Theological Review* (Dallax, TX) 6 (1992) 3-14. [NTA 37, 1252]

**CRUMP, F.J.**
1955 *Pneuma in the Gospels* (CUA. Studies in Sacred Theology, II/82). Washington, DC: CUA, 1955, 58 p.

**CRUZ HERNÁNDEZ, Miguel**
1990 El "Padrenuestro" de Jesús de Nazaret. — *Religión y Cultura* (Madrid) 36 (1990) 61-66. [NTA 35, 133]

**CRYER, Frederick H.**
1993 Eben Bohan. Det længe savnede hebræiske Matthæusevangelium? [Eben Bohan. The long lost Hebrew Gospel of Matthew?] — *DanskTeolTids* 56 (1993) 209-215. [NTA 38, 1351] → G. Howard 1987

**CULBERTSON, Philip**
1988 Reclaiming the Matthean Vineyard Parables. [20,1-16; 21,28-32.33-46] — *Encounter* 49 (1988) 257-283. [NTA 33, 615]

1995 *A Word Fitly Spoken: Context, Transmission, and Adoption of the Parables of Jesus* (SUNY Series in Religious Studies). Albany, NY: State University of New York Press, 1995, XVI-390 p.

**CULLMANN, Oscar**
1948R *Die Tauflehre des Neuen Testaments. Erwachsenen- und Kindertaufe* [1948] (ATANT, 12). Zürich: Zwingli, ²1958, 76 p. Esp. 11-12 [3,16-17; 12,17]; 66-70 [3,14].
Le baptême des enfants et la doctrine biblique du baptême [1948]. — ID., *Des sources de l'Évangile à la formation de la théologie chrétienne*, Neuchâtel-Paris: Delachaux et Niestlé, 1969, 97-148.
*Baptism in the New Testament*, trans. J.K.S. Reid (Studies in Biblical Theology, 1). London: SCM, 1950, 84 p. Esp. 16-17; 75-77 [3,14]; ¹¹1978.
Trans. Swedish 1952; Italian 1971.

1950*  & MENOUD, P. (eds.), *Aux sources de la tradition chrétienne. Mélanges offerts à Maurice Goguel à l'occasion de son soixante-dixième anniversaire* (Bibliothèque théologique). Neuchâtel-Paris: Delachaux & Niestlé, 1950, XVI-280 p. → Eppel, Héring, Reicke, K.L. Schmidt

1952   *Petrus. Jünger – Apostel – Märtyrer. Das historische und das theologische Petrusproblem.* Zürich: Zwingli, 1952, 282 p.; Zürich–Stuttgart: Zwingli, ²1960, 287 p. ("umgearbeitet und ergänzt"). Esp. 18-34: "Petrus der Jünger"; 35-77: "Petrus der Apostel"; 179-271: "Die exegetisch-theologische Frage" [16,17-19]; (Siebenstern-Taschenbuch, 90-91), München–Hamburg: Siebenstern Taschenbuch Verlag, 1967, 281 p. → Cipriani 1953, Citrini 1983, Corti 1956, Fernández Jiménez 1957, Gaechter 1953b, Gilg 1955, Javierre 1954, O. Karrer 1953, Lattanzi 1957, Meinertz 1953a, Molland 1954, Vögtle 1954

    C.K. BARRETT, *JTS* 4 (1953) 311-313; M. BURROWS, *JBL* 73 (1954) 48-50; F.W. DANKBAAR, *NTT* 7 (1952-53) 307-308; E. FASCHER, *Zeitschrift für Kirchengeschichte* (Stuttgart) 64 (1952-53) 334-338; R.M. GRANT, *TTod* 10 (1953) 271-273; S.L. GREENSLADE, *ScotJT* 6 (1953) 203-207; K. HEUSSI, *Deutsche Literaturzeitung* (Berlin) 74 (1953) 273-275; G. HILLERDAL, *SvenskTKvart* 29 (1953) 139-140; J. MULDERS, *Bijdragen* 17 (1956) 221-222; J. MUNCK, *DanskTeolTids* 19 (1956) 115-121; F. ORTIZ DE URTARAN, *Lumen* (Vitoria) 3 (1954) 350-361; K.H. SCHELKLE, *TQ* 133 (1953) 103-104; H.J. SCHOEPS, *ZRelGeist* 5 (1953) 80-81; E. TOMASZEWSKI, *RuBi* 7 (1954) 220-227.
    *BibOr* 5 (1963) 195-196; S. AALEN, *TidsTeolKirk* 34 (1963) 194-195; P. BENOIT, *RB* 69 (1962) 442-443; H. FRIES, *MüTZ* 15 (1964) 154-155; F.W. GROSHEIDE, *GTT* 61 (1961) 62-63; E. NEUHÄUSLER, *ZMiss* 48 (1964) 236-238; E. RASCO, *Greg* 44 (1963) 881; B. STEIERT, *FZPT* 10 (1963) 344-345; A. VIARD, *RSPT* 46 (1962) 268-270; E.A. WEIS, *TS* 23 (1962) 280-282.

    *Saint Pierre. Disciple – Apôtre – Martyr. Histoire et théologie*, trans. É. Trocmé (Bibliothèque théologique). Neuchâtel–Paris: Delachaux & Niestlé, 1952, 229 p. Esp. 13-27; 28-60; 139-214. → Beaupère 1955, P. Benoit 1953c, P. Bonnard 1953a, F.-M. Braun 1953, Dejaifve 1953, Goguel 1955, Journet 1953, J. Schmitt 1954
    M.-É. BOISMARD, *LumièreV* 11 (1953) 194-198; *VSp* 89 (1953) 429-430; M. BOUTTIER, *FoiVie* 51 (1953) 497-517; L. BOUYER, *BibVieChrét* 2 (1953) 119-121; L. CERFAUX, *RHE* 48 (1953) 809-813; J. COPPENS, *ETL* 29 (1953) 558; G.M. GAGOV, *MiscFranc* 55 (1955) 283-285; J. GIBLET, *CollMech* 23 (1953) 598-604; B.M. LEMEER, *Ang* 31 (1954) 161-179; G. MITCHELL, *IrTQ* 21 (1954) 201-212; C. SPICQ, *RSPT* 37 (1953) 180-183.

    *Peter. Disciple – Apostle – Martyr. A Historical and Theological Study*, trans. F.V. Filson. London: SCM; Philadelphia, PA: Westminster, 1953, 252 p.; ²1958. Esp. 17-32; 33-69; 155-238. → Butler 1958, Flood 1958, Gundry 1964
    J.W. BAILEY, *JBR* 22 (1954) 211-212; F.F. BRUCE, *EvQ* 26 (1954) 45-46; R.H. FULLER, *Theology* 57 (1954) 28-30; A.H.N. GREEN-ARMYTAGE, *DownR* 72 (1954) 201-204; F. JOHNSTON, *CanJournTheol* 1 (1955) 53-55; J.E. JONES, *RExp* 51 (1954) 583-584; G.W.H. LAMPE, *ChurchQR* 155 (1954) 176-178; J.F. MCCONNELL, *CBQ* 16 (1954) 362-366; F.X. MURPHY, *IrEcclRec* 81 (1954) 436-443; W. NEIL, *ScotJT* 7 (1954) 207-210; E.A. RYAN, *TS* 15 (1954) 129-130; K. SMYTH, *Studies* 44 (1954) 271-284; N.B. STONEHOUSE, *WestTJ* 16 (1954) 183-189; V. TAYLOR, *ExpT* 66 (1954-55) 7; A. WIKGREN, *JRel* 35 (1955) 252-254.
    F.E. ELMO, *DunRev* 3 (1963) 255-258; S. LESSLY, *JRel* 43 (1963) 345; A.P. O'HAGAN, *AusBR* 11 (1963) 60-61.

    *San Pietro. Discepolo – Apostolo – Martire. — ID.*, et al., *Il primato di Pietro nel pensiero contemporaneo*, trans. G. Conte, Bologna: Il Mulino, 1965, 1-349.

    Trans. Swedish 1953, ²1956; Japanese 1965; Catalan 1967.

1957a  *Die Christologie des Neuen Testaments.* Tübingen: Mohr, 1957, VIII-352 p.; ²1958; ³1963. Esp. 11-49: "Jesus der Prophet"; 50-81: "Jesus der leidende Gottesknecht"; 111-137: "Jesus der Messias"; 138-198: "Jesus der Menschensohn"; 200-244: "Jesus der Herr"; 276-313: "Jesus der Gottessohn".
    *Christologie du Nouveau Testament*, trans. J.J. von Allmen & D. Appia (Bibliothèque théologique). Neuchâtel–Paris: Delachaux & Niestlé, 1958, ²1966, ³1968, 300 p. Esp. 18-47; 48-73; 97-117; 118-166; 169-205; 234-265.
    *The Christology of the New Testament*, trans. S.C. Guthrie & C.A.M. Hall (The New Testament Library). London: SCM; Philadelphia, PA: Westminster, 1959; ²1963, XVII-346 p. Esp. 13-50; 51-82; 111-136; 137-192; 195-237; 270-305.
    *Cristologia del Nuovo Testamento*, trans. M. Ravà & A. Soggin. Bologna: Il Mulino, 1970, 507 p.

1957b Que signifie le sel dans la parabole de Jésus? Les évangélistes, premiers commentateurs du logion. — *RHPR* 37 (1957) 36-43. Esp. 41-43 [5,13]. [NTA 2, 33]; = ID., *La foi et le culte de l'Église primitive*, Neuchâtel–Paris: Delachaux & Niestlé, 1963, 211-220. Esp. 218-220.

Das Gleichnis vom Salz. Zur frühesten Kommentierung eines Herrenwortes durch die Evangelisten. — ID., *Vorträge und Aufsätze*, 1966, 192-201. Esp. 199-201.

1959a L'apôtre Pierre instrument du diable et instrument de Dieu. La place de Matt. 16:16–19 dans la tradition primitive. — HIGGINS, A.J.B. (ed.), *New Testament Essays*. FS T.W. Manson, 1959, 94-105.

Petrus, Werkzeug des Teufels und Werkzeug Gottes. Die Stellung von Mt. 16,17-19 in der ältesten Überlieferung. — ID., *Vorträge und Aufsätze*, 1966, 202-213.

1959b Kindheitsevangelien. — HENNECKE, E. – SCHNEEMELCHER, W. (eds.), *Neutestamentliche Apokryphen*, I, ³1959, 272-311 (ET, 363-417). → 1987

1960 Das Thomasevangelium und die Frage nach dem Alter der in ihm enthaltenen Tradition. — *TLZ* 85 (1960) 321-334. Esp. 330.331-335. [NTA 5, 541]; = ID., *Vorträge und Aufsätze*, 1966, 566-588. Esp. 581.582-588. → North 1962

*TDig* 9 (1961) 175-181.

The Gospel of Thomas and the Problem of the Age of the Tradition Contained Therein. A Survey. — *Interpr* 16 (1962) 418-438. Esp. 431-432.433-438. [NTA 3, 929]

1962 Le douzième apôtre. [10,2-4] — *RHPR* 42 (1962) 133-140. [NTA 7, 506]

Der zwölfte Apostel. — ID., *Vorträge und Aufsätze*, 1966, 214-222.

1966a *Le Nouveau Testament* (Que sais-je?, 1231). Paris: PUF, 1966, 127 p. Esp. 21-26; ²1967; ³1976; ⁴1982; ⁶1991.

*The New Testament. An Introduction for the General Reader*, trans. D. Pardee. Philadelphia, PA: Westminster; London: SCM, 1968, 138 p.

*Einführung in das Neue Testament*, trans. I. Vogelsanger-de Roche (Siebenstern-Taschenbuch, 115). München–Hamburg: Siebenstern Taschenbuch Verlag, 1968, 155 p. Esp. 34-39; ²1984.

*Introduzione al Nuovo Testamento* (Saggi, 73). Bologna: Il Mulino, 1968, 160 p.

*El Nuevo Testamento*, trans. M. Mayoral & A. Amorós (El futuro de la verdad, 42). Madrid: Taurus, 1971, 196 p.

Trans. Japanese 1967; Polish 1968.

1966b *Vorträge und Aufsätze 1925-1962*, ed. K. Fröhlich. Tübingen: Mohr; Zürich: Zwingli, 1966, 723 p. → 1957b, 1959a, 1960, 1962

1970 *Jesus und die Revolutionären seiner Zeit. Gottesdienst, Gesellschaft, Politik*. Tübingen: Mohr, 1970, 82 p.

*Jésus et les révolutionnaires de son temps. Culte, société, politique*. Neuchâtel: Delachaux & Niestlé, 1970, 87 p.; ²1971.

*Jesus and the Revolutionaries*, trans. G. Putnam. New York: Harper, 1970, XI-84 p.

*Gesù e i rivoluzionari del suo tempo. Culto, società, politica*, trans. G. Stella. Brescia: Morcelliana, 1971, 79 p.

*Jesús y los revolucionarios de su tiempo. Culto, sociedad, política*, trans. D.E. Requena Calvo. Madrid: Studium, 1971, 76 p.; ²1973.

Trans. Swedish 1970; Portuguese 1972.

1987 Kindheitsevangelien. — HENNECKE, E. – SCHNEEMELCHER, W. (eds.), *Neutestamentliche Apokryphen*, I, ⁵1987, 330-372. → 1959b

1992 Beten und Sorgen. Zur vierten Bitte des Vaterunsers. [6,11] — *TZ* 48 (1992) 62-64.

1994 *Das Gebet im Neuen Testament. Zugleich ein Versuch einer vom Neuen Testament aus zu erteilenden Antwort auf heutige Fragen*. Tübingen: Mohr, 1994, 194 p.

*Prayer in the New Testament*, trans. J. Bowden (Overtures to Biblical Theology). Minneapolis, MN: Fortress, 1995, XVII-190 p.

*La prière dans le Nouveau Testament. Essai de réponse à des questions contemporaines* (Théologies). Paris: Cerf, 1995, 260 p.

CULVER, Robert Duncan
1967   What Is the Church's Commission? Some Exegetical Issues in Matthew 28:16-20. —
       *BEvTS* 10 (1967) 115-126. [NTA 12, 169]
       What Is the Church's Commission? — *BS* 125 (1968) 239-253. [NTA 13, 180]

CUMINETTI, Mario
1973   Commento a Matteo. [traduzione B. Corsani] — TOURN, G., et al., *Evangelo secondo
       Matteo*, 1973, 97-315.
1985   "Ero in carcere e siete venuti a trovarmi" Mt 25,36. — *Servitium* 39 (1985) 5-11.

CUMMINGS, J.T.
1980   The Tassel of His Cloak: Mark, Luke, Matthew – and Zechariah. [9,20] — LIVING-
       STONE, E.A. (ed.), *Studia Biblica 1978*, II, 1980, 47-61.

CUNNINGHAM, A.
1995   *The New Testament Text of Saint Cyril of Alexandria.* Diss. Manchester, 1995 (C.M.
       Tuckett).

CUNNINGHAM, Philip A.
1988   *Jesus and the Evangelists. The Ministry of Jesus and Its Portrayal in the Synoptic
       Gospels.* New York – Mahwah, NJ: Paulist, 1988, X-240 p. Esp. 46-78: "The Matthean Jesus:
       wisdom of God incarnate"; 117-118; [2]1993.
1993   The Synoptic Gospels and Their Presentation of Judaism. — EFROYMSON, D.P., et al.
       (eds.), *Within Context. Essays on Jews and Judaism in the New Testament*,
       Philadelphia, PA: American Interfaith Institute, 1993, 41-6. Esp. 51-57: "The gospel of
       Matthew".

CUNNINGHAM, Scott
1986   The Synoptic Problem. A Summary of the Leading Theories. — *African Journal of
       Biblical Studies* (Ibadan, Nigeria) 1 (1986) 48-58. Esp. 49-51 [Mk priority]; 51-52 [Q]; 52-55
       [Griesbach]. [NTA 33, 102]
1987   & BOCK, D.L., Is Matthew Midrash? — *BS* 144 (1987) 157-180. [NTA 31, 1049]

CURETON, Kenneth M.
1993   *Jesus as Son and Servant. An Investigation of the Baptism and Testing Narratives and
       Their Significance for Cohesion, Plot, and Christology in Matthew* [3,7-12; 4,1-11]. Diss.
       Southwestern Baptist Theol. Sem., Fort Worth, TX, 1993, 353 p. (L. Cranford). —
       *DissAbstr* 54 (1993-94) 1407.

CURRIE, Stuart D.
1964   Matthew 5:39a. Resistance or Protest? — *HTR* 57 (1964) 140-145. [NTA 9, 148]

CURTI, Carmelo
1968a  (ed.), *Due commentari inediti di Salonio ai Vangeli di Giovanni e di Matteo. Tradizione
       manoscritta, fonti, autore.* Torino: Bottega d'Erasmo, 1968, 70 p.
       E. GRIFFE, *BullLitEccl* 70 (1969) 71-72; R. ÉTAIX, *RHE* 65 (1970) 133-135; *Bulletin des Facultés
       catholiques de Lyon* 45 (1968) 67-68; A. PENNA, *RivBib* 18 (1970) 310-313.
1968b  (ed.), *Salonii, episcopi genavensis, De Evangelio Iohannis. De Evangelio Matthaei.*
       Torino: Bottega d'Erasmo, 1968, 160 p.
       E. GRIFFE, *BullLitEccl* 70 (1969) 71-72; A. PENNA, *RivBib* 18 (1970) 310-313.

CURTIS, Arthur H.
1954   *The Vision and Mission of Jesus. A Literary and Critical Investigation Based Specially
       upon the Baptismal and Temptation Narratives and Their Old Testament Background*
       [3,13-17; 4,1-11]. Edinburgh: Clark, 1954, LIII-388 p.

**CURTIS, K. Peter G.**

1972 Three Points of Contact between Matthew and John in the Burial and Resurrection Narratives. — *JTS* 23 (1972) 440-444. [NTA 17, 523]

1973 In Support of Q. — *ExpT* 84 (1972-73) 309-310. [NTA 18, 450]

**CURTIS, P.**

1970 The Biblical Work of Doctor Farrer. — *Theology* 73 (1970) 292-301. [NTA 15, 38] → Farrer 1954-55

**CUTRONE, Emmanuel J.**

1993 The Lord's Prayer and the Eucharist. The Syrian Tradition. — CARR, E., et al. (eds.), *Εὐλογήμα. Studies in Honor of Robert Taft* (Studia Anselmiana, 110; Analecta Liturgica, 17), Roma: Pont. Ateneo S. Anselmo, 1993, 93-106.

**CUVILLIER, Élian**

1991 *Parabolē* dans la tradition synoptique. — *ETR* 66 (1991) 25-44. Esp. 37-40: "*Parabolē* dans l'évangile de Matthieu". [NTA 36, 687]

1992a Marc, Justin, Thomas et les autres. Variations autour de la péricope du denier à César. — *ETR* 67 (1992) 329-344. Esp. 334-336 [22,15-22]. [NTA 37, 180]

1992b Tradition et rédaction en Marc 7:1-23. — *NT* 34 (1992) 169-192. Esp. 170-171: "Les traditions parallèles" [15,1-20]. [NTA 37, 173]

1993a *Le concept de παραβολή dans le second évangile. Son arrière-plan littéraire, sa signification dans le cadre de la rédaction marcienne, son utilisation dans la tradition de Jésus* (Études bibliques, NS 19). Paris: Gabalda, 1993, 282 p. Esp. 125-134 [12,22-32/Mk]; 212-216: "Παραβολή dans l'évangile de Matthieu". — Diss. Montpellier, 1991 (F. Vouga).

1993b Matthieu et le judaïsme: chronique d'une rupture annoncée. — *FoiVie* 92/5 = *Cahiers bibliques* 32 (1993) 41-54. Esp. 43-45; 45-47 [10]; 47-51: "La narration évangélique"; 51-52 [23]. [NTA 38, 741]

1994 *Qui donc es-tu Marie? Les différents visages de la mère de Jésus dans le Nouveau Testament.* Poliez-le-Grand: Éd. du Moulin, 1994, 100 p.

1995 Le baptême chrétien dans le Nouveau Testament: Éléments de réflexion. — *ETR* 70 (1995) 161-177. Esp. 172-174 [28,16-20].

**CYSTER, R.F.**

1961 The Lord's Prayer and the Exodus Tradition. — *Theology* 64 (1961) 377-381. [NTA 6, 453]

**CYWINSKI, E.**

1958 A Tentação de Jesus, Mt 4,1-11 par. — *RevistCuBíb* 2 (1958) 137-148.

**CZAJKÓWSKI, Michal**

1994 Czy jest antyzydowska Ewangelia najbardziej zydowska? [Is the most Jewish gospel the most anti-Jewish?] — *CollTheol* 64/2 (1994) 43-52. [NTA 39, 787]

**CZARNIAK, Władysław**

1986 *Sprawiedliwość w nauczaniu św. Pawła i w Ewangelii św. Mateusza* (La justice dans l'enseignement de saint Paul et dans l'évangile de saint Matthieu). Diss. Lublin, 1986, XXIV-266 p. (H. Langkammer).

**CZERSKI, Janusz**

1969 Chrystocentryzm Kościola w Ewangelii św. Mateusza. — *CollTheol* 39/3 (1969) 35-48. [NTA 14, 845]
Christozentrische Ekklesiologie im Matthäusevangelium. — *BibLeb* 12 (1971) 55-66.

**DAHLBERG, Bruce T.**
1975 The Typological Use of Jeremiah 1:4-19 in Matthew 16:13-23. — *JBL* 94 (1975) 73-80. [NTA 19, 955]

**DAHMS, John V.**
1974 "Lead us not into temptation". — *JEvTS* 17 (1974) 223-230. [NTA 19, 532]

**DAHMUS, Joseph**
1985 *The Puzzling Gospels. Suggested Explanations of Puzzling Passages in Matthew, Mark, Luke and John* (Basics of Christian Thought, 3). Chicago, IL: Thomas More, 1985, 168 p. Esp. 9-94: "The gospel according to Matthew".

**DALARUN, Jacques**
1991 La Scrittura alla lettera. De pericolo di una lettura letterale della Bibbia (Matteo III,2, e IV,17). — *Studi Medievali* (Spoleto) 32 (1991) 659-683.

**DALBESIO, Anselmo**
1976 Il Vangelo di Matteo e la Chiesa. — *Catechesi* 45/15 (1976) 13-28.
1993 La vita religiosa come attuazione della sequela radicale di Cristo secondo il Nuovo Testamento. — *Ant* 68 (1993) 300-326. Esp. 305-312 [19,16-22]; 312-314 [19,10-12]. [NTA 38, 1584]

**DAL COVOLO, Enrico**
1986 L'episodio del giovane ricco in Clemente e Origene. [19,16-22] — *Per foramen acus. Il cristianesimo antico di fronte alla pericope evangelica del "giovane ricco"* (Studia patristica mediolanensia, 14), Milano: Vita e Pensiero, 1986, 79-108. Esp. 101-107: "Il 'Commento a Matteo'".

**DALMAIS, Irenée-Henri**
1966 L'introduction et l'embolisme de l'Oraison dominicale dans la célébration eucharistique. — *La Maison-Dieu* (Paris) 85 (1966) 92-100. [NTA 11, 204]

**DALMAN, Gustaf**
1922[R] *Jesus-Jeschua. Die drei Sprachen Jesu. Jesus in der Synagoge, auf dem Berge, beim Passahmahl, am Kreuz* [1922]. Im Anhang: *Ergänzungen und Verbesserungen zu Jesus-Jeschua.* Darmstadt: Wissenschaftliche Buchgesellschaft, 1967, VIII-239 p. Esp. 52-79: "Der Bergprediger"; 200-209: "Jüdische Sprichwörter und Sentenzen".
*Jesus-Jeshua. Studies in the Gospels* [1929], trans. P.P. Levertoff. New York: Ktav, 1971, XIV-256 p. Esp. 56-85; 223-232.

1930[R] *Die Worte Jesu. Mit Berücksichtigung des nachkanonischen jüdischen Schrifttums und der aramäischen Sprache.* I: *Einleitung und wichtige Begriffe* [1898; ²1930]. Mit Anhang: A. *Das Vaterunser.* B. *Nachträge und Berichtigungen.* Darmstadt: Wissenschaftliche Buchgesellschaft, 1965, X-410 p. Esp. 83-119 [kingdom]; 113-116 [11,12-13]; 125-127 [αἰών]; 127-132 [ζωή]; 136-138 [κόσμος]; 146-147.269-272 [κύριος]; 155-159 [πατήρ]; 159-162 [θεός]; 168-180 [οὐρανός]; 208-219 [Son of Man]; 224-237 [Son of God]; 248-249 [χριστός]; 262-266 [Son of David]; 276-279 [διδάσκαλος]; 283-365: "Das Vaterunser".

**DALY, Robert J.**
1982 The New Testament and the Early Church. — CULLITON, J.T. (ed.), *Non-Violence – Central to Christian Spirituality: Perspectives from Scripture to the Present* (Toronto Studies in Theology, 8), Toronto, Ont.: Mellen, 1982, 33-62. Esp. 50-58: "The New Testament love commandment and the call to non-violence".
The New Testament Love Commandment and the Call to Non Violence. — ID. (ed.), *Christian Biblical Ethics*, 1984, 211-219.

1984 *Christian Sacrifice. The Judaeo-Christian Background before Origen* (CUA Studies in Christian Antiquity, 18). Washington, DC: CUA, 1978, XVI-587 p. Esp. 209-225: "The synoptics" [2,11; 5,23-24; 12,1-8; 20,28; 21,42; 26,26-29]. — Diss. Würzburg, 1972 (J. Betz).

1984* et al. (eds.), *Christian Biblical Ethics. From Biblical Revelation to Contemporary Christian Praxis: Method and Content.* New York – Mahwah, NJ: Paulist, 1984, IV-332 p. → Daly 1982, Schuele, Topel

### DAMBRICOURT, G.

1966 *Les traditions du Pentateuque et les évangiles synoptiques.* Paris: Spes, 1966, 297 p. Esp. 19-37: "La question synoptique"; 99-181: "Matthieu et la tradition élohiste-deutéronomiste".

1977 *Matthieu. Structures, sacrements, expérience des personnes divines.* Toulouse: Privat, 1977, 228 p.
F. BRÄNDLE, *EstJos* 34 (1980) 244; J. PINTARD, *EVie* 88 (1978) 13-14.

### DAMBRINE, Liliane

1971 Guérison de la femme hémoroïsse et résurrection de la fille de Jaïre. Un aspect de la lecture d'un texte: Marc 5,21-43; Matthieu 9,18-26; Luc 8,40-56. — *Reconnaissance à Suzanne de Diétrich*, 1971, 75-81. Esp. 78.

### DAMERAU, Rudolf

1966a *Das Herrengebet nach einem Kommentar des Gabriel Biel* (Studien zu den Grundlagen der Reformation, 3). Gießen: Schmitz, 1966, 176 p. Esp. 20-39: "Die Vaterunserauslegung"; 40-128: "Das Vaterunser". → Guyot 1969

1966b (ed.), *Der Herrengebetskommentar eines Unbekannten. 53 Auslegungen des Herrengebets des Karthäuserpriors Johannes Hagen († 1475). Textkritische Ausgabe* (Studien zu den Grundlagen der Reformation, 4). Gießen: Schmitz, 1966, 115 p. Esp. 9-56 [Anon.]; 57-114 [J. Hagen]

### D'ANCONA, M. → Thiede 1996a

### D'ANGELO, Francesco

1958 A proposito del testo di Matteo V,32 e XIX,9. — *Asprenas* 5 (1958) 81-89.

### D'ANGELO, Mary Rose

1984 Images of Jesus and the Christian Vocation in the Gospels of Mark and Matthew. — *Spirituality Today* (Chicago, IL) 36 (1984) 220-235. [NTA 29, 112]

1992a *Abba* and "Father": Imperial Theology and the Jesus Traditions. — *JBL* 111 (1992) 611-630. Esp. 617-618: "'Father' as an address to God" [Q]; 628-630. [NTA 37, 1198]

1992b Theology in Mark and Q: *Abba* and "Father" in Context. — *HTR* 85 (1992) 149-174. Esp. 162-173: "Q: as your Father does" [5,48; 6,9-13; 11,25-27].

### DANIEL, Constantin

1966 Esséniens, zélotes et sicaires et leur mention par paronyme dans le N.T. — *Numen* 13 (1966) 88-115. Esp. 91-96 [11,7]; 103-104 [7,15]; 112-114 [12,20].

1967a Les Esséniens et "Ceux qui sont dans les maisons des rois" (*Matthieu* 11,7-8 et *Luc* 7,24-25). — *RQum* 6 (1967) 261-277. [NTA 12, 871]

1967b → Negoiţā 1967

1968 Esséniens et eunuques (Matthieu 19,10-12). — *RQum* 6 (1968) 353-390. [NTA 13, 174]

1969 "Faux prophètes": Surnom des Esséniens dans le Sermon sur la montagne. — *RQum* 7 (1969) 45-79. Esp. 55-56.71-76 [7,15-20]. [NTA 15, 368]

1972 The Riddle of the Fig Tree and the Zealots (Mt 21,18-20; Mc 11,12-14; Lc 13,6-9; Jn 1,25-31). [Roumanian] — *Studii Teologice* 24 (1972) 45-58.

**DANIEL, Elinor Perkins**

1994    *A Rhetorical Analysis of the Resurrection Appearance Narratives in the Christian Gospels*. Diss. Georgia State Univ., 1994, 125 p. (G. Pullman). — *DissAbstr* 55 (1994-95) 2867-2868.

**DANIEL, Felix Harry**

1976    *The Transfiguration (Mark 9:2-13 and Parallels). A Redaction-critical and Traditio-historical Study*. Diss. Vanderbilt Univ., Nashville, TN, 1976, X-268 p. (P.W. Meyer). Esp. 97-157: "The role and function of the transfiguration pericope in Matthew's redaction of the synoptic tradition". — *DissAbstr* 37 (1976-77) 2241-2242.

**DANIELI, Ezechiele**

1969    "Eccetto in caso di fornicazione" (Mt. 5,32; 19,9). — *PalCl* 48 (1969) 1297-1300. [NTA 14, 482]

1981    Come leggere il Vangelo di Matteo. — *Spirito e Vita* 14 (1981) 101-104.

**DANIELI, Giuseppe**

1964    Alcune considerazioni sull'argomento "ex vaticiniis V.T." nell'apologetica di s. Matteo. — *DivThom* 67 (1964) 335-347. [NTA 9, 517]

1966    Significato di "profezia messianica" presso s. Matteo. — CANFORA, G. (ed.), *Il Messianismo* (Atti della XVIII Settimana Biblica), Brescia: Paideia, 1966, 219-231. Esp. 225-226 [2,23].

1967    Traditiones Evangelii Infantiae secundum Matthaeum earumque origo. — *VD* 45 (1967) 337-341. [NTA 13, 153] — Diss. Pont. Inst. Bib., Roma.

1968a   Esegesi dei vangeli sinottici. I: I Vangeli dell'Infanzia. — CANFORA, G., et al. (eds.), *Il Messaggio della Salvezza*, IV, 1968, 149-203.

1968b   L'influsso reciproco di tradizioni narrative e commenti profetici nel Vangelo di Matteo. — *DivThom* 71 (1968) 169-209. Esp. 171-185 [3,3]; 175-179 [4,15-16]; 179-182 [8,17]; 182-184 [12,18-21]; 184-185 [13,35]; 186-190 [21,5]; 190-193 [27,9-10]; 195-199 [1,22]; 199-201 [2,5]; 201-203 [2,15]; 203-205 [2,17-18]; 205 [2,23]. [NTA 13, 147] → 1969a

1968c   Matteo 1–2 e l'intenzione di narrare fatti accaduti. — *RivBib* 16 (1968) 187-199. [NTA 13, 561]

1969a   *Le tradizioni di Mt 1–2 e loro origine*. Piacenza: "Divus Thomas", 1969, 66 p. — Diss. Commissio Biblica, Roma, 1967. → = 1968c + 1969b
        J.M. ALONSO, *EphMar* 21 (1971) 139-140; J.A. CARRASCO, *EstJos* 24 (1970) 73-74; B. CHIESA, *BibOr* 14 (1972) 95; R. GAUTHIER, *EstJos* 20 (1972) 298-299; P.M. LUSTRISSIMI, *Marianum* 34 (1972) 145-146.

1969b   A proposito delle origini della tradizione sinottica sulla concezione verginale. — *DivThom* 72 (1969) 312-331. Esp. 313-318 [1,18-25]. [NTA 14, 470] → 1969a

1969c   Le sette parabole del Regno (Mt 13,1-52). — *ParVi* 14 (1969) 280-295.

1969d   Venuta del Figlio dell'uomo (Mt 24–25). — *Ibid.*, 308-316.

1971    Storicità di Matteo I-II: Stato presente della discussione. — *EstJos* 25 = *CahJos* 19 (1971) 53-61. [NTA 16, 846]

1973    Analisi strutturale ed esegesi di Matteo. A proposito del recente libro di J. Radermakers. — *RivBib* 21 (1973) 433-439. [NTA 19, 524r] → Radermakers 1972

1975    Ipotesi recenti sull'indissolubilità del matrimonio nel Nuovo Testamento. — *Asprenas* 22 (1975) 148-168. Esp. 154-161: "Le clausole di Matteo" [5,32; 19,9].

1979    → Martini 1979b

1980    *Matteo* (Leggere oggi la Bibbia, 2/1). Brescia: Queriniana, 1980, 95 p. [NTA 26, p. 82] *Mateus* (Pequeno Com. Bíb.). São Paolo: Paulinas, 1983, 142 p.

1984 "Elì, Elì, lamà sabactani?". Riflessioni sull'origine e il significato della suprema invocazione di Gesù secondo Matteo (Mt. 27,46). — ID. (ed.), *Gesù e la sua morte* (Atti della XXVII Settimana Biblica), Brescia: Paideia, 1984, 29-49.

1992 I Magi a Betlemme: origine e genere letterario di Mt 2,1-12. — SERRA, A. – VALENTINI, A. (eds.), *I Vangeli dell'infanzia*, I, 1992, 77-95.

**DANIÉLOU, Jean**

1957 L'étoile de Jacob et la mission chrétienne à Damas. — *VigChr* 11 (1957) 121-138. Esp. 137-138 [2,2]. [NTA 2, 447]

1958 *Histoire des doctrines chrétiennes avant Nicée. I: Théologie du judéo-christianisme* (Bibliothèque de Théologie). Paris: Desclée, 1958, 457 p. Esp. 237-247 [2,2]; 257-267 [27,51-53]; ²1991.

   *The Development of Christian Doctrine Before the Council of Nicaea. I: The Theology of Jewish Christianity*, trans. J.A. Baker. London: Darton, Longman & Todd, 1964, XVI-446 p. Esp. 218-224; 233-240.

   *La teologia del giudeo-cristianesimo*, trans. C. Prandi (Collana di stud religiosi). Bologna: Il Mulino, 1974, LXV-595 p.

1967 *Les Évangiles de l'enfance.* Paris: Seuil, 1967, 141 p. Esp. 11-20 [1,1-17]; 43-58 [1,18-25]; 79-106 [2,1-12]. [NTA 12, p. 255] → Delorme 1968a, Journet 1968

   P. BENOIT, *RB* 78 (1971) 626-627; G.-M. BERTRAND, *CahJos* 16 (1968) 347-348; A. DRÈZE, *LumVit* 23 (1968) 384-385; J. GUILLET, *Études* 328 (1968) 743-744; R. LAJRENTIN, *RSPT* 52 (1968) 485; M.-É. LAUZIÈRE, *RThom* 68 (1968) 450-451; C.M. MARTINI, *CC* 119/1 ⁻1968) 607-608; S. MUÑOZ IGLESIAS, *EstBíb* 27 (1968) 88-89; J. RADERMAKERS, *NRT* 100 (1968) 675-6⁻6; É. TROCMÉ, *RHPR* 48 (1968) 396-397; B. ZWEIFEL, *RTP* 21 (1971) 181.

   *The Infancy Narratives*, trans. R. Sheed. New York: Herder & Herder; London: Burns & Oats, 1968, 127 p. Esp. 11-19; 39-52; 71-95. [NTA 13, p. 267]

   J.M.T. BARTON, *CleR* 54 (1969) 912-913; R.C. CORREIA, *Theologica* 5 (1970) 254; M. DAVIS, *NBlackfr* 50 (1968-69) 661-662; A. HICKLING, *Theology* 71 (1968) 514-515; V. KESICH, *St. Vladimir's Theological Quarterly* (Tuckahoe, NY) 13 (1969) 165-167; F. STOOP, *Verbum Caro* (Taizé) 22 (1968) 63; J.R. VIDIGAL, *REB* 22 (1969) 1005; J. VOLCKAERT, *The Clergy Monthly* (Ranchi, India) 34 (1970) 176-177.

   *I vangeli dell'infanzia*, trans. G. Bacchiarello (Coll. "Il Pellicano"). Brescia: Morcelliana, 1968, 128 p.

   B. PRETE, *Sacra Doctrina* (Bologna) 14 (1969) 127-128.

   *Os evangelhos da infância*, trans. J.M. de Paiva. Petrópolis: Vozes, 1969, 86 p.

   *Los evangelios de la infancia.* Barcelona: Herder, 1969, 122 p.

   *Lumen* (Vitoria) 19 (1970) 93-94; F.J.R. BEN GÈS, *EstFranc* 72 (1971) 144-145; J.A. CARRASCO, *EstJos* 24 (1970) 245; EZQUERRA, *RazFe* 182 (1970) 524-525; J. FERRERAS, *Revista agustiniana de espiritualidad* (Calahorra) 11 (1970) 242; T. HANSON, *TVida* 11 (197⁻) 290-291; J.S. ROLDÁN, *Religión y Cultura* (Madrid) 16 (1970) 240; J. SALVADOR, *RevistCuBíb* 7 (1970) 113.

1968 Fels. — *RAC* 7/53 (1968) 723-731. Esp. 725-726 [16,17].

1969 *La Résurrection.* Paris: Seuil, 1969, 139 p.

**DANIEL-ROPS, Henri**

1961 À la base de toute connaissance de Jésus: l'Évangile. — AMIOT, F., et al., *Les sources de l'histoire de Jésus* (Je sais – je crois, 67), Paris: Fayard, 1961, 29-85. Esp. 42-49.

   *The Gospel: Basis of All Our Knowledge of Jesus.* — AMIOT, F., et al., *The Sources for the Life of Christ* (Faith and Fact Books, 67), London: Burns & Oates, 1962, 33-96. Esp. 50-59.

   Trans. Italian 1962.

**DANIELS, Boyd L.**

1967* & SUGGS, M.J. (eds.), *Studies in the History and Text of the New Testament in Honor of Kenneth Willis Clark Ph.D.* (Studies and Documents, 29). Salt Lake City, UT: Univ. of Utah Press, 1967, XI-187 p. → M.P. Brown, W.R. Farmer, Rife

**DANIELS, Jon B.**

1989 *The Egerton Gospel: Its Place in Early Christianity.* Diss. Claremont Graduate School, 1989, IX-301 p. (J.M. Robinson). Esp. 39-65: "The Egerton Gospel and its synoptic parallels" [8,2-3; 15,7-8].

**DANKER, Frederick W.**

1958    Luke 16,16 – An Opposition Logion. — *JBL* 77 (1958) 231-243. Esp. 239-243 [11,12-15]. [NTA 3, 369]

1970a   The Demonic Secret in Mark: A Reexamination of the Cry of Dereliction (15,34). — *ZNW* 61 (1970) 48-69. Esp. 58-61 [4,1-11]. [NTA 15, 531]

1970b   Fresh Perspectives on Matthean Theology. A Review Article. — *ConcTM* 41 (1970) 478-490. [NTA 15, 505r] → Kingsbury 1969

1973    Hardness of Heart. A Study in Biblical Thematic. [13,14-15] — *ConcTM* 44 (1973) 89-100. [NTA 18, 649]

1992    God With Us: Hellenistic Christological Perspectives in Matthew. — *CurrTMiss* 19 (1992) 433-439. [NTA 37, 702] → 1994

1994    Matthew: A Patriot's Gospel. — EVANS, C.A. - STEGNER, W.R. (eds.), *The Gospels and the Scriptures of Israel*, 1994, 94-115. Esp. 95-100: "Judean audition"; 100-114: "Greco-Roman". → 1992

**DANNER, Dan G.**

1983    The "Q" Document and the Words of Jesus. A Review of Theodore R. Rosché, "The Words of Jesus and the Future of the 'Q' Hypothesis". — *RestQ* 26 (1983) 193-201. [NTA 29, 73] → Rosché 1960

**DANOVE, Paul**

1993    The Theory of Construction Grammar and Its Application to New Testament Greek. — PORTER, S.E. - CARSON, D.A. (eds.), *Biblical Greek Language and Linguistics. Open Questions in Current Research* (JSNT SS, 80), Sheffield: JSOT, 1993, 119-151. Esp. 138-151 [ἀκούω].

**DANTEN, Jean**

1955    La révélation du Christ sur Dieu dans les paraboles. — *NRT* 77 (1955) 450-477. Esp. 452-453 [18,10-14]; 453-455 [13,1-9]; 455-457 [21,33-46]; 457 [21,28-32]; 457-459 [20,1-16]; 461 [18,23-35]; 461-462 [25,14-30]; 463-466 [22,1-14].

**DARBY, Robert R.**

1953    *A Study of the Variations of the Gethsemane Sayings of Jesus Common to the Synoptics* [26,36-46]. Diss. New Orleans Baptist Theol. Sem., 1953.

**DARR, John A.**

1993    The Gospels, and Early Christianity: A Response to René Girard. [*Ibid.*, 339-352] — *BibInt* 1 (1993) 357-367. Esp. 364-367 [22,1-13]. [NTA 38, 1310]

**DA SILVA, A.P.**

1974    Ajuda uma teoria sobre Mt 5,32 e 19,9? (No atual debate sobre o divórcio). — *RevistCuBíb* 11 (1974) 112-119. [NTA 19, 950]

**DA SILVA GORGULHO, G.** → A.F. Anderson 1973

**DA SORTINO, Placido M.**

1967    La vocazione di Pietro secondo la tradizione sinottica e secondo San Giovanni. — CANFORA, G. (ed.), *San Pietro*, 1967, 27-57. Esp. 40-50 [4,18-22]; 51-55 [16,18].

**DA SPINETOLI, Ortensio**

1964    I "poveri del Signore". — *BibOr* 6 (1964) 3-16. Esp. 10-12 [πτωχοί]. [NTA 9, 66]

1966    L'impostazione del problema escatologico in S. Matteo. — *BibOr* 8 (1966) 185-211. [NTA 11, 689]

1967a   *Introduzione ai Vangeli dell'infanzia* (Esegesi biblica, 2). Brescia: Paideia, 1967, 127 p.; Assisi: Cittadella, [2]1976, 163 p. Esp. 17-64. [NTA 12, p. 255] → Landucci 1967
J.A. CARRASCO, *EstJos* 21 (1968) 261-262; A. DA LINGUACLOSSA, *Laur* 9 (1968) 103-104; R. GAUTHIER, *CahJos* 20 (1972) 293-294; S. GONZÁLEZ DE CAREEA, *NatGrac* 15 (1968) 441-442; G. LEONARDI, *Studia Patavina* 15 (1968) 348; C.M. MARTINI, *CC* 119/1 (1968) 505-506; S. MUÑOZ IGLESIAS, *EstBíb* 26 (1967) 412; B. PRETE, *Sacra Doctrina* (Bologna) 13 (1968) 149; E. RASCO, *Greg* 49 (1968) 362-365; H.H. ROWLEY, *ExpT* 81 (1969-70) 31; G. SCICLONE, *Protestantesimo* 24 (1970) 252-253; R. SILVA, *Compostellanum* 12 (1967) 465-466; M. ZERWICK, *VD* 47 (1969) 49-50.

1967b   La portata ecclesiologica di Mt. 16,18-19. — *Ant* 42 (1967) 357-375. [NTA 12, 878]

1967c   I problemi letterari di Matt. 16,13-20. — CANFORA, G. (ed.), *San Pietro*, 1967, 79-92.

1969   *Il Vangelo del Primato* [16,13-20] (Esegesi biblica). Brescia: Paideia, 1969, 123 p. [NTA 14, p. 244]

1970   [URBANELLI, O.], Evangeli dell'infanzia. — *Enciclopedia delle Religioni* (Firenze) 2 (1970) 1388-1398.

1971   *Matteo. Commento al "Vangelo della Chiesa"*. Assisi: Cittadella, 1971, 718 p.; [2]1973, 753 p. [NTA 17, p. 30]; [3]1976. → Leonardi 1972
J. DUPONT, *Paroisse et liturgie* (Ottignies) 52 (1971) 568; F. MONTAGNINI, *Humanitas* 27 (1972) 565; G. RINALDI, *BibOr* 14 (1972) 94-95; L. SABOURIN, *BTB* 1 (1971) 336-337; P. ZARRELLA, *Laur* 13 (1972) 121-123.
J.A. CARRASCO, *EstJos* 34 (1980) 242-243; R. GAUTHIER, *CahJos* 26 (1978) 247.
*Matteo. Il Vangelo della Chiesa* (Commenti e studi biblici). Assisi: Cittadella, 4th rev. ed., 1983, 805 p. [NTA 29, p. 88]; [4]1985.
L. DE LORENZI, *Benedictina* 31 (1984) 250-253; V. PASQUETTO, *Teresianum* 37 (1986) 241-242.

1974   Les généalogies de Jésus et leur signification. Mt 1,1-25; Lc 3,23-28. — *AssSeign* II/9 (1974) 6-19. [NTA 19, 943]

1983   Il segno eucaristico nel racconto della moltiplicazione dei pani (Mt, Lc e Gv). — *ParSpirV* 7 (1983) 99-111. Esp. 101-106 [14,19; 26,26].

1992   I problemi di Matteo 1-2 e Luca 1-2. Orientamenti e proposte. — SERRA, A. - VALENTINI, A. (eds.), *I Vangeli dell'infanzia*, I, 1992, 7-44.

## DASSMANN, Ernst

1979   *Der Stachel im Fleisch. Paulus in der frühchristlichen Literatur bis Irenäus*. Münster: Aschendorff, 1979, XI-335 p. Esp. 102-106: "Gesetzeserfüllung und Christusnachfolge im Matthäusevangelium".

## DATTLER, Frederico

1966   *Sinopse evangélica*. São Paulo: Paulinas, 1966; [2]1967, 317 p.

1971   A Mixná no Nôvo Testamento. — VOIGT, S. - VIER, F. (eds.), *Atualidades Bíblicas. Miscelânea em memória de Frei João José Pedreira de Castro, o.f.m.*, Petrópolis: Vozes, 1971, 392-402. Esp. 397 [23,23]; 399-400 [19,3-9]; 400 [23,16-22].

1981   *Os evangelhos da infância de Jesús segundo Lucas e Mateus*. São Paulo: Paulinas, 1981, 166 p.

## DAUBE, David

1944a[R]   The Last Beatitude. [1944] — ID., *The New Testament and Rabbinic Judaism*, 1956, 196-201 (revised).

1944b[R]   Eye for Eye. [1944] — ID., *The New Testament and Rabbinic Judaism*, 1956, 254-265 (revised).

1945[R]   Reconstruction of the "Aramaic Gospels" [Divorce]. [1945] — ID., *The New Testament and Rabbinic Judaism*, 1956, 71-86 (revised). Esp. 83-85.

1946[R]   Public Retort and Private Explanation. [19,3-9] [1946] — ID., *The New Testament and Rabbinic Judaism*, 1956, 141-150 (revised).

1950    The Anointing at Bethany. — *ATR* 32 (1950) 186-199. Esp. 193-196 [26,6-13].
        Disgrace. — ID., *The New Testament and Rabbinic Judaism*, 1956, 301-324 (revised). Esp. 320-321.

1956a   *The New Testament and Rabbinic Judaism* (Jordan Lectures 1952). London: Athlone,
        1956, XVIII-460 p. → 1944a-b, 1945, 1946, 1950, 1956b-e

1956b   "Ye have heard – but I say unto you". — *Ibid.*, 55-62.

1956c   Basic Commandments. — *Ibid.*, 247-253.

1956d   Violence to the Kingdom. [11,12] — *Ibid.*, 285-300. Esp. 285-294: "The saying"; 294-300: "The context".

1956e   Two Incidents after the Last Supper. — *Ibid.*, 330-335. Esp. 332-335 [26,45].

1959    The Earliest Structure of the Gospels. — *NTS* 5 (1958-59) 174-187. Esp. 184-185 [2,13-18].
        [NTA 4, 50]

1964a   *Suddenness and Awe in Scripture* (Tenth Robert Waley Cohen Memorial Lecture,
        1963). London: Council of Christians and Jews, 1964, 20 p.

1964b   *The Sudden in the Scriptures*. Leiden: Brill, 1964, 86 p. Esp. 39.60-62.

1972    Responsibilities of Master and Disciples in the Gospels. — *NTS* 19 (1972-73) 1-15. Esp.
        4-8.11-13 [12,1-8]; 8-9 [15,1-20]; 9-10 [21,15-16]; 13-15 [17,24-27]. [NTA 17, 854]

1985    Zukunftsmusik: Some Desirable Lines of Exploration in the New Testament Field. —
        *BJRL* 68 (1985-86) 53-75. Esp. 53-56 [εὐθύς]; 68-69 [φιμόω]. [NTA 31, 4]; = DUNGAN, D.L.
        (ed.), *The Interrelations of the Gospels*, 1990, 360-380. Esp. 362-364; 373-374.

1987    Temple Tax. [17,24-27] — SANDERS, E.P. (ed.), *Jesus, the Gospels, and the Church*. FS
        W.R. Farmer, 1987, 121-134; = ID., *Appeasement or Resistance and Other Essays on
        New Testament Judaism*, Berkeley, CA: University of California Press, 1987, 39-58.

1994    Judas. — *California Law Review* 82 (1994) 95-108.

**DAUER, Anton**

1967    Das Wort des Gekreuzigten an seine Mutter und den "Jünger, den er liebte". Eine
        traditionsgeschichtliche und theologische Untersuchung zu Joh 19,25-27. — *BZ* 11
        (1967) 222-239. Esp. 223-235 [27,55-56/Jn]. [NTA 12, 602]; 12 (1968) 80-93. [NTA 12, 930]

1972    *Die Passionsgeschichte im Johannesevangelium. Eine traditionsgeschichtliche und
        theologische Untersuchung zu Joh 18,1–19,30* (SANT, 30). München: Kösel, 1972, 375
        p. Esp. 50-53 [Mt/Jn 18,1-11]; 96-97 [Mt/Jn 18,12-27]; 154-155 [Mt/Jn 18,28–19,16a]; 217-222 [Mt/Jn
        19,16b-30]. — Diss. Würzburg, 1968-69 (R. Schnackenburg). → Neirynck 1977b, Sabbe 1977, 1991c

1984    *Johannes und Lukas. Untersuchungen zu den johanneisch-lukanischen Parallelperikopen
        Joh 4,46-54 / Lk 7,1-10 – Joh 12,1-8 / Lk 7,36-50; 10,38-42 – Joh 20,19-29 / Lk
        24,36-49* (FzB, 50). Würzburg: Echter, 1984, 505 p. Esp. 42-44 [8,5-13/Jn]; 76-116.337-365:
        "Tradition und Redaktion in Lk 7,1-10 (und Mt 8,5-13)". — Diss. Würzburg, 1981-82 (R. Schnackenburg).
        → Neirynck 1984e, D.M. Smith 1992a

1992    Spuren der (synoptischen) Synedriumsverhandlung im 4. Evangelium. — DENAUX, A.
        (ed.), *John and the Synoptics*, 1992, 307-339. Esp. 317-320 [26,57-68/Jn].

**DAUMOSER, Innozenz**

1954    *Berufung und Erwählung bei den Synoptikern. Ein Beitrag zur biblischen Theologie des
        Neuen Testamentes*. Meisenheim: Hain; Stuttgart: Katholisches Bibelwerk, 1954, 256 p.
        Esp. 68-133: "Die Berufung bei den Synoptikern" [3,1-17; 20,1-16; 22,1-14]; 134-234: "Die Erwählung bei
        den Synoptikern" [13,10-17; 16,18; 22,14]. — Diss. Pont. Univ. Greg., Roma.

**DAUNER, Max**

1983    *À quoi comparerons-nous le règne de Dieu? Étude des principales paraboles de
        Matthieu et Marc*. Gigean: Horizons Chrétiens, 1983, 105 p.

**DAUTZENBERG, Gerhard**

1966 *Sein Leben bewahren.* Ψυχή *in den Herrenworten der Evangelien* (SANT, 14). München: Kösel, 1966, 181 p. Esp. 51-65 [16,25/Mk 8,35; 1C,39/Q]; 68-82 [16,26/Mk 8,36]; 92-97 [6,25/Q 12,22-23]; 98-107 [20,28/Mk 10,45]; 114-123 [22,37/Mk 12,30]; 124-133 [26,37-38/Mk 14,33-34]; 134-137 [11,29]; 138-153 [10,28]. — Diss. Würzburg, 1964 (R. Schnackenburg).

1969 Der Verzicht auf das apostolische Unterhaltsrecht. Eine exegetische Untersuchung zu 1 Kor 9. — *Bib* 50 (1969) 212-232. Esp. 216-217 [10,10/1 Cor 9,12]. [NTA 14, 264]

1977 Die Zeit des Evangeliums. Mk 1,1-15 und die Konzeption des Markusevangeliums. — *BZ* 31 (1977) 219-234. [NTA 22, 100]; 22 (1978) 76-91. Esp. 79-81 [εὐαγγέλιον]. [NTA 23, 114]

1979* & MERKLEIN, H. – MÜLLER, K. (eds.), *Zur Geschichte des Urchristentums* [FS R. Schnackenburg] (QDisp, 87). Freiburg: Herder, 1979. 160 p. → Dautzenberg, Merklein, Waibel

1979 Der Wandel der Reich-Gottes-Verkündigung in der urchristlichen Mission. — *Ibid.*, 11-32. Esp. 15-31: "Beobachtungen zur nachösterlichen Reich-Gottes-Verkündigung"; = ID., *Studien*, 1995, 16-37. Esp. 20-36.

1981 Ist das Schwurverbot Mt 5,33-37; Jak 5,12 ein Beispiel für die Torakritik Jesu? — *BZ* 25 (1981) 47-66. Esp. 48-50: "Die Traditionsgeschichte des Schwurverbots nach G. Strecker"; 50-53: "Zu Form und Intention des Schwurverbots"; 53-56: "Das Schwurverbot und die jüdische Eidkritik"; 57-60: "Das Schwurverbot und die Beteuerungsformeln der synoptischen Tradition"; 61-65: "Zur Wirkungsgeschichte des Schwurverbots im Urchristentum". [NTA 26, 91]; = ID., *Studien*, 1995, 38-62. Esp. 39-41; 42-45; 45-50; 50-55; 55-61. → A. Ito 1991

1983* & MERKLEIN, H. – MÜLLER, K. (eds.), *Die Frau im Urchristentum* (QDisp, 95). Freiburg: Herder, 1983, 358 p. → J. Blank, R. Geiger, R. Mahoney, Ritt

1983 Psalm 110 im Neuen Testament. — BECKER, H. – KACZYNSKI, R. (eds.), *Liturgie und Dichtung. Ein interdisziplinäres Kompendium.* I: *Historische Präsentation* (Pietas liturgica, 1), St. Ottilien: EOS, 1983, 141-171. Esp. 149-152 [22,41-46]; 152-154 [26,63-64]; = ID., *Studien*, 1995, 63-97. Esp. 73-75; 75-78.

1986 Gesetzeskritik und Gesetzesgehorsam in der Jesustradition. — KERTELGE, K. (ed.), *Das Gesetz im Neuen Testament*, 1986, 46-70. Esp. 62-69: "Zum Gesetzesverständnis der Logienquelle" [Q 11,39-52; 16,16-17.18]; = ID., *Studien*, 1995, 106-131. Esp. 122-128.

1988 Mt 5,43c und die antike Tradition von der jüdischen Misanthropie. — SCHENKE, L. (ed.), *Studien zum Matthäusevangelium.* FS W. Pesch, 1988, 47-77. Esp. 49-58 [5,43]; 58-77 [Judaism]; = ID., *Studien*, 1995, 156-187. Esp. 156-166 166-186.

1990 Mk 4,1-34 als Belehrung über das Reich Gottes. Beobachtungen zum Gleichniskapitel. — *BZ* 34 (1990) 38-62. Esp. 42-44 [13,11]; 50-52 [7,2]; 52 [13,31-32]. [NTA 34, 1153]; = ID., *Studien*, 1995, 188-221. Esp. 193-196; 204-206; 207.

1991a Jesus und der Tempel. Beobachtungen zur Exegese der Perikope von der Tempelsteuer (Mt 17,24-27). — OBERLINNER, L. – FIEDLER, P. (eds.), *Salz der Erde*. FS A. Vögtle. 1991, 223-238. Esp. 224-227: "Probleme der formgeschichtlichen Klassifikation der Überlieferung"; 227-231: "Die Einheitlichkeit von Mt 17,24-27"; 231-236: "Der traditionsgeschichtliche Ort"; 236-238: "Mt 17,24-27 im Rahmen der mt Redaktion"; = ID., *Studien*, 1995, 263-282. Esp. 264-268; 268-272; 273-279; 279-281.

1991b Jesus und die Tora. — *Orientierung* 55 (1991) 229-232, 243-246. Esp. 230-232 [Q 9,59-60; 11,39-41.42; 16,18]; = ID., *Studien*, 1995, 334-351. Esp. 337-342.

1992 Tora des Menschensohnes? Kritische Überlegungen zu Daniel Kosch. — *BZ* 36 (1992) 93-103. [NTA 36, 1240r]; = ID., *Studien*, 1995, 283-300. → Kosch 1989a

1995 *Studien zur Theologie der Jesustradition* (Stuttgarter Biblische Aufsatzbände, 19). Stuttgart: Katholisches Bibelwerk, 1995, XI-423 p. → 1979, 1981, 1983, 1986, 1988, 1990, 1991a-b, 1992

**DAUVILLIER, Jean**

1957 La parabole du trésor et les droits orientaux. [13,44-46] — *RevIntDroitsAnt* 4 (1957) 107-115.

1964 L'indissolubilité du mariage dans la nouvelle Loi. — *L'Orient Syrien* (Paris) 9 (1964) 265-289. Esp. 273-280. [NTA 9, 147]

1970 *Les Temps Apostoliques. 1ᵉʳ siècle* (Histoire du Droit et des Institutions de l'Église en Occident, 2). Paris: Sirey, 1970, XVIII-744 p. Esp. 394-405: "Explications proposées de l'incise de saint Matthieu".

**DAVENPORT, Gene L.**

1988 *Into the Darkness: Discipleship in the Sermon on the Mount.* Nashville, TN: Abingdon, 1988, 302 p. [NTA 33, p. 383]
      E. FRANKLIN, *ExpT* 101 (1989-90) 121; D. HILL, *JSNT* 40 (1990) 115.

**DAVEY, F. Noel**

1931 → Hoskyns 1931

1964 Healing in the New Testament. — RAMSEY, I.T., et al., *The Miracles and the Resurrection. Some Recent Studies* (SPCK Theological Collections, 3), London: SPCK, 1964, 50-63.

**DAVID, Jean-Eudes**

1967 Τὸ αἱμά μου τῆς διαθήκης. Mt 26:28: Un faux problème. — *Bib* 48 (1967) 291-292. [NTA 12, 165]

**DAVIDS, Peter H.**

1985 James and Jesus. — WENHAM, D. (ed.), *The Jesus Tradition Outside the Gospels*, 1985, 63-84. Esp. 66-67, 70-77.

1991 *More Hard Sayings of the New Testament.* Downers Grove, IL: InterVarsity, 1991, 312 p.

**DAVIDSON, F.**

1953 & STIBBS, A.M. – KEVAN, E.F. (eds.), *The New Bible Commentary.* Leicester: Inter-Varsity, 1953, ²1954, 1200 p. → France 1994b, Guthrie 1970

**DAVIDSON, J.A.**

1970 *The Lord's Prayer* (World Inspirational Books). New York: World Press, 1970, 60 p.

**DAVIDSON, Maxwell J.**

1992 Angels. — *DJB*, 1992, 8-11. Esp. 9-10.

**DAVIDSON, Robert** → Leaney 1970

**DAVIES (PAMMENT), Margaret**

1981a Empty Tomb and Resurrection. [27,55-28,20] — *NBlackfr* 62 (1981) 488-493. [NTA 26, 481]

1981b The Kingdom of Heaven according to the First Gospel. — *NTS* 27 (1980-81) 211-232. Esp. 211-229: "The Kingdom of heaven" [3,2; 4,17; 5-7; 8,11-12; 11,11-12; 13; 24-25]; 229-232: "The kingdom of God" [6,10; 12,24-28; 19,24; 21,31.43]. [NTA 25, 845]

1981c Moses and Elijah in the Story of the Transfiguration. — *ExpT* 92 (1980-81) 338-339. [NTA 26, 119] → Moiser 1985a

1981d Witch-Hunt. [Pharisees, Scribes] — *Theology* 84 (1981) 98-106. [NTA 25, 846]

1983a Singleness and Matthew's Attitude to the Torah. — *JSNT* 17 (1983) 73-86. Esp. 73-75 [25]; 75-76 [5,17-18; 11,12-13]; 77 [12,1-14; 15,1-20]; 78-79 [23]; 80 [19,3-22]. [NTA 27, 906]

1983b The Son of Man in the First Gospel. — *NTS* 29 (1983) 116-129. Esp. 118-119 [8,20]; 119-120 [9,6]; 120-121 [10,22-23; 11,19; 12,8]; 121-122 [12,32.40]; 122-123 [13,41-42; 16,13]; 123-124 [16,27-28; 19,28; 20,18-19]; 125 [24,30]; 126 [25,31]. [NTA 27, 504]

1989 → E.P. Sanders 1989

1993 *Matthew* (Readings: A New Biblical Commentary). Sheffield: JSOT, 1993, 224 p. [NTA 38, p. 118]
D. CATCHPOLE, *EpworthR* 21 (1994) 112-113; E. CUVILLIER, *ETR* 71 (1996) 83-84; J.C. FENTON, *JTS* 45 (1994) 648; H.B. GREEN, *NBlackfr* 75 (1994) 336-338; P. MEAGHER, *Vidyajyoti* 58 (1994) 400-401.

1995 On Prostitution. — CARROLL R., M.D. – CLINES, D.J.A. – DAVIES, P.R. (eds.), *The Bible in Human Society. Essays in Honour of John Rogerson* (JSOT SS, 200), Sheffield: JSOT, 1995, 225-248. Esp. 236-238 [5,32; 19,9; 21,31-32].

**DAVIES, Paul Ewing**

1957 Did Jesus Die as a Martyr-Prophet? — *BR* 2 (1957) 19-30. Esp. 24-25 [23,29-39]. [NTA 2, 520]
Did Jesus Die as a Martyr-Prophet? — *BR* 19 (1974) 37-47. Esp. 42. [NTA 19, 912]

1962 Experience and Memory. The Role of the Exalted Christ in the Life and the Experience of the Primitive Church. — *Interpr* 16 (1962) 181-192. Esp. 188-189 [11,27]. [NTA 7, 22]

**DAVIES, Philip R.**

1990* & WHITE, R.T. (eds.), *A Tribute to Geza Vermes. Essays on Jewish and Christian Literature and History* (JSOT SS, 100). Sheffield: JSOT, 1990, 406 p. → J. Barr, M. Black, Millar

**DAVIES, Rupert E.**

1970 Christ in Our Place – The Contribution of the Prepositions. — *TyndB* 21 (1970) 71-91. Esp. 72-81 [ἀντί]. [NTA 15, 445]

**DAVIES, Stevan L.**

1981 Who Is Called Bar Abbas? [23,7-10; 27,17] — *NTS* 27 (1980-81) 260-262. [NTA 25, 817]

1983 *The Gospel of Thomas and Christian Wisdom.* New York: Seabury, 1983, 182 p. Esp. 100-104 [Q/Th]; 121-124 [11,25-30/Th].

1988 *The New Testament. A Contemporary Introduction.* San Francisco, CA: Harper & Row, 1988, XI-207 p.
*New Testament Fundamentals.* Sonoma, CA: Polebridge, 1994, 250 p. Esp. 127-154.

1992 The Christology and Protology of the *Gospel of Thomas.* — *JBL* 111 (1992) 663-682. Esp. 663-664.682. [NTA 37, 1644]

1995 *Jesus the Healer. Possession, Trance, and the Origins of Christianity.* London: SCM, 1995, 216 p.

**DAVIES, W.J.**

1950 Was His Father Lying Dead at Home? [8,21] — *ExpT* 62 (1950-51) 92. → H.G. Howard 1950

**DAVIES, William David**

1953 "Knowledge" in the Dead Sea Scrolls and Matthew 11:25-30. — *HTR* 46 (1953) 113-139. Esp. 114-118; 136-139; = ID., *Christian Origins and Judaism*, 1962, 119-144. Esp. 120-124; 141-144.

1956* & DAUBE, D. (eds.), *The Background of the New Testament and Its Eschatology. In Honour of Charles Harold Dodd.* Cambridge: University Press, 1956, XIX-555 p. → G. Bornkamm, R.P. Casey, W.D. Davies, Feuillet, Schweizer

1956a Reflections on Archbishop Carrington's 'The Primitive Christian Calendar'. [P. Carrington, 1952] — *Ibid.*, 124-152. Esp. 139-142 [place]; 149-152: "Note on Levertoff's treatment of Matthew" [1928]; = ID., *Christian Origins and Judaism*, 1962, 68-95. Esp. 84-85; 92-95.

1956b Dödahavsrullarna och kristendomens ursprung. — *SEÅ* 21 (1956) 5-26. Esp. 11-12 [18,15-17]. [NTA 3, 259]
The Dead Sea Scrolls and Christian Origins. — *RelLife* 26 (1957) 246-264. Esp. 251-252; = ID., *Christian Origins and Judaism*, 1962, 99-117. Esp. 103.

1957 Matthew, 5,17-18. — *Mélanges bibliques*. FS A. Robert, 1957, 428-456. Esp. 429-430 [πληρόω]; 431-433 [5,17-20]; 433-438 [antitheses]; 438-456 [5,17-18]; = ID., *Christian Origins and Judaism*, 31-66. Esp. 32-34; 34-37, 37-43; 43-66.

1962a *Christian Origins and Judaism*. London: Darton, Longman & Todd, 1962, IX-261 p.
→ 1953, 1956a-b, 1957

1962b Law in the New Testament. — *IDB* 3 (1962) 95-102. Esp. 95-97: "The law in the synoptic gospels"; = ID., *Jewish and Pauline Studies*, 1984, 227-242 (notes, 368-370). Esp. 227-232.

1963a *The Setting of the Sermon on the Mount*. Cambridge: University Press, 1963, XIV-547 p. [NTA 8, p. 464]; repr. 1966; (Brown Judaic Studies, 186). Atlanta, GA: Scholars, 1989. Esp. 14-108: "The setting in Matthew"; 191-315: "The setting in the contemporary Judaism"; 316-414: "The setting in the Early Church"; 415-435: "The setting in the ministry of Jesus"; 443-444 [1-2: genre]; 451-453 [6,9-13]; 457-460: "'Wisdom' sayings of Jesus"; 463-434 [5,15; 6,1-6; 7,24; 18,23/Jn]. [NTA 34, p. 244] → Allison 1993a, Brandon 1965, Carlston 1985, J.M. Ford 1967b, Westerholm 1991
*ExpT* 75 (1963-64) 289-290; R.S. BARBOUR, *ScotJT* 19 (1966) 238-242; J.M.T. BARTON, *CleR* 50 (1965) 528-530; F.W. BEARE, *JBL* 88 (1969) 88-91; P. BENOIT, *RB* 72 (1965) 595-601; R.E. BROWN, *TS* 25 (1964) 640-643; F.F. BRUCE, *JSS* 10 (1965) 285-286; *EvQ* 37 (1965) 57-59; J. CARMIGNAC, *RQum* 5 (1965) 285-287; B. CORSANI, *Protestantesimo* 24 (1969) 50-54; G.E.P. COX, *Theology* 67 (1964) 412-414; J. DANIÉLOU, *RSR* 53 (1965) 124-127; F. DREYFUS, *RSPT* 50 (1966) 98-100; J. DUPONT, *RivStoLR* 3 (1967) 314-322; R.E. HIGGINSON, *TSF Bulletin* (London) 41 (1965) 27-29; S.E. JOHNSON, *ChrCent* 81 (1964) 368; W. KOESTER, *TheolPhil* 41 (1966) 119-121; X. LÉON-DUFOUR, *RSR* 53 (1965) 616-623; B. LINDARS, *JTS* 17 (1966) 135-138; J. MAIER, *Judaica* 21 (1965) 191-192; J.-C. MARGOT, *RTP* 17 (1967) 197-198; J.E. MÉNARD, *RHR* 168 (1965) 200-201; F.L. MORIARTY, *Greg* 45 (1964) 826-828; V. NIKIPROVETZKY, *RevÉtudJuiv* 123 (1964) 518-526; D.J. O'C., *IrEcclRec* 104 (1965) 381-383; B. PEARSON, *VigChr* 21 (1967) 63-65; 23 (1969) 307; N. PERRIN, *JRel* 45 (1965) 54; L. POIRIER, *CBQ* 27 (1965) 57-59; J. RADERMAKERS, *NRT* 89 (1967) 696; L.F. RIVERA, *RevistBíb* 29 (1967) 126; S. SANDMEL, *TTod* 23 (1966-67) 290-294; L.H. SILBERMAN, *Judaism* 13 (1964) 506-510; W. SIMON, *ChurchQR* 165 (1964) 512-513; G. STRECKER, *NTS* 13 (1966-67) 105-112; H.M. TEEPLE, *JBR* 33 (1965) 170-172; É. TROCMÉ, *RHPR* 44 (1964) 255-256; S. VIRGULIN, *EuntDoc* 17 (1964) 159-160; D.H. WALLACE, *ChrTod* 8 (1963-64) 605-607; P. WINTER, *ATR* 47 (1965) 302-307; *Gnomon* (München) 38 (1966) 102-103; M. ZERWICK, *VD* 42 (1964) 199-203.

1963b Matthew, Gospel according to. — HASTINGS, J. (ed.), *Dictionary of the Bible* [1909], ed. F.C. Grant & H.H. Rowley, Edinburgh: Clark, ²1963, 630-633.

1966a *The Sermon on the Mount*. Cambridge: University Press, 1966, VIII-163 p. Esp. 1-32: "The setting in Matthew"; 65-90: "The setting in the contemporary Judaism"; 91-125: "The setting in the early church"; 126-150: "The setting in the ministry of Jesus". [NTA 11, p. 272]; (Resource Book). Nashville, TN – New York: Abingdon, ²1968, 163 p.
F.W. BEARE, *JBL* 88 (1969) 88-91; F.L. MORIARTY, *Greg* 48 (1967) 371; J. NEVES, *Itinerarium* 14 (1968) 161-162; G.G. O'COLLINS, *HeythJ* 8 (1967) 456; J. RADERMAKERS, *NRT* 86 (1967) 696; L.F. RIVERA, *RevistBíb* 31 (1969) 56-57; A. SALAS, *CiudDios* 180 (1967) 459; S.E. SMITH, *CBQ* 29 (1967) 612-613; S.D. TOUSSAINT, *BS* 124 (1967) 360-361.
*Die Bergpredigt. Exegetische Untersuchung ihrer jüdischen und frühchristlichen Elemente*, trans. G. & G. Reim. München: Claudius, 1970, 199 p.
R. BAUMANN, *BK* 26 (1971) 94-95; K. NIEDERWIMMER, *TLZ* 96 (1971) 686-688.
*Pour comprendre "le Sermon sur la montagne"*, trans. É. McGraw (Parole de Dieu, 4). Paris: Seuil, 1970, 192 p.
P. BONNARD, *RTP* 21 (1971) 265-266; M. BOUTTIER, *ETR* 45 (1970) 392-393; H. COUSIN, *VSp* 124 (1971) 634; J. DECROIX, *BiBTS* 127 (1971) 22-23; J. DUPONT, *RHE* 66 (1971) 704-705; X. JACQUES, *NRT* 94 (1972) 1098-1099; B. JAY, *RHPR* 51 (1971) 386-387; M.É. LAUZIÈRE, *RThom* 71 (1971) 678-679; S. LÉGASSE, *BullLitEccl* 73 (1972) 283-284; J.É. MÉNARD, *RHR* 181 (1972) 210-212; *RevSR* 46 (1972) 81-82; M. MORLET, *EVie* 81 (1971) 435.

*El sermón de la montaña.* Madrid: Cristiandad, 1975, 245 p.
*Bergspredikan. Ett bidrag till fördjupad förståelse,* trans. S. Lindhaven. Stockholm: Verbum, 1971, 176 p.
*Capire il Sermone sul monte. Il quadro storico, teologico e culturale,* trans. A. Comba (Piccola biblioteca teologica, 8). Torino: Claudiana, 1975, 188 p.
    G. BERNINI, *CC* 127/1 (1976) 518-519; M. CAPRIOLI, *EphCarm* 27 (1976) 308; G.G. GAMBA, *Sal* 37 (1975) 861; G. LEONARDI, *Studia Patavina* 22 (1975) 651; C.C. MAECHESELLI, *Asprenas* 22 (1975) 446-448; C. MATEOS, *EstAgust* 10 (1975) 316; G. MOLLICA, *Augustinianum* 15 (1975) 500-501; S. RONCHI, *Protestantesimo* 31 (1976) 113-114; P. ZERAFA, *Angelicum* 53 (1976) 112-113.

1966b  *Invitation to the New Testament. A Guide to Its Main Witnesses.* Garden City, NY: Doubleday, 1966; London: Darton, Longman & Todd, 1967, XII-540 p. Esp. 84-96: "The sources of the gospels"; 209-218: "The gospel of Matthew".
    *Aproximación al Nuevo Testamento. Guía para una lectura ilustrada y creyente,* trans. J. Valiente Malla. Madrid: Cristiandad, 1979, 478 p.

1969    The Relevance of the Moral Teaching of the Early Church. — ELLIS, E.E. – WILCOX, M. (eds.), *Neotestamentica et Semitica.* FS M. Black, 1969, 30-44. Esp. 32-33; = ID., *Jewish and Pauline Studies,* 1984, 289-302 (notes, 399-404). Esp. 293-294. → 1972

1972    The Moral Teaching of the Early Church. — EFIRD, J.M. (ed.), *The Use of the Old Testament in the New.* FS W.F. Stinespring, 1972, 310-332. Esp. 325-329; = ID., *Jewish and Pauline Studies,* 1984, 278-288 (notes, 387-399). Esp. 285-287. → 1969

1974    *The Gospel and the Land. Early Christianity and Jewish Territorial Doctrine.* Berkeley, CA: Univ. of California Press, 1974, XV-521 p. Esp. 221-243: "The land in Mark and Matthew" [11,20-24]; 336-365: "Jesus and the land" [5,5; 19,28; 25,14-30]. → 1975

1975    Jérusalem et la terre dans la tradition chrétienne. — *RHPR* 55 (1975) 491-533. Esp. 497-500 [5,3-12; 19,28]. → 1974

1984    *Jewish and Pauline Studies.* London: SPCK; Minneapolis MN: Fortress, 1984, XI-419 p. → 1962b, 1969, 1972

1988    → Allison 1988a

1990    A Different Approach to Jamnia: The Jewish Sources of Matthew's Messianism. — FORTNA, R.T. – GAVENTA, B.R. (eds.), *The Conversation Continues. Studies in Paul & John. In Honor of J. Louis Martyn,* Nashville, TN: Abingdon, 1990, 378-395. Esp. 380-382: "The new creation" [1,1]; 382-385: "The Son of David"; 385-387: "The Son of Abraham"; 387-394: "The greater Moses".
    The Jewish Sources of Matthew's Messianism. — CHARLESWORTH, J.H., et al. (eds.), *The Messiah,* 1992, 494-511. Esp. 496-498; 499-501; 501-503; 503-511.

1991a  → Allison 1988a/91

1991b  & ALLISON, D.C., Jr., Reflections on the Sermon on the Mount. — *ScotJT* 44 (1991) 283-309. Esp. 284-293: "Some traditional approaches"; 294-309: "Eight theses". [NTA 36, 709]

1992    & ALLISON, D.C., Jr., Matt. 28:16-20: Texts Behind the Text. — *RHPR* 72 (1992) 89-98. [NTA 36, 1285]

1997    → Allison 1988a/97

**DAVIS, Carl Judson**
1996    *The Name and Way of the Lord. Old Testament Themes. New Testament Christology* (JSNT SS, 129). Sheffield: JSOT, 1996, 227 p. Esp. 87-101: "Isaiah 40.3 in the New Testament: New Testament data". — Diss. Sheffield, 1993 (R.P. Martin).

**DAVIS, Charles Thomas**
1967    *Tradition and Redaction in Matthew 1-2.* Diss. Emory Univ., Atlanta, GA, 1967, 193 p. — *DissAbstr* 28 (1967-68) 1887-1888.

1971    Tradition and Redaction in Matthew 1:18-2:23. — *JBL* 90 (1971) 404-421. Esp. 404-406: "Current state of research"; 406-411: "The unity of formal structure and language in Matthew 1-2" [2,22-23; 4,12-17]; 411-419: "The unity of quotation and narration" [1,1-17.23; 2,6.15.18.23]. [NTA 16, 849]

1973    The Fulfillment of Creation. A Study of Matthew's Genealogy. — *JAAR* 41 (1973) 520-
        535. Esp. 522-537: "The Matthean vision of history" [1,1-17]. [NTA 18, 848]

**DAVIS, Christian R.**
1988    Structural Analysis of Jesus' Narrative Parables: A Conservative Approach. — *GraceTJ*
        9 (1988) 191-204. [NTA 33, 1101]

**DAVIS, James J.**
1971    Saint Joseph in the "Postillae" of Hugh of St. Cher. — *EstJos* 24 = *CahJos* 19 (1971)
        296-317. Esp. 298-301, 303-308, 312.

**DAVIS, Philip George**
1994    Divine Agents, Mediators, and New Testament Christology. — *JTS* 45 (1994) 479-503.
        Esp. 488-489. [NTA 39, 1021]

**DAVIS, Stephen T.**
1993    *Risen Indeed. Making Sense of the Resurrection.* London: SPCK; Grand Rapids, MI:
        Eerdmans, 1993, XII-220 p. Esp. 62-84.

**DAVIS, William Hersey**
1962    *Davis' Notes on Matthew.* Nashville, TN: Broadman, 1962, 109 p. [NTA 7, p. 265]
            R.D. CONGDON, *BS* 120 (1963) 280-281.

**DAVISON, James E.**
1985    *Anomia* and the Question of an Antinomian Polemic in Matthew. — *JBL* 104 (1985)
        617-635. Esp. 626-633: "*Anomia* in the gospel of Matthew" [7,21-23; 13,41; 23,28; 24,10-12]. [NTA 30,
        1037]

**DAYTON, Wilbert T.**
1953    *The Greek Perfect Tense in Relation to John 20:23, Matthew 16:19 and Matthew 18:18.*
        Diss. Northern Bapt. Theol. Sem., 1953.

**D'CRUZ, Peter**
1988    "The Rock" in the New Testament. — *Vidyajyoti* 52 (1988) 285-292. [NTA 33, 347]

**DE AMBROGGI, Pietro**
1952    et al., Matteo, apostolo, evangelista. — *Enciclopedia Cattolica* (Città del Vaticano) 8
        (1952) 485-495. Esp. 486-493.

**DEAN, Margaret E.**
1993a   *Reading Matthew's Treasure Map: Territoriality in Matthew's Five Sermons.* Diss.
        Phillips Graduate Sem., 1993.

1993b   → B.B. Scott 1993b

**DE ANDIA, Ysabel**
1984    La beatitudine dei miti (Mt V,5) nell'interpretazione di Ireneo. — *RivStoLR* 20 (1984)
        275-286. → 1989

1989    L'interprétation irénéenne de la béatitude des doux: "Bienheureux les doux, ils
        recevront la terre en héritage" (Mt 5:5). — *Studia Patristica* 18/3 (1989) 85-102. → 1984

1990    Le mystère de la Transfiguration. — LÉTHEL, F.-M. (ed.), *L'Évangile de Jésus. Ren-
        contre spirituelle et théologique 1989* (Spiritualité, 6), Venasque: Carmel, 1990, 45-78.

**DEAN-OTTING, Miriam**
1993    & ROBBINS, V.K., Biblical Sources for Pronouncement Stories in the Gospels. —
        *Semeia* 64 (1993) 95-113. Esp. 96-99 [9,10-13]; 103-105 [12,5-7]. [NTA 39, 778]

**DEARDORF, James W.**

1992 *The Problems of New Testament Gospel Origins. A Glasnost Approach.* San Francisco, CA: Mellen Research University Press, 1992, IX-228 p. Esp. 9-32 [Papias]; 70-73; 75-91 [Urgospel]; 94-103 [Lk/Mt]; 140-150 [minor agreements]; 150-155: "Further evidence that E2 edited Matthew"; 157-175: "Deficiencies of the Griesbach hypothesis"; 185-202: "Speculations of the *Logia's* contents".
F. NEIRYNCK, *ETL* 69 (1993) 180-181.

**DEARING, Vinton A.**

1979 The Synoptic Problem: Prolegomena to a New Solution. — O'FLAHERTY, W.D. (ed.), *The Critical Study of Sacred Texts* (Berkeley Religious Studies Series), Berkeley, CA: Graduate Theological Union, 1979, 121-137.

**DE BAAR, H.**

1961 *De Bijbel over de wederkomst van Christus* (De Bijbel over..., 7). Roermond–Maaseik: Romen, 1961, 115 p. Esp. 27-33.60-67.

**DE BEAUMONT, Pierre**

1967 *L'Évangile selon saint Matthieu.* Paris: Fayard-Mame, 1967, 163 p.

**DE BEUS, Charles**

1953 *Jezus en de Wet* (Verkenning en Verklaring, 3). Amsterdam: Uitgeversmaatschappij Holland, 1953, 128 p. Esp. 20-28 [righteousness]; 29-35 [5,17-20]; 36-48 [5,21-26]; 49-58 [5,27-32]; 60-63 [5,33-37]; 64-69 [5,38-42]; 70-80 [love]; 81-95 [law].

1955 Achtergrond en inhoud van de uitdrukking "de Zoon des Mensen" in de synoptische evangeliën. — *NTT* 9 (1954-55) 272-295.

1960 Een onderzoek naar formulecitaten bij Mattheüs met het oog op het vroegste christologische denken volgens het Nieuwe Testament. — *NTT* 14 (1960) 401-419. [NTA 5, 702]

1979 *Komst en toekomst van het Koninkrijk. Studie over het Koninkrijk Gods en het Koningschap van Jezus, volgens de Evangeliën.* Voorburg: Protestantse Stichting Bibliotheekwezen, 1979, 269 p. Esp. 49-90: "Het evangelie van Mattheüs" [4,23; 5,3.10.17-20.48; 6,10.33; 8,11-12; 9,35; 10,5-42; 12,28; 18; 19,12.23-24; 20,21; 21,31.43; 23,13; 24,14]; 145-165: "De gelijkenissen van het Koninkrijk" [13,3-9.31-32/Mk; 13,24-30.36-43.44-46.47-50; 20 1-16; 22,1-14; 25,1-13.14-30]; 179-182 [6,10]; 217-223 [25,31-46]; 225-231 [28,18-20]; 233-237 [21,43].

**DE BOER, Martinus C.**

1988 Ten Thousand Talents? Matthew's Interpretation and Redaction of the Parable of the Unforgiving Servant (Matt 18:23-35). — *CBQ* 50 (1988) 214-232. Esp. 214-219: "Ten thousand talents?"; 219-228: "Matthew's interpretation and redaction". [NTA 32, 1116]

1993* (ed.), *From Jesus to John: Essays on Jesus and New Testament Christology in Honour of Marinus de Jonge* (SNTS SS, 84). Sheffield: JSOT, 1993, 363 p. → Catchpole, H.J. de Jonge 1991, Stanton, Tuckett

**DE BRUIN, Cebus Cornelis**

(ed.), *Corpus Sacrae Scripturae Neerlandicae Medii Aevi.* Leiden: Brill, 1970-1984.
*Series minor.* Tomus I. *Harmoniae evangeliorum – Evangeliënharmonieën.* 4 vols., 1970.
Vol. I: *Diatessaron Leodiense – Het Luikse Diatessaron*, XLII-312 p.; Vol. II: *Diatessaron Haarense – Het Haarense Diatessaron*, VII-123 p.; Vol. III: *Diatessaron Cantabrigiense – Het Diatessaron van Cambridge*, V-64 p.; Vol. IV: *Diatessaron Theodiscum – Das Leben Jhesu*, ed. C. Gerhardt, XXII-180 p.
*Series minor.* Tomus II. *Lectionaria.* 2 vols., 1970/73.
Vol. I: *Lectionarium Amstelodamense – Het Amsterdamse Lectionarium*, 1970, IX-330 p.; Vol. II: *Lectionarium Gruuthusianum – Het Lectionarium van Gruuthuse*, 1973, X-252 p.
*Miscellanea.* 2 vols., 1984.

Vol. III: *Diatessaron Leodiense. Indices – Het Luikse Diatessaron. Registers*, XVIII-40 p.; Vol. IV: *Fragmenta – Fragmenten*, XIII-187 p. Esp. 116-133.
*Series maior*. Tomus II. *Novum Testamentum*. 2 vols., 1971/79.
Vol. I: *Novum Testamentum in linguam belgicam meridionalem versum. Pars prior: Evangelica – De Zuidnederlandse vertaling van het Nieuwe Testament. Eerste stuk: Evangeliën*, 1971, X-145 p. Esp. 1-42.
Vol. II: *Novum Testamentum Devotionis Modernae – Het Nieuwe Testament van de Moderne Devotie*, 1979, XII-337 p. Esp. 1-41.

**DEBRUNNER, Albert**
1913[R] BLASS, F. – DEBRUNNER, A., *Grammatik des neutestamentlichen Griechisch* [[1]1913, [5]1921, [6]1931, [7]1943, [8]1949]. Göttingen: Vandenhoeck & Ruprecht, [9]1954, [10]1959, XVIII-368 p.; [11]1961, [12]1965 (mit Ergänzungsheft von David TABACHOVITZ, 56 p.); [13]1970. →
Rehkopf 1976
*A Greek Grammar of the New Testament and Other Early Christian Literature. A Translation and Revision of the Ninth-Tenth German Edition* [1954/1959] *Incorporating Supplementary Notes of A. Debrunner by Robert W. Funk*. Chicago, IL – London: University of Chicago Press, 1961, XXXVIII-325 p.

1952 *"Epiousios"* und kein Ende. — *Museum Helveticum* (Basel) 9 (1952) 60-62.

**DE BURGOS NUÑEZ, Miguel**
1982 La resurrección de Jesús, revelación escatológica del poder de Dios sobre la muerte. — *Communio* (Sevilla) 15 (1982) 155-193. Esp. 176-178 [28,1-10]. [NTA 27, 489]

**DE CHALENDAR, Xavier**
1981 Et l'argent... Matthieu 19,30–20,16. — *Christus* 28 (1981) 450-456.

**DE CHAZAL, Nancy**
1994 The Women in Jesus' Family Tree. — *Theology* 97 (1994) 413-419. [NTA 39, 793]

**DÉCLAIS, Jean-Louis**
1995 Les ouvriers de la onzième heure, ou la parabole du salaire contesté. De l'évangile au midrash et au hadith. [20,1-16] — *Islamocristiana* 21 (1995) 43-63.

**DE CLERCK, Paul**
1990 Les origines de la formule baptismale. [28,19] — ID. – PALAZZO, É. (eds.), *Rituels. Mélanges offerts à Pierre-Marie Gy, o.p.*, Paris: Cerf, 1990, 199-213.

**DE CONICK, April D.**
1990 The Yoke Saying in the *Gospel of Thomas* 90. [11,28-30] — *VigChr* 44 (1990) 280-294. [NTA 35, 993]

**DEDEN, D.**
1962 *De Bijbel over de Kerk* (De Bijbel over..., 13). Roermond–Maaseik: Romen, 1962, 106 p. Esp. 26-33 [16,17-19].

**DE DIEGO, J.**
1978 The Infancy Gospels and Christology. [Chinese] — *ColcTFu* 10/36 (1978) 241-258.

**DE DIÉTRICH, Suzanne**
1961 *The Gospel according to Matthew*, trans. D.G. Miller (The Layman's Bible Commentary, 16). Richmond, VA: Knox, 1961, 152 p. [NTA 6, p. 267]; Atlanta, GA: Knox, 1977.
P.L. HAMMER, *Interpr* 17 (1963) 214; S.D. TOUSSAINT, *BS* 119 (1962) 186.
*Mais moi, je vous dis. Commentaire de l'Évangile de Matthieu*. Neuchâtel: Delachaux & Niestlé, 1965, 191 p.
S.S., *BibOr* 9 (1967) 217-218; F. SALVONI, *RicBibRel* 2 (1967) 79-80.

**DEEKS, David G.**
1977 Papias Revisited. — *ExpT* 88 (1976-77) 296-301, 324-329. Esp. 298-299. [NTA 22, 289]

**DEER, Donald S.**

1967   The Implied Agent in Greek Passive Verb Forms in the Gospel of Matthew. — *BTrans* 18 (1967) 164-167. [NTA 12, 548]

1975   The Interpretation and Translation of Constructions with a Passive Meaning in the Greek of the Synoptic Gospels. — *BTrans* 26 (1975) 338-346. [NTA 20, 71]

1987   Supplying "Only" in Translation. — *BTrans* 38 (1987) 227-234. Esp. 227-228. [NTA 32, 54]

**DE FOUCAULT, Jules-Albert**

1970   Notre pain quotidien. — *RevÉtudGrecq* 83 (1970) 56-62.

**DE FRAINE, Jan**

1960a  *Bijbels bidden. De Bijbelse achtergrond van grote gebeden.* Brugge: Beyaert, 1960, 256 p. Esp. 7-95: "Het Onze Vader"; 175-253: "De acht zaligheden".
*Prier avec la Bible.* Brugge: Beyaert, 1961.
*Praying with the Bible. The Biblical Bases of Great Christian Prayers,* trans. J.W. Saul [French, 1961]. New York: Desclée, 1964, VIII-182 p. Esp. 1-64; 127-182.

1960b  Oraison dominicale. — *DBS* 6/33 (1960) 788-800. Esp. 788-790: "Critique textuelle"; 790-793: "Critique littéraire"; 793-795: "Les sources".

**DE FREITAS FERREIRA, José**

1980   *Conceição virginal de Jesus. Análise crítica da pesquisa liberal protestante, desde a "Declaração de Eisenach" até hoje, sobre o testemunho de Mt 1,18-25 e Lc 1,26-38* (AnGreg, 217). Roma: Pont. Univ. Greg., 1980, 535 p. Esp. 13-89: "A Conceição virginal em Mt 1,18-25"; 219-268: "Uma única tradição – dois testemunhos independentes". [NTA 25, p. 301] — Diss. Pont. Univ. Greg., Roma, 1977 (J. Galot). → Aranda Pérez 1982
D. AMATO, *Sal* 47 (1985) 335-336; D. FERNÁNDEZ, *EphMar* 32 (1982) 124-125; J. GALOT, *CC* 132/4 (1981) 614-615; R. GAUTHIER, *CahJos* 28 (1980) 271-272; R. LAURENTIN, *Didaskalia* 12/1 (1982) 195-199; S. LÉGASSE, *BullLitEccl* 86 (1985) 223; M.-V. LEROY, *RThom* 85 (1985) 137-139; E.M. PERETTO, *Marianum* 47 (1985) 605-607; G. SEGALLA, *Studia Patavina* 28 (1981) 650-651; F. URICCHIO, *MiscFranc* 83 (1983) 368-372.

**DE FUENTERRABÍA, Felipe**

1956   Doctrina del Nuevo Testamento y del judaísmo contemporáneo sobre la remisión de los pecados más allá de la muerte. — *La escatología individual neotestamentaria a la luz de las ideas en los tiempos apostolicos. Otros estudios* (XVI Semana Biblica Española), Madrid: Consejo Superior de Investicagiones Científicas, 1956, 187-224. Esp. 213-217 [12,31-32].

1956   La imagen parabólica del matrimonio y la parábola de las diez vírgenes. — *EstFranc* 57 (1956) 321-362. Esp. 322-324 [9,14-17]; 324-328 [22,1-14]; 331-362 [25,1-13].

**DE GAIFFIER, Baudouin**

1962a  Hagiographie salernitaine. La translation de S. Matthieu. — *AnBoll* 80 (1962) 82-110. → Atenolfi 1958

1962b  La commémoration de S. Matthieu au 6 mai dans le martyrologe hiéronymien. — *Ibid.*, 111-115.

**DE GOEDT, Michel**

1959   L'explication de la parabole de l'ivraie (Mt. XIII,36-43). Création matthéenne, ou aboutissement d'une histoire littéraire? — *RB* 66 (1959) 32-54. Esp. 34-44: "Le point de vue littéraire"; 44-49: "Le 'Sitz im Leben' de Mt., XIII,36-43"; 49-54: "Le 'passé' de Mt., XIII,36-43". [NTA 4, 81]

1970   Jésus parle aux foules en paraboles. Mt 13,24-43. — *AssSeign* II/47 (1970) 18-27.

1988    Élie le prophète dans les Évangiles synoptiques. — WILLEMS, G.F. (ed.), *Élie le prophète. Bible, tradition, iconographie. Colloque des 10 et 11 novembre 1985, Bruxelles* (Publications de l'Institutum Iudaicum), Leuven: Peeters, 1988, 69-90. Esp. 78-81 [3,1-6.11-12; 11,2-15; 14,1-2; 17,1-13; 27,45-54].

**DE GRAAF, Johannes**

1971    *In gesprek met de bergrede*. Den Haag: Boekencentrum, 1971, 67 p.
        *Mit der Bergpredigt leben* (Siebenstern, 1057). Gütersloh: Mohn, 1982, 79 p. → Frankemölle 1983c

**DE GROOT, Adriaan**

1961    *De Bijbel over het wonder* (De Bijbel over..., 11). Roermond–Maaseik: Romen, 1961, 111 p. Esp. 62-80: "Het wonder als verkondiging en lering in het Mattheüsevangelie" [8,2-17.23-27; 9,2-8; 15,21-28].

1964    *De Bijbel over het heil der volken* (De Bijbel over..., 21). Roermond–Maaseik: Romen, 1964, 124 p. Esp. 71-72 [10,5-6; 15,24]; 73-79 [universalism]; 84-87 [28,18-20].

**DE HAES, Paul**

1953    *La Résurrection de Jésus dans l'apologétique des cinquante dernières années* (AnGreg, 59). Roma: Pont. Univ. Greg., 1953, XII-318 p.

1961    Maria en Jozef volgens Mattheus I.18-25. — *De Mariapassages uit het Matthaüsevangelie* (Verslagboek der achttiende Mariale Dagen), Tongerlo: Norbertijner-abdij, 1961, 93-104; = *De Standaard van Maria* 38 (1962) 62-71.

**DE HALLEUX, André**

1963    *Philoxène de Mabbog. Sa vie, ses écrits, sa théologie* (Universitas Catholica Lovaniensis. Dissertationes, III/8). Leuven: Orientaliste, 1963, X-571 p. Esp. 134-142: "Fragments du commentaire de *Matthieu*" [1,15.17; 2,1.14-15; 3,1-16; 4,1-11; 5,17; 11,11; 13,16-17; 16,16-17; 22,29-32; 25,14-30; 26,26-29.36-44; 27,45-53].

1980    Le commentaire de Philoxène sur *Matthieu* et *Luc*. Deux éditions récentes. — *Muséon* 93 (1980) 5-35. → Fox 1979, J.W. Watt 1978

**DEHANDSCHUTTER, Boudewijn**

1971    Les paraboles de l'Évangile selon Thomas. La parabole du trésor caché (log. 109). — *ETL* 47 (1971) 199-219. Esp. 211-219 [13,44-46/Th 109]. [NTA 16, 409]

1974    La parabole des vignerons homicides (Mc., XII,1-12) et l'Évangile selon Thomas. — SABBE, M. (ed.), *L'Évangile selon Marc*, 1974, 203-219; ²1988 (note additionnelle, 219-220). Esp. 205-212 [Th 63-64].

1977    *Martyrium Polycarpi. Een literair-kritische studie* (BETL, 52). Leuven: Universitaire Pers, 1977, 296 p. Esp. 233-258: "Verwijzingen naar het Nieuwe Testament".

1979    La parabole de la perle (Mt 13,45-46) et l'Évangile selon Thomas. — *ETL* 55 (1979) 243-265. Esp. 249-258: "La rédaction du logion 76"; 258-265: "L'interprétation de la parabole". [NTA 24, 1051]

1982a   L'Évangile de Thomas comme collection de paroles de Jésus. — DELOBEL, J. (ed.), *Logia*, 1982, 507-515. Esp. 507-510 [Th/Q].

1982b   The Gospel of Thomas and the Synoptics: the Status Quaestionis. — *Studia Evangelica* 7 (1982) 157-160. Esp. 158-160.

1986    → Massaux 1950/86, 799-850

1989    Polycarp's Epistle to the Philippians. An Early Example of "Reception". — SEVRIN, J.-M. (ed.), *The New Testament in Early Christianity*, 1989, 275-291. Esp. 286-290.

1991    L'adoration des Mages dans le commentaire syriaque du Diatessaron. [2,1-12] — *Muséon* 104 (1991) 251-264.

1992 Recent Research on the Gospel of Thomas. — VAN SEGBROECK, F., et al. (eds.), *The Four Gospels 1992*. FS F. Neirynck, 1992, III, 2257-2262. Esp. 2258-2260 [Thomas/Q].

**DEICHGRÄBER, Reinhard**
1967 *Gotteshymnus und Christushymnus in der frühen Christenheit. Untersuchungen zu Form, Sprache und Stil der frühchristlichen Hymnen* (SUNT, 5). Göttingen: Vandenhoeck & Ruprecht, 1967, 251 p. Esp. 25-36 [doxologies: 6,13].

**DEIDENBACH, H.**
1990 *Zur Psychologie der Bergpredigt* (Fischer Taschenbuch, 10259). Frankfurt/M: Fischer, 1990, 250 p.

**DEIDUN, Thomas**
1976 The Parable of the Unmerciful Servant (Mt 18:23-35). — *BTB* 6 (1976) 203-224. Esp. 203-209: "Two recent interpretations" [Dietzfelbinger 1972, Deiss 1974]; 210-219: "The original meaning of the parable"; 220-224: "Matthew's interpretation". [NTA 21, 84]

**DEISS, Lucien**
1963a *Synopse de Matthieu, Marc et Luc avec les parallèles de Jean*. I: *Introduction, notes et vocabulaire*. II: *Texte*. Brugge: Desclée De Brouwer, 1964/1963, 192 and 239 p. Esp. I, 23-33: "Introduction à l'évangile de Matthieu"; 57-59 [1-2]; 64-69 [3-4]; 69-79 [5-7]; 79-82 [8-9]; 82-85 [10-11,1]; 86-89 [11,2-12,21]; 92-109 [12,22-19,1]; 122-134 [19-23]; 134-139 [24-25]; 139-148 [26-27]; 149-152 [28]. → 1991; → Léon-Dufour 1972c

1963b Matthieu 10,5-16. Le livret missionnaire des Douze. — *Spiritus* (Paris) 4 (1963) 245-256.

1964 La parabole du débiteur impitoyable. [18,23-35] — *AssSeign* I/76 (1964) 29-41.

1966a "Va d'abord te réconcilier avec ton frère". [5,20-24] — *AssSeign* I/59 (1966) 33-46.

1966b La parabole des dix vierges. [25,1-13] — *AssSeign* I/95 (1966) 33-57.

1970 La loi nouvelle. Mt 5,38-48; cf. Lc 6,27-38. — *AssSeign* II/38 (1970) 60-78. → 1971a

1971a La loi nouvelle. Mt 5,17-37. — *AssSeign* II/37 (1971) 19-33. → 1970

1971b La parabole des dix vierges. Mt. 25,1-13. — *AssSeign* II/63 (1971) 20-32.

1974 Le pardon entre frères. Mt 18,21-35. — *AssSeign* II/55 (1974) 16-24. [NTA 19, 538] → Deidun 1976

1991 *Synopse des Évangiles. Matthieu – Marc – Luc – Jean*. Nouvelle édition. Paris: Desclée De Brouwer, 1991, 421 p. Esp. 23-238: "Texte de Matthieu, Marc, Luc"; 311-325: "Introduction à Matthieu". → 1963

**DEISSLER, Alfons**
1974 Der Geist des Vaterunsers im alttestamentlichen Glauben und Beten. — BROCKE, M., et al. (eds.), *Das Vaterunser*, 1974, 129-150.
The Spirit of the Lord's Prayer in the Faith and Worship of the Old Testament. — BROCKE, M. – PETUCHOWSKI, J.J. (eds.), *The Lord's Prayer*, 1978, 3-17

**DEIST, Ferdinand E.**
1993 Die teken van Jona en Jesus as Messias (The sign of Jonah and Jesus as Messiah). — *Skrif en Kerk* (Pretoria) 14 (1993) 20-27 (English summary, 27). Esp. 20-22 [12,39-41]. [NTA 38, 766]

**DEJAIFVE, Georges**
1953 M. Cullmann et la question de Pierre. — *NRT* 75 (1953) 365-379. Esp. 373-377. → Cullmann 1952

**DE JONG, H.**
1977 Mattheüs 25 en het diakonaat. — *KerkT* 28 (1977) 46-52.

**DE JONGE, Henk Jan**

1980    De nieuwe Nestle: N²⁶. — *NTT* 34 (1980) 307-322. → K. Aland [Nestle-Aland 1979]

1991    De visie van de historische Jezus op zichzelf. — WEVERS, H.E., et al. (eds.), *Jezus' visie op zichzelf. In discussie met de Jonge's christologie*, Nijkerk: Callenbach, 1991, 48-64.
        The Historical Jesus' View of Himself and of His Mission. — DE BOER, M.C. (ed.), *From Jesus to John.* FS M. de Jonge, 1993, 21-37.

1992    Augustine on the Interrelations of the Gospels. — VAN SEGBROECK, F., et al. (eds.), *The Four Gospels 1992.* FS F. Neirynck, 1992, III, 2409-2417.

**DE JONGE, Marinus**

1966    De berichten over het scheuren van het voorhangsel bij Jezus' dood in de synoptische evangeliën. — *NTT* 21 (1966-67) 90-114. Esp. 90-97.106 [27,51]; 111-112 [23,37-39]. [NTA 11, 1040] → 1986

1967    Het motief van het gescheurde voorhangsel van de tempel in een aantal vroegchristelijke geschriften. [27,51] — *Ibid.*, 257-276. [NTA 12, 168] → 1986

1975    The Use of ὁ Χριστός in the Passion Narratives. — DUPONT, J. (ed.), *Jésus aux origines de la christologie*, 1975, 169-192; ²1989 (additional note, 420). Esp. 183-184; = ID., *Jewish Eschatology*, 1991, 63-86. Esp. 77-78.

1985    Jezus als profetische Zoon van David. — GARCÍA MARTÍNEZ, F. - DE GEUS, C.H.J. - KLIJN, A.F.J. (eds.), *Profeten en profetische geschriften* [FS A.S. van der Woude], Kampen: Kok; Nijkerk: Callenbach, 1985, 157-166. Esp. 165-166.

1986    Matthew 27:51 in Early Christian Exegesis. — *HTR* 79 (1986) 67-79. Esp. 69-72: "Matt 27:51 in its Matthean context"; 72-74: "Related apocryphal gospels"; 74-79: "Second- and third-century christian writers on the rending of the temple veil". [NTA 31, 596] → 1966, 1967

1988    *Christology in Context. The Earliest Christian Response to Jesus.* Philadelphia, PA: Westminster, 1988, 276 p. Esp. 71-88: "The sayings of Jesus in Q"; 91-96: "The christology of Matthew".
        *Christologie in Context. Jezus in de ogen van zijn eerste volgelingen.* Maarssen: De Ploeg, 1992. Esp. 96-119; 126-132.
        *Christologie im Kontext. Die Jesusrezeption des Urchristentums*, trans. R. Luipold - L. Visschers. Neukirchen-Vluyn: Neukirchener, 1995, IX-245 p. Esp. 57-73; 79-84.

1989    Jesus, Son of David and Son of God. — DRAISMA, S. (ed.), *Intertextuality in Biblical Writings.* FS B. van Iersel, 1989, 95-104. Esp. 100; = ID., *Jewish Eschatology*, 1991, 135-144.

1991a   *Jewish Eschatology, Early Christian Christology and the Testaments of the Twelve Patriarchs. Collected Essays* (SupplNT, 63). Leiden: Brill, 1991, XIX-342 p. → 1975, 1989

1991b   De visie van de jood Jezus op zijn opdracht. — BAARDA, T., et al. (eds.), *Jodendom en vroeg christendom*, 1991, 9-27. Esp. 14-15, 20-21, 26 [Q].

1992    Christ. — *ABD* 1 (1992) 914-921. Esp. 917-918.

**DEKKER, W.**

1961    De "geliefde Zoon" in de synoptische evangeliën. — *NTT* 16 (1961-62) 94-106. Esp. 102-105. [NTA 6, 751]

**DE KRUIJF, Theodorus C.**

1961    "Filius Dei Viventis" (Mt 16,16). Collationes ad christologiam evangelii secundum Matthaeum. — *VD* 39 (1961) 39-43. [NTA 6, 128]

1962    *Der Sohn des lebendigen Gottes. Ein Beitrag zur Christologie des Matthäusevangeliums* (AnBib, 16). Roma: Pontifical Biblical Institute, 1962, XVII-187 p. Esp. 41-115: "'Sohn

Gottes' bei Matthäus: Analyse der Texte" [2,15; 3,17; 4,3.6; 8,29; 11,27; 14,33; 16,16; 17,5; 24,36; 26,63; 27,40.43.54; 28,19]; 117-168: "Der Sohn des lebendigen Gottes". [NTA 8, p. 287] — Diss. Pont. Inst. Bibl., Roma, 1960 (M. Zerwick).

M.-É. BOISMARD, *RB* 71 (1964) 449-450; B. BRINKMANN, *Scho'astik* 39 (1964) 616-617; F. DREYFUS, *RSPT* 48 (1964) 318-319; J.A. FITZMYER, *TS* 25 (1964) 427-430 J.T. FORESTELL, *CBQ* 25 (1963) 447-450; P. GAECHTER, *ZKT* 86 (1964) 222-223; G.G. GAMBA, *Sai* 27 (1965) 465-466; S. GONZÁLEZ DE CARREA, *EstBíb* 24 (1965) 167-169; H.B. GREEN, *JTS* 15 (1964) 126-129; P. SEIDENSTICKER, *Franziskanische Studien* (Paderborn) 45 (1963) 189-191.

1974    Das Volk Gottes im Neuen Testament. — *Theologische Berichte* (Zürich) 3 (1974) 119-133. Esp. 122-126.

1985    & POORTHUIS, M., *Abinoe Onze Vader: Over de joodse achtergronden van het Onze Vader*. Utrecht: Secretariaat RK Kerkgenootschap in Nederland, 1985, 105 p.
        P.W. VAN DER HORST, *NTT* 39 (1985) 243-244.

1993    Go Therefore and Make Disciples of All Nations: Mt 28,19. — *Bijdragen* 54 (1993) 19-29. [NTA 38, 170]

**DE LA CALLE, Francisco**

1974    → Pikaza 1974a

1979    El evangelio ¿nuevo módulo de reconciliación? El mensaje de Jesús en la teología de Mateo. — *BibFe* 5 (1979) 34-46. [NTA 23, 807]

1980    José, el esposo. — *BibFe* 6 (1980) 293-303. [NTA 25, 453]

1983    Padre, que se lleve a cabo tu voluntad. [6,10] — *BibFe* 9 (1983) 36-43.

**DE LA CAMPA, H.**

1955    La estrella de los Magos. — *Proyección* (Granada) 7 (1955) 3-37.

**DE LA FUENTE, Alfonso**

1995    A favor o en contra de Jesús. El logion de Mc 9,40 y sus paralelos. — *EstBíb* 53 (1995) 449-459. Esp. 450-452, 457-459 [12,30]. [NTA 40, 1482]

**DE LA GAZZA, Rogelio**

1995    *Las parabolas en la exégesis de Juan Maldonado*. Diss. Athenaeum Romanum S. Crucis Fac. Theol., Roma, 1995, VIII-303 p. (M.A. Tabet – B. Estrada). Esp. 41-76: "El comentario al evangelio de San Mateo"; 205-232 [25,1-13]; 233-266 [25,14-30].

**DEL AGUA PÉREZ, Agustín**

1984    Derás cristológico del Salmo 110 en el Nuevo Testamento. — FERNÁNDEZ MARCOS, N., et al. (eds.), *Simposio bíblico español. Salamanca 1982*, Madrid: Complutense, 1984, 637-662.

1987    Aproximación al relato de los evangelios desde el micrás/derás. — *EstBíb* 45 (1987) 257-284. Esp. 279-280 [1,1]. [NTA 33, 78]
        Die "Erzählung" des Evangeliums im Lichte der Derasch Methode. — *Judaica* 47 (1991) 140-154. Esp. 149-150. [NTA 36, 688]

1988    El derás del "reino de Dios" en la tradición sinóptica. Sugerencias tras la lectura de O. Camponovo. [*Königtum, Königsherrschaft und Reich Gottes in den frühjüdischen Schriften*, 1984] — *EstBíb* 46 (1988) 173-186. Esp. 184-185. [NTA 33, 1100r]

1992    Derás narrativo del sobrenombre de "Pedro" en el conjunto de Mt 16,17-19. Un caso particular de la escuela exegética de Mateo. — *Salmanticensis* 39 (1992) 11-33 (English summary, 33). Esp. 13-14: "El consenso crítico"; 14-19 [Peter-Cephas]; 20-31 [Cephas]. [NTA 37, 149]

1994    Los evangelios de la infancia: ¿Verdad histórica o verdad teológica? — *RazFe* 230 (1994) 381-399. Esp. 388-395. [NTA 40, 811]

**DE LANG, Marijke H.**

1993 *De opkomst van de historische en literaire kritiek in de synoptische beschouwing van de evangeliën van Calvijn (1555) tot Griesbach (1774).* Leiden: Faculteit Theologie, 1993, 335 p. Esp. 23-99 [16th cent.]; 103-201 [17th cent.]; 205-270 [18th cent.]; 271-288. — Diss. Leiden, 1993 (H.J. de Jonge).
F. NEIRYNCK, *ETL* 69 (1993) 174-175.

1993 The Prehistory of the Griesbach Hypothesis. — *ETL* 69 (1993) 134-139. [NTA 38, 133]

**DE LANGHE, Robert**

1954 Judaïsme ou hellénisme en rapport avec le Nouveau Testament. — RIGAUX, B. (ed.), *L'attente du Messie* (Recherches bibliques, 1), Brugge: Desclée De Brouwer, 1954, ²1958, 154-183. Esp. 163 [2,11; 7,6]; 164 [22,14]; 165-166 [5,13]; 170 [5,11]; 171 [6,11]; 173-174 [3,15].

**DE LA POTTERIE, Ignace**

1967* (ed.), *De Jésus aux Évangiles. Tradition et rédaction dans les Évangiles synoptiques. Donum natalicium Josepho Coppens septuagesimum annum complenti d.d.d. collegae et amici*, vol. II (BETL, 25). Gembloux: Duculot; Paris: Lethielleux, 1967, XV-271 p.
→ P. Bonnard, A.-M. Denis, Didier, Léon-Dufour, McLoughlin, Neirynck, Rasco, Sabbe, van Iersel
*Da Gesù ai Vangeli. Tradizione e redazione nei vangeli sinottici.* Assisi: Cittadella, 1971, 237 p.

1983 La preghiera di Gesù nei vangeli. — DE GENNARO, G. (ed.), *La preghiera nella Bibbia. Storia, struttura e pratica dell'esperienza religioso* (Pubblicazioni dello studio biblico-teologico Aquilano), Napoli: Dehoniane, 1983, 41-67.

1985 La parabole du prétendant à la royauté (Lc 19,11-28). — GANTOY, R. (ed.), *À cause de l'Évangile.* FS J. Dupont, 1985, 613-641. Esp. 619-631 [25,14-30].

**DE LA SERNA, Eduardo**

1989 ¿Divorcio en Mateo? — *RevistBíb* 51 (1989) 91-110. Esp. 94-98: "El texto de Mt 19"; 98-99: "El texto de Mt 5"; 101-105 [πορνεία]. [NTA 34, 1135]

**DELCOR, Mathias**

1970 À propos de la traduction œcuménique du "Notre Père". — *BullLitEccl* 71 (1970) 127-130.

1981 Un manuscrit hébraïque inédit des quatre évangiles conservé à la Bibliothèque Vaticane (Hebr. 100). — *Anuario de filología* (Barcelona) 7 (1981) 201-219.

1993 La reine de Saba et Salomon. Quelques aspects de l'origine de la légende et de sa formation, principalement dans le monde juif et éthiopien, à partir des textes bibliques. — RAURELL, F., et al. (eds.), *Tradició i traducció.* FS G. Camps, 1993, 307-324. Esp. 310-311 [6,29].

**DELĒBANĒS, A.D.**

1990 *The Sermon on the Mount – The Lord's Prayer* [Greek]. Athens: S. Basilopoulos, 1990, 182 p. [NTA 36, p. 421]

**DELEBECQUE, Édouard**

1959 À propos de Mt 5,3. — *BBudé* 4 (1959) 326-331; 4 (1960) 104-105. → Casanova 1960, Vernotte 1960

1982 "Secouez la poussière de vos pieds...". Sur l'hellénisme de Luc, IX,5. — *RB* 89 (1982) 177-184. Esp. 178 [10,14]. [NTA 27, 552]; = ID., *Études*, 1995, 81-88.

1995a *Études sur le Grec du Nouveau Testament.* Aix-en-Provence: Univ. de la Provence, 1995, 489 p. → 1982, 1995b

1995b   L'Évangile de Matthieu, chapitres 1–8. — *Ibid.*, 405-466. Esp. 406-441 [text]; 442-466 [notes].

**DELESPESSE, Max**

1958    L'évangile selon saint Matthieu. — *Feu Nouveau* 1958/2: 3, 8-14; 4, 9-18 [1]; 5, 8-18 [2]; 6, 7-14 [3,1-12]; 1959/2: 7, 2-14 [3,13–4,25]; 8, 7-19 ⁚5,1-12]; 9, 6-17 [5,13-20]; 10, 7-15 [5,31-46]; 11, 9-20 [6,1-18]; 12, 9-16 [6,19-34]; 13, 9-2⁚ [7]; 14, 3-13 [8,1-22]; 15, 5-15 [8,23–9,17]; 16, 6-16 [9,18–10,4]; 17, 6-17 [10,5-20]; 18, 6-18 [10,21-33]; 19, 9-20 [10,34-42]; 20, 10-20 [11,1-19]; 21, 14-25 [11,20–12,21]; 22, 10-24 [12,22-50]; 1959/3: 1, 11-22 [13,1-23]; 2, 7-17 [13,24-43]; 3, 10-18 [13,44-52]; 4, 12-20 [13,53–14,12]; 5, 9-19 [14,13-36]; 6, 13-22 [15,1-20]; 1960/3: 7, 12-22 [15,21–16,12]; 9, 11-20 [16,13-20]; 10, 2-13 [16,21–17,9]; 11, 9-18 [17,10-27]; 12, 9-17 [18,1-9]; 13, 11-19 [18,10-18]; 14, 9-16 [18,19-35]; 15, 13-22 [19,1-12]; 16, 5-16 [19,13-30]; 17, 5-11 [20,1-16]; 18, 1-13 [20,17-34]; 19, 9-18 [21,1-17]; 20, 9-19 [21,18-32]; 21, 11-21 [21,33-46]; 22, 14-22 [22,1-14]; 1960/4: 2, 8-20 [22,15-33]; 3, 1-10 [22,34-46]; 4, 9-17 [23,1-12]; 5, 13-18 [23,13-22]; 6, 1-10 [23,23-32]; 1961/4: 7, 9-22 [23,33-39]; 8, 4-15 [24,1-14]; 9, 9-16 [24,15-28]; 10, 8-16 [24,29-3⁚]; 11, 12-21 [24,36-44]; 12, 9-20 [24,45–25,13]; 13, 13-25 [25,14-46]; 14, 14-21 [26,1-5.14-16]. 15, 2-14 [26,6-13.17-25]; 16, 16-26 [26,26-29]; 17, 10-21 [26,30-46]; 18, 9-23 [26,47-75]; 19. 12-24 [27,1-26]; 20, 3-15 [27,27-44]; 21, 11-24 [27,45-61]; 22, 4-22 [27,62–28,20].

**DE LETTER, Prudent**

1964    The Day of Judgment. — *The Clergy Monthly* (Ranchi, India) 28 (1964) 369-379. [NTA 9, 926]

**DELGADO, Ana María**

1983    ¡Felices, los mansos! [5,5] — *BibFe* 9 (1983) 137-149.

**DELHAYE, Philippe**

1966    Dossier néo-testamentaire de la charité. — *Studia Montiₛ Regii* (Montréal) 9 (1966) 155-175. Esp. 156-160: "Le discours évangélique de s. Matthieu".

1975    Les normes particulières du Sermon de la montagne d'après les commentaires de S. Thomas. — *EVie* 85 (1975) 33-43, 49-58.

1986    Le Sermon sur la montagne (Mt 5.6.7; Lc 6). Suggestions théologiques et péda-gogiques. — PINCKAERS, S. – PINTO DE OLIVEIRA, C.J. (eds.), *Universalité*, 1986, 408-441. Esp. 422-430 [5,43-48].

**DELLAGIACOMA, Vittore**

1959    Il matrimonio presso gli Ebrei. — *RivBib* 7 (1959) 230-241. Esp. 239-241 [5,32; 19,9]. [NTA 4, 385]

**DELLING, Gerhard**

1955    Das Verständnis des Wunders im Neuen Testament. — *Zeitschrift für systematische Theologie* (Berlin) 24 (1955) 265-280; = ID., *Studien zum Neuen Testament*, 1970, 146-159; = SUHL, A. (ed.), *Der Wunderbegriff im Neuen Testament*, 1980, 300-317.

1956    Das Logion Mark. x 11 [und seine Abwandlungen] im Neuen Testament. — *NT* 1 (1956) 263-274. Esp. 267-268 [5,32]; 268-270 [19,9]. [NTA 2, 293]; = ID., *Studien zum Neuen Testament*, 1970, 226-235. Esp. 229-231; 231-232.

1958*   (ed.), *Gott und die Götter. Festgabe für Erich Fascher zum 60. Geburtstag*. Berlin: Evangelische Verlagsanstalt, 1958, 158 p. → Eissfeldt, Lanczkowski, Stauffer

1960    Botschaft und Wunder im Wirken Jesu. — RISTOW, H. – MATTHIAE, K. (eds.), *Der historische Jesus und der kerygmatische Christus*, 1960, 389-402. Esp. 390-391 [16,4]; 394-397 [11,5-6].

1963    *Die Taufe im Neuen Testament*. Berlin: Evangelische Verlagsanstalt, 1963, 165 p.

1964   *Jesus nach den drei ersten Evangelien*. Berlin: Evangelische Verlagsanstalt, 1964, 111 p.

1970   *Studien zum Neuen Testament und zum hellenistischen Judentum. Gesammelte Aufsätze 1950-1968*, ed. F. Hahn, T. Holtz and N. Walter. Göttingen: Vandenhoeck & Ruprecht, 1970, 463 p. → 1955, 1956

1971   *Wort Gottes und Verkündigung im Neuen Testament* (SBS, 53). Stuttgart: Katholisches Bibelwerk, 1971, 166 p. Esp. 49-66: "Der Geltungsansprach des Wortes Jesu" [11,5-6; ἐξουσία; ἀμήν]; 67-72: "Jesustradition und Verkündigung".

1972   *Der Kreuzestod Jesu in der urchristlichen Verkündigung*. Göttingen: Vandenhoeck & Ruprecht, 1972, 187 p. Esp. 174-182: "Matthäus- und Lukas-Evangelium".

1977   Die "Söhne (Kinder) Gottes" im Neuen Testament. — SCHNACKENBURG, R., et al. (eds.), *Die Kirche des Anfangs*. FS H. Schürmann, 1977, 615-631. Esp. 620-621 [5,9.44-45; 17,26].

**DELL'OCA, R.**

1962   Estudio del Evangelio de la infancia en S. Matteo (1-2). — *RevistBíb* 24 (1962) 84-91.

**DELL'OCCA, E.C.**

1963   Camello por el ojo de una aguja. [19,24] — *RevistBíb* 25 (1963) 43-46. [NTA 9, 157]

**DEL MEDICO, H.E.**

1959   Les ruines de Qumran. — *Studia Evangelica* 1 (1959) 580-581.

**DELMONTE, Carlos**

1979   *Sobre todo el reino. La predicación de Jesús en el Sermón de la montaña*. Buenos Aires: Aurora, 1979, 202 p.
       R. OBERMÜLLER, *CuadTeol* 6 (1980) 86-87.

**DEL NIÑO JESÚS, Julio Felix**

1960   Consideraciones acerca del Evangelio de la Infancia según san Mateo. — *EstJos* 14 (1960) 29-39.

**DELOBEL, Joël**

1966   L'onction par la pécheresse. La composition littéraire de *Lc.*, VII,36-50. — *ETL* 42 (1966) 415-475. Esp. 449-453 [Q 7,18-35]; 453-457 [Q 7,1-10]. [NTA 11, 1065]

1973   La rédaction de Lc., IV, 14-16a et le "Bericht vom Anfang". — NEIRYNCK, F. (ed.), *L' Évangile de Luc*, 1973, 203-223. Esp. 206-207 [4,12-17/Mk]; 210-218 [4,12-17/Lk 4,14-16]; [2]1989, 113-133 (note additionnelle, 306-312). Esp. 116-117; 120-128. → Schürmann 1964, Tuckett 1982a

1977   → Neirynck 1977a

1979   → Neirynck 1979a

1982*  (ed.), *Logia. Les paroles de Jésus - The Sayings of Jesus. Mémorial Joseph Coppens* (BETL, 59). Leuven: University Press / Peeters, 1982, 647 p. [NTA 27, p. 328] → Carlston, Dehandschutter, Delobel, Denaux, Dupont, R.A. Edwards, Fusco, Hickling, A.D. Jacobson, Lambrecht, Légasse, Neirynck 1982d-e, R.A. Piper, J.M. Robinson, Sabbe, Schürmann, Tuckett, van Cangh, Vassiliadis, Vögtle, Wrege, Zeller; → Kevers 1981
       D.R. CATCHPOLE, *JSNT* 22 (1984) 110-112; A.-M. DENIS, *RHE* 80 (1985) 257-259; E.J. EPP, *JBL* 103 (1984) 494-495; C. FOCANT, *RTL* 15 (1984) 99-102; A. FUCHS, *SNTU* 8 (1983) 173-176; T. HOLTZ, *TLZ* 109 (1984) 124-125; J.-C. INGELAERE, *RHPR* 64 (1984) 186-187; J.S. KLOPPENBORG, *CBQ* 46 (1984) 381-383; F. LANGLAMET, *RB* 91 (1984) 301.

1982a  The Sayings of Jesus in the Textual Tradition. Variant Readings in the Greek Manuscripts of the Gospels. — *Ibid.*, 431-457. Esp. 445.447-449.454-455 [lists].

1982b  The Sayings of Jesus. Colloquium Biblicum Lovaniense XXXII (1981). — *ETL* 58 (1982) 197-200. Esp. 197-199: "The problems of the Q source".

1985 Luke 6,5 in Codex Bezae: The Man Who Worked on Sabbath. — GANTOY, R. (ed.), *À cause de l' Évangile*. FS J. Dupont, 1985, 453-477. Esp. 475-476: "Deviations of Mt 12,1-14 D from N[26]".

1989a Extra-Canonical Sayings of Jesus: Marcion and Some "Non-received" Logia. — PETERSEN, W.L. (ed.), *Gospel Traditions*, 1989, 105-116. Esp. 108-109 [Lk 11,2]; 109-111 [Marcion]. → Magne 1988

1989b The Lord's Prayer in the Textual Tradition. A Critique of Recent Theories and Their View on Marcion's Role. [Lk 11,2-4] — SEVRIN, J.-M (ed.), *The New Testament in Early Christianity*, 1989, 293-309. → Amphoux 1987

**DELOFFRE, Jean**

1989 *L'enfant et le Royaume. Recherche sur l'interprétation de Mt 18,3 à partir du Nouveau Testament et des œuvres de saint Augustin*. Diss. Paris, 1989, 286 p. (J. Lévêque).

**DE LORENZI, Lorenzo**

1981 La preghiera del discepolo (Mt 6,9-13). — *ParSpirV* 3 (1981) 106-121.

1983 La croce "segno" del cristiano. Note di spiritualità origeniana a proposito di Mt 16,24. — *Benedictina* (Roma) 30 (1983) 9-30.

1985 "Godete ed esultate" (Mt. 5,11-12). La gioia nelle tribolazioni per il Regno secondo Origene. — *Testimonium Christi*. FS J. Dupont, 1985, 151-176.

**DELORME, Jean**

1956a Sens du texte de S. Matthieu (V,31-32) sur le divorce. — *AmiCler* 66 (1956) 772-774. [NTA 2, 44]

1956b Marie habitait-elle chez Joseph? [1,19] — *Ibid.*, 774. [NTA 2, 43]

1956c La pratique du baptême dans le Judaïsme contemporain des origines chrétiennes. — *LumièreV* 26 (1956) 21-60 = 165-204. Esp. 43-54 [3,13-17]. [NTA 1, 160]

1957 Évangiles. Note complémentaire sur les évangiles synoptiques. — *Dictionnaire de théologie catholique*. Tables générales, I, Paris: Letouzey & Ané, 1957, col. 1434-1450. Esp. 1440-1444 [synoptic problem]; 1446-1448 [5,32; 16,18-19; 19,9].

1961 À propos des Évangiles de l'enfance. — *AmiCler* 71 (1961) 760-764. [NTA 6, 757]

1966 La prière du Seigneur. Pour une catéchèse biblique du "Notre Père". À propos de la nouvelle traduction. — *AmiCler* 76 (1966) 225-236. [NTA 11, 203]

1968a Les Évangiles de l'enfance du Christ. — *AmiCler* 78 (1968) 755-762. [NTA 13, 855] → Daniélou 1967, A. Paul 1968, Perrot 1967

1968b Pour une approche méthodique des évangiles. — *FoiVie* 67/4 = *Cahiers bibliques* 6 (1968) 3-71. Esp. 10-16 [18,12-14]; 21-23 [8,14-15]; 23-33 [6,25-34].

1970 & BONNARD, P., Quelques récits évangéliques relatifs au Ressuscité. — *FoiVie* 69/1 = *Cahiers bibliques* 8 (1970) 29-59. Esp. 39-41 [28,16-20]; 43-44.

1972 *Des Évangiles à Jésus* (Collection "Jeunesse de la foi", 9). Paris: Fleurus, 1972, 127 p. Esp. 37-53 [6,25-33]; 109-110 [26,26-29/Mk].
*De los Evangelios a Jesús*, trans. J.M. Yurrita. Bilbao: Mensajero, 1973, 166 p.

1974* (ed.), *Le ministère et les ministères selon le Nouveau Testament. Dossier exégétique et réflexion théologique* (Parole de Dieu). Paris: Seuil, 1974, 541 p. → Bony, Légasse, Sesboüé
*El ministerio y los ministerios según el Nuevo Testamento*. Madrid: Cristiandad, 1975, 484 p.

1985 Sémiotique du récit et récit de la passion. — *RSR* 73 (1985) 85-109. Esp. 95-99: "L'ouverture du récit selon Matthieu (26,1-16)". [NTA 30, 87]

1988 La théologie du salut dans le Nouveau Testament. I. Le salut dans les Évangiles synoptiques et les Actes des Apôtres. — *DBS* 11/62 (1988) 584-689. Esp. 605-619 [8,25; 9,21-22; 10,22; 14,30.36; 16,25; 19,25; 24,13.22; 27,40-49].

1989*  (ed.), *Les paraboles évangéliques. Pespectives nouvelles. XII<sup>e</sup> Congrès de l'ACFEB, Lyon (1987)* (LD, 135). Paris: Cerf, 1989, 452 p. → Cazeaux, Légasse, Marguerat, Sevrin

1991  *Au risque de la parole. Lire les évangiles* (Parole de Dieu, 31). Paris: Seuil, 1991, 248 p. Esp. 125-160.231-237: "Parole pour le temps de l'absence. La parabole des talents: Matthieu 25,14-30".

1993  Signification d'un récit et comparaison synoptique (Marc 9,14-29 et parallèles). [17,14-21] — FOCANT, C. (ed.), *The Synoptic Gospels*, 1993, 531-547.

**DEL PÁRAMO, Severiano**

1943<sup>R</sup>  Multi enim sunt vocati... (Mt 20,16b par). [1943] — ID., *Temas bíblicos*, II, 1967, 209-217.

1953  El fin de las parábolas de Cristo y el Salmo 77. — *MiscCom* 20 (1953) 233-255. Esp. 242-252 [13,34-35/OT]; = *Valoración sobrenatural del "cosmos". La inspiración bíblica. Otros estudios* (XIV Semana Biblica Española), Madrid: Consejo Superior de Investigaciones Científicas, 1954, 341-364. Esp. 350-362.

1955  Un problema de exégesis neotestamentaria. *Quidam autem dubitaverunt* (Mt. 28,17). — *EstBíb* 14 (1955) 281-296; = ID, *Temas bíblicos*, II, 1967, 125-143.

1964  Evangelio de San Mateo. — LEAL, J. - DEL PÁRAMO, S. - ALONSO, J. (eds.), *La Sagrada Escritura. Nuevo Testamento.* I: *Evangelios* (Biblioteca de autores cristianos, 207), Madrid: BAC, 1964, 1-315. Esp. 3-15 [introduction]; 16-308 [commentary].
*Vangelo secondo Matteo*, trans. A. Marchesi (Nuovo Testamento, 1). Roma: Città Nuova, 1970, 433 p. Esp. 25-39; 40-428. [NTA 17, p. 120]

1967  *Temas bíblicos.* Vol. II: *Temas evangélicos.* Santander: Sal Terrae / Univ. Pont. Comillas, 1967, 261 p. → 1943, 1955

1974  La Anunciación a San José (Mt. 1,18-25). — *EstJos* 28 (1974) 153-158.

**D'ELPIDIO, R.**

1969  *Le beatitudini, oggi.* Napoli: Domenicane Italiane, 1969, 182 p.

**DEL VERME, Marcello**

1984  I "guai" di Matteo e Luca e le decime dei farisei (*Mt.* 23,23; *Lc.* 11,42). — *RivBib* 32 (1984) 273-314. Esp. 277-281 [23,23]; 281-298 [23,23-24]; 298-308 [Q 11,42]. [NTA 29, 940]

1989  *Giudaismo e Nuovo Testamento: Il caso delle decime* [23,23] (Studi sul giudaismo e cristianesimo antico, 1). Napoli: D'Auria, 1989, 282 p. → 1991

1991  Le decime giudaiche negli scritti di Flavio Giuseppe e nel Nuovo Testamento. — *RivBib* 39 (1991) 175-191. Esp. 183-191 [23,23; Q 11,42]. [NTA 36, 473] → 1989

**DE MAAT, Paul** → Lukken 1983

**DÉMANN, Paul**

1951  Le premier Évangile est-il antijuif? — *Cahiers sioniens* (Paris) 5 (1951) 240-257.

**DE MARGERIE, Bertrand**

1992  *Praeparatio cordis ad plura perferenda.* S. Augustin, *De Sermone Domini in Monte* I,19,59 et 20,66 (*Mt* 5,39ss). — *Augustinianum* 32 (1992) 145-160.

**DE MARTIN DE VIVIES, P.**

1995  *Jésus et le Fils de l'homme. Emplois et significations de l'expression "Fils de l'homme" dans les Évangiles.* Lyon: Profac, 1995, v-173 p.

**DE MEEÛS, Xavier**

1961  Composition de Lc., XIV et genre symposiaque. — *ETL* 37 (1961) 847-870. Esp. 849-852 [Q 14,16-24]. [NTA 7, 165]

**DEMEULENARE, Roland**

1991a (ed.), *Le sermon* LXXVI *de saint Augustin sur la marche de Jésus et de Pierre sur les eaux. Édition critique.* [14,25-32] — BARTELINK, G.J.M. - HILHORST, A. - KNEEPKENS, C.H. (eds.), *Eulogia. Mélanges offerts à Antoon A.R. Bastiaensen* (Instrumenta Patristica, 24), Steenbrugge - Den Haag: Nijhoff, 199_, 51-63.

1991b (ed.), *Le sermon 84 de saint Augustin sur l'invitation de Jésus au jeune homme riche. Édition critique.* [19,17] — VAN UYTFANGHE, M. - DEMEULENAERE, R. (eds.), *Aevum inter utrumque. Mélanges offerts à Gabriel Sanders* (Instrumenta Patristica, 23), Steenbrugge: St. Pietersabdij - Den Haag: Nijhoff, 1991, 67-73.

**DEMING, Will**

1990 Mark 9.42-10.12, Matthew 5.27-32, and *B. Nid.* 13b: A First Century Discussion of Male Sexuality. — *NTS* 36 (1990) 130-141. Esp. 136-141. [NTA 34, 653]

**DEMMER, H.**

1969 et al., *Streit um Jesus. Vorträge und Bibelarbeit in der Arbeitsgruppe Streit um Jesus des 14. Deutschen Evangelischen Kirchentags Stuttgart 1969.* Stuttgart–Berlin: Kreuz, 1969, 104 p. [NTA 14, p. 244] → Suhl; → Bannach 1969

**DE MOOR, Johannes C.**

1988 The Reconstruction of the Aramaic Original of the Lord's Prayer. — VAN DER MEER, W. — DE MOOR, J.C. (eds.), *The Structural Analysis of Biblical and Canaanite Poetry* (JSOT SS, 74), Sheffield: JSOT, 1988, 397-422.

**DENAUX, Adelbert**

1982 Der Spruch von den zwei Wegen im Rahmen des Epilogs der Bergpredigt (Mt 7,13-14 par. Lk 13,23-24). Tradition und Redaktion. — DELOBEL, J. (ed.), *Logia*, 1982, 305-335. Esp. 305-307: "Mt 7,13-27 eine literarische Einheit"; 307-315 "Synchronische Analyse von Mt 7,13-27"; 315-329: "Diachronische Analyse von Mt 7,13-14"; 331-335: ' Parallelismus".

1986 & VERVENNE, M., *Synopsis van de eerste drie evangeliën.* Turnhout: Brepols; Leuven: Vlaamse Bijbelstichting, 1986, LXV-332 p.; ²1989, LXV-334 p. Esp. XXIV-LXV: "De synoptische kwestie". → Lambrecht 1986a, Neirynck 1986c

1992* (ed.), *John and the Synoptics* (BETL, 101). Leuven: University Press / Peeters, 1992, XXII-696 p. → Boismard, Caragounis, Dauer, Denaux, G. Geiger, Goulder, Lindars, Menken, Neirynck, Painter, Sabbe 1991c, Schenk, Thyen, Verheyden

1992 The Q-Logion Mt 11,27 / Lk 10,22 and the Gospel of John. — *Ibid.*, 163-199. Esp. 167-176: "Matthew 11,25-27 / Luke 10,21-22 in their different contexts"; 176-187: "Johannine parallels to Matthew 11,27 / Luke 10,22".

1995 Criteria for Identifying Q-Passages: A Critical Review of a Recent Work by T. Bergemann. — *NT* 37 (1995) 105-129. Esp. 107-116: "Presentation of the work"; 116-129: "Critical evaluation". [NTA 40, 139r] → Bergemann 1993

**DENAUX, Joris**

1969 & GROLLENBERG, L. - VAN ENGELEN, G.C., *Sleutel op de Evangeliën en de Handelingen.* Boxtel: Katholieke Bijbelstichting; 's Hertogenbosch: Malmberg, 1969, 171 p. Esp. 42-49 (J. Denaux).

**DEN HEYER, Cornelis Jacobus**

1986a *De messiaanse weg. II. Jezus van Nazaret.* Kampen: Kok, 1986, 270 p. Esp. 84-93 [infancy narratives]; 107-111 [John the Baptist]; 116-117 [3,13-17]; 141-145 [3,10-12; 11,2-19]; 176-185 [5,17-48]. → 1991

1986b Die Versuchungserzählung in den Evangelien. [4,1-11] — *ZDialTheol* 2 (1986) 10-20.

1988 'Toen werd het woord van de profeet vervuld...'. Oudtestamentisch-joodse achtergronden van de geboorteverhalen in het Nieuwe Testament. — WEREN, W., et al., *Geboorteverhalen van Jezus*, 1988, 31-60.

1991 *De messiaanse weg*. III. *De Christologie van het Nieuwe Testament*. Kampen: Kok, 1991, 314 p. Esp. 93-100 [Q: christology]; 208-222 [infancy narratives]; 223-235 [fulfilment quotations]; 242-250 [Moses typology]. → 1986a

1992 'Want Hij is het, die zijn volk zal redden van hun zonden' (Mat. 1:23). Jezus als redder én als rechter in het evangelie naar Matteüs. — BAARLINK, H., et al., *Christologische perspectieven*. FS H. Baarlink, 1992, 194-220. Esp. 195-196 [anti-Judaism]; 196-198 [judgment]; 198-203 [author]; 203-205 [style]; 205-209 [christology]; 209-212 [sources]; 213-217 [titles]; 217-220 [salvation].

1994 Matteüs en de *fiscus judaicus*. Matteüs 17,24-27 en de situatie van de joodse christenen ten tijde van het schisma Jodendom-Christendom. — *Ter Herkenning* (Breda) 22 (1994) 93-107.

**DENIS, Albert-Marie**

1957 L'investiture de la fonction apostolique par "apocalypse". Étude thématique de *Gal.*, I,16. — *RB* 64 (1957) 335-362, 492-515. Esp. 492-498 [11,25-27/Gal 1,15-16]; 498-500 [11,25-27]; 500-512 [16,17-18]. [NTA 2, 603]

1960 L'adoration des Mages vue par s. Matthieu. — *NRT* 82 (1960) 32-39. [NTA 4, 641]

1961 De parabels over het koninkrijk (Mt. 13). — *TijdTheol* 1 (1961) 273-288 (French summary, 287-288). Esp. 275-282 [genre]; 282-286 [13,3-9.18-23]. [NTA 6, 773]
Les paraboles du royaume, révélation de mystère (Matt., 13). — *Communio* (Sevilla) 1 (1968) 327-346. Esp. 330-338; 339-344. [NTA 14, 143]

1967 La marche de Jésus sur les eaux. Contribution à l'histoire de la péricope dans la tradition évangélique. [14,22-33] — DE LA POTTERIE, I. (ed.), *De Jésus aux Évangiles*. FS J. Coppens, 1967, 233-247. Esp. 233-241. (IT, 1971, 290-307).
Jesus' Walking on the Waters. A Contribution to the History of the Pericope in the Gospel Tradition. — *LouvSt* 1 (1966-67) 284-297. Esp. 286-294. [NTA 12, 556]

**DENIS, M.**

1968 *La relation du Christ avec les pauvres. Essai d'une étude exégétique et théologique de Mt 25,40*. Diss. Academia Alfonsiana, Roma, 1968.

**DENIS, Philippe**

1978 Le recours à l'Écriture dans les Églises de la Réforme au XVIe siècle: Exégèse de Mt 18,15-17 et pratique de la discipline. — FATIO, O. - FRAENKEL, P. (eds.), *Histoire de l'exégèse au XVIe siècle. Textes du Colloque international tenu à Genève en 1976*, Genève: Droz, 1978, 286-298.

**DENIS-BOULET, Noële Maurice**

1966 La place du Notre Père dans la liturgie. — *La Maison-Dieu* (Paris) 85 (1966) 69-91. [NTA 11, 204]

**DENKER, Jürgen**

1975 *Die theologiegeschichtliche Stellung des Petrusevangeliums. Ein Beitrag zur Frühgeschichte des Doketismus* (EHS, XXIII/36). Frankfurt/M: Lang, 1975, 257 p. Esp. 43-48: "Das Verhältnis des Petrusevangeliums zu Mt"; 93-125: "Zur Christologie im Petrusevangelium".

1985 La fuente de los logia (Q). — *RevistBíb* 47 (1985) 185-206 (English summary, 247). [NTA 30, 1034]

**DENZLER, Georg**

1970 et al., *Zum Thema Petrusamt und Papsttum*. Stuttgart: Katholisches Bibelwerk, 1970, 114 p. → Christ, Stockmeier, Trilling

**DEPROOST, Paul-Augustin**

1989 La mort de Judas dans l'*Historia apostolica* d'Arator (I,83-102). [27,3-10] — *RevÉtudAug* 35 (1989) 135-150.

**DEPUYDT, Leo**

1985 Two Notes on the Coptic Language. [26,36] — *OrLovPer* 16 (1985) 131-140. [NTA 30, 1066]

**DE RIDDER, Richard R.**

1971 *The Dispersion of the People of God. The Covenant Basis of Matthew 28:18-20 against the Background of Jewish, Pre-Christian Proselytizing and Diaspora, and the Apostleship of Jesus Christ.* Kampen: Kok, 1971, VIII-239 p. Esp. 120-127 [23,15]; 128-200: "The apostle, Jesus Christ"; 201-224: "The commissioned Church".
   D.W.B. ROBINSON, *RTR* 31 (1972) 61-63.
   *Discipling the Nations (Mt 28,18-20). Its Covenant Basis against the Background of Jewish Proselyting and the Apostleship of Jesus Christ.* Grand Rapids, MI: Baker, 1975, 252 p.
   S.C. KNAPP, *WestTJ* 32 (1976-77) 175-182.

**DERMIENCE, Alice**

1981 *La péricope de la Cananéenne: Matth. 15,21-28. Sources, rédactions, théologie.* Diss. Louvain-la-Neuve, 1981, XIX-235 p. (J. Giblet). → 1982

1982 La péricope de la Cananéenne (Mt 15,21-28). Rédaction et théologie. — *ETL* 58 (1982) 25-49. [NTA 27, 101] → 1981

1985 Rédaction et théologie dans le premier évangile. Une perspective de l'exégèse matthéenne récente. — *RTL* 16 (1985) 47-64. Esp. 48-49 [G. Bornkamm 1956b]; 49 [Nepper-Christensen 1958]; 50-51 [Strecker 1962]; 51-53 [Trilling 1959a/64]; 53-54 [Hummel 1963/66]; 55-56 [R. Walker 1967]; 56-58 [Frankemölle 1974a]; 58-59 [Goulder 1974]; 59-61 [Zumstein 1977]; 61-62 [Schweizer 1974a]; 62-63 [Marguerat 1981]. [NTA 30, 101]

1994 Les récits de guérisons dans les évangiles synoptiques. Signification anthropologique et théologique. — *FoiTemps* 24 (1994) 197-216. Esp. 2.2-216.

**DE ROSA, Giuseppe**

1955 Matrimonio e divorzio nel Vangelo di Matteo. — *PalCl* 34 (1955) 913-918.

1978 Storia e teologia nei racconti dell'infanzia di Gesù. — *CC* 129/2 (1978) 521-537. [NTA 23, 817]

**DEROUSSEAUX, Louis**

1974 Lier – Délier. [16,18; 18,18] — *Catholicisme* 7/30 (1974) 738-740.

**DERRETT, J. Duncan M.**

1963a Fresh Light on the Wicked Vinedressers. [21,33-46] — *RevIntDroitsAnt* 10 (1963) 11-41.
   The Parable of the Wicked Vinedressers. — ID., *Law*, 1970, 286-312 (revised and corrected version).

1963b Law in the New Testament: The Treasure in the Field (Mt. XIII,44). — *ZNW* 54 (1963) 31-42. [NTA 8, 578]
   The Treasure in the Field. — ID., *Law*, 1970, 1-16.

1963c Peter's Penny: Fresh Light on Matthew xvii 24-7. — *NT* 6 (1963) 1-15. [NTA 8, 948]
   Peter's Penny. — ID., *Law*, 1970, 247-265.

1964 The Anointing at Bethany. [26,6-13] — *Studia Evangelica* 2 (1964) 174-182.
   The Anointing at Bethany and the Story of Zacchaeus. — ID., *Law*, 1970, 266-285. Esp. 266-275 (= 1964).

1965a Herod's Oath and the Baptist's Head. (With an Appendix on Mk IX.12-13, Mal III.24, Micah VII.6). — *BZ* 9 (1965) 49-59, 233-246. Esp. 242-244 [17,11-12]; 245-246 [10,34-36]. [NTA 10, 135/533]; = ID., *Law*, 1970, 339-362. Esp. 358-360; 361-362.

1965b  Law in the New Testament: The Parable of the Talents and Two Logia. [13,12; 25,14-28.29] — *ZNW* 56 (1965) 184-195. [NTA 10, 916]
The Parable of the Talents and Two Logia. — ID., *Law*, 1970, 17-31.

1965c  Law in the New Testament. The Parable of the Unmerciful Servant. [18,23-34] — *RevIntDroitsAnt* 12 (1965) 3-19.
The Parable of the Unmerciful Servant. — ID., *Law*, 1970, 32-47.

1966  The Light under a Bushel: The Hanukkah Lamp? [5,15] — *ExpT* 78 (1966-67) 18. [NTA 11, 696] → 1970d

1968a  "The stone that the builders rejected". [21,42] — *Studia Evangelica* 4 (1968) 180-186; = ID., *Studies*, II, 1978, 60-67.

1968b  "You build the tombs of the prophets" (Lk. 11,47-51, Mt. 23,29-31). — *Ibid.*, 187-193; = ID., *Studies*, II, 1978, 68-75.

1970a  Κορβᾶν, ὅ ἐστιν δῶρον. [15,4-6] — *NTS* 16 (1969-70) 364-368. [NTA 15, 163]; = ID., *Studies*, I, 1977, 112-117.

1970b  *Law in the New Testament*. London: Darton, Longman & Todd, 1970, XLVI-503 p. → 1963a-c, 1964, 1965a-c, 1970c-e

1970c  The Parable of the Great Supper. [22,1-14] — *Ibid.*, 126-155.

1970d  The Lamp Which Must Not Be Hidden (Mc iv.21). — *Ibid.*, 189-207. Esp. 200-202 [5,15]; 204-205 [6,22-23]. → 1966

1970e  The Teaching of Jesus on Marriage and Divorce. — *Ibid.*, 363-388. Esp. 367-369 [19,9]. → W.J. Harrington 1972a

1971a  Law in the New Testament: The Palm Sunday Colt. — *NT* 13 (1971) 241-258. Esp. 242-243.256 [21,5]. [NTA 16, 886]; = ID., *Studies*, II, 1978, 165-183. Esp. 166-167.181.

1971b  The Parable of the Two Sons. [21,28-32] — *StudTheol* 25 (1971) 109-116. [NTA 16, 865]; = ID., *Studies*, I, 1977, 76-84.

1971c  La parabola delle vergini stolte (Mt 25:1-13). — *Conoscenza religiosa*, 1971, 394-406; = ID., *Studies*, I, 1977, 128-142.

1972  La nascita di Gesù. Storie patristiche e *haggadot* ebraiche. — *Conoscenza religiosa*, 1972, 221-225. Esp. 222-223; = ID., *Studies*, II, 1978, 33-38. Esp. 34-35 [1,18.25].

1973a  *Jesus' Audience. The Social and Psychological Environment in which He Worked. Prolegomenon to a Restatement of the Teaching of Jesus*. London: Darton, Longman & Todd, 1973, 240 p. Esp. 175-177 [13,52]; 187-191 [11,12].

1973b  Figtrees in the New Testament. — *HeythJ* 14 (1973) 249-265. Esp. 251-252 [21,19]; 254-255 [21,21-22]. [NTA 18, 58]; = ID., *Studies*, II, 1978, 148-164. Esp. 150-151; 153-155.

1973c  Law in the New Testament: *Si scandalizaverit te manus tua abscinde illam* (Mk. IX.42) and Comparative Legal History. [5,29-30; 18,6-9] — *RevIntDroitsAnt* 20 (1973) 11-36; = ID., *Studies*, I, 1977, 4-31.

1973d  Law in the New Testament: The Syro-Phoenician Woman and the Centurion of Capernaum. — *NT* 15 (1973) 161-186. Esp. 162-174 [15,21-28]; 174-183 [8,5-13]. [NTA 18, 876]; = ID., *Studies*, I, 1977, 143-169. Esp. 144-156; 156-165.

1974a  Gesù maestro della legge. — *Conoscenza religiosa*, 1974, 49-63. Esp. 58-62; = ID., *Studies*, II, 1978, 76-91. Esp. 85-89 [5,21-48].

1974b  Workers in the Vineyard: A Parable of Jesus. [20,1-16] — *JJS* 25 (1974) 64-91. [NTA 18, 860]; = ID., *Studies*, I, 1977, 48-75.

1975a  Further Light on the Narratives of the Nativity. — *NT* 17 (1975) 81-108. Esp. 95-105: "The Magi". [NTA 20, 114]; = ID., *Studies*, II, 1978, 4-32. Esp. 18-28.

1975b Midrash in Matthew. — *HeythJ* 16 (1975) 51-56. [NTA 19, 936r]; = ID., *Studies*, II, 1978, 205-210. → Goulder 1974

1977 *Studies in the New Testament*. Vol. I: *Glimpses of the Legal and Social Presuppositions of the Authors*. Leiden: Brill, 1977, XXVI-220 p. → 1970a, 1971b-c, 1973c-d, 1974b

1978a *Studies in the New Testament*. Vol. II: *Midrash in Action and as a Literary Device*. Leiden: Brill, 1978, X-229 p. → 1968a-b, 1971a, 1972, 1973t, 1974a, 1975a-b

1978b Spirit-possession and the Gerasene Demoniac. [8,28-34] — *Man* NS (London) 14 (1978) 286-293.

1978c I porci di Gerasa. [8,28-34] — *Conoscenza religiosa*, 1978, 232-266.

1979a Fresh Light on the Lost Sheep and the Lost Coin. — *NTS* 26 (1979-80) 36-60. Esp. 48-52 [12,11-12]. [NTA 24, 824]; = ID., *Studies*, III, 1982, 59-84. Esp. 71-75.

1979b "Have nothing to do with that just man!" (Matt. 27,19). Haggadah and the Account of the Passion. — *DownR* 97 (1979) 308-315. [NTA 24, 430]; = ID., *Studies*, III, 1982, 184-192.

1979c 'Where two or three are convened in my name...': A Sad Misunderstanding. [18,19-20] — *ExpT* 91 (1979-80) 83-86. [NTA 24, 426]; = ID., *Studies*, III, 1982, 230-233.

1980a Ἦσαν γὰρ ἁλιεῖς (Mk i 16). Jesus's Fishermen and the Parable of the Net. — *NT* 22 (1980) 108-137. Esp. 109-121: "The calling of the first apostles in Mark and Matthew"; 125-131 [13,47-49]. [NTA 24, 805]; = ID., *Studies*, III, 1982, 1-30. Esp. 2-14; 18-24.

1980b The Iscariot, *mᵉsîrâ*, and the Redemption. [26,48] — *JSNT* 8 (1980) 2-23. [NTA 25, 50]; = ID., *Studies*, III, 1982, 161-183.

1981a Mt 23,8-10 a Midrash on Is 54,13 and Jer 31,33-34. — *Bib* 62 (1981) 372-386. Esp. 373-375: "The texts"; 375-384: "Christian use of the passages"; 384-386 "Misunderstandings". [NTA 26, 98]; = ID., *Studies*, III, 1982, 215-229.

1981b Miscellanea: a Pauline Pun and Judas' Punishment. [27,3-10] — *ZNW* 72 (1981) 131-133. [NTA 26, 693]; = ID., *Studies*, IV, 1986, 187-189.

1981c Why and How Jesus Walked on the Sea. [14,22-33] — *NT* 23 (1981) 330-348. [NTA 26, 500]; = ID., *Studies*, IV, 1986, 92-110. → Klatt 1990

1982a *Studies in the New Testament*. Vol. III: *Midrash, Haggadah, and the Character of the Community*. Leiden: Brill, 1982, XII-261 p. → 1979a-c, 1980a-b, 1981a

1982b *The Anastasis: The Resurrection of Jesus as an Historical Event*. Shipston-on-Stour, UK: Drinkwater, 1982, XIV-166 p. Esp. 47-70; 108-109.

1982c The Merits of the Narrow Gate (Mt. 7:13-14, Lk. 13:24). — *JSNT* 15 (1982) 20-29. [NTA 27, 99]; = ID., *Studies*, IV, 1986, 147-156.

1983a Binding and Loosing (Matt 16:19; 18:18; John 20:23). — *JBL* 102 (1983) 112-117. [NTA 27, 924]; = ID., *Studies*, IV, 1986, 190-195. → Basser 1985b, Hiers 1985

1983b Peace, Sandals and Shirts (Mark 6:6b-13 *par*.). — *HeythJ* 24 (1983) 253-265. Esp. 264-265: "Synoptic comparison". [NTA 28, 112]; = ID., *Studies*, IV, 1986, 62-74. Esp. 73-74.

1983c Why Jesus Blessed the Children (Mk 10:13-16 par.). — *NT* 25 (1983) 1-18. Esp. 12-13.17-18 [19,13-15]. [NTA 27, 948]; = ID., *Studies*, IV, 1986, 111-128. Esp. 122-123.127-128.

1984 Palingenesia (Matthew 19.28). — *JSNT* 20 (1984) 51-58. [NTA 29, 109]; = ID., *Studies*, IV, 1986, 139-146.

1985a Taking up the Cross and Turning the Cheek. — HARVEY, A.E. (ed.), *Alternative Approaches to New Testament Study*, 1985, 61-78. Esp. 64 [10,38; 16,24]; 69 [5,39-40]; 70 [5,42]; = ID., *Studies*, V, 1989, 41-58. Esp. 44; 49; 50.

1985b  Two "Harsh" Sayings of Christ Explained. — *DownR* 103 (1985) 218-229. Esp. 218-221 [18,6]; 221-223 [8,22]. [NTA 30, 603]; = ID., *Studies*, V, 1989, 71-82. Esp. 71-74; 74-76.

1986a  *Studies in the New Testament*. Vol. IV: *Midrash, the Composition of Gospels, and Discipline*. Leiden: Brill, 1986, X-244 p. → 1981b-c, 1982c, 1983a-c, 1984

1986b  The Homelessness of the Religious Leader. [8,20] — *Adyar Library Bulletin* (Madras) 50 (1986) 198-217.

1986c  Receptacles and Tombs (Mt 23,24-30). — *ZNW* 77 (1986) 255-266. [NTA 31, 593]; = ID., *Studies*, V, 1989, 59-70.

1987   Birds of the Air and Lilies of the Field. [6,25-34] — *DownR* 105 (1987) 181-192. [NTA 32, 595]; = ID., *Studies*, V, 1989, 24-35.

1988a  Christ and Reproof (Matthew 7.1-5 / Luke 6.37-42). — *NTS* 34 (1988) 271-281. [NTA 32, 1107]; = ID., *Studies*, V, 1989, 85-95.

1988b  Moving Mountains and Uprooting Trees (Mk 11:22; Mt 17:20, 21:21; Lk 17:6). — *BibOr* 30 (1988) 231-244. [NTA 33, 1165]; = ID., *Studies*, VI, 1995, 28-41.

1988c  New Creation: Qumran, Paul, the Church, and Jesus. — *RQum* 13 (1988) 597-608. Esp. 603-607 [church].

1988d  "Thou art the stone, and upon this stone…". — *DownR* 106 (1988) 276-285. [NTA 33, 613]; = ID., *Studies*, VI, 1995, 6-15.

1989a  *The Ascetic Discourse: An Explanation of the Sermon on the Mount*. Eilsbrunn: Ko'amar, 1989, 112 p. [NTA 34, p. 245] → 1994a
       J. FISCH, *TRev* 86 (1990) 201; E. FRANKLIN, *ExpT* 101 (1989-90) 121; D. HILL, *JSNT* 40 (1990) 115-116; J.-M. ROUSÉE, *RB* 96 (1989) 474; U. SCHNELLE, *TLZ* 115 (1990) 268.

1989b  *Studies in the New Testament*. Vol. V: *The Sea-Change of the Old Testament in the New*. Leiden: Brill, 1989, XII-245 p. → 1985a-b, 1986c, 1987, 1988a

1989c  Der Wasserwandel in christlicher und buddhistischer Perspektive. [14,22-33] — *ZRelGeist* 41 (1989) 193-214. [NTA 34, 126]

1990   Ambivalence: Sowing and Reaping at Mark 4,26-29. — *EstBíb* 48 (1990) 489-510. Esp. 502-504: "Matthew and Luke". [NTA 36, 179]; = ID., *Studies*, VI, 1995, 42-63. Esp. 55-57.

1992   The Light and the City: Mt 5:14. — *ExpT* 103 (1991-92) 174-175. [NTA 36, 1262]; = ID., *Studies*, VI, 1995, 1.

1994a  *Sermon on the Mount. A Manual for Living*. Northampton, UK: Pilkington, 1994, V-112 p. → 1989a
       A.E. HARVEY, *Theology* 98 (1995) 60-61; L. HOULDEN, *ExpT* 106 (1994-95) 54.

1994b  Jesus as a Seducer (πλάνος = *mat'eh*). [27,63-64] — *Bijdragen* 55 (1994) 43-55. Esp. 47, 51. [NTA 39, 766]; = ID., *Studies*, VI, 1995, 202-214. Esp. 206, 210. *TDig* 42 (1995) 25-29.

1995a  *Studies in the New Testament*. Vol. VI: *Jesus Among Biblical Exegetes*. Leiden: Brill, 1995, X-251 p. → 1988b.d, 1990, 1992, 1994b

1995b  Akeldama (Acts 1:19). — *Bijdragen* 56 (1995) 122-132. Esp. 125-129 [27,3-10]. [NTA 40, 284]

1995c  The Evil Eye in the New Testament. — ESLER, P.F. (ed.), *Modelling Early Christianity*, 1995, 65-72. Esp. 68-69 [6,22-23; 20,15].

1995d  Luke 6:5D Reexamined. — *NT* 37 (1995) 232-248. Esp. 245-247 [23,3.13]. [NTA 40, 874]

DE RU, G.

1966   The Conception of Reward in the Teaching of Jesus. [20,1-16] — *NT* 8 (1966) 202-222. [NTA 11, 643]

**DESAUTELS, L.**

1986    La mort de Judas (*Mt* 27,3-10; *Ac* 1,15-26). — *SE* 38 (1986) 221-239. [NTA 31, 595]

**DESCAMPS, Albert L.**

1950    *Les Justes et la Justice dans les évangiles et le christianisme primitif hormis la doctrine*
        *proprement paulinienne* (Universitas Catholica Lovaniensis. Dissertationes, II/43).
        Leuven: Publ. Universitaires; Gembloux: Duculot, 1950, XIX-335 p. Esp. 31-53: "L'attente
        messianique des justes de l'Ancien Testament" [1,18-25; 3,15; 10,41; 13,16-17; 21,32; 23,29-35]; 94-110:
        "Le privilège des pécheurs dans l'accès du Royaume" [9,13]; 111-122: "L'accomplissement de la justice et
        la promulgation de la Loi" [3,15; 5,17]; 157-163: "La souffrance des chrétiens" [5,6.10; 23,29-35]; 164-206:
        "Les exhortations à la justice dans le Sermon sur la montagne" [5,6.45; 6,33; 23,27-28]; 207-245: "Les justes
        dans le Royaume" [10,40-42; 13,24-43.47-50]; 250-269: "Les chrétiens dans le cadre du jugement sur les
        œuvres" [25,31-46]; 270-285: "La rétribution divine" [20,1-16]. → Lyonnet 1954

1951    Le jugement des chrétiens d'après *Mt.*, XXV,31-46. — *RevDiocTournai* 6 (1951) 506-
        509.

1952a   Bienheureux les pauvres. — *RevDiocTournai* 7 (1952) 53-61.

1952b   Justice et charité dans les évangiles synoptiques. — *Ibid.*, 239-245.

1952c   Le détachement des richesses dans les synoptiques. — *Ibid.*, 331-337.

1953    Perspectives actuelles dans l'exégèse des Synoptiques. — *RevDiocTournai* 8 (1953) 3-
        16, 401-414, 495-523. Esp. 408-414 [28,1-10]; 495-502 [passion narrative]; 502-515 [eschatology]; 515-
        519 [miracles]; 520-521 [infancy narrative].

1954a   Le messianisme royal dans le Nouveau Testament. — RIGAUX, B. (ed.), *L'attente du*
        *Messie* (Recherches bibliques, 1), Brugge: Desclée De Brouwer, 1954, ²1958, 57-84.
        Esp. 58-64 [Son of David]; 71-73 [Son of David: Mt 1-2]; 77-78 [k ngdom].

1954b   Moïse dans les évangiles et dans la tradition apostolique. — *Cahiers sioniens* (Paris) 8
        (1954) 289-315; = CAZELLES, H., et al., *Moïse, l'homme de l'alliance*, Paris: Desclée,
        1955, 171-187. Esp. 171-180.

1954c   La morale des synoptiques. — BRAUN, F.M., et al., *Morale chrétienne et requêtes*
        *contemporaines* (Cahiers de l'actualité religieuse), Tournai–Paris: Casterman, 1954, 27-
        46.

1957    Du discours de Marc., IX,33-50 aux paroles de Jésus. — HEUSCHEN, J. (ed.), *La*
        *formation des évangiles*, 1957, 152-177. Esp. 160-162.164-169.172-174 [18,1-9].

1959a   Essai d'interprétation de Mt. 5,17-48. "Formgeschichte" ou "Redaktionsgeschichte"?
        — *Studia Evangelica* 1 (1959) 156-173. Esp. 160-166: "Les interventions rédactionnelles en Mt.
        5,17-48"; 167-169: "L'état de la tradition dans les communautés"; 169-173: "Origine de la tradition: les
        paroles de Jésus".

1959b   La structure des récits évangéliques de la résurrection. — *Bib* 40 (1959) 726-741. Esp.
        728-729: "Le tombeau vide" [28,1-8]; 729-731: "Les apparitions de Jésus aux femmes et à certains disciples"
        [28,9-10]; 737-738: "La succession chronologique 'Jérusalem–Gali ée–Jérusalem'" [28,7.18-20]; 738-740:
        "La succession chronologique 'Galilée–Jérusalem'" [28,16-20]. [NTA 3, 621]; = *Studia Biblica et*
        *Orientalia*, II, 1959, 158-173. Esp. 160-161; 161-163; 169-170; 170-172; = ID., *Jésus et*
        *l'Église*, 1987, 242-257. Esp. 244-245; 245-247; 253-254; 254-256.

1960    Le péché dans le Nouveau Testament. — DELHAYE, P., et al., *Théologie du péché*
        (Bibliothèque de Théologie, II/7). Tournai: Desclée, 1960, 49-124. Esp. 63-85: "Le péché
        dans le message de Jésus".
        Sin in the New Testament. — *Sin in the Bible*, trans. C. Schaldenbrand, New York: Desclée, 1964, 43-140.
        Esp. 63-89.

1961    Maria in het Kindheidsevangelie van Mattheüs. — *De Mariapassages uit het*
        *Matthaüsevangelie* (Verslagboek der achttiende Mariale Dagen), Tongerlo: Norbertijner-
        abdij, 1961, 119-129.

1970*  & DE HALLEUX, A. (eds.), *Mélanges bibliques en hommage au R.P. Béda Rigaux*.
       Gembloux: Duculot, 1970, XXVIII-618 p. → Agourides, C.K. Barrett, Beasley-Murray, M. Black,
       Blinzler, P. Bonnard, Dupont, Linton, Menoud, Schnackenburg, Schürmann, Trilling

1970   Les origines de l'Eucharistie. — VERGOTE, A. - DESCAMPS, A. - HOUSSIAU, A. (eds.),
       *L'Eucharistie. Symbole et réalité* (Réponses chrétiennes, 12), Gembloux: Duculot;
       Paris: Lethielleux, 1970, 57-125. Esp. 67-69; 76-80; 87-90; = ID., *Jésus et l'Église*, 1987,
       455-496. Esp. 461-462; 466-469; 473-475.
       Le origini dell'Eucharistia. — VERGOTE, A. - DESCAMPS, A. - HOUSSIAU, A. (eds.), *L'Eucharistia, simbolo
       e realtà*, trans. Sr. Colomba, Bologna: Dehoniane, 1973, 53-111.

1971   Aux origines du ministère. La pensée de Jésus. — *RTL* 2 (1971) 3-45. Esp. 28-29 [8,19-22].
       [NTA 16, 467]; 3 (1972) 121-159. Esp. 123-126 [13,10-15]; 129-132 [10,17]; 132-133 [23,34]; 137-138
       [23,8]; 139-143 [16,17-19]; 148-150 [18,15-18]; 155-158 [19,28]. [NTA 17, 57]; = ID., *Jésus et
       l'Église*, 1987, 373-454. Esp. 398-399; 418-421; 424-427; 427-428; 432-433; 434-438; 443-445; 450-
       453.

1972   Rédaction et christologie dans le récit matthéen de la Passion. — DIDIER, M. (ed.),
       *L'Évangile selon Matthieu*, 1972, 359-415. Esp. 363-381: "Modifications purement formelles";
       381-393: "Modifications de la teneur historique"; 393-412: "Éléments de christologie matthéenne"; = ID.,
       *Jésus et l'Église*, 1987, 185-241. Esp. 189-207; 207-219; 219-238.

1978   Les textes évangéliques sur le mariage. — *RTL* 9 (1978) 259-286; 11 (1980) 5-50. Esp.
       5-10 [19,3-8]; 10-22 [19,9]; 22-25 [19,10-12]; 25-30 [5,31-32]; 31-34 [Q 16,18]; 46-47. [NTA 23, 470; 24,
       965]; = ID., *Jésus et l'Église*, 1987, 510-583. Esp. 538-543; 543-555; 555-558; 558-563; 564-567;
       579-580.
       The New Testament Doctrine on Marriage. — MALONE, R. - CONNERY, J.R. (eds.), *Contemporary
       Perspectives on Christian Marriage. Propositions and Papers from the International Commission*, Chicago,
       IL: Loyola University Press, 1984, 217-273 (notes, 347-363).

1981   Le Discours sur la montagne. Esquisse de théologie biblique. — *RTL* 12 (1981) 5-39.
       Esp. 5-7: "La composition du discours"; 7-21: "Mt 5: forme littéraire et message"; 21-25: "Mt 6: le
       message"; 25-31: "Mt 7: le message"; 31-39: "Conclusion générale". [NTA 26, 87]; = PINCKAERS, S.
       - PINTO DE OLIVEIRA, C.J. (eds.), *Universalité*, 1986, 43-73. Esp. 43-45; 45-57; 58-61; 61-
       67; 67-73; = ID., *Jésus et l'Église*, 1987, 134-168. Esp. 134-136; 136-150; 150-154; 154-160;
       160-168.

1987   *Jésus et l'Église. Études d'exégèse et de théologie*, ed. F. Neirynck (BETL, 77).
       Leuven: University Press / Peeters, 1987, XLV-641 p. → 1959b, 1970, 1971, 1972, 1978, 1981

**DESMEDT, M.**

1979   *Chapître II de l'Évangile de s. Matthieu. Essai d'une procédure de lecture*. Diss.
       Louvain-la-Neuve, 1979, 99 p. (G. Lafon).

**DE SOLAGES, Bruno**

1959   *Synopse grecque des Évangiles. Méthode nouvelle pour résoudre le problème
       synoptique*. Leiden: Brill; Toulouse: Institut Catholique, 1959, 1128 p. Esp. 609-791:
       "Duplex traditio 'X'"; 805-867: "Marcus et Matthaeus"; 917-925: "Matthaei simplex traditio"; 957-995:
       "Textus a Matthaeo geminati"; 996-1011: "Textus geminati in Luca et in Matthaeo simul"; 1051-1086:
       "Solution du problème synoptique: mots communs"; 1087-1117: "Ordre commun des péricopes". → Courcier
       1974, Duthoit 1960, Léon-Dufour 1972b, J. Schmid 1961
       A Greek Synopsis of the Gospels. A New Way of Solving the Synoptic Problem, trans. J. Baissus. Leiden:
       Brill; Toulouse: Institut Catholique, 1959, 1128 p. → O'Rourke 1974
           P. BENOIT, RB 67 (1960) 93-102.

1960   Mathématiques et Évangiles. Réponse au R.P. Benoit. — *BullLitEccl* 61 (1960)
       287-311. Esp. 294-296 [13,31-32]; 296-298 [22,34-40]; 299 [11,1]; 300-301 [10,17-22].

1970   Le témoignage de Papias. — *BullLitEccl* 71 (1970) 3-14. [NTA 14, 836]; = ID., *Critique*,
       1972, 61-73.

1971    Réflexions sur les Évangiles de l'enfance. — *BullLittEccl* 72 (1971) 37-42. [NTA 16, 144]

1972    *Critique des Évangiles et méthode historique. L'exégèse des synoptiques selon R. Bultmann.* Toulouse: É. Privat, 1972, 219 p. → 1970

1973a    *Comment sont nés les Évangiles. Marc. Luc. Matthieu.* Toulouse: É. Privat, 1973, 206 p. Esp. 41-64: "Les paroles du Seigneur recueillies par l'apôtre Matthieu"; 129-141: "Les compléments matthéens" [Sondergut]; 143-175: "La composition de l'évangile de Matthieu: ses tendances et ses procédés". *Cómo se escribieron los evangelios.* Bilbao: Mensajero, 1975, 238 p.

1973b    *La composition des Évangiles de Luc et de Matthieu et leurs sources.* Leiden: Brill, 1973, 320 p. Esp. 11-32: "La solution du problème synoptique par l'ordre des péricopes"; 52-101: "Procédés de composition de Luc et de Matthieu"; 102-152: "Les transformations du texte de Marc dans les paraphrases de Luc et de Matthieu"; 153-182: "Procédés de composition de Luc et de Matthieu: Leur utilisation de X. Essai de reconstitution de cette source"; 183-210: "Comparaison des paraphrases de X par Luc et par Matthieu"; 211-221: "Les sources propres à Luc ou à Matthieu"; 222-228: "Les doublets"; 229-263: "Sources écrites et traditions orales"; 264-304: "La composition des ensembles"; 305-318: "Un phénomène synoptique de convergence" [minor agreements].
          M.-É. BOISMARD, *RB* 80 (1973) 588-593; K. GRAYSTON, *ExpT* 85 (1973-74) 311; S. LÉGASSE, *BullLittEccl* 74 (1973) 296-298; L. SABOURIN, *BTB* 5 (1975) 93-94; C.H. TALBERT, *JBL* 93 (1974) 464-465.

1973c    Une question de méthode: À propos de la théorie synoptique du P. M.-É. Boismard. — *BullLittEccl* 74 (1973) 139-141. [NTA 18, 56r] → Boismard 1972

1975    À propos de la "Théorie" des deux sources. Réponse au R.P. Boismard. — *BullLittEccl* 76 (1975) 61-64. Esp. 61-63 [17,18]; 63 [3,1-6]; 63-64 [10,5-1€]. [NTA 19, 921] → Boismard 1972

1976    *Christ est ressuscité. La résurrection selon le Nouveau Testament.* Toulouse: É. Privat, 1976, 167 p. Esp. 98-99; 106-110; 115-116; 163 [28,17]. *Cristo ha resucitado. La resurrección según el Nuevo Testamento,* trans. A. Martínez de Lapera. Barcelona: Herder, 1979, 214 p.

1979a    *Jean et les Synoptiques.* Leiden: Brill, 1979, 270 p. Esp. 50-66: "Logia se correspondant"; 99-113: "Jean et Matthieu"; 159-169: "Jean et X (la *Quelle*)"; 170-185: "Attitude de Jean vis-à-vis de la tradition synoptique". → D.M. Smith 1982
          F. NEIRYNCK, *ETL* 56 (1980) 176-179.

1979b    L'Évangile de Thomas et les Évangiles canoniques. L'ordre des péricopes. — *BullLittEccl* 80 (1979) 102-108. Esp. 104-106. [NTA 24, 71]

**DE SOUZA, Bento**

1970    The Coming of the Lord. — *SBF/LA* 20 (1970) 166-203. Esp. 176-196: "The day of the Lord in the New Testament". [NTA 15, 891]

**DESPINA, M.**

1973    Que ton nom soit sanctifié. — *Rencontre Chrétiens et Juifs* (Paris) 7 (1973) 179-187.

**DES PLACES, Édouard**

1982    *Eusèbe de Césarée commentateur. Platonisme et Écriture sainte* (Théologie historique, 63). Paris: Beauchesne, 1982, 196 p. Esp. 114, 152-153, 179-183 [1,23].

**DE STRYCKER, Émile**

1961    *La forme la plus ancienne du Protévangile de Jacques. Recherches sur le Papyrus Bodmer 5 avec une édition critique du texte grec et une traduction annotée* (Subsidia hagiographica, 33). Brussel: Société des Bollandistes, 1961, X-480 p. Esp. 429-433.

1965    Une ancienne version latine du Protévangile de Jacques, avec des extraits de la Vulgate de Matthieu 1-2 et Luc 1-2. — *Analecta Bollandiana* (Brussel) 83 (1965) 365-402 (402-410: J. Gribomont, Appendice: Couleur textuelle des extraits bibliques).

**DE SURGY, Paul**

1975    Rendez à César ce qui est à César, et à Dieu ce qui est à Dieu. Mt 22,15-21. —
*AssSeign* II/60 (1975) 16-25. [NTA 20, 89]

**DE TUYA, Manuel**

1955    La "agonía" de Jesucristo en el Gethsemaní. — *CiTom* 82 (1955) 519-567. Esp. 526-546:
"La cuestion exegetica".

1957    La doctrina eucarística de los Sinópticos. — *CiTom* 84 (1957) 217-281. Esp. 218-251:
"Valoración exegetica". [NTA 2, 521]

1964    *Evangelios* (Biblia Comentada, 5). Madrid: Católica, 1964, VIII-1329 p.

1967    & SALGUERO, J., *Introducción en la Biblia*. I: *Inspiración bíblica, canon, texto,
versiones*; II: *Hermenéutica bíblica, historia de la interpretación de la Biblia,
instituciones israelitas, geografía de Palestina* (Biblioteca de autores cristianos, 49-50).
Madrid: Católica, 1967, XX-615 and XX-631 p.

**DEUBLER, A.**

1987    Struktur und Theologie der matthäischen "Kindheitsgeschichte". — PAUL, E. – STOCK,
A. (eds.), *Glauben ermöglichen. Zum gegenwärtigen Stand der Religionspädagogik.
Festschrift für Günter Stachel*, Mainz: Grünewald, 1987, 160-182.

**DEUTSCH, Celia**

1987    *Hidden Wisdom and the Easy Yoke: Wisdom Torah and Discipleship in Matthew
11.25-30* (JSNT SS, 18). Sheffield: JSOT, 1987, 205 p. Esp. 21-53.150-161: "Critical analyses
of Mt 11.25-30: composition, redaction, source and form"; 55-112.161-174: "Comparative studies of the
themes in the Q saying (vv. 25-27)"; 113-139.174-179: "Comparative studies of the themes in the M sayings
(vv. 28-30)". [NTA 32, p. 241] — Diss. School of Theology, Toronto, Ont. (R.N. Longenecker).
    S. FOWL, *JSNT* 35 (1989) 121-122; D. FRANCE, *Themelios* 14 (1988-89) 66; D.E. GARLAND, *RExp* 87
(1990) 645-646; D.J. GOOD, *JBL* 108 (1989) 526-528; D.J. HARRINGTON, *CBQ* 50 (1988) 526-527; J.D.
KINGSBURY, *Interpr* 43 (1989) 102.104; C.R.A. MORRAY-JONES, *JJS* 43 (1992) 318-319; T.
PRENDERGAST, *Bib* 69 (1988) 587-588; G. STANTON, *ExpT* 99 (1987-88) 311; B.T. VIVIANO, *RB* 97
(1990) 613-614.

1990    Wisdom in Matthew: Transformation of a Symbol. — *NT* 32 (1990) 13-47. Esp. 31-45:
"Matthean wisdom texts" [11,19.25-30; 23,34-39]. [NTA 34, 1121]

1991    Torah, Jesus and Discipleship in the Gospel of Matthew. — *SIDIC* 24/2-3 (1991) 43-52.
[NTA 36, 1250]
Jésus, Torah et la qualité de disciple dans l'Évangile de Matthieu. — *SIDIC* 24/2-3 (1991) 46-56.

1992    Christians and Jews in the First Century: The Gospel of Matthew. — *Thought* (Bronx,
NY) 67 (1992) 399-408. [NTA 38, 143]

**DE VAULX, Jules**

1956    Les témoins du Fils de Dieu. 2. Jésus-Christ, fils de David, fils d'Abraham. L'Évangile
selon saint Matthieu. — *Évangile* 22 (1956) 29-58.

**DE VILLIERS, P.G.R.**

1982    Configuration and Plot in Mt 19–22. Aspects of the Narrative Character of the Gospel
of Matthew. — *Neotestamentica* 16 (1982) 56-73 (addendum, 22-37).

**DE VIRGILIO, Giuseppe**

1991    La ἐκκλησία come "società alternativa". Ricezione dell'opera di G. Lohfink. — *RivBib*
39 (1991) 467-475. Esp. 471-472. [NTA 36, 913r] → Lohfink 1982a

**DEVISCH, Michel**

1972    Le document Q, source de Matthieu. Problématique actuelle. — DIDIER, M. (ed.),
*L'Évangile selon Matthieu*, 1972, 71-97. Esp. 73-86: "Le point de départ"; 86-89: "La méthode";
89-95: "La théologie"; 95-97: "Le 'Sitz im Leben'".

1974    La relation entre l'évangile de Marc et le document Q. — SABBE, M. (ed.), *L'Évangile selon Marc*, 1974, 59-91; ²1988 (note additionnelle, 91). Esp. 60-64: "L'importance du problème"; 65-69: "Le problème"; 69-83: "Les diverses solutions"; 83-89: "La controverse au sujet de Béelzébul".

1975a   *De geschiedenis van de Quelle-hypothese*. I. *Inleiding*; II. *Van J.G. Eichhorn tot B.H. Streeter*; III. *De recente exegese* (2 vols.). Diss. Leuven, 1975, 80, 198, 561 p. (F. Neirynck). Esp. II, 2-36 [origin of the hypothesis]; 37-73 [H.J. Holtzmann]; 74-139 [C. Weizsäcker; B. Weiß; A. Resch; P. Wernle]; 140-195 [A. Harnack; B.H. Streeter]; III, 8-41 [Lk dependence on Mt]; 42-64 [oral tradition]; 95-94 [aramaic Mt]; 95-115 [Mk–Q]; 116-137 [sources in Q]; 138-181 [arguments pro Q]; 182-255 [reconstruction]; 256-265 [structure]; 266-278 [genre]; 278-298 [Thomas]; 317-338.344-401 [theology–redaction]; 339-341 [Sitz im Leben]; 402-532 [Q 3,1-22]; 533-561 [S. Schulz].

1975b   La source dite des Logia et ses problèmes. — *ETL* 51 (1975) 82-89. [NTA 21, 63]

**DE VOOGHT, Paul**

1957    L'argument patristique dans l'interprétation de *Matth.* 16,18 de Jean Huss. — *RSR* 45 (1957) 558-566. [NTA 2, 528]; = ID., *Hussiana* (Bibliothèque de la Revue d'histoire ecclésiastique, 35), Leuven: Publ. universitaires, 1960, 95-101; = ID., *L'hérésie de Jean Huss*, II (Bibliothèque de la RHE, 35bis), Leuven: Publ. universitaires, 1975, 616-624.

**DEVREESSE, Robert**

1963    *Les Évangiles et l'Évangile* (Sous la main de Dieu, 6). Paris: Fleurus, 1963, 251 p. Esp. 13-55: "Les premières étapes de la rédaction des évangiles" [proto-Mt]; 93-106: "L'évangile selon saint Matthieu".
        *Los evangelios y el evangelio*. Buenos Aires: Paulinas, 1964, 220 p.
        *I vangeli e il vangelo*, trans. L. Rosadoni. Milano: Paoline, 1965, 339 p.

**DEVRIES, Simon J.**

1983    The Vision on the Mount: Moses, Elijah and Jesus. — *Proceedings EGLBS* 3 (1983) 1-25.

**DEVULDER, Gérard**

1988    *L'évangile du bonheur. Les béatitudes* (Petite encyclopédie moderne du christianisme). Paris: Desclée De Brouwer, 1988, 48 p.
        M. DUMAIS, *ÉglT* 30 (1989) 479-480.
        *Il vangelo della felicità. Le beatitudine*, trans. T. Tosatti. Brescia: Queriniana, 1990, 78 p.
        *BibOr* 33 (1991) 58-59.

**DE WAARD, Jan**

1966    *A Comparative Study of the Old Testament Text in the Dead Sea Scrolls and in the New Testament* (Studies on the Texts of the Desert of Judah 4), Leiden: Brill, 1966, 101 p. Esp. 6-8 [13,14-15]; 9-10 [1,23]; 30-34 [19,4]; 34-37 [19,19; 22,39]; 37-41 [26,31]; 48-53 [3,3]. 68-70 [12,20].

1982    → D.J. Clark 1982

**DEWAILLY, Louis-Marie**

1965    "Vart fåfängligt ord" i svenska bibelöversättningar (Mt 12,36). ["Every careless word" in Swedish Bible translations (Mt 12,36)] — *Lumen* (København) 8 (1965) 93-99.

1967    La parole sans œuvre (Mt 12,36). — *Mélanges offerts à M.-D. Chenu* (Bibliothèque Thomiste, 37), Paris: Vrin, 1967, 203-219. [NTA 12, 554]

1980a   Vilket bröd avses i Fader vår? [Which bread is meant in the Lord's prayer?] — *SEÅ* 45 (1980) 77-89. Esp. 77 [4,2-4]; 78 [15,37; 26,26]. [NTA 25, 473]

1980b   "Donne-nous notre pain": Quel pain? Notes sur la quatrième demande du Pater. — *RSPT* 64 (1980) 561-588. Esp. 565-575 [Fathers]; 575-577 [Middle Ages]. [NTA 26, 469]

1987    Rabâchage et insistance. [6,7-8] — *VSp* 141 (1987) 4-9. [NTA 31, 1072]

**DEWEY, Arthur J.**

1989a A Prophetic Pronouncement. Q 12:42-46. — *Forum* 5/2 (1989) 99-108. Esp. 99-100: "Preliminary literary analysis"; 101-102: "The 'parable' of 12:42-44"; 102-106: "Formal considerations"; 106-107: "Q 12:48b: a Lukan elaboration". [NTA 34, 172]

1989b Quibbling over Serifs. Observations on Matt 5:18 / Luke 16:17. — *Ibid.*, 109-120. Esp. 109-115: "Preliminary observations"; 115-118: "Q 16:17: an impossible aphorism?". [NTA 34, 178]

1989c The Synoptic Use of πίστις: An Appeal for a Context-Sensitive Translation. — *Forum* 5/4 (1989) 83-86. Esp. 84. [NTA 35, 606]

1989d → J.D. Crossan 1985

1990 → J.D. Crossan 1988a

1992 The Unkindest Cut of All? Matt 19:11-12. — *Forum* 8 (1992) 113-122. Esp. 113-115: "Redactional notes"; 116-117: "Formal considerations"; 117-120: "The social-historical setting". [NTA 39, 158]

**DEWEY, Joanna**

1987 Order in the Synoptic Gospels: A Critique. — *SecCent* 6 (1987-88) 68-82. [NTA 34, 99r]
→ R.H. Fuller 1987, Longstaff 1977, 1987, W.O. Walker 1987b

1993 Jesus' Healings of Women: Conformity and Non-Conformity to Dominant Cultural Values as Clues for Historical Reconstruction. — *SBL 1993 Seminar Papers*, 178-191. Esp. 185-186 [8,14-15]; 186-188 [9,18-26]; 189-191 [15,21-28]; = *BTB* 24 (1994) 123-131. [NTA 39, 126]

**DEY, Joseph**

1953 Beobachtungen an den Bedingungssätzen synoptischer Parallelen. — SCHMID, J. — VÖGTLE, A. (eds.), *Synoptische Studien*. FS A. Wikenhauser, 1953, 78-82. Esp. 79-80 [4,3-9]; 80 [5,46-47]; 80-81 [17,20; 21,21].

**DEYOUNG, James B.**

1994 The Function of Malachi 3.1 in Matthew 11.10: Kingdom Reality as the Hermeneutic of Jesus. — EVANS, C.A. - STEGNER, W.R. (eds.), *The Gospels and the Scriptures of Israel*, 1994, 66-91. Esp. 67-73: "The problem of Jesus' use of Malachi 3.1 in Matthew 11.10"; 73-86: "Possible solutions to the problem"; 86-90: "A proposed solution: actualization of essential reality".

**DE YOUNG, James Calvin**

1960 *Jerusalem in the New Testament. The Significance of the City in the History of Redemption and in Eschatology.* Kampen: Kok, 1960, XII-168 p. Esp. 1-27: "The name Jerusalem in the New Testament"; 28-74: "Jerusalem, God's chosen city" [4,5; 5,34-35; 21,5; 23,21; 27,52-53]. — Diss. Amsterdam, 1960 (R. Schippers).

**DE ZAN, Renato**

1987 Regno, chiesa e mondo nei sinottici. — *ParSpirV* 15 (1987) 175-186.

**DHANIS, Édouard**

1974* (ed.), *Resurrexit. Actes du symposium international sur la Résurrection de Jésus (Rome 1970)*. Città del Vaticano: Libreria Editrice Vaticana, 1974, XV-766 p. → Blinzler, Dupont, Ghiberti, Kremer; → Ghiberti 1975

**DHAVAMONY, Mariasusai**

1987 The Lord's Prayer in the Sanskrit Bible. — *Greg* 68 (1987) 639-670 (French summary, 670). [NTA 32, 594]

**DHÔTEL, Jean-Claude**

1965 Note sur les anciennes traductions françaises du *Pater*. — *La Maison-Dieu* (Paris) 83 (1965) 148-157. [NTA 10, 906]

**Díaz, J. Manuel**

1955 La indisolubilidad del matrimonio en el Nuevo Testamento. — *Cathedra* 9 (1955) 257-275.

1956 ¿Real o aparente contradicción entre san Mateo (xiv,32-33) y san Marcos (vi,51-52) y entre los dos y san Juan (vi,20-21)? — *Cathedra* 10 (1956) 337-342.

**Díaz, Romualdo M.**

1953* (ed.), *Miscellanea Biblica B. Ubach* (Scripta et Documenta, 1). Montserrat, 1953, XI-474 p. → Bover, Colunga, Vandervorst

**Díaz Esteban, F.**

1968 Confirmación hebrea de que hay una errónea traducción en la versión castellana del Padrenuestro. [6,13] — *CuBíb* 25 (1968) 300-302.

**Díaz Mateos, Manuel**

1981 Oración del Señor, oración del Reino. — *Revista Teológica* (Lima) 15 (1981) 53-68; = *Páginas* 6/41 (1981) 1-12.

**Díaz Ortega, José Luis**

1983 Reflexiones sobre el matrimonio a la luz del Nuevo Testamento. — *Persona y Derecho* (Pamplona) 10 (1983) 367-398.

**Di Bianco, Nicola**

1992 *Il problema della struttura letteraria del Vangelo di Matteo*. Diss. Napoli, 1992, 93 p. (V. Fusco).

**Dibelius, Martin**

1926[R] *Geschichte der urchristlichen Literatur* [1926; ET, 1936], ed. F. Hahn (Theologische Bücherei, 58). München: Kaiser, 1975, 188 p. Esp. 37: "Die Kindheitsgeschichten"; 38-39: "Erzählungs- und Spruchsammlungen"; 39-41: "Die synoptische Frage"; 42-43: "Das Matthäusevangelium"; 43-45: "Das Papiasbericht".

1933[R] *Die Formgeschichte des Evangeliums* [1919, ²1933, IV-315 p.], 3rd rev. ed., ed. G. Bornkamm, with a "Nachtrag" by Gerhard Iber (302-312: "Neuere Literatur zur Formgeschichte"). Tübingen: Mohr, ³1959, V-327 p. Esp. 197-200 [passion narrative]; 244-265 [paraenesis: 5,21-48; 11,16-17; 13,24-30.33; 25,1-13.14-30]; ⁴1961; ⁵1966; ⁶1972.
*From Tradition to Gospel* [²1933] (The Library of Theological Translations), Greenwood, SC: Attic; London: Clarke, 1971, XV-311 p. Esp. 196-199; 243-265.
*La historia de las formas evangélicas* [= ⁶1972] (Clásicos de la ciencia bíblica, 2). Valencia: Edicep, 1984, 315 p.

1935[R] Evangelienkritik und Christologie. [English, 1935] — ID., *Botschaft und Geschichte*, I, 1953, 293-358. Esp. 305-317: "Die Bildung der Evangelientradition"; = HAHN, F. (ed.), *Zur Formgeschichte des Evangeliums* (Wege der Forschung, 81), Darmstadt: Wissenschaftliche Buchgesellschaft, 1985, 52-117. Esp. 64-76.

1940a[R] Die Bergpredigt. [English, 1940] — ID., *Botschaft und Geschichte*, I, 1953, 79-174. Esp. 79-87: "Das Christentum und die Bergpredigt"; 87-98: "Der Charakter der Bergpredigt"; 99-107: "Die alte Überlieferung der Predigt Jesu"; 107-121: "Die Sprüche Jesu"; 121-130: "Das jüdische Gesetz und das Gesetz des Gottesreichs"; 130-147: "Die Bergpredigt und Christi Sendung"; 147-174: "Die Bergpredigt und die heutige Welt".

1940b[R] Die dritte Bitte des Vaterunsers. [1940] — ID., *Botschaft und Geschichte*, I, 1953, 175-177.

1953 *Botschaft und Geschichte. Gesammelte Aufsätze von Martin Dibelius. I: Zur Evangelienforschung*, ed. G. Bornkamm & H. Kraft, Tübingen: Mohr, 1953, VIII-380 p. → 1935, 1940a-b

**DICHARRY, Warren**

1990 *Human Authors of the New Testament*. Vol. I: *Mark, Matthew, and Luke*. Collegeville, MN: Liturgical Press, 1990, 223 p. [NTA 35, p. 239]

**DICKSON, David**

1647R *A Brief Exposition of the Evangel of Jesus Christ according to Matthew* [1647] (Geneva Series of Commentaries). Edinburgh: Banner of Truth, 1981, X-416 p.

    A.T.B. McGOWAN, *EvQ* 56 (1984) 119.

**DIDIER, Jean-Charles**

1952 D'une interprétation récente de l'expression "lier–délier". [G. Lambert, 1945] — *MSR* 9 (1952) 55-62.

**DIDIER, Marcel**

1959 Les paraboles de Jésus. Le discours de Mt., XIII. — *RevDiocNamur* 13 (1959) 633-641.

1960a Les paraboles du semeur et de la semence qui croît d'elle-même. — *RevDiocNamur* 14 (1960) 185-196. Esp. 185-193 [13,3-9.18-23].

1960b Les paraboles de l'ivraie et du filet. — *Ibid.*, 491-504. Esp. 491-500 [13,24-30.36-43]; 500-504 [13,47-50].

1961 Les paraboles du grain de sénevé et du levain. — *RevDiocNamur* 15 (1961) 385-394. Esp. 386-393 [13,31-32]; 393-394 [13,33].

1962 Les paraboles du trésor et de la perle (*Mt.*, XIII,44-46). — *RevDiocNamur* 16 (1962) 296-302. Esp. 296-299 [13,44]; 300-302 [13,45-46].

1963 Simple explication du "Notre Père". — *RevDiocNamur* 17 (1963) 213-225.

1965 La parabole des talents. [25,14-30] — *AssSeign* I/93 (1965) 32-44; = *RevDiocNamur* 20 (1966) 171-187. Esp. 171-176: "Contexte littéraire"; 176-187: "Analyse" (= 1965).

1967a La parabole du voleur. — *RevDiocNamur* 21 (1967) 1-13. Esp. 1-5 [24,42-44].

1967b La parabole du serviteur-intendant. — *Ibid.*, 75-86. Esp. 75-80 [24,45-51].

1967c La révélation de Dieu par Jésus. — *Ibid.*, 159-183. Esp. 162-180.

1967d La parabole des talents et des mines. — DE LA POTTERIE, I. (ed.), *De Jésus aux Évangiles*. FS J. Coppens, 1967, 248-271. Esp. 252-257 [25,14-30]; 257-264 [Q 19,11-27 (Lk)]. (IT, 1971, 308-336).

1969 La parabole du semeur. — TROISFONTAINES, C. (ed.), *Au service de la Parole de Dieu*. FS A.-M. Charue, 1969, 21-41. Esp. 33-37 [13,18-23].

1970a Journées bibliques de Louvain 1970. L'Évangile selon Matthieu. — *ETL* 46 (1970) 433-440; = ID., *L'Évangile selon Matthieu*, 1972, 11-19.

1970b La parabole des vierges (*Mt.*, XXV,1-13). — *FoiTemps* 3 (1970) 329-350. Esp. 330-342: "Signification de la parabole pour l'évangéliste"; 343-347: "La parabole dans l'enseignement de Jésus".

1972* (ed.), *L'Évangile selon Matthieu. Rédaction et théologie* (BETL, 29). Gembloux: Duculot, 1972, 428 p. [NTA 17, p. 119] → Cothenet, Descamps, Devisch, M. Didier 1970a, Dupont, Gatzweiler, Hartman, Kahmann, Lambrecht, Légasse, Martini, Neirynck, Senior, Smit Sibinga, Strecker 1971, Van Segbroeck, Vögtle; → Raurell 1970, Sabourin 1973

    J.A. FITZMYER, *JBL* 92 (1973) 322; H. FRANKEMÖLLE, *TRev* 69 (1973) 109-110; I. GOMÁ CIVIT, *EstBíb* 33 (1974) 199-201; K. GRAYSTON, *ExpT* 84 (1972-73) 297; H.B. GREEN, *JTS* 24 (1973) 224-225; J.-C. INGELAERE, *RHPR* 53 (1973) 84-85; X. JACQUES, *CC* 124/1 (1974) 617-618; *NRT* 95 (1973) 847-849; J. MURPHY-O'CONNOR, *RB* 83 (1976) 301-302; G.W.E. NICKELSBURG, *CBQ* 35 (1973) 525-527; P. POKORNÝ, *ComViat* 15 (1972) 267-268; J. PONTHOT, *RTL* 1 (1970) 475-48; 3 (1972) 362; B. RIGAUX, *RHE* 68 (1973) 972-974; J.M. TISON, *Bijdragen* 34 (1972) 213-214; J. ZUMSTEIN, *RTP* 23 (1973) 401-402.

**DIEHL, Douglas Alan**

1991    *The Significance of Almsgiving in Primitive Christianity as a Means of Understanding New Testament Piety* [6,1-6.16-18]. Diss. Southwestern Baptist Theol. Sem., Fort Worth, TX, 1991, 235 p. (V. Gideon). — *DissAbstr* 52 (1991-92) 2588.

**DIEKHANS, Mariano**

1968    Mt 19,9 (5,32). — *REB* 28 (1968) 425-427. [NTA 13, 173]

**DIETERLE, Christiane**

1965    *Les petits et les enfants dans les Évangiles synoptiques*. Diss. Lausanne, 1965, 101 p.

**DIETRICH, Wolfgang**

1973*   & FREIMARK, P. – SCHRECKENBERG, H. (eds.), *Festgabe für Karl Heinrich Rengstorf zum 70. Geburtstag* (Theokratia. Jahrbuch des Institutum Judaicum Delitzschianum, 2). Leiden: Brill, 1973, VIII-444 p. → Braumann, Schwark, Völkel

**DIETZFELBINGER, Christian**

1972    Das Gleichnis von der erlassenen Schuld. Eine theologische Untersuchung von Matthäus 18,23-35. — *EvT* 32 (1972) 437-451. [NTA 17, 916] → Deidun 1976

1975    *Die Antithesen der Bergpredigt* (Theologische Existenz heute, NF 186). München: Kaiser, 1975, 85 p. Esp. 14-53: "Exegese der einzelnen Antithesen"; 54-85: "Die Frage nach dem Sinn der Antithesen". [NTA 20, p. 106]
        T. RYAN, *CBQ* 38 (1976) 377-378.

1979    Die Antithesen der Bergpredigt im Verständnis des Mattäus. — *ZNW* 70 (1979) 1-15. Esp. 1-6: "Die Aussage des Ganzen"; 6-14: "Die einzelnen Antithesen"; 14-15: "Rückfragen". [NTA 24, 420]

1983    Das Gleichnis von den Arbeitern im Weinberg als Jesuswort. [20,1-16] — *EvT* 43 (1983) 126-137. [NTA 28, 99]

1984    Die Frömmigkeitsregeln von Mt 6,1-18 als Zeugnisse frühchristlicher Geschichte. — *ZNW* 75 (1984) 184-201. Esp. 185-188 [6,2-4]; 188-196 [6,2-4 5-6.16-18]; 197-201 [6,1-18 and Jesus]. [NTA 30, 114]

1989    Das Gleichnis von den anvertrauten Geldern. [25,14-30] — *BTZ* 6 (1989) 222-233. [NTA 34, 636]

**DIEZ, Karlheinz**

1987    *Christus und seine Kirche. Zum Kirchenverständnis des Petrus Canisius* (Konfessionskundliche und kontroverstheologische Studien, 51). Paderborn: Bonifatius, 1987, 389 p. Esp. 343-356 [16,18-19]. — Diss. Pont. Univ. Greg., Roma, 1985 (A. Antón).

**DÍEZ ARAGON, Ramon Alfonso**

1993    La madre con el niño en la casa. Un estudio narratologico. [2,1-12] — *EphMar* 43 (1993) 47-60. [NTA 37, 154]

**DÍEZ MACHO, Alejandro**

1964    Targum y Nuevo Testamento. — *Mélanges Eugène Tisserant*, 1964, I, 153-185. Esp. 157-158 [2,1-8]; 163-164 [16,19; 18,18]; 173 [16,17]; 183 [2,5-6]; 184 [15,26].

1965    → Malo 1965

1975    Děráš y exégesis del Nuevo Testamento. — *Sefarad* 35 (1975) 37-89. Esp. 43-53: "Historia por paralelos en el Evangelio de la Infancia de Mateo"; 65 [6,1-21] 72-75; 81-83. [NTA 22, 11] → 1977a

1977a   *La historicidad de los Evangelios de la infancia. El entorno de Jesús* (Colección "Santiago Apostol", 4). Madrid: Católica, 1977, 132 p. [NTA 23, p. 92] → 1975
        R. GAUTHIER, *CahJos* 28 (1980) 269-270; D. MONTERO, *NatGrac* 24 (1977) 533-534.

1977b   Cristo instituyó el matrimonio indisoluble. — *Sefarad* 37 (1977) 261-291. Esp. 265-268 [19,1-9]; 271-275.289-291 [5,32; 19,9]; 275-282 [19,3]. [NTA 23, 831]

1978 *Indisolubilidad del matrimonio y divorcio en la Biblia. La sexualidad en la Biblia.* Madrid: Católica, 1978, 346 p. Esp. 28-47.213-217 [5,32; 19,9]; 217-222; 223-230 [19,3]; 232-250; 308-311.

1979 *W$^e$qara't* de Isaías 7,14 y la traducción *kai kalésousin* de Mateo 1,23. — *Miscelánea de Estudios Arabes y Hebraicos* 26-28 (1977-79) 31-42.

1980 Qaddis y Padrenuestro. — *El Olivo* 12 (1980) 23-46.

1981 Jesús *"Ho Nazoraios"*. — *Quaere Paulum. Miscelánea homenaje a monseñor doctor Lorenzo Turrado* (Bibliotheca Salmanticensis. Estudios, 39), Salamanca: Universidad Pontificia, 1981, 9-26. Esp. 25-26 [2,23].

**DIEZ MERINO, Luis**

1983 Testimonios judíos sobre la existencia de un evangelio arameo. — *EstBíb* 41 (1983) 157-163.

1984 ¿Un evangelio arameo de Mateo en la universidad de Barcelona? (Manuscritto BUB n. 350). — *Anuario de filología* (Barcelona) 10 (1984) 65-88.

**DIGNATH, Walter**

1965 *Weihnachtstexte im Unterricht.* Gütersloh: Mohn, 1965, 192 p. Esp. 36.51-56.65-66.103-115.136-138.172-180 [2]. — Diss. Mainz, 1961 (M. Metzger).

1966 Die Verklärung Jesu (Markus 9,2-13; vgl. Matthäus 17,1-13; Lukas 9,28-37). — ID. - WIBBING, S., *Taufe – Versuchung – Verklärung* (Handbücherei für den Religionsunterricht, 3), Gütersloh: Mohn, 1966, 55-80. Esp. 64-68.

**DIHLE, Albrecht**

1962 *Die Goldene Regel. Eine Einführung in die Geschichte der antiken und frühchristlichen Vulgärethik* (Studien zur Altertumswissenschaft, 7). Göttingen: Vandenhoeck & Ruprecht, 1962, 135 p. Esp. 103-109: "Die goldene Regel in der antiken und der christlichen Tradition"; 109-127: "Die goldene Regel und das Nächstenliebegebot".

1981 Goldene Regel. — *RAC* 11 (1981) 930-940. Esp. 937-938.

**DI LELLA, Alexander A.**

1989 The Structure and Composition of the Matthean Beatitudes. — HORGAN, M.P. - KOBELSKI, P.J. (eds.), *To Touch the Text*. FS J.A. Fitzmyer, 1989, 237-242.

**DILLEMORE, F.W.**

1965 The Gospel according to Matthew. — *Westminster Study Bible*, New York: Collins, 1965, 23-65.

**DILLERSBERGER, Josef**

1949$^R$ *Der Neue Mensch. Seligpreisungen und Tugendleben* [1949] (Licht vom Licht: eine Sammlung geistlicher Texte, 9). Einsiedeln: Benziger, 1951, 168 p.

1952 *Matthäus. Das Evangelium des heiligen Matthäus in theologischer und heilsgeschichtlicher Schau. I: Sein Kommen in Vielfalt (Die Vorgeschichte).* Salzburg: Müller, 1953, 172 p.; II: *Der Meister in Wort und Wunder*, 1952, 177 p.; III: *Der Kirche entgegen*, 1953, 187 p.; IV: *Das grosse Zeigen seines Leidens*, 1953, 169 p.; V: *Die letzten Tage in Jerusalem*, 1953, 197 p.; VI: *Die messianische Vollendung*, 1954, 164 p.

  E. BERBUIR, *Wort und Wahrheit* (Wien) 35 (1954) 304; P. GAECHTER, *ZKT* 75 (1953) 488; 76 (1954) 360-361; K.H. SCHELKLE, *TQ* 134 (1954) 126; A. STÖGER, *TPQ* 102 (1954) 167-168.

**DILLMAN, Charles Norman**

1980 *A Study of Some Theological and Literary Comparisons of the Gospel of Matthew and the Epistle of James*. Diss. Edinburgh, 1980, 341 p. (H. Anderson).

**DILLMANN, Rainer**

1984 *Das Eigentliche der Ethik Jesu. Ein exegetischer Beitrag zur moraltheologischen Diskussion um das Proprium einer christlichen Ethik* (Tübinger theologische Studien, 23). Mainz: Matthias-Grünewald, 1984, 132 p. Esp. 77-81 [19,16-30/Mk]. — Diss. Frankfurt, 1981 (F. Lentzen-Deis).

**DILLON, E.I.**

1964 *The Good News to the Poor in the Kerygma of Jesus (Mt 11,5 et Lc 7,22; Lc 4,18s)*. Diss. Pont. Univ. Greg., Roma, 1964-65.

**DILLON, Gerald F.**

1963 *A Study of the Literary Form and Underlying Theology of the Transfiguration Narratives* [17,1-9]. Diss. St. Michael's College, Toronto, Ont., 1963.

**DILLON, John**

1983 "Jesus Went into His House": Origen's Exegesis of Matthew 13:36-52. — *ProcIrBiblAss* 7 (1983) 60-73.

**DILLON, Richard J.**

1966 Towards a Tradition-History of the Parables of the True Israel (Matthew 21,33–22,14). — *Bib* 47 (1966) 1-42. Esp. 8-12: "Mt 22,1-14 in the context of recent Matthean study"; 12-37: "'The wicked husbandmen': origins of its Matthean application"; 37-41: "A common *Sitz-im-Leben der Kirche*?". [NTA 11, 215]

1975 The Law of Christ and the Church of Christ according to Saint Matthew. — *Communio* (Notre Dame, IN) 2 (1975) 32-53. [NTA 20, 76]

1983 Early Christian Experience in the Gospel Sayings. — *BiTod* 21 (1983) 83-88. [NTA 27, 970]

1985 On the Christian Obedience of Prayer (Matthew 6:5-13). — *Worship* 59 (1985) 413-426. [NTA 30, 571]

1991 Ravens, Lilies, and the Kingdom of God (Matthew 6:25-33 / Luke 12:22-31). — *CBQ* 53 (1991) 605-627. Esp. 608-617: "Regaining the Q text"; 617-626: "Exposition of the argument". [NTA 36, 719]

**DI MARCO, Angelico-Salvatore**

1976 Der Chiasmus in der Bibel, 3. Teil. — *LingBib* 39 (1976) 37-85. Esp. 38-57. [NTA 21, 338]

1980 *Il chiasmo nella Bibbia. Contributi di stilistica strutturale* (Ricerche e proposte, 1). Torino: Marietti, 1980, 215 p.

1981 *Il "Perfetto" nei Vangeli. Grammatica ed esegesi* (Ricerche e proposte, 2). Torino: Marietti, 1981, 128 p.

1993 La recezione del Nuovo Testamento nei padri apostolici. — *ANRW* II.27.1 (1993) 724-762. Esp. 741-746: "Sinottici".

**DI NICOLA, Angelo**

1989 Il prologo di *Tractatus in Matthaeum* di Cromazio. — *Chromatius Episcopus*, 1989, 81-116.

**DINKLER, Erich**

1954 Jesu Wort vom Kreuztragen. — ELTESTER, W. (ed.), *Neutestamentliche Studien*. FS R. Bultmann, 1954, 110-129. Esp. 110-111 [Q 14,27/Mk]; 115-117 [11,28-30]; = ID., *Signum Crucis*, 1967, 77-98. Esp. 78-79; 83-85.

1955 The Idea of History in Earliest Christianity. — *The Idea of History in the Ancient Near East*, New Haven, CT: Yale University Press, 1955, 169-214. Esp. 194-195; = ID., *Signum Crucis*, 1967, 313-350. Esp. 332-333.

1959  Die Petrus-Rom-Frage. Ein Forschungsbericht. — *TR* 25 (1959) 189-230, 289-335. Esp.
195-198 [16,17-19]. [NTA 5, 535]; 27 (1961) 33-64; 31 (1966) 232-253.

1964*  (ed.), *Zeit und Geschichte. Dankesgabe an Rudolf Bultmann zum 80. Geburtstag.*
Tübingen: Mohr, 1964, XI-749 p. [English → J.M. Robinson 1971*]. → G. Bornkamm, Dinkler,
Kümmel, J.M. Robinson

1964  Petrusbekenntnis und Satanswort. Das Problem der Messianität Jesu. — *Ibid.*, 127-153.
Esp. 131.135 [16,17]; 144 [11,12]; 149-150 [Q 14,27]; = ID., *Signum Crucis*, 1967, 283-312.
Esp. 288.292; 301; 308.
Peter's Confession and the 'Satan' Saying. The Problem of Jesus' Messiahship. — ROBINSON, J.M. (ed.), *The
Future of Our Religious Past.* FS R. Bultmann, 1971, 169-202. Esp. 175.179; 190; 198.

1967  *Signum Crucis. Aufsätze zum Neuen Testament und zur Christlichen Archäologie.*
Tübingen: Mohr, 1967, VIII-403 p. → 1954, 1955, 1964

1971  Die Taufaussagen des Neuen Testaments. Neu untersucht im Hinblick auf Karl Barths
Tauflehre. — VIERING, F. (ed.), *Zu Karl Barths Lehre von der Taufe*, Gütersloh:
Mohn, 1971, 60-153. Esp. 62-70; = MERK, O. – WOLTER, M. (eds.), *Im Zeichen des
Kreuzes. Aufsätze von Erich Dinkler* (BZNW, 61), Berlin: de Gruyter, 1992, 39-132.
Esp. 41-49.

**DINTER, Paul E.**

1990  Disabled for the Kingdom. Celibacy, Scripture & Tradition. — *Commonweal* 117
(1990) 571-577. Esp. 571-573 [19,12]. [NTA 35, 631]

**DIPBOYE, Carolyn**

1995  Matthew 25:14-30 – To Survive or to Serve? — *RExp* 92 (1995) 507-512.

**DI PINTO, Luigi**

1973  "Seguire Gesù" secondo i vangeli sinottici. Studio di teologia biblica. — CANFORA, G.
(ed.), *Fondamenti biblici*, 1973, 187-251.

1980  Amore e giustizia. Il contributo specifico del Vangelo di Matteo. — DE GENNARO, G.
(ed.), *Amore e Giustizia* (L'Aquila), Napoli: Dehoniane, 1980, 328-455.

1981  L'uomo visto da Gesù di Nazaret. — DE GENNARO, G. (ed.), *L'antropologia biblica*
(Studio Biblico Teologico Aquilano), Napoli: Dehoniane, 1981, 645-706 (discussion, 707-
716). Esp. 655-677 [6,25-34; 12,9-14].

1983  Il giudizio finale sul servizio ai fratelli (Mt 25,31-46): punto focale del discorso
escatologico. — *ParSpirV* 8 (1983) 175-199.

**DI SANTE, Carmine**

1993  "Dacci oggi il nostro pane quotidiano". La storia del pane. [6,11] — *RasT* 34 (1993)
322-330. [NTA 40, 1460]

**DITTMAR, Wilhelm**

1899ᴿ  *The Old Testament in the New* [German, 1899]. Grand Rapids, MI, 1987.

**DOBBELER, Stephanie VON**

1988  *Das Gericht und das Erbarmen Gottes. Die Botschaft Johannes des Täufers und ihre
Rezeption bei den Johannesjüngern im Rahmen der Theologiegeschichte des Frühjuden-
tums* (BBB, 70). Frankfurt/M: Athenäum, 1988, 258 p. Esp. 45-62: "Rekonstruktion des Grund-
textes der Umkehrpredigt auf der Basis von Mt 3,7-12 par Lk 3,7-9.16f"; 63-82: "Synchrone Analyse des
Grundtextes"; 83-150: "Traditionsgeschichtliche Einordnung des Täufers"; 223-236: "Messias, Elia, Prophet?
Johannes der Täufer in Joh 1,1-34 und Mt 11,7-13 par Lk 7,24-28". — Diss. Bonn, 1987 (H. Merklein).

**DOBLE, Peter**

1960  The Temptations. [4,1-11] — *ExpT* 72 (1960-61) 91-93. [NTA 5, 708] → W. Powell 1961

**DOBSCHÜTZ, Ernst VON**

1928[R] Matthäus als Rabbi und Katechet. [1928] — LANGE, J. (ed.), *Das Matthäus-Evangelium*, 1980, 52-64. Esp. 53-60 [style]; 60-63 [Lk dep. on Mt; date].
Matthew as Rabbi and Catechist. — STANTON, G. (ed.), *The Interpretation of Matthew*, 1983, 19-29. Esp. 20-26; 26-29; [2]1995, 27-38. Esp. 28-34; 34-37.

**DOCKX, Stanislas**

1976 *Chronologies néotestamentaires et Vie de l'Église primitive. Recherches exégétiques.* Paris-Gembloux: Duculot, 1976, VIII-303 p.; Leuven: Peeters, [2]1984, VIII-413 p. Esp. 233-253 ([2]1984, 277-297): "Étapes rédactionnelles du récit des apparitions aux saintes femmes"; [2]1984, 299-308: "La genèse du 'Notre Père' replacée dans le cadre de l'histoire".

**DODD, Charles Harold**

1935[R] *The Parables of the Kingdom* [1935]. London: Nisbet, repr. 1950, 214 p.; rev. ed., 1961, XI-176 p. Esp. 1-20: "The nature and purpose of the gospel parables"; 21-59: "The Kingdom of God" [8,11; 10,34-36; 11,2-11; 12,28; 23,34-36.37-38]; 60-84: "The day of the Son of Man" [10,15.32-33; 12,41-47; 19,28; 24,37-39]; 85-121: "The 'setting-in-life'" [5,13.15.17-48; 8,19-22; 13,44-46; 18,12-14; 20,1-16; 22,1-14; 25,14-30]; 122-139: "Parables of crisis" [7,22-23; 24,43-44.45-51; 25,1-12]; 140-156: "Parables of growth" [13,24-30.31-32.33.47-50]; (Scribner Library, 125), New York: Scribner, 1965. → Newell 1972
*Le parabole del Regno*, trans. F. Ronchi (Studi biblici, 10). Brescia: Paideia, 1970, 202 p.
*Las parábolas del Reino*, trans. A. de la Fuente Adánez. Madrid: Cristiandad, 1974, 180 p.
*Les paraboles du Royaume de Dieu*, trans. H. Perret & S. deBussy (Parole de Dieu, 14). Paris: Seuil, 1977, 187 p.
Die Gleichnisse der Evangelien. [1935, 1-20] — HARNISCH, W. (ed.), *Gleichnisse Jesu*, 1982, 137-153.

1938[R] *History and the Gospel* [1938]. London: Nisbet, repr. 1952; 1960, 189 p. Esp. 77-110: "Historical criticism of the gospels".
*Évangile et histoire*, trans. P. Noury (Lire la Bible, 39). Paris: Cerf, 1974, 176 p.
*Storia ed evangelo*, trans. A. Ornella (Biblioteca minima di cultura religiosa, 27). Brescia: Paideia, 1976, 152 p.

1947[R] Matthew and Paul. [1947] — ID., *New Testament Studies*, Manchester: University Press, 1953, 53-66.

1952 *According to the Scriptures. The Sub-structure of New Testament Theology.* London: Nisbet, 1952, 145 p. Esp. 48-49 [21,5]; 53 [11,5]; 64-65 [Zech]; 75-77 [Hos]; 79 [1,23]; 80-81 [4,15-16]; 89 [12,18-21].

1953 *The Interpretation of the Fourth Gospel.* Cambridge: University Press, 1953, XI-478 p. Esp. 390-396; 440-441.
*L'interpretazione del quarto vangelo* (Biblioteca teologica, 11). Brescia: Paideia, 1974, 580 p.
*L'interprétation du quatrième évangile*, trans. M. Montabrut (LD, 82). Paris: Cerf, 1975, 598 p.

1955a The Appearances of the Risen Christ: An Essay in Form-Criticism of the Gospels. — NINEHAM, D.E. (ed.), *Studies in the Gospels*. FS R.H Lightfoot, 1955, 9-35. Esp. 11-13 [28]; = ID., *More New Testament Studies*, 1968, 102-133. Esp. 104-106.
Die Erscheinungen des Auferstandenen Christus. Ein Essay zur Formkritik der Evangelien. — HOFFMANN, P. (ed.), *Zur neutestamentlichen Überlieferung von der Auferstehung Jesu*, 1988, 297-330. Esp. 299-302.

1955b Some Johannine 'Herrenworte' with Parallels in the Synoptic Gospels. — *NTS* 2 (1955-56) 75-86. Esp. 76-78 [10,24-25]; 78-81 [10,39; 16,25]; 81-85 [10,40]; 85-86 [18,18]. → 1963, 335-365

1957 The Beatitudes. — *Mélanges bibliques*. FS A. Robert, 1957, 404-410.
The Beatitudes: A Form-Critical Study. — ID., *More New Testament Studies*, 1968, 1-10.

1959 The Primitive Catechism and the Sayings of Jesus. — HIGGINS, A.J.B. (ed.), *New Testament Essays*. FS T.W. Manson, 1959, 106-118 Esp. 111-112; 114 [24,43-44]; 116-117 [5,16]; = ID., *More New Testament Studies*, 1968, 11-29. Esp. 17-18; 23; 27-28.

1961 Some Problems of New Testament Translation. — *ExpT* 72 (1960-61) 268-274. Esp. 268 [6,19; 20,26-27; 24,43]; 273 [11,19]. [NTA 6, 41]

1962 T.W. Manson and His Rylands Lectures. — *ExpT* 73 (1961-62) 302-303. Esp. 303 [Q].

1963 *Historical Tradition in the Fourth Gospel.* Cambridge: University Press, 1963, XII-454 p. Esp. 23-25 [26,1-16/Mk]; 27 [26,4/Jn]; 32 [26–27/OT]; 78-79 [26,52/Jn]; 170-172 [9,27-31]; 188-195 [8,5-13/Jn]; 208-211 [15,29-31/Jn]; 218-219 [12,38/Jn]; 266-269 [3,11/Jn]; 271-278 [Jn 1,19-37]; 288-301 [John the Baptist]; 333-334 [6,9-13/Jn]; 335-365: "Sayings common to John and the synoptics" [7,7; 10,24-25.39.40; 11,27; 13,16; 16,24; 18,3.18; 21,22; 28,18/Jn] (→ 1955b); 366-368 [5,13; 6,22-23/Jn]; 396-397 [16,2-3/Jn]; 409-410 [24,9/Jn]; 410-412 [10,17-19/Jn]. → J. Bligh 1964

1967 The Portrait of Jesus in John and in the Synoptics. — FARMER, W.R., et al. (eds.), *Christian History and Interpretation.* FS J. Knox, 1967, 183-198. Esp. 190-193 [7,24-27; 8,5-13; 11,21-22; 12,39-42; 28,18].

1968 *More New Testament Studies.* Manchester: University Press; Grand Rapids, MI: Eerdmans, 1968, VII-157 p. → 1955a, 1957, 1959

1976 New Testament Translation Problems. — *BTrans* 27 (1976) 301-311. Esp. 301-305 [1,23]; 307-310 [5,3]; 28 (1977) 101-116. [NTA 21, 19/324]

**DÖMER, Michael**

1978 *Das Heil Gottes. Studien zur Theologie des lukanischen Doppelwerkes* (BBB, 51). Köln–Bonn: Hanstein, 1978, XLVII-233 p. Esp. 37-40 [11,12-13/Q 16,16]. — Diss. Bonn, 1977-78 (H. Zimmermann).

**DOEVE, Jan Willem**

1953 *Jewish Hermeneutics in the Synoptic Gospels and Acts* (Van Gorcum's Theologische Bibliotheek, 24). Assen: Van Gorcum, 1953, 232 p. Esp. 91-118: "Jewish interpretation of Scripture and the New Testament" [13]; 119-161: "The kingdom of God – the Son of Man – the Messiah"; 177-205: "The examination of Scripture and the fixation of traditional material". — Diss. Leiden, 1953 (J. de Zwaan).

1955 Purification du Temple et dessèchement du figuier. Sur la structure du 21ème chapitre de Matthieu et parallèles (Marc xi.1-xii.12, Luc xix.28-xx.19). — *NTS* 1 (1954-55) 297-308.

1957 Le rôle de la tradition orale dans la composition des évangiles synoptiques. — HEUSCHEN, J.M. (ed.), *La formation des évangiles*, 1957, 70-84.

1959 Die Gefangennahme Jesu in Gethsemane. Eine traditionsgeschichtliche Untersuchung. [26,36-46] — *Studia Evangelica* 1 (1959) 458-480.

**DOHNA, Lothar**

1986* & MOKROSCH, R. (eds.), *Werden und Wirkung der Reformation* (Wissenschaft und Technik, 19). Darmstadt: Technische Hochschule, 1986, 288 p. → J. Blank, Geyer, Mokrosch

**DOIGNON, Jean**

1972 La scène évangélique du baptême de Jésus commentée par Lactance (*Divinae institutiones*, 4,15) et Hilaire de Poitiers (*In Matthaeum*, 2,5-6). — FONTAINE, J. – KANNENGIESSER, C. (eds.), *Epektasis.* FS J. Daniélou, 1972, 63-73. Esp. 68-73.

1975a L'argumentation d'Hilaire de Poitiers dans l'Exemplum de la Tentation de Jésus (*In Matthaeum*, 3,1-5). — *VigChr* 29 (1975) 296-308.

1975b Citations singulières et leçons rares du texte latin de l'Évangile de Matthieu dans l'"*In Matthaeum*" d'Hilaire de Poitiers. — *BullLitEccl* 76 (1975) 187-196. [NTA 20, 426]

1977 Une addition éphémère au texte de l'Oraison dominicale chez plusieurs Pères latins. Recherches sur son origine et son histoire (seconde moitié du IV^e siècle – début du V^e siècle). [6,13] — *BullLitEccl* 78 (1977) 161-180. Esp. 162-166 [Hilarius of Poitiers]; 166-169 [Jerome].

1978    (ed.), *Hilaire de Poitiers. Sur Matthieu.* I: *Introduction, texte critique, traduction et notes*; II: *Texte critique, traduction, notes, index et appendice* (SC, 254 and 258). Paris: Cerf, 1978-79, 305 and 299 p. Esp. 19-86: "Introduction"; 89-303 and 7-261: "Texte et traduction".
→ Simonetti 1979, Smulders 1983
        C. BASEVI, *ScriptTheol* 13 (1981) 295-299; D.A. BERTRAND, *RHPR* 61 (1981) 284-285; R. BRAUN, *Revue des études anciennes* (Bordeaux) 86 (1984) 383-384; W.J. BURGHARDT, *TS* 40 (1979) 789; E. CATTANEO, *OCP* 46 (1980) 247-249; H. CROUZEL, *BullLitEccl* 81 (1980) 212-213; I.-H. DALMAIS, *La Maison-Dieu* (Paris) 142 (1980) 115-116; G. DE DURAND, *RSPT* 55 (1981) 443-444; Y.-M. DUVAL, *Latomus* 40 (1981) 396-399; J. FONTAINE, *Revue des études latines* (Paris) 57 (1979) 455-457; C. GRANADO, *EstE* 55 (1980) 385-386; R. GRYSON, *RTL* 10 (1979) 266; É. JUNOD, *RTP* 31 (1981) 184; C. KANNENGIESSER, *RSR* 70 (1982) 584-585; D. LADARIA, *RevistEspTeol* 38 (1978) 186-187; J. LEMARIÉ, *RBén* 90 (1980) 335-337; C. MARTIN, *NRT* 101 (1979) 758-759; C. MORESCHINI, *Aevum* 55 (1981) 341-342; P. NAUTIN, *RHR* 198 (1981) 85; G. PELLAND, *SE* 31 (1979) 409-410; M. PERRIN, *MSR* 38 (1981) 144-146; P.-H. POIRIER, *LavalTP* 38 (1982) 89-90; H. SAVON, *RevÉtudAug* 27 (1981) 187-191; J. SCHAMP, *Revue belge de philologie et d'histoire* (Bruxelles) 60 (1982) 213-214; L. VERHEIJEN, *Antiquité classique* 51 (1982) 478-479.

1979a   Chromatiana. À propos de l'édition de l'œuvre de Chromace d'Aquilée. — *RSPT* 63 (1979) 241-250. → Étaix 1974a

1979b   Rhétorique et exégèse patristique; la defensio de l'apôtre Pierre chez Hilaire de Poitiers. — CHEVALLIER, R. (ed.), *La rhétorique à Rome. Colloque des 10-11 décembre 1977, Paris* (Caesarodunum, 14bis; Calliope, 1), Paris: Les Belles Lettres, 1979, 141-152.

1982a   "Erat in Iesu Christo *homo totus*" (Hilaire de Poitiers, *In Matthaeum* 2,5). Pour une saine interprétation de la formule. — *RevÉtudAug* 28 (1982) 201-207.

1982b   Pierre "Fondement de l'Église" et foi de la confession de Pierre "Base de l'Église" chez Hilaire de Poitiers. — *RSPT* 66/3 (1982) 417-425.

1983    La comparaison de *Matth.* 23,37 *sicut gallina ... sub alas suas* dans l'exégèse d'Hilaire de Poitiers. Une mise au point à propos de la *sollicitude* du Christ. — *LavalTP* 39 (1983) 21-26. → Børresen 1982

1984a   Quatre formules énigmatiques dans l'exégèse d'Hilaire de Poitiers. — *VigChr* 38 (1984) 371-384. Esp. 31-374 [15,21-28]; 374-376 [19,10].

1984b   Le sens d'une formule relative à Jean-Baptiste dans l'*In Matthaeum* d'Hilaire de Poitiers. [11,12-13] — *VetChr* 21 (1984) 27-32.

1985    L'exégèse latine de la parabole des deux fils (Matth. 21,28-31): Hilaire de Poitiers devant le problème de l'obéissance à Dieu. — *RHPR* 65 (1985) 53-59.

1987    Les Capitula de l'*In Matthaeum* d'Hilaire de Poitiers. Édition critique et commentaire. — DUMMER, J. (ed.), *Texte und Textkritik. Eine Aufsatzsammlung* (TU, 133), Bonn: Akademie, 1987, 87-96.

1990    La "lectio" de textes d'Hilaire de Poitiers à la lumière d'études récentes. [9,2; 11,5] — *Wiener Studien* 103 (1990) 179-191.

1991    Hilaire de Poitiers témoin latin le plus ancien d'un texte rare du logion "Matthieu" 10,38. — *RBén* 101 (1991) 28-31.

1995    De l'absence à la présence d'Origène dans l'exégèse d'Hilaire de Poitiers: Deux cas typiques. [5,8; 20,1-6] — DORIVAL, G. - LE BOULLUEC, A. (eds.), *Origeniana Sexta*, 1995, 693-699.

**DOMASZEWICZ, Lidia** → Urbaniak 1984

**DOMERIS, W.R.**

1987    et al., *Portraits of Jesus. A Contextual Approach to Bible Study. Matthew.* London: Collins, 1987, 88 p. [NTA 33, p. 384]

1990    "Blessed are you ..." (Matthew 5:1-12). — *JTSouthAfr* 73 (1990) 67-76. [NTA 35, 1127]

**DONAHUE, John Raymond**

1971  Tax Collectors and Sinners. An Attempt at Identification. — *CBQ* 33 (1971) 39-61. Esp. 57-58 [11,19; 18,17]. [NTA 15, 828]

1986a  The "Parable" of the Sheep and the Goats: A Challenge to Christian Ethics. [25,31-46] — *TS* 47 (1986) 3-31. Esp. 9-11: "The question of genre"; 11-16: "The literary context" [28,16-20]; 16-28: "The theological context". [NTA 30, 1064]

1986b  Recent Studies on the Origin of "Son of Man" in the Gospels. — *CBQ* 48 (1986) 484-498. Esp. 486-490: "The Fitzmyer/Vermes debate"; 490-496: "After the debate". [NTA 31, 325]

1988  *The Gospel in Parable. Metaphor, Narrative, and Theology in the Synoptic Gospels.* Philadelphia, PA: Fortress, 1988, XI-254 p. Esp. 63-125: "The parables of Matthew"; 199-203: "Eschatology, ethics, and the good news of the Kingdom: Matthew's gospel in parable".

1990  Parables of Jesus. — BROWN, R.E., et al. (eds.), *The New Jerome Biblical Commentary*, 1990, 1364-1369. Esp. 1368.
Le parabole di Gesù. — BROWN, R.E., et al., *Nuovo grande commentario biblico*, 1997, 1794-1799. Esp. 1799.

1994  Redaction Criticism: Has the *Hauptstrasse* Become a *Sackgasse*? — MALBON, E.S. – McKNIGHT, E.V., *The New Literary Criticism and the New Testament* (JSNT SS, 109), Sheffield: JSOT, 1994, 27-57. Esp. 34-36: "Redaction criticism and the gospels of Matthew and Luke"; 36-38: "Redaction criticism of Q and John".

**DONALDSON, James**

1973  The Title Rabbi in the Gospels – Some Reflections on the Evidence of the Synoptics. — *JQR* 63 (1972-73) 287-291. [NTA 18, 834]

**DONALDSON, Terence L.**

1985  *Jesus on the Mountain. A Study in Matthean Theology* (JSNT SS, 8). Sheffield: JSOT, 1985, XVI-326 p. Esp. 87-104.242-250: "The mountain of temptation"; 105-121.250-256: "The mountain of teaching"; 122-135.256-263: "The mountain of feeding"; 136-156.263-271: "The mountain of transfiguration"; 157-169.271-275: "The Mount of Olives and the olivet discourse"; 170-190.275-283: "The mountain of commissioning"; 193-202.283-284: "The mountain of motif in Matthew's gospel"; 203-213.284-287: "The mountain motif and the Matthean redaction". [NTA 30, p. 94] — Diss. School of Theology, Toronto, Ont., 1981 (R.N. Longenecker). → Allison 1993a
R.A. EDWARDS, *CBQ* 48 (1986) 740-741; R. GUNDRY, *Bib* 67 (1986) 402-404; J.D. KINGSBURY, *Interpr* 41 (1987) 102.104; W.L. KYNES, *JTS* 37 (1986) 524-526; J.P. MEIER, *JBL* 106 (1987) 539-541; G. STANTON, *ExpT* 97 (1985-86) 212-213; B.T. VIVIANO, *RB* 96 (1989) 461; F. VOUGA, *ETR* 62 (1987) 434-435; D. WENHAM, *EvQ* 59 (1987) 168-170.

1990  The Law That "Hangs" (Mt. 22:40): Rabbinic Formulation and Matthean Social World. — *SBL 1990 Seminar Papers*, 14-33. Esp. 14-20: "Rabbinic formulation and Matthean usage"; 20-27: "Tensions in Matthew and the problem of interpretation"; 27-33: "Matt 22:40 in cognitive dissonance perspective".

1991  The Mockers and the Son of God (Matthew 27.37-44): Two Characters in Matthew's Story of Jesus. — *JSNT* 41 (1991) 3-18. Esp. 3-7: "From redactional to narrative analysis"; 7-12: "The mockers, the son, and Matthew's sequence of events"; 12-18: "The mockers, the son, and the plot of Matthew's gospel". [NTA 36, 161]

1995  The Law That Hangs (Matthew 22:40): Rabbinic Formulation and Matthean Social World. — *CBQ* 57 (1995) 689-709. Esp. 689-698: "Rabbinic formulation and Matthean usage"; 696-703: "Tensions in Matthew"; 704-709: "Mt 22:40 in the perspective of cognitive dissonance". [NTA 40, 1467]

**DONDORP, A.**

1951  *De verzoekingen van Jezus Christus in de woestijn* [4,1-11]. Kampen: Kok, 1951, 186 p. Esp. 9-43 [synoptic problem]; 44-79 [history of interpretation]; 125-186 [analysis]. — Diss. Amsterdam, 1951 (F.W. Grosheide).

**DONELSON, Lewis R.**

1988    "Do Not Resist Evil" and the Question of Biblical Authority. [5,21-48] — *HorizonsBT*
        10/1 (1988) 33-46. [NTA 33, 1125]

1995    The Sermon on the Mount: The Stripping of Ideology. — *Insights* (Austin, TX) 110/2
        (1995) 43-53. [NTA 40, 160]

**DONFRIED, Karl Paul**

1974a   *The Setting of Second Clement in Early Christianity* (SupplNT, 38). Leiden: Brill, 1974,
        X-240 p. Esp. 56-82: "Conscious quotations from the gospel tradition" [5,44-46; 7,21-23; 9,13;
        10,16.28.32; 12,49-50; 13,42-43; 16,26]— Diss. Heidelberg, 1968 (G. Bornkamm).

1974b   The Allegory of the Ten Virgins (Matt 25:1-13) as a Summary of Matthean Theology.
        — *JBL* 93 (1974) 415-428. Esp. 417-419 [interpretation]; 419-422 [relation with Mt 24–25]; 422-425
        [relation with Mt 5–7]; 425-427 ["oil"]. [NTA 19, 543]
            *TDig* 23 (1975) 106-110; *SelT* 15 (1976) 127-132.

1992    Peter. — *ABD* 5 (1992) 251-263. Esp. 256-258.

**DONN, T.M.**

1950    'Let the dead bury their dead' (Mt viii.22, Lk ix.60). — *ExpT* 61 (1949-50) 384. → M.
        Black 1950a

**DONNE, Brian K.**

1977    The Significance of the Ascension of Jesus Christ in the New Testament. — *ScotJT* 30
        (1977) 555-568. Esp. 559-560 [28,16-20]. [NTA 22, 533]

**DONNER, Herbert**

1980    Der Redaktor. Überlegungen zum vorkritischen Umgang mit der Heiligen Schrift. —
        *Henoch* 2 (1980) 1-30. Esp. 16-23 [28,1-2].

**DOOHAN, Leonard**

1985    Images of God in Matthew. — *Milltown Studies* (Dublin) 16 (1985) 65-84. Esp. 65-67
        [God as father]; 67-80 [Christ]; 80-82 [spirit]. [NTA 31, 104]

1986    Ecclesial Sharing in Matthew's Gospel. — *BiTod* 24 (1986) 254-259. [NTA 31, 103]

1987    Matthew's Challenge to Spiritual Renewal. — *Emmanuel* 93 (1987) 284-290. [NTA 32,
        106]

1988    Mission and Ministry. — *BiTod* 26 (1988) 243-247. [NTA 33, 120]

**DORAN, Robert**

1987    A Complex of Parables: GTh 96-98. — *NT* 29 (1987) 347-352. Esp. 348 [13,33/Th 96].
        [NTA 32, 978]

1991    The Divinization of Disorder: The Trajectory of Matt 8:20 // Luke 9:58 // *Gos. Thom.*
        86. — PEARSON, B.A., et al. (eds.), *The Future of Early Christianity*. FS H. Koester,
        1991, 210-219.

**DORÉ, Joseph**

1993*   & THEOBALD, C. (eds.), *Penser la foi. Recherches en théologie aujourd'hui. Mélanges
        offerts à Joseph Moingt*. Paris: Cerf/Azsas, 1993, 1096 p. → Aletti, Brieskorn, J. Guillet, J.-L.
        Lemaire

**DORIANI, Daniel**

1994    The Deity of Christ in the Synoptic Gospels. — *JEvTS* 37 (1994) 333-350. [NTA 39, 779]

**DORIVAL, Gilles**

1995*   & LE BOULLUEC, A. (eds.), *Origeniana Sexta. Origène et la Bible / Origen and the
        Bible. Actes du Colloquium Origenianum Sextum. Chantilly, 30 août – 3 septembre
        1993* (BETL, 118). Leuven: University Press / Peeters, 1995, XII-865 p. → Bammel, Bastit,
        Doignon

**DORMAN, William E.**

1971 *Matthew: A Theology for Active Discipleship.* Diss. Vanderbilt Divinity School, Nashville, TN, 1971, 139 p. — *DissAbstr* 32 (1971-72) 2175.

**DORMEYER, Detlev**

1974 Literarische und theologische Analyse der Parabel Lukas 14,15-24. — *BibLeb* 15 (1974) 206-219. Esp. 208-211: "Traditionsgeschichte". [NTA 19, 986]

1989 Das Verständnis von Arbeit im Neuen Testament im Horizont der Naherwartung. [20,1-16] — *HervTS* 45 (1989) 801-814.

1992 Mt 1,1 als Überschrift zur Gattung und Christologie des Matthäus-Evangeliums. — VAN SEGBROECK, F., et al. (eds.), *The Four Gospels 1992.* FS F. Neirynck, 1992, II, 1361-1383. Esp. 1361-1363: "Die Überschrift 1,1"; 1363-1366: "Jesus als Sohn Davids und Sohn Abrahams"; 1366-1371: "Die Hoheitstitel Sohn Gottes, Christus, Menschensohn"; 1371-1373: "Der Prophet"; 1373-1379: "Der Lehrer und Herr Jesus im Matthäusevangelium"; 1379-1383: "Das 'Buch' einer christlichen Idealbiographie von Jesus Christus".

1993 *Das Neue Testament im Rahmen der antiken Literaturgeschichte. Eine Einführung.* Darmstadt: Wissenschaftliche Buchgesellschaft, 1993, XI-314 p. Esp. 64-124 [sayings]; 140-159 [parables]; 166-176 [miracles]; 212-220 [biography: Q]; 225-226 [Mt].

1994 Metaphorik und Erzähltextanalyse als Zugänge zu apokalyptischen Texten. — KLAUCK, H.-J. (ed.), *Weltgericht und Weltvollendung.* FS R. Schnackenburg, 1994, 182-205. Esp. 182-193: "Der Menschensohn in Lk 12,8f / Mt 10,32f; Mk 8,38 par.".

**DORNEICH, Monica**

1982 (ed.), *Das Vater-Unser. Bibliographie — The Lord's Prayer. A Bibliography* (Veröffentlichungen der Stiftung Oratio Dominica). Freiburg: Herder, 1982, 240 p. [NTA 28, p. 82] → 1988

    H.J. SIEBEN, *TheolPhil* 58 (1983) 572-573; L.V., *NRT* 105 (1983) 784.

1988 (ed.), *Vater-Unser. Bibliographie – The Lord's Prayer. A Bibliography. Neue Folge.* (Veröffentlichungen der Stiftung Oratio Dominica). Freiburg: Herder, 1988, 136 p. Esp. 65-115. [NTA 34, p. 108] → 1982; → Faust

**DORNSEIFF, Franz**

1956 Ἐπιούσιος im Vaterunser. — *Glotta* 34 (1956) 145-149; = ID., *Sprache und Sprechender* (Kleine Schriften, 2), Leipzig: Koehler und Amelang, 1964, 248-255.

**DOSKOCIL, Walter**

1958 *Der Bann in der Urkirche. Eine rechtsgeschichtliche Untersuchung* (Münchener Theologische Studien, III/11). München: Zink, 1958, XV-220 p. Esp. 30-38: "Das Vorgehen gegen den sündigenden Bruder (Mt 18,15-18)".

**DOS SANTOS, Elmar Camillo**

1985 & LINDSEY, R.L., *A Comparative Greek Concordance of the Synoptic Gospels.* Jerusalem: Dugith, 3 vols., I, 1985, XVI-451 p.; II, 1988, 327 p.; III, 1989, 300 p. (collator and compiler: J.L. Burnham). → Neirynck 1987c

**DOTY, William G.**

1971 An Interpretation: Parables of the Weeds and Wheat. [13,24-30] — *Interpr* 25 (1971) 185-193. [NTA 16, 176]

**DOUGLAS, Rees Conrad**

1981 On the Way Out: Matthew's Anti-Pharisaic Polemic. — *SBT* 11 (1981) 151-176. Esp. 152-153 [3,7]; 153-154 [5,17-20]; 155-156 [9,9-13]; 157-158 [15,1-20]; 158-160 [12,1-8]; 162-163 [19,3-12; 22,15-46]; 165-166 [22,1-14]; 166-170 [23].

1990    *Family, Power, Religion: A Discussion of the Background and Functions of References to God as Father in the Gospel of Matthew.* Diss. Claremont Graduate School, 1990, 494 p. (B.L. Mack). — *DissAbstr* 51 (1990-91) 1261.

1995    "Love Your Enemies". Rhetoric, Tradents, and Ethos. — KLOPPENBORG, J.S. (ed.), *Conflict and Invention*, 1995, 116-131.

**DOUGLAS, Robert**

1960    The Neglected Commandment II (Matthew 22:34-40). — *SWJT* 3 (1960) 74-77. → C.A. Clark 1960

**DOUIE, Decima Langworthy**

1975    Olivi's Postilla super Matthaeum. — *Franciscan Studies* (New York) 35 (1975) 66-92.

**DOWDA, Robert Ellis**

1972    *The Cleansing of the Temple in the Synoptic Gospels.* Diss. Duke Univ., Durham, NC, 1972, 411 p. (W.D. Davies). — *DissAbstr* 33 (1972-73) 5815.

**DOWN, M.J.**

1978    The Matthaean Birth Narratives: Matthew 1,18–2,23. — *ExpT* 90 (1978-79) 51-52. [NTA 23, 426]

1984    The Sayings of Jesus about Marriage and Divorce. [5,31-32; 19,3-9] — *ExpT* 95 (1983-84) 332-334. [NTA 29, 491]

**DOWNING, F. Gerald**

1965    Towards the Rehabilitation of Q. — *NTS* 11 (1964-65) 169-181. Esp. 171-176 [12,22-45]; 176-177 [3,1-4,11]; 177 [9,35-10,16]; 177-180 [24-25]. [NTA 9, 858]; = BELLINZONI, A.J., Jr., et al. (eds.), *The Two-Source Hypothesis*, 1985, 269-285. Esp. 271-277; 278-280; 280-283. → Farrer 1955

1980    Redaction Criticism: Josephus' *Antiquities* and the Synoptic Gospels. — *JSNT* 8 (1980) 46-65; 9 (1980) 29-48. Esp. 29-48: "Luke and the other two synoptists". [NTA 25, 327/441]

1984a   Contemporary Analogies to the Gospels and Acts: 'Genres' or 'Motifs'? — TUCKETT, C.M. (ed.), *Synoptic Studies*, 1984, 51-65. Esp. 56-59 [genre: Q]; 59-62 [Mt].

1984b   Cynics and Christians. — *NTS* 30 (1984) 584-593. [NTA 29, 797]

1985    Ears to Hear. — HARVEY, A.E. (ed.), *Alternative Approaches to New Testament Study*, 1985, 97-121. Esp. 105-108 [Q/Cynics].

1988a   *Christ and the Cynics. Jesus and other Radical Preachers in First-Century Tradition* (JSOT Manuals, 4). Sheffield: JSOT, 1988, XIII-232 p. Esp. 6-87: "The 'Q' Material (in the Lukan order)"; 88-116: "Material in Matthew only". → H.D. Betz 1994

1988b   Quite like Q. A Genre for 'Q': The 'Lives' of Cynic Philosophers. — *Bib* 69 (1988) 196-225. Esp. 197-203: "A formal comparison"; 203-219: "A comparison of content"; 219-222: "Possible objections"; 223-224: "The 'trajectory' of 'Q'". [NTA 33, 104] → 1992a; → Tuckett 1989a

1988c   Compositional Conventions and the Synoptic Problem. — *JBL* 107 (1988) 69-85. Esp. 82-85: "Either 'Q' or total novelty". [NTA 32, 1092]

1992a   *Cynics and Christian Origins.* Edinburgh: Clark, 1992, IX-377 p. Esp. 115-142: "Christians and cynics in the 50's: the Q document"; 154-162: "Jesus as cynic". → 1988b
        G. HUELIN, *ExpT* 105 (1993-94) 28; F. WILLIAMS, *IBS* 16 (1994) 138-144.

1992b   A Paradigm Perplex: Luke, Matthew and Mark. — *NTS* 38 (1992) 15-36. Esp. 16-23 [implicit picture of Luke in Goulder]; 23-25 [parallels in ancient sources?]; 25-34 [inconsistencies in Goulder's Luke]. [NTA 36, 1231] → Goulder 1989, 1993a

1992c   The Woman from Syrophoenicia and Her Doggedness: Mark 7:24-31 (Matthew 15:21-28). — BROOKE, G.J. (ed.), *Women in the Biblical Tradition* (Studies in Woman and Religion, 31), Lewiston, NJ: Mellen, 1992, 129-149.

1994    A Genre for Q and a Socio-Cultural Context for Q: Comparing Sets of Similarities with
        Sets of Differences. — *JSNT* 55 (1994) 3-26. [NTA 39, 780]

**DOYLE, Brian Rod**

1984a   *Matthew's Wisdom. A Redaction-critical Study of Matthew 11.1–14.13a.* Diss. Univ.
        of Melbourne, Australia, 1984, 572 p. — *DissAbstr* 46 (1985-86) 1318-1319.

1984b   "Crowds" in Matthew: Texts and Theology. — *Catholic Theological Review* (Clayton,
        Australia) 6 (1984) 28-33. [NTA 30, 557]

1984c   Disciples as Sages and Scribes in Matthew's Gospel. — *Word in Life* (North Sydney,
        NSW) 32 (1984) 4-9. [NTA 29, 512]

1985    Matthew 11:12. A Challenge to the Evangelist's Community. — *Colloquium* 18 (1985)
        20-30. [NTA 30, 574]

1986    A Concern of the Evangelist: Pharisees in Matthew 12. — *AusBR* 34 (1986) 17-34. Esp.
        19-22 [12,17-21]; 22-30 [12,22-37]. [NTA 32, 1109]

1988    Matthew's Intention as Discerned by His Structure. — *RB* 95 (1988) 34-54. Esp. 35-37:
        "The present situation"; 37-47: "A proposal"; 48-53: "Why a 'disciple' structure?". [NTA 32, 1099]

1992    Disciples in Matthew: A Challenge for the Church Today. — *East Asian Pastoral
        Review* (Quezon City) 29 (1992) 306-329. Esp. 309-310 [28,16-20]; 313-314 [10,24-25]. [NTA
        39, 130]

1994    The Place of the Parable of the Labourers in the Vineyard in Matthew 20:1-16. —
        *AusBR* 42 (1994) 39-58. Esp. 42-47 [19,1–20,34]; 47-51 [20,1-16]; 55-58: "Matthew develops
        expressions from his sources, Mk and Q". [NTA 40, 832]

**DOYLE, P.Y.**

1967    *A Study of the Text of Matthew's Gospel in the Book of Mulling and of the
        Palaeography of the Whole Manuscript.* Diss. Dublin, 1967 (L. Bieler).

**DOZOIS, C.**

1960    *Le "Pater" chez saint Thomas d'Aquin. Essai d'histoire littéraire et doctrinale.* Ottawa,
        1960, XI-249 p. Esp. 183-212 [ed. In Mt 6,9-15].

**DRAISMA, Sipke**

1989*   (ed.), *Intertextuality in Biblical Writings. Essays in Honour of Bas van Iersel.* Kampen:
        Kok, 1989, 207 p. → M. de Jonge, Farla, Standaert, van Tilborg

**DRANE, John W.**

1987    *Introducing the New Testament.* San Francisco, CA: Harper & Row, 1987, 479 p.

1990    *An Introduction to the Bible.* Oxford: Lion Publishing; San Francisco, CA: Harper &
        Row; Sidney: Albatross, 1990, 816 p.

**DRAPER, H. Mudie**

1956    Did Jesus Speak Greek? [5,39-40] — *ExpT* 67 (1955-56) 317. [NTA 1, 25] → Argyle 1955,
        R.McL. Wilson 1957a

**DRAPER, Jonathan Alfred**

1985    The Jesus Tradition in the Didache. — WENHAM, D. (ed.), *The Jesus Tradition Outside
        the Gospels*, 1985, 269-287. Esp. 273-279 [5,25-26.38-48/Did 1,3-2,1]; 279 [6,1-13/Did 8]; 280-283
        [24/Did 16]; = ID., *The Didache in Modern Research*, 1996, 72-91 (updated). Esp. 79-85;
        85-86; 86-90.

1989    Lactantius and the Jesus Tradition in the Didache. — *JTS* 40 (1989) 112-116. Esp. 114-
        115 [5,48/Did]. [NTA 33, 1484]

1991   Torah and Troublesome Apostles in the Didache Community. — *NT* 33 (1991) 347-372.
       Esp. 354-355: "The relation between Didache and Matthew"; 356-360: "The instructions of *Didache* 11:1-2
       and Matthew 5:17-20"; 364-365 [11,29-30]; 366-367 [5,48; 19,16-22]; 369-370 [7,15.23; 26,74]. [NTA 36,
       1085]; = ID., *The* Didache *in Modern Research*, 1996, 340-363. Esp. 346-348; 348-352; 356;
       357-358; 360-361.

1992   Christian Self-Definition against the "Hypocrites" in *Didache* 8. — *SBL 1992 Seminar
       Papers*, 362-377. Esp. 366-367 [6,16]; 369-370 [6,9-13]; 371-372 [7,6]; 372-373 [6,1-18]; = ID.,
       *The* Didache *in Modern Research*, 1996, 223-243. Esp. 231-232; 235-238; 239-240; 241-242.

1993   The Development of "the Sign of the Son of Man" in the Jesus Tradition. — *NTS* 39
       (1993) 1-21. Esp. 13-17: "The sign of the Son of Man in Didache and Matthew" [24,30-31]. [NTA 37,
       1188]

1996   *The* Didache *in Modern Research* (Arbeiten zur Geschichte des antiken Judentums und
       des Urchristentums, 37). Leiden: Brill, 1996, XVIII-445 p. → 1985, 1991, 1992; → Tuckett
       1989c

**DREHER, Bruno**
1967   Die Verkündigung der Wunder Jesu in der Katechese. — *BK* 22 (1967) 47-57.

**DREW, Douglas Laurel**
1951   Two Literary Puzzles from Palestine: 1. Jewish Protest in *Contra Apionem 2,49*; 2.
       John the Baptist's Desert Food and Clothes (Mt. 3,1-4). — *Bulletin of the Faculty of
       Arts* (Cairo) 13 (1951) 53-60.

**DREWERMANN, Eugen**
1992   *Das Matthäusevangelium*. Erster Teil: *Mt 1,1-7,29. Bilder der Erfüllung*. Olten-
       Freiburg: Walter, 1992, 848 p. Esp. 16-43: "Jesus und die Kirche"; 44-69: "Von Zwang und Freiheit
       oder: Gesetz und Evangelium"; 70-101: "Wie glaubt man Jesus als den Christus"; 102-139: "Von Juden und
       Heiden oder: Das Galiläa der Völker"; 140-184: "Der kommende Menschensohn"; 185-217: "Fragen der
       Übersetzung oder: Aramäisch auf Griechisch". [NTA 38, p. 118] → G.-M. Bertrand 1994, J. Ernst 1992
           E. GLOSSE, *MüTZ* 43 (1992) 239-250; R. HOPPE, *BK* 48 (1993) 166-167; B. KAEMPF, *RHPR* 74 (1994)
           103; H.-J. KLAUCK, *WissWeish* 56 (1993) 89-92; R. OBERFORCHER, *ZKT* 116 (1994) 217-219; U. RUH,
           *Herder Korrespondenz* 46 (1992) 194.
       Zweiter Teil: *Mt 8,1-20,19. Bilder der Erfüllung*. Solothurn–Düsseldorf: Walter, 1994,
       648 p. [NTA 40, p. 338]
       Dritter Teil: *Mt 20,20-28,20. Bilder der Erfüllung*. Solothurn–Düsseldorf: Walter,
       1995, 431 p.

1993   *Das Vaterunser*. München: Kösel, 1993, 159 p. [NTA 38, p. 119]
           H. ROEFFAERS, *Streven* 60 (1993) 859.

**DREWES, B.F.**
1971   The Composition of Matthew 8-9. — *The South East Asia Journal of Theology*
       (Singapore) 12 (1971) 92-101. [NTA 16, 154]

**DREYFUS, François**
1959   Saint Matthieu et l'Ancien Testament. — *VSp* 101 (1959) 121-135. [NTA 4, 71]

**DREYFUS, Paul**
1955   La Primauté de Pierre à la lumière de la théologie biblique du reste d'Israël. — *Istina*
       (Paris) 2 (1955) 338-346. Esp. 339-342 [16,17-19].

**DRIJVERS, Han J.W.**
1988   & REININK, G.J., Taufe und Licht. Tatian, Ebionäerevangelium und Thomasakten. —
       BAARDA, T., et al. (eds.), *Text and Testimony*. FS A.F.J. Klijn, 1988, 91-110. Esp. 95-
       98.102-103 [3,11].

**DRISCOLL, Jeremy**

1984    The Transfiguration in Hilary of Poitiers' Commentary on Matthew. — *Augustinianum*
24 (1984) 395-420. — Diss. Roma 1983.

**DRIVER, Godfrey Rolles**

1965    Two Problems in the New Testament. — *JTS* 16 (1965) 327-337. Esp. 327-31 [28,1]. [NTA
10, 524]

**DRIVER, Juan (John)**

1986    Sal, luz, ciudad. [5,13-16] — *Mision* (Buenos Aires) 5 (1986) 116-121.

**DRIVER, Tom F.**

1966    The Gospel according to St. Matthew. — *Christianity and Crisis* (New York) 26 (1966)
95-97. [NTA 11, 189]

**DROGE, Arthur J.**

1983    Call Stories in Greek Biography and the Gospels. — *SBL 1983 Seminar Papers*, 245-
257. Esp. 254-255 [8,19-22]. → Butts 1987d

**DROMWRIGHT, H.L.**

1962    The Ethical Motif in Matthew 5–7. — *SWJT* 5 (1962) 65-76.

**DROUZY, Maurice**

1955    Le "Pater", prière du Christ. — *VSp* 93 (1955) 115-134.

**DRURY, John**

1976    *Tradition and Design in Luke's Gospel. A Study in Early Christian Historiography.*
London: Darton, Longman & Todd; Atlanta, GA; Knox, 1976, XIII-208 p. Esp. 120-173:
"Using Matthew"; 191-192 [time indications in Mt].

1985    *The Parables in the Gospels. History and Allegory.* London: SPCK; New York:
Crossroad, 1985, IX-180 p. Esp. 70-107.

**D'SA, Francis X.**

1979    "Dhvani" as a Method of Interpretation. [6,25-33] — *Bible Bhashyam* 5 (1979) 276-294.
[NTA 24, 791]

**DSCHULNIGG, Peter**

1988    *Rabbinische Gleichnisse und das Neue Testament. Die Gleichnisse der PesK im Vergleich mit den Gleichnissen Jesu und dem Neuen Testament* (Judaica et Christiana, 12).
Bern–Frankfurt/M: Lang, 1988, XVII-654 p. Esp. 39-527: "Die Gleichnisse der PesK im Vergleich
mit dem NT" [7,24-27; 11,16-19; 13,24-30.31-33.44.45-46.47-50.52; 18,12-14.23-35; 20,1-16; 21,28-32.33-
44; 22,1-14; 24,37-39.45-51; 25,1-13.14-30]. — Diss. Luzern, 1988 (C. Thoma). → 1991

1989a   Gestalt und Funktion des Petrus im Matthäusevangelium. — *SNTU* 14 (1989) 161-183.
Esp. 162-178: "Die Szenen mit Petrus im MtEv" [4,18-20; 8,14-15; 10,2-4; 14,28-32; 15,15; 16,16-19.21-
23; 17,1-8.24-27; 18,21-22; 19,27-28; 26,30-35.36-46.69-75]. [NTA 35, 124]

1989b   Der theologische Ort des zweiten Petrusbriefes. — *BZ* 33 (1989) 161-177. Esp. 168-176:
"Zur Näherbestimmung des Judenchristentums des Verfassers". [NTA 34, 794]

1991    Rabbinische Gleichnisse und Gleichnisse Jesu. Ein Vergleich aufgrund der Gleichnisse
aus Pesiqta de Rab Kahana (PesK). — *Judaica* 47 (1991) 185-197. Esp. 188-189 [18,12-14].
[NTA 36, 1232] → 1988

1993    Schöpfung im Licht des Neuen Testaments. Neutestamentliche Schöpfungsaussagen und
ihre Funktion (Mt, Apg, Kol, Offb). — *FZPT* 40 (1993) 125-145. Esp. 126-127 [5,43-48];
127-129 [6,25-34]; 129-130 [10,28-31]; 130-131 [11,25-27]. [NTA 38, 419]

1995 Die Zerstörung des Tempels in den synoptischen Evangelien. — LAUER, S. – ERNST, H. (eds.), *Tempelkult und Tempelzerstörung (70 n. Chr.). Festschrift für Clemens Thoma zum 60. Geburtstag* (Judaica et Christiana, 15), Bern: Lang, 1995, 167-187. Esp. 171-173.

**DUBARLE, André-Marie**

1955a Le péché originel dans les suggestions de l'Évangile. — *RSPT* 39 (1955) 603-614. [NTA 1, 112]; = ID., *Le péché originel dans l'Écriture* (LD, 20) Paris: Cerf, 1958, 105-119.

1955b La Primauté de Pierre à la lumière de l'Ancien Testament. — *Istina* (Paris) 2 (1955) 335-338.

1964 Mariage et divorce dans l'Évangile. — *L'Orient Syrien* (Paris) 9 (1964) 61-73. Esp. 63-70. [NTA 8, 938]
*SelT* 9 (1970) 259-261.

1978 La conception virginale et la citation d'Is., VII,14 dans l'Évangile de Matthieu. — *RB* 85 (1978) 362-380. Esp. 362-367: "Le motif de l'embarras de Joseph"; 367-369: "Le rôle de la citation d'Is., VII,14"; 373-378: "Spéculations possibles sur la conception virginale?". [NTA 24, 78]

1987 Les textes évangéliques sur le mariage et le divorce. — CAZELLES, H. (ed.), *La vie de la Parole*. FS P. Grelot, 1987, 333-344. Esp. 334-335 [5,32]; 335-337 [19,3-12].

**DUBOIS, Jean Daniel**

1979* (ed.), L'Évangile de Matthieu. En reconnaissance à Pierre Bonnard. — *FoiVie* 78/3 = *Cahiers bibliques* 18 (1979) 3-129. → Cambe, Charpentier, Combet-Galland, Escande, Ingelaere, Marguerat 1979b-c, Smyth, Zumstein

1989 Une variante copte de Matthieu 27,49 tirée du Codex Scheide. — ROSENSTIEHL, J.-M. (ed.), *Troisième Journée d'études coptes, Musée du Louvre 23 mai 1986* (Cahiers de la Bibliothèque Copte, 4), Leuven: Peeters, 1989, 32-45.

1994 La mort de Zacharie. Mémoire juive et mémoire chrétienne. — *RevÉtudAug* 40 (1994) 23-38. Esp. 32-36 [23,35].

**DU BUIT, F. Michel**

1967a Le discours des paraboles. [13] — *Évangile* 67 (1967) 5-57. [NTA 12, 873]

1967b Les paraboles du jugement. — *Évangile* 68 (1967) 5-59. Esp. 5-18 [13,44-50]; 19-27 [22,1-14]; 28-35 [25,1-13]; 36-48 [24,31-46]. [NTA 12, 875]

1968 Les paraboles de l'attente et de la miséricorde. — *Évangile* 72 (1968) 5-27. Esp. 13-18 [24,45-51]; 19-27 [25,14-30]. [NTA 13, 840]

1969 Notre Père. — *Évangile* 75 (1969) 5-46. [NTA 14, 484]

1977 *En tous les temps Jésus-Christ*. Tome 3: *Sermon sur la montagne*. Mulhouse: Salvator, 1977, 189 p. [NTA 22, p. 212]

**DUCK, Ruth C.**

1991 *Gender and the Name of God. The Trinitarian Baptismal Formula*. Cleveland, OH: Pilgrim Press, 1991, X-219 p. Esp. 60-62 [11,25]; 127-128 [28,19].

**DUCKWORTH, R.**

1980 (ed.), *This is the Word of the Lord. Year A: The Year of Matthew*. London: Bible Reading Fellowship; Oxford: University Press, 1980, XII-174 p. [NTA 25, p. 218]

**DÜRIG, Walter**

1968 Die Bedeutung der Brotbitte des Vaterunser bei den lateinischen Vätern bis Hieronymus. — *Liturgisches Jahrbuch* (Münster) 18 (1968) 72-86.

1972 Die Exegese der vierten Vaterunser-Bitte bei Augustinus. — *Liturgisches Jahrbuch* 22 (1972) 49-61.

**DUFF, Nancy J.**

1985 Wise and Foolish Maidens, Matthew 25:1-13. — *USQR* 40/3 (1985) 55-58.

**DUFRASNE, Dieudonné**

1983 Va d'abord te réconcilier... [5,23-24] — *ComLtg* 65 (1983) 115-117. [NTA 28, 93]

**DUFTON, Francis**

1989 The Syrophoenician Woman and her Dogs. [15,27] — *ExpT* 100 (1988-89) 417. [NTA 34, 147]

**DULAEY, Martine**

1993 La parabole de la brebis perdue dans l'Église ancienne: De l'exégèse à l'iconographie. [18,12-14] — *RevÉtudAug* 39 (1993) 3-22. [NTA 38, 771]

**DULIÈRE, W.L.**

1954 La péricope sur le "pouvoir des clés"'. Son absence dans le texte de Matthieu aux mains d'Irénée. Son incorporation au canon vers l'an 190. — *La nouvelle Clio* (Bruxelles) 6 (1954) 73-90.

1955 La révélation par songe dans l'Évangile de Matthieu. — *Mélanges Isidore Lévy* (Annuaire de l'Institut de philologie et d'histoire orientales et slaves, 13), Bruxelles: ULB, 1955, 665-669.

1959 Inventaire de quarante-et-un porteurs du nom de Jésus dans l'histoire juive écrite en grec. — *NT* 3 (1959) 180-217. Esp. 216-217. [NTA 4, 824]

1968 Les textes évangéliques sur des visées temporelles de Jésus. Alternances de concepts autoritaires et de concepts iréniques. — *StudTheol* 22 (1968) 107-148. Esp. 109.112 [11,12]; 110 [21,19]; 115-116 [26,59-61]; 116-117 [27,39-40]; 119-120 [22,41-46]; 122 [27,16]; 139-143. [NTA 13, 801]

**DULING, Dennis C.**

1978 The Therapeutic Son of David: An Element in Matthew's Christological Apologetic. — *NTS* 24 (1977-78) 392-410. Esp. 393-399: "The therapeutic Messiah of deed in Matthew" [4,23; 8,16-17; 9,35; 11,5]; 399-407: "The therapeutic Son of David in Matthew" [9,27-31; 12,22-24; 15,21-28; 20,29-34; 21,1-16; 22,41-46]; 407-410: "Matthew's therapeutic Son of David and Judaism". [NTA 22, 752]

1982 → N. Perrin 1974b

1983 Matthew and the Problem of Authority: Some Preliminary Observations. — *Proceedings EGLBS* 3 (1983) 59-68.

1984 Norman Perrin and the Kingdom of God: Review and Response. — *JRel* 64 (1984) 468-483. → N. Perrin 1976

1987 Binding and Loosing: Matthew 16:19; Matthew 18:18; John 20:23. — *Forum* 3/4 (1987) 3-31. Esp. 3-4.25-26 [16,19]; 4.17-18 [18,18]; 5-6 [16,13-23]; 6-17.19-24 [16,17-19]. [NTA 33, 124]

1990 Against Oaths. Crossan *Sayings Parallels* 59. — *Forum* 6 (1990) 99-138. Esp. 101-103: "The antithetical form 'But I say to you'"; 103-106: "The parallels"; 106-109: "Similarities and contrasts"; 110-129: "Five representative hypotheses" [Minear, Guelich, Strecker, Dautzenberg, Suggs]. [NTA 37, 140] → J.D. Crossan 1986a

1991 "[Do not Swear...] by Jerusalem because It Is the City of the Great King" (Matt 5:35). — *JBL* 110 (1991) 291-309. Esp. 291-293 [5,33-37]; 293-296.305-309 [5,35]. [NTA 36, 141]

1992a Kingdom of God, Kingdom of Heaven. — *ABD* 4 (1992) 56-59. Esp. 57-58.

1992b Matthew. — *Ibid.*, 618-622.

1992c Matthew's Plurisignificant "Son of David" in Social Science Perspective: Kinship, Kingship, Magic, and Miracle. — *BTB* 22 (1992) 99-116. Esp. 109-113. [NTA 37, 703]

1993 Matthew and Marginality. — *SBL 1993 Seminar Papers*, 642-671. Esp. 652-656 [marginals]; 659-663 [community leaders]; = *HervTS* 51 (1995) 358-387. [NTA 40, 802].

1995 The Matthean Brotherhood and Marginal Scribal Leadership. — ESLER, P.F. (ed.), *Modelling Early Christianity*, 1995, 159-182. Esp. 164-172: "The Matthean brotherhood" [5,21-26; 7,1-5; 12,46-50; 18,15-22; 23,8-10; 25,40; 28,10]; 172-175: "Scribes in the gospel of Matthew" [8,19; 13,52; 24,34]; 178-180.

**DUMAIS, Marcel**

1993 Sermon sur la montagne. — *DBS* 12/68-69 (1993-94) 699-938. Esp. 699-703: "Bibliographie"; 703-729: "Interprétation du Sermon au cours des âges"; 729-735: "Problème littéraire des deux versions"; 735-749: "Le Sermon dans son contexte évangélique"; 749-764: "Structure et genre littéraire du Sermon"; 764-772: "Arrière-plan du Sermon"; 772-932: "Interprétation des sections"; 932-938: "Conclusions". → Stramare 1995
*Le Sermon sur la montagne. État de la recherche, interprétation, bibliographie.* Paris: Letouzey et Ané, 1995, 331 p.
    E. CUVILLIER, *ETR* 71 (1996) 92-93; R.A. EDWARDS, *CBQ* 59 (1997) 768-769.

1995 *Le Sermon sur la montagne (Matthieu 5–7)* (Cahiers Évangile, 94). Paris: Cerf, 1995, 76 p. [NTA 40, p. 338]

**DUMAS, Benoit A.**

1984 *Los milagros de Jesús. Los signos mesiánicos e la teología de la liberación* (Cristianismo y sociedad, 4). Bilbao: Desclée De Brouwer, 1984, 362 p.

**DUMBRELL, William J.**

1981 The Logic of the Role of the Law in Matthew v 1-20. — *NT* 23 (1981) 1-21. Esp. 4-5 [4,23-25]; 6-9 [5,3]; 10 [5,10-12]; 11-16 [5,13-16]; 16-21 [5,17-20]. [NTA 25, 852]

**DUMERMUTH, Fritz**

1964 Bemerkung zu Jesu Menschwerdung. [1,18-25] — *TZ* 20 (1964) 52-53.

**DUMONT, C.-J.**

1953 Les Béatitudes et l'esprit d'unité. — *VSp* 88 (1953) 5-19.

**DUNCKER, Petrus G.**

1963 Biblical Criticism. — *CBQ* 25 (1963) 22-33. Esp. 25-27 [16,16-19]; = RYAN, M.R. (ed.), *Contemporary New Testament Studies*, 1965, 21-31. Esp. 24-26.

**DUNDERBERG, Ismo**

1994 *Johannes und die Synoptiker. Studien zu Joh 1–9* (Annales Academiae Scientiarum Fennicae. Dissertationes Humanarum Litterarum, 69). Helsinki: Suomalainen Tiedeakatemia, 1994, 225 p. Esp. 23-30: "Zum Vergleich von Joh und den Synoptikern"; 50-71: "Der Vergleich mit den Synoptikern" [3,1-17; 16,17-19/Jn 1,19-51]; 84-91 [8,5-13/Jn 4,46-54]; 91-96 [8,14-15; 13,57; 15,21-28/Jn]; 148-154 [14,12-21/Jn]; 154-156 [15,29-31/Jn]; 170-172 [16,13-28/Jn]; 187 [23,15-26/Jn]. — Diss. Helsinki, 1994, 228 p. (K. Syreeni).
    F. NEIRYNCK, *ETL* 72 (1996) 454-456.

1995 Q and the Beginning of Mark. — *NTS* 41 (1995) 501-511. [NTA 40, 794]

**DUNGAN, David Laird**

1970 Mark – The Abridgement of Matthew and Luke. — BUTTRICK, D.G. (ed.), *Jesus and Man's Hope.* I, 1970, 51-97. Esp. 54-81: "Critique of the main arguments for Mark's priority as formulated by B.H. Streeter"; 81-88: "Other hypotheses" [Augustinian hypothesis; Urgospel; Two-Document hypothesis]; 88-97: "The Griesbach hypothesis". [NTA 15, 153]
Critique of the Main Arguments for Mark's Priority as Formulated by B.H. Streeter. [1970, 54-74] — BELLINZONI, A.J., Jr., et al. (eds.), *The Two-Source Hypothesis*, 1985, 143-161.
Critique of the Q Hypothesis. [1970, 74-80] — *Ibid.*, 427-433.

1971   *The Sayings of Jesus in the Churches of Paul. The Use of the Synoptic Tradition in the Regulation of Early Church Life.* Oxford: Blackwell, 1971, XXXIII-180 p. Esp. 41-75: "The mission instructions in the synoptic gospels" [10,1-16]; 102-131: "The sayings on divorce in the synoptic gospels" [19,3-9].

1980   Theory of Synopsis Construction. — *Bib* 61 (1980) 305-329. Esp. 323-324 [5,3-12]; 324-326 [12,22-30]. [NTA 25, 442]

1984   A Griesbachian Perspective on the Argument from Order. — TUCKETT, C.M. (ed.), *Synoptic Studies*, 1984, 67-74. → Neirynck 1982b

1985a  Insights from Sociology for New Testament Christology: A Test Case. — *SBL 1985 Seminar Papers*, 351-368. Esp. 365-368.

1985b  Synopses of the Future. — *Bib* 66 (1985) 457-492. Esp. 459-460 [19,21]; 465-476: "Where should the Sermon on the Mount be paralleled to Mark?". [NTA 30, 993]; = ID. (ed.), *The Interrelations of the Gospels*, 1990, 317-347. Esp. 318-319; 324-333. → Neirynck 1986c

1987   Jesus and Violence. — SANDERS, E.P. (ed.), *Jesus, the Gospels, and the Church.* FS W.R. Farmer, 1987, 135-162. Esp. 144-146 [5,38-42]; 146-147 [26,51-54]; 151-153.

1990*  (ed.), *The Interrelations of the Gospels. A Symposium Led by M.-É. Boismard - W.R. Farmer - F. Neirynck, Jerusalem 1984* (BETL, 95). Leuven: University Press / Peeters, 1990, XXX-672 p. → Abogunrin 1987, Boismard 1990a-c, Borgen 1990a-b, Daube 1985, Dungan 1985b, 1990a, J.K. Elliott 1989b, W.R. Farmer 1990b, Gerhardsson 1986a, McNicol, Merkel, Neirynck 1990b-f, Orchard, Peabody, Reicke, Shuler, Stuhlmacher, Tuckett

1990a  Response to the Two-Source Hypothesis. — *Ibid.*, 201-216. → Neirynck 1990b

1990b  → W.R. Farmer 1990b

1992a  Two-Gospel Hypothesis. — *ABD* 6 (1992) 671-679.

1992b  → W.R. Farmer 1992a/93/94/95

1995   *'Eppur Si Muove'*: Circumnavigating the Mythical Recensions of Q. — *Soundings* (Knoxville, TN) 78 (1995) 541-570. [NTA 40, 1445]

**DUNKERLEY, Roderic**

1951   The Textual Critic in the Pulpit. — *ExpT* 63 (1951-52) 75-77, 101-104. Esp. 103-104 [27,16-17; 18,11].

1963   Was Barabbas also Called Jesus? [26,16-17] — *ExpT* 74 (1962-63) 126-127. [NTA 7, 792] → Nevius 1963

1964   The Etiquette of the Kingdom. [20,28] — *LondQuartHolRev* 33 (1964) 151-153. [NTA 8, 950]

**DUNN, James D.G.**

1970a  *Baptism in the Holy Spirit. A Re-examination of the New Testament Teaching on the Gift of the Spirit in Relation to Pentecostalism Today* (Studies in Biblical Theology, II/15). London: SCM, 1970; [2]1977, VIII-248 p. Esp. 8-22: "The expectation of John the Baptist" [3,11]; 23-37: "The experience of Jesus at Jordan". — Diss. Cambridge, 1968 (C.F.D. Moule). *El bautismo del Espíritu santo.* Buenos Aires: La Aurora, 1977, 296 p.

1970b  Spirit and Kingdom. — *ExpT* 82 (1970-71) 36-40. [NTA 15, 665]; = ID., *The Christ and the Spirit*, II, 1998, 133-141.
       *TDig* 19 (1971) 247-250.

1972   Spirit-and-Fire Baptism. [3,11] — *NT* 14 (1972) 81-92. [NTA 17, 139]; = ID., *The Christ and the Spirit*, II, 1998, 93-102.

1975   *Jesus and the Spirit. A Study of the Religious and Charismatic Experience of Jesus and the First Christians as Reflected in the New Testament.* London: SCM; Philadelphia, PA: Westminster, 1975, XII-515 p. Esp. 27-34 [11,27]; 36-37 [Q 22,28-30]; 44-49 [12,28]; 49-53 [12,31-32]; 55-62 [5,3-6; 11,2-6]; 77-78 [8,9-10]; 123-125 [28,17]; 126-128 [28,8-10].

1977 *Unity and Diversity in the New Testament. An Inquiry into the Character of Earliest Christianity.* London: SCM, 1977, XVII-470 p. Esp. 35-40.70-74.219-221.283-288 [Q]; 94-96 [2,23; 27,9-10/OT]; 246-252 [law]; London: SCM; Philadelphia, PA: Trinity Press International, [2]1990, XLI-482 p.

1978a The Birth of a Metaphor – Baptized in Spirit. — *ExpT* 89 (1977-78) 134-138, 173-175. Esp. 135-136: "John the Baptist" [3,11]; 136-137 [11,2-6]. [NTA 22, 915]; = ID., *The Christ and the Spirit,* II, 1998, 103-117. Esp. 104-107; 107-108.

1978b Prophetic 'I'-Sayings and the Jesus Tradition: The Importance of Testing Prophetic Utterances within Early Christianity. — *NTS* 24 (1977-78) 175-198. Esp. 185-187 [24,11]; 193-196 [12,32]. [NTA 22, 383]; = ID., *The Christ and the Spirit,* II, 1998, 142-169. Esp. 154-156; 164-166. → Boring 1983

1980a *Christology in the Making. An New Testament Inquiry into the Origins of the Doctrine of the Incarnation.* London: SCM, 1980, XVII-443 p. Esp. 197-206 [11,19.25-30; 23,34-36.37-39]; [2]1989.

1980b & TWELFTREE, G.H., Demon-Possession and Exorcism in the New Testament. — *Churchman* (London) 94 (1980) 210-225; = ID., *The Christ and the Spirit,* II, 1998, 170-186.
La possession démoniaque et l'exorcisme dans le Nouveau Testament. — *Hokhma* 51 (1992) 34-52.

1981 Models of Christian Community in the New Testament. — BITTLINGER, A. (ed.), *The Church is Charismatic: The World Council of Churches and the Charismatic Renewal,* Genève: World Council of Churches, 1981, 99-116; = ID., *The Christ and the Spirit,* II, 1998, 245-259. Esp. 256-257: "The Matthean church: the Law-abiding brotherhood".

1983 Jesus and the Constraint of Law. — *JSNT* 17 (1983) 10-28. Esp. 16-17. [NTA 27, 882r]

1985 Jesus and Ritual Purity. A Study of the Tradition History of Mk 7,15. — GANTOY, R. (ed.), *À cause de l'Évangile.* FS J. Dupont, 1985, 251-276. Esp. 261-263 [15,11]; 263-264 [15,11/Th]; = ID., *Jesus, Paul and the Law,* 1990, 37-58 (additional note, 58-60). Esp. 42-43; 43-44.

1987 *The Living Word.* London: SCM, 1987, IX-196 p. Esp. 25-43: "The gospels as oral tradition"; 46-55: "Jesus and the Old Testament" [5,17-18.38-41]; 96-97 [5,18].

1988a Matthew 12:28/Luke 11:20 – A Word of Jesus? — GLOER, W.H. (ed.), *Eschatology and the New Testament. Essays in Honor of George Raymond Beasley-Murray,* Peabody, MA: Hendrickson, 1988, 29-49. Esp. 34-37: "Jesus the exorcist – the sayings"; 38-42: "Mt 12:28/Lk 11:20 – the criterion of double dissimilarity"; 42-46: "Mt 12:28/Lk 11,20 – the criterion of coherence"; = ID., *The Christ and the Spirit,* II, 1998, 187-204. Esp. 191-194; 194-198; 198-201.

1988b Pharisees, Sinners and Jesus. — NEUSNER, J., et al. (eds.), *The Social World of Formative Christianity and Judaism.* FS H.C. Kee, Philadelphia, PA: Fortress, 1988, 264-289; = ID., *Jesus, Paul and the Law,* 1990, 61-86 (additional note, 86-88). Esp. 86-87.

1989 Paul's Knowledge of the Jesus Tradition. The Evidence of Romans. — KERTELGE, K., et al. (eds.), *Christus bezeugen.* FS W. Trilling, 1989, 193-207. Esp. 199 [8,17/Rom 15,1]; 201 [5,43-44/Rom 12,14]; 203 [7,1/Rom 14,13]; 204 [12,28/Rom 14,17].

1990 *Jesus, Paul and the Law. Studies in Mark and Galatians.* London: SPCK, 1990, X-277 p. → 1985, 1988b

1991a *The Partings of the Ways Between Christianity and Judaism and Their Significance for the Character of Christianity.* London: SCM; Philadelphia, PA: Trinity Press International, 1991, XVI-368 p. Esp. 37-56: "Jesus and the temple"; 151-156: "The evidence of Matthew – church and synagogue in dispute"; 163-182: "Jesus and the one God"; 213-215 [christology].

1991b  John and the Oral Gospel Tradition. — WANSBROUGH, H. (ed.), *Jesus and the Oral Gospel Tradition*, 1991, 351-379. Esp. 359-363 [8,5-13/Jn 4,46-54]; 365-368 [26,6-13/Jn 12,1-8]; 370-371 [9,37-38; 18,3/Jn 3,3.5; 4,35-38].

1992*  (ed.), *Jews and Christians: The Parting of the Ways A.D. 70 to 135. The Second Durham–Tübingen Research Symposium on Earliest Christianity and Judaism (Durham, September, 1989)* (WUNT, 66). Tübingen: Mohr, 1992, X-408 p. → Birdsall, J.D.G. Dunn, Stanton

1992a  The Question of Anti-Semitism in the New Testament Writings of the Period. — *Ibid.*, 177-211. Esp. 203-210: "Is Matthew 'anti-semitic'?" [27,25].

1992b  Christology. — *ABD* 1 (1992) 979-991. Esp. 980-982.
New Testament Christology. — ID., *The Christ and the Spirit*, I, 1998, 3-29. Esp. 8-11.

1992c  Matthew's Awareness of Markan Redaction. — VAN SEGBROECK, F., et al. (eds.), *The Four Gospels 1992*. FS F. Neirynck, 1992, II, 1349-1359.

1992d  Prayer. — *DJG*, 1992, 617-625. Esp. 619-623 [Lord's prayer].

1993  Christology as an Aspect of Theology. — MALHERBE, A.J. - MEEKS, W.A. (eds.), *The Future of Christology. Essays in Honor of Leander E. Keck*, Minneapolis, MN: Fortress, 1993, 202-212. Esp. 207-208 [1,23]; = ID., *The Christ and the Spirit*, I, 1998, 377-387. Esp. 382-383.

1994a  *Christian Liberty. A New Testament Perspective* (The Didbury Lectures). Carlisle: Paternoster, 1993; Grand Rapids, MI: Eerdmans, 1994, XI-115 p. Esp. 27-52: "Jesus and authority".

1994b  Jesus Tradition in Paul. — CHILTON, B. - EVANS, C.A. (eds.), *Studying the Historical Jesus*, 1994, 155-178. Esp. 159-168 [Paul/Mt]; = ID., *The Christ and the Spirit*, I, 1998, 169-189. Esp. 173-180.

1994c  John the Baptist's Use of Scripture. — EVANS, C.A. - STEGNER, W.R. (eds.), *The Gospels and the Scriptures of Israel*, 1994, 42-54. Esp. 43-46 [3,3]; 46-47 [3,4]; 47-53 [3,7-12]; = ID., *The Christ and the Spirit*, II, 1998, 118-129. Esp. 119-122; 122; 123-128.

1998  *The Christ and the Spirit. Collected Essays*. Vol. I: *Christology*; Vol. II: *Pneumatology*. Edinburgh: Clark, 1998, XIX-462 and XVI-382 p.; I: → 1992b, 1993, 1994b; II: → 1970b, 1972, 1978a-b, 1980b, 1981, 1988a, 1994c

**DUNN, Mark R.**

1990  *An Examination of the Textual Character of Codex Ephraemi Syri Rescriptus (C,04) in the Four Gospels*. Diss. Southwestern Baptist Theol. Sem., Fort Worth, TX, 1990, VIII-327 p. Esp. 43-115: "The textual character of C in Matthew". — *DissAbstr* 51 (1990-91) 2409-2410.

**DUPLACY, Jean**

1957  Où en est la critique textuelle du Nouveau Testament? — *RSR* 45 (1957) 419-441; 46 (1958) 270-313; 430-462. Esp. 289-292. [NTA 2, 236; 3, 24/312]

1961  La foi qui déplace les montagnes (Mt., XVII,20; XXI,21 et par.). — BARUCQ, A., et al. (eds.), *À la rencontre de Dieu*. FS A. Gelin, 1961, 273-287.

1962  Le maître généreux et les ouvriers égoïstes (Matthieu 20,1-16). — *BibVieChrét* 44 (1962) 16-30. [NTA 7, 139]

1967  Et il y eut un grand calme... La tempête apaisée (Matthieu 8,23-27). — *BibVieChrét* 74 (1967) 15-28. [NTA 12, 155]

1987a  *Études de critique textuelle du Nouveau Testament*, ed. J. Delobel (BETL, 78). Leuven: University Press / Peeters, 1987, XXVII-431 p. → 1987b-c

1987b  L'histoire la plus ancienne et la forme originale du texte en *Luc* 22,43-44. [26,39] — *Ibid.*, 349-385. Esp. 350-355, 360-363, 379.

1987c  Note sur les variantes et le texte original de *Matthieu* 19,9. — *Ibid.*, 387-412.

**DUPLANTIER, Jean-Pierre**

1970   *Les récits synoptiques de la Transfiguration. Étude sur la composition et le "milieu" littéraire de Mc 9,2-8; Mt 17,1-9; Lc 9,28-36*. Diss. Strasbourg, 1970, 323 p.

**DU PLESSIS, Isak J.**

1967   The Ethics of Marriage according to Matt. 5:27-32. — *Neotestamentica* 1 (1967) 16-27. [NTA 18, 104]

1986   Contextual Aid for an Identity Crisis: An Attempt to Interpret Luke 7:35. — PETZER, J.H. – HARTIN, P.J. (eds.), *A South African Perspective on the New Testament*. FS B.M. Metzger, 1986, 112-127. Esp. 115-116 [Q 7,1-10]; 119-126 [Q 7,18-35].

1990   Philanthropy or Sarcasm? – Another Look at the Parable of the Dishonest Manager (Luke 16:1-13). — *Neotestamentica* 24 (1990) 1-20. Esp. 15-16 [Q 16,13]. [NTA 35, 679]

**DU PLESSIS, J.G.**

1987   Pragmatic Meaning in Matthew 13:1-23. — *Neotestamentica* 21 (1987) 33-56. [NTA 33, 122]

1988   Mark's Priority: The Nature and Structure of the Argument from Order. — MOUTON, J., et al. (eds.), *Paradigms and Progress in Theology* (Human Sciences Research Council Studies in Research Methodology, 5), Pretoria: HSRC, 1988, 295-308.

**DU PLESSIS, Paul Johannes**

1959   *Τέλειος. The Idea of Perfection in the New Testament* (Theologische Academie, Kampen). Kampen: Kok, 1959, 255 p. Esp. 123-124 [τελέω]; 163-166 [24–25]; 168-173 [5,48; 19,21]. — Diss. Kampen, 1959 (H.N. Ridderbos).

1967   Love and Perfection in Matt. 5:43-48. — *Neotestamentica* 1 (1967) 28-34. [NTA 18, 105]

**DUPONT, Jacques**

1954   *Les Béatitudes. Le problème littéraire. Le message doctrinal*. Brugge: St. Andriesabdij; Leuven: Nauwelaerts, 1954, 327 p. Esp. 19-74: "Le Sermon sur la montagne"; 79-123: "Les béatitudes"; 127-180: "La bonne nouvelle messianique"; 183-244: "Les pauvres et les riches"; 245-299: "La justice chrétienne". → 1958a, 1969a, 1973; → Léon-Dufour 1970a, Sabbe 1959a, Zarrella 1970a
   P. BENOIT, *RB* 62 (1955) 420-424; P. BONNARD, *RTP* 4 (1954) 292-295; B. BRINKMANN, *Scholastik* 31 (1956) 308-309; R.E. BROWN, *CBQ* 17 (1955) 522-525; C. BUTLER, *DownR* 73 (1955) 82-83; J. CAMBIER, *ETL* 33 (1957) 97-98; I. DE LA POTTERIE, *Bijdragen* 16 (1955) 91-92; H. DUESBERG, *BibVieChrét* 8 (1954-55) 121-122; P. GAECHTER, *ZKT* 77 (1955) 342-344; A. GELIN, *AmiCler* 64 (1954) 375-376; G. LAMBERT, *NRT* 77 (1955) 540; H. MUSURILLO, *TS* 16 (1955) 132-133; J. LEAL, *EstBíb* 14 (1955) 467-469; C. PERROT, *Cahiers sioniens* (Paris) 9 (1955) 174-177; J. PONTHOT, *IrEcclRec* 85 (1956) 186; B. RIGAUX, *RHE* 50 (1955) 671-672; J.N. SANDERS, *NTS* 2 (1955-56) 147-148; C. SPICQ, *FZPT* 2 (1955) 227-228; Y.B. TRÉMEL, *LumièreV* 22 (1955) 103-110/532-534; A. VIARD, *RSPT* 39 (1955) 292-293; D.E.H. WHITELEY, *JTS* 6 (1955) 130; M. ZERW CK, *VD* 33 (1955) 298-300.

1956   Le nom d'Apôtres: a-t-il été donné aux Douze par Jésus? — *L'Orient Syrien* (Paris) 1 (1956) 267-290, 425-444. Esp. 286-290: "Le témoignage de saint Matthieu".[NTA 1, 113/182]; = ID., *Études sur les Évangiles synoptiques*, II, 1985, 976-1018 (note additionnelle, 1018). Esp. 995-999.

1957a  L'arrière-fond biblique du récit des tentations de Jésus. [4,1-11] — *NTS* 3 (1956-57) 287-304. [NTA 2, 270]

1957b  La parabole des ouvriers de la vigne (Matthieu, XX,1-16). — *NRT* 79 (1957) 785-797. [NTA 2, 279]

1957c  Le paralytique de Capharnaüm. [9,1-8] — *LumièreV* 35 (1957) 12-19. [NTA 2, 280]

1958a  *Les Béatitudes*. [I] *Le problème littéraire. Les deux versions du Sermon sur la montagne et des Béatitudes*. Brugge: St. Andriesabdij; Leuven: Nauwelaerts, ²1958 (new ed.), 387 p. Esp. 41-204: "Le Sermon sur la montagne" (61-128: "Les matériaux propres à Matthieu"; 129-187: "Le discours de Matthieu"); 205-345: "Les deux versions des béatitudes" (209-250: "Les béatitudes parallèles chez Matthieu"; 251-264: "Les béatitudes propres à Matthieu"). → 1954, 1969a, 1973

M.-É. BOISMARD, *RB* 66 (1959) 613-615; M.M. BOURKE, *TS* 20 (1959) 457-459; J. CABALLERO, *EstE* 37 (1962) 109-111; A. COLUNGA, *Salmanticensis* 6 (1959) 247-248; J. DELORME, *AmiCler* 73 (1963) 664-665; J. GIBLET, *CollMech* 44 (1959) 451-452; X. LÉON-DUFOUR, *RSR* 46 (1958) 253-260; J.F. McCONNELL, *CBQ* 21 (1959) 374-375; J. RADERMAKERS, *NRT* 83 (1961) 86; R. SCHNACKENBURG, *BZ* 5 (1961) 144-146; M. ZERWICK, *VD* 38 (1960) 48-51.

1958b "Vous n'aurez pas achevé les villes d'Israël avant que le Fils de l'homme ne vienne" (Mat. X 23). — *NT* 2 (1957-58) 228-244. Esp. 231-233: "Matthieu x 23 et Marc XIII 10"; 233-238: "Le v. 23b et le discours de mission"; 238-244: "La venue du Fils de l'homme". [NTA 4, 78]

1959a *Mariage et divorce dans l'Évangile. Matthieu 19,3-12 et parallèles*. Brugge: Abbaye de Saint-André/Desclée De Brouwer, 1959, 239 p. Esp. 27-35: "Le récit de Matthieu"; 37-49: "L'enchaînement des sentences"; 51-77: "Répudiation et remariage" [53-57; 64-69; 73-75]; 81-92: "Origine des incises"; 93-114: "Une exception" [5,32; 19,9]; 115-157: "La répudiation pour inconduite"; 161-174: "Tous ne comprennent pas cette parole"; 175-190: "Ceux qui comprennent"; 191-220: "Les exigences du royaume". → Neirynck 1960a, Zerwick 1960

M.-É. BOISMARD, *RB* 67 (1960) 463-464; A. BOUTRY, *BibVieChrét* 34 (1960) 88; J.L. D'ARAGON, *ScEccl* 12 (1960) 271-276; J. DELORME, *AmiCler* 73 (1963) 665-667; J. GIBLET, *CollMech* 45 (1960) 180-181; K. GIERATHS, *FZPT* 7 (1960) 195-197; S. GRZYBEK, *RuBi* 14 (1961) 177-179; A. JANSSEN, *ETL* 36 (1960) 726-727; P.J. KING, *TS* 22 (1961) 466-468; J. LEGRAND, *Études* 307 (1960) 132; X. LÉON-DUFOUR, *RSR* 50 (1962) 102-104; E. O'DOHERTY, *CBQ* 22 (1960) 343-345; L.M. ORRIEUX, *LumièreV* 50 (1960) 131-134; L.F. RIVERA, *RivBib* 23 (1961) 152; C. SPICQ, *FZPT* 8 (1961) 386-387; A. VANDENBUNDER, *Bijdragen* 21 (1960) 312-313; A. VIARD, *RSPT* 44 (1960) 293-294; M.R. WEJERS, *RThom* 62 (1962) 116-119; T. WORDEN, *Scripture* 12 (1960) 57-59.

1959b De armen van geest. [5,3] — *Getuigenis* 3 (1959) 268-276. → 1963
Les pauvres en esprit. — BARUCQ, A., et al. (eds.), *À la rencontre de Dieu*. FS A. Gelin, 1961, 265-272.

1959c Ressuscité "le troisième jour". — *Bib* 40 (1959) 742-761. Esp. 742-745 [16,21; 17,23; 20,19]. [NTA 4, 622]; = *Studia Biblica et Orientalia*, II, 1959, 174-193. Esp. 174-177; = ID., *Études sur les Actes des Apôtres* (LD, 45), Paris: Cerf, 1967, 321-336. Esp. 321-324.
Risuscitato "il terzo giorno" (1 Cor 15,4; At 10,40). — ID., *Studi sugli Atti degli apostoli*, trans. A. Girlanda, Roma: Paoline, Cor 15,4; At 10,40). — ID., *Studi sugli Atti degli apostoli*, trans. A. Girlanda, Roma: Paoline, 1971, ²1973, ³1975, 547-574.
Resuscitou "ao terceiro dia" (1 Cor 15,4; At 10,40). — ID., *Estudios sobre os Atos dos apostolos*, Sâo Paolo: Paulinas, 1974, 320-335.

1959d "Soyez parfaits" (Mt., V,48). "Soyez miséricordieux" (Lc., VI,36). — COPPENS, J., et al. (eds.), *Sacra Pagina*, 1959, II, 150-162. → 1966a

1960a L'entrée de Jésus à Jérusalem dans le récit de saint Matthieu (XXI,1-17). — *LumièreV* 48 (1960) 1-8. [NTA 5, 83]

1960b Le paralytique pardonné (Mt 9,1-8). — *NRT* 82 (1960) 940-958. Esp. 940-943 [9,1-2]; 944-948 [9,3-7]; 948-958 [9,8]. [NTA 5, 712]

1961a L'ambassade de Jean-Baptiste (Matthieu 11,2-6; Luc 7,18-23). — *NRT* 83 (1961) 805-821, 943-959. Esp. 806-813: "La question de Jean"; 814-821: "Celui qui vient"; 943-951: "La réponse de Jésus"; 951-958: "Le scandale". [NTA 6, 771]
"Art thou he who is to come?". — *TDig* 12 (1964) 42-47.

1961b Es-tu celui qui vient? [11,2-10] — *AssSeign* I/4 (1961) 35-50.
¿Eres tú el que ha de venir? — McCARTHY, D.J. - CALLEN, W.B. (eds.), *Estudios modernos sobre la Biblia* ("Palabra Inspirada", 8), Santander: Sal Terrae, 1969, 123-132.

1962a La genealogia di Gesù secondo Matteo 1,1-17. — *BibOr* 4 (1962) 3-6. [NTA 6, 760]

1962b Les tentations de Jésus dans le désert. [4,1-11] — *AssSeign* I/26 (1962) 37-53.

1962c Le paralytique pardonné. [9,1-8] — *AssSeign* I/73 (1962) 34-46.

1963 Les πτωχοὶ τῷ πνεύματι de Matthieu 5,3 et les ‏ רוח ‎ ‏ ענוי ‎ de Qumrân. — BLINZLER, J., et al. (eds.), *Neutestamentliche Aufsätze*. FS J. Schmid, 1963, 53-64; = ID., *Études sur les Évangiles synoptiques*, II, 1985, 779-792 (note additionnelle, 792). → 1959b

1964a Le logion des douze trônes (Mt 19,28; Lc 22,28-30). — *Bib* 45 (1964) 355-392. Esp.
355-370: "Problèmes littéraires"; 370-389: "L'objet de la promesse" [esp. 377-379.386-389]. [NTA 9, 539];
= ID., *Études sur les Évangiles synoptiques*, II, 1985, 706-743 (note additionnelle, 743). Esp.
706-721; 721-740 (esp. 728-730; 737-740).

1964b La révélation du Fils de Dieu en faveur de Pierre (*Mt* 16 17) et de Paul (*Ga* 1,16). —
*RSR* 52 (1964) 411-420. Esp. 412-414: "Dépendance de Matthieu"; 415-417 [16,16-18]; 417-420
[16,17/Gal 1,16]. [NTA 9, 536]; = ID., *Études sur les Évangiles synoptiques*, II, 1985, 929-
938 (note additionnelle, 939). Esp. 930-932; 933-935; 935-938.

1964c "Le Royaume des cieux est semblable à ...". — *BibOr* 6 (1964) 247-253. [NTA 9, 859]

1965a Les ouvriers de la vigne. [20,1-16] — *AssSeign* I/22 (1965) 28-51.

1965b L'entrée messianique de Jésus à Jérusalem. [21,1-17] — *AssSeign* I/37 (1965) 46-62.

1966a L'appel à imiter Dieu en Mt 5,48 et Lc 6,36. — *RivBib* 14 (1966) 137-158. Esp. 144-145
[19,21]; 150 [18,12-14]; 151 [6,14-15]; 152-153 [18,23-35]; 154-156 [5,48]; 156-158 [Q 6,36]. [NTA 11,
697]; = ID., *Études sur les Évangiles synoptiques*, II, 1985, 529-550 (note additionnelle,
550). Esp. 536-537; 542; 543; 544-545; 546-548; 548-550. → 1959d

1966b "Béatitudes" égyptiennes. — *Bib* 47 (1966) 185-222. [NTA 11, 695]; = ID., *Études sur
les Évangiles synoptiques*, II, 1985, 793-830 (note additionnelle, 831).

1966c L'interprétation des Béatitudes. — *FoiVie* 65/4 = *Cahiers bibliques* 4 (1966) 17-39. Esp.
18-21 [Mt]; 21-25 [Lk]; 25-31: "Le problème littéraire"; 31-39: "La signification originelle".

1966d & BONNARD, P., Le Notre Père. Notes exégétiques. — *La Maison-Dieu* (Paris) 85
(1966) 7-35. [NTA 11, 204]; = *FoiVie* 65/4 = *Cahiers bibliques* 4 (1966) 51-79; = ID.,
*Études sur les Évangiles synoptiques*, II, 1985, 832-860 (note additionnelle, 861).
Le Notre Père. Commentaire exégétique. — BONNARD, P., et al. (eds.), *Notre Père qui es aux cieux*, 1968,
77-115.

1966e L'origine du récit des tentations de Jésus au désert. [4,1-11] — *RB* 73 (1966) 30-76. Esp.
34-48: "Les deux traditions"; 48-58: "L'hypothèse de l'origine communautaire"; 58-73: "Raisons d'attribuer
le récit à Jésus". [NTA 11, 194]
The Origin of the Narrative of Jesus' Temptation. — *TDig* 15 (1967) 230-235.
*SelT* 6 (1967) 267-278.

1967a "Beaucoup viendront du levant et du couchant..." (*Matthieu* 8,11-12; *Luc* 13,28-29). —
*ScEccl* 19 (1967) 153-167. Esp. 154-158: "Critique littéraire"; 158-161: "Le point de vue de Jésus";
162-164: "Le point de vue de Matthieu". [NTA 12, 154]; = ID., *Études sur les Évangiles
synoptiques*, II, 1985, 568-582 (note additionnelle, 582). Esp. 569-573; 573-576; 577-579.

1967b Bergpredigt. — *Sacramentum Mundi* (Freiburg) 1 (1967) 493-496.
Sermon on the Mount. — *Sacramentum Mundi* (London – New York) 5 (1970) 71-73.

1967c "Ce que Dieu a uni". [19,3-6] — *AssSeign* I/97 (1967) 31-41.

1967d Le chapitre des paraboles. — *NRT* 89 (1967) 800-820. Esp. 811-819: "La version de Matthieu".
[NTA 12, 555]; = ID., *Études sur les Évangiles synoptiques*, I, 1985, 215-235 (note
additionnelle, 235). Esp. 226-234.
*SelT* 7 (1968) 239-246.

1967e Les paraboles du sénevé et du levain. — *Ibid.*, 897-913. Esp. 897-910 [13,31-32]; 911-913
[13,33]. [NTA 12, 874]; = ID., *Études sur les Évangiles synoptiques*, II, 1985, 592-608.
Esp. 592-605; 606-608. → 1975b
*SelT* 7 (1968) 237-239.

1967f La parabole de la semence qui pousse toute seule (*Marc* 4,26-29). — *RSR* 55 (1967)
367-392. Esp. 390. [NTA 12, 564]; = ID., *Études sur les Évangiles synoptiques*, I, 1985,
295-320 (note additionnelle, 320). Esp. 318.

1967g La parabole du semeur. — *FoiVie* 66/5 = *Cahiers bibliques* 5 (1967) 3-25. Esp. 21-24;
= ID., *Études sur les Évangiles synoptiques* I, 1985, 236-258 (note additionnelle, 258). Esp.
254-257.
*SelT* 9 (1970) 73-78.

1967h  Les "simples" *(petâyim)* dans la Bible et à Qumrân. À propos des νήπιοι de Mt. 11,25;
Lc. 10,21. — *Studi sull'Oriente e la Bibbia*. FS G. Rinaldi, 1967, 329-336; = ID.,
*Études sur les Évangiles synoptiques*, II, 1985, 583-590 (note additionnelle, 591).

1968a  *Les tentations de Jésus au désert* (Studia Neotestamentica, Studia 4). Brugge: Desclée
De Brouwer, 1968, 152 p. Esp. 9-42: "Le récit de Matthieu"; 73-130: "L'origine du récit".
> J. MURPHY-O'CONNOR, *RB* 77 (1970) 449-450.
> *Die Versuchungen Jesu in der Wüste*, trans. A. van Dülmen (SBS, 37). Stuttgart: Katholisches Bibelwerk,
> 1969, 132 p. Esp. 9-41; 70-126.
>> J.D. KINGSBURY, *CBQ* 32 (1970) 445-446; B. PIEPIÓRKA, *ZKT* 93 (1971) 229; A. SALAS, *EstBíb* 29
>> (1970) 297-298; F.J. STEINMETZ, *GL* 43 (1973) 73; WEISS, *BK* 24 (1969) 151.
> *Le tentazioni di Gesù nel deserto*, trans. E. Bovone (Studi biblici, 11). Brescia: Paideia, 1970, 160 p.; 1985,
> 170 p.
>> V. FUSCO, *RasT* 15 (1974) 394-395.

1968b  Jésus et la prière liturgique. — *La Maison-Dieu* 95 (1968) 16-49. Esp. 25-28 [6,9-13]; 30-35
[6,2-4.5-6.16-18]; 38-40 [6,7-8]. [NTA 13, 538]; = ID., *Études sur les Évangiles synoptiques*,
I, 1985, 146-179 (note additionnelle, 179). Esp. 155-158; 160-165; 168-170.

1968c  Nova et vetera (Matthieu 13:52). — *L'Évangile hier et aujourd'hui. Mélanges offerts
au Professeur Franz-J. Leenhardt*, Genève: Labor et Fides, 1968, 55-63; = ID., *Études
sur les Évangiles synoptiques*, II, 1985, 920-928 (note additionnelle, 928).

1968d  In parabola magni convivii (Matth. 22,2-14; Luc. 14,16-24) historia salutis delineatur.
— SCHÖNMETZER, A. (ed.), *Acta Congressus Internationalis de Theologia Concilii
Vaticani II (Romae, 1966)*, Città del Vaticano: Typis Polyglottis Vaticanis, 1968, 455-
459.

1968e  La parabole de la brebis perdue (Matthieu 18,12-14; Luc 15,4-7). — *Greg* 49 (1968)
265-287. Esp. 266-269 [Mt]; 269-273 [Lk]; 273-279: "Critique littéraire", 279-287: "La parabole dans le
ministère de Jésus". [NTA 13, 172]; = ID., *Études sur les Évangiles synoptiques*, II, 1985,
624-646. Esp. 625-628; 628-632; 632-638; 638-346. → 1975a

1968f  La parabole du figuier qui bourgeonne *(Mc, XIII,28-29 et par.)*. — *RB* 75 (1968) 526-
548. Esp. 533 [24,32-33]; 544 [11,5; 12,28]; 544-545 [16,2-3]. [NTA 13, 890]; = ID., *Études sur les
Évangiles synoptiques*, I, 1985, 474-497 (note additionnelle, 497). Esp. 481; 492-493.
> La parabola del fico che germoglia (Marco 13,28-29 par.). — ID., *Distruzione del tempio*, 1979, 183-224. Esp.
> 196; 216-217.

1968g  Les paraboles du trésor et de la perle. [13,44-46] — *NTS* 14 (1967-68) 408-418. Esp. 410-
413: "Le problème"; 413-415: "La pointe des récits"; 415-416: "L'application"; 416-418: "Le point de vue
de Matthieu". [NTA 13, 165]; = ID., *Études sur les Évangiles synoptiques*, II, 1985, 908-918
(note additionnelle, 919). Esp. 910-913; 913-915; 915-916; 916-918.

1969a  *Les Béatitudes. I. Le problème littéraire. Les deux versions du Sermon sur la montagne
et des Béatitudes* (Études bibliques). Paris: Gabalda [1958], repr. 1969, 387 p. → 1958a
II. *La Bonne Nouvelle* (Études bibliques). Paris: Gabalda, 1969, 426 p. → 1954, 1973; →
Coppens 1974b
> M. BENÉITEZ, *EstE* 45 (1970) 281-282; J. DECROIX, *BibTS* 121 (1970) 23; A. DESCAMPS, *RTL* 1 (1970)
> 338-343; M. GILBERT, *NRT* 92 (1970) 91-92; I. GOMÁ CIVIT, *EstBíb* 30 (1971) 373-375; É. JACQUEMIN,
> *La Maison-Dieu* 100 (1969) 192-193; J. KAHMANN, *TijdTheol* 11 (1971) 313; J. LAMBRECHT, *Bijdragen*
> 32 (1971) 76-77; M.-É. LAUZIÈRE, *RThom* 71 (1971) 133; F. MONTAGNINI, *ParVi* 14 (1969) 395-396;
> M. MORLET, *EVie* 80 (1970) 97-100; J.J. O'ROURKE, *CBQ* 32 (1970) 112-113; B. PRETE, *Sacra
> Doctrina* (Bologna) 15 (1970) 310; L.F. RIVERA, *RevistBíb* 32 (1970) 366-367; T. SNOY, *RBén* 79 (1969)
> 445-447; A. TURCK, *Paroisse et Liturgie* (Ottignies) 556-558; L. TURRADO, *Salmanticensis* 18 (1971)
> 409-410; P. ZARELLA, *ScuolC* 99 (1971) 481-482.
> *Le Beatitudini*. I: *Il problema letterario. La buona novella* [= vol. I-II], trans. G. Gandolfi & A. Girlanda
> (Parola di Dio, 7). Roma: Paoline, 1972, ²1973, 1212 p.
>> R.G., *RivAscM* 24 (1973) 86-87; G. LEONARDI, *Studia Patavina* 20 (1973) 418; J. WIMMER,
>> *Augustinianum* 18 (1978) 399-400.

1969b  Le Christ et son Précurseur. Mt 11,2-11. — *AssSeign* II/7 (1969) 16-26.
       Cristo e il suo Precursore (Matteo 11,2-11). — *Per l'Assemblea Festiva* (Brescia) 4 (1969) 33-47.
       Cristo y su Precursor (Mt 11,2-11). — *Esqucha Israel* (Barcelona) 7 (1969) 27-43.

1969c  La lampe sur le lampadaire dans l'évangile de saint Luc (Lc VIII,16; XI,33). —
       TROISFONTAINES, C. (ed.), *Au service de la Parole de Dieu*. FS A.-M. Charue, 1969,
       43-59. Esp. 44-49: "Le texte"; 55-58 [Q 11,33]; = ID., *Études sur les Évangiles synoptiques*,
       II, 1985, 1032-1048. Esp. 1033-1038; 1044-1047. → 1982

1969d  Matthieu 18,3: ἐὰν μὴ στραφῆτε καὶ γένησθε ὡς τὰ παιδία. — ELLIS, E.E. -
       WILCOX, M. (eds.), *Neotestamentica et Semitica*. FS M. Black, 1969, 50-60.
       Ἐὰν μὴ στραφῆτε καὶ γένησθε ὡς τὰ παιδία (Mt 18,3). — ID., *Études sur les Évangiles synoptiques*, II,
       1985, 940-950 (note additionnelle, 950).

1969e  La parabole des talents. Mt 25,14-30. — *AssSeign* II/64 (1969) 18-28. → 1969f

1969f  La parabole des talents (Mat. 25:14-30) ou des mines (Luc 19:12-27). — *RTP* 19 (1969)
       376-391. Esp. 379-385: "Interprétation chrétienne de la parabole"; 386-391: "La parabole dans la
       prédication de Jésus". [NTA 14, 861]; = ID., *Études sur les Évangiles synoptiques*, II, 1985,
       744-760 (note additionnelle, 760). Esp. 747-753; 754-759. → 1969e

1970a  Beati i puri di cuore perchè vedranno Dio (Mt 5,8). — *FarVi* 15 (1970) 301-316.

1970b  La parabole du maître qui rentre tard dans la nuit (Mc 13,34-36). — DESCAMPS, A.L.
       - DE HALLEUX, A. (eds.), *Mélanges bibliques*. FS B. Rigaux, 1970, 89-116. Esp. 92-93
       [Mk/Mt]; 97-98 [25,14-15]; 108-111 [24,43-44]; = ID., *Études sur les Évangiles synoptiques*,
       I, 1985, 498-526 (note additionnelle, 526). Esp. 501-502; 506-507; 517-520.
       La parabola del padrone che rientra nel corso della notte (Marco 13,34-36). — ID., *Distruzione del tempio*,
       1979, 225-275. Esp. 232-233; 240-241; 259-261.

1971a  Les deux fils dissemblables. Mt 21,28-32. — *AssSeign* II/57 (1971) 20-32.

1971b  Les pauvres et la pauvreté dans les Évangiles et les Actes. — GEORGE, A., et al. (eds.),
       *La pauvreté*, 1971, 37-63. Esp. 45-53: "Le privilège des pauvres".
       Poor and Poverty in the Gospels and Acts. — GEORGE, A., et al. (eds.), *Gospel Poverty*, 1977, 25-52.

1971c  Renoncer à tous ses biens (*Luc 14,33*). — *NRT* 93 (1971) 561-582. Esp. 562-567: "Luc
       14,26-27 et Matthieu 10,37-38". [NTA 16, 200]; = ID., *Études sur les Évangiles synoptiques*,
       II, 1985, 1076-1097 (note additionnelle, 1097). Esp. 1077-1082.

1972a  Encore des paraboles. Mt 13,44-52. — *AssSeign* II/48 (1972) 16-26.
       Ancora parabole (Mt 13,44-52). — *Per l'Assemblea Festiva* 45 (1972) 32-46.

1972b  Le point de vue de Matthieu dans le chapitre des paraboles. — DIDIER, M. (ed.),
       *L'Évangile selon Matthieu*, 1972, 221-259. Esp. 223-229: "Les Fils du Royaume et les Fils de
       Mauvais"; 229-249: "Les disciples et la foule"; 250-259: "Enseignement et paraboles"; = ID., *Études
       sur les Évangiles synoptiques*, II, 1985, 869-907 (note additionnelle, 907). Esp. 871-877; 877-
       898; 898-907.

1973   *Les Béatitudes*. III. *Les évangélistes* (Études bibliques). Paris: Gabalda, 1973, 743 p.
       Esp. 207-667: "La version de Matthieu" (213-305: "La justice chrétienne"; 307-384: "Les béatitudes de la
       justice"; 385-471: "Les pauvres en esprit"; 473-555: "Les doux et les affligés"; 557-667: "Trois béatitudes
       nouvelles"). → 1954, 1958a, 1969a
       J. ALONSO DÍAZ, *EstE* 50 (1975) 141-142; G. BAGET BOZZO, *Renovatio* 9 (1974) 408-414; P.M.
       BOGAERT, *RBén* 84 (1974) 413-415; G. DANIELI, *RivBib* 24 (1976) 308-314; A. GEORGE, *RTL* 5 (1974)
       220-224; M. GILBERT, *NRT* 96 (1974) 618-619; H.C. KEE, *JBL* 94 (1975) 132-134; X. LÉON-DUFOUR,
       *RSR* 62 (1974) 267-271; D. LÜHRMANN, *TRev* 71 (1975) 29-30; J.J. O'ROURKE, *CBQ* 37 (1975) 110-
       112; J. SALGUERO, *Angelicum* 52 (1975) 410-412; G. SCHNEIDER, *BZb* 56 (1975) 281-284; S. TALAVERO,
       *Salmanticensis* 22 (1975) 581-583; A. TURCK, *ComLtg* 57 (1975) 87-90; J. WINANDY, *VSp* 128 (1974)
       943-944.
       *Le Beatitudini*. II. *Gli evangelisti* [= vol. III], trans. D. Danna (Parola di Dio, 14). Roma: Paoline, 1977,
       1146 p.; Milano–Cinisello Balsamo: Paoline, ⁴1979.
       G.G. GAMBA, *Sal* 40 (1978) 688-689; J.F. WIMMER, *Augustinianum* 18 (1978) 399-400.

1974a "Assis à la droite de Dieu". L'interprétation du Ps 110,1 dans le Nouveau Testament. — DHANIS, É. (ed.), *Resurrexit*, 1974, 340-422. Esp. 358-364: "La déclaration de Jésus devant le Sanhédrin en Mt 26,64"; 413-416: "Fils de David et Fils de Dieu: Mt 22,41-46"; = ID., *Nouvelles études sur les Actes des Apôtres* (LD, 118), Paris: Cerf, 1984, 210-295. Esp. 230-237; 289-292.

1974b L'opzione pastorale nella parabola della pecora amarrita (Mt 18,12-14). — *Chiesa per il mondo*. I: *Saggi storico-biblici. Miscellanea teologico-pastorale M. Pellegrino*, Bologna: Dehoniane, 1974, 97-104.

1974c Le semeur est sorti pour semer. Mt 13,1-23. — *AssSeign* II/46 (1974) 18-27. [NTA 19, 89]

1974d Les ouvriers de la onzième heure. Mt 20,1-16. — *AssSeign* II/56 (1974) 16-27. [NTA 19, 539]
Gli operai dell'undicesima ora (Matteo 20,1-16a). — *Per l'Assemblea Festiva* 53 (1975) 26-42.

1975* (ed.), *Jésus aux origines de la christologie* (BETL, 40). Gembloux: Duculot; Leuven: University Press, 1975, 375 p.; Leuven: University Press / Peeters, ²1989, 458 p. → P. Benoit, M. de Jonge, Dupont, Fitzmyer, George, Léon-Dufour, Linnemann, Neirynck; ²1989 → Lambrecht 1977

1975a Les implications christologiques de la parabole de la brebis perdue. — *Ibid.*, 331-350. Esp. 331-336: "Les versions évangéliques"; 336-342: "Problèmes de méthode"; 342-345: "La parabole dans le ministère de Jésus"; 346-350: "La portée christologique de la parabole"; = ID., *Études sur les Évangiles synoptiques*, II, 1985, 647-666 (note additionnelle, 666). Esp. 647-652; 652-658; 658-661; 662-666. → 1968e

1975b Le couple parabolique du sénevé et du levain. Mt 13,31-33; Lc 13,18-21. — STRECKER, G. (ed.), *Jesus Christus in Historie und Theologie*. FS H. Conzelmann, 1975, 331-345. Esp. 333-336 [Q 13,18-19]; 336-338 [Mk 4,30-32/Mt]; 338-341 [Mk/Q]; = ID., *Études sur les Évangiles synoptiques*, II, 1985, 609-623 (note additionnelle, 623). Esp. 611-614; 614-616; 616-619. → 1967e

1975c L'évangile de saint Matthieu: quelques clés de lecture. — *ComLtg* 57 (1975) 3-40. Esp. 6-7 [fulfilment quotations]; 7-9 [christological titles]; 11-13 [Lord]; 17-21 [Son of God]; 21-25 [church]; 25-27 [7,21; 12,49-50; 28,18-20]; 27-30 [righteousness]; 30-32 [love]; 35-37 [11,28-30]; 32-35 [disciples]; 37-40 [judgement]. [NTA 19, 934]

1976 Introduction aux Béatitudes. — *NRT* 98 (1976) 97-108. Esp. 103-107: "Les Béatitudes dans la version de Matthieu". [NTA 20, 773]
*SelT* 17 (1978) 323-329.
Introdução às bem-aventuranças. — *Convergência* (Rio de Janeiro) 12 (1979) 67-74.
Introducción a las bienaventuranzas. — *Páginas* 6/35 (1981) 1-8.

1977a *Pourquoi des paraboles? La méthode parabolique de Jésus* (Lire la Bible, 46). Paris: Cerf, 1977, 120 p. → 1980b
*Il metodo parabolico di Gesù*, trans. U. Mattioli (Biblioteca minima di cultura religiosa, 28). Brescia: Paideia, 1978, 85 p.
*Por que parábolas? O método parabólico de Jesus*. Petrópolis: Vozes, 1980, 90 p.
*Per què en paràboles? El métode parabólic de Jesús*, trans. D. Codina. Abadia de Montserrat, 1981, 83 p.

1977b La persécution comme situation missionnaire (Marc 13,9-11). — SCHNACKENBURG, R., et al. (eds.), *Die Kirche des Anfangs*. FS H. Schürmann, 1977, 97-114. Esp. 99 [24,9-14]; 101-102 [10,17-22]; 102-104 [Q 12,11-12]; 105-106 [10,17-22/Mk]; 106-107 [10,17-22/Lk]; 107-111 [Q 12,11-12/Mk]; = ID., *Études sur les Évangiles synoptiques*, I, 1985, 456-473 (note additionnelle, 473). Esp. 458; 460-461; 464-465; 465-466.
La persecuzione come situazione missionaria (Marco 13,9-11). — ID., *Distruzione del tempio*, 1979, 149-181. Esp. 153-154; 158-161; 161-165; 166-168; 168-170; 170-174.

1977c La ruine du Temple et la fin des temps dans le discours de Mc 13. — ACFEB (ed.), *Apocalypses et théologie de l'espérance. Congrès de Toulouse (1975)* (LD, 95), Paris:

Cerf, 1977, 207-269. Esp. 263-265: "La version de Matthieu"; = ID., *Études sur les Évangiles synoptiques*, I, 1985, 368-433 (note additionnelle, 433). Esp. 424-426.
La distruzione del Tempio e la fine del mondo nel discorso di Marco 13. — ID., *Distruzione del tempio*, 1979, 13-114. Esp. 101-104.

1978*  et al. (eds.), *La parabola degli invitati al banchetto. Dagli evangelisti a Gesù* (Testi e ricerche di Scienze religiose, 14). Brescia: Paideia, 1973, 352 p. → Barbaglio, Beatrice, Buzzetti, Dupont, Fabris, Gaeta, Pesce
       H. BOJORGE, *RevistBíb* 42 (1980) 116-119; E.J. EPP, *JBL* 98 (1979) 310; G.G. GAMBA, *Sal* 41 (1979) 560-561.

1978a  La parabola degli invitati al banchetto nel ministero di Gesù. — *Ibid.*, 279-329. Esp. 285-290: "Il racconto parabolico"; 290-311: "Situazione della parabola nel ministero di Gesù"; 311-329: "Significato della parabola nel ministero di Gesù".
       La parabole des invités au festin dans le ministère de Jésus. — ID., *Études sur les Évangiles synoptiques*, II, 1985, 667-704 (note additionnelle, 704-705). Esp. 671-675; 675-691; 691-704.

1978b  *Le message des béatitudes* (Cahiers Évangile, 24). Paris: Cerf, 1978, 65 p. Esp. 38-58: "Les Béatitudes selon saint Matthieu".
       *El mensaje de las bienaventuranzas* (Cuadernos Bíblicos, 24). Estella: Verbo Divino, 1978, 64 p.; ²1980.
           F. PASTOR, *EstE* 55 (1980) 138.
       *Il messaggio delle Beatitudini* (Bibbia oggi, 10). Torino: Gribaudi, 1979, 60 p.

1978c  Jésus annonce la bonne nouvelle aux pauvres. — CANFORA, G. (ed.), *Evangelizare pauperibus* (Atti della XXIV Settimana Biblica, 1976), Brescia: Paideia, 1978, 127-189. Esp. 164-171: "La béatitude des pauvres (*Mt.* 5,3; *Lc.* 6,20)"; 171-183: "La réponse de Jésus aux envoyés de Jean (*Mt.* 11,2-6; *Lc.* 7,18-23)"; = ID., *Études sur les Évangiles synoptiques*, I, 1985, 23-85 (note additionnelle, 85). Esp. 60-67; 67-79.
       A benaventurança dos pobres. — *Liturgia e Vida* (Rio de Janeiro) 25 (1978) 33-40.

1979   *Distruzione del tempio e fine del mondo. Studi sul discorso di Marco 13*, trans. C. Danna (La parola di Dio, 20). Roma: Paoline, 1979, 279 p. → 1968f, 1970b, 1977b-c

1980a  *Gesù e la famiglia nei Vangeli* (Quaderni de "La nostra Assemblea"). Roma: Comunità di S. Egidio, 1980, 20 p.
       Jésus et la famille dans les Évangiles. — *ComLtg* 62 (1980) 477-491. Esp. 485 [10,37]; 485-486 [8,19-22]. [NTA 25, 818]; = ID., *Études sur les Évangiles synoptiques*, I, 1985, 131-145 (note additionnelle, 145). Esp. 139-140.

1980b  Actualiteit van de parabelmethode van Jezus. — BULCKENS, J. (ed.), *Parabels meerstemmig*, 1980, 151-175. → 1977a
       El mètode parabòlic de Jesús avui. — *QüestVidaCr* 104 (1980) 7-24.
       La méthode parabolique de Jésus aujourd'hui. — ID., *Études sur les Évangiles synoptiques*, I, 1985, 197-212.

1981   La prière et son efficacité dans l'évangile de Luc. — *RSR* 69 (1981) 45-56. Esp. 50-54: "Luc et Matthieu" [7,7-11]. [NTA 25, 885]; = ID., *Études sur les Évangiles synoptiques*, II, 1985, 1055-1065. Esp. 1060-1064.
       The Efficacy of Prayer in Luke's Gospel. — *TDig* 30 (1982) 25-26.

1982   La transmission des paroles de Jésus sur la lampe et la mesure dans Marc 4,21-25 et dans la tradition Q. — DELOBEL, J. (ed.), *Logia*, 1982, 201-236. Esp. 209-226: "Comparaison de la version de Marc avec la version Q"; 226-235: "Les logia interprétés par leur contexte Q"; = ID., *Études sur les Évangiles synoptiques*, I, 1985, 259-294. Esp. 267-284; 284-293. → 1969c

1983a  *O Sermâo da montanha. Introduçâo, interpretaçâo e estruttura* (Sermâo da montanha, 1). São Paulo: Paulinas, 1983, 31 p.; vol. 2-7, 1983-84.

1983b  Pregando, non siate come i pagani (Mt 6,7-8). — *Silenzio e Parola. Miscellanea M. Pellegrino*, Torino-Leumann: Elle Di Ci, 1983, 55-63.
       "En priant ne ressemblez pas aux païens" (Mt 6,7-8). — ID., *Études sur les Évangiles synoptiques*, II, 1985, 862-868.

1983c Vivere nell'attesa del Signore (Lc 12,35-48). — *ParSpirV* 8 (1983) 146-158. Esp. 153-155 [Q 12,41-46].

1984a Dieu ou Mammon (Mt 6,24; Lc 16,13). — *CrnStor* 5 (1984) 441-461. Esp. 444-449: "La sentence comme unité littéraire autonome"; 449-456: "La sentence comme unité littéraire homogène"; 456-461: "La sentence dans la prédication de Jésus". [NTA 29, 933]; = ID., *Études sur les Évangiles synoptiques*, II, 1985, 551-567 (note additionnelle, 567). Esp. 553-558; 558-563; 563-567.

1984b Évangiles et tradition apostolique. À propos d'un ouvrage de Pierre Grelot. — *RTL* 15 (1984) 462-467. [NTA 29, 884] → Grelot 1984a

1984c Gesù Messia dei poveri, Messia povero. — ID. – HAMMAN, A.G. – MICCOLI, G., *Seguire Gesù povero* (Parola e Storia), Magnano: Communità di Bose, 1984, 7-87. Esp. 24-26 [11,5]; 27-31 [5,3].
Jésus Messie des pauvres, Messie pauvre. — ID., *Études sur les Évangiles synoptiques*, I, 1985, 86-130 (note additionnelle, 130). Esp. 95-97; 97-99.
*Jesus, messias dos pobres, messias pobre* (Col. A Palavra viva). São Paulo: Paulinas, 1985, 93 p.

1985a *Études sur les Évangiles synoptiques*. Présentées par F. Neirynck (BETL, 70A-B). Leuven: University Press / Peeters, 1985, 2 vols., XXI-526 and IX-527-1210 p.
I → 1967d.f-g, 1968b.f, 1970b, 1977b-c, 1978c, 1980a-b, 1982, 1984c
II → 1956, 1963, 1964a-b, 1966a-b.d, 1967a.e.h, 1968c.e.g, 1969c-d.f, 1971c, 1972b, 1975a-b, 1978a, 1981, 1983b, 1984a, 1985b

1985b Le langage symbolique des directives éthiques de Jésus dans le Sermon sur la montagne. — *Ibid.*, II, 763-778. Esp. 772-773 [6,1-6.16-18]; 773-775 [5,39]; 775-778 [5,21-22]; = PINCKAERS, S. – PINTO DE OLIVEIRA, C.J. (eds.), *Universalité*, 1986, 74-89. Esp. 83-84; 85-87; 87-89.

1985c *Les trois apocalypses synoptiques. Marc 13; Matthieu 24–25; Luc 21* (LD, 121). Paris: Cerf, 1985, 149 p. Esp. 49-97: "Le discours sur la parousie du Fils de l'homme. Matthieu 24–25".
H. GIESEN, *SNTU* 12 (1987) 219-221; X. JACQUES, *NRT* 108 (1986) 752-753; J. LAMBRECHT, *TLZ* 112 (1987) 188-189; R. PESCH, *TRev* 82 (1986) 199; R.D. WITHERUP, *CBQ* 48 (1986) 741-743.
*Le tre apocalissi sinottiche. Marco 13; Matteo 24–25; Luca 21*, trans. R. Tufariello (Studi biblici, 14). Bologna: Dehoniane, 1987, 159 p.

1988a Beatitudine / Beatitudini. — ROSSANO, P. – RAVASI, G. – GIRLANDA, A. (eds.), *Nuovo Dizionario di Teologia biblica*, Cinisello Balsamo: Paoline, 1988, 155-161.

1988b "Laisse là ton offrande, devant l'autel..." (Mt 5,23-24). — FARNEDI, G. (ed.), *Traditio et progressio. Studi liturgici in onore del Prof. Adrien Nocent, OSB* (Studia Anselmiana, 95. Analecta liturgica, 12), Roma: Pontificio Ateneo S. Anselmo, 1988, 205-214.

**DUPRAZ, Louis**

1966 *De l'association de Tibère au principat à la naissance du Christ. Trois études* (Studia Friburgensia, NS 43). Freiburg/Schw: Éd. universitaires, 1966, x-267 p. Esp. 100-142: "L'année de la naissance du Christ" [2].

**DUPREZ, Antoine**

1973a Le programme de Jésus, selon Matthieu. Mt 4,12-23. — *AssSeign* II/34 (1973) 9-18. [NTA 18, 852]

1973b Le jugement dernier. Mt 25,31-46. — *AssSeign* II/65 (1973) 17-28. [NTA 18, 861]

1974a Les récits évangéliques de miracles. — *LumièreV* 119 (1974) 49-69. Esp. 61-62 [12,9-14]. [NTA 19, 923]

1974b → Charpentier 1974a

**DUPUY, Bernard** → Charpentier 1974a

**DUQUOC, Christian**

1961 La tentation du Christ. — *LumièreV* 53 (1961) 21-41. Esp. 26-32 [4,1-11]. [NTA 6, 450]

1968   *Christologie. Essai dogmatique*. I. *L'homme Jésus* (Cogtatio fidei, 29). Paris: Cerf, 1968, 338 p. Esp. 23-41: "Les enfances du Christ"; 43-126: "Le temps de la prédication"; 131-170: "Le Christ prophète"; 188-208: "Jésus, Fils de l'homme".
Los evangelios de la infancia: ¿descripción histórica o expresión de fe? — *SalT* 61 (1973) 943-949.

1987   Une parabole de l'agir de Dieu. — *LumièreV* 183 (1987) 85-96. → Ansaldi 1987

**DURAND, Alfred**
1924[R]  & HUBY, J., *Vangelo secondo san Matteo* [French, 1924, ²¹1929], trans. U. Massi ("Verbum Salutis"). Roma: Editrice Studium, 1955, XIX-593 p.
G.G. GAMBA, *Sal* 18 (1956) 193; E. RAVAROTTO, *Ant* 32 (1957) 270-271.
*The Word of Salvation. Translation and Explanation of the Gospel according to St. Matthew and the Gospel according to St. Mark*, trans. J.J. Heenan. Milwaukee, WI: Bruce, 1957, XVII-936 p.
E. MAY, *TS* 18 (1957) 606-607; G.S. SLOYAN, *CBQ* 20 (1958) 123; J. VOLCKAERT, *The Clergy Monthly* (Ranchi, India) 21 (1957) 387.
*Evangelio según San Mateo*, trans. D. Servando Montaña (Verbum Salutis). Madrid: Paulinas, 1963, XV-529 p. [NTA 9, p. 142]
S. DEL PÁRAMO, *SalT* 52 (1964) 379; O. GARCÍA DE LA FUENTE, *CiudDios* 177 (1964) 147.

**DURKEN, Daniel**
1990   Mountains and Matthew. — *BiTod* 28 (1990) 304-307. [NTA 35, 125]

**DURLAND, William Reginald**
1977   *No King but Jesus: Matthew 25 and the Biblical Basis of Christian Non-Violent Assistance*. Diss. Union Graduate School, Cleveland, OH, 1977, 447 p. — *DissAbstr* 39 (1978-79) 6828-6829.

**DU ROY, Jean-Baptiste**
1959   Le dernier repas de Jésus. [26,26-29] — *BibVieChrét* 26 (1959) 44-52. [NTA 4, 92]

**DURRWELL, François-Xavier**
1950   *La résurrection de Jésus. Mystère de salut. Étude Biblique*. Paris – Le Puy: Mappus, 1950, 397 p.; ²⁻³1954, 431 p.; ⁵1960; ⁶1961. Esp. 96-97 [26,29]; 186-187.303-304 [26,64]; 187-188 [21,33-44]; 353-354 [12,39]; 361-362 [3,11-12]; Paris: Cerf, ¹⁰1976.
*Die Auferstehung Jesu als Heilsmysterium. Eine bibeltheologische Untersuchung*, trans. E. Kretz. Salzburg: Müller, 1958, 440 p.
*The Resurrection. A Biblical Study*, trans. R. Sheed. New York: Sheed and Ward, 1960, XXVI-371 p. Esp. 75-76; 154-157; 311-313.
*La resurrección de Jesús misterio de salvación*, trans. M. Rodriguez del Palacio. Barcelona: Herder, 1962, 392 p.; ⁴1979.
*La risurrezione di Gesù mistero di salvezza. Teologia biblica della risurrezione*, trans. V. Ricci (Biblioteca di cultura religiosa, 2). Roma: Paoline, 1962, 524 p.; ³1969, 543 p.; ⁷1993.
Trans. Japanese 1975.

**DURSTON, Christopher**
1988   Historical Interpretations of the Sermon on the Mount. — *ScriptB* 18 (1988) 42-49. [NTA 33, 598]

**DUSSAUT, Louis**
1972   *L'Eucharistie. Pâques de toute la vie. Diachronie symbolique de l'Eucharistie* (LD, 74). Paris: Cerf, 1972, 329 p. Esp. 59-60 [11,25-30]; 92-96; 131-133; 236-238.

**DUTHEIL, Michel**
1956   Le baptême de Jésus. (Éléments d'interprétation). — *SBF/LA* 6 (1955-56) 85-124. Esp. 109-112 [3,13-17].

1961   *Le baptême de Jésus dans le Jourdain d'après les évangiles synoptiques*. Diss. Strasbourg, 1961.

**DUTHOIT, R.**

1960  Une nouvelle synopse des Évangiles. — *NRT* 82 (1960) 247-268. Esp. 259-268: "Solution du problème synoptique". [NTA 5, 287r] → de Solages 1959
A New Approach to the Synoptic Problem. — *TDig* 9 (1961) 14.

**DU TOIT, Andries B.**

1965  *Der Aspekt der Freude im urchristlichen Abendmahl.* Winterthur: Keller, 1965, IX-188 p. Esp. 76-102 [26,26-29]. — Diss. Basel, 1959 (B. Reicke).

1966  The Nature of the Witness of the Church in the World according to Mt. 5:13-16. — VAN ZYL, A.H. (ed.), *Biblical Essays 1966*, Potchefstroom: Herald Beperk, 1966, 200-218.

1967  The Self-Revelation of Jesus in Matthew 5–7. — *Neotestamentica* 1 (1967) 66-72. [NTA 18, 101]

1977  Analysis of the Structure of Mt 4:23–5:48. — *Neotestamentica* 11 (1977) 32-47 (addendum, 8-11).

1986  Enkele gedachtes oor Matteus se gebruikmaking van die Ou Testament in Matteus 2:15. — *HervTS* 42 (1986) 386-396. → Prinsloo 1986

1994  Liggaamstaal in gebed: 'n Nuwe-Testamentiese perspektief (Bodily posture in prayer: a New Testament perspective). — *Skrif en Kerk* (Pretoria) 15 (1994) 264-279. Esp. 268-269.272 [6,5-6]. [NTA 39, 1691]

**DUVEKOT, Willem S.**

1972  *Heeft Jezus zichzelf voor de Messias gehouden? Een exegetisch-historisch onderzoek, in het bijzonder met het oog op het ontkennend antwoord op deze vraag door Bultmann en zijn leerlingen* (Van Gorcum's Theologische Bibliotheek, 45). Assen: Van Gorcum, 1972, XI-352 p. Esp. 96-98 [16,13-23]; 105-116 [16,17-19]; 215-218 [11,27].

s.d.  *Kunnen wij Jezus kennen?* (Bijbel en Gemeente, 14). Kampen: Kok, [s.d.], 176 p. Esp. 149-153 [6,9-13]; 125-128 [anti-semitism].

**DVORÁČEK, J.A.**

1968  Nebojti se! Ev. podle Matouše 10,27-31. — *Theologická příloha – Křest'anské revue* (Praha) 35 (1968) 73-76.
Fürchtet euch nicht. Das Evangelium nach Mt 10,27-31. — *Deutsches Pfarrerblatt* (Essen) 69 (1969) 482-488.

**DYER, Charles H.**

1981  Do the Synoptics Depend on Each Other? — *BS* 138 (1981) 230-245. [NTA 26, 76]

**DYSON, Robert A.** → Leeming 1956

# E

**EAGER, B.**

1960 The Lord Is with You. [28,18-20] — *Scripture* 12 (1960) 48-54. [NTA 5, 403]

**EAKIN, Frank E. Jr.**

1972 Spiritual Obduracy and Parable Purpose. — EFIRD, J.M. (ed.), *The Use of the Old Testament in the New*. FS W.F. Stinespring, 1972, 87-109. Esp. 99-109 [13,10-15].

**EARLE, Ralph**

1964 & BLANEY, H.J.S. – CARTER, C.W., *Matthew–Mark–Luke–John–Acts* (Wesleyan Bible Commentary, 4). Grand Rapids, MI: Eerdmans, 1964, VII-749 p. [NTA 9, p. 271]

1980 *Word Meanings in the New Testament*. 2 vols., I: *Matthew, Mark and Luke*. Grand Rapids, MI: Baker, 1980, 285 p. [NTA 25, p. 301]

1985 Matthew. — *The New International Version Study Bible*, Grand Rapids, MI: Zondervan, 1985, 1439-1489.

**EASTWELL, R.**

1956 Except for Adultery? A Comment on the Exegesis of Mt 5,32 and 19,9. — *Bellarmine Commentary* (London) 1 (1956) 6-10.

**EBELING, Gerhard**

1961 Der Grund christlicher Theologie. Zum Aufsatz Ernst Käsemanns über "Die Anfänge christlicher Theologie". — *ZTK* 58 (1961) 227-244. [NTA 6, 669] → Käsemann 1960

1973* & JÜNGEL, E. – SCHUNACK, G. (eds.), *Festschrift für Ernst Fuchs*. Tübingen: Mohr, 1973, XV-361 p. → Biser, Linnemann, Möller

**EBERSOHN, Michael**

1993 *Das Nächstenliebegebot in der synoptischen Tradition* (Marburger theologische Studien, 37). Marburg: Elwert, 1993, 280 p. Esp. 182-211: "Das Nächstenliebegebot bei Matthäus" [5,43-47; 19,16-22; 22,34-40]. — Diss. Marburg, 1992 (D. Lührmann).

**EBERTZ, Michael N.**

1987 *Das Charisma des Gekreuzigten. Zur Soziologie der Jesusbewegung* (WUNT, 45). Tübingen: Mohr, 1987, XI-308 p. Esp. 126-151; 165-195; 225-253: "Die radikaltheokratische Stellungnahme des Propheten Jesu". — Diss. Konstanz, 1985 (G. Simmel).

**ECKERT, Willehad Paul**

1967* et al. (eds.), *Antijudaismus im Neuen Testament? Exegetische und systematische Beiträge* (Abhandlungen zum christlich-jüdischen Dialog, 2). München: Kaiser, 1967, 214 p. → Gnilka, Harder, Kümmel, Mussner, Schelkle 1966d

**EDDY, G.T.**

1990 The Resurrection of Jesus. A Consideration of Professor Cranfield's Argument. — *ExpT* 101 (1989-90) 327-329. [NTA 35, 111] → Cranfield 1990

**EDER, Gottfried**

1956 *Der göttliche Wundertäter. Ein exegetischer und religionswissenschaftlicher Versuch*. Passau: Privately published, 1956, 231 p. Esp. 43-46: "Matthäus".

**EDGAR, S.L.**

1962 Respect for Context in Quotations from the Old Testament. — *NTS* 9 (1962-63) 55-62. Esp. 57-58 [1,23; 2,15.18; 4,15-16; 27,9]; 60 [12,1-8]. [NTA 7, 464] → Mead 1964

**EDGAR, Thomas Randall**

1969 *An Analysis of the Synoptic Problem.* Diss. Theol. Sem., Dallas, TX, 1969.

**EDLUND, Conny**

1952 *Das Auge der Einfalt. Eine Untersuchung zu Matth. 6,22-23 und Luk. 11,34-35* (Acta Seminarii Neotestamentici Upsaliensis, 19). Lund: Gleerup; København: Munksgaard, 1952, 143 p. Esp. 103-122: "Exegese des Logions vom Auge" [6,22-23; Q 11,34-35]. — Diss. Uppsala, 1952 (A. Fridrichsen).
  CC 105/1 (1954) 327; *LumièreV* 7 (1952) 24; P. BENOIT, *RB* 60 (1953) 603-605; P. BONNARD, *RTP* 4 (1954) 147-148; J. DANIÉLOU, *RSR* 43 (1955) 567-569; J. DELORME, *AmiCler* 66 (1956) 84; J. HEMPEL, *ZAW* 66 (1954) 120; L. JAMISON, *JBL* 72 (1953) 204-205; S.L. JOHNSON, Jr., *BS* 110 (1953) 277; P.H. MENOUD, *ETR* 27 (1952) 73; E. SCHWEIZER, *TLZ* 78 (1953) 25; C. SPICQ, *RSPT* 37 (1953) 167-168; J. VAN DER PLOEG, *Studia catholica* (Nijmegen) 30 (1955) 153-154; J. WENNEMER, *Scholastik* 29 (1954) 612-613.

**EDMONDS, Peter**

1980 The Lucan Our Father: A Summary of Luke's Teaching on Prayer? — *ExpT* 91 (1979-80) 140-143. [NTA 24, 823]

**EDSMAN, Carl-Martin**

1964 *Die weise Jungfer* [25,1-13] (Horae Soederblomianae, 6). Lund: Gleerup, 1964, 82 p.

**EDWARDS, David L.**

1992 *The Real Jesus.* London: HarperCollins, 1992. Esp. 33-107: "Eight gospels" (64-70: "The gospel in Q").

**EDWARDS, David Darnell**

1992 *Jesus and the Temple. A Historico-Theological Study of Temple Motifs in the Ministry of Jesus.* Diss. Southwestern Baptist Theol. Sem., Fort Worth, TX, 1992, 287 p. — *DissAbstr* 53 (1992-93) 1959.

**EDWARDS, George R.**

1972 *Jesus and the Politics of Violence.* New York – London: Harper & Row, 1972, VI-186 p. Esp. 17-43: "Jesus and the Zealots: a Matthean approach".

**EDWARDS, James R.**

1987 The Use of προσέρχεσθαι in the Gospel of Matthew. — *JBL* 106 (1987) 65-74. Esp. 67-72 [Mt]; 73-74 [Jesus as subject]. [NTA 31, 1050]

**EDWARDS, Richard Alan**

1969 The Eschatological Correlative as a *Gattung* in the New Testament. — *ZNW* 60 (1969) 9-20. Esp. 9-13 [Q]; 12-13 [13,40-41]; 16-17 [24,27.37]; 17-18 [12,40]; 18-19 [24,39-40]; 19-20 [10,32]. [NTA 14, 464]

1971a *The Sign of Jonah in the Theology of the Evangelists and Q* (Studies in Biblical Theology, II/18). London: SCM, 1971, XI-122 p. Esp. 1-24: "A history of criticism"; 25-70: "Redaction criticism of the gospels and Q" [30-34: Mt; 41-70: Q]; 71-107: "The history of the tradition of the sign of Jonah". [NTA 17, p. 161] — Diss. Univ. of Chicago, 1968. → D. Schmidt 1977
  P.D. MEYER, *JBL* 91 (1972) 557-558; H. WANSBROUGH, *NBlackfr* 52 (1971) 524-525.

1971b An Approach to a Theology of Q. — *JRel* 51 (1971) 247-269. Esp. 250-252: "Eschatology"; 253-257: "Prophecy"; 257-266: "Wisdom christology". [NTA 16, 518]

1975 *A Concordance to Q* (SBL Sources for Biblical Study, 7). Missoula, MT: SBL/Scholars, 1975, 186 p. [NTA 20, p. 106]

E. BEST, *ScotJT* 31 (1978) 295; M.-É. BOISMARD, *RB* 83 (1976) 633-634; M. BOUTTIER, *ETR* 51 (1976) 234; C.B. CRAWFORD, *JAAR* 47 (1979) 307-308; D.L. JONES, *CBQ* 39 (1977) 147-148; E. KRENTZ, *CurrTMiss* 3 (1976) 188; X. LÉON-DUFOUR, *RSR* 64 (1976) 428; D. MARGUERAT, *RTP* 30 (1980) 195-196; I.A. MOIR, *JTS* 27 (1976) 452-453; W. SCHENK, *TLZ* 102 (1977) 586-587; R. SCHNACKENBURG, *BZ* 20 (1976) 315.

1976a    *A Theology of Q. Eschatology, Prophecy, and Wisdom.* Philadelphia, PA: Fortress, 1976, XIII-173 p. Esp. 32-43: "Eschatology"; 44-57: "Prophecy in Q"; 58-79: Wisdom in Q" [Q 6,20-23; 7,18-23; 10,13-15.23-24; 11,39-52; 12,42-44; 13,34-35; 17,1-2]; 80-145: "The interaction of themes in Q". [NTA 20, p. 359]
     M. BARRIOS, *TVida* 21 (1980) 96-97; M.-É. BOISMARD, *RB* 85 (1978) 631; M. BOUTTIER, *ETR* 54 (1979) 314-315; S. BROWN, *JBL* 96 (1977) 599-601; J.L. CLARK, *LuthQ* 28 (1976) 386-387; H.B. GREEN, *JTS* 28 (1977) 151-153; J.D. KINGSBURY, *Interpr* 31 (1977) 318.320; J. KODELL, *TS* 37 (1976) 525; H. MYRE, *SE* 28 (1976) 340-341; W. NEIL, *ExpT* 88 (1976-77) 29; L. SABOURIN, *BTB* 6 (1976) 295-298; D.M. SMITH, *JAAR* 45 (1977) 372.374; L.J. TOPEL, *CBQ* 39 (1977) 148-150; E.S. WEHRLI, *CurrTMiss* 4 (1977) 52.

1976b    Christian Prophecy and the Q Tradition. — *SBL 1976 Seminar Papers*, 119-126. Esp. 123-126.

1982    Matthew's Use of Q in Chapter Eleven. — DELOBEL, J. (ed.), *Logia*, 1982, 257-275. Esp. 257-263: "Preliminary comments and starting point"; 263-269 [11,2-19]; 269-273 [11,21-27].

1985a    *Matthew's Story of Jesus.* Philadelphia, PA: Fortress, 1985, 95 p. Esp. 11-18 [1,1-4,22]; 19-25 [4,23-7,29]; 26-36 [8,1-11,1]; 37-67 [11,2-18,35]; 68-84 [19,1-25,46]; 85-95 [26-28]. [NTA 29, p. 323] → M.A. Powell 1992d
     K.A. BARTA, *BTB* 19 (1989) 109-110; H.J.B. COMBRINK, *Neotestamentica* 20 (1986) 75; A.T. KENEALY, *CurrTMiss* 16 (1989) 386-387; S.D. MOORE, *Forum* 3'3 (1987) 43-49.

1985b    Uncertain Faith: Matthew's Portrait of the Disciples. — SEGOVIA, F.F. (ed.), *Discipleship in the New Testament*, Philadelphia, PA: Fortress, 1985, 47-61.

1989    Reading Matthew: The Gospel as Narrative. — *Listening* 24 (1989) 251-261. Esp. 253-255 [1,18-25]; 255-258 [disciples]; 258-260 [γάρ]. [NTA 34, 597]

1990    Narrative Implications of *Gar* in Matthew. — *CBQ* 52 (1990) 636-655. Esp. 636-638: "*Gar* in the synoptics"; 638-641: "Matthew's use of *gar*" [classification; organized by speaker]; 641-651: "Narrative significance" [in framework; in sayings]; 652-655: "List of *gars* in Matthew". [NTA 35, 615]

1992    Characterization of the Disciples as a Feature of Matthew's Narrative. — VAN SEGBROECK, F., et al. (eds.), *The Four Gospels 1992.* FS F. Neirynck, 1992, II, 1305-1323. Esp. 1306-1308: "Implied reader"; 1308-1310: "Character"; 1310-1312: "Character-shaping incidents"; 1313-1317 [4,18-22]; 1317-1319 [8,18-27]; 1319-1322 [5-7]; 1322-1323 [8,1-15].

**EFFERIN, H.**

1993    The Sabbath Controversy Based on Matthew 12:1-8. — *Stulos Theological Journal* (Bandung) 1 (1993) 43-48. [NTA 38, 1367]

**EFIRD, James M.**

1972*    (ed.), *The Use of the Old Testament in the New and Other Essays. Studies in Honor of William Franklin Stinespring.* Durham, NC: Duke University Press, 1972, XV-332 p.
     → W.D. Davies, Eakin, D.M. Smith

1980    *The New Testament Writings. History, Literature and Interpretation.* Atlanta, GA: Knox, 1980, XII-223 p.

1981    Matthew 16:21-27. — *Interpr* 35 (1981) 284-289.

**EGAN, George A.**

1983    *An Analysis of the Biblical Quotations of Ephrem in "An Exposition of the Gospel" (Armenian Version)* (CSCO, 443). Leuven: Peeters, 1983, XII-55 p. Esp. 6-7; 37; 38-46.

**EGAWA, Ken**

1991    The Question about Paying Tribute (Mt 22,15-22). [Japanese] — *Nanzan Journal of Theological Studies* 14 (1991) 83-124.

1992a   The Question about the Resurrection (Mt 22,23-33). [Japanese] – *Nanzan Journal of Theological Studies* 15 (1992) 1-26.

1992b   The Great Commandment (Mt 22,34-40). [Japanese] — WAFS, K.-K. (ed.), *Shu no subete ni yori hito wa ikuru. Festschrift für K.H. Walkenhorst zum 65. Geburtstag*, Tokyo: Lithon, 1992, 257-280.

1994    *Incredulity and Judgment. Disputation About the Authority of Jesus in Mt 21,23–22,14.* Roma: Pont. Univ. Greg., 1994, 542 p. Esp. 17-140: "Disposition of the text of Mt 21,23–22,14 respecting Mt 21,23–22,46 in the wider context of Mt 19–25"; 142-176 [21,23-27]; 177-215 [21,28-32]. 216-268 [21,33-46]; 269-321 [22,1-14]; 323-360 [21,23-27]; 361-459 [21,28–22,14]. — Diss. Pont. Univ. Greg., Roma, 1993 (F. Lentzen-Deis).

**EGELKRAUT, Helmuth L.**

1976    *Jesus' Mission to Jerusalem: A Redaction Critical Study of the Travel Narrative in the Gospel of Luke, Lk 9:51–19:48* (EHS, XXIII/80). Frankfurt/M–Bern: Lang, 1976, X-257 p. Esp. 134-196: "The double tradition in the TN". — Diss. Princeton Theol. Sem., Princeton, NJ, 1975 (W.R. Murdock).

**EGG, Gottfried**

1968    *Adolf Schlatters kritische Position gezeigt an seiner Matthäusinterpretation* (Arbeiten zur Theologie, II/14). Stuttgart: Calwer, 1968, 264 p. Esp. 135-238. — Diss. Erlangen-Nürnberg, 1966 (G. Friedrich).

**EGGER, Wilhelm**

1969    Die Verborgenheit Jesu in Mk 3,7-12. — *Bib* 50 (1969) 466-490. Esp. 474-476: "Vergleich mit Mt" [4,25; 12,15-21]. [NTA 14, 868]

1977    *Einer ist euer Lehrer. Ein Arbeitsheft zum Matthäusevangelium* (Gespräche zur Bibel, 2). Klosterneuburg: Österreichisches Katholisches Bibelwerk, 1977, 32 p. [NTA 23, p. 92]
        *Incontri biblici sul vangelo di Matteo. Sussidio popolare per gruppi biblici.* Bologna, 1977, 47 p.
        Trans. Hungarian 1980.
                G.G. GAMBA, *Sal* 40 (1978) 689.

1978a   *Kleine Bibelkunde zum Neuen Testament.* Innsbruck: Tyrolia, 1978, 159 p.; ²1981; ³1984; ⁴1987. Esp. 41-45.
        *Primo approccio al Nuovo Testamento*, trans. F. Frezza (Collana 'Biblica'). Torino: Marietti, 1980, 128 p.
        Trans. Hungarian 1981; Polish 1991.

1978b   Faktoren der Textkonstitution in der Bergpredigt. — *Laur* 19 (1978) 177-198. Esp. 178-183: "Einleitung der Bergpredigt in Absätze"; 183-186: "Verknüpfung der Absätze"; 186-198: "Einheit der Bergpredigt". [NTA 23, 92]

1981    Überschriften in Bibelausgaben als Lesehilfe. Überlegungen zur Überschriftenredaktion anhand der Bergpredigt. — *Konferenzblatt für Theologie und Seelsorge* (Brixen) 92 (1981) 93-102.
        I titoli delle pericopi bibliche come chiave di lettura. Considerazioni sulla redazione di titoli per il discorso della montagna. — *RivBib* 29 (1981) 33-43. [NTA 26, 88]

1984    Handlungsorientierte Auslegung der Antithesen Mt 5,21-48. — KERTELGE, K. (ed.), *Ethik im Neuen Testament*, 1984, 119-144.

1987    *Methodenlehre zum Neuen Testament. Einführung in linguistische und historisch-kritische Methoden.* Freiburg: Herder, 1987, 234 p. Esp. 87-89 [18,15-17; 28,18-20]; ²1990.
        *Metodologia del Nuovo Testamento. Introduzione allo studio scientifico del Nuovo Testamento*, trans. G. Forza (Studi biblici, 16). Bologna: Dehoniane, 1989, 256 p.; ²1991.

*Lecturas del Nuevo Testamento. Metodología lingüística histórico-crítica*, trans. C. Ruiz Garrido (Estudios bíblicos). Estella: Verbo Divino, 1990, 283 p.

**EGIDO LÓPEZ, Teófanes**

1973  San José y el Evangelio de la Infancia. XI Semana de Estudios Josefinos (11-14 septiembre de 1973). — *Teologia Espiritual* (Valencia) 17 (1973) 405-407; = *EstAgust* 8 (1973) 563-565; = *EstE* 49 (1974) 117-119; = *RevistEspTeol* 34 (1974) 107-109.
El evangelio de la infancia en la XI Semana de Estudios Josefinos (Zaragoza, 11-14 septiembre de 1973). — *Marianum* 36 (1974) 106-107.

1975  San José en los dos primeros capítulos de Mateo y Lucas. — *EstJos* 29 (1975) 231-236; = *Marianum* 37 (1975) 537-539; = *EstE* 51 (1976) 129-131.
San José en los primeros capítulos de Mateo y Lucas (XII Semana ce Estudios Josefinos Madrid, 30 de septiembre al 3 de octubre de 1975). — *EphMar* 26 (1976) 356-358.

**EHLER, Bernhard**

1986  *Die Herrschaft des Gekreuzigten. Ernst Käsemanns Frage nach der Mitte der Schrift* (BZNW, 46). Berlin: de Gruyter, 1986, XV-365 p. Esp. 242-254 [genre; kingdom]. — Diss. Augsburg, 1984 (H. Leroy).

**EHRHARDT, Arnold A.T.**

1952  Lass die Toten ihre Toten begraben. — *StudTheol* 6 (1952) 128-164.

1953  Greek Proverbs in the Gospel. — *HTR* 46 (1953) 59-77. Esp. 64-66 [11,17]; 66-72 [24,28]; = ID., *The Framework of the New Testament Stories*, Manchester: University Press, 1964, 44-63. Esp. 51-53; 53-58.

1964a  The Disciples of Emmaus. — *NTS* 10 (1963-64) 182-201. Esp. 189-191 [ἵνα πληρωθῇ]; 191-192 [11,11-12]. [NTA 8, 989]

1964b  Judaeo-Christians in Egypt, the Epistula Apostolorum and the Gospel of the Hebrews. — *Studia Evangelica* 3 (1964) 360-382. Esp. 375-377 [18,17].

**EHRMAN, Bart D.**

1986  *Didymus the Blind and the Text of the Gospels* (The New Testament in the Greek Fathers, 1). Atlanta, GA: Scholars, 1986, XII-288 p. Esp. 38-87: "Text and apparatus: Gospel of Matthew"; 190-194: "Didymus's affinities in Matthew"; 268-270 [N²⁶]; 274 [UBS³]. — Diss. Princeton Theol. Sem., Princeton, NJ, 1985 (B.M. Metzger).

1993  *The Orthodox Corruption of Scripture. The Effect of Early Christological Controversies on the Text of the New Testament.* New York – Oxford: University Press, 1993, XIV-314 p. Esp. 54-59.75-76.137-139 [1,16.18.25]; 91-92 [24,36]; 135-136 [12,30]; 141-142 [3,16]; 158-159 [28,19]; 159-160 [16,20]; 194-195 [27,49]; 196-197 [17,12-13].

**EICHHOLZ, Georg**

1963  *Einführung in die Gleichnisse* (Biblische Studien, 37). Neukirchen-Vluyn: Neukirchener, 1963, 110 p. Esp. 54-77 [22,1-14/Q 14,16-24].

1964  Verkündigung und Tradition. — *EvT* 24 (1964) 565-586. Esp. 578-580; = ID., *Tradition und Interpretation*, 1965, 11-34. Esp. 24-26.

1965a  *Auslegung der Bergpredigt* (Biblische Studien, 46). Neukirchen-Vluyn: Neukirchener, 1965, 165 p.; ²1970; ³1975; ⁴1978; ⁵1982.
NVet 45 (1970) 151; G. SCHIWY, *TheolPhil* 43 (1968) 624.

1965b  *Tradition und Interpretation. Studien zum Neuen Testament und zur Hermeneutik* (Theologische Bücherei, 29). München: Kaiser, 1965, 233 p. → 1964, 1965c

1965c  Die Aufgabe einer Auslegung der Bergpredigt. — *Ibid.*, 35-56. Esp. 39-43: "Die Rahmen von Mt. 5-7"; 43-46: "Tradition und Interpretation"; 46-51: "Die Bergpredigt im Rahmen der Theologie des Matthäus"; 51-56: "Matthäus und Paulus".

1971 *Gleichnisse der Evangelien. Form, Überlieferung, Auslegung.* Neukirchen-Vluyn: Neukirchener, 1971, 239 p. Esp. 85-108 [20,1-16]; 109-125 [13,44-46]; 126-147 [22,1-14]; [2]1975; [3]1979. → Klauck 1972

1984 *Das Rätsel des historischen Jesus und die Gegenwart Jesu Christi,* ed. G. Sauter (Theologische Bücherei, 72). München: Kaiser, 1984, 166 p. Esp. 15-78: "Christus und der Bruder" [10,40-42; 18,23-35; 25,31-46].

**EICHINGER, Matthias**
1969 *Die Verklärung Christi bei Origenes. Die Bedeutung des Menschen Jesus in seiner Christologie* (Wiener Beiträge zur Theologie, 23). Wien: Herder, 1969, 203 p. Esp. 19-21, 163-168. — Diss. Pont. Univ. Greg., Roma, 1968 (A. Orbe).
C. KANNENGIESSER, *RSR* 58 (1970) 616-620.

**EID, Volker** → Hoffmann 1975, Merklein 1994b

**EIGO, Francis A.**
1995 (ed.), *New Perspectives on the Beatitudes* (Proceedings of the Theology Institute of Villanova University, 27). Villanova, PA: University Press, 1995, XI-221 p. [Crosby, d'Angelo, Hellwig, Hinsdale, Muto, Reid]

**EISING, Hermann**
1964 Schriftgebrauch und Schriftverständnis in den Matthäus-Homilien des Johannes Chrysostomus. — *Oriens Christianus* (Wiesbaden) 48 (1964) 84-106.

**EISSFELDT, Otto**
1958 Biblos geneseos. — DELLING, G. (ed.), *Gott und die Götter.* FS E. Fascher, 1958, 31-40; = ID., *Kleine Schriften,* III, ed. R. Sellheim – F. Maas, Tübingen: Mohr, 1966, 458-470.

1970 Πληρῶσαι πᾶσαν δικαιοσύνην in Matthäus 3,15. — *ZNW* 61 (1970) 209-215. [NTA 15, 844]; = ID., *Kleine Schriften,* V, ed. R. Sellheim – F. Maas, Tübingen: Mohr, 1973, 179-184. → Ljungman 1954

**EJDER, Bertil**
1978 Om språket i Herrens bön på svenska i äldre tid. [The Lord's Prayer in Old-Swedish] — *SvenskTeolKvart* 54 (1978) 110-118.

**EKKA, Martin**
1995 *The Ecclesial Perspective of Matthew and Tribal (Oraon) Community Life.* Diss. Ranchi, India, 1995, XI-213 p.

**ELANSKAYA, Alla Ivanova**
1994 *The Literary Coptic Manuscripts in the A.S. Pushkin State Fine Arts Museum in Moscow* (Supplements to Vigiliae Christianae, 18). Leiden: Brill, 1994, VII-529 p. (+ 192 plates). Esp. 421-426 [1,23–3,16]; 427-428 [11,17-19.23-24]; 429-430 [22,30.39-40].

**ELBERT, Paul**
1974 The Perfect Tense in Matthew 16:19 and Three Charismata. — *JEvTS* 17 (1974) 149-155. [NTA 19, 536] → Mantey 1973

**ELDERING-JONCKERS NIEBOER, Ida**
1980 Een vrouw die wint. Matteüs 15:21-28. — *Schrift* 69 (1980) 89-92.

**ELDRIDGE, Lawrence Allen**
1969 *The Gospel Text of Epiphanius of Salamis* (Studies and Documents, 41). Salt Lake City, UT: Univ. of Utah Press, 1969, III-191 p. Esp. 90-114: "The textual character of Epiphanius'

quotations from the gospel of Matthew"; 169-172. — Diss. Princeton Theol. Sem., Princeton, NJ, 1967 (B.M. Metzger).

**ELDRIDGE, V.**

1982 Typology. The Key to Understanding Matthew's Formula Quotations? — *Colloquium* 15 (1982) 43-51. [NTA 27, 904]

1983 Second Thoughts on Matthew's Formula Quotations. [2,23; 13,35; 27,9-10] — *Colloquium* 15 (1983) 45-47. [NTA 28, 86]

**ELKINS, Jorge**

1984 Análisis lingüístico estructural de la parábola del siervo s.n entrañas (Mt 18,21-35). — *CuBíb* 39 (1984-86) 68-77.

**ELLENA, Domenico**

1973 Thematische Analyse der Wachstumsgleichnisse. [13,24-30.33.47-50] — *LingBib* 23-24 (1973) 48-62. [NTA 18, 92]

**ELLICOT, C.J.**

1971 Matthew. — *Ellicott's Bible Commentary in One Volume*, Grand Rapids, MI: Zondervan, 1971, 681-757.

**ELLINGTON, John**

1979 The translation of *humnéo*, "Sing a Hymn" in Mark 14.26 and Matthew 26.30. — *BTrans* 30 (1979) 445-446. [NTA 25, 881]

1987 Where is the Other Side? — *BTrans* 38 (1987) 221-226. Esp. 222-223, 224-226 [4,15; 19,1]. [NTA 32, 55]

**ELLINGWORTH, Paul**

1989 "In secret"? (Matthew 6.4, 6, 18). — *BTrans* 40 (1989) 446-447. [NTA 34, 620]

1993 Understanding and Applying the Bible Today. Two Test Cases. [19,12] — *EpworthR* 20 (1993) 80-90.

**ELLIOTT, James Keith**

1969 The Use of ἕτερος in the New Testament. — *ZNW* 60 (1969) 140-141. [NTA 14, 414]

1971 The Synoptic Problem and the Laws of Tradition: A Cautionary Note. — *ExpT* 82 (1970-71) 148-152. [NTA 15, 829] → E.P. Sanders 1969a

1972 Κηφᾶς. Σίμων Πέτρος. ὁ Πέτρος: An Examination of New Testament Usage. — *NT* 14 (1972) 241-256. Esp. 242-248; 250-251; 252-256 [anarthrous Peter]. [NTA 17, 836]

1974 The Anointing of Jesus. [26,6-13] — *ExpT* 85 (1973-74) 105-107. [NTA 18, 881]

1976* (ed.), *Studies in New Testament Language and Text. Essays in Honour of George D. Kilpatrick on the Occasion of his Sixty-Fifth Birthday* (SupplNT, 44). Leiden: Brill, 1976, X-400 p. → Burrows, Geerlings, B.M. Metzger, Reicke

1977a Jerusalem in Acts and the Gospels. — *NTS* 23 (1976-77) 462-469. Esp. 467-469. [NTA 22, 152]

1977b The Two Forms of the Third Declension Comparative Adjectives in the New Testament. — *NT* 19 (1977) 234-239. Esp. 235-236 [23,19]; 237 [26,53]. [NTA 22, 345]

1978a Textual Variation Involving the Augment in the Greek New Testament. — *ZNW* 69 (1978) 247-252. Esp. 248 [δύναμαι]. [NTA 23, 759]

1978b The Third Edition of the United Bible Societies' Greek New Testament. — *NT* 20 (1978) 242-277. [NTA 24, 28] → K. Aland [GNT 1975]

1979 Mathētēs with a Possessive in the New Testament. — *TZ* 35 (1979) 300-304. Esp. 301-302. [NTA 24, 766]

1980 Textual Criticism, Assimilation and the Synoptic Gospels. — *NTS* 26 (1979-80) 231-242. Esp. 236-237 [μαθητὴς αὐτοῦ]; 238-239 [compound verbs]. [NTA 24, 767]

1981 An Examination of the Twenty-Sixth Edition of Nestle-Aland *Novum Testamentum Graece*. — *JTS* 32 (1981) 19-49. [NTA 25, 791] → K. Aland [Nestle-Aland 1979]

1986 An Examination of the Text and Apparatus of Three Recent Greek Synopses. — *NTS* 32 (1986) 557-582. Esp. 560-568 [Huck-Greeven; Aland]; 568-571 [Orchard]. [NTA 31, 95] → K. Aland [Synopsis 1985], Greeven 1981, Orchard 1983a

1987 *A Survey of Manuscripts Used in Editions of the Greek New Testament* (SupplNT, 57). Leiden: Brill, 1987, XXXVII-280 p. Esp. 221-257: "Huck-Greeven's sundries".

1989a *A Bibliography of Greek New Testament Manuscripts* (SNTS MS, 62). Cambridge: University Press, 1989, XXI-210 p.

1989b L'importance de la critique textuelle pour le problème synoptique. — *RB* 96 (1989) 56-70. Esp. 59 [13,8; 23,38]; 60-62 [19,24]; 66 [24,27.34]. [NTA 34, 97]
The Relevance of Textual Criticism to the Synoptic Problem. — DUNGAN, D.L. (ed.), *The Interrelations of the Gospels*, 1990, 348-359. Esp. 350; 351-352; 356.

1991 Which is the Best Synopsis? — *ExpT* 102 (1990-91) 200-204. Esp. 203-204 [Q-synopsis: Kloppenborg 1988, Neirynck 1988a]. [NTA 35, 1090] → K. Aland [Synopsis 1985], Boismard 1986a, Funk 1985a, Greeven 1981, Orchard 1983a

1992a New Testament Linguistic Usage. — BLACK, D.A. (ed.), *Scribes and Scripture. New Testament Essays in Honor of J. Harold Greenlee*, Winona Lake, IN: Eisenbrauns, 1992, 41-48. Esp. 42 [ἐκεῖνος].

1992b Printed Editions of Greek Synopses and Their Influence on the Synoptic Problem. — VAN SEGBROECK, F., et al. (eds.), *The Four Gospels 1992*. FS F. Neirynck, 1992, I, 337-357. Esp. 339-340: "Types of changes"; 341-344: "Where the parallels occur in only two gospels"; 348-349: "The triple tradition".

1993a El problema de la existencia de tres evangelios sinopticos. ¿Quién copió de quién? — PIÑERO, A. (ed.), *Fuentes del cristianismo*, 1993, 95-115.

1993b Resolving the Synoptic Problem Using the Text of Printed Greek Synopses. — *FilolNT* 6 (1993) 51-58. Esp. 52 [11,9]; 52-53 [11,23]; 54 [21,27]; 54-55 [14,6]; 55 [19,24]; 56 [21,44]; 56-57 [22,32]; 57 [9,6]; 57-58 [16,25]. [NTA 38, 1344]

1994a The Fourth Edition of the United Bible Societies' Greek New Testament. — *TRev* 90 (1994) 9-20. [NTA 39, 35] → K. Aland [GNT 1993]

1994b The Twentyseventh Edition of Nestle-Aland's Novum Testamentum Graece. — *Ibid.*, 19-24. [NTA 39, 37] → K. Aland [Nestle-Aland 1993]

1994c The New Testament in Greek: Two New Editions. — *TLZ* 119 (1994) 493-496. [NTA 39, 36] → K. Aland [GNT 1993, Nestle-Aland 1993]

1995 & MOIR, I., *Manuscripts and the Text of the New Testament. An Introduction for English Readers*. Edinburg: Clark, 1995, X-111 p. Esp. 40-43 [6,13b; 16,2-3; 27,49b]; 54-55 [17,4; 18,14]; 61 [24,36]; 64-68 [1,7-8; 5,44; 8,28; 10,3.25; 11,19; 14,24; 15,39; 20,16.22; 26,68; 27,16-17]; 74 [21,28-32]; 76 [11,19].

1996 A Comparison of Two Recent Greek New Testaments. — *ExpT* 107 (1995-96) 105-106. → K. Aland [GNT 1993, Nestle-Aland 1993]

**ELLIOTT, John H.**

1968 Law and Eschatology. The Antitheses of the "Sermon on the Mount". — *Lutheran World* (Genève) 15 (1968) 16-24. [NTA 12, 867]
Die Antithesen der Bergpredigt. Gesetz und Eschatologie. — *LuthRundschau* 18 (1968) 19-29. [NTA 12, 867]

1992 Matthew 20:1-15: A Parable of Invidious Comparison and Evil Eye Accusation. — *BTB* 22 (1992) 52-65. [NTA 37, 150]

1994   The Evil Eye and the Sermon on the Mount. Contours of a Pervasive Belief in Social
       Scientific Perspective. — *BibInt* 2 (1994) 51-84. Esp. 65-68.74-80 [6,22-23]. [NTA 39, 146]

**ELLIOTT, M.A.**

1992   Israel. — *DJG*, 1992, 356-363. Esp. 358-359.

**ELLIOTT, Neil**

1993   The Silence of the Messiah: The Function of "Messianic Secret" Motifs across the
       Synoptics. — *SBL 1993 Seminar Papers*, 604-622. Esp. 607-610: "Alignment of secrecy motifs";
       610-615: "The silence of the Messiah in Matthew".

**ELLIS, E. Earle**

1955   A Note on Pauline Hermeneutics. — *NTS* 2 (1955-56) 127-133. Esp. 128, 132-133 [Old
       Testament]. → Stendahl 1954

1963   Luke xi.49-51: An Oracle of a Christian Prophet? [23,34-35] — *ExpT* 74 (1962-63) 157-
       158. [NTA 7, 808]

1966   *The Gospel of Luke* (The Century Bible). London: Nelson, 1966, XXI-300 p. Esp. 21-30:
       "The formation of the gospels – the sources of Luke".

1969*  & WILCOX, M. (eds.), *Neotestamentica et Semitica. Studies in Honour of Matthew
       Black*. Edinburgh: Clark, 1969, XXI-297 p. → Baarda, W.D. Davies, Dupont, Stauffer

1971   Midraschartige Züge in den Reden der Apostelgeschichte. — *ZNW* 62 (1971) 94-104.
       Esp. 101-103 [21,33-44]. [NTA 16, 231]
       Midrashic Features in the Speeches of Acts. — ID., *Prophecy and Hermeneutic*, 1978, 198-208. Esp. 205-
       207.

1975a  The Composition of Luke 9 and the Sources of Its Christology. — HAWTHORNE, G.F.
       (ed.), *Current Issues in Biblical and Patristic Interpretation*. FS M.C. Tenney, 1975,
       121-127 [Q influence in Lk 9].

1975b  New Directions in Form Criticism. — STRECKER, G. (ed.), *Jesus Christus in Historie
       und Theologie*. FS H. Conzelmann, 1975, 299-315. Esp. 310-314 [Mk 12,1-12.28-31/Q]; =
       ID., *Prophecy and Hermeneutic*, 1978, 237-253. Esp. 248-252.

1977a  How the New Testament Uses the Old. — MARSHALL, I.H. (ed.), *New Testament
       Interpretation*, 1977, 199-219. Esp. 209-212; = ID., *Prophecy and Hermeneutic*, 1978,
       147-172. Esp. 157-159.

1977b  Prophecy in the New Testament Church – and Today. — PANAGOPOULOS, J. (ed.),
       *Prophetic Vocation in the New Testament and Today* (SupplNT, 45), Leiden: Brill,
       1977, 46-57. Esp. 46-49.

1978   *Prophecy and Hermeneutic in Early Christianity* (WUNT. 18). Tübingen: Mohr, 1978,
       XVII-289 p. → 1971, 1975b, 1977a

1983   Gospels Criticism. A Perspective on the State of the Art. — STUHLMACHER, P. (ed.),
       *Das Evangelium und die Evangelien*, 1983, 27-54. Esp. 34-38 [Q]; = STUHLMACHER, P.
       (ed.), *The Gospel and the Gospels*, 1991, 26-52. Esp. 33-37.

1989   How Jesus Interpreted His Bible. — *Criswell Theological Review* (Dallas, TX) 3 (1988-
       89) 341-351. [NTA 34, 82]; = ID., *The Old Testament in Early Christianity. Canon and
       Interpretation in the Light of Modern Research* (WUNT, 54), Tübingen: Mohr, 1991,
       125-138 (revised).

1991   The Making of Narratives in the Synoptic Gospels. — WANSBROUGH, H. (ed.), *Jesus
       and the Oral Gospel Tradition*, 1991, 310-333. Esp. 314-317 [miracles: survey]; 318-327: "The
       structure of the narrative episodes"; 331-332 [compositional tendency].

**ELLIS, I.P.**

1968   'But Some Doubted'. [28,17] — *NTS* 14 (1967-68) 574-580. [NTA 13, 181]

**ELLIS, Peter F.**

1974a   *Matthew. His Mind and His Message*. Collegeville, MN: Liturgical Press, 1974, X-179
p. Esp. 3-25: "Rabbinic Matthew"; 27-98: "Meticulous Matthew"; 99-155: "Theological Matthew". [NTA
18, p. 382]
> B.J. HUBBARD, *CBQ* 37 (1975) 248-249; L. SABOURIN, *BTB* 5 (1975) 322; W.G. THOMPSON, *TS* 35
> (1974) 335-337; L.J. TOPEL, *HomPastR* 75/9 (1974-75) 77-79.

1974b   Matthew: His Mind and His Message. The Sermon on the Mount – the Authority of
Jesus 'in Word'. Mt 5:1–7:29. — *BiTod* 70 (1974) 1483-1491. [NTA 18, 853]

**ELLISON, C.S.S.**

1950   Was His Father Lying Dead at Home? [8,21] — *ExpT* 62 (1950-51) 92. → H.G. Howard
1950

**ELLISON, H.L.**

1969   The Gospel according to Matthew. — *A New Testament Commentary*, Grand Rapids,
MI: Zondervan, 1969, 141-176.

**ELLUL, Danielle**

1992   Dérives autour d'un figuier: Matthieu 21,18-22. — *FoiVie* 91/5 (1992) 69-76. [NTA 37,
735]

**ELLUL, Jacques**

1952   L'argent. — *ETR* 27 (1952) 29-66. Esp. 31. → Martin-Achard 1953
1973   Du texte au sermon (18). Les talents. Matthieu 25/13-30. — *ETR* 48 (1973) 125-138.
[NTA 18, 475]
1991   *Si tu es le Fils de Dieu. Souffrances et tentations de Jésus*. Zürich: Brockhaus; Paris:
Centurion, 1991, 110 p.

**ELMORE, W. Emory**

1987   Linguistic Approaches to the Kingdom. — WILLIS, W. (ed.), *The Kingdom of God*,
1987, 53-65. Esp. 62-64.

**ELSAS, Christoph**

1994*   et al. (eds.), *Tradition und Translation. Zum Problem der interkulturellen
Übersetzbarkeit religiöser Phänomene. Festschrift für Carsten Colpe zum 65.
Geburtstag*, Berlin – New York: de Gruyter, 1994, XXXVI-565 p. → Pokorný, J.M.
Robinson, W. Strothmann

**ELTESTER, Walther**

1954*   (ed.), *Neutestamentliche Studien für Rudolf Bultmann zu seinem siebzigsten Geburtstag
am 20. August 1954* (BZNW, 21). Berlin: Töpelman, 1954, ²1957, 304 p. → G.
Bornkamm, Clavier, Dinkler, Fascher, E. Fuchs, F.C. Grant

1954   Bericht über den Berliner Theologentag 1954. — *ZNW* 45 (1954) 129-144. Esp. 133-134.
→ G. Bornkamm 1954c

1960*   (ed.), *Judentum, Urchristentum, Kirche. Festschrift für Joachim Jeremias* (BZNW, 26).
Berlin: Töpelmann, 1960, 259 p.; ²1964, XXX-259 p. → P. Benoit, Hunzinger, Lohse, O.
Michel, Rengstorf, Schweizer, Stendahl

1962   "Freund, wozu du gekommen bist" (Mt. xxvi 50). — *Neotestamentica et Patristica*. FS
O. Cullmann, 1962, 70-91. Esp. 72-74 [textual criticism]; 74-82 [patristic exegesis]; 82-90; 90-91
[Vulgate].

**EMERTON, John A.**

1962a   Τὸ αἷμα μου τῆς διαθήκης: The Evidence of the Syriac Versions. [26,28] — *JTS* 13
(1962) 111-117. [NTA 7, 144]

1962b   Binding and Loosing. Forgiving and Retaining. [16,19] — *Ibid.*, 325-331. [NTA 7, 785]

**ENGELBRECHT, Edgar**

1985   *Missions and Righteousness in the Gospel of Matthew* [Afrikaans]. Diss. Pretoria, 1985 (G.M.M. Pelser). — *DissAbstr* 46 (1985-86) 3064; *SBT* 14 (1986) 192.

**ENGELBRECHT, Johan**

1984   Wonders in die Nuwe Testament. [Miracles in the New Testament] — *TheolEvang* 17 (1984) 4-11. [NTA 29, 883]

1988   Trends in Miracle Research. — *Neotestamentica* 22 (1988) 139-161. Esp. 146-147. [NTA 34, 1083]

1990a  The Language of the Gospel of Matthew. — *Neotestamentica* 24 (1990) 199-213. Esp. 200-202: "Matthew's sources"; 202-206: "Matthew's language"; 206-208: "Matthew's vocabulary"; 208-211 [6,24; 8,14-15; 9,32-34; 12,22-24; 13,44]. [NTA 36, 129]

1990b  'n Nuwe benadering tot die styl van Matteus. [A new approach to the style of Matthew] — *Scriptura* 35 (1990) 26-34. [NTA 35, 616]

1993   Die historiese Jesus as wonderwerker. [The historical Jesus as miracle worker] — *HervTS* 49 (1993) 119-134. [NTA 38, 704]

1994   Die maagdelike ontvangenis van Jesus Christus: Opmerkings oor 'n belangrike debat. [The virginal conception of Jesus Christ. Remarks on an important debate] — *HervTS* 50 (1994) 296-310. [NTA 39, 741]

1995a  Are All the Commentaries on Matthew Really Necessary? — *Religion & Theology / Religie & Teologie* (Pretoria) 2 (1995) 206-215. [NTA 40, 803]

1995b  Die rol van die dissipels in die Christologie van Matteus. [The role of the disciples in the Christology of Matthew). — *HervTS* 51 (1995) 134-146. [NTA 40, 150]

**ENGELEN, Jan C.M.**

1981   *Mattheüs. Hoofdstuk 1-4* (Verklaring van een Bijbelgedeelte). Kampen: Kok, 1981, 88 p. [NTA 27, p. 93]

**ENGELHARDT, Paulus**

1969   "Selig, die Verfolgung leiden um der Gerechtigkeit willen, denn ihrer ist das Himmelreich". — MÜSSLE, M. (ed.), *Der "politische" Jesus*, 1969, 103-116.

**ENGLAND, James**

1988   Matthew 25:31-46. — *RExp* 85 (1988) 317-320.

**ENGLEZAKIS, Benedict**

1979   *Thomas*, Logion 30. [18,20] — *NTS* 25 (1978-79) 262-272. [NTA 23, 723]

**ENNULAT, Andreas**

1994   *Die "Minor Agreements". Untersuchungen zu einer offenen Frage des synoptischen Problems* (WUNT, II/62). Tübingen: Mohr, 1994, VII-594 p. Esp. 1-34: "Grundsätzliche Vorüberlegungen"; 35-416: "Textanalysen" [Mk 1,1-15; 1,16-3,19; 3,20-35; 4,1-34; 4,35-8,26; 8,27-10,52; 11,1-13,37; 14,1-16,8]; 417-430: "Ergebnisse"; 471-594: "Textblätter zu den Textanalysen". [NTA 39, p. 136] — Diss. Bern, 1990 (U. Luz). → T.A. Friedrichsen 1991, A. Fuchs 1994d, Neirynck 1991g
       D.L. DUNGAN, *CRBR* 9 (1996) 199-201; R.L. MOWERY, *CBQ* 58 (1996) 153-155; C.M. TUCKETT, *NT* 37 (1995) 197-199.

**ENOUT, J.E.**

1988   As tentações de Jesus como tema teológico. [4,1-11] — *Liturgia e Vida* (Rio) 209 (1988) 1-9.

**ENSLIN, Morton Scott**

1967   Luke and Matthew. — *JQR* 75th Anniversary Volume (1967) 178-191. → 1985

1972 How the Story Grew: Judas in Fact and Fiction. [26,14-16; 27,3-10] — BARTH, E.H. - COCROFT, R.E. (eds.), *Festschrift to Honor F. Wilbur Gingrich*, 1972, 123-141. Esp. 127.

1975 John and Jesus. — *ZNW* 66 (1975) 1-18. Esp. 4-8. [NTA 20, 398]

1985 Luke and Matthew: Compilers or Authors? — *ANRW* II.25.3 (1985) 2357-2388. Esp. 2360-2361: "The double tradition"; 2361-2362: "Papias' words about Matthew and Mark"; 2363-2365: "Q, arguments for and against"; 2366-2387: "Critical examination of nine sections in Matthew and Luke which suggest Luke's direct use and alteration of Matthew" [4,1-11.12-17; 8,1-4.5-13; 10,2.5-6; 14,14; 22,34-40; 25,14-30; 28,16-20]. → 1967

**ENSOR, Peter W.**

1996 *Jesus and His 'Works'. The Johannine Sayings in Historical Perspective* (WUNT, II/85). Tübingen: Mohr, 1996, XI-337 p. Esp. 13-16; 53-56; 91-94; 118-120 [12,27-28]; 179-181 [12,11]; 207-212 [11,27]; 246-251 [11,2-6]; 251-254 [11,20-24]. — Diss. Aberdeen, 1993 (R.B. Edwards).

**ENTRICH, Manfred**

1992 *Die Bergpredigt als Ausbildungsordnung. Der katechetische Entwurf einer 'ratio formationis' bei Albert dem Grossen* (Studien zur Theologie und Praxis der Seelsorge, 10). Würzburg: Echter, 1992, XXIV-347 p. — Diss. Salzburg, 1991, 394 p. (A. Biesinger)

**EPP, Eldon Jay**

1981* & FEE, G.D. (eds.), *New Testament Textual Criticism. Its Significance for Exegesis. Essays in Honour of Bruce M. Metzger*. Oxford: Clarendon, 1981, XXVIII-410 p. → K. Aland, Frede, Hirunuma, Kilpatrick, Klijn, Logachev, Rhodes, Smit Sibinga

1987 Mediating Approaches to the Kingdom: Werner Georg Kümmel and George Eldon Ladd. — WILLIS, W. (ed.), *The Kingdom of God*, 1987, 35-52. Esp. 40, 42, 48-50.

1989* & MACRAE, G.W. (eds.), *The New Testament and Its Modern Interpreters* (The Bible and Its Modern Interpreters, 3). Philadelphia, PA: Fortress; Atlanta, GA: Scholars, 1989, XXXII-601 p. → H.C. Kee, E.V. McKnight, Murphy-O'Connor, Reumann, Saldarini

**EPPEL, Robert**

1950 L'interprétation de Matthieu 16.18b. — CULLMANN, O. - MENOUD, P. (eds.), *Aux sources de la tradition chrétienne*. FS M. Goguel, 1950, 71-73. → J.B. Bauer 1953b

**Erasmus**

1705[R] Adnotationes. [1705] — *Opera Omnia VI*, Hildesheim: Olms, 1962, 1-148.

1706[R] In Evangelium Matthaei Paraphrasis. [1706] — *Opera Omnia VII*, Hildesheim: Olms, 1962, 1-146.

**ERDMAN, Charles R.**

1966 *The Gospel of Matthew*. Philadelphia, PA: Westminster, 1966.

**ERDOZÁIN, Luis**

1968 *La función del signo en la fe según el cuarto evangelio. Estudio crítico exegético de las perícopas Jn VI,46-54 y Jn XX,24-29* (AnBib, 33). Roma: Pontificio Instituto Bíblico, 1968, XV-56 p. Esp. 9-24 [Jn 4,46-54/Q 7,1-10]. — Diss. Pont. Univ. Greg., Roma, 1965 (D. Mollat).

**ERLEMANN, Kurt**

1988 *Das Bild Gottes in den synoptischen Gleichnissen* (BWANT, 126). Stuttgart: Kohlhammer, 1988, 308 p. Esp. 56-75 [13,24-30]; 76-92 [18,23-35]; 93-114 [20,1-16]; 115-130 [25,1-13]; 170-195 [22,1-14]; 196-221 [25,14-30]; 222-241 [21,33-46]. — Diss. Heidelberg, 1987 (K. Berger).

1995 *Naherwartung und Parusieverzögerung im Neuen Testament. Ein Beitrag zur Frage religiöser Zeiterfahrung* (TANZ, 17). Tübingen: Francke, 1995, XV-511 p. Esp. 143-150 [Mt]; 150-157 [Q]. — Diss. Heidelberg, 1993 (K. Berger).

**ERNST, Cornelius**

1969    The Primacy of Peter. Theology and Ideology. — *NBlackfr* 50 (1969) 347-355; 51 (1969) 399-404. [NTA 13, 867]

**ERNST, Josef**

1970    Die Einheit von Gottes- und Nächstenliebe in der Verkündigung Jesu. — *TGl* 60 (1970) 3-14. Esp. 11-12 [5,43]. [NTA 15, 169]

1972    *Anfänge der Christologie* (SBS, 57). Stuttgart: Katholisches Bibelwerk, 1972, 173 p. Esp. 14-56: "Die Hoheitstitel"; 125-145: "Jüngerschaft und Nachfolge" [4,18-22; 8,19-22; 9,9; 10,37-38; 19,10-12.21.27-29]; 145-158: "Der Nonkonformismus Jesu" [5,32.39-42; 9,15; 12,8; 15,1-20; 19,9].

1978    *Herr der Geschichte. Perspektiven der lukanischen Eschatologie* (SBS, 88). Stuttgart: Katholisches Bibelwerk, 1978, 127 p. Esp. 28-31 [Q 3,9.17 (Lk)]; 31-37 [Q 10,9.11 (Lk)]; 40-42 [Q 12,45-46 (Lk)]; 81-82.101 [Q 12,4-5]; 104-105 [Q 12,22].

1982    Datierung oder Rück-Datierung des Neuen Testamentes? Ein Bericht. — *TGl* 72 (1982) 384-401. [NTA 27, 829] → J.A.T. Robinson 1976, R. Wegner 1982

1984    Öffnet die Türen dem Erlöser. Johannes der Täufer – seine Rolle in der Heilsgeschichte. — *TGl* 74 (1984) 137-165. [NTA 29, 50]

1989a   *Johannes der Täufer. Interpretation – Geschichte – Wirkungsgeschichte* (BZNW, 53). Berlin – New York: de Gruyter, 1989, XV-427 p. Esp. 39-80: "Johannes der Täufer in der Logienquelle" [Q 3,7-9.16-17; 11,2-19]; 155-185: "Johannes der Täufer in der Matthäusredaktion" [3,1-6.7-12.13-17; 4,12; 9,14-17; 11,22-19; 14,3-12; 17,10-13; 21,23-27.28-32]. → Lupieri 1994

1989b   *Matthäus. Ein theologisches Portrait.* Düsseldorf: Patmos, 1989, 152 p. [NTA 36, p. 263] *Matteo, un ritratto teologico*, trans. U. Proch. Brescia: Morcelliana, 1992, 190 p. J.J. BARTOLOMÉ, *Sal* 55 (1993) 792-793; A. PITTA, *Asprenas* 40 (1993) 117-118.

1989c   War Jesus ein Schüler Johannes' des Täufers? — FRANKEMÖLLE, H. – KERTELGE, K. (eds.), *Vom Urchristentum zu Jesus*. FS J. Gnilka, 1989, 13-33. Esp. 19-21 [3,11]; 21-25 [2,23]; 25-27 [11,7-19].

1991    Der Spruch von den "frommen" Sündern und den "unfrommen" Gerechten (Lk 7,29f). Geschichte der Deutung eines umstrittenen Logions. — BUSSMANN, C. – RADL, W. (eds.), *Der Treue Gottes trauen.* FS G. Schneider, 1991, 197-213. Esp. 201-205: "Die literarische Erklärung des Logions"; 205: "Mt 21,32 – Leitquelle für Lk 7,29f?"; 206-207: "Gehört das Logion zur Sonderquelle des Lukas?"; 207-210: "Die redaktionsgeschichtliche Erklärung des Logions"; 210-212: "Lk 7,29f – ein redaktioneller Übergangsvers des Lukas".

1992    Anmerkungen zum "Matthäus-Roman" von Eugen Drewermann. — *TGl* 82 (1992) 352-358. [NTA 37, 1237r] → Drewermann 1992

1994    *Johannes der Täufer – der Lehrer Jesu?* (Biblische Bücher, 2). Freiburg: Herder, 1994, 168 p.

1995*   & LEIMGRUBER, S. (eds.), *Surrexit Dominus vere. Die Gegenwart des Auferstandenen in seiner Kirche. Festschrift für Erzbischof Dr. Johannes Joachim Degenhardt.* Paderborn: Bonifatius, 1995, 574 p. → Backhaus, J. Ernst, Frankemölle, Lindemann, G. Lohfink

1995    Die Kirche des Auferstandenen und der historische Jesus. Hat Jesus die Kirche gewollt? — ERNST, J. – LEIMGRUBER, S. (eds.), *Surrexit Dominus vere.* FS J.J. Degenhardt, 1995, 93-105. Esp. 100-102 [16,17-19].

**ERNST, Michael**

1991    Hellenistische Analogien zu ntl. Gleichnissen. Eine Sammlung von Vergleichstexten sowie Thesen über die sich aus der parabolischen Redeweise ergebenden gesellschaftspolitischen Konsequenzen. — REITERER, F.V. (ed.), *Ein Gott, eine Offenbarung. Beiträge zur biblischen Exegese, Theologie und Spiritualität. Festschrift für Notker Füglister OSB zum 60. Geburtstag*, Würzburg: Echter, 1991, 461-480. Esp. 464-465 [10,16; 11,16; 24,27]; 471 [21,28-32]; 472-473 [13,47-50].

**ERNST, Wilhelm**

1977*  & FEIEREIS, K. – HOFFMANN, F. (eds.), *Dienst der Vermittlung. Festschrift zum 25-jährigen Bestehen des Philosophisch-theologischen Studiums im Priesterseminar Erfurt* (ErfTS, 37). Leipzig: St. Benno, 1977, 689 p. → Christian, Löbmann, Trilling

**ESCANDE, Jacques**

1979   Judas et Pilate prisonniers d'une même structure (Mt 27,1-26). — *FoiVie* 78/3 = *Cahiers bibliques* 18 (1979) 92-100. [NTA 24, 429]

**ESCOBAR, Samuel**

1982   Notas para el estudio e interpretación de Mateo 25:31-46. — *Boletin teologico. Fraternidad teologica latinoamericana* (México) 5 (1982) 122-130.

**ESLER, Philip F.**

1994   Response to K.C. Hanson: Mountaineering in Matthew. — *Semeia* 67 (1994) 171-177. → K.C. Hanson 1994b

1995*  (ed.), *Modelling Early Christianity. Social-scientific Studies of the New Testament in Its Context.* London – New York: Routledge, 1995, XV-349 p. → Derrett, Duling, Neyrey

**ESPEJA, Jesús**

1994   Jesucristo, justicia y violencia de Dios. — *CiTom* 121 (1994) 47-77. Esp. 66-69, 71-72.

**ESPINEL MARCOS, José Luis**

1975   El Padre Nuestro, resumen de los ideales por los que murió Jesús. — *CuBíb* 32 (1975) 243-253.

1977   El optimismo de Jesús respecto del Reino de Dios. [beatitudes] — *CuBíb* 34 (1977) 47-54.

1980   *La eucaristía del Nuevo Testamento* (Estudio teológico de San Esteban. Glosas, 7). Salamanca: San Esteban, 1980, 300 p. Esp. 269-283: "El 'Padre Nuestro' en la liturgia".

1984   El pacifismo de Jésus. — *CiTom* 75 (1984) 229-250. Esp. 237-240 [11,12]; 243-245 [5,39-42].

1986   *La poesía de Jesús* (Estudio teológico de San Esteban. Glosas, 10). Salamanca: San Esteban, 1986, 295 p. Esp. 83-156: "Teopoética de las parábolas de Jesús"; 157-187: "Las escenificaciones proféticas y poéticas de Jesús".

1989   Nuevo Testamento y Pacifismo. — *RazFe* 219 (1989) 67-79. Esp. 71-73.

1992   *El pacifismo del Nuevo Testamento* (Facultad de Teología de San Esteban. Paradosis, 8). Salamanca: San Esteban, 1992, 237 p. Esp. 61-63 [11,5-6]; 71-73.75-78 [11,12]; 79-84 [10,34-36]; 101-102 [5,21-48]; 112-113 [5,43-45]; 114-115 [Q 6,27-36 (Lk)]; 122-126 [5,39-42]; 132-133: "Matteo y Lucas"; 133-136: "Matteo y el pacifismo" [5,9; 10,16; 25,31-46; 28,16].

1995   Inventario de palabras históricas de Jesús en escritos canónicos y apócrifos. — *CiTom* 122 (1995) 147-160. [NTA 41, 139] → J.D. Crossan 1991a/94

**ESSAME, W.G.**

1961   Matthew x.23. — *ExpT* 72 (1960-61) 248. [NTA 6, 125]

1964   Matthew xxvii.51-54 and John v.25-29. — *ExpT* 76 (1964-65) 103. [NTA 9, 551]

**ESSINGER, Helmut**

1969   Die Weihnachtsgeschichte als Ausdruck frühchristlicher Bekenntnisse. — *EvErz* 21 (1969) 473-482.

**ESTÉVEZ, Elisa**

1990   Significado de σπλαγχνίζομαι en el NT. — *EstBíb* 48 (1990) 511-541. Esp. 515-516 [minor agreements]; 519; 521-522; 529-530, 537-539. [NTA 36, 117]

**ESTRADA BARBIER, Bernardo**

1987 Il comandamento dell'amore e le sue conseguenze alla luce di *Mt* 5,17-20. — *Annales theologici* 1 (1987) 107-129. Esp. 107-116: "Il primo comandamento"; 116-129: "I singoli precetti". [NTA 32, 1103]

1988 Il binomio "kalein-akolouthein" nei vangeli sinottici. La vocazione al ministero gerarchico e alla santità nel proprio stato. — *DivThom* 91 (1988) 72-91. [NTA 34, 1113]

1989 L'importanza delle antitesi del primo Vangelo. — *Annales theologici* 3 (1989) 99-119. Esp. 99-107: "Il loro posto nel discorso della montagna"; 107-119: "Il valore delle antitesi".

1992 Lo sfondo rabbinico di Matteo 1,1-18. — SERRA, A. - VALENTINI, A. (eds.), *I Vangeli dell'infanzia*, I, 1992, 103-109.

1994 *El Sembrador. Perspectivas filológico-hermenéuticas de una parábola* (Bibliotheca Salmanticensis. Estudios, 165). Salamanca: University Press, 1994, VII-250 p. Esp. 87-116 [13,1-52]; 117-183 [13,3-9].

**ÉTAIX, Raymond**

1960a *Fragments nouveaux du commentaire sur Matthieu de saint Chromace d'Aquilée*. Diss. Lyon, 1960, 270 p.

1960b "Tractatus in Matheum" partiellement inédits, pouvant être attribués à Chromace d'Aquilée. — *RBén* 70 (1960) 469-503.

1966 & LEMARIÉ, J., La tradition manuscrite des *Tractatus in Mathaeum* de saint Chromace d'Aquilée. — *Sacris Erudiri* (Steenbrugge) 17 (1966) 302-354.

1974a & LEMARIÉ J. (eds.), *Chromatii Aquileiensis Opera. Tractatus in Mathaeum* (CC SL, 9A). Turnhout: Brepols, 1974, XLIX-610 p.; *Supplementum*, 1978, 611-661 p. Esp. XXVIII-XLI [introduction]; 184-498 [text]; 618-643 [supplement]. → Doignon 1979a, Hoste 1957, Simonetti 1975 H. CROUZEL, *BullLitEccl* 80 (1979) 70-71.

1974b Fragments inédits de l'"Opus imperfectum in Matthaeum". — *RBén* 84 (1974) 271-300.

1981 Un "Tractatus in Matheum" inédit de saint Chromace d'Aquilée. [12,38-40] — *RBén* 91 (1981) 225-230.

1982 Textes inédits tirés des homiliaires de la Bibliothèque capitulaire de Bénévent. — *RBén* 92 (1982) 324-357. Esp. 337-338 [16,17-19].

1989 L'homéliaire d'Épinal. B.M. 20(3). — *Recherches augustiniennes* (Paris) 24 (1989) 165-198. Esp. 196-198: "Fragments d'un commentaire carolingien sur Matthieu"; = ID., *Homéliaires patristiques latins. Recueil d'études de manuscrits médiévaux* (Collection des études augustiniennes. Série Moyen-Âge et Temps modernes, 29), Paris: Institut d'études augustiniennes, 1994, 341-374. Esp. 372-374.

1994 L'homéliaire carolingien d'Angers. — *RBén* 104 (1994) 148-190. Esp. 184-189 [18,23-35; 22,34–23,9; 25,14-23].

**[Évangile]**

1964 *L'Évangile selon saint Matthieu*. Tournai: Centre diocésain de documentation, 1964, 120 p.

**EVANS, Christopher Francis**

1963 *The Lord's Prayer* (Seraph Books). New York: Seabury; London: SPCK, 1963, VII-103 p. [NTA 8, p. 287]

1970a *Resurrection and the New Testament* (Studies in Biblical Theology, II/12). London: SCM, 1970; repr. 1981, IX-190 p. Esp. 81-91: "Matthew".

1970b The New Testament in the Making. — ACKROYD, P.R. - EVANS, C.F. (eds.), *The Cambridge History of the Bible*. Vol. 1: *From the Beginnings to Jerome*, Cambridge: University Press, 1970, 232-284. Esp. 271-273.

1977    The Passion of Christ. — ID., *Explorations in Theology*, 2, London: SCM, 1977, 3-49. Esp. 7-12; 21-22; 29-30.

1979    Goulder and the Gospels. — *Theology* 82 (1979) 425-432. [NTA 24, 396r] → Goulder 1974, 1978a

1990    *Saint Luke* (TPI New Testament Commentaries). Philadelphia, PA: Trinity Press International; London: SCM, 1990, XXI-933 p. Esp. 21-26 [Q].

**EVANS, Craig A.**

1989a   *Life of Jesus Research: An Annotated Bibliography* (New Testament Tools and Studies, 13). Leiden: Brill, 1989, XIII-207 p. Esp. 100-167; rev. ed. (New Testament Tools and Studies, 24), 1996, XVII-335 p. Esp. 127-255, 300-318.

1989b   Jesus' Action in the Temple: Cleansing or Portent of Destruction? — *CBQ* 51 (1989) 237-270. Esp. 246-247 [3,7]. [NTA 333, 1163]

1992a   *Jesus* (IBR Bibliographies, 5). Grand Rapids, MI: Baker, 1992, 152 p.

1992b   *Noncanonical Writings and New Testament Interpretation*. Peabody, MA: Hendrickson, 1992, XV-281 p. Esp. 179-182 [25,14-30]; 190-193 [OT quotations: survey]; 221-223 [NT and pseudepigraphal gospel parallels]; 227-231 [Jesus' parables and Rabbi's parables].

1992c   Hardness of Heart. — *DJG*, 1992, 298-299.

1992d   Midrash. — *Ibid.*, 544-548. Esp. 546.

1992e   Old Testament in the Gospels. — *Ibid.*, 578-590. Esp. 585-586.

1992f   Predictions of the Destruction of the Herodian Temple in the Pseudepigrapha, Qumran Scrolls, and Related Texts. — *Journal for the Study of the Pseudepigrapha* (Sheffield) 10 (1992) 89-147. Esp. 105-107 [Q 13,34-35].

1993    From Public Ministry to the Passion: Can a Link Be Found between the (Galilean) Life and the (Judean) Death of Jesus? — *SBL 1993 Seminar Papers*, 460-472. Esp. 462-469 [Kingdom]; 469-470 [27,37]; = ID., *Jesus and His Contemporaries*, 1995, 301-318. Esp. 304-313; 314-315.

1994*   & STEGNER, W.R. (eds.), *The Gospels and the Scriptures of Israel* (JSNT SS, 104; Studies in Scripture in Early Judaism and Christianity, 3). Sheffield: JSOT, 1994, 505 p. → D.A. Carson, Danker, DeYoung, J.D.G. Dunn, A.E. Harvey, O'Rourke, R. Pesch, J.A. Sanders, Trumbower

1994a   Appendix: The Recently Published Dead Sea Scrolls and the Historical Jesus. — CHILTON, B. - EVANS, C.A. (eds.), *Studying the Historical Jesus*, 1994, 547-565. Esp. 552-553 [4Q521]; 559-560 [4Q525]. → 1995b

1994b   → Charlesworth 1994c

1994c   → Chilton 1994b

1995a*  & PORTER, S.E. (eds.), *The Historical Jesus. A Sheffield Reader* (The Biblical Seminar, 33). Sheffield: JSOT, 1995, 314 p. → Allison 1983, 1987b, Bauckham 1985a, M. Black 1990a, Chilton 1982b, Cohn-Sherbok 1979, 1981a, A. Ito 1991, Kilpatrick 1982, Lindars 1985, Moo 1984, E.P. Sanders 1983

1995b*  & PORTER, S.E. (eds.), *The Synoptic Gospels. A Sheffield Reader* (The Biblical Seminar, 31). Sheffield: JSOT, 1995, 313 p. → D. Hill 1980, 1984a, Hurtado 1990, A. Ito 1992, Kingsbury 1984, 1985

1995a   *Jesus and His Contemporaries: Comparative Studies* (Arbeiten zur Geschichte des Antiken Judentums und des Urchristentums, 25). Leiden: Brill, 1995, XIII-532 p. → 1993, 1995b-c

1995b   Jesus and the Messianic Texts from Qumran: A Preliminary Assessment of the Recently Published Materials. — *Ibid.*, 83-154. Esp. 127-129 [4Q521]. → 1994a

1995c Jesus and Rabbinic Parables, Proverbs, and Prayers. — *Ibid.*, 251-297. Esp. 252-255; 269-276; 287-288 [11,25-26].

**EVANS, Henry M.**

1987 Current Exegesis on the Kingdom of God. A Review Article. — *PerspRelSt* 14 (1987) 67-77. [NTA 31, 1008r] → Beasley-Murray 1986a

**EVANS, Owen E.**

1951 The Negative Form of the Golden Rule in the Diatessaron. [7,12] — *ExpT* 63 (1951-52) 31-32.

1957 The Unforgivable Sin. [12,31-32] — *ExpT* 68 (1956-57) 240-244. [NTA 2, 271]

1961 Synoptic Criticism since Streeter. — *ExpT* 72 (1960-61) 295-299. Esp. 297-298 [Q]. [NTA 6, 441]

**EVANS, P.W.**

1953 The Baptismal Commission in Matthew 28,19. — *The Baptist Quarterly* (Philadelphia, PA) 15 (1953) 19-28.

**EVERDING, H. Edward**

1992 A Response to Arthur J. Bellinzoni. — *SecCent* 9 (1992) 259-263. → Bellinzoni 1992

**EWALD, Marie Liguori**

1966 (trans.), *The Homilies of Saint Jerome*. Vol. 2 *(Homilies 60-96)* (The Fathers of the Church. A New Translation, 57). Washington, DC: CUA, 1966, X-295 p. Esp. 195-199 [18,7-9].

**EXBRAYAT, I.**

1955 *Notre Père, ou la prière révolutionnaire*. Genève: Labor et Fides, 1955, 173 p.

# F

**FABBRI, E.**

1956a El bautismo de Jesús en el Evangelio de los Hebreos y en el de los Ebionitos. — *Revista teológica* (Rio de Janeiro) 6 (1956) 36-56.

1956b El bautismo de Jesús y la unción del Espiritu en la teologia de S. Ireneo. — *Ciencia y fe* (Buenos Aires) 12/45 (1956) 7-42; 12/48 (1956) 39-63.

**FABER VAN DER MEULEN, Harry E.**

1978 De christologische relevantie van de zaligsprekingen bij Matteüs. — GROSHEIDE, H.H., et al. (eds.), *De knechtsgestalte van Christus*. FS H.N. Ridderbos, 1978, 47-53.

1993 Gods openbaring in Jezus als de "Nederige": Mattheus' versie van de zaligsprekingen en een rabbijnse opvatting van ' Anawah. [5,3-12] — *HervTS* 49 (1993) 477-501. [NTA 38, 1361]

**FABRIS, Rinaldo**

1969a Il discorso missionario nell'Evangelo di Matteo (Mt 10,1-42). — *ParVi* 14 (1969) 194-204.

1969b Il discorso del monte (Mt 5-7). — *Ibid.*, 243-259.

1977a *Leggi della libertà in Giacomo* (Supplementi alla Rivista Biblica, 8). Brescia: Paideia, 1977, 306 p. Esp. 184-190 [11,28-30]; 212-224: "La 'legge perfetta' in Giacomo e la tradizione di Matteo" [5,17.48; 19,21].

1977b → Festorazzi 1977

1978 La parabola degli invitati alla cena. Analisi redazionale di *Lc.* 14,16-24. — DUPONT, J., et al. (eds.), *La parabola degli invitati al banchetto*, 1978, 127-166.

1982 *Matteo. Traduzione e commento* (Commenti biblici). Roma: Borla, 1982, 674 p. [NTA 28, p. 312]
L. DE LORENZI, *Benedictina* 30 (1983) 578-579; B. MARCONCINI, *ParVi* 29 (1984) 413-415; V. PASQUETTO, *Teresianum* 34 (1983) 518; G. SEGALLA, *Studia Patavina* 31 (1984) 451-452; N. URICCHIO, *CC* 135/2 (1984) 611-613.

1983 Il metodo esegetico di Cromazio di Aquileia nei *Tractatus in Matthaeum*. — *Varietas indivisa. Teologia della chiesa locale. Studi in onore di Pietro Bertolla e Aldo Moretti* (Scuola superiore di teologia di Udine e Gorizia, 1), Brescia: Paideia, 1983, 91-117.

1984 La parabola della pecora perduta (Mt 18,12-14; Lc 15,4-7). — *ParSpirV* 10 (1984) 105-119. Esp. 106-108.113-115 [18,12-14]; 108-110.115-116 [Q 15,4-7].

1985 "Gli eunuchi per il Regno dei cieli" (Mt 19,12). — *ParSpirV* 12 (1985) 128-142. Esp. 132-134 [19,10-12]; 134-142 [19,12].

1987 Il lievito e il seme: il Regno nel tempo. — *ParSpirV* 15 (1987) 157-174. Esp. 159-162 [13,31-32.33].

1988a La chiave della conoscenza (Lc 11,52 par.). — *ParSpirV* 18 (1988) 113-126. Esp. 119-124: "Il contesto letterario e tematico di Matteo".

1988b Risurrezione. — ROSSANO, P. - RAVASI, G. - GIRLANDA, A. (eds.), *Nuovo Dizionario di Teologia Biblica*, Cinisello Balsamo: Paoline, 1988, 1342-1361.

1989a Il Dio di Gesù Cristo nella teologia di Matteo. — *ScuolC* 117 (1989) 121-148. Esp. 122-125: "Il vocabulario teologico nel vangelo di Matteo"; 126-137: "Dio Padre nelle sentenze di Gesù"; 138-143: "L'immagine di Dio nelle parabole di Gesù"; 143-146: "Lo stile di Dio nei gesti e scelte di Gesù". [NTA 34, 598]

1989b La vergogna redenta. Mt 1,1-17. — *ParSpirV* 20 (1989) 89-103.

1991 Gesù e la legge: compimento profetico. — *ParSpirV* 24 (1991) 113-127. Esp. 116-124 [5,17-48]; 124-126 [19,19].

1993a Il discorso parabolico in Matteo (Mt 13,1-52). — *Credere oggi* 74 (1993) 61-71.

1993b I pagani in Matteo (21,43). — *ParSpirV* 27 (1993) 109-120.

**FABRIZIUS, Karl Frederick**

1994 *Rupert of Deutz on Matthew. A Study in Exegetical Method.* Diss. Marquette Univ., Milwaukee, WI, 1994, 264 p. — *DissAbstr* 55 (1994-95) 2437-2438.

**FACCIO, Hyacinthus**

1950 De Thesauro abscondito (Mt. 13,44). — *VD* 28 (1950) 237-242.

**FÄRNSTRÖM, E.**

1962 *Jesu bergspredikan och vår tid* [The Sermon on the Mount and our time] (Bibelstudieplan, 28). Stockholm: Studiebokförlaget, 1962, 52 p.

**FAHEY, Michael Andrew**

1971 *Cyprian and the Bible: A Study in Third-Century Exegesis* (Beiträge zur Geschichte der biblischen Hermeneutik, 9). Tübingen: Mohr, 1971, VI-656 p. Esp. 259-330 [quotations and allusions]; 684-687 [index]. — Diss. Tübingen, 1970 (K.H. Schelkle).

**FAHNER, Christian**

1981 *Synopsis van de vier evangeliën. Mattheüs, Markus, Lukas, Johannes. Met een inleiding tot het synoptisch probleem.* Utrecht: De Banier, 1981, 452 p. Esp. 433-446 [synoptic problem].

**FAHY, Thomas**

1955 Notes on the Gospels. — *IrEcclRec* 84 (1955) 396-401. Esp. 399 [21,9]; 400-401 [9,16].

1956 St. John and Elias. — *IrTQ* 23 (1956) 285-286. [NTA 1, 207]

1957a St. Matthew, 19:9 – Divorce or Separation? — *Ibid.*, 173-174. [NTA 2, 281]

1957b The Marriage of Our Lady and St. Joseph (St. Luke 1:26ff; St. Matthew 1:18ff). — *IrTQ* 24 (1957) 261-267. [NTA 2, 272]

**FAIRCHILD, Mark Robin**

1989 *Eschatology in the Q Source.* Diss. Drew University, Madison, NJ, 1989, VI-242 p. (D. Doughty). Esp. 47-93: "Kingdom of God sayings" [Q 6,20-23; 7,18-28; 10,2-5; 11,2-7.14-20.39-52; 12,22-31; 13,18-32.23-30; 14,16-24; 16,16; 22,28-30]; 94-142: "The judgment" [Q 3,7-9.16-17; 6,37-38; 10,12-15; 11,29-32.39-52; 12,39-46.57-59; 13,23-30; 14,16-24; 17,23-24.26-30; 19,12-27; 22,28-30]; 143-179: "The Son of Man sayings" [Q 6,22; 7,34; 9,58; 11,30; 12,8-9.10.40; 17,24.26.30]; 180-217: "The mission of the Q community" [Q 3,7-9; 7,1-10.31-35; 10,2-15; 11,29-32 39-52; 13,23-30; 14,16-24; 15,4-7; 17,1-4; 22,28-30]. — *DissAbstr* 51 (1990-91) 196.

**FALCKE, Heino**

1984 Die Seligpreisungen der Bergpredigt und das gesellschaftliche Zeugnis der Kirche. — *ZEvEth* 28 (1984) 376-401.

**FALCONE, Sebastian A.**

1976 The Kind of Bread We Pray for in the Lord's Prayer. [6,11] — MCNAMARA, R.F. (ed.), *Essays in Honor of Joseph P. Brennan*, Rochester, NY: St. Bernard's Seminary, 1976, 36-59.

**FALK, Harvey**

1985 *Jesus the Pharisee. A New Look at the Jewishness of Jesus.* New York – Mahwah, NJ: Paulist, 1985, VII-175 p. Esp. 148-161: "Understanding the Christian Bible through Bet Shammai and Bet Hillel".

1990 A Reply to Reviews by Chernick and Levine of Sigal's *The Halakhah of Jesus of Nazareth according to the Gospel of Matthew*. — *JEcuSt* 27 (1990) 347-354. [NTA 36, 130] → Sigal 1986, Swidler 1989
Replies: CHERNICK, *Ibid.*, 355-360; LEVINE, *Ibid.*, 360-364.

**FALK, Zeev W.**

1966 On Talmudic Vows. [15,5] — *HTR* 59 (1966) 309-312. [NTA 11, 700] → G.W. Buchanan 1965

**FALLA, Terry C.**

1994 Questions Concerning the Content and Implications of the Lexical Work *A Key to the Peshitta Gospels*. [Falla, 1991] — LAVENANT, R. (ed.), *VI Symposium Syriacum 1992. University of Cambridge, Faculty of Divinity 30 August - 2 September 1992* (Orientalia Christiana Analecta, 247), Roma: Pontificio Istituto Orientale, 1994, 85-99. Esp. 97-98 [4,1; 11,17; 25,11].

**FALLON, Francis T.**

1988 & CAMERON, R., The Gospel of Thomas: A Forschungsbericht and Analysis. — *ANRW* II.25.6 (1988) 4195-4251. Esp. 4213-4224: "Relationship to the canonical gospels".

**FALLON, M.**

1980 *The Four Gospels. An Introductory Commentary* (The Winston Commentary on the Gospels). Minneapolis, MN: Winston Press, [1980], VIII-469 p.

**FANDER, Monika**

1992 Frauen im Urchristentum am Beispiel Palästinas. — *JbBT* 7 (1992) 165-185. Esp. 169-172 [Q 10,1-12].

**FANG CHIH-JUNG, M.**

1976 An Essay of Interpreting Mt 5:45.48 through 1 Ching, ch. I: On Heaven. [Chinese] — *ColcTFu* 8/29 (1976) 329-346.

**FANIN, Luciano**

1974 Le parabole evangeliche in Tertulliano. — *Laur* 15 (1974) 402-433. Esp. 404-407 [3,12; 13,30]; 407-408 [17,3]; 414-416 [13,24-30]; 417-419 [6,11]; 427-429 [6,12]; 429-431 [18,23-35].

**FANNING, Buist M.**

1990 *Verbal Aspect in New Testament Greek* (Oxford Theological Monographs). Oxford: Clarendon, 1990, XIV-471 p. — Diss. Oxford, 1987 (G.B. Caird - J. Ashton).

**FANNON, Patrick**

1962 The Four Gospels. 2. St Matthew's Gospel. — *CleR* 47 (1962) 481-491. [NTA 7, 122]
1964 *The Four Gospels. A Short Introduction to Their Making and Message* (Stagbooks, 8/6). London: Sheed & Ward, 1964, 113 p.; (A Fides Dome Book). Notre Dame, IN: Fides, 1966, X-113 p.
*Die vier Evangelien. Legende oder Wahrheit?*, trans. M. Zehnder. Stuttgart: Katholisches Bibelwerk, 1966, 99 p.
*Los cuatro evangelios. Breve introducción a su estructura y mensaja*. Barcelona: Herder, 1970, 144 p.
1965 Matthew Revisited. — *Scripture* 17 (1965) 97-103. [NTA 10, 896] → G. Bornkamm 1959a/63, Strecker 1962, Trilling 1959a

**FARAHIAN, Edmund**

1991 Relire Matthieu 25,31-46. — *Greg* 72 (1991) 437-457. Esp. 442-452: "Le contenu". [NTA 36, 157]

**FARBSTEIN, David**

1952 Waren die Pharisäer und die Schriftgelehrten Heuchler? — *Judaica* 8 (1952) 193-207. Esp. 202-207 [23,35].

**FARKASFALVY, Denis**

1983 → W.R. Farmer 1983d

1992a Matthew's Gospel in the Second Century: Response to Arthur J. Bellinzoni. — *SecCent* 9 (1992) 271-275. → Bellinzoni 1992

1992b The Presbyter's Witness on the Order of the Gospels as Reported by Clement of Alexandria. — *CBQ* 54 (1992) 260-270. Esp. 265-267 [1,2-17]. [NTA 37, 84]

**FARLA, Piet Jacobus**

1978 *Jezus' oordeel over Israel. Een form- en redaktionsgeschichtliche analyse van Mc 10,46–12,40.* Kampen: Kok, 1978, XI-581 p. Esp. 102-105 [17,20]; 173-174 [21,33-46]; 241-254 [22,34-40]; 285-287 [23,1-12]; 291-295 [23,6-7]. — Diss. Nijmegen, 1978 (B. van Iersel).

1982 Trouw in liefde en vrijheid. De betekenis van de synoptische teksten over het huwelijk. — *Schrift* 79 (1982) 16-32.

1989 'The two shall become one flesh'. Gen. 1.27 and 2.24 in the New Testament Marriage Texts. — DRAISMA, S. (ed.), *Intertextuality in Biblical Writings*. FS B. van Iersel, 1989, 67-82. Esp. 70-72 [19,3-12].

**FARMER, Ron**

1987 The Kingdom of God in the Gospel of Matthew. — WILLIS, W. (ed.), *The Kingdom of God*, 1987, 119-130.

**FARMER, Ronald Lynn**

1982 *The Significance of the Transfiguration for the Synoptic Accounts of the Ministry of Jesus.* Diss. Southwestern Baptist Theol. Sem., Fort Worth, TX, 1982. — *DissAbstr* 43 (1982-83) 1588; *SBT* 13 (1983) 93.

**FARMER, William Reuben**

1961 A 'Skeleton in the Closet' of Gospel Research. — *BR* 6 (1961) 18-42. Esp. 24-26 [Lachmann's argument]; 20-30 [19th cent.]; 30-40 [Holtzmann]. [NTA 6, 442]

1962 Notes on a Literary and Form-Critical Analysis of Some of the Synoptic Material Peculiar to Luke. — *NTS* 8 (1961-62) 301-316. Esp. 301-303 [18,12-14]; 308-309 [18,21-22]. [NTA 7, 164]

1964a *The Synoptic Problem. A Critical Analysis.* New York: Macmillan; London: Collier-Macmillan, 1964, XI-308 p.; Dillsboro, NC: Western North Carolina Press; Macon, GA: Mercer University Press, ²1976. Esp. 199-232: "A new introduction to the problem". → R.H. Fuller 1975b, Léon-Dufour 1972b, Meynell 1963/67, Mitton 1965, Snape 1966
  F.W. BEARE, *JBL* 84 (1965) 295-297; T.A. BURKILL, *ChrCert* 81 (1964) 1430; B. CORSANI, *Protestantesimo* 24 (1969) 47-49; S. CUTT, *Theology* 69 (1966) 255-257; F., *BibOr* 9 (1967) 217; F.C. GRANT, *Interpr* 19 (1965) 352-354; W.E. HULL, *RExp* 65 (1968) 490-492; J.H. LUDLUM, *ChrTod* 9 (1964-65) 306; M. RESE, *VerkFor* 12/2 (1967) 34-38; H. RHYS, *ATR* 48 (1966) 92-94; W. SCHMITHALS, *TLZ* 92 (1967) 424-425.
  M.-É. BOISMARD, *RB* 85 (1978) 628-629; F.F. BRUCE, *EvQ* 49 (1977) 225-226; G.G. GAMBA, *Sal* 40 (1978) 184-186; M. HUBAUT, *RTL* 8 (1977) 235; X. JACQUES, *NRT* 100 (1978) 265-266; R. KUGELMAN, *TS* 38 (1977) 564-565; A.J. MCNICOL, *RestQ* 24 (1981) 247-250; D. NINEHAM, *JTS* 28 (1977) 548-551; B. REICKE, *TZ* 33 (1977) 176-177; A. RODRÍGUEZ CARMONA, *EstBib* 44 (1986) 239-240; L. SABOURIN, *BTB* 7 (1977) 187-188; P.B. SANTRAM, *IndianJT* 29 (1980) 55-63; D. WENHAM, *EvQ* 54 (1982) 242-244.
  A New Introduction to the Problem. [²1976, 199-232] — BELLINZONI, A.J., Jr., et al. (eds.), *The Two-Source Hypothesis*, 1985, 163-197.

1964b Some Thoughts on the Provenance of Matthew. — VARDAMAN, E.J. – GARRETT, J.L., Jr. (eds.), *The Teacher's Yoke. Studies in Memory of Henry Trantham*, Waco, TX: Baylor University Press, 1964, 109-116.

1966a The Synoptic Problem and the Contemporary Theological Chaos. — *ChrCent* 83 (1966) 1204-1206.

1966b  The Two-Document Hypothesis as a Methodological Criterion in Synoptic Research.
       — *ATR* 48 (1966) 380-396. [NTA 11, 1025]

1967*  & MOULE, C.F.D. – NIEHBUHR, R.R. (eds.), *Christian History and Interpretation:*
       *Studies Presented to John Knox.* Cambridge: University Press, 1967, XXXV-428 p. →
       Beare, Dodd, W.R. Farmer

1967a  An Historical Essay on the Humanity of Jesus Christ. — *Ibid.*, 101-126. Esp. 112-121
       [20,1-16]; 121-124 [Sondergut].

1967b  The Problem of Christian Origins: A Programmatic Essay. — DANIELS, B.L. – SUGGS,
       M.J. (eds.), *Studies in the History and Text of the New Testament.* FS K.W. Clark,
       1967, 81-88. Esp. 82-84.

1968   'The Lachmann Fallacy'. — *NTS* 14 (1967-68) 441-443. [NTA 13, 139] → N.H. Palmer 1967

1969   *Synopticon. The Verbal Agreement between the Greek Texts of Matthew, Mark and Luke*
       *Contextually Exhibited.* Cambridge: University Press, 1969, XI-229 p.
              A.M. ARTOLA, *Lumen* (Vitoria) 20 (1971) 273; W. ELLIS, *AusBR* 18 (1970) 49; C.F. EVANS, *Theology*
              73 (1970) 225-226; J.A. FITZMYER, *TS* 30 (1969) 742-743; M. GARCIA CORDERO, *Salmanticensis* 20
              (1973) 678-679; T.J. HERTER, *WestTJ* 32 (1969) 219-220; H.W. HOEHNER, *BS* 126 (1969) 353-354;
              B.M. METZGER, *CBQ* 32 (1970) 118-119; C.L. MITTON, *ExpT* 81 (1969-70) 131-132; J.W. OLLEY, *The*
              *South East Asia Journal of Theology* (Singapore) 11 (1971) 114-115; A. SALAS, *CiudDios* 183 (1970)
              460-461; R.F. SMITH, *RRel* 28 (1969) 1042-1043; H.F.D. SPARKS, *JTS* 22 (1971) 189-192.

1971   Redaction Criticism and the Synoptic Problem. — *SBL 1971 Seminar Papers*, I, 239-
       250. Esp. 241-243 [minor agreements: 13,12; 25,29]; 243-245 [4,23; 9,35]; 248 [4,12-17].

1973   A Response to Robert Morgenthaler's *Statistische Synopse* — *Bib* 54 (1973) 417-433.
       Esp. 422-424 [3,10; 4,1-12.17; 10,17-23; 24,42]; 431 [14,14]; 432 [11,10]. [NTA 18, 837r] → Morgenthaler
       1971

1975a  A Fresh Approach to Q. — NEUSNER, J. (ed.), *Christianity, Judaism and Other Greco-*
       *Roman Cults. Studies for Morton Smith at Sixty.* Part One: *New Testament* (Studies in
       Judaism in Late Antiquity, 12/1), Leiden: Brill, 1975, 39-50. Esp. 45-50: "Luke's treatment
       of Matthew on the Griesbach hypothesis"; = BELLINZONI, A.J., Jr., et al. (eds.), *The Two-*
       *Source Hypothesis*, 1985, 397-408. Esp. 404-408. → A. Fuchs 1980c

1975b  Jesus and the Gospels: A Form-critical and Theological Essay. — *PerkJourn* 28/2
       (1975) 1-62. Esp. 5-35: "The origin and development of the gospel tradition"; 35-61: "From the gospel
       tradition to the gospel genre". [NTA 19, 890]

1976a  → 1964a

1976b  Matthew and the Bible: An Essay in Canonical Criticism. — *LexTQ* 11 (1976) 57-66.
       [NTA 20, 768]

1976c  The Post-Sectarian Character of Matthew and Its Post-War Setting in Antioch of Syria.
       — *PerspRelSt* 3 (1976) 235-247. [NTA 21, 369]

1977   Modern Developments of Griesbach's Hypothesis. — *NTS* 23 (1976-77) 275-295. Esp.
       276-279: "Historical background"; 279-280: "Present situation"; 281-283: "New developments of Griesbach's
       hypothesis"; 283-293: "Objections to Griesbach's hypothesis answered". [NTA 21, 708]

1978a  Basic Affirmation with Some Demurrals: A Response to Roland Mushat Frye. —
       WALKER, W.O., Jr. (ed.), *The Relationships among the Gospels*, 1978, 303-322 Esp.
       304-312: "On sequence and dependence: the Griesbach hypothesis". → Frye 1978, Tyson 1978b

1978b  Kritik der Markushypothese. — *TZ* 34 (1978) 172-174. [NTA 23, 416r] → 1980b; → Stoldt 1977

1978c  The Present State of the Synoptic Problem. — *PerkJourn* 32/2 (1978) 1-7. [NTA 23, 407]

1979   Who Are the 'Tax Collectors and Sinners' in the Synoptic Tradition? — HADIDIAN,
       D.Y. (ed.), *From Faith to Faith.* FS D.G. Miller, 1979, 167-174. Esp. 170-171 [11,16-19].

1980a  *Occasional Notes on Some Points of Interest in New Testament Studies.* Macon, GA: Mercer University Press, 1980, 30 p. Esp. 7-14: "Notes for a compositional analysis on the Griesbach hypothesis of the Empty Tomb stories in the synoptic gospels". [NTA 25, 377]

1980b  The Stoldt–Conzelmann Controversy: A Review Article. — *PerspRelSt* 7 (1980) 152-162. → 1978b; → Stoldt 1977, 1980

1980c  The Synoptic Problem. The Inadequacies of the Generally Accepted Solution. — *PerkJourn* 33/4 (1980) 20-27. [NTA 25, 54]

1982  *Jesus and the Gospel. Tradition, Scripture, and Canon.* Philadelphia, PA: Fortress, 1982, XIV-300 p. Esp. 11-19: "Matthew and the Bible"; 93-134: "The sequence of the gospels"; 134-138 [date, provenance]; 138-140: "Literary method of Matthew (Mt 4,12-25)"; 146-148: "Isaiah and the healing motif in Matthew"; 149-154: "The wisdom motif"; 154-159: "The motif of martyrdom and the passion of Jesus"; 159-161: "Son of God christology".

1983*  (ed.), *New Synoptic Studies. The Cambridge Gospel Conference and Beyond* [FS J.B. Orchard]. Macon, GA: Mercer University Press, 1983, XLI-533 p. → P.W. Agnew, G.W. Buchanan, Cope, W.R. Farmer 1983a-c, Gamba, Kingsbury, Orchard, P. Parker, Peabody, Reicke, Shuler, Sigal, W.O. Walker Jr.; → Powers 1980, Riesner 1980

1983a  Introduction. — *Ibid.*, VII-XLI.

1983b  The Patristic Evidence Reexamined: A Response to George Kennedy. — *Ibid.*, 3-15. Esp. 3-6 [Papias]; 6-9 [Clement of Alexandria]; 9-12 [Irenaeus]; 13-14 [Origen]. → G.A. Kennedy 1978

1983c  A Response to Joseph Fitzmyer's Defence of the "Two-Document Hypothesis". — *Ibid.*, 501-523. Esp. 506-512: "Excursus on Griesbach and the phenomenon of order"; 512-517: "Excursus on Lachmann and the phenomenon of order"; 517-523: "Fitzmyer's defence of Q". → Fitzmyer 1970

1983d  & FARKASFALVY, D.M., *The Formation of the New Testament Canon. An Ecumenical Approach* (Theological Inquiries). New York: Paulist, 1983, 182 p.

1984a  Certain Results Reached by Sir John C. Hawkins and C.F. Burney Which Make More Sense if Luke Knew Matthew, and Mark Knew Matthew and Luke. — TUCKETT, C.M. (ed.), *Synoptic Studies*, 1984, 75-98. Esp. 75-85 [Hawkins]; 85-91 [Burney]; 91-95 [24/Lk]; 95-98 [24/Mk]. → Goulder 1984a

1984b  Reply to Michael Goulder. — *Ibid.*, 105-109. → Goulder 1984a

1984c  The Import of the Two-Gospel Hypothesis. — *ConcTQ* 48 (1984) 55-59. [NTA 28, 900]

1984d  Is Streeter's Fundamental Solution to the Synoptic Problem Still Valid? — WEINRICH, W.C. (ed.), *The New Testament Age*. FS B. Reicke, 1984, I, 147-164. Esp. 152-158 [Mk priority]; 158-164 [Q]. → Fitzmyer 1970

1986a  The Church's Stake in the Question of 'Q'. — *PerkJourn* 39/3 (1986) 9-19. [NTA 31, 96]

1986b  The Sermon on the Mount: A Form-Critical and Redactional Analysis of Matt 5:1–7:29. — *SBL 1986 Seminar Papers*, 56-87. Esp. 56-63: "The evangelist Matthew and the Sermon on the Mount"; 63-87: "Organizing principles of 5:3–7:27".

1987a  Luke's Use of Matthew: A Literary Inquiry. — *African Journal of Biblical Studies* (Ibadan, Nigeria) 2 (1987) 7-24. [NTA 34, 655]

1987b  Luke's Use of Matthew. A Christological Inquiry. — *PerkJourn* 40/3 (1987) 39-50. [NTA 32, 153] → W. Baird 1987

1988  Source Criticism: Some Comments on the Present Situation. — *USQR* 42/1-2 (1988) 49-57. Esp. 52-55 [Q]. [NTA 32, 1093]

1990a  & KERESZTY, R., *Peter and Paul in the Church of Rome. The Ecumenical Potential of a Forgotten Perspective* (Theological Inquiries). New York: Paulist, 1990, IX-186 p. Esp. 53-81.140-146: "Peter and Paul in the theologies of Irenaeus and Tertullian".

1990b & DUNGAN, D.L. – McNICOL, A.J. – PEABODY, D.B. – SHULER, P.L., Narrative Outline of the Markan Composition according to the Two Gospel Hypothesis. — *SBL 1990 Seminar Papers*, 212-239.

1990c The Passion Prediction Passages and the Synoptic Problem: A Test Case. — *NTS* 36 (1990) 558-570. Esp. 559-560.568 [16,21-23]; 561-563.569 [17,22-23];563-566.570 [20,17-19]. [NTA 35, 608] → Neirynck 1991d

1990d The Two-Gospel Hypothesis. The Statement of the Hypothesis. — DUNGAN, D.L. (ed.), *The Interrelations of the Gospels*, 1990, 125-156. Esp. 125-130: "The tradition of the church"; 132-136: "Literary evidence"; 147-151: "An historical account of the composition of the gospels" [Mt].

1991 The Minor Agreements of Matthew and Luke Against Mark and the Two Gospel Hypothesis. A Study of These Agreements in Their Compositional Contexts. — *SBL 1991 Seminar Papers*, 773-815. Esp. 774-811; 811-813; = STRECKER, G. (ed.), *Minor Agreements*, 1993, 163-208. Esp. 164-203: "Markan networks absent in Matthew and Luke" [πάλιν: 9,1.9.18; 12,9-10.21-24; 13,1-3; 15,10.29-30.32; 16,4-6; 19,1-2.6-9; 20,17; 21,23]; 203-205: "Other networks in Mark. The structure of Matthew in Mark". → Luz 1993c

1992a & COPE, L. – DUNGAN, D.L. – McNICOL, A.J. – PEABODY, D.B. – SHULER, P.L., Narrative Outline of the Composition of Luke according to the Two Gospel Hypothesis. — *SBL 1992 Seminar Papers*, 98-120; *SBL 1993 Seminar Papers*, 303-333; *SBL 1994 Seminar Papers*, 516-573; *SBL 1995 Seminar Papers*, 636-687. → cf. McNicol 1996a, 71-78.80-108; 108-149; 151-244, 245-317 (revised)

1992b State *Interesse* and Marcan Primacy 1870-1914. — VAN SEGBROECK, F., et al. (eds.), *The Four Gospels 1992*. FS F. Neirynck, 1992, III, 2477-2498; = REVENTLOW, H. – FARMER, W.R. (eds.), *Biblical Studies and the Shifting of Paradigms, 1850-1914* (JSOT SS, 192), Sheffield: JSOT, 1995, 15-49 (slightly revised).

1994 *The Gospel of Jesus. The Pastoral Relevance of the Synoptic Problem*. Louisville, KY: Westminster/Knox, 1994, XIV-240 p. Esp. 15-38: "What is the Two-Gospel hypothesis?"; 41-122: "What difference does it make for worship, theology, and ethics?"; 125-160: "How, why, where, and when did the idea of Markan primacy originate?"; 163-173: "What is behind the current interest in Q?"; 202-208: "The Two-Source hypothesis as a methodological criterion in synoptic research".
M.D. HOOKER, *JTS* 46 (1995) 815-816; C.M. TUCKETT, *ExpT* 106 (1994-95) 120.

**FARRER, Austin M.**

1954 *St Matthew and St Mark* (The Edward Cadbury Lectures 1953-54). Westminster: Dacre, 1954, ²1966, XIII-236 p. Esp. 38-56: "Matthaean reconstruction, I"; 116-130: "Matthaean reconstruction, II"; 160-176: "The Sermon on the Mount"; 177-197: "St Matthew's great discourses". → P. Curtis 1970, Hefling 1983, Huston 1957, Muddiman 1983, J.S. Roberts 1965, R.McL. Wilson 1959b
A.W. ARGYLE, *HibbJourn* 53 (1954-55) 302-303; C.K. BARRETT, *JTS* 7 (1956) 107-110; F.W. BEARE, *JRel* 35 (1955) 254-255; C. MOELLER, *ETL* 31 (1955) 689; C. PERROT, *Cahiers sioniens* (Paris) 9 (1955) 136-137; E.K. WINTER, *Judaica* 11 (1955) 190-191.

1955 On Dispensing with Q. — NINEHAM, D.E. (ed.), *Studies in the Gospels*. FS R.H. Lightfoot, 1955, 55-88. Esp. 55-62 [Q]; 63-66.66-73 [Lk 10,25–18,30 dependent on Mt]; 73-82 [structure]; 82-86 [Lk arrangement of Mt]; 87-88 [1,1-17]; = BELLINZONI, A.J., Jr., et al. (eds.), *The Two-Source Hypothesis*, 1985, 321-356. Esp. 322-330; 330-341; 341-349; 349-353; 353-354. → Bradby 1957, P. Curtis 1970, Downing 1965, N. Turner 1969

1956a An Examination of Mark XIII.10. [10,17-20] — *JTS* 7 (1956) 75-79. [NTA 1, 45] → Kilpatrick 1958

1956b Q. — *Theology* 59 (1956) 247-248. [NTA 1, 33] → W.H.B. Martin 1956

1965 *The Triple Victory. Christ's Temptations according to Saint Matthew*. London: Faith, 1965, 96 p.

**FASCHER, Erich**

1951 *Das Weib des Pilatus (Matthäus 27,19). Die Auferweckung der Heiligen (Matthäus 27,51-53). Zwei Studien zur Geschichte der Schriftauslegung* (Hallische Monographien, 20). Halle: Niemeyer, 1951, 51 p. Esp. 1-31 [27,19]; 32-51 [27,51-53].
C.O'C. SLOANE, *CBQ* 14 (1952) 387-389; C. SPICQ, *RSPT* 37 (1953) 153-154.

1953 *Textgeschichte als hermeneutisches Problem.* Halle/Saale: Niemeyer, 1953, 108 p. Esp. 14 [3,9]; 15 [3,2-3]; 16 [3,11]; 17 [3,17]; 18 [17,1.5]; 48-50 [1,16-2,5]; 52-53 [13,58]; 58-59 [16,27-28]; 71-72 [17,26]; 75-76 [9,24; 10,12.38]; 76-78 [6,13b]; 78-79 [7,11]; 80-81 [5,37; 23,26.31].

1954a Jesus der Lehrer. Ein Beitrag zur Frage nach dem "Quellort der Kirchenidee". — *TLZ* 79 (1954) 325-342.

1954b Theologische Beobachtungen zu δεῖ. — ELTESTER, W. (ed.), *Neutestamentliche Studien.* FS R. Bultmann, 1954, 228-254. Esp. 238 [24,6]; 239 [16,21]. 242 [20,28; 26,53].

1957 Bergpredigt. II. Auslegungsgeschichtlich. — *RGG* 1 (³1957) 1050-1053.

1964 "Von dem Tage aber und von der Stunde weiß niemand...". Der Anstoß in Mark. 13,32 (Matth. 24,36). Eine exegetische Skizze zum Verhältnis von historisch-kritischer und christologischer Interpretation. — *Ruf und Antwort. Festgabe für Emil Fuchs zum 90. Geburtstag*, Leipzig: Koehler & Amelang, 1964, 475-483. → 1968c

1968a *Frage und Antwort. Studien zur Theologie und Religionsgeschichte.* Berlin: Evangelische Verlagsanstalt, 1968, 231 p. → 1968b-c

1968b Jesus, der Arzt. — *Ibid.*, 9-41. Esp. 28-31.

1968c Probleme der Zukunftserwartung nach Markus 13,32 und Matthäus 24,36. — *Ibid.*, 68-84. → 1964

1968d Mündliche Überlieferung als Prozess der Textauslegung. — *Ibid.*, 85-116. Esp. 102-114.

**FAUST, Ludwig Maria**

1988 Das verheißene Brot. Die Bergpredigt mit dem Vaterunser als neutestamentliches Lehrgedicht, dargestellt von Annemarie Scholl. — DORNEICH, M. (ed.), *Vater-Unser*, 1988, 9-64.

**FAUX, Jean-Marie**

1977 *La foi du Nouveau Testament.* Brussel: Institut d'études théologiques, 1977, 402 p. Esp. 132-149: "La foi des évangiles"; 158-165: "Saint Matthieu"; 359-364: "Le discours eschatologique chez saint Matthieu"; 375-386: "Mt 28,20".

**FAWCETT, Thomas**

1973 *Hebrew Myth and Christian Gospel.* London: SCM, 1973, IX-325 p. Esp. 75-81 [light]; 102-103 [14,28-33]; 138-152: "The nativity stories"; 193-194 [12,39-40]; 199-201 [27,51-53]; 241 [7,24-27].

**FEDALTO, Giorgio**

1976 *San Pietro e la sua Chiesa tra i padri d'Oriente e d'Occidente nei primi secoli.* Roma: Città Nuova, 1976, 118 p.

**FEE, Gordon D.**

1976 The Genre of New Testament Literature and Biblical Hermeneutics. — SCHULTZ, S.J. – INCH, M.A. (eds.), *Interpreting the Word of God. Festschrift in Honor of Steven Barabas*, Chicago, IL: Moody, 1976, 105-127. Esp. 121-123 [20,1-16].

1978 Modern Text Criticism and the Synoptic Problem. — ORCHARD, B. – LONGSTAFF, T.R.W. (eds.), *J.J. Griesbach: Synoptic and Text-critical Studies*, 1978, 154-169, 214-218. Esp. 163-166 [3,1-2; 4,17; 22,44].
Modern Textual Criticism and the Synoptic Problem: On the Problem of Harmonization in the Gospels. — EPP, E.J. – FEE, G.D., *Studies in the Theory and Method of New Testament Textual Criticism* (Studies and Documents, 45), Grand Rapids, MI: Eerdmans, 1993, 174-182. Esp. 175-178.

1980    A Text-Critical Look at the Synoptic Problem. — *NT* 22 (1980) 12-28. Esp. 14-16
[argument from order]; 17-23 [24,15-20/Mk 13,14-18]; 23-28 [7,2]. [NTA 24, 768] → M. Lowe 1982a

**FEGHALI, Joseph**
1959    À propos de l'incise de s. Matthieu (V,32; XIX,9). — *L'Année canonique* (Paris) 6
(1959) 117-119.

**FEILER, Paul Frederick**
1983    The Stilling of the Storm in Matthew: A Response to Günther Bornkamm. — *JEvTS* 26
(1983) 399-406. [NTA 29, 99] → G. Bornkamm 1959a/63

**FELD, Helmut**
1973*   & NOLTE, J. (eds.), *Wort Gottes in der Zeit. Festschrift Karl Hermann Schelkle zum 65.
Geburtstag dargebracht von Kollegen, Freunden, Schülern.* Düsseldorf: Patmos, 1973,
509 p. → Rolf Baumann, O. Betz, Limbeck, Smitmans

**FELDMEIER, Reinhard**
1983    Die Darstellung des Petrus in den synoptischen Evangelien. — STUHLMACHER, P. (ed.),
*Das Evangelium und die Evangelien*, 1983, 267-271. Esp. 268-269.
Excursus. The Portrayal of Peter in the Synoptic Gospels. — HENGEL, M., *Studies in the Gospel of Mark*,
London: SCM, 1985, 59-63. Esp. 60-61; = STUHLMACHER, P. (ed.), *The Gospel and the Gospels*, 1991,
252-256. Esp. 253-254.

1987    *Die Krisis des Gottessohnes. Die Gethsemaneerzählung als Schlüssel der Markuspassion*
(WUNT, II/21). Tübingen: Mohr, 1987, XII-299 p. Esp. 9-11; 20-31 [26,36-46/Mk]. — Diss.
Tübingen, 1986 (M. Hengel).

**FELDTKELLER, Andreas**
1993    *Identitätssuche des syrischen Urchristentums. Mission, Inkulturation und Pluralität im
ältesten Heidenchristentum* (NTOA, 25). Freiburg/Schw: Universitätsverlag; Göttingen:
Vandenhoeck & Ruprecht, 1993, IX-266 p. Esp. 71-74: "Innerjüdisches Selbstverständnis des
Matthäusevangeliums"; 149-152: "Die petrinisch-matthäische Synthese". — Diss. Heidelberg, 1992 (G.
Theissen).

**FELICI, Sergio**
1994*   *Esegesi e catechesi nei Padri (secc. IV-VII). Convegno di studio e aggiornamento.
Facoltà di Lettere cristiane e classiche (Pontificium Institutum Altioris Latinitatis).
Roma 25-27 marzo 1993* (Biblioteca di scienze religiose, 112). Roma: LAS, 1994, 287
p. → Girardi, Maritano, Nuñez Moreno, Riggi

**FÉLIERS, Jeanne**
1970    L'exégèse de la péricope des porcs de Gérasa dans la patristique latine. [8,28-36] —
*Studia Patristica* 10 (1970) 225-229.

**FENDLER, Folkert**
1991    *Studien zum Markusevangelium. Zur Gattung, Chronologie, Messiasgeheimnistheorie
und Überlieferung des zweiten Evangeliums* (Göttinger theologische Arbeiten, 49).
Göttingen: Vandenhoeck & Ruprecht, 1991, 208 p. Esp. 147-190: "Deuteromarkus – die erste
Bearbeitung des Markusevangeliums? Eine Analyse der minor agreements in den synoptischen Evangelien".
— Diss. Göttingen, 1990 (G. Strecker). → A. Fuchs 1993, Neirynck 1991g

**FENEBERG, Wolfgang**
1990    *Jesus, der nahe Unbekannte.* München: Kösel, 1990, 139 p.

**FENSHAM, F. Charles**
1960    The Legal Background of Mt. vi 12. — *NT* 4 (1960) 1-2. [NTA 6, 124]

1965   Judas' Hand in the Bowl and Qumran. [26,23] — *RQum* 5 (1965) 259-261. [NTA 10, 125]
1967   The Good and Evil Eye in the Sermon on the Mount. [6,22-23] — *Neotestamentica* 1
       (1967) 51-58. [NTA 18, 107]

**FENSKE, Wolfgang**

1997   *"Und wenn ihr betet..." (Mt. 6,5). Gebete in der zwischenmenschlichen Kommunikation
       der Antike als Ausdruck der Frömmigkeit* (SUNT, 21). Göttingen: Vandenhoeck &
       Ruprecht, 1997, 348 p. Esp. 63-66 [6,9-15]; 90-93.201-203 [11,25-27]; 90-91.156-157 [9,37-38]; 196-
       198.238-269 [6,9-13]. — Diss. München, 1994 (H.-W. Kuhn).

**FENTON, John C.**

1959   Inclusio and Chiasmus in Matthew. — *Studia Evangelica* 1 (1959) 174-179.
1963   *The Gospel of St Matthew* (Pelican Gospel Commentaries). Harmondsworth: Penguin,
       1963, 487 p. Esp. 9-27: "Introduction"; 31-453: "Commentary". [NTA 8, p. 291]; repr. *Saint
       Matthew*, Philadelphia, PA: Westminster, 1978, 487 p. → Ziesler 1985
       ExpT 75 (1963-64) 226; H.J. CADBURY, JTS 17 (1966) 138-139; LACE, M., DownR 82 (1964) 247-248;
       S.B. MARROW, Bib 47 (1966) 298-299; H.K. MOULTON, BTrans 15 (1964) 204.
1966   Expounding the Parables. IV. The Parables of the Treasure and the Pearl (Mt 13,44-
       46). — *ExpT* 77 (1965-66) 178-180. [NTA 11, 212]
1968   Raise the Dead. [10,8] — *ExpT* 80 (1968-69) 50-51. [NTA 13, 570]
1980   Matthew and the Divinity of Jesus: Three Questions Concerning Matthew 1:20-23. —
       LIVINGSTONE, E.A. (ed.), *Studia Biblica 1978*, II, 1980, 79-82.
1993   The Four Gospels: Four Perspectives on the Resurrection. — AVIS, P. (ed.), *The
       Resurrection of Jesus Christ*, London: Darton, Longmann & Todd, 1993, 39-49. Esp.
       44-45 [28,1-10].

**FERNÁNDEZ, Aurelio**

1987   "No temáis a los que matan el cuerpo, pero no pueden matar el alma". Interpretación
       patrística de Mt 10,28. — *Burgense* 28 (1987) 85-108. Esp. 90-92 [Justin]; 92-94 [Irenaeus];
       94-95 [2 Clem]; 95-97 [Clement of Alexandria]; 97-102 [Tertullian]; 102-103 [Hippolyte]; 103-104
       [Novatian]; 104-105 [Cyprian]; 106-107 [Ps.Clem]; 107 [Peter of Alexander; Didasc. Apost.].

**FERNÁNDEZ, Domiciano**

1990   Natus ex Maria Virgine. Reflexiones sobre el nacimiento de Jesús. — Κεχαριτωμένη.
       FS R. Laurentin, 1990, 291-308. Esp. 298-300 [1,23].

**FERNÁNDEZ, Víctor Manuel**

1993   El Antiguo Testamento como mensaje actual. — *RevistBíb* 55 (1993) 225-234. Esp. 228-
       230 [1,23/OT].

**FERNÁNDEZ CARVAJAL, Francisco**

1974   *El evangelio de san Mateo.* Madrid: Palabra, 1974, ⁴1979, 464 p.

**FERNÁNDEZ JIMÉNEZ, Manuel**

1957   ¿Fué en Cesarea de Filipo donde Jesús prometió a Pedro el primado? [16,17-19] — *CuBíb*
       14 (1957) 106-112. → Cullmann 1952

**FERNÁNDEZ LAGO, José**

1995   Deja que los muertos entierren a sus muertos. [8,22] — *Compostellanum* 40 (1995) 7-27.

**FERNÁNDEZ RAMOS, Felipe**

1985   Los relatos de la pasión. — *Studium Legionense* (León) 25 (1985) 9-78.
1989   *El Nuevo Testamento. I-II: Presentación y contenido.* Madrid: Atenas, 1989, 396 and
       446 p.

1990  La sal de tierra. [5,13] — *Studium Legionense* 31 (1990) 63-85.

1993  La luz del mundo. — *Studium Legionense* 34 (1993) 11-73. Esp. 20-23.30-38 [5,14-16]; 25-30
      [Q 11,33].

**FERNÁNDEZ Y FERNÁNDEZ, Juan**

1962  Vocación de Mateo "el publicano". [9,9-13] — *CuBíb* 19 (1962) 45-50. [NTA 7, 132]

**FERRARI D'OCCHIEPPO, Konradin**

1965  Der Messiasstern unter neuen astronomischen und archäologischen Gesichtspunkten. —
      *Religion, Wissenschaft, Kultur* 15 (1965) 3-19.

1969  *Der Stern der Weisen – Geschichte oder Legende?* Wien: Herold, 1969, 136 p.; [2]1977,
      171 p. → 1991
         H.T. BRIK, *TPQ* 118 (1970) 188-189; P. GAECHTER, *ZKT* 92 (1970) 233.
         C. SCHEDL, *TPQ* 126 (1978) 393-394.

1989  The Star of the Magi and Babylonian Astronomy. — VARDAMAN, J. - YAMAUCHI,
      E.M. (eds.), *Chronos, Kairos, Christos*. FS J. Finegan, 1989, 41-53.

1991  *Der Stern von Bethlehem in astronomischer Sicht. Legende oder Tatsache?* Gießen:
      Brunnen, 1991; [2]1994, 186 p. (revised and expanded). → 1969

**FERRARO, Giuseppe**

1973  Il termine 'ora' nei vangeli sinottici. — *RivBib* 21 (1973) 383-400. [NTA 19, 517]

**FERREIRA, Paulo**

1969  Ein Unzialblatt vom Sinai (089 + [092a]). [26,2-12] — ALAND, K. (ed.), *Materialien*,
      1969, 134-143.

**FERREIRA-MARTINS, José Miguel**

1992  *As fontes de Mt 1–2: contributos para a exegese do Evangelho da Infancia de Mateus*.
      Diss. Pamplona, 1992, 318 p. (J.M. Casciaro). Esp. 11-20; 70-134: "As fontes de Mt 1-2"; 215-
      296: "Breves notas para a exegese".

**FESTORAZZI, Franco**

1961  Populus Israel estne maledictus et repudiatus a Deo? — *VD* 39 (1961) 255-271. Esp. 258-
      261 [23]; 261-262 [20,1-16]; 262-263 [21,18-22]; 263-264 [21,28-32]; 264-266 [22,1-14]; 266-270 [21,33-
      46]. [NTA 7, 146]

1963  Matrimonio e verginità nella Bibbia. — COLOMBO, C., et al. (eds.), *Matrimonio e
      Verginità. Saggi di Teologia* (Hildephonsiana, 3), Varese: "La Scuola Cattolica", 1963,
      51-158. Esp. 92-95 [19,3-19].

1972a L'ipocrisia farisaica e la giustizia cristiana. — *RivClerIt* 53 (1972) 747-752.

1972b Matrimonio e verginità secondo Mt 19. — *ParVi* 17 (1972) 325-333.

1973a Cristo e la giustizia divina. — *RivClerIt* 54 (1973) 171-176.

1973b Cristo giustizia del Padre e la giustizia cristiana. — *Ibid.*, 335-341.

1977  & FABRIS, R., Modelli interpretativi della salvezza nella Bibbia. — *RivBib* 25 (1977)
      245-296. Esp. 278-290: "Modelli interpretativi della morte di Gesù nella tradizione sinottica" (R. Fabris);
      291-296. [NTA 23, 977]

1985  "Ecco, ora qui c'è più di Salomone!" (Mt. 12,42). — *Testimonium Christi*. FS J.
      Dupont, 1985, 193-203. Esp. 194-195: "Logia sapienziali di Gesù"; 195-197: "Logia sapienziali del
      discorso della montagna (*Mt.* 5–7)"; 198-203: "Qualità della sapienza e insegnamento di Gesù".

1991  Messianismo senza Messia? Ipotesi di lavoro sulla questione messianica. — *RivBib* 39
      (1991) 157-165. Esp. 162-164 [12,28.42; 26,64]. [NTA 36, 371]

**FEUILLET, André**

1949 La synthèse eschatologique de saint Matthieu (XXIV-XXV). — *RB* 56 (1949) 340-364. Esp. 342-360: "La 'fin' de Jérusalem et le triomphe de Jésus (XXIV,1-44˙"; 57 (1950) 62-91. Esp. 62-86: "La 'fin' individuelle des disciples et leur association à l'œuvre et aux destinées de Jésus (XXIV,45-XXV,30)"; 180-211. Esp. 180-200: "La fin du monde et le Royaume du Père (XXV,31-46 et par.).

1954 L'ἐξουσία du Fils de l'homme (d'après Mc. II, 10-28 et parr.). — *RSR* 42 (1954) 161-192.

1955 Jésus et la Sagesse divine d'après les évangiles synoptiques. — *RB* 62 (1955) 161-196. Esp. 164-168 [11,18-19]; 169-195 [11,25-30].

1956 Le sens du mot Parousie dans l'Évangile de Matthieu. Comparaison entre Matth. xxiv et Jac. v,1-11. — DAVIES, W.D. – DAUBE, D. (eds.), *The Background of the New Testament*. FS C.H. Dodd, 1956, 261-280. Esp. 262-272: "La parousie dans le contexte de Matthieu".

1958 Les perspectives propres à chaque évangéliste dans les récits de la transfiguration. — *Bib* 39 (1958) 281-301. Esp. 292-299 [17,1-9]. [NTA 3, 348]

1959a ROBERT, A. – FEUILLET, A. (eds.), *Introduction à la Bible*. II. *Nouveau Testament*. Tournai: Desclée, 1959, XXIII-939 p. → Feuillet 1959b, Léon-Dufour 1959a; → Tricot 1939
*Einleitung in die Heilige Schrift*. II: *Neues Testament*. Wien: Herder, 1964, ²1965, XXIV-840 p.
*Introduction to the New Testament*, trans. P.W. Skehan. New York – Tournai: Desclée, 1965, XVIII-912 p.
*Introducción a la Biblia*. II: *Nuevo Testamento*. Barcelona: Herder, 1965, 831 p.
Trans. Portuguese 1967.

1959b Quelques thèmes moyens du Nouveau Testament, étudiés à la lumière de l'Ancien Testament. — *Ibid.*, 763-918. Esp. 771-818: "Le Règne de Dieu et la personne de Jésus d'après les évangiles synoptiques".

1959c Les grandes étapes de la fondation de l'Église d'après les évangiles synoptiques. — *ScEccl* 11 (1959) 5-21. Esp. 10-14: "La promesse faite à Pierre" [NTA 3, 571]

1959d La participation actuelle à la vie divine d'après le quatrième Évangile. Les origines et le sens de cette conception. — *Studia Evangelica* 1 (1959) 295-309. Esp. 302-307. [11,25-30]; = ID., *Études johanniques*, 1962, 175-189. Esp. 181-187.
Participation in the Life of God according to the Fourth Gospel. — ID., *Johannine Studies*, 1964, 169-180. Esp. 174-178.

1959e Le récit lucanien de la tentation (Lc 4,1-13). [4,1-11] — *Bib* 40 (1959) 613-631. Esp. 613-616: "L'ordre primitif des tentations; confrontation des deux traditions matthéenne et lucanienne". [NTA 4, 671]; = *Studia Biblica et Orientalia*, II, 1959, 345-363.

1959f Les témoignages de saint Paul, saint Marc et saint Matthieu relatifs à la Vierge Marie. — *BibVieChrét* 30 (1959) 45-54. Esp. 49-54. [NTA 4, 623]

1960a Parousie. — *DBS* 6/35 (1960) 1331-1419. Esp. 1337-1354: "Les évangiles synoptiques".

1960b Les thèmes bibliques majeurs du discours sur le pain de vie (Jn 6). — *NRT* 82 (1960) 803-822, 918-939, 1040-1062. Esp. 812-814 [4,1-11]; 931-939: "Les allusions des Synoptiques aux rapports de Jésus avec la Sagesse". [NTA 5, 746]; = ID., *Études johanniques*, 1962, 47-129. Esp. 59-61; 91-99.
The Principal Biblical Themes in the Discourse on the Bread of Life. — ID., *Johannine Studies*, 1964, 53-128. Esp. 64-66; 95-102.

1961 Les origines et la signification de Mt 10,23[b]. Contribution à l'étude du problème eschatologique. — *CBQ* 23 (1961) 182-198. Esp. 182-189: "L'origine du *logion*"; 189-197: "L'interprétation du *logion*". [NTA 6, 126]
Pochodzenie i sens wersetu 10,23b Ew. św. Mt. Przyczynek do studium problematyki eschatologicznej (Ursprung und Sinn von Mt 10,23). — *Studia biblijne i archeologiczne*, Poznań: Księg. sw. Wojciecha, 1963, 107-122.

1962a  *Études johanniques* (Museum Lessianum: Section biblique, 4). Paris–Brugge: Desclée
De Brouwer, 1962, 315 p. → 1959d, 1960b
*Johannine Studies.* Staten Island, NY: Alba House, 1964, 292 p.

1962b  Le triomphe du Fils de l'homme d'après la déclaration du Christ aux Sanhédrites (*Mc.*,
XIV,62; *Mt.*, XXVI,64; *Lc.*, XXII,69). — MASSAUX, É. (ed.), *La venue du Messie*, 1962,
149-171. Esp. 155-160 [minor agreements].

1964a  Le Nouveau Testament et le cœur du Christ. Étude des principaux textes évangéliques
utilisés par la liturgie du Sacré-Cœur. — *AmiCler* 74 (1964) 321-333. Esp. 321-325 [1,28-
30]. [NTA 9, 152]

1964b  Le baptême de Jésus. [3,13-17] — *RB* 71 (1964) 321-352. [NTA 9, 555]
The Baptism of Jesus. — *TDig* 14 (1966) 207-212.
*SelT* 4 (1965) 228-234.

1967a  La coupe et le baptême de la passion (*Mc*, X,35-40; cf. *Mt*, XX,20-23; *Lc*, XII,50). —
*RB* 74 (1967) 356-391. Esp. 366-368. [NTA 12, 566]

1967b  Les trois grandes prophéties de la passion et de la résurrection des évangiles
synoptiques. — *RThom* 67 (1967) 533-560; 68 (1968) 41-74. [NTA 13, 195]

1968  La controverse sur le jeûne (*Mc 2*, 18-20; *Mt 9*, 14-15; *Lc 5*, 33-35). — *NRT* 90 (1968)
113-136, 252-277. Esp. 115-124: "Les problèmes littéraires"; 124-136.252-262: "L'exégèse du texte";
262-269: "La question de l'historicité". [NTA 13, 190]
*SelT* 7 (1968) 181-183.

1970a  "Chercher à persuader Dieu" (Ga i 10ᵃ). Le début de l'Épître aux Galates et la scène
matthéenne de Césarée de Philippe. — *NT* 12 (1970) 350-360. Esp. 354-359 [16,13-23].
[NTA 15, 951]

1970b  La personnalité de Jésus entrevue à partir de sa soumission au rite de repentance du
Précurseur. [3,13-17] — *RB* 77 (1970) 30-49. [NTA 15, 87]

1971  Morale ancienne et morale chrétienne d'après Mt v.17-20; comparaison avec la doctrine
de l'Épître aux Romains. — *NTS* 17 (1970-71) 123-137. Esp. 124-129: "Brève analyse"; 129-
136: "La morale évangélique". [NTA 15, 846]

1972  *Le mystère de l'amour divin dans la théologie johannique* (Études bibliques). Paris:
Gabalda, 1972, 293 p. Esp. 133-177: "Comparaison avec les synoptiques. L'hymne de jubilation (Mt
11,25-30; Lc 10,21-22)".

1976  Il significato fondamentale dell'agonia del Getsèmani. [26,32-42] — *La sapienza della
croce oggi. Atti del Congresso internazionale, Roma, 13-18 ottobre, 1975*. I: *La
sapienza della croce nella rivelazione e nell' ecumenismo*, Torino-Leumann: Elle Di Ci,
1976, 69-85.

1977  *L'agonie de Gethsémani. Enquête exégétique et théologique suivie d'une étude du
"Mystère de Jésus" de Pascal.* Paris: Gabalda, 1977, 345 p. Esp. 67-76: "Le problème
synoptique"; 77-142: "Commentaire des récits de l'agonie de saint Marc (14,32-42) et de saint Matthieu
(26,36-46)".

1978a  I due aspetti della giustizia nel Sermone della montagna. — *Communio* (Milano) 38
(1978) 21-29.
Die beiden Aspekte der Gerechtigkeit in der Bergpredigt. — *IKZ/Communio*
(Rodenkirchen) 7 (1978) 108-115. Esp. 112-113 [3,15]; 113-115 [5,17-20/Paul]. [NTA 22, 761]

1978b  Le caractère purement religieux et universel du Règne de Dieu d'après les évangiles
synoptiques. — *Divinitas* 22 (1978) 153-175. Esp. 159-167 [10,23; 15,24]; 173-174 [28,19-20].
[NTA 23, 59]

1979a  Les ouvriers envoyés à la vigne (Mt. XX,1-16). Le service désintéressé et la gratuité de
l'alliance. — *RThom* 79 (1979) 5-24. [NTA 24, 94]

1979b   Die Versuchungen Jesu. — *IKZ/Communio* (Rodenkirchen) 8 (1979) 226-237. [NTA 24, 81]

1980a   Le caractère universel du jugement et la charité sans frontières en *Mt* 25,31-46. — *NRT* 102 (1980) 179-196. Esp. 180-186: "Les tentatives de limitations de la perspective universaliste"; 186-192: "L'exclusion de toute limitation"; 192-196: "Observations générales". [NTA 24, 796]

1980b   Loi de Dieu, loi du Christ et loi de l'Esprit d'après les épîtres pauliniennes. Les rapports de ces trois lois avec la Loi mosaïque. — *NT* 22 (1980) 29-65. Esp. 45-51: "Les références explicites ou implicites aux enseignements de Jésus". [NTA 24, 861]

1981    Règne de Dieu. III. Évangiles synoptiques. — *DBS* 10/54 (1981) 61-165. Esp. 61-121; 141-152 [24-25]; 152 [10,23]; 152-153 [16,28]; 153-154 [19,28].

1982    Los relatos evangélicos de la infancia de Jesús. — *Tierra Santa* (Jerusalem) 57 (1982) 13-17.
        I racconti evangelici sull'infanzia di Gesù. — *Terra Santa* (Jerusalem) 58 (1982) 9-13.

1984    Les épousailles messianiques et les références au Cantique des cantiques dans les évangiles synoptiques. — *RThom* 84 (1984) 181-211, 399-424. Esp. 197-211: "Le roi qui offre un festin pour les noces de son fils" [22,1-14]; 399-417: "La parabole des dix vierges" [25,1-13]. [NTA 29, 75/534]

1985    L'indissolubilité du mariage et le monde féminin d'après la doctrine évangélique et quelques autres données bibliques parallèles. — *ScriptTheol* 17 (1985) 415-461. Esp. 428-453: "Les textes du premier évangile". [NTA 30, 1276]

1988    Observations sur les deux généalogies de Jésus-Christ de saint Matthieu (1,1-17) et de saint Luc (3,23-38). — *EVie* 98 (1988) 294, 605-608. [NTA 33, 594]

1990    Le Sauveur messianique et sa mère dans les récits de l'enfance de saint Matthieu et de saint Luc. — *Divinitas* 34 (1990) 17-52, 103-150. Esp. 21-49. [NTA 34, 1127]; = (Collezione Teologica, 4). Città del Vaticano: Pontificia Academia Teologica Romana – Libreria Editrice Vaticana, 1990, 88 p.
        J.J. BARTOLOMÉ, *Sal* 53 (1991) 582-583; M. GESTEIRA, *RevistEspTeol* 51 (1991) 106-107; G. PÉREZ, *Salmanticensis* 37 (1990) 366-367; É. RICAUD, *EVie* 100 (1990) 571; A. ROLLA, *Asprenas* 37 (1990) 513-514.

1991    La primauté et l'humilité de Pierre. Leur attestation en *Mt* 16,17-19, dans l'Évangile de Marc et dans la Première Épître de Pierre. — *NVet* 66 (1991) 3-24. Esp. 4-12, 16-18. [NTA 35, 1136] → G. Claudel 1988

1992a   *La primauté de Pierre (Essai).* Tournai: Desclée; Paris: Bégédis, 1992, 106 p.

1992b   La date de composition et les caractéristiques de chacun des quatre évangiles. — *Divinitas* 36 (1992) 3-18. Esp. 9-11. [NTA 36, 1194]

1992c   La connaissance de Jésus d'après la double tradition synoptique et johannique. — *Ibid.*, 103-118. Esp. 107-110 [11,25-30]; 110-111 [16,17-19]. [NTA 37, 85]

**FICHTNER, Rudolf**

1994    *Taufe und Versuchung Jesu in den* Evangeliorum libri quattuor *des Bibeldichters Juvencus (1,346-408)* (Beiträge zur Altertumskunde, 50). Stuttgart: Teubner, 1994, 222 p.

**FIDALGO HERRANZ, José-Antonio**

1984    La SS. Trinidad en la Suma contra los gentiles: Fuentes bíblicas. — *EstBíb* 42 (1984) 363-389; 44 (1986) 147-193. Esp. 181-184 [28,19]

**FIEBIG, Paul**

1904R   Die Chronologie der jüdischen Gleichnisse und die Originalität der Gleichnisse Jesu. [1904] — HARNISCH, W. (ed.), *Gleichnisse Jesu*, 1982, 20-57. Esp. 51-56 [13,24-30.36-43]. → Jülicher 1899

**FIEDERLEIN, Friedrich Martin**

1988  *Die Wunder Jesu und die Wundererzählungen der Urkirche*. München: Don Bosco, 1988, 264 p. Esp. 29-37: "Die Wundererzählungen im Matthäusevangelium"; 79-84 [9,27-31; 20,29-34]; 107-108 [9,32-34]; 118-122 [15,21-28]; 122-127 [8,5-13]; 188-189 [14,28-31].

**FIEDLER, Martin Johannes**

1957  *Der Begriff* δικαιοσύνη *im Matthäus-Evangelium, auf seine Grundlagen untersucht*. Diss. Halle-Wittenberg, 1957, 168 and 134 p. → Rohde 1965
      *TLZ* 83 (1958) 591-592.

1977  "Gerechtigkeit" im Matthäus-Evangelium. — *TVers* 8 (1977) 63-75. Esp. 65-70: "Einzeluntersuchung des Begriffs 'Gerechtigkeit' bei Matthäus".

**FIEDLER, Peter**

1969  *Die Formel "Und siehe" im Neuen Testament* (SANT, 20). München: Kösel, 1969, 96 p. Esp. 23-29; 51-59. — Diss. Freiburg, 1968 (A. Vögtle).

1970  Die übergebenen Talente. Auslegung von Mt 25,14-30. — *BibLeb* 11 (1970) 259-273. [NTA 15, 859]

1975*  & ZELLER, D. (eds.), *Gegenwart und kommendes Reich. Schülergabe Anton Vögtle zum 65. Geburtstag* (SBB). Stuttgart: Katholisches Bibelwerk, 1975, 189 p. → P. Fiedler, Maisch, Oberlinner, Zeller

1975  Der Sohn Gottes über unserem Weg in die Gottesherrschaft. Gegenwart und Zukunft der βασιλεία im Mattäusevangelium. — *Ibid.*, 91-100. Esp. 91-95: "'Christologisierung' der βασιλεία-Verkündigung"; 96-100: "'Ethisierung' der βασιλεία-Verkündigung".

1976  *Jesus und die Sünder* (BET, 3). Frankfurt/M: Lang, 1976, 413 p. Esp. 136-147 [11,16-19; Q 7,31-35]; 173-184 [20,1-15]; 185-195 [5,38-48]; 195-204 [18,23-35]; 205-211 [6,12]; 211-215 [12,27-28]; 233-238 [21,28-32]; 238-241 [22,1-10]; 255-259 [6,13]. — Diss. Freiburg, 1975 (A. Vögtle).

1981  Geschichten als Theologie und Verkündigung – die Prologe des Matthäus- und Lukas-Evangeliums. — PESCH, R. (ed.), *Zur Theologie der Kindheitsgeschichten*, 1981, 11-26. Esp. 17-21.

1986  Die Tora bei Jesus und in der Jesusüberlieferung. — KERTELGE, K. (ed.), *Das Gesetz im Neuen Testament*, 1986, 71-87. → G. Klein 1984

1991  Die Passion des Christus. — OBERLINNER, L. - FIEDLER, P. (eds.), *Salz der Erde*. FS A. Vögtle, 1991, 299-319. Esp. 299-302: "Das Gefüge der Matthäus-Passion"; 302-314: "Die Botschaft der Matthäus-Passion"; 314-319: "Probleme der Matthäus-Passion".

1994  Das Matthäusevangelium und "die Pharisäer". — MAYER, C., et al. (eds.), *Nach den Anfängen fragen*. FS G. Dautzenberg, 1994, 199-218. Esp. 200-204 [5,21-48]; 204-205 [12,9-14]; 205-207 [15,1-20]; 207-208 [19,1-9].

**FIEGER, Michael**

1991  *Das Thomasevangelium. Einleitung, Kommentar und Systematik* (NTAbh, NF 22). Münster: Aschendorff, 1991, XIX-296 p. Esp. 6-7: "Das Verhältnis zu den Synoptikern"; 291-294: "Parallelen zu den kanonischen Evangelien". — Diss. München, 1988-89 (J. Gnilka).

**FIGURA, Michael**

1984  *Das Kirchenverständnis des Hilarius von Poitiers* (Freiburger theologische Studien, 127). Freiburg: Herder, 1984, 382 p. Esp. 238-243 [5,31-32; 19,3-12]. — Diss. Freiburg (K. Lehmann).

**FILAS, Francis L.**

1956  The Star of the Magi. — *IrEcclRec* 85 (1956) 432-433. → Marsh-Edwards 1956

**FILIPPINI, Roberto**

1987  "Ma io vi dico...". — *ParVi* 32 (1987) 244-253.

**FILSON, Floyd V.**

1956 Broken Patterns in the Gospel of Matthew. [1,1-16; 5,3-12.21-48; 13,1-53; 23,13-36] — *JBL* 75 (1956) 227-231. [NTA 1, 391]
Gebrochene Formen im Matthäusevangelium. — LANGE, J. (ed.), *Das Matthäus-Evangelium*, 1980, 265-272.

1960 *A Commentary on the Gospel according to St. Matthew* (Black's New Testament Commentaries). London: Black, 1960, VII-319 p. Esp. 1-44: "Introduction"; 45-47: "Selected bibliography"; 49-306: "Translation and commentary". [NTA 6, p. 123]; repr. 1971. → Ziesler 1985
*The Gospel according to St. Matthew* (Harper's New Testament Commentary). New York: Harper, 1961, 314 p.
E. ANDREWS, *Interpr* 16 (1962) 109-111; H.A. BLAIR, *CQR* 162 (1961) 490-491; J. BLIGH, *HeythJ* 2 (1961) 176-180; B.S. BROWN, *AusBR* 9 (1961) 46; R.B. BROWN, *RExp* 58 (1961) 372; T.A. BURKILL, *JRel* 44 (1964) 75-76; G.E.P. COX, *Theology* 64 (1961) 166-167; H.B. GREEN, *JTS* 12 (1961) 317-319; R. MASSON, *Angelicum* 38 (1961) 452; P. NEPPER-CHRISTENSEN, *TLZ* 87 (1962) 114-115; P. PARKER, *JBL* 81 (1962) 80-83; J.S. STEWART, *ScotJT* 15 (1962) 95-97; V. TAYLOR, *ExpT* 72 (1960-61) 105; A. VIARD, *RSPT* 45 (1961) 287-288.

1964 *A New Testament History. The Story of the Emerging Church.* Philadelphia, PA: Westminster, 1964, XI-435 p. Esp. 83-84, 365-367.
*Geschichte des Christentums in neutestamentlicher Zeit*, trans. F.J. Scherse (Kommentare und Beiträge zum Alten und Neuen Testament). Düsseldorf: Patmos, 1967, XIII-461 p. Esp. 95-96, 393-396.

1972 Capitalization in English Translations of the Gospel of Matthew. — AUNE, D.E. (ed.), *Studies in New Testament*. FS A.P. Wikgren, 1972, 25-30.

1982 Gospels, Synoptic. — BROMILEY, G.W., et al. (eds.), *The International Standard Bible Encyclopedia*, II, Grand Rapids, MI: Eerdmans, 1982, 532-536.

**FINDLAY, J. Alexander**

1950 *Jesus and His Parables.* London: Epworth, 1950, 158 p.

**FINKBEINER, Douglas**

1991 An Examination of "Make Disciples of All Nations" in Matthew 28:18-20. — *Calvary Baptist Theological Journal* (Lansdale, PA) 7/1 (1991) 12-42; 7/2 (1991) 1-10.

**FINKEL, Asher**

1963 Jesus' Sermon at Nazareth (Luk. 4,16-30). — BETZ, O., et al. (eds.), *Abraham unser Vater*. FS O. Michel, 1963, 106-115. Esp. 112-114 [5,3-12].

1964 *The Pharisees and the Teacher of Nazareth. A Study of Their Background, Their Halachic and Midrashic Teachings, the Similarities and Differences* (Arbeiten zur Geschichte des Spätjudentums und Urchristentums, 4). Leiden: Brill, 1964, XIII-184 p. Esp. 129-175: "The message of Jesus in the light of Pharisaic teachings" [5-7; 5,3-12; 12,1-8.9-14].

1981* & FRIZZELL, L. (eds.), *Standing before God. Studies on Prayer in Scriptures and in Tradition with Essays In Honor of John M. Oesterreicher.* New York: Ktav, 1981, 410 p. → Finkel, Sievers, Zeller

1981 The Prayer of Jesus in Matthew. — *Ibid.*, 131-170. Esp. 145-152: "The redaction of Matthew"; 152-158: "The meaning of Pater Noster".

**FINKENZELLER, Josef**

1964 Auf diesen Felsen will ich meine Kirche bauen (Mt 16,18). — SCHMAUS, M. – LÄPPLE, A. (eds.), *Wahrheit und Zeugnis. Aktuelle Themen der Gegenwart in theologischer Sicht*, Düsseldorf: Patmos, 1964, 624-634. Esp. 624-625 [16,18-19; 18,18]

**FIORENZA, Elisabeth SCHÜSSLER**

1972 *Priester für Gott. Studien zum Herrschafts- und Priestermotiv in der Apokalypse* (NTAbh, NF 7). Münster: Aschendorff, 1972, VIII-450 p. Esp. 188-192 [24,30/Ap 1,7].

1977 The Quest for the Johannine School: The Apocalypse and the Fourth Gospel. — *NTS* 23 (1976-77) 402-427. Esp. 419-424 [Apoc/Mt]. [NTA 22, 208]; = ID., *The Book of Revelation. Justice and Judgment*, Philadelphia, PA: Fortress, 1985, 85-113. Esp. 101-106.

1983 *In Memory of Her. A Feminist Theological Reconstruction of Christian Origins.* New York: Crossroad; London: SCM, 1983, XXV-357 p. Esp. 118-130: "The basileia vision of Jesus"; 130-140: "The sophia-God"; 149-150 [23,8-12]; [2]1990. → F.W. Hughes 1987
*En mémoire d'elle. Essai de reconstruction des origines chrétiennes selon la théologie féministe* (Cogitatio Fidei, 136). Paris: Cerf, 1986, 482 p. Esp. 183-200; 200-214; 225-227.
*Ter herinnering aan haar. Een feministisch theologische reconstructie van de oorsprongen van het christendom*, trans. T. van der Stap. Hilversum: Gooi en Sticht, 1987, 384 p.
*Zu ihrem Gedachtnis... Eine feministisch-theologische Rekonstruktion der christlichen Ursprünge.* München: Kaiser; Mainz: Grünewald, 1988, 426 p. Esp. 162-177; 177-189; 199-202.
*En memoria de ella...* Bilbao: Desclée De Brouwer, 1989, 415 p.

1989 Les Douze dans la communauté des disciples égaux: contradiction ou malentendu? — *FoiVie* 88/5 = *Cahiers bibliques* 28 (1989) 13-24. Esp. 17-18 [19,28]. [NTA 34, 828]

1995 Jesus – Messenger of Divine Wisdom. — *StudTheol* 49 (1995) 231-252. Esp. 234-238: "The earliest sophialogical Jesus traditions"; 239-242: "Feminist interpretations of Q's wisdom dicourses"; 242-246 [Q 10,21-22]. [NTA 40, 1658]

**FIRPO, Giulio**

1983 *Il problema cronologico della nascita di Gesù* (Biblioteca di cultura religiosa, 42). Brescia: Paideia, 1983, 302 p. Esp. 89-118 [2,1-23]. [NTA 28, p. 313]
A. BARZANÒ, *VetChr* 21 (1984) 389-393; C. BERNAS, *JBL* 105 (1986) 149-150; R. DELLA CASA, *Sal* 46 (1984) 554-555; J.-C. INGELAERE, *RHPR* 64 (1984) 183-184; X. JACQUES, *Études classiques* 52 (1984) 264; A. PASSONI DELL'ACQUA, *ParVi* 29 (1984) 339-342.

1986 Addenda e puntualizzazione sulla cronologia della nascita di Gesù. — *Paideia* (Genova) 41 (1986) 63-70.

**FISCHBACH, Stephanie M.**

1992 *Totenerweckungen. Zur Geschichte einer Gattung* (FzB, 69). Würzburg: Echter, 1992, XIV-345 p. Esp. 198-211 [9,18-26]. — Diss. Würzburg, 1991 (H.-J. Klauck).

**FISCHER, Balthasar**

1972 Die acht Seligkeiten als Gesangs- und Gebetstext in Vergangenheit und Gegenwart. — *TTZ* 81 (1972) 276-284.

**FISCHER, Bonifatius**

1980 Ein altlateinisches Evangelienfragment. — BRECHT, M. (ed.), *Text – Wort – Glaube. Studien zur Überlieferung, Interpretation und Autorisierung biblischer Texte Kurt Aland gewidmet* (Arbeiten zur Kirchengeschichte, 50), Berlin – New York: de Gruyter, 1980, 84-111. Esp. 86-89; = ID., *Beiträge zur Geschichte der lateinischen Bibeltexte* (Vetus Latina. Aus der Geschichte der lateinischen Bibel, 12), Freiburg: Herder, 1986, 275-307.

1988 *Die lateinischen Evangelien bis zum 10. Jahrhundert. I. Varianten zu Matthäus* (Vetus Latina. Aus der Geschichte der lateinischen Bibel, 13). Freiburg: Herder, 1988, 48*-496 p.
G.M. BARTELINK, *VigChr* 44 (1990) 303; P.-M. BOGAERT, *RHE* 84 (1989) 505-506; *Bulletin d'ancienne littérature chrétienne latine* (Maredsous) 6 (1993) 275-278; J.K. ELLIOTT, *JTS* 41 (1990) 637-640; M. GESTEIRA, *RevistEspTeol* 51 (1991) 111; W.J. GOCHEE, *JBL* 109 (1990) 530-533; X. JACQUES, *NRT* 111 (1989) 751-752; J.C. HAELEWYCK, *Scriptorium* (Brussel) 45 (1991) 34-35; S. LÉGASSE, *BullLitEccl* 91 (1990) 291; C. MUNIER, *RevSR* 64 (1990) 335; J.-M. ROUSÉE, *RB* 96 (1989) 312.

**FISCHER, G.** → Hasitschka 1995

**FISCHER, Karl Martin**

1970 Redaktionsgeschichtliche Bemerkungen zur Passionsgeschichte des Matthäus. — *TVers*

2 (1970) 109-128. Esp. 109-115: "Die Hoheit Jesu"; 115-121: "Der Sinn des Todes Jesu"; 121-123: "Die Jünger".

1978 *Das Ostergeschehen* (Aufsätze und Vorträge zur Theologie und Religionswissenschaft, 71). Berlin: Evangelische Verlagsanstalt, 1978, 124 p. Göttingen: Vandenhoeck & Ruprecht, [2]1980.

1979 → H.-M. Schenke 1979

1985 *Das Urchristentum* (Kirchengeschichte in Einzeldarstellungen, I/1). Berlin: Evangelische Verlagsanstalt, 1985, [2]1991, 200 p. Esp. 73-77: "Die Wandermissionare und ihre Theologie nach der Logienquelle".

**FISHER, Eugene J.**

1993 The Passion and Death of Jesus of Nazareth: Catechetical Approaches. — EFROYMSON, D.P., et al. (eds.), *Within Context. Essays on Jews and Judaism in the New Testament*, Philadelphia, PA: American Interfaith Institute, 1993, 104-122. Esp. 118-122: "Matthew's passion narrative".

**FISHER, F.L.**

1976 *The Sermon on the Mount*. Nashville, TN: Broadman, 1976, 154 p. [NTA 21, p. 326]

**FISHER, N.F.**

1979 *The Parables of Jesus. Glimpses of the New Age*. 1979.
*The Parables of Jesus. Glimpses of God's Reign*. New York: Crossroad, rev. ed., 1990, XIV-178 p. [NTA 35, p. 240]

**FITCH, William**

1962 *The Beatitudes of Jesus*. Grand Rapids, MI: Eerdmans, 1962, 132 p.; Glasgow: Pickering & Inglis, 1962, 144 p.
   M. ZERWICK, *VD* 43 (1965) 46-47.

**FITZER, Gottfried**

1957 Die Sünde wider den Heiligen Geist. — *TZ* 13 (1957) 161-182. Esp. 170-172 [12,31-32].

**FITZGERALD, John T.**

1972 The Temptation of Jesus. The Testing of the Messiah in Matthew. — *RestQ* 15 (1972) 152-160. [NTA 18, 100]

1995 The Problem of Perjury in Greek Context: Prolegomena to an Exegesis of Matthew 5:33; 1 Timothy 1:10; and *Didache* 2.3. — WHITE, L.M. – YARBROUGH, O.L. (eds.), *The Social World of the First Christians. Essays in Honor of Wayne A. Meeks*, Minneapolis, MN: Fortress, 1995, 156-177. Esp. 171-172.176-177.

**FITZMYER, Joseph A.**

1957 "4Q Testimonia" and the New Testament. — *TS* 18 (1957) 513-537. Esp. 515-518: "The formula quotations". [NTA 2, 653]; = ID., *Essays*, 1971, 59-89. Esp. 63-65.

1959a The Aramaic Qorbān Inscription from Jebel Ḥallet et-Ṭûri and Mark 7,11 / Matt 15,5. — *JBL* 78 (1959) 60-65. [NTA 4, 88]; = ID., *Essays*, 1971, 93-100.

1959b The Oxyrhynchus *Logoi* of Jesus and the Coptic Gospel according to Thomas. — *TS* 20 (1959) 505-560. Esp. 511-529 [POxy 654]; 529-543 [POxy 1]; 543-551 [POxy 655]. [NTA 4, 813]; = ID., *Essays*, 1971, 355-433 (426-433: "Additional Bibliography 1969"). Esp. 364-387; 387-404; 404-414.

1961a *An Introductory Bibliography for the Study of Scripture* (Woodstock Papers: Occasional Essays for Theology, 5), Westminster, MD: Newman, 1961, XIX-135 p.; (Subsidia Biblica, 3), Roma: Biblical Institute Press, [2]1981, XI-154 p.; [3]1990, XV-217 p.

1961b  The Use of Explicit Old Testament Quotations in Qumran Literature and in the New Testament. — *NTS* 7 (1960-61) 297-333. Esp. 299-305: "The introductory formulae"; 309 [4,1-11]; 316 [4,15-16]; 329 [7,23]. [NTA 6, 315]; = ID., *Essays*, 1971, 3-58. Esp. 7-16; 21; 32; 52.

1962   Memory and Manuscript: The Origins and Transmission of the Gospel Tradition. — *TS* 23 (1962) 442-457. Esp. 450-454. [NTA 7, 705r] → Gerhardsson 1961

1963   The Name Simon. — *HTR* 56 (1963) 1-5. [NTA 7, 783]; = ID., *Essays*, 1971, 105-110. → C. Roth 1961, 1964

1965   Anti-Semitism and the Cry of "All the People" (Mt 27:25). — *TS* 26 (1965) 667-671. [NTA 10, 920]

1966   The Son of David Tradition and Matthew 22,41-46 and Parallels. — *Concilium* (New York) 20 (1966) 75-87. Esp. 83-87. [NTA 11, 705]; = ID., *Essays*, 1971, 113-126. Esp. 122-126.
       La tradition du Fils de David en regard de Mt 22,41-46 et des écrits parallèles. — *Concilium* (Paris) 2/20 (1966) 67-78. Esp. 74-78.
       Die Davidssohn-Überlieferung und Mt 22,41-46 (und die Parallelstellen). — *IZT/Concilium* (Mainz) 2/10 (1966) 780-786. Esp. 784-786.

1970   The Priority of Mark and the "Q" Source in Luke. — BUTTRICK, D.G. (ed.), *Jesus and Man's Hope*. I, 1970, 131-170. Esp. 134-147: "The priority of Mark"; 147-156: "Luke's use of Q"; 156-163: "Other solutions" [Vaganay, Léon-Dufour, Farmer]. [NTA 15, 119]; = ID., *To Advance the Gospel*, 1981, 3-40. Esp. 5-16; 16-23; 23-29; 29-30 ("Postscript"). → W.R. Farmer 1983c, 1984d
       The Priority of Mark. [1970, 134-147.164-166]. — BELLINZONI, A.J., Jr., et al. (eds.), *The Two-Source Hypothesis*, 1985, 37-52.
       Luke's Use of Q. [1970, 147-156]. — *Ibid.*, 245-257.

1971   *Essays on the Semitic Background of the New Testament*. London: Chapman, 1971, XIX-524 p.; (Sources of Biblical Study, 5), Missoula, MT: Scholars, 1974; = *The Semitic Background of the New Testament. Combined Edition of* Essays on the Semitic Background of the New Testament *and* A Wandering Aramean. Collected Aramaic Essays, Grand Rapids, MI / Cambridge: Eerdmans; Livonia, MI: Dove, 1997. → 1957, 1959a-b, 1961b, 1963, 1966, C. Roth 1964

1972   The Use of ἄγειν and φέρειν in the Synoptic Gospels. — BARTH, E.H. - COCROFT, R.E. (eds.), *Festschrift to Honor F. Wilbur Gingrich*, 1972, 147-160. Esp. 150-153 [φέρω]; 153-155 [ἄγω].

1973   The Virginal Conception of Jesus in the New Testament. — *TS* 34 (1973) 541-575. Esp. 550-552, 560-566. [NTA 18, 422]; = ID., *To Advance the Gospel*, 1981, 41-78. Esp. 46-47; 51-53; 61-65 ("Postscript"). → R.E. Brown 1972

1975   Methodology in the Study of the Aramaic Substratum of Jesus' Sayings in the New Testament. — DUPONT, J. (ed.), *Jésus aux origines de la christologie*, 1975, 73-102; [2]1989 (additional note, 418-419). Esp. 94-95 [7,6].
       The Study of the Aramaic Background of the New Testament. — ID., *A Wandering Aramean*, 1979, 1-27 (slightly revised). Esp. 14-15.

1976   The Matthean Divorce Texts and Some New Palestinian Evidence. — *TS* 37 (1976) 197-226. Esp. 200-202 [Q 16,18]; 202-203 [5,31-32]; 205-207 [19,3-9]; 207-211 [5,32; 19,9]; 221-223 [Qumran/19,9]. [NTA 21, 76]; = ID., *To Advance the Gospel*, 1981, 79-111. Esp. 82-83; 83-84; 86-87; 87-89; 97-99.

1978   Crucifixion in Ancient Palestine, Qumran Literature, and the New Testament. — *CBQ* 40 (1978) 493-513. Esp. 508 [27,35]; 512-513 [27,39-43]. [NTA 23, 396]; = ID., *To Advance the Gospel*, 1981, 125-146. Esp. 136; 139.

1979a  *A Wandering Aramean. Collected Aramaic Essays* (SBL MS, 25). Missoula, MT: Scholars, 1979, XVII-290 p. → 1975, 1979b; → 1971/97

1979b The New Testament Title "Son of Man" Philologically Considered. — *Ibid.*, 143-160. Esp. 144; 154.

1979c Aramaic Kepha' and Peter's Name in the New Testament. — BEST, E.- WILSON, R.McL. (eds.), *Text and Interpretation.* FS M. Black, 1979, 121-132. Esp. 130; = ID., *To Advance the Gospel,* 1981, 112-124. Esp. 118.

1981a *The Gospel According to Luke. Introduction, Translation and Notes.* Vol. I: *I-IX;* Vol. II: *X-XXIV* (The Anchor Bible, 28/28A). New York: Doubleday, 2 vols., 1981/1985, XXVI-837 and XXVI-839-1642 p. Esp. 73-75: "Luke's supposed dependence on Matthew"; 75-81: "Luke's dependence on 'Q'".
Trans. Spanish 1986/87.

1981b *To Advance the Gospel. New Testament Studies.* New York: Crossroad, 1981, XIII-265 p.; (The Biblical Resource Series), Grand Rapids, MI / Cambridge: Eerdmans; Livonia, MI: Dove, [2]1998, XVII-421 p. (Appendix, 382-384) → 1970, 1973, 1976, 1978, 1979c; → 1987b

1981c The Dead Sea Scrolls and the New Testament after Thirty Years. — *TDig* 29 (1981) 351-367. Esp. 361-363 [5,32; 19,3-12]. [NTA 26, 1093]
Dödahavsrullarna och Nya testamentet efter trettio år. — *SvenskTeolKvcrt* 58 (1982) 117-130. Esp. 126-128. [NTA 27, 1190]

1981d Nouveau Testament et christologie. Questions actuelles. — *NRT* 103 (1981) 18-47; 187-208. Esp. 31-35 [sayings of Jesus]; 187-189 [1,18-25]; 192-194 [28]. [NTA 25, 1033]

1985a → 1981a

1985b *Abba* and Jesus' Relation to God. — GANTOY, R. (ed.), *À cause de l'Évangile.* FS J. Dupont, 1985, 15-38. Esp. 35-37 [Q 10,21-22].

1987a Aramaic Evidence Affecting the Interpretation of *Hosanna* in the New Testament. — HAWTHORNE, G.F. – BETZ, O. (eds.), *Tradition and Interpretation.* FS E.E. Ellis, 1987, 110-118. Esp. 114-115 [21,9.15].

1987b The Resurrection of Jesus Christ according to the New Testament. — *The Month* (London) 248 (1987) 402-410. Esp. 406 [28,1-20]; = ID., *To Advance the Gospel* [1981], [2]1998, 369-381.

1988 The Qumran Scrolls and the New Testament after Forty Years. — *RQum* 13 (1988) 609-620. Esp. 617-618.

1992 A Palestinian Collection of Beatitudes. — VAN SEGBROECK, F., et al. (eds.), *The Four Gospels 1992.* FS F. Neirynck, 1992, I, 509-515.

1995 The Dead Sea Scrolls and Early Christianity. — *TDig* 42 (1995) 303-319. Esp. 311-315 [4Q521]. → Neirynck 1997d, É. Puech 1992, 1993, 1994, Tabor 1992a

**FJÄRSTEDT, Biörn**

1968 Fråga och svar i Matt. 19,3-12. [Question and answer in Matt. 19,3-12] — *SEÅ* 33 (1968) 118-140. [NTA 14, 145]

1974 *Synoptic Tradition in 1 Corinthians. Themes and Clusters of Theme Words in 1 Corinthians 1-4 and 9.* Uppsala: University Press, 1974, XX-191 p. Esp. 88-94 [25,14-30/1 Cor 9,19-27]; 122-129 [Q 12,39-46/1 Cor 4]; 129-133 [25,31-46/1 Cor 4]; 133-135 [5,1-16/1 Cor 4]; 145-150 [11,25-27/1 Cor 2]; 150-152 [12,38-42/1 Cor 1,20-24]; 157-160 [21,33-46/1 Cor 3]; 161 [7,24-27/1 Cor 3]; 162-163 [10,40-42/1 Cor 3,6-7]; 163-164 [Q 17,28-31/1 Cor]; 165-167 [13,24-30.36-43/1 Cor 3]. — Diss. Uppsala, 1974 (L. Hartman).

**FLACKE, Maria Luise**

1983 Das ist aber ungerecht! Die Parabel von den Arbeitern im Weinberg (Matth. 20,1-15), Primarstufe. — *Religion Heute* (Hannover) 6 (1983) 228-242.

**FLANAGAN, Donal**

1982    There Was a Birth Certainly... – The Infancy Narratives. — *Furrow* 33 (1982) 131-136; = DRURY, R., *The New Testament as Personal Reading*, Springfield, IL: Templegate, 1983, 42-52.

**FLANAGAN, Neal M.**

1978    *Mark, Matthew, and Luke: A Guide to the Gospel Parallels. A Companion for Individuals and Study Groups to the* Gospel Parallels *of Burton H. Throckmorton, Jr.* Collegeville, MN: Liturgical Press, 1978, XII-91 p. [NTA 23, p. 347] → Throckmorton 1967

**FLEDDERMANN, Harry T.**

1981    The Discipleship Discourse (Mark 9:33-50). — *CBQ* 43 (1981) 57-75. Esp. 61-64 [10,40]; 64-66 [12,30]; 67-69 [18,6-7]; 72-73 [5,13]. [NTA 25, 879]

1982    A Warning about the Scribes (Mark 12:37b-40). — *CBQ* 44 (1982) 52-67. Esp. 57-61 [23,6-7]. [NTA 26, 869]

1984    John and the Coming One (Matt 3:11-12 // Luke 3:16-17). — *SBL 1984 Seminar Papers*, 377-384.

1985    The Beginning of Q. — *SBL 1985 Seminar Papers*, 153-159.

1986    The Householder and the Servant Left in Charge. [Q 12,39-40.42-46] — *SBL 1986 Seminar Papers*, 17-26. Esp. 17-24: "The reconstruction"; 24-26: "The interpretation".

1987    The Q Saying on Confessing and Denying. [Q 12,8-9] — *SBL 1987 Seminar Papers*, 606-616. Esp. 607-612: "The reconstruction"; 612-616: "The interpretation".

1988    The Cross and Discipleship in Q. [Q 14,26-27] — *SBL 1988 Seminar Papers*, 472-482. Esp. 472-479: "The reconstruction"; 479-482: "Tradition history and interpretation".

1989    The Mustard Seed and the Leaven in Q, the Synoptics, and Thomas. [Q 13,18-21] — *SBL 1989 Seminar Papers*, 216-236. Esp. 217-224: "The Q reconstruction"; 224-236: "Formal correspondence, tradition history, and interpretation".

1990    The End of Q. [Q 22,28-30] — *SBL 1990 Seminar Papers*, 1-10. Esp. 1-7: "The reconstruction"; 7-10: "The interpretation".

1992    The Demands of Discipleship. Matt 8,19-22 par. Luke 9,57-62. — VAN SEGBROECK, F., et al. (eds.), *The Four Gospels 1992*. FS F. Neirynck, 1992, I, 541-561. Esp. 542-552: "The Q reconstruction"; 552-561: "The interpretation".

1995    *Mark and Q. A Study of the Overlap Texts*. With an Assessment by F. Neirynck (BETL, 122). Leuven: University Press / Peeters, 1995, XI-307 p. Esp. 1-23: "The overlap texts"; 25-31 [Q 7,27]; 31-39 [Q 3,16-17]; 41-66 [Q 11,14-15.17-26]; 66-73 [Q 12,10]; 75-80 [Q 11,33]; 81-84 [Q 12,2]; 85-87 [Q 12,31]; 87-90 [Q 19,26]; 90-99 [Q 13,18-19]; 101-126 [Q 10,2-16]; 126-134 [Q 11,16.29-32]; 135-141 [Q 14,27]; 142-145 [Q 17,33]; 145-152 [Q 12,8-9]; 153-157 [Q 10,16]; 157-159 [Q 11,23]; 159-166 [Q 17,1-2]; 166-169 [Q 14,34-35]; 171-174 [Q 16,18]; 174-177 [Q 13,30]; 178-182 [Q 17,6]; 182-186 [Q 11,10]; 186-189 [Q 11,43]; 191-195 [Q 12,11-12]; 195-199 [Q 12,51-53]; 199-201 [Q 17,23]; 201-206 [Q 16,17]; 206-208 [Q 12,40]; 209-218: "The relationship of Mark and Q". [NTA 40, p. 339] → Neirynck 1995h, 1996d, Verheyden 1996
        E. FRANKLIN, *ExpT* 107 (1995-96) 378; M.D. GOULDER, *NT* 39 (1997) 193-194; E.C. MALONEY, *CBQ* 59 (1997) 578-580; C.M. TUCKETT, *Bib* 78 (1997) 279-283.

**FLEMING, Thomas V.**

1963    Christ and Divorce. [19,9] — *TS* 24 (1963) 106-120. Esp. 106-113: "Augustine's interpretation"; 113-114: "The common protestant interpretation"; 115-116: "The classical interpretation"; 116-119: "The rabbinic hypothesis". [NTA 7, 780]

**FLENDER, Helmut**

1965    Lehren und Verkündigung in den synoptischen Evangelien. — *EvT* 25 (1965) 701-714. Esp. 704-706. [NTA 10, 893]

1968 *Die Botschaft Jesu von der Herrschaft Gottes.* München: Kaiser, 1968, 113 p. Esp. 32-34 [8,11-12]; 37-38 [13,24-30.36-43]; 48-51 [kingdom]; 63-64 [23,8-10]; 76-79 [10,32-33]; 80-81 [11,11-12]; 81.85 [12,32]; 85-86 [8,20]; 86 [11,19].

**FLESSEMAN-VAN LEER, Ellen**
1967 Die Interpretation der Passionsgeschichte vom Alten Testament aus. — CONZELMANN, H., et al., *Zur Bedeutung des Todes Jesu. Exegetische Beiträge* (Schriftenreihe des Theologischen Ausschusses der Evangelischen Kirche der Union), Gütersloh: Mohn, 1967, 79-96. Esp. 83-88, 91-94.
1976 Nogmaals "De arbeiders in de wijngaard". [20,1-16] — *Ter Herkenning* (Breda) 4 (1976) 120-121. → Zuidema 1976
1980 Dat is niet eerlijk! Uitleg van Matteüs 20,1-16. — *Schrift* 68 (1980) 64-69.

**FLETCHER, Donald R.**
1964 Condemned to Die. The Logion on Cross-Bearing: What Does It Mean? [10,38-39] — *Interpr* 18 (1964) 156-164. [NTA 9, 170]

**FLOOD, Edmund**
1958 One of the Promises to Peter. [16,17-19] — *CleR* 43 (1958) 584-594. [NTA 3, 357] → Cullmann 1952/53
1981a *Parables of Jesus.* New York - Toronto, Ont.: Paulist, [1981], 64 p.
1981b *Parables for Now. More Parables for Now.* London: Darton, Longman & Todd, 1981, 2 vols., VI-98 p. and VI-102 p.

**FLORER, Warren W.**
1951 The Language of Luther's Version. [5] — *CBQ* 13 (1951) 257-267.

**FLORQUIN, C.**
1978 L'évangile selon saint Luc est-il indépendant de celui selon saint Matthieu? — *CahRenan* 26-106 (1978) 105-125. [NTA 23, 408]

**FLOWERS, H.J.**
1953 Ἐν πνεύματι ἁγίῳ καὶ πυρί. [3,11] — *ExpT* 64 (1952-53) 155-156. → Schweizer 1953
1961 Matthew xxiii.15. — *ExpT* 73 (1961-62) 67-69. [NTA 6, 780] → Hoad 1962

**FLUSSER, David**
1960 Blessed are the Poor in Spirit... [5,3-5] — *IsrExplJourn* 10 (1960) 1-13. [NTA 5, 393]
1961 Mt 17,24-27 and the Dead Sea Sect. [Hebrew] — *Tarbiz* (Jerusalem) 31 (1961-62) 150-156.
1967a The Conclusion of Matthew in a New Jewish Christian Source. [28,19] — *ASTI* 5 (1966-67) 110-120; = ID., *Judaism and Christianity: Collection of Articles*, Jerusalem: Akademon, 1973, 300-310; = ID., *Jewish Sources*, 1979, 50-59. → Kosmala 1965b Der Schluß des Matthäusevangeliums in einer neuen judenchristlichen Quelle. — ID., *Entdeckungen*, 1987, 68-77.
1967b The Pesher of Isaiah and the Twelve Apostles. [Hebrew] [10,2-4] — *Eretz-Israel* (Jerusalem) 8 (1967) 52-62, 69*-70*; = ID., *Jewish Sources*, 1979, 283-304.
1973 Die Tora in der Bergpredigt. — KREMERS, H. (ed.), *Juden und Christen lesen dieselbe Bibel* (Duisburger Hochschulbeiträge, 2), Duisburg: Braun, 1973, 102-113; = ID., *Jewish Sources*, 1979, 226-234; = ID., *Tussen oorsprong en schisma. Artikelen over Jezus, het Jodendom en het vroege Christendom*, trans. T. de Bruin, P.J. Tomson & W.A.C. Whitlau (Informatie Jodendom, 2), Hilversum: Folkertsma Stichting voor Talmudica, 1984, 192-203; = ID., *Entdeckungen*, 1987, 21-31. Esp. 21-24 [5,21-48]; 24-27 [5,17-20].

1975 Two Anti-Jewish Montages in Matthew. — *Immanuel* 5 (1975) 37-45. Esp. 37-39 [23,32-36]; 39-43 [7,21-23; 8,11-12]; 43-45 [21,33-46]. [NTA 20, 427]; = ID., *Judaism*, 1988, 552-560. Esp. 552-554; 554-558; 558-560.
Zwei Beispiele antijüdischer Redaktion bei Matthäus. — ID., *Entdeckungen*, 1987, 78-96 (87-96, expanded). Esp. 78-81; 81-84; 84-87.

1976 → Safrai 1976

1978 Some Notes to the Beatitudes (Matthew 5:3-12, Luke 6:20-26). — *Immanuel* 8 (1978) 37-47. [NTA 23, 93]; = ID., *Judaism*, 1988, 115-125.

1979a *Jewish Sources in Early Christianity. Studies and Essays* [Hebrew]. Tel Aviv: Sifri'at Po'alim, 1979, 486 p. → 1967a-b, 1973, 1979b

1979b Die literarischen Beziehungen zwischen den synoptischen Evangelien. — *Ibid.*, 28-49 [Hebrew]; = ID., *Entdeckungen*, 1987, 40-67. Esp. 46-49 [12,12-14]; 49-51 [22,34-40]; 51-53 [12,28-29]; 53-56 [22,15-22]; 58-60 [20,20-23]; 60-67 [10,34-36].

1979c Do You Prefer New Wine? [9,14-17] — *Immanuel* 9 (1979) 26-31. [NTA 24, 132]
Mögen Sie etwa lieber neuen Wein? — ID., *Entdeckungen*, 1987, 108-114.
¿Te gusta más el vino nuevo? — *El Olivo* 2 (1978) 63-72.

1981 *Die rabbinischen Gleichnisse und der Gleichniserzähler Jesus. 1. Teil: Das Wesen der Gleichnisse* (Judaica et Christiana, 4). Bern – Frankfurt/M: Lang, 1981, 336 p. Esp. 31-49: "Strukturen der Gleichnisse"; 51-62: "Ästhetik der Gleichnisse"; 63-117: "Der Rahmen und die Deutungen der Gleichnisse in den Evangelien"; 119-139: "Die wirkliche und die vermeintliche Allegorese"; 141-160: "Ursprung und Vorgeschichte der jüdischen Gleichnisse"; 161-175: "Das Sujet der Gleichnisse und sein Zweck"; 177-192: "Die zehn Jungfrauen" [25,1-13]; 193-233: "Die synoptische Frage und die Gleichnisse Jesu"; 235-263: "Die Gleichnisse Jesu, ein Mittel zur Verstockung?"; 265-281: "Jubelruf und selige Augenzeugen" [11,25-27; 13,10-15]; 283-318: "Der epische Stil der Gleichnisse Jesu".

1983 → M. Lowe 1983

1985 The Ten Commandments and the New Testament. [1985] — SIGAL, B.-Z. (ed.), *The Ten Commandments in History and Tradition* (Publications of the Perry Foundation for Biblical Research), Jerusalem: Magness Press, The Hebrew Univ., 1990, 219-246. Esp. 221-223 [19,16-22]; 227-228 [7,12]; 229-232 [22,34-40]; 232-240 [5,17-48].

1986a Die Sünde gegen den Heiligen Geist. [12,31] — EHRLICH, E.L. - KLAPPERT, B. - AST, U. (eds.), *"Wie gut sind deine Zelte, Jaakow...". Festschrift zum 60. Geburtstag von Reinhold Mayer*, Gerlingen: Bleicher Verlag, 1986, 139-144.

1986b "Who Is It that Struck You?" [26,68] — *Immanuel* 20 (1986) 27-32; = ID., *Judaism*, 1988, 604-609.

1987a *Entdeckungen im Neuen Testament. Band 1: Jesusworte und ihre Überlieferung*, ed. M. Majer. Neukirchen-Vluyn: Neukirchener, 1987, VIII-260 p. → 1967a, 1973, 1975, 1979b-c, 1987b
*Ontdekkingen in het Nieuwe Testament. Woorden van Jesus en hun overlevering*, trans. P.J. Booij. Baarn: Ten Have, 1988, 168 p.

1987b "Ich bin mitten unter ihnen". [18,20] — *Ibid.*, 97-107.
"I am in the Midst of Them" (Mt 18,20). — ID., *Judaism*, 1988, 515-525.

1988a *Judaism and the Origins of Christianity*, ed. B. Young. Jerusalem: Magness Press, 1988, XXVIII-725 p. → 1975, 1978, 1986b, 1987b, 1988b-f, Safrai 1976

1988b Johanan ben Zakkai and Matthew. — *Ibid.*, 490-493.

1988c A Rabbinic Parallel to the Sermon on the Mount. — *Ibid.*, 494-508.

1988d Jesus and the Sign of the Son of Man. [12,38-42] — *Ibid.*, 526-534.

1988e A Lost Jewish Benediction in Matthew 9,8. — *Ibid.*, 535-542.

1988f Matthew's "Verus Israel". — *Ibid.*, 561-574.

1989a  Aesop's Miser and the Parable of the Talents. [25,14-30] — THOMA, C. — WYSCHOGROD, M. (eds.), *Parable and Story*, 1989, 9-25.

1989b  Die Versuchung Jesu und ihr jüdischer Hintergrund. — *Judaica* 45 (1989) 110-128. Esp. 111-113 [4,1-11]; 113-116 [Q/Mk 1,12-13]. [NTA 34, 115]

1992a  "Den Alten ist gesagt". Zur Interpretation der sog. Antithesen der Bergpredigt. — *Judaica* 48 (1992) 35-39. [NTA 37, 139]
"It is Said to the Elders". On the Interpretation of the So-Called Antitheses in the Sermon on the Mount. — *Mishkan* (Jerusalem) 17-18 (1992-93) 115-119. [NTA 37, 1255]

1992b  Jesus and Judaism: Jewish Perspectives. — ATTRIDGE. H.W. - HATA, G. (eds.), *Eusebius, Christianity, and Judaism* (Studia Post-Biblica, 42), Leiden: Brill, 1992, 80-109. Esp. 85-86 [6,9-10/rabbinism].

1995  Die beiden wichtigen Gebote bei den Griechen. [22,34-40] — *Freiburger Rundbrief* 2/1 (1995) 27-30. [NTA 39, 1458]

**FLYNN, L.B.**

1993  *Four Faces of Jesus: The Uniqueness of the Gospel Narratives.* Grand Rapids, MI: Kregel, 1993, 175 p.

**FOCANT, Camille**

1985  Tromper le mamon d'iniquité (Lc 16,1-13). — GANTOY, R. (ed.), *À cause de l'Évangile*. FS J. Dupont, 1985, 547-569. Esp. 562-563 [Q :6,13].

1988  La chute de Jérusalem et la datation des évangiles. — *RTL* 19 (1988) 17-37. Esp. 18-29: "Les apocalypses synoptiques" [24,1-3.15-22]; 31-36 [22,1-14]. [NTA 32, 1094] → J.A.T. Robinson 1976

1992  The Synoptic Gospels. Source Criticism and the New Literary Criticism. Colloquium Biblicum Lovaniense XLI (1992). — *ETL* 68 (1992) 494-499. → 1993* (Introduction, 3-8) Les Évangiles synoptiques. Critique des sources et nouvelles approches littéraires: Colloquium Biblicum Lovaniense XLI. — *RTL* 24 (1993) 282-290.

1993*  (ed.), *The Synoptic Gospels. Source Criticism and the New Literary Criticism* (BETL, 110). Leuven: University Press / Peeters, 1993, XXXIX-670 p. → Baarda, Bammel, Breytenbach, Delorme, Focant, Frankemölle, R.A. Friedrichsen, H.B. Green, Kingsbury, H. Klein, Kühschelm, März, Marguerat, Neirynck, Robbins, Rolland, Schenk, Tuckett, van Cangh; → 1992 A. FUCHS, *SNTU* 20 (1995) 205-208.

1993  Mc 7,24-31 par. Mt 15,21-29. Critique des sources et/ou étude narrative. — *Ibid.*, 39-75. Esp. 39-42: "La question synoptique"; 53-60 [15,21-29].

**FODOR, György**

1988  "Wenn ihr nicht wie Kinder werdet..." (Mt 18,3). — *TBud* 22 (1988) 204-207.

**FOERSTER, Werner**

1952  *Grundriß des Neuen Testaments. Kurzgefaßtes Repetitorium der urchristlichen Schriften* (Stundenbücher, 60). Stuttgart: Kohlhammer, 1952; Hamburg: Furche, ²1966, 133 p. Esp. 12-15: "Die Synoptiker"; 23-31: "Das Matthäusevangelium".

1953  Das Gleichnis von den anvertrauten Pfunden. [25,14-30] — ID. (ed.), *Verbum Dei manet in aeternum. Festschrift für Otto Schmitz zu seinem siebzigsten Geburtstag am 16 Juni 1953*, Witten: Luther-Verlag, 1953, 37-56.

1959  Die Grundzüge der ptolemaeischen Gnosis. — *NTS* 6 (1959-60) 16-31. Esp. 29-30 [26,32]. [NTA 4, 522]

**FOLLET, R.**

1951  "Constituerunt ei triginta argenteos" (ad Mt 26,15). — *VD* 29 (1951) 98-100.

**FOLLIET, Georges**

1954  Les trois catégories de chrétiens à partir de Luc (17,34-36), Matthieu (24,40-41) et Ézéchiel (14,14). — *Augustinus Magister. Congrès international augustinien, Paris, 21-24 septembre 1954*, II, Paris: Études augustiniennes, 1954, 631-644.

**FONTAINE, Jacques**

1972*  & KANNENGIESSER, C. (eds.), *Epektasis. Mélanges patristiques offerts au Cardinal Jean Daniélou*. Paris: Beauchesne, 1972, XII-689 p. → Canivet, Doignon, Leclercq

**FORCE, Paul**

1993  Encore les incises de Matthieu! — *BullLitEccl* 94 (1993) 315-327. Esp. 318-326 [5,32; 19,9]. [NTA 38, 1371]

**FORD, Desmond**

1979  *The Abomination of Desolation in Biblical Eschatology*. Washington, DC: University Press of America, 1979, XIV-334 p. Esp. 23-25 [10,17-22; 24/Mk]; 27-29 [Q 17,22-37]. — Diss. Manchester, 1972 (F.F. Bruce).

**FORD, J. MASSINGBERD**

1965a  St Paul, the Philogamist (1 Cor. vii in Early Patristic Exegesis). — *NTS* 11 (1964-65) 326-348. Esp. 338-345 [19,12]. [NTA 10, 601]

1965b  "Thou Art 'Abraham' and Upon this Rock...". [16,16-19] — *HeythJ* 6 (1965) 289-301. [NTA 10, 520]
          *TDig* 15 (1967) 134-137.

1967a  The Parable of the Foolish Scholars (Mt. xxv 1-13). — *NT* 9 (1967) 107-123. [NTA 12, 164]

1967b  Reflections on W.D. Davies, *The Setting of the Sermon on the Mount*. — *Bib* 48 (1967) 623-628. [NTA 13, 159r] → W.D. Davies 1963a

1967c  Yom Kippur and the Matthean Form of the Pater Noster. — *Worship* 41 (1967) 609-619. [NTA 12, 869]

1968a  The Forgiveness Clause in the Matthaean Form of the Our Father. [6,12] — *ZNW* 59 (1968) 127-131. [NTA 13, 163]

1968b  "The Son of Man" – A Euphemism? — *JBL* 87 (1968) 257-266. Esp. 259-261 [8,29; 14,33; 16,16; 26,64; 27,40]; 264-265 [12,6]. [NTA 13, 522]

1973  Mary's Virginitas Post-Partum and Jewish Law. [1,20-23] — *Bib* 54 (1973) 269-272. [NTA 18, 463]

1976  Money "Bags" in the Temple (Mk 11,16). — *Bib* 57 (1976) 249-253. Esp. 252 [10,9-10]. [NTA 21, 400]

**FORESI, Pasquale**

1979a  Il celibato in Matteo. [19,3-12] — *Nuova umanità* (Roma) 1/1 (1979) 29-50.

1979b  La preghiera del Signore. [6,9-13] — *Nuova umanità* 1/6 (1979) 3-22.

**FORESTELL, J. Terence**

1979  *Targumic Traditions and the New Testament. An Annotated Bibliography with a New Testament Index* (SBL Aramaic Studies, 4). Chico, CA: Scholars, 1979, XIII-137 p. Esp. 71-80.

1991  *As Ministers of Christ. The Christological Dimension of Ministry in the New Testament. An Exegetical and Theological Study*. New York – Mahwah, NJ: Paulist, 1991, VIII-199 p. Esp. 29-30 [11,27]; 39-40 [28,16-20]; 41-43 [10,5-40]; 44-45 [9,1-8]; 45-47 [18,15-20]; 47-48 [16,17-19].

**FORESTI, Fabrizio**

1984 Maria, genitrice del sabato escatologico. Considerazioni sul significato di *Mt.* 1,1-17. — *BibOr* 26 (1984) 31-43. [NTA 29, 83]
*SelT* 24 (1985) 79-82.

**FORKMAN, Göran**

1972 *The Limits of the Religious Community. Expulsion from the Religious Community within the Qumran Sect, within Rabbinic Judaism, and within Primitive Christianity* (ConBibNT, 5). Lund: Gleerup, 1972, 257 p. Esp. 116-132.:63-170.178-179.187-190[18,1-35]. — Diss. Lund, 1972 (B. Gerhardsson).

**FORMOSA, Mary J.**

1988 The Synoptics and the Holy Spirit. — *Augustinian Panorama* (La Valletta) 5-7 (1988-90) 87-107. Esp. 98-107.

**FORNBERG, Tord**

1977 *An Early Church in a Pluralistic Society. A Study of 2 Peter*, trans. J. Gray (ConBibNT, 9). Lund: Gleerup, 1977, 175 p. Esp. 109-110 [12,43-45]; 140 [10,1-16]. — Diss. Uppsala, 1977 (L. Hartman).

1981 *Evangelium enligt Matteus.* Uppsala: Privately published, 1981, VIII-338 p. [NTA 26, p. 196]
H. KVALBEIN, *SEÅ* 48 (1983) 168-171.

1983 Petrus – det nya förbundets överstepräst? [16,17-19] — *Religion och Bibel* (Uppsala) 42-43 (1983-84) 39-44. [NTA 30, 1056]
Peter – the High Priest of the New Covenant? — *East Asia Journal of Theology* (Singapore) 4 (1986) 113-121. [NTA 30, 1057]

1984 Matthew and the School of Shammai. A Study in the Matthean Antithesis. — *Theology and Life* (Hong Kong) 7 (1984) 35-59. [NTA 30, 568]; = ID., *Jewish-Christian Dialogue*, 1988, 11-31.

1988 *Jewish-Christian Dialogue and Biblical Exegesis* (Studia Missionalia Upsaliensia, 47). Uppsala: Teol. Institutionen, 1988, 74 p. Esp. 11-31 (→ 1984) 32-46: "Anti-Pharisaic polemic and Jewish-christian dialogue" [5,21-48; 11,2-6; 27,25.51-53; 28,16-20]; 55-58 [5,23-24].
R. DE SMET, *Vidyajyoti* 52 (1992) 240-241; L. ERIKSSON, *SEÅ* 55 (1990) 128-130; B. FJÄRSTEDT, *SvenskTeolKvart* 65 (1989) 30-32; Z. GARBER, *JEcuST* 27 (1990) :27-128; L. LEGRAND, *IndianTS* 27 (1990) 361-362; T. STORDALEN, *TidsTeolKirk* 61 (1990) 310; B.T VIVIANO, *RB* 100 (1993) 633-634.

1989 *Matteusevangeliet 1:1-13:52* (Kommentar till Nya Testamentet, 1A). Uppsala: EFS-förlaget, 1989, 260 p. [NTA 35, p. 240]
S. BYRSKOG, *SvenskTeolKvart* 67 (1991) 88-91; H. KVALBEIN, *Svensk Pastoraltidskrift* 32 (1990) 463-465; K. SYREENI, *SEÅ* 56 (1991) 128-129.

1995* & HELLHOLM, D. (eds.), *Texts and Contexts. Biblical Texts in Their Textual and Situational Contexts. Essays in Honor of Lars Hartman.* Oslo: Scandinavian University Press; Lewiston, NY: Mellen, 1995, XXIX-1070 p. → Bovon, Freyne, Hagner, Hellholm, Hultgren, Kieffer, Pokorný

1995 The Figure of Peter in Matthew and in 2 Peter. — *IndianTS* 32 (1995) 237-249. Esp. 237-245 [16,17-19]. [NTA 40, 1450]

**FORTE, Anthony John**

1991 *A Critical Edition of a Hiberno-Latin Commentary on Matthew 1-8 (Codex Vindobonensis 940).* Diss. Univ. of California, 1991, IV-263 p. (B. Löfstedt). — *DissAbstr* 52 (1991-92) 954-955.

**FORTNA, Robert Tomson**

1987 Sayings of the Suffering and Risen Christ. The Quadruple Tradition. — *Forum* 3/3 (1987) 63-69. Esp. 63-64 [26,50]; 64-65 [26,51-54]; 66 [26,54-65]. [NTA 32, 543]

1990    "You have made them equal to us!" (Mt 20:1-16). — *JTSouthAfr* 72 (1990) 66-72.
        [NTA 35, 633]

1992    Reading Jesus' Parable of the Talents Through Underclass Eyes. Matt 25:14-30. —
        *Forum* 8 (1992) 211-228. [NTA 40, 835]

**FORTUNA, Marida**

1989    Hebrajska Ewangelia św Mateusza ze średniowiecznego traktatu zydowskiego. [The
        Hebrew gospel of Matthew according to a Jewish medieval source] — *RuBi* 42 (1989)
        241-249. → G. Howard

**FOSSION, André**

1995    "Donnez-leur vous-mêmes à manger": Lecture de Mt 14,13-21. — *LumVit* 50 (1995)
        7-16. [NTA 40, 171]

**FOSTER, L.A.**

1964    The "Q" Myth in Synoptic Studies. — *BEvTS* 7 (1964) 111-119. [NTA 9, 491]

**FOULKES, Pamela A.**

1994    "To Expound Discipline or Judgement": The Portrait of the Scribe in Ben Sira. —
        *Pacifica* 7 (1994) 75-84. [NTA 38, 1730] → Trainor 1991

**FOULKES, Ricardo**

1987    La gran comisión de Mateo 28:16-20. — *Vida y Pensamiento* (San José) 5 (1987) 56-
        67. → P.A. Jimenez 1987

**FOURNELLE, G.G.**

1956    Our Lady's Marriage to Saint Joseph. — *Marian Studies* (Washington, DC) 7 (1956)
        122-129.

**FOWLER, Robert M.**

1986    Reading Matthew Reading Mark: Observing the First Steps toward Meaning-as-
        Reference in the Synoptic Gospels. — *SBL 1986 Seminar Papers*, 1-16. Esp. 12-16. → cf.
        1991, 237-254

1991    *Let the Reader Understand. Reader-Response Criticism and the Gospel of Mark.*
        Augsburg, MN: Fortress, 1991, XIII-279 p. Esp. 228-260: "The history of reading Mark". → 1986

**FOX, Douglas J.**

1979    *The "Matthew-Luke Commentary" of Philoxenus. Text, Translation and Critical
        Analysis* (SBL DS, 43). Missoula, MT: Scholars, 1979, VII-319 p. Esp. 24-36; 43-177 [text-
        translation]; 211-246: "Biblical quotations in the manuscript". [NTA 24, p. 80] — Diss. Toronto, Ont., 1975
        (E.G. Clarke). → de Halleux 1980
                J.F. COAKLEY, *JTS* 31 (1980) 631-633; A. DE HALLEUX, *ETL* 56 (1980) 187-188; C. KANNENGIESSER,
                *RSR* 71 (1983) 555; R. KÖBERT, *Bib* 61 (1980) 430-432.

**FOYE, E.J.**

1964a   "You shall indeed share my cup". Mt 20,23. — *FrontLine* (Baltimore, MD) 3 (1964)
        29-44.

1964b   The Three Kings. A Projection. — *Ibid.*, 90-96.

**FRADES, Eduardo**

1974    Para leer y predicar hoy el evangelio de S. Mateo. — *Mision Abierta* (Madrid) 9
        (1974) 19-42.

**FRAEYMAN, Marcel**

1955    S. Eucharistia in narrationibus institutionis (Mt 26,26-29 par). — *CollBrugGand* 1
        (1955) 78-86.

**FRAHIER, Louis-Jean**

1987 L'interprétation du récit du jugement dernier (Mt 25,31-46) dans l'œuvre d'Augustin. — *RevÉtudAug* 33 (1987) 70-84.

1992 *Le jugement dernier. Implications éthiques sur le bonheur de l'homme: Mt 25,31-46* (Recherches morales. Synthèses, 17). Paris: Cerf, 1992, 426 p. [NTA 38, p. 460] — Diss. Paris, 1991. → Wattiaux 1993
    J. DIJKMAN, *TijdTheol* 33 (1993) 293-294; J.J. LAVOIE, *StudRel/SciRel* 23 (1994) 119-120.

**FRANCE, Richard Thomas**

1968 The Servant of the Lord in the Teaching of Jesus. — *TynaB* 19 (1968) 26-52. Esp. 40-41 [3,15]; 42-43 [11,4-5]. [NTA 14, 457]

1971 *Jesus and the Old Testament. His Application of Old Testament Passages to Himself and His Mission.* London: Tyndale; Downers Grove, IL: Inter-Varsity, 1971, XII-13-286 p. Esp. 38-82: "Typological use of the OT" [4,1-11; 5,5.48; 8,11-12; 11,23; 12,5-6.40.42; 17,17; 19,28; 23,38; 24,31]; 83-162: "The use of OT prediction" [3,15; 6,8; 8,11-12; 10,23; 11,5.10.14; 13,41; 19,28; 24,30; 25,16.31.32; 28,18]; 240-258: "A detailed study of the text-form of the OT quotations". — Diss. Bristol, 1966 (K. Grayston).

1975 Old Testament Prophecy and the Future of Israel: A Study of the Teaching of Jesus. — *TyndB* 26 (1975) 53-78. Esp. 55-58.63-65.69-71. [NTA 21, 342]

1976 The Authenticity of the Sayings of Jesus. — BROWN, C. (ed.), *History, Criticism and Faith. Four Exploratory Studies*, Leicester, UK: Inter-Varsity, 1976, 101-143.

1977 Exegesis in Practice: Two Samples. — MARSHALL, I.H. (ed.), *New Testament Interpretation*, 1977, 252-281. Esp. 252-263 [8,5-13]. → Goldingay 1977

1979a God and Mammon. — *EvQ* 51 (1979) 3-21. Esp. 10-12 [5,3-12]. [NTA 23, 786]

1979b Herod and the Children of Bethlehem. — *NT* 21 (1979) 98-120. Esp. 99-113: "The literary question"; 114-120: "The historical question". [NTA 24, 80]

1980* & WENHAM, D. (eds.), *Studies of History and Tradition in the Four Gospels* (Gospel Perspectives, 1). Sheffield: JSOT, 1980, 263 p. → Chilton, R.H. Stein

1980a Jésus devant Caïphe. [26,64] — *Hokhma* 15 (1980) 20-35. [NTA 25, 495]

1980b The 'Massacre of Innocents' – Fact or Fiction? [2,16] — LIVINGSTONE, E.A. (ed.), *Studia Biblica 1978*, II, 1980, 83-94.

1981* & WENHAM, D. (eds.), *Studies of History and Tradition in the Four Gospels* (Gospel Perspectives, 2). Sheffield: JSOT, 1981, 375 p. → Aune, France, G. Maier, Payne, D. Wenham

1981a Scripture, Tradition and History in the Infancy Narratives of Matthew. — *Ibid.*, 239-266. Esp. 239-243: "Matthew 1-2 as history"; 243-246: "Matthew 1-2 as midrash"; 246-248: "Midrash and history"; 248-250: "Did Matthew make it all up?"; 250-255: "Scripture and tradition"; 255-260: "Verisimilitude and historicity".

1981b The Formula-Quotations of Matthew 2 and the Problem of Communication. — *NTS* 27 (1980-81) 233-251. Esp. 234-237: "Scripture and tradition in Matthew 2"; 237-240: "The purpose and message of Matthew 2"; 241-249: "The four formula quotations in Matthew 2" [2,6-7.15.18-23]. [NTA 25, 849]

1983* & WENHAM, D. (eds.), *Studies in Midrash and Historiography* (Gospel Perspectives, 3). Sheffield: JSOT, 1983, 299 p. → Bauckham, Moo, Morris. Payne

1984 Matthieu, Marc, Luc. — LADD, G.E., *Théologie du Nouveau Testament*, 1984, 271-306 (supplementary chapter). → Ladd 1974a
Matthew, Mark, and Luke. — LADD, G.E., *Theology of the New Testament*, 1993, 212-245. Esp. 218-228.

1985 *The Gospel according to Matthew. An Introduction and Commentary* (The Tyndale New Testament Commentaries, 1). Leicester: Inter-Varsity: Grand Rapids, MI: Eerdmans; 1985, repr. 1987, 416 p. Esp. 15-62: "Introduction"; 68-416: "Commentary". [NTA 33, p. 245] → G. Maier 1987

1986   Chronological Aspects of 'Gospel Harmony'. — *Vox Evangelica* (London) 16 (1986) 33-59.

1989a   *Matthew: Evangelist and Teacher*. Grand Rapids, MI: Zondervan; Exeter: Paternoster, 1989, 345 p. Esp. 13-49: "The first gospel"; 50-80: "Who was 'Matthew'?"; 81-122: "The setting of the gospel"; 123-165: "Literary character of the gospel"; 166-205: "Fulfilment"; 206-241: "Matthew and Israel"; 242-278: "Matthew's gospel and the church"; 279-317: "Matthew's portrait of Jesus". [NTA 34, p. 245]
    S. McKNIGHT, *JEvTS* 35 (1992) 424-426.

1989b   Matthew's Gospel in Recent Study. — *Themelios* 14/2 (1989) 41-46. [NTA 33, 1108]

1992a   Faith. — *DJG*, 223-226. Esp. 224.

1992b   Servant of Yahweh. — *Ibid.*, 744-747. Esp. 746.

1994a   Jesus the Baptist? — GREEN, J.B. - TURNER, M.B.B. (eds.), *Jesus of Nazareth*. FS I.H. Marshall, 1994, 94-111. Esp. 103-104 [3,14-15]; 109-110 [28,19-20].

1994b   Matthew. — CARSON, D.A., et al. (eds.), *New Bible Commentary. 21st Century Edition*, Leicester / Downers Grove, IL: Inter-Varsity, ⁴1994, 904-945. → F. Davidson 1953, Guthrie 1970

**FRANCKE, Johannes**

1973   *Van sabbat naar zondag. De rustdag in Oud en Nieuw Testament*. Amsterdam: Bolland, 1973, II-210 p. Esp. 131-137.

**FRANCO, C.A.**

1976a   Un ejemplo de exégesis moderna y meditación de los evangelios. La parábola de los diez virgenes (Mt 25,1-13). — *CuadEv* 3/23 (1976) 5-27.

1976b   → Herranz Marco 1976a

**FRANGIPANE, D.**

1954   *Della interpretazione letterale eucaristica della parabola del lievito Mt 13,33; Lc 13,20s*. Barcelona: Congreso Eucar. Intern., Sessiones de Estudio 1, 1954, 487-494.

**FRANK, Karl Suso**

1980   Die Vaterunser-Erklärung der Regula Magistri. — DASSMANN, E. - FRANK, K.S. (eds.), *Pietas. Festschrift für Bernhard Kötting* (Jahrbuch für Antike und Christentum, Ergänzungsband 8). Münster: Aschendorff, 1980, 458-471.

**FRANKEMÖLLE, Hubert**

1971   Die Makarismen (Mt 5,1-12; Lk 6,20-23). Motive und Umfang der redaktionellen Komposition. — *BZ* 15 (1971) 52-75. Esp. 54-58: "Der literarische Befund"; 59-61: "Die atl Tradition in Q"; 61-63: "Die Gattung der Makarismen"; 63-73: "Die Redaktion"; 73-75: "Redaktion und Gemeindetheologie". [NTA 15, 845]

1973   Amtskritik im Matthäus-Evangelium? — *Bib* 54 (1973) 247-262. Esp. 251-254: "Zum matthäischen Kirchenverständnis"; 254-257: "Die Christen als Jünger"; 257-260: "Die Typisierung des Petrus". [NTA 18, 460]
    Amtskritik im Matthäusevangelium. Ein Zeichen für kirchlichen Unfrieden? — ID., *Friede und Schwert*, 1983, 115-129. Esp. 119-121; 121-124; 124-127.

1974a   *Jahwebund und Kirche Christi. Studien zur Form- und Traditionsgeschichte des "Evangeliums" nach Matthäus* (NTAbh, 10). Münster: Aschendorff, 1974, X-429 p. Esp. 7-83: "Die christo-logische und theo-logische Basis der Gemeinde nach Mt (μεθ᾽ ὑμῶν)" [1,23; 17,17; 18,20; 26,29.38.10; 28,16-20]; 84-190: "Individuell-personale Begriffe in der mt Ekklesiologie"; 191-256: "Kollektiv-bildliche Begriffe in der mt Ekklesiologie" [16,18; 18,17-18]; 257-307: "Heilszusage und Heilsbewährung in der mt Theologie"; 308-400: "Das MtEv als Geschichtsdeutung (Zur Form des mt 'Evangeliums')". [NTA 19, p. 111]; ²1984, XX-429 p. [NTA 29, p. 89] — Diss. Münster, 1972 (J. Gnilka). → Dermience 1985

H. BOJORGE, *RevistBíb* 36 (1974) 347-350; B.R. DOYLE, *AusBR* 25 (1977) 42; V. HASLER, *TZ* 32 (1976) 33-34; J.D. KINGSBURY, *Bib* 56 (1975) 434-437; P.-G. MÜLLER, *BK* 30 (1975) 35; J. MURPHY-O'CONNOR, *RB* 83 (1976) 302-303; K.H. SCHELKLE, *TQ* 155 (1975) 71; G. SCHNEIDER, *BZ* 21 (1977) 127-129; E. SCHWEIZER, *TRev* 70 (1974) 368-370; D. SENIOR, *CBQ* 38 (1976) 230-232; W. TRILLING, *TLZ* 101 (1976) 580-583.
A. FUCHS, *SNTU* 10 (1985) 204-205; K.H. SCHELKLE, *Freiburger Rundbrief* 35-36 (1983-84) 122-123; B.T. VIVIANO, *RB* 92 (1985) 631-632.

1974b  Neutestamentliche Christologien vor dem Anspruch alttestamentlicher Theologie. — *BibLeb* 15 (1974) 258-273. Esp. 264-266. [NTA 20, 590]; = ID., *Jüdische Wurzeln*, 1998, 45-55. Esp. 51-55.

1977  *In Gleichnissen Gott erfahren* (Biblisches Forum, 12). Stuttgart: Katholisches Bibelwerk, 1977, 144 p. Esp. 43-45 [13,44]; 46-50 [13,31-33]; 84-87 [1,23]; 99-103 [25,31-46]; 103-107 [18,21-35]; 108-110 [5,13-16]; 121-125 [13,14-43]; 125-130 [21,33-46]; 130-133 [22,11-13].

1979a  Evangelist und Gemeinde. Eine methodenkritische Besinnung (mit Beispielen aus dem Mattäusevangelium). — *Bib* 60 (1979) 153-190. Esp. 155-159: "Zur forschungsgeschichtlichen Situation"; 159-162: "Das Verhältnis des Evangelisten zur Gemeinde als bewußtes methodisches Problem"; 162-190: "Fakten, Aporien und methodologische Thesen". [NTA 24, 47]; = ID., *Biblische Handlungsanweisungen*, 1983, 50-79. Esp. 51-54; 55-57; 57-79.

1979b  Menschlichkeit. Impulse aus den Evangelien zu einem Grundwert des Lebens. — *BK* 34 (1979) 90-95. Esp. 92 [11,25]; 93 [20,15]; = ID., *Biblische Handlungsanweisungen*, 1983, 222-231. Esp. 225-226; 228-229.

1979c  'Pharisäismus' in Judentum und Kirche. Zur Tradition und Redaktion in Matthäus 23. — GOLDSTEIN, H. (ed.), *Gottesverächter und Menschenfeinde? Juden zwischen Jesus und frühchristlicher Kirche*, Düsseldorf: Patmos, 1979. 123-189. Esp. 124-134: "Zur Relevanz des Themas" (128-134: "Zum vorausgesetzten Textverständnis"); 134-142: "Die matthäischen Vorlagen bei Markus und in der Logienquelle"; 142-148: "Beispiele innerjüdischer Fremd- und Selbstkritik"; 149-172: "Zum kompositorischen Verfahren des Matthäus"; 172-185: "Mt 23 als innerchristliche Kritik"; 185-188: "Intention und Wirkungsgeschichte eines Textes"; = ID., *Biblische Handlungsanweisungen*, 1983, 133-190. Esp. 134-139; 139-147; 147-153; 153-176; 176-188; 188-190.

1980  Die Offenbarung an die Unmündigen. Pragmatische Impulse aus Mt 11,25f. — THIELE, J. — BECKER, R. (eds.), *Chancen und Grenzen religiöser Erziehung*, Düsseldorf: Patmos, 1980, 97-127. Esp. 98-103: "Die historischen Verhaltensmuster"; 104-109: "Parallelen zu Mt 11,25f"; 109-120: "Dan 2,19-23 als 'Gegentext' zu Mt 11,25f"; 120-127: "Die pragmatische Provokation 'Jesu'"; = ID., *Biblische Handlungsanweisungen*, 1983, 80-108. Esp. 81-86; 86-91; 91-102; 102-108.

1982a  Zur Theologie der Mission im Matthäusevangelium. — KERTELGE, K. (ed.), *Mission im Neuen Testament* (QDisp, 93), Freiburg: Herder, 1982, 93-129. Esp. 94-100: "Der Begriff Mission und seine Synonyme im Matthäusevangelium"; 100-125: "Juden- und Heidenmission im Matthäusevangelium" [10,5-6.23; 15,24; 28,16-20]; 125-129: "Die missionarische Praxis Jesu und seiner Jünger im Matthäusevangelium"; = ID., *Biblische Handlungsanweisungen*, 1983, 191-221. Esp. 192-196; 197-217; 217-221.

1982b  Umkehr zur wahren Gerechtigkeit. Neutestamentliche Anregungen zur Gestaltung von Fastenzeit und Ostern. — ID., et al., *"Wenn unsere Gerechtigkeit nicht grösser ist..."*, Hamm: KSA, 1982, 3-6.
Umkehr zur wahren Gerechtigkeit. Eine christlich-jüdische Selbstbesinnung zu Mt 5,20. — ID., *Friede und Schwert*, 1983, 136-143.

1983a  *Biblische Handlungsanweisungen. Beispiele pragmatischer Exegese*. Mainz: Matthias-Grünewald, 1983, 248 p. → 1979a-c, 1980, 1982a

1983b  *Friede und Schwert. Frieden schaffen nach dem Neuen Testament* (Grünewald Reihe, 11). Mainz: Matthias-Grünewald, 1983, 172 p. → 1973, 1982b

1983c  Neue Literatur zur Bergpredigt. — *TRev* 79 (1983) 177-198. Esp. 180-182 [Schweizer 1982a]; 182-184 [Berner 1979]; 184-186 [Moltmann 1981*]; 186-189 [Lapide 1982a]; 188-189 [Kantzenbach 1982]; 189 [de Graaf 1971/82]; 190-191 [Borne 1982a]; 191-192 [Hochgrebe 1982*]; 193-198 [Schnackenburg 1982*]. [NTA 28, 88]

1984   Evangelium als theologischer Begriff und sein Bezug zur literarischen Gattung 'Evangelium'. — DORMEYER, D. - FRANKEMÖLLE, H., Evangelium als literarische Gattung und als theologischer Begriff. Tendenzen und Aufgaben der Evangelienforschung im 20. Jahrhundert, mit einer Untersuchung des Markusevangeliums in seinem Verhältnis zur antiken Biographie. — *ANRW* II.25.2 (1984) 1543-1704, pp. 1635-1704. Esp. 1659-1660.1664 [11,5]. → 1988a

1988a  *Evangelium – Begriff und Gattung. Ein Forschungsbericht* (SBB, 15). Stuttgart: Katholisches Bibelwerk, 1988, VI-255 p. Esp. 137-138 [Q 7,22]; 149-155: "'Evangelium' im Matthäusevangelium"; [2]1994 ("aktualisiert und stark erweitert"), XII-307 p. Esp. 141-149: "'Evangelium' in der Logienquelle"; 171-180: "'Evangelium' im Matthäusevangelium". → 1984

1988b  Die Geburt im Stall. Die "Weinachtsgeschichte" im Widerstreit zwischen tiefenpsychologischer und historisch-kritischer Auslegung. — *Diakonia* 19 (1988) 402-410. [NTA 33, 591]

1989*  & KERTELGE, K. (eds.), *Vom Urchristentum zu Jesus. Für Joachim Gnilka.* Freiburg: Herder, 1989, 536 p. → S. Brown, J. Ernst, Frankemölle, Kremer, H.-W. Kuhn, Löning, Luz, Roloff, Schnackenburg, Weder

1989a  Jesus als deuterojesajanischer Freudenbote? Zur Rezeption von Jes 52,7 und 61,1 im Neuen Testament, durch Jesus und in den Targumim. — *Ibid.*, 34-67. Esp. 47-49: "Das mt 'Evangelium von der Gottesherrschaft'"; 49-50 [5,3]; 50-53 [11,5]; = ID., *Jüdische Wurzeln*, 1998, 131-159. Esp. 142-143; 143-144; 144-147.

1989b  Christlich glauben in ambivalenter Wirklichkeit. Handlungsanweisungen durch Wundergeschichten (am Beispiel von Mt 8–9). — *KatBlät* 114 (1989) 419-425.

1989c  Die "Praxis Christi" (Mt 11,2) und die handlungsorientierte Exegese. — KOCH, D.-A., et al. (eds.), *Jesu Rede von Gott.* FS W. Marxsen, 1989, 142-164. Esp. 144-152: "Die Praxis Jesu Christi nach Matthäus (im historisch-kritischen Ansatz)"; 158-164: "Die Praxis Jesu Christi nach Matthäus (im handlungsorientierten, pragmatischen Ansatz)".

1991   Evangelium und Wirkungsgeschichte. Das Problem der Vermittlung von Methodik und Hermeneutik in neueren Auslegungen zum Matthäusevangelium. — OBERLINNER, L. - FIEDLER, P. (eds.), *Salz der Erde.* FS A. Vögtle, 1991, 31-89. Esp. 33-37: "Methodik und/oder Hermeneutik? Zur Situation"; 38-62: "Textliche und historische Aspekte bei der Auslegung des MtEv"; 63-84: "Rezeptionsorientierte Aspekte"; 84-89: "Die Theozentrik des matthäischen Evangeliums".

1992   Jüdisch-christlicher Dialog. Interreligiose und innerchristliche Aspekte. — *Catholica* 46 (1992) 114-139; = ID., *Jüdische Wurzeln*, 1998, 407-430. Esp. 423 [11,2-6]; 425-426 [ἐκκλησία].

1993   Das Matthäusevangelium als heilige Schrift und die heilige Schrift des früheren Bundes. Von der Zwei-Quellen- zur Drei-Quellen-Theorie. — FOCANT, C. (ed.), *The Synoptic Gospels*, 1993, 281-310. Esp. 287-306: "Das Matthäusevangelium als 'heilige Schrift'" [1,1.22.23; 5,19.21-48; 6,10; 24,14; 26,1; 28,20]; 306-310: "Zur Gattung des Matthäusevangeliums"; = ID., *Jüdische Wurzeln*, 1998, 233-259. Esp. 239-256; 256-259.

1994a  *Matthäus: Kommentar I (bis 9,35).* Düsseldorf: Patmos, 1994, 332 p. [NTA 39, p. 323] M. LIMBECK, *BK* 50 (1995) 248-249; W. WIEFEL, *TLZ* 119 (1994) 883-885. *Matthäus: Kommentar II [9,36–28,20].* Düsseldorf: Patmos, 1997, 560 p.

1994b  Mose in Deutungen des Neuen Testaments. — *Kirche und Israel* 9 (1994) 70-86. Esp. 77-81; = ID., *Jüdische Wurzeln*, 1998, 91-107. Esp. 99-103.

1994c  Die sogenannten Antithesen des Matthäus (5,21ff). Hebt Matthäus für Christen das "Alte" Testament auf? Von der Macht der Vorurteile. — ID. (ed.), *Die Bibel. Das bekannte Buch – das fremde Buch*, Paderborn: Schön.ngh, 1994, 61-92; = ID., *Jüdische Wurzeln*, 1998, 295-328. Esp. 295-300: "Überwundene Vorurteile?"; 300-302: "Wo liegt das Problem, wenn nicht im Philologischen?"; 303-310: "Vor der Last unserer christlichen Auslegungsgeschichte der Bibel" [Marcion]; 310-317: "Die Antithesen (5,21-48) in der Deutung des Matthäus"; 317-320: "Zur Sprechsituation des Matthäus"; 321-328: "Von der Notwendigkeit des Verzichts auf diskriminierende Vorurteile".

1995a  Ehescheidung und Wiederverheiratung von Geschiedenen im Neuen Testament. — SCHNEIDER, T. (ed.), *Geschieden – wiederverheiratet – abgewiesen? Antworten der Theologie* (QDisp, 157), Freiburg: Herder, 1995, 28-50. Esp. 35-38 [5,32; 19,9].

1995b  Matthäus. — GÖRG, M. – LANG, B. (eds.), *Neues Bibel-Lexikon*, II/10, Zürich: Benziger, 1995, 736-737.

1995c  Matthäusevangelium. — *Ibid.*, 737-744.

1995d  Die "Kirche Gottes in Christus". Zum Verhältnis von Christentum und Judentum als Anfrage an christliches Selbstverständnis. — ERNST, J. – LEIMGRUBER, S. (eds.), *Surrexit Dominus vere*. FS J.J. Degenhardt, 1995, 381-394. Esp. 386, 393 [ἐκκλησία]; = ID., *Jüdische Wurzeln*, 1998, 431-444. Esp. 436, 443.

1995e  Die Antithesen der Bergpredigt. Glaubensbotschaft oder moralische Überforderung? — *Lebendige Seelsorge* (Würzburg) 46 (1995) 9-14.

1997  → 1994a

1998  *Jüdische Wurzeln christlicher Theologie. Studien zum biblischen Kontext neutestamentlicher Texte* (BBB, 116). Bodenheim: Philo, 1998, 466 p. (including four articles on mt published in 1996-1998). → 1974b, 1989a, 1992, 1993, 1994b-c, 1995d

**FRANKFURTER, David T.M.**

1990  The Origin of the Miracle-List Tradition and Its Medium of Circulation. — *SBL 1990 Seminar Papers*, 344-374. Esp. 350-352 [Q 7,22].

**FRANKLIN, Eric**

1994  *Luke: Interpreter of Paul, Critic of Matthew* (JSNT SS, 92). Sheffield: JSOT, 1994, 414 p. Esp. 163-278: "Luke and Matthew"; 279-375: "Luke's use of Matthew".
  C.J.A. HICKLING, *Theology* 98 (1995) 141-142; J. NOLLAND, *JTS* 46 (1995) 263-269.

**FRANKOVIC, Joseph**

1994  Remember Shiloh! [21,12-13] — *Jerusalem Perspective* 46-47 (1994) 24-31. [NTA 39, 1457]

1995  The Power of Parables. — *Jerusalem Perspective* 48 (1995) 10-15. [NTA 40, 141]

**FRANQUESA, Pere**

1993  Los hermanos de Jesús: Mt 12,46-50; Mt 13,55. — *EphMar* 43 (1993) 81-90. [NTA 38, 161]

**FRANSEN, Irénée**

1954  La charte du Royaume des cieux. Le Sermon sur la montagne (Matth. 5,1-7,29). — *BibVieChrét* 6 (1954) 68-82.

1957  Le Discours en Paraboles (Matthieu 11,2-13,53). — *BibVieChrét* 18 (1957) 72-84. [NTA 2, 282]

1961  La charte de l'apôtre (Matth. 8,1-11,1). — *BibVieChrét* 37 (1961) 34-45. [NTA 5, 711]

1962  L'avènement du Fils de l'Homme (Matthieu 19,1-25,46). — *BibVieChrét* 48 (1962) 27-38. [NTA 7, 787]

**FRANZ, G.**

1995 The Parable of the Two Builders. [7,24-27] — *Archaeology in the Biblical World* (Shafter, CA) 3 (1995) 6-11 [NTA 40, 1462]

**FRANZMANN, Majella H.**

1960 Studies in Discipleship. — *ConcTM* 31 (1960) 607-625, 670-689. [NTA 5, 390]

1961 *Following Jesus. Discipleship according to St. Matthew.* St. Louis, MO: Concordia, 1961, IX-240 p.
    V. BARTLING, *ConcTM* 33 (1962) 45-46; W.E. HULL, *RExp* 59 (1962) 93; E.J. MOELLER, *Springfielder* (Missouri, MT) 26 (1962) 63-64; O.A. PIPER, *PrincSemB* 55/3 (1961-62) 89-90; I.K. STORAASLI, *LuthQ* 14 (1962) 181-182; E.S. TANNER, *JBL* 80 (1961) 398.

1992 Of Food, Bodies, and the Boundless Reign of God in the Synoptic Gospels. — *Pacifica* 5 (1992) 17-31. Esp. 17-24 [11,18-19]; 24-27 [15,10-20]. [NTA 36, 1273]

**FREDE, Hermann J.**

1981 Neutestamentliche Zitate in Zeno von Verona. — EPP, E.J. - FEE, G.D. (eds.), *New Testament Textual Criticism.* FS B.M. Metzger, 1981, 297-304. Esp. 303-304.

**FREDRIKSEN, Paula**

1988 *From Jesus to Christ. The Origins of the New Testament Images of Jesus.* New Haven, CT - London: Yale University Press, 1988, XII-256 p. Esp. 36-43: "Matthew: the Christ of the Scriptures"; 187-191; 208-209.
    *De Jésus aux Christs. Les origines des représentations de Jésus dans le Nouveau Testament,* trans. M.-O. Fortier-Masek (Jésus depuis Jésus). Paris: Cerf, 1992, 345 p. Esp. 68-78; 275-279; 303-304.

1995 What You See Is What You Get: Context and Content in Current Research on the Historical Jesus. — *TTod* 52 (1995-96) 75-97. Esp. 79-85. [NTA 39, 1405] → J.D. Crossan 1991a, Mack 1993

**FREED, Edwin D.**

1961 The Entry into Jerusalem in the Gospel of John. [21,9.15] — *JBL* 80 (1961) 329-338. [NTA 6, 816] → D.M. Smith 1963

1965 *Old Testament Quotations in the Gospel of John* (SupplNT, 11). Leiden: Brill, 1965, XIV-130 p. Esp. 1-3 [3,3]; 44-47 [2,6]; 66-68 (→ D.M. Smith 1963); 68-72 [21,9]; 86-88 [13,14-15]; 115-116 [24,30].

1986 *The New Testament. A Critical Introduction.* Belmont, CA: Wadsworth, 1986, XIII-449 p.; ²1991, XVII-462 p. Esp. 44-58: "Synoptic problem"; 116-139: "The gospel of Matthew".

1987 The Women in Matthew's Genealogy. — *JSNT* 29 (1987) 3-19. Esp. 7-8 [1,3]; 8-10 [1,5]; 14-18 [1,18-25]. [NTA 31, 1058]

1992 Jn 1,19-27 in Light of Related Passages in John, the Synoptics, and Acts. — VAN SEGBROECK, F., et al. (eds.), *The Four Gospels 1992.* FS F. Neirynck, 1992, III, 1943-1961. Esp. 1956-1957 [3,11/Jn 1,26-27]; 1958-1959 [Q 11,2-6/Jn 1,30].

**FREEDMAN, David Noel**

1960 → R.M. Grant 1960

1964 The Hebrew Old Testament and the Ministry Today. An Exegetical Study of Leviticus 19:18b. [22,39] — *Pittsburgh Perspective* 5 (1964) 9-14, 30. [NTA 8, 952]

1971 → J.A. Baird

**FRENSCHKOWSKI, Marco**

1995 *Offenbarung und Epiphanie.* Band 1: *Grundlagen des spätantiken und frühchristlichen Offenbarungsglaubens* (WUNT, II/79). Tübingen: Mohr, 1995, IX-481 p. Esp. 354-359. — Diss. Mainz, 1994 (O. Böcher).

**FRENZ, Albrecht**

1971 Mt xxi 5.7. — *NT* 13 (1971) 259-260. [NTA 16, 864]

**FRESENIUS, Wilhelm**

1960 Beobachtungen und Gedanken zum Gebet des Herrn. — *EvT* 20 (1960) 235-239. [NTA 5, 76]

**FREUDENBERG, J.**

1972 *Die synoptische Weherede: Tradition und Redaktion in Mt 23 par.* Diss. Münster, 1972-73, III-136 and 96 p.

**FREUDENBERGER, Rudolf**

1969 Zum Text der zweiten Vaterunserbitte. — *NTS* 15 (1968-69) 419-432. Esp. 421-422 [6,10]; 426.430 [12,28]; 430-432 [6,9-13]. [NTA 14, 183]

**FREY, Louis**

1972 *Analyse ordinale des évangiles synoptiques* (École Pratique des Hautes Études. VI: Sciences économiques et sociales. Mathématiques et sciences de l'homme, 11). Paris: Mouton Gauthier-Villars, 1972, 383 p. Esp. 17-41 [permutations]; 42-66 [insertions]; 67-99 [doublets]; 149-168 [omissions]; 199-287: "Regards sur les synoptiques" [246-247: doublets]; 356-361.366-368 [doublets]. → Aletti 1972, Bouhours 1972, Causse 1977, Courcier 1974, Léon-Dufour 1972b

**FREYNE, Seán**

1967 The Twelve Apostles. An Essay in Redaction Criticism. — *IrTQ* 34 (1967) 242-253. Esp. 248-249 [10,1-2]. [NTA 12, 539]

1968 *The Twelve: Disciples and Apostles. A Study in the Theology of the First Three Gospels.* London–Sydney: Sheed & Ward, 1968, X-278 p. Esp. 151-206: "Matthew and the twelve disciples". — Diss. Angelicum, Roma, 1965 (P. Zerafa).

1970 The Exercise of Christian Authority according to the New Testament. — *IrTQ* 37 (1970) 93-117. Esp. 105-109: "Peter". [NTA 15, 291]

1971 & WANSBROUGH, H., *Mark and Matthew* (Scripture Discussion Commentary, 7). London–Sydney: Sheed & Ward; Chicago, IL: ACTA Foundation, 1971, VIII-245 p. Esp. 137-242.

1985 Vilifying the Other and Defining the Self: Matthew's and John's Anti-Jewish Polemic in Focus. — NEUSNER, J. – FRERICHS, E.S. (eds.), *"To See Ourselves as Others See Us". Christians, Jews, "Others" in Late Antiquity* (Scholars Press Studies in the Humanities), Chico, CA: Scholars, 1985, 117-143. Esp. 119-123; 129-140.

1988a *Galilee, Jesus and the Gospels. Literary Approaches and Historical Investigations.* Dublin: Gill and Macmillan; Philadelphia, PA: Fortress, 1988, VIII-311 p. Esp. 70-90: "Matthew".

1988b Oppression from the Jews. Matthew's Gospel as an Early Christian Response. — *Concilium* (London) 200 (1988) 47-54. [NTA 34, 599]
L'oppression de la part des juifs. L'évangile de Matthieu, réaction chrétienne des origines. — *Concilium* (Paris) 220 (1988) 57-65.
Unterdrückung von seiten der Juden: Das Matthäusevangelium als eine frühe christliche Antwort. — *IZT/Concilium* (Mainz) 24 (1988) 462-467.

1995 Jesus and the Urban Culture of Galilee. — FORNBERG, T. – HELLHOLM, D. (eds.), *Texts and Contexts.* FS L. Hartman, 1995, 597-622. Esp. 610-616.

**FRIDRICHSEN, Anton**

1922a[R] The Logion Concerning "To Carry One's Cross". A Critical-exegetical Study. [Norwegian, 1922] — ID., *Exegetical Writings*, 1994, 33-45. Esp. 33-38: "Luke 14:27 and Matt. 10:37-39"; 38-40: "Matt. 10:38 and Mark 8:34".

1922b[R]  The Tripartite Formula in Matt. 28:19 and Baptism in the Three Names. [Norwegian, 1922] — *Ibid.*, 46-57.

1925[R]  *The Problem of Miracle in Primitive Christianity* [French, 1925], trans. R.A. Harrisville & J.S. Hanson, ed. K. Stendahl. Minneapolis, MN: Augsburg, 1972, 174 p.

1944[R]  Excepta fornicationis causa. [Swedish, 1944] [5,32] — *Ibid.*, 116-119.

1946[R]  Neutestamentliche Wortforschung. Zu Matth. 11,11-15. [1946] — *Ibid.*, 120-121.

1950  → Lindeskog 1950a

1953*  et al. (eds.), *The Root of the Vine. Essays in Biblical Theology.* Edinburgh: Dacre, VII-160 p. → Reicke, Riesenfeld 1951, Stendahl

1953  Eine unbeachtete Parallele zum Heilandsruf. Zu Mt 11,28ff. — SCHMID, J. — VÖGTLE, A. (eds.), *Synoptische Studien.* FS A. Wikenhauser, 1953, 83-85.

1994  *Exegetical Writings. A Selection*, trans. and ed. C.C. Caragounis & T. Fornberg (WUNT, 76). Tübingen: Mohr, 1994, XIII-314 p. → 1922a-b, 1944, 1946

**FRIEDL, Alfred**

1996  *Das eschatologische Gericht in Bildern aus dem Alltag. Eine exegetische Untersuchung von Mt 24,40f par Lk 17,34f* (Österreichische Bibelstudien, 14). Frankfurt/M: Lang, 1996, 355 p. Esp. 20-26 [context]; 40-48 [textual criticism]; 75-215: "Synchrone Analyse"; 245-304: "Wirkungsgeschichte"; 309-319: "Theologische Interpretation". — Diss. Wien, 1993-94 (J. Kremer)

**FRIEDLANDER, Gerald**

1911[R]  *The Jewish Sources of the Sermon on the Mount* [1911] (The Library of Biblical Studies). New York: Ktav, 1969, LVIII-301 p. Esp. 11-23 [5,3-12]; 24-34 [5,11-16]; 35-45 [5,17-20]; 46-90 [5,21-48]; 91-107 [6,1-6.16-18]; 123-136: "The fatherhood of God in Judaism and Christianity"; 137-151: "The kingdom of God"; 152-165: "The Old Testament as the original source of the Lord's Prayer"; 166-196 [6,19-34]; 197-211 [6,24]; 212-225 [7,1-6]; 226-238 [7,7-12]; 239-266 [7,13-27]. [NTA 14, p. 108] → S. Zeitlin 1969

   *Asbury Seminarian* (Wilmore, KY) 24/3 (1970) 46; G.J. BAHR, *CBQ* 32 (1970) 284-285; M. BOUTTIER, *ETR* 45 (1970) 391-392; G. FOHRER, *ZAW* 82 (1970) 157-157; J. KAHMANN, *TijdTheol* 10 (1970) 306-307; A.F.J. KLIJN, *NT* 12 (1970) 318; K. MÜLLER, *BZ* 15 (1971) 148; J. MURPHY-O'CONNOR, *RB* 79 (1972) 314.

**FRIEDRICH, Gerhard**

1956  Beobachtungen zur messianischen Hohepriestererwartung in den Synoptikern. — *ZTK* 53 (1956) 265-311. Esp. 282-284 [3,17]; 292-293 [16,17-19]; = ID., *Auf das Wort kommt es an. Gesammelte Aufsätze. Zum 70. Geburtstag*, ed. J.H. Friedrich, Göttingen: Vandenhoeck & Ruprecht, 1978, 56-102. Esp. 73-75; 83-84.

1977  *Sexualität und Ehe. Rückfragen an das Neue Testament* (Biblisches Forum, 11). Stuttgart: Katholisches Bibelwerk, 1977, 157 p. Esp. 58-61 [19,10-12]; 133-134 [19,3-9]; 135-139 [5,32].

1983  Die formale Struktur von Mt 28,18-20. — *ZTK* 80 (1983) 137-183. Esp. 151-162 [28,16-20]; 162-170.171-183 [28,18-20]. [NTA 28, 102]

**FRIEDRICH, Johannes H.**

1977  *Gott im Bruder? Eine methodenkritische Untersuchung von Redaktion, Überlieferung und Traditionen in Mt 25,31-46* (Calwer theologische Monographien, A7). Stuttgart: Calwer, 1977, XXI-307-196 p. Esp. 9-45: "Wortstatistische Untersuchungen"; 46-110: "Parallelen im Neuen Testament" [10,40-42; 13,36-43.49-50; 16,27; 19,28]; 220-257: "Einzelprobleme [ἀδελφοί; ἐλάχιστοι; πάντα τὰ ἔθνη]; 271-297: "Zur Überlieferungsgeschichte" [25,31-46]. [NTA 22, p. 88] — Diss. Tübingen, 1976 (P. Stuhlmacher).

   K. GRAYSTON, *ExpT* 91 (1979-80) 150; D. MARGUERAT, *RTP* 30 (1980) 196-197.

1978 Wortstatistik als Methode am Beispiel der Frage einer Sonderquelle im Matthäusevangelium. — BAYER, O. - G.U. WANZECK (eds.), *Festgabe für Friedrich Lang zum 65. Geburtstag am 6. September 1978*, Tübingen: Univ. Ev.-Theol. Sem., 1978; = ZNW 76 (1985) 29-42 ("stark überarbeitet"). Esp. 39-41 [13,24-30.36-43.47-50; 25,31-46]. [NTA 30, 102]

**FRIEDRICHSEN, G.W.S.**

1962 Notes on the Gothic Bible. — *NTS* 9 (1962-63) 39-55. Esp. 39-40 [9,20]; 42 [9,10; 17,1-4]; 43 [15,32-39]. [NTA 7, 436]

**FRIEDRICHSEN, Timothy A.**

1989a The Matthew-Luke Agreements against Mark. A Survey of Recent Studies: 1974-1989. — NEIRYNCK, F. (ed.), *L'Évangile de Luc*, 1989, 335-392. Esp. 345-350: "Mark: conflation of Matthew and Luke"; 350-354: "Proto-Matthew and Proto-Luke"; 365-367: "Luke's knowledge of Matthew"; 367-384: "Dependence of Luke upon Matthew". → 1992a

1989b The Minor Agreements of Matthew and Luke against Mark. Critical Observations on R.B. Vinson's Statistical Analysis. — *ETL* 65 (1989) 395-408. [NTA 34, 1114] → 1992a, 270-283; → Vinson 1984

1989c → Neirynck 1989a

1991 New Dissertations on the Minor Agreements. — *ETL* 67 (1991) 373-394. Esp. 373-385 [Ennulat 1994/89]; 385-390 [Rauscher 1990]; 391-394 [Yoon 1986]. [NTA 36, 1233] → 1992a

1992a *The Matthew-Luke Agreements against Mark 1974-1991.* Diss. Leuven, 1992, VII-316 and VI-312 p. (F. Neirynck). Esp. I, 113-215: "The Matthew-Luke agreements against Mark. A critical survey of recent studies: 1974-1991" (→ 1989a); 216-265: "Matthew-Luke agreements against Mk 4,30-32" (→ 1992b); 270-283 (→ 1989b); 284-288: "Note on Luke 9,22" (→ Neirynck 1989a); 289-291 [→ H. Riley 1989]; 292-313: "New dissertations" (→ 1991); II, 1-296: "A cumulative list"; 297-308: "The minor agreements in four synopses".

1992b 'Minor' and 'Major' Matthew-Luke Agreements against Mk 4,30-32. — VAN SEGBROECK, F., et al. (eds.), *The Four Gospels 1992. FS* F. Neirynck, 1992, I, 649-676. Esp. 653-662: "Did Mark know Q?"; 662-675: "The double question: Mk 4,30 / Lk 13,18". → 1992a, 216-265

1993 Alternative Synoptic Theories on Mk 4,30-32. — FOCANT, C. (ed.), *The Synoptic Gospels*, 1993, 427-450. Esp. 427-430: "The Griesbach hypothesis"; 430-440: "Deuteromarkus"; 440-450: "Lucan dependence on Matthew".

**FRIELING, Rudolf**

1963 "Die Werke der Barmherzigkeit". Matthäus 25,31-46. — *Die Christengemeinschaft* 35 (1963) 354-358; = ID., *Christologische Aufsätze*, 1982, 315-321.

1964 Das Gleichnis von der königlichen Hochzeit. Matthäus 22,1-14. — *Die Christengemeinschaft* 36 (1964) 289-293; = ID., *Christologische Aufsätze*, 1982, 265-273.

1965a Der Sohn Gottes. Eine Sinn-Figur im Gewebe des Matthäus-Evangeliums. — *Die Christengemeinschaft* 37 (1965) 65-70; = ID., *Christologische Aufsätze*, 1982, 35-44.

1965b "Kommet her zu mir alle...". Matthäus 11,28-30. — *Ibid.*, 353-356; = ID., *Christologische Aufsätze*, 1982, 69-76.

1966 Die Arbeiter im Weinberg und ihr Lohn. Matthäus 20,1-16. — *Die Christengemeinschaft* 38 (1966) 129-133; = ID., *Christologische Aufsätze*, 1982, 283-289.

1969a *Die Verklärung auf dem Berge. Eine Studie zum Evangelienverständnis* (Schriften zur Religionserkenntnis). Stuttgart: Urachhaus, 1969; = ID., *Studien zum Neuen Testament* (Gesammelte Aufsätze zum Alten und Neuen Testament, 4), Stuttgart: Urachhaus, 1986, 183-311. Esp. 231-268: "Nach Matthäus".

1969b  Im Zeichen des Menschensohnes. [24,29-30] — *Die Christengemeinschaft* 41 (1969) 33-38;  = ID., *Christologische Aufsätze*, 1982, 45-53.
1973  Werde und stirb – stirb und werde. Matthäus 1,1-17. — *Die Christengemeinschaft* 45 (1973) 33-38; = ID., *Christologische Aufsätze*, 1982, 16-24.
1982  *Christologische Aufsätze. Der Weg des Christus Jesus – Heilungen – Gleichnisse – Apostelzeugnisse* (Gesammelte Schriften zum Alten und Neuen Testament, 3). Stuttgart: Urachhaus, 1982, 402 p. → 1963, 1964, 1965a-b, 1966, 1969b, 1973

**FRIESEN, B.**
1981  Approaches to the Interpretation and Application of the Sermon on the Mount. — *Direction* (Fresno, CA) 10/2 (1981) 19-25. [NTA 25, 851]

**FRIGGENS, M.A.**
1982  The Relationship of the Prophetic Quotations in Matthew ii in the Light of the Triennial Lectionary Cycle. — *Studia Evangelica* 7 (1982) 183-188.

**FRINGS, Christian**
1971  *Untersuchungen zu den Texten vom Kreuztragen in der Synopse* [10,37-38; 16,24; Q 14,26-27]. Roma: Pont. Univ. Greg, 1971, 54 p.

**FRIZZI, Giuseppe**
1973  Carattere originale e rilevanza degli "apostoli inviati" in Q/*Lc.* 11,49-51; 13,34-35 / *Mt.* 23,34-36.37-39. — *RivBib* 21 (1973) 401-412. Esp. 402-409 [23,34-36]; 409-412 [23,37-39]. [NTA 19, 582]
1974  L'ἀπόστολος delle tradizioni sinottiche (Mc, Q, Mt, Lc, e Atti). — *RivBib* 22 (1974) 3-37. Esp. 9-12 [10,2]; 16-17 [Q 11,49]; 24-26 [Q: ἀπόστολος]. [NTA 19, 519]

**FRÖHLICH, Karlfried**
1963  *Formen der Auslegung von Mt 16,13-18 im lateinischen Mittelalter.* Diss. Basel, 1963, VI-177 p.
1989  Saint Peter, Papal Primacy, and the Exegetical Tradition, 1150-1300. — RYAN, C.J. (ed.), *The Religious Role of the Papacy: Ideals and Realities, 1150-1300* (Papers in Mediaeval Studies, 8), Toronto, Ont.: Pontifical Institute of Mediaeval Studies, 1989, 3-44.
1992  The Lord's Prayer in Patristic Literature. — *PrincSemB* suppl. 2 (1992) 71-87.

**FRÖR, Kurt**
1957  Bergpredigt. III. Im Predigt und Unterricht. — *RGG* 1 (³1957) 1053-1054.
1961  *Biblische Hermeneutik. Zur Schriftauslegung in Predigt und Unterricht.* München: Kaiser, 1961, ²1964, 397 p. Esp. 278-286 [infancy narrative]; 292-308 [parables]; 308-318 [Sermon on the Mount]; 318-332 [miracles].

**FROST, G.**
1963  The Word of God in the Synoptic Gospels. — *ScotJT* 16 (1963) 186-194. [NTA 8, 80]

**FRUTIGER, Simone**
1983  Les lectures d'Évangile ou les textes disjoints. Matthieu 16,13 à 25,46. — *FoiVie* 82/4 = *Cahiers bibliques* 22 (1983) 59-75.

**FRY, E. McGregor**
1967  A Provisional New Translation of the Lord's Prayer. — *BTrans* 18 (1967) 123-125. [NTA 12, 151]

**FRYE, Roland Mushat**

1978 The Synoptic Problem and Analogies in Other Literatures. — WALKER, W.O., Jr. (ed.), *The Relationships among the Gospels*, 1978, 261-302. Esp. 262-286: "On sequence and dependence: the Griesbach hypothesis". → W.R. Farmer 1978a, Tyson 1978b

1979 The Jesus of the Gospels: Approaches Through Narrative Structure. — HADIDIAN, D.Y. (ed.), *From Faith to Faith*. FS D.G. Miller, 1979, 75-89. Esp. 79-81 [16,13-23]; 81-86 [4,1-11].

1991 On Praying "Our Father". The Challenge of Radical Feminist Language for God. — *ATR* 73 (1991) 388-402. Esp. 398-401. [NTA 36, 716]

**FRYER, M.S.L.**

1987 Matthew 13:14-21. The Feeding of the Five Thousard. A Grammatico-Historical Exegesis. — *In die Skriflig* 21 (1987) 27-42.

**FUCHS, Albert**

1966 *Die Tradition von Johannes dem Täufer im Matthäusevangelium. Quellenuntersuchung. Exegese und Redaktionstheologie*. Diss. Salzburg, 1966, XV-155 p.

1971 *Sprachliche Untersuchungen zu Matthäus und Lukas. Ein Beitrag zur Quellenkritik* (AnBib, 49). Roma: Biblical Institute Press, 1971, X-217 p. Esp. 18-37.45-170 [9,27-31; 20,29-34]; 37-44.171-175 [Q 12,11-12]. — Diss. Salzburg, 1968 (E. Schächer). → Neirynck 1980b
F.H. BORSCH, *Interpr* 26 (1972) 102-103; J. COPPENS, *ETL* 47 (1971) 606-607; B.R. DOYLE, *AusBR* 20 (1972) 59-60; J. ERNST, *TGl* 66 (1976) 239; H. FRANKEMÖLLE *TRev* 68 (1972) 375; A. GABOURY, *JBL* 91 (1972) 553-554; M. GOULDER, *JTS* 23 (1972) 197-200; K. GRAYSTON, *ExpT* 83 (1971-72) 308; X. JACQUES, *NRT* 95 (1973) 412; U. LUZ, *TZ* 30 (1974) 112; H. MERKEL, *TLZ* 97 (1972) 190-192; A. SALAS, *CiudDios* 185 (1972) 727; A. SAND, *TPQ* 120 (1972) 68-69; G. SCHNEIDER, *BZ* 17 (1973) 268-269; A. SEGOVIA, *ArchTeolGran* 34 (1971) 232-233; W.G. THOMPSON, *CBQ* 34 (1972) 75-76.

1976 Intention und Adressaten der Bußpredigt des Täufers bei Mt 3,7-10. — *SNTU* 1 (1976) 62-75.

1978 Die Behandlung der mt/lk Übereinstimmungen gegen Mk durch S. McLoughlin und ihre Bedeutung für die Synoptische Frage. — *SNTU* 3 (1978) 24-57. Esp. 29-42 [survey]; 42-57 [12,22-30]. → McLoughlin 1967, Neirynck 1980b

1980a *Die Entwicklung der Beelzebulkontroverse bei den Synoptikern. Traditionsgeschichtliche und redaktionsgeschichtliche Untersuchung von Mk 3,22-27 und Parallelen, verbunden mit der Rückfrage nach Jesus* (SNTU, B5). Linz: SNTU, 1980, 279 p. Esp. 21-29: "Die Doppelüberlieferung Mt 12,22-24 / Q 32-34 und die Lk-Parallele 11,14-15"; 29-35: "Die Übereinstimmungen gegen Mk"; 35-121: "Deuteromarkinische Redaktion"; 121-169: "Die Redaktion der Großevangelisten in Mt 12,22-34 / 9,32-34 und Lk 11,14-15"; 169-249: "Literaturdiskussion". — Diss. Regensburg, 1977 (F. Mußner). → Neirynck 1980b

1980b Die Überschneidungen von Mk und "Q" nach B.H. Streeter und E.P. Sanders und ihre wahre Bedeutung (Mk 1,1-8 Par.). — HAUBECK, W. – BACHMANN, M. (eds.), *Wort in der Zeit*. FS K.H. Rengstorf, 1980, 28-81. Esp. 29-56 [Mk/Q]; 57-78 [DeuteroMk]. → Neirynck 1980b, E.P. Sanders 1973

1980c Die Wiederbelebung der Griesbachhypothese oder Wissenschaft auf dem Holzweg. — *SNTU* 5 (1980) 139-149. [NTA 28, 475] → W.R. Farmer 1975a

1982 Entwicklungsgeschichtliche Studie zu Mk 1,29-31 par Mt 8,14-15 par Lk 4,38-39. Macht über Fieber und Dämonen. — *SNTU* 6-7 (1981-82) 21-76. Esp. 22-25: "Die Quellenfrage"; 25-28: "Methodische Überlegungen"; 28-66: "Synoptischer Einzelvergleich". [NTA 28, 932]

1983 Durchbruch in der Synoptischen Frage. Bemerkungen zu einer "neuen" These und ihren Konsequenzen. — *SNTU* 8 (1983) 5-17. [NTA 30, 1035] → Strecker 1983a

1984 Versuchung Jesu. — *SNTU* 9 (1984) 95-159. Esp. 99-101 [Mk/Mt]; 101-114: "Deuteromarkinische agreements"; 114-139: "Redaktion des Mt und des Lk"; 139-146: "Zugehörigkeit zu Q?". [NTA 30, 1073]

1990a Offene Probleme der Synoptikerforschung. Zur Geschichte der Perikope Mk 2,1-12 par Mt 9,1-8 par Lk 5,17-26. — *SNTU* 15 (1990) 73-99. Esp. 74-82: "Analyse"; 84-95: "Literarkritischer Ausblick". [NTA 36, 175]

1990b Die "Seesturmperikope" Mk 4,35-41 parr im Wandel der urkirchlichen Verkündigung. — STAUDINGER, F. - WURZ, H. (eds.), *Weihbischof Dr. Alois Stöger Exeget zwischen Bibelkommission und Offenbarungskonstitution*, St. Pölten, 1990, 59-86; = *SNTU* 15 (1990) 101-133 (revised). Esp. 104-123: "Analyse der agreements". [NTA 36, 180]; = STRECKER, G. (ed.), *Minor Agreements*, 1993, 65-92. Esp. 68-85. → Schenk 1993a
La perícopa de la "tempestad calmada" (Mk 4,35-41 par.) en el kerigma de la Iglesia primitiva. — *EstBíb* 48 (1990) 433-460. Esp. 436-451. [NTA 36, 180]

1991 Die Last der Vergangenheit. Bemerkungen zu J. Kiilunen, *Das Doppelgebot der Liebe in synoptischer Sicht. Ein redaktionskritischer Versuch über Mk 12,28-34 und die Parallelen.* — *SNTU* 16 (1991) 151-168. [NTA 37, 181r] → Kiilunen 1989

1992a Schrittweises Wachstum. Zur Entwicklung der Perikope Mk 5,21-43 par Mt 9,18-26 par Lk 8,40-56. — *SNTU* 17 (1992) 5-53. Esp. 14-40: "Einzelanalyse der agreements". [NTA 37, 1286]

1992b Aufwind für Deuteromarkus. — *Ibid.*, 55-76. [NTA 37, 1238] → Luz 1985a/90

1992c Die synoptische Aussendungsrede in quellenkritischer und traditionsgeschichtlicher Sicht. — *Ibid.*, 77-168. Esp. 80-115 [minor agreements: 10,1.7-11.14]; 115-157 [survey of literature]. [NTA 37, 1287]

1993 Das Elend mit der Zweiquellentheorie. Eine Auseinandersetzung mit zwei neueren Dissertationen zum Thema der minor agreements. — *SNTU* 18 (1993) 183-243. Esp. 186-190 [10,1.7-11.14]; 190-196 [3,1-12]; 196-202 [12,22-30]; 202-208: "Konsequenzen der Analyse"; 218-225 [minor agreements: 9,7; 12,1; 13,11; 14,13; 16,21; 26,68]; 227-232 [13,31-32]; 232-234 [17,1-9]. [NTA 39, 127] → Fendler 1991, Schüling 1991

1994a Die Sehnsucht nach der Vergangenheit. — *SNTU* 19 (1994) 69-111. Esp. 73-77 [Q 10,2-12 (Lk)]; 77-86 [11,24-40]; 86-108 [Q 11,14-23 (Lk)]. [NTA 39, 873] → Schürmann 1994b

1994b Die Sünde wider den Heiligen Geist. Mk 3,28-30 par Mt 12,31-32 par Lk 12,10. — *Ibid.*, 113-130. [NTA 39, 823]

1994c Das Zeichen des Jona. Vom Rückfall. — *Ibid.*, 131-160. Esp. 131-146: "Quellenkritische und traditionsgeschichtliche Analyse"; 146-156: "Traditionsgeschichtliche Folgerungen". [NTA 39, 805]

1994d Bevormundung oder Die Arroganz der halben Wahrheit. Zu einer neuen agreement-Dissertation. — *Ibid.*, 161-172. [NTA 39, 781r] → Ennulat 1994

1995 Exegese im elfenbeinernen Turm. Das quellenkritische Problem von Mk 1,2-8 par Mt 3,1-12 par Lk 3,1-17 in der Sicht der Zweiquellentheorie und von Deuteromarkus. — *SNTU* 20 (1995) 23-149. [NTA 40, 1476] → Neirynck 1996b

FUCHS, Éric

1973 Trace de Dieu: la parabole. — *Bulletin du Centre protestant d'études* (Genève) 25 (1973) 19-39. [NTA 18, 451]

1978 L'imaginaire et le symbolique. Réflexions hasardeuses sur Matthieu 5,17-20. — *Bulletin du Centre protestant d'études* 30 (1978) 21-28. [NTA 23, 96]

1992 L'éthique du Sermon sur la montagne. — BÉLANGER, R. - PLOURDE, S. (eds.), *Actualiser la morale. Mélanges offerts à René Simon*, Paris: Cerf, 1992, 317-332.

FUCHS, Ernst

1954a *Hermeneutik*. Bad Cannstadt: Müllerschön, 1954; Tübingen: Mohr, [4]1970, v-270 p. Esp. 211-230: "Die Analogie".
Die Analogie. — HARNISCH, W. (ed.), *Die neutestamentliche Gleichnisforschung*, 1982, 1-19.

1954b  Bemerkungen zur Gleichnisauslegung. — *TLZ* 79 (1954) 345-348. Esp. 346-347 [20,1-15];
= ID., *Zur Frage nach dem historischen Jesus*, 1960, 136-142. Esp. 139-140; =
HARNISCH, W. (ed.), *Gleichnisse Jesu*, 1982, 256-261. Esp. 258-259.

1954c  Jesu Selbstzeugnis nach Matthäus 5. — *ZTK* 51 (1954) 14-34. Esp. 17-24: "Historisch-
kritische Analyse von Matthäus 5"; 24-29: "Christologische Interpretation"; 29-34: "Das hermeneutische
Problem"; = ID., *Zur Frage nach dem historischen Jesus* 1960, 100-125. Esp. 105-112;
113-120; 120-125.

1954d  Die vollkommene Gewißheit. Zur Auslegung von Matthäus 5,48. — ELTESTER, W.
(ed.), *Neutestamentliche Studien*. FS R. Bultmann, 1954 130-136; = ID., *Zur Frage
nach dem historischen Jesus*, 1960, 126-135.

1958   Die der Theologie durch die historisch-kritische Methode auferlegte Besinnung. [20,1-16]
— *EvT* 18 (1958) 256-268; = ID., *Zur Frage nach dem historischen Jesus*, 1960, 219-
237.

1959a  The Parable of the Unmerciful Servant (Matt. 18,23-35). — *Studia Evangelica* 1 (1959)
487-494.

1959b  Das Sprachereignis in der Verkündigung Jesu, in der Theologie des Paulus und im
Ostergeschehen. — ID., *Zum hermeneutischen Problem in der Theologie. Die
existentiale Interpretation* (Gesammelte Aufsätze, 1), Tübingen: Mohr, 1959, 281-305.
Esp. 286-289 [5,21-48].

1959c  Was wird in der Exegese des Neuen Testaments interpretiert? — *ZTK* 56 (1959) 31-48.
Esp. 36-39 [13,31-32]; 39-40 [13,44]; = ID., *Zur Frage nach dem historischen Jesus*, 1960,
280-303. Esp. 287-291; 291-293.

1960a  Die Verkündigung Jesu. Der Spruch von den Raben. [Q 12,24] — RISTOW, H. -
MATTHIAE, K. (eds.), *Der historische Jesus und der kerygmatische Christus*, 1960,
385-388. → 1960c, 305-310

1960b  *Zur Frage nach dem historischen Jesus* (Gesammelte Aufsätze, 2). Tübingen: Mohr,
1960, X-458 p. → 1954b-d, 1958, 1959c, 1960c
*Studies of the Historical Jesus* (Studies in Biblical Theology, 42). London: SCM; Naperville, IL: Allenson,
1964, 240 p.

1960c  Das Zeitverständnis Jesu. — *Ibid.*, 304-376. Esp. 305-310 (= 1960a); 310-313 [5,25-26]; 313-
318 [25,31-46]; 327-328 [13,44-46]; 330-332 [13,18-23]; 340-341 [13,24-30.36-43]; 341-342 [13,33]; 343-
344 [11,5-6]; 350-351 [5,21-48]; 360-361 [18,23-35]; 361-364 [20,1-16]; 367-368 [7,16].

1961   Über die Aufgabe einer christlicher Theologie. Zum Aufsatz Ernst Käsemanns über
"Die Anfänge christlicher Theologie". — *ZTK* 58 (1961) 245-267. [NTA 7, 24]; = ID.,
*Wagnis des Glaubens*, 1979, 182-201. → Käsemann 1960

1966   Kanon und Kerygma. Ein Referat. — *ZTK* 63 (1966) 410-433. Esp. 415-419; = ID.,
*Wagnis des Glaubens*, 1979, 21-41. Esp. 25-28 [20,1-16].

1971   *Jesus. Wort und Tat*. Tübingen: Mohr, 1971, IX-159 p. Esp. 19-25 [20,1-16]; 28-46: "Der
Standpunkt Jesu" [18,23-35]; 62-67 [5,21-48].

1979   *Wagnis des Glaubens. Aufsätze und Vorträge*, ed. E. Grötzinger. Neukirchen-Vluyn:
Neukirchener, 1979, 285 p. → 1961, 1966

**FUCHS, Josef**

1991   Die schwierige Goldene Regel. [7,12] — *Stimmen der Zeit* (München) 209 (1991) 773-
781. [NTA 36, 722]

**FUCHS, Werner**

1987   Meditaçäu sobre Mateus 25:31-46. — *Estudos Teológicos* (São Leopoldo) 27 (1987) 81-
186.

**FUELLENBACH, John**

1995 *The Kingdom of God. The Message of Jesus Today*. Maryknoll, NY: Orbis, 1995, XI-340 p. Esp. 273-293: "The Lord's prayer as a summary of the kingdom message".

**FÜLLKRUG-WEITZEL, Cornelia**

1986 Die kanaanäische Frau und die Verheißung Israels, Mt. 15,21-28. — *TK* 31-32 (1986) 40-60.

**FÜRST, Heinrich**

1985 Utopien im Neuen Testament. — *Franziskanische Studien* (Paderborn) 67 (1985) 3-18. Esp. 3-5: "Die Utopie der Bergpredigt".

**FÜSSEL, Kuno**

1977 Was heisst materialistische Lektüre der Bibel. — *Una Sancta* 32 (1977) 46-54. Esp. 52-54 [20,1-16]. [NTA 21, 642]

**FUETER, Paul D.**

1986 The Therapeutic Language of the Bible. — *BTrans* 37 (1986) 309-319. Esp. 315-318 [5,1-16.17-42.43-47]. [NTA 31, 21]

**FUJITA, Neil S.**

1986 *A Crack in the Jar. What Ancient Jewish Documents Tell Us about the New Testament*. New York – Mahwah, NJ: Paulist, 1986, VIII-308 p. Esp. 109-157: "The significance of the Judaean finds for New Testament studies".

**FULIGA, Jose B.**

1994 The Temptations of Jesus: A Class Struggle. [4,1-11] — *AsiaJT* 8 (1994) 172-185. [NTA 40, 853]

**FULLER, Daniel P.**

1980 *Gospel and Law: Contrast or Continuum? The Hermeneutics of Dispensationalism and Covenant Theology*. Grand Rapids, MI: Eerdmans, 1980, XIII-217 p. Esp. 59-62 [18,23-35].

**FULLER, G.C.**

1966 The Olivet Discourse. An Apocalyptic Time-Table. [24] — *WestTJ* 28 (1966) 157-163. [NTA 11, 217]

**FULLER, Reginald Horace**

1954 *The Mission and Achievement of Jesus. An Examination of the Presuppositions of New Testament Theology* (Studies in Biblical Theology, 12). London: SCM, 1954; repr. 1956, 1960, 1970, 128 p. Esp. 20-49: "The kingdom of God in the proclamation of Jesus"; 50-78: "The kingdom of God and the death of Jesus"; 79-117: "The raw materials of Christology" [christological titles].

1956 The Virgin Birth: Historical Fact or Kerygmatic Truth? — *BR* 1 (1956) 1-8. [NTA 2, 522]

1963 *Interpreting the Miracles*. Philadelphia, PA: Westminster, 1963; London: SCM, 1966, 128 p.; repr. 1968. Esp. 25-27 [12,27]; 27-28 [11,4-6]; 28-29 [13,16-17]; 47-48: "The tradition in Q"; 77-82: "Ten miracles in Matthew" [8-9]; 114-116 [11,2-10].
  *Die Wunder Jesu in Exegese und Verkündigung*, trans. mit einem Vor- und Nachwort von F.J. Schierse (Theologische Perspektiven). Düsseldorf: Patmos, 1967, ²1968, ³1969, 144 p.
  *De interpretatie van de wonderen van Jezus*, trans. K. Van Dun. Antwerpen–Utrecht: Patmos, 1971, 124 p.

1964 The Clue to Jesus' Self-understanding. — *Studia Evangelica* 3 (1964) 58-66. Esp. 63-64 [Q 12,8-9]; = ID., *Christ and Christianity: Studies in the Formation of Christology*, ed. R. Kahl, Valley Forge, PA: Trinity, 1994, 37-46. Esp. 42-43.

1965 *The Foundations of New Testament Christology.* London: Lutterworth; New York: Scribner, 1965, 268 p.; (The Fontana Library. Theology & Philosophy), London–Glasgow: Collins, 1969, 268 p. Esp. 108-129.155-173.184-197 [christological titles]; ²1972.
*Fundamentos de una cristología neotestamentaria.* Madrid: Cristiandad 1978, 286 p.

1966 *A Critical Introduction to the New Testament.* London: Duckworth & Co., 1966, IX-221 p. Esp. 69-80: "The synoptic problem"; 113-118: "The gospel o⁻ Matthew".

1967 The 'Thou Art Peter' Pericope and the Eastern Appearances. [16,17-19] — *McCormick Quarterly* (Chicago, IL) 20 (1967) 309-315. [NTA 12, 159]

1971 *The Formation of the Resurrection Narratives.* New York: Macmillan, 1971; London: SPCK, 1972, XIV-225 p. Esp. 71-93: "The resurrection narratives in Matthew"; Philadelphia, PA: Fortress, ²1980.

1973 The Choice of Matthias. — *Studia Evangelica* 6 (1973) 140-146. Esp. 143 [27,3-10/Acts 1,18-19].

1975a Das Doppelgebot der Liebe. Ein Testfall für die Echtheitskriterien der Worte Jesu. [22,34-40] — STRECKER, G. (ed.), *Jesus Christus in Historie und Theologie.* FS H. Conzelmann, 1975, 317-329.
The Double Commandment of Love. Test Case for the Criteria of Authenticity. — SCHOTTROFF, L., et al. (eds.), *Essays on the Love Commandment,* 1978, 41-56.

1975b & SANDERS, E.P. – LONGSTAFF, T.R.W., The Synoptic Problem: After Ten Years. — *PerkJourn* 28/2 (1975) 63-74. Esp. 63-68 [Fuller]; 68-71 [Sanders]; 72-74 [Longstaff]. [NTA 19, 924r] → W.R. Farmer 1964a

1978a Baur versus Hilgenfeld: A Forgotten Chapter in the Debate on the Synoptic Problem. — *NTS* 24 (1977-78) 355-370. [NTA 22, 748]

1978b Classics and the Gospels: The Seminar. — WALKER, W.O., Jr. (ed.), *The Relationships among the Gospels,* 1978, 173-192. Esp. 176-183 [Papias]. → G.A. Kennedy 1978

1978c Die neuere Diskussion über das synoptische Problem. — *TZ* 34 (1978) 129-148. [NTA 23, 409]

1983 Christology in Matthew and Luke. — ID. – PERKINS, P., *Who Is This Christ? Gospel Christology and Contemporary Faith,* Philadelphia, PA: Fortress, 1983, 81-95. Esp. 81-86.

1985 The Son of Man: A Reconsideration. — GROH, D.E. – JEWETT, R. (eds.), *The Living Text.* FS E.W. Saunders, 1985, 207-217. Esp. 210-211; 213-214 [Q 12,8-9]; 215-216 [Q 11,30; Q 12,40; Q 17,24.30].

1987 Order in the Synoptic Gospels: Summary. — *SecCent* 6 (1987-88) 107-109. → J. Dewey 1987, Longstaff 1987, W.O. Walker Jr. 1987b

1988 Matthew. — MAYS, J.L. (ed.), *Harper's Bible Commentary,* San Francisco, CA: Harper & Row, 1988, 951-982.

1989 The Decalogue in the New Testament. — *Interpr* 43 (1989) 243-255. Esp. 243-250: "The Decalogue in the Jesus tradition" [5,27-48; 12,11-12; 19,16-22]. [NTA 34, 352]

1990 *He That Cometh: The Birth of Jesus in the New Testament.* Harrisburg, PA – Wilton, CT: Morehouse, 1990, X-117 p.

1993 4QMicah: A Small Fragment of a Manuscript of the Minor Prophets from Qumran, Cave IV. [2,6] — *RQum* 16 (1993) 193-202. [NTA 39, 1130⁻]

**FUNK, Robert Walter**
1959 The Wilderness. — *JBL* 78 (1959) 205-214. Esp. 209-213. [NTA 4, 343]
1961 → Debrunner 1913

1966  *Language, Hermeneutic, and Word of God. The Problem of Language in the New Testament and Contemporary Theology*. New York: Harper & Row, 1966, XVI-317 p. Esp. 133-162: "The parable as metaphor"; 163-187: "The parable of the great supper: text and context"; 188-198: "The parable of the great supper: a reading and theses". Das Gleichnis als Metapher. — HARNISCH, W. (ed.), *Die neutestamentliche Gleichnisforschung*, 1982, 20-58.

1969  The Temporal Horizon of the Kingdom. — *Journal for Theology and the Church* 6 (1969) 175-171; = ID., *Parables and Presence*, 1982, 67-79. Esp. 73-75.

1971  Beyond Criticism in Quest of Literacy: The Parable of the Leaven. [13,33] — *Interpr* 25 (1971) 149-170. [NTA 16, 157]
      The Parable of the Leaven: Away-From-Here as the Destination. — ID., *Jesus as Precursor*, ed. E.F. Beutner (SBL Semeia Supplements, 2), Philadelphia, PA: Fortress; Missoula, MT: Scholars, 1975; Sonoma, CA: Polebridge, rev. ed., 1994, 51-72.

1974  Structure in the Narrative Parables of Jesus. — *Semeia* 2 (1974) 51-73. [NTA 19, 926]
      Die Struktur der erzählenden Gleichnisse Jesu. — HARNISCH, W. (ed.), *Die neutestamentliche Gleichnisforschung*, 1982, 224-247.

1977  The Narrative Parables: The Birth of a Language Tradition. — JERVELL, J. - MEEKS, W.A. (eds.), *God's Christ and His People. Studies in Honour of Nils Alstrup Dahl*, Oslo-Bergen-Tromsö: Universitetsforlaget, 1977, 43-50; = ID., *Parables and Presence*, 1982, 19-28.

1982  *Parables and Presence. Forms of the New Testament Tradition*. Philadelphia, PA: Fortress, 1982, XIV-206 p. → 1969, 1977

1985a  *New Gospel Parallels*. Volume 1: *The Synoptic Gospels*; Volume 2: *John and the Other Gospels* (Foundations and Facets: New Testament, 5). Philadelphia, PA: Fortress, 1985, XX-492 p. and XX-396 p.

1985b  Polling the Pundits. — *Forum* 1/1 (1985) 31-50. Esp. 33-37 [3,2; 4,17]; 37-47 [9,9-13]. [NTA 30, 529]

1985c  From Parable to Gospel. Domesticating the Tradition. — *Forum* 1/3 (1985) 3-24. Esp. 8-11 [12,46-50]. [NTA 31, 560]
      Addendum: J.F. DECHOW, *Ibid.*, 25-30.

1986a  Poll on the Parables. — *Forum* 2/1 (1986) 54-80.

1986b  The Beatitudes and Turn the Other Cheek. Recommendations and Polling. — *Forum* 2/3 (1986) 103-128. Esp. 104-110 [5,3-12]; 110-113 [5,42]; 113-122: "Polling categories"; 122-125: "The development of the gospel tradition: assumptions". [NTA 31, 1069] → Boring 1985, J.D. Crossan 1988c

1988  & SCOTT, B.B. - BUTTS, J.R., *The Parables of Jesus. Red Letter Edition* (Jesus Seminar Series, 1). Sonoma, CA: Polebridge, 1988, XX-108 p. Esp. 25-75: "The parables of Jesus". → Hoover 1988

1989  Unraveling the Jesus Tradition. Criteria and Criticism. [Q 6,27-35] — *Forum* 5/2 (1989) 31-62. Esp. 32: "The Q text"; 32-41: "Rhetorical structure and sequence analysis"; 41-43: "The aphoristic tradition"; 43-45 [Q 6,30b]; 45-46: "Verbal and structural agreements"; 46-50: "Matthew and Luke edit Q"; 50-58: "Earlier stages of the tradition and Jesus". [NTA 34, 163]

1993a  & HOOVER, R.W. (eds.), *The Five Gospels. The Search for the Authentic Words of Jesus* ("A Polebridge Press Book"). Sonoma, CA: Polebridge; New York: Macmillan, 1993, XXII-553 p. Esp. 9-16: "A map of synoptic relationships"; 129-270: "The gospel of Matthew"; 271-400: "The gospel of Luke"; 471-532: "The gospel of Thomas".

1993b  On Distinguishing Historical from Fictive Narrative. — *Forum* 9 (1993) 179-216. Esp. 198-211: "John the Baptist: fact or fiction?". [NTA 41, 732]

**FURFEY, Paul Hanly**

1955  Christ as *Tektôn*. [13,55] — *CBQ* 17 (1955) 324-335 (204-215). Esp. 333-335.

**FURNISH, Victor Paul**

1972 *The Love Command in the New Testament.* Nashville, TN – New York: Abingdon, 1972, 240 p. Esp. 30-34 [22,34-40]; 45-54 [5,43-48]; 54-59 [Q 6,27-36 (Lk)]; 59-69: "Love in Jesus' teachings"; 74-84: "The settings in the synoptic gospels: Matthew".

1976 Griesbach Hypothesis. — *IDBS*, 1976, 381.

1982 Love of Neighbor in the New Testament. [22,34-40] — *Journal of Religious Ethics* (Knoxville, TN) 10 (1982) 327-334. [NTA 27, 709]

1984 War and Peace in the New Testament. — *Interpr* 38 (1984) 363-379. Esp. 369-370 [10,34]. [NTA 29, 698]

**FUSCO, Vittorio**

1975 Gesù il liberatore, che vive nella sua Chiesa (Mt 8,1-9,34). — *ParVi* 20 (1975) 114-126.

1980 Il "vissuto" della Chiesa in Matteo – Appunti metodologici con esemplificazione da Mt 7,15-23. — *Asprenas* 27 (1980) 3-26. Esp. 5-14: "Appunti metodologici"; 15-18: "Aspetti fondamentali del 'vissuto' ecclesiale in Mt"; 18-26 [7,15-23].

1981 Il segreto messianico nell'episodio del lebbroso (*Mc.* 1,40-45). — *RivBib* 29 (1981) 273-313. Esp. 275-278 [minor agreements]; 307-309 [9,27-31/Mk 1,40-45]. [NTA 26, 858]

1982 L'accord mineur Mt 13,11a / Lc 8,10a contre Mc 4,11a. — DELOBEL, J. (ed.), *Logia*, 1982, 355-361.

1983 *Oltre la parabola. Introduzione alle parabole di Gesù* (Kyrios). Roma: Borla, 1983, 202 p. [13,1-9.13-20.24-30.31-32.36-43.44.45-46; 18,12-14.23-35; 20,1-16; 21,28-32.33-46; 22,1-14; 24,32-34.43-44; 25,1-13].

1985a Carità, Chiesa, mondo, nella descrizione del giudizio finale (Mt 25,31-46). — *RasT* 26 (1985) 270-274.

1985b Il rito interrotto (Mt 5,23-24). — *Jesus caritas* 7/19 (1985) 8-15.

1986 Settanta volte sette (Mt 18,1-35). — *Jesus caritas* 8/21 (1986) 5-19.

1987 Consensi e dissensi nella questione sinottica. — *CrnStor* 8 (1987) 591-607. [NTA 32, 1091] → Bellinzoni 1985*

1988a L'incredulità del credente: un aspetto dell'ecclesiologia di Matteo. — *ParSpirV* 17 (1988) 118-142. Esp. 124-125 [6,30]; 125-127 [8,23-27]; 127-134 [14,28-31]; 134-136 [16,5-12]; 136-139 [17,14-20].

1988b Matteo. — ROSSANO, P. – RAVASI, G. – GIRLANDA, A. (eds.), *Nuovo Dizionario di Teologia Biblica*, Cinisello Balsamo: Paoline, 1988, 930-937.

1990a Dalla missione di Galilea alla missione universale. La tradizione del discorso missionario (Mt 9,35-10,42; Mc 6,7-13; Lc 9,1-6; 10,1-16). — GHIBERTI, G. (ed.), *La missione nel mondo antico e nella Bibbia* (Atti della XXX Settimana Biblica) = *Ricerche storico-bibliche* 2/1 (1990) 101-125.

1990b L'invettiva e il lamento. Mt 23,1-39. — *ParSpirV* 21 (1990) 153-172.

1991 *Povertà e sequela. La pericope sinottica della chiamata del ricco (Mc. 10,17-31 parr.)* [19,16-30] (Studi biblici, 94). Brescia: Paideia, 1991, 147 p.

1993 La Scrittura nella tradizione sinottica e negli Atti. — NORELLI, E. (ed.), *La Bibbia nell'antichità cristiana.* I: *Da Gesù a Origene* (La Bibbia nella storia, 15), Bologna: Dehoniane, 1993, 105-149. Esp. 119-125: "Matteo".

1994a *La casa sulla roccia: Temi spirituali di Matteo* (Spiritualità biblica). Magnano: Qiqajon, 1994, 140 p. [NTA 39, p. 504]

1994b Introduzione generale ai Sinottici. — LÀCONI, M. (ed.), *Vangeli sinottici*, 1994, 33-132. Esp. 37-98: "La questione sinottica".

1994c  Un racconto di miracolo: la guarigione del cieco Bartimeo (Mc 10,46-52; Mt 20,29-34; Lc 18,35-43). — *Ibid*., 213-225. Esp. 219-221.

1994d  Una parabola: la pecora smarrita (Mt 18,12-14; Lc 15,4-7). — *Ibid*., 305-315. Esp. 307-309, 312-315.

**FUTTERLIEB, Hartmut**

1988   Die Götzen des Verwirrers. Eine Unterrichtsskizze zur Versuchungserzählung (Mt 4,1-11). — *Schönberger Hefte* (Frankfurt/M) 18/2 (1988) 1-29.

# G

**GABEL, John B.**

1986 & WHEELER, C.B., *The Bible as Literature. An Introduction.* Oxford: University Press, 1986, XIV-278 p. Esp. 182-194.196-198.

**GABOURY, Antonio**

1970 *La structure des évangiles synoptiques. La structure-type à l'origine des Synoptiques* (SupplNT, 22). Leiden: Brill, 1970, IX-226 p. Esp. 24-31: "La priorité de Matthieu"; 63-65: "Comparaison entre synoptiques"; 66-67; 79-83; 120-139: "Indices ce différents stades d'insertion dans l'évangile de Matthieu". — Diss. Commissio Biblica, Roma, 1962 (X. Léon-Dufour). → Courcier 1974, Léon-Dufour 1970b, 1972b, López Fernández 1971, Neirynck 1972d, Rolland 1984a

1972 Christological Implications Resulting from a Study of the Structure of the Synoptic Gospels. — *SBL 1972 Seminar Papers*, I, 97-146.

**GÄBLER, Ulrich**

1992 Das Vaterunser in der Basler Reformation. — *TZ* 48 (1992) 118-126.

**GAECHTER, Paul**

1953a *Maria im Erdenleben. Neutestamentliche Marienstudien.* Innsbruck: Tyrolia, 1953, 260 p.; [2]1954. Esp. 109-116 [1,18-25].
*María en el Evangelio*, trans. M. Villanueva (Stella Matutina, 6). Bilbao: Desclée De Brouwer, 1959, 369 p. Esp. 171-181.

1953b Petrus und seine Nachfolge. Zum Petrusbuch von Prof. Oskar Cullmann. — *ZKT* 75 (1953) 331-337. → Cullmann 1952

1964 *Das Matthäus-Evangelium. Ein Kommentar.* Innsbruck: Tyrolia, 1964, 978 p. Esp. 13-21: "Einleitung"; 23-972 [commentary]. [NTA 8, p. 464]
*BK* 21 (1968) 132; J.S. CROATTO, *Stromata* (San Míguel, Arg.) 21 (1965) 615-617; M.S.J. D., *VoxTheol* 39 (1969) 188; J. DILLERSBERGER, *Oesterreichisches Klerus-Blatt* 97 (1964) 228; F. DREYFUS, *RB* 75 (1968) 621; *RSPT* 50 (1966) 100-101; J.A. FITZMYER, *TS* 26 (1965) 300-303; P. GAECHTER, *ZKT* 86 (1964) 220-221; J.M. GUIRAU, *Augustinianum* 5 (1965) 397-399; V. HASLER, *TZ* 22 (1966) 216-217; J. HUERGO, *CiTom* 94 (1967) 130-132; A.K., *Freiburger Rundbrief* 16-17 (1965-66) 113-114; W. KOESTER, *Scholastik* 40 (1965) 264-267; M. LÀCONI, *Angelicum* 52 (1965) 511-513; G. LEONARDI, *Studia Patavina* 11 (1964) 507-509; X. LÉON-DUFOUR, *RSR* 53 (1965) 604-610; M. MÍGUENS, *Ant* 42 (1967) 128-131; F. MUSSNER, *TTZ* 74 (1965) 60-61; J. RADEEMAKERS, *NRT* 89 (1967) 656; P. ROSSANO, *RivBib* 12 (1964) 428-429; H.H. ROWLEY, *ExpT* 77 (1965-66) 122-123; A. SALAS, *CiudDios* 178 (1965) 143-144; B. SCHWANK, *ErbAuf* 42 (1966) 343; B. STEIERT, *FZPT* 12 (1965) 368-369; A. STÖGER, *TPQ* 113 (1965) 196-198; B. VAWTER, *CBQ* 26 (1964) 485-486; J. VÍLCHEZ, *ArchTeolGran* 28 (1965) 327-328; F. ZEHRER, *BLtg* 38 (1964-65) 154-155; M. ZERWICK, *VD* 42 (1964) 261-268.

1966 *Die literarische Kunst im Matthäus-Evangelium* (SBS, 7). Stuttgart: Katholisches Bibelwerk, 1966, 82 p. Esp. 12-25: "Anordnung nach einfachen Zahlenverhältnissen"; 26-32: "Symmetrie und Chiasmus in Erzählungsreihen"; 33-35: "Geschlossene symmetrische Formen im Leidensbericht"; 36-44: "Chiastische Symmetrie in den Unterweisungsreden"; 45-48: "Kunstvolle Zweiteilung in Mt 18"; 49-53: "Kunstvolle Wortstellungen"; 54-59: "Doppelfunktionen"; 60-65: "Der Inhalt und Aufbau des Matthäus-Evangeliums"; 66-69: "Apologetik und literarische Form im Leidens- und Auferstehungsbericht"; 70-74: "Symmetrie und Inhalt"; 75-79: "Licht in Dunkel". [NTA 12, p. 134]
*BK* 21 (1966) 132; G.G. GAMBA, *RivBib* 14 (1966) 322-327; J.L.C. ILARRI, *EstBíb* 27 (1968) 89; J. MURPHY-O'CONNOR, *RB* 75 (1968) 621-622; L. SABOURIN, *VD* 45 (1967) 247.

1967 Die Engelerscheinungen in den Auferstehungsberichten. Untersuchungen einer "Legende". — *ZKT* 89 (1967) 191-202. [NTA 12, 115] → Gutwenger 1966

1968 Die Magierperikope (Mt 2,1-12). — *ZKT* 90 (1968) 257-295. Esp. 258-267: "Astrologisches"; 267-281: "Midrasch"; 281-293: "Der Text". [NTA 13, 562]

**GÄRTNER, Bertil E.**

1954    The Habakkuk Commentary (DSH) and the Gospel of Matthew. — *StudTheol* 8 (1954)
1-24. Esp. 13-22 [12,18-21; 15,5; 27,9/OT].
Der Habakuk-Kommentar (1 Qp Hab) und das Matthäus-Evangelium. — LANGE, J. (ed.), *Das Matthäus-Evangelium*, 1980, 174-204. Esp. 191-198.

1956    Judas Iskariot. — *SEÅ* 21 (1956) 50-81. Esp. 62-66 [26,14-16]. [NTA 3, 51] → 1957
*Iscariot*, trans. V.I. Gruhn (Facet Books. Biblical Series, 29). Philadelphia, PA: Fortress, 1971, XVI-46 p.

1957    *Die rätselhaften Termini Nazoräer und Iskariot* (Horae Soederblomianae, 4). Lund:
Gleerup, 1957, 68 p. Esp. 5-18 [1,20-21; 2,23]; 46-50 [26,6-16.50; 27,9]. → 1956

1965    *The Temple and the Community in Qumran and the New Testament. A Comparative
Study in the Temple Symbolism of the Qumran Texts and the New Testament* (SNTS MS,
1). Cambridge: University Press, 1965, XII-164 p. Esp. 105-122: "Jesus and the temple in the
gospel tradition".

**GAERTNER, C.A.**

1965    New Testament Teachings and 20th Century Church Practice with Special Reference
to Relations with Missions and Sister Churches. [28,19-20] — *ConcTM* 36 (1965) 239-
242. [NTA 9, 936]

**GAETA, Giancarlo**

1978    Invitati e commensali al banchetto escatologico. Analisi letteraria della parabola di Luca
(14,16-24). [22,1-14] — DUPONT, J., et al. (eds.), *La parabola degli invitati al
banchetto*, 1978, 103-125.

**GAGER, John G.**

1975    *Kingdom and Community. The Social World of Early Christianity* (Prentice-Hall Studies
in Religion). Englewood Cliffs, NJ: Prentice-Hall, 1975, XIII-158 p. Esp. 19-65: "The end
of time and the rise of community".
Das Ende der Zeit und die Entstehung von Gemeinschaften [1975, 19-49; 57-64] — MEEKS, W.A. (ed.), *Zur
Soziologie des Urchristentums. Ausgewählte Beiträge zum frühchristlichen Gemeinschaftsleben in seiner
gesellschaftlichen Umwelt*, trans. G. Memmert (Theologische Bücherei, 62), München: Kaiser, 1979, 88-130.

1983    *The Origins of Anti-Semitism. Attitudes Toward Judaism in Pagan and Christian
Antiquity*. Oxford: University Press, 1983, VIII-312 p. Esp. 137-141 [Q]; 141-142 [SgMt]; 147-
148 [Mt].

**GAGNON, Robert A.J.**

1993    Statistical Analysis and the Case of the Double Delegation in Luke 7:3-7a. — *CBQ* 55
(1993) 709-731. Esp. 711-715 [8,5-10.13]. [NTA 38, 1411]

1994a   Luke's Motives for Redaction in the Account of the Double Delegation in Luke 7:1-10.
— *NT* 36 (1994) 122-145. Esp. 124-127 [Q 7,1-10]. [NTA 39, 216]

1994b   The Shape of Matthew's Q Text of the Centurion at Capernaum: Did It Mention
Delegations? [8,5-13] — *NTS* 40 (1994) 133-142. Esp. 135-139: "A reconstruction of Matthew's
Q account"; 139-142: "Other objections to Matthean abbreviation". [NTA 38, 1365]

**GAIDE, Gilles**

1968    *Jérusalem, voici ton Roi (Commentaire de Zacharie 9–14)* (LD, 49). Paris: Cerf, 1968,
202 p. Esp. 174-176 [21,5/Zach 9,9]; 181-186 [27,9/Zach 11,13].

1974a   Jésus et Pierre marchent sur les eaux. Mt 14,22-33. — *AssSeign* II/50 (1974) 23-31.
[NTA 19, 91]

1974b   "Tu es le Christ" ... "Tu es Pierre". Mt 16,13-20. — *AssSeign* II/52 (1974) 16-26.
[NTA 19, 92]

**GALBIATI, Enrico**

1959 Gesù perfeziona il quinto comandamento (*Matteo* 5,20-24). Il tributo a Cesare (*Matt.* 22,15.22). La domanda del Battista (*Matt.* 11,2-10). — *BibOr* 1 (1959) 96/12-96/15; 160/22-160/25; 192/33-192/36.

1960 Il granello di senape: il lieveto (*Matt.* 13,1-31). Il primato di Pietro (*Matt.* 16,13-19). I falsi profeti (*Matt.* 7,15-21). Gli invitati alle nozze (*Matt.* 22,1-14). — *BibOr* 2 (1960) 25-26; 94-99; 166-169; 173-177.

1961 Le tentazioni di Gesù (*Matt.* 4,1-11). La trasfigurazione (*Matt.* 17,1-9). Il paralitico di Cafarnao (*Matteo* 9,1-8). Il debitore spietato (*Matteo* 18,23-35). Fine di un mondo e fine del mondo (*Matt.* 24,15-35). — *BibOr* 3 (1961) 26-31; 146-151; 190-193; 193-195; 214-222.

1962 L'adorazione dei magi (*Matt.* 2,1-12). L'ingresso messianico in Gerusalemme (*Matt.* 21,1-9). — *BibOr* 4 (1962) 20-29. [NTA 6, 761]; 60-63.

1963 Gli operai nella vigna (*Matt.* 20,1-16). — *BibOr* 5 (1963) 22-29. [NTA 7, 790]

1964 Gesù guarisce l'emorroissa e risuscita la figlia di Giairo (*Matt.* 9,18-26). — *BibOr* 6 (1964) 225-230. [NTA 9, 531]

1966 L'episodio evangelico dei magi. Storia della salvezza e profezia. [2,1-12] — *RivClerIt* 47 (1966) 723-730.

1973 Genere letterario e storia in Matteo 1–2. — *BibOr* 15 (1973) 3-16. [NTA 18, 462]

1979 *Scritti minori*. Brescia: Paideia, 1979, 2 vols., 847 p. [NTA 24, p. 181]

**GALBIATI, G.**

1981 "Nel deserto preparate la via..." (Isaia 40,3 e sue citazioni). — *RicBibRel* 16 (1981) 7-46. Esp. 41-44. [NTA 26, 307]

**GALILEA, Segundo**

1984 *La misión según las bienaventuranzas*, 1984.
*The Beatitudes. To Evangelize as Jesus Did*, trans. R. Barr. Dublin: Gill & Macmillan; Maryknoll, NY: Orbis, 1984, 108 p. Esp. 33-103.
*ExpT* 96 (1984-85) 222.

**GALITIS, Georges A.**

1965 The Exegetical Problems of the Parallel Accounts of the Death of Judas (Mt 27,3-10; Act 1,18-20). [Greek] — Θεολογία (Athens) 36 (1965) 270-281, 436-447.

1972 "You are Peter...". [Greek] [16,18] — *Gregorios Palamas* (Thessaloniki) 55 (1972) 193-197.

**GALIZZI, Mario**

1971 La Chiesa nel suo mistero (Mt 13,1-52). — *ParVi* 16 (1971) 4-16.

1972 *Gesù nel Getsemani (Mc 14,32-42; Mt 26,36-46; Lc 22,39-46)* (Biblioteca di scienze religiose, 4). Zürich: PAS, 1972, XVI-317 p. Esp. 91-135: "La narrazione di Mt 26,36-46"; 241-248 [26,36-46/Mk]; 248-255 [26,36-46/Lk]. — Diss. Commissio Biblica, Roma, 1971.

1975 Lettura della Passione secondo Matteo. — *ParVi* 20 (1975) 127-138.

1987 Beati i non-violenti. [5,5] — *ParVi* 32 (1987) 254-261.

1988 I quattro vangeli. — CIMOSA, M. - MOSETTO, F. (eds.), *Parole e vita. Una introduzione alla Bibbia*, Torino: Elle Di Ci, 1988, 212-297.

1990 *Il vangelo secondo Matteo. I: Oltre ogni frontiera. II: Un popolo che si dice Chiesa. III: Il coraggio di guardare avanti* (Commenti al Nuovo Testamento, 1-3). Torino-Leumann: Elle Di Ci, 1990, 3 vols., 256, 134 and 156 p.

**GALL, Robert**

1970　Heutige Exegese des Scheidungsverbotes Jesu. [5,32; 19,9] — *Schweizerische Kirchen-zeitung* (Luzern) 138 (1970) 512-514, 528-531, 549-551.

**GALLEGO, Epifanio**

1986　La eucaristía. Perspectiva sinóptica. [26,26-29] — *BibFe* 12 (1986) 158-173.

**GALLMAN, R. Lee**

1955　*The Purpose of the Gospel of Matthew*. Diss. New Orleans Baptist Theol. Sem., New Orleans, LA, 1955.

**GALLUS, Tibor**

1952　Primatus *infallibilitatis* in metaphora "petrae" indicatus (Mt 16,18). — *VD* 30 (1952) 193-204. Esp. 193-199.

1955　De primatu infallibilitatis ex Mt 16,13-18 eruendo. — *VD* 33 (1955) 209-214. [NTA 1, 26]

1965　Ist Mt 18,18 in seiner überlieferten Form ein Logion Jesu? — *Österreichisches Klerus-Blatt* 48 (1965) 196-198.

1976a　Ist Mt 18,18 ein Herrenwort? — NEUMANN, M. (ed.), *Vorstösse. Festschrift zum 70. Geburtstag des P. Tibor Gallus SJ*, Klagenfurt: Carinthia, 1976, 51-54.

1976b　Der "Fels" der Kirche (Mt 16,18). — *Ibid.*, 55-65.

**GALOT, Jean**

1958　*Marie dans l'Évangile* (Museum Lessianum. Section théologique, 53). Paris–Leuven: Desclée De Brouwer, 1958, 197 p.
　　　*Mary in the gospel*, trans. Maria Constance. Westminster: Newman, 1965, VIII-231 p.
　　　Trans. Spanish 1960; Portuguese 1961; Italian 1964.

1968　La conception virginale du Christ. — *Greg* 49 (1968) 637-666. Esp. 650-655.

1969　*Être né de Dieu. Jean 1,13* (AnBib, 37). Roma: Institut biblique pontifical, 1969, 135 p. Esp. 52-55 [Origen: Jn 1,13/Mt 1,20]; 121-122: "Rapports avec les récits de Matthieu et de Luc".

1972　La motivation évangélique du célibat. — *Greg* 53 (1972) 731-758 (English summary, 758). Esp. 736-750 [19,10-12]. [NTA 17, 919]

1974　"Qu'il soit pour toi comme le paien et le publicain". — *NRT* 96 (1974) 1009-1030. Esp. 1009-1016 [18,15-18]; 1021-1024 [18,17]; 1025-1028 [18,18]. [NTA 19, 956] → Centi 1975

1975a　Le fondement évangélique du vœu religieux de pauvreté. — *Greg* 56 (1975) 441-467 (English summary, 466-467). Esp. 443-445.454-457 [19,16-22]. [NTA 20, 461]

1975b　Un messaggio sconvolgente di riconciliazione. [18,15-18] — *CC* 126/2 (1975) 42-51.
　　　La conscience de la mission rédemptrice. — *Didaskalia* 14 (1984) 139-155. [NTA 31, 545]

1981　Il potere conferito a Pietro. — *CC* 132/2 (1981) 15-29. [NTA 26, 95]
　　　Le pouvoir donné à Pierre. — *EVie* 98 (1988) 33-40. [NTA 32, 1111]

1984　La prière au Père. — *Telema* 37 (1984) 53-66.
　　　La preghiera al Padre. — *CC* 136/1 (1985) 222-235. [NTA 29, 1108]

1987　Il "Padre Nostro" nella vita consacrata. — *VCons* 23 (1987) 1-14, 97-106, 204-214, 261-270, 592-702, 789-800.

1988　Giuseppe "il Giusto" e la vita consacrata. — *VCons* 24 (1988) 177-190.

1991　Soffereza e beatitudine. — BALLIS, G. (ed.), *Il mondo dell'uomo nascosto*, 1991, 49-61.

**GAMBA, Giuseppe Giovanni**

1964　In margine all'autenticità di Mt. 28,19. — *Sal* 26 (1964) 463-474.

1965　Considerazioni in margine alla poetica dei vangeli. — *RivBib* 13 (1965) 289-302. [NTA 10, 868]

1966 Gesù Cristo il sì di Dio Padre. Considerazioni in margine al significato dottrinale dei primi due capitoli del Vangelo di S. Matteo. — *Rivista di pedagogia e scienze religiose* (Torino) 4 (1966) 72-91.

1967 "Al monte, ove Gesù aveva dato loro i comandamenti" (Mt. 28,16). — *Studi sull'Oriente e la Bibbia*. FS G. Rinaldi, 1967, 349-360.

1968 Agonia di Gesù. — *RivBib* 16 (1968) 159-166. [NTA 13, 505]

1969a Annotazioni in margine alla struttura letteraria ed al significato dottrinale di Matteo I-II. — *Jalones de la Historia de la Salvación en el Antiguo y Nuevo Testamento* (XXVI Semana Biblica Española), Madrid: Consejo Superior de Investigaciones Científicas, 1969, 59-99. Esp. 60-70: "Struttura letteraria e significato dottrinale di Mt. 1,1-17"; 70-97: "Struttura letteraria e significato dottrinale di Mt. 1,18-2,23"; = *BibOr* 11 (1969) 5-24, 65-76, 109-123.

1969b Struttura letteraria e significato funzionale di Mt. 3,1-4. — *Sal* 31 (1969) 234-264 (French summary, 264). Esp. 235-237 [3,1-4,11]; 237-238 [structure of 3,1-4]; 238-249: "Analisi redazionale"; 249-262: "Contenuto dottrinale e significato funzionale".

1971 La passione di Gesu in Mt (I). Considerazioni in margine alla struttura letteraria ed al significato dottrinale di Mt 27,27-56. — *BibOr* 13 (1971) 159-190.

1974 Gesù si stabilisce a Cafarnao. Annotazioni in margine alla struttura letteraria ed al significato dottrinale e funzionale di *Mt.* 4,12-16 ed al piano d'insieme del Vangelo di Matteo. — *BibOr* 16 (1974) 109-132. [NTA 19, 945]

1977 La testimonianza di S. Ireneo in *Adversus Haereses III,1,1* e la data di composizione dei quattro vangeli canonici. — *Sal* 39 (1977) 545-585. Esp. 563-574: "Ciò che Ireneo afferma a proposito del Vangelo di Matteo". [NTA 23, 54]

1980 La "eunuchia" per il Regno dei Cieli. Annotazioni in margine a Matteo 19,10-12. — *Sal* 42 (1980) 243-287 (French summary, 287). Esp. 244-245 [Greek text]; 245-248 [formal analysis]; 249-253 [19,10-12/19,3-9]; 253-255 [19,3-9]; 256-258: "Portata dottrinale e funzionale" [19,10-12]; 258-282 [19,11-12]. [NTA 25, 78]

1982 La disposizione "Matteo, Luca, Marco, Giovanni" nella tradizione antica. Contributo alla soluzione della Questione Sinottica. — MARCHESELLI, C.C. (ed.), *Parola e Spirito*. FS S. Cipriani, 1982, I, 25-36.

1983 A Further Reexamination of Evidence from the Early Tradition. — FARMER, W.R. (ed.), *New Synoptic Studies*, 1983, 17-35. Esp. 18-20 [Papias]; 20-21 [Clement of Alexandria]; 21-26 [monarchian prologues]; 26-29 [Jerome]; 29-34 [Irenaeus]; 34-35 [Origen].

1995 Matteo: il vangelo della Chiesa-madre. — STRUS, A. (ed.), *Tra giudaismo e cristianesimo. Qumran - Giudeocristiani* (Ieri Oggi Domani, 17), Roma: LAS, 1995, 131-174.

**GAMBER, Klaus**

1980 Fragmentblätter eines Regensburger Evangeliars aus dem Ende des 8. Jahrhunderts. [23,35-26,25] — *Scriptorium* (Gent) 34 (1980) 72-77.

**GAMBLE, Harry Y.**

1985 *The New Testament Canon. Its Making and Meaning*. Philadelphia, PA: Fortress, 1985, 95 p. Esp. 24-27 [Papias].

**GANCHO HERNÁNDEZ, Claudio**

1957 Las citaciones del A.T. en los Sinópticos y en los Rabinos. — *Salmanticensis* 4 (1957) 289-359. Esp. 296-316, 329-343.
Las citaciones del A.T. en los Evangelios sinópticos y en los rabinos. — *Generos literarios en los evangelios. Otros estudios* (XVII Semana Biblica Española), Madrid: Consejo Superior de Investigaciones Científicas, 1958, 3-82. Esp. 21-36, 50-65.

1965    Infancia, Evangelio de la. — *Enciclopédia de la Bíblia* (Barcelona) 4 (1965; ²1969) 162-
175. Esp. 162-169.

**GANDER, Georges**

1966    *La notion primitive d'Église d'après l'Évangile selon Matthieu, chapitre 16, versets 18
et 19* (Études évangéliques, 1966). Aix-en-Provence: Faculté libre de théologie
protestante, 1966, 143 p. [NTA 13, p. 155]

1968    *L'Évangile de l'Église. Commentaire de l'Évangile selon Matthieu.* I: *Chapitres 1 à 20*
(Études évangéliques, 1967-68). Aix-en-Provence: Faculté libre de théologie
protestante, 1968, 318 p. [NTA 13, p. 400]; II: *Chapitres 21 à 28. Tables générales*
(Études évangéliques, 1969-70), 1970, 312 p.; Genève: Labor et Fides, 1970, 2 vols.,
318 and 319-629 p.
         M. BOUTTIER, *ETR* 45 (1970) 393; J.D. KINGSBURY, *TZ* 28 (1972) 448; É. TROCMÉ, *RHPR* 51 (1971)
         387-388; J. ZUMSTEIN, *RTP* 21 (1971) 265.

**GANGEL, Kenneth O.**

1987    Leadership: Coping with Cultural Corruption. [11,25-30] — *BS* 144 (1987) 450-460.

**GANOCZY, Alexandre**

1968    Jean Major, exégète gallican. — *RSR* 56 (1968) 457-495. Esp. 462-488: "Le commentaire de
1518" [16,13-19; 18,15-18]; 488-495: "Le commentaire de 1529".

**GANTOY, Robert**

1985*   (ed.), *À cause de l'Évangile. Études sur les Synoptiques et les Actes offertes au P.
Jacques Dupont, O.S.B. à l'occasion de son 70ᵉ anniversaire* (LD, 123). Paris: Cerf;
Brugge: Publications de Saint-André, 1985, XI-832 p. → C.K. Barrett, Bouttier, Broer, de la
Potterie, Delobel, J.D.G. Dunn, Fitzmyer, Focant, Gnilka, Gourgues, Grelot, Kertelge, Léon-Dufour, März,
Puig i Tàrrech, Schlosser, Schnackenburg, G. Schneider, Zeller

**GARCÍA, José Antonio**

1986    "Sed perfectos...". Canto y compromiso en el acercamiento salvador de Dios. [5,48] —
*SalT* 74 (1986) 703-713.

**GARCÍA, Santiago**

1979    Evangelios sinópticos. Hechos. — UBIETA, J.A. (ed.), *Iniciación a la lectura del Nuevo
Testamento* (Temas bíblicos), Bilbao: Desclée De Brouwer, 1979, 109-153.

**GARCÍA BURILLO, Jesús**

1977    El ciento por uno (Mc 10,29-30 par). Historia de las interpretaciones y exégesis. —
*EstBíb* 36 (1977) 173-203. Esp. 183-188 [19,27-28]. [NTA 24, 114]; 37 (1978) 29-55. Esp. 29-31
[19,16-30]; 34-36 [19,27-30]; 52-53 [19,28]; 53-54 [19,30]. [NTA 25, 101]

**GARCÍA CORDERO, Maximiliano**

1971    Conceptión jerárquica de la Iglesia en el Nuevo Testamento. — *Salmanticensis* 18
(1971) 233-287. Esp. 247-265: "La promesa de la primacía jerárquica (Mt 16,17-19)". [NTA 17, 270]

1994    Las esperanzas mesiánicas judías y el mesianismo de Jesús. — ARANDA, G., et al.
(eds.), *Biblia, Exegesis y Cultura.* FS J.M. Casciaro, 1994, 221-247. Esp. 235-247.

1995    La correlación de la fe y las obras en la justificación del creyente según los escritos del
Nuevo Testamento. — *CiTom* 122 (1995) 219-255, 439-476. [NTA 40, 1686]

**GARCÍA DE HARO, Ramón**

1981    Las bienaventuranzas y la moral cristiana. — *Doctor Communis* (Roma) 34 (1981) 209-
219. → Pinckaers 1979
         A moral do evangelho. — *Theologica* 17 (1982) 496-514.

**GARCÍA DEL MORAL, Antonio**

1981   "Los eunucos que a sí mismos se hicieron tales por el reino de los cielos" (Mt 19,12) ¿para ocupar los puestos de responsabilidad y servicio? — *CuBíb* 38 (1981) 171-198.
→ Vera Arrechea 1981

**GARCÍA MARTÍNEZ, Florentino**

1989   La reprensión fraterna en Qumrán y Mt 18,15-17. — *Filo!NT* 2 (1989) 23-40. Esp. 33-37.
[NTA 34, 129]
Brotherly Rebuke in Qumran and Mt 18:15-17. — ID. – TREBOLLE BARRERA, J., *The People of the Dead Sea Scrolls. Their Writings, Beliefs and Practices*, Leiden: Brill, 1995, 221-232. Esp. 227-230.

**GARCÍA MIRALLES, Manuel**

1977   San José en "Commentaria in Evangelium Divi Matthaei" de Alfonso de Avendaño. — *EstJos* 31 = *CahJos* 25 (1977) 119-140.

1978   Mt 1–2 y Lc 1–2 en San Alberto Magno. — *EstJos* 32 (1978) 147-164. Esp. 150-158.

**GARCÍA PAREDES, Jose Crislo Rey**

1993   La génesis de Jesús el Cristo (Mt 1,18-25). — *EphMar* 43 (1993) 29-45. [NTA 38, 153]

**GARDNER, Richard B.**

1973   *Jesus' Appraisal of John the Baptist. An Analysis of the Sayings of Jesus Concerning John the Baptist in the Synoptic Tradition.* Diss. Würzburg, 1973, 331 p. (R. Schnackenburg).

1991   *Matthew* (Believers Church Bible Commentary). Scottdale, PA – Waterlooo, Ont.: Herald, 1991, 446 p. [NTA 36, p. 109]
I. BROER, *TLZ* 117 (1992) 749; F.W. BURNETT, *CRBR* 5 (1992) 200-202; D.L. TURNER, *GraceTJ* 12 (1991) 298-299.

**GARDNER-SMITH, Percival**

1953   St John's Knowledge of Matthew. — *JTS* 4 (1953) 31-35. → H.F.D. Sparks 1952b

**GARGANO, Innocenzo**

1981   Il Padre nostro e la preghiera nell'esegesi di san Cipriano. — *ParSpirV* 3 (1981) 199-211.

1989   *"Lectio divina" su il vangelo di Matteo* (Conversazioni bibliche). Bologna: Dehoniane, 1989, 136 p. [NTA 36, p. 109]

1992   *Iniziazione alla "Lectio divina". Indicazioni metodologiche con l'esemplificazione di alcuni brani presi dal Vangelo secondo Matteo* [8-9] (Conversazioni bibliche). Bologna: Dehoniane, 1992, 144 p. [NTA 38, p. 119]

**GARITTE, Gérard**

1960a  Les "Logoi" d'Oxyrhynque et l'apocryphe copte dit "Évangile de Thomas". — *Muséon* 73 (1960) 151-172. Esp. 168-169 [5,14/Oxy fr 2]. [NTA 5, 227]

1960b  Les "Logoi" d'Oxyrhynque sont traduits du copte. — *Ibid.*, 335-349. Esp. 342-343 [5,14/Oxy fr 2]. [NTA 5, 241] → Guillaumont 1960

**GARLAND, David Ellsworth**

1979   *The Intention of Matthew 23* (SupplNT, 52). Leiden: Brill, 1979, XII-255 p. Esp. 8-33: "The composition and structure of Mt 23"; 34-63 [23,1-12]; 64-90: "The intention of the woes in Mt 23"; 91-123: "The charge of hypocrisy"; 124-162: "The exegesis of the individual woes in Mt 23:13-28"; 163-209 [23,29-39]. [NTA 24, p. 81] — Diss. Southern Baptist Theol. Sem., Louisville, KY, 1976 (F. Stagg).
A. FUCHS, *SNTU* 6-7 (1981-82) 258-261; D.R.A. HARE, *CBQ* 44 (1982) 323-325; U. LUZ, *TLZ* 107 (1982) 347-348; J.R. MICHAELS, *JBL* 100 (1981) 302-304; C.F.D. MOULE, *JTS* 32 (1981) 227-229; J. MURPHY-O'CONNOR, *RB* 90 (1983) 304-305; E. SCHWEIZER, *RExp* 77 (1980) 561-562.

1987a Matthew's Understanding of the Temple Tax (Matt 17:24-27). — *SBL 1987 Seminar Papers*, 190-209. Esp. 190-196; 201-209.
The Temple Tax in Matthew 17:24-25 and the Principle of not Causing Offense. — BAUER, D.R. - POWELL, M.A. (eds.), *Treasures New and Old*, 1996, 69-98. Esp. 69-78; 85-98.

1987b A Biblical View of Divorce. — *RExp* 84 (1987) 419-432. Esp. 421-426 [5,32; 19,9]. [NTA 32, 348]

1989 *One Hundred Years of Study on the Passion Narrative* (NABPR Bibliographic Series, 3). Macon, GA: Mercer University Press, 1989, XVIII-174 p.

1992a Blessing and Woe. — *DJG*, 1992, 77-81. Esp. 79-80.

1992b The Lord's Prayer in the Gospel of Matthew. — *RExp* 89 (1992) 215-228. [NTA 37, 729]

1993 *Reading Matthew. A Literary and Theological Commentary on the First Gospel* (Reading the New Testament Series). New York: Crossroad, 1993, XVI-269 p. [NTA 38, p. 119]
D.C. ALLISON, *Interpr* 48 (1994) 410-414; F.W. BURNETT, *CRBR* 7 (1994) 189-190; R.F. COLLINS, *LouvSt* 18 (1993) 383-384; D. GREENE, *PerspRelSt* 22 (1995) 198-199; E. KRENTZ, *CurrTMiss* 21 (1994) 373; S.C. MUIR, *TorontoJT* 11 (1995) 95-96; R.L. OMANSON, *BTrans* 45 (1994) 152-153; K. SNODGRASS, *RExp* 91 (1994) 440-441; F.S. SPENCER, *CBQ* 56 (1994) 795-796.

**GARLINGTON, Don B.**

1994 Jesus, the Unique Son of God: Tested and Faithful. — *BS* 151 (1994) 284-308. Esp. 291-303 [4,1-11]. [NTA 39, 138]

1995 Oath-Taking in the Community of the New Age (Matthew 5:33-37). — *TrinJ* 16 (1995) 139-170. Esp. 151-165. [NTA 40, 1458]

**GARNET, Paul**

1983 The Parable of the Sower: How the Multitudes Understood It. — FURCHA, E.J. (ed.), *Spirit within Structure. Essays in Honor of George Johnston on the Occasion of his Seventieth Birthday*, Allison Park, PA: Pickwick, 1983, 39-54.

**GAROFALO, Salvatore**

1957 Parate viam Domino. [3,3] — *Studi S. Mallardi*, Napoli, 1957, 27-31.

1958 "Preparare la strada al Signore". [3,3] — *RivBib* 6 (1958) 131-134. [NTA 3, 349]

1964 *Pietro nell'Evangelo*. Roma: Coletti, 1964, 175 p.
*San Pedro*. Buenos Aires: Claretiana, 1982, 80 p.

1972 De vinculo matrimonii in Novo Testamento. — *Periodica de re morali, canonica, liturgica* (Roma) 61 (1972) 225-250. Esp. 229-235 [19,3-12/Mk]; 235-237 [5,3]; 237-246: "De clausulis Matthaei" [5,32; 19,9].

1979 *Il Vangelo del Padre Nostro. Riflessioni bibliche*. Milano: Áncora, 1979, 94 p.

**GARRIDO, Julio**

1957 Un nouveau papyrus de l'Évangile de saint Matthieu en copte sahidique. — *Les Cahiers coptes* (Cairo) 15 (1957) 5-16.
Hallazgo de un papiro del Nuevo Testamento en copto sahídico. [16,21] — *EstBíb* 17 (1958) 107-108. [NTA 3, 26]

**GARRIDO BONAÑO, Manuel**

1976 Mt. 1–2 y Lc. 1–2 en la liturgía. — *EstJos* 30 (1976) 19-39.

**GARRIGA, P.**

1977 El baptisme de Jesús segons Joan Baptista. — *QüestVidaCr* 87 (1977) 88-95.

**GARRISON, Roman**

1979 *Matthew 11:25-27 = Luke 10:21,22. A Bridge between the Synoptic and Johannine*

*Traditions*. Diss. Oxford, 1979, XIV-357 p. Ep. 101-105 [22,44/Ps 110,1]; 106-111 [24,64/Ps 110,1]; 124-130 [text: 11,25-27]; 131-144: "The differences between Mt 11:25-27 and Lk 10:21,22"; 145-195: "The background of the logion"; 196-216: "Features of the logion which support its genuineness"; 217-257: "The synoptic 'parallels' to the logion" [13,10-17; 16,17-19; 28,18]; 314-321: "John 10 and the synoptic tradition" [9,36; 10,6.16; 12,11-12.30; 15,24; 18,10-14; 23,35; 26,31]

1993    *Redemptive Almsgiving in Early Christianity* (JSNT SS, 77). Sheffield: JSOT, 1993, 177 p. Esp. 60-66: "The sayings of Jesus". — Diss. Toronto, 1991 (P. Richardson).

**GARRY, Laurie**

1993    & HOWSARE, R., Form Criticism and the Parable of the Sower (Matt. 13:1-23 and par.). — ALBL, M.C., et al. (eds.), *Directions in New Testament Methods*, 1993, 23-29.

**GARSHOWITZ, Libby**

1993    Shem Tov ben Isaac Ibn Shaprut's Gospel of Matthew. — WALFISH, B. (ed.), *Frank Talmage. Memorial Volume* 1, Haifa: University Press, 1992-93, 297-322. → G. Howard

**GAST, Frederick**

1968    Synoptic Problem. — BROWN, R.E., et al. (eds.), *The Jerome Biblical Commentary*, II, 1968, 1-6.
El problema sinóptico. — BROWN, R.E., et al. (eds.), *Comentario Bíblico "San Jerónimo"*, III, 1972, 11-24.

**GASTON, Lloyd**

1962    Beelzebul. [10,25; 12,24] — *TZ* 18 (1962) 247-255. [NTA 7, 508]

1973    *Horae Synopticae Electronicae. Word Statistics of the Synoptic Gospels* (SBL Sources for Biblical Study, 3). Missoula, MT: SBL, 1973, III-101 p.

1975    The Messiah of Israel as Teacher of the Gentiles. The Setting of Matthew's Christology. — *Interpr* 29 (1975) 24-40. Esp. 27-33 [Messiah]; 33-39 [gentile mission]. [NTA 19, 935]; = MAYS, J.L. (ed.), *Interpreting*, 1981, 78-96.

**GATTI, Enzo**

1979    *La chiesa delle beatitudini. Lettura catechetica del discorso delle beatitudini in prospettiva ecclesiale e missionaria*. Bologna: Dehoniane, 1979, 128 p.

**GATTI, Florence M.** → Cortés 1968

**GATZWEILER, Karl**

1967    La résurrection de Jésus, ses répercussions dans l'histoire. — *RevEcclLiège* 53 (1967) 257-284. Esp. 267-269 [28,1-10]; 278-279 [28,16-20].

1972a   La guérison du démoniaque gérasénien. — *FoiTemps* 2 (1972) 461-476. Esp. 469-471 [8,28-34].

1972b   Un pas vers l'universalisme: la Cananéenne. Mt 15,21-28. — *AssSeign* II/51 (1972) 15-24.

1972c   Les récits de miracles dans l'Évangile selon saint Matthieu. — DIDIER, M. (ed.), *L'Évangile selon Matthieu*, 1972, 209-220. Esp. 211-214 [form criticism]; 214-215 [8-9]; 215-218 [8,28-34]; 218-219 [8,5-13]. → Held 1959/70

1979    L'exégèse historico-critique. Une guérison à Capharnaüm. Mt 8,5-13; Lc 7,1-10; Jn 4,46-54. — *FoiTemps* 9 (1979) 297-315. Esp. 304-307, 313-314.

1983    Jésus en prière. Textes du Pater. — *LumVit* 38 (1983) 379-392.
Jesus in Prayer. Texts of the Our Father. — *LumVit* 39 (1984) 141-154. [NTA 29, 96]

1992    L'Église, une communauté fraternelle, d'après Matthieu 18. — *Le semeur sortit pour semer ...*, Liège: Dricot, 1992, 81-94.

**GAUTHIER, Roland**

1971 Saint Joseph d'après deux séries d'homélies latines du VIᵉ siècle sur S. Matthieu (le pseudo-Chrysostome et le pseudo-Origène). — *EstJos* 25 = *CahJos* 19 (1971) 161-182.

**GAVENTA, Beverly Roberts**

1993 & CROSSAN, J.D., The Challenge of Christmas. Two Views. — *ChrCent* 110 (1993) 1270-1278. [NTA 38, 746]

1995 *Mary. Glimpses of the Mother of Jesus* (Studies on Personalities of the New Testament). Columbia, SC: University Press, 1995, XIV-164 p.

**GAY, G.A.**

1970 *Matthew's Unique Presentation of the Kingdom.* Diss. Manchester, 1970-71.

**GAY, George**

1978 The Judgment of the Gentiles in Matthew's Theology. — GASQUE, W.W. - LASOR, W.S. (eds.), *Scripture, Tradition and Interpretation. Essays Presented to Everett F. Harrison by his Students and Colleagues in Honor of his 75th Birthday*, Grand Rapids, MI: Eerdmans, 1978, 199-215.

**GEDEN, A.S.** → H.K. Moulton 1978 [Moulton-Geden 1897]

**GEERLINGS, Jacob**

1961a *Family 13 - The Ferrar Group. The Text according to Matthew* (Studies and Documents, 19). Salt Lake City, UT: Univ. of Utah Press, 1961, V-108 p. Esp. 21-94: "Text and apparatus criticus".
      C.M. MARTINI, *Bib* 46 (1965) 103-104.

1961b *Family 13 (The Ferrar Group). The Text according to Luke* (Studies and Documents, 20). Salt Lake City, UT: Univ. of Utah Press, 1961, VIII-155 p. Esp. 153-155: "Codex 230 in Matthew".

1966 → Champlin 1966

1968a *Family E and Its Allies in Mark. Appendices A and B: Studies of Lectionary 767 and Codex 2633 (Spyridon Loverdou 4)* (Studies and Documents, 31). Salt Lake City, UT: Univ. of Utah Press, 1968, V-102 p. Esp. 75-78 [lect. 767]; 88-93 [Codex 2633].

1968b *Family E and Its Allies in Luke. Appendix A: Collation of Sinai 148 (Greg. 1185) by K.W. Ogden* (Studies and Documents, 35). Salt Lake City, UT: Univ. of Utah Press, 1968, III-164 p. Esp. 107-119.145-149 [lect. 1185; Mt 23]

1976 Codex 1386 and the Iota PHIᴿ Group. — ELLIOTT, J.K. (ed.), *Studies in New Testament Language and Text*. FS G.D. Kilpatrick, 1976, 209-234. Esp. 211-215 [collation]; 228-234 [5].

**GEIGER, Georg**

1992 Die ἐγώ εἰμι-Worte bei Johannes und den Synoptikern. Eine Rückfrage nach dem historischen Jesus. — DENAUX, A. (ed.), *John and the Synoptics*, 1992, 466-472.

1997 Falsche Zitate bei Matthäus und Lukas. — TUCKETT, C.M. (ed.), *The Scriptures in the Gospels*, 1997, 479-486. Esp. 479-482 [1,23; 2,6.23; 4,10; 26,31; 27,9].

**GEIGER, Ruthild**

1983 Die Stellung der geschiedenen Frau in der Umwelt des Neuen Testaments. — DAUTZENBERG, G., et al. (eds.), *Die Frau im Urchristentum*, 1983, 134-157. Esp. 147-148 [5,32]; 149-150 [19,3-9].

**GEISELMANN, Josef Rupert**

1965 *Jesus der Christus. I. Teil: Die Frage nach dem historischen Jesus*. München: Kösel, 1965, 237 p. Esp. 201-231 [christological titles].

**GEISLER, Norman L.**

1983a    Methodological Unorthodoxy. — *JEvTS* 26 (1983) 87-94. [NTA 28, 480r] → Gundry 1982, 1983c-d

1983b    Is There Madness in the Method? A Rejoinder to Robert H. Gundry. — *Ibid.*, 101-108.
→ Gundry 1982, 1983c-d

**GEIST, Heinz**

1970    Jesusverkündigung im Matthäusevangelium. — PESCH, W. (ed.), *Jesus in den Evangelien* (SBS, 45), Stuttgart: Katholisches Bibelwerk, 1970, 105-126. Esp. 105-107: "Die Gemeinde des ersten Evangeliums"; 107-108: "Der lebendige Herr inmitten seiner Gemeinde"; 108-123: "Der volmächtige Herr der Gemeinde"; 123-126: "Der Auftrag des Herrn an die Gemeinde".
La prédication de Jésus dans l'Évangile de Matthieu. — *Jésus dans les Évangiles*, trans. A. Liefooghe (Lire la Bible, 29), Paris: Cerf, 1971, 91-116. Esp. 91-93; 93-95; 95-113; 113-116.

1974    Die Warnung vor den falschen Propheten – eine ernste Mahnung an die heutige Kirche. Zu Mt 7,15-23; 24,11f.24. — MERKLEIN, H. – LANGE, J. (eds.), *Biblische Randbemerkungen*. FS R. Schnackenburg, 1974, 139-149. Esp. 139-142 [7,15-23]; 140; 142-143 [24,11-12.24].

1986    *Menschensohn und Gemeinde. Eine redaktionskritische Untersuchung zur Menschensohnprädikation im Matthäusevangelium* (FzB, 57). Würzburg: Echter, 1986, XV-517 p. Esp. 14-31: "Zur Relevanz der Menschensohntexte im ersten Evangelium"; 33-71: "Menschensohnvorstellungen in der Zeit des Frühjudentums bis zur Abfassung des Matthäusevangeliums" [52-58: Q; 62-66: Mt]; 73-370: "Literarische und theologische Analyse der Menschensohntexte des Matthäusevangeliums" [5,11-12; 8,20; 9,6; 10,23.32-33; 11,19; 12,8.32.40; 13,36-43; 16,13-28; 17,12-13.22-23; 19,28-29; 20,18-19; 24–25; 26,2.24.45.64; 28,16-20]; 371-411: "Die mt Menschensohnvorstellung und ihr Verhältnis zu anderen christologischen Aussagen des ersten Evangeliums"; 413-439: "Die Relevanz der Menschensohntradition für Matthäus und seine Gemeinde". [NTA 31, p. 362] — Diss. Würzburg, 1985 (R. Schnackenburg).
R. BARTNICKI, *CollTheol* 58/3 (1988) 166-167; F. GONZÁLEZ GARCÍA, *EstBíb* 48 (1990) 428-430; R. LEIVESTAD, *NorskTeolTids* 90 (1989) 180-181; R.D. WITHERUP, *CBQ* 50 (1988) 530-531.

**GELDARD, M.**

1978    Jesus' Teaching on Divorce. Thoughts on the Meaning of *Porneia* in Matthew 5:32 and 19:9. — *Churchman* (London) 92 (1978) 134-143. [NTA 23, 97]

**GELDENHUYS, J. Norval**

1953    *Supreme Authority. The Authority of the Lord, His Apostles and the New Testament.* Grand Rapids, MI: Eerdmans, 1953, 128 p. Esp. 18-30; 53-61 [apostle].

**GELIN, Albert**

1953    *Les pauvres de Yahvé* (Témoins de Dieu, 14). Paris: Cerf, 1953, 182 p. Esp. 131-132; 142-148: "La béatitude de la pauvreté chez saint Luc et saint Matthieu"; ²1954; ³1956.
*Les pauvres que Dieu aime* (Foi Vivante, 41). Paris, 1967, 172 p. Esp. 133-139.
*Die Armen, sein Volk*, trans. J. Keppi. Mainz: Matthias-Grünewald, 1957, 149 p.
*The Poor of Yahweh*, trans. K. Sullivan. Collegeville, MN: Liturgical Press, 1964, 125 p.

1955    Messianisme. — *DBS* 5/28 (1955) 1165-1212. Esp. 1206-.211.

**GEMÜNDEN, Petra VON**

1993    *Vegetationsmetaphorik im Neuen Testament und seiner Umwelt. Eine Bildfelduntersuchung* (NTOA, 18). Freiburg/Schw: Universitätsverlag; Göttingen: Vandenhoeck & Ruprecht, 1993, XI-541 p. Esp. 122-265: "Vegetationsmetaphern in den Evangelien" [3,7-10.12; 6,26-30; 7,16-20; 12,33-37; 13,24-30.36-43; 15,13; 21,43]. — Diss. Heidelberg, 1989 (G. Theißen).

1994    L'arbre et son fruit. Analyse d'un corpus d'images comme méthode exégétique. [7,17; 12,33] — *ETR* 69 (1994) 315-327. [NTA 39, 148]

**GENCH, Frances Taylor**

1997   *Wisdom in the Christology of Matthew*. Lanham, MD – New York – Oxford: Univ.
Press of America, 1997, XII-229 p. — Diss. Union Theol. Sem., Virginia, GA, 1988.

**GENEST, Olivette**

1985a  Le discours de l'exégèse biblique sur la mort de Jésus. — COUTURIER, G. – CHARRON,
A. – DURAND, G. (eds.), *Essais sur la mort: travaux d'un séminaire de recherche sur
la mort* (Héritage et Projet, 29), Montreal: Fides, 1985, 123-176.

1985b  Évangiles et femmes. — *SE* 37 (1985) 275-295. Esp. 275-287. [NTA 30, 995]

1987   La sémiotique et les femmes du Nouveau Testament. — CHENÉ, A., et al., *De Jésus
et des femmes. Lectures sémiotiques* (Recherches, NS 14), Montreal: Bellarmin; Paris:
Cerf, 1987, 189-207. Esp. 193-194 [15,21-28].

**GENNARINI, S.**

1972   Le principali interpretationi postliberali della pericope della trasfigurazione di Gesù.
[17,1-9] — *RivStoLR* 8 (1972) 80-132. [NTA 17, 537]

**GENTHE, Hans Jochen**

1977   *Kleine Geschichte der neutestamentlichen Wissenschaft*. Göttingen: Vandenhoeck &
Ruprecht, 1977, 354 p. Esp. 99-101; 118-121 [Q].

**GENUYT, François**

1987   Du règne de la Loi à la loi du Royaume. — *LumièreV* 183 (1987) 41-56. Esp. 42-44: "Le
cadre et les acteurs"; 45-56: "Le discours sur la loi et le royaume". [NTA 32, 589]

1991   Évangile de Matthieu. Chapitres 3–4,11; 4,12–7,29; 8–9,8; 9,9-26. — *SémBib* 61
(1991) 23-34; 62 (1991) 2-20; 63 (1991) 3-17; 64 (1991) 3-14. [NTA 36, 138/723/1271]

1992   Évangile de Matthieu 10,1-42. Le discours apostolique. Chapitre 11. — *SémBib* 65
(1992) 3-17; 68 (1992) 3-14. [NTA 36, 1272; 37, 1263]

1993   Matthieu chapitre 12,1-21. Évangile de Matthieu 12,22-50. — *SémBib* 70 (1993) 41-54;
71 (1993) 39-48. [NTA 38, 159/1368]

1994   Matthieu 13: L'enseignement en paraboles. Matthieu 14. Matthieu 15. — *SémBib* 73
(1994) 30-44; 74 (1994) 30-41; 75 (1994) 29-36. [NTA 39, 152/153/807]

1995   Matthieu 16,1-20; 16,21-23 [16,21-17,9]; 17,10-27. — *SémBib* 78 (1995) 35-46; 79
(1995) 35-46; 80 (1995) 51-58. [NTA 40, 831/1464]

1996   CALLOUD, J. – GENUYT, F., *L'Évangile de Matthieu*. I: *Lecture sémiotique des
chapitres 1 à 10*. La Tourette: Centre Thomas More; Lyon: Centre pour l'Analyse du
Discours Religieux, 1996, 112 p.

**GÉOLTRAIN, Pierre**

1966   Les récits de la passion dans les Synoptiques. — *FoiVie* 65/4 = *Cahiers bibliques* 4
(1966) 41-49. Esp. 45-47.

1967   Notes sur Matthieu 24–25. — *FoiVie* 66/5 = *Cahiers bibliques* 5 (1967) 26-35.

1969   Dans l'ignorance du jour, veillez. Mt 24,37-44. — *AssSeign* II/5 (1969) 17-28.

**GEORGE, Augustin**

1956a  Le Père et le Fils dans les évangiles synoptiques. — *LumièreV* 29 (1956) 27-40(=603-
616). [NTA 1, 389]

1956b  Heureux les cœurs purs! Ils verront Dieu! (Matth. 5,8). — *BibVieChrét* 13 (1956) 74-
79.

1957a  La "forme" des Béatitudes jusqu'à Jésus. — *Mélanges bibliques*. FS A. Robert, 1957,
398-403.

1957b Les miracles de Jésus dans les évangiles synoptiques. — *LumièreV* 33 (1957) 7-24(=295-312). [NTA 2, 274]

1957c Soyez parfaits comme votre Père céleste (Matth. 5,17-48). — *BibVieChrét* 19 (1957) 84-90. [NTA 2, 283]

1959a La justice à faire dans le secret (Matthieu 6,1-6 et 16-18). — *Bib* 40 (1959) 590-598. [NTA 4, 649]; = *Studia Biblica et Orientalia*, II, 1959, 22-30.

1959b Le sens de la parabole des semailles (*Mc.*, IV, 3-9 et parallèles). — COPPENS, J., et al. (eds.), *Sacra Pagina*, 1959, II, 163-169.

1960 Parabole. — *DBS* 6/34 (1960) 1149-1177. Esp. 1155-1165: "Les paraboles des Synoptiques", 1175.

1961 Jésus et les Psaumes. — BARUCQ, A., et al. (eds.), *À la rencontre de Dieu*. FS A. Gelin, 1961, 297-308. Esp. 303 [21,16]; 304 [5,5; 27,46]; 305-306 [5,35]; 306 [22,43-44]; 306 [26,64]; 307 [21,42; 23,39].

1962 La seigneurie de Jésus dans le Règne de Dieu d'après les Évangiles synoptiques. — *LumièreV* 57 (1962) 22-42. [NTA 7, 92]; = LACAN, M.-F., et al., *L'espérance du Royaume* (Paroles de vie), Paris: Mame, 1966, 33-54.

1965 La méthode des paraboles. — *AssSeign* I/15 (1965) 32-44. Esp. 36-43.

1966a Ne nous soumets pas à la tentation... Note sur la traduction nouvelle du Notre Père. [6,13] — *BibVieChrét* 71 (1966) 74-79. [NTA 11, 698]

1966b Note sur quelques traits lucaniens de l'expression "Par le doigt de Dieu" (Lc XI,20). — *ScEccl* 18 (1966) 461-466. [NTA 11, 1067]
"Par le doigt de Dieu" (Lc 11,20). — ID., *Études sur l'œuvre de Luc*, 1978, 127-132.

1968 "Qui veut sauver sa vie, la perdra; qui perd sa vie, la sauvera". [16,25] — *BibVieChrét* 83 (1968) 11-24. [NTA 13, 572]

1969 Les récits d'apparition aux onze à partir de Luc 24,36-53. — DE SURGY, P., et al., *La Résurrection du Christ et l'exégèse moderne* (LD, 50), Paris: Cerf 1969, 75-104. Esp. 86-90 [28,16-20].

1971* et al. (eds.), *La pauvreté évangélique* (Lire la Bible, 27). Paris: Cerf, 1971, 189 p. → Dupont, Légasse, Rigaux
*Gospel Poverty. Essays in Biblical Theology*, trans. M.D. Guinan. Chicago, IL: Franciscan Herald Press, 1977.

1971 Comment Jésus a-t-il perçu sa propre mort? — *LumièreV* 101 (1971) 34-59. [NTA 16, 121]

1972a Guérison de l'esclave d'un centurion. Lc 7,1-10. — *AssSeign* II/40 (1972) 66-77. Esp. 69-73 [8,5-13]. [NTA 17, 973]

1972b La venue de Jésus, cause de division entre les hommes. Lc 12,49-53. — *AssSeign* II/51 (1972) 62-71. Esp. 66-67 [10,34-36].

1974 Les paraboles. — *LumièreV* 119 (1974) 35-48. Esp. 40-43 [18,10-14]. [NTA 19, 927]

1975 Paroles de Jésus sur ses miracles (Mt 11,5.21; 12,27.28 et par.). — DUPONT, J. (ed.), *Jésus aux origines de la christologie*, 1975, 283-301; ²1989 (note additionnelle, 429-430). Esp. 286-292 [11,5/Q 7,22]; 293-296 [11,21/Q 10,13]; 296-300 [12,27-28/Q 11,19-20].

1978a *Études sur l'œuvre de Luc* (Sources bibliques). Paris: Gabalda, 1978, 487 p. → 1966b, 1978b-d

1978b Les anges. — *Ibid.*, 149-183. Esp. 170-171 [Q 12,8-9].

1978c Le Règne de Dieu. — *Ibid.*, 285-306. Esp. 296-299 [Q 7,28; 11,20; 13,18-21].

1978d La prière. — *Ibid.*, 395-427. Esp. 411-413 [Q].

**GERBER, Wolfgang**

1967 Die Metamorphose Jesu, Mark. 9,2f. par. [17,2] — *TZ* 23 (1967) 385-395. [NTA 12, 889]

**GERHARDSSON, Birger**

1959 Matteusevangeliet och judekristendomen. [The gospel of Matthew and Jewish Christianity] — *SEÅ* 24 (1959) 97-110. → Nepper-Christensen 1958

1961 *Memory and Manuscript. Oral Tradition and Written Transmission in Rabbinic Judaism and Early Christianity* (Acta Seminarii Neotestamentici Upsaliensis, 22). Lund: Gleerup; København: Munksgaard, 1961, 379 p. Esp. 324-335: "The origins and transmission of the gospel tradition"; ²1964. — Diss. Uppsala, 1961 (H. Riesenfeld). → Fitzmyer 1962, McEleney 1972

1966a *The Testing of God's Son (Matt 4:1-11 & Par). An Analysis of an Early Christian Midrash*, trans. J. Toy (ConBibNT, II/1). Lund: Gleerup, 1966, 83 p. Esp. 19-24 "The Son of God"; 36-70: "The temptation narrative (Matt 4:1-11) and Deut 6-8"; 71-83: "The temptation narrative (M) and Deut 6:5". [NTA 11, p. 274; 13, p. 563]
J.A. BERGQUIST, *IndianJT* 18 (1969) 222-223; P. BONNARD, *RTP* 17 (1967) 67; P. BORGEN, *JBL* 86 (1967) 361-362; M. BOUTTIER, *ETR* 42 (1967) 237-238; F. DREYFUS, *RB* 75 (1968) 636-637; J.H. ELLIOTT, *CBQ* 29 (1967) 624; F.R.C. RevistBíb 33 (1971) 183-184; K. GÁBRIŠ, *ComViat* 10 (1967) 82-83; I. GOMÁ CIVIT, *EstBíb* 26 (1967) 310-312; T.B. JENSEN, *DanskTeolTids* 31 (1968) 153-154; J. JEREMIAS, *TLZ* 93 (1968) 262; J. KAHMANN, *TijdTheol* 7 (1967) 441; H.A. KELLY, *TS* 29 (1968) 528-531; F.W. KOESTER, *TheolPhil* 44 (1969) 595-596; E. LARSSON, *TidsTeolKirk* 38 (1967) 52-53; M.É. LAUZIÈRE, *RThom* 67 (1967) 483; J.É. MÉNARD, *RHR* 174 (1968) 88-90; E. NEUHÄUSLER, *TRev* 65 (1969) 193; B. PIEPIÓRKA, *ZKT* 91 (1969) 223-224; L.F. RIVERA CRUZ, *RevistBíb* 33 (1971) 183-184; J.N. SEVENSTER, *NTT* 21 (1966-67) 316; J. SEYNAEVE, *RHE* 69 (1974) 968-969; D.M. SMITH, *Interpr* 22 (1968) 349-350; É. TROCMÉ, *RHPR* 47 (1967) 182-183; *ExpT* 78 (1966-67) 211; W. WEISSENBUEHLER, *LuthQ* 19 (1967) 327-328; P. ZARELLA, *ScuolC* 97 (1969) 423-424.
The Temptation Narrative (M) and Deut 6:5. [1966, 71-83] — ID., *The Shema*, 1996, 13-23 (additional note, 23). Esp. 18-21.

1966b Liknelsen om fyrahanda sädesåker och dess uttydning. — *SEÅ* 31 (1966) 80-113. Esp. 85-86; 86-88; 88-97.104-111. [NTA 12, 158]; = ID., *Hör, Israel*, 1979, 12-45.
The Parable of the Sower and its Interpretation. — *NTS* 14 (1967-68) 165-193. Esp. 169-170 [22,34-40]; 170-171 [4,1-11]; 172-179.185-191 [13,1-52]. [NTA 12, 872]; = ID., *The Shema*, 1996, 24-52. Esp. 28-29; 29-31; 31-38.44-50.

1967 Utlämnad och övergiven. Till förståelsen av passionshistorien i Matteusevangeliet. — *SEÅ* 32 (1967) 92-120. Esp. 107-108 [26,36-56]; 110-113 [27,33-56]. [NTA 13, 148]; = ID., *Hör, Israel*, 1979, 85-113.
Jésus livré et abandonné d'après la Passion selon saint Matthieu. — *RB* 76 (1969) 206-227. Esp. 217-218; 219-222. [NTA 14, 130]
Jesus, ausgeliefert und verlassen - nach dem Passionsbericht des Matthäusevangeliums. — LIMBECK, M. (ed.), *Redaktion und Theologie des Passionsberichtes*, 1981, 262-291. Esp. 273-275; 277-280; = ID., *The Shema*, 1996, 109-138. Esp. 121-122; 124-127.

1969 De sju liknelserna i Matteus 13. — *SEÅ* 34 (1969) 77-106. Esp. 78-79; 79-81; 81-89.91-95; 89-91; 95-97; 97-99; 100-103; 103-106. [NTA 15, 504]; = ID., *Hör, Israel*, 1979, 46-75.
The Seven Parables in Matthew xiii. — *NTS* 19 (1972-73) 16-37. Esp. 17: "The parables and the 'secrets'"; 17-19 [pattern]; 19-29 [structure]; 29-31: "The expositions"; 31-32: "The secrets of the kingdom"; 33-36: "Nature and authenticity"; 36-37: "The 'kingdom of heaven'". [NTA 17, 913]; = ID., *The Shema*, 1996, 53-74. Esp. 54; 54-56; 56-66; 66-68; 68-69; 70-73; 73-74.

1970 Ur Matteusevangeliet. [Commentary on Mt 1-2.5-7.26-28] — HARTMAN, L. (ed.), *Ur Nya Testamentet. Kommentarer till valda texter*, Lund: Gleerup, 1970, 113-155, 167-206; ²1972, 108-150, 163-201.

1971a Andlig offertjänst enligt Matt. 6:1-6, 16-21. — *SEÅ* 36 (1971) 117-125. [NTA 17, 907]; = ID., *Hör, Israel*, 1979, 76-84.
Geistiger Opferdienst nach Matth 6,1-6.16-21. — BALTENSWEILER, H. - REICKE, B. (eds.), *Neues Testament und Geschichte*. FS O. Cullmann, 1972, 69-77; = ID., *The Shema*, 1996, 75-83.

1971b Bibelns ethos. — WINGREN, G. (ed.), *Etik och kristen tro* [Ethic and christian belief], Lund: LiberLäromedel; København: Gyldendal, 1971, 13-92. Esp. 34-54: "Enligt Matteus".

1972 Du Judéo-christianisme à Jésus par le Shema'. — *RSR* 60 (1972) 23-36. Esp. 27-28 [4,1-11]; 28-31 [27,33-50]; 32-33 [22,34-40]; 33-35 [13,3-9.18-23]. [NTA 17, 70]; = ID., *The Shema*, 1996, 286-299. Esp. 290-291; 291-294; 295-296; 296-298.
*SelT* 13 (1974) 66-75.

1973a Gottes Sohn als Diener Gottes. Messias, Agape und Himmelsherrschaft nach dem Matthäusevangelium. — *StudTheol* 27 (1973) 73-106. Esp. 74-79 [3,1-4,11]; 81-88 [ἐξουσία]; 88-90 [10,16-39]; 94-96 [26,36-46]; 98-103 [27,33-50]; 103-106 [Mess ah]. [NTA 18, 839]; = ID., *The Shema*, 1996, 139-172. Esp. 140-145; 147-154; 154-156; 160-162; 164-169; 169-172. → D. Hill 1980 Guds son som Guds tjänare. Messias, agape och himlens herravälde enligt Matteusevangeliet. — ID, *Hör, Israel*, 1979, 114-146.

1973b Monoteism och högkristologi i Matteusevangeliet. [Monotheism and high christology in the gospel of Matthew] — *SEÅ* 37-38 (1972-73) 125-144. Esp. 127-129 [28,19]. [NTA 18, 862]; = ID., *Hör, Israel*, 1979, 171-190.

1974 Sacrificial Service and Atonement in the Gospel of Matthew. — BANKS, R. (ed.), *Reconciliation and Hope. New Testament Essays on Atonement and Eschatology Presented to L.L. Morris on his 60th Birthday*, Grand Rapids, MI: Eerdmans, 1974, 25-35. Esp. 25 [1,21; 20,28; 26,27-28]; 28-29 [12,5-7]; 29-31 [διακονεῖν-λατρεύειν]; = ID., *The Shema*, 1996, 98-108. Esp. 98; 101-102; 102-104.

1975 Det hermeneutiska programmet i Matt. 22:37-40. — *SEÅ* 40 (1975) 66-89. Esp. 68-71 [22,34-40/Mk]; 71-80.84-89 [22,37-40]; 80-81 [5,17-48]; 82-83 [13,14-15.51-52]. [NTA 20, 781]; = ID., *Hör, Israel*, 1979, 147-170.
The Hermeneutic Program in Matthew 22:37-40. — HAMERTON-KELLY, R. - SCROGGS, R. (eds.), *Jews, Greeks and Christians. Religious Cultures in Late Antiquity. Essays in Honor of William David Davies* (Studies in Judaism in Late Antiquity, 21), Leiden: Brill, 1976, 129-150. Esp. 133-136; 136-142.145-150; 142-143. 143-144; = ID., *The Shema*, 1996, 202-223. Esp. 206-209; 209-215.218-223; 215-216; 216-217.

1977 *Die Anfänge der Evangelientradition* (Glauben und Denken, 919). Wuppertal: Brockhaus, 1977, 69 p.
*Evangeliernas förhistoria.* Lund: Håkan Ohlssons, 1977, 59 p.; Lund: Novapress, ²1991, 88 p.
*Préhistoire des évangiles*, trans. A. Liefooghe (Lire la Bible, 48). Paris: Cerf, 1977, 126 p.
*Evangeliernes forhistorie*, trans. P. Baekgaard. Aarhus: Forlaget Aros, 1978, ²1985, 71 p.
*The Origins of the Gospel Traditions.* Philadelphia, PA: Fortress, 1979; London: SCM, 1980, 95 p.
*Le origini delle tradizioni evangeliche. — Nuovo Testamento e critica*, II/5 (1979) 4-108.
*Prehistoria de los evangelios.* Santander: Sal Terrae, 1980, 94 p.

1978 Fader vår i Nya testamentet. — *SvenskTeolKvart* 54 (1978) 93-102. [NTA 23, 435]
The Matthaean Version of the Lord's Prayer (Matt 6:9b-13): Some Observations. — WEINRICH, W.C. (ed.), *The New Testament Age*. FS B. Reicke, 1984, I, 207-220. Esp. 207-209: "The context"; 209-210: "The structure of the prayer"; 210-214: "The 'thou-petitions'"; 214-217: "The 'we-petitions'"; 217-218: "The invocation"; 218-220: "Some characteristics of the Lord's prayer"; = ID., *The Shema*, 1996, 84-97. Esp. 84-86; 86-87; 87-91; 91-94; 94-95; 95-97.

1979a *The Mighty Acts of Jesus according to Matthew* (Scripta Minora Regiae Societatis Humaniorum Litterarum Lundensis 1978-1979, 5). Lund: Gleerup, 1979, 94 p. Esp. 11-19: "The general terminology"; 20-37: "The summarizing accounts of Jesus' therapeutic activity in Israel"; 38-51: "The pericopes of Jesus' therapeutic miracles in individual cases"; 52-67: "The pericopes of Jesus' non-therapeutic miracles"; 68-81: "Material concerning resistance and controversies"; 82-92: "The christological appellations in our material". [NTA 24, p. 300] → 1979d-e, 1980, 1981b
G. DELLING, *SEÅ* 46 (1981) 180-181; H. KVALBEIN, *TidsTeolKirk* 54 (1983) 308-309; J.P. MEIER, *Interpr* 35 (1981) 89-90; B. OLSSON, *SvenskTeolKvart* 58 (1982) 152-154; J.M. REESE, *CBQ* 43 (1981) 293-294; J.A. ZIESLER, *ExpT* 92 (1980-81) 24-25.

*Jesu maktgärningar i Matteusevangeliet.* Lund: Novapress, 1991, 135 p. Esp. 121-132: "Undren och Himlaväldet: 'Gud med oss'". → 1994
H.K. NIELSEN, *SvenskTeolKvart* 67 (1991) 136-138.

1979b "*Hör, Israel!*" *Om Jesus och den gamla bekännelsen* ["Hear, Israel!" On Jesus and the early creed]. Lund: LiberLäromedel, 1979, 224 p. [NTA 25, p. 78] → 1966b, 1967, 1969, 1971a, 1973a-b, 1975

1979c "*Med hela ditt hjärta*". *Om Bibelns ethos.* Lund: LiberLäromedel, 1979, 143 p.; Lund: Novapress, [2]1996.
*The Ethos of the Bible*, trans. S. Westerholm. Philadelphia, PA: Fortress, 1981; London: Darton, Longman & Todd, 1982, VIII-152 p. Esp. 33-62: "Early christianity's ethos according to Matthew".

1979d Jesu maktgärningar. Om de urkristna berättarnas val av termer. [Jesus' mighty deeds: early Christian narrators' choice of terms]. — *SEÅ* 44 (1979) 122-133. Esp. 123-124 [τέρας]; 124-127 [σημεῖον]; 128-129 [θαυμάσιον-ἔργον]; 129-130 [δύναμις]. [NTA 24, 721] → 1979a

1979e Jesus – Israels läkare. Om de s k summarierna i Matteusevangeliet. [Jesus – Israel's healer. On the so-called summaries in the gospel of Matthew]. — ASHEIM, I., et al. (eds.), *Israel – Kristus – Kirken*, Oslo–Bergen–Tromsø: Universitetsforlaget, 1979, 77-90. → 1979a

1980 Kristi makt och den undermottagande tron. De matteiska perikoperna om Jesu terapeutiska under. [Christ's power and miracle-receiving faith. The Matthean pericopes about Jesus' therapeutic miracles]. — *SEÅ* 45 (1980) 58-76. Esp. 59-61 [8-9]. [NTA 25, 453] → 1979a

1981a Confession and Denial before Men: Observations on Matt. 26:57–27:2. — *JSNT* 13 (1981) 46-66. Esp. 53-55.60-63 [26,69-75]; 55-60 [26,59-64]. [NTA 26, 480]
Bekännelse och förnekelse inför människorna. Jesus och Petrus i Matt 26:57–27:2. — *SEÅ* 47 (1982) 151-171. Esp. 157-160.166-168; 160-166. [NTA 27, 931]

1981b Kristi exousia och den undergörande tron. De matteiska perikoperna om Jesu icke-terapeutiska under. [Christ's exousia and miracle-working faith. The Matthean pericopes on Jesus' non-therapeutic miracles] — *SEÅ* 46 (1981) 74-94. Esp. 77-78 [8,23-27]; 78-80 [14,13-21; 15,29-39]; 80-81 [14,22-33]; 81-83 [21,18-22]; 83-84 [17,24-27]. [NTA 27, 905] → 1979a

1982 "An ihren Früchten sollt ihr sie erkennen". Die Legitimitätsfrage in der matthäischen Christologie. — *EvT* 42 (1982) 113-126. Esp. 113-15; 115-117; 117-124; 124-126. [NTA 27, 92]; = ID., *The Shema*, 1996, 173-186. Esp. 173-175; 175-177; 177-184; 184-186.
*SelT* 23 (1984) 335-340.

1983 Der Weg der Evangelientradition. — STUHLMACHER, P. (ed.), *Das Evangelium und die Evangelien*, 1983, 79-102.
The Path of the Gospel Tradition. — STUHLMACHER, P. (ed.), *The Gospel and the Gospels*, 1991, 75-96.

1984 Eleutheria ("frihet") i bibliskt tänkande. — *SvenskTeolKvart* 60 (1984) 118-129. [NTA 29, 700]. Esp. 123 [17,24-27].
*Eleutheria* ('freedom') in the Bible. — THOMPSON, B.P. (ed.), *Scripture: Meaning and Method. Essays Presented to Anthony Tyrrell Hanson for His Seventieth Birthday*, Hull: University Press, 1987, 3-23. Esp. 11-12.

1986a *The Gospel Tradition* (ConBibNT, 15). Malmö: Gleerup, 1986, 57 p. Esp. 40 [13]; 54 [28,16-20]. → W.H. Kelber 1983
The Gospel Tradition. — DUNGAN, D.L. (ed.), *The Interrelations of the Gospels*, 1990, 497-545. Esp. 529; 542-543.

1986b Enhetsskapande element i Bibelns etiska mångfald. [Unifying elements in the ethical multiplicity of the Bible] — *SvenskTeolKvart* 62 (1986) 49-58. Esp. 52-53 [7,12]; 53 [22,37-40]; 53 [5,17-48]. [NTA 31, 819]
Agape and Imitation of Christ. — SANDERS, E.P. (ed.), *Jesus, the Gospels, and the*

*Church.* FS W.R. Farmer, 1987, 163-176. Esp. 167-168 [7, .2]; 168-169 [22,37-40]; 169 [5,17-48]; = ID., *The Shema*, 1996, 272-285. Esp. 276-277; 277-278; 278.

1986c  Jesus och Torah. [Jesus and the Torah] — HIDAL, S., et al. (eds.), *Judendom och kristendom under de första århundradena. Nordiskt patristikerprojekt 1982-1985*, Stavanger–Oslo–Bergen–Tromsø:Universitetsforlaget, 1986, 124-144. Esp. 132-136 [5,17-48]; 136-137 [22,34-40]; 137-139 [15,1-20].

1987  Mysteriet med saltet. Ett kryptiskt Jesusord (Matt 5:13a). [The mystery of the salt. A cryptic saying of Jesus] — ECKERDAL, L., et al. (eds.), *Kyrka och universitet. Festskrift till Carl-Gustaf Andrén*, Stockholm: Verbum, 1987, 113-120.

1988  The Narrative Meshalim in the Synoptic Gospels. A Comparison with the Narrative Meshalim in the Old Testament. — *NTS* 34 (1988) 339-363. Esp. 359-361 [minor agreement: 13,11]; 362 [6,24-34]. [NTA 33, 105]
De berättande maschalerna i de synoptiska evangelierna. En jämförelse med samma textsort i Gamla testamentet. — *SEÅ* 53 (1988) 36-62. Esp. 58-60; 61. [NTA 33, 586]

1989  The Narrative Meshalim in the Old Testament Books anc in the Synoptic Gospels. — HORGAN, M.P. – KOBELSKI, P.J. (eds.), *To Touch the Text*. FS J.A. Fitzmyer, 1989, 289-304. Esp. 294-300.

1991a  If We Do Not Cut the Parables Out of Their Frames. — *NTS* 37 (1991) 321-335. Esp. 324-325 [βασιλεία]; 328 [13]; 330-331 [25,31-46]; 334-335 [22,34-40]. [NTA 36, 118]; = ID., *The Shema*, 1996, 224-238. Esp. 227-228; 231; 233-234; 237-238.
Om vi inte skär ut liknelserna ur ramarna. — *SEÅ* 56 (1991) 29-44. Esp. 32-33; 36-37; 38-39; 43-44. [NTA 37, 690]

1991b  Illuminating the Kingdom. Narrative Meshalim in the Synoptic Gospels. — WANSBROUGH, H. (ed.), *Jesus and the Oral Gospel Tradition*, 1991, 266-309. Esp. 268; 285-287; 291-292.

1992a  The Shema ' in Early Christianity. — VAN SEGBROECK, F., et al. (eds.), *The Four Gospels 1992*. FS F. Neirynck, 1992, I, 275-293. Esp. 279-281 [4,1-11]; 281-282 [27,33-54]; 282 [13,1-9.18-23]; 283 [13,24-33.44-48]; 283-284 [6,1-6.16-21]; 291 [Mt]; = ID., *The Shema*, 1996, 300-318. Esp. 304-306; 306-307; 307; 308; 308-309; 316.

1992b  Tillbakablick: avskedsföreläsning. [In retrospect: a fare-well lecture] — *SvenskTeol-Kvart* 68 (1992) 97-108. [NTA 37, 637]. Esp. 106: "Matteusevangeliet".

1994  Mighty Acts and Rule of Heaven: 'God is with Us'. — SCHMIDT, T.E. – SILVA, M. (eds.), *To Tell the Mystery*. FS R.H. Gundry, 1994, 34-43. Esp. 38-41 [1,18-25]; 42-43 [4,1-11]; 43-46 [miracles]; = ID., *The Shema*, 1996, 187-201. Esp. 191-194; 195-196; 196-199. → 1979a/91

1995  Mashalen om de tio bröllopstärnorna (Matt 25:1-13). [The mashal on the ten wedding-maidens (Matt 25:1-13)]. — *SEÅ* 60 (1995) 83-94. [NTA 40, 1470]

1996  *The Shema in the New Testament. Deut 6:4-5 in Significan: Passages*. Lund: Novapress, 1996, 324 p. → 1966a, 1966b/68, 1967/81, 1969/72, 1971a/72, 1972, 1973a, 1974, 1975/76, 1978/84, 1982, 1986b/87, 1991a, 1992a, 1994

**GERHARTZ, Johannes Günter**

1971  Bergpredigt und Grundgesetz. Gedanken zur Möglichkeit und Sinnhaftigkeit eines Grundgesetzes der Kirche. — *GL* 44 (1971) 382-391.

**GERLEMAN, Gillis**

1983  *Der Menschensohn* (Studia Biblica, 1). Leiden: Brill, 1983, IX-79 p. Esp. 20-64: "Der Menschensohn im Neuen Testament".

**GERMANO, José M.**

1968  Nova et vetera in pericopam de sancto Ioseph (Mt 1,18-25). — *VD* 46 (1968) 351-360. [NTA 14, 134]

1969 Privilegium nominis messianici a S. Ioseph imponendi (Is 7,14; Mt 1,21.23.25). — *VD* 47 (1969) 151-162. [NTA 15, 131]

1973 "Et non cognoscebat eam donec...". Inquisitio super sensu spirituali seu mystico Mt 1,25. — *Marianum* 35 (1973) 184-240. Esp. 186-218: "Excursus historicus"; 218-240: "Analysis systematica". [NTA 18, 851]

**GERO, Stephen**

1981 The Gates or the Bars of Hades? A Note on Matthew 16.18. — *NTS* 27 (1980-81) 411-414. [NTA 25, 861]

**GESE, Hartmut**

1968 Psalm 22 und das Neue Testament. Der älteste Bericht vom Tode Jesu und die Entstehung des Herrenmahles. — *ZTK* 65 (1968) 1-22. Esp. 15 [27,46-54]. [NTA 13, 506]; = ID., *Vom Sinai zum Zion*, 1974, 180-201. Esp. 194.
Psalm 22 and the New Testament. — *TDig* 18 (1970) 237-243.

1971 Natus ex virgine. — WOLFF, H.W., *Probleme biblischer Theologie. Gerhard von Rad zum 70. Geburtstag*, München: Kaiser, 1971, 73-89. Esp. 74-77; = ID., *Vom Sinai zum Zion*, 1974, 130-146. Esp. 131-134.

1974 *Vom Sinai zum Zion: Alttestamentliche Beiträge zur biblischen Theologie* (BEvT, 64). München: Kaiser, 1974, 258 p. → 1968, 1971

1979 Die Weisheit, der Menschensohn und die Ursprünge der Christologie als konsequente Entfaltung der biblischen Theologie. — *SEÅ* 44 (1979) 77-114. Esp. 98-101 [11,25-27; 12,41-42; 23,34-39]. [NTA 24, 941]

**GESTEIRA GARZA, Manuel**

1991 "Christus medicus". Jesus ante el problema del mal. — *RevistEspTeol* 51 (1991) 253-300. Esp. 262-267; 267-300.

**GEWALT, Dietfried**

1966 *Petrus. Studien zur Geschichte und Tradition des frühen Christentums*. Diss. Heidelberg, 1966, IV-146 and II-134 p. (E. Dinkler). — *TLZ* 94 (1969) 628-629. [NTA 14, 808]

1973 Matthäus 25,31-46 im Erwartungshorizont heutiger Exegese. — *LingBib* 25-26 (1973) 9-21. [NTA 18, 477]

1986 Die Heilung Blinder und Lahmer im Tempel (Matthäus 21,14). — *Dielheimer Blätter zum Alten Testament und seiner Rezeption in der Alten Kirche* (Heidelberg) 23 (1986) 156-173. Esp. 157-162 [21,10-17]; 165-173 [21,14].

**GEYER, Hans-Georg**

1983 Luthers Auslegung der Bergpredigt. — ID., et al. (eds.), *"Wenn nicht jetzt, wann dann?" Aufsätze für Hans-Joachim Kraus zum 65. Geburtstag*, Neukirchen-Vluyn: Neukirchener, 1983, 283-293.

1986 Luthers Auslegung der Bergpredigt. — DOHNA, L. - MOKROSCH, R. (eds.), *Werden und Wirkung der Reformation*, 1986, 139-146.

**GEYSER, A.S.**

1960 Un essai d'explication de Rom. xv.19. — *NTS* 6 (1959-60) 156-159. Esp. 158 [16,18-19]. [NTA 4, 726]

1978 Jesus, the Twelve and the Twelve Tribes in Matthew. — *Neotestamentica* 12 (1978) 1-19. [NTA 26, 459]

1980 Some Salient New Testament Passages on the Restoration of the Twelve Tribes of Israel. [1,17.23; 3,15; 10,1-8; 15,24] — LAMBRECHT, J. (ed.), *L'Apocalypse johannique et l'Apocalyptique dans le Nouveau Testament* (BETL, 53), Gembloux: Duculot; Leuven: University Press, 1980, 305-310.

**GHERARDINI, Brunero**

1979   Pietro, la roccia. — *Divinitas* 23 (1979) 335-345. [NTA 25, 476] → Subilia 1978

1993   A proposito dei fondamenti biblici del papato. — *Divinitas* 37 (1993) 278-284. Esp. 279-280 [16,17-19]. [NTA 38, 989]

**GHIBERTI, Giuseppe**

1968   Esegesi dei racconti della risurrezione. — ID. (ed.), *Il Messaggio della Salvezza*. V: *Scritti apostolici*, Torino-Leumann: Elle Di Ci, 1968, 1-92.

1969   Bibliografia sull'esegesi dei racconti pasquali e sul problema della risurrezione di Gesù (1957-1968). — *ScuolC* 97 (1969) 68*-84*. Esp. 71 [28]. [NTA 14, 449] → 1974a, 1993

1972   *I racconti pasquali del cap. 20 di Giovanni confrontati con le altre tradizioni neotestamentarie* (Studi biblici, 19). Brescia: Paideia, 1972, 171 p. Esp. 57-78: "I racconti sinottici"; 143-167: "Giov. 20,23 et Mt. 16,19; 18,18".

1974a   Bibliografia sulla risurrezione di Gesù (1920-1973). — DHANIS, É. (ed.), *Resurrexit*, 1974, 645-764. Esp. 672-674 [28]. → 1969, 1993

1974b   "Per il regno dei cieli" (Mt 19,12). Riflessioni su un paradosso biblico. — *Chiesa per il mondo*. I: *Saggi storico-biblici. Miscellanea teologico-pastorale M. Pellegrino*, Bologna: Dehoniane, 1974, 61-72.

1975   Resurrexit. Gli Atti di un simposio e la discussione successiva. — *RivBib* 23 (1975) 413-440. Esp. 428. [NTA 20, 754] → Dhanis 1974*

1976   Discussione sulla risurrezione di Gesù. — *RivBib* 24 (1976) 57-93. Esp. 73-75. [NTA 23, 401]

1977   "Apparve a Cefa". Pietro nei racconti pasquali. — *ParVi* 22 (1977) 216-230; = GALIZZI, M. (ed.), *Il servizio di Pietro. Appunti per una riflessione interconfessionale*, Torino-Leumannn: Elle Di Ci, 1978, 161-178.

1979   Sepolcro, sepoltura e panni sepolcrali di Gesù. Riconsiderando i dati biblici relativi alla Sindone di Torino. — *RivBib* 27 (1979) 123-158. Esp. 127-130 [27,57-61]; 138.148-150 [27,59]. [NTA 24, 755] → 1982b

1982a   *La risurrezione di Gesù* (Biblioteca minima di cultura religiosa, 30). Brescia: Paideia, 1982, 196 p.

1982b   *La sepoltura di Gesù. I Vangeli e la Sindone* (Studia taurinensia, 3). Roma: Marietti, 1982, 115 p. Esp. 17-62: "Sepolcro, sepoltura e panni sepolcrali di Gesù". → 1979

1984a   Gesù e la sua morte secondo i racconti della cena. Alcune interpretazioni del XX secolo. — DANIELI, G. (ed.), *Gesù e la sua morte* (Atti della XXVII Settimana Biblica), Brescia: Paideia, 1984, 129-153.

1984b   La testimonianza biblica su Pietro e il suo servizio. Momenti del recente dialogo ecumenico. [16,17-19] — SARTORI, L. (ed.), *Papato e istanze ecumeniche. Atti del convegno tenuto a Trento il 19-20 maggio 1982* (Scienze religiose, 6), Bologna: Dehoniane, 1984, 11-49, 51-59 (discussion). Esp. 11-17, 23-27, 33-36.

1987   "Fate discepole tutte le genti" (Mt 28,16-20). — *ParSpirV* 16 (1987) 153-169. Esp. 159-165 [mission].

1988   "Lo avvolse in un candido lenzuolo" (Matteo 27,59). — RONDANTE, S. (ed.), *La Sindone, indagini scientifiche. Atti del IV Congresso nazionale di studi sulla Sindone, Siracusa 17-18 ottobre 1987*, Cinisello Balsamo: Paoline, 1988, 370-380.

1992   L'Apostolo Pietro nel Nuovo Testamento. La discussione e i testi. — *ANRW* II.26.1 (1992) 462-538. Esp. 483-490: "La scena matteana di Cesarea (Mt 16,17-19)"; 499-517: "Lettura dei testi".

1993  & BORGONOVO, G., Bibliografia sulla risurrezione di Gesù (1973-1992). — *ScuolC* 121 (1993) 171-287. Esp. 196-202. [NTA 38, 128] → 1969, 1974a

1994  Le "grandi" apparizioni del Risorto nei racconti sinottici. — LÀCONI, M. (ed.), *Vangeli sinottici*, 1994, 411-428. Esp. 416-420 [28,16-20].

**GHIDELLI, Carlo**

1968  Bibliografía Bíblica Petrina. — *ScuolC* 96 (1968) 62\*-110\*. Esp. 69-72. [NTA 13, 90]

1977  Rileggendo insieme il Nuovo Testamento. Una comunità che si interroga sul suo passato: Matteo. — *RivClerIt* 58 (1977) 13-22.

1981  *La parola e le Scritture. Introduzione al Nuovo Testamento* (Fede e mondo moderno, 10). Milano: Vita e Pensiero, 1981, 202 p.

1994  Gesù e Giovanni il battezzatore (Lc 7,18-35 par. Mt 11,2-6). — LÀCONI, M. (ed.), *Vangeli sinottici*, 1994, 289-303. Esp. 301-303.

**GIAMBERARDINI, Gabriele**

1983  Ruolo di S. Giuseppe nella Fuga in Egitto. Matt. 2,13 secondo la tradizione copta. — *EstJos* 37 (1983) 73-100.

**GIARDINI, F.**

1963  Conversione e fede nei Sinottici. — *Tabor* (Roma) 32 (1963) 40-70.

**GIAVINI, Giovanni**

1965  Abbiamo forse in *Mt.* 6,19-7,11 il primo commento al "Pater Noster"? — *RivBib* 13 (1965) 171-177. [NTA 10, 514] → 1972b

1968  "Donec eiciat ad victoriam iudicium": Mt. *12,20c* nel suo contesto. — *RivBib* 16 (1968) 201-205. [NTA 13, 571]

1971a  Introduzione al Vangelo di Matteo. — *RivClerIt* 52 (1971) 48-55.

1971b  Nuove e vecchie vie per la lettura delle clausole di Mt. sul divorzio. — *ScuolC* 99 (1971) 83-93. Esp. 85-88 [5,32]; 88-89 [19,3-10]. [NTA 16, 533]

1972a  Le norme etiche della Bibbia e l'uomo d'oggi. — *ScuolC* 100 (1972) 5-15, 83-97. Esp. 83-97: "Il Discorso della montagna nella problematica attuale circa il valore delle norme etiche nel Nuovo Testamento". [NTA 17, 685]
       Il Discorso della montagna e il valore delle norme etiche del Nuovo Testamento. — CANFORA, G. (ed.), *Fondamenti biblici*, 1973, 253-272.

1972b  Lo schema di *Mt.* 6,5-7,12: una precisazione. — *RivBib* 20 suppl. (1972) 575-587. [NTA 19, 86] → 1965

1973a  Il messaggio morale del Discorso della montagna. — GHIBERTI, G. (ed.), *Rivelazione e morale* (Biblioteca di cultura religiosa, 22), Brescia: Paideia, 1973, 97-111.

1973b  La risurrezione di Gesù come problema esegetico. — *ScuolC* 101 (1973) 217-237. Esp. 222-223 [28]. [NTA 18, 438]

1974  *La risurrezione di Gesù* (Problemi di Fede e di Morale, 4). Padova–Milano: Daverio, 1974, 139 p.

1977  L'"inizio del Vangelo" et la "voce celeste" al battesimo di Gesù. [3,16-17] — *ScuolC* 105 (1977) 478-486. [NTA 22, 775r] → Poppi 1976

1980  *Tra la folla al Discorso della montagna. Esegesi e vita* (Conoscere il Vangelo, 7). Padova: Messaggero, 1980, 201 p. [NTA 26, p. 83]
      *Ma io vi dico. Esegesi e vita attorno al Discorso della montagna* (Aggiornamenti teologici, 8). Milano: Àncora, ²1985, 211 p.

1983  Un altro libro sul divorzio secondo Gesù e secondo Matteo. — *ScuolC* 111 (1983) 218-222. [NTA 28, 72r] → Marucci 1982

**GIBBS, James M.**

1964 Purpose and Pattern in Matthew's Use of the Title 'Son of David'. — *NTS* 10 (1963-64) 446-464. Esp. 447-448 [1,1.20]; 449-453 [ἐλέησον, ὄχλος, τυφλός/κωφός]; 453-462 [9,27-31.32-34; 12,22-24; 15,21-28; 20,27-34; 21,1-9.14-15; 22,41-46; 23,1-36]. [NTA 9, 139]

1968 The Son of God as the Torah Incarnate in Matthew. — *Studia Evangelica* 4 (1968) 38-46.

1973 Mark 1,1-15, Matthew 1,1-4,16, Luke 1,1-4,30, John 1,1-51. The Gospel Prologues and their Function. — *Studia Evangelica* 6 (1973) 154-188. Esp. 157, 159-160, 178-181.

1976 Matthew's Use of 'Kingdom', 'Kingdom of God' and 'Kingdom of Heaven'. — *BangalTF* 8/1 (1976) 60-79. Esp. 62-66 [kingdom]; 66-68 [kingdom of God]; 68-74 [kingdom of heaven]. [NTA 21, 716]

**GIBBS, Jeffrey Alan**

1987 Parables of Atonement and Assurance: Matthew 13:44-46. — *ConcTQ* 51 (1987) 19-43. Esp. 27-36 [13,44]; 36-40 [13,45-46]. [NTA 32, 124]

1995 *"Let the Reader Understand": The Eschatological Discourse of Jesus in Matthew's Gospel*. Diss. Union Theol. Sem., Virginia, GA, 1995, 636 p. — *DissAbstr* 56 (1995-96) 1828.

**GIBERT, Pierre**

1975 *La résurrection du Christ. Le témoignage du Nouveau Testament. De l'histoire à la foi* (Croire aujourd'hui). Paris: Desclée; Montréal: Bellarmin, 1975, 106 p. Esp. 45-52.

1990 *Le récit biblique de rêve. Essai de confrontation analytique* (PROFAC Série biblique, 3). Lyon: Profac, 1990, 124 p. Esp. 15-22: "Première approche: les rêves de Joseph dans l'Évangile de Matthieu (Mt 1-2)".

**GIBLET, Jean**

1957 Les promesses de l'Esprit et la mission des Apôtres dans les évangiles. — *Irénikon* 30 (1957) 5-43. Esp. 8-17 [10,20]. [NTA 2, 18]

1962 Jésus, Fils de David. — *LumièreV* 57 (1962) 3-21. Esp. 8-10 [21,9]; 10-13 [22,41-46]; 18-19 [1,1-17]. [NTA 7, 106]

1963 Pénitence. Nouveau Testament. — *DBS* 7/38 (1963) 671-687. Esp. 673-678.

1965 Les douze. Histoire et théologie. — ID. (ed.), *Aux origines de l'Église* (Recherches bibliques, 7), Brugge: Desclée De Brouwer, 1965, 51-64. Esp. 61-63 [19,28].
Die Zwölf. Geschichte und Theologie. — ID. (ed.), *Vom Christus zur Kirche. Charisma und Amt im Urchristentum*, trans. M. Lehne, Freiburg: Herder, 1966, 61-78. Esp. 75-77.

1966 Les lignes de faîte de la morale néo-testamentaire. — *RevDiocNamur* 20 (1966) 266-281. Esp. 270-274 [5,17].

1967 Le sens de la mission dans le Nouveau Testament. — *AssSeign* I/98 (1967) 42-53. Esp. 48-49 [28,16-20].

**GIBLIN, Charles Homer**

1968 Theological Perspective and Matthew 10:23b. — *TS* 29 (1968) 637-661. Esp. 641-646: "Those addressed"; 646-649: "The verbal elements in Mt 10:23b"; 649-654: "The coming of the Son of Man"; 654-659: "The cities of Israel". [NTA 13, 866]

1971 "The Things of God" in the Question Concerning Tribute to Caesar (Lk 20:25; Mk 12:17; Mt 22:21). — *CBQ* 33 (1971) 510-527. Esp. 515-520. [NTA 16, 574]

1975a A Note on Doubt and Reassurance in Mt 28:16-20. — *CBQ* 37 (1975) 68-75. [NTA 19, 959]

1975b Structural and Thematic Correlations in the Matthean Burial-Resurrection Narrative (Matt. xxvii.57–xxviii.20). — *NTS* 21 (1974-75) 406-420. Esp. 406-408 [structure]; 409-411

[28,1-10]; 411-413 [27,57.62; 28,1]; 413-419: "Thematic correlations: narrative and predictions". [NTA 20, 96] → Senior 1992c

1985 *The Destruction of Jerusalem According to Luke's Gospel: A Historical-Typological Moral* (AnBib, 107). Roma: Biblical Institute Press, 1985, x-123 p. Esp. 33-34 [Q 10,13-15.16]; 34-36 [Q 11,29-32]; 37-43 [Q 13,34-35]; 43-44 [Q 17,37]; 44-46 [Q 19,12-27].

**GIBSON, J.**

1981 Hoi Telōnai kai hai Pornai. [21,31-32] — *JTS* 32 (1981) 429-433. [NTA 26, 479]

**GIBSON, Jeffrey B.**

1995 *The Temptations of Jesus in Early Christianity* (JSNT SS, 112). Sheffield: JSOT, 1995, 370 p. Esp. 25-41: "The tradition of Jesus' wilderness temptations: the accounts and their relationship"; 83-118: "Jesus' wilderness temptation according to Q"; 119-157: "The tradition of Jesus' temptation in the demand for a 'sign'"; 196-211: "The 'sign' demand temptation according to Q"; 264-268 [19,1-9]. — Diss. Oxford, 1993 (J. Muddiman).

L.R. DONELSON, *CRBR* 9 (1996) 213-215; E.M. WAINWRIGHT, *CBQ* 59 (1997) 379-381.

**GIDEON, V.E.**

1962 Preaching Values in Matthew 5. — *SWJT* 5 (1962) 77-88.

**GIERTZ, Bo**

1984 *Förklaringar till Nya Testamentet. Första delen Matteus, Markus, Lukas* [Explanations of the New Testament. Part I: Matthew, Mark, Luke]. Stockholm: Verbum; Göteborg: Pro Caritate, 1984, 377 p.

1990 *Matteus: selitys evankeliumi in Matteuksen mukaan*, trans. S. Asunta. Helsinki: SLEY-kirjat, 1990, 201 p.

**GIESEN, Heinz**

1970 *Zum Problem der Exkommunikation nach dem Matthäus-Evangelium.* Exc. ex diss. Pontif. Athenaei S. Anselmi de Urbe, Roma, 1970, 120 p.; = *Studia Moralia* (Roma) 8 (1970) 185-269. Esp. 189-220 [18,15-18]; 220-250 [16,19; 18,18]; 252-259 [18,8-9]; 259-267 [13,24-30.36-43.47-50]; = ID., *Glaube und Handeln*, I, 1983, 17-83. Esp. 19-39; 39-60; 61-66; 66-71.

1980 "Herrschaft der Himmel" und Gericht. Zum Gerichtsverständnis des Matthäusevangeliums. — *Studia Moralia* 18 (1980) 195-221. Esp. 199-206: "Die 'Herrschaft der Himmel' im Matthäusevangelium"; 207-218 [25,1-13]; = ID., *Glaube und Handeln*, I, 1983, 85-104. Esp. 86-93; 93-102.

1982a *Christliches Handeln. Eine redaktionskritische Untersuchung zum* δικαιοσύνη-*Begriff im Matthäus-Evangelium* (EHS, XXIII/181). Frankfurt/M–Bern: Lang, 1982, 319 p. Esp. 21-77: "Δικαιοσύνη in der sogenannten Täufertradition (3,15; 21,32)"; 79-196: "Δικαιοσύνη in der Bergpredigt"; 197-235: "Gerechtigkeit und Vaterwille" [7,21-23; 13,41.43; 23,28; 24,12]; 237-263: "Die Gerechtigkeit nach Matthäus und Paulus. Ein Vergleich". [NTA 27, p. 330] — Diss. Pont. Inst. Bib., Roma, 1979 (I. de la Potterie).

C. BISSOLI, *Sal* 46 (1984) 357; R.A. EDWARDS, *CBQ* 46 (1982) 571-572; A. FUCHS, *SNTU* 8 (1983) 183-184; J.D. KINGSBURY, *JBL* 104 (1985) 339-340; G. LOHFINK, *TQ* 164 (1984) 221-222; F. ZEILINGER, *TGeg* 27 (1984) 187-188.

1982b Josef der Gehorsame. Warum Matthäus Josef gerecht nennt (Mt 1,19). — *TGeg* 25 (1982) 344-347; = ID., *Glaube und Handeln*, I, 1983, 11-15.

1983 *Glaube und Handeln.* Band 1: *Beiträge zur Exegese und Theologie des Matthäus- und Markus-Evangeliums* (EHS, XXIII/205). Frankfurt/M–Bern: Lang, 1983, 172 p. → 1970, 1980, 1982b

E.J. EPP, *JBL* 105 (1986) 176-177; A. FUCHS, *SNTU* 9 (1984) 253-254; X. JACQUES, *NRT* 106 (1984) 427-428.

1987a Naherwartung im Neuen Testament? — *TGeg* 30 (1987) 151-164. Esp. 158 [10,23].

1987b Matthäus und seine Gemeinde. Neue Kommentare zum Matthäus-Evangelium. — *TGeg* 30 (1987) 257-266. → Gnilka 1986, Limbeck 1986, Luz 1985a, Sand 1986, Schnackenburg 1985a

1988 Jesu Krankenheilungen im Verständnis des Matthäusevangeliums. — SCHENKE, L. (ed.), *Studien zum Matthäusevangelium*. FS W. Pesch, 1988, 79-106. Esp. 83-104: "Jesu Botschaft von der Herrschaft Gottes und das Leiden"; 104-106: "Die Krankenheilungen Jesu – Machtvolle Zeichen der messianischen Heilszeit".

1994 Christusnachfolge als Weg zum Heil. Zum matthäischen Verständnis des Logions vom engen Tor (Mt 7,13f). — MAYER, C., et al. (eds.), *Nach den Anfängen fragen*. FS G. Dautzenberg, 1994, 251-276.

1995 *Herrschaft Gottes – heute oder morgen? Zur Heilsbotschaft Jesu und der synoptischen Evangelien* (BibUnt, 26). Regensburg: Pustet, 1995, 162 p. Esp. 23-34: "Jesus und Johannes der Täufer"; 35-44: "Die Herrschaft der Himmel im Matthäusevangelium"; 64-66 [12,28/Q 11,20]; 66-68 [13,16/Q 10,23-24]; 68-69 [12,41-42/Q 11,31-32]; 69-70 [11,5-6/Q 7,22-23]; 123-124 [10,23]; 125-126.

**GIGLIOLI, Alberto**

1962 Il giorno dell'ultima cena e l'anno della morte di Gesù. — *RivBib* 10 (1962) 156-181. [NTA 8, 954] → Jaubert 1957

**GIGNAC, Francis T.**

1986 Morphological Phenomena in the Greek Papyri Significant for the Text and Language of the New Testament. — *CBQ* 48 (1986) 499-511. Esp. 499-503 [nouns]; 503-504 [adjectives]; 504-505 [pronouns]; 505-506 [numerals]; 506-511 [verbs]. [NTA 31, 56]

**GIGUÈRE, P.-A.**

1981 L'historicité des récits de l'enfance. — *PrêtreP* 84 (1981) 654-661.

**GIL, Luis**

1988 Versiones del *Pater Noster* al castellano en el Siglo de Oro. — *FilolNT* 1 (1988) 175-191. [NTA 33, 1126]

**GILBERT, Maurice**

1984a La figure de Salomon en Sg 7–9. — KUNTZMANN, R. – SCHLOSSER, J. (eds.), *Études sur le judaïsme hellénistique. Congrès de Strasbourg (1983)* (LD, 119), Paris: Cerf, 1984, 225-249. Esp. 244-245 [12,42].

1984b La loi du talion. — *Christus* 31 (1984) 73-82. Esp. 81-82 [5,38-42]. [NTA 28, 915]

**GIL DE SANTIVAÑEZ, Agustín**

1978 Indisolubilidad matrimonial, ¿ley o ideal neotestamentario? — *Religión y Cultura* (Madrid) 24 (1978) 199-215.

**GILG, Arnold**

1955 Die Petrusfrage im Lichte der neuesten Forschung. — *TZ* 11 (1955) 185-206. Esp. 196-199 [16,17-19]. → Cullmann 1952

**GILL, D.**

1991 Socrates and Jesus on Non-Retaliation and Love of Enemies. [5,44] — *Horizons* (Villanova, PA) 18 (1991) 246-262. [NTA 36, 1263]

**GILL, David W.**

1986 *Peter the Rock. Extraordinary Insights from an Ordinary Man*. Downers Grove, IL: Inter-Varsity, 1986, 206 p.

**GILL, W.**

1965 The Historic Jesus and Ecumenical Endeavor. [14,15-21] — *LondQuartHolRev* 34 (1965) 279-284. [NTA 10, 517]

**GILLES, Jean**

1979 *Les "frères et sœurs" de Jésus. Pour une lecture fidèle des évangiles* (Questions religieuses). Paris: Aubier, 1979, 127 p. Esp. 29-32 [1,25].
*I "fratelli e sorelle" di Gesù. Per una lettura fedele dei vangeli*, trans. Mirella Corsani (Piccola biblioteca teologica, 16). Torino: Claudiana, 1985, 112 p.

**GILLMAN, Florence Morgan**

1992 The Wife of Pilate (Matthew 27:19). — *LouvSt* 17 (1992) 152-165. Esp. 154-159: "Exegetical analyses of Matthew 27:19"; 159-164: "Matthean dreams and Matthew 27:19". [NTA 36, 1284]

**GILS, Félix**

1957 *Jésus prophète d'après les évangiles synoptiques* (Orientalia et Biblica Lovaniensia, 2). Leuven: Publications Universitaires, 1957, XI-196 p. Esp. 9-23 [13,57; 14,2; 16,14; 26,28]; 24-25 [21,11.46]; 35-40 [Moses]; 49-73 [3,13-17]; 73-78 [17,1-9]; 78-82 [11,25-30]; 89-91 [3,7-12]; 92-98 [13,10-15]; 98-100 [13,31-33]; 100-103 [13,24-30.36-43.47-50]; 103 [22,10]; 104-105 [10,17-39]; 106-107 [16,24-28]; 107 [20,23]; 107-108 [23,29-36]; 108-109 [5,10-12]; 109-110 [22,6]; 111 [21,19-20]; 111-112 [21,28-32]; 112-113 [21,33-44]; 113 [22,2-16]; 113-114 [20,1-16]; 114-115 [10,18]; 115-117 [24,14]; 117-118 [26,13]; 121 [21,12-17]; 122-124 [18,18]; 124-125 [16,17-19]; 126-133 [24–25]; 134-141 [passion predictions]; 136-139 [Is 53/Mt]; 142-149 [resurrection narr.].

1962 "Le sabbat a été fait pour l'homme et non l'homme pour le sabbat" (*Mc*, II, 27). Réflexions à propos de *Mc*, II,27-28. — *RB* 69 (1962) 506-523. Esp. 512-513 [Mk 2,27-28/Mt]; 515-517 [12,1-8]; 517-518 [12,9-14]; 518 [19,1-9]; 519-521 [22,34-40]. [NTA 7, 794]

**GINZEL, Günther B.**

1985 *Die Bergpredigt: jüdisches und christliches Glaubensdokument. Eine Synopse* (Lambert Schneider Taschenbücher. Zur Sache, 3). Heidelberg: Scheider, 1985, 147 p. [NTA 30, p. 352]
P. VON DER OSTEN-SACKEN, *TLZ* 111 (1986) 888-889; S. SCHREINER, *Judaica* 42 (1986) 258-259; T. SÖDING, *TRev* 82 (1986) 119-120; M. WYSCHOGROD, *JEcuSt* 25 (1988) 106-107.

**GIOCARINIS, Kimon** → Post 1955

**GIORGI DELL'AMICO, Anna Maria**

1992 *'Aprí loro la mente all'intelligenza delle Scritture'. Categorie bibliche interpretative della morte e risurrezione di Gesù nei vangeli sinottici* (Studi e ricerche bibliche). Roma: Borla, 1992, 255 p.

**GIRARDI, Mario**

1994a Catechesi ed esegesi nel monachesimo antico: le "fraternità" di Basilio di Cesarea. — FELICI, S. (ed.), *Esegesi e catechesi nei Padri*, 1994, 13-32. Ep. 23-30: "Presenza preponderante di Matteo" [5-7; 10,16].

1994b *Erotapokriseis* neotestamentarie negli *Ascetica* di Basilio di Cesarea. Evangelismo e paolinismo nel monachesimo delle origini. — *AnStoEseg* 11 (1994) 461-490. Esp. 470-475: "La presenza di Matteo".

1994c Fra esigenze di perfezione e rapporti con i fratelli: Basilio di Cesarea e le beatitudini. — *Nicolaus. Rivista di teologia ecumenico-patristica* (Bari) 21 (1994) 95-132.

1995a Annotazioni alla esegesi di Gregorio Nisseno nel *De beatitudinibus*. — *Augustinianum* 35 (1995) 161-182.

1995b Basilio e Gregorio Nisseno sulle beatitudini. — *VetChr* 32 (1995) 91-130.

**GIRLANDA, A.**

1992 *Nuovo Testamento. Iniziazione biblica* (Universo teologia, 10). Milano: Paoline, 1992, 334 p.

**GIROD, Robert**

1970 (ed.), *Origène. Commentaire sur l'Évangile selon Matthieu.* Tome 1: *Livres X et XI. Introduction, traduction et notes* (SC, 162). Paris: Cerf, 1970, 394 p. Esp. 7-137: "Introduction"; 139-387: "Texte et traduction" [13,36–15,38]. [NTA 17, p. 409]
P. BONNARD, *RTP* 23 (1973) 259-260; H. CROUZEL, *ETR* 58 (1983) 99-100; C.P. HAMMOND, *JTS* 24 (1973) 252-256; R. HENRY, *Revue belge de philologie et d'histoire* (Bruxelles) 49 (1971) 1343-1345; C. MARTIN, *NRT* 93 (1971) 710-711; P. NAUTIN, *RHR* 181 (1972) 218-220; I. ORTIZ DE URBINA, *OCP* 39 (1973) 247; F. SALVONI, *RicBibRel* 6 (1971) 115-116; J.C.M. VAN WINDEN, *VigChr* 27 (1973) 68.

1975 La traduction latine anonyme du Commentaire sur Matthieu. — CROUZEL, H., et al. (eds.), *Origeniana. Premier colloque international des études origéniennes (Montserrat, 18-21 septembre 1973)* (Quaderni di "Vetera Christianorum", 12), Bari: Istituto di Letteratura Cristiana Antica, 1975, 125-138.

**GIROUD, Jean-Claude**

1987a & PANIER, L., *Sémiotique. Une pratique de lecture et d'analyse des textes bibliques* (Cahiers Évangile, 59). Paris: Cerf, 1987, 68 p. Esp. 9-25: "La parabole des ouvriers de la vigne (Matthieu 20,1-15)".

1987b La porte étroite du Royaume ou le secret de l'impossible. [7,13-14] — *LumièreV* 183 (1987) 57-65. [NTA 32, 593]

**GISPERT-SAUCH, George**

1978 St Peter Walking on the Ganges? [14,28-33] — *Vidyajyoti* 42 (1978) 468-472. [NTA 23, 830]

1983 The Lord's Prayer in Sanskrit. — *Indica* (Bombay) 20 (1983) 1-12. [NTA 28, 494]
La "preghiera del Signore" in Sanscrito. — *Studi di Ricerche dell'Oriente Cristiano* (Roma) 9 (1986) 209-215.

**GIULIANO, Raffaele**

1988 "Perché sarà tolto il regno di Dio a voi". Il dramma d'Israele in Mt 21,33-46. — *Rivista di Scienze Religiose* (Molfetta) 2 (1988) 13-27.

**GIURISATO, Giorgio**

1972a Due diatribe fra Gesù e i Farisei (Mt 15,1-20; 16,1-12) — *ParVi* 17 (1972) 267-281.

1972b "Non sono stato mandato, se non alle pecore perdute della casa di Israele" (Mt 15,24). — *Ibid.*, 293-302.

**GIUSTOZZI, Enzo**

1975 ¿Hay un sistema de normas en el Sermón de la montaña? — *RevistBíb* 37 (1975) 235-243. [NTA 20, 435]

1982 → Levoratti 1982

**GIVERSEN, Søren**

1986 Mattæusevangeliet og De apostoloske Fædre. [The Gospel of Matthew and the Apostolic Fathers] — NISSEN, J. - SIMONSEN, H. (eds.), *Teologi og kirke. Festskrift til Poul Nepper-Christensen*, København, 1986, 104-117.

**GLANCY, Jennifer Ann**

1990 *Satan in the Synoptic Gospels.* Diss. Columbia Univ., 1990, 250 p. (R.E. Brown). — *DissAbstr* 52 (1991-92) 569.

**GLASSON, Thomas Francis**

1945[R] *The Second Advent. The Origin of the New Testament Doctrine* [1945, ²1947]. London: Epworth, rev. ed., ³1963, XV-254 p. Esp. 56-62 [26,64]; 66-70 [parousia]; 78-84 [Q 17,22-37 (Lk)]; 87-90 [25]; 94-99 [23,37-39]; 99-100 [10,23]; 100-101 [25,31]; 130-131 [11,20-24]; 131-134 [25,31-46]; 144-145 [19,28]; 198-200 [24,30-31].

1956  Water, Wind and Fire (Luke iii.16) and Orphic Initiation. [3,11] — *NTS* 3 (1956-57) 69-71. [NTA 2, 59]

1957  Chiasmus in St. Matthew vii.6. — *ExpT* 68 (1956-57) 302. [NTA 2, 284]

1960  The Reply to Caiaphas (Mark xiv.62). — *NTS* 7 (1960-61) 88-93. Esp. 89-90 [26,64]. [NTA 5, 411] → McArthur 1958

1961  Anti-Pharisaism in St. Matthew. — *JQR* 51 (1960-61) 316-320. [NTA 6, 447]

1962  Carding and Spinning: Oxyrhynchus Papyrus No. 655. [6,28] — *JTS* 13 (1962) 331-332. [NTA 7, 781] → P. Katz 1954

1964  The Ensign of the Son of Man (Matt. XXIV.30). — *JTS* 15 (1964) 299-300. [NTA 9, 546]

1966a  Did Matthew and Luke Use a 'Western' Text of Mark? [8,1-4; 9,5; 12,4; 18,1-5; 22,17] — *ExpT* 77 (1965-66) 120-121. [NTA 10, 894]

1966b  An Early Revision of the Gospel of Mark. — *JBL* 85 (1966) 231-233. [NTA 11, 235] → J.P. Brown 1959

1971  The Uniqueness of Christ: The New Testament Witness. [11,25-27] — *EvQ* 43 (1971) 25-35. [NTA 15, 801]

1974  Davidic Links with the Betrayal of Jesus. [27,5] — *ExpT* 85 (1973-74) 118-119. [NTA 18, 816]

1980  *Jesus and the End of the World*. Edinburgh: St. Andrew Press, 1980, IX-145 p.

1982  The Last Judgment – In Rev. 20 and Related Writings. — *NTS* 28 (1982) 528-539. Esp. 528-530 [25,31-46]. [NTA 27, 686]

1988  Theophany and Parousia. — *NTS* 34 (1988) 259-270. Esp. 265-266. [NTA 32, 1321]

**GLASSWELL, Mark Errol**

1976  The Parable of the Labourers in the Vineyard (Matthew 20,1-16). — *ComViat* 19 (1976) 61-64. [NTA 21, 85]

1981  St. Matthew's Gospel – History or Book? — *ComViat* 24 (1981) 41-45. Esp. 41-42 [1,1]; 42-45 [OT]. [NTA 26, 460]

**GLAUE, Paul**

1958  Einige Stellen, die die Bedeutung des Codex D charakterisieren. — *NT* 2 (1957-58) 310-315. Esp. 311 [6,22; 14,6; 26,74]; 313 [12,11]; 314 [16,18; 19,28]; 315 [20,17]. [NTA 4, 23]

**GLAZENER, Clyde Gorman**

1974  *An Investigation of Jesus' Usage of the Term "Son of Man". A Possible Interpretive Key to the Gospel of Matthew*. Diss. Southwestern Baptist Theol. Sem., Fort Worth, TX, 1974.

**GLICKMAN, Steven Craig**

1983  *The Temptation Account in Matthew and Luke*. Dallas, TX: Swift, 1983, X-539 p. Esp. 14-102: "The prelude of the baptism" [3,13-17]; 103-216: "The significance of the circumstances"; 217-258: "The analysis of the testing"; 259-277: "The preliminary ethico-theological assessment of the account"; 279-357: "The perspective of Matthew: Jesus is the true Israel"; 358-382: "The consequent ethico-theological perspective of Matthew". — Diss. Basel, 1983 (B. Reicke – J.M. Lochman).

**GLOBE, Alexander**

1980  Some Doctrinal Variants in Matthew 1 and Luke 2, and the Authority of the Neutral Text. — *CBQ* 42 (1980) 52-72. Esp. 62-70 [1,16.18.19.20.24.25]. [NTA 24, 782]

1983  *The Dialogue of Timothy and Aquila* as Witness to a Pre-Caesarean Text of the Gospels. — *NTS* 29 (1983) 233-246. Esp. 235-239. [NTA 27, 1242]

1984  Serapion of Thmuis as Witness to the Gospel Text Used by Origen in Caesarea. — *NT* 26 (1984) 97-127. Esp. 101-102.103-104.104-107.110-111.113-118.123-125. [NTA 29, 32]

**GLÖCKNER, Richard**

1979 *Biblischer Glaube ohne Wunder?* (Sammlung Horizonte, NF 14). Einsiedeln: Johannes, 1979, 132 p. Esp. 35-50: "Bedeutung und Darstellungsweise der Wunder Jesu in den Evangelien"; 96-102 [3,13-17].

**GLOEGE, Gerhard**

1955 Vom Ethos der Ehescheidung. — HÜBNER, F. (ed.), *Gedenkschrift für D. Werner Elert. Beiträge zur historischen und systematischen Theologie*, Berlin: Lutherisches Verlagshaus, 1955, 335-358. Esp. 339-343 [5,32; 19,9].

**GLOMBITZA, Otto**

1961 Der Perlenkaufmann (Eine exegetische Studie zu Matth. xiii.45-6). — *NTS* 7 (1960-61) 153-161. [NTA 5, 716]

1962a Das Grosse Abendmahl. Luk. xiv 12-24. [22,1-14] — *NT* 5 (1962) 10-16. [NTA 7, 166]

1962b Das Zeichen des Jona (Zum Verständnis von Matth. xii 38-42). — *NTS* 8 (1961-62) 359-366. [NTA 7, 134]

1971 Die christologische Aussage des Lukas in seiner Gestaltung der drei Nachfolgeworte Lukas ix 57-62. — *NT* 13 (1971) 14-23. Esp. 16-17 [8,18-22]. [NTA 16, 198]

**GLORIEUX, Palémon**

1972 Deux éloges de la Sainte Écriture par Pierre d'Ailly. — *MSR* 29 (1972) 113-129. Esp. 122-129 [16,18].

**GLOVER, F.C.**

1975 Workers for the Vineyard. [20,4] — *ExpT* 86 (1974-75) 310-311. [NTA 20, 87]

**GLOVER, Richard**

1956 *A Teacher's Commentary on the Gospel of St. Matthew.* London: Marshall, Morgan & Scott, 1956, 338 p.
W. BARCLAY, *ExpT* 68 (1956-57) 171-172; A. ROSS, *EvQ* 29 (1957) 114-115.

1958 The Didache's Quotations and the Synoptic Gospels. — *NTS* 5 (1958-59) 12-29. Esp. 13 [7,12; 22,37-39]; 14 [5,39.44.46]; 15 [5,40-42]; 16 [5,26]; 17 [5,5; 19,18]; 18 [6,16; 15,19; 24,4]; 19 [6,9-13; 7,6]; 20 [12,31; 21,9]; 21 [10,10; 24,42.44; 25,13]; 23 [24,10.11-12.24]; 24 [24,21.24.30-31]. [NTA 3, 739]

1985 Patristic Quotations and Gospel Sources. — *NTS* 31 (1985) 234-251. Esp. 236-245 [Justin]. [NTA 30, 97]

**GLYNN, Leo Edward**

1971 *The Use and Meaning of* ἔλεος *in Matthew.* Diss. Graduate Theological Union, 1971, 227 p. — *DissAbstr* 32 (1971-72) 3410.

**GNILKA, Joachim**

1959a "Mein Gott, mein Gott, warum hast du mich verlassen?" (Mk 15,34 Par.) [27,46] — *BZ* 3 (1959) 294-297. [NTA 4, 405] → M. Rehm 1958

1959b "Parusieverzögerung" und Naherwartung in den synoptischen Evangelien und in der Apostelgeschichte. — *Catholica* 13 (1959) 277-290. [NTA 4, 635] → Grässer 1957

1961a *Die Verstockung Israels. Isaias 6,9-10 in der Theologie der Synoptiker* (SANT, 3). München: Kösel, 1961, 229 p. Esp. 90-102: "Das Wort von der Verstockung im Verständnis des Matthäus"; 103-115: "Die matthäische Parabelauffassung"; 151. — Diss. Würzburg, 1959 (R. Schnackenburg). → Lambrecht 1963

1961b Die essenischen Tauchbäder und die Johannestaufe. [3,1-12] — *RQum* 3 (1961) 185-207. Esp. 197-200 [John the Baptist]; 200-202 [μετάνοια]. [NTA 6, 582]

1961c Zur Theologie des Hörens nach den Aussagen des Neuen Testaments. — *BibLeb* 2 (1961) 71-81. Esp. 71-77.

1963 Die Kirche des Matthäus und die Gemeinde von Qumrân. — *BZ* 7 (1963) 43-63. Esp. 45 [11,25-27]; 46 [22,1-14]; 49 [13,36-43]; 51-57 [structure]; 53 [18,12-14]; 54 [18,15-17]; 57 [5,3.6]; 60 [5,43-48]; 61 [19,16-26]. [NTA 8, 118]

1964 Synoptiker. — *LTK* 9 (²1964) 1240-1249. Esp. 1245-1246: "Theologie der Spruchquelle".

1967 Das Verstockungsproblem nach Matthäus 13,13-15. — ECKERT, W.P., et al. (eds.), *Antijudaismus*, 1967, 119-128, 206-207.

1968 Der Missionsauftrag des Herrn nach Mt 28 und Apg 1. — *BibLeb* 9 (1968) 1-9. [NTA 13, 179]

1970 *Jesus Christus nach frühen Zeugnissen des Glaubens* (Biblische Handbibliothek, 8). München: Kösel, 1970, 180 p. Esp. 110-126: "Das Christusbild der Spruchquelle".

1974* (ed.), *Neues Testament und Kirche. Für Rudolf Schnackenburg.* Freiburg: Herder, 1974, 580 p. → J. Blank, Hoffmann, Kertelge, Kilpatrick, Minear, Reuss, Schlier, Schweizer, Vögtle

1976 Wie urteilte Jesus über seinen Tod? — KERTELGE, K. (ed.), *Der Tod Jesu*, 1976, 13-50. Esp. 26-29 [Q 13,34-35].

1977 Martyriumsparänese und Sühnetod in synoptischen und jüdischen Traditionen. — SCHNACKENBURG, R., et al. (eds.), *Die Kirche des Anfangs.* FS H. Schürmann, 1977, 223-246. Esp. 230-235: "Martyriumsparänese: die synoptischen Evangelien".

1985a & RÜGER, H.P. (eds.), *Die Übersetzung der Bibel – Aufgabe der Theologie* (Texte und Arbeiten zur Bibel, 2). Bielefeld: Luther, 1985, 315 p. Esp. 224-256: "Zur Übersetzung von Matthäus 13,24-52 und Römer 8" [K. Haacker, 225-226; K.-P Hertzsch, 240-242; A. Stock, 246-247].

1985b Das Kirchenbild im Matthäusevangelium. — GANTOY, R. (ed.), *À cause de l'Évangile.* FS J. Dupont, 1985, 127-143. Esp. 128-131: "Der geographische Ort der Kirche des Mt"; 131-135: "Das Selbstverständnis der Kirche des Mt"; 135-138: "Die Lebens- und Glaubenspraxis der Kirche des Mt"; 138-140: "Die inneren Strukturen der Kirche des Mt".

1986 *Das Matthäusevangelium.* I. Teil: *Kommentar zu Kap. 1,1-13,58* (HTKNT, I/1). Freiburg–Basel–Wien: Herder, 1986, XVI-518 p. Esp. 22-33: "Die Jungfrauengeburt"; 60-62: "Das literarische Genus von Matthäus 2"; 285-295: "Die Auslegungsproblemen der Bergpredigt"; 348-351: "Intentionen der Wunderzyklus". [NTA 31, p. 99] → Giesen 1987b, H. Riniker 1987
X. ALEGRE, *ActBibl* 25 (1988) 63; R. BARTNICKI, *CollTheol* 57/4 (1987) 175-181; E. BEST, *ExpT* 98 (1986-87) 301; J. BEUTLER, *TheolPhil* 63 (1988) 255-256; C. BISSOLI, *Sal* 51 (1989) 357-358; J. ERNST, *TGl* 77 (1987) 381; A. FUCHS, *SNTU* 12 (1987) 223-224; P. JAUMANN, *GL* 60 (1987) 318; J. KUHL, *ZMiss* 71 (1987) 236-237; M. MÜLLER, *DanskTeolTids* 51 (1988) 63; P.-G. MÜLLER, *BK* 42 (1987) 84; S. SABUGAL, *Revista Agustiniana* (Madrid) 29 (1988) 740; A. SAND, *TRev* 83 (1987) 194-196; G. SCHMAHL, *TTZ* 97 (1988) 66-67; A. SEGOVIA, *ArchTeolGran* 50 (1987) 451; A. STÖGER, *BLtg* 59 (1986) 236-237; A. VARGAS-MACHUCA, *EstE* 63 (1988) 371-372.

*Das Matthäusevangelium.* II. Teil: *Kommentar zu Kap. 14,1-28,20 und Einleitungsfragen* (HTKNT, I/2). Freiburg–Basel–Wien: Herder, 1988, VIII-552 p. Esp. 71-80: "Die Petrusverheißung in Geschichte und Gegenwart"; 513-551: "Das Matthäusevangelium. Einleitungsfragen". [NTA 33, p. 246]; ²1992. → Allison 1989a
E. BEST, *ExpT* 100 (1988-89) 377-378; J. BEUTLER, *TheolPhil* 65 (1990) 590-591; C. BISSOLI, *Sal* 51 (1989) 357-358; T. BÖHM, *MüTZ* 43 (1992) 113-114; J. ERNST, *TGl* 79 (1989) 620-621; B. ESTRADA, *Annales theologici* 4 (1990) 435-440; A. FUCHS, *SNTU* 14 (1989) 244-245; D.J. HARRINGTON, *CBQ* 52 (1990) 155-156; X. JACQUES, *NRT* 111 (1989) 428-429; O. KNOCH, *TPQ* 138 (1990) 186-187; J. KUHL, *ZMiss* 74 (1990) 83-84; M. MÜLLER, *DanskTeolTids* 53 (1990) 231; P.-G. MÜLLER, *BK* 43 (1988) 178-179; F. NEIRYNCK, *ETL* 67 (1991) 167-169; S. SABUGAL, *Revista Agustiniana* (Madrid) 30 (1989) 696-697; A. SAND, *TRev* 85 (1989) 200; G. SCHMAHL, *TTZ* 100 (1991) 159; A. VARGAS-MACHUCA, *EstE* 65 (1990) 94-95.

*Il vangelo di Matteo*, trans. S. Cavallini (Commentario teologico del Nuovo Testamento, 1). Brescia: Paideia, I, 1990, 755 p.; II, 1991, 809 p.
S. CIPRIANI, *Asprenas* 38 (1991) 109-111; E. CUVILLIER, *ETR* 66 (1991) 120-121; M. LÀCONI, *ParVi* 38 (1993) 67-68.

1987 "Tu es, Petrus". Die Petrus-Verheißung in Mt 16,17-19. — *MüTZ* 38 (1987) 3-17. Esp. 3-4: "Der Text"; 4-6: "Seligpreisung"; 6-7: "Kephas/Petrus"; 8-11: "Die Überlieferung"; 11-15: "Interpretation"; 15-17: "Das Petrusbild des Matthäusevangelium". [NTA 32, 126]

1988a → 1986

1988b Der Prozeß Jesu nach den Berichten des Markus und Matthäus mit einer Rekonstruktion des historischen Verlaufs. — KERTELGE, K. (ed.), *Der Prozeß gegen Jesus. Historische Rückfrage und theologische Deutung* (QDisp, 112), Freiburg: Herder, 1988, ²1989, 11-40. Esp. 21-25: "Der Matthäus-Bericht"; 25-39: "Die historische Frage - Versuch einer Rekonstruktion".

1988c "Selig, die reinen Herzens sind". [5,8] — *IKZ/Communio* (Rodenkirchen) 17 (1988) 385-391. [NTA 33, 600]

1989a *Neutestamentliche Theologie. Ein Überblick* (Die Neue Echter Bibel, NT-Ergänzungsband, 1). Würzburg: Echter, 1989, 158 p. Esp. 11-22: "Jesus"; 23-28: "Die Spruchquelle"; 41-49: "Das Matthäusevangelium".
*Teologia del Nuovo Testamento*, trans. E. Gatti (Biblioteca biblica, 9). Brescia: Queriniana, 1992, 180 p.

1989b Apokalyptik und Ethik. Die Kategorie der Zukunft als Anweisung für sittliches Handeln. — MERKLEIN, H. (ed.), *Neues Testament und Ethik*. FS R. Schnackenburg, 1989, 464-481. Esp. 477-480 [24-25].

1989c "Selig, die Frieden stiften". [5,9] — *IKZ/Communio* 18 (1989) 97-103. [NTA 33, 1121]

1990 *Jesus von Nazaret. Botschaft und Geschichte* (HTKNT, Supplementband, 3). Freiburg: Herder, 1990, 331 p. Esp. 79-86 [John the Baptist]; 89-97 [20,1-16]; 99-100 [18,23-35]; 100-102 [25,14-30]; 118-141 [miracles]; 141-165 [kingdom]; 166-193 [disciples]; 213-225 [law]; ²1993.
*Jesús de Nazaret. Mensaje e historia*, trans. C. Ruiz Garrido. Barcelona: Herder, 1993, 400 p.
*Gesù di Nazaret. Annuncia e storia* (Commentario teologico del Nuovo Testamento. Supplementi, 3). Brescia: Paideia, 1993, 431 p.
*Jesus of Nazareth. Message and History*, trans. S. Schatzmann. Peabody, MA: Hendrickson, 1997, XIV-346 p.

1992 Zum Gottesgedanken in der Jesusüberlieferung. — KLAUCK, H.-J. (ed.), *Monotheismus und Christologie. Zur Gottesfrage im hellenistischen Judentum und im Urchristentum* (QDisp, 138), Freiburg: Herder, 1992, 144-162. Esp. 154-158: "Zum Gottesgedanken des Matthäusevangeliums".

1994 *Theologie des Neuen Testaments* (HTKNT, Supplementband 5). Freiburg: Herder, 1994, 470 p. Esp. 133-143: "Die Spruchquelle"; 174-196: "Das theologische Konzept des Matthäus".

**GNUSE, Robert K.**

1990 Dream Genre in the Matthean Infancy Narratives. — *NT* 32 (1990) 97-120. Esp. 98-104: "Dream report genres"; 104-114: "Matthean dream reports"; 114-120: "Matthew's use of dream reports". [NTA 34, 1128]

**GÖGLER, Rolf**

1980 'Ωφέλεια dans le *Commentaire sur Matthieu* d'Origène. — CROUZEL, H. – QUACQUARELLI, A. (eds.), *Origeniana Secunda*, 1980, 199-203.

**GOEHRING, James E.**

1990* et al. (eds.), *Gospel Origins & Christian Beginnings. In Honor of James M. Robinson* (Forum Fascicles, 1). Sonoma, CA: Polebridge, 1990, XXIX-214 p. → H.D. Betz, Kloppenborg, Koester, Mack, Sieber

**GOENAGA, José Antonio**

1979 Celebración de la navidad y crítica de los Evangelios de la infancia. — *ScriptVict* 26 (1979) 241-298; = *Phase* 19 (1979) 397-418.

**GÖRG, Manfred**

1994 Heinrich Corrodi und die Anfänge der historisch-kritischen Arbeit am Neuen Testament. [5-7] — *BibNot* 73 (1994) 13-17.

**GOERGEN, Aloys**

1980   Der Neue Bund als österliche Gemeinde Jesu Christi. Das Oster- und Pfingstereignis
       nach Psalm 22 und nach Matthäus. — *TGeg* 23/3 (1980) 3-5.

**GOFFI, Tullo**

1957   Il divorzio nella legge rivelata. [5,32] — *RivClerIt* 38 (1957) 317-320.

**GOGUEL, Maurice**

1932[R]  *Jésus* [1932]. Paris: Payot, [2]1950 (rev. ed.), 479 p. Esp. 101-107: "Les évangiles synopt.ques";
       228-234 [Sermon on the Mount: style]; 369-386 [passion narrative].

1955   Le livre d'Oscar Cullmann sur saint Pierre. – *RHPR* 35 (1955) 196-209. → Cullmann 1952

**GOITA, José**

1956   La noción dinámica del πνεῦμα en los libros sagrados. — *EstBíb* 15 (1956) 147-185;
       341-380. Esp. 341-348: "El pneûma en la infancia de Jesús"; 348-366: "El pneûma en la vida pública de
       Jesús"; 16 (1957) 115-159. Esp. 121-126: "La personalidad del pneûma en los evangelios sinopticos".
       [NTA 2, 393]

**GOLDHAHN-MÜLLER, Ingrid**

1989   *Die Grenze der Gemeinde. Studien zum Problem der Zweiten Buße im Neuen Testament
       unter Berücksichtigung der Entwicklung im 2. Jh. bis Tertullian* (Göttinger theologische
       Arbeiten, 39). Göttingen: Vandenhoeck & Ruprecht, 1989, IX-406 p. Esp. 163-196: "Die
       Überwindung der Sünde durch institutionalisiertes Handeln der Gemeinde des Mt" [18,15-20]. — Diss.
       Göttingen, 1987-88 (G. Strecker).

**GOLDINGAY, John**

1977   Expounding the New Testament. — MARSHALL, I.H. (ed.), *New Testament
       Interpretation*, 1977, 351-365. Esp. 352-357 [8,5-13]. → France 1977

1982   The Old Testament and Christian Faith. Jesus and the Old Testament in Matthew 1–5.
       — *Themelios* 8/1 (1982) 4-10; 8/2 (1983) 5-12. [NTA 27, 507/909]

1994   *Models for Scripture*. Grand Rapids, MI: Eerdmans; Carlisle: Paternoster, 1994, XI-420
       p. Esp. 89-92 [4,1-11].

1995   *Models for Interpretation of Scripture*. Grand Rapids, MI: Eerdmans; Carlisle:
       Paternoster, 1995, X-328 p. Esp. 141-151 [1–2].

**GOLDSMITH, Dale**

1989   'Ask, and it will be given...'. Toward Writing the History of a Logion. [7,7-11.12] —
       *NTS* 35 (1989) 254-265. Esp. 255-258: "An independent logion"; 258-263: "Retracing 'steps'"; 262-
       264: "Meaning potential". [NTA 33, 1130]

**GOLLINGER, Hildegard**

1970   "Ihr wißt nicht, an welchem Tag euer Herr kommt". Auslegung von Mt 24,37-51. —
       *BibLeb* 11 (1970) 238-247. Esp. 239-243 [24,37-42]; 243-244 [24,43-44]; 245-247 [24,45-51]. [NTA
       15, 857]

1991   "... und diese Lehre verbreitete sich bei Juden bis heute". Mt 28,11-15 als Beitrag zum
       Verhältnis von Israel und Kirche. — OBERLINNER, L. - FIEDLER, P. (eds.), *Salz der
       Erde*. FS A. Vögtle, 1991, 357-373. Esp. 359-362: "Einige Beobachtungen am Text"; 362-364: "Zu
       Herkunft und Bedeutung der Perikope"; 364-373: "Zur Funktion der Perikope in der Konzeption des
       Matthäus".

**GOLLWITZER, Helmut**

1981   Bergpredigt und Zwei-Reiche-Lehre. — MOLTMANN, J. (ed.), *Nachfolge und
       Bergpredigt*, 1981, 89-120. Esp. 91-96 [Luther]; 96-99 [law].

1983   Die Bergpredigt in der Sicht Luthers. — GEYER, H.-G., et al. (eds.), *"Wenn nicht jetzt, wann dann?" Aufsätze für Hans-Joachim Kraus zum 65. Geburtstag*, Neukirchen-Vluyn: Neukirchener, 1983, 295-304.

**GOMÁ CIVIT, Isidro**

1962   Y les habló en parábolas. [13,1-3] — *CuBíb* 19 (1962) 131-137. [NTA 7, 511]

1963a  La parábola del sembrador. [13,3-9] — *CuBíb* 20 (1963) 33-36. [NTA 8, 135]

1963b  "El que oye la Palabra...". [13,18-23] — *Ibid.*, 263-273. [NTA 8, 945]

1964   La gracia de conocer y entender. [13,10-17] — *CuBíb* 21 (1964) 195-204. [NTA 9, 534]

1966a  *El Evangelio según San Mateo (1-13). Traducción y commentario* (Comentario al Nuevo Testamento, III/1; Colectanea San Paciano, XXII/1). Madrid: Marova, 1966, XXXII-774 p. [NTA 12, p. 256]
       J.A. CARRASCO, *EstJos* 21 (1967) 263-266; J.M. CASCIARO, *EstBíb* 30 (1971) 117-119; B. CELADA, *CuBíb* 25 (1968) 40-42; J.J. DAVIS, *CBQ* 31 (1969) 256; F. DREYFUS, *RB* 76 (1969) 607-608; C. FARINA, *BZ* 12 (1968) 312-313; P. FRANQUESA, *EphMar* 17 (1967) 220-221; M. HACKETT, *Theology* 70 (1967) 372-373; E. LÁKATOS, *RevistBíb* 29 (1967) 183-184; C. LO GIUDICE, *CC* 118/2 (1967) 168; C. MATEOS, *EstAgust* 3 (1968) 144-145; E. RASCO, *Greg* 49 (1968) 762-763; A. SALAS, *CiudDios* 180 (1967) 451-452; C. SOLTERO, *VD* 45 (1967) 181-184; J. SZLAGA, *RuBi* 22 (1969) 52-53; S.S., *BibOr* 9 (1967) 217; G. TESTA, *DivThom* 73 (1970) 364-365; J. VÍLCHEZ, *ArchTeolGran* 30 (1967) 377; J.L. Z., *HeythJ* 10 (1969) 222-223.
       *El Evangelio según San Mateo. Volumen segundo (14-28)* (Comentario al Nuevo Testamento, III/2; Colectanea San Paciano, XXII/2). Madrid: Marova, 1976, XXIII-784 p. [NTA 21, p. 86]
       F. BRÄNDLE, *EstJos* 32 (1978) 100; J.J. DAVIS, *CBQ* 40 (1978) 126; J. ESQUERDA BIFET, *EuntDoc* 29 (1976) 595-596; G.G. GAMBA, *Sal* 40 (1978) 689-690; A. MAZZOLA, *VetChr* 16 (1979) 320-321; F. MONTAGNINI, *RivBib* 25 (1977) 332-334; F. NEIRYNCK, *ETL* 54 (1978) 190-191; F. RAURELL, *RevistCatTeol* 3 (1978) 205-206; A. RODRÍGUEZ CARMONA, *EstBíb* 35 (1976) 119-120; L. SABOURIN, *Bib* 58 (1977) 454-455; *BTB* 8 (1978) 93-94; A. SALAS, *BibFe* 2 (1976) 374-375; J. SANCHEZ BOSCH, *RevistCatTeol* 1 (1976) 531-534; A. SEGOVIA, *ArchTeolGran* 39 (1979) 280-281.

1966b  Sous le regard de Dieu. [6,1-6.16-18] — *AssSeign* I/25 (1966) 33-45.

1970   Fraternité et service pastoral. Mt 23,1-12. — *AssSeign* II/62 (1970) 21-32.

1972   Esprit et ordre dans la famille de Dieu. Mt 18,15-20. — *AssSeign* II/54 (1972) 16-26.

1976   → 1966a

**GOMES, M.**

1950   A argumentação de Jesus no Sermão da montanha. — *REB* 10 (1950) 333-352.

**GONNET, Giovanni**

1986   L'incidence du Sermon de la montagne sur l'éthique des Vaudois du moyen âge. — *ComViat* 29 (1986) 119-127.
       The Influence of the Sermon on the Mount Upon the Ethics of the Waldensians in the Middle Ages. — *Brethren Life and Thought* (Chicago, IL) 35 (1990) 34-40.

**GONZÁLEZ, A.**

1969   Prière. — *DBS* 8/44 (1969) 555-606. Esp. 597-599 [Lord's prayer].

**GONZÁLEZ, N.**

1965   En torno al Jesús de Pasolini. — *RazFe* 171 (1965) 629-634. [NTA 10, 107]

**GONZÁLEZ ECHEGARAY, Joaquín**

1992   Las tres ciudades de los Evangelios de la Infancia de Jesús: Nazaret, Belén y Jerusalén. — *EstBíb* 50 (1992) 85-102. Esp. 86-89: "Nazaret"; 89-93: "Belén"; 93-99: "Jerusalén".

**GONZÁLEZ FAUS, José Ignacio**

1972  Las tentaciones de Jesús y la tentación cristiana. [4,1-11] — *EstE* 47 (1972) 155-188. Esp. 158-166: "Aproximación historica"; 169-183 [theology]. [NTA 17, 140]

1977  Jesús y los demonios. Introducción cristológica a la lucha por la justicia. — *EstE* 52 (1977) 487-519. Esp. 500-510 [exorcisms]. [NTA 22, 731]

1982  *Clamor del Reino. Estudio sobre los milagros de Jesús* (Verdad e Imagen, 79). Salamanca: Sígueme, 1982, 214 p.

1990  La autoridad de Jesús. — *Revista Latinoamericana de Teologia* (San Salvador) 7 (1990) 189-206. [NTA 37, 1203]

1992  Jesús y la mentira. — *Revista Latinoamericana de Teologia* 9 (1992) 231-242. [NTA 37, 1204]

1993  Hacia una cultura del perdón. La misericordia y las bienaventuranzas como carta magna del creyente. — *Revista Latinoamericana de Teologia* 10 (1993) 171-187. [NTA 38, 755]

**GONZÁLEZ GARCÍA, Faustino**

1990  Oralidad y textualidad en la composición de Mc. Aproximación a la teoría de Werner H. Kelber. — *EstBíb* 48 (1990) 351-373. Esp. 367-370 [Q]. [NTA 36, 164] → W.H. Kelber 1983

**GONZÁLEZ LAMADRID, Antonio**

1958  Género escatológico-apocalíptico en los Evangelios. — *Generos literarios en los evangelios. Otros estudios* (XVII Semana Biblica Española), Madrid: Consejo Superior de Investigaciones Científicas, 1958, 115-132. Esp. 126-129.

**GONZÁLEZ RAPOSO, J.**

1987  As mulheres na genealogia de Jesus Cristo no evangelho segundo são Mateus. [1,1-17] — *RevistCuBíb* 11 (1987) 59-68.

**GONZÁLEZ RUIZ, José María**

1952  El divorcio en Mt. 5,32 y 19,9. — *La enciclica Humani generis* (XII Semana Biblica Española), Madrid: Consejo Superior de Investigaciones Científicas, 1952, 513-528. Esp. 515-518: "Cuestiones críticas"; 518-520: "Historia de la exégesis"; 521-527: "Principios de solución".

1977  El divorci en el Nou Testament. — *QüestVidaCr* 86 (1977) 19-30.

1983  *Mateo. El judaísmo se realiza en el cristianismo.* Madrid: Católica, 1983, 59 p.

**GONZÁLEZ SILVA, Santiago**

1974  El seguimiento de Cristo en los logia ἀκολουθεῖν. — *Claretianum* (Roma) 14 (1974) 115-162. Esp. 119-124 [16,24]; 124-126 [10,38]; 127-135 [19,21]; 135-147 [19,28].

**GOOCH, Peter** → P. Richardson 1985

**GOOD, Deirdre**

1990  The Verb ἀναχωρέω in Matthew's Gospel. — *NT* 32 (1990) 1-12. Esp. 1-2 [2,12-15.22-23]; 2-3 [4,12-18]; 3-4 [12,15-21]; 4 [14,12-14]; 4-5 [15,21-28; 27,5-10]. [NTA 34, 1122]

1991  The Canaanite Woman: Patristic Exegesis of *Matthew* 15,21-28. — *Figures du Nouveau Testament chez les Pères* (Cahiers de Biblia Patristica, 3), Strasbourg: Centre d'analyse et de documentation patristiques, 1991, 169-177.

**GOODACRE, Mark S.**

1996  *Goulder and the Gospels: An Examination of a New Paradigm* (JSNT SS, 133). Sheffield: JSOT, 1996, 416 p. Esp. 17-39: "Goulder and his critics"; 42-88: "QC words and characteristic vocabulary"; 89-130: "The minor agreements and characteristic language"; 131-291: "Luke's special material"; 293-369: "The lectionary theory". — Diss. Oxford, 1994 (J. Muddiman). → Neirynck 1997a

**GOODING, D.W.**

1978 Structure littéraire de Matthieu, XIII,53 à XVIII,35. — *RB* 85 (1978) 227-252. [NTA 23, 829] → Murphy-O'Connor 1975

**GOODMAN, F.W.**

1961 Sources of the First Two Chapters in Matthew and Luke. — *ChurchQR* 162 (1961) 136-143. [NTA 6, 117]

**GOODRICK, E.W.** → Kohlenberger 1995

**GOODSPEED, Edgar J.**

1952 Problems of New Testament Translation. — *BTrans* 3 (1952) 68-71. Esp. 68-69 [21,9].

1959 *Matthew, Apostle and Evangelist.* Philadelphia, PA: Winston, 1959, X-166 p. [NTA 4, p. 97]

 M.J. GIACCHI, *BibOr* 4 (1962) 77-78; C.F. NESBITT, *Interpr* 14 (1960) 111-112.

**GOPPELT, Leonhard**

1939[R] *Typos. Die typologische Deutung des Alten Testaments im Neuen* [1939] (Beiträge zur Förderung christlicher Theologie, II/43). Gütersloh: Bertelsmann, [2]1969, IX-255 p. Esp. 70-126: "Jesus Christus"; Darmstadt: Wissenschaftliche Buchgesellschaft, 1973, XI-299 p. *Typos. The Typological Interpretation of the Old Testament in the New*, trans. D.H. Madvig. Grand Rapids, MI: Eerdmans, 1982, XXIII-264 p.

1954 *Christentum und Judentum im ersten und zweiten Jahrhundert. Ein Aufriss der Urgemeinde der Kirche* (Beiträge zur Förderung christlicher Theologie, II/55). Gütersloh: Bertelsmann, 1954, XI-328 p. Esp. 30-70: "Jesus und das Judentum". *Les origines de l'Église. Christianisme et judaïsme aux deux premiers siècles* (Bibliothèque historique). Paris: Payot, 1961, 293 p. *Jesus, Paul and Judaism. An Introduction to New Testament Theology*, trans. E. Schroeder. New York: Nelson, 1964, 192 p. (= 1954, first part). Esp. 39-96.

1960 Der verborgene Messias. Zu der Frage nach dem geschichtlichen Jesus. — RISTOW, H. - MATTHIAE, K. (eds.), *Der historische Jesus und der kerygmatische Christus*, 1960, 371-384. Esp. 377-381; = ID., *Christologie und Ethik*, 1968, 11-26. Esp. 19-23.

1963 Zum Problem des Menschensohns. Das Verhältnis von Leidens- und Parusieankündigung. — SIERIG, H. (ed.), *Mensch und Menschensohn. Festschrift für Bischof Professor D Karl Witte*, Hamburg: Wittig, 1963, 20-32. Esp. 21-22.28-30 [Q]; = ID., *Christologie und Ethik*, 1968, 66-78. Esp. 67-68; 73-75.

1967 Die Herrschaft Christi und die Welt. — *LuthRundschau* 17 (1967) 22-50. Esp. 23-28; = ID., *Christologie und Ethik*, 1968, 102-136. Esp. 103-103.

1968a *Die Bergpredigt und die Wirklichkeit dieser Welt* (Calwer Hefte, 96). Stuttgart: Calwer, 1968, 32 p. Das Problem der Bergpredigt. Jesu Gebot und die Wirklichkeit dieser Welt. — ID., *Christologie und Ethik*, 1968, 27-43. Esp. 33-36 [5,17-20]; 27-33.36-43 [5,21-48].

1968b *Christologie und Ethik. Aufsätze zum Neuen Testament.* Göttingen: Vandenhoeck & Ruprecht, 1968, 276 p. → 1960, 1963, 1967, 1968a.c

1968c Begründung des Glaubens durch Jesus. — *Ibid.*, 44-65. Esp. 47-50.

1975 *Theologie des Neuen Testaments. Erster Teil: Jesu Wirken in seiner theologischen Bedeutung*, ed. J. Roloff. Göttingen: Vandenhoeck & Ruprecht, 1975, 312 p.; Zweiter Teil: *Vielfalt und Einheit des apostolischen Christuszeugnisses*, 1977, 313-669 p.; [3]1980 (in one vol.). Esp. 62-65: "Die Quellen"; 94-127: "Das Kommen der Gottesherrschaft"; 128-170: "Die Umkehr als Forderung (Die ethischen Weisungen Jesu)"; 171-188: "Die Umkehr als Geschenk der Gottesherrschaft"; 189-206: "Jesu Heilswirken als Ausdruck der eschatologischen Erneuerung"; 207-253: "Das Selbstverständnis Jesu"; 254-270: "Jesus und die Kirche"; 271-299: "Jesu Ausgang"; 543-568: "Die

Deutung der Erscheinung Jesu durch Matthäus".

*Theology of the New Testament*. Volume One: *The Ministry of Jesus in its Theological Significance.* trans. J.E. Alsup. Grand Rapids, MI: Eerdmans, 1981, XXVI-292 p.

Trans. Portuguese 1976 (I), 1988 (II); Spanish 1982 (I-II), ³1988 (I).

### GORDINI, G.D.

1967    & RAGGI, A.M., Magi, adoratori di Gesù, santi. [2,1-12] — *Bibl. Sanct. Lateran.* 8 (1967) 494-528.

### GORDON, Barry

1989    *The Economic Problem in Biblical and Patristic Thought* (Supplements to Vigiliae Christianae, 9). Leiden: Brill, 1989, X-144 p. Esp. 43-47: "The Sermon on the Mount"; 50-51.57-58 [labour]; 70-76 [wealth].

### GORDON, Cyrus H.

1977    Paternity at Two Levels. [1,1-16] — *JBL* 96 (1977) 101. [NTA 21, 718]

1978    The Double Paternity of Jesus. — *BibArchRev* 4/2 (1978) 26-27. [NTA 23, 90]

### GORDON, T. David

1994    Critique of Theonomy: A Taxonomy. — *WestTJ* 56 (1994) 23-43. Esp. 28-33 [5,17-20]. [NTA 39, 142]

### GORI, Franco

1986    La bontà di Dio nell'esegesi gnostica di Mc 10,18 (e paralleli). — *AnStoEseg* 3 (1986) 163-171.

1987    Dio, sommo bene, nell'esegesi patristica di Mc 10,18 (e paralleli). — *AnStoEseg* 4 (1987) 21-66.

### GORMAN, Frank H.

1989    When Law Becomes Gospel: Matthew's Transformed Torah. — *Listening* 24 (1989) 227-240. Esp. 235-238: "Law in the Gospel of Matthew". [NTA 34, 601]

### GOUDOTE, Benoît

1986    Ponce Pilate, Procurator Provinciae Judaeae. — *Apollinaris* 59 (1986) 335-368; 66 (1993) 613-652; 67 (1994) 207-318. Esp. 266-302.

### GOULD, Graham E.

1989    Basil of Caesarea and Gregory of Nyssa on the Beatitudes. — *Studia Patristica* 23 (1989) 14-22.

### GOULDER, Michael D.

1963    The Composition of the Lord's Prayer. — *JTS* 14 (1963) 32-45. [NTA 8, 131]

1968    Characteristics of the Parables in the Several Gospels. — *JTS* 19 (1968) 51-69. [NTA 13, 140]

1974    *Midrash and Lection in Matthew* (The Speaker's Lectures in Biblical Studies, 1969-71). London: SPCK, 1974, XV-528 p. Esp. 3-27: "A scribe discipled"; 28-46: "The midrashic method"; 47-69: "The midrashic parable"; 70-94: "Matthew's poetry"; 95-115: "Matthaean imagery"; 116-136: "Language and use of Scripture"; 139-152: "The non-Marcan traditions"; 153-170: "Matthew and Paul"; 171-201: "Matthew and the Jewish year"; 227-249 [1-4]; 250-269 [5-7]; 270-289 [5,3-26]; 290-311 [5,27-7,27]; 312-337 [8-9; 12]; 338-363 [10-11]; 364-382 [13-16,12]; 383-406 [16,13-19]; 407-430 [20-23]; 431-451 [24-28]; 452-473: "Luke's use of Mark and Matthew"; 476-485: "Matthew's vocabulary". [NTA 20, p. 107]
→ P.S. Alexander 1984, Dermience 1985, Derrett 1975b, C.F. Evans 1979, Morris 1983
   G. ASHBY, *JTSouthAfr* 12 (1975) 73-74; D.R. CATCHPOLE, *EvQ* 47 (1975) 239-240; R. CROTTY, *AusBR* 23 (1975) 44; B. GERHARDSSON, *SEÅ* 45 (1980) 147-149; A.E. HARVEY, *JTS* 27 (1976) 188-195; C.L. MITTON, *ExpT* 86 (1974-75) 97-99.192; J. MURPHY-O'CONNOR, *RB* 83 (1976) 304-305; B.M. NOLAN, *IrTQ* 42 (1975) 223-225; J. ROLOFF, *TLZ* 103 (1978) 589-591; L. SABOURIN, *BTB* 6 (1976) 91-93; E.P.

SANDERS, *JBL* 96 (1977) 453-455; J.A. SANDERS, *Interpr* 30 (1976) 91.94; J.A. SHERLOCK, *TS* 36 (1975) 338-340; M. SMITH, *JAAR* 43 (1975) 604.606. A. SNELL, *RTR* 33 (1974) 84-86; G.N. STANTON, *Themelios* 1 (1975-76) 31-32.

1978a  *The Evangelists' Calendar. A Lectionary Explanation of the Development of Scripture* (The Speaker's Lectures in Biblical Studies, 1972). London: SPCK, 1978, XIV-334 p. Esp. 48-50; 212-240: "Matthew, the O.T. cycles and the Epistle". [NTA 24, p. 188] → C.F. Evans 1979

1978b  On Putting Q to the Test. — *NTS* 24 (1977-78) 218-234. Esp. 219-221 [4,13; 13,54]; 221-222 [4,13-22]; 222-223 [9,2]; 223-224 [10,2]; 224-225 [11,10]; 226 [10,1; 17,5]; 226-228 [26,67-68]; 228-229 [26,75]; 229-230 [27,1]; 230-231 [27,59-60]; 231-233 [28,1]. [NTA 22. 385] → Neirynck 1982d, Romaniuk 1982, Tuckett 1984c

1978c  Mark xvi.1-8 and Parallels. — *Ibid.*, 235-240. Esp. 235 [28,1-10/Mk]; 236-240 [28,1-10/Lk]. [NTA 22, 417]

1980  Farrer on Q. — *Theology* 83 (1980) 190-195. [NTA 25, 56]

1983  → Tuckett 1983b

1984a  Some Observations on Professor Farmer's "Certain Results...". — TUCKETT, C.M. (ed.), *Synoptic Studies*, 1984, 99-104. → W.R. Farmer 1984a-b

1984b  The Order of a Crank. — *Ibid.*, 111-130.

1985  A House Built on Sand. — HARVEY, A.E. (ed.), *Alternative Approaches to New Testament Study*, 1985, 1-24. Esp. 7-11: "The Matthaean vocabulary fallacy"; 16-22: "An alternative paradigm"; = ID., *Luke*, 1989, 3-26.179-182. Esp. 11-15; 22-26.

1989  *Luke. A New Paradigm*. Vol. I: *The Argument. Commentary Luke 1.1–9.50*; Vol. II: *Commentary Luke 9.51–24.53* (JSNT SS, 20). Sheffield: JSOT, 1989, 2 vols. XI-452 and 453-824 p. Esp. 27-71.182-188: "Q"; 147-177.192-194: "The calendar in the synoptics". → 1985; → Downing 1992b, Neirynck 1989a
       F. NEIRYNCK, *ETL* 67 (1991) 434-436.

1992a  John 1,1–2,12 and the Synoptics. — DENAUX, A. (ed.), *John and the Synoptics*, 1992, 201-237. Esp. 224-226 [21,12/Jn 2,14-15; 26,61/Jn 2,19]; 235-237 [8,5-13/Jn 4,43-54].

1992b  Translation and Exegesis. Some Reflections on the Swedish Translations of 1917 and 1981. — *SEÅ* 57 (1992) 102-114. Esp. 102-103 [6,22]. [NTA 37, 628]

1993a  Luke's Compositional Options. — *NTS* 39 (1993) 150-152. [NTA 37, 1303] → Downing 1992b

1993b  Luke's Knowledge of Matthew. — STRECKER, G. (ed.), *Minor Agreements*, 1993, 143-162. Esp. 144-150 [4,12-17]; 150 [9,2]; 150-151 [10,2]; 151-152 [11,10]; 153-155 [26,67-68]; 155-156 [26,75]; 156-158 [27,58-61]; 158-159 [28,1]. → Tuckett 1993c

1994  Already? — SCHMIDT, T.E. - SILVA, M. (eds.), *To Tell the Mystery*. FS R.H. Gundry, 1994, 21-33. Esp. 28-33 [eschatology].

## GOURGUES, Michel

1978  *À la droite de Dieu. Résurrection de Jésus et actualisation du Psaume 110:1 dans le Nouveau Testament* (Études bibliques). Paris: Gabalda, 1978, 270 p. Esp. 127-143 [22,44]; 143-163 [26,64]. [NTA 23, 242] — Diss. Paris, 1976 (P. Grelot - C. Perrot).

1979a  *Jésus devant sa passion et sa mort* (Cahiers Évangile, 30). Paris: Cerf, 1979, 64 p. Esp. 48-50 [11,19]; 50-51 [11,25].
       *Jesús ante su pasión y su muerte*. Estella: Verbo Divino, 1980, 63 p.
       *Gesù davanti alla sua passione e alla sua morte*. Torino: Gribaudi, 1981, 60 p.
       *Jesus diante de sua paixão e morte*. São Paulo: Paulinas, 1985.

1979b  Jésus et la violence. — *SE* 31 (1979) 125-146. Esp. 135-145: "Essai d'inventaire et de regroupement des données synoptiques". [NTA 23, 788]

1985a  *Le défi de la fidélité. L'expérience de Jésus* (Lire la Bible, 70). Paris: Cerf, 1985, 143 p. Esp. 19-53: "La tentation au désert ou l'option de départ (Mc 1 12s. par.)".
       *La sfida della fedeltà. L'esperienza di Gesù*. Roma: Borla, 1987, 148 p.

1985b Deux miracles, deux démarches de foi (Marc 5,21-43 par.). — GANTOY, R. (ed.), *À cause de l'Évangile*. FS J. Dupont, 1985, 229-249. Esp. 231-232: "Le récit de Matthieu" [9,18-26].

1987 Halakâh et Haggadâh chrétiennes. Les indications de Marc 2,23-28 et parallèles (les épis arrachés) sur le "sens chrétien de l'Ancien Testament". — CAZELLES, H. (ed.), *La vie de la Parole*. FS P. Grelot, 1987, 195-209. Esp. 204-205 [12,5-6]; 206-208 [12,7].

1989 *Le Crucifié. Du scandale à l'exaltation* (Collection "Jésus et Jésus Christ", 38). Paris: Desclée; Montréal: Bellarmin, 1989, 178 p. Esp. 31-39 [26–27]; 147-153 [16,24]; 153-156 [10,38].

1993 Le bonheur des Béatitudes est-il "exportable"? [5,3-12] — *VSp* 147 (1993) 547-560.

1994 "Il entendit de son temple ma voix". Échos du "cantique de David" (Ps 18 = 2S 22) en *Mt* 27,50-51 et dans le Nouveau Testament. — PETIT, J.-C. – CHARRON, A. – MYRE, A. (eds.), *"Où demeures-tu?" (Jn 1,38). La maison depuis le monde biblique. En hommage au professeur Guy Couturier à l'occasion de ses soixante-cinq ans*, Montréal: Fides, 1994, 323-341. Esp. 326-333.

1995 *Foi, bonheur et sens de la vie. Relire aujourd'hui les béatitudes* (Lire la Bible, 42). Montréal/Paris: Médiaspaul, 1995, 102 p.

**GOVENDER, Shun**

1987 The Sermon on the Mount (Matt 5-7) and the Question of Ethics. — TLHAGALE, B. – MOSALA, I. (eds.), *Hammering Swords into Ploughshares. Essays in Honor of Archbishop Mpilo Desmond Tutu*, Grand Rapids, MI: Eerdmans; Trenton, NJ: Africa World Press, 1987, 173-184.

**GRADARA, R.**

1992 *Matteo: il Vangelo della comunità*. Bologna: Dehoniane, 1992, 92 p. [NTA 37, p. 278]

**GRADY, L. Augustine**

1970 *The History of the Exegesis of Matthew 27.25: A Study of Early Medieval Commentaries (650-1000) on Matthew's Gospel*. Diss. Fordham Univ., Bronx, NY, 1970, 307 p. — *DissAbstr* 31 (1971) 5508-5509.

**GRAEF, Hilda C.**

1954 (trans.), *St. Gregory of Nyssa: The Lord's Prayer – The Beatitudes* (Ancient Christian Writers, 18). Westminster, MD: Newman; London: Longman–Green, 1954, VI-210 p. *LumièreV* 22 (1953) 31; E. BOULARAND, *BullLitEccl* 57 (1956) 49-50; J.L. MCKENZIE, *CBQ* 16 (1954) 381; R. WEIJENBORG, *Ant* 33 (1958) 164-165.

**GRÄSSER, Erich**

1957 *Das Problem der Parusieverzögerung in den synoptischen Evangelien und in der Apostelgeschichte* (BZNW, 22). Berlin: Töpelmann, 1957, VIII-234 p. Esp. 95-113 [6,9-15]; 113-127 [24,42–25,30]; 128-131 [24,34]; 131-137 [16,28]; 137-141 [10,23]; 141-149 [13,3-9.24-30.31-33.47-50]; 152-170 [24]; 2nd rev. ed., 1960, VIII-256 p.; Berlin: de Gruyter, 3rd enl. ed., 1977, XXXIV-237 p. — Diss. Marburg, 1955 (W.G. Kümmel). → Gnilka 1959b

1973a *Die Naherwartung Jesu* (SBS, 61). Stuttgart: Katholisches Bibelwerk, 1973, 146 p. Esp. 17-23 [24,43-51; 25,1-13]; 109-112 [23,37-39].

1973b Nachfolge und Anfechtung bei den Synoptikern. — ALSEN, V., et al. (eds.), *Angefochtene Nachfolge. Beiträge zur theologischen Woche 1972* (Bethel, 11), Bethel: Verlagshandlung der Anstalt, 1973, 44-57. Esp. 48-52 [Q 9,57-60; 14,27]; = ID., *Der Alte Bund im Neuen*, 1985, 168-182. Esp. 172-176.

1974 Zum Verständnis der Gottesherrschaft. — *ZNW* 65 (1974) 3-26. Esp. 7-11 [12,28]. [NTA 19, 489]

On Understanding the Kingdom of God. — CHILTON, B.D. (ed.), *The Kingdom of God*, 1984, 52-71. Esp. 54-56.

1975 Jesus und das Heil Gottes. Bemerkungen zur sog. "Individualisierung des Heils". — STRECKER, G. (ed.), *Jesus Christus in Historie und Theologie*. FS H. Conzelmann, 1975, 167-184. Esp. 176-178 [15,24]; = ID., *Der Alte Bund im Neuen*, 1985, 183-200. Esp. 192-194.

1979 Neutestamentliche Grundlagen des Papsttums? Ein Diskussionsbeitrag. — *Papsttum als ökumenische Frage*, München: Kaiser; Mainz: Matthias–Grünewald, 1979, 33-58. Esp. 39-43 [16,18-19].

1984 Rechtfertigung des Einzelnen – Rechtfertigung der Welt: Neutestamentliche Erwägungen. — WEINRICH, W.C. (ed.), *The New Testament Age*. FS B. Reicke, 1984, I, 221-236. Esp. 225-230.

1985 *Der Alte Bund im Neuen. Exegetische Studien zur Israelfrage im Neuen Testament* (WUNT, 35). Tübingen: Mohr, 1985, VIII-345 p. → 1975b, 1975

**GRAF, Ernest**
1952 Exit "Q". — *HomPastR* 53 (1952) 143-146. → Butler 1957

**GRAFFI, Adrian**
1984 *A Prophet Confronts His People. The Disputation Speech in the Prophets* (AnBib, 104). Roma: Biblical Institute Press, 1984, XI-148 p. Esp. 124-129: "Disputation speeches of the prophet Jesus?" [5,21-48].

**GRAGG, Douglas Lloyd**
1990 *The Parable of the Workers in the Vineyard and Its Use in the Gospel of Matthew*. Diss. Emory Univ., 1990, 222 p. (H. Boers). — *DissAbstr* 51 (1990-91) 3434.

**GRAHAM, Eric**
1961 The Temptation in the Wilderness. — *ChurchQR* 162 (1961) 17-32. [NTA 6, 118]

**GRAHAM, Holt Hutton**
1951 Community in the Synoptic Gospels. — JOHNSON, S.E. (ed.), *The Joy of Study. Papers on New Testament and Related Subjects Presented to Honor Frederick Clifton Grant*, New York: Macmillan, 1951, 31-42. Esp. 35-40 [community]; 40-42 [Kingdom].

1959 *The Reflection of the Church in Mark, Matthew, Paul's Letters and Acts*. Diss. Union Theol. Sem., New York, 1959, 154 p.

**GRAHAM, Susan Lochrie**
1997 A Strange Salvation. Intertextual Allusion in Mt 27,39-44. — TUCKETT, C.M. (ed.), *The Scriptures in the Gospels*, 1997, 501-511.

**GRAHAM, W.F.**
1968 *The Secret of Happiness. Jesus' Teaching on Happiness as Expressed in the Beatitudes* (Waymark Books, W9). Garden City, NY: Doubleday, 1968, 117 p.

**GRAMS, Rollin**
1991 The Temple Conflict Scene: A Rhetorical Analysis of Matthew 21–23. — WATSON, D.F. (ed.), *Persuasive Artistry*. FS G.A. Kennedy, 1991, 41-65. Esp. 42-47: "An overview of Matthew's rhetoric: invention, arrangement, and style"; 47-64: "Rhetorical analysis of the Temple conflict scene (Mt. 21–23)".

**GRANADO BELLIDO, Carmelo**
1980 La oración de Jesús. [11,25-26] — *Proyección* (Granada) 27 (1980) 3-9.

**GRANADOS FERNÁNDEZ, Consolación**

1981 ¿Mateo evangelista en Macrobio, Sat. II 4,11? — *Emerita* (Madrid) 49 (1981) 361-363.

1985 Macrobius y la Biblia. [12,10-12] — *Emerita* 53 (1985) 115-125.

**GRANATA, Giovanni**

1982 La 'sinapis' del Vangelo: Nicotiana glauca Graham o senape nera? [13,31-32] — *BibOr* 24 (1982) 175-177. [NTA 27, 520] → Pace 1980

1983 Some More Information about Mustard and the Gospel. [13,31-32] — *BibOr* 25 (1983) 105-106. [NTA 28, 96]

**GRÁNDEZ, Rufino Maria**

1989 Las tinieblas en la muerte de Jesús. Historia de la exégesis de Lc 23,44-45a (Mt 27,45; Mc 15,33). — *EstBíb* 47 (1989) 177-223. Esp. 180-185 [patristic-medieval age]; 186-198 [16-18th cent.]; 198-201 [hellenism]; 201-209 [19th cent.]; 210-218 [20th cent.]. [NTA 34, 673]

**GRANFIELD, Patrick**

1970* & JUNGMANN, J.A. (eds.), *Kyriakon. Festschrift Johannes Quasten*. Münster: Aschendorff, 1970, 2 vols., 498 and 499-972 p. → Cremer, McNally, B.M. Metzger, Musurillo, Quacquarelli

**GRANGER, John Wayne**

1990 *Matthew's Use of Apocalyptic*. Diss. New Orleans Baptist Theological Seminary, 1990, 188 p. (B.E. Simmons). — *DissAbstr* 52 (1991-92) 185.

**GRANT, Frederick Clifton**

1953 What is Exegesis? A Study of Matthew 5:3. — AUSEKLIS. Societas theologorum Universitatis Latviensis (ed.), *Spiritus et Veritas*. [FS K. Kundziņš], Eutin: Ozolin, 1953, 75-82.

1954 The Authenticity of Jesus' Sayings. — ELTESTER, W. (ed.), *Neutestamentliche Studien*. FS R. Bultmann, 1954, 137-143.

1955 *The Gospel of Matthew in the King James Version with Introduction and Critical Notes* (Harper's Annotated Bible Series, 10-11). New York: Harper & Brothers, 1955, 2 vols., 69 and 61 p.
    J.B. CLOWER, JR., *Interpr* 9 (1955) 475-476; S.E. JOHNSON, *ATR* 37 (1955) 143-145.

1957 *The Gospels. Their Origin and Their Growth*. New York: Harper; London: Faber & Faber, 1957, VIII-216 p. Esp. 134-153: "The ecclesiastical gospel: Matthew".

1962a (ed.), *New Testament. Matthew–Acts* (Nelson's Bible Commentary Based on the Revised Standard Version, 6). New York – Edinburgh: Nelson, 1962, 518 p.

1962b Biblical Theology and the Synoptic Problem. — KLASSEN, W. - SNYDER, G.F. (eds.), *Current Issues in New Testament Interpretation. Essays in Honor of Otto A. Piper*, New York: Harper; London: SCM, 1962, 79-90. Esp. 83-85 [jewishness]; 86-87 [Q].

1962c Matthew, Gospel of. — *IDB* 3 (1962) 302-313.

**GRANT, Michael**

1977 *Jesus*. London: Weidenfeld and Nicholson, 1977, 261 p. Esp. 184-188 [sources of Mt].

**GRANT, Robert M.**

1960 & FREEDMAN, D.N., *The Secret Sayings of Jesus*. Garden City, NY: Doubleday, 1960, 206 p.
    *Die Geheime Worte Jesu. Das Thomas-Evangelium*, trans. S. George (& H. Quecke). Frankfurt/M: Scheffler, 1960, 228 p. Esp. 114-180: "Das Thomas-Evangelium: Übersetzung und Kommentar".

*Het Thomas-evangelie. Vertaling en toelichting*, trans. J. Mooy (Aula-boeken, 87). Utrecht: Spectrum, 1962, 190 p.

1961 *The Earliest Lives of Jesus.* London: SPCK, 1961, IX-134 p. Esp. 50-79: "Origen and the gospels"; 80-110: "Origen and the life of Jesus".

1963a *A Historical Introduction to the New Testament.* New York – Evanston, IL: Harper & Row, 1963, 447 p. Esp. 113-117: "Q"; 127-132: "The gospel of Matthew".
*Introduction historique au Nouveau Testament* (Bibliothèque historique). Paris: Payot, 1969, 357 p.

1963b Scripture and Tradition in St. Ignatius of Antioch. — *CBQ* 25 (1963) 322-335. Esp. 325-327. [NTA 8, 327]; = ID., *After the New Testament*, Philadelphia, PA: Fortress, 1967, 37-54. Esp. 41-43.

1965 *The Formation of the New Testament.* New York: Harper & Row, 1965, 194 p. Esp. 65-68; 100-101; 127-128; 146-147; 152-154; 176-177.
*La formazione del Nuovo Testamento.* Brescia: Paideia, 1973.

1978 The Sermon on the Mount in Early Christianity. — *Semeia* 12 (1978) 215-231. [NTA 23, 430]

**GRAPPE, Christian**

1992a *D'un Temple à l'autre. Pierre et l'Église primitive de Jérusalem* (Études d'histoire et de philosophie religieuses, 71). Paris: PUF, 1992, 371 p. Esp. 93-103 [16,18/OT]; 103-112 [16,17-19]; 177-179 [16,21-23]; 226-229 [14,28-31]. — Diss. Strasbourg, 1989 (É. Trocmé).

1992b Mt 16,17-19 et le récit de la Passion. — *RHPR* 72 (1992) 33-40. [NTA 36, 1276]

1993 Le logion des douze trônes. Éclairages intertestamentaires. — PHILONENKO, M. (ed.), *Le Trône de Dieu* (WUNT, 69), Tübingen: Mohr, 1993, 204-212. Esp. 204-210 [19,28].

1995 *Images de Pierre aux deux premiers siècles* (Études d'histoire et de philosophie religieuses, 75). Paris: PUF, 1995, 349 p.

**GRASS, Hans**

1956 *Ostergeschehen und Osterberichte.* Göttingen: Vandenhoeck & Ruprecht, 1956, 301 p.; ²1962, 346 p. ("Nachträge", 289-328). Esp. 23-32: "Die Ostergeschichten des Matthäus"; 173-183 [27,57-58]; ⁴1970.

**GRASSI, Joseph A.**

1964a Emmaus Revisited (Luke 24,13-35 and Acts 8,26-40). — *CBQ* 26 (1964) 463-467. Esp. 465-466 [25,31-46]. [NTA 9, 572]

1964b The Five Loaves of the High Priest (Mt xii,1-8; Mk ii,23-28; Lk vi,1-5; I Sam xxi,1-6). — *NT* 7 (1964-65) 119-122. [NTA 9, 909]

1965 Ezekiel xxxvii.1-14 and the New Testament. [27,51-54] — *NTS* 11 (1964-65) 162-164. [NTA 9, 894]

1967a Beatitudes (in the Bible). — *NewCathEnc* 2 (1967) 193-195.

1967b Our Father. — *NewCathEnc* 10 (1967) 829-831.

1967c Sermon on the Mount. — *NewCathEnc* 13 (1967) 119-121.

1975 *Underground Christians in the Earliest Church.* Santa Clara, CA: Diakonia, 1975, 142 p. Esp. 57-72: "Matthew: conflict in a divided community".

1977 The Last Testament-Succession. Literary Background of Matthew 9:35–11:1 and its Significance. — *BTB* 7 (1977) 172-176. [NTA 22, 399]

1978 "You yourselves give them to eat". An Easily Forgotten Command of Jesus (Mk. 6:37; Mt. 14:16; Lk. 9:13). — *BiTod* 97 (1978) 1704-1709. [NTA 23, 116]

1981 "I was hungry and you gave me to eat." (Matt. 25:35ff). The Divine Identification Ethic in Matthew. — *BTB* 11 (1981) 81-84. [NTA 26, 99]

1987    *Rediscovering the Impact of Jesus' Death. Clues From the Gospel Audiences*. Kansas City, MO: Sheed & Ward, 1987, II-123 p.

1989a   *The Hidden Heroes of the Gospels. Female Counterparts of Jesus*. Collegeville, MN: Liturgical Press, 1989, 143 p.

1989b   Matthew as a Second Testament Deuteronomy. [24,14; 26,13] — *BTB* 19 (1989) 23-29. [NTA 33, 1109]

1989c   Matthew's Gospel as Live Performance. — *BiTod* 27 (1989) 225-232. [NTA 34, 105]

1991    *Loaves and Fishes: The Gospel Feeding Narratives* (Zacchaeus Studies: New Testament). Collegeville, MN: Liturgical Press, 1991, 104 p. Esp. 6-11: "The four feeding narratives"; 51-60: "The Matthaean version: the teacher and the giver of bread".

1992    Child, Children. — *ABD* 1 (1992) 904-907. Esp. 906.

**GRASSO, Domenico**

1951    "Tu es Petrus". Questioni sul primato. — *CC* 102/4 (1951) 637-650.

**GRASSO, Santi**

1994    *Gesù e i suoi fratelli. Contributo allo studio della cristologia e dell'antropologia nel Vangelo di Matteo* (Supplementi alla Rivista Biblica, 29). Bologna: Dehoniane, 1994, 307 p. Esp. 15-77: "Gesù e i suoi fratelli. Mt 12,46-50"; 79-141: "Il figlio dell'uomo e i suoi fratelli. Mt 25,31-46"; 143-194: "Il risorto e i suoi fratelli. Mt 28,1-10"; 195-236: "Prospettive della fraternità nel Vangelo di Matteo". [NTA 39, p. 138] — Diss. Pont. Inst. Bibl., Roma, 1991 (K. Stock).
         M. GRILLI, *CC* 146/3 (1995) 545-546; G. LEONARDI, *ParVi* 39/4 (1994) 55-56; F. MARTÍNEZ, *Carthaginensia* 11 (1995) 436-437; J. PELAEZ, *FilolNT* 16 (1995) 235; E. VALLAURI, *RivBib* 43 (1995) 294-295.

1995    *Il Vangelo di Matteo* (Collana Biblica). Roma: Dehoniane, 1995, 696 p.
         J.M. DIAZ RODELAS, *EstBíb* 55 (1997) 550-552.

**GRAVES, Thomas H.**

1987    A Story Ignored. An Exegesis of Matthew 2:13-23. — *Faith and Mission* (Wake Forest, NC) 5/1 (1987) 66-76. [NTA 32, 581]

1989    Matthew 1:1-17. — *RExp* 86 (1989) 595-600.

**GRAY, James R.**

1991    *Prophecy on the Mount* [24]. Chandler, AZ: Borean Advocate Ministries, 1991, 141 p.
         J.F. WALVOORD, *BS* 149 (1992) 250-251.

**GRAY, John**

1979    *The Biblical Doctrine of the Reign of God*. Edinburgh: Clark, 1979, XIII-401 p. Esp. 317-357: "The kingdom of God in the mission of Jesus".

**GRAY, Sherman W.**

1989    *The Least of My Brothers: Matthew 25:31-46. A History of Interpretation* (SBL DS, 114). Atlanta, GA: Scholars, 1989, XXII-462 p. Esp. 11-148: "The patristic period"; 149-189: "The middle ages"; 191-240: "The renaissance and reformation"; 241-330: "The modern era". [NTA 34, p. 246] — Diss. Catholic University of America, Washington, DC, 1987 (J.A. Fitzmyer). → Cranfield 1994
         D.J. HARRINGTON, *CBQ* 53 (1991) 326-327; G. HAUFE, *TLZ* 116 (1991) 828-829; W.C. LINSS, *CurrTMiss* 19 (1992) 295-296; G. ROBBINS, *JRel* 72 (1992) 96-97; J.-M. ROUSÉE, *RB* 97 (1990) 315; D.C. SIM, *AusBR* 40 (1992) 84-87; J.L. THOMPSON, *CRBR* 4 (1991) 195-197; B.T. VIVIANO, *RB* 101 (1994) 452-454.

**GRAYSON, Bobby Kent**

1989    *Is Reincarnation Compatible with Christianity? A Historical, Biblical, and Theological Evaluation* [11,7-14; 16,13-16; 17,9-13]. Diss. Southwestern Baptist Theol. Sem., Fort Worth, TX, 1989, 328 p. — *DissAbstr* 51 (1990-91) 188.

**GRAYSTON, Kenneth**

1962 Sermon on the Mount. — *IDB* 4 (1962) 279-289.

1973 Matthieu 1:18-25. Essai d'interprétation. — *RTP* 23 (1973) 221-232. [NTA 18, 464]

1979 Matthew 5:16. An Interpretation. — *EpworthR* 6 (1979) 61-63. [NTA 24, 85]

1984 The Translation of Matthew 28.17. — *JSNT* 21 (1984) 105-109. [NTA 29, 111] → K.L. McKay 1985b, van der Horst 1986

1990 *Dying, We Live. A New Enquiry into the Death of Christ in the New Testament.* London: Darton, Longman & Todd, 1990, VIII-496 p. Esp. 164-228: "Mark and the other synoptics" (194-198; 209-210); 353-355.

1993 The Decline of Temptation – and the Lord's Prayer. [πειρασμός] — *ScotJT* 46 (1993) 279-295. [NTA 38, 762]

**GRAYSTONE, Geoffrey**

1950 "I Have Come to Cast Fire on the Earth…". [10,34] — *Scripture* 4 (1950) 135-141.

1953 Bibliography of Christ and the Gospels. — *Scripture* 5 (1953) 153-160. Esp. 154-155.

**GRECH, Prosper**

1981 Escatologia e storia nel Nuovo Testamento. — FABRIS, R. (ed.), *Problemi e prospettive di scienze bibliche*, Brescia: Queriniana, 1981, 407-426. Esp. 417-418.

**GREEN, H. Benedict**

1968a The Structure of St Matthew's Gospel. — *Studia Evangelica* 4 (1968) 47-59.

1968b The Command to Baptize and Other Matthaean Interpolations. — *Ibid.*, 60-63.

1975 *The Gospel according to Matthew in the Revised Standard Version* (New Clarendon Bible. New Testament). Oxford: University Press, 1975, XIV-264 p. Esp. 1-48: "Introduction"; 49-232: "Commentary"; 232-256: "Detached notes" [Son of Man; kingdom; Peter; marriage; trial]. [NTA 20, p. 360]; repr. 1980; 1987. → Ingelaere 1981, Ziesler 1985
M. GOULDER, *JTS* 27 (1976) 449-452; G.V. JONES, *ScotJT* 31 (1973) 492-494; C.L. MITTON, *ExpT* 87 (1975-76) 321-322; A.M. WEDDERBURN, *HeythJ* 17 (1976) 481.

1982 Solomon the Son of David in Matthaean Typology. — *Studia Evangelica* 7 (1982) 227-230.

1984a The Credibility of Luke's Transformation of Matthew. — TUCKETT, C.M. (ed.), *Synoptic Studies*, 1984, 131-155.

1984b Matthew 12.22-50 and Parallels: An Alternative to Matthaean Conflation. — *Ibid.*, 157-176.

1989a Matthew, Clement and Luke: Their Sequence and Relationship. — *JTS* 40 (1989) 1-25. Esp. 4-12 [1 Clem 13,2/Mt]; 12-25 [1 Clem 46,8/Mt]. [NTA 33, 1486]

1989b Matthew 28:19, Eusebius, and the *lex orandi*. — WILLIAMS, R. (ed.), *The Making of Orthodoxy. Essays in Honour of Henry Chadwick*, Cambridge: University Press, 1989, 124-141.

1993 Matthew 11,7-15: Redaction or Self-Redaction? — FOCANT, C. (ed.), *The Synoptic Gospels*, 1993, 459-466.

**GREEN, Joel B.**

1987 The Gospel of Peter: Source for a Pre-Canonical Passion Narrative? — *ZNW* 78 (1987) 293-301. Esp. 296-298 [Gospel of Peter 4,10-13]; 298-301: "The gospel of Peter and the Matthean passion narrative". [NTA 32, 972]

1988 *The Death of Jesus. Tradition and Interpretation in the Passion Narrative* (WUNT, II/33). Tübingen: Mohr, 1988, XVI-351 p. Esp. 20-23: "The gospel of Matthew"; 46-48 [19,28]; 221-313: "Jesus' suffering and death in the passion narrative" [Mk/Mt]. — Diss. Aberdeen, 1985 (I.H. Marshall).

1992a & MCKNIGHT, S. (eds.), *Dictionary of Jesus and the Gospels*. Downers Grove, IL – Leicester, UK: Inter-Varsity, 1992, XXV-934 p. → Allison 1992b, Barton 1992a-b, D.R. Bauer 1992c-d, D.A. Black, Blackburn, Blomberg 1992b, Broyles, F.W. Burnett 1992b-c, Calvert, Caragounis, B. Corley, M.J. Davidson, J.D.G. Dunn 1992d, M.A. Elliott, C.A. Evans 1992c-e, France 1992a-b, Garland 1992a, J.B. Green 1992b-c, W.R. Herzog, Huffmann, D.L. Hurst, Hurtado 1992a-c, D.H. Johnson, Liefeld, Losie, Lunde, Marshall 1992a-c, S. McKnight 1992a-c, Moo 1992a, G.R. Osborne, Painter 1992a-b, Riesner 1992a-b, Scholer 1992, Snodgrass 1992b, Stanton 1992i-j, R.H. Stein 1992a-b, Travis, Trites 1992b, M.M.B. Turner, Twelftree 1992a-c, D.F. Watson, Weatherly, Westerholm 1992a-c, Wilkins 1992b-c, D.J. Williams, Witherington 1992b-d

1992b & HEARON, H.E., Anointing. — *Ibid.*, 11-13. Esp. 12 [12,6-13].

1992c Death of Jesus. — *Ibid.*, 146-163. Esp. 154-157.

1994* & TURNER, M.B.B. (eds.), *Jesus of Nazareth: Lord and Christ. Essays on the Historical Jesus and New Testament Christology [FS I.H. Marshall]*. Grand Rapids, MI: Eerdmans; Carlisle: Paternoster, 1994, XXI-536 p. → D.A. Carson, France, Schnabel, Stanton, D. Wenham

1995 → J.T. Carroll 1995a

**GREEN, Michael**

1989 *Matthew for Today. Expository Study of New Testament*. Irving, TX: Word, 1989, 304 p.

    *ExpT* 101 (1989-90) 191; N.E.B. HOFSTETTER, *WestTJ* 54 (1992) 183-185.

**GREENFIELD, Guy**

1992 The Ethics of the Sermon on the Mount. — *SWJT* 35 (1992) 13-19. [NTA 37, 133]

**GREENLEE, J. Harold**

1955 *The Gospel Text of Cyril of Jerusalem* (Studies and Documents, 17). København: Munksgaard, 1955, 100 p. Esp. 38-64: "Cyril's text of Matthew".

1960 Εἰς μνημόσυνον αὐτῆς, 'For her memorial': Mt xxvi.13, Mk xiv.9. — *ExpT* 71 (1959-60) 245. [NTA 5, 85]

1964 *Introduction to New Testament Textual Criticism*. Grand Rapids, MI: Eerdmans, 1964; London: S. Bagster, 1976, 160 p. Esp. 119-121 [Lk 11,2]; 132-133; Peabody, MA: Hendrickson, 1995.

1968 *Nine Uncial Palimpsests of the Greek New Testament* (Studies and Documents, 39). Salt Lake City, UT: Univ. of Utah Press, 1968, 131 p. Esp. 22-34 [0104]; 50-90 [0135].

**GREENWOOD, David**

1970 Moral Obligation in the Sermon on the Mount. — *TS* 31 (1970) 301-309. [NTA 15, 137]

**GREER, Rowan A.**

1989 *The Fear of Freedom. A Study of Miracles in the Roman Imperial Church*. Philadelphia, PA: University Press, 1989, 212 p. Esp. 8-34: "The wonderworker in the gospels".

**GREEVEN, Heinrich**

1952 "Wer unter euch..."? — *WDienst* 3 (1952) 86-101. Esp. 93-94 [7,9-11]; 95-96 [12,11]; 97-98 [18,12-14]; 98-99 [6,27]; = HARNISCH, W. (ed.), *Gleichnisse Jesu*, 1982, 238-255. Esp. 246-248; 248-250 251-252; 252-253.

1955 Die Heilung des Gelähmten nach Matthäus. [9,1-8] — *WDienst* 4 (1955) 65-78; = LANGE, J. (ed.), *Das Matthäus-Evangelium*, 1980, 205-222.

1957 Zu den Aussagen des Neuen Testaments über die Ehe. — *ZEvEth* 1 (1957) 109-125.

1960 Erwägungen zur synoptischen Textkritik. — *NTS* 6 (1959-60) 281-296. Esp. 288-290, 290-292 [16,24]; 292-295 [2,7.13]; 295-296 [21,23]. [NTA 5, 386]

1969 Ehe nach dem Neuen Testament. — *NTS* 15 (1968-69) 365-388. Esp. 369-372 [19,10-12]; 374-375 [10,37]; 376-381 [19,3-9]; 381-387 [5,32]. [NTA 14, 306]; = KREMER, G. – MUMM, R. (eds.), *Theologie der Ehe*, Regensburg: Pustet; Göttingen: Vandenhoeck & Ruprecht, 1969, 37-79.

1978 The Gospel Synopsis from 1776 to the Present Day. — ORCHARD, B. – LONGSTAFF, T.R.W. (eds.), *J.J. Griesbach: Synoptic and Text-critical Studies*, 1978, 22-49, 189-198.

1981 *Albert Huck Synopse der drei ersten Evangelien mit Beigabe der johanneischen Parallelstellen. Synopsis of the First Three Gospels with the Addition of the Johannine Parallels.* Tübingen: Mohr, [13]1981, XLI-298 p. → Huck 1936; → J.K. Elliott 1986, 1991, Neirynck 1982c, 1984a (451-464), 1985b

**GREGANTI, Germano**

1969 *La vocazione individuale nel Nuovo Testamento. L'uomo di fronte a Dio* (Corona Lateranensis, 13). Roma: Pont. Univ. Lateranense, 1969, 456 p. Esp. 61-77: "Vocazione nei Vangeli".

**GRÉGOIRE, Réginald**

1970a Un commentaire latin inédit des Béatitudes. — *RevÉtudAug* 16 (1970) 147-158.

1970b Nouveau témoin du commentaire de Remi d'Auxerre sur s. Matthieu. — *Ibid.*, 283-287.

**GREIG, James C.G.**

1968 Abba and Amen: Their Relevance to Christology. — *Studia Evangelica* 5 (1968) 3-13. Esp. 10-12 (ἀμήν).

1973 The Problem of the Messianic Interpretation of Jesus's Ministry in the Primitive Church. — *Studia Evangelica* 6 (1973) 197-220. Esp. 213-218.

**GREIJDANUS, Seakle**

1943[R] *De toestand der eerste christelijke gemeente in zijn betekenis voor de synoptische kwestie* [1943]. Kampen: Kok, 1973, 48 p. (33-48: postface J. van Bruggen). Esp. 21-32.

**GRELOT, Pierre**

1972 La naissance d'Isaac et celle de Jésus. Sur une interprétation "mythologique" de la conception virginale. — *NRT* 94 (1972) 462-487, 561-585. Esp. 462-471: "Position du problème"; 579-585. [NTA 17, 71]

1979 La quatrième demande du 'Pater' et son arrière-plan sémitique. [6,11] — *NTS* 25 (1978-79) 299-314. Esp. 300-302: "Le sens de la quatrième demande"; 302-305: "La demande du pain et l'épisode de la manne"; 305-311: "Original hébreu ou araméen?"; 311-313: "Retour vers l'arrière-plan sémitique du 'Pater'". [NTA 23, 423] → 1984b

1981 *Les Poèmes du Serviteur. De la lecture critique à l'herméneutique* (LD, 103). Paris: Cerf, 1981, 282 p. Esp. 164-170 [8,17; 12,18-21]; 158-161 [20,28].

1982 Paul et Pierre fondateurs de la "primauté" romaine. — *Istina* (Paris) 27 (1982) 228-268. Esp. 257-259 [16,16-19].

1983 *Les Évangiles. Origine, date, historicité* (Cahiers Évangile, 45). Paris: Cerf, 1983, 76 p. Esp. 28-29 [date]; 68-69 [passion narratives].
*Los evangelios. Origen, fechas, historicidad*, trans. N. Darrical (Cuadernos Bíblicos, 45). Estella: Verbo Divino, 1984, 74 p.

1984a *Évangiles et tradition apostolique. Réflexions sur un certain "Christ hébreu"* ("Apologique"). Paris: Cerf, 1984, 197 p. Esp. 62-70 [semitisms]; 90-94 [date]; 105-114 [22,1-14]; 148-166 [2,1-23]. → 1986a; → Tresmontant 1983; → Carmignac 1984 Dupont 1984b, Rasco 1986, Rossé 1988
    F. NEIRYNCK, *ETL* 60 (1984) 405-406.

1984b L'arrière-plan araméen du "Pater". — *RB* 91 (1984) 531-556. Esp. 532-538: "Examen d'une question de principe"; 538-541: "Les parallèles du 'Pater' dans le récit de Gethsémani"; 542-553: "Examen des diverses demandes"; 553-556: "Essai de retraduction araméenne". [NTA 29, 931] → 1979

1985a L'origine de Matthieu 16,16-19. — GANTOY, R. (ed.), *À cause de l'Évangile*. FS J. Dupont, 1985, 91-105. Esp. 92-95: "Notes critiques sur les textes synoptiques"; 95-99: "Origine araméenne de Mt 16,16-19"; 99-105: "Le cadre vivant du texte primitif".

1985b Sacré. III. La sainteté consacrée dans le Nouveau Testament. — *DBS* 10/59 (1985) 1432-1483. Esp. 1436-1439, 1477-1479.

1986a *L'origine des évangiles. Controverse avec J. Carmignac* ("Apologique"). Paris: Cerf, 1986, 154 p. Esp. 71-72 [Papias]; 98-99 [date]; 108-111: "Matthieu grec". → 1984a; → Carmignac 1984, Casalini 1987, Rasco 1986, Rossé 1988, Rubino 1986
   F. NEIRYNCK, *ETL* 63 (1987) 434-436.
   *L'origine dei vangeli: Controversia con J. Carmignac*. Roma: Libreria Editrice Vaticana, 1989, 166 ϱ.

1986b *Évangiles et histoire* (Introduction à la Bible. Édition nouvelle. Le Nouveau Testament, 6). Paris: Desclée, 1986, 338 p. Esp. 145-147 [4,1-11]; 150-159 [2,1-12]; 161-164 [14,13-16,12/Mk]; 226-232 [1,20-21; 3,13-17].
   *Los evangelios y la historia*, trans. I. Arias. Barcelona: Herder, 1987, 327 p.
   *Vangeli e storia*, trans. C. Valentino (Introduzione al Nuovo Testamento, 6). Roma: Borla, 1988, 313 p.

1986c *Les paroles de Jésus Christ* (Introduction à la Bible. Édition nouvelle. Le Nouveau Testament, 7). Paris: Desclée, 1986, 364 p. Esp. 69-73 [10,37-39/Mk]; 89-94.121-125 [24/Mk]; 158-164 [11,2-19]; 174-205: "Sur la fonction propre de Pierre" [16,16-19]; 236-241.246-249.256-257 [22,1-14]; 278-280 [6,9-13]; 281-291 [11,25-27]; 320-324 [5-7].
   *Las palabras de Jesucristo*, trans. A. Martínez de Lapera. Barcelona: Herder, 1988, 386 p.
   *Le parole di Gesù Cristo* (Introduzione al Nuovo Testamento, 7). Roma: Borla, 1988, 329 p.

1986d Michée 7,6 dans les évangiles et dans la littérature rabbinique. — *Bib* 67 (1986) 363-377. Esp. 365-366 [10,21-22]. [NTA 31, 97]

1987 "Sur cette pierre je bâtirai mon Église" (*Mt 16*,18b). — *NRT* 109 (1987) 641-659. [NTA 32, 607]

1989a *Homélies sur l'Écriture à l'époque apostolique* (Introduction à la Bible. Édition nouvelle. Le Nouveau Testament, 8). Paris: Desclée, 1989, 320 p. Esp. 75-86: "Les antithèses dans le Discours sur la montagne"; 89-94: "Les récits de la tentation".
   *Homilías sobre la Escritura en la época apostólica*, trans. I. Arias. Barcelona: Herder, 1991, 300 p.

1989b Sur Matthieu 16,16-19: de la promesse de Jésus à la fonction de l'église de Rome dans l'Église universelle. — *Unité et Diversité dans l'Église. Texte officiel de la Commission Biblique Pontificale et travaux personnels des membres* (Teologia e filosofia, 15), Città del Vaticano: Libreria Editrice Vaticana, 1989, 183-197.

1992a Sémitismes (dans le Nouveau Testament). — *DBS* 12/67 (1992) 333-424. Esp. 413-414.

1992b La tradition apostolique. — *RB* 99 (1992) 163-204. Esp. 168-173: "La notion de tradition dans le Nouveau Testament"; 179-182 [oral tradition]; 184 [1-2]. [NTA 37, 3]

1994a *Dieu, le Père de Jésus Christ* ("Jésus et Jésus-Christ", 60). Paris: Desclée, 1994, 368 p. Esp. 63-197: "La tradition des synoptiques".

1994b La conception virginale de Jésus et sa famille. — *EVie* 104 (1994) 625-633. [NTA 39, 744]

1995a *La condition de la femme d'après le Nouveau Testament*. Paris: Desclée De Brouwer, 1995, 167 p.

1995b "Celui qui vient" (Mt 11,3 et Lc 7,19). — KUNTZMANN, R. (ed.), *Ce Dieu qui vient. Études sur l'Ancien et le Nouveau Testament offertes au Professeur Bernard Renaud à l'occasion de son soixante-cinquième anniversaire* (LD, 159), Paris: Cerf, 1995, 275-290. Esp. 276-279: "Le sens de la question posée", 279-287: "La réponse de Jésus".

1995c Notes sur les propositions du Pr Carsten Peter Thiede. — *RE* 102 (1995) 589-591. [NTA 40, 1363] → Thiede 1995c

1995d Remarques sur un manuscrit de l'évangile de Matthieu. [P⁶⁴] — *RSR* 83 (1995) 403-405. [NTA 40, 717] → Thiede 1995c

1995e Les tentations de Jésus. — *NRT* 117 (1995) 501-516. [NTA 40, 817]

**GRESE, William C.**

1979 *Corpus Hermeticum XIII and Early Christian Literature* (Studia ad Corpus Hellenisticum Novi Testamenti, 5). Leiden: Brill, 1979, XIII-229 p. Esp. 59-197: "Corpus Hermeticum XIII and early christian literature".

**GRGEC, Radovan**

1972 Prvo blaženstvo. (La première béatitude chez Mt). [5,3] — *Bogoslovska Smotra* (Zagreb) 42 (1972) 450-452.

**GRIESBACH, Johann Jakob**

1789ᴿ Commentatio qua Marci Evangelium totum e Matthaei et Lucae commentariis decerptum esse monstratur. [1789] — ORCHARD, B. - LONGSTAFF, T.R.W. (eds.), *J.J. Griesbach: Synoptic and Text-critical Studies*, 1978, 68-102, 201-207 (Introduction by B. Reicke, 68-73).
Demonstration that Mark was Written after Matthew and Luke (Translation by B. Orchard). — *Ibid.*, 103-135, 207-214.

**GRIFFITHS, D.R.**

1951 St. Matthew iii.15: Ἄφες ἄρτι· οὕτω γὰρ πρέπον ἐστὶν ἡμῖν πληρῶσαι πᾶσαν δικαιοσύνην. — *ExpT* 62 (1950-51) 155-157.

**GRIFFITHS, J. Gwyn**

1960 Wisdom about Tomorrow. [6,34] — *HTR* 53 (1960) 219-221.

1970 The Disciple's Cross. [10,38; 16,24] — *NTS* 16 (1969-70) 358-364. [NTA 15, 164]

**GRILL, Severin**

1955 *Das Neue Testament nach dem syrischen Text*. Klosterneuburg–München, 1955, 120 p.

1959 Selbstsüchtige und selbstlose Nachfolger Jesu. Erklärung von Matth. 8,19-22. — *Der Seelsorger* (Wien) 30 (1959) 77-79.

**GRILLI, Massimo**

1992 *Comunità e missione. Le direttive di Matteo. Indagine esegetica su Mt 9,35–11,1* (EHS, XXIII/458). Frankfurt/M: Lang, 1992, 369 p. Esp. 31-75: "Organizzazione di Mt 9,35–11,1"; 79-100: "Mt 9,35–10,5a: lo sfondo ermeneutico del discorso"; 101-122: "Mt 10,5b-15: il compito degli inviati"; 123-155: "Mt 10,16-33: invio e persecuzione"; 157-174: "Mt 10,34-42: le implicazioni del mandato"; 179-219: "Mt 9,35–10,5a: i fondamenti dell'annuncio"; 221-285: "Mt 10,5b-42: i 'modelli d'azione' nell'espletamento della missione". [NTA 38, p. 120] — Diss. Pont. Inst. Bibl., Roma, 1991 (F. Lentzen-Deis).
L. RUBIO, *EstBib* 53 (1995) 140-142; G.F. SNYDER, *CRBR* 7 (1994) 191-192; B.T. VIVIANO, *CBQ* 56 (1994) 374-375; *RB* 101 (1994) 617-618.

**GRILLMEIER, Aloys**

1956 *Der Logos am Kreuz. Zur christologischen Symbolik der älteren Kreuzigungsdarstellung*. München: Hüber, 1956, XII-151 p. Esp. 6-10: "Ein interpolierter Matthäus-Text" [27,49-50].

**GRIMM, Werner**

1970 Selige Augenzeugen, Luk. 10,23f. Alttestamentlicher Hintergrund und ursprünglicher Sinn. — *TZ* 26 (1970) 172-183. Ep. 172, 179-180 [Q 10,23-24].

1972    Zum Hintergrund von Mt 8,11f / Lk 13,28f. — *BZ* 16 (1972) 255-256. [NTA 17, 516] →
        Zeller 1971

1973    Der Dank für die empfangene Offenbarung bei Jesus und Josephus. — *BZ* 17 (1973)
        249-256. Esp. 249-250: "Parallelen zu Mt 11,25-27"; 252-253 [Dan 2,19-23; Fl. Josephus]; 253-256:
        "Jesus und Daniel". [NTA 18, 470] (= *Das Institutum Judaicum der Universität Tübingen
        1971-72*, Tübingen, 1972, 69-78).

1976    *Weil Ich dich liebe. Die Verkündigung Jesu und Deuterojesaja* (Arbeiten zum Neuen
        Testament und Judentum, 1). Frankfurt/M: Lang, 1976, XI-321 p. Esp. 68-77 [5,3-12/Q
        6,20-23]; 78-82 [22,1-10/Q 14,16-24]; 93 [Q 11,21-22]; 94-96 [11,12]; 96-97 [12,28]; 102-110 [11,28-30];
        110-111 [8,16-17]; 112-124 [13,16-17/Q 10,23-24]; 124-130 [11,2-6/Q 7,18-23]; 146-147 [26,28-29]; 152
        [6,6; 7,11/Q 11,13]; 152-154 [7,7/Q 11,9]; 157-159 [10,28-31/Q 12,4-7]; 159-160 [6,19-21/Q 12,33-34];
        160-161 [17,20]; 166 [13,51-52]; 171-177 [11,25-27/Q 10,21-22]; 183-186 [5,39/Q 6,29]; 186-188 [5,14-16];
        188-190 [6,33/Q 12,31]; 190-191 [25,35-36]; 192-196 [8,11-12/Q 13,28-29]; 277-280 [Q 12,49-50].
        *Die Verkündigung Jesu und Deuterojesaja*, 2nd rev. and enl. ed., 1981, XI-360 p.
        ("Nachwort", 346-360).

1977    → O. Betz 1977b

1980a   *Der Ruhetag. Sinngehalte einer fast vergessenen Gottesgabe* (Arbeiten zum Neuen Tes-
        tament und Judentum, 4). Frankfurt/M: Lang, 1980, 94 p. Esp. 46 [11,28]; 49-50 [12,11-12];
        59-60 [12,1-8]; 80-82 [sabbat].

1980b   Die Hoffnung der Armen. Zu den Seligpreisungen Jesu. — *TBeitr* 11 (1980) 100-113.
        [NTA 25, 72]

1984    *Jesus und das Danielbuch.* I: *Jesu Einspruch gegen das Offenbarungssystem Daniels (Mt
        11,25-27; Lk 17,20-21)* (Arbeiten zum Neuen Testament und Judentum, 6/1).
        Frankfurt/M: Lang, 1984, 110 p. Esp. 1-69: "Jesus – Intimus Gottes. Eine Auslegung von Mt.
        11,25-27 / Lk. 10,21f"; 91-100: "Jesus und Daniels Apokalyptik".

1992    *Die Motive Jesu. Das Vaterunser kommentiert und ausgelegt* (Biblisch-theologische
        Grundlagen, 1). Stuttgart: Calwer, 1992, 142 p. [NTA 37, p. 115]

**GRINBERGS, E.D.**

1974    *A Study of the Concept and Experience of Temptation in the Synoptic Gospels.* Diss.
        Durham, 1974.

**GRINDEL, John A.**

1967    Matthew 12,18-21. — *CBQ* 29 (1967) 110-115. [NTA 11, 1033]

1969    Another Characteristic of the *Kaige* Recension: נצח‎/νικος. — *CBQ* 31 (1969) 499-513.
        Esp. 511 [12,18-21].

**GRINTZ, Jehoshua M.**

1960    Hebrew as the Spoken and Written Language in the Last Days of the Second Temple.
        — *JBL* 79 (1960) 32-47. Esp. 33-42 [12,42; 15,21; 16,17; 23,2; 28,1]. [NTA 5, 239] → E. Vogt 1960

**GRIVEC, Franciscus**

1954    De exegesi S. Cyrilli Thessalonicensis. — *OCP* 20 (1954) 137-150. Esp. 139-148 [16,18;
        18,15]; 148-150 [7,17; 12,33].

**GROBEL, Kendrick**

1962    How Gnostic Is the Gospel of Thomas? — *NTS* 8 (1961-62) 367-373. Esp. 368 [9,37/Th
        73³]; 368-369 [10,26/Th 6]; 369 [10,27/Th 33³]; 371 [7,3-5/Th 26]; 371-372 [6,3/Th 62]; 372 [13,44-45/Th
        25].

**GROBLER, J.D.**

1977    *Die Heilige Gees by die sinoptiese Evangelies en Johannes. 'n Vergelykende studie.*
        Diss. Univ. of Pretoria, 1977.

**GROENEWALD, Evert Philippus**

1959 Grond vir Egskeiding volgens Mt. [Reasons for divorce] — *NduitseGT* 1 (1959) 5-12.

1961 'n Aantekening oor Matt 2,2. [On Mt 2,2] — *NduitseGT* 2 (1961) 204-205.

1967 God and Mammon. [6,24] — *Neotestamentica* 1 (1967) 59-66. [NTA 18, 108]

**GROGAN, G.W.**

1967 The New Testament Interpretation of the Old Testament: A Comparative Study. — *TyndB* 18 (1967) 54-76. Esp. 54-59: "The hermeneutics of the gospel of Matthew".

**GROH, Dennis E.**

1985* & JEWETT, R. (eds.), *The Living Text. Essays in Honor of Ernest W. Saunders*. Lanham, MD: Univ. Press of America, 1985, X-261 p. → R.H. Fuller, Ringgren, J.T. Sanders

**GROLLENBERG, Lucas H.**

1968 *Nieuwe kijk op het oude Boek. Een verkenning van de moderne bijbeluitleg.* Amsterdam–Brussel: Elsevier, 1968, ²1969, ³1972; ⁵1977, 367 p. Esp. 345-348 [Mt]; 335-339 [sayings].

1969 → J. Denaux 1969

1983 *Geloven is zo gek nog niet. Een manier van bijbellezen.* Baarn: Ten Have, 1983, 204 p. Esp. 107-110 [26,47-56]; 140-145 [1,18-25].
*Believe Makes Sense. A Way of Reading the Bible*, trans. J. Bowden. London: SCM, 1983, VII-182 p. Esp. 95-98; 125-129.

1987 *Onverwachte Messias. De Bijbel kan ook misleidend zijn.* Baarn: Ten Have, 1987, 224 p. Esp. 158-167 [anti-Judaism].
*Unexpected Messiah, or How the Bible Can Be Misleading*, trans. J.L. Bowden. London: SCM, 1988, VIII-199 p. Esp. 136-144.

**GROMACKI, Robert Glenn**

1974 *The Virgin Birth. Doctrine of Deity.* Nashville, TN – New York: Nelson, 1974, 202 p. Esp. 76-82: "Testimony of Matthew"; Grand Rapids, MI: Baker, 1981.

**GRONKOWSKI, Witold**

1959 Przyjacielu, jakże zu wszedłes, nie mając szaty godowej? ["Friend, how did you come in here?"] [22,12]. — *RuBi* 12 (1959) 24-28.

**GROSHEIDE, Frederik Willem**

1922ᴿ *Het Heilig Evangelie volgens Mattheüs* [1922] (Commentaar op het Nieuwe Testament, 1). Kampen: Kok, 2nd, rev. and enlarged ed., 1954, 464 p. Esp. 7-16 [introduction]; 17-458 [commentary].
N.B. STONEHOUSE, *WestTJ* 17 (1954-55) 230-231; M.R. WEIJERS, *RB* 62 (1955) 453-454.

1952 *Wat leert het Nieuwe Testament inzake de tucht?* (Exegetica I, 3). Delft: van Keulen, 1952, 62 p. Esp. 35-42 [16,19]; 42-48 [18,15-18].

1953 *De Openbaring Gods in het Nieuwe Testament.* Kampen: Kok, 1953, 268 p. Esp. 215-218.

**GROSHEIDE, Herman Hendrik**

1978* et al. (eds.), *De knechtsgestalte van Christus. Studies door collega's en oud-leerlingen aangeboden aan Prof. Dr. H.N. Ridderbos.* Kampen: Kok. 1978, 351 p. → Baarlink, Faber van der Meulen, Rothuizen

**GROS LOUIS, Kenneth R.R.**

1982 The Jesus Birth Stories. — ID. - ACKERMAN, J.S. (eds.), *Literary Interpretations of Biblical Narratives*, II, Nashville, TN: Abingdon, 1982, 273-284.

1985 Different Ways of Looking at the Birth of Jesus. — *BibReview* 1/1 (1985) 33-40. [NTA 29, 927]

**GROSS, Gerhard**

1964  Die "geringsten Brüder" Jesu in Mt 25,40 in Auseinandersetzung mit der neueren Exegese. — *BibLeb* 5 (1964) 172-180. [NTA 9, 547]

**GROSS, Julius**

1957  Die Schlüsselgewalt nach Haimo von Auxerre. [16,16-19] — *ZRelGeist* 9 (1957) 30-41.

**GROSSI, Vittorino**

1980  Il contesto battesimale dell'oratio dominica nei commenti di Tertulliano, Cipriano, Agostino. [6,9-13] — *Augustinianum* 20 (1980) 205-220.

1982  La ricerca cristiana della verità nel sec. III: Problemi di metodo. — MARCHESELLI, C.C. (ed.), *Parole e Spirito*. FS S. Cipriani, 1982, I, 833-846. Esp. 840-844 [7,7].

**GROSSOUW, Willem K.**

1954  *Bijbelse vroomheid. Beschouwingen over de spiritualiteit van het Nieuwe Testament.* Utrecht–Antwerpen: Spectrum, 1954, $^{2-3}$1955, $^4$1956, 239 p.; $^5$1959, $^6$1964, 243 p. Esp. 49-63 [Sermon on the Mount]; 103-105 [11,25-30].
*Biblische Frömmigkeit. Betrachtungen zum Geist des Neuen Testaments*, trans. O. Karrer. München: Ars Sacra, 1956, 239 p. Esp. 46-60; 100-102.
*La piedad bíblica en el Nuevo Testamento.* Buenos Aires: Lohlé, 1959, 197 p. Esp. 38-49; 79-80.
*Spiritualité du Nouveau Testament* (Lire la Bible, 2). Paris: Cerf, 1964, 227 p. Esp. 45-58; 94-96.

**GROSVENOR, Mary** → Zerwick 1953/74

**GROUNDS, Vernon C.**

1971  Mountain Manifesto. [5,3-12] — *BS* 128 (1971) 135-141. [NTA 16, 148]

**Groupe de Bergerac**

1980  Lecture critique de Matthieu 6/9-13. — *ETR* 55 (1980) 556-559.

**Groupe de Cadir**

1977  La communication parabolique. Matthieu 13,1-53. — *SémBib* 5 (1977) 29-40 (H.J. Striker); 41-45 (J. Escande); 6 (1977) 5-9.10-12 (É. Maréchal); 13-26 (I. Darrault).

**GRUBER, Mayer I.**

1993  The Meaning of Biblical Parallelism: A Biblical Perspective. [21,1-11] — *Prooftexts* 13 (1993) 289-293. [NTA 38, 1372]

**GRÜHNBERG, Madeleine**

1967  *The West-Saxon Gospels: A Study of the Gospel of St. Matthew with the Text of the Four Gospels.* Amsterdam: Scheltema & H., 1967, 382 p.
P. MERTENS-FONCK, *English Studies* (Amsterdam) 54 (1973) 59-60; J. ROSSIER, *Anglia* (Tübingen) 92 (1974) 229-231.

**GRÜNDEL, Johannes**

1982  Die Bergpredigt als Orientierung für unser Handeln. Zur Erneuerung der Moraltheologie "aus der Lehre der Schrift". — SCHNACKENBURG, R. (ed.), *Die Bergpredigt*, 1982, 81-112. Esp. 93-98 [5,21-48]; 100-103 [5,32; 7,16].

**GRUENLER, Royce Gordon**

1981  Implied Christological Claims in the Core Sayings of Jesus: An Application of Wittgenstein's Phenomenology. — *SBL 1981 Seminar Papers*, 65-77. Esp. 71 [12,28]; 74 [11,16-19].

1982  *New Approaches to Jesus and the Gospels. A Phenomenological and Exegetical Study of Synoptic Christology.* Grand Rapids, MI: Baker, 1982, 261 p.

1983  Mapping Jesus' Logically Odd Use of "I" as a Clue to His Intentionality. — *SBL 1983 Seminar Papers*, 55-60. Esp. 59-60.

**GRUNDMANN, Walter**

1940[R]   Die Arbeit des ersten Evangelisten am Bilde Jesu. [1940] — LANGE, J. (ed.), *Das Matthäus-Evangelium*, 1980, 73-102. Esp. 74-80 [salvation history]; 80-84 [Israel]; 84-87 [law]; 88-93 [God]; 93-95 [OT]; 95-98 [Messiah]; 98-100 [Church].

1957   *Die Geschichte Jesu Christi*. Berlin: Evangelische Verlagsanstalt, 1957, 422 p.; [2]1959; [3]1961, 448 p. (Anhang, 425-448). Esp. 30-32 [Q 3,7-9.16-17]; 38-41 [11,7-19]; 70-72 [7,7-11]; 96-100 [5,3-12]; 100-106 [5,38-48]; 119-131 [5,21-48]; 148-153 [Q 11,33-36]; 179-182 [6,25-33]; 208-210 [Q 17,22-37 (Lk)]; 340-343 [27,3-10]; 378 [28,20]; 401-402 [1,2-17]; 402-409 [1,18-2,23].

1959a   Die Bergpredigt nach der Lukasfassung. — *Studia Evangelica* 1 (1959) 180-189.

1959b   Die νήπιοι in der urchristlichen Paränese. — *NTS* 5 (1958-59) 188-205. Esp. 201-204 [11,25]. [NTA 4, 189]

1965   Matth. xi.27 und die johanneischen 'Der Vater – Der Sohn'-Stellen. — *NTS* 12 (1965-66) 42-49. [NTA 10, 515]

1968   *Das Evangelium nach Matthäus* (Theologischer Handkommentar zum Neuen Testament, 1). Berlin: Evangelische Verlagsanstalt, 1968, XX-580 p. Esp. 1-58: "Einleitung"; 59-580: "Auslegung" ["Exkurse": 71-73; 80-81; 107-109; 115-118; 181-190; 204-206; 236-242; 281-283; 364-365; 392-396; 497-499]. [NTA 13, p. 268]; [3]1972; [6]1986, XX-586 p. (581-586: Bibliography; Register).
     B. CELADA, *CuBíb* 26 (1969) 230-234; H. DROZD, *RuBi* 22 (1959) 160-162; R. PESCH, *Freiburger Rundbrief* 21 (1969) 90; L.F. RIVERA, *RevistBíb* 32 (1970) 92; G. STRECKER, *TLZ* 95 (1970) 817-823.

1973   *Die frühe Christenheit und ihre Schriften. Umwelt, Entstehung und Eigenart der neu-testamentlichen Bücher*. Berlin: Evangelische Haupt-Bibelgesellschaft, 1973; (Calwer Paperback), Stuttgart: Calwer, 1983, 142 p. Esp. 67-73 [Q]; 97-100 [Mt].

1977   Weisheit im Horizont des Reiches Gottes. Eine Studie zur Verkündigung Jesu nach der Spruchüberlieferung Q. — SCHNACKENBURG, R., et al. (eds.), *Die Kirche des Anfangs*. FS H. Schürmann, 1977, 175-199. Esp. 176-183 [Q 7,31-35; 9,58; 10,21-22; 11,31-32.49-51; 13,34-35]; 183-188 [Q 7,12-23.31-35; 11,9-11]; 188-193 [Q 6,20-49]; 193-198 [Q 3,7-9.16-17; 4,1-13; 9,58; 12,28-32; 14,16-24; 17,22-37]. → 1988

1988   *Weisheit im Horizont des Reiches Gottes. Erwägungen zur Christusbotschaft und zum Christusverständnis im Lichte der Weisheit in Israel*. Stuttgart: Evangelische Kirche, 1988, 411 and 104 p. Esp. 130-239 + 26-55: "Die Botschaft innerhalb der Spruch-Q-Tradition in ihrem Bezug zur Weisheit in Israel"; 239-307 + 56-78: "Die 'eschatologische Weisheit' Jesu in der Bergpredigt". → 1977

**GRYGLEWICZ, Feliks**

1950   Character socialis Orationis Dominicae. [Polish] — *RuBi* 3 (1950) 207-219.

1956   Praca ewangelistów nad przypowieściami o robotnikach w winnicy i o synu marno-trawnym (Die Arbeit der Evangelisten an den Gleichnissen von den Arbeitern im Weinberg und vom verlorenen Sohn). [20,1-16] — *RoczTK* 3 (1956) 226-240.

1957   The Gospel of the Overworked Workers. [11,28-30; 20,1-16] — *CBQ* 19 (1957) 190-198. [NTA 2, 35]

1961   Reguła wojny z Qumran a Księgi Machabejskie i Ewangelia Mateusza (Die Kriegsregel von Qumran, die Makkabäer-Bücher und das Matthäusevangelium). — *Zeszyty Naukowe Katolickiego Uniwersytetu Lubelskiego* (Lublin) 4/2 (1961) 41-60.

1962   Pierwotny tekst Modlitwy Pańskiej (Le texte primitif de l'oraison dominicale). — *Zeszyty Naukowe Katolickiego Uniwersytetu Lubelskiego* 5/2 (1962) 17-31.

1965   The St Adalbert Codex of the Gospels. — *NTS* 11 (1964-65) 256-278. Esp. 259, 263-265, 268-271, 273. [NTA 10, 60]

1978   Jezus przed Piłatem. [Jesus before Pilate] [27,11-14] — ID. (ed.), *Męka Jezusa Chrystusa*, Lublin: Catholic University, 1978, 47-57.

**GRYSON, Roger**

1965 À propos du témoignage de Papias sur Matthieu. Le sens du mot *λόγιον* chez les Pères du second siècle. — *ETL* 41 (1965) 530-547. Esp. 533-536 [1 Clem]; 537 [Polycarp]; 538-539 [2 Clem]; 539-540 [Justin]; 540 [Tatian]; 541-545 [Irenaeus]; 545-546 [Clement of Alexandria]. [NTA 10, 897]

1988 La vieille-latine, témoin privilégié du texte du Nouveau Testament. L'exemple de Matthieu 13,13-15. — *RTL* 19 (1988) 413-432. [NTA 33, 611]

1993* (ed.), *Philologia Sacra. Biblische und patristische Studien für Hermann J. Frede und Walter Thiele zu ihrem siebzigsten Geburtstag* (Vetus Latina. Aus der Geschichte der lateinischen Bibel, 24/1-2). Freiburg: Herder, 1993, 2 vols., 10*-674 p. → Leloir, McNamara 1992, H.J. Vogt

**GUBLER, Marie-Louise**

1977 *Die frühesten Deutungen des Todes Jesu. Eine motivgeschichtliche Darstellung aufgrund der neueren exegetischen Forschung* (Orbis Biblicus et Orientalis, 15). Freiburg/Schw: Universitätsverlag; Göttingen: Vandenhoeck & Ruprecht, 1977, XV-424 p. Esp. 16-27: "Die Prophetenaussage der Logienquelle" [Q 6,22; 7,33-35; 11,31-32.47-48.49-51; 13,34-35]; 43-70: "Aufnahme und Verwendung der dtr Prophetengeschickvorstellung im palästinischen Urchristentum" [Q]. — Diss. Freiburg/Schw, 1975.

1988 Wo nehmen wir den Stern her? Gedanken zur Weihnachtsbotschaft nach Mattäus. — *Diakonia* 19 (1988) 410-415. [NTA 33, 596]

**GUELICH, Robert A.**

1973 Mt 5,22: Its Meaning and Integrity. — *ZNW* 64 (1973) 39-52. Esp. 39-47: "Lexical questions"; 47-49: "Questions of integrity"; 50-52: "Questions of meaning". [NTA 18, 467]

1976a The Antitheses of Matthew v.21-48: Traditional and/or Redactional? — *NTS* 22 (1975-76) 444-457. [NTA 21, 75]

1976b The Matthean Beatitudes: "Entrance-Requirements" or Eschatological Blessings? — *JBL* 95 (1976) 415-434. Esp. 416-419: "Form-critical observations"; 419-426: "The question of source"; 426-431: "Redaction-critical considerations". [NTA 21, 377]

1981 The Gospels: Portraits of Jesus and His Ministry. — *JEvTS* 24 (1981) 117-125. [NTA 26, 439]

1982 *The Sermon on the Mount. A Foundation for Understanding*. Waco, TX: Word, 1982, 451 p. Esp. 41-61: "The setting of the Sermon on the Mount" [4,23–5,2]; 62-118: "The gospel of the kingdom" [5,3-12]; 119-133: "The role of discipleship" [5,13-16]; 134-174: "Jesus and the law" [5,17-20]; 175-271: "The greater righteousness" [5,21-48]; 272-320: "On doing righteousness" [6,1-18]; 321-381: "The life of prayer" [6,9-7,12]; 382-413: "The narrow gate" [7,13-27]; 414-421: "Epilogue" [7,28-29]. [NTA 27, p. 208] — Diss. Hamburg, 1967. → Carlston 1985, Nolland 1983, D. Wenham 1983
  H.D. BETZ, *JBL* 103 (1984) 479-481; L. CHOUINARD, *RestQ* 27 (1984) 111-114; R.H. GUNDRY, *The Reformed Journal* (Grand Rapids, MI) 33/1 (1983) 18-20; L.E. KECK, *RelStR* 9 (1983) 273; J. REUMANN, *Interpr* 39 (1985) 419-422; D.P. SCAER, *ConcTQ* 48 (1984) 78; D.L. SCOTT, *SWJT* 25/2 (1982-83) 131-132.

1983 The Gospel Genre. — STUHLMACHER, P. (ed.), *Das Evangelium und die Evangelien*, 1983, 183-219. Ep. 190-192; = STUHLMACHER, P. (ed.), *The Gospel and the Gospels*, 1991, 173-208. Esp. 180-182.

1987 Interpreting the Sermon on the Mount. — *Interpr* 41 (1987) 117-130. [NTA 31, 1063]

1993 Golden Rule. — METZGER, B.M. - COOGAN, M.D. (eds.), *The Oxford Companion to the Bible*, 1993, 257-258.

**GÜNTHER, Hartmut**

1971 Die Gerechtigkeit des Himmelreiches in der Bergpredigt. — *KerDog* 17 (1971) 113-126. Esp. 115-116 [δικαιοσύνη]; 117-120 [5,21-48]; 120-121 [6,1-18]; 122-123 [6,19-34]; 123-124 [5,6.10]. [NTA 16, 146]

1980 Das Vaterunser: Gebet im Namen Jesu. — *Lutherische Theologie und Kirche* (Oberwisel) 4 (1980) 34-41.

1987 "Wer diese meine Worte hört und tut sie..." (Mt 7,24). Zum Verständnis der Bergpredigt. — *Lutherische Theologie und Kirche* 11 (1987) 1-16.

**GUENTHER, Heinz O.**

1989a Greek: Home of Primitive Christianity. — *TorontoJT* 5 (1989) 247-279. [NTA 34, 1084]

1989b When 'Eagles' Draw Together. — *Forum* 5/2 (1989) 140-150. Esp. 142-143: "Q 17:37b in Matthean perspective"; 143: "Q 17:37b in Lukan perspective"; 144-145: "The 'eagle' saying in Q"; 146-147: "The proverbial wisdom of Q 17:37b"; 147-149: "The authenticity of Q 17:37b". [NTA 34, 181]

1990 A Fair Face is Half the Portion. The Lot Saying in Luke 17:28-29. — *Forum* 6 (1990) 56-66. Esp. 57-60: "Special plea for inclusion in Q"; 60-64: "Authenticity". [NTA 36, 771]

1992 The Sayings Gospel Q and the Quest for Aramaic Sources. Rethinking Christian Origins. — *Semeia* 55 (1992) 41-76. Esp. 44-62 [Aramaic hypothesis]; 62-70 [Greek provenance of Q; literary genre]. [NTA 36, 1234]

**GÜTTGEMANNS, Erhardt**

1971 *Studia linguistica neotestamentica. Gesammelte Aufsätze zur linguistischen Grundlage einer neutestamentlichen Theologie* (BEvT, 60). München: Kaiser, 1971, ²1973, VIII-243 p. Esp. 99-183: "Die linguistisch-didaktische Methodik der Gleichnisse Jesu".

1972a Bemerkungen zur linguistischen Analyse von Matthäus 13,24-30.36-43. — GÜLICH, E. — RAIBLE, W. (eds.), *Textsorten. Differenzierungskriterien aus linguistischer Sicht* (Athenaion-Skripten Linguistik, 5). Frankfurt/M: Athenaion, 1972, ²1975, 81-97 (Diskussion, 90-97).

1972b Strukturale Meditation über Mt 4,1-11. — GERBER, U. - GÜTTGEMANNS, E. (eds.), *"Linguistische" Theologie: biblische Texte, christliche Verkündigung und theologische Sprachtheorie* (Forum theologiae linguisticae: Interdisziplinäre Schriftenreihe für Theologie, Semiotik und Linguistik, 3), Bonn: Linguistica biblica, 1972, 173-175.

1973a Narrative Analyse synoptischer Texte. — *LingBib* 25-26 (1973) 50-73. Esp. 54-55 [25,14-30]; 56-58 [18,21-35]; 58-62 [25,1-13]; 63-65 [22,1-14]; 65-66 [20,1-16]; 68-69 [25,31-46]. [NTA 18, 452]; = HARNISCH, W. (ed.), *Die neutestamentliche Gleichnisforschung*, 1982, 179-223 (überarbeitet). Esp. 188-190; 192-195; 195-203; 205-209; 209-210; 215-216.
Narrative Analysis of Synoptic Texts. — *Semeia* 6 (1976) 127-179. Esp. 136-138; 140-144; 144-152; 153-158; 158-160; 165-167. [NTA 21, 645]

1973b Die synoptische Frage im Licht der modernen Sprach- und Literaturwissenschaft. — *LingBib* 29-30 (1973) 2-40. [NTA 18, 835]

1977 Narrative Analyse des Streitgesprächs über den "Zinsgroschen". [22,15-22] — *LingBib* 41-42 (1977) 88-105. [NTA 22, 781] → Jason 1977

1983 *Fragmenta semiotico-hermeneutica. Eine Texthermeneutik für den Umgang mit der Hl. Schrift* (Forum theologiae linguisticae: Interdisziplinäre Schriftenreihe für Theologie, Semiotik und Linguistik, 9). Bonn: Linguistica biblica, 1983, 347 p. Esp. 171-204: "F.D.E. Schleiermacher: Hermeneutik als strukturale Linguistik (am Beispiel des Synoptikerproblems)".

**GUIDETTI, Armando**

1954 *Evangelium secundum Matthaeum. Gesù Messia. Introduzione, coordinamenti et note.* Milano: Ed. Letture, 1954, 227 p.
    P. NOBER, *VD* 32 (1954) 244.

**GUIJARRO OPORTO, Santiago**

1983 El signo de Jonás. [12,38-42] — *EstAgust* 18 (1983) 39-50.
    The Sign of Jonah. — *TDig* 32 (1985) 49-53.

1987a  *La buena noticia de Jesús. Introducción a los Evangelios sinópticos y a los Hechos de los Apóstoles.* Madrid: Sociedad de Educación Atenas, 1987, 268 p.

1987b  Mat 28,16-20, la clave de un evangelio. — COLLADO BERTOMEU, V. (ed.), *Actas del II Simposio Bíblico Español (Córdoba, 1985)*, Córdoba-Valencia: Fundación Bíblica Española, 1987, 429-440.

1989   *Evangelio según San Mateo, comentario* (El Mensaje del Nuevo Testamento, 1). Salamanca: Sígueme, 1989, 229 p.

**GUILBERT, Pierre**

1975   *Il ressuscita le troisième jour* (Foi chrétienne). Paris: Centurion, 1975, 261 p. Esp. 107-110 [28,9-10]; 148-157: "Le témoignage de Matthieu" [28,1-8]; (Racines), Paris: Nouvelle Cité, 1988, 256 p.

**GUILLAUME, A.**

1951   Mt. xxvii,46 in the Light of the Dead Sea Scroll of Isaiah. — *PEQ* 83 (1951) 78-80. E. VOGT, *Bib* 33 (1952) 305.

**GUILLAUMONT, Antoine**

1960   Les *Logia* d'Oxyrhynchos sont-ils traduits du copte? — *Muséon* 73 (1960) 325-333. Esp. 331-332 [5,14/Oxy fr 2]. [NTA 5, 840] → Garitte 1960b

1981   Les sémitismes dans l'Évangile selon Thomas. Essai de classement. — VAN DEN BROEK, R. – VERMASEREN, M.J. (eds.), *Studies in Gnosticism and Hellenistic Religions Presented to Gilles Quispel on the Occasion of his 65th Birthday* (Études préliminaires aux religions orientales dans l'empire romain, 91), Leiden: Brill, 1981, 190-204. Esp. 192 [10,37/Th 55; 18,1/Th 12]; 194 [24,28/Th 56]; 197 [12,35/Th 45; 13,46/Th 76; 13,48/Th 8; 19,19/Th 25]; 198 [13,4/Th 9]; 16,3/Th 91]; 199 [18,19/Th 48]; 199-200 [18,12-13/Th 107]; 200 [6,25/Th 36]; 202 [22,19/Th 100].

**GUILLEMETTE, Nil**

1980   *Introduction à la lecture du Nouveau Testament. Au soir du troisième jour* (Initiations). Paris: Cerf, 1980, 417 p.

1995   The Sermon on the Mount: Feasible Ethics? — *Landas* (Manila) 9 (1995) 209-236. [NTA 40, 818]

**GUILLEMETTE, Pierre**

1980   La forme des récits d'exorcisme de Bultmann. Un dogme à reconsidérer. — *ÉglT* 11 (1980) 177-193. Esp. 192-193 [9,32-34]. [NTA 25, 57]

1987   & BRISEBOIS, M., *Introduction aux méthodes historico-critiques* (Héritage et Projet, 35). Montreal: Fides, 1987, 507 p. Esp. 461-465 [6,9-13].

**GUILLEMIN, Elaine**

1979   *Matthew 5:17-20. Some Jewish and Christian Perspectives.* Diss. Ottawa, 1979, v-160 p. (M. Dumais).

**GUILLET, Jacques**

1961   À propos des titres de Jésus: Christ, Fils de l'homme, Fils de Dieu. — BARUCQ, A., et al. (eds.), *À la rencontre de Dieu.* FS A. Gelin, 1961, 309-317. Esp. 309-315 [Son of Man]; 615-617 [Christ; Son of God].

1969   Jésus et la politique. — BESSIÈRE, G. (ed.), *Que dites-vous du Christ?*, 1969, 223-233.

1971   *Jésus devant sa vie et sa mort* (Intelligence de la foi). Paris: Aubier, 1971, 255 p. Esp. 33-45 [John the Baptist]; 61-73 [kingdom]; 83-93: "Le discours sur la montagne"; 95-116: "La loi nouvelle"; ³1976; (Théologie), Paris: Desclée De Brouwer, 1991, 253 p. *Jesus vor seinem Leben und Tod*, trans. H.U. von Balthasar (Theologia romanica, 2). Einsiedeln: Johannes, 1973, 247 p.

1975 De l'Ancien Testament à l'évangile. Une expérience globale. — *RSR* 63 (1975) 397-406. Esp. 401-405 [antitheses]. [NTA 20, 942]

1976 *L'Évangile de Jésus-Christ selon les quatre évangélistes. Textes présentés et commentés.* Paris: Cerf, 1976, 336 p.

1981 Luc 22,29. Une formule johannique dans l'évangile de Luc? — *RSR* 69 (1981) 113-122. Esp. 118-122 [19,28]. [NTA 25, 902]

1986a L'Évangile. Du bonheur à la joie. — *Quatre Fleuves* (Paris) 23-24 (1986) 21-31. Esp. 24-25 [7,12]. [NTA 31, 997]

1986b Saint Esprit. II. Nouveau Testament. 1. Le Saint Esprit dans les évangiles synoptiques. — *DBS* 11/60 (1986) 172-182.

1987 Justice – Foi – Loi. — CAZELLES, H. (ed.), *La vie de la Parole.* FS P. Grelot, 1987, 345-353. Esp. 352 [3,15].

1993 Justifiés par la foi du Christ. L'Évangile selon Paul et selon Matthieu. — DORÉ, J. – THEOBALD, C. (eds.), *Penser la foi.* FS J. Moingt, 1993, 107-115. Esp. 113-115.

1995 *Jésus dans la foi des premiers disciples.* Paris: Desclée De Brouwer, 1995, 257 p. Esp. 91-107 [Beatitudes]; 109-122: "La justice selon Matthieu".

**GUILLET, P.-E.**

1977 Entrée en scène de Pilate. — *CahRenan* 24/98 (1977) 1-24. [NTA 21, 700]

**GUINDON, Henri-Marie**

1976 L'angoisse de S. Joseph. — *CahJos* 24 (1976) 187-210.

**GUINDON, Roger**

1955a Le caractère évangélique de la morale de saint Thomas d'Aquin. — *RevUnivOtt* 25 (1955) 145*-167*. Esp. 150*-153*: "Lectura super Matthaeum".

1955b La "Lectura super Matthaeum incompleta" de saint Thomas. — *Ibid.*, 213*-219*.

1958 Le "De Sermone Domini in monte" de S. Augustin dans l'œuvre de S. Thomas d'Aquin. — *RevUnivOtt* 28 (1958) 57*-85*. Esp. 60*-67* [Lectura super Mt].

**GUIRAU, José Manuel**

1966 Mt. 27,46 y la interpretación del Ps. 21 en el Nuevo Testamento. — *CiudDios* 179 (1966) 383-430. Esp. 395-400, 409-422: "Mt 27,46 y el ciclo de la crucifixión". [NTA 11, 1041]

**GUITTON, Jean**

1954 La force de la Vierge. — *LumièreV* 16 (1954) 77-94. Esp. 77-80 [1,18-25].

**GUNDRY, Robert Horton**

1964 The Narrative Framework of Matthew xvi 17-19. A Critique of Professor Cullmann's Hypothesis. — *NT* 7 (1964-65) 1-9. [NTA 9, 915] → Cullmann 1952/53

1967a *The Use of the Old Testament in St. Matthew's Gospel. With Special Reference to the Messianic Hope* (SupplNT, 18). Leiden: Brill, 1967, XV-252 p. Esp. 9-150: "Examination of the text-form" [formal quotations Mt/Mk (9-28); allusive quotations Mt/Mk (28-66); formal quotations Mt/Lk (66-68); allusive quotations Mt/Lk (69-89); formal quotations peculiar to Mt (89-127); allusive quotations peculiar to Mt (127-147)]; 151-185: "Explanation of the text-form"; 189-204: "The question of historicity"; 205-234: "The problem of legitimacy". [NTA 13, p. 44] — Diss. Manchester, 1964 (F.F. Bruce). → Van Segbroeck 1972b, Ware 1981

    P.L. BRATSIOTIS, Θεολογία (Athens) 38 (1967) 673; G.W. BUCHANAN, *CBQ* 30 (1968) 450-451; E.D. FREED, *Bib* 52 (1971) 583-591; D.M. HAY, *JBL* 88 (1969) 95-96; J. LINDARS, *JTS* 20 (1969) 282-284; I.H. MARSHALL, *EvQ* 40 (1968) 237-239; A. SALAS, *CiudDios* 182 (1969) 91; G. SCHILLE, *TZ* 25 (1969) 137-138; A. SUHL, *TLZ* 94 (1969) 590-592.

1967b 'Verba Christi' in I Peter: Their Implications Concerning the Authorship of I Peter and the Authenticity of the Gospel Tradition. — *NTS* 13 (1966-67) 336-350. Esp. 340 [5,16; 17,26-27]; 342 [5,10]. [NTA 12, 654] → 1974a; → G. Maier 1985

1970    *A Survey of the New Testament*. Grand Rapids, MI: Zondervan, 1970, ²1975; ³1994; Exeter: Paternoster, 1979, XVI-400 p. Esp. 83-93.

1974a   Further *Verba* on *Verba Christi* in First Peter. — *Bib* 55 (1974) 211-232. Esp. 221-222 [21,42/1 Pe 2,4.7]; 222 [16,18/1 Pe 2,4.6]; 223-224 [6,20/1 Pe 1,4]; 225 [24,45/1 Pe 4,10]; 225-226 229 [5,11-12.16/1 Pe 4,13-14]; 226 [5,46/1 Pe 2,19-20]; 228-229 [5,10.45; 13,17; 23,29/1 Pe 3,14]; 230 [17,25-27/1 Pe 2,13-17]. [NTA 19, 703] → 1967b; → E. Best 1970a

1974b   Recent Investigations into the Literary Genre "Gospel". — LONGENECKER, R.N. - TENNEY, M.C. (eds.), *New Dimensions*, 1974, 97-114. Esp. 104-106 [Q].

1982    *Matthew: A Commentary on His Literary and Theological Art*. Grand Rapids, MI: Eerdmans, 1982, XVIII-652 p.; repr. 1983. Esp. 1-11: "Introduction"; 13-597: "The commentary proper"; 599-622: "Some higher-critical conclusions"; 623-640: "A theological postscript"; 641-649: "Greek index" [vocabulary]. [NTA 26, p. 318] → D.A. Carson 1982b, Geisler 1983a-b, Moo 1983b-c, Nolland 1983, Payne 1983, J.W. Scott 1985, Ziesler 1985

R. BARTNICKI, *CollTheol* 57/2 (1987) 187-189; H.J.B. COMBRINK, *WestTJ* 45 (1983) 426-430; L. COPE, *ATR* 65 (1983) 218-220; R.T. FRANCE, *Themelios* 8/3 (1982-83) 31-32; G. GREENFIELD, *SWJT* 25/2 (1982-83) 129-131; U. LUZ, *TLZ* 112 (1987) 505-507; D.L. MEALAND, *ScotJT* 37 (1984) 255-257; J.P. MEIER, *America* 147 (1982) 37-38; *JBL* 103 (1984) 475-477; F. NEIRYNCK, *ETL* 63 (1987) 408-410; D.P. SCAER, *ConcTQ* 46 (1982) 247-248; D.E. SMITH, *JAAR* 52 (1984) 171-172; D.M. SWEETLAND, *CBQ* 46 (1984) 160-162; D. TROTTER, *JEvTS* 27 (1984) 95-99; R. YARBROUGH, *EvQ* 55 (1983) 183-185.

*Matthew: A Commentary on His Handbook for a Mixed Church under Persecution*. Grand Rapids, MI: Eerdmans, rev. ed., 1994, XLII-685 p. Esp. 1-11; 13-597; 599-622; 623-640; 641-647: "A dialogue with Dan O. Via, Jr., on hypocrisy in Matthew" (→ Via 1990); 648-673: "Endnotes"; 674-682: "Greek index". [NTA 39, p. 323]

E. CUVILLIER, *ETR* 71 (1996) 81-82; S.A. HUNT, *JSNT* 59 (1995) 123; F. NEIRYNCK, *ETL* 71 (1995) 218-221.

1983a   A Response to "Matthew and Midrash". — *JEvTS* 26 (1983) 41-56. → Moo 1983b-c

1983b   A Surrejoinder to Douglas J. Moo. — *Ibid.*, 71-86. → Moo 1983b-c

1983c   A Response to "Methodological Unorthodoxy". — *Ibid.*, 95-100. → Geisler 1983a-b

1983d   A Surrejoinder to Norman L. Geisler. — *Ibid.*, 109-115. → Geisler 1983a-b

1985    On Interpreting Matthew's Editorial Comments. — *WestTJ* 47 (1985) 319-328. [NTA 30, 558] → J.W. Scott 1985

1987    The Hellenization of Dominical Tradition and Christianization of Jewish Tradition in the Eschatology of 1–2 Thessalonians. [24] — *NTS* 33 (1987) 161-178. Esp. 161-169: "Hellenization of dominical tradition"; 169-172: "Christianization of Jewish tradition". [NTA 31, 1225]

1991    A Responsive Evaluation of the Social History of the Matthean Community in Roman Syria. — BALCH, D.L. (ed.), *Social History of the Matthean Community*, 1991, 62-67. → A.J. Saldarini 1991, Segal 1991a, Stark 1991

1992    Matthean Foreign Bodies in Agreements of Luke with Matthew against Mark Evidence that Luke Used Matthew. [minor agreements] — VAN SEGBROECK, F., et al. (eds.), *The Four Gospels 1992*. FS F. Neirynck, 1992, II, 1467-1495. Esp. 1468-1469 [10,1]; 1470 [10,2]; 1470-1471 [13,11.13]; 1471 [13,19]; 1471-1472 [12,47]; 1472-1473 [8,26-27]; 1473-1474 [10,1.7-8]; 1474 [10,10]; 1474-1475 [14,13-14]; 1475-1478 [16,21]; 1479 [16,28; 20,19]; 1479-1480 [18,1]; 1480-1482 [22,35-37]; 1482-1483 [12,25]; 1483 [12,30]; 1483-1484 [19,21]; 1484 [20,17]; 1484-1485 [21,24-26]; 1485 [21,38.39]; 1486 [21,42]; 1486-1487 [21,44]; 1487-1488 [26,39]; 1488-1489 [26,64]; 1489-1490 [27,54]; 1490 [27,55-56]; 1490-1491 [27,58]; 1491-1492 [28,4]; 1492 [28,6]; 1493 [28,8]. → 1995

1994a   → 1982

1994b   On True and False Disciples in Matthew 8.18-22. — *NTS* 40 (1994) 433-441. [NTA 39, 149]

1995    A Rejoinder on Matthean Foreign Bodies in Luke 10,25-28. [22,34-40] — *ETL* 71 (1995) 139-150. [NTA 40, 230] → 1992; → Neirynck 1995a

**GUNTEN, F. VON**

1966    La doctrine de Cajétan sur l'indissolubilité du mariage. — *Angelicum* 43 (1966) 62-72. Esp. 65-67 [5,32; 19,9].

**GUTBROD, Karl**

1967a   *Ein Weg zu den Gleichnissen Jesu*. Stuttgart: Calwer, 1967, 50 p.
*Guida alle parabole di Gesù*, trans. D. Merli (Studi biblici, 52). Brescia: Paideia, 1980, 73 p.

1967b   *Die Wundergeschichten des Neuen Testaments. Dargestellt nach den ersten drei Evangelien*. Stuttgart: Calwer, 1967, ²1968, 70 p. Esp. 17-19 [8,23-27; 12,22-24]; 38-41 [8–9]; 53-55 [15,29-39].

1969    *Die Auferstehung Jesu im Neuen Testament*. Stuttgart: Calwer, 1969, 88 p. Esp. 55-59 [28,1-10].

1971    *Die "Weihnachtsgeschichten" des Neuen Testaments*. Stuttgart: Calwer, 1971, 92 p. Esp. 31-50; 76-92.
     J. PIKAZA, *Salmanticensis* 22 (1975) 580-581.

**GUTHRIE, Donald**

1965    *New Testament Introduction*. I: *The Gospels and Acts*. London: Tyndale; Chicago, IL: Inter-Varsity, 1965, 380 p. Esp. 19-48: "Matthew's gospel"; 114-177: "The synoptic problem".
*New Testament Introduction* [in one volume]. Downers Grove, IL: Inter-Varsity; Leicester: Apollos, ³1970, 1054 p.; ⁴1990, 1161 p. Esp. 28-60; 136-208.

1970    & MOTYER, J.A. (eds.), *The New Bible Commentary Revised*. Leicester – Grand Rapids, MI: Inter-Varsity, 1970, XIV-1310 p. → F. Davidson 1953, France 1994

1981    *New Testament Theology*. Downers Grove, IL – Leicester: Inter-Varsity, 1981, 1064 p. Esp. 75-115: "God"; 122-130: "The world"; 151-158: "Man"; 187-193: "Man in relation to God"; 238-243: "Messiah"; 253-256: "Son of David"; 260-263: "Servant"; 270-282: "Son of Man"; 303-312: "Son of God"; 365-369: "Virgin birth"; 409-425: "Kingdom"; 436-447: "Salvation"; 514-526: "Holy Spirit"; 602-609: "Grace"; 675-680: "Law"; 702-720: "Ecclesiology/Church"; 791-798: "Eschatology"; 818-823: "Death–Resurrection"; 848-853: "Judgment"; 875-877.887-890: "Heaven–Hell"; 896-907: "Ethics"; 955-964: "Scripture".

**GUTWENGER, Engelbert**

1966    Zur Geschichtlichkeit der Auferstehung Jesu. — *ZKT* 88 (1966) 257-282. [NTA 11, 648] → Gaechter 1967
The Narration of Jesus' Resurrection. — *TDig* 16 (1968) 8-13.

**GUTZKE, Manford George**

1966    *Plain Talk on Matthew*. Grand Rapids, MI: Zondervan, 1966, 245 p.
     S.D. TOUSSAINT, *BS* 124 (1967) 279.

**GUTZWILLER, Richard**

1960    *Die Gleichnisse des Herrn*. Einsiedeln: Benziger, 1960, 163 p. Esp. 23-28 [20,1-16]; 32-35 [13,31-32]; 41-45 [13,33]; 46-49 [13,44]; 49-51 [13,45-46]; 59-65 [13,4-9.18-23]; 66-70 [22,2-14]; 71-75 [Q 14,16-24]; 84-88 [21,28-32]; 88-91 [21,33-44]; 92-95 [25,14-30]; 107-110 [18,23-35]; 147-153 [13,24-30.36-43]; 156-159 [25,1-13].
*Le parabole di Gesù*. Milano: Paoline, 1962, 262 p.
*De gelijkenissen van Onze Heer*, trans. J. Krol. Hilversum: Brand; Hasselt: Heideland, 1962, 165 p.
*The Parables of the Lord*, trans. A Swidler. New York: Herder; Montreal: Palm, 1964, 144 p.
*Le Royaume de Dieu est semblable …; les paraboles du Seigneur*, trans. É. Saillard. Mulhouse: Salvator, 1965, 158 p.

**GUY, Harold A.**

1952    *The Study of the Gospels*. London: Macmillan, 1952, VII-158 p.

1955    *A Critical Introduction to the Gospels*. New York: St. Martin's Press, 1955.

1959    The Golden Rule. [7,12] — *ExpT* 70 (1958-59) 184. [NTA 4, 76] → B.M. Metzger 1958b

1960    *The Synoptic Gospels*. New York: St. Martin's Press, 1960, VII-183 p.

1968    The Origin of the Virgin Birth Tradition. [1,23] — *ExpT* 79 (1967-68) 183. [NTA 12, 360]

1971    *The Gospel of Matthew*. London: Macmillan, 1971, VIII-151 p. Esp. 1-27: "Introduction"; 34-149 [commentary]. [NTA 17, p. 245]

1972    Did Luke Use Matthew? — *ExpT* 83 (1971-72) 245-247. [NTA 17, 156]

**GUYOT, Bertrand-Georges**

1969    À propos de quelques commentaires sur le "Pater Noster". — *RSPT* 53 (1969) 245-255; 56 (1972) 423-432. → E. Bauer 1966, Damerau 1966a

**GWYNN, John**

1989    Hippolytus on St. Matthew 24,15-22. — *Hermathena* (Dublin) 7 (1989) 137-150.

# H

### HAACKE, Hrabanus

1979 (ed.), *Ruperti Tuitiensis De gloria et honore Filii hominis super Mattheum* (CC CM, 29). Turnhout: Brepols, 1979, XXI-458 p. Esp. IX-XXI [introduction]; 1-421 [text]. L.-J. BATAILLON, *RSPT* 69 (1984) 624; C. MARTIN, *NRT* 103 (1981) 421; H. SILVESTRE, *BTAM* 13 (1981) 69-71; *RHE* 76 (1981) 661-663; *Scriptorium* 36 (1982) 346-348; J. VAN EUGEN, *Speculum* 57 (1982) 426-428; P. VERBRAKEN, *RBén* 91 (1981) 410.

### HAACKER, Klaus

1971a Ehescheidung und Wiederverheiratung im Neuen Testament. — *TQ* 151 (1971) 28-38. Esp. 33-35 [5,32; 19,9]. [NTA 16, 335]

1971b Das hochzeitliche Kleid von Mt. 22,11-13 und ein palästinisches Märchen. — *ZDPV* 87 (1971) 95-97. [NTA 16, 161]

1977 Der Rechtssatz Jesu zum Thema Ehebruch (Mt 5,28). — *BZ* 21 (1977) 113-116. [NTA 22, 86]

1985 Zur Übersetzung von Matthäus 13,24-52 und Römer 8. Stellungnahme des neutestamentlichen Exegeten. — GNILKA, J. – RÜGER, H.P. (eds.), *Die Übersetzung der Bibel – Aufgabe der Theologie. Stuttgarter Symposion 1984* (Texte und Arbeiten zur Bibel, 2), Bielefeld: Luther-Verlag, 1985, 224-238. Esp. 225-226.

1986 "Sein Blut über uns". Erwägungen zu Matthäus 27,25. — *Kirche und Israel* (Neukirchen) 1 (1986) 47-50.

1992 Feindesliebe kontra Nächstenliebe? Bemerkungen zu einer verbreiteten Gegenüberstellung von Christentum und Judentum. [5,43-48] — MATHEUS, F. (ed.), *"Dieses Volk schuf ich mir, daß es meinen Ruhm verkünde". Dieter Vetter zum 60. Geburtstag*, Duisburg, 1992, 47-51.

### HAAG, Ernst

1991 *Vom Sabbat zum Sonntag. Eine bibeltheologische Studie* (Trierer theologische Studien, 52). Trier: Paulinus, 1991, VIII-199 p. Esp. 129-131 [12,1-14].

### HAAG, Herbert

1963 Die biblischen Wurzeln des Minjan. — BETZ, O., et al. (eds.), *Abraham unser Vater. FS O. Michel*, 1963, 235-242. Esp. 240 [18,20]; = ID., *Das Buch des Bundes. Aufsätze zur Bibel und zu ihrer Welt*, ed. B. Lang (Kommentare und Beiträge zum Alten und Neuen Testament), Düsseldorf: Patmos, 1980, 88-93. Esp. 91-92.

### HAAPA, Esko

1953 De jubilo in sermone montano commentatio. — *Talenta Quinque* (Helsinki), 1953, 55-60.

1983 Zur Selbsteinschätzung des Hauptmanns von Kapharnaum im Lukasevangelium. [Q 7,1-10] — KIILUNEN, J., et al. (eds.), *Glaube und Gerechtigkeit. FS R. Gyllenberg*, 1983, 69-76.

### HAAS, Jakob

1953 *Die Stellung Jesu zu Sünde und Sünder nach den vier Evangelien* (Studia Friburgensia, NF 7). Freiburg/Schw: Universitätsverlag, 1953, XXV-254 p. Esp. 210-223: "Die Übertragung der Vergebungsvollmacht an die Apostel" [16,19; 18,18]. — Diss. Freiburg/Schw, 1952 (F.-M. Braun).

**HABBE, J.**
1996   *Palästina zur Zeit Jesu. Die Landwirtschaft in Galiläa als Hintergrund der synoptischen Evangelien* (Neukirchener theologische Dissertationen und Habilitationen, 6). Neukirchen-Vluyn: Neukirchener, 1996, X-126 p. — Diss. Erlangen-Nurnberg, 1994 (O. Merk).

**HADDAD, Victor**
1987   *Jesus em Mateus*. Aparecida: Santuário, 1987, 128 p.

**HADFIELD, P.**
1959   Matthew and the Apocalyptic Editor. — *LondQuartHolRev* 28 (1959) 128-132. [NTA 4, 72]

**HADIDIAN, Dikran Y.**
1958   The Meaning of ἐπιούσιος and the Codices Sergii. [6,11] — *NTS* 5 (1958-59) 75-81. [NTA 3, 582]

1979*  (ed.), *From Faith to Faith. Essays in Honor of Donald G. Miller on his Seventieth Birthday* (Pittsburgh Theological MS, 31). Pittsburgh, PA: Pickwick, 1979, XXXII-446 p. → W.R. Farmer, Frye, Reicke

1982   The Lord's Prayer and the Sacraments of Baptism and of the Lord's Supper in the Early Church. — *Studia Liturgica* 15 (1982-83) 132-144. Esp. 134-139 [Fathers]; 139-140 [6,13]. [NTA 30, 1047]

**HADIWARDOYO, A. Purwa**
1986   The Principles of Christian Ethics according to Matthew. [Indonesian] — *Orientasi* 18 (1986) 100-113.

**HÄFNER, Gerd**
1992   Gewalt gegen die Basileia? Zum Problem der Auslegung des "Stürmerspruches" Mt 11,12. — *ZNW* 83 (1992) 21-51. Esp. 21-25: "Problemlage und Lösungsvorschläge"; 26-37 [βιάζομαι–βιαστής–ἁρπάζω]; 37-47: "Probleme der Interpretation *in malam partem*"; 47-51: "Die Vorzüge der Deutung *in bonam partem*". [NTA 37, 144]

1993   "Jene Tage" (Mt 3,1) und der Umfang des matthäischen "Prologs". Ein Beitrag zur Frage nach der Struktur des Mt-Ev. — *BZ* 37 (1993) 43-59. Esp. 43-45: "Abgrenzungen des ersten Teils des Mt-Ev."; 45-52: "Die verschiedenen Deutungen 'jener Tage' in Mt 3,1"; 52-54: "Der Bezug 'jener Tage' auf die Zeit des Wohnens Jesu in Nazareth"; 54-59: "Folgerungen". [NTA 37, 1247]

1994   *Der verheißene Vorläufer. Redaktionskritische Untersuchung zur Darstellung Johannes des Täufers im Matthäus-Evangelium* (SBB, 27). Stuttgart: Katholisches Bibelwerk, 1994, XIII-443 p. Esp. 4-34 [3,1-6]; 34-85 [3,7-12]; 86-115 [3,13-17]; 115-118 [4,12]; 119-127 [5,6]; 127-135 [5,10]; 135-147 [3,15]; 147-151 [21,32]; 159-191 [11,2-6]; 191-243 [11,7-15]; 244-280 [11,15-19]; 280-287 [11,2-19]; 288-305 [14,1-13]; 306-320 [17,10-13]; 386-400 [21,28-32]. [NTA 39, p. 505] — Diss. Freiburg, 1993 (L. Oberlinner).
       A. FUCHS, *SNTU* 20 (1995) 210-211.

**HAENCHEN, Ernst**
1951   Matthäus 23. — *ZTK* 48 (1951) 38-61; = ID., *Gott und Mensch*, 1965, 29-54; = LANGE, J. (ed.), *Das Matthäus-Evangelium*, 1980, 134-163.

1959a  Faith and Miracle. [8,5-13] — *Studia Evangelica* 1 (1959) 495-498.

1959b  Johanneische Probleme. — *ZTK* 56 (1959) 19-54. Esp. 23-31 [8,5-13/Jn]; 31-34 [14,13-21/Jn]; 41-46 [21,12-27/Jn]. [NTA 4, 677]; = ID., *Gott und Mensch*, 1965, 78-113. Esp. 82-90; 90-93; 100-105.

1962a  Literatur zum Thomasevangelium. — *TR* 28 (1962) 147-178, 306-338. Esp. 162-178: "Quellenprobleme". [NTA 6, 564; 7, 324]

1962b  Spruch 68 des Thomasevangeliums. [5,11] — *Muséon* 75 (1962) 19-29. [NTA 7, 643]

1963 Die Komposition von Mk viii 27–ix 1 und Par. — *NT* 6 (1963) 81-109. Esp. 96-103 [16,13-28]. [NTA 8, 964]
Leidensnachfolge. Eine Studie zu Mk. 8,27–9,1 und den kanonischer Parallelen. — ID., *Die Bibel und wir*, 1968, 102-134. Esp. 120-126.

1965 *Gott und Mensch. Gesammelte Aufsätze.* Tübingen: Mohr, 1965, 488 p. → 1951, 1959b

1968a *Die Bibel und wir. Gesammelte Aufsätze. Zweiter Band.* Tübingen: Mohr, 1968, 423 p. → 1963, 1968b

1968b Das Gleichnis vom grossen Mahl. — *Ibid.*, 135-155.

1973 Die Anthropologie des Thomas-Evangeliums. — BETZ, H.D. – SCHOTTROFF, L. (eds.), *Neues Testament und christliche Existenz. Festschrift für Herbert Braun zum 70. Geburtstag am 4. Mai 1973*, Tübingen: Mohr, 1973, 207-227. Esp. 217-218 [6,25/Th 36]; 218 [11,7/Th 78]; 218-219 [24,43-44/Th 103]; 221 [7,3/Th 26].

1980 *Das Johannesevangelium. Ein Kommentar*, ed. U. Busse. Tübingen: Mohr, 1980, XXXIV-614 p. Esp. 74-85 [John and the synoptics].
*John*, trans. F.W. Funk (Hermeneia). Philadelphia, PA: Fortress, 2 vols., 1984, XXX-308 and XVIII-366 p. Esp. I, 74-86.

### HAENDLER, Gert

1956 Die drei großen nordafrikanischen Kirchenväter über Mt. 16,18-19. — *TLZ* 81 (1956) 361-364.

1976 Zur Frage nach dem Petrusamt in der Alten Kirche. [16,17-19] — *StudTheol* 30 (1976) 89-122.

### HÄRING, Bernhard

1967 The Normative Value of the Sermon on the Mount. — *CBQ* 29 (1967) 375-385/69-79. [NTA 12, 148]
Valor normativo do Sermão da montanha. — *Theologica* 2 (1967) 7-17.

1968a *Liebe ist mehr als Gebot. Lebenserneuerung aus dem Geist der Bergpredigt.* München-Freiburg: Wewel, 1968, 208 p.
*La morale del Discorso della montagna* (I Libri della famiglia cristiana, 7). Roma: Paoline, 1968, 284 p.

1968b *Zusage an die Welt* (Theologische Brennpunkte: aktuelle Schriftenreihe, 14). Bergen-Enkheim: Kaffke, 1968, 79 p.
Amore come apertura secondo il Discorso della montagna. — ID., *Il cristiano nel mondo*, trans. C. Mariani (Punti scottanti di teologia, 29), Roma: Paoline, 1969, 95-116.

1976 *The Beatitudes: Their Personal and Social Implications.* Slough: St. Paul Publications, 1976, 98 p.
*Blessed are the Pure in Heart. The Beatitudes.* New York: Crossroad, 1977, 111 p.
*Bienaventuranzas. Vida y testimonio.* Buenos Aires: Paulinas, 1979, 80 p.

### HÄRING, E.

1971 *Die Struktur und die theologische Bedeutung der beiden neutestamentlichen Genealogien, unter besonderer Berücksichtigung der literarischen Gattung "Genealogie" im Alten Testament und im Judentum.* Diss. Salzburg, 1971, 132 p.

### HÄUSSLING, Angelus A.

1985 Mt 18,20 in der Texttradition der lateinischen Liturgie. — *Archiv für Liturgiewissenschaft* (Regensburg) 27 (1985) 405-407. → Lona 1985

### HAGEDORN, Dieter

1966 & MERKELBACH, R., Ein neues Fragment aus Porphyrios "Gegen die Christen". [17,20] — *VigChr* 20 (1966) 86-90.

1978 → Kramer 1978

**HAGEMEYER, Oda**

1976 "Wenn dir jemand einen Streich gibt auf deine rechte Backe..." (Matthäus 5,39). Beispiele heutiger Interpretation der Bergpredigt. — JASPERT, B. - MOHR, R. (eds.), *Traditio - Krisis - Renovatio aus theologischer Sicht. Festschrift Winfried Zeller zum 65. Geburtstag*, Marburg: Elwert, 1976, 10-23.

**HAGER, J.**

1959 *Das Verbum πιστεύω in den vier Evangelien.* Diss. Graz, 1959.

**HAGG, Gregory Dean**

1988 *The Interrelationship between the New Testament and Tannaitic Judaism.* Diss. Univ. of New York, 1988, 346 p. (C.H. Gordon). — *DissAbstr* 49 (1988-89) 1176.

**HAGNER, Donald Alfred**

1973 *The Use of the Old and New Testaments in Clement of Rome* (SupplNT, 34). Leiden: Brill, 1973, X-393 p. Esp. 135-178: "Clement's knowledge of synoptic material" (135-151 [5,7; 6,14; 7,1-2.12/1 Clem 13,2]; 152-164 [18,6; 26,24/1 Clem 46,8]; 164-171 [allusions: 5,18; 7,13-14.21; 11,29-30; 13,3; 26,28; OT/15,8]); 277-283: "Allusion and quotation. The synoptic gospels" [Apostolic Fathers].

1976 The Old Testament in the New Testament. — SCHULTZ, S.J. - INCH, M.A. (eds.), *Interpreting the Word of God. Festschrift in Honor of Steven Barabas*, Chicago, IL: Moody, 1976, 78-104. Esp. 89-91; 94 [1,23]; 95 [2,15.18.23]; 95-96 [12,40]; 96 [27,9-10].

1985a Apocalyptic Motifs in the Gospel of Matthew: Continuity and Discontinuity. — *HorizonsBT* 7/2 (1985) 53-82. Esp. 57-59: "The life-setting of Matthew's readers"; 60-68: "The apocalyptic viewpoint of Matthew"; 68-73: "Matthew's altered apocalyptic"; 73-77: "The role of apocalyptic in Matthew". [NTA 31, 105]

1985b The Sayings of Jesus in the Apostolic Fathers and Justin Martyr. — WENHAM, D. (ed.), *The Jesus Tradition Outside the Gospels*, 1985, 233-268. Esp. 234-239 [5-7/1 Clem 13,2; 18,6; 26,24/1Clem 46,8]; 239-240 [10,16/Ignatius, Polyc. 2,2]; 240 [26,41/Polycarp, Phil. 2,3]; 240-242 [7,6/Did 9,5; 6,16/Did 8,1; 22,37-39/Did 1,2]; 242 [Barnabas]; 243-244 [Hermas]; 244-246 [2 Clem]. 246-249 [Justin].

1985c The *Sitz im Leben* of the Gospel of Matthew. — *SBL 1985 Seminar Papers*, 243-269. Esp. 244-246: "Tensions in Matthew"; 246-254: "The relation to contemporary Judaism"; 254-259: "The *Sitz im Leben* of Matthew's community"; 259-264: "Distinctive emphases in Matthew"; 264-266: "The date and provenance of the gospel"; 266-269: "Matthew in the context of first century christianity"; = BAUER, D.R. - POWELL, M.A. (eds.), *Treasures New and Old*, 1996, 27-68. Esp. 29-32; 32-45; 45-53; 53-60; 60-64; 64-68.

1986 Matthew. — BROMILEY, G.W., et al. (eds.), *The International Standard Bible Encyclopedia*, III, Grand Rapids, MI: Eerdmans, 1986, 280.
Matthew, Gospel according to. — *Ibid.*, 280-288.

1992 Righteousness in Matthew's Theology. — WILKINS, M.J. - PAIGE, T. (eds.), *Worship, Theology and Ministry in the Early Church. Essays in Honor of Ralph P. Martin* (JSNT SS, 87), Sheffield: JSOT, 1992, 101-120. Esp. 102-105: "The Law"; 105-107: "Grace"; 107-118: "Righteousness".

1993 *Matthew 1–13* (Word Biblical Commentary, 33A). Dallas, TX: Word, 1993, LXXVII-407 p. Esp. XXXIX-LXXVII: "Introduction". [NTA 38, p. 293]
    M. ALVAREZ, *Ant* 70 (1995) 696-697; S.A. HUNT, *JSNT* 57 (1995) 121; S. JURIĆ, *Angelicum* 71 (1994) 450-451; A.-J. LEVINE, *JBL* 115 (1996) 354-356; R.K. MCIVER, *AusBR* 43 (1995) 85.
*Matthew 14–28* (Word Biblical Commentary, 33B). Dallas, TX: Word, 1995, XXXIX-408-935 p. [NTA 40, p. 340]
    D.C. ALLISON, *JBL* 116 (1997) 363-141.

1994 Matthew's Eschatology. — SCHMIDT, T.E. - SILVA, M. (eds.), *To Tell the Mystery*. FS R.H. Gundry, 1994, 49-71. Esp. 50-64: "The data"; 64-70: "Theses concerning Matthew's eschatology".

1995a  → 1993

1995b  Imminence and Parousia in Matthew. — FORNBERG, T. - HELLHOLM, D. (eds.), *Texts and Contexts*. FS L. Hartman, 1995, 77-92. Esp. 78-79 [24,3]; 79-80 [10,23]; 82-86 [εὐθέως]; 86-88 [24,15-22]; 88-89 [date].

1995c  Writing a Commentary on Matthew: Self-Conscious Ruminations of an Evangelical. — *Semeia* 72 (1995) 51-72. Esp. 61-65 [historical Jesus]; 65-69 [anti-Judaism]. → 1993/95

**HAHN, Ferdinand**

1963a  *Christologische Hoheitstitel. Ihre Geschichte im frühen Christentum* (FRLANT, 83). Göttingen: Vandenhoeck & Ruprecht, 1963; [4]1974, 442 p. Esp. 13-53: "Menschensohn" [24,27.37-39]; 67-125: "Kyrios" [7,21-23; 8,8.19-22; 10,24-25; 23,8; 25,1-13]; 133-225: "Christos" [4,8-10; 10,34; 11,2-6; 25,31-46]; 242-279: "Davidssohn" [1,1-17.18-25; 2,1-12]; 280-333: "Gottessohn" [1,18-25; 11,27; 28,18-20]; 351-404: "Der eschatologische Prophet" [11,2-6.7-19]; (Uni-Taschenbücher, 1873), [5]1995, 488 p. — Diss. Heidelberg, 1961 (G. Bornkamm). → Vielhauer 1965a.d
*The Titles of Jesus in Christology. Their History in Early Christianity*, trans. H. Knight & G. Ogg. London: Lutterworth; New York: World Publ. Times Mirror, 1969, 415 p.

1963b  *Das Verständnis der Mission im Neuen Testament* (WMANT, 13). Neukirchen-Vluyn: Neukirchener, 1963; [2]1965, 168 p. Esp. 24-28 [8,5-13]; 33-36 [10,5-16]; 44-45 [10,5-6.23]; 54-57 [28,18-20]; 103-111 [24,14]. — Diss. Heidelberg, 1962 (G. Bornkamm).
*Mission in the New Testament* (Studies in Biblical Theology, 47). London: SCM, 1965, 184 p. Esp. 41-46; 54-56; 65-68; 120-128.

1967a  Die Nachfolge Jesu in vorösterlicher Zeit. — ID. - STROBEL, A. - SCHWEIZER, E., *Die Anfänge der Kirche im Neuen Testament* (Evangelisches Forum, 8), Göttingen: Vandenhoeck & Ruprecht, 1967, 7-36. Esp. 35-36 [16,18-19].

1967b  Der urchristliche Gottesdienst. — *Jahrbuch für Liturgie und Hymnologie* 12 (1967) 1-44.
*Der urchristliche Gottesdienst* (SBS, 41). Stuttgart: Katholisches Bibelwerk, 1970, 101 p. Esp. 17-31: "Jesu Stellung zum Gottesdienst" [5,17-48; 6,5-8.16-18].
*The Worship of the Early Church*, trans. D.E. Green. Philadelphia, PA: Fortress, 1973, XXVI-118 p.
*Le culte dans l'Église primitive*. — *SE* 46 (1994) 309-332. Esp. 314-321; 47 (1995) 189-213. [NTA 39, 1699; 40, 1092]

1970a  Das Gleichnis von der Einladung zum Festmahl. — BÖCHER, O. - HAACKER, K. (eds.), *Verborum Veritas*. FS G. Stählin, 1970, 51-82. Esp. 51-60 [22,1-10]; 60-65 [22,1/Th 64], 65-82 [interpretation].

1970b  Die Petrusverheissung Mt 16,18f: eine exegetische Skizze. — *Materialdienst des Konfessionskundlichen Instituts Bensheim* 21 (1970) 8-13; = KERTELGE, K. (ed.), *Das kirchliche Amt*, 1977, 543-563. Esp. 545-547 [origin]; 547-549 [historical Jesus]; 549-553 [16,18]; 554-558 [16,19]; = ID., *Exegetische Beiträge*, 1986, 185-200. Esp. 186-188; 188-189; 190-193; 193-196.

1971  Die Bildworte vom neuen Flicken und vom jungen Wein (Mk. 2,21f parr). — *EvT* 31 (1971) 357-375. Esp. 357-364 [9,16-17/Mk]. [NTA 16, 548]

1973a  Neutestamentliche Grundlagen für eine Lehre vom kirchlichen Amt. — ID., et al., *Dienst Wort und Amt. Überlebensfrage der Kirchen*, Regensburg: Pustet, 1973, 7-40. Esp. 36-40 [16,18-19]; = ID., *Exegetische Beiträge*, 1986, 159-184. Esp. 181-184.

1973b  Die Worte vom Licht Lk 11,33-36. — HOFFMANN, P., et al. (eds.), *Orientierung an Jesus*. FS J. Schmid, 1973, 107-138. Esp. 107-117 [Q 11,33-36]; 117-119 [5,13-16]; 120-124 [10,26/Mk 4,22]; 124-127 [6,19-24]; 132-134 [Q 11,29-32].

1980  Der Sendungsauftrag des Auferstandenen. Matthäus 28,16-20. — SUNDERMEIER, T., et al. (eds.), *Fides pro mundi vita. Missiontheologie heute. Hans-Werner Gensichen zum 65. Geburtstag* (Missionswissenschaftliche Forschungen, 14), Gütersloh: Mohn, 1980, 28-43.

1982 Urchristliche Lehre und neutestamentliche Theologie. Exegetische und fundamental-theologische Überlegungen zum Problem christlicher Lehre. — KERN, W. (ed.), *Die Theologie und das Lehramt* (QDisp, 91), Freiburg: Herder, 1982, 63-115. Esp. 74; 79-83 [διδάσκω].

1983 Mt 5,17: Anmerkungen zum Erfüllungsgedanken bei Matthäus. — LUZ, U. - WEDER, H. (eds.), *Die Mitte des Neuen Testaments*. FS E. Schweizer, 1983, 42-54. Esp. 42-43.47-48 [5,17]; 44-45 [OT fulfilment quotations]; 45-46 [5,21-48].

1985 Jesu Wort vom bergeversetzenden Glauben. — *ZNW* 76 (1985) 149-169. Esp. 150-152; 153-160 [17,20; 21,21]; 160-161 [7,7-8]. [NTA 30, 1083]

1986a *Exegetische Beiträge zum ökumenischen Gespräch. Gesammelte Aufsätze*, I. Göttingen: Vandenhoeck & Ruprecht, 1986, 354 p. → 1970b, 1973a

1986b Ist das textkritische Problem von 2 Kor 1,17 lösbar? — SCHRAGE, W. (ed.), *Studien zum Text und zur Ethik das Neuen Testaments*. FS H. Greeven, 1986, 158-165. Esp. 159-162 [5,37].

1988 Die eschatologische Rede Matthäus 24 und 25. — SCHENKE, L. (ed.), *Studien zum Matthäusevangelium*. FS W. Pesch, 1988, 107-126. Esp. 110-112 [Mark; Q]; 112-114 [structure]; 114-115 [23]; 115-120 [24,1-33]; 120-121 [24,34-41]; 122 [24,42-44.45-51]; 122-123 [25,1-13]; 123 [25,14-30]; 123-124 [25,31-46]; 124-126 [eschatology].

1989 Prophetie und Lebenswandel. Bemerkungen zu Paulus und zu zwei Texten der Apostolischen Väter. — MERKLEIN, H. (ed.), *Neues Testament und Ethik*. FS R. Schnackenburg, 1989, 527-537. Esp. 531-534 [Didache/Mt].

**HAHN, Paul Douglas**

1990 *Structure in Rhetorical Criticism and the Structure of the Sermon on the Plain (Luke 6:20-49)*. Diss. Marquette Univ., Milwaukee, WI, 1990, 483 p. — *DissAbstr* 52 (1991-92) 569.

**HAHN, S.R.**

1951 Βασιλεία *and Its Cognates in the New Testament*. Diss. Southern Baptist Theol. Sem., Louisville, KY, 1951.

**HAHNEMAN, Geoffrey Mark**

1992 *The Muratorian Fragment and the Development of the Canon* (Oxford Theological Monographs). Oxford: Clarendon, 1992, XI-237 p. Esp. 93-95 [Papias]; 183-187 [gospel order]. → Kaestli 1994

**HAIBLE, Eberhard**

1963 Die Kirche als Wirklichkeit Christi im Neuen Testament. — *TTZ* 72 (1963) 65-83. Esp. 77-83: "Die Aüßerung der Christus-wirklichkeit (Mt)". [NTA 8, 287]

**HAINTHALER, Theresia**

1988 *"Von der Ausdauer Ijobs habt ihr gehört" (Jak 5,11). Zur Bedeutung des Buches Ijob im Neuen Testament* (EHS, XXIII/337). Frankfurt/M-Bern: Lang, 1988, 465 p. Esp. 84-140: "Die Parallelen im Mt-Evangelium" [6,26; 7,25; 11,11; 13,7; 16,18; 24,28; 25,8.35.42]. — Diss. Frankfurt/M, 1986 (J. Beutler).

**HAINZ, Josef**

1992* (ed.) *Theologie im Werden. Studien zu den theologischen Konzeptionen im Neuen Testament. [In Memoriam Otto Kuss]*. Paderborn: Schöningh, 1992, 463 p. → Hofrichter, Sand 1992a-b

**HALL, Craig L.**

1994 *Biblical Hermeneutics and the Sociology of Knowledge: The Parable of the Pounds according to C.H. Dodd and Itumeleng J. Mosala* [25,14-30]. Diss. Baylor Univ., Waco, TX, 1994, 289 p. (M.C. Parsons). — *DissAbstr* 55 (1994-95) 3879.

**HALL, Douglas John**

1992 The Theology and Ethics of the Lord's Prayer. — *PrincSemB* suppl. 2 (1992) 125-136.

**HALL, Randy**

1987 God Knows Your Name. Matthew 10:26-33. — *RestQ* 29 (1987) 235-237.

**HALL, Stuart G.**

1987 Synoptic Transfigurations: Mark 9,2-10 and Partners. — *King's College Theological Review* (London) 10 (1987) 41-44. [NTA 32, 627]

**HALL, T. Hartley**

1975 An Exposition of Matthew 4:12-23. — *Interpr* 29 (1975) 63-67.

**HALSON, B.R.**

1964 A Note on the Pharisees. — *Theology* 67 (1964) 248-251. Esp. 249-250. [NTA 9, 72]

**HALVERSON, John**

1994 Oral and Written Gospel: A Critique of Werner Kelber. — *NTS* 40 (1994) 180-195. Esp. 189-191.195 [Mk/Q]. [NTA 38, 1379] → W.H. Kelber 1983

**HAMANN, H.P.**

1970 *Sic et Non*: Are We So Sure of Matthean Dependence on Mark? — *ConcTM* 41 (1970) 462-469. [NTA 15, 484]

1977 The Ten Virgins. An Exegetical-Homiletical Study. [25,1-13] — *LuthTJ* 11 (1977) 68-72. [NTA 22, 92]

1984 *Chi Rho Commentary on the Gospel according to Matthew*. Adelaide, S. Australia: Lutheran Publishing House, 1984, 320 p. [NTA 30, p. 230]

**HAMEL, Eduardo**

1958 Loi naturelle et loi du Christ. — *ScEccl* 10 (1958) 49-76. Esp. 69-73: "Les antithèses du Sermon sur la montagne". → 1964

1964 *Loi naturelle et loi du Christ* (Studia. Recherches de philosophie et de théologie, 17). Brugge–Paris: Desclée De Brouwer, 1964, 171 p. Esp. 1-43: "Loi naturelle et loi du Christ" (→ 1958); 128-142: "Le Décalogue dans le Nouveau Testament".

1969 *Les dix paroles. Perspectives bibliques* (Essais pour notre temps. Section de théologie, 7). Bruxelles–Paris: Desclée; Montréal: Bellarmin, 1969, 169 p. Esp. 102-122: "Le Décalogue dans les Synoptiques".

1986 A não-violência em S. Mateus. Reflexões bíblico-teológicas. [Non-violence in Mt. Biblical-theological reflexions] — *Brotéria* (Rio de Janeiro) 123 (1986) 554-560.

**HAMERTON-KELLY, Robert G.**

1965 A Note on Matthew xii.28 par. Luke xi.20. — *NTS* 11 (1964-65) 167-169. [NTA 9, 910]

1972 Attitudes to the Law in Matthew's Gospel: A Discussion of Matthew 5:18. — *BR* 17 (1972) 19-32. [NTA 17, 905]

1973 *Pre-existence, Wisdom, and the Son of Man. A Study of the Idea of Pre-Existence in the New Testament* (SNTS MS, 21). Cambridge: University Press, 1973, XII-310 p. Esp. 22-102: "Pre-existence in the synoptic tradition" [22-47: Q 6,22; 7,33-35; 9,58; 11,29-32.49-51; 12,8.10; 13,34-35; 67-83: Mt 1–2; 11,28-30; 13,35.41-42; 25,31].

1976 Matthew, Gospel of. — *IDBS*, 1976, 580-583.

1979 *God the Father. Theology and Patriarchy in the Teaching of Jesus* (Overtures to Biblical Theology). Philadelphia, PA: Fortress, 1979, XVI-128 p. Esp. 70-81: "Jesus and the Divine Father" [6,9-13; 11,25-27]; 88-93: "The Church as the united family of God: Matthew".

**HAMILTON, Robert**

1975  *The Delay of the Parousia as a Factor in New Testament Salvation History: A Consideration with Special References to the Synoptic Gospels.* Diss. Manchester, 1975.

**HAMM, M. Dennis**

1990  *The Beatitudes in Context. What Luke and Matthew Meant* (Zacchaeus Studies: New Testament). Wilmington, DE: Glazier, 1990, VII-120 p. Esp. 27-67: "The beatitudes (and woes) according to Luke"; 68-109: "The beatitudes according to Matthew". [NTA 34, p. 384]

**HAMMAN, Adalbert**

1951  Le baptême par le feu. [3,11] — *MSR* 8 (1951) 285-292; = ID., *Études patristiques. Méthodologie – Liturgie – Histoire – Théologie* (Théologie historique, 85), Paris: Beauchesne, 1991, 79-86.

1952  *Le Pater expliqué par les Pères.* Paris: Éd. franciscaines, 1952, 164 p.; exp. ed., 1962, 232 p.; new ed. 1995, 224 p.
      A. BENOÎT, *RHPR* 34 (1954) 294-295; C. MOHRMANN, *VigChr* 10 (1956) 53-54.

1955  La prière de Jésus. — *BibVieChrét* 10 (1955) 7-21. Esp. 16-17 [11,25-26].
      The Prayer of Jesus. — *Way* 3 (1963) 174-183.

1957  *La prière.* I. *Le Nouveau Testament* (Bibliothèque de théologie). Paris–Tournai: Desclée, 1957, 484 p. Esp. 59-169: "La prière dans les évangiles synoptiques" [5,44; 6,1-8.9-13; 7,7-11; 11,25-26; 26,39-44; 27,46].

1958  (ed.), *Ambrosiaster, In Mattheaum XXIV fragmenta* (Patrologiae Latinae Supplementum, 1). Paris: Garnier, 1958, 655-668.

1966  Le Notre Père dans la catéchèse des Pères de l'Église. — *La Maison-Dieu* (Paris) 85 (1966) 41-68. [NTA 11, 204]

1978  *Explication du Sermon sur la montagne* (Les Pères dans la foi, 5). Paris: Desclée De Brouwer, 1978, 166 p.

1985  → Landry

**HAMMER, Paul L.**

1962  Principles of Interpretation in Matthew. — *Theology and Life* (Lancaster, PA) 5 (1962) 25-36. Esp. 28-32: "Christ and the Old Testament". [NTA 7, 495]

**HAMMER, R.A.**

1970  Elijah and Jesus: A Quest for Identity. — *Judaism* 19 (1970) 207-218. [NTA 15, 92]

**HAMMER, Wolfgang**

1980  L'intention de la généalogie de Matthieu. [1,1] — *ETR* 55 (1980) 305-306. [NTA 25, 70]
      → Chopinau 1978

**HAMMOND BAMMEL, Caroline Penrose**

1973  Some Textual Points in Origen's *Commentary on Matthew.* — *JTS* 24 (1973) 380-404. Esp. 381-382 [5,14]; 382-393 [13,44]; 393-395 [13,50; 15,8-9]; 395-404 [15,10-20]; = ID., *Origeniana et Rufiniana* (Vetus Latina. Die Reste der altlateinischen Bibel. Aus der Geschichte der lateinischen Bibel, 29), Freiburg: Herder, 1996, 380-404.

**HAMPEL, Volker**

1989  "Ihr werdet mit den Städten Israels nicht zu Ende kommen". Eine exegetische Studie über Matthäus 10,23. — *TZ* 45 (1989) 1-31. Esp. 3-4: "Mt 10,23 in seinem heutigen Kontext"; 4-8: "Tradition und matthäische Redaktion"; 8-11: "Mt 10,23 und seine traditionsgeschichtlichen Grundlagen im Alten Testament und im Judentum"; 15-18: "Mt 10,23 und die Vorhersagen über das Erleben der Heilsvollendung"; 18-20: "Mt 10,23 und seine Deutung bei Matthäus"; 20-24: "Mt 10,23 und seine Deutung in der palästinischen Kirche"; 24-27: "Mt 10,23 im Mund Jesu"; 27-28: "Mt 10,23 – ein Irrtum Jesu?". [NTA 33, 1132]

1990   *Menschensohn und historischer Jesus. Ein Rätselwort als Schlüssel zum messianischen Selbstverständnis Jesu.* Neukirchen-Vluyn: Neukirchener, 1990, XIV-418 p. Esp. 51-187: "Die Logien von der zukünftigen Hoheit des Menschensohns" [8 11-12; 10,23.32-33; 12,38-40; 19,28; 24,27.37-39]; 188-211; 212-245: "Die Logien von der gegenwärtigen Niedrigkeit des Menschensohns" [8,19-20; 11,16-19]. — Diss. Tübingen, 1983 (O. Betz).

**HANHART, Karel**
1970   The Structure of John I 35–IV 54. — *Studies in John.* FS J.N. Sevenster, 1970, 22-46. Esp. 24-26.28 [Jn 1,43-51/Mt].

**HANIG, Roman**
1993   Christus als "wahrer Salomo" in der frühen Kirche. — *ZNW* 84 (1993) 111-134. Esp. 120-121 [6,29; 12,42]; 126-134 [12,42]. [NTA 38, 387]

**HANKS, Thomas D.**
1986   La navidad según san Mateo. [2,1-12] — *Mision* (Buenos Aires) 5 (1986) 95-101.
1992   Poor, Poverty (NT). — *ABD* 5 (1992) 414-424.

**HANSEN, Theo**
1969   *De overeenkomsten Mattheüs-Lucas tegen Marcus in de drievoudige traditie. I. Historisch overzicht van de problematiek met cumulatieve lijst van overeenkomsten. II. Onderzoek van Mc 1 en parallelteksten.* Diss. Leuven, 1969, XXIII-237 and XXV-202 p. (F. Neirynck).
1974   → F. Neirynck 1974a

**HANSON, Anthony Tyrrell**
1957   *The Wrath of the Lamb.* London: SPCK, 1957, X-249 p. Esp. 112-131: "Judgement in the synoptic gospels and Acts".
1978   Rahab the Harlot in Early Christian Tradition. — *JSNT* 1 (1978) 53-60. Esp. 53-54 [1,5]. [NTA 23, 725]
1980   *The New Testament Interpretation of Scripture.* London: SPCK, 1980, XI-237 p. Esp. 122-156: "The scriptural background to the doctrine of the *Descensus ad inferos*" [12,38-41].
1983   *The Living Utterances of God. The New Testament Exegesis of the Old.* London: Darton, Longman & Todd, 1983, VI-250 p. Esp. 70-78: "The use of scripture in Matthew's gospel" [1,23; 2,17-18.23; 8,17; 11,25-29; 12,7.18-21; 13,43; 21,4-5; 27,9-10]; 150-151 [5,8-9]; 179-180 [1,22-23].

**HANSON, John S.**
1980   Dreams and Visions in the Graeco-Roman World and Early Christianity. — *ANRW* II.23.2 (1980) 1395-1427. Esp. 1421-1422.

**HANSON, J.K.**
1994   *The Star of Bethlehem. The History, Mystery, and Beauty of the Christmas Star.* New York: Hearst Books, 1994, 64 p. [NTA 39, p. 324]

**HANSON, K.C.**
1993   Greco-Roman Studies and the Social-Scientific Study of the Bible: A Classified Periodical Bibliography (1970-1994). — *Forum* 9 (1993) 63-119. [NTA 41, 538]
1994a  'How Honorable! How Shameful!' A Cultural Analysis of Matthew's Makarisms and Reproaches. — *Semeia* 68 (1994) 81-111. Esp. 87-99 [macarisms]; 99-101 [5,3-10]; 101-103 [23,13-36]. [NTA 41, 202]
1994b  Transformed on the Mountain: Ritual Analysis and the Gospel of Matthew. — *Semeia* 67 (1994) 147-170. Esp. 152-157: "Mountains in Matthew"; 157-160 [4,1-12]; 160-161 [4,25-8,1]; 161-163 [15,29-31]; 164-165 [17,1-8]; 165-167 [28,16-20]. [NTA 40, 804] → Esler 1994

**HANSSEN, Olav**

1970    Zum Verständnis der Bergpredigt. Eine missionstheologische Studie zu Mt 5,17-18. — LOHSE, E., et al. (eds.), *Der Ruf Jesu*. FS J. Jeremias, 1970, 94-111. Esp. 95-99: "Die Bedeutung der Didache Jesu nach dem Missionsbefehl"; 99-104: "Versuch einer literarkritische Analyse der Bergpredigt"; 104-110: "Das Doppelgebot der Liebe als Erfüllung des Gesetzes"; 110-111: "Die Bedeutung der Didache Jesu für die Mission".

**HANSSLER, Bernhard**

1984    Das Jünger-Ethos der Bergpredigt im Verhältnis zu den allgemeinen Moralprinzipien. — *Renovatio* (Bonn) 40 (1984) 82-95. [NTA 29, 90]

**HARAGUCHI, Takaaki**

1991    *The Prohibition of Oath-Taking in the Gospel of Matthew* [5,33-37]. Diss. Lutheran School of Theology, Chicago, IL, 1991, 249 p. (W.C. Linss). — *DissAbstr* 52 (1991-92) 1389.

1993    Das Unterhaltsrecht des frühchristlichen Verkündigers. Eine Untersuchung zur Bezeichnung ἐργάτης im Neuen Testament. — *ZNW* 84 (1993) 178-195. Esp. 186-193 [9,37-38; 10,10]. [NTA 38, 990]

**HARDER, Günther**

1967    Jesus und das Gesetz (Matthäus 5,17-20). — ECKERT, W.P., et al. (eds.), *Antijudaismus*, 1967, 105-118, 205-206.

**HARDING, Mark**

1994    The Lord's Prayer and Other Prayer Texts of the Greco-Roman Era. A Bibliography. — CHARLESWORTH, J.H., et al., *The Lord's Prayer*, 1994, 101-257. Esp. 186-201: "Lord's prayer"; 202: "Matthew".

**HARE, Douglas R.A.**

1967    *The Theme of Jewish Persecution of Christians in the Gospel according to Matthew* (SNTS MS, 6). Cambridge: University Press, 1967, XIV-204 p. Esp. 80-129: "References to Jewish persecution of Christians in the gospel according to St Matthew" [5,10-12; 10,16-33; 22,6; 23,29-39]; 130-145: "Matthew's understanding of the causes of persecution" [5,10-12]; 146-166: "The Christian response to persecution by the Jews as evidenced by Matthew". [NTA 12, p. 393] — Diss. Union Theol. Sem., New York, 1965 (W.D. Davies).

> P.B. BARNETT, *AusBR* 16 (1968) 62-63; C.K. BARRETT, *JTS* 21 (1970) 166-168; E. BEST, *ScotJT* 21 (1968) 359-360; G.B. CAIRD, *ExpT* 79 (1967-68) 238-239; J. COPPENS, *ETL* 44 (1968) 584; I. GOMÁ CIVIT, *EstBíb* 27 (1968) 257-259; R.M. GRANT, *VigChr* 24 (1970) 143-144; K. GRAYSTON, *The Church Quarterly* 1 (1968) 71-72; R. GROB, *TZ* 26 (1970) 441-442; R.H. GUNDRY, *JBL* 87 (1968) 346-347; C. HAUFE, *TLZ* 96 (1971) 113-114; J HIGGENS, *RHE* 64 (1969) 269-270; B. JAY, *RHPR* 49 (4969) 374-375; S.E. JOHNSON, *ATR* 50 (1968) 209; G. JOHNSTON, *Perspective* (Pittsburg, PA) 9/2 (1968) 167-170; R. JONES, *RExp* 57 (1970) 233-234; L.E. KECK, *RelLife* 37 (1968) 636-637; R.P. MARTIN, *EvQ* 40 (1968) 178-180; N.J. McELENEY, *CBQ* 30 (1968) 618-620; J. MURPHY-O'CONNOR, *RB* 76 (1969) 597-601; J. NEVES, *Itinerarium* 15 (1969) 568-569; V. NIKIPROWETZKY, *RevÉtudJuiv* 129 (1970) 261-273; M. PLESSNER, *Bibliotheca Orientalis* 28 (1971) 389-390; J.S. POBEE, *Theology* 71 (1968) 416-417; L.F. RIVERA, *RevistBíb* 31 (1969) 57; S. SANDMEL, *JEcuSt* 5 (1968) 769-770; K.H. SCHELKLE, *Bib* 49 (1968) 585-587; T. SNOY, *RBén* 38 (1968) 344; M.J. SUGGS, *JAAR* 36 (1968) 396-399; L. SWEETMAN, Jr., *CalvTJ* 4 (1969) 99-104; M. V.d.H., *Irénikon* 44 (1971) 442-443.

1975    & HARRINGTON, D.J., "Make Disciples of All the Gentiles" (Mt 28:19). — *CBQ* 37 (1975) 359-369. Esp. 361-363: "The appearances of *ethnos/ethnē* in Matthew"; 363-366: "The case for *panta ta ethnē* including Israel"; 366-367: "'Jews' and 'Gentiles' in Matthean theology"; 367-368: "Some patristic interpretations of Mt 28:19". [NTA 20, 447]; = HARRINGTON, D.J., *The Light*, 1982, 110-123. Esp. 114-116; 117-120; 120-121; 121-123. → J.P. Meier 1977a

1979    The Rejection of the Jews in the Synoptic Gospels and Acts. — DAVIES, A. (ed.), *Antisemitism and the Foundations of Christianity*, New York: Paulist, 1979, 27-47. Esp.

32-40: "Gentilizing anti-Judaism only in Matthew"; 40-43: "Is there a relationship between gentilizing anti-Judaism and christology in Matthew?"; 43-46: "Toward a hermeneutic of Matthean anti-Judaism".

1984    The Quest of the Son of Man: A Progress Report. — *Proceedings EGLBS* 4 (1984) 166-180.

1990a   *The Son of Man Tradition.* Minneapolis, MN: Fortress, 1990, XIV-316 p. Esp. 113-182: "Matthew" [7,22-23; 8,20; 9,36; 10,23; 11,19, 12,8.32.40; 13,37.41; 16,13.27-28; 17,9.12.22-23; 19,28; 24,27.30-31.37-39; 25,31; 26,2.24.45.64; 28,16-20]; 214-225: "The Q material" [Q 7,33-35; 12,8-9]; 257-282: "Jesus" [Q 7,34; 9,58; 11,30; 12,8-9.10].

1990b   "The mountain where Jesus laid down rules for them" (Matt. 28:16). — CURRY, R.C. – KELSO, T.J. – MAUE, C.S. (eds.), *He Came Here And Loved Us. A Festschrift for William F. Orr*, Watsontown, PA: W.F. Orr Festschrift Foundation, 1990, 167-173.

1993    *Matthew* (Interpretation. A Bible Commentary for Teaching and Preaching). Louisville, KY: Knox, 1993, XIII-338 p. [NTA 37, p. 437]
D.C. ALLISON, *Interpr* 48 (1994) 410-414; L. COPE, *TS* 55 (1994) 175-176; E. CUVILLIER, *ETR* 71 (1996) 84; D. GREENE, *PerspRelSt* 22 (1995) 198; A.V. MCNICOL, *RestQ* 36 (1994) 55-56; G.T. MONTAGUE, *CBQ* 56 (1994) 595-596; P. PRZYBYLSKI, *CRBR* 7 (1994) 198-199; J.D. SMALL, *HorizonsBT* 16 (1994) 100-101.

**HARGREAVES, John**
1968    *A Guide to the Parables* (TEF Study Guide, 1). London: SPCK, 1968, [2]1970, XI-132 p. Esp. 43-50 [20,1-16]; 80-86 [13,44-46]; 87-94 [18,23-35]; 103-111 [25,1-13]; 112-122 [25,14-30].
*Las parábolas evangélicas: orientación para una mejor comprensión,* trans. J. Martínez Aduriz. Santander: Sal Terrae, 1973, 206 p.

**HARL, Marguerite**
1988    La Septante aux abords de l'ère chrétienne. Sa place dans le Nouveau Testament. — DORIVAL, G. – HARL, M. – MUNNICH, O., *La Bible grecque des Septante. Du judaïsme hellénistique au christianisme ancien* ("Initiations au christianisme ancien"), Paris: Cerf/CNRS, 1988, 269-288. Esp. 277-280.288.

1990    Références philosophiques et références bibliques du langage de Grégoire de Nysse dans ses *Orationes in Canticum Canticorum.* — EISENBERGER, H. (ed.), Ἑρμηνεύματα. *Festschrift für H. Hörner zum sechzigsten Geburtstag,* Heidelberg, 1990, 117-131; = ID., *La langue de Japhet. Quinze études sur la Septante et le grec des chrétiens,* Paris: Cerf, 1994, 235-249. Esp. 245-246 [3,10]; 248-249 [24,12].

**HARLÉ, Paul-André**
1966a   Le problème synoptique. — *FoiVie* 65/4 = *Cahiers bibliques* 4 (1966) 3-16.

1966b   La tempête apaisée. Notes exégétiques sur cette péricope synoptique à trois témoins. — *Ibid.,* 81-88. Esp. 85-86 [8,23-27].

**HARMS, Ray**
1966    *The Matthean Weekday Lessons in the Greek Gospel Lectionary* (Studies in the Lectionary Text of the Greek New Testament, II/6). Chicago, IL: University Press, 1966, 55 p. — Diss. Princeton Theol. Sem., Princeton, NJ, 1963.
D.C. PELLETT, *JBL* 86 (1967) 118-119.

**HARNER, Philip B.**
1975    *Understanding the Lord's Prayer.* Philadelphia, PA: Fortress, 1975, X-149 p. Esp. 1-22: "The versions of the prayer"; 23-56: "The address"; 57-82: "The 'thou' petitions"; 83-113: "The 'we' petitions"; 114-119: "The doxology"; 120-122: "The Lord's prayer and christian faith". [NTA 20, p. 236]

1987    Matthew 6:5-15. — *Interpr* 41 (1987) 173-178.

**HARNISCH, Wolfgang**

1974 Die Sprachkraft der Analogie. Zur These vom 'argumentativen Charakter' der Gleichnisse Jesu. — *StudTheol* 28 (1974) 1-20. Esp. 16-20. [NTA 19, 79]; = ID. (ed.), *Gleichnisse Jesu*, 1982, 390-413. Esp. 408-413.

1977 The Metaphorical Process in Matthew 20:1-15. — *SBL 1977 Seminar Papers*, 231-250. Esp. 239-246.

1979 Die Metapher als heuristisches Prinzip: Neuerscheinungen zur Hermeneutik der Gleichnisreden Jesu. — *VerkFor* 24 (1979) 53-89.

1982a* (ed.), *Gleichnisse Jesu. Positionen der Auslegung von Adolf Jülicher bis zur Form- geschichte* (Wege der Forschung, 366). Darmstadt: Wissenschaftliche Buchgesellschaft, 1982, XIII-457 p. → M. Black 1960, Dodd 1935, Fiebig 1904, E. Fuchs 1954b, Greeven 1952, Harnisch 1974, J. Jeremias 1947, Jüngel 1962, E. Lohmeyer 1938, Madsen 1929, Schoedel 1972

1982b* (ed.), *Die neutestamentliche Gleichnisforschung im Horizont von Hermeneutik und Literaturwissenschaft* (Wege der Forschung, 575). Darmstadt: Wissenschaftliche Buchgesellschaft, 1982, IX-441 p. → J.D. Crossan 1972, E. Fuchs 1954a/70, Funk 1966, 1974, Güttgemanns 1973a, L. Marin 1971b, Via 1971

1985 *Die Gleichniserzählungen Jesu. Eine hermeneutische Einführung* (Uni-Taschenbücher, 1343). Göttingen: Vandenhoeck & Ruprecht, 1985, [2]1990, [3]1995, 332 p. Esp. 177-200 [20,1-16]; 230-253 [22,2-14]; 253-271 [18,23-35].
*Las parábolas de Jesús. Una introducción hermenéutica*, trans. M. Olasagasti (Biblioteca de estudios bíblicos, 66). Salamanca: Sígueme, 1989, 296 p.

1989 Der bezwingende Vorsprung des Guten. Zur Parabel von den bösen Winzern (Markus 12,1ff. und Parallelen). [21,33-46] — WEDER, H. (ed.), *Die Sprache der Bilder. Gleichnis und Metapher in Literatur und Theologie* (Gütersloher Taschenbücher Siebenstern, 558), Gütersloh: Gütersloher Verlagshaus, 1989, 22-38.

1994 Beiträge zur Gleichnisforschung (1984-1991). — *TR* 59 (1994) 346-387. Esp. 353-354; 357-371 [20,1-16]. [NTA 39, 1436]

**HARRELL, I.B.**

1988 & BENSON, A.H. (eds.), *This Man Jesus. The Gospel Narrative of His Life and Ministry*. Grand Rapids, MI: Zondervan, 1988, 215 p.

**HARRINGTON, Daniel J.**

1972 Baptism in the Holy Spirit. — *ChSt* 11 (1972) 31-44. Esp. 34-35 [3,11]; = ID., *The Light*, 1982, 46-60. Esp. 49-50.

1974 New Testament Perspectives on the Ministry of the Word. — *ChSt* 13 (1974) 65-76. Esp. 70-72 [10]. [NTA 19, 258]; = ID., *The Light*, 1982, 79-92. Esp. 84-86.

1975a Matthean Studies since Joachim Rohde. — *HeythJ* 16 (1975) 375-388. Esp. 376-379 [composition]; 379-383 [community]; 383-388 [theology]. [NTA 20, 428]; = ID., *The Light*, 1982, 93-109. Esp. 95-98; 98-104; 104-106.

1975b → Hare 1975

1979 *Interpreting the New Testament. A Practical Guide* (New Testament Message, 1). Dublin: Veritas; Wilmington, DE: Glazier, 1979, XI-149 p. Esp. 21-22 [6,33]; 49-53 [28,19]; 79-81 [13,31-33]; 100-105 [8,18-27]; 134-139 [22,34-40].

1982 *The Light of All Nations. Essays on the Church in New Testament Research* (Good News Studies, 3). Wilmington, DE: Glazier, 1982, 201 p. → 1972, 1974, 1975a-b

1983 *The Gospel according to Matthew* (Collegeville Bible Commentary, 1). Collegeville, MN: Liturgical Press, 1983, 128 p. [NTA 28, p. 77]; 1989 [NTA 33, p. 375]
K.A. BARTA, *BTB* 15 (1985) 34.

*Vangelo secondo Matteo*, trans. M.M. Di Vicinio (La Bibbia per tutti, 26). Brescia: Queriniana, 1992, 161 p.
M. LÀCONI, *RivBib* 42 (1994) 227-229.
*El Evangelio de San Mateo*, trans. J.I. Alfaro (Comentario Bíblico de Collegeville. Nuevo Testamento, 1).
Collegeville, MN: Liturgical Press, 1994, 120 p. [NTA 39, p. 505]
B.T. VIVIANO, *RB* 101 (1994) 457.

1985 *The New Testament: A Bibliography* (Theological and Biblical Resources, 2). Wilmington, DE: Glazier, 1985, 242 p. Esp. 59 [Q]; 63-66 [Mt].

1986 The Synoptic Gospels. — COLLINS, J.J. - CROSSAN, J.D. (eds.), *The Biblical Heritage In Modern Catholic Scholarship* [FS B. Vawter], Wilmington, DE: Glazier, 1986, 131-155. Esp. 134-135 [purpose, audience]; 137 [structure]; 139 [theology]; 140 [disciples]; 141-144 [Q]; 144-146 [oral tradition; Sondergut]; 147-148 [historical Jesus]; 149-150 [teaching of Jesus]; 150-151 [virginal conception]; 151-152 [resurrection account].

1989a Birth Narratives in Pseudo-Philo's Biblical Antiquities and the Gospels. — HORGAN, M.P. - KOBELSKI, P.J. (eds.), *To Touch the Text*. FS J.A. Fitzmyer, 1989, 316-324. Esp. 321-324.

1989b A Dangerous Text. Matthew and Judaism. — *Canadian Catholic Review* (Saskatoon) 7 (1989) 135-142. [NTA 33, 1110]

1989c New and Old in New Testament Interpretation: The Many Faces of Matthew 1:18-25. — *NewTheolRev* 2/1 (1989) 39-49. [NTA 33, 1114]

1989d "Not to abolish, but to fulfill". [5,17-20] — *BiTod* 27 (1989) 333-337. [NTA 34, 619]

1990a The Mixed Reception of the Gospel: Interpreting the Parables in Matt 13:1-52. — ATTRIDGE, H.W. - COLLINS, J.J. - TOBIN, T.H. (eds.), *Of Scribes and Scrolls. Studies on the Hebrew Bible, Intertestamental Judaism, and Christian Origins Presented to John Strugnell on the Occasion of his Sixtieth Birthday* (College Theology Society Resources in Religion, 5), Lanham, MD: University Press of America, 1990, 195-201.

1990b Polemical Parables in Matthew 24–25. — *USQR* 44 (1990) 287-298. [NTA 36, 729]

1991a *The Gospel of Matthew* (Sacra Pagina Series, 1). Collegeville, MN: The Liturgical Press - Glazier, 1991, XIII-429 p. Esp. 1-25: "Introduction"; 27-417: "Translation, notes, interpretation". [NTA 36, p. 264]
D.C. ALLISON, *Bib* 75 (1994) 115-118; D.L. BOCK, *BS* 150 (1993) 246; J. BRENNAN, *DoctLife* 44 (1994) 509-510; M.C. DIPPENAAR, *Neotestamentica* 27 (1993) 438-439; R.A. EDWARDS, *CBQ* 55 (1993) 581-583; T. FORNBERG, *SEÅ* 58 (1993) 171-172; A. FUCHS, *SNTU* 18 (1993) 255-257; J. GALOT, *Greg* 75 (1994) 161-162; R.B. GARDNER, *CRBR* 6 (1993) 251-252; D. GREENE, *PerspRelSt* 22 (1995) 197; M. HASITSCHKA, *ZKT* 115 (1993) 185-186; M. LÀCONI, *RivBib* 42 (1994) 227-229; J. LAMBRECHT, *LouvSt* 18 (1993) 72-73; P. MEAGHER, *Vidyajyoti* 58 (1994) 398-399; F. NEIRYNCK, *ETL* 68 (1992) 439-441; J.F. O'GRADY, *ChSt* 33 (1994) 83-85; C.S. RODD, *ExpT* 104 (1992-93) 150; D.C. SIM, *AusBR* 42 (1994) 75-76; M.L. SOARDS, *Interpr* 47 (1993) 410-411; B.T. VIVIANO, *RB* 101 (1994) 457; J. WOOD, *EvQ* 65 (1993) 89-90.

1991b Sabbath Tensions: Matthew 12:1-14 and Other New Testament Texts. — ESKENAZI, T., et al. (eds.), *The Sabbath in Jewish and Christian Traditions*, New York: Crossroad, 1991, 45-56.

1992 The Rich Young Man in Matthew 19,16-22. Another Way to God for Jews? — VAN SEGBROECK, F., et al. (eds.), *The Four Gospels 1992*. FS F. Neirynck, 1992, II, 1425-1432. Esp. 1425-1427: "State of research"; 1427-1429: "Mt 19,16-22: redactional analysis"; 1429-1431: "Confirmation from context"; 1431-1432: "Theological significance".

1993a Matthew as a Jewish Book. — *Priests & People* (London) 7 (1993) 240-244. [NTA 38, 145]

1993b Matthew as a Christian Gospel. — *Ibid.*, 284-288. [NTA 38, 144]

**HARRINGTON, Jay M.**

1982    *Matthew 28:16-20 and the Feast of the Ascension. An Investigation into a Biblico-liturgical Relationship.* Diss. (Master's) Catholic Theol. Union, Chicago, IL, 1982, V-339 p. (D. Senior). Esp. 9-91.285-300: "Literary analysis of Matthew 28:16-20"; 92-228.300-320: "Dominant themes proclaimed in Matthew 28:16-20"; 244-282.609-627: "Matthew 28:16-20 and the feast of the ascension".

**HARRINGTON, Wilfrid J.**

1962    *Formation of the Gospels. The Gospel of St Matthew* (Doctrine and Life Series, 1). Dublin: Dominican Publications, 1962, 57 p. [NTA 7, p. 137]

1963    *Explaining the Gospels* (Deus Books). Glen Rock, NJ: Paulist, 1963, 190 p.

1964    *A Key to the Parables* (Deus Books). New York – Glen Rock, NJ: Paulist, 1964, 160 p. Esp. 29-35 [22,1-14]; 39-44 [20,1-16]; 46-53 [25,14-30]; 121-122 [18,12-14]; 138-140 [7,24-27].
*He Spoke in Parables.* Dublin: Helicon, 1964, 127 p.
*Il parlait en paraboles*, trans. J. Mignon (Lire la Bible, 10). Paris: Cerf, 1967, 152 p. Esp. 30-35; 39-43; 46-51; 121-122; 131-133.
*Hij sprak in parabels*, trans. J. Verstraeten. Bilthoven: Nelissen, 1967, 140 p.

1970    Jesus' Attitude towards Divorce. — *IrTQ* 37 (1970) 199-209. Esp. 203-207 [5,31-32; 19,3-9]. [NTA 15, 667] → 1972a

1972a   The New Testament and Divorce. — *IrTQ* 39 (1972) 178-187. Esp. 178-184: "The Matthaean clauses: a new look". [NTA 17, 520] → 1970; → Derrett 1970e

1972b   The Parables in Recent Study (1960-1971). — *BTB* 2 (1972) 219-241. Esp. 233-236 [18,23-35; 24,45-51]; 236-238 [13]. [NTA 17, 495] → Kingsbury 1969, Weiser 1971
Les paraboles: études récentes. — *BTB* 2 (1972) 219-242.

1974    *Parables Told by Jesus. A Contemporary Approach to the Parables.* Staten Island, NY: Alba House, 1974, VII-135 p.

1975    Hidden Treasure. [13,44-46] — *Furrow* 26 (1975) 523-529. [NTA 20, 441]

**HARRIS, Murray J.**

1983    *Raised Immortal. Resurrection and Immortality in the New Testament.* London: Morgan & Scott, 1983; Grand Rapids, MI: Eerdmans, 1985, XIV-304 p. Esp. 18-22 [28,1-20]; 174-175 [25,31-46].

1986    'The dead are restored to life': Miracles of Revivification in the Gospels. — WENHAM, D. – BLOMBERG, C. (eds.), *The Miracles of Jesus*, 1986, 295-326. Esp. 304-310: "The daughter of Jairus" [9,18-26].

**HARRIS, Xavier J.**

1988    Discipleship in the Gospels. — *BiTod* 26 (1988) 75-79. Esp. 75-77 [passion predictions]. [NTA 32, 1071]

**HARRISON, C.H.**

1991    "Are not two strouths for an assar bought?" Notes on the Principles of Bible Translation. [10,29] — *Notes on Translation* (Dallas, TX) 5/3 (1991) 1-14. [NTA 36, 1160]

**HARRISON, Everett F.**

1959    The Christology of the Fourth Gospel in Relation to the Synoptics. [11,27/Jn] — *BS* 116 (1959) 303-309. [NTA 4, 419]

1973    Did Christ Command World Evangelism? [28,18-20] — *ChrTod* 18 (1973) 210-214. [NTA 18, 481]

**HARRISVILLE, Roy A.**

1966    The Woman of Canaan. A Chapter in the History of Exegesis. [15,21-28] — *Interpr* 20 (1966) 274-287. [NTA 11, 213]

1969  Jesus and the Family. — *Interpr* 23 (1969) 425-438. Esp. 428-429 [10,34-35]; 429-430 [10,37]; 432-433 [8,21-22]. [NTA 14, 428]

1993  In Search of the Meaning of "the Reign of God". — *Interpr* 47 (1993) 140-151. Esp. 143-144 [11,12]; 149-150 [13]. [NTA 37, 1476]

**HART, H. St. J.**

1984  The Coin of "Render unto Caesar..." (A Note on Some Aspects of Mark 12:13-17; Matt. 22:15-22; Luke 20:20-26). — BAMMEL, E. - MOULE, C.F.D. (eds.), *Jesus and the Politics of His Day*, 1984, 241-248.

**HART, John Francis**

1986  *A Chronology of Matthew 24:1-44*. Diss. Grace Theol. Sem., Winona Lake, IN, 1986, XII-275 p. (J. Sproule – D. Turner – G. Meadors). Esp. 25-48: "Structures and chronological approaches to Mt 24"; 49-76: "The context and setting of Mt 24"; 77-121 [24,3-14]; 122-180 [24,15-28]; 181-221 [24,29-35]; 222-248 [24,36-44]. — *DissAbstr* 47 (1986-87) 2188; *SBT* 15 (1987) 116.

**HARTENSTEIN, Karl**

1951  *Wann wird das geschehen? Der Versuch einer Auslegung von Matthäus 24 und 25*. Stuttgart: Evang. Missionsverlag, 1951, 68 p.

**HARTIN, Patrick John**

1987  The Pharisaic Roots of Jesus and the Early Church. — *Neotestamentica* 21 (1987) 113-124. Esp. 115-117 [23,4-36]; 117 [15,3-6]; 119-121 [5,31-32]. [NTA 33, 442]

1989  James and the Q Sermon on the Mount/Plain. — *SBL 1989 Seminar Papers*, 440-457. Esp. 440-442: "Development of the Sermon on the Mount"; 442-451: "James and the beatitudes"; 452-456: "James and other aspects of the Q Sermon on the Mount".

1991  *James and the Q Sayings of Jesus* (JSNT SS, 47). Sheffield, JSOT, 1991, 266 p. Esp. 44-80: "The role of Wisdom in James and Q: paraenetical advice"; 116-137: "The personification of Wisdom in Q" [Q 7,31-35; 10,21-22; 11,31.49-51; 13,34-35]; 140-172: "James and the Sermon on the Mount/Plain: a comparative examination" [Q 6,20-26.27-33.36.43-45.47-49]; 173-198: "James and the Jesus traditions" [Q 11,9-13; 12,33-34; 14,11; 16,13.17; 17,3; Mt 5,33-37; 25,34-35]; 199-217: "The Wisdom theme of perfection in James and the Jesus traditions" [5,48.17-19; 11,28-30; Q 10,21-22]; 220-227: "The Q community"; 227-233: "The Matthean community". — Diss. University of South Africa, Pretoria, 1988 (I. du Plessis). → G. Jenkins 1994

> R. BAUCKHAM, *JTS* 44 (1993) 298-301; D.R. CATCHPOLE, *ExpT* 103 (1991-92) 26-27; B. COYAULT, *ETR* 67 (1992) 110-111; P.M. HEAD, *Themelios* 18/1 (1992) 29-30; M. HÜNEBURG, *TLZ* 119 (1994) 1078-1080; J.S. KLOPPENBORG, *CBQ* 54 (1992) 567-568; R.A. PIPER, *EvQ* 65 (1993) 84-86; H.B. RAMSEY, *Interpr* 47 (1993) 84.86; R. TREVIANO ETCHEVERRíA, *Salmanticensis* 39 (1992) 308-310.

1993  The Religious Nature of First-Century Galilee as a Setting for Early Christianity. — *Neotestamentica* 27 (1993) 331-350. Esp. 345-347 [Q: setting]. [NTA 38, 1652]

1994  The Wisdom and Apocalyptic Layers of the Sayings Gospel Q: What is Their Significance? — *HervTS* 50 (1994) 556-582. [NTA 39. 1437] → Kloppenborg 1987a

1995  "Yet Wisdom is justified by her children" (Q 7:35). A Rhetorical and Compositional Analysis of Divine Sophia in Q. — KLOPPENBORG, J.S. (ed.), *Conflict and Invention*, 1995, 151-164. Esp. 153-156 [Q 7,31-35]; 156-158 [Q 11,49-51]; 159-161 [Q 10,21-22].

**HARTKE, Wilhelm**

1961  *Vier urchristliche Parteien und ihre Vereinigung zur Apostolischen Kirche* (Deutsche Akademie der Wissenschaften. Schriften der Sektion für Altertumswissenschaft, 24). Berlin: Akademie, 1961, 2 vols., XIV-401 and 402-792 p. Esp. 278-290: "Das Verhältnis des Lc zu Mt"; 290-345: "Feststellung der Einwirkung des Ur-Lc auf RMc und durch diesen auf Mt"; 371-381: "Q – ein zu Lebzeiten Jesu geführtes Tagebuch"; 381-401: "Die Einstimmigkeit des Gesamtaufrisses der drei letzten Jahre Jesu bei UrJoh und Q mit Ur-Mc".

**HARTMAN, Lars**

1963   *Testimonium Linguae. Participial Constructions in the Synoptic Gospels. A Linguistic Examination of Luke 21,13* (Coniectanea Neotestamentica, 19). Lund: Gleerup; København: Munksgaard, 1963, 75 p. Esp. 28-36.

1966   *Prophecy Interpreted. The Formation of Some Jewish Apocalyptic Texts and of the Eschatological Discourse Mark 13 par.*, trans. N. Tomkinson & J. Gray (ConBibNT, 1). Lund: Gleerup, 1966, 299 p. Esp. 145-177 [24,4-25.29-31]; 219-226 [24,1-3.32-36]; 242-245. — Diss. Uppsala, 1966 (H. Riesenfeld).

1970   "Såsom det är skrivet". Några reflexioner över citat som kommunikationsmedel i Matteusevangeliet. ["As it is written". Some reflections on citations as a means of communication in the gospel of Matthew] — *SEÅ* 35 (1970) 33-43. Esp. 34 [4,14-16]; 36 [24,6]; 36-38 [2]; 39-41 [26,64]; 41-43 [17,17]. [NTA 16, 843] → 1972

1971   Dopet "till Jesu namn" och tidig kristologi. Några trevande överväganden. — *SEÅ* 36 (1971) 136-163. Esp. 139-142 [kingdom]; 142-144 [John the Baptist]. [NTA 17, 1090]
       Baptism "Into the Name of Jesus" and Early Christology. Some Tentative Considerations. — *StudTheol* 28 (1974) 21-48. Esp. 31-33 [John the Baptist]; 33-35 [kingdom]. [NTA 19, 250] → 1974, 1992a

1972   Scriptural Exegesis in the Gospel of St. Matthew and the Problem of Communication. — DIDIER, M. (ed.), *L'Évangile selon Matthieu*, 1972, 131-152. Esp. 135 [24,6]; 137-141 [2,18]; 142-146 [Mt/Is 53; Dan 7]; 147 [9,36; 17,17]; 148-151 [Midrash]. → 1970

1973   Dop, ande och barnaskap. Några traditionshistoriska överväganden till Mk 1:9-11 par. — *SEÅ* 37-38 (1972-1973) 88-106. Esp. 93-95 [Mk 1,9-11/Q]; 104-105 [John the Baptist]. [NTA 18, 869]
       Taufe, Geist und Sohnschaft. Traditionsgeschichtliche Erwägungen zu Mk 1,9-11 par. — *SNTU* 1 (1976) 89-109. Esp. 95-97; 107-108.

1974   'Into the Name of Jesus'. A Suggestion Concerning the Earliest Meaning of the Phrase. — *NTS* 20 (1973-74) 432-440. Esp. 434-435 [28,19]; 438 [10,41; 18,20]. [NTA 19, 444] → 1971, 1992a

1982   "Your will be done on earth as it is in heaven". — *AfTJ* 11 (1982) 209-218. [NTA 28, 496]

1992a  *"Auf den Namen des Herrn Jesus". Die Taufe in den neutestamentlichen Schriften* (SBS, 148). Stuttgart: Katholisches Bibelwerk, 1992, 164 p. Esp. 14-31: "Die Taufe Johannes des Täufers"; 136-141: "Das Matthäusevangelium". → 1971, 1974
       *"Till Herrens Jesu namn"* (Tro & Tanke, 4). Uppsala: Svenska Kyrkans Forskningsråd, 1993, 146 p. Esp. 120-124.
       *"Into the Name of the Lord Jesus". Baptism in the Early Church.* Edinburgh: Clark, 1997, x-214 p. Esp. 147-153.

1992b  Baptism. — *ABD* 1 (1992) 583-594. Esp. 583-585, 590.

**HARTMANN, Gert**

1964   Die Vorlage der Osterberichte in Joh 20. — *ZNW* 55 (1964) 197-220. Esp. 202-210 [28,8-9]; 210-215 [28,10.16-20]. [NTA 9, 977]

**HARVEY, Anthony E.**

1970   *The New English Bible. Companion to the New Testament.* Cambridge: University Press; Oxford: University Press, 1970, VIII-850 p.; 1971; 1973; 1979. Esp. 17-110: "The gospel according to Matthew"

1982   "The workman is worthy of his hire". Fortunes of a Proverb in the Early Church. [10,10] — *NT* 24 (1982) 209-221. [NTA 27, 138]

1985*  (ed.), *Alternative Approaches to New Testament Study.* London: SPCK, 1985, x-144 p. → Derrett, Downing, Goulder, A.E. Harvey

1985   Forty Strokes Save One: Social Aspects of Judaizing and Apostasy. — *Ibid.*, 79-96. Esp.
       90-94: "Matthew".

1990   *Strenuous Commands. The Ethic of Jesus.* London: SCM; Philadelphia, PA: Trinity,
       1990, VIII-248 p. Esp. 68-70 [beatitudes]; 71-73 [5,40-41]; 7?-75 [5,25-26]; 76-80 [antitheses]; 80-82
       [5,27-28]; 82-89 [5,31-32]; 89-91 [5,33-37]; 92-96 [5,38-42]; 96-110 [5,43-48]; 112-114 [forgiveness]; 116-
       139 [poverty/wealth].

1993   Marriage, Sex and the Bible. — *Theology* 96 (1993) 364-372, 461-468. Esp. 366-369.
       [NTA 38, 758/1013]

1994   Genesis versus Deuteronomy? Jesus on Marriage and Divorce. — EVANS, C.A. –
       STEGNER, W.R. (eds.), *The Gospels and the Scriptures of Israel,* 1994, 55-65.

**HARVEY, Graham**

1996   *The True Israel. Uses of the Names Jew, Hebrew and Israel in Ancient Jewish and
       Early Christian Literature* (Arbeiten zur Geschichte des Antiken Judentums und des
       Urchristentums, 35). Leiden: Brill, 1996, XVII-303 p. Esp. 234-238 [Israel]. — Diss. Newcastle,
       1991 (J.F.A. Sawyer).

**HARY, P.**

1985   Reflexión sobre la parábola de los talentos. [25,14-30] — *Verbo* (Buenos Aires) 251
       (1985) 87-96.

**HASENFRATZ, Hans-Peter**

1975   *Die Rede von der Auferstehung Jesu Christi. Ein methodologischer Versuch* (Forum
       Theologiae Linguisticae, 10). Bonn: Linguistica Biblica, 1975, 271 p. Esp. 70-72.75-77
       [Mk/Q]; 189-195: "Q und das Auferstehungskerygma" [Q 11,29-32; 13,34-35; 14,27]; 226-238 [5,3-12/Q];
       238-243 [5,44-48/Q].

**HASHIMOTO, Shigeo**

1978   The Parable of Sheep and Goats (Mt 25,31-46) and the Ecclesiology in Matthew.
       [Japanese] — *Kirisutokyō Kenkyū* 42 (1978) 36-50.

1981   Sophia-Christology and the Gospel of Matthew. [Japanese] — *Kirisutokyō Kenkyū* 44
       (1981) 1-29.

1986   Position of Gentiles in the Gospel according to Matthew. [Japanese] — *Kirisutokyō
       Kenkyū* 47 (1986) 16-45.

1990   Temple Tax in the Matthean Tradition. An Exegetical Study on Mt 17,24-27. [Japanese]
       — *Kirisutokyō Kenkyū* 52 (1990) 1-18.

1991   The Gospel according to Matthew. [Japanese] — *New Testament Commentary on the New
       Interconfessional Bible*, 1991, I, 29-165.

**HASITSCHKA, Martin**

1975   *Traditionsgeschichtliche Einordnung der synoptischen Berichte von der Versuchung
       Jesu.* Diss. Innsbruck, 1975, XIII-247 p. (N. Kehl). — *ZKT* 97 (1975) 502-503.

1995   FISCHER, G. – HASITSCHKA, M., *Auf dein Wort hin. Berufung und Nachfolge in der
       Bibel.* Innsbruck–Wien: Tyrolia, 1995, 150 p.

1997   Die Verwendung der Schrift in Mt 4,1-11. — TUCKETT, C.M. (ed.), *The Scriptures in
       the Gospels*, 1997, 487-490.

**HASKIN, Richard Webb**

1968   *The Call to Sell All. The History of the Interpretation of Mark 10,17-23 and Parallels.*
       Diss. Columbia Univ., New York, 1968, 489 p. — *DissAbstr* 32 (1971-72) 526-527.

**HASLER, Victor**

1952 *Gesetz und Evangelium in der alten Kirche bis Origenes. Eine auslegungsgeschichtliche Untersuchung.* Zürich–Frankfurt/M: Gotthelf, 1952, XVIII-135 p. Esp. 9-26: "Die Untersuchung des synoptischen Textbestandes" [5,17-20.21-48; 7,12; 12,1-8.9-14; 15,2; 19,16-22; 22,34-40]. — Diss. Zürich, 1952 (D. Lerch).

1959 Das Herzstück der Bergpredigt. Zum Verständnis der Antithesen in Matth. 5,21-48. — *TZ* 15 (1959) 90-106. [NTA 4, 384]

1962 Die königliche Hochzeit, Matth. 22,1-14. — *TZ* 18 (1962) 25-35. [NTA 7, 140]

1968 Judenmission und Judenschuld. — *TZ* 24 (1968) 173-190. Esp. 184-190. [NTA 13, 265]

1969 *Amen. Redaktionsgeschichtliche Untersuchung zur Einführungsformel der Herrenworte "Wahrlich ich sage euch".* Zürich–Stuttgart: Gotthelf, 1969, 207 p. Esp. 55-76: "Die Logien in der Redequelle" [Q 3,8; 6,27; 7,9.26.28; 10,12.24; 11,51; 12,4-5.8.22.27.44.51.59; 13,35; 15,7; 19,26; Mt 5,18; 8,11-12; 11,22-24; 17,20]; 77-99: "Das Sondergut des Matthäus" [5,20.22.28.32.34.39; 6,2.5.16; 10,23; 12,6.36; 18,10.18.19; 21,31.43; 25,12.40.45]; 126-138: "Die Formeln bis Matthäus" [5,18; 8,11; 11,24; 17,20; 19,9.23.24.28; 24,2; 26,29.64]; 159-165: "Die gemeinsamen Formeln in Q"; 162.165-167 [Sondergut Mt]; 180-187 [historical Jesus]. → K. Berger 1970a

**HASTINGS, Francis**

1991 How the Synoptic Gospels Came to Be Written. — *Priests & People* 5 (1991) 73-76, 78. Esp. 74-78: "The two-gospel hypothesis". [NTA 35, 1118]

**HASTOUPIS, Athanasios P.**

1986 The Passages Matth. 6.6 and John 20.16-17. [Greek] — Θεολογία (Athens) 57 (1986) 855-856.

**HAUBECK, Wilfrid**

1980* & BACHMANN, M. (eds.), *Wort in der Zeit. Neutestamentliche Studien. Festgabe für Karl Heinrich Rengstorf zum 75. Geburtstag.* Leiden: Brill, 1980, VIII-293 p. → Bachmann, P.-R. Berger, Correns, A. Fuchs, Haubeck, Orchard

1980 Zum Verständnis der Parabel von den Arbeitern im Weinberg (Mt 20,1-15). — *Ibid.*, 95-107.

**HAUDEBERT, Pierre**

1987 La *métanoia*, des Septante à saint Luc. — CAZELLES, H. (ed.), *La vie de la Parole*. FS P. Grelot, 1987, 355-366. Esp. 362 [3,2; 4,17]; 363 [Q 10,13-15; Q 11,29-32].

**HAUERWAS, Stanley**

1988 The Sermon on the Mount, Just War and the Quest for Peace. — *Concilium* (London) 195 (1988) 36-43. [NTA 34, 614]

Le Sermon sur la montagne. Guerre juste et recherche de la paix. — *Concilium* (Paris) 215 (1988) 51-59.

**HAUFE, Günter**

1964 "Soviel ihr getan habt einem dieser meiner geringsten Brüder...". [25,31-46] — *Ruf und Antwort. Festgabe für Emil Fuchs zum 90. Geburtstag*, Leipzig: Koehler & Amelang, 1964, 484-493.

1968 *Vom Werden und Verstehen des Neuen Testaments. Eine Einführung.* Gütersloh: Mohn, 1968, 160 p. Esp. 58-59 [Q]; 65-67 [Mt].

1979 Das Kind im Neuen Testament. — *TLZ* 104 (1979) 625-638. [NTA 24, 970]

1985 Reich Gottes bei Paulus und in der Jesustradition. — *NTS* 31 (1985) 467-472. Esp. 470-472. [NTA 30, 212]

1986 Individuelle Eschatologie des Neuen Testaments. — *ZTK* 83 (1986) 436-463. Esp. 441-443: "Sondergut und Redaktion bei Matthäus und Lukas". [NTA 30, 820]

1989   Umstrittene Bergpredigt – Positionen ihrer Auslegungs- und Wirkungsgeschichte. — *TVers* 17 (1989) 35-43.

**HAUG, Martin**
1975   Mission: Was ist das? – Wie geschieht das? Eine Befragung von Matthäus 9,35–10,8. — *TBeitr* 6 (1975) 185-191. [NTA 20, 439]

**HAULOTTE, Edgar**
1966   *Symbolique du vêtement selon la Bible* (Théologie, 65)  Paris: Aubier, 1966, 352 p. Esp. 278-319: "La robe nuptiale" [22,1-14].

**HAUSER, Alan J.** → D.F. Watson 1994

**HAVENER, Ivan**
1983   Jesus in the Gospel Sayings. — *BiTod* 21 (1983) 77-82. [NTA 27, 894]

1987   *Q. The Sayings of Jesus. With a Reconstruction of Q by A. Polag* (Good News Studies, 19). Wilmington, DE: Glazier, 1987, 176 p. Esp. 17-107: "An introduction to Q"; 115-165: "The text of Q". [NTA 31, p. 231] → Polag 1979
       H.T. FLEDDERMANN, *BTB* 18 (1988) 34-35; J.G. LODGE, *CBQ* 51 (1989) 152-153; J.M. REESE, *TS* 48 (1987) 786; T.A. ROBINSON, *Religious Studies and Theology* (Edmonton, Alberta) 7/2-3 (1987) 96-97; P. SELLEW, *CRBR* 1 (1988) 224-226.

**HAWKINS, John Cesar**
1909[R]   *Horae Synopticae. Contributions to the Study of the Synoptic Problem* [1899, [2]1909]. Oxford: Clarendon; Grand Rapids, MI: Baker, 1968, XVI-223 p. Esp. 3-10; 30-34: "Words and phrases characteristic of St Matthew's gospel"; 54-113: "Indications of sources" [identities in language; words differently applied; transpositions of the order; doublets; the source largely used by Matthew and Luke apart from Mark]; 154-173: "Further statistics and observations"; 199-200: "Words peculiar to Matthew"; 208-212 [minor agreements]. → Neirynck 1970

**HAWKINS, Peter S.**
1983   Parable as Metaphor. [13,44] — *Christian Scholar's Review* (Grand Rapids, MI) 12 (1983) 226-236. [NTA 27, 923] → J.W. Sider 1984

**HAWKINS, R.A.**
1969   Covenant Relations of the Sermon on the Mount. — *RestQ* 12 (1969) 1-9. [NTA 14, 477]

**HAWTHORN, T.**
1954   The Gerasene Demoniac: A Diagnosis. Mark v.1-20. Luke viii.26-39. (Matthew viii.28-34). — *ExpT* 66 (1954-55) 79-80.

**HAWTHORNE, Gerald F.**
1975*   (ed.), *Current Issues in Biblical and Patristic Interpretation. Studies in Honor of Merrill C. Tenney Presented by His Former Students*. Grand Rapids, MI: Eerdmans, 1975, 377 p. → Aune, E.E. Ellis, W.C. Kaiser, Keylock, Longenecker, Mare

1987*   & BETZ, O. (eds.), *Tradition and Interpretation in the New Testament. Essays in Honor of E. Earle Ellis for His 60th Birthday*. Grand Rapids, MI: Eerdmans; Tübingen: Mohr, 1987, XXI-369 p. → Borgen, Catchpole, Fitzmyer, Hawthorne, S. Kim, Luz, P. Richardson, D.M. Smith, Stanton, Strecker

1987   The Role of Christian Prophets in the Gospel Tradition. — *Ibid.*, 119-133. Esp. 122-126.

**HAY, David M.**
1973   *Glory at the Right Hand. Psalm 110 in Early Christianity* (SBL MS, 18). Nashville, TN – New York: Abingdon, 1973, 176 p. Esp. 68-69 [26,64]; 116-117 [21,41-46]. — Diss. Yale Univ., New Haven, CT, 1965 (P.W. Meyer).

1990    Moses through New Testament Spectacles. — *Interpr* 44 (1990) 240-252. Esp. 240-241
        [17,1-8]; 242 [4,2]; 243 [2,13-14]; 247 [5,21-48]. [NTA 35, 336]

**HAYES, John H.**
1973    *Introduction to the Bible*. London: SPCK, 1973, XVI-515 p. Esp. 424-437: "The gospel
        according to Matthew"; 325-329: "Synoptic problem".

**HEAD, Peter M.**
1990    Observations on Early Papyri of the Synoptic Gospels, Especially on the "Scribal
        Habits". — *Bib* 71 (1990) 240-247. [NTA 36, 613]
1992    On the Christology of the Gospel of Peter. — *VigChr* 46 (1992) 209-224. Esp. 213-215
        [26,64/GP 19]; 215-218 [passion narr.]. [NTA 37, 1088]
1993    Christology and Textual Transmission: Reverential Alterations in the Synoptic Gospels.
        — *NT* 35 (1993) 105-129. Esp. 116-118 [1,16.18-25]; 119-120 [7,28; 8,18; 9,35; 15,30]. [NTA 38,
        46]
1995a   The Date of the Madgalen Papyrus of Matthew (*P.Magd.Gr.* 17 = P[64]): A Response to
        C.P. Thiede. — *TyndB* 46 (1995) 251-285. [NTA 40, 1364] → Thiede 1995c
1995b   The Self-Offering and Death of Christ as a Sacrifice in the Gospels and the Acts of the
        Apostles. — BECKWITH, R.T. – SELMAN, M.J. (eds.), *Sacrifice in the Bible*, Carlisle:
        Paternoster; Grand Rapids, MI: Baker, 1995, 111-129. Esp. 115-116.
1997    *Christology and the Synoptic Problem. An Argument for Markan Priority* (SNTS MS,
        94). Cambridge: University Press, 1997, XVIII-337 p. Esp. 49-65 [19,16-22]; 66-83 [13,53-58];
        84-96 [14,22-33]; 133-137 [passion narr.]; 140-147 [Mt/Mk]; 156-160.165-169.180-186.200-214.227-231
        [christological titles]. — Diss. Cambridge, 1994 (M.D. Hooker).
             *TyndB* 46 (1995) 197-200.

**HEALEY, John F.**
1989    Models of Behavior: Matt 6:26 (// Luke 12:24) and Prov 6:6-8. — *JBL* 108 (1989)
        497-498. [NTA 34, 622]

**HEALEY, Phyllis**
1990    & HEALEY, Alan, Greek Circumstantial Participles: Tracking Participants with Parti-
        ciples in the Greek New Testament. — *OPTAT* 4 (1990) 177-259. Esp. 251-255 [sources of
        data]. [NTA 35, 1069]

**HEARD, Richard G.**
1950    *An Introduction to the New Testament*. London: Black, 1950; New York: Harper, 1951,
        XII-268 p. Esp. 49-52 [Q]; 64-73: "The gospel of Matthew".
1954a   The ἀπομνημονεύματα in Papias, Justin, and Irenaeus. — *NTS* 1 (1954-55) 122-129.
        Esp. 122-123 [Papias]; 123-127 [Justin]; 127-129 [Irenaeus]. → C.F.D. Moule 1955a
1954b   Papias' Quotations from the New Testament. — *NTS* 1 (1954-55) 130-134. Esp. 131-132.

**HEARON, H.E.** → J.B. Green 1992b

**HEATER, Homer, Jr.**
1983    Matthew 2:6 and Its Old Testament Sources. — *JEvTS* 26 (1983) 395-397. [NTA 29, 84]
        → Petrotta 1985

**HEAWOOD, Percy J.**
1951    The Time of the Last Supper. [26,17-18] — *JQR* 42 (1951) 37-44.

**HEBART, Friedemann**
1984    Die Bedeutung des Vaterunsers für Luthers Theologie des Gebets. — *Luther* (Hamburg)
        55 (1984) 112-127.

**HEBBLETHWAITE, Peter**

1985 St. Augustine's Interpretation of Matthew 5,17. — *Studia Patristica* 16 (1985) 511-516.

**HEBERT, A. Gabriel**

1961 The Problem of the Gospel according to Matthew. — *ScotJT* 14 (1961) 403-413. Esp.
406-413 [date; purpose; mission; law; christology; eschatology]. [NTA 6, 756]

**HEDINGER, Ulrich**

1976 Jesus und die Volksmenge. Kritik der Qualifizierung der *óchloi* in der Evangelien-
auslegung. — *TZ* 32 (1976) 201-206. [NTA 21, 359]

**HEDRICK, Charles W.**

1979 Resurrection: Radical Theology in the Gospel of Matthew. — *LexTQ* 14 (1979) 40-45.
[NTA 24, 74]

1986 The Treasure Parable in Matthew and Thomas. — *Forum* 2/2 (1986) 41-56. Esp. 43-49:
"The argument for Matthew's revision of the tradition"; 49-52: "The illegality/immorality motif in the
treasure (Matt 13:44)"; 52-54: "The argument for Thomas' preservation of the tradition". [NTA 31, 1075]

1987 Parables and the Kingdom. The Vision of Jesus in Fiction and Faith. — *SBL 1987
Seminar Papers*, 368-393. Esp. 370-376.382-387 [inventory of parables]; 377-378 [Mt].

1989 Thomas and the Synoptics: Aiming at a Consensus. — *SecCent* 7 (1989-90) 39-56. Esp.
39-42: "Options for explaining the relationship between *Thomas* and the synoptics"; 52-56. [NTA 34, 1492]

1990 On Moving Mountains. Mark 11:22b-23 / Matt 21:21 and Parallels. — *Forum* 6 (1990)
219-237. Esp. 222-223 [21,21/Mk 11,21-33]; 223-225 [17,20/Lk 17,6]; 225 [17,20/Th 48; 106]; 225-227
[17,20/Didascalia 15]; 227-230: "Structural analysis". [NTA 38, 190]

1994 *Parables as Poetic Fictions: The Creative Voice of Jesus* [13,44-50]. Peabody, MA:
Hendrickson, 1994, XXXIX-277 p.

**HEER, Josef**

1970 Der Bethlehemspruch Michas und die Geburt Jesu (Mich 5,1-3). — *BK* 25 (1970) 106-
109. Esp. 108-109 [2,6]. [NTA 15, 841]

**HEFLING, Charles C., Jr.**

1983 Origen *Redivivus*: Farrer's Scriptural Divinity. — EATON, J.C. – LOADES, A. (eds.),
*For God and Clarity. New Essays in Honor of Austin Farrer* (Pittsburgh Theological
Monographs, NS 4), Allison Park, PA: Pickwick, 1983, 35-50. Esp. 46-48. → Farrer 1954

**HEGER, Klaus**

1967 *Die Bibel in der Romania: Matthäus 6,5-13* (Romanische Paralleltexte, 1). Tübingen:
Niemeyer, 1967, XVI-38 p.
J. MASSOT MUNTANER, *Studia Monastica* (Montserrat) 12 (1970) 355.

**HEICKE, J.**

1965 *De Bijbel over geloven* (De Bijbel over..., 28). Roermond–Maaseik: Romen, 1965, 112
p. Esp. 52-59 [8,23-27; 14,22-33].

**HEIDT, William**

1951 Translating New Testament Imperatives. — *CBQ* 13 (1951) 253-256. Esp. 253-254 [6,9-13].

**HEIL, Christoph**

1994 *Die Ablehnung der Speisegebote durch Paulus. Zur Frage nach der Stellung des
Apostels zum Gesetz* (BBB, 96). Weinheim: Beltz Athenäum, 1994, XV-386 p. Esp. 107-
108: "Johannes der Täufer"; 109-115: "Jesus von Nazareth"; 267-268: "Logienquelle Q"; 273-274:
"Matthäusevangelium". — Diss. Bonn, 1993 (H. Merklein).

**HEIL, John Paul**

1979    Significant Aspects of the Healing Miracles in Matthew. — *CBQ* 41 (1979) 274-287.
        Esp. 275-279: "Miracles in Matthew?" [9,1-8; 12,9-14]; 279-282: "Significance of a miracle" [8,1-4]; 283-
        285: "Healing activity leads to death-resurrection"; 285-287: "Healing and Matthew's readers". [NTA 24,
        75]

1981    *Jesus Walking on the Sea. Meaning and Gospel Functions of Matt 14:22-33, Mark 6:45-
        52 and John 6:15b-21* (AnBib, 87). Roma: Biblical Institute Press, 1981, XII-200 p. Esp.
        8-17: "The sea-walking as an epiphany"; 31-67: "Exegesis of Matt 14:22-33"; 84-117: "Function of the sea-
        walking epiphany in Matthew". — Diss. Pont. Inst. Bibl., Roma, 1979 (F. Lentzen-Deis).
        M.-É. BOISMARD, *RB* 93 (1986) 472-473; J.D.M. DERRETT, *HeythJ* 24 (1983) 218-220; P.F. ELLIS,
        *CBQ* 45 (1983) 136-137; D. HILL, *ExpT* 93 (1981-82) 120; H.C. KEE, *JBL* 103 (1984) 481-482; L.
        LÓPEZ DE LAS HERAS, *Studium* (Madrid) 22 (1982) 167; F. NEIRYNCK, *ETL* 58 (1982) 162-163; P.
        PERKINS, *TS* 43 (1982) 175-176; R. RIESNER, *TZ* 40 (1984) 84-85; G. STRECKER, *TLZ* 109 (1984) 512-
        514; H. WANSBROUGH, *ScriptB* 12 (1981-82) 72.

1991a   *The Death and Resurrection of Jesus. A Narrative-Critical Reading of Matthew 26-28.*
        Minneapolis, MN: Fortress, 1991, XI-126 p. Esp. 23-56 [26,1-56]; 57-89 [26,57-27,54]; 91-110
        [27,55-28,20]. [NTA 36, p. 422] → Senior 1992c
        E. CUVILLIER, *ETR* 68 (1993) 581-582; P. MEAGHER, *Vidyajyoti* 58 (1994) 401-402; C. MERCER, *RelStR*
        19 (1993) 355; C.M. TUCKETT, *JSNT* 47 (1992) 127; R.D. WITHERUP, *CBQ* 55 (1993) 583-584.

1991b   The Blood of Jesus in Matthew: A Narrative-Critical Perspective. — *PerspRelStud* 18
        (1991) 117-124. Esp. 117-118 [23,29-36]; 118-119 [26,28]; 119-122 [27,3-10]; 122-124 [27,24-25].
        [NTA 36, 131]

1991c   The Narrative Structure of Matthew 27:55-28:20. — *JBL* 110 (1991) 419-438. Esp. 420-
        422 [narrative structure]; 422-437 [implied reader]. [NTA 36, 731] → Senior 1992c

1991d   The Narrative Roles of the Women in Matthew's Genealogy. — *Bib* 72 (1991) 538-545.
        Esp. 538-540 [1,3]; 540-541 [1,5]; 541-542 [1,6]; 542-544 [1,16]. [NTA 36, 1254]

1993    Ezekiel 34 and the Narrative Strategy of the Shepherd and Sheep Metaphor in Matthew.
        — *CBQ* 55 (1993) 698-708. Esp. 699-700 [2,6]; 700-701 [9,36]; 701-702 [10,6]; 702-703 [10,16];
        703-704 [14,14; 15,24.32]; 704 [18,12-14]; 705 [25,31-46]; 706-707 [26,31-32]. [NTA 38, 1352]

**HEILIGENTHAL, Roman**

1983a   *Werke als Zeichen. Untersuchungen zur Bedeutung der menschlichen Taten im Früh-
        judentum, Neuen Testament und Frühchristentum* (WUNT, II/9). Tübingen: Mohr,
        1983, XIV-374 p. Esp. 52-58 [7,15-23]; 59-65 [23,1-12]; 115-123 [5,13-16]. — Diss. Heidelberg, 1981-
        82 (K. Berger).

1983b   Werke der Barmherzigkeit oder Almosen? Zur Bedeutung von ἐλεημοσύνη. — *NT* 25
        (1983) 289-301. Esp. 291-292 [25,31-46]; 294-295.297 [26,6-13]. [NTA 28, 442]

1985    Goldene Regel. II. Neues Testament und frühes Christentum. — *TRE* 13 (1985) 573-
        575.

**HEIN, Kenneth**

1971    Judas Iscariot: Key to the Last-Supper Narratives? — *NTS* 17 (1970-71) 227-232. [NTA
        15, 879]

**HEINE, Susanne**

1989    Eine Person von Rang und Namen. Historische Konturen der Magdalenerin. — KOCH,
        D.-A., et al. (eds.), *Jesu Rede von Gott.* FS W. Marxsen, 1989, 179-194. Esp. 186 [28,8-
        10].

**HEINEN, Heinz**

1990    Göttliche Sitometrie: Beobachtungen zur Brotbitte des Vaterunsers. — *TTZ* 99 (1990)
        72-79. [NTA 34, 1136]

**HEINIMANN, Siegfried**

1988    *Oratio dominica romanice. Das Vaterunser in den romanischen Sprachen von den Anfängen bis ins 16. Jahrhundert mit den griechischen und lateinischen Vorlagen* (Beihefte zur Zeitschrift für romanische Philologie, 219). Tübingen: Niemeyer, 1988, XII-224 p.
W. GROSS, *TQ* 169 (1989) 140-141.

**HEINRICH, Rolf**

1981    Gott – rücksichtslos der Gott der Armen. Leben mit Matthäus 5, Vers 3. — MOLT-MANN, J. (ed.), *Nachfolge und Bergpredigt*, 1981, 73-88.

**HEINZE, M.**

1967    Das "Zeichen des Jona". Mt 12,38-40; 16,1-4; Lk 11,29f.; Mk 8,11f. — BENCKERT, H., et al. (eds.), *Wort und Gemeinde. Festschrift für Erdmann Schott zum 65. Geburtstag* (Aufsätze und Vorträge zur Theologie und Religionswissenschaft, 42), Berlin: Evangelische Verlagsanstalt, 1967, 77-82.

**HEISING, Alkuin**

1964    Exegese und Theologie der alt- und neutestamentlichen Speisewunder. — *ZKT* 86 (1964) 80-96. Esp. 90-96: "Die Brotvermehrung im Neuen Testament". [NTA 9, 153]

1966    *Die Botschaft der Brotvermehrung. Zur Geschichte und Bedeutung eines Christus-bekenntnisses im Neuen Testament* (SBS, 15). Stuttgart: Katholisches Bibelwerk, 1966; ²1967, 83 p. Esp. 72-74: "Eucharistie und kirchlicher Dienst – die Brotvermehrung im Matthäus-Evangelium".
*De boodschap van de broodvermenigvuldiging. Bijdrage tot geschiedenis en zin van een Christus-getuigenis in het Nieuwe Testament*, trans. S. Antheunis (De christen in de tijd, 39). Antwerpen: Patmos, 1968, 98 p.
*La moltiplicazione dei pani*, trans. I. Perini (Studi biblici, 12). Brescia: Paideia, 1970, 103 p.

1967    *"Gott wird Mensch". Eine Einführung in die Aussageabsicht und Darstellungsweise von Mt 1-2; Lk 1-2; 3,23-38* (Kreuzring-Bücherei, 45). Trier: J.J. Zimmer, 1967, 111 p.
Esp. 22-28; 29-33 [1,1-17]; 36-55 [1,18-2,23]. [NTA 11, p. 374]
F. DATTLER, *RevistCuBíb* 4 (1967) 155; W. RAUSCH, *RevistBíb* 29 (1967) 245; A. SALAS, *CiudDios* 181 (1968) 343-344; M.W. SCHOENBERG, *CBQ* 29 (1967) 632-633; B. SCHWANK, *ErbAuf* 43 (1967) 339-340; R. SILVA, *Burgense* 10 (1968) 521-522; P. VANDEN BERGHE, *CollBrugGand* 13 (1967) 424; F. ZEILINGER, *TPQ* 116 (1968) 282.

**HEISTER, Maria-Sybilla**

1984    *Frauen in der biblischen Glaubensgeschichte*. Göttingen: Vandenhoeck & Ruprecht, 1984, 226 p.

**HELD, Heinz Joachim**

1959    Matthäus als Interpret der Wundergeschichten. — BORNKAMM, G., et al., *Überlieferung und Auslegung*, 1959, 155-287. Esp. 155-199: "Die Neuerzählung der Wundergeschichten durch Matthäus"; 200-234: "Die Form der Wundergeschichten im Matthäusevangelium"; 234-262: "Die Wundergeschichten als Zeugnisse für die Christologie des Matthäus"; 263-284: "Die Interpretation des Glaubens in den Wundergeschichten durch Matthäus"; 284-287: "Matthäus als Tradent und Interpret". — Diss. Heidelberg, 1957 (G. Bornkamm).
Matthew as Interpreter of the Miracle Stories. — BORNKAMM, G., et al., *Tradition and Interpretation*, 1963, 165-299. Esp. 165-211; 211-246; 246-275; 275-296; 296-299.
Matthieu, interprète des récits de miracles. — *FoiVie* 69/3 = *Cahiers bibliques* 9 (1970) 91-110. → Gatzweiler 1972c

1993    Hoffen auf Gott und Entschlossenheit zum Guten. Unterweisung auf dem Weg der Gerechtigkeit in Psalm 37 und in der Bergpredigt. — MOMMER, P., et al. (eds.), *Gottes Recht als Lebensraum. Festschrift Hans Jochen Boecker*, Neukirchen-Vluyn: Neukirchener, 1993, 293-302. Esp. 301-302.

**HELEWA, Giovanni**

1978    "Non giudicate". La misericordia nella comunione fraterna. [7,1-2] — *Presenza del Carmelo* (Roma) 15 (1978) 10-20.

1990    "Beati gli operatori di pace". I. "Cristo la nostra pace"; II. "Le opere della pace"; III. La preghiera; pace del Cristo nel cuore; IV. "Beati gli afflitti". — *Rivista di vita spirituale* (Roma) 44 (1990) 9-24, 123-137, 374-388, 561-577.

**HELLEMO, Geir**

1985    Transfigurasjonen og det kristologiske paradoks. [The transfiguration and the christological paradox] [17,1-8] — *NorskTeolTids* 86 (1985) 65-78. [NTA 30, 576]

**HELLESTAM, Sigvard**

1990    Mysteriet med saltet. [The mystery of the salt]. [5,13] — *SEÅ* 55 (1990) 59-63. [NTA 35, 624]

**HELLHOLM, David**

1987    En textgrammatisk konstruktion i Matteusevangeliet. [A text-grammatical construction in the gospel of Matthew] [7,28; 11,1; 13,53; 19,1; 26,1] — *SEÅ* 51-52 (1986-87) 80-89. [NTA 31, 571]

1994    "Rejoice and Be Glad, for Your Reward is Great in Heaven": An Attempt at Solving the Structural Problem of Matt 5:11-12. — *Festschrift Günter Wagner. Edited by Faculty of Baptist Theological Seminary Rüschlikon/Switzerland* (International Theological Studies: Contributions of Baptist Scholars, 1), Bern: Lang, 1994, 47-86. Esp. 47-48: "A proposal of a series of ten makarisms in the Sermon on the Mount"; 48-77: "Examination of the proposal".

1995    Substitutionelle Gliederungsmerkmale und die Komposition des Matthäusevangeliums. — FORNBERG, T. - HELLHOLM, D. (eds.), *Texts and Contexts*. FS L. Hartman, 1995, 11-76. Esp. 11-15: "Einige Strukturmerkmale an der Textoberfläche des Matthäusevangeliums"; 15-33: "Sprachwissenschaftliche Grundlagenüberlegungen"; 33-64: "Einige substitutionelle Gliederungsmerkmale im Matthäusevangelium".

**HELMBOLD, Heinrich**

1953    *Vorsynoptische Evangelien*. Stuttgart: Klotz, 1953, 110 p. Esp. 33-39 [14,13-21]; 42-47 [18,1-5]; 52-58 [8,5-13]; 58-97 [Mt/Q].

**HELMS, Randel**

1988    *Gospel Fictions*. Amherst, NY: Prometheus Books, 1988, 154 p. Esp. 35-37 [John the Baptist]; 43-60: "Nativity legends"; 61-81: "Miracles: the synoptic narratives"; 113-116 [27,3-10]; 134-142 [28,1-20].

**HEMELSOET, Ben P.M.**

1982    Jesus en Jeruzalem, niet gescheiden, niet gedeeld. — *Amsterdamse Cahiers* 3 (1982) 86-98 (English summary, 168). Esp. 86-89 [24,28; Q 17,37].

1985    De berg van de bergrede. Een hoogtepunt in de theologie van Mattheüs. — *Amsterdamse Cahiers* 6 (1985) 174-187 (English summary, 196). Esp. 174-178 [5,1-2]; 178-180 [4,12-17]; 183-185 [Mt/Lk 6,12].

1988    De verzoeking van Jezus in de woestijn. — *Amsterdamse Cahiers* 9 (1988) 97-116 (English summary, 140-141). Esp. 97-112 [Mt]; 112-114 [Mt/Lk].

1989    De Zoon des Mensen, die niet heeft dat Hij zijn hoofd neerlegge, die macht heeft op de aarde om zonden te vergeven, volgens Mattheüs. — *Amsterdamse Cahiers* 10 (1989) 88-102 (English summary, 149). Esp. 90-99 [8,19–9,8]; 92-93 [8,18-22]; 96-97 [9,1-8].

1992    De Zoon des Mensen, de Heer van de Sabbat, de Knecht des Heren, volgens Mattheüs. — *Amsterdamse Cahiers* 11 (1992) 84-100 (English summary, 152). Esp. 85-94 [12,1-21]; 94-100 [11,25-30].

**HEMER, Colin J.**

1984  'Επιούσιος. — *JSNT* 22 (1984) 81-94. [NTA 29, 522]; = PORTER, S.E. – EVANS, C.A. (eds.), *New Testament Text and Language. A Sheffield Reader* (The Biblical Seminar, 44), Sheffield: JSOT, 1997, 222-234.

**HEMMERDINGER, Bertrand**

1972  Un élément pythagoricien dans le Pater. [6,11] — *ZNW* 63 (1972) 121. [NTA 17, 909]

**HEMMERDINGER-ILIADOU, Democracie E.**

1973  Les citations évangéliques de l'Éphrem grec. — Βυζαντινά (Thessaloniki) 5 (1973) 313-393.

**HEMPEL, Johann**

1958  Heilung als Symbol und Wirklichkeit im biblischen Schrifttum. — *Nachrichten der Akademie der Wissenschaften in Göttingen* 3 (1958) 237-314.

**HEMPELMANN, Heinzpeter**

1990  "Das dürre Blatt im Heilgen Buch". Mt 1,1-17 und der Kampf wider die Erniedrigung Gottes. — *TBeitr* 21 (1990) 6-23. [NTA 34, 1130]

**HENAUT, Barry W.**

1987  Matthew 11:27. The Thunderbolt in Corinth? — *TorontoJT* 3 (1987) 282-300. Esp. 283-285: "Richardson and the thunderbolt in Q"; 285-287: "The thunderbolt and its context in Q"; 288-289: "The wisdom christology of Q"; 289-293: "The logion's conceptual background and origin"; 294-296: "The thunderbolt in Corinth". [NTA 32, 603] → P. Richardson 1984

1988  Is Q but the Invention of Luke and Mark? Method and Argument in the Griesbach Hypothesis. — *Religious Studies and Theology* (Edmonton, Alberta) 8/3 (1988) 15-32. [NTA 35, 117]

1993  *Oral Tradition and the Gospels. The Problem of Mark 4* (JSNT SS, 82). Sheffield: JSOT, 1993, 335 p. Esp. 251-265 [Mk 4,30-32; Q 13,18-19; Th 20]; 270-271 [Mk 4,21; Q 11,33; Th 33]; 278-283 [Mk 4,22; Q 12,2; Th 5,6b]; 284-288 [Mk 4,24b; Q 6,38]; 288-292 [Mk 4,25; Q 19,26; Th 41]; 292-294 [Mk 4,23; Q 14,35; Th 8]. — Diss. Toronto, Ont., 1991 (H.O. Guenther).

**HENDERSON, Ian H.**

1991  Gnomic Quatrains in the Synoptics: An Experiment in Genre Definition. — *NTS* 37 (1991) 481-498. Esp. 487-498 [6,22-24; 7,6; 10,24-27]. [NTA 36, 691]

1992  *Didache* and Orality in Synoptic Comparison. — *JBL* 111 (1992) 283-306. Esp. 286-288: "Authorship" [13,52; 23,34-39]; 288-291: "Literary genre"; 291-295: "Genre and oral sensibility"; 295-298: "Orality and repressed literacy" [6,2-4.7-15]; 298-304: "Orality and literary unity". [NTA 37, 1089]

1995  Style-Switching in the *Didache*: Fingerprint or Argument? — JEFFORD, C.N. (ed.), *The Didache in Context*, 1995, 177-209. Esp. 179-185; 187-188 [5,39].

1996  *Jesus, Rhetoric and Law* (Biblical Interpretation Series, 20). Leiden – New York – Köln: Brill, 1996, 437 p. Esp. 1-72: "Introduction" [23-25.48-55: Gnomic-Q]; 73-155: "Defining gnome"; 156-195: "Gnome and wisdom saying" [179-188: Q]; 196-235: "Logia, aphorisms and authenticity"; 236-291: "Gnomai in tradition and redaction: Distribution and distinctness"; 292-352: "Discipleship, eschatology and the projection of character in synoptic gnomai"; 353-406: "Gnomic normativity and law in synoptic and in Pauline reception"; 410-413: "Appendix: A catalogue of synoptic gnomai". — Diss. Oxford, 1988 (E.P. Sanders).

**HENDRICKX, Herman**

1975  *The Infancy Narratives*. Manila: East Asian Pastoral Institute, 1975, VI-136 p. [NTA 22, p. 213]; (Studies in the Synoptic Gospels), London: Chapman, 1984, VIII-145 p. Esp. 8-21: "The infancy narrative of Matthew"; 22-52 [1-2]; 117-123. [NTA 29, p. 324]

   E. PERETTO, *Marianum* 40 (1978) 199; R.A. WILD, *CBQ* 40 (1978) 275-276.

*CahJos* 34 (1986) 121; H.B. GREEN, *NBlackfr* 67 (1986) 147-148; D. HILL, *JSNT* 26 (1986) 121-125; B.M. NOLAN, *IBS* 8 (1986) 47-48; J. STEYN, *Neotestamentica* 21 (1987) 95-96.
*Los relatos de la infancia*, trans. E. Requena Calvo (La palabra de Dios A). Madrid: Paulinas, 1986, 175 p.
E. BARÓN, *Proyección* 34 (1987) 242; P. BLÁZQUEZ, *Studium* (Madrid) 29 (1989) 552; J.A. CARRASCO, *EstJos* 42 (1988) 233-234.

1977   *The Passion Narratives of the Synoptic Gospels*. Manila: East Asian Pastoral Institute, 1977, VIII-173 p. [NTA 22, p. 213]; (Studies in the Synoptic Gospels), London: Chapman, 1984, X-192 p. Esp. 10-16 [26,47-56]; 35-44 [26,57-75]; 44-52 [27,1-10]; 68-78 [27,11-31]; 101-114 [27,32-56]; 133-135 [27,57-61]; 142-146. [NTA 29, p. 324]
       *Los relatos de la pasión. Estudio sobre los evangelios sinópticos*, trans. E. Requena Calvo (La palabra de Dios A). Madrid: Paulinas, 1986, 228 p.

1978   *The Resurrection Narratives of the Synoptic Gospels*. Manila: East Asian Pastoral Institute, 1978, VII-159 p. [NTA 23, p. 227]; (Studies in the Synoptic Gospels), London: Chapman, 1984, VIII-150 p. Esp. 20-38 [27,62-28,15]; 47-65.118-121 [28,16-20]. [NTA 29, p. 324]
       *Los relatos de la resurrección. Estudio sobre los evangelios sinópticos*, trans. E. Requena Calvo (La palabra de Dios). Madrid: Paulinas, 1987, 181 p.

1979   *The Sermon on the Mount*. Manila: East Asian Pastoral Institute, 1979, VIII-219 p. [NTA 24, p. 189]; (Studies in the Synoptic Gospels), London: Chapman, 1984, X-210 p. Esp. 8-9 [5,1-2]; 10-36 [5,3-12]; 37-43 [5,13-16]; 44-58 [5,17-20]; 59-96 [5,21-48]; 97-127 [6,1-18]; 128-148 [6,29-34]; 149-159 [7,1-12]; 160-174 [7,13-27]; 175-176 [7,28-29]; 177-183: "The practicability of the Sermon on the Mount". [NTA 29, p. 324]
       J.M. COURT, *ExpT* 96 (1974-75) 371.
       H.B. GREEN, *NBlackfr* 67 (1986) 147-148.
       *El sermón de la montaña*, trans. E. Requena Calvo (La palabra de Dios A). Madrid: Paulinas, 1986, 246 p.
       A. SALAS, *BibFe* 14 (1988) 149.

1983a  *The Parables of Jesus Then and Now*. Manila: St. Paul Publications, 1983, IX-382 p. *The Parables of Jesus* (Studies in the Synoptic Gospels). London: Chapman; San Francisco, CA: Harper & Row, rev. ed. 1986, XII-291 p. Esp. 30-39.42-43 [13,31-32]; 45-81 [13,33]; 52-63 [13,24-30]; 63-73 [13,36-43]; 108-137 [22,1-14].

1983b  Eight Beatitudes? [Chinese] — *ColcTFu* 55 (1983) 69-78.

1987   *The Miracle Stories of the Synoptic Gospels* (Studies in the Synoptic Gospels). London: Chapman; San Francisco, CA: Harper & Row, 1987, X-310 p. Esp. 73-79 [8,14-15]; 96-99 [8,1-4]; 134-142 [9,1-8]; 159-164 [12,9-14]; 193-199 [8,23-27].

1990   Matthew's Community. [Chinese] — *Theology Annual* (Hong Kong) 12 (1990-91) 141-153. [NTA 36, 1251] → 1992a

1991   *From One Jesus to Four Gospels*. Quezon City: Maryhill School of Theology/Claretian Publications, 1991, XI-164 p. Esp. 79-103 [introduction].

1992a  *The Household of God. The Communities Behind the New Testament Writings*. Quezon City: Claretian Publications, 1992, X-142 p. Esp. 49-69: "Matthew's community". → 1990

1992b  *A Key to the Gospel of Matthew*. Quezon City: Claretian Publications, 1992, VI-58 p.

**HENDRIKS, Wilhelmus Maria Antonius**

1974   Zur Kollektionsgeschichte des Markusevangeliums. — SABBE, M. (ed.), *L'Évangile selon Marc*, 1974, 35-57; ²1988 ("Nachtrag", 57). Esp. 43-53: "Das praesens historicum in den synoptischen Evangelien".

1986   *Karakteristiek woordgebruik in de synoptische evangelies*. Nijmegen: Universitaire pers, 1986, 3 vols., 596 p. — Diss. Nijmegen, 1986 (B. van Iersel).

1994   Zoek het Koninkrijk der hemelen: Tekst en tekstgeschiedenis van Mattheus 6,33. — AKERBOOM, D., et al. (eds.), *Broeder Jehosjoea*. FS B. Hemelsoet, 1994, 137-150. Esp. 143-149 [Church fathers].

**HENDRIKSEN, William**

1973a New Testament Commentary. Expositon of the Gospel according to Matthew. Grand Rapids, MI: Baker; Edinburgh: Banner of Truth, 1973, VIII-1015 p. [NTA 18, p. 383]; ²1989.

F.F. BRUCE, EvQ 47 (1975) 191-192; W.B. WALLIS, WestTJ 36 (1973-74) 405-407; A.J.M. WEDDERBURN, ScotJT 28 (1975) 486-488; D. WILLIAMS, RTR 34 (1975) 90-91.
Comentario del Nuevo Testamento. Exposición del evangelio según Mateo. Grand Rapids, MI: SLC, 1986, 1066 p.

1973b The Beauty of Matthew's Gospel. — WestTJ 35 (1973) 115-120. [NTA 17, 897]

**HENDRY, George S.**

1983 Judge Not: A Critical Test of Faith. [7,1] — TTod 40 (1983-84) 113-129. [NTA 28, 95]

**HENGEL, Martin**

1959 & HENGEL, Rudolf, Die Heilungen Jesu und medizinisches Denken. — CHRISTIAN, P. - RÖSSLER, D. (eds.), Medicus Viator. Fragen und Gedanken am Wege Richard Siebecks. Eine Festgabe seiner Freunde und Schüler zum 75. Geburtstag, Tübingen: Mohr; Stuttgart: Thieme, 1959, 331-361. Esp. 343 [8,5-13]; 344 [9,2-8; 12,9-13]; = SUHL, A. (ed.), Der Wunderbegriff im Neuen Testament, 1980, 338-373. Esp. 352-354.

1963 Maria Magdalena und die Frauen als Zeugen. — BETZ, O., et al. (eds.), Abraham unser Vater. FS O. Michel, 1963, 243-256. Esp. 252.255 [28,9-10].

1968 Nachfolge und Charisma. Eine exegetisch-religionsgeschichtliche Studie zu Mt 8,21f. und Jesu Ruf in die Nachfolge (BZNW, 34). Berlin: Töpelmann, 1968, VIII-116 p. Esp. 3-17: "Zur Auslegung von Mt 8,21-22 par.". [NTA 13, p. 156]

L. ÁLVAREZ VERDES, Pentecostés 8 (1970) 107-108; H.D. BETZ, JBL 88 (1969) 116-117; G. DAUTZENBERG, TRev 66 (1970) 19-20; E. ESKING, TZ 26 (1970) 287; G. FOHRER, ZAW 30 (1968) 433; S. GONZÁLEZ DE CARREA, NatGrac 17 (1970) 218-219; E. GRÄSSER, TLZ 95 (1970) 275-277; G.F. HASEL, Bibliotheca Orientalis 26 (1969) 262-264; A.F.J. KLIJN, NT 11 (1969) 318; E. LARSSON, Bib 53 (1972) 445-457; X. LÉON-DUFOUR, RSR 59 (1971) 610-611. R. MORGAN, ScriptB 3/1 (1971) 14; J. MURPHY-O'CONNOR, RB 79 (1972) 631-632; B.A. PEARSON, VigChr 24 (1971) 304-306; Q. QUESNELL, CBQ 31 (1969) 432-434; G. RINALDI, BibOr 11 (1969) 228-229; L.F. RIVERA, RevistBíb 35 (1973) 89; A. SALAS, CiudDios 182 (1969) 421-422; K.H. SCHELKLE, TQ 149 (1969) 95-96; R. SCHNACKENBURG, BZ 15 (1971) 276-277; E. SCHWEIZER, EvT 30 (1970) 624-625; F. SEN, RQum 7 (1970) 297-298; J. SUDBRACK, GL 42 (1969) 152-153.
The Charismatic Leader and His Followers, trans. J.C.G. Greig. Edinburgh: Clark, 1981, 111 p.; paperback, 1996.

E. BEST, JSNT 17 (1983) 114-115; R.E. CLEMENTS, JSS 27 (1982) 308-309; D. FRANCE, EvQ 55 (1983) 53-54; S. FREYNE, IBS 6 (1984) 145-147; M.D. HOOKER, NBlackfr 63 (1982) 489-490; É. TROCMÉ, RHPR 63 (1983) 341.
Seguimiento y carisma. La radicalidad de la llamada de Jesús (Presencia Teológica, 7). Santander: Sal Terrae, 1981, 132 p.

P. FERNANDEZ, CiTom 108 (1981) 598.
Sequela e carisma. Studio esegetico e di storia delle religioni su Mt 8,21s. e la chiamata di Gesù alla sequela (Studi biblici, 90). Brescia: Paideia, 1990, 177 p.

J.J. BARTOLOMÉ, Sal 53 (1991) 582-583; C. CIPRIANI, Asprenas 38 (1991) 395-396; G. DOGLIANI SALADINI, RivStoLR 28 (1992) 694-695; V. FUSCO, CC 142/3 (1991) 448; S. RONCHI, Protestantesimo 47 (1992) 327-328.

1970 Leben in der Veränderung. Ein Beitrag zum Verständnis der Bergpredigt. — EvKom 3 (1970) 647-651. [NTA 15, 487]

1971 Kerygma oder Geschichte? Zur Problematik einer falschen Alternative in der Synoptikerforschung aufgezeigt an Hand einiger neuer Monographien. — TQ 151 (1971) 323-336. Esp. 333-336 [Q]. [NTA 16, 837] → Roloff 1970

1973a Eigentum und Reichtum in der frühen Kirche. Aspekte einer frühchristlichen Sozialgeschichte. Stuttgart: Calwer, 1973, 96 p. Esp. 31-38: "Die Verkündigung Jesu".

*Property and Riches in the Early Church. Aspects of a Social History of Early Christianity*, trans. J. Bowden. Philadelphia, PA: Fortress, 1974, 96 p. Esp. 23-30.
*Propriedad y riqueza en el cristianismo primitivo.* Bilbao: Desclée De Brouwer, 1983, 108 p.

1973b   & MERKEL, H., Die Magier aus dem Osten und die Flucht nach Ägypten (Mt 2) im Rahmen der antiken Religionsgeschichte und der Theologie des Matthäus. — HOFFMANN, P., et al. (eds.), *Orientierung an Jesus. FS J.* Schmid, 1973, 139-169. Esp. 140-142: "Zur Analyse der Erzählung"; 142-153 [2,1-6]; 153-156 [2,7-12]; 156-158 [2,13-15]; 158-160 [2,16-18]; 161-164 [2,19-23]; 164-166: "Das theologische Anliegen des Evangelisten in Mt 2".

1978   Jesus und die Tora. — *TBeitr* 9 (1978) 152-172. [NTA 23, 390]

1979   Jesus als messianischer Lehrer der Weisheit und die Anfänge der Christologie. — *Sagesse et Religion, Colloque de Strasbourg (octobre 1976)* (Bibliothèque des Centres d'études supérieures spécialisés), Paris: PUF, 1979, 144-188. Esp. 149-160: "Die Sprüche von der Weisheit in der Logienquelle" [Q 7,31-35; 10,21; 11,31-32.49; 13,34-35]; 160-162: "Zum Heilandsruf Matthäus 11,28-30".
Jesus as Messianic Teacher of Wisdom and the Beginnings of Christology. — ID., *Studies*, 1995, 73-118. Esp. 75-87; 87-89.

1983   Die Bergpredigt im Widerstreit. — *TBeitr* 14 (1983) 53-67. Esp. 54-60: "Der Text der Bergpredigt". [NTA 27, 911]

1984   *Die Evangelienüberschriften* (Sitzungsberichte der Heidelberger Akademie der Wissenschaften. Philosophisch-historische Klasse, 1984, 3). Heidelberg: C. Winter Universitätsverlag, 1984, 52 p. Esp. 8-9, 17-20.
The Titles of the Gospels and the Gospel of Mark. — ID., *Studies in the Gospel of Mark*, London: SCM, 1985, 64-84, 192-182. Esp. 65, 68-71.

1987   Zur matthäischen Bergpredigt und ihrem jüdischen Hintergrund. — *TR* 52 (1987) 327-400. Esp. 329-362: "Die Aporie der matthäischen Seligpreisungen"; 362-400: "Zur Auslegung der Bergpredigt". [NTA 32, 586] → Broer 1986a, Neirynck 1997d, Strecker 1984, Weder 1985a

1992   Jesus, der Messias Israels. Zum Streit über das 'messianische Sendungsbewußtsein' Jesu. — GRUENWALD, I., et al. (eds.), *Messiah and Christos. Studies in the Jewish Origins of Christianity Presented to David Flusser on the Occasion of His Seventy-Fifth Birthday* (Texte und Studien zum antiken Judentum, 32), Tübingen: Mohr, 1992, 155-176. → 1995b

1995a   *Studies in Early Christology.* Edinburgh: Clark, 1995, XIX-402 p. → 1979, 1995b

1995b   Jesus, the Messiah of Israel. — *Ibid.*, 1-72. → 1992

**HENNE, Philippe**

1994   L'Évangile des Ébionites. Une fausse harmonie. Une vraie supercherie. — KESSLER, A. - RICKLIN, T. - WURST, G. (eds.), *Peregrina curiositas: Eine Reise durch den orbis antiquus. Zu Ehren von Dirk Van Damme* (NTOA, 27), Freiburg/Schw: Universitätsbibliothek; Göttingen: Vandenhoeck & Ruprecht, 1994, 57-75. Esp. 59-65.67-74 [3,13-17].

**HENNECKE, Edgar** → Schneemelcher 1959*, 1964*, 1987*, 1989*

**HENRY, A.**

1966a   La visite des Mages (Mt 2,1-12). — *Terre Sainte* (Jerusalem) 1 (1966) 2-4.

1966b   La tentation de Jésus. — *Terre Sainte* 3 (1966) 65-67.

1966c   Les béatitudes. — *Terre Sainte* 11 (1966) 257-266.

**HENRY, Carl F.H.**

1992   Reflections on the Kingdom of God. — *JEvTS* 35 (1992) 39-49. Esp. 43-44.

**HENRY, Jerry Michael**

1983 *The Parable of the Pounds. A Study in Parable Hermeneutics* [25,14-30]. Diss. Southwestern Baptist Theol. Sem., Fort Worth, TX, 1983. — *DissAbstr* 44 (1983-84) 1829.

**HENSHAW, Thomas**

1952 *New Testament Literature in the Light of Modern Scholarship.* London: Allen & Unwin, 1952, 454 p. Esp. 79-92: "The synoptic problem"; 111-129: "The gospel according to Matthew".

**HENZE, Clemens M.**

1950 De prima narratione evangelica (Mt. 1,18-25), tanti pro vita B.M.V. momenti. — *Marianum* 12 (1950) 285-291. → Maltempi 1951

1951 Brevis replicatio. — *Marianum* 13 (1951) 185-186. → Maltempi 1951

1953 Bezeichnet "desponsata" in Mt 1,18 und Lk 1,27 und 2,5 eine Verlobte oder eine Vermählte? — *TPQ* 101 (1953) 308-313.

1964 Das Problem der Ehe Mariens und Josephs. — *FZPT* 11 (1964) 298-307. [NTA 10, 145]

**HERBST, Karl**

1979 *Was wollte Jesus selbst? Die vorkirchlichen Jesusworte in den Evangelien.* Düsseldorf: Patmos, 2 vols., I, 1979, ³1986, 275 p.; II, 1981, ²1986, 295 p.

**HERGESEL, Tomasz**

1979 Adoracja cudotwórcy – Mateuszowa interpretacja cudów Jezusa. [The adoration of the miracle-worker. Matthew's interpretation of the miracles of Jesus] — *RuBi* 32 (1979) 104-114.

1984 Syn Maryi Synem Bożym. Postać Maryi w Mateuszowej Ewangelii dzieciństwa. [Son of Mary or Son of God. Mary in Mt 1-2] — SZLAGA, J. (ed.), *U boku Syna*, Lublin: Catholic University, 1984, 65-73.

**HÉRING, Jean**

1950 Un texte oublié: Matthieu 18.10. À propos des controverses récentes sur le pédobaptisme. — CULLMANN, O. - MENOUD, P. (eds.), *Aux sources de la tradition chrétienne.* FS M. Goguel, 1950, 95-102.

1959 Simples remarques sur la prière à Gethsémané. Matthieu 26,36-46; Marc 14,32-42; Luc 22,40-46. — *RHPR* 39 (1959) 97-102. [NTA 4, 84] → 1962b

1962a Le Sermon sur la montagne dans la nouvelle traduction anglaise de la Bible. [NEB] — *RHPR* 42 (1962) 122-132. [NTA 7, 503]

1962b Zwei exegetische Probleme in der Perikope von Jesus in Gethsemane (Markus XIV 32-42; Matthaeus XXVI 36-46; Lukas XXII 40-46). — *Neotestamentica et Patristica.* FS O. Cullmann, 1962, 64-69. Esp. 64-65 [26,41]; 65-68 [26,38]. → 1959

1966 Remarques sur les bases araméennes et hébraïques des Évangiles synoptiques. Prolégomènes à une nouvelle traduction, rédigés en mémoire de l'enseignement de Charles Jaeger. — *RHPR* 46 (1966) 17-33. Esp. 18-19 [2,9-11]; 19 [4,8]; 20 [8,12]; 20-21 [8,22]; 21-22 [10,11.27.29.31.34]; 22 [11,19]; 23 [12,38-42]; 24 [13,4]; 27 [10,38]; 28 [11,21]; 31 [21,41; 24,51]; 31-32 [21,32]; 32 [26,45]. [NTA 11, 183]

**HERMANN, Ingo**

1960 Aussageformen im Neuen Testament. — *BibLeb* 1 (1960) 110-117. Esp. 111-114 [genre].

1969 "Selig, die den Frieden schaffen, denn sie werden Söhne Gottes heißen". — MÜSSLE, M. (ed.), *Der "politische" Jesus*, 1969, 91-102.

**HERMANS, L.J.M.**

1960 *De Bijbel over Jezus' geboorte en jeugd* (De Bijbel over ..., 5). Roermond–Maaseik: Romen, 1960, 115 p. Esp. 19-37: "Een vergelijking tussen Mt. 1-2 en Lc. 1-2".

> A. DRUBBEL, *Ons Geestelijk Leven* 38 (1961) 313-314; P. PAS, *CollMech* 47 (1962) 203; P. VAN DIEMEN, *RB* 69 (1962) 127-128.
>
> *The Bible on the Childhood of Jesus*, trans. H.J.J Vaughan. De Pere, WI: St. Norbert Abbey Press; London: Sheed and Ward, 1965, 122 p.
>
> G.M. BERTRAND, *CahJos* 16 (1968) 349; J. BLIGH, *HeythJ* 8 (1967) 223; J.A. CARRASCO, *EstJos* 24 (1970) 74-75; E. RASCO, *Greg* 48 (1967) 368-369; L. SWAIN, *CleR* 51 (1966) 404; J. VOLCKAERT, *The Clergy Monthly* (Ranchi, India) 31 (1967) 33-34.
>
> *Jesu Geburt und Jugend im Zeugnis der Bibel* (Zeugnis der Bibel, 13). Salzburg: O. Müller, 1968, 105 p.
>
> *L'infanzia di Gesù nella Bibbia* (La Bibbia e i problemi dell'uomo d'oggi, 14). Bari: Paoline, 1969, 133 p.
>
> V. FUSCO, *RasT* 11 (1970) 427; G. SEGALLA, *RivBib* 19 (1971) 258-259.

**HERMANT, Dominique**

1989 La deuxième annonce de la Passion (Histoire du texte). [17,22-23] — *BLOS* 1 (1989) 14-18.

> J. MAGNE, *BLOS* 2 (1989) 15.

1990a La première scène d'enfants (Mt 18,1-5; Mc 9,33-37; Lc 9,46-48). — *BLOS* 3 (1990) 7-11.

1990b La purification du lépreux (Mt 8,1-4; Mc 1,40-45; Lc 5,12-16). — *BLOS* 4 (1990) 13-22. → Amphoux 1990, Rolland 1990b

1990c La femme au flux de sang et la fille de Jaïre (Mt 9,18-26; Mc 5,22-43; Lc 8,41-56). — *BLOS* 5 (1990) 8-16.

**HERNÁNDEZ, Juan F.**

1954 Teoría y práctica de las bienaventuranzas. [5,3-12] — *CuBíb* 11 (1954) 79-83.

**HERRÁN, Laurentino M.**

1978 La infancia de Jesús según San Mateo en el villancico y poesía popular de España. [1-2] — *EstJos* 32 (1978) 37-59.

**HERRANZ MARCO, Mariano**

1969 Las espigas arrancadas en sábado (Mt 12,1-8 par.) Tradición y elaboración literaria. — *EstBíb* 28 (1969) 313-348. Esp. 313-322: "Forma primitiva de la respuesta de Jesús"; 323-345: "Forma primitiva de la introducción". [NTA 15, 503]

> Las espigas arrancadas en sábado (Mt. 12,1-8 par.). Tradición y elaboración redaccional. — *La Etica Bíblica* (XXIX Semana Bíblica Española), Madrid: Consejo Superior de Investigaciones Científicas, 1971, 289-322. Esp. 289-298; 298-319.

1970 El Jordán y el mar de Galilea en el marco geográfico de los Evangelios. — *EstBíb* 29 (1970) 327-352. Esp. 328-331.335-338 [19,1]. [NTA 15, 779]

1974 El género literario de los evangelios. — *CuadEv* 1/15 (1974) 7-30.

1975a Los milagros de Jesús. I. Su historicidad. II. Los relatos evangélicos. III. La curación de un leproso (Mc 1,40-45). IV. Signos que anuncian el Reino de Dios. — *CuadEv* 2/15 (1975) 5-25; 2/16 (1975) 5-26; 2/17 (1975) 5-24; 2/18 (1975) 5-23.

1975b Los relatos pascuales. El sepulchro vacío y las apariciones. [28,1-10] — *CuadEv* 2/20 (1975) 5-30.

1976a & FRANCO, C.A., El Evangelio según S. Mateo. — *CuadEv* 3/25 (1976) 5-29.

1976b El proceso ante el Sanhedrin. II. El escandaloso perdon de los pecados (Mc 2,1-12 par.). — *EstBíb* 35 (1976) 49-78, 187-221. Esp. 207-219: "La versión de Mateo (9,1-8)". [NTA 23, 398]; 36 (1977) 35-55. [NTA 24, 108]

1979 Substrato arameo en el relato de la Anunciación a José I: "Inventa est in utero habens de Spiritu Sancto" (Mt 1,18). II: "Et non cognoscebat eam donec peperit filium" (Mt 1,25). — *EstBíb* 38 (1979-80) 35-55, 237-268. [NTA 26, 84]

1980 "No me veréis hasta que digás: Bendito el que viene en el nombre del Señor" (Mt 23,39; Lc 13,35). — *Cuadernos Bíblicos* (Valencia) 4 (1980) 56-71.

**HERRENBRÜCK, Fritz**

1981 Wer waren die 'Zöllner'? — *ZNW* 72 (1981) 178-194. Esp. 180-181 [5,46]. [NTA 26, 455] → 1990

1990 *Jesus und die Zöllner. Historische und neutestamentlich-exegetische Untersuchungen* (WUNT, II/41). Tübingen: Mohr, 1990, XII-380 p. Esp. 244-246 [18,17]; 246-349 [5,46-47]; 255-261 [Q 7,31-35]; 262-267 [21,28-32]. — Diss. Tübingen, 1979 (M. Hengel). → 1981

**HERRMANN, Léon**

1981 Correction du *k* en *a* dans une phrase de Jésus. [8,22] — *Revue des études anciennes* (Bordeaux) 83 (1981) 283. [NTA 29, 525]

**HERRMANN, Volker**

1991 Anmerkungen zum Verständnis einiger Paralleltexte zu Mt 25,31ff aus der altägyptischen Religion. — *BibNot* 59 (1991) 17-22. [NTA 37, 154]

**HERRMANN, Wolfram**

1961 *Das Wunder in der evangelischen Botschaft. Zur Interpretation der Begriffe* blind *und* taub *im Alten und Neuen Testament* (Aufsätze und Vorträge zur Theologie und Religionswissenschaft, 20). Berlin: Evangelische Verlagsanstalt, 1961, 32 p. Esp. 5-20 [τύφλος, κωφός]; 28-32 [11,5].

**HERTIG, Paul A.**

1995 *The Messiah at the Margins: A Missiology of Transformation Based on the Galilee Theme in Matthew.* Diss. Fuller Theol. Sem., Pasadena, CA, 1995, 379 p. (C. Van Engen). — *DissAbstr* 56 (1995-96) 1829.

**HERZ, Johannes**

1960 Die Gleichnisse der Evangelien Matthäus, Markus und Lukas in ihrer geschichtlichen Überlieferung und ihrem religiös-sittlichen Inhalt. — AMBERG, E.-H. – KÜHN, U. (eds.), *Bekenntnis zur Kirche. Festgabe für Ernst Sommerlath zum 70. Geburtstag*, Berlin: Evang. Verlagsanstalt, 1960, 52-93.

**HERZOG, John Joseph**

1972 *An Investigation of J. Arthur Baird's Program of Audience Criticism: The Analysis of Audience as a Critical Approach to the Synoptic Sayings of Jesus.* Diss. Sem. Foundation, Hartford, CT, 1972, 237 p. — *DissAbstr* 34 (1973-74) 406. → J.A. Baird 1969

**HERZOG, William R., II**

1992 Temple Cleansing. — *DJG*, 1992, 817-821. Esp. 818-819 [21,12-13].

1994 *Parables as Subversive Speech. Jesus as Pedagogue of the Oppressed* [18,23-35; 20,1-16; 25,14-30]. Louisville, KY: Westminster/Knox, 1994, X-299 p.

**HESTER, James D.**

1992 Socio-Rhetorical Criticism and the Parable of the Tenants. [21,33-46] — *JSNT* 45 (1992) 27-57. Esp. 29-34: "The parable"; 34-54: "The interpretation". [NTA 37, 152]

**HETH, William Alexander**

1982 Another Look at the Erasmian View of Divorce and Remarriage. — *JEvTS* 25 (1982) 263-272. Esp. 266-272 [19,9.12]. [NTA 27, 916]

1984a & WENHAM, G.J., *Jesus and Divorce: Towards an Evangelical Understanding of New Testament Teaching*. London: Hodder & Stoughton, 1984, 287 p. *Jesus and Divorce. The Problem with the Evangelical Consensus*. Nashville, TN: Nelson, 1985, 287 p.

1984b The Meaning of Divorce in Matthew 19:3-9. — *Churchman* (London) 98 (1984) 136-152. [NTA 29, 108]

1986 *Matthew's "Eunuch Saying" (19:12) and Its Relationship to Paul's Teaching on Singleness in 1 Corinthians 7*. Diss. Theol. Sem., Dallas, TX, 1986, IX-348 p. Esp. 139-198: "Matthew 19:10-12: meaning and function"; 255-266 [19,11-12/1 Cor 7,7]. — *DissAbstr* 48 (1987-88) 147; *SBT* 16 (1988) 130-131.

1987 Unmarried "for the sake of the kingdom" (Matthew 19:12) in the Early Church. — *GraceTJ* 8 (1987) 55-88. [NTA 32, 128]

1990 The Changing Basis for Permitting Remarriage after Divorce for Adultery: The Influence of R.H. Charles. — *TrinJ* NS 11 (1990) 143-159. [NTA 35, 1156]

1995 Divorce and Remarriage: The Search for an Evangelical Hermeneutic. — *TrinJ* 16 (1995) 63-100. Esp. 68-76 [5,31-32]; 76-82 [1,18-25]; 93-97 [19,9]. [NTA 40, 430r] → Keener 1991

**HEUBERGER, Josef**

1980 *Sämann und Gotteswort. Beitrag zu einer Geschichte der Auslegung des Sämanns-gleichnisses in der griechischen Patristik*. Graz: Dbv-Verlag, 1980, 369 p. — Diss. Graz, 1980 (J.B. Bauer).

1987 Samenkörner Christi des Sämanns auf griechischem Ackerboden. Zur pragmatischen Wirkungsgeschichte von Mt 13,23 parr. — BROX, N., et al. (eds.), *Anfänge der Theologie*. FS J.B. Bauer, 1987, 155-174.

**HEUBÜLT, Christine**

1980 Mt 5,17-20. Ein Beitrag zur Theologie des Evangelisten Matthäus. — *ZNW* 71 (1980) 143-149. [NTA 26, 466]

**HEUSCHEN, Josef Maria**

1950a De Bergrede bij Mattheus en Lucas. — *RevEcclLiège* 37 (1950) 27-33. Esp. 28-30.

1950b De leer der acht zaligheden. — *Ibid.*, 97-99.

1951 Excepta fornicationis causa (Mt 5,32). — *RevEcclLiège* 38 (1951) 312-317.

1955 Le thème de la pauvreté dans les béatitudes. — *RevEcclLiège* 42 (1955) 97-103, 173-180, 220-232, 276-285. Esp. 97-103, 276-285.

1957* (ed.), *La formation des évangiles. Problème synoptique et Formgeschichte* (Recherches bibliques, 2). Brugge: Desclée De Brouwer, 1957, 222 p. → Cambier, Cerfaux, Descamps, Doeve, Heuschen, Léon-Dufour, Levie, Rigaux 1955, van Bohemen, van Unnik

1957 La formation des évangiles. — *Ibid.*, 11-23.

**HEYDER, Gebhard M.**

1964 *Evangelium Jesu Christi. Synopsen. Harmonie mit lebensnaher Erklärung. I: Jugend-geschichte. II: Beginn des öffentlichen Lebens bis Parabelpredigt. III: Aussendung der Apostel bis Endweissagungen. IV: Passions- und Verherrlichungsgeschichte*. Regensburg: Habel, ²1964, 140 p.; 1966, 340 p.; 1968, 576 p.; 1967, 216 p.

**HEZSER, Catherine**

1990 *Lohnmetaphorik und Arbeitswelt in Mt 20,1-16. Das Gleichnis von den Arbeitern im Weinberg im Rahmen rabbinischer Lohngleichnisse* (NTOA, 15). Freiburg/Schw: Universitätsverlag; Göttingen: Vandenhoeck & Ruprecht, 1990, X-342 p. Esp. 133-136 [μισθός]; 157-236: "Mt 20,1-15 im Rahmen rabbinischer Lohngleichnisse – religionsgeschichtlicher Vergleich"; 237-244: "Auslegung des Gleichnisses von den Arbeitern im Weinberg"; 246-250: "Zur Frage

nach der Authentizität von Mt 20,1-15"; 251-290: "Die Bedeutung des Gleichnisses von den Arbeitern im Weinberg für Matthäus und seine Gemeinde – Redaktionsgeschichte"; 291-295: "Die Rezeption des Gleichnisses in den ersten fünf Jahrhunderte". [NTA 35, p. 383] — Diss. Heidelberg, 1985 (G. Theißen).
    E. BEST, *ExpT* 103 (1991-92) 184; A. FUCHS, *SNTU* 16 (1991) 213-215; R.H. GUNDRY, *JBL* 111 (1992) 340-341; X. JACQUES, *NRT* 113 (1991) 761-763; C. KÄHLER, *TLZ* 117 (1992) 911-914; J. LAMBRECHT, *TRev* 90 (1994) 216-217; P. PEZZOLI, *RivBib* 41 (1993) 224-227.

### HICKLING, Colin J.A.

1976    Reading, and Reading About, Matthew's Gospel. [Survey] — *EpworthR* 3 (1976) 103-108. [NTA 21, 69]

1982a   Conflicting Motives in the Redaction of Matthew: Some Considerations on the Sermon on the Mount and Matthew 18:15-20. — *Studia Evangelica* 7 (1982) 247-260.

1982b   The Plurality of "Q". — DELOBEL, J. (ed.), *Logia*, 1982, 425-429.

1990    Baptism in the First-Century Churches: A Case for Caution. — CLINES, D.A.J., et al. (eds.), *The Bible in Three Dimensions*, 1990, 249-267. Esp. 262-264 [28,19].

### HICKS, John M.

1984    The Sabbath Controversy in Matthew. An Exegesis of Matthew 12:1-14. — *RestQ* 27 (1984) 79-91. [NTA 30, 119]

### HIEBERT, David Edmond

1975    *An Introduction to the New Testament.* Vol. 1: *The Gospels and Acts.* Chicago, IL: Moody, 1975, 298 p.

1992    An Expository Study of Matthew 28:16-20. — *BS* 149 (1992) 338-354. [NTA 37, 156]

### HIERS, Richard H.

1966    Eschatology and Methodology. — *JBL* 85 (1966) 170-184. Esp. 171-173. [NTA 11, 453]

1968    *Jesus and Ethics. Four Interpretations.* Philadelphia, PA: Westminster, 1968, 208 p. Esp. 115-124 [10,17-22; 11,12-13; 12,28; 24,45-51; 25,1-12.14-30].

1970    *The Kingdom of God in the Synoptic Tradition* (University of Florida Humanities Monograph, 33). Gainesville, FL: University of Florida Press, 1970, 107 p. Esp. 30-35 [12,28/Q 11,20]; 36-42 [11,12]; 57-65 [11,11/Q 7,28]; 66-71 [10,23]; 72-77 [parables: kingdom]; 78-82.90-92 [kingdom: Mt/Q].

1973    *The Historical Jesus and the Kingdom of God. Present and Future in the Message and Ministry of Jesus* (University of Florida Humanities Monograph, 38). Gainesville, FL: University of Florida Press, 1973, VIII-128 p. Esp. 11-46: "Jesus' message, beliefs, and expectations"; 47-70: "Jesus' Galilean ministry".

1974    Satan, Demons, and the Kingdom of God. [12,28] — *ScotJT* 27 (1974) 35-47. [NTA 18, 803]

1981    *Jesus and the Future. Unresolved Questions for Understanding and Faith.* Atlanta, GA: Knox, 1981, XV-160 p. Esp. 24-30: "Q" [Q 3,7-9.16-17; 6,20-23.37-38.47-49; 10,2-12.13-15; 11,29-32.49-51; 12,8-9.33.39-40.42-46.57-59;13,23-24.28-29; 17,26-27; 19,12-27; 22,28-30]; 30-34: "M" [5,5-10; 7,21-23; 10,23; 11,23-24; 12,36-37; 13,47-50; 18,23-35; 22,13; 25,1-13.31-46; 16,27-28]; 38-41; 69-71 [Q 11,20]; 73-74 [Q 13,28-29]; 75 [Q 12,29-31]; 76 [6,11].

1985    "Binding" and "Loosing": The Matthean Authorizations. — *JBL* 104 (1985) 233-250. Esp. 237-239 [12,29]; 240-248 [16,19; 18,18]. [NTA 30, 122] → Derrett 1983a

1987    Pivotal Reactions to the Eschatological Interpretations: Rudolf Bultmann and C.H. Dodd. — WILLIS, W. (ed.), *The Kingdom of God*, 1987, 15-33. Esp. 19 [12,28].

### HIGGINS, Angus John Brockhurst

1952    The Persian Gospel Harmony as a Witness to Tatian's Diatessaron. — *JTS* 3 (1952) 83-87. Esp. 86-87 [5,45].

1959*   (ed.), *New Testament Essays. Studies in Memory of Thomas Walter Manson, 1893-1958.*
Manchester: University Press, 1959, XV-327 p. → M. Black, Bowman, Cullmann, Dodd, V.
Taylor, van Unnik

1959    The Persian and Arabic Gospel Harmonies. — *Studia Evangelica* 1 (1959) 793-810. Esp.
795 [1,19; 27,34]; 801 [26,15]; 802-803 [26,49; 27,4; 28,10]; 806 [26,58; 27,5]; 809-810 [26,55.73; 27,3].

1960a   Non-Gnostic Sayings in the Gospel of Thomas. — *NT* 4 (1960) 292-306. Esp. 296-301:
"Non-gnostic sayings of synoptic form and content" [13,31-32/Th 20; 7,5/Th 27; 13,12; 25,29/Th42; 11,11-
12/Th 47; 5,3/Th 55; 10,37-38/Th 56; 21,33-41/Th 66; 8,20/Th 86; 13,33/Th 96]. [NTA 6, 695]

1960b   The Old Testament and Some Aspects of New Testament Christology. —
*CanJournTheol* 6 (1960) 200-210. [NTA 5, 525]; = BRUCE, F.F. (ed.), *Promise and
Fulfilment. Essays Presented to Professor S.H. Hooke in Celebration of His Ninetieth
Birthday 21st January 1964*, Edinburgh: Clark, 1963, 128-141. Esp. 129-131 [Son of David];
132-135 [Son of God].

1963    The Sign of the Son of Man (Matt. xxiv.30). — *NTS* 9 (1962-63) 380-382. [NTA 8, 138]

1964    *Jesus and the Son of Man.* London: Lutterworth, 1964; Philadelphia, PA: Fortress,
1965, 223 p. Esp. 97-118: "The Son of Man in Matthew" [13,37.41; 16,27-28; 19,28; 24,30; 25,31;
26,2]; 119-142: "The Son of Man in Q" [Q 6,22; 7,34; 9,58; 12,8.10; 11,30; 12,40; 17,24.26]; 185-209:
"Jesus and the Son of Man". → Tödt 1959/65

1968    The Son of Man Concept and the Historical Jesus. — *Studia Evangelica* 5 (1968) 14-20.
Esp. 16-18 [11,27].

1975    "Menschensohn" oder "ich" in Q: Lk 12,8-9 / Mt 10,32-33? — PESCH, R., et al.
(eds.), *Jesus und der Menschensohn*. FS A. Vögtle, 1975, 117-123.

1980    *The Son of Man in the Teaching of Jesus* (SNTS MS, 39). Cambridge: University Press,
1980, X-177 p. Esp. 29-49: "The Son of Man in the synoptic gospels in recent study"; 56-72 [Q
17,24.26.30]; 75-77 [10,23]; 80-84 [Q 12,8-9]; 84-90.116-117 [Q 12,10]; 90-113.118-119 [Q 11,29-30]; 113
[Q 6,22]; 113-114 [16,13]; 114 [16,28]; 115 [Q 22,28-30].

**HIGGINS, Martin J.**

1961    New Testament Result Clauses with Infinitive. — *CBQ* 23 (1961) 233-241. Esp. 234-237.
[NTA 6, 65]

**HILD, Helmut**

1981    Die Bergpredigt – Wegweisung in unserer Zeit. — BÖCHER, O., et al., *Die Bergpredigt
im Leben der Christenheit*, 1981, 41-55.

**HILGERT, Earle**

1962    *The Ship and Related Symbols in the New Testament.* Assen: Van Gorcum, 1962, 158
p. — Diss. Basel, 1962.

1967    Symbolismus und Heilsgeschichte in den Evangelien. Ein Beitrag zu den Seesturm- und
Gerasenererzählungen.— CHRIST, F. (ed.), *Oikonomia. Heilsgeschichte als Thema der
Theologie. Oscar Cullmann zum 65. Geburtstag gewidmet*, Hamburg–Bergstedt: Reich,
1967, 51-56. Esp. 54-55 [8,23-34].

**HILHORST, Anton**

1988    Biblical Metaphors Taken Literally. — BAARDA, T., et al. (eds.), *Text and Testimony*.
FS A.F.J. Klijn, 1988, 123-131. Esp. 123-124 [7,13-14/TestAbrah]; 124-125 [2,2/Num 24,17].

**HILL, David**

1965a   Δίκαιοι as a Quasi-Technical Term. — *NTS* 11 (1964-65) 296-302. Esp. 297 [23,29]; 297-
298 [13,17]; 298-299 [10,41]; 299-300 [13,43]. [NTA 10, 108]

1965b   A Note on Matthew i.19. — *ExpT* 76 (1964-65) 133-134. [NTA 9, 900] → Spicq 1964

1967 *Greek Words and Hebrew Meanings: Studies in the Semantics of Soteriological Terms* (SNTS MS, 5). Cambridge: University Press, 1967, XV-333 p. Esp. 120-139 [δίκαιος-δικαιοσύνη]; 241-253 [πνεῦμα]. — Diss. St. Andrew's Univ. 1964 (M. Black – R.McL. Wilson).

1972 *The Gospel of Matthew* (New Century Bible). London: Oliphants, 1972, 367 p. Esp. 21-72: "Introduction"; 73-362: "Commentary". [NTA 17, p. 245]; Grand Rapids, MI: Eerdmans, 1981. → Ziesler 1985

    D.J. ATKINSON, *Theology* 76 (1973) 544-545; D.J. CLARK, *BTrans* 25 (1974) 360; J.F. LAVOE, *ATR* 56 (1974) 229-230; I.H. MARSHALL, *EvQ* 45 (1973) 58-59.

1974 On the Evidence for the Creative Role of Christian Prophets. — *NTS* 20 (1973-74) 262-274. Esp. 271 [10,32]. [NTA 19, 373]

1976 False Prophets and Charismatics: Structure and Interpretation in Matthew 7,15-23. — *Bib* 57 (1976) 327-348. Esp. 327-333: "A review of proposed identifications of the false prophets"; 333-340: "The case for and against the 'antinomian hypothesis'"; 340-348: "The identity of the two separate groups: 'false prophets and charismatics'". [NTA 21, 723]

1977 On the Use and Meaning of Hosea vi.6 in Matthew's Gospel. — *NTS* 24 (1977-78) 107-119. Esp. 107-108.113-116 [12,7]; 110 [23,23]; 110-113 [9,13]. [NTA 22, 398]

1979a *New Testament Prophecy* (Marshall's Theological Library, 3). London: Marshall, Morgan & Scott; Atlanta, GA: Knox, 1979, XIV-241 p. Esp. 43-47 [John the Baptist]; 58-69 [Jesus as prophet]; 152-154 [Q: Prophecy]; 154-156 [Mt]. → Boring 1983

1979b Some Recent Trends in Matthaean Studies. — *IBS* 1 (1979) 139-149. [NTA 24, 401]

1980 Son and Servant: An Essay on Matthean Christology. — *JSNT* 6 (1980) 2-16. Esp. 4-12 (Kingsbury 1975a); 12-15 (Gerhardsson 1973a). [NTA 24, 778]; = EVANS, C.A. – PORTER, S.E. (eds.), *The Synoptic Gospels*, 1995, 13-27. Esp. 13-25; 25-27. → Allison 1987d

1983 "Our daily bread" (Matt. 6.11) in the History of Exegesis. — *IBS* 5 (1983) 2-10. [NTA 27, 918]

1984a The Figure of Jesus in Matthew's Story: A Response to Professor Kingsbury's Literary-Critical Probe. — *JSNT* 21 (1984) 37-52. Esp. 37-42 [literary criticism]; 42-48 [structure]; 48-51 [Son of Man]; = EVANS, C.A. – PORTER, S.E. (eds.), *The Synoptic Gospels*, 1995, 81-96. Esp. 81-89; 89-93; 93-96. → Allison 1987d, Kingsbury 1984, 1985

1984b The Meaning of the Sermon on the Mount in Matthew's Gospel. — *IBS* 6 (1984) 120-133. [NTA 29, 91]

1985 Matthew 27:51-53 in the Theology of the Evangelist. — *IBS* 7 (1985) 76-87. [NTA 30, 127]

1986a The Conclusion of Matthew's Gospel: Some Literary-Critical Observations. — *IBS* 8 (1986) 54-63. [NTA 31, 126]

1986b In Quest of Matthean Christology. — *Ibid.*, 135-142. [NTA 31, 106] → Allison 1987d

**HILL, Robert**

1987 Synoptic "Basileia" and Pauline "Mysterion". [13,11] — *EstBíb* 45 (1987) 309-324. [NTA 33, 106]

**HILLERDAL, Gunnar**

1983 *Simon Petrus*. Stockholm: EFS-förlaget, 1983, 118 p.

**HILLMANN, Willibrord**

1956 Perfectio evangelica. Neutestamentlich-theologische Grundlagen des Ordenslebens. — *WissWeish* 19 (1956) 161-172.

**HILLS, Julian V.**

1990 Tradition, Redaction, and Intertextuality: Miracle Lists in Apocryphal Acts as a Test Case. — *SBL 1990 Seminar Papers*, 375-390. Esp. 378-379 [4,23-24; 10,7-8; 15,30-31; Q 7,22].

1991 The Three "Matthean" Aphorisms in the *Dialogue of the Savior* 53. [6,34; 10,10.25] — *HTR* 84 (1991) 43-58. [NTA 36, 1646]

1994 The Acts of the Apostles in the *Acts of Paul*. — *SBL 1994 Seminar Papers*, 24-54. Esp. 29-39: "Gospels and Epistles" [Mt/Acts of Paul]; 51.

**HILLYER, N.**

1964 Matthew's Use of the Old Testament. — *EvQ* 36 (1964) 12-26. [NTA 8, 932]

**HILTON, Marvin J.**

1958 *A Textual Evaluation of the Gospel according to Matthew (Chapters 1-7)*. Diss. Midwestern Baptist Theol. Sem., Kansas City, KS, 1958.

**HIMMELFARB, Martha**

1965 On Reading Matthew. — *Commentary* 40/4 (1965) 56-65. [NTA 10, 503]

**HINNEBUSCH, Paul**

1972 The Messianic Meaning of the Beatitudes. — *BiTod* 59 (1972) 707-717. [NTA 16, 852]

1980 *St. Matthew' Earthquake. Judgment and Discipleship in the Gospel of Matthew*. Ann Arbor, MI: Servant Books, 1980, XII-150 p. [NTA 25, p. 196]

**HIRSCH, Emanuel**

1941[R] *Frühgeschichte des Evangeliums*. II. *Die Vorlagen des Lukas und das Sondergut des Matthäus* [1941]. Tübingen: Mohr, [2]1951, XXXIX-269 p., 445 p. Esp. 73-170: "Q (Lu I) in Luk 3–21"; 284-338: "Zur Analyse des Matthäusevangeliums"; 352-354: "Das Evangelium MaS"; 354-362: "Die Evangelisten Luk und Matth"; 428-439: "Die Worte Jesu aus MaS". → M. Lehmann 1970

**HIRSCH, Selma**

1950 Studien zu Matthäus 11,2-26. Zugleich ein Beitrag zur Geschichte Jesu und zur Frage seines Selbstbewußtseins. — *TZ* 6 (1950) 241-260. Esp. 241-245 [11,2-9]; 245-249 [11,6.13-15.19]; 250-254 [11,18.20-24]; 254-257 [11,12.25-26]; 257-260 [11,11].

**HIRT, Oscar Herbert**

1985 *Interpretation in the Gospels: An Examination of the Use of Redaction Criticism in Mark 8:27–9:32 (par. Matthew 16:13–17:23; Luke 9:18-45)*. Diss. Theol. Sem., Dallas, TX, 1985, 337 p. — *DissAbstr* 46 (1985-86) 2725; *SBT* 14 (1986) 196.

**HIRUNUMA, Toshio**

1970- The Praxis of NT Textual Criticism. [Japanese] — *Shinyaku Kenkyū (= Studia Textus NT)* 49-104 (1970-75) [1,18.25; 2,18; 3,7.12.15.16; 4,17; 5,22]; 116-138 (1976-78) [8,13.18.21. 23.25.28; 9,4.8.14.18.26.34; 10,3.4.8.23.37.42; 11,2.9.15.17.19.23; 12,4.15.25.30.31.47; 13,9.13.35.40. 43.44.55; 14,3.9.10.12.15.16.22.24.27.28.30; 15,2.4.5.6.14.15.23.26.30.31]; 139 (1978) 1153-1155 [15]; 145-150 (1978-79) 1204-1245 [18,7–19,22]; 167 (1980) 1389-1396 [26]; 168 (1980) 1399-1412; 171 (1980) 1429-1430 [26,63–27,4; 27,35.40]; 173 (1981) 1442-1446 [27,49–28,14]; 174 (1981) 1450-1452 [28,15.17.20]

1980 National Museum, Berlin P 16 388 (Ts 25) Papyrus 35. [Japanese] — *Shinyaku Kenkyū* 165 (1980) 1373-1376, 1381-1388.

1981 Matthew 16:2b-3. — EPP, E.J. — FEE, G.D. (eds.), *New Testament Textual Criticism*. FS B.M. Metzger, 1981, 35-45.

1987 ἄνευ τοῦ πατρός. [Japanese] — *Shinyaku Kenkyū* 252 (1987) 2089-2100. ἄνευ τοῦ πατρός. "Without (of) the Father". — *FilolNT* 3 (1990) 53-62. Esp. 53-54 [10,29]. [NTA 35, 141]

**HJÄRPE, Jan**

1971 "Pärlor åt svin". Ett "Jesusord" i arabisk tradition. ["Pearls to swine". A "saying of Jesus" in Arabic tradition] [7,6] — *SEÅ* 36 (1971) 126-135. [NTA 17, 910]

**HJERL-HANSEN, Børge**

1959 Did Christ Know the Qumran Sect? Jesus and the Messiah of the Desert. An Observation Based on Matthew 24,26-28. — *RQum* 1 (1959) 495-508. [NTA 4, 657]

**HOAD, John**

1962 On Matthew xxiii.15: A Rejoinder. — *ExpT* 73 (1961-62) 211-212. [NTA 7, 142] → Flowers 1961

**HOBBS, Edward Craig**

1980 A Quarter-Century without "Q". — *PerkJourn* 33/4 (1980) 10-19. [NTA 25, 58]

**HOBBS, Herschel H.**

1961 *The Gospel of Matthew* (Proclaiming the New Testament). Grand Rapids, MI: Baker, 1961, 135 p. [NTA 6, p. 268]

1962 The Miraculous Element in Matthew. — *SWJT* 5 (1962) 41-54.

1965 *An Exposition of the Gospel of Matthew*. Grand Rapids, MI: Baker, 1965, 422 p.
F.F. BRUCE, *EvQ* 37 (1965) 249-250.
*An Exposition of the Four Gospels*. Volume 1: *The Gospel of Matthew*. Nashville, TN: Broadman, 1977, 422 p. [NTA 23, p. 24]

**HOBBS, T. Raymond**

1990 Crossing Cultural Bridges. The Biblical World. [18,3] — *McMaster Journal of Theology* (Hamilton, Ont.) 1 (1990) 1-21. [NTA 36, 1278]

**HOCHGREBE, Volker**

1982* (ed.), *Provokation Bergpredigt. Mit dem Text von Matthäus 5-7 in der Übersetzung von Walter Jens und mit Beiträgen von Josef Blank et al.* Stuttgart: Kreuz, 1982, 158 p. [NTA 27, p. 209] → J. Blank, L. Schottroff, Walf, Zink; → Frankemölle 1983c

**HODGES, Zane C.**

1964 The Centurion's Faith in Matthew and Luke. — *BS* 121 (1964) 321-332. [NTA 9, 530]

1965 The Blind Men at Jericho. [20,29-34] — *BS* 122 (1965) 319-330. [NTA 10, 521]

1966 The Women and the Empty Tomb. [28,1-10] — *BS* 123 (1966) 301-309. [NTA 11, 714]

1982 & FARSTAD, A.L. (eds.), *The Greek New Testament according to the Majority Text*. Nashville, TN: Nelson, 1982, XLVI-810 p. Esp. 1-103; [2]1985.

**HODGSON, Robert, Jr.**

1979 The Testimony Hypothesis. — *JBL* 98 (1979) 361-378. Esp. 366-367.372-375 [fulfilment quotations]; 371 [13,14-15]; 374 [12,18-21]. [NTA 24, 338]

1984 The Christmas Story. — *BiTod* 22 (1984) 355-360. Esp. 356-358 [1-2]. [NTA 29, 516]

1985 On the Gattung of Q: A Dialogue with James M. Robinson. — *Bib* 66 (1985) 73-95. Esp. 73-75: "Introduction"; 75-76: "Q as a collection of sapientia sayings"; 76-77: "Q and the testimony hypothesis"; 77-85: "Q and the Old Testament"; 85-90: "Organizaional principles in Q's material"; 90-93: "The Herodian pharisees". [NTA 29, 916] → J.M. Robinson 1964/71, 1982b

**HÖFER, Albert**

1962 Weihnachtliches Christentum. Das christliche Dasein nach den Kindheitsberichten (Mt 1-2; Lk 1-2). — *BLtg* 36 (1962-63) 78-83.

**HOEHNER, Harold W.**

1972 *Herod Antipas* (SNTS MS, 17). Cambridge: University Press, 1972, XVI-437 p. Esp. 114-117 [14,3-12]; 184-191 [14,1-2]; 211-213 [16,5-12]. — Diss. Cambridge, 1968 (E. Bammel).

**HOERBER, R.G.**

1981 Implications of the Imperative in the Sermon on the Mount. — *Concordia Journal* (St.

Louis, MO) 7 (1981) 100-103. [NTA 26, 89]; = ID., *Studies in the New Testament*, Cleveland, OH: Biblion, 1991.

1986 *Reading the New Testament for Understanding* [Jesus and the New Israel]. St. Louis, MO: Concordia, 1986, 211 p.

**HÖRSTER, Gerhard**

1988 Die eschatologische Ethik der Bergpredigt. — BURKHARDT, H. (ed.), *Begründung ethischer Normen. Bericht von der 5. Theologischen Studienkonferenz des Arbeitskreises für evangelikale Theologie (AfeT) vom 9.-12. September 1987 in Tübingen* (Monographien und Studienbücher, 339), Wuppertal: Brockhaus; Gießen-Basel: Brunner, 1988, 99-114.

**HOET, Rik**

1982 *"Omnes autem vos fratres estis", Étude du concept ecclésiologique des "frères" selon Mt 23,8-12* (AnGreg, 232). Roma: Università Gregoriana, 1982, IX-226 p. Esp. 7-34: "Analyses critiques"; 35-94: "Analyse du contexte" [23,2-39]; 95-111: "Analyse de la structure"; 113-141.143-187: "Analyse sémantique"; 189-211: "Interprétation théologique de Mt 23,8c". [NTA 28, p. 313] — Diss. Pont. Univ. Greg., Roma, 1980 (E. Rasco).
   *TLZ* 108 (1983) 598; J. DUPONT, *RTL* 14 (1983) 468-469; A. SEGOVIA, *ArchTeolGran* 47 (1984) 381; K. STOCK, *ZKT* 106 (1984) 197; C.M. TUCKETT, *JTS* 35 (1984) 508-509.

**HOFFMAN, R. Joseph**

1984 *Jesus Outside the Gospels*. Buffalo, NY: Prometheus Books, 1984, 132 p. Esp. 86-97: "Q".

**HOFFMANN, Paul** → IQP

1967 Πάντες ἐργάται ἀδικίας. Redaktion und Tradition in Lk 13,22-30. — *ZNW* 58 (1967) 188-214. Esp. 195-196 [7,13-14]; 200-203 [7,22-23]; 205-210 [8,11-12]. [NTA 12, 900]; = ID., *Tradition und Situation*, 1995, 135-161. Esp. 141-142; 146-149; 152-156.

1969a Die Anfänge der Theologie in der Logienquelle — SCHREINER, J. - DAUTZENBERG, G. (eds.), *Gestalt und Anspruch*, 1969, 134-152. Esp. 135-137: "Überblick"; 137-141: "Die Boten Jesu"; 141-143: "Die Nähe der Herrschaft Gottes"; 143-147: "Jesus der Menschensohn"; 147-152: "Die Auslegung der Botschaft Jesu in Q".
   Gli inizi della teologia nella fonte dei logia. — PENNA, R. (ed.), *Introduzione letteraria e teologica al Nuovo Testamento*, Roma, 1982, 224-253.

1969b Die Stellung der Bergpredigt im Matthäusevangelium. Auslegung der Bergpredigt I. — *BibLeb* 10 (1969) 57-65. Esp. 58-59 [5-7/Mk]; 59-61 [4,14-17]; 61-62 [4,23; 9,35]; 62-64 [28,18-20]. [NTA 14, 137]

1969c "Selig sind die Armen...". Auslegung der Bergpredigt II (Mt 5,3-16). — *Ibid.*, 111-122. [NTA 14, 139]

1969d Die bessere Gerechtigkeit. Auslegung der Bergpredigt III (Mt 5,17-37). — *Ibid.*, 175-189. Esp. 176-180 [5,17-20]; 180-189 [5,21-37]. [NTA 14, 479]

1969e Die bessere Gerechtigkeit. Die Auslegung der Bergpredigt IV (Mt 5,38-48). — *Ibid.*, 264-275. Esp. 265-268 [5,38-42]; 269-271 [5,43-48]. [NTA 14, 853] → 1970d

1969f Die Versuchungsgeschichte in der Logienquelle. Zur Auseinandersetzung der Judenchristen mit dem politischen Messianismus. — *BZ* 13 (1969) 207-223. Esp. 208-209: "Zur Rekonstruktion des Textes der Logienquelle"; 209-213: "Methodische Vorüberlegungen"; 213-219: "Die zeitgeschichtliche Erklärung der einzelnen Szenen"; 220-222: "Die Versuchungsgeschichte im Rahmen der Logienquelle". [NTA 14, 475]; = ID., *Tradition und Situation*, 1995, 193-207. Esp. 193-194; 195-198; 199-204; 204-206.

1970a Jesusverkündigung in der Logienquelle. — PESCH, W. (ed.), *Jesus in den Evangelien* (SBS, 45), Stuttgart: Katholisches Bibelwerk, 1970, 50-70. Esp. 50-54: "Allgemeine

Charakteristik der Logienquelle"; 54-56: "Jesus Bote des Weisheit" 56-64: "Jesus der Menschensohn"; 65-66: Jesus und Johannes der Täufer"; 67-70: "Die Auslegung der Botschaft Jesu in der Logienquelle". La prédication de Jésus dans la source des Logia. — *Jésus dans les Évangiles*, trans. A. Liefooghe (Lire la Bible, 29), Paris: Cerf, 1971, 25-49. Esp. 26-31; 31-33; 33-41; 43-45; 45-48.

1970b **Jesu Wort von der Ehescheidung und seine Auslegung in der neutestamentlichen Überlieferung.** — *IZT/Concilium* (Mainz) 6 (1970) 326-332.

Jesus' Saying about Divorce and Its Interpretation in the New Testament Tradition. — *Concilium* (London) 6/5 (1970) 51-66.

Paroles de Jésus à propos du divorce avec l'interprétation qui en a été donnée dans la tradition néotestamentaire. — *Concilium* (Paris) 55 (1970) 49-62.

1970c **Die Offenbarung des Sohnes. Die apokalyptischen Voraussetzungen und ihre Verarbeitung im Q-Logion Mt 11,27 par Lk 10,22.** — *Kairos* 12 (1970) 270-288. [NTA 16, 537]

1970d **Der ungeteilte Dienst. Die Auslegung der Bergpredigt V (Mt 6,1–7,27).** — *BibLeb* 11 (1970) 89-104. Esp. 89-94 [6,1-18]; 94-96 [6,19-34]; 97 [7,1-5]; 97-98 [7,6]; 98-100 [7,7-11]; 100 [7,13-14]; 100-101 [7,15-20]; 101-102 [7,21-23]; 102 [7,24-27]. [NTA 15, 496] → 1969e

1971 **Lk 10,5-11 in der Instruktionsrede der Logienquelle.** — *EKK NT Vorarbeiten*, 3, 1971, 37-53. Esp. 39-42 [Q 10,10-11]; 42-50 [Q 10,8].

1972 *Studien zur Theologie der Logienquelle* (NTAbh, NF 8). Münster: Aschendorff, 1972, VIII-357 p.; [2]1975; [3]1982, VIII-366 p. ("Bibliographischer Nachtrag", 352-360). Esp. 15-33: "Die Gerichtspredigt des Johannes in der Logienquelle" [Q 3,7-9.16-27]; 34-50: "Die Naherwartung in der Logienquelle"; 50-79: "Die Deutung der Zeit seit Johannes in der Logienquelle" [11,12-13/Q 16,16]; 82-102: "Jesus, der Menschensohn. Die Fragestellung" [Son of Man in Q]; 102-142: "Die Apokalypsis des Sohnes" [Q 10,21-22]; 142-158: "Die Identifizierung Jesu mit dem Menschensohn" [Q 6,22-23; 7,34; 9,57-58; 12,10]; 158-190: "Propheten-Tradition und Menschensohnbekenntnis" [Q 6,22-23; 7,33-35; 9,58; 11,31-32.47-48.49-51; 13,34-35]; 190-233: "Johannes und der Menschensohn Jesus" [Q 7,18-23.24-28.31-35]; 237-287: "Die Rekonstruktion des Q-Textes der Botenrede" [Q 10,2-16.21-22]; 287-311: "Die Botenrede in der Logienquelle" [Q 10,2-16]; 312-331: "Die eschatologisch-charismatische Eigenart des Auftretens der Boten" [Q 10,4]. — Diss. Münster, 1968 (J. Gnilka). → Luz 1973, Sabourin 1973

D.E. AUNE, *CBQ* 35 (1973) 93-95; M.-É. BOISMARD, *RB* 80 (1973) 615; F. CHRIST, *TZ* 29 (1973) 438-439; J. DUPONT, *TRev* 69 (1973) 198-199; R.A. EDWARDS, *JBL* 92 (1973) 606-608; M. MEES, *VetChr* 9 (1972) 398-400; H. MERKLEIN, *BZ* 18 (1974) 112-114; N., *RevistBíb* 35 (1973) 281-282; B. PIEPIÓRKA, *ZKT* 95 (1973) 227; L. SABOURIN, *BTB* 3 (1973) 287-292; G. SCHMAHL, *TTZ* 82 (1973) 183-184; W. SCHMITHALS, *TLZ* 98 (1973) 348-350; A. SUHL, *Fre.burger Rundbrief* 25 (1973) 136-137. E. BAASLAND, *TidsTeolKirk* 47 (1976) 58-59: W. TRILLING, *Kairos* 17 (1975) 154-157.

1973* & BROX, N. - PESCH, W. (eds.), *Orientierung an Jesus. Zur Theologie der Synoptiker. Für Josef Schmid.* Freiburg: Herder, 1973, 431 p. → Brox, F. Hahn, Hengel, Hoffmann, Kilpatrick, Mussner, Neirynck, W. Pesch, Schelkle, Schürmann, Schweizer, Vögtle

1973 **Mk 8,31. Zur Herkunft und markinischen Rezeption einer alten Überlieferung.** — *Ibid.*, 170-204. Esp. 179-180.189 [Q 17,1-2]; 182-183 [Q 10,21-22]; = ID., *Tradition und Situation*, 1995, 281-312. Esp. 290-291.299; 293-294.

1974 **Der Petrus-Primat im Matthäusevangelium.** — GNILKA, J. (ed.), *Neues Testament und Kirche.* FS R. Schnackenburg, 1974, 94-114. Esp. 95-98 [16,17-19]; 98 [23,13]; 98-102 [16,19; 18,18]; 102-106 [16,18]; 106-108 [16,23-28]; 108-110 [Peter]; 110-113 [ecclesiology]; = DENZLER, G. (ed.), *Das Papsttum in der Diskussion*, Regensburg: Pustet, 1974, 9-35; = LANGE, J. (ed.), *Das Matthäus-Evangelium*, 1980, 414-440. Esp. 416-418; 419; 419-422; 422-425; 425-427; 427-429; 429-432; = ID., *Studien*, 1994, 326-349.

1975 & EID, V., *Jesus von Nazareth und eine christliche Moral. Sittliche Perspektiven der Verkündigung Jesu* (QDisp, 66). Freiburg: Herder, 1975, 259 p. Esp. 27-58: "Die Basileia-Verkündigung Jesu" [3,7-10; 5,3-12]; 73-94: "Die Überwindung gesetzhafter Sittlichkeit in der Auseinandersetzung Jesu mit jüdisch-pharisäischen Gesetzesverständnis" [5,21-48]; 109-131: "Jesu Stellungnahme zur Ehescheidung und ihre Auswirkungen im Urchristentum" [5,31-32; 19,3-9]; 147-166: "Der Feind als 'Nächster'" [5,39-42.44-45]; 186-230: "Jesu Forderung, auf Vorrang und Herrschaft zu verzichten" [18,1-5; 23,11]; [2]1976; [3]1978; = ID., *Studien*, 1994, 41-130.

1978a  Die Bedeutung des Petrus für die Kirche des Mattäus. Redaktionsgeschichtliche Beobachtungen zu Mt 16,17-19. — RATZINGER, J. (ed.), *Dienst an der Einheit. Zum Wesen und Auftrag des Petrusamts* (Schriften der Katholischen Akademie in Bayern, 85), Düsseldorf: Patmos, 1978, 9-26. Esp. 9-12: "Zur Fragestellung"; 12-15: "Mt 16,17-19 im Kontext des Mattäusevangeliums"; 25-26: "Mattäus und die Primatsfrage".

1978b  "Eschatologie" und "Friedenshandeln" in der Jesusüberlieferung. — LIEDKE, G., et al. (eds.), *Eschatologie und Frieden*. II: *In biblischen Texten* (Texte und Materialien der Forschungsstatte der Evangelischen Studiengemeinschaft, A7), Heidelberg: FES, 1978, 283-298; = *Eschatologie und Friedenshandeln. Exegetische Beiträge zur Frage christlicher Friedensverantwortung* (SBS, 101), Stuttgart: Katholisches Bibelwerk, 1981, 115-152. Esp. 120-138; 144-146.

1979   Auferstehung Jesu Christi. II/1. — *TRE* 4 (1979) 478-513. Esp. 500-503 [28,1-10]; = ID., *Studien*, 1994, 188-251.

1981   "Er weiß, was ihr braucht..." (Mt 6,7). Jesu einfache und konkrete Rede von Gott. — "*Ich will euer Gott werden*". *Beispiele biblischen Redens von Gott* (SBS, 100), Stuttgart: Katholisches Bibelwerk, 1981, 151-176; = ID, *Studien*, 1994, 15-40.

1984a  Bergpredigt und christliche Verantwortung für den Frieden. — *KatBlät* 109 (1984) 266-273. Esp. 266-268.

1984b  Tradition und Situation. Zur "Verbindlichkeit" des Gebots der Feindesliebe in der synoptischen Überlieferung und in der gegenwärtigen Friedensdiskussion. — KERTELGE, K. (ed.), *Ethik im Neuen Testament*, 1984, 50-118. Esp. 51-63.64-81 [Q 6,27-36]; 82-93 [5,3-12.39-48]; = ID., *Tradition und Situation*, 1995, 3-61. Esp. 4-15; 15-30; 31-40.

1985   Der garstige breite Graben. Zu den Anfängen der historisch-kritischen Osterdiskussion. — KERN, H. (ed.), *Zeit und Stunde. Festschrift für Aloys Goergen*, Münster: Mäander, 1985, 79-106; = ID., *Tradition und Situation*, 1995, 341-372. → 1988a-c

1986   Kirchliches Amt unter der Herausforderung der Botschaft Jesu. Zur Entwicklung der Gemeindestrukturen im frühen Christentum. — HIEROLD, A.E., et al. (eds.), *Die Kraft der Hoffnung. Gemeinde und Evangelium. Festschrift für Alterzbischof DDr. Josef Schneider zum 80. Geburtstag*, Bamberg: St. Otto, 1986, 48-61. Esp. 58-59: "Die Gemeinde als Bruderschaft des Messias Jesus im Matthäusevangelium".

1987   Priestertum und Amt im Neuen Testament. Eine Bestandsaufnahme. — ID. (ed.), *Priesterkirche* (Theologie zur Zeit, 3), Düsseldorf: Patmos, 1987, 12-61. Esp. 56-58: "Die matthäische Alternative: Kirche als Gemeinschaft der Schwestern und Brüder des Messias Jesus"; = ID., *Studien*, 1994, 274-325. Esp. 320-323.

1988*  (ed.), *Zur neutestamentlichen Überlieferung von der Auferstehung Jesu* (Wege der Forschung, 522). Darmstadt: Wissenschaftliche Buchgesellschaft, 1988, VII-499 p. → M. Albertz 1922, J. Becker 1975, P. Benoit 1960, Dodd 1955a, Hoffmann 1988a-c, McArthur 1971c; → Bloem 1987

1988a  Die historisch-kritische Osterdiskussion von H.S. Reimarus bis zu Beginn des 20. Jahrhunderts. [1986] — *Ibid.*, 15-67. → 1985

1988b  Das Zeichen für Israel. Zu einem vernachlässigten Aspekt der matthäischen Ostergeschichte. [1986] — *Ibid.*, 416-452. Esp. 416-423 [12,39-40; 27,63-65]; 423-434 [12,40; 27,63]; 434-443 [27,57-28,20]; 443-447 [28,1-8]; 447-452 [27,39-43.51-54]; = ID., *Tradition und Situation*, 1995, 313-340. Esp. 313-318; 318-326; 326-333; 333-336; 336-340. → 1985

1988c  Chronologische Auswahlbibliographie zur Auferstehung Jesu. — *Ibid.*, 453-483. → 1985

1988d Der Q-Text der Sprüche vom Sorgen. Mt 6,25-33 / Lk 12,22-31. Ein Rekonstruktionsversuch. — SCHENKE, L. (ed.), *Studien zum Matthäusevangelium*. FS W. Pesch, 1988, 127-155. Esp. 131-133: "Die Stellung der Sprüche in Q"; 133-134 [6,25/Q 12,22.23]; 134-138 [6,26.28b-30/Q 12,24.27-28]; 139-140 [6,27.28a/Q 12,25.26]; 140-154 [6,31-33(34)/Q 12,29-31(32)]; = ID., *Tradition und Situation*, 1995, 62-87. Esp. 64-65; 65-66; 66-70; 70-72; 72-85. → 1989c

1989a Die Auferweckung Jesu als Zeichen für Israel. Mt 12,39f und die matthäische Ostergeschichte. — KERTELGE, K., et al. (eds.), *Christus bezeugen*. FS W. Trilling, 1989, 110-123. Esp. 110-112: "Die Geschichte von der Wache des Pilatus als apologetische Legende"; 112-115: "Der Schlüssel zu einem weiterführenden Verständnis: Das Jona-Zeichen"; 115-119: "Die matthäische Ostergeschichte"; 119-120: "Heilsgeschichtliche contra eschatologische Interpretation"; 120-123: "Die Zeichen bei Jesu Tod und die Ostergeschichte".

1989b Jesu "Verbot des Sorgens" und seine Nachgeschichte in der synoptischen Überlieferung. — KOCH, D.-A., et al. (eds.), *Jesu Rede von Gott*. FS W. Marxsen, 1989, 116-141. Esp. 118-124: "Der auf Jesus zurückgehende Grundbestand der Spruchkomposition: Mt 6,25bc.26.28b-30.31.32b"; 124-127: "Die Rezeption der Sprüche in der Logienquelle"; 127-131: "Die Rezeption der Sprüche durch Matthäus"; = ID., *Tradition und Situation*, 1995, 107-134. Esp. 109-115; 115-119; 119-123.

1989c Die Sprüche vom Sorgen (Mt 6,25-33 / Lk 12,22-31) in der vorsynoptischen Überlieferung. — HIERDEIS, H. - ROSENBUSCH, H.S. (eds.), *Artikulation der Wirklichkeit*. *Festschrift für Siegfried Oppolzer zum 60. Geburtstag*, Frankfurt/M: Lang, 1989, 73-94. Esp. 75-76: "Der vorausgesetzte Q-Text"; 77-80: "Zur Struktur des Q-Textes"; 80-88: "Literarische Analyse der Texteinheit"; = ID., *Tradition und Situation*, 1995, 88-106. Esp. 88-90; 90-93; 93-105. → 1988d

1991 Jesus versus Menschensohn. Mt 10,32f und die synoptische Menschensohnüberlieferung. — OBERLINNER, L. - FIEDLER, P. (eds.), *Salz der Erde*. FS A. Vögtle, 1991, 165-202. Esp. 165-167 [Q 12,8-9]; 167-170 [Q 12,8]; 171-172 [Q 12,9]; 172-180 [Son of Man]; 180-184 [10,26-32; Q 12,2-9]; 185-186 [10,32-33/Mk 8,38]; 190-193 [Q 12,8-9]; 193-200 [authenticity]; = ID., *Tradition und Situation*, 1995, 208-242. Esp. 208-210; 210-213; 213-215; 215-222; 222-227; 227-228; 232-235; 235-242.

1992a Logienquelle. — *EKL* 3 (³1992) 175-176.

1992b QR und der Menschensohn. Eine vorläufige Skizze. — VAN SEGBROECK, F., et al. (eds.), *The Four Gospels 1992*. FS F. Neirynck, 1992, I, 421-456. Esp. 422-428: "Die Grundlegung der neueren Diskussion" [→ O.H. Steck 1967, Tödt 1959]; 428-434: "Erste Versuche einer Redaktionskritik" [→ Lührmann 1969]; 434-435: "Die weisheitliche-deuteronomistische Redaktion in Q" [→ A.D. Jacobson 1978]; 446-449: "Zwei neuerer alternative Entwürfe" [Kloppenborg 1987a, Sato 1988]; 450-456: "Der Menschensohn und der Fall Jerusalems"; = ID., *Tradition und Situation*, 1995, 243-278. Esp. 244-250; 250-256; 256-268; 268-272; 272-278. The Redaction of Q and the Son of Man: A Preliminary Sketch. — PIPER, R.A. (ed.), *The Gospel Behind the Gospels*, 1995, 159-198. Esp. 160-167; 167-173; 173-186; 186-190; 190-198.

1993 "Gekreuzigt unter Pontius Pilatus". Jesu Hinrichtung in der Deutung der Evangelienüberlieferung. — *Orientierung* 57 (1993) 65-70. Esp. 67-68. [NTA 38, 125]; = ID., *Studien*, 1994, 172-187.

1994a *Studien zur Frühgeschichte der Jesus-Bewegung* (Stuttgarter biblische Aufsatzbände. NT, 17). Stuttgart: Katholisches Bibelwerk, 1994, 368 p.; ²1995. → 1974, 1975, 1979, 1981, 1987, 1993

1994b Q 6,22 in der Rezeption durch Lukas. — MAYER, C., et al. (eds.), *Nach den Anfängen fragen*. FS G. Dautzenberg, 1994, 293-326. Esp. 296-302: "Lk 6,22a: der allgemeine Menschenhaß"; 312-317: "Die 'Ausgrenzung' der Jünger"; = ID., *Tradition und Situation*, 1995, 162-189. Esp. 165-170; 180-184.

1995a   *Tradition und Situation. Studien zur Jesusüberlieferung in der Logienquelle und den synoptischen Evangelien* (NTAbh, NF 28). Münster: Aschendorff, 1995, V-390 p. [NTA 39, p. 506] → 1967, 1969f, 1973, 1984b, 1985, 1988b.d, 1989b-c, 1991, 1992b, 1994b R.F. HOCK, *RelStR* 22 (1996) 68; J.S. KLOPPENBORG, *CRBR* 9 (1996) 231-233; F. LANGLAMET, *RB* 103 (1996) 119; A. MÉHAT, *RHR* 212 (1995) 479-480; F. NEIRYNCK, *ETL* 71 (1995) 463.

1995b   "Dienst" als Herrschaft oder "Herrschaft" als Dienst? [18,1-5; 20,25-28; 23,8-12] — *BK* 50 (1995) 146-152. [NTA 40, 796]

**HOFIUS, Otfried**

1978   Agrapha. — *TRE* 2 (1978) 103-110. Esp. 107-109.

1983   "Unbekannte Jesusworte". — STUHLMACHER, P. (ed.), *Das Evangelium und die Evangelien*, 1983, 355-382. Esp. 369-379 [Th 8; 48; Agrapha]. "Unknown Sayings of Jesus". — STUHLMACHER, P. (ed.), *The Gospel and the Gospels*, 1991, 336-360. Esp. 348-357.

1991   Nächstenliebe und Feindeshaß. Erwägungen zu Mt 5,43. — DEGENHARDT, J.J. (ed.), *Die Freude an Gott - unsere Kraft. Festschrift für Otto Bernhardt Knoch zum 65. Geburtstag*, Stuttgart: Katholisches Bibelwerk, 1991, 102-109.

1993   Ist Jesus der Messias? Thesen. — *JbBT* 8 (1993) 103-129. Esp. 120, 126-127, 129. → Stuhlmacher 1993

**HOFMANN, Frank-Matthias**

1983   Rückblick auf zwei "Jahre der Bergpredigt". — *Reformatio* 32 (1983) 28-33.

**HOFMANS, F.**

1962   Maria altijd maagd. — *CollBrugGand* 8 (1962) 475-494. Esp. 477-482 [1,18-25]; 487-490 [1,1-17]; 9 (1963) 53-78. [1,25]. [NTA 8, 571]

**HOFRICHTER, Peter**

1986   *Im Anfang war der "Johannesprolog". Das urchristliche Logosbekenntnis - die Basis neutestamentlicher und gnostischer Theologie* (BibUnt, 17). Regensburg: Pustet, 1986, 481 p. Esp. 264-269: "Die synoptischen Kindheitsgeschichten als midraschim zum Text des Logosbekenntnisses. Die matthäische Interpretation".

1992   Von der zweifachen Speisung des Markus zur zweifachen Aussendung des Lukas. Die Auseinandersetzung um die Heidenmission in der Redaktionsgeschichte der Evangelien. — HAINZ, J. (ed.), *Theologie im Werden*. FS O. Kuss, 1992, 143-155. Esp. 153-154: "Die Stellung des Matthäusevangeliums" [14,13-21; 16,1-8].

**HOGAN, Larry P.**

1992   *Healing in the Second Temple Period* (NTOA, 21). Freiburg/Schw: Universitätsverlag; Göttingen: Vandenhoeck & Ruprecht, 1992, 337 p. Esp. 268-275: "Matthew". — Diss. Jerusalem, 1991 (D. Flusser).

**HOGNESTAD, Helge**

1978a   *Forkynnelse til oppbrudd. Studier i Matteusevangeliet og kirkens bruk av det* [Preaching for action. Studies in the gospel of Matthew and its use in the church]. Oslo–Bergen–Tromsø: Universitetsforlaget, 1978, 2 vols., 155 and 149 p. [NTA 24, p. 189] — Diss. Oslo, 1978.

1978b   Troverdig forkynnelse - fir hvem? Svar til Wingren, Jervell og Lønning. [Credible preaching - for whom? Answers to Wingren, Jervell and Lønning] — *NorskTeolTids* 79 (1978) 267-284. Esp. 280-284. → Jervell 1979, Lønning 1978, Wingren 1978, 1979

**HOLL, Adolf**

1960   *Augustins Bergpredigtexegese. Nach seinem Frühwerk De Sermone Domini in Monte*

*Libri Duo*. Wien: Herder, 1960, 74 p. — Diss. Wien, 1954.

> E. BOULARAND, *BullLitEccl* 62 (1961) 74-75; F. SCHIERSE, *Scholastik* 35 (1960) 621-622; J. SINT, *ZKT* 83 (1961) 492.

### HOLLAND, Glenn S.

1985 Let no one deceive you in any way: 2 Thessalonians as a Reformulation of the Apocalyptic Tradition. — *SBL 1985 Seminar Papers*, 327-341. Esp. 337-339 [24/2 Thess].

1987 Augustine's Hermeneutics as Polemic and Apologetic: The Case of *De Sermone Domini in Monte*. — *Proceedings EGLBS* 7 (1987) 117-129.

### HOLLEMAN, Joost

1995 *Resurrection and Parousia. A Traditio-Historical Study of Paul's Eschatology in 1 Cor. 15:20-23*. Leiden: Univ. Leiden, 1995, XIV-235 p. Esp. 79-83 [Q 7,22; 10,13-15; 11,29-32; 13,28-29; 22,30]; 88-89; 97-99 [Q 12,8-9.40; 13,35; 17,24.26.30; 22,28-30]; 108-113; 132-133 [27,52]. — Diss. Leiden, 1995 (H.J. de Jonge – M. de Jonge).

### HOLLENBACH, Paul W.

1979 Social Aspects of John the Baptizer's Preaching Mission in the Context of Palestinian Judaism. — *ANRW* II.19.1 (1979) 850-875. Esp. 860-861 [3,7-10]; 865-866 [3,11-12].

1982 The Conversion of Jesus: From Jesus the Baptizer to Jesus the Healer. — *ANRW* II.25.1 (1982) 196-219. Esp. 208 [9,14-15]; 212-214 [11,2-19].

1992 John the Baptist. — *ABD* 3 (1992) 887-899. Esp. 888-889.

### HOLLERAN, J. Warren

1973 *The Synoptic Gethsemane. A Critical Study* (AnGreg, 191). Roma: Pont. Univ. Greg., 1973, XXXII-222 p. Esp. 69-82: "Literary analysis of Matthew 26:36-46"; 146-169: "Editorial history of Matthew 26:36-46"; 211-214: "Theology". — Diss. Pont. Univ. Greg., Roma, 1973 (D. Mollat).

### HOLLY, David

1983 *Comparative Studies in Recent Greek New Testament Texts. Nestle-Aland's 25ᵗʰ and 26ᵗʰ Editions* (Subsidia Biblica, 7). Roma: Biblical Institute Press, 1983, XII-149 p. Esp. 3-8 [changes N-A²⁵ᐟ²⁶]; 62-91: "Catalogue"; 121-124 [statistics].

> F. NEIRYNCK, *ETL* 59 (1983) 370-371.

### HOLMAN, Charles L.

1973 The Idea of an Imminent Parousia in the Synoptic Gospels. — *SBT* 3 (1973) 15-31. Esp. 16-18; 20-23 [16,28/Mk 9,1]; 23-26 [24,34/Mk 13,30]; 27-28 [26,64/Mk 14,62]; 28-29 [10,23].

### HOLMAN, Wilbur A.

1954 *Right and Wrong according to the Gospel of Matthew*. Diss. Midwestern Baptist Theol. Sem., Kansas City, KS, 1954.

### HOLMES, Michael W.

1984 *Early Editorial Activity and the Text of Codex Bezae in Matthew*. Diss. Theol. Sem., Princeton, NJ, 1984, VII-346 p. (B.M. Metzger). Esp. 70-114.115-203: "Evidence of early editorial activity in the text of Matthew in codex Bezae"; 204-237: "Is there a theological tendency in codex Bezae in Matthew?"; 259-282: "An analysis of the textual relationships of P⁴⁵ in Matthew"; 283-310: "A preliminary analysis of the textual relationships of codex Scheide". — *DissAbstr* 45 (1984-85) 1426; *SBT* 14 (1986) 86.

1986 The Text of Matthew 5.11. — *NTS* 32 (1986) 283-286. [NTA 31, 116]

1990 The Text of the Matthean Divorce Passages: A Comment on the Appeal to Harmonization in Textual Decisions. — *JBL* 109 (1990) 651-664. Esp. 652-656 [26,73/Mk 14,70]; 656-663 [5,32; 19,9]. [NTA 35, 1141]

HOLOTIK, Gerhard

1984 Grundzüge eines eschatologischen Ethos. Anstösse durch die Bergpredigt. — *Verbum caro factum est. Festschrift für Weihbischof Dr. Alois Stöger zum 80. Geburtstag*, St. Pölten–Wien: Niederösterreichisches Pressehaus, 1984, 209-218.

HOLST, Robert

1971 The Temptation of Jesus. [4,3.6] — *ExpT* 82 (1970-71) 343-344. [NTA 16, 532]

1972 Reexamining Mk 3,28f. and Its Parallels. [12,32] — *ZNW* 63 (1972) 122-124. [NTA 17, 941]

HOLTZ, Traugott

1977a "Euer Glaube an Gott". Zu Form und Inhalt von 1 Thess 1,9f. — SCHNACKENBURG, R., et al. (eds.), *Die Kirche des Anfangs*. FS H. Schürmann, 1977, 459-488. Esp. 465-467 [1 Thess 1,10/Q 12,8]; 478-480 [1 Thess 1,9-10/Q 3,9; 16,13]; = ID., *Geschichte und Theologie*, 1991, 270-296. Esp. 276-277; 287-290.

1977b Grundzüge einer Auslegung der Bergpredigt. — *Die Zeichen der Zeit* (Berlin) 31 (1977) 8-16; = ID., *Geschichte und Theologie*, 1991, 365-377.

1983 Traditionen im 1. Thessalonicherbrief. — LUZ, U. - WEDER, H. (eds.), *Die Mitte des Neuen Testaments*. FS E. Schweizer, 1983, 55-78. Esp. 67 [24,43-44/1Thess 5,2]; = ID., *Geschichte und Theologie*, 1991, 246-269. Esp. 262.

1991 *Geschichte und Theologie des Urchristentums. Gesammelte Aufsätze*, ed. E. Reinmuth & C. Wolff (WUNT, 57). Tübingen: Mohr, 1991, IX-492 p. → 1977a-b, 1983

HOLTZCLAW, William Brooks

1972 A Note on Matthew 5.21-48. — BARTH, E.H. - COCROFT, R.E. (eds.), *Festschrift to Honor F. Wilbur Gingrich*, 1972, 161-163.

HOMBURG, Klaus

1974 Consideraçoes exegéticas e homiléticas sobre Mateus 17:1-9. — *Estudos Teologicos* (São Leopoldo) 14 (1974) 34-39.

HOMEAU, H.A.

1974 On Fishing for Staters: Matthew 17,27. — *ExpT* 85 (1973-74) 340-342. [NTA 19, 537]

HOMERSKI, Józef

1976 "Panujacy" z Betlejem (Interpretacja perykopy Mich 5,1-5) (Le "souverain" de Bethleem. Interprétation de la péricope Mich 5,1-5). — *RoczTK* 23 (1976) 5-16. Esp. 14-15 [2,15-16].

1977 Starotestamentalne cytaty w Ewangelii Mateusza (Alttestamentliche Zitaten in dem Matthäus-Evangelium). — *RoczTK* 24/1 (1977) 31-39. [NTA 23, 808]

1978 Teologiczne aspekty kompozycji literackiej Mateuszowej Ewangelii Dzieciństwa (Aspects théologiques de la composition littéraire de l'Évangile de l'enfance de Matthieu). — *RoczTK* 25/1 (1978) 51-57. [NTA 24, 414]

1979a *Ewangelia według św. Mateusza. Wstęp, przekład z oryginału, komentarz* [Gospel according to St. Matthew. Introduction, new translation, commentary] (Pismo Święte Nowego Testamentu, 3/1). Poznań–Warszawa: Pallottinum, 1979, 409 p. [NTA 26, p. 196]

1979b Starotestamentalne cytaty i aluzje w ewangelicznych opisach męki i śmierci Jezusa (Old Testament quotations and allusions in the Gospel descriptions of the passion and death of Christ). — *RoczTK* 26/1 (1979) 13-24. Esp. 15-17 [27,9-10]; 17 [26,31]; 18-19 [26,64]; 19-20 [27,43]; 20 [27,46]. [NTA 26, 452]

**HOMMEL, Gisela**

1969   "Selig die Trauernden, denn sie werden getröstet werden". — MÜSSLE, M. (ed.), *Der "politische" Jesus*, 1969, 31-40.

**HOMMEL, Hildebrecht**

1954   Das Wort Karban und seine Verwandten. — *Philologus* (Berlin) 98 (1954) 132-149. Esp. 139-140; = ID. (ed.), *Wege zu Aischylos*. I: *Zugang. Aspekte der Forschung. Nachleben* (Wege der Forschung, 87), Darmstadt: Wissenschaftliche Buchgesellschaft, 1974, 368-387. Esp. 376-377 [15,3-6]; = ID., *Sebasmata*, II, 1984, 10-31. Esp. 18-19.

1963   Profectio Mariae. Zur Ikonographie der "Flucht nach Ägypten". — *TViat* 9 (1963) 95-112; = ID., *Sebasmata*, II, 1984, 258-275 ("Nachträge", 276-279).

1966   Herrenworte im Lichte sokratischer Überlieferung. — *ZNW* 57 (1966) 1-23. Esp. 4-8 [5,27-32]; 8-11 [8,21-22; 10,37]; 17-18 [5,29; 18,8-9]. [NTA 11, 145]; = ID., *Sebasmata*, II, 1984, 51-73 ("Nachträge", 73-74). Esp. 54-58; 58-61; 67-68.

1976   Delphisch-sokratische und neutestamentliche Moral. — GLADIGOW, B. (ed.), *Religion und Moral* (Patmos Paperbacks), Düsseldorf: Patmos, 1976, 203-220. Esp. 210-213 [5,27-32; 8,21-22; 10,37; 18,8-9]; = ID., *Sebasmata*, II, 1984, 32-49 ("Nachträge", 50). Esp. 39-42.

1984   *Sebasmata. Studien zur antiken Religionsgeschichte und zum frühen Christentum.* Band II (WUNT, 32). Tübingen: Mohr, 1984, X-415 p. → 1954, 1963, 1966, 1976

1989   Die Tore des Hades. [16,18] — *ZNW* 80 (1989) 124-125. [NTA 34, 127]

**HONEYMAN, A.M.**

1954   Matthew v.18 and the Validity of the Law. — *NTS* 1 (1954-55) 141-142.

**HONG, John Sungchul**

1994   On the Great Commission. — *EvJ* 12 (1994) 67-74. [NTA 39, 815]

**HONINGS, Bonifacio**

1976   I Padri latini e l'indissolubilità del matrimonio cristiano. Contributo alla teologia sulla clausola matteana. — *Lateranum* 42 (1976) 70-121. Esp. 72-87 [Nautin 1974], 87-121: "La tesi 'tramandata' dai Padri".

**HONORÉ, A.M.**

1968   A Statistical Study of the Synoptic Problem. — *NT* 10 (1968) 95-147. Esp. 98-103 [two-document hypothesis]; 103-106 [two-source hypothesis]; 106-110: "The sequence of sections"; 110-118 [verbal agreements]; 118-121: "Quantitative use of sources"; 121-132: "Variation in distribution of common material"; 132-135: "The Q hypothesis"; 136-147: "Division of gospels into sections". [NTA 13, 553] → Carlston 1971, O'Rourke 1974

**HOOD, R.T.**

1961   The Genealogies of Jesus. — WIKGREN, A. (ed.), *Early Christian Origins. Studies in Honor of H.R.W. Willoughby*, Chicago, IL: Quadrangle Books, 1961, 1-15.

**HOOGASIAN, Berge A.**

1958   *The Dead Sea Scrolls and the Gospel of Matthew. A Structural Comparison.* Diss. Southern Bapt. Theol. Sem., Louisville, KY, 1958.

**HOOKE, Samuel Henry**

1957   Jesus and the Centurion: Matthew viii.5-10. — *ExpT* 69 (1957-58) 79-80. [NTA 2, 529]

1961   *Alpha and Omega. A Study in the Pattern of Revelation.* Digwell Place: Nisbet, 1961, XVI-304 p. Esp. 142-150: "Comparison between the three blocks of the Mosaic Torah and the three Matthaean blocks of Jesus' teaching".

1967   *The Resurrection of Christ as History and Experience*. London: Darton, Longman &
       Todd, 1967, XI-209 p. Esp. 23-31: "Resurrection in the synoptic gospels"; 40-42: "The Matthaean
       account".

**HOOKER, Morna Dorothy**

1959   *Jesus and the Servant. The Influence of the Servant Concept of Deutero-Isaiah in the
       New Testament*. London: SPCK, 1959, XIV-230 p. Esp. 62-102: "The servant in the synop:ic
       gospels". — Diss. Bristol, 1955-56.

1971   Uncomfortable Words. X. The Prohibition of Foreign Missions (Mt 10,5-6). — *ExpT*
       82 (1970-71) 361-365. [NTA 16, 536]

1975*  & HICKLING, C. (eds.), *What about the New Testament? Essays in Honour of Chris-
       topher Evans*. London: SCM, 1975, IX-242 p. → Borsch, Hooker, Stanton

1975   In His Own Image? — *Ibid.*, 28-44. Esp. 29-30, 33-34.

1979   *Studying the New Testament*. London: Epworth, 1979; Minneapolis, MN: Augsburg,
       1982, 224 p. Esp. 70-92: "The true Israel – St. Matthew".

1986   *Continuity and Discontinuity. Early Christianity in Its Jewish Setting*. London: Epworth,
       1986, IV-76 p. Esp. 28-33 [controversy].

1988   Traditions about the Temple in the Sayings of Jesus. — *BJRL* 70/1 (1988) 7-19. Esp. 11-
       13. [NTA 33, 80]

1992   The Son of Man and the Synoptic Problem. — VAN SEGBROECK, F., et al. (eds.), *The
       Four Gospels 1992*. FS F. Neirynck, 1992, I, 189-201. Esp. 195 [10,32-33; 16,27]; 195-196
       [24,30; 26,64]; 196-197 [10,23]; 197 [16,28; 19,28]; 198 [24,27.37.39]. → W.O. Walker Jr. 1982a

1993   The Beginning of the Gospel. — MALHERBE, A.J. – MEEKS, W.A. (eds.), *The Future
       of Christology. Essays in Honor of Leander E. Keck*, Minneapolis, MN: Fortress, 1993,
       18-28. Esp. 24-25 [3,1-4,17].

1994   *Not Ashamed of the Gospel. New Testament Interpretations of the Death of Christ* (The
       Didsbury Lectures). Carlisle: Paternoster, 1994; Grand Rapids, MI: Eerdmans, 1995,
       143 p. Esp. 68-77: "Matthew".

**HOOSE, Bernard**

1987   Imitating Jesus and Allowing Divorce. — *Priests & People* (London) 1 (1987) 210-212.
       [NTA 32, 353]

**HOOVER, Roy W.**

1988   Sayings from Q, Parables Round Two. — *Forum* 4/4 (1988) 109-128. [NTA 33, 1102] →
       Funk 1988

**HOPHAN, Otto**

1946R  *Die Apostel* [1946]. Luzern: Räber, [2]1952; [3]1955, 435 p. Esp. 171-192: "Matthäus".
       *Los apóstoles*. Madrid: Palabra, 1982, 475 p.

**HOPKINS, Martin K.**

1964   *God's Kingdom in the New Testament*. Chicago, IL: Regnery Co, 1964, XXV-247 p.
       Esp. 88-94; 96-99; 103-111; 113-119; 123-126.

**HOPPE, Leslie J.**

1987   *Being Poor. A Biblical Study* (Good News Studies, 20). Wilmington, DE: Glazier,
       1987, VIII-191 p. Esp. 151-153.

**HOPPE, Rudolf**

1977   *Der theologische Hintergrund des Jakobusbriefes* (FzB, 28). Würzburg: Echter, 1977,
       III-170 p. Esp. 119-148: "Jakobusbrief und Jesusüberlieferung" [5,3-12.17-19; 11,25-27]. — Diss.
       Freiburg, 1976 (A. Vögtle).

1984 Gleichnis und Situation. Zu den Gleichnissen vom guten Vater (Lk 15,11-32) und gütigen Hausherrn (Mt 20,1-15). — *BZ* 28 (1984) 1-21. Esp. 13-20 [20,1-15]. [NTA 28, 966]

1991 Vollkommenheit bei Matthäus als theologische Aussage. — OBERLINNER, L. - FIEDLER, P. (eds.), *Salz der Erde*. FS A. Vögtle, 1991, 141-164. Esp. 142-151 [5,17-20]; 152-159 [5,21-48]; 159-164 [19,16-29].

1993 Der unausweichliche Konflikt – Überlegungen zur urchristlichen Rezeption der Jesus-verkündigung im Spannungsfeld zwischen Widerspruch und Anpassung. — *BibNot* 66 (1993) 83-97. Esp. 87-92: "Die Q-Gruppe". [NTA 37, 1478]

### HORBURY, William

1974 New Wine in Old Wine-Skins: IX. The Temple. — *ExpT* 86 (1974-75) 36-42. Esp. 39. [NTA 19, 739]

1984 The Temple Tax. [17,24-27] — BAMMEL, E. - MOULE, C.F.D. (eds.), *Jesus and the Politics of His Day*, 1984, 265-286.

1986 The Twelve and the Phylarchs. — *NTS* 32 (1986) 503-527. Esp. 504-505.523-525 [19,28]. [NTA 31, 339]

1997 The Hebrew Text of Matthew in Shem Tob Ibn Shaprut's *Eben Bohan*. — ALLISON, D.C. - DAVIES, W.D., *Commentary on Matthew XIX–XXVIII*, 1997, 729-738. → G. Howard 1987/95
    W.L. PETERSEN, *NTS* 44 (1998) 490-512.

### HORGAN, Maurya P.

1989* & KOBELSKI, P.J. (eds.), *To Touch the Text. Biblical and Related Studies in Honor of Joseph A. Fitzmyer, S.J.* New York: Crossroad, 1989, XIV-418 p. → Carmody, A.Y. Collins, Di Lella, Gerhardsson, D.J. Harrington

### HORMAN, John

1979 The Source of the Version of the Parable of the Sower in the Gospel of Thomas. [13,1-9] — *NT* 21 (1979) 326-343. [NTA 24, 435]

### HORN, Friedrich Wilhelm

1983 *Glaube und Handeln in der Theologie des Lukas* (Göttinger theologische Arbeiten, 26). Göttingen: Vandenhoeck & Ruprecht, 1983; [2]1986, 400 p. Esp. 66-70 [12,22-31]; 122-130 [5,3-12]; 204-205 [23,12]. — Diss. Göttingen, 1982 (G. Strecker).

1991 Christentum und Judentum in der Logienquelle. — *EvT* 51 (1991) 344-364. Esp. 347-349: "Das älteste Spruchgut"; 349-352: "Frühe Sammlungen"; 352-357: "Die Hauptsammlung"; 357-363: "Die Redaktion". [NTA 36, 692]

### HORNSCHUH, Manfred

1962 Das Gleichnis von den zehn Jungfrauen in der Epistula Apostolorum. — *Zeitschrift für Kirchengeschichte* (Stuttgart) 73 (1962) 1-8. → 1965

1965 *Studien zur Epistula Apostolorum* (Patristische Texte und Studien, 5). Berlin: de Gruyter, 1965, III-136 p. Esp. 21-29 (= 1962); 121-124.

### HORSLEY, G.H.R.

*New Documents Illustrating Early Christianity.* → Llewelyn

1981 1. *A Review of the Greek Inscriptions and Papyri Published in 1976.* Sydney, NSW: Macquarie Univ., 1981, V-155 p. Esp. 96-97 [5,6.11].

1982 2. *[1977]*, 1982, IV-224 p. Esp. 126-127 [10,17-20.21-23.25-32]. → K. Treu 1966

1983 3. *[1978]*, 1983, IV-182 p. Esp. 102; 103-105 [6,9-13].

1987 4. *[1979]*, 1987, VI-297 p. Esp. 191-192 [6,11-13]

1990 "Tί" at Matthew 7:14: "Because", Not "How". — *FilolNT* 3 (1990) 141-143. [NTA 36, 146] → D.A. Black 1989a

**HORSLEY, Richard A.**

1986  Ethics and Exegesis. "Love your Enemies" and the Doctrine of Non-Violence. — *JAAR* 54 (1986) 3-31. Esp. 11-12: "The text of the sayings in Matthew, Luke, and Q"; 12-15: "Misconceptions in interpretation of Luke 6:27-36 / Matthew 5:38-48"; 15-16: "The character of the sayings"; 85-89: "The social-economic context". [NTA 31, 117];  = SWARTLEY, W.M. (ed.), *The Love of Enemy*, 1992, 72-101. Esp. 80-81; 81-83; 83-85; 85-89.

1987  *Jesus and the Spiral of Violence. Popular Jewish Resistance in Roman Palestine.* San Francisco, CA: Harper & Row, 1987, XI-355 p.; paperback 1993.
       R.A. HORSLEY, Jesus and the Spiral of Violence. A Summary. — *Forum* 5/4 (1989) 3-17.

1989a  *The Liberation of Christmas. The Infancy Narratives in Social Context.* New York: Crossroad, 1989, XIV-201 p. Esp. 21-60: "The infancy narratives in historical context: the rulers"; 61-123: "The people"; 125-161: "Analogy and critical understanding"; 162-172: "Legends of the birth of the hero: a critical appraisal". [NTA 33, p. 248]
       C.L. BLOMBERG, *WestTJ* 52 (1990) 373-375; B. ESTRADA, *Annales theologici* 5 (1991) 417-419; R. GAUTHIER, *CahJos* 38 (1990) 268-269; P. HOLLENBACH, *BTB* 20 (1990) 170-172; R. PELLY, *ATR* 71 (1989) 209-211; J.J. PILCH, *CBQ* 52 (1990) 347-348; R.A. RAMSARAN, *JBL* 110 (1991) 159-162; S.H. RINGE, *TTod* 46 (1989-90) 222.224.226.

1989b  *Sociology and the Jesus Movement.* New York: Crossroad, 1989, VII-178 p. Esp. 105-129: "The Jesus movement in Jewish Palestine: a provisional sketch" [Q]; New York: Continuum, [2]1994.

1989c  Questions about Redactional Strata and the Social Relations Reflected in Q. — *SBL 1989 Seminar Papers*, 186-203. Esp. 186-195: "Questions about the formation of Q"; 195-200: "Social context and social relations indicated in Q"; 201-203: "Movement, leadership, and writing"  → Kloppenborg 1987a, 1989a

1991a  Logoi Prophētōn? Reflections on the Genre of Q. — PEARSON, B.A., et al. (eds.), *The Future of Early Christianity.* FS H. Koester, 1991, 195-209. Esp. 196-200: "The question of apocalyptic and sapiential strata in Q"; 200-207: "Characteristics of Q complexes"; 207-209: "Q and community instruction".

1991b  The Q People. Renovation, Not Radicalism. — *Continuum* (New York) 1 (1991) 49-63. [NTA 36, 693]

1992a  Jesus and Judaism: Christian Perspectives. — ATTRIDGE, H.W. - HATA, G. (eds.), *Eusebius, Christianity, and Judaism* (Studia Post-Biblica, 42), Leiden: Brill, 1992, 53-79. Esp. 63-66 [kingdom: Q]; 66-69 [law: Q]; 69-71 [pharisees: Q].

1992b  Q and Jesus: Assumptions, Approaches, and Analyses. — *Semeia* 55 (1992) 175-209. Esp. 175-183 [clusters]; 184-186 [Q 6,20-49]; 186-187 [Q 7,18-35]; 187-189 [Q 9,57-62; Q 10,2-16]; 189-191 [Q 11,2-4.9-13]; 191-194 [Q 11,14-26.29-32.33-36.39-52]; 194-195 [Q 12,2-12.22-31.33-34]; 195-196 [Q 13,28-30.34-35; Q 14,16-24]; 163 [Q 17,23-37; Q 22,28-30]; 196-209: "Q and Jesus". [NTA 36, 1235] → Attridge 1992

1992c  Response to Walter Wink, "Neither Passivity Nor Violence: Jesus' Third Way". — SWARTLEY, W.M. (ed.), *The Love of Enemy*, 1992, 126-132. → Wink 1988

1992d  Tradition and Innovation in Gospel Studies. — *RelStR* 18 (1992) 290-295. Esp. 291-293: "Sayings traditions". [NTA 37, 1190r] → Koester 1990a, Theissen 1989/91

1994  Wisdom Justified by All Her Children: Examining Allegedly Disparate Traditions in Q. — *SBL 1994 Seminar Papers*, 733-751.

1995  Social Conflict in the Synoptic Sayings Source Q. — KLOPPENBORG, J.S. (ed.), *Conflict and Invention*, 1995, 37-52.

**HORSTMANN, Maria**

1969  *Studien zur markinischen Christologie. Mk 8,27–9,13 als Zugang zum Christusbild des zweiten Evangeliums* (NTAbh, NF 6). Münster: Aschendorff, 1969, [2]1973, IV-150 p. Esp. 35-41: "Zur Echtheitsfrage der Logien vom kommenden Menschensohn"; 41-54: "Vergleich von Mk 8,38 mit der Parallele in der Quelle Q (Lk 12,8f / Mt 10,32f)". — Diss. Münster, 1969 (J. Gnilka).

**HORTON, Fred L., Jr.**
1987 Parenthetical Pregnancy: The Conception and Birth of Jesus in Matthew 1:18-25. — *SBL 1987 Seminar Papers*, 175-189. Esp. 175-179 [1,1-16]; 179-186 [1,18-25].

**HORTON, H.**
1961 The Gates of Hades Shall Not Prevail Against It. [16,18] — *RestQ* 5 (1961) 1-5.

**HORVÁTH, J.**
1970 Máté evangelista bizonyságtétele Krisztus szenvedéséröl. [Matthew's testimony of the passion of Christ] — *Református Szemle* (Kolozsvár) 63 (1970) 1970, 202-214.

**HORVATH, Tibor**
1979 *The Sacrificial Interpretation of Jesus' Achievement ir the New Testament. Historical Development and Its Reasons.* New York: Philosophical Library, 1979, VII-100 p. Esp. 37-40: "Matthew's theology of sacrifice".

**HOSKYNS, Edwyn C.**
1931[R] & DAVEY, N., *The Riddle of the New Testament* [1931]. London: Faber & Faber, [3]1952, 238 p. Esp. 76-82: "The synoptic problem"; 83-104: "Matthew and Luke".
*Das Rätsel des Neuen Testaments*, trans. H. Bolewski (Theologische Bücherei, 7). München: Kaiser, 1957, 199 p. Esp. 76-82; 81-107.
*Het raadsel van het Nieuwe Testament* (Bibliotheek van boeken bij de Bijbel, 6). Baarn: Bosch en Keuning, s.d., 175 p.

**HOSTE, Anselme**
1957 (ed.), *Chromatii Aquileiensis episcopi quae supersun:. Sermo de octo beatitudinibus. Tractatus XVII in evangelium Matthaei. Praefatio orationis dominicae* (CC SL, 9). Turnhout: Brepols, 1957, 371-447. Esp. 381-388 [5,3-12]; 389-442 [sermons]; 443-444 [6,9-13].
→ Étaix 1974a, Lemarié 1974a

**HOSTETLER, J.J.**
1988 *Matthew Explained: The Gospel Story of Jesus as King.* Scottdale, PA: Herald, 1988, 176 p.

**HOSTETLER, M.S.**
1952 *The Place of B.H. Streeter in the Study of the Synoptic Problem.* Diss. Hartford Sem., Stafford Springs, CT, 1952, 220 p.

**HOUK, Cornelius B.**
1966 Πειρασμός. The Lord's Prayer, and the Massah Tradition. — *ScotJT* 19 (1966) 216-225. [NTA 11, 208]

**HOULDEN, James Leslie**
1973 *Ethics and the New Testament* (Penguin Books). London: Penguin, 1973; London-Oxford: Mowbray, 1975, IX-134 p.; Edinburgh: Clark, 1992. Esp. 47-54: "Matthew"; 78-79 [5,32; 19,3-15]; 91 [19,16-30]; 95; 106-108.

1977 *Patterns of Faith. A Study in the Relationship between the New Testament and Christian Doctrine.* London: SCM; Philadelphia, PA: Fortress, 1977, VII-87 p. Esp. 38-40.

1979 The Development of Meaning. — *Theology* 82 (1979) 251-259. Esp. 253-255 [12,30]. [NTA 24, 92]

1987 *Backward into Light. The Passion and Resurrection of Jesus according to Matthew and Mark.* London: SCM, 1987, X-84 p. Esp. 1-12: "Hearing the gospels"; 13-19: "Matthew among the gospels"; 20-40 [27,45-54; 28,1-10]; 41-54 [27,3-10]; 55-65 [27,62-66; 28,2-4.11-15]. [NTA 32, p. 103]
K. GRAYSTON, *NBlackfr* 68 (1987) 576-577.

1992 Lord's Prayer. — *ABD* 4 (1992) 356-362.

1994    The Puzzle of Matthew and the Law. — PORTER, S.E., et al. (eds.), *Crossing the Boundaries*. FS M.D. Goulder, 1994, 115-131. Esp. 120-131: "Christology" [8,22; 9,9-13.14-17; 12,1-8; 16,12].

**HOUSSIAU, Albert**

1953    L'exégèse de Matthieu XI,27B, selon saint Irénée. — *ETL* 29 (1953) 328-354. Esp. 329-330 [Ptolemaeus]; 331-332 [Marcion]; 332-350 [Irenaeus, adv. haer. 2,6,1-3; 4,6,1; 4,6-7]; 350-352 [Justin]; 352-354 [Ps-Clem. Recog.].

1955    *La christologie de saint Irénée* (Universitas Catholica Lovaniensis. Dissertationis, III/1). Leuven: Publications Universitaires de Louvain; Gembloux: Duculot, 1955, XII-277 p. Esp. 72-86 [11,27].

**HOWARD, Fred David**

1966    *Interpreting the Lord's Parables*. Nashville, TN: Broadman, 1966, 72 p.

**HOWARD, George**

1967    The Meaning of Petros-Petra. — *RestQ* 10 (1967) 217-221. [NTA 12, 876]

1978    Stylistic Inversion and the Synoptic Tradition. — *JBL* 97 (1978) 375-389. [NTA 23, 410]

1980    Harmonistic Readings in the Old Syriac Gospels. — *HTR* 73 (1980) 473-491. Esp. 479-491. [NTA 25, 811]

1986a   Shem-Tob's Hebrew Matthew. — *Proceedings of the Ninth World Congress of Jewish Studies*, Jerusalem: World Union of Jewish Studies, 1986, 223-230.

1986b   The Textual Nature of an Old Hebrew Version of Matthew. [1553] — *JBL* 105 (1986) 49-63. [NTA 30, 1038]

1986c   Was the Gospel of Matthew Originally Written in Hebrew? — *BibReview* 2/4 (1986) 15-25. [NTA 31, 572]

1987    *The Gospel of Matthew according to a Primitive Hebrew Text*. Macon, GA: Mercer; Leuven: Peeters, 1987, XII-228 p. Esp. 1-151: "Shem-Tob's Hebrew Matthew. Text and translation"; 153-221: "Analysis and commentary". [NTA 32, p. 242] → Cryer 1993
        D.J. HARRINGTON, *CBQ* 50 (1988) 717-718; W. HORBURY, *JTS* 43 (1992) 166-169; D.K. LOWERY, *BS* 146 (1989) 470; W.L. PETERSEN, *JBL* 108 (1989) 722-726; R. WINANDY, *RTAM* 56 (1989) 238-239.
        *Hebrew Gospel of Matthew*. Macon, GA: Mercer, ²1995, XIV-240 p. [NTA 40, p. 143] → 1995; → Horbury 1997

1988a   The Gospel of the Ebionites. — *ANRW* II.25.5 (1988) 4034-4053.

1988b   A Note on the Short Ending of Matthew. — *HTR* 81 (1988) 117-120. [NTA 32, 1123]

1988c   A Primitive Hebrew Gospel of Matthew and the Tol'doth Yeshu. — *NTS* 34 (1988) 60-70. [NTA 32, 576]

1989    The Textual Nature of Shem-Tob's Hebrew Matthew. [1380] — *JBL* 108 (1989) 239-257. Esp. 246-247 [Old Syriac; Old Latin]; 247-249 [Gospel of Thomas]; 253-256 [Q]. [NTA 34, 107]

1992a   Matthew, Hebrew Version of. — *ABD* 4 (1992) 642-643.

1992b   A Note on Codex Sinaiticus and Shem-Tob's Hebrew Matthew. — *NT* 34 (1992) 46-47. [NTA 36, 1252]

1992c   A Note on Shem-Tob's Hebrew Matthew and the Gospel of John. — *JSNT* 47 (1992) 117-126. Esp. 120-122: "John's agreements with the Hebrew Matthew"; 122-126: "John the Baptist". [NTA 37, 786]

1994    The Pseudo-Clementine Writings and Shem-Tob's Hebrew Matthew. — *NTS* 40 (1994) 622-628. [NTA 39, 788]

1995    Hebrew Gospel of Matthew. A Report. — *Journal of Higher Criticism* (Madison, NJ) 2 (1995) 53-67. [NTA 42, 1653] → 1987/95

**HOWARD, H.G.**

1950 Was His Father Lying Dead at Home? A Question of Exegesis. [8,21] — *ExpT* 61 (1949-50) 350. → W.J. Davies 1950, C.S.S. Ellison 1950

**HOWARD, J. Keir**

1967 The Baptism of Jesus and Its Present Significance. [3,13-17] — *EvQ* 39 (1967) 131-138. [NTA 12, 103]

1985 New Testament Exorcism and Its Significance Today. — *ExpT* 96 (1984-85) 105-109. Esp. 106 [8,28-34]; 107 [9,32-33; 12,22; 15,21-28; 17,14-21]. [NTA 29, 504]

**HOWARD, Tracy L.**

1986 The Use of Hosea 11:1 in Matthew 2:15: An Alternative Solution. — *BS* 143 (1986) 314-328. [NTA 31, 582]

**HOWARD, Virgil P.**

1975 *Das Ego Jesu in den synoptischen Evangelien. Untersuchung zum Sprachgebrauch Jesu* (Marburger theologische Studien, 14). Marburg: Elwert, 1975, X-317 p. Esp. 149-184: "Q-Texte" [Q 7,1-10; 10,3; 11,9.19-20.49; 12,8-9; 22,28-30]; 185-212: "Matthäusevangelium" [5,21-48; 11,28-30; 16,17-19]. — Diss. Marburg, 1973-74 (W.G. Kümmel).

**HOWELL, David B.**

1990 *Matthew's Inclusive Story. A Study in the Narrative Rhetoric of the First Gospel* (JSNT SS, 42). Sheffield: JSOT, 1990, 292 p. Esp. 55-92: "The use of 'salvation history' in the interpretation of Matthew: a reader response critique"; 93-160: "Narrative temporal ordering, and emplotment, in Matthew's inclusive story"; 161-203: "Implied author, narrator, and point of view"; 205-248: "The implied reader"; 249-259: "Jesus as exemplary for discipleship". [NTA 35, p. 102] — Diss. Oxford, 1988 (R.C. Morgan).

> D.R. BAUER, *TTod* 48 (1991-92) 376-377; R.A. EDWARDS, *CBQ* 54 (1990) 570-571; R.M. FOWLER, *CRBR* 5 (1992) 218-220; H.B. GREEN, *JTS* 42 (1991) 51-54; J.D. KINGSBURY, *Bib* 72 (1991) 280-283; U. LUZ, *TLZ* 117 (1992) 189-191; G. STANTON, *ExpT* 103 (1991-92) 24-25; A.A. TRITES, *RExp* 88 (1991) 267-268.

**HOWSARE, Rodney** → Garry 1993

**HOWTON, John**

1962 The Sign of Jonah. — *ScotJT* 15 (1962) 288-304. Esp. 288-292, 300-303 [12,38-42]. [NTA 7, 509]

**HOYT, Thomas, Jr.**

1980 The Poor/Rich Theme in the Beatitudes. [5,3] — *Journal of Religious Thought* (Washington, DC) 37 (1980) 31-41. [NTA 25, 471]

**HRE KIO, S.**

1990 Understanding and Translating "Nations" in Mt 28.19. — *BTrans* 41 (1990) 230-238. [NTA 35, 151]

**HRUBÝ, Kurt**

1972 Las Horas de Oración en el Judaismo de la Epoca de Jesús. [6,5-6] — *RevistBíb* 34 (1972) 55-72. [NTA 17, 337]

**HUANG, Caleb T.**

1986 *Jesus' Teaching on "Entering the Kingdom of Heaven" in the Gospel according to Matthew*. Diss. Concordia Theol. Sem., St. Louis, MO, 1986.

**HUBAUT, Michel**

1975 La parabole des vignerons homicides: son authenticité, sa visée première. [21,33-46] — *RTL* 6 (1975) 51-61. [NTA 19, 957] → 1976a

1976a  *La parabole des vignerons homicides* (Cahiers de la Revue Biblique, 16). Paris: Gabalda, 1976, 155 p. Esp. 13-103: "La comparaison synoptique"; 105-141: "La transmission de la parabole". — Diss. Louvain-la-Neuve, 1974 (A. Descamps). → 1975
   J. COPPENS, *ETL* 53 (1977) 224-226; A. DESCAMPS, *RTL* 8 (1977) 75-80; J. DRURY, *JTS* 29 (1978) 194-195; J. DUPONT, *Bib* 59 (1978) 139-141; M. GILBERT, *NRT* 98 (1976) 702; X. LÉON-DUFOUR, *RSR* 66 (1978) 118-121; J. SMIT, *TijdTheol* 17 (1977) 301-302.

1976b  Jésus et la Loi de Moïse. — *RTL* 7 (1976) 401-425. Esp. 411-414. [NTA 21, 344]

### HUBBARD, Benjamin Jerome

1974  *The Matthean Redaction of a Primitive Apostolic Commissioning: An Exegesis of Matthew 28:16-20* (SBL DS, 19). Missoula, MT: SBL – Scholars, 1974, XIII-187 p. Esp. 69-99: "Matthew 28:16-20. A form critical and exegetical analysis"; 101-136: "The Matthean redaction of a primitive apostolic commissioning"; 151-175: "The authenticity of the triadic baptismal formula (Mt. 28:19)". [NTA 19, p. 390] — Diss. Univ. of Iowa, 1973 (G.W.E. Nickelsburg). → Abramowski 1984, Meier 1977b
   K. BERGER, *TRev* 72 (1976) 22-24; E. KRENTZ, *CurrTMiss* 2 (1975) 364.366; X. LÉON-DUFOUR, *RSR* 64 (1976) 433-435; H.K. MCARTHUR, *CBQ* 38 (1976) 107-108; J. MURPHY-O'CONNOR, *RB* 83 (1976) 97-102; L. SABOURIN, *BTB* 6 (1976) 101-102; G. SCHILLE, *TLZ* 101 (1976) 586-588; D. SENIOR, *JBL* 95 (1976) 488-489; C. WANAMAKER, *JEvTS* 19 (1976) 132-134.

### HUBER, Wolfgang

1982  Feindschaft und Feindesliebe. Notizen zum Problem des "Feindes" in der Theologie. — *ZEvEth* 26 (1982) 128-158. Esp. 133-136 [5,43-44].

### HUBY, Joseph

1924[R]  → Durand 1924

1929[R]  *L'Évangile et les évangiles* [1929; 1940] (Verbum Salutis, 11). Paris: Beauchesne, 1954 ("revue et augmentée par X. Léon-Dufour"), VIII-304 p. Esp. 99-133: "L'Évangile selon saint Matthieu".

1939[R]  Les livres du Nouveau Testament. [1939] — TRICOT, A. (ed.), *Initiation biblique*, ³1954, 204-279. Esp. 210-216 [Mt].
   The Books of the New Testament. — TRICOT, A. (ed.), *Guide to the Bible*, 1960, 382-474. Esp. 389-396.

### HUCK, Albert

1936[R]  & LIETZMANN, H. – OPITZ, H.G., *Synopse der drei ersten Evangelien* [⁹1936]. Tübingen: Mohr, ¹⁰1950, ¹²1975, XX-213 p. → Greeven 1981, Throckmorton 1967
   & LIETZMANN, H., *A Synopsis of the First Three Gospels. English Edition* [1936], ed. F.L. Cross. Oxford: Blackwell, 1952, XX-213 p. → Beare 1962

### HÜBNER, Hans

1973  *Das Gesetz in der synoptischen Tradition. Studien zur These einer progressiven Qumranisierung und Judaisierung innerhalb der synoptischen Tradition*. Witten: Luther, 1973, 261 p.; Göttingen: Vandenhoeck & Ruprecht, ²1986, 277 p. Esp. 15-39: "Das Programm: Mt 5,17-20"; 60-112: "Die Antithesen als Konkretisierung"; 123-128 [12,1-8/Mk 2,23-28]; 136-141 [12,9-14]; 176-182 [15,1-20]; 196-207: "Matthäus als Redaktor"; 212-213 [Q]. — Diss. Bochum, 1971 (H. Greeven – E. Grässer).

1981  Biblische Theologie und Theologie des Neuen Testaments. — *KerDog* 27 (1981) 2-19. Esp. 12-15 [fulfilment quotations]. [NTA 25, 1029]

1992  New Testament, OT Quotations in the. — *ABD* 4 (1992) 1096-1104. Esp. 1099-1100.

1995  *Biblische Theologie des Neuen Testaments*. Band 3: *Hebräerbrief, Evangelien und Offenbarung. Epilegomena*. Göttingen: Vandenhoeck & Ruprecht, 1995, 322 p. Esp. 96-119: "Das Matthäus-Evangelium"; 246-247; 258-261 [12,28].

**HÜBSCH, Bruno**

1991 Le Notre Père, quand la prière devient mémorial. [6,9-13] — *Ta parole est ma joie. Mélanges bibliques offerts au Père Léonard Ramaroson*, Antananarivo, Madagascar: Institut supérieur de théologie, 1991, 20-31.

**HÜLSBUSCH, Werner**

1972 Wenn der Menschensohn in seiner Herrlichkeit kommt. Predigtvorschlag für das Christkönigsfest nach Mt 25,31-46. — *BibLeb* 13 (1972) 207-214. Esp. 208-210: "Exegetische Anmerkungen".

**HUFFMAN, Norman A.**

1978 Atypical Features in the Parables of Jesus. — *JBL* 97 (1978) 207-220. Esp. 208-210 [20,1-16]; 211 [18,12-14]; 211-212 [13,3-8.31-33]; 213 [13,44.46; 18,23-25]; 213-214 [22,1-10]; 215-216 [25,1-13.14-30]; 217 [13,24-30]; 217-218 [21,33-41]. [NTA 23, 77]

**HUFFMANN, Douglas S.**

1992 Genealogy. — *DJG*, 1992, 253-259. Esp. 254-256 [1,1-17].

**HUGGINS, Ronald V.**

1992 Matthean Posteriority: A Preliminary Proposal. — *NT* 34 (1992) 1-22. Esp. 5-9: "The phenomenon of order"; 9-13: "Matthean redactional procedures"; 14-15: "The limited extent of Matthew's use of Luke"; 15-17: "Luke/Mark disagreements in order"; 17-22: "The infancy and resurrection narratives". [NTA 36, 1236]

**HUGHES, Frank Witt**

1987 Feminism and Early Christian History. — *ATR* 69 (1987) 287-299. Esp. 290-292 [Q]. [NTA 33, 536r] → Fiorenza 1983

**HUGHES, John H.**

1972 John the Baptist: The Forerunner of God Himself. — *NT* 14 (1972) 191-218. Esp. 195-200.204 [3,10-12]; 201 [3,3]; 202.206-212 [11,2-6.7-10.11-12.16-19]. [NTA 17, 453]

**HUGHES, Kirk T.**

1991 Framing Judas. — *Semeia* 54 (1991) 223-238. [NTA 36, 1196]

**HUGHES, Michael B.**

1994 *The Sermon on the Mount as a Paradigm for Effective Christian Discipleship*. Diss. Fuller Theol. Sem., Pasadena, CA, 1994, 299 p. (R. Redman). — *DissAbstr* 55 (1994-95) 3875.

**HULL, John M.**

1974 *Hellenistic Magic and the Synoptic Tradition* (Studies in Biblical Theology, II/28). London: SCM, 1974, XII-192 p. Esp. 116-141.165-169: "Matthew: the tradition purified of magic" [2,1-12; 12,31-32.38-42; 28,2-4].

**HULL, William E.**

1962 A Teaching Outline of the Gospel of Matthew. — *RExp* 59 (1962) 433-444. [NTA 7, 496]

**HULSBOSCH, Ansfried**

1963 *De Bijbel over bekering* (De Bijbel over..., 20). Roermond–Maaseik: Romen, 1963, 111 p. Esp. 45-54 [11-13].

**HULTGREN, Arland J.**

1974 The Double Commandment of Love in Mt 22:34-40. Its Sources and Compositions. — *CBQ* 36 (1974) 373-378. [NTA 19, 542]

1979 *Jesus and His Adversaries. The Form and Function of the Conflict Stories in the Synoptic Tradition*. Minneapolis, MN: Augsburg, 1979, 223 p. Esp. 45-46 [22,41-46]; 46-47

[12,38-42]; 47-50 [22,34-40]; 68-75 [21,23-27/Mk 11,27-33]; 75-78 [22,15-22/Mk 12,13-17]; 78-82 [9,14-15/Mk 12,18-20]; 82-84 [12,9-13/Mk 3,1-5]; 100-106 [12,22-32/Mk 3,22-30]; 106-109 [9,1-8/Mk 2,1-12]; 109-111 [9,10-13/Mk 2,1-12]; 111-115 [12,1-8/Mk 2,23-28]; 115-119 [15,1-9/Mk 7,1-8]; 119-123 [19,3-9/Mk 10,2-9]; 123-131 [22,23-33/Mk 12,18-29]; 184-190: "Matthew's use of the conflict stories". — Diss. Union Theol. Sem., New York, 1971 (R.H. Fuller).

1988    *New Testament Christology. A Critical Assessment and Annotated Bibliography* (Bibliographies and Indexes in Religious Studies, 12). Westport, CT – London – New York: Greenwood Press, 1988, XV-485 p. Esp. 70-80 [OT; christology]; 115-212 [christological titles]; 225-226 [Q]; 227-236 [Mt]; 353-448 [christological themes].

1990*    & HALL, B. (eds.), *Christ and His Communities. Essays in Honor of Reginald Fuller*. Cincinatti, OH: Forward Movement Publications, 1990, XXVIII-153 p. → Hultgren, S.E. Johnson, Schweizer

1990    The Bread Petition of the Lord's Prayer. — *Ibid.* = *ATR* SS 11 (1990) 41-54. Esp. 41-43: "Textual observations"; 43-48: "Proposed meanings"; 48-54: "*Epiousios artos*". [NTA 34, 1137]

1991    Jesus and Gnosis. The Saying on Hindering Others in Luke 11:52 and Its Parallels. — *Forum* 7 (1991) 165-182. Esp. 165-170: "The synoptic parallels"; 170-176: "Extra-canonical versions" [Th 39; POxy 655]; 176-178: "Assessments". [NTA 38, 835]

1992    Things New and Old at Matthew 13:52. — ID. – JUEL, D.H. – KINGSBURY, J.D. (eds.), *All Things New. Essays in Honor of Roy A. Harrisville* (Word & World SS, 1), St. Paul, MN: Word & World, 1992, 109-117.

1994    *The Rise of Normative Christianity*. Minneapolis, MN: Fortress, 1994, XIII-213 p. Esp. 31-41: "The Q community"; 56-65: "Developments in Syria".

1995    Liturgy and Literature: The Liturgical Factor in Matthew's Literary and Communicative Art. — FORNBERG, T. – HELLHOLM, D. (eds.), *Texts and Contexts*. FS L. Hartman, 1995, 659-673. Esp. 660-666: "Liturgically formed materials"; 666-670: "Literary and communicative functions".

**HUMBERT, Alphonse**

1954    Essai d'une théologie du scandale dans les Synoptiques. — *Bib* 35 (1954) 1-28. Esp. 6-11: "Dans les synoptiques" [13,41; 16,23; 18,7; 24,10].
The Notion of "Scandal" in the Synoptics. — *TDig* 3 (1955) 108-112.

**HUMMEL, Reinhart**

1963    *Die Auseinandersetzung zwischen Kirche und Judentum im Matthäusevangelium* (BEvT, 33). München: Kaiser, 1963, 166 p. Esp. 11-33: "Die Kirche des Matthäus und das zeitgenössische Judentum"; 34-75: "Das Gesetz" [5,17-20.21-48; 9,1-8.9-13; 12,1-8.9-14; 15,1-20; 16,18-19; 18,15-20; 19,1-9; 22,34-40]; 76-108: "Tempel und Opferkult" [5,23-24; 8,4; 12,5-7; 17,27-27; 23,16-22; 26,61]; 109-142: "Der Messias" [12,22-45]; 143-161: "Israel und die Kirche". [NTA 7, p. 391]; [2]1966, 183 p. Esp. 1-161 (= 1963); 162-173: "Zum Problem einer Theologie des Matthäusevangeliums". — Diss. Kiel, 1960 (E. Lohse). → Dermience 1985, Rohde 1965, Trilling 1959a
T. BAARDA, *VoxTheol* 35 (1965) 93-94; M.-É. BOISMARD, *RB* 71 (1964) 450; F. DREYFUS, *RSPT* 48 (1964) 317-318; P. GAECHTER, *ZKT* 87 (1965) 337-339; S. GONZÁLEZ DE CARREA, *NatGrac* 11 (1964) 336-337; K. HRUBY, *Judaica* 24 (1968) 192; C. MATEOS, *EstAgust* 4 (1969) 161; R. SCHIPPERS, *GTT* 65 (1965) 55-56; E. SCHWEIZER, *EvT* 23 (1963) 613; W. TRILLING, *TLZ* 90 (1965) 433-437; P. WINTER, *ATR* 46 (1964) 119-120; M. ZERWICK, *VD* 41 (1963) 217-222.

**HUMPHREY, Hugh Minear**

1977    *The Relationship of Structure and Christology in the Gospel of Matthew*. Diss. Fordham Univ., Bronx, NY, 1977, 282 p. — *DissAbstr* 38 (1977-78) 340.

1989    Mt 5:9: "Blessed are the peacemakers, for they shall be called sons of God". — TAMBASCO, A.J. (ed.), *Blessed Are the Peacemakers. Biblical Perspectives on Peace and Its Social Foundations*, New York – Mahwah, NJ: Paulist, 1989, 62-78.

1991    Temptation and Authority: Sapiential Narratives in Q. — *BTB* 21 (1991) 43-50. Esp. 45-47 [4,1-11]; 47-48 [8,5-13]. [NTA 36, 119] → Kloppenborg 1987a

**HUMPHREYS, Colin J.**

1991    The Star of Bethlehem, a Comet in 5 BC and the Date of Christ's Birth. — *Quarterly Journal of the Royal Astronomical Society* (London) 32 (1991) 389-407; = *TyndB* 43 (1992) 31-56 (revised). [NTA 37, 129]

**HUMPHRIES, Michael Lawrence**

1990    *The Language of the Kingdom of God in the Beelzebul Discourse* [12,22-30]. Diss. Graduate School, Claremont, CA, 1990, 394 p. (B.L. Mack). — *DissAbstr* 51 (1990-91) 2048.

1993    The Kingdom of God in the Q Version of the Beelzebul Controversy. Q 11:14-26. — *Forum* 9 (1993) 121-150. Esp. 126-140: "The exposition of an elaborated chreia"; 140-146: "A reassessment of the kingdom language in Q 11:20". [NTA 41, 276]

**HUMPHRIES-BROOKS, Stephenson**

1989    Apocalyptic Paraenesis in Matthew 6.19-34. — MARCUS, J. – SOARDS, M.L. (eds.), *Apocalyptic and the New Testament.* FS J.L. Martyn, 1989, 95-112.

1991    Indicators of Social Organization and Status in Matthew's Gospel. — *SBL 1991 Seminar Papers*, 31-49. Esp. 37-46: "Plot, characters, and the genre of the first gospel"; 46-47: "Textual audience vs. empirical audience".

1993    Spatial Form and Plot Disruption in the Gospel of Matthew. — *Essays in Literature* 20 (1993) 54-69.

1994    Matthew. — MILLS, W.E. – WILSON, R.F. (eds.), *Mercer Commentary on the Bible*, Macon, GA: Mercer, 1994; = *Mercer Commentary on the Bible.* VI: *The Gospels*, Macon, GA: Mercer, 1996. [NTA 41, p. 149]

**HUNT, Tony**

1983    Le "sensus moralis" du *Sponsus*. [25,1-13] — *Cahiers de civilisation médiévale* (Poitiers) 26 (1983) 327-334.

**HUNTER, Archibald M.**

1945[R]   *Introducing the New Testament* [1945]. Philadelphia, PA: Westminster, 2nd rev. and enlarged ed., 1957, 208 p.; 3rd rev. ed., 1973, VIII-216 p.

1950    *The Work and Words of Jesus.* London: SCM, 1950; Philadelphia, PA: Westminster, 1951, 196 p. Esp. 131-146: "The text of Q"; 147-168: "The text of M"; rev. ed. 1973, 230 p.

1951    *Interpreting the New Testament 1900-1950.* London: SCM, 1951, 144 p. Esp. 40-46 [Q].

1952a   *Design for Life. An Exposition of the Sermon on the Mount, Its Making, Its Exegesis and Its Meaning.* London: SCM, 1952.
     W. BARCLAY, *ExpT* 64 (1952-53) 201.
     *A Pattern for Life. An Exposition of the Sermon on the Mount. Its Making, Its Exegesis and Its Learning.* Philadelphia, PA: Westminster, 1954, 124 p.; repr. 1966.
     J.C. SWAIN, *Interpr* 9 (1955) 227.
     *Design for Life. The Sermon on the Mount* (Living Church Book). London: SCM, 1965, 128 p.
     *Un idéal de vie. Le Sermon sur la montagne*, trans. P. Noury (Lire la Bible, 44). Paris: Cerf, 1976, 154 p. [NTA 21, p. 198]
     S.R., *BibOr* 19 (1977) 36-37.

1952b   The Meaning of the Sermon on the Mount. — *ExpT* 63 (1951-52) 176-179.

1957    *Introducing New Testament Theology.* London: SCM; Philadelphia, PA: Westminster, 1957, 160 p. Esp. 13-51 [kingdom]; 52-61 [resurrection].
     *Introduction à la théologie du Nouveau Testament*, trans. C. Tunmer (Lire la Bible, 13). Paris: Cerf, 1968, 168 p. Esp. 15-55; 57-66.

1958    The Interpretation of the Parables. — *ExpT* 69 (1957-58) 100-104. [NTA 2, 513]

1960    Interpreting the Parables. I. The Interpreter and the Parables. The Centrality of the Kingdom; II. The Gospel in Parables. The Coming of the Kingdom; III. The Gospel in Parables. The Men and the Crisis of the Kingdom; IV. The Proclamation of the Kingdom. Preaching the Parables. — *Interpr* 14 (1960) 70-84, 167-185, 315-332, 440-454. Esp. 70-77: "Basic questions"; 77-84: "The history of exegesis"; 167-174: "The coming of the Kingdom"; 174-185: "The grace of the Kingdom"; 315-322: "The men of the Kingdom"; 322-332: "The crisis of the Kingdom"; 441-444 [allegory]; 444-446 [moral interpretation]; 447-454 [Sitz im Leben]. [NTA 5, 59/380]
The Interpreter and the Parables. The Centrality of the Kingdom. — BATEY, R. (ed.), *New Testament Issues*, 1970, 71-87. Esp. 72-79; 79-87.

1961    *Interpreting the Parables*. Philadelphia, PA: Westminster, 1961, 126 p.; [2]1974; 1976 (paperback); London: SCM, 1964, 128 p.

1962    Crux Criticorum – Matt. xi.25-30 – A Re-appraisal. — *NTS* 8 (1961-62) 241-249. [NTA 7, 133]

1983    *The Parables for Today*. London: SCM, 1983, 83 p. Esp. 13-16 [13,24-30]; 17-20 [13,44-46]; 29-32 [20,1-15]; 52-55 [25,14-30]; 71-73 [25,1-13]; 74-76 [25,31-46]; 77-80 [7,24-27].

1986    Rite of Passage. The Implications of Matthew 4:1-11 for an Understanding of the Jewishness of Jesus. — *Christian-Jewish Relations* (London) 19 (1986) 7-22. [NTA 33, 1117]

**HUNZINGER, Claus-Hunno**

1960    Unbekannte Gleichnisse Jesu aus dem Thomas-Evangelium. — ELTESTER, W. (ed.), *Judentum, Urchristentum, Kirche*. FS J. Jeremias, 1960, 209-220. Esp. 217-220 [Th/Mt 13,45-46]. [NTA 5, 843] → J.B. Bauer 1962

**HURAULT, B.**

1980    *Sinopsis Pastoral de Mateo-Marcos-Lucas-(Juan) con notas exegéticas y pastorales*. Madrid: Paulinas, 1980, 311 p. [NTA 26, p. 197]

**HURD, John Coolidge, Jr.**

1966    *A Bibliography of New Testament Bibliographies*. New York: Seabury Press, 1966, 75 p. Esp. 31.

**HURLEY, James B.**

1981    *Man and Woman in Biblical Perspective*. Grand Rapids, MI: Zondervan, 1981, 288 p. Esp. 93-109: "Women in the teaching of Jesus" [19,3-12].

**HURST, David**

1955    (ed.), *Bedae Venerabilis Opera. III. Opera homiletica. Homeliarum evangelii libri II* (CC SL, 122). Turnhout: Brepols, 1955, XXI-403 p. Esp. 32-36 [1,18-25]; 68-72 [2,13-23]; 80-87 [3,13-17]; 88-94 [19,27-29]; 141-147 [16,13-19]; 148-155 [9,9-13]; 156-160 [15,21-28]; 170-177 [16,27–17,9]; 200-206 [21,1-9]; 225-232 [28,1-10]; 233-238 [28,16-20]; 335-341 [20,20-23]; 349-357 [24,1-12].

1969    & ADRIAEN, M. (eds.), *S. Hieronymi Presbyteri opera. Pars I. Opera exegetica. 7. Commentariorum in Matheum libri IV* (CC SL, 77). Turnhout: Brepols, 1969, XVI-316 p. Esp. 1-283 [text].

**HURST, Lincoln D.**

1992    Ethics of Jesus. — *DJG*, 1992, 210-222.

**HURTADO, Larry Weir**

1990    The Gospel of Mark: Evolutionary or Revolutionary Document? — *JSNT* 40 (1990) 15-32. Esp. 18-19.22-23 [Q: genre]. [NTA 35, 1147]; = EVANS, C.A. – PORTER, S.E. (eds.), *The Synoptic Gospels*, 1995, 196-211. Esp. 200-201.205-206.

1992a   Christ. — *DJG*, 1992, 106-117. Esp. 112.

1992b   God. — *Ibid.*, 270-276. Esp. 273.

1992c   Gospel (genre). — *Ibid.*, 276-282. Esp. 280-281.

**HUSTON, Hollis W.**

1957   The "Q"-Parties at Oxford. — *JBR* 25 (1957) 123-128. → Farrer 1954

**HUTCHINSON, Arno M.**

1977   Christian Prophecy and Matthew 12:38-42. A Test Exegesis. — *SBL 1977 Seminar Papers*, 379-385.

**HUTTER, Manfred**

1984   Ein altorientalischer Bittgestus in Mt 9,20-22. — *ZNW* 75 (1984) 133-135. [NTA 29, 100]

1991   Mt 25:31-46 in der Deutung Manis. — *NT* 33 (1991) 276-282. [NTA 36, 158]

**HUTTON, Delvin Dwayne**

1969   *The Resurrection of the Holy Ones (Mt 27:51b-53). A Study of the Theology of the Matthean Passion Narrative*. Diss. Divinity School, Harvard, MA, 1969-70, VIII-198 p.

**HUTTON, W.R.**

1952   The Kingdom of God has Come. — *ExpT* 64 (1952-53) 89-91. Esp. 90-91 [26,45]. → Staples 1959

1964   Make a Tree Good? — *ExpT* 75 (1963-64) 366-367. [NTA 9, 532]

**HVALVIK, Reidar**

1996   *The Struggle for Scripture and Covenant. The Purpose of the Epistle of Barnabas and Jewish-Christian Competition in the Second Century* (WUNT, II/82). Tübingen: Mohr, 1996, XIII-415 p. Esp. 292-296 [23,15/Barnabas]. — Diss. Oslo, 1994 (O. Skarsaune).

**HYLDAHL, Niels**

1961   Die Versuchung auf der Zinne des Tempels (Matth 4,5-7 ≠ Luk 4,9-12). — *StudTheol* 15 (1961) 113-127. Esp. 114-118 [πτερύγιον]. [NTA 8, 126]

# I

**IACONO, V.**

1955   Caratteristiche dell'Evangelo di S. Matteo. — *RivBib* 3 (1955) 32-48.

**IBAÑEZ ARANA, Andrés**

1968   Sobre los Evangelios de la infancia de Jesús. — *Lumen* (Vitoria) 17 (1968) 128-140.

1969   El Evangelio de la infancia en Mt 1-2. — *Lumen* 18 (1969) 3-25.

**IBER, Gerhard**

1953   *Überlieferungsgeschichtliche Untersuchungen zum Begriff des Menschensohnes im Neuen Testament.* Diss. Heidelberg, 1953, IX-190 p. (G. Bornkamm).

1959   → Dibelius 1933

**IMBERT, Jean**

1980   *Le procès de Jésus* (Que sais-je?, 1896). Paris: PUF, 1980, ²1984, 128 p.
Il processo di Gesù, trans. M.M. Velleda. Brescia: Morcelliana, 1984, 184 p.

**INCH, Morris A.**

1971   Matthew and the House-Churches. — *EvQ* 43 (1971) 196-202. [NTA 16, 525]

**INFANTE, Lorenzo**

1990   Il Battista chiama al ritorno. — *ParSpirV* 22 (1990) 127-140. Esp. 130-133 [3,1-6]; 134-135 [3,7-10]; 135-137 [3,11-12].

1994   Il battesimo di Gesù (Mt 3,13-17 par.). — LÀCONI, M. (ed.), *Vangeli sinottici*, 1994, 199-212.

**INGELAERE, Jean-Claude**

1970   La "parabole" du Jugement Dernier (Matthieu 25/31-46). — *RHPR* 50 (1970) 23-60. Esp. 24-32: "La venue du Fils de l'homme"; 32-44: "Le jugement des nations"; 45-50: "Les attendus du jugement"; 50-59: "Les plus petits frères du Fils de l'homme". [NTA 15, 149]

1979   Structure de Matthieu et histoire du salut. État de la question — *FoiVie* 78/3 = *Cahiers bibliques* 18 (1979) 10-33. Esp. 12-16 [Bacon]; 16-20 [geography]; 20-24 [Kingsbury]. [NTA 24, 402]

1981   Chronique matthéenne. — *RHPR* 61 (1981) 67-79. Esp. 68-69 [Sabourin 1975a/77]; 69-70 [Sabourin 1978a]; 70-71 [H.B. Green 1975]; 72 [Rist 1978]; 72-74 [Kingsbury 1975a]; 74-75 [Kingsbury 1977a]; 75-77 [Zumstein 1977]; 77-79 [Künzel 1978]. [NTA 25, 844]

1995   Universalisme et particularisme dans l'Évangile de Matthieu: Matthieu et le Judaïsme. — *RHPR* 75 (1995) 45-59. [NTA 40, 151]

**INGRANUS, L.**

1968   & KINGSTON, P. – PARSONS, P.J. – REA, J.R. (eds.), *Oxyrhynchus Papyri XXXIV.* London: Egypt Exploration Society, 1968. Esp. 1-3 [P⁷⁷].

**INRIG, J. Gary**

1983   Called to Serve: Toward a Philosophy of Ministry. — *BS* 140 (1983) 335-349. Esp. 338-339 [18,1-5; 20,20-28; 23,8-12]. [NTA 28, 682]

**IPOLY, Otho N.**

1987   On the Priority of Mark's Gospel. — *Josephinum Journal of Theology* (Columbus, OH) 6 (1987) 3-16. [NTA 32, 99]

**IQP – The International Q Project**
1990  ROBINSON, J.M., Work Session 17 November 1989. — *JBL* 109 (1990) 499-501. [Q 11,2-4; 12,2-7; 16,13.17-18]. [NTA 35, 611]
1991  ROBINSON, J.M., Work Session 16 November 1990. — *JBL* 110 (1991) 494-498. [Q 4,16; 6,41-42.46-49; 10,2-4; 11,9.11-13; 12,10; 13,18-21.28-29; 14,34-35; 17,1-4.6] [NTA 36, 697]
1992  ASGEIRSSON, J.M. – ROBINSON, J.M., Work Sessions 12-14 July, 22 November 1991. — *JBL* 111 (1992) 500-508. [Q 3,1.2-3.4; 6,20-21.39-40; 11,14 33-36.39-44.46.47-48.52; 14,5.15.16-21.22.23.24.26-27; 17,24.26-27.28-29.30.34-35.37]. [NTA 37, 688] → Neirynck 1993a
1993  MORELAND, M. – ROBINSON, J.M., Work Sessions 31 July – 2 August, 20 November 1992. — *JBL* 112 (1993) 500-506. [NTA 38, 733]
1994  MORELAND, M. – ROBINSON, J.M., Work Sessions 6-8 August, 18-19 November 1993. — *JBL* 113 (1994) 495-499. [NTA 39, 783]
1995  MORELAND, M. – ROBINSON, J.M., Work Sessions 23-27 May, 22-26 August, 17-18 November 1994. — *JBL* 114 (1995) 475-485. [NTA 40, 799]
1997  MORELAND, M. – ROBINSON, J.M., Editorial Board Meetings 1-10 June, 16 November 1995, 16-23 August, 22 November 1996. Work Sessions 17 November 1995, 23 November 1996. — *JBL* 116 (1997) 521-525.

Reconstruction of Q
New Project Launched. — *Bulletin of the Institute for Antiquity and Christianity* 10/4 (1983) 6; The New Q Project Goes Public. — *Ibid.*, 11/1 (1984) 9; A Computerized Q. — *Ibid.*, 12/2 (1985) 9; The Jesus Movement in Galilee: Reconstructing Q. — *Ibid.*, 14/3 (1987) 4-5; [S. Carruth] Scholar in Focus – James M. Robinson. — *Ibid.*, 16/1 (1989) 4-6; Scholar in Focus: Shawn Carruth. — *Ibid.*, 17/3 (1990) 12-13; Institute to Host Q Conference. — *Ibid.*, 18/2 (1991) 10-11; [S. Anderson] Reconstructing Q. — *Ibid.*, 18/3 (1991) 6-8. [S. Anderson] IQP in Bamberg and Claremont. — *Ibid.*, 20/1 (1993) 10-11.

*Documenta Q: Reconstructions of Q Through Two Centuries of Gospel Research Excerpted, Sorted, and Evaluated*, ed. J.M. ROBINSON, P. HOFFMANN, J.S. KLOPPENBORG. Leuven: Peeters, 1996-
*The Database of the International Q Project:*
*Q 11,2b-4*, 1996, XII-206 p.
      F. NEIRYNCK, *ETL* 72 (1996) 418-424; J. VERHEYDEN, *LouvSt* 22 (1997) 183-186.
*Q 4,1-13.16*, 1996, XVIII-479 p. → Neirynck 1997b
      J. VERHEYDEN, *LouvSt* 23 (1998) 283-286.
*Q 12,8-12*, 1997, XIX-812 p.
*Q 12,49-59*, 1997, XVII-434 p.
      F. NEIRYNCK, *ETL* 73 (1997) 458-459; J. VERHEYDEN, *LouvSt* 23 (1998) 286-287.

**IRIARTE, Lázaro**
1978  Testi del Nuovo Testamento particolarmente cari a san Francesco. — *Laur* 19 (1978) 261-274. Esp. 262-265 [5,3-12]; 265 [7,12]; 266 [8,20]; 266-267 [20,25-28].
Textos del Nuevo Testamento preferidos por san Francisco. — *Selecciones de franciscanismo* (Valencia) 9 (1980) 137-150.

**IRIARTE, María Eugenia**
1980  José, el justo. [1,19] — *BibFe* 6 (1980) 281-292. [NTA 25, 466]
1983  ¡Padre, venga tu reino! [6,10] — *BibFe* 9 (1983) 24-35.

**IRMSCHER, Johannes**
1960  Σὺ λέγεις (Mk 15,2; Mt 27,1; Lc 23,3). — *Studii Clasice* (Bucuresti) 2 (1960) 151-158.

**IRWIN, Kevin W.**

1971 The Supper Text in the Gospel of Saint Matthew. [26,26-29] — *DunRev* 11 (1971) 170-184. [NTA 16, 164]

**IRWIN, Kathleen M.**

1985 *The Liturgical and Theological Correlations in the Associations of Representations of the Three Hebrews and the Magi in the Christian Art of Late Antiquity.* Diss. Graduate Theol. Union, Berkeley, CA, 1985.

**IRWIN, M.E.**

1991 Considering the Lilies. [6,28-30] — *McMaster Journal of Theology* (Hamilton, Ont.) 2 (1991) 20-28. [NTA 36, 1269]

**ISAAC, Jules**

1953 De quelques abus dans la traduction et l'interprétation des textes. — *RHPR* 33 (1953) 52-65. Esp. 54-56 [11,12-14]; 57-59 [21,18-22]; 60-63 [22,1-14]; 64-65 [8,11-12].

**ISAKSSON, Abel**

1965 *Marriage and Ministry in the New Temple. A Study with Special Reference to Mt. 19.3-12 and 1. Cor. 11.3-16,* trans. N. Tomkinson (Acta Seminarii Neotestamentici Upsaliensis, 24). Lund: Gleerup; København: Munksgaard, 1965, 210 p. Esp. 15-152: "Marriage in the New Temple. Mt 19.3-12". [NTA 10, p. 138] — Diss. Uppsala, 1965 (H. Riesenfeld).
    H. BALTENSWEILER, *TZ* 23 (1967) 356-358; J.L. CUNCHILLOS, *EstBíb* 26 (1967) 209-212; G. DELLING, *TLZ* 92 (1967) 276-277; L. DE LORENZI, *RQum* 5 (1965) 446-452; J.D.M. DERRETT, *JBL* 85 (1966) 98-99; F. DREYFUS, *RB* 76 (1969) 303-304; J.A. FITZMYER, *TS* 27 (1966) 451-454; J.M. FORD, *JTS* 18 (1967) 197-200; R.M. GRANT, *VigChr* 22 (1968) 223-224; E. LARSSON, *SvenskTeolKvart* 44 (1968) 181-185; P. NOBER, *VD* 45 (1967) 52-57; J.S. RUEF, *Interpr* 20 (1966) 356; J. SWETNAM, *Bib* 47 (1966) 297-298; E. UTNEM, *TidsTeolKirk* 38 (1967) 67-68.

**ISBELL, Charles D.**

1977 Does the Gospel of Matthew Proclaim Mary's Virginity? — *BibArchRev* 3/2 (1977) 18-19, 52.

**ISHIWATA, Koji**

1994 A Reflection on the Christology and Theology of Matthew Observed in Mt 11,28-30. [Japanese] — *Shinyakugaku Kenkyu (New Testament Studies)* 22 (1994) 1-11.

**ISIDRO ALVES, Manuel**

1984 A morte de Cristo à luz da figura do Servo de Jahvé. [The death of Jesus in light of the figure of the Servant of Jahwe] — *Didaskalia* 14 (1984) 157-168. [NTA 31, 803]

**ISRAEL, Martin**

1968 *The Record of Christ's Life and Doctrine Related by Saint Matthew. Interpretation and Comments.* Jericho, NY: Exposition, 1968, IX-190 p. [NTA 13, p. 269]

**ITO, Agnes Y.**

1994 Les sept montagnes de Jésus dans saint Matthieu. — *LumVit* 49 (1994) 413-423. [NTA 39, 1440]

**ITO, Akio**

1989 *Matthew's Understanding of the Law with Special Reference to the Fourth Antithesis* [5,38-42]. Diss. Oxford, 1989, 361 p. — *DissAbstr* 51 (1990-91) 192.

1991 The Question of the Authenticity of the Ban on Swearing (Matthew 5.33-37). — *JSNT* 43 (1991) 5-13. [NTA 36, 714]; = EVANS, C.A. - PORTER, S.E. (eds.), *The Historical Jesus,* 1995, 140-147. → Dautzenberg 1981

1992  Matthew and the Community of the Dead Sea Scrolls. — *JSNT* 48 (1992) 23-42. Esp.
25-33: "The possible Matthean parallels" [5,3.33-35.43.48; 13,35.26-43; 16,17-19; 18,10.15-17]; 33-42:
"Assessment". [NTA 37, 1239]; = EVANS, C.A. – PORTER, S.E. (eds.), *The Synoptic
Gospels*, 1995, 28-46. Esp. 30-38; 38-46.

ITTEL, **Gerhard Wolfgang**

1967  *Ostern und das leere Grab*. Gütersloh: Mohn, 1967, 54 p. Esp. 12-18: "Vergleich der vier
Evangelienberichte".

1970  *Jesus und die Jünger*. Gütersloh: Mohn, 1970, 135 p. Esp. 14-18 [4,18-22]; 28-41 [10,1-4];
43-45 [8,23-27]; 56-59 [10,1-15]; 64-67 [14,22-33]; 72-75 [16,13-23]; 85-88 [17,1-13]; 94-95 [20,20-28];
102-112: "Die kleingläubigen Jünger (Matthäus)".

IULIANO, **Giuseppe**

1982  *"È risorto come ha parlato!" (Mt 28,6). La Chiesa orante annuncia e celebra il
Signore. Temi teologici spirituali e mistagogici missionari della notte pasquale*. Parma,
1982, LXXI-734 p. Esp. 22-40. — Diss. Pont. Univ. Urbaniana, Roma, 1982 (T. Federici).

# J

**JACKS, Clive Franklin, Jr.**

1966 *The Epiphany Narratives in Mark and Matthew. A Study in Cultic and Literary Tradition*. Diss. Union Theol. Sem., New York, 1966, 404 p. — *DissAbstr* 27 (1966-67) 1913.

**JACKSON, David R.**

1985 The Priority of the Son of Man Sayings. — *WestTJ* 47 (1985) 83-96. Esp. 85-86 [16,28/Mk]; 87-88 [24/Rev]. [NTA 30, 311]

**JACKSON, Glenna Sue**

1993 *"Have Mercy on Me": The Canaanite Woman in Matthew 15:21-28*. Diss. Marquette Univ., Milwaukee, WI, 1993, 222 p. — *DissAbstr* 54 (1993-94) 4135.

1994 A Source for Matthew's Story of the Canaanite Woman. — *Proceedings EGLBS* 14 (1994) 47-56.

**JACKSON, S.A.**

1993 The Lord's Prayer in St. Augustine. — *Studia Patristica* 27 (1993) 311-321.
El Padrenuestro en san Agustín. — *Augustinus* (Madrid) 40 (1995) 125-137.

**JACOB, Günter**

1981 Die Proklamation der messianischen Gemeinde. Zur Auslegung der Makarismen in der Bergpredigt. — *TVers* 12 (1981) 47-75. Esp. 47-49: "Redaktionsgeschichtliche und kompositorische Aspekte"; 49-52: "Die messianische Dimension"; 52-61 [5,3-6]; 62-69 [5,7-9]; 69-74 [5,10-12].

**JACOB, René**

1973 *Les péricopes de l'entrée à Jérusalem et de la préparation de la cène. Contribution à l'étude du problème synoptique* (Église nouvelle – Église ancienne. Études bibliques, 2). Paris: Beauchesne, 1973, 162 p. Esp. 28-35 [26,17-19]; 67-78 [21,1-9]; 78-81 [minor agreements: Mt 21,1-9]; 103-107 [21,1-9]; 107-113 [21,1-9/Jn]. — Mémoire École Biblique, Jerusalem, 1970.

**JACOB, Thomas**

1976 The Daily Bread in the Teaching of Jesus. — *Jeevadhara* 6 (1976) 187-197. [NTA 21, 78]

**JACOBS, Manfred**

1981 Die Bergpredigt in der Geschichte der Kirche. — BÖCHER, O., et al., *Die Bergpredigt im Leben der Christenheit*, 1981, 17-40.

**JACOBSON, Arland Dean**

1978 *Wisdom Christology in Q*. Diss. Graduate School, Claremont, CA, 1978, XIII-259 p. Esp. 24-126: "The first section of Q" [Q 3,1-6.7-9.16-17.21-22; 4,1-13; 6,20-49; 7,1-10.18-35]; 127-155: "The second section of Q" [Q 9,57-60; 10,2-16.21-22]; 156-209: "The third section of Q" [Q 11,14-32.33-36.39-52]; 210-214: "The last wisdom pericope: Luke 13:34-35/Matthew 23:37-39"; 215-224: "The final redaction of Q". — *DissAbstr* 39 (1978-79) 3653. → 1992a; → Hoffmann 1992b

1982a The Literary Unity of Q. Lc 10,2-16 and Parallels as a Test Case. — DELOBEL, J. (ed.), *Logia*, 1982, 419-423.

1982b The Literary Unity of Q. — *JBL* 101 (1982) 365-389. Esp. 365-371: "The synoptic problem" (= 1992a, 13-18); 371-388: "The literary unity of Q" (= 1992a, 61-76) [form criticism; traditions Mk/Q; source]. [NTA 27, 494]; = KLOPPENBORG, J.S. (ed.), *The Shape of Q*, 1994, 98-115 (= 1982b, 371-388).

1987    The History of the Composition of the Synoptic Sayings Source, Q. — *SBL 1987 Seminar Papers*, 285-294. (286-290 = 1992a, 49-51). → Kloppenborg 1987a

1991    The Sayings Gospel Q. — MILLER, R.J. (ed.), *The Complete Gospels. Annotated Scholars Version*, Sonoma, CA: Polebridge, 1991, [2]1992, 249-300.

1992a   *The First Gospel. An Introduction to Q.* Sonoma, CA: Polebridge, 1992, XI-309 p. Esp. 5-18: "Source criticism" (13-18 = 1982b, 365-371); 19-32: "From source to gospel"; 33-60: "Recent Q research" (49-51 = 1987, 286-290); 61-76: "The literary unity of Q" (= 1982b, 371-388); 77-129: "John and Jesus"; 130-151: "Mission and reception"; 152-183: "Against this generation"; 184-250: "To the community" (77-250 → 1978). [NTA 38, p. 120] → Patterson 1993b
     D. CATCHPOLE, *ExpT* 105 (1993-94) 284-285; H.T. FLEDDERMANN, *JBL* 113 (1994) 334-336; R.J. MILLER, *CBQ* 56 (1994) 376-378; F. NEIRYNCK, *ETL* 69 (1993) 177-179.

1992b   Apocalyptic and the Synoptic Sayings Source Q. — VAN SEGBROECK, F., et al. (eds.), *The Four Gospels 1992.* FS F. Neirynck, 1992, I, 403-419. Esp. 403-412: "Some recent perspectives on Q and apocalyptic"; 412-419: "Apocalyptic in Q".

1995    Divided Families and Christian Origins. — PIPER, R.A. (ed.), *The Gospel Behind the Gospels*, 1995, 361-380. Esp. 361-363 [Q 9,59-60]; 363-364 [Q 14,26]; 364-367 [Q 12,51-53]; 367-369 [Q 16,13]; 369-373 [Q 16,18]; 374-375 [Q 17,26-27].

**JACOBSON, Delmar**

1975    An Exposition of Matthew 13:44-52. — *Interpr* 29 (1975) 277-282.

**JACQUEMIN, Edmond**

1963    Les béatitudes. [5,1-12] — *AssSeign* I/89 (1963) 34-53.

1964    Les options du chrétien. [6,24-33] — *AssSeign* I/68 (1964) 31-44; cf. II/39 (1972) 18-27. [NTA 17, 515]

1965    La Prière du Seigneur. [6,9-13] — *AssSeign* I/48 (1965) 47-64.

1969    Le baptême du Christ. Mt 3,13-17; Mc 1,6b-11; Lc 3,15s.21s. — *AssSeign* II/12 (1969) 48-65. Esp. 55-58.

1973    Les béatitudes selon saint Matthieu. Mt 5,1-12a. — *AssSeign* II/66 (1973) 50-63. [NTA 18, 466]

**JACQUES, Victor**

1950    Quelques réflexions à partir du discours sur la montagne. — *RevDiocNamur* 5 (1950) 110-118.

1951a   Les disciples de Jésus dans le premier évangile. — *RevDiocNamur* 6 (1951) 20-37.

1951b   Jésus-docteur ou Jésus-seigneur dans le premier évangile. — *Ibid.*, 169-181.

1951c   Consignes missionnaires (Mt., X). — *Ibid.*, 289-305. Esp. 294-300 [10,5-16]; 300-302 [10,17-23]; 302-305 [10,24-39].

1968    À propos des évangiles de l'enfance. — *FoiTemps* 1 (1968) 103-110.

**JACQUES, Xavier**

1969    *Index des mots apparentés dans le Nouveau Testament. Complément des Concordances et Dictionnaires.* Roma: Biblical Institute Press, 1969, 124 p.
     *List of New Testament Words Sharing Common Elements. Supplement to Concordance or Dictionary.* Roma: Biblical Institute Press, 1969, 124 p.

**JÄRVELÄINEN, Matti**

1985    Die geringsten Brüder im Weinberg. Mt 20,1-16 und Jesu Botschaft von Gottes Solidarität. — *Diakonie* (Stuttgart) 11 (1985) 356-359.

**JAHNKE, Vernon J.**

1988    "Love your enemies". The Value of New Perspectives. — *CurrTMiss* 15 (1988) 267-273. [NTA 32, 1105]

**JAKI, Stanley L.**

1989 The Virgin Birth and the Birth of Science. — *DownR* 107 (1989) 255-273.

**JAMES, J.L.**

1994 *The Day of Christ's Return: Interpreting Selected Synoptic Sayings about the Time of Second Coming.* Diss. Mid-America Baptist Theol. Sem., 1994, 188 p. — *DissAbstr* 56 (1995-96) 235.

**JAMIESON, J.G.**

1951 *The Gospel of the Kingdom in the Sermon on the Mount.* London: Hodge, 1951, 118 p.

**JANKOWSKI, Bogdan**

1954 Regnum venturum quod adest. De genuino sensu eschatologico, quem nonnulla "logia" Matthaeana de Regno Dei prae se ferunt. — *CollTheol* 25 (1954) 147-161. [5,3-10.19-20; 6,10.33; 7,21; 19,14.23-24; 25,34]. [NTA 1, 38r]

1956 Dokoła tzw. lauzul rozwodowych pierwszej Ewangelii (Mt 5,32; 19,9) (Über die sogenannte "Scheidungsklauseln" bei Matthäus). — *RoczTK* 3 (1956) 401-416.

**JANKOWSKI, Gerhard**

1987 Die Taufe des Messias im Jordan. — *TK* 35 (1987) 17-44. Esp. 26-34 [3,13-17].

**JANNASCH, Wilhelm** → J. Jeremias 1962c

**JANSEN, John Frederick**

1980 *The Resurrection of Jesus Christ in New Testament Theology.* Philadelphia, PA: Westminster, 1980, 187 p.

**JANSSEN, Friedrich**

1973 Die synoptischen Passionsberichte. Ihre theologische Konzeption und literarische Komposition. — *BibLeb* 14 (1973) 40-57. Esp. 45. [NTA 18, 81]

**JARRETT, Paul Daniel**

1992 *Eusebius of Caesarea and the Text of the Gospels.* Diss. Southwestern Baptist Theol. Sem., Fort Worth, TX, 1992, 266 p. (L. Cranford). — *DissAbstr* 53 (1992-93) 1960.

**JARVIS, Cynthia A.**

1988 Matthew 28:1-10. — *Interpr* 42 (1988) 63-68.

**JARVIS, Peter G.**

1966 Expounding the Parables. V. The Tower-builder and the King Going to War (Luke 14,25-33). — *ExpT* 77 (1965-66) 196-198. Esp. 196 [10,37-38]; 198 [τίς ἐξ ὑμῶν]. [NTA 11, 264]

**JASIŃSKI, S. Andrzej**

1986 Αἰών w Nowym Testamencie. [Αἰών in the New Testament] — *RoczTK* 33/1 (1986) 79-99. Esp. 85, 90. [NTA 35, 1070]

**JASON, Heda**

1977 Der Zinsgroschen: Analyse der Erzählstruktur. — *LingBib* 41-42 (1977) 49-87. Esp. 67-68 [22,15-22]. [NTA 22, 780] → Güttgemanns 1977

**JAUBERT, Annie**

1957 *La date de la Cène. Calendrier biblique et liturgie chrétienne* (Études bibliques). Paris: Gabalda, 1957, 159 p. Esp. 105-136 [26,17-19]. → M. Black 1959, Giglioli 1962, Mendoza Ruiz 1964, Ogg 1959, Ruckstuhl 1963, M.H. Shepherd 1961, N. Walker 1963b
*The Date of the Last Supper*, trans. I. Rafferty. Staten Island, NY: Alba, 1965; London: Herder, 1966, 176 p.

1960 Jésus et le calendrier de Qumrân. — *NTS* 7 (1960-61) 1-30. Esp. 11-15: "Jésus et certains groupes palestiniens"; 18-19 [temple]. [NTA 5, 364]

1964 Les séances du sanhédrin et les récits de la passion. — *RHR* 166 (1964) 143-169; 167 (1965) 1-33. Esp. 144-161. [NTA 9, 933; 10, 129]

1968 Le mercredi où Jésus fut livré. — *NTS* 14 (1967-68) 145-164. Esp. 145-152.155-160 [26,2-5]. [NTA 12, 830]

1972 Écho du Livre de la Sagesse en Barnabé 7,9. — *RSR* 60 (1972) 193-198. Esp. 196-197 [27,54]. [NTA 17, 230]

**JAVIERRE, Antonio M.**

1954 Sucesión apostólica. Cielos de actitudes protestantes en torno a su concepto. — *Sal* 16 (1954) 77-108. Esp. 98-100 [16,17-19] → Cullmann 1952

1958a La sucesión primacial y apostólica en el evangelio de Mateo. Resultado de una encuesta. [16,17-19; 18,18] — *Sal* 20 (1958) 27-71.
*La sucesión primacial y apostólica en el Evangelio de Mateo. Resultado de una encuesta. Datos para el problema de la Sucesión Apostólica*, I (Biblioteca del "Salesianum", 49). Torino: Società editrice internazionale, 1958, 68 p. → Brandenburg 1960
B. BRINKMANN, *Scholastik* 34 (1959) 583; J. COLLANTES, *EstE* 36 (1961) 494; G. D., *NRT* 83 (1961) 777; G. OGGIONI, *ScuolC* 87 (1959) 224-226; I. ORTIZ DE URBINA *OCP* 24 (1958) 416-417; V. PROAÑO GIL, *RevistEspTeol* 19 (1959) 83-84; A. VIARD, *RSPT* 43 (1959) 305.

1958b "Caeci vident". — *Sal* 20 (1958) 508-541. Esp. 513-517 [9,27-31].

**JEANNE D'ARC, Sœur**

1962 Les Béatitudes, apprivoisement à la béatitude. — *VSp* 107 (1962) 356-367. [NTA 7, 504]

1987 *Les Évangiles. Évangile selon Matthieu. Présentation du texte grec, traduction et notes* (Nouvelle collection des textes et documents. Association Guillaume Budé). Paris: Les Belles Lettres – Desclée De Brouwer, 1987, XIII-199 and 25 p. [NTA 32, p. 101]
B. AMATA, *Sal* 51 (1989) 356; M. BOUTTIER, *ETR* 64 (1989) 635-636; N. GUEUNIER, *Études* 368 (1988) 136; M.-É. LAUZIÈRE, *RThom* 88 (1988) 131-133; J. POMS, *ETR* 63 (1988) 607.

1990 Miettes d'Évangile. — Κεχαριτωμένη. FS R. Laurentin, 1990, 153-164. Esp. 153-155 [11,11]; 162-164 [27,55-61].

**JEFFORD, Clayton N.**

1989a *The Sayings of Jesus in the Teaching of the Twelve Apostles* (Supplements to Vigiliae Christianae, 11). Leiden: Brill, 1989, XVI-185 p. Esp. 22-29 [7,13-14/Did 1,1]; 29-38 [7,12; 22,37-39/Did 1,2]; 38-52 [5,38-48/Did 1,3b–2,1]; 55-57 [19,18/Did 2,2]; 63-69 [5,21-37/Did 3,1-6]; 73-81 [5,5/Did 3,7]; 85-92 [24/Did 16]; 93-95 [11,28-30/Did 6,2]; 118-122: 'The Matthean community"; 130-135 [M source]; 135-138 [6,1-18/Did]; 146-159 [Q 13,23-24]. — Diss. Graduate School, Claremont, CA, 1988 (J.E. Goehring).

1989b The Dangers of Lying in Bed. Luke 17:34-35 and Parallels. — *Forum* 5/1 (1989) 106-110. [NTA 34, 180]

1995* (ed.), *The* Didache *in Context. Essays on Its Text, History and Transmission* (SupplNT, 77). Leiden: Brill, 1995, XVIII-420 p. → Henderson, Klopperborg, Tuilier

**JENKINS, Geoffrey**

1994 A Written Jerusalem Gospel "Y": Reflections on the Socio-Politics of the Synoptic Problem. — *Pacifica* 7 (1994) 309-323. [NTA 39, 1438] → Hartin 1991

**JENKINS, R.G.**

1993 A Note on the Syriac Text of Matthew 20:23-31 in Sinai Ar. 514. — *New Testament Textual Research Update* (Sydney) 1 (1993) 3-4. → Brock 1992

**JENKS, Gregory C.**

1990 *The Origins and Early Development of the Antichrist Myth* [24,23-24] (BZNW, 59).

Berlin: de Gruyter, 1990, XVIII-416 p. Esp. 199-207: "The synoptic gospels". — Diss. Univ. Queensland, 1989 (M. Lattke).

**JENNI, Ernst**

1992 Kausativ und Funktionsgefüge. Sprachliche Bemerkungen zur Bitte: "Führe uns nicht in Versuchung". — *TZ* 48 (1992) 77-88.

**JENNINGS, Theodore W., Jr.**

1990* (ed.), *Text and Logos. The Humanistic Interpretation of the New Testament. [FS H.W. Boers]* (Scholars Press homage series). Atlanta, GA: Scholars, 1990, XVI-306 p. → H.D. Betz, Patte, Weder

**JENSEN, Joseph**

1978 Does *porneia* Mean Fornication? A Critique of Bruce Malina. — *NT* 20 (1978) 161-184. Esp. 179-183 [5,32; 15,19; 19,9; 21,31-32]. [NTA 23, 42] → Malina 1972

**JENSON, Philip P.**

1995 Models of Prophetic Prediction and Matthew's Quotation of Micah 5:2. — SATTERTHWAITE, P.E. (ed.), *The Lord's Anointed: Interpretation of Old Testament Messianic Texts*, Carlisle: Paternoster, 1995, 189-211. Esp. 204-206, 209-211.

**JEONG WOO KIM**

1991 *The Function and Meaning of the Lord's Prayer in the Sermon on the Mount.* Diss. Calvin Sem., Grand Rapids, MI, 1991 (D. Holwerda).

**JEPSEN, Alfred**

1972 Anmerkungen eines Aussenseiters zum Synoptikerproblem. — *NT* 14 (1972) 106-114. Esp. 109-114 [Ur-Mt/Ur-Mk]. [NTA 17, 105]

**JEREMIAS, Gert**

1971* & KUHN, H.-W. - STEGEMANN, H. (eds.), *Tradition und Glaube. Das frühe Christentum in seiner Umwelt. Festgabe für Karl Georg Kuhn zum 65. Geburtstag.* Göttingen: Vandenhoeck & Ruprecht, 1971, 434 p. → Carmignac, Colpe, Schweizer, H. Stegemann

**JEREMIAS, Joachim**

1923ᴿ *Jerusalem zur Zeit Jesu. Eine kulturgeschichtliche Untersuchung zur neutestamentlichen Zeitgeschichte* [1923-1937]. Göttingen: Vandenhoeck & Ruprecht, ²1958; ³1962 ("neubearbeitet"), X-429 p. Esp. ; 155-157 [27,7]; 324-331 [1,1-17].
*Jérusalem au temps de Jésus. Recherches d'histoire économique et sociale pour la période néo-testamentaire*, trans. J. le Moyne. Paris: Cerf, 1967, 525 p.; ³1980. Esp. 197-199; 384-392.
*Jerusalem in the Time of Jesus. An Investigation into Economic and Social Conditions during the New Testament Period.* London: SCM, 1969, XVI-405 p. Esp. 138-140; 290-297.

1930ᴿ Zur Hypothese einer schriftlichen Logienquelle. [1930] — ID., *Abba*, 1966, 90-92.

1935ᴿ *Die Abendmahlsworte Jesu* [1935, 99 p.; ²1949, 128 p.]. Göttingen: Vandenhoeck & Ruprecht, ³1960 ("völlig neu bearbeitet"), 275 p.; ⁴1967 ("durchgesehen"). Esp. 153-165: "Vergleich der Texte" [26,26-29].
*The Eucharistic Words of Jesus*, trans. A. Ehrhardt. Oxford: Blackwell, 1955, IX-195 p. [= German ²1949]; trans. N. Perrin (The New Testament Library), London: SCM; New York: Scribner, 1966, 278 p. [= German ³1960]. Esp. 160-173; London: SCM, 1976; Philadelphia, PA: Fortress, 1977.
*La dernière Cène. Les paroles de Jésus*, trans. M. Benzerath & R. Henning (LD, 75). Paris: Cerf, 1972, 337 p. Esp. 190-205.
*Le parole dell'ultima cena*, trans. M. Verdesca (Biblioteca di cultura religiosa, 23). Brescia: Paideia, 1973, 365 p.

1937ᴿ "Laß allda deine Gabe" (Mt. 5,23f.). [1937] — ID., *Abba*, 1966, 103-107.

1940ᴿ Die Lampe unter dem Scheffel. [1940] — ID., *Abba*, 1966, 99-102.

1947[R]  *Die Gleichnisse Jesu* [1947, 119 p.] (ATANT, 11). Zürich: Zwingli, [2]1952 ("völlig neu bearbeitet"), 174 p. Esp. 16-90: "Von der Urkirche zu Jesus zurück" [5,25-26; 13,18-23.36-43.49-50; 18,12-14; 20,1-16; 21,28-32.33-44; 22,1-14; 23,43-51; 24,42; 25,1-13.14-30]; 91-162: "Die Botschaft der Gleichnisse Jesu" [5,13; 6,24-34; 7,9-11; 9,16-17; 11,5-6.16-19; 12,43-45; 13,3-8.24-30.31-32.33.44-46.47-48; 18,3-4.23-35; 20,1-16; 25,31-46]; Göttingen: Vandenhoeck & Ruprecht, [3]1954 ("durchgesehen"), 176 p.; [4]1956 ("neu bearbeitet"), 208 p. Esp. 17-97; 98-193; [5]1958 ("unverändert"); [6]1962 ("neu bearbeitet"), 242 p. Esp. 19-114; 115-226; [7]1965 ("durchgesehen"); [8]1970; [9]1979; [10]1984. → 1965a; → Jurgens 1983, Little 1976, Newell 1972

  *The Parables of Jesus*, trans. S.H. Hooke (The New Testament Library). London: SCM; New York: Scribner, 1954, 178 p. [= German [2]1952]; rev. ed., 1963 [= German [6]1962], [2]1969, 248 p. Esp. 23-114; 115-229.

  *Les paraboles de Jésus*, trans. B. Hübsch. Le Puy: Mappus, 1964, 237 p. [= German [6]1962]; (Livre de Vie, 85-86), Paris: Seuil, 1968, 320 p.

  *Le parabole di Gesù*, trans. G. Capra & M.A. Colao Pellizzari (Biblioteca di cultura religiosa, 3). Brescia: Paideia, 1967, 300 p.; [2]1973 [= German [7]1965]

  *Las parábolas de Jesús*, trans. F.J. Calvo (Biblia y Kerygma, 3). Estella: Verbo Divino, 1970, 304 p.; [6]1981. Trans. Japanese 1969; Portuguese 1976; Danish 1978, [2]1981.

  Von der Urkirche zu Jesus zurück. [1947, 15-74] — HARNISCH, W. (ed.), *Gleichnisse Jesu*, 1982, 180-237.

1952  The Gentile World in the Thought of Jesus. — *Bulletin SNTS* 3 (1952; [2]1963) 18-28. Esp. 18-19 [23,15]; 19 [15,24]; 21 [10,5-6.23]; 25-26 [8,11-12]; 27-28 [25,31-32]; 27-28 [5,14]; 28 [5,35].

1953  Kennzeichen der ipsissima vox Jesu. — SCHMID, J. – VÖGTLE, A. (eds.), *Synoptische Studien*. FS A. Wikenhauser, 1953, 86-93. Esp. 90-92; = ID., *Abba*, 1966, 145-152. Esp. 148-150.

  Characteristics of the *ipsissima vox Jesu*. — ID., *The Prayers*, 1967, 108-115. Esp. 112-113.

1956  *Jesu Verheissung für die Völker. Franz Delitzsch-Vorlesungen, 1953.* Stuttgart: Kohlhammer, 1956, 69 p.; [2]1959. Esp. 15-16 [23,15-16]; 16-17.22-24 [10,5-6]; 19-20 [24,14]; 22-29 [15,21-28]; 29-30 [8,5-13]; 32-33 [28,18-20]; 54-55 [25,31-46].

  *Jésus et les païens*, trans. J. Carrère (Cahiers théologiques, 39). Neuchâtel: Delachaux & Niestlé, 1956, 71 p.

  *Jesus' Promise to the Nations. The Franz Delitzsch Lectures for 1953*, trans. S.H. Hooke (Studies in Biblical Theology, 24). London: SCM; Naperville, IL: Allenson, 1958, [2]1967, 84 p. Esp. 17-18; 19-20.26-28; 23-24; 26-35; 34-35; 38-39; 47-48.

  *La promesa de Jesús a los paganos.* Madrid: Fax, 1974, 125 p.

1958  *Heiligengräber in Jesu Umwelt (Mt. 23,29; Lk 11,47). Eine Untersuchung zur Volksreligion der Zeit Jesu.* Göttingen: Vandenhoeck & Ruprecht, 1958, 155 p. Esp. 67-73 [23,35]; 121.126 [23,29].

1959a  *Die Bergpredigt* (Calwer Hefte zur Förderung biblischen Glaubens und christlichen Lebens, 27). Stuttgart: Calwer, 1959; [3]1961; [5]1965, 31 p. Esp. 1-13: "Das Problem"; 13-17: "Die Entstehung der Bergpredigt"; 17-21: "Die Bergpredigt als urchristlicher Katechismus"; 21-30: "Die einzelnen Worte Jesu"; 30-31: "Nicht Gesetz, sondern Evangelium"; = ID., *Abba*, 1966, 171-189. Esp. 171-177; 177-180; 180-183; 183-189; 189. → 1963a, 13-48.

  *Bib* 42 (1961) 111; *BibOr* 2 (1960) 224; P. BENOIT, *RB* 67 (1960) 626; P. NOBER, *VD* 37 (1959) 368.

  *The Sermon on the Mount*, trans. N. Perrin. London: Athlone, 1961, 34 p.; (Facet Books, Biblical Series, 2). Philadelphia, PA: Fortress, 1963, IX-38 p.

  *ExpT* 73 (1961-62) 258-259.

  *Il Discorso della montagna*, trans. M. Bellincioni (Biblioteca minima di cultura religiosa, 6). Brescia: Paideia, 1963, 45 p.

  G. RINALDI, *BibOr* 4 (1962) 150-151.

  Trans. Danish 1969, [2]1984; Portuguese 1976.

1959b  Die Muttersprache des Evangelisten Matthäus. — *ZNW* 50 (1959) 270-274. Esp. 271-272 [22,37]; 272-274 [21,9.15]. [NTA 4, 640]; = ID., *Abba*, 1966, 255-260. Esp. 257-258; 258-260.

1960  The Lord's Prayer in Modern Research. — *ExpT* 71 (1959-60) 141-146. [NTA 4, 651]; = BATEY, R. (ed.), *New Testament Issues*, 1970, 88-101. → 1962a

Le pater et la recherche moderne sur le Nouveau Testament. — *Nouvelles chrétiennes d'Israël* (Jerusalem) 14 (1963) 9-13.

1962a  *Das Vater-Unser im Lichte der neueren Forschung* (Calwer Hefte zur Förderung biblischen Glaubens und christlichen Lebens, 50). Stuttgart: Calwer, 1962, 31 p. Esp. 1-7: "Das Vater-Unser in der ältesten Kirche"; 8-16: "Der älteste Text des Vater-Unsers"; 16-30: "Der Sinn des Vater-Unsers"; ³1965; ⁴1967; = *Zeichen der Zeit* 16 (1962) 1-13; = (Tradition und Gegenwart), Berlin: Evangelische Verlagsanstalt, 1962, 7-34; = ID., *Abba*, 1966, 152-171. Esp. 152-154; 155-160; 161-171. → 1960; 1963a, 49-79.

> A. IBAÑEZ, *ScriptVict* 10 (1963) 341-342; F. LUCIANI, *BibOr* 7 (1965) 89.
> Fader vår i den nyare forskningens ljus. — *SEÅ* 27 (1962) 33-54. Esp. 33-35; 35-42; 52-54. [NTA 9, 528]
> *The Lord's Prayer*, trans. J. Reumann (Facet Books, Biblical Series 8). Philadelphia, PA: Fortress, 1964, XVII-37 p.
> The Lord's Prayer in the Light of Recent Research. — ID., *The Prayers*, 1967, 82-107. Esp. 82-85; 85-94; 94-107.
> *O pai-nosso. A oração do Senhor*. São Paulo: Paulinas, 1976, 58 p.

1962b  Die Deutung des Gleichnisses vom Unkraut unter dem Weizen (Mt. xiii 36-43). — *Neotestamentica et Patristica*. FS O. Cullmann, 1962, 59-63; = ID., *Abba*, 1966, 261-265.

1962c  & JANNASCH, W., Vaterunser. — *RGG* 6 (³1962) 1235-1238.

1963a  *Paroles de Jésus. Le Sermon sur la montagne – Le Notre Père dans l'exégèse actuelle*, trans. M. Mailhé (LD, 38). Paris: Cerf, 1963, 79 p. (= 1959a + 1962a). Esp. 13-48 [15-24; 25-29; 31-35; 37-45; 47-48]; 49-79 [51-54; 55-63; 65-79]; = (Foi Vivante), Paris, 1965, 103 p. Esp. 15-60; 61-101.

> M.-É. BOISMARD, *RB* 72 (1965) 306-307; M. CAMBE, *VSp* 112 (1965) 605-607; J. COPPENS, *ETL* 40 (1964) 208; J. DUPONT, *Paroisse et Liturgie* (Ottignies) 46 (1964) 460; B.H., *Verbum Caro* (Taizé) 18 (1964) 109; M.É. LAUZIÈRE, *RThom* 64 (1964) 465-466; X. LÉON-DUFOUR, *RSR* 53 (1965) 627-630; R. MEHL, *RHPR* 46 (1966) 88-89; E. PASCUAL, *EstBíb* 24 (1965) 273-274; P. PROULX, *Bib* 45 (1964) 577-578; J. RADERMAKERS, *NRT* 87 (1965) 421-422; *NRT* 89 (1967) 891; L.F. RIVERA, *RevistBíb* 26 (1964) 230-232; S. VOIGT, *REB* 25 (1965) 164-165; J. ZALOTAY, *CBQ* 96 (1964) 374-375; M. ZERWICK, *VD* 43 (1965) 91-99.
> *Palabras de Jesús. El Sermón de la montaña. El Padre Nuesto*, trans. J.M. Bernáldez Montalvo (Actualidad Bíblica, 7). Madrid: Fax, 1968; ²1970; ³1974, 185 p.
> *TVida* 11 (1970) 68; L. ÁLVAREZ VERDES, *Pentecostés* 8 (1970) 224; M.A. BRAND MESA, *RevistBíb* 32 (1970) 92-93; B. CELADA, *CuBíb* 24 (1972) 111-112; C. FLORES, *RazFe* 179 (1968) 220-221; P.E. GALLEGO, *Religión y Cultura* (Madrid) 15 (1969) 450-451; M. GALLART, *ScriptTheol* 1 (1969) 558; S. GONZÁLEZ DE CARREA, *NatGrac* 17 (1970) 290-291; R. SILVA, *Burgense* 10 (1969) 524; *Compostellanum* 15 (1970) 136; *RevistEspTeol* 31 (1971) 216; J.I. VICENTINI, *Stromata* (San Míguel, Arg.) 25 (1969) 602-603; E.A. WCELA, *CBQ* 33 (1971) 588-589.
> *The Sermon on the Mount, the Lord's Prayer and the Problem of the Historical Jesus*. Bangalore: Theological Publications in India, 1976, 146 p.

1963b  Matthäus 7,6a. — BETZ, O., et al. (eds.), *Abraham unser Vater*. FS O. Michel, 1963, 271-275; = ID., *Abba*, 1966, 83-87.

1965a  *Die Gleichnisse Jesu* (Siebenstern-Taschenbuch, 43). München–Hamburg: Siebenstern-Taschenbuch, 1965, 157 p. (= short edition → 1947/⁶1962), ²1966, ³1969; (Kleine Vandenhoeck Reihe, 1500), Göttingen: Vandenhoeck & Ruprecht, ¹⁰1988.

> *Rediscovering the Parables*. London: SCM, 1966, 191 p.; New York: Scribner, 1967 (= short edition of ET 1963).
> *De gelijkenissen van Jesus*, trans. B. Meuwissen. Bilthoven: Nelissen, 1968, 174 p.
> *Interpretación de la parábolas*, trans. F.J. Calvo (Buena noticia, 12). Estella: Verbo Divino, 1971, 216 p.; ²1982; ⁴1991.

1965b  *The Central Message of the New Testament*. London: SCM; New York: Scribner, 1965, 95 p.; Philadelphia, PA: Fortress, 1981. Esp. 9-30: "Abba" [11,27] → 1966b

> *Le message central du Nouveau Testament* (Lire la Bible, 8). Paris: Cerf, 1966, 126 p. Esp. 7-29; (Foi

Vivante, 175), ²1976, 124 p. Esp. 9-29.
*Il messaggio centrale del Nuovo Testamento*, trans. A. Ornella (Biblioteca minima di cultura religiosa, 19). Brescia: Paideia, 1968, 143 p.
*Abba. El mensaje central del Nuevo Testamento*, trans. F.M. Goñi (Biblioteca de estudios bíblicos, 30). Salamanca: Sígueme, 1981, 355 p.

1965c Λαμπάδες Mt 25,1.3f.7f. — *ZNW* 56 (1965) 196-201 [NTA 10, 915]
Lampades in Matthew 25:1-13. — RICHARDS, J.McD. (ed.), *Soli Deo Gloria. New Testament Studies in Honor of William Childs Robinson*, Richmond, VA: Knox, 1968, 83-87, 147-149. → Waller 1981

1966a *Abba. Studien zur neutestamentlichen Theologie und Zeitgeschichte.* Göttingen: Vandenhoeck & Ruprecht, 1966, 371 p. → 1930, 1937, 1940, 1953, 1959a-b, 1962a-b, 1963b, 1966b
*Abba. Jésus et son père* (Parole de Dieu, 8). Paris: Seuil, 1972, 141 ɔ.

1966b Abba. — *Ibid.*, 15-67. Esp. 33-56: "Vater als Bezeichung Gottes in den Logien Jesu"; 56-67: "Die Vateranrede in den Gebeten Jesu". → 1965b
Abba. — ID., *The Prayers*, 1967, 11-65. Esp. 29-54; 54-65.

1967a *The Prayers of Jesus* (Studies in Biblical Theology, II/6). London: SCM, 1967, 124 p. → 1953, 1962a, 1966b

1967b Die älteste Schicht der Menschensohn-Logien. — *ZNW* 58 (1967) 159-172. Esp. 159-160.162.165-167. [NTA 12, 851]

1971 *Neutestamentliche Theologie. Erster Teil: Die Verkündigung Jesu.* Gütersloh: Mohn, 1971, ²1973, 314 p. Esp. 13-49: "Zur Frage nach der Zuverlässigkeit der Überlieferung der Worte Jesu"; 50-80: "Die Sendung"; 81-123: "Der Anbruch der Heilszeit"; 124-156: "Die Gnadenfrist"; 157-238: "Das neue Gottesvolk"; 239-284: "Das Hoheitsbewußtsein Jesu"; 285-295: "Ostern".
*New Testament Theology. Part One: The Proclamation of Jesus*, trans. J. Bowden (The New Testament Library). London: SCM; New York: Scribner's, 1971, ²1972, XVII-330 p. Esp. 1-41; 42-75; 76-121; 122-158; 159-249; 250-299; 300-311.
*Teologia del Nuovo Testamento. I: La predicazione di Gesù*. Brescia: Paideia, 1972, 391 p.; ²1976.
*Théologie du Nouveau Testament. Première partie: La prédication de Jésus*, trans. J. Alzin & A. Liefooghe (LD, 76). Paris: Cerf, 1973, 420 p. Esp. 7-55; 57-97; 99-125; 157-200; 201-309; 311-373; 375-388.
*Teología del Nuevo Testamento. I: La predicación de Jesús*, trans. C. Ruiz Garrido (Biblioteca de estudios bíblicos, 2). Salamanca: Sígueme, 1974, 378 p.
Trans. Portuguese 1977, ²1981.

**JERVELL, Jacob**

1960 Herodes Antipas og hans plass i evangelieoverleveringen. [Herod Antipas and his place in the gospel tradition] — *NorskTeolTids* 61 (1960) 28-40. Esp. 34-36 [14,1-12]. [NTA 5, 60]

1961 Skilsmisse og gjengifte etter Det nye testamente. [Divorce and remarriage according to the New Testament]. — *NorskTeolTids* 62 (1961) 195-210. [NTA 6, 767]

1962 *Den historiske Jesus*. Oslo: Land og Kirke, 1962, 107 p. ²1969, 116 p.; ³1978, 146 p.
*The Continuing Search for the Historical Jesus*, trans. H.E. Kaasa. Minneapolis, MN: Augsburg, 1965, 106 p.

1968 Jesu blods aker. *Matt.* 27,3-10. — *NorskTeolTids* 59 (1968) 158-162. [NTA 13, 574]

1979 Matteusevangeliet? — *NorskTeolTids* 80 (1979) 241-248. [NTA 24, 403] → Hognestad 1978b

1980 The Mighty Minority. — *StudTheol* 34 (1980) 13-38. Esp. 34-35 [Jewish-christians]. [NTA 25, 376]

**JESKE, Richard**

1972 Wisdom and the Future in the Teaching of Jesus. [7,24-27; 24,45-51; 25,1-13] — *Dialog* (Minneapolis, MN) 11 (1972) 108-117. [NTA 16, 839]

**The Jesus Seminar**

1990 Voting Records Sorted by Gospel, Chapter, and Verse; by Weighted Average; by Gospel, by Weighted Average; by Grouped Parallels, by Weighted Average. — *Forum* 6 (1990) 3-55. Esp. 33-47; 139-191; 245-298. Esp. 276-290; 299-352. [NTA 37, 93; 38, 95/96]

1991 Voting Records Sorted by Clusters, by Weighted Average; Alphabetically by Title. — *Forum* 7 (1991) 51-104; 105-158. [NTA 38, 97/98]

**JIMÉNEZ, Humberto**
1978 La base cristológica y teológica de la comunidad según Mateo ("meth' hymôn"). — *Cuestiones Teológicas* (Medellín) 13 (1978) 139-153.

**JIMENEZ, J.** → D. O'Connor 1977

**JIMENEZ, Pablo A.**
1987 Diálogo exegético con Mateo y con Ricardo Foulkes. — *Vida y Pensamiento* (San José) 5 (1987) 68-70. → R. Foulkes 1987

**JIMÉNEZ FONT, L.M.**
1950 (ed.), *Comentarios al Evangelio de San Mateo* (Biblioteca de autores cristianos, 59). Madrid: Católica, 1950, VIII-1160 p.
      L. TURRADO, *EstBíb* 10 (1951) 481.

**JOCZ, Jakob**
1970 Jesus and the Law. — *Judaica* 26 (1970) 105-124. Esp. 109-116.

**JÖRNS, Klaus-Peter**
1970 Die Gleichnisverkündigung Jesu. Reden von Gott als Wort Gottes. [20,1-16] — LOHSE, E., et al. (eds.), *Der Ruf Jesu*. FS J. Jeremias, 1970, 157-178. → Klauck 1972
1987 "Armut, zu der der Geist hilft" (Mt 5,3) als *nota ecclesiae*. — *TZ* 43 (1987) 59-70. Esp. 59-68: "Mt 5,3 im Rahmen des Matthäusevangeliums ausgelegt". [NTA 31, 1068]

**JOEST, Christoph**
1994 *Bibelstellenkonkordanz zu den wichtigsten älteren Mönchsregeln* (Instrumenta Patristica, 9). Steenbrugge: St. Pietersabdij; Den Haag: Nijhoff, 1994, XLV-149 p. Esp. 73-89.

**JOHANNY, Raymond**
1966 La prière du Seigneur chez les Pères. — *Parole & pain* (Marseille) 12 (1966) 5-33.

**JOHN, Mathew P.**
1980 Give us this day our ... bread (Matthew 6.11). — *BTrans* 31 (1980) 245-247. [NTA 25, 74]

**JOHNE, Karin**
1981 *Meditieren mit dem Mattäus-Evangelium. Meditationsanregungen zu den Leseabschnitten des Mattäus-Evangeliums. Mit dem Text der Einheitsübersetzung*. Zürich: Benziger; Stuttgart: Calwer, 1981, 260 p.
      H.B.C., *RevistBíb* 45 (1983) 55; J. SUDBRACK, *GL* 54 (1981) 319-320.

**JOHNSON, Allan E.**
1989 Rhetorical Criticism in Eusebius' *Gospel Questions*. [1,1-17] — *Studia Patristica* 18/1 (1989) 33-39.
1992 → Arias 1992

**JOHNSON, Benjamin Arlen**
1965 *Empty Tomb Tradition in the Gospel of Peter*. Diss. Harvard Univ., Cambridge, MA, 1965, 132 p. (H. Koester). Esp. 37-56: "The guard at the tomb story in Mt"; 57-105: "The form and function of the story in Mt and GP"; 106-119: "Tendencies in the tradition".
      Empty Tomb Tradition in the Gospel of Peter. — *HTR* 59 (1966) 447-448. [NTA 11, 713]

**JOHNSON, David H.**
1992 Shepherd, Sheep. — *DJG*, 1992, 750-754. Esp. 753-754 [25,31-46].

**JOHNSON, Donald Duane**

1978 *Beyond Consumption. An Economic Perspective Based on Matthew 6:19-21, 6:24 and 6:25-34*. Diss. School of Theology, Claremont, CA, 1978, 102 p. — *DissAbstr* 39/3 (1978-79) 1662.

**JOHNSON, Edgar Albert**

1985 *Aspects of the Remnant Concept in the Gospel of Matthew*. Diss. Andrews Univ., Berrien Springs, MI, 1985, 417 p. (A. Terian). — *DissAbstr* 46 (1985-86) 1321.

**JOHNSON, E. Elizabeth**

1988 Jews and Christians in the New Testament. John, Matthew and Paul. — *Reformed Review* (New Brunswick, NJ) 42/2 (1988-89) 113-128. [NTA 33, 866]

**JOHNSON, Elizabeth A.**

1985 Jesus, the Wisdom of God. A Biblical Basis for Non-Androcentric Christology. — *ETL* 61 (1985) 261-294. Esp. 280-284: "Q and Matthew". [NTA 30, 1253]

**JOHNSON, Luke Timothy**

1986 *The Writings of the New Testament. An Interpretation*. London: SCM; Philadelphia, PA: Fortress, 1986, XXI-593 p. Esp. 172-196: "The gospel of Matthew".

**JOHNSON, Marshall D.**

1969 *The Purpose of the Biblical Genealogies. With Special Reference to the Setting of the Genealogies of Jesus* (SNTS MS, 8). Cambridge: University Press, 1969, X-310 p. Esp. 139-228: "The genealogy of Jesus in Matthew"; 273-275. [NTA 13, p 402]; [2]1988, XXXIV-310 p.

J. BARR, *JSS* 16 (1971) 104-106; R.P. BODE, *The South East Asic Journal of Theology* (Singapore) 11 (1970) 107-108; H. BOERS, *Interpr* 24 (1970) 521-522; G.B. CAIRD, *JTS* 21 (1970) 159-160; J.A. FITZMYER, *TS* 30 (1969) 700-704; F.R.C., *RevistBíb* 33 (1971) 184-185; S. GONZÁLEZ DE CARREA, *EstBíb* 31 (1972) 228-229; H.W. HOEHNER, *BS* 127 (1970) 270; S.E. ISENBERG, *JBL* 89 (1970) 368-370; T. LARRIBA, *ScriptTheol* 2 (1970) 225-229; A.R.C. LEANEY, *Theology* 73 (1970) 140; I.H. MARSHALL, *ExpT* 81 (1969-70) 56; F. MARTIN, *CBQ* 32 (1970) 131-134; H.K. MCARTHUR, *JAAR* 38 (1970) 430-432; R.F. MCCASLIN, *RRel* 28 (1969) 1014-1015; J. MCHUGH, *CleR* 56 (1971) 293-294; J. MURPHY-O'CONNOR, *RB* 77 (1970) 627; J. POLHILL, *RExp* 67 (1970) 99-100; L. SABOURIN, *Bib* 51 (1970) 288-290; A. SALAS, *CiudDios* 183 (1970) 199-200; A. VÖGTLE, *LuthRundschau* 20 (1970) 110-111. S. GREENHALGH, *ScriptB* 21 (1991) 25; J.-M. ROUSÉE, *RB* 96 (1989) 317.

1974 Reflections on a Wisdom Approach to Matthew's Christology. — *CBQ* 36 (1974) 44-64. Esp. 45-53 [OT wisdom/Mt]; 53-64 [Q/Mt]. [NTA 18, 847r] → Suggs 1970

**JOHNSON, S. Lewis, Jr.**

1955 The Argument of Matthew. [kingdom] — *BS* 112 (1955) 143-153.

1956 The Message of John the Baptist. — *BS* 113 (1956) 30-35.

1965 The Genesis of Jesus. [1,18-25] — *BS* 122 (1965) 331-342. [NTA 10, 505]

1966a The Baptism of Christ. — *BS* 123 (1966) 220-229. Esp. 224-229 [3,13-17]. [NTA 11, 193]

1966b The Temptation of Christ. [4,1-11] — *Ibid.*, 342-352. [NTA 11, 693]

1967a The Transfiguration of Christ. [17,1-8] — *BS* 124 (1967) 133-143. [NTA 12, 160]

1967b The Triumphal Entry of Christ. [21,1-11] — *Ibid.*, 218-229. [NTA 12, 106]

1967c The Agony of Christ. [26,36-46] — *Ibid.*, 303-313. [NTA 12, 559]

1968 The Death of Christ. [27,45-46] — *BS* 125 (1968) 10-19. [NTA 12, 881]

**JOHNSON, Sherman Elbridge**

1951a The Gospel according to St. Matthew. Introduction and Exegesis by S.E. Johnson. Exposition by G.A. Buttrick. — BUTTRICK, G.A. (ed.), *The Interpreter's Bible*, VII, 1951, 229-625.

P. Benoit, *RB* 60 (1953) 445-446; W. Bieder, *TZ* 9 (1953) 372-375; L. Cerfaux, *ETL* 29 (1953) 97-98; F.V. Filson, *JBL* 72 (1953) 69-70; A.J.B. Higgins, *TTod* 10 (1953) 118-122; C.F.W. Smith, *ATR* 35 (1953) 37-41.

1951b Jesus and First-Century Galilee. — Schmauch, W. 5ED.), *In Memoriam Ernst Lohmeyer*, 1951, 73-88. Esp. 76-82 [Pharisees: 11,12; 12,22-32; 19,3-12; 23,23]; 82-84 [Galilee]; 84-86 [violence-peace]; 87-88 [eschatology].

1955 King Parables in the Synoptic Gospels. [17,24-27; 18,23-25; 20,1-15; 22,1-14; 25,31-46] — *JBL* 74 (1955) 37-39.

1966 *The Theology of the Gospels*. London: Duckworth, 1966, VIII-199 p. Esp. 50-64 [Mt]; 83-89 [Q: christology]; 92-95 [Sondergut]; 109-128 [kingdom]; 129-147 [God]; 147-172 [christological titles].

1968 The Davidic-Royal Motif in the Gospels. — *JBL* 87 (1968) 136-150. Esp. 140-143. [NTA 13, 98]

1990 The Message of Jesus to the Poor and the Powerful. — Hultgren, A.J. – Hall, B. (eds.), *Christ and His Communities*. FS R.H. Fuller = *ATR* SS 11 (1990) 16-28. Esp. 17-18 [5,3]; 18-21 [parables]; 22-23 [Q]. [NTA 34, 1115]

1991 *The Griesbach Hypothesis and Redaction Criticism* (SBL MS, 41). Atlanta, GA: Scholars, 1991, VII-172 p. Esp. 41-52: "The shape and theology of Matthew"; 77-84: "The reign of God"; 85-90: "The parables discourse"; 91-112: "Christology" [91-97: Mt; 105-112: Q]. [NTA 36, p. 110]
    O.W. Allen, *JBL* 113 (1994) 332-334; F. Neirynck, *ETL* 68 (1992) 436-437; D.C. Sim, *AusBR* 40 (1992) 82-84; C.M. Tuckett, *JSNT* 45 (1992) 121.

### Johnston, George

1976 New Testament Christology in a Pluralistic Age. — McKay, J.R. – Miller, J.F. (eds.), *Biblical Studies*. FS. W. Barclay, 1976, 178-193. Esp. 186-187 [Son of Man].

1992 Should the Synoptic Evangelists Be Considered as Theologians? — *StudRel/SciRel* 21 (1992) 181-190. Esp. 185-187. [NTA 37, 691]

### Johnston, Peter J.

1990 The Textual Character of the Textus Receptus (Received Text) where It Differs from the Majority Text in the Gospels of Matthew and Mark. — *Bulletin of the Institute for Reformed Biblical Studies* (Fort Wayne, IN) 2 (1990) 4-9. [NTA 35, 537]

### Johnston, Robert M.

1982 "The least of the commandments". Deuteronomy 22:6-7 in Rabbinic Judaism and Early Christianity. [5,19] — *AndrUnS* 20 (1982) 205-215. [NTA 27, 512]

### Jolliffe, Ronald L.

1990 *The Woes on the Pharisees: A Critical Text and Commentary on Q 11:46,43,52,42,39-40,44,47-48*. Diss. Graduate School, Claremont, CA, 1990, 203 p. (J.M. Robinson). — *DissAbstr* 51 (1990-91) 188.

### Joly, Robert

1968 *Le vocabulaire chrétien de l'amour est-il original? Φιλεῖν et ἀγαπᾶν dans le grec antique* (Institut d'histoire du christianisme). Brussel: Presses universitaires, 1968, 63 p. Esp. 51-53 [6,24; 10,37].

### Jones, Alan H.

1983 *Independence and Exegesis. The Study of Early Christianity in the Work of Alfred Loisy (1857-1940), Charles Guignebert (1857-1939), and Maurice Goguel (1880-1955)* (Beiträge zur Geschichte der biblischen Exegese, 26). Tübingen: Mohr, 1983, XI-302 p. Esp. 173-175 [Guignebert on Mt].

**JONES, Alexander**

1953    The Gospel of Jesus Christ according to Saint Matthew. — ORCHARD, B. – SUTCLIFFE, E.F. – FULLER, R.C. – RUSSELL, R. (eds.), *A Catholic Commentary on Holy Scripture*, Edinburgh: Nelson, 1953, ²1963, 851-904.

1965    *The Gospel according to St Matthew. A Text and Commentary for Students*. New York: Sheed & Ward, 1965, 334 p. Esp. 17-39: "Introduction"; 41-321: "The text of the gospel". [NTA 9, p. 431]

        H.B. GREEN, *Theology* 69 (1966) 471-472; S.K., *IrEcclRec* 105 (1966) 68-69; J. RYAN, *IrTQ* 33 (1966) 173-174; B. VAWTER, *CBQ* 27 (1965) 446-447; H.H. WERNECKE, *Interpr* 20 (1966) 111-112.

**JONES, C.**

1970    *Messianic Law. A Study of the "Law of Christ" in the Writings of Matthew and Paul against its Judaic Background*. Diss. Sheffield, 1970-71.

**JONES, Geraint Vaughan**

1964    *The Art and Truth of the Parables. A Study in Their Literary Form and Modern Interpretation*. London: SPCK, 1964, XII-250 p. Esp. 42-54 [formcritical]; 141-161 [classification]; 230-240 [gospel of Thomas].

**JONES, Ivor H.**

1985    Recent Work on the Parables. [13,34-43] — *EpworthR* 12 (1985) 89-96. [NTA 29, 917]

1994    *The Gospel of Matthew* (Epworth Commentaries). London: Epworth, 1994, XXII-175 p. [NTA 39, p. 325]

        N. CLARK, *ExpT* 106 (1994-95) 87.

1995    *The Matthean Parables. A Literary and Historical Commentary* (SupplNT, 80). Leiden: Brill, 1995, IX-602 p. Esp. 110-169: "The function of the Matthean parables"; 173-281: "The summary parables" [7,24-27; 11,16-19; 12,43-45; 13,52; 18,12-14.23-35; 25 31-46]; 282-358: "The chapter of parables"; 359-424: "Parables and Marcan contexts" [5,13-16; 20,1-16; 21,28-32.33-46; 22,1-14]; 425-481: "The eschatological parables" [24,32-33.42-44.45-51; 25,1-13.14-30]; 482-520: "The genitive absolute". [NTA 40, p. 340]

        N. CLARK, *ExpT* 106 (1994-95) 87.

**JONES, James L.**

1959    References to John the Baptist in the Gospel according to St. Matthew. — *ATR* 41 (1959) 298-302. [NTA 4, 381]

**JONES, John Mark**

1994    Subverting the Textuality of Davidic Messianism: Matthew's Presentation of the Genealogy and the Davidic Title. — *CBQ* 56 (1994) 256-272. Esp. 261-266 [1,17-23]; 266-270 [1,1-16]. [NTA 39, 794]

1995    "Think of the lilies" and Prov 6:6-11. — *HTR* 88 (1995) 175-177. [NTA 40, 877]

**JONES, J.E.**

1956    The Temptation Narrative. — *RExp* 53 (1956) 303-313.

**JONES, Peter Rhea**

1982    *The Teaching of the Parables*. Nashville, TN: Broadman, 1982, 263 p.

**JÓNSSON, Jakob**

1965    *Humour and Irony in the New Testament. Illuminated by Parallels in Talmud and Midrash*. Reykjavik: Menningarsjóds, 1965, 299 p. Esp. 90-165: "The synoptic gospels"; (Beihefte der Zeitschrift für Religions- und Geistgeschichte, 28), Leiden: Brill, 1985, 315 p.

**JOOSTEN, Jan**

1990    The Old Testament Quotations in the Old Syriac and Peshitta Gospels. A Contribution
        to the Study of the Diatessaron. — *Textus* (Jerusalem) 15 (1990) 55-76. Esp. 60-68. [NTA
        36, 94]

1991a   The Text of Matthew 13.21a and Parallels in the Syriac Tradition. — *NTS* 37 (1991)
        153-159. [NTA 35, 1135]

1991b   West Aramaic Elements in the Old Syriac and Peshitta Gospels. — *JBL* 110 (1991) 271-
        289. Esp. 272-281: "West Aramaic elements"; 281-283: "Evaluation"; 286-289: "Tatian's fifth source?".
        [NTA 36, 95]

1992    Two West Aramaic Elements in the Old Syriac and Peshitta Gospels. — *BibNoi* 61
        (1992) 17-21. Esp. 18-19 [10,38]; 20-21 [26,47]. [NTA 37, 87]

1996    *The Syriac Language of the Peshitta and Old Syriac Versions of Matthew. Syntactic
        Structure, Inner-Syriac Developments and Translation Technique* (Studies in Semitic
        Langages and Linguistics, 22). Leiden: Brill, 1996, XII-223 p. Esp. 5-30: "The Old-Syriac
        and Peshitta versions of Matthew" 31-76; "Syntax of the nominal phrase"; 77-96: "Syntax of the non-verbal
        clause"; 97-108: "Syntax of the *'it* clause"; 109-142: "Verbal syntax"; 143-152: "Inner Syriac
        developments"; 153-179: "Syntax and translation technique"; 181-213: "The non-verbal clauses contained in
        PCS of Matthew". [NTA 41, p. 146] — Diss. Jerusalem, 1988 (M.H. Goshen-Gottstein).

**JORDAN, Clarence**

1970    *Sermon on the Mount.* Valley Forge, PA: Judson, 1970, 126 p.
            R.D. CONGDON, *BS* 128 (1971) 183.

**JOSSA, Giorgio**

1989    *Dal Messia al Cristo. Le origini della cristologia* (Studi biblici, 88). Brescia: Paideia,
        1989, 191 p. Esp. 41-53 [prophet]; 53-79 [Messiah]; 122-128 [Son of Man]; 128-135 [Lord]; 125-150
        [Son of God]; 153-158 [parousia].

1991    *I cristiani e l'impero romano. Da Tiberio a Marco Aurelio* (Studi sul Giudaismo e sul
        Cristianesimo antico, 2). Napoli: D'Auria, 1991, 286 p. Esp. 72-76.

**JOUBERT, Stephan J.**

1993a   A Bone of Contention in Recent Scholarship: The "Birkat ha-Minim" and the
        Separation of Church and Synagogue in the First Century AD. — *Neotestamentica* 27
        (1993) 351-363. Esp. 356-357. [NTA 38, 1740]

1993b   Jesus van Nazaret se bevrydende visie vir 'n geweldadige samelewing (Jesus of
        Nazareth's liberating vision for a violent society). — *Skrif en Kerk* (Pretoria) 14 (1993)
        222-235. Esp. 229-231 [5,21-48]. [NTA 38, 1318]

1995    Much ado about Nothing? In Discussion with the Study of Evert-Jan Vledder: "Conflict
        in the Miracle Stories in Matthew 8 and 9: A Sociological and Exegetical Study". —
        *HervTS* 51 (1995) 245-253. [NTA 40, 170] → Vledder 1997/94

**JOURNET, Charles**

1953    *Primauté de Pierre dans la perspective protestante et dans la perspective catholique*
        (Sagesse et cultures). Paris: Alsatia, 1953, 153 p. Esp. 55-60 [28,16-20]; 85-114 [16,16-19]. →
        Cullmann 1952

1966    Le mariage indissoluble. — *NVet* 41 (1966) 44-62. Esp. 48-50; 53-57. [NTA 11, 447]

1968    Les Évangiles de l'Enfance et la critique historique. — *NVet* 43 (1968) 65-72. [NTA 13,
        154r] → Daniélou 1967

**JOUSTEN, Alois**

1967    La signification profonde de la foi chez les Synoptiques. — *RevEcclLiège* 53 (1967)
        374-382. Esp. 378-380 [8,5-13; 15,21-28]; 381-382 [8,18-27; 14,22-33].

De diepe betekenis van het geloof bij de synoptiekers. — *Diocesaan tijdschrift voor het bisdom Luik* 53 (1967) 227-236.

**JÓŹWIAK, Franciszek**

1974    "Jezusa kazał ubiczować i wydał na ukrzyżowanie". ["Jesus delivered to crucifixion"]. — *Ateneum Kaplanskie* (Wroclaw) 83 (1974) 29-43.

**JUDGE, Peter J.**

1989    Luke 7,1-10. Sources and Redaction. — NEIRYNCK, F. (ed.), *L'Évangile de Luc*, 1989, 473-490. Esp. 473-474: "Luke 7,1-10 as the tradition"; 477-478: "Mt 8,5-13 used by Luke"; 479-489: "Mt 8,5-10.13 closer to Q"; 489-490: "The context in Q".

1995    *Mt 8,5-13 / Lk 7,1-10: The Centurion from Capernaum. A History of Modern Interpretation.* Diss. Leuven, 1995, XXXII-223 p. (F. Neirynck).

**JÜCHEN, Aurel VON**

1985    *Jesus zwischen Reich und Arm. Mammonworte und Mammongeschichten im Neuen Testament* [6,24]. Stuttgart: Alektor, 1985, 129 p.

**JUEL, Donald H.**

1978    & ACKERMAN, J.S. – WARSHAW, T.S., *An Introduction to New Testament Literature.* Nashville, TN: Abingdon, 1978, 368 p.

1988    *Messianic Exegesis. Christological Interpretation of the Old Testament in Early Christianity.* Philadelphia, PA: Fortress, 1988, XII-193 p. Esp. 158-162 [Dan 7].

1992    The Lord's Prayer in the Gospels of Matthew and Luke. — *PrincSemB* suppl. 2 (1992) 56-70. [NTA 37, 143]

**JÜLICHER, Adolf**

1899R    *Die Gleichnisreden Jesu* [I, 1886, ²1899; II, 1899]. Darmstadt: Wissenschaftliche Buchgesellschaft, 1963, VII-328 p. and VIII-643 p. Esp. I, 1-25: "Die Echtheit der Gleichnisreden Jesu"; 25-118: "Das Wesen der Gleichnisreden"; 118-148: "Der Zweck"; 148-182: "Der Wert"; 183-202: "Die Aufzeichnung"; 202-322: "Geschichte der Auslegung"; II, 3-11 [24,32-33]; 23-36 [11,16-19]; 36-44 [7,9-11]; 44-50 [10,24-25]; 50-57 [15,10-20]; 67-91 [5,13.14-15]; 91-97 [10,26-27]; 98-115 [6,22-23.24]; 116-128 [7,16-20; 12,33-37]; 128-133 [13,52]; 133-161 [24,28.43-44.45-51]; 174-202 [9,12-13.14-15.16-17]; 214-240 [12,22-30.43-45]; 240-246 [5,25-26]; 254-259 [15,26-27]; 259-268 [7,24-27]; 302-333 [18,10-14.21-35]; 365-406 [21,28-32.33-46]; 407-433 [22,1-14]; 448-459 [25,1-13]; 459-471 [20,1-16]; 472-495 [25,14-30]; 514-538 [13,3-9.18-23]; 546-585 [13,24-30.31-33.36-43.44-46.47-50]. → Fiebig 1904

1938R    (ed.), *Matthäus-Evangelium* [1938] (Itala. Das Neue Testament in altlateinischer Überlieferung, 1), ed. W. Matzkow & K. Aland. Berlin – New York: de Gruyter, 2nd rev. ed., 1972, VIII-214 p.

> P.-M. BOGAERT, *RBén* 82 (1972) 240-241; *Bulletin d'ancienne littérature chrétienne latine* (Maredsous) 5 (1974) 240-241; J. DUPLACY, *Bib* 54 (1973) 97; I. GOMÁ CIVIT, *EstBíb* 33 (1974) 90-92; C. MARTIN, *NRT* 94 (1972) 649-650; R. SCHNACKENBURG, *BZ* 16 (1972) 258-259; J. VAN AMERSFOORT, *Bijdragen* 33 (1972) 453-454.

**JÜNGEL, Eberhard**

1962    *Paulus und Jesus. Eine Untersuchung zur Präzisierung der Frage nach dem Ursprung der Christologie* (Hermeneutische Untersuchungen zur Theologie, 2). Tübingen: Mohr, 1962, ²1964, ³1967, ⁵1979, XI-319 p. Esp. 87-215: "Jesus und die Gottesherrschaft" [13,24-30.44-46.47-48; 20,1-16]; 215-262: "Jesus und der Menschensohn" [10,23.32-33; 12,40; 19,28; 24,27.37-39.44]. Die Problematik der Gleichnisrede Jesu. [1962, 87-132] — HARNISCH, W. (ed.), *Gleichnisse Jesu*, 1982, 281-342.

**JULLIEN DE POMEROL, Patrice**

1980    *Quand un évangile nous est conté. Analyse morphologique du récit de Matthieu* (Collection "écritures", 3). Bruxelles: Lumen Vitae, 1980, 240 p. Esp. 31-200: "Analyse syntagmatique"; 201-223: "Vérification sur l'axe paradigmatique". [NTA 25, p. 86] — Diss. Paris, 1979 (M. Meslin – M. Houis).

X. A*legre*, *ActBibl* 19 (1982) 79-80; L.-M. ANTONIOTTI, *RThom* 82 (1982) 513-516; J. CALLOUD, *SémBib* 23 (1981) 57-60; J. DUPONT, *ComLtg* 62 (1980) 549-550; G. GAETA, *CrnStor* 6 (1985) 395-397; J. GUILLET, *RSR* 68 (1980) 581-584; A. PASQUIER, *Études* 353 (1980) 426; Y. SIMOENS, *NRT* 103 (1981) 773.

*Il vangelo come racconto. Analisi morfologica del vangelo di Matteo* (Bibbia/Linguaggio/Cultura, 5). Torino: Elle Di Ci, 1983, 248 p.

R. DELLA CASA, *Sal* 46 (1984) 355; S. MIGLIASSO, *ParVi* 30 (1985) 70-73.

**JUNACK, Klaus**

1969    Ein weiteres neutestamentliches Unzialfragment aus Damaskus (0255). — ALAND, K. (ed.), *Materialien*, 1969, 209-217.

1970    Zu einem neuentdeckten Unzialfragment des Matthäus-Evangeliums. [087] — *NTS* 16 (1969-70) 284-288. [NTA 15, 132] → I.A. Sparks 1969

**JURGENS, D.W.**

1983    *The Least. Contemporary Interpretations of the Judgment in Matthew 25:31-46.* Iowa City, IA: Privately published, 1983, XIV-156 p. Esp. 8-15 [J. Jeremias 1947]; 16-26 [J.A.T. Robinson 1956]; 27-60 [Catchpole 1979]; 61-70 [Michaels 1965]; 71-74 [Stendahl 1962]; 75-82 [Cope 1969]; 83-91 [Lambrecht 1972].

# K

**K'ADJAIA, Lamara**

1989    *Die älteste georgische Vier-Evangelien-Handschrift*. I. *Prolegomena*, trans. H. Greeven – M. Job. Bochum: Brockmyere, 1989, XI-99 p.

**KÄHLER, Christoph**

1974    *Studien zur Form- und Traditionsgeschichte der biblischen Makarismen* [5,3-12]. Diss. Jena, 1974, III-272 p. → 1976

1976    Zur Form- und Traditionsgeschichte von Matth. xvi.17-19. — *NTS* 23 (1976-77) 36-58. Esp. 36-46: "Zu Mar. viii.27-33 und Matth. xvi.13-23"; 46-55: "Die formgeschichtlichen Parallelen zu Matth. xvi.17-19" [4 Ezra 10,57; JosAsen 16,14; Henoch 4,9; Memar Marqah 2,9; EvBarthol 1,8; ApocPauli; Pistis Sophia; ApocMariae]. [NTA 21, 382] → 1974

1989    Kirchenleitung und Kirchenzucht nach Matthäus 18. — KERTELGE, K., et al., *Christus bezeugen*. FS W. Trilling, 1989, 136-145. Esp. 136 [18,17] 136-137 [Qumran]; 138-139 [18,15-17]; 139-145 [ἁμαρτάνω].

1994    Satanischer Schriftgebrauch: Zur Hermeneutik von Mt 4,1-11/Lk 4,1-13. — *TLZ* 119 (1994) 857-868. [NTA 39, 798]

1995    *Jesu Gleichnisse als Poesie und Therapie. Versuch eines integrativen Zugangs zum kommunikativen Aspekt von Gleichnissen Jesu* (WUNT, 78). Tübingen: Mohr, 1995, IX-265 p. Esp. 117-134 [22,1-14]; 164-190 [25,14-30]. — Diss. Jena, 1992.

**KÄHLER, Martin**

1892[R]    *Der sogenannte historische Jesus und der geschichtliche, biblische Christus* [1892, ²1896] (Theologische Bücherei, 2), ed. E. Wolf. München: Kaiser, 1953, 80 p.; ²1956, 126 p. *The So-Called Historical Jesus and the Historic Biblical Christ*, trans. & ed. with an Introduction by C.E. Braaten [1-38], foreword by P.J. Tillich (Seminar Editions). Philadelphia, PA: Fortress, 1964, 153 p. Trans. Italian 1992.

**KÄSEMANN, Ernst**

1955    Sätze heiligen Rechtes im Neuen Testament. — *NTS* 1 (1954-55) 248-260. Esp. 256-257 [10,32-33]; = ID., *Exegetische Versuche und Besinnungen*, II, 1964, 69-82. Esp. 78-79; = ID., *Exegetische Versuche und Besinningen. Auswahl*, 1936, 96-109. Esp. 105-106. → K. Berger 1970b
Sentences of Holy Law in the New Testament. — ID., *New Testament Questions*, 1969, 66-81. Esp. 77.
Un droit sacré dans le Nouveau Testament. — ID., *Essais exégétiques*, 1972, 227-241. Esp. 237-238.

1960    Die Anfänge christlicher Theologie. — *ZTK* 57 (1960) 162-185. Esp. 164-165 [23,8-10]; 165-166 [5,17-20]; 172-173 [10,13-15]. [NTA 5, 703]; = ID., *Exegetische Versuche und Besinnungen*, II, 1964, 82-104. Esp. 84-85; 85-86; 93-94; = ID., *Exegetische Versuche und Besinningen. Auswahl*, 1986, 110-132. Esp. 112-113; 113-114; 121-122. → Ebeling 1961, E. Fuchs 1961
The Beginnings of Christian Theology. — ID., *New Testament Questions*, 1969, 82-107. Esp. 84-85; 85-86; 94-95.
Les débuts de la théologie chrétienne. — ID., *Essais exégétiques*, 1972, 174-198. Esp. 176-177; 177-178; 186-187.

1964    *Exegetische Versuche und Besinnungen. Zweiter Band*. Göttingen: Vandenhoeck & Ruprecht, 1964, 304 p. → 1955, 1960
*Exegetische Versuche und Besinnungen. Erster und zweiter Band*. Göttingen: Vandenhoeck & Ruprecht, 1964 (I³ + II), 1965 (I⁴ + II²), 1967 (I⁵ + II³), 1970 (I⁶ + II⁴).
*Exegetische Versuche und Besinnungen. Auswahl*. Göttingen: Vandenhoeck & Ruprecht, 1986, 194 p.

*New Testament Questions of Today*, trans. W.J. Montague (The New Testament Library). London: SCM, 1969, XIII-305 p.

*Essais exégétiques*, trans. D. Appia (Le Monde de la Bible, 3). Neuchâtel: Delachaux & Niestlé, 1972, 271 p.

*Ensayos exegéticos*. Salamanca: Sígueme, 1978, 299 p.

**KAESTLI, Jean-Daniel**

1994 La place du *Fragment de Muratori* dans l'histoire du canon. À propos de la thèse de Sundberg et Hahneman. [A.C. Sundberg, *HTR* 66 (1973) 1-41] — *CrnStor* 15 (1994) 609-634. Esp. 630-634 [Chromatius of Aquileia]. [NTA 39, 1279] → Hahneman 1992

**KAHANE, Henry**

1957 & KAHANE, Renée, Pearls Before Swine? A Reinterpretation of Matt. 7.6. — *Traditio* (New York) 13 (1957) 421-424. [NTA 3, 73]

**KAHL, Werner**

1994 *New Testament Miracle Stories in their Religious-Historical Setting. A religions-geschichtliche Comparison from a Structural Perspective* (FRLANT, 163). Göttingen: Vandenhoeck & Ruprecht, 1994, 259 p. Esp. 91-93.166-173.177-185 [8,5-13]; 91-93.108-109 [15,21-28]; 133-135 [9,18-26]; 185-187 [9,27-31]; 197-201 [17,14-20]. — Diss. Emory Univ., Atlanta, GA, 1992 (H.W. Boers).

**KAHLE, Paul E.**

1954 *Bala 'izah I*. London, 1954. Esp. 399-402 [7,28-29; 8,3-4.7-9].

**KAHLEFELD, Heinrich**

1959 Die Oster-Evangelien. Bericht und Verkündigung. — FISCHER, B. – WAGNER, J. (eds.), *Paschatis Sollemnia. Festschrift für J.A. Jungmann*, Freiburg: Herder, 1959, 25-31. Esp. 30-31 [28,16-20]; = ID., *Kleine Schriften*, 1984, 9-22. Esp. 20-22.

1961 *Der Jünger. Eine Auslegung der Rede Lk 6,20-49*. Frankfurt/M: Knecht, 1961, 156 p. Esp. 12-21.

1962 Was fordert die Bergpredigt? — *TJb*, 1962, 210-223.

1963 *Gleichnisse und Lehrstücke im Evangelium*. Frankfurt/M: Knecht, 1963, 2 vols., 192 and 197 p. Esp. I, 26-28 [13,33]; 53-62 [13,24-30]; 63-65 [13,47-50]; 65-72 [13,36-43]; 79-93 [21,33-41]; 93-114 [22,1-14]; 122-126 [24,45-51]; 131-140 [25,1-13]; 149-170 [25,14-30]; 171-176 [13,44-46]; II, 13-22 [21,28-32]; 35-45 [20,1-15]; 128-136 [18,23-35]; 138-149 [kingdom].
*Parables and Instructions in the Gospels*, I, trans. A. Swidler. Montreal: Palm, 1966, 174 p. Esp. 26-27; 51-58; 58-60; 60-66; 72-80; 80-102; 108-112; 117-124; 132-150; 150-155.
*Parábolas y ejemplos del evangelio*, trans. R. Velasco. Estella: Verbo Divino, 1967, 333 p.
*Paraboles et leçons dans l'évangile*, trans. G. Bret (LD, 55-56). Paris: Cerf, I, 1969, 152 p. Esp. 20-22; 44-50; 50-53; 53-59; 66-77; 77-93; 100-103; 108-115; 125-142; 142-146; II, 1970, 144 p. Esp. 9-17; 27-35; 102-108; 111-118.

1970 Die Gestalt des Täufers in den Evangelien. — *BK* 25 (1970) 20-23. [NTA 15, 70]; = ID., *Kleine Schriften*, 1984, 161-169.

1981 *Die Gestalt Jesu in den synoptischen Evangelien*. Frankfurt/M: Knecht, 1981, 264 p. Esp. 170-183 [Sermon on the Mount].

1984 *Kleine Schriften. Aufsätze aus den Jahren 1959 bis 1979*. Frankfurt/M: Knecht, 1984, 344 p. → 1959, 1970

**KAHMANN, Johannes J.A.**

1961 Het volgen van Christus door zelfverloochening en kruisdragen. Een beschouwing van Mk. 8,34-38 en parallelplaatsen. — *TijdTheol* 1 (1961) 205-226 (French summary, 225-226). Esp. 221-222 [16,24-27/Mk]. [NTA 6, 789]

1964 *Het Evangelie van het Koninkrijk. Hoofdstuk 5: De Bergrede* (De Bazuin, 47). Nijmegen, 1964, 23 p.

1972 Die Verheissung an Petrus. *Mt.*, XVI,18-19 im Zusammenhang des Matthäusevangeliums. — DIDIER, M. (ed.), *L'Évangile selon Matthieu*, 1972, 261-280. Esp. 261-264:
"Simon als Fels und Petrus als Satan"; 264-269 [16,18/OT–Qumran]; 270-272 [14,28-31; 16,18-19; 17,24-
27]; 272-280: "Sitz im Leben".

**KAHN, Jean Georges**

1971 La parabole du figuier stérile et les arbres récalcitrants de la Genèse. — *NT* 13 (1971)
38-45. Esp. 39-41 [21,18-22]; 45 [10,9]. [NTA 16, 183]

**KAISER, Odilo**

1970 *Die ersten drei Evangelien. Einführung in ihre literarische und theologische Gestalt*
(Der Christ in der Welt, VI. Reihe, Das Buch der Bücher, 8b/c). Aschaffenburg:
Pattloch, 1970, 269 p. Esp. 42-52: "*Evangelium* in der Verkündigungsschrift des Matthäus"; 67-69;
97-131: "Die Aufschlüsselung der Stoffe der evangelischen Überlieferung"; 163-207: "Das Beispiel des
Matthäus-Evangeliums".

1975 Menschensohn, Menschensohnforschung und praktische Verkündigung. Überlegungen
zur Dialektik von Autonomie und Finalisierung neutestamentlicher Wissenschaft. —
PESCH, R., et al. (eds.), *Jesus und der Menschensohn*. FS A. Vögtle, 1975, 435-488.
Esp. 464-469: "Eine Paradigmatik: das entfaltete Modell der Menschensohnchristologie im
Matthäusevangelium"; 469-475: "Zur 'Rückführung' eines entfalteten (matthäischen) Modells der
Menschensohnchristologie auf den historischen Jesus".

**KAISER, Walter C.**

1975 The Weighthier and Lighter Matters of the Law: Moses, Jesus, and Paul. —
HAWTHORNE, G.F. (ed.), *Current Issues in Biblical and Patristic Interpretation*. FS
M.C. Tenney, 1975, 176-192. Esp. 183-185 [22,36; 23,23].

1982 The Promise of the Arrival of Elijah in Malachi and the Gospels. — *GraceTJ* 3 (1982)
221-233. Esp. 229-233. [NTA 27, 478]

**KAI-YUNG CHANG, Anna**

1993a *Il Padre Nostro nei principali commenti patristici e il suo uso nella liturgia latina*
(Pontificium Athenaeum S. Anselmi in Urbe. Theses ad lauream, 181). Roma: San
Anselmo, 1993, 330 p.
E. BEST, *ExpT* 105 (1993-94) 218.

1993b Il rito della consegna del *Padre nostro* (Mt 6,9-13) nei *Sermoni LVI-LIX* di
Sant'Agostino di Ipona. — *Ecclesia Orans* 10 (1993) 287-312.

**KALIN, Everett R.**

1988 Matthew 9:18-26: An Exercise in Redaction Criticism. — *CurrTMiss* 15 (1988) 39-47.
[NTA 32, 598]

**KALLAS, James Gus**

1961 *The Significance of the Synoptic Miracles* (SPCK Biblical Monographs, 2). London:
SPCK, 1961, VIII-118 p. Esp. 9-13.24-37 [kingdom]; 80-81.100-101.

1968a *Jesus and the Power of Satan*. Philadelphia, PA: Westminster, 1968, 215 p. Esp. 28-32:
"The special interest of Matthew"; 94-101: "The virgin birth narratives"; 141-151: "The sermon and the
parables".

1968b *John and the Synoptics – A Discussion of Some of the Differences between Them*. Diss.
Univ. of Southern California, 1968, IV-557 p. Esp. 105-112; 118-120; 286-289 [3,14-15/Jn]. —
*DissAbstr* 29 (1968-69) 319.

**KALLIKUZHUPPIL, John**

1984 The Greater Righteousness. — *Bible Bhashyam* 10 (1984) 89-105. [NTA 29, 519]

1985 The Church and the Kingdom of God in the Synoptic Gospels. A Comparative and Synthetic Study. — *Jeevadhara* 15 (1985) 85-93. [NTA 30, 554]

**KALUZA, Zénon**

1985 Le traité de Pierre d'Ailly sur l'Oraison dominicale. — *FZPT* 32 (1985) 273-293.

**KAMLAH, Ehrhard**

1963 Die Parabel vom ungerechten Verwalter (Luk. 19,1ff.) im Rahmen der Knechtsgleichnisse. — BETZ, O., et al. (eds.), *Abraham unser Vater*. FS O. Michel, 1963, 276-294. Esp. 284-286.290-293.

1964 *Die Form der katalogischen Paränese im Neuen Testament* (WUNT, 7). Tübingen: Mohr, 1964, VIII-245 p. Esp. 24-26 [5,3-12; 25,31-46]. — Diss. Mainz, 1961 (O. Michel).

1968 Kritik und Interpretation der Parabel von den anvertrauten Geldern. Mt. 25,14ff.; Lk. 19,12ff. — *KerDog* 14 (1968) 28-38. [NTA 13, 178]

**KAMPEN, John**

1990 A Reexamination of the Relationship between Matthew 5:21-48 and the Dead Sea Scrolls. — *SBL 1990 Seminar Papers*, 34-59. Esp. 36-44: "The form of the antitheses"; 44-58: "The content of the antitheses". → 1994b

1994a The Matthean Divorce Texts Reexamined. [5,31-32; 19,1-9] — BROOKE, G.J. (ed.), *New Qumran Texts and Studies. Proceedings of the First Meeting of the International Organization for Qumran Studies, Paris 1992* (Studies on the Texts of the Desert of Judah, 15), Leiden: Brill, 1994, 149-167.

1994b The Sectarian Form of the Antitheses within the Social World of the Matthean Community. — *Dead Sea Discoveries* (Leiden) 1 (1994) 338-363. Esp. 343-357: "Rhetorical analysis of the antitheses". [NTA 39, 1447] → 1990

**KAMPHAUS, Franz**

1965 Die Wunderberichte der Evangelien. — *BibLeb* 6 (1965) 122-135. [NTA 10, 473] *SelT* 9 (1970) 86-88.

1968 *Von der Exegese zur Predigt. Über die Problematik einer schriftgemäßen Verkündigung der Oster-, Wunder- und Kindheitsgeschichten.* Mainz: Matthias-Grünewald, 1968, ²1968, 363 p. Esp. 33-35 [28,1-10]; 43-45 [28,16-20]; 124-125.178-180 [9,1-8]; 129-131.189-191 [8,23-27]; 140-142 [14,13-21; 15,32-39]; 232-240 [1-2]; 280-296 [2,1-12]. — Diss. Münster, 1967 (T. Filthaut). *De paasverhalen*, trans. H. Biezeno (Van exegese tot verkondiging, 1). Boxtel: Katholieke Bijbelstichting, 1970, 102 p; ²1973; = 1968, 21-112. *De Kindsheidverhalen bij Lucas en Matteüs* (Van exegese tot verkondiging, 2). Boxtel: Katholieke Bijbelstichting, 1970, 112 p.; ²1974; = 1968, 209-306. *De wonderverhalen in de evangelies* (Van exegese tot verkondiging, 3). Boxtel: Katholieke Bijbelstichting, 1971, 99 p.; ²1973; = 1968, 113-208.

1971 Zwischen Abfall und Nachfolge. Auslegung und Besinnung zu Mt 16,21-28. — *BibLeb* 12 (1971) 48-54. [NTA 16, 540]

**KAMPLING, Rainer**

1984 *Das Blut Christi und die Juden. Mt 27,25 bei den lateinischsprachigen christlichen Autoren bis zu Leo dem Grossen* (NTAbh, NF 16). Münster: Aschendorf, 1984, VIII-260 p. Esp. 16-61: "Mt 27,25 bei Autoren des zweiten und dritten Jahrhunderts"; 62-117: "Mt 27,25 bei Ambrosius, Hieronymus und Augustinus"; 197-218: "Mt 27,25 in Predigten des fünften Jahrhunderts – Ps-Augustinus und Leo der Große"; 219-231: "Hauptmotive des Verständnisses von Mt 27,25". [NTA 29, p. 205] — Diss. Münster, 1983 (K. Kertelge).

E. BAMMEL, *TRev* 84 (1988) 369-370; J. DOIGNON, *RHPR* 66 (1986) 352-353; W.-D. HAUSCHILD, *Zeitschrift für Kirchengeschichte* (Stuttgart) 98 (1987) 411-412; L. LIES, *ZKT* 115 (1993) 209; M. PARMENTIER, *Bijdragen* 49 (1988) 450-452; K.H. SCHELKLE, *Freiburger Rundbrief* 35-36 (1983-84) 127; R. VICENT, *Sal* 47 (1985) 322.

1986 Jesus von Nazareth – Lehrer und Exorzist. — *BZ* 30 (1986) 237-248. Esp. 241.247 [12,27-28]. [NTA 31, 548]

1990 Neutestamentliche Text als Bausteine der späteren Adversus-Judaeos-Literatur. — FROHNHOFEN, H. (ed.), *Christlicher Antijudaismus und jüdischer Antipaganismus: ihre Motive und Hintergründe in den ersten drei Jahrhunderten* (Hamburger theologische Studien, 3), Hamburg: Steinmann, 1990, 121-138.

**KANG, Chang-Hee**

1987 *The Literary Affinities of the Sermon on the Mount with Special Reference to Deuteronomic Features.* Diss. Fuller Theol. Sem., Pasadena, CA, 1987, 340 p. — *DissAbstr* 48 (1987-88) 156; *SBT* 16 (1988) 129-130.

**KANNENGIESSER, Charles**

1974 *Foi en la résurrection. Résurrection de la foi* (Le point théologique, 9). Paris: Beauchesne, 1974, 156 p. Esp. 122-124 [28,1-10].

**KANTZENBACH, Friedrich W.**

1982 *Die Bergpredigt. Annäherung – Wirkungsgeschichte.* Stuttgart: Kohlhammer, 1982, 158 p. [NTA 27, p. 332] → Frankemölle 1983c
W. LÖSER, *TheolPhil* 58 (1983) 247-248; W. SOMMER, *ZRelGeis*‧ 36 (1984) 381-382; A. STÖGER, *BLtg* 56 (1983) 123.

**KANY, Roland**

1995 Die Frau des Pilatus und ihr Name: Ein Kapitel aus der Geschichte neutestamentlicher Wissenschaft. [27,19] — *ZNW* 86 (1995) 104-110. [NTA 40, 179]

**KAPELRUD, Arvid S.**

1980 The Gates of Hell and the Guardian Angels of Paradise. [16,18] — *Journal of the American Oriental Society* (New Haven, CT) 70 (1980) 151-156; = ID., *God and His Friends in the Old Testament*, Oslo: Universitetsforlaget, 1979, 191-194.

**KARAVIDÓPOULOS, Johannes D.**

1968 The Power of the Salt in the Logion of Jesus in Mark 9,49-50; Luke 14,34-35; Matt. 5,13. [Greek] — *Θεολογία* (Athens) 39 (1968) 386-393.

1969 The Parable of the Lamp in the Synoptic Gospels. [Greek] [5,15] — *Gregorios Palamas* (Thessaloniki) 52 (1969) 165-172.

1971 Ein Agraphon in einem liturgischen Text der griechischen Kirche. [18,21-22] — *ZNW* 62 (1971) 299-300. [NTA 16, 1027] → G. Schwarz 1985b

1992 Le rôle de Pierre et son importance dans l'Église du Nouveau Testament: problématique exégétique contemporaine. — *Nicolaus. Rivista di teologia ecumenico-patristica* (Bari) 19 (1992) 13-29. Esp. 18-21.

1994 Citation de Zacharie dans le Nouveau Testament. [21,5; 26,3; 27,9-10] — *DeltBM* 23/1 (1994) 48-55. [NTA 39, 731]

**KARLEEN, Paul Stuart**

1980 *The Syntax of the Participle in the Greek New Testament.* Diss. Univ. of Pennsylvania, 1980, VI-244 p. (H. Hiz).

**KARNETZKI, Manfred**

1955 *Die alttestamentlichen Zitate in der synoptischen Tradition.* Diss. Tübingen, 1955, X-316 p. — *TLZ* 81 (1956) 492-493.

1956 Textgeschichte als Überlieferungsgeschichte. — *ZNW* 47 (1956) 170-180. Esp. 171-174; 176-179. [NTA 2, 5]

**KARPIŃSKI, Ryszard**

1965 Nierozerwalność małżeństwa w Nowym Testamencie. Mt 5,32 i 19,9. [The indissolubility of marriage in the New Testament] — *RuBi* 18 (1965) 77-88. [NTA 10, 114]

1968 'Εξουσία à la base de l'enseignement de Jésus et de la mission apostolique selon S. Matthieu (Studia ecclesiastica, 9. Biblica, 1). Roma: Institutum studiorum ecclesiasticorum, 1968, XVII-110 p. — Diss. Angelicum, Roma, 1968.
F. KŁONIECKI, *Studia Gnesnensia* (Gniezno) 1 (1975) 283-284; B. PIEPIÓRKA, *ZKT* 93 (1971) 221-222.

1969 Władza nauczycielska Chrystusa w Ewangelii św. Mateusza. [Christ as teacher in Matthew]. — *RuBi* 22 (1969) 206-213. [NTA 14, 468]

**KARRER, Martin**

1990 *Der Gesalbte. Die Grundlagen des Christustitels* (FRLANT, 151). Göttingen: Vandenhoeck & Ruprecht, 1990, 482 p. Esp. 280-283 [Son of David]. — Diss. Erlangen-Nürnberg, 1988-89 (J. Roloff).

1992 Der lehrende Jesus. Neutestamentliche Erwägungen. — *ZNW* 83 (1992) 1-20. Esp. 4-5 [Q 6,40]; 16-18 [διδάσκαλος]. [NTA 37, 348]

1993 Christliche Gemeinde und Israel. Beobachtungen zur Logienquelle. — MOMMER, P., et al. (eds.), *Gottes Recht als Lebensraum. Festschrift Hans Jochen Boecker*, Neukirchen-Vluyn: Neukirchener, 1993, 145-163. Esp. 146-153 [Temple]; 153-156 [John the Baptist]; 156-159 [Q 7,1-10]; 159-160 [Q 22,28-30].

**KARRER, Otto**

1953 *Um die Einheit der Christen. Die Petrusfrage. Ein Gespräch mit Emil Brunner, Oskar Cullmann, Hans von Campenhausen.* Frankfurt/M: Knecht/Carolusdruckerei, 1953, 228 p. Esp. 91-105: "Der Primat des Petrus". → Cullmann 1952
*Peter and the Church. An Examination of Cullmann's Thesis*, trans. R. Walls (QDisp, 8). London – New York: Herder & Herder, 1963, 141 p.

1955 Apostolische Nachfolge und Primat. Ihre biblischen Grundlagen im Licht der neueren Theologie. — *ZKT* 77 (1955) 129-168. Esp. 151-163: "Zur Primatsverheißung Mt 16,17-19".

1968 Simon Petrus, Jünger, Apostel, Felsenfundament. — *BK* 23 (1968) 37-43. Esp. 38-40 [16,13-19]. [NTA 13, 167]

**KASSELOURIS, H.**

1994 The Narrative on the Confession of Peter (Mt 16,13-20 par.) and on the Anointing of Jesus (Mt 26,6-13 par.). Parallel Messianic Narratives?. [Greek] — *DeltBM* 23 (1994) 27-33. [NTA 40, 174]

**KASSER, Rodolphe**

1962 (ed.), *Papyrus Bodmer XIX. Évangile de Matthieu XIV,28–XXVIII,20. Épître aux Romains I,1–II,3 en sahidique.* Cologny–Genève: Bibliotheca Bodmeriana, 1962, 256 p. Esp. 47-229.

**KASSING, Altfrid**

1965 Die Glaubensentscheidungen Jesu (Mt 4,1-11). — *Am Tisch des Wortes* (Stuttgart) 8 (1965) 30-40.

1969 *Auferstanden für uns. Eine Auslegung der neutestamentlichen Osterbotschaft.* Mainz: Matthias-Grünewald, 1969, 176 p. Esp. 56-59 [28,1-10]; 73-76 [28,16-20].

**KASTING, Heinrich**

1969 *Die Anfänge der urchristlichen Mission. Eine historische Untersuchung* (BEvT, 55). München: Kaiser, 1969, 158 p. Esp. 34-38 [28,18-20].

**KASTNER, Joseph M.**

1967 *Moses im Neuen Testament. Eine Untersuchung der Mosestraditionen in den neutestamentlichen Schriften.* Diss. München, 1967, 385 p.

**KATZ, Friedrich**

1973 *Luke 9,52–11,36. Beobachtungen zur Logienquelle und ihrer hellenistisch-judenchristlichen Redaktion.* Diss. Mainz, 1973, III-337 p. (F. Hahn).

**KATZ, Peter**

1954 Πῶς αὐξάνουσιν Matt. VI.28. — *JTS* 5 (1954) 207-209. → Glasson 1962

**KAVANAGH, Denis J.**

1951 (trans.), *Saint Augustine. Commentary on the Lord's Sermon on the Mount. With Seventeen Related Sermons* (The Fathers of the Church. A New Translation, 11). New York: Fathers of the Church Inc., 1951, VI-388 p.; repr. Washington, DC: CUA, 1963, 1977, VI-382 p. Esp. 17-199 [5–7]; 201-208 [Retractationes: 5–7]; 211-226 [LIII: 5,3-8]; 227-232 [LIV: 5,16; 6,1]; 233-238 [LV: 5,23]; 239-257 [LVI: 6,9-13]; 259-292 [LX-LXI.LXXII: on almsgiving]; 293-295 [XCIV: 25,14-30]; 295-299 [CIX: 5,25]; 357-371 [XI: 5,3-10].

**KAY, Richard** → Post 1955

**KAYALAPARAMPIL, Thomas**

1984 The Missionary Discourse in the Gospel of Matthew. — *Bible Bhashyam* 10 (1984) 247-256. [NTA 30, 118]

1990 Passion and Resurrection in the Gospel of Matthew. — *Bible Bhashyam* 16 (1990) 41-51. Esp. 44-50 [28,1-10]. [NTA 35, 149]

**KAYE, Bruce N.**

1990 "One Flesh" and Marriage. [19,4-5] — *Colloquium* 22 (1990) 46-57. [NTA 35, 163]

**KAZMIERSKI, Carl R.**

1979 *Jesus, the Son of God. A Study of the Markan Tradition and Its Redaction by the Evangelist* (FzB, 33). Würzburg: Echter, 1979, XV-247 p. Esp. 50-53 [12,18]; 131-133.145.148-149 [11,25-27]. — Diss. Würzburg, 1977 (R. Schnackenburg).

1987 The Stones of Abraham: John the Baptist and the End of Torah (Matt 3,7-10 par. Luke 3,7-9). — *Bib* 68 (1987) 22-40. Esp. 22-25: "Problems and prospects"; 25-29: "Unpacking the tradition"; 30-34: "The origin of the apocalyptic tradition about John the Baptist"; 34-38: "The social context of the development of the Baptist tradition"; 38-39: "Patterns of development". [NTA 32, 113]

**KEA, Perry V.**

1983 *Discipleship in the Great Sermon. A Literary-critical Approach.* Diss. Univ. of Virginia, Charlotteville, VA, 1983, 425 p. — *DissAbstr* 47 (1986-87) 1369-1370.

1986 The Sermon on the Mount: Ethics and Eschatological Time. — *SBL 1986 Seminar Papers*, 88-98. Esp. 92-98.

1990 Salting the Salt. Q 14:34-35 and Mark 9:49-50. — *Forum* 6 (1990) 239-244. [NTA 38, 214]

1991 Dan Via as New Testament Critic in the Existentialist Mode. A Review Article. — *PerspRelSt* 18 (1991) 249-259. [NTA 36, 833] → Via 1990

1994 Writing a *bios*: Matthew's Genre Choices and Rhetorical Situation. — *SBL 1994 Seminar Papers*, 574-586.

**KEALY, Sean P.**

1979 The Modern Approach to Matthew. — *BTB* 9 (1979) 165-178. [NTA 24, 404]

1990   *Jesus and Politics* (Zacchaeus Studies: New Testament). Collegeville, MN: Liturgical Press, 1990, 96 p.

**KEARNEY, Peter J.**

1980   He Appeared to 500 Brothers (1 Cor. xv 6). — *NT* 22 (1980) 264-284. Esp. 274 [28,16-20]. [NTA 25, 197]

**KEARNS, Rollin**

1986   *Das Traditionsgefüge um den Menschensohn. Ursprünglicher Gestalt und älteste Veränderung im Urchristentum.* Tübingen: Mohr, 1986, V-202 p. Esp. 8-20.

1988   *Die Entchristologisierung des Menschensohnes. Die Übertragung des Traditionsgefüges um den Menschensohn auf Jesus.* Tübingen: Mohr, 1988, V-209 p. Esp. 49-56 [24,27.37]; 71-86 [8,20; 11,19; 12,32]; 97-99 [Q 6,22(Lk)]; 110-113: "Die matthäische Redaktion" [13,37; 17,9; 26,2]; 127-130: "Die Redaktion der Spruchsammlung Q" [Q 17,30]; 130-134 [Q 12,8(Lk)]; 137-149: "Die matthäische Redaktion" [10,23; 13,41; 25,31].

**KEARSLEY, R.A.** → Llewelyn 1992, 1994a

**KEATING, John P.**

1969   The Moral Teaching of Jesus in the Synoptics. — *BiTod* 45 (1969) 3114-3118. [NTA 14, 465]

**KECK, Leander E.**

1962   An Exegesis of Matthew 16:13-20. — *Foundations* (Rochester, NY) 5 (1962) 226-237.

1965   The Poor among the Saints in the New Testament. — *ZNW* 56 (1965) 100-129. Esp. 112-116. [NTA 10, 458]

1970   The Spirit and the Dove. — *NTS* 17 (1970-71) 41-67. Esp. 53-54.58-61 [3,16]. [NTA 15, 518]

1971   The Sermon on the Mount. — MILLER, D.G. - HADIDIAN, D.Y. (eds.), *Jesus and Man's Hope.* II, 1971, 311-322.

1980   Ethos and Ethics in the New Testament. — GAFFNEY, J. (ed.), *Essays in Morality and Ethics. The Annual Publication of the College Theology Society,* New York: Paulist, 1980, 29-49. Esp. 38-45.

1983   Ethics in the Gospel according to Matthew. — *Iliff Review* (Denver, CO) 40 (1983) 39-56. [NTA 28, 908]

1995   Matthew and the Spirit. — WHITE, L.M. - YARBROUGH, O.L. (eds.), *The Social World of the First Christians. Essays in Honor of Wayne A. Meeks,* Minneapolis, MN: Fortress, 1995, 145-155. Esp. 147-149 [28,16-20]; 149-153: "Ambivalence toward spirit activity".

**KEE, Alistair**

1969   The Question about Fasting. [9,14-15] — *NT* 11 (1969) 161-173. [NTA 14, 504]

1970   The Old Coat and the New Wine. A Parable of Repentance. [9,16-17] — *NT* 12 (1970) 13-21. [NTA 14, 867]

**KEE, Howard Clark**

1957   & YOUNG, F.W., *Understanding the New Testament.* Englewood Cliffs, NJ: Prentice Hall, 1957, [2]1963, XVIII-492 p. Esp. 320-322: "The Jewishness of Matthew's gospel".
       & YOUNG, F.W. - FROELICH, K. [3]1973, XV-446 p. Esp. 422-423: "Appendix II: A reconstruction of Q" (F.C. Grant).
       [4]1983, X-408 p. Esp. 86-96: "The Q Source"; 391-393: "Appendix III: The Q Source: A Formal Analysis"; [5]1993, X-436 p.
       *De wereld van het Nieuwe Testament,* trans. S.G. Oosterhoff (Bibliotheek van boeken bij de Bijbel, 24/27/32). Baarn: Bosch en Keuning, s.d., 216, 148 and 176 p.; 1979, 535 p.

1963   "Becoming a Child" in the Gospel of Thomas. — *JBL* 82 (1963) 307-314. Esp. 309 [11,12/Th 46]. [NTA 8, 748]

1970  *Jesus in History. An Approach to the Study of the Gospels.* New York: Harcourt, Brace
      & World, 1970, VIII-280 p. Esp. 62-103: "Jesus as God's eschatological messenger: The Q document";
      144-161: "Jesus in the history of the church: the gospel of Matthew"; New York: Harcourt, Brace,
      Jovanovich, [2]1977, VIII-312 p. Esp. 76-120; 166-185.

1971  The Gospel according to Matthew. — LAYMAN, C.M (ed.), *The Interpreter's One-
      Volume Commentary on the Bible*, Nashville, TN – New York: Abingdon, 1971, 609-
      643.

1980  *Christian Origins in Sociological Perspective.* London: SCM, 1980, 206 p. Esp. 135-137
      [Q]; 140-143 [Mt].

1982  Christology and Ecclesiology: Titles of Christ and Models of Community. — *SBL 1982
      Seminar Papers*, 227-242. Esp. 237-239 [Q]; 239-240 [2,1-12]: = *Semeia* 30 (1984) 171-192.
      Esp. 185-188; 188-189. [NTA 30, 312]
           Response: D.C. DULING, *Semeia* 30 (1984) 193-199.

1983  *Miracle in the Early Christian World. A Study in Sociohistorical Method.* New Haven,
      CT: Yale University Press, 1983, XI-320 p. Esp. 156-159: "The Q source"; 183-190: "Portent
      in the gospel of Matthew".

1985a Messiah and the People of God. — BUTLER, J.T. – CONRAD, E.W. – OLLENBURGER,
      B.C. (eds.), *Understanding the Word. Essays in Honor of Bernhard W. Anderson* (JSOT
      SS, 37), Sheffield: JSOT, 1985, 341-358. Esp. 344-345 [Son of Man]; 348-353 [Son of God].

1985b New Rule of God, New People of God. — *HorizonsBT* 7/2 (1985) 21-51. Esp. 42-45
      [covenant]. [NTA 31, 340]

1989  Synoptic Studies. — EPP, E.J. – MACRAE, G.W. (eds.), *The New Testament and Its
      Modern Interpreters*, 1989, 245-269. Esp. 245-248: "Challenges to common assumptions"; 248-252:
      "Attacks on and alternatives to the two-source theory"; 253-258: "Gospel genre"; 261.

1990a *What Can We Know about Jesus?* (Understanding Jesus Today Series). Cambridge:
      University Press, 1990, V-122 p. Esp. 59-88. [NTA 35, p. 102]
      *¿Qué podemos saber sobre Jesús?*, trans. R. Godoy (Entorno al Nuevo Testamento, 16). Cordóba: Almendro,
      1992, 158 p.

1990b The Transformation of the Synagogue after 70 C.E. Its Import for Early Christianity.
      — *NTS* 36 (1990) 1-24. Esp. 14-19: "The synagogue in the gospel tradition"; 20-24: "The gospel of
      Matthew as evidence of an *Auseinandersetzung* between concurrently emergent *synagoge* and *ekklesia*". [NTA
      34, 736]

1995  *Who Are the People of God? Early Christian Models of Community.* New Haven, CT
      – London: Yale University Press, 1995, VII-280 p. Esp. 97-120: "The structure and strategy of
      the gospel of Matthew" [law]; 56-62: "The Q source".

**KEECH, Finley Morris**

1959  *The Agreements of Matthew and Luke against Mark in the Triple Tradition.* Madison,
      NJ (for private circulation only), 1959, XII-31 p.

**KEEGAN, Terence J.**

1977  Discipleship in Matthew. — HEYER, R. (ed.), *Scripture and the Church*, New York:
      Paulist, 1977.

1982  Introductory Formulae for Matthean Discourses. — *CBQ* 44 (1982) 415-430. Esp. 417-
      420: "Jesus sat (on a mountain)"; 420-424: "The disciples come to Jesus"; 424-425: "The disciples"; 425-
      428: "The crowds". [NTA 27, 94]

**KEENER, Craig S.**

1987  Matthew 5:22 and the Heavenly Court. — *ExpT* 99 (1987-88) 46. [NTA 32, 591]

1991  *... And Marries Another. Divorce and Remarriage in the Teaching of the New
      Testament.* Peabody, MA: Hendrickson, 1991, XII-256 p. Esp. 12-14.121-123 [19,3-12]. →
      Heth 1995

**KEERANKERI, George**

1994　The Social World of Matthew's Gospel and Community. — *Vidyajyoti* 57 (1994) 192-199. [NTA 39, 133r] → Overman 1990a

**KEGEL, Günter**

1970　*Auferstehung Jesu – Auferstehung der Toten. Eine traditionsgeschichtliche Untersuchung zum Neuen Testament*. Gütersloh: Mohn, 1970, 132 p. Esp. 72-80: "Die Funktionalisierung der urchristlichen Auferstehungstraditionen im Matthäusevangelium". — Diss. Münster, 1967.

**KELBER, W.**

1958　Die Essäer-Schriften von Qumran und das Matthäus-Evangelium. — *Die Christengemeinschaft* (Stuttgart) 30/4 (1958) 127.

**KELBER, Werner H.**

1983　*The Oral and the Written Gospel. The Hermeneutics of Speaking and Writing in the Synoptic Tradition, Mark, Paul and Q*. Philadelphia, PA: Fortress, 1983, XVIII-254 p. Esp. 191-192 [Q/Passion predictions]; 199-203 [Q/oral tradition]; 207-209 [Q/Mk]; Indiana University Press, ²1994. → Gerhardsson 1986a, González García 1990, Halverson 1994
　　　*Tradition orale et écriture*, trans. J. Prignaud (LD, 145). Paris: Cerf, 1991, 332 p. Esp. 271-273; 283-290; 296-300.

1992　Die Anfangsprozesse der Verschriftlichung im Frühchristentum. — *ANRW* II.25.1 (1992) 3-62. Esp. 29-33: "Die Redequelle (Q)"; 36-42: "Die synoptische Tradition".

1994　Jesus and Tradition: Words in Time, Words in Space. — *Semeia* 65 (1994) 139-167. Esp. 145-146.148.154-157. [NTA 40, 769]
　　　Response: J.M. FOLEY, *ibid*., 169-180; B.B. SCOTT, *ibid*., 181-191.

**KELLAS, Carol**

1994　The Healing of the Leper: The Accounts in the Synoptic Gospels and Papyrus Egerton 2, Papyrus Köln 255. — *IBS* 16 (1994) 161-173. [NTA 39, 1453] → Neirynck 1985a

**KELLER, Christian**

1985　Das Urteil des Königs über die Weltstämme. Matthäus 25,31-46. — *TK* 28 (1985) 32-51.

**KELLOGG, Alfred L.**

1960　& TALBERT, E.W., The Wyclifite *Pater Noster* and the *Ten Commandments*, with Special Reference to English MSS. 85 and 90 in the John Rylands Library. — *BJRL* 42 (1959-60) 345-377. Esp. 358-363. [NTA 5, 77]

**KELLY, Balmer H.**

1975　An Exposition of Matthew 4:1-11. — *Interpr* 29 (1975) 57-62.

**KELLY, H.A.**

1964　The Devil in the Desert. [4,1-11] — *CBQ* 26 (1964) 190-220. Esp. 196-202: "The *peirasmos*"; 202-213: "The figure of Satan"; 214-220: "The gospel narrative". [NTA 9, 146]

**KELLY, James L.**

1994　*Conscientious Objections. Toward a Reconstruction of the Social and Political Philosophy of Jesus of Nazareth* [5-7] (Toronto Studies in Theology, 68). Lewiston, NY – Queenston, Ont.: Mellen, 1994, X-458 p.

**KELLY, Joseph F.**

1981　Frigulus. An Hiberno-Latin Commentator on Matthew. — *RBén* 91 (1981) 363-373.

1984　The Virgin Birth in Hiberno-Latin Theology. — *Studia Patristica* 15 (1984) 328-335.

1988　A Catalogue of Early Medieval Hiberno-Latin Biblical Commentaries. — *Traditio* (New York) 44 (1988) 537-571; 45 (1989-90) 393-434. Esp. 395-404 [gospels]; 404-415 [Matthew]. [NTA 36, 31]

1993 The Würzburg Saint Matthew. — *Würzburger Diözesangeschichtsblätter* 55 (1993) 5-12.

**KELLY, L.G.**
1970 Cultural Consistency in Translation. [18,23-35] — *BTrans* 21 (1970) 170-175.

**KELLY, M.**
1977 The Woes against the Scribes and Pharisees. — *SIDIC* 10/2 (1977) 17-22. [NTA 22, 91]

**KEMMER, Alfons**
1981 *Gleichnisse Jesu. Wie man sie lesen und verstehen soll* (Herderbücherei, 875). Freiburg: Herder, 1981, 128 p.; ²1983.
Las hablaba en parábolas; cómo leerlas y entenderlas, trans. F. Palacios (Alcance, 28). Santander: Sal Terrae, 1982, 198 p.
Le parabole di Gesù. Come leggerle, come conprenderle, trans. P. Giombini (Studi biblici, 93). Brescia: Paideia, 1990, 158 p.

**KEMP, Ian S.**
1982 The Blessing. Power and Authority of the Church. A Study in Matthew 16:17-19. — *Evangelical Review of Theology* (Exeter) 6 (1982) 9-22.

**KEMPTHORNE, Renatus**
1977 The Marcan Text of Jesus' Answer to the High Priest (Mark xiv 62). — *NT* 19 (1977) 197-208. Esp. 206-208 [26,64]. [NTA 22, 416]

**KENDALL, Daniel**
1987 → G. O'Collins 1987b
1993 & O'COLLINS, G., Christ's Resurrection and the Aorist Passive of ἐγείρω. — *Greg* 74 (1993) 725-735. [NTA 38, 728]

**KENNEDY, Eugene**
1985 *The Choice to Be Human. Jesus Alive in the Gospel of Matthew*. Garden City, NY: Doubleday, 1985, 263 p.
R.C. LESLIE, *RelStR* 12 (1986) 293.

**KENNEDY, George A.**
1978 Classical and Christian Source Criticism. — WALKER, W.O., Jr. (ed.), *The Relationships among the Gospels*, 1978, 125-155. Esp. 147-152 [Papias]. → W.R. Farmer 1983b, R.H. Fuller 1978b, Meeks 1978
1983 An Introduction to the Rhetoric of the Gospels. — *Rhetorica* (Berkeley, CA) 1 (1983) 17-31. [NTA 30, 51]
1984 *New Testament Interpretation through Rhetorical Criticism* (Studies in Religion). Chapel Hill, NC: University Press, 1984, X-171 p. Esp. 39-72: "Deliberative rhetoric: the Sermon on the Mount, the Sermon on the Plain, and the rhetoric of Jesus"; 97-113: "The rhetoric of the gospels" [1-4].

**KENNEDY, Gerald**
1960 Nothing Without a Parable. — MCARTHUR, H.K. (ed.), *New Testament Sidelights. Essays in Honor of Alexander Converse Purdy*, Hartford: Hartford Seminary Foundation Press, 1960, 10-26.

**KENNY, Anthony**
1957 The Transfiguration and the Agony in the Garden. — *CBQ* 19 (1957) 444-452. Esp. 445-448 [17,1-13; 26,36-46]. [NTA 2, 275]
1986 *A Stylometric Study of the New Testament*. Oxford: Clarendon, 1986, XII-127 p.

**KENSKY, A.**
1993 Moses and Jesus: The Birth of the Savior. — *Judaism* 42 (1993) 43-49. [NTA 37, 1246]

**KENT, Homer A.**

1964 Matthew's Use of the Old Testament. — *BS* 121 (1964) 34-43. [NTA 8, 933]

**KER, Donald**

1988 Jesus and the Mission to the Gentiles. — *IBS* 10 (1988) 89-101. Esp. 91, 95-96 [8,11-12]. [NTA 33, 92]

**KER, Neil Ripley**

1962 Fragments of Jerome's Commentary on St. Matthew. — *Medievalia et Humanistica* (Boulder, Colarado) 14 (1962) 7-14.

**KERESZTY, Roch** → W.R. Farmer 1990a

**KERMODE, Frank**

1987 Matthew. — ALTER, R. - KERMODE, F. (eds.), *The Literary Guide to the Bible*, Cambridge, MA: Harvard University Press - Belknap, 1987, 387-401.

**KERRIGAN, Alexander**

1956 Animadversiones in Novum Testamentum documentis Qumrân illustratum. — *Ant* 31 (1956) 51-82. Esp. 61-64: "De methodo exegetica a sancto Matthaeo applicata". [NTA 1, 163]

**KERTELGE, Karl**

1968 Zur Interpretation der Wunder Jesu. Ein Literaturbericht. — *BibLeb* 9 (1968) 140-153. Esp. 142.147-148. [NTA 13, 99]

1971 Neutestamentliche Ethik. Ein Literaturbericht. — *BibLeb* 12 (1971) 126-140. Esp. 135-137. [NTA 16, 336]

1972a *Gemeinde und Amt im Neuen Testament* (Biblische Handbibliothek, 10). München: Kösel, 1972, 176 p. Esp. 40-41.135-139 [16,17-19]; 62.68-70 [28,18-20]; 136-137 [18,18].

1972b Jesus und die Gemeinde. — MÜLLER, K. (ed.), *Die Aktion Jesu und die Reaktion der Kirche. Jesus von Nazareth und die Anfänge der Kirche*, Würzburg: Echter, 1972, 101-117. Esp. 112-116 [16,17-19].

1972c Der sogenannte Taufbefehl Jesu (Mt 28,19). — AUF DER MAUR, H. - KLEINHEYER, B. (eds.), *Zeichen des Glaubens. Studien zu Taufe und Firmung. Balthasar Fischer zum 60. Geburtstag*, Einsiedeln: Benziger; Freiburg: Herder, 1972, 29-40.

1973 Die Bergpredigt als Thema heutiger Verkündigung. — KNOCH, O., et al. (eds.), *Das Evangelium auf dem Weg zum Menschen*. FS H. Kahlefeld, 1973, 25-34. Esp. 25-27: "Die Bergpredigt – eine Sittenlehre?"; 27-31: "Der Wille Gottes"; 31-34: "Die Feindesliebe".

1974a Apokalypsis Jesou Christou (Gal 1,12). — GNILKA, J. (ed.), *Neues Testament und Kirche*. FS R. Schnackenburg, 1974, 266-281. Esp. 276-279: "Vergleich mit Mt 16,17 und 11,25-27".

1974b Sündenvergebung an Stelle Gottes. Eine neutestamentlich-theologische Darlegung. — *Dienst der Versöhnung. Umkehr, Buße und Beichte – Beiträge zu ihrer Theologie und Praxis* (Trierer theologische Studien, 31), Trier: Paulinus, 1974, 27-44.

1974c Die Überlieferung der Wunder Jesu und die Frage nach dem historischen Jesus. — ID. (ed.), *Rückfrage nach Jesus. Zur Methodik und Bedeutung der Frage nach dem historischen Jesus* (QDisp, 63), Freiburg: Herder, 1974, 174-193. Esp. 183-189 [11,2-6].

1976* (ed.), *Der Tod Jesu. Deutungen im Neuen Testament* (QDisp, 74). Freiburg: Herder, 1976, 234 p. → Gnilka, R. Pesch, Vögtle

1977* (ed.), *Das kirchliche Amt im Neuen Testament* (Wege der Forschung, 189). Darmstadt: Wissenschaftliche Buchgesellschaft, 1977, VII-574 p. → F. Hahn 1970b, Rigaux 1960, Trilling 1970a

1977 Offene Fragen zum Thema "Geistliches Amt" und das neutestamentliche Verständnis von der "repraesentatio Christi". — SCHNACKENBURG, R., et al. (eds.), *Die Kirche des Anfangs*. FS H. Schürmann, 1977, 583-605. Esp. 588-590: "Die Sendung der Jünger durch Jesus" [10,40].

1984* (ed.), *Ethik im Neuen Testament* (QDisp, 102). Freiburg: Herder, 1984, 214 p. → Egger, Hoffmann, G. Lohfink 1983

1984 Handeln aus Glauben. Zum Verständnis der Bergpredigt. — *Renovatio* (Bonn) 40 (1984) 73-81. [NTA 29, 92]

1985 Das Doppelgebot der Liebe im Markusevangelium. — GANTOY, R. (ed.), *À cause de l'Évangile*. FS J. Dupont, 1985, 303-322. Esp. 307-312: "Zur traditionsgeschichtlichen Situation"; = *TTZ* 103 (1994) 38-55. Esp. 42-47.

1986* (ed.), *Das Gesetz im Neuen Testament* (QDisp, 108). Freiburg: Herder, 1986, 240 p. → Broer, Dautzenberg, P. Fiedler

1987 "Selig, die verfolgt werden um der Gerechtigkeit willen" (Mt 5,10). — *IKZ/Communio* (Rodenkirchen) 16 (1987) 97-106. Esp. 100-105: "Die doppelte Seligpreisung der Verfolgten in Mt 5,10.11f.". [NTA 31, 1070]

1989* & HOLTZ, T. - MÄRZ, C.-P. (eds.), *Christus bezeugen. Festschrift für Wolfgang Trilling zum 65. Geburtstag* (ErfTSt, 59). Leipzig: St. Benno, 1989; Freiburg: Herder, 1990, 319 p. → J.B. Bauer, Baumbach, J.D.G. Dunn, Hoffmann, C. Kähler, H. Klein, Luz, März, Schweizer, Zeilinger

1990 "Ihr alle aber seid Brüder" (Mt 23,8). — HAGEMANN, L. - PULSFORT, E. (eds.), *"Ihr alle aber seid Brüder". Festschrift für A.Th. Khoury zum 60. Geburtstag* (Würzburger Forschungen zur Missions- und Religionswissenschaft. Abt. 2: Religionswissenschaftliche Studien, 14), Würzburg: Echter; Altenberge: Oros, 1990, 17-25.

1991a *Grundthemen paulinischer Theologie*. Freiburg: Herder, 1991, 244 p. Esp. 56-61 [11,25-27; 16,17/Paul].

1991b "Selig die Trauernden..." (Mt 5,4). — *IKZ/Communio* 20 (1991) 387-392. [NTA 36, 711]

**KERTSCH, Manfred**

1992 L'esegesi di Mt 19,11-12 in Gregorio Nazianzeno e Giovanni Crisostomo. — MORESCHINI, C. - MENESTRINA, G. (eds.), *Gregorio Nazianzeno teologo e scrittore* (Pubblicazioni dell'Istituto di Scienze Religiose di Trento, 17), Bologna: Dehoniane, 1992, 103-114.

**KESICH, Veselin**

1960 The Problem of Peter's Primacy in the New Testament and the Early Christian Exegesis. — *St. Vladimir's Seminary Quarterly* (New York) 4/2-3 (1960) 2-25. Esp. 5-12; 12-16 [16,17-19]. [NTA 5, 397]

1961a Christ's Temptation in the Apocryphal Gospels and Acts. — *St. Vladimir's Seminary Quarterly* 5/4 (1961) 3-9. Esp. 5-6 [Gospel of the Hebrews].

1961b Empire-Church Relations and the Third Temptation. [4,8-10] — *Studia Patristica* 4 (1961) 465-471.

1965 Hypostatic and Prosopic Union in the Exegesis of Christ's Temptation. — *St. Vladimir's Seminary Quarterly* 9 (1965) 118-137. [NTA 10, 902]

1966 The Antiocheans and the Temptation Story. [4,1-11] — *Studia Patristica* 7 (1966) 496-502. [NTA 11, 694]

1971 *The Gospel Image of Christ*. Crestwood, NY: St. Vladimir's Sem. Press, 1971; rev. ed., 1992, 214 p. Esp. 48-49; 73-75; 88-92 [Q].

**KESSLER, Hans**

1970   *Die theologische Bedeutung des Todes Jesu. Eine traditionsgeschichtliche Untersuchung*
       (Themen und Thesen der Theologie). Düsseldorf: Patmos, 1970, ²1971, 347 p. — Diss.
       Münster, 1969.

1985   *Sucht den Lebenden nicht bei den Toten. Die Auferstehung Jesu Christi in biblischer,*
       *fundamentaltheologischer und systematischer Sicht.* Düsseldorf: Patmos, 1985, 422 p.
       Esp. 79-108; Würzburg: Echter, 1995 (Neuausgabe), 427 p. Esp. 79-108.
       *La resurrección de Jesús. Aspecto bíblico, teológico y sistemático,* trans. M. Olasagasti (Lux Mundi, 65).
       Salamanca: Sígueme, 1989, 373 p.

**KEULERS, Josef**

1935ᴿ  *Het Evangelie van Mattheus* [1935] (Boeken van het Nieuwe Testament, 1).
       Roermond–Maaseik: Romen, ²1951, 515 p.
       I. DE LA POTTERIE, *Bijdragen* 13 (1952) 440; W. GROSSOUW, *ScuolC* 27 (1952) 103-104.

1958   *Synopsis van de eerste drie Evangeliën.* Roermond–Maaseik: Romen, 1958, 262 p.

**KEVERS, Paul**

1980   De gelijkenis van het onkruid tussen de tarwe (Mt. 13,24-30.36-43). — BULCKENS, J.
       (ed.), *Parabels meerstemmig,* 1980, 116-121.

1981   Bijbelse studiedagen te Leuven over Jezus' "logia". — *TijdTheol* 21 (1981) 424-425.
       → Delobel 1982*

**[Κεχαριτωμένη]**

1990*  *Κεχαριτωμένη. Mélanges René Laurentin.* Paris: Desclée, 1990, 735 p. → Calkins 1988,
       Cazelles, D. Fernández, Jeanne d'Arc

**KEYLOCK, Leslie Robert**

1975   Bultmann's Law of Increasing Distinctness. — HAWTHORNE, G.F. (ed.), *Current Issues*
       *in Biblical and Patristic Interpretation.* FS M.C. Tenney, 1975, 193-210. Esp. 202-206
       [Tables: Mt more/less precise than Mk]; 209. → 1995

1995   *Luke and Matthew as Editors: An Evaluation of Bultmann's Law of Increasing*
       *Distinctness.* Diss. Trinity Evangelical Divinity School, 1995, 346 p. (S. McKnight).
       — *DissAbstr* 56 (1995-96) 2280. → 1975

**KGATLA, S.T.**

1989   Church Discipline according to Matthew. — *TViat* 17 (1989) 150-162.

**KHALIL, S.**

1976   Note sur le fonds sémitique commun de l'expression "un chameau passant par le trou
       d'une aiguille". [19,24] — *Arabica* (Leiden) 23 (1976) 89-94. → Schub 1976

**KHIOK-KHNG, Yeo**

1992   The Mother and Brothers of Jesus (Lk 8:19-21; Mk 3:31-35; Mt 12:46-50). — *AsiaJT*
       6 (1992) 311-317. [NTA 37, 773]

**KIDDER, S.J.**

1983   "This Generation" in Matthew 24:34. — *AndrUnS* 21 (1983) 203-209. [NTA 28, 501]

**KIEFFER, René**

1969   Vishet och välsignelse som grundmotiv i saligprisningarna hos Matteus och Lukas. —
       *SEÅ* 34 (1969) 107-121. Esp. 112-121 [5,3-12]. [NTA 15, 490]
       Wisdom and Blessing in the Beatitudes of St. Matthew and St. Luke. — *Studia*
       *Evangelica* 6 (1973) 291-295.
       Weisheit und Segen als Grundmotive der Seligpreisungen bei Mattäus und Lukas. — *SNTU* 2 (1977) 29-43.
       Esp. 36-43.

1972    *Essais de méthodologie néo-testamentaire* (ConBibNT, 4). Lund: Gleerup, 1972, 86 p. Esp. 26-50 [5,1-12].

1977    *Nytestamentlig teologi* [New Testament theology]. Stockholm: Verbum; Lund: Ohlsson, 1977; Stockholm: Skeab; Lund: Berling, [2]1979; Stockholm: Verbum, [3]1991. Esp. 65-74.
*Die Bibel deuten – das Leben deuten. Einführung in die Theologie des Neuen Testaments*, trans. M. Hofmann. Regensburg: Pustet, 1987.
*Jésus raconté: théologie et spiritualité des évangiles* (Lire la Bible, 108). Paris: Cerf, 1996, 209 p.

1978    Fader vår i äldre kyrklig traditionen. [The Lord's prayer in early church tradition] — *SvenskTeolKvart* 54 (1978) 103-109.

1979a   Jesus och den mänskliga gemenskapen. Föreningen Lärare i Religionskunskap. [1-2] — *Årsbok* 12 (1979) 161-172.

1979b   "Mer-än"-kristologin hos synoptikerna. — *SEÅ* 44 (1979) 134-147. Esp. 135-143 [1,1-17; 3,11; 6,25.30; 11,7-15; 12,1-8.38-42; 14,1-2; 16,1-4.13-20; 17,1-9; 22,41-46]. [NTA 24, 770]
La christologie de supériorité dans les évangiles synoptiques. — *ETR* 54 (1979) 579-591. Esp. 580-587. [NTA 24, 769]
A Christology of Superiority in the Synoptic Gospels. — *Religious Studies Bulletin* (Sudbury, Ont.) 3 (1983) 61-75. [NTA 28, 81]

1987    Judiska reningar och det dop som Jesus kommer med. [Jewish purifications and the baptism Jesus brought] — *SEÅ* 51-52 (1986-87) 116-126. [NTA 31, 823]

1995    Traditions juives selon Mc 7,1-23. — FORNBERG, T. - HELLHOLM, D. (eds.), *Texts and Contexts*. FS L. Hartman, 1995, 675-688. Esp. 675-678 [15,1-20/Mk].

**KIEHL, E.H.**

1981    Jesus Taught in Parables. [13,24-30.36-43] — *Concordia Journal* (St. Louis, MO) 7 (1981) 221-228. [NTA 26, 473]

1990    Why Jesus Spoke in Parables. — *Concordia Journal* 16 (1990) 245-257. [NTA 35, 118]

**KIENLE, Bettina VON**

1993    *Feuermale. Studien zur Wortfelddimension "Feuer" in den Synoptikern, im pseudophilonischen Liber Antiquitatum Biblicarum und im 4. Esra* (BBB, 89). Bodenheim: Athenäum/Hain/Hanstein, 1993, 305 p. Esp. 50-155: "Das Matthäusevangelium" [3,7-12; 5,13-16.21-22.27-30; 6,28-30; 7,16-20; 8,14-15; 10,28-31; 12,9-14; 13,3-9.18-23.24-30.36-43.47-50; 17,14-20; 17,24-18,14; 23,15.32-33; 25,31-46]. — Diss. Heidelberg, 1992 (C. Burchard).

**KIILUNEN, Jarmo**

1983*   & RIEKKINEN, V. - RÄISÄNEN, H. (eds.), *Glaube und Gerechtigkeit. In Memoriam Rafael Gyllenberg (18.6.1893–29.7.1982)* (Schriften der Finnischen Exegetischen Gesellschaft, 38). Helsinki: Finnish Exegetical Society, 1983, VIII-222 p. → Haapa, Lindeskog, Nikolainen, Schweizer, Sollamo

1989    *Das Doppelgebot der Liebe in synoptischer Sicht. Ein redaktionskritischer Versuch über Mk 12,28-34 und die Parallelen* (Annales Academiae Scientiarum Fennicae, B/250). Helsinki: Suomalainen Tiedeakatemia, 1989, 110 p. Esp. 33-47 [22,34-40]; 79-89 [Synoptic problem]. → A. Fuchs 1991, Neirynck 1995a
F. NEIRYNCK, *ETL* 67 (1991) 432-433.

1991    Der nachfolgewillige Schriftgelehrte. Matthäus 8.19-20 im Verständnis des Evangelisten. — *NTS* 37 (1991) 268-279. [NTA 35, 1131] → Kingsbury 1988a

**KIKAWADA, Isaac M.**

1975    Literary Convention of the Primaeval History. — *AJBI* 1 (1975) 3-21. Esp. 18-21 [1-3].

**KILEY, Mark**

1984    Why "Matthew" in Matt 9,9-13? — *Bib* 65 (1984) 347-351. [NTA 29, 526]

1994 The Lord's Prayer and Matthean Theology. — CHARLESWORTH, J.H., et al., *The Lord's Prayer*, 1994, 15-27.

**KILGALLEN, John J.**

1980 To What Are the Matthean Exception-Texts (5,32 and 19,9) an Exception? — *Bib* 61 (1980) 102-105. [NTA 24, 789]

1990 *A Brief Commentary on the Gospel of Matthew.* New York: Paulist, 1990; Lewiston, NY: Mellen, 1992, IX-231 p. [NTA 37, p. 280]

**KILPATRICK, George Dunbar**

1943[R] Western Text and Original Text in the Gospels and Acts. [1943] — ID., *Principles and Practice*, 1990, 113-127. Esp. 118-120 [minor agreements: 21,44; 22,35; 26,68].

1944[R] Matthew iv.4. [1944] — ID., *Principles and Practice*, 1990, 259-260.

1946[R] *The Origins of the Gospel according to St. Matthew* [1946]. Oxford: Clarendon, repr. 1950, 151 p. Esp. 8-36: "The documentary sources"; 37-58: "The peculiar narratives"; 59-71: "The liturgical background"; 72-100: "The liturgical character of the gospel"; 101-123: "The gospel and Judaism"; 124-134: "The community of the gospel"; 135-139: "The evangelist".
E.K. WINTER, *Judaica* 9 (1953) 250-254.

1947[R] Φρόνιμος, σοφός and συνετός in Matthew and Luke. [11,25] [1947] — ID., *Principles and Practice*, 1990, 225-226.

1950 Scribes, Lawyers, and Lucan Origins. — *JTS* 1 (1950) 56-60. Esp. 56-57 [22,35]; = ID., *Principles and Practice*, 1990, 245-249. Esp. 245-246.

1958 Mark XIII.9-10. — *JTS* 9 (1958) 81-86. Esp. 83-85 [10,17-20/Mk]. [NTA 3, 84]; = ID., *Principles and Practice*, 1990, 299-304. Esp. 301-302. → Farrer 1956a

1959 *Matthew. A Greek-English Diglot for the Use of Translators.* London: The British and Foreign Bible Society, 1959, IV-77 p. → Rodgers 1992

1962 The Order of Some Noun and Adjective Phrases in the New Testament. [12,18; 23,35] — *NT* 5 (1962) 111-114. [NTA 7, 450]; = *BTrans* 16 (1965) 117-119. [NTA 10, 459]; = ID., *Principles and Practice*, 1990, 163-166.

1963 Atticism and the Text of the Greek New Testament. — BLINZLER, J., et al. (eds.), *Neutestamentliche Aufsätze*. FS J. Schmid, 1963, 125-137. Esp. 129-130 [19,19]; 133-135 [Atticism]; = ID., *Principles and Practice*, 1990, 15-32. Esp. 21-22; 29-30.

1964 Dura-Europos: The Parchments and the Papyri. [0212] — *Greek, Roman and Byzantine Studies* (Cambridge, MA) 5 (1964) 215-225.

1967a The Aorist of γαμεῖν in the New Testament. — *JTS* 18 (1967) 139-140. [NTA 12, 199]; = ID., *Principles and Practice*, 1990, 187-188.

1967b Ἰδού and ἴδε in the Gospels. — *Ibid.*, 425-426. Esp. 426. [NTA 12, 561]; = ID., *Principles and Practice*, 1990, 205-206. Esp. 206.

1968 "Kurios" in the Gospels. — *L'Évangile hier et aujourd'hui. Mélanges offerts au Professeur Franz-J. Leenhardt*, Genève: Labor et Fides, 1968, 65-70. Esp. 65-66; = ID., *Principles and Practice*, 1990, 207-212. Esp. 206-207.

1970 What John Tells Us about John. — *Studies in John*. FS J.N. Sevenster, 1970, 75-87. Esp. 76-77, 80-81, 83, 86-87; = ID., *Principles and Practice*, 1990, 333-344. Esp. 334-335, 338, 344.

1973 Κύριος Again. — HOFFMANN, P., et al. (eds.), *Orientierung an Jesus*. FS J. Schmid, 1973, 214-219. Esp. 217; = ID., *Principles and Practice*, 1990, 216-222. Esp. 219.

1974 Eucharist as Sacrifice and Sacrament in the New Testament. — GNILKA, J. (ed.), *Neues Testament und Kirche*. FS R. Schnackenburg, 1974, 429-433. Esp. 431 [26,28].

1977a The Historic Present in the Gospels and Acts. — *ZNW* 58 (1977) 258-262. Esp. 258-259. [NTA 22, 722]; = ID., *Principles and Practice*, 1990, 169-176. Esp. 169-170.

1977b Some Thoughts on Modern Textual Criticism and the Synoptic Gospels. — *NT* 19 (1977) 275-292. Esp. 281 [27,4]; 283 [17,17]; 283-284 [4,7]; 287 [26,67-68]; 288 [26,75]; 288-289 [13,11]. [NTA 23, 39]; = ID., *Principles and Practice*, 1990, 80-97. Esp. 86; 88; 88-89; 92; 93; 93-94.

1979 Three Problems of New Testament Text. — *NT* 21 (1979) 289-292. Esp. 289-290 [4,8]. [NTA 24, 364]; = ID., *Principles and Practice*, 1990, 241-244. Esp. 241-242.

1981 Conjectural Emendation in the New Testament. — EPP, E.J. – FEE, G.D. (eds.), *New Testament Textual Criticism*. FS B.M. Metzger, 1981, 349-360. Esp. 353 [6,32; 23,37]; 354 [22,10]; 355 [8,18; 15,35]; = ID., *Principles and Practice*, 1990, 98-109. Esp. 102; 103; 105.

1982 Jesus, His Family and His Disciples. — *JSNT* 15 (1982) 3-19. Esp. 8-10 [Mt]; 18 [Q]. [NTA 27, 68]; = EVANS, C.A. – PORTER, S.E. (eds.), *The Historical Jesus*, 1995, 13-28. Esp. 18-20; 27.

1983 *The Eucharist in Bible and Liturgy* (The Moorhouse Lectures 1975). Cambridge: University Press, 1983, VII-115 p. Esp. 1-12 [26,26-29].

1984 Matthew on Matthew. — TUCKETT, C.M. (ed.), *Synoptic Studies*, 1984, 177-185. Esp. 177-178 [9,9]; 181-182 [19,24]; = ID., *Principles and Practice*, 1990, 250-258. Esp. 250-251; 252-253.

1990 *The Principles and Practice of New Testament Textual Criticism. Collected Essays*, ed. J.K. Elliott (BETL, 96). Leuven: University Press / Peeters, 1990, XXXVIII-489 p. → 1943, 1944, 1947, 1950, 1958, 1962, 1963, 1967a-b, 1968, 1970, 1973, 1977a-b, 1979, 1981, 1984

**KIM, Chan-Hie**

1975 The Papyrus Invitation. [22,3] — *JBL* 94 (1975) 391-402. [NTA 20, 630]

**KIM, Duk Ki**

1992 *A Postmodern Ethical-Political Interpretation of Jesus' Sayings and Parables in Light of Derrida, Foucault, and Ricœur* [11,12; 20,1-16]. Diss. Drew Univ., Madison, WI, 1992, 348 p. (D.J. Doughty). — *DissAbstr* 53 (1992-93) 1960.

**KIM, Ki Kon**

1994 *The Signs of the Parousia. A Diachronic and Comparative Study of the Apocalyptic Vocabulary of Matthew 24:27-31*. Diss. Andrews Univ., Berrien Springs, MI, 1994, 491 p. (R.M. Johnston). — *DissAbstr* 55 (1994-95) 1295.

**KIM, K.W.**

1950 Codices 1582, 1739, and Origen. — *JBL* 69 (1950) 167-175.

1953 Origen's Text of Matthew in his *Against Celsus*. — *JTS* 4 (1953) 42-49.

**KIM, Myung-Soo**

1990 *Die Trägergruppe von Q – Sozialgeschichtliche Forschung zur Q-Überlieferung in den synoptischen Evangelien* (Wissenschaftliche Beiträge aus europäischen Hochschulen, I/1). Ammersbek-Hamburg: Lottbek/Jensen, 1990, 389 p. Esp. 81-94: "Ein Überblick über die Anwendung der sozialgeschichtlichen Fragestellung auf Q"; 95-136 [5,3-4.6/Q 6,20-21]; 137-170 [5,38-48; 7,12/Q 6,27-36]; 171-204 [11,2-6/Q 7,18-23]; 205-241 [8,18-22/Q 9,57-62]; 243-304 [9,37-10,16/Q 10,2-12]; 305-359: "Die Jesusbewegung der Q-Gemeinde". [NTA 35, p. 243] — Diss. Hamburg, 1990 (H. Paulsen).

**KIM, Seyoon**

1983 *"The 'Son of Man'" as the Son of God* (WUNT, 30). Tübingen: Mohr, 1983; Grand Rapids, MI: Eerdmans, 1985, X-118 p. Esp. 3.87-94 [Son of Man]; 76-78 [kingdom].

1987 Jesus – The Son of God, the Stone, the Son of Man, and the Servant: The Role of Zechariah in the Self-Identification of Jesus. — HAWTHORNE, G.F. - BETZ, O. (eds.), *Tradition and Interpretation*. FS E.E. Ellis, 1987, 134-148. Esp. 136.142 [21,44].

**KIM, Young Bong**

1993 *Jesus and the Scriptures. An Inquiry into Jesus' Self-Understanding*. Diss. McMaster Univ., Toronto, Ont., 1993, 270 p. (S. Westerholm). — *DissAbstr* 55 (1994-95) 1591.

**KINDER, Ernst**

1959 Die Ehe. — SUCKER, W., et al. (eds.), *Die Mischehe. Handbuch für die evangelische Seelsorge*, Göttingen: Vandenhoeck & Ruprecht, 1959, 9-35. Esp. 11-14.

**KING, J.R.**

1991 The Parables of Jesus. A Social Psychological Approach. — *Psychology and Theology* (LaMirada, CA) 19 (1991) 257-267. [NTA 36, 694]

**KING, Karen**

1987 Kingdom in the Gospel of Thomas. — *Forum* 3/1 (1987) 48-97. Esp. 83 [13,47-50/Th 8]. [NTA 31, 1420]

**KING, Nicholas**

1982 *What is a Gospel?* Leigh-on-Sea: K. Mayhew, 1982, 132 p. Esp. 10-16 [1,1-17]; 37-41 [28]; 85-101: "Matthew: the apprentice scribe" [18,10-14; 14,22-33; 16,13-28; 18,15-18].

**KING, Philip A.**

1962 Matthew and Epiphany. — *Worship* 36 (1961-62) 89-95. [NTA 6, 758]

**KINGSBURY, Jack Dean**

1966 The "Jesus of History" and the "Christ of Faith". In Relation to Matthew's View of Time – Reactions to a New Approach. — *ConcTM* 37 (1966) 500-510. [NTA 11, 658] → Strecker 1962

1969 *The Parables of Jesus in Matthew 13. A Study in Redaction-Criticism*. Richmond, VA: Knox; London: SPCK, 1969, ²1971, XII-180 p. Esp. 1-11: "Modern trends in parable interpretation"; 12-16: "Matthew 13: structure and context"; 17-21: "Matthew's concept of 'the kingdom of heaven'"; 22-91: "Jesus' parables to the Jewish crowds beside the sea (13.1-35)"; 92-129: "Jesus' parables to the disciples in privat (13.36-52)"; 130-137: "Observations and conclusions". [NTA 14, p. 109] — Diss. Basel, 1966. → Danker 1970b, W.J. Harrington 1972b
   R.P. BOTO, *EstAgust* 5 (1970) 706-707; C.B. COUSAR, *Interpr* 24 (1970) 518; F.W. DANKER, *ConcTM* 42 (1971) 241-242; G. DAUTZENBERG, *BZ* 19 (1975) 118-119; E. ESKING, *TZ* 26 (1970) 287-288; T.F. GLASSON, *Theology* 72 (1969) 559-560; M.D. GOULDER, *JTS* 21 (1970) 164-166; J.A. GRINDEL, *CBQ* 32 (1970) 135-136; X. JACQUES, *NRT* 92 (1970) 699-700; J. JEREMIAS, *TLZ* 96 (1971) 270-271; G.J. KUIPER, *JAAR* 39 (1971) 384-385; M. MAXWELL, *AndrUnS* 9 (1971) 170-172; J. MURPHY-O'CONNOR, *RB* 78 (1971) 128-130; K.F. NICKLE, *RRel* 29 (1970) 175; R. POTTER, *NBlackfr* 51 (1970) 201-202; A. SALAS, *CiudDios* 183 (1970) 300; A. SEGOVIA, *ArchTeolGran* 32 (1969) 265-266; H.F.G. SWANSTON, *ScriptB* 2/1 (1970) 24; D.O. VIA, Jr., *JBL* 89 (1970) 370-371; S. ZEDDA, *RivBib* 20 (1972) 229-231.
   *The Parables in Matthew 13. A Study in Redaction Criticism*. London: SPCK, 1977, 180 p.
   G.V. JONES, *ScotJT* 32 (1979) 94-96.

1970 Ernst Fuchs' Existentialist Interpretation of the Parables. — *LuthQ* 22 (1970) 380-395. [NTA 15, 830]

1971 Major Trends in Parable Interpretation. — *ConcTM* 42 (1971) 579-596. [NTA 16, 470]

1972 The Parables of Jesus in Current Research. — *Dialog* (Minneapolis, MN) 11 (1972) 101-107. [NTA 16, 840]

1973a Matthew's Redefinition of the Gospel. — *Dialog* 12 (1973) 32-37. [NTA 17, 898]

1973b The Structure of Matthew's Gospel and His Concept of Salvation-History. — *CBQ* 35 (1973) 451-474. Esp. 453-459 [1,1-4,16]; 459-466 [4,17-16,20; 16,21-28,20]; 466-474 [salvation history]. [NTA 18, 461] → 1975a; → Neirynck 1988c

1974  The Composition and Christology of Matt 28:16-20. — *JBL* 93 (1974) 573-584. Esp. 573-579: "The composition of Matt 28:16-20"; 579-584: "The christology of Matt 28:16-20". [NTA 19, 548]

1975a  *Matthew: Structure, Christology, Kingdom.* Philadelphia, PA: Fortress, 1975, XIV-178 p. Esp. 1-39: "The structure of Matthew's gospel and his concept of salvation-history"; 40-83: "The christology of Matthew: the title Son of God"; 84-127: "The christology of Matthew: other titles"; 128-160: "Matthew's view of the Son of God and the kingdom of heaven". [NTA 20, p. 236]; ²1989. → 1973b; → Allison 1993a, D. Hill 1980, Ingelaere 1981, Meier 1979, Neirynck 1988c, Slater 1980

> J. ASHTON, *Month* 238 (1977) 28; F.H. BORSCH, *Interpr* 31 (1977) 73-76; M. BOUTTIER, *ETR* 54 (1979) 315-316; F. BRÄNDLE, *EstJos* 33 (1979) 114; J.A. CARRASCO, *EstJos* 34 (1980) 246-247; J. FENTON, *Theology* 80 (1977) 58-60; G.A. GAY, *Themelios* 2 (1976-77) 90; M.A. GETTY, *CBQ* 39 (1977) 580-581; M.D. GOULDER, *JTS* 28 (1977) 144-146; H.B. GREEN, *ExpT* 87 (1975-76) 376; *NBlackfr* 57 (1976) 521; D.R.A. HARE, *JBL* 96 (1977) 307-308; T. LEWAN ROBERTZ, *SvenskTeolKvart* 58 (1982) 150-152; F.L. MORIARTY, *Greg* 57 (1976) 578-579; J. MURPHY-O'CONNOR, *RB* 83 (1976) 306-307; J.M. REDFORD, *CleR* 62 (1977) 161-162; J.M. REESE, *BTB* 7 (1977) 45-46; L. SABOURIN, *BTB* 6 (1976) 280-282; A. SALAS, *CiudDios* 190 (1977) 380-381; J.A. SHERLOCK, *TS* 37 (1976) 317-318; S.S. SMALLEY, *EvQ* 49 (1977) 128; A. SNELL, *RTR* 36 (1977) 21-22; G.N. STANTON, *HeythJ* 19 (1978) 182-183; W.R. STEGNER, *ATR* 59 (1977) 462-465; J.W. THOMPSON, *RestQ* 21 (1978) 118-119; W. WILKENS, *TZ* 37 (1977) 177-178.

1975b  Form and Message of Matthew. — *Interpr* 29 (1975) 13-23. Esp. 13-15: "The form of the gospel"; 15-18: "The form of the gospel reconsidered"; 19-22: "The message of the gospel". [NTA 19, 937]; = MAYS, J.L. (ed.), *Interpreting*, 1981, 66-77.

1975c  Preaching the Sermon on the Mount. — *BiTod* 80 (1975) 504-509.

1975d  The Title "Kyrios" in Matthew's Gospel. — *JBL* 94 (1975) 246-255. Esp. 248-249 [application]; 249 [7,21-22; 24,42]; 250-254 [relation with other titles]. [NTA 20, 77]

1975e  The Title "Son of God" in Matthew's Gospel. — *BTB* 5 (1975) 3-31. Esp. 5-13 [1,1-4,16]; 13-22 [4,17-16,20]; 22-29 [16,21-28,20]. [NTA 19, 938]

1975f  The Title "Son of Man" in Matthew's Gospel. — *CBQ* 37 (1975) 193-202. Esp. 193-195 [Son of God: 1,18-25; 27,54]; 196-202 [Son of Man: 8,19-22; 16,13-21; 20,24-25; 26,20-25]. [NTA 20, 78]

1976  The Title "Son of David" in Matthew's Gospel. — *JBL* 95 (1976) 591-602. Esp. 592-593 [application]; 593-597 [Son of David; Son of God]; 597-601 [purpose]. [NTA 21, 370]

1977a  *Matthew* (Proclamation Commentaries. The New Testament Witnesses for Preaching). Philadelphia, PA: Fortress, 1977, XII-116 p. [NTA 22, p. 89]; ²1986, X-133 p. Esp. 1-29: "Towards an understanding of Matthew"; 30-57: "Matthew's understanding of Christ"; 58-77: "Matthew's understanding of God"; 78-106: "Matthew's understanding of the Church". [NTA 31, p. 101] → Ingelaere 1981, Ziesler 1985

> D.E. GARLAND, *RExp* 74 (1977) 567-568; R.W. KLEIN, *CurrTMiss* 4 (1977) 364; H.C. WAETJEN, *Interpr* 32 (1978) 434.436.

*Matthew, a Commentary for Preachers and Others.* London: SPCK, 1978, 118 p.

> R. LUNT, *ExpT* 89 (1977-78) 376.

1977b  Retelling the "Old, Old Story". The Miracle of the Cleansing of the Leper as an Approach to the Theology of Matthew. — *CurrTMiss* 4 (1977) 342-349. [NTA 22, 397]

1978a  Observations on the "Miracle Chapters" of Matthew 8-9. — *CBQ* 40 (1978) 559-573. Esp. 560-562: "Arrangement"; 562-566: "Christology"; 566-568: "Context"; 568-572: "Paradigmatic function". [NTA 23, 436]

1978b  The Verb *Akolouthein* ("To Follow") as an Index of Matthew's View of His Community. — *JBL* 97 (1978) 56-73. Esp. 57-62 [exegesis: 4,20.22; 8,19-22; 9,9.27; 19,27-29; 20,34; 21,9]; 62-70 [Church]. [NTA 22, 753]

1979a  The Figure of Peter in Matthew's Gospel as a Theological Problem. — *JBL* 98 (1979) 67-83. Esp. 69-76 [analysis]; 76-80 [synthesis]. [NTA 24, 76]

1979b  The Gospel in Four Editions. — *Interpr* 33 (1979) 363-375. Esp. 367-370 [christology]. [NTA 24, 382]

1981    *Jesus Christ in Matthew, Mark, and Luke* (Proclamation Commentaries. The New
        Testament Witnesses for Preaching). Philadelphia, PA: Fortress, 1981, IX-134 p. Esp.
        1-27: "The document of Q"; 61-93: "Matthew" [Jesus; mission of Jesus; discipleship; soteriology].

1983    The Theology of St. Matthew's Gospel according to the Griesbach Hypothesis. —
        FARMER, W.R. (ed.), *New Synoptic Studies*, 1983, 331-361. Esp. 335-343 [1,18-25]; 343-347
        [1,1-4,16]; 347-353 [4,17-16,20]; 353-355 [Lord]; 355-359 [Son of Man].

1984    The Figure of Jesus in Matthew's Story: A Literary-Critical Probe. — *JSNT* 21 (1984)
        3-36. Esp. 7-11 [1,1-4,16]; 11-14 [4,17-16,20]; 14-20 [16,21-28,20]; 22-32 [Son of Man]. [NTA 29, 80];
        = EVANS, C.A. - PORTER, S.E. (eds.), *The Synoptic Gospels*, 1995, 47-80. Esp. 53-57;
        57-60; 60-66; 68-80. → Allison 1987d, D. Hill 1984a

1985    The Figure of Jesus in Matthew's Story. A Rejoinder to David Hill. — *JSNT* 25 (1985)
        61-81. Esp. 61-63 [literary criticism]; 65-74 [christology]; 75-79 [structure]. [NTA 30, 559]; = EVANS,
        C.A. - PORTER, S.E. (eds.), *The Synoptic Gospels*, 1995, 97-117. Esp. 97-99; 101-111; 111-
        116. → D. Hill 1984a

1986a   *Matthew as Story*. Philadelphia, PA: Fortress, 1986, X-149 p. Esp. 1-40: "Understanding
        Matthew: a literary-critical approach"; 41-56: "The presentation of Jesus (1:1-4:16)"; 57-77: "The ministry
        of Jesus to Israel and Israel's repudiation of Jesus (4:17-16,20)"; 78-94: "The journey of Jesus to Jerusalem
        and his suffering, death, and resurrection (16:21-28,20)"; 95-102: "Jesus as the Son of Man"; 103-119: "The
        disciples of Jesus"; 120-133: "The community of Matthew". [NTA 30, p. 354]; ²1988, X-181 p. [NTA
        33, p. 107] → M.A. Powell 1992d
        F.W. BURNETT, *TTod* 43 (1986-87) 438.440; D. DULING, *Interpr* 41 (1987) 187-190; R.A. EDWARDS,
        *CBQ* 49 (1987) 505-506; J.L. HOULDEN, *JSNT* 29 (1987) 125; A. ITO, *Themelios* 13 (1987-88) 61-62;
        S. McKNIGHT, *JEvTS* 30 (1987) 369-371; P.M. MEAGHER, *Vidyajyoti* 53 (1989) 631-632; S.D. MOORE,
        *Forum* 3/3 (1987) 32-33; R.L. MOWERY, *BTB* 18 (1988) 86.
        D.A. BLACK, *FilolNT* 1 (1988) 221; M. DESJARDINS, *Religious Studies and Theology* (Edmonton) 10/2
        (1990) 113; L.A. KAUPPL, *CurrTMiss* 16 (1989) 130-131; H.A. MOELLERING, *ConcTQ* 56 (1992) 55-58;
        D. SENIOR, *CRBR* 3 (1990) 211-213.

1986b   The Parable of the Wicked Husbandmen and the Secret of Jesus' Divine Sonship in
        Matthew: Some Literary-Critical Observations. — *JBL* 105 (1986) 643-655. Esp. 644-646
        [21,33-46 as allegory]; 646-652 [21,33-46 in structure of Mt]. [NTA 31, 1081]

1987a   The Developing Conflict between Jesus and the Jewish Leaders in Matthew's Gospel:
        A Literary-Critical Study. — *CBQ* 49 (1987) 57-73. Esp. 58-60 [term]; 60-64 [character]; 64-66
        [correlation Jesus-leaders: 1,1-4,16]; 66-70 [4,17-16,20]; 70-72 [16,21-28,20]. [NTA 31, 1051]; =
        STANTON, G. (ed.), *The Interpretation of Matthew*, ²1995, 179-197. Esp. 180-182; 182-186; 186-189; 189-
        192; 192-194; 194-196.

1987b   The Place, Structure, and Meaning of the Sermon on the Mount within Matthew. —
        *Interpr* 41 (1987) 131-143. [NTA 31, 1064]

1988a   On Following Jesus: The 'Eager' Scribe and the 'Reluctant' Disciple (Matthew
        8.18-22). — *NTS* 34 (1988) 45-59. Esp. 45-46 [structure]; 46-47 [setting: 8,18]; 47-52 [8,19-20];
        52-53 [8,21-22]. [NTA 32, 597] → Kiilunen 1991

1988b   Reflections on 'the Reader' of Matthew's Gospel. — *Ibid.*, 442-460. Esp. 457-458 [10,5-6].
        [NTA 33, 112]

1989    Matthew. — ANDERSON, B.W. (ed.), *The Books of the Bible*. II: *The Apocrypha and
        the New Testament*, New York: Scribner's, 1989, 125-147.

1991    Conclusion: Analysis of a Conversation. — BALCH, D.L. (ed.), *Social History of the
        Matthean Community*, 1991, 259-269. Esp. 259-263: "Considerations regarding methodology"; 263-
        265: "The character and makeup of Matthew's community"; 265-266: "The use of source theories".

1992a   Matthäusevangelium. — *EKL* 3 (³1992) 341-343.

1992b   The Plot of Matthew's Story. — *Interpr* 46 (1992) 347-356. Esp. 347-349 [1,1-4,16]; 349-352
        [4,17-16,20]; 352-355 [16,21-28,20]. [NTA 37, 704]

1992c The Stilling of the Storm (Matthew 8:23-27). — HULTGREN, A.J. – JUEL, D.H. – KINGSBURY, J.D. (eds.), *All Things New. Essays in Honor of Roy A. Harrisville* (Word & World SS, 1), St. Paul, MN: Word & World, 1992, 101-108.

1993a Matthew, The Gospel according to. — METZGER, B.M. – COOGAN, M.D. (eds.), *The Oxford Companion to the Bible*, 1993, 502-506.

1993b The Significance of the Cross within the Plot of Matthew's Gospel. A Study in Narrative Criticism. — FOCANT, C. (ed.), *The Synoptic Gospels*, 1993, 263-279. Esp. 272-278 [27,38-54]; 264-272 [controversies].
Korsets betydelse i Matteusevangeliets "Plot". — *SEÅ* 58 (1993) 85-98. Esp. 85-93: 93-97. [NTA 38, 1353]

1995 The Rhetoric of Comprehension in the Gospel of Matthew. — *NTS* 41 (1995) 358-377. Esp. 361-364 [1,1-4,16]; 364-367 [4,17-16,20]; 367-371 [16,21-28,20]; 371-376 [christological titles]. [NTA 40, 152]

**KINNIBURGH, E.**

1963 Hard Sayings. III. Matthew 23.23. — *Theology* 66 (1953) 414-416. [NTA 8, 585]

**KINZER, Mark Stephen**

1995 *"All Things under His Feet": Psalm 8 in the New Testament and in Other Jewish Literature of Late Antiquity.* Diss. Univ. of Michigan, 1995, 310 p. (J. Fossum). — *DissAbstr* 56 (1995-96) 3165.

**KIPPER, João Balduino**

1977 Quanto valem os 10.000 Talents da Parábola (Mt 18,23-35). — *RevistCuBíb* 1 (1977) 83-89. [NTA 21, 727]

1981 *Taryaq ou 613 preceitos de Moisés: 248 mandamentos e 365 proibições.* [11,28-30] — *RevistCuBíb* 5 (1981) 208-216.

**KIRAZ, George Anton**

1993 *A Computer-Generated Concordance to the Syriac New Testament According to the British and Foreign Bible Society's Edition. Based on the SEDRA Database.* Volumes I-VI. Leiden: Brill, 1993, XXXV-758; 759-1590; 1591-2399; 2400-3138; 3139-3911; 3912-4639 p. → 1996

1996 *Comparative Edition of the Syriac Gospels. Aligning the Sinaiticus, Curetonianus, Peshîtta and Harklean Versions.* Volume I: *Matthew* (New Testament Tools and Studies, 21/1). Leiden: Brill, 1996, LXXXV-454 p. [NTA 41, p. 147] → 1993

**KIRBAN, S.**

1972 *Matthew. The Beginning of Sorrows.* Chicago, IL: Moody, 1972, 142 p.

**KIRCHERT, Klaus**

1991 Philologisch-exegetische Grundlagen der Bibelübersetzung im Mittelalter. [2,1-12] — REINITZER, H. (ed.), *Deutsche Bibelübersetzungen des Mittelalters* (Vestigia bibliae: Jahrbuch des Deutschen Bibel-Archivs Hamburg, 9-10), Bern: Lang, 1991, 13-33.

**KIRCHGÄSSNER, Alfons**

1950 *Erlösung und Sünde im Neuen Testament.* Freiburg: Herder, 1950, XI-321 p. Esp. 175-207: "Die synoptischen Evangelien".

1973 "Im Herzen der Erde". Zur Symbolsprache von Mt 12,40 Eine Meditation. — KNOCH, O., et al. (eds.), *Das Evangelium auf dem Weg zum Menschen.* FS H. Kahlefeld, 1973, 101-108.

**KIRCHHEVEL, Gordon D.**

1994 He That Cometh in Mark 1:7 and Matt 24:30. — *Bulletin for Biblical Research* (Winona Lake, IN) 4 (1994) 105-111. [NTA 39, 819]

**KIRCHSCHLÄGER, Walter**

1972 *Der Satan der Evangelien als Versucher. Eine Untersuchung über Mt 4,1-11 par. unter besondere Berücksichtigung der Gestalt und der Funktion Satans.* Diss. Wien, 1972, XII-172 p. (J. Kremer).

1980 *Die Evangelien vorgestellt* (Reihe b4). Klosterneuburg: Österreichisches Katholisches Bibelwerk, 1980, 48 p.

1981 *Jesu exorzistisches Wirken aus der Sicht des Lukas. Ein Beitrag zur lukanischen Redaktion* (Österreichische Biblische Studien, 3). Klosterneuburg: Österreichisches Katholisches Bibelwerk, 1981, 331 p. Esp. 229-236: "Texte aus dem Bereich der Quelle Q" [Q 7,21; 11,14-23.24-26]. — Diss. Wien, 1981 (J. Kremer).

1983 Die Friedensbotschaft der Bergpredigt. Zu Mt 5,9.17-48; 7,1-5. — *Kairos* 25 (1983) 223-237. Esp. 224-227 [5,9]; 227-231 [5,17-48]; 231 [7,3-5]. [NTA 29, 95]

1987a *Ehe und Ehescheidung im Neuen Testament. Überlegungen und Anfragen zur Praxis der Kirche.* Wien: Herold, 1987, 111 p. Esp. 30-32.59-69 [5,27-32]; 72-76 [5,33-37/James].

1987b Das Geistwirken in der Sicht des Neuen Testaments. Dargestellt an seinen Hauptzeugen. — *Theologische Berichte* (Zürich) 16 (1987) 15-52. Esp. 32-37: "Das matthäische Verständnis des Geistwirkens".

1990 *Das Phänomenon des Bösen. Beiträge zu einem theologischen Problem.* Luzern: Rex, 1990, 114 p.

1992 Satan et démons dans le Nouveau Testament. — *DBS* 12/66 (1992) 25-47. Esp. 28-34.

1995 Die Entwicklung von Kirche und Kirchenstruktur zur neutestamentlichen Zeit. — *ANRW* II.26.2 (1995) 1277-1356. Esp. 1326-1328.

**KIRK, Alan**

1994 Examining Priorities: Another Look at the *Gospel of Peter*'s Relationship to the New Testament Gospels. — *NTS* 40 (1994) 572-595. Esp. 583-583 [27,54/Gospel of Peter]; 586-594 [27,62-66; 28,2-4.11-15/Gospel of Peter]. [NTA 39, 1252]

**KIRK, Albert**

1978 & OBACH, R.E., *A Commentary on the Gospel of Matthew.* New York – Ramsey, NJ – Toronto, Ont.: Paulist, 1978, IV-296 p. [NTA 24, p. 83]
D.A. CARSON, *JEvTS* 23 (1980) 357; A. SALAS, *CiudDios* 194 (1981) 641.

**KIRK, J. Andrew**

1969 The Meaning of Wisdom in James: Examination of a Hypothesis. — *NTS* 16 (1969-70) 24-38. Esp. 24-25 [7,7]. [NTA 14, 967]

1972 The Messianic Role of Jesus and the Temptation Narrative: A Contemporary Perspective. — *EvQ* 44 (1972) 11-29, 91-102. [NTA 16, 874; 17, 115]

**KIRSCH, Ludwig**

1982 *Das Vaterunser als Schule des Gebetes (Mt 6,9-13 par Lk 11,2-4).* Diss. Würzburg, 1982, X-227 p.

**KIRSCH, Paul J.**

1982 The Gospel Passion Narratives and Jews. — THOMPSON, N.H. – COLE, B.K. (eds.), *The Future of Jewish-Christian Relations*, Schenectady: Character Research, 1982, 185-204.

**KISNER, G.D.**

1993 Jesus' Encounter with the Rich Young Ruler and Its Implications for Theology and Development. [19,16-30] — *Journal of Religious Thought* (Washington, DC) 49/2 (1992-93) 81-86. [NTA 39, 809]

**KISSINGER, Warren S.**

1975 *The Sermon on the Mount: A History of Interpretation and Bibliography* (American Theological Library Association Bibliography Series, 3). Metuchen, NJ: Scarecrow Press / ATLA, 1975, XIII-296 p. Esp. 1-125: "History of interpretation"; 127-275: "Bibliography". [NTA 20, p. 363]
    E.J. EPP, *JBL* 101 (1982) 148-150; N.J. MCELENEY, *CBQ* 38 (1976) 567; D. SENIOR, *TS* 37 (1976) 362.

1979 *The Parables of Jesus. A History of Interpretation and Bibliography* (American Theological Library Association Bibliography Series, 4). Metuchen, NJ: Scarecrow Press / ATLA, 1979, XXIV-439 p. Esp. 1-230: "History of interpretation"; 231-415: "Bibliography".

1985 *The Lives of Jesus. A History and Bibliography.* New York – London: Garland, 1985, XIII-230 p. Esp. 115-230: "The bibliography".

**KISTEMAKER, Simon J.**

1972 *The Gospels in Current Study.* Grand Rapids, MI: Baker, 1972, 171 p.; ²1980, 181 p.

1978 The Lord's Prayer in the First Century. — *JEvTS* 21 (1978) 323-328. [NTA 23, 822]

1980 *The Parables of Jesus.* Grand Rapids, MI: Baker, 1980. XXVI-301 p.

**KISTER, Menahem**

1982 The Sayings of Jesus and the Midrash. [Hebrew] — *Jerusalem Studies in Jewish Thought* 2 (1982) 7-17. [NTA 27, 86]; [English] = *Immanuel* 15 (1982-83) 39-50. Esp. 43-47 [5,17-20.27-32]; 47-49 [23,23-27]. [NTA 29, 505]

1990 Plucking on the Sabbath and Christian-Jewish Polemic. [12,1-8] — *Immanuel* 24-25 (1990) 35-51.

**KITCHENS, Ted G.**

1989 *Church Discipline: An Exegetical and Theological Inquiry* [18,15-20]. Diss. Theol. Sem., Dallas, TX, 1989, 247 p. — *DissAbstr* 51 (1990-91) 889-890.

**KITTEL, Gerhard**

1950 Der Jakobusbrief und die Apostolischen Väter. — *ZNW* 43 (1950-51) 54-112. Esp. 83-109: "Die Herrenwort-Zitationen und -Anklänge bei den Apostolischen Vätern und im Jakobusbrief".

**KITZMANN, Harold Louis**

1985 *The Fulfilling of Righteousness. Matthew 3:13-15: A Redactional Study.* Diss. Lutheran School of Theol., Chicago, IL, 1985, 391 p. — *DissAbstr* 46 (1985-86) 1980-81-A; *SBT* 14 (1986) 193-194.

**KJÄRGAARD, Mogens Stiller**

1986 *Metaphor and Parable. A Systematic Analysis of the Specific Structure and Cognitive Function of the Synoptic Similes and Parables qua Metaphors* (Acta theologica Danica, 20). Leiden: Brill, 1986, 262 p. Esp. 133-197: "The metaphor in modern parable research".

**KJAER-HANSEN, Kai**

1982 *Studier i navnet Jesus* [Studies in the name of Jesus]. Aarhus: Menighetsfakultetet, 1982, VI-422 p. Esp. 269-368. — Diss. Lund, 1982 (B. Gerhardsson).

**KJESETH, Peter**

1984 Preaching from Matthew in 1983-84. — *CurrTMiss* 11 (1984) 69-78.

**KLAIBER, Walter**

1992 Proexistenz und Kontrastverhalten. Beobachtungen zu einer Grundstruktur neutestamentlicher Ekklesiologie. — *JbBT* 7 (1992) 125-144. Esp. 143-144 [23,8-12].

**KLASSEN, William**

1992a "Love Your Enemies": Some Reflections on the Current Status of Research. — SWARTLEY, W.M. (ed.), *The Love of Enemy*, 1992, 1-31. Esp. 7-14 [5,43-48].

1992b Judas Iscariot. — *ABD* 3 (1992) 1091-1096. Esp. 1093.

1992c Love (NT and Early Jewish). — *ABD* 4 (1992) 381-396. Esp. 385-389.

1996 *Judas. Betrayer or Friend of Jesus?* London: SCM; Minneapolis, MN: Fortress, 1996, XIV-238 p. Esp. 96-115: "Judas as portrayed by the gospel of Matthew"; 160-176 [27,3-10].

**KLASSEN-WIEBE, Sheila**

1992 Matthew 1:18-25. — *Interpr* 46 (1992) 392-395.

**KLATT, N.**

1990 *Jesus und Buddhas Wasserwandel. Walking on the Water of Jesus and of the Buddha. A Presentation of the Case in English. With a Critical Discussion of the Opinion of J. Duncan M. Derrett in German.* Göttingen: Klatt, 1990, 62 p. → Derrett 1981c

**KLAUCK, Hans-Josef**

1970 Das Gleichnis vom Mord im Weinberg (Mk 12,1-12; Mt 21,33-46; Lk 20,9-19). — *BibLeb* 11 (1970) 118-145. Esp. 121-126 [Mk/Mt]; 128-131 [Mt/Lk]; 142-143 [Mt]. [NTA 15, 529]

1972 Neue Beiträge zur Gleichnisforschung. — *BibLeb* 13 (1972) 214-230. [Eichholz 1971, Jörns 1970, Via 1967/70, Weiser 1971]. [NTA 17, 889]

1978 *Allegorie und Allegorese in synoptischen Gleichnistexten* (NTAbh, NF 13). Münster: Aschendorff, 1978, VIII-410 p. Esp. 158 [9,12]; 167-168 [9,15]; 173 [9,16-17]; 174-179 [Q 11,17]; 179-182 [Q 11,21-22]; 210-212 [13,31-32]; 227-229 [Q 11,33]; 235-236 [Q 12,2]; 239-240 [13,12]; 240-259 [Mt/Mk 4,1-34]; 264-265 [15,11]; 279-280 [15,26-27]; 281 [Q 14,34-35]; 289-291 [21,33-46]; 311-313 [21,28-32.33-46; 22,1-14]; 324 [24,33]; 328-329 [25,14]; 347-348 [8,23-27]; [2]1986, 427 p. — Diss. München, 1977 (J. Gnilka).

1981a *Hausgemeinde und Hauskirche im frühen Christentum* (SBS, 103). Stuttgart: Katholisches Bibelwerk, 1981, 120 p. Esp. 56-62: "Die synoptischen Evangelien" [8,21-22; 10,10-13.37].

1981b Die Frage der Sündenvergebung in der Perikope von der Heilung des Gelähmten (Mk 2,1-12 parr). — *BZ* 25 (1981) 223-248. Esp. 246-247 [9,1-8]. [NTA 26, 495]; = ID., *Gemeinde - Amt - Sakrament. Neutestamentliche Perspektiven*, Würzburg: Echter, 1989, 286-312. Esp. 310-311.

1987 *Judas - ein Jünger des Herrn* (QDisp, 111). Freiburg: Herder, 1987, 160 p. Esp. 33-70: "Die synoptische Überlieferung (traditio triplex)"; 92-101 [27,3-10].

1992a "Christus, Gottes Kraft und Gottes Weisheit" (1 Kor 1,24). Jüdische Weisheitsüberlieferungen im Neuen Testament. — *WissWeish* 55 (1992) 1-22. Esp. 12-14. [NTA 37, 918]; = ID., *Alte Welt und neuer Glaube. Beiträge zur Religionsgeschichte, Forschungsgeschichte und Theologie des Neuen Testaments* (NTOA, 29), Freiburg/Schw: Universitätsverlag; Göttingen: Vandenhoeck & Ruprecht, 1994, 251-275. Esp. 263-265 [Q 7,35; 11,49; Mt 11,28-30].

1992b Judas der 'Verräter'? Eine exegetische und wirkungsgeschichtliche Studie. — *ANRW* II.26.1 (1992) 717-740. Esp. 725-728; 731.

1994* (ed.), *Weltgericht und Weltvollendung. Zukunftsbilder im Neuen Testament [FS R. Schnackenburg]* (QDisp, 150). Freiburg: Herder, 1994, 268 p. → Dormeyer, März, Schlosser

**KLAWEK, Aleksy**

1964 Najstarszy rękopis Ewangelii św. Mateusza. [An old manuscript of the gospel of Matthew] [P⁶⁴] — *RuBi* 17 (1964) 50-51. [NTA 9, 140] → Roca-Puig 1956/62

**KLEIN, Günter**

1960    Wunderglaube und Neues Testament. — *Das Gespräch* (Wuppertal) 28 (1960); = ID., *Ärgernisse. Konfrontationen mit dem Neuen Testament*, München: Kaiser, 1970, 13-57. Esp. 42-45: "Die Spruchquelle".

1964    Die Prüfung der Zeit (Lukas 12,54-56). — *ZTK* 61 (1964) 373-390. Esp. 385-390 [16,1-4]. [NTA 10, 155]

1972    Die Verfolgung der Apostel, Luk 11,49. — BALTENSWEILER, H. – REICKE, B. (eds.), *Neues Testament und Geschichte*. FS O. Cullmann, 1972, 113-124.

1984    Gesetz. III. Neues Testament. — *TRE* 13 (1984) 58-75. Esp. 58-61: "Jesus". → P. Fiedler 1986

1993    "Über das Weltregiment Gottes". Zum exegetischen Anhalt eines dogmatischen Lehrstücks. — *ZTK* 90 (1993) 251-283. Esp. 269 [11,25-27]; 269-270 [28,18-20]. [NTA 38, 1015]

**KLEIN, Hans**

1982    Das Glaubensverständnis im Matthäusevangelium. — HAHN, F. – KLEIN, H. (eds.), *Glaube im Neuen Testament. Studien zu Ehren von Hermann Binder anläßlich seines 70. Geburtstags* (Biblisch-Theologische Studien, 7), Neukirchen-Vluyn: Neukirchener, 1982, 29-42. Esp. 29-33 [4,17; 8,26; 9,2.18; 13,58; 15,28; 16,8; 17,20; 18,6; 20,34; 21,21; 22,21-22; 27,42/Mk]; 33-35 [Q 11,42; 17,5-6.23]; 35-42 [faith].

1989a   Judenchristliche Frömmigkeit im Sondergut des Matthäus. — *NTS* 35 (1989) 466-474. Esp. 467-469 [will of God]; 469-471 [judgment]; 471-473 [ecclesiology]. [NTA 34, 108]

1989b   Zur Traditionsgeschichte von Mt 16,16b.17. Zugleich ein Beitrag zur Frühgeschichte der christlichen Taufe. — KERTELGE, K., et al. (eds.). *Christus bezeugen*. FS W. Trilling, 1989, 124-135. Esp. 124-127 [16,16-19]; 127-131 [16,13-23]; 131-133 [16,16/1 Thess 1,9-10; 16,17/Gal 1,14-15]; 133-134 [16,17/JosephAsenat].

1991    Christologie und Anthropologie in den Petruslegenden des matthäischen Sondergutes. — BREYTENBACH, C. – PAULSEN, H. (eds.), *Anfänge der Christologie*. FS F. Hahn, 1991, 209-220. Esp. 209-214 [17,24-27]; 214-216 [14,28-31]; 216-217 [11,28-30; 16,16-17; 18,20].

1993    Zur Methode der Erforschung vormarkinischer Quellen. — FOCANT, C. (ed.), *The Synoptic Gospels*, 1993, 503-517. Esp. 505-506 [9,18-26]; 508 [19,13-15]; 509-510.

**KLEIN, Peter**

1980    Die lukanischen Weherufe Lk 6,24-26. — *ZNW* 71 (1980) 150-159. Esp. 150-152 [5,3-12]. [NTA 26, 520]

**KLEINE, Richard**

1953    Die Bergpredigt des Herrn in ihrer grundlegenden Bedeutung für den Aufbau des Reiches Gottes. — *ZMiss* 37 (1953) 175-187, 269-274.

1962    "Ich bin nicht gekommen, aufzuheben, sondern die Fülle zu bringen" (Mt 5,17). Ein praktischer Aufweis heilsgeschichtlicher-kerygmatischer Verkündigung. — *Anzeiger für die katholische Geistlichkeit* (Freiburg) 71 (1962) 414-424.

1963a   Die Seligpreisungen des Herrn (Mt 5,3-9). — *Anzeiger für die katholische Geistlichkeit* 72 (1963) 222-228, 526-534.

1963b   "Ihr seid das Salz der Erde"... (Mt 5,13-16). — *Ibid.*, 462-470.

**KLEINKNECHT, Karl Theodor**

1985    Johannes 13, die Synoptiker und die "Methode" der johanneischen Evangelienüber-lieferung. — *ZTK* 82 (1985) 361-388. Esp. 369-374 [26/Jn 13]; 380-381 [10,24.40/Jn 13,16.20]. [NTA 30, 191]

**KLEMM, Hans G.**

1969    Das Wort von der Selbstbestattung der Toten. Beobachtungen zur Auslegungsgeschichte von Mt. viii.22 Par. — *NTS* 16 (1969-70) 60-75. [NTA 14, 356]

**KLEMM, Matthys**

1977 *Eiρήνη im neutestamentlichen Sprachsystem. Eine Bestimmung von lexikalischen Bedeutungen durch Wortfeld-Funktionen und deren Darstellung mittels EDV* (Forum Theologiae Linguisticae, 8). Bonn: Linguistica Biblica, 1977, 294 p. Esp. 55-57 [10,12-13.34].

**KLIJN, Albertus Frederik Johannes**

1959a Scribes, Pharisees, Highpriests and Elders in the New Testament. — *NT* 3 (1959) 259-267. Esp. 259-262 [par Mk]; 262-263 [par Lk]; 263 [Sondergut]; 265-266 [passion narrative]. [NTA 5, 62]

1959b Die Wörter "Stein" und "Felsen" in der syrischen Übersetzung des Neuen Testaments. — *ZNW* 50 (1959) 99-105. Esp. 100-102 [16,18; 27,51.60]. [NTA 4, 82]

1961 *Inleiding tot het Nieuwe Testament* (Aula, 66). Utrecht–Antwerpen: Spectrum, 1961, 224 p.; Roermond–Maaseik: Romen, ²1963, VIII-369 p. → 1982

1965a *De wordingsgeschiedenis van het Nieuwe Testament* (Aula, 207). Utrecht–Antwerpen: Spectrum, 1965, 256 p. Esp. 22-30: "Het synoptisch probleem"; 42-49: "Mattheus"; ²1968; ³1971; ⁴1974; ⁵1976; ⁶1978; ⁷1983; rev. ed., ⁸1987.
*An Introduction to the New Testament*, trans. M. van der Vathorst-Smit. Leiden: Brill, 1967; rev. ed., 1980 [= ⁶1978], XIV-237 p. Esp. 8-16; 28-35.

1965b Some Remarks on the Quotations of the Gospels in Gregory of Nyssa's "De instituto christiano" and Macarius' "Epistula magna". — *VigChr* 19 (1965) 164-168. [NTA 10, 734] → A. Baker 1964, 1966, Quispel 1964

1966 The Question of the Rich Young Man in a Jewish-Christian Gospel. [19,16-30] — *NT* 8 (1966) 149-155. [NTA 11, 703]

1969 *A Survey of the Researches into the Western Text of the Gospels and Acts*. Part Two: *1949-1969* (SupplNT, 21). Leiden: Brill, 1969, 86 p. Esp. 5-28: "The Diatessaron".

1972 Jerome's Quotations from a Nazoraean Interpretation of Isaiah. — *RSR* 60 (1972) 241-255. Esp. 245-247.251-255 [4,15-16]. [NTA 17, 763]

1979 Patristic Evidence for Jewish Christian and Aramaic Gospel Tradition. — BEST, E. - WILSON, R.McL. (eds.), *Text and Interpretation*. FS M. Black, 1979, 169-177.

1981 Matthew 11:25 // Luke 10:21. — EPP, E.J. - FEE, G.D. (eds.), *New Testament Textual Criticism*. FS B.M. Metzger, 1981, 3-14.

1982 *Inleiding tot de studie van het Nieuwe Testament*. Kampen: Kok, 1982, 225 p. → 1961

1988 Das Hebräer- und das Nazoräerevangelium. — *ANRW* II.25.5 (1988) 3997-4033. Esp. 4008-4020: "Hieronymus"; 4021-4024: "To Ioudaïkon".

1992a *Jewish-Christian Gospel Tradition* (Supplements to Vigiliae Christianae, 17). Leiden: Brill, 1992, VII-156 p. Esp. 3-26: "The evidence for Jewish-christian gospels"; 56-60 [Origen]; 60-65 [Eusebius]; 65-77 [Epiphanius]; 86-94.120-126 [CommMt: Jerome, Sedulius Scottus, Rabanus Maurus, P. Radbertus]; 105-115 [Codices NT 4, 566, 899, 1424]; 138-139 [Hugo of St. Cher].

1992b De kanonisatie van de vier evangeliën. — BAARLINK, H., et al., *Christologische perspectieven*. FS H. Baarlink, 1992, 257-267. Esp. 259-260, 263-264 [Papias].

1995 *Het ontstaan van een Nieuw Testament*. Nijkerk: Callenbach, 1995, 184 p.

**KLINE, Leslie L.**

1975a *The Sayings of Jesus in the Pseudo-Clementine Homilies* (SBL DS, 14). Missouli, MT: SBL/Scholars, 1975, IX-198 p. Esp. 13-84: "Harmonized and conflated readings"; 86-116: "Matthew". — Diss. Harvard Univ., Cambridge, MA, 1971 (H. Koester).

1975b Harmonized Sayings of Jesus in the Pseudo-Clementine Homilies and Justin Martyr. — *ZNW* 66 (1975) 223-241. Esp. 225-229: "Conflations of inner-Matthean texts" [6,8.32; 7,15-16; 22,37-38; 24,5; 25,30.41]; 229-239: "Harmonizations of synoptic texts" [5,39-41.44.45; 8,11; 10,28; 11,27; 19,16-17]. [NTA 20, 996] → Strecker 1958, 1978b

**KLINGELE, O.H.**

1962 Jene drei Männer, die zur Krippe zogen. — *Das Heilige Land* (Köln) 94 (1962) 33-42.

1963 Die Flucht der Heiligen Familie. — *Das Heilige Land* 95 (1963) 42-45.

**KLINGHARDT, Matthias**

1988 *Gesetz und Volk Gottes. Das lukanische Verständnis des Gesetzes nach Herkunft, Funktion und seinem Ort in der Geschichte des Urchristentums* (WUNT, II/32). Tübingen: Mohr, 1988, VIII-371 p. Esp. 17-19 [Q 16,17]; 20-22 [Q 16,18]; 314-315. — Diss. Heidelberg, 1986-87 (K. Berger).

1996 *Gemeinschaftsmahl und Mahlgemeinschaft. Soziologie und Liturgie frühchristlicher Mahlfeiern* (TANZ, 13). Tübingen: Francke, 1996, XI-633 p. Esp. 395-399 [21,9.15/Did 10,6]. — Diss. Heidelberg, 1994 (K. Berger).

**KLINKENBERG, Hans Martin**

1955 Der römische Primat im 10. Jahrhundert. — *Zeitschrift der Savigny-Stiftung für Rechtsgeschichte* (Weimar) 72 (1955) 1-57. Esp. 12-1: "Römische Quellen"; 16-24: "Rather von Veronica"; 25-30: "Atto von Vercelli"; 30-40: "Gerbert von Aurillac"; 41-47: "Odo von Cluny"; 52-57: "Abbo von Fleury".

**KLINZING, Georg**

1971 *Die Umdeutung des Kultus in der Qumrangemeinde und im Neuen Testament* (SUNT, 7). Göttingen: Vandenhoeck & Ruprecht, 1971, 248 p. Esp. 202-210: "Die Synoptiker" [16,18; 21,14; 26,61].

**KLOPPENBORG, John S.** → IQP

1978 Wisdom Christology in Q. — *LavalTP* 34 (1978) 129-147. Esp. 132-135 [Q 10,21-22: reconstruction]; 135-146: "Form and tradition-critical observations". [NTA 23, 102]

1979 Didache 16,6-8 and Special Matthaean Tradition. — *ZNW* 70 (1979) 54-67. Esp. 57-59 [25,31]; 59-66 [24,30-31]. [NTA 24, 657]

1984 Tradition and Redaction in the Synoptic Sayings Source. — *CBQ* 46 (1984) 34-62. Esp. 35-36: "Multiple documents"; 36-45: "Form criticism and tradition-history"; 45-47: "Thematic analyses"; 47-54: "Redaction-critical studies"; 54-57: "Reflections on method"; 57-62: "Genre and redaction". [NTA 28, 477]

1985a Bibliography on Q. — *SBL 1985 Seminar Papers*, 103-126.

1985b A Synopsis for Q [11:14-26]. — *Ibid.*, 127-132.

1985c Q 11:14-26: Work Sheets for Reconstruction. — *Ibid.* 133-151.

1986a Blessing and Marginality. The 'Persecution Beatitude' in Q, Thomas & Early Christianity. — *Forum* 2/3 (1986) 36-56. Esp. 38-44: "Reconstruction of Q 6:22-23"; 44-46: "The redaction of Q 6:22-23"; 46-49: "Tradition-history"; 49-54: "Authenticity". [NTA 31, 1117]

1986b The Formation of Q and Antique Instructional Genres. — *JBL* 105 (1986) 443-462. Esp. 443-449 [Q/Thomas]; 449-455: "The formative component in Q"; 456-462: "The formative component of Q as 'instruction'". [NTA 31, 561]; = ID. (ed.), *The Shape of Q*, 1994, 138-155. Esp. 138-144; 144-149; 150-155.

1986c The Function of Apocalyptic Language in Q. — *SBL 1986 Seminar Papers*, 224-235. Esp. 226-227: "Non-apocalyptic configurations in Q"; 227-233: "Q's use of apocalyptic language"; 234-235: "The function of apocalyptic language in Q". → 1987b

1987a *The Formation of Q. Trajectories in Ancient Wisdom Collections* (Studies in Antiquity and Christianity, 2). Philadelphia, PA: Fortress, 1987, XVIII-377 p. (Foreword, J.M. Robinson, XI-XIV). Esp. 1-40: "Introduction" [genre]; 41-88: "The document Q" [written/oral; languange; order; extent]; 89-101: "The composition of Q"; 102-170 "The announcement of judgment in Q" [Q 3,7-9.16-17; 7,1-10.18-23.24-26.31-35; 11,24-26.29-32.33-36.39-52; 12,39-40.42-46.49.51-53.54-56.57-59; 16,16; 17,23.24.26-30.34-35.37]; 171-245: "Sapiential speeches in Q" [Q 6,20-49; 9,57-62; 10,2-16.21-

24; 11,2-4.9-13; 12,2-12.22-34; 13,24-30.34-35; 14,16-24.26-27.34-35; 17,33]; 246-262: "The temptation story in Q" [Q 4,1-13]; 263-316: "Q and ancient sayings collections"; 317-329: "Conclusion" [instruction; chriae; final recension]. — *The Literary Genre of the Synoptic Sayings Source*. Diss. Univ. of St. Michael's College, Toronto, Ont., 1984. → 1989a; → M. Black 1990a, Hartin 1994, Hoffmann 1992b, R.A. Horsley 1989c, Humphrey 1991, A.D. Jacobson 1987, Vaage 1994, J.G. Williams 1988

    H. BOERS, *Interpr* 43 (1989) 200-201; A.Y. COLLINS, *CBQ* 50 (1988) 720-722; J.H. CRENSHAW, *RelStR* 15 (1989) 159-160; M.R. FAIRCHILD, *JEvTS* 34 (1991) 123-124; D. HILL, *ExpT* 99 (1987-88) 152-153; R. HODGSON, JR., *Bib* 70 (1989) 282-285; A.D. JACOBSON, *JBL* 108 (1989) 150-152; D. LÜHRMANN, *TLZ* 113 (1988) 435-437; A. MORAL, *Religión y Cultura* (Madrid) 38 (1992) 615-616; A. OSIANDER, *TorontoJT* 4 (1988) 308-309; T. PRENDERGAST, *StudRel/SciRel* 17 (1988) 227-228; C.M. TUCKETT, *JSNT* 32 (1988) 119-120; R. URO, *TAik* 94 (1989).

    *The Composition of Q* (Occasional Papers, 9). Claremont, CA: The Institute for Antiquity and Christianity, Claremont Graduate School, 1987 (= *The Formation*, pp. XI-XIV and 89-101).

1987b  Symbolic Eschatology and the Apocalypticism of Q. — *HTR* 80 (1987) 287-306. Esp. 291-292: "Eschatological wisdom in Q"; 292-294: "Nonapocalyptic configurations in Q"; 294-303: "Q's use of apocalyptic language"; 303-306: "Symbolic eschatology and apocalypticism". [NTA 32, 100] → 1986c

1988    *Q Parallels. Synopsis, Critical Notes & Concordance* (Foundations & Facets Reference Series: New Testament). Sonoma, CA: Polebridge, 1988, XXXV-249 p. Esp. 1-203: "The synoptic sayings source: synopsis and critical notes"; 207-238: "Concordance". → 1992b; → J.K. Elliott 1991, Neirynck 1988d

    M.E. BORING, *JBL* 108 (1989) 720-722; J.K. ELLIOTT, *TLZ* 114 (1989) 428-429; *NT* 32 (1990) 191-192; A. FUCHS, *SNTU* 16 (1991) 205-208; J.G. LODGE, *CBQ* 52 (1990) 559-561; C.M. TUCKETT, *JSNT* 36 (1989) 125.

1989a  *The Formation of Q* Revisited: A Response to Richard Horsley. — *SBL 1989 Seminar Papers*, 204-215. Esp. 204-211: "Stratigraphy"; 211-215: "The social context". → 1987a; → R.A. Horsley 1989c

1989b  The Q Sayings on Anxiety (Q 12:2-7). — *Forum* 5/2 (1989) 83-98. [NTA 34, 170]

1990a  & MEYER, M.W. – PATTERSON, S.J. – STEINHAUSER, M.G., *Q – Thomas Reader*. Sonoma, CA: Polebridge, 1990, X-166 p. Esp. 1-74: "The sayings gospel Q". → 1990b, Patterson 1990b, Steinhauser 1990a

    W. BRAUN, *Studies in Religion* 22 (1993) 258-259; J.A. FITZMYER, *BibReview* 7/1 (1991) 10-11; H. GUENTHER, *TorontoJT* 8 (1992) 336-339; F.J. MATERA, *CBQ* 54 (1992) 394-395; F. NEIRYNCK, *ETL* 69 (1993) 175-177; H.-M. SCHENKE, *TLZ* 117 (1992) 359-360; C.M. TUCKETT, *JSNT* 43 (1991) 125; R. WINTERHALTER, *Journal of Religious and Psychical Research* 17 (1994) 51-52.

1990b  Translation and Notes. — *Ibid.*, 35-74.

1990c  Alms, Debt and Divorce: Jesus' Ethics in Their Mediterranean Context. — *TorontoJT* 6 (1990) 182-200. Esp. 189-196: "Listening to Jesus' sayings" [6,1-6.16-18]. [NTA 35, 1100]

1990d  "Easter Faith" and the Sayings Gospel Q. — *Semeia* 49 (1990) 71-99. Esp. 73-76: "Catechesis and missionary preaching in the 'second sphere'"; 76-82: "The synoptic passion narratives and Q"; 82-92: "Resurrection and the hermeneutical horizon of Q". [NTA 35, 119]

    Response: B.L. MACK, *ibid.*, 169-176.

1990e  City and Wasteland: Narrative World and the Beginning of the Sayings Gospel (Q). — *Semeia* 52 (1990) 145-160. Esp. 147-151: "Reconstructing the beginning of Q"; 151-152: "The beginning of Q and the story of Lot"; 152-153: "The social map of Q"; 154-157: "Spatiality and the narrative map of Q". [NTA 35, 1119] → Neirynck 1995g, 1996b

    Response: E.S. MALBON, *ibid.*, 177-184; R.C. TANNEHIL, *ibid.*, 190.

1990f  *Nomos* and *Ethos* in Q. — GOEHRING, J.E., et al. (eds.), *Gospel Origins*. FS J.M. Robinson, 1990, 35-48. Esp. 37-43: "Pharisaic halakah and the Q-woes"; 43-79: "Q 16:16-18"; 46-47: "A nomocentric redaction of Q?"; 47-48: "Law and salvation in Q".

1992a  & VAAGE, L.E., Early Christianity, Q and Jesus: The Sayings Gospel and Method in the Study of Christian Origins. — *Semeia* 55 (1992) 1-14. Esp. 2-3 [Q–synoptic problem]; 3-4 [Q–Jesus]; 4-5 [form-criticism]; 5-8 [message of Q]; 8-9 [redaction in Q]; 9-10 [Q and special description]. [NTA 36, 1238] → J.D. Crossan 1992a

1992b Literary Convention, Self-Evidence and the Social History of the Q People. — *Ibid.*, 77-102. Esp. 79-81: "From text to social entity"; 81-91: "The instructional layer and its audience"; 91-99: "Rejection and rationalization"; 99-100: "The final redaction and its public". [NTA 36, 1237] → 1988

1992c The Theological Stakes in the Synoptic Problem. — VAN SEGBROECK, F., et al. (eds.), *The Four Gospels 1992*. FS F. Neirynck, 1992, I, 93-120. Esp. 97-108 [Two-document hypothesis]; 109-112 [Son of Man]; 113-119 [Q].

1993 The Sayings Gospel Q: Recent Opinion on the People Behind the Document. — *Currents in Research: Biblical Studies* (Sheffield) 1 (1993) 9-34. Esp. 12-21: "Sociohistorical description"; 21-28: "Source critical reflections". [NTA 38, 1347]

1994* (ed.). *The Shape of Q. Signal Essays on the Sayings Gospel.* Minneapolis, MN: Augsburg Fortress, 1994, VIII-224 p. [NTA 40, p. 341] → Bultmann 1913, A.D. Jacobson 1982b, Kloppenborg 1986b, 1994, Koester 1968/71, Lührmann 1969, R.A. Piper 1982, J.M. Robinson 1964/71, Sato 1988, Schürmann 1975b, Zeller 1982
F. NEIRYNCK, *ETL* 70 (1994) 163-164.

1994 Introduction. — *Ibid.*, 1-21. Esp. 7-10: "Q as kerygma"; 10-15: "Wisdom genres and the sayings gospel"; 15-20: "The shape of Q".

1995* (ed.), *Conflict and Invention. Literary, Rhetorical, and Social Studies on the Sayings Gospel Q.* Valley Forge, PA: Trinity Press International, 1995, IX-245 p. [NTA 40, p. 341] → Arnal, Carruth, Cotter, R.C. Douglas, Hartin, R.A. Horsley, Kloppenborg, R.A. Piper, Reed, Vaage 1989a, 1995a
F. NEIRYNCK, *ETL* 72 (1996) 442-443.

1995a Conflict and Invention. Recent Studies on Q. — *Ibid.*. 1-14. Esp. 3-6: "The social location of the Q people"; 6-11: "Invention and arrangement" [composition].

1995b Jesus and the Parables of Jesus in Q. — PIPER, R.A. (ed.), *The Gospel Behind the Gospels*, 1995, 275-319. Esp. 281-290: "Between Jesus and the parables in Q"; 290-300: "Parables in the secondary layer" [Q 7,31-32; 12,42-46; 14,16-24; 19,12-27]; 300-317: "The formative stratum" [Q 12,16-21; 13,18-21; 15,4-7.8-10].

1995c The Transformation of Moral Exhortation in *Didache* 1-5. — JEFFORD, C.N. (ed.), *The Didache in Context*, 1995, 88-109. Esp. 102-104 [7,12; 22,34-40/Did]; 106-108.111-112 [5,21/48/Did].

**KLOPPENBURG, B.**

1957 Sessão espirita no Monte Tabor? (Mt 17,1-8 par). — *REB* 17 (1957) 116-118.

**KLOSTERMANN, Erich**

1909R *Matthäus* (Handbuch zum Neuen Testament. II. Die Evangelien) [1909]; *Das Matthäusevangelium* (Handbuch zum Neuen Testament, 4) [²1927; ³1938]. Tübingen: Mohr, ⁴1971, VIII-233 p. [NTA 16, p. 240]

1933R (ed.), *Origenes Werke XII. Origenes Matthäuserklärung. II: Die lateinische Übersetzung der Commentariorum Series* [1933], ed. U. Treu (GCS, 38). Berlin: Akademie, ²1976, X-307 p.
A. LE BOULLUEC, *RevÉtudGrecq* 92 (1979) 277-278.

1955 & FRÜCHTEL, L. (eds.), *Origenes Werke XII. Origenes Matthäuserklärung. III: Fragmente und Indices. 2. Hälfte* (GCS, 41/2). Berlin: Akademie, 1955, 490 p. Esp. 1-22: "Einführung in die Arbeiten des Origenes zum Matthäus" (Klostermann); 23-53: "Zur altlateinischen Übersetzung von Origenes' Matthäus-Kommentar" (Früchtel); 53-79: "Nachträge" (Früchtel); 81-83: "Vergleich der Zählung der Katenen-Fragmente in TU 47,2" (G. Perl); 85-490: "Gesamtregister" (Früchtel); ed. U. Treu, ²1968, 409 p. Esp. 1-406: "Nachträge"; 407-409: "Vergleich".
W. BAUER, *TLZ* 80 (1955) 539-540; É. DES PLACES, *VD* 34 (1956) 124; C. MARTIN, *NRT* 80 (1958) 199-200.

1956 Zum Verständnis von Mt 6,2. — *ZNW* 47 (1956) 280-281. [NTA 2, 46]

1964 *Epilog zu Origenes' Kommentar zum Matthäus* (Sitzungsberichte der deutschen Akademie der Wissenschaften zu Berlin. Klasse für Sprachen, Literatur und Kunst, 1964/4). Berlin: Akademie, 1964, 35 p.
C. MARTIN, *NRT* 87 (1965) 988.

**KLUG, Heinrich**

1976 *Das Evangelium als Geschichtsquelle und Glaubensverkündigung. Zugang zum historischen Jesus und zur göttlichen Offenbarung.* Stein am Rhein/Schw: Christiana, 1976, 526 p. Esp. 47-57: "Matthäus, Verfasser der Logia"; 427-500: "Kindheitsevangelien".

**KLUMBIES, Paul-Gerhard**

1992 *Die Rede von Gott bei Paulus in ihrem zeitgeschichtlichen Kontext* (FRLANT, 155). Göttingen: Vandenhoeck & Ruprecht, 1992, 289 p. Esp. 107-109 [6,9-13]. — Diss. Bethel-Bielefeld, 1988 (A. Lindemann).

**KNACKSTEDT, Joseph**

1960 Manifestatio SS. Trinitatis in Baptismo Domini? — *VD* 38 (1960) 76-91. [NTA 5, 63]

1963 De duplici miraculo multiplicationis panum. [14,13-22; 15,32-39] — *VD* 41 (1963) 39-51, 140-153. [NTA 8, 579]

1964 Die beiden Brotvermehrungen im Evangelium. — *NTS* 10 (1963-64) 309-335. Esp. 310-320: "Literarkritik"; 320-328: "Moderne Exegese auf Grund der genera litteraria"; 328-331: "Nochmals der Rückverweis bei Mt. und Mk.". [NTA 9, 154]

**KNAK, Siegfried**

1954 Neutestamentliche Missionstexte nach neuerer Exegese. — *TViat* 5 (1953-54) 27-50. Esp. 29-32.41-46 [28,16-20].

**KNEPPER, Maria**

1953 Die "Armen" der Bergpredigt Jesu. — *BK* 8/1 (1953) 19-27.

**KNIBB, Michael A.**

1979 The Date of the Parables of Enoch: A Critical Review. — *NTS* 25 (1978-79) 345-359. Esp. 356-357 [19,28; 13,40-43; 25,31]. [NTA 23, 1042]

**KNIGHT, George A.F.**

1960 "Thou art Peter". [16,18] — *TTod* 17 (1960-61) 168-180. [NTA 5, 718]

**KNIGHT, Jonathan**

1996 *Disciples of the Beloved One. The Christology, Social Setting and Theological Context of the Ascension of Isaiah* (Journal for the Study of the Pseudepigrapha, SS 18). Sheffield: JSOT, 1996, 354 p. Esp. 276-278, 291-294. — Diss. Cambridge, 1991 (C. Rowland).

**KNOCH, Otto**

1963 *Ein Sämann ging aus. Botschaft der Gleichnisse. Eine Handreichung* (Werkhefte zur Bibelarbeit, 2). Stuttgart: Katholisches Bibelwerk, 1963, 160 p.; ²1964, 192 p. Esp. 25; 30-58 [13]; 59-61 [11,16-17]; 68-80 [22,1-14]; 81-86 [21,33-46]; 103-107 [25,1-13]; 108-112 [20,1-16]; 137-142 [18,23-35].
*Le parabole*, trans. C. Vivaldelli. Roma: Città Nuova, 1969, 217 p.

1964 *Eigenart und Bedeutung der Eschatologie im theologischen Aufriß des ersten Clemensbriefes. Eine auslegungsgeschichtliche Untersuchung* (Theophaneia, 17). Bonn: Hanstein, 1964, 483 p. Esp. 69-75: "Die synoptischen Evangelien". — Diss. Tübingen, 1959 (K.H. Schelkle).

1966 *Einer ist euer Meister. Jüngerschaft und Nachfolge* (Werkhefte zur Bibelarbeit, 10). Stuttgart: Katholisches Bibelwerk, 1966, 206 p. Esp. 74-80 [8,19-22]; 99-102 [10,37]; 109-118 [19,10-12]; 119-125 [10,38; 16,24]; 136-139 [19,29]; 140-142 [19,28]; 142 [8,11-12]; 142-143 [22,1-10]; 143-144 [25,31-46]; 144-145 [25,14-30].

1968   Die Deutung der Primatstelle Mt 16,18 im Lichte der neueren Diskussion. Eine
       Übersicht. — *BK* 23 (1968) 44-46. [NTA 13, 170]

1969   Gott als Anwalt des Menschen. Mitmenschlichkeit als Aufgabe der Christen nach Mt
       25,31-46. — *BK* 24 (1969) 82-84. [NTA 14, 490]

1970   Die Botschaft des Matthäusevangeliums über Empfängnis und Geburt Jesu vor dem
       Hintergrund der Christusverkündigung des Neuen Testaments. — *Zum Thema
       Jungfrauengeburt*, Stuttgart: Katholisches Bibelwerk, 1970, 37-59. Esp. 39-48: "Aufbau und
       Eigenart der Kindheitsgeschichte des Matthäusevangeliums".

1971   "Machet alle Völker zu meinen Jüngern!" Die Botschaft des Evangeliums nach Mattäus.
       — *BK* 26 (1971) 65-69. [NTA 16, 526]

1973*  & MESSERSCHMID, F. – ZENNER, A. (eds.), *Das Evangelium auf dem Weg zum
       Menschen. Zur Vermittlung und zum Vollzug des Glaubens [Heinrich Kahlefeld zum 70.
       Geburtstag]*. Frankfurt/M.: Knecht, 1973, XIII-359 p. → Kertelge, Kirchgässner, Knoch, H.
       Leroy, Trilling, E. Walter

1973   "Denn ich bin sanftmütig und demütig von Herzen" (Mt 11,28). Das Ringen um eine
       sinngetreue Übersetzung von Mt 11,28-30 als Voraussetzung für eine sachgemässe
       Auslegung. — *Ibid.*, 87-100.

1980   *Begegnung wird Zeugnis. Werden und Wesen des Neuen Testamentes* (Biblische Basis
       Bücher, 6). Stuttgart: Katholisches Bibelwerk; Kevelaer: Butzon & Bercker, 1980, 260
       p. Esp. 44-56: "Das Matthäusevangelium".

1981   Die Wunder Jesu. Biblische Gesichtspunkte. — *TGeg* 24 (1981) 203-211.

1983a  *Wer Ohren hat, der höre. Die Botschaft der Gleichnisse Jesu. Ein Werkbuch zur Bibel.*
       Stuttgart: Katholisches Bibelwerk, 1983, 346 p. Esp. 71-76 [13,1-9/Mk]; 77-84 [13,18-23/Mk];
       91-94 [13,31-32/Mk]; 95-99 [13,33/Q 13,20]; 101-105 [13,24-30]; 107-112 [13,36-43]; 113-118 [13,47-50];
       119-123 [13,44-46]; 125-128 [11,16-17/Q 7,31-32]; 137-144 [22,1-10/Q 14,16-24]; 145-149 [22,11-13]; 151-
       159 [21,33-46/Mk]; 171-176 [24,45-51/Q 12,42-46]; 177-181 [24,43-44/Q 12,39-40]; 183-187 [5,25-26/Q
       12,58-59]; 189-193 [24,37-39/Q 17,26-30]; 195-201 [25,1-13]; 203-210 [20,1-16]; 227-236 [25,14-30/Q
       19,12-27]; 237-242 [18,12-14/Q 15,4-7]; 261-267 [21,28-32]; 295-301 [18,23-35].

1983b  Charisma und Amt: Ordnungselemente der Kirche Christi. — *SNTU* 8 (1983) 124-161.
       Esp. 144-145. [NTA 30, 1262]

1984   Maria in der Heiligen Schrift. — BEINERT, W. – PETRI, H. (eds.), *Handbuch der
       Marienkunde*, Regensburg: Pustet, 1984, 15-92. Esp. 30-40: "Die marianischen Aussagen des
       Matthäusevangeliums" [1-2; 12,46-50; 13,54-58; 27,55-56.61; 28,1]; 76-79; 88-92.

1986   *Dem, der glaubt, ist alles möglich. Die Botschaft der Wundererzählungen der Evan-
       gelien. Ein Werkbuch zur Bibel.* Stuttgart: Katholisches Bibelwerk, 1986, 584 p. Esp.
       147-256: "Wunderbare Heilungen" [8,1-4.5-13.14-15; 9,1-8.20-22.27-31; 12,9-14; 20,29-34]; 257-326:
       "Dämonenaustreibungen" [8,28-34; 9,32-34; 12,22-24; 15,21-28; 17,14-21]; 327-350: "Totenerweckungen"
       [9,18-24]; 351-400: "Messianische Zeichenhandlungen" [14,13-21; 15,29-39; 17,1-9; 21,18-22]; 401-409:
       "Vollmachtswunder" [17,24-27]; 477-502: "Rettungswunder" [8,23-27; 14,22-33].

1988a  *Vollständige Synopse der Evangelien. Nach dem Text der Einheitsübersetzung. Mit
       wichtigen außerbiblischen Parallelen.* Stuttgart: Katholische Bibelanstalt, 1988, XXIV-
       325 p. → Peisker 1983
       F. NEIRYNCK, *ETL* 67 (1991) 164-165.

1988b  Kenntnis und Verwendung des Matthäus-Evangeliums bei den Apostolischen Vätern.
       — SCHENKE, L. (ed.), *Studien zum Matthäusevangelium*. FS W. Pesch, 1988, 157-177.
       Esp. 159-162: "Der Stand der Forschung"; 162-175: "Die einzelnen Schriften und ihre Auswertung des
       Matthäusevangeliums".

1991   Petrus im Neuen Testament. — MACCARRONE, M. (ed.), *Il primato del vescovo di
       Roma nel primo millennio. Ricerche e testimonianze. Atti del Symposium storico-*

*teologico Roma, 9-13 Ottobre 1989* (Pontificio comitato di scienze storiche. Atti e documenti, 4), Città del Vaticano: Ed. Vaticana, 1991, 3-52. Esp. 27-31: "Das Petrusbild des Matthäusevangeliums".

1994 Die "andere" Maria: Eine von den "Frauen um Jesus". [27,61; 28,1] — *Bausteine für die Einheit der Christen* (Gersfeld-Dalherda) 34/134 (1994) 3-6. [NTA 38, 1375]

KNOCKAERT, André

1984 Redécouvrir le discours sur la "fin du temps" (Mt 24-25). — *LumVit* 39 (1984) 407-418. A Fresh Look at the Eschatological Discourse (Mt 24-25). — *LumVit* 40 (1985) 167-179. [NTA 30, 125]

KNÖRZER, Wolfgang

1966 *Vater unser. Das Gebet der Christenheit. Mitte von Frömmigkeit und Lehre. Gebets- und Lebensordnung des Christen nach Mt 6,1-18 und Lk 10,25-11,13* (Werkhefte zur Bibelarbeit, 6). Stuttgart: Katholisches Bibelwerk, 1966, 130 p.; [2]1969, 117 p.

1967a *Wir haben seinen Stern gesehen. Die Kindheitsevangelien nach Lukas und Matthäus* (Werkhefte zur Bibelarbeit, 11). Stuttgart: Katholisches Bibelwerk, 1967, 272 p. [NTA 12, p. 394]; [2]1968, 240 p. Esp. 177-235: "Das Kindheitsevangelium nach Matthäus".

1967b Unser Vater im Himmel. Das Gebet des Herrn als Inbegriff des Evangeliums. — *BK* 22 (1967) 79-86. [NTA 12, 553]

1967c Thesen zur Praxis des Vaterunserbetens. — *Ibid.*, 93-94.

1968 *Die Bergpredigt. Modell einer neuen Welt* (Biblisches Forum, 2). Stuttgart: Katholisches Bibelwerk, 1968, 104 p. [NTA 14, p. 109]
   J. DE JESÚS MARIA, *EstJos* 26 (1972) 111-112; WEISS, *BK* 24 (1969) 72.

KNOPP, R.

1989 *Finding Jesus in the Gospels. A Companion to Mark, Matthew, Luke and John.* Notre Dame, IN: Ave Maria Press, 1989, 326 p. [NTA 34, p. 247]

KNOTZINGER, K.

1967 Die Seligpreisungen bei Bernhard von Clairvaux. — *Jahrbuch für Mystische Theologie* 13 (1967-68) 11-42.

KNOWLES, Michael

1993 *Jeremiah in Matthew's Gospel. The Rejected Prophet Motif in Matthaean Redaction* (JSNT SS, 68). Sheffield: JSOT, 1993, 376 p. Esp. 19-95: "Matthew's three explicit references to Jeremiah" [2,17-18; 16,14; 27,9-10]; 96-161: "The deuteronomistic rejected-prophet motif in Matthew"; 162-222: "Textual allusions in Matthew to Jeremiah traditions"; 223-246: "Typological references in Matthew to Jeremiah traditions"; 247-264: "The Jeremiah of Matthew's day"; 265-311: "Matthew's vision of Jeremiah"; 312-323: "A deuteronomistic outlook and the provenance of Matthew's gospel". [NTA 38, p. 121] — Diss. School of Theology, Toronto, Ont., 1991 (R.N. Longenecker).
   R. CARROLL, *ExpT* 105 (1993-94) 247; G. CLAUDEL, *Bib* 76 (1995) 427-430; E. CUVILLIER, *ETR* 71 (1996) 87-88; B.R. DOYLE, *AusBR* 42 (1994) 76-77; D.R.A. HARE, *CRBR* 8 (1995) 238-240; D.J. HARRINGTON, *CBQ* 56 (1994) 601-602; A. MELLO, *SBF/LA* 43 (1993) 559-560; W. WIEFEL, *TLZ* 119 (1994) 652-654.

KNOX, D. Broughton

1975 The Five Comings of Jesus: Matthew 24 and 25. — *RTR* 34/2 (1975) 44-54. [NTA 20, 445]

KNOX, John

1958 *The Death of Christ. The Cross in New Testament History and Faith.* New York – Nashville, TN: Abingdon, 1958, 190 p. Esp. 88-107 [Son of Man sayings in the synoptic gospels]; London: Collins, 1959; (The Fontana Library. Theology and Philosophy, 8/6), 1967, 160 p. Esp. 71-91.

**KNOX, Ronald**

1952  *A Commentary on the Gospels*. New York: Sheed & Ward, 1952, XVIII-284 p.
*A New Testament Commentary for English Readers. I. The Gospels*. London: Burns,
Oates and Washbourne; New York: Sheed and Ward, 1953, XV-276 p. Esp. 1-72: "The
gospel according to St. Matthew".

**KNOX, Wilfred Lawrence**

1957  *The Sources of the Synoptic Gospels*. II. *St Luke and St Matthew*, ed. H. Chadwick.
Cambridge: University Press, 1957, IX-170 p. Esp. 1-36: "The question of Q" [5-7]; 119-137:
"The sources of Matthew" [1-2; 13; 18]. [NTA 3, p. 306-307]
A.E. BARNETT, *Interpr* 12 (1958) 248.250; F.V. FILSON, *JBL* 76 (1957) 322-323; H. GREEVEN, *TLZ*
85 (1960) 589-592; A. VIARD, *RSPT* 42 (1958) 325; A. WIKGREN, *JRel* 32 (1958) 272-273; P. WINTER,
*TZ* 13 (1957) 367-369; S. ZEITLIN, *JQR* 45 (1954-55) 268-270.

**KNUTH, Hans Christian**

1971  *Zur Auslegungsgeschichte von Psalm 6* (Beiträge zur Geschichte der biblischen Exegese,
11). Tübingen: Mohr, 1971, XI-430 p. Esp. 21-22 [7,23/Ps 6,9].

**KOBELSKI, Paul J.**

1981  *Melchizedek and Melchireša'* (CBQ MS, 10). Washington, DC: CBAA, 1981, IX-166
p. Esp. 130-137: "11Q Melchizedek and the Son of Man question".

**KOCH, Dietrich-Alex**

1975  *Die Bedeutung der Wundererzählungen für die Christologie des Markusevangeliums*
(BZNW, 42). Berlin: de Gruyter, 1975, XII-217 p. Esp. 155-157 [16,1-4; Q 11,29-32/Mk]; 173-
175 [Q 11,20/Mk]. — Diss. Göttingen, 1973 (H. Conzelmann).

1989*  & SELLIN, G. – LINDEMANN, A. (eds.), *Jesu Rede von Gott und ihre Nachgeschichte
im frühen Christentum. Beiträge zur Verkündigung Jesu und zum Kerygma der Kirche.
Festschrift für Willi Marxsen zum 70. Geburtstag*, Gütersloh: Mohn, 1989, 476 p. →
Frankemölle, Heine, Hoffmann, Lindemann, Schüller

1992a  Source Criticism. — *ABD* 6 (1992) 165-171. Esp. 166-169: "The Synoptic Gospels".

1992b  Der Täufer als Zeuge des Offenbarers. Das Täuferbild von Joh 1,19-34 auf dem
Hintergrund von Mk 1,2-11. — VAN SEGBROECK, F.. et al. (eds.), *The Four Gospels
1992*. FS F. Neirynck, 1992, III, 1963-1984. Esp. 1974-1975 [3,11/Jn 1,26]; 1975-1978 [3,11
minor agreements].

**KOCH, Gerhard**

1959  *Die Auferstehung Jesu Christi* (Beiträge zur historischen Theologie, 27). Tübingen:
Mohr, 1959, ²1965, 338 p. Esp. 23-75: "Die Osterbotschaft des Neuen Testamentes".

**KOCH, Klaus**

1964  *Was ist Formgeschichte? Neue Wege der Bibelexegese*. Neukirchen-Vluyn:
Neukirchener, 1964, ²1967, XIII-260 p. Esp. 7-9.21-22.46-48.64-68 [5,3-12].
*Was ist Formgeschichte? Methoden der Bibelexegese*. Neukirchen-Vluyn: Neukirchener,
³1974, XV-342 p. Esp. 7-9.50-55-74-78 [5,3-12].
*The Growth of the Biblical Tradition. The Form-Critical Method*, trans. S.M. Cupitt. London: Black, 1969,
XV-233 p. Esp. 6-8.39-44.59-62.

1968  Der Schatz im Himmel. — LOHSE, B. – SCHMIDT, H.P. (eds.), *Leben angesichts des
Todes. Beiträge zum theologischen Problem des Todes. Helmut Thielicke zum 60.
Geburtstag*, Tübingen: Mohr, 1968, 47-60. Esp. 50-52 [6,19-21].

**KOCH, Robert**

1957  Die Wertung des Besitzes im Lukasevangelium. — *Bib* 38 (1957) 151-169. Esp. 152.158-
161 [5,3-6]; 166-167 [6,19-20; 7,13-14]. [NTA 2, 36]

1959   Die religiös-sittliche Umkehr (metanoia) nach den drei ältesten Evangelien und der Apostelgeschichte. — *Anima* (Freiburg/Schw) 14 (1959) 296-307. Esp. 300-304.

1987   L'appello alla santità di Lv 19,2 alla luce di Mt 5,48 e Lc 6,36. — NALEPA, M. — KENNEDY, T. (eds.), *La coscienza morale oggi. Omaggio al Prof. Domenico Capone* (Quaestiones morales, 3), Roma: Editiones Academiae Alphonsianae, 1987, 25-38. Esp. 32-34 [5,48]; 35-38 [Q 6,36].

**KODELL, Jerome**

1969   Luke's Use of *Laos*, "People," Especially in the Jerusalem Narrative (Lk 19,28–24,53). — *CBQ* 31 (1969) 327-343. Esp. 328-331: "The *laos* and the leaders"; 333-335: "The use of *laos* in Matthew". [NTA 14, 529]

1978   The Celibacy Logion in Matthew 19:12. — *BTB* 8 (1978) 19-23. [NTA 22, 403]

1988   *The Eucharist in the New Testament* (Zacchaeus Studies NT). Wilmington, DE: Glazier, 1988, 142 p.

**KODJAK, Andreij**

1986   *A Structural Analysis of the Sermon on the Mount* (Religion and Reason, 34). Berlin – New York: de Gruyter; Amsterdam: Mouton, 1986, X-234 p. Esp. 1-40: "Author's point of view and method"; 41-74 [5,3-12]; 75-102 [5,13-48]; 103-136 [6]; 137-149 [7,1-12]; 151-164 [7,13-27]; 165-212: "The structure and the message of Christ's standard sermon". [NTA 31, p. 364]

　　　X. ALEGRE, *ActBibl* 26 (1989) 43-44; G. HALLBÄCK, *DanskTeolTids* 51 (1988) 151-152.

**KÖBERT, Raimund**

1959   Zwei Fassungen von Mt. 16,18 bei den Syrern. — *Bib* 40 (1959) 1018-1020. [NTA 4, 655]

**KÖHLER, Wolf-Dietrich**

1987   *Die Rezeption des Matthäusevangeliums in der Zeit vor Irenäus* (WUNT, II/24). Tübingen: Mohr, 1987, XVI-605 p. Esp. 19-56 [Didache]; 57-72 [1 Clement]; 73-96 [Ignatius]; 97-110 [Polycarp]; 111-123 [Barnabas]; 125-128 [Hermas]; 129-149 [2 Clement]; 151-158 [Papias]; 159 [Diognetus]; 161-265 [Justin]; 270-271 [Gospel of the Hebrews]; 272-287 [Gospel of the Ebionites]; 288-300 [Gospel of the Nazoraeans]; 303-308 [Ascension of Isaiah]; 309-313 [Orac. Sibyllina]; 314-318 [Apoc. of Peter]; 319-324 [Testaments of the XII Patriarchs]; 325-336 [5 Ezra]; 337 [Ps.-Clem. Recogn.]; 340-350 [Ptolemaeus]; 351-354 [Heracleon]; 355-365 [Valentinus]; 365-368 [Theodotus]; 369-370 [Gospel of Mary]; 371-372 [Odes of Salomon]; 373-376 [Basilides]; 379-428 [Nag Hammadi]; 429-436 [Protev. Jacobi]; 437-448 [Gospel of Peter]; 449-450 [Infancy Gospel (of Thomas)]; 451-452 [Pap. Eg. 2]; 453-454 [Pap. Eg. 3]; 455 [Pap. Cairo. 10735]; 456 [Pap. Copt. Strasb.]; 457 [Agrapha]; 458 [P. Oxy 840; 1224]; 459-460 [Acts of Andrew]; 461-465 [Acts of John]; 463-466 [Acts of Paul]; 467-470 [Acts of Peter]; 471-483 [Ep. Apostolorum]; 484-485 [1 Peter]; 486 [2 Peter]; 487-489 [MartPol]; 490-492 [Acts of the martyrs]; 493 [Aristides]; 494-498 [Athenagoras]; 499 [Tatian]; 500-504 [Theophilus of Antiochia]; 505-507 [Melito of Sardes]; 508 [Sentences of Sextus]; 509 [Hegesippus]; 510-511 [Apollinaris of Hierapolis]; 512-513 [Apollonius, c. Montanum]; 514 [Dionysius of Corinth]; 515-516 [Theodotus]; 539-571: "Tabellarischer Überblick über die Rezeption des Mt vor Irenäus". [NTA 32, p. 372] — Diss. Bern, 1986 (U. Luz).

　　　T. FORNBERG, *SEÅ* 55 (1990) 172-173; H. GIESEN, *TGeg* 32 (1989) 77-78; P. GRECH, *CrnStor* 11 (1990) 376-378; J.D. KINGSBURY, *CRBR* 2 (1989) 213-215; S. MOYSA, *CollTheol* 58/3 (1988) 185; M. MÜLLER, *DanskTeolTids* 52 (1989) 222-223; M. PARMENTIER, *Bijdragen* 51 (1990) 85-86; W.R. SCHOEDEL, *CBQ* 51 (1989) 562-564; A. SEGOVIA, *ArchTeolGran* 50 (1987) 476-477; C.M. TUCKETT, *JSNT* 38 (1990) 127.

**KOEKEMOER, P.J.T.**

1972   Die getuienis van die evangelie volgens Mattheus oor die maagdelike geboorte van Jesus Christus. [1,18-25] — *HervTS* 28 (1972) 63-87.

**KÖNIG, A.**

1980   Nog eens oor die betekenis van gelykenisse. [Once again concerning the meaning of parables] — *NduitseGT* 21 (1980) 307-312. [NTA 25, 863]

**KOENIG, John**

1979  *Jews and Christians in Dialogue. New Testament Foundations.* Philadelphia, PA: Westminster, 1979, 185 p. Esp. 16-18 [19,16-22/Mk]; 21-25 [Jewish leaders]; 25-29 [law]; 82-96.166-167: "Matthew: a claim on Israel's leadership".

1985  *New Testament Hospitality. Partnership with Strangers as Promise and Mission* (Overtures to Biblical Theology, 17). Philadelphia, PA: Fortress, 1985, XIII-158 p. Esp. 20-26 [11,16-19]; 26-38.

**KÖPPEN, Klaus-Peter**

1961  *Die Auslegung der Versuchungsgeschichte unter besonderer Berücksichtigung der Alten Kirche. Ein Beitrag zur Geschichte der Schriftauslegung* (Beiträge zur Geschichte der biblischen Exegese, 4). Tübingen: Mohr, 1961, 126 p. Esp. 4-66.79-93 [Early Church]; 94-103 [Middle Ages]; 104-113 [Luther].
R.P.C. HANSON, *JTS* 13 (1962) 412-413; N. PERRIN, *JBL* 81 (1962) 426-427.

1989  The Interpretation of Jesus' Temptations (Mt. 4,1-11; Mk. 1,12f; Lk. 4,1-13) by the Early Church Fathers. — *Patristic and Byzantine Review* (Kingston, NY) 8 (1989) 41-43.

**KÖRKEL-HINKFOTH, R.**

1994  *Die Parabel von den klugen und törichten Jungfrauer (Mt 25,1-13) in der bildenden Kunst und im geistlichen Schauspiel* (EHS, XXVIII/190). Frankfurt/M: Lang, 1994.

**KÖRTNER, Ulrich H.J.**

1983  *Papias von Hierapolis. Ein Beitrag zur Geschichte des frühen Christentums* (FRLANT, 133). Göttingen: Vandenhoeck & Ruprecht, 1983, 371 p. Esp. 203-206: "Das Mt-Fragment". — Diss. Bethel-Bielefeld, 1981 (D. Lührmann).

**KOESTER, Helmut**

1957a  *Synoptische Überlieferung bei den apostolischen Vätern* (TU, 65). Berlin: Akademie, 1957, XVII-274 p. Esp. 4-23 [1 Clem]; 24-61 [Ignatius]; 62-11: [2 Clem]; 112-123 [Polycarp; EpPhil]; 124-158 [Barnabas]; 159-241 [Didache]; 242-256 [Hermas]. — Diss. Marburg, 1954 (R. Bultmann). → Bellinzoni 1992

1957b  Die ausserkanonischen Herrenworte als Produkte der christlichen Gemeinde. — *ZNW* 48 (1957) 220-237. Esp. 223-225 [1 Clem]; 225-226 [Polycarp Phil]; 226-229 [Gospel of the Hebrews]; 229-230 [Ps-Clementine Hom]; 231-233 [Gospel of the Nazoraeans]; 233-235 [24,30-31/1Thess 4,15-17]; 235-236 [18,20/P. Aboth 3,2].
The Extracanonical Sayings of the Lord as Products of the Christian Community. — *Semeia* 44 (1988) 57-77. [NTA 33, 987] Esp. 60-63; 63-64; 64-66; 66-68; 69-70; 71-73; 74-75.
Une production de la communauté chrétienne: les paroles du Seigneur. — ID. - BOVON, F. (eds.), *Genèse de l'écriture chrétienne* (Mémoires premières), Turnhout: Brepols, 1991, 23-58. Esp. 28-31; 31-34; 34-38; 39-41; 44-47; 48-51; 51-52; 55-56 (Postface).

1965  Γνωμαὶ διάφοροι. The Origin and Nature of Diversfication in the History of Early Christianity. — *HTR* 58 (1965) 279-316. Esp. 287-290 [Peter]; 293-304 [Th]. [NTA 10, 712]; = ROBINSON, J.M. - KOESTER, H. (eds.), *Trajectories*, 1971, 114-157. Esp. 123-126; 128-143.
Γνωμαὶ διάφοροι. Ursprung und Wesen der Mannigfaltigkeit in der Geschichte des frühen Christentums. — *ZTK* 65 (1968) 160-203. Esp. 167-172; 176-190. [NTA 13, 411]; = ROBINSON, J.M. - KOESTER, H. (eds.), *Entwicklungslinien*, 1970, 107-146.

1968  One Jesus and Four Primitive Gospels. — *HTR* 61 (1968) 203-247. Esp. 203-211: "The problem of the 'historical' Jesus and the question of primitive gospel forms"; 211-230: "Collections of sayings". [NTA 13, 100]; = ROBINSON, J.M. - KOESTER, H. (eds.), *Trajectories*, 1971, 158-204. Esp. 158-166; 166-187.
Ein Jesus und vier ursprüngliche Evangeliengattungen. — ROBINSON, J.M. - KOESTER, H. (eds.), *Entwicklungslinien*, 1970, 147-190.

The Synoptic Sayings Source and the *Gospel of Thomas*. [1971, 166-187] — KLOPPENBORG, J.S. (ed.), *The Shape of Q*, 1994, 158-204.

1980a  *Einführung in das Neue Testament im Rahmen der Religionsgeschichte und Kultur-geschichte der hellenistischen und römischen Zeit* (de Gruyter Lehrbuch). Berlin – New York: de Gruyter, 1980, XIX-801 p. Esp. 477-482: "Die synoptische Frage und die Quellen der Evangelien"; 584-586 [Q]; 607-614 [Mt].
*Introduction to the New Testament*. Vol. I: *History, Culture, and Religion of the Hellenistic Age*; Vol. II: *History and Literature of Early Christianity* (Hermeneia: Foundations and Facets). Berlin – New York: de Gruyter; Philadelphia, PA: Fortress, 1982, XXX-429 p. and XXX-365 p. Esp. II, 44-49; 147-149; 171-177. *Introducción al Nuevo Testamento*, trans. J. Lacarra & A. Piñero (Biblioteca de estudios bíblicos, 59). Salamanca: Sígueme, 1988, 905 p.

1980b  Apocryphal and Canonical Gospels. — *HTR* 73 (1980) 105-130. Esp. 112-119: "The synoptic sayings source and the gospel of Thomas"; 126-130: "The gospel of Peter and the passion narrative". [NTA 25, 738]
Évangiles apocryphes et évangiles canoniques. — ID. - BOVON, F. (eds.), *Genèse de l'écriture chrétienne* (Mémoires premières), Turnhout: Brepols, 1991, 59-106. Esp. 70-80.

1980c  Gnostic Writings as Witnesses for the Development of the Sayings Tradition. — LAYTON, B. (ed.), *The Rediscovery of Gnosticism. Proceedings of the International Conference on Gnosticism at Yale New Haven, Connecticut, March 28-31, 1978*. I. *The School of Valentinus* (Studies in the History of Religions. Supplements to *Numen*, 41/1), Leiden: Brill, 1980, 238-261. Esp. 238-244 [Q 11,9-13/Th 94]; 244-250 [11,28-30; Q 10,21-24/Th 90].

1983a  Formgeschichte/Formkritik. II. Neues Testament. — *TRE* 11 (1983) 286-299. Esp. 289-293: "Der Redenstoff der Evangelien"; 293-295: "Der Erzählungsstoff der Evangelien".

1983b  History and Development of Mark's Gospel (From Mark to *Secret Mark* and "Canonical" Mark). — CORLEY, B. (ed.), *Colloquy on New Testament Studies. A Time for Reappraisal and Fresh Approaches*, Macon, GA: Mercer University Press, 1983, 35-57 (discussion, 59-85). Esp. 42-54 [minor agreements]. → Peabody 1983b

1983c  Three Thomas Parables. — LOGAN, A.H.B. - WEDDERBURN, A.J.M. (eds.), *The New Testament and Gnosis: Essays in Honour of Robert McL. Wilson*, Edinburgh: Clark, 1983, 195-203. Esp. 195-197 [13,3-9/Th 9]; 197-198 [22,1-14/Th 64]; 199-200 [21,33-41/Th 65].

1984   Überlieferung und Geschichte der frühchristlichen Evangelienliteratur. — *ANRW* II.25.2 (1984) 1463-1542. Esp. 1480-1481 [gospel genre]; 1497-1500.1538 [Jewish-christian gospels]; 1512-1515 [Q]; 1529-1531 [sources/composition]; 1539-1542 [Diatessaron].

1989a  From the Kerygma-Gospel to Written Gospels. — *NTS* 35 (1989) 361-381. Esp. 367-368 [εὐαγγέλιον]; 370-373 [2nd cent.]; 374-375 [Papias]. [NTA 34, 76]

1989b  The Text of the Synoptic Gospels in the Second Century. — PETERSEN, W.L. (ed.), *Gospel Traditions*, 1989, 19-37. Esp. 20-25: "Evidence for Matthew's and Luke's use of Mark" [13,11; 16,21; 17,14-21; 22,34-40]; 26-28: "Evidence from the apostolic fathers"; 28-33: "Justin Martyr" [27,29.40].

1990a  *Ancient Christian Gospels. Their History and Development*. Philadelphia, PA: Trinity Press International; London: SCM, 1990, XXXII-448 p. Esp. 84-113: "The gospel of Thomas and the synoptic tradition" [Th/Q: 86-99; Th/Mt: 103-107]; 128-171: "The synoptic sayings source"; 314-332: "The gospel of Matthew"; 360-402: "The gospel quotations of Justin Martyr". → Petersen; → R.A. Horsley 1992b, Neirynck 1991e, Tuckett 1991
W.G. MOORE, *ExpT* 102 (1990-91) 315.

1990b  Q and Its Relatives. — GOEHRING, J.E., et al. (eds.), *Gospel Origins*. FS J.M. Robinson, 1990, 49-63. Esp. 50-53: "The 1 Corinthians complex"; 53-55: "The esoteric wisdom of the parables"; 55-63: "Q and the gospel of Thomas".

1993   Recovering the Original Meaning of Matthew's Parables. — *BibReview* 9/3 (1993) 11.52.

1994a  Jesus' Presence in the Early Church. — *CrnStor* 15 (1994) 541-557. Esp. 541-546 [Q].
[NTA 39, 1667]

1994b  Written Gospels or Oral Tradition? — *JBL* 113 (1994) 293-297. [NTA 39, 88] → Massaux
1950/86

**KOGLER, Franz**

1988  *Das Doppelgleichnis vom Senfkorn und vom Sauerteig in seiner traditionsgeschichtlichen
Entwicklung. Zur Reich-Gottes-Vorstellung Jesu und ihren Aktualisierungen in der
Urkirche* (FzB, 59). Würzburg: Echter, 1988, 295 p. Esp. 18-28: "Die Texte und ihr Kontext";
31-42: "Forschungsüberblick"; 63-76: "Agreements"; 179-187 [13,33/Lk 13,20]; 206-208 [Mt redaction].
— Diss. Linz, 1987 (A. Fuchs).
   J. ERNST, *TGl* 79 (1989) 622; V. FUSCO, *RivBib* 38 (1990) 532-534; H. GIESEN, *TGeg* 34 (1991) 153-
154; G. NEBE, *TRev* 86 (1990) 201-203; F. NEIRYNCK, *ETL* 65 (1989) 440-441; A. PUIG I TÀRRECH,
*Bib* 71 (1990) 134-137; U. SCHNELLE, *SNTU* 14 (1989) 277-278; M.L. SOARDS, *CBQ* 52 (1990) 751-
752; G. STRECKER, *TLZ* 115 (1990) 810-812; C.M. TUCKETT, *JSNT* 39 (1990) 119-120.

**KO HA FONG, Maria**

1984  *Crucem tollendo Christum sequi. Untersuchung zum Verständnis eines Logions Jesu in
der Alten Kirche* (Münsterische Beiträge zur Theologie, 52). Münster: Aschendorff,
1984, VII-148 p. Esp. 9-25: "Das Logion vom Kreuztragen in den synoptischen Evangelien" [10,38;
16,24]. — Diss. Münster, 1982-83 (B. Kötting).

**KOHLENBERGER, John R.**

1995  & GOODRICK, E.W. – SWANSON, J.A., *The Exhaustive Concordance to the Greek New
Testament.* Grand Rapids, MI: Zondervan, 1995, XV-1056 p.

**KOHLER, Werner**

1983  Der Vater und die Väter. Das Unser-Vater im Horizont einer vaterlosen Gesellschaft.
— LUZ, U. – WEDER, H. (eds.), *Die Mitte des Neuen Testaments.* FS E. Schweizer,
1983, 119-130. Esp. 124-127.

**KOKKINOS, Nikos**

1989  Crucifixion in *A.D.* 36: The Keystone for Dating the Birth of Jesus. — VARDAMAN, J.
– YAMAUCHI, E.M. (eds.), *Chronos, Kairos, Christos.* FS J. Finegan, 1989, 133-163.
Esp. 157-162: "Matthew and the datum of the star".

**KOKOT, Miroslaw**

1978  *Znaczenie obłoku w synoptycznych opisach Przemienienia Pańskiego* [The significance
of the cloud in the synoptics]. Diss. Lublin, 1978, XII-259 p. (F. Gryglewicz).

**KOLLMANN, Bernd**

1990a  *Ursprung und Gestalten der frühchristlichen Mahlfeier* (Göttinger theologische Arbeiten,
43). Göttingen: Vandenhoeck & Ruprecht, 1990, 296 p. Esp. 181-184 [26,26-29]; 208-212
[22,1-14]; 213-215 [8,11-12]; 221 [11,19]; 259-260 [28,18-20]; 260-261 [16,18-19]; 261-262 [10,34-36]. —
Diss. Göttingen, 1989 (H. Stegemann).

1990b  Lk 12,35-38 – ein Gleichnis der Logienquelle. [24,42-44; 25,1-13] — *ZNW* 81 (1990)
254-261. [NTA 35, 677]

1996  *Jesus und die Christen als Wundertäter. Studien zu Magie, Medizin und Schamanismus
in Antike und Christentum* (FRLANT, 170). Göttingen: Vandenhoeck & Ruprecht,
1996, 438 p. Esp. 174-215: "Dämonenaustreibungen Jesu" [10,5-16; 12,22-30.43-45; 17,14-21]; 215-271:
"Krankenheilungen Jesu" [8,5-13; 11,2-6; 12,11; 13,16-17]; 271-281: "Naturwunder" [17,24-27]; 281-287:
"Die Verweigerung demonstrativer Machterweise" [4,1-11; 12,38-42; 15,1-4]; 292-294 [Mt redaction]; 316-
321 [Q 10,1-15]; 330-335 [7,15-23]. — Diss. Göttingen, 1994 (H. Stegemann).

**KOLPING, Adolf**

1981 *Fundamentaltheologie*. III: *Die katholische Kirche als die Sachwalterin der Offenbarung Gottes*. I. Teil: *Die geschichtliche Anfänge der Kirche Christi*. Münster: Regensberg, 1981, XXV-875 p. Esp. 76-86: "Die Q-Tradition"; 94-102: "Das Mattäus-Evangelium"; 216-229: "Jüngerschaft zur Zeit des irdischen Jesus nach der Redenquelle (Q)" [Q 9,57-60; Q 10,2-12; Q 22,28-30]; 298-302: "Jünger in der Sicht des Mattäus"; 322-379: "Der Kreis der Jünger um den historischen Jesus von Nazaret"; 484-486 [27,57-66]; 525-526.529-534 [28,16-20].

**KONCZ, Lajos**

1987 Biblische Theologie der Nächstenliebe. [Hungarian] — *Teologia* (Budapest) 21 (1987) 210-215.

**KONINGS, Johan**

1974 *Jesus nos Evangelhos Sinóticos* (Subsídios, 3). Porto Alegre: Pont. Univ. Católica do Rio Grande do Sul, 1974, 161 p. Esp. 24-25; 27-36 [kingdom]; 37-68 [5-7]; 72-74 [20,1-16]; 87-91 [24-25]; Petrópolis: Vozes, 1977, 149 p.

1978 Quem é quem na "parábola do último juizo" (Mt 25,31-46)? — *Perspectiva Theologica* (São Leopoldo) 10 (1978) 367-402.

**KOOLE, Jan Leunis**

1953 *Gaven der genezing* (Exegetica I, 5). Delft: van Keulen, 1953, 61 p. Esp. 7-31 [healing miracles].

**KOOLMEISTER, Richard**

1954 Selbstverleugnung, Kreuzesaufnahme und Nachfolge. Eine historische Studie zu Mt 16,24. — *Charistêria Iohanni Kõpp octogenario oblata* (Papers of the Estonian Theological Society in Exile, 7), Stockholm, 1954, 64-94.

**KOOP, Raymond Carl**

1989 *God as Father in the Synoptic Gospels and Pauline Literature: A Comparison and Differentiation*. Diss. Golden Gate Baptist Theol. Sem., 1989, 359 p. (O.S. Brooks). — *DissAbstr* 50 (1989-90) 2539.

**KOOREN, J.G.**

1963 Wet en Evangelie. [5,17] — *Homiletica en Biblica* (Den Haag) 22 (1963) 200-205. [NTA 9, 904]

**KOOYMAN, Arie C.**

1992 *De joodse kontekst van Mattheüs 5:31-32. Een bijdrage aan het debat over het gebruik van rabbijnse teksten voor de bestudering van het Nieuwe Testament*. Diss. Utrecht, 1992, VI-219 p. (P. van der Horst). Esp. 9-78: "Een historisch overzicht van het gebruik van rabbijnse parallellen voor de uitleg van Mattheüs 5:17-48"; 79-124: "Methodische problemen rond het gebruik van rabbijnse teksten voor de bestudering van Mattheüs 5:17-49"; 125-179: "De derde antithese (Mattheüs 5:31-32) en een rabbijnse parallel (Gittin 9:10)"; 187-190: "Summary".
B.J. KOET, *NTT* 48 (1994) 241-242; M. POORTHUIS, *Bijdragen* 54 (1993) 93-94.

**KOPAS, Jane**

1990 Jesus and Women in Matthew. — *TTod* 47 (1990-91) 13-21. [NTA 34, 1123]

**KOPP, Clemens**

1953 Die Stätte der Bergpredigt und Brotvermehrung. — *BK* 8/3 (1953) 10-16.

1959 *Die heiligen Stätten der Evangelien*. Regensburg: Pustet, 1959, 504 p. Esp. 16-21 [Betlehem].
*The Holy Places of the Gospels*. Edinburgh, 1963.

**KORNFELD, Walter**

1979 Die Liebeswerke Mt 25,35f.42f. in alttestamentlicher Überlieferung. — SCHMIDT-LAUBER, H.-C. (ed.), *Theologia scientia eminens practica. Fritz Zerbst zum 70. Geburtstag*, Wien–Freiburg–Basel: Herder, 1979, 255-265.

**KORTING, Georg**

1989 Binden oder lösen. Zu Verstockungs- und Befreiungstheologie in Mt 16,19; 18,18.21-35 und Joh 15,1-17; 20,23. — *SNTU* 14 (1989) 39-91. Esp. 39-43; 63-81 [18]; 82-89 [16,19]. [NTA 35, 144]

**KOSCH, Daniel**

1985 *Die Gottesherrschaft im Zeichen des Widerspruchs. Traditions- und redaktionsgeschichtliche Untersuchung von Lk 16,16 // Mt 11,12f bei Jesus, Q, und Lukas* (EHS, XXIII/257). Bern – Frankfurt/M – New York: Lang, 1985, 142 p. Esp. 12-18.86-91: "Literarkritik: synoptischen Vergleich und Quellenkritik"; 19-64.92-127: "Zur Traditionsgeschichte von Lk 16,16//Mt 11,12f". [NTA 30, p. 230]
    A. FUCHS, *SNTU* 12 (1987) 219.

1989a *Die eschatologische Tora des Menschensohnes. Untersuchungen zur Rezeption der Stellung Jesu zur Tora in Q* (NTOA, 12). Freiburg/Schw: Universitätsverlag; Göttingen, Vandenhoeck & Ruprecht, 1989, 512 p. Esp. 61-212: "Wehe euch Pharisäern…' (Lk 11,39b-41.42 // Mt 23,23-25f)"; 213-426: 'Liebet eure Feinde…' (Lk 6,27-35 // Mt 5,38-48)"; 427-444: "Das Gesetz und die Propheten bei Johannes…' (Lk 16,16-28 // Mt 11,12f; 5,18.32)"; 445-483: "Die Rezeption der Stellung Jesu zur Tora in Q". — Diss. Freiburg/Schw, 1988 (H.-J. Venetz). → Dautzenberg 1992, Neirynck 1990a
    A. FUCHS, *SNTU* 15 (1990) 205-206; V. FUSCO, *RivBib* 41 (1993) 227-228; F. GONZÁLEZ GARCÍA, *EstBib* 49 (1991) 559-561; J.S. KLOPPENBORG, *JBL* 110 (1991) 525-527; D. LÜRHMANN, *TLZ* 117 (1992) 191-192; C.-P. MÄRZ, *BK* 46 (1991) 90-91; P. MAGNE, *ETR* 67 (1992) 107-108; J.-M. ROUSÉE, *RB* 97 (1990) 314; P.W. VAN DER HORST, *NTT* 46 (1992) 162-163; R.D. WITHERUP, CBQ 54 (1992) 357-358; D. ZELLER, *TRev* 88 (1992) 28-29.

1989b Q: Rekonstruktion und Interpretation. Eine methodenkritische Hinführung mit einem Exkurs zur Q-Vorlage des Lk. — *FZPT* 36 (1989) 409-425. Esp. 412-416: "Rekonstruktions-Probleme"; 416-420: "Zum Profil von Q^Lk"; 421-424: "Interpretations-Probleme". [NTA 34, 1116] → Neirynck 1990a

1992 Q und Jesus. — *BZ* 36 (1992) 30-58. Esp. 30-31: "Zur Deutung von Q für die Jesusforschung"; 31-32: "Differenzen zwischen dem 'gängigen Jesusbild' und Q"; 32-38: "Zur Eigenart von Q"; 39-40: "Methodologische Konsequenzen für die Rückfrage nach Jesus"; 40-57: "Zum Jesusbild von Q". [NTA 36, 1239]

**KOSCHEL, Ansgar**

1982 *Dialog um Jesus mit Ernst Bloch und Milan Machovec* (EHS, XXIII/170). Frankfurt/M–Bern: Lang, 1982, V-587 p. Esp. 96-110 [1–2]; 110-122 [3,1-17]; 122-127 [4,1-11]; 152-186 [24]; 187-198 [parables]; 199-238 [5–7]; 238-261 [6,9-13]; 276-289 [miracles]; 289-359 [passion narr.]; 359-387 [resurrection narr.].

**KOSKENNIEMI, Erkki**

1994 *Apollonios von Tyana in der neutestamentlichen Exegese* (WUNT, II/61). Tübingen: Mohr, 1994, IX-273 p. Esp. 190-193 [1,18-25]. — Diss. Åbo, 1992 (J. Thurén).

**KOSMALA, Hans**

1960 Mt xxvi 52 – A Quotation from the Targum. — *NT* 4 (1960) 3-5. [NTA 6, 134]; = ID., *Studies, Essays & Reviews*, II, 1978, 73-75.

1965a The Three Nets of Belial. A Study in the Terminology of Qumran and the New Testament. — *ASTI* 4 (1965) 91-113. Esp. 109-111 [13,22]. [NTA 12, 902]; = ID., *Studies, Essays, & Reviews*, II, 1978, 115-137.

1965b The Conclusion of Matthew. [28,19] — *Ibid.*, 132-147. Esp. 133-134 [text]; 141-142 [ὄνομα]; 142-145 [12,18-21]. [NTA 11, 716]; = ID., *Studies, Essays & Reviews*, II, 1978, 1-16. → Flusser 1967a

1967	"In My Name". — *ASTI* 5 (1966-67) 87-109. Esp. 88 [7,22]; 97-105 [ἐξουσία].

1970	"His blood on us and on our children" (The Background of Mat. 27,24-25). — *ASTI* 7 (1968-69) [1970] 94-126. Esp. 94-97; 111-112 [26,57-66]; 120-121 [5,10-11]. [NTA 16, 165]; = ID., *Studies, Essays & Reviews*, II, 1978, 82-114.

1978	*Studies, Essays, & Reviews*. II: *New Testament*. Leiden: Brill, 1978, X-231 p. → 1960, 1965a-b, 1970

**KOSNETTER, Johannes**

1958	Die Busspredigt in der Verkündigung Jesu. — *Der Seelsorger* (Wien) 29 (1958) 200-205.

1965	Das Thomasevangelium und die Synoptiker. — KISSER, J., et al. (eds.), *Wissenschaft im Dienste des Glaubens. Festschrift für Hermann Peichl* (Studien der Wiener katholischen Akademie, 4), Wien: Katholische Akademie, 1965, 29-49.

1971	Der Geschichtswert der Kindheitsgeschichte (Mt 1-2; Luk 1-2). — KOVÁCS, E. (ed.), *Festschrift Franz Loidl zum 65. Geburtstag* (Sammlung "Aus Christentum und Kultur", 3), Wien: Hollinek, 1971, 73-93.

**KOSSEN, H.B.**

1956	Quelques remarques sur l'ordre des paraboles dans Luc xv et sur la construction de Matthieu xviii 8-14. — *NT* 1 (1956) 75-80. [NTA 1, 51]

1960	*Op zoek naar de historische Jezus. Een studie over Albert Schweitzers visie op Jezus' leven* (Van Gorcum's Theologische Bibliotheek, 34). Assen: Van Gorcum, 1960, 300 p. Esp. 58-59.73-74.227-232.246-247 [10,23]; 113-116.242-245 [11,12]; 223-225 [8,11]; 216-217 [10,5-6]. → Schweitzer 1906

**KOTHES, Heinrich**

1951	Die Ehe im Neuen Testament. Bericht über ein schwedisches Buch. — *TGl* 41 (1951) 266-270. → Lövestam 1950

**KOTTACKAL, Joseph**

1984	The Righteous Required of the Followers of Christ (Mt ch. VII). — *Bible Bhashyam* 10 (1984) 132-139. [NTA 29, 524]

**KOTZÉ, P.P.A.**

1977	The Structure of Matthew One. — *Neotestamentica* 11 (1977) 1-9 (addendum, 1).

**KOWALCZYK, Andrzej**

1980	Niektóre problemy literackie i egzegetyczne Kazania na Górze, Mt 5-7 (Alcuni problemi letterari e esegetici del Discorso della montagna [Mt 5-7]) — *Studia Gdańskie* (Gdańsk) 4 (1980) 119-133.

1982	Krytyka fałszywych pojęć mesjańskich w opisie kuszenia Jezusa (Mt 4,1-11) (La critique des fausses conceptions messianiques dans le récit de la tentation de Jésus [Mt 4,1-11]). — *Miesięcznik Diecezji Gdański* 1-3 (1982) 63-66.

1985	Rola tematu "Działalność Jezusa - nowym wyjściem i nowym podbojem Ziemi Obiecanej" w redakcji Ewangelii św. Mateusza. [Role of the theme "activity of Jesus - the New Exodus and New Conquest of the Promised Land" in the redaction of Matthew] — *RuBi* 38 (1985) 134-159.

1986	Mowa eschatologiczna w Ewangelii św. Mateusza. [The eschatological sermon in the gospel of Matthew] — *Studia Gdańskie* 6 (1986) 179-207.

1987	Wpływ Heksateuchu na dobór perykop w częściach narracyjnych Ewangelii Mateusza. [On the influence of the Hexateuch on the gospel of Matthew] — *RuBi* 40 (1987) 26-39.

1993 Próba wyjaśnienia różnic w kompozycji Mt–Mk (Attempt to explain the differences in the composition of Mt–Mk). – *StudTheolVars* 31/1 (1993) 77-116. Esp. 91-105 [Sondergut; Q]; 105-112 [8,14-17.22-34; 9,18-26; 10,5-16; 12,1-16; 21,12-13.18-22/Mk]. [NTA 39, 165]

**KOWALCZYK, Mirosław**

1990 Historical Significance of the Nations in the Light cf the Biblical and Dogmatical Sources, with a Special Regard to Matthew's Gospel [Polish]. Diss. Lublin, 1990, 328 p. (C. Bartnik).

1991 Teologiczny sens *ethnos* w ewangelii świętego Mateusza. [The theological sense of *ethnos* in the gospel according to saint Matthew] — *RoczT* 38-39/2 (1991-92) 65-74. [NTA 38, 1354]

**KOWALSKI, Thomas W.**

1972 Les sources pré-synoptiques de Marc 1,32-34 et parallèles. Phénomènes d'amalgame et indépendance mutuelle immédiate des évangélistes synoptiques. — *RSR* 60 (1972) 541-573. Esp. 544-550: "Matthieu 8,16"; 550-554: "Matthieu 4,24b"; 561-569: "Marc 1,32-34". [NTA 17, 938]

**KOZAR, Joseph Vlcek**

1993 The Tragedy of Israel's Religious History as Portrayed in the Story of Matthew's Gospel. — *Proceedings EGLBS* 13 (1993) 47-54.

**KRAELING, Carl H.**

1951 *John the Baptist*. New York – London: Scribner, 1951, XII-218 p. Esp. 67-71 [3,1-2]; 45-50.71-75 [3,7-10]; 53-63 [3,11-12]; 131-135.154-155 [3,13-17]; 127-131 [11,2-6]; 138-141 [11,7-11]; 155-157 [11,12-13].

1961 Seek and you will find. [7,7-8] — WIKGREN, A. (ed.), *Early Christian Origins. Studies in Honor of H.R.W. Willoughby*, Chicago, IL: Quadrangle Books, 1961, 24-34.

**KRÄMER, Helmut**

1981 Eine Anmerkung zum Verständnis von Mt 15,6a. — *WDienst* 16 (1981) 67-70. [NTA 26, 474]

1986 Zur explikativen Redeweise im neutestamentlichen Griechisch. — SCHRAGE, W. (ed.), *Studien zum Text und zur Ethik des Neuen Testaments*. FS H. Greeven, 1986, 212-216. Esp. 214 [ὥστε + inf.; τοῦ + inf.]; 215 [πρός + inf.].

**KRÄMER, Michael**

1964a Die Menschenwerdung Jesu Christi nach Matthäus (Mt 1). Sein Anliegen und sein literarisches Verfahren. — *Bib* 45 (1964) 1-50. Esp. 4-22: "Die globale Analyse des Stiles in Mt 1,18-25"; 22-45: "Die Diskussion der Schwierigkeiten im Einzelner." [1,20.25]; 45-50: "Das apologetische Anliegen des Evangelisten". [NTA 9, 142]

1964b Zwei Probleme aus Mt. 1,18-25. — *Sal* 26 (1964) 303-333. Esp. 309-324 [1,18-21]; 324-332 [1,25].

1976 Hütet euch vor den falschen Propheten. Eine überlieferungsgeschichtliche Untersuchung zu Mt 7,15-23 / Lk 6,43-46 / Mt 12,33-37. — *Bib* 57 (1976) 349-377. Esp. 349-362.369-372 [7,15-23]; 362-366 [Q]; 373-376: "Der Überlieferungsprozess des Stoffes". [NTA 21, 724]

1977 Ihr seid das Salz der Erde ... Ihr seid das Licht der Welt. Die vielgestaltige Wirkkraft des Gotteswortes der Heiligen Schrift für das Leben der Kirche aufgezeigt am Beispiel Mt 5,13-16. — *MüTZ* 28 (1977) 133-157. Esp. 133-136: "Die Bildworte"; 136-147: "Die Überlieferungsgeschichte". [NTA 22, 85]

1983 Die Parabelrede in den synoptischen Evangelien. Eine überlieferungsgeschichtliche Untersuchung der parallelen Stellen Mt 13,1-53 – Mk 4,1-34 – Lk 8,4-18. — BODEM, A. – KOTHGASSER, A. M. (eds.), *Theologie und Leben. Festgabe für Georg Söll zum 70.*

*Geburtstag* (Biblioteca di Scienze Religiose, 58), Roma: LAS, 1983, 31-53. Esp. 34-43 [13,1-23/Mk 4,1-20]; 46-49 [13,1-23].

1991 *Die Gleichnisrede in den synoptischen Evangelien. Eine synoptische Studie zu Mt 13,1-52; Mk 4,1-34; Lk 8,4-21* (Deutsche Hochschulschriften, 461). Egelsbach: Hänsel-Hohenhausen, 1991, IX-69 p.
  M.C. DE BOER, *CBQ* 57 (1995) 400-401.

1992 *Die Überlieferungsgeschichte der Bergpredigt. Eine synoptische Studie zu Mt 4,23-7,29 und Lk 6,17-49* (Deutsche Hochschulschriften, 433). Egelsbach: Hänsel-Hohenhausen, 1992, XXIV-246 p.; ³1994, XXIII-270 p.
  K.-M. BULL, *TLZ* 120 (1995) 659-661; H.T. WREGE, *Sal* 57 (1995) 372-373.

**KRAFT, Heinrich**
1981 *Die Entstehung des Christentums*. Darmstadt: Wissenschaftliche Buchgesellschaft, 1981, VII-289 p. Esp. 1-43 [John the Baptist]; 96-103 [4,1-11]; 162-164 [8,20]; 167-168 [11,16-19]; 168-169 [12,32].

**KRAFT, Robert A.**
1972 *Eis nikos* = Permanently/Successfully: 1 Cor 15.54, Matt 12.20. — ID. (ed.), *Septuagintal Lexicography* (Septuagint and Cognate Studies, 1), Missoula, MT: University Press, 1972, 153-156.

**KRAMER, Barbel**
1978 & HAGEDORN, D., *Kölner Papyri 2* (Papyrologica Coloniensia, 7/2). Köln, 1978. Esp. 88-89 [P⁸⁶].

**KRATZ, Reinhard**
1973 *Auferweckung als Befreiung. Eine Studie zur Passions- und Auferstehungstheologie des Matthäus (besonders Mt 27,62-28,15)* (SBS, 65). Stuttgart: Katholisches Bibelwerk, 1973, 93 p. Esp. 22-24 [17,1-9]; 37-56: "Die Verwertung des Erdbeben-Motivs durch den Evangelisten Matthäus" [8,23-27; 21,1-11; 27,51-54]; 57-83: "Überlegungen zur Passions- und Auferstehungstheologie des Matthäus" [27,62-28,15]. [NTA 19, p. 112]
  E.L. BODE, *CBQ* 36 (1974) 602; G. GHIBERTI, *RivBib* 24 (1976) 199-200; R. PESCH, *BK* 29 (1974) 108.

1974 Der Seewandel des Petrus (Mt 14,28-31). — *BibLeb* 15 (1974) 86-101. [NTA 19, 535]

1975 → R. Pesch 1975a

1979 *Rettungswunder. Motiv-, traditions- und formkritische Aufarbeitung einer biblischen Gattung* (EHS, XXIII/123). Frankfurt/M–Bern: Lang, 1979, XI-559 p. Esp. 220-246 [8,23-27]; 292-310 [14,22-33]; 511-541 [27,62-28,15]. — Diss. Frankfurt/M, 1978 (R. Pesch).

1992 Die Gnade des täglichen Brots. Späte Psalmen auf dem Weg zum Vaterunser. — *ZTK* 89 (1992) 1-40. Esp. 7-13 [6,11]. [NTA 36, 1266]

**KRAUSE, Christiaan**
1968 Der Bergpredigt in den ökumenischen Studien seit dem Zweiten Weltkrieg. — *LuthRundschau* 18 (1968) 65-74. [NTA 12, 865]
  The Sermon on the Mount in Ecumenical Thought Since World War II. — *Lutheran World* (Genève) 15 (1968) 52-59. [NTA 12, 865]

**KRAUSE, Gerhard**
1970 Sch'ma Jisrael – Sch'mone Esre – Pater noster. Glaubensbekenntnisse und Pflichtgebete in klingenden Äusserungen. — *Deutsches Pfarrerblatt* (Essen) 70 (1970) 273-277, 405-406.

**KRAUTTER, Bernhard**
1973 *Die Bergpredigt im Religionsunterricht. Eine exegetisch-didaktische Erschließung zu*

*Mattäus 5–7* (Religionspädagogische Praxis, 12). München: Kösel; Stuttgart: Calwer, 1973, 104 p. [NTA 18, p. 243] — Diss. Freiburg, 1973.

**KREDEL, Elmar M.**

1956   Der Apostelbegriff in der neueren Exegese. Historisch-kritische Darstellung. — *ZKT* 78 (1956) 169-193, 257-305. Esp. 291-292 [16,18].

**KREIDER, Eugene Charles**

1976   *Matthew's Contribution to the Eschatological-Ethical Perspective in the Life of the Early Church. A Redaction-Critical Study of Matthew 18.* Diss. Vanderbilt Univ., Nashville, TN, 1976 (P.W. Meyer). — *DissAbstr* 37 (1976-77) 2246-2247.

**KREIER, Johannes Joachim**

1994   *Eunuchie und Reich Gottes. Eine Studie zum Eunuchenspruch, Mt 19,12.* Diss. Salzburg, 1994, 278 p. (W. Beilner).

**KREMER, Jacob**

1968   *Die Osterbotschaft der vier Evangelien. Versuch einer Auslegung der Berichte über das leere Grab und die Erscheinungen des Auferstandenen* (Biblisches Forum, 1). Stuttgart: Katholisches Bibelwerk, 1968, ²1968, ³1969, 144 + 11 p. Esp. 32-53: "Die Osterberichte des Matthäusevangeliums". → 1977

1970   Die Voraussagen des Pfingstgeschehens in Apg 1,4-5 und 8. Ein Beitrag zur Deutung des Pfingstberichts. — BORNKAMM, G. - RAHNER, K. (eds.), *Die Zeit Jesu.* FS H. Schlier, 1970, 145-168. Esp. 154-158 [Q 3,16].

1974a  "Neues und Altes". Jesu Wort über den christlichen "Schriftgelehrten" (Mt 13,52). — ID. — SEMMELROTH, O. — SUDBRACK, J. (eds.), *Neues und Altes. Zur Orientierung in der augenblicklichen Situation der Kirche,* Freiburg: Herder, 1974, 11-33, 83-87; = ID., *Die Bibel beim Wort genommen,* 1995, 13-29. Esp. 13-18: "Eigenart und Sinn des Logions"; 19-26: "Bibeltheologische Aussage".

1974b  Zur Diskussion über "das leere Grab". — DHANIS, É. (ed.), *Resurrexit,* 1974, 137-161 (discussion, 161-168). Esp. 153-155 [28,1-8].

1975   "Heilt Kranke ... treibt Dämonen aus!" (Mt 10,8). Zur Bedeutung von Jesu Auftrag an die Jünger für die heutige Pastoral. — WIENER, J. — ERHARTER, H. (eds.), *Zeichen des Heils. Leitideen künftiger Sakramentenpastoral. Österreichische Pastoraltagung 2.- 4. Januar 1975,* Wien: Herder, 1975, 33-52; = *Art und Christ* (Salzburg) 23/1 (1977) 1-17.

1977a  *Die Osterevangelien – Geschichten um Geschichte.* Stuttgart: Katholisches Bibelwerk; Klosterneuburg: Österreichisches Katholisches Bibelwerk, 1977, 240 p.; ²1981. Esp. 55-95: "Die Osterevangelien des Matthäus". → 1968
*De Paasevangeliën. Verhalen rond een gebeurtenis,* trans. J. Krol. Boxtel: Katholieke Bijbelstichting, 1979, 210 p. Esp. 52-87.

1977b  Jesu Verheissung des Geistes. Zur Verankerung der Aussage von Joh 16,13 im Leben Jesu. — SCHNACKENBURG, R., et al. (eds.), *Die Kirche des Anfangs.* FS H. Schürmann, 1977, 247-276. Esp. 262-267: "Zu den verwandten Logien bei den Synoptikern" [10,19-20]; = ID., *Die Bibel beim Wort genommen,* 1995, 133-160. Esp. 147-152.

1979   Die Bergpredigt – Weisung Jesu Christi. — *Lebendige Seelsorge* (Würzburg) 30 (1979) 157-162.

1986   Einfache und wissenschaftliche Lesung der Bergpredigt. — *BLtg* 59 (1986) 47-50. [NTA 30, 1045]

1988   *Die Bibel. Gottes Wort an alle. Kleine Anleitungen zum Lesen der Heiligen Schrift.* Leipzig: St. Benno, 1988, 160 p.

*De Schrift. Woord van God voor iedereen. Aanwijzingen voor het Bijbellezen*, trans. L. Geysels. Leuven: VBS/Acco; 's-Hertogenbosch: KBS, 1992, 144 p. Esp. 112-119 [27,45-56]; 119-124 [5,38-42].

1989 Mahnungen zum innerkirchlichen Befolgen des Liebesgebotes. Textpragmatische Erwägungen zu Lk 6,37-45. — FRANKEMÖLLE, H. - KERTELGE, K. (eds.), *Vom Urchristentum zu Jesus.* FS J. Gnilka, 1989, 231-245. Esp. 232-242 [Q 6,37-45].

1990a Das Erfassen der bildsprachlichen Dimension als Hilfe für das rechte Verstehen der biblischen "Kindheitsevangelien" und ihre Vermittlung als lebendiges Wort Gottes. — KERTELGE, K. (ed.), *Metaphorik und Mythos im Neuen Testament* (QDisp, 126), Freiburg: Herder, 1990, 78-109. Esp. 80-85; = ID., *Die Bibel beim Wort genommen*, 1995, 30-58. Esp. 32-36.

1990b Viele "Kirchen" – eine "Kirche". Biblische Aussagen und ihre frühchristliche Wirkungsgeschichte (unter besonderer Berücksichtigung von Mt 16,17-19). — KÖNIG, F. (ed.), *Zentralismus statt Kollegialität? Kirche im Spannungsfeld* (Schriften der Katholischen Akademie in Bayern, 134), Düsseldorf: Patmos, 1990, 16-54. Esp. 34-48; = ID., *Die Bibel beim Wort genommen*, 1995, 381-408. Esp. 394-404.

1993a Konflikte und Konfliktlösungen in der Urkirche und frühen Christenheit. — GRÜNDEL, J., et al. (eds.), *Zwischen Loyalität und Widerspruch. Christsein mit der Kirche*, Regensburg: Pustet, 1993, 9-34; = ID., *Die Bibel beim Wort genommen*, 1995, 361-380. Esp. 371-372 [18,15-17].

1993b Was bleibt von den Weihnachtsevangelien übrig? — GL 66 (1993) 413-418. Esp. 414-415. [NTA 38, 1358]

1995a *Die Bibel beim Wort genommen: Beiträge zu Exegese und Theologie des Neuen Testaments*, ed. R. Kühschelm - M. Stowasser. Freiburg: Herder, 1995, 496 p. → 1974a, 1977b, 1990a-b, 1993a

1995b Jesu Wort zur Ehescheidung: Bibeltheologische Überlegungen zum Schreiben der Päpstlichen Glaubenskongregation vom 14.9.1994. — SCHNEIDER, T. (ed.), *Geschieden - Wiederverheiratet - Abgewiesen? Antworten der Theologie* (QDisp, 157), Freiburg: Herder, 1995, 51-67. Esp. 54-58 [5,32; 19,3-12]; = *Stimmen der Zeit* 213 (1995) 89-105.

**KRENTZ, Edgar**

1964 The Extent of Matthew's Prologue. Toward the Structure of the First Gospel. — *JBL* 83 (1964) 409-414. [NTA 9, 895]

Der Umfang des Matthäus-Prologs. Ein Beitrag zum Aufbau des ersten Evangeliums. — LANGE, J. (ed.), *Das Matthäus-Evangelium*, 1980, 316-325.

1977 The Egalitarian Church of Matthew. — *CurrTMiss* 4 (1977) 333-341. [NTA 22, 389]

1983 None Greater among Those Born from Women: John the Baptist in the Gospel of Matthew. — *CurrTMiss* 10 (1983) 333-338. [NTA 28, 481]

1987 Community and Character: Matthew's Vision of the Church. — *SBL 1987 Seminar Papers*, 565-573. Esp. 565-566 [23,8-10]; 568-571 [23,1-12].

1992 More Than Many Lessons. On Preaching Matthew. — *CurrTMiss* 19 (1992) 440-452. [NTA 37, 705]

**KRETZER, Armin**

1971 *Die Herrschaft der Himmel und die Söhne des Reiches. Eine redaktionsgeschichtliche Untersuchung zum Basileiabegriff und Basileiaverständnis im Matthäusevangelium* (Stuttgarter Biblische Monographien, 10). Stuttgart: Katholisches Bibelwerk; Würzburg: Echter, 1971, 358 p. Esp. 19-63: "Grundlegende Beobachtungen zum mt Basileiabegriff"; 65-224: "Die theologische Entfaltung des mt Basileiaverständnisses" [1-2; 3,1-12; 4,13-17; 11,11-15; 13; 21,28-32.33-46; 22,1-14; 25,1-13.14-30.31-46]; 225-260: "Der 'ekklesiologische' Ort des mt Basileiaverständnisses" [16,18-19; 18,12-14.23-35]; 261-302: "Der besondere Typus des mt Basileiaverständnisses" [19,30; 20,1-16]. [NTA

18, p. 108] — Diss. Würzburg, 1968 (R. Schnackenburg). → Sabourin 1973
J.D. KINGSBURY, *Bib* 55 (1974) 117-119; A. SEGOVIA, *ArchTeclGran* 35 (1972) 329.

1974 Die Frage: Ehe auf Dauer und ihre mögliche Trennung nach Mt 19,3-12. — MERKLEIN,
H. – LANGE, J. (eds.), *Biblische Randbemerkungen*. FS R. Schnackenburg, 1974, 218-
230. Esp. 221-228: "Zum Problem der Ehescheidung nach Mt 19,3-12".

1980 Christsein in dieser Welt. Das Matthäusevangelium – heute. — *BK* 35 (1980) 130-138.
[NTA 25, 454]

**KRIEGER, Klaus-Stefan**

1986 Das Publikum der Bergpredigt (Mt 4,23-25). Ein Beitrag zu der Frage: Wem gilt die
Bergpredigt? — *Kairos* 28 (1986) 98-119. Esp. 100-101: "Der Rahmen"; 101-110: "Das
Summarium 4,23-25 und die unmittelbaren Rahmenverse 5,1f; 7,28f und 8,1"; 110-111 [8,5-13]. [NTA 31,
1060] → G. Lohfink 1983, 1988c

1990 Fordert Mt 5,39b das passive Erdulden von Gewalt? Ein kleiner Beitrag zur
Redaktionskritik der 5. Antithese. — *BibNot* 54 (1990) 28-32. [NTA 36, 142]

**KRIEGER, Norbert**

1956a Barfuss Busse tun. [3,11] — *NT* 1 (1956) 227-228. [NTA 1, 379]

1956b Ein Mensch in weichen Kleidern. [11,8] — *Ibid.*, 228-230. [NTA 1, 410]

**KRISTEN, Peter**

1995 *Familie, Kreuz und Leben. Nachfolge Jesu nach Q und dem Markusevangelium*
(Marburger theologische Studien, 42). Marburg: Elwert, 1995, IX-248 p. Esp. 55-155:
"Nachfolge Jesu nach dem Spruchevangelium Q" [Q 9,57-60; 10,1-15; 12,49-53; 14,26-27; 17,33]. — Diss.
Marburg, 1995 (D. Lührmann).

**KROGMANN, Willy**

1960 Heliand, Tatian und Thomasevangelium. — *ZNW* 51 (1960) 255-268. Esp. 259 [5,21]; 259-
260 [27,34]; 262-263 [13,47-48]; 265-266 [5,14-15]. [NTA 5, 844]

1964 Heliand und Thomasevangelium. [5,43; 6,28; 13,4.28; 22,21] — *VigChr* 18 (1964) 65-73.
→ Quispel 1962

**KRONHOLM, Tryggve**

1982 Polygami och monogami i Gamla testamentet. Med en utblick över den antika
judendomen och Nya testamentet. [Polygamy and monogamy in the Old Testament.
With notes on early Judaism and the New Testament] — *SEÅ* 47 (1982) 48-92. Esp. 86-86
[5,32]; 86-88 [19,3-12].

1989 Den kommande Hiskia. Ett försök att förstå den messianska interpretationen (Matt 1,18-
25) av Immanuelsprofetian (Jes 7,14) i ljuset av några rabbinska texter. [The coming
Hezekiah] — *SEÅ* 54 (1989) 109-117. Esp. 110-111.117 [1,18-25]. [NTA 34, 609]

**KRÜGER, Friedhelm**

1986 *Humanistische Evangelienauslegung. Desiderius Erasmus von Rotterdam als Ausleger
der Evangelien in seinen Paraphrasen* (Beiträge zur historischen Theologie, 68).
Tübingen: Mohr, 1986, IX-260 p. Esp. 177-204: "Die Auslegung von Matthäus 5-7".

**KRÜGER, René**

1992 Humilde, montado en um burrito. Mateo 21,1-11 y el recurso escrituristico. —
*RevistBíb* 54 (1992) 65-83.

**KRUSE, Heinz**

1968 "Pater Noster" et Passio Christi. — *VD* 46 (1968) 3-29. [NTA 13, 162]
The Lord's Prayer and the Passion of Christ. [Japanese] — *Katorikku Shingaku* (Tokyo) 7 (1968) 20-61.
[NTA 13, 161]

1977 Das Reich Satans. — *Bib* 58 (1977) 29-61. Esp. 37-44 [12,26]; 44-59 [4,1-11]. [NTA 22, 102]

1989 The Temptations of Jesus. [Japanese] — *Katorikku Kenkyu* (Tokyo) 28 (1989) 1-33. [NTA 34, 141]

1992 Jesus and Mission. [Japanese] [28,19-20] — *Katorikku Kenkyu* 31/2 (1992) 1-13. [NTA 37, 1209]

1995 Gold und Weihrauch und Myrrhe (Mt 2,11). — *MüTZ* 46 (1995) 203-213. [NTA 40, 158]

**KUBO, Sakae**

1965 *P72 and the Codex Vaticanus* (Studies and Documents, 27). Salt Lake City, UT: Univ. of Utah Press, 1965, III-196 p. Esp. 162-170 [Geerlings: codex 904].

1971 *A Reader's Greek-English Lexicon of the New Testament* (Andrews University Monographs, 4). Leiden: Brill, 1971, IX-284 p. Esp. 1-27: "Gospel of Matthew".

**KUDASIEWICZ, Józef**

1965 Chrzest Chrystusa (Le baptême du Christ). — *Ateneum Kaplanskie* (Wroclaw) 68 (1965) 151-164.

1970 Ewangelie dzieciństwa Jezusa (Les évangiles de l'enfance). — *CollTheol* 40 (1970) 161-170. Esp. 166-168. [NTA 16, 145]

1971 Centralne tematy teologiczno-etyczne Kazania na Górze (Mt 5-7). [Central themes of the Sermon on the Mount] — *Ateneum Kaplanskie* 77 (1971) 80-90.

1974a Mesjasz, Syn Dawida i Abrahama, w Ewangelii Dziecięctwa według Mateusza (Le Messie fils de David, fils d'Abraham d'après Mt 1-2). — ŁACH, S. - FILIPIAK, M. (eds.), *Mesjasz w biblijnej historii zbawienia*, Lublin: Catholic University, 1974, 307-327.

1974b Nauka o Bogu w ewangeliach synoptycznych. [God in the synoptic gospels] — BEJZE, B. (ed.), *O Bogu dziś Warszawa*, Wydo SS. Loretaner, 1974, 171-181.

1975a Kazanie na Górze (Mt 5-7). Problematyka literacka i teologiczna. [Sermon on the Mount. Literary and theological problems] — *Znak* (Warszawa) 24 (1975) 567-583.

1975b "Miłosierdzia chcę a nie ofiary" (Oz 6,6; Mt 9,13; 12,7). ["I require mercy, not sacrifice"] — *Powołanie człowieka* (Poznań) 4 (1975) 123-142.

1977 Evangelia dzieciństwa Jezusa – historia czy legenda? [The infancy-gospel – history or legend?] — *Biblia w ręku chrześcijan. - "W drodze"* 5/12 (1977) 41-48.

1978 Narodzenie Pana Jezusa. [The birth of Jesus]. — *Kielecki Przegląd Diecezjalny* (Kielce) 54 (1978) 296-320.

1986 *Teologia Nowego Testamentu. 1: Teologia Ewangelii synoptycznych* [Theology of the New Testament. 1: Theology of the Synoptic Gospels]. Lublin: Catholic University, 1986, 127 p.

1994 "Królestwo Boze będzie wam zabrane, a dane narodowi, który wyda jego owoc" (Mt 21,43). ["The kingdom of God will be taken away from you, and be given to a nation producing the fruit of it" (Mt 21,43)]. — *RoczT* 41/1 (1994) 79-84. [NTA 40, 176]

**KÜCHLER, Max**

1979 *Frühjüdische Weisheitstraditionen. Zum Fortgang weisheitlichen Denkens im Bereich des frühjüdischen Jahweglaubens* (Orbis Biblicus et Orientalis, 26). Freiburg/Schw: Universitätsverlag; Göttingen: Vandenhoeck & Ruprecht, 1979, 703 p. Esp. 553-592: "Christliche Weisheit, jesuanische Weisheit" [Q 7,31-35; 10,21-22; 11,49-51; genre]; 386-402: "Achikar und die neutestamentlichen Schriften" [5,38-48; 7,12; 24,45-51; 25,14-30; 27,5].

1989 "Wir haben seinen Stern gesehen..." (Mt 2,2). — *BK* 44 (1989) 179-186. Esp. 185-186. [NTA 34, 611]

**KÜHLWEIN, K.**

1992 *Familienbeziehung und Bergpredigt-Weisungen* (EHS, XXIII/435). Frankfurt/M–Bern: Lang, 1992, 347 p. [NTA 37, p. 280] — Diss. Frankfurt/M, 1991 (R. Lay).

**KÜHNEWEG, Uwe**

1993 *Das neue Gesetz. Christus als Gesetzgeber und Gesetz. Studien zu den Anfängen christlicher Naturrechtslehre im 2. Jahrhundert* (Marburger theologische Studien, 36). Marburg: Elwert, 1993, VIII-358 p. Esp. 280-284; 297-301 [5,17-20]. — Diss. Marburg, 1989 (W. Bienert).

**KÜHSCHELM, Roman**

1983 *Jüngerverfolgung und Geschick Jesu. Eine exegetisch-bibeltheologische Untersuchung der synoptischen Verfolgungsankündigungen Mk 13,9-13 par und Mt 23,29-36 par* (Österreichische Biblische Studien, 5). Klosterneuburg: Österreichisches Katholisches Bibelwerk, 1983, 337 p. Esp. 14-33: "Texte, Kontexte"; 34-72 "Sprachliche Analyse"; 73-90: "Form- und Gattungskritik"; 91-107: "Traditions- und Motivkritik"; 108-162: "Literarkritik, Überlieferungskritik, Redaktionskritik"; 163-259: "Versweise Einzelauslegung"; 260-309: "Theologische Auslegung" [10,16-23; 23,29-36; 24,9-14; Q 11,47-51; 12,11-11]. — Diss. Wien, 1981 (J. Kremer).
   H.-T. WREGE, *TLZ* 111 (1986) 105-107.

1986 Das Verhältnis von Kirche und Israel bei Matthäus. — *BLtg* 59 (1986) 165-176. Esp. 166-171 [8,10-13; 21,40-45; 22,1-14; 23,37-39; 27,23-26]. [NTA 31, 573]

1993 Angelophanie - Christophanie in den synoptischen Grabesgeschichten Mk 16,1-8 par. (unter Berücksichtigung von Joh 20,11-18). [28,9-10] — FOCANT, C. (ed.), *The Synoptic Gospels*, 1993, 556-565. → Neirynck 1995b

**KÜMMEL, Werner Georg**

1934R Jesus und der jüdische Traditionsgedanke. [1934] — ID., *Heilsgeschehen und Geschichte*, 1965, 15-35. Esp. 33-35 [5,17-20].

1943R *Kirchenbegriff und Geschichtsbewußtsein in der Urgemeinde und bei Jesus* [1943]. Göttingen: Vandenhoeck & Ruprecht, ²1968, 63 p. Esp. 21-24 [ἐκκλησία]; 32-42 [16,18-19].

1945R *Verheissung und Erfüllung. Untersuchungen zur eschatologischen Verkündigung Jesu* [1945] (ATANT, 6). Zürich: Zwingli, ²1953 ("völlig neu bearbeitet"), 156 p. Esp. 13-80: "Die nahe Zukunft der Gottesherrschaft" [10,14-15.23.32-33; 11,25-30; 12,28.38-39; 23,37-39; 25,1-13.31-46]; 98-132: "Die Gegenwart der Gottesherrschaft" [11,2-6.12-13; 12,41-42; 13,24-30.36-43.47-50; 16,18-19]; ³1956, 158 p.
*Promise and Fulfilment. The Eschatological Message of Jesus* (Studies in Biblical Theology, 23). London: SCM, 1957, 168 p.; ²1961; repr. 1974. Esp. 19-87; 105-140.

1953 Jesus und die Anfänge der Kirche. — *StudTheol* 7 (1953) 1-27. Esp. 12-13 [26,64]; 14-26 [16,17-19]; = ID., *Heilsgeschehen und Geschichte*, 1965, 289-309. Esp. 298-299; 299-308.

1958 *Das Neue Testament. Geschichte der Erforschung seiner Probleme* (Orbis Academicus, III/3). Freiburg-München: Karl Alber, 1958, VIII-596 p.; ²1970, VIII-613 p. ("Anmerkungen, Literaturverzeichnis und Biographischer Anhang: völlig neu bearbeitet"). → 1969b
*Il Nuovo Testamento. Storia dell'indagine scientifica sul problema neotestamentario*, trans. V. Benassi. Bologna: Il Mulino, 1976, 620 p.

1963a *Einleitung in das Neue Testament*. Heidelberg: Quelle & Meyer, (Feine-Behm¹²)1963, XVI-458 p. Esp. 13-44: "Die synoptische Frage"; 57-72: "Das Matthäusevangelium"; ¹³1964, XVI-461 p.; ¹⁴1965, XVI-467 p.; ¹⁶1969. → 1973; → (Feine-)Behm 1936
*Introduction to the New Testament*, trans. A.J. Mattill Jr. (The New Testament Library). Nashville, TN: Abingdon; London: SCM, 1966 [= German, ¹⁴1965], 444 p. Esp. 33-60; 72-86; ²1975.

1963b Die neutestamentliche Exegese. — KAISER, O. (ed.), *Einführung in die exegetischen Methoden*, München: Kaiser, 1963, ²1964, 37-67. Esp. 57-67 [12,22-37].

New Testament Exegesis. — KAISER, O. - KÜMMEL, W.G. (eds.), *Exegetical Method. A Student's Handbook*, trans. E.V.N. Goetchius, New York: Seabury, 1967, 35-69. Esp. 58-69.

1964　Die Naherwartung in der Verkündigung Jesu. — DINKLER, E. (ed.), *Zeit und Geschichte*. FS R. Bultmann, 1964, 31-46. Esp. 41-45 [10,23]; = ID., *Heilsgeschehen und Geschichte*, 1965, 457-470. Esp. 465-469.

Eschatological Expectation in the Proclamation of Jesus. — ROBINSON, J.M. (ed.), *The Future of Our Religious Past*. FS R. Bultmann, 1971, 29-48. Esp. 41-46; = CHILTON, B.D. (ed.), *The Kingdom of God*, 1984, 36-51. Esp. 42-43; 49.

1965　*Heilsgeschehen und Geschichte. Gesammelte Aufsätze 1933-1964*, ed. E. Grässer - O. Merk - A. Fritz (Marburger theologische Studien, 3). Marburg: Elwert, 1965, XI-512 p. → 1934, 1953, 1964

1966　Jesusforschung seit 1950. — *TR* 31 (1966) 15-46, 289-315. [NTA 11, 146/1001]; = ID., *Dreißig Jahre Jesusforschung*, 1985, 1-32, 33-59.

1967　Die Weherufe über die Schriftgelehrten und Pharisäer (Matthäus 23,13-36). — ECKERT, W.P., et al. (eds.), *Antijudaismus*, 1967, 135-147, 208-209; = ID., *Heilsgeschehen und Geschichte*, II, 1978, 29-38.

1969a　*Die Theologie des Neuen Testaments nach seinen Hauptzeugen, Jesus, Paulus, Johannes* (Grundrisse zum Neuen Testament. NTD Ergänzungsreihe, 3). Göttingen: Vandenhoeck & Ruprecht, 1969, [5]1987, 312 p. Esp. 20-85: "Die Verkündigung Jesu nach den drei ersten Evangelien".

*The Theology of the New Testament according to Its Major Witnesses Jesus - Paul - John*, trans. J.E. Steely. Nashville, TN - New York: Abingdon, 1973, 350 p.

*Síntese teológica do Novo Testamento de acordo com as Testemunhas Principais: Jesu, Paulo, João*, trans. S. Schneider & W. Fuchs. São Leopoldo: Sinodal, 1974, 380 p.

*La teologia del Nuovo Testamento. Gesù - Paolo - Giovanni*, trans. F. Tomasoni. Brescia: Paideia, 1976, 462 p.

Japanese trans.

1969b　Die exegetische Erforschung des Neuen Testaments in diesem Jahrhundert. — VORGRIMLER, H. - VAN DER GUCHT, R. (eds.), *Bilanz der Theologie im 20. Jahrhundert. Perspektiven, Strömungen, Motive in der christlichen und nichtchristlichen Welt*, Freiburg: Herder, 1969, II, 279-371. Esp. 285-293 (FT, 1970). → 1958

*Das Neue Testament im 20. Jahrhundert. Ein Forschungsbericht* (SBS, 50). Stuttgart: Katholisches Bibelwerk, 1970, 159 p. Esp. 33-44.

1970　"Das Gesetz und die Propheten gehen bis Johannes" - Lukas 16,16 im Zusammenhang der heilsgeschichtlichen Theologie der Lukasschriften. — BÖCHER, O. - HAACKER, K. (eds.), *Verborum Veritas*. FS G. Stählin, 1970, 89-102. Esp. 94-98 [Q 16,16].

1973　*Einleitung in das Neue Testament*. Heidelberg: Quelle & Meyer, [17]1973, XIX-548 p. Esp. 13-53: "Die synoptische Frage"; 73-92: "Das Matthäusevangelium"; [21]1983, XIX-593 p. → 1963a

*Introduction to the New Testament*, trans. H.C. Kee. Nashville, TN: Abingdon; London: SCM, 1975, 629 p. Esp. 38-80; 101-121; [5]1984.

In Support of Markan Priority. [1975, 56-63] — BELLINZONI, A.J., Jr., et al. (eds.), *The Two-Source Hypothesis*, 1985, 53-62.

In Support of Q. [1975, 63-67] — *Ibid.*, 227-243.

*Introdução ao Novo Testamento*. São Paolo: Paulinas, 1982, 790 p.

1974　Jesu Antwort an Johannes den Täufer. Ein Beispiel zum Methodenproblem in der Jesusforschung. — *Sitzungsberichte der wissenschaftlichen Gesellschaft an der J.W. Goethe-Universität* (Frankfurt/M) 11/4 (1974) 129-159. Esp. 149-159 [11,2-6]; Wiesbaden: Steiner, 1974, 35 p. Esp. 25-35; = ID., *Heilsgeschehen und Geschichte*, II, 1978, 177-200.

1975a　Ein Jahrzehnt Jesusforschung (1965-1975). — *TR* 40 (1975) 289-336. [NTA 20, 746]; 41 (1976) 197-258, 295-363: "Die Lehre Jesu". [NTA 21, 346]; 43 (1978) 105-161, 233-265:

"Bergpredigt-Gleichnisse-Wunderberichte". [NTA 23, 60/391]; 45 (1980) 40-84, 293-337. Esp. 40-50: "Der persönliche Anspruch Jesu"; 50-84: "Die Menschensohnfrage"; 293-337: "Der Prozess und der Kreuzestod Jesu". [NTA 24, 742; 25, 427]; = ID., *Dreißig Jahre Jesusforschung*, 1985, 61-108, 109-170, 171-239, 240-296, 297-329, 330-374, 375-419. Esp. 330-340; 340-374.

1975b Das Verhalten Jesus gegenüber und das Verhalten des Menschensohns. Markus 8,38 par und Lukas 12,8f par Mattäus 10,32f. — PESCH, R., et al. (eds.), *Jesus und der Menschensohn*. FS A. Vögtle, 1975, 210-224. Esp. 213-216 [10,32-33]; 216-219 [Q/Mk 8,38]; 219-224 [Son of Man]; = ID., *Heilsgeschehen und Geschichte*, II, 1978, 201-214.

1978 *Heilsgeschehen und Geschichte*. Band 2. *Gesammelte Aufsätze 1965-1977*, ed. E. Grässer – O. Merk (Marburger theologische Studien, 16). Marburg: Elwert, 1978, XII-279 p. → 1967, 1974, 1975b

1981 Jesusforschung seit 1965: Nachträge 1975-1980. — *TR* 46 (1981) 317-363. [NTA 26, 824]; 47 (1982) 136-165, 348-383. Esp. 136-165: "Die Lehre Jesu"; 349-369: "Bergpredigt-Gleichnisse-Wunderberichte"; 369-378: "Der persönliche Anspruch Jesu"; 378-383: "Der Prozess und der Kreuzestod Jesu". [NTA 27, 69/883]; = ID., *Dreißig Jahre Jesusforschung*, 1985, 421-467, 468-497, 498-533. Esp. 468-497; 499-519; 519-528; 528-533.

1984 Jesus der Menschensohn. — *Sitzungsberichte der wissenschaftlichen Gesellschaft an der J.W. Goethe-Universität* (Frankfurt/M) 20/3 (1984) 147-188.

1985 *Dreißig Jahre Jesusforschung (1950-1980)*, ed. H. Merklein (BBB, 60). Königstein/Ts.–Bonn: Hanstein, 1985, X-549 p. → 1966, 1975a, 1981; → 1994

1988 Jesusforschung seit 1981. — *TR* 53 (1988) 229-249. [NTA 33, 91]; 54 (1989) 1-53. [NTA 33, 1081]; 55 (1990) 21-45: "Die Lehre Jesu". [NTA 34, 109C]; 56 (1991) 27-53: "Gleichnisse". [NTA 35, 1120]; 56 (1991) 391-420: "Der persönliche Anspruch sowie der Prozeß und Kreuzestod Jesu". [NTA 36, 374]; = ID., *Vierzig Jahre Jesusforschung*, 1994, 535-690. Esp. 609-633; 634-660; 661-690.

1994 *Vierzig Jahre Jesusforschung (1950-1990)*, ed. H. Merklein (BBB, 91). Weinheim: Beltz-Athenäum, 1994, X-706 p. → 1985, 1988

## KÜNZEL, Georg

1978 *Studien zum Gemeindeverständnis des Matthäus-Evangeliums* (Calwer theologische Monographien, A10). Stuttgart: Calwer, 1978, 295 p. Esp. 11-44: "Zur Auslegungsgeschichte des Mt-ev unter ekklesiologischem Aspekt"; 45-70: "Der geschichtstheologische Aspekt der mt Theologie"; 71-120: "Jesusgeschehen als Gottesgeschichte"; 121-166: "Das Selbstverständnis der Gemeinde"; 167-179: "Funktionen in der Gemeinde"; 180-217: "Petrus und die Vollmacht der Gemeinde"; 218-250: "Ende und Vollendung – das Wortfeld τέλος im Mt-ev"; 251-257: "Zur Herkunft des Mt-ev". [NTA 23, p. 94] — Diss. Erlangen, 1975 (O. Merk). → Ingelaere 1981
X. ALEGRE, *ActBibl* 17 (1980) 319-320; G. DELLING, *TLZ* 106 (1981) 336-337; H. FRANKEMÖLLE, *Bib* 63 (1982) 129-132; W. TRILLING, *TRev* 75 (1979) 26-27.

## KÜNZI, Martin

1970 *Das Naherwartungslogion Matthäus 10,23. Geschichte seiner Auslegung* (Beiträge zur Geschichte der biblischen Exegese, 9). Tübingen: Mohr, 1970, VII-201 p. Esp. 4-8 [10,23]; 11-36 [Early Church]; 37-48 [Middle Ages]; 49-77 [16-17th cent.]; 78-115 [18th-19th cent.]; 115-163 [20th cent.]. [NTA 15, p. 120] — Diss. Basel, 1967 (O. Cullmann).
*Studia Patavina* 18 (1971) 237; C. BRÜTSCH, *TZ* 28 (1972) 365-366; G. DE RU, *KerkT* 21 (1970) 406-408; J.-C. INGELAERE, *RHPR* 53 (1973) 86-87; E. KRENTZ, *ConcTM* 43 (1972) 461; D. LOSADA, *RevistBib* 34 (1972) 86-87; F. MARTIN, *CBQ* 33 (1971) 270-272; J.R. MICHAELS, *JBL* 90 (1971) 122-123; A. SEGOVIA, *ArchTeolGran* 33 (1970) 323-324.

1977 *Das Naherwartungslogion Markus 9,1 par. Geschichte seiner Auslegung mit einem Nachwort zur Auslegungsgeschichte von Markus 13,30 par.* [10,23; 16,27] (Beiträge zur Geschichte der biblischen Exegese, 21). Tübingen: Mohr, 1977, VII-247 p.

KÜNZLE, Beda O.

1984 *Das altarmenische Evangelium / L'Évangile arménien ancien. I. Edition zweier altarmenischer Handschriften / Édition de deux manuscrits arméniens anciens* [cod. Matenadaran 6200 and 2374]. II. *Lexikon / Lexique* (EHS, XXI/33). Bern: Lang, 1984, 144*-293 and 29*-703 p. Esp. I, 1-82.

KÜRZINGER, Josef

1959 Zur Komposition der Bergpredigt nach Matthäus. — *Bib* 40 (1959) 569-589. [NTA 4, 645]; = *Studia Biblica et Orientalia*, II, 1959, 1-21.

1960 Das Papiaszeugnis und die Erstgestalt des Matthäusevangeliums. — *BZ* 4 (1960) 19-38. [NTA 5, 69]; = ID., *Papias von Hierapolis*, 1983, 9-32.

1963 Irenäus und sein Zeugnis zur Sprache des Matthäusevangeliums. — *NTS* 10 (1963-64) 108-115. Esp. 109-110 [Papias]; 110-115 [Irenaeus]; 112-114 [1,23]. [NTA 8, 934]; = ID., *Papias von Hierapolis*, 1983, 33-42. Esp. 34-35; 35-40; 36-38.

1977 Die Aussage des Papias von Hierapolis zur literarischen Form des Markusevangeliums. — *BZ* 21 (1977) 245-264. Esp. 260-264. [NTA 22, 97]; = ID., *Papias von Hierapolis*, 1983, 43-67. Esp. 57-61.

1979 Papias von Hierapolis: Zu Titel und Art seines Werkes. — *BZ* 23 (1979) 172-186. Esp. 174-178.182-184. [NTA 24, 659]; = ID., *Papias von Hierapolis*, 1983, 69-87. Esp. 71-75.79-81.

1981 Das "Wort, das ergeht durch Gottes Mund" (Mt 4,4). Zum Verständnis der ersten Versuchung Jesu. — HÜBNER, R.M., et al. (eds.), *Der Dienst für den Menschen in Theologie und Verkündigung. Festschrift für Aloïs Brems Bischof von Eichstätt zum 75. Geburtstag* (Eichstätter Studien, NF 13), Regensburg: Pustet, 1981, 157-164.

1983a *Papias von Hierapolis und die Evangelien des Neuen Testaments. Gesammelte Aufsätze. Neuausgabe und Übersetzung der Fragmente. Kommentierte Bibliographie* (Eichstätter Materialien. Abteilung Philosophie und Theologie, 4). Regensburg: Pustet, 1983, 250 p. → 1960, 1963, 1977, 1979, 1983b; → Cirillo 1986

1983b Kommentierte Bibliographie 1960-1981 (E. König - M. Vinzent). — *Ibid.*, 139-244. Esp. § 37, 43, 44.

KUHN, Hans-Jürgen

1988 *Christologie und Wunder. Untersuchungen zu Joh 1,35-51* (BibUnt, 18). Regensburg: Pustet, 1988, XV-679 p. Esp. 12-25.201-207 [Mt/Jn 1,35-51]; 315-317 [Jesus as prophet]; 370-374.378-380 [Son of God]; 400-410.447-452.473-474.492-494 [miracles].

KUHN, Heinz-Wolfgang

1966 *Enderwartung und gegenwärtiges Heil. Untersuchungen zu den Gemeindeliedern von Qumran mit einem Anhang über Eschatologie und Gegenwart in der Verkündigung Jesu* (SUNT, 4). Göttingen: Vandenhoeck & Ruprecht, 1966, 242 p. Esp. 189-204 [11,5-6; 12,28; 13,16-17].

1980 Nachfolge nach Ostern. — LÜHRMANN, D. - STRECKER, G. (eds.), *Kirche. Festschrift für Günther Bornkamm zum 75. Geburtstag*, Tübingen: Mohr, 1980, 105-132. Esp. 113-119 [Q 7,9; Q 9,57-62; Q 14,26-27; Q 22,28-30]; 125-129 [Q 12,51-53].

1989 Das Liebesgebot Jesu als Tora und als Evangelium. Zur Feindesliebe und zur christlichen und jüdischen Auslegung der Bergpredigt. — FRANKEMÖLLE, H. - KERTELGE, K. (eds.), *Vom Urchristentum zu Jesus. FS J. Gnilka*, 1989, 194-230. Esp. 204-210 [5,17-20; 7,12]; 210-211 [ἔλεος]; 211-220 [5,17-20]; 220-222 [εὐαγγέλιον]; 222-230 [historical Jesus].

1995 Bethsaida in the Gospels: The Feeding Story in Luke 9 and the Q Saying in Luke 10. [Q 10,13-15] — ARAV, R. - FREUND, R.A. (eds.), *Bethsaida. A City by the North Shore of the Sea of Galilee* (Bethsaida Excavations Project, 1), Kirksville, MO: Jefferson Univ. Press, 1995, 243-256.

**KUHN, K.H.**

1960 Some Observations on the Coptic Gospel according to Thomas. — *Muséon* 73 (1960) 317-323. Esp. 319-321 [5,14/Th Oxy fr 2]; 321-323 [10,37-38/Th 55; 16,26/Th 25; 11,28-30/Th 90]. [NTA 5, 845]

1985 *Kakie kakôs* in the Sahidic Version of Matthew 21:41. — *JTS* 36 (1985) 390-393. [NTA 30, 580]

**KUHN, Karl Georg**

1950 *Achtzehngebet und Vaterunser und der Reim* (WUNT, 1). Tübingen: Mohr, 1950, III-51 p. Esp. 30-40 [6,9-13]; 40-46.
    J. BLINZLER, *MüTZ* 5 (1954) 216-219; J. BONSIRVEN, *Bib* 31 (1950) 517; E.L. DIETRICH, *TLZ* 76 (1951) 291-293; F.V. FILSON, *JBL* 70 (1951) 255-256; K. GALLING, *VerkFor* 1951-52/3 (1954) 221-223; F.C. GRANT, *ATR* 33 (1951) 62-63; H. GREEVEN, *Zeitschrift für Kirchengeschichte* (Stuttgart) 64 (1952-53) 192-194; O. KUSS, *TGl* 41 (1951) 45-46; J. LEVIE, *NRT* 72 (1950) 1102; P. NOBER, *VD* 32 (1954) 54-55; H. SAHLIN, *SEÅ* 16 (1951) 85-87; K. STENDAHL, *SvenskTeolKvart* 27 (1951) 61-64; J.L. TEICHER, *JJS* 2 (1951) 111-112.

1952 Jesus in Gethsemane. — *EvT* 12 (1952-53) 260-285. Esp. 267-268 [26,36-46]; = LIMBECK, M. (ed.), *Redaktion und Theologie des Passionsberichtes nach den Synoptikern*, 1981, 81-111.

**KUNKEL, Fritz**

1946[R] *Creation Continues. A Psychological Interpretation of the Gospel of Matthew* [1946]. New York – Mahwah, NJ: Paulist, [2]1973; [3]1987, 286 p. [NTA 32, p. 243]
    B.T. VIVIANO, *RB* 97 (1990) 615.
    *Die Schöpfung geht weiter. Eine psychologische Untersuchung des Matthäus-Evangeliums*. Konstanz: Bahn, 1957, xv-312 p.
    G. HOLTZ, *TLZ* 84 (1959) 107-108.

**KUNTZ, Manfred**

1988 Eine Skizze zum Sabbatverständnis des Matthäusevangeliums. — BAUMGARTNER, M. (ed.), *Theologische Kaprizen. Hans Friedrich Geisser zum 60. Geburtstag*, Zürich: Univ. Theol. Fak. Inst. Hermeneutik, 1988, 358-361.

**KUNZ, Ulrich**

1954 *Das Matthäus-Evangelium*. Stuttgart: Quell-Verlag, 1954, 104 p.

**KUPFERSCHMID, A.**

1963 *Das Kommen Christi und unsere Zukunft. Eine Auslegung von Matthäus 24 und 25*. Basel: Reinhardt, 1963, 140 p. [NTA 9, p. 274]

**KUPP, David D.**

1996 *Matthew's Emmanuel. Divine Presence and God's People in the First Gospel* (SNTS MS, 90). Cambridge: University Press, 1996, XIX-252 p. Esp. 28-48: "Matthew's narrative art"; 49-108: "Reading Matthew's story of divine presence"; 157-175: "Matthew 1: the birth of the 'God-with-us' Messiah"; 176-200: "Matthew 18.1-20: the presence of Jesus and his ἐκκλησία"; 201-219: "Matthew 28.16-20: the presence of the risen Jesus"; 220-233: "Jesus' presence and Matthew's christology". — Diss. Durham, 1992 (J.D.G. Dunn).

**KURICHIANIL, John**

1975 The Temptations of Christ, Their Meaning. — *Bible Bhashyam* 1 (1975) 106-125. [NTA 20, 434]

**KUSCHKE, Arnulf**

1950 Das Idiom der "relativen Negation" im NT. [6,19; 9,13; 15,24; 18,21-22] — *ZNW* 43 (1950-51) 263.

**Kuss, Otto**

1955    Bemerkungen zu dem Fragenkreis: Jesus und die Kirche im Neuen Testament. — *TQ* 135 (1955) 28-55, 150-183. Esp. 43-51 [16,17-19]; = ID., *Auslegung und Verkündigung*, I, 1963, 25-77. Esp. 38-45.

1959    Zum Sinngehalt des Doppelgleichnisses vom Senfkorn und Sauerteig. — *Bib* 40 (1959) 641-653. Esp. 644-646 [13,31-33]. [NTA 4, 636]; = *Studia Biblica et Orientalia*, II, 1959, 73-85. Esp. 76-78; = ID., *Auslegung und Verkündigung*, I, 1963, 85-97. Esp. 88-90.

1963    *Auslegung und Verkündigung. I: Aufsätze zur Exegese des Neuen Testaments.* Regensburg: Pustet, 1963, XI-384 p. → 1955, 1959

1967    Das Vaterunser. — ID., *Auslegung und Verkündigung. II: Biblische Vorträge und Meditationen*, Regensburg: Pustet, 1967, 277-333.

**KUTHIRAKKATTEL, Scaria**

1990    *The Beginning of Jesus' Ministry according to Mark's Gospel (1,14–3,6): A Redaction Critical Study* (AnBib, 123). Roma: Pontificio istituto biblico, 1990, XXVI-300 p. Esp. 84-85 [4,12-17/Mk 1,14-15]; 103 [4,18-22/Mk 1,16-20]; 117-118 [7,28-29/Mk 1,22]; 141-142 [8,14-15/Mk 1,29-31]; 149-150 [8,16/Mk 1,32-34]; 161-162 [8,1-4/Mk 1,40-45]; 177-178 [9,1-8/Mk 2,1-12]; 198-199 [9,9-13/Mk 2,13-17]; 211 [9,14-17/Mk 2,18-22]; 219 [12,1-8/Mk 2,23-28]; 227 [12,9-14/Mk 3,1-6]. — Diss. Pont. Univ. Greg., Roma, 1987 (I. de la Potterie).

**KUTSCH, Ernst**

1960    "Eure Rede aber sei ja ja, nein nein". — *EvT* 20 (1960) 206-218. Esp. 208-214 [5,37]. [NTA 5, 75]

1978    *Neues Testament – Neuer Bund? Eine Fehlübersetzung wird korrigiert.* Neukirchen-Vluyn: Neukirchener, 1978, X-179 p. Esp. 107-109; 113-118: "Das Deutewort zum Wein Mk 14,24 / Mt 26,28".

**KVALBEIN, Hans**

1969    *Matteusevangeliet: forelesninger over "tekster til mer inngående studium".* Oslo: Universitetsforlaget, 1969, [2]1977, [3]1986, 237 p.

1981    *Jesus og de fattige. Jesu syn på de fattige og hans bruk av ord for "fattig"* [Jesus and the poor. Jesus' view of the poor and his use of words for "poor"]. Oslo: Luther forlag, 1981, 2 vols., 431 and 120 p. Esp. 308-319 [11,2-6]. — Diss. Oslo, 1981 (E. Larsson).

1987    Jesus and the Poor. Two Texts and a Tentative Conclusion. — *Themelios* 12/3 (1987) 80-87. [NTA 32, 70]

1988    Go Therefore and Make Disciples... The Concept of Discipleship in the New Testament. — *Themelios* 13/2 (1988) 48-53. [NTA 32, 1122]

1990    *Matteus-evangeliet I-II.* Oslo: Nye Luther / Lunde, 1990, 328 and 311 p.
        T. FORNBERG, *TidsTeolKirk* 62 (1991) 226-227.

**KWIK, Robert J.**

1966    Some Doubted. [28,17] — *ExpT* 77 (1965-66) 181. [NTA 11, 233]

**KWON, Sung-Soo**

1988    "*Your reward in heaven is great*". A Study on Gradation of Reward in Matthew. Diss. Westminster Theol. Sem., 1988, 283 p. (R.B. Gaffin). — *DissAbstr* 49 (1988-89) 1843.

**KYNES, W.L.**

1991    *A Christology of Solidarity. Jesus as the Representative of His People in Matthew.* Lanham, MD – New York – London: University Press of America, 1991, XIII-247 p. [NTA 36, p. 422] — Diss. Cambridge, 1986 (M.D. Hooker).

# L

**LAANSMA, Jon**

1997 *"I will give you rest". The Rest Motif in the New Testament with Special Reference to Mt 11 and Heb 3-4* (WUNT, II/98). Tübingen: Mohr, 1997, xv-459 p. Esp. 2-9; 159-208: "Mt 11,28-30 and Matthew's wisdom christology"; 209-251: "The meek king and God's promise of rest" [1,1-17; 11,25-30; 12,6; 21,5]. — Diss. Aberdeen, 1995 (I.H. Marshall).

**LABARRIÈRE, Pierre-Jean**

1969 L'homme des Béatitudes. — *Christ* 16 (1969) 352-365.

**LA BONNARDIÈRE, Anne-Marie**

1955 Les commentaires simultanés de *Mat.* 6,12 et *I Jo.* 1,8 dans l'œuvre de saint Augustin. — *RevÉtudAug* 1 (1955) 129-147.

1961 *Tu es Petrus*. La péricope "Matthieu 16,13-23" dans l'œuvre de saint Augustin. — *Irénikon* 34 (1961) 451-499. [NTA 6, 775]

1964 En marge de la "Biblia Augustiniana": une rétractation. — *RevÉtudAug* 10 (1964) 305-307.

1967 La Chananéenne. Préfiguration de l'Église des Gentils d'après saint Augustin. — *Augustinus* 12 (1967) 209-238.

**LABOSIER, Brian C.**

1990 *Matthew's Exception Clause in the Light of Canonical Criticism: A Case Study in Hermeneutics*. Diss. Westminster Theol. Sem., 1990, 339 p. (M. Silva). — *DissAbstr* 51 (1990-91) 1661.

**LACAN, Marc-François**

1960 Conversion et royaume dans les Évangiles synoptiques. — *LumièreV* 47 (1960) 25-47. Esp. 36-41: "Les fruits de la conversion d'après saint Matthieu". [NTA 5, 70]; = ID., et al., *L'espérance du royaume* (Paroles de vie), Paris: Mame, 1966, 7-32. Esp. 20-25.

1964 "Mon Dieu, mon Dieu, pourquoi?" (Matthieu, 27,46). — *LumièreV* 66 (1964) 33-53. Esp. 44-46 [6,25-34]. [NTA 8, 957]

**ŁACH, Jan**

1974 Mt 5,17: non veni solvere. — ŁACH, S. (ed.), *Biblia księga zycia*, Lublin: Catholic University, 1974, 70-90. → 1980

1976 Pokłon Magów (Mt2,1-12). (Adoratio magorum [Mat. 2,1-12]) — *RuBi* 29 (1976) 260-270.

1977 Historyczność genealogii Chrystusa w Mt 1,1-17 (Geschichtlichkeit des Stammbaumes Jesu bei Mt 1,1-17). — *StudTheolVars* 15/1 (1977) 19-35. [NTA 22, 81]

1978a Logion Jezusa o przestrzeganiu starotestamentalnego Prawa (Mt 5,17) (Logion Jesu über die Befolgung des Gesetzes des Alten Testament [Mt 5,17]). — *StudTheolVars* 16/1 (1978) 3-17. [NTA 23, 95]

1978b Ze studiów nad teologia ewangelii dziecięctwa (Études sur les Évangiles d'enfance de Jésus). — *Studia z biblistyki* 1 (1978) 155-322.323-325.

1980 Nie sadźcie, że przyszedłem rozwiązać Prawo albo proroków (Mt 5,17). (Nolite cogitare quod veni solvere legem au prophetas). — ŁACH, S. – FILIPIAK, M. (eds.), *Biblia, Księga Ludu Bożego*, Lublin: Catholic University, 1980, 79-89. → 1974

1982a   Ewangelia dziecięctwa – historia czy legenda (Les Évangiles de l'enfance. Histoire ou légende). — *Ateneum Kaplanskie* (Wroclaw) 99 (1982) 304-316.

1982b   "Sól ziemi" (Mt 5,13) (Salz der Erde). — *CollTheol* 52/4 (1982) 47-56. [NTA 27, 912]

1986    Obowiązek pojednania i miłości (Mt 5,43-48). — *RuBi* 39 (1986) 231-243.
        Die Pflicht zur Versöhnung und Liebe (Mt 5,43-48). — *CollTheol* 57 (special issue, 1987) 57-69. [NTA 33, 118]

1988a   Jezus zrodzony z Marii Dziewicy (Jesus natus ex Maria Virgine). [1,18-25] — *RuBi* 41 (1988) 242-252. Esp. 244-246.

1988b   Relacja "złotej zasady postępowania" (Mt 7,12) do nakazu miłości nieprzyjaciół (Mt 5.43-48). [On the relation beween 7,12 and 5,43-48] — *Ibid.*, 457-465.

1990a   "Nikt nie może dwom panom służyć" (Mt 6,24) ("Nul ne peut servir deux maîtres" [Mt 6,24]). — *StudTheolVars* 28/2 (1990) 38-50. [NTA 36, 1267]

1990b   Gdy cię ktoś uderzy w prawy policzek, nadstaw mu i drugi (Mt 5,39). ("Wenn dich einer auf die rechte Wänge schlägt, dann halt ihm auch die andere hin" [Mt 5,39]). — CHMIEL, J. - MATRAS, T. (eds.), *Studium scripturae anima theologiae. Prace ofiarowane Ksiedzu Profesorowi Stanisławowi Grzybkowi*, Kraków: Polskie Towarzystwo Teologiczne, 1990, 167-174.

1993    The Teachings of Jesus on Marriage according to the Sermon on the Mount (Mt 5,27-32). [Polish] — *Agnus et Sponsa* [FS A. Jankowski], Krakow: Benedyktynow, 1993, 196-215.

**LACHS, Samuel Tobias**

1975a   John the Baptist and His Audience. — *Gratz College Annual of Jewish Studies* (Philadelphia, PA) 4 (1975) 28-32. [NTA 23, 91]

1975b   On Matthew vi.12. — *NT* 17 (1975) 6-8. [NTA 19, 952]

1975c   On Matthew 23:27-28. — *HTR* 68 (1975) 385-388. [NTA 21, 731]

1977    Studies in the Semitic Background to the Gospel of Matthew. — *JQR* 67 (1976-77) 195-217. Esp. 195-197 [1,16]; 197-199 [3,7]; 199-203 [5,14-16]; 203-207 [5,46-47; 6,5-7; 18,15-17]; 207-211 [7,6]; 211-213 [10,15-17]; 213 [10,22]; 214-215 [26,50]; 215 [22,12]. [NTA 22, 77]

1978    Some Textual Observations on the Sermon on the Mount. — *JQR* 69 (1978-79) 98-111. Esp. 99-101 [5,1]; 101-103 [5,10]; 103-105 [6,1-4]; 106-108 [5,18]; 108-109 [5,29-30]; 109-110 [7,11]; 110-111 [6,26-29]. [NTA 23, 819]

1980    Hebrew Elements in the Gospels and Acts. — *JQR* 71 (1979-80) 31-43. Esp. 36-38 [5,7-8]; 38-39 [11,5]; 39-40 [15,21-28]. [NTA 25, 32] → G. Schwarz 1985a

1987    *A Rabbinic Commentary on the New Testament: The Gospels of Matthew, Mark, and Luke.* Hoboken, NJ: Ktav; New York: Anti-Defamation League of B'nai B'rith, 1987, XXIX-468 p. Esp. 1-14: "The Matthean infancy narrative"; 67-151: "The Sermon on the Mount".
        D.J. HARRINGTON, *CBQ* 50 (1988) 331-332; F.L. HORTON, *JEcuSt* 25 (1988) 460-461; J.M. LIEU, *ExpT* 99 (1987-88) 216; S. SCHREINER, *Judaica* 45 (1989) 71-72; G. VERMES, *JJS* 39 (1988) 123-124; B.L. VISOTSKY, *JQR* 78 (1987-88) 340-343; W. WIEFEL, *TLZ* 113 (1988) 266-268.

**LACKMANN, Max**

1961    Beiträge zum Amt des Petrus im NT. — *Bausteine für die Einheit der Christen* (Gersfeld-Dalherda) 1/4 (1961) 1-5; 2/5 (1962) 1-4; 2/6 (1962) 1-5; 3/9 (1963) 1-4.

1968    Die Deutung des "Felsen" und der "Schlüssel" des Himmelreichs. — *Bausteine* 8/31 (1968) 11-12. [NTA 13, 171]

**LÀCONI, Mauro**

1968a   Esegesi dei vangeli sinottici. II: La vita pubblica. — CANFORA, G., et al. (eds.), *Il*

*Messaggio della Salvezza*, IV, 1968, 205-442. Esp. 281-363: "Il discorso della montagna"; 365-391: "Il discorso missionario"; 393-402: "Il discorso delle parabole"; 421-432: "Il discorso escatologico".

1968b I Vangeli dell'Infanzia nella duplice presentazione di Matteo (cc. 1. 2.) e di Luca (cc. 1. 2.). — *RivAscM* 13 (1968) 31-43. [NTA 13, 156]

1968c Le caratteristiche del racconto della passione nei singoli evangelisti. — *Ibid.*, 149-164. [NTA 13, 101]

1968d La risurrezione di Cristo nella diversa narrazione e interpretazione dei quatro evangelisti. — *Ibid.*, 224-241. [NTA 13, 124]

1972a La passione secondo Matteo nella tradizione evangelica. — *ParVi* 17 (1972) 83-93.

1972b La nuova giustizia dei discepoli di Gesù nel Discorso della montagna di S. Matteo. — *Ibid.*, 163-173.

1977 "Tu sei Pietro e su questa pietra edificherò la mia Chiesa" (Mt 16,16-18). — *ParVi* 22 (1977) 173-187.

1982 Vangeli sinottici: un discorso pastorale alle Chiese. — *Sacra Doctrina* (Bologna) 27 (1982) 322-339. Esp. 330-332: "La catechesi di Matteo". [NTA 27, 495]

1987 Il discorso missionario (Mt 10). — *ParSpirV* 16 (1987) 115-127.

1989 "Ma liberaci dal male" (Mt 6,13). — *ParSpirV* 19 (1989) 97-107.

1994* (ed.), *Vangeli sinottici e Atti degli Apostoli* (Logos. Corso di studi biblici, 5). Torino-Leumann: Elle Di Ci, 1994, 584 p. → Buzzetti 1994a-b, Fusco 1994b-d, Ghiberti, Ghidelli, Infante, Làconi 1994a-b, Mosetto, Orsatti 1994a-b, Panimolle, Vallauri, Zedde

1994a Introduzione speciale. — *Ibid.*, 133-192. Esp. 170-173: "Matteo: uno stile chiraro e solenne".

1994b Il messaggio dottrinale dei Sinottici e degli Atti. — *Ibid.*, 547-579. Esp. 557-564: "Matteo: la catechesi del 'Dio con noi'".

**LACY, John A.**

1968 Ἠγέρθη – He Has Risen. — *BiTod* 36 (1968) 2532-2535.

**LADARIA, Luis F.**

1989a *La cristología de Hilario de Poitiers* (AnGreg, 255). Roma: Pont. Univ. Greg., 1989, XX-322 p. Esp. 40-47, 105-129, 131-135, 162-165, 185-190, 219-223, 265-270.

1989b El bautismo y la unción de Jesús en Hilario de Poitiers. — *Greg* 70 (1989) 277-290.

1990 Adán y Cristo. Un motivo soteriológico del *In Matthaeum* de Hilario de Poitiers. — ROMERO-POSE, E. (ed.), *Pléroma. Salus carnis. Homenaje a Antonio Orbe, S.J.*, Santiago de Compostella, 1990, 443-460. Esp. 443-451 [4,1-11]; 451-454 [9,2-8]; 454-457 [18,12-14]; 457-458 [27,45-50].

**LADD, George Eldon**

1959 More Light on the Synoptics. — *ChrTod* 3 (1959) 12-16. [NTA 3, 572]

1962a Consistent or Realized Eschatology in Matthew. — *SWJT* 5 (1962) 55-63.

1962b The Kingdom of God – Reign or Realm? — *JBL* 81 (1962) 230-238. [NTA 7, 465]

1964a *Jesus and the Kingdom. The Eschatology of Biblical Realism.* New York: Harper & Row, 1964, XV-367 p. Esp. 3-38 [eschatology]; 101-300 [kingdom].

1964b The *Sitz im Leben* of the Parables of Matthew 13: the Soils. — *Studia Evangelica* 2 (1964) 203-210.

1967 *The New Testament and Criticism.* Grand Rapids, MI: Eerdmans, 1967, 222 p. Esp. 126-127 [Q]; 130.132 [Papias]; 166-168 [Mt/Mk].

1968 *The Pattern of New Testament Truth.* Grand Rapids, MI: Eerdmans, 1968, 119 p. Esp. 41-63: "The synoptic pattern: the Kingdom of God".

1974a    *A Theology of the New Testament*. Grand Rapids, MI: Eerdmans, 1974, 661 p. Esp. 13-
         210: "The synoptic gospels"; rev. ed. D.A. Hagner, 1993, XIV-764 p. Esp. 29-245. → France
         1984, D. Wenham 1993
         *Théologie du Nouveau Testament* (Collection théologique Hokhma), trans. J.M. Sordet et al., Lausanne:
         Presses Bibliques Universitaires; Paris: Sator, 1984, 3 vols., XXVII-922 p.

1974b    The Parable of the Sheep and the Goats in Recent Interpretation. [25,31-46] —
         LONGENECKER, R.N. – TENNEY, M.C. (eds.), *New Dimensions*, 1974, 191-199.

1975     *I Believe in the Resurrection of Jesus*. Grand Rapids, MI: Eerdmans, 1975, 156 p. Esp.
         79-103: "The witness of the gospels".

**LÄPPLE, Alfred**

1993     *Kindheitsgeschichte Jesu. Kanonische und ausserkanonische Überlieferungen*
         (Akademie-Vorträge, 39). Schwerte: Katholische Akademie, 1993, 106 p.

**LAEUCHLI, Samuel**

1953     Origen's Interpretation of Judas Iscariot. [27,3-10]— *Church History* 22 (1953) 253-268.

1992     *Jesus und der Teufel: Begegnung in der Wüste. Imagination, Spiel und Therapie in der
         Versuchungsgeschichte*. Neukirchen-Vluyn: Neukirchener, 1992, VI-161 p.

**LAFON, Guy**

1988     La gratuité de Dieu. — *RSR* 76 (1988) 485-497. Esp. 490-496 [6,19-34]. [NTA 33, 604]

1994     Dans l'alliance humaine, l'origine de Jésus-Christ. [1,18-25] — *Études* 380 (1994) 647-
         656. [NTA 39, 136]

**LAFONT, Ghislain**

1986     *Dieu, le temps et l'être* (Cogitatio fidei, 139). Paris: Cerf, 1986, 373 p. Esp. 160-167: "Les
         femmes, les gardes et les disciples (Mt 27,57–28,20)".

1987     Fraternal Correction in the Augustinian Community. A Confrontation between the
         Praeceptum IV,6-9 and Matthew 18:15-17. — *Word and Spirit* (Still River, MA) 9
         (1987) 87-91.

**LAGE, Francisco**

1981     Las Bienaventuranzas: Texto e interpretación. — *Communio* (Madrid) 3/6 (1981) 574-
         585. Esp. 575-582: "El texto"; 582-587: "La redaccion y el género literario"; 587-590: "La interpretación".

**LAGO TOIMIL, M.**

1968     "Allora il re dirà...". Cristo Re, in Mt. 25,31-46. — *PalCl* 47 (1968) 1318-1321. [NTA
         13, 573]

**LAGRAND, James**

1980     How was the Virgin Mary "Like a Man" ( *'yk gbr* ')? A Note on Mt. i 18b and Related
         Syriac Christian Texts. — *NT* 22 (1980) 97-107. [NTA 24, 783]

**LAGRAND, James, Jr.**

1995     *The Earliest Christian Mission to "All Nations" in the Light of Matthew's Gospel* [10,5-
         42; 28,16-20] (University of South Florida International Studies in Formative Christianity
         and Judaism, 1). Atlanta, GA: Scholars, 1995, XI-288 p. Esp. 133-139 [10,5-6]; 145-156
         [23,15]; 157-186: "The nations in the design of the gospel"; 187-210: "Proclamation in word and deed"
         [4,18-22; 8,5-13; 10,5-42; 12,38-42; 13,1-23; 15,21-28]; 211-233: "Establishment of the kingdom" [26–28];
         235-247 [28,16-20]. [NTA 41, p. 148] — Diss. Basel, 1989 (E. Stegemann – R. Brändle).
         D.C. ALLISON, *JBL* 116 (1997) 742-744.

**LAGRANGE, Marie-Joseph**

1928[R]  *L'Évangile de Jésus-Christ* [1928]. *Avec la Synopse évangélique traduite par le P. C.*

*Lavergne* (Études bibliques). Paris: Gabalda, nouvelle édition, 1954, XIV-713 p.
*The Gospel of Jesus Christ*, trans. R. Ginns. Bangalore: Theological Publications of India, 1992, XXV-350 p.

**LAI, Pham Huu**

1973  Production du sens par la foi. Autorités religieuses contestées/fondées. Analyse structurale de Matthieu 27,57-28,20. — *RSR* 61 (1973) 65-96. [NTA 18, 114]
Sinn-Erzeugung durch den Glauben – widerlegte und begründete religiöse Autoritäten. Strukturale Analyse von Matt 27,57-28,20. — *LingBib* 32 (1974) 1-37. [NTA 19, 546]

**LAKE, Kirsopp**

1941[R]  & LAKE, Silva, *Family 13 (The Ferrar Group). The Text according to Mark. With a Collation of Codex 28 of the Gospels* [1941] (Studies and Documents, 11). Salt Lake City, UT: University of Utah Press, 1968, XI-161 p. Esp. 117-123: "A collation of Codex 28" [Mt].

**LAMARCHE, Paul**

1962  Le "blasphème" de Jésus devant le Sanhédrin. — *RSR* 50 (1962) 74-85. Esp. 76-81 [26,63-65]. [NTA 7, 145]; = ID., *Révélation de Dieu chez Marc*, 1976, 105-118. Esp. 110-115. → 1966
*SelT* 2 (1963) 197-199.

1965  La guérison de la belle-mère de Pierre et le genre littéraire des évangiles. — *NRT* 87 (1965) 515-526. Esp. 522-524 [8,14-15]. [NTA 10, 117]; = ID., *Révélation de Dieu chez Marc*, 1976, 47-60. Esp. 57-60.

1966  *Christ vivant. Essai sur la christologie du Nouveau Testament* (LD, 43). Paris: Cerf, 1966, 181 p. Esp. 51-53 [1,23; 11,25-27]; 149-156 [26,63-65]. → 1962
*Cristo vivo. Ensayo sobre la Cristología del Nuovo Testamento* (Col. Henneni, 60). Salamanca: Sígueme, 1968, 200 p.

1968  Le possédé de Gérasa (*Mt* 8,28-34; *Mc* 5,1-20; *Lc* 8,26-39). — *NRT* 90 (1968) 581-597. Esp. 593-597 [8,28-34]. [NTA 13, 569]; = ID., *Révélation de Dieu chez Marc*, 1976, 79-103. Esp. 98-103 [8,28-34].
*SelT* 9 (1970) 83-85.

1976  *Révélation de Dieu chez Marc* (Le point théologique, 20). Paris: Beauchesne, 1976, 159 p. → 1962, 1965, 1968

1983  L'indissolubilité selon Matthieu. Matthieu 19,9. — *Christus* 30 (1983) 475-482. [NTA 28, 500]

1990  Hypothèses à propos des divergences théologiques dans le Nouveau Testament. — THÉOBALD, C. (ed.), *Le Canon des Écritures. Études historiques, exégétiques et systématiques* (LD, 140), Paris: Cerf, 1990, 441-491. Esp. 450-455 [christology]; 455-458 [God]; 460-469 [law: 5,17-20; 7,15-23; 13,24-43; 28,16-20]; 472-476 [authority].

**LAMBERIGTS, Sylvester**

1975  De zaligsprekingen. Belofte en levensweg. — *Collationes* 5 (1975) 203-225.

1977  *De bergrede: grondwet van het kristendom.* Leuven: Davidsfonds, 1977, 96 p.

1980  De parabel van de tien bruidsmeisjes (Mt. 25,1-13). — BULCKENS, J. (ed.), *Parabels meerstemmig*, 1980, 122-132.

**LAMBERT, Bernard**

1969  *Bibliotheca Hieronymiana Manuscripta. La tradition manuscrite des œuvres de saint Jérome* (Instrumenta Patristica, 4). Steenbrugge: St. Pietersabdij – Den Haag: Nijhoff, II, 1969, IX-519 p. Esp. 191-208: "Commentarii in Matthaeum"; 209-260: "Homiliae excerptae ex commentariis in Matthaeum"; 315-318: "Homilia in Evangelium secundum Matthaeum XVIII,7-9 (Ps.-Chrysostomus)"; IIIB, 1970, XIV-255-790 p. Esp. 360-373: "Expositio quattuor evangeliorum; De oratione dominica".

**LAMBERT, Gustave**

1955 "Mon joug est aisé et mon fardeau léger". Note d'exégèse. — *NRT* 77 (1955) 963-969. Esp. 967-968 [11,28-30]. [NTA 1, 25]

**LAMBERTZ, Max**

1953 Die Toledoth in Mt. 1,1-17 und Lc. 3,23b ff. — KUSCH, H. (ed.), *Festschrift Franz Dornseiff zum 65. Geburtstag*, Leipzig: VEB Bibliographisches Institut, 1953, 201-225.

**LAMBIASI, Francesco**

1976a *L'autenticità storica dei vangeli. Studio di criteriologia* (Studi biblici, 4). Bologna: Dehoniane, 1976, 272 p.; [2]1987. — Diss. Pont. Univ. Greg., Roma, 1975 (R. Latourelle). *Autenticidade histórica dos evangelhos. Estudos de criteriologia*. São Paulo: Paulinas, 1978, 272 p.

1976b L'autenticità storica delle controversie con i Farisei. — *BibOr* 18 (1976) 3-27. [NTA 21, 64]

**LAMBRECHT, Jan**

1963 De theologische betekenis van de parabels. — *Bijdragen* 24 (1963) 314-318. Esp. 315-316 [13,11-12]. → Gnilka 1961a

1966 Die Logia-Quellen von Markus 13. — *Bib* 47 (1966) 321-360. [NTA 11, 1052] → 1967a

1967a *Die Redaktion der Markus-Apokalypse. Literarische Analyse und Strukturuntersuchung* (AnBib, 28). Roma: Päpstliches Bibelinstitut, 1967, XXIX-321 p. Esp. 76-78 [Q 13,35-36/Mk 13,2]; 100-105 [Q 17,23/Mk 13,5-6.21-22]; 115-136 [Q 12,11-12/Mk 13,9-13]; 168-173 [Q 17,23/Mk 13,21-23]; 203-204 [Q 11,51/Mk 13,30]; 211-226 [Q 16,17/Mk 13,31]; 235-252 [Q 12,35-46/Mk 13,32-36]; 257-259. — Diss. Pont. Inst. Bibl., Roma, 1965 (I. de la Potterie). → 1966

1967b L'évangile de Matthieu. — *RClerAfr* 22 (1967) 481-491.

1968a Les "dix vierges" (Mt 25,1-3). — *RClerAfr* 23 (1968) 225-233.

1968b Ware verwantschap en eeuwige zonde. Ontstaan en structuur van Mc. 3,20-35. — *Bijdragen* 29 (1968) 114-150, 234-258, 369-393 (English summary, 149-150, 258). Esp. 121-148: "De Q-tekst"; 234-257: "Mc. 3,20-35 en de Q-reconstructie". [NTA 13, 191/584/880]; = ID., *Marcus Interpretator. Stijl en boodschap in Mc. 3,20–4,34*, Brugge–Utrecht: Desclée De Brouwer, 1969, 19-97 Esp. 22-49; 50-73.

1971 Geen politieke Messias (Mt. 4,1-11). — *Getuigenis* 16 (1971-72) 116-123.

1972 The Parousia Discourse. Composition and Content in *Mt.*, XXIV-XXV. — DIDIER, M. (ed.), *L'Évangile selon Matthieu*, 1972, 309-342. Esp. 310-313: "A survey"; 313-341: "Discussion".

1974a The Message of the Good Samaritan (Lk 10:25-37). — *LouvSt* 5 (1974-75) 121-135. Esp. 124-127 [Q 10,25-28(Lk)]. [NTA 19, 980]

1974b The Relatives of Jesus in Mark. — *NT* 16 (1974) 241-258. Esp. 246-248 [12,22-30]; 248-250 [12,31-32]. [NTA 19, 965] → J.D. Crossan 1973a

1975 Jezus en het Gebed. — *Tijdschrift voor Geestelijk Leven* (Leuven) 31 (1975) 649-672. Esp. 658-660 [6,1-6.16-18]; 661-666 [6,9-13]. Jesus and Prayer. — *LouvSt* 6 (1976-77) 128-143. Esp. 135-136; 136-139. [NTA 21, 687]

1976a *Terwijl Hij tot ons sprak. Parabels van Jezus*. Tielt–Amsterdam: Lannoo, 1976, 295 p.; [3]1981. Esp. 17-41: "Parabels in de synoptische evangeliën"; 56-67 [18,12-14]; 87-90 [Q 10,25-28(Lk)]; 150-152 [Q 11,14-23]; 183-207 [25,1-13]; 209-240 [25,14-30]; 241-286 [25,31-46]. → 1976b *Parables of Jesus. Insight and Challenge*, trans. R. Van de Walle & C. Begg. Bangalore: Theological Publications in India, 1978, 346 p. Esp. 19-49; 65-79; 102-105; 175-178; 213-242; 243-280; 281-335. *Tandis qu'Il nous parlait. Introduction aux paraboles*, trans. M. Claes ("Le Sycomore", Série "Chrétiens aujourd'hui", 7). Paris: Lethielleux; Namur: Culture et Vérité, 1980, 302 p. Esp. 17-43; 58-70; 92-97; 154-157; 187-212; 213-244; 245-290. Les paraboles dans les Synoptiques. [1980, 17-43] — *NRT* 102 (1980) 672-691. [NTA 25, 446] *Once More Astonished. The Parables of Jesus*. New York: Crossroad, 1981, XIV-245 p. Esp. 1-23; 35-45; 64-66; 118-120; 146-166; 167-195; 196-235. *Le parabole di Gesù* (Bibbia e catechesi, 8). Bologna: Dehoniane, 1982, 318 p.

1976b Parabels over "het verlorene" (Lc. 15). — *Collationes* 6 (1976) 449-479. Esp. 460-470 [18,12-14]. [NTA 21, 424] → 1976a

1977a Jesus and the Law. An Investigation of Mk 7,1-23. — *ETL* 53 (1977) 24-82. Esp. 43-60 [Q/Mk 7,1-16]. [NTA 22, 104]; = DUPONT, J. (ed.), *Jésus aux origines de la christologie*, ²1989, 358-415 (additional note, 428-429).

1977b Parabels in Mt. 13. — *TijdTheol* 17 (1977) 25-47 (English summary, 47). Esp. 26-29: "De compositie van Mt. 13"; 30-42: "De redactie van Matteüs"; 42-46: 'De theologie van Matteüs". [NTA 21, 726]

1980 "Are you the one who is to come, or shall we look for another?". The Gospel Message of Jesus Today. — *LouvSt* 8 (1980-81) 115-128. Esp. 116-120: "Literary analysis"; 120-124: "Exegesis of the text"; 124-128: "Relevancy of the text". [NTA 25, 860]
"Zijt Gij de komende of hebben we een ander te verwachten?". Jezus en zijn boodschap vandaag. — *Collationes* 27 (1981) 130-146. [NTA 26, 92]; ID., *Één is onze meester*, 1994, 160-176. Trans. Polish 1989.

1982 Q-Influence on Mark 8,34-9,1. — DELOBEL, J. (ed.), *Logia*, 1982, 277-304. Esp. 278-292 [Mk/Q 12,9; 14,27; 17,33]; 293-303 [Q 12,8-9; 14,26-27; 17,33]. → Neirynck 1982d

1983a *Maar Ik zeg u. De programmatische rede van Jezus (Mt. 5-7; Lc. 6,20-49)*. Leuven: Vlaamse Bijbelstichting / Acco, 1983, 296 p. Esp. 21-48 [5-7; Q 6,20-49]; 49-87 [5,3-16]; 89-134 [5,17-48]; 135-170 [6,1-18]; 178-203 [6,19-7,12]; 205-230 [7,13-27]. [NTA 27, p. 332]
A. DERMIENCE, *RTL* 15 (1984) 375-376; F. VAN SEGBROECK, *Ons Geestelijk Leven* 60 (1983) 280.
*Ich aber sage euch. Die Bergpredigt als programmatische Rede Jesu (Mt 5-7; Lk 6,20-49)*, trans. L. Hug. Stuttgart: Katholisches Bibelwerk, 1984, 252 p. Esp. 19-42; 43-75; 77-115; 117-142; 143-170; 171-191. [NTA 29, p. 206]
E. BEST, *ExpT* 96 (1984-85) 332-333; L. DEVILLERS, *RThom* 86 (1986) 309-312; H. FRANKEMÖLLE, *TRev* 81 (1985) 198-199; A. FUCHS, *SNTU* 9 (1984) 244-245; G. GEIGER, *BLtg* 57 (1984) 273; H.B. GREEN, *JTS* 37 (1986) 175-177; J. GUILLET, *RSR* 74 (1986) 244; H. HAUSER, *EVie* 95 (1985) 155-157; J.D. KINGSBURY, *CBQ* 48 (1986) 145-146; O. KNOCH, *BK* 39 (1984) 186; H. KVALBEIN, *TidsTeolKirk* 60 (1989) 143-144; F. NEIRYNCK, *ETL* 60 (1984) 408-410; G. SEGALLA, *Studia Patavina* 33 (1986) 439-440; K. STOCK, *Bib* 68 (1987) 122-124; W. TRILLING, *TLZ* 110 (1985) 819-821; M. VANLANGENAEKER, *Collationes* 14 (1984) 486-487; B.T. VIVIANO, *RB* 93 (1986) 156-157.
*The Sermon on the Mount. Proclamation and Exhortation* (Good News Studies, 14). Wilmington, DE: Glazier, 1985, 255 p. [NTA 30, p. 98]
C. BERNAS, *TS* 47 (1986) 342-343; H.D. BETZ, *JBL* 106 (1987) 541-543; M. FITZPATRICK, *AusBR* 34 (1986) 73-74; R.L. MOWERY, *BTB* 17 (1987) 36; M.G. REDDISH, *RExp* 83 (1986) 460-461.
*"Eh bien! Moi je vous dis". Le discours-programme de Jésus (Mt 5-7; Lc 6,20-49)*, trans. A. Dermience (LD, 125). Paris: Cerf, 1986, 265 p. Esp. 15-40; 41-76; 77-117; 119-147; 149-178; 179-222.
M. DUMAIS, *ÉglT* 19 (1988) 101-102; B. ESTRADA, *Annales theologici* 3 (1989) 156-159; E. FARAHIAN, *Greg* 70 (1989) 785-786; C. FOCANT, *FoiTemps* 19 (1987) 285; H.-M. GUINDON, *LavalTP* 44 (1988) 123-124; M. HUBAUT, *MSR* 43 (1986) 212; A.J. LEVORATTI, *RevistBíb* 49 (1987) 191-192; D. MUÑOZ LEÓN, *EstBíb* 47 (1989) 424-425; F. NEIRYNCK, *ETL* 63 (1987) 430-431; J. PONTHOT, *RTL* 18 (1987) 85; L. SABOURIN, *SE* 39 (1987) 252-253; B.T. VIVIANO, *RB* 95 (1988) 146; N. WASWANDI, *RAfrT* 13 (1989) 110-114.
*Pero yo os digo ... El sermón programático de Jesús (Mt 5-7; Lc 5,20-49)* (Biblioteca de estudios bíblicos, 81). Salamanca: Sígueme, 1994, 302 p. Esp. 15-42; 43-79; 81-123; 125-155; 157-190; 191-216.
P. BARRADO FERNANDEZ, *RevistEspTeol* 54 (1994) 469-470; J L. ESPINEL, *CiTom* 122 (1995) 418-419; U. GIL ORTEGA, *Lumen* 44 (1995) 169-171; A.J. LEVORATTI, *RevistBíb* 57 (1995) 121-123; J. O'CALLAGHAN, *ActBibl* 63 (1995) 56-57; R. SANZ VALDIVIESO, *Carthaginensia* 11 (1995) 439-440.

1983b Righteousness in the Bible and Justice in the World. — *RAfrT* 7 (1983) 19-27. Esp. 21-26. [NTA 30, 111]; = *TheolEvang* 21 (1988) 6-13. [NTA 32, 1104]

1983c Zal de Wet niet vergaan? [5,18] — *Ons Geestelijk Leven* 60 (1983) 92-97.

1984a Het gebed des Heren. — *Innerlijk Leven* 38 (1984) 324-337, 415-430; = ID., *Één is onze meester*, 1994, 114-136.
*Het gebed des Heren. Uitleg en bezinning*. Mechelen: Kerk en Wereld, n.d., 32 p. [NTA 30, p. 98]

1984b Het matteaanse lijdensverhaal. — *Collationes* 14 (1984) 161-190. [NTA 29, 110]; = ID., *Één is onze meester*, 1994, 206-235.

1984c "Gij zijt Petrus". Mt. 16,16-19 en het pausschap. — *Collationes* 14 (1984) 389-419. Esp. 392-399; 400-410; 410-419. [NTA 29, 937]; = ID., *Één is onze meester*, 1994, 177-205. "Du bist Petrus". Mt 16,16-19 und das Papsttum. — *SNTU* 11 (1986) 5-32. Esp. 8-14; 14-24; 24-32. [NTA 31, 589]

1986a Een nieuwe Nederlandse Synopsis. Het gebruik ervan toegelicht door een analyse van Mt. 8,18-27. — *Collationes* 16 (1986) 405-428. [NTA 31, 1043r]; = ID., *Één is onze meester*, 1994, 137-159. → Denaux 1986

1986b "Je serai leur Dieu et ils seront mon peuple". — *NRT* 108 (1986) 481-498. Esp. 491-494 [28,18-20]. [NTA 31, 357]

1987 The Sayings of Jesus on Nonviolence. — *LouvSt* 12 (1987) 291-305. Esp. 293-295 [5,38-42]; 295-300 [historical Jesus]. [NTA 32, 592]; = BURGGRAEVE, R. – VERVENNE, M. (eds.), *Swords into Plowshares. Theological Reflections on Peace* (Louvain Theological & Pastoral Monographs, 8), Leuven: Peeters, 1991, 127-143. Esp. 129-132; 132-137.
Jesus' uitspraken over geweldloosheid. — BURGGRAEVE, R. (ed.), *Pacifisme: De politiek van Jezus?* (Cahiers voor Vredestheologie, 1), Leuven: VBS/Acco, 1987, 11-31. Esp. 14-15.16-20; = ID., *Één is onze meester*, 1994, 97-113.

1989a Bewerkers van vrede. [5,9] — *IKT/Communio* (Gent) 14 (1989) 81-86.

1989b Het bruiloftsmaal (Mt. 22,1-14). — *Jota* 3 (1989) 25-36.

1991a *Nieuw en oud uit de schat. De parabels in het Matteüsevangelie.* Leuven: Vlaamse Bijbelstichting/Acco; Boxtel: Katholieke Bijbelstichting, 1991, ²1992, 294 p. Esp. 15-27: "Matteaanse parabels"; 33-48 [18,12-14]; 49-64 [18,23-35]; 65-83 [20,1-16]; 89-101 [21,28-32]; 103-123 [21,33-44]; 125-140 [22,2-14]; 145-175 [13,1-52]; 185-193 [24,45-51]; 195-211 [25,1-13]; 213-239 [25,14-30]; 256-279 [25,31-46].
P. BEENTJES, *Streven* 59 (1992-93) 659; S.J. NOORDA, *TijdTheol* 33 (1993) 185; M. STEEN, *Collationes* 22 (1992) 323-324; H. VAN DE SANDT, *NTT* 47 (1993) 248-249.
*Out of the Treasure. The Parables in the Gospel of Matthew* (Louvain Theological & Pastoral Monographs, 10). Leuven: Peeters; Grand Rapids, MI: Eerdmans, 1992, 299 p. Esp. 19-31; 37-52; 53-68; 69-88; 93-104; 105-125; 127-142; 149-179; 189-198; 199-215; 217-244; 249-284. [NTA 37, p. 116]
B. BEAUMONT – É. COTHENET, *EVie* 103 (1993) 618; E. CUVILLIER, *ETR* 68 (1993) 581; A. DE LA FUENTE, *EstBíb* 53 (1995) 139-140; L. DEVILLERS, *RThom* 95 (1995) 316-319; D.J. HARRINGTON, *LouvSt* 17 (1992) 409-411; I.H. JONES, *JTS* 46 (1995) 257-258; C. KÄHLER, *TLZ* 118 (1993) 926-928; J.D. KINGSBURY, *CRBR* 7 (1994) 216-217; P. MEAGHER, *Vidyajyoti* 58 (1994) 401; G. STANTON, *ExpT* 104 (1992-93) 218; B.T. VIVIANO, *RB* 101 (1994) 616-617.

1991b Tussen God en mens. Engelen in het Matteüs-evangelie. — *Jota* 11 (1991) 25-33.

1992 John the Baptist and Jesus in Mark 1.1-15: Markan Redaction of Q? — *NTS* 38 (1992) 357-384. Esp. 359-361: "Structure and line of thought"; 361-370: "A search for Q in Mark 1.1-15" [3,1-6.11.13-17; 4,1-11]. [NTA 37, 166] → Neirynck 1996b

1993 Willibrord herzien: een bijgewerkte vertaling van het Nieuwe Testament. — *Bijdragen* 54 (1993) 407-429. Esp. 412-413. [NTA 38, 1271]

1994a *Één is onze meester. Luisteren naar het Matteüsevangelie.* Averbode: Altiora; Den Bosch: Katholieke Bijbelstichting, 1994, 357 p. Esp. 20-93: "Tekst en context" [homiletics]; 237-340: "Bijbelse overwegingen" [homiletics]. → 1980/81, 1984a-c, 1986a, 1987

1994b Is Active Nonviolent Resistance Jesus' Third Way? An Answer to Walter Wink. [5,39-42] — *LouvSt* 19 (1994) 350-351. [NTA 39, 1448] → Wink 1993

1995 The Great Commandment Pericope and Q. — PIPER, R.A. (ed.), *The Gospel Behind the Gospels*, 1995, 73-96. Esp. 78-88: "Minor agreements and Q" [22,34-40]; 88-95: "Markan redaction of Q".

**LAMMENS, G.N.**

1965 Zalige honger, Mt 5,6. — *Homiletica en Biblica* (Den Haag) 24 (1965) 19-22.

**LAMMERS, Klaus**

1966   *Hören, Sehen und Glauben im Neuen Testament* (SBS, 11). Stuttgart: Katholisches Bibelwerk, 1966, 113 p. Esp. 28-36. — Diss. Tübingen, 1966.

**LAMOUILLE, Arnauld** → Boismard 1986a

**LAMPE, Geoffrey William Hugo**

1973   St. Peter's Denial. — *BJRL* 55 (1972-73) 346-368. Esp. 355.362-363 [10,32-33]; 356-357 [12,32]. [NTA 18, 126]

**LAMPE, Peter**

1979   Das Spiel mit dem Petrusnamen – Matt. xvi.18. — *NTS* 25 (1978-79) 227-245. Esp. 242-245. [NTA 23, 437]

1983   & LUZ, U., Diskussionsüberblick. — STUHLMACHER, P. (ed.), *Das Evangelium und die Evangelien*, 1983, 413-431.
Overview of the Discussion. — STUHLMACHER, P. (ed.), *The Gospel and the Gospels*, 1991, 387-404.

**LAMPE, Stephen J.**

1992   Authority and Power in the Synoptics. — *BiTod* 30 (1992) 271-277. [NTA 37, 120]

**LANA, Horacio**

1989   La bienaventuranza a los pobres (Lc 6,20b; Mt 5,3). — *Proyecto Centro Salesiano de Estudios* (Buenos Aires) 1/1 (1989) 7-39.

**LANCELLOTTI, Angelo**

1975   *Matteo. Versione – introduzione – note* (Nuovissima versione della Bibbia dai testi originali, 33). Torino: Paoline, 1975, ²1978; ³1981, 414 p. [NTA 23, p. 228]
*Comentário ao Evangelho de São Mateus*, trans. A. Angonese & E. Ferreira Alves (Comentários exegéticos). Petrópolis: Vozes, 1980, 262 p.
S. VOIGT, *REB* 40 (1980) 805-806.

1977   Il Vangelo di Matteo (presentazione). — *La guida liturgica delle diocesi di Roma e del Lazio*, Roma, 1977, 42-70.

1983   La casa di Pietro a Cafarnao nei vangeli sinottici. Redazione e tradizione. — *Ant* 58 (1983) 48-69. Esp. 50-53 [Mt/Mk: οἶκος-οἰκία]. [NTA 28, 925]

**LANCZKOWSKI, Günter**

1958   Neutestamentliche Parallelen zu Láo-tsés Tao-te-king. — DELLING, G. (ed.), *Gott und die Götter*. FS E. Fascher, 1958, 7-15. Esp. 10-12 [5,3.48; 16,26; 18,3; 20,16; 23,11-12]; 15 [5,44].

**LANDES, George M.**

1967   The "Three Days and Their Nights" Motif in Jonah 2,1. — *JBL* 86 (1967) 446-450. Esp. 446-447 [12,40].

1983   Matthew 12:40 as an Interpretation of 'The Sign of Jonah' against Its Biblical Background. — MEYERS, C.L. - O'CONNOR, M. (eds.), *The Word of the Lord Shall Go Forth. Essays in Honor of David Noel Freedman in Celebration of His Sixtieth Birthday* (Americal Schools of Oriental Research, Special Volume Series, 1), Winona Lake, IN: Eisenbrauns, 1983, 665-684. Esp. 665-669 [traditional interpretations]; 669-671 [context]; 671-672 [12,40/Jn 5,25-29; 1 Pe 3,18-22; 4,5-6]; 673-674 [Justin; Irenaeus]; 674-678 [interpretation].

**LANDIS, Stephan**

1994   *Das Verhältnis des Johannesevangeliums zu den Synoptikern. Am Beispiel von Mt 8,5-13; Lk 7,1-10; Joh 4,46-54* (BZNW, 74). Berlin – New York: de Gruyter, 1994, IX-76 p. Esp. 4-17; 38-56. → Neirynck 1995d
M.-É. BOISMARD, *RB* 103 (1996) 614-615.

**LANDRY, Baptista**

1985 *L'évangile selon Matthieu commenté par les Pères* [Préface A.G. Hamman] (Les Pères dans la foi). Paris: Desclée De Brouwer, 1985, 173 p. [NTA 30, p. 231]
É. COTHENET, *EVie* 95 (1985) 336; H. CROUZEL, *BullLitEccl* 87 (1986) 309-310; A. VICIANO 17 (1984) 941-943.

**LANDUCCI, Pier Carlo**

1967 Il dramma della esegesi moderna. — *PalCl* 46 (1967) 1268-1274, 1338-1343, 1380-1386. [NTA 12, 551r] → da Spinetoli 1967a

1968 La promessa del primato. [16,16-19] — *PalCl* 47 (1968) 212-222. [NTA 12, 877]

1983 Un S. Matteo troppo intraprendente. — *Renovatio* 18 (1983) 475-477. → Marucci 1982

**LANE, William L.**

1969 Matthew – Blessing on the Nations. — BARKER, G.W. - LANE, W.L. - MICHAELS, J.R., *The New Testament Speaks*, New York: Harper & Row, 1969, 260-274.

**LANEY, J. Carl**

1981 *The Divorce Myth. A Biblical Examination of Divorce and Remarriage.* Minneapolis, MN: Bethany House, 1981, 160 p.

**LANG, Bernhard**

1982 Grußverbot oder Besuchsverbot? Eine sozialgeschichtliche Deutung von Lukas 10,4b. — *BZ* 26 (1982) 75-79. Esp. 78 [10,12]. [NTA 26, 890]

**LANG, Friedrich**

1975 Erwägungen zur eschatologischen Verkündigung Johannes des Täufers. — STRECKER, G. (ed.), *Jesus Christus in Historie und Theologie*. FS H. Conzelmann, 1975, 459-473. Esp. 461-466 [3,7-12]; 467 [3,11].

**LANG, Harald**

1952 Was is mit dem Felsen in Mt 16,18? — *Für Arbeit und Besinnung* 6 (1952) 90-93.

1976 Verschränkung von narrativer Syntax und kommunikativen Einheiten und ihre Abhängigkeit vom sozio-kulturellen Kontext, dargestellt am Beispiel der Bergpredigt. — *LingBib* 37 (1976) 16-30. Esp. 22-30. [NTA 21, 73]

**LANGE, Harvey**

1978 The Greater Righteousness: Theological Reflections on Matthew 5:17-20. — *CurrTMiss* 5 (1978) 116-121. [NTA 22, 763]

**LANGE, Joachim**

1973 *Das Erscheinen des Auferstandenen im Evangelium nach Mattäus. Eine traditions- und redaktionsgeschichtliche Untersuchung zu Mt 28,16-20* (FzB, 11). Würzburg: Echter, 1973, 573 p. Esp. 24-178: "Ἐδόθη μοι πᾶσα ἐξουσία ἐν οὐρανῷ καὶ ἐπὶ [τῆς] γῆς (Mt 28,18b)" [4,8-9; 6,10; 7,29; 8,9; 9,6-8; 10,1; 11,27; 12,8; 16,19; 18,18.19-20; 21,23-27]; 179-246: "Das christologische Konzept in und hinter Mt 28,18b(-20)" [11,27; 13,36-43; 22,41-46; 26,64]; 247-326: "Πορευθέντες οὖν μαθητεύσατε πάντα τὰ ἔθνη (Mt 28,19-20a)" [4,15; 6,32; 10.5.18; 12,18-21; 20,19.25; 21,43; 24,7.9.14; 25,32]; 327-356: "Καὶ ἰδοὺ ἐγὼ μεθ᾿ ὑμῶν εἰμι πάσας τὰς ἡμέρας ἕως τῆς συντελείας τοῦ αἰῶνος (Mt 28,20b)" [1,23; 8,23-27; 9,14-15; 17,19; 18,20; 23,39; 26,64]; 357-446: "Der Ort der Begegnung mit dem Auferstandenen (Γαλιλαία; ὄρος)" [2,22; 3,13; 4,8.12.15.18.23-25; 5,1; 14,23; 15,29; 17,1.22; 19,1; 21,11; 26,32; 27,55; 28,7.10.16]; 471-486: "Die Begegnung mit dem Auferstandenen (Mt 28,17.18a)". [NTA 18, p. 385] — Diss. Würzburg, 1973 (R. Schnackenburg). → Coppens 1974c, Meier 1977b
E.L. BODE, *CBQ* 37 (1975) 125-126; J. ERNST, *TGl* 66 (1976) 346-347; G. GHIBERTI, *RivBib* 24 (1976) 73-75; V. HASLER, *TZ* 31 (1975) 370; H. LEROY, *TRev* 71 (1975) 190-191; J. MURPHY-O'CONNOR, *RB* 83 (1976) 97-102; R. PESCH, *Freiburger Rundbrief* 27 (1976) 97; K.H. SCHELKLE, *TQ* 155 (1975) 71-72; G. SCHNEIDER, *BZ* 21 (1977) 125-127; A. SEGOVIA, *ArchTeolGran* 37 (1974) 290; N. WALTER, *TLZ* 102 (1977) 503-506.

1974 Zur Ausgestaltung der Szene vom Sterben Jesu in den synoptischen Evangelien. [27,45-54] — MERKLEIN, H. - LANGE, J. (eds.), *Biblische Randbemerkungen*. FS R. Schnackenburg, 1974, 40-55.

1980* (ed.), *Das Matthäus-Evangelium* (Wege der Forschung, 525). Darmstadt: Wissenschaftliche Buchgesellschaft, 1980, VI-464 p. [NTA 25, p. 303] → Bacon 1918, G. Bornkamm 1948, 1956b, K.W. Clark 1947, von Dobschütz 1928, Filson 1956, Gärtner 1954, Greeven 1955, Grundmann 1940, Haenchen 1951, Hoffmann 1974, Krentz 1964, J. Lange, Luz 1971, O. Michel 1950, C.F.D. Moule 1962, Schweizer 1952a, 1970, Sickenberger 1933, Stendahl 1960, Strecker 1966, Trilling 1959b
F. BRÄNDLE, *EstJos* 36 (1982) 158; E.J. EPP, *JBL* 100 (1981) 498-499; H. GIESEN, *TGeg* 23/4 (1980) 58; X. JACQUES, *NRT* 103 (1981) 772-773; G. RAVASI, *Henoch* 4 (1982) 425-427; R. SCHNACKENBURG, *BZ* 25 (1981) 154; K. STOCK, *ZKT* 104 (1982) 205-206.

1980 Einführung. — *Ibid.*, 1-40.

**LANGER, A.**

1969 Die Goldene Regel – ein Schlüssel zum Frieden. [7,12] — REISS, K. - SCHÜTZ, H. (eds.), *Kirche, Recht und Land. Festschrift Weihbischof Adolf Kindermann*, Taunus: Königstein, 1969, 67-74.

**LANGEVIN, Paul-Émile**

1972 *Bibliographie biblique. Biblical Bibliography*. I. *(1930-1970)*. Québec: Les Presses de l'Université Laval, 1972, XXVIII-941 p. Esp. 253-256 [synoptic problem]; 262-293 [Mt]; II. *(1930-1975)*, 1978, LXV-1591 p. Esp. 602-606 [synoptic problem]; 612-654 [Mt]; III. *(1930-1983)*, 1985, LIII-1901 p. Esp. 791-797 [synoptic problem]; 798-840 [Mt].

**LANGKAMMER, Hugolin**

1968 Der Ursprung des Glaubens an Christus den Schöpfungsmittler. — *SBF/LA* 18 (1968) 55-93. Esp. 60-74 [Ps 110,1/Mt]. [NTA 14, 117]

1983 Jedna teologia dwuwarstwowej Ewangelii. Wokół Ewangelii według św. Mateusza (Eine Theologie im Zweischichten-Evangelium des Matthäus). — *RoczTK* 30/1 (1983) 65-76. [NTA 31, 574]

1988a Dziewicza Matka. Rzeczywistość czy ideologia? (Mater virgo. Realitas an ideologia?). — *RuBi* 41 (1988) 471-486.

1988b Maryja – Matka Zbawiciela (Maria – die Mutter der Erlösers). — *RoczTK* 35/1 (1988) 65-80. Esp. 72-74 [2,13-23]. [NTA 38, 436]

1991 "Przyjdź królestwo Twoje!" ("Zu uns komme Dein Reich!"). — *RoczT* 38-39/1 (1991-92) 75-83. Esp. 75-76 [6,9-13]. [NTA 38, 1413]

**LANGLAMET, François**

1977 Rahab. — *DBS* 9/51 (1977) 1065-1092. Esp. 1085-1091 "Rahab, ancêtre du Messie (Mt., 1,5)".

**LANGLEY, James A.**

1957 *A Critique of the Contemporary Interpretations of the Sermon on the Mount, with Special Reference to Albert Schweitzer, Reinhold Niebuhr, and C.H. Dodd*. Diss. Southwestern Baptist Theol. Sem., Fort Worth, TX, 1957, 170 p.

**LANIER, David E.**

1992 The Lord's Prayer: Matt 6:9-13 - A Thematic and Semantic-Structural Analysis. — *Criswell Theological Review* (Dallas, TX) 6 (1992) 57-72. Esp. 58-62: "Thematic analysis"; 62-66: "Semantic-structural". [NTA 37, 1259]

**LAPIDE, Pinchas E.**

1973a Die Bergpredigt: Theorie und Praxis. [H. van Oyen, *ZEvEth* 15 (1971) 98-117] — *ZEvEth* 17 (1973) 369-372.

1973b   Hidden Hebrew in the Gospels. — *Immanuel* 2 (1973) 28-34. Esp. 28-29 [1,21]; 30-31 [7,28-29]. [NTA 18, 93]

1974   Der "Prüfstein" aus Spanien. Die einzige rabbinische Hebraisierung des Mt-Evangelium. — *Sefarad* 34 (1974) 227-272. [NTA 20, 79]

1977   Hebräisch im Evangelium. — *Judaica* 33 (1977) 7-29. Esp. 14-16, 18-21. [NTA 21, 679]

1980   & VON WEIZSÄCKER, C.F., *Die Seligpreisungen. Ein Glaubensgespräch.* Stuttgart: Calwer; München: Kösel, 1980, 102 p. [NTA 25, p. 197]
*De zaligsprekingen. Een geloofsgesprek.* Kampen: Kok, 1987, 85 p.
J. LACH, *CollTheol* 52/4 (1982) 187-189; U. LUZ, *TLZ* 107 (1982) 516-517.

1981   Es geht um die Entfeindungsliebe. Realpolitik, wie sie die Bergpredigt eigentlich meint. — *Lutherische Monatshefte* (Hamberg) 20 (1981) 505-508. [NTA 26, 467]

1982a   *Die Bergpredigt – Utopie oder Programm?* Mainz: Grünewald, 1982, 144 p.; [3]1983, 153 p. Esp. 32-43 [5,3-12]; 44-141 [5,21-48]. [NTA 27, p. 332] → Frankemölle 1983c
J.-F. COLLANGE, *RHPR* 65 (1985) 211-212; B. DE ARMELLADA, *NatGrac* 30 (1983) 452-453; J. ERNST, *TGl* 73 (1983) 490; H. GIESEN, *TGeg* 27 (1984) 184; J. THOMAS, *TZ* 42 (1986) 83-84.
*De Bergrede – Utopie of program?* Baarn: Ten Have, 1984, 143 p. Esp. 31-42; 43-131.
P. BEENTJES, *Streven* 52/7 (1984-85) 562.
*The Sermon on the Mount. Utopia or Program for Action?*, trans. A. Swidler. Maryknoll, NY: Orbis, 1986, VII-148 p. Esp. 25-37; 39-135. [NTA 30, p. 354]
J.M. CASCIARO RAMIREZ, *ScriptTheol* 19 (1987) 937-941; J.T. PAWLIKOWSKI, *JEcuSt* 24 (1987) 127; R.J. RAJA, *Vidyajyoti* 51 (1987) 338; P. VAN BUREN, *Commonweal* 113 (1986) 564-565.
*O Sermão da montanha. Utopia o programma?* Petrópolis: Vozes, 1986, 136 p.

1982b   What Did Jesus Ask? A Jewish Reading of the Sermon on the Mount. — *Christianity and Crisis* (New York) 42 (1982) 139-142.

1984a   *Wie liebt man seine Feinde? Mit einer Neuübersetzung der Bergpredigt (Mt 5-7) unter Berücksichtigung der rabbinischen Lehrmethoden und der jüdischen Muttersprache Jesu.* Mainz: Grünewald, 1984, 103 p. [NTA 29, p. 91]
F. REISINGER, *TPQ* 133 (1985) 165-166.
*Hoe heeft men zijn vijanden lief? Met een nieuwe vertaling van de Bergrede*, trans. J. van den Berg. Kampen: Kok, 1984, 87 p.

1984b   *Er wandelte nicht auf dem Meer. Ein jüdischer Theologe liest die Evangelien* (Gütersloher Taschenbücher Siebenstern, 1410). Gütersloh: Mohn, 1984, 126 p. Esp. 51-86: "Das Vaterunser – ein christliches oder ein jüdisches Gebet?".
*Das Vaterunser – ein jüdisches oder ein christliches Gebet? — Renovatio* (Bonn) 47 (1991) 108-110. [NTA 36, 144]

1986   The Beatitudes. — *Emmanuel* 92 (1986) 322-329.355. [NTA 31, 115]

1987   *Wer war schuld an Jesu Tod?* (Gütersloher Taschenbücher Siebenstern, 1419). Gütersloh: Mohn, 1987, 123 p. Esp. 11-42 [Judas].

**LAPOORTA, J.**

1989   "Whatever you did for one of the least of these … You did for me" (Matt. 25:31-46). — *JTSouthAfr* 68 (1989) 103-109. [NTA 34, 637]

**LARCHER, Charles**

1962   *L'actualité chrétienne de l'Ancien Testament d'après le Nouveau Testament* (LD, 34). Paris: Cerf, 1962, 533 p. Esp. 82-89 [kingdom]; 90-96 [christological titles]; 98-114 [Messiah]; 158-176 [servant]; 186-192 [Son of Man]; 218-255 [law].

**LARIDON, Valere**

1953   De Oratione Dominica. — *CollBrug* 49 (1953) 414-422.

**LARMER, Robert A.H.**

1987   *Water into Wine? An Investigation of the Concept of Miracle.* Kingston: McGill; Montreal: Queen's Univ., 1987, XI-155 p.

**LaRondelle, Hans K.**

1971 *Perfection and Perfectionism. A Dogmatic-Ethic Study of Biblical Perfection and Phenomenal Perfectionism* (Andrews University Monographs. Studies in Religion, 3). Berrien Springs, MI: Andrews University Press, 1971, [4]1984, VII-364 p. Esp. 159-182: "Christ and perfection" [5,48; 19,21].

**Larrain, Christian**

1970 *L'Opus imperfectum in Matthaeum: son utilisation selon les siècles, son contenu, son texte biblique.* Diss. Paris, 1970.

**Larson, Stan**

1986 The Sermon on the Mount. What Its Textual Transformation Discloses Concerning the Historicity of the Book of Mormon. — *TrinJ* NS 7 (1986) 23-45. [NTA 31, 1065]

**Larsson, Edvin**

1966 Dopet och Andens insegel. [Baptism and seal of the Spirit] [3,13-17] — *TidsTeolKirk* 37 (1966) 1-14.

**LaSor, William Sanford**

1972 *The Dead Sea Scrolls and the New Testament.* Grand Rapids, MI: Eerdmans, 1972, 281 p. Esp. 142-153 [John the Baptist]; 206-236 [Jesus]; 238-244 [Sermon on the Mount].

**Lasserre, Guy**

1996 *Les synopses: élaboration et usage* (Subsidia Biblica, 19). Roma: Pont. Istituto Biblico, 1996, VIII-134 p. Esp. 1-30: "Les synopses évangéliques et leur méthodologie". — Diss. Lausanne, 1993. F. Neirynck, *ETL* 72 (1996) 439-442; A. Poppi, *RivBib* 44 (1996) 361-364; C.M. Tuckett, *NT* 39 (1997) 192-193.

**Lategan, Bernard C.**

1969 Die Botsing tussen Jesus en die Fariseërs volgens Matt. 23. [The conflict between Jesus and the Pharisees according to Mt 23] — *NduitseGT* 10 (1969) 217-230. [NTA 14, 489]

1977 Structural Interrelations in Matthew 11-12. — *Neotestamentica* 11 (1977) 115-129 (addendum, 28-34).

1982 Structure and Reference in Mt 23. — *Neotestamentica* 16 (1982) 74-87 (addendum, 38-41).

**Latham, James E.**

1982 *The Religious Symbolism of Salt* (Théologie historique, 64). Paris: Beauchesne, 1982, 256 p. Esp. 193-202: "The basic logion"; 203-211: "The parable in Matthew" [5,13].

**Latourelle, René**

1973 Authenticité historique des miracles de Jésus. Essai de critériologie. — *Greg* 54 (1973) 225-262 (English summary, 261-262). [NTA 18, 427]

1986 *Miracles de Jésus et théologie du miracle* (Recherches, NS 8). Montreal: Bellarmin; Paris: Cerf, 1986, 393 p. Esp. 59-71: "Les miracles de Jésus selon Jésus" [11,2-6.20-24; 12,28]; 93-269: "Récits particuliers et test d'historicité"; 287-289. → Levorati 1988
*Miracoli di Gesù e teologia del miracolo.* Assisi: Cittadella, 1987. 464 p.
*The Miracles of Jesus and the Theology of Miracles,* trans. M.J. O'Connell. New York – Mahwah, NJ: Paulist, 1988, VI-371 p.
*Milagros de Jesús y teología del milagro* (Verdad y Imagen, 112) Salamanca: Sígueme, 1990, 382 p.

**Lattanzi, Ugo Emilio**

1957 Il primato di Pietro nella interpretazione di O. Cullmann. — *Divinitas* 1 (1957) 54-70. → Cullmann 1952

1967 Eschatologici sermonis Domini logica interpretatio (Mt. 24,1-36; Mc. 13,1-37; Lc. 21,5-35). — *Divinitas* 11 (1967) 71-92. [NTA 13, 177]

1968 L'Évangile de l'Enfance: vérité historique ou mythe? — *Itinéraires* 121 (1968) 271-288. Il Vangelo dell'Infanzia è verità o mito? — *De cultu B.V. Mariae respectu habito ad mythologiam et libros apocryphos* (De primordiis cultus mariani. Acta congressus mariologici-mariani in Lusitania anno 1967 celebrati, V/4), Roma: Pont. Acad. Mariana Int., 1970, 31-46.

**LATTEY, Cuthbert**

1950 The Evidence for the Belief That Our Lord Himself Claimed to Be Divine. [8,1-4; 9,1-8] — *ExpT* 62 (1950-51) 31. → Argyle 1950

1952 How Is Matt V,17-18 to Be Reconciled with the Abolition in the New Law of the Jewish Ritual Observances, the Sabbath Rest... — *Scripture* 5 (1952) 50-51.

1953 Camelus per foramen acus. [19,24] — *VD* 31 (1953) 291-292.

**LATTKE, Michael**

1984 Salz der Freundschaft in Mk 9,50c. — *ZNW* 75 (1984) 44-59. Esp. 44-48 [5,13]. [NTA 29, 127]

1994 Glückselig durch den Geist (Matthäus 5,3). — MAYER, C., et al. (eds.), *Nach den Anfängen fragen*. FS G. Dautzenberg, 1994, 363-382. Esp. 364-374 [5,3/Qumran]; 375-380: "Exegetische Begründung des Übersetzungsvorschlags".

**LAU, Franz**

1951 *Das Matthäus-Evangelium übersetzt und ausgelegt* (Bibelhilfe für die Gemeinde. NT, 1). Berlin: Evangelische Verlagsanstalt, 1951, 223 p. Esp. 7-15.218-222 [introduction]; 16-217 [commentary].

**LAUER, Stewart E.**

1993 Must We Obey the Law? [5,17-20] — *Kerux* 8/3 (1993) 3-18.

**LAUER, W.G.**

1971 *Jesu Stellung zur Ehe nach Mt 19,3-12 (als Beitrag zu seiner Lehre über Schöpfung, Gesetz und Reich Gottes)*. Diss. München, 1971-72.

**LAUFEN, Rudolf**

1980 *Die Doppelüberlieferungen der Logienquelle und des Markusevangeliums* (BBB, 54). Königstein/Ts.–Bonn: Hanstein, 1980, 614 p. Esp. 59-92.388-404: "Einleitung"; 93-125.405-426: "Die Ankündigung des Messias durch Johannes den Täufer" [Q 3,16]; 126-155.427-455: "Das Streitgespräch über den Vorwurf des Teufelsbündnisses" [Q 11,15-18]; 156-173.456-469: "Das Offenbarwerden des Verborgenen" [Q 12,2]; 174-200.470-490: "Das Gleichnis vom Senfkorn" [Q 13,18-19]; 201-301.491-545: "Die Aussendungsrede" [Q 10,1-12.16]; 302-342.546-572: "Die Worte vom Kreuznehmen und Lebenverlieren/Lebenfinden" [Q 14,27; 17,33]; 343-360.573-594: "Das Wort von Ehescheidung und Ehebruch" [Q 16,18]; 361-384.595-613: "Die Warnung vor falschen Messiassen" [Q 17,23]. — Diss. Bonn, 1976-77 (H. Zimmermann).

M.-É. BOISMARD, *RB* 90 (1983) 624-625; C.E. CARLSTON, *CBQ* 43 (1981) 473-475; A. FUCHS, *SNTU* 5 (1980) 169-175; M.D. GOULDER, *JTS* 33 (1982) 242-245; F. NEIRYNCK, *ETL* 57 (1981) 181-183; H. RITT, *BZ* 25 (1981) 270-272; K. STOCK, *Bib* 62 (1981) 569-570; D. ZELLER, *BK* 35 (1980) 34.

Βασιλεία und ἐκκλησία. Eine traditions- und redaktionsgeschichtliche Untersuchung des Gleichnisses vom Senfkorn. [1980, 174-200.470-490] — ZMIJEWSKI, J. – NELLESSEN, E. (eds.), *Begegnung mit dem Wort*. FS H. Zimmermann, 1980, 105-140.

1985 Die Logienquelle Q. — *Religionsunterricht an höheren Schulen* 28 (1985) 275-291.

**LAUNDERVILLE, Dale**

1983 Jacob's Well. [The Synoptic Problem and "Q"]. — *BiTod* 21 (1983) 74-76.

**LAURENTIN, René**

1974 Les Évangiles de l'enfance. — *LumièreV* 119 (1974) 84-105. Esp. 84-90 [historical Jesus]; 91-93 [1,1-17]. [NTA 19, 940] → Cousin 1974b
Os evangelhos da infância. — *RevistCuBíb* 12 (1975) 88-108.

1979    Exégèses réductrices des Évangiles de l'enfance. — *Marianum* 41 (1979) 76-100. [NTA
        24, 779r] → R.E. Brown 1977

1981    Approche structurale de Matthieu 1-2. — CARREZ, M. - DORÉ, J. - GRELOT, P. (eds.),
        *De la Tôrah au Messie. Études d'exégèse et d'herméneutique bibliques offertes à Henri
        Cazelles pour ses 25 années d'enseignement à l'Institut Catholique de Paris (Octobre
        1979)*, Paris: Desclée, 1981, 383-416. Esp. 384-386: "Structure littéraire"; 386-411: "Approche
        sémiotique".

1982a   *Les Évangiles de l'Enfance du Christ. Vérité de Noël au-delà des mythes. Exégèse et
        sémiotique, historicité et théologie.* Paris: Desclée De Brouwer, 1982, 633 p. Esp. 299-
        356: "Matthieu 1-2"; 379-384; 393-425: "Les généalogies"; 470-506: "La conception virginale". [NTA 28,
        p. 83]; [2]1984. → 1983, 1985; → Berton 1983, Blanco Pacheco 1983, R.E. Brown 1985a-b, Calabuig 1985,
        Carmignac 1985, Ols 1985, Segalla 1983a
            M. ALCALÁ, *EstE* 60 (1985) 496-497; D. BERTETTO, *Sal* 46 (1984) 142; B. BILLET, *EVie* 95 (1985) 262-
        263; M.M. BOURKE, *CBQ* 46 (1984) 579-582; J.A. CARRASCO, *EstJos* 37 (1983) 250-251; L. CIGNELLI,
        *SBF/LA* 35 (1985) 481-485; J. GALOT, *Greg* 65 (1984) 173-174; G. GIRONÉS, *Anales Valentinos* 10
        (1984) 205-209; J. GUILLET, *RSR* 71 (1983) 411-414; J. MASSONET, *LumièreV* 183 (1987) 99-100; L.
        MONLOUBOU, *EVie* 93 (1983) 647-649; M.-J. NICOLAS, *RThom* 84 (1984) 479-487; L. PANIER, *SémBib*
        34 (1984) 38-43; T. SIUDI, *RuBi* 38 (1985) 466-468; J. WINANDY, *NRT* 106 (1984) 257-258.
            *I vangeli dell'infanzia di Cristo, la verità del Natale al di là dei miti. Esegesi e semiotica, storicità e teologia*,
        trans. C. Danna (Parola di Dio, 2/1). Milano – Cinisello Balsamo: Paoline, 1985, [2]1986, 713 p.; [3]1989, 698
        p.
            *BibOr* 33 (1991) 187; C. BISSOLI, *Sal* 52 (1990) 742; M. LÀCONI, *ParVi* 31 (1986) 383-385; G.
        SEGALLA, *Studia Patavina* 33 (1986) 441.
            *The Truth of Christmas. Beyond the Myths. The Gospels of Infancy of Christ*, trans. M.J. Wrenn, et al.
        (Studies in Scripture). Petersham, MA: St. Bede's Publications, 1986, XX-569 p. [NTA 31, p. 102]

1982b   Analyse sémiotique des Évangiles de Marie. Bilan et prospective. — *EphMar* 32 (1982)
        53-80. Esp. 69-72 [1-2].

1982c   Concepito dallo Spirito santo. La critica, l'esegesi e il senso. — *ParSpirV* 6 (1982) 74-
        92. Esp. 76-78.80-83 [1,18-25].

1983    Vérité des Évangiles de l'enfance. — *NRT* 105 (1983) 691-710. [NTA 28, 486] → 1982a

1985    *Les Évangiles de Noël.* Paris: Desclée, 1985, 235 p. Esp. 175-209: "Matthieu 1-2"; 210-214
        [Mt/Lk]. [NTA 30, p. 354] → 1982a
            *I vangeli del Natale.* Casale Monferrato: Piemme, 1987, 268 p.
            B. ESTRADA, *Annales theologici* 3 (1989) 154-156.

1995    La foi de Marie: Réflexions exégétiques sur les écrits du Nouveau Testament. — *Études
        Mariales* 51 (1995) 51-85.

**LAVERDIERE, Eugene A.**

1966    La Prière de la Nouvelle Alliance. — *Parole et pain* (Marseille) 16 (1966) 397-420.

1976    & THOMPSON, W.G., New Testament Communities in Transition: A Study of Matthew
        and Luke. — *TS* 37 (1976) 567-597. Esp. 571-582 [Judaism; mission; community; judgement].
        [NTA 21, 371]

1982    God as Father. — *Emmanuel* 88 (1982) 545-550. [NTA 27, 555]

1983    *When We Pray ... Meditation on the Lord's Prayer.* Notre Dame, IN: Ave Maria Press,
        1983, 172 p.

1986a   Looking Ahead to the Year of Matthew. — *Emmanuel* 92 (1986) 498-503, 527. [NTA
        31, 576]

1986b   A Garment of Camel's Hair. [3,4] — *Ibid.*, 545-551. [NTA 31, 583]

1987a   God is with Us. [1,18-25] — *Emmanuel* 93 (1987) 26-31, 60. [NTA 31, 575]

1987b   The Passion Story as Prophecy. — *Ibid.*, 85-90. [NTA 31, 1084]

1987c   The Resurrection according to Matthew. — *Ibid.*, 126-135. [NTA 31, 1087]

1987d His Mother Mary. [12,46-50; 13,54-58] — *Ibid.*, 191-197. [NTA 31, 1052]

1987e The Holy Spirit in Matthew's Gospel. — *Ibid.*, 272-277, 290. [NTA 32, 107]

1987f The Discourse on the Mountainside. — *Ibid.*, 315-323. [NTA 32, 114]

1987g The Parables in Matthew's Gospel. — *Ibid.*, 446-453. [NTA 32, 108]

1988 The Lord's Prayer in Literary Context. — OSIEK, C. – SENIOR, D. (eds.), *Scripture and Prayer, a Celebration for Caroll Stuhlmueller*, Wilmington, DE: Glazier, 1988, 104-116.

1993 They Shall Name Him Emmanuel, Which Means "God Is With Us". — *Emmanuel* 99 (1993) 544-551. [NTA 38, 749]

1994a The Eucharist in the New Testament and the Early Church. I. Before Ever There Was a Name. Our Daily Bread. [6,11] — *Emmanuel* 100 (1994) 4-13. [NTA 38, 1364]

1994b The Eucharist in the New Testament and the Early Church. IV. For the Forgiveness of Sins. The Eucharist in Matthew's Gospel. — *Ibid.*, 196-206. [NTA 39, 159]

**LAWLER, Thomas C.**

1972 Some Observations on the Brown Article on the Virginal Conception of Jesus. — *HomPastR* 73/3 (1972) 61-66. [NTA 17, 465] → R.E. Brown 1972

**LAWLOR, George L.**

1974 *The Beatitudes Are for Today.* Grand Rapids, MI: Baker, 1974, 131 p.

**LAWTON, T.A.D.**

1967 A Buried Treasure in the Gospels (Mt 19,16-22 par). — *EvQ* 39 (1967) 93-101. [NTA 12, 91]

**LAYMON, Charles M.**

1968 *The Lord's Prayer in Its Biblical Setting.* Nashville, TN – New York: Abingdon, 1968, 160 p. [NTA 13, p. 270]

**LAYTON, Bentley**

1968 The Sources, Date and Transmission of *Didache* 1.3b–2.1. — *HTR* 61 (1968) 343-383. Esp. 352-361 [5,38-48/Did]; 361-363 [5,25-26/Did]; 373-375 [5,48/Did]. [NTA 13, 718]

**LÁZARO RECALDE, Ricardo**

1981 Las bienaventuranzas: Evangelio y programa de vida. — *Communio* (Madrid) 3/6 (1981) 615-629.

**LEA, Thomas D.**

1992 Understanding the Hard Sayings of Jesus. [Sermon on the Mount] — *SWJT* 35 (1992) 20-27. [NTA 37, 134]

**LEAL, Juan**

1952 La Virgen en el Evangélio: III. José, su marido, como era bueno y no quería afrentarla, tenía pensado dejarla ocultamente (Mt. 1,19). — *CuBíb* 9 (1952) 215-217.

1954 *Sinopsis concordada de los cuatro evangelios* (Biblioteca de autores cristianos, 124). Madrid: Católica, 1954, xx-353 p. → 1975

1956 Nota al problema sinóptico. Con motivo del libro del señor Vaganay. — *EstE* 30 (1956) 469-479. → Vaganay 1954a

1957 Forma, historicidad y exegesis de las sentencias evangélicas. — *EstE* 31 (1957) 267-325. Esp. 278-325 [sayings]. [NTA 2, 260]

1965 Valor eclesiológico y sacramental de Mt 9,8b: "Qui dedit potestatem talem hominibus". — *EstBíb* 24 (1965) 245-253. [NTA 12, 157]

1966 "Qui dedit potestatem talem hominibus" (Mt 9,8). — *VD* 44 (1966) 53-59. [NTA 11, 210]

1969 La Misión de San José en la historia de Jesús (Mt 1,18-25). — *Manresa* 41 (1969) 209-216. [NTA 14, 471]

1975 *Sinopsis concordada de los cuatro evangelios. Nueva versión del original griego, en columnas paralelas y con notas críticas* (Biblioteca de autores cristianos, 124). Madrid: Católica, 1975, 334 p. → 1954

**LEANEY, Alfred Robert Clare**

1954a Dominical Authority for the Ministry of Healing. — *ExpT* 65 (1953-54) 121-123. Esp. 122 [10,7-8].

1954b Jesus and the Symbol of the Child (Luke ix.46-48). [18,1-5] — *ExpT* 66 (1954-55) 91-92.

1955 The Authorship of Egerton Papyrus No. 3. — *VigChr* 9 (1955) 212-217. → Chadwick 1956

1956 The Lucan Text of the Lord's Prayer (Lk xi 2-4). — *NT* 1 (1956) 103-111. Esp. 103-105 [6,9-11]. [NTA 1, 49]

1958 *A Commentary on the Gospel according to St. Luke* (Black's New Testament Commentaries). London: Black, 1958, [2]1966, XII-300 p. Esp. 12-33: "Luke and his sources".

1962 The Birth Narratives in St Luke and St Matthew. — *NTS* 8 (1961-62) 158-166. Esp. 163-166 [1,3.5.6.16.21]. [NTA 6, 759]

1965 The Gospels as Evidence for First-Century Judaism. — NINEHAM, D.E., et al. (eds.), *Historicity and Chronology*, 1965, 28-45. Esp. 34-37: "Matthew – the duty to rebuke".

1970 DAVIDSON, R. - LEANEY, A.R.C., *Biblical Criticism* (The Pelican Guide to the Bible, 3; Pelican Books, A1050). Harmondsworth: Penguin, 1970, 393 p. Esp. 233-265: "New methods: the synoptic gospels".

1972 *The New Testament* (Knowing Christianity). London: Hodder & Stoughton, 1972, 256 p. Esp. 37-48: "The gospel of Matthew".

**LEBEAU, Paul**

1966a *Le vin nouveau du Royaume. Étude exégétique et patristique sur la Parole eschatologique de Jésus à la Cène* (Museum Lessianum. Section biblique, 5). Paris–Brugge: Desclée De Brouwer, 1966, 319 p. Esp. 69-184: "Le vin nouveau et l'avènement du Royaume dans les Synoptiques" [26,29]; 185-294: "L'exégèse patristique du logion eschatologique". [NTA 12, p. 136] — Diss. Paris, 1964.

1966b La parole eschatologique de Jésus à la Cène (Mt. 26,29) dans l'exégèse patristique. — *Studia Patristica* 7 (1966) 516-523. [NTA 11, 711]

**LE BRAS, Gabriel**

1967 Commentaires bibliques et droit canon. Matthieu au *Corpus Juris Canonici*. — *Mélanges offerts à M.-D. Chenu* (Bibliothèque Thomiste, 37), Paris: Vrin, 1967, 325-343.

**LEBRETON, Jules**

1947[R] *Lumen Christi. La doctrine spirituelle du Nouveau Testament* [1947] (Verbum Salutis). Paris: Beauchesne, [21]1956, 386 p. Esp. 141-157: "Le Sermon sur la montagne".

**LECKIE, Joseph Logan**

1980 *The Criteria of Judgment in the Gospel according to Matthew*. Diss. St. Andrews, Faculty of Divinity, 1980 (R. McL. Wilson).

**LECLERCQ, Jean**

1972 "Scopis mundatam" (*Matth. 12,44; Lc. 11,25*). Le balai dans la Bible et dans la liturgie d'après la tradition latine. — FONTAINE, J. - KANNENGIESSER, C. (eds.), *Epektasis*. FS

J. Daniélou, 1972, 129-137.

La escoba en la Biblia y en la liturgia según la tradición latina. — *Cuadernos mónasticos* (Buenos Aires) 12 (1977) 459-466.

**LE DÉAUT, Roger**

1962    Goûter le calice de la mort. [20,20-23] — *Bib* 43 (1962) 82-86.

1963    *La nuit pascale. Essai sur la signification de la Pâque juive à partir du Targum d'Exode XII 42* (AnBib, 22). Roma: Institut biblique pontifical, 1963, 423 p. Esp. 311-315 [Mt/Ex].

1964    *Actes* 7,48 et *Matthieu* 17,4 (par.) à la lumière du Targum palestinien. — *RSR* 52 (1964) 85-90. Esp. 87-90. [NTA 9, 219]

1968    Le substrat araméen des évangiles: scolies en marge de l'*Aramaic Approach* de Matthew Black. — *Bib* 49 (1968) 388-399. Esp. 390 [18,3]; 391-392 [6,11]; 395 [16,16]. → M. Black 1946/67

1974    Targumic Literature and New Testament Interpretation. — *BTB* 4 (1974) 243-289. Esp. 249-251 [19,6]. [NTA 19, 805]

**LEDRUS, Michel**

1970    & SARTORI, R., Padre nostro, che sei nei cieli. — *ParVi* 15 (1970) 94-108.

1971    Il salario evangelico (nella parabola dei braccianti: Mt. 20,1-16). — *PalCl* 50 (1971) 14-27. [NTA 15, 854]

**LE DU, Jean**

1977    *La tentation de Jésus ou l'économie des désirs* (Série Évangile, 2). Saint-Brieux: Sofec, 1977, 86 p.

**LEE, Bernard J.**

1988    *Conversation on the Road Not Taken.* Vol. 1: *The Galilean Jewishness of Jesus: Retrieving the Jewish Origins of Christianity* (Studies in Judaism and Christianity, 1). New York – Mahwah, NJ: Paulist, 1988, VI-158 p. Esp. 139-141 [Q].

1993    *Conversation on the Road Not Taken.* Vol. 2: *Jesus and the Metaphors of God: The Christs of the New Testament* (Studies in Judaism and Christianity: A Stimulus Book). New York – Mahwah, NJ: Paulist, 1993, VIII-204 p.

**LEE, Dorothy A.**

1993    Presence or Absence? The Question of Women Disciples at the Last Supper. — *Pacifica* 6 (1993) 1-20. Esp. 10-13. [NTA 37, 1218]

**LEE, Edwin Kenneth**

1963a   Hard Sayings. I. *Be ye therefore perfect, even as your Father which is in heaven is perfect.* Matthew 5.48. — *Theology* 66 (1963) 318-320. [NTA 8, 130] → G.A. Robson 1963

1963b   Hard Sayings. II. — *Ibid.*, 462. [NTA 8, 576] → G.A. Robson 1963

**LEE, G.M.**

1950    'Whosoever hath, to him shall be given...'. [13,12] — *ExpT* 61 (1949-50) 159.

1954    Matthew xvi.26. — *ExpT* 65 (1953-54) 251.

1965    Studies in Texts: Matthew 17.24-27. — *Theology* 68 (1965) 380-381. [NTA 10, 119]

1966    St. Peter on the Water (Matthew, xiv,28-31). — *The Modern Churchman* (Oxford) 9 (1966) 163-165. [NTA 10, 911]

1968    The Inscription on the Cross. [27,37] — *PEQ* 100 (1968) 144. [NTA 13, 891]

1969a   The Guard at the Tomb. — *Theology* 72 (1969) 169-175. [NTA 13, 871]

1969b   Matthew xxvi.50 Ἑταῖρε, ἐφ' ὃ πάρει; — *ExpT* 81 (1969-70) 55. [NTA 14, 492]

**LEE, John A.L.**

1992   The United Bible Societies' Lexicon and Its Analysis of Meanings. — *FilolNT* 5 (1992) 167-189. Esp. 175 [4,3; 5,34]; 178-179 [26,15]. [NTA 38, 50] → Louw 1993

**LEEMING, Bernard**

1956   & DYSON, R.A., Except It Be for Fornication? [5,32; 19,9] — *Scripture* 8 (1956) 75-82. [NTA 1, 39] → Vaccari 1955b, Vawter 1954

**LEENHARDT, Franz J.**

1969   Les femmes aussi... À propos du billet de répudiatior.. — *RTP* 19 (1969) 31-40. Esp. 32-35 [5,27-28]; 38-39 [19,1-12]. [NTA 14, 140]

**LEFEVRE, Frans**

1984   Nederlandstalige boeken rond het Onzevader. — *Collctiones* 14 (1984) 460-470. [NTA 29, 932]

**LE GALL, Robert**

1981   *La liturgie dans la Nouvelle Alliance.* Chambray: CLD, 1981, 267 p. Esp. 49-54: "Matthieu: l'Église rassemblée autour de l'Emmanuel".

**LÉGASSE, Simon**

1960   La révélation aux νήπιοι. — *RB* 67 (1960) 321-348. Esp. 321-325 [11,25-30]; 325-333 [13,11-15]. [NTA 5, 714]

1961   Scribes et disciples de Jésus. — *RB* 68 (1961) 321-345, 481-506. Esp. 323-333 [23,34-36]; 333-339 [23,8-10]; 339-340 [28,19]; 340-345 [8,19-20]; 481-489 [22,34-40]; 489-496 [13,52]. [NTA 6, 753]

1962   Les pauvres en esprit et les 'volontaires' de Qumran. — *NTS* 8 (1961-62) 336-345. Esp. 336.344 [5,3]. [NTA 7, 125]

1964   Jésus a-t-il annoncé la conversion finale d'Israël? (À propos de Marc x.23-7). — *NTS* 10 (1963-64) 480-487. Esp. 481-483 [7,13-14]. [NTA 9, 172]

1966   *L'appel du riche (Marc 10,17-31 et parallèles). Contribution à l'étude des fondements scripturaires de l'état religieux* (Verbum Salutis. Collection annexe, 1). Paris: Beauchesne, 1966, 294 p. Esp. 113-146: "La perfection selon Matthieu" [5,17-48]; 147-183: "Perfection et détachement chez Matthieu" [6,19-21.22-23.24.25-34; 13,18-23.44-46]; 184-214: "Le 'jeune homme riche'"; 233-246: "Le conseil de pauvreté et Mt 19,16-26".

1968   Les faux prophètes. Matthieu 7,15-20. — *ÉtFranc* 18 (1968) 205-218. [NTA 13, 568]

1969   *Jésus et l'enfant. "Enfants", "petits" et "simples" dans la tradition synoptique* (Études bibliques). Paris: Gabalda, 1969, 375 p. Esp. 32-36.215-231.323-326[18,1-5]; 41-43.215-231.326-333 [19,13-15]; 43-50 [21,14-16]; 54-55 [18,6]; 55-62 [18,12-14; Q 15,4-7]; 62-63.71-72 [18,10]; 76-85 [10,42]; 85-100 [25,31-46]; 122-151 [11,25-30; Q 10,21-22]; 151-185 [11,25-26]; 215-268: "La figure de l'enfant chez Matthieu" [11,25-30; 18,1-5; 19,13-15; 21,15-16]; 289-317 [11,16-19; Q 7,31-35]. — Diss. Pont. Com. Bibl., Roma, 1964-65.

1971   L'appel du riche. — GEORGE, A., et al. (eds.), *La pauvreté*, 1971, 65-91. Esp. 82-88. The Call of the Rich Man. — GEORGE, A., et al. (eds.), *Gospel Poverty*, 1977, 53-80.

1972a   L'"antijudaïsme" dans l'Évangile selon Matthieu. — DIDIER, M. (ed.), *L'Évangile selon Matthieu*, 1972, 417-428.

1972b   L'épisode de la Cananéenne d'après Mt. 15,21-28. — *BullLitEccl* 73 (1972) 21-40. [NTA 17, 124]

1972c   Jésus et l'impôt du temple (Matthieu 17,24-27). — *SE* 24 (1972) 361-377. [NTA 17, 519]

1974a   *Les pauvres en esprit. Évangile et non-violence* (LD, 78). Paris: Cerf, 1974, 122 p. Esp. 9-15: "Le Sermon sur la montagne"; 19-53 [5,3-12]; 57-74 [5,2.-26]; 77-86 [5,38-42]; 89-98 [5,43-47]. [NTA 19, p. 112]

X. JACQUES, *NRT* 97 (1975) 690-691.

*I poveri di spirito. Vangelo e non violenza*, trans. A. Balestrieri Secchi (Studi biblici, 37). Brescia: Paideia, 1976, 102 p.

1974b Les chrétiens, "sel de la terre", "lumière du monde". Mt 5,13-16. — *AssSeign* II/36 (1974) 17-25. [NTA 18, 854]

1974c L'Évangile selon Matthieu. — DELORME, J. (ed.), *Le ministère et les ministères*, 1974, 182-206. Esp. 188-197: "La vie d'une communauté chrétienne"; 197-205: "Charges et organisation".

1974d Jésus devant le Sanhédrin. Recherche sur les traditions évangéliques. — *RTL* 5 (1974) 170-197. Esp. 179-181 [26,59-66]. [NTA 19, 117]

1974e → Charpentier 1974

1976a Jésus et les prostituées. — *RTL* 7 (1976) 137-154. Esp. 142-146 [21,28-32]. [NTA 21, 46]

1976b Le logion sur le Fils révélateur (*Mt.*, XI,27 par. *Lc.*, X,22). Essai d'analyse prérédactionnelle. — COPPENS, J. (ed.), *La notion biblique de Dieu* (BETL, 41), Gembloux: Duculot; Leuven: University Press, 1976; repr. 1985, 245-274. Esp. 247-249: "Critique littéraire: le logion et son contexte"; 249-250: "Construction et unité de Mt., XI,27 par."; 250-264: "Analyse du logion"; 264-273: "Quelques orientations concernant l'origine du logion".

1977a Le baptême de Jésus et le baptême chrétien. — *SBF/LA* 27 (1977) 51-68. Esp. 58-60 [12,18]; 65-66 [3,13-17]. [NTA 22, 774]

1977b L'étendue de l'amour interhumain d'après le Nouveau Testament: limites et promesses. — *RTL* 8 (1977) 137-159, 293-304. Esp. 154-159 [5,43-47]; 298-300 [22,34-40]. [NTA 22, 239/564] → 1984b, 1989a
Interhuman Love: New Testament Limits and Promise. — *TDig* 27 (1979) 9-13.

1977c Jésus historique et le Fils de l'homme. Aperçu sur les opinions contemporaines. — ACFEB (ed.), *Apocalypses et théologie de l'espérance. Congrès de Toulouse (1975)* (LD, 95), Paris: Cerf, 1977, 271-298. Esp. 281.287 [8,20].

1977d Les miracles de Jésus selon Matthieu. — LÉON-DUFOUR, X. (ed.), *Les miracles de Jésus*, 1977, 227-247. Esp. 228-230: "La forme littéraire"; 230-238: "Le thème christologique"; 238-244: "Le thème de la foi"; 244-247: "Le thème ecclésial".

1980 Mt 5,17 et la prétendue tradition paracanonique. — ZMIJEWSKI, J. — NELLESSEN, E. (eds.), *Begegnung mit dem Wort*. FS H. Zimmermann, 1980, 11-21.

1982a L'oracle contre "cette génération" (Mt 23,34-36 par. Lc 11,49-51) et la polémique judéo-chrétienne dans la Source des Logia. — DELOBEL, J. (ed.), *Logia*, 1982, 237-256. Esp. 237-239: "Le contenu de l'oracle dans la source"; 240-245: "Le texte du passage dans la source"; 245-248: "Jésus et 'cette génération' dans la source des Logia"; 248-256 ["Sitz im Leben"].

1982b Richesse. — *DBS* 10/56 (1982) 645-687. Esp. 672-675, 679-685.

1983a Oraison dominicale. — *Catholicisme* 10/44 (1983) 112-124.

1983b Le refroidissement de l'amour avant la fin (Mt 24,12). — *SNTU* 8 (1983) 91-102. [NTA 30, 1063]

1984a Matthieu 23,2-3, une incongruité? — PROVERA, L. (ed.), *Gesù Apostolo e Sommo Sacerdote*. FS T. Ballarini, 1984, 63-72.

1984b Morale hellénistique et morale chrétienne primitive: les rapports interhumains. — KUNTZMANN, R. - SCHLOSSER, J. (eds.), *Études sur le judaïsme hellénistique. Congrès de Strasbourg (1983)* (LD, 119), Paris: Cerf, 1984, 321-338. Esp. 333-336 [5,44]; 336-338 [5,39-48]. → 1977b, 1989a

1989a *"Et qui est mon prochain?" Étude sur l'objet de l'agapè dans le Nouveau Testament* (LD, 136). Paris: Cerf, 1989, 183 p. Esp. 65-67 [22,34-40]; 91-102: "L'amour des ennemis dans les évangiles: Matthieu" [5,21-48]; 103-111 [Q 6,27-36 (Lk)]; 118-124: "La source des 'Logia'". [NTA 33, p. 407] → 1977b, 1984b

1989b La parabole des dix vierges (Mt 25,1-13). Essai de synthèse historico-littéraire. — DELORME, J. (ed.), *Les paraboles évangéliques*, 1989, 349-360.

1991 "Scribes et Pharisiens". De l'anamnèse à Jésus. — MARGUERAT, D. - ZUMSTEIN, J. (eds.), *La mémoire et le temps*. FS P. Bonnard, 1991, 47-53. Esp. 48-49.

1992a L'autre "baptême" (Mc 1,8; Mt 3,11; Lc 3,16; Jn 1,26.31-33). — VAN SEGBROECK, F., et al. (eds.), *The Four Gospels 1992*. FS F. Neirynck, 1992, I, 257-273. Esp. 259-261 [3,11]; 262-265 [Q 3,7-9.16-17]; 266-268 [3,7-12].

1992b Scribes. III. Nouveau Testament. — *DBS* 12/67 (1992) 266-281. Ep. 272-275.

1993 *Naissance du Baptême*. Paris: Cerf, 1993, 174 p. Esp. 27-56: "Le baptême de Jean"; 57-69: "Le baptême de Jésus et le baptême chrétien"; 71-87: "Jésus baptiste".

1994 *Le procès de Jésus*. I: *L'histoire* (LD, 156). Paris: Cerf, 1994, 196 p. Esp. 40-42 [26,48]; 39-40 [26,14-16]; 80-81 [26,67-79]; 123-126 [27,27-31].

1995 *Le procès de Jésus*. II: *La passion dans les quatre évangiles* (LD, Commentaires, 3). Paris: Cerf, 1995, 632 p. Esp. 158-319: "Matthieu".

**LEGAULT, André**

1954 An Application of the Form-Critique Method to the Anointings in Galilee (Lk 7,36-50) and Bethany (Mt 26,6-13; Mk 14,3-9; Jn 12,1-8). — *CBQ* 16 (1954) 131-145. Esp. 135-140 [26,6-13].

1961 Le baptême de Jésus et la doctrine du Serviteur souffrant. — *ScEccl* 13 (1961) 147-166. Esp. 150-152, 161. [NTA 6, 136]

1962 L'authenticité de Mt 16,17-19 et le silence de Marc et de Luc. — *L'Église dans la Bible. Communications présentées à la XVII<sup>e</sup> réunion annuelle de l'ACÉBAC* (Studia. Recherches de philosophie et de théologie, 13), Brugge: Desclée De Brouwer, 1962, 35-52.

1969 Christophanies et angélophanies dans les récits évangéliques de la résurrection. — *SE* 21 (1969) 443-457. Esp. 448, 450, 456. [NTA 14, 450]

**LEGRAND, Lucien**

1959 Vidimus stellam ejus in Oriente. [2,1-12] — *The Clergy Monthly* (Ranchi, India) 23 (1959) 377-384. [NTA 4, 643]

1963 *The Biblical Doctrine of Virginity*. London: Chapman, 1963, 167 p. Esp. 38-44 [19,3-12]; 114-115 [1,1.18].
*La virginité dans la Bible* (LD, 39). Paris: Cerf, 1964, 160 p. Esp 34-41; 107-109.

1964 Matthew, Chapter 19, and the Three Vows. — *RRel* 23 (1964) 705-714. Esp. 706-708 [19,16-30]; 709-710 [19,13-15]; 710-712 [19,12]. [NTA 9, 538]

1965 The Harvest is Plentiful (Mt 9:37). — *Scripture* 17 (1965) 1-9. [NTA 9, 907]

1973 Jesus and the Gospel. — ID. - PATHRAPANKAL, J. - VELLANICKAL, M., *Good News and Witness. The New Testament Understanding of Evangelization*, Bangalore: Theological Publications of India, 1973, 1-60. Esp. 27-46: "Announcing the gospel".

1979 Bare Foot Apostles? The Shoes of St Mark (Mk. 6:8-9 and parallels). — *IndianTS* 16 (1979) 201-219. Esp. 203-205 [10,10]. [NTA 24, 436]

1984 Images de la Mission dans le Nouveau Testament. [28,19] — *Spiritus* (Paris) 25 (1984) 17-24.

1986 The Missionary Command of the Risen Christ. I. Mission and Resurrection. — *IndianTS* 23 (1986) 290-309. Esp. 302-304 [28,18-20]. [NTA 31, 1034] → 1987

1987 The Missionary Command of the Risen Lord. Mt 28:16-20. — *IndianTS* 24 (1987) 5-28. Esp. 6-13: "Structure"; 13-26: "The text". [NTA 32, 133] → 1986

1988 *Le Dieu qui vient. La mission dans la Bible*. Paris: Desclée, 1988, 235 p. Esp. 66-68 [11,2-6]; 77-79 [10,5-6.23; 15,24]; 106-112 [28,16-20].

1993 The Way of the Magi and the Way of the Shepherds. A Christmas Meditation. [2,1-12] — *IndianTS* 30 (1993) 313-318. [NTA 39, 137]

**LE GUILLOU, Marie-Joseph**

1964 La Primauté de Pierre. — *Istina* 10 (1964) 93-102. Esp. 94-98. [NTA 9, 916]

**LEHMANN, Hans**

1953 "Du bist Petrus...". Zum Problem von Matthäus 16,13-26[20]. — *EvT* 13 (1953) 44-67.

**LEHMANN, Henning**

1985 Bygger det armeniske ny Testamente på syrisk eller graesk forlaeg? Et forsknings-historisk rids. [Is the Armenian New Testament based upon a Syriac or a Greek source? An outline of the history of research] — *DanskTeolTids* 48 (1985) 25-50, 153-171. Esp. 33 [5,18; 10,10]; 43-44 [3,15; 11,28]; 156-157 [5,28; 11,28]; 157 [3,3]. [NTA 30, 40]

**LEHMANN, Manfred R.**

1960 Gen 2,24 as the Basis for Divorce in Halakhah and New Testament. — *ZAW* 72 (1960) 263-267. [NTA 5, 720]

**LEHMANN, Martin**

1970 *Synoptische Quellenanalyse und die Frage nach dem historischen Jesus. Kriterien der Jesusforschung untersucht in Auseinandersetzung mit Emanuel Hirschs* Frühgeschichte des Evangeliums (BZNW, 38). Berlin: de Gruyter, 1970, XII-218 p. Esp. 24-27 [Q]; 29-32 [Mt]; 73-76 [13,24-30/Mk 4,26-29]; 117-137: "Authentisches Jesusgut in der Quelle Q"; 153-159 [13,44-46; 20,1-16; 21,28-32]; 163-205: "Kriterien der Jesusforschung". → E. Hirsch 1941

**LEIVESTAD, Ragnar**

1952 An Interpretation of Matt 11,19. — *JBL* 71 (1952) 179-181.

1954 *Christ the Conqueror. Ideas of Conflict and Victory in the New Testament*. London: SPCK, 1954, XII-320 p. Esp. 27-80: "The synoptic gospels".

1966 Ταπεινός - ταπεινόφρων. — *NT* 8 (1966) 36-47. Esp. 43-44 [11,29]. [NTA 11, 91]

1968 Der apokalyptische Menschensohn ein theologisches Phantom? — *ASTI* 6 (1968) 49-105. Esp. 67-98: "Die synoptischen Menschensohnsprüche [9,8; 10,23.32-33; 11,19; 12,6-8.32; 13,37.41; 16,13.21.27; 17,9; 19,28; 20,28; 24,30.37; 26,63-64]". [NTA 14, 810] → 1972
Er den apokalyptiske menneskesønn en moderne teologisk oppfinnelse? — *NorskTeolTids* 70 (1969) 221-235. [NTA 14, 811]

1972 Exit the Apocalyptic Son of Man. — *NTS* 18 (1971-72) 243-267. Esp. 256-258 [16,13]; 258-259 [9,8; 12,32]; 261-262 [10,32-33]. [NTA 17, 77] → 1968; → Lindars 1975

1982a *Hvem ville Jesus vaere?* Oslo: Land og Kirke - Gyldendal, 1982, 194 p.
*Jesus in his Own Perspective. An Examination of His Sayings, Actions, and Eschatological Titles*, trans. D.E. Aune. Minneapolis, MN: Augsburg, 1987, 192 p. Esp. 31-40: "John the Baptist"; 68-72: "The servant of the Lord"; 124-127 [miracles]; 153-168 [Son of Man].

1982b Jesus - Messias - Menschensohn. Die jüdischen Heilandserwartungen zur Zeit der ersten römischen Kaiser und die Frage nach dem messianischen Selbstbewußtsein Jesu. — *ANRW* II.25.1 (1982) 220-264. Esp. 220-232 [Messiah]; 232-236.246-255 [Son of Man]; 240-246 [self-consciousness].

1985 Betydningen av uttrykket "menneskesønnen". [The meaning of the expression "Son of Man"] — *DanskTeolTids* 48 (1985) 172-194. Esp. 184-185 [24,30]; 185-186 [26,64]; 187 [28,18]; 187 [13,37-43]; 190 [16,13]. → M. Müller 1984

**LEJEUNE, Charles**

1990 Les oiseaux et les lis. Lecture "écologique" de Matthieu 6,25-34. — *Hokhma* 44 (1990) 2-20. [NTA 35, 1130]

**LEKAI, Emery Aniano**

1974 *The Theology of the People of God in Ernst Lohmeyer's Commentaries on the Gospels of Mark and Matthew*. Diss. Catholic Univ. of America, Washington, DC, 1974, 272 p. — *DissAbstr* 35 (1974-75) 1744-45. → E. Lohmeyer 1956a

**LELOIR, Louis**

1953   *Saint Éphrem. Commentaire de l'Évangile concordant version arménienne* (CSCO, 137/145). Leuven: Durbecq, 1953, XI-364 p. [text]; 1954, VI-261 p. [translation].

1957   Éphrem et l'ascendance davidique du Christ. [1,1-17] — *Studia Patristica* 1 (1957) 389-394.

1958   *L'Évangile d'Éphrem d'après les œuvres éditées. Recueil des textes* (CSCO, 180). Leuven: CSCO, 1958, VIII-159 p. Esp. 1-60: "Témoignage de Matthieu".

1961   *Doctrines et méthodes de s. Éphrem d'après son Commentaire de l'Évangile concordant (original syriaque et version arménienne)* (CSCO, 220). Leuven: CSCO, 1961, VIII-72 p. Esp. 1-22: "Le Diatessaron de Tatien et son commentaire par Éphrem".

1962a   (ed. and trans.), *Commentaire de l'Évangile concordant. Texte syriaque* (Chester Beatty Monographs, 8). Dublin: Hodges Figgis, 1962, 261 p. → 1990

1962b   *Le témoignage d'Éphrem sur le Diatessaron* (CSCO, 227). Leuven: CSCO, 1962, XX-261 p. Esp. 1-69: "Le texte du Diatessaron d'après le commentaire d'Éphrem"; 70-231: "La portée du témoignage du commentaire de l'Évangile concordant".

1966   (ed.), *Commentaire de l'Évangile concordant ou Diatessaron traduit du syriaque et de l'arménien. Introduction, traduction et notes* (SC, 121). Paris: Cerf 1966, 438 p. Esp. 11-39: "Introduction"; 41-400: "Texte".

1967   *Citations du Nouveau Testament dans l'ancienne tradition arménienne. I,A. L'évangile de Matthieu, I-XII. I,B. XIII-XXVIII* (CSCO, 283-284). Leuven: CSCO, 1967, XIII-184 and 185-363 p.
   J. DUPLACY, *Bib* 49 (1968) 550-551.

1976   La version arménienne des Actes apocryphes d'André, et le Diatessaron. — *NTS* 22 (1975-76) 115-139. Esp. 122-127 [3,16-17; 8,23-27; 10,9-10.25-27; 11,5; 17,1-9; 24,29; 25,41]. [NTA 20, 997]

1987   Le commentaire d'Éphrem sur le Diatessaron. Quarante et un folios retrouvés. — *RB* 94 (1987) 481-518. → 1990

1988   Éphrem. Le texte de son commentaire du Sermon de la montagne. — *Mémorial Dom Jean Gribomont (1920-1986)* (Studia Ephemeridis "Augustinianum", 27), Roma: Institutum Patristicum Augustinianum, 1988, 361-391

1990   *Saint Éphrem, Commentaire de l'Évangile concordant. Texte syriaque (Manuscrit Chester Beatty 709). Folios additionnels* (Chester Beatty Monographs, 8). Leuven–Paris: Peeters, 1990, XXIV-157 p. → 1962a, 1987

1993   Les citations évangéliques dans la version arménienne des Actes apocryphes. — GRYSON, R. (ed.), *Philologia Sacra*. FS J. Frede - W. Thiele, 1993, 364-377. Esp. 375-377.

**LEMAIRE, André**

1973   The Ministries in the New Testament. Recent Research. — *BTB* 3 (1973) 133-166. Esp. 148-150. [NTA 18, 275]

**LEMAIRE, Jean-Louis**

1993   Histoire et exégèse dans l'*In Mattheum* d'Hilaire de Poitiers. — DORÉ, J. - THEOBALD, C. (eds.), *Penser la foi*. FS J. Moingt, 1993, 437-447.

**LEMARIÉ, Joseph**

1962   Homélies inédites de saint Chromace d'Aquilée. — *RBén* 72 (1962) 201-277. Esp. 246-249 [6,22-23]; 257-259 [22,1-10]; 266-267 [23,37]. → 1974

1966a   Un nouveau sermon de saint Chromace d'Aquilée et fragments provenant d'homiliaires bavarois. — *RBén* 76 (1966) 7-40. Esp. 33-40 [5,3-12].

1966b → Étaix 1966

1969 (ed.), *Chromace d'Aquilée. Sermons. Introduction, texte critique, notes*. Tome I *(Sermons 1-17A)*; Tome II *(Sermons 18-41)*, trans. H. Tardif (SC, 154/164). Paris: Cerf, I, 1969, 282 p.; II, 1971, 290 p. Esp. I, 9-122: "Introduction"; 123-279 and II, 9-290: "Texte et traduction".

   A.-G. MARTIMORT, *BullLitEccl* 71 (1970) 304-306; 72 (1971) 301-302; C. VOGEL, *VigChr* 27 (1973) 154-155.

1972a À propos des sermons XVIII et XXXIII de Chromace d'Aquilée. — *Sacris Erudiri* (Steenbrugge) 21 (1972-73) 35-42.

1972b Un sermon inédit sur *Matthieu 16,13-19* de l'école de Fulgence de Ruspe. — *RevÉtudAug* 18 (1972) 116-123.

1974a (ed.) *Chromatii Aquileiensis Opera. Sermones* (CC SL, 9A). Turnhout: Brepols, 1974, XLIX-610 p. Esp. 23-26 [5,1-12]; 27-29 [6,22-23]; 58-60 [23,37]; 168-170 [5,1-12]; 171-173 [6,9-13]; 174-180 [5,1-12]. → Hoste 1957

1974b → Étaix 1974a

1975 Les homiliaires de Bobbio et la tradition textuelle de l'"Opus Imperfectum in Matthaeum". — *RBén* 85 (1975) 358-362.

1977 Un nouveau témoin important des *Tractatus in Matthaeum* de saint Chromace d'Aquilée: l'homéliaire de San Silvestro de Fabriano. — *RevÉtudAug* 23 (1977) 124-154.

1978 Homélies composées sur Matthieu de l'homéliaire de Ripoll. — *Miscellània litúrgica catalana*, I, Barcelona: Soc. Cat. d'Estudis Liturgics, 1978, 92-107.

1980 Le commentaire de saint Chromace d'Aquilée sur la transfiguration. — *RivStoLR* 16 (1980) 213-222.

1989 L'apport des nouveaux manuscrits témoins des sermons et du commentaire sur Matthieu de Chromace. — *Chromatius Episcopus*, 1989, 63-80.

1994 Nouveaux fragments de sermons attribuables à un Pseudo-Fulgence. — *RBén* 104 (1994) 191-203. Esp. 195-198 [18,23-35].

**LEMCIO, Eugene E.**

1981 The Gospels and Canonical Criticism. — *BTB* 11 (1981) 114-122. Esp. 117-119 [5,1-12]. [NTA 26, 441]; = WALL, R.W. - LEMCIO, E.E., *The New Testament as Canon*, 1992, 28-47. Esp. 36-41.

   Response: J.A. SANDERS, *ibid.*, 122-124.

1986 The Parables of the Great Supper and the Wedding Feast: History, Redaction and Canon. — *HorizonsBT* 8/1 (1986) 1-26. Esp. 4-7 [22,1-14; Q 14,16-24]; 7-11.13-17 [historicity]; 11-13 [Lk redaction]; 17-19 [Mt redaction]. [NTA 31, 1082]; = WALL, R.W. - LEMCIO, E.E., *The New Testament as Canon*, 1992, 48-66. Esp. 51-53; 53-57.59-62; 57-59; 63-66.

1988 *Pirke 'Abot* 1,2(3) and the Synoptic Redactions of the Commands to Love God and Neighbor. — *Asbury Theological Journal* (Wilmore, KY) 43/1 (1988) 43-53. Esp. 44-46, 52-53 [22,34-40].

   The Commands to Love God and Neighbor: History, Redaction and Canon. — WALL, R.W. - LEMCIO, E.E., *The New Testament as Canon*, 1992, 67-77. Esp. 68-70, 76-77.

1991 *The Past of Jesus in the Gospels* (SNTS MS, 68). Cambridge: University Press, 1991, XIV-190 p. Esp. 49-73.145-150: "Matthew".

**LEMOINE, Bernadette**

1994 Étude comparée des quatre récits de la Cène. [26,26-29/Mk] — *EphLtg* 108 (1994) 52-72. [NTA 38, 1394]

**LÉMONON, Jean-Pierre**

1981  *Pilate et le gouvernement de la Judée. Textes et monuments* (Études bibliques). Paris: Gabalda, 1981, 313 p. Esp. 177-203: "Pilate dans les récits de la Passion de Jésus de Nazareth (Mt., XXVII et paral.)". — Diss. Lyon, 1979 (J. Rougé).

**LE MOYNE, Jean**

1964  → A. Michel 1964

1972  *Les Sadducéens* (Études bibliques). Paris: Gabalda, 1972, 464 p. Esp. 122-129.

**LENHARDT, Pierre** → Collin 1990

**LENKEY, Klára**

1983  Die Sündenvergebung, die Fünfte Bitte des Vaterunsers, Mt 6,12. [Hungarian] — *TSzem* 26 (1983) 68-74.

**LENSSEN, F.A.**

1964  *De Bijbel over de uittocht* (De Bijbel over..., 24). Roermond–Maaseik: Romen, 1964, 126 p. Esp. 85-89: "Jezus, de nieuwe Mozes: Mattheüs".

**LENTZEN-DEIS, Fritzleo**

1968  Die Evangelien zwischen Mythos und Geschichtlichkeit – dargestellt an den Berichten über die Taufe Jesu. [3,13-17] — *Theologische Akademie* (Frankfurt/M) 5 (1968) 82-113; = *TJb*, 1970, 81-98.
The Gospel between Myth and Historicity – as Demonstrated in the Accounts about the Baptism of Jesus. — *Tantur Yearbook*, 1980-81, 165-186. [NTA 27, 533]

1969  Das Motiv der "Himmelsöffnung" in verschiedenen Gattungen der Umweltliteratur des Neuen Testaments. — *Bib* 50 (1969) 301-327. Esp. 326-327 [3,16]. [NTA 14, 707] → 1970

1970  *Die Taufe Jesu nach den Synoptikern. Literarkritische und gattungsgeschichtliche Untersuchungen* (Frankfurter theologische Studien, 4). Frankfurt/M: Knecht, 1970, VIII-324 p. Esp. 27-57: "Literar-Analyse der synoptischen Texte"; 82-84 [11,2-19]; 85-86 [3,7-10]; 282-284 [3,13-17]. — Diss. Pont. Inst. Bibl., Roma, 1969 (I. de la Potterie). → 1969

1980  Entwicklungen in der synoptischen Frage? — *TheolPhil* 55 (1980) 559-570. [NTA 25, 447] → Stoldt 1977

1990  Alcuni aspetti dell'"ingresso di Gesù a Gerusalemme" secondo gli evangeli sinottici alla luce dello sfondo giudaico. [21,1-9] — *Giudaismo e cristianesimo*, Torino: Federazione Interreligiosa per gli Studi Teologici, 1990, 53-68.

**LENZ, E.**

1990  *Betrachtungen über das Matthäus-Evangelium. Studien zur Komposition und Initiation im ersten Evangelium.* Stuttgart: Urachhaus, 1990, 140 p.

**LEONARDI, Giovanni**

1964  Le tentazioni di Gesù nel Nuovo Testamento (prescindendo da quelle sinottiche nel deserto). — *Studia Patavina* 11 (1964) 169-200. — Diss. Pont. Inst. Bibl., Roma, 1964. → 1968, 1969b

1968  Le tentazioni di Gesù nella interpretazione patristica. — *Studia Patavina* 15 (1968) 229-262. [NTA 13, 564] → 1964, 1969b

1969a  Discorso apostolico (Mt 10,6-42). — *ParVi* 14 (1969) 260-279.

1969b  Il racconto sinottico delle tentazioni di Gesù: fonti, ambiente e dottrina. — *Studia Patavina* 16 (1969) 391-429. [NTA 15, 134] → 1964, 1968

1972  Pregi e limiti del recente commento a Matteo di Ortensio da Spinetoli. — *PalCl* 51 (1972) 475-486. [NTA 17, 111r] → da Spinetoli 1971

1975 *L'infanzia di Gesù nei Vangeli di Matteo e di Luca* (Conoscere il Vangelo, 2). Padova: Messaggero, 1975, 282 p. Esp. 17-104: "L'infanzia di Gesù nel Vangelo di Matteo". [NTA 20, p. 237] → 1990

A. BONORA, *Studia Patavina* 22 (1975) 596-599; J.A. CARRASCO, *EstJos* 30 (1976) 114-115; G.J. DIAMOND, *AusBR* 25 (1977) 42; G. GHIBERTI, *ParVi* 21 (1976) 152-153; K. GRAYSTON, *ExpT* 87 (1975-76) 261; J. KAHMANN, *TijdTheol* 16 (1976) 218; E. LUPIERI, *RivBib* 29 (1981) 119-120; A. MODA, *RHPR* 57 (1977) 107-108; E. PERETTO, *Marianum* 38 (1976) 541-542; J. PONTHOT, *RTL* 7 (1976) 238-239; B. PRETE, *Sacra Doctrina* (Bologna) 22 (1977) 521; A. SALAS, *CiudDios* 190 (1977) 183; N. URICCHIO, *CC* 127/3 (1976) 543-544.

1980 "Cercate e troverete ... lo Spirito Santo" nell'unità letteraria di Luca 11,1-13. — DANIELI, G. (ed.), *Quaerere Deum* (Atti della XXV Settimana Biblica), Brescia: Paideia, 1980, 261-288. Esp. 267-271 [6,9-13]; 275-284 [7,7-11].

1982 Venuti per servire, non per essere serviti. Il ministero di Gesù e dei cristiani nelle comunità del Nuovo Testamento. — MARCHESELLI, C.C. (ed.), *Parole e Spirito*. FS S. Cipriani, 1982, I, 163-194. Esp. 177 [23,37-39]; 178 [26,28]; 178-179 [20,28]; 186-187 [8,17; 12,18-21].

1990 I Vangeli dell'infanzia di Matteo e di Luca. XXXI Settimana Biblica Nazionale dell'ABI (10-14 settembre 1990). — *Studia Patavina* 37 (1990) 737-749. [NTA 35, 1123] → 1975; → Serra 1992

1991 Il discorso della montagna e del pianoro. Struttura letteraria e teologica (Mt cc. 5-7; Lc 6,12-7,1). — *Credere oggi* 11 (1991) 5-19.

1995 "I dodici" e "gli apostoli" nei Vangeli sinottici e Atti: Problemi e prospettive. — *Studia Patavina* 42 (1995) 163-195. [NTA 40, 142]

**LÉON-DUFOUR, Xavier**
1954 → Huby 1929
1956 *Concordance des Évangiles synoptiques*. Paris: Desclée, 1956, 20 p.
*Concordance of the Synoptic Gospels*, trans. R.J. O'Connell. New York – Paris: Desclée, 1957, 21 p.
Pour approfondir les Évangiles synoptiques: un nouvel instrument de travail. — *NRT* 79 (1957) 296-302.

1957a L'annonce à Joseph. — *Mélanges bibliques*. FS A. Robert, 1957, 390-397. → 1959b, 1965c

1957b L'épisode de l'enfant épileptique. — HEUSCHEN, J. (ed.), *La formation des évangiles*, 1957, 85-115. Esp. 89-94 [Mt]; 101-113: "Histoire de la tradition"; = ID., *Études d'évangile*, 1965, 183-227 ("révisé"). Esp. 191-201; 210-227.

1958 Livre de la genèse de Jésus-Christ. — *VieChrét* 12 (1958) 15-19. → 1965b

1959a Les Évangiles synoptiques. — ROBERT, A. - FEUILLET, A. (eds.), *Introduction à la Bible. II. Nouveau Testament*, 1959, 143-334. Esp. 163-195: "L'évangile selon saint Matthieu". → 1976; → McLoughlin 1965
The Synoptic Gospels [ET, 1965] — MCARTHUR, H.K. (ed.), *In Search of the Historical Jesus*, 1969, 54-67.

1959b Le juste Joseph. [1,18-25] — *NRT* 81 (1959) 225-231. [NTA 4, 73] → 1957a, 1965c

1959c Matthieu et Marc dans le récit de la Passion. — *Bib* 40 (1959) 684-696. Esp. 686-687: "La présentation des matériaux"; 688-689: "L'expression"; 689-690: "'Glissements' étranges de Mc à Mt"; 690-694: "Les accords Mt-Lc contre Mc"; 694-695: "Les accords Mt-Jn contre Mc". [NTA 4, 637]; = *Studia Biblica et Orientalia*, II, 1959, 129-140.

1960 Passion (Récits de la). — *DBS* 6/35 (1960) 1419-1492. Esp. 1424-1479: "Formation littéraire des récits évangéliques" [Mt: 1450-1454, 1474-1476]; 1479-1492: "Historicité des récits évangéliques".

1963a *Les évangiles et l'histoire de Jésus* (Parole de Dieu, 1). Paris: Seuil, 1963, 526 p.; [10]1986, 528 p. Esp. 144-165: "L'évangile selon saint Matthieu" [ecclesiology; style; audience]; 225-241: "Des évangiles aux traditions présynoptiques"; 346-349 [1-2]; 460-462 [passion narrative].
*Die Evangelien und der historische Jesus*. Aschaffenburg: Pattloch, 1966, XII-599 p.

*Los evangelios y la historia de Jesús*, trans. D. Darnell, revis. por J. Martínez Escalera (Col. Theologia, 3). Barcelona: Estela, 1966, ²1967, XII-457 p.
*I vangeli e la storia di Gesù*, trans. P. Rossano & A. Girlanda (La Parola di Dio, 1). Milano: Paoline, 1967, ²1968, 739 p.; Roma: Paoline, ³1970, 739 p.; Cinisello Balsamo: Paoline, 1986, 544 p.
*The Gospels and the Jesus of History*, trans. & ed. J. McHugh. New York – Tournai: Desclée, 1968, 288 p. (abridged); (Doubleday Image Books), 1970; London: Collins, 1968; (Fontana Library), 1970. → McLoughlin 1969
Trans. Portuguese 1972.

1963b  La Transfiguration de Jésus. [17,1-9] — *AssSeign* I/28 (1963) 27-44; = ID., *Études d'évangile*, 1965, 83-122.

1963c  Vers l'annonce de l'Église. Matthieu 14,1–16,20. — *L'homme devant Dieu. Mélanges Henri de Lubac. Exégèse et patristique* (Théologie, 56), Paris: Aubier, 1963, 37-49; = ID., *Études d'évangile*, 1965, 229-254.

1965a  *Études d'évangile* (Parole de Dieu, 2). Paris: Seuil, 1965, ²1969, 397 p. → 1957b, 1963b-c, 1965b-g
*Studi sul vangelo*, trans. P. Rossano. Milano: Paoline, 1967, 550 p.
*Estudios de evangelio*, trans. J. López de Castro (Colección Teología, 15). Barcelona: Estela, 1969, XXVIII-408 p.; Madrid: Cristiandad, ²1982, 366 p.
Trans. Portuguese 1972; Japanese 1977.

1965b  Livre de la genèse de Jésus-Christ. — *Ibid.*, 47-63. Esp. 51-55: "Le genre littéraire des généalogies"; 55-60: "Jésus, à la fin de l'histoire sainte (Mt 1,2-17)'; 60-63: "Jésus-Christ, fin de l'histoire (Mt 1,1)". → 1958
Libro della genesi di Gesù Cristo. — *RivBib* 13 (1965) 223-237. [NTA 10, 899]

1965c  L'annonce à Joseph. [1,18-25] — *Ibid.*, 65-81. → 1957a, 1959b

1965d  La parabole du semeur. — *Ibid.*, 255-301. Esp. 268-285 [Mt/Mk]; 292-301: "Matthieu et l'interprétation de la parabole".

1965e  La guérison de la belle-mère de Simon-Pierre. [8,14-15] — *EstBíb* 24 (1965) 193-216. Esp. 200-210 [8,14-15]. [NTA 11, 209]; = ID., *Études d'évangile*, 1965, 123-148. Esp. 132-143.

1965f  La parabole des vignerons homicides. — *ScEccl* 17 (1965) 365-396. Esp. 371-387: "Vers la parabole originelle"; 387-390: "La perspective pré-synoptique"; 392-396: "La perspective de Matthieu". [NTA 10, 913]; = ID., *Études d'évangile*, 1965, 303-344. Esp. 315-331; 332-335; 338-344.
The Murderous Vineyard-Workers. — *TDig* 15 (1967) 30-36.

1965g  La tempête apaisée. — *NRT* 87 (1965) 897-922. Esp. 908-912 [8,18-27]; 913-922: "Esquisse d'une histoire de la tradition". [NTA 10, 909]; = ID., *Études d'évangile*, 1965, 149-182. Esp. 165-170; 170-182.

1965h  Le point de vue de l'historien (sur le film "L'Évangile de Matthieu" de P.P. Pasolini). — *France Catholique*, Paris, 12 mars 1965, 3.

1966  Comparaison synoptique avec les séquences du film de Pasolini "L'Évangile selon saint Matthieu" et analyse des thèmes. — *Centre culturel du Cinéma*, Lyon, 1966, 14.

1967  Interprétation des Évangiles et problème synoptique. — *ETL* 43 (1967) 5-16. [NTA 12, 137]; = DE LA POTTERIE, I. (ed.), *De Jésus aux Évangiles*. FS J. Coppens, 1967, 5-16. (IT, 1971, 17-31).

1970a  L'exégète et l'événement historique. — *RSR* 58 (1970) 551-560. Esp. 555-559 [5,37]. [NTA 15, 752] → Dupont 1954

1970b  Redaktionsgeschichte of Matthew and Literary Criticism. — BUTTRICK, D.G. (ed.), *Jesus and Man's Hope*. I, 1970, 9-35. Esp. 11-17: "A working hypothesis"; 17-23: "Matthew 4–13 and its sources"; 23-27: "Conclusion". [NTA 15, 127] → Gabour 1970

1971  *Résurrection de Jésus et message pascal* (Parole de Dieu, 7). Paris: Seuil, 1971, 390 p.; ⁴1985. Esp. 137-144.195-197 [28,16-20]; 151-162 [28,1-8]; 164-166 [27,62-66; 28,1-4.11-15]; 188-195 [27,62-28,15]. → J. Schmitt 1973

*Resurrección de Jesús y mensaje pascual*, trans. R. Silva Costoyas (Biblioteca de estudios bíblicos, 1). Salamanca: Sigueme, 1973, ⁵1992, 399 p.

*Risurrezione di Gesù e messagio pasquale*, trans. R. Arrighi (Parola di Dio). Cinisello Balsamo – Milano: Paoline, 1973, 528 p.; ²1987, 381 p.

*Resurrection and the Message of Easter*, trans. R.N. Wilson. London: Chapman, 1974; New York: Holt, Rinehart & Winston, 1975, XXII-330 p. Esp. 94-100; 106-116; 117-120; 139-149.

Trans. Japanese 1974.

1972a  *L'évangile selon S. Matthieu. Lectures: enfance, tentation, béatitudes, Sermon sur la montagne, paraboles, vers Jérusalem* (Conférences Faculté de Théologie catholique de Fourvière-Lyon). Lyon: Profac, 1972, 159 p.

   J.A. CARRASCO, *EstJos* 34 (1980) 241; R. GAUTHIER, *CahJos* 26 (1978) 247-248.

1972b  Autour de la question synoptique. — *RSR* 60 (1972) 491-518. Esp. 492-501: "Les hypothèses" [W.R. Farmer 1964a; Gaboury 1970]; 501-506: "Critique littéraire" [E.P. Sanders 1969a; Boismard 1972]; 506-517: "Ordonnance des synoptiques" [E.P. Sanders 1969a; Gaboury 1970; de Solages 1959; Morgenthaler 1971; Frey 1972]. [NTA 17, 890]

1972c  Synopses évangéliques. — *RSR* 60 (1972) 615-632. [NTA 17, 891] → K. Aland [Synopsis 1963], P. Benoit 1965, Deiss 1963a, R.J. Swanson 1975

1975  Jésus devant sa mort à la lumière des textes de l'institution eucharistique et des discours d'adieu. — DUPONT, J. (ed.), *Jésus aux origines de la christologie*, 1975, 141-168; ²1989 (note additionnelle, 419-420).

   Jesus' Understanding of His Death. — *TDig* 24 (1976) 293-300.

1976  Les Évangiles synoptiques. — ID. - PERROT, C., *L'annonce de l'Évangile* (Introduction à la Bible. Édition nouvelle. Tome III, Le Nouveau Testament, 2), Paris: Desclée, 1976, pp. 11-237. Esp. 73-108: "L'évangile selon saint Matthieu"; 143-185: "Le fait synoptique". → 1959a; → Neirynck 1979d

   I vangeli sinottici. — ID. - PERROT, C., *L'annuncio del vangelo* (Introduzione al Nuovo Testamento, III/2), Roma: Borla, 1978, 9-224.

1977*  (ed.), *Les miracles de Jésus selon le Nouveau Testament* (Parole de Dieu, 16). Paris: Seuil, 1977, 396 p. → Carrez, Légasse, Léon-Dufour

   *Los milagros de Jesús según el Nuevo Testamento*. Madrid: Cristiandad, 1979, 371 p.; ²1986.

   *I miracoli di Gesù secondo il Nuovo Testamento* (Strumenti, 15). Brescia: Queriniana, 1980, 328 p.

1977  Structure et fonction du récit de miracle. — *Ibid.*, 289-353.

1978  Jésus face à la mort menaçante. — *NRT* 100 (1978) 802-821. Esp. 809-813: "Le sort tragique des prophètes" [Q 11,47-51; 23,34-35]. [NTA 23, 392]; = ID., *Face à la mort*, 1979, 73-100 (revised).

   How Did Jesus See His Death? — *TDig* 29 (1981) 57-60.

1979a  Jésus à Gethsémani. Essai de lecture synchronique. — *SE* 31 (1979) 251-268. Esp. 260-262 [26,36-46/Mk]. [NTA 24, 393]; = ID., *Face à la mort*, 1979, 123-143 (revised).

1979b  *Face à la mort. Jésus et Paul* (Parole de Dieu, 18). Paris: Seuil, 1979, 320 p. Esp. 36-38 [10,28-31]; 52-54 [25,31-46]; 62-68 [10,39; 16,24-25]; 101-113 [26,26-29/Mk]; 147-166 [27,45-54/Mk]; ³1982. → 1978, 1979a; → Segalla 1982a

   *Als der Tod seinen Schrecken verlor. Die Auseinandersetzung Jesu mit dem Tod und die Deutung des Paulus. Ein Befund*, trans. H.-W. Eichelberger. Olten–Freiburg: Walter Verlag, 1981, 370 p.

   *Jesús y Pablo ante la muerte*. Madrid: Cristiandad, 1982, 302 p.

   *Di fronte alla morte, Gesù e Paolo*. Torino: Elle Di Ci, 1982, 246 p.

   *Life and Death in the New Testament. The Teaching of Jesus and Paul*. San Francisco, CA: Harper & Row, 1986, 316 p.

   Trans. Japanese 1986.

1982  *Le partage du pain eucharistique selon le Nouveau Testament* (Parole de Dieu, 21). Paris: Seuil, 1982, 380 p.; ⁴1990. Esp. 62-70 [26,26-29/Mk]; 103-105 [26,29/Mk].

   *Abendmahl und Abschiedsrede im Neuen Testament*, trans. H.-W. Eichelberger. Stuttgart: Katholisches Bibelwerk, 1983, 405 p.

*La fracción del pan. Culto y existencia en el Nuevo Testamento.* Madrid: Cristiandad, 1983, 397 p.
*Condividere il pane eucaristico secondo il Nuovo Testamento.* Torino: Elle Di Ci, 1983, 311 p.
*Sharing the Eucharistic Bread. The Witness of the New Testament,* trans. M.J. O'Connell. New York –
Mahwah, NJ: Paulist, 1987, iv-391 p.
Trans. Portuguese 1984.

1985 Présence du Seigneur ressuscité (Mt 28,16-20). — GANTOY, R. (ed.), *À cause de l'Évangile.* FS J. Dupont, 1985, 195-209. Esp. 195-199: "Le texte du récit"; 199-207: "En quête du genre littéraire"; 207-209: "Vers le sens".

1989 Introduction à l'Évangile selon St. Matthieu. — *Traduction œcuménique de la Bible,* Paris: Cerf – Société biblique française, 1989, 41-47.

**L'ÉPLATTENIER, Charles**

1978 La séquence matthéenne de Jésus au Temple, Mt 21/10-24/2. — *ETR* 53 (1978) 514-518.

**LE POITTEVIN, P.** → Charpentier 1974

**LERLE, Ernst**

1955 *Das Raumverständnis im Neuen Testament.* Berlin: Evangelische Verlagsanstalt; Stuttgart: Lutheraner, 1955, 123 p. Esp. 68 [4,17]; 70-71 [18,10]; 76-77 [6,19-21]; 78-79 [23,23]; 83-84 [8,20]; 84 [18,20].

1960 *Proselytenwerbung und Urchristentum.* Berlin: Evangelische Verlagsanstalt, 1960, 155 p. Esp. 63-66 [23,15.23]; 68-74 [25,31-46]; 84-86 [8,11]; 86-87 [15,29-31]; 95-99 [28,16-20]; 130-131 [10,5].

1970 Realisierbare Forderungen der Bergpredigt? — *KerDog* 16 (1970) 32-40. Esp. 32-37 [7,12]. [NTA 15, 138]

1981 Die Ahnenverzeichnisse Jesu. Versuch einer christologischen Interpretation. — *ZNW* 72 (1981) 112-117. Esp. 113-114 [1,1]. [NTA 26, 519]

**LEROY, François-Joseph** → Aubineau 1993

**LEROY, Herbert**

1964 "Sein Name wird sein Emmanuel!" Die Kindheitsgeschichte nach Matthäus. — *BK* 19 (1964) 110-117. [NTA 9, 896]

1973 "Mein Blut ... zur Vergebung der Sünden" (Mt 26,28). Zur matthäischen Interpretation des Abendmahles. — KNOCH, O., et al. (eds.), *Das Evangelium auf dem Weg zum Menschen.* FS H. Kahlefeld, 1973, 43-53. Esp. 43-45: "Textanalyse, Text- und Literarkritisches"; 45-51: "Traditionsgeschichtliches".

1974 *Zur Vergebung der Sünden. Die Botschaft der Evangelien* (SBS, 73). Stuttgart: Katholisches Bibelwerk, 1974, 114 p. Esp. 29-62: "Das Matthäusevangelium" [9,1-8; 16,16-19; 18,18; 26,28]; 98-101.

**LESKE, Adrian M.**

1991 The Beatitudes, Salt and Light in Matthew and Luke. — *SBL 1991 Seminar Papers,* 816-839. Esp. 816-819: "The beatitudes in recent scholarship"; 820-835: "Matthew's introduction to the Sermon on the Mount"; 835-839: "Matthew 5:13-16: Salt and Light".

1994 The Influence of Isaiah 40-66 on Christology in Matthew and Luke: A Comparison. — *SBL 1994 Seminar Papers,* 897-916. Esp. 898-900 [1-2]; 902-905 [3,16]; 905-906 [8,17]; 906-907 [11,2-6]; 907-908 [11,25-30]; 908-911 [12,15-21]; 911-912 [16,13-23]; 912 [17,5]; 912-913 [20,28]; 913-914 [26,28].
The Influence of Isaiah on Christology in Matthew and Luke. — FARMER, W.R. (ed.), *Crisis in Christology: Essays in Quest of Resolution,* Livonia, MI: Dove Booksellers, 1995, 241-269. Esp. 242-244; 248-251; 251-252; 252-253; 253-255; 255-258; 258-260; 260; 261; 262.

**LESLIE, Robert C.** → Wuellner 1984

**LESSMANN, P.G.**

1965    *The Lord's Prayer and the Lord's Passion.* St. Louis, MO: Concordia, 1965, 109 p.

**LÉTHEL, François-Marie**

1982    La prière de Jésus à Gethsémani dans la controverse monothélite. [26,36-46] — HEINZER,
F. - SCHÖNBORN, C. (eds.), *Maximus Confessor. Actes du Symposium sur Maxime le
Confesseur, Fribourg, 2-5 septembre 1980* (Paradosis, 27), Freiburg/Schw: Éd.
universitaires, 1982, 207-214.

**LEUBA, Jean-Louis**

1950    *L'institution et l'événement. Les deux modes de l'œuvre de Dieu selon le Nouveau
Testament. Leur différence, leur unité* (Bibliothèque théologique). Neuchâtel–Paris:
Delachaux et Niestlé, 1950, 141 p. Esp. 7-45: "Le Christ".
*Institution und Ereignis. Gemeinsamkeiten und Unterschiede der beiden Arten von Gottes Wirken nach dem
Neuen Testament.* Göttingen: Vandenhoeck & Ruprecht, 1957, 144 p. Esp. 9-51.

**LEVIE, Jean**

1954    L'évangile araméen de S. Matthieu est-il la source de l'évangile de S. Marc? — *NRT*
76 (1954) 689-715, 812-843. Esp. 690-704 [two-source hyp.]; 704-715 [Mk/Mt]; 814-843 [Lk-Mt/Mk;
816-833 [minor agreements: 3,1-6; 14,13-22; 17,14-21]; 838-843 [structure]; = (Cahiers de la NRT, 11),
Tournai–Paris: Casterman, 1954, 64 p. → Cerfaux 1954b, McCool 1956, Ponthot 1958, Vaganay 1954a,
1955a, Weijers 1956
     B. BRINKMANN, *Scholastik* 30 (1955) 260; B.C. BUTLER, *DownR* 73 (1955) 281-283; J. CAMBIER, *ETL*
35 (1959) 633-634; H. CONZELMANN, *TZ* 13 (1957) 140-141; F.V. FILSON, *JBL* 74 (1955) 202; P.
GAECHTER, *ZKT* 77 (1955) 362; C. PERROT, *Cahiers sioniens* (Paris) 9 (1955) 132-136; H. SUASSO,
*Bijdragen* 16 (1955) 421-422; A. VIARD, *RSPT* 39 (1955) 278.

1955    La complexité du problème synoptique. — *ETL* 31 (1955) 619-636. Esp. 620-622 [Q]; 624-
633: "La réfutation de l'hypothèse de travail de M. Vaganay". → Vaganay 1954a, 1955a

1957    Critique littéraire évangélique et l'évangile araméen de l'apôtre Matthieu. —
HEUSCHEN, J.M. (ed.), *La formation des évangiles*, 1957, 34-69. Esp. 41-58: "Comparaison
des trois évangiles synoptiques"; 58-69: "Comparaison des textes de la double tradition — L'évangile araméen
de l'apôtre Matthieu".

**LEVIN, Saul**

1988    A Camel or a Cable through a Needle's Eye? [19,24] — EMBLETON, S. (ed.), *Fourteenth
Lacus Forum 1987*, Linguistic Association of Canada and the United States, 1988, 406-
415.

**LEVINE, Amy-Jill**

1988    *The Social and Ethnic Dimensions of Matthean Salvation History. "Go nowhere among
the Gentiles..." (Matt. 10:5b)* (Studies in the Bible and Early Christianity, 14).
Lewiston, NY - Queenston, Ont., 1988, XII-319 p. [NTA 33, p. 249] — Diss. Duke Univ.,
Durham, NC, 1984 (D.M. Smith).
     S. BROWN, *TorontoJT* 7 (1991) 130-131; T.L. DONALDSON, *JBL* 109 (1990) 723-725; D.E. GARLAND,
*RExp* 87 (1990) 646-648; B.J. MALINA, *BTB* 20 (1990) 129-130; B.T. VIVIANO, *CBQ* 52 (1990) 754-
755.

1989    → Swidler 1989

1990    Who's Catering the Q Affair? Feminist Observations on Q Paraenesis. — *Semeia* 50
(1990) 145-161. Esp. 146-147: "The form of Q"; 147-153: "Liminal vs. marginal". [NTA 35, 609] →
Robbins 1990

1992    Matthew. — NEWSOM, C.A. - RINGE, S.H. (eds.), *The Women's Bible Commentary*,
London: SPCK; Louisville, KY: Westminster/Knox, 1992, 252-262.

1994 Second Temple Judaism, Jesus, and Women. Yeast of Eden. — *BibInt* 2 (1994) 8-33. Esp. 22-26; 26-33 [Q]. [NTA 39, 561]

1996 Discharging Responsibility: Matthean Jesus, Biblical Law, and Hemorrhaging Woman. [9,18-26] — BAUER, D.R. - POWELL, M.A. (eds.), *Treasures New and Old*, 1996, 379-397.

**LEVINE, Etan**

1976 The Sabbath Controversy according to Matthew. — *NTS* 22 (1975-76) 480-483. [NTA 21, 81]

**LEVISON, Jack**

1982 A Better Righteousness: The Character and Purpose of Matthew 5:21-48. — *SBT* 12 (1982) 171-194. Esp. 171-176 [5,17-20]; 176-180 [5,21-26]; 180-183 [5,27-30]; 183-185 [5,31-32]; 185-188 [5,33-37]; 188-192 [5,38-42]; 192-194 [5,43-48].

**LEVISON, John R.**

1987 Responsible Initiative in Matthew 5:21-48. — *ExpT* 98 (1986-87) 231-234. [NTA 32, 119]

**LEVORATTI, Armando J.**

1982 & GIUSTOZZI, E. - RUBINO, M., La buena noticia según Mateo. — *Palabra y Vida* (Buenos Aires) 9 (1982) 3-32.

1988 Milagros de Jesús y teología del milagro. — *RevistBíb* 50 (1988) 1-32. Esp. 5-10 [kingdom]. [NTA 32, 1072] → Latourelle 1986

**LÉVY, S.**

1976 Le Chema Israël, une prière juive citée dans les Évangiles (Mt 22,35). — *Rencontre Chrétiens et Juifs* (Paris) 10 (1976) 296-302.

**LEWIS, J.J.**

1974 The Wilderness Controversy and Peirasmos. [6,13] — *Colloquium* 7 (1974) 42-44. [NTA 19, 951]

**LEWIS, Jack P.**

1976 *The Gospel according to Matthew*. Part I: *1:1-13:52*. Part II: *13:53-28:20* (Living Word Commentary, 2). Austin, TX: Sweet Publishing Co., 1976, 191 and 174 p. [NTA 24, p. 191]

1995 "The gates of hell shall not prevail against it" (Matt 16:18): A Study of the History of Interpretation. — *JEvTS* 38 (1995) 349-367. Esp. 353-362 [Church fathers]; 362-363 [Middle Ages]; 363-367 [modern period]. [NTA 41, 213]

**LEWIS, James Newton, Jr.**

1973 *The Church in the Synoptic Tradition*. Diss. Southern Baptist Theol. Sem., Louisville, KY, 1973, 170 p. (W.E. Ward). — *DissAbstr* 34 (1973-74) 6098.

**LICHTENBERGER, Hermann**

1987 Täufergemeinden und frühchristliche Täuferpolemik im letzten Drittel des 1. Jahrhunderts. — *ZTK* 84 (1987) 36-57. Esp. 53-57. [NTA 31, 1410]

**LIE, Hwa-Sun**

1973 *Der Begriff Skandalon im Neuen Testament und der Wiederkehrgedanke bei Laotse* (EHS, XXIII/24). Bern–Frankfurt/M: Lang, 1973, 252 p. Esp. 22-71: "Das Begriff Skandalon bei den Synoptikern" [4,17; 5,29; 11,6; 13,21.41.53-58; 15,12-14 16,23; 17,24-27; 18,6-7; 24,10; 26,31-33].

**LIEBENBERG, J.**

1993 The Function of the *Standespredigt* in Luke 3:1-20. A Response to E.H. Scheffler's *The*

*Social Ethics of the Lukan Baptist (Lk 3:10-14).* — *Neotestamentica* 27 (1993) 55-67. Esp. 58-59 [Q 3,7-9]; 62-63 [Q 3,17]. [NTA 38, 826] → Scheffler 1990

**LIEBERS, Reinhold**

1993 *"Wie geschrieben steht". Studien zu einer besonderen Art frühchristlichen Schriftbezuges.* Berlin – New York: de Gruyter, 1993, VIII-445 p. Esp. 10-16 [2,23; 11,14; 16,27; 17,12; 26,51-54]. — Diss. Kiel, 1991 (U. Luck).

**LIEBHART, Leopold**

1954 Die Seltenheit der Himmelserscheinung des Jahres 7 vor Christus. — *TPQ* 102 (1954) 12-20.

**LIEBSTER, W.**

1966 Die Gültigkeit des Gesetzes und die Frage der neuen Gerechtigkeit in der Bergpredigt. — *Kirche in der Zeit* 21 (1966) 368-373.

**LIEFELD, Walter L.**

1986 Lord's Prayer. — BROMILEY, G.W., et al. (eds.), *The International Standard Bible Encyclopedia*, III, Grand Rapids, MI: Eerdmans, 1986, 160-164.

1992 Transfiguration. — *DJG*, 1992, 834-841. Esp. 834-835 [17,1-9].

**LIENEMANN, Wolfgang**

1982 *Gewalt und Gewaltverzicht. Studien zur abendländischen Vorgeschichte der gegenwärtigen Wahrnehmung von Gewalt* (Forschungen und Berichte der Evangelischen Studiengemeinschaft, 36). München: Kaiser, 1982, 295 p. Esp. 48-77: "Gewalt und Gewaltverzicht im Neuen Testament".

**LIENHARD, Marc**

1992 Luther et Calvin commentateurs du Notre Père. — *RHPR* 72 (1992) 73-88.

**LIES, Lothar**

1979 Origenes und die Eucharistiekontroverse zwischen Paschasius Radbertus und Ratramnus. [26,26-29] — *ZKT* 101 (1979) 414-426.

1980 Die dreigestaltige Eucharistieauffassung nach SerMt 85 u. 86. — CROUZEL, H. – QUACQUARELLI, A. (eds.), *Origeniana Secunda*, 1980, 205-214.

**LIETAERT PEERBOLTE, Lambertus Johannes**

1996 *The Antecedents of Antichrist. A Traditio-Historical Study of the Earliest Christian Views on Eschatological Opponents* (Supplements to the Journal for the Study of Judaism). Leiden: Brill, 1996, XV-380 p. Esp. 51-54 [24-25]; 59-60; 173-174. — Diss. Leiden, 1995 (M. de Jonge – H.J. de Jonge).

**LIETZMANN, Hans**

1932R Matthaeus 25,34 in den Freisinger Denkmälern. [1932] — ID., *Kleine Schriften*, II, 1958, 189-190.

1935R Neue Evangelienpapyri. [1935] [Pap. Eg. 2] — ID., *Kleine Schriften*, II, 1958, 180-188.

1936R → Huck 1936

1958 *Kleine Schriften.* II: *Studien zum Neuen Testament*, ed. K. Aland (TU, 68). Berlin: Akademie, 1958, X-303 p. → 1932, 1935

**LIFSHITZ, Baruch**

1970 Notes d'épigraphie grecque. — *RB* 77 (1970) 76-83. Esp. 77-78 [11,28]. [NTA 15, 335]

**LIGHTFOOT, John**

1859R *A Commentary on the New Testament from the Talmud and Hebraica. Matthew – 1*

*Corinthians* [1859], ed. R. Gandell. Vol. 2: *Matthew–Mark*. Grand Rapids, MI: Baker, 1979, 480 p. Esp. 7-384: "Hebrew and talmudical exercitations upon the gospel of St. Matthew". [NTA 24, p. 183]; Peabody, MA: Hendrickson, repr. 1989.

**LIGHTFOOT, Robert Henry**

1938[R] *Locality and Doctrine in the Gospels* [1938]. Ann Arbor, MI – London: Univ. Microfilms Intern., 1979, X-166 p. Esp. 66-72 [28,1-20]; 126-131.

**LILLIE, Betty Jane**

1989 Matthew's Wisdom Theology: Old Things and New. — *Proceedings EGLBS* 9 (1989) 124-137. Esp. 127-128 [24,45]; 128-129 [7,24-25]; 130-131 [1.,16-19]; 131-135 [11,25-30]; 135-136 [23,34-39].

**LILLIE, William**

1965 The Empty Tomb and the Resurrection. — NINEHAM D.E., et al. (eds.), *Historicity and Chronology*, 1965, 117-134. Esp. 127-129. [NTA 11, 232]

**LIMBECK, Meinrad**

1972 *Von der Ohnmacht des Rechts. Untersuchungen zur Gesetzeskritik des Neuen Testaments* (Theologische Perspektiven). Düsseldorf: Patmos, 1972, 112 p. Esp. 61-83: "Die Gesetzeskritik Jesu".

1973 Beelzebul – eine ursprüngliche Bezeichnung für Jesus? — FELD, H. – NOLTE, J. (eds.), *Wort Gottes in der Zeit*. FS K.H. Schelkle, 1973, 31-42. Esp. 34-35.39-40 [10,25]; 37-38 [12,27].

1974a Das Recht des Herkömmlichen. Tradition und Fortschritt im Mattäusevangelium. — *BK* 29 (1974) 80-85. [NTA 19, 523]

1974b Satan und das Böse im Neuen Testament. — HAAG, H. (ed.), *Teufelsglaube*, Tübingen: Katzman, 1974; [2]1980, 271-388. Esp. 277-282: "Mattäisches Sondergut"; 290-293: "Die Parallele Mk 8,33 und Mt 16,23"; 293-308 [4,1-11; 12,22-31; 13,18-23]; 308-313: "Jesu exorzistisches Wirken" [8,28-34; 15,21-28; 17,14-21]; 327-334: "Mattäusevangelium".

1975 Bemerkungen zur neuen Einheitsübersetzung. Übersetzungsfehler im Mattäusevangelium. — *TQ* 155 (1975) 327-330.

1976 Das Judasbild im Neuen Testament aus christlicher Sicht. — GOLDSCHMIDT, H.L. – LIMBECK, M. *Heilvoller Verrat? Judas im Neuen Testament*, Stuttgart: Katholisches Bibelwerk, 1976, 37-101. Esp. 60-74: "Judas im Verständnis des Mattäusevangeliums".

1977 et al., *Die bessere Gerechtigkeit: Mattäusevangelium* (Bibelauslegung für die Praxis, 16). Stuttgart: Katholisches Bibelwerk, 1977, 206 p.
G.G. GAMBA, *Sal* 41 (1979) 171-172; O. KNOCH, *BK* 33 (1978) 138-139.

1980a *Von Jesus beten lernen. Das Vaterunser auf dem Hintergrund des Alten Testamentes*. Stuttgart: Religiöse Bildungsarbeit, 1980, 133 p. [NTA 26, p. 198]

1980b Auserwählt – doch nicht für den Himmel! — *BK* 35 (1980) 17-22. Esp. 18-19 [5,13-16].

1981* (ed.), *Redaktion und Theologie des Passionsberichtes nach den Synoptikern* (Wege der Forschung, 481). Darmstadt: Wissenschaftliche Buchgesellschaft, 1981, VIII-428 p. →
Bultmann 1931, Dahl 1955, Gerhardsson 1967, K.G. Kuhn 1952, Limbeck, Vanhoye 1967

1981 Einführung. — *Ibid.*, 1-16. Esp. 12-13: "Die Matthäuspassion".

1982 "Stecke dein Schwert in die Scheide...!". Die Jesusbewegung im Unterschied zu den Zeloten. — *BK* 37 (1982) 98-104. [NTA 27, 70]

1985 Um Gottes willen – für den Menschen! Neutestamentliche Kriterien für eine christliche Ethik. — *BK* 40 (1985) 107-115. Esp. 112-113 [12,1-8]; 114-115 [22,34-40]. [NTA 30, 818]

1986 *Matthäus-Evangelium* (Stuttgarter Kleiner Kommentar. Neues Testament, 1). Stuttgart: Katholisches Bibelwerk, 1986, 312 p. Esp. 9-17: "Einleitung"; 19-303: "Kommentar". [NTA 31,

p. 232]; ²1988. → Giesen 1987b

A. FUCHS, *SNTU* 12 (1987) 227; U. LUZ, *TLZ* 114 (1989) 592-593; A. SAND, *TRev* 84 (1988) 23-24; A. STÖGER, *BLtg* 60 (1987) 43-45.

1988 Die nichts bewegen wollen! Zum Gesetzesverständnis des Evangelisten Matthäus. — *TQ* 168 (1988) 299-320. Esp. 301-309 [23,1-4]; 309-311 [16,19]; 311-313 [11,28-30]; 314-317 [12,1-14]; 318-319 [mercy]. [NTA 33, 617]

1989a Der kleine Weg der größeren Gerechtigkeit. Die Inkarnation Gottes als Ausgangspunkt einer neuen Schöpfung. — *BK* 44 (1989) 158-163. Esp. 160 [28,16-20]. [NTA 34, 602]

1989b Vom rechten Gebrauch des Gesetzes. — *JbBT* 4 (1989) 151-169. Esp. 164-168: "Matthäus – die Schlüssel des Himmelreichs".

1992 "... der das Wort hört und versteht ..." (Mt 13,23). Zur Verkündigung des Matthäus-Evangeliums (I). — *BLtg* 65 (1992) 236-239. [NTA 37, 730]

1993a "Es geschehe dein Wille!" (Mt 6,10). Zur Verkündigung des Matthäus-Evangeliums (1). — *BLtg* 66 (1993) 50-53. [NTA 37, 1240]

1993b Auf der Suche nach dem Himmelreich. (2). — *Ibid.*, 111-114. [NTA 38, 147]

1993c Die Chance des Wohl-Stands. (3). [18–25] — *Ibid.*, 169-174. [NTA 38, 770]

1993d Wer zu spät kommt...! (4). — *Ibid.*, 251-256. [NTA 38, 1355]

1994 Zugänge zu Matthäus. — *TQ* 174 (1994) 235-239. [NTA 39, 789] → Luz 1985a/90, Oberlinner 1991a, L. Schenke 1988a

**LINCOLN, Andrew T.**

1982 From Sabbath to Lord's Day: A Biblical and Theological Perspective. — CARSON, D.A. (ed.), *From Sabbath to Lord's Day: A Biblical, Historical, and Theological Investigation* (Contemporary Evangelical Perspectives), Grand Rapids, MI: Zondervan, 1982, 343-412. Esp. 362-364, 371-374.

1990 Matthew – A Story for Teachers? — CLINES, D.A.J., et al. (eds.), *The Bible in Three Dimensions*, 1990, 103-125. Esp. 106-111 [16,13-20]; 111-115 [28,16-20]; 115-118: "Disciples, implied readers and the teaching discourses"; 119-121: "Disciples and the story-line about Israel and the gentiles"; 112-124: "Disciples and the story-line about Jesus".

**LINDARS, Barnabas**

1958 Matthew, Levi, Lebbaeus and the Value of the Western Text. [9,9; 10,3] — *NTS* 4 (1957-58) 220-222.

1961a *New Testament Apologetic. The Doctrinal Significance of the Old Testament Quotations.* London: SCM, 1961, 303 p. Esp. 86-88.153-154 [8,17]; 113-114 [21,5]; 116-122 [27,3-10]; 122-127 [24,30]; 144-152 [12,18-21]; 156-158 [13,35]; 167-169 [21,19]; 192-194 [2,6]; 194-196 [2,23]; 196-199 [4,15-16]; 213-216 [1,18-23]; 216-217 [2,15]; 217-218 [2,18]; 259-265: "Formula-quotations in Matthew".

1961b The Composition of John xx. — *NTS* 7 (1960-61) 142-147. Esp. 144-146 [28,1-10]. [NTA 5, 755]; = ID., *Essays*, 1992, 3-8.

1964 Books of Testimonies. — *ExpT* 75 (1963-64) 173-175. Esp. 173-174. [NTA 8, 861]

1975 Re-enter the Apocalyptic Son of Man. — *NTS* 22 (1975-76) 52-72. Esp. 65-72. [NTA 20, 594] → Leivestad 1972

1980 Jesus as Advocate: A Contribution to the Christology Debate. — *BJRL* 62 (1979-80) 476-497. Esp. 484-486 [10,32-33]. [NTA 25, 491]

1981a Discourse and Tradition: The Use of the Sayings of Jesus in the Discourses of the Fourth Gospel. — *JSNT* 13 (1981) 83-101. Esp. 85-86 [18,3/Jn 3,3.5]; 88 [6,11/Jn 6,34]; 91-92 [11,27/Jn 3,3.5]. [NTA 26, 530]; = ID., *Essays*, 1992, 113-129. Esp. 115-116; 118; 122.

1981b John and the Synoptic Gospels: A Test Case. [18,3/Jn 3,3.5] — *NTS* 27 (1980-81) 287-294. [NTA 25, 922]; = ID., *Essays*, 1992, 105-112. → Neirynck 1992b (29-31), Pryor 1991b

1981c The New Look on the Son of Man. — *BJRL* 63 (1980-31) 437-462. Esp. 443-446 [Q 7,34; 9,58; 12,8-9.10]. [NTA 26, 653]

1981d The Persecution of Christians in John 15:18-16:4a. — HORBURY, W. - MCNEIL, B. (eds.), *Suffering and Martyrdom in the New Testament. Studies Presented to G.M. Styler by the Cambridge New Testament Seminar*, Cambridge: University Press, 1981, 48-69. Esp. 58-63 [Jn/Mt]; = ID., *Essays*, 1992, 131-152. Esp. 141-146.

1983 *Jesus Son of Man. A Fresh Examination of the Son of Man Sayings in the Gospels in the Light of Recent Research*. London: SPCK; Grand Rapids, MI: Eerdmans, 1983, XI-244 p. Esp. 17-28: "The Son of Man in the sayings of Jesus"; 29-59: "Six Son of Man sayings in Mark and Q" [8,20; 10,32-33; 11,16-19; 12,32-40]; 85-100: "The future Son of Man in Q" [Q 12,40; 17,22-37]; 115-131: "Matthew and the parousia of the Son of Man" [10,23; 13,24-30; 19,28; 24,30; 25,31]; 158-189: "The Son of Man and christology" [8,20; 10,32-33; 11,18-19; 12,32.40]. → Bauckham 1985a, M. Black 1984, P.M. Casey 1987
*Credi tu nel Figlio dell'uomo? I testi evangelici su Gesù Figlio dell'uomo alla luce delle ultime ricerche*. Milano: Paoline, 1987, 269 p.

1985 Response to Richard Bauckham: The Idiomatic Use of Bar Enasha. — *JSNT* 23 (1985) 35-41. Esp. 38-41 [8,20; 11,19; 12,32]; = EVANS, C.A. - PORTER, S.E. (eds.), *The Historical Jesus*, 1995, 256-261. Esp. 259-261. → Bauckham 1985a, P.M. Casey 1987

1988 The New Testament. Part III. — ROGERSON, J. - ROWLAND, C. - LINDARS, B., *The Study and Use of the Bible* (The History of Christian Theology, 2), Basingstoke - Grand Rapids, MI, 1988, 227-397. Esp. 334-337: "Synoptic problem".

1992a Capernaum Revisited. John 4,46-53 and the Synoptics. — VAN SEGBROECK, F., et al. (eds.), *The Four Gospels 1992*. FS F. Neirynck, 1992, III, 1985-2000. Esp. 1988-1996: "John and the Centurion's servant"; 1996-1998: "The underlying story"; = ID., *Essays*, 1992, 199-214. Esp. 202-210.

1992b Rebuking the Spirit. A New Analysis of the Lazarus Story of John 11. — *NTS* 38 (1992) 89-104. Esp. 98-99 [ἐμβριμάομαι]. [NTA 36, 1362]; = ID., *Essays*, 1992, 183-198. Esp. 192-193; = DENAUX, A. (ed.), *John and the Synoptics* 1992, 542-547 (short version).

1992c *Essays on John*, ed. C.M. Tuckett (SNTA, 17). Leuven: University Press / Peeters, 1992, XVII-233 p. → 1961b, 1981a-b.d, 1992a-b

**LINDEMANN, Andreas**

1975 → Conzelmann 1975

1979 *Paulus im ältesten Christentum. Das Bild des Apostels und die Rezeption der paulinischen Theologie in der frühchristlichen Literatur bis Marcion* (Beiträge zur historischen Theologie, 58). Tübingen: Mohr, 1979, XL-449 p. Esp. 154-158. — Diss. Göttingen, 1977 (H. Conzelmann).

1980 Zur Gleichnisinterpretation im Thomas-Evangelium. — *ZNW* 71 (1980) 214-243. Esp. 216-219 [13,45-50/Th 8]; 219-220 [13,45/Th 76]; 222-224 [13,3-8/Th 9]; 224-226 [13,31/Th 20]; 226-227 [13,33/Th 96]; 229-232 [22,1-14/Th 64]; 233-234 [13,44/Th 109] 234-238 [21,33-46/Th 65-66]; 238-240 [18,12-13/Th 107]; 240-242 [13,24-30/Th 57]. [NTA 26, 773]

1984 Literaturbericht zu den synoptischen Evangelien 1978-1983. — *TR* 49 (1984) 223-276, 311-371. Esp. 246-257: "Das synoptische Problem"; 257-263: "Die Logienquelle Q"; 331-346: "Matthäusevangelium". [NTA 29, 76/506] → 1994; → Conzelmann 1978

1986a Erwägungen zum Problem einer "Theologie der synoptischen Evangelien". — *ZNW* 77 (1986) 1-33. Esp. 24-30 [Q]. [NTA 31, 100]

1986b Gottesherrschaft und Menschenherrschaft. Beobachtungen zum neutestamentlichen Basileia-Zeugnis und zum Problem einer theologischen Ethik des Politischen. — *TGl* 76 (1986) 69-94. Esp. 71-75. [NTA 30, 1287]

1986c Herrschaft Gottes / Reich Gottes. IV. Neues Testament und spätantikes Judentum. — *TRE* 15 (1986) 196-218. Esp. 201-207: "Jesus von Nazareth"; 209-210: "Matthäusevangelium".

1989 Die Versuchungsgeschichte Jesu nach der Logienquelle und das Vaterunser. — KOCH, D.-A., et al. (eds.), *Jesu Rede von Gott.* FS W. Marxsen, 1989, 91-100. Esp. 92-96 [4,1-11]; 96-100 [6,9-13].

1993 Samaria und Samaritaner im Neuen Testament. — *WDienst* 22 (1993) 51-76. Esp. 52-57 [10,5]. [NTA 39, 480]

1994 Literatur zu den synoptischen Evangelien 1984-1991. — *TR* 59 (1994) 41-100, 113-185, 252-284. Esp. 69-77: "Das 'synoptische Problem'"; 77-88: "Die Logienquelle Q"; 147-185: "Das Matthäusevangelium". [NTA 38, 1348; 39, 128] → 1984

1995 "... ex Maria virgine". Konfessionsspezifische Interpretationen der biblischen Aussage der Jungfrauengeburt? — ERNST, J. - LEIMGRUBER, S. (eds.), *Surrexit Dominus vere.* FS J.J. Degenhardt, 1995, 365-379. Esp. 372-379 [1,18-25].

**LINDESKOG, Gösta**

1950a & FRIDRICHSEN, A. - RIESENFELD, H., *Inledning till Nya Testamentet.* Stockholm: Diakonistyrelsen, 1950, ²1958, ³1964, ed. K. Stendahl, 398 p. Esp. 23-57: "Den synoptiska frågan"; 57-66 "Evangelium enligt Matteus".

1950b Logia-Studien. — *StudTheol* 4 (1950) 129-189. Esp. 134-136.141-143.146-148.155-162[13,12]; 136-137.143-145.146-148.155-162[25,29]; 165-181: "Logien als 'Wanderer' in der synoptischen Tradition" [Q 6,39.40.43-45; 10,16; 11,23.29-32.43; 12,6-7.9.10.40; 13,30; 14,11.27.34-35; 16,13.17.18; 17,6.23.33; 18,14].

1961 Israel in the New Testament. Some Few Remarks on a Great Problem. — *SEÅ* 26 (1961) 57-92. Esp. 60 [23,39]; 72 [16,18]; 83-84 [10,5; 13,14]. [NTA 7, 747]

1964 Christianity as Realized Judaism. — *Pistis kai erga [FS R. Gyllenberg]* (Horae Sœderblomianae, 6), Lund: Gleerup, 1964, 15-36. Esp. 19 [OT quotations]; 24.26 [law]; 28-29 [prophecy]; 33 [Messiah].

1967 Människosonens gåta. [The riddle of the Son of Man] — *Religion och Bibel* (Uppsala) 26 (1967) 1-13. → 1968

1968 Das Rätsel des Menschensohnes. — *StudTheol* 22 (1968) 149-175. Esp. 151-153 [9,35-10,33]. [NTA 13, 839] → 1967

1974 Autorität und Tradition im Neuen Testament. Einige Bemerkungen. — *ASTI* 9 (1973) [1974] 42-63. Esp. 42-43 [5,45; 7,29]. [NTA 19, 3]

1980 (ed.), *Studiebibel: Nya Testamentet. Bibelkommentar på uppdrag av Religionspedagogiska Institutet* [A study Bible: The New Testament. A biblical commentary written for the Religionspedagogiska Institutet]. Stockholm: Skeab, 1980, 247 p. Esp. 9-87.

1983a Johannes der Täufer. Einige Randbemerkungen zum heutigen Stand der Forschung. — *ASTI* 12 (1983) 55-83. Esp. 60-64 [3,11-12]; 64-66 [3,13-17]; 67-68 [16,13-14]; 68-71 [22,2-14]; 70-71 [17,9-13]; 71-72 [9,14-17]; 72-73 [21,23-27]. [NTA 29, 487]

1983b Das Kamel und das Nadelöhr. — KIILUNEN, J., et al. (eds.), *Glaube und Gerechtigkeit.* FS R. Gyllenberg, 1983, 109-122. Esp. 116-122 [19,24].

**LINDHAGEN, Stig**

1966 *Utläggning av Matteus' Evangelium. För studium och uppbyggelse* [An exposition of the gospel according to Matthew. For study and devotion] (Bibeltjänsts korta bibelkommetarer, 1). Stockholm: Diakonistyrelsen, 1966, 216 p.

**LINDIJER, Coert H.**

1966 De tekenen bij Jezus' dood. [27,45-53] — *Homiletica en Biblica* (Den Haag) 25 (1966) 55-59. [NTA 11, 230]

1970 Die Jungfrauen in der Offenbarung des Johannes XIV 4. — *Studies in John*. FS J.N. Sevenster, 1970, 124-142. Esp. 138 [19,12].

**LINDNER, Helgo**

1993 Johannes Hyrkan und der Reiche Jüngling. Scheitern an der Einlaßbedingung bei den Pharisäern und in der Jesustradition (Ant 13,291 und Mt 19,21). — KOCH, D.-A. - LICHTENBERGER, H. (eds.), *Begegnung zwischen Christentum und Judentum in Antike und Mittelalter. Festschrift für Heinz Schreckenberg* (Schriften des Institutum Judaicum Delitzschianum, 1), Göttingen: Vandenhoeck & Ruprecht, 1993, 263-270.

**LINDSAY, Dennis Ray**

1991 *"Pistis" und "pisteuein" als Glaubensbegriffe in den Schriften des Flavius Josephus und im Neuen Testament*. Diss. Tübingen, 1991, 243 p. (O. Betz).

**LINDSEY, Robert Lisle**

1963 A Modified Two-Document Theory of the Synoptic Dependence and Interdependence. — *NT* 6 (1963) 239-263. Esp. 240-244 [Q]; 244.253-257 [minor agreements]; 244-247 [independence]; 247-248.259-260 [Mk/Mt relationship]; 253-257 [14,1-2]. [NTA 9, 112]

1971 A New Approach to the Synoptic Gospels. — *Christian News from Israel* (Jerusalem) 22 (1971) 56-63.
Aperçu nouveau sur les Évangiles. — *Nouvelles chrétiennes d'Israël* (Jerusalem) 22 (1971) 56-64.

1985 → dos Santos 1985

1993 A New Approach to the Synoptic Gospels. — *Mishkan* (Jerusalem) 17-18 (1992-93) 87-106. [NTA 37, 1231]

1995 Unlocking the Synoptic Problem. Four Keys for Better Understanding Jesus. — *Jerusalem Perspective* 49 (1995) 10-17, 38. [NTA 40, 797]

**LING, Trevor**

1961 *The Significance of Satan. New Testament Demonology and Its Contemporary Relevance* (SPCK Biblical Monographs). London: SPCK, 1961, VI-114 p. Esp. 18-26.61-62.

**LINK, Charles E.**

1995 *Jesus' Epilogue to the Sermon on the Mount. A Study of the Lord's Prayer*. Lima, OH, 1995, 88 p.

**LINMANS, Adrianus J.M.** → van Iersel 1978

**LINNEMANN, Eta**

1960 Überlegungen zur Parabel vom großen Abendmahl. Lc 14,15-24 / Mt 22,1-14. — *ZNW* 51 (1960) 246-255. [NTA 5, 735]

1961 *Gleichnisse Jesu. Einführung und Auslegung*. Göttingen: Vandenhoeck & Ruprecht, 1961, 196 p. Esp. 70-72 [18,12-14]; 87-94 [20,1-16]; 94-103 [22,1-14]; 103-111 [13,44-46]; 111-119 [18,23-35]; 130-134 [25,1-13]; [2]1962; 3rd rev. and enlarged ed., 1964, 207 p.; [5]1969; [6]1975.
*The Parables of Jesus. Introduction and Exposition*, trans. J. Sturdy. London: SPCK; New York – Evanston, IL: Harper & Row, 1966, XV-218 p.
*Le parabole di Gesù. Introduzione e interpretazione*, trans. L. Pusci. Brescia: Queriniana, 1982, 165 p.

1969 Der (wiedergefundene) Markusschluß. — *ZTK* 66 (1969) 255-287. Esp. 269-278 [28,16-20]. [NTA 14, 878] → Schmithals 1972b

1970 *Studien zur Passionsgeschichte* (FRLANT, 102). Göttingen: Vandenhoeck & Ruprecht, 1970, 187 p. Esp. 32-34 [26,36-46]. — Diss. Marburg, 1970 (W. Lorenz).

1973 Jesus und der Täufer. — EBELING, G., et al. (eds.), *Festschrift für Ernst Fuchs*, 1973, 219-236. Esp. 227-228 [21,31-32]; 230 [3,7-10; 7,7-11].

1975a Hat Jesus Naherwartung gehabt? — DUPONT, J. (ed.), *Jésus aux origines de la christologie*, 1975, ²1989, 103-110. Esp. 105-107.

1975b Zeitansage und Zeitvorstellung in der Verkündigung Jesu. — STRECKER, G. (ed.), *Jesus Christus in Historie und Theologie*. FS H. Conzelmann, 1975, 237-263. Esp. 239 [7,24-27; 24,37-39; 25,1-12]; 240 [10,23]; 241 [24,45-51]; 247 [12,28]; 247-248 [11,5-6].

1992 *Gibt es ein synoptisches Problem?* (Theologie für die Gemeinde, 2). Stuttgart: Hänssler, 1992, ²1995, 192 p.

> *Is There a Synoptic Problem? Rethinking the Literary Dependence of the First Three Gospels*, trans. R.W. Yarbrough. Grand Rapids, MI: Baker, 1992, 219 p.

1995 Q – das verlorene Evangelium? Fantasie oder Faktum? — *Jahrbuch für evangelische Theologie* (Wuppertal) 9 (1995) 43-61.

> Is There a Gospel of Q? — *BibReview* 11/3 (1995) 18-23, 42-43. [NTA 40, 143] → Patterson 1995b

**LINSKENS, John**

1983 A Pacifist Interpretation of Peace in the Sermon on the Mount? — *Concilium* (London) 164 (1983) 16-25. Esp. 16-17; 17-23. [NTA 28, 493]

> Une interprétation pacifiste de la paix dans le Sermon sur la montagne? — *Concilium* (Paris) 184 (1983) 37-52. Esp. 38-39; 39-49.
>
> Ein pazifistisches Verständnis des Friedens in der Bergpredigt? — *IZT/Concilium* (Mainz) 19 (1983) 263-272. Esp. 263-264; 264-270.

**LINSS, William C.**

1955 *The Four Gospels' Text of Didymus the Blind*. Diss. Union School of Theol., Boston, 1955, 199 p. — *DissAbstr* 15 (1954-55) 1268.

**LINTON, Olof**

1952a Matteus. — ENGNELL, I. - FRIDRICHSEN, A. (eds.), *Svenskt Bibliskt Uppslagsverk*, Gävle: Skolboksförlaget, 1952, c. 222; Stockholm: Nordiska Uppslagsböcker, ²1963, c. 55-56.

1952b Matteus' evangelium. — *Ibid.*, 1952, c. 222-226; ²1963, c. 56-59.

1952c Synoptiker. — *Ibid.*, 1952, c. 1296-1307; ²1963, c. 1122-1134.

1961 The Trial of Jesus and the Interpretation of Psalm cx. — *NTS* 7 (1960-61) 258-262. Esp. 258-259 [26,64]. [NTA 6, 142]

1964 St. Matthew 5,43. — *StudTheol* 18 (1964) 66-79. [NTA 9, 149]

1965 The Demand for a Sign from Heaven (Mk 8,11-12 and Parallels). [12,38-39; 16,1-4] — *StudTheol* 19 (1965) 112-129. [NTA 11, 242]

1970 Le *parallellismus membrorum* dans le Nouveau Testament. Simples remarques. — DESCAMPS, A.L. - DE HALLEUX, A. (eds.), *Mélanges bibliques*. FS B. Rigaux, 1970, 489-507. Esp. 493 [21,7]; 497-498 [10,26]; 498 [7,16; 23,29]; 498-500 [10,37-39]; 499 [6,25-34]; 501-504 [5,44-46]; 502-503 [7,1-2]; 505-506 [10,24]; 506-507 [10,29].

1972a The Q-Problem Reconsidered. — AUNE, D.E. (ed.), *Studies in New Testament*. FS A.P. Wikgren, 1972, 43-59.

1972b Den synoptiske forsknings dilemma. — *DanskTeolTids* 35 (1972) 47-62. [NTA 18, 94] Das Dilemma der synoptischen Forschung. — *TLZ* 101 (1976) 881-892 ("bearbeitet"). Esp. 886-890. [NTA 22, 76]

1973 Sonen och sönerna. [The Son and the sons] — *SEÅ* 37-38 (1972-73) 185-195. Esp. 185-193 [11,25-27]. [NTA 18, 1018]

1976a Origen and the Interpretation of the Baptist's Call to Repentance. [3,7-12] — *Studia Patristica* 14 (1976) 148-159.

1976b The Parable of the Children's Game. Baptist and Son of Man (Matt. xi.16-19 = Luke vii.31-35): A Synoptic Text-critical, Structural and Exegetical Investigation. — *NTS* 22 (1975-76) 159-179. [NTA 20, 776]

1980 Coordinated Sayings and Parables in the Synoptic Gospels: Analysis versus Theories. — *NTS* 26 (1979-80) 139-163. Esp. 140-159 [4,1-11; 5,3-12.13-16.21-48; 6,18-18.25-34; 8,18-22; 10,5-6.26-33.37-38; 11,18-19.20-24; 12,41-42; 13,31-33.44-46; 18,12-14; 24,27-28]; 159-163 [Mk/Q]. [NTA 24, 771]

**LIPIŃSKI, Éduard**

1959 Namaszczenie w Betanii (De unctione peracta Bethaniae). — *RuBi* 12 (1959) 220-229. [NTA 4, 364]

**LIPS, Hermann VON**

1988 Schweine füttert man, Hunde nicht – ein Versuch, das Rätsel von Matthäus 7,6 zu lösen. — *ZNW* 79 (1988) 165-186. Esp. 165-171: "Auslegungsgeschichte – Interpretationsprobleme – Neuansatz"; 171-174: "Klärungen anhand synchroner Analyse"; 174-180: "Klärungen im Kontext antiker und orientalischer Sprichwörter"; 180-183: "Mt 7,6 als Wort des historischen Jesus?; 184-186: "Mt 7,6 im Kontext des Matthäusevangeliums und in nach-ntl. Zeit". [NTA 33, 605]

1990 *Weisheitliche Traditionen im Neuen Testament* (WMANT, 64). Neukirchen-Vluyn: Neukirchener, 1990, XII-512 p. Esp. 197-227: "Weisheitlicher Einfluß in der Logienquelle (Q)"; 227-234: "Weisheitsmaterial in Mk und im synoptischen Sondergut"; 234-240: "Gesamtsicht der weisheitlichen Materials in den synoptischen Evangelien (einschließlich Q)"; 240-257: "Weisheit in der Verkündigung Jesu"; 267-290: "Ansätze weisheitlicher Christologie in den synoptischen Evangelien (insbesondere Q)".

1991 Christus als Sophia? Weisheitliche Traditionen in der urchristlichen Christologie. — BREYTENBACH, C. – PAULSSEN, H. (eds.), *Anfänge der Christologie*. FS F. Hahn, 1991, 75-95. Esp. 85-87.92-93 [Q].

**LISCHER, Richard**

1987 The Sermon on the Mount as Radical Pastoral Care. — *Interpr* 41 (1987) 157-169. [NTA 31, 1066]

**LITTLE, James Crickton**

1976 Parable Research in the Twentieth Century. I. The Predecessors of J. Jeremias. II. The Contribution of J. Jeremias. III. Developments since J. Jeremias. — *ExpT* 87 (1975-76) 356-360; 88 (1976-77) 40-44, 71-75. [NTA 21, 65/360/361] → J. Jeremias 1947

**LITWAK, Kenneth D.**

1983 The Use of Quotations from Isaiah 52:13–53:12 in the New Testament. — *JEvTS* 26 (1983) 385-394. Esp. 388-389 [8,17].

**LIU, Peter**

1986 *The Poor and the Good News. A Study of the Motif of εὐαγγελίζεσθαι πτωχοῖς in Isaiah 61 and Luke–Acts*. Diss. Fuller Theol. Sem., Pasadena, CA, 1986, 381 p. (R. Martin – F. Bush). — *DissAbstr* 47 (1986-87) 2622-2623.

**LIVERMORE, P.**

1975 Reflections on the Sermon on the Mount. — *Asbury Seminarian* (Wilmore, KY) 30/1 (1975) 20-31.

**LIVINGSTONE, Elizabeth A.**

1980* (ed.), *Studia Biblica 1978. II. Papers on the Gospels. Sixth International Congress on Biblical Studies, Oxford 3-7 April 1978* (JSNT SS, 2). Sheffield: JSOT, 1980, 350 p. → Boyd, Cummings, Fenton, France, Marsh, Russell, Sherriff, Wanamaker

**LIVIO, J.B.**

1968 → Soares-Prabhu 1968

1978 La signification théologique de la "montagne" dans le premier évangile. — *Bulletin du Centre protestant d'études* (Genève) 30 (1978) 13-20. [NTA 23, 82]

LI YOUNG-HÚN

1989 The Exegetical Interpretation of the Gospel of Matthew 5:17-20. [Korean] — *Sinhak Jonmang* (Kwangju) 85 (1989) 2-13.

**LJUNGMAN, Henrik**

1954 *Das Gesetz erfüllen. Matth. 5,17ff. und 3,15 untersucht* (Lunds Univ. Årsskrift 50/6). Lund: Gleerup, 1954, 140 p. → Eissfeldt 1970

   J.S. BARR, *ScotJT* 9 (1956) 314-315; J. BIENECK, *TZ* 13 (1957) 304-305; M.-É. BOISMARD, *RB* 62 (1955) 455; P. BONNARD, *RTP* 5 (1955) 220-221; A. DESCAMPS, *ETL* 31 (1955) 139-140; E. HAAPA, *TAik* 61 (1956) 144-145; E. KÄSEMANN, *TLZ* 81 (1956) 547-548; C. MAURER, *Judaica* 11 (1955) 123-125; E.S. TANNER, *JBL* 75 (1956) 68-69; A. VIARD, *RSPT* 40 (1956) 144-145.

1958 En Sifre-text till Matt. 11,18f. par. [A text from the Siphre for Mt 11,18f. par.] — *SEÅ* 22-23 (1957-58) 238-242. [NTA 3, 586]

1964 Matthäusevangelium. — REICKE, B. - ROST, L. (eds.), *Biblisch-historisches Handwörterbuch*, II, Göttingen: Vandenhoeck & Ruprecht, 1964, 1171-1172.

**LJUNGVIK, Herman**

1965 Översättningsförslag och språkliga förklaringar till skilda ställen i Nya Testamentet. [Proposals for translation and linguistic explanations to various NT passages] — *SEÅ* 30 (1965) 102-120. Esp. 110 [7,4; 18,21]; 113 [10,26]; 115 [23,31]; 32 (1967) 121-147. Esp. 128 [7,12]; 140-141 [27,64]; 144-145 [20,12]. [NTA 12, 814]; 33 (1968) 149-174. Esp. 149 [6,24; 7,15]; 149-150 [8,20]; 150 [21,41]; 150-151 [26,29]; 151 [26,40]; 152 [6,30]. [NTA 14, 70]

1969 Randanmärkningar till 1963 års bibelkommittés översättningsförslag. [Marginal notes on the proposed translation of the 1963 Bible committee] — *SEÅ* 34 (1969) 147-169. Esp. 167 [5,19; 6,33; 7,6]. [NTA 15, 30]

1974 Zu Mt 27,14. — *Eranos* 72 (1974) 71-73.

**LLAMAS, Román**

1974 El anuncio de San José comparado con los demás anuncios tanto del Antiguo como del Nuevo Testamento. — *EstJos* 28 (1974) 15-31. Esp. 17-24 [1,18-25].

**LLAMAS MARTÍNEZ, Enrique**

1977 San José en las genealogías de Jesús en la época del renacimiento. Nuevas soluciones. — *EstJos* 31 = *CahJos* 25 (1977) 55-77. Esp. 57-61 [1,1-17]; 61-75 [16th cent.].

1986 San José y la Virgen María. [1,18-25] — *EstJos* 40 (1986) 185-203.

**LLEWELYN, Stephen R.**

1989 Mt 7:6a: Mistranslation or Interpretation? — *NT* 31 (1989) 97-103. [NTA 34, 120]

   & KEARSLEY, R.A., *New Documents Illustrating Early Christianity.* → G.H.R. Horsley
1992 6. *A Review of the Greek Inscriptions and Papyri Published in 1980-81*. Sydney, NSW: Macquarie University, 1992, VII-227 p. Esp. 16 [5,32]; 68 [ellipse]; 82-86 [8,27]; 86-105 [21,33-44].

1994a 7. *[1982-83]*, 1994, V-287 p. Esp. 86-87 [5,41]; 130-162: "Forcible acquisition and the meaning of Matt. 11.12"; 222-224 [5,25-26]; 257-262.

1994b The *Traditionsgeschichte* of Matt. 11:12-13, par. Luke 16:16. — *NT* 36 (1994) 330-349. Esp. 334-338: "The thematic unity of Luke 16:14-18"; 338-342: "Luke's modification of v. 16b"; 342-346: "Matthew's supposed modification". [NTA 39, 804]

**LLOMPART, G.**

1972 La cruz y las cruces. La iconografía y el folklore en la interpretación del Evangelio de S. Matteo 16,24. — *Revista del etnografia* 16 (1972) 273-322.

**LO, Ping-Cheung**

1990 *Love and Imitation in the New Testament and Recent Christian Ethics*. Diss. Yale Univ., Durham, NC, 1990, 477 p. (G. Outka). — *DissAbstr* 51 (1990-91) 2784.

**LOADER, James Alfred**

1990 *A Tale of Two Cities, Sodom and Gomorrah in the Old Testament, Early Jewish and Early Christian Traditions* (Contributions to Biblical Exegesis and Theology, 1). Kampen: Kok, 1990, 150 p. Esp. 118 [10,15]; 120 [11,23-24].

**LOADER, William R.G.**

1978 The Apocalyptic Model of Sonship: Its Origin and Development in New Testament Tradition. — *JBL* 97 (1978) 525-554. Esp. 529 [19,28]; 530 [22,11-13; 25,31-46]; 530-531 [13,36-43]; 536-537 [11,27; 28,18-19]; 537-538 [16,16-18]; 540 [4,1-11]; 546-548 [11,27]. [NTA 23, 978]

1982a Son of David, Blindness, Possession, and Duality in Matthew. — *CBQ* 44 (1982) 570-585. Esp. 572 [9,27-31]; 572-573 [9,32-34; 12,22-24]; 573 [20,29-34]; 574 [21,1-9]; 574-578 [9,27-31.32-34; 12,22-24]; 578-580 [15,21-28; 20,29-34; 21,1-9]; 580-582 [8,28-34]. [NTA 27, 502]

1982b → McGinlay 1982

1984 The Central Structure of Johannine Christology. — *NTS* 30 (1984) 188-216. Esp. 204-209: "Precursors of Johannine christology". [NTA 28, 988]

1989 Jesus Left Loose Ends. — *Pacifica* 2 (1989) 210-228. Esp. 215-218 [gentile mission]. [NTA 34, 84]

**LOBEL, Edgar**

1957 & ROBERTS, C.H. – TURNER, E.G. – BARNS, J.W.B. (eds.), *The Oxyrhynchus Papyri XXIV*. London: Egypt Exploration Society, 1957, XIII-216 p. Esp. 4-5 [P⁷⁰]; 5-6 [P⁷¹]

**LOCHER, Gottfried W.**

1990 'Wie auch wir...'. Die Unser-Vater-Bitte um Vergebung (Mt vi,12) bei Luther, Zwingli und Calvin. — BACKUS, I. – HIGMAN, F. (eds.), *Théorie et pratique de l'exégèse. Actes du III<sup>e</sup> Colloque international sur l'histoire de l'exégèse biblique au XVI<sup>e</sup> s. (Genève, 31 août – 2 septembre 1988)* (Études de philologie et d'histoire, 43), Genève: Droz, 1990, 287-301.

**LOCHMAN, Jan Milič**

1967 Div vánoc (Mt 1,18-25). — *Theologická příloha – Křest'anské revue* (Praha) 34 (1967) 97-102.

1988 *Unser Vater, Auslegung*. Göttingen, 1988, 152 p.
  A. JÄGER, *TZ* 45 (1989) 378-380.
  *The Lord's Prayer*, trans. G.W. Bromiley. Grand Rapids, MI: Eerdmans, 1990, X-180 p. [NTA 35, p. 103]
  A.C. WINN, *Interpr* 46 (1992) 206.

**LOCKMANN, Paulo D.**

1987 Mt 5,17-20. A justiça e o justo. — *Estudos Biblicos* (Petrópolis) 14 (1987) 44-50.

**LODGE, John G.**

1986 Matthew's Passion-Resurrection Narrative. — *ChSt* 25 (1986) 3-20. [NTA 30, 1065]

**LODS, Marc**

1958 Le "Tu es Petrus" dans l'exégèse patristique. — *Église et théologie* (Paris) 21 (1958) 15-34. [NTA 3, 587]; = ID., *Protestantisme et tradition de l'Église*, ed. J.-N. Pérès – J.-N. Dubois (Patrimoines. Christianisme), Paris: Cerf, 1988, 3-21.

**LÖBMANN, Benno**

1977 Das Ehescheidungsverbot Jesu im Hinblick auf die Eheauffassung in der orientalischen und lateinischen Kirche. — ERNST, W., et al. (eds.), *Dienst der Vermittlung*, 1977, 673-689. Esp. 677-679 [5,32]; 681-683: "Die Unzuchtsklauseln bei Mt 5,32 und 19,9".

**LÖFSTEDT, Bengt**

1983 Notizen zu Hieronymus' Matthäuskommentar. [21,1.21.46] — *Aevum* (Milano) 57 (1983) 123-124.

1988a Adnotatiunculae patristicae. — *Aevum* 62 (1988) 169-170.

1988b Zu Augustins Schrift "De sermone Domini in Monte". — *Orpheus* (Catania) 9 (1988) 96-97.

1989 *Sedulius Scottus, Kommentar zum Evangelium nach Matthäus 1,1-11,1* (Vetus Latina. Aus der Geschichte der lateinischen Bibel, 14). Freiburg: Herder, 1989, 306 p. *Sedulius Scottus, Kommentar zum Evangelium nach Matthäus. 11,2 bis Schluß. Anhang, Register* (Vetus Latina, 19). Freiburg: Herder, 1991, 307-706 p.

> G.J.M. BARTELINK, *VigChr* 44 (1990) 396-397; 48 (1994) 99; P.-M. BOGAERT, *RBén* 104 (1994) 431; J.-P. BOUHOT, *Revue des études latines* (Paris) 68 (1990) 195-196; A. CODY, *CBQ* 53 (1991) 333-334; R. ÉTAIX, *RHE* 85 (1990) 735-739; 87 (1992) 794-795; J. FONTAINE, *Revue des études latines* 67 (1989) 277-278; M. GESTEIRA, *RevistEspTeol* 50 (1990) 106-107; X. JACQUES, *NRT* 112 (1990) 594; 114 (1992) 743-744; J. MEYERS, *Latomus* (Bruxelles) 51 (1992) 658-659; 53 (1994) 422-423; J.-M. ROUSÉE, *RB* 96 (1989) 640; M. WINTERBOTTOM, *JTS* 41 (1990) 729-731; 44 (1993) 495-496.

**LÖNING, Karl**

1989 Die Füchse, die Vögel und der Menschensohn (Mt 8,19f par Lk 9,57f). — FRANKEMÖLLE, H. – KERTELGE, K. (eds.), *Vom Urchristentum zu Jesus*. FS J. Gnilka, 1989, 82-102. Esp. 83-86: "Literarkritik"; 86-93: "Formkritik"; 93-99: "Motivkritik".

**LOESCHKE, Gerhard**

1908R *Die Vaterunser-Erklärung des Theophilus von Antiochien. Eine Quellenuntersuchung zu den Vaterunser-Erklärungen des Tertullian, Cyprian, Chromatius und Hieronymus* [1908] (Neue Studien zur Geschichte der Theologie und der Kirche, 4). Aalen: Scientia, 1973, 51 p.

**LÖVESTAM, Evald**

1950 *Äktenskapet i Nya Testamentet* [Marriage in the New Testament. With a summary in English] [19,3-12]. Lund: Gleerup, 1950, 235 p. → Kothes 1951

> P. BENOIT, *RB* 58 (1951) 296-297; L. FENDT, *TLZ* 77 (1952) 161-162; P.P. NOBER, *Bib* 34 (1953) 246-250.

1958 Till förståelsen av Luk. 7:35. [A contribution to the understanding of Lk 7,35] — *SEÅ* 22-23 (1957-58) 47-63. Esp. 55-57 [23,34-39]; 58-59 [22,1-10]. [NTA 3, 600]

1961a *Son and Saviour. A Study of Acts 13,32-37. With an Appendix: 'Son of God' in the Synoptic Gospels* (Coniectanea Neotestamentica, 18). Lund: Gleerup; København: Munksgaard, 1961, 134 p. Esp. 88-112.

1961b Die Frage des Hohenpriesters (Mark. 14,61, par. Matth. 26,63). — *SEÅ* 26 (1961) 93-107. [NTA 7, 798]

1961c "Masculum et feminam fecit eos deus". [19,4] — *TidsTeolKirk* 32 (1961) 74-84.

1962a Die Davidssohnfrage. [22,41-46] — *SEÅ* 27 (1962) 72-82. [NTA 9, 545]

1962b Ἀπολύειν - en gammalpalestinensisk skilsmässoterm. [Ἀπολύειν - an old Palestinian divorce term] [5,31-32; 19,9] — *Ibid.*, 132-135. [NTA 9, 526]

1962c Wunder und Symbolhandlung. Eine Studie über Matthäus 14,28-31. — *KerDog* 8 (1962) 124-135. [NTA 7, 136]

1963 *Spiritual Wakefulness in the New Testament* (Lunds Universitets Årsskrift, NF, 1.55/3). Lund: Gleerup, 1963, 170 p. Esp. 95-107 [24,43-51]; 108-122 [25,1-13].

1964 En problematisk eskatologisk utsaga: Mark. 13:30 par. [A problematic eschatological statement: Mark 13,30 par.] — *SEÅ* 28-29 (1963-64) 64-80. Esp. 75-77 [24,34]. [NTA 10, 140] → 1980

1968a *Spiritus Blasphemia. Eine Studie zu Mk 3,28f par Mt 12,31f, Lk 12,10* (Scripta Minora Regiae Societatis Humaniorum Litterarum Lundensis, 1966-1967, 1). Lund: Gleerup, 1968, 88 p. Esp. 35-68.

    E. BAMMEL, *JTS* 22 (1971) 192-194; M.A. CHEVALLIER, *RHPR* 52 (1972) 370-371; J. DUPONT, *RHE* 65 (1970) 328; J. LÄHNEMANN, *TLZ* 94 (1969) 759-761; F. LENTZEN-DEIS, *Bib* 51 (1970) 587-590; X. LÉON-DUFOUR, *RSR* 59 (1971) 611-612.

1968b Logiet om hädelse mot den helige Ande (Mark. 3:28f. par. Matt. 12:31f.; Luk. 12:10). [The logion on blasphemy against the Holy Spirit] — *SEÅ* 33 (1968) 101-117. [NTA 14, 162]; = ID., *Axplock*, 1988, 39-50.

1973 Davids-son-kristologin hos synoptikerna. — *SEÅ* 37-33 (1972-1973) 196-210. Esp. 197-206 [12,22-30]. [NTA 18, 836]; = ID., *Axplock*, 1988, 27-38. Esp. 28-35.
    Jésus Fils de David chez les Synoptiques. — *StudTheol* 28 (1974) 97-109. Esp. 98-105. [NTA 19, 521]
    *SelT* 15 (1976) 132-134.

1977 Die funktionale Bedeutung der synoptischen Jesusworte über Ehescheidung und Wiederheirat. [5,31-32; 19,9] — *SNTU* 2 (1977) 19-28.
    De synoptiska Jesus-orden om skilsmässa och omgifte: referensramar och implikationer. — *SEÅ* 43 (1978) 65-73. [NTA 23, 471]

1980 The ἡ γενεὰ αὕτη Eschatology in Mk 13,30 parr. [24,34] — LAMBRECHT, J. (ed.), *L'Apocalypse johannique et l'Apocalyptique dans le Nouveau Testament* (BETL, 53), Gembloux: Duculot; Leuven: University Press, 1980, 403-413. → 1964
    This "Generation" Will Not Pass Away Before All These Things Take Place. — ID., *Axplock*, 1987, 91-101.

1981 Divorce and Remarriage in the New Testament. [5,31-32; 19,9] — *Jewish Law Annual* (Leiden) 4 (1981) 47-65. [NTA 28, 703]; = ID., *Axplock*, 1988, 61-69.

1984 Eschatologie und Tradition im 2. Petrusbrief. — WEINRICH, W.C. (ed.), *The New Testament Age*. FS B. Reicke, 1984, II, 287-300. Esp. 295-299 [24,34-51/2 Pe].

1986 Urkyrkans skriftförståelse. [OT quotations] — HIDAL, S., et al. (eds.), *Judendom och kristendom under de första århundradena. Nordiskt patristikerprojekt 1982-1985*, Stavanger–Oslo–Bergen–Tromsø: Universitetsforlaget, 1986, 259-267.

1988 *Axplock. Nytestamentliga studier*. Lund: Teologiska Institutionen, 1988, 124 p. → 1968b, 1973, 1980, 1981

1995 *Jesus and "This Generation". A New Testament Study* (ConBibNT, 25). Stockholm: Almqvist & Wiksell, 1995, 130 p. Esp. 21-37: "The synoptic texts of the demand for a sign" [12,38-42; 16,1-4]; 38-45 [11,16-19/Q 7,31-35]; 46-55 [17,14-20/Mk 9,14-29]; 59-66 [Q 17,22-37 (Lk)]; 67-80 [23,34-36/Q 11,49-51]; 81-87 [24,34/Mk 13,30].

**LOEWEN, Howard J.**

1978 The Great Commission. [28,16-20] — *Direction* (Fresno, CA) 7/2 (1978) 33-35. [NTA 22, 769]

**LÖWENSTEIN, Kathrin** → Schramm 1986

**LOGACHEV, K.I.**

1981 Greek Lectionaries and Problems in the Oldest Slavonic Gospel Translations. — EPP, E.J. - FEE, G.D. (eds.), *New Testament Textual Criticism*. FS B.M. Metzger, 1981, 345-348. Esp. 348.

**LOHFINK, Gerhard**

1974a Gab es im Gottesdienst der neutestamentlichen Gemeinden eine Anbetung Christi? —

*BZ* 18 (1974) 161-179. Esp. 164-165 [προσκυνέω]. [NTA 19, 729]; = ID., *Studien zum Neuen Testament*, 1989, 245-265. Esp. 249-250.

1974b Jesus und die Ehescheidung. Zur Gattung und Sprachintention von Mt 5,32. — MERKLEIN, H. - LANGE, J. (eds.), *Biblische Randbemerkungen*. FS R. Schnackenburg, 1974, 207-217.

1975 Zur Möglichkeit christlicher Naherwartung. — GRESHAKE, G. - LOHFINK, G., *Naherwartung, Auferstehung, Unsterblichkeit*. *Untersuchungen zur christlichen Eschatologie* (QDisp, 71), Freiburg: Herder, 1975, 38-81. Esp. 41-50: "Die Naherwartung Jesu".

1976a Die Parabel von den zehn Mädchen (Mt. 25,1-13). — *KatBlät* 101 (1976) 130-133.

1976b Der Ursprung der christlichen Taufe. — *TQ* 156 (1976) 35-54. Esp. 44-45 [3,11-12]. [NTA 21, 233]; = ID., *Studien zum Neuen Testament*, 1989, 173-198. Esp. 184-186.

1977 Universalismus und Exklusivität des Heils im Neuen Testament. — KASPER, W. (ed.), *Absolutheit des Christentums* (QDisp, 79), Freiburg: Herder, 1977, 63-82. Esp. 74-82: "Die Rede vom Weltgericht in Mt 25".

1981 Hat Jesus eine Kirche gestiftet? — *TQ* 161 (1981) 81-97. Esp. 83-84.86 [16,17-19]. [NTA 26, 131]
   *SelT* 22 (1983) 179-186.

1982a *Wie hat Jesus Gemeinde gewollt? Zur gesellschaftlichen Dimension des christlichen Glaubens*. Freiburg: Herder, 1982, 223 p.; [2]1983. Esp. 17-41: "Jesus und Israel" [3,7-10; 6,9-10; 8,11-12; 10,5-6; 11,5.21-22; 12,41-42]; 42-88: "Jesus und seine Jünger" [Sermon on the Mount; 5,13-16.39-42; 7,24-27; 11,28-30; 13,44-46; 23,8-12]. → De Virgilio 1991
   *Jesus and Community. The Social Dimension of Christian Faith*, trans. J.P. Galvin. Philadelphia, PA: Fortress; New York: Paulist, 1984, XII-211 p. Esp. 7-29; 31-73.
   *L'Église que voulait Jésus*, trans. J.P. Bagot. Paris, 1985, 196 p.
   *La Iglesia que Jesús quería. Dimension comunitaria de la fe cristiana*. Bilbao, 1986, 202 p.
   *Gesù come voleva la sua comunità? La chiesa quale dovrebbe essere*, trans. A. Rizzi. Roma, 1987, [2]1990, 247 p.

1982b Der ekklesiale Sitz im Leben der Aufforderung Jesu zum Gewaltverzicht (Mt 5,39b-42/Lk 6,29f). — *TQ* 162 (1982) 236-253. Esp. 239-243 [Q 6,29-30]; 243-250 [5,39-42]. [NTA 27, 98]; = *TJb*, 1984, 194-209. Esp. 195-199; 199-206.
   *SelT* 23 (1984) 3-13.
   Wer kann die Gewaltlosigkeit leben? — ID., *Wem gilt die Bergpredigt?*, 1988, 39-53, 213-214 ("leicht überarbeitet"). Esp. 42-48 [5,39-42].

1983 Wem gilt die Bergpredigt? Eine redaktionskritische Untersuchung von Mt 4,23–5,2 und 7,28f. — *TQ* 163 (1983) 264-284. Esp. 267-271: "Die Struktur des Rahmens"; 272-273: "Die Literargeschichte des Rahmens"; 273-281; "Die Theologie des Rahmens". [NTA 28, 490]; = KERTELGE, K. (ed.), *Ethik im Neuen Testament*, 1984, 145-167. Esp. 148-153; 153-154; 154-163. → 1988c; → K.-S. Krieger 1986
   Wem gilt die Bergpredigt? — ID., *Wem gilt die Bergpredigt?*, 1988, 15-38, 210-213 ("leicht überarbeitet"). Esp. 18-24; 24-25; 25-35.

1984 Gesetzeserfüllung und Nachfolge. Zur Radikalität des Ethischen im Matthäusevangelium. — WEBER, H. (ed.), *Der ethische Kompromiß* (Studien zur theologischen Ethik, 11), Freiburg/Schw: Universitätsverlag; Freiburg: Herder, 1984, 15-58. Esp. 20-28.32-41 [5,48]; 28-32 [11,28-30; 13,44-46; 19,16-30].
   Worin besteht die Radikalität der Bergpredigt? — ID., *Wem gilt die Bergpredigt?*, 1988, 65-98, 214-220 ("geringfügig überarbeitet"). Esp. 69-75.78-85; 75-78.

1985 Die Korrelation von Reich Gottes und Volk Gottes bei Jesus. — *TQ* 165 (1985) 173-183. Esp. 176-177 [5,43-48]; 182 [8,11-12]. [NTA 30, 538]; = ID., *Studien zum Neuen Testament*, 1989, 77-90. Esp. 81-82; 89.

1986  "Schwerter und Pflugscharen". Die Rezeption von Jes 2,1-5 par Mi 4,1-5 in der Alten
Kirche und im Neuen Testament. — *TQ* 166 (1986) 184-209. Esp. 203-204 [5,14]. [NTA 31,
827]
Wo werden die "Schwerter zu Plugscharen"? — ID., *Wem gilt die Bergpredigt?*, 1988, 161-192, 225-229
("leicht überarbeitet"). Esp. 186-188.

1987  Jesu Verbot der Ehescheidung und seine Adressaten. — *TQ* 167 (1987) 144-146.
Wem gilt das Ehescheidungsverbot Jesu? — ID., *Wem gilt die Bergpredigt?*, 1988, 193-198.

1988a  *Wem gilt die Bergpredigt? Beiträge zu einer christlichen Ethik.* Freiburg: Herder, 1988,
238 p. [NTA 32, p. 373] → 1982b, 1983, 1984, 1986, 1987, 1988b; → Oberlinner 1990
G. ABBÀ, *Sal* 51 (1989) 136-137; M. HELSPER, *BK* 43 (1988) 125-126; E. LOHSE, *TLZ* 113 (1988) 897-
899; M. SCHEUER, *TPQ* 141 (1993) 416-417.
*El sermón de la montaña. ¿Para quién?*, trans. V.A. Martínez de Lapera. Barcelona: Herder, 1989, 274 p.
X. ALEGRE, *ActBibl* 27 (1990) 197-198; J.L. ESPINEL, *CiTom* 117 (1990) 383-384; F.F. RAMOS,
*NatGrac* 37 (1990) 317; J. VITÓRIO, *Perspectiva Teológica* (Sao Leopoldo) 21 (1989) 400-402.
*Per chi vale il discorso della montagna? Contributi per un'etica cristiana*, trans. G. & M. Gillini (Biblioteca
biblica, 3). Brescia: Queriniana, 1990, 229 p.
L. CILIA, *RivBib* 39 (1991) 61-63. S. CIPRIANI, *Asprenas* 38 (1991) 540-542; C. GHIDELLI, *ParVi* 36
(1991) 335-336; V. PASQUETTO, *Teresianum* 43 (1992) 288-289.

1988b  Weshalb verlangt die Bergpredigt notwendig eine Kontrastgesellschaft? — *Ibid.*, 99-160,
221-224. Esp. 99-104: "Auslegungsaporien"; 107-109 [4,23–5,2]; 110-119: "Die Bergpredigt und das
Gesetz vom Sinai" [5,1.17-20.43-48]; 119-132: "Kontrastive Forderungen" [5,23-24.38-42; 6,25-34]; 132-
138: "Das kontrastive Gottesbild"; 138-142 [5,13]; 142-147 [5,14-16]; 147-160: "Mißverständnisse von
Kontrastgesellschaft".

1988c  Das Publikum der Bergpredigt. Eine Auseinandersetzung mit Klaus-Stefan Krieger. —
*Ibid.*, 199-209. → 1983; → K.-S. Krieger 1986

1988d  Die Not der Exegese mit der Reich-Gottes-Verkündigung Jesu. — *TQ* 168 (1988) 1-15.
Esp. 6-7 [13,44-46]; 8-9 [25,14-30]. [NTA 32, 1327]; = ID., *Studien zum Neuen Testament*,
1989, 383-402. Esp. 389-391; 391-393.
The Exegetical Predicament Concerning Jesus' Kingdom of God Proclamation. — *TDig* 36 (1989) 103-110.

1989a  Der präexistente Heilsplan. Sinn und Hintergrund der dritten Vaterunserbitte. —
MERKLEIN, H. (ed.), *Neues Testament und Ethik*. FS R. Schnackenburg, 1989,
110-133. Esp. 110-119 [6,10]; 124-126 [11,25-27; 26,42]; 132 [7,21]; = ID., *Studien zum Neuen
Testament*, 1989, 49-75. Esp. 49-59; 64-67; 73-74.

1989b  *Studien zum Neuen Testament* (Stuttgarter Biblische Aufsatzbände. Neues Testament,
5). Stuttgart: Katholisches Bibelwerk, 1989, 408 p. → 1974a, 1976b, 1985, 1988d, 1989a

1995  & PESCH, R., Volk Gottes als "Neue Familie". — ERNST, J. - LEIMGRUBER, S. (eds.),
*Surrexit Dominus vere*. FS J.J. Degenhardt, 1995, 227-242. Esp. 239-242: "Das Vaterunser
als Gebet der 'neuen Familie'".

### LOHFINK, Norbert

1977  Das Ethos des Neuen Testaments – erhabener als das des Alten? — ID., *Unsere großen
Wörter. Das Alte Testament. Zu Themen dieser Jahre*, Freiburg: Herder, 1977, 225-
240. Esp. 236-238 [5,38-42].

1987  Psalm 6: Beobachtung beim Versuch, ihn "kanonisch" auszulegen. — *TQ* 167 (1987)
277-288. Esp. 286-287 [7,23]. → 1988b

1988a  Der Messiaskönig und seine Armen kommen zum Zion. Beobachtungen zu Mt 21,1-17.
— SCHENKE, L. (ed.), *Studien zum Matthäusevangelium*. FS W. Pesch, 1988, 179-200.
Esp. 183-185: "Die narrative Verkoppelung von 'Einzug' und 'Reinigung'"; 185-186: "Der Anfang der
Einheit"; 186-188: "Erzählungsinterne Einheitssignale"; 188-191: "Die innere Handlung"; 191-193: "Mt
21,12-14 als zusammengehörige Aussage"; 194-196: "Die Präsenz des matthäischen Anawim-Wortfeldes";
197-199: "Die Ablehnung des 'armen Messias' vorher und nachher"; 199-200: "Hermeneutische Nach-

gedanken"; = ID., *Studien zur biblischen Theologie*, 1993, 294-314. Esp. 296-298; 298-300; 300-301; 301-304; 304-307; 307-310; 310-313; 313-314.

1988b Was wird anders bei kanonischer Schriftauslegung? Beobachtungen am Beispiel von Psalm 6. — *JbBT* 3 (1988) 29-53. Esp. 43-48 [7,23]; = ID., *Studien zur biblischen Theologie*, 1993, 263-293. Esp. 280-286. → 1987

1993 *Studien zur biblischen Theologie* (Stuttgarter Biblische Aufsatzbände. Altes Testament, 16). Stuttgart: Katholisches Bibelwerk, 1993, 325 p. → 1988a-b

**LOHMEYER, Ernst**

1937[R] Die Versuchung Jesu. [1937] — ID., *Urchristliche Mystik*, 1956, [2]1958, 81-122.

1938[R] Vom Sinn der Gleichnisse Jesu. [1938] — ID., *Urchristliche Mystik*, 1956, [2]1958, 123-157. Esp. 125-132; = HARNISCH, W. (ed.), *Gleichnisse Jesu*, 1982, 154-179. Esp. 156-161.

1945[R] *Gottesknecht und Davidssohn* [1945] (FRLANT, 61). Göttingen: Vandenhoeck & Ruprecht, [2]1953, 155 p. Esp. 8-14 [12,18-21]; 40-46 [1–2]; 69-75 [Son of David].

1946[R] *Das Vater-unser* (ATANT, 23) [1946]. Zürich: Zwingli, [3]1952, 216 p.; Göttingen: Vandenhoeck & Ruprecht, [4]1961; [5]1962.

   P. BONNARD, *RTP* 4 (1954) 146-147.

   *The Lord's Prayer*, trans. J. Bowden. London: Collins, 1965, 309 p.

   *"Our Father". An Introduction to the Lord's Prayer*, trans. J. Bowden. New York: Harper & Row, 1966, 320 p.

   P.J. ACHTEMEIER, *ChrCent* 83 (1966) 113; J. BLIGH, *HeythJ* 7 (1966) 465-466; F.F. BRUCE, *EvQ* 38 (1966) 174-175; W.E. HULL, *RExp* 64 (1967) 85-86; I.H. MARSHALL, *ExpT* 77 (1965-66) 238; E. MARY, *Theology* 70 (1967) 187-188; N. PERRIN, *Interpr* 20 (1966) 475-476; D. REES, *DownR* 85 (1967) 352-353; E.F. SIEGMAN, *TS* 27 (1966) 725-726; W.W., *ChurchQR* 167 (1966) 382-383.

1951 "Mir ist gegeben alle Gewalt!" Eine Exegese von Mt. 28,16-20. — SCHMAUCH, W. (ed.), *In Memoriam Ernst Lohmeyer*, 1951, 22-49. Esp. 23-28 [form-genre]; 28-33 [Eusebius]; 33-43 [structure-theology]; 43-49 [mission].

1956a *Das Evangelium des Matthäus. Nachgelassene Ausarbeitungen und Entwürfe*, ed. W. Schmauch (KEK, Sonderband). Göttingen: Vandenhoeck & Ruprecht, 1956, 429 p.; [2]1958; [3]1962, 12*-429 p.; [4]1967. → Lekai 1974

   C.K. BARRETT, *JTS* 9 (1958) 356-358; P. BENOIT, *RB* 64 (1957) 433-434; H. BRAUN, *VerkFor* 1956-57/1-2 (1957) 158-160; K.H. SCHELKLE, *TQ* 137 (1957) 88-89; F.J. SCHIERSE, *Scholastik* 32 (1957) 616.

1956b *Urchristliche Mystik. Neutestamentliche Studien*. Darmstadt: Gentner, 1956; [2]1958, 181 p. → 1937, 1938

**LOHMEYER, Monika**

1995 *Der Apostelbegriff im Neuen Testament. Eine Untersuchung auf dem Hintergrund der synoptischen Aussendungsreden* (SBB, 29). Stuttgart: Katholisches Bibelwerk, 1995, XI-472 p. Esp. 155-159 [ἀπόστολος/ἀποστέλλειν]; 160-293: "Die synoptischen Aussendungsreden" [Q 10,2-12: reconstruction; composition; analysis]; 294-343: "Gesandte in der Tradition der Logienquelle und die Gesandten der Aussendungsrede" [Q 7,24-28.31-35; 9,57-62; 11,49-51; 13,34-35]; 364-394: "Apostel bei Mt: Missionare für Israel" [9,36–10,42; 28,16-20]; 396-403 [Q 9,57–10,24]. — Diss. Siegen, 1994 (I. Broer).

**LOHR, Charles H.**

1961 Oral Techniques in the Gospel of Matthew. — *CBQ* 23 (1961) 403-435. Esp. 405-408: "Formulaic language: the traditional style"; 408-419: "Repetitive devices for the elaboration of unifying themes"; 419-434: "Principles of structure". [NTA 6, 448]

   Oral Techniques in Matthew's Gospel. — *TDig* 12 (1964) 92-98; = RYAN, M.R. (ed.), *Contemporary New Testament Studies*, 1965, 252-260; = MCCARTHY, D.J. – CALLEN, W.B. (eds.), *Modern Biblical Studies. An Anthology from Theology Digest*, Milwaukee, WI: Bruce, 1967.

   Técnicas orales en el Evangelio de Mateo. — *SelT* 1/3 (1962) 36-42; = MCCARTHY, D.J. – CALLEN, W.B. (eds.), *Estudios modernos sobre la Biblia* ("Palabra Inspirada", 8), Santander: Sal Terrae, 1969, 133-143.

**LOHSE, Eduard**

1958 Matthäusevangelium. — *EKL* 2 (1958) 1272-1274.

1960 Jesu Worte über den Sabbat. — ELTESTER, W. (ed.), *Judentum, Urchristentum, Kirche.* FS J. Jeremias, 1960, 79-89. Esp. 86-88 [12,11-12]. [NTA 5, 690]; = ID., *Die Einheit des Neuen Testaments*, 1973, 62-72. Esp. 69-71.

1963 Hosianna. — *NT* 6 (1963) 113-119. Esp. 117-118 [21,9]. [NTA 8, 965]; = ID., *Die Einheit des Neuen Testaments*, 1973, 104-110. Esp. 108-109.

1964 *Die Geschichte des Leidens und Sterbens Jesu Christi.* Gütersloh: Mohn, 1964, [2]1967, [3]1973, 102 p.; (Gütersloher Taschenbücher/Siebenstern, 316), [4]1984, 100 p.
*History of the Suffering and Death of Jesus Christ*, trans. M.O. Dietrich. Philadelphia, PA: Fortress, 1967, VIII-120 p.
*La storia della passione e morte di Gesù Cristo.* Brescia: Paideia, 1975, 119 p.
*A história de paixão e morte de Jesus Cristo.* Sâo Paolo: Paulinas, 1977, 153 p.

1970* & BURCHARD, C. - SCHALLER, B. (eds.), *Der Ruf Jesu und die Antwort der Gemeinde. Exegetische Untersuchungen. Joachim Jeremias zum 70. Geburtstag gewidmet von seinen Schülern.* Göttingen: Vandenhoeck & Ruprecht, 1970, 289 p. → Burchard, Colpe, Hanssen, Jörns, Lohse, Schaller, Storch, Wrege

1970 "Ich aber sage euch". — *Ibid.*, 189-203; = ID., *Die Einheit des Neuen Testaments*, 1973, 73-87.

1972 *Die Entstehung des Neuen Testaments* (Theologische Wissenschaft, 4). Stuttgart: Kohlhammer, 1972, 159 p.; [2]1976, [3]1979, [4]1983. Esp 76-83: "Die synoptische Frage"; 87-91: "Das Matthäusevangelium".
*Introduccion al Nuevo Testamento.* Madrid: Cristiandad, 1975, 274 p.; [2]1986, 264 p.
*The Formation of the New Testament*, trans. M.E. Boring. Nashville, TN: Abingdon, 1981, 256 p.
Trans. Portuguese 1980; Finnish 1986.

1973 *Die Einheit des Neuen Testaments. Exegetische Studien zur Theologie des Neuen Testaments.* Göttingen: Vandenhoeck & Ruprecht, 1973, [2]1976, 355 p. → 1960, 1963, 1970

1974 *Grundriß der neutestamentlichen Theologie* (Theologische Wissenschaft, 5/1). Stuttgart: Kohlhammer, 1974; [2]1979; [3]1984; [4]1989, 171 p. Esp. 18-50: "Die Verkündigung Jesu"; 119-122: "Das Matthäusevangelium".
*Teología del Nuevo Testamento.* Madrid: Cristiandad, 1978, 286 p.
*Compendio di teologia del Nuovo Testamento*, trans. G. Poletti. Brescia: Queriniana, 1987, 241 p.
*Théologie du Nouveau Testament.* Genève: Labor et Fides, 1987, 287 p.
Trans. Japanese 1974; Greek 1980; Finnish 1983.

1975 Christus als der Weltenrichter. — STRECKER, G. (ed.), *Jesus Christus in Historie und Theologie.* FS H. Conzelmann, 1975, 475-486. Esp. 481-482; = ID., *Die Vielfalt des Neuen Testaments*, 1982, 70-81. Esp. 76-77.

1978 Glauben im Neuen Testament. — HERMISSON, H.-J. - LOHSE, E., *Glauben* (Biblische Konfrontationen. Kohlhammer Taschenbücher, 1005), Stuttgart: Kohlhammer, 1978, 79-132. Esp. 89-102.

1979a *Die Urkunde der Christen. Was steht im Neuen Testament?* Stuttgart–Berlin: Kreuz, 1979, 190 p.
*Het getuigschrift van de christenen: wat staat er in het Nieuwe Testament?* Kampen: Kok, 1982, 124 p. Esp. 53-58 [Sermon on the Mount]; 116-117.
*The First Christians. Their Beginnings, Writings, and Beliefs*, trans. M.E. Boring. Philadelphia, PA: Fortress, 1983, 126 p.

1979b *Glaube und Wunder. Ein Beitrag zur theologia crucis in den synoptischen Evangelien.* — ANDRESEN, C. - KLEIN, G. (eds.), *Theologia Crucis - Signum Crucis. Festschrift für Erich Dinkler zum 70. Geburtstag*, Tübingen: Mohr, 1979, 335-350. Esp. 343-347; = ID., *Die Vielfalt des Neuen Testaments*, 1982, 29-44. Esp. 37-41.

1982   *Die Vielfalt des Neuen Testaments. Exegetische Studien zur Theologie des Neuen Testaments II.* Göttingen: Vandenhoeck & Ruprecht, 1982, 255 p. → 1975, 1979b

1984   *Die Ethik der Bergpredigt und was sie uns heute zu sagen hat* (Vorlagen, 21). Hannover: Lutherhaus Verlag, 1984, 26 p. [NTA 31, p. 102]

1988   *Theologische Ethik des Neuen Testaments* (Theologische Wissenschaft, 5/2). Stuttgart: Kohlhammer, 1988, 145 p. Esp. 44-51: "Die Ethik der Bergpredigt".
       *Theological Ethics of the New Testament,* trans. M.E. Boring. Minneapolis, MN: Fortress, 1991, VIII-236 p.

1991   "Vollkommen sein". Zur Ethik des Matthäusevangeliums. [5,48; 19,21] — OBERLINNER, L. - FIEDLER, P. (eds.), *Salz der Erde.* FS A. Vögtle, 1991, 131-140.

## LOI, Vincenzo

1974   *Vetus latina,* "testo occidentale" dei Vangeli, *Diatessaron* nelle testimonianze di Novaziano. — *Augustinianum* 14 (1974) 201-221. Esp. 203-204; 208-209 [1,23; 19,17]; 215-216 [10,29.33; 16,17]; 218 [28,20]. [NTA 19, 471]

## LOIMARANTA, L.K.

1992   Matteus 19:30–20:16. Kiastinen tekstian alyysi. [chiastic structures] — *TAik* 97 (1992) 113-120.

## LONA, Horacio E.

1985   "In meinem Namen versammelt". Mt 18,20 und liturgisches Handeln. — *Archiv für Liturgiewissenschaft* (Regensburg) 27 (1985) 373-404. Esp. 374-390: "Der exegetische Befund"; 390-399: "Wirkungsgeschichte von Mt 16,20 in der Alten Kirche". [NTA 30, 1061] → Häussling 1985

1995   Perdón y reconciliación en el evangelio de Mateo. — *Proyecto Centro Salesiano de Estudios* (Buenos Aires) 20 (1995) 37-54.

## LONGENECKER, Richard N.

1968   Some Distinctive Early Christological Motifs. — *NTS* 14 (1967-68) 526-545. Esp. 534-535 [ὄνομα]. [NTA 13, 134]

1969   "Son of Man" as a Self-Designation of Jesus. — *JEvTS* 12 (1969) 151-158. Esp. 154-156: "In the gospels". [NTA 14, 118]

1970   *The Christology of Early Jewish Christianity* (Studies in Biblical Theology, II/17). London: SCM, 1970, XI-178 p. Esp. 63-119: "Messiahship and its implications".

1974*  & TENNEY, M.C. (eds.), *New Dimensions in New Testament Study.* Grand Rapids, MI: Zondervan, 1974, XIII-386 p. → Gundry, Ladd, Van Elderen

1975a  *Biblical Exegesis in the Apostolic Period.* Grand Rapids, MI: Eerdmans, 1975, 246 p. Esp. 51-78: "Jesus and the Old Testament"; 133-137; 140-152: "The quotations of Matthew" [1,23; 2,15.18.23; 3,3; 4,15-16; 8,17; 12,18-21; 13,35; 21,5; 27,9-10].

1975b  Literary Criteria in Life of Jesus Research: An Evaluation and Proposal. — HAWTHORNE, G.F. (ed.), *Current Issues in Biblical and Patristic Interpretation.* FS M.C. Tenney, 1975, 217-229. Esp. 227-228.

1985   The Nature of Paul's Early Eschatology. — *NTS* 31 (1985) 85-95. Esp. 90-92 [24,8.43-44/1 Thess 5,1-11; 24,15/2 Thess 2,1-2]. [NTA 29, 1064]

## LONGO, Fausto

1969   Il discorso ecclesiastico (Mt 18). — *ParVi* 14 (1969) 296-307.

## LONGOBARDO, Luigi

1988   (trans.), *Ilario di Poitiers, Commentario a Matteo* (Collana di testi patristici, 74). Roma: Città Nuova, 1988, 326 p.
       M. DIEGO SÁNCHEZ, *Teresianum* 42 (1991) 640-646; A. FERRUA, *CC* 140/3 (1989) 203-204.

**LONGSTAFF, Thomas Richmond Willis**

1975a   The Minor Agreements: An Examination of the Basic Argument. — *CBQ* 37 (1975) 184-192. [NTA 20, 73] → 1979; → Throckmorton 1977

1975b   → R.H. Fuller 1975b

1976   A Critical Note in Response to J.C. O'Neill. — *NTS* 23 (1976-77) 116-117. [NTA 21, 362] → O'Neill 1975

1977   *Evidence of Conflation in Mark? A Study in the Synoptic Problem* (SBL DS, 28). Missoula, MT: Scholars, 1977, X-245 p. Esp. 129-140 [8,14-15/Mk]; 140-152 [8,16-17/Mk]; 153-167 [12,9-14/Mk]; 168-178 [10,42/Mk]; 178-188 [21,12-13/Mk]; 183-201 [26,17-25/Mk]. — Diss. Columbia Univ., 1973 (J.L. Martyn). → J. Dewey 1987, W.O. Walker Jr. 1987b
         E. BEST, *ScotJT* 32 (1979) 96; M.-É. BOISMARD, *RB* 85 (1978) 629-630; D.L. DUNGAN, *CBQ* 41 (1979) 163-164; E.V. MCKNIGHT, *JBL* 98 (1979) 143-145; V. MORA, *SBF/LA* 39 (1989) 363-364; M.T. NORWOOD, *JAAR* 46 (1978) 370; R. PESCH, *TRev* 75 (1979) 108-109; C.S. RODD, *ExpT* 89 (1977-78) 353-355; M.E. THRALL, *JTS* 29 (1978) 535-536; R. TREVIJANO ETCHEVERRÍA, *Salmanticensis* 26 (1979) 312-313.

1978   → Tyson 1978a

1979   Mark and Roger of Hovedon: A Response. — *CBQ* 41 (1979) 118-120. [NTA 23, 800] → 1975a; → Throckmorton 1977

1981   The Women at the Tomb: Matthew 28:1 Re-examined. — *NTS* 27 (1980-81) 277-282. [NTA 25, 869]

1987   Order in the Synoptic Gospels: A Response. — *SecCent* 6 (1987-88) 98-106. → J. Dewey 1987, R.H. Fuller 1987, W.O. Walker Jr. 1987b

1988   & THOMAS, P.A., *The Synoptic Problem. A Bibliography, 1716-1988* (New Gospel Studies, 4). Macon, GA: Mercer University Press, 1988, XXVIII-235 p.

**LØNNING, Per**

1978   Om ikke-bevisstgjort normativitet. [On a non-conscious normativity] — *NorskTeolTids* 79 (1978) 249-266. → Hognestad 1978b

**LOOSLEY, Ernest G.**

1964   *The Challenge from the Mount.* London: Epworth, 1964, 78 p. [NTA 9, p. 274]

**LÓPEZ CASUSO, Jesús A.**

1975   Aportación trinitaria de la "Teología de los evangelios de Jesus". — *EstTrin* 9 (1975) 293-308. Esp. 296-298. → Pikaza 1974a

**LÓPEZ FERNÁNDEZ, Enrique**

1971   Nueva solución al problema sinóptico. La teoría de Antonio Gaboury: hipótesis, argumentos y crítica. — *EstBíb* 30 (1971) 313-343; 31 (1972) 43-81. Esp. 318-343; 43-70: "La solución de Gaboury"; 71-80: "Observaciones críticas". [NTA 16, 834; 17, 96] → Gaboury 1970

1975   Las fuentes de los Evangelios sinópticos. Estado actual de la cuestión. — *StOvet* 3 (1975) 121-202. [NTA 20, 760]

1983   El yugo de Jesús (Mt 11,28-30). Historia y sentido de una metáfora. — *StOvet* 11 (1983) 65-118. [NTA 31, 1074]

1995   Nazoraios y sus problemas en torno a Mt 2,23. — *StOvet* 23 (1995) 17-102.

**LÓPEZ MELÚS, Francisco María**

1962   *Perspectivas de las bienaventuranzas* (Colección Selección Bíblica, 4). Madrid: Centro Bíblico Hispano Americano, 1962, 158 p.; Madrid: Casa de la Biblia, ²1967, 191 p. → Celada 1962
         F.F. RAMOS, *Studium Legionense* (León) 5 (1964) 276-278.

1965   Bienaventuranzas, Las. — *Enciclopédia de la Bíblia* (Barcelona) 1 (1965; ²1969) 1210-1212.

1976    *Las bienaventuranzas. Ley del reino* (Biblia "a distancia"). Madrid: Edicabi, 1976, 172 p. → 1978
      A. SALAS, *BibFe* 3 (1977) 108-109.

1978    *Las bienaventuranzas. Ley fundamental de la vida cristiana.* Madrid: Privately published, 1978, 368 p.; Zaragoza: Privately published, [7]1982, 549 p.; (Nueva alianza, 109), Salamanca: Sígueme, 1988, 588 p. → 1976
      G. ARANDA, *ScriptTheol* 12 (1980) 259-262; J. BEOBIDE, *EstTrin* 13 (1979) 384; J. DE GOITIA, *EstE* 55 (1980) 133-134; J.L. ESPINEL, *CiTom* 108 (1981) 180-181; A. SALAS, *BibFe* 5 (1979) 321-323. A.M. ARTOLA, *ScriptVict* 32 (1985) 443-444; F. ORTIZ DE U., *Lumen* (Vitoria) 31 (1982) 380; G. PÉREZ, *Salmanticensis* 30 (1983) 100-102; F.F. RAMOS, *Studium Legionense* (León) 24 (1983) 282-284; A. SALAS, *BibFe* 8 (1982) 303-304; J. SALGUERO, *Angelicum* 60 (1983) 293-295; S. VERGÉS, *SelT* 19 (1982) 258-259.
      G. ABBÀ, *Sal* 55 (1993) 408; J.M. CASCIARO RAMIREZ, *ScriptTheol* 22 (1990) 273-275; R. DE SIVATTE, *ActBibl* 26 (1989) 242-243; L. JULIÁ, *QüestVidaCr* 145 (1989) 146; D. NATAL, *EstAgust* 24 (1989) 259-260; V. PASQUETTO, *Teresianum* 40 (1989) 624-625; F.F. RAMOS, *NatGrac* 35 (1988) 438-439; L.-J. RENARD, *NRT* 111 (1989) 940; J. SALGUERO, *Angelicum* 67 (1990) 138-140.

1983    ¡Felices los limpios de corazón! [5,8] — *BibFe* 9 (1983) 178-186.

**LÓPEZ PULIDO, Francisco**

1977    *La nueva buena. Ocurrencias marginales al evangelio de Mateo.* Salamanca: Sígueme, 1977, 128 p.

**LÓPEZ RIVERA, Francisco**

1980    Mt 25,31-46 y la teología sinóptica. — *Christus* (México) 45 (1980) 26-30.

**LÓPEZ ROSAS, Ricardo**

1989    San José en la Sagrada Escritura. La justicia de San José según Mateo 1,18ss. — *EfMex* 7 (1989) 179-193. [NTA 34, 113]

**LOPTON, G.P.**

1954    *Greek Text Problems of Mt 16,13-20.* Diss. Theol. Sem., Dallas, TX, 1954.

**LORD, Albert Bates**

1978    The Gospels as Oral Traditional Literature. — WALKER, W.O., Jr. (ed.), *The Relationships among the Gospels*, 1978, 33-91. Esp. 45-52: "The birth stories"; 58-89: "Parallel sequences and verbal correspondences" [3–13/Mk].
      Response: C.A. TALBERT, *ibid.*, 93-102.

**LORENZEN, Thorwald**

1973    Ist der Auferstandene in Galiläa erschienen? Bemerkungen zu einem Aufsatz von B. Steinseifer. — *ZNW* 64 (1973) 209-221. Esp. 213-214 [28,16-20]. [NTA 19, 71] → Steinseifer 1971

1995    *Resurrection and Discipleship. Interpretive Models, Biblical Reflections, Theological Consequences.* Maryknoll, NY: Orbis, 1995, X-358 p. Esp. 167-181: "The empty tomb narratives"; 303-305 [28,16-20].

**LORENZMEIER, Theodor**

1973    Zum Logion Mt 12,28; Lk 11,20. — BETZ, H.D. - SCHOTTROFF, L. (eds.), *Neues Testament und christliche Existenz. Festschrift für Herbert Braun zum 70. Geburtstag am 4. Mai 1973*, Tübingen: Mohr, 1973, 289-304. Esp.289-291: "Zur Frage der Authentizität"; 291-293: "Zum Exorzismus Jesu"; 294-296: "Zum Selbstbewußtsein Jesu"; 296-302: "Zum Gegenwärtigkeit der Gottesherrschaft"; 302-304: "Zum Verständnis der Gottesherrschaft".

**LORES, Rubén**

1987    Estudio exegético de la gran comisión, según Mateo 28:18-19. — *Vida y Pensamiento* (San José) 5 (1987) 31-38.

**LORIA, R.**

1967 "Legare e sciogliere" nella Chiesa primitiva alla luce della dottrina del Corpo Mistico. [16,18-20; 18,15-18] — *PalCl* 46 (1967) 978-996. [NTA 12, 557]

**LORVEGLIO, G.**

1970 Una discrepanza tra i Sinottici per un errore di traduzione. [4,1-3] — *BibOr* 12 (1970) 221-222.

**LOSADA, Diego Adolfo**

1974 Modelo de la sinopsis griego-castellano. — *Boletín de la SAPSE* 8 (1974) 37-41.

1975 ¿Una inversión de todo orden? [19,13-15] — *RevistBíb* 37 (1975) 245-255. [NTA 20, 391]

1976 Jesús camina sobre las aguas. Un relato apocalíptico. [14,22-33] — *RevistBíb* 38 (1976) 311-319. [NTA 21, 749]

1977 El llamado grupo de los "Doce" y el de los "Siete". — *RevistBíb* 39 (1977) 97-115. [NTA 22, 910]

1978 La venida imprevista del Señor. — *RevistBíb* 40 (1978) 201-216. Esp. 213-215 [25,1-13]; 216 [24,43-44]. [NTA 23, 993]

1979 Bienaventurados los mansos porque ello heredarán la tierra. [5,5] — *RevistBíb* 41 (1979) 239-243. [NTA 24, 786]

1983 La paz y el amor a los enemigos. [5,43-48] — *RevistBíb* 45 (1983) 1-15. [NTA 28, 91]

**LOSIE, Lynn Allan**

1985 *The Cleansing of the Temple. A History of a Gospel Tradition in Light of Its Background in the Old Testament and in Early Judaism* [21,10-17]. Diss. Fuller Theol. Sem., Pasadena, CA, 1985, 383 p. (D. Hagner). — *DissAbstr* 46 (1985-86) 1323.

1992 Triumphal Entry. — *DJG*, 1992, 854-859. Esp. 856-857 [21,1-10].

**LOSKI, Tadeusza**

1995 *Ewangelia według św. Mateusza: 2 Komentarzem.* Katowice: Wyd. Ksiegarnia św. Jacka, 1995, 316 p.

**LOUW, Johannes P.**

1967 Δικαιοσύνη. [5,6.10.20; 6,1.33] — *Neotestamentica* 1 (1967) 35-41. [NTA 18, 102]

1977 The Structure of Mt 8:1–9:35. — *Neotestamentica* 11 (1977) 91-97 (addendum, 18-24).

1993 The Analysis of Meaning in Lexicography. — *FilolNT* 6 (1993) 139-148. Esp. 141-142 [4,3; 5,34; 26,15]. [NTA 38, 1255] → J.A.L. Lee 1992

**LOVE, Stuart L.**

1993 The Household: A Major Social Component for Gender Analysis in the Gospel of Matthew. — *BTB* 23 (1993) 21-31. [NTA 37, 1241]

1994 The Place of Women in Public Settings in Matthew's Gospel: A Sociological Inquiry. — *BTB* 24 (1994) 52-65. [NTA 39, 1441]

**LOVISON, Tino**

1971 La pericopa della Cananea *Mt*. 15,21-28. — *RivBib* 19 (1971) 273-305. Esp. 274-272 [14,13-16,12]; 282-285 [structure 15,21-28]; 285-303 [15,21-28]. [NTA 16, 862]

**LOVSKY, Fadiey**

1959 A Rendering May Be Anti-Semitic. [27,25] — *BTrans* 10 (1959) 47.

1987 Comment comprendre "Son sang sur nous et nos enfants"? — *ETR* 62 (1987) 343-362. [NTA 32, 609]

**LOWE, John**

1956 *Saint Peter*. Oxford: Clarendon, 1956, 65 p. Esp. 46-65: "The primacy of Peter".

1962 *The Lord's Prayer*. Oxford: University Press; London: Clarendon, 1962, IX-68 p. [NTA 7, p. 392]
B. FRID, *SvenskTeolKvart* 43 (1967) 50.

**LOWE, Malcolm**

1976 Who Were the Ἰουδαῖοι? — *NT* 18 (1976) 101-130. Esp. 110-111 [Israel]; 112-114 [Judea]; 118-119 [King of the Jews]; 126-127 [28,15]. [NTA 21, 328]

1982a The Demise of Arguments from Order for Markan Priority. — *NT* 24 (1982) 27-36. [NTA 26, 834] → Fee 1980

1982b From the Parable of the Vineyard to a Pre-Synoptic Source. — *NTS* 28 (1982) 257-263. [NTA 26, 847]

1983 & FLUSSER, D., Evidence Corroborating a Modified Proto-Matthean Synoptic Theory. — *NTS* 29 (1983) 25-47. Esp. 28-30 [8,5-10.13]; 30-33 [12,9-14]; 33-35 [14,1-2]; 35-40 [13,1-23.31-35]. [NTA 27, 496]

1987 Real and Imagined Anti-Jewish Elements in the Synoptic Gospels and Acts. — *JEcuSt* 24 (1987) 267-284. Esp. 271-276, 282. [NTA 32, 571]

1990 A Hebraic Approach to the Parable of the Laborers in the Vineyard. [21,33-46] — *Immanuel* 24-25 (1990) 109-117.

**LOWERY, David K.**

1987 *God as Father with Special Reference to Matthew's Gospel*. Diss. Univ. Aberdeen, 1987, 392 p. — *DissAbstr* 50 (1989-90) 3989-3990.

**LOZA, José**

1989 *Las Palabras de Yahve. Estudio del Decalogo*. Mexico: Univ. Pont. de Mexico, 1989, 388 p. Esp. 319-329: "En los Evangelios".

**LUCAS, Nico** → Cambe 1979

**LUCK, Ulrich**

1967 Herrenwort und Geschichte in Matth. 28,16-20. — *EvT* 27 (1967) 494-508. [NTA 12, 560]

1968 *Die Vollkommenheitsforderung der Bergpredigt. Ein aktuelles Kapitel der Theologie des Matthäus* (Theologische Existenz heute, NF 150). München: Kaiser, 1968, 62 p. Esp. 13-19: "Die Bergpredigt im Matthäusevangelium"; 20-38: "Die Voraussetzungen der Bergpredigt"; 39-48: "Das theologische Ziel des Evangelisten Matthäus"; 49-56: "Jesus und Matthäus". [NTA 13, p. 270]

1975 Weisheit und Christologie in Mt 11,25-30. — *WDienst* 13 (1975) 35-52.

1979 Inwiefern ist die Botschaft von Jesus Christus "Evangelium"? — *ZTK* 76 (1979) 24-41. Esp. 37-39 [Q 7,22].

1986 Die Frage nach dem Guten. Zu Mt 19,16-30 und Par. — SCHRAGE, W. (ed.), *Studien zum Text und zur Ethik des Neuen Testaments*. FS H. Greeven, 1986, 282-297.

1993 *Das Evangelium nach Matthäus* (Zürcher Bibelkommentare, 1). Zürich: Theologischer Verlag, 1993, 324 p. Esp. 13-17: "Das Matthäusevangelium und sein Verfasser"; 19-318: "Auslegung". [NTA 38, p. 462]
E. CUVILLIER, *ETR* 71 (1996) 82-83; A. FUCHS, *SNTU* 19 (1994) 215-216.

**LUCK, William F.**

1987 *Divorce and Remarriage. Recovering the Biblical View*. San Francisco, CA: Harper & Row, 1987, XII-317 p. Esp. 86-110.284-287 [5,31-32a]; 111-129.287-290 [5,32b/Lk 16,18]; 130-158.290-294 [19,3-12/Mk].

**LUCKHART, Robert**

1953 Matthew 11,27 in the "Contra Haereses" of St. Irenaeus. — *RevUnivOtt* 23 (1953) 65*-79*.

**LUDLUM, John H.**

1958 New Light on the Synoptic Problem. — *ChrTod* 3/3 (1958) 6-9; 3/4 (1958) 10-14.

1959 Are We Sure of Mark's Priority? — *ChrTod* 3/24 (1959) 11-14; 3/25 (1959) 9-10. [NTA 4, 375]

**LUDOLPHY, Ingetraut**

1973 Zur Geschichte der Auslegung des Evangelium infantium. — KRAUSE, G. (ed.), *Die Kinder im Evangelium* (Praktische Schriftauslegung, 10). Stuttgart–Göttingen: Klotz, 1973, 31-51. Esp. 34-35.39-50 [19,13-15].

**LUDWIG, Joseph**

1952 *Die Primatworte Mt 16,18.19 in der altkirchlichen Exegese* (NTAbh, 19/4). Münster: Aschendorff, 1952, VIII-112 p. Esp. 7-36: "Mt 16,18.19 in der Exegese des Abendlandes bis zum Tode Cyprians"; 37-57: "Mt 16,18.19 in der Exegese des Morgenlandes bis zum Tode des Johannes Chrysostoms"; 58-94: "Mt 16,18.19 im Abendland von Papst Stephan I. bis zu Papst Leo I"; 95-112: "Epilog". — Diss. Würzburg, 1946.
    H. BACHT, *Scholastik* 28 (1953) 281-283; P. BENOIT, *RB* 61 (1954) 310-311; B. BOTTE, *RTAM* 6 (1953) 574-575; P.T. CAMELOT, *RSPT* 37 (1953) 499-500; P. GAECHTER, *ZKT* 74 (1952) 485; B. LEMER, *Angelicum* 30 (1953) 296; P. NOBER, *Bib* 36 (1955) 529-532.

**LUDWIG, Martina**

1994 *Wort als Gesetz. Eine Untersuchung zum Verständnis von "Wort" und "Gesetz" in israelitisch-frühjüdischen und neutestamentlichen Schriften. Gleichzeitig ein Beitrag zur Theologie des Jakobusbriefes* (EHS, XXIII/502). Frankfurt/M: Lang, 1994, 217 p. Esp. 92-94 [15,1-9]; 95-97 [ϑέλημα]; 99-100 [7,24-27; Q 6,47-49]; 100-10ι [5,18; Q 16,17]; 102 [24,35]; 103-104 [19,16-22]; 104-107 [22,34-40]; 107-108 [law]. — Diss. Heidelberg, 1991 (H.-W. Kuhn).

**LÜDEMANN, Gerd**

1994 *Die Auferstehung Jesu. Historie, Erfahrung, Theologie* Göttingen: Vandenhoeck & Ruprecht; Stuttgart: Radius, 1994, 275 p. Esp. 138-153: "Die Ostergeschichten bei Matthäus".
    *The Resurrection of Jesus. History, Experience, Theology.* London: SCM; Minneapolis, MN: Fortress, 1994, VIII-263 p.

1995 *Was mit Jesus wirklich geschah. Die Auferstehung historisch betrachtet.* Stuttgart: Radius, 1995, 139 p.
    *What Really Happened to Jesus: A Historical Approach to the Resurrection*, trans. J. Bowden. London: SCM, 1995, IX-147 p. Esp. 48-60: "The Easter event according to Matthew".

**LÜHRMANN, Dieter**

1969 *Die Redaktion der Logienquelle* (WMANT, 33). Neukirchen-Vluyn: Neukirchener, 1969, 138 p. Esp. 24-48: "Jesus und 'dieses Geschlecht'" [Q 3,7-9.17; 7,18-35; 11,14-26.29-32.39-52]; 49-68: "Die Gemeinde" [Q 6,20-49; 7,1-10; 9,57-62; 10,2-12.13-15.21-22; 12,2-9]; 69-83: "Die Eschatologie" [Q 12,39-40.42-46; 17,24.26-30.34-35.37; 19,12-27]; 84-104: "Q in der Geschichte des Urchristentums"; 105-121: "Zur weiteren Überlieferung der Logienquelle". — Diss. Heidelberg, 1968 (G. Bornkamm). → Hoffmann 1992b, Luz 1973
    H.D. BETZ, *TLZ* 96 (1971) 428-429; G. DAUTZENBERG, *WissWeish* 35 (1972) 232-233; J. DUPONT, *RivStoLR* 6 (1970) 399-402; H.K. MCARTHUR, *CBQ* 33 (1971) 445-447; P.D. MEYER, *JBL* 89 (1970) 367-368; J. MURPHY-O'CONNOR, *RB* 80 (1973) 132-133; R. SCHNACKENBURG, *BZ* 15 (1971) 279-281; E. SCHWEIZER, *EvT* 30 (1970) 624-626.

    Q in the History of Early Christianity. [1969, 84-104] — KLOPPENBORG, J.S. (ed.), *The Shape of Q*, 1994, 59-73.

1972a Liebet eure Feinde (Lk 6,27-36 / Mt 5,39-48). — *ZTK* 69 (1972) 412-438. [NTA 17, 972]

1972b   Noah und Lot (Lk 17,26-29) – ein Nachtrag. [24,37-39] — *ZNW* 63 (1972) 130-132. [NTA 17, 977]

1976   *Glaube im frühen Christentum.* Gütersloh: Mohn, 1976, 99 p. Esp. 17-30: "Jesus" [8,5-13; 17,20; 21,21].

1977   Jesus und seine Propheten. Gesprächsbeitrag. — PANAGOPOULOS, J. (ed.), *Prophetic Vocation in the New Testament and Today* (SupplNT, 45), Leiden: Brill, 1977, 210-217. Esp. 210-214.

1984   *Auslegung des Neuen Testaments* (Zürcher Grundrisse zur Bibel). Zürich: Theologischer Verlag, 1984, ²1987, 122 p.
       *An Itinerary for New Testament Study.* London: SCM, 1989, IX-131 p.

1987   Das Bruchstück aus dem Hebräerevangelium bei Didymos von Alexandrien. — *NT* 29 (1987) 265-279. [NTA 32, 472]

1989   The Gospel of Mark and the Sayings Collection Q. — *JBL* 108 (1989) 51-71. Esp. 51-60: "The history of research"; 63-66: "Christology"; 66-69: "Eschatology"; 69-71: "Ecclesiology". [NTA 33, 1104]

1993   POx 4009: ein neues Fragment des Petrusevangeliums? — *NT* 35 (1993) 390-410. Esp. 392-401 [10,16.28]. [NTA 39, 1179]

1995   Q: Sayings of Jesus or Logia? — PIPER, R.A. (ed.), *The Gospel Behind the Gospels*, 1995, 97-116. Esp. 98-102 [Papias]; 102-112 [genre]; 112-116 [POxy/Th].

**LÜLSDORFF, Raimund**

1990   Vom Stein zum Felsen. Anmerkungen zur biblischen Begründung des Petrusamtes nach Mt 16,18. — *Catholica* 44 (1990) 274-283. [NTA 35, 1137]

**LÜTHI, Kurt**

1956   Das Problem des Judas Iskariot – neu untersucht. — *EvT* 16 (1956) 98-114. Esp. 99-108: "Synoptisches".

**LÜTHI, Walter**

1936ᴿ   & BRUNNER, R., *The Sermon on the Mount* [German, 1936], trans. K. Schoenenberger. Edinburgh–London: Oliver and Boyd, 1963, X-172 p. [NTA 8, p. 467]
       J. BLIGH, *HeythJ* 5 (1964) 356-357; C. HAY, *AusBR* 12 (1965) 60-61.

1946ᴿ   *The Lord's Prayer. An Exposition* [German, 1946], trans. K. Schoenenberger. Edinburgh–London: Oliver & Boyd, 1961, 103 p.; Richmond, VA: Knox, 1962, VII-103 p.
       *ExpT* 73 (1961-62) 129-130; J. BISHOP, *PrincSemB* 55/3 (1961-62) 100-101; J. GARRETT, *AusBR* 10 (1962) 48-49; I.H. MARSHALL, *EvQ* 34 (1962) 49; J.T. MUELLER, *ChrTod* 6 (1961-62) 648-649.

1962   & BRUNNER, R., *Die Seligpreisungen ausgelegt für die Gemeinde.* Basel: Reinhardt, 1962, 130 p.
       *Les Béatitudes*, trans. R. Revet (La foi et la vie). Neuchâtel–Paris: Delachaux et Niestlé, 1963, 126 p.
       I. MAUSOLF, *CBQ* 26 (1964) 146.

**LUIS IGLESIAS, Angel**

1974   San José en Mt 1-2 según el pensamiento de El Tostado. — *EstJos* 28 (1974) 199-245.

1976   Mt 1-2 en Maldonado. — *EstJos* 30 (1976) 41-70. Esp. 46-70.

1985   Paternidad de San José en Francisco de Toledo y Juan de Maldonado. — *EstJos* 39 (1985) 47-70. Esp. 63-70 [Maldonatus].

**LUKE, K.**

1985   The Ethiopic Version of the Bible. — *Bible Bhashyam* 11 (1985) 170-188, 236-253. Esp. 245-247.252. [NTA 30, 974]

1986   The Georgian Version of the Bible. — *Bible Bhashyam* 12 (1986) 59-79, 248-262. Esp. 249-252. [NTA 31, 53/979]

1990 The Syriac Text of Matthew 11:29b and John 1:32-33. — *Bible Bhashyam* 16 (1990) 250-267. Esp. 250-254 [text]; 254-265 [Syriac tradition]. [NTA 35, 1133]

1992 The Old Syriac Version of the Bible. — *Bible Bhashyam* 18 (1992) 105-123. Esp. 119-121. [NTA 37, 1151]

1993 The Syriac Versions of the New Testament. — *Bible Bhashyam* 19 (1993) 300-314. Esp. 306-312 [11,28-29]. [NTA 38, 1247]; 20 (1994) 124-138. Esp. 136-138. [NTA 39, 1345]

1994 The Thirty Pieces of Silver. [26,15] — *IndianTS* 31 (1994) 156-158. [NTA 39, 813]

**LUKKEN, Gerard**

1983 & DE MAAT, P. - RIJKHOFF, M. - TROMP, N., Matteüs 2. Een semiotische analyse. — *Reflecties op Schrift. Opstellen voor prof. dr. Gijs Bouwman svd bij gelegenheid van zijn afscheid als hoogleraar in de uitleg van het Nieuwe Testament aan de Theologische Faculteit Tilburg* (Cahiers voor levensverdieping, 44), Averbode–Apeldoorn: Altiora, 1983, 65-100.

**LUND, Nils W.**

1942R *Chiasmus in the New Testament. A Study in Formgeschichte* [1942]. Chapel Hill: Univ. of North Carolina Press, 1970.
*Chiasmus in the New Testament. A Study in the Form and Function of Chiastic Structures.* Peabody, MA: Hendrickson, 1992, xxx-428 p. Esp. 240-261: "The Sermon on the Mount"; 262-271: "The missionary discourse"; 272-281: "Discourses on authority and the law" [12,22-45; 15,1-20]; 282-301: "The discourse against the Pharisees".

**LUNDE, Jonathan**

1992 Repentance. — *DJG*, 1992, 669-673. Esp. 672.

**LUNDMARK, Knut**

1950 Till frågan om Messiasidéns och den nytestamentliga eskatologiens ursprung och utveckling. — *SvenskTeolKvart* 26 (1950) 346-368. Esp. 352-354 [2,1-12].
*Sur le problème de l'origine et de l'évolution de l'idée du Messie et de l'eschatologie du Nouveau Testament* (Lunds Universitets Årsskrift, NF 2,49/11; Kungl. Fysiografiska Sällskapets Handlingar, NF 64/11). Lund: Gleerup, 1954, 25 p. Esp. 9-10.

**LUNDSTRÖM, Gösta**

1947R *The Kingdom of God in the Teaching of Jesus. A History of Interpretation from the Last Decades of the Nineteenth Century to the Present Day* [Swedish, 1947], trans. J. Bulman. Edinburgh: Oliver & Boyd, 1963, XIV-300 p.

**LUNNY, William J.**

1989 *The Sociology of the Resurrection.* London: SCM, 1989, IX-146 p. Esp. 11-13 [28,1-10].

**LUPIERI, Edmondo**

1984a L'arconte dell'utero. Contributo per una storia dell'esegesi della figura di Giovanni Battista, con particolare attenzione alle problematiche emergenti nel secondo secolo. — *AnStoEseg* 1 (1984) 165-199. Esp. 189-191 [3,16-17].

1984b John the Baptist, the First Monk. — *Word and Spirit* (Still River, MA) 6 (1984) 11-23.

1988a *Giovanni Battista fra storia e leggenda* (Biblioteca di cultura religiosa, 53). Brescia: Paideia, 1988, 475 p. Esp. 97-118: "Matteo".

1988b *Giovanni Battista nelle tradizioni sinottiche* (Studi biblici, 82). Brescia: Paideia, 1988, 126 p.

1992a El bautismo de Juan entre judaismo y cristianismo. — *EstTrin* 25 (1992) 225-247.

1992b John the Baptist in New Testament Traditions and History. — *ANRW* II.26.1 (1992) 430-461. Esp. 447-449: "Matthew's redaction".

1994  Una recente pubblicazione su Giovanni Battista. — *CrnStor* 15 (1994) 137-144. [NTA 39, 83r] → J. Ernst 1989a

**LUSCOMB, J.A.**

1987  The Hebraic Background of Jesus' Beatitudes (Matthew 5,1-10). Diss. Oral Roberts University, 1987, 253 p.

**LUTER, Asa Boyd**

1992  Great Commission, The. — *ABD* 2 (1992) 1090-1091. Esp. 1091.

1995  Women Disciples and the Great Commission. — *TrinJ* 16 (1995) 171-185. Esp. 172-177 [28,16-20]. [NTA 40, 1471]

**LUTTIKHUIZEN, Gerard P.**

1991  Vroeg-christelijk jodendom. — BAARDA, T., et al. (eds.), *Jodendom en vroeg christendom*, 1991, 163-189. Esp. 170-171 [law]; 174-179 [Jewish-christian gospels].

**LUX, Rüdinger**

1991  Das Erbe der Gewaltlosen. Überlegungen zu Mt 5,5 und seiner Vorgeschichte. — MEINHOLD, A. - LUX, R. (eds.), *Gottesvolk. Beiträge zu einem Thema biblischer Theologie*. [FS Siegfried Wagner], Berlin: Evangelische Verlagsanstalt, 1991, 75-90. Esp. 76-81 [5,5]; 81-82 [Qumran]; 83-85 [Ps 37].

**LUZ, Ulrich**

1970  Einige Erwägungen zur Auslegung Gottes in der ethischen Verkündigung Jesu. — *EKK NT Vorarbeiten*, 2, 1970, 119-130; = *Universitas* 28 (1973) 273-282.

1971  Die Jünger im Matthäusevangelium. — *ZNW* 62 (1971) 141-171. Esp. 142-152 [disciples: historicity – idealisation];152-159 [miracle stories]; 159-165 [terminology]; 165-171 [tradition]. [NTA 16, 844]; = LANGE, J. (ed.), *Das Matthäus-Evangelium*, 1980, 377-414. Esp. 378-386; 386-391; 391-397; 397-401 (401-414, notes).
The Disciples in the Gospel according to Matthew. — STANTON, G. (ed.), *The Interpretation of Matthew*, 1983, 98-128. Esp. 99-105; 105-110; 110-114; 115-119 (119-128, notes); ²1995, 115-148. Esp. 116-123; 123-128; 128-133; 133-137 (138-148, notes).

1973  Die wiederentdeckte Logienquelle. — *EvT* 33 (1973) 527-533. [NTA 18, 453r] → Hoffmann 1972, Lührmann 1969, Polag 1977/69, S. Schulz 1972a

1975  Das Jesusbild der vormarkinischen Tradition. — STRECKER, G. (ed.), *Jesus Christus in Historie und Theologie*. FS H. Conzelmann, 1975, 347-374. Esp. 352-359: "Die Eschatologie der vormarkinischen Überlieferung".

1978  Die Erfüllung des Gesetzes bei Matthäus (Mt 5,17-20). — *ZTK* 75 (1978) 398-435. Esp. 401-412; 412-431 [5,17-20]; 431-435: "Matthäus und Paulus". [NTA 23, 820]

1981a  Die Bergpredigt im Spiegel ihrer Wirkungsgeschichte. — MOLTMANN, J. (ed.), *Nachfolge und Bergpredigt*, 1981, 37-72. Esp. 39-47 [5,3-12]; 47-62 [5,17-48].

1981b  Gesetz. III. Das Neue Testament. — SMEND, R. - LUZ, U., *Gesetz* (Kohlhammer Taschenbücher - Biblische Konfrontationen, 1015), Stuttgart: Kohlhammer, 1981, 58-139. Esp. 79-86: "Das Gesetz bei Matthäus".

1982  Jesus und die Pharisäer. — *Judaica* 38 (1982) 229-246. [NTA 27, 884]

1983*  & WEDER, H. (eds.), *Die Mitte des Neuen Testaments. Einheit und Vielfalt neutestamentlicher Theologie. Festschrift für Eduard Schweizer zum siebzigsten Geburtstag*. Göttingen: Vandenhoeck & Ruprecht, 1983, XI-437 p. → F. Hahn, Holtz, Kohler, S. Schulz, Stalder, I. Yamauchi

1983a  Sermon on the Mount/Plain: Reconstruction of Q^Mt and Q^Lk. — *SBL 1983 Seminar Papers*, 473-479.

1983b  → P. Lampe 1983

1984    Q 3-4. — *SBL 1984 Seminar Papers*, 375-376.

1985a   *Das Evangelium nach Matthäus*. 1. Teilband: *Mt 1-7* (EKK NT, I/1). Zürich: Benziger; Neukirchen-Vluyn: Neukirchener, 1985, XI-420 p. [NTA 30, p. 98]; ²1989. Esp. 15-82: "Einleitung"; 83-420. → Giesen 1987b, G. Maier 1987, Neidhardt 1986, H. Riniker 1987

P. BEENTJES, *Streven* 53 (1985-86) 380-381; S. BROWN, *CBQ* 49 (1987) 150-151; A. FUCHS, *SNTU* 12 (1987) 221-223; G. LOHFINK, *TQ* 165 (1985) 244-245; C. MINETTE DE TILLESSE, *RevistBíbBras* 4 (1987) 169-170; M. MÜLLER, *DanskTeolTids* 49 (1986) 300-301; F. NEIRYNCK, *ETL* 63 (1987) 410-413; V. PASQUETTO, *Teresianum* 37 (1986) 503-504; R. PENNA, *Greg* 68 (1987) 392-394; E. SCHWEIZER, *EvT* 45 (1985) 91-92; A. STÖGER, *BLtg* 59 (1986) 141-142; S. VAN TILBORG, *TijdTheol* 26 (1986) 295; F. VOUGA, *ETR* 61 (1986) 429-430.

*Matthew 1-7. A Commentary*, trans. W.C. Linss. Minneapolis, MN: Augsburg, 1989, 460 p. [NTA 35, p. 103]

H.J.B. COMBRINK, *Neotestamentica* 25 (1991) 445-446; M. DAVIES, *NBlackfr* 72 (1991) 346-347; E. FARAHIAN, *Greg* 76 (1995) 382-385; D.A. HAGNER, *JBL* 111 (1992) 539-542; D.E. HOLWERDA, *CalvTJ* 29 (1994) 211-212; P.M. MEAGHER, *Vidyajyoti* 55 (1991) 228-230; C.J. MONAGHAN, *Pacifica* 4 (1991) 346-350; R. OBERFORCHER, *ZKT* 113 (1991) 299-300; M.A. POWELL, *Interpr* 45 (1991) 294-296; J.-M. ROUSÉE, *RB* 97 (1990) 635-636; C.M. TUCKETT, *ScotJT* 45 (1992) 114-116.

*El Evangelio segun San Mateo. Mt 1-7*, trans. M. Olasagasti Gaztelumendi (Biblioteca de estudios bíblicos, 74). Salamanca: Sígueme, 1993, 589 p.

X. ALEGRE, *ActBibl* 31 (1994) 220-221; P. BARRADO FERNANDEZ, *RevistEspTeol* 53 (1993) 493-497; S. CARILLO-ALDAY, *EphMex* 12 (1994) 263-265; R.A. DÍEZ, *EstAgust* 29 (1994) 170; J.L. ESPINEL, *CiTom* 121 (1994) 199-200; F.F. RAMOS, *NatGrac* 40 (1993) 164; S. SABUGAL, *Revista Agustiniana* (Madrid) 35 (1994) 740-741; R. SANZ VALDIVIESO, *Carthaginensia* 10 (1994) 454-455.

Trans. Japanese 1990.

*Das Evangelium nach Matthäus*. 2. Teilband: *Mt 8-17* (EKK NT, I/2). Zürich: Benziger; Neukirchen-Vluyn: Neukirchener, 1990, XIII-537 p. Esp. 5-537: "Kommentar". [NTA 36, p. 111] → A. Fuchs 1992b, Limbeck 1994

A. FUCHS, *SNTU* 16 (1991) 209-211; M. MÜLLER, *DanskTeolTids* 55 (1992) 151-152; F. NEIRYNCK, *ETL* 67 (1991) 169-171; J. PAINTER, *AusBR* 40 (1992) 88-89; C.S. RODD, *ExpT* 104 (1992-93) 150; A. SALAS, *BibFe* 20 (1994) 175.

*Das Evangelium nach Matthäus*. 3. Teilband: *Mt 18-25* (EKK NT, I/3). Zürich: Benziger; Neukirchen-Vluyn: Neukirchener, 1997, XII-561 p. → Neirynck 1998

1985b   Q 10:2-16; 11:14-23. — *SBL 1985 Seminar Papers*, 101-102.

1985c   Wirkungsgeschichtliche Exegese. Ein programmatischer Arbeitsbericht mit Beispielen aus der Bergpredigtexegese. — *BTZ* 2 (1985) 18-32. [NTA 31, 508]

1987    Die Wundergeschichten von Mt 8-9. — HAWTHORNE, G.F. – BETZ, O. (eds.), *Tradition and Interpretation*. FS E.E. Ellis, 1987, 149-165. Esp. 149-152 [structure]; 152-155 [context]; 155-158 [plot]; 158-159.159-161.

1989a   Charisma und Institution in neutestamentlicher Sicht. — *EvT* 49 (1989) 76-94. Esp. 89-90. [NTA 33, 1033]

      *SelT* 29 (1990) 17-28.

1989b   Die Jüngerrede des Matthäus als Anfrage an die Ekklesiologie oder: Exegetische Prolegomena zu einer dynamischen Ekklesiologie. — KERTELGE, K., et al. (eds.), *Christus bezeugen*. FS W. Trilling, 1989, 84-101. Esp. 84-89: "Die grundsätzliche Gültigkeit der Aussendungsrede"; 89-97: "Grundlegende 'notae' der Kirche nach Mt 10"; 97-101: "Die ekklesiologische Bedeutung der matthäischen Jüngerrede".

1989c   Das Matthäusevangelium und die Perspektive einer biblischen Theologie. — *JbBT* 4 (1989) 233-248. Esp. 236-237.241-242 [prophets]; 237-238.242-244 [law]; 238-239 [christology]; 239-240.244-246 [OT].

1989d   Vom Taumellolch im Weizenfeld. Ein Beispiel wirkungsgeschichtlicher Hermeneutik. — FRANKEMÖLLE, H. – KERTELGE, K. (eds.), *Vom Urchristentum zu Jesus*. FS J. Gnilka, 1989, 154-171. Esp. 158-163: "Die matthäische Deutung" [13,36-43]; 164-171: "Überlegungen zur Wirkungsgeschichte".

1990 → 1985a

1991a L'évangéliste Matthieu: un judéo-chrétien à la croisée des chemins. Réflexions sur le plan narratif du premier évangile. — MARGUERAT, D. - ZUMSTEIN, J. (eds.), *La mémoire et le temps*. FS P. Bonnard, 1991, 77-92. Esp. 77-81: "Composition"; 81-88: "Histoire"; 88-92: "Narration".

1991b Jesus der Menschensohn zwischen Juden und Christen. — MARCUS, M., et al. (eds.), *Israel und Kirche heute. Beiträge zum christlich-jüdischen Dialog [Für Ernst Ludwig Ehrlich]*, Freiburg–Basel–Wien: Herder, 1991, 212-223.

1991c The Primacy Text (Mt. 16:18). — *PrincSemB* 12 (1991) 41-55. Esp. 42-44: "Hermeneutical presuppositions"; 44-49: "Exegetical remarks"; 49-52: "The history of effects of Mt. 16:18"; 52-55: "Hermeneutical conclusions". [NTA 35, 1138] → 1991d

1991d Das Primatwort Matthäus 16.17-19 aus wirkungsgeschichtlicher Sicht. — *NTS* 37 (1991) 415-433. Esp. 415-417: "Das Problem"; 417-422: "Zur Wirkungsgeschichte"; 422-427: "Zur Exegese"; 427-433: "Hermeneutische Überlegungen". [NTA 36, 154] → 1991c

1991e Eine thetische Skizze der matthäischen Christologie. — BREYTENBACH, C. — PAULSEN, H. (eds.), *Anfänge der Christologie*. FS F. Hahn, 1991, 221-235. Esp. 221-223: "Die narrative Christologie"; 223-226: "Der Davidssohn"; 226-231: "Menschensohn"; 231-234: "Gottessohn".

1992a Matthew's Anti-Judaism. Its Origin and Contemporary Significance. — *CurrTMiss* 19 (1992) 405-415. [NTA 37, 734]
Der Antijudaismus im Matthäusevangelium als historisches und theologisches Problem. Eine Skizze. — *EvT* 53 (1993) 310-327. Esp. 310-312; 312-317 [21–28]; 317-323: "Historische Überlegungen"; 323-326: "Entlastungsversuche"; 326-327. [NTA 38, 774]
L'antigiudaismo nel vangelo di Matteo come problema storico e teologico: uno schizzo. — *Greg* 74 (1993) 425-445. Esp. 425-428; 428-433; 433-441; 441-444; 444-445. [NTA 38, 167]
Le problème historique et théologique de l'antijudaïsme dans l'évangile de Matthieu. — MARGUERAT, D. (ed.), *Le déchirement. Juifs et chrétiens au premier siècle* (Le Monde de la Bible, 32), Genève: Labor et Fides, 1996, 127-150. Esp. 128-130; 130-136; 136-145; 145-148; 148-150.

1992b The Son of Man in Matthew: Heavenly Judge or Human Christ. — *JSNT* 48 (1992) 3-21. Esp. 7-10: "The meaning of the expression 'son of the man'"; 10-17: "Son of the man in the Matthean narrative". [NTA 37, 1242]

1993a *Die Jesusgeschichte des Matthäus*. Neukirchen-Vluyn: Neukirchener, 1993, 181 p. Esp. 11-32: "Das Buch"; 33-53 [1–4]; 54-74 [5–7]; 96-115 [12,1–16,20]; 116-132 [16,21–20,34]; 133-149 [21–25]; 150-158 [26–28]. [NTA 38, p. 463]
I. BROER, *TLZ* 120 (1995) 343-344; W.C. LINNS, *CRBR* 7 (1994) 223-224; T. SÖDING, *TRev* 90 (1994) 381-383.
*The Theology of the Gospel of Matthew*, trans. J.B. Robinson (New Testament Theology). Cambridge: University Press, 1995, xiv-166 p. [NTA 40, p. 145]
J.T. CARROLL, *Interpr* 51 (1997) 297-299; W. CARTER, *JBL* 116 (1997) 145-146; S.P. KEALY, *CBQ* 59 (1997) 155-156.

1993b Fiktivität und Traditionstreue im Matthäusevangelium im Lichte griechischer Literatur. — *ZNW* 84 (1993) 153-177. Esp. 155-162: "Der Befund bei Matthäus". [NTA 38, 742]

1993c Korreferat zu W.R. Farmer, The Minor Agreements of Matthew and Luke against Mark and the Two Gospel Hypothesis. — STRECKER, G. (ed.), *Minor Agreements*, 1993, 209-220. Esp. 213-219: "Zu den Modeltexten". → W.R. Farmer 1991/93

1994 *Matthew in History: Interpretation, Influence and Effects* [10; 16,17-19]. Philadelphia, PA: Fortress; Minneapolis, MN: Augsburg, 1994, 108 p. [NTA 40, p. 145]

1996 The Final Judgment (Matt 25:31-46): An Exercise in "History of Influence" Exegesis. — BAUER, D.R. - POWELL, M.A. (eds.), *Treasures New and Old*, 1996, 271-310. Esp. 273-286: "History of interpretation and history of influence of Matt 25:31-46"; 286-292: "Analysis"; 292-308: "Interpretation"; 308-310: "Towards the sense of the text for today".

1997 → 1985a

**LUZARRAGA, Jesús**

1973 *Las tradiciónes de la nube en la Biblia y en el judaismo primitivo* (AnBib, 54). Roma: Biblical Institute Press, 1973, 306 p. Esp. 212-220 [17,5]; 227-228 [24,30; 26,64]. — Diss. Pont. Inst. Bibl., Roma, 1971 (R. Le Déaut).

1977 Discernimiento espiritual en las tentaciones de Jesús y de la Iglesia. — *Manresa* 49 (1977) 129-142. [NTA 22, 82]

1994 Lo simbólico de la mujer en la genealogía mateana. [1,1-17] — ARANDA, G., et al. (eds.), *Biblia, Exegesis y Cultura*. FS J.M. Casciaro, 1994, 295-310.

**LYBAEK, Lena**

1997 Matthew's Use of Hosea 6,6 in the Context of the Sabbath Controversies. — TUCKETT, C.M. (ed.), *The Scriptures in the Gospels*, 1997, 491-499.

**LYNCH, William E.**

1967 *Jesus in the Synoptic Gospels* (Impact Books). Milwaukee, WI: Bruce, 1967, XVI-132 p.

**LYON, Jeffrey Paul**

1994 *Syriac Gospel Translations: A Comparison of the Language and Translation Method Used in the Old Syriac, the Diatessaron, and the Peshitto* (CSCO, 548). Leuven: Peeters, 1994, XXIV-235 p. Esp. 41-74 [18,1-20]; 212-214 [.9,16-24]. — Diss. Univ. of California, 1991 (S. Stegert).

**LYON, Robert W.**

1959 A Re-examination of Codex Ephraemi Rescriptus. — *NTS* 5 (1958-59) 260-272. Esp. 266-267. [NTA 4, 333]

**LYONNET, Stanislas**

1950 *Les origines de la version arménienne et le Diatessaron* (Biblica et Orientalia, 13). Roma: Pontificio Istituto Biblico, 1950, 9*-302 p. Esp. 17-20 [11,28]; 20-22 [12,40]; 32-43: "Citations de S. Matthieu"; 101-110: "Chrysostome: les homélies sur S. Matthieu"; 206-224: "Leçons d'Aphraate syriaque" [2,9; 3,9; 5,18; 6,12; 7,1.14.25.27; 8,25; 13,1-9.45-46; 16,26; 24,2; 25,21.23.41]; 225-234: "Leçons non harmonisantes".

1954 L'étude du milieu littéraire et l'exégèse du Nouveau Testament. À propos de quelques publications récentes. — *Bib* 35 (1954) 480-502. Esp. 488-489 [3,15]; 36 (1955) 202-212; 37 (1956) 1-38. → Descamps 1950

1970 & SABOURIN, L., *Sin, Redemption, and Sacrifice. A Biblical and Patristic Study* (AnBib, 48). Roma: Biblical Institute Press, 1970, XVI-351 p. Esp. 31-36 [sin]; 87-90.112-115 [redemption].

1972 L'eucaristia sacrificio della Nuova Alleanza (Mt 26,68 par; 1 Cor 11,23). — ID., *Il Nuovo Testamento alla luce dell'Antico. VII Settimana Biblica del Clero, Napoli, Luglio 1968* (Studi Biblici Pastorali dell'Associazione Biblica Italiana, 3), Brescia: Paideia, 1972, 67-85.

**LYS, Daniel**

1970 Mon corps, c'est ceci (Notule sur Mt 26/26-28 et par.). — *ETR* 45 (1970) 389. [NTA 15, 509]

1989 Contre le salut par les œuvres dans la prédication des talents. [25,14-30] — *ETR* 64 (1989) 331-340. [NTA 34, 132]

# M

**MAAN, P.J.**

1962 Die Exegese von Matth. 16,18-19. — *Internationale kirchliche Zeitschrift* (Bern) 52 (1962) 100-107.

**MAARTENS, Pieter Jacobus**

1977 The Cola Structure of Matthew 6. — *Neotestamentica* 11 (1977) 48-76 (addendum, 12-15).

1982 The Structuring Principles in Mt 24 and 25 and the Interpretation of the Text. — *Neotestamentica* 16 (1982) 88-117 (addendum, 22-37).

1991 Critical Dialogue in Theory and Practice of Literary Interpretation: A Study of Semiotic Relations in Matthew 5:11 and 12. — *LingBib* 65 (1991) 5-24. [NTA 36, 139]

**MAAS, Paul**

1931ᴿ Ev. Matth. 26,50. [1931] — ID., *Kleine Schriften*, ed. W. Buchwald, München: Beck, 1973, 110-111.

1932ᴿ Weiteres zu Matth. 26,50. [1932] — *Ibid.*, 111-112.

**MAAS, Wilhelm**

1979 *Gott und die Hölle. Studien zum Descensus Christi* (Sammlung Horizonte, NF 14). Einsiedeln: Johannes Verlag, 1979, 339 p. Esp. 67-69 [12,40]; 73-97 [27,51b-53]. — Diss. Freiburg (M. Lehmann).

**MABAKA MA MBUMBA**

1990 *La spécificité de l'agir chrétien selon le Sermon sur la montagne (Mt 5-7). Problème des critères et des fondements*. Diss. Pont. Univ. Lateranensis, Roma, 1990, v-137 p. (L. Alvarez-Verdes). Esp. 12-36: "Structuration de Mt 5-7 au niveau de l'expression formelle"; 37-84: "au niveau sémantique"; 85-108: "au niveau de la composition"; 109-123: "Réflexion herméneutique".

**MACARTHUR, John F., Jr.**

1980 *Kingdom Living Here and Now*. Chicago, IL: Moody, 1980, 191 p.
   W.J. LARKIN, *JEvTS* 23 (1980) 373-374.

1985 *Matthew 1-7* (MacArthur New Testament Commentary). Chicago, IL: Moody, 1985, 505 p.
   W.J. LARKIN, *JEvTS* 30 (1987) 83-84; G.H. LOVIK, *Calvary Baptist Theological Journal* (Lansdale, PA) 3/1 (1987) 70-71; J.F. WALVOORD, *BS* 144 (1987) 236-237.
   *Matthew 8-15*, 1987, 497 p.
   G.S. SHOGREN, *JEvTS* 34 (1991) 418-419.
   *Matthew 24-28*, 1989, VIII-360 p.
   J.F. WALVOORD, *BS* 148 (1991) 126-127.

**MACCAFFREY, James**

1986 Prayer and the Fatherhood of God in Matthew. — *CleR* 71 (1986) 135-141. [NTA 30, 1039]

**MACCOBY, Hyam Z.**

1969 Jesus and Barabbas. — *NTS* 16 (1969-70) 55-60. Esp. 56-58 [ὄχλος]. [NTA 14, 863]

1982 The Washing of Cups. [23,25-26] — *JSNT* 14 (1982) 3-15. [NTA 26, 848]

**MACCORKLE, Douglas Beals**

1961 *Interpretive Problems of the Gospel of Matthew*. Diss. Theol. Sem., Dallas, TX, 1961, 175 p.

**MACCOULL, Leslie S.B.**

1983 Three Coptic Papyri in the Duke University Collection. [1,1] — *Bulletin of the American Society of Papyrologists* (New York) 20 (1983) 137-140.

1989 More Coptic Papyri from the Beinecke Collection. — *Archiv für Papyrusforschung* (Leipzig) 35 (1989) 25-35. Esp. 32-33 [20,1-20].

**MACDONALD, D.**

1989 The Worth of the Assarion. [10,29] — *Historia* (Stuttgart) 38 (1989) 120-123. [NTA 34, 1139]

**MACDOUGALL, Daniel W.**

1988 *The Fig and Fig Tree Imagery in the Gospel of Matthew* [7,16-20; 21,18-22]. Diss. Calvin Sem., Grand Rapids, MI, 1988, III-159 p. (B. Van Elderen).

**MACH, Michael**

1992 Christus mutans: Zur Bedeutung der 'Verklärung Jesu' im Wechsel von jüdischer Messianität zur neutestamentlichen Christologie. — GRUENWALD, I., et al. (eds.), *Messiah and Christos. Studies in the Jewish Origins of Christianity Presented to David Flusser on the Occasion of His Seventy-Fifth Birthday* (Texte und Studien zum antiken Judentum, 32), Tübingen: Mohr, 1992, 177-198.

**MACHINEK, Marian**

1995 *Gesetze oder Weisungen? Die Frage nach der sittlichen Verbindlichkeit neutestamentlicher Aussagen über Moral, verdeutlicht am Beispiel des Scheidungsverbotes Jesu* (Moraltheologische Studien. Systematische Abteilung, 21). St. Ottilien: EOS, 1995, 384 p. Esp. 151-165: "Die neutestamentlichen Scheidungslogien" [5,32; 19,9; Q 16,18]; 165-173: "Das Streitgespräch mit den Pharisäern" [19,3-9]; 174-183: "Die sogenannte Unzuchtsklausel (Mt 5,32; 19,9)". — Diss. Augsburg, 1994 (D. Piegsa).

**MACHOLZ, Christian**

1990 Das "Passivum divinum", seine Anfänge im Alten Testament und der "Hofstil". — *ZNW* 81 (1990) 247-253. Esp. 247-248 [5,4.6.7.9]. [NTA 35, 546]

**MACINA, Robert**

1984 Jean le Baptiste était-il Élie? Examen de la tradition néotestamentaire. — *Proche Orient Chrétien* (Jerusalem) 34 (1984) 209-232. Esp. 214-216 [3,4-6].

**MACK, Burton L.**

1988 The Kingdom That Didn't Come: A Social History of the Q Tradents. — *SBL 1988 Seminar Papers*, 608-635. Esp. 610-620: "A comparison of the literary profiles (Q1 and Q2)"; 620-632: "A reconstruction of social behavior and formation". → H.D. Betz 1994

1989 → Robbins 1989a-d

1990a *Rhetoric and the New Testament* (Guides to Biblical Scholarship. New Testament Series). Minneapolis, MN: Fortress, 1990, 110 p. Esp. 53-54 [5,43-48]; 81-85 [5-7].

1990b Lord of the Logia. Savior or Sage? — GOEHRING, J.E., et al. (eds.), *Gospel Origins*. FS J.M. Robinson, 1990, 3-18. Esp. 5-9: "Apocalyptic and the teachings of Jesus"; 9-12: "Wisdom and the authority of Jesus"; 12-17: "The Holy Spirit and the sayings of Jesus".

1992a The Christ and Jewish Wisdom. — CHARLESWORTH, J.H., et al. (eds.), *The Messiah*, 1992, 192-221. Esp. 209-215.

1992b Q and the Gospel of Mark: Revising Christian Origins. — *Semeia* 55 (1992) 15-39. Esp. 15-21: "Q and the kerygma of christian origins"; 21-30: "Q and the gospel of Mark"; 31-38: "Christian origins after Q". [NTA 36, 1241] → Attridge 1992

1993    *The Lost Gospel. The Book of Q & Christian Origins*. San Francisco, CA:
        HarperCollins, 1993, VII-275 p. Esp. 15-70: "The discovery of a lost gospel"; 71-104: "The text of
        a lost gospel"; 105-190: "The recovery of social experiment"; 191-244: "The reconception of christian
        origins". [NTA 37, p. 439] → G.A. Boyd 1995, Fredriksen 1995, Oakman 1994, Patterson 1993b, J.M.
        Robinson 1995a
            M. BARKER, *HeythJ* 35 (1994) 444-446; S.R. BECHTLER, *PrincSemB* 14 (1993) 302-304; M.E. BORING,
            *Interpr* 49 (1995) 108.110; H.T. COOK, *ATR* 75 (1993) 567-569; M.R. FAIRCHILD, *Christian Scholar's
            Review* 24 (1994) 93-95; A.D. JACOBSON, *CRBR* 8 (1995) 253-257; D.T. LANDRY, *TTod* 50 (1993-94)
            650-652; R.K. MCIVER, *Andrews University Seminary Studies* 33 (1995) 132-134; M. MORELAND,
            *Bulletin of the Institute for Antiquity and Christianity* 20/1 (1993) 13; C. OSIEK, *NewTheolRev* 7/2 (1994)
            104-105; P. PERKINS, *ChrCent* 110 (1993) 749-751.

1995    *Who Wrote the New Testament? The Making of the Christian Myth*. San Francisco, CA:
        HarperCollins, 1995, XI-326 p. Esp. 47-60: "The sayings source Q"; 312-313: "The contents of Q".

**MACKENZIE, Roderick A.F.**

1957    The Messianism of Deuteronomy. — *CBQ* 19 (1957) 299-305. Esp. 303-304.

1960    *Introduction to the New Testament* (The New Testament Reading Guide, 1).
        Collegeville, MN: Liturgical Press, 1960, 47 p.; [2]1965, 64 p.
        *Introducción al Nuevo Testamento* (Conoce la Biblia. Nuevo Testamento, 1). Santander: Sal Terrae, 1967,
        76 p.

**MACKIN, Theodore**

1989    *Marriage in the Catholic Church. The Marital Sacrament*. New York – Mahwah, NJ:
        Paulist, 1989, XI-701 p. Esp. 62-64: "Matthew's account of Jesus' teaching".

**MACKRELL, G.F.**

1979    The Rich Young Man. [19,16-22] — *NBlackfr* 60 (1979) 84-89. [NTA 23, 833]

**MACKY, Peter W.**

1988    Exploring the Depths of Artistic Biblical Metaphors. — *Proceedings EGLBS* 8 (1988)
        167-176. Esp. 169-176 [11,28-30].
        *Metaphor in the Bible*. Queenston, Ont.: Mellen, 1989. Esp ch. 11: "Reaching the depths: participating in
        a speaker's metaphorical thinking" (revised version).

**MACLAURIN, E.C.B.**

1978    Beelzeboul. [10,25; 12,24] — *NT* 20 (1978) 156-160. [NTA 23, 101]

1980    The Canaanite Background of the Doctrine of the Virgin Mary. [1,20-23] — *Religious
        Traditions* (Sydney) 3/2 (1980) 1-11. [NTA 26, 686]

**MACPHAIL, J.R.**

1956    *The Gospel according to St. Matthew. Introduction and Commentary*. Madras: Christian
        Literature Society, 1956.
        *ExpT* 68 (1956-57) 44.

**MACRAE, George Winsor**

1960    The Gospel of Thomas – *Logia Iesou?* — *CBQ* 22 (1960) 56-70. Esp. 59-64: "The sayings
        of the synoptic type". [NTA 4, 816]

1973    New Testament Perspectives on Marriage and Divorce. — WRENN, L.G. (ed.), *Divorce
        and Remarriage in the Catholic Church*, New York: Newman, 1973, 1-15. Esp. 4-5.7-11
        [5,32; 19,9]; = ID., *Studies in the New Testament and Gnosticism*, ed. D.J. Harrington
        & S.B. Marrow (Good News Studies, 26), Wilmington, DE: Glazier, 1987, 115-129.
        Esp. 119-120.122-126.

1987    Messiah and Gospel. — NEUSNER, J. – GREEN, W.S. – FRERICHS, E.S. (eds.),
        *Judaisms and Their Messiahs at the Turn of the Christian Era*, Cambridge: University
        Press, 1987, 169-185. Esp. 179-181.

**MADDEN, Nicholas**

1982 The Commentary on the Pater Noster. An Example of the Structural Methodology of Maximus the Confessor. — HEINZER, F. – SCHÖNBORN, C. (eds.), *Maximus Confessor. Actes du Symposium sur Maxime le Confesseur, Fribourg, 2-5 septembre 1980* (Paradosis, 27), Freiburg/Schw: Éd. universitaires, 1982, 147-155.

1995a Maximus Confessor: On the Lord's Prayer. — FINAN, T. – TWOMEY, V. (eds.), *Scriptural Interpretation in the Fathers: Letter and Spirit*, Blackrock (Ireland): Four Courts Press, 1995, 119-141.

1995b A Patristic Salutation: The Prologue to the Pater Noster of Maximus Confessor. — *IrTQ* 61 (1995) 239-249.

**MADDEN, Patrick J.**

1997 *Jesus' Walking on the Sea. An Investigation of the Origin of the Narrative Account* (BZNW, 81). Berlin – New York: de Gruyter, 1997, X-156 p. Esp. 6-7; 79-82; 103-106 [14,22-33]; 134-135 [15,32-39/Mk]. — Diss. Washington, DC, 1995 (J.A. Fitzmyer).

**MADDOX, Robert J.**

1965 Who are the "Sheep" and the "Goats"? A Study of the Purpose and Meaning of Matthew xxv:31-46. — *AusBR* 13 (1965) 19-28. [NTA 11, 218]

1968 The Function of the Son of Man according to the Synoptic Gospels. — *NTS* 15 (1968-69) 45-74. Esp. 52-55 [10,23; 16,28; 24,27]; 58-60 [12,32; 16,17-19]; 64-66 [8,20; 11,19]; 68-72 [17,9-12; 20,28; 26,2.45]. [NTA 13, 842]

1971 The Quest for Valid Methods in "Son of Man" Research. — *AusBR* 19 (1971) 36-51. [NTA 16, 802] → Borsch 1967, Colpe 1969, N. Perrin 1968
Methodenfragen in der Menschensohnforschung. — *EvT* 32 (1972) 143-160. [NTA 17, 78]

**MADEC, Goulven**

1990 (ed.), *Saint Bonaventure. Le Christ Maître. Édition, traduction et commentaire du sermon universitaire "Unus est magister noster Christus"* [23,10] (Bibliothèque des textes philosophiques). Paris: Vrin, 1990, 144 p.

**MADIGAN, Kevin J.**

1992 *Peter Olivi's "Lectura supra Matthaeum" in Medieval Exegetical Context*. Diss. Chicago, IL, 1992 (B. McGinn).

1995 Ancient and High-Medieval Interpretations of Jesus in Gethsemane: Some Reflections on Tradition and Continuity in Christian Thought. — *HTR* 88 (1995) 157-173. [NTA 40, 837]

**MADSEN, Iver K.**

1929R Zur Erklärung der evangelischen Parabeln. [1929] — HARNISCH, W. (ed.), *Gleichnisse Jesu*, 1982, 102-115. Esp. 103-110 [22,1-14]; 110-113 [13,3-8].

**MAERTENS, Thierry**

1959 *Le souffle de l'Esprit de Dieu* (Thèmes bibliques). Brugge: Desclée De Brouwer, 1959, 144 p. Esp. 92-94; 133-134 [3,11].

**MÄRZ, Claus-Peter**

1980 *"Siehe, dein König kommt zu Dir...". Eine traditionsgeschichtliche Untersuchung zur Einzugsperikope* (ErfTSt, 43). Leipzig: St. Benno, 1980, XXXVI-248 p. Esp. 4-8 [21,1-9]; 94-96 [21,1-9/Mk].

1985 "Feuer auf die Erde zu werfen, bin ich gekommen...". Zum Verständnis und zur Entstehung von Lk 12,49. — GANTOY, R. (ed.), *À cause de l'Évangile*. FS J. Dupont, 1985, 479-511. Esp. 480-487: "Literarische Analyse"; 488-493: "Lk 12,49 im Zusammenhang der

Redequelle"; 493-501: "Traditionskritische Erwägungen zu Lk 12,49"; = ID., *"... laßt eure Lampen brennen!"*, 1991, 9-31. Esp. 9-15; 15-20; 20-31.

1986 Lk 12,54b-56 par Mt 16,2b.3 und die Akoluthie der Redequelle. — *SNTU* 11 (1986) 83-96. Esp. 83-87: "Zum vorlukanischen Zusammenhang von Lk 12,54b-56"; 87-95: "Mt 16,2b-3 - eine synoptische Parallele zu Lk 12,54b-56?". [NTA 31, 634]; = ID., *"... laßt eure Lampen brennen!"*, 1991, 32-43. Esp. 32-35; 35-43.

1987 Zur Vorgeschichte von Lk 12,49-59. — *SNTU* 12 (1987) 69-84. Esp. 70-75: "Eine vorlukanische Spruchgruppe"; 75-83: "Zur Komposition". [NTA 33, 181]; = ID., *"...laßt eure Lampen brennen!"*, 1991, 44-57. Esp. 44-49; 49-56.

1989 Zur Vorgeschichte von Lk 12,35-48. Beobachtungen zur Komposition der Logientradition in der Redequelle. — KERTELGE, K., et al. (eds.), *Christus bezeugen.* FS W. Trilling, 1989, 166-178. Esp. 166-172: "Lk 12,35-38.39f.42-46 Q - eine vorlukanische Spruchgruppe"; 172-178: "Zur Komposition und Einordnung von Lk 12,35.36-38.39f.42-46 Q"; = ID., *"... laßt eure Lampen brennen!"*, 1991, 58-71. Esp. 58-64; 64-71.

1991a *"... laßt eure Lampen brennen!"*. *Studien zur Q-Vorlage von Lk 12,35-14,24* (Erfurter Theologische Schriften, 20). Leipzig: St. Benno, 1991, 124 p. [NTA 36, p. 265] — Vorwort, 5-6; Epilog, 114-117. → 1985, 1986, 1987, 1989, 1991b

1991b Zur Q-Vorlage von Lk 13,22-14,24. — *Ibid.*, 72-113. Esp. 72-81: "Lk 13,22-14,24 und die Q-Akoluthie"; 81-95: "Zur Rekonstruktion des Textbestandes von Lk 13,24.25-30; 14,16-24 Q"; 95-104: "Zur Bedeutung von Lk 13,24.25-30; 14,16-24 Q"; 104-113: "Zur Kompositionsgeschichte".

1992 Das Gleichnis vom Dieb. Überlegungen zur Verbindung von Lk 12,39 par Mt 24,43 und 1 Thess 5,2.4. — VAN SEGBROECK, F., et al. (eds.), *The Four Gospels 1992.* FS F. Neirynck, 1992, I, 633-648. Esp. 634-639 [survey of research]; 639-644 [Q 12,39-48]; 644-648 [1 Thess 5,1-11/Mt-Lk].

1993 Zur Q-Rezeption in Lk 12,35-13,35 (14,1-24). Die Q-Hypothese und ihre Bedeutung für die Interpretation des lukanischen Reiseberichtes. — FOCANT, C. (ed.), *The Synoptic Gospels*, 1993, 177-208. Esp. 185-193: "Literarkritische Orientierung"; 193-198: "Struktur, Bedeutung und Zusammenhang der Q-Vorlage"; 198-203: "Die Q-Rezeption in Lk 12,35-14,24"; 203-205: "Rekonstruktion der Q-Vorlage".

1994 Zum Verständnis der Gerichtspredigt in Q. — KLAUCK, H.-J. (ed.), *Weltgericht und Weltvollendung.* FS R. Schnackenburg, 1994, 128-148. Esp. 130-136: "Der 'Ort' der Gerichtspredigt in Q"; 136-145: "Die theologischen Akzente der Gerichtspredigt in Q" [Q 3,7-9.16-17; 6,46; 10,13-15; 11,49-51; 12,35-46.49-58; 13,24-30.34-35; 17,23-37]; 145-148: "Zur Funktion der Gerichtspredigt in Q".

**MAESTRI, Gabriella**

1992 Un contributo alla conoscenza dell'antica liturgia egiziana: studio dell'anafora del santo evangelista Matteo. — *Memoriam sanctorum venerantes. Miscellanea in onore di Monsignor Victor Saxer* (Studi di Antichità cristiana, 48), Città del Vaticano: Pont. Istituto di Archeologia cristiana, 1992, 525-537.

**MAGASS, Walter**

1972 Zur Semiotik der signifikanten Orte in den Gleichnissen Jesu. — *LingBib* 15-16 (1972) 3-21. [NTA 17, 106]

1973a "Der Schatz im Acker" (Mt 13,44): Von der Kirche als einem Tauschphänomen - Paradigmatik und Transformation. — *LingBib* 21-22 (1973) 2-18. [NTA 17, 915]

1973b "Er aber schlief" (Mt 8,24). Ein Versuch über die Kleinigkeit (meloč). — *LingBib* 29-30 (1973) 55-59. [NTA 18, 857]

1975 Die magistralen Schlußsignale der Gleichnisse Jesu. — *LingBib* 36 (1975) 1-20. Esp. 6-7.17-18 [21,33-44]; 18-19 [13]. [NTA 20, 761]

1977 Die Kirche und ihre Legitimation (Mt 9,9-13). — *LingBib* 41-42 (1977) 5-20. [NTA 22, 765]

1978 Bemerkungen zur Gleichnisauslegung. — *Kairos* 20 (1978) 40-52. [NTA 23, 411]

1979 Zum Verständnis des Gleichnisses von den spielenden Kindern (Mt 11,16-19). — *LingBib* 45 (1979) 59-70. [NTA 24, 91]

1981 Theologie und Wetterregel. Semiotische Variationen über Arats "Phainomena". — *LingBib* 49 (1981) 7-26. Esp. 17-20 [16,2-3]; 20-22 [24,27]. [NTA 26, 353]

1983 *Hermeneutik und Semiotik. Schrift – Predigt – Emblematik* (Forum theologiae linguisticae, 15). Bonn: Linguistica biblica, 1983, 108 p. Esp. 31-43: "Die Geschichte mit den drei Horizonten. Am Beispiel der Syrophönizerin Mt 15,21-28".

## MAGAZZÙ, Cesare

1994 Motivi encratiti nell'*Opus Imperfectum in Matthaeum*. — SFAMENI GASPARRO, G. (ed.), Ἀγαθὴ ἐλπίς. *Studi storico-religiosi in onore di Ugo Bianchi* (Storia della Religione, 11), Roma: L'"Erma" di Bretschneider, 1994, 427-442.

## MAGEE, John

1988 Note on Boethius, "Consolatio" I,1,5; 3,7: A New Biblical Parallel. [27,35] — *VigChr* 42 (1988) 79-82.

## MAGGI, Alberto

1990 Nota sull'uso di "τῷ σῷ ὀνόματι" e "ἀνομία" in Mt 7,21-23. — *FilolNT* 3 (1990) 145-149. [NTA 36, 147]

1995 *Padre dei poveri: Traduzione e commento delle Beatitudini e del Padre Nostro di Matteo*. Volume 1: *Le Beatitudini* (Orizzonti biblici). Assisi: Cittadella, 1995, 232 p.
V. PASQUETTO, *Teresianum* 46 (1995) 664-667.

## MAGGIONI, Bruno

1970 La passion nécessaire du Christ et de son disciple. Mt 16,21-27. — *AssSeign* II/53 (1970) 15-26.

1981 *Il racconto di Matteo* (Bibbia per tutti). Assisi: Cittadella Editrice, 1981, 375 p. [NTA 26, p. 85]
*PalCl* 61 (1982) 534.
*El relato de Mateo*, trans. E. Requeña Calvo. Madrid: Paulinas, 1982, 310 p.
X. ALEGRE, *ActBibl* 20 (1983) 102; L. DE LORENZI, *Benedictina* 29 (1982) 281-282; V. MUNIZ, *NatGrac* 31 (1984) 190-191; J.A. CARRASCO, *EstJos* 37 (1983) 252.

1987 Eunuchi per il Regno. [19,12] — *ParVi* 32 (1987) 281-289.

1991 Le molte forme del primato di Dio. Una lettura delle beatitudini. — *Credere oggi* 11 (1991) 20-28.

1993 Il Figlio dell'uomo non ha dove pesare il capo. Mt 8,20; Lc 9,58. — *ParSpirV* 28 (1993) 103-116.

1994 *I racconti evangelici della passione* (Commenti e studi biblici). Assisi: Cittadella, 1994, 329 p.; ²1995.
*Los relatos evangélicos de la pasión*. Salamanca: Sígueme, 1995, 308 p.

1995 *Padre Nostro* (Sestante, 7). Milano: Vita e pensiero, 1995, 130 p.

## MAGNE, Jean

1958 Répétitions de mots et exégèse dans quelques psaumes et le Pater. — *Bib* 39 (1958) 177-197. Esp. 196-197.

1973 Le pain de la multiplication des pains et des disciples d'Emmaüs comme preuve de l'origine gnostique des sacrements, de l'Église et du Sauveur. — *Studia Evangelica* 6 (1973) 341-347. Esp. 343-344 [7,6; 13,45-46].

1975 *Sacrifice et sacerdoce* (Origines chrétiennes, 2). Paris: Privately published, 1975, 219 p. Esp. 95-128: "Les conditions primitives du salut chrétien et l'origine de la vie commune" [6,19-21; 10,34-36.37-39; 13,44-46; 19,1-9].

1982 Pauvreté et célibat dans les évangiles. — RIES, J. (ed.), *Gnosticisme et monde hellénistique. Actes du colloque de Louvain-la-Neuve (11-14 mars 1980)* (Publications de l'Institut Orientaliste de Louvain, 27), Louvain-la-Neuve: Université catholique, 1982, 319-325.

1988 La réception de la variante "Vienne ton esprit saint sur nous et qu'il nous purifie" (Lc 11,2) et l'origine des épiclèses, du baptême et du "Notre Père". — *EphLtg* 102 (1988) 81-106. Esp. 82-85 [Lk 11,2(Q)]; 100-105: "L'origine du Notre Père". [NTA 33, 179] → Delobel 1989a

1990a La vocation de Matthieu. [9,9-13] — *BLOS* 3 (1990) 3-6.

1990b Le repas avec les pécheurs. [9,9-13] — *BLOS* 5 (1990) 17-20.

1991a La non-guérison du lépreux dans les évangiles synoptiques. — *Revue de la Société Ernest-Renan* 40 (1990-91) 43-66.

1991b Les récits de la cène et la date de la Passion. — *EphLtg* 105 (1991) 185-236. Esp. 187-189 [26,29]; 207-211: "Les récits de *Mt* et de *Mc*"; 211-214: "La source commune à *Mt* et à *Mc* (S–MtMc); 214-218 [26,6-13/Mk]; 220-228 [26,1-5/Mk]. [NTA 36, 109]

1992 Les récits de la multiplication des pains à la lumière de la solution nouvelle du problème synoptique proposée par Philippe Rolland. — *EphLtg* 106 (1992) 477-525. Esp. 478-517: "Analyse des récits" [14]. [NTA 37, 1289] → Rolland 1984a

**MAHER, Michael**
1975 'Take my yoke upon you' (Matt. xi.29). — *NTS* 22 (1975-76) 97-103. [NTA 20, 440]

**MAHNKE, Hermann**
1978 *Die Versuchungsgeschichte im Rahmen der synoptischen Evangelien. Ein Beitrag zur frühen Christologie* (BET, 9). Frankfurt/M: Lang, 1978, 445 p. Esp. 55-103 [4,1-4/Q 4,1-4]; 104-126 [4,5-7/Q 4,9-12]; 127-152 [4,8-10/Q 4,5-8]; 153-169 [4,11/Q 4,13]; 170-205: "Allgemeine Probleme der Versuchungsgeschichte: Reihenfolge / Verhältnis zu Q / Inhalt, Form und 'Sitz im Leben'". — Diss. Kiel, 1977 (W.H. Schmidt).
    A. FUCHS, *SNTU* 5 (1980) 175-177; G.G. GAMBA, *Sal* 42 (1980) 936-937; J. GUILLET, *RSR* 68 (1980) 586-588; R.L. JESKE, *CBQ* 44 (1982) 680-682.

**MAHONEY, Aidan**
1968 A New Look at the Divorce Clauses in Mt 5,32 and 19,9. — *CBQ* 30 (1968) 29-38. Esp. 30-32 [textual-linguistic evidence]; 32-35 [19,9 in context]; 35-36 [1 Cor 7,10]; 36-38 [par. Mk 10,12; Lk 16,18]. [NTA 12, 868]

**MAHONEY, Robert**
1974 *Two Disciples at the Tomb. The Background and Message of John 20.1-10* (Theologie und Wirklichkeit, 6). Frankfurt/M: Lang, 1974, 344 p. Esp. 46-48 [27,49]; 118-121 [27,57-61]; 161-165 [28,1-8]; 194-227: "Analysis: comparison with the synoptics" [Jn 20,1-18]. — Diss. Würzburg, 1973 (R. Schnackenburg). → Neirynck 1977b

1983 Die Mutter Jesu im Neuen Testament. — DAUTZENBERG, G., et al. (eds.), *Die Frau im Urchristentum*, 1983, 92-116. Esp. 97-103: "Maria im Matthäusevangelium" [1,1-17.18-25; 2,1-23; 12,46-50; 13,53-58].

**MAHYUE, R.L.**
1995 For What Did Christ Atone in Isa 53:4-5? [8,17] — *Master's Seminary Journal* (Sun Valley, CA) 6 (1995) 121-141. [NTA 40, 827]

**MAIA, Pedro Américo**
1987 As bem-aventuranças ou os critérios de Jesus. [The beatitudes and the criteria of Jesus] — *Atualização* (Belo Horizonte) 18 (1987) 47-59.

**MAIER, Anneliese**

1968 Der Kommentar Benedikts XII. zum Matthaeus-Evargelium. — *Archivum Historiae Pontificiae* 6 (1968) 397-405; = ID., *Ausgehendes Mittelalter. Gesammelte Aufsätze zur Geistesgeschichte des 14. Jahrhunderts*, III, ed. A. Paravicini (Storia e letteratura. Raccolta di studi e testi, 138), Roma: Ed. di storia e etteratura, 1977, 591-600.

**MAIER, Friedrich Wilhelm**

1965 *Jesus – Lehrer der Gottesherrschaft.* Würzburg: Echter, 1965, 190 p. Esp. 25-98: "Die Predigt vom Gottesreich"; 99-140: "Die Forderungen der Gottesherrschaft"; 141-188: "Selbstoffenbarung des Menschensohns".

**MAIER, Gerhard**

1979 *Matthäus-Evangelium.* Neuhausen–Stuttgart: Hänsler, 2 vols., 1979-1980, 575 and 503 p. [NTA 25, p. 303]

1981 Johannes und Matthäus. Zwiespalt oder Viergestalt des Evangeliums? — FRANCE, R.T. – WENHAM, D. (eds.), *Studies of History and Tradition*, 1981, 267-291. Esp. 267-270: "Zum Problem"; 270-275: "Duktus und Struktur bei Matthäus und Johannes"; 275-286: "Einzelvergleiche" [ἐγώ εἰμι, son of..., Messiah, spirit, σημεῖον, ἄρτος].

1984 The Church in the Gospel of Matthew: Hermeneutical Analysis of the Current Debate. [16,17-19] — CARSON, D.A. (ed.), *Biblical Interpretation and the Church: Text and Context*, Exeter: Paternoster, 1984; Nashville, TN: Nelson, 1985, 45-63.
Die Kirche im Matthäusevangelium: Hermeneutische Analyse der gegenwärtigen Debatte über das Petrus-Wort Mt 16,17-19. — THIEDE, C.P. (ed.), *Das Petrusbild in der neueren Forschung* (Theologische Verlagsgemeinschaft, Monographien), Wuppertal: Brockhaus, 1987, 171-191.

1985 Jesustradition im 1. Petrusbrief? — WENHAM, D. (ed.), *The Jesus Tradition Outside the Gospels*, 1985, 85-128. Esp. 86-102. → E. Best 1970a, Gundry 1967b

1987 Three Commentaries on Matthew. A Review. — *Themelios* 12/3 (1987) 89-93. [NTA 32, 109] → D.A. Carson 1984, France 1985, Luz 1985a

1988 L'esegesi dei miracoli neotestamentari nel corso degli ultimi due secoli. — *Studi di Teologia dell'Istituto Biblico Evangelico* (Padova) 11 (1988) 9-51.

**MAIER, John P.**

1986 Matthew 15:21-28. — *Interpr* 40 (1986) 397-402.

**MAIER, Paul L.**

1975 The Infant Massacre – History or Myth? — *ChrTod* 20 (1975) 299-302. [NTA 20, 433]

1989a The Date of the Nativity and the Chronology of Jesus' Life. — VARDAMAN, J. – YAMAUCHI, E.M. (eds.), *Chronos, Kairos, Christos*. FS J. Finegan, 1989, 113-130. Esp. 115-118 [2,1]; 119-120 [2,1-12].

1989b Herod and the Babes of Bethlehem. A Pious Myth? — *Liberty* (Hagerstown, MD) 84 (1989) 6-8. [NTA 34, 612]

**MAILLOT, Alphonse**

1978 Quelques remarques sur la naissance virginale du Christ. — *FoiVie* 77/4 (1978) 30-44. Esp. 43-44. [NTA 23, 863]

**MAIO, Eugene**

1959 The Synoptic Problem and the Vaganay Hypothesis. — *IrTQ* 26 (1959) 167-181. [NTA 4, 376] → Vaganay 1954a

**MAISCH, Ingrid**

1970 Das Gleichnis von den klugen und törichten Jungfrauen. Auslegung von Mt 25,1-13. — *BibLeb* 11 (1970) 247-259. Esp. 249-254: "Zur Form- und Traditionsgeschichte des Textes Mt

25,1-13"; 255-258: "Die Aussageabsicht des Gleichnisses Mt 25,1-12"; 258-259: "Gestalt und Aussage des Gleichnisses bei Matthäus". [NTA 15, 858]

1975 Die Botschaft Jesu von der Gottesherrschaft. — FIEDLER, P. - ZELLER, D. (eds.), *Gegenwart und kommendes Reich*. FS A. Vögtle, 1975, 27-41. Esp. 31-35 [13,31-32]; 35-36 [13,33]; 38-40 [13,44-46].

1986 Die österliche Dimension des Todes Jesu. Zur Osterverkündigung in Mt 27,51-54. — OBERLINNER, L. (ed.), *Auferstehung Jesu - Auferstehung der Christen. Deutungen des Osterglaubens*. [FS Anton Vögtle zum 75. Geburtstag] (QDisp, 105), Freiburg: Herder, 1986, 96-123. Esp. 97-98: "Synoptischer Vergleich (Mk 15,38.39; Mt 27,51-54)"; 99-115: "Die Verse 51b-53 in der Diskussion"; 116-121: "Der Text Mt 27,51-54"; 121-123: "Tod und Auferstehung".

1991 Christsein in Gemeinschaft (Mt 18). — OBERLINNER, L. - FIEDLER, P. (eds.), *Salz der Erde*. FS A. Vögtle, 1991, 239-266. Esp. 240-243: "Der literarische Rahmen (Mt 18,1 und 19,1)"; 244-246: "Ziel und Anliegen von Mt 18"; 247-251: "Zur Aufteilung von Mt 18"; 251-253 [18,1-5]; 253-257 [18,6-14]; 257-262 [18,15-20]; 263-264 [18,21-35].

**MAIWORM, Josef**

1955 Umgekehrte Gleichnisse. — *BK* 10 (1955) 82-85. Esp. 82 [18,23-35].

**MAJERNIK, Jan**

1990 *The Parable of the Servant Left in Charge in Mt 24,45-51. The Exegesis and History of Interpretation*. Diss. Studium Biblicum Franciscanum, Jerusalem, 1990, VI-281 p. (G. Bissoli).

**MAKARA, J.**

1950 Initium Ev. S. Matthaei. — *Ateneum Kaplanskie* (Wroclaw) 53 (1950) 144-151.

**MAKRIS, S.G.**

1966 The Sermon on the Mount. [Greek] — Θρησκευτικη και Ηθικη Εγκυκλοπαιδιεια (Athens) 9 (1966) 973-976.

**MALAN, François Stephanus**

1989 Salvation in the New Testament. Emphases of the Different Writers. — *TViat* 17 (1989) 1-20. [NTA 35, 838]

**MALEVEZ, Léopold**

1968 Foi existentielle et foi doctrinale. — *NRT* 90 (1968) 137-154. Esp. 137-145: "Les évangiles synoptiques" [8,23-27; 9,1-8.18-26.27-31; 14,22-33.34-36; 17,14-21; 21,18-22]. [NTA 13, 346]

**MALI, Franz**

1987 Zum Verhältnis von Matthäuskommentar des Origenes und *Opus Imperfectum in Matthaeum*. Mt 19,3-11, die Frage der Ehescheidung. — BROX, N., et al. (eds.), *Anfänge der Theologie*. FS J.B. Bauer, 1987, 243-256.

1991 *Das "Opus imperfectum in Matthaeum" und sein Verhältnis zu den Matthäuskommentaren von Origenes und Hieronymus* (Innsbrucker theologische Studien, 34). Innsbruck–Wien: Tyrolia, 1991, 397 p. Esp. 16-90: "Einführung"; 91-323: "Textvergleich" [1,1-8,10; 10,16-13,13; 19,1-22,13; 22,34-25,44]; 324-353: "Ergebnis". — Diss. Graz, 1990 (J.B. Bauer). 
    J. DOIGNON, *RHPR* 75 (1995) 234-235; H.J. SIEBEN, *TheolPhil* 67 (1992) 590-591; R.B. VAGGIONE, *JTS* 46 (1995) 359-360.

1995 → van Banning 1995a

**MALILLOS, J.L.** → P. Benoit 1965/75

**MALINA, Bruce J.**

1967 Matthew 2 and Is 41,2-3: a Possible Relationship? — *SBF/LA* 17 (1967) 290-302. Esp. 290-294: "The contribution of Gk Mt"; 294-301: "The source(s) of Gk Mt". [NTA 12, 862]

1970 The Literary Structure and Form of Matt. xxviii.16-20. — *NTS* 17 (1970-71) 87-103.
Esp. 88-96: "Literary form"; 97-101: "Literary structure"; 101-103: "Literary form and exegesis". [NTA 15, 510]

1972 Does *Porneia* Mean Fornication? — *NT* 14 (1972) 10-17. Esp. 11, 14. [NTA 16, 770] →
Jensen 1978

1986 Normative Dissonance and Christian Origins. — *Semeia* 35 (1986) 35-59. Esp. 45-47:
"Inconsistency in the gospel story" (46-47: In Matthew). [NTA 31, 29]

1987 Wealth and Poverty in the New Testament and Its World. — *Interpr* 41 (1987) 354-367.
Esp. 362-363.366 [6,25-32]. [NTA 32, 358]

1988a & NEYREY, J.H., *Calling Jesus Names. The Social Value of Labels in Matthew*
(Foundations & Facets. Social Facets). Sonoma, CA: Polebridge, 1988, XVIII-174 p.
Esp. 1-32: "Jesus the witch" [12]; 33-67: "Jesus the deviant" [12]; 59-91: "Jesus on trial" [26-27]; 93-131:
"Jesus proclaimed" [26-27]; 152-157 [list of labels in Matthew]. [NTA 32, p. 374]
F.W. BURNETT, *CBQ* 52 (1990) 165-166; R. HODGSON, *BTB* 20 (1990) 171-172; B.T. VIVIANO, *RB* 101
(1994) 455.

1988b Patron and Client. The Analogy behind Synoptic Theology. — *Forum* 4/1 (1988) 2-32.
Esp. 9-11 [God as Father]. [NTA 33, 587]

1992 & ROHRBAUGH, R.L., *Social Science Commentary on the Synoptic Gospels*.
Minneapolis, MN: Fortress, 1992, VIII-422 p. Esp. 19-169: "Matthew".

**MALIPURATHU, Thomas**

1994 *The Beatitudes according to Luke. An Exegetico-Theological Study of Luke 6,20-26 in
the Perspective of the Sermon on the Plain and of the Designation of Luke as the
"Evangelist of the Poor"*. Roma: Pont. Univ. Greg., 1994, X-487 p. Esp. 191-333: "The
interpretation of the text"; 344-346: "Luke and Q". — Diss. Pont. Univ. Greg., Roma, 1994 (U. Vanni).

**MALO, Adrien-M.**

1962 L'Évangile de saint Matthieu, évangile ecclésiastique. — *L'Église dans la Bible.
Communications présentées à la XVII^e réunion annuelle de l'ACÉBAC* (Studia.
Recherches de philosophie et de théologie, 13), Brugge: Desclée De Brouwer, 1962,
19-34.

1965 & DÍEZ MACHO, A., Sermon de la montaña (Mt 5,1-7,29). — *Enciclopédia de la
Bíblia* (Barcelona) 6 (1965; ²1969) 630-639.

**MALONEY, Elliott Charles**

1991 "We have given up everything to follow you". — *BiTod* 29 (1991) 210-214. Esp. 212-213.
[NTA 36, 120]

**MALTEMPI, B.M.**

1951 Animadversiones quaedam in articulum R.P. Clementis M. Henze, C.SS.R. Brevis
replicatio. — *Marianum* 13 (1951) 184. → Henze 1950, 1951

**MALTMANN, Nicholas**

1979 Light in and on the Digby Mary Magdalene. [27,56] — KING, M.H. – STEVENS, W.M.
(eds.), *Saints, Scholars, and Heroes. Studies in Medieval Culture in Honor of Charles
W. Jones*, Collegeville, MN: St. John's Univ., 1979, I, 257-280.

**MAŁUNOWICZ, Leokadia**

1982 Citations bibliques dans l'évangile grecque. — *Studia Evangelica* 7 (1982) 333-337. Esp.
335.

**MANDAC, Marijan**

1977 Jesus in the First Chapter of Matthew. [Serbo-Croatian] — *Bogoslovska Smotra* (Zagreb)
47 (1977) 45-62 (French summary, 62).

**MANDRUZZATO, Enzo**

1989  (ed.), *Il buon messaggio seguendo Matteo* (Il soggetto e la scienza, 7). Pordenone: Biblioteca dell'Immagine, 1989, XLV-186 p.
      V. FUSCO, *CC* 141/4 (1990) 514-515; B. MARRA, *RasT* 31 (1990) 525-526.

**MÁNEK, Jindřich**

1957  Fishers of Men. [4,19] — *NT* 2 (1957-58) 138-141. [NTA 3, 355]

1959  The Biblical Concept of Time and Our Gospels. — *NTS* 6 (1959-60) 45-51. Esp. 47 [21,34]; 50. [NTA 4, 366]

1967  On the Mount – On the Plain (Mt. v 1 – Lk. vi 17). — *NT* 9 (1967) 124-131. [NTA 12, 149]

1970  Composite Quotations in the New Testament and Their Purpose. [2,6; 21,5; 24,30; 27,10] — *ComViat* 13 (1970) 181-188. [NTA 16, 49]

1973  Mit wem identifiziert sich Jesus? Eine exegetische Rekonstruktion ad Matt. 25:31-46. — LINDARS, B. - SMALLEY, S.S. (eds.), *Christ and Spirit in the New Testament. In Honour of Charles Francis Digby Moule*, Cambridge: University Press, 1973, 15-25.

1977  ... *Und brachte Frucht. Die Gleichnisse Jesu*, trans. J. & U. Dachsel. Stuttgart: Calwer, 1977, 119 p.

**MANFREDI, A.**

1968  Matteo cap. 24: Discorso escatologico o discorso profetico? Contributo ad un confronto sinottico fra Matteo cap. 24 (e passi paralleli) e alcuni passi profetici dell'AT. — *Ricerche religiose* 1 (1968) 5-23.

**MANFREDI, Manfredo**

1983  (ed.), *Trenta testi greci da papiri letterari e documentari, editi in occasione del XVII Congresso Internazionale di Papirologia, Napoli 19-26 maggio 1983* (PSI, 17). Firenze: Ist. Papir. 'G. Vitelli', 1983. Esp. 7-9 [14,22.28-29].

**MANGAN, Celine**

1984  *Can We Still Call God "Father"? A Woman Looks at the Lord's Prayer Today* (Ways of Prayer, 12). Wilmington, DE: Glazier; Dublin: Dominican Publications, 1984, 110 p. [NTA 29, p. 206]

**MANGATT, George**

1977  At the Tomb of Jesus. — *Bible Bhashyam* 3 (1977) 91-96. [NTA 22, 110]

1980  Reflections on the Apostolic Discourse (Mt 10). — *Bible Bhashyam* 6 (1980) 196-206. [NTA 25, 477]

1984  The Kingdom of God and Detachment (Mt 6:19-34). — *Bible Bhashyam* 10 (1984) 122-131. [NTA 29, 523]

1990  The Public Ministry of Jesus in the Gospel of Matthew. — *Bible Bhashyam* 16 (1990) 20-40. Esp. 20-28: "Jesus the Messiah of Israel"; 28-32: "Rejection of the Messiah by Israel"; 32-40: "The Messiah and his Church". [NTA 35, 126]

1991  The Family of Nazareth. — *Bible Bhashyam* 17 (1991) 181-195. Esp. 181-188.191-194 [1,18-25]. [NTA 36, 1197]

1993  Jesus and Religion. — *Bible Bhashyam* 19 (1993) 249-282. Esp. 254-256 [love]; 262-264 [6,1-18]. [NTA 38, 1322]

1994  Jesus' Teaching on Marriage and Divorce. — *Bible Bhashyam* 20 (1994) 88-107. Esp. 98-101 [5,32; 19,9]. [NTA 39, 1411]

**MANI, A.**

1980  Introduction to the Gospel of Matthew. — *Bible Bhashyam* 6 (1980) 177-195. [NTA 25, 455]

**MANICARDI, Ermenegildo**

1981 *Il cammino di Gesù nel Vangelo di Marco. Schema narrativo e tema cristologico* (AnBib, 96). Roma: Biblical Institute Press, 1981, X-221 p. Esp. 40-42.65-68.84-86.109-110.135-137: "Confronto con Matteo e Luca". — Diss. Pont. Inst. Bibl., Roma, 1980 (F. Lentzen-Deis).

1987 Gesù, la sapienza e la legge nel Vangelo secondo Matteo: un sondaggio in Mt 11-13. — FANULI, A. (ed.), *Sapienza e Torah* (Atti della XXIX Settimana Biblica), Bologna: Dehoniane, 1987, 99-126. Esp. 102-107 [11,2-19]; 107-112 [11,25-30]; 112-117 [12,1-21]; 117-118 [12,42]; 118-121 [13,34-35]; 121-123 [13,53-58].

1993 Il discorso di Gesù per l'invio dei Dodici a Israele nel Vangelo secondo Matteo. — ID. (ed.), *Teologia ed evangelizzazione. Saggi in onore di mons. Serafino Zardoni* (Studi e saggi della Sezione Seminario regionale dello Studio teologico accademico bolognese), Bologna: Dehoniane, 1993, 81-108. Esp. 85-89 [10,5-15]; 89-94 [10,16-23]; 95-102 [10,24-33]; 102-105 [10,34-42]; 106-108 [23,34-39].

**MANN, Christopher Stephen**

1958 Epiphany – Wise Men or Charlatans? — *Theology* 61 (1958) 495-500.

1965 The Historicity of the Birth Narratives. — NINEHAM, D.E., et al. (eds.), *Historicity and Chronology*, 1965, 46-58. Esp. 47-53. [NTA 11, 191]

1971 → Albright 1971

1986 *Mark. A New Translation with Introduction and Commentary* (The Anchor Bible, 27). New York: Doubleday, 1986, XXVI-715 p. Esp. 47-71: "Synoptic relationships and the supposed priority of Mark".

**MANNS, Frédéric**

1978 La Halakah dans l'Évangile de Matthieu. — *Ant* 53 (1978) 3-22. Esp. 17-22. [NTA 23, 83] → 1983
*Halakah* in Matthew's Gospel. — *TDig* 27 (1979) 151-154.

1980a L'arrière-plan socio-économique de la parabole des ouvriers de la onzième heure et ses limites. — *Ant* 55 (1980) 258-268. Esp. 265-268 [20,1-16]. [NTA 25, 79]

1980b Un midrash chrétien: le récit de la mort de Judas. — *RevSR* 54 (1980) 197-203. [NTA 25, 545]

1983 La Halakah dans l'Évangile de Matthieu. Note sur Mt. 16,16-19. — *BibOr* 26 (1983) 129-135. [NTA 28, 499] → 1978

1988 Une tradition rabbinique réinterprétée dans l'évangile de Mt 22,1-10 et en Rm 11,30-32. — *Ant* 63 (1988) 416-426. Esp. 423-434. [NTA 33, 615]

1991 La parabole des talents. Wirkungsgeschichte et racines juives. — *RevSR* 65 (1991) 343-362. Esp. 346-358: "L'histoire de l'interprétation"; 358-362: "Les racines juives du texte". [NTA 36, 730]

**MANRIQUE, Andrés**

1978 Jesús de Nazaret ante el divorcio. — *BibFe* 4 (1978) 33-46. Esp. 39-46. [NTA 22, 735]

1983 ¡Padre, libranos del maligno!. [6,13] — *BibFe* 9 (1983) 75-83.

**MANSON, Thomas Walter**

1931[R] *The Teaching of Jesus. Studies of Its Form and Content* [1931, ²1935]. Cambridge: University Press, 1951, XII-352 p.; repr. 1955, 1963, 1967. Esp. 27-34 [Q]; 34-38 [M]; 82-83 [12,28; Q 11,20]; 83-86 [22,1-14]; 89-115 [God as father]; 116-141.160-10.196-211 [kingdom]; 211-234 [Son of Man]; 260-284 [eschatology].

1937[R] *The Sayings of Jesus as Recorded in the Gospels according to St. Matthew and St. Luke Arranged with Introduction and Commentary* [1937; 1949]. London: SCM, 1950; 1954; Grand Rapids, MI: Eerdmans, 1979, 352 p. Esp. 15-21: "The document Q"; 21-26: "The matter peculiar to Matthew"; 39-148: "The document Q"; 149-252: "Teaching peculiar to Matthew". [NTA 24, p. 191]

*I detti di Gesù nei vangeli di Matteo e Luca* (Biblioteca teologica, 17). Brescia: Paideia, 1980, 562 p. [NTA 25, p. 110]

    A. AMATO, *Sal* 43 (1981) 695-696; A. BODRATO, *Humanitas* 36 (1981) 629-630; V. PASQUETTO, *Teresianum* 34 (1983) 515-516; A. PASSONI DELL'ACQUA, *RivBib* 31 (1983) 253-255; D. TOMASETTO, *Protestantesimo* 37 (1982) 170-172.

1946[R]  The Gospel according to St. Matthew. [1946] — ID., *Studies in the Gospels and Epistles*, ed. M. Black, Manchester: University Press; Philadelphia, PA: Westminster, 1962, 68-104. Esp. 69-87: "Traditions regarding Mt". (pp. 75-83 = McARTHUR, H.K. (ed.), *In Search of the Historical Jesus*, 1969, 28-32).

1953a  *The Servant-Messiah. A Study of the Public Ministry of Jesus.* Cambridge: University Press, 1953, VII-104 p. Esp. 55-58 [4,1-11]; 59-60 [9,37-10,16]; 66-67 [11,18-19]; 98-99 [28,19].

1953b  John the Baptist. — *BJRL* 36 (1953-54) 395-412. Esp. 401-404.

1955  The Lord's Prayer. — *BJRL* 38 (1955-56) 99-113; 436-448.

1960  *Ethics and the Gospel*, ed. R. Preston. London: SCM, 1960; repr. 1962, 109 p. Esp. 43-57: "Jesus and the law of Moses"; 99-101.

### MANSON, William

1937[R]  The Imperative of Jesus. A Study of the "Sermon on the Mount" and the Gospel Ethics. [1937] — ID., *Jesus and the Christian*, 1967, 50-57.

1943[R]  *Jesus the Messiah. The Synoptic Tradition of the Revelation of God in Christ with Special Reference to Form-Criticism* [1943]. London: Hodder & Stoughton, repr. 1952, XII-200 p. Esp. 30-32 [5,39-40]; 38-39 [11,2-19; Q 11,14-23/Mk]; 51-53 [Son of God]; 53-55 [13,11/Mk]; 71-76 [11,25-30]; 78-93 [Sermon on the Mount]; 110-112 [servant]; 113-119 [Son of Man].
*Bist Du der da kommen soll? Das Zeugnis der drei ersten Evangelien von der Offenbarung Gottes in Christo unter Berücksichtigung der Formgeschichte.* Zürich: Evangelischer Verlag, 1952, 238 p. Esp. 43-44; 52-53; 69-70; 71-72; 89-95; 98-114; 133-136; 136-144.

1952  Principalities and Powers: The Spiritual Background of the Work of Jesus in the Synoptic Gospels. — *Bulletin SNTS* 3 (1952; ²1963) 7-17. Esp. 12-13 [11,12; 16,18-20]; = ID., *Jesus and the Christian*, 1967, 77-88. Esp. 82-83.

1967  *Jesus and the Christian*. Grand Rapids, MI: Eerdmans; London: J. Clarke, 1967, 236 p. → 1937, 1952

### MANTEY, Julius Robert

1951a  The Causal Use of *eis* in the New Testament. [3,11; 12,41; 14,31] — *JBL* 70 (1951) 45-48. → R. Marcus 1951, 1952

1951b  On Causal *eis* Again. — *Ibid.*, 309-311. → R. Marcus 1951, 1952

1969  What of Priestly Absolution? [16,19] — *ChrTod* 13 (1969) 388-391.

1973  Evidence that the Perfect Tense in John 20:23 and Matthew 16:19 Is Mistranslated. — *JEvTS* 16 (1973) 129-138. [NTA 18, 474] → Elbert 1974

1981  Distorted Translations in John 20:23; Matthew 16:18-19 and 18:18. — *RExp* 78 (1981) 409-416. [NTA 26, 179]

### MANUS, Chris Ukachukwu

1991a  "King-Christology". Reflections on the Figure of the Matthean *Endzeit* Discourse Material (Mt 25:31-46) in the African Context. — *Acta theologica* 11 (1991) 19-41.

1991b  "King-Christology". The Result of a Critical Study of Matt 28:16-20 as an Example of Contextual Exegesis in Africa. — *Scriptura* 39 (1991) 25-42. [NTA 36, 1286] → Combrink 1991b

1992  → Nwachkwu 1992

1993a    *Christ, the African King: New Testament Christology* (Studien zur interkulturellen Geschichte des Christentums – Études d'histoire interculturelle du christianisme – Studies in the Intercultural History of Christianity, 82). Frankfurt/M: Lang, 1993, 280 p. Esp. 169-173 [1-2]; 206-207 [11,16-19].

1993b    Universalism and Mission. Mt 28,16-20. — ADESO, P., et al., *5ième Congrès des biblistes africains. Universalisme et mission dans la Bible, Abidjan 16-23.VII.1991*, Nairobi: Kath. Jungschar Österreichs – Cath. Biblical Centre for Africa and Madagascar, 1993, 86-111.

**MANZONI, Giuseppe**

1993    *Le Beatitudini*. Roma: Dehoniane, 1993, 396 p.
     V. PASQUETTO, *Teresianum* 44 (1993) 748-749.

**MARA, Maria Grazia**

1973    *Évangile de Pierre. Introduction, texte critique, traduction, commentaire et index* (SC, 201). Paris: Cerf, 1973, 238 p. Esp. 69-212: "Commentaire"; 226-227.

1990    Colet et Érasme au sujet de l'exégèse de Mt 26,39. — BACKUS, I. – HIGMAN, F. (eds.), *Théorie et pratique de l'exégèse. Actes du III^e Colloque international sur l'histoire de l'exégèse biblique au XVI^e s. (Genève, 31 août – 2 septembre 1988)* (Études de philologie et d'histoire, 43), Genève: Droz, 1990, 259-272.

**MARAFIOTI, Domenico**

1994    Verginità e matrimonio in Mt 19 e 1Cor 7. — *RasT* 35 (1994) 663-686. Esp. 666-668 [19,3-12]; 668-670 [19,10-12]. [NTA 40, 1465]

**MARANGON, Antonio**

1969    Il cinque discorsi del Vangelo di Matteo. Presentazione. — *ParVi* 14 (1969) 241-242.

**MARCATO, Giorgio**

1972    Il figlio e il padre. L'interpretazione di *Mt* 11,25-30. — *ParVi* 17 (1972) 218-225.

**MARCEL, Pierre Charles**

1950    Gethsémané. Matthieu XXVI,36-46 – Marc XIV,32-41 – Luc XXII,39-46. — *RRéf* 1/1 (1950) 21-33.

1958    Our Lord's Use of Scripture. — HENRY, C.F.H. (ed.), *Revelation and the Bible. Contemporary Evangelical Thought*, London: Tyndale, 1958, 119-134.

1964    "Frères et sœurs" du Christ. — *RRéf* 15/4 (1964) 18-30. Esp. 25-27 [18,1-5]; 16/1 (1965) 12-26. Esp. 12-22 [25,31-46]. [NTA 10, 122/123]

1983    La parabole des talents (Matthieu 25:14-30). — *RRéf* 34 (1983) 49-54. [NTA 28, 502]

**MARCHAND, Geraldus**

1958    *Matthieu 18,20 dans la tradition des six premiers siècles*. Diss. Pont. Univ. Greg., Roma, 1958. — *GregLA* 406 (1959) 235.

**MARCHEL, Witold**

1963a    *Abba, Père! La prière du Christ et des chrétiens. Étude exégétique sur les origines et la signification de l'invocation à la divinité comme père, avant et dans le Nouveau Testament* (AnBib, 19). Roma: Institut biblique pontifical, 1963, XLIV-290 p. Esp. 133-137.147-177 [11,25-27]; 137-138 [26,39.42]; 191-202 [6,9; Q 11,2]; (AnBib, 19A), nouvelle édition entièrement refondue, 1971, 272 p. Esp. 125-130.139-167 [11,25-27]; 179-189 [6,9; Q 11,2]. — Diss. Pont. Inst. Bibl., Roma, 1961 (S. Lyonnet).

1963b    *Abba, Vater! Die Vaterbotschaft des Neuen Testaments* (Die Welt der Bibel). Düsseldorf: Patmos, 1963, 126 p.

*Dieu Père dans le Nouveau Testament*, trans. M. Cé. Paris: Cerf, 1966, 142 p.
*De Bijbel over God, de Vader*, trans. J. Mertens (De Bijbel over..., 23). Roermond–Maaseik: Romen, 1964, 128 p. Esp. 44-98 [God as father].

### MARCHESELLI, Casale Cesare

1977    "Beati i miti" (*Mt* 5,5a) (Studio di storia della redazione). — *Asprenas* 24 (1977) 119-145. Esp. 120-124 [12,17-21]; 125-128 [21,5]; 130-140 [9,35-38]; 141-143 [5,5].

1978    Il Vangelo di Matteo. Riflessioni in margine a una recente opera di Leopold Sabourin. — *Asprenas* 25 (1978) 179-192. → Sabourin 1975a

1981    Il Servo di Jahweh, profeta e messia. Saggio di *Kritikform* su *Dt-Is* 42,1a-4c = *Mt* 12,18-21. — *Asprenas* 28 (1981) 3-28. Esp. 27-28.

1982*   (ed.), *Parola e Spirito. Studi in onore di Settimio Cipriani*. Brescia: Paideia, 1982, 2 vols., XLVII-920 and 939-1601 p. → Bordoni, Gamba, Grossi, Leonardi, Mongillo, Wilckens

1985    "Andate e annunciate a Giovanni ciò che udite e vedete" (Mt. 11,4; Lc. 7,22). — *Testimonium Christi*. FS J. Dupont, 1985, 257-288. Esp. 259-264 [11,3]; 264 [11,5]; 278-281 [11,6.12]; 282-283 [11,16-19]; 284-286 [7,13-14].

### MARCONCINI, Benito

1971    Tradizione e redazione in *Mt*. 3,1-12. — *RivBib* 19 (1971) 165-186. [NTA 16, 851]

1972a   La predicazione del Battista in Marco e Luca confrontata con la redazione di Matteo. — *RivBib* 20 suppl. (1972) 451-466. Esp. 460-466: "Matteo come redazione più antica". [NTA 19, 102]

1972b   Dal Battista 'storico' al Battista 'giovanneo': Interpretazione esistenziale. [3,1-12] — *Ibid.*, 467-480. [NTA 19, 155]

1973    La predicazione del Battista. Interpretazione storica e applicazioni. — *BibOr* 15 (1973) 49-60. [NTA 18, 465]

### MARCU, G.

1966    Homophony or Paradox? Exegetical-theological Discussion of Mt 29,24 and Par. [Roumanian] — *Mitropolia Ardealuliu*, 1966, 267-278.

### MARCUS, Joel

1988a   Entering into the Kingly Power of God. — *JBL* 107 (1988) 663-675. Esp. 671-672 [19,23-28]. [NTA 33, 1364]

1988b   The Gates of Hades and the Keys of the Kingdom (Matt 16:18-19). — *CBQ* 50 (1988) 443-455. [NTA 33, 123] → Basser 1990

1989*   & SOARDS, M.L. (eds.), *Apocalyptic and the New Testament. Essays in Honor of J. Louis Martyn* (JSNT SS, 24). Sheffield: JSOT, 1989, 351 p. → Cope, Humphries-Brooks, Scroggs

1995    The Old Testament and the Death of Jesus: The Role of Scripture in the Gospel Passion Narratives. — CARROLL, J.T. - GREEN, J.B. (eds.), *The Death of Jesus*, 1995, 205-233. Esp. 210-211 [27,43]; 214-215 [26,24]; 215-219 [26.28]; 215-217 [27,57]; 224-226 [26,31]; 226-228 [27,9-10.34.48].

### MARCUS, Ralph

1951    On Causal *eis*. [3,11; 12,41; 14,31] — *JBL* 70 (1951) 129-130. → Mantey 1951a-b

1952    The Elusive Causal *eis*. — *JBL* 71 (1952) 43-44. → Mantey 1951a-b

### MARE, W. Harold

1968    The Smallest Mustard Seed: Matthew 13:32. — *Grace Journal* (Winona Lake, IN) 9/1 (1968) 3-9.

1972 The Role of the Note-taking Historian and His Emphasis on the Person and Work of Christ. — *JEvTS* 15 (1972) 107-121. Esp. 111-114. [NTA 17, 60]

1975 A Study of the New Testament Concept of the Parousia. — HAWTHORNE, G.F. (ed.), *Current Issues in Biblical and Patristic Interpretation.* FS M.C. Tenney, 1975, 336-345. Esp. 337-341 [parousia]; 343-344 [10,23]; 344 [19,28].

1990 Genre Criticism and the Gospels. — SKILTON, J.H. (ed.), *The Gospels Today*, 1990, 82-101.

**MAREŠ, Francis Wenceslas**

1972 Zu den Wiener kirchenslavischen Glossen. [12,7] — *Anzeiger der Österreichische Akademie der Wissenschaften in Wien. Philosophisch-historische Klasse* (Wien) 109/15 (1972) 125-126.

**MARGOT, Jean-Claude**

1967 L'indissolubilité du mariage selon le Nouveau Testament. — *RTP* 17 (1967) 391-403. Esp. 394-399 [5,32; 19,3-12]. [NTA 12, 1037]. Die Unauflöslichkeit der Ehe nach dem Neuen Testament. — DAVID, J. – SCHMALZ, F. (eds.), *Wie unauflöslich ist die Ehe? Eine Dokumentation*, Aschaffenburg: Pattloch, 1969, 223-236. Esp. 227-232.

1979 *Traduire sans trahir. La théorie de la traduction et son application aux textes bibliques.* Lausanne: L'âge d'homme, 1979, 389 p. Esp. 167-186 [17,24-27]. — Diss. Lausanne, 1978 (P. Bonnard).

**MARGUERAT, Daniel**

1978a L'Église et le monde en Matthieu 13,36-43. — *RTP* 28 (1978) 111-129. [NTA 23, 103] Church and World in Mt 13:36-43. — *TDig* 27 (1979) 158-160.

1978b Matthieu 5/21-26. Les conflits. — *ETR* 53 (1978) 508-513.

1979a L'existence chrétienne selon Matthieu. — *RTP* 29 (1979) 291-299. [NTA 24, 410r] → Zumstein 1977

1979b Jésus et la Loi, selon Matthieu. — *FoiVie* 78/3 = *Cahiers bibliques* 18 (1979) 53-76. Esp. 54-56.74-76 [Paul/Mt]; 56-68: "La loi en faveur du prochain"; 68-72: "Jésus, maître de la loi". [NTA 24, 406]

1979c L'étude biblique: un dialogue entre l'auteur du texte et le lecteur. — *Ibid.*, 107-112. Esp. 109-111 [4,1-11].

1979d Bibliographie sélective. — *Ibid.*, 123-129. [NTA 24, 405]

1981 *Le Jugement dans l'Évangile de Matthieu* (Le monde de la Bible, 6). Genève: Labor et Fides, 1981, 598 p. Esp. 11-63: "Le jugement dans l'évangile"; 55-235: "Christ et la loi" [5,17-20.21-48; 7,13-27; 16,24-28]; 237-407: "L'église et l'échec d'Israel" [8,10-12; 10,15; 11,20-24; 12,41-42; 21,28-32.33-46; 22,1-14; 23,29-24,2]; 409-475: "L'église face au jugement" [13,10-17.24-30.36-43; 18,15-18; 19,27-30; 20,1-16]; 477-561: "Être vigilant" [24,37-44.45-51; 25,1-13.14-30.31-46]. [NTA 26, p. 321]; ²1995, IV-624 p. [NTA 40, p. 145] — Diss. Lausanne, 1981 (P. Bonnard). → Dermience 1985
    F. BAUDRAZ, *RTP* 33 (1983) 217-218; L. DEVILLERS, *RThom* 86 (1986) 315-319; J. DUPONT, *RTL* 13 (1982) 82-84; R.A. EDWARDS, *CBQ* 45 (1983) 499-500; V. FUSCO, *RasT* 24 (1983) 185-187; M.D. GOULDER, *JTS* 34 (1983) 248-251; K. GRAYSTON, *ExpT* 94 (1982-83) 148; J. GUILLET, *RSR* 71 (1983) 403-408; P.-É. LANGEVIN, *SE* 36 (1984) 376-378; S. LÉGASSE, *ETR* 57 (1982) 641-643; J. MURPHY-O'CONNOR, *RB* 90 (1983) 305-306; A. SAND, *TRev* 79 (1983) 24-27; V. SORIA, *CuBíb* 38 (1981) 233-237.
    E. CUVILLIER, *ETR* 71 (1996) 91-92; N. COCHAND, *RTP* 45 (1995) 415.

1982 L'avenir de la loi: Matthieu à l'épreuve de Paul. — *ETR* 57 (1982) 361-373. Esp. 362-364: "Le choc Matthieu–Paul". [NTA 27, 95]
    *SelT* 23 (1984) 196-204.

1989 La parabole, de Jésus aux évangiles: une histoire de réception. — DELORME, J. (ed.), *Les paraboles évangéliques*, 1989, 61-88.

1990a  *Le Dieu des premiers chrétiens* (Essais bibliques, 16). Genève: Labor et Fides, 1990, 223 p. Esp. 51-67: "Le Dieu du jugement" [7,15-20; 18,23-35; 25,31-46]; 85-87 [28,17].

1990b  *L'homme qui venait de Nazareth. Ce qu'on peut aujourd'hui savoir de Jésus*. Aubonne: Poulin, 1990, 212 p.; ²1993.

1991*  & ZUMSTEIN, J. (eds.), *La mémoire et le temps. Mélanges offerts à Pierre Bonnard* (Le monde de la Bible, 23). Genève: Labor et Fides, 1991, 322 p. → Légasse, Luz, Marguerat, Ruegg, Strecker 1966

1991a  Jésus et la loi dans la mémoire des premiers chrétiens. — *Ibid.*, 55-74. Esp. 66-71.

1991b  *Parabole* (Cahiers Évangile, 75). Paris: Cerf, 1991, 68 p. Esp. 46-49 [20,1-16]; 57-60 [13,10-15].
       *Parábola*, trans. N. Darrical (Cuadernos Bíblicos, 75). Estella: Verbo Divino, 1992, 66 p.

1993   La construction du lecteur par le texte (Marc et Matthieu). — FOCANT, C. (ed.), *The Synoptic Gospels*, 1993, 239-262. Esp. 245-253 [Mk/Mt: christology]; 253-259 [Mk/Mt: faith]; 259-261 [Mk/Mt: law].

1995   Le Nouveau Testament est-il anti-juif? L'exemple de Matthieu et du livre des Actes. — *RTL* 26 (1995) 145-164. Esp. 147-154: "La violence théologique de Mt"; 154-159: "Matthieu et le judaïsme sectaire". [NTA 40, 153]

**MARIADASAN, Varuvel**

1978   *Le triomphe messianique de Jésus et son entrée à Jérusalem. Étude critico-littéraire des traditions évangéliques (Mc 11:1-11; Mt 21:1-11; Lc 19:28-38; Jn 12:12-16)*. Tindivanam, India: Catechetical Centre, 1978, X-66 p. Esp. 27-56 [21,1-11]. — Diss. Louvain-la-Neuve, 1977 (J. Giblet).
       L. LEGRAND, *IndianTS* 17 (1980) 285-286; F. NEIRYNCK, *ETL* 55 (1979) 411-412.

**MARIANI, Bonaventura**

1960   L'origine dei vangeli sinottici secondo L. Vaganay e V. Taylor. — MARINI, O., et al., *I vangeli nella critica moderna*, 1960, 37-88. → Vaganay 1954a

**MARIMÓN BATLLO, Ricardo**

1980   Relectura y diálogo con el autor de un artículo sobre la infancia de Jesús. — *NatGrac* 27 (1980) 147-167. → Scheifler 1977

**MARIN, D.**

1970   "Per molti" non "per tutti" (Mt 26,27). — *Studia Florentina. Alessandro Ronconi oblata*, Frankfurt, 1970, 221-231.

**MARIN, Louis**

1971a  *Sémiotique de la Passion. Topiques et figures* (Bibliothèque de sciences religieuses). Paris: Aubier Montaigne/Cerf/Delachaux & Niestlé/Desclée De Brouwer, 1971, 252 p. Esp. 62-63; 79-87; 122-131; 141-157 [Judas]; 159-160.
       *Semiotik der Passionsgeschichte. Die Zeichensprache der Ortsangaben und Personennamen*, trans. S. Virgils (BEvT, 70). München: Kaiser, 1976, VIII-202 p. (E. Güttgemanns, "Nachwort", 188-196). Esp. 54-55; 70-76; 107-115; 124-139; 141-142.
       *The Semiotics of the Passion Narrative. Topics and Figures*, trans. A.M. Johnson (Pittsburgh Theological Monograph Series, 25). Pittsburgh, PA: Pickwick, 1980, XII-263 p.

1971b  Essai d'analyse structurale d'un récit-parabole: Matthieu 13/1-23. — *ETR* 46 (1971) 35-74. Esp. 38-41: "Le problème de la clôture du texte"; 41-46: "Le problème du corpus"; 46-74: "Propositions pour un modèle d'analyse structurale". [NTA 16, 539]; = CHABROL, C. - MARIN, L. (eds.), *Le récit évangélique*, 1974, 93-134. Esp. 95-98; 99-104; 104-134.
       Versuch zur strukturalen Analyse des Gleichnis-Berichts Matthäus 13,1-23. — HARNISCH, W. (ed.), *Die neutestamentliche Gleichnisforschung*, 1982, 76-126. Esp. 76-79; 79-86; 86-126.

1971c  Les femmes au tombeau. Essai d'analyse structurale d'un texte évangélique. — CHABROL, C. - MARIN, L. (eds.), *Sémiotique narrative: récits bibliques* (Langages 6/22), Paris: Didier-Larousse, 1971, 39-50; = ID., *Études sémiologiques: écritures, peintures* (Collection d'esthétique, 11), Paris: Klincksieck, 1971, 221-231.

Die Frauen am Grabe. Versuch einer Strukturanalyse an einem Text des Evangeliums. — CHABROL, C. - MARIN, L. (eds.), *Erzählende Semiotik nach Berichten der Bibel*, trans. K.H. Neufeld, München: Kösel, 1973, 67-85.

The Women at the Tomb: A Structural Analysis Essay of a Gospel Text. — JOHNSON, A.M. (ed.), *The New Testament and Structuralism. A Collection of Essays* (Pittsburgh Theological Monograph Series, 11), Pittsburgh, PA: Pickwick, 1976, 73-96.

1971d  Jésus devant Pilate. — *Ibid.*, 51-74; = ID., *Études sémiologiques*, 1971, 233-263.

Jesus vor Pilatus. Versuch einer Strukturanalyse. — CHABROL, C. - MARIN, L., *Erzählende Semiotik*, 1973, 87-122.

Jesus before Pilate: A Structural Analysis Essay. — JOHNSON, A.M. (ed.), *The New Testament and Structuralism*, 1976, 97-144.

### MARIN, Marcello

1973  Le vergini prudenti e le vergini stolte (Mt. 25,1-13) nell' esegesi di S. Agostino. — *VetChr* 10 (1973) 263-289; 11 (1974) 31-63; 12 (1975) 61-100.

1977  "De corporis puritate"? Hier. *In Matheum* IV (25,12) CC 77, 238, ll. 793-794. — *VetChr* 14 (1977) 169-175.

1978  Esegesi patristica di Matteo (1976-1977). — *VetChr* 15 (1978) 136-147.

1980a  Gerusalemme e la casa deserta (Mt 23,37-39; Lc 13,34-35) nell'esegesi origeniana. — CROUZEL, H. - QUACQUARELLI, A. (eds.), *Origeniana Secunda*, 1980, 215-227.

1980b  *Irrisio.* Note di letteratura agostiniana. [25,9] — *VetChr* 17 (1980) 370-380.

1981a  *Ricerche sull'esegesi agostiniana della parabola delle dieci vergini (Mt 25,1-13)* (Quaderni di "Vetera Christianorum", 16). Bari: Edipuglia, 1981, 344 p. Esp. 15-46: "Cronologia e metodo esegetico"; 47-64: "'Ista parabola vel similitudo'"; 65-83: "Dalla 'lectio' all' 'enarratio'"; 85-122: "Dieci vergini incontro allo sposo"; 123-132: "Le lampade"; 133-172: "'Oleum'"; 173-186: "Sonno e risveglio"; 187-194: "'Consuetudo'"; 195-220: "'Humilitas' e 'irrisio'. La caratterizzazione delle prudenti"; 221-258: "'Sera et infructuosa paenitentia'".

B. AMATA, *Sal* 45 (1983) 722; H. CROUZEL, *BullLitEccl* 85 (1984) 92; J. DEN BOEFT, *VigChr* 37 (1983) 405-407; R.J. DESIMONE, *Augustinian Studies* (Villanova, PA) 15 (1984) 129-131; C. SCAGLIONI, *CrnStor* 7 (1986) 609-611.

1981b  Note sulla fortuna dell'esegesi agostiniana di *Mt* 25,1-13. — *VetChr* 18 (1981) 33-79.

1985  Note di filologia patristica. — *VetChr* 22 (1985) 317-329. Esp. 322-325 [Origen: 25,1-5].

1988  *Pendula expectatio.* Un *topos* stoico nei Padri latini. [24,36] — *VetChr* 25 (1988) 407-411.

1991  L'esclusione degli eletti. Gregorio e la parabola delle dieci vergini. [25,1-13] — GIORDANO, L. (ed.), *Gregorio Magno. Il Maestro della communicazione spirituale e la tradizione gregoriana in Sicilia. Atti del Convegno (Vizzini, 10-11 marzo 1991)*, Catania: CUECM, 1991, 143-155.

### MARINELLI, Giovanni

1994  La donna nella Chiesa. "Ministra" o "mediatrice"? — *Sacra Doctrina* (Bologna) 39/3-4 (1994) 3-284. Esp. 60-74 [apostles - twelve]; 74-79 [women].

### MARÍN HEREDIA, Francisco

1973  Más sobre Mt 19,12. — *SalT* 61 (1973) 533-546. → Ruiz 1973

1977  Un recurso obligado a la tradición presinóptica. [19,10-12] — *EstBíb* 36 (1977) 205-216.
[NTA 24, 93]

1987 Valor midráshico de la prueba de José (Mt 1,18-25). — *Carthaginensia* 3 (1987) 171-178.

1988a Nueva perspectiva para Mc 1,12-13. — *Carthaginensia* 4 (1988) 97-105. Esp. 99-100 [4,1-11].

1988b Revisionismo necesario. Puntualización de textos bíblicos. — *Ibid.*, 223-233. Esp. 231-232 [2,4].

1991 Más allá de las apariencias: Mt 2,1-23. — *Carthaginensia* 7 (1991) 319-330.

**MARINI, O.**

1960* et al., *I vangeli nella critica moderna. Primo Congresso Biblico Franciscano d'Italia, Roma 1957*. Torino: Elle Di Ci, 1960, 243 p. → B. Benassi, Mariani, Marini

1960 I manoscritti di Qumrân e San Matteo. — *Ibid.*, 1-16.

**MARITANO, Mario**

1994 Il "lector" nel "Commento al Vangelo di Matteo" di Girolamo. — FELICI, S. (ed.), *Esegesi e catechesi nei Padri*, 1994, 33-63.

**MARKLOWSKI, Konrad**

1965 "Przyjdz Królestwo Twoje". Sens eschatologiczny czy historyczny? (Dein Reich komme, eschatologischer oder historischer Sinn). [6,10] — *RoczTK* 12/1 (1965) 45-48. [NTA 10, 1048]

**MARLOW, Ransom**

1966 The *Son of Man* in Recent Journal Literature. — *CBQ* 28 (1966) 20-30. [bibliography]. [NTA 10, 885]

**MARMER BIGORRA, S.**

1956 Sub potestate constitutus (Mt 8,9; Lc 7,8). — *Helmántica* (Salamanca) 7 (1956) 391-399.

**MAROT, Hilaire**

1967 Pierre, fondement de l'Église. [16,16-19] — *AssSeign* I/84 (1967) 47-58.

**MARQUARDT, Generosus**

1958 Die Bergpredigt des Matthäus-Evangeliums, eine meisterlich disponierte Komposition des Evangelisten. — *BK* 13 (1958) 81-84.

**MARQUET, Claudette**

1983 Ne vous faites pas appeler "maître". Matthieu 23,8-12. — *Christus* 30 (1983) 88-102. [NTA 27, 928]

**MARRION, Malachy**

1974 *Petitionary Prayer in Mark and in the Q Material* [Q 17,6/Mk 11,23-24]. Diss. Catholic Univ. of America, Washington, DC, 1974, 356 p. — *DissAbstr* 35 (1974-75) 1745-46.

**MARROW, Stanley B.**

1979 *The Words of Jesus in Our Gospels. A Catholic Response to Fundamentalism*. New York: Paulist, 1979, V-152 p. Esp. 33-35 [6,9-13]; 37-38 [5,3]; 43-45 [13,18-23]; 88-105: "The book of Matthew".

1988 Marriage and Divorce in the New Testament. — *ATR* 70 (1988) 3-15. Esp. 10-12 [5,32; 19,9]. [NTA 33, 872]

**MARSH, J.**

1980 Meditations in Matthew. — LIVINGSTONE, E.A. (ed.), *Studia Biblica 1978*, II, 1980, 129-149.

**MARSH-EDWARDS, J.C.**

1956    The Magi in Tradition and Art. — *IrEcclRec* 85 (1956) 1-9. → Filas 1956

**MARSHALL, I. Howard**

1963    *Eschatology and the Parables*. London: Tyndale, 1963, 48 p.

1966    The Synoptic Son of Man Sayings in Recent Discussion. — *NTS* 12 (1965-66) 327-351.
        Esp. 339-340 [11,19]; 340-341 [8,20]; 345 [24,44]. [NTA 11, 662]; = ID., *Jesus the Saviour*, 1990,
        73-99. Esp. 85-86; 90.

1967    The Divine Sonship of Jesus. — *Interpr* 21 (1967) 87-103. Esp. 91-95 [11,27]; 95-96 [16,17];
        96-97 [19,28]. [NTA 11, 1003]; = ID., *Jesus the Saviour*, 1990, 134-149. Esp. 137-140; 140-141;
        141-142.

1969    Son of God or Servant of Yahweh? A Reconsideration of Mark i.11. — *NTS* 15 (1968-
        69) 326-336. Esp. 330 [8,8.9]; 332-333 [12,18]. [NTA 13, 878]; = ID., *Jesus the Saviour*, 1990,
        121-133. Esp. 125; 128-129.

1970a   The Son of Man in Contemporary Debate. — *EvQ* 42 (1970) 67-87. [NTA 15, 96]; = ID.,
        *Jesus the Saviour*, 1990, 100-120.

1970b   Uncomfortable Words. VI. 'Fear him who can destroy both soul and body in hell' (Mt
        10,28 R.S.V.). — *ExpT* 81 (1969-70) 276-280. [NTA 15, 143]

1973a   The Meaning of the Verb "To Baptize". — *EvQ* 45 (1973) 130-140. [NTA 18, 50]

1973b   New Wine in Old Wine-Skins: V. The Biblical Use of the Word 'Ekklēsia'. — *ExpT*
        84 (1972-73) 359-364. Esp. 361 [18,17]. [NTA 18, 637]

1977*   (ed.), *New Testament Interpretation. Essays on Principles and Methods*. Exeter:
        Paternoster, 1977, 406 p.; rev. ed., 1979, 412 p. → Catchpole, E.E. Ellis, France, Goldingay,
        S.S. Smalley, Travis, D. Wenham

1977    *I Believe in the Historical Jesus*. London: Hodder & Stoughton, 1977; Grand Rapids,
        MI: Eerdmans, 253 p. Esp. 143-163: "The nature of the gospels".

1980    *Last Supper and Lord's Supper*. Exeter: Paternoster, 1980; Grand Rapids, MI:
        Eerdmans, 1981, 191 p. Esp. 99-101: "The Last Supper in the gospel of Matthew".

1984    How to Solve the Synoptic Problem: Luke 11:43 and Parallels. — WEINRICH, W.C.
        (ed.), *The New Testament Age*. FS B. Reicke, 1984, II, 313-325. Esp. 313-317 [synoptic
        problem]; 319-324 [23,6-7].

1987    The Hope of a New Age: The Kingdom of God in the New Testament. — DEASLEY,
        A.R.G. – SHELTON, R.L. (eds.), *The Spirit and the New Age*, London: Warner, 1987,
        319-355; = ID., *Jesus the Saviour*, 1990, 213-238. Esp. 218-219; 224-225 [Q]; 229-230 [16,18].

1990a   *Jesus the Saviour. Studies in New Testament Theology*. Downers Grove, IL: Inter-
        Varsity, 1990, 329 p. → 1966, 1967, 1969, 1970a, 1987

1990b   *The Origins of New Testament Christology*. Downers Grove, IL: InterVarsity, 1990.

1992a   Church. — *DJG*, 1992, 122-125. Esp. 123-124 [16,18; 18,17].

1992b   Salvation. — *Ibid.*, 719-724. Esp. 721-722.

1992c   Son of Man. — *Ibid.*, 775-781. Esp. 776.

1994    The Synoptic "Son of Man" Sayings in the Light of Linguistic Study. — SCHMIDT,
        T.E. – SILVA, M. (eds.), *To Tell the Mystery*. FS R.H. Gundry, 1994, 72-94. Esp. 84-85.

**MARTELET, Gustave**

1956    Remets-nous nos dettes, comme nous remettons les leurs à ceux qui nous doivent. [6,12]
        — *Verbum Caro* (Neuchâtel) 10/3 (1956) 79-84.

**MARTENS, Allan Wayne**

1995 *The Compositional Unity of Matthew 21:12–24:2. Redaction-Critical, Literary-Rhetorical and Thematic Analyses*. Diss. Toronto School of Theology, Toronto, Ont., 1995 (R. Longenecker).

**MARTIN, Alain**

1983 P. Vindob. L. 91, un fragment du *Pater* latin. — *Latomus* (Bruxelles) 42 (1983) 412-418.

**MARTIN, Brice Lemuel**

1977 *Matthew and Paul on Christ and the Law: Compatible or Incompatible Theologies?* Diss. McMaster Univ., Toronto, Ont., 1977.

1983 Matthew on Christ and the Law. — *TS* 44 (1983) 53-70. Esp. 54-58: "The validity of the Mosaic Torah" [5,17-48; 19,3-9]; 58-60: "The validity of the halakah"; 60-61 [5,20]; 62-63 [5,48]; 63-64 [5,43-47; 22,34-40]; 64-69 [5,17-18]. [NTA 27, 913]

**MARTIN, Francis**

1975 The Image of Shepherd in the Gospel of Matthew. — *SE* 27 (1975) 261-301. Esp. 271-285: "The analysis of the shepherd figure in Matthew, ch. 1-20" [2,6; 9,36; 10,6; 12,9-14.22-30; 14,14; 15,21-28; 18,12-14; 20,29-34]; 285-297: "The use of the shepherd theme in Matthew 21–28" [21,1-12; 24,30; 25,31; 26,15.28.31.56; 27,3-10]. [NTA 20, 429]

1984 Le baptême dans l'Esprit. Tradition du Nouveau Testament et vie de l'Église. — *NRT* 106 (1984) 23-58. Esp. 23-28 [3,11]. [NTA 28, 1134]

1988 *Narrative Parallels to the New Testament* (SBL Resources for Biblical Study, 22). Atlanta, GA: Scholars, 1988, X-266 p.

**MARTIN, François**

1982 Le signe du fils de l'homme. Analyse des chapitres 24 et 25 de l'Évangile de Matthieu. — *LumièreV* 160 (1982) 61-77. Esp. 63-70 [24,4-41]; 70-75 [24,42-25,30]; 75-77 [25,31-46]. [NTA 27, 929]

1987 & PANIER, L., Dévoilement du péché et salut dans le récit de la passion selon saint Matthieu. — *LumièreV* 185 (1987) 72-88. Esp. 73-77: "Une hypothèse de lecture"; 78-87: "Récit de la passion: dévoilement du péché". [NTA 32, 1120]

1988a Parole écriture accomplissement dans l'Évangile de Matthieu. — *SémBib* 50 (1988) 27-51. Esp. 31-37 [1: structure]; 38-41 [1,18-25]; 41-48 [1,23]. [NTA 33, 113]

1988b Naître entre juifs et païens. Matthieu 2. — *SémBib* 51 (1988) 8-21. Esp. 8-13 [2,1-12]; 13-21 [2,13-23]. [NTA 33, 595]
Naître entre juifs et païens. — *FilolNT* 1/1 (1988) 77-93. Esp. 78-82.82-90.

1988c Parler. Matthieu 13. — *SémBib* 52 (1988) 17-33. [NTA 33, 1135]

1989a Mourir. Matthieu 26–27. — *SémBib* 53 (1989) 18-48. Esp. 35-40 [27,3-10]. [NTA 33, 1137]

1989b Sortir du livre. [fulfilment quotations] — *SémBib* 54 (1989) 1-18. [NTA 34, 109]

1993 Figures et transfiguration. [17,1-8] — *SémBib* 70 (1993) 3-12. [NTA 38, 359]

**MARTIN, Hugh**

1937[R] *The Parables of the Gospels* [1937]. London: SCM, 1962, 256 p.

1953 *The Beatitudes*. New York: Harper and Brothers; London: SCM, 1953, 92 p.
W. BARCLAY, *ExpT* 63 (1951-52) 330-331; B. BOYD, *Interpr* 8 (1954) 104.106.

**MARTIN, James P.**

1975 The Church in Matthew. — *Interpr* 29 (1975) 41-56. Esp. 43-46: "The problem of the church"; 46-52: "The character of the church"; 52-56: "The shape of the Matthean church". [NTA 19, 939]; = MAYS, J.L. (ed.), *Interpreting*, 1981, 97-114.

**MARTIN, John**

1986    Dispensational Approaches to the Sermon on the Mount. — TOUSSAINT, S.D. – DYER,
        C.H. (eds.), *Essays in Honor of J. Dwight Pentecost*, Chicago, IL: Moody, 1986, n.p.

**MARTIN, José Pablo**

1987    El cristiano y la espada. Variaciones hermenéuticas en los primeros siglos. [10,34] —
        *RevistBíb* 49 (1987) 17-52.

**MARTIN, Ralph Philip**

1964    *Worship in the Early Church*. London–Edinburgh: Marshall, Morgan and Scott, 1964,
        144 p. Esp. 91 [3,13-17]; 94-97 [28,19-20].

1969    St. Matthew's Gospel in Recent Study. — *ExpT* 80 ‾1968-69) 132-136. Esp. 133-134
        [redaction criticism]; 134-135 [Papias]. [NTA 13, 853]

1975    *New Testament Foundations: A Guide for Christian Students*. Vol. 1: *The Four Gospels*.
        Grand Rapids, MI: Eerdmans; Exeter: Paternoster, ‾975, 326 p. Esp. 139-160: "The
        synoptic problem"; 224-243: "The gospel of Matthew"; 291-298: "The great thanksgiving and invitation
        (Matthew 11:25-30)".

1978    The Pericope of the Healing of the "Centurio's" Servant/Son (Mt 8,5-13 par. Luke 7,1-
        10): Some Exegetical Notes. — GUELICH, R.A. (ed.), *Unity and Diversity in New
        Testament Theology. Essays in Honor of George E. Ladd*, Grand Rapids, MI:
        Eerdmans, 1978, 14-22.

1988    Q. — BROMILEY, G.W., et al. (eds.), *The International Standard Bible Encyclopedia*,
        IV, Grand Rapids, MI: Eerdmans, 1988, 1-4.

**MARTIN, Raymond A.**

1987a   *Syntax Criticism of the Synoptic Gospels* (Studies in the Bible and Early Christianity,
        10). Lewiston, NY – Queenston, Ont.: Mellen, 1987, IX-219 p. Esp. 37-87: "Mark 1–10 and
        parallels in Luke and Matthew"; 89-103: "Q material"; 113-118.123-125: "Special Matthew"; 193-201 [Mk
        1–10/Mt–Lk]; 203-206 [Q]; 210-211 [Sondergut Mt].

1987b   Semitic Traditions in Some Synoptic Accounts. — *SBL 1987 Seminar Papers*, 295-335.
        Esp. 322-323.

1989    *Syntax Criticism of Johannine Literature, the Catholic Epistles, and the Gospel Passion
        Accounts* (Studies in the Bible and Early Christianity, 18). Lewiston, NY – Lampeter,
        UK – Queenston, Ont.: Mellen, 1989, X-185 p.

1995    *Studies in the Life and Ministry of the Historical Jesus*. Lanham, MD – New York –
        London: University Press of America, 1995, X-161 p.

**MARTIN, Vincent**

1995    *A House Divided. The Parting of the Ways Between Synagogue and Church* (Studies in
        Judaism and Christianity). New York – Mahwah, NJ: Paulist, 1995, VII-194 p. Esp. 120-
        131.

**MARTIN, W.H. Blyth**

1956    The Indispensability of Q. — *Theology* 59 (1956) 182-188. [NTA 1, 32] → Farrer 1956b

**MARTIN-ACHARD, Robert**

1953    Notes sur Mammon et la parabole de l'économe infidèle. — *ETR* 28 (1953) 137-141.
        → J. Ellul 1952

**MARTINDALE, Cyril Charlie**

1957    *The Gospel according to Saint Matthew* (Stonyhurst Scripture Manuals). Westminster,
        MD: Newman, 1957, XXVII-224 p.
            J.A. GRISPINO, *CBQ* 20 (1958) 407-408.

**MARTINEZ, Ernest R.**

1961   The Interpretation of *'oi mathētai* in Matthew 18. — *CBQ* 23 (1961) 281-292. Esp. 281: "The problem"; 281-285: "Various opinions"; 285-290: "Suggested solution". [NTA 6, 457]

1971   *The Gospel Accounts of the Death of Jesus. A Study in the Death Accounts Made in the Light of the New Testament Traditions, the Redaction and the Theology of the Four Evangelists.* Diss. Pont. Univ. Greg., Roma, 1971. Excerpta 1970, 65 p. — *GregLA*, 1971, 570.

**MARTÍNEZ, Gabriel B.**

1974   Un caso literario sobre la resurrección de Jesús de Nazaret. — *Veritas* (Buenos Aires) 19 (1974) 330-358.

1985   Galilea en los Evangelios de Mateo, Marcos y Lucas: La equivocidad del término Galilea. — *EstBíb* 43 (1985) 331-371. Esp. 331-348: "El nombre Galilea en el evangelio de Mateo". [NTA 30, 1031]

**MARTÍNEZ DALMAU, Eduardo**

1964   *A Study on the Synoptic Gospels. A New Solution to an Old Problem: The Dependence of the Greek Gospels of St. Matthew and St. Luke upon the Gospel of St. Mark.* New York: Speller, 1964, XIII-122 p. [NTA 9, p. 429]

**MARTÍNEZ DE LAHIDALGA AGUIRRE, Jose**

1973a  Indisolubilidad y divorcio en la teología de Tomás Sánchez. — *Lumen* (Vitoria) 22 (1973) 336-355.

1973b  Indisolubilidad y *porneia* en la teología de Sánchez. — *Ibid.*, 442-463.

1974   El divorcio vincular y la *porneia* en la teología de Tomás Sánchez. — *ScriptVict* 21 (1974) 70-92.

**MARTÍNEZ SANZ, Alfons**

1974   *Jesús, hijo de Dios, en el Evangelio de Mateo.* Diss. Pamplona, 1974, 340 p. (J.M. Casciaro). Esp. 84-101 [3,17]; 102-127 [17,5]; 129-167 [11,25-27]; 168-181 [22,41-46]; 182-194 [24,36]; 195-213 [26,63-64]; 214-238 [28,19-20]; 240-252 [14,32-33]; 253-269 [16,16]; 271-280 [27,40-43]; 281-289 [27,54]; 290-305 [4,3]; 306-317 [8,29].

**MARTINI, Carlo Maria**

1959   *Il problema storico della risurrezione negli studi recenti* (AnGreg, 104). Roma: Pont. Univ. Greg., 1959, XI-174 p.; ²1980. Esp. 42-75: "Le condizioni letterarie delle narrazioni evangeliche sulla risurrezione"; 76-113: "Il contenuto storico del messaggio pasquale primitivo"; 114-145: "Il contenuto storico delle narrazioni evangeliche".

1968a  Introduzione ai vangeli sinottici. — CANFORA, G., et al. (eds.), *Il Messaggio della Salvezza*, IV, 1968, 1-145. → 1979a

1968b  → K. Aland [GNT² 1968]

1969   Les signes de la résurrection. Mt 28,1-10. — *AssSeign* II/21 (1969) 48-57; = GANTOY, R. (ed.), *La Bonne Nouvelle de la Résurrection* (Lire la Bible, 66), Paris: Cerf, 1981; ²1984, 114-123.
       I segni della Risurrezione (Mt 28,1-10). — GANTOY, R. (ed.), *La buona novella della risurrezione*, trans. E. De Rosa (Letture Bibliche), Roma: Borla, 1985, 138-152.

1972   La problématique générale du texte de Matthieu. — DIDIER, M. (ed.), *L'Évangile selon Matthieu*, 1972, 21-36. Esp. 23-27: "Vue d'ensemble sur le matériel"; 27-31: "Problèmes du choix des variantes"; 31-35: "Problème de l'histoire du texte"; = ID., *La Parola di Dio alle origini della Chiesa* (AnBib, 93), Roma: Biblical Institute Press, 1980, 129-144. Esp. 131-135, 135-139, 139-143.

1979a Introduzione generale ai vangeli sinottici. — ID., et al. (eds.), *Il Messaggio della Salvezza. Corso completo di studi biblici.* VI: *Matteo, Marco e Opera Lucana,* Torino-Leumann: Elle Di Ci, [4]1979, 15-107. [NTA 24, p. 301] → 1968a

1979b Matteo, Marco e Opera Lucana. — *Ibid.,* 109-531. [G. Danieli: 5-7; G. Tosatto: 26,47-57].

1981 *Gli Esercizi Ignaziani alla luce del Vangelo di San Matteo.* Roma: Communità di vita cristiana, 1981, 184 p.
    G. ARLEDLER, *CC* 133/2 (1982) 616.
    *El Evangelio eclesial de san Mateo. Los ejercicios de san Ignacio a la luz del Evangelio de San Mateo.* Bogotá: Paulinas, 1984, 272 p.
    *Ich bin bei euch. Leben im Glauben nach dem Matthäusevangelium,* trans. A. Berz. Freiburg: Herder, 1985, 240 p.
    R. BARTNICKI, *CollTheol* 57/2 (1987) 185-187; M. BEHNISCH, *TLZ* 111 (1986) 769-770; K. STOCK, *BLtg* 60 (1987) 191.

**MARTÍN RAMOS, Nicasio**
1990 La eucaristía, misterio de reconciliación. — *Communio* (Sevilla) 23 (1990) 31-73, 209-248, 333-354. Esp. 32-38: "Mt 26,28 y 1 Cor 11,23-29".

**MARTORELL, José**
1980 *Los milagros de Jesús* (Series Academica, 2). Valencia: Facultad de Teología "San Vicente Ferrer", 1980, 94 p.

**MARTUCCI, Jean**
1975 Les récits de miracle: influence des récits de l'Ancien Testament sur ceux du Nouveau. — *SE* 27 (1975) 133-146. [NTA 20, 43]

**MARTY, William Henry**
1984 *The New Moses.* Diss. Theol. Sem., Dallas, TX, 1984, 303 p. — *SBT* 14 (1986) 85-86.

**MARUCCI, Corrado**
1982 *Parole di Gesù sul divorzio. Ricerche scritturistiche previe ad un ripensamento teologico, canonistico e pastorale della dottrina cattolica dell'indissolubilità del matrimonio* (Aloisiana, 16). Brescia: Morcelliana, 1982, 452 p. Esp. 169-406: "Le parole di Gesù contro il ripudio" [1,18-19; 5,31-32; 19,1-12]. [NTA 27, p. 210] — Diss. Frankfurt, 1979 (J. Beutler). → Aznar Gil 1983, Cannizzo 1983, Giavini 1983, Landucci 1983, Neudecker 1984

1990a Clausole matteane e critica testuale. In merito alla teoria di H. Crouzel sul testo originale di Mt 19,9. — *RivBib* 38 (1990) 301-325. [NTA 35, 630] → Crouzel 1971a, 1972

1990b Clausole matteane e matrimoni misti. Osservazioni critiche ad un saggio di T. Stramare. — *RasT* 31 (1990) 74-85. [NTA 36, 713r] → Stramare 1986

1993 Influssi latini sul greco del Nuovo Testamento. — *FilolNT* 6 (1993) 3-30. Esp. 4-7. [NTA 38, 1256]

1995 Immagini e problemi della Chiesa nel Nuovo Testamento: Il merito da un recente volume di J. Roloff. — *CC* 146/3 (1995) 399-412. Esp. 403-405. [NTA 40, 1068r] → Roloff 1993

**MARX, Werner G.**
1979 Money Matters in Matthew. — *BS* 136 (1979) 148-157. [NTA 23, 809]

1992 *Proof Positive. A Fresh Look at Synoptic Origins.* Lima, OH: Fairway, 1992, 117 p.

**MARXSEN, Willi**
1955 Bemerkungen zur "Form" der sogenannten synoptischen Evangelien. — *ZNW* 46 (1955) 274-275. → 1956b

1956a *Der Evangelist Markus. Studien zur Redaktionsgeschichte des Evangeliums* (FRLANT, 67). Göttingen: Vandenhoeck & Ruprecht, 1956, [2]1959 151 p. Esp. 26-30 [3,1-6; 4,1-

11/Mk]; 62-64 [Mt/Mk: geography]; 92-95 [Mt/Mk: εὐαγγέλιον]; 135-139 [24/Mk 13].
*Mark the Evangelist. Studies on the Redaction History of the Gospel*, trans. J. Boyce, et al.
Nashville, TN – New York: Abingdon, 1969, 222 p.
*El evangelista Marcos; estudio sobre la historia de la redación del evangelio*, trans. M. Balasch (Biblioteca
de estudios bíblicos, 33). Salamanca: Sígueme, 1981, 211 p.

1956b   Bemerkungen zur "Form" der sogenannten synoptischen Evangelien. — *TLZ* 81 (1956)
        345-348. Esp. 347-348. → 1955

1958    *Der "Frühkatholizismus" im Neuen Testament* (Biblische Studien, 21). Neukirchen-
        Vluyn: Neukirchener, 1958; repr. 1964, 75 p. Esp. 39-54: "Der Fels der Kirche (Matth. 16,13-
        20)".

1960    *Anfangsprobleme der Christologie*. Gütersloh: Mohn, 1960, 111 p.; ²1964, 55 p. Esp.
        20-34 [Son of Man]; 34-43 [faith].
        *The Beginnings of Christology: A Study in Its Problems*, trans. P.J. Achtemeier (Facet Books. Biblical Series,
        22). Philadelphia, PA: Fortress, 1969, XII-81 p. → N.M. Watson 1985
        *Alle origini della cristologia*, trans. B. Liverani (Epifania della Parola, 4). Bologna: Dehoniane, 1969, 163 p.

1962    Bibelarbeit über Mk 5,21-43 / Mt 9,18-26. — *Fragen der wissenschaftlichen Er-
        forschung der Heiligen Schrift. Sonderdruck aus dem Protokoll der Landessynode der
        Ev. Kirche im Rheinland (Tagung vom 2. bis 5. Januar 1962)*, Düsseldorf, 1962, 10-23.
        Esp. 17-23; = ID., *Der Exeget als Theologe. Vorträge zum Neuen Testament*, Gütersloh:
        Mohn, 1968, 171-182. Esp. 177-182.

1963    *Einleitung in das Neue Testament. Eine Einführung in ihre Probleme*. Gütersloh: Mohn,
        1963, ²⁻³1964, 240 p. Esp. 101-107: "Das synoptische Problem"; 130-136: "Matthäus-Evangelium";
        ⁴1978 (völlig neu bearbeitet), 295 p. Esp. 120-126; 149-156.
        *Introduction to the New Testament. An Approach to Its Problems*, trans. G. Buswell. Oxford: Blackwell;
        Philadelphia, PA: Fortress, 1968, XIV-284 p.
        *Introducción al Nuevo Testamento. Una iniciación a sus problemas*, trans. M. Legido López (Biblioteca de
        estudios bíblicos, 38). Salamanca: Sígueme, 1983, 290 p.
        Trans. Japanese 1984.

1964    *Die Auferstehung Jesu als historisches und als theologisches Problem*. Gütersloh: Mohn,
        1964, ²⁻³1965, ⁴1966, 35 p.; = ID., et al., *Die Bedeutung der Auferstehungsbotschaft
        für den Glauben an Jesus Christus*, Gütersloh: Mohn, ⁵1967, 9-40. → 1968
        *The Resurrection of Jesus as a Historical and Theological Problem. — MOULE, C.F.D. (ed.), The Significance
        of the Message of the Resurrection for Faith in Jesus Christ* (Studies in Biblical Theology, II/8), London:
        SCM; Naperville, IL: Allenson, 1968, 15-50.
        *La resurreción de Jesús como problema histórica y teológico*, trans. P. Velasco Beteta (Pedal, 95). Salamanca:
        Sígueme, 1979, 68 p.
        Trans. Japanese 1974.

1968    *Die Auferstehung Jesu von Nazareth*. Gütersloh: Mohn, 1968, ²1972; (Gütersloher
        Taschenbücher Siebenstern, 66), ³1978, 191 p. Esp. 47-51: "Matthäus-Evangelium". → 1964
        *The Resurrection of Jesus of Nazareth*, trans. M. Kohl. London: SCM; Philadelphia, PA: Fortress, 1970,
        191 p.
        *La resurrezione di Gesù di Nazareth*, trans. B. Liverani (Epifania della Parola, 6). Bologna: Dehoniane, 1970,
        248 p.
        *La resurreción de Jesús de Nazaret*, trans. A.E. Lator Ros. Barcelona: Herder, 1974, 236 p.

1983    Die Geschichte des Abendmahls im Neuen Testament. — *Die Zeichen der Zeit* (Berlin)
        37 (1983) 248-252.

1986    Der Streit um die Bergpredigt – ein exegetisches Problem? Anmerkungen zum Umgang
        mit der Sprache. — SCHRAGE, W. (ed.), *Studien zum Text und zur Ethik des Neuen
        Testaments*. FS. H. Greeven, 1986, 315-324.

1989    *"Christliche" und christliche Ethik im Neuen Testament*. Gütersloh: Mohn, 1989, 272
        p. Esp. 79-82 [11,2-6]; 96-104.211-212 [5,43-44]; 204-217: "Die Ethik des Matthäus" [4,17; 5,17-20; 23].

**MARZOTTO, Damiano**

1972 Quando verrà il Figlio dell'uomo... (Analisi strutturale di *Mt.* 24–25). — *RivBib* 20 suppl. (1972) 547-570. [NTA 19, 96]

1982 Il celibato nel Nuovo Testamento. — *ScuolC* 110 (1982) 333-370. Esp. 337-338.354-358 [19,12]. [NTA 27, 720]

**MASER, Peter**

1983 Sonne und Mond. Exegetische Erwägungen zum Fortleben der spätantik-jüdischen in der frühchristlichen Kultur. — *Kairos* 25 (1983) 41-67. Esp. 49-50 [24,29-31]. [NTA 28, 709]

**MASIÁ, Juan**

1989 Id y aprended de todas las gentes. [28,16-20] — *SalT* 77 (1989) 665-672. *SelT* 29 (1990) 129-131.

**MASINI, Mario**

1966 Le iscrizioni dei vangeli. — *ParVi* 11 (1966) 172-180.

1983 (ed.), *La passione secondo i quattro vangeli* (Universale teologica, 5). Brescia: Queriniana, 1983, 106 p.

1992 I "Vangeli dell'Infanzia" di Gesù: traguardi e prospettive. — *Marianum* 54 (1992) 451-460. [NTA 38, 815r] → Muñoz Iglesias 1990a

1995 Lectio divina su Mt 1,1-16. — *Theotokos* 3/1 (1995) 173-194.

**MASON, Steve**

1990a & ROBINSON, T., *An Early Christian Reader*. Toronto, Ont.: Canadian Scholar's Press, 1990, XIII-605 p. Esp. 120-142: "'Q': A lost sayings source".

1990b Pharisaic Dominance Before 70 CE and the Gospel's Hypocrisy Charge (Matt 23:2-3). — *HTR* 83 (1990) 363-381. [NTA 36, 728]

1992a *Josephus and the New Testament*. Peabody, MA: Hendrickson, 1992, VII-248 p. Esp. 151-163 [John the Baptist: 3,7-12; 11,2-6].

1992b Fire, Water and Spirit: John the Baptist and the Tyranny of Canon. — *StudRel/SciRel* 21 (1992) 163-180. Esp. 164-166: "The tendencies of the tradition"; 168-179: "Historical reconstruction" [Q 3,7-9.16-17; 7;18-23]. [NTA 37, 661]

**MASSAUX, Édouard**

1950 *Influence de l'évangile de saint Matthieu sur la littérature chrétienne avant saint Irénée* (Diss. ad grad. magistri, 42). Leuven: Publications Universitaires; Gembloux: Duculot, 1950, XLVII-730 p. — Diss. Leuven, 1950 (L. Cerfaux); repr. ed. F. Neirynck (BETL, 75), Leuven: University Press / Peeters, 1986, XXVII-850 p. Esp. 7-35 [1 Clem]; 66-83 [Barnabas]; 94-107 [Ignatius]; 139-148 [2 Clem]; 165-172 [Polycarpus, EpPhil]; 189-191 [MartPol]; 196-198 [Ascension of Isaiah]; 206-209 [Odes of Salomon]; 227-241 [Orac. Sib.]; 248-258 [ApocPeter]; 261-284 [Pastor of Hermas]; 328-329 [PapEg]; 341-345 [Gospel of the Hebrews]; 347-355 [Gospel of the Ebionites]; 357-358 [Gospel of the Egyptians]; 358-373 [Gospel of Peter]; 390-393 [Protev. Jacobi]; 400-402 [Kerygma Petri]; 406-419 [Agrapha]; 422-423 [Basilides]; 425-426 [Valentinus]; 426-434 [Heracleon]; 439-448 [Ptolemaeus]; 462-463 [Aristides]; 466-505 [Justin, Apol]; 510-555 [Justin, Dial]; 571-572 [Tatian]; 577-579 [Apollinaris of Hierapolis]; 580-585.590-591 [Athenagoras]; 594-598 [Theophilus of Antioch]; 604-641 [Didache]; 725-762: "Appendice" (→ 1952); 799-850: "Supplément. Bibliographie 1950-1985" (B. Dehandschutter). [NTA 31, p. 365] → Bellinzoni 1992, Koester 1994b, Neirynck 1986e

J.-P. AUDET, *RB* 58 (1951) 600-608; B. BOTTE, *BTAM* 6 (1951) 197-198; J. CAMBIER, *ETL* 30 (1954) 478-480; J. DANIÉLOU, *RSR* 38 (1950) 600-601; J. HÉRING, *RHPR* 33 (1953) 74-75; G.D. KILPATRICK, *JTS* 2 (1951) 199-200.

D.A. BERTRAND, *RHPR* 67 (1987) 309-310; P.-M. BOGAERT, *RBén* 97 (1987) 329; I. BROER, *TRev* 84 (1988) 116-121; R.F. COLLINS, *LouvSt* 13 (1988) 190-191; X. JACQUES, *NRT* 109 (1987) 742; G. MICHIELS, *BTAM* 14 (1988) 414; P. PERKINS, *SecCent* 8 (1991) 247-248; J. PONTHOT, *RTL* 18 (1987) 383-384; W.R. SCHOEDEL, *CBQ* 51 (1989) 562-564; B. SESBOÜÉ, *RSR* 76 (1988) 602-603; C.M. TUCKETT, *JSNT* 31 (1987) 128; B.T. VIVIANO, *RB* 96 (1989) 146-147.

*The Influence of the Gospel of Saint Matthew on Christian Literature before Saint Irenaeus*. Book I: *The First Ecclesiastical Writers*; Book II: *The Later Christian Writings*; Book III: *The Apologists and the Didache*, edited and with an Introduction and Addenda by A.J. Bellinzoni; trans. N.J. Belval & S. Hecht (New Gospel Studies, 5/1-3). Macon, GA: Mercer; Leuven: Peeters, I, 1990, XXVI-172 p. Esp. 7-32 [1 Clem]; 59-74 [Barnabas]; 85-96 [Ignatius]; 123-162 [bibliography]. [NTA 35, p. 384]; II, 1992, XXVIII-366 p. Esp. 3-12 [2 Clem]; 28-33 [Polycarpus, EpPhil]; 46-49 [MartPol]; 55-57 [Ascension of Isaiah]; 63-66 [Odes of Salomon]; 81-94 [Orac. Syb.]; 99-109 [ApocPeter]; 111-130 [Pastor of Hermas]; 173-174 [PapEg]; 183-189 [Gospel of the Hebrews]; 192-198 [Gospel of the Ebionites]; 200-201 [Gospel of the Egyptians]; 201-214 [Gospel of Peter]; 228-231 [Protev. Jacobi]; 243-245 [Kerygma Petri]; 249-261 [Agrapha]; 265 [Basilides]; 267-268 [Valentinus]; 268-275 [Heracleon]; 279-287 [Ptolemaeus]; 298-346 [bibliography]. [NTA 37, p. 281]; III, 1993, XXVIII-258 p. Esp. 6-7 [Aristides]; 11-45 [Justin, Apol]; 49-89 [Justin, Dial]; 110-111 [Tatian]; 116-118 [Apollinaris of Hierapolis]; 120-125.129 [Athenagoras]; 134-138 [Theophilus of Antioch]; 144-176 [Didache]; 190-230 (→ 1952); 232-245 [bibliography]. [NTA 38, p. 463]
  A. CHESTER, *Theological Book Review* (Guilford, Surrey) 7/3 (1994-95) 24-25; I.H. JONES, *ExpT* 106 (1994-95) 883; F. NEIRYNCK, *ETL* 69 (1993) 172-173; 71 (1995) 221-222; S.E. PORTER, *JSNT* 66 (1997) 119; D.P. SCAER, *ConcTQ* 58 (1994) 190-193; A.A. TRITES, *RExp* 89 (1992) 428-429.

1952  Le texte du Sermon sur la montagne de Matthieu utilisé par saint Justin. Contribution à la critique textuelle du premier évangile. — *ETL* 28 (1952) 411-448. Esp. 414-416: "Textes où Justin coïncide pratiquement avec *Mt.*" [5,20; 7,19.20]; 416-428: "Textes où de simples changements de style apparaissent" [5,28-29.32.34.37; 6,19-20; 7,15-16.22-23]; 428-443: "Textes où la dépendance de *Mt.* pourrait être plus éloignée" [5,16.41-42.44-46; 6,1.21.25-26.31-33]. → 1950/86, 725-762 The Text of Matthew's Sermon on the Mount Used by Saint Justin. A Contribution to the Textual Criticism of the First Gospel. — ID. *The Influence of the Gospel of Saint Matthew*, III, 1993, 190-230. Esp. 193-196; 196-208; 209-225.

1954  Collation du Codex 1185 (Sinaï 148) du Nouveau Testament. — *Muséon* 67 (1954) 1-42. Esp. 2-10.

1958  Les relations entre la Loi Ancienne et la Loi Nouvelle selon Mt., V,17-48. — *RevDiocNamur* 12 (1958) 265-283. Esp. 265-269 [5,17-20]; 269-281 [5,21-48].

1962*  (ed.), *La venue du Messie. Messianisme et eschatologie* (Recherches bibliques, 6). Brugge: Desclée De Brouwer, 1962, 260 p. → Feuillet, Quecke, Riesenfeld, Rigaux, Sabbe, van Iersel

1986  → 1950

**MASSEY, Isabel Ann**

1991  *Interpreting the Sermon on the Mount in the Light of Jewish Tradition as Evidenced in the Palestinian Targums of the Pentateuch. Selected Themes* (Studies in the Bible and Early Christianity, 25). Lewiston, NY – Queenston, Ont. – Lampeter, UK: Mellen, 1991, XX-209 p. [NTA 36, p. 424] — Diss. St. Michael's College, Toronto, Ont., 1980 (T. Forestell).

**MASSON, Charles**

1957  Le reniement de Pierre. Quelques aspects de la formation d'une tradition. — *RHPR* 37 (1957) 24-35. Esp. 29-31 [26,69-75]. [NTA 2, 38]; = ID., *Vers les sources*, 1961, 87-101. Esp. 94-96.

1961a  *Vers les sources d'eau vive. Études d'exégèse et de théologie du Nouveau Testament* (Publications de la Faculté de Théologie. Université de Lausanne, 2). Lausanne: Payot, 1961, X-249 p. → 1957, 1961b-c

1961b  Le démoniaque de Gérasa. Marc 5:1-20 (Matthieu 8:28-34; Luc 8:26-39). — *Ibid.*, 20-37.

1961c  Des pains oubliés au levain des Pharisiens et d'Hérode (Marc 8:14-21; Matthieu 16:5-12). — *Ibid.*, 70-86.

1964  Un nouveau commentaire de l'Évangile selon saint Matthieu. — *RTP* 14 (1964) 155-158. → P. Bonnard 1963

**MASSON, Jacques**

1982 *Jésus fils de David dans les généalogies de saint Matthieu et de saint Luc.* Paris: Téqui, 1982, XII-589 p. [NTA 27, p. 333] — Diss. Pont. Univ. S. Thoma, Roma, 1979 (K. Gieraths).
   X. ALEGRE, *ActBibl* 22 (1985) 94; J.A. CARRASCO, *EstJos* 37 (1983) 114-115; J. GUILLET, *RSR* 71 (1983) 415-416; A. MODA, *BibOr* 26 (1984) 250-252; E.M. PERETTO, *Marianum* 47 (1985) 368-370; J. PONTHOT, *RTL* 16 (1985) 374-375; A. VIARD, *RSPT* 67 (1983) 348.

**MASSONNET, Jean**

1991 Sanhédrin. — *DBS* 11/65 (1991) 1353-1413. Esp. 1361-1372.

**MASTIN, Brian A.**

1969 The Date of the Triumphal Entry. [21,8] — *NTS* 16 (1969-70) 76-82. [NTA 14, 860]

1984 Latin Mam(m)ona and the Semitic Languages: A False Trail and a Suggestion. [6,24] — *Bib* 65 (1984) 87-90. [NTA 28, 916]

**MASTON, Thomas Bufford**

1982 *Biblical Ethics. A Guide to the Ethical Message of the Scriptures from Genesis through Revelation.* Cleveland, OH: World Publications, 1967; repr. Atlanta, GA: Mercer, 1982, XX-300 p. Esp. 145-175: "The synoptic gospels".

**MATEOS, Ciriaco**

1972 Uso e interpretación de Zacarías 9,9-10 en el Nuevo Testamento. — *EstAgust* 7 (1972) 471-493; 8 (1973) 3-29.

1978 *Los relatos evangélicos de la passión de Jesús* (Orientación teológica-pastoral). Valladolíd: Estudio Agustiniano, 1978, 161 p.; = *EstAgust* 13 (1978) 3-54; 195-250.

**MATEOS, Juan**

1976 & ALONSO SCHÖKEL, L., Generosidad Mt 6,22-23. — *CuBíb* 33 (1976) 197-201.

1977a *Estudios de Nuevo Testamento.* I: *El aspecto verbal en el Nuevo Testamento* (Institución San Jeronimo. Estudios y monografías, 1). Madrid: Cristiandad; Valencia: Institución San Jeronimo, 1977, 171 p.

1977b & ALEPUZ, M., El imperfecto sucesivo en el Nuevo Testamento. — URBÁN FERNANDEZ, A., et al., *Estudios de Nuevo Testamento*, II, 1977, 65-101. Esp. 78-82.

1977c Eὐθύς y sinonimos en el Evangelio de Marcos y demas escritos del Nuevo Testamento. — *Ibid.*, 103-139. Esp. 129-131 [Mt/Mk]; 132 [Sondergut].

1981 & CAMACHO, F., *El Evangelio de Mateo. Lectura comentada* (Lectura del Nuevo Testamento, 2). Madrid: Cristiandad, 1981, 292 p. Esp. 11-16 [introduction]; 17-287 [commentary]. [NTA 29, p. 326]
   R. DE ANDRÉS, *RazFe* 207 (1983) 102-103.

1989 Análisis semántico de los lexemas σκανδαλίζω y σκάνδαλον. — *FilolNT* 2 (1989) 57-92. Esp. 62-63 [13,57; 15,12; 17,27]; 66-67 [11,6; 26,31.33]; 70-71 [18,6]; 71-73 [5,29-30]; 76 [24,10]; 82 [16,23]; 85-86 [13,41; 18,7]. [NTA 34, 57]

1990 Σάββατα, σάββατον, προσάββατον, παρασκευή. — *FilolNT* 3 (1990) 19-38. Esp. 23-24, 35-36. [NTA 35, 71]

1991 *El sermón del monte* (Biblia y pueblo, 4). México: Centro de Reflexión teológica, 1991.

1995 & CAMACHO, F., *El Hijo del hombre. Hacia la plenitud humana* (En los origenes del cristianismo, 9). Córdoba: El Almendro – Fundación Épsilon, 1995, XIV-360 p. Esp. 38-39; 45-47 [9,6]; 51-52 [12,8]; 57 [20,28]; 58-60 [8,20]; 61-62 [11,19]; 63-64 [12,32]; 65-67 [13,37]; 67-68 [16,13]; 77-78 [16,21]; 82 [17,22]; 85 [20,18]; 88 [26,24]; 90 [26,45]; 94 [17,9]; 97 [17,12]; 97-99 [12,40]; 101-102 [26,2]; 117-118 [16,27]; 128-129 [24,30]; 135 [26,64]; 136-137 [24,27]; 138-139 [24,37-39]; 141-142 [24,44]; 143-145 [10,23]; 145-147 [13,41]; 147-148 [16,28]; 148-150 [19,28]; 150-152 [25,31]; 191-198: "Matteo".

**MATERA, Frank John**

1984    Matthew 27:11-54. — *Interpr* 38 (1984) 55-59.

1986    *Passion Narratives and Gospel Theologies. Interpreting the Synoptics through Their Passion Stories* (Theological Inquiries). New York – Mahwah, NJ: Paulist, 1986, XI-256 p. Esp. 80-85: "The passion according to Matthew: overview"; 86-120: "Commentary"; 121-149: "Matthew's gospel theology" [Messiah; church; righteousness].

1987a   The Passion according to Matthew. Part One: Jesus Unleashes the Passion, 26:1-75. — *CleR* 72 (1987) 93-97. [NTA 31, 1085]

        Part Two: Jesus Suffers the Passion, 27:1-66. — *Priests & People* (London) 1 (1987) 13-17. [NTA 31, 1086]

1987b   The Plot of Matthew's Gospel. — *CBQ* 49 (1987) 233-253. Esp. 235-240 [plot, event, arrangement]; 240-243 [plot in Mt]; 243-246 [kernel of Mt's plot]; 246-252 [narrative blocks in Mt]. [NTA 31, 1053] → Carter 1992, M.A. Powell 1992d, A. Williams 1992

1989a   "His blood be on us and on our children". [27,25] — *BiTod* 27 (1989) 345-350. [NTA 34, 638]

1989b   The Ethics of the Kingdom in the Gospel of Matthew. — *Listening* 24 (1989) 241-250. Esp. 242-244: "Jesus and the law"; 244-249: "The more abundant righteousness". [NTA 34, 615]

1989c   The Incomprehension of the Disciples and Peter's Confession (Mark 6,14–8,30). — *Bib* 70 (1989) 153-172. Esp. 166-167 [14,28-31; 16,5-12]. [NTA 34, 144]

1991    The Trial of Jesus. Problems and Proposals. — *Interpr* 45 (1991) 5-16. Esp. 6-7 [26,57–27,26]; 9-11. [NTA 35, 598]

**MATEU Y LLOPIS, Felipe**

1986    Talentum argenti y talenta auri. Del Evangelio de san Mateo a los diplomas hispanos anteriores a 1126. — MUÑOZ LEÓN, D. (ed.), *Salvación en la palabra. Targum – Derash – Berith. En memoria del profesor Alejandro Díez Macho*, Madrid: Cristiandad, 1986, 735-748. Esp. 735-739.

**MATHAVADIAN, Christudhas**

1995    *The ἐξουσία of Jesus in the Gospel of Matthew*. Diss. Pont. Univ. Urbaniana, Roma, 1995, XV-365 p. (S. Virgulin). Esp. 6-29: "ἐξουσία (authority)"; 32-78: "Teaching as one having authority (Mt 7:28-29)"; 79-127: "Authority to forgive sins (Mt 9:1-8)"; 128-175: "Sending the disciples with authority (Mt 10:1-15)"; 176-211: "Do not be like the rulers of the gentiles (Mt 20:20-28)"; 212-234: "Who gave you this authority? (Mt 21:23-27)"; 235-291: "All authority to Jesus (Mt 28:16-20)"; 293-322: "Theological synthesis".

**MATHER, P. Boyd**

1977    Christian Prophecy and Matthew 28:16-20. A Test Exegesis. — *SBL 1977 Seminar Papers*, 103-116.

**MATHEW, Parackel Kuriakose**

1979    *The Setting of the Resurrection Narrative in the Gospel according to St. Matthew*. Diss. McGill, Montréal, 1979 (J.C. Kirby). — *DissAbstr* 40 (1979-80) 3371.

1985    Authority and Discipline. Matt. 16.17-19 and 18.15-18 and the Exercise of Authority and Discipline in the Matthean Community. — *ComViat* 28 (1985) 119-125. [NTA 31, 123]

**MATTAM, Joseph**

1993    The Our Father: The Revolutionary Prayer of Commitment to the Kingdom of God. — *AfEcclRev* 35 (1993) 69-78. [NTA 38, 158]

**MATTER, H.M.**

1980    *Wederkomst en wereldeinde. De zin van de "parousia" in het Nieuwe Testament*. Kampen: Kok, 1980, 157 p. Esp. 33-57: "Woordgebruik bij Matteüs" [παρουσία].

**MATTERA, R.**

1995 Kingdom Theology in the Synoptic Gospels: Towards a Socio-Political Ethic. — *Journal from the Radical Reformation* (Morrow, GA) 4 (1995) 31-41. [NTA 40, 144]

**MATTHEWS, A.D.**

1967 St Matthew's Gospel: A Problem in Identity. — *ChurchQR* 168 (1967) 153-162. [NTA 12, 144]

**MATTHEWS, Victor H.**

1991 & BENJAMIN, D.C., The Stubborn and the Fool. — *BiTod* 29 (1991) 222-226. Esp. 225-226 [5,21-26]. [NTA 36, 140]

**MATTHEWS, Walter Robert**

1960 *The Lord's Prayer. An Exposition for To-day*. London. Hodder & Stoughton, 1960. W. BARCLAY, *ExpT* 71 (1959-60) 236-237.

**MATTHEY, J.**

1980 The Great Commission according to Matthew. [28,16-20] — *International Review of Mission* (Genève) 69 (1980) 161-173. [NTA 24, 797]

**MATTILA, Sharon Lea**

1994 A Problem Still Clouded: Yet Again – Statistics and 'Q'. — *NT* 36 (1994) 313-329. Esp. 314-319: "The problem with the basic argument"; 319-324: "A purified Matt-Luke triple tradition"; 324-329: "A 'purified' Q?". [NTA 39, 782] → Carlston 1971

1995 A Question Too Often Neglected. — *NTS* 41 (1995) 199-217. Esp. 199-206: "Prediatessaronic synoptic harmonies?" [10,2-4]. [NTA 39, 1439]

**MATTILL, A.J., Jr.**

1974 Matthew 25:31-46 Relocated. — *RestQ* 17 (1974) 107-114. [NTA 19, 98]

1979 "The Way of Tribulation". [7,13-14] — *JBL* 98 (1979) 531-546. Esp. 531-534; 540-546. [NTA 24, 792]

1983 *Jesus and the Last Things. The Story of Jesus the Suffering Servant*. Gordo, AL: Flatwoods, 1983, VI-141 p.

1986 The Sermon on the Mount. How Not to Live. — *American Rationalist* (St. Louis, MO) 31 (1986) 95-98. [NTA 31, 111]

**MATTISON, Robin Dale**

1989 God/Father. Tradition and Interpretation. — *Reformed Review* (New Brunswick, NJ) 42/3 (1988-89) 189-206. [NTA 33, 1112]

1995 *To Beget or Not to Beget: Presuppositions and Persuasion in Matthew Chapter One*. Diss. Vanderbilt Univ., Nashville, TN, 1995, 442 p. (D. Patte). — *DissAbstr* 56 (1995-96) 4819.

**MATURA, Thaddée**

1974 Les invités à la noce royale. Mt 22,1-14. — *AssSeign* II/59 (1974) 16-27. [NTA 19, 541]

1975 Le célibat dans le Nouveau Testament d'après l'exégèse récente. — *NRT* 97 (1975) 481-500, 593-604. Esp. 487-496 [19,10-12]; 496-498 [19,29/Mk]; 498-500 [22,30/Mk]. [NTA 20, 616]

1978 *Le radicalisme évangélique. Aux sources de la vie chrétienne* (LD, 97). Paris: Cerf, 1978, 210 p. Esp. 19-30: "Présentation des textes radicaux"; 33-50: "Exigences radicales à l'égard des disciples" [8,19-22; 10,21-22; 18,1-5; 23,8-12]; 51-69: "Ensembles sur le renoncement" [10,37-39; 19,10-12]; 69-110: "Attitude à l'égard des biens matériels" [5,3; 6,19-34; 13,44-46; 19,16-22; 21,31-46]; 111-138: "Radicalisation de la loi" [5,3-12.21-48; 6,1-18; 7,1-2]; 139-154: "Paroles détachées" [7,13-14; 10,34-36; 11,12; 12,30; 22,14].

MATZKOW, Walter → Jülicher 1938/72

MAUL, S.
1965    La Mesio-prediko de Johano-Baptisto (Mt 3,11-12 par). — *Biblia Revuo* (Melbourne)
        2 (1965) 1-6.

MAURER, Christian
1959    Petrusevangelium. — HENNECKE, E. - SCHNEEMELCHER, W. (eds.), *Neutestamentliche
        Apokryphen*, [3]1959, 118-124 (ET, 179-187). → Schneemelcher 1987b

MAUROMATES, G.
1989    *The Exegesis of the "Lord's Prayer" in the Greek Fathers* [Greek]. Katerine: Tertio,
        1989, 211 p.

MAUSER, Ulrich W.
1963    *Christ in the Wilderness. The Wilderness Theme in the Second Gospel and Its Basis in
        the Biblical Tradition* (Studies in Biblical Theology, 39). London: SCM, 1963, 159 p.
        Esp. 144-146: "The wilderness in Matthew".
1986    Christian Community and Governmental Power in the Gospel of Matthew. — *Ex Auditu*
        (Princeton, NY) 2 (1986) 46-54.
1987    "Heaven" in the World View of the New Testament. — *HorizonsBT* 9/2 (1987) 31-51.
        Esp. 37-43 [heaven]; 43-46 [kingdom of heaven]. [NTA 33, 873]

MAXWELL-STUART, P.G.
1978    A Note on Matthew 16,2-3. — *Liverpool Classical Monthly* 3 (1978) 259-260.
1979    'Do not give what is holy to the dogs.' (Mt 7,6). — *ExpT* 90 (1978-79) 341. [NTA 24,
        90]

MAY, David M.
1991    *Social Scientific Criticism of the New Testament: A Bibliography* (NABPR Bibliographic
        Series, 4). Macon, GA: Mercer, 1991, xv-91 p.

MAY, Eric E.
1956    Translation of Monetary Terms in St. Matthew's Gospel. — *CBQ* 18 (1956) 140-143.

MAY, G. Lacey
1951    Temple or Shrine? [23,35; 27,5] — *ExpT* 62 (1950-51) 346-347.

MAY, John
1979    Fehlt dem Christentum ein Verhältnis zur Natur? Eine Analyse der Seligpreisungen (Mt
        5,2-12) und der Feuerpredigt des Buddha (Samy. XXXV,28). — *Una Sancta* 34 (1979)
        159-171. Esp. 160-166. [NTA 24, 83]

MAYENCE, Étienne
1965    *La parole de Jésus sur le serment (Mt 5,33-37; Jc 5,12). Tradition et rédaction dans
        l'Évangile de Matthieu*. Diss. Leuven, 1965, XXV-263 p. (F. Neirynck). Esp. 12-30: "Le
        logion sur le serment en Mt 5,33-37"; 31-38: "Jc 5,12 et Mt 5,33-37"; 39-65: "Le lemme d'introduction en
        Mt 5,33"; 72-121: "Les allusions à l'Écriture dans le récit de la passion en Mt"; 122-133: "Mt 18,15-17.21-
        22"; 134-182: "Les ajoutes matthéennes en finale de péricope"; 183-240: "Περισσός et πονηρός dans Mt";
        241-247: "Tradition et rédaction en Mt 5,33-37"; 215-257: "Les témoignages patristiques"; 258-260: "Mt
        23,16-22".

MAYER, Cornelius
1994*   & MÜLLER, K. - SCHMALENBERG, G. (eds.), *Nach den Anfängen fragen. Herrn Prof.
        Dr. theol. Gerhard Dautzenberg zum 60. Geburtstag am 30. Januar 1994* (Gießener
        Schriften zur Theologie und Religionspädagogik, 8). Gießen: Fachbereich Evangelische

Theologie und Katholische Theologie, 1994, 810 p. → Beutler, Fiedler, Giesen, Hoffmann, Lattke, Schweizer

**MAYER, I.**

1959   "Buch der Genesis Jesu Christi...". [1,1] — *Der große Entschluß* (Wien) 14 (1959) 511-513.

**MAYORDOMO-MARÍN, Moisés**

1992   Jak 5,2.3a: Zukünftiges Gericht oder gegenwärtiger Zustand? — *ZNW* 83 (1992) 132-137. Esp. 135-136 [6,19]. [NTA 37, 330]

**MAYS, James Luther**

1981*  (ed.), *Interpreting the Gospels*. Philadelphia, PA: Fortress, 1981, X-307 p. → Carlston 1975b, Gaston 1975, Kingsbury 1975b, J.P. Martin 1975

**MBENA, Romanus Rocky**

1995   *A Call to the Wedding Banquet and Membership of the Kingdom of God. A Biblical-Theological Study of* Mt *22,1-14*. Diss. Pont. Univ. Urbaniana, Roma, 1995, XV-207 p. (T. Federici). Esp. 38-71: "Preliminary Questions on *Mt* 22,1-14"; 72-147: "Analysis of *Mt* 22,1-14"; 148-158: "The parable and the Matthean community"; 159-191: "Theological themes".

**MCARTHUR, Harvey K.**

1958   Mark xiv.62. — *NTS* 4 (1957-58) 156-158. Esp. 157 [26,64]. [NTA 2, 536] → Glasson 1960

1960a  *Understanding the Sermon on the Mount*. New York: Harper, 1960, 192 p.; repr. Westport, CT: Greenwood, 1978. Esp. 11-25: "The sermon as problem"; 26-57: "The sermon and the Mosaic tradition"; 58-104: "The sermon and the Pauline tradition"; 105-148: "The sermon and ethics". [NTA 5, p. 244]
       S.M. GILMOUR, *JBL* 80 (1961) 100.

1960b  The Dependence of the Gospel of Thomas on the Synoptics. — *ExpT* 71 (1959-60) 286-287. [NTA 5, 230] → R.McL. Wilson 1960c

1960c  The Gospel according to Thomas. [5,15/Th 33a; 15,14/Th 34] — ID. (ed.), *New Testament Sidelights. Essays in Honor of Alexander Converce Purdy*. Hartford: Hartford Seminary Foundation Press, 1960, 43-77.

1964   Basic Issues. A Survey of Recent Gospel Research. — *Interpr* 18 (1964) 39-55. Esp. 40-42 [Q]; 47-51 [authenticity]. [NTA 8, 893]; = ID. (ed.), *In Search of the Historical Jesus*, 1969, 139-144.

1965   The Eusebian Sections and Canons. — *CBQ* 27 (1965) 250-256. [NTA 10, 62]

1969*  (ed.), *In Search of the Historical Jesus* (Scribner Source Books in Religion). New York: Scribner, 1969; London: SPCK, 1970, XIII-284 p. → G. Bornkamm 1956a/60, Léon-Dufour 1959a/65, T.W. Manson 1946/62, McArthur 1964, V. Taylor 1954

1971a  The Burden of Proof in Historical Jesus Research. — *ExpT* 82 (1970-71) 116-119. [NTA 15, 803]

1971b  The Parable of the Mustard Seed. [13,31-32] — *CBQ* 33 (1971) 198-210. Esp. 198-202: "The various versions"; 202-205: "The language of the parable and the OT"; 205-208: "The primitive form of the parable and its meaning"; 209-210: "The relation of the parable to the teaching of Jesus". [NTA 15, 869]

1971c  'On the Third Day'. — *NTS* 18 (1971-72) 81-86. Esp. 82.85. [NTA 16, 630] "Am dritten Tag". 1 Kor 15,4b und die rabbinische Interpretation von Hosea 6,2. — HOFFMANN, P. (ed.), *Zur neutestamentlichen Überlieferung von der Auferstehung Jesu*, 1988, 94-202. Esp. 195.200-201.

1973   "Son of Mary". — *NT* 15 (1973) 38-58. Esp. 49-50 [13,55]. [NTA 17, 947]

1977   The Origin of the 'Q' Symbol. — *ExpT* 88 (1976-77) 119-120. [NTA 21, 363]

**MCBRIDE, Alfred**

1977   *The Kingdom and the Glory of St. Matthew*. New York: Arena Lettres, 1977, 208 p. [NTA 22, p. 91]

**McCAFFREY, U.P.**

1981 Psalm Quotations in the Passion Narratives of the Gospels. — *Neotestamentica* 14 (1981) 73-89. Esp. 78-83 [Ps 22]; 83-86 [26,3-4.64; 27,34.38.48]. [NTA 27, 76] — Diss. Univ. of South Africa, Pretoria, 1979.

**McCANE, Byron R.**

1990 "Let the dead bury their own dead": Secondary Burial and Matt 8:21-22. — *HTR* 83 (1990) 31-43. [NTA 35, 1132]

1992a *Jews, Christians, and Burial in Roman Palestine* [8,11-12; 23,27-28]. Diss. Duke Univ., Durham, NC, 1992, 268 p. (E.M. Meyers – D.M. Smith, Jr.). — *DissAbstr* 53 (1992-93) 3249.

1992b Is a Corpse Contagious? Early Jewish and Christian Attitudes toward the Dead. — *SBL 1992 Seminar Papers*, 378-388. Esp. 384-385 [23,27-28].

1993 "Where no one had yet been laid": The Shame of Jesus' Burial. — *SBL 1993 Seminar Papers*, 473-484. Esp. 482 [27,60].

**McCANT, Jerry W.**

1978 *The Gospel of Peter. The Docetic Question Re-examined.* Diss. Emory Univ., Atlanta, GA, 1978, 287 p. (L.E. Keck) — *DissAbstr* 39 (1978-79) 4332-33.

1984 The Gospel of Peter: Docetism Reconsidered. — *NTS* 30 (1984) 258-273. Esp. 259-262 [26,63]; 262-265 [27,46]; 265-267 [27,50]; 267-268 [κύριος]. [NTA 28, 1236]

**McCARTHY, Carmel**

1991 Gospel Exegesis from a Semitic Church: Ephrem's Commentary on the Sermon on the Mount. — NORTON, G.J. – PISANO, S. (eds.), *Tradition of the Text. Studies Offered to Dominique Barthélemy in Celebration of his 70th Birthday* (Orbis Biblicus et Orientalis, 109), Freiburg/Schw: Universitätsverlag; Göttingen: Vandenhoeck & Ruprecht, 1991, 103-123.
St. Ephrem's Commentary on Tatian's Diatessaron. Reflecting on Chester Beatty Syriac Manuscript 709. — *ProcIrBibAss* 14 (1991) 79-92. [NTA 36, 665]

1993 *Saint Ephrem's Commentary on Tatian's Diatessaron* (JSS Supplements, 2). Oxford: University Press, 1993, VII-381 p.

**McCARTY, S.**

1992 Beatitudes and Gifts as Formative for Spiritual Guidance. — *Studies in Formative Spirituality* (Pittsburgh, PA) 13 (1992) 203-220. [NTA 37, 720]

**McCASLAND, S. Vernon**

1953 "Abba, Father". — *JBL* 72 (1953) 79-91. Esp. 87-88.

1957 Signs and Wonders. — *JBL* 76 (1957) 149-152. Esp. 152 [12,39-41; 16,4]. [NTA 2, 136]

1958 "The Way". — *JBL* 77 (1958) 222-230. Esp. 226-228 [3,3]. [NTA 3, 485]

1961 Matthew Twists the Scriptures. [1,1-17; 5,27-31; 20,29-34; 21,1-11; 28,1-10] — *JBL* 80 (1961) 143-148. [NTA 6, 116]

**McCAUGHEY, J. Davis**

1960 Two Synoptic Parables in the Gospel of Thomas. [21,33-46/Th 65; 22,1-10/Th 64] — *AusBR* 8 (1960) 24-28. [NTA 8, 137]

1972a Marriage and Divorce. Some Reflections on the Relevant Passages in the New Testament. — *Colloquium* 4 (1972) 24-39. [NTA 17, 288] → Powers 1972

1972b Marriage and Divorce. A Response to Dr. Powers' Comments. — *Colloquium* 5 (1972) 42-43. [NTA 17, 918] → Powers 1972

1985    Matthew 6.13A. The Sixth Petition in the Lord's Prayer. — *AusBR* 33 (1985) 31-40.
[NTA 32, 1106]

### MCCONNELL, Richard Sterling

1969    *Law and Prophecy in Matthew's Gospel. The Authority and Use of the Old Testament in the Gospel of St. Matthew* (Theologische Dissertationen, 2). Basel: Reinhardt, 1969, VII-224 p. Esp. 6-58: "Jesus' fulfillment of the Law" [5,17-20.21-48]; 59-85: "Jesus' rejection of certain elements of the Mosaic Law" [5,33-37; 12,1-14; 15,1-20; 17,24-27; 19,7-8; 23,2-3.23]; 86-94: "Did Jesus bring a new Law?"; 95-100: "The authority of Jesus and the authority of the Old Testament law"; 101-141: "The formula quotations"; 142-146: "The use of Old Testament prophetic quotations which are ascribed to Jesus" [11,4-5.10; 12,40; 13,13-15; 21,42; 26,31]; 147-168: "Jesus and the expectation of the Messiah"; 169-13: "Jesus and the suffering servant"; 194-214: "Jesus and the Son of Man". [NTA 16, p. 167] — Diss. Basel, 1964 (B. Reicke). → Van Segbroeck 1972b
      E. BEST, *ScotJT* 23 (1970) 493; F.H. BORSCH, *Interpr* 25 (1971) 221-222; C. DIETERLÉ, *RTP* 21 (1971) 189-190; G. GANDER, *TZ* 27 (1971) 140; J. KAHMANN, *TijdTheol* 11 (1971) 83-84; C. MATEOS, *EstAgust* 6 (1971) 278-279; B. SALOMONSEN, *DanskTeolTids* 33 (1970) 307; A. SUHL, *TLZ* 96 (1971) 271-272.

### MCCONVERY, Brendan

1995    The Death of the Messiah. — *DoctLife* 45 (1995) 297-306. [NTA 40, 133r] → R.E. Brown 1994a

### MCCOOL, Francis J.

1956    Revival of Synoptic Source-Criticism. — *TS* 17 (1956) 459-493. [NTA 1, 185] → Cerfaux 1954b, Levie 1954, Vaganay 1954a

1967    Synoptic Problem. — *NewCathEnc* 13 (1967) 886-891.

### MCCORD, H.

1957    The Synoptic Problem. — *RestQ* 1 (1957) 51-69.

### MCCRACKEN, David

1994    *The Scandal of the Gospels. Jesus, Story, and Offense.* Oxford: University Press, 1994, XII-204 p. Esp. 76-89 [20,1-16]; 92-106 [13]; 110-127 [17,22-18,35].

### MCCULLOUGH, John C.

1982    Early Syriac Commentaries on the New Testament. — *Theological Review* (Beirut) 5 (1982) 14-33, 79-126.

### MCCUMBER, W.E.

1975    *Matthew* (Beacon Bible Expositions, 1). Kansas City, MO: Beacon Hill Press, 1975, 224 p. [NTA 21, p. 89]

### MCDERMOTT, John M.

1977    Luke, XII,8-9: Stone of Scandal. [10,32] — *RB* 84 (1977) 523-537. [NTA 23, 137] → 1978

1978    Luc, XII,8-9: Pierre angulaire. — *RB* 85 (1978) 381-401. [NTA 24, 134] → 1977

1981    Jesus and the Son of God Title. — *Greg* 62 (1981) 277-318 (French summary, 317-318). Esp. 280-288 [24,36/Mk]; 288-292 [11,27]; 293-296 [21,37/Mk]. [NTA 26, 265]

1984    Mt. 10:23 in Context. — *BZ* 28 (1984) 230-240. Esp. 231-232: "The Matthaean context"; 232-236: "The context of Mt. 10"; 236-240: "The source and meaning of Mt. 10:23". [NTA 29, 101]

### MCDONALD, James Ian Hamilton

1978    The Concept of Reward in the Teaching of Jesus. — *ExpT* 89 (1977-78) 269-273. Esp. 270-271. [NTA 23, 64]

1987    → Chilton 1987a

1989    *The Resurrection. Narrative and Belief.* London: SPCK, 1989, XII-161 p. Esp. 78-94: "Power and presence (Matthew)".

1993     The Great Commandment and the Golden Rule. — AULD, A.G. (ed.), *Understanding Poets and Prophets. Essays in Honour of George Wishart Anderson* (JSOT SS, 152), Sheffield: JSOT, 1993, 213-226. Esp. 213-216 [7,12; 22,34-40].

**McDONNELL, Kilian**
1991     → Montague 1991
1995     Jesus' Baptism in the Jordan. — *TS* 56 (1995) 209-236. [NTA 40, 632]

**McELENEY, Neil J.**
1972     Authenticating Criteria and Mark 7:1-23. — *CBQ* 34 (1972) 431-460. Esp. 432-448: "The criteria". [NTA 17, 535] → Gerhardsson 1961, E.P. Sanders 1969a
1976     Mt 17:24-27 – Who Paid the Temple Tax? A Lesson in Avoidance of Scandal. — *CBQ* 38 (1976) 178-192. Esp. 179-182: "The temple tax"; 182-192: "Matthew 17:24-27". [NTA 20, 779]
1979a    *The Growth of the Gospels.* New York – Ramsey, NJ – Toronto, Ont.: Paulist, 1979, VII-88 p.
1979b    The Principles of the Sermon on the Mount. — *CBQ* 41 (1979) 552-570. Esp. 554-563: "Matthew 5:17 and 5:20 as structural prinicples of the sermon"; 563-567: "Authenticity and Mt 5:17-20"; 567: "Jesus, the Law and Christian ethic". [NTA 24, 419]
1981     The Beatitudes of the Sermon on the Mount/Plain. — *CBQ* 43 (1981) 1-13. Esp. 2-3: "A textual question" [5,3.5]; 3-13: "Stages in the development of the Sermon's beatitudes". [NTA 25, 853]
1985     Does the Trumpet Sound or Resound? An Interpretation of Matthew 6,2. — *ZNW* 76 (1985) 43-46. [NTA 30, 115]
1990a    Peter's Denials – How Many? To Whom? — *CBQ* 52 (1990) 467-472. Esp. 468: "Matthew's penchant for pluralizing". [NTA 35, 150]
1990b    The Sermon on the Mount. Then and Now. [5,17-20] — *LivLight* 27 (1990) 30-35. [NTA 35, 622]
1994     The Unity and Theme of Matthew 7:1-12. — *CBQ* 56 (1994) 490-500. [NTA 39, 1452]

**McFALL, Leslie**
1994     Tatian's *Diatessaron*: Mischievous or Misleading? — *WestTJ* 56 (1994) 87-114. Esp. 97-99: "Why did Tatian omit the genealogies of Jesus?"; 106-114. [NTA 39, 90]

**McGAUGHY, Lane C.**
1975     The Fear of Yahweh and the Mission of Judaism: A Postexilic Maxim and Its Early Christian Expansion in the Parable of the Talents. — *JBL* 92 (1975) 235-245. Esp. 236-239: "An apocalyptic warning"; 239-241: "A parenetic pronouncement"; 241-243: "The original parable"; 243-245: "A postexilic maxim". [NTA 20, 93]
1992     A Short History of Parable Interpretation. Part I. — *Forum* 8 (1992) 229-245. [NTA 40, 798]

**McGING, Brian C.** → Skeat 1991

**McGINLAY, Hugh**
1982     (ed.), *The Year of Matthew.* Northcote, Australia: Desbooks; Melbourne: Joint Board of Christian Education of Australia and New Zealand, 1982-85, V-85 p. [F.J. Moloney: Mt 1-2; W.R.G. Loader: Mt 4-7]. [NTA 31, p. 234]

**McGINN, Sheila E.**
1995     "Not counting [the] women…". A Feminist Reading of Matthew 26–28. — *SBL 1995 Seminar Papers*, 168-176.

**McGOVERN, John J.**
1960     There I am in the midst of them. [18,20] — *Worship* 34 (1959-60) 450-453. [NTA 5, 81]

**McGRAW, Larry Ray**

1983　*An Examination of the Literary Context of the Great Commission in Matthew 28:16-20.* Diss. Southwestern Baptist Theol. Sem., Fort Worth, TX, 1983. — *DissAbstr* 44 (1983-84) 3720; *SBT* 14 (1986) 87-88.

**McGUCKIN, John Anthony**

1984　Jesus Transfigured: A Question of Christology. — *CleR* 69 (1984) 271-279. [NTA 29, 124]

1986　*The Transfiguration of Christ in Scripture and Tradition* (Studies in the Bible and Early Christianity, 9). Lewiston, NY – Queenston, Ont.: Mellen, 1986, XVI-333 p. Esp. 99-128: "The patristic interpretation of the transfiguration"; 145-248: "The Greek fathers"; 249-322: "The Latin fathers".

1989　The Patristic Exegesis of the Transfiguration. — *Studia Patristica* 18/1 (1989) 335-341.

**McHUGH, John**

1973a　The Origins and Growth of the Gospel Traditions. — *CleR* 58 (1973) 2-9, 83-95, 162-175. Esp. 84-87 [8,23-27]; 94-95 [14,22-33]. [NTA 17, 855/856/880]

1973b　The Literary Origins of the Gospels. — *Ibid.*, 421-428. Esp. 425-426. [NTA 18, 57] → Boismard 1972

1975　*The Mother of Jesus in the New Testament.* London: Darton, Longman & Todd; Garden City, NY: Doubleday, 1975, XLVIII-510 p. Esp. 157-163 [1,18]; 164-172 [1,19]; 200-254: "The brothers of Jesus"; 278-283 [1,23]. → R.E. Brown 1985a
　　　*La mère de Jésus dans le Nouveau Testament*, trans. J. Winandy (LD. 90). Paris: Cerf, 1977, 493 p. Esp. 201-207; 208-216; 244-298; 321-326.
　　　*La madre de Jesús en el Nuevo Testamento*, trans. J. Goitia (Nueva biblioteca de teologia, 42). Bilbao: Desclée De Brouwer, 1979, 551 p.

1978　A New Approach to the Infancy Narratives. — *Marianum* 40 (1978) 277-287. Esp. 278-282. [NTA 24, 412r] → R.E. Brown 1977

1980　Exegesis and Dogma. A Review of Two Marian Studies. — *The Ampleforth Review* (York) 85 (1980) 43-57. Esp. 47-49: "The Matthean infancy narrative". → R.E. Brown 1977, 1978
　　　Response: R.E. BROWN, *ibid.*, 57-60.

1991　Galatians 2:11-14: Was Peter Right? — HENGEL, M. – HECKEL, U. (eds.), *Paulus und das antike Judentum. Tübingen-Durham-Symposium im Gedenken an den 50. Todestag Adolf Schlatters († 19 Mai 1938)* (WUNT, 58), Tübingen: Mohr, 1991, 319-330. Esp. 326-328. → Meier 1983

**McIVER, Robert Kerry**

1989　*The Problem of Synoptic Relationships in the Development and Testing of a Methodology for the Reconstruction of the Matthean Community.* Diss. Andrews Univ., Berrien Springs, MI, 1989, 731 p. (R. Johnston). — *DissAbstr* 50 (1989-90) 3259-3260.

1994　One Hundred-Fold Yield – Miraculous or Mundane? Matthew 13.8,23; Mark 4.8,20; Luke 8.8. — *NTS* 40 (1994) 606-608. [NTA 39, 806]

1995a　The Parable of the Weeds among the Wheat (Matt 13:24-30,36-43) and the Relationship between the Kingdom and the Church as Portrayed in the Gospel of Matthew. — *JBL* 114 (1995) 643-659. Esp. 644-648: "The universalist interpretation"; 648-653: "The ecclesiastical interpretation"; 654-657: "Kingdom as either reign or realm"; 657-659: "Matthean theology of the kingdom". [NTA 40, 830]

1995b　The Sabbath in the Gospel of Matthew. A Paradigm for Understanding the Law in Matthew? — *AndrUnS* 33 (1995) 231-243 [NTA 40, 1463]

**McKAY, Heather A.**

1992　From Evidence to Edifice: Four Fallacies about the Sabbath. — CARROLL, R.P. (ed.),

*Text as Pretext. Essays in Honour of Robert Davidson* (JSOT SS, 138), Sheffield: JSOT, 1992, 179-199. Esp. 196-198 [6,5].

1994 *Sabbath and Synagogue. The Question of Sabbath Worship in Ancient Judaism* (Religions in the Graeco-Roman World, 122). Leiden: Brill, 1994, XI-279 p. Esp. 132-151; 159-161: "Discussion on synagogues in Matthew"; 172 [6,5].

**MCKAY, Johnston R.**

1976* & MILLER, J.F. (eds.), *Biblical Studies. Essays in Honour of William Barclay*. London: Collins; Philadelphia, PA: Westminster, 1976, 223 p. → M. Black, G. Johnston, Neil

**MCKAY, K.L.**

1981 On the Perfect and Other Aspects in New Testament Greek. — *NT* 23 (1981) 289-329. — *NT* 23 (1981) 289-329. Esp. 292 [18,20; 26,43]; 299-301 [20,25]; 303 [9,30]; 305 [16,3]; 306 [27,18]; 310-311 [2,5.20; 3,2; 5,32; 7,25; 10,6]; 313 [9,29]; 316 [24,25-26]; 318 [21,4]; 320 [13,46]; 322 [7,25; 25,26]. [NTA 26, 416]

1985a Aspect in Imperatival Constructions in New Testament Greek. — *NT* 27 (1985) 201-226. Esp. 207-214 [2nd p.]; 214-216 [3rd p.]; 216-219 [prohibitions]; 219-220 [future]; 220-222 [exhortation]; 222-223 [infinitive]; 223-224 [ἵνα]; 224-226 [participles]. [NTA 30, 45] → Thorley 1989

1985b The Use of *hoi de* in Matthew 28.17. A Response to K. Grayston. — *JSNT* 24 (1985) 71-72. [NTA 30, 129] → Grayston 1984, van der Horst 1986

1992 Time and Aspect in New Testament Greek. — *NT* 34 (1992) 209-228. Esp. 215 [23,23]; 219 [25,24]; 221 [7,24-27]; 222-223 [13,3-9.44-46]. [NTA 37, 621] → S.E. Porter 1989

**MCKEATING, Henry**

1961 The Prophet Jesus. — *ExpT* 73 (1961-62) 4-7, 50-53. [NTA 6, 436]

**MCKEE, Elsie Anne**

1991 Some Reflections on Relating Calvin's Exegesis and Theology. — BURROWS, M.S. - ROREM, P. (eds.), *Biblical Hermeneutics in Historical Perspective. Studies in Honor of Karlfried Froehlich on His Sixtieth Birthday*, Grand Rapids, MI: Eerdmans, 1991, 215-226. Esp. 221-222 [18,15-18].

1992 John Calvin's Teaching on the Lord's Prayer. — *PrincSemB* suppl. 2 (1992) 88-106.

**MCKELVEY, R.J.**

1969 *The New Temple. The Church in the New Testament* (Oxford Theological Monographs). Oxford: University Press, 1969, XIX-238 p. Esp. 58-74: "The synoptic gospels"; 193-194 [16,18].

**MCKENNA, Thomas F.**

1979 Matthew on Church Authority. Guidelines Toward a Healthy Image. — *BiTod* 102 (1979) 2035-2041. [NTA 23, 810]

**MCKENZIE, Alyce Mundi**

1994 *Preaching on Proverbial Wisdom in Proverbs, Qohelet and the Synoptic Jesus through the Reader Response Theory of Wolfgang Iser* [Q: wisdom]. Diss. Theol. Sem., Princeton, NJ, 1994, 297 p. (T.G. Long). — *DissAbstr* 55 (1994-95) 2003.

**MCKENZIE, John L.**

1964 Signs and Power. The New Testament Presentation of Miracles. — *ChSt* 3 (1964) 5-18. [NTA 9, 114]

1968 The Gospel according to Matthew. — BROWN, R.E., et al. (eds.), *The Jerome Biblical Commentary*, II, 1968, 62-114.
    J. MURPHY-O'CONNOR, *RB* 77 (1970) 420-421.
    Evangelio según San Mateo. — BROWN, R.E., et al. (eds.), *Comentario Bíblico "San Jeronimo"*, III, 1972, 163-293.
    Il Vangelo secondo Matteo. — BROWN, R.E., et al. (eds.), *Grande commentario biblico*, 1973, 899-968.

1983    The Mother of Jesus in the New Testament. — *Concilium* (London) 168 (1983) 3-11.
Esp. 4-5. [NTA 28, 713]
La mère de Jésus dans le Nouveau Testament. — *Concilium* (Paris) 188 (1983) 25-38. Esp. 27-28.
Die Mutter Jesu im Neuen Testament. — *IZT/Concilium* (Mainz) 19 (1983) 595-603. Esp. 596-597.

**MCKENZIE, R.A.**
1985    *The First Day of the Week. The Mystery and Message of the Empty Tomb.* New York:
Paulist, 1985, III-87 p.

**MCKERRAS, R.**
1988    Who is "This Generation"? An Alternative View. — *Notes on Translation* (Dallas, TX)
2/1 (1988) 57-58. [NTA 33, 1055]

**MCKIBBENS, Thomas R.**
1982    The Exegesis of John Chrysostom: Homilies on the Gospels. — *ExpT* 93 (1981-82) 264-
270.

**MCKIM, Donald K.**
1982    Karl Barth on the Lord's Prayer. — *Center Journal* (South Bend) 2 (1982) 81-99. → K.
Barth 1965

**MCKNIGHT, Edgar V.**
1969    *What is Form Criticism?* (Guides to Biblical Scholarship. New Testament Series).
Philadelphia, PA: Fortress, 1969, ³1971, X-86 p. Esp. 67-78: "Examples of the application of
form criticism" [Q].
1971    → C.H. Talbert 1971
1989    Form and Redaction Criticism. — EPP, E.J. – MACRAE, G.W. (eds.), *The New
Testament and Its Modern Interpreters*, 1989, 149-174. Esp. 153-154, 157-159, 160-161.

**MCKNIGHT, Scot**
1986a   *New Shepherds for Israel: An Historical and Critical Study of Matthew 9.35–11.1.* Diss.
Nottingham, 1986.
1986b   Jesus and the End-Time: Matthew 10:23. — *SBL 1986 Seminar Papers*, 501-520. Esp.
505-507: "The structural placement of Matt 10.23"; 507-509: "Redactional analysis of Matt 10.23"; 510-517:
"The original location of Matt 10.23"; 517-520: "A redactional interpretation of Matt 10.23".
1988    *Interpreting the Synoptic Gospels* (Guides to New Testament Exegesis, 2). Grand
Rapids, MI: Baker, 1988, 141 p.
1992a   Gentiles. — *DJG*, 1992, 259-265. Esp. 261-262.
1992b   Justice, Righteousness. — *Ibid.*, 411-416. Esp. 413-414.
1992c   Matthew, Gospel of. — *Ibid.*, 526-541. Esp. 526-528 [introduction]; 529-532 [structure]; 532-541
[theology].
1993    A Loyal Critic: Matthew's Polemic with Judaism in Theological Perspective. — EVANS,
C.A. – HAGNER, D.A. (eds.), *Anti-Semitism and Early Christianity. Issues of Polemic
and Faith*, Minneapolis, MN: Fortress, 1993, 55-79. Esp. 58-62: "Matthew's supposed anti-
semitism"; 62-70: "Theological foundations"; 70-77: "Matthew's polemical implications".

**MCLEAN, Bradley**
1995    On the Gospel of Thomas and Q. — PIPER, R.A. (ed.), *The Gospel Behind the Gospels*,
1995, 321-345. Esp. 322-333: "The relationship of the gospel of Thomas to the synoptic gospels"; 333-
342: "The gospel of Thomas and Q stratigraphy"; 342-345: "The gospel of Thomas, Q, and Christian
origins".

**MCLOUGHLIN, Swithun**
1965    *The Synoptic Theory of Xavier Léon-Dufour. An Analysis and Evaluation.* Diss. Leuven,

1965, V-555 p. (F. Neirynck). Esp. 1-70: "Introduction to the synoptic question"; 71-505: "The synoptic solution of X. Léon-Dufour"; 507-516: "Further horizons" [Mk/Q]. → 1967; → Léon-Dufour 1959a, Neirynck 1979d

1967    Les accords mineurs Mt-Lc contre Mc et le problème synoptique. Vers la théorie des Deux Sources. — *ETL* 43 (1967) 17-40. Esp. 18-21: "Les accords mineurs Mt-Lc"; 21-28: "La rareté des accords significatifs"; 28-35: "L'absence totale d'accords significatifs" [9,7.20; 17,2.17; 26,68; 27,75]; 36-38: "Critique textuelle". [NTA 12, 138]; = DE LA POTTERIE, I. (ed.), *De Jésus aux Évangiles*. FS J. Coppens, 1967, 17-40. (IT, 1971, 32-59). → 1965; → A. Fuchs 1978

1969    The Gospels and the Jesus of History. — *DownR* 87 (1969) 183-200. [NTA 14, 84] → Léon-Dufour 1963a/68, Meynell 1963/97

1972    A Reply. — *DownR* 90 (1972) 201-206. [NTA 17, 108] → Meynell 1972

**MCMENOMY, Bruce Alan**

1993    *The Matthew Commentary of Claudius Bishop of Turin. A Critical Edition of the Sections Pertaining to Matthew 1-4*. Diss. UCLA, 1993, 282 p. (B. Löfstedt). — *DissAbstr* 54 (1993-94) 927.

**MCMURRY, Berta Ward**

1992    *Testing in the Wilderness: A Comparative Study of Matt 4:1-11 in the Light of Deut 6-8 and Midrashic Interpretations*. Diss. Southwestern Baptist Theol. Sem., Fort Worth, TX, 1992, 289 p. (T.C. Urrey). — *DissAbstr* 53 (1992-93) 4369.

**MCNALLY, Robert E.**

1959    *The Bible in the Early Middle Ages*. Westminster, MD: Newman, 1959; Atlanta, GA: Scholars, 1986, 121 p. Esp. 105-107.

1970    The Three Holy Kings in the Early Irish Latin Writing. — GRANFIELD, P. - JUNGMANN, J.A. (eds.), *Kyriakon*. FS J. Quasten, 1970, II, 667-690.

**MCNAMARA, Martin**

1966    *The New Testament and the Palestinian Targum to the Pentateuch* (AnBib, 27). Roma: Pontifical Biblical Institute, 1966, XXIV-285 p. Esp. 126-131 [5,21/Tg Gen 9,6]; 133-138 [5,48/Tg Ps-Jon Lev 22,28]; 138-142 [7,2/Pal Tg Gen 38,26]; 142-145: "The synoptic problem and the Palestinian Targum"; 160-163 [23,35/Tg Lam 2,22]; 240-242 [13,17/Pal Tg]; [2]1978 (with supplement, 287-303). — Diss. Pont. Inst. Bibl., Roma, 1964 (S. Lyonnet).

1968a   God's Living Word: The Infancy Narratives and Midrash. — *DoctLife* 18 (1968) 701-705. [NTA 13, 856]

1968b   Were the Magi Essenes? — *IrEcclRec* 110 (1968) 305-328. Esp. 323-328 [2,1-12]. [NTA 13, 860]

1970    Jewish Law and the Gospels. — *BiTod* 47 (1970) 3237-3243. Esp. 3238-3239 [1-2]. [NTA 14, 812]

1972    *Targum and Testament. Aramaic Paraphrases of the Hebrew Bible: A Light on the New Testament*. Shannon: Irish Univ. Press, 1972. 227 p. Esp. 91-169: "The Palestinian Targum and New Testament Studies".

1983    *Palestinian Judaism and the New Testament* (Good News Studies, 4). Wilmington, DE: Glazier, 1983, 279 p. Esp. 159-204: "Rabbinic tradition and the New Testament" [21,16; 23,16-22.23].

1990    *Studies on Texts of Early Irish Latin Gospels (A.D. 600-1200)* (Instrumenta Patristica, 20). Steenbrugge: Sint-Pietersabdij; Dordrecht: Kluwer, 1990, XV-248 p. Esp. 30-33; 38-55: "Echternach gospels marginalia"; 106-107; 113-123: "St Gallen 51"; 179-181: "Cadmug"; 207-209: "MS Ambrosiana I.61sup."; 216-228: "Catechesis celtica".

1992    Non-Vulgate Readings of Codex AMB I.61 Sup. I. The Gospel of Matthew. — *Sacris Eruditi* (Steenbrugge) 33 (1992-93) 183-257. [NTA 37, 1243]

Non-Vulgate Readings of Codex Ambrosianus I 61 Sup. The Gospel of Matthew. — GRYSON, R. (ed.), *Philologia Sacra*. FS J. Frede – W. Thiele, 1993, 177-192.

**MCNEIL, Brian**

1983    The Odes of Solomon and the Scriptures. — *Oriens Christianus* (Wiesbaden) 67 (1983) 104-122. Esp. 116-118 [16,18/OdSal 22,11-12].

**MCNICOL, Allan James**

1987    The Two-Gospel Hypothesis under Scrutiny. A Response to C.M. Tuckett's Analysis of Recent Neo-Griesbachian Gospel Criticism. — *PerkJourn* 40/2 (1987) 5-13. [NTA 32, 101] → Tuckett 1983a, W.O. Walker Jr. 1987c

1989    Discipleship as Mission. A Missing Dimension in Contemporary Discussion on Matt 28:18-20. — *Christian Studies* 10 (1989) 27-47.

1990a   The Two-Gospel Hypothesis. Textual Discussion. The Composition of the Synoptic Eschatological Discourse. — DUNGAN, D.L. (ed.), *The Interrelations of the Gospels*, 1990, 157-200. Esp. 159-182: "Luke's use of Matthew 24 as a major source in the composition of his eschatological discourses" [5,18; 10,17-22; 24,1-41.42-51]; 182-200: "Mark's use of Matthew 24–25 and Luke 21". → 1996b; → Boismard 1990c, Neirynck 1990d, Tuckett 1990a

1990b   → W.R. Farmer 1990b

1992    → W.R. Farmer 1992a/93/94/95

1996a   & DUNGAN, D.L. – PEABODY, D.B. (eds.), *Beyond the Q Impasse – Luke's Use of Matthew. A Demonstration by the Research Team of the International Institute for Gospel Studies*, with a Preface by William R. Farmer. Valley Forge, PA: Trinity Press International, 1996, XVI-333 p. Esp. 13-24: "Luke's use of Matthew". → W.R. Farmer 1992a/93/94/95

1996b   *Jesus' Directions for the Future. A Source and Redaction-History Study of the Use of the Eschatological Traditions in Paul and in the Synoptic Accounts of Jesus' Last Eschatological Discourse* (New Gospel Studies, 9). Macon, GA: Mercer, 1996, XIV-219 p. Esp. 19-21.29-31.48-54 [24/1 Thess]; 67-114: "The Matthean version of the Last Eschatological Discourse". → 1990a

**MCQUILLAN, J.**

1956    The Magi in the Gospels. — *IrEcclRec* 85 (1956) 119-121.

**MCTERNAN, O.J.**

1989    *A Call to Witness: Reflections on the Gospel of St. Matthew*. Collegeville, MN: Liturgical Press, 1989, 104 p. [NTA 34, p. 112]

**MCVANN, Mark**

1989    The Making of Jesus the Prophet. Matthew 3:13–4:25. — *Listening* 24 (1989) 262-277. [NTA 34, 613]

1991    Uno de los profetas. Interpretación del relato de las tentaciones en Mateo como rito de iniciación. — *EstBíb* 49 (1991) 191-208. Esp. 196-197: "La estructura ritual de Mateo 3,13–4,25"; 197-199: "Puesta en marcha del proceso ritual"; 199-201: "Las tentaciones"; 201-203: "La función del diablo y las tentaciones"; 203-204: "Función de la Sagrada Escritura". [NTA 36, 1259]
        One of the Prophets: Matthew's Testing Narrative as a Rite of Passage. — *BTB* 23 (1993) 14-20. [NTA 37, 1249]

**MCVEY, Kathleen E.**

1990    The Anti-Judaic Polemic of Ephrem Syrus' Hymns on the Nativity. — ATTRIDGE, H.W. – COLLINS, J.J. – TOBIN, T.H. (eds.), *Of Scribes and Scrolls. Studies on the Hebrew Bible, Intertestamental Judaism, and Christian Origins Presented to John Strugnell on the Occasion of his Sixtieth Birthday* (College Theology Society Resources in Religion, 5), Lanham, MD: University Press of America, 1990, 229-240.

**MEAD, Richard T.**

1964  A Dissenting Opinion about Respect for Context in Old Testament Quotations. — *NTS* 10 (1963-64) 279-289. Esp. 281-287. [NTA 8, 862] → S.L. Edgar 1962

**MEADORS, Edward Paul**

1992  The Orthodoxy of the 'Q' Sayings of Jesus. — *TyndB* 43 (1992) 233-257. Esp. 239-249: "'Q' and Deuteronomistic theology" [Q 11,47-51; 13,34-35; 14,27]; 249-255: "Quotations and allusions to the Old Testament within Q" [Q 7,22-23; 11,21-22]. [NTA 37, 692]

1995  *Jesus the Messianic Herald of Salvation* (WUNT, II/72). Tübingen: Mohr, 1995, XI-387 p. Esp. 1-16: "The study of Mark and Q"; 17-35: "The Q community hypothesis"; 36-71: "Wisdom christology in Q" [Q 7,30-35; 10,21-22; 11,49-51; 13,34-35]; 72-96: "Jesus the prophet in Q"; 124-145: "The Son of Man and the Q material"; 146-233: "The kingdom of God in Q" [Q 6,20; 7,22-23.28; 10,9; 11,2-4.20; 12,29-31; 13,18-21.28-29; 16,16]; 234-293: "The kingdom of God in Mark compared with Q"; 294-315: "Is Q from a 'second sphere' of Christianity?" [Q 7,22-23; 11,21-22.47-51; 13,34-35; 14,27]. — Diss. Aberdeen, 1993 (I.H. Marshall).
S.J. PATTERSON, *JBL* 116 (1997) 138-141; C.M. TUCKETT, *NT* 38 (1996) 296-297.

**MEADORS, Gary T.**

1985  The "Poor" in the Beatitudes of Matthew and Luke. — *GraceTJ* 6 (1985) 305-314. [NTA 30, 627]

**MEAGHER, John C.**

1975  *The Way of the Word. The Beginning and the Establishing of Christian Understanding.* New York: Seabury, 1975, V-234 p. Esp. 66-70; 78-84 [18,15-20; 23,8-10].

**MEAGHER, Paul Kevin** → Vann 1957

**MEALAND, David L.**

1980  *Poverty and Expectation in the Gospels.* London: SPCK, 1980, VIII-136 p. Esp. 12-37.109-115: "The evangelists and their sources"; 38-60.115-119: "Hostility to wealth and the oral tradition"; 61-87.119-126: "Poverty and the kingdom of God".

**MEARNS, Chris**

1985  The Son of Man Trajectory and Eschatological Development. — *ExpT* 97 (1985-86) 8-12. Esp. 9 [5,11; 8,20; 11,19]; 10-11 [10,32; 14,32.40; 24,27.37]. [NTA 30, 786]

1987  Realized Eschatology in Q? A Consideration of the Sayings in Luke 7.22, 11.20 and 16.16. — *ScotJT* 40 (1987) 189-210. Esp. 194-196: "Q's theology"; 196-201 [Q 16,16]; 201-203 [Q 7,22]; 203-208 [Q 11,20]. [NTA 32, 102]

**MĘDALA, Stanisław**

1989  Nowe źródło do badań przekazu Ewangelii Mateusza. (De novo fonte ad traditionem investigandam evangelii secundum Matthaeum). — *RuBi* 42 (1989) 249-259.

**MÉDEBIELLE, Alexis**

1951  "Quoniam Nazaraeus vocabitur" (Mt. II,23). — METZINGER, A. (ed.), *Miscellanea Biblica et Orientalia R.P. Athanasio Miller o.s.b. Secretario Pontificiae Commissionis Biblicae completis LXX annis oblata* (Studia Anselmiana, 27-28), Roma: Orbis Catholicus – Herder, 1951, 301-326. Esp. 305-312: "Nazareth et Ναζωραῖος"; 312-315: "Nazareth et les Nazaréens"; 315-319: "Nazaréen–Naziréen"; 319-326: "Nazaraeus–Nêṣer".

**MEDISCH, Richard**

1979  Ein neuer Kommentar zu den Kindheitsgeschichten. — *TGeg* 22 (1979) 242-247. [NTA 24, 413r] → R.E. Brown 1977

1988  Der historische Judas – und was aus ihm gemacht wurde. — *TGeg* 31 (1988) 50-54. Esp. 53-54 [27,3-10].

**MEEKS, Wayne A.**

1978 Hypomnēmata from an Untamed Sceptic: A Response tɔ George Kennedy. — WALKER, W.O., Jr. (ed.), *The Relationships among the Gospels*, 1978, 157-172. Esp. 163-166 [Papias]. → G.A. Kennedy 1978

1986 *The Moral World of the First Christians* (Library of Early Christianity, 6). Philadelphia, PA: Westminster, 1986, 182 p. Esp. 136-143: "Messianic biography as community-forming literature: the gospel of Matthew".

1993 *The Origins of Christian Morality. The First Two Centuries*. New Haven, CT: Yale University Press, 1993, X-275 p. Esp. 199-203.

**MEES, Michael**

1966 Matthäus 5,1-26 in den altlateinischen Bibelübersetzungen. *Emendare* und *traducere* in ihrem Einfluss. — *VetChr* 3 (1966) 85-100.

1967 Die Änderungen und Zusätze im Matthäus-Evangelium des Codex Bezae. — *VetChr* 4 (1967) 107-129. Esp. 118-129 [3,15-17; 4,24; 5,12.22.41.44; 6,4.5.8; 9,14-15.17; 10,3.12.23.42; 13,13.14.24-25.45-46.47-48.54; 14,2; 15,1.8.11.33; 17,2.12-13; 18,10; 19,6.25; 20,28; 21,39; 22,13; 23,27; 24,31.41; 25,1.41; 27,32; 28,10].

1968 Das Matthäus-Evangelium in den Werken des Clemens von Alexandrien. — *Divinitas* 12 (1968) 675-698. Esp. 682-683; 683-695; 696-698. [NTA 14, 132]

1970a *Die Zitate aus dem Neuen Testament bei Clemens von Alexandrien* (Quaderni di "Vetera Christianorum", 2). Bari: Istituto di Letteratura Cristiara Antica, 1970, I, XI-217 and II, IV-267 p.: "Die Texte" (in 1 vol.). Esp. I, 12-54: "Die Zitate aus dem Matthäusevangelium" [cod. B; cod. Sinaiticus]; 190-200: "Scheinbare Zitate aus dem Matth -Evangelium"; 207-212: "Platon und das Neue Testament" [4,8; 6,20; 10,23; 15,14; 19,21.23; 20,17; 22,35; 23,13]; 213-217: "Die von Clemens selbst geformten Logia" [3,11; 5,44; 7,16]; II, 1-58: "Die Texte" [Mt]. — Diss. Pont. Inst. Bibl., Roma, 1966 (É. des Places – C.M. Martini).

1970b Der älteste Textzeuge für Mt 23,30-39. — *Orient-Press* (Roma) 1 (1970) 79-84.

1970c Mt 5,44. Einige Überlegungen zur Überlieferung der Herrenworte. — *Ibid.*, 119-128.

1970d Rassegna di "logia" e "sentenze" nelle ricerche degli ultimi anni. — *VetChr* 7 (1970) 389-396. → 1971d
Zur Frage der Logienquelle. — *TGeg* 14 (1971) 103-106. [NTA 16, 522]

1971a Die Bezeugung von Mt. 26,20-40 auf Papyrus (P$^{64}$, P$^{53}$, P$^{45}$, P$^{37}$) und ihre Bedeutung. — *Augustinianum* 11 (1971) 409-431. [NTA 16, 867]

1971b Die Bedeutung der Sentenzen und ihrer *auxesis* für die Formung der Jesuworte nach *Didaché* 1,3b-2,1. [5,38-48] — *VetChr* 8 (1971) 55-76.

1971c Schema und Dispositio in ihrer Bedeutung für die Formung der Herrenworte aus dem 1. *Clemensbrief*, Kap. 13,2. [7,1] — *Ibid.*, 257-272.

1971d Rassegna di "logia" e "sentenze" nella ricerche degli anni 1968-1970. — *Ibid.*, 322-331. → 1970d

1972a Das Herrenwort aus dem Ersten Clemensbrief, Kap 46,8 und seine Bedeutung für die Überlieferung der Jesusworte. — *Augustinianum* 12 (1972) 233-256. Esp. 242-246, 251-256 [18,6-7/1 Clem 46,8].

1972b Das Paradigma vom reichen Mann und seiner Berufung nach den Synoptikern und dem Nazaräerevangelium. [19,16-30] — *VetChr* 9 (1972) 245-265. [NTA 18, 494]

1973 Ausserkanonische Parallelstellen zu den Gerichtsworten Mt. 7,21-23; Lk. 6,46; 13,26-28 und ihre Bedeutung für die Formung der Jesusworte. — *VetChr* 10 (1973) 79-102. Esp. 85-87 [Lk 6,46]; 88-95 [7,21]; 95-100 [7,22-23/Lk 13,26-27]. [NTA 20, 438]

1974a Die moderne Deutung der Parabeln und ihre Probleme. — *VetChr* 11 (1974) 416-433. [NTA 20, 420]

1974b Das Sprichwort Mt. 6,21 / Lk. 12,34 und seine ausserkanonischen Parallelen. — *Augustinianum* 14 (1974) 67-89. Esp. 74-85: "Unseren Evangelien ähnliche Formen"; 85-89: "Abweichende Formen". [NTA 19, 87]

1974c Formen, Strukturen und Gattungen ausserkanonischer Herrenworte. — *Ibid.*, 459-488. Esp. 463-464 [10,12-13]; 470-473 [4,17]; 473-788 [10,37-38; 16,24]. [NTA 20, 75]

1975 *Ausserkanonische Parallelstellen zu den Herrenworten und ihre Bedeutung* (Quaderni di "Vetera Christianorum", 10). Bari: Istituto di Letteratura Cristiana Antica, 1975, 189 p. Esp. 25-46 [11,4-6]; 46-51 [5,4-5]; 52-59 [13,16-17]; 59-71 [8,11-12]; 71-81 [23,27-29]; 81-87 [23,29-39]; 87-94 [10,32-33]; 97-109 [5,27-29]; 109-127 [5,38-42]; 129-133 [8,19-22]; 133-141 [6,19-21]; 142-150 [8,21-22].

1977 Form und Komposition der Herrenworte in Justin, Apol. 1,15-17. — *Augustinianum* 17 (1977) 283-306. Esp. 292-296 [5,28-29.44-46; 18,8-9. 19,11-12]; 299-300 [5,38-42].

1983 Herrenworte und Erzählstoff in den judenchristlichen Evangelien und ihre Bedeutung. — *Augustinianum* 23 (1983) 187-212. Esp. 199-201 [3,13-15/Nazoreans]; 201-202 [5,22]; 202-204 [7,21-23]; 206-207 [18,22]; 208-210.

**MEGIVERN, James**

1966 Forgive Us Our Debts. — *Scripture* 18 (1966) 33-47. Esp. 33-39: "The text" [6,12]; 39-46: "Synoptic comparison". [NTA 11, 206]

**MEHLMANN, Joannes**

1960 Elias e seu carro na transfiguração de Jesus (Mt 17,3 par.). — *RevistCuBíb* 4 (1960) 160-161.

**MEIER, John Paul**

1975 Salvation-History in Matthew: In Search of a Starting Point. — *CBQ* 37 (1975) 203-215. Esp. 204-207: "Relation between 10:5-6; 15:24; and 28:16-20"; 207-210: "The death-resurrection as *die Wende der Zeit*" [5,18-19; 27,51-54; 28,2-3]; 210-215: "A second look at 28:16-20 – 'Proleptic parousia?'". [NTA 20, 80]; = ID., *The Mission of Christ and His Church*, 1990, 125-139 (afterword, 140). Esp. 126-130; 130-134; 134-139. → cf. 1976, 25-40

1976 *Law and History in Matthew's Gospel. A Redactional Study of Mt. 5:17-48* (AnBib, 71). Roma: Biblical Institute Press, 1976, XI-206 p. Esp. 25-40: "Salvation-history in Matthew: in search of a starting point" (→ 1975, revised); 41-124: "Matthew 5:17-20 – tradition and redaction"; 125-161: "The antitheses – confirmation of a thesis". [NTA 22, p. 91] — Diss. Pont. Inst. Bib., Roma, 1975 (M. Zerwick).

J. COPPENS, *ETL* 53 (1977) 221; G. GIAVINI, *ScuolC* 106 (1978) 114-115; J. MURPHY-O'CONNOR, *RB* 84 (1977) 470-472; B. RINALDI, *RivBib* 25 (1977) 435-437; C.S. RODD, *ExpT* 88 (1976-77) 129-130; J.P. SAMPLEY, *JBL* 97 (1978) 140-142; D. SENIOR, *CBQ* 39 (1977) 438-440; G. STANTON, *JTS* 30 (1979) 267-270; N. WALTER, *TLZ* 104 (1979) 111-112.

1977a Nations or Gentiles in Matthew 28:19? — *CBQ* 39 (1977) 94-102. Esp. 95-101: "The occurrences of *ethnos/ethnē* in Matt". [NTA 21, 733]; = ID., *The Mission of Christ and His Church*, 1990, 141-151 (afterword, 151-152). Esp. 142-149. → Hare 1975

1977b Two Disputed Questions in Matt 28:16-20. — *JBL* 96 (1977) 407-424. Esp. 407-416: "Tradition and redaction"; 416-424: "The question of Gattung". [NTA 22, 405r]; = ID., *The Mission of Christ and His Church*, 1990, 153-178 (afterword, 178-179). Esp. 154-166; 166-178. → Hubbard 1974, J. Lange 1973

1979 *The Vision of Matthew. Christ, Church, and Morality in the First Gospel* (Theological Inquiries). New York – Ramsey, NJ – Toronto, Ont.: Paulist, 1979, X-270 p. Esp. 5-39: "Remodeling the form of the gospel: from Mark to Matthew" [27,51-54; 28,2-3.16-20]; 41-219: "Remodeling the message of gospel: a mini-commentary on the gospel of Matthew"; 221-264: "Remodeling morality: the eschatological demand of Christ" [5,17-20.21-48]. [NTA 24, p. 85]; New York: Crossroad, 1991, VIII-270 p. [NTA 36, p. 113] → Kingsbury 1975a

D.A. CARSON, *JEvTS* 23 (1980) 357-358; C.H. FELDER, *TTod* 37 (1980-81) 145; D.E. GARLAND, *RExp* 79 (1982) 522-524; B.J. HUBBARD, *JBL* 100 (1981) 122-123; J. KODELL, *TS* 41 (1980) 439; P. MEAGHER, *Vidyajyoti* 58 (1994) 399-400; J.M. REESE, *BTB* 9 (1979) 139; F.F. SEGOVIA, *CBQ* 43 (1981) 139-140; D. SENIOR, *Horizons* (Villanova, PA) 7 (1980) 325-326; R.H. SMITH, *CurrTMiss* 8 (1981) 250-251.

1980a   *Matthew* (New Testament Message, 3). Wilmington, DE: Glazier; Dublin: Veritas, 1980, XII-377 p. [NTA 25, p. 88]; Collegeville, MN: Liturgical Press, 1990, XII-377 p. [NTA 35, p. 104] → Ziesler 1985

    C. BERNAS, *CBQ* 43 (1981) 304-305; F.F. BRUCE, *ExpT* 96 (1984-85) 54-55; R.H. GUNDRY, *JBL* 101 (1982) 289-291; B.M. NOLAN, *IrTQ* 48 (1981) 138-140.

1980b   *The Gospel according to Matthew* (An Access Guide for Scripture Study). New York – Chicago, IL – Los Angeles, CA: Sadlier, 1980, X-118 p. [NTA 25, p. 304]; 1983, 174 p.

1980c   John the Baptist in Matthew's Gospel. — *JBL* 99 (1980) 383-405. Esp. 387-392 [3,1-17]; 392-399 [11,2-19]; 399-400 [14,3-12]; 400-401 [17,10-13]; 401 [21,28-32]; 401-405 [interpretation]. [NTA 25, 456]; = ID., *The Mission of Christ and His Church*, 1990, 180-207 (afterword, 207-208). Esp. 185-191; 191-199; 199-200; 201; 202-207.

1983   Antioch. — BROWN, R.E. – MEIER, J.P., *Antioch and Rome*, 1983, 11-86. Esp. 15-27: "Locating Matthew's church in time and space"; 45-72: "The Antiochene church of the second Christian generation" (A.D. 70-100 – Matthew)"; 73-84 [Ignatius; Didache/Mt]. → McHugh 1991
Antioche. — *Antioche et Rome*, 1988, 29-117. Esp. 35-49; 71-100; 101-113.

1986   Matthew 15:21-28. — *Interpr* 40 (1986) 397-402.
The Canaanite Woman in Matthew 15:21-28 and the Problem of World Religions. — ID., *The Mission of Christ and His Church*, 1990, 209-215 (afterword, 215-216).

1990a   *The Mission of Christ and His Church. Studies in Christology and Ecclesiology* (Good News Studies, 30). Wilmington, DE: Glazier, 1990, XI-327 p. → 1975, 1977a-b, 1980c, 1986

1990b   Jesus. — BROWN, R.E., et al. (eds.), *The New Jerome Biblical Commentary*, 1990, 1316-1328.
Gesù. — BROWN, R.E., et al., *Nuovo grande commentario biblico*, 1997, 1730-1746.

1990c   Jesus in Josephus: A Modest Proposal. — *CBQ* 52 (1990) 76-103. Esp. 94 [10,5-6; 28,16-20]. [NTA 34, 1449]

1990d   Matthew 5:3-12. — *Interpr* 44 (1990) 281-285.

1991a   *A Marginal Jew. Rethinking the Historical Jesus.* Vol. I: *The Roots of the Problem and the Person* (The Anchor Bible Reference Library). New York: Doubleday, 1991, X-484 p. Esp. 41-45; 115-117; 132-139; 160-162; Vol. II: *Mentor, Message, and Miracles*, 1994, XVI-1118 p. Esp. 27-40: "The Q tradition of John's words and deeds" [3,7-10.11-12]; 130-163: "The second Baptist-block in Q"; 167-170 [21,31-32]; 177-181: "Excursus on the Q document" [Baptist]; 291-302 [6,10]; 309-317 [8,11-12]; 317-336 [5,3-12]; 339-341 [10,23]; 407-423 [12,28]; 434-439 [13,16-17]; 656-657 [9,32-33; 12,22-23]; 685.718-726 [8,5-13]; 698.832-837 [11,5]; 777-788 [9,18-26/Mk]; 880-884 [17,24-27]; 905-923 [14,22-33/Mk]; 924-933 [8,23-27/Mk]; 950-967 [14,13-21/Mk]. → Bauckham 1994
Portuguese trans., vol. I, 1992.
    J. SCHLOSSER, *BZ* 37 (1993) 131-133; 41 (1997) 262-266.

1991b   Matthew and Ignatius: A Response to William R. Schoedel. — BALCH, D.L. (ed.), *Social History of the Matthean Community*, 1991, 178-186. → Schoedel 1991

1992a   The Brothers and Sisters of Jesus in Ecumenical Perspective. — *CBQ* 54 (1992) 1-28. Esp. 8-15: "Relevant texts in Matthew: 1:25; 13:55; 12:46-50".

1992b   Matthew, Gospel of. — *ABD* 4 (1992) 622-641. Esp. 622-627 [introduction]; 627-639 [structure; content]; 637-640 [theology].

1994   → 1991a

1995a   "Happy the eyes that see": The Tradition, Message, and Authenticity of Luke 10:23-24 and Parallels. — BECK, A.B., et al. (eds.), *Fortunate the Eyes That See. Essays in*

*Honor of David Noel Freedman in Celebration of His Seventieth Birthday*, Grand Rapids, MI: Eerdmans, 1995, 467-477. Esp. 474-477: "The original Q form of the beatitude".

1995b The Eucharist at the Last Supper: Did It Happen? — *TDig* 42 (1995) 335-351. Esp. 341-342 [26,26-28]. [NTA 40, 1426]

**MEINERTZ, Max**

1912[R] *Einleitung in das Neue Testament* [A. Schaefer, 1898]; [²1912, ³1921, ⁴1932] (Wissenschaftliche Handbibliothek, I/15). Paderborn: Schöningh, ⁵1950, 354 p. Esp. 165-178: "Das Matthäusevangelium"; 202-215: "Die synoptische Frage".

1950 *Theologie des Neuen Testamentes* (Die Heilige Schrift des Neuen Testamentes. Ergänzungsband 1). Bonn: Hanstein, 1950, 2 vols., XII-248 and VIII-389 p. Esp. I, 15-27 [John the Baptist]; 30-56 [kingdom]; 56-69 [eschatology]; 69-79 [church]; 80-115 [ethics]; 115-126 [God]; 138-146 [passion]; 147-156 [Jesus]; 156-176 [Messiah]; 176-191 [Son of Man]; 191-198 [Son of God]; 198-211 [virgin birth; resurrection].
*Teologia de Nuevo Testamento*. Madrid: Fax, 1963, XXX-658 p.

1953a Ein neues Buch über den Apostel Petrus. [16,17-19] — *ZMiss* 37 (1953) 235-239. → Cullmann 1952

1953b Die Tragweite des Gleichnisses von den zehn Jungfrauen. [25,1-13] — SCHMID, J. — VÖGTLE, A. (eds.), *Synoptische Studien*. FS A. Wikenhauser, 1953, 94-106.

1957 "Dieses Geschlecht" im Neuen Testament. [11,16; 12,39.41-42; 16,4; 17,17; 23,35-36; 24,34] — *BZ* 1 (1957) 283-289. [NTA 2, 524]

1959 Zum Ursprung der Heidenmission. [8,11-12; 22,1-14; 23,15] — *Bib* 40 (1959) 762-777. [NTA 4, 627]; = *Studia Biblica et Orientalia*, II, 1959, 194-209.

**MEISINGER, Hubert**

1996 *Liebesgebot und Altruismusforschung. Ein exegetischer Beitrag zum Dialog zwischen Theologie und Naturwissenschaft* (NTOA, 33). Freiburg/Schw: Universitätsverlag; Göttingen: Vandenhoeck & Ruprecht, 1996, VII-320 p. Esp. 35-51: "Das Liebesgebot in den synoptischen Evangelien: Das Matthäusevangelium" [5,17-20.43-48; 19,16-22; 22,34-40]. — Diss. Heidelberg 1994-95 (G. Theissen).

**MEISTAD, Tore**

1987 Martin Luther and John Wesley on the Sermon on the Mount. — BøCKMAN, P.W. - KRISTIANSEN, R.E. (eds.), *Context. Festskrift til Peder Johan Borgen. Essays in Honour of Peder Johan Borgen* ("Relieff", 24), Trondheim: Tapir, 1987, 137-151.

**MEJÍA, Jorge**

1978 Los "Evangelios de la Infancia" en un libro reciente. — *Teología* 15 (1978) 175-184. → R.E. Brown 1977

**[Mélanges bibliques]**

1957* *Mélanges bibliques rédigés en l'honneur de André Robert* (Travaux de l'Institut Catholique de Paris, 4). Paris: Bloud & Gay, 1957, 580 p. → Bloch, W.D. Davies, Dodd, George, Léon-Dufour

**[Mélanges E. Tisserant]**

1964* *Mélanges Eugène Tisserant*. Vol. I: *Écriture sainte – Ancien orient* (Studi e Testi, 231). Città del Vaticano: Biblioteca apostolica Vaticana, 1964, XXI-487 p. → Cerfaux, Díez Macho, Schnackenburg

**MELBOURNE, Bertram Lloyd**

1988 *Slow to Understand. The Disciples in Synoptic Perspective*. Lanham, MD – New York – London: University Press of America, 1988, XVII-206 p. Esp. 24-27; 58-72: "The Matthean portrait of the disciples"; 158-159. — Diss. Andrews University, 1986 (A. Terian).

**MELIÁ, Juan**

1978 *Misión Galilea y mision universal en los Sinópticos.* Ðiss. Valencia, 1978 (E. Pax). — *Cuadernos Bíblicos* (Valencia) 2 (1978) 1-101 (also separately published). Esp. 7-18; 25-40 [9,37–10,16]; 50-72: "La tradición literaria primitiva de los relatos de la misión".

**MELINSKY, Hugh**

1966 *The Modern Reader's Guide to the Gospels. Matthew* (A Libra Book). London: Darton, Longman and Todd, 1966, 96 p.
J.E. BRUNS, *CBQ* 28 (1966) 356-357.

**MELL, Ulrich**

1994a *Die "anderen" Winzer. Eine exegetische Studie zur Vollmacht Jesu Christi nach Markus 11,27–12,34* (WUNT, 77). Tübingen: Mohr, 1994, XIII-438 p. Esp. 314-320: "Die Frage nach dem obersten Gebot nach der Logienquelle Q (Mt 22,35-40; Lk 10,25-28)". — Diss. Kiel, 1993 (J. Becker).

1994b Gehört das Vater-Unser zur authentischen Jesus-Tradition? (Mt 6,9-13; Lk 11,2-4). — *BTZ* 11 (1994) 148-180. Esp. 150-159: "Zur Rekonstruktion des ursprünglichen Gebetstextes"; 159-162: "Zur Bestimmung authentischer Jesus-Tradition"; 162-169: "Die Gebetsanrede Gottes als 'Vater!'"; 174-180: "Die Dreiheitsbitte um Gottes Barmherzigkeit über Israel". [NTA 39, 1450]

**MELLO, Alberto**

1995 *Evangelo secondo Matteo. Commento midrashico e narrativo* (Spiritualità biblica). Magnano: Qiqajon, 1995, 332 p.

**MELLON, Christian**

1973 La parabole. Manière de parler, manière d'entendre. — *RSR* 61 (1973) 49-63. Esp. 51-59 [13,10-17]; 59-63 [13,18-23]. [NTA 18, 110]; = CHABROL, C. - MARIN, L. (eds.), *Le récit évangélique*, 1974, 147-161. Esp. 149-157; 157-161.

**MELONI, Pietro**

1979 "Beati gli affamati e assetati di giustizia". L'interpretazione patristica. — *Sandalion* (Sassari) 2 (1979) 143-219.

1980a "Beati i perseguitati per la giustizia". L'interpretazione patristica. — *Sandalion* 3 (1980) 191-250.

1980b Fame e sete della Parola di Dio nell'interpretazione patristica della quarta beatitudine. [5,6] — *ParSpirV* 1 (1980) 206-225.

1990 Le beatitudini nei Padri della chiesa. — *ParSpirV* 21 (1990) 221-240.

**MEN, A.**

1962 Das Geheimnis der Magier. [Russian] — *Journal des Moskauer Patriarchats* 1 (1962) 60-67.

**MENA, Jesus M.**

1983 El Padrenuestro, cifra de fe y oración en San Agustín. El Padrenuestro en la reflexión agustiniana. — *Mayeútica* 9 (1983) 215-226.

**MENAHEM, R.**

1987 A Jewish Commentary on the New Testament: A Sample Verse. [3,9] — *Immanuel* 21 (1987) 43-54. [NTA 32, 582]

1990 *Epitropos/Paqid* in the Parable of the Laborers in the Vineyard. [20,8] — *Immanuel* 24-25 (1990) 118-131.

**MÉNARD, Jacques-É.**

1957 *Pais Theou* as Messianic Title in the Book of Acts. — *CBQ* 19 (1957) 83-92. Esp. 84-88:

"Jesus, the suffering prophet of the synoptics". [NTA 1, 415]

Un titre messianique propre au livre des Actes: le *pais theou*. — *Studia Montis Regii* (Montréal) 1 (1958) 213-224. Esp. 214-218. [NTA 3, 384]

1965   Logia. — *Enciclopédia de la Bíblia* (Barcelona) 4 (1965; [2]1969) 1063-1066.

1975   *L'Évangile selon Thomas* (Nag Hammadi Studies, 5). Leiden: Brill, 1975, X-252 p. Esp. 75-210: "Commentaire".

1976   Les problèmes de l'Évangile de Thomas. — *Studia Patristica* 14 (1976) 209-228. Esp. 211-224 [6,24; 7,3.5.12; 8,20; 11,11; 17,20; 18,3; 23,25].

1981   La tradition synoptique et l'Évangile selon Thomas. — PASCHKE, F., et al. (eds.), *Überlieferungsgeschichtliche Untersuchungen* (TU, 125), Berlin: Akademie, 1981, 411-426. Esp. 416-417 [8,20/Th 107]; 419 [22,10-14/Th 75]; 424-425 [5,11.15; 13,25; 23,13/Th].

**MENDNER, Siegfried**

1956   Die Tempelreinigung. — *ZNW* 47 (1956) 93-112. Esp. 94-95 [21,12-13]; 101 [26,61; 27,40]. [NTA 2, 22]

1958   Zum Problem 'Johannes und die Synoptiker'. [14,13-21] — *NTS* 4 (1957-58) 282-307. Esp. 289 [15,29-31]. [NTA 3, 101]

**MENDOZA EGUARAS, Angela**

1987   Inscripción mozárabe de la Zubia (Granada). [24,15] — *Cuadernos de prehistoria y arqueología* (Madrid) 13-14 (1986-87) 277-279.

**MENDOZA RUIZ, Fernando**

1964   El jueves día de la Ultima Cena. — *EstBíb* 23 (1964) 5-40, 151-171, 259-294; 24 (1965) 85-106. Esp. 260-272 [21-25]; 272-294 [26-27]. [NTA 9, 930; 10, 917; 11, 221] → Jaubert 1957

**MENESTRINA, Giovanni**

1976   Matteo 5-7 e Luca 6,20-49 nell'Evangelo di Tommaso. — *BibOr* 18 (1976) 65-67. [NTA 21, 74]

1977   Sicut in caelo et in terra (Nota a *Matteo* 6,10). — *BibOr* 19 (1977) 5-8. [NTA 21, 722]

1979   Καταθεματίζω. [26,74] — *BibOr* 21 (1979) 12.

**MENIS, Gian Carlo**

1983   Il signum Ionae in un nuovo tractatus di Cromazio e nella tradizione esegetica e iconografica aquileiese. [12,40] — *Varietas indivisa. Teologia della chiesa locale. Studi in onore di Pietro Bertolla e Aldo Moretti* (Scuola superiore di teologia di Udine e Gorizia, 1), Brescia: Paideia, 1983, 119-150.

**MENKEN, Maarten J.J.**

1984   The References to Jeremiah in the Gospel according to Matthew (Mt 2,17; 16,14; 27,9). — *ETL* 60 (1984) 5-24. Esp. 6-12 [2,17-18; 27,9-10]; 12-23 [16,14]. [NTA 29, 86]

1985   The Quotation from Isa 40,3 in John 1,23. [3,3] — *Bib* 66 (1985) 190-205. Esp. 195-199 [ἑτοιμάζω]. [NTA 30, 180]
       "I Am the Voice of One Crying in the Wilderness..." (John 1:23). — ID., *Old Testament Quotations*, 1996, 21-35. Esp. 26-29.

1989   Die Redaktion des Zitates aus Sach 9,9 in Joh 12,15. — *ZNW* 80 (1989) 193-209. Esp. 193-197 [21,5/Jn 12,15]. [NTA 34, 706]
       "Do Not Fear, Daughter Zion..." (John 12:15). — ID., *Old Testament Quotations*, 1996, 79-97. Esp. 79-83.

1992   The Quotations from Zech 9,9 in Mt 21,5 and in Jn 12,15. — DENAUX, A. (ed.), *John and the Synoptics*, 1992, 571-578. Esp. 571-575: "Zech 9,9 in Mt 21,5"; 577-578 [21,5/Jn 12,15].

1994   Het gesprek van Jezus met de rijke jongeman (Matteüs 19,16-22) en de uitleg ervan in *Veritatis splendor*. — RIKHOF, H.W.M. - VOSMAN, F.J.H. (eds.), *De schittering van de waarheid. Theologische reflecties bij de encycliek Veritatis splendor*, Zoetermeer: Meinema, 1994, 62-77.

1996 *Old Testament Quotations in the Fourth Gospel. Studies in Textual Form* (Contributions to Biblical Exegesis and Theology, 15). Kampen: Kok Pharos, 1996, 255 p. → 1985, 1989

**MENNINGER, Richard E.**

1986 The Concept of the Remnant in the Gospel of Matthew. — *SBT* 14 (1986) 5-35. Esp. 10-13 [3,7-12]; 13-15 [11,25-30]; 15-18 [12,46-50]; 19-23 [2,6]; 23-25 [9,36]; 25-26 [25,32-33]; 26-28 [26,31]; 28-33 [πτωχός].

1994 *Israel and the Church in the Gospel of Matthew* (American University Studies. VII. Theology and Religion, 162). New York: Lang, 1994, X-204 p. Esp. 23-62: "The historical relationship between Israel and Matthew's church"; 63-102: "Jesus the Messiah of Israel"; 103-133: "The 'Law' of the True Israel"; 135-166: "The church as the True Israel of God". [NTA 40, p. 145] — Diss. Fuller Theol. Sem., Pasadena, CA, 1991 (D.A. Hagner).
W. CARTER, *CRBR* 9 (1996) 242-244; E. CUVILLIER, *ETR* 71 (1996) 90-91.

**MENOUD, Philippe-H.**

1970 Le sens du verbe βιάζεται dans Lc 16,16. — DESCAMPS, A.L. - DE HALLEUX, A. (eds.), *Mélanges bibliques*. FS B. Rigaux, 1970, 207-212. Esp. 207-209 [Q 16,16]; = ID., *Jésus-Christ et la Foi. Recherches néotestamentaires* (Bibliothèque théologique), Neuchâtel–Paris: Delachaux & Niestlé, 1975, 125-130. Esp. 125-126.

**MENSA I VALLS, Jaume**

1989 Les citacions bíbliques en Català en les obres d'Arnau de Vilanova. — *RevistCatTeol* 14 (1989) 517-526 (English summary, 526). Esp. 519-521.

**MENZIES, Robert P.**

1991 *The Development of Early Christian Pneumatology. With Special Reference to Luke–Acts* (JSNT SS, 54). Sheffield: JSOT, 1991, 375 p. Esp. 178-180 [Q 10,21]; 180-185 [Q 11,13]; 185-189 [Q 11,20]; 190-198 [Q 12,10.12]. — Diss. Aberdeen, 1990 (I.H. Marshall).

**MERCIER, Gérard**

1971 Saint Joseph dans les commentaires bibliques et les homéliaires du IX^e siècle. — *EstJos* 25 = *CahJos* 19 (1971) 220-261.

**MERCURIO, Roger**

1959 A Baptismal Motif in the Gospel Narratives of the Burial. — *CBQ* 21 (1959) 39-54. Esp. 40-45: "Genesis and analysis of the burial narratives" [27,57-61]; 48-50: "Baptismal motif in the synoptics". [NTA 3, 562]

1960 Some Difficult Marian Passages in the Gospels. — *Marian Studies* (Washington, DC) 11 (1960) 104-122. [NTA 5, 693]

1961 "And then they will fast". [9,16] — *Worship* 35 (1960-61) 150-154. [NTA 5, 713]

**MEREDITH, Anthony**

1984 The Evidence of Papias for the Priority of Matthew. — TUCKETT, C.M. (ed.), *Synoptic Studies*, 1984, 187-196.

**MERENDINO, Rosario Pius**

1987 Testi anticotestamentari in Mc 1,2-8. — *RivBib* 35 (1987) 3-25. Esp. 11-22. [NTA 32, 619]

**MERENTITIS, Konstantinos I.**

1958 The Sermon on the Mount. [Greek] — *Festschrift Hamilcar Alivisatos*, Athens, 1958, 242-261.

**MERK, Augustin**

1933[R]  *Novum Testamentum Graece et Latine* [1933]. Roma: Pont. Inst. Bibl., [7]1951, [8]1957, [9]1964, 47*-875 p. Esp. 2-108: "Κατὰ Ματϑαῖον".

**MERK, L.**

1967   Exegese über Mt 28,18-20. — *Estudos Teologicos* (São Leopoldo) 7 (1967) 87-93.

**MERK, Otto**

1991   Begegnen und Erkennen. Das Matthäusevangelium im Werk Anton Vögtles. — OBERLINNER, L. - FIEDLER, P. (eds.), *Salz der Erde.* FS A. Vögtle, 1991, 11-29. Esp. 16-18 [16,17-19]; 19-21 [10,5-6; 28,18-20]; 23-24 [12,40]; 24-25 [22,1-10]; 25 [11,2-6]; 26-27 [5,39-42].

**MERKEL, Helmut**

1968   Jesus und die Pharisäer. — *NTS* 14 (1967-68) 194-208. Esp. 197-201; 202-207 [9,14-17; 12,1-8; 15,1-20; 19,3-9]. [NTA 12, 837]

1971   *Die Widersprüche zwischen den Evangelien. Ihre polemische und apologetische Behandlung in der Alten Kirche bis zu Augustin* (WUNT, 13). Tübingen: Mohr, 1971, VI-295 p. — Diss. Erlangen–Nürnberg 1971 (W. von Loewenich).

1974   Das Gleichnis von den 'ungleichen Söhnen' (Matth. xxi.28-32). — *NTS* 20 (1973-74) 254-261. Esp. 255-257 [Mt redaction]; 257-258 [tradition]; 258-261 [interpretation]. [NTA 19, 95]

1978   (ed.), *Die Pluralität der Evangelien als theologisches und exegetisches Problem in der Alten Kirche* (Traditio Christiana, 3). Bern – Frankfurt/M – Las Vegas: Lang, 1978, XXX-172 p.
*La pluralité des Évangiles comme problème théologique et exégétique dans l'Église ancienne*, trans. J.-L. Maier (Traditio Christiana, 3). Bern – Frankfurt/M – Las Vegas: Lang, 1978, XXX-172 p.
*La pluralità dei Vangeli* (Traditio Christiana, 5). Torino: Soc. Ed. Int., 1990, XXXI-182 p.

1984a  Clemens Alexandrinus über die Reihenfolge der Evangelien. — *ETL* 60 (1984) 382-385. [NTA 29, 886]

1984b  The Opposition between Jesus and Judaism. — BAMMEL, E. - MOULE, C.F.D. (eds.), *Jesus and the Politics of His Day*, 1984, 129-144.

1990   Die Überlieferungen der Alten Kirche über das Verhältnis der Evangelien. — DUNGAN, D.L. (ed.), *The Interrelations of the Gospels*, 1990, 566-590. Esp. 567-572 [Papias]; 572-573 [Justin]; 573-575 [Irenaeus]; 577-582 [Clement of Alexandria]; 585-589 [Augustin]. → Neirynck 1990f, Orchard 1990b

1991   Die Gottesherrschaft in der Verkündigung Jesu. — HENGEL, M. - SCHWEMER, A.M. (eds.), *Königsherrschaft Gottes und himmlischer Kult im Judentum, Urchristentum und in der hellenistischen Welt* (WUNT, 55), Tübingen: Mohr, 1991, 119-161. Esp. 123-128.142-144 [12,28]; 136-137 [10,7]; 148-149 [11,12-13]; 149 [13,44-46]; 150-151 [18,23-35].

**MERKELBACH, Reinhold** → Hagedorn 1966

**MERKLEIN, Helmut**

1972   Der Jüngerkreis Jesu. — MÜLLER, K. (ed.), *Die Aktion Jesu und die Re-Aktion der Kirche. Jesus von Nazareth und die Anfänge der Kirche*, Würzburg: Echter, 1972, 65-100. Esp. 73-75 [10,37-38]; 78 [8,20].

1974*  & LANGE, J. (eds.), *Biblische Randbemerkungen. Schülerfestschrift für Rudolf Schnackenburg zum 60. Geburtstag.* Würzburg: Echter, 1974, XX-386 p. → Ambrozic, Geist, Kretzer, J. Lange, G. Lohfink, K. Müller, Rieger, Steinhauser

1978   *Die Gottesherrschaft als Handlungsprinzip. Untersuchung zur Ethik Jesu* (FzB, 34). Würzburg: Echter, 1978, 339 p.; [2]1981; [3]1984. Esp. 56-64 [8,21-22]; 64-69 [13,44-46]; 72-80.91-96 [5,17-20]; 80-90 [11,12-13/Q]; 135-137 [7,13-14.15-20.22-23.24-27]; 174-183 [6,25-33/Q 12,22-31]; 186-192 [18,12-14/Q 15,4-7]; 222-237 [5,44-48/Q 6,27-36]; 237-242 [18,23-35]; 243-246 [7,12/Q 6,31]; 247-249 [18,21-22/Q 17,3-4]; 253-291 [5,21-48]. — Diss. Würzburg, 1977 (R. Schnackenburg).

1979    Zur Entstehung der urchristlichen Aussage vom präexistenten Sohn Gottes. — DAUTZENBERG, G., et al. (eds.), *Zur Geschichte des Urchristentums*. FS R. Schnackenburg, 1979, 33-62. Esp. 35-37: "Sophia-Logien"; 46-47; 55; 57-58; 60; = ID., *Studien zu Jesus und Paulus*, 1987, 247-276. Esp. 249-251; 260-261; 269; 271-272; 274.

1981a    Die Auferweckung Jesu und die Anfänge der Christologie (Messias bzw. Sohn Gottes und Menschensohn). — *ZNW* 72 (1981) 1-26. Esp. 22-25 [Q]. [NTA 26, 654]; = ID., *Studien zu Jesus und Paulus*, 1987, 221-246. Esp. 242-245.

1981b    Die Umkehrpredigt bei Johannes dem Täufer und Jesus von Nazaret. — *BZ* 25 (1981) 29-46 Esp. 31-38 [3,7-12]; 39 [11,20-21; 12,41]; 43 [18,12-14]. [NTA 26, 60]; = ID., *Studien zu Jesus und Paulus*, 1987, 109-126. Esp. 111-118; 119-120; 123.

1983a    *Jesu Botschaft von der Gottesherrschaft. Eine Skizze* (SBS, 111). Stuttgart: Katholisches Bibelwerk, 1983, 189 p. Esp. 18-19 [kingdom: Q]; 22-23 [kingdom: Mt]; 28-33 [3,7-12]; 45-46.48-51 [5,3-12]; 55-56 [10,23]; 63-68 [Q 7,22-23; 10,23-24; 11,20]; 73-74 [Q 13,18-19]; 76-77 [13,44-46]; 103-116 [5,21-48]; 121-122 [18,23-35]; 122-124 [5,39-40]; 162-164 [Q 12,8-9; 17,26-30]; ²1984 [= (Die Botschaft Gottes, II/36), Leipzig: St. Benno, 1989, 228 p.]; ³1989, 199 p. *La signoria di Dio nell'annuncio di Gesù* (Studi biblici, 107). Brescia: Paideia, 1994, 249 p.

1983b    Die Antithesen der Bergpredigt (Mt 5) nach der Intention Jesu. [5,21-48] — REIKERSTORFER, J. (ed.), *Gesetz und Freiheit*, Wien–Freiburg–Basel: Herder, 1983, 65-84. Esp. 66-70: "Zur Rekonstruktion der ursprünglichen Jesusworte".

1984    Politische Implikationen der Botschaft Jesu? — *Lebendige Seelsorge* 35 (1984) 112-121. Esp. 115-117 [5,38-48]; = ID., *Studien zu Jesus und Paulus*, 1987, 192-205. Esp. 196-198.

1985    Jesus, Künder des Reiches Gottes. — KERN, W. – POTTMEYER, H.J. – SECKLER, M. (eds.), *Handbuch der Fundamentaltheologie*, II, Freiburg: Herder, 1985, 145-174. Esp. 147-148 [3,7-12]; 150-152 [5,3-12]; 154-156 [12,28]; 162-163 [5,21-48]; = ID., *Studien zu Jesus und Paulus*, 1987, 127-156. Esp. 129-130; 132-134; 136-138; 144-145.

1986    Basileia und Ekklesia. Jesu Botschaft von der Gottesherrschaft und ihre Konsequenzen für die Kirche. — HIEROLD, A.E., et al. (eds.), *Die Kraft der Hoffnung. Gemeinde und Evangelium. Festschrift für Alterzbischof Dr. Josef Schneider zum 80. Geburtstag*, Bamberg: St. Otto, 1986, 35-47. Esp. 36-38; 40-42; = ID., *Studien zu Jesus und Paulus*, 1987, 207-220. Esp. 208-211; 214-217.

1987a    *Studien zu Jesus und Paulus* (WUNT, 43). Tübingen: Mohr, 1987, X-479 p. → 1979, 1981a-b, 1984, 1985, 1986

1987b    Die Einzigkeit Gottes als die sachliche Grundlage der Botschaft Jesu. — *JbBT* 2 (1987) 13-32. Esp. 19-23; = ID., *Studien zu Jesus und Paulus*, II, 1998, 154-173. Esp. 160-164.

1987c    Eschatologie im Neuen Testament. — ALTHAUS, H. (ed.), *Apokalyptik und Eschatologie. Sinn und Ziel der Geschichte*, Freiburg–Basel–Wien: Herder, 1987, 11-42. Esp. 24-25; = ID., *Studien zu Jesus und Paulus*, II, 1998, 82-113. Esp. 99.

1988a    Der Prozeß der Barmherzigkeit. Predigtmeditation zu Mt 18,21-35. — SCHENKE, L. (ed.), *Studien zum Matthäusevangelium*. FS W. Pesch, 1988, 201-207.

1988b    Die Reich-Gottes-Verkündigung Jesu. — GORDAN, P. (ed.), *Säkulare Welt und Reich Gottes*, Graz: Styria, 1988, 51-79. Esp. 60-70: "Der Gehalt der Botschaft Jesu"; = ID., *Studien zu Jesus und Paulus*, II, 1998, 125-153. Esp. 134-144.

1989*    (ed.), *Neues Testament und Ethik. Für Rudolf Schnackenburg*. Freiburg: Herder, 1989, 597 p. → Beasley-Murray, J. Becker, Gnilka, F. Hahn, G. Lohfink, R. Pesch, Roloff, G. Schneider, Vögtle

1990    Gericht und Heil. Zur heilsamen Funktion des Gerichts bei Johannes dem Täufer, Jesus und Paulus. — *JbBT* 5 (1990) 71-92. Esp. 72-76 [3,7-12]; = ID., *Studien zu Jesus und Paulus*, II, 1998, 60-81. Esp. 61-65.

1993    Jerusalem – bleibendes Zentrum der Christenheit? Der neutestamentliche Befund. —
        HAHN, F., et al. (eds.), *Zion Ort der Begegnung*. *Festschrift für Laurentius Klein zur
        Vollendung des 65. Lebensjahres* (BBB, 90), Bodenheim: Athenäum/Hain/Hanstein,
        1993, 47-61. Esp. 48-50.

1994a   *Die Jesusgeschichte – synoptisch gelesen* (SBS, 156). Stuttgart: Katholisches Bibelwerk,
        1994, 246 p. Esp. 20-27 [3,1-4,11]; 33-40 [1-2]; 63-65 [4,12-25]; 86-95 [5-7]; 95-99 [8-9]; 103-105
        [12,22-37]; 112-118 [13]; 125-128 [9,35-11,30]; 130-132 [14,13-33]; 133-136 [15,1-39]; 137-141 [16,1-20];
        150-157 [16,21-20,34]; 183-189 [21-23]; 197-202 [24-25]; 214-218 [27,15-56]; 225-235 [28].

1994b   & EID, V. – RIDEZ, L., Bergpredigt. — *LTK* 2 (³1994) 253-258.

1998    *Studien zu Jesus und Paulus*, II (WUNT, 105). Tübingen: Mohr, 1998, XIV-455 p. →
        1987b-c, 1988b, 1990

**MERLI, Dino**

1972    Il segno di Giona. [12,38-39; 16,1-4] — *BibOr* 14 (1972) 61-77. [NTA 18, 491]

1973    *Fiducia e fede nei miracoli evangelici* (Quaderni della rivista "Bibbia e Oriente", 5).
        Genova: Studio e Vita, 1973, 380 p. Esp. 143-221: "Matteo" [4,15-16; 8,17; 9,32-34; 11,2-19;
        12,22-24.39-40; 14,22-33; 21,14-16; 27,51-56.62-66; 28,1-10].
            *BibLeb* 14 (1973) 210-215. [NTA 19, 44]

**MERRILL, Eugene H.**

1980    The Sign of Jonah. [12,38-42; 16,1-4] — *JEvTS* 23 (1980) 23-30. [NTA 25, 120]

**MERRIMAN, E.H.**

1954    Matthew xxii.1-14. — *ExpT* 66 (1954-55) 61.

**MERRITT, Robert L.**

1985    Jesus Barabbas and the Paschal Pardon. [27,17] — *JBL* 104 (1985) 57-68. [NTA 30, 145]

**MERTENS, Herman-Emiel**

1957    *L'Hymne de jubilation chez les Synoptiques. Matthieu XI,25-30 – Luc X,21-22*. Gem-
        bloux: Duculot, 1957, 79 p. Esp. 19-50: "L'authenticité"; 51-78: "Le Père et le Fils". — Diss. Pont.
        Univ. Greg., Roma, 1954 (É. Dhanis).
            M.-É. BOISMARD, *RB* 65 (1958) 302-303; J. COPPENS, *ETL* 34 (1958) 390; P. DELHAYE, *MSR* 15 (1958)
            157; J. DUPONT, *LumièreV* 37 (1958) 32; P.Y. E., *Verbum Caro* 12 (1958) 95; P. GAECHTER,
            *ZKT* 80 (1958) 344; H. MERTENS, *Greg* 405 (1957-58) 215-216; J. PONTHOT, *RevDiocTournai* 13 (1958)
            381; J.N. SANDERS, *JTS* 10 (1959) 130; L. TURRADO, *Salmanticensis* 5 (1958) 257; A. VIARD, *RSPT*
            342; M. ZERWICK, *Bib* 40 (1959) 122.

**MESCHKE, Kurt**

1972    Matteusevangeliets mitt. [The middle of the gospel of Matthew] — *SvenskTeolKvart* 48
        (1972) 119-121. [NTA 17, 507]

**MESSANA, Vincenzo**

1977    L'economia nel *Quis dives salvetur*. Alcune osservazione filologiche. [19,21] —
        *Augustinianum* 17 (1977) 133-143.

**MESSERSCHMIDT, L.**

1967    Jesus stiller stormen på søen. Myte eller frelseshistorisk virkelighed? [Jesus stills the
        storm on the lake. Myth or a reality of salvation-history?] — *Catholica* (København)
        24 (1967) 45-54. [NTA 12, 156]

1968    Dommedagstalen hos Matthaeus. De teologiske hovedtanker i Matthaeusevangeliet kap.
        24,1-31. [Judgment day in Matthew. The principal theological ideas in Mt 24,1-31]. —
        *Catholica* 25 (1968) 47-59. [NTA 13, 176]

**MESSINA, Giuseppe**

1951    *Diatessaron persiano. I. Introduzione. II. Testo e traduzione* (Biblica et Orientalia, 14). Roma: Pontificio Istituto Biblico, 1951, CXIV-389 p. Esp. XXXV-LI; LII-LXXXIV; XCVIII-CIV: "Lezioni tazianee nel c. I dell'Armonia Persiana".

**MESTERS, Carlos**

1973    *O Sermão da montanha* (Círculos Bíblicos, 17-20; 21-24). Petrópolis: Vozes, 1973, 3 vols., 35, 32 and 38 p.

**METTAYER, Arthur**

1995    L'Esprit descendit du ciel tel une colombe ou, lorsque le déplacement détermine le choix de la métaphore. [3,16-17] — *StudRel/SciRel* 24 (1995) 433-439.

**METZ, Johannes Baptist**

1964*   et al. (eds.), *Gott in Welt. Festgabe für Karl Rahner*. Freiburg: Herder, 1964, I,83*-667 p. → Mussner, Schnackenburg, Vögtle; II, 8*-964 p. → Congar, E. Wolf
        *God en Wereld*, trans H. & R. Wagemans. I. *Structuur van Verbond en Kerk*; IV. *Eschatologie in het bewustzijn van Jezus en van de Kerk*. Hilversum–Antwerpen: Brand, 1965, I, 160 p. → E. Wolf; IV, 181 p. → Schnackenburg, Vögtle
        *Le message de Jésus et l'interprétation moderne. Mélanges Karl Rahner* (Cogitatio Fidei, 37). Paris: Cerf, 1969, III-235 p. → Mussner, Schnackenburg, Vögtle

**METZGER, Bruce M.**

1950    Tatian's Diatessaron and a Persian Harmony of the Gospels. — *JBL* 69 (1950) 261-280. Esp. 269-270, 278 [11,17].

1951a   *Index of Articles on the New Testament and the Early Church Published in Festschriften* (JBL MS, 5). Philadelphia, PA: SBL, 1951, XV-182 p. Esp. 66-68; Supplement, 1955, VIII-20 p. Esp. 11.

1951b   The Language of the New Testament. — BUTTRICK, G.A. (ed.), *The Interpreter's Bible*, VII, 1951, 43-59. Esp. 49-50.

1954    Scriptural Quotations in Q Material. — *ExpT* 65 (1953-54) 125. → Argyle 1953, 1954

1955    *Annotated Bibliography of the Textual Criticism of the New Testament, 1914-1939* (Studies and Documents, 16). København: Munksgaard, 1955, XVIII-133 p. Esp. 103-105.

1956    Num bis relata sit, extra orationem Dominicam vox *epiousios*? — *VD* 34 (1956) 349-350.
        How Many Times Does 'epiousios' Occur Outside the Lord's Prayer? — *ExpT* 69 (1957-58) 52-54. [NTA 2, 285]; = ID., *Historical and Literary Studies*, 1968, 64-66.

1958a   On the Citation of Variant Readings of Matt 1,16. — *JBL* 77 (1958) 361-363. [NTA 3, 577] → Throckmorton 1959

1958b   The Designation 'The Golden Rule'. — *ExpT* 69 (1957-58) 304. [NTA 3, 74] → Guy 1959

1962    The New Testament View of the Church. — *TTod* 19 (1962-63) 369-380. Esp. 371-374 [16,17-19]. [NTA 7, 605]

1963    Explicit References in the Works of Origen to Variant Readings in New Testament Manuscripts.— BIRDSALL, J.N. – THOMSON, R.W. (eds.), *Biblical and Patristic Studies. In Memory of Robert Pierce Casey*, Freiburg: Herder, 1963, 78-95. Esp. 81-85 [4,17; 8,28; 16,20; 18,1; 21,5; 24,19; 27,16-17]; 91-92 [5,45; 6,1]; = ID., *Historical and Literary Studies*, 1968, 88-103. Esp. 91-94; 100-101.

1964    *The Text of the New Testament. Its Transmission, Corruption, and Restoration*. Oxford: Clarendon, 1964, XI-268 p. Esp. 153-154 [27,9]; 186-206: "The causes of error in the transmission of the text of the New Testament"; 190-191 [11,16]; 239-240 [22,34-35]; ²1968, XI-284 p.; Oxford: University Press, ³1992, XI-310 p.

*Der Text des Neuen Testaments. Eine Einführung in die neutestamentliche Textkritik*, trans. E. Lohse. Stuttgart: Kohlhammer, 1966, XI-272 p.
Trans. Korean 1979; Chinese 1981; Japanese 1973.

1965    *The New Testament. Its Background, Growth, and Content*. New York – Nashville, TN: Abingdon, 1965, 288 p. Esp. 73-166: "Aspects of the life and teaching of Jesus Christ"; Nashville, TN: Abingdon, ²1983, 309 p.
Trans. Chinese 1976.

1966a   *Index to Periodical Literature on Christ and the Gospels* (New Testament Tools and Studies, 6). Leiden: Brill, 1966, XXIII-602 p. Esp. 9-10 [historical Jesus]; 129-131 [Q]; 131-134 [literary criticism]; 176 [form criticism]; 205-206 [literary style]; 209-267: "Critical and exegetical studies of passages in Matthew"; 390-391.

1966b   The Christianization of Nubia and the Old Nubian Version of the New Testament. — *Studia Patristica* 7 (1966) 531-542. Esp. 540-541 [1,24-25]. [NTA 11, 606]; = ID., *Historical and Literary Studies*, 1968, 111-122. Esp. 121.

1966c   → K. Aland [GNT, 1966]

1968    *Historical and Literary Studies. Pagan, Jewish, and Christian* (New Testament Tools and Studies, 8). Leiden: Brill, 1968, X-170 p. [NTA 14, p. 104] → 1956, 1963, 1966b

1970    Names for the Nameless in the New Testament. A Study in the Growth of Christian Tradition. — GRANFIELD, P. - JUNGMANN, J.A. (eds.), *Kyriakon*. FS J. Quasten, 1970, I, 79-99. Esp. 80-85 [2,1-12]; = ID., *New Testament Studies*, 1980, 23-43 (addenda, 44-45). Esp. 24-29.

1971    *A Textual Commentary on the Greek New Testament. A Companion Volume to the United Bible Societies' Greek New Testament (Third Edition)*. London – New York: United Bible Societies, 1971, XXXI-775 p. Esp. 1-72: "The gospel according to Matthew". → Royse 1983
*A Textual Commentary on the Greek New Testament (Fourth Revised Edition)*. Stuttgart: Deutsche Bibelgesellschaft, ²1994, XIV-16*-696 p. Esp. 1-61.
F. NEIRYNCK, *ETL* 71 (1995) 453-454.

1972    The Text of Matthew 1.16. — AUNE, D.E. (ed.), *Studies in New Testament*. FS A.P. Wikgren, 1972, 16-24; = ID., *New Testament Studies*, 1980, 105-113.

1975    The Practice of Textual Criticism among the Church Fathers. — *Studia Patristica* 12 (1975) 340-349. Esp. 342-345 [5,22; 27,16-17; 28,1]; = ID., *New Testament Studies*, 1980, 189-198. Esp. 191-194.

1976    An Early Coptic Manuscript of the Gospel according to Matthew. — ELLIOTT, J.K. (ed.), *Studies in New Testament Language and Text*. FS G.D. Kilpatrick, 1976, 301-312; = ID., *New Testament Studies*, 1980, 93-104.

1979    St Jerome's Explicit References to Variant Readings in Manuscripts of the New Testament. — BEST, E. - WILSON, R.McL. (eds.), *Text and Interpretation*. FS M. Black, 1979, 179-190. Esp. 180-182 [5,22; 6,25; 11,19.23; 13,35; 16,2-3; 21,31; 24,36]; 188-190; = ID., *New Testament Studies*, 1980, 199-210. Esp. 200-202; 208-210.

1980    *New Testament Studies. Philological, Versional, and Patristic* (New Testament Tools and Studies, 10). Leiden: Brill, 1980, X-234 p. → 1970, 1972, 1975, 1976, 1979

1983    The Prayer That Jesus Taught His Disciples. — ROGERS, P. (ed.), *Sowing the Word. Biblical-Liturgical Essays*, Dublin: Dominican, 1983, 125-134.

1987    *The Canon of the New Testament. Its Origin, Development, and Significance*. Oxford: Clarendon, 1987, X-326 p. Esp. 39-73: "The Apostolic Fathers"; 1997, X-336 p.
*Der Kanon des Neuen Testaments. Entstehung, Entwicklung, Bedeutung*. Düsseldorf: Patmos, 1993, 304 p. Esp. 48-80.

1993* & COOGAN, M.D. (eds.), *The Oxford Companion to the Bible*. Oxford: University Press, 1993, XXI-874 p. → Coggan, Guelich, Kingsbury, Neirynck, Overman, Styler, van Daalen

1994 → 1971

**METZGER, Thérèse**

1965 Note sur le motif de la "poule et des poussins" dans l'iconographie juive (Mt 23,37). — *Cahiers archéologiques* (Paris) 14 (1965) 245-248.

**METZNER, Rainer**

1995 *Die Rezeption des Matthäusevangeliums im 1. Petrusbrief. Studien zum traditionsgeschichtlichen und theologischen Einfluß des 1. Evangeliums auf den 1. Petrusbrief* (WUNT, II/74). Tübingen: Mohr, 1995, X-340 p. Esp. 7-106: "Der literarische Einfluß des Matthäusevangeliums auf den 1. Petrusbrief" [4,1-11; 5,10.11-12.16.38-48; 6,25-34]; 107-264: "Der theologische Einfluß des Matthäusevangeliums auf den 1. Petrusbrief" [Peter; ecclesiology; christology; eschatology]; 265-282: "Das Kriterium der Bezeugung des Matthäusevangeliums in der frühchristlichen Schriften des 1. und 2. Jahrhunderts". [NTA 40, p. 342] — Diss. Berlin, 1994 (C. Wolff).
P.H. DAVIDS, *CBQ* 59 (1997) 387-389; J.H. ELLIOTT, *JBL* 116 [1997) 379-382.

**MEURER, Hermann-Josef**

1997 *Die Gleichnisse Jesu als Metaphern. Paul Ricœurs Hermeneutik der Gleichniserzählung Jesu im Horizont des Symbols "Gottesherrschaft / Reich Gottes"* (BBB, 111). Bodenheim: Philo, 1997, 783 p. Esp. 151-178: "Das 'ultra-strukturalistische' Modell von Louis Marin" [13,1-23]; 536-542 [3,7-12]; 545-550 [5,3-12]; 581-618 [12,28]; 619-644 [13,31-32]; 710-719 [18,23-35]; 727-729 [22,1-10]. — Diss. Münster, 1995-96 (H. Vorgrimler).

**MEURER, Siegfried**

1972 *Das Recht im Dienst der Versöhnung und des Friedens. Studie zur Frage des Rechts nach dem Neuen Testament* (ATANT, 63). Zürich: Theologischer Verlag, 1972, 194 p. Esp. 29-44: "Zur Beziehung der Gerechtigkeit Gottes zum Recht. Dazu Auslegung von Mt 20,1-16"; 45-48 [18,1-5.6-9.12-14]; 48-58 [18,15-18]; 59-60 [18,19-20]; 60-62 [18,21-35]; 63-64 [7,1]; 64-70 [5,38-42]; 70-76 [5,25-26]; 76-79 [13,24-30.36-43]; 79-81 [18,15/Did 15,3].

**MEYE, Robert Paul**

1968 The Christological Conclusion of Matthew's Gospel. — *Foundations* (Rochester, NY) 11 (1968) 9-26.

**MEYER, A.**

1959 & BAUER, W., Jesu Verwandtschaft. — HENNECKE, E. – SCHNEEMELCHER, W. (eds.), *Neutestamentliche Apokryphen*, I, ³1959, 312-321. Esp. 319-321. (ET, 418-432). → Bienert 1987

**MEYER, Ben F.**

1965 Jesus and the Remnant of Israel. — *JBL* 84 (1965) 123-130. Esp. 125-127. [NTA 10, 84]

1979 *The Aims of Jesus*. London: SCM, 1979, 335 p. Esp. 185-197: "In the region of Caesarea Philippi" [16,17-19].

1990 Many (= All) Are Called, but Few (= Not All) Are Chosen. [22,14] — *NTS* 36 (1990) 89-97. [NTA 34, 632]; = ID., *Christus Faber: The Master Builder and the House of God* (Princeton Theological Monograph Series, 29). Allison Park, PA: Pickwick, 1992.

1992 Jesus. — *ABD* 3 (1992) 773-796.

1993a Master Builder and Copestone of the Portal: Images of the Mission of Jesus. — *TorontoJT* 9 (1993) 187-209. [NTA 38, 717]

1993b The Temple: Symbol Central to Biblical Theology. — *Greg* 74 (1993) 223-240. Esp. 231-237: "Jesus and the Temple". [NTA 38, 381]

1994    *Five Speeches That Changed the World* [5-7; 10,5-11,1; 13,1-52; 18; 24-25]. Collegeville, MN: Liturgical Press, 1994, 139 p. [NTA 39, p. 141]

**MEYER, Eduard**

1921[R]    *Ursprung und Anfänge des Christentums*. Band I: *Die Evangelien* [1921]. Darmstadt: Wissenschaftliche Buchgesellschaft, 1962, XII-340 p. Esp. 212-263: "Die übrigen Quellen und das Matthaeusevangelium".

**MEYER, Marvin W.**

1983    *Who Do People Say I Am? Interpretation of Jesus in the New Testament Gospels*. Grand Rapids, MI: Eerdmans, 1983, VI-89 p.

1990a    The Beginning of the Gospel of Thomas. — *Semeia* 52 (1990) 161-173. Esp. 161-163: "Q and Thomas as sayings gospels"; 169-171. [NTA 35, 1495]
Response: R.C. TANNEHILL, *ibid*., 191.

1990b    → Kloppenborg 1990a

**MEYER, Paul Donald**

1967    *The Community of Q*. Diss. Univ. of Iowa, 1967, IV-98 p. (C.E. Carlston). Esp. 7-28: "The gentile mission"; 29-49: "Opposition and persecution"; 50-64: "Eschatology"; 65-82: "The present kingdom of God". — *DissAbstr* 28 (1968-68) 3256.

1970    The Gentile Mission in Q. — *JBL* 89 (1970) 405-417. Esp. 405-410 [12,38-42]; 410-411 [8,5-10]; 411-412 [8,11-12]; 412-414 [22,1-10]; 415-416 [23,34-39]. [NTA 15, 831]

**MEYER, Paul W.**

1986    Matthew 21:1-11. — *Interpr* 40 (1986) 180-185.

1988    Context as a Bearer of Meaning in Matthew. [13,44-46; 25,31-46] — *USQR* 42/1-2 (1988) 69-72. [NTA 32, 100]

**MEYNELL, Hugo**

1963    The Synoptic Problem: Some Unorthodox Solutions. — *The Life of the Spirit* (London) 17 (1963) 451-459. [NTA 8, 85]; = *Theology* 70 (1967) 386-397. [NTA 12, 542] → Butler 1951, W.R. Farmer 1964a, McLoughlin 1969, P. Parker 1953, Streeter 1924

1972    A Note on the Synoptic Problem. — *DownR* 90 (1972) 196-200. [NTA 17, 107] → McLoughlin 1972

**MEYNET, Roland**

1983    Qui donc est "le plus fort"? Analyse rhétorique de Mc 3,22-30; Mt 12,22-37; Luc 11,14-26. — *RB* 90 (1983) 334-350. Esp. 337-342: "La parole chez Matthieu". [NTA 28, 934]

1993    *Passion de notre Seigneur Jésus-Christ selon les évangiles synoptiques* [26-27] (Lire la Bible, 99). Paris: Cerf, 1993, 232 p.

**MICHAEL, M.**

1967    In the Steps of St. Matthew. [Juvencus] — *AustralasCR* 44 (1967) 96-106. [NTA 12, 145]

**MICHAELIS, Christine**

1968    Die Π-Alliteration der Subjektsworte der ersten 4 Seligpreisungen in Mt. v 3-6 und ihre Bedeutung für den Aufbau der Seligpreisungen bei Mt., Lk. und in Q. — *NT* 10 (1968) 148-161. Esp. 149-153 [structure]; 153-160 [alliteration]. [NTA 13, 565]

**MICHAELIS, Wilhelm**

1939[R]    *Die Gleichnisse Jesu. Eine Einführung* [*Das hochzeitliche Kleid*, 1939] (Die urchristliche Botschaft, 32). Hamburg: Furche, [3]1956, 272 p.

1946[R]    *Einleitung in das Neue Testament. Die Entstehung, Sammlung und Überlieferung der Schriften des Neuen Testaments* [1946]. Bern: Berchthold Haller Verlag, [2]1954, XI-410 p.; [3]1961. Esp. 24-40: "Matthäus-Evangelium"; 74-87: "Die synoptische Frage".

1950 *Versöhnung des Alls. Die Frohe Botschaft von der Gnade Gottes*. Gümligen (Bern): Siloah, 1950, 198 p. Esp. 43-44; 49-53 [12,32]; 56-63 [18,8-9; 25,41.46].

1953 Kennen die Synoptiker eine Verzögerung der Parusie? — SCHMID, J. – VÖGTLE, A. (eds.), *Synoptische Studien*. FS A. Wikenhauser, 1953, 107-123. Esp. 116-121 [25,1-13]; 121 [24,45-51]; 121-122 [25,14-30].

1955 Die Gleichnisse Jesu und die Verzögerung der Parousie. — *KirchRefSchweiz* 111 (1955) 193-197, 210-212.

1960 Die Davidssohnschaft Jesu als historisches und kerygmatisches Problem. — RISTOW, H. – MATTHIAE, K. (eds.), *Der historische Jesus und der kerygmatische Christus*, 1960, 317-330. Esp. 318-321.

**MICHAELS, J. Ramsey**

1965 Apostolic Hardships and Righteous Gentiles. A Study of Matthew 25,31-46. — *JBL* 84 (1965) 27-37. [NTA 9, 927] → Jurgens 1983

1968 The Parable of the Regretful Son. [21,28-32] — *HTR* 61 (1968) 15-26. [NTA 12, 880]

1976 Christian Prophecy and Matthew 23:8-12. A Test Exegesis. — *SBL 1976 Seminar Papers*, 305-310.

1981 *Servant and Son. Jesus in Parable and Gospel*. Atlanta, GA: Knox, 1981, XIII-322 p. Esp. 5-10 [3,7-12]; 29-30 [3,13-17]; 46-51 [4,1-11]; 66-109 [kingdom]; 114-139 [13]; 157-163 [8,28-34]; 163-166 [15,21-28]; 183-184 [12,9-14]; 231-240 [5–7]; 246-247 [22,1-14]; 276-279 [7,7-11]; 279-283 [6,9-13]; 284-291 [Son of Man]; 291-302 [24–25].

1987 The Kingdom of God and the Historical Jesus. — WILLIS, W. (ed.), *The Kingdom of God*, 1987, 109-118. Esp. 110-111 [Mt]; 112-113 [Q]; 116 [8,11-12].

**MICHALON, Pierre**

1953 Le témoignage du Nouveau Testament sur la mère de Jésus. — *LumièreV* 10 (1953) 109-126. Esp. 112-114.

**MICHAUD, Jean-Paul**

1991 *Marie des Évangiles* (Cahiers Évangile, 77). Paris: Cerf, 1991, 76 p. Esp. 15-28: "Marie vue par Matthieu".

**MICHEL, A.**

1964 & LE MOYNE, J., Pharisiens. — *DBS* 7/39-40 (1964-65) 1022-1115. Esp. 1068-1100: "Jésus et les Pharisiens"; 1100-1110: "Les Pharisiens et la mort de Jésus".

**MICHEL, Otto**

1950 Der Abschluß des Matthäusevangeliums. Ein Beitrag zur Geschichte der Osterbotschaft. — *EvT* 10 (1950-51) 16-26; = LANGE, J. (ed.), *Das Matthäus-Evangelium*, 1980, 119-133.
The Conclusion of Matthew's Gospel. A Contribution to the History of the Easter Message. — STANTON, G. (ed.), *The Interpretation of Matthew*, 1983, 30-41; ²1995, 39-51.

1952 Binden und Lösen (rechtstheologische Ausdrücke). — *RAC* 2/11 (1952) 374-380. Esp. 375-376 [16,19; 18,18].

1959a Eine philologische Frage zur Einzugsgeschichte. [21,2.5.7] — *NTS* 6 (1959-60) 81-82. [NTA 4, 367]

1959b Polemik und Scheidung. Eine biblische und religionsgeschichtliche Studie. — HERMELINK, J. – MARGULL, H.J. (eds.), *Basileia. Walter Freytag zum 60. Geburtstag*, Stuttgart: Evang. Missionsverlag, 1959; Darmstadt: Wissenschaftliche Buchgesellschaft, ²1961, 185-198. Esp. 188-190 [3,7]; = *Judaica* 15 (1959) 193-212. Esp. 197-200.

1960 & BETZ, O., Von Gott gezeugt. — ELTESTER, W. (ed.), *Judentum, Urchristentum, Kirche*. FS J. Jeremias, 1960, 1-23. Esp. 17-18 [1,18-25].

1969    Zur Methodik der Forschung. — ID., et al., *Studies on the Jewish Background of the New Testament*, Assen: van Gorcum, 1969, 1-11. Esp. 9-10 [5,48].

1971a   Der Menschensohn in der Jesusüberlieferung. — *TBeitr* 2 (1971) 119-128. [NTA 18, 260]

1971b   Der Menschensohn. Die eschatologische Hinweisung. Die apokalyptische Aussage. Bemerkungen zum Menschensohn-Verständnis des N.T. — *TZ* 27 (1971) 81-104. Esp. 97-100. [NTA 16, 112]

1972    Zeuge und Zeugnis. Zur neutestamentlichen Traditionsgeschichte. — BALTENSWEILER, H. - REICKE, B. (eds.), *Neues Testament und Geschichte*. FS O. Cullmann, 1972, 15-31. Esp. 22-23 [Q].

### MICHIELS, Robrecht

1965    La conception lucanienne de la conversion. — *ETL* 41 (1965) 42-78. Esp. 62-67 [3,7-12]; 67-68 [Q 10,13-15]; 69-71 [Q 11,31-32]. [NTA 10, 144]

1971    De kerkelijke rede uit het Matteüsevangelie (hfd. 18). — *Tijdschrift voor Geestelijk Leven* (Leuven) 27 (1971) 441-452.

1972    Het beeld van Jezus in de geboorteverhalen van Matteüs en Lucas. [1-2] — *Getuigenis* 17 (1972-73) 46-56.

1974    Het evangelie volgens Matteüs. — *Tijdschrift voor Geestelijk Leven* 30 (1974) 595-629; 31 (1975) 98-121, 162-201.

1986    *Evangelie en evangelies* (Nikè-reeks: Didachè. Het Nieuwe Testament leren lezen, 1). Leuven–Amersfoort: Acco, 1986, 184 p. Esp. 76-79 [redaction criticism]; 92-96 [4,1-11].

1993    Church of Jesus Christ: An Exegetical-Ecclesiological Consideration. — *LouvSt* 18 (1993) 297-317. Esp. 314-317 [16,18; 18,17]. [NTA 38, 1590]

### MICHL, Johann

1969    Die Jungfrauengeburt im Neuen Testament. — BROSCH, H.J. - HASENFUSS, J. (eds.), *Jungfrauengeburt gestern und heute* (Mariologische Studien, 4), Essen: Driewer, 1969, 145-184. Esp. 147-148 [1,16]; 149-155 [1,18-25]; 170-172.

1970    Da trat der Versucher an ihn heran. Die Überlieferung von den Versuchungen Jesu im Neuen Testament. — *BK* 25 (1970) 1-5. Esp. 2-3 [4,1-11]. [NTA 15, 135]

1973    Sündenbekenntnis und Sündenvergebung in der Kirche des Neuen Testaments. — *MüTZ* 24 (1973) 189-207. Esp. 196-200 [16,19; 18,18]. [NTA 18, 639]

### MIEGGE, Giovanni

1960    Le "Notre Père", prière du temps présent. — *ETR* 35 (1960) 237-253. [NTA 6, 123]

1970    *Il Sermone sul monte. Commentario esegetico. Revisione, note e bibliografia a cura di Bruno Corsani* (Collana della Facoltà Valdese di Teologia, 10). Torino: Claudiana, 1970, 284 p. Esp. 19-24 [4,25-5,2]; 25-66 [5,3-12]; 67-81 [5,13-16]; 83-161 [5,17-48]; 165-177 [6,1-6]; 179-225 [6,7-15]; 227-243 [6,19-34]; 245-256 [7,1-12]; 257-272 [7,13-29]. [NTA 15, p. 240]
        G. BERTRAM, *TLZ* 97 (1972) 123-124; S. CARTECHINI, *Greg* 52 (1971) 571-573; F. CHRIST, *TZ* 27 (1971) 137-138; T. DA CANALNOVO, *PalCl* 49 (1970) 1327-1328; J. DUPONT, *RivBib* 18 (1970) 432; *RivStoLR* 7 (1971) 180-181; G.G. GAMBA, *Sal* 34 (1972) 174-175; G. GIAVINI, *ScuolC* 100 (1972) 347; K. GRAYSTON, *ExpT* 82 (1970-71) 278; J.-C. INGELAERE, *RHPR* 53 (1973) 86; J. LLAMAS, *CiudDios* 184 (1971) 126; C. MATEOS, *EstAgust* 6 (1971) 127; F. MONTAGNINI, *ParVi* 16 (1971) 158; J. SALGUERO, *Angelicum* 49 (1972) 118; G. SEGALLA, *Studia Patavina* 18 (1971) 528; P. ZARRELLA, *Laur* 12 (1971) 111-112.

### MIEGGE, Mario

1969    *I talenti messi a profitto. L'interpretazione della parabola dei denari affidati ai servi dalla Chiesa Antica a Calvino* [25,14-30]. Urbino: Argalia, 1969, 142 p.

**MIGLIORE, Daniel L.**

1993* (ed.), *The Lord's Prayer. Perspectives for Reclaiming Christian Prayer.* Grand Rapids, MI: Eerdmans, 1993, 151 p. [NTA 38, p. 464]; = *PrincSemB* suppl. 2 (1992) → Froehlich, D.J. Hall, Juel, McKee
R. LUNT, *ExpT* 105 (1993-94) 348.

**MIGUÉNS, Manuel**

1955 Anotaciones sobre Mateo cc. 24–25. — *SBF/LA* 6 (1955-56) 125-195. Esp. 126-159: "Exegesis patristica"; 160-175: "El problema textual" [10,17-22; 24.3.7.9-14.26-28.36-41].

1959 La predicazione di Gesù in parabole (*Mc.* 4; *Lc.* 8,4-18; *Mt.* 13). [12,15-21; 13,10-11] — *BibOr* 1 (1959) 35-40. [NTA 4, 79]

1963 *El Paráclito (Jn 14–16)* (Studi Biblici Franciscani Analecta, 2). Jerusalem: SBFA, 1963, XIII-277 p. Esp. 107-121 [10,17-22/Mk].

1967 Kephâs, Ho Pétros y el primado de Pedro. — *SBF/LA* 17 (1967) 348-364. Esp. 362-363. [NTA 12, 831]

1974 La virginidad de María. El silencio del Nuevo Testamento. — *EstBíb* 34 (1974) 245-264, 357-381. Esp. 253-259 [13,53-58]. → 1975
Mary, a Virgin? Alleged Silence in the New Testament. — *Marian Studies* (Washington, DC) 26 (1975) 26-179. [NTA 20, 57]

1975 *The Virgin Birth. An Evaluation of Scriptural Evidence.* Westminster, MD: Christian Classics, 1975, IV-170 p. → 1974
M.A. CHEVALLIER, *RHPR* 57 (1977) 106-107; J.M. DOWD, *Marianum* 42 (1980) 343-345; R. GAUTHIER, *CahJos* 28 (1980) 270-271; S.B. MARROW, *CBQ* 38 (1976) 576-577; J. MURPHY-O'CONNOR, *RB* 84 (1977) 469-470; B. PENNACCHINI, *Ant* 51 (1986) 331-334.

1976 *Church Ministries in New Testament Times.* Arlington, VA: Christian Culture Press; Westminster, MD: Christian Classics, 1976, XVII-221 p. Esp. 3-19: "Ministry in the Synoptic Gospels"; 80-82 [18,15-20]; 91-95 [16,18-19]; 85-91 [Peter].

1980 The Infancy Narratives and Critical Biblical Method. — *Communio* (Notre Dame, IN) 7 (1980) 24-54. [NTA 24, 780r] → R.E. Brown 1977

**MÍGUEZ, Néstor O.**

1986 Continuidad y ruptura. Confrontación y conflicto. Elementos para una aproximación socio-política a Mateo 23–24. — *RevistBíb* 48 (1986) 153-167. [NTA 31, 591]

**MIKRE-SELLASSIE, G. Ammanuel**

1988 Problems in Translating Pronouns from English Versions. — *BTrans* 39 (1988) 230-237. Esp. 233-237 [6,1-2; 25,3-13]. [NTA 33, 68]

**MILAVEC, Aaron A.**

1978 Matthew's Integration of Sexual and Divine Begetting. — *BTB* 8 (1978) 108-116. [NTA 23, 87]

1989 A Fresh Analysis of the Parable of the Wicked Husbandmen in the Light of Jewish-Catholic Dialogue. — THOMA, C. — WYSCHOGROD, M. (eds.), *Parable and Story*, 1989, 81-117. Esp. 87-94 [21,33-46/Mk]. → Boadt 1989, D. Stern 1989

1995 The Social Setting of "Turning the Other Cheek" and "Loving One's Enemies" in Light of the *Didache*. [5,38-48] — *BTB* 25 (1995) 131-143. [NTA 40, 821]

**MILIKOWSKY, Chaim**

1988 Which Gehenna? Retribution and Eschatology in the Synoptic Gospels and in Early Jewish Texts. — *NTS* 34 (1988) 238-249. Esp. 242-244 [5,29-30; 10,14-15.28]. [NTA 32, 1095]

**MILLAR, Fergus**

1990 Reflections on the Trials of Jesus. — DAVIES, P.R. - WHITE, R.T. (eds.), *A Tribute to Geza Vermes*, 1990, 355-381. Esp. 357-358 [genre]; 366-367 [26,17-29; 27,1-10].

**MILLER, Donald G.**

1971* & HADIDIAN, D.Y. (eds.), *Jesus and Man's Hope*. II (A Perspective Book). Pittsburgh, PA: Pittsburgh Theological Seminary, 1971, 362 p. → Keck, Schweizer, Voegelin

**MILLER, J. Hillis**

1982 Parable and Performative in the Gospels and in Modern Literature. — TUCKER, G.B. – KNIGHT, D.A. (eds.), *Humanizing America's Iconic Book. SBL Centennial Addresses 1980, Dallas* (SBL Scholarship in North America, 6), Chico, CA: Scholars, 1982, 57-71.

**MILLER, Merrill P.**

1974 *Scripture and Parable. A Study of the Function of the Biblical Features in the Parable of the Wicked Husbandmen and Their Place in the History of the Tradition*. Diss. Columbia Univ., 1974, 500 p. — *DissAbstr* 36 (1975-76) 948.

**MILLER, Robert J.**

1988 The Rejection of the Prophets in Q. — *JBL* 107 (1988) 225-240. Esp. 226-233 [23,29-32.34-36]; 233-240 [23,37-39]. [NTA 33, 108]

1989a The Inside Is (Not) the Outside. Q 11:39-41 and GThom 89. — *Forum* 5/1 (1989) 92-105. Esp. 92-98: "A history of the tradition"; 98-104: "The issue of authenticity". [NTA 34, 169]

1989b The Lord's Prayer and Other Items from the Sermon on the Mount. — *Forum* 5/2 (1989) 177-186. Esp. 177-178 [6,2-4.5-8.16-18]; 178 [5,21-22.27-28.33-37.43-44; 6,25-33]; 179-183 [6,9-13]; 184-186: "Voting results". [NTA 34, 116]

1992 Historical Method and the Deeds of Jesus: The Test Case of the Temple Demonstration. — *Forum* 8 (1992) 5-30. Esp. 25 [Q/historical Jesus]. [NTA 39, 187]

**MILLET, Gabriel**

1956 Doura et El-Bagawat. La parabole des vierges. [25,1-13] — *Cahiers archéologiques* (Paris) 8 (1956) 1-8.

**MILLING, D.H.**

1969 The Interpretation of the Lord's Prayer in Terms of Future Eschatology. — *BangalTF* 3/1 (1969) 13-25.

**MILLINGTON, Fr. C.**

1959 A Spoilt Masterpiece. [5,32; 19,9] — *Studia Evangelica* 1 (1959) 506-509.

**MILLS, Watson E.**

1993 *The Gospel of Matthew* (Bibliographies for Biblical Research. New Testament Series, 1). Lewiston, NY – Queenston, Ont. – Lampeter, UK: Mellen, 1993, XXIII-279 p. [NTA 39, p. 141]

**MILTON, A. Edward**

1995 "Deliver Us from the Evil Imagination": Matt. 6:13B in Light of the Jewish Doctrine of the *Yêṣer Hârâ '*. — *Religious Studies and Theology* (Saskatoon) 13-14 (1995) 52-67. [NTA 40, 168]

**MILTON, Helen**

1962 The Structure of the Prologue to St. Matthew's Gospel. [1,16.17.20.23] — *JBL* 81 (1962) 175-181. [NTA 7, 123]

**MILWARD, Peter**

1961 The Prophetic Perspective and the Primacy of Peter. — *AmEcclRev* 144 (1961) 122-129. [NTA 5, 717]

1963 The Rock of the New Testament. — *AmEcclRev* 148 (1963) 73-97. [NTA 7, 749]

**MIMOUNI, Simon C.**

1995   Controverse ancienne et récente autour d'une apparition du Christ ressuscité à la vierge
Marie. [27,61; 28,1] — *Marianum* 57 (1995) 239-268. [NTA 40, 1441]

**MINASSIAN, Martiros**

1987   Critique des variantes de Matthieu 1-5 dans les Bibles arméniennes de 1805, 1860,
1895. — *Revue des études arméniennes* (Paris) 20 (1986-87) 109-122.

**MINEAR, Paul S.**

1950a  *The Interpreter and the Birth Narratives* (Symbolae Biblicae Upsalienses. Suppl. *SEÅ*,
13). Uppsala: Wretmans Boktryckeri, 1950, 22 p.

1950b  The Interpreter and the Nativity Stories. — *TTod* 7 (1950-51) 358-375. → 1982, 152-164

1953a  The Coming of the Son of Man (An Exegesis of Mt 25:31-46). — *TTod* 9 (1952-53)
489-493. → 1982, 180-184

1953b  The Covenant and the Great Commission. — GOODALL, N. (ed.), *Missions under the
Cross*, London: Edinburgh House, 1953, 64-80. → 1982, 184-189

1954   *Christian Hope and the Second Coming.* Philadelphia, PA: Westminster, 1954, 219 p.
Esp. 97-110 [parousia]. → 1982, 173-180

1960   *Images of the Church in the New Testament.* Philadelphia, PA: Westminster, 1960;
London: Lutterworth, 1961, 294 p.

1971   Yes or No: The Demand for Honesty in the Early Church. — *NT* 13 (1971) 1-13. Esp.
1-4 [5,33-37]; 4-6 [23,16-22]; 8 [12,34-37]; 8-9 [15,18-20]. [NTA 16, 151]

1972   *Commands of Christ.* Nashville, TN – New York: Abingdon; Edinburgh: St. Andrews
Press, 1972, 190 p. Esp. 31-34.37-38 [5,34-35]; 34-36 [23,16-22]; 47-68 [6,1-6.16-18] (→ 1982, 164-
173); 113-131 [7,7-11]; 132-151 [6,25-34]; 69-82 [Q 6,27-36 (Lk)].

1973   Matthew, Evangelist, and Johann, Composer. — *TTod* 30 (1973-74) 243-255. [NTA 18,
479] → 1982, 189-193

1974a  The Disciples and the Crowds in the Gospel of Matthew. — *ATR* SS 3 (1974) 28-44.
[NTA 19, 82]

1974b  False Prophecy and Hypocrisy in the Gospel of Matthew. — GNILKA, J. (ed.), *Neues
Testament und Kirche.* FS R. Schnackenburg, 1974, 76-93. Esp. 76-79: "Three theses"; 80-86:
"The editing of 7,15-27"; 86-93: "The editing of 23,29-39".

1977   *To Die and to Live. Christ's Resurrection and Christian Vocation* (A Crossroad Book).
New York: Seabury, 1977, VI-162 p.

1981   The Bible's Authority in the Congregation. — *TTod* 38 (1981-82) 350-356. Esp. 352-356
[6,9-13]. [NTA 26, 401]

1982   *Matthew. The Teacher's Gospel.* New York: Pilgrim, 1982, X-194 p. Esp. 3-28:
"Introduction"; 29-142 [commentary]; 152-164: "On interpreting the birth stories" (→ 1950b); 164-173: "On
secret piety" [6,1-6.16-18] (→ 1972, 47-68); 173-180: "The expectation of Christ's return" (→ 1954, 97-110);
180-184: "The parable of final judgment" (→ 1953a); 184-189: "The covenant and great commission" (→
1953b); 189-193: "J.S. Bach's interpretation of the Matthean passion" (→ 1973). [NTA 27, p. 96]
R.A. BARTELS, *WWorld* 4 (1984) 217-218; F.W. BURNETT, *Interpr* 38 (1984) 320.322; D. HILL, *ScotJT*
38 (1985) 445-446; R. LUNT, *ExpT* 96 (1984-85) 55; J. MUDDIMAN *Theology* 88 (1985) 142-143; J.A.
WILLIAMS, *RelStR* 10 (1984) 178.

1984   Matthew 28:1-10. — *Interpr* 38 (1984) 59-63.

1995   The Messiah Forsaken ... Why? — *HorizonsBT* 17 (1995) 62-83. Esp. 72-73 [24,29]; 74-80
[27,51-54]. [NTA 40, 177]

**MINETTE DE TILLESSE, Gaëtan**

1988   O problema sinótico. — *RevistBíbBras* 5 (1988) 3-22.

1990a A fonte de Lógia. — *RevistBíbBras* 7 (1990) 157-205. [NTA 35, 120] → Neirynck 1988a

1990b Uma tradiçâo batista? — *Ibid.*, 213-248. [NTA 35, 581]

**MINK, Gerd** → Schmitz 1986

**MINNERATH, Roland**

1987 *Jésus et le pouvoir* (Le point théologique, 46). Paris: Beauchesne, 1987, 231 p. Esp. 39-41 [24,44]; 73-74 [19,28]; 99-113 [11,25-27]; 123-125 [18,3]; 130-132 [23,8-9]; 187-189 [28,19-20].

1992 L'exégèse de Mt 16,18.19 chez Tertullien. — *RHPR* 72 (1992) 61-72.

1994 *De Jérusalem à Rome. Pierre et l'unité de l'Église apostolique* (Théologie historique, 101). Paris: Beauchesne, 1994, 616 p. Esp. 26-36 [16,13-28]; 60-62 [16,18-19]; 112-125: "Le problème synoptique"; 126-129: "L'évangile araméen de Matthieu"; 277-298: "La communauté matthéenne" [18; 23,8-10].

**MINOR, Mark**

1992 *Literary-Critical Approaches to the Bible. An Annotated Bibliography*. West Cornwall, CT: Locust Hill Press, 1992, XXXI-520 p. Esp. 376-389: "Matthew"; *A Bibliographical Supplement*, 1996, XVII-310 p.

**MINUTI, Riccardo**

1966 & MONTI, F. (trans.), *S. Giovanni Crisostomo. Commento al Vangelo di San Matteo.* Roma: Città Nuova, 1966-67, 3 vols., 395, 426 and 382 p.
    A. FERRUA, *CC* 120/2 (1969) 302; B. PRETE, *Sacra Doctrina* (Bologna) 13 (1968) 148-149.

**MIQUEL, Pierre**

1961 Le mystère de la transfiguration. — *Questions Liturgiques et Paroissiales* (Leuven) 42 (1961) 194-223. Esp. 195-213 [17,1-8]. [NTA 6, 546]
    The Mystery of the Transfiguration. — *TDig* 11 (1963) 159-164.

**MIRKES, Renée**

1993 The Matthean Author's Use of Redaction. An Exegesis of Matthew 8:18-27. — ALBL, M.C., et al. (eds.), *Directions in New Testament Methods*, 1993, 31-37.

**MITCHELL, Curtis C.**

1990 The Practice of Fasting in the New Testament. — *BS* 147 (1990) 455-469. Esp. 457-460 [6,16-18]. [NTA 35, 842]

**MITTON, Charles Leslie**

1956 Present Justification and Final Judgment. A Discussion of the Parable of the Sheep and the Goats. — *ExpT* 68 (1956-57) 46-50. Esp. 47 [25,31-46].

1957 The Law and the Gospel. — *ExpT* 68 (1956-57) 312-315. [NTA 2, 396]

1960 The Will of God. In the Synoptic Tradition of the Words of Jesus. — *ExpT* 72 (1960-61) 68-71. Esp. 70-71 [7,21]. [NTA 5, 700]

1961 *The Good News: Matthew, Mark, Luke*. London: Lutterworth, 1961, 96 p.

1964 Threefoldness in the Teaching of Jesus. — *ExpT* 75 (1963-64) 228-230. [NTA 9, 115] → Ackroyd 1964

1965 Notes of Recent Exposition. — *ExpT* 77 (1965-66) 1-3. → W.R. Farmer 1964a

1966 Expounding the Parables. VII. The Workers in the Vineyard (Matthew 20,1-16). — *ExpT* 77 (1965-66) 307-311. [NTA 11, 214]

1971 Uncomfortable Words. IX. Stumbling-block Characteristics in Jesus. [11,6] — *ExpT* 82 (1970-71) 168-172. [NTA 15, 850]

1973 New Wine in Old Wine-Skins: IV. Leaven. — *ExpT* 84 (1972-73) 339-343. Esp. 340-341 [13,33]. [NTA 18, 664]

1979    Matthew's Disservice to Jesus. [23] — *EpworthR* 6 (1979) 47-54. [NTA 24, 427]

**MIYOSHI, Michi**

1974    *Der Anfang des Reiseberichts. Lk 9,51–10,24. Eine redaktionsgeschichtliche Untersuchung* (AnBib, 60). Roma: Biblical Institute Press, 1974, X-176 p. Esp. 33-44 [Q 9,57-62]; 59-76 [Q 10,1-16]; 120-134 [Q 10,21-24]. — Diss. Pont. Inst. Eibl., Roma, 1973 (I. de la Potterie).

1984    Zur Entstehung des Glaubens an die jungfräuliche Geburt Jesu in Mt 1 und Lk 1. — *AJBI* 10 (1984) 33-62. Esp. 37-44. [NTA 29, 926]

1986    "Undivided Heart" in Matthew 5:8 and Chap. 6. [Japanese] — *Shinyakugaku Kenkyu (New Testament Studies)* 14 (1986) 2-14.

1989    Die Theologie der Spaltung und Einigung Israels in der Geburts- und Leidensgeschichte nach Matthäus. [2,6.10; 27,3-10.51-53] — *AJBI* 15 (1989) 27-52. [NTA 34, 1124]

**MIZUGAKI, W.**

1967    Seeking and Finding. A Study of the Gnostic and Early Christian Interpretation of Mt. 7,7. [Japanese] — *Nihonno Shingaku (Theological Studies in Japan)* 6 (1967) 175-184.

**MIZZI, J.**

1954a   The Latin Text of Matt V–VII in St. Augustine's *De Sermone Domini in monte*. — COURCELLE, P., et al. (eds.), *Augustiniana. Sexto decimo exacto saeculo a die natali S. Aurelii Augustini 354-1954*, Leuven: Institut Historique Augustinien, 1954, 450-494.

1954b   Mt VI,13 and a Peculiar Augustinian Reading. — *MelTheol* 7 (1954) 17-19.

1962    The Latin Text of the Gospel Quotations in St. Augustine's "De Diversis Quaestionibus LXXXIII Liber Unus". — *Augustiniana* 12 (1962) 245-290. Esp. 275-281.

1965    A Comparative Study of Some Portions of Cod. Palatinus and Cod. Bobiensis. — *RBén* 75 (1965) 7-39.

1968    The African Element in the Latin Text of Mt. XXIV of Cod. Cantabrigiensis. — *RBén* 78 (1968) 33-66. [NTA 13, 59]

**MLADIN, Nicola**

1967    "As you did it to one of the least of my brethren, you did it to me" (Mt 25,40). [Roumanian] — *Mitropolia Moldovei si Sucevei* (Iasi) 43 (1967) 259-270.

**M'NEILE, Alan Hugh**

1915[R]  *The Gospel according to St. Matthew. The Greek Text with Introduction, Notes, and Indices* [1915]. London: MacMillan; New York: St. Martin's, repr. 1951, 1955, 1965, XXXVI-448 p. Esp. XI-XXXII: "Introduction"; XXXIII-XXXIV: "Old Testament quotations and allusions"; 1-439: "Text and notes"; Appendices: 4-5 [1,16]; 5 [genealogy]; 10-13 [virgin birth]; 22-24 [2]; 33-37 [3,1-12]; 54-55 [5,12]; 79-80 [ἐπιούσιος]; 99-101 [Sermon on the Mount]; 114-115 [8,28-34]; 128-129 [9,27-33]; 163-166 [11,27]; 191-192 [13,10-15]; 195-196 [13,18-23]; 202-203 [13,37-43]; 211-213 [John the baptist: death]; 215-217 [14,13-21]; 219-220 [14,22-33]; 224-225 [15,1-6]; 237-238 [14,13–16,12]; 251-252 [17,1-9]; 262-263 [αἰώνιος]; 297-298 [21,1-10]; 299-300 [21,11-17]; 323-324 [Sadducees]; 326 [22,34-40]; 340-341 [23,35]; 376 [26,6-13]; 383-386 [26,26-29]; 408-409 [27,3-10]; 437-439 [resurrection narr.]; (Thornapple Commentaries), Grand Rapids, MI: Baker, 1980, 448 p.

1927[R]  *An Introduction to the Study of the New Testament* [1927, repr. 1950], revised by C.S.C. Williams. Oxford: Clarendon, 1953, VIII-486 p. Esp. 3-45: "The synoptic gospels"; 59-91 "The synoptic problem".

**MODA, Aldo**

1991    Il discorso della montagna attualità o utopia? Un sondaggio sulle risposte dei secoli passati. [5-7] — *Credere oggi* 11 (1991) 80-100.

**MOE, Steinar**

1976 *Matteusevangeliet i hovedtrekk*. Oslo: Universitetsforlaget, 1976, 32 p.

**MÖDRITZER, Helmut**

1994 *Stigma und Charisma im Neuen Testament und seiner Umwelt. Zur Soziologie des Urchristentums* (NTOA, 28). Freiburg/Schw: Universitätsverlag; Göttingen: Vandenhoeck & Ruprecht, 1994, 335 p. Esp. 56-67: "Die Verkündigung des Täufers als Ausdruck provokatorischer Selbststigmatisierung" [3,7-12]; 110-123: "Jesu Mahnung zu Feindesliebe und Gewaltverzicht" [5,38-48]; 123-132: "Aggressionsüberwindung durch Selbststigmatisierung" [5,39-42]. — Diss. Heidelberg, 1992-93 (G. Theissen).

**MÖLLER, Christian**

1973 Welche Bedeutung hat der biblische Text für die Predigt? — EBELING, G., et al. (eds.), *Festschrift für Ernst Fuchs*, 1973, 263-279. Esp. 275-278 [1,1].

**MOESER, Annelies G.**

1992 The Death of Judas. [27,3-10] — *BiTod* 30 (1992) 145-151. [NTA 37, 155]

**MOFFATT, James**

1918[R] *An Introduction to the Literature of the New Testament* [1911, [2]1912, [3]1918, revised] (International Theological Library). Edinburgh: Clark, 1961, XXXIX-659 p. Esp. 177-217: "The synoptic problem"; 243-261: "Gospel of Matthew".

**MOHRLANG, Roger**

1984 *Matthew and Paul. A Comparison of Ethical Perspectives* (SNTS MS, 48). Cambridge: University Press, 1984, XIII-242 p. Esp. 7-26.42-47: "Law" [5,17-19.21-48; 12,1-14; 15,1-20; 19,3-9; 22,34-40; 23,1-36]; 48-57.67-71: "Reward and punishment"; 72-81.89-93: "Relationship to Christ and the role of grace"; 94-100.106-110: "Love"; 111-114.123-125: "Inner forces". — Diss. Oxford, 1979 (J.L. Houlden). → Allison 1993a
   J. BARCLAY, *Themelios* 11/2 (1985-86) 63-64; H.D. BETZ, *JRel* 66 (1986) 206; S. BROWN, *CBQ* 47 (1985) 738-739; D.R. CATCHPOLE, *JTS* 38 (1987) 503-505; J.M. COURT, *HeythJ* 28 (1987) 456; J.L. ESPINEL, *CiTom* 113 (1986) 589-590; C. EVANS, *Theology* 88 (1985) 145-146; L. GROLLENBERG, *TijdTheol* 24 (1984) 304; X. JACQUES, *NRT* 107 (1985) 886-887; L.E. KECK, *Interpr* 40 (1986) 95-96; J. MURPHY O'CONNOR, *RB* 92 (1985) 463; G. SEGALLA, *Studia Patavina* 32 (1985) 132-135; H. WANSBROUGH, *ScriptB* 16/1 (1985-86) 24; J.A. ZIESLER, *ExpT* 95 (1983-84) 344.

**MOINGT, Joseph**

1968 Le divorce "pour motif d'impudicité" (Matthieu 5,32; 19,9). — *RSR* 56 (1968) 337-384. Esp. 338-349: "Interprétations anciennes"; 349-356: "Exégèses contemporaines"; 356-375: "La pensée de Jésus et celle de Matthieu"; 375-384: "L'économie". [NTA 13, 567] → Crouzel 1969, Pelland 1972 Ehescheidung "auf Grund von Unzucht" (Matth 5,32; 19,9). — DAVID, J. - SCHMALZ, F. (eds.), *Wie unauflöslich ist die Ehe? Eine Dokumentation*, Aschaffenburg: Pattloch, 1969, 178-222. Esp. 179-190; 190-196; 197-214; 214-222.

**MOIR, Ian**

1956 *'Codex Climaci Rescriptus Graecus'. A Study of Portions of the Greek New Testament Comprising the Underwriting of Part of a Palimpsest in the Library of Westminster College, Cambridge (Ms. Gregory 1561, L)* (Texts and Studies, 2). Cambridge: University Press, 1956, XI-117 p. Esp. 15-16 [content]; 27-30; 35-38; 47-50; 57-59; 69-72 [transcription]; 75-76.111-112 [collations]; 85-8.101.105 [discussion of the text].

1995 → J.K. Elliott 1995

**MOISDON, R.**

1975 *Les évangiles et le Christ au travail. 2: Sociologie divino-humaine du Christ des évangiles à travers Matthieu et Marc*. Bescond: Saint-Pierre-sur-Dives, 1975.

**MOISER, Jeremy**

1985a Moses and Elijah. [17,9-13] — *ExpT* 96 (1984-85) 216-217. [NTA 30, 577] → M. Davies 1981c

1985b The Structure of Matthew 8–9: A Suggestion. — *ZNW* 76 (1985) 117-118. [NTA 30, 117]

1995 The Resurrection. Recent Official Pronouncements and Recent Exegesis. — *DownR* 113 (1995) 235-247. Esp. 238-239. [NTA 40, 787]

**MOITEL, Pierre**

1980 Travailler le texte. [5,3-10; 23,13-32; 25,32-46] — *SémBib* 20 (1980) 17-42.

**MOKROSCH, Reinhold**

1986 Liebe und Glaube. Wird Luthers Auslegung der Bergpredigt dem Anspruch Jesu und des Matthäus-Evangeliums gerecht? — DOHNA, L. - MOKROSCH, R. (eds.), *Werden und Wirkung der Reformation*, 1986, 153-156.

**MOLARI, Carlo**

1991 L'intreccio ideale delle Beatitudini. — BALLIS, G. (ed.), *Il mondo dell'uomo nascosto*, 1991, 5-20.

**MOLIN, Georg**

1968 Matthäus 5,43 und das Schrifttum von Qumran. — WAGNER, S. (ed.), *Bibel und Qumran. Beiträge zur Erforschung der Beziehungen zwischen Bibel- und Qumranwissenschaft: Hans Bardtke zum 22.9.1966*, Berlin: Evangelische Haupt-Bibelgesellschaft, 1968, 150-152.

**MOLITOR, Joseph**

1953 Das Adysh-Tetraevangelium. Neu übersetzt und mit altgeorgischen Paralleltexten verglichen. — *Oriens Christianus* (Wiesbaden) 37 (1953) 30-55. [1–7]; 38 (1954) 11-40 [8–16]; 39 (1955) 1-32 [17–25]; 40 (1956) 1-15 [26–28].

1956a *Monumenta iberica antiquiora. Textus Chanmeti et Haemeti ex inscriptionibus S. Bibliis et patribus* (CSCO, 166). Leuven: Durbecq, 1956, XVIII-165 p. Esp. 9-17 [6,30-34; 7,1-16; 24,29-35; 28,7-20]; 40-46 [9,24-26; 11,2-6; 12,10-15; 14,2-11; 17,1-17; 18,9-10].

1956b Evangelienzitate in einem altgeorgischen Väterfragment. — *Oriens Christianus* 40 (1956) 16-21. Esp. 16-19 [3,15; 12,14-15; 21,5.9.15-16; 22,18-19].

1957a Chanmetifragmente. Ein Beitrag zur Textgeschichte der altgeorgischen Bibelübersetzung. — *Oriens Christianus* 41 (1957) 22-34. Esp. 22-27 [6,30-7,16]; 27-29 [24,29-35]; 29-31 [28,7-20].

1957b Mt 15,5 in einer altgeorgischen Fassung. — *BZ* 1 (1957) 130-132. [NTA 2, 286]

1963 Das Haemeti-Palimpsestfragment Tiflis 1329 und sein Verhältnis zum altgeorgischen Evangelientext. — BLINZLER, J., et al. (eds.), *Neutestamentliche Aufsätze*. FS J. Schmid, 1963, 175-184. Esp. 176-178: "Die Matthäusfragmente"; 183 [17,1-5].

1964 Synoptische Evangelienzitate in Sinai-Mravalthair. — *Oriens Christianus* 48 (1964) 180-190. [3,3; 5,40; 8,8.22; 9,15; 10,31; 11,3.27; 13,31-32; 14,3.4; 15,4; 16,16.26; 17,1.4.5.9; 19,5; 20,22; 21,1.7.9.44; 22,44; 23,37; 24,35; 26,41].

1965 *Synopsis latina evangeliorum ibericorum antiquissimorum secundum Matthaeum, Marcum, Lucam desumpta e codicibus Adysh, Opiza, Tbeth necnon fragmentis biblicis et patristicis quae dicuntur Chanmeti et Haemeti* (CSCO, 256). Leuven: CSCO, 1965, VI-301 p.

1967 Σῴζω und σωτηρία in syrisch-georgischer Evangelienübersetzung. — *BZ* 11 (1967) 258-265. Esp. 259-261 [1,21; 9,21-22; 10,22; 16,25; 19,25; 24,13.22; 27,40]. [NTA 12, 494]

1968 *Grundbegriffe der Jesusüberlieferung im Lichte ihrer orientalischen Sprachgeschichte* (Kommentare und Beiträge zum Alten und Neuen Testament). Düsseldorf: Patmos,

1968, 112 p. Esp. 16-22 [1,21; 9,21-22; 10,22; 16,25; 19,25; 24,13.22; 27,40]; 36-38 [3,2.8.11; 4,17; 9,13; 11,21; 12,41]; 45-72 [1,24; 2,12.13.14.19-21; 3,9; 8,15.25-26; 9,5-7.9; 9,19.33; 11,5.11; 12,41; 14,2; 16,21; 17,7.9.23; 20,19.32; 22,23; 24,7.11; 25,7; 26,32.46.62; 27,63-64; 28,6.9]; 96-101 [10,22-23; 11,1; 13,39.40.49.53; 17,11; 19,1.25; 24,3.6.13; 26,1; 28,20].

1969    Tatians Diatessaron und sein Verhältnis zur altsyrischen und altgeorgischen Über-lieferung. — *Oriens Christianus* 53 (1969) 1-88; 54 (1970) 1-75; 55 (1971) 1-61.

**MOLL, Helmut**

1975    *Die Lehre von der Eucharistie als Opfer. Eine dogmengeschichtliche Untersuchung vom Neuen Testament bis Irenäus von Lyon* (Theophaneia, 26). Köln–Bonn: Hanstein, 1975, 208 p. Esp. 54-60 [26,26-29]. — Diss. Regensburg, 1973-74 (J. Ratzinger).

**MOLLAND, Einar**

1954    Cullmans Petrus-bok. — *NorskTeolTids* 55 (1954) 1-15. Esp. 10-14 [16,17-19]. → Cullmann 1952

**MOLLDREM, Mark J.**

1991    A Hermeneutic of Pastoral Care and the Law / Gospel Paradigm Applied to the Divorce Texts of Scripture. — *Interpr* 45 (1991) 43-54. Esp. 46-48 [5,32; 19,3-9]; 51-52 [Law-gospel]. [NTA 35, 629]

**MØLLER, Jens Glebe**

1966    Jesu forkyndelse og dagligsprogets logik. [Jesus' preaching and the logic of everyday language]. [18,21-35] — *DanskTeolTids* 29 (1966) 42-51. [NTA 11, 153]

**MOLONEY, Francis J.**

1979a    Matthew 19,3-12 and Celibacy. A Redactional and Form Critical Study. — *JSNT* 2 (1979) 42-60. Esp. 43-49: "The significance of Matt. 19,12 within the context of 19,3-12. A redactional study"; 49-53: "The significance of Matt. 19,12 on the lips of Jesus. A form critical study". [NTA 23, 832]

1979b    The Infancy Narratives. Another View of Raymond Brown's "The Birth of the Messiah". — *CleR* 64 (1979) 161-166. [NTA 24, 77r] → R.E. Brown 1977

1980    The End of the Son of Man? — *DownR* 98 (1980) 280-290. [NTA 25, 621] → P.M. Casey 1979

1982    → McGinlay 1982

1986    *The Living Voice of the Gospel. The Gospels Today.* Melbourne: Collins Dove; New York – Mahwah, NJ: Paulist, 1986, XII-251 p. Esp. 117-158: "The gospel of Matthew" [27,32-28,20; 28,16-20].
*Quattro vangeli, una Parola*, trans. S. Fissore (Religione). Torino: SEI, 1992, 198 p.

1990    *A Body Broken for a Broken People. Eucharist in the New Testament* [14,13-21; 15,32-39; 26,20-35]. Melbourne: Collins Dove, 1990, VIII-143 p. [NTA 36, p. 130]

1992    Beginning the Gospel of Matthew. Reading Matthew 1:1–2:23. — *Sal* 54 (1992) 341-359. Esp. 343-346: "The shape of the narrative"; 347-358: "Reading the narrative". [NTA 37, 127]

**MOLONEY, Raymond**

1990    The Temptations of Christ. What Do We Mean When We Say Christ Was Tempted? — *Priests & People* (London) 4 (1990) 54-56. [NTA 34, 1338]

**MOLTMANN, Jürgen**

1981*    (ed.), *Nachfolge und Bergpredigt* (Kaiser Traktate, 65). München: Kaiser, 1981; ²1982, 120 p. [NTA 26, p. 321] → Gollwitzer, Heinrich, Luz; → Frankemölle 1983c

**MOLTMANN-WENDEL, Elisabeth**

1980    *Ein eigener Mensch werden. Frauen um Jesus* (Gütersloher Taschenbücher/Siebenstern, 1006). Gütersloh: Mohn, 1980, 150 p. Esp. 123-133: "Matthäus und die Mütter".

*The Women around Jesus*, trans. J. Bowden, 1982. New York: Crossroad, XII-148 p. Esp. 119-129.
*Bij Jezus tellen vrouwen mee. Evangelieverhalen doorbreken gevestigde patronen*, trans. A. Rademaker-Brey. Baarn: Ten Have, 1982, 145 p. Esp. 119-130.

**MONGEAU, M.**

1994    Saint Joseph, époux "bien accordé" à Marie. — *CahJos* 42 (1994) 173-216. [NTA 39, 1445]

**MONGILLO, Dalmazio**

1982    "... in remissione dei peccati" (Mt 26,28). La condizione umana in prospettiva storico-salvifica. — MARCHESELLI, C.C. (ed.), *Parola e Spirito*. FS S. Cipriani, 1982, II, 1279-1288. Esp. 1280.

1994    Les Béatitudes et la béatitude. Le dynamisme de la *Somme de théologie* de Thomas d'Aquin: une lecture de Iª-IIᵃᵉ q. 69. — *RSPT* 78 (1994) 373-388. Esp. 373-376: "L'interprétation de *Matthieu* 5,1-10 par Thomas d'Aquin".

**MONLOUBOU, Louis**

1971    *Lire aujourd'hui les évangiles de l'enfance* (Prière et vie. Croire aujourd'hui, 14). Paris: Sénevé, 1971, 109 p. [NTA 16, p. 372]
        H.-P. BERGERON, *CahJos* 26 (1978) 242-243.

1977    *Lire, prêcher l'Évangile de Matthieu. Homélies Année A*. Mulhouse: Salvator, 1977, 304 p. [NTA 22, p. 331]
        L. WALTER, *EVie* 88 (1978) 685-686.
        *Leer y predicar el Evangelio de Mateo*. Santander: Sal Terrae, 1981, 314 p.
        A. SALAS, *BibFe* 8 (1982) 201-202.

**MONNERET DE VILLARD, Ugo**

1952    *Le leggende orientali sui Magi evangelici* (Studi e testi, 163). Città del Vaticano: Biblioteca apostolica Vaticana, 1952, 262 p. Esp. 3-68: "I primitivi testi siriaci".

**MONRO, A.**

1994    Alterity and the Canaanite Woman: A Postmodern Feminist Theological Reflection on Political Action. — *Colloquium* 26 (1994) 32-43. [NTA 39, 808]

**MONSARRAT, Violaine**

1977    Matthieu 24-25. Du Temple au démunis. — *FoiVie* 76/5 = *Cahiers bibliques* 16 (1977) 67-80. Esp. 69-75 [24,1-3; 25,31-46]; 75-79 [24,4-25,30]. [NTA 24, 98]

**MONSENGWO PASINYA, Laurent**

1988    Lokola biso tokolimbisaka baninga (Mt 6,9 par). Incidence théologique d'une traduction. — *RAfrT* 12 (1988) 15-21. [NTA 33, 1129]

**MONTAGNINI, Felice**

1970    Il comando missionario. [28,19] — *ParVi* 15 (1970) 12-28.

1983    Echi del discorso del monte nella Didaché. — *BibOr* 26 (1983) 137-143. [NTA 28, 813]

1985    "Va', mostrati al sacerdote... per testimonianza...". — *Testimonium Christi*. FS J. Dupont, 1985, 317-328.

**MONTAGUE, George T.**

1976    *The Holy Spirit: Growth of a Biblical Tradition*. New York: Paulist, 1976, IX-374 p. Esp. 302-310: "The discreet pneumatology of Matthew".

1989    *Companion God. A Cross-Cultural Commentary on the Gospel of Matthew*. New York – Mahwah, NJ: Paulist, 1989, III-330 p. [NTA 34, p. 249]
        K.A. BARTA, *TS* 51 (1990) 736-737; A. BONORA, *RivBib* 39 (1991) 251-252; B.E. BOWE, *CBQ* 54 (1992) 361-362; D.M. MAY, *BTB* 21 (1991) 81-82; J.-M. ROUSÉE, *RB* 97 (1990) 635.

1991 MCDONNELL, K. – MONTAGUE, G.T., *Christian Initiation and Baptism in the Holy Spirit. Evidence from the First Eight Centuries.* Collegeville, MN: Liturgical Press, 1991, XIV-354 p. Esp. 3-14: "Fire and power. Spirit-baptism in Q and Mark"; 15-22: "Works of mercy and righteousness: Spirit-baptism in Matthew".
*Baptême dans l'Esprit et initiation chrétienne. Témoignage des huit premiers siècles* (Chemin neuf). Paris: Desclée De Brouwer, 1993, 371 p.

MONTEFIORE, Claude Goldsmid
1927[R] *The Synoptic Gospels Edited with an Introduction and a Commentary* [1909, 38-392; [2]1927] (The Library of Biblical Studies). New York: Ktav, 1968, 2 vols., 18-CXLVI-411 p. and XII-678 p. Esp. II, 1-359.

1930[R] *Rabbinic Literature and Gospel Teachings* [1930] (The Library of Biblical Studies). New York: Ktav, 1970, XLII-442 p. Esp. 1-341 [5-28].

MONTEFIORE, Hugh W.
1956 God as Father in the Synoptic Gospels. — *NTS* 3 (1956-57) 31-46. Esp. 37-41 [Mt/Lk]; 41-42 [Mt]. [NTA 2, 39]

1960 Josephus and the New Testament. — *NT* 4 (1960) 139-160; 307-318. Esp. 140-148 [2,1-12]. [NTA 6, 70/711]

1961 A Comparison of the Parables of the Gospel according to Thomas and of the Synoptic Gospels. — *NTS* 7 (1960-61) 220-248. Esp. 225-228: "Embellishment" [13,23.31-32.45; 18,12; 21,33; 22,5-6]; 229-230: "Change of audience" [13,31; 21,33]; 230-232: "The hortatory use of parables by the Church"; 232-235: "The influence of the Church's situation" [11,28; 13,44-47; 15,14; 18,13; 22,4-5]; 235-238: "Allegorization" [13,18-23.36-43; 21,33.39; 22,1-11]; 238-244: "Collection and conflation of parables" [5,14-15; 9,16-17; 12,33-34; 13,1-9.44-47.47-50]; 244-248: "The setting" [11,25-27; 13,33.44.49-50; 16,2-3; 21,33-46]. [NTA 6, 308]; = TURNER, H.E.W. – MONTEFIORE, H.W., *Thomas and the Evangelists* (Studies in Biblical Theology, 35), London: SCM, 1962, 40-78.

1962 Thou Shalt Love the Neighbour as Thyself. — *NT* 5 (1962) 157-170. Esp. 159-160 [5,43]. [NTA 7, 623]

1964 Jesus and the Temple Tax. — *NTS* 11 (1964-65) 60-71. Esp. 64-71 [17,24-27]. [NTA 9, 537]

1971 Jesus on Divorce and Remarriage. — *Marriage, Divorce, and the Church. The Report of a Commission Appointed by the Archbischop of Canterbury to Prepare a Statement on the Christian Doctrine of Marriage,* London: SPCK, 1971, 79-95, 169-170. Esp. 83-85 [19,3-9]; 85-87 [πορνεία]; 87-88 [5,31-32].

MONTERO, Domingo
1978 Para una mejor comprensión de Mt 14,22-33. — *NatGrac* 25 (1978) 251-269. Esp. 256-267.

1979a Discurso de la misión (Un acercamiento a Mt 9,35–11,1). — *NatGrac* 26 (1979) 7-48. Esp. 20-33 [10,1-15]; 33-41 [10,17-36]; 41-47 [10,37-42].

1979b En torno a una polémica: ¿una nueva comprensión del dogma de la concepción virginal? — *NatGrac* 26 (1979) 373-399. Esp. 384-390 [1,18-25].

1988 Las bienaventuranzas. — *Nuevo Mundo* (Caracas) 139 (1988) 447-456.

1989 "Ekklēsía" y "Ekklēsíai" en el Nuevo Testamento. [16,18] — *Unité et Diversité dans l'Église. Texte officiel de la Commission Biblique Pontificale et travaux personnels des Membres* (Teologia e filosofia, 15), Città del Vaticano: Libreria Editrice Vaticana, 1989, 113-126.

MONTGOMERY, T.A.
1955 *A Linguistic Study of the Book of Matthew in Manuscript I.i.6 of the Escorial Bible.* Diss. Univ. of Wisconsin, 1955.

MONTI, F. → Minuti 1966

**MONTIZAMBERT, Eric**
1955    *The Flame of Life. An Interpretation of the Sermon on the Mount*. Greenwich, CT:
        Seabury, 1955, 114 p.
            E.E. TILDEN, JR., *Interpr* 11 (1957) 75.

**MOO, Douglas J.**
1981    "Gospel Origins": A Reply to J.W. Wenham. — *TrinJ* NS 2 (1981) 24-36. Esp. 25-27.
        [NTA 26, 48] → J.W. Wenham 1978, 1981

1983a   *The Old Testament in the Gospel Passion Narratives*. Sheffield: Almond Press, 1983,
        XI-468 p. Esp. 79-172: "The use of the Isaianic servant songs in the gospel passion texts" [passion
        predictions; 3,17; 9,15; 20,28; 26,28.63.67-68; 27,12.14.30.38.57]; 173-224: "The use of Zechariah 9–14
        in the gospel passion texts" [21,4-5; 26,15.31.32; 27,3-10]; 225-300: "The use of the lament psalms in the
        gospel passion texts" [26,3-4.38; 27,34.35.46.55]; 301-311 [26,26-29]; 331-350: "Miscellaneous Old
        Testament passages" [12,40; 21,42; 26,4; 27,45.51-53]; 375-380 [27,9-10]; 383-387 [πληρόω]. — Diss. St.
        Andrews, 1979 (M. Black – R.McL. Wilson).

1983b   Matthew and Midrash: An Evaluation of Robert H. Gundry's Approach. — *JEvTS* 26
        (1983) 31-39. [NTA 28, 480r] → Gundry 1982, 1983a-b

1983c   Once Again, "Matthew and Midrash": A Rejoinder to Robert H. Gundry. — *JEvTS* 26
        (1983) 57-70. → Gundry 1982, 1983a-b

1983d   Tradition and Old Testament in Matt 27:3-10. — FRANCE, R.T. – WENHAM, D. (eds.),
        *Studies in Midrash and Historiography*, 1983, 157-175. Esp. 157-161: "The quotation"; 161-
        166: "Narrative and quotation"; 166-168: "A Midrash?".

1984    Jesus and the Authority of the Mosaic Law. — *JSNT* 20 (1984) 3-49. Esp. 8-10.16-17 [7,12;
        9,13; 12,3-4.7]; 11 [23,23]; 13 [19,16-22]; 15 [15,11]; 17-23 [5,17-48; 11,13]; 24-28 [5,17-19; 24,34-35].
        [NTA 29, 63]; = EVANS, C.A. – PORTER, S.E. (eds.), *The Historical Jesus*, 1995, 83-
        128. Esp. 95-97.103-105; 97; 99-100; 102; 106-118; 118-126.

1992a   Law. — *DJG*, 1992, 450-461. Esp. 458-459.

1992b   → D.A. Carson 1992

**MOODY, D.**
1954    On the Virgin Birth of Jesus Christ. — *RExp* 51 (1954) 435-462.

**MOORE, A.L.**
1966    *The Parousia in the New Testament* (SupplNT, 13). Leiden: Brill, 1966, 248 p. Esp. 143-
        146.187-190 [10,23]; 128-130 [16,28]; 199-201 [24–25].

**MOORE, Bruce R.**
1993    *Doublets in the New Testament*. Dallas, TX: Summer Institute of Linguistics, 1993, 67
        p. Esp. 21-25.

**MOORE, P.A.**
1970    Quinque prudentes virgines. [25,1-13] — *Studies in Comparative Religion* (Bedford) 4
        (1970) 80-95.

**MOORE, W. Ernest**
1964    One Baptism. — *NTS* 10 (1963-64) 504-516. Esp. 506 [3,13-17]. [NTA 9, 258] → J.A.T.
        Robinson 1953/62

1975    Βιάζω, ἁρπάζω and Cognates in Josephus. — *NTS* 21 (1974-75) 519-543. Esp. 540-543:
        "Some suggestions on the interpretation of Matt. xi.12". [NTA 20, 318]

1989    Violence to the Kingdom. Josephus and the Syrian Churches. [11,12] — *ExpT* 100 (1988-
        89) 174-177. [NTA 33, 609]

1991    'Lead us not into temptation'. [6,13] — *ExpT* 102 (1990-91) 171-172. [NTA 35, 1129] → P.S.
        Cameron 1990, S.E. Porter 1990

**MORA, Gaspar**

1989    El regne de Déu, concepte clau de les benaurances. — *RevistCatTeol* 14 (1989)
        279-290.

**MORA, Vincent**

1983    *Le signe de Jonas* (Lire la Bible, 63). Paris: Cerf, 1983, 151 p.
        J.-C. INGELAERE, *RHPR* 65 (1985) 212-213.

1986    *Le refus d'Israël. Matthieu 27,25* (LD, 124). Paris: Cerf, 1986, 182 p. Esp. 17-41: "Le
        refus d'Israël: le fait"; 43-81: "Les conséquences du refus pour Israël" [2,1-13; 8,5-13; 21,18-22.28-32.33-
        46; 22,1-10; 23,21-39]; 83-118: "Les conséquences du refus d'Israël pour l'Église chrétienne: le statut
        théologique d'Israël" [12,1-14; 15,1-20; 23]; 119-133: "Les causes divines du refus d'Israël" [13,10-17]; 135-
        150: "Les causes humaines du refus d'Israël"; 151-164: "Son sang pour nous. Histoire ou mythe?"; 165-173:
        "Les visées de Matthieu". [NTA 30, p. 355] — Diss. Studium Biblicum Franciscanum, Jerusalem, 1970.
                X. ALEGRE, *ActBibl* 24 (1987) 215-216; L. DEVILLERS, *RThom* 88 (1988) 481-484; E. FARAHIAN, *Greg*
        68 (1987) 394; C. FOCANT, *RTL* 18 (1987) 85-86; R.H. FULLER, *CRBR* 2 (1989) 229-230; V. FUSCO,
        *CC* 137/3 (1986) 541; L. GROLLENBERG, *TijdTheol* 27 (1987) 405; D.J. HARRINGTON, *CBQ* 49 (1987)
        346-347; I.H. JONES, *JTS* 38 (1987) 167-169; S. LÉGASSE, *BullLitEccl* 89 (1988) 295-296; *EVie* 96
        (1986) 555-556; M. MORGEN, *RevSR* 63 (1989) 150-151; F. MUSSNER, *TRev* 82 (1986) 457-459; G.
        PÉREZ, *Salmanticensis* 34 (1987) 232-234; M. PETIT, *RevÉtudJuiv* 146 (1987) 168-170; J.-M. POFFET,
        *VSp* 141 (1987) 491; A. PUIG I TÀRRECH, *RevistCatTeol* 12 (1987) 229-231; J. SALGUERO, *Angelicum*
        64 (1987) 526-527; V. SERRA, *EstFranc* 88 (1987) 222-223; J.-Y. THÉRIAULT, *SE* 39 (1987) 261-263;
        A. TORNOS, *EstE* 63 (1988) 249-250; B.T. VIVIANO, *RB* 96 (1989) 147-148; W. WEREN, *Bijdragen* 48
        (1987) 343-344.

1991    *La symbolique de la création dans l'évangile de Matthieu* (LD, 144). Paris: Cerf, 1991,
        236 p. Esp. 17-124: "Les sept montagnes" [4,1-11; 5-7; 15,29-39; 17,1-9; 21,1-17; 24-25; 26,36-46;
        27,32-44; 28,16-20]; 125-182: "La symbolique de la mer" [4,12-17.18-22; 8,19-9,1; 13; 14,22-33; 15,29-
        39]; 183-192: "Le bestiaire de l'évangile selon Matthieu"; 193-217: "Les signes cosmiques dans l'évangile
        de Matthieu" [2,1-12; 24,29-31; 27,45-53; 28,1-8]. [NTA 35, p. 384]
                R. CAPOEN, *Telema* 19 (1993) 92-93; E. FARAHIAN, *Greg* 74 (1993) 573-575; C. FOCANT, *RTL* 25
        (1994) 372-373; M. GIRARD, *SE* 44 (1992) 231-232; L. GROLLENBERG, *TijdTheol* 32 (1992) 312; A.
        SEGOVIA, *ArchTeolGran* 54 (1991) 376-377; P. TERNANT, *Proche Orient Chrétien* (Jerusalem) 41 (1991)
        177-178; L. WALTER, *EVie* 102 (1992) 213-215.

**MORALDI, Luigi**

1962*   & LYONNET, S. (eds.), *Introduzione alla Bibbia. Corso sistematico di studi biblici. IV.
        I vangeli.* Torino: Marietti, 1962, 574 p.; ²1973. → Algisi, Moraldi, Saldarini 1962a-b
        *Introdução a Bíblia.* IV: *Os Evangelhos*, trans. J.E.M. Terra. Petrópolis: Vozes, 1972, 589 p.

1962a   La questione sinottica. — *Ibid.*, 385-395.

1962b   → Saldarini 1962b

1965    Evangelio de Mateo. — *Enciclopédia de la Bíblia* (Barcelona) 4 (1965; ²1969) 1360-
        1373.

**MORALES, José**

1974    La conversión en el evangelio de S. Mateo. — *Christus* (México) 39 (1974) 46-50.

**MORELAND, Milton** → IQP

**MORENO MARTÍNEZ, José Luis**

1989    El molino de los dos Testamentos. Un símbolo de la exégesis patrística y medieval. —
        *EstBíb* 47 (1989) 559-568. Esp. 561-563 [24,41/Dt 24,6]; 563-568: "La exégesis alegórica de Mt
        24,41".

**MORERA, Manuel**

1976 (trans.), *Agustín, El Sermon de la montaña. Jesucristo predicando*. Madrid: Palabra, 1976, 222 p.

**MORETON, Michael J.**

1964 The Genealogy of Jesus. — *Studia Evangelica* 2 (1964) 219-224.

**MORGAN, Barry E.**

1987 *The Synoptic Pericopes Concerning Divorce and Remarriage: An Exegetical and Hermeneutical Study*. Diss. Southwestern Baptist Theol. Sem., Fort Worth, TX, 1987, 282 p. — *DissAbstr* 48 (1987-88) 946.

**MORGAN, C. Shannon**

1970 *The Comparative Influence of the Gospels of Matthew and Luke on Christian Literature before Irenaeus*. Diss. Harvard, 1970-71.

1979 "When Abiathar was High Priest" (Mark 2:26). — *JBL* 98 (1979) 409-410. [NTA 24, 434]

**MORGAN, G. Campbell**

1929^R *The Gospel according to Matthew* [1929, 1946] (Marshall's Study Library). London: Marshall, Morgan and Scott, 1976, 321 p.

**MORGAN, Robert**

1994 Which Was the Fourth Gospel? The Order of the Gospels and the Unity of Scripture. — *JSNT* 54 (1994) 3-28. Esp. 11-14 [Q]. [NTA 39, 91]

**MORGAN-WYNNE, J.E.**

1976 Matthew the Pastor. — *The Baptist Quarterly* (Philadelphia, PA) 26 (1975-76) 294-304.

**MORGEN, Michèle**

1980 *Le Fils de l'homme dans les Synoptiques. Méthode historico-critique et sémiotique littéraire*. Diss. Institut Catholique, Paris, 1980, 2 vols., 337 and 96 p. (C. Perrot).

1981 *Analyse littéraire et interprétation d'un thème apocalyptique. Le Fils de l'homme*. Diss. Nanterre, Paris, 1981, 2 vols., 353 and 97 p. (P. Géoltrain).

1993 *Afin que le monde soit sauvé. Jésus révèle sa mission de salut dans l'évangile de Jean* (LD, 154). Paris: Cerf, 1993, 401 p. Esp. 293-298 [13,15/Jn 12,40].

**MORGENTHALER, Robert**

1958 *Statistik des neutestamentlichen Wortschatzes*. Zürich–Frankfurt/M: Gotthelf, 1958, ³1982, 188 p. Esp. 33-37.170-172 [vocabulary: Mk/Mt; Mt/Lk]; 49-51.181 ["Vorzugswörter"]. *Beiheft zur 3. Auflage*. Zürich: Gotthelf, 1982, 24 p. Esp. 8; 15-17.

1971 *Statistische Synopse*. Zürich–Stuttgart: Gotthelf, 1971, 328 p. Esp. 70-84: "Die Q-Tradition"; 85: "Traditionsmischungen Mk–Q"; 86: "S-Mt"; 90-102: "Mt (Mk Mt + QMt + SMt)"; 122-123: "Wortfolgen: Q-Logien"; 125-126: "Mischlogien Mk–Q"; 128-160: "Dublettenlogien"; 164-167 [conclusion]; 190-198: "Satzfolgen: Q-Tradition"; 198 [SgMt]; 198-211: "Traditionsmischungen in den Satzfolgen: Logiensammlungen" [3,1-12; 5-7; 9,35-11,1; 13,1-52; 18; 23; 24-25]. 220-221: "Perikopenintarsien"; 250-262: "Abschnittfolgen: Q-Tradition"; 262-264: "S-Tradition"; 264-274: "Traditionsmischungen"; 290-300: "Das Rätsel 'Q'"; 300-305: "Kannte Lk Mt?". → W.R. Farmer 1973, Léon-Dufour 1972b, Neirynck 1973b

1993 *Lukas und Quintilian. Rhetorik als Erzählkunst*. Zürich: Gotthelf, 1993, 433 p. Esp. 258-281: "Rhetorisierung des Q-Stoffes" [Q 6,20-49; 11,34-36.46; 12,4-5.11-12.51-53.58-59; 13,24.28-30; 22,28-30].

**MORIN, Émile**

1969 Les premiers portraits de Jésus. — BESSIÈRE, G. (ed.), *Que dites-vous du Christ?*, 1969, 31-57. Esp. 31-37: "Le Jésus de saint Matthieu".

**MORIN, J.-Alfred**

1973  Les deux derniers des Douze: Simon le Zélote et Judas Iskariôth. — *RB* 80 (1973) 332-358. Esp. 349-358 [Judas]. [NTA 19, 45]

**MORK, Carol**

1989  Revelation and Response. Matthean Texts for Christmas and Epiphany. — *WWorld* 9 (1989) 394-399.

**MORLOT, François**

1974  "Heureux les pauvres": béatitude ou conseil? — *La Vie Consacrée* (Paris–Brussel) 46 (1974) 204-216.
Beati i poveri: beatitudine o consiglio? — *VCons* 11 (1975) 46-55.

**MOROSCO, Robert E.**

1979  Redaction Criticism and the Evangelical. Matthew 10 a Test Case. — *JEvTS* 22 (1979) 323-331. [NTA 24, 793]

1984  Matthew's Formation of a Commissioning Type-Scene Out of the Story of Jesus' Commissioning of the Twelve. — *JBL* 103 (1984) 539-556. Esp. 541-543: "Matthew and type-scenes"; 543-546: "The idea of the commissioning story as a type-scene"; 546-555: "Matt 9:35–11:1 as a commissioning type-scene". [NTA 29, 935]

**MORREALE, Margherita**

1964  Apostillas a un glosario de la Biblia Medieval romanceada. — *Nueva Revista de Filología Hispánica* (Madrid) 17 (1963-64) 338-351.

**MORRICE, William G.**

1975  New Wine in Old Wine-Skins: XI. Covenant. — *ExpT* 86 (1974-75) 132-136. Esp. 134-135 [26,28]. [TNA 19, 1086]

1984a  *Joy in the New Testament.* Exeter: Paternoster, 1984, 173 p. Esp. 100-104: "Joy in Matthew and Mark".

1984b  The Parable of the Dragnet and the Gospel of Thomas. [13,47-50] — *ExpT* 95 (1983-84) 269-273. [NTA 29, 104]

1987  The Parable of the Tenants and the Gospel of Thomas. [21,33-46] — *ExpT* 98 (1986-87) 104-107. [NTA 31, 944]

**MORRIS, Leon L.**

1965  *The Cross in the New Testament.* Grand Rapids, MI: Eerdmans, 1965; repr. 1967; (Mount Radford Reprints, 19), Exeter: Paternoster, 1976, ²1979, 454 p. Esp. 13-62: "The cross in Matthew and Mark".
*¿Por qué murió Jesús?* Buenos Aires: Certezza, 1976, 104 p.

1969  The Relationship of the Fourth Gospel to the Synoptics. — ID., *Studies in the Fourth Gospel*, Grand Rapids, MI: Eerdmans; Exeter: Paternoster, 1969, 15-64. Esp. 31-34 [26,6-13/Jn]; 40-62: "An interlocking tradition".

1974  *Luke. An Introduction and Commentary* (Tyndale New Testament Commentaries). Leicester, UK: Inter-Varsity; Grand Rapids, MI: Eerdmans, 1974; repr. 1977, 1986, 350 p. Esp. 47-59: "The synoptic problem"; rev. ed., 1988, 382 p. Esp. 51-63.

1981  *Testaments of Love. A Study of Love in the Bible.* Grand Rapids, MI: Eerdmans, 1981, X-298 p.

1983  The Gospels and the Jewish Lectionaries. — FRANCE, R.T. - WENHAM, D. (eds.), *Studies in Midrash and Historiography*, 1983, 129-156. Esp. 131-133; 142-147. → Goulder 1974

1986  *New Testament Theology.* Grand Rapids, MI: Zondervan, 1986, 368 p. Esp. 114-143: "The gospel of Matthew".

1992a  *The Gospel according to Matthew* (Pillar New Testament Commentary). Grand Rapids, MI: Eerdmans; Leicester, UK: Inter-Varsity, 1992, XVII-781 p. [NTA 37, p. 118]
E.J. BURSEY, *AndrUnS* 32 (1994) 294-295; E. CUVILLIER, *ETR* 68 (1993) 574-575; D.E. GARLAND, *CRBR* 7 (1994) 240-241; D.R.A. HARE, *HorizonsBT* 16 (1994) 184-186; W.C. HEISER, *TDig* 40 (1993) 178; J.D. KINGSBURY, *CBQ* 55 (1993) 814-816; D. PETERSON, *The Reformed Theological Review* (Hawthorne) 53 (1994) 39-40; M.L. REID, *Interpr* 48 (1994) 90.92; S.D. TOUSSAINT, *BS* 151 (1994) 371; D. WENHAM, *The European Journal of Theology* (Carlisle) 2 (1993) 177-178; J. WOOD, *EvQ* 67 (1995) 90-92.

1992b  → D.A. Carson 1992

### MOSBECH, Holger
1953  The Ethics of the Sermon on the Mount. — AUSEKLIS. Societas theologorum Universitatis Latviensis (ed.), *Spiritus et Veritas*. [FS K. Kundzinš], Eutin: Ozolin, 1953, 121-134.

### MOSCHNER, Franz M.
1953  *Das Himmelreich in Gleichnissen. Betrachtungen zu neutestamentlichen Texten.* Freiburg: Herder, 1953, XIII-348 p.

### MOSES, A.D.A.
1996  *Matthew's Transfiguration Story and Jewish-Christian Controversy* (JSNT SS, 122). Sheffield: JSOT, 1996, 294 p. Esp. 20-49: "A critical survey of scholarship on the transfiguration"; 85-113: "Matthew 17.1-13 in the light of literary parallels and Daniel 7 – Sinai considerations"; 114-160: "An exegesis of Matthew 17.1-13 in the light of source and redaction critical issues"; 161-207: "Matthew's transfiguration pericope in the light of the Jesus-Moses and Exodus-Sinai parallelism elsewhere in the first gospel". [NTA 40, p. 524] — Diss. Oxford, 1992 (D. Wenham – N.T. Wright).
R.H. GUNDRY, *JBL* 116 (1997) 560-562; M.A. POWELL, *CBQ* 59 (1997) 585-587.

### MOSETTO, Francesco
1986  Rassegna bibliografica sul Vangelo di Matteo. — *ParVi* 31 (1986) 438-443.
1994  La parabola dei vignaiuoli ribelli (Mc 12,1-12 parr.). [21,33-46] — LÀCONI, M. (ed.), *Vangeli sinottici*, 1994, 243-259.

### MOSLEY, A.W.
1963  Jesus' Audiences in the Gospels of St Mark and St Luke. — *NTS* 10 (1963-64) 139-149. Esp. 143 [Mt/Mk]; 145-149 [Q]. [NTA 8, 959]

### MOSZORO DABROWSKI, Stefan A.
1984  *Mt 27,46 en la Cristología de Tertuliano, S. Hilaric de Poitiers y S. Ambrosio de Milán.* Diss. Pamplona, 1984, 378 p. (L.F. Mateo-Seco). Esp. 13-53 [Tertullian]; 54-216 [Hilary of Poitiers]; 217-334 [Ambrosius].

### MOTTE, A.R.
1981  La structure du logion de Matthieu, XI,28-30. — *RB* 88 (1981) 226-233. [NTA 26, 844]

### MOTTÉ, Magda
1970  "Mann des Glaubens". Die Gestalt Josephs nach dem Neuen Testament. — *BibLeb* 11 (1970) 176-189. Esp. 178; 179-186: "Die Gestalt Josephs nach den Kindheitsgeschichten" [1,18-25]. [NTA 15, 790]

### MOTTU, Henry
1978  & VOUGA, F., La passion de la parole. Jésus, prophète invectivant et souffrant. — *Bulletin du Centre protestant d'études* (Genève) 30 (1978) 38-46. [NTA 23, 105]

### MOULDER, J.
1978  Who Are My Enemies? An Exploration of the Semantic Background of Christ's Command. [5,43-48] — *JTSouthAfr* 25 (1978) 41-49. [NTA 24, 790]

**MOULE, A.W. Handley**

1971  The Pattern of the Synoptists. [structure: OT] — *EvQ* 43 (1971) 162-171. [NTA 16, 137]

**MOULE, Charles Francis Digby**

1953  *An Idiom Book of New Testament Greek.* Cambridge: University Press, 1953, X-241 p.; ²1959, XII-246 p.

1955a  & STEPHENSON, A.M.G., R.G. Heard on Q and Mark. — *NTS* 2 (1955-56) 114-118. Esp. 116-118 [Q]. [NTA 1, 30] → Heard 1954a

1955b  Some Reflections on the 'Stone' *Testimonia* in Relation to the Name Peter. [16,18] — *NTS* 2 (1955-56) 56-58.

1962  *The Birth of the New Testament* (Black's New Testament Commentaries. Companion Volume, 1). London: Black; (Harper's New Testament Commentaries), San Francisco, CA: Harper & Row, 1962, XII-252 p.; ²1966. Esp. 86-91 [genre]; 194-196 [apostolic fathers]; 215-219: "Translation Greek and original Greek in Matthew"; 3rd rev. ed., San Francisco, CA: Harper & Row, 1981; Toronto, Ont.: Fitzhenry & Whiteside, 1982, XII-382 p. → Styler
Übersetzungsgriechisch und Originalgriechisch im Matthäusevangelium. [1962, 215-219] — LANGE, J. (ed.), *Das Matthäus-Evangelium*, 1980, 312-315.
*Het Nieuwe Testament in de Oude Kerk*, trans. L.A. Rood (Aula, 299). Utrecht–Antwerpen: Spectrum, 1966, 288 p. Esp. 90-94; 198-200; 219-224.
*La genèse du Nouveau Testament*, trans. R. Mazerand. Neuchâtel: Delachaux & Niestlé, 1971, 218 p.
*Le origini del Nuovo Testamento*, trans. P. Spanu, rev. by F. Ronchi (Studi biblici, 15). Brescia: Paideia, 1971, 219 p.
*El nacimiento del Nuevo Testamento*, trans. R.V. del Toro. Estella: Verbo Divino, 1974, 404 p.
*As origens do Novo Testamento.* São Paulo: Paulinas, 1979, 272 p.

1963  Commentaries on the Gospel according to St Matthew. — *Theology* 66 (1963) 140-144. [NTA 7, 776]

1964  St. Matthew's Gospel: Some Neglected Features. — *Studia Evangelica* 2 (1964) 91-99. Esp. 92 [9,9]; 92-93 [anti-Pharisaic]; 95-96 [5,13-14.22; 12,31-32; 16,22; 23,8.10; 27,3-10]; 98 [13,52]; = ID., *Essays*, 1982, 67-74. Esp. 68; 68-69; 71-72; 73-74.

1968  Fulfilment-Words in the New Testament: Use and Abuse. — *NTS* 14 (1967-68) 293-320. Esp. 312; 313-316 [5,17]; = ID., *Essays*, 1982, 3-36. Esp. 28-32.

1969  Uncomfortable Words. I. The Angry Word: Matthew 5,21f. — *ExpT* 81 (1969-70) 10-13. [NTA 14, 480]

1974  An Unsolved Problem in the Temptation-Clause in the Lord's Prayer. — *RTR* 33/3 (1974) 65-75. [NTA 19, 953]

1976  The Fulfilment Theme in the New Testament. — *JTSouthAfr* 14 (1976) 6-16. [NTA 21, 210]

1977  *The Origin of Christology.* Cambridge: University Press, 1977, X-187 p. Esp. 11-46 [christological titles]; 127-128 [fulfilment].

1978  '... As we forgive...': A Note on the Distinction between Deserts and Capacity in the Understanding of Forgiveness. — BAMMEL, E. - BARRETT, C.K. - DAVIES, W.D. (eds.), *Donum gentilicium. New Testament Studies in Honour of David Daube*, Oxford: Clarendon, 1978, 68-77. Esp. 68-69 [6,12]; 70.76 [5,23]; = ID., *Essays*, 1982, 278-286. Esp. 278-279; 279.285.

1982  *Essays in New Testament Interpretation.* Cambridge: University Press, 1982, XIV-327 p. → 1964, 1968, 1978

**MOULTON, Harold K.**

1978  MOULTON, W.F. — GEDEN, A.S., *A Concordance to the Greek Testament according to the Texts of Westcott and Hort, Tischendorf and the English Revisers* [1897], ed.

H.K. Moulton. Edinburg: Clark, ⁵1978, XVI-1110 p. Pp. 1035-1110: "Supplement" (ἀπό, εἰς, ἐκ/ἐξ, ἐν, ὅτι, οὖν, σύν).

**MOULTON, James Hope**

1909ᴿ New Testament Greek in the Light of Modern Discovery. [1909] — PORTER, S.E. (ed.), *The Language of the New Testament: Classic Essays* (JSNT SS, 60), Sheffield: JSOT, 1991, 60-97. Esp. 79-81 [symmetry].

**MOUNCE, Robert H.**

1965 Synoptic Self-portraits. — *EvQ* 37 (1965) 212-217. [NTA 10, 502]

1985 *Matthew* (A Good News Commentary). San Francisco, CA: Harper & Row, 1985, XVII-292 p. [NTA 30, p. 231]
    S. KISTEMAKER, *CalvTJ* 21 (1986) 320.
    *Matthew* (New International Biblical Commentary, 1). Peabody, MA: Hendrickson, 1991, XIII-288 p. [NTA 35, p. 385]

1988 Sermon on the Mount. — BROMILEY, G.W., et al. (eds.), *The International Standard Bible Encyclopedia*, IV, Grand Rapids, MI: Eerdmans, 1988, 411-416.

**MOURLON BEERNAERT, Pierre**

1992 *Marthe, Marie et les autres. Les visages féminins de l'Évangile* (Écritures, 5). Brussels: Lumen Vitae, 1992, 256 p.

1993 Jésus appelle Matthieu à le suivre: Analyse à un double niveau. — *LumVit* 48 (1993) 429-441. [NTA 38, 1366]

**MOUSON, Jean**

1951 Adveniat regnum tuum (Mt. VI,10a). — *CollMech* 21 (1951) 597-599.

1952 De locutione "filius hominis" apud Matthaeum. — *CollMech* 22 (1952) 627-631.

1953 Explicatur baptismus Iesu secundum Matth. III,13-17. — *CollMech* 23 (1953) 687-690.

1954 De structura Evangelii secundum Matthaeum. — *CollMech* 24 (1954) 176-178.

1955 De tribus praedictionibus passionis apud synopticos. — *CollMech* 25 (1955) 709-714. [NTA 1, 66]

1957 Explicatur parabola de operariis in vineam missis (Mt. XX,1-16). — *CollMech* 27 (1957) 611-615. [NTA 2, 530]

1958a "Non veni vocare justos, sed peccatores" (Mt. IX,13 = Mc. II,17 = Lc. V,32). — *CollMech* 28 (1958) 134-139. [NTA 3, 61]

1958b Explicatur parabola de magno convivio (Mt. XXII,1-14; Lc. XIV,16-24). — *Ibid.*, 610-613. [NTA 3, 588]

1959a Explicatur parabola de zizaniis in agro (Mt. XIII,24-30,36-43). — *CollMech* 29 (1959) 171-175. [NTA 4, 80]

1959b De sanatione pueri Centurionis (Mt. VIII,5-13). — *Ibid.*, 633-636. [NTA 4, 388]

**MOWERY, Robert L.**

1986 The Articular References to the Holy Spirit in the Synoptic Gospels and Acts. — *BR* 31 (1986) 26-45. Esp. 33-35 [Q]; 36-37 [Mt]. [NTA 31, 525]

1988 God, Lord and Father: The Theology of the Gospel of Matthew. — *BR* 33 (1988) 24-36. Esp. 25-27 [θεός, κύριος]; 27-29 [πατήρ]. [NTA 33, 114]

1989 The Activity of God in the Gospel of Matthew. — *SBL 1989 Seminar Papers*, 400-411. Esp. 401-404: "Communication" [revelation]; 404-407: "Three activities of the Father"; 407-411: "The activity of the Lord, God and Father in Matt 1–7".

1990 Subtle Differences: The Matthean "Son of God" References. — *NT* 32 (1990) 193-200. [NTA 35, 127]

1994 The Matthean References to the Kingdom. Different Terms for Different Audiences. — *ETL* 70 (1994) 398-405. Esp. 399-400 [kingdom of heaven]; 401-402 [kingdom of the Father]; 402-403 [kingdom of God]. [NTA 39, 1442]

**MOWRY, Lucetta**
1962 Beatitudes. — *IDB* 1 (1962) 369-371.

**MOXNES, Halvor**
1988 *The Economy of the Kingdom. Social Conflict and Economic Relations in Luke's Gospel* (Overtures to Biblical Theology). Philadelphia, PA: Fortress, 1988, XXII-183 p. Esp. 15-16 [pharisees].

**MOYLE, Frank W.**
1956 *About the Bible.* London: Bles, 1956, IX-182 p. Esp. 113-127: "According to Matthew".

**MUDDIMAN, John B.**
1983 John's Use of Matthew. A British Exponent of the Theory. — *ETL* 59 (1983) 333-337. [NTA 28, 976] → Farrer 1954

**MÜHLENBERG, Ekkehard**
1990 Das Gleichnis von den Arbeitern im Weinberg (Matthäus 20,1-16) bei den Vätern. — EISENBERGER, H. (ed.), *Hermēneumata. Hadwig Hörner zum 60. Geburtstag* (Bibliothek der klassischen Altertumswissenschaften, II/79), Heidelberg: Winter, 1990, 11-26.

**MÜLHAUPT, Erwin**
1938R (ed.), *D. Martin Luthers Evangelien-Auslegung.* I: *Die Weihnachts- und Vorgeschichten bei Matthäus und Lukas (Matth. 1-2 und Lk. 1-2; 3,23-38)* [1938]. Göttingen: Vandenhoeck & Ruprecht, ³1955; ⁴1964 (vermehrte Auflage), 8*-318 p.; ⁵1984.
1947R (ed.), *D. Martin Luthers Evangelien-Auslegung.* II: *Das Matthäus-Evangelium (Kap. 3-25)* [1947]. Göttingen: Vandenhoeck & Ruprecht, ²1954; ³1960, 890 p.

**MÜLLER, Burkhard**
1988 Politik der Bergpredigt? — *Wege zum Menschen* (Göttingen) 40 (1988) 142-156.

**MÜLLER, Gerhard Ludwig**
1989 *Was heisst: Geboren von der Jungfrau Maria? Eine theologische Deutung* (QDisp, 119). Freiburg: Herder, 1989, 124 p. Esp. 62-72: "Die Aussageintention des christologischen Prologs bei Matthäus und Lukas".

**MÜLLER, Gotthold**
1982 Der Dekalog im Neuen Testament. Vor-Erwägungen zu einer unerledigten Aufgabe. — *TZ* 38 (1982) 79-97. Esp. 88-93: "Der Dekalog in den synoptischen Evangelien". [NTA 27, 722]

**MÜLLER, Hans-Peter**
1960 Die Verklärung Jesu. Eine motivgeschichtliche Studie. [17,1-9] — *ZNW* 51 (1960) 56-64. [NTA 5, 408]

**MUELLER, James R.**
1980 The Temple Scroll and the Gospel Divorce Texts. — *RQum* 10 (1980) 247-256. Esp. 255-256 [5,32; 19,9]. [NTA 25, 684]

**MÜLLER, Karlheinz**
1974 Jesus und die Sadduzäer. — MERKLEIN, H. – LANGE, J. (eds.), *Biblische Rand-bemerkungen.* FS R. Schnackenburg, 1974, 3-24. Esp. 9-10 [15,1-20]; 11-12 [23,13-22].

**MÜLLER, Mogens**

1977 Om udtrykket "menneskesønnen" i evangelierne. — *DanskTeolTids* 40 (1977) 1-17.
[NTA 23, 235]
Über den Ausdruck "Menschensohn" in den Evangelien. — *StudTheol* 31 (1977) 65-82.
[NTA 22, 902]

1983 Jesu brug af udtrykket "menneskesønnen". — *DanskTeolTids* 46 (1983) 201-220. Esp.
214, 220 [Q]. [NTA 28, 676]
The Expression 'the Son of Man' as Used by Jesus. — *StudTheol* 38 (1984) 47-64. Esp.
53-55. [NTA 29, 263]

1984 *Der Ausdruck "Menschensohn" in den Evangelien. Voraussetzungen und Bedeutung*
(Acta theologica Danica, 17). Leiden: Brill, 1984, XI-279 p. Esp. 104-123: "Das
Matthäusevangelium" [10,23; 13,37.41; 16,27-28; 19,28; 24,30.37-39; 25,31; 26,64; 28,18-20]; 152-154
[24,30-31/Did 16]; 163-167 [Son of Man – historical Jesus]; 187-200 [8,20; 11,19; 12,31-32.40; 16,13;
26,2]; 219-232 [Son of Man – aramaic]. — Diss. København, 1984. → Leivestad 1985

1987 Mattæusevangeliets messiasbillede: Et forsøg på at bestemme Mattæusevangeliets
forståelse af Jesu messianitet. [Matthew's portrayal of the Messiah: an attempt to
determine the understanding of Jesus' Messiahship in the gospel of Matthew] [5,13-26;
13,38; 28,18-20] — *SEÅ* 51-52 (1986-87) 168-179. [NTA 31, 577]

1988 *Mattæusevangeliet fortolket* (Det Danske Bibelskabs kommentarserie). København: Det
Danske Bibelskab, 1988, 362 p.

1992 The Gospel of St Matthew and the Mosaic Law: A Chapter of a Biblical Theology. —
*StudTheol* 46 (1992) 109-120. [NTA 38, 1356]

1993 Frelseshistorie i Matthæusevangeliet. Et eksempel på bibelsk teologi. — *DanskTeolTids*
56 (1993) 131-152. Esp. 133-135 [salvation-history]; 136-137 [fulfilment]; 137-138 [covenant]; 138-140
[revelation]; 140-143 [church]; 143-147 [Israel]; 147-150 [gentiles].
Salvation-History in the Gospel of Matthew. An Example of Biblical Theology. —
PEDERSEN, S. (ed.), *New Directions in Biblical Theology. Papers of the Aarhus
Conference, 16-19 September 1992* (SupplNT, 76), Leiden: Brill, 1994, 58-76. Esp. 59-
61; 62-63; 64; 65-66; 66-68; 69-72; 72-75.

**MÜLLER, Paul-Gerhard**

1973 Χριστὸς ἀρχηγός. *Der religionsgeschichtliche und theologische Hintergrund einer
neutestamentlichen Christusprädikation* (EHS, XXIII,28). Bern–Frankfurt/M: Lang,
1973, 432 p. Esp. 320-328: "Jesus als messianischer Anführer des neuen Israel bei Mattäus" [2,6; 15,14;
21,1-11]. — Diss. Regensburg, 1972 (F. Mussner).

1982 *Der Traditionsprozeß im Neuen Testament. Kommunikationsanalytische Studien zur
Versprachlichung des Jesusphänomens*. Freiburg: Herder, 1982, 364 p. Esp. 139-146: "Der
Traditionswille der Logienquelle Q"; 157: "Der matthäische Traditionswille". — Diss. Regensburg, 1976 (F.
Mussner).

**MÜLLER, Ulrich B.**

1977 Vision und Botschaft. Erwägungen zur prophetischen Struktur der Verkündigung Jesu.
— *ZTK* 74 (1977) 416-448. Esp. 429-432 [5,21-48]; 432-435 [11,11]; 435-437 [5,44-45]. [NTA 22,
375]

1978 Krankheit und Heilung. B. Neues Testament. — SEYBOLD, K. - MÜLLER, U.B.,
*Krankheit und Heilung* (Biblische Konfrontationen. Kohlhammer Taschenbücher, 1008),
Stuttgart: Kohlhammer, 1978, 80-162. Esp. 95-147.

**MUELLER, W.A.**

1956 Self-Defense and Retaliation in the Sermon on the Mount. [5,38-48] — *RExp* 53 (1956)
46-54.

**MÜSSLE, Marianne**

1969* (ed.) *Der "politische" Jesus. Seine Bergpredigt* (Pfeiffer-Werkbücher, Abteilung "Geistliches Leben", 76). München: Pfeiffer, 1969, 131 p. → F. Betz, O. Betz, Engelhardt, Hermann, G. Hommel, Sartory, Sartory-Reidick, Spaemann, J. Thomas F. MUSSNER, *TPQ* 118 (1970) 191.

**MUGARUKA MUGARUKA NGABO, Richard**

1991 *La traduction de la Bible comme moment d'inculturation du message révélé. Application à la version Shi des Béatitudes en Mt 5,1-12.* Diss. Louvain-la-Neuve, 1991, 411 p. (J. Ponthot).

1992 La traduction de la Bible comme moment d'inculturation du message révélé: Application à la version shi de Mt 5,1-2. — *RAfrT* 16 (1992) 5-32.

**MULDER, Harm**

1952 *Het synoptisch vraagstuk* (Exegetica I, 2). Delft: van Keulen, 1952, 88 p. Esp. 8-25: "Schreef Mattheüs in het Grieks?".

1956 De prediking van Petrus en het synoptisch vraagstuk. — *GTT* 56 (1956) 22-29, 65-77. Esp. 71-75.

1964 Mattheüs' appèl op de bevolking van Jeruzalem. — *Homiletica en Biblica* (Den Haag) 23 (1964) 158-161. [NTA 9, 518]

1977 *De verwoesting van Jeruzalem en haar gevolgen* (Exegetica II, 5). Amsterdam: Bolland, 1977, 148 p. Esp. 15-21 [24,15-22].

**MULHOLLAND, M. Robert**

1981 The Infancy Narratives in Matthew and Luke – of History, Theology and Literature. A Review Article of Raymond E. Brown's Monumental *The Birth of the Messiah.* — *BibArchRev* 7/2 (1981) 46-59. [NTA 25, 848r] → R.E. Brown 1977

**MULLEN, Rodene Lynn**

1994 *Cyril of Jerusalem and the Text of the New Testament in Fourth-Century Palestine.* Diss. Univ. of North Carolina at Chapel Hill, 1994, 430 p. (B.D. Ehrman). — *DissAbstr* 55 (1994-95) 1591-1592.

**MULLINS, Terence Y.**

1973 Ascription as a Literary Form. — *NTS* 19 (1972-73) 194-205. Esp. 201-205 [οὐαί]. [NTA 17, 842]

1976 New Testament Commission Forms, Especially in Luke-Acts. — *JBL* 95 (1976) 603-614. Esp. 603-605 [28,16-20]; 605-609: "Instances". [NTA 21, 307]

1991 Jesus, the "Son of David". [9,29-34; 12,22-24; 15,22-31; 20,30; 21,9.15] — *AndrUnS* 29 (1991) 117-126. [NTA 36, 700]

**MULLOOR, Augustine**

1989 *Jesus' Prayer of Praise: A Study of the Meaning and Function of Mt 11,25-30 in the First Gospel.* Diss. Pont. Inst. Bibl., Roma, 1989, 585 p. (F. Lentzen-Deis). Esp. 2-23: "Status quaestionis"; 24-56: "Mt 11,25-30 as a coherent whole"; 57-108: "The theme of Mt 11,25-30 and its development in the rest of the gospel"; 109-239: "Analysis of the individual elements of Mt 11,25-30"; 240-376: "Mt 11,2-30 as 'interfatio' of the gospel narrative"; 377-400: "The communicative function of Mt 11,25-30 in the first gospel".

1994 The Blind, the Lame and the Children in the Temple. Mt 21,14-17 as a Model of Action. — *Bible Bhashyam* 20 (1994) 29-41. Esp. 32-34: "Syntactic analysis"; 34-39: "Semantic analysis"; 39-40: "Narrative analysis". [NTA 39, 810]

**MUNCEY, R.W.**

1959 *The New Testament Text of St. Ambrose* (Texts and Studies, NS 4). Cambridge: University Press, 1959, LXXVIII-119 p. Esp. XXVI-XXVII; XXVIII-XLI; LXXV; 3-19.

**MUNCK, Johannes**

1950a   Israel and the Gentiles in the New Testament. — *Bulletir SNTS* 1 (1950; ²1963) 26-38. Esp. 36-37; = *JTS* 2 (1951) 3-16. Esp. 13-14.
Israel og Hedningerne i det Ny Testamente. — *DanskTeolTids* 14 (1951) 65-81.

1950b   Matthaeusevangeliet. [The gospel of Matthew] — *Illustreret Religionsleksikon* 2 (1950) 560.

1950c   Q, d.v.s. "Quelle". — *Illustreret Religionsleksikon* 3 (1950) 170.

1958   Presbytere og Herrens disciple hos Papias. Exegetiske bemærkninger til Euseb, h.e. III, 39. — *SEÅ* 22-23 (1957-58) 172-190. Esp. 176-177. [NTA 3, 741]
Presbyters and Disciples of the Lord in Papias. Exegetical Comments on Eusebius, Ecclesiastical History, III,39. — *HTR* 52 (1959) 223-243. Esp. 227-228. [NTA 4, 525]

1962   Die Tradition über das Matthäusevangelium bei Papias. — *Neotestamentica et Patristica*. FS O. Cullmann, 1962, 249-260.

**MUÑOZ, Jesús M.**

1985   An Introduction to the Gospel according to St. Matthew [Chinese] — *ColcTFu* 65 (1985) 327-352.

**MUÑOZ IGLESIAS, Salvador**

1954   Géneros literarios en los Evangelios. — *EstBíb* 13 (1954) 289-318. Esp. 297.311-312 [1-2]; = *Los géneros literarios de la Sagrada Escritura. Congresso de Ciencias Eclesiásticas, con ocasión del VII centenario de la Universidad de Salamanca (29 abril – 7 mayo de 1954)*, Barcelona: Flors, 1957, 219-244.

1957   Los Evangelios de la Infancia, y las infancias de los héroes. — *EstBíb* 16 (1957) 5-36. Esp. 24-28. [NTA 2, 40]; = *Generos literarios en los evangelios. Otros estudios* (XVII Semana Biblica Española), Madrid: Consejo Superior de Investigaciones Científicas, 1958, 83-113. Esp. 102-106.

1958   El género literario del Evangelio de la Infancia en San Mateo. — *EstBíb* 17 (1958) 243-273. Esp. 244-269: "Principales 'motivos' del evangelio de la infancia en san Mateo"; 270-273: "Estructura literaria de Mateo I–II". [NTA 3, 576]
El evangelio de la infancia en S. Mateo. — COPPENS, J., et al. (eds.) *Sacra Pagina*, 1959, II, 121-149. Esp. 122-146; 146-149.
Literary Genre of the Infancy Gospel in St. Matthew. — *TDig* 9 (1961) 15-20; = RYAN, M.R. (ed.), *Contemporary New Testament Studies*, 1965, 246-252.

1960   El Evangelio de Tomás y algunos aspectos de la cuestión sinóptica. — *EstE* 34 (1960) 883-894. Esp. 885 [7,7-8]; 885-886 [13,9]; 889-890 [5,18]; 890-891 [20,16]; 891-894 [10,26-27]. [NTA 6, 566]; = *Miscelanea Biblica Andres Fernandez*, 1960, 579-590.

1962   Venez, adorons-le. [2,1-12] — *AssSeign* I/13 (1962) 31-44.

1968   *Los generos literarios y la interpretación de la Biblia* (La Biblia hoy). Madrid: Casa de la Biblia, 1968, 167 p. Esp. 113-123 [gospel genre]; 144-146 [genealogy].

1969   Les mages et l'étoile. Mt 2,1-12. — *AssSeign* II/12 (1969) 19-31.

1972   Midráš y Evangelios de la Infancia. — *EstE* 47 (1972) 331-359. Esp. 331-335. [NTA 18, 98]

1978   La concepción virginal de Cristo en los Evangelios de la Infancia. I. Postura negativa de algunas autores católicas recientes. II. Crítica de una postura. — *EstBíb* 37 (1978) 5-28, 213-241. Esp. 10-14 [Pikaza 1976]; 14-15 [R.E. Brown 1973b]; 16-18 [Scheifler 1977]. [NTA 25, 69]

1989   Derás en Mt 1-2. — *RevistCatTeol* 14 (1989) 111-12_ (English summary, 121). Esp. 114-115 [1,17]; 115-116 [1,21-23]; 116-117 [2,1-12]; 117-118 [2,6]; 118-119 [2,13-21]; 120 [2,23].

1990a   *Los Evangelios de la Infancia. IV. Nacimiento e infancia de Jesús en San Mateo* (Biblioteca de autores cristianos, 509). Madrid: Católica, 1990, XVI-443 p. [NTA 36, p.

113] → Masini 1992, Muñoz León 1992

S. BLANCO, *EphMar* 42 (1992) 202-203; R.E. BROWN, *JBL* 112 (1993) 341-343; J.M. CASCIARO RAMIREZ, *ScriptTheol* 24 (1992) 335-336; M. DE BURGOS, *Communio* (Sevilla) 24 (1991) 104-105; J.L. ESPINEL, *CiTom* 121 (1994) 412-413; R. KRÜGER, *RevistBíb* 54 (1992) 117-120; G. MARCONI, *Greg* 73 (1992) 146-148; F. MARTIN, *CBQ* 54 (1992) 794-795; G. PÉREZ, *Salmanticensis* 38 (1991) 374-376.

1990b Tradición y redacción en la infancia de Jesús según Mateo 1–2 (A proposito de un libro reciente del prof. G. Segalla). — *Marianum* 52 (1990) 228-235. [NTA 36, 137r] → Segalla 1987b

1994 Lexemas y estilomas en Mateo 1–2. — ARANDA, G., et al. (eds.), *Biblia, Exegesis y Cultura*. FS J.M. Casciaro, 1994, 285-294.

### MUÑOZ LEÓN, Domingo

1982 El principio Trinitario inmanente y la interpretación del Nuevo Testamento (A propósito de la cristología epifánica restrictiva). — *EstBíb* 40 (1982) 19-48, 277-312; 41 (1983) 241-283. Esp. 37-38: "Evangelio de Mateo". [NTA 28, 281/677; 30, 315]

1988 Jesus y la apocalíptica pesimista (A propósito de Lc 18,8b y Mt 24,12). — *EstBíb* 46 (1988) 457-495. Esp. 481-489: "El enfriamiento de la caridad: Examen de Mt 24,12 en el contexto del discurso escatológico sinóptico". [NTA 33, 1192]

1989 "Allí estoy yo en medio de ellos" (Mt 18,20). Un ejemplo mateano de derás de traspaso. — *RevistCatTeol* 14 (1989) 133-148 (English summary, 148). Esp. 134-142 [18,20/OT]; 143-145 [derash].

1990 "Iré delante de vosotros a Galilea" (Mt 26,32 y par). Sentido mesiánico y posible sustrato arameo del logion. — *EstBíb* 48 (1990) 215-241. Esp. 216-219: "Presentación de los textos"; 219-223: "Dificultades de las soluciones propuestas"; 224-230: "¿Qué significa 'caminar delante'?; 230-235: "Possibilidad de una mala inteligencia en la formulación base del logion"; 235-240: "¿Prioridad de Marcos o de Mateo en el logion?". [NTA 35, 635]

1992 Derás e historia. La distinción entre acontecimiento-base y artificio literario en los relatos derásicos. Una discusión con el Prof. Muñoz Iglesias en su obra "Los Evangelios de la Infancia". — *EstBíb* 50 (1992) 123-148. Esp. 143-147: "Derás y historia en el nacimiento e infancia de Jesús en s. Mateo". → Muñoz Iglesias 1990a

### MURAOKA, Takamitsu

1973 Purpose or Result? ″Ωστε in Biblical Greek. — *NT* 15 (1973) 205-219. Esp. 214-215 [13,54]. [NTA 18, 776]

1975 On the Nominal Clause in the Old Syriac Gospels. — *JSS* 20 (1975) 28-37. [NTA 20, 373]

### MUR ESTEVAN, Antonio

1973 *Mito y Biblia. Historicidad de los Evangelios*. Zaragoza: Hechos y dichos, 1973, V-271 p. Esp. 235-254: "Los evangelios de la infancia".

### MURPHY, Harold S.

1954 Eusebius' NT Text in the *Demonstratio Evangelica*. — *JBL* 73 (1954) 162-168. Esp. 163-164.

### MURPHY, Roland E.

1956 The Dead Sea Scrolls and New Testament Comparisons. — *CBQ* 18 (1956) 263-272. Esp. 265-266. [NTA 1, 164]

### MURPHY-O'CONNOR, Jerome

1967 Sin and Community in the New Testament. — O'CALLAGHAN, D. (ed.), *Sin and Repentance. Papers of the Maynooth Union Summer School 1966*, Dublin: Gill, 1967, 18-50. Esp. 34-36 [6,9-13]; 38-40 [18,1-14]; 46-48 [5,21-22; 18,18].
*TDig* 16 (1968) 120-125.
Péché et communauté dans le Nouveau Testament. — *RB* 74 (1967) 161-193 (texte développé). Esp. 168-170

[18,17]; 176-177; 179-181; 188-190; 190-192. [NTA 12, 384]
Sünde und Gemeinde im Neuen Testament. — *TGeg* 11 (1968) 75-81. Esp.77-78 [18,18].

1975 The Structure of Matthew XIV–XVII. — *RB* 82 (1975) 360-384. Esp. 362-371: "Proposed structures of Matthew XIV–XVII"; 371-384: "An alternative structure". [NTA 20, 777] → Gooding 1978

1989 Qumran and the New Testament. — EPP, E.J. - MACRAE, G.W. (eds.), *The New Testament and Its Modern Interpreters*, 1989, 55-71. Esp. 57-60.

**MURRAY, Gregory**

1981 A New Look on the Synoptic Problem. — *CleR* 66 (1981) 213-217. [NTA 26, 80r] → Orchard 1976a

1983 Order in St Mark's Gospel. — *DownR* 101 (1983) 182-186. [NTA 28, 104]

1984a Mark the Conflator. — *DownR* 102 (1984) 157-162. [NTA 29, 507]

1984b The Questioning of Jesus. — *Ibid.*, 271-275. [NTA 29, 952]

1985a The Rich Young Man. — *DownR* 103 (1985) 144-146. [NTA 30, 123]

1985b Saint Peter's Denials. — *Ibid.*, 296-298. [NTA 30, 582]

1988 What Defiles a Man? [15,1-20] — *DownR* 106 (1988) 297-298. [NTA 33, 612]

1989 The Sign of Jonah. — *DownR* 107 (1989) 224-225. [NTA 34, 666]

1990 Five Gospel Miracles. — *DownR* 108 (1990) 79-90. [NTA 35, 121]

1994 New Light on St Matthew's Gospel. — *DownR* 112 (1994) 34-43. [NTA 39, 134r] → H. Riley 1992

**MURRAY, John**

1977 The Interadvental Period and the Advent. Matthew 24 and 25. — ID., *Collected Writings. Select Lectures in Systematic Theology*, II, Philadelphia, PA: Banner of Truth, 1977, 401-417.

**MURRAY, Robert**

1964 The Rock and the House on the Rock. A Chapter in the Ecclesiological Symbolism of Aphraates and Ephrem. [7,24-27; 16,18-19] — *OCP* 30 (1964) 315-362. Esp. 317-325 [Aphraates]; 325-350 [Ephrem].

1974 The Exhortation to Candidates for Ascetical Vows at Baptism in the Ancient Syriac Church. — *NTS* 21 (1974-75) 59-80. Esp. 65-71 [10,34]. [NTA 19, 839]

1975 *Symbols of Church and Kingdom: A Study in Early Syriac Tradition*. Cambridge: University Press, 1975, XV-394 p. Esp. 228-236; 324-329 [16,18].

**MUSSIES, Gerard**

1963 The Declension of the -(ί)ων Comparatives in New Testament Greek. — *NT* 6 (1963) 233-238. Esp. 234 [26,53]. [NTA 9, 84]

1972 *Dio Chrysostom and the New Testament* (Studia ad Corpus Hellenisticum Novi Testamenti, 2). Leiden: Brill, 1972, XII-257 p. Esp. 33-87: "Matthew".

1984 The Use of Hebrew and Aramaic in the Greek New Testament. — *NTS* 30 (1984) 416-432. Esp. 424-425 [5,22; 15,5; 21,9]; 429 [27,46]. [NTA 28, 34]

1986 Parallels to Matthew's Version of the Pedigree of Jesus. [1,2-17] — *NT* 28 (1986) 32-47. Esp. 32-36 [1,1]; 37-38 [1,2]; 38-39 [1,3]; 39 [1,6]; 39-44 [1,12]; 44-45 [1,16]; 45-47 [1,17]. [NTA 30, 1041]; = VAN DER HORST, P.W. - MUSSIES, G., *Studies*, 1990, 49-64. Esp. 49-53; 54-55; 55-56; 56; 56-61; 61-62; 62-64.

1988a Joseph's Dream (Matt 1,18-23) and Comparable Stories. — BAARDA, T., et al. (eds.), *Text and Testimony*. FS A.F.J. Klijn, 1988, 177-186; = VAN DER HORST, P.W. - MUSSIES, G., *Studies*, 1990, 86-95.

1988b  Vernoemen in de antieke wereld. De historische achtergrond van Luk. 1,59-63. — *NTT*
42 (1988) 114-125. [NTA 32, 1159]
Name Giving after Relatives in the Ancient World. The Historical Background of Luke I 59-63 in Connection
with Matt. I 16 and XIII 55. — VAN DER HORST, P.W. - MUSSIES, G., *Studies*, 1990, 65-85. Esp. 76-81.

1990   → van der Horst 1990

1995   Some Astrological Presuppositions of Matthew 2: Oriental, Classical and Rabbinical
Parallels. — VAN DER HORST, P.W. (ed.), *Aspects of Religious Contact and Conflict
in the Ancient World* (Utrechtse theologische Reeks, 31), Utrecht: Faculteit der
Godgeleerdheid, 1995, 25-44.

MUSSNER, Franz

1953   "Gib uns heute unser Brot für morgen". — *TTZ* 62 (1953) 164-166.

1956a  Das "Gleichnis" vom gestrengen Mahlherrn (Lk 13,22-30). Ein Beitrag zum
Redaktionsverfahren und zur Theologie des Lukas. — *TTZ* 65 (1956) 129-143. Esp. 130-
133 [Q 13,23-30]; = ID., *Praesentia Salutis*, 1967, 113-124. Esp. 114-117.

1956b  Schatz und Perle. [13,44-46] — *KatBlät* 81 (1956) 62-64.

1956c  Unkraut und Fischnetz. [13,24-30.47-48] — *Ibid.*, 137-139.

1959a  Jesus und die Pharisäer. — *KatBlät* 84 (1959) 433-440, 490-495. Esp. 438-439 [5,17-20];
493-494; = ID., *Praesentia Salutis*, 1967, 99-112. Esp. 104-105; 110.

1959b  Der nicht erkannte Kairos (Mt 11,16-19 = Luke 7,31-35). — *Bib* 40 (1959) 599-612.
Esp. 599-601: "Das Gleichnis"; 601-605: "Das Logion"; 605-606: "Der Zusammenhang"; 606-612: "Die
Perikope im Zusammenhang ihrer Akoluthie". [NTA 4, 653]; = *Studia Biblica et Orientalia*, II,
1959, 31-44.

1961   *Die Botschaft der Gleichnisse Jesu* (Schriften zur Katechetik, 1). München: Kösel,
1961, 102 p.; ²1964. Esp. 18-20 [13,4-9/Mk]; 21-25 [13,44-46]; 29-32 [13,31-33/Mk; Q 13,18-21]; 33-
37 [13,24-30.47-48]; 46-50 [22,1-14/Q 14,16-24]; 65-68 [20,1-16]; 80-83 [11,16-17/Q 7,31-32]; 84-87
[21,33-44/Mk]; 88-92 [25,14-30/Q 19,12-27]; 93-96 [25,1-13].
*The Use of Parables in Catechetics*. Notre Dame, IN: University Press, 1965, 107 p.
*Il messaggio delle parabole di Gesù*, trans. M. Masini (Universale teologica, 18). Brescia: Queriniana, 1971,
²1986, 106 p.
Trans. Japanese 1966.

1964   "Evangelium" und "Mitte des Evangeliums". Ein Beitrag zur Kontroverstheologie. —
METZ, J.B., et al. (eds.), *Gott in Welt*. FS K. Rahner, 1964, I, 492-514. Esp. 504; =
*TJb*, 1966, 219-239. Esp. 230; = ID., *Praesentia Salutis*, 1967, 159-177. Esp. 169.
"Évangile" et "centre de l'Évangile". Une contribution à la théologie de controverse. — *Le message de Jésus*,
1969, 151-176. Esp. 164-165.

1967a  *Praesentia Salutis. Gesammelte Studien zu Fragen und Themen des Neuen Testamentes*
(Kommentare und Beiträge zum Alten und Neuen Testament). Düsseldorf: Patmos,
1967, 299 p. → 1956a, 1959a, 1964

1967b  *Die Wunder Jesu. Eine Hinführung* (Schriften zur Katechetik, 10). München: Kösel,
1967, 90 p. Esp. 25-28 [11,20-24]; 28-31 [12,35-37]; 50-51 [8,28-34]; 61-68 [14,22-33]. → R. Pesch
1970a
*The Miracles of Jesus. An Introduction*, trans. A. Wimmer (Contemporary Catechetics, PL-23). Notre Dame,
IN: University Press, 1968, XI-105 p.; Shannon: Ecclesia Pr., 1970, XI-105 p.
*I miracoli di Gesù - Problemi preliminari*, trans. B. Alemanno (Giornale di Teologia, 38). Brescia:
Queriniana, 1969, 99 p.
*Los milagros de Jesús. Una orientación*, trans. J. Urbán (Annuntia, 15). Estella: Verbo Divino; Madrid: PPC,
1970, 69 p.

1967c  Die bösen Winzer nach Matthäus 21,33-46. — ECKERT, W.P., et al. (eds.),
*Antijudaismus*, 1967, 129-134, 207-208.

1968    Wege zum Selbstbewußtsein Jesu. Ein Versuch. — *BZ* 12 (1968) 161-172. Esp. 165-171: "Ausgeführte Beispiele aus der Logienquelle" [10,34; 11,25-26; 12,41-42]. [NTA 13, 543]

1970    Jesu Lehre über das kommende Leben nach den Synoptikern. — *IZT/Concilium* (Mainz) 6 (1970) 692-695.
The Synoptic Account of Jesus' Teaching on the Future Life. — *Concilium* (London) 6/10 (1970) 46-53. [NTA 15, 832]
L'enseignement de Jésus sur la vie future d'après les Synoptiques. — *Concilium* (Paris) 60 (1970) 43-50.

1971    Biblische Theologie des Tauf- und Missionsbefehls in Mt 28,18-20. — SUTTNER, E.C. (ed.), *Taufe und Firmung. Zweites Regensburger Ökumenisches Symposion*, Regensburg: Pustet, 1971, 179-190.

1973    Gab es eine "galiläische Krise"? — HOFFMANN, P. (ed.), *Orientierung an Jesus*. FS J. Schmid, 1973, 238-252. Esp. 244-248 [10,1-16].

1976    *Petrus und Paulus – Pole der Einheit. Eine Hilfe für die Kirchen* (QDisp, 76). Freiburg: Herder, 1976, 143 p. Esp. 11-22: "Petrus in der matthäischen Redaktion" [16,18-19].

1978a    Die Beschränkung auf einen einzigen Lehrer. Zu einer wenig beachteten *differentia specifica* zwischen Judentum und Christentum. — MÜLLER, G. (ed.), *Israel hat dennoch Gott zum Trost. Festschrift für Schalom Ben-Chorin*, Trier: Paulinus, 1978, 33-43. Esp. 36-37 [23,8-10].

1978b    Petrusgestalt und Petrusdienst in der Sicht der späten Urkirche. Redaktionsgeschichtliche Überlegungen. — RATZINGER, J. (ed.), *Dienst an der Einheit. Zum Wesen und Auftrag des Petrusamts* (Schriften der Katholischen Akademie in Bayern, 85), Düsseldorf: Patmos, 1978, 27-45. Esp. 28-34 [16,17-19].

1979    *Traktat über die Juden*. München: Kösel, 1979, 399 p. Esp. 185-193 [5,17-20]; 198-208 [6,9-13]; 216-264 [Pharisees]; 305-310 [27,24-25].
*Traité sur les Juifs*, trans. R. Givord (Cogitatio fidei, 109). Paris: Cerf, 1981, 439 p. Esp. 196-206; 211-222; 280-283; 328-333.
*Tractate on the Jews. The Significance of Judaism for Christian Faith*. London – Phildadelphia, PA: Fortress, 1984, XII-339 p.

1983    Gesetz und Evangelium, paulinisch und jesuanisch gesehen. — REIKERSTORFER, J. (ed.), *Gesetz und Freiheit*, Wien–Freiburg–Basel: Herder, 1983, 85-97. Esp. 90-95 [5,17-20; Q 16,16.17].

1988    Die Stellung zum Judentum in der "Redenquelle" und in ihrer Verarbeitung bei Matthäus. — SCHENKE, L. (ed.), *Studien zum Matthäusevangelium*. FS W. Pesch, 1988, 209-225. Esp. 211-213: "Konsequenzen der Trennung der Kirche von Israel für die Jesusüberlieferung"; 213-222: "Israelkritische Logien in Q"; 222-224: "Antijüdische Akzente in der Q-Rezeption durch den Mt-Evangelisten?"; = ID., *Dieses Geschlecht wird nicht vergehen. Judentum und Kirche*, Freiburg: Herder, 1991, 87-100.

1993    *Die Mutter Jesu im Neuen Testament*. St. Ottilien: EOS, 1993, 156 p.

**MUSURILLO, Herbert**

1970    John Chrysostom's *Homilies on Matthew* and the Version of Annianus. — GRANFIELD, P. – JUNGMANN, J.A. (eds.), *Kyriakon*. FS J. Quasten, 1970, I, 452-460.

**MUSZYŃSKI, Henryk**

1976    Kuszenie Chrystusa w tradycji synoptycznej (Die Versuchung Jesu in der synoptischen Tradition). — *CollTheol* 46/3 (1976) 17-41. [NTA 21, 719]

**MUTO, Susan Annette**

1982    *Blessings that Make Us Be. A Formative Approach to Living the Beatitudes*. New York: Crossroad, 1982, X-137 p.

**MUTZENBECHER, Almut**

1967 (ed.), *Sancti Aurelii Augustini De Sermone Domini in monte libros duos post Maurinorum recensionem* (CC SL, 35). Turnhout: Brepols, 1967, LVII-241 p. Esp. 1-188 [text].
     B.V.E. JONES, *JTS* 20 (1969) 324-327.

1980 (ed.), *Sancti Aurelii Augustini Quaestiones evangeliorum cum appendice quaestionum XVI in Matthaeum* (CC SL, 44B). Turnhout: Brepols, 1980, LXII-178 p.

**MYHRE, Klara**

1984 "Paktens blod" i vinordet. En undersøkelse av henspillingen på Ex 24,8 i Mark 14,24/Matt 26,28. ["Blood of the covenant" in the saying concerning the wine. A study of the allusion to Ex 24,8 in Mk 14,24/Mt 26,28] — *TidsTeolKirk* 55 (1984) 271-286. [NTA 29, 964]

**MYRE, André**

1973 Dix ans d'exégèse sur le divorce dans le Nouveau Testament. — *Le divorce. L'Église catholique ne devrait-elle pas modifier son attitude séculaire à l'égard de l'indissolubilité du mariage? Travaux du Congrès de la Société canadienne de théologie tenu à Montréal du 21 au 24 août 1972* (Héritage et Projet, 6), Montréal: Fides, 1973, 139-163. Esp. 143-144.147-151 [5,32]; 145-146 [19,3-12].

1994 Jésus avait-il une maison? — PETIT, J.-C. – CHARRON, A. – MYRE, A. (eds.), *"Où demeures-tu?" (Jn 1,38). La maison depuis le monde biblique. En hommage au professeur Guy Couturier à l'occasion de ses soixante-cinq ans*, Montréal: Fides, 1994, 305-322. Esp. 308-311 [9,9-10].

**MYRES, William Venting**

1958 *The Psychological Elements of the Sermon on the Mount.* Diss. Southwestern Baptist Theol. Sem., Fort Worth, TX, 1958, 172 p.

# N

**NAADLAND, Jakob**
1954 Ordet om sverder Mt 26,52. — *NorskTeolTids* 55 (1954) 162-173.

**NAASTEPAD, Thomas Johannes Marie**
1978 *Acht Gelijkenissen uit Mattheüs en Lukas* (Verklaring van een Bijbelgedeelte). Kampen: Kok, 1978, 138 p. Esp. 20-34 [7,1-12]; 35-46 [21,23-32]; 47-6⁻ [25,14-30].

**NACPIL, Emerito P.**
1983 The Way to Life. Matt. 7:13-14. — *The East Asia Journal of Theology* (Singapore) 1/1 (1983) 130-132.

**NAEGELE, J.**
1986 Translation of *talanton* "talent". — *BTrans* 37 (1986) 441-443. [NTA 31, 594]

**NAGANO, Paul M.**
1976 An Exegesis of Matthew 25:31-46. — *Foundations* (Rochester, NY) 19 (1976) 216-222.

**NAGEL, Peter**
1989 Editionen koptischer Bibeltexte seit Till 1960. — *Archiv für Papyrusforschung* (Leipzig) 35 (1989) 43-100. Esp. 62 [sa], 80-81 [bo], 84, 89.

**NAGEL, Walter**
1960 Neuer Wein in alten Schläuchen (Mt 9,17). — *VigChr* 14 (1960) 1-8. [NTA 5, 78]
1961 Gerechtigkeit – oder Almosen? (Mt 6,1). — *VigChr* 15 (1961) 141-145. [NTA 6, 451]

**NAGÓRNY, Janusz**
1985 Kazanie na Górze (Mt 5-7) jako moralne orędzie Nowego Przymierza (Die Bergpredigt [Matth. 5-7] als sittliches Manifest des neuen Bundes). — *RoczTK* 32/3 (1985) 5-21. [NTA 35, 1126]

**NALDINI, Mario**
1964 (ed.), *Documenti dell'Antichità cristiana. Papiri e pergamene greco-egizie della raccolta Fiorentina*. Firenze: Le Monnier, 1964, 39 p.; ²1965, 45 p. Esp. no. 14 [P³⁵].
1975 Nuovi frammenti del Vangelo di Matteo. [P⁷⁰] — *Prometheus* (Firenze) 1 (1975) 193-200.

**NANAKOS, S.**
1967 *The Temptations of Jesus in the Desert* [Greek]. Thessaloniki: Society of Bible Transl. 1967, 167-VIII p.

**NARDI, Carlo**
1979 Chrysostomus Hom. 59 (60) in Mt 7: motivi socratici e pseudoplutarchei. — LIVREA, E. – G.A. PRIVITERA (eds.), *Studi in onore di Anthos Ardizzoni* (Filologia e Critica, 25), Roma: Ateneo & Bizzarri, 1979, II, 615-638.

**NARDONI, Enrique**
1970 Amor – Liberdad – Autenticidad. En el evangelio según s. Mateo. — *RevistBíb* 32 (1970) 303-315. [NTA 16, 141]
1992 Interaction of Orality and Textuality: Response to Arthur J. Bellinzoni. — *SecCent* 9 (1992) 265-270. → Bellinzoni 1992

**NASH, S.**

1992    (ed.), *The Sermon on the Mount. Studies and Sermons* (Kerygma and Church). Greenville, SC: Smyth & Helwys, 1992, X-182 p. [NTA 37, p. 440]

**NAU, Arlo J.**

1992    *Peter in Matthew. Discipleship, Diplomacy, and Dispraise ... with an Assessment of Power and Privilege in the Petrine Office* (Good News Studies, 36). Collegeville, MN: Liturgical Press, 1992, XVI-184 p. Esp. 43-45 [18,21-22]; 46-49 [14,28-30]; 49-56 [16,17-19]; 56-58 [17,24-27]; 59-66: "Redaction criticism: Matthean omissions"; 67-91: "Marcan Petrine references in Matthew" [4,18-22; 8,14-15; 10,2-4; 17,1-8; 19,27-30; 26,30-35.36-46.57-75]; 92-121: "Petrine references unique to Matthew" [14,22-33; 15,10-20; 16,13-23; 17,24-27; 18,21-22]; 122-143: "Peter in Matthew". [NTA 37, p. 282]
    E. FRANKLIN, *ExpT* 105 (1993-94) 51-52; D.J. HARRINGTON, *CBQ* 55 (1993) 816-817; M. KNOWLES, *TorontoJT* 10 (1994) 261-263; W.C. LINSS, *JBL* 113 (1994) 143-145; E. WAINWRIGHT, *NewTheolRev* 7/3 (1994) 87-88.

**NAUCK, Wolfgang**

1952    Salt as a Metaphor in Instructions for Discipleship. — *StudTheol* 6 (1952) 165-178. Esp. 177-178 [5,13].

1955    Freude im Leiden. Zum Problem einer urchristlichen Verfolgungstradition. — *ZNW* 46 (1955) 68-80. Esp. 69-70 [5,11-12].

1956    Die Bedeutung des leeren Grabes für den Glauben an den Auferstandenen. — *ZNW* 47 (1956) 243-267. Esp. 254-255. [NTA 2, 23]

**NAUROY, Gérard**

1989    Chromace, disciple critique de l'exégèse d'Ambroise. Réalités et limites de l'influence de l'*In Lucam* sur les *Tractatus in Matthaeum*. — *Chromatius Episcopus*, 1989, 117-149.

**NAUTIN, Pierre**

1972    L'"Opus imperfectum in Matthaeum" et les Ariens de Constantinople. — *RHE* 67 (1972) 381-408, 745-766.

1973    Le canon du concile d'Arles de 314 sur le remariage après divorce. — *RSR* 61 (1973) 353-362. → Crouzel 1974a

1974    Divorce et remariage dans la tradition de l'Église latine. [19,9] — *RSR* 62 (1974) 7-54. Esp. 9-14 [Tertullian]; 14-17 [Lactantius]; 18-20 [Council of Elvira]; 20-21 [Council of Arles]; 21-26 [Hilarius of Poitiers]; 27-30 [Ambrosiaster]; 30-39 [Ambrosius]; 39-41 [Chromatius of Aquileia]; 42-44 [Innocentius I]; 44-47 [Victorinus of Pettau]; 47-54 [5-9th cent.]. [NTA 19, 94] → Crouzel 1974b, Honings 1976

1983    Divorce et remariage chez saint Épiphane. — *VigChr* 37 (1983) 157-173. → Crouzel 1984

**NAVONE, John**

1984    *Gospel Love. A Narrative Theology* (Good News Studies, 12). Wilmington, DE: Glazier, 1984, 159 p. Esp. 31-32; 36-41; 66-75.
    *L'amore evangelico. Una teologia narrativa*. Roma: Borla, 1986, 204 p.

1986    & COOPER, T., *The Story of the Passion*. Roma: Pont. Univ. Greg., 1986, 415 p. Esp. 170-209: "The passion according to Matthew".

**NEALE, David**

1993    Was Jesus a *Mesith*? Public Response to Jesus and His Ministry. — *TyndB* 44 (1993) 89-101. Esp. 94-98 [10,19-21]. [NTA 38, 115]

**NEBE, Gerhard-Wilhelm**

1987    Die lateinisch-christliche Inschrift in der St. Vartan Kapelle der Grabeskirche in Jerusalem, ein neutestamentliches Zitat? [8,25] — *ZNW* 78 (1987) 153-161. [NTA 32, 392]

**NEBE, Gottfried**

1989 *Prophetische Züge im Bilde Jesu bei Lukas* (BWANT, 127). Stuttgart: Kohlhammer, 1989, 302 p. Esp. 71-77; 165-169 [Q 6,47-49]; 169-174 [Q 7,31-35]; 182-186 [Q 13,18-21].

**NECHUTOVÁ, Jana**

1990 & CEGNA, R. (eds.), *Nicolae Dresdensis. Expositio super Pater Noster* (Mediaevalia Philosophica Polonorum, 30). Wraclaw-Warszawa-Krakau, 1990, 212 p.

**NEE, Watchman**

1978 *The King and the Kingdom of Heaven: A Study of Matthew.* New York: Christian Fellowship Publishers, 1978, 386 p.

**NEERAKKAL, Cyriac**

1991 *The Concept of 'Perfect' in the Gospel of Matthew: An Exegetico-Theological Investigation.* Diss. Pont. Univ. Greg., Roma, 1991, 382 p. (K. Stock). Esp. 147-229: "'Teleios' in the context of the Sermon on the Mount" [5,17-48]; 230-295: "'Teleios' in a context of discipleship" [19,16-22].

**NEGOITÄ, Athanase**

1967 & DANIEL, C., L'énigme du levain. Ad Mc. viii 15; Mt. xvi 6; et Lc. xii 1. — *NT* 9 (1967) 306-314. Esp. 306-308.310-111. [NTA 12, 888]

**NEIDHART, Walter**

1986 Wissenschaftliche Erklärung des Matthäus und Probleme heutiger christlicher Praxis. — *Reformatio* 35 (1986) 2-7. → Luz 1985a

**NEIL, William**

1976 Five Hard Sayings of Jesus. — MCKAY, J.R. - MILLER, J.F. (eds.), *Biblical Studies.* FS W. Barclay, 1976, 157-171. Esp. 157-160 [10,34]; 160-163 [5,39.44]; 163-166 [17,20].

1981 & TRAVIS, S.H., *More Difficult Sayings of Jesus.* London-Oxford: Mowbray, 1981, VIII-128 p. Esp. 3-6 [5,4]; 7-10 [5,13-14]; 11-14 [5,12]; 15-18 [11,19]; 23-26 [16,23]; 27-30 [7,6]; 31-34 [6,8]; 65-68 [5,17]; 69-72 [6,34]; 73-76 [10,16]; 77-80 [11,27]; 81-84 [20,15]; 85-88 [25,41].

**NEILL, Stephen**

1964 *The Interpretation of the New Testament 1861-1961. The Firth Lectures, 1962.* London - New York - Toronto, Ont.: Oxford University Press, 1964 (paperback 1966), ⁶1985, VII-360 p. Esp. 104-136: "Jesus and the gospel".
*De interpretatie van het Nieuwe Testament* (Aula, 353). Utrecht-Antwerpen: Spectrum, 1968, 427 p.
& WRIGHT, T., *The Interpretation of the New Testament, 1861-1986. Second edition.* Oxford: University Press, 1988, XI-464 p. Esp. 112-146.

1976 *Jesus through Many Eyes. Introduction to the Theology of the New Testament.* Philadelphia, PA: Fortress, 1976, IX-214 p. Esp. 94-103.

**NEIRYNCK, Frans**

1958 Het evangelisch echtscheidingsverbod. — *CollBrugGand* 4 (1958) 25-46. Esp. 29-34 [5,32]; 34-39 [19,9]; 40-43 [Q 16,18]. [NTA 3, 62] → 1972c, 1996a

1960 Huwelijk en echtscheiding in het evangelie. — *CollBrugGand* 6 (1960) 123-130. [NTA 5, 290r] → Dupont 1959a

1966 Mc 9,33-50 en de overlevering van de Jezuswoorden. — *Concilium* (Hilversum) 2/10 (1966) 62-73. Esp. 67-71 [18,1-14]; = ID., *Evangelica*, 1982, 811-820. Esp. 816-819. → 1991a, 804
The Tradition of the Sayings of Jesus: Mk 9,33-50. — *Concilium* (London) 2/10 (1966) 62-74. Esp. 68-72. [NTA 11, 724]
La tradition des paroles de Jésus et Mc 9,33-50. — *Concilium* (Paris) 20 (1966) 57-66.

1967a Synoptica. Het argument van de acoloethie in de synoptische kwestie (Studiorum Novi Testamenti Auxilia, 5). Leuven, 1967, 53 p. Esp. 5-21 [argument from order]; 22-40 [absence of the Sermon on the Mount in Mk]; 41-51 [double tradition].

1967b La rédaction matthéenne et la structure du premier évangile. — ETL 43 (1967) 41-73. Esp. 43-51 [redaction criticism; synoptic problem]; 51-72 [structure]. [NTA 12, 146]; = DE LA POTTERIE, I. (ed.), De Jésus aux Évangiles. FS J. Coppens, 1967, 41-73. (IT, 1971, 60-96); = ID., Evangelica, 1982, 3-35 (note additionnelle, 35-36). Esp. 5-13; 13-34. → 1988c

1968 Une nouvelle théorie synoptique (À propos de Mc., 1,2-6 et par.). Notes critiques. — ETL 44 (1968) 141-153. Esp. 143-148 [Mt/Gospel of the Ebionites]; 148-151 [3,1-6/Mk]. [NTA 13, 188]; = ID., Jean et les Synoptiques, 1979, 299-311. Esp. 301-306; 306-309. → Boismard 1966a

1969 Les femmes au tombeau: Étude de la rédaction matthéenne (Matt. xxviii.1-10). — NTS 15 (1968-69) 168-190. Esp. 168-170 [28,5-7]; 170-176 [28,2-4]; 176-184 [28,9-10]; 184-189 [Jn/Mt]. [NTA 13, 872]; = ID., Evangelica, 1982, 273-295 (note additionnelle, 296). Esp. 273-275; 275-281; 281-289; 289-294. → 1991a, 797

1970 Hawkins's Additional Notes to His "Horae Synopticae". — ETL 46 (1970) 78-111. Esp. 83 [characteristics of Mt]; 86-87.90-93.101-105 [Mt]; 109-110 [Lt/Lk agreements]. [NTA 15, 122] → J.C. Hawkins 1909/68

1972a Duality in Mark. Contributions to the Study of the Markan Redaction (BETL, 31). Leuven: University Press, 1972, 214 p.; Leuven: University Press / Peeters, ²1988, 252 p. (revised edition with Supplementary Notes, 215-252). → 1972b; 1988b

1972b Duplicate Expressions in the Gospel of Mark. — ETL 48 (1972) 150-209. Esp. 159-161: "Avoidance of pleonasm and repetition"; 174-181: "Duplicate expressions and the original text of the gospel"; 196-200 [Mk/Mt: οὐ ... ἀλλά]; 200-208 [Mk/Mt: oratio obliqua/recta]. [NTA 17, 133]; = ID., Duality in Mark, 1972, 13-72. Esp. 22-24; 37-44; 59-63; 63-71; = ID., Evangelica, 1982, 83-142 (additional note, 142). Esp. 92-94; 107-114; 129-133; 133-141.

1972c De Jezuswoorden over echtscheiding. — HEYLEN, V. (ed.), Mislukt huwelijk en echtscheiding. Een multi-disciplinaire verkenning (Sociologische Verkenningen, 2), Leuven: University Press, 1972, 127-141. Esp. 131-134.136-138 [5,32; Q 16,18]; = ID., Evangelica, 1982, 821-834. Esp. 823-827.829-832 (note, 833-834).→ 1991a, 804; → van Tilborg 1970

1972d The Gospel of Matthew and Literary Criticism. A Critical Analysis of A. Gaboury's Hypothesis. — DIDIER, M. (ed.), L'Évangile selon Matthieu, 1972, 37-69. Esp. 38-40: "The argument from the order of incidents"; 40-49.51-53 [Mk 1,14-6,1/Mt]; 49-50: "The phenomenon of order"; 54-56: "The Q source in Matthew"; 56-67: "The summaries in Matthew"; = SBL 1972 Seminar Papers, I, 147-179 Esp. 148-150; 150-159.161-163; 159-160; 164-166; 166-167; = ID., Evangelica, 1982, 691-723 (additional note, 723). Esp. 692-694; 694-703.705-707; 703-705; 708-710; 710-721. → 1991a, 802-803; → Gaboury 1970

1973* (ed.), L'Évangile de Luc. Problèmes littéraires et théologiques. Mémorial Lucien Cerfaux (BETL, 32). Gembloux: Duculot, 1973, 385 p. → 1989*; → Cerfaux, Delobel, Neirynck

1973a La matière marcienne dans l'évangile de Luc. — Ibid., 157-201 (162-166 = ID., Jean et les Synoptiques, 1979, 313-317). Esp. 193-194 [minor agreements]; ²1989, 67-111 (note additionnelle, 304-305). Esp. 103-104; = ID., Evangelica, 1982, 37-81 (note additionnelle, 81-82). Esp. 73-74. → 1991a, 793-794

1973b The Argument from Order and St. Luke's Transpositions. — ETL 49 (1973) 784-815. Esp. 785-790: "The agreements Matthew-Luke against Mark"; 790-799: "The absence of agreement and its significance"; 799-804: "The position of R. Morgenthaler". [NTA 19, 522]; = ID., The Minor Agreements, 1974, 291-322. Esp. 292-297; 297-306; 306-311; = ID., Evangelica, 1982, 737-768 (additional note, 768). Esp. 738-743; 743-752; 752-757. → 1991a, 803; → Morgenthaler 1971, E.P. Sanders 1969b

1973c Minor Agreements Matthew-Luke in the Transfiguration Story. — HOFFMANN, P., et al. (eds.), *Orientierung an Jesus*. FS J. Schmid, 1973, 253-266. Esp. 256-260 [17,2]; 260-264 [17,5]; = ID., *Evangelica*, 1982, 797-809 (additional note, 809-810: "The Study of the Minor Agreements"). Esp. 800-804; 804-808. → 1991a, 804

1974a & HANSEN, T. - VAN SEGBROECK, F., *The Minor Agreements of Matthew and Luke against Mark, with a Cumulative List* (BETL, 37). Leuven: University Press, 1974, 330 p. Esp. 11-48: "The study of the minor agreements"; 49-195: "A cumulative list of the minor agreements"; 197-288: "A classification of stylistic agreements with comparative material from the triple tradition". → 1973b; 1991b; → Causse 1977

M.-É. BOISMARD, *RB* 83 (1976) 635; M. CAUSSE, *ETR* 52 (1977) 125-127; R.T. FRANCE, *JEvTS* 19 (1976) 134; K. GRAYSTON, *ExpT* 87 (1975-76) 261; J.-C. INGELAERE, *RHPR* 57 (1977) 105-106; X. LÉON-DUFOUR, *RSR* 64 (1976) 428-429; U. LUZ, *TZ* 33 (1977) 49; E.V. MCKNIGHT, *JBL* 96 (1977) 140-141; L. SABOURIN, *BTB* 6 (1976) 105-106; W. SCHENK, *TLZ* 102 (1977) 439-441.

1974b Les accords mineurs et la rédaction des évangiles. L'épisode du paralytique (*Mt.*, IX,1-8 / *Lc.*, V,17-26, par. *Mc.*, II,1-12). — *ETL* 50 (1974) 215-230. Esp. 216-223 [minor agreements]; 223-230 [καὶ ἰδού]. [NTA 19, 954]; = ID., *Evangelica*, 1982, 781-796. Esp. 782-789; 789-796. → 1991a, 803-804; → Vargas-Machuca 1969b

1974c Urmarcus redivivus? Examen critique de l'hypothèse ces insertions matthéennes dans Marc. — SABBE, M. (ed.), *L'Évangile selon Marc*, 1974, 103-145; ²1988 (note additionnelle, 145-146). Esp. 105-118: "Additions rédactionnelles simultanées dans Mt et Mc (à propos de Mc., 1,2-3)" [3,1-3; 14,26; 26,55-56]; 118-144: "Influences du Mt-intermédiaire sur l'ultime rédaction de Mc" [4,24-25; 8,16-17; 10,19-20; 12,15-16; 16,13-20; 26,18.50-57.58; 27,12-14.55]; = ID., *Jean et les Synoptiques*, 1979, 319-361. Esp. 321-334; 334-360. → Boismard 1972, 1974

1975 Jesus and the Sabbath. Some Observations on Mark II.27. — DUPONT, J. (ed.), *Jésus aux origines de la christologie*, 1975, 227-270. Esp. 232-235 [12,1-8/Mk]; ²1989 (additional note, 422-427); = ID., *Evangelica*, 1982, 637-680. Esp. 642-645.

1976a La nouvelle Concordance du Nouveau Testament. — *ETL* 52 (1976) 134-142; 54 (1978) 323-345. [NTA 23, 769]; 55 (1979) 152-155; 56 (1980) 132-138. [NTA 25, 34]; 57 (1981) 360-362, 438-442; = ID., *Evangelica*, 1982, 955-1002. → 1984a; 1991a, 807-808; → K. Aland [Concordance 1978]

1976b The Sermon on the Mount in the Gospel Synopsis. — *ETL* 52 (1976) 350-357. [NTA 21, 375]; = ID., *Jean et les Synoptiques*, 1979, 375-383; = ID., *Evangelica*, 1982, 729-736. → 1991a, 803

1976c Note on the Codex Bezae in the Textual Apparatus of the Synopsis. — *Ibid.*, 358-363. Esp. 360-361. [NTA 21, 364]; = ID., *Evangelica*, 1982, 941-946. Esp. 943-944. → 1991a, 807; → K. Aland [Synopsis 1976]

1976d The Synoptic Gospels according to the New Textus Receptus. — *Ibid.*, 364-379. Esp. 365-369 [GNT³/N²⁶]; 377-379 [minor agreements]. [NTA 21, 365]; = ID., *Evangelica*, 1982, 883-898. Esp. 884-888; 896-898. → 1991a, 804-805; → K. Aland [Synopsis 1976; GNT 1975]

1976e Q. — *IDBS*, 1976, 715-716.

1976f Synoptic Problem. — *Ibid.*, 845-848; = BELLINZONI, A.J., Jr., et al. (eds.), *The Two-Source Hypothesis*, 1985, 85-93.

1977a & VAN BELLE, G. - VAN SEGBROECK, F. - DELOBEL J. - SNOY, T., L'Évangile de Jean. Examen critique du commentaire de M.-É. Boismard et A. Lamouille. — *ETL* 53 (1977) 363-478. Esp. 451-478: "Foi et miracle. Le fonctionnaire royal de Capharnaüm en 4,46-54". [NTA 22, 435r]; = ID., *Jean et les Synoptiques*, 1979, 7-120. Esp. 93-120.

1977b John and the Synoptics. — DE JONGE, M. (ed.), *L'Évangile de Jean. Sources, rédaction, théologie* (BETL, 44), Gembloux: Duculot; Leuven: University Press, 1977; Leuven: University Press / Peeters, ²1987, 73-106. Esp. 82-93 [Jn/Mt agreements]; 96-98 [28,9-

10/Jn] (82-93 = ID., *Jean et les Synoptiques*, 1979, 363-374); = ID., *Evangelica*, 1982, 365-398 (additional note, 398-400). Esp. 374-385; 388-390. → 1991a, 798-799; 1984b, 1992b; → Dauer 1972, R. Mahoney 1974

1978    The Symbol Q (= Quelle). — *ETL* 54 (1978) 119-125. [NTA 23, 79]; = ID., *Evangelica*, 1982, 683-689. → 1979c, 1991h

1979a    & DELOBEL, J. – SNOY, T. – VAN BELLE, G. – VAN SEGBROECK, F., *Jean et les Synoptiques. Examen critique de l'exégèse de M.-É. Boismard* (BETL, 49). Leuven: University Press, 1979, XI-428 p. Esp. 188-194 [16,16-18/Jn 1,41-42]; 385-387 [synopsis]. → 1968, 1973a, 1974c, 1976b, 1977a-b; → P. Benoit 1965, Boismard 1972, D.M. Smith 1982

1979b    L'édition du texte de Q. — *ETL* 55 (1979) 373-381. [NTA 24, 774r]; = ID., *Evangelica*, 1982, 925-933 (note additionnelle, 933). → Polag 1979

1979c    Once More: The Symbol Q. — *Ibid.*, 382-383. [NTA 24, 772]; = ID., *Evangelica*, 1982, 689-690. → 1978, 1991h; → J.J. Schmitt 1981, Silberman 1979

1979d    Les Évangiles synoptiques. X. Léon-Dufour. — *Ibid.*, 405-409; = ID., *Evangelica*, 1982, 724-728. → Léon-Dufour 1976, McLoughlin 1965

1980a    Marc 16,1-8. Tradition et rédaction. — *ETL* 56 (1980) 56-88. Esp. 78-80: "Mc 16,8 et l'accord de Mt/Lc". [NTA 25, 105]; = ID., *Evangelica*, 1982, 239-271 (note additionnelle, 271-272). Esp. 261-263. → 1991a, 796-797

1980b    Deuteromarcus et les accords Matthieu-Luc. — *Ibid.*, 397-408. Esp. 398-400: "La liste des accords mineurs"; 403-407: "Deutéro-Marc et Q". [NTA 25, 840]; = ID., *Evangelica*, 1982, 769-780. Esp. 770-772; 775-779. → 1991a, 803; → Aichinger 1976, 1978, A. Fuchs 1971, 1978, 1980a-b

1980c    Studies on Q since 1972. — *Ibid.*, 409-413. [NTA 25, 841] → 1982d-e, 1986d

1982a    *Evangelica. Gospel Studies – Études d'évangile. Collected Essays*, ed. F. Van Segbroeck (BETL, 60). Leuven: University Press / Peeters, 1982, XIX-1033 p. → 1966, 1967b, 1969, 1972b-d, 1973a-c, 1974b, 1975, 1976a-d, 1977b, 1978, 1979b-d, 1980a-b; → 1991a (Appendix, 791-808)
         A. DENAUX, *ETL* 60 (1984) 124-133; X. JACQUES, *NRT* 102 (1983) 593; G.D. KILPATRICK, *NT* 25 (1983) 382-383; F. MONTAGNINI, *RivBib* 31 (1983) 352.

1982b    The Griesbach Hypothesis: The Phenomenon of Order. — *ETL* 58 (1982) 111-122. Esp. 112-113 [Lachmann]; 115-121 [argument from order]. [NTA 27, 88]; = ID., *Evangelica II*, 1991, 281-292 (additional note, 292). Esp. 282-283; 285-291. → Dungan 1985b

1982c    & VAN SEGBROECK, F., Greeven's Text of the Synoptic Gospels. — *Ibid.*, 123-135. Esp. 124-125; 126-128. [NTA 27, 85r]; = ID., *Evangelica II*, 1991, 377-388. Esp. 378-379; 380-382. → 1984a; → Greeven 1981

1982d    Recent Developments in the Study of Q. — DELOBEL, J. (ed.), *Logia*, 1982, 29-75. Esp. 31-35: "Q and the synoptic problem"; 35-41: "The reconstruction of Q"; 41-53: "Mark and Q"; 54-74: "The redaction of Q"; = ID., *Evangelica II*, 1991, 409-461 (Bibliographical Supplement, 1990, 462-463; Additional Notes, 463-464). Esp. 411-415; 415-421; 421-433; 434-454. → 1980c, 1986d → Goulder 1978b, Lambrecht 1982

1982e    & VAN SEGBROECK, F., Q Bibliography. — *Ibid.*, 561-586. → 1980c, 1986d; → Scholer

1983a    & VAN SEGBROECK, F., The Westcott-Hort Marginal Readings in the Concordance. — *ETL* 59 (1983) 114-126. [NTA 28, 41]; = ID., *New Testament Vocabulary*, 1984, 465-477. → K. Aland [Concordance 1978]

1983b    Les expressions doubles chez Marc et le problème synoptique. — *Ibid.*, 303-330. Esp. 315-325: "L'argument synoptique". [NTA 28, 928]; = ID., *Evangelica II*, 1991, 293-320 (note additionnelle, 320). Esp. 305-315. → Rolland 1982, 1983a-b

1984a    & VAN SEGBROECK, F., *New Testament Vocabulary. A Companion Volume to the Concordance* (BETL, 65). Leuven: University Press / Peeters, 1984, XVI-494 p. Esp.

23-202: "Compounds and derivates"; 205-334: "Synoptic parallels"; 335-422: "Synonyms and substitutes"; 437-487: "The text of the synoptic gospels" [N, N²⁶, GNT¹⁻³, Greeven, WH]; 489-494: "The double-tradition text (Q reconstructions)". → 1976a, 1982c, 1983a, 1986b; → K. Aland [Concordance 1978], Greeven 1981 E. BEST, *ExpT* 96 (1984-85) 374; J. BEUTLER, *TheolPhil* 62 (1987) 259-260; C.C. CARAGOUNIS, *SEÅ* 53 51988° 121-122; F.W. DANKER, *CBQ* 47 (1985) 739-740; A. DENAUX, *Collationes* 15 (1985) 122-123; J. DUPONT, *RHE* 80 (1985) 558-559; J.K. ELLIOTT, *NT* 26 (1984) 380-382; P.J. FARLA, *TijdTheol* 24 (1984) 412-413; J. GUTTIÉREZ, *CiudDios* 200 (1987) 125-126; J.-C. INGELAERE, *RHPR* 65 (1985) 206-207; X. JACQUES, *Études classiques* 53 (1985) 514-515; *NRT* 107 (1985) 882-884; B.J. KOET, *Bijdragen* 46 (1985) 438; W.G. KÜMMEL, *TR* 50 (1985) 100; G. MUSSIES, *NTT* 39 (1985) 332-338; T.P. OSBORNE, *RTL* 16 (1985) 232-233; A. RODRÍGUEZ CARMONA, *EstBíb* 44 (1986) 242-243; C.M. TUCKETT, *ETL* 61 (1985) 391-393.

1984b   John and the Synoptics. The Empty Tomb Stories. — *NTS* 30 (1984) 161-187. Esp. 166-172: "John 20.11-18 and Mt. 28,9-10". [NTA 28, 1000]; = ID., *Evangelica II*, 1991, 571-599 (additional note, 597, 600). Esp. 579-588. → 1977b; → D.M. Smith 1992a

1984c   The Matthew-Luke Agreements in Mt 14,13-14 / Lk 9,10-11 (par. Mk 6,30-34). The Two-Source Theory Beyond the Impasse. — *ETL* 60 (1984) 25-44. Esp. 27-32 [14,13-21]; 41-43 [14,13-14]. [NTA 29, 105]; = ID., *Evangelica II*, 1991, 75-93 (additional note, 94). Esp. 77-82; 91-93. → 1990d; → Boismard 1979
   A. FUCHS, Die Agreement-Redaktion von Mk 6,32-44 par. Mt 14,13-21 par. Lk 9,10b-17. Ein vorläufiger Entwurf. — *SNTU* 22 (1997) 181-203.

1984d   Réponse à P. Rolland. [4,1; 8,23; 9,4; 13,10; 14,13.17] — *Ibid.*, 363-366. L'arrière-fond sémitique des Évangiles synoptiques. — ID., *Evangelica II*, 1991, 321-324 (note additionnelle, 324). → Rolland 1984b

1984e   John 4,46-54. Signs Source and/or Synoptic Gospels. — *Ibid.*, 367-375. Esp. 371-375. [NTA 29, 1000]; = ID., *Evangelica II*, 1991, 679-687 (additional note, 687-688). Esp. 682-687. → 1995d; → Dauer 1984

1985a   Papyrus Egerton 2 and the Healing of the Leper. — *ETL* 61 (1985) 153-160. Esp. 157-158 [8,3]. [NTA 30, 134]; = ID., *Evangelica II*, 1991, 773-780 (additional notes, 780-783). Esp. 776-777. → Boismard 1981, Kellas 1994

1985b   The Order of the Gospels and the Making of a Synopsis. — *Ibid.*, 161-166. [NTA 30, 69r]; = ID., *Evangelica II*, 1991, 357-362 (additional note, 362). → 1986c; → Greeven 1981, Orchard 1982, 1983a, 1986

1986a   Mt 12,25a / Lc 11,17a et la rédaction des évangiles. — *ETL* 62 (1986) 122-133. Esp. 125-133: "La source Q". [NTA 31, 587]; = ID., *Evangelica II*, 1991, 481-492 (note additionnelle, 492). Esp. 484-492. → Rolland 1986

1986b   New Testament Vocabulary. Corrections and Supplement. — *Ibid.*, 134-140. [NTA 31, 526] → 1984a

1986c   Once More: The Making of a Synopsis. — *Ibid.*, 141-154. Esp. 141-145 [Aland]; 145-147 [Denaux-Vervenne]. [NTA 31, 537]; = ID., *Evangelica II*, 1991, 363-376 (additional note, 376). Esp. 363-367; 367-369. → 1985b; → K. Aland [Synopsis 1985], Denaux 1986, Dungan 1985b

1986d   & VAN SEGBROECK, F., Q Bibliography. Additional List 1981-1985. — *Ibid.*, 157-165. [NTA 31, 565] → 1980c, 1982d-e

1986e   L'influence de l'Évangile de Matthieu. À propos d'une réimpression. — *Ibid.*, 399-403. [NTA 31, 1054] → Massaux 1950/86

1986f   Paul and the Sayings of Jesus. — VANHOYE, A. (ed.), *L'apôtre Paul. Personnalité, style et conception du ministère* (BETL, 73), Leuven: University Press / Peeters, 1986, 265-321. Esp. 268-281: "List of parallels"; 281-306: "Paul and pre-synoptic sources"; = ID., *Evangelica II*, 1991, 511-567 (additional note, 567-568). Esp. 514-527; 527-552. → 1996c; → Allison 1982, N. Walter 1985

1987a   Τίς ἐστιν ὁ παίσας σε. Mt 26,68 / Lk 22,64 (diff. Mk 14,65). — *ETL* 63 (1987) 5-47. Esp. 28-41 [26,67-68]; 33-36 [28,17]. [NTA 32, 132]; = ID , *Evangelica II*, 1991, 95-137 (additional note, 138). Esp. 118-131; 123-126. → 1991f; → P. Benoit 1962, van der Horst 1986, Wheeler 1985

1987b Le texte des évangiles dans la Synopse de Boismard-Lamouille. — *Ibid.*, 119-135. Esp. 124, 128-132. [NTA 32, 66r]; = ID., *Evangelica II*, 1991, 389-405 (additional note, 405). Esp. 394, 398-402. → Boismard 1986a

1987c A Concordance of the Synoptic Parallels. — *Ibid.*, 375-383. Esp. 377-380: "Mark and parallels"; 380-382: "Matthew-Luke parallels". [NTA 33, 103r] → 1984a; → dos Santos 1985

1988a *Q-Synopsis. The Double Tradition Passages in Greek* (Studiorum Novi Testamenti Auxilia, 13). Leuven: University Press / Peeters, 1988, 63 p. [NTA 33, p. 110]; 1995, 79 p. (revised ed., with appendix → 1990a, 1993a). [NTA 40, p. 146] → 1988d; → J.K. Elliott 1991, Minette de Tillesse 1990a, Sanz Valdivieso 1990
   A. BONORA, *RivBib* 37 (1989) 245-246; L. DEVILLERS, *RThom* 89 (1989) 490; J. DUPONT, *RHE* 84 (1989) 528-529; J. GUILLET, *RSR* 77 (1989) 387; E.C. MALONEY, *CBQ* 52 (1990) 567-568; A. RODRÍGUEZ CARMONA, *EstBíb* 48 (1990) 431.
   A. FUCHS, *SNTU* 20 (1995) 208-209; A. POPPI, *RivBib* 44 (1996) 367-368.

1988b Supplementary Notes. — ID., *Duality in Mark*, [2]1988, 215-252. Esp. 227-235: "Duplicate expressions and synoptic problem". → 1972a

1988c Ἀπὸ τότε ἤρξατο and the Structure of Matthew. — *ETL* 64 (1988) 21-59. Esp. 25-46: "The beginning at Mt 4,12-17"; 46-57: "Matthew 16,13-23". [NTA 33, 115]; = ID., *Evangelica II*, 1991, 141-179 (additional note, 180-182). Esp. 145-166; 166-177. → 1967b; → D.R. Bauer 1988a, Kingsbury 1973b, 1975a

1988d A Synopsis of Q. — *Ibid.*, 441-449. [NTA 33, 1103r]; = ID., *Evangelica II*, 1991, 465-473 (additional note, 473). → 1988a; → Kloppenborg 1988

1988e Le lexique de Bauer-Aland. — *Ibid.*, 450-454. [NTA 33, 1050r]; = ID., *Evangelica II*, 1991, 785-790 (additional note, 790). → K. Aland [Bauer-Aland 1988]

1989* (ed.), *L'Évangile de Luc - The Gospel of Luke. Revised and Enlarged Edition* (BETL, 32). Leuven: University Press / Peeters, 1989, X-590 p. → 1973*; → T.A. Friedrichsen, Judge, Neirynck, Schreck, Verheyden

1989a & FRIEDRICHSEN, T.A., Note on Luke 9,22. A Response to M.D. Goulder. [16,21] — *Ibid.*, 393-398; = *ETL* 65 (1989) 390-394. [NTA 34, 1179]; = ID., *Evangelica II*, 1991, 43-48 (additional note, 48). → Goulder 1989

1989b Marc 6,14-16 et par. — *ETL* 65 (1989) 105-109. [NTA 34, 143]; = ID., *Evangelica II*, 1991, 325-329 (note additionnelle, 329). → Rolland 1989b

1990a Q[Mt] and Q[Lk] and the Reconstruction of Q. — *ETL* 66 (1990) 385-390. [NTA 35, 1121]; = ID., *Evangelica II*, 1991, 475-480 (additional note, 480). → 1988a/95; → Kosch 1989a-b, Sato 1988

1990b The Two-Source Hypothesis. — DUNGAN, D.L. (ed.), *The Interrelations of the Gospels*, 1990, 3-22. Esp. 7-8.19-22 [argument of order]; 10-11 [minor agreements]; 12-14 [doublets]; 14-18 [different solutions]. → Dungan 1990a

1990c The Two-Source Hypothesis. Textual Discussion. Matthew 4:23–5:2 and the Matthean Composition of 4:23–11:1. — *Ibid.*, 23-46. Esp. 26-36: "Analysis of Mt 4:23–5:2"; 36-38: "The setting of the sermon in Q"; 38-39: "The composition of Mt 4:23–8:17"; 40-42: "Mt 4:23–11:1 and the relative order of Mark"; 42-46: "The doublets of Mt 4:25 and 12:15(-16)".

1990d Response to the Multiple-Stage Hypothesis. I. The Introduction to the Feeding Story. Mt 14:13-14; Mk 6:30-34; Lk 9:10-11. II. The Healing of the Leper. Mt 8:2-4; Mk 1:40-44; Lk 5:12-14. III. The Eschatological Discourse. — *Ibid.*, 81-93, 94-107, 108-124. Esp. 81-82 [14,13-14]; 96-104 [8,2-4]; 108-117: "A new debate: Q or Proto-Luke" [Q 3,7-9; 7,18-35; 17,27]; 118-124: "Mark 13 and Proto-Matthew" [10,17-20; 24,1-3.9-14.23-25.29-31.34.36]. → 1984c; → Boismard 1979, 1981, 1990b, 1990c, McNicol 1990a
   The Eschatological Discourse. [1990, 108-124] — ID., *Evangelica II*, 1991, 493-509 (additional note, 510). Esp. 494-502; 503-509.

1990e John and the Synoptics: Response to P. Borgen. — *Ibid.*, 438-450. Esp. 442-447 [12,1-8/Jn 5,1-18]; 447-450 [21,10-12/Jn 2,12-22] John 5,1-18 and the Gospel of Mark. — ID., *Evangelica II*, 1991, 699-711 (additional note, 711-712). Esp. 703-708; 708-710; = BORGEN, P., *Early Christianity*, 1996, 159-173. Esp. 163-170; 170-172. → Borgen 1990a-b, 1996

1990f Note on Patristic Testimonies. — *Ibid.*, 605-606. → Merkel 1990, Orchard 1990b

1990g Synoptic Problem. — BROWN, R.E., et al. (eds.), *The New Jerome Biblical Commentary*, 1990, 587-595. Esp. 590-592: "The Q Source". La questione sinottica. — BROWN, R.E., *Nuovo grande commentario biblico*, 1997, 765-775. Esp. 769-771.

1991a *Evangelica II. 1982-1991. Collected Essays*, ed. F. Van Segbroeck (BETL, 99). Leuven: University Press / Peeters, 1991, XIX-874 p. (Appendix *Evangelica* [1982], 791-808). → 1982b-d, 1983b, 1984b-e, 1985a-b, 1986a.c.f, 1987a-b, 1988c-e, 1989a-b, 1990a.d-e, 1991c-f.h; → 1982a
E. BEST, *ExpT* 103 (1992-93) 103; R.F. COLLINS, *LouvSt* 17 (1992) 73-74; E. CUVILLIER, *ETR* 67 (1992) 461-462; T.C. DE KRUIJF, *Bijdragen* 55 (1997) 85-86; A. GARCÍA MORENO, *ScriptTheol* 24 (1992) 1088-1089; M. GOULDER, *NT* 35 (1993) 199-202; J. MUDDIMAN, *JTS* 44 (1993) 658-659; J. PONTHOT, *RTL* 25 (1994) 370-371; S.E. PORTER, *FilolNT* 5 (1992) 213-214.

1991b *The Minor Agreements in a Horizontal-Line Synopsis* (Studiorum Novi Testamenti Auxilia, 15). Leuven: University Press / Peeters, 1991. 103 p. → 1974a
R.F. COLLINS, *LouvSt* 17 (1992) 74-75; E. CUVILLIER, *ETR* 67 (1992) 461-462; L. DEVILLERS, *RThom* 93 (1993) 319; J.K. ELLIOTT, *NT* 34 (1992) 412-413; A. FUCHS, *SNTU* 16 (1991) 204; V. FUSCO, *RivBib* 41 (1993) 100; X. JACQUES, *NRT* 115 (1993) 909-910; J.-F. RACINE, *LavalTP* 49 (1993) 376; J. SMIT SIBINGA, *NTT* 47 (1994) 248; T. SÖDING, *TRev* 90 (1994) 380-381.

1991c Luke 14,1-6. Lukan Composition and Q Saying. — BUSSMANN, C. - RADL, W. (eds.), *Der Treue Gottes trauen*. FS G. Schneider, 1991, 243-263. Esp. 243-246 [Lk 14,1-6: Q?]; 246-251 [Lk 14,3: minor agreement]; 251-256; 257-260 [Q 14,5]; = ID., *Evangelica II*, 1991, 183-203 (additional note, 203-204). Esp. 183-187; 187-193; 193-199.199-203.

1991d The Minor Agreements. Note on a Test Case. A Response to W.R. Farmer. — *ETL* 67 (1991) 73-81. Esp. 74-75 [16,21]; 75-77 [17,22]; 78-80 [20,17-19]. [NTA 36, 121]; = ID., *Evangelica II*, 1991, 49-58 (additional note, 58). Esp. 50-51; 51-54; 54-58. → W.R. Farmer 1990d

1991e The Minor Agreements and Proto-Mark. A Response to H. Koester. — *ETL* 67 (1991) 82-94. Esp. 83-89: "The minor agreements" [17,18; 19,24; 28,5]. [NTA 36, 168]; = ID., *Evangelica II*, 1991, 59-73. Esp. 60-68. → Koester 1990a

1991f The Minor Agreements and the Two-Source Theory. — ID., *Evangelica II*, 1991, 3-42. Esp. 5-9: "Current solutions"; 10-28: "Significant agreements" [9,20; 13,11; 17,17; 26,68]; 29-40: "Independent redaction" [14,13-14; 17,1-9] (additional note, 41-42); = STRECKER, G. (ed.), *Minor Agreements*, 1993, 25-63. Esp. 27-31; 32-50; 50-61. → 1987a, 1991g

1991g A Symposium on the Minor Agreements. — *ETL* 67 (1991) 361-372. [NTA 36, 1242] → 1991f; → Ennulat 1994, Fendler 1991, Strecker 1993*

1991h Note on the Siglum Q. — ID., *Evangelica II*, 1991, 474. → 1978, 1979c

1992a & VERHEYDEN, J. - VAN SEGBROECK, F., et al., *The Gospel of Mark. A Cumulative Bibliography* (BETL, 102; COBRA, 3). Leuven: University Press / Peeters; Brussel: Koninklijke Academie voor Wetenschappen, Letteren en Schone Kunsten van België, 1992, XII-717 p. Esp. 647: "Mark and Q"; 648: "Mark and Matthew".

1992b John and the Synoptics: 1975-1990. — DENAUX, A. (ed.), *John and the Synoptics*, 1992, 3-62. Esp. 16-35: "John and Matthew" [10,24-25; 18,3; 21,5; 26,39.42.52; 28,9-10]. → 1977b; → Lindars 1981b, D.M. Smith 1963, 1992a, H.F.D. Sparks 1952b

1993a The International Q Project. — *ETL* 69 (1993) 221-225. Esp. 222-224: "Narrative elements in Q"; 224-225: "The reconstructed text" [Q 6,20-21; 10,4]. [NTA 38, 135] → 1988a/95; → IQP 1992

1993b Literary Criticism, Old and New. — FOCANT, C. (ed.), *The Synoptic Gospels*, 1993, 11-38. Esp. 13-16: "Matthew and Mark"; 16-18: "The minor agreements and Lukan redaction"; 19-27: "The passion and resurrection narratives"; 27-35: "The sayings source Q".

1993c Gospel, Genre of. — METZGER, B.M. - COOGAN, M.D. (eds.), *The Oxford Companion to the Bible*, 1993, 258-259.

1994a The Historical Jesus. Reflections on an Inventory. — *ETL* 70 (1994) 221-234. Esp. 222-224 [Q]; 226-229 [Gospel of Peter]. [NTA 39, 102] → R.E. Brown 1994a, J.D. Crossan 1991a

1994b Gospel Issues in the Passion Narratives. Critical Note on a New Commentary. — *Ibid.*, 406-416. Esp. 410-415 [minor agreements]. [NTA 39, 1427] → R.E. Brown 1994a

1994c Luke 10:25-28: A Foreign Body in Luke? — PORTER, S.E., et al. (eds.), *Crossing the Boundaries*. FS M.D. Goulder, 1994, 149-165. Esp. 150-157 [νομικός]; 157-164: "Agreements and disagreements". → 1995a

1995a The Minor Agreements and Lk 10,25-28. — *ETL* 71 (1995) 151-160. Esp. 152-154 [22,34-40/Mk]. [NTA 40, 231] → 1994c; → Gundry 1995, Kiilunen 1989

1995b Note on Mt 28,9-10. — *Ibid.*, 161-165. [NTA 40, 180] → R.E. Brown 1994a, Kühschelm 1993

1995c Urmarcus révisé. La théorie synoptique de M.-É. Boismard nouvelle manière. — *Ibid.*, 166-175. Esp. 168-169: "La source Q". [NTA 40, 187] → Boismard 1994

1995d Jean 4,46-54. Une leçon de méthode. — *Ibid.*, 176-184. Esp. 176-181 [Q 7,1-10/Jn 4,46-54]. [NTA 40, 264r] → 1984e; → Boismard 1992c, Landis 1994

1995e Q: From Source to Gospel. — *Ibid.*, 421-430. Esp. 422-424; 424-427 [Q 7,22]; 427-429 [Thomas]. [NTA 40, 1446]

1995f The Divorce Saying in Q 16:18. — *LouvSt* 20 (1995) 201-218. Esp. 201-203: "The study of the divorce sayings"; 204-206: "The reconstruction of the Q saying"; 206-211 [5,32]; 212-218 [Q 16,18]. [NTA 40, 237] → 1996a

1995g The Minor Agreements and Q. — PIPER, R.A. (ed.), *The Gospel Behind the Gospels*, 1995, 49-72. Esp. 54-64: "Mark, not Q, in Luke's central section" [16,6; 18,6; 22,34-40; 24,17-18]; 65-71: "The beginning of Q" [3,1-6.13-17]. → Kloppenborg 1990e, J.M. Robinson 1995b, Schlosser 1983a

1995h Assessment. — FLEDDERMANN, H.T., *Mark and Q*, 1995, 261-307. Esp. 268-270 [Q 7,27]; 270-271 [Q 3,16-17]; 271-275 [Q 11,14-15.17-26]; 275-277 [Q 12,10]; 277 [Q 11,33; 12,2.31; 19,26]; 277-278 [Q 13,18-19]; 279-280 [Q 10,2-16]; 280-281 [Q 11,16.29-32]; 282-283 [Q 14,27]; 283-284 [Q 17,33]; 284-285 [Q 12,8-9]; 285 [Q 10,16]; 286 [Q 11,23]; 286-287 [Q 17,1-2]; 288 [Q 14,34-35; 16,18]; 289 [Q 13,30]; 289-290 [Q 17,6]; 290-291 [Q 11,10]; 291-292 [Q 11,43]; 292-293 [Q 12,11-12]; 293-294 [Q 12,51-53]; 294 [Q 17,23]; 295 [Q 16,17]; 295-296 [Q 12,40]. → 1996d; → Verheyden 1996

1996a De echtscheidingslogia in de evangeliën. — *Academiae Analecta* (Brussel) 58 (1996) 21-42. → 1958, 1972c, 1995f; → Baumert 1992

1996b The First Synoptic Pericope: The Appearance of John the Baptist in Q? — *ETL* 72 (1996) 41-74. Esp. 41-46: "A synoptic source diff. Mk 1,1-6"; 46-51: "Retrospect"; 52-70: "The minor agreements"; 70-74: "How Q begins". [NTA 41, 182] → Catchpole 1992a, A. Fuchs 1995, Kloppenborg 1990e, Lambrecht 1992, J.M. Robinson 1995b, N. Walter 1992

1996c The Sayings of Jesus in 1 Corinthians. — BIERINGER, R. (ed.), *The Corinthian Correspondence* (BETL, 125), Leuven: University Press / Peeters, 1996, 141-176. Esp. 166-171. → 1986f; → Baumert 1992, D. Wenham 1985

1996d The Sayings Source Q and the Gospel of Mark. — CANCIK, H. - LICHTENBERGER, H. — SCHÄFER, P. (eds.), *Geschichte - Tradition - Reflexion. Festschrift für Martin Hengel zum 70. Geburtstag*. III: *Frühes Christentum*, ed. H. Lichtenberger, Tübingen: Mohr, 1996, 125-145. Esp. 127-131 [Lk 11,21-22; 13,30; 17,2.33(Q)]; 131-139: "Redactional Q" [Q 7,27; 11,10.29-30; 12,40; 14,27/Mk]; 139-142: "Mark and Q". → 1995h; → Fleddermann 1995

1997a Goulder and the Minor Agreements. — *ETL* 73 (1997) 84-93. → Goodacre 1996

1997b Note on Q 4,1-2. — *Ibid.*, 94-102. → IQP (*Documenta Q 4,1-13.16*)

1997c Notes on the Argument(s) from Order. — *Ibid.*, 386-392. → Neville 1994

1997d Q 6,20b-21; 7,22 and Isaiah 61. — TUCKETT, C.M. (ed.), *The Scriptures in the Gospels*, 1997, 27-64. Esp. 29-45 [Q 6,20-21]; 45-62 [Q 7,22]. → Broer 1986a, Fitzmyer 1995, Hengel 1987, É. Puech 1992, J.M. Robinson 1992b, 1995b

1998    The Sources of Matthew: Annotations to U. Luz's Commentary. — *ETL* 74 (1998) 109-126. → Luz 1985a/97

**NEL, C.**

1994    & VAN AARDE, A.G., Die etiek van Jesus in die lig van Q: Eskatologies of wysheidsteologies begrond? [The ethics of Jesus in the Light of Q: Rooted in eschatology or sapiential theology?] — *HervTS* 50 (1994) 936-952. [NTA 39, 1414]

1995    & VAN AARDE, A.G., Tendense in die studie van die kultuur van oraliteit: Implikasies vir die verstaan van die Matteusevangelie. [Tendencies in the study of orality: Implications for the understanding of the gospel of Matthew]. — *HervTS* 51 (1995) 409-437. [NTA 40, 806]

**NELLER, Kenneth V.**

1983    *The Gospel of Thomas and the Earliest Texts of the Synoptic Gospels*. Diss. St. Andrews, 1983, 351 p. (R.McL. Wilson).

**NELLESSEN, Ernst**

1969a    *Das Kind und seine Mutter. Struktur und Verkündigung des 2. Kapitels im Matthäusevangelium* (SBS, 39). Stuttgart: Katholisches Bibelwerk, 1969, 160 p. Esp. 13-16: "Die Stellung der Kindheitsgeschichten bei Matthäus und Lukas innerhalb des neutestamentlichen Schrifttums"; 17-21: "Matthäus 1-2 im Vergleich mit Lukas 1-2"; 22-28: "Matthäus 2 im Ganzen des Matthäusevangeliums"; 29-57: "Der Anteil des Evangelisten an der Gestalt des 2. Kapitels"; 58-80: "Die literarische Art"; 81-97: "Die theologische Aussage"; 97-112: "Jungfrauengeburt – ein Theologumenon?"; 113-125: "Der Bezug zur Geschichte"; 126-143: "Zur Verkündigung heute und morgen". [NTA 14, p. 350] J.M. ALONSO, *EphMar* 20 (1970) 415; 21 (1971) 340; J.A. DE ALDAMA, *ArchTeolGran* 33 (1970) 326-327; T. EGIDO, *EstJos* 26 (1972) 110; R. GAUTHIER, *CahJos* 22 (1974) 265; P.M. LUSTRISSIMI, *Marianum* 34 (1972) 288-289; C. MATEOS, *EstAgust* 5 (1970) 418; J. MURPHY-O'CONNOR, *RB* 80 (1973) 282-285; J.M. TISON, *Bijdragen* 32 (1971) 196-197.

1969b    Die Verkündigung der Menschwerdung in Mt 2. — BROSCH, H.J. - HASENFUSS, J. (eds.), *Jungfrauengeburt gestern und heute* (Mariologische Studien, 4), Essen: Driewer, 1969, 185-204.

1969c    Zu den Kindheitsgeschichten bei Matthäus und Lukas. Bericht über neuere deutschsprachige Literatur. — *TTZ* 78 (1969) 305-309. [NTA 14, 851]

1975    Tradition und Schrift in der Perikope von der Erwählung des Mattias (Apg 1,15-26). — *BZ* 19 (1975) 205-218. Esp. 207-211: "Die Tradition vom Ende des Judas und vom Blutacker" [27,3-10]. [NTA 20, 150]

**NELSON, Diedrick A.**

1975    An Exposition of Matthew 20:1-16. — *Interpr* 29 (1975) 288-292.

**NELSON, Jimmie L.**

1992    Preaching Values in the Sermon on the Mount (Matthew 5-7). — *SWJT* 35 (1992) 28-33. [NTA 37, 135]

**NELSON, Neil D., Jr.**

1995    "This Generation" in Matt 24:34: A Literary Critical Perspective. — *JEvTS* 38 (1995) 369-385. Esp. 370-373: "Characterization of the disciples"; 373-377: "Characterization of 'this generation'"; 377-380 [24,4-28]; 380-384: "'This generation'". [NTA 41, 217]

**NELSON, Peter K.**

1993    Luke 22:29-30 and the Time Frame for Dining and Ruling. — *TyndB* 44 (1993) 351-361. Esp. 353-355 [19,28]. [NTA 38, 842]

1994    *Leadership and Discipleship. A Study of Luke 22:24-30* (SBL DS, 138). Atlanta, GA: Scholars, 1994, XVII-330 p. Esp. 173-179: "Sources for Luke 22:28-30".

**NEMBACH, Ulrich**

1970 Ehescheidung nach alttestamentlichem und jüdischem Recht. — *TZ* 26 (1970) 161-171. Esp. 169-171 [5,32; 19,9]. [NTA 17, 514]

**NÉMETH, Tamás**

1985 Ethics in the Sermon on the Mount. — *TSzem* 28 (1985) 146-148.

**[Neotestamentica et Patristica]**

1962* *Neotestamentica et Patristica. Eine Freundesgabe, Herrn Professor Dr. Oscar Cullmann zu seinem 60. Geburtstag überreicht* (SupplNT, 6). Leiden: Brill, 1962, XIX-330 p. → P. Benoit, Eltester, Héring, J. Jeremias, Munck, Riesenfeld 1961

**NEPPER-CHRISTENSEN, Poul**

1958 *Das Matthäusevangelium ein judenchristliches Evangelium?* (Acta theologica Danica, 1). Aarhus: Universitetsforlaget, 1958, 231 p. Esp. 13-36: "Forschungsstatus"; 37-75: "Altkirchliche Traditionen über Matthäus und das Matthäusevangelium"; 76-100: "Ist unser kanonisches Matthäusevangelium die Übersetzung einer semitischen Urschrift?"; 101-135: "Die sprachlichen Verhältnisse zu Beginn unserer Zeitrechnung"; 136-162: "Der Erfüllungsbegriff im Matthäusevangelium, seine Gestaltung und seine Rolle"; 163-179: "Die typologische Betrachtungsweise im Matthäusevangelium"; 180-201: "Der jüdische Horizont des Matthäusevangeliums"; 202-207: "Das Matthäusevangelium ein judenchristliches Evangelium?". [NTA 4, p. 97] — Diss. Aarhus, 1956 (J. Munck). → Dermience 1985, Gerhardsson 1959 P. BENOIT, *RB* 66 (1959) 438-440; W.D. DAVIES, *JBL* 79 (1960) 88-91; W.G. KÜMMEL, *TLZ* 90 (1965) 114-115; X. LÉON-DUFOUR, *RSR* 50 (1962) 98-101; F. MONTAGNINI, *BibOr* 3 (1961) 114; B. NOACK, *DanskTeolTids* 22 (1959) 54-57.

1969 Utugtsklausulen og Josef i Matthaeusevangeliet. [The fornication clause and Joseph in the gospel of Matthew] — *SEÅ* 34 (1969) 122-146. Esp. 122-123 [5,31-32; 19,9]; 123-124 [15,19]; 124 [21,31]; 124-133 [5,31-32]; 133-138 [19,3-12]; 139-146 [1,18-25]. [NTA 15, 493]

1985 Die Taufe im Matthäusevangelium. Im Lichte der Traditionen über Johannes den Täufer. — *NTS* 31 (1985) 189-207. Esp. 189-192: "Verschiedene 'Bilder' vom Täufer"; 192-195: "Die Täufertraditionen im Matthäusevangelium"; 195-198: "Die Situation der Matthäusgemeinde"; 198-201: "Jesu Taufe"; 201-203: "Die Taufe der Matthäusgemeinde". [NTA 30, 103]

1988 *Matthæusevangeliet; en kommentar* [The gospel of Matthew; a commentary]. Aarhus: ANIS, 1988, 323 p. H. KVALBEIN, *TidsTeolKirk* 60 (1989) 58; H. SIMONSEN, *DanskTeolTids* 52 (1989) 149-151.

1990 Hvem var den discipel, som Jesus elskede? [Who was the disciple whom Jesus loved?] — *DanskTeolTids* 53 (1990) 81-105. Esp. 84-87 [20,20-23]; 96-101; 104-105. [NTA 35, 187]

1991 Apostlen Matthæus og Matthæusevangeliet. [The apostle Matthew and Matthew's gospel] — *DanskTeolTids* 54 (1991) 95-112. Esp. 95-101 [Jerome]; 102-103 [10,2-4]; 103-106.110-112 [Papias]; 108-109 [Q]; 109-111 [9,9]. [NTA 36, 701]

1995 Matth 10,23 - et crux interpretum? — *DanskTeolTids* 58 (1995) 161-175. [NTA 40, 829]

**NERBURN, Kent Michael**

1980 *John the Baptist according to Matthew: An Exercise in Visual Theology*. Diss. Graduate Theol. Union, 1980, 90 p. (J. Dillenberger). — *DissAbstr* 40 (1980-81) 4074; *SBT* 11 (1981) 233-234.

**NEREPARAMPIL, Lucius**

1984a Jesus and the Nations. — *Jeevadhara* 14/80 (1984) 136-150. Esp. 138-144 [2,1-12; 5,43-48; 6,7-13; 8,5-13; 10,5; 12,14-21; 15,21-28]. [NTA 29, 64]

1984b The Theology of Redemption in the Synoptic Gospels. — *Bible Bhashyam* 10 (1984) 149-159. Esp. 150-151 [20,28]. [NTA 29, 918]

**NESTLE, Erwin**

1950 *Novum Testamentum Graece cum apparatu critico curavit †D. Eberhard Nestle novis* *curis elaboravit D. Erwin Nestle.* Stuttgart: Württembergische Bibelanstalt, [20]1950, [21]1952, 110*-671 p. Esp. 1-83: "Κατὰ Μαϑϑαῖον". → K. Aland [Nestle-Aland 1956]

**NETTELHORST, Robin P.**

1988    The Genealogy of Jesus. — *JEvTS* 31 (1988) 169-172. [NTA 33, 116]

**NEUDECKER, Reinhard**

1983    The Sermon on the Mount as a Witness to Inculturation. — ROEST CROLLIUS, A.A. (ed.), *Bible and Inculturation*, 3, Roma: Pont. Greg. Univ., 1983, 73-89.

1984    Wie steht es heute mit den Worten Jesu zur Ehescheidung? — *Greg* 65 (1984) 719-724. [NTA 29, 496r] → Marucci 1982

1994    Das "Ehescheidungsgesetz" von Dtn 24,1-4 nach altjüdischer Auslegung. Ein Beitrag zum Verständnis der neutestamentlichen Aussagen zur Ehescheidung. — *Bib* 75 (1994) 350-387. Esp. 384-387: "Anhang: Dtn 28,1-4 bei Matthäus". [NTA 39, 1202]

**NEUFELD, Vernon**

1963    *The Earliest Christian Confessions* (New Testament Tools and Studies, 5). Leiden: Brill, 1963, XIII-166 p. Esp. 108-117: "The homologia in the synoptic gospels".

**NEUGEBAUER, Fritz**

1972    *Jesus der Menschensohn. Ein Beitrag zur Klärung der Wege historischer Wahrheitsfindung im Bereich der Evangelien* (Arbeiten zur Theologie, 50). Stuttgart: Calwer, 1972, 72 p. Esp. 39-40 [3,11-12]; 45-47 [11,4-6].

1974    Die Davidssohnfrage (Mark xii.35-7 parr.) und der Menschensohn. — *NTS* 21 (1974-75) 81-108. Esp. 82-90: "Verdeutlichung der Texte"; 91-96: "Davidssohn und Menschensohn – ihre semantische Analogie"; 96-101: "Ihre messianologische Differenz"; 101-106: "Die Herkunft der Davidssohnfrage". [NTA 19, 563]

1985    Die dargebotene Wange und Jesu Gebot der Feindesliebe. Erwägungen zu Lk 6,27-36 / Mt 5,38-48. — *TLZ* 110 (1985) 865-876. [NTA 30, 1103]

1986a    *Jesu Versuchung. Wegentscheidung am Anfang.* Tübingen: Mohr, 1986, VI-120 p. Esp. 7-18: "Jesu Versuchung als Teil der Jesusüberlieferung"; 29-32: "Das dreifache der Versuchung in Mt 4,1-11 par."; 33-38 [4,1-2]; 39-52 [4,3-4]; 53-62 [4,4]; 63-68 [4,3-7]; 69-74 [4,7]; 75-88 [4,8-10]; 99-114: "Jesu Versuchung als außerordentliche Erfahrung"; 115-120: "Jesu Versuchung – die Entscheidung am Anfang".
         R. DAL ZILIO, *Sal* 50 (1988) 228; W. VOGLER, *TLZ* 113 (1988) 437-438.

1986b    Die wunderbare Speisung (Mk 6,30-44 parr.) und Jesu Identität. — *KerDog* 32 (1986) 254-277. Esp. 270-273 [14,13-21]. [NTA 31, 608]

**NEUHÄUSLER, Engelbert**

1962    *Anspruch und Antwort Gottes. Zur Lehre von den Weisungen innerhalb der synoptischen Jesusverkündigung.* Düsseldorf: Patmos, 1962, 263 p. Esp. 17-26 [11,25-30]; 45-52 [5,43-48]; 53-55 [6,25-34]; 56-58 [7,16-20]; 58-63 [6,1-6.16-18]; 72-74 [25,14-30]; 80-81 [6,33]; 81 [22,1-14]; 81-86 [11,12]; 86-89 [19,11-12]; 89-91 [13,44-46]; 93-95 [6,19-21]; 101-103 [6,24]; 103-104 [25,14-30]; 104-106 [21,28-32]; 114-118 [22,34-40]; 119-120 [19,16-26]; 125-127 [3,2]; 134-135 [18,3]; 138-140 [11,25-30]; 141-169 [5,1-12]; 170-171 [6,19-21]; 187-190 [10,37-39]; 194-197 [7,13-14]; 199-200 [8,11-12]; 200-202 [11,21-24]; 209-210 [10,42]; 210-212 [25,31-46]; 216-218 [22,11-13]; 225-234 [25,1-13].
         *Exigence de Dieu et morale chrétienne. Études sur les enseignements moraux de la prédication de Jésus dans les Synoptiques,* trans. F. Schanen (LD, 70). Paris: Cerf, 1971, 369 p. Esp. 22-32; 62-74; 74-78; 89,82; 82-89; 103-106; 113-115; 115-116; 117-124; 124-127; 128-131; 134-136; 143-146; 146-147; 147-152; 163-170; 170-173; 179-182; 196-198; 198-200; 203-245; 247-249; 272-276; 283-286; 291-292; 292-295; 304-305; 305-308; 315-317; 331-341.

1970    Mit welchem Maßstab mißt Gott die Menschen? Deutung zweier Jesussprüche. — *BibLeb* 11 (1970) 104-113. Esp. 105-108 [13,12; 25,29]; 108-111 [7,1-2]. [NTA 15, 508]

1971    Jesu Stellung zum Sabbat. Versuch einer Interpretation. — *BibLeb* 12 (1971) 1-16. Esp. 13-15 [12,5-7]. [NTA 16, 523]

**NEUMANN, Charles William**

1962    *The Virgin Mary in the Works of Saint Ambrose* (Paradosis, 17). Freiburg/Schw: Universitätsverlag, 1962, XVI-280 p. Esp. 91-100: "Ambrose on Mt. 1:24"; 240-244 [1,18]; 244-248 [1,25]; 248-251 [1,19]; 252 [1,24].

**NEUMANN, Frederick**

1983    *The Proper Self-Concern. Matthew* (Selective Homiletical Commentary on the New Testament, 1). Allison Park, PA: Pickwick, 1983, 337 p.

**NEUSNER, Jacob**

1976    'First cleanse the inside'. The 'Halakhic' Background of a Controversy-Saying. [23,25-26] — *NTS* 22 (1975-76) 486-495. [NTA 21, 87]

1993a   *A Rabbi Talks with Jesus: An Intermillennial Interfaith Exchange.* New York – London: Doubleday, 1993, XVIII-154 p. [NTA 37, p. 441]
    R.J. HUTCHINSON, What the Rabbi Taught Me About Jesus. — *ChrTod* 37 (1993) 27-29. [NTA 38, 743r]
    P. TRUDINGER, The Contemporary Rabbi and Jesus. — *St Mark's Review* (Canberra) 157 (1994) 19-23. [NTA 39, 131r]

1993b   *Are There Really Tannaitic Parallels to the Gospels? A Refutation of Morton Smith* (South Florida Studies in the History of Judaism, 80). Atlanta, GA: Scholars, 1993, XIII-186 p. → M. Smith 1951

1995    → Chilton 1995

**NEVILLE, David J.**

1994    *Arguments from Order in Synoptic Source Criticism. A History and Critique* (New Gospel Studies, 7). Macon, GA: Mercer, 1994, XIV-270 p. Esp. 14-38 [J.J. Griesbach]; 39-58 [K. Lachmann]; 60-82 [F.H. Woods]; 83-94 [W.C. Allen]; 94-103 [J.C. Hawkins]; 105-112 [H.G. Jameson]; 112-123 [J.F. Springer]; 124-146 [B.H. Streeter]; 148-167 [B.C. Butler]; 168-189 [W.R. Farmer]; 190-222 [C.M. Tuckett]. → Neirynck 1997c

**NEVIUS, Richard C.**

1963    A Reply to Dr. Dunkerley. [26,16-17] — *ExpT* 74 (1962-63) 255. [NTA 8, 141] → Dunkerley 1963

1964    *The Divine Names in Mark* (Studies and Documents, 25). Salt Lake City, UT: Univ. of Utah Press, 1964, V-84 p. Esp. 64-68 [Codex 1510: E. Schneider].

1967    *The Divine Names in the Gospels. Appendices D and E: Studies of Codex 1,6 in the Gennadian Library and Codex 1867 (Catholic and Pauline Epistles) by Jacob Geerlings* (Studies and Documents, 30). Salt Lake City, UT: Univ. of Utah Press, 1967, V-135 p. Esp. 42-59: "The divine names in St. Matthew" ['Ιησοῦς; Χριστός; Κύριος]; 104-109 [apparatus criticus]; 117-120 [lect. 1679: Geerlings].

**NEW, David S.**

1991a   The Injunctive Future and Existential Injunctions in the New Testament. — *JSNT* 44 (1991) 113-127. Esp. 118-119.125-127. [NTA 23, 1142]; = PORTER, S.E. – EVANS, C.A. (eds.), *New Testament Text and Language. A Sheffield Reader* (The Biblical Seminar, 44), Sheffield: JSOT, 1997, 130-144. Esp. 135-136.141-144.

1991b   The Occurrence of αὐτῶν in Matthew 13.15 and the Process of Text Assimilation. — *NTS* 37 (1991) 478-480. [NTA 36, 152]

1993    *Old Testament Quotations in the Synoptic Gospels, and the Two-Document Hypothesis* (SBL Septuagint and Cognate Studies, 37). Atlanta, GA: Scholars, 1993, VII-140 p. Esp. 11-22: "Holtzmann's argument"; 23-37: "Grouping citations in the synoptics by text-type" [survey of research]; 39-87: "Quotations appearing in more than one synoptic gospel" [3,3; 4,4.6.7.10; 11,10; 15,4.8-9; 19,4.5.18-19; 21,13.42; 22,32.37.39.44; 26,31]; 89-115: "Quotations appearing in only one synoptic gospel" [1,23; 2,15.18; 4,15-16; 5,21.27.31.33.38.43; 8,17; 9,13; 12,7.18-21; 13,14-15.35; 21,5.16]. — Diss.

McMaster University, Toronto, Ont., 1990 (S.R. Westerholm).
L. COPE, *JBL* 114 (1995) 516-517; T.R. HATINA, *JSNT* 56 (1994) 121; F. NEIRYNCK, *ETL* 70 (1994) 167-168.

### NEWELL, Jane E.

1972 & NEWELL, Raymond R., The Parable of the Wicked Tenants. [21,33-41] — *NT* 14 (1972) 226-237. [NTA 17, 541] → Dodd 1935, J. Jeremias 19≤7

### NEWLANDS, George McLeod

1978 *Hilary of Poitiers: A Study in Theological Method* (EHS, XXIII/108). Bern–Frankfurt/M: Lang, 1978, IX-216 p. Esp. 42-99: "The Law and the Gospel: The early period: the commentary on St. Matthew". — Diss. Edinburgh, 1970 (T.F. Torrance – D.F. Wright).

### NEWMAN, Barclay M.

1970 Towards a Translation of "the Son of Man" in the Gospels. — *BTrans* 21 (1970) 141-146. [NTA 15, 476]

1974 Translating "the Kingdom of God" and "the Kingdom of Heaven" in the New Testament. [3,2; 4,23; 5,3.19.20] — *BTrans* 25 (1974) 401-404. [NTA 19, 448]

1975 Some Translational Notes on the Beatitudes. Matthew 5.1-12. — *BTrans* 26 (1975) 106-120. [NTA 19, 947]

1976a Matthew 1.1-18: Some Comments and a Suggested Restructuring. — *BTrans* 27 (1976) 209-212. [NTA 20, 771]

1976b The Kingdom of God/Heaven in the Gospel of Matthew. — *Ibid.*, 427-434. [NTA 21, 372]

1980 Some Problems with "Us" and "We". [8,25] — *BTrans* 31 (1980) 441-443. [NTA 25, 476]

1983 To Teach or Not to Teach (A Comment on Matthew 13.1-3). — *BTrans* 34 (1983) 139-143. [NTA 27, 922]

1988 & STINE, P.C., *A Translator's Handbook on the Gospel of Matthew* (Helps for Translators). London – New York – Stuttgart: United Bible Societies, 1988, X-939 p. [NTA 33, p. 251] → Bratcher 1981
C.M. TUCKETT, *JSNT* 39 (1990) 120.

### NEWMAN, Robert C.

1981 The Synoptic Problem! A Proposal for Handling Both Internal & External Evidence. — *WestTJ* 43 (1981) 132-151. [NTA 26, 78]

1982 Jesus' Self-Understanding according to the So-Called Q Material. — SKILTON, J.H. — LADLEY, C.A. (eds.), *The New Testament Student and His Field* (The New Student, 5), Phillipsburg, NJ: Presbyterian and Reformed Publ. Co., 1982, 70-97. Esp. 73-84: "Jesus' understanding of his person"; 84-88: "Jesus' understanding of his mission and message"; 88-94: "Jesus' understanding of his destiny".

### NEWPORT, Kenneth G.C.

1990 A Note on the "Seat of Moses" (Matthew 23:2). — *AndrUnS* 28 (1990) 53-58. [NTA 35, 147]

1995 *The Sources and* Sitz im Leben *of Matt 23* (JSNT SS, 117). Sheffield: JSOT, 1995, 205 p. Esp. 15-60: "Compositional theories"; 61-79: "The *Sitz im Leben* of Matthew 23"; 80-116: "Pre-70 CE Jewish customs and practices in Matthew 23"; 157-181: "Links between Matthew 23 and other material in the Gospel". [NTA 40, p. 344] — Diss. Oxford, 1988 (E.P. Sanders).
K.A. BARTA, *CBQ* 59 (1997) 389-390.

### NEYREY, Jerome H.

1981 Decision Making in the Early Church. The Case of the Canaanite Woman (Mt 15:21-28). — *SE* 33 (1981) 373-378. [NTA 26, 475]

1982    The Thematic Use of Isaiah 42,1-4 in Matthew 12. — *Bib* 63 (1982) 457-473. [NTA 27, 519]

1985    *Christ Is Community. The Christologies of the New Testament* (Good News Studies, 13). Wilmington, DE: Glazier, 1985, 295 p. Esp. 65-104: "The christologies in Matthew's gospel".

1988a   *The Resurrection Stories* (Zacchaeus Studies: New Testament). Wilmington, DE: Glazier, 1988, 109 p. [NTA 33, p. 252]

1988b   → Malina 1988a

1995    Loss of Wealth, Loss of Family and Loss of Honour. The Cultural Context of the Original Makarisms in Q. — ESLER, P.F. (ed.), *Modelling Early Christianity*, 1995, 139-158. Esp. 144-148: "Honour and the Matthean makarisms"; 149-153: "Loss of family in the Q source".

### NG, E.Y.L.

1987    The Structure of the Sermon on the Mount. [Chinese] — *CGST Journal* (Hong Kong) 3 (1987) 57-72. [NTA 32, 115]

### NGALAME, Edward E.

1989    *Peace according to Matthew and the Jewish Teaching Confronted with the Bakossi Tradition*. Diss. Pont. Univ. Urbaniana, Roma, 1989, XIV-230 p. (M. Erbetta). Esp. 11-91: "Peace in the gospel of Matthew" [5,1-12.23-24; 6,12; 10,12-13.34-36].

### NGAYIHEMBAKO, Samuel

1994    *Les temps de la fin. Approche exégétique de l'eschatologie du Nouveau Testament* (Le monde de la Bible, 29). Genève: Labor et Fides, 1994, 430 p. Esp. 169-189: "Le vocabulaire de la 'fin' dans l'évangile de Matthieu". — Diss. Genève, 1993 (F. Bovon).

### NICHOLL, Donald

1982    Discipline for a New Community – The Gospel according to St Matthew. — *Furrow* 33 (1982) 67-75. [NTA 26, 837]; = DRURY, R. (ed.), *The New Testament as Personal Reading*, Springfield, IL: Templegate, 1983, 28-41.

### NICKELS, Peter

1967    *Targum and New Testament. A Bibliography together with a New Testament Index*. Roma: Pontifical Biblical Institute, 1967, XI-88 p. Esp. 15-23.

### NICKELSBURG, George W.E.

1977    Good News / Bad News: The Messiah and God's Fractured Community. — *CurrTMiss* 4 (1977) 324-332.

1981a   *Jewish Literature between the Bible and the Mishnah. A Historical and Literary Introduction*. Philadelphia, PA: Fortress, 1981, XX-332 p. Esp. 303-305 [OT pseudepigrapha].

1981b   Enoch, Levi, and Peter: Recipients of Revelation in Upper Galilee. — *JBL* 100 (1981) 575-600. Esp. 590-600: "Peter's commissioning at Caesarea Philippi". [NTA 26, 1118]

1992a   Passion Narratives. — *ABD* 5 (1992) 172-177. Esp. 174.

1992b   Resurrection (Early Judaism and Christianity). — *Ibid.*, 684-691. Esp. 689-690.

1992c   Son of Man. — *ABD* 6 (1992) 137-150. Esp. 142-143 [Q]; 144-145 [Mt].

1993    Jews and Christians in the First Century: The Struggle over Identity. — *Neotestamentica* 27 (1993) 365-390. Esp. 382, 386. [NTA 38, 1657]

### NICKLIN, T.

1950    The Messiah's Baptism and the Holy Ghost. — *ChurchQR* 149 (1950) 127-137.

**NICLÓS ALBARRACÍN, J.V.**

1995 Aspectos cristológicos y haláquicos de carácter polémico en la traducción y comentario al Evangelio de San Mateo de Shem Tob Ben Shaprut. — *Escritos del Vedat* (Torrent) 25 (1995) 199-246. [NTA 41, 191] → G. Howard

**NICOL, Willem**

1977 The Structure of Matthew Seven. — *Neotestamentica* _1 (1977) 77-90 (addendum, 15-18).

**NICOLAS, Albert**

1960 La relation avec l'ennemi. Étude biblique. — *FoiVie* 59 (1960) 235-251. Esp. 243-246 [5,38-42]; 246-251 [5,43-48]. [NTA 5, 396]

**NICOLAU, Francesc**

1989 Nota sobre l'aspecte verbal de l'imperfet en el grec del Nou Testament. — *RevistCatTeol* 14 (1989) 273-278. Esp. 276.

**NICOLÁU, Miguel**

1975 Virginidad y continencia en la Sagrada Escritura. [19,10-12] — *Manresa* 47 (1975) 19-40. [NTA 20, 279]

**NIEBERGALL, Alfred**

1985 *Ehe und Ehescheidung in der Bibel und in der Geschichte der Alten Kirche*, ed. A.M. Ritter (Marburger theologische Studien, 18). Marburg: Elwert, 1985, XXV-267 p. Esp. 77-88: "Die Eheauffassung Jesu".

**NIEBUHR, Karl-Wilhelm**

1997 Die Werke des eschatologischen Freudenboten (4Q521 und die Jesusüberlieferung). — TUCKETT, C.M. (ed.), *The Scriptures in the Gospels*, 1997, 637-646. Esp. 640-641.

**NIEDERBERGER, Gero**

1963 Die Leidensweissagungen bei Matthäus 16,21; 17,22-23; 20,17-19 – Ihr theologischer Sinn. — *Laur* 4 (1963) 3-26, 171-203. Esp. 6-10: "Die Leidensweissagungen in ihren Kontext"; 10-21: "Die Struktur der drei Leidensweissagungen im Vergleich zueinander"; 22-26.171-196: "Philologisch-theologische Analyse".

**NIEDERWIMMER, Kurt**

1966 *Der Begriff Freiheit im Neuen Testament* (Theologische Bibliothek Töpelmann, 11). Berlin: Töpelmann, 1966, IV-240 p. Esp. 150-168: "Die Freiheit der Gottesherrschaft (Jesus)" [6,1-18; 17,24-27].

1968 *Jesus*. Göttingen: Vandenhoeck & Ruprecht, 1968, 95 p. Esp. 53-70 [Law].

1975 *Askese und Mysterium. Über Ehe, Ehescheidung und Eheverzicht in den Anfängen des christlichen Glaubens* (FRLANT, 113). Göttingen: Vandenhoeck & Ruprecht, 1975, 267 p. Esp. 13-24.49-52 [5,32; 19,9]; 24-29 [5,28]; 30-32 [5,29-30]; 54-58 [19,10-12]; 60-61 [25,1-13]; 170-171.

**NIEDNER, Frederick A., Jr.**

1989 Rereading Matthew on Jerusalem and Judaism. — *BTB* 19 (1989) 43-47. [NTA 33, 1111]

**NIELEN, Josef Maria**

1937R *Gebet und Gottesdienst im Neuen Testament. Eine Studie zur biblischen Liturgie und Ethik* [1937]. Freiburg: Herder, ²1963, XXIV-357 p. Esp. 2-14 [prayer]; 29-36 [Lord's prayer]; 53-60 [Law].

**NIELSEN, Helge Kjaer**

1976 Kriterier til bestemmelse af autentiske Jesusord. — PEDERSEN, S. (ed.), *Nytestamentlige Studier. Udgivelse fra Institut for Ny Testamente ved Aarhus Universitet* (Teologiske

Studier, 4), Aarhus: Forlaget Aros, 1976, 9-33.

Kriterien zur Bestimmung authentischer Jesusworte. — *SNTU* 4 (1979) 5-26. Esp. 12-15 [11,2-6; 13,16-17]; 15-18; 18-21. [NTA 25, 419]

1986    Forståelsen af helbredelse i Mattæusevangeliet (Das Verständnis der Heilung im Matthäusevangelium). — NISSEN, J. - SIMONSEN, H. (eds.), *Teologi og kirke. Festskrift til Poul Nepper-Christensen*, København, 1986, 43-58.

1987    *Heilung und Verkündigung. Das Verständnis der Heilung und ihres Verhältnisses zur Verkündigung bei Jesus und in der ältesten Kirche* (Acta theologica Danica, 22). Leiden: Brill, 1987, XI-302 p. Esp. 28-46 [12,28]; 51-57 [13,16-17]; 57-65 [11,2-6]; 65-71 [11,20-24]; 71-90 [10,7-16]; 124-137: "Das Matthäusevangelium" [28,16-20]. — Diss. Aarhus, 1986 (S. Pedersen).

1990    Er den "dovne" tjener doven? Om oversættelsen af ὀκνηρός i Matth 25,26. [Is the "lazy" servant lazy? Concerning the translation of ὀκνηρός in Mt 25,26] — *DanskTeolTids* 53 (1990) 106-115. [NTA 35, 148]

**NIELSEN, J.T.**

1971    *Het Evangelie naar Mattheüs* (De prediking van het Nieuwe Testament). Nijkerk: Callenbach, 3 vols., I, 1971, 262 p.; II, 1973, 267 p.; III, 1974, 234 p. A.F.N. LEKKERKERKER, *KerkT* 23 (1971) 125-126.

**NIELSEN, Kirsten**

1990    Intertextuality and Biblical Scholarship. — *Scandinavian Journal of the Old Testament* (Århus) 4 (1990) 89-95. [NTA 35, 525]

**NIEMAND, Christoph**

1989a    *Studien zu den Minor Agreements der synoptischen Verklärungsperikopen. Eine Untersuchung der literarkritischen Relevanz der gemeinsamen Abweichungen des Matthäus und Lukas von Markus 9,2-10 für die synoptische Frage* (EHS, XXIII/352). Frankfurt/M–Bern: Lang, 1989, 345 p. Esp. 15-51: "Forschungsgeschichtlicher Überblick zu einzelnen minor agreements der Verklärungsperikopen"; 52-59: "Zur Fragestellung und zur Methode"; 60-268: "Einzelanalysen"; 269-300: "Bewertung der Analyseergebnisse und Folgerungen für die synoptische Frage". — Diss. Linz, 1987 (A. Fuchs).
F. NEIRYNCK, *ETL* 65 (1989) 441-442; U. SCHNELLE, *SNTU* 16 (1991) 208-209.

1989b    Bemerkungen zur literarkritischen Relevanz der minor agreements. Überlegungen zu einigen Aufgaben und Problemen der agreement-Forschung. — *SNTU* 14 (1989) 25-38. [NTA 35, 122]

1993a    *Die Fusswaschungserzählung des Johannesevangeliums. Untersuchungen zu ihrer Entstehung und Überlieferung im Urchristentum* (Studia Anselmiana, 114). Roma: Pont. Atheneo S. Anselmo, 1993, XIV-460 p. Esp. 295-307 [3,11-12]; 323-330 [11,2-19]. — Diss. Linz, 1993 (A. Fuchs).

1993b    Die Täuferlogien Mk 1,7-8 parr. Traditions- und redaktionsgeschichtliche Überlegungen und ihre Bedeutung für die Synoptische Frage. — *SNTU* 18 (1993) 63-96. Esp. 69-77: "Synoptische Textbeobachtungen"; 77-79: "Zur ursprünglichen Form der Sprüche"; 79-85 [πνεύματι καὶ πυρί]; 85-94: "Folgerungen für ein synoptisches Erklärungsmodell". [NTA 39, 174]

1994    Nationalismus in der Bibel? — *TPQ* 142 (1994) 263-275. Esp. 269-275: "Zum kirchlichen Selbstverständnis im Matthäusevangelium". [NTA 39, 790]

**NIETO, T.** → Silva Costoya 1964

**NIEWCZAS, Bogusław Józef**

1980    Wezwanie do naśladowania Chrystusa według Mt 16,24 i tekstów paralelnych. (L'appel à l'imitation du Christ selon Mt 16,24 par.). — *Studia z Biblistyki* 2 (1980) 194-320.

**NIEWIADOMSKI, Jósef** → Schwager 1983

**NIEYVIAERTS, Jacques**

1992 *L'entrée de Jésus à Jérusalem. Lecture de Mt XXI,1-17. Approche narrative et théologique de la christologie de Matthieu.* Diss. Toulouse, 1992.

**NIKITOPOULOS, P.**

1993 Pietro e la pietra della fede. Un riferimento interpretativo negli atti del Niceno II su "Mt. 16,18". — *Nicolaus. Rivista di teologia ecumenico-patristica* (Bari) 20 (1993) 163-166.

**NIKOLAINEN, Aimo T.**

1983a *Matteuksen evankeliumi: Kuninkaan asialla.* Helsinki: Kirjapaja, 1983, 233 p.

1983b Exegetisch-theologische Probleme bei der Übersetzungsarbeit der Bibel. — KIILUNEN, J., et al. (eds.), *Glaube und Gerechtigkeit.* FS R. Gyllenberg, 1983, 123-130 [πορνεία, τέλειος, δίκαιος/-σύνη, σῴζω, μακάριος, ἀφίημι, ἐπιούσιος].

**NIKOLAKOPOULOS, C.**

1994 The Hymnic Texts of Matthew. Extensions of Meaning on the Basis of Rhetorical Forms. [Greek] — *DeltBM* 23/2 (1994) 34-50. [NTA 40, 154]

**NIN, Manuel**

1992 Il commento di Giovanni il Solitario a Mt. 5:3. — *The Harp* (Kerala) 5 (1992) 29-37.

**NINEHAM, Dennis Eric**

1955* (ed.), *Studies in the Gospels. Essays in Memory of R.H. Lightfoot.* Oxford: Blackwell, 1955, XVI-262 p. → Dodd, Farrer, H.F.D. Sparks

1965* et al. (eds.), *Historicity and Chronology in the New Testament* (Theological Collections, 6). London: SPCK, 1965, VIII-160 p. → Leaney, W. Lillie, Mann

1976 The Genealogy in St. Matthew's Gospel and Its Significance for the Study of the Gospels. — *BJRL* 58 (1975-76) 421-444. [NTA 21, 71]; = ID., *Explorations in Theology*, 1, London: SCM, 1977, 166-187, 204-206.

**NISCOVEANU, Mircea**

1965 Doctrina Sfîntului Ioan Gura de Aur în Comentariul sau la "Predica de pe Munte" (La doctrine de St. J. Chrysostome dans son commentaire au Sermon sur la montagne (Mt V–VII). — *Studii Teologice* 17 (1965) 541-570.

**NISIN, Arthur**

1960 *Histoire de Jésus.* Paris: Seuil, 1960, 413 p. Esp. 122-128 [infancy narr.]; 177-196 [Sermon on the Mount].

**NISSEN, Johannes**

1995 The Distinctive Character of the New Testament Love Command in Relation to Hellenistic Judaism. Historical and Hermeneutical Reflections. — BORGEN, P. – GIVERSEN, S. (eds.), *The New Testament and Hellenistic Judaism*, Aarhus: University Press, 1995, 123-150. Esp. 130-131 [22,34-40]; 133-136 [7,12].

**NIXON, R.E.**

1970 Matthew. — GUTHRIE, D., et al. (eds.), *New Bible Commentary Revised*, London: Inter-Varsity, ³1970, 813-850.

**NJOROGE, Peter D.**

1989 *An Exegetical Study of "Interiority: A Dimension in the Mission of Jesus" in Selected Texts in the Gospel of Matthew.* Diss. Pont. Univ. Greg., Roma, 1989, 397 p. (E. Rasco).

**NOACK, Bent**

1954 *Zur johanneischen Tradition. Beiträge zur Kritik an der literarkritischen Analyse des vierten Evangeliums.* København: Rosenskilde og Bagger, 1954, 172 p. Esp. 89-109: "Synoptische Logien" [3,11/Jn 1,27; 13,55/Jn 6,42; 13,57/Jn 4,44; 10,24-25/Jn 13,16 and 15,20; 10,40/Jn 12,44-45; 26,42/Jn 18,10; 26,34/Jn 13,38]; 16,17-18/Jn 1,42]; 16,19; 18,18/Jn 20,23; 27,40/Jn 2,19; 26,21/Jn 13,21; 26,39/Jn 12,27; 26,31/Jn 16,32]; 109-111.

1963 En konstrueret lignelse refereret og kritiseret. [An invented parable, reported and criticized]. [13,44-46] — *DanskTeolTids* 26 (1963) 238-243. [NTA 9, 535]

1969 *Om Fadervor* [On the Lord's prayer]. København: Gad, 1969, 236 p.
B. FRID, *SvenskTeolKvart* 50 (1974) 173-174; B. SALOMONSEN, *DanskTeolTids* 33 (1970) 67-68.

1971 *Matthæusevangeliets folkelighed* [The popular character of the gospel of Matthew]. København: Gad, 1971, 170 p.
H. IVARSSON, *SEÅ* 40 (1975) 127-129; P. NEPPER-CHRISTENSEN, *DanskTeolTids* 35 (1972) 137-139.

1992 *Fra det exegetiske vaerksted: artikles og notater* [Collected essays]. København: Gad; Aarhus: Institut for Ny Testamente, 1992, 309 p.

**NOBER, Petrus**

1958 Mt 27,15. — *Freiburger Rundbrief* 11 (1958) 73-77.

1963 "Que o seu sangue caia sôbre nós e sôbre nossos filhos" (Mt. 27,25). — *RevistCuBíb* 7 (1963) 17-28. [NTA 9, 162]

**NOËL, Filip**

1994 *De compositie van het Lucasevangelie in zijn relatie tot Marcus. Het probleem van de "grote weglating"* (Verhandelingen van de Koninklijke Academie voor Wetenschappen, Letteren en Schone Kunsten van België, 150). Brussel: Paleis der Academiën, 1994, 291 p. Esp. 57-63: "De hypothese van de Matteüsprioriteit"; 132-134; 146-152 [Deutero-Mk; minor agreements]; 171-177 [Lk dependent on Mt]. — Diss. Leuven, 1992 (F. Neirynck).
J. VERHEYDEN, *ETL* 72 (1996) 240-241.

**NOEMI, Juan**

1967 *El significado de Mt 25,40 y 45.* Santiago: Univ. Católica de Chile, 1967, 19 p.

**NÖTSCHER, Friedrich**

1950 "Das Reich (Gottes) und seine Gerechtigkeit" (Mt 6,33 vgl. Lc 12,31). — *Bib* 31 (1950) 237-241; = ID., *Vom Alten zum Neuen Testament. Gesammelte Aufsätze* (BBB, 17), Bonn: Hanstein, 1962, 226-230.

**NOLAN, Brian M.**

1969 Some Observations on the Parousia and New Testament Eschatology. — *IrTQ* 36 (1969) 283-314. Esp. 290-300: "The Parousia in the Synoptics". [NTA 14, 675]
*TDig* 18 (1970) 150-153.

1979 *The Royal Son of God. The Christology of Matthew 1-2 in the Setting of the Gospel* (Orbis Biblicus et Orientalis, 23). Freiburg/Schw: Éd. universitaires; Göttingen: Vandenhoeck & Ruprecht, 1979, 282 p. Esp. 16-22: "The possible sources of Mt 1-2"; 23-47: "The Old Testament resonance of Mt 1-2"; 48-91: "The first century Jewish resonance of Mt 1-2"; 92-97: "The situation of Matthew"; 98-113: "The relationship of Mt 1-2 with the rest of the gospel"; 114-144: "The subjective discussion: the Christ with us"; 145-240: "The objective dimension: the royal Son of God". [NTA 24, p. 86] — Diss. Freiburg/Schw, 1975 (C. Spicq).
J.A. CARRASCO, *EstJos* 36 (1982) 120-121; J.C. FENTON, *JTS* 31 (1980) 587-588; K. GRAYSTON, *ExpT* 91 (1979-80) 150; R. GUNDRY, *Bib* 61 (1980) 585-588; D. HILL, *JSNT* 9 (1980) 66-69; X. JACQUES, *NRT* 102 (1980) 904-905; P.-É. LANGEVIN, *SE* 32 (1980) 241-244; L. LEGRAND, *IndianTS* 17 (1980) 389-392; B. LINDARS, *ScriptB* 11 (1980-81) 20-21; J.P. MEIER, *CBQ* 42 (1980) 418-419; E.M. PERETTO, *Marianum* 47 (1985) 365-368; R. PESCH, *TRev* 77 (1981) 106-107; D. SENIOR, *TS* 41 (1980) 586-587; W.B. TATUM, *JBL* 100 (1981) 125-127; D. ZELLER, *BZ* 25 (1981) 272-273.

1980    The Heir Unapparent: Detecting the Royal Theology in the Parable of the Master's Son
        (Matthew 21:33-46). — *ProcIrBibAss* 4 (1980) 84-95. [NTA 25, 483]

1981    The Figure of David as a Focus for the Christology of Matthew. — *ScriptB* 12 (1981)
        46-49. [NTA 27, 503]

1992    Rooting the Davidic Son of God of Matthew 1-2 in the Experience of the Evangelist's
        Audience. — *EstBíb* 50 (1992) 149-156. Esp. 149-152: "The pastoral setting of Matthew 1-2";
        153-154: "The Son of David of popular expectation"; 154-156: "The Son of God of embarrassing lowliness".

**NOLL, Rudolf**

1967    Ein Goldglas mit Bibelzitat. [28,20] — *Jahrbuch für Antike und Christentum* (Münster)
        10 (1967) 121-123.

**NOLLAND, John**

1979    Proselytism or Politics in Horace *Satires* I,4,138-143? [23,15] — *VigChr* 33 (1979) 347-
        355. [NTA 24, 608]

1983    Recent Studies in Matthew. A Review Article. — *Crux* 19/2 (1983) 25-29. [NTA 29, 510r]
        → Beare 1981, Guelich 1982, Gundry 1982

1989    *Luke 1-9:20*; *Luke 9:21-18:34*; *Luke 18:35-24:53* (Word Biblical Commentary, 35A-
        C). Dallas, TX: Word, 1989/1993/1993, LXVI-454, LIX-455-896 and LXI-897-1293 p.

1993    → 1989

1995    The Gospel Prohibition of Divorce: Tradition History and Meaning. — *JSNT* 58 (1995)
        19-35. Esp. 21-25 [5,32]; 25-27 [19,9]; 27-30 [Q 16,18]; 30-31 [19,9/Mk]. [NTA 40, 164]

**NOLLI, Gianfranco**

1981    (ed.), *Novum Testamentum Graece et Latine. Textus Graecus, cum apparatu critico-
        exegetico, Vulgata Clementina et Neovulgata.* Città del Vaticano: Libreria Editrice
        Vaticana, 1981, XLIX-1387 p. Esp. 1-173: "Εὐαγγέλιον κατὰ Μαθθαῖον".

1988    *Evangelo secondo Matteo. Testo greco, Neovolgata latina, analisi filologica, traduzione
        italiana.* Città del Vaticano: Libreria Editrice Vaticana, 1988, XLVI-958 p.
        G.P. COLÒ, *ScuolC* 22 (1988) 821.

**NOME, John**

1951    Bergprekenens betydning i den kristne etikk. [The meaning of the Sermon on the Mount
        for christian ethics] — *TidsTeolKirk* 22 (1951) 49-68.

**NOORDA, Sijbolt Jan**

1991    & WEREN, W.J.C., Christelijke schriftgeleerdheid. De vervullingscitaten in Mt. 8,17
        en 12,17-21. — BAARDA, T., et al. (eds.), *Jodendom en vroeg christendom*, 1991, 81-
        101. Esp. 83-88 [8,17]; 88-96 [12,17-21].

**NOORDEGRAAF, Albert**

1982    *De bergrede.* Apeldoorn: Willem de Zwijgerstichting, 1982, 56 p.

**NOORDMANS, Oepke**

1925R   De achtergrond van de bergrede. [1925, unpublished] — ID., *Verzamelde werken.* II:
        *Dogmatische peilingen. Rondom Schrift en Belijdenis*, Kampen: Kok, 1979, 36-56.

1935R   Dingen die verborgen waren. [1935] — *Ibid.*, 57-83. Esp. 62-73 [13,3-9]; 73-83 [20,1-16].

**NORDSIECK, Reinhardt**

1980    *Reich Gottes – Hoffnung der Welt. Das Zentrum der Botschaft Jesu* (Neukirchener
        Studienbücher, 12). Neukirchen-Vluyn: Neukirchener, 1980, 224 p.

**NORDSTOKKE, Kjell**

1991 "Salige er de fattige i ånden, for himmelriket er deres". En tolkning av "fattige" i saligprisninge etter Matteus, sett i frigjøringsteologisk perspektiv. ["Blessed are the poor, for they will inherit the kingdom". An analysis of "poor" and blessing in Mt from a liberation-theological perspective] — *NorskTeolTids* 92 (1991) 157-169.

**NORELLI, Enrico**

1980 La resurrezione di Gesù nell'Ascensione di Isaia. — *CrnStor* 1 (1980) 315-366. Esp. 324-331 [27,51-53.62-66; 28,2-4.11-15/AscIs]. [NTA 25, 1140]

1994a *L'Ascensione di Isaia. Studi su un apocrifo al crocevia dei cristianesimi* (Collana Origini. NS, 1). Bologna: Dehoniane, 1994, 359 p. Esp. 69-78: "AI 1 e l'Opus imperfectum in Matthaeum"; 115-166: "L'AI e il vangelo di Matteo" [1,18-25; 27,51-53.62-66; 28,2-4.11-15]; 213-219: "AI 4,16 e la parabola del ritorno del padrone (Lc 12,36-38)" [Q 12,36-38.42-46; 17,7-10 (Lk)]. → Verheyden 1989a

1994b Avant le canonique et l'apocryphe: Aux origines des récits de la naissance de Jésus. — *RTP* 44 (1994) 305-324. Esp. 310-320 [1,18-25/AscIs]; 320-322 [1,18-25/Protev. James]. [NTA 39, 1894]

**NORLIN, Dennis** → Carlston 1971

**NORMANN, Friedrich**

1967 *Christos Didaskalos. Die Vorstellung von Christus als Lehrer in der christlichen Literatur des ersten und zweiten Jahrhunderts* (Münsterische Beiträge zur Theologie, 32). Münster: Aschendorff, 1967, VIII-192 p. Esp. 23-45: "Matthäus" [5-7; 23,8]. — Diss. Münster, 1965 (B. Kötting).

**NORTH, Robert**

1950 "Humilis corde" in luce Psalmorum. — *VD* 28 (1950) 153-161. Esp. 153-155 [11,29].

1962 Chenoboskion and Q. — *CBQ* 24 (1962) 154-170. [NTA 7, 325] → Cullmann 1960

1978 The Gospel Infancy Narratives. — *Cross Currents* 27 (1977-78) 464-467. → R.E. Brown 1977

1985 Violence and the Bible: The Girard Connection. — *CBQ* 47 (1985) 1-27. Esp. 16-21. [NTA 29, 848]

**NORTJÉ, L.**

1994 Matthew's Motive for the Composition of the Story of Judas's Suicide in Matthew 27:3-10. — *Neotestamentica* 28 (1994) 41-51. Esp. 42-46: "The role of the twelve disciples"; 46-51 [27,3-10]. [NTA 39, 814]

**NORTJE, S.J.**

1989 John the Baptist and the Resurrection Traditions in the Gospels. — *Neotestamentica* 23 (1989) 349-358. Esp. 354-355. [NTA 34, 1085]

**NORTON, Arthur M.**

1959 *Motives to Which Christ Appealed in the Sermon on the Mount.* Diss. Midwestern Baptist Theol. Sem., Kansas City, KS, 1959.

**NORTON, David**

1993 *A History of the Bible as Literature.* I: *From Antiquity to 1700.* II: *From 1700 to the Present Day.* Cambridge: University Press, 1993, XVII-375 and XII-493 p. Esp. I, 314-317 [Rendering of Mt 4,18-25]; 320-323 [7]; II, 449-454 [7].

**NOTHOMB, Dominique**

1960 La nature du pouvoir de jurisdiction du confesseur. — *NRT* 82 (1960) 470-482. Esp. 473-475 [16,19].

**NÜTZEL, Johannes Maria**

1973    *Die Verklärungserzählung im Markusevangelium. Eine redaktionsgeschichtliche Untersuchung* (FzB, 6). Würzburg: Echter, 1973, V-311 p. Esp. 231-234: "Die Chronologie des Matthäusevangeliums" [26–27]; 275-288: "Die Verklärung Jesu nach Matthäus 17,1-9". — Diss. Freiburg, 1972 (A. Vögtle).

1986    Elija- und Elischa-Traditionen im Neuen Testament. — *BK* 41 (1986) 160-171. [NTA 31, 831]

1991    "Darf ich mit dem Meinen nicht tun, was ich will?" (Mt 20,15a). — OBERLINNER, L. – FIEDLER, P. (eds.), *Salz der Erde*. FS A. Vögtle, 1991, 267-284. Esp. 237-270: "Die Antwort des Weinbergbesitzers"; 270-279: "Gesichtspunkte zur Auslegung auf der Ebene der Botschaft Jesu"; 280-284: "Die Auswertung der Parabel bei Matthäus".

**NÚÑEZ, Helio Maria**

1966    ʽĀnî, πτωχός, pobre. (Métodos para el entronque del vocabulario griego-hebreo). — *EstBíb* 25 (1966) 193-205. Esp. 201, 204-205. [NTA 12, 74]

**NUÑEZ MORENO, José M.**

1994    Il "De Baptismo" di Paciano di Barcellona. Un modello di esegesi biblica nella catechesi ispana del secolo IV. — FELICI, S. (ed.), *Esegesi e catechesi nei Padri*, 1994, 93-119. Esp. 108 [4,3].

**NUNN, H.P.V.**

1952    *The Authorship of the Fourth Gospel*. Oxford: Alden & Blackwell, 1952, XII-152 p. Esp. 120, 122-123 [11,25/Jn].

**NUTZ, Earl Glen**

1972    *Unity of the Sermon on the Mount*. Diss. B. Jones Univ., 1972, 331 p.

**NWACHKWU, Fortunatus**

1992    & MANUS, U.C., Forgiveness and Non-Forgiveness in Matthew 12:31-32: Exegesis against the Background of Early Jewish and African Thought Forms. — *AfTJ* 21 (1992) 57-77. Esp. 58-62. [NTA 38, 160]

**NYGREN, Anders**

1956    Bergpredigt. — *EKL* 1 (1956) 392-395.

**NYIREDY, Maurus**

1987    "Was ihr für einen meiner geringsten Brüder getan habt, das habt ihr mir getan". [Hungarian] — *Teologia* (Budapest) 21 (1987) 197-201.

# O

**OAKLEY, Ivor J.W.**

1969    *The Concept of Grace in the Gospel of Matthew with Special Reference to the Prologue.* Diss. Queen's College, Belfast, 1969-70.

1984    *The Heightened Ethical Imperative in the Matthaean Tradition.* Diss. Queen's Univ., Belfast, 1984, 433 p. — *DissAbstr* 46 (1985-86) 1524.

1985    "Hypocrisy" in Matthew. [23] — *IBS* 7 (1985) 118-138. [NTA 30, 104]

**OAKMAN, Douglas Edward**

1985    Jesus and Agrarian Palestine: The Factor of Debt. — *SBL 1985 Seminar Papers*, 57-73. Esp. 68-73 [5,25; 6,12; 18,23-35].

1986    *Jesus and the Economic Questions of His Day* (Studies in the Bible and Early Christianity, 8). Lewiston, NY – Queenston, Ont.: Mellen, 1986, XV-319 p. Esp. 114-123 [13,24-30]; 123-128 [13,31-32]; 149-150 [18,27]; 160-161 [6,25-34]; 161-163 [7,1-5]; 164-165 [20,1-16]; 165-166 [22,1-10]; 166-167 [13,44-46]. — Diss. Graduate Theol. Union, Berkeley, CA, 1986 (H. Waetjen).

1988    Rulers' Houses, Thieves, and Usurpers. The Beelzebul Pericope. [Q 11,14-23] — *Forum* 4/3 (1988) 109-123. [NTA 33, 1187]

1993    Cursing Fig Trees and Robbers' Dens. Pronouncement Stories within Social-Systemic Perspective: Mark 11:12-25 and Parallels. — *Semeia* 64 (1993) 253-272. Esp. 254-256 [21,18-19/Mk]. [NTA 39, 830]

1994    The Archaeology of First-Century Galilee and the Social Interpretation of the Historical Jesus. — *SBL 1994 Seminar Papers*, 220-251 Esp. 233-240. → Mack 1993

**OBACH, Robert E.** → A. Kirk 1978

**OBENG, E.A.**

1992    The Significance of the Miracles of Resuscitation and Its Implications for the Church in Africa. — *Bible Bhashyam* 18 (1992) 83-95. Esp. 85-87 [9,18-26]. [NTA 37, 1191]

**OBERLINNER, Lorenz**

1975a    *Historische Überlieferung und christologische Aussage. Zur Frage der "Brüder Jesu" in der Synopse* (FzB, 19). Stuttgart: Katholisches Bibelwerk, 1975, XI-396 p. Esp. 51-57 [1,25]; 93-97 [27,56-62]; 243-248 [12,46-50]; 352-354 [13,54-58]. — Diss. Freiburg, 1974 (A. Vögtle).

1975b    Die Stellung der "Terminworte" in der eschatologischen Verkündigung des Neuen Testaments. — FIEDLER, P. – ZELLER, D. (eds.), *Gegenwart und kommendes Reich.* FS. A. Vögtle, 1975, 51-66. Esp. 64-65 [10,23].

1980    *Todeserwartung und Todesgewißheit Jesu. Zum Problem einer historischen Begründung* (SBB, 10). Stuttgart: Katholisches Bibelwerk, 1980, 190 p. Esp. 42-44.96-97 [11,2-6]; 86-93 [11,21-24]; 97-102 [5,11-12; 11,16-17; 23,29-31.34-36.37-39]; 169-171 [10,38].

1990    Wem gilt die Bergpredigt? — *BZ* 34 (1990) 104-108. [NTA 34, 1132r] → G. Lohfink 1988a

1991*    & FIEDLER, P. (eds.) *Salz der Erde – Licht der Welt. Exegetische Studien zum Matthäusevangelium. Festschrift für Anton Vögtle zum 80. Geburtstag.* Stuttgart: Katholisches Bibelwerk, 1991, 423 p. [NTA 36, p. 114] → Broer, Dautzenberg, Fiedler, Frankemölle, Gollinger, Hoffmann, Hoppe, Lohse, Maisch, O. Merk, Nützel, Oberlinner, Riedl, Schlosser, Schnackenburg, Schweizer; → Limbeck 1994
    J.J. BARTOLOMÉ, *Sal* 54 (1992) 159-160; A. FUCHS, *SNTU* 16 (1991) 179-180.

1991 "... sie zweifelten aber" (Mt 28,17b). Eine Anmerkung zur matthäischen Ekklesiologie.
— *Ibid.*, 375-400. Esp. 377-389: "Fragen zur Übersetzung und zur Bedeutung von οἱ δὲ ἐδίστασαν";
389-400: "Der Zweifel der Jünger in der Deutung des Mt".

**OBERMÜLLER, Rodolfo**

1972 "¿Cuando te vimos?" Observaciones exegéticas en el evangelio de Mateo 25:31-46. —
*CuadTeol* 2 (1972) 197-212.

1973 ¿Donde estuviste? [25,31-46] — *RevistBíb* 35 (1973) 14-21. [NTA 18, 478]

**OBERWEIS, Michael**

1989 Beobachtungen zum AT-Gebrauch in der matthäischen Kindheitsgeschichte. — *NTS* 35
(1989) 131-149. Esp. 131-134: "Unstimmiges in Mt 2"; 134-141: "Verborgener AT-Gebrauch in Mt";
141-146: "Jes 7.14 im Kontext des Prophetenbuches" [1,23]; 146-143: "Mt 1/2 und die Divergenzen zwischen
Hebräischem und Griechischem AT". [NTA 33, 593]

**O'BRIEN, Peter T.**

1976 The Great Commission of Matthew 28:18-20. A Missionary Mandate or Not? — *RTR*
35/3 (1976) 66-78. [NTA 21, 386]

**OBRIST, Franz**

1961 *Echtheitsfragen und Deutung der Primatsstelle Mt 16,18f. in der deutschen
protestantischen Theologie der letzten dreissig Jahre* (NTAbh, 21/3-4). Münster:
Aschendorff, 1961, XVI-203 p. Esp. 27-41: "Der Kirchenspruch im Rahmen der Messiasfrage"; 42-
47: "Die Verheißung an Petrus und die Echtheitsfrage"; 48-67: "Der Wahrheitsgehalt des Kirchenspruchs im
Urteil der protestantischen Kritik"; 78-137: "Petrus, der Fels in protestantischer Deutung"; 138-179: "Die
im zweiten Teil des Petruspruches (V. 19) enthaltenen petrinischen Vollmachten in protestantischer
Auslegung"; 180-203: "Die in Mt 16,18f verheißene Vormachtstellung des Petrus im Lichte ihrer
geschichtlichen Erfüllung". [NTA 6, p. 415]. — Diss. Pont. Univ. Greg., Roma, 1956 (D. Grasso).
J. BEUMER, *Scholastik* 36 (1961) 595; M.-É. BOISMARD, *RB* 69 (1962) 431; J. COPPENS, *ETL* 37 (1961)
606-607; P. GAECHTER, *ZKT* 83 (1961) 487; J. GNILKA, *BZ* 7 (1963) 313-314; G. KLEIN, *Zeitschrift für
Kirchengeschichte* (Stuttgart) 74 (1963) 142-144; D.J. UNGER, *TS* 22 (1961) 707; A. VIARD, *RSPT* 46
(1962) 270; M. ZERWICK, *VD* 39 (1961) 295-296; *Bib* 43 (1962) 537-540; H. ZIMMERMANN, *TGl* 52
(1962) 55-56.

**O'CALLAGHAN, José**

1971 ¿Mt 2,14 en el fragmento adéspota de P¹? — *Studia Papyrologica* 10 (1971) 87-92.

1974a *Los papiros griegos de la cueva 7 de Qumrân* (Biblioteca de autores cristianos, 353).
Madrid: Católica, 1974, 99 p. Esp. 98-99: "7Q5 = Mt 1,2-3". → P. Parker 1972

1974b Sobre la identificación de 7Q4. — *Studia Papyrologica* 13 (1974) 45-55. Esp. 50-51
[2,15.17-18].

1977 BOVER, J.M. – O'CALLAGHAN, J., *Nuevo Testamento Trilingüe* (Biblioteca de autores
cristianos, 400). Madrid: Católica, 1977, LXIII-1380 p. Esp. 3-174: "Evangelio de Mateo". →
Bover 1943

1981 La variante εισ/ελθων en Mt 9,18. — *Bib* 62 (1981) 104-106. [NTA 25, 857]

1983a Mt 8,1. Discusión crítica. — *MiscCom* 78-79 (1983) 133-134.

1983b Nota crítica a Mc 8,36. [16,26] — *Bib* 64 (1983) 116-117. [NTA 27, 944]

1984 Discusión crítica en Mt 17,4. — *Bib* 65 (1984) 91-93. [NTA 28, 919]

1985a Mt 17,7: revisión crítica. — *Bib* 66 (1985) 422-423. [NTA 30, 578]

1985b Reflexions crítiques sobre Mt 9,20 i 13,4. — *RevistCatTeol* 10 (1985) 319-322. Esp. 319-
320 [9,20]; 321-322 [13,4]. [NTA 31, 120]

1986a La variente 'cielo, -os' en Mt. 18:18. — *Faventia* (Barcelona) 8 (1986) 67-68.

1986b La variante *etelesen/syn-* en Mt 7,28. — *Emerita* (Madrid) 54 (1986) 295-296.

1986c La variante neotestamentaria "levadura de los panes". [16,12] — *Bib* 67 (1986) 98-100. [NTA 30, 1055]

1986d Consideraciones críticas sobre Mt 15,35-36a. — *Ibid.*, 360-362. [NTA 31, 122]

1986e Sobre tres variants de Mt 14,6.15.18. — *RevistCatTeol* 11 (1986) 27-30. Esp. 27-28 [14,6]; 28-29 [14,15]; 29-30 [14,18]. [NTA 31, 588]

1986f La variante "se gritan ... diciendo", de Mt 11,16-17. — *EstE* 61 (1986) 67-70. [NTA 30, 1051]

1986g La variante "palabra" o "precepto" en Mt 15,6. — *Ibid.*, 421-423. [NTA 31, 1077]

1987a La variante "ahogaron" en Mt 13,7. — *Bib* 68 (1987) 402-403. [NTA 32, 604]

1987b Dos retoques antioquenos: Mt 10,10; Mc 2,20. — *Ibid.*, 564-567. Esp. 564-565. [NTA 32, 601]

1988a Armonizaciones en Mt 11,8.10.16. — *Emerita* 56 (1988) 117-119.

1988b Dissensio crítica in Mt 10,42. — *Eranos* (Stockholm) 86 (1988) 163-164. [NTA 33, 1133]

1988c Examen crítico de Mt 19,24. — *Bib* 69 (1988) 401-405. [NTA 33, 125]

1988d Probabile armonizzazione in *Mt* 10,14. — *RivBib* 36 (1988) 79-80. [NTA 32, 1108]

1989a Consideracions crítiques sobre Mt 19,20-21. — *RevistCatTeol* 14 (1989) 149-154 (English summary, 154). Esp. 149-152 [19,20]; 152-154 [19,21].

1989b Tres casos de armonización en Mt 9. — *EstBíb* 47 (1989) 131-134. Esp. 131-132 [9,6]; 132-133 [9,13]; 133-134 [9,14]. [NTA 34, 626]

1990a Discusión crítica en Mt 17,25. — *FilolNT* 3 (1990) 151-153. [NTA 36, 155]

1990b Dos variantes en la parábola del sembrador (Mt 13,4.7). — *EstBíb* 48 (1990) 267-270. Esp. 267-269 [13,4]; 269-270 [13,7]. [NTA 35, 628]

1990c Nota crítica sobre Mt 19,30. — *Ibid.*, 271-273. [NTA 35, 632]

1990d Fluctuación textual en Mt 20,21.26.27. — *Bib* 71 (1990) 553-558. Esp. 553-555 [20,21]; 555-556 [20,26]; 557-558 [20,27]. [NTA 35, 1143]

1992 Dos minucias textuales en Mt (18,19.35). — *Emerita* 60 (1992) 111-114.

1993 Detalls crítics en Mt 21,1-3. — RAURELL, F., et al. (eds.), *Tradició i traducció*. FS G. Camps, 1993, 283-286.

1994a Discusión de dos lecturas mateanas. [20,31.34] — PRIVITERA, G.A. (ed.), *Paideia cristiana. Studi in onore di Mario Naldini* (Scritti in onore, 2), Roma: Gruppo editoriale internazionale, 1994, 36.

1994b Reflexiones críticas sobre Mt 21,7. — ARANDA, G., et al. (eds.), *Biblia, Exegesis y Cultura*. FS J.M. Casciaro, 1994, 249-252.

**OCHAGAVÍA, Juan**

1964 *Visibile patris filius. A Study of Irenaeus' Teaching on Revelation and Tradition* (Orientalia Christiana Analecta, 171). Roma: Pontificium Institutum Orientalium Studiorum, 1964, XI-208 p. Esp. 62-69 [11,27].

**OCKER, Christopher**

1991 The Fusion of Papal Ideology and Biblical Exegesis in the Fourteenth Century. [16,18-19] — BURROWS, M.S. - ROREM, P. (eds.), *Biblical Hermeneutics in Historical Perspective. Studies in Honor of Karlfried Froehlich on His Sixtieth Birthday*, Grand Rapids, MI: Eerdmans, 1991, 131-151.

**O'COLLINS, Gerald**

1973 *The Easter Jesus*. London: Darton, Longman & Todd, 1973, XIV-142 p. Esp. 18-28: "Easter in the gospels"; [2]1980, VI-233 p.

*The Resurrection of Jesus Christ*. Valley Forge, PA: Judson, 1973, XIV-142 p.

*Il Gesù pasquale*. Assisi: Cittadella, 1975, 195 p.

1978    *What Are They Saying about the Resurrection?* (Deus Books). New York – Ramsey, NJ – Toronto, Ont.: Paulist, 1978, V-120 p.

1981    Peter as Easter Witness. — *HeythJ* 22 (1981) 1-18. Esp. 10-15. [NTA 25, 832]
        Easter Witness and Peter's Ministry. — *HeythJ* 26 (1985) 177-178. [NTA 30, 95]

1987a   *The Resurrection. What Actually Happened and What Does It Mean?* London: Darton, Longman & Todd, 1987, VIII-233 p.
        *Jesus Risen. An Historical, Fundamental, and Systematic Examination of Christ's Resurrection*. New York – Mahwah, NJ: Paulist, 1987, VI-233 p.
        *Jesús resucitado. Estudio histórico, fundamental y sistemático*. Barcelona: Herder, 1988, 332 p.
        *Gesù risorto. Un'indagine biblica, storica e teologica sulla risurrezione di Gesù*. Brescia: Queriniana, 1989, 265 p.

1987b   & KENDALL, D., Mary Magdalene as Major Witness to Jesus' Resurrection. — *TS* 48 (1987) 631-646. Esp. 643-644. [NTA 32, 568]

1988    *Interpreting the Resurrection. Examining the Major Problems in the Stories of Jesus' Resurrection*. New York – Mahwah, NJ: Paulist, 1988, 88 p. Esp. 32-35.

1991*   & MARCONI, G. (eds.), *Luca–Atti. Studi in onore di P. Emilio Rasco nel suo 70° compleanno* (Commenti e studi biblici, NS). Assisi: Cittadella, 1991. → Bovon, Caba, Vanni
        *Luke and Acts. [FS E. Rasco]*, trans. M.J. O'Connell. New York – Mahwah, NJ: Paulist, 1993, VI-295 p.

1993a   *The Resurrection of Jesus Christ: Some Contemporary Issues* (The Père Marquette Lecture in Theology, 24). Milwaukee, WI: Marquette University Press, 1993, V-50 p.

1993b   → Kendall 1993

1995    *Christology. A Biblical, Historical, and Systematic Study of Jesus Christ*. Oxford: University Press, 1995, XI-333 p. Esp. 82-112: "The resurrection; 113-135: "The Son of God".
        *Cristologia. Uno studio biblico, storico e sistematico su Gesù Cristo* (Biblioteca di teologia contemporanea, 90). Brescia: Queriniana, 1997, 333 p. Esp. 85-115; 116-137.

**O'COLLINS, John J.**

1993    Apocalypticism, and Generic Compatibility. — PERDUE, L.G., et al. (eds.), *In Search of Wisdom*. FS J.G. Gammie, 1993, 165-185. Esp. 181-185 [Q].

**O'CONNELL, Laurence J.**

1978    Boismard's Synoptic Theory: Exposition and Response. — *TDig* 26 (1978) 325-342. [NTA 23, 827] → Boismard 1972

**O'CONNOR, D.**

1977    & JIMENEZ, J., *The Images of Jesus. Exploring the Metaphors in Matthew's Gospel*. Minneapolis, MN: Winston, 1977, 187 p. [NTA 23, p. 231]

**O'CONNOR, Edward Dennis**

1961    *Faith in the Synoptic Gospels. A Problem in the Correlation of Scripture and Theology*. Notre Dame, IN: University Press, 1961, XX-164 p. Esp. 1-80: "The synoptic texts on faith" [1,21; 6,25-34; 8,5-13.23-27; 9,18-26.27-31; 13,1-23.53-58; 14,25-33; 15,21-28; 16,5-12; 17,14-21; 18,6; 21,18-22.23-32; 23,23; 24,1-27; 27,39-44]; 81-113: "The synoptic conception of faith". — Diss. Pont. Univ. S. Thomae, Roma.

**Ó CRÓINÍN, D.**

1989    Würzburg, Universitätsbibliothek, M.p.th.f. 61 and Hiberno-Latin Exegesis in the VIIIth Century. [18,1] — LEHNER, A. – BERSCHIN, W. (eds.), *Lateinische Kultur im VIII. Jahrhundert. Traube-Gedenkschrift*, St. Ottilien: EOS, 1989, 209-216.

**O'DAY, Gail R.**

1989 Surprised by Faith: Jesus and the Canaanite Woman. [15,21-28] — *Listening* 24 (1989) 290-301. [NTA 34, 628]

**ODENKIRCHEN, P. Cornelius**

1968 "Praecedam vos in Galilaeam" (Mt 26,32 cf. 28,7.10; Mc 14,28; 16,7 cfr. Lc 24,6). — *VD* 46 (1968) 193-223. Esp. 195-200 [26,32/Mk 14,28]; 200-205 [28,7/Mk 16,7]; 213-223 [Galilee]. [NTA 14, 491]

**ODERO, José M.**

1986 El debate de Jesús con Satán (Mt 4,5-7; Lc 4,9-12) (Cuestiones teológicas sobre fe y hermenéutica). — CASCIARO, J.M. (ed.), *Biblia y hermenéutica. VII simposio internacional de teología de la Universidad de Navarra, 10-12 abril 1985*, Pamplona: Univ. Navarra, 1986, 241-255.

**O'DONNELL, A.M.**

1991 Philology, Typology, and Rhetoric in Tyndale's *Exposition upon the V, VI, VII Chapters of Matthew*. — *"Moreana"* 106-107 (1991) 155-164.

**O'DONNELL, Patrick James**

1979 A Literary Analysis of Matthew 8: Jesus' First Gentile Mission. Diss. Iliff School of Theology, 1979, 223 p. — *DissAbstr* 41 (1980-81) 293; *SBT* 11 (1981) 107-108.

**OEGEMA, Gerbern S.**

1994 *Der Gesalbte und sein Volk. Untersuchungen zum Konzeptualisierungsprozeß der messianischen Erwartungen von den Makkabäern bis Bar Koziba* (Schriften des Institutum Judaicum Delitzschianum, 2). Göttingen: Vandenhoeck & Ruprecht, 1994, 351 p. Esp. 136-148: "Logienquelle 'Q' und die synoptische Redaktion" [Q 3,16-17; 6,22; 11,30; 12,8-9; 17,24.26.30]; 157-158 [Q/Paul]; 165-169 [24/Mk]. — Diss. Berlin 1989-90 (P. Schäfer).

**ÖHLER, Markus**

1997 *Elia im Neuen Testament. Untersuchungen zur Bedeutung des alttestamentlichen Propheten im frühen Christentum* (BZNW, 88). Berlin – New York: de Gruyter, 1997, XVII-374 p. Esp. 48-69 [Q 3,7-9.16-17; Q 7,18-23.24-28]; 70-77 [3,3-4; 11,7-15; 17,9-13]; 154-163 [Q 9,57-62]; 163-175 [16,14; 17,1-9; 27,46-50]; 292-293.— Diss. Wien, 1995 (K. Niederwimmer).

**O'FLYNN, John A.**

1951 The Eschatological Discourse (Matthew cc. 24–25; Mark c. 13; Luke c. 21). — *IrTQ* 18 (1951) 277-281.

**OGAWA, Akira**

1970 History in the Theology of Matthew. [Japanese] — *Seisho-gaku ronshū* (Tokyo) 7 (1970) 63-92.

1977 Le problème de l'actualisation chez Matthieu. — *AJBI* 3 (1977) 84-131. Esp. 84-98: "Actualisation des récits de miracles"; 98-116: "Les disciples et les chrétiens". [NTA 22, 754]

1978 The Mission of the Disciples in the Gospel of Matthew. [Japanese] — *Seisho-gaku ronshū* 13 (1978) 70-94.

1979a *L'histoire de Jésus chez Matthieu. La signification de l'histoire pour la théologie matthéenne* (EHS, XXIII/116). Frankfurt/M–Bern: Lang, 1979, 512 p. Esp. 15-72.296-332: "L'histoire du salut chez Matthieu" [2,1-12; 4,12-17; 12,18-21.38-45; 27,51-54]; 73-110.332-359: "La vie terrestre de Jésus sous le rapport de l'histoire du salut" [1,1-17.18-25; 2,23; 27,3-10; 28,18-20]; 111-145.360-386: "Jésus et la loi" [5,17-20.21-48; 12,1-8.10-12; 15,1-20; 19,1-12; 22,34-40]; 147-176.386-419: "L'eschatologie et l'histoire du salut" [13; 24; 25,14-30.31-46]; 177-202.419-433: "L'Église et le peuple de Dieu" [5,1-10; 21,28-32.33-44; 22,1-14]; 203-246.433-467: "L'Église combattante" [5,11-16; 10,5-42; 11,20-

24; 12,38-42; 17,24-27]; 247-281.467-494: "L'histoire de Jésus et le temps présent de l'Église" [23,35-36; 26,29.64]. [NTA 25, p. 199] — Diss. Strasbourg, 1975 (É. Trocmé).

    G.G. GAMBA, *Sal* 42 (1980) 938-939; L. MORALDI, *Henoch* 8 (1986) 253-256; P. POKORNÝ, *TLZ* 109 (1984) 194-195; É. TROCMÉ, *RHPR* 57 (1977) 419-420.

1979b    Paraboles de l'Israël véritable? Reconsidération critique de Mt. xxi 28–xxii 14. — *NT* 21 (1979) 121-149. Esp. 121-127 [21,28-32]; 127-139 [21,33-44]; 139-149 [22,1-14]. [NTA 24, 95]

1993    Action-motivating Faith. The Understanding of 'Faith' in the Gospel of Matthew. — *AJBI* 19 (1993) 53-86. Esp. 60-67 [9,18; 17,20; 21,21-22/Mk]; 67-83 [5,24-34; 9,1-8; 18,6]. [NTA 39, 132]

**OGG, George**

1959    Review: Mlle Jaubert, *La date de la Cène*. — *NT* 3 (1959) 149-160. Esp. 152-153 [12,40]. [NTA 4, 862r] → Jaubert 1957

**O'GRADY, John F.**

1989    *The Four Gospels and the Jesus Tradition*. New York – Mahwah, NJ: Paulist, 1989, IV-275 p. Esp. 153-209: "The Jesus tradition and the Church: Matthew".

1991    *Disciples and Leaders. The Origins of Christian Ministry in the New Testament*. Mahwah, NJ: Paulist, 1991, VII-137 p. Esp. 30-31 [resurrection]; 42-46 [authority]; 69-71.74-76 [Peter]; 96-100: "The church of Matthew".

1994    *Models of Jesus Revisited*. New York – Mahwah, NJ: Paulist, 1994, V-233 p. Esp. 56-63.

**O'HAGAN, Angelo**

1966    "Greet no one on the way" (Lk 10,4b). — *SBF/LA* 16 (1965-66) 69-84. [NTA 12, 198]

1972    Divorce – Marriage in Tension with This Age. — *SBF/LA* 22 (1972) 95-108. Esp. 98-99 [5,32; 19,9]. [NTA 18, 667]

**O'HARA, John**

1967    Christian Fasting (*Mt.* 6,16-18). — *Scripture* 19 (1967) 3-18. [NTA 12, 153]

**OH KYONG, Ran**

1995    *The New Covenant in the NT as Fulfilment of the OT Covenant*. Roma: Pont. Univ. Urbaniana, 1995, VIII-209 p. (S. Virgulin). Esp. 129-157 [26,28].

**O'KEEFE, Vincent T.**

1959    Towards Understanding the Gospels. — *CBQ* 21 (1959) 171-189. Esp. 173-176: "Light from synoptic research"; 176-182: "Form criticism". [NTA 4, 58]
        *TDig* 9 (1961) 9-14.
    The Gospels Read as Gospels. — HEANEY, J.J. (ed.), *Faith, Reason, and the Gospels. A Selection of Modern Thought on Faith and the Gospels*, Westminster, MD: Newman, 1961, 227-252.

**OKEKE, George E.**

1987    The Temptations of Jesus Christ. — *The Living Word* (Kerala) 93 (1987) 395-407.

1988    The After-Life in St. Matthew as an Aspect of Matthean Ethic. — *ComViat* 31 (1988) 159-168. Esp. 162-165 [13,36-43]. [NTA 34, 110]; = *Melanesian Journal of Theology* (Papua, New Guinea) 4 (1988) 35-44.

**OKORIE, A.M.**

1995    El reino de Dios en el ministerio de Jesús. — *RevistBíb* 57 (1995) 19-28. Esp. 23-28.

**OLAREWAJU, Samuel Ayo**

1995    *Oath-Taking in the New Testament* [5,33-37]. Diss. Trinity Evangelical Divinity School, 1995, 246 p. — *DissAbstr* 56 (1995-96) 2281.

**O'LEARY, Patrick**

1986    New Testament Foundations for Primacy. — *Centro Pro Unione* (Roma) 30 (1986) 44-51. [NTA 31, 1265]

**OLIVAR, Alexandre**

1976 Le sermon pour la Toussaint sur *Beati qui persecutionem patiuntur* de Jean Gerson. [5,10] — *BullLitEccl* 77 (1976) 265-285. Esp. 270-285 [edition].

1982 Trois nouveaux fragments en onciale du commentaire de saint Jérôme sur l'évangile de Matthieu. — *RBén* 92 (1982) 76-81.

**OLIVEIRA, F.**

1991 Interpretación derásica de *Mt* 1,18-25. — *Mayéutica* 17 (1991) 281-304. [NTA 36, 1255]

**OLIVEIRA DE AZEVEDO, Walmor**

1987 "Dai-lhes vós mesmos de comer". Desafio, crise e partilha. [14,13-21] — *Estudos Biblicos* (Petrópolis) 15 (1987) 47-56.

**OLIVER, Harold H.**

1961 *The Text of the Four Gospels as Quoted in the Moralia of Basil the Great*. Diss. Emory Univ., Atlanta, GA, 1961.

**OLIVIER, André**

1960 *Apocalypse et Évangiles* (Cahiers de littérature sacrée). Saint-Maurice: Privately published, 2 vols., 1960, 140 and 16 p. Esp. 99-114: "Vers la solution du problème synoptique".

1964 *L'Évangile au premier siècle*. Vol. I: *Évangile de saint Matthieu, 1re partie (Chap. I-XI). Introduction, Commentaire, Étude comparative, Annexes I-III* (Études sur le Nouveau Testament). Saint-Maurice: Privately published, 1964, 120-10 p. [NTA 10, p. 283]

1969 *Évangile et critique moderne*. Saint Maurice: Privately published, 1969, 2 vols., VI-236 and III-71 p. Esp. I, 40-57: "Matthieu et Marc strophiques"; 57-74: "Matthieu et Luc strophiques"; 82-89: "Accords Mt.-Lc. contre Marc"; 90-123: "Sermon sur la montagne et discours de mission"; 125-131 [18,1-14]; 131-133 [18,21-35]; 160-166 [3,1-17]; 179-187 [16,13-28]; 188-192 [17,1-13]; 201-228 [24]; II, 5-52: "Composition littéraire des évangiles".

**OLS, Daniel**

1985 Deux annotations à propos d'un grand livre. — *Marianum* 47 (1985) 208-215. [NTA 30, 562r] → Laurentin 1982a

**OLSEN, Vigo Norskov**

1971 *The New Testament Logia on Divorce. A Study of Their Interpretation from Erasmus to Milton* (Beiträge zur Geschichte der biblischen Exegese, 10). Tübingen: Mohr, 1971, VI-161 p. — Diss. Basel, 1968 (B. Reicke).

**OLSSON, Birger**

1980 En textorienterad läsning av Bibeln. [A text-oriented reading of the Bible] [1,18-25] — *SEÅ* 45 (1980) 110-121; = KIEFFER, R. - OLSSON, B. (eds.), *Exegetik idag. Nya frågor till gamla texter* (Religio. Skrifter utgivna av Teologiska Institutionen i Lund, 11), Lund: Teologiska Institutionen, 1983, 33-45.

**OLSTHOORN, M.F.**

1975 *The Jewish Background and the Synoptic Setting of Mt 6,25-33 and Lk 12,22-31* (Studium Biblicum Franciscanum. Analecta, 10). Jerusalem: Franciscan Printing Press, 1975, 88 p. Esp. 7-18: "Common tradition and editorial variations in Mt 6,25-33 and Lk 12,22-31"; 19-31 [6,25/Q 12,22-23]; 32-54 [6,26-30/Q 12,24-28]; 55-78 [6,31-33/Q 12,29-31]. [NTA 20, p. 364] — Diss. Studium Biblicum Franciscanum/Antonianum, Jerusalem/Roma, 1970 (E. Pax).

I. ARIAS, *NatGrac* 24 (1977) 142-143; L. DE LORENZI, *RivBib* 25 (1977) 208-210; G. GIAVINI, *ScuolC* 105 (1977) 264; A. JAUBERT, *RHR* 196 (1979) 96; X. LÉON-DUFOUR, *RSR* 64 (1976) 430-432; P. TERNANT, *Proche Orient Chrétien* (Jerusalem) 26 (1976) 190; F. URICCHIO, *MiscFranc* 77 (1977) 233.

**OLUWAFEMI, Titus Oluwafipide**

1979  *Jesus' Resurrection as the Ultimate "Sign" of His Messianic Authority. A Special Reference Study of the Jonah-Sign in Matthew–Luke ar.d the Temple Sign in John.* Diss. Baylor Univ., Waco, TX, 1979, 174 p. — *DissAbstr* 41 (1980-81) 704; *SBT* 11 (1981) 108-109.

**O'MALLEY, T.P.**

1967  *Tertullian and the Bible. Language – Imagery – Exegesis* (Latinitas Christianorum Primaeva, 21). Nijmegen: Dekker & van de Vegt, 19€7, XVI-186 p. Esp. 45-46 [8,17]; 46-50 [13,35]; 53-54 [27,9].

**OMANSON, Robert L.**

1988  A Gentile Palaver. — STINE, P.C. (ed.), *Issues in Bible Translation* (United Bible Societies, MS 3). London – New York – Stuttgart: UBS, 1988, 274-286. Esp. 281-284 [πορνεία].

**OMANSON, Roger Lee**

1990  What Do Those Parentheses Mean? — *BTrans* 41 (1€90) 205-214. Esp. 207-208 [24,15]. [NTA 35, 88]

1991  A Question of Harmonization – Matthew 9.18-25. — *BTrans* 42 (1991) 241. [NTA 36, 148]

**OÑATE OJEDA, Juan Angel**

1965a  Las tentaciones del Señor (Mt 4,1-11; Mc 1,12-13; Lc 4,1-13). — *CuBíb* 22 (1965) 218-226.

1965b  Sermon de la montaña (Mt 5,1-7,29). — *Enciclopédia de la Bíblia* (Barcelona) 6 (1965; ²1969) 630-642.

1991  Pues, así como el relámpago... [24,27] — *Burgense* 32 (1991) 569-572. [NTA 36, 1282]

**O'NEILL, John C.**

1969  The Silence of Jesus. — *NTS* 15 (1968-69) 153-167. Esp. 158 [26,63]; 160-161 [10,32]. [NTA 13, 822]
       *TDig* 18 (1970) 24-28.

1975  The Synoptic Problem. — *NTS* 21 (1974-75) 273-285. [NTA 19, 928] → Longstaff 1976

1981  Did Jesus Teach That His Death Would Be Vicarious as well as Typical? — HORBURY, W. – McNEIL, B. (eds.), *Suffering and Martyrdom in the New Testament. Studies Presented to G.M. Styler by the Cambridge New Testament Seminar*, Cambridge: University Press, 1981, 9-27. Esp. 15 [10,38]; 17-18 [16,28]; 21-24 [20,20-27].

1983  The Unforgivable Sin. [12,32] — *JSNT* 19 (1983) 37-42. [NTA 28, 497]

1985  The Study of the New Testament. — SMART, N., et al. (eds.), *Nineteenth Century Religious Thought in the West*, III, Cambridge: University Press, 1985, 143-178. Esp. 159-164.

1988  The Source of the Parables of the Bridegroom and the Wicked Husbandmen. [21,33-46] — *JTS* 39 (1988) 485-489. [NTA 33, 606]

1989a  The Origins of Monasticism. — WILLIAMS, R. (ed.), *The Making of Orthodoxy. Essays in Honour of Henry Chadwick*, Cambridge: University Press, 1989, 270-287. Esp. 280-281 [19,12].

1989b  The Rules Followed by the Editors of the Text Found in the Codex Vaticanus. — *NTS* 35 (1989) 219-228. Esp. 225 [1,18]. [NTA 33, 1048]

1991  The Lost Written Records of Jesus' Words and Deeds behind Our Records. — *JTS* 42 (1991) 483-504. [NTA 36, 696]

1993a  'Good Master' and the 'Good' Sayings in the Teaching of Jesus. — *IBS* 15 (1993) 167-178. Esp. 169-175 [19,16-17]. [NTA 38, 799]

1993b   The Kingdom of God. — *NT* 35 (1993) 130-141. Esp. 134-137. [NTA 38, 444]

1993c   The Lord's Prayer. — *JSNT* 51 (1993) 3-25. [NTA 38, 759]

1995    *Who Did Jesus Think He Was?* (Biblical Interpretation Series, 11). Leiden: Brill, 1995, 238 p. Esp. 84-85; 125-132 [Son of Man]; 136-163 [Messiah].

**ONUKI, Takashi**

1977    Die johanneischen Abschiedsreden und die synoptische Tradition — eine traditionskritische und traditionsgeschichtliche Untersuchung. — *AJBI* 3 (1977) 157-268. Esp. 188-189 [26,20-25]; 220-222 [26,31-35]; 235-236 [26,36-46]. [NTA 22, 812]

**ONWU, Nlenanya**

1985    Jesus and the Canaanite Woman (Matt. 15:21-28). Toward a Relevant Hermeneutics in African Context. — *Bible Bhashyam* 11 (1985) 130-143. [NTA 30, 1054]

1987    Righteousness in Matthew's Gospel: Its Social Implications. — *Bible Bhashyam* 13 (1987) 151-178. Esp. 152-160: "Analysis of *dikaiosune* texts" [3,15; 5,6.10.21-48; 6,1.33; 21,32]; 160-169: "Jesus' social attitudes in Matthew" [12,1-8.9-14; 15,1-20; 18,23-35; 20,20-28; 22,15-22; 25,31-46]. [NTA 32, 577]

1988    Righteousness and Eschatology in Matthew's Gospel: A Critical Reflection. — *IndianTS* 25 (1988) 213-235. Esp. 216-229: "Matthew's understanding of the kingdom of heaven/God"; 229-235: "The temporal framework in Matthew's gospel". [NTA 33, 589]

**OPITZ, Hans-Georg** → Huck 1936

**OPPEL, Dagmar**

1995    *Heilsam erzählen – erzählend heilen. Die Heilung der Blutflüssigen und die Erweckung der Jairustochter in Mk 5,21-43 als Beispiel markinisches Erzählfertigkeit* (BBB, 102). Weinheim: Beltz Athenäum, 1995, 274 p. Esp. 188-194 [Hilary of Poitiers, *in Mt*]; 227-231 [John Chrysostom, *in Mt*]. — Diss. München, 1993 (J. Gnilka).

**OPPERMANN, Ralf**

1987    Eine Beobachtung in bezug auf das Problem des Markusschlusses. — *BibNot* 40 (1987) 24-29. Esp. 27-29 [28,7-10]. [NTA 32, 1148]

**ORBÁN, Arpad Peter**

1970    *Les dénominations du monde chez les premiers auteurs chrétiens* (Graecitas Christianorum Primaeva, 4). Nijmegen: Dekker & van de Vegt, 1970, XIX-243 p. Esp. 16-17; 111-116; 151-152.

1995    Juvencus als Bibelexeget und als Zeuge der "afrikanischen" Vetus-Latina-Tradition. Untersuchungen der Bergpredigt (Mt. 5,1-48) in der Vetus Latina und in der Versifikation des Juvencus (I 452-572). — *VigChr* 49 (1995) 334-352.

**ORBE, Antonio**

1956    *Los primeros herejes ante la persecución. Estudios Valentinianos, V* (AnGreg, 83). Roma: Pont. Univ. Greg., 1956, XI-314 p. Esp. 1-159: "Heracleón y la exegesis de *Mt*. 10,32-3".

1970    La revelación del Hijo por el Padre según san Ireneo (Adv. haer. IV 6). (Para la exegesis prenicena de Mt. 11,27). — *Greg* 51 (1970) 5-86 (English summary, 83-86). Esp. 7-15 [Valentinus]; 16-24.31-51 [Irenaeus]; 24-30 [Origen]; 52-73 [Irenaeus: 16,17]. [NTA 15, 144]

1971    San Ireneo y la parábola de los obreros de la viña: Mt. 20,1-16. — *EstE* 46 (1971) 35-62, 183-206. Esp. 35-37 [gnosis]; 37-39 [Tertullian]; 39-42 [Clement of Alexandria]; 43-45 [Origen]; 183-206 [Irenaeus]. [NTA 16, 159/541]

1972a   *Parábolas evangélicas en San Ireneo* (Biblioteca de autores cristianos, 331-332). Madrid: Católica, 1972, XII-460 and VIII-515 p. Esp. I, 75-105 [7,24-27]; 228-270 [21,33-46]; 288-386 [13,24-30.36-43]; 411-460 [20,1-16]; II, 3-84 [25,14-30]; 84-105 [21,28-32]; 117-181 [18,12-14]; 220-313 [22,1-14]; 444-450 [24,45-51]; 451-456 [24,28].

1972b  Ecclesia, sal terrae, según San Ireneo. [5,13] — *RSR* 60 (1972) 219-240. [NTA 17, 765]

1973   Supergrediens angelos (S. Ireneo, Adv. haer. V,36,3). — *Greg* 54 (1973) 5-59 (English summary, 58-59). Esp. 28-31 [18,10].

1976   La tentación de Jesús. — ID., *Cristología gnóstica. Introducción a la soteriologia de los siglos II y III* (Biblioteca de autores cristianos, 385), Madrid: Católica, 1976, 3-15.

1977   El Hijo del hombre come y bebe (Mt 11,19; Lc 7,34). — *Greg* 58 (1977) 523-555 (English summary, 554-555). Esp. 524-533 [Valentinus; Clement of Alexandria]; 537-552 [Irenaeus]. [NTA 22, 401]

1987   *Introducción a la teología de los siglos II y III* (AnGreg, 248). Roma: Pont. Univ. Greg., 1987, XIX-1053 p. Esp. 575-609: "En torno a los Magos"; 678-701: "Las tentaciones".

1988   El "Padrenuestro" según Marción. — *Compostellanum* (Santiago de Compostela) 33 (1988) 301-304.

1995   El Espíritu en el bautismo de Jesús (en torno a san Ireneo). [3,13-17] — *Greg* 76 (1995) 663-699.

**ORCHARD, J. Bernard**

1973   The Meaning of *ton epiousion* (Mt 6:11 = Lk 11:3). — *BTB* 3 (1973) 274-282. [NTA 18, 855]

1976a  *Matthew, Luke & Mark* (Griesbach Solution to the Synoptic Question, 1). Manchester: Koinonia, 1976, VIII-168 p. → G. Murray 1981
       D.L. DUNGAN, *Bib* 59 (1978) 584-587; B.J. MALINA, *CBQ* 39 (1977) 443-444; D.E. NINEHAM, *JTS* 28 (1977) 548-551; G. O'COLLINS, *Month* 238 (1977) 319; B. REICKE, *TZ* 33 (1977) 176-177; J.M. RIST, *JBL* 98 (1979) 137-138; C.S. RODD, *ExpT* 88 (1976-77) 257-260; M. WARD, *DownR* 25 (1977) 151-153.

1976b  J.A.T. Robinson and the Synoptic Problem. — *NTS* 22 (1975-76) 346-352. [NTA 21, 86] → J.A.T. Robinson 1975

1978*  & LONGSTAFF, T.R.W. (eds.), *J.J. Griesbach: Synoptic and Text-critical Studies 1776-1976* (SNTS MS, 34). Cambridge: University Press, 1978, XVI-224 p. → Fee, Greeven, Griesbach 1789, Reicke 1976a; → Causse 1980
       M.-É. BOISMARD, *RB* 87 (1980) 450-451; F.F. BRUCE, *EvQ* 51 (1979) 117-118; B.D. CHILTON, *ScotJT* 33 (1980) 185-187; L. COPE, *CBQ* 43 (1981) 142-143; G.G. GAMBA, *Sal* 41 (1979) 901; D. LOSADA, *RevistBíb* 44 (1982) 117.

1978   Are All Gospel Synopses Biassed? — *TZ* 34 (1978) 149-162. [NTA 23, 412]

1979   Why *three* Synoptic Gospels? A Statement of the Two-Gospel Hypothesis. — *IrTQ* 46 (1979) 240-255. [NTA 25, 59]

1980a  The Making of a Synopsis. — HAUBECK, W. – BACHMANN, M. (eds.), *Wort in der Zeit*. FS K.H. Rengstorf, 1980, 24-27.

1980b  The Two-Gospel Hypothesis or, Some Thoughts on the Revival of the Griesbach Hypothesis. — *DownR* 98 (1980) 267-279. [NTA 25, 443]

1982   *A Synopsis of the Four Gospels in a New Translation. Arranged according to the Two-Gospel Hypothesis*. Macon, GA: Mercer, 1982, XXV-294 p. → Neirynck 1985b
       B.M. METZGER, *Interpr* 38 (1984) 79-81; J.C. TURRO, *CBQ* 46 (1984) 588.

1983a  *A Synopsis of the Four Gospels in Greek Arranged according to the Two-Gospel Hypothesis*. Macon, GA: Mercer; Edinburgh: Clark, 1983, XXXIV-342 p. → J.K. Elliott 1986, 1991, Neirynck 1985b, Prior 1986
       I.H. MARSHALL, *ExpT* 95 (1983-84) 56-57.

1983b  The "Common Step" Phenomenon in the Synoptic Pericopes. [8,2-4.5-13; 14,1-2.3-12; 27,57-60] — FARMER, W.R. (ed.), *New Synoptic Studies*, 1983, 393-407.

1986   The "Neutrality" of Vertical-column Synopses. — *ETL* 62 (1986) 155-156. [NTA 31, 542] → Neirynck 1985b

1987a & RILEY, H., *The Order of the Synoptics. Why Three Synoptic Gospels?* Macon, GA: Mercer; Leuven: Peeters, 1987, XIV-294 p. → Orchard 1987b-c, H. Riley 1987
D.L. AKIN, *Criswell Theological Review* (Dallas, TX) 2 (1988) 441-443; D.L. DUNGAN, *Bib* 70 (1989) 555-558; J.K. ELLIOTT, *NT* 32 (1990) 383-384; J. ERNST, *TGl* 79 (1989) 623; P. FITZGERALD-LOMBARD, *HeythJ* 29 (1988) 510-512; A. FUCHS, *SNTU* 13 (1988) 214-215; F.J. MATERA, *CBQ* 50 (1988) 539-540; J. MCPOLIN, *IrTQ* 55 (1989) 77-78; J. MUDDIMAN, *JTS* 40 (1989) 554-556; A.G. MURRAY, *DownR* 106 (1988) 67-77; D.E. NINEHAM, *JTS* 40 (1989) 554-556; C. TUCKETT, *ScotJT* 42 (1989) 572; W.O. WALKER, Jr., *JBL* 108 (1989) 521-522; H.-T. WREGE, *TLZ* 114 (1989) 189-191.

1987b The Historical Tradition. — *Ibid.*, 109-226. Esp. 118-122: "The Matthean tradition before A.D. 150"; 123-156 [patristic witnesses: 2nd-3rd cent.]; 157-199 [Eusebius]; 200-214 [4th cent.].

1987c How the Synoptic Gospels Came into Existence. — *Ibid.*, 227-277. Esp. 233-236; 239-245: "The composition of the gospel of Matthew".

1987d The Solution of the Synoptic Problem. — *ScriptB* 18 (1987) 2-14. Esp. 4-12: "A critique of Markan priority" [8,1-4.5-13; 14,1-2.3-12]; 12-13: "The credibility of the two-gospel hypothesis". [NTA 32, 1097]

1987e Some Reflections on the Relationship of Luke to Matthew. — SANDERS, E.P. (ed.), *Jesus, the Gospels, and the Church*. FS W.R. Farmer, 1987, 33-46.

1988 The Formation of the Synoptic Gospels. — *DownR* 106 (1988) 1-16. Esp. 7-9 [Mt]; 10-16 [Mt/Mk]. [NTA 32, 1096]

1990a *Dei Verbum* and the Synoptic Gospels. — *DownR* 108 (1990) 199-214. [NTA 35, 610]

1990b Response to H. Merkel. — DUNGAN, D.L. (ed.), *The Interrelations of the Gospels*, 1990, 591-604. Esp. 592-598. → Merkel 1990, Neirynck 1990f

**ORDON, Hubert**

1984 Jezusowa interpretacja zakazu cudzołóstwa (Mt 5,27-28) (Das Ehebruchverbot in der Interpretation Jesu [Mt 5,27-28]). — *RoczTK* 31/1 (1984) 81-90. [NTA 33, 1122]

1990 Kuszenie Jezusa w świątyni w relacji Łk 4,9-12 (par. Mt 4,5-7) a śmierć Jakuba, brata Pańskiego (Die Versuchung Jesu auf "der Zinne" des Tempels [Lk 4,9-12; vgl. Mt 4,5-7] und der Tod des Jakobus Herrenbruders). — *RoczTK* 37/1 (1990) 63-75. Esp. 63-66. [NTA 38, 204]

**ORGE RAMIREZ, Manuel**

1967 "Percutiam pastorem et dispergentur oves" (Mc. 14,27; Mt. 26,31). De momento scandali crucis genesi fidei christianae. — *Claretianum* (Roma) 7 (1967) 271-291.

**ORLANDI, Tito**

1974 *Koptische Papyri theologischen Inhalts. Papiri copti di contenuto teologico. Edizione e traduzione* (Mitteilungen aus der Österreichischen Nationalbibliothek Papyrus Erzherzog Rainer, NS 9). Wien: Hollinek, 1974, V-221 p. Esp. 49-51 [3,10-12.13-15].

**ORNELLA, Antonio**

1972 Les chrétiens seront jugés. Mt 7,21-27. — *AssSeign* II/40 (1972) 16-27. [NTA 17, 911]

**O'ROURKE, John J.**

1962 The Fulfillment Texts in Matthew. — *CBQ* 24 (1962) 394-403. [NTA 7, 498]

1964a Explicit Old Testament Citations in the Gospels. — *Studia Montis Regii* (Montreal) 7 (1964) 37-60. Esp. 37-38 [2,5-6]; 38 [3,3]; 40 [4,6-10]; 41 [5,21.32.33.38.43]; 42-44 [13,14-15]; 44-45 [15,4]; 45-46 [15,7-8]; 46 [19,4]; 46-47 [19,17]; 47-48 [21,13.16.42]; 49 [22,24]; 50 [22,31-32.37]; 51 [22,42-43]; 52-53 [24,15]; 53-54 [26,31]; 58-60. [NTA 9, 117]

1964b A Note on an Exception: Mt 5:32 (19:9) and 1 Cor 7:12 Compared. — *HeythJ* 5 (1964) 299-302. [NTA 9, 527]

1970 The Military in the NT. — *CBQ* 32 (1970) 227-236. Esp. 227-228 [8,7]; 229 [27,27]; 230 [27,54]; 231 [28,12]; 232 [27,62-66]. [NTA 15, 45]

1974 Some Observations on the Synoptic Problem and the Use of Statistical Procedures. — *NT* 16 (1974) 272-277. [NTA 19, 929] → de Solages 1959, Honoré 1968

1975 The Article as a Pronoun in the Synoptic Gospels. — *CBQ* 37 (1975) 492-499. Esp. 493-494.497-498. [NTA 20, 763]

1994 Possible Uses of the Old Testament in the Gospels: An Overview. — EVANS, C.A. – STEGNER, W.R. (eds.), *The Gospels and the Scriptures of Israel*, 1994, 15-25. Esp. 16-18.

**ORSATTI, Mauro**

1980 *Un saggio di teologia della storia. Esegesi di Mt. 1,1-17* (Studi biblici, 55). Brescia: Paideia, 1980, 112 p. [NTA 25, p. 200]
A. BONORA, *Humanitas* 36 (1981) 894-895; A. BOTTINO, *Marianum* 47 (1985) 370-371; B. CORSANI, *Henoch* 7 (1985) 97; J. DUPONT, *TRev* 78 (1982) 454; F.C.D., *RivBib* 30 (1982) 285; P. ZILONKA, *CBQ* 44 (1982) 342-343.

1994a I Vangeli dell'Infanzia (Mt 1-2 e Lc 1-2). — LÀCONI, M. (ed.), *Vangeli sinottici*, 1994, 443-457.

1994b La visita dei Magi: Mt 2,1-12. — *Ibid.*, 459-472.

1995 Gesù Cristo, Figlio di Davide, di Abrahamo ... di Maria: Una nota mariologica nella cristologia di Mt 1,1-17. — *Theotokos* 3/1 (1995) 13-38.

**ORTEGA, Ofelia**

1980 Tres parábolas de Jesús sobre pobreza y justicia. [13,24-30.36-43; 20,1-15] — *Cristianismo y Sociedad* 18 (1980) 121-128.

**ORTIZ VALDIVIESO, Pedro**

1981 *Introducción a los evangelios* (Colección Profesores, 11). Bogotá: Pontificia Universidad Javeriana, 1981, 152 p.

**ORTON, David E.**

1989 *The Understanding Scribe. Matthew and the Apocalyptic Ideal* (JSNT SS, 25). Sheffield: JSOT, 1989, 280 p. Esp. 15-38.177-187: "The scribes in Matthew"; 137-163.230-238: "The scribal ideal and Matthew's disciples" [13,51-52; 23,34]; 165-176.238-240: "Matthew as scribe". [NTA 34, p. 113] — Diss. Sheffield, 1986 (P.R. Davies – B.D. Chilton).
W. ADLER, *JQR* 83 (1992-93) 184-186; I. BROER, *TLZ* 115 (1990) 812-813; G. CLAUDEL, *Bib* 72 (1991) 119-123; E. CUVILLIER, *ETR* 65 (1990) 450; M. DAVIES, *ExpT* 101 (1989-90) 121; B.R. DOYLE, *RB* 98 (1991) 626-627; D.E. GARLAND, *RExp* 87 (1990) 648; C.J.A. HICKLING, *JTS* 42 (1991) 189-191; L. HOULDEN, *Theology* 93 (1990) 159-160; A.-Y. LEVINE, *JBL* 110 (1991) 527-529; B.F. MEYER, *CBQ* 53 (1991) 503-504; J. NOLLAND, *EvQ* 63 (1991) 268-270; J.-M. ROUSÉE, *RB* 96 (1989) 636-637; C. SCHANS, *JJS* 45 (1994) 140-142; H. WANSBROUGH, *ScriptB* 22/1 (1992) 25-26.

1994 Matthew and Other Creative Jewish Writers. [OT pseudepigrapha] — PORTER, S.E., et al. (eds.), *Crossing the Boundaries*. FS M.D. Goulder, 1994, 133-140.

**ORY, Georges**

1983 Saint Pierre, ce célèbre inconnu. — *CahRenan* 31 (1983) 121-134. [NTA 28, 1238]

**OSBORN, Eric F.**

1976 Origen and Justification: The Good is One. There is None Good but God (Matt. 19.17 et par.) — *AusBR* 24 (1976) 18-29.

**OSBORNE, Grant R.**

1976 Redaction Criticism and the Great Commission. A Case Study Toward a Biblical Understanding of Inerrancy. — *JEvTS* 19 (1976) 73-85. Esp. 73-83: "A redactional study". [NTA 21, 385]

1979 Redactional Trajectories in the Crucifixion Narrative — *EvQ* 51 (1979) 80-96. Esp. 86-88 [27,33-54]. [NTA 23, 795]

1984 *The Resurrection Narratives. A Redactional Study.* Grand Rapids, MI: Baker, 1984, 344 p. Esp. 73-98: "Matthew's resurrection narrative"; 195-219: "The empty tomb narratives". — Diss. Aberdeen, 1975 (I.H. Marshall).

1992 Resurrection. — *DJG,* 1992, 673-688. Esp. 679-681.

**OSBORNE, Robert E.**

1973 The Provenance of Matthew's Gospel. — *StudRel/SciRel* 3 (1973-74) 220-235. [NTA 18, 840]

**OSBURN, Carroll D.**

1981 The Present Indicative in Matthew 19:9. — *RestQ* 24 (1981) 193-203. [NTA 26, 845]

**O'SHEA, William J.**

1970 Marriage and Divorce: The Biblical Evidence. — *AustralasCR* 47 (1970) 89-109. Esp. 94-109: "St. Matthew's version". [NTA 15, 995]
    *TDig* 19 (1971) 4-8.

**OSIEK, Carolyn**

1981 The Ransom of Captives. Evolution of a Tradition. — *HTR* 74 (1981) 365-386. Esp. 367-368 [25,36.39.43].

1983 *Rich and Poor in the Shepherd of Hermas. An Exegetical-Social Investigation* (CBQ MS, 15). Washington, DC: Catholic Biblical Association, 1983, XI-184 p. Esp. 24-32 [Q]; 68-72. — Diss. Harvard Univ., 1981 (H. Koester).

1989 The Resurrection: Prism of New Testament Faith. — *BiTod* 27 (1989) 133-139. Esp. 135-136 [Mt]. [NTA 33, 1094]

**OSSEGE, Manfred**

1975 Einige Aspekte zur Gliederung des neutestamentlichen Wortschatzes (am Beispiel von δικαιοσύνη bei Matthäus). — *LingBib* 34 (1975) 37-101. Esp. 61-63, 85, 88-100. [NTA 20, 24]

**OSSOLA, Carlo**

1973 Un contributo alla storia della spiritualità valdesiana in Italia: Tradizione e traduzione del *Commento a Matteo* di Juan de Valdés. — *RivStoLR* 9 (1973) 62-68.

1985 & CAVALLARIN, A.M. (eds.), *Juan de Valdés. Lo evangelio di San Matteo* [1539; Spanish ed. 1880; Italian trans. 1930] (Biblioteca del Cinquecento. Europa delle corti, 31). Roma: Bulzoni, 1985, 540 p.
    T. BOZZA, *Protestantesimo* 42 (1987) 56-58; G. FRAGNITO, *RivStoLR* 23 (1989) 171-176.

**OTADUY, Esteban Inciarte**

1967 Die evangelische Geschichte Christi des Königs. Untersuchung eines Mißverständnisses. [2,2] — ROSENKRANZ, G. (ed.), *Theologische Stimmen aus Asien, Afrika und Lateinamerika* (Beiträge zur biblischen Theologie, 2), München: Kaiser, 1967, 164-192. Esp. 172-176 [2,2].

**OTRANTO, Giorgio**

1969 Matteo 7,15-16a e gli ψευδοπροφῆται nell'esegesi patristica. — *VetChr* 6 (1969) 33-45.

**OTT, Wilhelm**

1965 *Gebet und Heil. Die Bedeutung der Gebetsparänese in der lukanischen Theologie* (SANT, 12). München: Kösel, 1965, 160 p. Esp. 92-123: "Die Gebetsunterweisungen in Lk 11,1-13" [Q]. — Diss. Würzburg, 1963-64 (R. Schnackenburg).

**OTTO, Rudolf**

1933[R] *Reich Gottes und Menschensohn. Ein religionsgeschichtlicher Versuch* [1933]. München:

Beck, [3]1954, XI-326 p. Esp. 48 [3,2]; 50 [11,28-30]; 79-82 [11,11-13]; 93 [13,33]; 94-96 [13,47-50]; 96-98 [13,44-46]; 104-111 [13,10-17]; 180 [16,13]; 185-186 [11,25-27]; 252-255 [26,26-29]; 295-296 [16,17-19]; 297 [23,13].

**OUDERSLUYS, R.C.**

1973 The Parable of the Sheep and Goats (Mt 25:31-46): Eschatology and Mission, Then and Now. — *Reformed Review* (New Brunswick, NJ) 26 (1972-73) 151-161.

**OUTTIER, Bernard**

1972 Un feuillet du lectionnaire géorgien hanmeti à Paris. [28,4-7] — *Muséon* 85 (1972) 399-402. [NTA 17, 834] → Tarchnišvili 1942/60

**OVERMAN, John Andrew**

1990a *Matthew's Gospel and Formative Judaism. The Social World of the Matthean Community*. Minneapolis, MN: Fortress, 1990, IX-174 p. Esp. 6-34: "The background and horizon of Matthean and formative Judaism"; 72-149: "The social development of the Matthean community"; 150-161: "The nature and world of the Matthean community". [NTA 35, p. 245] — Diss. Boston, 1988-89 (H.C. Kee). → Keerankeri 1994

    S.C. BARTON, *ExpT* 102 (1990-91) 315-316; B.E. BOWE, *CBQ* 54 (1992) 362-363; F.W. BURNETT, *JBL* 110 (1991) 725-726; L. COPE, *TS* 52 (1991) 388; B.R. DOYLE, *Pacifica* 6 (1993) 335-337; J. ENGELBRECHT, *Neotestamentica* 27 (1993) 195-197; P.F. ESLER, *BibInt* 1 (1993) 255-258; R.A.J. GAGNON, *NT* 34 (1992) 294-297; D. HARRINGTON, *NewTheolRev* 5/3 (1992) 107-108; S. JOUBERT, *BTB* 22 (1992) 42-43; M.P. KNOWLES, *TorontoJT* 8 (1992) 191-192. S.P. SAUNDERS, *JQR* 84 (1993-94) 356-358; A.A. TRITES, *RExp* 88 (1991) 268-269; B.T. VIVIANO, *RB* 99 (1992) 607-609; M.I. WEGENER, *Interpr* 46 (1992) 200-201.

1990b Heroes and Villains in Palestinian Lore: Matthew's Use of Traditional Jewish Polemic in the Passion Narrative. — *SBL 1990 Seminar Papers*, 592-602. Esp. 593-597: "The Palestinian setting of Matthean polemics"; 597-601: "Traditional polemic in Matthew's passion narrative".

1993 Matthew. — METZGER, B.M. – COOGAN, M.D. (eds ), *The Oxford Companion to the Bible*, 1993, 501-502.

1995 Matthew's Parables and Roman Politics. The Imperial Setting of Matthew's Narrative with Special Reference to His Parables. — *SBL 1995 Seminar Papers*, 425-439.

**OVERNEY, Max**

1953 Le cadre historique des paroles de Jésus sur la primauté de saint Pierre. — *NVet* 28 (1953) 206-229.

**OVERSTREET, R. Larry**

1981 Difficulties of New Testament Genealogies. — *GraceTJ* 2 (1981) 303-326. [NTA 26, 462]

**OWEN, H.P.**

1959 The Parousia of Christ in the Synoptic Gospels. — *ScotJT* 12 (1959) 171-192. Esp. 175-176 [10,23]; 177-178 [23,37-39]; 178-179 [25,14-30]; 179-181 [24,42-51]. [NTA 4, 66]

**OWEN-BALL, David T.**

1993 Rabbinic Rhetoric and the Tribute Passage (Mt. 22:15-22; Mk. 12:13-17; Lk. 20:20-26). — *NT* 35 (1993) 1-14. [NTA 37, 1270]

**OWENS, L.G.**

1967 Virgin Birth. — *NewCathEnc* 14 (1967) 692-697.

# P

**PACE, Giuseppe**

1980    La senapa del Vangelo. [13,31-32] — *BibOr* 22 (1980) 119-123. [NTA 25, 480] → Granata 1982

**PACIOREK, Antoni**

1973    Mt 16,17-19 przedredakcyjna jednostka literacka (De influxu traditionis primitivae in Mt 16,17-19). — *RoczTK* 20/1 (1973) 59-67. [NTA 19, 93]

1978    Kilka uwag o literackich problemach obietnicy prymatu (Mt 16,17-19). [Literary-critical problems on the primacy (Mt 16,17-19)] — ŁACH, S. - SZLAGA, J. (eds.), *Studio lectionem facere*, Lublin: Catholic University, 1978, 165-168.

**PADILLA, Carmen**

1990    Sobre el verbo ἀποκρίνομαι en el Nuevo Testamento. — *FilolNT* 3 (1990) 67-74. [NTA 35, 72]

**PAFFENROTH, Kim**

1992    The Stories of the Fate of Judas and Differing Attitudes towards Sources. — *Proceedings EGLBS* 12 (1992) 67-81. Esp. 68-71 [27,3-10].

1994    Science or Story? The Star of Bethlehem. [2,9] — *ExpT* 106 (1994-95) 78-79. [NTA 39, 796]

**PAGANI, Sergio**

1978    Le versioni latine africane del Nuovo Testamento: considerazioni su *Mt.* 10,32-33 in Tertulliano e Cipriano. — *BibOr* 20 (1978) 255-270. Esp. 264-270. [NTA 23, 825]

**PAGE, Homer Ansburn, Jr.**

1991    *An Investigation of the Concept of Reward in the Gospel of Matthew.* Diss. New Orleans Baptist Theological Seminary, 1991, 206 p. (B.E. Simmons). — *DissAbstr* 53 (1992-93) 185.

**PAGELS, Elaine**

1992    The Social History of Satan. Part 2: The Human Face(s) of Satan in the Gospels. — *SBL 1992 Seminar Papers*, 320-345. Esp. 327-331. → 1994

1994    The Social History of Satan. Part 2: Satan in the New Testament Gospels. — *JAAR* 62 (1994) 17-58. Esp. 22-23 [Q]; 29-35 [Mt]. [NTA 39, 93] → 1992

1995    *The Origin of Satan.* New York: Random, 1995, XXIII-214 p. Esp. 63-88: "Matthew's campaign against the Pharisees: Deploying the Devil".
    *L'origine de Satan*, trans. C. Cantoni-Fort. Paris: Bayard, 1997, 271 p. Esp. 85-114.

**PAGENKEMPER, Karl Edmond**

1990    *An Analysis of the Rejection Motif in the Synoptic Parables and Its Relationship to Pauline Soteriology.* Diss. Theol. Sem., Dallas, TX, 1990, 421 p. (D.L. Bock). — *DissAbstr* 52 (1991-92) 969.

**PAGNOTTA, Umberto**

1973    Tu sei Pietro. Considerazioni della filologia del testo del Vangelo di Matteo (16,13-20), considerato titolo giuridico del Primato Pontificio: sua autenticità e legittimità. — *RicBibRel* 8/1 (1973) 71-77. [NTA 18, 471]

**PAINTER, John**

1989    Tradition and Interpretation in John 6. — *NTS* 35 (1989) 421-450. Esp. 422-426: "John and the Synoptics". [NTA 34, 213]

1991 Quest Stories in John 1–4. — *JSNT* 41 (1991) 33-70. Esp. 56 [18,3/Jn 3,3.5]; 65-68 [8,5-13/Jn 4,46-54]. [NTA 36, 231]

1992a Bread. — *DJG*, 1992, 83-86. Esp. 84-85.

1992b World. — *Ibid.*, 887-891. Esp. 887-889.

1992c Quest Stories in John and the Synoptics. — DENAUX, A. (ed.), *John and the Synoptics*, 1992, 498-506. Esp. 501-505 [Jn 1,19-34].

**PAJOR, Piotr**

1967 Znaczenie chrztu Duchem Świętym i ogniem (La signification du baptême de l'Esprit Saint et du feu). [3,11] — *RoczTK* 14/1 (1967) 49-64. [NTA 12, 698] — Diss. Lublin, 1966.

**PALATTY, Paul**

1985 Discipleship in the Synoptic Gospels. — *Bible Bhashyam* 11 (1985) 224-235. [NTA 31, 101]

**PALMER, Darryl**

1974 The Resurrection of Jesus and the Mission of the Church. — BANKS, R. (ed.), *Reconciliation and Hope. New Testament Essays on Atonement and Eschatology Presented to L.L. Morris on his 60th Birthday*, Grand Rapids, MI: Eerdmans, 1974, 205-223. Esp. 206-208 [28,1-10]; 209 [28,16-20]; 215-216 [28,9-10.16-20].

**PALMER, N. Humphrey**

1967 Lachmann's Argument. — *NTS* 13 (1966-67) 368-378. [NTA 12, 544]; = BELLINZONI, A.J., Jr., et al. (eds.), *The Two-Source Hypothesis*, 1985, 119-131. → W.R. Farmer 1968

1968 *The Logic of Gospel Criticism. An Account of the Methods and Arguments Used by Textual, Documentary, Source and Form Critics of the New Testament*. London: Macmillan – New York: St. Martin's, 1968, X-260 p. Esp. 112-137.138-163: "Placing the books"; 167-174: "Proving a source" [Q]; 225-231 [Mark].

1976 Just Married, Cannot Come. — *NT* 18 (1976) 241-257. Esp. 245-247: "Matthew's tale"; 253-255: "Matthew's much-revised version" [22,1-14]; 255-256 [22,13]. [NTA 21, 730]

**PALMERO, María Dolores**

1983 ¡Felices, los misericordiosos! [5,7] — *BibFe* 9 (1983) 170-177.

**PALOMERO DÍAZ, Gabriel**

1951a Valor del "cum esset justus" in Mt. 1,19. — *EstJos* 5 (1951) 67-73.

1951b La paternidad de San José en los Evangelios. — *Ibid.*, 143-175.

**PAMMENT, M.** → DAVIES (PAMMENT), M.

**PANČOVSKI, J.G.**

1968 Zeniti v rodoslovieto na Iisusa Christa (Frauen in der Genealogie Jesu Christi). — *Duchovna Kultura* (Sofia) 48/1 (1968) 26-32.

**PANIER, Louis**

1984 *Récit et commentaires de la tentation de Jésus au désert. Approche sémiotique du discours interprétatif*. Paris: Cerf, 1984, V-381 p. Esp. 19-110.365-369: "La composante narrative du récit de commentaire"; 111-272.370-376: "La composante discursive du discours de commentaire"; 273-298.376-378: "Esquisse sur l'énonciation dans le commentaire". — Diss. Paris–Nanterre, 1976 (A.J. Greimas). → Giroud 1987a, F. Martin 1987

   C. FOCANT, *RTL* 17 (1986) 89-90; C.J.A. HICKLING, *JTS* 38 (1987) 166-167; É. NODET, *RB* 93 (1986) 613-614; D. PATTE, *JBL* 106 (1987) 335-339; W. VOGELS, *CBQ* 47 (1985) 741-742.

1987 → F. Martin 1987

1993 Le Fils de l'homme et les nations. Lecture de Mt 25,31-46. — *SémBib* 69 (1993) 39-52. [NTA 38, 169]

**PANIKKAR, Raimon**

1972 El sujeto de la infalibilidad. Solipsismo y verificación. — *Revista de Occidente* (Madrid) 108 (1972) 315-340.

**PANIMOLLE, Salvatore Alberto**

1985a L'amore dei nemici. — *ParSpirV* 11 (1985) 111-125. Esp. 119-125 [5,43-48].

1985b La struttura del discorso della montagna (Mt. 5-7). — *Testimonium Christi*. FS J. Dupont, 1985, 329-350.

1986 *Il discorso della montagna (Mt 5-7). Esegesi e vita* (Fame e sete della parola, 5). Torino: Paoline, 1986, 230 p. [NTA 32, p. 108]
    V. FUSCO, *RivBib* 36 (1988) 113-115; S. SABUGAL, *Revista Agustiniana* (Madrid) 30 (1989) 741.

1987 Voi siete il sale della terra e la luce del mondo (Mt 5,13-16). — *ParSpirV* 15 (1987) 139-155.

1990a "Beati...! Guai...!". Lc 6,20ss. — *ParSpirV* 21 (1990) 117-151. Esp. 123-135: "La struttura di Mt 5,3-12"; 135-141 [Q 6,20-23].

1990b Storicità dell'incarnazione del Verbo e Vangelo dell'Infanzia nel *Dialogo con Trifone* di san Giustino. — *Marianum* 52 (1990) 63-85. Esp. 74-79.

1992 Il Vangelo dell'Infanzia negli scritti de S. Giustino. — SERRA, A. - VALENTINI, A. (eds.), *I Vangeli dell'infanzia*, I, 1992, 97-102.

1994 La legge della comunità cristiana (Mt 5,21-48; Lc 6,27-36). — LÀCONI, M. (ed.), *Vangeli sinottici*, 1994, 319-335.

**PANOSIAN, E.W.**

1967 et al., Focus on Matthew. — *Biblical Viewpoint* (Greenville, SC) 1/2 (1967) 75-149.

**PANTELIS, Jorge**

1989 Los pobres en espíritu. Bienaventurados en el Reino de Dios. Mateo 5,3-12. — *RevistBíb* 51 (1989) 1-9. [NTA 34, 1134]

**PANTLE-SCHIEBER, Klaus**

1989 Anmerkungen zur Auseinandersetzung von ἐκκλησία und Judentum im Matthäus-evangelium. — *ZNW* 80 (1989) 145-162. Esp. 146-153 [ἐκκλησία-συναγωγή]; 253-161 [γραμματεῖς-Φαρισαῖοι]. [NTA 34, 603]

**PAPONE, Paolo**

1990 Il regno dei cieli soffre violenza? (Mt 11,12). — *RivBib* 38 (1990) 375-376. [NTA 35, 626]

**PAPPAS, Harry S.**

1980 The "Exhortation to Fearless Confession" - Mt. 10.26-33. — *The Greek Orthodox Theological Review* (Brookline, MA) 25 (1980) 239-248. [NTA 25, 859]

**PARENTE, Pietro**

1983 Teologia del "Padre Nostro". — *PalCl* 62 (1983) 1322-1335.

**PARETSKY, Jeremy Albert**

1985 *Jewish Eschatological Expectation and the Transfiguration of Christ*. Diss. Pont. Univ. S. Thomae, Roma, 1985, XII-352 p. (J. Salguero). Esp. 224-230.

1991 The Transfiguration of Christ: Its Eschatological and Christological Dimensions. — *NBlackfr* 72 (1991) 313-324.

**PARISI, Serafino**

1994 Mt 5,17-48: giustizia superiore e fede "estroversa". La morale sociale da "un punto di vista" della Scrittura. — *Vivarium* (Catanzaro) 2 (1994) 45-62. [NTA 39, 143]

**PARK, Eung Chung**

1995    *The Mission Discourse in Matthew's Interpretation* (WUNT, II/81). Tübingen: Mohr, 1995, VIII-219 p. Esp. 32-60: "Establishment of the text"; 61-79: "Literary analysis"; 80-166: "Interpretation"; 167-186: "Matthew's theology of mission". [NTA 41, p. 150] — Diss. Chicago, IL, 1991 (H.D. Betz).

**PARK, Tae-Sik**

1994    *Ὄχλος im Neuen Testament*. Diss. Göttingen, 1994, 262 p. (G. Strecker). Esp. 73-138: "Ὄχλος im Matthäusevangelium".

**PARKER, David C.**

1985    The Translation of οὖν in the Old Latin Gospels. — *NTS* 31 (1985) 252-276. Esp. 253-261: "The translation of the gospels into Latin"; 261-267: "The Greek texts represented in the Latin witnesses" [6,33]; 267-275: "Codex Bezae" [13,28; 18,26; 21,26; 25,3; 26,24]. [NTA 30, 43]

1992    *Codex Bezae. An Early Christian Manuscript and Its Text*. Cambridge: University Press, 1992, XXIII-349 p. Esp. 198-203: "The gospel of Matthew"; 287-288; 291-293 [Scrivener]. — Diss. Leiden, 1989 (M. de Jonge).

1993    The Early Traditions of Jesus' Sayings on Divorce. — *Theology* 96 (1993) 372-383. Esp. 373-374 [5,27-32]; 376-378 [19,3-9]. [NTA 38, 757]

1995    Was Matthew Written Before 50 CE? The Magdalen Papyrus of Matthew. — *ExpT* 107 (1995-96) 40-43. [NTA 40, 718] → Thiede 1995c

**PARKER, Pierson**

1953    *The Gospel before Mark*. Chicago, IL: University Press, 1953, IX-266 p. Esp. 7-24: "The text of M"; 27-31: "The language of M and Q compared"; 32-39 "The language of M and Matthew's Markan material"; 47-51: "The gaps in M"; 60-69: "Matthew's method with Q"; 70-84: "The extent of Q in Matthew"; 123-128: "The effect of Q in Matthew"; 129-138: "Matthew and the age of Domitian"; 141-155: "What was the K document?"; 163-172: "K and the synoptic solution"; 175-235: "The reconstruction of K"; 239-249: "Appendices". → 1979; → Butler 1955b, Meynell 1963, C.W.F. Smith 1954, Zerwick 1955 M.E. ANDREWS, *JBR* 22 (1954) 64-65; A.E. BARNETT, *JBL* 73 (1954) 184-185; M.-É. BOISMARD, *RB* 61 (1954) 454-455; H.J. CADBURY, *The Review of Religion* (New York) 19 (1954-55) 209-211; J.T. GRIFFIN, *CBQ* 16 (1954) 259-261; X. LÉON-DUFOUR, *RSR* 42 (1954) 572-576; J. LEVIE, *NRT* 77 (1955) 536-537; T.W. MANSON, *JTS* 8 (1957) 143-145; B.M. METZGER, *Interpr* 8 (1954) 330-332; C. PERROT, *Cahiers sioniens* (Paris) 9 (1955) 124-127; J. SCHMID, *TRev* 52 (1956) 55-56; M. SMITH, *ATR* 36 (1954) 210-213; V. TAYLOR, *Theology* 57 (1954) 228-229; A. VIARD, *RSPT* 39 (1955) 275; A. WIKGREN, *JRel* 35 (1955) 180-181; E.K. WINTER, *Judaica* 10 (1954) 123-127; H.G. WOOD, *HibbJourn* 52 (1953-54) 312-314.

1963    Luke and the Fourth Evangelist. — *NTS* 9 (1962-93) 317-336. Esp. 326-334 [Mt/Jn]. [NTA 8, 152]

1970    Mark, Acts, and Galilean Christianity. — *NTS* 16 (1969-70) 295-304. Esp. 301-302 [Mt/Acts]. [NTA 15, 156]

1972    7Q5. Enthält das Papyrusfragment 5 aus der Höhle 7 von Qumrân einen Markustext? [1,2-3] — *ErbAuf* 48 (1972) 467-469. [NTA 17, 830] → O'Callaghan 1974a

1976    *Good News in Matthew*. Matthew *in Today's English Version*. Cleveland, OH: Collins & World/Fount Books, 1976, 283 p. [NTA 23, p. 96]

1979    A Second Look at *The Gospel before Mark*. — *SBL 1979 Seminar Papers*, I, 147-168. Esp. 147-150 [central thesis; some departures]; 163-166 [Lk and Q]; = *JBL* 100 (1981) 389-413 (revised). Esp. 389-395; 408-411. [NTA 26, 835] → 1953

The Second Gospel is Secondary. [1979, 151-161 = 1981, 395-405] — BELLINZONI, A.J., Jr., et al. (eds.), *The Two-Source Hypothesis*, 1985, 205-217.

1983    The Posteriority of Mark. — FARMER, W.R. (ed.), *New Synoptic Studies*, 1983, 67-142. Esp. 92-103: "Mark and Matthew"; 103-115: "Mark, Matthew, and Luke".

**PARKER, S. Thomas**

1975 The Decapolis Reviewed. — *JBL* 94 (1975) 437-441. [NTA 20, 631]

**PARKHURST, L.G.**

1979 Matthew 28,16-20 Reconsidered. — *ExpT* 90 (1978-79) 179-180. [NTA 23, 835]

**PARKMAN, Joel Willam**

1994 *Adam Christological Motifs in the Synoptic Traditions.* Diss. Baylor Univ., Waco, TX, 1994, 221 p. (N.H. Keathley). — *DissAbstr* 55 (1994-95) 996.

**PARKS, S.K.**

1993 *A Theological Rationale for a Worldwide Mission: A Critical Evaluation of Jesus' Use of Old Testament Themes Concerning the Nations.* Diss. Southern Baptist Theol. Sem., Louisville, KY, 1993, 347 p. (J.C. Anderson). — *DissAbstr* 54 (1993-94) 1427.

**PARRATT, J.K.**

1971 The Holy Spirit and Baptism. Part I. The Gospels and the Acts of the Apostles. — *ExpT* 82 (1970-71) 231-235. Esp. 232-234 [3,11-17]. [NTA 16, 78]

**PARRINDER, Geoffrey**

1992 *Son of Joseph. The Parentage of Jesus.* Edinburgh: Clark, 1992, VII-129 p. Esp. 1-9 [1,1-17]; 10-25: "Annunciation and nativity – Matthew".

**PARROTT, H.W.**

1960 Blind Bartimaeus Cries out Again. [9,27-31; 20,29-34] — *EvQ* 32 (1960) 25-29.

**PARROTT, Rod**

1989 Entering the Narrow Door. Matt 7:13-14 / Luke 13:22-24. — *Forum* 5/1 (1989) 111-120. Esp. 114-117 [7,13-14]; 117-118 [Q 13,24a]. [NTA 34, 121]

**PARUZEL, H.**

1975 La infanceo de Jesuo. — *Biblia Revuo* (Ravenna) 11 (1975) 133-149. [NTA 20, 770]

**PARVIS, Paul**

1984 The Teaching of the Fathers: Chrysostom and the Reading of Matthew's Gospel. — *CleR* 69 (1984) 97-99.

**PASCHE, M.**

1976 Du complot à la résurrection. En priant avec S. Matthieu. — *Les Échos de Saint-Maurice* 72 (1976) 99-113.

**PASCUAL CALVO, Enrique**

1964 La Genealogía de Jesús según S. Mateo. — *EstBíb* 23 (1964) 109-149. Esp. 109-114.118-124 [1,1]; 125-146 [1,2-17]. [NTA 9, 899]

**PASQUETTO, Virgilio**

1977 I racconti evangelici dell'infanzia di Gesù. — *Rivista di vita spirituale* (Roma) 31 (1977) 32-51.

1978a Il discorso della montagna. — *Rivista di vita spirituale* 32 (1978) 27-52, 146-168.

1978b Il privilegio di "essere piccoli" nell'insegnamento di Matteo. — *Ibid.*, 249-270.

**PASQUIER, Jean Marc**

1984 Présence d'Élie dans le Nouveau Testament. — *SIDIC* 17/3 (1984) 26-30.
     The Presence of Elijah in the New Testament. — *SIDIC* 17/3 (1984) 22-25. [NTA 32, 1112]

**PASSONI DELL'ACQUA, Anna**

1980  Frammenti inediti del Vangelo secondo Matteo. — *Aegyptus* 60 (1980) 96-119. Esp. 97-102 [*l* 1354]; 102-106 [0275]; 107-109 [6,9]; 110-119 [0204]. [NTA 26, 82]

1993  Pietro e la roccia. Puntualizzazione dell'analisi filologca di un libro recente. — *RivBib* 41 (1993) 189-199. [NTA 38, 164r] → Caragounis 1990

**PATHRAPANKAL, Joseph**

1980  Aspects of Discipleship in the Sermon on the Mount. — *Jeevadhara* 10 (1980) 148-158. [NTA 25, 71] → 1982, 7-18

1982  *Christian Life. New Testament Perspectives.* Bangalore: Dharmaram, 1982, VII-114 p. Esp. 7-18 (= 1980); 46-47; 51-52.

**PATRÔNOS, G.P.**

1975  The Call of the Disciples of Jesus according to the Gospel Tradition (Synoptic and Johannine). [Greek] — *Θεολογία* (Athens) 46 (1975) 882-900; 47 (1976) 114-125, 391-401.

**PATSCH, Hermann**

1971  Abendmahlsterminologie außerhalb der Einsetzungsberichte. Erwägungen zur Traditionsgeschichte der Abendmahlsworte. — *ZNW* 62 (1971) 210-231. Esp. 213-214 [26,26]; 214-215 [15,36]; 227-228. [NTA 16, 779]

1972  *Abendmahl und historischer Jesus* (Calwer theologische Monographien, A1). Stuttgart: Calwer, 1972, 390 p. Esp. 69-70 [26,26-29]; 111-114 [13,24-30]; 124-127 [10,23]; 200-202 [21,33-46]; 202-204 [12,39-40]. — Diss. München, 1969 (L. Goppelt).

**PATSCH, Joseph**

1957  Die Magier aus dem Morgenland. — *TPQ* 105 (1957) 1-8.

**PATTE, Daniel**

1982  Entering the Kingdom Like Children: A Structural Exegesis. — *SBL 1982 Seminar Papers*, 371-396. Esp. 376-378.389-390 [18,1-5]; 378.390-392 [19,13-15]; 381-383 [18,1-5/Th 22]. → J.D. Crossan 1982
Jesus' Pronouncement about Entering the Kingdom Like a Child: A Structural Exegesis. — *Semeia* 29 (1983) 3-42. Esp. 11-13.28-31; 14-15.31-33; 19-21; 39-40: "Conclusion: Entering the Kingdom like a child according to Matthew 18 & 19". [NTA 28, 939]
Response: B.B. SCOTT, *ibid.*, 118-130.

1987  *The Gospel according to Matthew. A Structural Commentary on Matthew's Faith.* Philadelphia, PA: Fortress, 1987, XVI-432 p. Esp. 1-15 "Introduction"; 16-405 [commentary]; 406-417: "Narrative oppositions in Matthew". [NTA 31, p. 235]
D.A. BLACK, *Criswell Theological Review* (Dallas, TX) 3 (1988-89) 218-220; F.W. BURNETT, *CBQ* 50 (1988) 144-145; M. CARREZ, *RHPR* 68 (1988) 248-249; W.R. DOMERIS, *Neotestamentica* 24 (1990) 373-376; J.D. EVERS, *TorontoJT* 6 (1990) 353-355; D. FRANCE, *Themelios* 13 (1987-88) 99; D.E. GARLAND, *RExp* 85 (1988) 135; D. HILL, *ExpT* 99 (1987-88) 23; J.D. KINGSBURY, *JBL* 107 (1988) 756-758; R.A. PIPER, *ScotJT* 42 (1989) 451-453; D. SENIOR, *CRBR* 3 (1990) 230-232; G. STANTON, *Interpr* 43 (1989) 184-186; W. WUELLNER, *CurrTMiss* 14 (1987) 451-452.

1988  Anti-Semitism in the New Testament. Confronting the Dark Side of Paul's and Matthew's Teaching. — *Chicago Theological Seminary Register* (Chicago, IL) 78 (1988) 31-52. [NTA 32, 1022]

1990a  Bringing Out the Gospel-Treasure. What Is New and What Is Old. Two Parables in Matthew 18–23. [18,21-35; 20,1-16] — *QuartRev* 10/3 (1990) 79-108. [NTA 35, 145]

1990b  "Love Your Enemies" – "Woe to You, Scribes and Pharisees". The Need for a Semiotic Approach in New Testament Studies. — JENNINGS, T.W. (ed.), *Text and Logos*. FS H.W. Boers, 1990, 81-96. Esp. 84-90, 94-96 [5,44-45; 23,13-35].

1993 Textual Constraints, Ordinary Readings, and Critical Exegesis: An Androcritical Perspective. — *Semeia* 62 (1993) 59-79. Esp. 70-75: "Diversified textual determinacy: critical interpretations of Matt. 8:17". [NTA 38, 645]

1995 *Ethics of Biblical Interpretation. A Reevaluation.* Louisville, KY: Westminster/Knox, 1995, XI-145 p. Esp. 37-54 [23,8-11].

**PATTEN, P.**

1991 & PATTEN, R., *The World of the Early Church: A Companion to the New Testament.* Lewiston, NY – Queenston, Ont. – Lampeter: Mellen, 1991, IX-263 p.

**PATTERSON, Stephen J.**

1988 *The Gospel of Thomas Within the Development of Early Christianity.* Diss. Claremont Graduate School, 1988, VIII-334 p. (J.M. Robinson). Esp. 5-69: "The Gospel of Thomas and the synoptic tradition. A *Forschungsbericht* and critique"; 70-163: "The Gospel of Thomas and the synoptic tradition. A solution".

1989 Fire and Dissension. Ipsissima Vox Jesu in Q 12:49,51-53? — *Forum* 5/2 (1989) 121-139. Esp. 122-126: "The Q text"; 126-130: "Tradition history in Q 12:49,51-53"; 130-134: "The question of attribution: criteria"; 134-138: "Recommendations". [NTA 34, 173]

1990a The Gospel of Thomas and the Historical Jesus. *Retrospectus* and *Prospectus*. — *SBL 1990 Seminar Papers*, 614-636. Esp. 624-627: "Jesus in the Synoptics" [13,47-50; 22,1-14; 24,23-28.37-42]; 628-629: "Wisdom sayings"; 629-633: "Social radicalism"; 633-639: "Parables". → 1990b

1990b The Gospel of Thomas. Introduction. — KLOPPENBORG, J.S., et al., *Q – Thomas Reader*, 1990, 77-127. Esp. 103-106: "The Gospel of Thomas and early christianity"; 114-120: "The Gospel of Thomas and the quest of the historical Jesus". → 1990a

1990c Q – Thomas Parallels. — *Ibid.*, 159.

1992a The Gospel of Thomas and the Synoptic Tradition: A Forschungsbericht and Critique. — *Forum* 8 (1992) 45-97. Esp. 45-69: "The early discussion" (50-63); 69-77: "The Robinson-Koester synthesis"; 77-90: "The more recent discussion" (79-82). [NTA 39, 129]

1992b Logia. — *ABD* 4 (1992) 347-348.

1993a *The Gospel of Thomas and Jesus.* Sonoma, CA: Polebridge, 1993, 275 p.

1993b Q – The Lost Gospel. — *BibReview* 9/5 (1993) 34-41, 61-62. [NTA 38, 732r] → A.D. Jacobson 1992a, Mack 1993

1993c Wisdom in Q and Thomas. — PERDUE, L.G., et al. (eds.), *In Search of Wisdom.* FS J.G. Gammie, 1993, 187-221. Esp. 188-189 [Q]; 189-191 [Thomas]; 191-193 [genre]; 193-194 [Q: composition]; 194-201 [common tradition]; 201-205 [kingdom]; 205-207 [wisdom]; 208-210 [Q/Th: redaction].

1995a The End of Apocalypse. Rethinking the Eschatological Jesus. — *TTod* 52 (1995-96) 29-48. Esp. 35-36: "Q and early christian wisdom"; 36-38 [Thomas/Q]. [NTA 39, 1416]

1995b Yes, Virginia, There Is a Q. — *BibReview* 11/3 (1995) 39-40. [NTA 40, 800] → Linnemann 1995

**PATZIA, Arthur G.**

1968 Did John the Baptist Preach a Baptism of Fire and the Holy Spirit? [3,11] — *EvQ* 40 (1968) 21-27. [NTA 12, 863]

**PAUL, André**

1968 *L'Évangile de l'Enfance selon saint Matthieu* (Lire la Bible, 17). Paris: Cerf, 1968, 191 p. Esp. 9-44 [1,1-17]; 45-94 [1,18-25]; 95-139 [2,1-12]; 141-169 [2,13-23]. [NTA 13, p. 402]; (Lire la Bible, 17bis), nouvelle édition rev. et corr., 1984, 181 p. → Delorme 1968a
    R.E. BROWN, *CBQ* 31 (1969) 597-598; J. DECROIX, *BibTS* 112 (1969) 23-24; R. DíAZ, *QüestVidaCr* 46 (1969) 102-103; P. FRANQUESA, *EphMar* 19 (1969) 608-609; J. GALOT, *Greg* 51 (1970) 213-214;

R. Gauthier, *CahJos* 20 (1972) 294-296; J. Huergo, *CiTom* 37 (1970) 172-173; R. Laurentin, *RSPT* 54 (1970) 270; M.-É. Lauzière, *RThom* 70 (1970) 121-122; S Légasse, *BullLitEccl* 1 (1970) 140-141; B. Piepiórka, *ZKT* 93 (1971) 220; B. Prete, *Sacra Doctrina* (Bologna) 14 (1969) 691; J. Radermakers, *NRT* 92 (1970) 172-173; S. R., *BibOr* 12 (1970) 44-45; A. Salas, *CiudDios* 182 (1969) 425-426; F. Salvoni, *RicBibRel* 6 (1971) 260; F. Stoop, *Verbum Caro* (Taizé) 19 (1969) 84; P. Ternant, *Proche Orient Chrétien* (Jerusalem) 20 (1970) 217; J.M. Tison *Bijdragen* 30 (1969) 316; M. Zerwick, *VD* 47 (1969) 47-49.

*Il vangelo dell'infanzia secondo san Matteo*, trans. G. Valentino. Roma: Borla, 1986, 200 p.
L. De Lorenzi, *Benedictina* 35 (1988) 226-227; M. Orsatti, *FarVi* 33 (1988) 158-159; E.M. Peretto, *Marianum* 51 (1989) 655-657; G. Segalla, *Studia Patavina* 33 (1986) 695.

1970 La guérison de l'aveugle (des aveugles) de Jéricho. — *FoiVie* 69/3 = *Cahiers bibliques* 9 (1970) 44-69. Esp. 44-49 [9,27-31]; 49-54 [20,29-34].

1971a La fuite en Égypte et le retour en Galilée. Mt 2,13-15.19-23. — *AssSeign* II/11 (1971) 19-28.

1971b L'entrée de Jésus à Jérusalem. Mc 11,1-10; Mt 21,1-11; Lc 19,28-40; Jn 12,12-19. — *AssSeign* II/19 (1971) 4-26. Esp. 15-20.

1985a La conception virginale dans la Bible. [1,18-25] — *LumièreV* 171 (1985) 55-66. [NTA 30,10]

1985b Matthieu 1 comme écriture apocalyptique. Le récit véritable de la 'crucifixion' de l'ἔρως. — *ANRW* II.25.3 (1985) 1952-1968. Esp. 1953-1959: "Matthieu 1: βίβλος γενέσεως ou apocalypse parfaite".

**PAUL, Maarten Jan**
1990 De Marcushypothese. — van den Brink, G., et al. (eds.), *Verkenningen in de evangeliën*, 1990, 39-45. Esp. 42 [Q].

**PAULI, Judith**
1994 Zur Rezeption der Bergpredigt in der Benediktsregel — *Regulae Benedicti Studia* (Hildesheim) 18 (1994) 167-175; = *ErbAuf* 70 (1994) 15-23.

**PAULSEN, Henning**
1991 Von der Unbestimmtheit des Anfangs. Zur Entstehung von Theologie im Urchristentum. — Breytenbach, C. - Paulsen, H. (eds.), *Anfänge der Christologie*. FS F. Hahn, 1991, 25-41. Esp. 29-30.

**PAULUS, Beda**
1984 (ed.), *Pascasii Radberti Expositio in Matheo libri XII* (CC CM, 56 and 56A-B). Turnhout: Brepols, 1984, LXI-462 (I-IV); 463-925 (V-VIII) and 926-1599 (IX-XII).
G. Mathon, *BTAM* 14 (1986) 48-49; M. Schneiders, *Bijdragen* 47 (1986) 336; H. Silvestre, *Scriptorium* 42 (1988) 113-115.

**PAWLIKOWSKI, John T.**
1989 Christian-Jewish Dialogue and Matthew. — *BiTod* 27 (1989) 356-362. [NTA 34, 604]

**PAX, Elpidius**
1955 Ἐπιφάνεια. *Ein religionsgeschichtlicher Beitrag zur biblischen Theologie* (Münchener theologische Studien, I/10). München: Zink, 1955, XXV-280 p. Esp. 189-193; 217-220 [παρουσία]; 252-253. — Diss. München, 1953 (J. Schmid).

1962 Beobachtungen zum biblischen Sprachtabu. — *SBF/LA* 12 (1961-62) 66-112. Esp. 92-110 [divine passive]. [NTA 7, 724]

1964a Archäologie und Exegese. — *BibLeb* 5 (1964) 256-266. Esp. 260-262 [2,16-18]; 265-266 [16,18]. [NTA 9, 1124]

1964b Spuren sog. "erlebter Rede" im Neuen Testament. — *SBF/LA* 14 (1963-64) 339-354. Esp. 344-345 [17,20]; 349-350 [4,3-4].

1968 Palästinensische Volkskunde im Spiegel der Kindheitsgeschichten. — *BibLeb* 9 (1968) 287-299. [NTA 13, 857]

1972 Probleme des neutestamentlichen Griechisch. — *Bib* 53 (1972) 557-564. Esp. 563-564 [3,11].

1974 Spuren der Nabatäer im Neuen Testament. — *BibLeb* 15 (1974) 193-206. Esp. 195-203 [2,1-12]. [NTA 19, 1106]

**PAYNE, Philip Barton**

1976 *Metaphor as a Model for Interpretation of the Parables of Jesus, with Special Reference to the Parable of the Sower.* Diss. Cambridge, 1976.

1981a The Authenticity of the Parables of Jesus. — FRANCE, R.T. - WENHAM, D. (eds.), *Studies of History and Tradition*, 1981, 329-344.

1981b Jesus' Implicit Claim to Deity in His Parables. — *TrinJ* NS 2 (1981) 3-23. Esp. 4-6 [13,3-9]; 7-8 [13,24-30.36-43]; 8-9 [7,24-27]; 9-10 [18,12-14]. [NTA 26, 61]

1983 Midrash and History in the Gospels with Special Reference to R.H. Gundry's *Matthew*. — FRANCE, R.T. - WENHAM, D. (eds.), *Studies in Midrash and Historiography*, 1983, 177-215. Esp. 180-194: "Evidence for midrashic intent in Matthew" [fulfilment quotations, genealogy, discrepancies between Mt and Mk or Lk, tendentious changes]; 194-209: "Literary problems with the thesis that Matthew is midrashic". → Gundry 1982

**PAYOT, Christian**

1969 Le baptême de Jésus dans les évangiles synoptiques. — *FoiVie* 68/3 = *Cahiers bibliques* 7 (1969) 3-20. Esp. 13-14.17-19 [3,13-17].

1970 Jean-Baptiste censuré. — *ETR* 45 (1970) 273-283. Esp. 276-277. [NTA 15, 461r] → Wink 1968

**PAZZINI, Domenico**

1993 & SANTI, F., *Le beatitudini in Agostino e Francesco*. Verrucchio (Forlì): Privately published, 1993, 55 p.

**PEABODY, David Barrett**

1978 A Pre-Markan Prophetic Sayings Tradition and the Synoptic Problem. — *JBL* 97 (1978) 391-409. Esp. 395-396 [Mt: ἀμὴν λέγω ὑμῖν]; 396-400: "The literary formulas within the synoptic tradition"; 400-405: "The Two Document hypothesis"; 405-408: "The Griesbach hypothesis". [NTA 23, 413]

1983a Augustine and the Augustinian Hypothesis. A Reexamination of Augustine's Thought in *De consensu evangelistarum*. — FARMER, W.R. (ed.), *New Synoptic Studies*, 1983, 37-64.

1983b The Late Secondary Redaction of Mark's Gospel and the Griesbach Hypothesis: A Response to Helmut Koester. — CORLEY, B. (ed.), *Colloquy on New Testament Studies. A Time for Reappraisal and Fresh Approaches*, Macon, GA: Mercer University Press, 1983, 87-132. Esp. 89-90 [Q]; 93-95 [Mt Sondergut]; 116-129 [minor agreements]. → Koester 1983b

1987 Chapters in the History of the Linguistic Argument for Solving the Synoptic Problem. The Nineteenth Century in Context. — SANDERS, E.P. (ed.), *Jesus, the Gospels, and the Church*. FS W.R. Farmer, 1987, 47-68.

1990a Response to the Multi-Stage Hypothesis. — DUNGAN, D.L. (ed.), *The Interrelations of the Gospels*, 1990, 217-230. Esp. 228-230 [14,13-21]. → Boismard 1990a

1990b → W.R. Farmer 1990b

1991 Repeated Language in Matthew: Clues to the Order and Composition of Luke and Mark. — *SBL 1991 Seminar Papers*, 647-686. Esp. 649-655 [4,23-7,29]; 655-657 [9,10-17; 12,1-13]; 657-667 [4,23-7,29; 10,1-4; 12,15-16]; 667-681 [5,29-30; 10,40.42; 18,1-14]; 682-686 [5,31-32; 18,3; 19,9.13-15].

1992   → W.R. Farmer 1992a/93/94/95

1995   H.J. Holtzmann and His European Colleagues: Aspects of the Nineteenth-Century European Discussion of Gospel Origins. — REVENTLƆW, H. - FARMER, W.R. (eds.), *Biblical Studies and the Shifting of Paradigms, 1850-1914* (JSOT SS, 192), Sheffield: JSOT, 1995, 1995, 50-131.

**PEACOCK, Heber F.**

1956   The Text of the Sermon on the Mount. — *RExp* 53 (1956) 9-23.

**PEARSON, Birger A.**

1991*  et al. (eds.), *The Future of Early Christianity. Essays in Honor of Helmut Koester*. Minneapolis, MN: Fortress, 1991, XX-509 p. → H.D. Betz, P.S. Cameron, Doran, R.A. Horsley, J.M. Robinson

**PEDERSEN, Sigfred**

1965   Zum Problem der vaticinia ex eventu. (Eine Analyse von Mt. 21,33-46 par.; 22,1-10 par.). — *StudTheol* 19 (1965) 167-188. Esp. 170-176 [21,33-46]; 176-180 [22,1-10]. [NTA 11, 216]

1975   Die Proklamation Jesu als des eschatologischen Offenbarungsträgers (Mt. xvii 1-13). — *NT* 17 (1975) 241-264. Esp. 242-247: "Traditionsgeschichtliche Unterschiede"; 247: "Der Aufbau der Perikope"; 247-250: "Die Vision"; 250-253: "Die Deutung des Petrus"; 253-262: "Die Deutung der Gottes-Stimme". [NTA 20, 778]

1987   Die Gotteserfahrung bei Jesus. [20,1-15] — *StudTheol* 41 (1987) 127-156. [NTA 32, 1080]

1995   Israel als integrierter Teil der christlichen Hoffnung (Matthäus 23). — *StudTheol* 49 (1995) 133-149; = HELLHOLM, D. - MOXNES, H. - SEIM, T.K. (eds.), *Mighty Minorities? Minorities in Early Christianity - Positions and Strategies. Essays in Honour of Jacob Jervell on His 70th Birthday 21 May 1995*, Oslo: Scandinavian University Press, 1995, 133-149. Esp. 135-136: "Kap. 23 als Teil einer kompositorischen Einheit"; 136-147: "Die einzelnen Abschnitte"; 147-149: "Kap. 23 als Teil der Ganzheit des Mt".

**PEEL, Malcolm L.**

1990   Q. — MILLS, W.E., et al. (eds.), *Mercer Dictionary of the Bible*, Macon, GA: Mercer University Press, 1990, 727-728.

**PEETERS, C.**

1975   Gotisch "*aflet uns thatei skulans sijaima*" (Mt 6,12). — *Zeitschrift für vergleichende Sprachforschung* (Göttingen) 88 (1975) 127-128.

**PEIFER, Claude J.**

1970   Jesus and Violence. — *BiTod* 46 (1970) 3204-3210.

1983   Jonah and Jesus: The Prophet as Sign. — *BiTod* 21 (1983) 377-383. Esp. 380-382 [12,38-42]. [NTA 28, 498]

**PEISKER, Carl Heinz**

1962   *Zürcher Evangelien-Synopse*. Wuppertal: Oncken, 1962, V-168(double)-XV p.; [3]1973; [18]1979; [24]1988, 558 p.

1983   *Evangelien-Synopse der Einheitsübersetzung*. Wuppertal–Kassel: Oncken; Stuttgart: Katholisches Bibelwerk, 1983, V-182(double)-XV p. → Knoch 1988a

**PELAEZ DEL ROSAL, Jesús**

1984   *Los milagros de Jesús en los Evangelios sinópticos. Morfología e interpretación* (Estudios de Nuevo Testamento, 3). Valencia: Institución San Jerónimo, 1984, 175 p. Esp. 96-120: "Analisis funcional de los relatos de milagro del Evangelio de Mateo con relacion a Marcos".

*Los milagros de Jesús. Siglas, fórmulas y corpus de texto.* Valencia: Institución San Jerónimo, 1984, 65 p.

1993 El evangelio de Mateo. Origen, forma y función. — PIÑERO, A. (ed.), *Fuentes del cristianismo*, 1993, 117-154. Esp. 118-135: "Origen"; 135-142: "Forma"; 142-154: "Función".

1995 → Piñero 1995

**PELC, Josip**

1973 On the translation of γενεά in Mt 24,34 (Mk 13,30 and Lk 21,32). [Serbo-Croatian] — *Bogoslovska Smotra* (Zagreb) 43 (1973) 483-492.

**PELCÉ, Francette**

1966 Jésus à Gethsémani. Remarques comparatives sur les trois récits évangéliques. — *FoiVie* 65/4 = *Cahiers bibliques* 4 (1966) 89-99. Esp. 91-93 [26,36-46].

**PELFRÈNE, J.-M.**

1966 "Tu aimeras ton prochain comme toi-même". — *AssSeign* I/66 (1966) 50-67. Esp. 57-61 [22,40].

**PELIKAN, Jaroslav Jan**

1951 The Temptation of the Church. A Study of Matthew 4:1-11. — *ConcTM* 22 (1951) 251-259.

**PELLAND, Gilles**

1972 Le dossier patristique relatif au divorce. Revue de quelques travaux récents. — *SE* 24 (1972) 285-312. Esp. 286-307 [Crouzel 1971a]; 307-312 [Moingt 1968].

1974 Le canon tridentin concernant le divorce. À propos d'un ouvrage récent [L. BRESSAN, *Il canone tridentino sul divorzio per adulterio*, 1973]. — *SE* 26 (1974) 341-377. Esp. 352-355 [19,9].

1979 Le thème biblique du Règne chez saint Hilaire de Poitiers. — *Greg* 60 (1979) 639-674 (English summary, 674). Esp. 639-644: "Au commentaire sur Matthieu".

**PELLEGRINO, Michele**

1969 La fede di Pietro secondo i Padri della Chiesa. — *Petrus et Paulus martyres. Commemorazione del XIX centenario del martirio degli Apostoli Pietro e Paolo*, Milano, 1969, 1-30; = ID., *Ricerche patristiche (1938-1980)*, II, Torino: Bottega d'Erasmo, 1982, 175-204.

**PELLETIER, André**

1966 L'annonce à Joseph. [1,20-21] — *RSR* 54 (1966) 67-68. [NTA 11, 192]

**PELLETIER, Anne-Marie**

1995 *Lectures bibliques. Aux sources de la culture occidentale* (Collection "réf."). Paris: Nathan/Cerf, 1995, 384 p. Esp. 249-260 [2,1-23]; 261-270 [5,38-48].

**PENATI BERNARDINI, Anna**

1992 (trans.), *Gregorio di Nissa, Commento al Nuovo Testamento. Le Beatitudini ed altri scritti* (Cultura e culture). Roma: Coletti, 1992, 181 p.

**PENN, Richard William**

1989 *The Call to Discipleship. A Matthean Model for Contemporary Evangelism.* Diss. Southern Baptist Theol. Sem., Louisville, KY, 1989, 281 p. (H.L. Poe). — *DissAbstr* 51 (1990-91) 198.

**PENNA, Angelo**

1954 *San Pietro discepolo, apostolo, maestro.* Brescia: Morcelliana, 1954, 350 p. *San Pedro*, trans. L.M. Jiménez Font. Madrid: Fax, 1958, 508 p.

*Saint Pierre. Le disciple, l'apôtre, le docteur de la foi*, trans. E. Viale & Y. del Pozzo. Paris: Alsatia, 1958, 480 p. Esp. 13-142.

1955 Il "De consensu evangelistarum" ed i "Canoni eusebiani". — *Bib* 36 (1955) 1-19. Esp. 11-17.

1972 *Amore nella Bibbia*. Brescia: Paideia, 1972, 172 p. Esp. 50-66.

**PENNA, Romano**

1989 *Letture evangeliche. Saggi esegetici sui quattro vangeli* (Studi e ricerche bibliche). Roma: Borla, 1989, 238 p. Esp. 31-84 [1-2.3-4.5-7].

1993 Il fatto sinottico e le sue soluzioni. Annotazioni in margine a una nuova Sinossi dei Vangeli. — *Lateranum* 59 (1993) 143-160. → Poppi 1992

**PENNACCHINI, Bruno**

1982 Le Beatitudini e le ammonizioni di S. Francesco. — BENEDETTI, G. (ed.), *Parola di Dio e Francesco d'Assisi* (Ricerche teologiche, 1), Assisi: Cittadella, 1982, 203-215.

**PENNELLS, Stephen**

1983 The Spear Thrust (Mt. 27.49b, *v.l.* / Jn 19.34). — *JSNT* 19 (1983) 99-115. [NTA 28, 504]

**PENNER, Erwin**

1989 & WALL, J., The Lord's Supper and the Church. — *Direction* (Fresno, CA) 18/2 (1989) 33-43. [NTA 34, 826]

**PENNER, James A.**

1995 Revelation and Discipleship in Matthew's Transfiguration Account. — *BS* 152 (1995) 201-210. [NTA 39, 1456]

**PENNING DE VRIES, Piet**

1967 "Ehelos um des Himmelreiches willen". [19,12] — *GL* 40 (1967) 410-422. Esp. 410-417.

**PENTECOST, J. Dwight**

1958 The Purpose of the Sermon on the Mount. — *BS* 115 (1958) 128-135, 212-217, 313-319. [NTA 3, 578]

1982 *The Parables of Jesus*. Grand Rapids, MI: Zondervan, 1982, 180 p.

**PEPPERMÜLLER, Rolf**

1969 Ein Unzialfragment auf dem Athos (Vatopediu und Protatu) und in Paris (0102 + [0138]). — ALAND, K. (ed.), *Materialien*, 1969, 144-176. Esp. 150-165 [21,24-24,15].

**PERARNAU I ESPELT, Josep**

1989 Sermó inèdit de sant Vicent Ferrer explicant el "Pare Nostre" (Barcelona, Biblioteca de Catalunya, Ms. 477). — *RevistCatTeol* 14 (1989) 527-540 (English summary, 540).

1994 Problemes i criteris d'autenticitat d'obres espirituals attribuïdes a Arnau de Vilanova. [Expositio super XXIV capi Matthaei] — *Arxiv des textos catalans antics* (Barcelona) 13 (1994) 25-103.

**PERCY, Ernst**

1953 *Die Botschaft Jesu. Eine traditionsgeschichtliche und exegetische Untersuchung* (Lunds Universitets Årsskrift 49/5). Lund: Gleerup, 1953, X-324 p. Esp. 40-108 [5,3-12]; 119-122 [5,17-19]; 123-164 [5,21-48]; 178-187 [12,28-29]; 191-202 [11,12-13].

**PERDUE, Leo G.**

1986 The Wisdom Sayings of Jesus. — *Forum* 2/3 (1986) 3-35. Esp. 7-12 [proverbs]; 14-16 [questions]; 16-18 [beatitudes: 5,3-12]; 18-19 [admonitions: 5,16; 22,21]; 19,25 [instructions: 5,23-25.34-37; 6,3-4.17-18; 11,28-30; Q 6,27-49; Q 11,9-13; Q 12,33-34]; 25-26 [disputations: 4,1-11]; 26-27 [wisdom psalms: 11,25-27]; 27-28 [wisdom poems: 11,16-19]; 28-32 [aphorisms]. [NTA 31, 1045]

1993*   & SCOTT, B.B. - WISEMAN, W.J. (eds.), *In Search of Wisdom. Essays in Memory of John G. Gammie*. Louisville, KY: Westminster/Knox, 1993, XVIII-318 p. → J.J. O'Collins, Patterson, B.B. Scott

## PERETTO, Elio (Licinio) M.

1955   *La mariologia del protovangelo di Giacomo* (Scripta Facultatis Theologicae "Marianum", 5). Roma: Marianum, 1955, 86 p.

1969   Ricerche su Mt 1-2. — *Marianum* 31 (1969) 140-247. Esp. 145-179: "Lettura esegetica di Mt 1-2"; 180-209: "Problema letterario"; 210-231: "Problema storico"; 232-244: "Problemi dottrinali". [NTA 14, 469]
    *Ricerche su Mt. 1-2* (Scripta Facultatis Theologicae "Marianum", 25). Roma: Marianum, 1970, 124 p. Esp. 9-46; 47-77; 78-99; 100-116. [NTA 17, p. 300]
    R.E. BROWN, *CBQ* 34 (1972) 239; M. CAMAGNI, *Humanitas* 27 (1972) 330-331; J.A. CARRASCO, *EstJos* 26 (1972) 231-232; J. COPPENS, *ETL* 47 (1971) 605-606; R. GAUTHIER, *CahJos* 22 (1974) 265-266; X. JACQUES, *NRT* 94 (1972) 1097-1098; A. MODA, *MSR* 30 (1973) 197; J. MURPHY-O'CONNOR, *RB* 80 (1973) 282-285; J. PONTHOT, *RTL* 2 (1971) 481-482; N. URICCHIO, *MiscFranc* 71 (1971) 496-497; *CC* 123/3 (1972) 86-87; L. ZANI, *RivBib* 20 (1972) 407-410; P. ZARRELLA, *Laur* 13 (1972) 255-256.
    *Lettura esegetica del racconto di Mt. 1-2 (Appunto)* (Facoltà teologica "Marianum". Sezione Diploma). Roma: Marianum, 1969, 54 p.

1970   Criteri d'impiego di alcune citazioni bibliche nel "Protevangelo di Giacomo". — *Atti del Congresso Mariologico Internazionale*, IV, Roma: PAMI, 1970, 274-293. Esp. 289-293: "Le citazioni di Matteo"; = ID., *Saggi di patristica*, 1997, 25-42. Esp. 39-42.

1972   La Madonna nel Nuovo Testamento. Le prospettive ideologiche di Mt 1-2. — *La Madonna e l'Ecumene, I° Simposio Mariano per l'Umbria 20-23 sett. 1971 al Santuario della Stella, Arcidiocesi di Spoleto*, San Gabriele/Teramo: ECO, 1972, 47-63.

1976   Loghia del Signore e Vangelo di Tommaso. — *RivBib* 24 (1976) 13-56. Esp. 31-32 [5,14/Th 32]; 32-33 [6,24; 9,16-17/Th 47]; 40-41 [7,7/Th 92]; 44-45 [6,3/Th 41]; 45-46 [7,6/Th 93]. [NTA 23, 726]; = ID., *Saggi di patristica*, 1997, 77-113. Esp. 92-93; 93-94; 103; 105; 106.

1977a   *La Giustizia. Ricerca su gli autori cristiani del II° secolo* (Scripta Facultatis Theologicae "Marianum", 29). Roma: Marianum, 1977, XI-348 p. Esp. 270-276.

1977b   *Evangelizare pauperibus* (Lc 4,18; 7,22-23) nella lettura patristica dei secoli II-III. — *Augustinianum* 17 (1977) 71-100. Esp. 91-99 [5,3/Lk 6,20; Thomas; Polycarp; Clement of Alexandria]; = ID., *Saggi di patristica*, 1997, 131-156. Esp. 147-155.

1979   Genere sapienziale e detti del Signore. — *Vichiana* 8 (1979) 307-328; = ID., *Saggi di patristica*, 1997, 191-211. Esp. 206-211 [11,25-30].

1985   Cristiano di Stavelot: cultura ed esegesi etimologica. — *Benedictina* (Roma) 32 (1985) 467-493. Esp. 477-493 [1,2-16]; = ID., *Saggi di patristica*, 1997, 321-344. Esp. 330-341.

1989   Testo biblico e sua applicazione nel *De obitu Valentiniani* di Ambrogio. — *Vichiana* 18 (1989) 99-170; = ID., *Saggi di patristica*, 1997, 457-528. Esp. 511-517 [5,3; 11,28-30; 16,19; 26,64].

1997   *Saggi di patristica e di filologia biblica* (Scripta Pont. Fac. Theol. Marianum, 52). Roma: Marianum, 1997, 764 p. → 1970, 1976, 1977b, 1979, 1985, 1989

## PÉREZ-COTAPOS LARRAÍN, Eduardo

1991   *Parabolas: Dialogo y experiencia. El metodo parabólico de Jesús según Dom Jacques Dupont* (Anales de la Facultad de Teologia. Pontificia Universidad Católica de Chile, 42). Santiago de Chile: Pontificia Universidad Católica, 1991, 272 p. Esp. 123-130, 138-149, 160-167. — Diss. Pont. Univ. Greg., Roma, 1990 (E. Rasco).

1992   Las parábolas de Jesús: su sentido y adecuada interpretación. — *TVida* 33 (1992) 165-178. [NTA 37, 1232]

**PÉREZ FERNÁNDEZ, Miguel**

1968 "Prope est aestas" (Mc 13,28; Mt 24,32; Lc 21,29). — *VD* 46 (1968) 361-369. [NTA 14, 170]

**PÉREZ GORDO, Ángel**

1976 Notas sobre los anuncios de la Pasión. — *Burgense* 17 (1976) 251-270. Esp. 251-254 [δεῖ]; 254-257 [ὁ υἱὸς τοῦ ἀνθρώπου]; 258-261 [παραδίδοται]; 261-264 [ἀποδοκιμάζειν]; 265-268 [ἀναστῆναι]; 268-270 [μετὰ τρεῖς ἡμέρας]. [NTA 21, 99] Gli annunci della passione. — *La sapienza della croce oggi. Atti del Congresso internazionale, Roma, 13-18 ottobre, 1975.* I: *La sapienza della croce nella rivelazione e nell' ecumenismo,* Torino-Leumann: Elle Di Ci, 1976, 106-125.

**PÉREZ RODRÍGUEZ, Gabriel**

1979 Lucas, Evangelio de exigencias radicales — *Servidor de la Palabra. Miscelánea bíblica en honor del P. Alberto Colunga o.p.,* Salamanca: San Esteban, 1979, 319-367. Esp. 330-333 [Q 4,1-13; Q 14,16-24]; 334-338 [21,18-22.33-46].

1983 Aportación de los sabios de Israel al matrimonio cristiano. — *MiscCom* 78-79 (1983) 357-368. Esp. 367-368 [5,32; 19,9/OT].

1990 *La infancia de Jesús (Mt 1-2; Lc 1-2)* (Teología en Diálogo, 4). Salamanca: Universidad Pontificia de Salamanca, 1990, 266 p. [NTA 37, p. 120] J.M. FERREIRA-MARTINS, *ScriptTeol* 24 (1992) 679-680; S. MUÑOZ IGLESIAS, *Salmanticensis* 38 (1991) 373-374.

1992 Dimensión existencial de Mt 1-2; Lc 1-2. — *EstBíb* 50 (1992) 161-175. Esp. 164.166-169 [1,1-16]; 172 [1,18-25].

1994 Bienaventurados los desprendidos (Mt 5,3). — ARANDA, G., et al. (eds.), *Biblia, Exegesis y Cultura.* FS J.M. Casciaro, 1994, 311-325.

**PERI, Israel**

1987 Der Weggefährte. [20,13; 22,12; 26,50] — *ZNW* 79 (1987) 127-131. [NTA 32, 131]

**PERKIN, J.R.C.**

1992 Introduction to the Parables and Preaching. — *McMaster Journal of Theology* (Hamilton, Ont.) 3 (1992) 5-16. [NTA 37, 122]

**PERKINS, Pheme**

1974 Peter in Gnostic Revelation. — *SBL 1974 Seminar Papers,* II, 1-13. Esp. 5-6.

1978 *Reading the New Testament. An Introduction.* New York – Mahwah, NJ: Paulist, 1978, VII-342 p.; [2]1988, VII-350 p. Esp. 214-228: "Matthew: Jesus, teacher of Israel"; 62-65 [Q].

1981 *Hearing the Parables of Jesus.* New York – Ramsey, NJ: Paulist, 1981, 224 p. Esp. 5-10 [13,10-17]; 26-28 [13,44]; 28-29 [13,45-50]; 29-32 [18,12-14]; 39-41 [5,15]; 41-43 [5,13]; 43-45 [11,16-19]; 42-43 [5,25-26]; 78-82 [13,3-8]; 83-85 [13,24-30]; 85-90 [13,31-32]; 94-98 [22,1-10]; 104-110 [25,1-13]; 123-134 [18,23-35]; 137-146 [20,1-16]; 146-151 [25,14-30]; 151-152 [24,45-51]; 158-165 [25,31-46]; 181-194 [21,33-44].

1982 *Love Commands in the New Testament.* New York – Ramsey, NJ: Paulist, 1982, V-130 p. Esp. 10-26 [22,34-40]; 27-41 [5,43-48].

1984a *Resurrection: New Testament Witness and Contemporary Reflection.* Garden City, NY: Doubleday, 1984, 504 p. Esp. 124-147 [28].

1984b Taxes in the New Testament. — *The Journal of Religious Ethics* (Knoxville, TN) 12 (1984) 182-200. Esp. 188-189 [22,15-22]; 189-190 [17,24-27] [NTA 32, 361]

1989 Christology and Mission: Matthew 28:16-20. — *Listening* 24 (1989) 302-309. Esp. 302-305: "Narrative climax"; 305-307: "Mission"; 307-309: "Judgement". [NTA 34, 639]

1990a *Jesus as Teacher* (Understanding Jesus Today, 2). Cambridge: University Press, 1990, V-177 p.

1990b  → Senior 1990c

1991   Gender Analysis: A Response to Antoinette Clark Wire. — BALCH, D.L. (ed.), *Social History of the Matthean Community*, 1991, 122-126. → Wire 1991

1992a  Ethics (NT). — *ABD* 2 (1992) 652-665. Esp. 658-660.

1992b  "I have seen the Lord" (John 20:18). Women Witnesses to the Resurrection. — *Interpr* 46 (1992) 31-41. Esp. 36-38 [28,9-10]. [NTA 36, 682]

1993a  Matthew 28:16-20, Resurrection, Ecclesiology and Mission. — *SBL 1993 Seminar Papers*, 574-588. Esp. 574-578: "The problem of genre"; 579-583: "Matthean composition in Matt. 28:16-20"; 583-586: "Commissioning sayings".

1993b  *Gnosticism and the New Testament*. Minneapolis, MN: Fortress, 1993, X-261 p.

1994   *Peter: Apostle for the Whole Church* (Studies on Personalities of the New Testament). Columbia, SC: University of South Carolina Press, 1994, VI-209 p.

1995   Jesus and Ethics. — *TTod* 52 (1995-96) 49-65. Esp. 51-54. [NTA 39, 1417]

**PERLER, Othmar**

1936ᴿ  Zur Datierung der beiden Fassungen des vierten Kapitels *De unitate Ecclesiae*. [1936] — ID., *Sapientia et Caritas. Gesammelte Aufsätze zum 90. Geburtstag* [O. Perler], eds. D. Van Damme, et al. (Paradosis, 29), Freiburg/Schw: Universitätsverlag, 1990, 13-56. Esp. 35-36; 42-45; 49-52 [16,18].

**PERLEWITZ, Miriam**

1988   *The Gospel of Matthew* (Message of Biblical Spirituality, 8). Wilmington, DE: Glazier, 1988, 191 p. [NTA 33, p. 252]
       P. ROGERS, *CBQ* 52 (1990) 358-359.

**PERNIGOTTI, Sergio**

1983   Frammenti del Nuovo Testamento in copto nella *Papyrussammlung* di Vienna. [26,2-3.9-11] — *Festschrift zum 100-jährigen Bestehen der Papyrussammlung der Österreichischen Nationalbibliothek: Papyrus Erzherzog Rainer*, Wien: Akademie, 1983, 185-187.

**PEROTTI, Pier Angelo**

1992   Commento al *Pater noster* (Mt. 6,9-13; Lc. 11,2-4). — *Maia* (Bologna) 44 (1992) 91-96. [NTA 38, 760]

**PERRIN, Louis**

1989   Interpréter, c'est recevoir un "plus": la révélation et la filiation. Une lecture de Mt, 16,1-20. — *SémBib* 55 (1989) 19-28. [NTA 34, 629]

1991   Chemins concrets d'interprétation. Matthieu 2,1-12. — *SémBib* 61 (1991) 35-42.

**PERRIN, Norman**

1963   *The Kingdom of God in the Teaching of Jesus* (The New Testament Library). London: SCM; Philadelphia, PA: Westminster, 1963, 215 p. Esp. 170-171.173 [12,28]; 171-174 [11,12-13]; 181-183 [5,3-12]; 183 [8,11]; 191-198.201-202 [6,9-13]; 202-204 [Sermon on the Mount]. — Diss. Göttingen, 1959 (J. Jeremias).

1967   *Rediscovering the Teaching of Jesus* (The New Testament Library). London: SCM, 1967, 272 p. Esp. 63-68 [12,28/Q 11,20]; 74-77 [11,12/Q 16,16]; 85-87 [11,16-19]; 87-90 [13,44-46/Th 76; 109]; 98-101 [18,12/Th 107]; 105-106 [11,16-19]; 106-108 [8,11]; 110-114 [22,1/Q 14,16/Th 64]; 116-118 [20,1-16]; 118-119 [21,28-32]; 119-121 [11,16-19/Q 7,31-35]; 125-126 [18,23-35]; 137-138 [17,20/Q 17,6]; 144-145 [7,13-14]; 146-148 [5,39-41]; 148-149 [5,44-48]; 157-158 [Mk/Q 13,18-19/Th 20]; 158-159 [13,33/Th 96]; 160-161 [6,10/Q 11,2]; 161-164 [8,11/Q 13,28-29]; 183-185 [24,30/Mk 13,26]; 185-191 [10,32-33/Q 12,8-9/Mk 8,38]; 191-195 [12,40/Q 11,30]; 195-197 [24,26-28/Q 17,23-24]; 201-202 [10,23]. *Was lehrte Jesus wirklich? Rekonstruktion und Deutung*, trans. P.-G. Nohl. Göttingen: Vandenhoeck & Ruprecht, 1972, 298 p.

1968   The Son of Man in the Synoptic Tradition. — *BR* 13 (1968) 3-25. Esp. 6-7; 9-10 [Q 17,26; 12,40]; 14-15 [Q 7,34; 12,10]. [NTA 13, 843]; = ID., *A Modern Pilgrimage*, 1974, 57-83 (Postscript 83-93). → Maddox 1971

1969   *What is Redaction Criticism?* (Guides to Biblical Scholarship. New Testament Series). Philadelphia, PA: Fortress, 1969, IX-86 p. Esp. 25-28: "G. Bornkamm and the Gospel of Matthew"; 57-62 [16,13-28].

Redaction Criticism at Work: A Sample. [1969, 40-63] — TOLLERS, V.L. - MAIER, J.R. (eds.), *The Bible in Its Literary Milieu. Contemporary Essays*, Grand Rapids, MI: Eerdmans, 1979, 344-361. Esp. 356-359 [16,13-28].

1971   The Modern Interpretation of the Parables of Jesus and the Problem of Hermeneutics. — *Interpr* 25 (1971) 131-148. Esp. 131-135 [A. Jülicher]; 135-137 [E. Fuchs]; 137-139 [A.N. Wilder]; 139-142 [R.W. Funk]; 142-147 [D.O. Via]. [NTA 16, 138]

1972   Wisdom and Apocalyptic in the Message of Jesus. — *SBL 1972 Seminar Papers*, II, 543-572. Esp. 559 [11,12]; 563 [5,39]; 565 [5,44-48; 7,13-14].

1974a  *A Modern Pilgrimage in New Testament Christology.* Philadelphia, PA: Fortress, 1974, X-148 p. → 1968

1974b  *The New Testament. An Introduction. Proclamation and Parenesis, Myth and History.* New York: Harcourt Brace Jovanovich, 1974, XII-385 p. Esp. 74-77 [Q]; 169-193: "The gospel of Matthew: Christianity as obedience to the new revelation"; & DULING, D.C., [2]1982, XXIII-516 p. Esp. 100-107; 263-291; [3]1993.

Apocalyptic Christianity. The Synoptic Source "Q"; The Apocalyptic Discourses; The Book of Revelation. [1974, 65-85] — HANSON, P.D. (ed.), *Visionaries and Their Apocalypses* (Issues in Religion and Theology, 2), Philadelphia, PA: Fortress; London: SPCK, 1983, 121-145. Esp. 131-134: "The source Q".

1976   *Jesus and the Language of the Kingdom. Symbol and Metaphor in New Testament Interpretation.* Philadelphia, PA: Fortress, 1976, XIII-225 p. Esp. 38-40; 41-54 [Q 11,20 (Lk); Mt 5,39-41.44-48; 6,9-13; 7,13-14; 11,12]; 57-60 [Q 17,22-37 (Lk)]. → Duling 1984

Jesus and the Language of the Kingdom. [1976, 16-32, 127-131, 197-199] — CHILTON, B.D. (ed.), *The Kingdom of God*, 1984, 92-106.

1977   *The Resurrection according to Matthew, Mark, and Luke.* Philadelphia, PA: Fortress, 1977, X-85 p.; [4]1984. Esp. 39-58: "The resurrection narratives in the gospel of Matthew".
*The Resurrection Narratives. A New Approach.* London: SCM, 1977, 86 p.

**PERRONE, Lorenzo**

1990   Le *Quaestiones evangelicae* di Eusebio di Cesarea. Alle origini di un genere letterario. [28,1-10] — *AnStoEseg* 7 (1990) 417-435.

**PERROT, Charles**

1959   Essai sur le discours eschatologique (*Mc. XIII*,1-37; *Mt. XXIV*,1-36; *Lc. XXI*,5-36). — *RSR* 47 (1959) 481-514. Esp. 483-506: "Le discours eschatologique saisi au niveau de M-Mg"; 506-514: "Le discours eschatologique au niveau de Mg. et des Évangiles canoniques". [NTA 4, 662] → Vaganay 1954

1961   La lecture synagogale d'Exode XXI,1-XXII,23 et son influence sur la littérature néo-testamentaire. — BARUCQ, A., et al. (eds.), *À la rencontre de Dieu*. FS A. Gelin, 1961, 223-239. Esp. 237-238 [21,13].

1967   Les récits d'enfance dans la Haggada antérieure au IIe siècle de notre ère. — *RSR* 55 (1967) 481-518. Esp. 509-518: "Les récits de l'enfance de Jésus". [NTA 12, 861] → Delorme 1968a

1968   La descente du Christ aux enfers dans le Nouveau Testament. — *LumièreV* 87 (1968) 3-29. Esp. 14-15 [12,40].

1975   Matthieu, le Messie annoncé par les prophètes. — BEAUDE, P.-M., *"... selon les Écritures"* (Cahiers Évangile, 12), Paris: Cerf, 1975, 27-30.

1976	*Les récits de l'enfance de Jésus. Matthieu 1-2; Luc 1-2* (Cahiers Évangile, 18). Paris: Cerf, 1976, 71 p. Esp. 17-34.
	*I racconti dell'infanzia di Gesù, Mt 1-2 e Lc 1-2.* Torino: Gribaudi, 1977, 72 p.
	N. URICCHIO, *CC* 130/2 (1979) 614.
	*Los relatos de la infancia de Jesús.* Estella: Verbo Divino, 1978, 72 p.; ⁴1980.
	J.A. CARRASCO, *EstJos* 33 (1979) 251-252; E.M. PERETTO, *Marianum* 46 (1984) 477-478.
	*As narrativas da infância de Jesus.* São Paulo: Paulinas, 1982, 110 p.

1979	*Jésus et l'histoire* (Collections "Jésus et Jésus-Christ", 11). Paris: Desclée, 1979, 336 p. Esp. 150-166 [law]; 171-200 [Jesus as prophet]; 201-240 [miracles]; 241-272 [Son of Man]; rev. ed., 1993, 287 p.

1982	Les prophètes de la violence et la nouveauté des temps. Matthieu 11,12-13. — DORÉ, J., et al., *L'Ancien et le Nouveau. Travaux de l'U.E.R. de théologie et de sciences religieuses* (Cogitatio fidei, 111), Paris: Cerf, 1982, 93-109. Esp. 94-95: "Le contexte de Mt 11,2-19"; 95-98: "Une reconstruction de la source Q?"; 98-107: "Le logion matthéen 11,12"; 107-109: "Mt 11,12 et la nouveauté du temps".

1984	& COTHENET, É., Matthieu (Évangile de). — POUPARD, P. (ed.), *Dictionnaire des Religions*, Paris: PUF, 1984, 1064-1066; ³1993, 1267-1269.

**PERRY, Alfred M.**

1951	The Growth of the Gospels. — BUTTRICK, G.A. (ed.), *The Interpreter's Bible*, VII, 1951, 60-74. Esp. 61-62 [syn. problem]; 63 [minor agreements]; 63-65 [Q]; 66 [Sondergut].

**PERRY, Charles Austin**

1986	*The Resurrection Promise. An Interpretation of the Easter Narratives.* Grand Rapids, MI: Eerdmans, 1986, IX-139 p. Esp. 36-47: "The pattern in Matthew 28:16-20".

**PERRY, John M.**

1986	The Three Days in the Synoptic Passion Predictions. — *CBQ* 48 (1986) 637-654. Esp. 638; 647-648 [27,63]; 651-653 [28,1-10]. [NTA 31, 566]

1993a	*Exploring the Resurrection of Jesus.* Kansas City, MO: Sheed & Ward, 1993, III-145 p.

1993b	*Exploring the Transfiguration Story.* Kansas City, MO: Sheed & Ward, 1993, III-59 p.

**PERRY, Michael C.**

1959	*The Easter Enigma. An Essay on the Resurrection with Special Reference to the Data of Psychical Research.* London: Faber and Faber, 1959, 264 p. Esp. 65-81: "According to the Scriptures".

**PERUMALIL, Augustine C.**

1972	The Gospel according to Matthew. — *IndianES* 11 (1972) 242-252. [NTA 17, 899]

1974a	St. Matthew and his Critics. — *HomPastR* 74/4 (1974) 31-32, 47-53. [NTA 18, 841]

1974b	Papias. — *ExpT* 85 (1973-74) 361-366. Esp. 363-365. [NTA 19, 842]

1980	Are Not Papias and Irenaeus Competent to Report on the Gospels? — *ExpT* 91 (1979-80) 332-337. [NTA 25, 45]

**PESCE, Mauro**

1978	Ricostruzione dell'archetipo letterario comune a *Mt.* 22,1-10 e *Lc.* 14,15-24. — DUPONT, J. (ed.), *La parabola degli invitati al banchetto*, 1978, 167-236. Esp. 170-182 [22,1-2/Q 14,15-16]; 182-199 [22,2b-3/Q 14,16b-18]; 199-209 [22,5/Q 14,18-20]; 209-220 [22,7-9/Q 14,21b]; 220-234 [22,10/Q 14,22-24].

1982	Discepolato gesuano e discepolato rabbinico. Problemi e prospettive della comparazione. — *ANRW* II.25.1 (1982) 351-389. Esp. 366-380.

**PESCH, Rudolf**

1966a Eine alttestamentliche Ausführungsformel im Matthäus-Evangelium. Redaktionsgeschichtliche und exegetische Beobachtungen. — *BZ* 10 (1966) 220-245. Esp. 222-226 [1,24-25; 21,6-7; 26,19; 28,15]; 234-239 [26,17-19]; 239-245 [21,1-7]. [NTA 11, 690]; 11 (1967) 79-95. Esp. 79-91 [1,18-25]; 91-95 [28,11-15]. [NTA 11, 1027]

1966b Umkehr, Glaube und Taufe. Zu Taufe und Taufformel im Neuen Testament. — *BibLeb* 7 (1966) 1-14. Esp. 8-11 [baptism]. [NTA 11, 441]

1967 Der Gottessohn im matthäischen Evangelienprolog (Mt 1-2). Beobachtungen zu den Zitationsformeln der Reflexionszitate. — *Bib* 48 (1967) 395-420. Esp. 398-408 ["Reflexionszitate"]; 408-419 [Son of God]. [NTA 13, 157]

1968a *Neuere Exegese – Verlust oder Gewinn?* Freiburg: Herder, 1968, 175 p. Esp. 100-101; 162-169 [8,14-15].

1968b Levi–Matthäus (Mc 2,14 / Mt 9,9 10,3). Ein Beitrag zur Lösung eines alten Problems. — *ZNW* 59 (1968) 40-56. Esp. 45-47 [9,9]; 47-49 [10,3]; 50-53 [μαθηταί; δώδεκα]; 53-54 [Mary, Joseph]; 54-55 [Salome]; 55-56 [Matthew]. [NTA 13, 164]

1969a Heilszukunft und Zukunft des Heils. Eschatologie und Apokalyptik in den Evangelien und Briefen. — SCHREINER, J. – DAUTZENBERG, G. (eds.), *Gestalt und Anspruch*, 1969, 313-329. Esp. 322-324: "Die Großevangelisten redigieren Mk 13".

1969b Kirche unter der Botschaft des Täufers (Mt 3,1-12). — *Am Tisch des Wortes* (Stuttgart) 101 (1969) 36-43.

1970a *Jesu ureigene Taten? Ein Beitrag zur Wunderfrage* (QDisp, 52). Freiburg: Herder, 1970, 166 p. Esp. 20-23 [12,22-27]; 36-44.46-48 [11,5/Q 7,22]; 44-45 [10,18]; 87-98 [8,1-4]. → Mussner 1967b

1970b Eschatologie und Ethik. Auslegung von Mt 24,1-36. — *BibLeb* 11 (1970) 223-238. Esp. 225-228 [24,1-2]; 228-236 [24,3-36]; 236-238: "Eschatologie und Ethik". [NTA 15, 856]

1971a *Freie Treue. Die Christen und die Ehescheidung.* Freiburg: Herder, 1971, 109 p. Esp. 37-43 [5,32]; 43-48 [5,31-32]; 49-56 [19,3-9].

1971b Manifestation de la miséricorde de Dieu. Mt 9,9-13. — *AssSeign* II/41 (1971) 15-24.

1971c The Position and Significance of Peter in the Church of the New Testament. A Survey of Current Research. — *Concilium* (London) 7/4 (1971) 21-35. Esp. 28-31 [16,17-19].

1972 *Der Besessene von Gerasa. Entstehung und Überlieferung einer Wundergeschichte* (SBS, 56). Stuttgart: Katholisches Bibelwerk, 1972, 70 p. Esp. 50-56: "Vom Markus- zum Matthäustext" [8,28-34].

1973 Jüngerschaft und Gottesvolk. Zum Kirchenbild der synoptischen Evangelien. — *BK* 28 (1973) 8-11. Esp. 9-10. [NTA 18, 95]

1975* & SCHNACKENBURG, R. – KAISER, O. (eds.), *Jesus und der Menschensohn. Für Anton Vögtle.* Freiburg: Herder, 1975, 488 p. → Broer, A.J.B. Higgins, O. Kaiser, Kümmel, Schneider, Schürmann

1975a & KRATZ, R., *So liest man synoptisch. Anleitung und Kommentar zum Studium der synoptischen Evangelien*, I. Frankfurt/M: Knecht, 1975, 95 p.; II. *Wundergeschichten*. Teil I: *Exorzismen – Heilungen – Totenerweckungen*, 1976, ²1978, 101 p.; III. *Wundergeschichten*. Teil II: *Rettungswunder. Geschenkwunder – Normenwunder – Fernheilungen*, 1976, ²1978, 99 p.; IV. *Gleichnisse und Bildreden*. Teil I: *Aus der dreifachen Überlieferung*, 1978, 96 p.; V. *Gleichnisse und Bildreden*. Teil II: *Aus der zweifachen Überlieferung*, 1978, 77 p.; VI. *Passionsgeschichte. Erster Teil*, 1979, 112 p.; VII. *Passionsgeschichte. Zweiter Teil*, 1980, 174 p.

1975b Die Zuschreibung der Evangelien an apostolische Verfasser. — *ZKT* 97 (1975) 56-71. Esp. 57, 63-64. [NTA 20, 393]

1976a Das Abendmahl und Jesu Todesverständnis. — KERTELGE, K. (ed.), *Der Tod Jesu*, 1976, 137-187. Esp. 145-148 [26,26-29]. → 1978; → Segalla 1982a

1976b Mt 10,2-9. — KAHLEFELD, H. - KNOCH, O. (eds.), *Episteln und Evangelien*. II: *Ehe und Familie*, Frankfurt/M: Knecht, 1976, 140-183.

1977a *Wie Jesus das Abendmahl hielt. Der Grund der Eucharistie.* Freiburg: Herder, 1977, [3]1979, 110 p. Esp. 18-21; 25-32: "Der mattäische Abendmahlstext".

1977b Über die Autorität Jesu. Eine Rückfrage anhand des Bekenner- und Verleugnerspruchs Lk 12,8f par. — SCHNACKENBURG, R., et al. (eds.), *Die Kirche des Anfangs*. FS H. Schürmann, 1977, 25-55. Esp. 26-41: "Geht der Bekenner- und Verleugnerspruch Lk 12,8f par auf Jesus zurück?"; 41-49: "Zur Interpretation des Bekenner- und Verleugnerspruchs"; 49-53: "Die eschatologische Autorität Jesu".

1978 *Das Abendmahl und Jesu Todesverständnis* (QDisp, 80). Freiburg: Herder, 1978, 125 p. Esp. 24-25 [26,26-29]. → 1976a

1980a *Simon-Petrus. Geschichte und geschichtliche Bedeutung des ersten Jüngers Jesu Christi* (Päpste und Papsttum, 15). Stuttgart: Hiersemann, 1980, VII-193 p. Esp. 96-104 [16,17-19]; 140-144: "Das matthäische Petrusbild".

1980b *Synoptisches Arbeitsbuch zu den Evangelien. Die vollständigen Synopsen nach Markus, nach Mattäus, nach Lukas, mit den Parallelen aus dem Johannes-Evangelium und den nicht-kanonischen Vergleichstexten sowie einer Auswahlkonkordanz.* Band 2: *Synopse nach Mattäus.* Zürich: Benziger; Gütersloh: Mohn, 1980, 111 p. → Wilckens 1970b
F. NEIRYNCK, *ETL* 57 (1981) 363-364.

1981* (ed.), *Zur Theologie der Kindheitsgeschichten. Der heutige Stand der Exegese* (Schriftenreihe der katholischen Akademie der Erzdiözese Freiburg). München–Zürich: Schnell & Steiner, 1981, 118 p. → Broer, Fiedler, Zeller

1988a *Der Prozeß Jesu geht weiter* (Herderbücherei, 1507). Freiburg: Herder, 1988, 126 p. Esp. 66-70 [27,24-25].

1988b "Wo zwei oder drei versammelt sind auf meinen Namen hin..." (Mt 18,20). Zur Ekklesiologie eines Wortes Jesu. — SCHENKE, L. (ed.), *Studien zum Matthäus-evangelium.* FS W. Pesch, 1988, 227-243. Esp. 229-232 [ecclesiology]; 233-236.240-243 [18,19-20].

1989 Jesus und das Hauptgebot. — MERKLEIN, H. (ed.), *Neues Testament und Ethik.* FS R. Schnackenburg, 1989, 99-109. Esp. 100-102 [6,24].

1992 "Er wird Nazoräer heißen". Messianische Exegese in Mt 1-2. — VAN SEGBROECK, F., et al. (eds.), *The Four Gospels 1992.* FS F. Neirynck, 1992, II, 1385-1401. Esp. 1385-1392 [1-2]; 1392-1394 [2,23]; 1394-1401 [1,1-17]. → 1994

1994 'He will be called a Nazorean': Messianic Exegesis in Matthew 1-2. — EVANS, C.A. - STEGNER, W.R. (eds.), *The Gospels and the Scriptures of Israel*, 1994, 129-178. Esp. 138-147 [1,1-17]; 147-164 [1,18-21]; 164-167 [2,6]; 167-170 [2,15]; 170-173 [2,18]; 173-176 [2,23]. → 1992

1995 → G. Lohfink 1995

**PESCH, Wilhelm**

1955 *Der Lohngedanke in der Lehre Jesu verglichen mit der religiösen Lohnlehre des Spätjudentums* (Münchener theologische Studien, I/7). München: Zink, 1955, X-156 p. Esp. 3-5 [6,1-6.16-18]; 5-6 [6,19-21]; 9-12 [20,1-16]; 27-29 [Q 12,42-46]; 29-39 [Q 19,12-17]; 40-43 [Q 11,39-52]; 44-47 [21,33-41/Mk]; 47-48 [21,28-32]; 49-50 [Q 13,34-35]; 53-55 [Q 6,20-26]; 55-57 [18,3/Mk]; 57-58 [Q 6,27-36]; 58-59 [18,23-35]; 59-61 [Q 6,47-49]; 61-62 [Q 12,8-9]; 63-64 [16,25/Mk]; 64-68 [25,31-46]; 68-70 [20,20-28/Mk]; 70-73 [19,27-30/Mk]; 73-76 [Q 22,28-30]; 76-78 [11,28-30]. — Diss. München, 1953 (J. Schmid).

1960a Zur Formgeschichte und Exegese von Lc 12,32. — *Bib* 41 (1960) 25-40. Esp. 31-34 [10,28.29-31]. [NTA 5, 100]

1960b  Zur Exegese von Mt 6,19-21 und Lk 12,33-34. — *Ibid.*, 356-378. Esp. 356-361 [Mt/Lk]; 361-366 [hellenistic parallels]; 366-373 [Mt]. [NTA 5, 710]

1963  Die sogenannte Gemeindeordnung Mt 18. — *BZ* 7 (1963) 220-235. Esp. 221-226 [18,1-14]; 226-229 [18,15-35]; 229-232 [Mk; Lk]. [NTA 8, 583]; = BAUER, J.B., *Evangelienforschung*, 1968, 177-197. Esp. 178-185; 185-189; 189-194.
Matthäus als Theologe. — *TGeg* 7 (1964) 23-26 (abridged). → 1989

1964a  *Der Ruf zur Entscheidung. Die Bekehrungspredigt des Neuen Testamentes* (Schriftenreihe des Instituts für missionarische Seelsorge, 4). Freiburg: Seelsorge, 1964, 77 p. Esp. 45-46.

1964b  Das Höchste aber ist die Liebe. Das Liebesgebot in der Verkündigung Jesu. — *BK* 19 (1964) 85-89. [NTA 9, 543]

1966  *Matthäus der Seelsorger. Das neue Verständnis der Evangelien dargestellt am Beispiel von Matthäus 18* (SBS, 2). Stuttgart: Katholisches Bibelwerk, 1966, 80 p. Esp. 17-33: "Von den Kindern und den Kleinen" [18,1-14]; 35-48: "Von der Bruderliebe" [18,15-35]; 49-57: "Die Worte Jesu für diese Kirche"; 59-65: "Matthäus der Schriftsteller"; 67-76: "Matthäus der Seelsorger".
J. COPPENS, *ETL* 43 (1967) 270-271; F. DREYFUS, *RB* 76 (1967) 606-607; E. GEMMINGEN, *ZKT* 89 (1967) 231; I. GOMÁ CIVIT, *EstBíb* 26 (1967) 309-310; F. HEINEMANN, *Ordens Korrespondenz* 8 (1967) 101; B.F. MEYER, *CBQ* 29 (1967) 279-280; J. SUDBRACK, *GL* 40 (1967) 233; W. WEISS, *BK* 22 (1967) 103.

1973  Theologische Aussagen der Redaktion von Matthäus 23. — HOFFMANN, P., et al. (eds.), *Orientierung an Jesus*. FS J. Schmid, 1973, 286-299. Esp. 287-290 [23,1-12]; 291-294 [23,13-33]; 294-296 [23,34-36]; 296-298 [Mt redaction].

1989  Matthäus als Gemeindetheologe und Seelsorger. [25,31-46] — *TGeg* 32 (1989) 277-289. → 1963

**PETER, Michał**

1979  "Mąż sprawiedliwy" (św. Józef według tekstu Mateusza 1,19). ["The just man" (St. Joseph according to Mt 1,19)] — *Biblia w ręku chrześcijan. - "W drodze"* 2 (1979) 48-56.

**PETERS, Albrecht**

1979  Das Vaterunser-Auslegung in Luthers Katechismen. — *Lutherische Theologie und Kirche* (Oberursel) 3 (1979) 101-115; 4 (1980) 66-82.

1992  *Kommentar zu Luthers Katechismen. 3. Das Vaterunser*, ed. G. Seebass. Göttingen: Vandenhoeck & Ruprecht, 1992, 198 p.
H.J.E. BEINTKER, *TZ* 50 (1994) 176-177; H. GÜNTHER, *Lutherische Theologie und Kirche* 17 (1993) 33-35; B. HÄGGLUND, *TLZ* 119 (1994) 257-258; M.J. HAEMIG, *LuthQ* NS 7 (1993) 473-475.

**PETERS, E.**

1961  Visão teológica do pecado segundo nos Sinóticos. — *RevistCuBíb* 5 (1961) 427-439.

**PETERSEN, William L.**

1981  The Parable of the Lost Sheep in the Gospel of Thomas and the Synoptics. [18,12-14] — *NT* 23 (1981) 128-147. Esp. 136-147. [NTA 25, 862]

1983  Romanos and the Diatessaron: Readings and Method. — *NTS* 29 (1983) 484-507. Esp. 491-492 [16,24]; 493-494 [8,4]; 494-502 [27,52-53]. [NTA 28, 438]

1985  *The Diatessaron and Ephrem Syrus as Sources of Romanos the Melodist* (CSCO, 475). Leuven: Peeters, 1985, XXXIII-216 p. Esp. 67-71 [1,24]; 71-76 [2,11]; 76-80 [3,15-16]; 80-83 [8,4]; 83-87 [16,24]; 87-88 [25,11]; 88-92 [26,33-35]; 92-95 [27,51]; 95-112 [27,52-53]. — Diss. Utrecht, 1984 (G. Quispel).

1986  New Evidence for the Question of the Original Language of the Diatessaron. — SCHRAGE, W. (ed.), *Studien zum Text und zur Ethik des Neuen Testaments*. FS H. Greeven, 1986, 325-343. Esp. 334-336 [2,18].

1989* (ed.), *Gospel Traditions in the Second Century. Origins, Recensions, Text, and Transmission* (Christianity and Judaism in Antiquity, 3). Notre Dame, IN: University Press, 1989, XI-174 p. → Baarda, Birdsall, Delobel, Koester, Wisse

1990a Tatian's Diatessaron. — KOESTER, H., *Ancient Christan Gospels*, 1990, 403-430. Esp. 422-423 [3,15-16]; 424 [8,4]; 424-426 [27,52-53]; 426-427 [5,29; 18,9].

1990b Textual Evidence of Tatian's Dependence Upon Justin's Ἀπομνημονεύματα. — *NTS* 36 (1990) 512-534. Esp. 516-520 [3,15-16]; 520-522 [5,29; 18,9]; 522-524 [19,17]; 524-525 [22,37]; 525-527 [23,23]; 527-528 [11,27]; 528 [5,45]; 528-529 [6,31-32].

1992 Ebionites, Gospel of the. — *ABD* 2 (1992) 261-626.

1994a *Tatian's Diatessaron. Its Creation, Dissemination, Significance, and History in Scholarship* (Supplements to Vigiliae Christianae, 25). Leiden: Brill, 1994, XIX-555 p. Esp. 14-20 [3,15-16]; 22-24 [8,4]; 79-80 [19,4]; 111-112 [21,17]; 131-132 [4,1-11]; 165-166.375-376 [10,9-10]; 226-228.364-365 [7,17-18]; 248-249 [27,51]; 273-274 [10,34]; 274-275 [23,13]; 351-355 [14,15-21]; 398-403 [28,1-8]; 404-414 [27,52]; 420-424 [22,37].

1994b What Can New Testament Textual Criticism Ultimately Reach? — ALAND, B. - DELOBEL, J. (eds.), *New Testament Textual Criticism, Exegesis and Church History. A Discussion of Methods* (Contributions to Biblical Exegesis and Theology, 7), Kampen: Kok, 1994, 136-151. Esp. 141-144 [19,17]; 145-147 [22,37].

**PÉTRÉ, Hélène**
1952 Les leçons du *Panem Nostrum Quotidianum*. — *RSR* 40 (1951-52) 63-79.

**PETRESCU, Nicolae**
1965 Exegetical Note on the Gospel of Matthew: Mt 28,17. [Roumanian] — *Mitropolia Olteniei* (Craiova) 17 (1965) 557-567.

**PETRIE, C. Stewart**
1959 'Q' is Only What You Make It. — *NT* 3 (1959) 28-33. [NTA 4, 378]
1967 The Authorship of 'The Gospel According to Matthew'. A Reconsideration of the External Evidence. — *NTS* 14 (1967-68) 15-32. [NTA 12, 549]

**PETROTTA, Anthony J.**
1985 A Closer Look at Matt 2:6 and Its Old Testament Sources. — *JEvTS* 28 (1985) 47-52. [NTA 30, 564] → 1990; → Heater 1983
1990 An even Closer Look at Matt 2:6 and Its Old Testament Sources. — *JEvTS* 33 (1990) 311-315. [NTA 35, 620] → 1985

**PETTEM, Michael Allan**
1985 Le premier récit de la multiplication des pains et le problème synoptique. — *StudRel/SciRel* 14 (1985) 73-83. [NTA 30, 599]
1989 *Matthew: Jewish Christian or Gentile Christian?* Diss. McGill Univ., Montreal, 1989, 397 p. (F. Wisse). — *DissAbstr* 51 (1990-91) 3107; 53 (1992-93) 185.

**PETTINGILL, W.L.**
1986 *Estudios sencillos sobre Mateo*. Barcelona: CLIE, 1986, 264 p.

**PETTY, M.**
1964 Evangelios de la infancia y ejercicios espirituales. — *Cien y Fe* (Buenos Aires) 20 (1964) 469-480. [NTA 10, 110]

**PETUCHOWSKI, Jacob J.** → Brocke 1974/78

**PETZER, Jakobus (= Kobus) Hendrik**
1986* & HARTIN, P.J. (eds.), *A South African Perspective on the New Testament. Essays by*

*South African New Testament Scholars Presented to Bruce Manning Metzger During his Visit to South Africa in 1985.* Leiden: Brill, 1986, XII-271 p. → I.J. du Plessis, van Aarde, Vorster

1991    Style and Text in the Lucan Narrative of the Institution of the Lord's Supper (Luke 22.19b-20). — *NTS* 37 (1991) 113-129. Esp. 122-124 [25,26-29]. [NTA 35, 1189]

**PETZKE, Gerd**

1970    *Die Traditionen über Apollonius von Tyana und das Neue Testament* (Studia ad Corpus Hellenisticum Novi Testamenti, 1). Leiden: Brill, 1970, XII-264 p. Esp. 162-167.179-182. — Diss. Mainz, 1968 (H. Braun).

1976    Die historische Frage nach den Wundertaten Jesu. Dargestellt am Beispiel des Exorzismus Mark. ix.14-29 Par. — *NTS* 22 (1975-76) 180-204. Esp. 198-202: "Die Wundertraditionen im Neuen Testament" [Q]. [NTA 20, 803]

**PETZOLDT, Martin**

1984    *Gleichnisse Jesu und christliche Dogmatik.* Göttingen: Vandenhoeck & Ruprecht, 1984, 180 p. Esp. 35-45 [21,33-46/Mk]; 46-51 [18,23-35]; 51-56 [20,1-16]; 56-63 [22,1-14/Q 14,16-24]; 63-68 [25,1-13]; 68-72 [25,14-30/Q 19,12-27]; 72-77 [25,31-46]. — Diss. Leipzig, 1975 (E.-H. Amberg).

**PFÄLTZER, N.**

1959    *Die deutschen Vaterunser-Auslegungen von den Anfängen bis ins zwölften Jahrhundert. Vergleichende Studie auf Grund von quellenkritischen Einzelinterpretation.* Diss. Frankfurt/M, 1959, 193 p.

**PFENDSACK, Werner**

1965    *Unser Vater. Eine Auslegung des Gebetes der Christenheit.* Basel: Reinhardt, 1965, 113 p.

1966    *Ihr seid das Salz der Erde. Eine Auslegung der Bergpredigt Jesu.* Basel: Reinhardt, 1966, 205 p.

1968    *Die Kirche bleibt nicht im Dorf. Gleichnisse des Matthäus-Evangeliums ausgelegt für die Gemeinde.* Basel: Reinhardt, 1968, 183 p.

**PFISTER, Xaver**

1979    Eingeladen zum Gewährenlassen. Das Unkraut unter dem Weizen (Mattäus 13,24-30). — STEINER, A. – WEYMANN, V. (eds.), *Gleichnisse Jesu,* 1979, 103-128.

**PFITZNER, Victor C.**

1982    Purified Community – Purified Sinner. Expulsion from the Community according to Matthew 18:15-18 and 1 Corinthians 5:1-5. — *AusBR* 30 (1982) 34-55. [NTA 27, 925]

**PHILBIN, Lester G.**

1973    The Contemporary Understanding of the Holy and Its Reflection in Matthew's Gospel. — *RelLife* 42 (1973) 508-513. [NTA 18, 842]

**PHILIPOSE, John**

1977    Off the Beaten Track: Some Problems of Translation. — *BTrans* 28 (1977) 312-326. Esp. 312-314 [introductory formula]; 314-315 [2,20]; 315-317 [3,.1]; 317-321 [5,1.17-18.21-22]; 321-322 [6,7]; 322-323 [7,6]; 323-324 [11,12]; 324-325 [21,7.9]; 325-326 [26,64; 27,11]; 326 [5,19]. [NTA 22, 78] → Ross 1978b

**PHILIPPART, Guy**

1972    Fragments palimpsestes latins du Vindobonensis 563 (V<sup>e</sup> siècle?): Évangile selon S. Matthieu, Évangile de l'Enfance selon Thomas, Évangile de Nicodème. — *AnBoll* 90 (1972) 391-411. Esp. 403-408.

**PHILLIPS, Gary Allen**

1981 *Enunciation and the Kingdom of Heaven: Text, Narration and Hermeneutic in the Parables of Matthew 13.* Diss. Vanderbilt Univ., Nashville, TN, 1981, 572 p. — *DissAbstr* 42 (1981-82) 4484.

1983 History and Text: The Reader in Context in Matthew's Parables Discourse. — *SBL 1983 Seminar Papers*, 415-437. Esp. 423-437: "Matt 13 as intertextuality and discourse"; = *Semeia* 31 (1985) 111-138. Esp. 119-137. [NTA 30, 120]

1984 Kingdom Speaking and Kingdom Hearing: Matthew's Interpretation of Jesus' Kingdom Tradition. — KOPAS, J. (ed.), *Interpreting Tradition. The Art of Theological Reflection* (The Annual Publication of the College Theology Society, 1983, 29), Chico, CA: Scholars, 1984, 73-91. Esp. 84-88: "Matthew's interpretation of Jesus' parabolic tradition".

1989 Training Scribes for a World Divided: Discourse and Division in the Religious System of Matthew's Gospel. — NEUSNER, J., et al. (eds.), *Religious Writings and Religious Systems. Systemic Analysis of Holy Books in Christianity, Islam, Buddhism, Greco-Roman Religions, Ancient Israel, and Judaism.* II: *Christianity* (Brown Studies in Religion, 1), Atlanta, GA: Scholars, 1989, 51-74.

**PHILONENKO, Marc**

1988 La parabole sur la lampe (Luc 11,33-36) et les horoscopes qoumrâniens. [6,22-23] — *ZNW* 79 (1988) 145-151. [NTA 33, 18]

1992 La troisième demande du "Notre Père" et l'hymne de Nabuchodonosor. — *RHPR* 72 (1992) 23-31. [NTA 36, 1265]

1993a Prêter serment par le trône de Dieu (à propos de Matthieu 5,34). — ID. (ed.), *Le Trône de Dieu* (WUNT, 69), Tübingen: Mohr, 1993, 243-251.

1993b Le sang du juste. (*I Hénoch* 47,1.4; *Matthieu* 27,24). — *RHPR* 73 (1993) 395-399. [NTA 38, 1374]

1995 "Que ton esprit saint vienne sur nous et qu'il nous purifie" (*Luc* 11,2): l'arrière-plan qoumrânien d'une variante lucanienne du "Notre Père". — *RHPR* 75 (1995) 61-66. [NTA 40, 232]

**PHILOTHEOS, P.**

1955 Analysis of Mt 6,19-33 in the Lord's Sermon on the Mount. [Greek] — *Orthodoxia* (Istanbul) 31 (1955) 324-335.

**PHIPPS, William E.**

1986 The Magi and Halley's Comet. — *TTod* 43 (1986) 88-92. [NTA 30, 1043]

**PICCIRILLO, Michele**

1983 "Date a Cesare quel che è di Cesare". La numismatica e il Vangelo. [22,15-22] — *ParVi* 28 (1983) 71-75.

**PICKERING, Stuart R.**

1993a Matthew 20:23-31, 1 Corinthians 15:51/52-57, Colossians 3:22. New Texts in Syriac and Greek. — *New Testament Textual Research Update* (Sydney) 1 (1993) 2-3. → Brock 1992

1993b Matthew 23:14. Devourers of Widows' Houses. — *Ibid.*, 4-5. → Ross 1992

1994a Gospel Transmission via the *Diatessaron* in Africa. [7,14] — *New Testament Textual Research Update* 2 (1994) 9-12. → Quispel 1993

1994b "Western Non-Interpolations": The View from the Perspective of UBS⁴/NA²⁷. — *Ibid.*, 34-38. Esp. 35 [27,49].

1994c  Transmission of Gospel Materials in the Second Century: Evidence of a New Fragment from Oxyrhynchus. — *Ibid.*, 105-110.

1994d  A New Papyrus Text of the Lord's Prayer. — *Ibid.*, 111-112.

1994e  Additions to the Lord's Prayer in the Textual Tradition. [6,13] — *Ibid.*, 112-118.

1995a  Additional Sayings of Jesus in Some Texts of the Gospel of Matthew. [10,23; 16,2-3; 17,21.26; 18,11; 20,28; 21,44] — *New Testament Textual Research Update* 3 (1995) 12-17.

1995b  Controversy Surrounding Fragments of the Gospel of Matthew in Magdalen College, Oxford. — *Ibid.*, 22-25. → Thiede 1995c

PIERPONT, W.G. → M.A. Robinson 1991

**PIETRANTONIO, Ricardo**

1982  Duda y adoración. *Hoi de edistasan* (Mt 28,17). — *RevistBíb* 44 (1982) 233-242. [NTA 27, 932]

1984  Un estudio bíblico sobre la Iglesia. Explicación de la metodología de los estudios bíblicos. — *RevistBíb* 46 (1984) 275-286. Esp. 280-283 [5,13-16]. [NTA 29, 684]

1986  ¿Está la justicia enraizada en el NT? — *RevistBíb* 48 (1986) 89-119. Esp. 98-99, 101-109 [δικαιοσύνη]. [NTA 31, 362]

1987  Aspectos evangelizadores de Mateo 10. Estudio Bíblico. — *RevistBíb* 49 (1987) 129-153. Esp. 134-139 [9,36–10,45]; 139-142 [10,5-15]; 142-148 [10,16-25]; 148-150 [10,26-33]; 150-153 [10,34-42]. [NTA 32, 600]

**PIETTRE, Monique**

1988  *Les paroles dures de l'Évangile.* Paris: Chalet, 1988, ²1989, 128 p.
*Le parole "dure" del Vangelo*, trans. P. Crespi (Universale teologica. 29). Brescia: Queriniana, 1990, 131 p.

**PIKAZA, Xavier**

1973  Hacia una visión de la trinidad partiendo del Nuevo Testamento. — *La Trinidad en la Biblia. Cristo, revelador del Padre y emisor del Espíritu en el Nuevo Testamento* (Semañas de estudios trinitarios, 6), Salamanca: Secretariado Trinitario, 1973, 9-71. Esp. 43-48; 50-53.

1974a  & DE LA CALLE, F., *Teología de los evangelios de Jesús* (Biblioteca de estudios bíblicos, 6). Salamanca: Sígueme, 1974, 505 p. Esp. 109-218: "Teología de Mateo"; ²1975; ⁴1980. → López Casuso 1975
*Leggere Matteo, il vangelo della catechesi* [1974, 109-218], trans. P. Ferraris & A. Giudíci (Azimut). Torino: Marietti, 1977, 140 p.
*PalCl* 57 (1978) 576; G.G. GAMBA, *Sal* 40 (1978) 692-693; G. RINALDI, *BibOr* 20 (1978) 308; 23 (1981) 235.
*Teologia de Mateus.* São Paulo, 1978, 160 p.

1974b  Mt 25,31-46 y la teología de la liberación. — *CuBíb* 31 (1974) 27-28.

1975  El origen de Jesús según el Nuevo Testamento. [1-2] — *Estudios* (Madrid) 31 (1975) 155-186.

1976  *Los orígines de Jesús. Ensayos de cristología bíblica* (Biblioteca de estudios bíblicos, 15). Salamanca: Sígueme, 1976, 525 p. Esp. 317-327: "El origen de Jesús en Mateo"; 112-118 [God as father]; 84-98 [12,28]; 269-307 [1,18-25]. → Muñoz Iglesias 1978
En torno a "Los orígenes de Jesús". — *Salmanticensis* 24 (1977) 351-361. [NTA 22, 903]

1977  Mateo 25,31-46: cristología y liberación. — VARGAS-MACHUCA, A. (ed.), *Jesucristo en la historia y en la fe*, Salamanca: Sígueme, 1977, 220-228.

1979a  Dios, hombre y Cristo en el mensaje de Jesús (Introducción al tema de la autenticidad jesuánica de Mt 25,31-46). — *Salmanticensis* 26 (1979) 5-50. Esp. 8-30: "El mensaje de Jesús"; 31-35: "Vida de Jesús"; 36-44: "Mt 25,31-46 en la historia de Jesús"; 44-50: "Valoración crítica". [NTA 24, 102]

1979b   La bendición y maldición del Hijo del Hombre (Trasfondo veterotestamentario del
        "Benditos-Malditos" de Mt 25,34.41). — *Salmanticensis* 26 (1979) 277-286. [NTA 24,
        428]

1979c   El juicio del Hijo del Hombre. Trasfondo veterotestamentario de Mt. 25,31c-33. —
        *NatGrac* 26 (1979) 249-297.

1979d   El hijo del hombre y las obras de diakonia. Trasfondo veterotestamentario y sentido de
        las obras de Mt 25,31-46. — *Estudios* 35 (1979) 197-230.

1980    Salvación y condena del Hijo del Hombre (Trasfondo veterotestamentario y judío de Mt
        25,34.41.46). — *Salmanticensis* 27 (1980) 419-438. Esp. 420-426 [25,34]; 426-434 [25,41];
        434-438 [25,46]. [NTA 25, 867]

1983    La estructura de Mt y su influencia en 25,31-46. — *Salmanticensis* 30 (1983) 11-40.
        Esp. 13-20: "Los cines discursos"; 20-27: "Los tres momentos del proceso narrativo"; 27-40: "Unidad de
        alianza". [NTA 27, 930]

1984    *Hermanos de Jesús y servidores de los mas pequeños (Mt 25,31-46). Juicio de Dios y
        compromiso histórico en Mateo* (Biblioteca de estudios bíblicos, 46). Salamanca:
        Sígueme, 1984, 460 p. [NTA 30, p. 232]
        X. ALEGRE, *ActBibl* 24 (1987) 84; V.J. ANSEDE ALONSO, *Communio* (Sevilla) 19 (1986) 248-450; P.
        BONATI, *DivThom* 88 (1985) 403-405; R. DE ANDRÉS, *RazFe* 212 (1985) 217; J.L. ESPINEL, *CiTom* 112
        (1985) 428-429; A.J. LEVORATTI, *RevistBíb* 47 (1985) 179-181; D. MONTERO, *NatGrac* 32 (1985) 80-81;
        F. ORTIZ DE URTARAN, *Lumen* (Vitoria) 34 (1985) 190.

1988    "Limpios de corazón". Reflexión bíblica sobre Mt 5,8. — *Communio* (Madrid) 10/6
        (1988) 502-520.

1992    *La figura de Jesús. Profeta, taumaturgo, rabino, mesías* (El mundo de la Biblia).
        Estella: Verbo Divino, 1992, 249 p.

1993    *Antropología bíblica. Del árbol del juicio al sepulcro de pascua* (Biblioteca de estudios
        bíblicos, 80). Salamanca: Sígueme, 1993, 537 p. Esp. 266-272 [Q 12,22-32]; 273-279 [5,45];
        289-292 [Q 6,37-42]; 292-302 [7,1-5]; 302-307 [Q 6,27-36]; 307-313 [5,38-48]; 319-324 [4,1-11]; 324-331
        [6,24]; 334-337 [Q 16,13]; 348-356 [12,18-21]; 356-360 [10,34-37]; 390-393 [27,3-10]; 435-441 [Q 11,47-
        51]; 463-468 [28,18-20].

1995    María: De la historia al símbolismo en el Nuevo Testamento. — *EphMar* 45 (1995)
        9-41. Esp. 25-33 [1,18-25; 2,1-12]. [NTA 40, 439]

        **PILCH, John J.**

1979    Marriage in the Lord. [19,3-12] — *BiTod* 102 (1979) 2010-2013.

1986    The Health Care System in Matthew: A Social Science Analysis. — *BTB* 16 (1986)
        102-106. Esp. 104-105 [8-9]. [NTA 31, 107]

1987    Teacher for a Troubled Church: Matthew's Jesus. — *BiTod* 25 (1987) 23-28. [NTA 31,
        578]

1988    Understanding Biblical Healing. Electing the Appropriate Model. — *BTB* 18 (1988) 60-
        66. Esp. 65 [8,1-4]. [NTA 32, 1024]

1989    Reading Matthew Anthropologically: Healing in Cultural Perspective. — *Listening* 24
        (1989) 278-289. [NTA 34, 624]

        **PILLARELLA, G.**

1962    "... conoscere i misteri" (Matt. 13,11). — *PalCl* 41 (1962) 418-422. [NTA 7, 135]

        **PINCKAERS, Servais**

1979    *La quête du bonheur*. Paris: Téqui, 1979, 191 p. → García de Haro 1981

1981    La Loi de l'Évangile ou Loi nouvelle selon S. Thomas. — ID. - RUMPF, L. (eds.), *Loi
        et évangile. Héritages confessionnels et interpellations contemporaines. Actes du 3e*

*cycle d'éthique des Universités de Suisse romande 1979-80* (Le champ éthique, 5), Genève: Labor et Fides, 1981, 57-79. Esp. 68-72: "Le Sermon sur la montagne, comme expression de la Loi nouvelle".

1985 La Loi évangélique, vie selon l'Esprit, et le Sermon sur la montagne. — *NVet* 60 (1985) 217-228. Esp. 224-228 [Thomas Aquinas].

1986* & PINTO DE OLIVEIRA, C.J. (eds.), *Universalité et permanence des Lois morales* (Études d'éthique chrétienne; Studien zur theologischen Ethik, 16), Freiburg/Schw: Éd. universitaires; Paris: Cerf, 1986, 454 p. → Delhaye, Descamps 1981, Dupont 1985b

**PIÑERO, Antonio**

1993* (ed.), *Fuentes del cristianismo. Tradiciones primitivas sobre Jesús.* Cordoba: El Almendro; Madrid: Univ. Complutense, 1993, 530 p. → J.K. Elliott, Pelaez del Rosal, Vargas-Machuca

1995 & PELÁEZ, J., *El Nuevo Testamento: Introducción al estudio de los primeros escritos cristianos* (En los origenes del cristianismo, 8). Córdoba: El Almendro / Fundación Épsilon, 1995, 569 p.

**PINTO, Evarist**

1974 Jesus as the Son of God in the Gospels. — *BTB* 4 (1974) 75-93. Esp. 80-83; 85-88 [11,25-27]. [NTA 18, 791]

1981 *Jesus the Son and Giver of Life in the Fourth Gospel.* Diss. Pont. Univ. Urbaniana, Roma, 1981, 274 p. (S. Virgulin). Esp. 74-85 [Son of God in the synoptics].

**PIPER, John S.**

1979 *'Love your enemies'. Jesus' Love Command in the Synoptic Gospels and in the Early Christian Paraenesis. A History of the Tradition and Interpretation of Its Uses* (SNTS MS, 38). Cambridge: University Press, 1979, XIV-273 p. Esp. 49-63.187-194 [5,38-48/Q 6,27-36]; 66-99.195-210: "Jesus' command of enemy love in the larger context of his message"; 134-170.220-233: "The gospel tradition of Jesus' command of enemy love and its use in Matthew and Luke". — Diss. München, 1974 (L. Goppelt); Grand Rapids, MI: Baker, 1991.

    J. DRURY, *JTS* 32 (1981) 218-220; D.L. DUNGAN, *CBQ* 44 (1982) 344-345; A.B. DU TOIT, *Skrif en Kerk* (Pretoria) 15 (1994) 328-329; P. EDMONDS, *HeythJ* 22 (1981) 336-337; B. EHRMAN, *JBL* 116 (1997) 178-179; R.T. FRANCE, *EvQ* 53 (1981) 62-63; R.H. FULLER, *ATR* 63 (1981) 320-322; L. GROLLENBERG, *TijdTheol* 21 (1981) 79-80; H.W. HOLLANDER, *NTT* 35 (1981) 241-242; X. JACQUES, *NRT* 102 (1980) 903-904; J.P. MEIER, *Interpr* 36 (1982) 208.210; G. O'GRADY, *CleR* 66 (1981) 68; G. SEGALLA, *Studia Patavina* 28 (1981) 415-417; H. WEDER, *TLZ* 106 (1981) 34-35.

**PIPER, Otto A.**

1957 Unchanging Promises. Exodus in the New Testament. — *Interpr* 11 (1957) 3-22. Esp. 6-8.16-20.

1962 Change of Perspective. Gnostic and Canonical Gospels. — *Interpr* 16 (1962) 402-417. Esp. 414 [Gospel of Thomas / 13,47-50]. [NTA 7, 932]

1964 The Virgin Birth. The Meaning of the Gospel Accounts. — *Interpr* 18 (1964) 131-148. [NTA 9, 143]

**PIPER, Ronald A.**

1982 Matthew 7,7-11 par. Luke 11,9-13. Evidence of Design and Argument in the Collection of Jesus' Sayings. — DELOBEL, J. (ed.), *Logia*, 1982, 411-418; = KLOPPENBORG, J.S. (ed.), *The Shape of Q*, 1994, 131-137.

1989 *Wisdom in the Q-Tradition. The Aphoristic Teaching of Jesus* (SNTS MS, 61). Cambridge: University Press, 1989, IX-325 p. Esp. 14-99.209-235: "Collections of aphoristic sayings in the double tradition" [Q 6,27-36.37-42.43-45; 11,9-13; 12,2-9.22-31]; 100-109.235-258: "The use of aphoristic sayings outside the aphoristic collections" [Q 3,9; 6,40; 7,24-35; 10,2.7; 11,14-23.33-36; 12,33-

34.58-59; 13,23-24; 14,34-35; 17,37; 19,26]; 161-192.258-271: "The place of aphoristic wisdom in the sapiential traditions of the double tradition" [Q 10,21-22]. [NTA 33, p. 389] — Diss. London, 1986 (G.N. Stanton).

    J.D. CROSSAN, *JBL* 110 (1991) 522-525; J.K. ELLIOTT, *ScriptB* 21 (1989) 22-23; H.T. FLEDDERMANN, *CBQ* 53 (1991) 715-716; R.T. FRANCE, *EvQ* 64 (1992) 174-175; P. HOFFMANN, *CrnStor* 13 (1992) 421-427; M.D. HOOKER, *NBlackfr* 71 (1990) 516-518; H.M. HUMPHREY, *BTB* 21 (1991) 127-128; J.S. KLOPPENBORG, *Bib* 71 (1990) 432-436; H. VON LIPS, *TRev* 87 (1991) 475-477; I.H. MARSHALL, *ExpT* 100 (1988-89) 431; S.E. PORTER, *FilolNT* 4 (1991) 77-79; J.-M. ROUSÉE, *RB* 96 (1989) 318; M.G. STEINHAUSER, *Religious Studies and Theology* (Edmonton) 10/2 (1990) 123-124; C.M. TUCKETT, *JSNT* 40 (1990) 118-119; *JTS* 41 (1990) 608-610.

1995\*  (ed.), *The Gospel Behind the Gospels. Current Studies on Q* (SupplNT, 75). Leiden: Brill, 1995, X-411 p. [NTA 39, p. 327] → Cotter, Hoffmann 1992b, A.D. Jacobson, Kloppenborg, Lambrecht, Lührmann, McLean, Neirynck, R.A. Piper, J.M. Robinson, Sato, L. Schottroff 1991, Tuckett, Uro, Vaage

    F. BURNETT, *RelStR* 22 (1996) 68; M.D. GOULDER, *NT* 38 (1996) 194-196; F. NEIRYNCK, *ETL* 72 (1996) 443-444.

1995a  In Quest of Q: The Direction of Q Studies. — *Ibid.*, 1-18.

1995b  The Language of Violence and the Aphoristic Sayings in Q. A Study of Q 6:27-36. — KLOPPENBORG, J.S. (ed.), *Conflict and Invention*, 1995, 53-72.

**PITTENGER, Norman**

1969  On Miracle. — *ExpT* 80 (1968-69) 104-107, 147-150. Esp. 147-148 [Virgin birth].

**PIZIVIN, Daniel**

1992  Scandale. — *DBS* 12/66 (1992) 49-66. Esp. 49-53.

**PIZZOLATO, Luigi Franco**

1978  *La dottrina esegetica di sant'Ambrogio* (Studia patristica mediolanensia, 9). Milano: Vita e Pensiero, 1978, XXI-359 p. Esp. 148-154: "Matteo e Marco".

**PIZZUTO, Antonio**

1978  *Tre parabole dell'attesa (Lc 12,35-46 // Mt 24,43-51). Dagli Evangelisti a Gesù attraversa la Fonte Q.* Diss. Napoli, 1978, 308 p. (V. Fusco).

**PLACKAL, Anthony O.**

1988  *Tradition and Redaction in the Matthean Beatitudes.* Diss. Catholic University of America, Washington, DC, 1988, 274 p. (M.A. Getty). — *DissAbstr* 49 (1989-90) 470.

**PLANK, Karl A.**

1990  The Human Face of Otherness: Reflections on Joseph and Mary (Matthew 1:18-25). — CARROLL, J.T., et al. (eds.), *Faith and History*. FS P.W. Meyer, 1990, 55-73.

**PLATT, Elizabeth E.**

1977  The Ministry of Mary of Bethany. — *TTod* 34 (1977-78) 29-39. Esp. 31-32 [26,6-13]. [NTA 21, 753]

**PLATZECK, Erhard-Wolfram**

1983  El centro del Padre nuestro. — *NatGrac* 30 (1983) 399-406.

**PLEVNIK, Joseph**

1978  The Trinitarian Formula in Mt 28,19b. — DUNNE, T.A. - LAPORTE, J.-M. (eds.), *Trinification of the World: A Festschrift in Honour of Frederick E. Crowe in Celebration of His 60th Birthday*, Toronto, Ont.: Regis College, 1978, 241-258. Esp. 242-245: "Mt 28,19b: formulation of the evangelist?"; 245-251: "Mt 28,19b in the pre-Matthean tradition"; 251-253: "Mt 28,19b and the risen Jesus"; 253-254: "Mt 28,19b in the gospel of Matthew"; 254-256: "Mt 28,19b in the emerging trinitarian doctrine".

1979    1 Thess 5,1-11: Its Authenticity, Intention and Message. — *Bib* 60 (1979) 71-90. Esp.
80-84 [1 Thess 5,2-3 / Mt 24,43-44]. [NTA 24, 189]

1983    Divine Call and Human Response. Praying with the Word. — *Way* 23 (1983) 148-159.
Esp. 148-154 [Lord's prayer]. [NTA 23, 1145]

1991    Son of Man Seated at the Right Hand of God: Luke 22,69 in Lucan Christology. — *Bib*
72 (1991) 331-347. Esp. 336-337: "Matthew's account of the trial, 26,63-66". [NTA 36, 774]

PLOCH, W.

1994    *Jesaja-Worte in der synoptischen Evangelientradition* (Dissertationen: Theologische
Reihe, 64). St. Ottilien: EOS, 1994, XIX-296 p. — Diss. München, 1992 (J. Gnilka).

PLUM, Karin Friis

1989a   The Female Metaphor. The Definition of Male and Female – an Unsolved Problem?
[1,1-16] — *StudTheol* 43 (1989) 81-89. [NTA 34, 532]

1989b   Genealogy as Theology. [1,1-17] — *Scandinavian Journal of the Old Testament* (Aarhus)
3/1 (1989) 66-92. Esp. 87-92: "The New Testament genealog es". [NTA 33, 1113]

1990    Det himmelske favntag. Bibelsk ægteskabs- og seksualmetaforik. [The heavenly
embrace. Biblical metaphors of marriage and sexuality] — *DanskTeolTids* 53 (1990)
161-182. Esp. 178-180 [9,14-15; 22,1-14; 25,1-13]. [NTA 35, £50]

PLUMMER, Alfred

1915R   *An Exegetical Commentary on the Gospel according to St. Matthew* [1909, ²1915]
(Thornapple Commentaries). Grand Rapids, MI: Baker, 1953; 1982, XLVI-451 p. [NTA
27, p. 212]
A.J. BANDSTRA, *CalvTJ* 18 (1963) 142; H.J. HOEFLINGER, *WestTJ* 16 (1953) 131-134.

POBEE, John S.

1987    *Who Are the Poor? The Beatitudes as a Call to Community* (The Risk Book Series).
Genève: WCC Publications, 1987, VII-71 p. Esp. 14-31 [Beatitudes]. [NTA 32, p. 108]
J. ANSALDI, *ETR* 63 (1988) 321-322; N.C. CAPULONG, *AsiaJT* 3 (1989) 358-361; K. NORDSTOKKE,
*NorskTeolTids* 88 (1987) 208; T. PRESLER, *ATR* 70 (1988) 285-286.

PÖHLMANN, Wolfgang

1993    *Der Verlorene Sohn und das Haus. Studien zu Lukas 15,11-32 im Horizont der antiken
Lehre von Haus, Erziehung und Ackerbau* (WUNT, 68). Tübingen: Mohr, 1993, X-222
p. Esp. 147-153: "Die Parabel von den ungleichen Söhnen (Mt 21.28-32) und die Parabel vom verlorenen
Sohn (Lk 15,11-32)".

POELMAN, Roger

1954    Lecture de l'Évangile selon saint Matthieu. — *Lumière V* 20 (1954) 16-24.

1963    La prière de Jésus. — *LumVit* 18 (1963) 625-656. Esp. 638-345: "Le Christ 'en' prière"; 646-
656: "Les prières explicites du Christ".
The Prayer of Jesus. — *LumVit* 19 (1964) 9-44.

1965    Saint Pierre et la Tradition. — *LumVit* 20 (1965) 632-648. Esp. 635-367 [5-7/1 Pet].

POKORNÝ, Petr

1969a   *Der Kern der Bergpredigt. Eine Auslegung* (Evangelische Zeitstimmen, 4). Hamburg-
Bergstedt: Reich, 1969, 62 p. [NTA 14, p. 111]
H.-J. KOSMAHL, *TZ* 27 (1971) 54-55; J. ROHDE, *TLZ* 95 (1970) 435-436.

1969b   Die Worte Jesu nach der Logienquelle im Lichte des zeitgenössischen Judentums. —
*Kairos* 11 (1969) 172-180. Esp. 175-180 [eschatology]. [NTA 15, 123]

1971    *Der Gottessohn. Literarische Übersicht und Fragestellung* (Theologische Studien, 109).
Zürich: Theologischer Verlag, 1971, 70 p. Esp. 30-31 [11,25-27]; 39-40.

1973   The Core of the Sermon on the Mount. — *Studia Evangelica* 6 (1973) 429-433.

1974   The Temptation Stories and Their Intention. — *NTS* 20 (1973-74) 115-127. Esp. 115-120.122-125. [NTA 18, 870]; = ID. — SOUČEK, J.B., *Bibelauslegung*, 1997, 275-287. Esp. 275-280.282-285.

1985   *Die Entstehung der Christologie. Voraussetzungen einer Theologie des Neuen Testaments.* Stuttgart: Calwer, 1985, 180 p. Esp. 21-31 [kingdom]; 69-73 [Q].

1986   Zur Entstehung der Evangelien. — *NTS* 32 (1986) 393-403. Esp. 398-401 [Mk/Q]. [NTA 31, 102]

1992   *Die Zukunft des Glaubens. Sechs Kapitel über Eschatologie* (Arbeiten zur Theologie, 72). Stuttgart: Calwer, 1992, 105 p. Esp. 38-48: "Jesus"; 49-68: "Das Evangelium".

1994   Griechische Sprichwörter im Neuen Testament. — ELSAS, C., et al. (eds.), *Tradition und Translation*. FS C. Colpe, 1994, 336-343. Esp. 338-339 [5,33; 10,16; 13,5; 15,20; 18,20; 21,19]; = ID. — SOUČEK, J.B., *Bibelauslegung*, 1997, 147-154. Esp. 146-150.

1995a  Die Bedeutung des Markusevangeliums für die Entstehung der christlichen Bibel. — FORNBERG, T. - HELLHOLM, D. (eds.), *Texts and Contexts*. FS L. Hartman, 1995, 409-427. Esp. 418-420 [Mk/Q]; = ID. — SOUČEK, J.B., *Bibelauslegung*, 1997, 255-273. Esp. 264-266.

1995b  From a Puppy to the Child. Some Problems of Contemporary Biblical Exegesis Demonstrated from Mark 7.24-30/Matt 15.21-8. — *NTS* 41 (1995) 321-337. [NTA 40, 199]; = ID. — SOUČEK, J.B., *Bibelauslegung*, 1997, 69-85.

1997   & SOUČEK, J.B., *Bibelauslegung als Theologie*, ed. P. Pokorný (WUNT, 100). Tübingen: Mohr, 1997, IX-372 p. → 1974, 1994, 1995a-b, Souček 1963

**POLAERT, André**

1966   La catéchèse du Notre Père aux hommes d'aujourd'hui. — *La Maison-Dieu* (Paris) 85 (1966) 117-139. [NTA 11, 204]

**POLAG, Athanasius**

1968   Zu den Stufen der Christologie in Q. — *Studia Evangelica* 4 (1968) 72-74.

1977   *Die Christologie der Logienquelle* (WMANT, 45). Neukirchen-Vluyn: Neukirchener, 1977, IX-213 p. Esp. 33-128: "Der christologische Aussagegehalt des Überlieferungsgutes"; 129-144: "Die christologischen Züge der Redaktion der Hauptsammlung"; 145-170: "Die christologischen Züge der späten Redaktion"; 171-197: "Das Verhältnis der Logienquelle zur frühen Gemeinde". [NTA 22, p. 214] — Diss. Trier, 1969 (F. Mussner – W. Thüsing). → Luz 1973
       P. HOFFMANN, *TRev* 79 (1983) 205-208; D. LÜHRMANN, *TLZ* 105 (1980) 193-194; F.J. MOLONEY, *Sal* 44 (1982) 848-849; L. MORALDI, *Henoch* 8 (1986) 102-103.

1979   *Fragmenta Q. Textheft zur Logienquelle.* Neukirchen-Vluyn: Neukirchener, 1979, 102 p.; ²1982, 104 p. → Havener 1987, Neirynck 1979b, Sanz Valdivieso 1990
       A. FUCHS, *SNTU* 6-7 (1981-82) 249-254; G.G. GAMBA, *Sal* 41 (1979) 902; D. LÜHRMANN, *TLZ* 105 (1980) 895-896; P.-G. MÜLLER, *Freiburger Rundbrief* 31 (1979) 122-123; R. PESCH, *TRev* 76 (1980) 114-115; K. SCHAUPP, *ZKT* 103 (1981) 213-214; D. ZELLER, *BK* 35 (1980) 33.

1983   Die theologische Mitte der Logienquelle. — STUHLMACHER, P. (ed.), *Das Evangelium und die Evangelien*, 1983, 103-111. Esp. 103-105: "Die Existenz von Q"; 105-107: "Zur Geschichte von Q"; 107-110: "Die theologische Mitte von Q"; 110-111: "Das Evangelium in Q".
       The Theological Center of the Sayings Source. — STUHLMACHER, P. (ed.), *The Gospel and the Gospels*, 1991, 97-105. Esp. 97-99; 99-101; 101-104; 104-105.

**POLITI, J.**

1992   "Not (Not I)". [26,31-33] — *Literature & Theology* (Oxford) 6 (1992) 345-355. [NTA 37, 738]

**POLKOW, Dennis**

1987  Method and Criteria for Historical Jesus Research. — *SBL 1987 Seminar Papers*, 336-356. Esp. 342-346 [13,31-32].

**POLLASTRI, Allesandra**

1979  Nota all'interpretazione di Matteo 13,33 / Luca 13,21 nel frammento "Incipit de tribus mensuris". — *Studi storico-religiosi* (Roma) 3 (1979) 61-78.

**PONTHOT, Joseph**

1958  Les évangiles et leur formation. Présentation de quelques ouvrages récents. — *RevDiocTournai* 13 (1958) 55-61. → Levie 1954, Vaganay 1954a

1964  L'évangile de l'Enfance selon saint Matthieu. Perspectives doctrinales de Mt, 1-2. — *RevDiocTournai* 19 (1964) 615-637. Esp. 615-621: "Situation de l'évangile de l'Enfance"; 621-636: "Commentaire de Mt., 1-2".

1965  Les traditions évangéliques sur la Résurrection du Christ. Perspectives théologiques et problèmes d'historicité. — *LumVit* 20 (1965) 649-673. Esp. 658-661 [28,16-20]; 668-669 [28,9-10]; 670-671 [28,1-8]; 671-672 [28,11-15]; 21 (1966) 99-110.
Les traditions évangéliques sur la résurrection du Christ. — *RevDiocTournai* 21 (1966) 97-123. Esp. 107-110; 118-119; 119-120; 121.
Gospel Traditions about Christ's Resurrection. Theological Perspectives and Problems of Historicity. — *LumVit* 21 (1966) 66-90, 205-224. [NTA 11, 157/158]

**POORTHUIS, Marcel** → de Kruijf 1985

**POPE, Marvin H.**

1988  Hosanna. What It Really Means. [21,9] — *BibReview* 4/2 (1988) 16-25. [NTA 32, 1117]

**POPKES, Wiard**

1967  *Christus traditus. Eine Untersuchung zum Begriff der Dahingabe im Neuen Testament* (ATANT, 49). Zürich–Stuttgart: Zwingli, 1967, 317 p. Esp. 143-145 [4,12/Mk 1,14]; 145-147 [10,17-22; 24,9-14/Mk 13,9-13]; 154-155 [17,22/Mk 9,31]; 156-157 [26,2/Mk 14,1]; 169-172 [20,28/Mk 10,45]; 174-175 [26,14-16; 27,3-10]. — Diss. Zürich, 1967 (E. Schweizer).

1983  Die Funktion der Sendschreiben in der Johannes-Apokalypse. Zugleich ein Beitrag zur Spätgeschichte der neutestamentlichen Gleichnisse. — *ZNW* 74 (1983) 90-107. Esp. 96-102: "Zur Spätgeschichte der Gleichnisse". [NTA 28, 266]

1986  *Adressaten, Situation und Form des Jakobusbriefes* (SBS, 125-126). Stuttgart: Katholisches Bibelwerk, 1986, 219 p. Esp. 156-176: "Die Bergpredigt-Tradition".

1989  Die Gerechtigkeitstradition im Matthäus-Evangelium. — *ZNW* 80 (1989) 1-23. Esp. 1-3; 4-8 [3,15; 5,6.10.20; 6,1.33; 21,32]; 8-17 [Mt/Paul]; 17-19 [5–7]; 20-23 [theology]. [NTA 34, 111]

1990  Die letzte Bitte des Vater-Unser. Formgeschichtliche Beobachtungen zum Gebet Jesu. — *ZNW* 81 (1990) 1-20. Esp. 1-3: "Der auffällige Schluß des Gebets"; 3-5: "Zur Anfechtungs-Thematik"; 6-7: "Zur Frühgeschichte des Vater-Unser"; 8-17: "Die Abba-Texte" [26,39]; 17-20: "Der Inhalt der letzten Bitte". [NTA 35, 136]

**POPPI, Angelico**

1970  *Vangeli a confronto. Sinossi didattico-pastorale dei quattro Vangeli.* Padova: Messaggero, 1970, 254 p.; ²1972, 319 p.

1976  *L'inizio del Vangelo. Predicazione del Battista, battesimo e tentazione di Gesù* ("Conoscere il Vangelo", 4). Padova: Messaggero, 1976, 205 p. Esp. 58-60.63-87 [3,7-12; John the baptist]; 94-97.109-110 [3,13-17]; 138-159 [4,1-11]. → Giavini 1977

1983  *Sinossi dei quattro Vangeli.* Vol. I: *Testo*, Padova: Messaggero, 1983, 325 p.; Vol. II: *Introduzione e commento*, 1988, 510 p. → 1990, 1992

1990 *Sinossi dei quattro Vangeli*. Vol. I: *Testo*; Vol. II: *Introduzione generale e ai singoli vangeli*. *Commento*. Padova: Messaggero, 2nd revised ed., 1990, 333 and 558 p. Esp. II, 43-171: "Vangelo secondo Matteo". → 1983, 1992
F. NEIRYNCK, *ETL* 67 (1991) 165.

1992 *Sinossi dei quattro Vangeli greco-italiano. Testo greco dal codice Vaticano (B, 03). (Duplice e Triplice Traduzione in evidenza)*. Volume I: *Testo*. Padova: Messaggero, 1992, 638 p. → 1983, 1990; → R. Penna 1993
J.K. ELLIOTT, *NT* 36 (1994) 200-202; M. LÀCONI, *RivBib* 41 (1993) 99; F. NEIRYNCK, *ETL* 68 (1992) 437-439; F. URICCHIO, *MiscFranc* 94 (1994) 167-173.

### PORSCH, Felix

1982 *Viele Stimmen – ein Glaube. Anfänge, Entfaltung und Grundzüge neutestamentlicher Theologie* (Biblische Basis Bücher, 7). Kevelaer: Butzon & Bercker; Stuttgart: Katholisches Bibelwerk, 1982, 284 p. Esp. 44-51: "Die Redequelle – Motive ihrer Entstehung und ihr christologisches Bekenntnis"; 55-87: "Die Botschaft und die Praxis Jesu"; 103-113: "Die Theologie des Matthäusevangeliums".

### PORTER, C.

1987 "Wise as Serpents: Innocent as Doves". How Shall We Live? [10,16] — *Encounter* 48 (1987) 15-26. [NTA 31, 586]

### PORTER, Stanley E.

1983 The Adjectival Attributive Genitive in the New Testament: A Grammatical Study. — *TrinJ* NS 4 (1983) 3-17. Esp. 6-7 [12,31]; 11 [1,18]; 12-13 [21,25]; 13-14 [26,28]. [NTA 28, 443]

1988 Vague Verbs, Periphrastics, and Matt 16:19. — *FilolNT* 1 (1988) 155-173. Esp. 155-162; 162-169; 169-171; 171-172. [NTA 33, 1136]; = ID., *Studies in the Greek New Testament*, 1996, 103-123. Esp. 104-112: "The context and grammar of Matthew 16:19"; 112-120: "The exegesis and theology of Matthew 16:19"; 120-121 [18,18]; 121-123: "The authenticity of Matthew 16:19".

1989 *Verbal Aspect in the Greek of the New Testament, with Reference to Tense and Mood* (Studies in Biblical Greek, 1). New York – Bern: Lang, 1989, XII-582 p. Esp. 471-474 [16,19; 18,18]. → K.L. McKay 1992

1990 Mt 6:13 and Lk 11:4: 'Lead us not into temptation'. — *ExpT* 101 (1989-90) 359-362. [NTA 35, 137] → P.S. Cameron 1990, W.E. Moore 1991

1991 & BUCHANAN, P., On the Logical Structure of Matt 19:9. — *JEvTS* 34 (1991) 335-339. [NTA 36, 727]

1992 Joseph, Husband of Mary. — *ABD* 3 (1992) 974-975.

1993 Did Jesus Ever Teach in Greek? — *TyndB* 44 (1993) 199-235. Esp. 225-226 [27,11-14]; 228 [8,5-13]; 229-235 [16,13-20]. [NTA 38, 719]
Did Jesus Ever Teach in Greek? A Look at Scholarly Opinion and the Evidence. — ID., *Studies in the Greek New Testament*, 1996, 139-171 (revised). Esp. 162-163; 165-166; 166-171.

1994* & JOYCE, P. - ORTON, D.E. (eds.), *Crossing the Boundaries. Essays in Biblical Interpretation in Honour of Michael D. Goulder* (Biblical Interpretation Series, 8). Leiden: Brill, 1994, XVIII-381 p. → Houlden, Neirynck, Orton

1994 Jesus and the Use of Greek in Galilee. — CHILTON, B. - EVANS, C.A. (eds.), *Studying the Historical Jesus*, 1994, 123-154. Esp. 151-152 [8,5-13/Jn].

1996 *Studies in the Greek New Testament. Theory and Practice* (Studies in Biblical Greek, 6). New York: Lang, 1996, VII-290 p. → 1988, 1993

### PORÚBČAN, Štefan

1964 Form Criticism and the Synoptic Problem. — *NT* 7 (1964-65) 81-118. [NTA 9, 860]

1967 The Consciousness of Peter's Primacy in the New Testament. — *Archivum Historiae Pontificiae* (Roma) 5 (1967) 9-39. Esp. 11-13.27-36 [16,17-19].

**PORUTHUR, Anto**

1994    Ahimsâ and the Love Commandment. — *Vidyajyoti* 58 (1994) 617-622. [NTA 40, 165]

**POST, Gaines**

1955    & GIOCARINIS, K. – KAY, R., The Medieval Heritage of a Humanistic Ideal: "Scientia donum Dei est, unde vendi non potest". — *Traditio* (New York) 11 (1955) 195-234. Esp. 224-231: "The patristic and medieval tradition of commentary on Matthew 10.8-10" (R. Kay).

**POTESTÀ, Gian Luca**

1994    Dall'annuncio dell'Anticristo all'attesa del Pastore Angelico. Gli scritti di Arnaldo di Villanova nel codice dell'Archivio Generale dei Carmelitani. [24] — *Arxiv des textos catalans antics* (Barcelona) 13 (1994) 287-344.

**POTIN, Jean**

1965    Guérison d'une hémoroïsse et résurrection de la fille de Jaïre. [9,18-26] — *AssSeign* I/78 (1965) 25-36.

**POTTER, R.**

1961    St. John the Baptist and the Desert. — *Life of the Spirit* (London) 16 (1961) 80-87. [NTA 6, 428]

**POTTHOFF, Harvey H.**

1984    Homiletical Resources. The Sermon as Theological Event: Interpretations of Parables. [13,1-23.24-43.44-51; 18,21-35] — *QuartRev* 4/2 (1984) 76-102.

**POUILLY, Jean**

1989    *Dieu notre Père. La révélation de Dieu Père et le "Notre Père"* (Cahiers Évangile, 68). Paris: Cerf, 1989, 68 p. Esp. 32-53: "Le Notre Père".

**POUSSET, Édouard**

1974    → Simoens 1974

1975a   Le trésor et la perle (Matthieu 13,44-46). — *VieChrét* 173 (1975) 12-16.

1975b   Le sénevé et le levain (Mt. 13,31-33). — *VieChrét* 174 (1975) 13-16.

**POWELL, Evan**

1994    *The Unfinished Gospel. Notes on the Quest for the Historical Jesus.* Westlake Village, CA: Symposium Books, 1994, 347 p. Esp. 236-256: "Gospel patterns"; 257-294: "The lost Gospel" [Q]. → 1995

1995    *The Myth of the Lost Gospel: A Layman's Letter to the Jesus Seminar* [Q]. Westlake Village, CA: Symposium Books, 1995, 39 p. [NTA 40, p. 147] → 1994

**POWELL, J. Enoch**

1982    Those "Lilies of the Field" Again. [6,28] — *JTS* 33 (1982) 490-492. [NTA 27, 516]

1991    The Genesis of the Gospel. — *JSNT* 42 (1991) 5-16. Esp. 8-9; 12-14 [6,1-18]. [NTA 36, 132]

1994    *The Evolution of the Gospel. A New Translation of the First Gospel with Commentary and Introductory Essay.* New Haven – London: Yale University Press, 1994, XXIX-224 p. Esp. XI-XXVIII: "Introduction"; 1-50: "Translation"; 51-221: "Commentary". [NTA 39, p. 327]
        J. ASHTON, *Tablet* 248 (1994) 1164; R.A. BURRIDGE, *Theology* 98 (1995) 227-228; I.H. JONES, *ExpT* 106 (1994-95) 212; M.H. SMITH, *CRBR* 8 (1995) 280-282.

**POWELL, Mark Allan**

1988    *The Religious Leaders in Matthew: A Literary-Critical Approach.* Diss. Union Theological Seminary, Richmond, VA, 1988, 276 p. (J.D. Kingsbury). — *DissAbstr* 51 (1990-91) 534.

1990a The Plot to Kill Jesus from Three Different Perspectives: Point of View in Matthew. — *SBL 1990 Seminar Papers*, 603-613. Esp. 604-606 [religious leaders: 12,14; 26,3; 27,1]; 606-607 [Pilate]; 607-609 [Jesus]; 612-613: "Implications for reading the passion narrative".

1990b The Religious Leaders in Luke: A Literary-Critical Study. — *JBL* 109 (1990) 93-110. Esp. 108-109: "A brief comparison with Matthew". [NTA 34, 1171]

1991 Direct and Indirect Phraseology in the Gospel of Matthew. — *SBL 1991 Seminar Papers*, 405-417. Esp. 408-410 [Jesus]; 410-412 [disciples]; 412-416 [religious leaders]. Characterization on the Phraseological Plane in the Gospel of Matthew. — BAUER, D.R. – POWELL, M.A. (eds.), *Treasures New and Old*, 1996, 161-177. Esp. 166-169; 169-171; 171-177.

1992a *The Bible and Modern Literary Criticism. A Critical Assessment and Annotated Bibliography* (Bibliographies and Indexes in Religious Studies, 22). New York – Westport, CT – London: Greenwood, 1992, XVII-470 p. Esp. 264-272: "The parables"; 272-285: "The gospel of Matthew".
    F. NEIRYNCK, *ETL* 68 (1992) 432-433.

1992b What is "Literary" about Literary Aspects? — *SBL 1992 Seminar Papers*, 40-48.

1992c Toward a Narrative-Critical Understanding of Matthew. — *Interpr* 46 (1992) 341-346. [NTA 37, 706]

1992d The Plot and Subplots of Matthew's Gospel. — *NTS* 38 (1992) 187-204. Esp. 187-189 [R.A. Edwards 1985a]; 189-192 [Matera 1987b]; 192-193 [Kingsbury 1986a]; 193-198: "Additional observations"; 198-203: "Proposal for a new description". [NTA 36, 1253]

1993 Expected and Unexpected Readings of Matthew: What the Reader Knows. — *Asbury Theological Journal* (Wilmore, KY) 48 (1993) 31-51. [NTA 38, 744]

1994 The Mission of Jesus and the Mission of the Church in the Gospel of Matthew. — *Trinity Seminary Review* (Columbus, OH) 16/2 (1994) 77-89. [NTA 40, 1455]

1995a *God With Us: A Pastoral Theology of Matthew's Gospel*. Minneapolis, MN: Fortress, 1995, XI-156 p. [NTA 40, p. 147]
    J.P. MEIER, *Interpr* 51 (1997) 91.

1995b Do and Keep What Moses Says (Matthew 23:2-7). — *JBL* 114 (1995) 419-435. Esp. 421-424: "Description of the problem(s)"; 424-431: "Survey of critical response"; 431-435: "A new idea". [NTA 40, 834]

1995c A Typology of Worship in the Gospel of Matthew. — *JSNT* 57 (1995) 3-17. [NTA 40, 155]

**POWELL, W.**

1956 'Lead us not into temptation'. — *ExpT* 67 (1955-56) 177-178.

1961 The Temptation. — *ExpT* 72 (1960-61) 248. [NTA 6, 119] → Doble 1960

**POWERS, B.W.**

1972 Marriage and Divorce. The Dispute of Jesus with the Pharisees, and its Inception. — *Colloquium* 5 (1972) 34-41. [NTA 17, 917] → McCaughey 1972a-b

1980 The Shaking of the Synoptics. A Report on the Cambridge Conference on the Synoptic Gospels, August 1979. — *RTR* 39/2 (1980) 33-39. [NTA 25, 60] → W.R. Farmer 1983*

1985 *The Writing of the Synoptic Gospels: A Study in the History and the Solution of the Synoptic Problem*. Petersham: Privately published, 1985.

**POZO, Candido**

1982 *La figura de Pedro* (Cuadernos BAC, 32). Madrid: Católica, 1982, 32 p.

**PRADO, Juan**

1964a Genealogías de Jesucristo. [1,1-17] — *Enciclopédia de la Bíblia* (Barcelona) 3 (1964; ²1969) 754-755.

1964b Trasfondo histórico de la reciente Instrucción de la P.C.B. sobre la verdad histórica de los Evangelios. — *EstBíb* 23 (1964) 235-258. Esp. 243-258 [1-2]. [NTA 10, 864]

1967 *Santos Evangelios. Traducidos y anotados.* Barcelona: Vallés; Madrid: "El perpetuo socorro", 1967, 764 p. Esp. 595-764: "Anotaciones exegéticos".

**PRAEDER, Susan M.**

1988 *The Word in Women's Worlds. Four Parables* [13,33; 25,1-13] (Zacchaeus Studies: New Testament). Wilmington, DE: Glazier, 1988, 120 p. [NTA 33, p. 253]

**PRAGER, Miriam**

1960 Die Parabeln Jesu. — *BLtg* 34 (1960-61) 6-15; 111-116 [21,42; 22,1-14]; 186-196 [13,3-9; 20,1-16]; 211-219.

**PRATSCHER, Wilhelm**

1989 Das neutestamentliche Bild Marias als Grundlage der Mariologie. — *KerDog* 35 (1989) 189-211. Esp. 194-196. [NTA 34, 373]

**PREGEANT, Russell**

1975 The Matthean Undercurrent: Process Hermeneutic and the "Parable of the Last Judgment". — *SBL 1975 Seminar Papers*, II, 143-159. Esp. 144-146 [25,31-46]; 145 [5,17-20; 10,40-42]; 146-147 [13,36-43]; 149-150 [11,25-30]; 151 [28,16-20].

1976 Matthew's "Undercurrent" and Ogden's Christology. — *Process Studies* (Claremont, CA) 6 (1976) 171-194. [NTA 21, 373]

1978 *Christology beyond Dogma. Matthew's Christ in Process Hermeneutic* (SBL Semeia Supplements, 7). Philadelphia, PA: Fortress; Missoula, MT: Scholars, 1978, 176 p. Esp. 47-60: "Christology and soteriology in Matthew's gospel"; 61-103: "The components of Matthew's christology: Torah, salvation, grace" [5,17-20; 11,25-30]; 105-128: "The undercurrent: an incipient universalism" [13,36-43; 25,31-46]; 129-141: "A fragmentary chris:ology". [NTA 22, p. 331]. — Diss. Vanderbilt Univ., Nashville, TN, 1970.
D.A. CARSON, *JEvTS* 24 (1981) 266-267; L.S. FORD, *JRel* 59 (1979) 364-366; J. GALOT, *Greg* 60 (1979) 183; A. GOUNELLE, *ETR* 57 (1982) 667-668; D.J. HARRINGTON – A.T. MOORE, *CBQ* 41 (1979) 165-167; U. LUZ, *TLZ* 107 (1982) 273-274; I.H. MARSHALL, *ExpT* 90 (1978-79) 119-120; V. MORA, *SBF/LA* 39 (1989) 363; D.A. NORLIN, *JAAR* 48 (1980) 115-116; D. SENIOR, *TS* 40 (1979) 177-178; H.C. WAETJEN, *JBL* 98 (1979) 601-602.

1990 The Wisdom Passages in Matthew's Story. — *SBL 1990 Seminar Papers*, 469-493. Esp. 470-476: "The case for a redactional emphasis: pro and con"; 476-489: "A reader-response analysis"; = BAUER, D.R. – POWELL, M.A. (eds.), *Treasures New and Old*, 1996, 197-232. Esp. 198-206; 206-225.

1995 *Engaging the New Testament. An Interdisciplinary Introduction.* Minneapolis, MN: Fortress, 1995, XXV-581 p. Esp. 200-235: "Matthew".

**PRETE, Benedetto**

1957 *Vangelo secondo Matteo* (Biblioteca Universale Rizzoli, 1119-1122). Milano: Rizzoli, 1957, 320 p.
M.-É. BOISMARD, *RB* 66 (1959) 138; F. MONTAGNINI, *BibOr* 1 (1959) 186.

1961 Tu sei Pietro. — ROSSI, G. (ed.), *Cento problemi biblici* 1961, 418-434.

1970a Il senso del "logion" di Gesù in Mt 21,31. — *BibOr* 12 (1970) 49-58.

1970b Il senso dell'espressione οἱ καθαροὶ τῇ καρδίᾳ (*Mt.* 5,8). — *RivBib* 18 (1970) 253-268. [NTA 15, 491]

1983 Motivazioni e contenuti della preghiera di Gesù nel Vangelo di Luca. — DE GENNARO, G. (ed.), *La preghiera nella Bibbia. Storia, struttura e pratica dell'esperienza religioso* (Pubblicazioni dello studio biblico-teologico Aquilano), Napoli: Dehoniane, 1983, 293-327; = ID., *L'opera di Luca*, 1986, 80-103. Esp. 95-99 [11,25-27].

1984    Il logion sulla lampada nella duplice attestazione di Luca 8,16 e 11,33. — PROVERA,
        L. (ed.), *Gesù Apostolo e Sommo Sacerdote*. FS T. Ballarini, 1984, 83-97; = ID.,
        *L'opera di Luca*, 1986, 185-203. Esp. 187-188; 190-191 [5,15].

1986a   *L'opera di Luca. Contenuti e prospettive*. Torino-Leumann: Elle Di Ci, 1986, 591 p.
        → 1983, 1984, 1986b

1986b   Stuttura del Vangelo di Luca. [1981, unpublished] — *Ibid.*, 34-79. Esp. 55-58: "La posizione
        dei critici sulla *Quelle* (= Q)". → J. Wenham 1981b

1993    Il messaggio cristologico nell'annuncio a Giuseppe (*Mt* 1,18-25). — *DivThom* 96/3
        (1993) 190-213.

**PREUSS, Horst Dietrich** → K. Berger 1980

**PRICE, James L.**

1958    The Servant Motif in the Synoptic Gospels. A New Appraisal. — *Interpr* 12 (1958) 28-
        38. Esp. 32-33, 34-35. [NTA 3, 65]

1961    *Interpreting the New Testament*. New York: Holt, Rinehart & Winston, 1961, XV-572
        p.; [2]1971.
        *The New Testament. Its History and Theology*. New York – London: Macmillan, rev.
        ed., [3]1987, XV-489 p. Esp. 104-106 [Q]; 106-111 [Griesbach-Farmer]; 145-162: "The gospel of
        Matthew".

**PRICE, Robert M.**

1989    Jesus' Burial in a Garden: The Strange Growth of the Tradition. — *Religious Traditions*
        (Montreal-Sydney) 12 (1989) 17-30. [NTA 34, 589]

**PRICE, Stephen Gregory**

1984    *The Accusation of Hypocrisy in Matthew's Gospel* [6,2.5.16; 7,5; 15,7; 22,18; 23,13-15; 24,51].
        Diss. Marquette Univ., Milwaukee, WI, 1984, 318 p. (R.A. Edwards). — *DissAbstr* 47
        (1986-87) 218; *SBT* 15 (1987) 115.

**PRICE, William Craig**

1989    *The Textual Relationships of Quotations from the Four Gospels in Irenaeus' Against
        Heresies*. Diss. Southwestern Baptist Theol. Sem., Fort Worth, TX, 1989, 209 p. —
        *DissAbstr* 50 (1989-90) 2934.

**PRICKETT, Stephen**

1977    What Do the Translators Think They Are Up To? — *Theology* 80 (1977) 403-410. Esp.
        408-410 [1,18]. [NTA 22, 353]

**PRIEST, John**

1992    A Note on the Messianic Banquet. — CHARLESWORTH, J.H., et al. (eds.), *The Messiah*,
        1992, 222-238. Esp. 229-234 [19,28; 22,1-10].

**PRIEUR, Alexander**

1996    *Die Verkündigung der Gottesherrschaft. Exegetische Studien zum lukanischen
        Verständnis von βασιλεία τοῦ θεοῦ* (WUNT, II/89). Tübingen: Mohr, 1996, VIII-336
        p. Esp. 193-197 [13,11.13]; 221-225 [Q 10,1-12]; 233-234 [Q 16,16]; 262-265 [Q 19,12-27]. — Diss.
        Tübingen, 1992-93 (G. Jeremias).

**PRIGENT, Pierre**

1961    *Les Testimonia dans le christianisme primitif. L'épître de Barnabé I-XVI et ses sources*
        (Études bibliques). Paris: Gabalda, 1961, 240 p. Esp. 147-157 [24/Barn 4]; 202-204 [27,35.46/Ps
        22].

1964 *Justin et l'Ancien Testament. L'argumentation scripturaire du traité de Justin contre toutes les hérésies comme source principale du dialogue avec Tryphon et de la première Apologie* (Études bibliques). Paris: Gabalda, 1964, 357 p. Esp. 165-168 [11,5/1 Ap 48,1-2].

1972 Les citations des Pères grecs et la critique textuelle du Nouveau Testament. — ALAND, K. (ed.), *Die alten Übersetzungen des Neuen Testaments, die Kirchenväterzitate und Lektionare. Der gegenwärtige Stand ihrer Erforschung und ihre Bedeutung für die griechische Textgeschichte* (Arbeiten zur neutestamentlichen Textforschung, 5), Berlin: de Gruyter, 1972, 436-454. Esp. 441-453 [6,21; 10,38; 13.35; 14,25-27; 16,4.24; 19,17].

**PRIGNAUD, Jean**

1992 Les cœurs purs, dans la Bible. [5,8] — *VSp* 146 (1992) 429-434. [NTA 37, 725]

**PRINSLOO, Willem S.**

1986 'Aanhalings' van die Ou Testament deur die Nuwe Testament: Hosea 11:1 / Matteus 2:15. — *HervTS* 42 (1986) 378-385. → du Toit 1986

**PRIOR, Michael P.**

1986 A "Copernican" Revolution, or Griesbach Re-buried. — *ScriptB* 17 (1986) 14-19. [NTA 31, 1000r] → Orchard 1983a

1988 Jesus' Teaching on the Mount. — *ScriptB* 18 (1988) 26-33. [NTA 33, 599]

**PRITCHARD, John Paul**

1972 *A Literary Approach to the New Testament.* Norman, OK: University of Oklahoma Press, 1972, XI-355 p. Esp. 66-98: "The gospel according to Matthew".

**PRITZ, Ray A.**

1988 *Nazarene Jewish Christianity. From the End of the New Testament Period Until Its Disappearance in the Fourth Century* (Studia Post-Biblica, 37). Jerusalem: Magnes; Leiden: Brill, 1988, 153 p. Esp. 11-14 [2,23]; 83-94: "The gospel according to the Hebrews".

1991 "He shall be called a Nazarene". [2,23] — *Jerusalem Perspective* (Jerusalem) 4 (1991) 3-4. [NTA 36, 1258]

**PROCKTER, L.J.**

1994 The Blind Spot: New Testament Scholarship's Ignorance of Rabbinic Judaism. [6,1-18] — *Scriptura* 48 (1994) 1-12. [NTA 39, 800]

**PROCOPÉ, J.P.**

1993 Mundate quae intus sunt. [23,26] — *Studia Patristica* 27 (1993) 383-387.

**PROCTER, David L.**

1985 *A Redaction-Critical Study of Synoptic Tendencies with Special Reference to Bultmann's Law of Increasing Distinctness.* Diss. Baylor Univ., Waco, TX, 1985, 437 p. — *DissAbstr* 46 (1985-86) 2336; *SBT* 14 (1986) 190-191.

**PROD'HOMME, Fernand**

1971 Les pauvres rassasiés au festin du Royaume. Mt 14,13-21. — *AssSeign* II/49 (1971) 17-26.

**PRONZATO, Alessandro**

1989 *Il Padre Nostro preghiera dei figli* (Le preghiere del cristiano). Torino: Gribaudi, 1989, 298 p.
*El Padrenuestro oración de los hijos*, trans. G. González & A. Ortiz (Pedal, 225). Salamanca: Sígueme, 1993, 340 p.
J.L. ESPINEL, *CiTom* 122 (1995) 421-422.

**PROULX, Pierre**

1978 & ALONSO SCHÖKEL, L., Las sandalias del Mesías Esposo. [3,11] — *Bib* 59 (1978) 1-37. Esp. 1-5, 12-16. [NTA 23, 152]

**PROVERA, Laura**

1984* (ed.), *Gesù Apostolo e Sommo Sacerdote. Studi biblici in memoria di P. Teodorico Ballarini*. Casale Monferrato: Marietti, 1984, XX-234 p. → Légasse, Prete, Virgulin

**PROVERA, Mario**

1975 *Le parabole evangeliche ed il loro messaggio* (Quaderni de "la Terra Santa"). Jerusalem: Franciscan Printing Press, 1975, 172 p.

**PRUNETTI, P.**

1983 (ed.), *Trenta testi greci da papiri letterari e documentari* (XVII Congresso internazionale di Papirologia, Napoli, 19-26 Maggio, 1983). Firenze: Vitelli, 1983, 132 p. Esp. 7-9 [0277].

**PRYKE, John**

1964 John the Baptist and the Qumran Community. — *RQum* 4 (1964) 483-496. [NTA 9, 521]

**PRYOR, John W.**

1991a The Great Thanksgiving and the Fourth Gospel. [11,25-27] — *BZ* 35 (1991) 157-179. [NTA 35, 786]

1991b John 3.3,5. A Study in the Relation of John's Gospel to the Synoptic Tradition. — *JSNT* 41 (1991) 71-95. Esp. 71-77: "Independent sayings of Jesus?"; 77-87: "Matthew 18.3 and the synoptic interrelationships"; 87-94: "John 3.3,5 and the synoptic tradition". [NTA 36, 233] → Lindars 1981b

1992 Justin Martyr and the Fourth Gospel. — *SecCent* 9 (1992) 153-169. Esp. 163-166 [18,3/1 Apol 61,4-5]. [NTA 37, 791]

**PRZYBYLA, E. Alfons**

1976 List rozwodowy w prawie Mojżesza (Lettre de divorce dans la loi mosaïque). [19,7] — *Życiei Myśl* (Warszawa) 26 (1976) 54-63. [NTA 21, 378]

**PRZYBYLSKI, Benno**

1974 The Role of Mt 3:13–4:11 in the Structure and Theology of the Gospel of Matthew. — *BTB* 4 (1974) 222-235. [NTA 19, 528]

1980 *Righteousness in Matthew and His World of Thought* (SNTS MS, 41). Cambridge: University Press, 1980, XIII-184 p. Esp. 1-12.124-126: "The problem of the meaning and significance of the Matthean concept of righteousness"; 77-104.147-157: "The meaning of *dikaiosunē*, *eleēmosynē* and *dikaios* in the gospel of Matthew" [3,15; 5,6.10.20; 6,1.33; 21,32]; 105-115.157-159: "The relative significance of the concept of righteousness"; 116-123.159: "The provisional function of the Matthean concept of righteousness". [NTA 25, p. 305] — Diss. McMaster Univ., Toronto, Ont., 1975 (E. Sanders).
C. BISSOLI, *Sal* 46 (1984) 562; F.W. BURNETT, *JBL* 102 (1983) 149-151; J. CARMIGNAC, *RQum* 10 (1981) 453-454; J.C. FENTON, *JTS* 33 (1982) 247-248; D.E. GARLAND, *RExp* 79 (1982) 149-151; H. GIESEN, *TRev* 79 (1983) 280-283; J.D. KINGSBURY, *CBQ* 45 (1983) 320-322; G. LOHFINK, *TQ* 164 (1984) 221-222; U. LUZ, *TLZ* 109 (1984) 264-265; M. PAMMENT, *NBlackfr* 62 (1981) 242-244; R.A. PIPER, *ScotJT* 36 (1983) 408-411; G. SEGALLA, *Studia Patavina* 30 (1983) 174-176; G. STANTON, *HeythJ* 23 (1982) 182-183; A. VARGAS-MACHUCA, *EstE* 61 (1986) 120-121; H.C. WAETJEN, *Interpr* 36 (1982) 315.320-321; J.A. ZIESLER, *ExpT* 92 (1980-81) 279.

1986 The Setting of Matthean Anti-Judaism. — RICHARDSON, P. — GRANSKOU, D. (eds.), *Anti-Judaism in Early Christianity*. I: *Paul and the Gospels* (Studies in Christianity and Judaism, 2), Waterloo, Ont.: Laurier, 1986, 181-200.

**PUDUSSERY, Paul**

1991 Jesus' Teaching on Family Life. — *Bible Bhashyam* 17 (1991) 217-241. Esp. 230-234 [19,9]. [NTA 37, 107]

**PUECH, Émile**

1988  Un hymne essénien en partie retrouvé et les Béatitudes; *1QH* V 12–VI 18 (= col. XIII–XIV 7) et *4QBéat*. — *RQum* 13 (1988) 59-88. Esp. 80.83-84.

1991  4Q525 et les péricopes des Béatitudes en Ben Sira et Matthieu. — *RB* 98 (1991) 80-106. Esp. 95-101.104-106. [NTA 35, 1402] → Viviano 1992, 1993

1992  Une apocalypse messianique *(4Q521)*. — *RQum* 15 (1991-92) 475-519. Esp. 487-495. [NTA 37, 1559] → 1993, 627-669 (revised); → Fitzmyer 1995, Neirynck 1997d, Tabor 1992a

1993  *La croyance des Esséniens en la vie future: immortalité, résurrection, vie éternelle? Historie d'une croyance dans le judaïsme ancien. I. La résurrection des morts et le contexte scripturaire. II. Les données qumraniennes et classiques* (Études bibliques, NS 21-22). Paris: Gabalda, 1993, 2 vols., XXVIII-324 and 325-956 p. Esp. I, 243-263: "Évangiles" [5,29-30; 10,28; 11,3-6; 12,41-42; 17,1-9; 19,28-29; 20,20-23; 22,23-33; 25,31-46]; II, 627-692: "Une apocalypse messianique (4Q521)" [627-669 → 1992; 669-692: "Commentaire général"]. → Fitzmyer 1995, Tabor 1992a

1994  Messianism, Resurrection, and Eschatology at Qumran and in the New Testament. — ULRICH, E. — VANDERKAM, J. (eds.), *The Community of the Renewed Covenant. The Notre Dame Symposium on the Dead Sea Scrolls* (Christianism and Judaism in Antiquity Series, 10), Notre Dame, IN: University Press, 1994, 235-256. Esp. 243-246 [4Q521]. → Fitzmyer 1995, Tabor 1992a

1995  Des fragments grecs de la grotte 7 et le Nouveau Testament? 7Q4 et 7Q5, et le Papyrus Magdalen Grec 17 = P$^{64}$. — *RB* 102 (1995) 570-584. Esp. 577-584. [NTA 40, 1366] → Thiede 1995c

**PUECH, Henri-Charles**

1959  Das Thomas-Evangelium. — HENNECKE, E. - SCHNEEMELCHER, W. (eds.), *Neutestamentliche Apokryphen*, I, $^3$1959, 199-223 (ET, 278-307). → Blatz 1987

**PUIGDOLLERS, Rodolfo**

1979  La historicidad de los relatos de la infancia. — *Analecta Calasanctiana* (Salamanca) 21 (1979) 13-43. → Scheifler 1977

**PUIG I TÀRRECH, Armand**

1980  La parabola de les dames d'honor de l'Espos (Mateu 25,1-13). — *QüestVidaCr* 104 (1980) 43-63.

1981  Temps i història en Mt 24–25. — *RevistCatTeol* 6 (1981) 299-335 (English summary, 335). Esp. 299-303 [23–25]; 303-307 [24,4b-35]; 307-328 [24,4b-14]; 328-335 [Mt on history]. [NTA 27, 522]

1982  Els sants que ressusciten (Mt 27,51b-53). — *Butlletí de l'Associacio Biblica de Catalunya. Suplement* 2 (1982) 41-65.

1983a  *La parabole des dix vierges (Mt 25,1-13)* (AnBib, 102). Roma: Biblical Institute Press; (Collectània Sant Pacià, 28). Barcelona: Facultat de Teologia, 1983, 308 p. Esp. 19-30: "Le contexte de Mt 25,1-13"; 31-50: "Analyse narrative de Mt 25,1-13"; 51-91: "Les intérêts du rédacteur de Mt 25,1-13"; 92-117: "Les motivations du rédacteur"; 123-141: "Le débat sur l'authenticité"; 142-187: "Tradition et rédaction"; 188-214: "Vers l'état primitif de la parabole"; 215-262: "La parabole dans le ministère de Jésus". [NTA 29, p. 92] — Diss. Commissio Biblica, Roma, 1982 (J. Dupont). E. CORTÈS, *EstFranc* 86 (1985) 384-387; J. DUPONT, *RTL* 16 (1985) 212-215; R.A. EDWARDS, *CBQ* 47 (1985) 560-561; I. GOMÁ CIVIT, *RevistCatTeol* 10 (1985) 201-202; J. GUILLET, *RSR* 74 (1986) 243-244; F. SARACINO, *RivBib* 33 (1985) 365-367; A. SEGOVIA, *ArchTeolGran* 48 (1985) 349-350; B.T. VIVIANO, *RB* 94 (1987) 425-428.

1983b  Jesús i els infants. [18,1-4] — *QüestVidaCr* 118 (1983) 25-37.

1985a  *Quatre comunitats davant Jesús*. Barcelona: Claret, 1985. Esp. 45-71.

1985b  La oración en el Nuevo Testamento. — *Phase* (Barcelona) 25 (1985) 269-282.

1985c  La parabole des talents (Mt 25,14-30) ou des mines (Lc 19,11-28). — *RevistCatTeol* 10 (1985) 269-317. Esp. 270-278: "La parabole des talents (Mt 25,14-30)"; 283-294: "Vers l'état primitif de la parabole"; 294-314: "La parabole de l'argent confié dans le ministère de Jésus". [NTA 31, 124]; = GANTOY, R. (ed.), *À cause de l'Évangile*. FS J. Dupont, 1985, 165-193 (abridged version). Esp. 166-170; 172-174;175-193.

1989   El rerefons de la declaració "la sang d'ell sobre nosaltres i els nostres fills" (Mt 27,25). [The background of the declaration "His blood be upon us and our children"]. — *La paraula al servei dels homes. XXV Jornades de biblistes catalans (1963-1985)*, Barcelona: Claret, 1989, 102-116.

1993   Les citacions de compliment en l'Evangeli segons Mateu. — RAURELL, F., et al. (eds.), *Tradició i traducció*. FS G. Camps, 1993, 119-132.

**PULEO, Enrico**

1987   *La morale delle antitesi. Considerazioni su Mt 5,17-48*. Diss. Pamplona, 1987, 245 p. (J.M. Casciaro). Esp. 47-83: "Il clima teologico del vangelo di Matteo"; 86-168: "Obbligatorietà nel messaggio morale delle antitesi"; 171-223: "Universalità nel messaggio morale delle antitesi".

**PUNGE, Manfred**

1961   *Endgeschehen und Heilsgeschichte im Matthäus-Evangelium*. Diss. Greifswald, 1961, 220 p. — *TLZ* 89 (1964) 711. → Rohde 1965

1970   "... bis an der Welt Ende". Einführende Bemerkungen zum Matthäus-Evangelium. — *Die Zeichen der Zeit* (Berlin) 24 (1970) 325-331.

**PUNNAKOTTIL, G.**

1977   The Passion Narrative according to Matthew. A Redaction Critical Study. — *Bible Bhashyam* 3 (1977) 20-47. [NTA 21, 732]

**PURDY, J.C.**

1989   *Returning God's Call. The Challenge of Christian Living* [4,17-22; 5,38-48; 6,1-18; 9,35-10,8; 12,46-50; 16,24-28; 19,3-9.16-22; 20,20-28; 28,16-20]. Louisville, KY: Westminster/Knox, 1989, 156 p. [NTA 33, p. 389]

**PUSKAS, Charles B.**

1989   *An Introduction to the New Testament*. Peabody, MA: Hendrickson, 1989, XXII-297 p. Esp. 118-126: "The biographical genre. A comparison with Matthew"; 213-214: "Matthean christianity".

**PUZICHA, Michaela**

1980   *Christus peregrinus. Die Fremdenaufnahme (Mt 25,35) als Werk der privaten Wohltätigkeit im Urteil der Alten Kirche* (Münsterische Beiträge zur Theologie, 47). Münster: Aschendorff, 1980, XII-200 p. Esp. 6-65: "Die praxisorientierte Paränese zu den Werken der Barmherzigkeit (Mt 25,35f) am Beispiel der Fremdenaufnahme"; 66-178: "Die Motivationen altkirchlicher Barmherzigkeit im Zusammenhang der Auslegung von Mt 25,35-40". [NTA 25, p. 200] — Diss. Münster, 1976-77 (B. Kötting).
    H. BACHT, *TheolPhil* 57 (1982) 294-295; A. BÖCKMANN, *TRev* 78 (1982) 26-28; J.H. ELLIOTT, *RelStR* 9 (1983) 78; G. HAENDLER, *TLZ* 107 (1982) 367-369; E. SAUSER, *TTZ* 93 (1984) 76-77.

**PYTEL, Jan**

1964   *Adveniat regnum tuum*. Historia interpretacji prośby ("Que votre règne arrive". Histoire de l'interprétation de cette prière). [6,10] — *RoczTK* 11/1 (1964) 57-69. [NTA 10, 116]

# Q

## QUACQUARELLI, Antonio

1953    *Il triplice frutto della vita cristiana: 100, 60 e 30 (Matteo XIII,8 nelle diverse interpretazioni)*. Roma: Coletti, 1953, 128 p.; Bari: Edipuglia, ²1989. [NTA 35, p. 106]
> A. BINI, *NRT* 76 (1954) 539-540; T. PISCITELLI, *Orpheus* (Catania) 11 (1990) 418-419; P. VERBRAKEN, *RBén* 100 (1990) 589-590.

1969    Gli incisi ellittici (5,32a e 19,9a) nella *compositio* di Matteo. — *VetChr* 9 (1969) 5-31; = ID., *Saggi patristici*, 1971, 345-377.

1970    L'esegesi di Tertulliano a Matteo 19.6. — GRANFIELD, P. - JUNGMANN, J.A. (eds.), *Kyriakon*. FS J. Quasten, 1970, II, 511-520; = ID., *Saggi patristici*, 1971, 327-344.

1971    *Saggi patristici. Retorica ed esegesi biblica* (Quaderni di "Vetera Christianorum", 5). Bari: Adriatica, 1971, 556 p. → 1969, 1970

1990    La vergine Maria nella esegesi di Cromazio. [1,18-25] — FELICI, S. (ed.), *La mariologia nella catechesi dei Patri (Età Postnicena). Convegno di studio e di aggiornamento. Facoltà di Lettere cristiane e classiche Roma, 10-11 marzo 1989* (Biblioteca di scienze religiose, 95), Roma: LAS, 1990; = ID., *Esegesi Biblica e Patristica fra tardo antico ed altomedioevo* (Quaderni di "Vetera Christianorum", 23), Bari: Edipuglia, 1991, 53-61.

## QUARLES, Charles Leland

1994    *An Analysis of Midrash Criticism as Applied to the Synoptic Birth Narratives*. Diss. Mid-America Baptist Theol. Sem., 1994, 243 p. — *DissAbstr* 55 (1994-95) 1592-1593.

## QUECKE, Hans

1962    L'Évangile de Thomas. État des recherches. — MASSAUX, É. (ed.), *La venue du Messie*, 1962, 217-241. Esp. 233-235 [22,1-14/Th].

1993    Die Schlußformeln zum Unservater bei den Kopten. — CARR, E., et al. (eds.), Εὐλόγημα. *Studies in Honor of Robert Taft, sj* (Studia Anselmiana, 110; Analecta Liturgica, 17), Roma: Pont. Ateneo S. Anselmo, 1993, 373-387.

## QUELLE, Constantino

1983    ¡Padre, no nos dejes caer en la tentación! [6,13] — *BibFe* 9 (1983) 64-74.

## QUÉRÉ, France

1982    *Les femmes de l'Évangile*. Paris: Seuil, 1982, 190 p. Esp. 126-131 (Mary); 85-97 [26,6-13].

1992    *Jésus enfant* (Jésus et Jésus-Christ, 55). Paris: Desclée De Brouwer, 1992, 253 p.

## QUESNEL, Michel

1989    Les citations de Jérémie dans l'évangile selon saint Matthieu. — *EstBíb* 47 (1989) 513-527. Esp. 515-519 [2,17-18]; 519-526 [27,9-10]. [NTA 36 133]

1991    *Jésus-Christ selon saint Matthieu. Synthèse théologique* (Coll. "Jésus et Jésus-Christ", 47). Paris: Desclée, 1991, 239 p. Esp. 13-64: "Les noms et titres de Jésus"; 65-112: "Jésus à travers sa parole et ses gestes"; 113-163: "Jésus et l'Ancien Testament"; 165-199: "Une christologie en récit"; 201-219: "Les circonstances historiques de la christologie matthéenne"; 221-230: "Ouvertures et postérité". [NTA 35, p. 245]
> É. COTHENET, *EVie* 101 (1991) 253-255; H. COUSIN, *VSp* 146 (1992) 396; E. CUVILLIER, *ETR* 68 (1993) 579-580; R. DORAN, *CBQ* 54 (1992) 584-585; L. LARROQUE, *RB* 101 (1994) 139-140; J.-Y. THÉRIAULT, *SE* 45 (1993) 235-237.

*Jesucristo según San Mateo. Sintesis teológica* (Estudios bíblicos). Estella: Verbo Divino, 1993, 234 p.
P. BARRADO FERNANDEZ, *RevistEspTeol* 53 (1993) 244-246; J.L. ESPINEL, *CiTom* 121 (1994) 414-415; J.I. GONZÁLEZ FAUS, *EstE* 68 (1993) 374.

1993 Le Règne de Dieu chez Matthieu. — BLANCHARD, Y.-M., et al., *Évangile et Règne de Dieu* (Cahiers Évangile, 84), Paris: Cerf, 1993, 33-43.

**QUESNELL, Quentin**

1968 "Made themselves eunuchs for the Kingdom of heaven" (Mt 19,12). — *CBQ* 30 (1968) 335-358. Esp. 340-348 [19,10-12]; 341-344.349-351 [19,9]; 345-346 [22,23-33]; 352-353 [19,3-9]. [NTA 13, 175]
*TDig* 17 (1969) 222-226; *SelT* 9 (1970) 265-271.
*Hacerse eunucos por el reino de los cielos*. Madrid: Rama Dorada, 1986, 52 p.
A. SALAS, *BibFe* 12 (1986) 368-369.

1969 *The Mind of Mark. Interpretation and Method through the Exegesis of Mark 6,52* (AnBib, 38). Roma: Pontifical Biblical Institute, 1969, XXIV-327 p. Esp. 112-114 [16,5-12/Mk 8,14-21]; 185-186 [13/Mk 4]; 244-246.256 [12,38-39; 16,1-4/Mk 8,11-13]. — Diss. Pont. Inst. Bibl., Roma, 1967 (A. Vanhoye).

**QUIN, J. Cosslett**

1987 The Infancy Narratives with Special Reference to Matt. 1 and 2. — *IBS* 9 (1987) 63-69. [NTA 32, 112]

**QUINLAN, John**

1967 Matthew, Gospel acc. to St. — *NewCathEnc* 9 (1967) 493-502.

**QUINN, John Francis**

1970 The Pilate Sequence in the Gospel of Matthew. [27,1-31] — *DunRev* 10 (1970) 154-177. [NTA 15, 151]

**QUINN, Jerome D.**

1962 Saint John Chrysostom on History in the Synoptics. [1,2-17] — *CBQ* 24 (1962) 140-147. [NTA 7, 94]

1981 Is 'Ραχάβ in Mt 1,5 Rahab of Jericho? — *Bib* 62 (1981) 225-228. [NTA 26, 83] → R.E. Brown 1982

**QUINSAT, Pierre**

1954 La manière dont Jésus parlait. — *La Maison-Dieu* (Paris) 39 (1954) 59-82. Esp. 62-82 [authority of Jesus; style].

**QUINZÁ LLEÓ, Xavier**

1990 La reflexión bíblica sobre los signos de los tiempos. — *EstBíb* 48 (1990) 317-334. Esp. 327-331: "Pretexto y contexto de Mt 16,1-4"; 331-334: "La topología textual de la perícopa: una interpretación". [NTA 36, 153]

**QUISPEL, Gilles**

1957a Das Hebräerevangelium im gnostischen Evangelium nach Maria. [6,21] — *VigChr* 11 (1957) 139-144. [NTA 2, 415]

1957b The Gospel of Thomas and the New Testament. — *Ibid.*, 189-207. Esp. 202-204. [NTA 2, 644]; = ID., *Gnostic Studies*, 1975, 3-16. Esp. 13-14.

1958 L'Évangile selon Thomas et les Clémentines. — *VigChr* 12 (1958) 181-196; = ID., *Gnostic Studies*, 1975, 17-29.

1959a L'Évangile selon Thomas et le Diatessaron. [5,15; 13,25] — *VigChr* 13 (1959) 87-117. [NTA 4, 238]; = ID., *Gnostic Studies*, 1975, 31-55.

1959b Some Remarks on the Gospel of Thomas. — *NTS* 5 (1958-59) 276-290. Esp. 279 [6,24/Th 47]; 279-280 [10,35/Th 10]; 287 [10,37/Th 55]. [NTA 4, 532] → H.-W. Bartsch 1960c

1960    L'Évangile selon Thomas et le "Texte Occidental" du Nouveau Testament. — *VigChr*
        14 (1960) 204-215. → 1975c

1962    Der Heliand und das Thomasevangelium. — *VigChr* 16 (1962) 121-151. Esp. 139-151
        [3,16; 5,11.14.15.43; 12,35; 13,4.5-6.47-48]. [NTA 8, 347]; = Id., *Gnostic Studies*, 1975, 70-97.
        Esp. 87-96. → Krogman 1964

1964    The Syrian Thomas and the Syrian Macarius. — *VigChr* 18 (1964) 226-235. Esp. 228-229
        [10,37/Th 55]; 233-234 [7,14; 25,10; Th 75]. [NTA 10, 349]; = Id., *Gnostic Studies*, 1975, 113-
        121. Esp. 115-116; 118-119. → Klijn 1965b

1967    *Makarius, das Thomasevangelium und das Lied von der Perle* (SupplNT, 15). Leiden:
        Brill, 1967, 126 p. Esp. 93-96 [21,21/Th 48; 10,37/Th 55].

1969    The Latin Tatian or the Gospel of Thomas in Limburg. — *JBL* 88 (1969) 321-330. Esp.
        326 [2,9]; 328 [1,19; 27,3]. [NTA 14, 688]; = Id., *Gnostic Studies*, 1975, 159-168. Esp. 164;
        166.

1971    Some Remarks on the Diatessaron Haarense. — *VigChr* 25 (1971) 131-139. Esp. 134-138
        [2,9; 5,21; 6,13; 22,21; 27,34]. [NTA 16, 452]

1974    Jewish-Christian Gospel Tradition. — *ATR* SS 3 (1974) 112-116. Esp. 115-116 [13,44-
        46/Th]. [NTA 19, 378]

1975a   *Tatian and the Gospel of Thomas. Studies in the History of the Western Diatessaron.*
        Leiden: Brill, 1975, X-200 p. Esp. 78-82 [Diat. OHG/Th/5,43]; 92-95 [Diat. OHG/Th/4,1-11]; 82-87
        [Diat. OHG/Th/8,20]; 95-107 [Diat OHG/Th/13,47-48]; 110-125: "Diatessaron readings in the Old High
        German version and the Latin codex Sangallensis" [1,18.19; 2,13.18; 3,17; 4,5.6.8.11; 5,43; 8,20; 10,27;
        13,33.47; 15,2.3.6; 16,17; 17,24; 27,20.40.65; 28,7.9.11]; 142-158: "Diatessaron readings in the *Vita Jesu
        Christi* of Ludolph of Saxony" [1,19; 2,9.11.14-16; 3,2.13-14; 4 1.5.8; 5,43; 6,13.14.18; 7,1; 8,11.23;
        10,16; 12,35; 13,48; 15,23.27; 17,27; 19,16.24.27; 20,5; 25,32.34; 26,38.48.64; 27,3; 28,6]; 174-190:
        "Variants common to the Diatessaron and the gospel of Thomas".

1975b   *Gnostic Studies*, II. Istanbul: Nederlands Historisch-Archaeologisch Instituut, 1975, III-
        307 p. → 1957b, 1958, 1959a, 1962, 1964, 1969, 1975c

1975c   The Gospel of Thomas and the Western Text: A Reappraisal. — *Ibid.*, 56-69. → 1960

1976    An Apocryphal Variant in Macarius. [23,25] — *OrLovPer* 6-7 (1975-76) 487-492. [NTA
        20, 444]

1993    A Diatessaron Reading in a Latin Manichean Codex. [7,14] — *VigChr* 47 (1993) 374-
        378. [NTA 38, 1248] → Pickering 1994a

# R

**RAASCH, J.**

1968    The Monastic Concept of Purity of Heart (Mt 5,8) and Its Sources. III. Philo, Clement of Alexandria and Origen. — *Studia Monastica* (Barcelona) 10 (1968) 7-55.

**RAATSCHEN, Johannes Heinrich**

1980    Empfangen durch den Heiligen Geist. Überlegungen zu Mt 1,18-25. — *TBeitr* 11 (1980) 262-277. Esp. 263-264: "Redaktionelle Zusätze"; 264-271: "Der überlieferte Bericht"; 271-277: "Die christologische Frage". [NTA 25, 465]

**RABACCHI, Stefano**

1983    Il Vangelo di Matteo. — *Sacra Doctrina* (Bologna) 28 (1983) 528-548. Esp. 529-531 [author]; 531-534 [date; audience]; 534-537 [sources; style]; 537-538 [structure]; 538-548 [characteristics]. [NTA 28, 482]

**RÁBANOS, Ricardo**

1954    El problema del divorcio. — *CuBíb* 11 (1954) 83-89, 161-168.

**RABIN, Chaim**

1966    Noṣerim. — *Textus. Annual of the Hebrew University Bible Project* (Jerusalem) 5 (1966) 44-52. Esp. 52 [2,23].

**RABINOWITZ, Jacob J.**

1956    The Sermon on the Mount and the School of Shammai. — *HTR* 49 (1956) 79.

**RACETTE, Jean**

1957    L'Évangile de l'enfance selon saint Matthieu. — *ScEccl* 9 (1957) 77-82. [NTA 2, 47]

**RACINE, Jean-François**

1995    Trois approches de la situation des femmes dans le document Q: Hal Taussig, Luise Schottroff et Amy-Jill Levine. — *Des femmes aussi faisaient route avec lui. Perspectives féministes sur la Bible* (Sciences bibliques, 2), Montréal: Médiaspaul, 1995, 133-152.

**RACZECK, E. VON**

1957    "Selig, die hungern und dursten nach der Gerechtigkeit, denn sie werden gesättigt werden" (Mt 5,6). — *Benediktinische Monatschrift* (Beuron) 33 (1957) 46-49. [NTA 2, 49]

**RADAELLI, Anselmo**

1980    I racconti dell'infanzia nel contesto del prologo all'Evangelo. — *RicBibRel* 15 (1980) 7-26, 199-227. Esp. 199-227 [1,1-4,24]. [NTA 25, 92/461]; 16 (1981) 292-330. [NTA 26, 884]

**RADERMAKERS, Jean**

1969    La prière de Jésus dans les évangiles synoptiques. — *LumVit* 24 (1969) 393-410. Esp. 402-403, 405-406; = *Confrontations* (Tournai) 2 (1969) 299-317. Esp. 309-312. The Prayer of Jesus in the Synoptic Gospels. — *LumVit* 24 (1969) 561-578. [NTA 14, 840]

1971    La Mission, engagement radical. Une lecture de *Mt 10*. — *NRT* 93 (1971) 1072-1085. [NTA 16, 860] → 1972, 133-148

1972    *Au fil de l'évangile selon saint Matthieu. 1. Texte. 2. Lecture continue.* Heverlee-Leuven: Institut d'études théologiques, 1972, 95 and 399 p.; ²1974 Esp. II, 9-24:

"Introduction"; 25-381 [commentary]. [NTA 17, p. 247] → 1971; → Danieli 1973, Sabourin 1973, Snoy 1972 M.-É. BOISMARD, *RB* 80 (1973) 616; J.A. CARRASCO, *EstJo* 28 (1974) 249; J. COPPENS, *ETL* 48 (1972) 630; É. COTHENET, *EVie* 82 (1972) 369-370; G. DANIELI, *RivBib* 21 (1973) 433-439; A. DESCAMPS, *RTL* 4 (1973) 217-225; L. DEVILLERS, *RThom* 84 (1984) 139-140; I. GOMÁ CIVIT, *EstBíb* 30 (1974) 300-302; K. GRAYSTON, *ExpT* 84 (1972-73) 297-298; J. GUILLET, *Études* 337 (1972) 315; D.R.A. HARE, *JBL* 93 (1974) 117-118; J.-C. INGELAERE, *RHPR* 53 (1973) 85-86; J. KAHMANN, *TijdTheol* 13 (1973) 343-344; J. LAMBRECHT, *Bijdragen* 34 (1972) 212-213; X. LÉON-DUFOUR, *RSR* 62 (1974) 263-264; P. MEAGHER, *The Clergy Monthly* (Ranchi, India) 37 (1973) 121-123; L. MONDEN, *Streven* 26 (1972-73) 407-408; R. PESCH, *Freiburger Rundbrief* 24 (1972) 75; B. PIEPIÓRKA, *ZKT* 95 (1973) 220; A. SEGOVIA, *ArchTeolGran* 35 (1972) 337-338; W.G. THOMPSON, *CBQ* 35 (1973) 265-267; J.M. TISON, *NRT* 94 (1972) 809-812; A. VANHOYE, *Bib* 55 (1974) 292-293; F. VAN SEGBROECK, *Ons Geestelijk Leven* 50 (1973) 126-127; J. ZUMSTEIN, *RTP* 24 (1974) 61.
*Lettura pastorale del vangelo di Matteo*, trans. R. Passini. Bologna: Dehoniane, 1974, 366 p.

1978 Matthieu (saint). — *DictSpir* 10/66-67 (1978) 779-797.

1981 Évangile de Matthieu. — AUNEAU, J., et al. (eds.), *Évangiles synoptiques et Actes des apôtres* (Petite bibliothèque des sciences bibliques. Nouveau Testament, 4), Paris: Desclée, 1981, 131-194. Esp. 135-147: "Structure"; 149-164: "La manière d'écrire de Matthieu"; 165-172: "La communauté de Matthieu"; 173-184: "La théologie"; 185-189: "Qui est Matthieu?".
Matteo. — AUNEAU, J., et al. (eds.), *Vangeli sinottici e Atti deg'i Apostoli*, trans. P. Mariotti (Piccola Enciclopedia Biblica, 9), Roma: Borla, 1983, 145-217.
Trans. Portuguese 1986, ²1991.

1987 Matthieu, Évangile. — BOGAERT, P.-M., et al. (eds.), *Dictionnaire encyclopédique de la Bible*, Turnhout: Brepols, 1987, 799-800.

**RADL, Walter**

1982 Der Tod Jesu in der Darstellung der Evangelien. — *TGl* 72 (1982) 432-446. Esp. 436-438 [27,45-54]. [NTA 27, 891]

1983 Zur Struktur der eschatologischen Gleichnisse Jesu. — *TTZ* 92 (1983) 122-133. Esp. 123-125.127-128.130-131 [22,1-14]; 125-126.128-130.131-133 [25,1-13]. [NTA 28, 100]

1988 *Das Lukas-Evangelium* (Erträge der Forschung, 261). Darmstadt: Wissenschaftliche Buchgesellschaft, 1988, XVIII-170 p. Esp. 28-33 [Q]; 36-38 [Lk dep. on Mt].

**RÄISÄNEN, Heikki**

1969 *Die Mutter Jesu im Neuen Testament* (Annales Academiae Scientiarum Fennicae, B/158). Helsinki: Suomalainen Tiedeakatemia, 1969, 217 p. Esp. 52-76: "Maria im Evangelium des Matthäus"; (B/247) ²1989. — Diss. Helsinki, 1969 (A.T. Nikolainen). → Alonso 1972

1973 *The Idea of Divine Hardening. A Comparative Study of the Notion of Divine Hardening, Leading Astray and Inciting to Evil in the Bible and the Qur'ān* (Publications of the Finnish Exegetical Society, 25). Helsinki: Finnish Exegetical Society, 1973, ²1976, 108 p. Esp. 90-91 [13,13; 22,14].

1983a *Paul and the Law* (WUNT, 29). Tübingen: Mohr, 1983, ²1987, X-320 p. Esp. 29-30.86-90.212-214 [5,17-18; 9,13; 12,7]; Philadelphia, PA: Fortress, 1986.

1983b "Werkgerechtigkeit": Eine frühkatholische Lehre? Überlegungen zum 1. Klemensbrief. — *StudTheol* 37 (1983) 79-99. Esp. 97-99; = ID., *The Torah and Christ. Essays in German and English on the Problem of the Law in Early Christianity* (Publications of the Finnish Exegetical Society, 45), Helsinki: Finnish Exegetical Society, 1986, , 1986, 307-333. Esp. 330-333.
"Righteousness by Works": An Early Catholic Doctrine? Thoughts on 1 Clement. — ID., *Jesus, Paul and Torah. Collected Essays*, trans. D.E. Orton (JSNT SS, 43), Sheffield: JSOT, 1992, 203-224. Esp. 222-224.

1991 Mahatma Gandhi and the Sermon on the Mount. — *Temenos* (Helsinki) 27 (1991) 83-108.

1992 Freiheit von Gesetz im Urchristentum. — *StudTheol* 46 (1992) 55-67. Esp. 58-59, 62 [5,17]. [NTA 37, 1489]
Freedom from the Law in Early Christianity. — *TDig* 40 (1993) 43-48.

**RAGAZ, Leonhard**
1945[R] *Die Bergpredigt Jesu* [1945] (Stundenbücher, 102). Hamburg: Furche, 1971, 199 p. [NTA 18, p. 111] → Rostig 1991

**RAGGI, A.M.** → Gordini 1967

**RAHNER, Karl**
1957 "Nimm das Kind und seine Mutter". Zur Verehrung des hl. Joseph. [1,18-25] — *GL* 30 (1957) 14-22. [NTA 2, 48]
"Take the Child and his Mother". — *TDig* 6 (1958) 169-173.

**RAJA, R.J.**
1992 Follow Me – Discipleship in the Synoptic Gospels. — *Vidyajyoti* 56 (1992) 513-533. Esp. 532. [NTA 37, 1233]

**RAJA RAO, T.J.**
1990 Proverbs Jesus Used in the Gospel according to Matthew. — *Jeevadhaara* 20 (1990) 133-150. [NTA 35, 128]

**RALLO FRENI, R.A.**
1986 Alcune osservazioni sul testo neotestamentario utilizzato nelle *Expositiunculae Arnobii episcopi in Evangelio Iohannis evangelistae, Matthaei et Lucae*. — *Atti della Accademia Peloritana dei Pericolanti* (Classe di Lettere, 62), Messina, 1986, 219-234.

**RALPH, Margareth Nutting**
1986 *"And God Said What?" An Introduction to Biblical Literary Forms for Bible Lovers*. New York – Mahwah, NJ: Paulist, 1986, VI-255 p. Esp. 138-142 [gospel genre]; 149-173 [parables].

1990 *Discovering the Gospels. Four Accounts of the Good News* (Discovering the Living World). New York – Mahwah, NJ: Paulist, 1990, VI-283 p. [NTA 35, p. 245]

**RAMAROSON, Leonard**
1971 Une nouvelle interprétation de la "clausule" de Mt 19,9. — *SE* 23 (1971) 247-251. [NTA 16, 158]
Una nuova interpretazione della "clausola" di Matteo 19,9. — *RasT* 12 (1971) 337-340.

1974 La structure du premier Évangile. — *SE* 26 (1974) 69-112. Esp. 69-75: "Plans proposés jusqu'ici"; 75-112: "Notre propos". [NTA 18, 843]

1988 "Parole–semence" ou "Peuple–semence" dans la parabole du Semeur? [13,3-9] — *SE* 40 (1988) 91-101. [NTA 33, 151]

1991 "Notre part de nourriture" (Mt 6,11). — *SE* 43 (1991) 87-115. Esp. 87-94: "Les Pères de l'Église"; 95-114: "Les modernes". [NTA 36, 145]

**RAMIREZ OLID, J.**
1988a Vulgarismo en el evangelio de Mateo de la Vetus Latina. — *Analecta Malacitana* (Málaga) 11 (1988) 257-272.

1988b La influencia griega en el texto de Mateo de la Vetus Latina. — *Ibid.*, 401-414.

**RAMLOT, Léon**
1964 Les généalogies bibliques. Un genre littéraire oriental. — *BibVieChrét* 60 (1964) 53-70. Esp. 63-70 [1,1-17]. [NTA 9, 898]

**RAMM, Bernard L.**

1962 The Exegesis of Matthew 16:13-20 in the Patristc and Reformation Period. — *Foundations* (Rochester, NY) 5 (1962) 206-216.

**RAMSEY, Arthur Michael**

1945[R] *The Resurrection of Christ. A Study of the Event and Its Meaning for the Christian Faith* [1945]. London–Glasgow: Collins, 1961, 127 p.
La résurrection du Christ. Essai de théologie biblique, trans. H. Savon (Christianisme en mouvement, 7). Tournai–Paris: Casterman, 1968, 160 p.
La risurrezione di Dio. Saggio di teologia biblica, trans. A. Milaneli Berti. Torino–Roma: Marietti, 1969, 157 p.

1949[R] *The Glory of God and the Transfiguration of Christ* [1949] (Libra Books). London: Darton, Longman & Todd, 1967, 160 p. Esp. 29-30 [glory]; 120-121 [17,1-9].
La gloire de Dieu et la transfiguration du Christ, trans. M. Maillé (LD, 40). Paris: Cerf, 1965, 198 p. Esp. 44.116; 149-150.
Doxa. Gottes Herrlichkeit und Christi Verklärung, trans. A. Gestner. Einsiedeln: Johannes, 1969, 211 p.

1962 *The Narratives of the Passion* (Contemporary Stud es in Theology, 2). London: Mowbrays, 1962, 28 p.
The Narratives of the Passion. — *Studia Evangelica* 2 (1964) 122-134. Esp. 128-129.

**RAND, James F.**

1954 *The Eschatology of the Olivet Discourse as Found in Matthew 24 and 25.* Diss. Theol. Sem., Dallas, TX, 1954.

1955 Problems in Literal Interpretation of the Sermon on the Mount. — *BS* 112 (1955) 28-38, 125-136.

1956 A Survey of the Eschatology of the Olivet Discourse. — *BS* 113 (1956) 162-173, 200-213.

**RANDELLINI, Lino**

1959 Recenti tentativi per risolvere la questione sinottica. — *RivBib* 7 (1959) 159-172, 242-257. [NTA 4, 379]

1960 Aspetti formali delle parabole evangeliche. — *BibOr* 2 (1960) 1-5. [NTA 4, 628]

1961 Gli Evangeli e gli Atti degli Apostoli. — RINALDI, G. - DE BENEDETTI, P. (eds.), *Introduzione al Nuovo Testamento* (Il Nuovo Testameno Commentato, 10), Brescia: Morcelliana, 1961, 45-303; 2nd rev. ed., 1971.

1974 L'inno di giubilo: *Mt.* 11,25-30; *Lc.* 10,20-24. — *RivBib* 22 (1974) 183-235. Esp. 185-195: "Autenticità e unità del brano"; 195-197 [11,25]; 197-203 [11,25-26]; 204-225 [11,27]. [NTA 19, 534]

**RANDOLPH, R.E.**

1968 *The Development of the Synoptic Tradition.* Diss. Emory Univ., Atlanta, GA, 1968, 225 p.

**RANON, Angelo**

1990 *Da Gesù ai vangeli. Introduzione al Nuovo Testamento.* Vol. I (Strumenti di scienze religiose). Padova: Messaggero, 1990, 251 p. [NTA 37, p. 120]

**RANSON, G.H.**

1956 Persecuted for Righteousness' Sake. [5,10] — *RExp* 53 (1956) 55-60.

**RAPISARDA, Emanuele**

1959* (ed.), *Convivium Dominicum. Studi sull'Eucarestia nei Padri della Chiesa Antica e Miscellanea patristica.* Catania: Centro di Studi sull'Antico Cristianesimo, 1959, 462 p. → Coassolo, Costanza, Vona

**RAPISARDA, Grazia**

1991 Cielo e terra, angeli e demoni nell'esegesi biblica di Cromazio di Aquileia. [CommMt] — *AnStoEseg* 8 (1991) 615-630.

1992 Ancora sull'esegesi biblica di Cromazio di Aquileio: le figure femminili. — *AnStoEseg* 9 (1992) 519-535.

**RAPONI, Santino**

1974 *Tentazione ed esistenza cristiana. Il racconto sinottico della tentazione di Gesù alla luce della storia della salvezza nella prima letteratura patristica* (Teologia Morale, 13). Roma: Paoline, 1974, 227 p.

1983 Cristo tentato e il cristiano. Le lezione dei Padri. [4,1-11] — *Studia Moralia* (Roma) 21 (1983) 209-237.

**RASCO, Emilio**

1967 Les paraboles de Luc XV. Une invitation à la joie de Dieu dans le Christ. — DE LA POTTERIE, I. (ed.), *De Jésus aux Évangiles*. FS J. Coppens, 1967, 165-183. Esp. 173-176 [Q 15,4-7]. (IT, 1971, 209-229).

1968 Matthew I–II: Structure, Meaning, Reality. — *Studia Evangelica* 4 (1968) 214-230. Esp. 215-222 [structure]; 222-226; 226-230 [1,23].

1969 "Cuatro" y "la fe" ¿quiénes y de quién? (Mc 2,3b.5a). — *Bib* 50 (1969) 59-67. Esp. 64. [NTA 14, 160]

1971 El anuncio a José (Mt 1,18-25). — *EstJos* 25 = *CahJos* 19 (1971) 84-103. [NTA 16, 848]

1986 Deformación y formación de los Evangelios. De Claude Tresmontant a Pierre Grelot. — *Greg* 67 (1986) 329-339. [NTA 30, 1000] → Carmignac 1984, Grelot 1984a, 1986a, Tresmontant 1983

**RASTROJO, J.M.**

1974 El padrenuestro. — *Proyección* (Granada) 21 (1974) 233-247.

**RATCLIFF, Edward C.**

1960 The Prayer of St Chrysostom: A Note on Cranmer's Rendering and Its Background. [18,19-20] — *ATR* 42 (1960) 1-9. → B. Taylor 1958

**RATHEY, Markus**

1991 Talion im NT? Zu Mt 5,38-42. — *ZNW* 82 (1991) 264-266. [NTA 36, 715]

**RAU, Christoph**

1976 *Das Matthäus-Evangelium. Entstehung – Gestalt – Essenischer Einfluß* (Schriften zur Religionserkenntnis. Beiträge zur theologischen Forschung). Stuttgart: Urachhaus, 1976, 157 p. [NTA 21, p. 200]

**RAU, Eckhard**

1990 *Reden in Vollmacht. Hintergrund, Form und Anliegen der Gleichnisse Jesu* (FRLANT, 149). Göttingen: Vandenhoeck & Ruprecht, 1990, 434 p. Esp. 107-171: "Die Reich-Gottes Gleichnisse in Mk und Q"; 172-182 [7,9-11/Q 11,11-13; 13,31-32/Q 13,18-19; 13,33/Q 13,20-21]. — Diss. Hamburg, 1987 (U. Wilckens).

**RAU, Gottfried**

1965 Das Volk in der lukanischen Passionsgeschichte. Eine Konjektur zu Lk 23,13. — *ZNW* 56 (1965) 41-51. Esp. 41-42 [ὄχλος]. [NTA 10, 546]

**RAUNIO, Antti**

1987 Die "goldene Regel" als theologisches Prinzip beim jungen Luther. — MANNERMAA, T., et al. (eds.), *Thesaurus Lutheri. Auf der Suche nach neuen Paradigmen der Luther-*

*Forschung. Referate des Luther-Symposiums in Finnland 11.-12. November 1986*, Helsinki, 1987, 309-327.

**RAURELL, Frederic**

1970 "L'Évangile selon Matthieu. Rédaction et théologie". [Spanish] — *EstFranc* 71 (1970) 345-373. → Didier 1972*

1993* & ROURE, D. – TRAGAN, P.-R. (eds.), *Tradició i traducció de la Paraula. Miscellània Guiu Camps* (Scripta et Documenta, 47). Montserrat: Publicaciones de l'Abadia, 1993, 447 p. → Delcor, O'Callaghan, Puig i Tàrrech, Sidera

**RAUSCH, Jerome**

1966 The Principle of Nonresistance and Love of Enemy in Mt 5,38-48. — *CBQ* 28 (1966) 31-41. [NTA 10, 903]
Non resistenza e amore dei nemici in Mt. 5,38-48. — *RasT* 8 (1967) 295-302.

**RAUSCHER, Johann**

1990 *Vom Messiasgeheimnis zur Lehre der Kirche. Die Entwicklung der sogenannten Parabeltheorie in der synoptischen Tradition (Mk 4,10-12 par Mt 13,10-17 par Lk 8,9-10)*. Diss. Linz, 1990, XII-392 p. (A. Fuchs). Esp. 37-40: "Die Mt/Lk Übereinstimmungen gegen Mk in der Perikope von der Parabeltheorie und ihre Bedeutung"; 42-106: "Die Matthäusredaktion: Mt 13,10-17"; 135-165: "Die Deuteromarkusredaktion"; 271-299: "Das Anliegen der Matthäus-Redaktion". → T.A. Friedrichsen 1991

1994 *Das Bildwort von der Öllampe in der synoptischen Tradition. Eine Auslegung von Mk 4,21f par Lk 8,16f; Mt 5,15; Lk 11,33*. Desselbrunn: Privately published, 1994, XII-436 p.

**RAVASI, Gianfranco**

1974a I Vangeli dell'infanzia. Gesù vero Messia e Figlio di Dio. I dittici di Mt 1-2. — *RivClerIt* 55 (1974) 355-363.

1974b I Vangeli dell'infanzia. Lettura di Mt. 2,1-23. — *Ibid.*, 512-519.

1992 *Das Evangelium nach Matthäus. Einführung und Erklärungen* [Italian, 1989], trans. S. Liesenfeld. München: Neue Stadt, 1992, 152 p.
J. ERNST, *TGl* 83 (1993) 498.

**RAVENS, David**

1995 *Luke and the Restoration of Israel* (JSNT SS, 119). Sheffield: JSOT, 1995, 287 p. Esp. 212-246: "Luke, Matthew and Israel". — Diss. Sheffield, 1994 (L. Alexander).

**RAY, Charles A.**

1992 The Beatitudes. Challenging Worldviews. — *Theological Educator* (New Orleans) 46 (1992) 97-104. [NTA 37, 721]

**RAY, Walter Alan**

1964 *The Relationship between Eschatology and Ecclesiology in the Gospel of Matthew. A Study in "Redaktionsgeschichte"*. Diss. Fuller Theol. Sem., Pasadena, CA, 1964, VIII-264 p. — *DissAbstr* 28 (1967-68) 2767.

**RAYBURN, Robert G.**

1952 *Matthew 13, Christ's Prophetic Picture of Christendom*. Diss. Theol. Sem., Dallas, TX, 1952, 1975 p.

**READ, David H.C.**

1951 The Mind of Christ. IX. His Way with Inquirers. — *ExpT* 63 (1951-52) 37-40. Esp. 37-38 [Jewish leaders].

**READER, William**

1980 Entdeckung von Fragmenten aus zwei zerstörten neutestamentlichen Minuskeln (338 und 612). — *Bib* 61 (1980) 407-411. Esp. 408-409 (338: Mt 15,27-16,9; 26,2-14]. [NTA 25, 404]

**REBELL, Walter**

1989a *Alles ist möglich dem, der glaubt. Glaubensvollmacht im frühen Christentum*. München: Kaiser, 1989, 167 p. Esp. 21-33 [Mk/Q]; 34-66: "Die synoptischen Evangelien".

1989b 'Sein Leben verlieren' (Mark 8.35 parr.) als Strukturmoment vor- und nachösterlichen Glaubens. [10,39; 16,25] — *NTS* 35 (1989) 202-218. [NTA 33, 1161]

1991 *Erfüllung und Erwartung. Erfahrungen mit dem Geist im Urchristentum*. München: Kaiser, 1991, 196 p. Esp. 11-23: "Jesus und der Geist"; 175 [10,20].

**REBIĆ, Adalbert**

1969 *Das Auftreten und die Predigt Johannes' des Täufers. Redaktions- und traditions-geschichtliche Arbeit in Mt 3,1-17 und Parallelen*. Diss. Pont. Univ. Greg., Roma, 1969, 68 p. (excerpt).

**RECHOWICZ, Marian**

1955 St. Jean Kanty a-t-il été l'auteur du commentaire conciliariste de St. Matthieu? — *CollTheol* 26 (1955) 13-45.

**RECKER, Robert**

1979 The Redemptive Focus of the Kingdom of God. — *CalvTJ* 14 (1979) 154-186. Esp. 165-168. [NTA 23, 604]

**[Reconnaissance]**

1971* *Reconnaissance à Suzanne de Diétrich* (FoiVie/Cahiers bibliques, no. hors série). Paris: Foi et Vie, 1971, 224 p. → Cousin, Dambrine, Wire

**REDFORD, John**

1979 The Quest of the Historical Epiphany. Critical Reflections on Raymond Brown's "The Birth of the Messiah". — *CleR* 64 (1979) 5-11. [NTA 23, 514r] → R.E. Brown 1977

1981 Preparing the Way. John the Baptist. — *CleR* 66 (1981) 193-200. [NTA 26, 162]

**REED, Jonathan Lee**

1993 *Places in Early Christianity: Galilee, Archaeology, Urbanization, and Q*. Diss. Graduate School, Claremont, CA, 1993, 172 p. — *DissAbstr* 54 (1993-94) 3478.

1995 The Social Map of Q. — KLOPPENBORG, J.S. (ed.), *Conflict and Invention*, 1995, 17-36.

**REEDY, Charles J.**

1983 Rhetorical Concerns and Argumentative Techniques in Matthean Pronouncement Stories. [28,16-20] — *SBL 1983 Seminar Papers*, 219-222.

**REESE, David George**

1985 *A Survey of References to the Demonic in the Gospel of Matthew*. Diss. Southern Baptist Theol. Sem., Louisville, KY, 1985, 243 p. (G.L. Borchert). — *DissAbstr* 46 (1985-86) 1981-A; *SBT* 14 (1986) 192-193.

**REESE, James M.**

1977 How Matthew Portrays the Communication of Christ's Authority. — *BTB* 7 (1977) 139-144. [NTA 22, 79]

1978 *Jesus, His Word and Work. The Gospels of Matthew, Mark and Luke* (God's Work Today, 5. A New Study Guide to the Bible). New York: Pueblo, 1978, VII-118 p.

1981   The Parables in Matthew's Gospel. — *BiTod* 19 (1981) 30-35. [NTA 25, 478]

1992   *The Student's Guide to the Gospels* (Good News Studies, 24). Collegeville, MN: Liturgical Press, 1992, 150 p.

**REEVES, Keith Howard**

1993   *The Resurrection Narrative in Matthew. A Literary-Critical Examination.* Lewiston, NY – Queenston, Ont. – Lampeter, UK: Mellen, 1993, IX-113 p. [NTA 40, p. 525] — Diss. Union Theol. Sem., Virginia, GA, 1988, 185 p. (J.D. Kingsbury). Esp. 14-37: "The structure of Mt 27:55–28:20"; 38-69: "The characters in Mt 27:55–28:20"; 70-73 [27,55-61]; 79-88 [27,62-66]; 89-106 [28,1-10]; 107-114 [28,11-15]; 115-143 [28,16-20].

**REFOULÉ, François**

1964   Primauté de Pierre dans les évangiles. — *RevSR* 38 (1964) 1-41. Esp. 4-21 [16,13-24]. [NTA 8, 897]

1968   La prière des chrétiens. — BONNARD, P., et al. (eds ), *Notre Père qui es aux cieux,* 1968, 9-51. Esp. 10-16: "Le Notre Père dans la tradition chrétienne"; 16-51: "Le Notre Père et l'exégèse moderne".

1992   Le parallèle Matthieu 16/16-17 – Galates 1/15-16 réexaminé. — *ETR* 67 (1992) 161-175. Esp. 164-171: "Paul a-t-il pu connaître le logion de Mt 16/16-17?"; 171-175: "Le vocabulaire de Matthieu et celui de Paul en Galates". [NTA 37, 147]

1993   Jésus, nouveau Moïse, ou Pierre, nouveau Grand Prêtre? (Mt 17,1-9; Mc 9,2-10). — *RTL* 24 (1993) 145-162. [NTA 38, 165]

**REGTIEN, M.**

1979   *Het leven van Jezus Christus. Een Synopsis van de vier evangeliën.* 's-Gravenhage: Boekencentrum, 1979, 235 p.

**REHKOPF, Friedrich**

1961   Mt 26,50: ἑταῖρε, ἐφ᾿ ὃ πάρει. — *ZNW* 52 (1961) 109-115. [NTA 6, 461]

1976   BLASS, F. – DEBRUNNER, A. – REHKOPF, F., *Grammatik des neutestamentlichen Griechisch.* Göttingen: Vandenhoeck & Ruprecht, [14]1976, XX-511 p.; [15]1979, XXI-511 p.; [16]1984; [17]1990. → Debrunner 1913
       *Grammatica del Greco del Nuovo Testamento,* trans. U. Mattioli & G. Pisi (Supplementi al "Grande Lessico del Nuovo Testamento", 3). Brescia: Paideia, 1982, 709 p.

1991   Walter Bauer und Bauer/Aland: Wörterbuch zum Neuen Testament. — *TR* 56 (1991) 428-436. → K. Aland [Bauer-Aland 1988]

**REHM, Martin**

1958   Eli, Eli, lamma sabacthani. [27,46] — *BZ* 2 (1958) 275-278. [NTA 3, 78] → Gnilka 1959a

**REHM, Ulrich**

1994   *Bebilderte Vaterunser-Erklärungen des Mittelalters.* Baden: Koerner, 1994, 339 p.

**REICKE, Bo**

1950a  The New Testament Conception of Reward. — CULLMANN, O. – MENOUD, P. (eds.), *Aux sources de la tradition chrétienne.* FS M. Goguel, 1950, 195-206. Esp. 200-201.205-206.

1950b  Den primära israelsmissionen och hednamissionen enligt synoptikerna. [The first mission to Israel and the gentile mission according to the synoptics] [10,17-23; 24,9-14; 28,16-20] — *SvenskTeolKvart* 26 (1950) 77-100.

1952   Nytt ljus över Johannes döparens förkunnelse. [New light on the preaching of John the Baptist] — *Religion och Bibel* (Uppsala) 11 (1952) 5-18.

1953    A Synopsis of Early Christian Preaching. — FRIDRICHSEN, A., et al. (eds.), *The Root of the Vine*, 1953, 128-160. Esp. 130-145.

1959    Instruction and Discussion in the Travel Narrative. — *Studia Evangelica* 1 (1959) 206-216.

1972    Synoptic Prophecies on the Destruction of Jerusalem. — AUNE, D.E. (ed.), *Studies in New Testament*. FS A.P. Wikgren, 1972, 121-134. Esp. 123 [22,7]; 124-125 [24,2.15-16]; 130-131 [24,4-8]; 131-133 [24,9-14].

1976a   Griesbach und die synoptische Frage. — *TZ* 32 (1976) 341-359. [NTA 21, 710]
        Griesbach's Answer to the Synoptic Question. — ORCHARD, B. - LONGSTAFF, T.R.W. (eds.), *J.J. Griesbach: Synoptic and Text-critical Studies*, 1978, 50-67, 198-200.

1976b   The Synoptic Reports on the Healing of the Paralytic. Matt. 9:1-8 with Parallels. — ELLIOTT, J.K. (ed.), *Studies in New Testament Language and Text*. FS G.D. Kilpatrick, 1976, 319-329.

1979    Christ's Birth and Childhood. — HADIDIAN, D.Y. (ed.), *From Faith to Faith*. FS D.G. Miller, 1979, 151-165. Esp. 153-157 [fulfilment quotations]; 161-165 [1-2].

1983    A Test of Synoptic Relationships: Matthew 10:17-23 and 24:9-14 with Parallels. — FARMER, W.R. (ed.), *New Synoptic Studies*, 1983, 209-229.

1984    Die Entstehungsverhältnisse der synoptischen Evangelien. — *ANRW* II.25.2 (1984) 1758-1791. Esp. 1759-1790: "Geschichte der Diskussion"; 1770-1775: "Streuung des Materials"; 1775-1789: "Ursprünge der Traditionen". → 1990

1986    *The Roots of the Synoptic Gospels*. Philadelphia, PA: Fortress, 1986, X-191 p.
        F. NEIRYNCK, *ETL* 63 (1987) 421-422; D.P. SCAER, *ConcTQ* 51 (1987) 255-260.

1987a   The Historical Setting of John's Baptism. — SANDERS, E.P. (ed.), *Jesus, the Gospels, and the Church*. FS W.R. Farmer, 1987, 209-224. Esp. 211 [14,2-4]; 214-219 [3,7-12]; 219-220 [3,13-17]; 221-222 [11,7-19].

1987b   From Strauss to Holtzmann and Meijboom. Synoptic Theories Advanced During the Consolidation of Germany, 1830-70. — *NT* 29 (1987) 1-21. [NTA 31, 1047]

1990    The History of the Synoptic Discussion. — DUNGAN, D.L. (ed.), *The Interrelations of the Gospels*, 1990, 291-316. → 1984, 1759-1770

**REID, Barbara E.**

1993    *The Transfiguration: A Source- and Redaction-Critical Study of Luke 9:28-36* (Cahiers de la Revue Biblique, 32). Paris: Gabalda, 1993, XIV-195 p. Esp. 27-28: "Matthean redaction"; 90-93: "Agreements of Luke and Matthew against Mark". — Diss. Catholic University of America, Washington, DC, 1988 (J.P. Meier).
        R.J. MILLER, Source Criticism and the Limits of Certainty: The Lukan Transfiguration Story as a Test Case. — *ETL* 74 (1998) 127-144.

**REILING, Jannes**

1965    The Use and Translation of καὶ ἐγένετο, 'And it Happened', in the New Testament. — *BTrans* 16 (1965) 153-163. Esp. 157.163: "Matthew and Mark". [NTA 10, 932]

**REIN, Matthias**

1995    *Die Heilung des Blindgeborenen (Joh 9). Tradition und Redaktion* (WUNT, II/73). Tübingen: Mohr, 1995, XI-401 p. Esp. 274-276 [15,14]; 320-323 [11,2-6]. — Diss. Halle-Wittenberg, 1993-94 (T. Holtz).

**REINBOLD, Wolfgang**

1994    *Der älteste Bericht über den Tod Jesu. Literarische Analyse und historische Kritik der Passionsdarstellungen der Evangelien* (Beihefte zur ZNW, 69). Berlin - New York: de Gruyter, 1994, XII-357 p. Esp. 27-48: "Das Verhältnis des Johannesevangeliums zu den Synoptikern"; 287-288 [27,3-10.19.24-25.62-66]. — Diss. Göttingen, 1993 (H. Stegemann).

**REINELT, Heinz**

1968 "Selig die Friedensmacher, denn sie werden Kinder Gottes genannt werden" Mt 5,9. — *Königsteiner Studien* 14 (1968) 173-180.

1980 Hrabanus Maurus als Exeget. [8,14] — BÖHNE, W. (ed à, *Hrabanus Maurus und seine Schule*, Fulda, 1980, 64-76.

**REINER, Erica**

1968 Thirty Pieces of Silver. — HALLO, W.W. (ed.), *Essays in Memory of Ephraim Avigdos Speiser* (American Oriental Series, 53), New Haven, CT: American Oriental Society, 1968, 186-190.

**REINHARDT, Wolfgang**

1995 *Das Wachstum des Gottesvolkes. Untersuchungen zum Gemeindewachstum im lukanischen Doppelwerk auf dem Hintergrund des Alten Testaments.* Göttingen: Vandenhoeck & Ruprecht, 1995, 387 p. Esp. 116-132 [Q 13,18-21]. — Diss. Wuppertal, 1992 (K. Haacker).

**REININK, Gerrit J.**

1979 *Studien zur Quellen- und Traditionsgeschichte des Evangelienkommentars der Gannat Bussame* (CSCO, 414). Leuven: CSCO, 1979, 21*-309 p. Esp. 17-18; 30-32 [3,15]; 52-56 [2,1-2]; 129-131 [6,1-13]; 133-157 [27]; 232-256 [4,1-11].

1980 Neue Fragmente zum Diatessaronkommentar des Ephraemschülers Aba. [2,7; 3,4.12; 4,5-6; 5,18.29-30; 17,20; 18,8-9] — *OrLovPer* 11 (1980) 117-133.

1985 Der Dämon "Sohn des Daches" in der syrischen exegetischen Literatur. [4,24; 17,15] — *Studia Patristica* 16 (1985) 105-113.

1988 → Drijvers 1988

1990 Fragmente der Evangelienexegese des Katholikos Henanišo' I. — LAVENANT, R. (ed.), *V Symposium Syriacum 1988. Katholieke Universiteit Leuven, 29-31 août 1988* (Orientalia Christiana Analecta, 236), Roma: Pont. Inst. Stud. Orient., 1990, 71-92.

**REISER, Marius**

1990 *Die Gerichtspredigt Jesu. Eine Untersuchung zur eschatologischen Verkündigung Jesu und ihrem frühjüdischen Hintergrund* (NTAbh, NF 23). Münster: Aschendorff, 1990, IX-359 p. Esp. 153-182: "Das Gericht in der Verkündigung des Täufers" [3,7-12]; 183-314: "Das Gericht in der Verkündigung Jesu" [5,25-26; 7,1-2; 8,11-12; 9,37; 11,21-24; 12,41-42; 18,23-35; 19,28; 22,2-14].

**REMBRY, Jean Gabriel**

1961 "Quoniam Nazaraeus vocabitur" (Mt 2/23). — *SBF/LA* 12 (1961-62) 46-65. Esp. 49-57 [ὅτι; λέγων]; 58-60 [26,54-56]; 61-65 [2,23]. [NTA 7, 778]

**REMUS, Harold E.**

1992 Miracle (NT). — *ABD* 4 (1992) 857-869. Esp. 862-863.

**RENARD, Jean-Pierre**

1983 La "Lectura super Matthaeum" V,20-48 de Thomas c'Aquin. Édition d'après le ms. Bâle, Univ. Bibl. B.V. 12. — *RTAM* 50 (1983) 145-190.

**RENARD, Philip**

1983 (ed.), *Jezus spreekt. De toespraken en dialogen van Jezus Christus volgens de evangeliën van Marcus, Matteüs, Lucas en Johannes.* Amsterdam: Karnak, 1983, 191 p.

**RENDALL, R.**

1964 Quotation in Scripture as an Index of Wider Reference. [21] — *EvQ* 36 (1964) 214-221. [NTA 9, 541]

**RENGSTORF, Karl Heinrich**

1960 Die Stadt der Mörder (Mt 22,7). — ELTESTER, W. (ed.), *Judentum, Urchristentum, Kirche*. FS J. Jeremias, 1960, 106-129. [NTA 5, 723]

1962 Old and New Testament Traces of a Formula of the Judaean Royal Ritual. — *NT* 5 (1962) 229-244. Esp. 237-240 [28,16-20]; 241-242 [4,1-11]. [NTA 7, 793]

1963 Die στολαί der Schriftgelehrten. Eine Erläuterung zu Mark. 12,38. — BETZ, O., et al. (eds.), *Abraham unser Vater*. FS O. Michel, 1963, 383-404. Esp. 383-387 [23,5].

1970 Das Vaterunser in seiner Bedeutung für unser Zusammenleben. — *Kerygma und Melos. Christhard Mahrenholz 70 Jahre*, Kassel: Bärenreiter; Berlin: Lutherisches Verlagshaus, 1970, 13-25.

**RENIÉ, J.**

1955 Une antilogie évangélique (Mc 6,51-52; Mt 14,32-33). — *Bib* 36 (1955) 223-226.

**RENNER, Rudolf**

1966 *Die Wunder Jesu in Theologie und Unterricht*. Lahr/Schwarzwald: Schauenburg, 1966, 239 p. Esp. 143-158 [8,23-27]; 159-172 [20,29-34].

**RENNES, Jean**

1969 À propos de Matthieu 25/31-46. — *ETR* 44 (1969) 233-234. [NTA 14, 147]

**RENOV, Israel**

1955 The Seat of Moses. [23,2] — *IsrExplJourn* 5 (1955) 262-267.

**REPO, Eero**

1954 *Der Begriff "Rhēma" im biblisch-griechischen. Eine traditionsgeschichtliche und semasiologische Untersuchung*. II. *"Rhēma" im Neuen Testament, unter Berücksichtigung seines Gebrauchs in der übrigen altchristlichen Literatur* (Annales Academiae Scientiarum Fennicae, 88). Helsinki: Suomalainen Tiedeakatemia, 1954, 214 p. Esp. 15-21.

**RESE, Martin**

1969 *Alttestamentliche Motive in der Christologie des Lukas* (Studien zum Neuen Testament, 1). Gütersloh: Mohn, 1969, 227 p. Esp. 165-168 [Q 7,27]; 188-191 [Q 13,15]. — Diss. Bonn, 1965 (P. Vielhauer).

1985 Das Lukas-Evangelium. Ein Forschungsbericht. — *ANRW* II.25.3 (1985) 2258-2328. Esp. 2275-2280.2284-2288: "Die Frage nach den Quellen des Lukas-Evangeliums".

**RESENHÖFFT, Wilhelm**

1980 Jesu Gleichnis von den Talenten, ergänzt durch die Lukas-Fassung. — *NTS* 26 (1979-80) 318-331. Esp. 318-324 [25,14-30]; 325-327 [22,1-10]. [NTA 25, 81]

**REUMANN, John H.**

1968a *Jesus in the Church's Gospels: Modern Scholarship and the Earliest Sources*. Philadelphia, PA: Fortress, 1968, XVIII-539 p. Esp. 99-109: "The Lord's prayer and the praying Lord"; 182-189 [parables]; 233-241 [Sermon on the Mount].

1968b "Jesus the Steward". An Overlooked Theme in Christology. — *Studia Evangelica* 5 (1968) 21-29. Esp. 27-28 [οἰκοδεσπότης].

1972 The Quest for the Historical Baptist. — ID. (ed.), *Understanding the Sacred Text. Essays in Honor of Morton S. Enslin on the Hebrew Bible and Christian Beginnings*, Valley Forge, PA: Judson, 1972, 181-199.

1974 Psalm 22 at the Cross. Lament and Thanksgiving for Jesus Christ. — *Interpr* 28 (1974) 39-58. Esp. 49-50 [27,46]. [NTA 18, 884]

1982 *"Righteousness" in the New Testament. "Justification" in the United States. Lutheran-Roman Catholic Dialogue*. Philadelphia, PA: Fortress; New York: Paulist, 1982, XVII-278 p. Esp. 125-135.

1989 Jesus and Christology. — EPP, E.J. – MACRAE, G.W. (eds.), *The New Testament and Its Modern Interpreters*, 1989, 501-564. Esp. 509-514: "Christological titles"; 514-520: "Special areas".

1991 *Variety and Unity in New Testament Thought* (Oxford Bible Series). Oxford: University Press, 1991, XIV-330 p. Esp. 53-56: "Matthew's book about Christ and the Church".

1992 Righteousness (NT). — *ABD* 5 (1992) 745-773. Esp. 750-752.754-756.

**REUSS, Joseph**

1952 Die Matthäuserklärung des Photius von Konstantinopel. — *Ostkirchliche Studien* (Würzburg) 1 (1952) 132-134.

1954 Die Evangelienkatenen im Cod. Archivio di S. Pietro Gr. B 59. — *Bib* 35 (1954) 207-216. Esp. 207-211.

1957 *Matthäus-Kommentare aus der griechischen Kirche aus Katenenhandschriften gesammelt und herausgegeben* (TU, 61). Berlin: Akademie, 1957, XLVII-463 p. Esp. 1-54 [Apollinaris of Laodicea]; 55-95 [Theodor of Heraclea]; 96-135 [Theodor of Mopsuestia]; 136-150 [Theodor]; 151-152 [Theophilos of Alexandria]; 153-269 [Cyril of Alexandria]; 270-337 [Photios of Constantinople].
K.H. SCHELKLE, *TLZ* 83 (1958) 762-764; J. SCHMID, *BZ* 3 (1959) 147-149.

1974 Evangelien-Erklärungen vom 4. bis 9. Jahrhundert in der griechischen Kirche. — GNILKA, J. (ed.), *Neues Testament und Kirche*. FS R. Schnackenburg, 1974, 476-496. Esp. 477-484: "Das Matthäus-Evangelium".

**REUTER, Hans-Richard**

1979 Die Bergpredigt als Orientierung unseres Menschseins heute. Ein kritischer Diskurs in ethischer Absicht. — *ZEvEth* 23 (1979) 84-105.

1982a Bergpredigt und politische Vernunft. — SCHNACKENBURG, R. (ed.), *Die Bergpredigt*, 1982, 60-80. Esp. 63-66 [5,3-12]; 66-71 [5,21-48]; 71-74 [7,12]; 74-80 [6,9-13].

1982b Liebet eure Feinde! Zur Aufgabe einer politischen Ethik im Licht der Bergpredigt. — *ZEvEth* 26 (1982) 159-187.

**RÉVEILLAUD, Michel**

1964 (ed.), *Saint Cyprien. L'Oraison dominicale. Texte, traduction, introduction et notes* (Études d'histoire et de philosophie religieuses, 58). Paris: PUF, 1964, VIII-216 p. Esp. 78-134 [text and translation]; 135-208 [commentary].

**REVENTLOW, Henning Graf**

1990 *Epochen der Bibelauslegung*. Band I: *Vom Alten Testament bis Origenes*. München: Beck, 1990, 224 p. Esp. 69-72: "Das Verheißene ist erfüllt: Matthäus".

**REY, Bernard**

1986 *Les tentations et le choix de Jésus* (Lire la Bible, 72). Paris: Cerf, 1986, 163 p. Esp. 45-101: "Les épreuves de Jésus fils d'Israël. Matthieu 4,1-11".

**REYERO, S.**

1975 Algo muy importante acerca del Padre Nuestro y la oración en general. Con el P. Alonso Díaz y otros profesores de Comillas. — *CuBíb* 32 (1975) 137-142.

**REYNOLDS, Philip Lyndon**

1994 *Marriage in the Western Church. The Christianization of Marriage During the Patristic and Early Medieval Periods* (Supplements to Vigiliae Christianae, 24). Leiden: Brill,

1994, XXX-436 p. Esp. 173-212: "The Matthean exception in the Fathers"; 213-226: "The Matthean exception and the doctrine of indissolubility".

**RHOADS, David**

1992  The Gospel of Matthew. The Two Ways: Hypocrisy or Righteousness. — *CurrTMiss* 19 (1992) 453-461. [NTA 37, 707]

**RHODES, Erroll F.**

1981  Conjectural Emendations in Modern Translations. — EPP, E.J. - FEE, G.D. (eds.), *New Testament Textual Criticism*. FS B.M. Metzger, 1981, 361-374. Esp. 363 [2,6; 7,25]; 366-367 [6,18; 7,15; 8,30; 23,8]; 370 [12,33].

**RHYS, Howard**

1992  Examples of Redaction by the Evangelists. — *Sewanee Theological Review* (Sewanee, TN) 36 (1992) 103-122. [NTA 37, 1234]

**RIBADEAU DUMAS, Odile** → Bacq 1983

**RICCA, Paolo**

1991  Il battesimo di Gesù nel Giordano. Storia e teologia. — TRAGAN, P.-R. (ed.), *Alle origini del battesimo cristiano. Radici del battesimo e suo significato nelle comunità apostoliche. Atti dell'VIII convegno di teologia sacramentaria. Roma, 9-11 marzo 1989* (Studia Anselmiana, 106), Roma: Pont. Ateneo S. Anselmo, 1991, 109-127. Esp. 116-126.

**RICCI, Carla**

1994  *Maria di Magdala e le molte altre: Donne sul cammino di Gesù*. Napoli: D'Auria, 1991.
*Mary Magdalene and Many Others. Women Who Followed Jesus*, trans. P. Burns. Tunbridge Wells: Burns & Oats; Minneapolis, MN: Fortress, 1994, 237 p. Esp. 163-177 [27,55-56].

**RICCIOTTI, Giuseppe**

1950  El elemento romano en los cuatro evangelios. — *RevistBíb* 12 (1950) 143-149.

**RICE, Charles**

1983  Ordinary People. Shaping Sermons by the Interplay of Text and Metaphor. [6,19-34] — WARDLAW, D.M. (ed.), *Preaching Biblically*, Philadelphia, PA: Westminster, 1983, 101-120.

**RICE, Frank A.**

1960  *A History of Interpretation of Matthew 16:13-20*. Diss. Golden Gate Baptist Theol. Sem., Mill Valley, CA, 1960.

**RICE, George E.**

1985  Is Bezae a Homogeneous Codex? — TALBERT, C.H. (ed.), *Perspectives on the New Testament. Essays in Honor of Frank Stagg*, Macon, GA: Mercer University Press, 1985, 39-54. Esp. 40-41: "The Bezan text of Matthew and Luke".

**RICE, John R.**

1955  *The King of the Jews. A Commentary on the Gospel according to Matthew*. Wheaton, IL: Sword of the Lord Publ., 1955, 504 p.

**RICHARD, Earl**

1988  *Jesus: One and Many. The Christological Concept of New Testament Authors*. Wilmington, DE: Glazier, 1988, 546 p. Esp. 85-94: "Excursus on the Q-Source"; 129-156: "The gospel of Matthew"; 404-410 [apocalyptic].

**RICHARD, Marcel**

1959   *Le mystère de la Rédemption* (Bibliothèque de théologie, I,1). Tournai: Desclée, 1959, XI-299 p. Esp. 39-53: "Le mystère de la rédemption dans les évangiles synoptiques".

**RICHARDS, C.**

1989   *According to Matthew.* Glasgow, Blackie, 1989, V-122 p. [NTA 34, p. 387]

**RICHARDS, Hubert J.**

1956   The Three Kings (Mt. II.1-12). — *Scripture* 8 (1956) 23-28. [NTA 1, 20]

1959   Christ on Divorce. — *Scripture* 11 (1959) 22-32. Esp. 28-32 [5,32; 19,9]. [NTA 3, 581]; = WORDEN, T. (ed.), *Sacraments in Scripture. A Symposium*, London–Dublin: Chapman, 1966, 247-264. Esp. 257-264.

**RICHARDS, L.**

1976   *The Servant King: the Life of Jesus on Earth. Studies in Matthew* (His Bible Alive Series). Elgin, IL: Cook, 1976, 278 p.

**RICHARDS, W. Larry**

1978   Another Look at the Parable of the Two Sons. [21,28-32] — *BR* 23 (1978) 5-14. [NTA 23, 834]

**RICHARDSON, Alan**

1941[R]   *The Miracle-Stories of the Gospels* [1941]. London: SCM, 1952, repr. 1963, VIII-149 p. Esp. 103-108: "St. Matthew's handling of the miracle-stories".
*Las narraciones evangélicas sobre los milagros.* Madrid: Fax, 1974. 180 p.

1958   *An Introduction to the Theology of the New Testament.* London: SCM, 1958, repr. 1961, 423 p.

**RICHARDSON, Peter**

1969   *Israel in the Apostolic Church* (SNTS MS, 10). Cambridge: University Press, 1969, XIII-257 p. Esp. 48-69: "Jesus and his disciples"; 188-194: "Post-Pauline developments: Matthew". — Diss. Cambridge, 1965 (C.F.D. Moule).

1984   The Thunderbolt in Q and the Wise Man in Corinth. — ID. – HURD, J.C. (eds.), *From Jesus to Paul. Studies in Honour of Francis Wright Beare*, Waterloo, Ont.: Wilfrid Laurier University Press; Atlantic Highlands, NJ: Humanities Press, 1984, 91-111. Esp. 95-101.107-110 [Q 10,21-24]. → Henaut 1987

1985   & GOOCH, P., Logia of Jesus in 1 Corinthians. — WENHAM, D. (ed.), *The Jesus Tradition Outside the Gospels*, 1985, 39-62. Esp. 45-52.

1987   Gospel Traditions in the Church in Corinth (with Apologies to B.H. Streeter). — HAWTHORNE, G.F. – BETZ, O. (eds.), *Tradition and Interpretation.* FS E.E. Ellis, 1987, 301-318. Esp. 301-303: "Introduction" [Q – Proto-Luke]; 303-301: "The problems in Corinth and the revision of Q"; 317-318 [index].

1992   Why Turn the Tables? Jesus' Protest in the Temple Precincts. — *SBL 1992 Seminar Papers*, 507-523. Esp. 519 [17,24-27].

**RICHARDSON, Robert Douglas**

1957   The Lord's Prayer as an Early Eucharistia. — *ATR* 39 (1957) 123-130. [NTA 2, 137]

**RICHES, John K.**

1980   *Jesus and the Transformation of Judaism.* London: Darton, Longman & Todd, 1980, X-254 p. Esp. 44-61: "The study of the synoptic tradition: sources, methods and criteria"; 87-111: "Jesus' preaching of the kingdom"; 149-150 [6,25-33]; 150-151 [7,7-11]; 183-184 [11,19].

1983    The Sociology of Matthew. Some Basic Questions Concerning Its Relation to the Theology of the New Testament. — *SBL 1983 Seminar Papers*, 259-271. Esp. 265-266 [6,25-33].

1987    Die Synoptiker und ihre Gemeinden. — BECKER, J., et al. (eds.), *Die Anfänge des Christentums. Alte Welt und neue Hoffnung*, Stuttgart: Kohlhammer, 1987, 160-184. Esp. 168-178: "Gemeinde und Evangelium des Matthäus".

1992    The Actual Words of Jesus. — *ABD* 3 (1992) 802-804.

**RICHTER, Georg**

1957    *Die eschatologischen Eliasvorstellungen im Neuen Testament und ihre Vorgeschichte* [17,1-13]. Diss. Freiburg, 1957, XIV-232 p. (A. Vögtle).

1962    "Bist du Elias?" (Joh. 1,21). — *BZ* 6 (1962) 79-92, 238-256. Esp. 244-256: "Is 40,3 bei den Synoptikern" [3,3; 11,10]; 7 (1963) 63-80. [NTA 7, 178/539]; = ID., *Studien zum Johannesevangelium*, 1977, 1-41. Esp. 16-27.

1977a   *Studien zum Johannesevangelium*, ed. J. Hainz (BibUnt, 13). Regensburg: Pustet, 1977, IX-458 p. → 1962, 1977b

1977b   Zur Frage von Tradition und Redaktion in Joh 1,19-34. — *Ibid.*, 288-314. Esp. 299-302 [3,11/Jn].

**RICŒUR, Paul**

1990    The Golden Rule. Exegetical and Theological Perplexities. [7,12] — *NTS* 36 (1990) 392-397. [NTA 35, 138] → C. Theobald 1995, Thomasset 1996

**RIDDERBOS, Herman Nicolaas**

1950    *De komst van het Koninkrijk. Jezus' prediking volgens de Synoptische Evangelien.* Kampen: Kok, 1950, ²1972, 459 p.
        *The Coming of the Kingdom*, trans. H. de Jongste, ed. R.O. Zorn. Philadelphia, PA: Presbyterian & Reformed Publishing Co., 1962, XXXIV-556 p.
        Trans. Indonesian 1971.

1951    *Het Evangelie naar Mattheus.* I: *Hoofdstuk 1:1–16:12.* II: *Hoofdstuk 16:13–28:20* (Korte Verklaring der Heilige Schrift). Kampen: Kok, [1951]
        *Matthew*, trans. R. Togtman (Bible Student's Commentary). Grand Rapids, MI: Zondervan, 1987, III-556 p. [NTA 32, p. 109]
        D.A. CARSON, *JEvTS* 34 (1991) 124-125.

1958    *Het verborgen koninkrijk. Handleiding tot het Evangelie van Mattheus.* Kampen: Kok, 1958, 109 p.
        G. SEVENSTER, *NTT* 13 (1958-59) 375.
        *Matthew's Witness to Jesus Christ. The King and the Kingdom.* New York: Assoc. Press, 1958, 94 p.

1971    Tradition and Editorship in the Synoptic Gospels. — GEEHAN, E.R. (ed.), *Jerusalem and Athens. Critical Discussions on the Theology and Apologetics of Cornelius Van Til*, Nutley, NJ: Presbyterian and Reformed Publishing Co., 1971, 244-259. Esp. 248-257 [8-9].

1975    Jezus en de apokalyptiek. — *Ad Interim. Opstellen over Eschatologie, Apocalyptiek en Ethiek aangeboden aan Prof. Dr. R. Schippers*, Kampen: Kok, 1975, 23-42. Esp. 31-32 [kingdom]; 32-37 [Son of Man].

**RIDEZ, Louis**

1979    *Die Bergpredigt. Mensch sein nach Jesus. Mit einem Geleitwort von Erich Feifel* (Glaubens-Seminar, 1). Zürich–Köln: Benziger, 1979, 195-25 p.
        X. ALEGRE, *ActBibl* 18 (1981) 345-346.

1994    → Merklein 1994b

**RIDGWAY, John K.**

1991  A Correlation between Healing and Peace in Matt 10 1-16, Jesus' Commission to the Twelve. — *Proceedings EGLBS* 11 (1991) 104-115.

**RIEBL, Maria**

1978  *Auferstehung Jesu in der Stunde seines Todes? Zur Botschaft von Mt 27,51b-53* (SBB, 8). Stuttgart: Katholisches Bibelwerk, 1978, 93 p. Esp. 15-17: "Textkritik und Literarkritik"; 18-24: "Sprachliche Gestalt des Textes"; 25-41: "Motive"; 42-48: "Gattung"; 49-74: "Redaktion und Tradition"; 75-83: "Bibeltheologische Folgerungen". [NTA 23, p. 232] — Diss. Wien, 1975 (J. Kremer). F. BRÄNDLE, *EstJos* 33 (1979) 268; A. FUCHS, *SNTU* 6-7 (1981-82) 290-291; D. SENIOR, *CBQ* 42 (1980) 582-583.

1982  Nachfolge Jesu nach Ostern. Eine didaktisch aufbereitete Auslegung von Mt 8,23-27. — *BLtg* 55 (1982) 221-225. [NTA 27, 920]

1986  Die Erzählungen vom leeren Grab. Exegetisch-bibeltheologische Hinführung und Ausblick auf die Lesung der Texte in der Osternacht. — *BLtg* 59 (1986) 36-46. Esp. 41-42 [28,1-10]. [NTA 30, 1033]

**RIEDEL-SPANGENBERGER, Ilona**

1978  *Die Trennung von Tisch, Bett und Wohnung (cc. 1128-1132 CIC) und das Herrenwort Mk 10,9. Eine Untersuchung zur Theologie und Geschichte des kirchlichen Ehetrennungsrechts* (EHS, XXIII/102). Frankfurt/M-Bern: Lang, 1978, 227 p. Esp. 42-57: "Das Eheverständnis des Neuen Testamentes". — Diss. Münster, 1977 (H. Herrmann).

**RIEDINGER, Utto**

1960  Neue Hypotyposen-Fragmente bei Pseudo-Caesarius und Isidor von Pelusium. — *ZNW* 51 (1960) 154-196. Esp. 193-195 [Clement of Alexandria].

**RIEDL, Johannes**

1961  Reflexiones sobre la historia de la formas y la redacción de la promesa del Primado de Cristo (Mt 16,17ss). — *RevistBíb* 23 (1961) 61-73.

1963  Selig, die das Wort Gottes hören und befolgen (Lk 11,28). Theologisch-biblische Adventsbesinnung. — *BibLeb* 4 (1963) 252-260. Esp. 256-260 [1,18-25].

1965  Sie fanden das Kind mit Maria, seine Mutter (Mt 2,1-12). — *Am Tisch des Wortes* (Stuttgart) 7 (1965) 27-43.

1968a  *Die Vorgeschichte Jesu. Die Heilsbotschaft von Mt 1-2 und Lk 1-2* (Biblisches Forum, 3). Stuttgart: Katholisches Bibelwerk, 1968, 79 p. Esp. 14-45 [1-2]. [NTA 14, p. 111] J.M. ALONSO, *EphMar* 21 (1971) 341; J. DE JESÚS MARÍA, *EstJos* 26 (1972) 111; P.M. LUSTRISSIMI, *Marianum* 34 (1972) 289; K. WEISS, *BK* 24 (1969) 28. *I primi avvenimenti di Gesù*, trans. G. Colavero (Problemi d'oggi) Assisi: Cittadella, 1973, 104 p. F. BRAMBILLA, *ScuolC* 102 (1974) 219-220; R. GAUTHIER, *CahJos* 22 (1974) 264-265; F. SALVONI, *RicBibRel* 11 (1976) 81-84; A.M. SERRA, *Marianum* 37 (1975) 554-555.

1968b  Die evangelische Leidensgeschichte und ihre theologische Aussage. — *BLtg* 41 (1968) 70-111. [NTA 13, 104]

1973  Neutestamentliche Beispiele missionarischer Anpassung. — *Verbum SVD* 14 (1973) 44-84. Esp. 61-83: "Die missionstheologische Aussage von Mt (1-2)".

1991  Mt 1 und die Jungfrauengeburt. — OBERLINNER, L. - FIEDLER, P. (eds.), *Salz der Erde*. FS A. Vögtle, 1991, 91-109. Esp. 92-99: "Mt 1: Aufbau und Auslegung"; 99-108: "Jungfrauenempfängnis bzw. -geburt oder Gottessohnschaft?".

**RIEDLINGER, Helmut**

1966  *Geschichtlichkeit und Vollendung des Wissens Christi* (QDisp, 32). Freiburg: Herder, 1966, 160 p. Esp. 41-48.

**RIEGER, Josef**

1974   Die Speisungsgeschichte der Evangelien: Überholt oder aktuell? — MERKLEIN, H. –
LANGE, J. (eds.), *Biblische Randbemerkungen*. FS R. Schnackenburg, 1974, 33-39. Esp.
36 [15,32-39].

**RIEKERT, S.J.P.K.**

1982   The Narrative Coherence in Matthew 26-28. — *Neotestamentica* 16 (1982) 118-150
(addendum, 53-74).

**RIENECKER, Fritz**

1938[R]   *Sprachlicher Schlüssel zum Griechischen Neuen Testament nach der Ausgabe von D.
Eberhard Nestle* [1938]. Gießen–Basel: Brunnen, [8]1952, XXIII-636 p. Esp. 1-82; [9]1956;
[10]1960.

A Linguistic Key to the Greek New Testament. Vol. I: Matthew through Acts, trans. C.L. Rogers, Jr. Grand
Rapids, MI: Zondervan, 1976, XIV-345 p. Esp. 1-87; [2]1977. [NTA 21, p. 200]

1954   *Das Evangelium des Matthäus* (Wuppertaler Studienbibel). Wuppertal: Brockhaus,
1954; [3]1966, 384 p. Esp. 3-12 [introduction]; 13-379 [commentary]; [7]1974; [9]1977.

**RIESENFELD, Harald**

1950   → Lindeskog 1950a

1951   Ämbetet i Nya Testamentet. — LINDROTH, H. (ed.), *En bok om kyrkans ämbete*,
Uppsala, 1951, 19-69.

The Ministry in the New Testament. ["abridged version"] — FRIDRICHSEN, A., et al. (eds.), *The Root of the
Vine*, 1953, 96-127. Esp. 96-115.

Le ministère dans le Nouveau Testament. — ID., *Unité et diversité dans le Nouveau
Testament*, trans. L.-M. Dewailly (LD, 98), Paris: Cerf, 1979, 125-172. Esp. 128-138:
"Le ministère de Jésus"; 139-144: "Le ministère des disciples de Jésus".

1959   Les paraboles dans la prédication de Jésus selon les traditions synoptique et johannique.
— *Église et théologie* (Paris) 22 (1959) 21-29.

Liknelserna i den synoptiska och i den johanneiska traditionen. — *SEÅ* 25 (1960) 37-61.
Esp. 43 [21,33-44]; 44 [13,24-30.36-43]; 46-47 [18,12-14]. [NTA 6, 91]

The Parables in the Synoptic and in the Johannine Traditions. — ID., *The Gospel
Tradition*, 1970, 139-169. Esp. 146-147; 147-148; 151.

1961   Om skattsamlande och andra bekymmer – ett tema i urkristen parenes. Till Mt. 6:19-
34. — *Religion och Bibel* (Uppsala) 20 (1961) 30-40.

Vom Schätzesammeln und Sorgen – Ein Thema urchristlicher Paränese. Zu Mt vi 19-
34. — *Neotestamentica et Patristica*. FS O. Cullmann, 1962, 47-58.

1962   Le caractère messianique de la tentation au désert. [4,1-11] — MASSAUX, É. (ed.), *La
venue du Messie*, 1962, 51-63.

The Messianic Character of the Temptation in the Wilderness. — ID., *The Gospel Tradition*, 1970, 75-93.

1969a   Den envisa änkan eller liljorna på marken. [The stubborn widow or the lilies on the
ground] [6,25-28] — *Vad är människan värd?*, Stockholm: Verbum, 1969, 11-23; = ID.,
*I bibliskt perspektiv*, Stockholm: Verbum, 1971, 168-177.

1969b   Translating the Gospel in New Testament Times. — *The Church Crossing Frontiers.
Studies in Honour of B.S. Sundkler*, Uppsala, 1969, 20-26; = *SEÅ* 34 (1969) 43-50.
Esp. 43-45 [3,2; 4,17]. [NTA 15, 46]

1969c   Till frågan om den historiske Jesus. [On the question of the historical Jesus] — *Ibid.*,
51-76. Esp. 64-65 [22,1-14]; 70 [14,22-33]; 73 [8,23-27]. [NTA 15, 469]

1970   *The Gospel Tradition. Essays*, trans. E.M. Rowley & R.A. Kraft. Oxford: Blackwell;
Philadelphia, PA: Fortress, 1970, X-214 p. → 1959, 1962

1977   Guds söner och de heligas församling. [Sons of God and the congregation of the Holy Ones] — *SEÅ* 41-42 (1976-77) 179-188. Esp. 179-180 [5,9]; 184-185 [kingdom]. [NTA 23, 431]

1981   *Nya Testamentet. Bibelkommissionens utgåva 1981.* Stockholm: Skeab Förlag, 1981, 752 p. Esp. 1-86. → Sahlin 1984

1982   NT 81 och grundtexten. [NT 81 and the original text] — *SvenskTeolKvart* 58 (1982) 17-23. Esp. 18 [27,16-17]; 20-21 [5,32; 19,9]; 21-22 [16,18; 18,21-22]. [NTA 27, 470]

**RIESNER, Rainer**

1977   Wie sicher ist die Zwei-Quellen-Theorie? — *TBeitr* 8 (1977) 49-73. [NTA 21, 711]

1978   Der Aufbau der Reden im Matthäus-Evangelium. — *TBeitr* 9 (1978) 172-182. [NTA 23, 422]

1980   Wie steht es um die synoptische Frage? Gedanken zur Cambridge Griesbach Conference 1979. — *TBeitr* 11 (1980) 80-83. [NTA 25, 61] → W.R. Farmer 1983*

1981a  *Jesus als Lehrer. Eine Untersuchung zum Ursprung der Evangelien-Überlieferung* (WUNT, II/7). Tübingen: Mohr, 1981, XI-614 p.; ²1984; ³1988. Esp. 246-352: "Die Autorität Jesu" [7,24-27; 10,24-25; 11,3-6.16-19.25-26.27.28-30; 12,42; 23,5-7.8-10.37-39; 24,35; 26,18]; 353-407: "Die öffentliche Lehre" [13,9.24]; 408-498: "Die Jüngerlehre" [5,19; 8,19-22; 10,16.26-27.40; 11,25-26; 13,11-13.16-17; 19,28]. — Diss. Tübingen, 1980 (O. Betz).

1981b  Präexistenz und Jungfrauengeburt. — *TBeitr* 12 (1981) 177-187. Esp. 180-181 [23,37-39]. [NTA 26, 266]

1991   Jesus as Preacher and Teacher. — WANSBROUGH, H. (ed.), *Jesus and the Oral Gospel Tradition*, 1991, 185-210. Esp. 186-188.208-210 [Jesus as teacher].

1992a  Archaeology and Geography. — *DJG*, 1992, 33-46.

1992b  Teacher. — *Ibid.*, 807-811. Esp. 807.

1994   Auferstehung, Archäologie und Religionsgeschichte. — *TBeitr* 25 (1994) 319-326. Esp. 325-326. [NTA 39, 1433]

**RIESS, Richard**

1970   Psychologische Erwägungen zur Perikope von der Versuchung Jesu. — *Wege zum Menschen* (Göttingen) 22 (1970) 275-281.

**RIEW, Yong K.**

1983   *Biblical Principles Regarding the Missionary Role Found in the Gospel of Matthew.* Diss. Fuller Theol. Sem., Pasadena, CA, 1983.

**RIFE, John Merle**

1967   Matthew's Beatitudes and the Septuagint. — DANIELS, B.L. - SUGGS, M.J. (eds.), *Studies in the History and Text of the New Testament.* FS K.W. Clark, 1967, 107-112.

1975   *The Nature and Origin of the New Testament.* New York: Philosophical Library, 1975, XII-158 p. Esp. 78-84: "Matthew".

**RIGA, Peter J.**

1968   Reflections on the Beatitudes. — *BiTod* 39 (1968) 2731-2739. [NTA 13, 566]

1973a  Poverty as Counsel and as Precept. — *BiTod* 65 (1973) 1123-1128. Esp. 1126-1128 [19,16-22]. [NTA 17, 950]

1973b  The Kingdom and Celibacy. — *BiTod* 69 (1973) 1378-1384. [NTA 18, 811]

**RIGATO, Maria Luisa**

1969   Tradizione e redazione in Mc. 1,29-31 (e paralleli). La guarigione della suocera di Simon Pietro. — *RivBib* 17 (1969) 139-174. Esp. 162-167 [8,14-15]. [NTA 14, 503]

1992a  Riflessioni sulla sezione dei magi (Mt 2,1-12). — SERRA, A. - VALENTINI, A. (eds.), *I Vangeli dell'infanzia*, I, 1992, 119-127.

1992b   "Sarà chiamato Nazoreo" (Mt 2,23). — *Ibid.*, 129-141.

**RIGAUX, Béda**

1955   La formation des évangiles. Problème synoptique et Formgeschichte. Mise au point des débats sur le problème synoptique. — *ETL* 31 (1955) 658-664; = HEUSCHEN, J. (ed.), *La formation des évangiles*, 1957, 215-222.

1958   Révélation des mystères et perfection à Qumrân et dans le Nouveau Testament. — *NTS* 4 (1957-58) 237-262. Esp. 248-349 [τέλειος: 5,48; 19,21]. [NTA 3, 268]

1959   Βδέλυγμα τῆς ἐρημώσεως. Mc 13,14; Mt 24,15. — *Bib* 40 (1959) 675-683. [NTA 4, 663]; = *Studia Biblica et Orientalia*, II, 1959, 107-115.

1960   Die "Zwölf" in Geschichte und Kerygma. — RISTOW, H. - MATTHIAE, K. (eds.), *Der historische Jesus und der kerygmatische Christus*, 1960, 468-486. Esp. 471-472 [οἱ δώδεκα]; 476-477 [19,28]; 477-478 [27,3-10]; = KERTELGE, K. (ed.), *Das kirchliche Amt*, 1977, 280-304. Esp. 284-285; 288-289; 289-290.

1962   La seconde venue de Jésus. — MASSAUX, É. (ed.), *La venue du Messie*, 1962, 173-216. Esp. 182-183; 188-199 [kingdom]; 199-212 [Son of Man].

1967a   *Témoignage de l'évangile de Matthieu* (Pour une histoire de Jésus, 2). Brugge–Paris: Desclée De Brouwer, 1967, 307 p. Esp. 13-31: "Prolégomènes"; 33-55: "Le bon scribe"; 57-94: "'Alors paraît Jésus' (Mt 3,13)"; 95-131: "Les discours"; 133-153: "Enfance, passion et résurrection"; 155-178: "Matthieu devant ses sources"; 179-190: "Eschatologie et Église"; 191-200: "Le rejet d'Israël"; 201-218: "L'Église de Matthieu"; 219-242: "Accomplir toute justice"; 243-266: "Jésus Christ"; 267-276: "Les titres du Messie"; 277-284: "Le fils du Dieu vivant"; 285-299: "Nova et vetera". [NTA 13, p. 159]
        M. BOUTTIER, *ETR* 43 (1968) 247-248; M.P. BROWN, JR., *JBL* 88 (1969) 219-220; J. COPPENS, *ETL* 44 (1968) 657-658; J. DUPONT, *RHE* 63 (1968) 226-227; M. FALLET, *RTP* 20 (1970) 120-121; P. FRANQUESA, *EphMar* 20 (1970) 500; H., *PalCl* 49 (1970) 254; X. JACQUES, *NRT* 93 (1971) 429-430; J. KAHMANN, *TijdTheol* 8 (1968) 451; A. KERRIGAN, *Ant* 51 (1976) 331-334; R. LAPOINTE, *RevUnivOtt* 40 (1970) 170-171; M.-É. LAUZIÈRE, *RThom* 68 (1968) 450; N.J. McELENEY, *CBQ* 31 (1969) 601-602; J. MURPHY O'CONNOR, *RB* 78 (1971) 155; B. PIEPIÓRKA, *ZKT* 91 (1969) 223; L. POIRIER, *Culture* (Québec) 29 (1968) 92-93; S. RABACCHI, *Sacra Doctrina* (Bologna) 14 (1969) 539-540; R.M. SALERNI, *Servitium* 4 (1970) 414; A. SAND, *MüTZ* 20 (1969) 347; R. WALKER, *TLZ* 94 (1969) 670-671.
        *The Testimony of St. Matthew*, trans. P.J. Oligny (Herald Scriptural Library). Chicago, IL: Franciscan Herald, 1968, XIII-223 p.
        *Het getuigenis van Matteüs*, trans. O. de Nobel (De geschiedenis van Jezus, 2). Brugge–Utrecht: Desclée De Brouwer, 1969, 373 p. Esp. 17-39; 41-68; 69-115; 117-161; 163-187; 189-217; 219-232; 233-244; 245-266; 267-295; 297-325; 327-338; 339-348; 349-366.
        L. SEYNHAEVE, *Librije* (Steenbrugge) 5/1 (1969) 9; J.M. TISON, *Bijdragen* 30 (1969) 315.
        *El testimonio del Evangelio de S. Mateo* (Para una historía de Jesús, 2; Temas bíblicos, 8). Bilbao: Desclée De Brouwer, 1969, 319 p.
        J.A. CARRASCO, *EstJos* 24 (1970) 245; J.M. CASCIARO, *EstBíb* 30 (1971) 120-121; B. CELADA, *CuBíb* 26 (1969) 227-230; S. GONZÁLEZ DE CARREA, *EstBíb* 31 (1972) 350-351; A. SALAS, *CiudDios* 182 (1969) 633; R.M. SANZ DE DIEGO, *RazFe* 181 (1970) 216-217; F. de B. VIZMANOS, *EstE* 46 (1971) 555.
        *Testimonianza del vangelo di Matteo*, trans. P. Pampaloni (Per una storia di Gesù, 2). Padova: Gregoriana, 1969, 334 p.
        L. TURRADO, *Salmanticensis* 18 (1971) 163.

1967b   Saint Pierre et l'exégèse contemporaine. — *Concilium* (Paris) 27 (1967) 129-152.
        Der Apostel Petrus in der heutigen Exegese. — *IZT/Concilium* (Mainz) 3 (1967) 585-600.
        De heilige Petrus en de hedendaagse exegese. — *Concilium* (Hilversum) 3/7 (1967) 135-166. Esp. 148-157.

1970   La petite apocalypse de Luc (XVII,22-37). — COPPENS, J. (ed.), *Ecclesia a Spiritu Sancto edocta. Lumen Gentium, 53. Mélanges théologiques. Hommage à Mgr Gérard Philips. Verzamelde theologische Opstellen aangeboden aan Mgr. Gérard Philips* (BETL, 27), Gembloux: Duculot, 1970, 407-438. Esp. 413-416 [Q 17,23-24]; 419-423 [Q 17,26-30]; 426-429 [Q 17,33-35]; 430-431 [Q 17,37].

1971 Le radicalisme du Règne. [8,18-23] — GEORGE, A., et al. (eds.), *La pauvreté*, 1971, 135-173. Esp. 150 [10,5-8]; 157-166: "Le Règne de Dieu" [7,1?-14; 8,21-22; 10,37-38; 19,12.27-30]. The Radicalism of the Kingdom. — GEORGE, A., et al. (eds.), *Gospel Poverty*, 1977, 123-162.

1972 Le célibat et le radicalisme évangélique. — *NRT* 94 (1972) 157-170. Esp. 166-168 [19,10-12]. [NTA 16, 1011]

1973 *Dieu l'a ressuscité. Exégèse et théologie biblique* (Studii Biblici Franciscani Analecta, 4). Gembloux: Duculot, 1973, XII-474 p. Esp. 24-39 [22,?3-33/Mk]; 200-204 [28,1-8]; 223 [28,9-10]; 254-258 [28,16-20].
*Dio l'ha risuscitato. Esegesi e teologia biblica*, trans. R. Penna (Parola di Dio, 13). Cinisello Balsamo-Milano: Paoline, 1976, 637 p.

1974 "Lier et délier". Les ministères de réconciliation dans l'Église des temps apostoliques. — *La Maison-Dieu* (Paris) 117 (1974) 86-135. Esp. 87-106: "Situation et exégèse de Matthieu 16"; 106-115: "Lier et délier dans Matthieu 18,18"; 115-124: "Extension et pouvoir du lier-délier". [NTA 19, 263]

**RIGGANS, Walter**
1985 The Use of the Tanach in the Gospel according to Matthew. — *Mishkan* (Jerusalem) 3 (1985) 27-36 (37-45, response S.A. Swanson).

1991 Jesus and the Scriptures: Two Short Notes. [26,11] — *Themelios* 16/2 (1991) 15-16. [NTA 35, 1153]

**RIGGI, Calogero**
1971 S. Epifanio divorzista? — *Sal* 33 (1971) 599-666. Esp. 602-613: "La nostra recostruzione di Haer. 59,4, secondo le risonanze matteane".

1994 La giuntura "Imperium immo Consilium" nell'esegesi di Cassiano alla pericope matteana sul giovane ricco (*Conl* 24.24). [19,16-22] — FELICI, S. (ed.), *Esegesi e catechesi nei Padri*, 1994, 121-146.

**RIGGS, Douglas**
1991 *A Rhetorical-Critical Interpretation of the Divorce and Remarriage Passages in the Synoptic Gospels*. Diss. Southwestern Baptist Theol. Sem., Fort Worth, TX, 1991, 267 p. (T. Urrey). — *DissAbstr* 52 (1991-1992) 2589.

**RIJK, Cornelius A.**
1974 Andere Gebete Jesu. — BROCKE, M., et al. (eds.), *Das Vaterunser*, 1974, 196-208.

**RIJKHOFF, Martien**
1967 Christus' maagdelijke geboorte volgens Lukas en Matteüs. — *Ons Geestelijk Leven* 43 (1967) 293-307. Esp. 296-299.

1971 Maar Ik zeg u... (Mt 5,21-48). — *Ons Geestelijk Leven* 48 (1971) 4-13.

1983 → Lukken 1983

**RILEY, Gregory J.**
1994 The *Gospel of Thomas* in Recent Scholarship. — *Currents in Research: Biblical Studies* (Sheffield) 2 (1994) 227-252. Esp. 232-236 [synoptics/Th]; 2?7-238 [Q/Th]; 240-243 [Mt/Th]. [NTA 39, 1274]

1995 Influence of Thomas Christianity on Luke 12:14 and 5:39. — *HTR* 88 (1995) 229-235. Esp. 232-234 [Q 5,39/Th]. [NTA 40, 1504]

**RILEY, Harold**
1987 Internal Evidence. — ORCHARD, B. - RILEY, H., *The Order of the Synoptics*, 1987, 1-108. Esp. 3-18: "The significance of order"; 19-35: "The thematic order of Matthew"; 36-50: "Matthew and Mark"; 100-104: "Styler's key passages" [9,14; 14,3-12; 19,16-22; 22,41-46; 24,3; 27,15-18].

1989 *The Making of Mark. An Exploration.* Macon, GA: Mercer University Press, 1989, XX-268 p. Esp. 238-246: "Authorship and date of the synoptics: Matthew".
T.A. FRIEDRICHSEN, *ETL* 66 (1990) 410-413; G. MURRAY, *DownR* 108 (1990) 225-229; C.M. TUCKETT, *JTS* 42 (1991) 193-195; W.O. WALKER, Jr., *JBL* 110 (1991) 346-348.

1992 *The First Gospel.* Macon, GA: Mercer, 1992, 130 p. Esp. 7-22: "Doublets"; 23-36: "Narrative continuity"; 37-45: "The apocalyptic discourse"; 47-59: "The apostolic commission"; 51-55: "The parable collection"; 57-59: "The discourse on true greatness"; 61-68: "The Sermon on the Mount"; 69-92: "Proto-Matthew"; 93-99: "Additions to Proto-Matthew"; 101-113: "Matthew and Luke"; 121-124: "Proto-Matthew – A tentative reconstruction". [NTA 37, p. 284] → G. Murray 1994
H.A. BREHM, *SWJT* 35/3 (1992-93) 45; M. DAVIES, *ExpT* 104 (1992-93) 279; J. KLOPPENBORG, *TorontoJT* 10 (1994) 126-127; E.C. MALONEY, *CBQ* 56 (1994) 383-385; F. NEIRYNCK, *ETL* 69 (1993) 179-180.

**RIMOLDI, Antonio**

1958 *L'Apostolo San Pietro fondamento della Chiesa, principe degli apostoli ed ostario celeste nella Chiesa primitiva dalle origine al Concilio di Calcedonia* (AnGreg, 96). Roma: Pont. Univ. Greg., 1958, XIX-356 p. Esp. 41-46, 53-58, 61-64, 67-72, 79-83, 87-91, 99-110, 114-120, 124-128, 134-137, 143-155, 160-198, 204-212, 214-224, 256-262, 271-282, 309-317, 321-324, 327-330, 335-338, 342-346 [16,13-19]. — Diss. Pont. Univ. Greg., Roma, 1957 (V. Monachino).

**RINALDI, Bonaventura**

1965 Venite a me mite e umile di cuore (Mt 11,29). — *Fonti Vive* 11 (1965) 137-147.

**RINALDI, Giancarlo**

1989 *Biblia gentium. Primo contributo per un indice delle citazioni, dei riferimenti e delle allusioni alla Bibbia negli autori pagani, greci e latini, di età imperiale. A First Contribution towards an Index of Biblical Quotations, References and Allusions Made by Greek and Heathen Writers of the Roman Imperial Times.* Roma: Libreria Sacre Scritture, 1989, 752 p. Esp. 422-491: "Matteo".

**RINALDI, Giovanni**

1954 Il messianesimo tra le Genti in San Matteo. — *RivBib* 2 (1954) 318-324.

1967 Onus meum leve. Osservazioni su *Ecclesiastico* 51 (v. 26, Volg. 34) e *Matteo* 11,25-30. — *BibOr* 9 (1967) 13-23. Esp. 20-23. [NTA 11, 1031]

1968 Παραλαμβάνω. [1,20.24] — *BibOr* 10 (1968) 140.

1972 "Sì, sì, no, no" (Mt 5,37; Giac. 5,12). — *BibOr* 14 (1972) 106.

**RINCON, Alfredo**

1972 *Tú eres Pedro. Interpretación de "piedra" en Mat. 16,18 y sus relaciones con el tema bíblico de la edificación* (Colección Teológica). Pamplona: Ediciones Universidad de Navarra, 1972, 163 p. Esp. 11-52: "Introducción"; 53-85: "Πέτρος"; 87-127: "El contexto de la construcción"; 129-146: "La piedra y la edificatión". [NTA 18, p. 387] — Diss. Pamplona, 1971 (J.M. Casciaro Ramirez).

**RING, R.E.**

1964 La komisiigo de Petro (Mt 16,17ss). — *Biblia Revuo* (Melbourne) 1 (1964) 52-54.

**RINGE, Sharon H.**

1985a *Jesus, Liberation, and the Biblical Jubilee. Images for Ethics and Christology* (Overtures to Biblical Theology, 19). Philadelphia, PA: Fortress, 1985, XVIII-124 p. Esp. 45-49 [11,2-6]; 51-54 [5,3-6]; 54-60 [Q 14,16-24 (Lk)]; 63-64 [26,6-13/Mk]; 71-74 [9,1-8/Mk]; 74-77 [18,21-35]; 77-80 [6,12.14-15]; 81-874 [6,9-13]. — Diss. Union Theol. Sem., New York, 1981 (R.E. Brown).

1985b A Gentile Woman's Story. [15,21-28] — RUSSELL, L.M. (ed.), *Feminist Interpretation of the Bible*, Philadelphia, PA: Westminster, 1985, 65-72.

**RINGGER, Johannes**

1959 Das Felsenwort. Zur Sinndeutung von Mt 16,18, vor allem im Lichte der Symbolgeschichte. — ROESLE, M. — CULLMANN, O. (eds.), *Begegnung der Christen.* FS O. Karrer, 1959, 271-347. Esp. 273-279 [πέτρα]; 279-285 [16,18: symbolic interpretation]; 285-291 [16,18/Qumran]; 291-298 [16,18/Hermas]; 298-304 [16,18/rabbinism]; 304-310 [interpretation].

**RINGGREN, Helmer**

1985 The Use of Psalms in the Gospels. — GROH, D.E. - JEWETT, R. (eds.), *The Living Text.* FS E.W. Saunders, 1985, 39-43. Esp. 40 [16,27; 21,16]; 40-41 [4,6]; 41 [13,35; 21,9].

**RINGSHAUSEN, Gerhard**

1986 Die Kinder der Weisheit. Zur Auslegung von Mk 10,13-16 par. — *ZNW* 77 (1986) 34-63. Esp. 50-53 [10,40.42; 18,6-9.10]; 60-63 [19,13-15]. [NTA 31, 140]

**RINIKER, Christian**

1992 *Die Gerichtsverkündigung Jesu.* Diss. Bern, 1992, 567 p. (U. Luz).

**RINIKER, H.**

1987 Die Bergpredigt heute. — *Reformiertes Forum* (Zürich-Basel) 1/33 (1987) 11-14. [NTA 32, 116] → Gnilka 1986, Luz 1985a, Weder 1985a

**RIOU, Alain**

1973 *Le monde et l'Église selon Maxime le Confesseur* (Théologie historique, 22). Paris: Beauchesne, 1973, 279 p. Esp. 214-239: "Traduction: Commentaire du Notre Père".

**RIPOLL, Francis**

1977 The Infancy Narratives and Mary. — *Bible Bhashyam* 3 (1977) 297-302. [NTA 22, 757]

1980 The Parabolic Teaching of Jesus on the Kingdom Based on Mt 13. — *Bible Bhashyam* 6 (1980) 207-212. [NTA 25, 479]

1984 The Beatitudes of the Kingdom. — *Bible Bhashyam* 10 (1984) 85-88. [NTA 29, 517]

**RIQUELME, Julián**

1974 Significación del bautismo de Jesús. [3,13-17] — *TVida* 15 (1974) 115-139. [NTA 19, 552]

**RIST, John M.**

1978 *On the Independence of Matthew and Mark* (SNTS MS, 32). Cambridge: University Press, 1978, VIII-132 p. Esp. 17-33: "The literary hypothesis: some preliminary tests (Mt 3:1–9:17)"; 34-55: "Vocabulary and sequence: Matthew's version of Mk 2:23–6:13"; 56-62: "More skimpings and bowollerizings in Matthew" [8,23-27; 9,18-26; 13,53-58; 17,14-20 19,16-30]; 63-67: "A turning point in the tradition (Mt 14:1; Mk 6:14; Lk 9:7)"; 68-71: "Some passages about Peter in Matthew" [14,28-31; 15,15; 16,17-19; 17,24-27; 18,21-22]; 72-88: "From Caesarea Philippi to the burial of Jesus"; 109-111: "M.D. Goulder on the synoptic problem". → Ingelaere 1981
J.W. CROWE, *AusBR* 27 (1979) 62-63; B. DEHANDSCHUTTER, *NTT* 33 (1979) 311-312; A. DERMIENCE, *RTL* 14 (1983) 114-115; A. FUCHS, *SNTU* 6-7 (1981-82) 242-246; M.D. GOULDER, *JTS* 30 (1979) 265-267); D. HILL, *ScotJT* 32 (1979) 583-584; C.R. KAZMIERSKI, *CBQ* 41 (1979) 494-495; T.R.W. LONGSTAFF, *JBL* 100 (1981) 127-130; J.B. ORCHARD, *HeythJ* 20 (1979) 191-192; V. PARKIN, *IBS* 2 (1980) 54-57; C.S. RODD, *ExpT* 89 (1977-78) 355-356; G. SEGALLA, *Studia Patavina* 27 (1980) 191-193; H.-H. STOLDT, *TZ* 35 (1979) 246-248; R. TREVIJANO, *Salmanticensis* 26 (1979) 313-315.

**RISTOW, Helmut**

1960* & MATTHIAE, K. (eds.), *Der historische Jesus und der kerygmatische Christus. Beiträge zum Christusverständnis in Forschung und Verkündigung.* Berlin: Evangelische Verlagsanstalt, 1960, ²1961, ³1964, 710 p. → Delling, E. Fuchs, Goppelt, W. Michaelis, Rigaux, Schnackenburg, Schürmann

**RITT, Hubert**

1983 Die Frauen und die Osterbotschaft. Synopse der Grabesgeschichten (Mk 16,1-8; Mt 27,62–28,15; Lk 24,1-12; Joh 20,1-18). — DAUTZENBERG, G., et al. (eds.), *Die Frau im Urchristentum*, 1983, 117-133. Esp. 119-121; 124-125.

1987 "Wer war schuld am Tod Jesu?" Zeitgeschichte, Recht und theologische Deutung. — *BZ* 31 (1987) 165-175. Esp. 167-169. [NTA 32, 88]

**RITTMUELLER, J.**

1981 The Hiberno-Latin Background of the Matthew Commentary of Maél-Brigte va Maéluanaig. — DOAN, J.E. - BUTTIMER, C.G. (eds.), *Proceedings of the Harvard Celtic Colloquium*, Cambridge, MA: Harvard University Press, 1981.

1983 The Gospel Commentary of Maél Brigte ua Maéluanaig and Its Hiberno-Latin Background. — *Peritia* (Cork) 2 (1983) 185-214.

1993 MS Vat. Reg. Lat. 49 Reviewed: A New Description and a Table of Textual Parallels with the *Liber Questionum in Evangeliis*. — *Sacris Erudiri* (Steenbrugge) 33 (1992-93) 259-305.

**RIUDOR, Ignacio**

1962 Réflexions de caractère didactique à propos de Mt. 18,18 et Lc. 22,32. — *Sal* 24 (1962) 260-265. Esp. 262-263 [18,18].

**RIUS-CAMPS, Josep**

1989* & SÁNCHEZ BOSCH, J. - PIÉ I NINOT, S. (eds.), *In medio ecclesiae. Miscellània en homenatge al Prof. Dr. Isidre Gomà I Civit* (Revista Catalana de Teologia, 14). Barcelona: Facultat de Teologia de Catalunya, 1989, 578 p. → Camps I Gaset, Casciaro Ramirez, Mensa I Valls, G. Mora, Muñoz Iglesias, Muñoz León, Nicolau, O'Callaghan, Perarnau I Espelt, Rovira Belloso, Taradach, Tena Montero, Villegas

**RIVA, Franco**

1983 Metodi d'esegesi strutturale dei racconti evangelici confronto per una discussione. — *RivBib* 31 (1983) 293-327. Esp. 299-301.304-306 [26,1-5]. [NTA 28, 851]

**RIVA, R.**

1990 Il pastore, ministro della mensa della Parola. Le omelie di san Giovanni Crisostomo su Mt 18. Criteri esegetici e indicazioni per l'ermeneutica biblica. — AUTIERO, A. - CARENA, O. (eds.), *Pastor bonus in populo. Figura, ruolo, e funzioni del vescovo nella Chiesa*, Roma: Citta Nuova, 1990, 241-263.

**RIVAS, Luis Heriberto**

1970a Los bienes y la justicia. La pobreza: opción de vida y precendencia de valores. — *RevistBíb* 32 (1970) 245-251. [NTA 15, 499]

1970b "Poner la otra mejilla". Estudio sobre la redacción de *Mt* 5,39-41 y *Lc* 6,29-30. — *Teología* 8 (1970) 62-69.

1972 El "Padre Nuestro" en el evangelio según san Mateo. — *Teología* 10 (1972-73) 16-24.

1977 *La oración que Jesús nos enseñó* (Esperanza, 24). Buenos Aires: Patria Granda, 1977, 96 p.

**RIVERA, Luis Fernando**

1953 Cristo y el divorcio. [5,32; 19,9] — *RevistBíb* 15 (1953) 5-9.

1958 "Abraham, Isaac y Jacob" y la Resurrección. [22,32] — *RevistBíb* 20 (1958) 199-202.

1964 El relato de la Transfiguración en Mateo. Estudio de crítica literaria. — *RevistBíb* 26 (1964) 31-40. [NTA 9, 156]

1970 La fe según el NT. — *RevistBíb* 32 (1970) 131-145. [NTA 15, 671]

1974 Conversión, arrepentimiento y penitencia. [28,20] — *RevistBíb* 36 (1974) 105-112. [NTA 19, 472]

**RIVKIN, Ellis**

1978 Scribes, Pharisees, Lawyers, Hypocrites: A Study in Synonymity. — *HUCA* 49 (1978) 135-142. Esp. 135-138. [NTA 24, 72]

**RIZZI, Armido**

1991 L'uomo d'oggi di fronte al discorso della montagna. Attualità o utopia? [5-7] — *Credere oggi* 11 (1991) 101-108.

**ROARK, Dallas M.**

1964 The Great Eschatological Discourse. — *NT* 7 (1964-65) 123-127. [NTA 9, 924]

**ROBBINS, Vernon K.**

1982 Pronouncement Stories and Jesus' Blessing of Children: A Rhetorical Approach. — *SBL 1982 Seminar Papers*, 407-430. Esp. 414-415 [19,13-15]; 425 [18,1-5]; = *Semeia* 29 (1983) 43-74. Esp. 53-55; 66-68. [NTA 28, 940]; = ID., *New Boundaries in Old Territory*, 1994, 155-184. Esp. 163-165; 177-178.

1984 A Rhetorical Typology for Classifying and Analyzing Pronouncement Stories. — *SBL 1984 Seminar Papers*, 93-122. Esp. 106 [12,1-8].

1985 Pragmatic Relations as a Criterion for Authentic Sayings. — *Forum* 1/3 (1985) 35-63. Esp. 38-56 [5,3-12]; 57-60 [5,38-42]. [NTA 31, 567]

1987a Rhetorical Argument about Lamps and Light in Early Christian Gospels. — BØCKMAN, P.W. – KRISTIANSEN, R.E. (eds.), *Context. Festskrift til Peder Johan Borgen. Essays in Honour of Peder Johan Borgen* ("Relieff", 24), Trondheim: Tapir, 1987, 177-195. Esp. 189-193 [5,15]; = ID., *New Boundaries in Old Territory*, 1994, 201-217. Esp. 212-215.

1987b The Woman Who Touched Jesus' Garment: Socio-rhetorical Analysis of the Synoptic Accounts. — *NTS* 33 (1987) 502-515. Esp. 504-507: "The Matthean version". [NTA 32, 599]; = ID., *New Boundaries in Old Territory*, 1994, 185-200. Esp. 188-192.

1988a The Chreia. — AUNE, D.E. (ed.), *Greco-Roman Literature and the New Testament. Selected Forms and Genres* (SBL. Source for Biblical Study, 21), Atlanta, GA: Scholars, 1988, 1-23.

1988b The Crucifixion and the Speech of Jesus. [27,11-54] — *Forum* 4/1 (1988) 33-46. [NTA 33, 581]

1988c Pronouncement Stories from a Rhetorical Perspective. — *Forum* 4/2 (1988) 3-32. Esp. 16 [9,20-22]; 24 [19,16-22]; 25-27 [12,22-37]. [NTA 33, 532]

1989a Chreia & Pronouncement Study in Synoptic Studies. — MACK, B.L. – ROBBINS V.K., *Patterns of Persuasion in the Gospels* (Foundations and Facets), Sonoma, CA: Polebridge, 1989, 1-29. Esp. 20-22 [4,12-17].

1989b Foxes, Birds, Burials & Furrows. — *Ibid.*, 69-84. Esp. 70-74 [8,18-22]; 74-83 [Q 9,57-62].

1989c Plucking Grain on the Sabbath. — *Ibid.*, 107-141. Esp. 110-119: "The common synoptic theory"; 132-139: "The version in Matt 12:1-8".

1989d Rhetorical Composition & the Beelzebul Controversy. — *Ibid.*, 161-193. Esp. 163-167: "The common synoptic tradition"; 167-171: "The earliest tradition (Matt 9:32-34)"; 177-185: "The version in Matt 12:22-37"; 185-191: "The version in Luke 11:18-28".

1990 A Socio-rhetorical Response: Contexts of Interaction and Forms of Exhortation. — *Semeia* 50 (1990) 261-271. Esp. 264-267 (A.-J. Levine 1990); 267-269 (J.G. Williams 1990).

1991a Beelzebul Controversy in Mark and Luke. Rhetorical and Social Analysis. — *Forum* 7 (1991) 261-277. Esp. 264-276 [Q 11,14-35]. [NTA 38, 794]

1991b  Writing as a Rhetorical Act in Plutarch and the Gospels. — WATSON, D.F. (ed.),
       *Persuasive Artistry*. FS G.A. Kennedy, 1991, 142-168. Esp. 151-153 [8,14-15]; 153-155 [4,18-
       22]; 160-166 [9,20-22].

1993a  Progymnastic Rhetorical Composition and Pre-Gospel Traditions: A New Approach. —
       FOCANT, C. (ed.), *The Synoptic Gospels*, 1993, 111-147. Esp. 137-140: "Mt 5,3-12 and Lk
       6,20-26".

1993b  Rhetoric and Culture: Exploring Types of Cultural Rhetoric in a Text. — PORTER, S.E.
       – OLBRICHT, T.H. (eds.), *Rhetoric in the New Testament. Essays from the 1992
       Heidelberg Conference* (JSNT SS, 90), Sheffield: JSOT, 1993, 443-463. Esp. 451-454 [Q:
       cynics].

1993c  → Dean-Otting 1993

1994   *New Boundaries in Old Territory. Form and Social Rhetoric in Mark* (Emory Studies
       in Early Christianity, 3). New York: Lang, 1994, XX-270 p. → 1982, 1987a-b

**ROBERT, André** → Tricot 1939

**ROBERT, René**
1987   Le témoignage d'Irénée sur la formation des évangiles. — *RThom* 87 (1987) 243-259.
       Esp. 246-248. [NTA 32, 72]

**ROBERTS, Colin H.**
1950   *The Antinoopolis Papyri*, I. London: Egypt Exploration Society, 1950, XII-119 p. Esp.
       23-24 [0231].

1953   An Early Papyrus of the First Gospel. [P⁶⁴·⁶⁷] — *HTR* 46 (1953) 233-237.

**ROBERTS, James Hall**
1964   *The Q Document*. New York: William Morrow, 1964; Greenwich, CT: Fawcett, 1965.

1967   The Sermon on the Mount and the Idea of Liberty. — *Neotestamentica* 1 (1967) 9-15.
       [NTA 18, 103]

**ROBERTS, J.S.**
1965   The Old Testament and the Historicity of the Gospels. — *LondQuartHolRev* 34 (1965)
       44-49. [NTA 9, 848] → Farrer 1954

**ROBERTS, J.W.**
1958   A Note on εἰς in Mt 12:41. — *RestQ* 2 (1958) 19-21.

1972   The Meaning of Ekklesia in the New Testament. — *RestQ* 15 (1972) 27-36. [NTA 17,
       446]

**ROBERTS, R.L.**
1963   An Evil Eye (Matthew 6:23). — *RestQ* 7 (1963) 143-147. [NTA 9, 151]

**ROBERTS, T.A.**
1958   Some Comments on Matthew x.34-36 and Luke xii.51-53. — *ExpT* 69 (1957-58) 304-
       306. [NTA 3, 75]

**ROBERTSON, Arthur**
1983   *Matthew*. Chicago, IL: Moody, 1983, 168 p.

**ROBERTSON, Malcolm J., III**
1990   The Present State of Matthaean Studies in Consequence of Fresh Perspectives. —
       SKILTON, J.H. (ed.), *The Gospels Today*, 1990, 38-50.

**ROBINSON, Bernard P.**
1984   Peter and his Successors: Tradition and Redaction in Matthew 16.17-19. — *JSNT* 21
       (1984) 85-104. Esp. 86-95: "Tradition"; 95-98: "Redaction". [NTA 29, 106]

**ROBINSON, Donald W.B.**

1964   The Eucharistic Sacrifice in the Sacrament of the Body and Blood of Christ. [26,26-29]
       — *RTR* 23/3 (1964) 65-74. [NTA 9, 931]

**ROBINSON, G.**

1995   The Sermon on the Mount and Eschatology. — *Banga!TF* 27/3-4 (1995) 30-41. [NTA 41, 201]

**ROBINSON, James M.** → IQP

1959   *A New Quest of the Historical Jesus* (Studies in Biblical Theology, 25). London: SCM, 1959, 128 p. Esp. 116-121 [11,2-19]; = ID, *A New Quest*, 1983, 9-125. Esp. 116-121.
       *Kerygma und historischer Jesus.* Zürich–Stuttgart: Zwingli, 1960, 192 p. Esp. 143-148; 161-166; ²1967, 264 p. [39-134 = 1960]. Esp. 207-214; 226-230.
       *Le kérygme de l'Église et le Jésus de l'histoire*, trans. E. de Peyer (Nouvelle série théologique, 11). Genève: Labor et Fides, 1961, 157 p.
       *Kerygma e Gesù storico*, trans. G. Torti (Biblioteca teologica, 12). Brescia: Paideia, 1977, 286 p.

1962a  Basic Shifts in German Theology. — *Interpr* 16 (1962) 76-97. Esp. 82-86 [Q]. [NTA 6, 677]

1962b  The Formal Structure of Jesus' Message. — KLASSEN, W. – SNYDER, G.F. (eds.),
       *Current Issues in New Testament Interpretation. Essays in Honor of Otto A. Piper*, New York: Harper; London: SCM, 1962, 91-110, 273-284. Esp. 102-105 [parallelism]; = ID.,
       *A New Quest*, 1983, 126-152. Esp. 140-144.

1964   Λογοὶ σοφῶν. Zur Gattung der Spruchquelle Q. — DINKLER, E. (ed.), *Zeit und Geschichte*. FS R. Bultmann, 1964, 77-96. Esp. 79-84 [Gnosis]; 84-91 [Quelle]; 91-96 [Jewish wisdom literature]; = ID. — KOESTER, H. (eds.), *Entwicklungslinien*, 1970, 67-106.
       Logoi Sophon: On the *Gattung* of Q. — ID. (ed.), *The Future of Our Religious Past*. FS R. Bultmann, 1971, 84-130 (enlarged version). Esp. 87-100: "Logia, logoi and gospel in the Coptic gnostic library"; 100-110: "Primitive christian collections of Jesus' sayings"; 111-119: "From the quotation formula to the collection of sayings"; 119-130: "Jewish wisdom literature and the Gattung *logoi sophon*"; = ID. — KOESTER, H. (eds.), *Trajectories*, 1971, 71-113. Esp. 74-85; 85-95; 95-103; 103-113. → Hodgson 1985
       Jewish Wisdom Literature and the Gattung, Logoi sophon. [1971, 103-113] — KLOPPENBORG, J.S. (ed.), *The Shape of Q*, 1994, 51-58.

1965   Kerygma und Geschichte im Neuen Testament. — *ZTK* 62 (1965) 294-337. Esp. 312-314 [1 Cor/Q]; 324-326 [Q 7,1-10]. [NTA 11, 66]; = ID. — KOESTER, H. (eds.), *Entwicklungslinien*, 1970, 20-66.
       Kerygma and History in the New Testament. — HYATT, J.P. (ed.), *The Bible in Modern Scholarship. Papers Read at the 100th Meeting of the Society of Biblical Literature. December 28-30, 1964*, Nashville, TN: Abingdon, 1965, 114-150 (responses D.M. Stanley, 151-159; F.V. Filson, 160-165). Esp. 129-130; 139-141; = ID. — KOESTER, H. (eds.), *Trajectories*, 1971, 20-70. Esp. 42-44; 56-58.

1970*  & KOESTER, H. (eds.), *Entwicklungslinien durch die Welt des frühen Christentums.*
       Tübingen: Mohr, 1970, XII-276 p. → 1964, 1965, Koester 1965, 1968
       *Trajectories through Early Christianity*. Philadelphia, PA: Fortress, 1971, XII-297 p. → 1964, 1965, Koester 1965, 1968
       Trans. Japanese 1975.

1971*  (ed.), *The Future of Our Religious Past. Essays in Honour of Rudolf Bultmann*, trans. C.E. Carlston & R.P. Scharlemann. London: SCM; New York: Harper & Row, 1971, XI-372 p. [German → Dinkler 1964*] → G. Bornkamm 1964, Dinkler 1964, Kümmel 1964, J.M. Robinson 1964

1975   Jesus as Sophos and Sophia: Wisdom Tradition and the Gospels. — WILKEN, R.L. (ed.), *Aspects of Wisdom*, 1975, 1-16.

1982a  Early Collections of Jesus' Sayings. — DELOBEL, J. (ed.), *Logia*, 1982, 389-394.

1982b  Jesus. From Easter to Valentinus (or to the Apostles' Creed). — *JBL* 101 (1982) 5-37.
       Esp. 22-24 [Q]. [NTA 27, 59] → Hodgson 1985

1983a The Nag Hammadi Library and the Study of the New Testament. — LOGAN, A.H.B. - WEDDERBURN, A.J.M. (eds.), *The New Testament and Gnosis: Essays in Honour of Robert McL. Wilson*, Edinburgh: Clark, 1983, 1-18. Esp. 6, 10, 14-15.

1983b The Sayings of Jesus: Q. — *Drew Gateway* (Madison, NJ) 54/1 (1983) 26-38. [NTA 29, 919]

1983c The Sermon on the Mount/Plain: Work Sheets for the Reconstruction of Q. — *SBL 1983 Seminar Papers*, 451-454.

1983d *A New Quest of the Historical Jesus and Other Essays*. Philadelphia, PA: Fortress, 1983, 215 p. → 1959, 1962b

1984 The Preaching of John: Work Sheets for the Reconstruction of Q. — *SBL 1984 Seminar Papers*, 305-346.

1985 The Mission and Beelzebul: Pap. Q 10:2-16; 11:14-23. — *SBL 1985 Seminar Papers*, 97-99.

1986a On Bridging the Gulf from Q to the Gospel of Thomas (or Vice Versa). — HEDRICK, C.W. - HODGSON, R., Jr. (eds.), *Nag Hammadi, Gnosticism, & Early Christianity*, Peabody, MA: Hendrickson, 1986, 127-175. Esp. 135-142: "The sociological substructure"; 142-164: "The dating of Q and the gospel of Thomas"; 164-175: "The genre of Q and the gospel of Thomas".

1986b The Gospels as Narrative Tradition. — MCCONNELL, F. (ed.), *The Bible and Narrative Tradition*, New York - Oxford: University Press, 1986, 97-112.

1986c Reconstructing Q: A Lost Collection of Jesus' Sayings. — *Connections* (Claremont, CA) 1/2 (1986) 2-6.

1987 Worksheets for Q 12. — *SBL 1987 Seminar Papers*, 586-605.

1988a The Study of the Historical Jesus after Nag Hammadi. — *Semeia* 44 (1988) 45-55. [NTA 33, 576]

1988b Very Goddess and Very Man: Jesus' Better Self. — KING, K.L. (ed.), *Images of the Feminine in Gnosticism* (Studies in Antiquity and Christianity), Philadelphia, PA: Fortress, 1988, 113-127. Esp. 120-123: "The inclusiveness of wisdom christology".
     Response: C.W. HEDRICK, *Ibid.*, 128-135.

1991 The Q Trajectory: Between John and Matthew via Jesus. — PEARSON, B.A., et al. (eds.), *The Future of Early Christianity*. FS H. Koester, 1991, 173-194. Esp. 174-178 [A. Schweitzer - apocalyptic]; 178-181 [P. Vielhauer - Son of Man]; 182-184 [G. Bornkamm - Q]; 184-189 [H. Koester - wisdom/Q]; 189-194 [pre-apocalyptic Q].

1992a A Critical Text of the Sayings Gospel Q. — *RHPR* 72 (1992) 15-22. Esp. 21-22 [Q 11,2-4]. [NTA 36, 1243]

1992b The Sayings Gospel Q. — VAN SEGBROECK, F., et al. (eds.), *The Four Gospels 1992*. FS F. Neirynck, 1992, I, 361-388. Esp. 362-366: "ὁ ἐρχόμενος Q 3,16; 7,18; 13,35"; 366-368: "πτωχοί Q 6,20; 7,22"; 368-370: "μακάριος Q 6,20.21a.21b.22; 7,23"; 370-372: "εὐαγγελίζονται Q 7,22"; 373-382: "[ Ναζαρά ] Q 4,16"; 382-385: "ὁ υἱός μου ὁ ἀγαπητός / υἱὸς ... τοῦ θεοῦ / ὁ υἱός Q 3,22; 4,3.9; 10,22"; 385-388: "τὸ πνεῦμα Q 3,16.22; 4,1". → Neirynck 1997d

1993a *The Jesus of the Sayings Gospel Q* (Occasional Papers, 28). Claremont, CA: The Institute for Antiquity and Christianity, 1993, 18 p.

1993b Die Logienquelle: Weisheit oder Prophetie? Anfragen an Migaku Sato, Q und Prophetie. — *EvT* 53 (1993) 367-389. Esp. 368-373: "Die prophetische Makrogattung"; 373-377: "Die prophetischen Mikrogattungen"; 377-378: "Die Botenformel"; 378-379: "Das Ringbuch"; 379-382: "Die prophetischen Redaktionen"; 382-384 [5-7]; 386-389: "Λόγοι σοφῶν oder λόγοι προφητῶν?". [NTA 38, 735] → Sato 1988, 1993

1994a Die Bedeutung der gnostischen Nag-Hammadi Texte für die neutestamentliche Wissenschaft. — BORMANN, L., et al. (eds.), *Religious Propaganda and Missionary*

*Competition.* FS D. Georgi, 1994, 23-41. Esp. 26-32 [Gospel of Thomas/Q]; 34-39 [Q].
The Significance of the Nag Hammadi Library for Contemporary Theology and Early Christianity. — HEDRICK, C.W. – KING, K. (eds.), *A Reader's Guide to the Nag Hammadi Library*, Sonoma, CA: Polebridge.
Il significato dei testi gnostici di Nag Hammadi per la scienza neotestamentaria. — *Protestantesimo* 49 (1994) 283-296.

1994b The Son of Man in the Sayings Gospel Q. — ELSAS, C., et al. (eds.), *Tradition und Translation*. FS C. Colpe, 1994, 315-335. Esp. 316-318: "Christological titles in the layering of Q"; 319-325: "Son of Man sayings referring to Jesus' public ministry"; 325-335: "The apocalyptic Son of Man".

1995a The History and Religious Taxonomy of Q: The Cynic Hypothesis. — PREISSLER, H. – SEIWERT, H. (eds.), *Gnosisforschung und Religionsgeschichte: Festschrift für Kurt Rudolph zum 65. Geburtstag*, Marburg: Diagonal-Verlag, 1995, 247-265. → Mack 1993

1995b The *Incipit* of the Sayings Gospel Q. — *RHPR* 75 (1995) 9-33. [NTA 40, 147] → Neirynck 1995g, 1996b, 1997d

1995c The Jesus of Q as Liberation Theologian. — PIPER, R.A. (ed.), *The Gospel Behind the Gospels*, 1995, 259-274.

**ROBINSON, John A.T.**

1947[R] The Temptations. [1947] — ID., *Twelve New Testament Studies*, 1962, 53-60.

1948[R] Hosea and the Virgin Birth. [1948] — ID., *Twelve More New Testament Studies*, 1984, 1-11.

1953 The One Baptism as a Category of New Testament Soteriology. — *ScotJT* 6 (1953) 257-274. Esp. 260-262 [3,13-17].
The One Baptism. — ID., *Twelve New Testament Studies*, 1962, 158-175. Esp. 161-162. → W.E. Moore 1964

1956 The 'Parable' of the Sheep and the Goats. — *NTS* 2 (1955-56) 225-237. [NTA 1, 41]; = ID., *Twelve New Testament Studies*, 1962, 76-93. → Jurgens 1983

1957 *Jesus and His Coming. The Emergence of a Doctrine.* London: SCM, 1957, [2]1978, 192 p.

1958 Elijah, John and Jesus: An Essay in Detection. — *NTS* 4 (1957-58) 263-281. Esp. 264-265 [3,7-12]; 275-276 [17,9-13]. [NTA 3, 53]; = ID., *Twelve New Testament Studies*, 1962, 28-52. Esp. 31; 45.

1962 *Twelve New Testament Studies* (Studies in Biblical Theology, 34). London, 1962, [2]1965, 180 p. → 1947, 1953, 1956, 1958

1975 The Parable of the Wicked Husbandmen: A Test of Synoptic Relationships. [21,33-46] — *NTS* 21 (1974-75) 443-461. [NTA 20, 88]; = ID., *Twelve More New Testament Studies*, 1984, 12-34. → Orchard 1976b

1976 *Redating the New Testament.* London: SCM; Philadelphia, PA: Westminster, 1976, XIII-369 p. Esp. 86-117: "Acts and the synoptic gospels"; [4]1981. → 1977; → Carmignac 1983, J. Ernst 1982, Focant 1988, Spadafora 1986, R. Wegner 1982
*Wann entstand das Neue Testament?*, trans. J. Madey. Paderborn: Bonifatius; Wuppertal: Brockhaus, 1986, 383 p.
*Re-dater le Nouveau Testament*, trans. M. de Mérode (Bible et Vie Chrétienne). Paris: Lethielleux, 1987, 488 p.

1977 *Can We Trust the New Testament?* Oxford: Mowbray; Grand Rapids, MI: Eerdmans, 1977, 142 p. Esp. 48-49; 58-60; 74-78. → 1976
*Peut-on se fier au Nouveau Testament?*, trans. G. Passelecq (Bible et Vie Chrétienne). Paris: Lethielleux, 1980, 157 p.

1984a *Twelve More New Testament Studies.* London: SCM, 1984, 184 p. → 1948, 1975, 1984b

1984b The Lord's Prayer. — *Ibid.*, 44-64.

ROBINSON, M.A.

1991 & PIERPONT, W.G., *The New Testament in the Original Greek According to the Byzantine/Majority Textform*. Atlanta, GA: Original Word, 1991, LVII-510 p.

ROBINSON, T. → Mason 1990a

ROBINSON, William Childs

1965 A Re-study of the Virgin Birth of Christ. God's Son was Born of a Woman: Mary's Son Prayed "Abba Father". — *EvQ* 37 (1965) 198-211. [NTA 10, 506]

1972 The Virgin Birth. A Broader Base. — *ChrTod* 17 (1972) 238-240. [NTA 17, 475]

ROBSON, Edward Alfred

1980 *Kαί-Configurations in the Greek New Testament*. Diss. Syracuse Univ., 1980, 3 vols., I, X-355 p.; II, 98 p.; III, 459 p. (L. Roberts). Esp. I, 52-128: "The καί-configurations in Matthew's gospel"; 193-200 [index]; III, 1-47: "The gospel according to Matthew".

ROBSON, G.A.

1963 Hard Sayings. [5,48] — *Theology* 66 (1963) 416-417. [NTA 8, 575] → E.K. Lee 1963a-b

ROCA-PUIG, Ramón

1956 *Un papiro griego del Evangelio de San Mateo*. Barcelona, 1956; ²1962, 60 p.
Nueva publicación del papiro numero uno de Barcelona. — *Helmántica* (Salamanca) 37 (1961) 5-20.
*Un papir grec de l'Evangeli de S. Mateu, amb una nota de C. Roberts*. Barcelona: Gremio Sindical de Maestros Impresores de Barcelona, 1962, 66 p. → Klawek 1964

1957 P. Barc. Inv. N. 1 (Mt III 9, 15; V 20-22, 25-28). — *Studi in onore di A. Calderini e R. Paribeni*, II, Milano, 1957, 87-96.

1959 Un pergamino griego del Evangelio de San Mateo (P. Cairo, Catálogo, núm. 71942. Mt. VIII 25-IV 2; XIII 32-38, 40-46). — *Emerita* (Madrid) 27 (1959) 59-73.

1985 *Dos Pergamins Bíblics. Salm. 14(15) i Mateu 26. Papirs de Barcelona, Inv. nᵒ 2 i nᵒ 4*. Barcelona, 1985, 20 p.

ROCHAIS, Gérard

1981 *Les récits de résurrection des morts dans le Nouveau Testament* (SNTS MS, 40). Cambridge: University Press, 1981, XV-252 p. Esp. 50-53 [9,1.18]; 83-86: "Les accords mineurs" [9,18-26]; 88-99 [9,18-26]. — Diss. Montréal, 1973 (L. Audet).

ROCKWELL, Hays H.

1982 Addendum on Matthew 5:17 and Anti-Semitism. — THOMPSON, N.H. - COLE, B.K. (eds.), *The Future of Jewish-Christian Relations*, Schenectady: Character Research, 1982, 277-280.

RODD, Cyril S.

1961 Spirit or Finger. — *ExpT* 72 (1960-61) 157-158. [NTA 5, 715]

RÓDENAS, Ángel

1972 Cristo revelador del Padre y del Espíritu en los sinópticos. — *EstTrin* 6 (1972) 23-62. Esp. 23-36 [God as father]; 36-43 [spirit]; 44-47 [3,13-17]; 47-54 [11,25-27]; 54-61 [28,16-20]; = *La Trinidad en la Biblia. Cristo, revelador del Padre y emisor del Espíritu en el Nuevo Testamento* (Semañas de estudios trinitarios, 6), Salamanca: Secretariado Trinitario, 1973, 95-136. Esp. 99-110; 110-117; 118-121; 121-128; 128-135.

1978 Las raíces bíblicas del culto a María. — *Analecta Calasanctiana* (Salamanca) 20 (1978) 323-375.

**RODGERS, Peter E.**

1992 The New Eclecticism. An Essay in Appreciation of the Work of Professor George D. Kilpatrick. — *NT* 34 (1992) 388-397. Esp. 389-392; 396-397 [27,35]. [NTA 37, 615] → Kilpatrick 1959

**RODRIGUES, A.F.**

1971 O divórcio e os incísos de Mateus. — *Theologica* 6 (1971) 9-35.

**RODRÍGUEZ, Félix**

1972 Mt. 18,18 en el canon décimo del Decreto Tridentino sobre la penitencia. — *Burgense* 13 (1972) 69-84.

**RODRÍGUEZ, Isidoro**

1986 "Padre nuestro, qui estás *en los cielos*". — *NatGrac* 33 (1986) 327-329.

1990 Dos notas filológicas. [16,24-28] — *Helmántica* 41 (1990) 5-13.

**RODRÍGUEZ, José David**

1988 The Parable of the Affirmative Action Employer. [20,1-16] — *CurrTMiss* 15 (1988) 418-424. [NTA 33, 126]

**RODRÍGUEZ CARMONA, Antonio**

1978 El Targum Palestinense del Pentateuco y el problema sinóptico de los evangelios. — *CuBíb* 35 (1978) 111-120.

1979 El vocabulario neotestamentario de resurrección a la luz del Targum y literatura intertestamentaria. — *EstBíb* 38 (1979-80) 97-113. Esp. 98-99, 104 [27,52]; 105 [27,53]; 107 [28,18]; 109 [13,45]. [NTA 26, 73]

1980 Origen de las formulas neotestamentarias de resurrección con *anistánai* y *egeírein*. — *EstE* 55 (1980) 27-58. Esp. 32-35 [passion predictions]; 39-41 [22,30/Mk]; 43-44 [10,8]; 49 [27,51-53]. [NTA 24, 762]

1981 "El Reino de Dios en el pensamiento de Jesús". — *EstBíb* 39 (1981) 249-284. Esp. 258-265; 267-268 [Q 13,18-19.20-21]; 272 [10,23]. [NTA 27, 72]

1990 Tradición targúmica y tradición evangélica. — *EstBíb* 43 (1990) 335-349. Esp. 342-345: "Principios de la tradición evangélicas"; 345-349: "Cuestión sinóptica". [NTA 36, 125]

1992 → Aguirre Monasterio 1992

1994 Los métodos histórico-críticos en el Nuevo Testamento a la luz de un ejemplo: Jesús purifica a un leproso (Mt 8,1-4)? — *Miscelánea de estudios árabes y hebraicos* (Granada) 43 (1994) 15-48.

**RODRIGUEZ PLAZA, Braulio**

1975 La critica literaria de los evangelios. I. El problema sinóptico. II. Teoria de las fuentes. III. Teoria del Mateo arameo. — *CuadEv* 2/16 (1975) 27-51; 2/17 (1975) 25-52; 2/18 (1975) 25-52.

1977 *El Sermón de la montaña. Introducción* (Cuadernos de Evangelio, 31). Madrid: Fe católica, 1977, 80 p.
    J.C. NEVES, *Didaskalia* 8 (1978) 418-420.

**RODRÍGUEZ RUIZ, Miguel**

1988 El evangelio de Pedro. ¿Un desafío a los evangelios canónicos? — *EstBíb* 46 (1988) 497-525. Esp. 506-510: "Conexiones entre el EvPe y Mt". [NTA 33, 1492]

**RODZIANKO, V.**

1964 The Meaning of Matth. 5,3. — *Studia Evangelica* 2 (1964) 229-235.

**ROEHRS, W.R.**

1964 God's Tabernacles Among Men. A Study of the Transfiguration. [17,1-8] — *ConcTM* 35 (1964) 18-25. [NTA 8, 581]

**RÖHSER, Günter**

1995 Jesus – der wahre "Schriftgelehrte": Ein Beitrag zum Problem der "Toraverschärfung" in den Antithesen der Bergpredigt. — *ZNW* 86 (1995) 20-33. [NTA 40, 163]

**RÖMELT, Josef**

1992 Normativität, ethische Radikalität und christlicher Glaube. Zur theologisch-ethischen Hermeneutik der Bergpredigt. — *ZKT* 114 (1992) 293-303. [NTA 37, 136]

**RÖSEL, Martin**

1991 Die Jungfrauengeburt des endzeitlichen Immanuel. Jesaja 7 in der Übersetzung der Septuaginta. — *JbBT* 6 (1991) 135-151. Esp. 150-151 [1,23].

**ROESLE, Maximilian**

1959* & CULLMANN, O. (eds.), *Begegnung der Christen. Studien evangelischer und katholischer Theologen. [Otto Karrer gewidmet zum siebzigsten Geburtstag].* Stuttgart: Evangelisches Verlagswerk; Frankfurt/M: Knecht, 1959, 696 p.; ²1960. → Ringger, J. Schmid, Vögtle

**ROGALEWSKI, Tadeusz**

1980 Nauka Jezusa o nierozerwalności małżeństwa w Ewangelii św. Mateusza. (Quid de indissolubilitate matrimonii secundum Mattheum Jesus docuerit?) — *Studia z Biblistyki* 2 (1980) 165-193.

**ROGERS, Cleon L., Jr.**

1973 The Great Commission. [28,19-20] — *BS* 130 (1973) 258-267. [NTA 18, 115]

1993 The Covenant of David in the New Testament. I. The Davidic Covenant in the Gospels. — *BS* 150 (1993) 458-478. Esp. 459-464 [Son of David]. [NTA 38, 982]

**ROGERS, E.W.**

1962 *Jesus the Christ. A Survey of Matthew's Gospel.* London: Pickering & Inglis, 1962, VII-148 p. [NTA 7, p. 268]

**ROGUET, A.-M.**

1966 Le nouveau texte français du Notre Père. — *VSp* 114 (1966) 5-24. [NTA 10, 907]

1981 Paraboles oubliées. — *VSp* 135 (1981) 334-360. Esp. 349-354 [5-7]. [NTA 26, 819]

**ROHDE, Joachim**

1965 *Die redaktionsgeschichtliche Methode. Einführung und Sichtung des Forschungsstandes* (Theologische Arbeiten, 22). Berlin: Evangelische Verlagsanstalt, 1965, 242 p.; Hamburg: Furche, 1966, 247 p. Esp. 44-97: "Die Behandlung des Matthäus-Evangeliums". — Diss. Berlin, 1962 (E. Fascher – J. Schneider). → G. Bornkamm 1959a, Fiedler 1957, Hummel 1963, Punge 1961, Strecker 1962, Trilling 1959a
*Rediscovering the Teaching of the Evangelists*, trans. D.M. Barton (The New Testament Library). London: SCM, 1968; Philadelphia, PA: Westminster, 1969, IX-278 p. Esp. 47-112.

**ROHRBAUGH, Richard L.**

1992 → Malina 1992

1993 A Peasant Reading of the Parable of the Talents/Pounds: A Text of Terror? [25,14-30] — *BTB* 23 (1993) 32-39. [NTA 37, 1272]

**ROHRHIRSCH, Ferdinand**

1990 *Markus in Qumran? Eine Auseinandersetzung mit den Argumenten für und gegen das Fragment 7Q5 mit Hilfe des methodischen Fallibilismusprinzips.* Wuppertal: Brockhaus, 1990, 152 p. Esp. 107-110 [1,2-3]

**ROKEAH, David**

1968 Notes on the Gospels. [Hebrew] [24,21-22] — *Tarbiz* (Jerusalem) 38 (1968-69) 394-396.

1969 Ben Stara is Ben Pantera. Towards the Clarification of a Philological-Historical Problem. [Hebrew] [1,18-25] — *Tarbiz* 39 (1969-70) 9-18.

**ROLLA, Armando**

1961a La concezione verginale di Gesù. — ROSSI, G. (ed.), *Cento problemi biblici*, 1961, 308-316.

1961b Pastori e Magi alla culla di Gesù. — *Ibid.*, 326-328.

1961c I sogni di Giuseppe. — *Ibid.*, 329-333.

**ROLLAND, Philippe**

1972 De la genèse à la fin du monde. Plan de l'évangile de Matthieu. — *BTB* 2 (1972) 157-178. Esp. 158-172 [structure]; 172-178 [OT]. → Salvoni 1972
From the Genesis to the End of the World. The Plan of Matthew's Gospel. — *BTB* 2 (1972) 155-176. Esp. 156-170; 170-176. [NTA 17, 509]

1982 Les prédécesseurs de Marc. Les sources présynoptiques de Mc, II,18-22 et parallèles. — *RB* 89 (1982) 370-405. Esp. 383-399. [NTA 27, 941] → Neirynck 1983b

1983a Marc, première harmonie évangélique? — *RB* 90 (1983) 23-79. Esp. 26-79 [minor agreements]. [NTA 28, 105] → Neirynck 1983b

1983b Les évangiles des premières communautés chrétiennes. — *Ibid.*, 161-201. Esp. 162-178: "Insuffisance du système de Griesbach"; 178-200: "Les quatre documents utilisés par Matthieu, Marc et Luc". [NTA 28, 904] → Neirynck 1983b

1984a *Les premiers évangiles. Un nouveau regard sur le problème synoptique* (LD, 116). Paris: Cerf, 1984, 260 p. Esp. 19-56: "Insuffisance des théories anciennes sur le problème synoptique"; 59-85: "La source dont dépendent Matthieu et Marc"; 158-180: "L'évangile des Craignant-Dieu, source commune à Matthieu et à Luc"; 189-202: "La rédaction de Matthieu"; 209-244: "Regard sur des solutions récentes" [Vaganay; Gaboury; Boismard]. → Magne 1992
M.-É. BOISMARD, *RB* 95 (1988) 97-101; M. DUMAIS, *ÉglT* 17 (1986) 388-390; A. FUCHS, *SNTU* 12 (1987) 201-205; J. GUILLET, *RSR* 74 (1986) 225-227; J.-C. INGELAERE, *RHPR* 65 (1985) 209-211; J.S. KLOPPENBORG, *CBQ* 47 (1985) 744-745; S. LÉGASSE, *BullLitEccl* 87 (1986) 145-146; F. NEIRYNCK, *ETL* 60 (1984) 404-405; G. NOVOTNY, *SE* 37 (1985) 254-256; F. VOLGA, *ETR* 59 (1984) 416-417.

1984b L'arrière-fond sémitique des évangiles synoptiques. [4,1; 8,23; 9,4; 13,10; 14,13.17] — *ETL* 60 (1984) 358-362. [NTA 29, 920] → Neirynck 1984d

1986 Jésus connaissait leurs pensées. [9,4; 12,25] — *ETL* 62 (1986) 118-121. [NTA 31, 568] → Neirynck 1986a

1987 Synoptique, Question. — BOGAERT, P.-M., et al. (eds.), *Dictionnaire encyclopédique de la Bible*, Turnhout: Brepols, 1987, 1227-1231.

1988 Je vous envoie (Mt 10,1-42; Mc 6,7-13; Lc 9,1-6; Lc 10,1-12). — *Spiritus* (Paris) 29 (1988) 359-365. [NTA 33, 607]

1989a Le procès de Jésus devant les autorités juives du point de vue de la critique littéraire. — *BLOS* 1 (1989) 3-13.
J. MAGNE, *BLOS* 2 (1989) 12-14.

1989b La question synoptique demande-t-elle une réponse compliquée? [M.-É. BOISMARD, *RB* 95 (1988) 97-101] — *Bib* 70 (1989) 217-223. [NTA 34, 100] → Neirynck 1989b

1990a  Préliminaires à la première multiplication des pains (Mt 14,12b-14 + 9,36; Mc 6,30-34; Lc 9,10-11). — *BLOS* 3 (1990) 12-18.

1990b  Propos intempestifs sur la guérison du lépreux (Mt 8,1-4; Mc 1,40-45; Lc 5,12-16). — *BLOS* 4 (1990) 23-27. → Amphoux 1990, Hermant 1990b

1990c  La guérison de l'enfant épileptique (Mt 17,14-18; Mc 9,14-27; Lc 9,37-43a). — *BLOS* 5 (1990) 3-7. → 1993

1990d  La découverte du tombeau vide (Mt 28,1-8; Mc 16,1-8; Lc 23,56–24,11). — *BLOS* 6 (1990) 3-10.

1990e  Jésus est mis en croix (Mt 27,33-44; Mc 15,22-32; Lc 23,32-43). — *Ibid.*, 11-17.

1993  Lecture par couches rédactionnelles de l'épisode de l'épileptique (Mc 9,14-29 et parallèles). — FOCANT, C. (ed.), *The Synoptic Gospels*, 1993, 451-458. → 1990c

1994  *L'origine et la date des évangiles. Les témoins oculaires de Jésus.* Paris: Saint-Paul, 1994, 175 p. Esp. 41-46: "La double tradition"; 65-69: "Pré-Matthieu ou l'évangile pétrinien"; 69-76: "Matthieu hébreu ou l'évangile des Douze"; 77-80: "Matthieu hébreu ou Matthieu araméen"; 117-128: "L'évangile de Matthieu".

**ROLLIN, Bertrand**

1984  "Laissant leur barque et leur père, ils le suivirent" *(Mt 4,22).* — *NRT* 106 (1984) 76-95. [NTA 28, 1143]

**ROLOFF, Jürgen**

1965  *Apostolat – Verkündigung – Kirche. Ursprung, Inhalt und Funktion des kirchlichen Apostelamtes nach Paulus, Lukas und den Pastoralbriefen.* Gütersloh: Mohn, 1965, 296 p. Esp. 138-168: "Zwölferkreis und Apostolat" [16,17-19; 19,28; οἱ δώδεκα]. — Diss. Hamburg, 1963-64 (L. Goppelt).

1970  *Das Kerygma und der irdische Jesus. Historische Motive in den Jesus-Erzählungen der Evangelien.* Göttingen: Vandenhoeck & Ruprecht, 1970, 289 p.; ²1973. Esp. 75-80 [12,1-14]; 100-101 [21,12-17]; 117-119 [17,24-27]; 119-120 [11,5-6]; 132-133 [20,29-34]; 133-134 [9,27-31]; 155-156 [8,10]; 159-161 [15,21-28]; 166-171 [17,20]; 206-207 [17,14-21]; 220 [26,6-13]; 236-237 [9,14-17]; 251-254 [14,13-21; 15,32-39; 16,5-12]. — Diss. Hamburg, 1967-68 (L. Goppelt). → Hengel 1971

1977  *Neues Testament* (Neukirchener Arbeitsbücher). Neukirchen-Vluyn: Neukirchener, 1977, ⁴1989, VIII-284 p. Esp. 77-135: "Zur Synoptiker-Exegese".

1978  Stationen urchristlicher Missionserfahrung. — *Zeitschrift für Mission* (Basel) 4 (1978) 3-8. Esp. 6-8.

1987  Ansätze kirchlicher Rechtsbildungen im Neuen Testament. — SCHLAICH, K. (ed.), *Studien zu Kirchenrecht und Theologie*, 1 (Texte und Materialien der Forschungsstätte der evangelischen Studiengemeinschaft, Reihe A, 26), Heidelberg, 1987, 83-142. Esp. 105-111 [law]; = ID., *Exegetische Verantwortung in der Kirche. Aufsätze*, ed. M. Karrer, Göttingen: Vandenhoeck & Ruprecht, 1990, 279-336. Esp. 299-305.

1989a  "Siehe, ich stehe vor der Tür und klopfe an". Beobachtungen zur Überlieferungsgeschichte von Offb 3,20. — FRANKEMÖLLE, H. - KERTELGE, K. (eds.), *Vom Urchristentum zu Jesus.* FS J. Gnilka, 1989, 452-466. Esp. 456-458 [Q 12,35-38].

1989b  Themen und Traditionen urchristlicher Amtsträgerparänese. — MERKLEIN, H. (ed.), *Neues Testament und Ethik.* FS R. Schnackenburg, 1989, 507-526. Esp. 511-512 [Q 17,7-10]; 515-516 [Q 16,13]; 521-523 [Q 12,42-47]; 523-524 [Q 12,35-38].

1990  Neutestamentliche Einleitungswissenschaft. Tendenzen und Entwicklungen. — *TR* 55 (1990) 385-423. Esp. 410-415: "Evangelien-Probleme". [NTA 35, 505] → Schmithals 1985

1992  Das Kirchenverständnis des Matthäus im Spiegel seiner Gleichnisse. — *NTS* 38 (1992) 337-356. Esp. 337-340 [Bornkamm]; 340-341 [compositional means]; 342-343 [18,12-14]; 343-345 [20,1-

16]; 345-348 [21,28-46]; 348-350 [22,1-14]; 350-352 [24,45-51]; 352 [25,14-30]; 354-356 [13]. [NTA 37, 125]

1993    *Die Kirche im Neuen Testament* (Grundrisse zum Neuen Testament. NTD Ergänzungsreihe, 10). Göttingen: Vandenhoeck & Ruprecht, 1993, 344 p. Esp. 144-168: "Jüngergemeinde in der Nachfolge Jesu: Das Matthäusevangelium". → Marucci 1995

1995    *Einführung in das Neue Testament* (Universal-Bibliothek, 9413). Stuttgart: Reclam, 1995, 267 p.

### ROMANIUK, Kazimierz

1964a   "Ciało i krew nie objawiły tobie, tylko Ojciec mój, który jest w niebiesiech" (Mt 16,17). ("Caro et sanguis non revelavit tibi, sed Pater meus, qui in caelis est" [Mt 16,17]). — *RuBi* 17 (1964) 346-354. [NTA 9, 913]

1964b   "Ja jestem, nie bójcie sie!". Przyczynek do nowotestamentalnej teologii bojaźni Boga (L'expression "c'est moi, n'ayez pas peur" dans le Nouveau Testament). — *CollTheol* 35 (1964) 63-72.

1966a   *Le sacerdoce dans le Nouveau Testament*. Le Puy – Lyon: Mappus, 1966, 238 p. Esp. 65-130: "Les disciples et les apôtres du Seigneur dans les quatre évangiles" [4,18-22; 9,9-10; 16,13-20].

1966b   Repentez-vous, car le Royaume des Cieux est tout proche (Matt. iv.17 par.). — *NTS* 12 (1965-66) 259-269. Esp. 260-263 [3,2]; 263-267 [4,17]. [NTA 11, 195]

1968    Le Livre de la Sagesse dans le Nouveau Testament. — *NTS* 14 (1967-68) 498-514. Esp. 498-499. [NTA 13, 73]

1980    "Józef, mąż sprawiedliwy..." (Mt 1,19). — *CollTheol* 50/3 (1980) 25-34. [NTA 25, 467] "Joseph, son époux, qui était un homme juste et ne voulait pas la dénoncer..." (Mt 1,19). — *CollTheol* 50 (special issue, 1980) 123-131. [NTA 26, 85]

1981    *Wiara w zmartwychwstanie, pusty grób i pojawienie się zmartwychwstałego Chrystusa* [Faith in the resurrection; the empty tomb and the apparitions] (Attende Lectioni, 6). Katowice: Księgawnia Św. Jacka, 1981, ²1985, 100 p.; ³1993, 167 p.

1982    Refleksje na temat pewnej krytyki źródła Q (Réflexions sur une critique de la source Q). — *CollTheol* 52/4 (1982) 31-46. [NTA 27, 898] → Goulcer 1978b

1983    *Co to jest źródło Q?* Warszawa: Akademia Teologii Katolickiej, 1983, 164 p. [NTA 28, p. 86]

1984    O najstaraszej postaci błogosławieństw, stanowiących wstęp do Kazania na Górze (The oldest form of the beatitudes forming the introduction to the Sermon on the Mount). — *Przegląd Tomistyczny* (Warszawa) 1 (1984) 75-86.

1987a   "Ani sandałów, ani laski" (Mk 6,8-9; Mt 10,9-10; Lk 9,3). ["With neither sandals nor staff"] — *CollTheol* 57/1 (1987) 5-14. [NTA 32, 624]

1987b   La Formgeschichte della formula del calice o del sangue. [26,26-29] — VATTIONI, F. (ed.), *Sangue e antropologia, riti e culto. Atti della V Settimana (Roma 26.XI-1.XII.1984)* (Centro Studi Sanguis Christi), Roma: Pia Unione Preziosissimo Sangue, 1987, 683-696.

1990    O naśladowaniu Jezusa (Mt 8,18-22; Łk 9,57-60) (De l'imitation de Jésus). — *CollTheol* 60/1 (1990) 5-14. [NTA 36, 724]

### ROMEO, Lorenzo

1985    Giudei e pagani nella storia di salvezza secondo il Commento a Matteo di Ilario di Poitiers. — *Studi e Materiali di Storia delle Religioni* (Roma) 51 (1985) 341-352.

### ROMERO POSE, Eugenio

1979    Ticonio y el sermón "in natali sanctorum innocentium" (Exégesis de Mt. 2). — *Greg* 60 (1979) 513-544 (English summary, 543-544).

**RONDET, Michel**

1982    Dans l'esprit des Béatitudes. — *Christus* 29 (1982) 306-315.

**RONDYANG, Yakobo**

1987    *"Your Kingdom Come" in the Traditional Religion of the Bari (Sudan) and in the Lord's Prayer. A Comparative Study.* Diss. Angelicum, Roma, 1987, XVII-123 p. (L. Borriello).

**RONNING (RONEN), Halvor**

1989    Word Statistics and the Minor Agreements of the Synoptic Gospels. — MULLER, C. (ed.), *Bible et informatique. Actes du colloque international. Jérusalem, 9-13 juin 1988. Méthodes, outils, résultats*, Paris–Genève: Champion–Slatkine, 1989, 501-516.

**ROOSEN, P.A.**

1964    *De Bijbel over openbaring en overlevering* (De Bijbel over..., 26). Roermond–Maaseik: Romen, 1964, 121 p. Esp. 70-84: "De synoptische evangeliën".

**ROPES, James Hardy**

1934[R]   *The Synoptic Gospels* [1934]. London: Oxford University Press, [2]1960 (with a new preface by D.E. Nineham), X-117 p. Esp. 33-58.

**RORDORF, Willy**

1962    *Der Sonntag. Geschichte des Ruhe- und Gottesdiensttages im ältesten Christentum* (ATANT, 43). Zürich: Zwingli, 1962, 336 p. Esp. 55-79: "Die Stellung Jesu zum Sabbat". — Diss. Basel, 1961 (O. Cullmann).
*Sunday. The History of the Day of Rest and Worship in the Earliest Centuries of the Christian Church.* London: SCM – New York: Westminster, 1968, XV-340 p.
*El Domingo. Historia del día de descanso y de culto en los primeros siglos de la Iglesia cristiana.* Madrid: Marova, 1971, 320 p.

1969    Marriage in the New Testament and in the Early Church. — *Journal of Ecclesiastical History* (Cambridge) 20 (1969) 193-210. Esp. 193-198. [NTA 14, 676]; = ID., *Lex orandi*, 1993, 300-317. Esp. 300-304.

1970    "Wie auch wir vergeben *haben* unsern Schuldnern" (Matth. VI,12b). — *Studia Patristica* 10 (1970) 237-241.

1976    Le "pain quotidien" (Matth. 6,11) dans l'histoire de l'exégèse. — *Didaskalia* 6 (1976) 221-235. Esp. 221-227 [Gregory of Nyssa]; 228-232 [Luther]; 232-233 [Bucer]; 233-235 [Calvin]. [NTA 22, 88]; = ID., *Liturgie*, 1986, 93-107. Esp. 93-99; 100-104; 104-105; 105-107.
Le 'pain quotidien' (Matth. 6,11) dans l'exégèse de Grégoire de Nysse. [1976, 221-229] — *Augustinianum* 17 (1977) 193-199.
'Our Daily Bread': Shifts in Exegesis. — *TDig* 28 (1980) 43-44.

1981a   The Lord's Prayer in the Light of its Liturgical Use in the Early Church. — *Studia Liturgica* 14/1 (1980-82) 1-19; = ID., *Lex orandi*, 1993, 86-104.

1981b   Le problème de la transmission textuelle de *Didachè* 1,3b-2,1. — PASCHKE, F., et al. (eds.), *Überlieferungsgeschichtliche Untersuchungen* (TU, 125), Berlin: Akademie, 1981, 499-513. Esp. 501-509 [5,43-48/Did 1,3-5]; = ID., *Liturgie*, 1986, 139-153. Esp. 141-149.

1986    *Liturgie, foi et vie des premiers chrétiens. Études patristiques* (Théologie historique, 75). Paris: Beauchesne, 1986, 520 p. → 1976, 1981b

1991    Does the Didache Contain Jesus Tradition Independently of the Synoptic Gospels? — WANSBROUGH, H. (ed.), *Jesus and the Oral Gospel Tradition*, 1991, 394-423. Esp. 396-412 [Did 1,1-6]; 412-421 [Did 16,1-8]; 421-423 [Did 1,5; 8,1-2; 9,5; 11,7]; = ID., *Lex orandi*, 1993, 330-359.

1993 *Lex orandi, lex credendi. Gesammelte Aufsätze zum 60. Geburtstag* (Paradosis, 36). Freiburg/Schw: Universitätsverlag, 1993, XVI-510 p. → 1969, 1981a, 1991

**ROSAZ, Monique**

1979 Passer sur l'autre rive. — *Christus* 26 (1979) 323-332. Esp. 329-332 [25,1-13]. [NTA 24, 135]

**ROSCHÉ, Theodore Roos**

1960 The Words of Jesus and the Future of the "Q" Hypothesis. — *JBL* 79 (1960) 210-220. [NTA 5, 387]; = BELLINZONI, A.J., Jr., et al. (eds.), *The Two-Source Hypothesis*, 1985, 357-369. — Diss. Columbia University, New York, 1959. → Carlston 1971, Danner 1983

**ROSE, André**

1962 L'influence des Psaumes sur les annonces et les récits de la passion et de la résurrection dans les évangiles. — DE LANGHE, R. (ed.), *Le Psautier. Ses origines. Ses problèmes littéraires. Son influence. Études présentées aux XIIᵉ Journées Bibliques (29-31 août 1960)* (Orientalia et Biblica Lovaniensia, 4), Leuven: Institut orientaliste, 1962, 297-356. Esp. 301-304 [26,1-5]; 305-307 [26,27-28]; 307-308 [26,21]; 308-309 [26,37-38]; 309-310 [26,59-60]; 310-312 [26,64]; 312-316 [27,33-36]; 318-320 [27,55]; 321-322 [27.4.24.51].

**ROSENAU, Hartmut**

1993 *Allversöhnung. Ein transzendentaltheologischer Grundlegungsversuch* (Theologische Bibliothek Töpelmann, 57). Berlin – New York: de Gruyter, 1993, X-544 p. Esp. 82-103: "'Doppelter Ausgang' (Mt 25,31-46)".

**ROSENBAUM, H.-U.** → K. Aland 1995

**ROSENBERG, Roy A.**

1972 The "Star of the Messiah" Reconsidered. — *Bib* 53 (1972) 105-109. [NTA 17, 114]

**ROSENBLATT, M.-E.**

1994 Got into the Party After All: Women's Issues and the Five Foolish Virgins. — *Continuum* 3 (1994) 107-137. [NTA 39, 811]

**ROS GARCÍA, Salvador**

1986 "Carpintero" e "Hijo del carpintero" (Mc 6,3; Mt 13,55). El oficio de José y de Jesús. Notas de Cristologia inductiva. — *EstJos* 40 (1986) 163-177.

**ROSS, J.M.**

1976 The United Bible Societies' Greek New Testament. — *JBL* 95 (1976) 112-121. [NTA 20, 713r] → K. Aland [GNT 1975]

1978a Epileptic or Moonstruck? [4,24; 17,15] — *BTrans* 29 (1978) 126-128. [NTA 22, 760]

1978b Problems of Translation in Matthew. [5,1-2.17-18; 6,7] — *Ibid.*, 336-337. [NTA 23, 84] → Philipose 1977

1983 Some Unnoticed Points in the Text of the New Testament. — *NT* 25 (1983) 59-72. Esp. 61-62 [5,4-5; 22,32; 23,14]. [NTA 27, 862]

1987 Which Zachariah? [23,34-36] — *IBS* 9 (1987) 70-73. [NTA 32, 129]

1990 Jesus's Knowledge of Greek. — *IBS* 12 (1990) 41-47. Esp 43-45 [ἐπιούσιος]. [NTA 34, 1093]

1991 The Son of Man. — *IBS* 13 (1991) 186-198. Esp. 187, 190-191, 197-198. [NTA 36, 903]

1992 Floating Words: Their Significance for Textual Criticism. — *NTS* 38 (1992) 153-156. Esp. 154 [23,14]. [NTA 36, 1135] → Pickering 1993b

**ROSSANO, Piero**

1960 La parabola del tesoro e il diritto orientale. [13,44] — *RivBib* 8 (1960) 365-366.

**ROSSÉ, Gérard**

1972 *Gesù in mezzo. Matteo 18,20 nell'esegesi contemporanea* (Collana scritturistica). Roma: Città Nuova, 1972, 160 p. Esp. 19-26: "Il capitolo 18 nel primo Vangelo"; 27-52: "Il discorso del capitolo 18"; 53-72: "I destinari del discorso"; 73-144: "Mt. 18,20 nel suo contesto immediato: vv. 15-22".

1983 *Il grido di Gesù in croce. Una panoramica esegetica e teologica.* Roma Città Nuva Editrice, 1983, 166 p.
*Jésus abandonné. Approches du mystère* (Racines, 1). Paris: Nouvelle Cité, 1983, 198 p. Esp. 157-159 [27,46].
*The Cry of Jesus on the Cross. A Biblical and Theological Study,* trans. S.W. Arndt. New York – Mahwah, NJ: Paulist, 1987, x-145 p.

1986 La scelta dei Dodici. — *Nuova umanità* (Roma) 8/46-47 (1986) 11-27.

1987a *L'ecclesiologia di Matteo. Interpretazione di Mt. 18,20* (Contributi di teologia, 6). Roma: Città Nuova, 1987, 116 p. [NTA 33, p. 112]

1987b Il "Dio-con-noi" nell'ecclesiologia matteana. — *Nuova umanità* 9/52-53 (1987) 13-22.

1987c Il "discorso comunitario" di Mt 18. — *Nuova umanità* 9/54 (1987) 13-24.

1988 La formazione dei vangeli. A proposito di una questione dibattuta. — *Nuova umanità* 10/56 (1988) 105-117. → Carmignac 1984, Grelot 1984a, 1986a, Tresmontant 1983

**ROSSETTO, Giovanni**

1995 La tensione del Regno: Tappe di un cammino di ricerca. — *RivBib* 43 (1995) 391-428. Esp. 399-403 [Mk/Q]; 404-411 [Mt]. [NTA 40, 441]

**ROSSI, Giovanni**

1961* (ed.), *Cento problemi biblici.* Assisi: Ed. Pro Civitate Christiana, 1961, 584 p. → Prete, Rolla 1961a-c, Spadafora

**ROSSI DE GASPERIS, Francesco**

1991 Le Beatitudini del vangelo secondo Matteo. — BALLIS, G. (ed.), *Il mondo dell'uomo nascosto,* 1991, 21-38.

**ROSSO, Stefano**

1995 Mt 1,1-25 nei lezionari attuali del Rito Romano. — *Theotokos* 3/1 (1995) 135-158.

**ROSSOL, Heinz**

1993 "The Desolating Sacrilege" and the Synoptic Problem (Matt 24:15-22 and par.). — ALBL, M.C., et al. (eds.), *Directions in New Testament Methods,* 1993, 13-18.

**ROSSOUW, P.J.**

1991 Eschatological Preaching. With Special Reference to Matthew 24:1-14. — *Acta theologica* 11 (1991) 72-78.

**ROSTIG, D.**

1991 *Bergpredigt und Politik. Zur Struktur und Funktion des Reiches Gottes bei Leonhard Ragaz* (EHS, XXIII/419). Frankfurt/M–Bern: Lang, 1991, XII-276 p. → Ragaz 1945

**ROSZKO, Casimir**

1973 Traces of the First Armenian Version of the Gospels in an Early Manuscript: An Analysis of Ms. C (A24) of the Walters Art Gallery in Baltimore. — *SBF/LA* 23 (1973) 151-166. Esp. 154-155; 156-157; 158-160; 163-164. [NTA 18, 792]

**ROTH, Cecil**

1961 Simon-Petrus. — *HTR* 54 (1961) 91-98. [NTA 6, 777] → 1964; → Fitzmyer 1963

1964  & FITZMYER, J.A., The Name Simon. A Further Discussion. — *HTR* 57 (1964) 60-61.
[NTA 8, 946]; = FITZMYER, J.A., *Essays on the Semitic Background of the New Testament*, 1971, 110-112. → 1961; → Fitzmyer 1963

**ROTH, Wolfgang M.W.**

1992  Moses and Matthew. — *BiTod* 30 (1992) 362-366. [NTA 37, 708]

**ROTHFUCHS, Wilhelm**

1968  Die sog. Antithesen des Matthäus-Evangeliums und ihr Gesetzesverständnis – untersucht im Zusammenhang von Mt 5,7-48. — *Lutherischer Rundblick* (Wiesbaden) 16 (1968) 95-109.

1969  *Die Erfüllungszitate des Matthäus-Evangeliums. Eine biblisch-theologische Untersuchung* (BWANT, 88). Stuttgart: Kohlhammer, 1969, 202 p. Esp. 27-56: "Die Formel ἵνα πληρωθῇ κτλ im Matthäus-Evangelium"; 57-109: "Die Erfüllungszitate im Matthäus-Evangelium"; 110-133: "Die theologischen Bezüge der Erfüllungszitate"; 134-177: "Die Eigenständlichkeit des Matthäus-Evangeliums hinsichtlich der Erfüllungszitate". [NTA 14, p. 243] — Diss. Münster, 1966 (K.H. Rengstorf). → Van Segbroeck 1972b
        B. CORSANI, *Protestantesimo* 40 (1985) 119-120; H. FRANKEMÖLLE, *TRev* 67 (1971) 33-34; X. JACQUES, *NRT* 92 (1970) 700-701; M. KARNETZKI, *TLZ* 95 (1970) 585-587; R. PESCH, *BZ* 17 (1973) 112-114; *Freiburger Rundbrief* 22 (1970) 115; B. SCHWANK, *TheolPhil* 45 (1970) 302-303; S. SEGALLA, *Studia Patavina* 18 (1971) 170-171.

**ROTHUIZEN, G.T.**

1960  *De hand aan de ploeg. Klein commentaar op de Bergrede.* Aalten: Uitgeverij de Graafschap, 1960, 110 p.

1978  Kerk en politiek. Matteüs 20:25-28 en de Twee Rijken leer. — GROSHEIDE, H.H., et al. (eds.), *De knechtsgestalte van Christus*. FS H.N. Ridderbos, 1978, 179-193.

**ROTOLA, Albert C.**

1968  Matthew's Gospel Today. [law, rabbinism] — *BiTod* 37 (1968) 2603-2607.

**ROTONDI, G.M.**

1968  *Dal Vangelo secondo san Matteo.* Roma: Studium, 1968, 254 p.

**ROUILLER, Grégoire**

1972  Pour mieux lire l'évangile selon S. Matthieu. — *Les Échos de Saint-Maurice* 68 (1972) 17-34.

1975  & VARONE, M.C., S. Matthieu. Père ... que soit faite ta Volonté. Fascicule rédigé en prolongement de la session d'études bibliques tenue à La Pelouse-sur-Bex, 1975. — *Les Échos de Saint-Maurice* 71 (1975) 143-270.

1992  *Et moi je vous dis... Paroles de Jésus sur la montagne* (Cahiers, 1). Freiburg/Schw: Association biblique catholique, 1992, 126 p.

**ROULIN, Placide**

1959a & CARTON, G., Le baptême du Christ. [3,13-17] — *BibVieChrét* 25 (1959) 39-48. [NTA 3, 573]

1959b Le péché contre l'Esprit-Saint. — *BibVieChrét* 29 (1959) 33-45. Esp. 41-42 [9,32-34; 12,22-32]. [NTA 4, 380]

**ROURE, Damià**

1990  *Jesús y la figura de David en Mc 2,23-26. Trasfondo bíblico, intertestamentario y rabínico* (AnBib, 124). Roma: Pontificio Istituto Biblico, 1990, X-172 p. Esp. 28-32 [12,1-4/Mk].

**ROUSÉE, Jourdain-Marie**

1986 & PIERRE, M.-J. (eds.), *Catalogue de la Bibliothèque de l'École Biblique de Jérusalem.* Tome 8: *mande–neh.* Paris: Gabalda, 1986, 656 p. Esp. 178-237; *Supplément*, 4 vols., 1988. → Schaub 1971

**ROUSSEAU, François**

1989 *La poétique fondamentale du texte biblique. Le fait littéraire d'un parallélisme élargi et omniprésent* (Recherches, NS 20). Montreal: Bellarmin; Paris: Cerf, 1989, 280 p. Esp. 61-64 [8,23-27]; 85-89 [1,18-25]; 96-98 [6,9-13].

**ROUSSEAU, John J.**

1993 Jesus, an Exorcist of a Kind. — *SBL 1993 Seminar Papers*, 129-153. Esp. 141-147 [4,11; 7,28-29; 8,16.28-34; 12,15-16.27; 15,21-28; 17,14-20].

**ROUSSEAU, P.**

1983 The Exegete as Historian. Hilary of Poitiers' Commentary on Matthew. — CROKE, B. - EMMETT, A.M. (eds.), *History and Historians in Late Antiquity*, Sydney: Pergamon, 1983, 107-115.

**ROUSSEL, L.**

1968 *L'Évangile de Matthieu. Texte grec. Traduction nouvelle. Commentaire.* I: *Chapitres 1-7.* Paris: Pavillon, 1968, 217 p.
M. BOUTTIER, *ETR* 44 (1969) 67-68; F. DREYFUS, *RB* 77 (1970) 473; M.-É. LAUZIÈRE, *RThom* 70 (1970) 121.

**ROUSTANG, F.**

1959 Le Christ, ami des pécheurs. [9,2.13] — *Christus* 6/21 (1959) 6-21. [NTA 3, 729]

**ROUX, Hébert**

1942[R] *L'Évangile du Royaume. Commentaire sur l'Évangile selon saint Matthieu* [1942]. Genève: Labor et Fides, [2]1956, 297 p.
F. BAUDRAZ, *RTP* 8 (1958) 145; M. CARREZ, *RHPR* 37 (1957) 116; S. CIPRIANI, *RivBib* 6 (1958) 184-186; A.M. HENRY, *VSp* 96 (1957) 538-539; P. MONCADA, *Protestantesimo* 12 (1957) 141-142; J. PRADO, *Pentecostés* 8 (1970) 93-98; M. THURIAN, *Verbum Caro* (Taizé) 11 (1956) 64-65; Y.B. TRÉMEL, *LumièreV* 41 (1959) 129-130; A. VIARD, *RSPT* 40 (1956) 257.

**ROVIRA BELLOSO, Josep M.**

1989 Benaurats els qui sofreixen persecucío per la justícia. [5,10] — *RevistCatTeol* 14 (1989) 291-307. Esp. 292-294 [analysis]; 294-305 [survey of research].

**ROWDON, Harold Hamilyn**

1982* (ed.) *Christ the Lord. Studies in Christology Presented to Donald Guthrie.* Leicester: Inter-Varsity, 1982, XVI-344 p. → F.F. Bruce, D.A. Carson, D. Wenham

**ROWLAND, Christopher**

1985 *Christian Origins. An Account of the Setting and Character of the Most Important Messianic Sect of Judaism.* London: SPCK, 1985, XX-428 p. Esp. 122-193: "Jesus".

1994 Apocalyptic, the Poor, and the Gospel of Matthew. — *JTS* 45 (1994) 504-518. [NTA 39, 791]

1995a "The Gospel, the Poor and the Churches": Attitudes to Poverty in the British Churches and Biblical Exegesis. — ROGERSON, J.W. et al. (eds.), *The Bible in Ethics. The Second Sheffield Colloquium* (JSOT SS, 207), Sheffield: JSOT, 1995, 213-231. Esp. 225-230 [25,31-46].

1995b The "Interested" Interpreter. — CARROLL R., M.D. - CLINES, D.J.A. - DAVIES, P.R. (eds.), *The Bible in Human Society. Essays in Honour of John Rogerson* (JSOT SS, 200), Sheffield: JSOT, 1995, 429-444. Esp. 436-443 [anti-Judaism].

**ROWLINGSON, Donald T.**

1962a  Q. — *IDB* 3 (1962) 973.

1962b  Synoptic Problem. — *IDB* 4 (1962) 491-495.

1963  *A Bibliographical Outline of New Testament Research and Interpretation*. Boston: Boston University Bookstore, 1963, ²1965, VII-59 p.

**ROY, Michel**

1981  Jugement, sanction et évangile. Matthieu 25,31-46, Luc 15,11-32; 16,19-31. — *Christus* 28 (1981) 440-449.

**ROYSE, James R.**

1979  Scribal Habits in the Transmission of New Testament Texts. — O'FLAHERTY, W.D. (ed.), *The Critical Study of Sacred Texts* (Berkeley Religious Studies Series), Berkeley, CA: Graduate Theological Union, 1979, 139-161. Esp. 145-148 [3,7.12].

1983  The Treatment of Scribal Leaps in Metzger's *Textual Commentary*. — *NTS* 29 (1983) 539-551. Esp. 540 [12,47; 26,28]; 541 [18,35; 27,24]; 546 [8,8; 20,16; 28,9]; 547 [12,15; 14,27]. [NTA 28, 439] → B.M. Metzger 1971

**ROYSTER, Dmitri**

1992  *The Kingdom of God. The Sermon on the Mount* (Tradition Books). Crestwood, NY: St. Vladimir Seminary Press, 1992, 128 p. [NTA 38, p. 124]

**ROZMAN, Francè**

1976a  The Temptations of Jesus (Mt 4,1-11; Mk 1,12-13; Lk 4,1-13). [Serbo-Croatian] — *Bogoslovni Vestnik* (Ljubljana) 36 (1976) 62-81.

1976b  You Are Peter. [Serbo-Croatian] — *Ibid.*, 365-383.

**RUATTI, D.**

1960  *Il giudizio universale e le opere di misericordia (Mt 25,31-46)*. Diss. Pont. Univ. Greg., Roma, 1960.

**RUBENSTEIN, Richard L.**

1963  Scribes, Pharisees and Hypocrites: A Study in Rabbinic Psychology. [23] — *Judaism* 12 (1963) 456-468. [NTA 9, 159]

**RUBINKIEWICZ, Ryszard**

1980  Przypowieść o szacie godowej (Mt 22,11-13) w świetle Hen 10,4 (La parabole de la robe nuptiale [Mt 22,11-13] à la lumière d'Hén 10,4). — *RoczTK* 27/1 (1980) 53-69. [NTA 27, 927]

1984  *Eschatologia Hen 9–11 a Nowy Testament*. Lublin, 1984.
*Die Eschatologie von Hen 9–11 und das Neue Testament*, trans. H. Ulrich (Österreichische Biblische Studien, 6). Klosterneuburg: Österreichisches Katholisches Bibelwerk, 1984, 175 p. Esp. 97-113 [22,13/1 Enoch 10,4].

**RUBINO, Marina**

1982  → Levoratti 1982

1986a  ¿Cómo nacieron los evangelios? — *Palabra y Vida* (Buenos Aires) 28 (1986) 3-16. → Grelot 1986a

1986b  Origen y destino de Jesús, el Mesías (Mt 1–2). — *Palabra y Vida* 29 (1986) 3-21.

**RUCKSTUHL, Eugen**

1963  *Die Chronologie des Letzten Mahles und des Leidens Jesu* (Biblische Beiträge NF, 4). Einsiedeln–Zürich–Köln: Benziger, 1963, 124 p. Esp. 53-54 [27,15-21]. → Jaubert 1957

*Chronology of the Last Days of Jesus. A Critical Study*, trans. V.J. Drapela. New York – Roma: Desclée, 1965, X-143 p.

1974    Jésus a-t-il enseigné l'indissolubilité du mariage? — *Tantur Yearbook*, 1973-74, 79-96. Esp. 81-83.89.
        Hat Jesus die Unauflöslichkeit der Ehe gelehrt? — ID., *Jesus im Horizont der Evangelien* (Stuttgarter Biblische Aufsatzbände, 3), Stuttgart: Katholisches Bibelwerk, 1988, 49-66 ("Nachtrag", 66-68). Esp. 51-53.59.

1992    Die Speisung des Volkes durch Jesus und die Seeüberfahrt der Jünger nach Joh 6,1-25 im Vergleich zu den synoptischen Parallelen. — VAN SEGBROECK, F., et al. (eds.), *The Four Gospels 1992*. FS F. Neirynck, 1992, III, 2001-2019. Esp. 2003-2011 [14,13-21/Jn 6,1-15]; 2011-2015 [14,22-33/Jn 6,16-21]; 2018-2019.

RUDHARDT, J.
1973    Un papyrus chrétien de la Bibliothèque publique et universitaire de Genève. — *Littérature, histoire, linguistique. Recueil d'études offert à Bernard Gagnebin*, Lausanne: Presses Universitaires, 1973, 165-188.

RÜGER, Hans Peter
1968    Zum Problem der Sprache Jesu. — *ZNW* 59 (1968) 113-122. Esp. 113 [11,11]; 113-114 [16,28]; 115-116 [26,73]; 117-118 [27,8]; 118 [10,2-4]; 122 [5,32]. [NTA 13, 114]

1969    "Mit welchem Mass ihr meßt, wird euch gemessen werden". [7,2] — *ZNW* 60 (1969) 174-182. [NTA 14, 855]

1973    Μαμωνας. [6,24] — *ZNW* 64 (1973) 127-131. [NTA 18, 468]

1981    Ναζαρέθ/Ναζαρά Ναζαρηνός/Ναζωραῖος. — *ZNW* 72 (1981) 257-263. Esp. 257-260 [2,23]; 259-260 [4,13]. [NTA 26, 419]

RUEGG, Ulrich
1991    À la recherche du temps de Jacques. — MARGUERAT, D. – ZUMSTEIN, J. (eds.), *La mémoire et le temps*. FS P. Bonnard, 1991, 235-257. Esp. 241-242 [James/Mt 5,21-48].

RÜSTOW, Alexander
1960    Ἐντὸς ὑμῶν ἐστιν. Zur Deutung von Lukas 17,20-21. — *ZNW* 51 (1960) 197-224. Esp. 203-205 [24,27-28]; 207 [24,26]; 210 [10,28]. [NTA 5, 736]

RUF, Sieglinde M.
1995    *Maria aus Magdala. Eine Studie der neutestamentlichen Zeugnisse und archäologischen Befunde* (Biblische Notizen. Beihefte, 9). München: Red. Biblische Notizen, 1995, 116 p. Esp. 18-21.

RUIJS, Raul C.M.
1972    Exegese "kerygmática" de algumas passagens sinóticas. [16,16-19; 17,1-9] — *RevistCuBíb* 9 (1972) 66-80. [NTA 18, 472]

RUIZ, Gregorio
1973    "Eunucos por el Reino" (Mt. 19,12): ¿Dos interpretaciones contradictorias? — *SalT* 61 (1973) 83-92. → Marín Heredia 1973

1974a   La lectura continua. Evangelio de S. Mateo, 5–13: la justicia del Reino, sus heraldos, su misterio. — *SalT* 62 (1974) 459-462.

1974b   La lectura continua: Mt. 14–25. La decisión radical. Ley fundamental de la comunidad. — *Ibid.*, 549-552.

RUIZ BUENO, Daniel
1955    (ed.), *Obras de S. Juan Crisóstomo. I: Homilías sobre S. Mateo* (1-45); II: *Homilías sobre S. Mateo* (46-90) (Biblioteca de autores cristianos, 141/146). Madrid: Católica,

1955/56, XX-864 and XII-778 p.
U. DOMINGUEZ DEL VAL, *RevistEspTeol* 16 (1956) 551; A.M. PRIEGO, *EstBíb* 15 (1956) 454-455.

**RUMAK, Jery**

1950 Adoratio Magorum (Mt 2,1-12). — *Ateneum Kaplanskie* (Wroclaw) 52 (1950) 391-399.

1962 Ewangelia dziecięctwa Pana Jezusa a krytycy (Evange ium Infantiae Jesu Christi apud criticos). — *RuBi* 15 (1962) 344-352.

**RUMIANEK, Ryszard**

1979 *Dio pastore d'Israele secondo Ezechiele 34 e l'applicazione messianica nel Vangelo di Matteo.* Diss. Pont. Univ. Greg., Roma, 1979, XXV-175 p. (R. North).

1988 Przykłady pasterskie w nauczaniu Jezusa w Ewangelii świętego Mateusza (Les exemples pastoraux dans l'enseignement de Jésus selon l'Évangile de Matthieu). — *StudTheolVars* 26/1 (1988) 245-249. Esp. 245-246 [12,11] ; 246-248 [18,12-14]. [NTA 33, 590]

**RUNACHER, Caroline**

1994 *Croyants incrédules. La guérison de l'épileptique Marc 9,14-29* (LD, 157). Paris: Cerf, 1994, 300 p. Esp. 115-122: "Le problème synoptique".

**RUNIA, K.**

1965 The Papal Claim of Petrine Succession. — *RTR* 24/1 (1965) 13-21.

**RUPPERT, Lothar**

1972 *Jesus als der leidende Gerechte? Der Weg Jesu im Lichte eines alt- und zwischentestamentlichen Motivs* (SBS, 59). Stuttgart: Katholisches Bibelwerk, 1972, 87 p. Esp. 42-71: "Das Motiv vom 'leidenden Gerechten' und seine Bedeutung für die neutestamentliche Christologie, speziell nach den Voraussagen und der Darstellung des Leidens Jesu".

**RUSAM, Dietrich**

1993 *Die Gemeinschaft der Kinder Gottes. Das Motiv der Gotteskindschaft und die Gemeinden der johanneischen Briefe* (BWANT, 133). Stuttgart: Kohlhammer, 1993, 262 p. Esp. 72-76: "Gott als Vater aller Menschen – Zur Konzeption im Matthäusevangelium". — Diss. Neuendettelsau, 1992 (W. Stegemann).

**RUSCHE, Helga**

1976a Das Glück der vielfach Hungrigen (Mt 5,6). — *Dienender Glaube* (Kevelaer) 52 (1976) 24-26.

1976b Wir dürfen schauen, der uns sieht (Nachdenkliches zur 6. Seligpreisung = Mt 5.8). — *Ibid.*, 178-180.

1977 Krisis. Zum Gleichnis von den zehn Brautjungfern (Mt 25,1-13). — *Dienender Glaube* 53 (1977) 225-229.

1979 Für das 'Haus Israel' vom 'Gott Israels' gesandt. Jesus und die Juden in der Deutung von Mt 15,21-28. — GOLDSTEIN, H. (ed.), *Gottesverächter und Menschenfeinde? Juden zwischen Jesus und frühchristlicher Kirche*, Düsseldorf: Patmos, 1979, 99-122. Esp. 101-103 [Mt]; 103-106 [Mk]; 107-120 [15,24].

**RUSSELL, E.A.**

1980 The Canaanite Woman and the Gospels (Mt 15.21-28; cf. Mk 7.24-30). — LIVINGSTONE, E.A. (ed.), *Studia Biblica 1978*, II, 1980, 263-300.

1982a Divine Healing and Scripture. — *IBS* 4 (1982) 123-157. Esp. 135-143. [NTA 27, 323]

1982b The Image of the Jew in Matthew's Gospel. — *Studia Evangelica* 7 (1982) 427-442; = *ProcIrBibAss* 12 (1989) 37-57 (revised and updated). [NTA 36, 702]

1986 "Antisemitism" in the Gospel of St. Matthew. — *IBS* 8 (1986) 183-196. [NTA 31, 579]

1991 Some Reflections on Humour in Scripture and Otherwise. — *IBS* 13 (1991) 199-210. Esp. 207-209. [NTA 36, 955]

**RUSTAD, Joel Olaf**

1976 *Matthew's Attitude toward the Law in Matt. 19:16-22.* Diss. Concordia Sem. - Lutheran School of Theology, Chicago, IL, 1976-79, IV-263 p. — *DissAbstr* 37 (1976-77) 7175.

**RUSTENHAVEN, William, Jr.**

1978 *Renewed Interest in Alternate Solutions to the Synoptic Problem: An Examination of the Griesbach Hypothesis since 1964.* Diss. Southwestern Baptist Theol. Sem., Fort Worth, TX, 1978.

**RUTH, Lester**

1994 The Early Roman Christmas Gospel: Magi, Manger, or *Verbum Factum?* — *Studia Liturgica* 24 (1994) 214-221. Esp. 218-220. → Coebergh 1966

**RYAN, M. Rosalie**

1965* (ed.), *Contemporary New Testament Studies.* Collegeville, MN: Liturgical, 1965, XIV-489 p. → Duncker 1963, Lohr 1961/64, Muñoz Iglesias 1958/61, Sloyan 1958, Stanley 1964a, Sutcliffe 1962a, Willaert 1960/62

**RYAN, T.J.**

1978 Matthew 15:29-31. An Overlooked Summary. — *Horizons* (Villanova, PA) 5 (1978) 31-42. [NTA 23, 104]

**RYCKMANS, Gonzague**

1951 De l'or (?), de l'encens et de la myrrhe. [2,11] — *RB* 58 (1951) 372-376.

**RYDBECK, Lars**

1967 *Fachprosa, vermeintliche Volkssprache und Neues Testament. Zur Beurteilung der sprachlichen Niveauunterschiede im nachklassischen Griechisch* (Acta Universitatis Upsaliensis. Studia Graeca Upsaliensia, 5). Uppsala: Almqvist och Wiksell, 1967, 221 p. Esp. 42-45 [5,14-15]; 159-166 [βαστάζω: 3,11; 8,17].

1969 Bemerkungen zu Periphrasen mit εἶναι + Präsens Partizip bei Herodot und in der Koine. — *Glotta* (Göttingen) 47 (1969) 186-201. Esp. 195 [19,22].

**RYKEN, Leland**

1984 (ed.), *The New Testament in Literary Criticism* (A Library of Literary Criticism). New York: Frederick Ungar Publishing Co., 1984, X-349 p.

1987 *Words of Life. A Literary Introduction to the New Testament.* Grand Rapids, MI: Baker, 1987, 182 p.

1993 (ed.), *A Complete Literary Guide to the Bible.* Grand Rapids, MI: Zondervan, 1993.

**RYLE, John Charles**

1856[R] *Expository Thoughts on the Gospels. Matthew* [1856]. London: Clarke, 1955, 428 p.; repr. Edinburgh: Banner of Truth, 1986, XII-414 p.; (Crossway Classic Commentaries, 1). Wheaton, IL: Crossway, 1993, XVIII-296 p.

**RYPINS, Stanley**

1956 Two Inedited Leaves of Codex N. [14,22-31; 15,38-16,7] — *JBL* 75 (1956) 27-39.

**RYRIE, Charles Caldwell**

1982 Biblical Teaching on Divorce and Remarriage. — *GraceTJ* 3 (1982) 177-192. Esp. 183-189 [5,32; 19,9]. [NTA 27, 725]

# S

**SAARNIVAARA, U.**

1954 The Genealogies of Jesus in Matthew & Luke. — *Luth.Q* 6 (1954) 348-350.

**SABATOWICH, Jerome J.**

1987 Christian Divorce and Remarriage. [5,32] — *BiTod* 25 (1987) 253-255. [NTA 32, 120]

**SABBE, Maurits**

1954a Het belang van de voorgeschiedenis van de evangeliën. — *CollBrug* 50 (1954) 362-369.
→ Vaganay 1954a

1954b De tentatione Iesu in deserto. — *Ibid.*, 459-466; = ID., *Studia Neotestamentica*, 1991, 3-10 (additional note, 10-12).

1958 De transfiguratie van Jezus. — *CollBrugGand* 4 (1958) 467-503. [NTA 3, 574] → 1962a; → Coune 1969

1959a De exegese van de zaligheden. — *CollBrugGand* 5 (1959) 85-88. [NTA 4, 383] → Dupont 1954

1959b De parabel van de maagden. [25,1-13] — *Ibid.*, 369-378. [NTA 4, 392]

1962a La rédaction du récit de la transfiguration. — MASSAUX, É. (ed.), *La venue du Messie*, 1962, 65-100. Esp. 66-75; 87-89; = ID., *Studia Neotestamentica*, 1991, 65-100 (additional note, 101-104). Esp. 66-75; 87-89. → 1958; → Coune 1969

1962b Het verhaal van Jezus' doopsel. — *CollBrugGand* 8 (1962) 456-474. Esp. 458-466 [3,14-15]; 9 (1963) 211-230, 333-365. Esp. 211-230 [3,17]. [NTA 9, 145] → 1967

1967 Le baptême de Jésus. Étude sur les origines littéraires du récit des Évangiles synoptiques. — DE LA POTTERIE, I. (ed.), *De Jésus aux Évangiles*. FS J. Coppens, 1967, 184-211. Esp. 184-185; 190-194; 197-200; 204-207. (IT, 1971, 230-264); = ID., *Studia Neotestamentica*, 1991, 105-132 (additional note, 133-135). Esp. 105-106; 111-115; 118-121; 125-128. → 1962

1974* (ed.), *L'Évangile selon Marc. Tradition et rédaction* (BETL, 34). Gembloux: Duculot; Leuven: University Press, 1974, 594 p.; Leuven: University Press / Peeters, ²1988, 601 p. → Boismard, Dehandschutter, Devisch, Hendriks, Neirynck

1977 The Arrest of Jesus in Jn 18,1-11 and Its Relation to the Synoptic Gospels. A Critical Evaluation of A. Dauer's Hypothesis. — DE JONGE, M. (ed.), *L'Évangile de Jean. Sources, rédaction, théologie* (BETL, 44), Gembloux: Duculot; Leuven: University Press, 1977; Leuven: University Press / Peeters, ²1987, 203-234. Esp. 230-232 [26,52/Jn 18,11]; = ID., *Studia Neotestamentica*, 1991, 355-386 (additional note, 387-388). Esp. 382-384. → Dauer 1972

1982a Can Mt 11,27 and Lk 10,22 Be Called a Johannine Logion? — DELOBEL, J. (ed.), *Logia*, 1982, 363-371; = ID., *Studia Neotestamentica*, 1991, 399-407 (additional note, 408).

1982b The Footwashing in Jn 13 and Its Relation to the Synoptic Gospels. — *ETL* 58 (1982) 279-308. Esp. 287-305: "The synoptic gospels as a literary background" [Jn/Mt 26,6-13.17-20.26-29]. [NTA 27, 1002]; = ID., *Studia Neotestamentica*, 1991, 409-438 (additional note, 439-441). Esp. 417-435.

1991a John 10 and Its Relationship to the Synoptic Gospels. — BEUTLER, J. - FORTNA, R.T. (eds.), *The Shepherd Discourse of John 10 and Its Context. Studies by Members of the Johannine Writings Seminar* (SNTS MS, 67), Cambridge: University Press, 1991, 75-93; = ID., *Studia Neotestamentica*, 443-464 (additional note, 465-466).

1991b  *Studia Neotestamentica. Collected Essays* (BETL, 98). Leuven: University Press / Peeters, 1991, XV-573 p. → 1954b, 1962a, 1967, 1977, 1982a-b, 1991a.c

1991c  The Trial of Jesus before Pilate in John and Its Relation to the Synoptic Gospels. — *Ibid.*, 467-513. Esp. 467-477 [Dauer 1972]; 477-503 [Baum-Bodenbender 1984]; 503-508; 508-512; = DENAUX, A. (ed.), *John and the Synoptics*, 1992, 341-385. Esp. 341-351; 351-375; 375-379; 380-383.

1992    The Anointing of Jesus in John 12,1-8 and Its Synoptic Parallels. — VAN SEGBROECK, F., et al. (eds.), *The Four Gospels 1992*. FS F. Neirynck, 1992, III, 2051-2082. Esp. 2054-2055: "The Matthean redaction"; 2074-2075.

**SABOURIN, Leopold**

1961    *Rédemption sacrificielle. Une enquête exégétique* (Studia. Recherches de philosophie et de théologie, 11). Montreal: Desclée De Brouwer, 1961, 492 p. Esp. 237-239 [12,18-21]; 342-345 [26,28].

      *Redención sacrifical. Encuesta exegetica.* Bilbao: Desclée De Brouwer, 1969, 494 p.

1963    *Les noms et les titres de Jésus. Thèmes de Théologie Biblique.* Brugge–Paris: Desclée De Brouwer, 1963, 327 p. Esp. 15-25: "Les noms de Jésus"; 29-61: "Titres messianiques simples"; 65-132: "Titres messianiques communautaires"; 135-190: "Titres sotériologiques"; 193-298: "Titres proprement christologiques".

      *Los nombres y títulos de Cristo*, trans. R.M. Hernández, et al. Salamanca: S. Esteban, 1965, 375 p.

      *The Names and Titles of Jesus. Themes of Biblical Theology*, trans. M. Carroll. New York: Macmillan, 1967, XVIII-334 p.

1970    → Lyonnet 1970

1971    The Miracles of Jesus (I). Preliminary Survey. — *BTB* 1 (1971) 59-80. [NTA 15, 791] → 1974, 1975b, 1977

      *Les miracles de Jésus (I). Aperçu préliminaire.* — *BTB* 1 (1971) 64-86.

      *Os milagres de Jesus. Avaliação preliminar.* — *RevistCuBíb* 23 (1980) 83-96.

1972    The Divorce Clauses (Mt 5:32; 19:9]. — *BTB* 2 (1972) 80-86. [NTA 16, 853]

      *Les incises sur le divorce (Mt 5:32; 19:9).* — *BTB* 2 (1972) 80-87.

1973    Recent Gospel Studies. — *BTB* 3 (1973) 283-315. Esp. 283-292: "The theology of Q" [S. Schulz 1972a; Hoffmann 1972]; 292-295: "The kingdom of God" [Kretzer 1971]; 296-306: "Other Matthean studies" [Albright–Mann 1971; Radermakers 1972; Didier 1972*]; 306-315: "The synoptic problem" [Boismard 1972]. [NTA 18, 838]

1974    The Miracles of Jesus (II). Jesus and the Evil Powers. — *BTB* 4 (1974) 115-175. Esp. 161-163 [12,22-30]. [NTA 19, 473] → 1971, 1975b, 1977

1975a  *Il Vangelo di Matteo. Teologia e esegesi.* I: *Introduzione generale. Commentario 1:1-4:16.* Roma: "Fede ed Arte", 1975, 333 p. Esp. 17-32: "Origine del primo vangelo"; 33-47: "Le caratteristiche letterarie"; 48-64: "La struttura del vangelo di Matteo"; 65-84: "Temi teologici centrali"; 85-112: "Il Regno dei cieli"; 113-129: "Essere discepolo"; 130-166: "La cristologia di Matteo"; 167-180: "Opinioni sulla questione sinottica". [NTA 20, p. 240] → Marcheselli 1978

      J.L. AURRECOECHEA, *EstTrin* 10 (1976) 330-331; H. BOJORGE, *RevistBíb* 37 (1975) 290-291; J.A. CARRASCO, *EstJos* 30 (1976) 479-480; V.P. DE MAGALHAES, *BTB* 5 (1975) 222-223; G.G. GAMBA, *Sal* 37 (1975) 863-864; A. MODA, *Nicolaus* (Bari) 6 (1978) 384; J. MURPHY-O'CONNOR, *RB* 83 (1976) 300-301; F. NEIRYNCK, *ETL* 54 (1978) 189-190; G. RAVASI, *ScuolC* 104 (1976) 293-294; A. RIVERA, *EphMar* 26 (1976) 492; J. SALGUERO, *Angelicum* 53 (1976) 269-270; N. URICCHIO, *CC* 126/4 (1975) 507-508; *MiscFranc* 76 (1976) 324-325.

      *Il Discorso della montagna nel Vangelo di Matteo. Introduzione letteraria. Commentario (Mt 4:17-7:27).* Marino: "Fede ed Arte", 1976, 184 p. [NTA 21, p. 90]

      F. BRÄNDLE, *EstJos* 34 (1980) 258.

      *Il Vangelo di Matteo. Teologia e esegesi.* I: *Introduzione generale. Commentario fino a 7:27.* Roma: Paoline, 1976, 496 p. (1-4,16: 1-333; 4,17-7,27: 335-496).

      H. BOJORGE, *RevistBíb* 39 (1977) 88; A. BONORA, *Studia Patavina* 24 (1977) 88-92; G. DANIELI, *RivBib* 25 (1977) 201-204; A. GIL DE SANTIVAÑEZ, *Religión y Cultura* (Madrid) 23 (1977) 357; N. URICCHIO, *CC* 128/3 (1977) 94.

*Il Vangelo di Matteo. Teologia e esegesi.* II: *Commentario da 7:28 a 28:20*, Roma: Paoline, 1977, XI-579 p. (= 501-1079). [NTA 22, p. 93] → Ingelaere 1981
H. BOJORGE, *RevistBíb* 40 (1978) 179; A. BONORA, *Studia Patavina* 25 (1978) 174-176; G. DANIELI, *RivBib* 27 (1979) 411-413; M. GALIZZI, *ParVi* 22 (1977) 486-487; A. GIL DE SANTIVAÑEZ, *Religión y Cultura* (Madrid) 23 (1977) 227; X. JACQUES, *NRT* 100 (1978) 266-268; X. PIKAZA, *EstTrin* 12 (1978) 161-162; G. RAVASI, *ScuolC* 106 (1978) 114; G. RINALDI, *BibOr* 20 (1978) 79-80; G. SCUDERI, *Protestantesimo* 34 (1979) 41-43; N. URICCHIO, *CC* 129/3 (1978) 299-300.
*The Gospel according to St. Matthew.* I: *General Introduction, Commentary 1:1–7:27.* II: *Commentary 7:28–28:20.* Bombay: St. Paul Publications; Washington, DC: Newman, 1982, 945 p. [NTA 29, p. 92]
B.R. DOYLE, *AusBR* 33 (1985) 49-50; J. VOLCKAERT, *Vidyajyoti* 48 (1984) 160-161.

1975b     The Miracles of Jesus (III). Healings, Resuscitations, Nature Miracles. — *BTB* 5 (1975) 146-200. Esp. 148-151 [9,27-31; 20,29-31]; 152-153 [12,9-14]; 153-156 [8,5-13; Q 7,1-10]; 157-160 [11,2-6]; 173-175 [9,18-26]; 194-196 [8,23-27]; 198-199 [17,24-27] [NTA 20, 394] → 1971, 1974, 1977

1975c     La venue prochaine du Fils de l'homme d'après Mt 10,23b. — ALVAREZ VERDES, L. – ALONSO HERNÁNDEZ, E.J. (eds.), *Homenaje a Juan Prado. Miscelánea de estudios bíblicos y hebraicos*, Madrid: Consejo Superior de Investigaciones Científicas, 1975, 373-386.
"You will not have gone through all the towns of Israel, before the Son of Man comes" (Mat 10:23b). — *BTB* 7 (1977) 5-11. [NTA 21, 379]

1976a     "Connaître les mystères du Royaume" (Mt 13,11). — *Studia Hierosolymitana in onore di P. Bellarmino Bagatti.* II. *Studi esegetici* (Studii Biblici Franciscani. Collectio Maior, 23), Jerusalem: Franciscan Printing, 1976, 58-63.

1976b     Matteo: il vangelo del Regno. — *RasT* 17 (1976) 460-472. Esp. 465-468 [christology]; 468-470 [Israel]. [NTA 21, 374]

1976c     The Parables of the Kingdom. — *BTB* 6 (1976) 115-160. Esp. 117-118 [13,14-15]; 122-128 [13,11]; 137-160: "The parables of Mt 13". [NTA 21, 82]

1977     *The Divine Miracles Discussed and Defended.* Roma: Officium libri catholici, 1977, 276 p. Esp. 105-106 [9,27-31; 20,29-34]; 107 [12,9-14]; 107-110 [8,5-13]; 110-111 [11,2-6; 12,22-30]; 122-123 [9,18-26]; 133-136 [8,23-27]; 137-138 [17,24-27]. → 1971, 1974, 1975b

1978a     *L'Évangile selon saint Matthieu et ses principaux parallèles.* Roma: Biblical Institute Press, 1978, 406 p. [NTA 24, p. 87] → Ingelaere 1981
H. BOJORGE, *RevistBíb* 41 (1979) 279; J. COPPENS, *ETL* 66 (1979) 205-207; X. JACQUES, *NRT* 102 (1980) 767-768; M.-V. LEROY, *RThom* 81 (1981) 129-132; L. WALTER, *EVie* 89 (1979) 508-509.

1978b     Il discorso sulla parousia e le parabole della vigilanza (Matteo 24–25). — *BibOr* 20 (1978) 193-211. Esp. 194-200 [24,4-25]; 200-203 [24,29-31]; 203-205 [24,32-36]; 205-211 [24,37–25,30]. [NTA 23, 438]

1978c     Matthieu 5,17-20 et le rôle prophétique de la Loi (cf. Mt 11,13). — *SE* 30 (1978) 303-311. [NTA 23, 432]

1978d     As sete palavras de Jesus na Cruz. [27,46] — *RevistCuBíb* 2 (1978) 299-303. [NTA 24, 68]

1980     Why is God Called "Perfect" in Mt 5:48? — *BZ* 24 (1980) 266-268. [NTA 25, 472]

1981     Traits apocalyptiques dans l'Évangile de Matthieu. — *SE* 33 (1981) 357-372. Esp. 361-372 [6,33; 7,13-14; 8,12.24; 9,6; 10,21; 11,23; 12,32; 13,11.32.35.36-43; 16,19.21.27-28; 17,1-9; 18,10; 19,28; 21,10; 22,14; 24; 25,30.31-46; 26,39; 27,51-53; 28,2-3.18-20]. [NTA 26, 461]
Apocalyptic Traits in Matthew's Gospel. — *Religious Studies Bulletin* (Sudbury, Ont.) 3 (1983) 19-36. Esp. 26-36. [NTA 27, 505]

1984     *Christology. Basic Texts in Focus.* New York: Alba House, 1984, XII-259 p. Esp. 15-28: "Christological texts form 'Q'".
*La christologie à partir de textes clés* (Recherches, NS 9). Montréal: Bellarmin; Paris: Cerf, 1986, 227 p. Esp. 25-36: "Textes christologiques de la source 'Q'" [Q 3,16; 4,3.9; 6,46; 7,18-35; 9,58; 11,29-32; 12,8]; 89-98: "L'Évangile de Matthieu, traits christologiques distinctifs" [1,1.16; 2,15; 14,33; 16,27; 25,32].
*La cristologia a partire da testi chiave.* Brescia: Queriniana, 1989.

1985a  *L'Évangile de Luc. Introduction et commentaire.* Roma: Pont. Univ. Greg., 1985, 412 p. Esp. 20-21 [Q].
*The Gospel According to St. Luke. Introduction and Commentary.* Bandra, Bombay: Better Yourself Books, 1985, 439 p.

1985b  Matthieu 10,23 et 16,28 dans la perspective apocalyptique. — *SE* 37 (1985) 353-364. Esp. 353-357 [10,23]; 357-360 [16,28]. [NTA 30, 1049]

1989  *Protocatholicisme et ministères. Commentaire bibliographique.* Montréal: Bellarmin, 1989, 121 p. Esp. 17-19 [16,17-19]. → S. Schulz 1976
*Early Catholicism and Ministries. Bibliographical Commentary.* Burlington, Ont.: Trinity, 1989.

**SABUGAL, Santos**

1972  Χριστός. *Investigación exegética sobre la cristología joannea.* Barcelona: Herder, 1972, XXXI-565 p. Esp. 66-112: "El título χριστός en los sinópticos" [1,17; 11,2-6; 16,16-19; 22,41-46; 26,64; 27,42]; 437-440 [Jn/Mt].

1973  La embajada mesiánica del Bautista (Mt 11,2-6 = Lc 7,18-23). Análisis histórico-tradicional. — *Augustinianum* 13 (1973) 215-278. Esp. 216-227: "Historia de la interpretación"; 227-278: "La redacción mateana: Mt 11,2-6". [NTA 18, 469]; 14 (1974) 5-39 [Lk 7,18-23]. [NTA 19, 129]; 17 (1977) 395-424 ["La fuente (Q) de Mt y Lc"]. [NTA 22, 90]; 511-539 ["Hacia el evento histórico"]. [NTA 22, 766] → 1980a

1980a  *La embajada mesiánica de Juan Bautista (Mt 11,2-6 = Lc 7,18-23). Historia, exégesis, teológica, hermenéutica.* Madrid: Privately published, 1980, XVI-274 p. → 1973
S.B. MARROW, *CBQ* 44 (1982) 159-161; W. WIEFEL, *TLZ* 108 (1983) 203-205.

1980b  El Padrenuestro, análisis histórico-tradicional. — *Religión y Cultura* (Madrid) 26 (1980) 635-647.

1980c  El "Padrenuestro": Tradición literaria y comentarios patrísticos. — *Revista Agustiniana* (Madrid) 21 (1980) 47-72. [NTA 25, 474]

1982a  *El Padrenuestro en la interpretación catequética antigua y moderna* (Nueva Alianza, 79). Salamanca: Sígueme, 1982, 448 p. Esp. 107-118; 151-155; 204-215; 258-261; 308-315; 359-364; 403-407; 432-434. [NTA 28, p. 204] → 1985a
S. CASTRO, *RevistEspir* 42 (1983) 359; D. FERNÁNDEZ, *EphMar* 33 (1983) 342, R. HERNÁNDEZ, *CiTom* 109 (1982) 623; *Teología* 19 (1982) 208-210; M.A. KELLER, *CiudDios* 196 (1983) 167; P. LANGA, *Religión y Cultura* (Madrid) 30 (1984) 112-113; A. MEIS, *TVida* 26 (1985) 308; C. PETINO, *Divinitas* 28 (1984) 93-94; N. SILANES, *EstTrin* 16 (1982) 131-132.
Notre pain quotidien: Mt 6,11. [1982, 308-315] — *SIDIC* 18/2 (1985) 11-14.
Our Daily Bread. Mt 6:11; Lk 11:3. — *SIDIC* 18/2 (1985) 12-15. [NTA 30, 1048]
*Il Padrenostro nella catechesi antica e moderna*, trans. M. Nicolosi (Cristianismo, 2). Palermo: Augustinus, 1985, 412 p.
L. FATICA, *Asprenas* 37 (1990) 122-123; A. FERRUA, *CC* 140/3 (1989) 306-307; A. LONGOBARDI, *RasT* 30 (1989) 490-491; S. RAPONI, *Studia Moralia* (Roma) 28 (1990) 257-258; M. RUIZ JURADO, *Greg* 71 (1990) 599-600; W. TUREK, *Sal* 54 (1992) 198.

1982b  La importancia del Padrenuestro. — *Revista Agustiniana* 23 (1982) 437-486. [NTA 28, 94]

1983  La redacción mateana del Padrenuestro (Mt 6,9-13). — *EstE* 58 (1983) 307-329. Esp. 308-310 [context]; 310-312 [redaction]; 312-315 [structure]; 315-329 [interpretation]. [NTA 28, 495]

1984a  Didajé VIII 2: El "Padre Nuestro". — *RevistBíb* 46 (1984) 287-297. [NTA 29, 810]

1984b  La primitiva forma literaria del Padrenuestro. — *EstTrin* 18 (1984) 393-412. → 1985d

1985a  *Abba' ... La oración del Señor (Historia y exégesis teológica)* (Biblioteca de autores cristianos, 467). Madrid: Catolica, 1985, XXIV-759 p. Esp. 81-131: "La interpretación antigua y moderna del Padrenuestro"; 152-195: "La redacción del evangelista Mateo"; 244-286: "La tradición prerredaccional del Padrenuestro"; 287-723: "La enseñanza del Padrenuestro por Jesús de Nazaret". [NTA 31, p. 103] → 1982a
J. GALOT, *Greg* 67 (1986) 773; D. GOLDSMITH, *JBL* 106 (1987) 717-719; P. GRECH, *Augustinianum*

26 (1986) 582-584; J. GUTIÉRREZ, *CiudDios* 200 (1987) 117-118; H.E. LONA, *BZ* 30 (1986) 268-270; V. PASQUETTO, *Teresianum* 38 (1987) 227; M. PÉREZ FERNÁNDEZ, *RB* 94 (1987) 135-137; A. SALAS, *BibFe* 12 (1986) 131-132; J. SALGUERO, *Angelicum* 63 (1986) 468-488; A. SEGOVIA, *ArchTeolGran* 50 (1987) 463.

1985b    *Pecado y reconciliación en el mensaje de Jesús* (Cristianismo. Collana di studi storico-religiosi, 1). Palermo: Augustinus, 1985, 187 p. Esp. 104-105 [18,18]; 143-161 [5,38-42].

1985c    Hacia el origen histórico del "Padrenuestro". — *Religión y Cultura* (Madrid) 31 (1985) 41-56. [NTA 30, 116]

1985d    La lengua y composición original del Padrenuestro. — *EstTrin* 19 (1985) 209-225. [NTA 31, 118] → 1984b

1985e    El Padrenuestro a lo largo de la historia. — *Nuevo Mundo* (Buenos Aires) 29 (1985) 79-101.

1985f    Reino y reinado de Dios en el mensaje de Jesús. — *EstAgust* 20 (1985) 273-293.

1985g    La tradición pre-redaccional del Padre-Nuestro. — *NatGrac* 32 (1985) 233-266. Esp. 234-246: "La forma textual"; 246-265: "Significado teológico".

1987    *La Iglesia sierva de Dios. Hacia una eclesiología servicial.* Zamora: Montecasino, 1987, 190 p. Esp. 50-140.
     *La Chiesa serva di Dio. Per una ecclesiologia del servizio.* Roma: Dehoniane, 1992, 211 p. Esp. 55-160.

1991a    La resurrección de Jesús en el Evangelio de Mateo (*Mt* 28,1-20). — *Sal* 53 (1991) 467-478. [NTA 36, 732]

1991b    La resurrección de la hija de Jairo (Mc 5,21-24a.35-43 par.). Análisis histórico-tradicional. [9,18-19.23-26] — *EstAgust* 26 (1991) 80-101 [NTA 36, 181]

1992    La transfiguración de Jesús: Adelanto de su Resurrección (Mc 9,1-10 par). [17,1-9] — *EstAgust* 27 (1992) 453-481.

1993    *Anástasis. Resucitó y resucitaremos* (Biblioteca de autores cristianos, 536). Madrid: BAC, 1993, xx-712 p.

1994    La mateana tradición histórica sobre las apariciones del Resucitado (Mt 28,9-10.16-20). — *EstAgust* 29 (1994) 217-242.

**SACCHI, Alessandro**

1969    "Se vuoi essere perfetto" (*Mt.* 19,21): perfezione e vita cristiana. — *RivBib* 17 (1969) 313-325. Esp. 313-318 [19,16-30]; 318-325 [5,17-48]. [NTA 14, 859]

**SACCHI, Paolo**

1956    *Alle origini del Nuovo Testamento. Saggio per la storia della tradizione e la critica del testo* (Pubblicazioni della Università degli Studi di Firenze, IV/2). Firenze: Le Monnier, 1956, XI-178 p. Esp. 37-42 [1,16]; 105-108; 145-146 [1,16; 6,8].

1986    I sinottici furono scritti in ebraico? Una valida ipotesi di lavoro. — *Henoch* 8 (1986) 67-78. [NTA 31, 569] → Carmignac 1984, Tresmontant 1983

**SACHOT, Maurice**

1981    *L'homélie pseudo-chrysostomienne sur la Transfiguration. CPG 4724, BHG 1975. Contextes liturgiques, Restitution à Léonce, prêtre de Constantinople, Édition critique et commentée, Traduction et études connexes* (EHS, XXIII/151). Frankfurt/M–Bern: Lang, 1981, 554 p. Esp. 289-329: "Texte et traduction"; 331-431 "Commentaire" [16,21–17,9].

1982    Saint Cyprien. De la tradition de l'Écriture à l'écriture de la Tradition. De *Mt.* 16,18-19 au *De Ecclesiae Catholicae Unitate*, c. iv. — AUBERT, J.-M., et al. (eds.), *Du texte à la parole* (Le point théologique, 40), Paris: Beauchesne, 1982, 11-40.

1983  Le réemploi de l'homélie 56 in *Matthaeum* de Jean Chrysostome (*BHG*$^a$ *1984*) dans deux homélies byzantines sur la Transfiguration (*BHG* 1980k et $^a$1985). — *RevSR* 57 (1983) 123-146.

**SAEBO, Magne**

1970  Overleverringshistoriske problemer i Judas-Perikopen hos Matt. [Tradition-historical problems in the Judas pericope in Matthew] — *TidsTeolKirk* 41 (1970) 249-265.

**SÄNGER, Dieter**

1995  "Von mir hat er geschrieben" (Joh 5,46): Zur Funktion und Bedeutung Mose im Neuen Testament. — *KerDog* 41 (1995) 112-135. Esp. 119-123. [NTA 40, 442]

**SAENZ DE SANTA MARÍA, Miguel**

1983  ¡Padre, santificado sea tu nombre! [6,9] — *BibFe* 9 (1983) 17-23.

**SAFRAI, Shmuel**

1976  & FLUSSER, D., The Slave of Two Masters. [6,24] — *Immanuel* 6 (1976) 30-33. [NTA 21, 79]; = FLUSSER, D., *Judaism*, 1988, 169-172.

**SAGGIN, L.**

1952  Magister vester unus est, Christus (Mt 23,10). — *VD* 30 (1952) 205-213.

**SAHLIN, Harald**

1952  Zum Verständnis von drei Stellen des Markus-Evangeliums (Mk 4,26-29; 7,18f; 15,34). — *Bib* 33 (1952) 53-66. Esp. 62-66 [27,46].

1956  Chassidische Parallelen zum Neuen Testament. — *Judaica* 12 (1956) 65-98. Esp. 68-81.

1959  Zwei Fälle von harmonisierendem Einfluss des Matthäus-Evangeliums auf das Markus-Evangelium. — *StudTheol* 13 (1959) 166-179. Esp. 167-172 [3,1-6]; 172-179 [26,6-13].

1970  Die drei Kardinalsünden und das neue Testament. — *StudTheol* 24 (1970) 93-112. Esp. 102-104 [4,1-11]; 104-106 [13,1-9]; 106-109 [5,21-48]. [NTA 15, 778]

1977  Zum Verständnis der christologischen Anschauung des Markusevangeliums. — *StudTheol* 31 (1977) 1-19. Esp. 10-12 [27,51-53]; 18-19 [28,17]. [NTA 22, 98]

1979  Traditionskritische Bemerkungen zu zwei Evangelienperikopen. — *StudTheol* 33 (1979) 69-84. Esp. 69-77 [5,38-42]; 77-84 [11,16-19]. [NTA 24, 87]

1982  Emendationsvorschläge zum griechischen Text des Neuen Testaments I. — *NT* 24 (1982) 160-179. Esp. 161-165 [1,1; 6,5.28; 12,31-32.44; 14,29; 18,10; 19,4; 21,9; 24,26]. [NTA 27, 60] → D.A. Black 1989b

1984  Några randanmärkingar till NT 81. [Some marginal notes to NT 81] — *SEÅ* 49 (1984) 74-82. Esp. 75-76 [10,5; 28,17]. [NTA 29, 478] → Riesenfeld 1981

1987  Ett svårt ställe i Bergspredikan (Mt 5:39-42). [A difficult passage in the Sermon on the Mount (Mt 5,39-42)] — *SEÅ* 51-52 (1986-87) 214-218. [NTA 31, 585]

**SAITO, Tadashi**

1977  *Die Mosevorstellungen im Neuen Testament* (EHS, XXIII/100). Bern–Frankfurt/M: Lang, 1977, IV-241 p. Esp. 51-72: "Die Moseanschauungen im Mt-Ev" [1,18-2,23; 4,1-11; 17,1-8; 23,2; 28,16-20]. — Diss. Zürich, 1976 (E. Schweizer).

**SALAS, Antonio**

1970  El mensaje del Bautista. Redacción y teología en Mt 3,7-12. — *EstBíb* 29 (1970) 55-72. Esp. 56-59: "El mensaje del Bautista en el primer evangelio"; 59-66: "La redacción de Mt 3,7-12"; 66-71: "Contenido teológico del mensaje del Bautista". [NTA 15, 843]

El mensaje del Bautista. Estudio histórico-redaccional de Mt 3,7-12. — *La Etica Biblica* (XXIX Semana Biblica Española), Madrid: Consejo Superior de Investigaciones Científicas, 1971, 271-287. Esp. 273-275; 275-282; 282-287.

1972    Jesús, esperanza de los Gentiles, en Mt 2,1-12. — *La esperanza en la Biblia* (XXX
        Semana Biblica Española), Madrid: Consejo Superio: de Investigaciones Científicas,
        1972, 109-130. Esp. 112-121: "El horizonte teológico de Mt 2,1-12"; 121-129: "Eclesiología y
        escatología en Mt".

1975    El tema de la "Montaña" en el primer evangelio. ¿Precisión geográfica o motivación
        teológica? — *CiudDios* 188 (1975) 3-17. Esp. 7-10 [4,1-11]; 10-12 [5,1]; 12-14 [17,1-8]; 14-15
        [28,16-20]. [NTA 20, 81]

1976    *La infancia de Jesus (Mt 1-2). ¿Historia o teología?* (Biblioteca Escuela Bíblica, 1).
        Madrid: Biblia y Fe, 1976, 250 p. [NTA 21, p. 232]

        I. ARIAS, *NatGrac* 24 (1977) 143; J.L. AURRECOECHEA, *EstTrin* 11 (1977) 101-102; C. BERNAS, *CBQ*
        40 (1978) 136-137; H. BOJORGE, *RevistBíb* 39 (1977) 349-350; J.A. CARRASCO, *EstJos* 30 (1976) 479-
        480; M. DE BURGOS NUÑEZ, *Communio* (Sevilla) 10 (1977) 471-472; J.L. ESPINEL, *CiTom* 105 (1978)
        654-655; J. GALOT, *Greg* 58 (1977) 572-573; A. GARCÍA MORENO, *ScriptTheol* 10 (1978) 315-319; W.
        KIRCHSCHLÄGER, *BLtg* 50 (1977) 277; P.É. LANGEVIN, *SE* 29 (1977) 338-339; X. LÉON-DUFOUR, *RSR*
        66 (1978) 126-127; A. MANRIQUE, *BibFe* 2 (1976) 368-370; A. RÓDENAS M., *EstTrin* 12 (1978) 482-
        483.

1979    La figura de María en los Evangelios de la infancia. — *CiudDios* 192 (1979) 337-354.
        Esp. 338-342. [NTA 24, 781]

1980a   Maria, la Madre. — *BibFe* 6 (1980) 184-204. Esp. 188-197 [1,18-25].

1980b   José, el padre. [1,21] — *Ibid.*, 304-332. [NTA 25, 468]

1982    *Biblia y catequesis. ¿Cultura y fe en diálogo? Nuevo Testamento III: Los Evangelios.*
        Madrid: Escuela Bíblica, 1982, 416 p.

1983a   El Evangelio de Navidad. — *RazFe* 208 (1983) 350-361. Esp. 351-352, 354-355 [1,18-25];
        358-360 [2,1-12]. [NTA 28, 911]

1983b   Judas de Iscariote. Aproximación crítica al discípulo traidor desde la teología evan-
        gélica. — *CiudDios* 196 (1983) 189-209. Esp. 193-195; 202-204. [NTA 28, 456]

1983c   ¡Padre, perdónas nuestras ofensas! [6,12] — *BibFe* 9 (1983) 52-63.

1983d   ¡Felices, los que cooperan a la paz! [5,9] — *Ibid.*, 187-199.

        **SALDARINI, Anthony J.**

1988    *Pharisees, Scribes and Sadducees in Palestinian Society. A Sociological Approach.*
        Wilmington, DE: Glazier, 1988; Edinburgh: Clark, 1989, X-325 p. Esp. 157-173: "The
        Pharisees, Scribes and Sadducees in Matthew".

1989    Judaism and the New Testament. — EPP, E.J. - MACRAE, G.W. (eds.), *The New
        Testament and Its Modern Interpreters*, 1989, 27-54. Esp. 37-39: "Midrash in Matthew".

1991    The Gospel of Matthew and Jewish-Christian Conflict. — BALCH, D.L. (ed.), *Social
        History of the Matthean Community*, 1991, 38-61. Esp. 41-44: "The identity of Matthew's
        community"; 48-54: "Deviance in the gospel of Matthew"; 54-60: "The Matthean community as a deviance
        association". → Gundry 1991

1992a   Delegitimation of Leaders in Matthew 23. — *CBQ* 54 (1992) 659-680. Esp. 668-672:
        "Analysis of Mt 23"; 672-678: "The seven woe oracles". [NTA 37, 1271]

1992b   The Gospel of Matthew and Jewish-Christian Conflict in the Galilee. — LEVINE, L.I.
        (ed.), *The Galilee in Late Antiquity*, New York: The Jewish Theological Seminary of
        America, 1992, 23-38.

1992c   Pharisees. — *ABD* 5 (1992) 289-303. Esp. 296.

1994    *Matthew's Christian-Jewish Community* (Chicago Studies in the History of Judaism).
        Chicago, IL - London: University of Chicago Press, 1994, VII-317 p. Esp. 11-26.215-225:
        "Matthew within first-century Judaism"; 27-43.225-234: "Matthew's people: Israel"; 44-67.234-248:
        "Matthew's opponents: Israel's leaders"; 68-83.248-253: "Matthew's horizon: the nations"; 84-123.253-267:
        "Matthew's group of Jewish believers-in-Jesus"; 124-164.267-285: "Matthew's torah"; 165-193.286-295:
        "Jesus Messiah and Son of God". [NTA 38, p. 466]

M.E. BORING, *TS* 56 (1995) 152-154; M. DAVIES, *BibInt* 3 (1995) 375-377; R.H. GUNDRY, *Cross Currents* 44 (1994-95) 508-511; D.R.A. HARE, *HorizonsBT* 18 (1996) 103-105; A.-J. LEVINE, *JBL* 114 (1995) 732-734; I.A. LEVINSKAYA, *Theological Book Review* (Guilford, Surrey) 7/2 (1994-95) 17; B.T. VIVIANO, *CBQ* 57 (1995) 607-609.

1995   Boundaries and Polemics in the Gospel of Matthew. — *BibInt* 3 (1995) 239-265. Esp. 244-247: "Social location of the gospel of Matthew and its audience"; 247-252: "Community boundaries, gentiles, and the law"; 252-256: "The nature of Matthew's group"; 256-260: "Polemics and presuppositions". [NTA 40, 807]

**SALDARINI, Giovanni**

1962a   La genealogia di Gesù. — MORALDI, L. - LYONNET, S. (eds.), *Introduzione alla Bibbia*, IV, 1962, 411-425. Esp. 411-418 [1,1-17].

1962b   & MORALDI, L., Battesimo di Cristo. [3,13-17] — *Ibid.*, 493-501.

1969   *Le beatitudini evangeliche.* Milano: Opera della Regalità di NSGC, 1969, 182 p.
A. PANTONI, *Humanitas* 25 (1970) 761.

1972   Le beatitudini secondo Luca e Matteo. — *Presenza Pastorale* 42 (1972) 403-409.

**SALERNO, Antonio**

1980   Un nuovo aspetto del primato di Pietro in Mt. 10,2 e 16,18-19. — *RivBib* 28 (1980) 435-439. [NTA 25, 858]

**SALGUERO, José**

1967   → de Tuya 1967

1972   Las bienaventuranzas evangélicas. — *CuBíb* 29 (1972) 73-90.

**SALOM, A.P.**

1958   The Imperatival Use of ἵνα in the New Testament. — *AusBR* 6 (1958) 123-141. Esp. 137 [2,33]. [NTA 4, 42]

**SALVADOR, Joaquim**

1964   São os Judeus de ontem e hoje responsáveis pela morte de Jesus? [Are the Jews alone responsible for the death of Jesus?] — *RevistCuBíb* 1 (1964) 109-153. [NTA 10, 167]

**SALVONI, Fausto**

1968a   "Eccetto il caso di fornicazione". Riflessioni su di una nuova interpretazione biblica. — *RicBibRel* 3 (1968) 138-147. →1968b

1968b   Una nuova interpretazione delle clausole mattaiche sul divorzio. — *Ibid.*, 245-253. → 1968a

1969   Finchè non ebbe partorito un figlio. — *RicBibRel* 4 (1969) 11-43

1970   Bestemmia contro lo Spirito Santo. — *RicBibRel* 5 (1970) 365-381. Esp. 67-70 [Q 12,8-12]; 70-72 [12,22-32].

1972   Matteo, contenuto del Vangelo. — *RicBibRel* 7 (1972) 331-334. → Rolland 1972

1975   Il vaticinio di Michea. — *RicBibRel* 10 (1975) 31-42. Esp. 38-42 [2,6]. [NTA 20, 432]

1979   La visita dei Magi e la fuga in Egitto. — *RicBibRel* 14 (1979) 171-201. [NTA 24, 418]

**SALIJ, Jacek**

1976   (ed.), Św. Tomasz z Akwinu: Ewangelia Ojców Kościola. [Thomas Aquinas: the gospel according to the Fathers] — *Biblia w ręku chrześcijan.* - *"W drodze"* 4 (1976) 2/33-38; 3/43-55; 4/45-48; 5/68-71; 6/58-61; 7/64-73; 8/35-40; 9/42-45; 10/74-78; 11/62-65; 12/35-38; 5 (1977) 1/22-25; 2/69-72; 3/20-22; 4/40-45; 5/65-68; 6/49-50; 7/55-58; 8/49-52; 9/68-70; 10/76-79; 11/73-76; 12/49-51.

**SAMAIN, Pierre**

1950   Les ouvriers de la vigne (Mt., XX,1-16). — *RevDiocTournai* 5 (1950) 25-27.

**SAMUEL, S. Johnson**

1988 Communalism or Commonalism: A Study of Matthew's Account of Jesus' Baptism (3:13-17). — *IndianTS* 25 (1988) 334-347. Esp. 337-34ᶜ. [NTA 33, 1116]

**SÁNCHEZ CETINA, Edesio**

1982 Jesucristo la Palabra encarnada: revelación des nombre y poder de Dios (Mt 11). — COSTAS, O. (ed.), *Predicación evangélica y teología hispana*, San Diego: Publ. de las Américas, 1982, 45-54.

**SÁNCHEZ MIELGO, Gerardo**

1983 *Evangelios sinópticos. Planteamientos críticos. Mensaje central.* Bogotá: USTA, 1983, 576 p.

**SANCHO ANDREU, Jaime**

1979 "Fide divites". "Bienaventurados los pobres de espíritu" en la interpretación de los Santos Padres, hasta Orígenes. — *Anales Valentinos* 5 (1979) 311-349. Esp. 314-321 [Apostolic Fathers]; 321-324 [Apologetes]; 324-329 [Tertullian]; 329-331 [Cyprian]; 331-338 [Clement of Alexandria]; 338-343 [Origen]; 343-348 [Didasc. Apost.].

**SAND, Alexander**

1969 Die Unzuchtsklausel in Mt 5,31.32 und 19,3-9. — *MüTZ* 20 (1969) 118-129. [NTA 14, 481]

1970 Die Polemik gegen "Gesetzlosigkeit" im Evangelium nach Matthäus und bei Paulus. Ein Beitrag zur neutestamentlichen Überlieferungsgeschichte. — *BZ* 14 (1970) 112-125. Esp. 115-117 [5,17-20]; 118-120 [ἀνομία]; 123-125. [NTA 15, 128]

1972 "Wie geschrieben steht...". Zur Auslegung der jüdischer Schriften in den urchristlichen Gemeinden. — ERNST, J. (ed.), *Schriftauslegung. Beiträge zur Hermeneutik des Neuen Testamentes und im Neuen Testament*, München–Paderborn: Schöningh, 1972, 331-357. Esp. 343-345.

1974 *Das Gesetz und die Propheten. Untersuchungen zur Theologie des Evangeliums nach Matthäus* (BibUnt, 11). Regensburg: Pustet, 1974, XIII-246 p. Esp. 2-9: "Literar- und quellenkritische Untersuchungen"; 10-16: "Begriffs- und überlieferungsgeschichtliche Studien"; 17-31: "Form- und redaktionsgeschichtliche Darstellungen"; 33-45: "Das Gesetz als die ganze Tora oder die Einzelvorschrift"; 46-56: "Die Antithesen der Bergrede"; 57-105: "Die Streitgespräche"; 106-124: "Das Tun des Gesetzes als Erfüllung des Willens Gottes"; 125-137: "Prophet(en) und Prophetenschicksal bei Matthäus"; 138-167: "Jesus der 'Prophet' und Messias"; 168-177: "Jünger und Propheten in der Gemeinde des Matthäus"; 178-182: "Die Überlieferung der Logienquelle: Mt 11,12-13 / Lk 16,16"; 183-193: "Die redaktionellen Aussagen über 'Gesetz' und 'Propheten' bei Matthäus"; 194-205: "Die bessere Gerechtigkeit als der entscheidende Inhalt von 'Gesetz und Propheten'". [NTA 19, p. 266] — Diss. München, 1969 (O. Kuss).

F. B., *RevistEspir* 34 (1975) 140; H. BOJORGE, *RevistBíb* 37 (1975) 308-309; T.C. DE KRUIJF, *Bijdragen* 36 (1975) 328; J. DUPONT, *RivStoLR* 12 (1976) 231-233; I. FLÓREZ, *ArchTeolGran* 37 (1974) 303; K. GRAYSTON, *ExpT* 86 (1974-75) 261; B.J. HUBBARD, *JBL* 95 (1976) 664-666; J. KAHMANN, *TijdTheol* 15 (1975) 325-326; G. LEONARDI, *Studia Patavina* 22 (1975) 651-652; C. MATEOS, *EstAgust* 11 (1976) 134; J.P. MEIER, *CBQ* 37 (1975) 602-604; H. MERKEL, *TLZ* 102 (1977) 196-199; R. PESCH, *Freiburger Rundbrief* 27 (1975) 100; G. RINALDI, *BibOr* 18 (1976) 82-83; A. SALAS, *CiudDios* 188 (1975) 123-124; A. STÖGER, *TPQ* 124 (1976) 388-389.

1976 Propheten, Weise und Schriftkundige in der Gemeinde des Matthäusevangeliums. — HAINZ, J., *Die Kirche im Werden. Studien zum Thema Amt und Gemeinde im Neuen Testament*, Paderborn–München: Schöningh, 1976, 167-184.

1978 Jesu Sprechen mit Gott und über Gott nach dem Zeugnis der Synoptiker. — BEINERT, W., et al. (eds.), *Sprache und Erfahrung als Problem der Theologie* (Schriften zur Pädagogik und Katechetik, 29), Paderborn: Schöningh, 1978, 109-120.

1983    *Reich Gottes und Eheverzicht im Evangelium nach Matthäus* (SBS, 109). Stuttgart: Katholisches Bibelwerk, 1983, 82 p. Esp. 23-44 [history of research: 19,10-12]; 45-60: "Analyse und Exegese von Mt 19,10-12"; 69-78: "Der Eur.uchenspruch im Kontext der matthäischen Gemeindetheologie".
    A. Fuchs, *SNTU* 9 (1984) 247-248; J.P. Meier, *CBQ* 47 (1985) 567-568; F.J. Stendebach, *BK* 39 (1984) 37.

1984    Überliefern und Bewahren. Zum Traditionsverständnis Jesu und der urchristlichen Gemeinden. — *SNTU* 9 (1984) 5-30. Esp. 16-17 [9,16-17]; 19-20 [15,1-20]; 21-22 [13,51-52]. [NTA 30, 1014]

1985    Das Evangelium des Matthäus, das Evangelium der Kirche. — *Forum Katholische Theologie* (Aschaffenburg) 1 (1985) 61-67. [NTA 30, 105]

1986    *Das Evangelium nach Matthäus* (Regensburger Neues Testament). Regensburg: Pustet, 1986, 679 p. Esp. 17-34: "Allgemeine Einleitung"; 35-604: "Auslegung". [NTA 31, p. 367] → Giesen 1987b
    X. Alegre, *ActBibl* 25 (1988) 73-74; J. Beutler, *TheolPhil* 63 (1988) 253-255; C. Bissoli, *Sal* 51 (1989) 362; C.E. Carlston, *CBQ* 50 (1988) 543-545; J. Ernst, *TGl* 77 (1987) 381-382; A. Fuchs, *SNTU* 12 (1987) 224-226; V. Fusco, *CrnStor* 10 (1989) 150-151; J.D. Kingsbury, *JBL* 107 (1988) 538-540; S. Légasse, *BullLitEccl* 89 (1988) 294-295; K. Limburg, *ScriptTheol* 21 (1989) 699; F. Marín Heredia, *Carthaginensia* 4 (1988) 178-179; J.P. Miranda, *BK* 42 (1987) 138-139; M. Nobile, *Ant* 64 (1989) 610-611; R. Penna, *Greg* 69 (1988) 772-773; R. Pesch, *TRev* 83 (1987) 460-461; B. Proietti, *Claretianum* 27 (1987) 420-421; A. Salas, *CiudDios* 201 (1988) 485; A. Segovia, *ArchTeolGran* 50 (1987) 447-448; K. Stock, *ZKT* 110 (1988) 194-195; A. Stöger, *BLtg* 60 (1987) 43-45; H. Welzen, *TijdTheol* 27 (1987) 404; W. Wiefel, *TLZ* 113 (1988) 110-113.
    *Il Vangelo di Matteo*. Brescia: Morcelliana, 1992, 1014 p.
    D. Scaiola, *CC* 145/1 (1994) 623-624.

1987    Fremde und Feinde in der Verkündigung Jesu. — *BK* 42 (1987) 60-65. Esp. 61-62: "Die Gemeindeparänese bei Matthäus". [NTA 32, 81]

1990    Die Gemeinde zwischen "jenen Tagen Jesu" und "dem Tag des Gerichts". Zum Geschichtsverständnis des Matthäusevangelium. — *TTZ* 99 (1990) 49-71. Esp. 64-70: "Das Geschichtsverständnis des Matthäusevangeliums". [NTA 34, 1125]

1991    *Das Matthäus-Evangelium* (Erträge der Forschung, 275). Darmstadt: Wissenschaftliche Buchgesellschaft, 1991, VIII-196 p. Esp. 1-42: "Literarische Fragen"; 43-43: "Gott"; 63-101: "Jesus von Nazaret"; 101-129: "Die Gemeinde"; 129-138: "Gegenwart und Zukunft"; 139-167: "Hermeneutische Fragen". [NTA 36, p. 268]
    A. Fuchs, *SNTU* 18 (1993) 254-255; M. Müller, *DanskTeolTids* 55 (1992) 152-153.

1992    "Abba - Vater" – Gotteserfahrung und Gottesglaube Jesu. — *Renovatio* 48 (1992) 204-218. [NTA 37, 1216]

1992a   "Schule des Lebens". Zur Theologie des Matthäusevangeliums. — Hainz, J. (ed.), *Theologie im Werden*. FS O. Kuss, 1992, 57-82. Esp. 57-61: "Der Verfasser und seine redaktionelle Tätigkeit"; 61-76: "Mt 28,16-20 als Summarium der theologischen Grundgedanken des MtEv"; 76-79: "Die Verheißung an die Gemeinde für 'die Zeit dazwischen'"; 79-82: "Die Wirkungsgeschichte des MtEv in der frühen Kirche".

1992b   Die Logia Jesu, die vier Evangelien und der Kanon der ntl Schriften. — *Ibid.*, 125-141. Esp. 126-129 [Q]; 130-131 [Mt].

1995    Mt 18: Weisungen für eine Gemeinde in der Bewährung. — Reinhardt, H.J.F. (ed.), *Theologia et Ius Canonicum. Festgabe für Heribert Heinemann zur Vollendung seines 70. Lebensjahres*, Essen: Ludgerus, 1995, 51-57.

**SANDEGREN, C.**

1950    "Be ye perfect!" [5,48] — *ExpT* 61 (1949-50) 383.

1952    Voro de "vise männen" från Österlandet verkligen hedningar? [Were the "wise men" from the East really gentiles?] — *Svensk Jerusalems Föreningens Tidskrift* 51 (1952) 13-22.

**SANDERS, Ed Parish**

1969a *The Tendencies of the Synoptic Tradition* (SNTS MS, 9). Cambridge: University Press, 1969, XIV-328 p. Esp. 46-87: "Increasing length as a possible tendency of the tradition" [OT quotations; speeches; dialogues]; 88-189: "Increasing detail"; 190-255: "Diminishing semitism"; 256-271: "Direct discourse and conflation"; 290-293. — Diss. Union Theol. Sem., Richmond, VA, 1966 (W.D. Davies). → 1972; → J.K. Elliott 1971, Léon-Dufour 1972b, McEleney 1972

Suggested Exceptions to the Priority of Mark. [1969, 290-293] — BELLINZONI, A.J., Jr., et al. (eds.), *The Two-Source Hypothesis*, 1985, 199-203.

1969b The Argument from Order and the Relationship between Matthew and Luke. — *NTS* 15 (1968-69) 249-261. Esp. 255-256 [minor agreements]; 257-261 [Mk/Q]. [NTA 13, 844]; = BELLINZONI, A.J., Jr., et al. (eds.), *The Two-Source Hypothesis*, 1985, 409-425. → Neirynck 1973b

1971 Mark 10.17-31 and Parallels. [19,16-30] — *SBL 1971 Seminar Papers*, I, 257-270.

1972 Priorités et dépendances dans la tradition synoptique. — *RSR* 60 (1972) 519-540. Esp. 520-530: "Marc 10,17-31 par."; 530-535: "Marc 2,23-28 par."; 535-536: "Marc 1,29-31 par.". [NTA 17, 894] → 1969a

1973 The Overlaps of Mark and Q and the Synoptic Problem — *NTS* 19 (1972-73) 453-465. Esp. 458-459 [3,7-12]; 459 [3,13-17]; 459-460 [4,1-11]; 460-461 [12,25-32]. [NTA 18, 457] → A. Fuchs 1980b

1975 → R.H. Fuller 1975b

1982 Jesus, Paul and Judaism. — *ANRW* II.25.1 (1982) 390-450. Esp. 405-408 [21,12-13]; 408-410 [26,60-61]; 413-416 [8,21-22]; 416-417 [15,1-20]; 417-418 [22,23-40]; 418-425 [sinners].

1983 Jesus and the Sinners. — *JSNT* 19 (1983) 5-36. Esp. 9-10 [9,9-13; 11,16-19]; 24-28 [11,18; 21,32]. [NTA 28, 466]; = EVANS, C.A. – PORTER, S.E. (eds.), *The Historical Jesus*, 1995, 29-60. Esp. 33-35; 53-56.

1985 *Jesus and Judaism*. London: SCM, 1985, XIV-444 p. Esp. 61-122: "The restoration of Israel"; 123-244: "The kingdom"; 245-318: "Conflict and death"; ²1987, ⁴1994.

1987* (ed.), *Jesus, the Gospels, and the Church. Essays in Honor of William R. Farmer*. Macon, GA: Mercer University Press, 1987, XXXVIII-236 p. → Bellinzoni, Daube, Dungan, Gerhardsson 1986b, Orchard, Peabody, Reicke, E.P. Sanders, Shuler, W.O. Walker Jr.

1987 Jesus and the Kingdom: The Restoration of Israel and the New People of God. — *Ibid.*, 225-239. Esp. 229 [8,11-12; 12,41-42]; 234-235 [19,28].

1989 & DAVIES, M., *Studying the Synoptic Gospels*. London: SCM; Philadelphia, PA: Trinity Press International, 1989, IX-374 p. Esp. 49-119 "The synoptic problem"; 121-197: "Form criticism"; 201-223: "Redaction criticism"; 224-239: "Structuralism and de-construction"; 240-251: "Rhetorical criticism"; 252-265: "The genre of the first gospel"; 299-344: "Research into the life and teaching of Jesus".

1990 When is a Law a Law? The Case of Jesus and Paul. — FIRMAGE, E.B. – WEISS, B.G. – WELCH, J.W. (eds.), *Religion and Law: Biblical-Judaic and Islamic Perspectives*, Winona Lake, IN: Eisenbrauns, 1990, 139-158. Esp. 146-151: "The saying on divorce".

**SANDERS, Jack T.**

1969 Ethics in the Synoptic Gospels. — *BR* 14 (1969) 19-32. Esp. 26-32 [NTA 14, 842]
The Synoptic Gospels and Acts. — ID., *Ethics*, 1975, 31-46. Esp. 40-45.

1970 The Question of the Relevance of Jesus for Ethics Today. — *JAAR* 38 (1970) 131-146. Esp. 133-134; 137-139. [NTA 15, 97]
Jesus. — ID., *Ethics*, 1975, 1-29. Esp. 5-6; 14-17 (revised).

1975 *Ethics in the New Testament. Change and Development*. Philadelphia, PA: Fortress, 1975, XIII-144 p. → 1969, 1970

1985  The Pharisees in Luke-Acts. — GROH, D.E. - JEWETT, R. (eds.), *The Living Text*. FS
      E.W. Saunders, 1985, 141-188. Esp. 167-172 [23]; 172-173 [22,35].

1992  Jewish Christianity in Antioch before the Time of Hadrian: Where Does the Identity
      Lie? — *SBL 1992 Seminar Papers*, 346-361. Esp. 351-358.

1993  *Schismatics, Sectarians, Dissidents, Deviants. The First One Hundred Years of Jewish-
      Christian Relations*. London: SCM, 1993, XXIII-404 p. Esp. 19-27: "Evidence from the gospel
      of Matthew (and 'Q')"; 154-159 [Place of origin].

**SANDERS, James A.**

1965  Ναζωραῖος in Matt 2,23. — *JBL* 84 (1965) 169-172. Esp. 169-170 [geographic]; 170-171
      [christological]. [NTA 10, 112] → 1994

1974  The Ethic of Election in Luke's Great Banquet Parable. — CRENSHAW, J.L. - WILLIS,
      J.T. (eds.), *Essays in Old Testament Ethics (J. Philip Hyatt, In Memoriam)*, New York:
      Ktav, 1974, 245-271. Esp. 251.261 [22,1-10].

1987  A New Testament Hermeneutic Fabric: Psalm 118 in the Entrance Narrative. —
      EVANS, C.A. - STINESPRING, W.F. (eds.), *Early Jewish and Christian Exegesis.
      Studies in Memory of William Hugh Brownlee* (Scholars Press homage series, 10),
      Atlanta, GA: Scholars, 1987, 177-190. Esp. 177-179 [21,5/Zech 9,9]; 179-190 [21,9/Ps 118,25-26].

1994  Ναζωραῖος in Matthew 2.23. — EVANS, C.A. - STEGNER, W.R. (eds.), *The Gospels
      and the Scriptures of Israel*, 1994, 116-128. → 1965

**SANDERS, J.O.**

1975  *Bible Studies in Matthew's Gospel*. Grand Rapids, MI: Zondervan, 1975, 153 p.

**SANDERS, Joseph Newbould**

1950  *The Foundations of the Christian Faith. A Study of the Teaching of the New Testament
      in the Light of Historical Criticism*. London: Black, 1950, XII-199 p. Esp. 45-47 [Papias];
      49-55: "The synoptic problem"; 64-112: "The life and teaching of Jesus"; New York: Philosophical
      Library, 1952.

**SANDERS, Wilm**

1972  Das Blut Jesu und die Juden. Gedanken zu Matth. 27,25. — *Una Sancta* 27 (1972) 168-
      171. [NTA 17, 920]

**SANDIFER, D. Wayne**

1991  The Humor of the Absurd in the Parables of Jesus. — *SBL 1991 Seminar Papers*, 287-
      297. Esp. 288-289 [5,15]; 289-290 [6,26.28-29]; 290 [7,3-4]; 290-291 [7,9-10]; 291-292 [7,16]; 293-294
      [22,1-10]; 294-296 [17,20; 21,21]; 296-297 [23,24].

**SANDMEL, Samuel**

1956  *A Jewish Understanding of the New Testament*. Cincinatti, OH: Hebrew Union College,
      1956, 321 p.; augmented ed., New York: Ktav, 1974; London: SPCK, 1977,
      XXXIV-336 p. Esp. 136-143: "Beyond the gospel according to Mark" [Q]; 144-168: "The gospel according
      to Matthew".

1978a *Anti-Semitism in the New Testament?* Philadelphia, PA: Fortress, 1978, XXI-168 p. Esp.
      49-70: "The gospel according to Matthew".

1978b *Judaism and Christian Beginnings*. New York: Oxford University Press, 1978, XVII-510
      p. Esp. 352-362: "The gospel according to Matthew".

**SANLÉS OLIVARES, Ricardo**

1975  Teología de las narraciones evangélicas sobre el Espíritu Santo. — *Estudios* (Madrid)
      31 (1975) 443-464.

1977 El bautismo cristiano según el evangelio de Mateo (Mt 28,19). — *Estudios* 33 (1977) 255-275.

**SANT, Carmelo**
1954 The Commentary of St. Thomas on Mt 24: the Destruction of Jerusalem. — *MelTheol* 7 (1954) 1-16.

**SANTE CENTI, Tito**
1993 (ed.), Girolamo Savonarola, Esposizione del Pater Noster. — *Sacra Doctrina* (Bologna) 38 (1993) 525-569.

**SANTI, Francesco** → Pazzini 1993

**SANZ VALDIVIESO, Rafael**
1990 La fuente Q. Publicaciones recientes. — *Carthaginensia* 6 (1990) 183-194. → Neirynck 1988a, Polag 1979/82, Uro 1987, Zeller 1984/86

**SARAGGI, G.**
1970 Il matrimonio: sacramento dell'unità. Messaggio del Nuovo Testamento. [19,3-12] — *PalCl* 49 (1970) 1166-1174, 1229-1235. [NTA 15, 673]

**SARMIENTO NOVA, Antonio José**
1988 Las bienaventuranzas, programa de la nueva humanidad. — *Reflexiones CIRE* 14 (1988) 43-56.

**SARTORI, R.** → Ledrus 1970

**SARTORY, Thomas**
1969 "Selig, die lauteren Herzens sind, denn sie werden Gott schauen". — MÜSSLE, M. (ed.), *Der "politische" Jesus*, 1969, 78-90.

**SARTORY-REIDICK, Gertrude**
1969 "Selig die hungern und dürsten nach Gerechtigkeit, denn sie werden gesättigt werden". — MÜSSLE, M. (ed.), *Der "politische" Jesus*, 1969, 52-64.

**SASS, Gerhard**
1957 *Der Fels der Kirche. Eine Auslegung von Matthäus 16* (Biblische Studien, 17). Neukirchen: Neukirchener, 1957, 47 p. Esp. 13-17 [16,1-4]; 17-18 [16,5-12]; 18-39 [16,13-20]; 40-42 [16,21-23]; 42-47 [16,24-28].

1968 *Ungereimtes bei Matthäus*. Düsseldorf: Presseverband der Evangelischen Kirche im Rheinland, 1968, VII-73 p.

**SASSE, Hermann**
1965 Peter and Paul. Observations on the Origin of the Roman Primacy. — *RTR* 24/1 (1965) 1-11. [NTA 9, 917]

**SATAKE, Akira**
1967 An Exegetical Analysis of Mt 12,1-8. [Japanese] — TAJIMA, N. (ed.), *Festschrift Isaburo Takayanagi*, Tokyo: Sōbun-sha, 1967, 93-111.

1976 Das Leiden der Jünger "um meinetwillen". — *ZNW* 67 (1976) 4-19. Esp. 4-5 [Q]; 7 [10,39]; 8-9 [16,25]; 9 [19,29]; 9-10 [10,22; 24,9]; 10 [5,11]; 10-11 [10,39]. [NTA 21, 66]

1978 Zwei Typen von Menschenbildern in den Gleichnissen Jesu. — *AJBI* 4 (1978) 45-84. Esp. 45-48 [20,1-15]; 48-51 [18,12-13]; 55-57 [22,1-10]; 58-59 [7,24-27]; 59-60 [25,1-12]; 63-65 [25,14-30]; 65-67 [24,45-51]. [NTA 23, 802]

**SATO, Migaku**

1988 *Q und Prophetie. Studien zur Gattungs- und Traditionsgeschichte der Quelle Q* (WUNT, II/29). Tübingen: Mohr, 1988, XIII-437 p. Esp. 16-68: "Die Gestalt der Q-Quelle"; 69-95: "Vergleich der Makrogattung der Q-Quelle mit den alttestamentlichen Prophetenbüchern"; 108-313: "Vergleich der Mikrogattungen zwischen den alttestamentlichen Prophetenbüchern und der Q-Quelle"; 371-408: "Die Träger der Q-Quelle". [NTA 32, p. 376] — Diss. Bern, 1984 (U. Luz). → Hoffmann 1992b, Neirynck 1990a, J.M. Robinson 1993b

E. BARÓN, *EstE* 65 (1990) 98-99; W.H. BERFLO, *TijdTheol* 29 (1989) 64; D. CATCHPOLE, *JTS* 42 (1991) 223-225; F.G. DOWNING, *Bib* 72 (1991) 127-132; A. FUCHS, *SNTU* 14 (1989) 239-241; J. GUILLET, *RSR* 77 (1989) 405-406; J.S. KLOPPENBORG, *CBQ* 52 (1990) 362-364; *JBL* 109 (1990) 137-139; R. SANZ VALDIVIESO, *Carthaginensia* 4 (1988) 364; A. SEGOVIA, *ArchTeolGran* 51 (1988) 299; A. SUHL, *TLZ* 114 (1989) 669-672.

The Shape of the Q-Source. [1988, 16-47.62-65] — KLOPPENBORG, J.S. (ed.), *The Shape of Q*, 1994, 156-179.

1993 Q: Prophetie oder Weisheit? Ein Gespräch mit J.M. Robinson. — *EvT* 53 (1993) 389-404. Esp. 393-395: "Zu den Mikrogattungen"; 395-397: "Zu den Redaktionen"; 396-403: "Zur Makrogattung"; 403-504: "Zur Trägerschaft von Q". → J.M. Robinson 1993b

1995 Wisdom Statements in the Sphere of Prophecy. — PIPER, R.A. (ed.), *The Gospel Behind the Gospels*, 1995, 139-158.

**SATZINGER, Helmut**

1968 *Koptische Urkunden* (Ägyptische Urkunden aus den Staatlichen Museen Berlin, III/2). Berlin: Akademie, 1968, 143 p. Esp. 88-89 [20,23-28; 21,8-12].

**SAUCY, Mark**

1994 The Kingdom-of-God Sayings in Matthew. — *BS* 151 (1994) 175-197. Esp. 175-182 [1–10]; 182-186 [11–12]; 186-193 [13]. [NTA 38, 1357]

**SAUER, Georg**

1987 Die Messias-Erwartung nach Mt 21 in ihrem Rückbezug auf das Alte Testament als Frage an die Methode einer Biblischen Theologie. — OEMING, M. – GRAUPNER, A. (eds.), *Altes Testament und christliche Verkündigung. Festschrift für Antonius H.J. Gunneweg zum 65. Geburtstag*, Stuttgart: Kohlhammer, 1987, 81-94.

**SAUER, Jürgen**

1985 Traditionsgeschichtliche Erwägungen zu den synoptischen und paulinischen Aussagen über Feindesliebe und Wiedervergeltungsverzicht. — *ZNW* 76 (1985) 1-28. Esp. 5-17: "Rekonstruktion der ältesten Überlieferungselemente der Q-Überlieferung" [5,38-48]; 23-27 [5,38-48/Rom 12,9-21]. [NTA 30, 113]

1991 *Rückkehr und Vollendung des Heils. Eine Untersuchung zu den ethischen Radikalismen Jesu* (Theorie und Forschung, 133; Philosophie und Theologie, 9). Regensburg: Roderer, 1991, XII-1009 p. — Diss. Göttingen, 1990 (H. Stegemann).

**SAUER, Ralph**

1984 Das Vaterunser als Modell für unser Sprechen von Gott und Mensch in der Glaubensvermittlung. — *TQ* 164 (1984) 294-305. Esp. 295-296: "Der exegetische Befund".

**SAUGET, Joseph-Marie**

1988 Une homélie syriaque sur la vocation de Matthieu attribuée à Jean Chrystostome. [9,9-13] — *Mélanges Antoine Guillaumont. Contributions à l'étude des christianismes orientaux* (Cahiers d'Orientalisme, 20), Genève: Cramer, 1988, 187-199.

**SAUNDERS, Ernest W.**

1963 A Trio of Thomas Logia. — *BR* 8 (1963) 43-59. Esp. 55-58 [6,22-23/Th 24]. [NTA 8, 1168]

1967   *Jesus in the Gospels*. Englewood Cliffs, NJ: Prentice Hall, 1967, XII-324 p.

1991   A Response to H.D. Betz on the Sermon on the Mount. — *BR* 36 (1991) 81-87. → H.D. Betz 1991b

**SAUNDERS, Stanley Paul**

1987   → J.L. Bailey 1987

1990   *"No One Dared Ask Him Anything More"*: Contextual Readings of the Controversy Stories in Matthew. Diss. Princeton Theol. Sem., Princeton, NJ, 1990, 503 p. (J.W. Dukes – S. Kraftchik). — *DissAbstr* 51 (1990-91) 2054.

**SAUSER, Ekkart**

1970   Ungewohnte Väteraussagen über Maria. [12,46-50] — *TTZ* 79 (1970) 306-313.

**SAVOCA, Gaetano**

1974   *Lettura esistenziale della Parola di Dio. La nuova ermeneutica biblica* [5,32; 19,9]. Napoli: Dehoniane, 1974, 126 p.

**SAVON, Hervé**

1988   Jérôme et Ambroise, interprètes du premier évangile. — DUVAL, Y.-M. (ed.) *Jérôme entre l'Occident et l'Orient. XVI<sup>e</sup> centenaire du départ de S. Jérôme de Rome et de son installation à Betléem. Actes du colloque de Chantilly (Sept. 1986)* (Études augustiniennes. Série Antiquité, 122), Turnhout: Brepols, 1988, 205-225.

**SAXER, Victor**

1992   Marie-Madeleine dans les évangiles. "La femme coupée en morceaux"? — *RThom* 92 (1992) 674-701, 818-833. Esp. 682-693, 825-826. [NTA 37, 1194]

**SAWICKI, Marianne**

1986   How to Teach Christ's Disciples: John 1:19-37 and Matthew 11:2-15. — *LexTQ* 21 (1986) 14-26. [NTA 30, 1138]

**SAYDON, P.P.**

1950   The Order of the Gospels. — *Scripture* 4 (1950) 190-196.

1953   The Jeremias-Zacharias Puzzle in Matthew 27,9. — *MelTheol* 6 (1953) 134. → Sutcliffe 1952a

1966   Some Biblico-Liturgical Passages Reconsidered. [Vulgate: 1,18; 6,27; 25,1-12] — *MelTheol* 18 (1966) 10-17. [NTA 11, 959]

**SAYER, Josef**

1991   "Ich hatte Durst, und ihr gabt mir zu trinken". Zum Ansatz einer Theologie der menschlichen Grundbedürfnisse nach Mt 25,31ff im Rahmen der Pastoral der Befreiung. — *MüTZ* 42 (1991) 151-167. Esp. 153-158. [NTA 36, 159]

**SAYÉS, José Antonio**

1983   La resurrección de Jesús y la historia. Problemática actual. — *Burgense* 24 (1983) 9-93. Esp. 39-40 [28,1-8]; 63-64 [28,16-20]. [NTA 28, 473]

**SAYLER, Gwendolyn B.**

1984   *Have the Promises Failed? A Literary Analysis of 2 Baruch* (SBL DS, 72). Chico, CA: Scholars, 1984, VII-171 p. Esp. 142-146: "The gospel of Matthew and 2 Baruch".

**SCAER, David P.**

1989   The Two Sacraments Doctrine as a Factor in Synoptic Relationships. — *Philosophy & Theology* (Milwaukee, WI) 3 (1989) 205-222. [NTA 34, 377]

1991 The Relation of Matthew 28:16-20 to the Rest of the Gospel. — *ConcTQ* 55 (1991) 245-266. [NTA 36, 1287]

**SCATTOLON, Alfredo**

1978 L'ἀγαπητός sinottico nella luce della tradizione giudaica. — *RivBib* 26 (1978) 3-32. Esp. 29. [NTA 23, 414]

**SCHABERG, Jane**

1982 *The Father, the Son and the Holy Spirit. The Triadic Phrase in Matthew 28:19b* (SBL DS, 61). Chico, CA: Scholars, 1982, XIV-367 p. Esp. 1-86: "Survey of critical opinion regarding the Matthean triadic phrase"; 87-110: "Methodological considerations"; 111-141: "Is Matt 28:18b an allusion to the Septuagint of Dan 7:14?"; 263-317: "New Testament passages related to Daniel 7 and pertinent to Matt 28:16-20"; 319-349: "Matt 28:16-20 and its triadic phrase". [NTA 27, p. 212] — Diss. Union Theol. Sem., New York, 1980 (J.L. Martyn).
  J.C. ANDERSON, *JRel* 69 (1989) 238-239; F.W. BURNETT, *Interpr* 38 (1975) 320.322; R.S. DIETRICH, *Interpr* 43 (1989) 208; C.A. EVANS, *JBL* 104 (1985) 731-732; M.A. GETTY, *Horizons* (Villanova, PA) 16 (1989) 377-378; J. GUILLET, *RSR* 74 (1986) 246; D. HILL, *IBS* 5 (1983) 161-163; P. PERKINS, *America* 158 (1988) 435-437; C.S. RODD, *ExpT* 94 (1982-83) 215; B.T. VIVIANO, *CBQ* 46 (1984) 177-179.

1987 *The Illegitimacy of Jesus. A Feminist Theological Interpretation of the Infancy Narratives*. San Francisco, CA: Harper & Row, 1987, XI-255 p. Esp. 20-77: "Matthew's account of Jesus' origin" [1,5.16.17.18-25]; 178-194: "The virginal conception". [NTA 32, p. 109]; (Biblical Seminar, 28). Sheffield: JSOT, 1995, XI-262 p. [NTA 40, p. 148]
  B. MALINA, *BTB* 18 (1988) 118-119; B.E. REID, *CBQ* 52 (1990) 364-365.

1989 The Foremothers and the Mother of Jesus. — *Concilium* (London) 206 (1989) 112-119. Esp. 113-114 [1,1-17]; 114-118 [1,18-25]. [NTA 36, 136]
  Les aïeules et la mère de Jésus. — *Concilium* (Paris) 226 (1989) 135-143. Esp. 137-138; 138-142.

**SCHABERT, Arnold**

1966 *Die Bergpredigt. Auslegung und Verkündigung*. München: Claudius, 1966, 236 p.

**SCHAEFER, Carol Johnson**

1961 *A Study in the Exegesis of Matthew 6:22 through Analysis of ἁπλοῦς*. Diss. Brown University, 1961, 105 p. — *DissAbstr* 28 (1967-68) 2768.

**SCHÄFER, Karl Theodor**

1938[R] *Grundriss der Einleitung in das Neue Testament* [1938]. Bonn: Hanstein, [2]1952, VI-185-8* p. Esp. 56-61: "Das Matthäus-Evangelium"; 70-76: "Die synoptische Frage".

1953 "...und dann werden sie fasten, an jenem Tage" (Mk 2,20 und Parallelen). — SCHMID, J. - VÖGTLE, A. (eds.), *Synoptische Studien*. FS A. Wikenhauser, 1953, 124-147. Esp. 125-127 [minor agreements: 9,14-17]; 142-143.

1960 Der Primat Petri und das Thomas-Evangelium. — CARSTEN, W. - FROTZ, A. - LINDEN, P. (eds.), *Die Kirche und ihre Ämter und Stände. Festgabe seiner Eminenz dem hochwürdigsten Herrn Joseph Kardinal Frings dargeboten*, Köln: Bachem, 1960, 353-363. Esp. 356-358.

**SCHAEFFER, Susan E.**

1990 *The "Gospel of Peter", the Canonical Gospels, and Oral Tradition*. Diss. Union Theol. Sem., New York, 1990 (R.E. Brown).

1991 The Guard at the Tomb (*Gos. Pet.* 8:28–11:49 and Matt 27:62-66; 28:2-4,11-16): A Case of Intertextuality? — *SBL 1991 Seminar Papers*, 499-507.

**SCHALLER, Berndt**

1970 Die Sprüche über Ehescheidung und Wiederheirat in der synoptischen Überlieferung.

— LOHSE, E., et al. (eds.), *Der Ruf Jesu.* FS J. Jeremias, 1970, 226-246. Esp. 227-238 [5,32].

**SCHAREN, Hans**

1991 *The Development of the Concept of Gehenna and Its Use in the Synoptics.* Diss. Theol. Sem., Dallas, TX, 1991, 305 p. — *DissAbstr* 53 (1992-93) 190-191.

1992 Gehenna in the Synoptics. Part 1. — *BS* 149 (1992) 324-337. Esp. 33-36 [5,29-30]. [NTA 37, 123]

**SCHARLEMANN, Martin H.**

1968 *Stephen: A Singular Saint* (AnBib, 34). Roma: Pontifical Biblical Institute, 1968, X-211 p. Esp. 175-179: "Stephen and Matthew".

**SCHATTENMANN, Johannes**

1965 *Studien zum neutestamentlichen Prosahymnus.* München: Beck, 1965, VIII-115 p. Esp. 40-48: "Das Logion Jesu, Matthäus 16 Vers 17-19, das Vaterunser und der Missionsbefehl".

1979 Jesus und Pythagoras. [5,19-30; 19,10-12] — *Kairos* 21 (1979) 215-220. [NTA 24, 788]

**SCHAUB, R. Thomas**

1971 (ed.), *A Periodical and Monographic Index to the Literature on the Gospels and Acts Based on the Files of the École Biblique in Jerusalem* (Bibliographia Tripotamopolitana, 3). Pittsburgh, PA: Pittsburgh Theological Seminary. 1971, XXIV-336 p. Esp. 1-77. → Rousée 1986

**SCHEDL, Claus**

1969 *Talmud, Evangelium, Synagoge.* Innsbruck: Tyrolia, 1969, 448 p. Esp. 289-335: "Die zehn Wunder nach Matthäus".

1974 *Baupläne des Wortes. Einführung in die biblische Logotechnik.* Wien: Herder, 1974, 246 p. Esp. 56-58 [16,18-19]; 77-79 [17,1-3]; 85-86 [28,5-7]; 107-111 [6,9-13].

1981 Die Salbung Jesu in Betanien. Zur Kompositionskunst von Mk 14,3-9 und Mt 26,6-13. — *BLtg* 54 (1981) 151-162. Esp. 157-161. [NTA 26, 505]

1982 Zur Ehebruchklausel der Bergpredigt im Lichte der neu gefundenen Tempelrolle. — *TPQ* 130 (1982) 362-365. [NTA 27, 515]

**SCHEELE, Paul-Werner**

1984 "Wer bist du Herr?" (Apg 9,5). Vom rechten Fragen nach dem 'Christus praesens'. [16,13-20] — LIES, L. (ed.), *Praesentia Christi. Festschrift Johannes Betz zum 70. Geburtstag dargebracht von Kollegen, Freunden, Schülern,* Düsseldorf: Patmos, 1984, 19-24.

**SCHEFFCZYK, Leo**

1976 *Auferstehung. Prinzip des christlichen Glaubens* (Sammlung Horizonte, NF 9). Einsiedeln: Johannes Verlag, 1976, 303 p. Esp. 81-88: "Die Ostererzählung nach Matthäus".

1978 "Jungfrauengeburt": Biblischer Grund und bleibender Sinn. — *IKZ/Communio* (Rodenkirchen) 7 (1978) 13-25. Esp. 14-18.

**SCHEFFER, Heinrich Otto**

1973 *The Concept of Man in the Gospel of Matthew.* Diss. Union Theol. Sem., Richmond, VA, 1973.

**SCHEFFLER, Eben H.**

1990 The Social Ethics of the Lucan Baptist (Lk 3:10-14). — *Neotestamentica* 24 (1990) 21-36. Esp. 21-25 [Q 3,7-9.16-17]. [NTA 35, 668] → Liebenberg 1995

**SCHEIFLER, José Ramon**

1964    *Asi nacierón los evangelios*. Bilbao: Mensajero del Corazón de Jesús, 1964, 421 p.

1965    El Salmo 22 y la Crucifixión del Señor. — *EstBíb* 24 (1965) 5-83. Esp. 19-29.70-77 [27,35]; 29-45 [27,38-44]; 45-70 [27,45-54]. [NTA 11, 229]

1977    La vieja navidad perdida. Estudio bíblico sobre la infancia de Jesús. — *SalT* 65 (1977) 835-851. → Marimón Batllo 1980, Muñoz Iglesias 1978, Puigdollers 1979

**SCHELBERT, Georg**

1960    Ehe und Ehescheidung nach dem Evangelium (Mt 19,3-12 par). — *Schweizerische Kirchenzeitung* (Luzern) 128 (1960) 481-483, 495-497.

1965    "Mir ist alle Gewalt gegeben" (Matth 28,18). Auferstehung und Aussendung durch den Erhöhten nach Matthäus. — *BK* 20 (1965) 37-39. [NTA 10, 478]

1994    Die apostolische Herkunft der Evangelien nach H.J. Schulz. — *FZPT* 41 (1994) 532-541. Esp. 533; 535-537 [Papias]; 537-539 [Irenaeus]. [NTA 39, 1394r] → H.-J. Schulz 1993

**SCHELKLE, Karl Hermann**

1956    *Maria, Mutter des Herrn. Ihre biblische Gestalt.* Leipzig: St. Benno, 1956, 87 p.
*Die Mutter des Erlösers. Ihre biblische Gestalt* (Die Welt der Bibel). Düsseldorf: Patmos, 1958, 96 p.
*De Bijbel over Maria* (De Bijbel over..., 2). Roermond-Maaseik: Romen, 1960, 95 p. Esp. 39-44 [1,23/Is 7,14].
*La Madre del Salvatore. La figura di Maria nel Nuovo Testamento.* Roma: Città Nuova Editrice, 1985, 87 p.

1963a   *Das Neue Testament. Seine literarische und theologische Geschichte* (Berckers Theologische Grundrisse, 2). Kevelaer: Butzon & Bercker, 1963, ²1964, ³1966, ⁴1970, 267 p. Esp. 43-47: "Die synoptische Frage"; 47-55: "Das Evangelium nach Matthäus".
*Oorsprong en theologische betekenis van het Nieuwe Testament*, trans. F. van der Heijden. Roermond-Maaseik: Romen, 1964, 263 p. Esp. 33-38; 38-45.
*Introduction au Nouveau Testament. Histoire littéraire et théologique*, trans. M. Grandclaudon. Mulhouse: Salvator, 1965, 334 p.
*Introduzione al Nuovo Testamento*, trans. G. Barbaglio. Brescia: Queriniana, 1967, 299 p.
*An Introduction to the New Testament*, trans. G. Kirsten. Cork: Mercier, 1969, 240 p.
Trans. Japanese 1967.

1963b   Die Frauen im Stammbaum Jesu. — *BK* 18 (1963) 113-115. [NTA 8, 570]

1966a   Ehe und Ehelosigkeit im Neuen Testament. — *WissWeish* 29 (1966) 1-15. [NTA 11, 449]; = ID., *Wort und Schrift*, 1966, 183-198.

1966b   *Wort und Schrift. Beiträge zur Auslegung und Auslegungsgeschichte des Neuen Testaments* (Kommentare und Beiträge zum Alten und Neuen Testament). Düsseldorf: Patmos, 1966, 322 p. → 1966a, 1966c
*Palabra y Escritura; estudios sobre exégesis, eclesiologia y moral del Nuevo Testamento* (Actualidad Bíblica, 20). Madrid: Fax, 1972, 292 p.

1966c   Die Kindheitsgeschichte Jesu. Form und Theologie. — *Ibid.*, 59-75. Esp. 62-72: "Christus und Maria in der Kindheitsgeschichte"; = *LebZeug* 22/1 (1967) 78-96. Esp. 82-93.
*Die Kindheitsgeschichte Jesu.* — SINT, J. (ed.), *Bibel und zeitgemässer Glaube.* II: *Neues Testament*, Klosterneuburg: Buch- und Kunstverlag, 1967, 11-36.

1966d   Die "Selbstverfluchung" Israels nach Mt 27,23-25. — *Freiburger Rundbrief* 18 (1966) 52-54; = ECKERT, W.P., et al. (eds.), *Antijudaismus*, 1967, 148-156, 209-210; = ID., *Die Kraft des Wortes*, 1983, 89-97.

1968    *Theologie des Neuen Testaments* (Kommentare und Beiträge zum Alten und Neuen Testament). Düsseldorf: Patmos. I: *Schöpfung. Welt–Zeit–Mensch*, 1968, 172 p. Esp. 27-33 [creation]; 81-87 [history]; 107-118 [anthropology]; II: *Gott war in Christus*, 1973, 326 p. Esp. 88-93 [exorcisms; healings]; 102-115 [passion]; 116-121 [salvation]; 168-182 [birth stories]; 192-232

[christological titles]; 320-321 [Trinity]; III: *Ethos*, 1970, ²1977, 347 p.; IV.1: *Vollendung von Schöpfung und Erlösung*, 1974, 124 p. Esp. 15-17; 20-21; 47-48 [24]; 62-63 [parousia]; IV.2: *Jüngergemeinde und Kirche*, 1976, 208 p. Esp. 95-103 [15,17-19; 18,18]; 161-162 [22,1-14]; 162-169 [23]; 187-196 [mission].
*Teologia del Nuovo Testamento* (Epifania della Parola, 3). Bologna: Dehoniane, I, trans. G. Frumento, 1969, VIII-207 p.; II, trans. G. Cappelli, 1980, 348 p.; III, trans. G. Cappelli, 1974, 379 p.; IV, trans. G. Forza & S. Mugnai Galassi, 1980, 374 p.
*Theology of the New Testament*, trans. W.A. Jürgens. Collegeville, MN: Liturgical, 1971-1978.
*Teología del Nuevo Testamento* (Biblioteca Herder: Sagrada Escritura, 145-148). Barcelona: Herder, I, trans. R. Puente, 1975, 228 p.; II, trans. M. Villanueva, 1977, 472 p.; III, trans. R. Puente, 1975, 504 p.; IV, trans. M. Villanueva, 1978, 514 p.
Trans. Portuguese 1977-79; Polish 1984.

1969    Lohn und Strafe nach dem Neuen Testament. — *BibLeb* 10 (1969) 89-95. Esp. 89-90. [NTA 14, 312]

1973    Jesus – Lehrer und Prophet. — HOFFMANN, P., et al. (eds.), *Orientierung an Jesus.* FS J. Schmid, 1973, 300-308. Esp. 302 [23,8-10]; 306-307; = ID., *Die Kraft des Wortes*, 1983, 43-51. Esp. 45; 49-50.

1974a    Königsherrschaft Gottes. — *BibLeb* 15 (1974) 120-135. Esp. 126-128 [10,23]. [NTA 19, 766]
1974b    Gericht. — *Ibid.*, 159-173. Esp. 162-167. [NTA 19, 1090]

1976    Grundzüge biblischer Eschatologie. 2. Neutestamentliche Eschatologie. — FEINER, J. – LÖHRER, M. (eds.), *Mysterium Salutis. Grundriß heilsgeschichtlicher Dogmatik.* V: *Zwischenzeit und Vollendung der Heilsgeschichte*, Zürich–Einsiedeln–Köln: Benziger, 1976, 723-778. Esp. 732-750: "Eschatologie der Synopse"; = ID., *Die Kraft des Wortes*, 1983, 147-207. Esp. 157-177.

1977a    *Der Geist und die Braut. Die Frau in der Bibel.* Düsseldorf: Patmos, 1977, 176 p. Esp. 82-85 [5,32; 19,9].

1977b    Israel und Kirche im Neuen Testament. — SCHNACKENBURG, R., et al. (eds.), *Die Kirche des Anfangs.* FS H. Schürmann, 1977, 607-614. Esp. 609-612; = ID., *Die Kraft des Wortes*, 1983, 79-87. Esp. 82-84.

1980    Charisma und Amt. — ZMIJEWSKI, J. – NELLESSEN, E. (eds.), *Begegnung mit dem Wort.* FS H. Zimmermann, 1980, 311-323. Esp. 316 [23,8-10]; 316-318 [ἀπόστολος]; = ID., *Die Kraft des Wortes*, 1983, 209-223. Esp. 215; 215-217.

1983a    *Die Kraft des Wortes. Beiträge zu einer biblischen Theologie.* Stuttgart: Katholisches Bibelwerk, 1983, 279 p. → 1966d, 1973, 1976, 1977b, 1980

1983b    Israel und Kirche im Anfang. — *TQ* 163 (1983) 86-95. Esp. 86-91: "Spruchquelle Q". [NTA 28, 83]

1985    *Israel im Neuen Testament.* Darmstadt: Wissenschaftliche Buchgesellschaft, 1985, XIX-136 p. Esp. 12-20: "Spruchquelle Q".

### SCHENK, Wolfgang

1963    "Den Menschen" Mt 9,8. — *ZNW* 54 (1963) 272-275. [NTA 8, 940]

1967    *Der Segen im Neuen Testament. Eine begriffsanalytische Studie* (Theologische Arbeiten, 25). Berlin: Evangelische Verlagsanstalt, 1967, 191 p. [25,34] → Westermann 1968

1972    *Studienheft zu sieben Texten über den Propheten Jona.* Berlin(-Ost): Evangelische Hauptbibelgesellschaft, 1972, 23 p. Esp. 20-23: "Die urchristlichen Jona-Sprüche".

1973    Naherwartung und Parusieverzögerung. Die urchristliche Eschatologie als Problem der Forschung. — *TVers* 4 (1973) 47-69. Esp. 56-61 [Q 12,8-9].

1976    Das Präsens Historicum als makrosyntaktisches Gliederungssignal im Matthäusevangelium. — *NTS* 22 (1975-76) 464-475. [NTA 21, 70]

1977    *Studienheft zu sieben Texten aus dem Matthäusevangelium.* Berlin: Evangelische
        Hauptbibelgesellschaft, 1977, 24 p.

1978    Auferweckung der Toten oder Gericht nach den Werken. Tradition und Redaktion in
        Mattäus xxv 1-13. — *NT* 20 (1978) 278-299. Esp. 278-279; 279-282 [Vorlage]; 282-283 [25,13];
        283-288 [25,10-12]; 288-290 [structure]; 290-292 [25,1-9]; 292-294 [25,1]; 294-298 [1 Thess 415-17]. [NTA
        24, 99]

1979    Der Einfluß der Logienquelle auf das Markusevangelium. — *ZNW* 70 (1979) 141-165.
        Esp. 143-145 [Mk 8,38; 4,31-32]; 146-160 [Mk 1,1; 3,28-30; 8,11-13; 10,45]; 160-163. [NTA 25, 90]

1981    *Synopse zur Redenquelle der Evangelien. Q-Synopse und Rekonstruktion in deutscher
        Übersetzung mit kurzen Erläuterungen.* Düsseldorf: Patmos, 1981, 138 p.
        A. Fuchs, *SNTU* 6-7 (1981-82) 254-258; O. Knoch, *BK* 37 (1982) 152.

1983a   *Evangelium – Evangelien – Evangeliologie. Ein "hermeneutisches" Manifest* (Theolo-
        gische Existenz heute, NF 216). München: Kaiser, 1983, 127 p. Esp. 11-21: "Das seman-
        tische Wortfeld 'Evangelium' in bezug zu Osterereignis und Ostertexten"; 59-61: "Matthäus".

1983b   Gefangenschaft und Tod des Täufers. Erwägungen zur Chronologie und ihren
        Konsequenzen. — *NTS* 29 (1983) 453-483. Esp. 453-456: "Das Zutrauen der Forschung zur
        synoptischen Chronologie"; 456-459: "Der Widerspruch des 4. Evangeliums". [NTA 28, 457]

1983c   Das "Matthäusevangelium" als Petrusevangelium. — *BZ* 27 (1983) 58-80. Esp. 59-67:
        "Was bezeichnete Papias mit 'Matthäus'?"; 68-77: "Das Selbstverständnis des 'Matthäusevangeliums'". [NTA
        27, 907]

1987    *Die Sprache des Matthäus. Die Text-Konstituenten in ihren makro- und mikro-
        strukturellen Relationen.* Göttingen: Vandenhoeck & Ruprecht, 1987, 493 p. [NTA 32,
        p. 109]
        X. Alegre, *ActBibl* 25 (1988) 218-219; J. Becker, *TLZ* 113 (1988) 592-593; E. Best, *ExpT* 99 (1987-
        88) 283-284; F.W. Burnett, *CBQ* 51 (1989) 164-165; A. Fuchs, *SNTU* 13 (1988) 229; F. Marín
        Heredia, *Carthaginensia* 4 (1988) 179; A. Méhat, *RHR* 205 (1988) 313-314; R.L. Mowery, *JBL* 108
        (1989) 341-342; F. Mussner, *TRev* 84 (1988) 22-23; F. Neirynck, *ETL* 63 (1987) 413-419; S.
        Sabugal, *Revista Agustiniana* (Madrid) 29 (1988) 743; G. Segalla, *Studia Patavina* 37 (1990) 195-
        196; J. Smit Sibinga, *NTT* 44 (1990) 260-261; G. Stanton, *JTS* 41 (1990) 181-182; H. Welzen,
        *TijdTheol* 29 (1989) 64-65; W. Weren, *Bijdragen* 51 (1990) 326.

1992    Die Um-Codierungen der matthäischen Unser-Vater-Redaktion in Joh 17. — Denaux,
        A. (ed.), *John and the Synoptics*, 1992, 587-607.

1993a   Zur Frage einer vierten Version der Seesturm-Erzählung in einer Mt/Lk-Agreement-
        Redaktions-Schicht ("Dt-Mk"): Versuch einer textsemiotischen Geltungsprüfung von
        A. Fuchs. — Strecker, G. (ed.), *Minor Agreements*, 1993, 93-118. Esp. 95-113:
        "Empirische Kritik"; 113-118: "Methodologische Kritik". → A. Fuchs 1990b

1993b   Die Verwünschung der Küstenorte Q 10,13-15. Zur Funktion der konkreten Orts-
        angaben und zur Lokalisierung von Q. — Focant, C. (ed.), *The Synoptic Gospels*,
        1993, 477-490. Esp. 477-481: "Der Wehe-Spruch"; 481-489: "Die Ortsnamen"; 489-490: "Zur
        Lokalisierung der Q-Redaktion".

## SCHENKE, Hans-Martin

1978    Die Tendenz der Weisheit zur Gnosis. — Aland, B. (ed.), *Gnosis. Festschrift für Hans
        Jonas*, Göttingen: Vandenhoeck & Ruprecht, 1978, 351-372. Esp. 359-365 [Q – wisdom
        christology].

1979    & Fischer, K.M., *Einleitung in die Schriften des Neuen Testaments. II. Die Evangelien
        und die anderen neutestamentlichen Schriften.* Gütersloh: Mohn, 1979, 360 p. Esp. 24-30:
        "Das Problem der Logienquelle Q"; 96-123: "Das Matthäus-Evangelium".

1981    (ed.), *Das Matthäus-Evangelium im mittelägyptischen Dialekt des Koptischen (Codex
        Scheide)* (TU, 127). Berlin: Akademie, 1981, XII-202 p. Esp. 1-50 [introduction]; 53-127 [text].
        [NTA 28, p. 86] → 1985; → Shisha-Halevy 1983

M.-É. BOISMARD, *RB* 90 (1983) 461; M.W. HOLMES, *Bibliotheca Orientalis* 40 (1983) 637-639; G.D. KILPATRICK, *TRev* 81 (1985) 376-377; M. LATTKE, *TLZ* 109 (1984) 812-813; T. ORLANDI, *VetChr* 20 (1983) 467-469; J. OSING, *Enchoria* 12 (1984) 205-207; H. QUECKE, *Orientalia* (Roma) 53 (1984) 250-253; F. WISSE, *JBL* 103 (1984) 658-659.

1985 Notes on the Editions of the Scheide Codex. — ORLANDI, T. – WISSE, F. (eds.), *Acts of the Second International Congress of Coptic Studies, Roma 22-26.IX.1980*, Roma: C.I.M., 1985, 313-321. → 1981

**SCHENKE, Ludger**

1983 *Die wunderbare Brotvermehrung. Die neutestamentlichen Erzählungen und ihre Bedeutung.* Würzburg: Echter, 1983, 176 p. Esp. 19-25 [14,13-21/Mk 6,30-44]; 30-33 [15,32-38/Mk 8,1-9]; 157-164: "Die Interpretation der Speisungsgeschichten im Matthäusevangelium".

1988* (ed.), *Studien zum Matthäusevangelium. Festschrift für Wilhelm Pesch* (Stuttgarter Bibelstudien). Stuttgart: Katholisches Bibelwerk, 1988, 317 p. → Böcher, Broer, Dautzenberg, Giesen, F. Hahn, Hoffmann, Knoch, N. Lohfink, Merklein, Mussner, R. Pesch, L. Schenke, Schnackenburg, G. Schneider, Zeller; → Limbeck 1994

   G. BALESTIER-STENGEL, *ETR* 64 (1989) 634; E.J. EPP, *JBL* 109 (1990) 742-743; A. FUCHS, *SNTU* 14 (1989) 246; J. GUILLET, *RSR* 77 (1989) 412; F. LANGLAMET, *RB* 96 (1989) 431; G. SCHMAHL, *TTZ* 100 (1991) 332; R.D. WITHERUP, *CBQ* 52 (1990) 377-378.

1988 Die Interpretation der Parabel von den "Arbeitern im Weinberg" (Mt 20,1-15) durch Matthäus. — *Ibid.*, 245-268. Esp. 248-252: "Der Kontext des Gleichnisses"; 253-259: "Die Bearbeitung des Gleichnisses durch Matthäus"; 259-267: "Das ursprüngliche Gleichnis"; 267-268: "Die Interpretation des Matthäus".

1989 Die literarische Entstehungsgeschichte von Joh 1,19-51. — *BibNot* 46 (1989) 24-57. Esp. 41-44: "Anklänge an die Synoptiker". [NTA 34, 210]

**SCHENKER, Adrian**

1982 Substitution du châtiment ou prix de la paix? Le don de la vie du Fils de l'homme en Mc 10,45 et par. à la lumière de l'Ancien Testament. [20,28] — BENZERATH, M. – SCHMID, A. – GUILLET, J. (eds.), *La Pâque du Christ. Mystère de salut. Mélanges offerts au P. F.-X. Durrwell pour son 70e anniversaire* (LD, 112), Paris: Cerf, 1982, 75-90.

**SCHERER, Paul E.**

1966 A Gauntlet with a Gift in It. From Text to Sermon on Matthew 15:21-28 and Mark 7:24-30. — *Interpr* 20 (1966) 387-399.

**SCHERMANN, Josef**

1985 Das Gleichnis vom viererlei Acker: Matthäus 13,1-9. — *BLtg* 58 (1985) 219-228. [NTA 30, 1052]

**SCHERSTEN LAHURD, Carol**

1985 Rhetorical Criticism, Biblical Criticism and Literary Criticism: Issues of Methodological Pluralism. — *Proceedings EGLBS* 5 (1985) 87-101 [rhetorical criticism: 5-7].

**SCHEUERMANN, Georg**

1996 *Gemeinde im Umbruch. Eine sozialgeschichtliche Studie zum Matthäusevangelium* (FzB, 77). Würzburg: Echter, 1996, XI-279 p. Esp. 139-195: "Mt 18 – Gemeinde in Verantwortung"; 196-234: "Mt 23 – Ringen um eine geschwisterliche Gemeinde"; 235-249: "'Lehren' in der Gemeinde des Mt-Ev" [5,17-20; 28,19-20]. — Diss. Würzburg, 1995 (H.J. Klauck).

   F. URICCHIO, *MiscFranc* 96 (1996) 547-560.

**SCHICK, Eduard**

1962 Schicksahl und heilsgeschichtliche Bedeutung Johannes des Täufers. — *BK* 17 (1962) 106-110. [NTA 7, 443]

**SCHIEBER, Hans**

1977 Konzentrik im Matthäusschluß. Ein form- und gattungskritischer Versuch zu Mt 28,16-20. — *Kairos* 19 (1977) 286-307. Esp. 287-291: "Die Struktur von Mt 28,16-20"; 291-301: "Gattungsbestimmungsmodelle bisheriger Forschung"; 301: "Konzentrik als prägendes Moment des Matthäusschlusses". [NTA 23, 107]
The Conclusion of Matthew's Gospel. — *TDig* 27 (1979) 155-158.

**SCHIERSE, Franz Joseph**

1955 Die Stadt auf dem Berge. Gedanken zur Bergpredigt. — *GL* 28 (1955) 321-325.

1960 Weihnachtliche Christusverkündigung. Zum Verständnis der Kindheitsgeschichten. — *BibLeb* 1 (1960) 217-222.

1968 *Patmos-Synopse. Übersetzung der wichtigsten synoptischen Texte mit Parallelen aus dem Johannesevangelium, den apokryphen Evangelien und der frühchristlichen Literatur.* Düsseldorf: Patmos, 1968, [2]1969, [4]1971, [19]1987, 159 p.
*Schul-Synopse. Übersetzung ... Literatur.* Hamburg: Furche, 1975, 159 p; 12th rev. and enl. ed., 1979, 172 p.
*Sinossi dei vangeli. Traduzione dei principali testi sinottici con paralleli dal vangelo di Giovanni, dai vangeli apocrifi e della prima letteratura cristiana,* trans. G. Zappalà. Roma: Città Nova, 1971, 173 p.

1970 Wenn du Gottes Sohn bist... Was sagen die Versuchungsüberlieferungen des Neuen Testaments über Jesus Christus? [4,1-11] — *BK* 25 (1970) 6-8. [NTA 15, 136]

1978 *Einleitung in das Neue Testament* (Leitfaden Theologie, 1). Düsseldorf: Patmos, 1978, [3]1984, [4]1987, 171 p. Esp. 83-87: "Das Evangelium nach Mattäus"; 92-94: "Die synoptische Frage".
*Introducción al Nuevo Testamento,* trans. A. Martínez de Lapera. Barcelona: Herder, 1983, 228 p.
*Introduzione al Nuovo Testamento* [[3]1984], trans. E. Gatti (Giornale di Teologia, 173). Brescia: Queriniana, 1987, 212 p.

**SCHILDENBERGER, Johannes**

1965 Der Einzug des Königs in seine Stadt (Mt 21,1-9). — *Am Tisch des Wortes* (Stuttgart) 9 (1965) 19-26.

1979 Die Vertauschung der Aussagen über Zeichen und Bezeichnetes. Eine hermeneutisch bedeutsame biblische Redeweise. — WINTER, A., et al. (eds.), *Kirche und Bibel. Festgabe für Bischof Eduard Schick,* Paderborn: Schöningh, 1979, 397-408. Esp. 401-407 [parousia].

**SCHILLE, Gottfried**

1957 Die Topographie des Markusevangeliums, ihre Hintergründe und ihre Einordnung. — *ZPDV* 73 (1957) 133-166. Esp. 143 [8,5-13]; 161-164: "Der galiläisch-judäische Charakter der Mt-Überlieferung".

1958 Bemerkungen zur Formgeschichte des Evangeliums. II. Das Evangelium des Matthäus als Katechismus. — *NTS* 4 (1957-58) 101-114. Esp. 102-110 [Didache]; 105-110 [Q]; 107-110 [5-7]; 110-112 [Mt/Mk]. [NTA 2, 531]

1966 *Anfänge der Kirche. Erwägungen zur apostolischen Frühgeschichte* (BEvT, 43). München: Kaiser, 1966, 238 p. Esp. 65 [8,5-13]; 174-175 [Joseph]. — Diss. Rostock, 1966 (K. Weiss).

1967 *Die urchristliche Kollegialmission* (ATANT, 48). Zürich–Stuttgart: Zwingli, 1967, 215 p. Esp. 114-116 [10,2-4].

1969 Anfänge der christlichen Mission. — *KerDog* 15 (1969) 320-339. Esp. 326-329. [NTA 14, 843]

1970a *Das vorsynoptische Judenchristentum* (Aufsätze und Vorträge zur Theologie und Religionswissenschaft, 48). Berlin: Evangelische Verlagsanstalt, 1970, 96 p; (Arbeiten zur Theologie, I/43), Stuttgart: Calwer, 1970, 96 p. Esp. 21-27; 65-72 [5,11-12]; 85-90 [10,5-16.23].

1970b Was ist ein Logion? — *ZNW* 61 (1970) 172-182. Esp. 177-179.181 [6,16-18]. [NTA 15, 833]

1972 Literarische Quellenhypothesen im Licht der Wahrscheinlichkeitsfrage. — *TLZ* 97 (1972) 331-340. Esp. 334-335: "Die Schriftlichkeit von Q"; 335-338: "Neue Argumente". [NTA 17, 498]

1987 Übergänge von Jesus zur Kirche. — *SNTU* 12 (1987) 85-98. Esp. 90-95. [NTA 33, 335]

**SCHILLEBEECKX, Edward**

1974 *Jezus, het verhaal van een levende.* Bloemendaal: Nelissen, 1974, ³1975, 641 p. Esp. 191-199: "Q- en Mc-tradities i.v.m. 'Jezus en de Wet'". → 1978
*Jesus, die Geschichte von einem Lebenden.* Freiburg: Herder, 1975.
*Jesus: An Experiment in Christology.* New York: Seabury; London: Collins, 1979. Esp. 233-243.
Trans. Italian 1976; Spanish 1981.

1978 *Tussentijds verhaal over twee Jezusboeken.* Bloemendaal: Nelissen; Brugge: Emmaüs, 1978, 144 p. Esp. 44-58: "Geen voorliefde voor de Q-traditie noch verwaarlozing van het johanneïsme en de kerkelijke traditie". → 1974
*Die Auferstehung Jesu als Grund der Erlösung. Zwischenbericht über die Prolegomena zu einer Christologie,* trans. H. Zulauf (QDisp, 78). Freiburg: Herder, 1979, 150 p. Esp. 46-60.
*Interim Report on the Books Jesus and Christ.* London: SCM; New York: Crossroad, 1980. Esp. 35-48.
Trans. Italian 1980; Spanish 1983.

**SCHILLING, Frederick A.**

1956 "Amen, I say to you". — *ATR* 38 (1956) 175-181.

1965 What Means the Saying about Receiving the Kingdom of God as a Little Child (τὴν βασιλείαν τοῦ θεοῦ ὡς παιδίον)? Mk x.15; Lk xviii.17. [18,3; 19,13-15] — *ExpT* 77 (1965-66) 56-58. [NTA 10, 534]

**SCHINDLER, Peter**

1947[R] *Petrus* [Danish, 1947], trans. A. Zucconi. Vicenza: Società anonima tipografica editrice, 1951, XVI-626 p. Esp. 3-138: "Pietro nei Vangeli".

**SCHIPPERS, Reinier**

1960 & BAARDA, T., *Het Evangelie van Thomas: Apocriefe woorden van Jezus* (Boeketreeks, 14). Kampen: Kok, 1960, 166 p. Esp. 55-131: "Kommentaar"; 135-155 (→ Baarda).

1962 *Gelijkenissen van Jezus.* Kampen: Kok, 1962, 198 p.

1964 The Mashal-character of the Parable of the Pearl. [13,45-46] — *Studia Evangelica* 2 (1964) 236-241.

1965 De zoon des mensen in Mt. 12,32 – Lk. 12,10, vergeleken met Mk. 3,28. — *Ex auditu verbi. Theologische opstellen aangeboden aan Prof. Dr. G.C. Berkouwer,* Kampen: Kok, 1965, 233-257. Esp. 242-244 [12,31]; 244-257 [12,32].
The Son of Man in Matt. xii.32 = Lk. xii.10, compared with Mk. iii.28. — *Studia Evangelica* 4 (1968) 231-235.

1966 The Pre-Synoptic Tradition in I Thessalonians II 13-16. — *NT* 8 (1966) 223-234. Esp. 231-234. [NTA 11, 816]

1969 *Jezus Christus in het historisch onderzoek.* I: *Van het verhaal naar de feiten* (Cahiers voor de gemeente, 5). Kampen: Kok, 1969, 88 p. Esp. 60-67: "Mattheüs, de componist" [1,1-17; Sadducees; composition].

**SCHIWY, Günther**

1965 *Weg ins Neue Testament. Kommentar und Material,* Band I: *Das Evangelium nach Matthäus, Markus und Lukas.* Würzburg: Echter, 1965, 391 p.
K. WENNEMER, *TheolPhil* 42 (1967) 305.
*Iniciación al Nuevo Testamento,* trans. D. Ruiz Bueno. I: *Mateo, Marco, Luca* (Col. "Lux mundi", 27). Salamanca, Sígueme, 1969, 531 p.
J. APECECHEA, *ScriptTheol* 2 (1970) 569-571; J.M. CABALLERO, *Burgense* 12 (1971) 407-408; V.

CASILLAS, *Revista agustiniana de espiritualidad* (Calahorra) 11 (1970) 241; M. DE BURGOS, *Communio* (Sevilla) 3 (1970) 324; J. DE JESÚS MARIA, *EstJos* 24 (1970) 79; S. GONZÁLEZ DE CARREA, *NatGrac* 17 (1970) 403-404; J. LLAMAS, *CiudDios* 183 (1970) 125-126; P. ORTIZ VALDIVIESO, *Revista Javeriana* (Bogotá) 71 (1970) 340; R. SILVA COSTOYAS, *Compostellanum* 15 (1970) 502; *RevistEspTeol* 31 (1971) 363; V. SORIA, *CuBíb* 28 (1971) 319-320; L. TURRADO, *Salmanticensis* 18 (1971) 408; J.I. VICENTINI, *Stromata* (San Míguel, Arg.) 26 (1970) 131-132.

*Introduzione al Nuovo Testamento. Commento, materiale e documenti storici*, trans. D. Merli. Roma: Città Nuova, 1971, 429 p.

G. GHIBERTI, *ParVi* 17 (1972) 477-478; F. SALVONI, *RicBibRel* 7 (1972) 370; A. STÖGER, *TPQ* 115 (1967) 388.

### SCHLATTER, Adolf

1916<sup>R</sup> *Das Evangelium nach Matthäus* [1916] (Erläuterungen zum Neuen Testament, 1). Stuttgart: Calwer, 1953; 1995, 425 p.

     B.J. LEFROIS, *CBQ* 18 (1956) 468.

1922<sup>R</sup> *Die Theologie der Apostel* [¹1922], ed. H. Stroh & P. Stuhlmacher. Stuttgart: Calwer, ³1977, 576 p. Esp. 64-87: "Die Befestigung der Erinnerungen an Jesus durch Matthäus".

1928<sup>R</sup> *Die Gabe des Christus. Eine Auslegung der Bergpredigt* [1928] (Theologie und Dienst, 30). Gießen-Basel: Brunnen, ²1982, 45 p. [NTA 26, p. 323]

     A. SALAS, *CiudDios* 195 (1982) 498.

1929<sup>R</sup> *Der Evangelist Matthäus. Seine Sprache, sein Ziel, seine Selbständigkeit. Ein Kommentar zum 1. Evangelium* [1929]. Stuttgart: Calwer, ⁴1957, XI-816 p.; ⁶1963.

     J. DUPONT, *LumièreV* 40 (1958) 30.

### SCHLATTER, Fredric W.

1972    The Problem of Jn 1:3b-4a. — *CBQ* 34 (1972) 54-58. Esp. 56-57 [1,20]. [NTA 16, 915]

1985    The *Opus Imperfectum in Matthaeum* and the *Fragmenta in Lucam*. — *VigChr* 39 (1985) 384-392. → Bouhot 1970

1987    The Pelagianism of the *Opus Imperfectum in Matthaeum*. — *VigChr* 41 (1987) 267-284.

1988    The Author of the *Opus Imperfectum in Matthaeum*. — *VigChr* 42 (1988) 364-375.

### SCHLIER, Heinrich

1955a   Der Ruf Gottes. Eine biblische Besinnung zum Gleichnis vom königlichen Hochzeitsmahl. [22,1-14] — *GL* 28 (1955) 241-247.

     Der Ruf Gottes (Mt 22,1-14). — ID., *Besinnung*, 1964, 219-226.
     The Call of God. — ID., *The Relevance*, 1968, 249-258.
     L'appel de Dieu (Mt 22,1-14). — ID., *Essays*, 1968, 255-262.

1955b   Die Verkündigung der Taufe Jesu nach den Evangelien. — *Ibid.*, 414-419. Esp. 415-416; = ID., *Besinnung*, 1964, 212-218. Esp. 214-215.

     The Baptism of Jesus as Presented by the Gospels. — ID., *The Relevance*, 1968, 239-248. Esp. 241-243.
     La présentation du Baptême de Jésus dans les Évangiles. — ID., *Essays*, 1968, 247-254. Esp. 249-250.

1958    Die Engel nach dem Neuen Testament. — *Archiv für Liturgiewissenschaft* (Regensburg) 6 (1958) 43-56; = ID., *Besinnung*, 1964, 160-175.

     The Angels according to the New Testament. — ID., *The Relevance*, 1968, 172-192.
     Les anges dans le Nouveau Testament. — ID., *Essays*, 1968, 187-204.

1964    *Besinnung auf das Neue Testament. Exegetische Aufsätze und Vorträge*, II. Freiburg: Herder, 1964, ²1967, 376 p. → 1955a-b, 1958

     *The Relevance of the New Testament*, trans. W.J.. O'Hara. New York: Herder; London: Burns & Oates, 1968, X-258 p. (= *Besinnung*, 1-226).
     *Essais sur le Nouveau Testament*, trans. A. Liefooghe (LD, 46). Paris: Cerf, 1968, 416 p.

1972    Ekklesiologie des Neuen Testaments. — FEINER, J. - LÖHRER, M. (eds.), *Mysterium Salutis. Grundriß heilsgeschichtlicher Dogmatik*. IV/1: *Das Heilsgeschehen in der*

*Gemeinde*, Zürich–Einsiedeln–Köln: Benziger, 1972, 101-221. Esp. 102-116: "Die Kirche nach Matthäus".

1974 Zur Frage: Wer ist Jesus? — GNILKA, J. (ed.), *Neues Testament und Kirche*. FS R. Schnackenburg, 1974, 359-370. Esp. 369 [16,17-19]; = ID., *Der Geist und die Kirche. Exegetische Aufsätze und Vorträge*, IV, eds. V. Kubina & K. Lehmann, Freiburg: Herder, 1980, 20-32. Esp. 31-32.

**SCHLOSSER, Jacques**

1980 *Le Règne de Dieu dans les dits de Jésus* (Études bibliques). Paris: Gabalda, 1980, 2 vols., VII-417 and 419-747 p. Esp. 127-153 [12,28/Q 11,20]; 155-178 [11,11/Q 7,28]; 247-322 [6,10/Q 11,2]; 423-450 [5,3/Q 6,20]; 451-476 [21,31]; 509-539 [11,12-13/Q 16,16]; 603-669 [8,11-12/Q 13,28-29]. — Diss. Strasbourg, 1978 (J. Schmitt).
*Les Logia du Règne. Étude sur le vocable "Basileia tou Theou" dans la prédication de Jésus*. Lille: Univ. de Lille III, 1982, X-714 p. Esp. 59-70.447-460; 71-83.461-471; 125-167.501-531; 227-242.575-586; 243-256.587-598; 273-291.615-626; 331-369.651-678.
Le Règne de Dieu dans les dits de Jésus. — *RevSR* 53 (1979) 164-176. [NTA 24, 64]

1982 La genèse de *Luc*, XXII,25-27. — *RB* 89 (1982) 52-70. Esp. 56-59 [23,11]. [NTA 27, 558]

1983a Lk 17,2 und die Logienquelle. — *SNTU* 8 (1983) 70-78. Esp. 70-73 [Mk/Q]; 73-76 [Q 17,2]; 76-78 [reconstruction]. [NTA 30, 1110] → Neirynck 1995g, 57-59

1983b Le Règne de Dieu, présent et à venir, dans la prédication de Jésus. — *RevDroitCan* 33 (1983) 201-212. Esp. 203-204 [5,3-6]; 205-207 [6,10]; 208 [11 12-13]; 209-210 [12,28]. [NTA 28, 468]

1985 Mc 11,25: tradition et rédaction. — GANTOY, R. (ed.), *À cause de l'Évangile*. FS J. Dupont, 1985, 277-301. Esp. 283-284: "Le parallèle matthéer" [6,14-15]; 289-291 [Mk/Mt]; 297-298.

1987 *Le Dieu de Jésus. Étude exégétique* (LD, 129). Paris: Cerf, 1987, 281 p. Esp. 140-150.157-175 [God as father: Q 6,35.36; 10,21-22; 11,2.11-13; 12,30; Mt 5,16; 6,1-6.7-8.16-18; 16,17; 18,10.19; 23,9]; 213-233 [20,1-15]; 235-260 [5,44-45].
*El Dios de Jesús. Estudio exegético*, trans. A. Ortiz (Biblioteca de estudios bíblicos, 82). Salamanca: Sígueme, 1995, 285 p.

1990 La parole de Jésus sur la fin du Temple. — *NTS* 36 (1990) 398-414. Esp. 403-405 [26,61; 27,40]. [NTA 35, 166]

1991 Des choses sacrées au Dieu vivant (Mt 23,16-22). — OBERLINNER, L. – FIEDLER, P. (eds.), *Salz der Erde*. FS A. Vögtle, 1991, 285-298. Esp. 286-287: "L'analyse littéraire"; 288-291: "La genèse"; 291-294: "La théologie du fragment traditionnel (23,16-19)"; 295-298: "La théologie de la rédaction (23,16-22)".

1992 Le logion de Mt 10,28 par. Lc 12,4-5. — VAN SEGBROECK, F., et al. (eds.), *The Four Gospels 1992*. FS F. Neirynck, 1992, I, 621-631. Esp. 622: "Critique littéraire de Lc 12,4-7 par."; 623-625: "La teneur du logion de Lc 12,4-5 dans la source"; 625-629: "Exégèse du fragment"; 629-631: "L'authenticité du texte".

1994a Le Règne de Dieu et le temps. — LEUBA, J.-L. (ed.), *Temps et eschatologie. Données bibliques et problématiques contemporaines* (Académie internationale des sciences religieuses), Paris: Cerf, 1994, 55-63. Esp. 57-60 [Q 11,20].

1994b Die Vollendung des Heils in der Sicht Jesu. — KLAUCK, H.-J. (ed.), *Weltgericht und Weltvollendung*. FS R. Schnackenburg, 1994, 54-84. Esp. 64-65 [Q 13,28-30]; 68-69 [Q 22,28-30].

**SCHMAHL, Günther**

1973 Gültigkeit und Verbindlichkeit der Bergpredigt. — *BibLeb* 14 (1973) 180-187. [NTA 19, 84]

1974a *Die Zwölf im Markusevangelium. Eine redaktionsgeschichtliche Untersuchung* (Trierer theologische Studien, 30). Trier: Paulinus, 1974, XIII-170 p. Esp. 29-36: "Die Zwölf nach Mt 19,28 / Lk 22,28-30"; 146-147. — Diss. Trier, 1971-72 (K. Kertelge).

1974b Die Antithesen der Bergpredigt. Inhalt und Eigenart ihrer Forderungen. — *TTZ* 83 (1974) 284-297. Esp. 287-295: "Die Forderungen im einzelnen". [NTA 19, 530]

1978 Magier aus dem Osten und die Heiligen Drei Könige. [2,1-12] — *TTZ* 87 (1978) 295-303. [NTA 23, 427]

### SCHMAUCH, Werner

1951* (ed.), *In Memoriam Ernst Lohmeyer*. Stuttgart: Evangelisches Verlagswerk, 1951, 376 p. → G. Bornkamm, S.E. Johnson, E. Lohmeyer, Schmauch

1951 In der Wüste. Beobachtungen zur Raumbeziehung des Glaubens im Neuen Testament. — *Ibid.*, 202-223. Esp. 209-211, 214-215, 217-221.

1952 Der Ölberg. Exegese zu einer Ortsangabe besonders bei Matthäus und Markus. [21,17] — *TLZ* 77 (1952) 391-396; = ID., ... *zu achten aufs Wort*, 1967, 47-56.

1956 *Orte der Offenbarung und der Offenbarungsort im Neuen Testament*. Göttingen: Vandenhoeck & Ruprecht; Berlin: Evangelische Verlagsanstalt, 1956, 140 p. Esp. 20-26 [Nazareth]; 34-47 [desert]; 58-80 [mountains]; 91-93 [Jerusalem]; 94-113 [temple].

1957 Reich Gottes und Existenz nach der Bergpredigt. — *Kirche in der Zeit* 12 (1957) 277-281.

1958a Reich Gottes und menschliche Existenz nach der Bergpredigt. — ID. - WOLF, E., *Königsherrschaft Christi. Der Christ im Staat* (Theologische Existenz heute, NF 64), München: Kaiser, 1958, 5-19.

1958b Vaterunser. — *EKL* 3 (1958) 1610-1611.

1967a ... *zu achten aufs Wort. Ausgewählte Arbeiten*, eds. C. Grengel – M. Punge – W.-C. Schmauch. Göttingen: Vandenhoeck & Ruprecht, 1967, 143 p. → 1952, 1967b

1967b Die Komposition des Matthäus-Evangeliums in ihrer Bedeutung für seine Interpretation. — *Ibid.*, 64-87.

### SCHMEING, Clemens

1963 "Sanft und demütig von Herzen". Gedanken P. Anselm Fischers OSB († 1714) zu Mt 11,29. — *ErbAuf* 39 (1963) 29-41. [NTA 7, 782]

### SCHMELLER, Thomas

1989 *Brechungen. Urchristliche Wandercharismatiker im Prisma soziologisch orientierter Exegese* (SBS, 136). Stuttgart: Katholisches Bibelwerk, 1989, 128 p. Esp. 93-98: "Die Q-Boten"; 98-103: "Wanderpropheten im Umfeld des Mt-Evangeliums"; 104-106.

1994a *Das Recht der Anderen. Befreiungstheologische Lektüre des Neuen Testaments in Lateinamerika* (NTAbh, NF 27). Münster: Aschendorff, 1994, X-301 p. Esp. 215-222, 226-229. — Diss. München, 1993 (J. Gnilka).

1994b Das Reich Gottes im Gleichnis. Eine Überprüfung neuerer Deutungen der Gleichnisrede und der Reich-Gottes-Verkündigung Jesu. — *TLZ* 119 (1994) 599-608. [NTA 39, 784]

### SCHMID, Hans Heinrich

1987 Probleme der Bibelübersetzung. [5,1-2] — *Reformiertes Forum* (Zürich-Basel) 1/4 (1987) 11-13. [NTA 31, 987]

### SCHMID, Josef

1948[R] *Das Evangelium nach Matthäus übersetzt und erklärt* (Regensburger Neues Testament, 1) [1948]. Regensburg, [2]1952, 309 p.; [3]1956, 401 p.; [4]1959.

P. ASHMANN, *Bijdragen* 20 (1959) 196-197; P. BENOIT, *RB* 64 (1957) 434-436; J.L. D'ARAGON, *ScEccl* 10 (1958) 107-108.

*L'Evangelo secondo Matteo* [[3]1956], trans. M. Bellincioni (Il Nuovo Testamento commentato, 1). Brescia: Morcelliana, 1957, 489 p.; 1965, 515 p.

G.G. Gamba, *Sal* 21 (1959) 197-198.
*Het Evangelie volgens Mattheüs*, trans. L. Witsenburg (Het Nieuwe Testament met Commentaar, 1).
Bilthoven: Nelissen; Antwerpen: Patmos, 1963, 486 p.
R. D'Hondt, *Streven* 17 (1963-64) 491; R. Schippers, *GTT* 64 (1964) 77; J.M. Tison, *Bijdragen* 25 (1964) 92.
*El Evangelio según San Mateo*, trans. M. González-Haba (Comentario de Ratisbona al NT, 1). Buenos Aires: Herder, 1967, 572 p.; Barcelona: Herder, ³1981.
J.M. Arróniz, *ScriptVict* 16 (1969) 236-238; J.A. Carrasco, *EstJos* 22 (1968) 263-264; J.A. del Niño Jesús, *EstJos* 22 (1968) 263-264; M. Guiran, *Augustinianum* 9 (1969) 158-159; P.J. Huergo, *CiTom* 95 (1968) 354-355; C. Mateos, *EstAgust* 3 (1968) 143-144; M. Mateos, *RazFe* 177 (1968) 429-431; L. Turrado, *Salmanticensis* 16 (1969) 459-461; S. Vergés, *EstE* 44 (1969) 274-276.

1949ᴿ  *Synopse der drei ersten Evangelien mit Beifügung der Johannes-Parallelen* [1949]. Regensburg: Pustet, 2nd rev. ed., 1956, IV-215 p.; ³1960; ⁵1968; ¹⁰1992.
*Sinossi dei tre primi evangeli con i passi paralleli di Giovanni* (Il Nuovo Testamento commentato), ed. ital. a cura di F. Montagnini. Brescia: Morcelliana, 1970, IV-219 p.
*Evangeliesynops. Jämte paralleler i Johannesevangeliet.* Redigerad efter den tyska upplagen av S. Lindhagen. Stockholm: Verbum, 1967; ²1972, 199 p.

1951  Das textgeschichtliche Problem der Parabel von den zwei Söhnen. Mt 21,28-32. — Adler, N. (ed.), *Vom Wort des Lebens*. FS M. Meinertz, 1951, 68-84. Esp. 69-78: "Die Textform II" [Western text]; 78-84: "Der vor der Textform II liegende Text"; = Bauer, J.B., *Evangelienforschung*, 1968, 199-220. Esp. 200-212; 213-220.

1953*  & Vögtle, A. (eds.), *Synoptische Studien Alfred Wikenhauser zum siebzigsten Geburtstag am 22. Februar 1953 dargebracht von Freunden, Kollegen und Schülern.* München: Zink, 1953, 293 p. → P. Benoit, Cerfaux, Dey, Fridrichsen, J. Jeremias, Meinerz, W. Michaelis, Schäfer, J. Schmid, Schnackenburg, Vögtle

1953  Markus und der aramäische Matthäus. — *Ibid.*, 148-183. Esp. 150-159 [structure of Proto-Mt]; 159-165 [minor agreements]; 165-183 [Mt originality]; = Bauer, J.B. (ed.), *Evangelienforschung*, 1968, 75-118. Esp. 76-87; 88-95; 95-118.

1959  Petrus "der Fels" und die Petrusgestalt der Urgemeinde. — Roesle, M. — Cullmann, O. (eds.), *Begegnung der Christen*. FS O. Karrer, 1959, 347-359. Esp. 355-359 [16,18-19]; = *TJb*, 1964, 71-81. Esp. 75-80; = Bauer, J.B., *Evangelienforschung*, 1968, 159-175. Esp. 170-175.

1960  Zwei unbekannte Gleichnisse Jesu. — *GL* 33 (1960) 423-433. Esp. 428-431 [21,28-32]. [NTA 5, 721]

1961  Um eine neue Lösung des synoptischen Problems. — *BZ* 5 (1961) 136-142. [NTA 6, 345r]
→ de Solages 1959, Vaganay 1954a

1962a  Matthäusevangelium. — *LTK* 7 (²1962) 176-179.

1962b  "Selig wer sich an mich nicht ärgert!" (Mt 11,6). Jesus, der verheißene Messias im Neuen Testament. — *BK* 17 (1962) 42-46. [NTA 7, 98]

1964a  Ich aber sage euch. Der Anruf der Bergpredigt. — *BK* 19 (1964) 75-79. [NTA 9, 523]

1964b  Seligpreisung. — *LTK* 9 (²1964) 639-642. Esp. 640-641.

1964c  Synoptiker. — *LTK* 9 (²1964) 1240-1249. Esp. 1240-1245: "Synoptische Frage".

1973  *Einleitung in das Neue Testament.* Freiburg: Herder, 6th rev. ed. 1973, XVI-677 p. Esp. 224-247: "Das Matthäusevangelium"; 272-289: "Die synoptische Frage". → Wikenhauser 1953
*Introducción al Nuovo Testamento* (Bibliotheca Herder, 56). Barcelona: Herder, 1978, 1005 p.
*Introduzione al Nuovo Testamento*, trans. G. Forza (Biblioteca teolcgica, 9). Brescia: Paideia, 1981, 734 p.

### Schmid, Norbert

1961  *Kleine ringförmige Komposition in den vier Evangelien und der Apostelgeschichte. Untersuchungen über eine Stilfigur.* Diss. Tübingen, 1961, IX-180 p. — *TLZ* 87 (1962) 787.

**SCHMIDT, Andreas**

1989    Zum Papyrus P. Köln II 80: καὶ καταπατεῖσϑαι oder καὶ πατεῖσϑαι als Aussage des
        Korrektors? [5,13] — *Archiv für Papyrusforschung* (Leipzig) 35 (1989) 13.

1991    Der mögliche Text von P. Oxy. III 405, Z. 39-45. [1,22-25] — *NTS* 37 (1991) 160. [NTA
        35, 1125]

**SCHMIDT, Bernhard**

1987    (ed.), *Alberti Magni Super Matthaeum. Capitula I-XIV.XV-XXVIII* (Opera Omnia, 21/1-2).
        Münster: Aschendorff, 1987, LXXVII-437 and 437-773 p.

        R. ESCOL, *NRT* 110 (1988) 260-261; D. GRONEMANN, *BTAM* 16 (1993) 255-256; K. REINHARDT, *TTZ*
        99 (1990) 157-158; C. VANSTEENKISTE, *Angelicum* 67 (1990) 241-248.

**SCHMIDT, Daryl D.**

1977    The LXX *Gattung* "Prophetic Correlative". — *JBL* 96 (1977) 517-522. [NTA 22, 750] →
        R.A. Edwards 1971a

**SCHMIDT, H.**

1957    *Der verheissene heilige Herrscher. Gottes gute Botschaft nach Matthäus-Bericht
        bearbeitet* (Christus heute. Eine Erklärung der neutestamentlichen Botschaft, 16).
        Stuttgart: Kreuz, 1957, 134 p.

**SCHMIDT, Karl Ludwig**

1919[R]  *Der Rahmen der Geschichte Jesu. Literarkritische Untersuchungen zur ältesten Jesus-
        überlieferung* [1919]. Darmstadt: Wissenschaftliche Buchgesellschaft, 1964, XVIII-322 p.

        Esp. 22-23 [3,1-6]; 25-26 [3,11-12]; 31 [4,1-11]; 34-36 [4,12-17]; 44-45 [4,18-22]; 56-57 [8,14-17]; 69-71
        [5-7]; 71-75 [8,5-13]; 79-80 [9,1-8]; 85-86 [9,9-13]; 88 [9,14-17]; 93-94 [12,1-8]; 101-102 [12,9-14]; 108
        [12,15-21]; 116-118 [11,2-19]; 123-126 [12,22-50]; 133-134 [13,1-52]; 138 [8,23-27]; 142-143 [8,28-34];
        148-150 [9,18-26]; 158 [13,53-58]; 165-166.170 [10,1-42]; 174 [14,1-2]; 176-177 [14,3-12]; 193 [14,13-21];
        194 [14,22-33]; 196-198 [15,1-20]; 199 [15,21-28]; 201 [9,27-31; 15,29-31]; 203 [16,1-4]; 204 [16,5-12];
        210-211 [11,20-24]; 217 [16,13-19]; 220 [16,22-23]; 221 [16.24-28]; 226 [17,9-13]; 229 [17,14-21]; 231-232
        [18,1-5]; 232-233 [17,24-27]; 233-237 [18,6-35]; 239-240 [19,1-12]; 242-244 [19,16-30]; 271-273 [23,37-39];
        280 [21,28-32; 22,1-14]; 282-283 [22,34-40]; 295-297 [21,1-2]; 309-310.315-316 [1-2].

1946[R]  Das Pneuma Hagion als Person und als Charisma. Eine lexikologische und biblisch-
        theologische Studie. [1946] — ID., *Neues Testament - Judentum - Kirche. Kleine
        Schriften*, ed. G. Sauter (Theologische Bücherei, 69), München: Kaiser, 1981, 215-263.
        Esp. 240-244 [28,19]

1950    'Ιησοῦς Χριστὸς κολαφιζόμενος und die "colaphisation" der Juden. — CULLMANN,
        O. - MENOUD, P. (eds.), *Aux sources de la tradition chrétienne*. FS M. Goguel, 1950,
        218-227. Esp. 218-219 [26,67-68]; 219-221 [27,27-31].

**SCHMIDT, Martin Anton**

1992    Thomas von Aquino zu Matthäus 6,9/10. — *TZ* 48 (1992) 46-55.

**SCHMIDT, Peter**

1990    *Woord van God - Boek van mensen. Inleiding tot de Evangeliën en de Handelingen.*
        Averbode-Apeldoorn: Altiora, 1990, 215 p. Esp. 85-126: "De synoptische kwestie"; 143-157:
        "Het evangelie van Matteüs".

        *How to Read the Gospels. Historicity and Truth in the Gospels and Acts*, trans. C. Vanhove-Romanik. Slough-
        Maynooth: St Pauls, 1993, 205 p. Esp. 82-121; 137-151.

**SCHMIDT, Philipp**

1955    Etwas über den Stern der Weisen. — *Klerusblatt* 35 (1955) 507-508.

**SCHMIDT, Thomas E.**

1987    *Hostility to Wealth in the Synoptic Gospels* (JSNT SS, 15). Sheffield: JSOT, 1987, 251

p. Esp. 121-134.208-214: "Hostility to wealth in the gospel of Matthew" [4,8-10.18-22; 5,3.42; 6,3-4.19-24.25-34; 10,9-10; 13,22.44-46; 16,24-27; 19,16-30; 25,14-30.31-46]. — Diss. Cambridge, 1985 (E. Bammel).

1988    Burden, Barrier, Blasphemy: Wealth in Matt 6:33, Luke 14:33, and Luke 16:15. — *TrinJ* NS 9 (1988) 171-189. Esp. 172-178 [6,33]. [NTA 34, 623]

1992a   Mark 10.29-30; Matthew 19.29: 'Leave houses ... and region'? — *NTS* 38 (1992) 617-620. [NTA 37, 748]

1992b   The Penetration of Barriers and the Revelation of Christ in the Gospels. — *NT* 34 (1992) 229-246. Esp. 233-234 [3,16-17]; 235-236 [17,1-8]; 236-238 [27,51-54]; 238-240 [1,18-21]; 241-242 [28,2-7]. [NTA 37, 665]

1994*   & SILVA, M. (eds.), *To Tell the Mystery. Essays on New Testament Eschatology in Honor of Robert H. Gundry* (JSNT SS, 100). Sheffield: JSOT, 1994, 266 p. →
Gerhardsson, Goulder, Hagner, Marshall

**SCHMIED, Augustin**

1985   Antijudaismus im Neuen Testament? — *TGeg* 28 (1985) 48-54. Esp. 51-52 [27,25].

**SCHMITHALS, Walter**

1972a   Die Gegenwart Jesu Christi in seiner Gemeinde. — *TViat* 11 (1966-72) 217-233. Esp. 227-228 [28,16-20].

1972b   Der Markusschluß, die Verklärungsgeschichte und die Aussendung der Zwölf. — *ZTK* 69 (1972) 379-411. Esp. 403-406 [28,16-20]. [NTA 17, 958] → Linnemann 1969

1978   Leistung im Neuen Testament. — GUNNEWEG, A.H.J. - SCHMITHALS, W., *Leistung* (Biblische Konfrontationen. Kohlhammer Taschenbücher, 1007), Stuttgart: Kohlhammer, 1978, 84-163. Esp. 121-124 [20,1-15].

1979a   *Das Evangelium nach Markus.* 1. *Kapitel 1–9,1*; 2. *Kapitel 9,2–16,18* (ÖTKNT, II/1-2). Gütersloh: Mohn; Würzburg: Echter, 1979, 1-397 and 398-760 p.; [2]1986, 1-397 and 398-788 p. Esp. I, 22-25 [Mk/Q].

1979b   Die Worte vom leidenden Menschensohn. Ein Schlüssel zur Lösung des Menschensohn-Problems. — ANDRESEN, C. - KLEIN, G. (eds.), *Theologia Crucis - Signum Crucis. Festschrift für Erich Dinkler zum 70. Geburtstag*, Tübingen: Mohr, 1979, 417-445. Esp. 435-436 [Mark 8,38; 13,26/Q]; 437-445 [Q].

1980a   Biblische Konfrontation mit Herrschaft. — GUNNEWEG, A.H.J. - SCHMITHALS, W., *Herrschaft* (Biblische Konfrontationen. Kohlhammer Taschenbücher, 1012), Stuttgart: Kohlhammer, 1980, 46-148. Esp. 137-148 [2,1-12].

1980b   Kritik der Formkritik. — *ZTK* 77 (1980) 149-185. Esp. 151-154 [Q]. [NTA 25, 62]

1982   Evangelien, Synoptische. — *TRE* 10 (1982) 570-626. Esp. 575-599: "Die synoptische Quellenkritik"; 600-609: "Die synoptische Traditionskritik"; 609-626: "Die synoptische Redaktionskritik" [616-620: Mt; 620-623: Q].

1984   *Neues Testament und Gnosis* (Erträge der Forschung, 208). Darmstadt: Wissenschaftliche Buchgesellschaft, 1984, IX-194 p. Esp. 125-126: "Die Spruchquelle (Q)"; 126-127: "Das Matthäusevangelium".

1985   *Einleitung in die drei ersten Evangelien* (de Gruyter Lehrbuch). Berlin - New York: de Gruyter, 1985, XI-494 p. Esp. 138-163: "Matthäus-Priorität"; 215-229: "Die Logiensammlung (Q)"; 229-233: "Das Verhältnis von MkEv und Q zueinander. Die Dubletten"; 246-318: "Mündliche Tradition vor dem MkEv und vor Q"; 318-332: "Schriftliche Tradition vor dem MkEv und vor Q sowie vor S[Mt] und S[Lk]"; 333-335: "Schriftstellerischer Ursprung des MkEv und von Q"; 369-384: "Das MtEv"; 384-404: "Die Spruchquelle Q". → Roloff 1990

1987   Der Konflikt zwischen Kirche und Synagoge in neutestamentlicher Zeit. — OEMING, M. - GRAUPNER, A. (eds.), *Altes Testament und christliche Verkündigung. Festschrift für Antonius H.J. Gunneweg zum 65. Geburtstag*, Stuttgart: Kohlhammer, 1987, 366-384. Esp. 375-377.

1992   Die Bedeutung der Evangelien in der Theologiegeschichte bis zur Kanonbildung. — VAN SEGBROECK, F., et al. (eds.), *The Four Gospels 1992*. FS F. Neirynck, 1992, I, 129-157. Esp. 144-146.

1994   *Theologiegeschichte des Urchristentums. Eine problemgeschichtliche Darstellung.* Stuttgart: Kohlhammer, 1994, 332 p. Esp. 234-236 [synagogue]; 256-257; 274-277 [ethics].

SCHMITT, Albert
1952   (trans.), *Augustinus zur Bergpredigt [De Sermone Domini in monte sec. Matthaeum libri 2]*. St. Ottilien: EOS, 1952, 192 p.

SCHMITT, Götz
1978   Das Zeichen des Jona. — *ZNW* 69 (1978) 123-129. [NTA 23, 868]

SCHMITT, John J.
1981   In Search of the Origin of the *Siglum* Q. — *JBL* 100 (1981) 609-611. [NTA 26, 836] → Neirynck 1979c, Silberman 1979

1986   You Adulteresses! The Image in James 4:4. — *NT* 28 (1986) 327-337. Esp. 328-330 [12,39; 16,4]. [NTA 31, 778]

SCHMITT, Joseph
1951   Le récit de la résurrection dans l'évangile de Luc. Étude de critique littéraire. — *RevSR* 25 (1951) 119-137, 219-242. Esp. 123-127 [28,1-10/Lk].

1952   La résurrection de Jésus dans la prédication apostolique et la tradition évangélique. — *LumièreV* 3 (1952) 35-60. Esp. 55-56.

1954   Saint Pierre et les origines chrétiennes d'après O. Cullmann — *RevSR* 28 (1954) 58-71. Esp. 62-70 [16,17-19]. → Cullmann 1952

1959   L'organisation de l'Église primitive et Qumrân. — VAN DER PLOEG, J. (ed.), *La secte de Qumrân et les origines du christianisme* (Recherches bibliques, 4), Brugge: Desclée De Brouwer, 1959, 217-231. Esp. 228-230.

1973   Les formulations primitives du mystère pascal. — *Bib* 54 (1973) 273-280. Esp. 274.279 [28,16-20]. [NTA 18, 439r] → Léon-Dufour 1971

1978   L'investiture de Pierre selon *Mt.*, *XVI*,17-19 et l'exégèse contemporaine. — *RevDroitCan* 28 (1978) 5-14.

1981   Résurrection de Jésus dans le kérygme, la tradition, la catéchèse. — *DBS* 10/55-56 (1981-82) 487-582. Esp. 557-570 [27,62-28,20].

SCHMITZ, Franz-Jürgen
1986   & MINK, G., *Liste der koptischen Handschriften des Neuen Testaments. I/1. Die sahidischen Handschriften der Evangelien* (Arbeiten zur neutestamentlichen Textforschung, 8). Berlin: de Gruyter, 1986, XXIII-471 p.; I/2.1 (Arbeiten, 13), 1989, X-449 p.; I/2.2 (Arbeiten, 15), 1991, XII-451-1279 p.

SCHNABEL, Eckhard J.
1994   Jesus and the Beginnings of the Mission to the Gentiles. — GREEN, J.B. – TURNER, M.B.B. (eds.), *Jesus of Nazareth*. FS I.H. Marshall, 1994, 37-58. Esp. 43-47 [mission]; 49-57 [gentiles].

SCHNACKENBURG, Rudolf
1950   Typen der Metanoia-Predigt im Neuen Testament. — *MüTZ* 1/4 (1950) 1-13. Esp. 4-7.
       Umkehr-Predigt im Neuen Testament. — ID., *Christliche Existenz*, 1967, I, 35-60. Esp. 38-47.
       The Penitential Sermon in the New Testament. — ID., *Christian Existence*, 1968, I, 33-66. Esp. 37-50.

1952 Der Sinn der Versuchung Jesu bei den Synoptikern. — *TQ* 132 (1952) 297-326. Esp. 300-305: "Die drei Berichte"; 311-319: "Der Hauptsinn der Versuchung Jesu bei Mt und Lk"; 319-321: "Die Eigenart des Mt-Berichtes"; = ID., *Schriften zum Neuen Testament*, 1971, 101-126 ("Nachwort", 126-128). Esp. 104-108; 113-120; 120-122.

1953 Mk 9,33-50. — SCHMID, J. – VÖGTLE, A. (eds.), *Synoptische Studien*. FS A. Wikenhauser, 1953, 184-206. Esp. 184-190: "Analyse von Mk 9,33-50 unter Vergleich der Parallelüberlieferung bei Mt und Lk"; 204-206: "Folgerungen für die synoptische Frage"; = ID., *Schriften zum Neuen Testament*, 1971, 129-152 ("Nachwort", 152-154). Esp. 129-135; 150-152.

1954 *Die sittliche Botschaft des Neuen Testamentes* (Handbuch der Moraltheologie, 6). München: M. Hueber, 1954, XII-284 p. Esp. 3-29: "Jesu Verkündigung der Königsherrschaft Gottes"; 30-55: "Die jüdische Sittenlehre und Jesu sittliche Forderungen. Die Bergpredigt" [5,17-20.21-48; 11,28-30; 23,16-22; Q 6,20-49]; 56-71: "Die Großtat Jesu" [5,48; 18,23-35]; 72-94: "Jesu Forderungen für das Leben" [5,32; 6,24; 19,3-9]; 95-112: "Jesu Motivierung seiner Forderungen" [5,3-10; 6,1-18; 20,1-16]; ²1962, XII-330 p. Esp. 3-35; 36-64; 65-81; 82-109; 110-128. → 1986
*Le message moral du Nouveau Testament*. Le Puy: Mappus, 1963, 367 p.
*The Moral Teaching of the New Testament*, trans. J. Holland-Smith & W.J. O'Hara. New York: Herder & Herder, 1965, 409 p. Esp. 15-53; 54-89; 90-109; 110-143; 144-167.
*El testimonio moral del Nuevo Testamento*, trans. J. Manzano (Enciclopedia de Etica y Moral cristiana). Madrid: Rialp, 1965, 340 p.
*Messagio morale del Nuovo Testamento*. Alba, ²1971; ³1981. Esp. 53-84.
Trans. Polish 1981.

1958 Bergpredigt. — *LTK* 2 (²1958) 223-226.

1959a *Gottes Herrschaft und Reich. Eine biblisch-theologische Studie*. Freiburg: Herder, 1959, ⁴1965, XVI-255 p. Esp. 49-76: "Die von Jesus verkündigte Gottesherrschaft" [3,7-12; 5-7; 8,11-12; 11,12-13; 25,31-46]; 77-109: "Die Anwesenheit der eschatologischen Gottesherrschaft im Wirken Jesu" [11,11.12-13; 13,24-30.36-43]; 110-148: "Das Kommen des vollendeten Gottesreiches" [10,23.32-33; 25,31-46]; 149-180: "Die Gottesherrschaft und die Heilsgeschichte Jesu" [16,18-19; 18,1-20; 21,43; 22,1-10].
*God's Rule and Kingdom*. New York: Herder & Herder; London: Burns and Oates, 1961, ²1968 [= German ⁴1965], 400 p. Esp. 77-113; 114-159; 160-214; 215-258.
*Règne et Royaume de Dieu. Essai de théologie biblique*, trans. R. Marlé (Études théologiques, 2). Paris: Éd. de l'Orante, 1965, 325 p. Esp. 65-95; 96-134; 135-180; 181-216.
*Reino y reinado de Dios*, trans. J. Cosgaya (Actualidad Bíblica, 3). Madrid: Fax, 1967, XXIV-368 p.
*Signoria e Regno di Dio*. Bologna: Il Mulino, 1971.

1959b Die Vollkommenheit des Christen nach den Evangelien. — *GL* 32 (1959) 420-433. Esp. 423-428: "Die Vollkommenheit nach der Bergpredigt"; 428-433: "Vollkommenheit und Nachfolge Jesu". [NTA 4, 648]; = *TJb*, 1961, 67-81. Esp. 70-76; 76-81.
Die Vollkommenheit des Christen nach Matthäus. — ID., *Christliche Existenz*, I, 1967, 131-155.
Christian Perfection according to Matthew. — ID., *Christian Existence*, I, 1968, 158-189. Esp. 167-179; 179-189.
La perfezione del cristiano secondo il vangelo di Matteo. — *ParVi* 15 (1970) 241-265; = ID., *L'esistenza cristiana*, 1971, 111-131.

1960 Zum Verfahren der Urkirche bei ihrer Jesusüberlieferung — RISTOW, H. – MATTHIAE, K. (eds.), *Der historische Jesus und der kerygmatische Christus*, 1960, 439-454. Esp. 447-451 [13,36-43; 24,43-51; 25,1-13; Q 12,8-9]; = ID., *Schriften zum Neuen Testament*, 1971, 155-174 ("Nachwort", 175-176). Esp. 164-171.

1961a *Die Kirche im Neuen Testament. Ihre Wirklichkeit und theologische Deutung, ihr Wesen und Geheimnis* (QDisp, 14). Freiburg: Herder, 1961, 172 p. Esp. 47-48 [28,18-20]; 54-56 [16,18-19]; 64-71: "Die Kirchengedanke bei Matthäus" [5,17-20; 18,1-20]; 119-121 [5-7/Qumran]; 139.
*De Kerk in het Nieuwe Testament. Haar werkelijkheid en theologische verklaring. Haar wezen en mysterie*. Antwerpen: Patmos, 1964, 178 p. Esp. 46-47; 54-56; 64-71; 121-123; 142.
*The Church in the New Testament*. New York: Seabury, 1965, 221 p.
*La Chiesa nel Nuovo Testamento. Realtà, interpretazione teologica, essenza e mistero*, trans. P. Borgomeo. Brescia: Morcelliana, 1968, 208 p.

1961b  *La théologie du Nouveau Testament. État de la question* (Studia Neotestamentica Subsidia, 1). Brugge: Desclée De Brouwer, 1961, 123 p. Esp. 48-57: "Théologie des évangiles synoptiques"; 60-61: "St Matthieu".
*Neutestamentliche Theologie. Der Stand der Forschung* (Biblische Handbibliothek, 1). München: Kösel, 1963; ²1965, 159 p. Esp. 58-74; 80-83.
*New Testament Theology Today*, trans. D. Askew. New York: Herder & Herder; London: Chapman; Montreal: Palm Publishers, 1963, 133 p. Esp. 54-66; 68-70.
*La Teología del Nuevo Testamento. Estado de la cuestion*, trans. I. Viar (Temas bíblicos, 6). Bilbao: Desclée, 1966, 159 p. Esp. 63-78; 81-83.

1964a  "Ihr seid das Salz der Erde, das Licht der Welt". Zu Matthäus 5,13-16. — *Mélanges Eugène Tisserant*, 1964, I, 365-387. Esp. 367-372: "Zur Traditionsgeschichte der beiden Logien"; 373-382: "Der Sinn der Logien in ihrer Stellung und Gestalt bei Matthäus"; 383-387: "Wort Jesu und Aufnahme durch die Kirche"; = BAUER, J.B., *Evangelienforschung*, 1968, 119-146. Esp. 122-128; 128-140; 140-146; = ID., *Schriften zum Neuen Testament*, 1971, 177-199 ("Nachwort", 199-200). Esp. 179-184; 184-194; 194-199.

1964b  Kirche und Parusie. — METZ, J.B., et al. (eds.), *Gott in Welt*. FS K. Rahner, 1964, I, 551-578. Esp. 553 [παρουσία]; 565-568 [Q]; = ID., *Schriften zum Neuen Testament*, 1971, 288-318 ("Nachwort", 318-320). Esp. 290-291; 305-307.
Kerk en parusie. — *God en Wereld*, 1965, IV, 127-155, 176-181. Esp. 131; 142-144.
Église et parousie. — *Le message de Jésus*, 1969, 7-39. Esp. 9; 24-26.

1964c  Zur Traditionsgeschichte von Joh 4,46-54. — *BZ* 8 (1964) 58-88. Esp. 70-76.82-85. [NTA 8, 1002]

1965  *Das Johannesevangelium* (HTKNT, 4/1-4). Freiburg: Herder. I. Teil: *Einleitung und Kommentar zu Kap. 1-4*, 1965, XXXV-524 p.; ²1967; ³1972, XXXV-535 p. (525-535: "Erster Nachtrag"); ⁴1978, XXXV-548 p. (537-548: "Zweiter Nachtrag"); ⁵1981. Esp. 15-32: "Verhältnis zu den Synoptikern"; 305 [3,17]; 502-506 [8,5-13]; II. Teil: *Kommentar zu Kap. 5-12*, 1971, XVI-544 p.; ²1977, XVI-557 p. (545-557: "Nachtrag"); ³1980. Esp. 28-30 [14,13-21]; 464-465 [26,6-13]; 474-475 [21,1-9]; III. Teil: *Kommentar zu Kap. 13-21*, 1975, XVI-477 p.; ²1976; ³1979; ⁴1982, XVI-484 p. (471-484: "Nachtrag"). Esp. 321-322 [27,56]; 358-360 [28,1-10]; 413-414 [16,18-19]; IV. Teil: *Ergänzende Auslegungen und Exkurse*, 1984, 236 p. Esp. 185 ("Erster Nachtrag", ³1972), 198 ("Zweiter Nachtrag", ⁴1978). → 1980
*The Gospel according to St John* (Herder's Theological Commentary on the New Testament). New York: Crossroad / Herder and Herder / Seabury; London: Burns & Oates. Vol. I: *Introduction and Commentary on Chapters 1-4*, trans. K. Smyth, 1968, 638 p. Esp. 26-43; 305-306; 471-475; Vol. II: *Commentary on Chapters 5-12*, trans. C. Hastings, 1980, 556 p. Esp. 21-22; 370-371; 378-379; Vol. III: *Commentary on Chapters 13-21*, trans. D. Smith & G.A. Kon, 1982, VIII-510 p. Esp. 276-277; 304-306; 347-348.
Trans. Italian 1973-77-81; Spanish 1980.

1966  The Challenge of the Sermon on the Mount. — ID., *Present and Future. Modern Aspects of New Testament Theology* (The Cardinal O'Hara Series. Studies and Research in Christian Theology at Notre Dame, 3), Notre Dame, IN: University Press, 1966, 21-43. Esp. 23-29: "Insufficient answers"; 29-37: "Jesus' demands in the framework of His message"; 38-43: "Jesus applied to our time and circumstances".
Le Sermon sur la montagne. Une interpellation aux hommes. — ID., *Présent et futur. Aspects actuels de la théologie du Nouveau Testament*, trans. J.-P. Bayard (Lire la Bible, 18), Paris: Cerf, 1969, 26-45. Esp. 28-33;33-40; 41-45.
Die Bergpredigt Jesu und der heutige Mensch. — ID., *Christliche Existenz*, 1967, I, 109-130. Esp. 111-118; 118-125; 125-130 (with notes added).
The Sermon on the Mount and Modern Man. — ID., *Christian Existence*, 1968, I, 128-157. Esp. 130-141; 141-150; 150-157.
Il Discorso della montagna e l'uomo oggi. — ID., *L'esistenza cristiana*, 1971, 91-110.

1967a  *Christliche Existenz nach dem Neuen Testament. Abhandlungen und Vorträge.* München: Kösel, I, 1967, 196 p. → 1950, 1959b, 1966

*Christian Existence in the New Testament*, trans. F. Wieck. Notre Dame, IN: University Press, I, 1968, VIII-233 p.

*L'existence chrétienne selon le Nouveau Testament*, trans. H. Rochais. Brugge: Desclée De Brouwer, I, 1971, 208 p.

*L'esistenza cristiana secondo il Nuovo Testamento*, trans. E. Gatti & G. Mion. Modena: Paoline, I, 1971, 253 p.

1967b   Die Kirche der Welt. Aspekte aus dem Neuen Testament. — *BZ* 11 (1967) 1-21. Esp. 2-9: "Die Kirche als Zeichen und Kraft Gottes in der Welt: Mt 5,13-16". [NTA 12, 350]

1969a   Zur Aussageweise "Jesus ist (von den Toten) auferstanden". - *BZ* 13 (1969) 1-17. Esp. 7-8 [27,51-53; 28,16-20]. [NTA 13, 832]
On the Expression "Jesus is risen (from the dead)". — *TDig* 18 (1970) 36-42.

1969b   Die Ehe nach dem Neuen Testament. — KREMER, G. - MUMM, R. (eds.), *Theologie der Ehe*, Regensburg: Pustet; Göttingen: Vandenhoeck & Ruprecht, 1969, 9-36. Esp. 11-18; = ID., *Schriften zum Neuen Testament*, 1971, 414-433 ("Nachwort", 433-434). Esp. 415-422.

1969c   Hermeneutik und Exegese. — STACHEL, G. (ed.), *Existentiale Hermeneutik. Zur Diskussion des fundamentaltheologischen und religionspädagogischen Ansatzes von Hubertus Halbfas* (Unterweisen und Verkünden, 6), Einsiedeln–Köln: Benziger, 1969, 140-160. Esp. 146-152 [14,22-33].

1970a   Christologie des Neuen Testaments. — FEINER, J. - LÖHRER, M. (eds.), *Mysterium Salutis. Grundriß heilsgeschichtlicher Dogmatik. III/1: Das Christusereignis*, Zürich–Einsiedeln–Köln: Benziger, 1970, 227-388. Esp. 285-296: "Matthäus".

1970b   Der eschatologische Abschnitt Lk 17,20-37. — DESCAMPS, A.L. - DE HALLEUX, A. (eds.), *Mélanges bibliques*. FS B. Rigaux, 1970, 213-234. Esp. 217-226: "Analyse des Abschnitts"; 228-232: "Die ursprüngliche Logiensammlung und die ukanische Bearbeitung"; = ID., *Schriften zum Neuen Testament*, 1971, 220-243 ("Nachwort", 242-243). Esp. 224-234; 237-240.

1970c   Mitmenschlichkeit im Horizont des Neuen Testaments. — BORNKAMM, G. - RAHNER, K. (eds.), *Die Zeit Jesu*. FS H. Schlier, 1970, 70-92. Esp. 32-85; = *TJb*, 1972, 201-218; = ID., *Schriften zum Neuen Testament*, 1971, 435-457 ("Nachwort", 458). Esp. 448-452.

1971a   *Schriften zum Neuen Testament. Exegese in Fortschritt und Wandel*. München: Kösel, 1971, 504 p. → 1952, 1953, 1960, 1964a-b, 1969b, 1970b-c
*La vita cristiana. Esegesi in progresso e in mutamento*, trans. L. Tosti. Milano: Jaca Book, 1977, 386 p.

1971b   Das Petrusamt. Die Stellung des Petrus zu den anderen Aposteln. — *Wort und Wahrheit* (Freiburg) 26 (1971) 206-216. Esp. 210-211 [16,18-19].
The Petrine Office: Peter's Relationship to the Other Apostles. — *TDig* 20 (1972) 148-152.

1977*   & ERNST, J. - WANKE, J. (eds.), *Die Kirche des Anfangs. Festschrift für Heinz Schürmann zum 65. Geburtstag* (ErfTSt, 38). Leipzig: St. Benno, 1977; Freiburg: Herder, 1978, 667 p. → Delling, Dupont, Gnilka, Grundmann, Holtz, Kertelge, Kremer, R. Pesch, Schelkle, G. Schneider, Thüsing, Trilling

1977   Die Stellung des Petrus zu den anderen Aposteln. — BRANDENBURG, A. - URBAN, H.J. (eds.), *Petrus und Papst. Evangelium, Einheit der Kirche, Papstdienst. Beiträge und Notizen*, Münster: Aschendorff, 1977, 20-35. Esp. 27-29.

1980   Tradition und Interpretation im Spruchgut des Johannesevangeliums. — ZMIJEWSKI, J. - NELLESSEN, E. (eds.), *Begegnung mit dem Wort*. FS H. Zimmermann, 1980, 141-159. Esp. 142-146: "Synoptische Logien im Johannesevangelium"; 147-153: "Johanneische Logien mit Anlehnung an synoptische Tradition". → 1965/84, IV, 72-89. Esp. 73-78, 78-84.

1981   Das Vollmachtswort vom Binden und Lösen, traditionsgeschichtlich gesehen. — MÜLLER, P.-G. - STENGER, W. (eds.), *Kontinuität und Einheit. Für Franz Mußner*, Freiburg: Herder, 1981, 141-157. Esp. 142-145: "Mt 18,18 im Kontext von Mt 18,15-20"; 149-152: "Mt 16,19"; 152-157: "Herkunft und Ursprung des Vollmachtswortes" [28,18-20].

1982* (ed.), *Die Bergpredigt. Utopische Vision oder Handlungsanweisung?* (Schriften der Katholischen Akademie in Bayern, 107). Düsseldorf: Patmos, 1982, ²1984, 124 p. [NTA 27, p. 334] → Gründel, Reuter, Schnackenburg; → Frankemölle 1983c

1982a Die Bergpredigt. — *Ibid.*, 13-59. Esp. 13-36: "Einführung und Übersicht"; 36-59: "Auslegungsgeschichte und Sinndeutung". → 1984

1982b Die Seligpreisung der Friedensstifter (Mt 5,9) im mattäischen Kontext. — *BZ* 26 (1982) 161-178. Esp. 162-163: "Zur Forschungslage"; 163-167: "Die Herkunft der Seligpreisung"; 167-170: "Die Seligpreisung der Friedensstifter im Rahmen der Bergpredigt"; 170-174: "Der weitere Kontext im Mattäusevangelium"; 174-177: "Interpretation im damaligen und heutigen Kontext". [NTA 27, 511]

1983 Glaubensvermittlung im Matthäusevangelium. — *Dynamik im Wort. Lehre von der Bibel. Leben aus der Bibel*, Stuttgart: Katholisches Bibelwerk, 1983, 183-199.

1984 *Alles kann, wer glaubt. Bergpredigt und Vaterunser in der Absicht Jesu*. Freiburg: Herder, 1984, 144 p. Esp. 15-84: "Die Bergpredigt"; 85-136: "Das Vaterunser". [NTA 29, p. 93] → 1982a

    G. GEIGER, *BLtg* 57 (1984) 273-274; S. MOYSA, *CollTheol* 56/2 (1989) 189; F. REISINGER, *TPQ* 133 (1985) 166; J. SUDBRACK, *GL* 57 (1984) 238.

    *Tutto è possibile a chi crede. Discorso della montagna e Padrenostro nell'intenzione di Gesù*, trans. V. De Marchi (Studi biblici, 89). Brescia: Paideia, 1989, 142 p.

    A. BONORA, *RivBib* 38 (1990) 254-255; R. PENNA, *Lateranum* 57 (1991) 228-229.

    *All Things Are Possible to Believers: Reflections on the Lord's Prayer and the Sermon on the Mount*, trans. J.S. Currie. Louisville, KY: Westminster/Knox, 1995, VIII-102 p. [NTA 39, p. 510]

1985a *Matthäusevangelium.* I: *1,1-16,20.* II: *16,21-28,20* (Die Neue Echter Bibel, 1/1-2). Würzburg: Echter, I, 1985, ²1991, 153 p. Esp. 5-16 [introduction]. [NTA 30, p. 232]; II, 1987, ²1994, 155-294 p. [NTA 31, p. 368] → Giesen 1987b, Staab 1951

    C. BISSOLI, *Sal* 50 (1988) 434; A. FUCHS, *SNTU* 11 (1986) 228-229; 16 (1991) 211-212; A. SEGOVIA, *ArchTeolGran* 50 (1987) 464-465; T. SÖDING, *BLtg* 62 (1989) 57-58; A. STÖGER, *BLtg* 59 (1986) 236-237.

    *O evangelho segundo S. Mateus*. Pétropolis: Vozes, 1974, 356 p.

1985b Petrus im Matthäusevangelium. — GANTOY, R. (ed.), *À cause de l'Évangile*. FS J. Dupont, 1985, 107-125. Esp. 109-115: "Die traditionellen Texte in ihrer mattäischen Redaktion"; 115-119: "Spezielle mattäische Petrustexte außer 16,16-20"; 120-124: "Mt 16,16-20 in seiner Bedeutung für das mattäische Petrusverständnis".

1986 *Die sittliche Botschaft des Neuen Testaments*. I: *Von Jesus zur Urkirche*; II: *Die urchristlichen Verkündiger* (HTKNT, Supplementband 1/1-2). Freiburg: Herder, 1986/1988, 2 vols., 271 and 285 p. Esp. I, 31-67: "Jesu Verkündigung der Gottesherrschaft und seine grundlegenden Forderungen"; 68-97: "Die alttestamentlich-jüdische Sittenlehre und Jesu sittliche Forderungen" [5,3-10.17-20.21-48; 7,12; 20,1-16; 22,34-40]; 98-124: "Die extremen sittlichen Forderungen Jesu: Die Bergpredigt"; 125-155: "Jesu Weisungen im gesellschaftlichen Bereich" [5,32; 6,19-21.24; 19,3-9; 20,1-15]; II, 122-134: "Matthäus [righteousness; Law; 5,13-16.17-20; 8,11-12; 18]. → 1954

    *Il messaggio morale del Nuovo Testamento*, trans. F. Tomagoni. I: *Da Gesù alla Chiesa primitiva*. II: *I primi predicatori cristiani* (Supplementi al "Commentario teologico del Nuovo Testamento", 1-2). Brescia: Paideia, 1989/1990, 345 and 370 p.

    *El mensaje moral del Nuevo Testamento*, I. Barcelona: Herder, 1989, 323 p.

1988 Großsein im Gottesreich. Zu Mt 18,1-5. — SCHENKE, L. (ed.), *Studien zum Matthäusevangelium*. FS W. Pesch, 1988, 269-282. Esp. 272-273: "Abgrenzung der Texteinheit"; 273-275 [Mk/Mt]; 275-277 [βασιλεία τῶν οὐρανῶν]; 277-279 [18,3]; 279-280 [18,4]; 280-282 [18,5].

1989a "Jeder Schriftgelehrte, der ein Jünger des Himmelreiches geworden ist" (Mt 13,52). — ALAND, K. — MEURER, S. (eds.), *Wissenschaft und Kirche. Festschrift für Eduard Lohse* (Texte und Arbeiten zur Bibel, 4), Bielefeld: Luther, 1989, 57-69. Esp. 57-61: "Der christliche 'Schriftgelehrte'"; 61-64: "Der ein Jünger des Himmelreiches geworden ist"; 65-68: "Das Bild vom Vorratslager; 'Neues und Altes'".

1989b Das Matthäusevangelium als Testfall für hermeneutische Überlegungen. — FRANKEMÖLLE, H. – KERTELGE, K. (eds.), *Vom Urchristentum zu Jesus*. FS J. Gnilka, 1989, 136-153. Esp. 137-142: "Beobachtungen zur Transformation von Jesusüberlieferungen bei Matthäus" [5,32; 13,18-23; 18,1-5; 19,9]; 143-148: "Der Einfluß der Wirkungsgeschichte auf den Verstehensprozeß" [5–7; 16,18-19]; 148-153: "Hermeneutische Folgerungen. Retrospektive und Prospektive". Matthew's Gospel as a Test Case for Hermeneutical Reflections. — BAUER, D.R. – POWELL, M.A. (eds.), *Treasures New and Old*, 1996, 251-269. Esp. 252-259; 259-263; 264-269.

1991a Lk 13,31-33. Eine Studie zur lukanischen Redaktion und Theologie. — BUSSMANN, C. – RADL, W. (eds.), *Der Treue Gottes trauen*. FS G. Schneider, 1991, 229-241. Esp. 231; 235-236 [Q 11,49-51; Q 13,34-35].

1991b "Siehe da mein Knecht, den ich erwählt habe..." (Mt 12,18). Zur Heiltätigkeit Jesu im Matthäusevangelium. — OBERLINNER, L. – FIEDLER, P. (eds.), *Salz der Erde*. FS A. Vögtle, 1991, 203-222. Esp. 204-210: "Vollmacht und Herr-Sein Jesu"; 210-214: "Der Dienst des Gottesknechtes"; 214-216: "Der Gottesknecht unter wachsenden Verdächtigungen 9,1-35"; 217-220: "Verschärfung der Auseinandersetzung und das zweite Erfüllungszitat 11,2–12,21"; 221-222: "Hoheit und Niedrigkeit im Bild Jesu".

1992 Synoptische und johanneische Christologie. Ein Vergleich. — VAN SEGBROECK, F., et al. (eds.), *The Four Gospels 1992*. FS F. Neirynck, 1992, III, 1723-1750. Esp. 1741 [Q 4,1-13/Jn]; 1741-1743 [Q 10,22/Jn]; 1745 [26,64/Jn 14,7]; 1746-1748 [John the Baptist].

1993 *Die Person Jesu Christi im Spiegel der vier Evangelien* (HTKNT, Supplementband 4). Freiburg: Herder, 1993, 357 p. Esp. 90-151: "Matthäus".
*Jesus in the Gospels. A Biblical Christology*, trans. O.C. Dean. Louisville, KY: Westminster/Knox, 1995, XV-383 p.
*La persona di Gesù Cristo nei quattro vangeli* (Commentario teologico del Nuovo Testamento. Supplementi, 4). Brescia: Paideia, 1995, 451 p.

### SCHNEEMELCHER, Wilhelm

1959* HENNECKE, E. – SCHNEEMELCHER, W. (eds.), *Neutestamentliche Apokryphen in deutscher Übersetzung* [1904]. I: *Evangelien*. Tübingen: Mohr, ³1959, VIII-377 p. → 1964*; → Cullmann, Maurer, A. Meyer, H.-C. Puech, Schneemelcher, Vielhauer
*New Testament Apocrypha*. I: *Gospels and Related Writings*, trans. R.McL. Wilson. London: SCM, 1963, ²1973, 531 p.

1959a Evangelien. Einleitung. — *Ibid.*, 41-51. Esp. 44-48: "Zur Entstehung der Evangelien" (ET, 71-84). → 1987a

1959b Bemerkungen zum Kirchenbegriff der apokryphen Evangelien. — *Ecclesia. FS J.N. Bakhuizen van den Brink*, 's Gravenhage: Nijhoff, 1959, 18-32. Esp. 24-26; = ID., *Gesammelte Aufsätze zum Neuen Testament und zur Patristik*, eds. W. Bienert – K. Schäferdiek (Analekta Blatadôn, 22), Thessaloniki: Patriarchal Institute for Patristic Studies, 1974, 139-153. Esp. 145-148.

1964* II. *Apostolisches. Apokalypsen und Verwandtes*, ³1964, X-661 p.; ⁴1968. → 1959*; → Vielhauer
II: *Writings Relating to the Apostles Apocalypses and Related Subjects*, trans. R.McL. Wilson. London: Lutterworth, 1965, 852 p.

1987* (ed.), *Neutestamentliche Apokryphen in deutscher Übersetzung*. I. *Evangelien*. Tübingen: Mohr, ⁵1987, X-442 p.; ⁶1990. → 1989*; → Bienert, Blatz, Cullmann, Schneemelcher 1987a-b, Strecker
*New Testament Apocrypha*. I: *Gospels and Related Writings*, trans. R.McL. Wilson. Cambridge: Clarke – Louisville, KY: Westminster/Knox, 1991, VII-560 p.

1987a Evangelien. Einleitung. — *Ibid.*, 65-75. → 1959a

1987b Petrusevangelium. — *Ibid.*, 180-188. Esp. 182-183. → Maurer 1959

1989* II. *Apostolisches. Apokalypsen und Verwandtes*, ⁵1989, VIII-704 p. → 1987*; → Strecker

II: *Writings Relating to the Apostles Apocalypses and Related Subjects*, trans. R.McL. Wilson. Cambridge: Clarke – Louisville, KY: Westminster/Knox, 1992, 771 p.

**SCHNEIDER, Gerhard**

1969a *Botschaft der Bergpredigt* (Der Christ in der Welt, VI. Reihe, Das Buch der Bücher, 8a). Aschaffenburg: Pattloch, 1970, 123 p. Esp. 7-22: "Einführung in das Verständnis der Bergpredigt"; 23-116: "Auslegung der Bergpredigt"; (Botschaft Gottes II/30), Leipzig: St. Benno, 1973, 174 p. [NTA 19, p. 267]
L. SABOURIN, *BTB* 5 (1975) 223; D. SENIOR, *CBQ* 37 (1975) 420-421; F. STAUDINGER, *TPQ* 123 (1975) 77; F.J. STEINMETZ, *GL* 43 (1970) 314-315; A. STÖGER, *BLtg* 48 (1975) 57-58.

1969b *Verleugnung, Verspottung und Verhör Jesu nach Lukas 22,54-71. Studien zur lukanischen Darstellung der Passion* (SANT, 22). München: Kösel, 1969, 245 p. Esp. 47-60.70-72 [minor agr.]. – Diss. Würzburg, 1967 (R. Schnackenburg). → F. NEIRYNCK, *ETL* 48 (1972) 570-573

1970 Das Bildwort von der Lampe. Zur Traditionsgeschichte eines Jesus-Wortes. — *ZNW* 61 (1970) 183-209. Esp. 184-186.189-190 [Q]; 199-202 [5,15]; 206-208 [5,15/Th 33b]. [NTA 15, 868]; = ID., *Jesusüberlieferung*, 1992, 116-142. Esp. 117-119.122-123; 132-135; 139-141.

1971a *Die Frage nach Jesus. Christus-Aussagen des Neuen Testaments.* Essen: Ludgerus, 1971, 165 p. Esp. 47-49; 63-74 [sayings]; 115-144 [christological titles].
*Cristologia del Nuovo Testamento*, trans. M. Rava (Letture bibliche, 10). Brescia: Paideia, 1994, 112 p.

1971b *Anfragen an das Neue Testament.* Essen: Ludgerus, 1971, 167 p. Esp. 52-53.71-83 [miracles]; 59-70 [teaching of Jesus]; 98-115 [virgin birth].

1971c Jesu Wort über die Ehescheidung in der Überlieferung des Neuen Testaments. — *TTZ* 80 (1971) 65-87. Esp. 70-71.75-76 [Q 16,18]; 78-82 [5,31-32]; 82-83 [19,3-12]. [NTA 16, 149]; = ID., *Jesusüberlieferung*, 1992, 187-209. Esp. 192-193.197-198; 200-204; 204-205.

1973a *Die Passion Jesu nach den drei älteren Evangelien* (Biblische Handbibliothek, 11). München: Kösel, 1973, 174 p. Esp. 31-32; 43-153: "Die Passionserzählung der drei synoptischen Evangelien"; 159-164: "Matthäus: Die Kirche Christi im Lichte seines Leidensweges".

1973b Biblische Begründung ethischer Normen. — *BibLeb* 14 (1973) 153-164. Esp. 156-158 [5,32; Q 16,18]; 161-162 [7,12]. [NTA 19, 300]
The Biblical Grounding of Ethical Norms. — *TDig* 22 (1974) 117-120.

1973c Die Neuheit der christlichen Nächstenliebe. — *TTZ* 82 (1973) 257-275. Esp. 266-267 [5,39-48]; 267-271 [7,12]. [NTA 18, 669]; = ID., *Jesusüberlieferung*, 1992, 168-186. Esp. 177-178; 178-182.

1974 Das Evangelium als kritische Instanz. — *BibLeb* 15 (1974) 151-159. Esp. 158 [4,1-11]. [NTA 19, 1091]

1975a *Parusiegleichnisse im Lukasevangelium* (SBS, 74). Stuttgart: Katholisches Bibelwerk, 1975, 106 p. Esp. 20-54: "Parusiegleichnisse aus der 'Logien'-Tradition" [Q 3,9.17; 10,5-11; 12,35-38.39-40.41-46; 17,26-30; 19,12-27].

1975b Jesus und die Apokalyptik. — STRECKER, G. (ed.), *Jesus Christus in Historie und Theologie.* FS H. Conzelmann, 1975, 59-85. Esp. 66-68; 77-81 [16,16-18]; 83-85 [Q].

1975c "Der Menschensohn" in der lukanischen Christologie. — PESCH, R., et al. (eds.), *Jesus und der Menschensohn.* FS A. Vögtle, 1975, 267-282. Esp. 272-273 [Q 6,22]; 273-274 [Q 12,8]; 278-279 [18,11]; = ID., *Lukas*, 1985, 98-113. Esp. 103-104; 104-105; 109-110.

1977 Christusbekenntnis und christliches Handeln. Lk 6,46 und Mt 7,21 im Kontext der Evangelien. — SCHNACKENBURG, R., et al. (eds.), *Die Kirche des Anfangs.* FS H. Schürmann, 1977, 9-24. Esp. 10-14 [Q-form]; 14-17 [Mt redaction]; 17-20 [Lk redaction]; = ID., *Lukas*, 1985, 114-129. Esp. 115-119; 119-122; 122-125.

1978 Die theologische Sicht des Todes Jesu in den Kreuzigungsberichten der Evangelien. — *TPQ* 126 (1978) 14-22. Esp. 18-19 [27,45-54]. [NTA 22, 741]; = ID., *Jesusüberlieferung*, 1992, 296-304. Esp. 300-301.

1980 Christologische Aussagen des "Credo" im Lichte des Neuen Testaments. — *TTZ* 89 (1980) 282-292. Esp. 288-289 [1,18-25]. [NTA 25, 626]

1982 Der Missionsauftrag Jesu in der Darstellung der Evangelien. — KERTELGE, K. (ed.), *Mission im Neuen Testament* (QDisp, 93), Freiburg: Herder, 1982, 71-92. Esp. 72-78, 85-87 [28,16-20]; = ID., *Lukas*, 1985, 184-205. Esp. 185-191; 198-200; = *TJb* 30 (1987) 374-388. Esp. 374-378; 384-385.

1985a *Lukas, Theologe der Heilsgeschichte. Aufsätze zum lukanischen Doppelwerk* (BBB, 59). Bonn: Hanstein, 1985, 328 p. → 1975c, 1977, 1982

1985b Das Vaterunser des Matthäus. — GANTOY, R. (ed.), *À cause de l'évangile.* FS J. Dupont, 1985, 57-90. Esp. 59-63: "Der wachsende 'Umfang' des Vaterunsers"; 63-69: "Der 'Wortlaut' des Vaterunsers in Q"; 70-79: "Die Erweiterungen des Vaterunsers in der Mt-Fassung"; 79-90: "Das Vaterunser im Kontext des Matthäus-Evangeliums"; = ID., *Jesusüberlieferung*, 1992, 52-85. Esp. 54-58; 58-64; 65-74; 74-85.

1986 Die Bitte um das Kommen des Geistes im lukanischen Vaterunser (Lk 11,2 v.l.). — SCHRAGE, W. (ed.), *Studien zum Text und zur Ethik des Neuen Testaments.* FS H. Greeven, 1986, 344-373. Esp. 367-371: "Geht die Geist-Bitte auf lukanische 'Redaktion' zurück?"; = ID., *Jesusüberlieferung*, 1992, 86-115. Esp. 109-113.

1987 Das Vaterunser – oratio dominica et judaica? — BAIER, W., et al. (eds.), *Weisheit Gottes – Weisheit der Welt. Festschrift für Joseph Kardinal Ratzinger zum 60. Geburtstag*, St. Ottilien: EOS, 1987, I, 405-417. Esp. 407-408: "Das Vaterunser in der Fassung Jesu"; 410-412: "Die beiden Du-Bitten"; 412-415: "Die drei Wir-Bitten". Das Gebet des Herrn, ein "jüdisches" Gebet? – ID., *Jesusüberlieferung*, 1992, 40-51. Esp. 41-42; 44-46; 46-49.

1988 "Im Himmel – auf Erden", eine Perspektive matthäischer Theologie. — SCHENKE, L. (ed.), *Studien zum Matthäusevangelium.* FS W. Pesch, 1988, 283-297. Esp. 286-287: "'Himmelreich' und 'Vater im Himmel'"; 287-292: "Die Vielfalt der Bedeutungen von 'Himmel'"; 292-297: "'Im Himmel – auf Erden'".

1989 Imitatio Dei als Motiv der "Ethik Jesu". — MERKLEIN, H. (ed.), *Neues Testament und Ethik.* FS R. Schnackenburg, 1989, 71-83. Esp. 77-80 [5,38-48]; 81-83 [5,44-45]; = ID., *Jesusüberlieferung*, 1992, 155-167. Esp. 161-164; 165-167.

1992a *Jesusüberlieferung und Christologie. Neutestamentliche Aufsätze 1970-1990* (NTSuppl, 67). Leiden – New York: Brill, 1992, IX-391 p. → 1970, 1971c, 1973c, 1978, 1985b, 1986, 1987, 1989, 1992b

1992b Gott, der Vater Jesu Christi, in der Verkündigung Jesu und im urchristlichen Bekenntnis. — *Ibid.*, 3-38. Esp. 4-7: "Der Befund der Konkordanz und der Synopse"; 10-17: "Die Gott-Vater-Aussagen der Logienquelle" [Q 6,36; 10,21-22; 11,2.13; 12,30; Mt 5,45; 6,26; 10,29; 18,14]; 17-20: "'Vater' und 'mein Vater' im Sondergut des Mt" [16,17; 18,19.19]; 23-25; 36-37 [28,19].

1992c Auf Gott bezogenes "Mein Vater" und "Euer Vater" in den Jesus-Worten der Evangelien. Zugleich ein Beitrag zum Problem Johannes und die Synoptiker. — VAN SEGBROECK, F., et al. (eds.), *The Four Gospels 1992.* FS F. Neirynck, 1992, III, 1751-1781. Esp. 1755-1761.1774-1775 [Q]; 1764-1771.1775-1776 [Mt]; 1778-1781 [Jn/Mt 28,9-10].

**SCHNEIDER, Johannes**

1952 *Die Taufe im Neuen Testament.* Stuttgart: Kohlhammer, 1952, 80 p. Esp. 25-28: "Die Taufe Jesu".

**SCHNELL, C.W.**

1985 Jesuslogia, aforismes en vertelde wereld. — *TheolEvang* 18 (1985) 28-35. [NTA 29, 921]

**SCHNELLE, Udo**

1983 → Strecker 1983a

1987 *Antidoketische Christologie im Johannesevangelium. Eine Untersuchung zur Stellung des vierten Evangeliums in der johanneischen Schule* (FRLANT, 144). Göttingen: Vandenhoeck & Ruprecht, 1987, 283 p. Esp. 101-104 [8,5-13/Jn 4,46-54].

1991 *Neutestamentliche Anthropologie. Jesus–Paulus–Johannes* (Biblisch-Theologische Studien, 18). Neukirchen-Vluyn: Neukirchener, 1991, IX-197 p. Esp. 13-43: "Das Bild des Menschen in der Verkündigung Jesu".
*The Human Condition: Anthropology in the Teachings of Jesus, Paul and John*, trans. O.C. Dean. Minneapolis, MN: Fortress, 1996, IX-173 p.

1994 *Einleitung in das Neue Testament* (Uni-Taschenbücher, 1830). Göttingen: Vandenhoeck & Ruprecht, 1994, 639 p. Esp. 195-214: "Das synoptische Problem"; 214-233: "Die Logienquelle"; 256-278: "Das Matthäusevangelium"; ²1996.

**SCHNIDER, Franz**

1970 & STENGER, W., *Die Ostergeschichten der Evangelien* (Schriften zur Katechetik, 13). München: Kösel, 1970, 160 p. Esp. 30-55: "Die Ostergeschichten des Matthäusevangeliums (Mt 28,1-20)".

1971 & STENGER, W., *Johannes und die Synoptiker. Vergleich ihrer Parallelen* (Biblische Handbibliothek, 9). München: Kösel, 1971, 182 p. Esp. 18-20: "Matthäus: Die Interpretation des Logienstoffs durch das Evangelium"; 54-88 [8,5-13; Q 7,1-10/Jn 4,46-54]; 134-141 [14,13-33].

1973 *Jesus der Prophet* (Orbis Biblicus et Orientalis, 2). Freiburg/Schw: Universitätsverlag; Göttingen: Vandenhoeck & Ruprecht, 1973, 298 p. Esp. 102-104 [21,1-11]; 133-136 [Q 6,22-23]; 136-142 [Q 11,47-51]; 142-147 [Q 13,34-35]; 158-163: "Das Motiv bei Matthäus" [Q 11,47-51; Mt 13,54-58; 21,33-43]; 174-181 [Q 10,23-24; 11,31-32; 16,16]. — Diss. Regensburg, 1972-73 (F. Mussner).

1977 *Das Gleichnis vom verlorenen Schaf und seine Redaktoren. Ein intertextueller Vergleich.* — *Kairos* 19 (1977) 146-154. Esp. 149-150 [18,12-14]; 150-151 [Gospel of Thomas]. [NTA 23, 140]

1978 → Stenger 1978

1979 & STENGER, W., Die Frauen im Stammbaum Jesu nach Mattäus. Strukturale Beobachtungen zu Mt 1,1-17. — *BZ* 23 (1979) 187-196. [NTA 24, 416]; = STENGER, W., *Strukturale Beobachtungen*, 1990, 39-48.

1981a & STENGER, W., "Mit der Abstammung Jesu Christi verhielt es sich so: ...". Strukturale Beobachtungen zu Mt 1,18-25. — *BZ* 25 (1981) 255-264. [NTA 26, 463]; = STENGER, W., *Strukturale Beobachtungen*, 1990, 49-59.

1981b Von der Gerechtigkeit Gottes. Beobachtungen zum Gleichnis von den Arbeitern im Weinberg (Mt 20,1-16). — *Kairos* 23 (1981) 88-95. [NTA 26, 478]

**SCHNIEWIND, Julius**

1937ᴿ *Das Evangelium nach Matthäus* (NTD, 2) [1937]. Göttingen: Vandenhoeck & Ruprecht, ⁵1950, 282 p.; ⁶1953; ⁷1954; ⁸1956; ⁹1960; ¹⁰1962; ¹¹1964; ¹³1984, 285 p. → Schweizer 1973a
J. CAMBIER, *ETL* 33 (1957) 96-97; T. EGIDO, *EstJos* 27 (1973) 268.
*Il vangelo secondo Matteo* [⁸1956], trans. M. Soffritti (Nuovo Testamento, 2). Brescia: Paideia, 1977, 495 p.
F. BRÄNDLE, *EstJos* 34 (1980) 243-244; G. RINALDI, *BibOr* 20 (1978) 311; G. SCUDERI, *Protestantesimo* 38 (1983) 637-639; G. TESTA, *DivThom* 82 (1979) 96; N. URICCHIO, *CC* 133/3 (1982) 308-309.

**SCHNURR, Klaus Bernhard**

1985 *Hören und Handeln. Lateinische Auslegungen des Vaterunsers in der Alten Kirche bis zum 5. Jahrhundert* (Freiburger theologische Studien, 132). Freiburg: Herder, 1985, 290 p. — Diss. Freiburg, 1984 (K. Frank).
B. AMATA, *Sal* 48 (1986) 447; K. OBRYCKI, *CollTheol* 57/1 (1987) 176-179; W. RORDORF, *RTP* 37 (1987) 391; H.J. SIEBEN, *TheolPhil* 62 (1987) 274; J. WALDRAM, *TijdTheol* 26 (1986) 298; F. WEISSENGROBER, *SNTU* 11 (1986) 257-259.

**SCHOCKENHOFF, Eberhard**

1994 Die verdrängte Gewalt: Theologisch-ethische Überlegungen zum Verständnis der Bergpredigt. — *Stimmen der Zeit* (München) 212 (1994) 239-253. Esp. 247-252: "Theologisch-biblische Interpretation". [NTA 39, 139]

**SCHOEDEL, William R.**

1972 Parables in the Gospel of Thomas: Oral Tradition or Gnostic Exegesis? — *ConcTM* 43 (1972) 548-560. [NTA 17, 767]
Gleichnisse im Thomasevangelium. Mündliche Tradition oder gnostische Exegese? — HARNISCH, W. (ed.), *Gleichnisse Jesu*, 1982, 369-389. Esp. 376-375 [13,47-50/Th 8]; 378-381 [13,24-30.36-42/Th 57]; 381-383 [18,12-14/Th 107]; 383-384 [13,33/Th 96]; 384-387 [21,33-41/Th 65]

1975 Jewish Wisdom and the Formation of the Christian Ascetic. — WILKEN, R.L. (ed.), *Aspects of Wisdom*, 1975, 169-199. Esp. 173-183 [Teachings of Silvanus].

1991 Ignatius and the Reception of the Gospel of Matthew in Antioch. — BALCH, D.L. (ed.), *Social History of the Matthean Community*, 1991, 129-177. Esp. 151-175: "Ignatius and the gospel"; 175-177: "Ignatius and Matthew". → Meier 1991b

1993 Papias. — *ANRW* II.27.1 (1993) 235-270. Esp. 262-267.

**SCHÖLLIG, Hugo**

1968 Die Zählung der Generationen im matthäischen Stammbaum. — *ZNW* 59 (1968) 261-268. [NTA 13, 858]

**SCHOENBERG, Martin**

1963 The Location of the Mount of Beatitudes. [5,1-2] — *BiTod* 4 (1963) 232-239. [NTA 7, 779]

**SCHOENBORN, Ulrich**

1977 Experiencia e interpretação: ensaio a partir de Mateus 8,5-13. — *Estudos Teologicos* (São Leopoldo) 17 (1977) 77-92.

**SCHÖNDORF, Harald**

1988 Jungfrau und Mutter. — *ZKT* 110 (1988) 385-413. Esp. 390-393: "Exegetische Probleme". [NTA 33, 880]

**SCHÖNLE, Volker**

1982 *Johannes, Jesus und die Juden. Die theologische Position des Matthäus und des Verfassers der Redenquelle im Lichte von Mt. 11* (BET, 17). Frankfurt/M: Lang, 1982, 288 p. Esp. 25-95: "Untersuchung der Überlieferungsstadien"; 96-149: "Darstellung der Bearbeitungstendenzen". [NTA 27, p. 334] — Diss. Kiel, 1980 (G. Friedrich – U. Luck).
F. MUSSNER, *TRev* 80 (1984) 192-194; S. VAN TILBORG, *TijdTheol* 23 (1983) 309-310; B.T. VIVIANO, *CBQ* 46 (1984) 589-590.

**SCHOEPS, Hans-Joachim**

1941[R] Jesus und das jüdische Gesetz. [1941] — ID., *Aus frühchristlicher Zeit*, 1950, 212-220. Esp. 213-216. → 1953

1943[R] Die jüdischen Prophetenmorde. [1943] [23,31-33] — ID., *Aus frühchristlicher Zeit*, 1950, 126-143.

1947[R] Restitutio principii als kritisches Prinzip der nova lex Jesu. [English, 1947] — ID., *Aus frühchristlicher Zeit*, 1950, 271-285. Esp. 276-282 [19,1-9].

1950 *Aus frühchristlicher Zeit. Religionsgeschichtliche Untersuchungen*. Tübingen: Mohr, 1950, VIII-320 p. → 1941, 1943, 1947

1953 Jésus et la Loi juive. — *RHPR* 33 (1953) 1-20. Esp. 4-8 [5,17-20]; 8-10 [12,1-14]; 10-13 [15,1-20]; 13-14 [19,1-9]; 15-16 [5-7]. → 1941
Jesus und das jüdische Gesetz. — ID., *Studien*, 1963, 41-61. Esp. 44-47; 47-49; 49-53; 53-55; 55-57.

1960 Ebionitische Apokalyptik im Neuen Testament. — *ZNW* 51 (1960) 101-111. Esp. 109-110 [4,14-16]. [NTA 5, 410]; = ID., *Studien*, 1963, 68-77. Esp. 75-76.

1963 *Studien zur unbekannten Religions- und Geistesgeschichte* (Veröffentlichungen der Gesellschaft für Geistesgeschichte, 3). Göttingen: Musterschmidt, 1963, 355 p. → 1953, 1960

**SCHOLER, David M.**

1986- Q Bibliography. — *SBL Seminar Papers*:
1981-1986: *1986*, 27-36; 1981-1988: *1988*, 483-495; 1981-1989: *1989*, 23-37; Supplement I: *1990*, 11-13; Supplement II: *1991*, 1-7; Supplement III: *1992*, 1-4; Supplement IV: *1993*, 1-5; Supplement V: *1994*, 1-8; Supplement VI: *1995*, 1-5; Supplement VII: *1996*, 1-7; Supplement VIII: *1997*, 750-756. → Neirynck 1982e

1992 Women. — *DJG*, 1992, 880-887. Esp. 885.

**SCHOLTISSEK, Klaus**

1992 *Die Vollmacht Jesu. Traditions- und redaktionsgeschichtliche Analysen zu einem Leitmotiv markinischer Christologie* (NTAbh, NF 25). Münster: Aschendorff, 1992, XII-340 p. Esp. 72-80: "'Vollmacht' in der Redenquelle" [Q 7,1-10; 11,21-22]. — Diss. Münster, 1990 (K. Kertelge).

**SCHOONHEIM, Pieter Leendert**

1953 *Een semasiologisch onderzoek van parousia met betrekking tot het gebruik in Mattheüs 24.* Aalten: de Boer, 1953, VII-316 p. Esp. 8-28: "Mattheüs 24:3 in vergelijking met de parallellen bij Markus en Lukas"; 29-93: "Mattheüs 24:27,37,39 – in vergelijking met Lukas 17:20-37". — Diss. Utrecht, 1953 (W.C. van Unnik).

**SCHOTTROFF, Luise**

1971 Das Gleichnis vom verlorenen Sohn. — *ZTK* 68 (1971) 27-52. Esp. 32-35 [Q 15,4-7]. [NTA 16, 201]

1975 Gewaltverzicht und Feindesliebe in der urchristlichen Jesustradition. Mt 5,38-48; Lk 6,27-36. — STRECKER, G. (ed.), *Jesus Christus in Historie und Theologie*. FS H. Conzelmann, 1975, 197-221. Esp. 213-220: "Die Liebe der Christen zu ihren Verfolgern – Umrisse eines gewaltfreien Widerstandes"; = ID., *Befreiungserfahrungen*, 1990, 12-35. Esp. 28-35. Non-Violence and the Love of One's Enemies. — ID., et al., *Essays on the Love Commandment*, 1978, 9-39.

1978a & STEGEMANN, W., *Jesus von Nazareth. Hoffnung der Armen* (Urban-Taschenbücher, 639). Stuttgart: Kohlhammer, 1978, 164 p. Esp. 30-32 [Q 6,20-22; Q 7,22]; 36-38 [19,30; 20,16]; 54-88: "Schafe unter Wölfen. Die Wanderpropheten der Logienquelle" [Q 4,1-13; 6,27-36; 7,18-23; 10,2-12; 12,4-7.22-31].
*Jesús de Nazaret, esperanza de los pobres.* Salamanca: Sígueme, 1981, 225 p.
*Jesus van Nazareth. Hoop van de armen.* Baarn: Ten Have, 1982, 182 p.
*Jesus and the Hope of the Poor*, trans. M.J. O'Connell. Maryknoll: Orbis, 1986, 134 p.
*Gesù di Nazareth, speranza dei poveri.* Torino: Claudiana, 1988, 125 p.

1978b et al., *Essays on the Love Commandment*. Philadelphia, PA: Fortress, 1978, 107 p. → Burchard 1975, R.H. Fuller 1975a, L. Schottroff 1975, Suggs 1975

1979a & STEGEMANN, W., Der Sabbat ist um des Menschen willen da. Auslegung von Markus 2:23-28. — SCHOTTROFF, W. – STEGEMANN, W. (eds.), *Der Gott der kleinen Leute*, II, 1979, 58-70. Esp. 59-62: "Die Deutung durch Matthäus".
The Sabbath Was Made for Man: The Interpretation of Mark 2:23-28. — SCHOTTROFF, W. – STEGEMANN, W. (eds.), *God of the Lowly*, 1984, 118-128. Esp. 119-122.

1979b Die Güte Gottes und die Solidarität von Menschen. Das Gleichnis von den Arbeitern im Weinberg. — *Ibid.*, 71-93. Esp. 71-79: "Die soziale und rechtliche Situation im Gleichnis Mt 20,1-16"; 79-84: "Aussageabsichten in Mt 20,1-15"; 84-91: "Der Sinn des Gleichnisses im Zusammenhang des

Matthäusevangeliums"; 91-92: "Im Kontext der ältesten Jesustradition"; = ID., *Befreiungs-erfahrungen*, 1990, 36-56. Esp. 36-43; 44-48; 48-54; 55-56.
Human Solidarity and the Goodness of God: The Parable of the Workers in the Vineyard. — SCHOTTROFF, W. – STEGEMANN, W. (eds.), *God of the Lowly*, 1984, 129-147. Esp. 129-135; 135-139; 139-145; 145-146.

1979c  Jesusnachfolge & Feindesliebe. [4,4; 5,44] — *TK* 3 (1979) 35-40.

1981  Die Seligpreisungen. — *Zur Rettung des Feuers. Solidaritätsschrift für Kuno Füssel*, Münster: Christen für den Sozialismus, 1981, 14-20.

1982a  Die enge Pforte. — HOCHGREBE, V. (ed.), *Provokation Bergpredigt*, 1982, 117-129.

1982b  Maria Magdalena und die Frauen am Grabe Jesu. — *EvT* 42 (1982) 3-25. Esp. 18-21
[27,55-28,20/Mk]. [NTA 26, 876]; = ID., *Befreiungserfahrungen*, 1990, 134-159. Esp. 155-157.
Mary Magdalene and the Women at Jesus' Tomb. — ID., *Let the Oppressed Go Free: Feminist Perspectives on the New Testament* (Gender and Biblical Tradition), Louisville, KY: Westminster/Knox, 1993, 168-203.

1983a  Die Gegenwart in der Apokalyptik der synoptischen Evangelien. — HELLHOLM, D. (ed.), *Apocalypticism in the Mediterranean World and the Near East. Proceedings of the International Colloquium on Apocalypticism, Uppsala, August 12-17, 1979*, Tübingen: Mohr, 1983, 707-728. Esp. 721-723 [24]; = ID., *Befreiungserfahrungen*, 1990, 73-95. Esp. 88-90.

1983b  Das geschundene Volk und die Arbeit in der Ernte Gottes nach dem Matthäus-evangelium. — ID. – SCHOTTROFF, W. (eds.), *Mitarbeiter der Schöpfung. Bibel und Arbeitswelt*, München: Kaiser, 1983, 149-206. Esp. 151-166: "Die Situation des Volkes nach dem Matthäusevangelium"; 167-198: "Arbeitende Menschen in der Darstellung des Matthäusevangeliums"; 198-205: "Arbeiter in der Ernte Gottes".

1984a  Antijudaismus im Neuen Testament. — *IZT/Concilium* (Mainz) 20 (1987) 406-412. Esp.
406-408; = ID., *Befreiungserfahrungen*, 1990, 217-228. Esp. 218-222.
Anti-Judaism in the New Testament. — *Concilium* (London) 175 (1984) 53-59. Esp. 53-56.

1984b  "Gebt dem Kaiser, was dem Kaiser gehört, und Gott, was Gott gehört". Die theologische Antwort der urchristlichen Gemeinden auf ihre gesellschaftliche und politische Situation. — MOLTMANN, J. (ed.), *Annahme und Widerstand*, München, 1984, 15-58; = ID., *Befreiungserfahrungen*, 1990, 184-216. Esp. 193-196 [5,38-48; 26,47-56].
"Give to Caesar what belongs to Caesar and to God what belongs to God": A Theological Response of the Early Christian Church to Its Social and Political Environment. — SWARTLEY, W.M. (ed.), *The Love of Enemy*, 1992, 223-257. Esp. 230-233.

1986  Bibelarbeit über Matthäus 20,1-16. — *Junge Kirche* (Bremen) 47 (1986) 322-325.

1987  Das Gleichnis vom großen Gastmahl in der Logienquelle. — *EvT* 47 (1987) 192-211.
Esp. 192-196 [reconstruction]; 197-199 [metaphor]; 206-209 [Q]. [NTA 32, 1119]

1988a  Ihr werdet zu diesem Berg sagen: bewege dich von hier nach dort... (Mt. 17,20). — ID. – SCHAUMBERGER, C., *Schuld und Macht. Studien zu einer feministischen Befreiungstheologie*, München: Kaiser, 1988, 125-151. Esp. 148-149 [13,31-32]

1988b  Matthäus 20,1-16. Die Letzten werden die Ersten sein. Ein Sonntag nach Trinitas. — SCHMIDT, E.R. – KORENHOF, M. – JOST, R. (eds.), *Feministisch gelesen. Ausgewählte Bibeltexte für Gruppen und Gemeinden, Gebete für den Gottesdienst*, Stuttgart: Kreuz, 1988, I, 163-169.

1989  Schöpfung im Neuen Testament. — ALTNER, G. (ed.), *Ökologische Theologie. Perspektiven zur Orientierung*, Stuttgart: Kreuz, 1989, 130-148. Esp. 136-139 [6,25-34; 10,28-31]; 147-148 [6,9-13].

1990  *Befreiungserfahrungen. Studien zur Sozialgeschichte des Neuen Testaments* (Theolo-gische Bücherei, 82). München: Kaiser, 1990, 381 p. → 1975, 1979b, 1982b, 1983a, 1984a-b

1991   Wanderprophetinnen. Eine feministische Analyse der Logienquelle. — *EvT* 51 (1991) 332-344. [NTA 36, 698]
       *Itinerant Prophetesses. A Feminist Analysis of the Sayings Source Q* (Occasional Papers, 21). Claremont, CA: The Institute for Antiquity and Christianity, 1991; = PIPER, R.A. (ed.), *The Gospel Behind the Gospels*, 1995, 347-360.

1994a  *Lydias ungeduldige Schwestern. Feministische Sozialgeschichte des frühen Christentums.* Gütersloh: Kaiser, 1994, 248 p. Esp. 120-137: "Frauenhände – die Arbeit von Frauen im Neuen Testament (Mt 13,33; Lk 13,20f)"; 206-227: "Armenevangelium und Option für die Frauen (Lk 6,20f par; Mt 11,25 par)"; 228-256: "Das verstockte Patriarchat und die Nähe Gottes (Mt 24,37-39; Lk 17,26-27.30 und Mk 13,28-33) – Zur Eschatologie des frühen Christentums".
       *Lydia's Impatient Sisters: A Feminist Social History of Early Christianity*, trans. B. and M. Rumscheidt. Louisville, KY: Westminster/Knox, 1995, XVI-298 p.

1994b  The Sayings Source Q. — FIORENZA, E.S. (ed.), *Searching the Scriptures.* II: *A Feminist Commentary*, New York: Crossroad, 1994; London: SCM, 1995, 510-534. Esp. 512-515 [Q 12,51-53]; 515-520 [Q 17,26-27.30]; 521-525 [Q 13,20-21]; 525-532 [Q 10,21-22].

## SCHOTTROFF, Willy

1979*  & STEGEMANN, W. (eds.), *Der Gott der kleinen Leute. Sozialgeschichtliche Bibelaus-legungen.* II: *Neues Testament.* München: Kaiser; Gelnhausen: Burckhardthaus-Laetare, 1979, 120 p. → L. Schottroff 1979a-b, W. Stegemann
       *God of the Lowly. Socio-historical Interpretations of the Bible*, trans. M.J. O'Connell. Maryknoll, NY: Orbis, 1984, IV-172 p.

## SCHRAGE, Wolfgang

1964a  *Das Verhältnis des Thomas-Evangeliums zur synoptischen Tradition und zu den koptischen Evangelienübersetzungen. Zugleich ein Beitrag zur gnostischen Synoptiker-deutung* (BZNW, 29). Berlin: Töpelmann, 1964, VIII-213 p. — Diss. Kiel, 1963 (H. Greeven).

1964b  Evangelienzitate in den Oxyrhynchus-Logien und im koptischen Thomas-Evangelium. — ELTESTER, W. - KETTLER, F.H. (eds.), *Apophoreta. Festschrift für Ernst Haenchen zu seinem siebzigsten Geburtstag am 10. Dezember 1964* (BZNW, 30), Berlin: Töpelmann, 1964, 251-268. Esp. 258-259 [19,30/Th 4]; 259-262 [10,26/Th 5-6]; 262 [7,5/Th 26]; 262-263 [18,20/Th 30]; 264-265 [5,14/Th 32]; 265-266 [10,26/Th 33]; 266-268 [6,25/Th 36].

1971   *Die Christen und der Staat nach dem Neuen Testament.* Gütersloh: Mohn, 1971, 83 p. Esp. 29-49: "Jesus und die Evangelien".

1977   Leiden im Neuen Testament. — GERSTENBERGER, G. - SCHRAGE, W., *Leiden* (Biblische Konfrontationen. Kohlhammer Taschenbücher, 1004), Stuttgart: Kohlhammer, 1977, 118-236.

1980   Frau und Mann im Neuen Testament. — GERSTENBERGER, E.S. - SCHRAGE, W., *Frau und Mann* (Biblische Konfrontationen. Kohlhammer Taschenbücher, 1013), Stuttgart: Kohlhammer, 1980, 92-188. Esp. 111-112 [1,1-17]; 114-119; 163-172.

1982a  *Ethik des Neuen Testaments* (Grundrisse zum Neuen Testament. NTD Ergänzungsreihe, 4). Göttingen: Vandenhoeck & Ruprecht, 1982, 340 p. Esp. 136-145: "Der Weg der 'besseren Gerechtigkeit' nach Matthäus"; ⁵1989, 378 p. → Wendland 1970
       *The Ethics of the New Testament*, trans. D.E. Green. Philadelphia, PA: Fortress, 1988, XIV-369 p.
       *Etica del Nuevo Testamento*, trans. J. Lacarra (Biblioteca de estudios bíblicos, 57). Salamanca: Sígueme, 1987, 443 p.

1982b  Aspekte heutiger Bergpredigt-Interpretation. — *EvErz* 34 (1982) 387-398. [NTA 27, 510]

1982c  Einige Beobachtungen zur Lehre im Neuen Testament. — *EvT* 42 (1982) 233-251. Esp. 244-245 [διδάσκειν]. [NTA 27, 324]

1986*  (ed.), *Studien zum Text und zur Ethik des Neuen Testaments. Festschrift zum 80. Geburtstag von Heinrich Greeven* (BZNW, 47). Berlin – New York: de Gruyter, 1986, IX-456 p. → F. Hahn, H. Krämer, Luck, Marxsen, Petersen, G. Schneider, Schrage, Schroeder 1978

1986a Ethische Tendenzen in der Textüberlieferung des Neuen Testaments. — *Ibid.*, 374-396.

1986b Heil und Heilung im Neuen Testament. — *EvT* 46 (1986) 197-214. [NTA 31, 360]; = BROER, I. – WERBICK, J. (eds.), *"Auf Hoffnung hin sind wir erlöst" (Röm 8,24)*. *Biblische und systematische Beiträge zum Erlösungsverständnis heute* (SBS, 128), Stuttgart: Katholisches Bibelwerk, 1987, 95-117.

**SCHRAMM, Tim**

1977 Fest und Freude im Neuen Testament. — OTTO, E. – SCHRAMM, T., *Fest und Freude* (Biblische Konfrontationen. Kohlhammer Taschenbücher, 1003), Stuttgart: Kohl-hammer, 1977, 77-162.

1986 & LÖWENSTEIN, K., *Unmoralische Helden. Anstößige Gleichnisse Jesu*. Göttingen: Vandenhoeck & Ruprecht, 1986, 204 p. Esp. 22-42 [21,33-46/Mk]; 42-49 [13,44]; 50-53 [24,43-44/Q 12,39]; 59-62 [5,25-26/Q 12,57-59]; 132-147 [kingdom].

**SCHRECK, Christopher**

1989 The Nazareth Pericope. Luke 4,16-30 in Recent Study. — NEIRYNCK, F. (ed.), *L'Évangile de Luc*, ²1989, 399-471. Esp. 414-417: "Tuckett's proposal: Q"; 417-420: "Ναζαρά".

**SCHRECKENBERG, Heinz**

1982 *Die christlichen Adversus-Judaeos-Texte und ihr literarisches und historisches Umfeld (1.-11. Jh.)* (EHS, XXIII/172). Frankfurt/M-Bern: Lang. 1982, 747 p. Esp. 92-93; 113-115 [pharisees]; 120-121 [21,33-46]; 121-122 [22,1-14]; 129-131 [27,24-25].

1984 Josephus und die christliche Wirkungsgeschichte seines 'Bellum Iudaicum'. — *ANRW* II.21.2 (1984) 1106-1217. Esp. 1116-1122 [24,2].

**SCHREIBER, Johannes**

1969 Das Schweigen Jesu. — WEGENAST, K. (ed.), *Theologie und Unterricht. Über die Repräsentanz des Christlichen in der Schule. Festgabe für Hans Stock zu seinem 65. Geburtstag*, Gütersloh: Mohn, 1969, 79-87. Esp. 83-84 [26,57-68]; = ID., *Die Markuspassion*, 1993, 260-269. Esp. 264-265.

1981 Die Bestattung Jesu. Redaktionsgeschichtliche Beobachtungen zu Mk 15 42-47 par. — *ZNW* 72 (1981) 141-177. Esp. 157-160 [27,57-61]. [NTA 26, 506]; = ID., *Die Markuspassion*, 1993, 273-308. Esp. 288-291.

1986 *Der Kreuzigungsbericht des Markusevangeliums. Mk 15,20b-41. Eine traditions-geschichtliche und methodenkritische Untersuchung nach William Wrede (1859-1906)* (BZNW, 48). Berlin: de Gruyter, 1986, XVI-517 p. Esp. 257-260 [27,31-56]. — Diss. Bonn, 1959 (P. Vielhauer).

1993 *Die Markuspassion. Eine redaktionsgeschichtliche Untersuchung* (BZNW, 68). Berlin: de Gruyter, 1993, XV-561 p. Esp. 154-155 [14,3-12/Mk]; 358-359; 404-407: "Markus und die Spruchquelle". → 1969, 1981

**SCHREINER, Josef**

1969* & DAUTZENBERG, G. (eds.), *Gestalt und Anspruch des Neuen Testaments*. Würzburg: Echter, 1969, ²1979, X-398 p. → Hoffmann, R. Pesch, A. Schulz, Trilling, Ziener
*Forma y propósita de Nuevo Testamento. Introducción a su problemática* (Biblioteca Herder, Sección de Sagrada Escritura, 129). Barcelona: Herder, 1973, 474 p.
*Forma ed esigenze del Nuovo Testamento*. Bari: Paoline, 1973; *Introduzione letteraria e teologica al Nuovo Testamento* (Parola di Dio). Roma: Paoline, ²1982, 663 p..
*Forma e exigencias do Novo Testamento*. São Paulo: Paulinas, 1977, 580 p.

**SCHROEDER, Hans-Hartmut**

1972 *Eltern und Kinder in der Verkündigung Jesu. Eine hermeneutische und exegetische Untersuchung* (Theologische Forschung, 53). Hamburg: Evangelischer Verlag, 1972, 191 p. Esp. 78-80 [8,18-22].

1978    ¿Tienen los dichos de Jesús referentes a la pobreza consecuencias éticas en la realidad social? — *Los pobres: encuentro y compromiso*, Buenos Aires: Aurora, 1978, 29-43. Haben Jesu Worte über Armut und Reichtum Folgen für das soziale Verhalten? — SCHRAGE, W. (ed.), *Studien zum Text und zur Ethik des Neuen Testaments*. FS. H. Greeven, 1986, 397-409. Esp. 399-404.

1979    "Oikos" y la justicia en los evangelios sinópticos. [10,37-38] — *RevistBíb* 41 (1979) 249-259. [NTA 24, 775]

**SCHROER, Silvia**
1990    Konkretionen zum Vaterunser. — *Una Sancta* 45 (1990) 110-113. [NTA 35, 134]

**SCHRÖTEN, Jutta**
1995    *Entstehung, Komposition und Wirkungsgeschichte des 118. Psalms* (BBB, 95). Weinheim: Beltz Athenäum, 1995, VII-180 p. Esp. 158-159 [21,7/Ps 118,22]; 165-166 [21,42/Ps 118,22]. — Diss. Münster (E. Zenger).

**SCHRÖTER, Jens**
1997    Erwägungen zum Gestzesverständnis in Q anhand von Q 16,16-18. — TUCKETT, C.M. (ed.), *The Scriptures in the Gospels*, 1997, 441-458. Esp. 443-449: "Zur Position der Logien in Q"; 449-450 [Q 16,16]; 450-452 [Q 16,17]; 453-457 [Q 16,18].

**SCHRUERS, Paul**
1959    *De situering van Gods vaderschap ten opzichte van de mensen bij Mattheüs*. Diss. Leuven, 1959, 221 p. (A. Descamps). → 1960a
1960a   La paternité divine dans Mt., V,45 et VI,26-32. — *ETL* 36 (1960) 593-624. Esp. 594-599; 602-604: "Bilan des textes matthéens"; 605-616 [5,45]; 616-623 [6,26-32]. [NTA 6, 122] → 1959
1960b   Gods vaderschap voor de mensen bij Mattheus. — *RevEcclLiège* 47 (1960) 193-217, 257-276. Esp. 195-203 [5,45]; 203-209 [6,25-34]; 210-213 [6,16-16.18]; 213-217 [23,8-10]; 257-259 [6,9]; 260-262 [7,11]; 262-264 [6,14-15]; 266-268 [13,43]; 269-272 [18,14]; 272-274 [10,20]; 274-276 [5,16].
1970    Immanentie en transcendentie van God onze Vader in het licht van het Evangelie. — COPPENS, J. (ed.), *Ecclesia a Spiritu Sancto edocta. Lumen Gentium, 53. Mélanges théologiques. Hommage à Mgr Gérard Philips. Verzamelde theologische Opstellen aangeboden aan Mgr. Gérard Philips* (BETL, 27), Gembloux: Duculot, 1970, 439-453. Esp. 443-445 [5,45-48]; 445-448 [6,1-6.18]; 448-449 [6,7]; 449-452 [6,25-34]; 452-453 [5,16].

**SCHUB, M.B.**
1976    It is easier for a camel to go through the eye of a needle than for a rich man to enter God's Kingdom. [19,24] — *Arabica* (Leiden) 23 (1976) 311-312. → Khalil 1976

**SCHUBERT, B. VON**
1970    Die Bergpredigt in der Oberstufe. — *Theologia Practica* (Hamburg) 5 (1970) 135-154.

**SCHUBERT, Kurt**
1955    Bergpredigt und Texte von 'En Fesha. — *TQ* 135 (1955) 320-337. Esp. 322-325 [5,17]; 326-329 [5,3]; 330-332 [5,12]; 332-335 [5,21-48].
        The Sermon on the Mount and the Qumran Texts. — STENDAHL, K. (ed.), *The Scrolls and the New Testament*, New York: Harper, 1957, 118-128. Esp. 119-121; 122-124; 124-125; 125-127.
1958    *Die Gemeinde vom Toten Meer. Ihre Entstehung und ihre Lehren*. München–Basel: Reinhardt, 1958, 144 p. Esp. 109-114 [John the Baptist]; 114-127 [Jesus tradition]; = MAIER, J. – SCHUBERT, K., *Die Qumran-Essener. Texte der Schriftrollen und Lebensbild der Gemeinde* (Uni-Taschenbücher, 224), München–Basel: Reinhardt, 1973, 9-141. Esp. 109-114; 114-127.
        *The Dead Sea Community. Its Origin and Teachings*, trans. J.W. Doberstein. New York: Harper, 1959, XI-178 p. Esp. 126-131; 131-147.

1964*   (ed.), *Vom Messias zum Christus. Die Fülle der Zeit in religionsgeschichtlicher und theologischer Sicht.* Freiburg: Herder, 1964, VIII-356 p. → Brox, Schürmann 1959a, Sint

1972    Die Kindheitsgeschichten Jesu im Lichte der Religionsgeschichte des Judentums. — *BLtg* 45 (1972) 224-240. Esp. 234-240. [NTA 17, 903]
Die Jungfrauengeburt im Lichte frühjüdischer Quellen. — *TGeg* 16 (1973) 193-199.

1973    *Jesus im Lichte der Religionsgeschichte des Judentums.* Wien: Herold, 1973, 200 p. Esp. 11-40: "Die Kindheitsgeschichten Jesu im Lichte der Religionsgeschichte des Judentums"; 41-52.62-70 [Pharisees]; 76-77 [Sadducees].
*Jésus à la lumière du judaïsme du premier siècle*, trans. A. Liefooghe (LD, 84). Paris: Cerf, 1974, 190 p. Esp. 11-39; 41-52.62-69; 76-77.

**SCHUELE, Frederick E.**

1984    Living Up to Matthew's Sermon on the Mount. An Approach. — DALY, R.J., et al. (eds.), *Christian Biblical Ethics*, 1984, 200-210.

**SCHÜLING, Joachim**

1991    *Studien zum Verhältnis von Logienquelle und Markusevangelium* (FzB, 65). Würzburg: Echter, 1991, 252 p. Esp. 17-55: "Botensendung" [Q 10,2-16/Mk 6,7-13]; 56-108: "Johannes der Täufer" [Q 3,7-9.16-17; 7,18-35/Mk 1,2-15]; 109-136: "Beelzebulstreit" [Q 11,14-23/Mk 3,22-30]; 137-164: "Nachfolge" [Q 14,26-27/Mk 8,34–9,1]; 167-187: "Literarische Eigenständigkeit von Markusevangelium und Logienquelle"; 188-200: "Traditionsgeschichtliche Differenzierungen"; 201-215: "Verschriftung". [NTA 36, p. 269] — Diss. Gießen, 1987 (G. Dautzenberg). → A. Fuchs 1993
J. BEUTLER, *TheolPhil* 69 (1994) 573-574; F.G. DOWNING, *Bib* 73 (1992) 276-279; A. FUCHS, *SNTU* 19 (1994) 213-214; A.D. JACOBSON, *JBL* 113 (1994) 724-726; W SCHENK, *TLZ* 117 (1992) 842-843; T. SÖDING, *TRev* 88 (1992) 376-377; B.T. VIVIANO, *RB* 101 (1994) 618-619.

**SCHÜLLER, Bruno**

1989    Zur Interpretation der Antithesen der Bergpredigt. — KOCH, D.-A., et al. (eds.), *Jesu Rede von Gott.* FS W. Marxsen, 1989, 101-115.

**SCHÜRMANN, Heinz**

1953    Die Dubletten im Lukasevangelium. Ein Beitrag zur Verdeutlichung des lukanischen Redaktionsverfahrens. [Q(Lk)] — *ZKT* 75 (1953) 338-345; = ID., *Traditionsgeschichtliche Untersuchungen*, 1968, 272-278.

1954    Die Dublettenvermeidungen im Lukasevangelium. Ein Beitrag zur Verdeutlichung des lukanischen Redaktionsverfahrens. — *ZKT* 76 (1954) 83-93. Esp. 87-90: "Die Matthäus–Lukas Tradition"; = ID., *Traditionsgeschichtliche Untersuchungen*, 1968, 279-289 ("Nachtrag", 289). Esp. 284-286.

1955a   *Der Einsetzungsbericht Lk 22,19-20. II. Teil einer quellenkritischen Untersuchung des lukanischen Abendmahlsberichtes Lk 22,7-38* (NTAbh, 20/4). Münster: Aschendorff, 1955, XII-153 p.; ²1970; ³1986. Esp. 2-7: "Mt 26,26-28 als Markus-Redaktion". → 1957b

1955b   *Worte des Herrn. Jesu Botschaft vom Königtum Gottes. Auf Grund der synoptischen Überlieferung zusammengestellt.* Leipzig: St. Benno, 1955, VIII-412 p.; ²1956 (Mainz: Grünewald, 1956); ³1960, VIII-440 p. (Herder-Bücherei, 89; Freiburg: Herder, 1961, 188 p.; ²1963; ³1964); ⁴1966, VIII-432 p. (Freiburg: Herder, 1968); ⁵1994.
*Parole del Signore. Messaggio di Gesù sul Regno di Dio* [⁴1966], trans. L. Benna. Torino-Leumann: Elle Di Ci, 1966, 440 p.
Polish trans. [³1964] 1969.

1957a   *Das Gebet des Herrn. Aus der Verkündigung Jesu erläutert* (Die Botschaft Gottes, II/6). Leipzig: St. Benno, 1957, 143 p.; ²1958 (Freiburg: Herder, 1958; ²1962; ³1966); ³1959; ⁴1961; ⁵1965.
*Das Gebet des Herrn als Schlüssel zum Verstehen Jesu*, ⁶1981, 219 p. (Freiburg: Herder, ⁴1981, 187 p.); ⁷1990.

Eine theologische Meditation über das "eigentümlich Jesuanische" im Gebet Jesu ("Nachtrag" ⁶1981, 153-178; = ⁴1981, 135-155).

Das "eigentümlich Jesuanische" im Gebet Jesu. Jesu Beten als Schlüssel für das Verständnis seiner Verkündigung. — ID., *Jesus - Gestalt und Geheimnis*, 1994, 45-63.

M.-É. BOISMARD, *RB* 67 (1960) 147; F. BUCK, *CBQ* 21 (1959) 248; W. KOESTER, *Scholastik* 34 (1959) 307; R. KUGELMAN, *TS* 20 (1959) 481-482; R. MARLÉ, *RSR* 47 (1960) 482; C.M. MARTINI, *CC* 112/2 (1961) 428; F. MUSSNER, *TTZ* 68 (1959) 185-186; W. PESCH, *TRev* 54 (1958) 214-215; *Bib* 41 (1960) 203; K.H. SCHELKLE, *TQ* 139 (1959) 87; T. SCHUERMANS, *CollMech* 34 (1959-60) 111-112; B. SCHWANK, *ErbAuf* 35 (1959) 430-431; J. SINT, *ZKT* 81 (1959) 243-244.

L. KIRSCH, *BZ* 26 (1982) 304.

*Padre Nuestro* [³1959], trans. C. Ruiz-Garridu (Perspectivas, 20). Madrid: Fax, 1961, 216 p.; (Mundo y Dios, 18), Salamanca: Trinitario, ²1982, 214 p. (App., 189-207).

L. ARNALDICH, *Salmanticensis* 11 (1964) 376; F. DOMÍNGUEZ, *Augustinus* (Madrid) 8 (1963) 143-144.

*Het Gebed des Heren, toegelicht uit de prediking van Jezus* [⁴1961], trans. J. Verstraeten. Roermond–Maaseik: Romen, 1961, 127 p.

M. DIERICKX, *CollMech* 49 (1964) 188-189; A. DRUBBEL, *Ons Geestelijk Leven* 39 (1962-63) 319; P. FRANSEN, *Bijdragen* 23 (1962) 313; J. KAHMANN, *Nederlandse Katholieke Stemmen* (Zwolle) 59 (1963) 202.

*Praying with Christ. The "Our Father" for Today* [⁴1961], trans. W.M. Ducey, et al. New York: Herder, 1964, VI-141 p.

E.J. JOYCE, *CBQ* 26 (1964) 403-404.

*La Prière du Seigneur à la lumière de la prédication de Jésus* [⁴1961], trans. F. Diverres & C. Richard (Études théologiques, 3). Paris: Éd. de l'Orante, 1965, 120 p.

P. BENOIT, *RB* 73 (1966) 639; S. DEL PÁRAMO, *EstE* 42 (1967) 275-276; M.É. LAUZIÈRE, *RThom* 66 (1966) 310-311; V. LO GIUDICE, *CC* 117/1 (1966) 470-471; *CC* 119/1 (1968) 199; R. MARLÉ, *Études* 323 (1965) 133; B. PRETE, *Sacra Doctrina* (Bologna) 12 (1967) 259-260; 550-551; L. SABOURIN, *VD* 45 (1967) 367-368..

*Il Padre nostro alla luce della predicazione di Gesù* [⁵1965], trans. P. Vicentini ("Collana scritturistica di Città Nuova"). Roma: Città Nuova, 1967, 172 p.

*Padre nostro, la preghiera del Signore* [⁶1981], trans. M. Limiroli (Già e non ancora, 65). Milano: Jaca, 1983, 200 p. (App., 169-195); ²1994, 151 p. (App. 129-147).

F. BOLGIANI, *RivStoLR* 21 (1985) 346-347; R. DAL ZILIO, *Sal* 46 (1984) 564.

*A Oração do Senhor. Como chave para a interpretação de Jesus* [⁶1981], trans. A. Bruxel. São Paulo: Loyola, 1983, 150 p.

Japanese trans. [⁵1965] 1967.

1957b    *Jesu Abschiedsrede Lk 22,21-38. III. Teil einer quellenkritischen Untersuchung des lukanischen Abendmahlsberichtes Lk 22,7-38* (NTAbh, 20/5). Münster: Aschendorff, 1957, XIV-162 p.; ²1977, XX-170 p. (Nachwort: "Bemerkungen über die Handhabung der redaktionsgeschichtlichen Methode", 161-170). Esp. 37-54: "Scheidung von vorlukanischer Tradition und lukanischer Redaktion in Lk 22,28-30"; 54-63: "Die vormalige Kombination von Lk 22,28-30 mit Lk 22,15-20a" [19,28]. → 1955a

1958    Die Sprache des Christus. Sprachliche Beobachtungen an den synoptischen Herren-worten. — *BZ* 2 (1958) 54-84. Esp. 64-78 [style]. [NTA 3, 67]; = ID., *Traditions-geschichtliche Untersuchungen*, 1968, 83-108 ("Nachtrag", 108). Esp. 90-105.

1959a    Eschatologie und Liebesdienst in der Verkündigung Jesu. — *Kaufet die Zeit aus. Beiträge zur christlichen Eschatologie. [FS Theoderich Kampmann zum 60. Geburtstag],* Paderborn: Schöningh, 1959, 39-71; = *TJb*, 1962, 320-340. Esp. 322-327 [Q 12,57-59(Lk)]; 328-339; = SCHUBERT, K. (ed.), *Vom Messias zum Christus*, 1964, 203-232. Esp. 205-210; 211-229; = ID., *Ursprung und Gestalt. Erörterungen und Besinnungen zum Neuen Testament* (Kommentare und Beiträge zum Alten und Neuen Testament), Düsseldorf: Patmos, 1970, 279-296 ("Nachtrag", 296-298). Esp. 281-285; 286-295; = ID., *Jesus - Gestalt und Geheimnis*, 1994, 105-128 ("Nachtrag", 128-130).

1959b    Zur Traditions- und Redaktionsgeschichte von Mt 10,23. — *BZ* 3 (1959) 82-88. [NTA 3, 585]; = ID., *Traditionsgeschichtliche Untersuchungen*, 1968, 150-155 ("Nachtrag", 156).

1960a  Das Gebet des Herrn. Ein Übertragungsversuch. — *BibLeb* 1 (1960) 261-265.

1960b  Sprachliche Reminiszenzen an abgeänderte oder ausgelassene Bestandteile der Spruchsammlung im Lukas- und Matthäusevangelium. — *NTS* 6 (1959-60) 193-210. Esp. 200-208: "Matthäische Reminiszenzen" [4,17; 5,20.43; 6,2.5.8.9-13.16.27; 7,17.18; 8,6.21; 10,6.16.23.25.26; 11,13; 13,31; 16,6; 18,6.8.10; 22,3; 23,13; 24,43-51]. [NTA 5, 72]; = ID., *Traditionsgeschichtliche Untersuchungen*, 1968, 111-125 (Nachtrag: "Der Redequelle", 125). Esp. 116-125.

1960c  Die vorösterlichen Anfänge der Logientradition. Versuch eines formgeschichtlichen Zugangs zum Leben Jesu. — RISTOW, H. - MATTHIAE, K. (eds.), *Der historische Jesus und der kerygmatische Christus*, 1960, 342-370. Esp. 344-368 [sayings]; = ID., *Traditionsgeschichtliche Untersuchungen*, 1968, 39-64 ("Nachtrag", 64-65). Esp. 50-63; = ID., *Das Geheimnis Jesu. Versuche zur Jesusfrage* (Die Botschaft Gottes, II/28), Leipzig: St. Benno, 1972, 14-68 ("Nachtrag", 69-72).

Versuch eines formgeschichtlichen Zugangs zum Leben Jesu. (Die vorösterlichen Anfänge der Logientradition I). — ID., *Jesus - Gestalt und Geheimnis*, 1994, 380-389 ("Nachtrag", 395-397); Jesus bringt Gottes letztes Wort in letzter Stunde (Die vorösterlichen Anfänge der Logientradition II). — *Ibid.*, 85-104.

*La tradizione dei detti di Gesù*, trans. F. Montagnini (Biblioteca minima di cultura religiosa, 14). Brescia: Paideia, 1966, 77 p.

*SelT* 9 (1970) 17-29.

1960d  "Wer daher eines dieser geringsten Gebote auflöst...". Wo fand Matthäus das Logion Mt 5,19? — *BZ* 4 (1960) 238-250. Esp. 240-246 [5,18-19]; 246-250 [5,19]. [NTA 3, 585]; = ID., *Traditionsgeschichtliche Untersuchungen*, 1968, 126-136 ("Nachtrag", 136). Esp. 127-132; 132-136.

1961  Protolukanische Spracheigentümlichkeiten? Zu Fr. Rehkopf, Die lukanische Sonderquelle. Ihr Umfang und Sprachgebrauch. — *BZ* 5 (1961) 266-286. Esp. 270-277.277-285 [Q-Sondergut]. [NTA 6, 619r]; = ID., *Traditionsgeschichtliche Untersuchungen*, 1968, 209-227. Esp. 212-220.220-227.

1963  Mt 10,5b-6 und die Vorgeschichte des synoptischen Aussendungsberichtes. — BLINZLER, J., et al. (eds.), *Neutestamentliche Aufsätze. FS J. Schmid*, 1963, 270-282. Esp. 272-275 [origin]; 275-282 [Q]; = ID., *Traditionsgeschichtliche Untersuchungen*, 1968, 137-149 ("Nachtrag", 149). Esp. 139-142; 142-149.

1964  Der "Bericht vom Anfang". Ein Rekonstruktionsversuch auf Grund von Lk. 4,14-16. — *Studia Evangelica* 2 (1964) 242-258. Esp. 244-245 [4,12/Lk 4,14a]; 245-249 [4,24; 9,26/Lk 4,14b]; 249-251 [4,23/Lk 4,15]; 251-252 [4,25/Lk 4,42]; 254-255 [4,13/Lk 4,16]; = ID., *Traditionsgeschichtliche Untersuchungen*, 1968, 69-79 ("Nachtrag", 79-80). Esp. 70-71; 71-73; 73-74; 74-75; 76-78. → Delobel 1973, Tuckett 1982a

1966  Die Warnung des Lukas vor der Falschlehre in der "Predigt am Berge" Lk 6,20-49. — *BZ* 10 (1966) 57-81. Esp. 63-68 [Q 6,39-42]; 68-72 [Q 6,43-45]; 74-78 [Q 6,20-26(Lk)]; 78-80 [Q 6,46-49]; = ID., *Traditionsgeschichtliche Untersuchungen*, 1968, 290-309 ("Nachtrag", 309). Esp. 295-298; 298-302; 303-307; 307-308.

1968  *Traditionsgeschichtliche Untersuchungen zu den synoptischen Evangelien. Beiträge* (Kommentare und Beiträge zum Alten und Neuen Testament). Düsseldorf: Patmos, 1968, 367 p. → 1953, 1954, 1958, 1959b, 1960b-d, 1961, 1963, 1964, 1966

1969  *Das Lukasevangelium. Erster Teil: Kommentar zu Kap. 1,1-9,50* (HTKNT, 3/1). Freiburg: Herder, 1969, XLVIII-591 p.; ²1982, LII-591 p.; ³1984; ⁴1990; Leipzig: St. Benno, 1970, XLVIII-591 p.; ²1971. Esp. 161 [Lk 3,3-6(Q)]; 181-183 [Q 3,7-9.16-17]; 204-220 [Q 4,1-13]; 241-244 [Lk 4,16-30(Q)]; 323 [Lk 6,12-16(Q)]; 323-386 [Q 6,20-49]; 395-397 [Q 7,1-10]; 405-429 [Q 7,18-35]. → 1994b

*Il vangelo di Luca. Parte prima: Testo greco e traduzione. Commentario ai capp. 1,1-9,50* [²1982], trans. V. Gatti (Commentario teologico del Nuovo Testamento). Brescia: Paideia, 1983, 923 p.

1970 Zur Traditionsgeschichte der Nazareth-Perikope Lk 4,16-30. — DESCAMPS, A.L. — DE HALLEUX, A. (eds.), *Mélanges bibliques*. FS B. Rigaux, 1970, 187-205. Esp. 201-202 [4,12-16/Lk 4,14-16]; 203-205 [Lk 4,17-21.23.25-27: Q].

1973 Wie hat Jesus seinen Tod bestanden und verstanden? Eine methodenkritische Besinnung. — HOFFMANN, P., et al. (eds.), *Orientierung an Jesus*. FS J. Schmid, 1973, 325-344. Esp. 328-329; 335-337; 339-342; 348; 351; = *TJb*, 1974, 128-163; = ID., *Jesu ureigener Tod*, 1975, ²1976, 16-65. Esp. 21-22; 30-32; 35-39; 48; 53. → Segalla 1982a
Comment Jésus a-t-il affronté et compris sa mort? Réflexions critiques sur la méthode. — ID., *Comment Jésus a-t-il vécu sa mort?*, 1977, 21-81.

1975a *Jesu ureigener Tod. Exegetische Besinnungen und Ausblick*. Freiburg: Herder, 1975, 155 p.; ²1976. → 1973
*Comment Jésus a-t-il vécu sa mort? Exégèse et théologie* [²1976], trans. A. Chazelle (LD, 93). Paris: Cerf, 1977, 190 p.
*¿Como entendió y vivió Jesús su muerte? Reflexiones exegéticas y panorámica* [²1976], trans. A. Martínez de Lapera (Biblioteca de estudios bíblicos, 42). Salamanca: Sígueme, 1982, 166 p.
*Gesù di fronte alla propria morte. Riflessioni esegetiche e prospettiva* [²1976], trans. G. Marcarini. Brescia: Morcelliana, 1983, 200 p.

1975b Beobachtungen zum Menschensohn-Titel in der Redequelle. Sein Vorkommen in Abschluß- und Einleitungswendungen. — PESCH, R., et al. (eds.), *Jesus und der Menschensohn*. FS A. Vögtle, 1975, 124-147. Esp. 125 [Mt]; 130-131 [Q 6,20-23]; 131-132 [Q 7,33-34]; 132-133 [Q 9,57-60]; 133-135 [Q 11,29-30]; 135-136 [Q 12,8-9]; 136-137 [Q 12,10]; 137-138 [10,23]; 138 [Q 12,40]; 139 [Q 17,24]; 139-140 [Q 17,26-30]; 140-147; = ID., *Gottes Reich – Jesu Geschick*, 1983, 153-182 ("überarbeitet"). Esp. 154-155; 160-161; 161-162; 162-163; 164-165; 165-167; 167-168; 169; 169-170; 170-171; 171; 172-182: "Traditionsgeschichtliche Auswertung". → Coppens 1981
Observations on the Son of Man Title in the Speech Source: Its Occurence in Closing and Introductory Expressions. — KLOPPENBORG, J.S. (ed.), *The Shape of Q*, 1994, 74-97. Esp. 75-76; 80-81; 81-82; 82-83; 83-84; 84-86; 86-87; 87; 87-88; 88; 88-89; 89-96.

1979 Neutestamentliche Marginalien zur Frage nach der Institutionalität, Unauflösbarkeit und Sakramentalität der Ehe. — WINTER, A., et al. (eds.), *Kirche und Bibel. Festgabe für Bischof Eduard Schick*, Paderborn: Schöningh, 1979, 409-430. Esp. 412-415 [19,3-8/Mk]; 415-421 [5,32; 19,9]; = *TJb*, 1981, 147-164. Esp. 149-152; 152-158; = ID., *Studien zur neutestamentlichen Ethik*, 1990, 119-146 ("Literaturnachtrag", 144-146). Esp. 123-126; 126-134.
*Studia Moralia* (Roma) 16 (1978) 31-45; *Theologische Blätter* 11 (1979) 249-251.

1982a Jesu ureigenes Basileia-Verständnis. — WALDENFELS, H. (ed.), *Theologie – Grund und Grenzen. Festgabe für Heimo Dolch zur Vollendung des 70. Lebensjahres*, Paderborn: Schöningh, 1982, 191-237; = ID., *Gottes Reich – Jesu Geschick*, 1983, 21-64 ("durchgesehen"); 1985, 19-68; = ID., *Jesus – Gestalt und Geheimnis*, 1994, 18-30.31-44.157-164.174-185.

1982b Die Verbindlichkeit konkreter sittlicher Normen nach dem Neuen Testament, bedacht am Beispiel des Ehescheidungsverbotes und im Lichte des Liebesgebotes. — KERBER, W. (ed.), *Sittliche Normen. Zum Problem ihrer allgemeinen und unwandelbaren Geltung*, Düsseldorf: Patmos, 1982, 107-123. Esp. 109-115 [19,3-12/Mk]; = ID., *Studien zur neutestamentlichen Ethik*, 1990, 147-167 ("Literaturnachtrag", 167-171). Esp. 150-157.

1982c Das Zeugnis der Redenquelle für die Basileia-Verkündigung Jesu. Eine traditionsgeschichtliche Untersuchung. — DELOBEL, J. (ed.), *Logia*, 1982, 121-200. Esp. 122-133: "Das Fragmentum Q als Kontext von Basileia-Worten"; 133-179: "Die traditionsgeschichtliche Ortung von Basileia-Worten im Fragmentum Q" [Q 6,20-21; Q 7,28; Q 9,61-62; Lk 10,9.11; Q 11,2.14.17.19-20; Lk 11,14.17; Q 12,29-31; Lk 12,32; Q 13,18-19; Q 13,20-21.28-29; Mt 5,19; Q 16,16; Q 11,52]; 179-191: "Rückschlüsse aus der nachösterlichen Basileia-Verkündigung im Fragmentum Q auf das vorösterliche Basileia-Verständnis Jesu"; = ID., *Gottes Reich – Jesu Geschick*, 1983, 65-152 ("durchgesehen"). Esp. 66-80; 80-135; 136-152.

1983a    *Gottes Reich – Jesu Geschick. Jesu ureigener Tod im Licht seiner Basileia-Verkündigung.* Freiburg-Basel-Wien: Herder, 1983, 269 p. → 1975b, 1982a.c, 1983b-c Teildruck: (Die Botschaft Gottes, II/34). Leipzig: St. Benno, 1985, 133 p. → 1982a, 1983b-c

1983b    Jesu ureigener Tod im Licht seiner Basileia-Verkündigung. — *Ibid.*, 11-18; 1985, 9-18; = ID., *Jesus – Gestalt und Geheimnis*, 1994, 168-174 ("gekürzt und ergänzt").

1983c    Jesu Basileia-Verkündigung und das christologische Kerygma als Mitte der Schrift. — *Ibid.*, 246-251; 1985, 93-99.

1986    Die Redekomposition wider "dieses Geschlecht" und seine Führung in der Redenquelle (vgl. Mt 23,1-39 par Lk 11,37-54). Bestand – Akoluthie – Kompositionsformen. — *SNTU* 11 (1986) 33-81. Esp. 34-41: "Der Bestand der Redekomposition in Q"; 42-64: "Akoluthie und Gesamtgestalt der Redekomposition in Q"; 65-81: "Kompositionsformen in der Redekomposition von Q". [NTA 31, 592]

1990    *Studien zur neutestamentlichen Ethik* (Stuttgarter Biblische Aufsatzbände, 7), ed. T. Söding. Stuttgart: Katholisches Bibelwerk, 1990, 382 p. → 1979, 1982b

1991    Zur Kompositionsgeschichte der Redenquelle. Beobachtungen an der lukanischen Q-Vorlage. — BUSSMANN, C. – RADL, W. (eds.), *Der Treue Gottes trauen.* FS G. Schneider, 1991, 325-342. Esp. 332: "Die Redekompositionen"; 332-334: "'Strukturierte Kompositionen'"; 334-338: "Spruch-Paare"; 338-339: "Spruch-Gruppen"; = ID., *Jesus – Gestalt und Geheimnis*, 1994, 398-419. Esp. 406-407; 407-409; 410-414; 414-416.

1992    QLk 11,14-36 kompositionsgeschichtlich befragt. — VAN SEGBROECK, F., et al. (eds.), *The Four Gospels 1992.* FS F. Neirynck, 1992, I, 563-586. Esp. 567-574: "Die Spruchkomposition Q 11,14-26"; 574-583: "Die Spruchkomposition Q 11,16.29-36".

1994a    *Jesus – Gestalt und Geheimnis. Gesammelte Beiträge*, ed. K. Scholtissek. Paderborn: Bonifatius, 1994, 456 p. → 1957a/81, 1959a, 1960c, 1982a, 1983b, 1991

1994b    *Das Lukasevangelium. Zweiter Teil. Erste Folge: Kommentar zu Kapitel 9,51–11,54* (HTKNT, 3/2,1). Freiburg: Herder, 1994, XXIV-360 p. Esp. 32-48 [Q 9,57-62]; 57-85.98-99 [Q 10,2-16]; 101-125 [Q 10,21-24]; 137-140 [Lk 10,25-28(Q)]; 172-206 [Q 11,2-4]; 212-221 [Q 11,9-13]; 222-253.261-264 [Q 11,14-26]; 268-290 [Q 11,29-32]; 290-302 [Q 11,33-35(36)]; 306-335 [Q 11,37-54(Lk)]. → 1969; → A. Fuchs 1994a

### SCHÜTZ, Christian

1969    Die Mysterien des Lebens Jesu. 3. Die Mysterien des öffentlichen Lebens und Wirkens Jesu. — FEINER, J. – LÖHRER, M. (eds.), *Mysterium Salutis. Grundriß heilsgeschichtlicher Dogmatik.* III/2: *Das Christusereignis*, Zürich–Einsiedeln–Köln: Benziger, 1969, 58-131 p. Esp. 58-75 [3,13-17]; 75-90 [4,1-11]; 90-97 [17,1-9]; 97-123 [miracles: 8,14-15.23-27; 9,18-26].

### SCHÜTZ, Roland

1967    *Johannes der Täufer* (ATANT, 50). Zürich–Stuttgart: Zwingli, 1967, 151 p. Esp. 70-82: "Die Reden des Täufers"; 100-108: "Jesus und der Täufer"; 108-113: "Fasten und Beten".

### SCHÜTZEICHEL, Heribert

1995    Die wahre Gerechtigkeit: Calvins Auslegung von Mt 5,1-12 / Lk 6,20-26. — ANGEL, H.-G. – REITER, J. – WIRTZ, H.-G. (eds.), *Aus reichen Quellen leben: Ethische Fragen in Geschichte und Gegenwart. Helmut Weber zum 65. Geburtstag*, Trier: Paulinus, 1995, 163-167.

### SCHULTZE, Bernhard

1961    Die ekklesiologische Bedeutung des Gleichnisses vom Senfkorn (Matth. 13,31-32; Mk. 4,30-32; Lk. 13,18-19). — *OCP* 27 (1961) 362-386. Esp. 363-373. [NTA 6, 774]

1974    Origenes über Bekenntnis und Fall des Petrus. — *OCP* 40 (1974) 286-313. Esp. 289-297 [16,13-20]; 297-302 [16,21-28]; 302-305 [18,15-18].

**SCHULZ, Anselm**

1962 *Nachfolgen und Nachahmen. Studien über das Verhältnis der neutestamentlichen Jüngerschaft zur urchristlichen Vorbildethik* (SANT, 6). München: Kösel, 1962, 349 p. Esp. 33-49: "Lehrer und Schüler in den Evangelien"; 63-133: "Die Nachfolge Jesu in den synoptischen Evangelien"; 158-161: "Spuren des urchristlichen μαϑητής-Begriff im Matthäus-Evangelium". — Diss. München, 1959 (J. Schmid).

1964 *Jünger des Herrn. Nachfolge Christi nach dem Neuen Testament*. München: Kösel, 1964, 120 p. Esp. 17-38: "Der ursprüngliche Sinn der Nachfolge"; 40-53: "Die Wandlungen des 'Nachfolge'- und 'Schülerbegriffs' in der Synopse".
*Suivre et imiter le Christ d'après le Nouveau Testament*, trans. J.L. Klein (Lire la Bible, 5). Paris: Cerf, 1966, 118 p.
*Discípulos del Señor*. Barcelona: Herder, 1967, 115 p.

1967 *Unter dem Anspruch Gottes. Das neutestamentliche Zeugnis von der Nachahmung* (Kleine Schriften zur Theologie). München: Kösel, 1967, 106 p. Esp. 19-23 [5,43-48].

1969 Grundformen urchristlicher Paränese. — SCHREINER, J. - DAUTZENBERG, G. (eds.), *Gestalt und Anspruch*, 1969, 249-261. Esp. 256-258.

**SCHULZ, Hans-Joachim**

1993 *Die apostolische Herkunft der Evangelien* (QDisp, 145). Freiburg: Herder, 1993, 411 p. Esp. 34-78: "Die überlieferten Verfasser und Datierungen der Evangelien"; 218-242: "Das Matthäusevangelium: Kirche und apostolische Autorität nach dem Martyrium Petri" [16,18-19; 17,24-27; 22,7; 24,2].
→ Schelbert 1994

**SCHULZ, Siegfried**

1962 Maranatha und Kyrios Jesus. — *ZNW* 53 (1962) 125-144. Esp. 139-143. [NTA 7, 768]

1967 *Die Stunde der Botschaft. Einführung in die Theologie der vier Evangelisten*. Hamburg: Furche, 1967, 392 p.; Zürich: Zwingli, ²1970; Bielefeld: Luther-Verlag, ³1982. Esp. 157-234: "Matthäus".

1972a *Q. Die Spruchquelle der Evangelisten*. Zürich: Theologischer Verlag, 1972, 508 p. Esp. 11-44: "Der Stand der Erforschung der Q-Quelle"; 45-53: "Die traditionsgeschichtliche Analyse von Q"; 55-489: "Das Kerygma der judenchristlichen Q-Gemeinden" (57-176: "A. Das Kerygma der ältesten Q-Gemeinde des Palästinensisch-Syrischen Grenzraumes" [Q 6,20-21.27-28.29-30.31.32-36.37-38.41-42; 11,1-4.9-13.39-52; 12,4-7.8-9.22-31.33-34; 16,18]; 177-489: "B. Das Kerygma der jüngeren Q-Gemeinden Syriens" [Q 3,7-18; 4,1-13; 6,22-23.39.40.43-45.46.47-49; 7,1-10.18-23.24-28.31-35; 9,57-60; 10,2-12.13-15.16.21-22.23-24; 11,14-23.24-26.29-32.33.34-35.49-51; 12,2-3.10.11-12.39-40.42-46.51-53.57-59; 13,18-19.20-21.23-24.26-27.28-29.34-35; 15,4-7; 16,13.16; 17,3-4.5-6.23-37; 18,14; 19,12-27; 22,28-30]). → Luz 1973, Sabourin 1973
> T. BAARDA, *GTT* 73 (1973) 181-182; E. BAASLAND, *TidsTeolKirk* 47 (1976) 58; M.-É. BOISMARD, *RB* 81 (1974) 141-142; M. BOUTTIER, *ETR* 50 (1975) 86-87; J. DUPONT, *TRev* 70 (1974) 107-109; R.A. EDWARDS, *JBL* 94 (1975) 609-612; P. HOFFMANN, *BZ* 19 (1975) 104-115; K. HRUBY, *Judaica* 29 (1973) 126-127; J. HUG, *Choisir* 16 (1975) 36-37; J. LINMANS, *TijdTheol* 14 (1974) 307-308; D. LÜHRMANN, *EvKom* 7 (1974) 244-245; G.P. LUTTIKHUIZEN, *VoxTheol* 45 (1975) 60; D.L. MEALAND, *ScotJT* 30 (1977) 486-487; O. MICHEL, *TBeitr* 5 (1974) 93-94; A. MYRE, *SE* 26 (1974) 340-341; H. RÄISÄNEN, *TAik* 78 (1973) 391-402; W. WILKENS, *TZ* 31 (1975) 41-42; J. ZUMSTEIN, *RTP* 24 (1974) 63.

1972b *Griechisch-deutsche Synopse der Q-Überlieferungen*. Zürich: Theologischer Verlag, 1972, 106 p.

1972c Die neue Frage nach dem historischen Jesus. — BALTENSWEILER, H. - REICKE, B. (eds.), *Neues Testament und Geschichte*. FS O. Cullmann, 1972, 33-42.

1973 "Die Gottesherrschaft ist nahe herbeigekommen" (Mt 10,7 / Lk 10,9). Der kerygmatische Entwurf der Q-Gemeinde Syriens. — BALZ, H. - SCHULZ, S. (eds.), *Das Wort und die Wörter. Festschrift Gerhard Friedrich zum 65. Geburtstag*, Stuttgart: Kohlhammer, 1973, 57-67.

1975 Der historische Jesus. Bilanz der Fragen und Lösungen. — STRECKER, G. (ed.), *Jesus Christus in Historie und Theologie.* FS H. Conzelmann, 1975, 3-25.

1976 *Die Mitte der Schrift. Der Frühkatholizismus im Neuen Testament als Herausforderung an den Protestantismus.* Stuttgart–Berlin: Kreuz, 1976, 464 p. Esp. 161-199: "Das Matthäusevangelium". → Sabourin 1989

1983 Die Anfänge urchristlicher Verkündigung. Zur Traditions- und Theologiegeschichte der ältesten Christenheit. — LUZ, U. – WEDER, H. (eds.), *Die Mitte des Neuen Testaments.* FS E. Schweizer, 1983, 254-271. Esp. 255-256: "Die Q-Gemeinde"; 258-259: "Die Matthäus-Sondergut-Gemeinde".

1987 *Neutestamentliche Ethik* (Zürcher Grundrisse zur Bibel). Zürich: Theologischer Verlag, 1987, 681 p. Esp. 37-55: "Die Heilsbedeutsamkeit des Mosegesetzes" [5,32.39-42.44-48; 7,12]; 55-83: "Der ethische Radikalismus Jesu" [5,45; 6,9-13.19-21.25-33; 7,1-5.7-11; 8,19-22; 10,5-6.28-31.34-36.38-39; 23; Q 6,20-21; 10,2-12]; 87-128: "Das von Jesus ausgelegte Mosegesetz als Heilsfaktor" [5,18-19.21-22.27-30.33-37.39-42; 6,10-18; 8,11-12; 10,5-6.23; 11,2-6.16-19; 12,5-6.11-12; 17,24-27; 21,28-32; 23,16-22; Q 13,34-35]; 128-135: "Der Weg Gottes" [4,8-9; 10,5-6]; 272-279 [gnostics; 7,16-27; 24,10-12]; 447-466: "Matthäus" [17,24-27; 28,18-20].

**SCHULZE, Wilhelm August**

1956 Das Vaterunser bei Rudolf Steiner. — *EvT* 16 (1956) 427-432.

1975 Zur Geschichte der Auslegung von Matth. 2,1-12. — *TZ* 31 (1975) 150-160. → 1983

1983 Nachtrag zum meinem Aufsatz: *Zur Geschichte der Auslegung von Matth. 2,1-12,* ThZ 31 (1975) 150-160. — *TZ* 39 (1983) 178-181. → 1975

**SCHUPPAN, C.**

1978 *Gottes Herrschaft und Gottes Wille. Eine Untersuchung zur Struktur der Rede von Gott in der Spruchquelle Q im Vergleich mit dem Frühjudentum und den Matthäus- und Lukasevangelien.* Diss. Greifswald, 1978, XXI-160 p.

**SCHURR, Viktor**

1962 Das Zeichen des Menschensohnes. [24,30] — *TGeg* 5 (1962) 113-114.

**SCHUSTER, Hermann**

1956 Die konsequente Eschatologie in der Interpretation des Neuen Testaments, kritisch betrachtet. — *ZNW* 47 (1956) 1-25. [NTA 2, 151]

**SCHUTTER, William L.**

1990 Luke 12:11-2 / 21:12-5 and the Composition of Luke-Acts. — *Proceedings EGLBS* 10 (1990) 236-250.

**SCHWAGER, Raymund**

1978 *Brauchen wir ein Sündenbock? Gewalt und Erlösung in den biblischer Schriften.* München: Kösel, 1978, 239 p. Esp. 156-160 [23]; 161-164 [10,34-36].

1983 & NIEWIADOMSKI, J., Bergpredigt – Gericht – Politik – Friede. — *Stimmen der Zeit* (München) 201 (1983) 687-699. [NTA 28, 491]

1985 Christ's Death and the Prophetic Critique of Sacrifice. — *Semeia* 33 (1985) 109-123. Esp. 111-113, 113-116, 118. [NTA 30, 546]

**SCHWANK, Benedikt**

1962 Die Matthäustexte des Lektionars 1837 im Palimpsestkodex Paris B.N. suppl. grec 1232. — *ZNW* 53 (1962) 194-205. [NTA 7, 777]

1966 Nur Gott (Mt 5,24-33). — *Am Tisch des Wortes* (Stuttgart) 12 (1966) 28-42.

1972 "Dort wird Heulen und Zähneknirschen sein". [8,12] — *BZ* 16 (1972) 121-122. [NTA 16, 859]

1987 Ein griechisches Jesuslogion? Überlegungen zur Antwort Jesu auf die Steuerfrage (Mk 12,16-17 parr.). — BROX, N., et al. (eds.), *Anfänge der Theologie*. FS J.B. Bauer, 1987, 61-64.

**SCHWANKL, Otto**
1987 *Die Sadduzäerfrage (Mk 12,18-27 parr)*. *Eine exegetisch-theologische Studie zur Auferstehungserwartung* (BBB, 66). Frankfurt/M: Athenäum, 1987, XIX-699 p. Esp. 439-442: "Die matthäische Redaktion" [22,23-33]; 525-534 [8,11-12/Q 13,28-29]; 534-539 [11,21-24/Q 10,12-15]; 539-544 [12,41-42/Q 11,31-32]; 545-548 [10,28/Q 12,4-5]; 548-550 [5,29-30]. — Diss. Würzburg, 1986 (R. Schnackenburg).

**SCHWARK, Jürgen**
1973 Matthäus der Schriftgelehrte und Josephus der Priester. Ein Vergleich. — DIETRICH, W., et al. (eds.), *Festgabe für K.H. Rengstorf*, 1973, 137-154.

**SCHWARTZ, Daniel R.**
1985 "Scribes and Pharisees, Hypocrites". Who Are the "Scribes" in the New Testament? — *Zion* (Jerusalem) 50 (1985) 121-132; = ID., *Studies in the Jewish Background of Christianity* (WUNT, 60), Tübingen: Mohr, 1992, 89-101.
1986 The End of the γῆ (Acts 1:8): Beginning or End of the Christian Vision? — *JBL* 105 (1986) 669-676. Esp. 675-676 [10,23]. [NTA 31, 1156]

**SCHWARTZMAN, Sylvan D.**
1953 How Well Did the Synoptic Evangelists Know the Synagogue? — *HUCA* 24 (1952-53) 115-132. Esp. 118-119, 130-132.

**SCHWARZ, Günther**
1969 Matthäus vi.9-13 / Lukas xi.2-4. Emendation und Rückübersetzung. — *NTS* 15 (1968-69) 233-247. [NTA 13, 863]
1970a Matthäus v.13a und 14a. Emendation und Rückübersetzung. — *NTS* 17 (1970-71) 80-86. [NTA 15, 492]
1970b Matthäus vii 13a. Ein Alarmruf angesichts höchster Gefahr. — *NT* 12 (1970) 229-232. [NTA 15, 500]
1972 Matthäus vii 6a. Emendation und Rückübersetzung. — *NT* 14 (1972) 18-25. [NTA 16, 856]
1975 Ἰῶτα ἓν ἢ μία κεραία (Matthäus 5,18). — *ZNW* 66 (1975) 268-269. [NTA 20, 774]
1977a 'Ihnen gehört das Himmelreich'? (Matthäus v.3). — *NTS* 23 (1976-77) 341-343. [NTA 21, 720]
1977b 'Unkenntliche Gräber'? (Lukas xi.44). [23,27] — *Ibid.*, 345-346. [NTA 21, 767]
1978 Καλον το αλας. [5,13] — *BibNot* 7 (1978) 32-35.
1979 Οτι εκρυψας ταυτα απο ... συνετων. [11,25] — *BibNot* 9 (1979) 22-25.
1980a Και βιασται αρπαζουσιν αυτην? (Matthäus 11,12). — *BibNot* 11 (1980) 43-44.
1980b Αγαπατε τους εχθρους υμων Mt 5,44a / Lk 6,27a(35a). Jesu Forderung *kat' exochen*. — *BibNot* 12 (1980) 32-34.
1980c Γαλιλαια των εθνων. [4,15] — *BibNot* 13 (1980) 55.
1980d Προσθεῖναι ἐπὶ τὴν ἡλικίαν αὐτοῦ πῆχυν ἕνα. [6,27] — *ZNW* 71 (1980) 244-247. [NTA 26, 470]
1981a Τὸ δὲ ἄχυρον κατακαύσει. [3,12] — *ZNW* 72 (1981) 264-271. [NTA 26, 464]
1981b Ἄφες τοὺς νεκροὺς θάψαι τοὺς ἑαυτῶν νεκρούς. [8,22] — *Ibid.*, 272-276. [NTA 26, 471]

1981c   Matthäus 10,28. Emendation und Rückübersetzung. — Ibid., 277-282. [NTA 26, 472]

1981d   Zum Vokabular von Matthäus 6,19f. — BibNot 14 (1981) 46-49.

1981e   Zum Vokabular von Matthäus xxv.1-12. — NTS 27 (1980-81) 270-276. [NTA 25, 866]

1983   Απο μακροθεν / επι της οδου. [21,19] — BibNot 20 (1983) 56-57.

1984a   Πιστιν ως κοκκον σιναπεως. — BibNot 25 (1984) 27-35. [NTA 29, 938]

1984b   Συροφοινίκισσα–Χαναναία (Markus 7.26 / Matthäus 15.22). — NTS 30 (1984) 626-628. [NTA 29, 549]

1985a   "Und Jesus sprach". Untersuchungen zur aramäischer Urgestalt der Worte Jesu (BWANT, 118). Stuttgart: Kohlhammer, 1985, ²1987, X-362 p. Esp. 5-51: "Aramäische Wörter im griechischen Grundtext"; 52-119: "Aramaismen, Übersetzungsfehler und Überlieferungsvarianten" [5,13.18.20; 6,27; 8,22; 9,18; 10,16.29; 11,19]; 158-281: "Emendation und Rückübersetzung" [5,3.4.6.11-12.21-22.23.25-26.28.39;6,2-6.9-13.16-18.19-20.22-23;7,6.13-14; 9,16-17; 10,28; 11,12.16-17.25; 12,36]; 303-307 [5,7.8; 11,5; 15,21-28]. → Lachs 1980

1985b   Έγειραι, καὶ σωθήσῃ. — ZNW 76 (1985) 129-130. [NTA 30, 464] → Karavidópoulos 1971

1986   Jesus "der Menschensohn". Aramaistische Untersuchungen zu den synoptischen Menschensohnworten Jesu (BWANT, 119). Stuttgart: Kohlhammer, 1986, X-352 p. Esp. 96-322: "Emendation–Rückübersetzung–Interpretation [5,11-12; 8,20; 9,5; 10,23.32-33; 11,18-19; 12,32.40; 13,37.41-42; 16,13.21.27.28; 17,9.11-12.22-23; 19,28; 20,18-19.28; 24,27.30.37-39.44; 25,31; 26,2.24. 45.64]

1987   Der Nachfolgespruch Markus 8.34b.c Parr. Emendation und Rückübersetzung. [16,24] — NTS 33 (1987) 255-265. [NTA 31, 1099]

1988   Jesus und Judas. Aramaistische Untersuchungen zur Jesus–Judas–Überlieferung der Evangelien und der Apostelgeschichte (BWANT, 123). Stuttgart: Kohlhammer, 1988, X-308 p. Esp. 35-118: "Die Leidens- und Todesansagen Jesu" [5.13; 16,21; 17,11-12.22-23; 20,18-19.22.28; 26,24.39.42.45]; 119-155: "Die Absichten der Feinde Jesu" [12,14; 21,45-46; 26,1-5]; 156-207: "Die Anti-Judas-Tendenz" [10,2.4; 26,14-16.20-25.45-46.47-50; 27,3-8].

1990   Ὁ βλέπων ἐν τῷ κρυπτῷ (κρυφαῖς)? (Matthäus 6,4b.6e.18b). — BibNot 54 (1990) 38-40. [NTA 36, 143]

1991a   Τῆς τροφῆς αὐτοῦ oder τοῦ μισθοῦ αὐτοῦ. [10,10] — BibNot 56 (1991) 25. [NTA 36, 150] → 1992d

1991b   Φίλιππον καὶ Βαρθολομαῖον? [10,2-4] — Ibid., 26-30. [NTA 36, 177]

1991c   Ἀρκετὸν τῷ μαθητῇ ἵνα γένηται ὡς ὁ διδάσκαλος αὐτοῦ? [10,25] — BibNot 58 (1991) 29. [NTA 36, 725]

1991d   Τὴν τροφὴν ([τὸ] σιτομέτριον) ἐν καιρῷ? Mt 24,45 / Lk 12,42. — BibNot 59 (1991) 44. [NTA 37, 153]

1992a   Τὸ πτερύγιον τοῦ ἱεροῦ (Mt 4,5 / Lk 4,9). — BibNot 61 (1992) 33-35. [NTA 37, 131]

1992b   Jesus und der Feigenbaum am Wege (Mk 11,12-14.20-25 / Mt 21,18-22). — Ibid., 36-37. [NTA 37, 178]

1992c   Καθελεῖν oder σώσων? (Mk 15,36 / Mt 27,49). — BibNot 64 (1992) 17. [NTA 37, 1301]

1992d   "Seiner Nahrung" oder "seines Lohnes"? (Mt 10,10e / Lk 10,7c). — BibNot 65 (1992) 40-41. [NTA 37, 1262] → 1991a

1992e   Ἀνοίξας τὸ στόμα αὐτοῦ? (Matthäus 17.27). — NTS 38 (1992) 138-141. [NTA 36, 1277]

1993a   Er "wird einem klugen/törichten Mann ähnlich werden"? (Matthäus 7,24b.26b). — BibNot 68 (1993) 24-25. [NTA 38, 763]

1993b   & SCHWARZ, Jörn, Das Gebet der Gebete (Mt 6,9-13 / Lk 11,2-4). — BibNot 70 (1993) 21-24. [NTA 38, 1363]

1994a   "Er berührte ihre Hand"? (Matthäus 8,15). — BibNot 73 (1994) 33-35. [NTA 39, 803]

1994b  "Ein grosses Beben entstand auf dem Meer"? (Matthäus 8,24). — *BibNot* 74 (1994) 31-32. [NTA 39, 1454]

1994c  "Gebt ... den Inhalt als Almosen"? (Lukas 11,40.41). — *BibNot* 75 (1994) 26-30. [NTA 39, 1495]

1994d  "Reinige ... das Innere des Bechers"? (Matthäus 23,26). — *Ibid.*, 31-34. [NTA 39, 1459]

**SCHWARZ, Virgilia**

1961   Das Menschenbild nach Matthäus. — *BLtg* 34 (1960-61) 117-123, 196-201, 297-300.

**SCHWARZ, Wolfgang**

1984   Die Doppelbedeutung des Judastodes. — *BLtg* 57 (1984) 227-233. Esp. 227-230 [27,3-10]. [NTA 29, 941]

**SCHWEITZER, Albert**

1901[R]  *Das Abendmahl im Zusammenhang mit dem Leben Jesu und der Geschichte des Urchristentums.* I. *Das Abendmahlsproblem auf Grund der wissenschaftlichen Forschung des 19. Jahrhunderts und der historischen Berichte* [1901, ²1929]; II. *Das Messianitäts- und Leidensgeheimnis. Eine Skizze des Lebens Jesu* [1901]. Tübingen: Mohr, ³1956, XII-109 p. Esp. 47.51 [26,26-29].
       *The Lord's Supper in Relationship to the Life of Jesus and the History of the Early Church.* I. *The Problem of the Lord's Supper according to the Scholarly Research of the Nineteenth Century and the Historical Accounts*, trans. A.J. Mattill, ed. J. Reumann. Macon, GA: Mercer University Press, 1982, XI-144 p. Esp. 117.124.
       *The Mystery of the Kingdom of God. The Secret of Jesus' Messiahship and Passion* [1914], trans. W. Lowrie. New York: Macmillan, 1950, XV-174 p.; (Schocken Books, 78), New York: Schocken Books, 1964, 275 p.; Buffalo, NY: Prometheus Books, 1985, XXII-174 p.

1906[R]  *Von Reimarus zu Wrede. Eine Geschichte der Leben-Jesu-Forschung* [1906]; *Geschichte der Leben-Jesu-Forschung* [1913]. Tübingen: Mohr, ⁶1951, XXVIII-659 p. Esp. 604-608: "Die synoptische Frage"; 610-612: "Der Stern der Weisen"; (Siebenstern-Taschenbuch), München-Hamburg: Siebenstern, 1966, 2 vols., 651 p. → Kossen 1960
       *The Quest of the Historical Jesus. A Critical Study of its Progress from Reimarus to Wrede* [1910; ²1911; repr. 1936], trans. W. Montgomery. New York: Macmillan, 1959, IX-413 p.
       *Storia della ricerca sulla vita di Gesù*, trans. F. Coppellotti (Biblioteca di storia e storiografia dei tempi biblici, 4). Brescia: Paideia, 1986, 786 p.
       V. FUSCO, *Una traduzione in ritardo di ottant'anni.* — *CC* 138/4 (1987) 573-576.
       *Investigación sobre la vida de Jesús*, trans. J.M. Rodelas (Clásicos de la ciencia biblica, 4/1). Valencia: Instituto San Jerónimo, 1990, 379 p.

1967   *Reich Gottes und Christentum*, ed. U. Neuenschwander. Tübingen: Mohr, 1967, XII-212 p. Esp. 74-145: "Das Reich Gottes bei Jesus" [74-79: "Die Evangelien des Matthäus und Markus als Quelle"].

**SCHWEIZER, Eduard**

1950   Eine hebraisierende Sonderquelle des Lukas? — *TZ* 6 (1950) 161-185. Esp. 170-172 [Q 11,14(Lk)].

1952a  Matth. 5,17-20 – Anmerkungen zum Gesetzesverständnis des Matthäus. — *TLZ* 77 (1952) 479-484; = ID., *Neotestamentica*, 1963, 399-406; = LANGE, J. (ed.), *Das Matthäus-Evangelium*, 1980, 164-173 ("Nachtrag" [1976], 168-169).

1952b  The Spirit of Power. The Uniformity and Diversity of the Concept of the Holy Spirit in the New Testament. — *Interpr* 6 (1952) 259-278. Esp. 260-264: "Mark and Matthew".

1953   "With the Holy Ghost and Fire". [3,11] — *ExpT* 65 (1953-54) 29. → Flowers 1953

1954   The Reinterpretation of the Gospel by the Fourth Evangelist. — *Interpr* 8 (1954) 387-403. Esp. 396-398 [8,5-13].

1955    *Erniedrigung und Erhöhung bei Jesus und seinen Nachfolgern* (ATANT, 28). Zürich:
        Zwingli, 1955, 167 p. Esp. 7-19: "Die synoptischen Nachfolgeworte" [8,19-22; 10,33.37-39]; ²1962,
        196 p.
        *Lordship and Discipleship* (Studies in Biblical Theology, 28). London: SCM; Naperville, IL: Allenson, 1960,
        136 p. Esp. 11-21.

1956    Gegenwart des Geistes und eschatologische Hoffnung bei Zarathustra, spätjüdischen
        Gruppen, Gnostikern und den Zeugen des Neuen Testamentes. — DAVIES, W.D. –
        DAUBE, D. (eds.), *The Background of the New Testament*. FS C.H. Dodd, 1956, 482-
        508. Esp. 501-502: "Markus und Matthäus"; = ID., *Neotestamentica*, 1963, 153-179. Esp. 172-
        173.

1959a   *Gemeinde und Gemeindeordnung im Neuen Testament* (ATANT, 35). Zürich: Zwingli,
        1959, 217 p. Esp. 44-54: "Die Gemeinde des Matthäus".
        *Church Order in the New Testament* (Studies in Biblical Theology, 32) London: SCM, 1961, 239 p. Esp.
        51-62.

1959b   Der Menschensohn (Zur eschatologischen Erwartung Jesu). — *ZNW* 50 (1959) 185-209.
        Esp. 185-202 [5,11; 8,20; 10,23.32-33; 11,19; 12,32.40; 19,28; 24,27.37.39.44]. [NTA 4, 784]; = ID.,
        *Neotestamentica*, 1963, 56-84. Esp. 56-75.
        The Son of Man. — *JBL* 79 (1960) 119-129. Esp. 120-121 (summary of 1959). [NTA 5, 209] → Vielhauer
        1963

1960    "Er wird Nazoräer heißen" (zu Mc 1.24 Mt 2.23). — ELTESTER, W. (ed.), *Judentum,
        Urchristentum, Kirche*. FS J. Jeremias, 1960, 90-93. [NTA 5, 727]; = ID., *Neo-
        testamentica*, 1963, 51-55.

1963a   The Son of Man Again. — *NTS* 9 (1962-63) 256-261. [NTA 8, 108]; = ID.,
        *Neotestamentica*, 1963, 85-92.

1963b   *Neotestamentica. Deutsche und englische Aufsätze 1951-1963. German and English
        Essays 1951-1963*. Zürich–Stuttgart: Zwingli, 1963, 448 p. → 1952a, 1956, 1959b, 1960,
        1963a

1968    *Jesus Christus im vielfältigen Zeugnis des Neuen Testaments* (Siebenstern-Taschenbuch,
        126). München–Hamburg: Siebenstern, 1968, ²1970, ³1971; Gütersloh: Mohn, ⁴1976,
        ⁵1979, 191 p. Esp. 132-136: "Matthäus. Jesus, Ausleger und Erfüller des Gesetzes".
        *Jesus*, trans. D.E. Green (The New Testament Library). London: SCM Richmond, VA: Knox, 1971, VIII-
        200 p.
        *La foi en Jésus Christ. Perspectives et langages du Nouveau Testament*, trans. M. Roy (Parole de Dieu, 11).
        Paris: Seuil, 1975, 247 p. Esp. 164-169.
        Trans. Japanese 1974.

1970    Gesetz und Enthusiasmus bei Matthäus. — ID., *Beiträge zur Theologie des Neuen
        Testaments. Neutestamentliche Aufsätze (1955-1970)*, Zürich: Zwingli, 1970, 49-70. Esp.
        50-53: "Das Gesetz"; 53-62: "Der Enthusiasmus"; 62-65: "Das Ende der Bergpredigt"; 65-69: "Die
        Gemeinde des Matthäus"; = LANGE, J. (ed.), *Das Matthäus-Evangelium*, 1980, 350-376
        ("Nachtrag" [1976], 368-369). Esp. 351-354; 354-362; 362-364; 364-367.
        Observance of the Law and Charismatic Activity in Matthew. — *NTS* 16 (1969-70) 213-230. Esp. 214-216;
        216-223; 224-226; 226-229. [NTA 15, 129] → 1974e

1971a   The Gospel of Matthew. — MILLER, D.G. – HADIDIAN, D.Y. (eds.), *Jesus and Man's
        Hope*. II, 1971, 339-341.

1971b   Zur Sondertradition der Gleichnisse bei Matthäus. — JEREMIAS, G., et al. (eds.),
        *Tradition und Glaube*. FS K.G. Kuhn, 1971, 277-282. Esp. 278 [13,24-30]; 278-279.281-282
        [7,24-27]; = ID., *Matthäus und seine Gemeinde*, 1974, 98-105. Esp. 99-100; 100.104-105.

1973a   *Das Evangelium nach Matthäus* (NTD, 2). Göttingen: Vandenhoeck & Ruprecht,
        ¹³1973, IV-370 p. Esp. 1-6: "Einführung"; 6-351 [commentary]; Appendices: 10-12: "Reflexionszitate";
        14-16: "Die Geburt Jesu von der Jungfrau"; 28-30: "Gerechtigkeit Gottes"; 33-34: "Zum Problem des

Bösen"; 45-46: "Seligpreisungen"; 55-56: "Söhne Gottes"; 114-117: "Propheten, Weise, Schriftgelehrte und Gerechte"; 124-135: "Die Bergpredigt"; 233-234: "Zum Aufbau von Kapitel 18"; 242-244: "Das Problem der Sünde"; 291-292: "Jesus als Weisheit Gottes"; 314-316: "Wiederkunft Christi"; 349-351: "Vater, Sohn und heiliger Geist". [NTA 18, p. 245]; $^{3/15}$1981; $^{4/16}$1986. → Schniewind 1937, Ziesler 1985
  G. DE RU, KerkT 25 (1974) 260-261; A. EKENBERG, SEÅ 39 (1974) 185-188; L. GROLLENBERG, TijdTheol 14 (1974) 307-308; X. JACQUES, NRT 96 (1974) 1102-1103; O. KAISER, Freiburger Rundbrief 25 (1973) 146; K. KARNER, TZ 31 (1975) 175-177; J. MURPHY-O'CONNOR, RB 83 (1976) 300; L. SABOURIN, Bib 56 (1975) 278-281; K.H. SCHELKLE, TQ 155 (1975) 72-73; J.M. SHERIDAN, CBQ 38 (1976) 593-595; J.A. SHERLOCK, TS 35 (1974) 368-369; W. TRILLING, TRev 70 (1974) 209-211; TLZ 101 (1976) 183-189; N.M. WATSON, AusBR 22 (1974) 41-43.
The Good News according to Matthew, trans. D.E. Green. Atlanta, GA: Knox, 1975, 572 p. Esp. 11-20; 21-536; 27-30; 32-35; 53-56; 61-62; 80-82; 94-95; 178-184; 193-209; 358-360; 372-374; 446-447; 480-482; 532-534. [NTA 20, p. 366]
  J. ASHTON, Month 238 (1977) 28; J.A. BROOKS, SWJT 20/1 (1977-78) 111-112; F.F. BRUCE, EvQ 48 (1976) 177-178; W.P. DE BOER, CalvTJ 14 (1979) 253-260; J. FENTON, Theology 80 (1977) 58-59; M.D. GOULDER, JTS 28 (1977) 277-278; J.W. PRYOR, RTR 36 (1977) 25-26; J.M. REDFORD, CleR 62 (1977) 161-162; G.N. STANTON, ExpT 87 (1975-76) 379; H. WANSBROUGH, ScriptB 7 (1976-77) 41; M. WARD, HeythJ 19 (1978) 306-307.
Matteuksen evangeliumi, transl. P. Luomanen. Helsinki: Kirjapaja, 1989, 384 p.

1973b  Formgeschichtliches zu den Seligpreisungen Jesu. — NTS 19 (1972-73) 121-126. [NTA 17, 971]; = ID., Matthäus und seine Gemeinde, 1974, 69-72.

1973c  Matthäus 21-25. — HOFFMANN, P., et al. (eds.), Orientierung an Jesus. FS J. Schmid, 1973, 364-371; = ID., Matthäus und seine Gemeinde, 1974, 116-125.

1973d  Matthew's View of the Church in his 18th Chapter. — AusBR 21 (1973) 7-14. [NTA 18, 858]
Die matthäische Sicht der Gemeinde in Kapitel 18. — ID., Matthäus und seine Gemeinde, 1974, 106-115.

1973e  Noch einmal Mt 5,17-20. — BALZ, H. - SCHULZ, S. (eds.), Das Wort und die Wörter. Festschrift Gerhard Friedrich zum 65. Geburtstag, Stuttgart: Kohlhammer, 1973, 69-73; = ID., Matthäus und seine Gemeinde, 1974, 78-85.

1974a  Matthäus und seine Gemeinde (SBS, 71). Stuttgart: Katholisches Bibelwerk, 1974, 182 p. [NTA 19, p. 392] → 1971b, 1973b-e, 1974b-d; → Dermience 1985
  F. BRÄNDLE, EstJos 34 (1980) 260; T. EGIDO, EstJos 29 (1975) 104; X. JACQUES, CC 126/2 (1975) 296; J. KAHMANN, TijdTheol 15 (1975) 447; G. LEONARDI, Studia Patavina 23 (1976) 596-597; W. MARXSEN, TLZ 101 (1976) 923-924; L. SABOURIN, Bib 57 (1976) 137-140; A. SALAS, CiudDios 190 (1977) 181; J.M. SHERIDAN, CBQ 38 (1976) 596-597; F. ZEILINGER, TPQ 123 (1975) 405.
Matteo e la sua comunità, trans. G. Delvai Golino (Studi biblici, 81). Brescia: Paideia, 1987, 220 p.
  F. ANTOLIN, EstJos 44 (1990) 280; G. CONTE, Protestantesimo 45 (1990) 220-221; V. PASQUETTO, Teresianum 39 (1988) 539.

1974b  Christus und Gemeinde im Matthäusevangelium. — Ibid., 9-68. Esp. 9-13: "Das Evangelium in der Auseinandersetzung mit Israel"; 15-31: "Der Aufriß des Evangeliums"; 31-42: "Die Gemeinde als das 'Volk das Früchte bringt'"; 42-57: "Die Gemeinde unter Gottes gutem Gesetz"; 57-68: "Die Gemeinde in der Nachfolge Jesu".

1974c  "Der Jude im Verborgenen ..., dessen Lob nicht von Menschen, sondern von Gott kommt". Zu Röm 2,28f und Mt 6,1-18. — Ibid., 86-97. Esp. 86-89.93-97; = GNILKA, J. (ed.), Neues Testament und Kirche. FS R. Schnackenburg, 1974, 115-124. Esp. 115-118.120-124.

1974d  Die Kirche des Matthäus. — Ibid., 138-170. Esp. 138-140: "Syrien als Heimat"; 140-148: "Die Propheten"; 148-151: "Die Schriftgelehrten"; 151-155: "Petrus"; 156-157: "Die Gerechten"; 157-159: "Die Kleinen"; 159-163: "Die Frage des Amtes".
Matthew's Church. — STANTON, G. (ed.), The Interpretation of Matthew, 1983, 129-155. Esp. 129-130; 130-133; 133-135; 135-137; 137-139; 139-141; 141-145; $^2$1995, 149-177. Esp. 149-150; 150-154; 154-155; 155-158; 158-160; 160-162; 162-167.

1974e  The 'Matthean' Church. — NTS 20 (1973-74) 216. [NTA 18, 844] → 1970

1974f  Zur Struktur der hinter dem Matthäusevangelium stehenden Gemeinde. — *ZNW* 65 (1974) 139. [NTA 19, 525]

1976  Christianity of the Circumcised and Judaism of the Uncircumcised. The Background of Matthew and Colossians. — HAMERTON-KELLY, R.G. - SCROGGS, R. (eds.), *Jews, Greeks and Christians. Religious Cultures in Late Antiquity. Essays in Honor of William David Davies* (Studies in Judaism in Late Antiquity, 21), Leiden: Brill, 1976, 245-260. Esp. 246-249 [prophets; law].

1982a  *Die Bergpredigt* (Kleine Vandenhoeck-Reihe, 1481). Göttingen: Vandenhoeck & Ruprecht, 1982, ²1984, 118 p. [NTA 27, p. 98] → Frankemölle 1983c
       E. BEST, *ExpT* 94 (1982-83) 276; L. HARTMAN, *SEÅ* 49 (1984) 191-192; G. SCHMAHL, *TTZ* 92 (1983) 332; V. SUBILIA, *Protestantesimo* 40 (1985) 53-54.
       *El sermón de la montaña*, trans. V.A. Martínez de Lapera (Biblia y catequesis, 12). Salamanca: Sígueme, 1990, 154 p.
       X. ALEGRE, *ActBibl* 27 (1990) 203-204; R. ROBLES, *NatGrac* 37 (1990) 318-319; E. RODRIGUEZ, *CiTom* 120 (1993) 395; R. SANZ VALDIVIESO, *Carthaginensia* 7 (1991) 259.
       *Il discorso della montagna. Matteo cap. 5-7*, trans. M. Fiorillo (Piccola collana moderna). Torino: Claudiana, 1991, 144 p.
       G. DE VIRGILIO, *BibOr* 34 (1992) 57-58; *ParVi* 38 (1993) 71-72; S. JURIÉ, *Angelicum* 69 (1992) 270-271; M. MAROTTOLI, *Protestantesimo* 48 (1993) 61-62; D. SCAIOLA, *CC* 143/3 (1992) 453-454; V. SCIPPA, *Asprenas* 40 (1993) 118-120.

1982b  Zur Frage der Quellenbenutzung durch Lukas. — ID., *Neues Testament und Christologie im Werden. Aufsätze*, Göttingen: Vandenhoeck & Ruprecht, 1982, 33-85. Esp. 35-41; 49-51; 52-54; 68-78.

1983  Mattäus 12,1-8: Der Sabbat – Gebot und Geschenk. Der Weg vom Text zur Predigt. — KIILUNEN, J., et al. (eds.), *Glaube und Gerechtigkeit*. FS R. Gyllenberg, 1983, 169-179.

1985a  Die Christologie von Phil 2,6-11 und Q. — *TZ* 41 (1985) 258-263. [NTA 30, 746]

1985b  The Testimony to Jesus in the Early Christian Community. — *HorizonsBT* 7/1 (1985) 77-98. Esp. 77-85 [Jesus]. [NTA 30, 1256]

1987a  Jesus Christus I. Neues Testament. — *TRE* 16 (1987) 670-726. Esp. 697-698 [Q]; 701-702 [Mt].

1987b  Jesus als das Gleichnis Gottes. — BSTEH, A. (ed.), *Dialog aus der Mitte christlicher Theologie* (Beiträge zur Religionstheologie, 5), Mödling: St. Gabriel, 1987, 85-103. Esp. 94-96 [18,12-14]; 97-98 [8,11-12; 25,34-40].

1989a  *Theologische Einleitung in das Neue Testament* (Grundrisse zum Neuen Testament. NTD Ergänzungsreihe, 2). Göttingen: Vandenhoeck & Ruprecht, 1989, 176 p. Esp. 39-46: "Vorstufen der Evangelien (Q)"; 121-128: "Das Evangelium nach Matthäus".
       *A Theological Introduction to the New Testament*, trans. O.C. Dean. Nashville, TN: Abingdon, 1991, 191 p.
       *Introduzione teologica al Nuovo Testamento*, trans. A. Balestrieri (Nuovo Testamento. Supplementi, 2). Brescia: Paideia, 1992, 203 p.

1989b  Auf W. Trillings Spuren zu Mt 22,1-14. — KERTELGE, K., et al. (eds.), *Christus bezeugen*. FS W. Trilling, 1989, 146-149. → Trilling 1960b

1990  What Q Could Have Learned from Reginald Fuller. — HULTGREN, A.J. - HALL, B. (eds.), *Christ and His Communities*. FS R.H. Fuller = *ATR* SS 11 (1990) 55-67. Esp. 55-56: "The christology of Q"; 56-59: "Son of God"; 59-61: "Servant"; 61-64: "Son of Man"; 64-66: "Wisdom". [NTA 34, 1119]

1991  Aufnahme und Gestaltung von Q bei Matthäus. — OBERLINNER, L. - FIEDLER, P. (eds.), *Salz der Erde*. FS A. Vögtle, 1991, 111-130. Esp. 111-113: "Apophthegmatisierung"; 113-117: "Die Scheidung der Jünger von Israel"; 117-120: "Jesus, Lehrer und Wundertäter"; 120-122: "Jesus, die Weisheit Gottes"; 123-125: "Jesus, der Herr seiner Gemeinde"; 126-129: "Jesus, der kommende Menschensohn und Richter".

1992a   Markus, Begleiter des Petrus? — VAN SEGBROECK, F., et al. (eds.), *The Four Gospels 1992*. FS F. Neirynck, 1992, II, 751-773. Esp. 770-771 [1 Peter/Q-Mt].

1992b   Ministry in the Early Church. — *ABD* 4 (1992) 835-842. Esp. 837-838.

1994a   *Jesus the Parable of God* – *What Do We Really Know about Jesus?* (Princeton Theological MS, 37). Allison Park, PA: Pickwick, 1994, IX-120 p.
*Jesus, das Gleichnis Gottes. Was wissen wir wirklich vom Leben Jesu?* (Kleine Vandenhoeck-Reihe, 1572). Göttingen: Vandenhoeck & Ruprecht, 1995, ²1996, 120 p.

1994b   Die Bergpredigt im Kontext des Matthäusevangeliums. — MAYER, C., et al. (eds.), *Nach den Anfängen fragen*. FS G. Dautzenberg, 1994, 607-617. Esp. 607-611 [christology]; 611-613 [ecclesiology].

1994c   Jesus – Made in Great Britain and U.S.A. — *TZ* 50 (1994) 311-321. Esp. 312-315. [NTA 39, 1418]

**SCHWIENHORST-SCHÖNBERGER, Ludger**

1990    "Auge um Auge, Zahn um Zahn". Zu einem antijüdischen Klischee. — *BLtg* 63 (1990) 163-175. Esp. 171-175 [5,38-39]. [NTA 35, 625]

**SCOBIE, Charles H.H.**

1964    *John the Baptist*. Philadelphia, PA: Fortress; London: SCM, 1964, 224 p.

1969    John the Baptist. — BLACK, M. (ed.), *The Scrolls and Christianity. Historical and Theological Significance* (Theological Collections, 11), London: SPCK, 1969, 58-69.

1984    Jesus or Paul? The Origin of the Universal Mission of the Christian Church. — RICHARDSON, P. - HURD, J.C. (eds.), *From Jesus to Paul. Studies in Honour of Francis Wright Beare*, Waterloo, Ont.: Wilfrid Laurier University Press; Atlantic Highlands, NJ: Humanities Press, 1984, 47-60. Esp. 55-56.

**SCOGNAMIGLIO, Rosario**

1987    "Anthropos apodemon" (Mt 25,14): Problema e stimoli per la cristologia di Origene. — LIES, L. (ed.), *Origeniana Quarta. Die Referate des 4. internationalen Origeneskongresses (Innsbruck, 2.-6. September 1985)* (Innsbrucker theologische Studien, 19), Innsbruck–Wien: Tyrolia, 1987, 194-200.

1989    Il "Padre nostro" nelle esegesi dei Padri. — *ParVi* 34 (1989) 56-59, 136-140, 205-209, 286-288, 378-382, 451-455.

1994    Grazia o profitto? La parabola dei talenti (Mt 25,14-30) nell'esegesi di Origene. — *Nicolaus. Rivista di teologia ecumenico-patristica* (Bari) 21 (1994) 239-261.

**SCORZA BARCELLONA, Francesco**

1978    L'interpretazione dei doni dei Magi nel sermone natalizio di (Pseudo) Ottato di Milevi. — *Studi storico-religiosi* (Roma) 2 (1978) 129-149.

1985    "Oro e incenso e mirra" (Mt 2,11): l'interpretazione cristologica dei tre doni e la fede dei magi. — *AnStoEseg* 2 (1985) 137-147; 3 (1986) 227-245.

1988    La parabola della zizzania in Agostino. A proposito di *Quaestiones in Matthaeum 11*. — *AnStoEseg* 5 (1988) 215-223.

**SCOTLAND, Nigel A.D.**

1986    Conceived by the Holy Spirit, Born of the Virgin Mary. [1,18-25] — *Evangelical Review of Theology* (Exeter) 10 (1986) 27-32.

**SCOTT, Bernard Brandon**

1981a   *Jesus, Symbol-Maker for the Kingdom*. Philadelphia, PA: Fortress, 1981, VIII-182 p.
Esp. 5-22: "Kingdom and parable"; 32-39 [22,1-14]; 39-47 [25,14-30]; 67-73.105-106 [13,31-32]; 73-77.106-107.116-117.173-174 [13,33]; 133-135 [5,39-41]; 135-138 [Q 6,20-23]; 145-148 [11,12]; 148-152 [6,9-13].

1981b  Parables of Growth Revisited: Notes on the Current State of Parable Research. — *BTB* 11 (1981) 3-9. [NTA 25, 449]

1985   The King's Accounting: Matthew 18:23-34. — *JBL* 104 (1985) 429-442. Esp. 429-431: "Matthew as interpreter"; 433-434 [structure]; 434-440 [analysis]. [NTA 30, 579]

1986   Essaying the Rock. The Authenticity of the Jesus Parable Tradition. — *Forum* 2/1 (1986) 3-53. Esp. 11-13 [13,24-30]; 14-15 [13,31-32]; 15 [13,33]; 15-16 [13,44-46]; 16 [13,47-50]; 16-17 [18,12-14]; 17-18 [18,23-35]; 18-20 [20,1-16]; 20-23 [21,33-46]; 23-26 [22,1-14]; 27-29 [25,1-13]; 29-33 [25,14-30]. [NTA 31, 1048]

1988a  Lost Junk, Found Treasure. [13,44-46] — *BiTod* 26 (1988) 31-34. [NTA 32, 605]

1988b  → Funk 1988

1989   *Hear Then the Parable. A Commentary on the Parables of Jesus.* Minneapolis, MN: Fortress, 1989, XII-465 p. Esp. 21-30 [παραβολή]; 30-35 [Thomas/parables]; 56-62 [kingdom]; 80-84 [21,28-32]; 161-174 [22,1-14/Q 14,16-24]; 205-212 [24,45-51]; 217-235 [25,14-30]; 241-242 [21,33-46]; 267-280 [18,23-35]; 281-298 [20,1-15]; 313-316 [13,47]; 316-319 [13,45-46]; 321-329 [13,33]; 343-363 [13,1-9/Mk]; 389-403 [13,44]; 405-407 [18,12-14].

1990   The Birth of the Reader: Matthew 1:1–4:16. — CARROLL, J.T., et al. (eds.), *Faith and History*. FS P.W. Meyer, 1990, 35-54. Esp. 37-43 [1,1-17]; 43-49 [1,18-25]; 49-54 [2].
       The Birth of the Reader. — *Semeia* 52 (1990) 83-102. Esp. 84-88, 88-93, 93-97. [NTA 35, 1124]
            Response: E.S. MALBON, *ibid.*, 176-178.

1991   The Gospel of Matthew. — MILLER, R.J. (ed.), *The Complete Gospels. Annotated Scholars Version*, Sonoma, CA: Polebridge, 1991, ²1992. 55-114.

1993a  The Gospel of Matthew: A Sapiential Performance of an Apocalyptic Discourse. — PERDUE, L.G., et al. (eds.), *In Search of Wisdom*. FS J.G. Gammie, 1993, 245-262. Esp. 249-262 [24: structure].

1993b  & DEAN, M.E., A Sound Map of the Sermon on the Mount. — *SBL 1993 Seminar Papers*, 672-725. Esp. 680-708 [5-7]; = BAUER, D.R. - POWELL, M.A. (eds.), *Treasures New and Old*, 1996, 311-378. Esp. 319-357.

1994   To Impose Is Not / To Discover. Methodology in John Dominic Crossan's *The Historical Jesus*. — CARLSON, J. - LUDWIG, R.A. (eds.), *Jesus and Faith*, 1994, 22-30. Esp. 25-28 [Q].

### SCOTT, Ernest Findlay

1951   *The Lord's Prayer.* New York: Scribner, 1951, VII-126 p.; Toronto, Ont.: Saunders, 1962.
            P.S. ELLIS, JR., *Crozer Quarterly* (Chester, PA) 28 (1951) 260; I.J. MARTIN, *JBR* 19 (1951) 159-160; C.W. QUIMBY, *Interpr* 5 (1951) 355-356; C.C. RYRIE, *BS* 111 (1954) 178.

### SCOTT, Janet W.

1985   Matthew's Intention to Write History. [fulfilment quotations] — *WestTJ* 47 (1985) 68-82. [NTA 30, 106] → Gundry 1982, 1985

### SCOTT, Julius J., Jr.

1990   Gentiles and the Ministry of Jesus: Further Observations on Matt 10:5-6; 15:21-28. — *JEvTS* 33 (1990) 161-169. [NTA 35, 140]

### SCOTT, R.B.Y.

1965   The Sign of Jonah. An Interpretation. [12,39; 16,4] — *Interpr* 19 (1965) 16-25. [NTA 9, 911]

### SCREECH, Michael Andrew

1978   The Magi and the Star (Matthew 2). — FATIO, O. - FRAENKEL, P. (eds.), *Histoire de l'exégèse au XVIe siècle. Textes du Colloque international tenu à Genève en 1976*, Genève: Droz, 1978, 385-409.

**SCRIBA, Albrecht**

1995 *Die Geschichte des Motivkomplexes Theophanie. Seine Elemente, Einbindung in Geschehensabläufe und Verwendungsweisen in altisraelitischer, frühjüdischer und frühchristlicher Literatur* (FRLANT, 167). Göttingen: Vandenhoeck & Ruprecht, 1995, 274 p. Esp. 183-184 [3,11]; 195-196 [24,3]; 200-201 [24,30]; 219-220 [24,37-39]. — Diss. Mainz, 1991-92 (E. Brandenburger).

**SCROGGIE, William Graham**

1948[R] *A Guide to the Gospels* [1948]. London–Glasgow: Pickering & Inglis, repr. 1952, 1958, 1962, 1965, 1967, 1972, 1973, 1979 (paperback), 679 p. Esp. 131-133 [authorship]; 239-328: "St. Matthew".

**SCROGGS, Robin**

1965 The Exaltation of the Spirit by Some Early Christians. — *JBL* 84 (1965) 359-373. Esp. 360-367 [12,32]. [NTA 10, 530]

1972 A New Old Quest? A Review Essay. — *JAAR* 40 (1972) 506-512. → Albright 1971

1989 Eschatological Existence in Matthew and Paul: *Coincidentia Oppositorum*. — MARCUS, J. – SOARDS, M.L. (eds.), *Apocalyptic and the New Testament*. FS J.L. Martyn, 1989, 125-146. Esp. 133-141 [4,12-5,1; 5,17-20.21-48; 11,25-30; 15,1-20; 19,16-22; 22,34-40; 23,23; 25,31-46]; 141-142 [Paul/Mt]; = ID., *The Text and the Times. New Testament Essays for Today*, Minneapolis, MN: Augsburg, 1993, 234-256. Esp. 243-254.

**SEBASTIAN, Vedamuthu**

1994 *Discipleship of the Lord Jesus. Luke 14:25-35. A Biblico-Theological Investigation.* Diss. Pont. Univ. Urbaniana, Roma, 1994, XXXIII-217 p. (T. Federici). Esp. 1-25: "Literary aspects"; 27-28 [Q]; 26-113: "Exegesis of Lk 14:25-35" (= Excerpt 1994, XL-68 p.).

**SEBOTHOMA, Wilfred A.**

1994 Why Did Paul Make So Little of the Birth of Jesus? — *HervTS* 50 (1994) 655-668. [NTA 39, 1566]

**SECCOMBE, David Peter**

1982 *Possessions and the Poor in Luke–Acts* (SNTU, B6). Linz: SNTU, 1982, 298 p. Esp. 84-93 [Q 6,20-23 (Lk)]; 100-101 [Q 14,26-27]; 146-147 [Q 12,22-34].

**SEEBASS, Horst**

1992 *Herrscherverheißungen im Alten Testament* (Biblisch-Theologische Studien, 19). Neukirchen-Vluyn: Neukirchener, 1992, VIII-95 p. Esp. 66-68 [21,5/Zech 9,9].

**SEELEY, David**

1989 Was Jesus like a Philosopher? The Evidence of Martyrological and Wisdom Motifs in Q, Pre-Pauline Traditions, and Mark. — *SBL 1989 Seminar Papers*, 540-549. Esp. 541-544: "The sayings source Q".

1991 Here and There. A Response to James G. Williams. — *Forum* 7 (1991) 243-260. [NTA 38, 736] → J.G. Williams 1989

1992a Blessings and Boundaries: Interpretations of Jesus' Death in Q. — *Semeia* 55 (1992) 131-146. Esp. 132-134 [Q 14,27]; 134-139 [Q 6,22-23]; 139-141 [Q 7,31-35]; 141-143 [Q 11,47-51]; 143-145 [Q 13,34-35]. [NTA 36, 1245]

1992b Jesus' Death in Q. — *NTS* 38 (1992) 222-234. Esp. 222-224: "The deuteronomistic-prophetic understanding of Jesus' death in Q"; 224-234: "A Cynic-Stoic understanding of Jesus' death in Q" [Q 14,27]. [NTA 36, 1246]

1994 *Deconstructing the New Testament* (Biblical Interpretation Series, 5). Leiden: Brill, 1994, XVI-201 p. Esp. 21-52: "Deconstructing Matthew" [5,17-48; 6,14-15; 7,21-23; 12,1-8.36-37; 16,25-27; 19,16-22; 25,31-46; 26,28; 28,19-20].

**SEETHALER, Angelika**

1990 Die Brotvermehrung – ein Kirchenspiegel? [15,32-39] — *BZ* 34 (1990) 108-112. [NTA 34, 1159]

**SEETHALER, Paula**

1972 Eine kleine Bemerkung zu den Stammbäumen Jesu nach Matthäus und Lukas. — *BZ* 16 (1972) 256-257. [NTA 17, 510]

**SEGAL, Alan F.**

1991a Matthew's Jewish Voice. — BALCH, D.L. (ed.), *Social History of the Matthean Community*, 1991, 3-37. Esp. 4-8: "Matthew's positive perspective on Torah" [12,1-8; 15,1-20; 22,34-40]; 8-11: "Peter in Matthew"; 14-23: "Matthew and the incident at Antioch"; 23-25: "Matthew's negative perspective on pharisaism and Jews"; 25-29: "The provenance of Matthew's gospel". → Gundry 1991

1991b Studying Judaism with Christian Sources. — *USQR* 44 (1991) 267-286. [NTA 36, 703]

**SEGALLA, Giuseppe**

1964 La volontà del Figlio e del Padre nella tradizione sinottica. — *RivBib* 12 (1964) 257-284. [NTA 9, 879]

1965 Il figlio non conosce il giorno della parusia (Mt 24,36; Mc 13,32). — *ParVi* 10 (1965) 250-254.

1966 Gesù rivelatore della volontà del Padre nella tradizione sinottica. [6,10; 7,21; 9,13; 12,7.50; 18,14; 20,13-15; 21,31; 22,3] — *RivBib* 14 (1966) 467-508. [NTA 12, 139]

1970 Il testo più antico sul celibato: Mt. 19,11-12. — *Studia Patavina* 17 (1970) 121-137. [NTA 15, 148]

1972a Gesù Messia e Servo Sofferente nella formazione dei discepoli alla fede (Mt 16,13-16.21-23). — *ParVi* 17 (1972) 247-256.

1972b La predicazione dell'amore nella tradizione presinottica. — *RivBib* 20 suppl. (1972) 481-528. Esp. 484-486 [23,23; 24,12]; 487-493 [3,17; 17,5]; 497-500 [10,37]; 500-507 [25,31-46]; 507-512 [22,34-40]; 512-516 [6,24]; 516-527 [5,43-48]. [NTA 19, 80]

1977 "Teologia dei Sinottici". — *Dizionario teologico interdisciplinare*, Torino: Marietti, III, 1977, 370-387. Esp. 371-375.

1979 La cristologia escatologica della *Quelle*. — *Teologia* 4 (1979) 119-168. [NTA 24, 398]

1980a La cristologia nella tradizione sinottica dei miracoli. — *Teologia* 5 (1980) 41-66. [NTA 25, 64]

1980b La cristologia soteriologica dei miracoli nei sinottici. — *Ibid.*, 145-182. [NTA 25, 450]

1980c La ricerca di Dio come ricerca del regno nei sinottici. — DANIELI, G. (ed.), *Quaerere Deum* (Atti della XXV Settimana Biblica), Brescia: Paideia, 1980, 213-233.

1981 Redazione e teologia dei vangeli sinottici. — FABRIS, R. (ed.), *Problemi e prospettive di scienze bibliche*, Brescia: Queriniana, 1981, 303-325. Esp. 314-316 [theology].

1982a Gesù e la sua morte. Rassegna bibliografica. — *RivBib* 30 (1982) 145-156. [NTA 27, 77] → Léon-Dufour 1979b, R. Pesch 1976a, Schürmann 1973

1982b La novità e la libertà della persona di Gesù negli apoftegmi della tradizione sinottica. — *Teologia* 7 (1982) 205-248. [NTA 27, 899]

1983a A proposito di due libri recenti sui Vangeli dell'infanzia. — *Studia Patavina* 30 (1983) 117-130. [NTA 28, 485r] → R.E. Brown 1977, Laurentin 1982a

1983b Tradizione e redazione in Matteo 1-2. Una ripresa metodologica. — *Teologia* 8 (1983) 109-136. [NTA 28, 487] → 1985b, 1986c, 1987b

1985a *La cristologia del Nuovo Testamento. Un saggio* (Studi biblici, 71). Brescia: Paideia, 1985, 208 p. Esp. 98-103 [Q]; 108-115 [Mt].

1985b Matteo 1,18–2,23: dalla tradizione alla storia. — *Teologia* 10 (1985) 170-202. Esp. 171-179: "Critica al metodo ed ai risultati del commento a Mt. 1–2 di R.E. Brown"; 179-184: "Il problema letterario: le tradizioni prematteane sono originali"; 184-195: "Il problema storiografico: storia o leggenda teologica all'origine delle tradizioni prematteana? (English summary, 202). [NTA 30, 563] → 1983b, 1986c, 1987b; → R.E. Brown 1977

1986a *Panorama letterario del Nuovo Testamento* ("Leggere oggi la Bibbia", III/6). Brescia: Queriniana, 1986, 247 p. Esp. 58-64: "Il vangelo di Matteo: un vangelo didattico"; 94-101: "Il problema sinottico".

1986b L'etica di Gesù da Dodd a Dillmann (1951-1984). Una rassegna. — *Teologia* 11 (1986) 24-37 (English summary, 67). [NTA 31, 367]

1986c Matteo 1–2: dalla narrazione teologica della tradizione alla teologia kerygmatica della redazione. — *Ibid.*, 197-225. Esp. 250-216: "La narrazione teologica della tradizione prematteana"; 216-223: "La teologia kerygmatica dell'evangelista". [NTA 31, 1057] → 1983b, 1985b, 1987b

1987a *Panorama teologico del Nuovo Testamento* ("Leggere oggi la Bibbia", III/7). Brescia: Queriniana, 1987, 147 p. Esp. 76-79.

1987b *Una storia annunciata. I racconti dell'infanzia di Matteo*. Brescia: Morcelliana, 1987, 155 p. [NTA 33, p. 253] → 1983b, 1985b, 1986c; → Muñoz Iglesias 1990b
   C. BASEVI, *ScriptTheol* 22 (1990) 1009-1010; A. MODA, *Nicolaus* (Bari) 18 (1991) 398-405; *Studia Patavina* 36 (1989) 168-174; M. ORSATTI, *Humanitas* 42 (1987) 616; *RivBib* 36 (1988) 110-112; M.A. TÁBET, *Annales theologici* 3 (1989) 151-154.

1988 La narración del Evangelio de la Infancia segn S. Mateo. — *Ecclesia* 2 (1988) 281-290.

1989 *Introduzione all'etica biblica del Nuovo Testamento. Problemi e storia* (Biblioteca biblica, 2). Brescia: Queriniana, 1989, 316 p. Esp. 272-275: "Critica al principio del taglione in *Mt*".

1991a Perdono "cristiano" e correzione fraterna nella comunità di "Matteo" (Mt 18,15-17.21-35). — *Studia Patavina* 38 (1991) 499-518. [NTA 36, 1279]

1991b La triplici funzione dell'esperienza nell'etica sapienziale di Gesù. — *Teologia* 16 (1991) 101-146. Esp. 118-122: "I DS della triplice tradizione"; 122-133: "I DS della fronte Q" [Q 6,27-36.39.41-42.43-45; 11,9-12.34-36; 12,6-7.22-31.33-34.54-56; 16,13; 19,26]; 133-135: "I DS presenti solo nel vangelo di Matteo" [6,34; 10,16; 19,12; 26,52]

1993a *Evangelo e Vangeli. Quattro evangelisti, quattro Vangeli, quattro destinatari* (La Bibbia nella storia, 10). Bologna: Dehoniane, 1993, 400 p. Esp. 41-117: "Il vangelo secondo Matteo".

1993b Quattro modelli di "uomo nuovo" nella letteratura neotestamentaria. — *Teologia* 18 (1993) 113-165. Esp. 116-123: "Il modello dell'uomo 'più che giusto', 'figlio del regno' in Matteo". [NTA 38, 1025]

1994 *Cento anni di studi biblici (1893-1993). L'interpretazione della Bibbia nella Chiesa* (Studia Patavina). Padova: Studia Patavina, 1994, 186 p.

**SEGERT, Stanislav**

1984 Semitic Poetic Structures in the New Testament. — *ANRW* II.25.2 (1984) 1433-1462. Esp. 1443 [5,3-12; 6,9-13; 11,17; 21,9; 24,29]; 1446-1453 [3,3; 5,3-12.13.43; 6,9-13; 7,6; 8,20; 11,17; 15,27; 20,16; 23,4].

**SEGUNDO, Juan Luis**

1982 *El hombre de hoy ante Jesus de Nazaret. II.1. Historia y actualidad: Sinópticos y Pablo*. Madrid: Cristiandad, 1982, 599 p. Esp. 67-284: "El Jesus histórico de los sinópticos".
   *Jesus of Nazareth Yesterday and Today*. II: *The Historical Jesus of the Synoptics*, trans. J. Drury. Maryknoll, NY: Orbis; Melbourne: Dove Communications; London: Sheed and Ward, 1985, IX-230 p. Esp. 45-188: "The historical Jesus of the synoptics".

1994 *El caso Mateo. Los comienzos de una ética judeocristiana* (Presencia teológica). Santander: Sal Terrae, 1994, 270 p.
   R. DE ANDRÉS, *RazFe* 230 (1994) 113.

**SÉGURET, Vincent**

1994   La signification spirituelle de la vie insulaire dans les Sermons d'Isaac de l'Étoile. [8,23-27] — *Collectanea Cisterciensia* 56 (1994) 343-358; 57 (1995) 75-92.

**SEIDELIN, Paul**

1951   Das Jonaszeichen. [12,38-42; 16,1-4] — *StudTheol* 5 (1951) 119-131. Jonategnet. — *DanskTeolTids* 15 (1952) 193-205.

**SEIDENSTICKER, Philipp**

1967a  *Die Auferstehung Jesu in der Botschaft der Evangelisten. Ein traditionsgeschichtlicher Versuch zum Problem der Sicherung der Osterbotschaft in der apostolischen Zeit* (SBS, 26). Stuttgart: Katholisches Bibelwerk, 1967, 160 p. Esp. 87-92: "Die Osterüberlieferung nach Matthäus". *La resurrezione di Gesù nel messaggio degli evangelisti. Il messaggio pasquale nell'età apostolica: studio storico-tradizionale del problema*, trans. B. Zappieri (Studi biblici, 45). Brescia: Paideia, 1978, 203 p.

1967b  *Zeitgenössische Texte zur Osterbotschaft der Evangelien* (SBS, 27). Stuttgart: Katholisches Bibelwerk, 1967, 76 p. Esp. 45 [28,17-20]; 50-52 [27,51-53; 28,2-5]. *Testi contemporanei al messaggio pasquale dei vangeli*, trans. B. Zappieri (Studi biblici, 46). Brescia: Paideia, 1978, 88 p.

**SEIM, Turid Karlsen**

1979   "Herre, frels! Vi går under...". Momenter till frelsesforståelsen i den sinoptiske evangelielitteratur. ["Save, Lord! We are perishing...". Elements of the understanding of salvation in the synoptic gospel literature]. — *NorskTeolTids* 80 (1979) 161-175. [NTA 24, 407]

1983   Gudsrikets overraskelse. Parablene om et sennepsfrø og en surdeig. [The surprise of the Kingdom. Parables of the mustard seed and the leaven] — *NorskTeolTids* 84 (1983) 1-17. Esp. 1-7 [13,31-32]; 7-11 [16,5-12]. [NTA 29, 121]

**SEITZ, Oscar J.F.**

1950   Upon this Rock: A Critical Re-examination of Matt 16,17-19. — *JBL* 69 (1950) 329-340. Esp. 334-340: "The interpolated logion, Matt 16,17-19".

1959   Peter's "Profanity". Mark 14,71 in the Light of Matthew 16,22. — *Studia Evangelica* 1 (1959) 516-519.

1960   "What Do These Stones Mean?" — *JBL* 79 (1960) 247-254. Esp. 251-253 [3,8-9]. [NTA 5, 392]

1964a  Gospel Prologues: A Common Pattern? — *JBL* 83 (1964) 262-268. Esp. 263-265: "Prophetic scriptures fulfilled". [NTA 9, 499]

1964b  James and the Law. — *Studia Evangelica* 2 (1964) 472-486. Esp. 474-475 [19,16-22].

1969a  The Commission of the Prophets and "Apostles". A Re-examination of Matthew 23,34 with Luke 11,49. — *Studia Evangelica* 4 (1969) 236-240.

1969b  Love your Enemies. The Historical Setting of Matthew v.43f.; Luke vi.27f. — *NTS* 16 (1969-70) 39-54. Esp. 39-40: "The settings supplied by the evangelists"; 40-42: "The setting implied by the sayings"; 42-45: "Counsels concerning 'loving' and 'hating'"; 49-54: "The Origin of the antithesis in Matthew v.43f.". [NTA 14, 854]

1982   The Rejection of the Son of Man: Mark Compared with Q. — *Studia Evangelica* 7 (1982) 451-465. Esp. 458-465: "Some rejection motifs in the Q tradition" [Q 6,22-23; 7,33-34; 9,58; 11,29-30; 12,10].

**SELBY, Donald Joseph**

1971   *Introduction to the New Testament. "The Word Became Flesh"*. New York – London: Macmillan, 1971, XXIII-530 p. Esp. 45-55: "The quest for sources"; 70-72 [Papias]; 110-145: "Matthew".

**SÉLIS, Claude**

1992    La répudiation dans le Nouveau Testament. — *LumièreV* 41 (1992) 39-49. Esp. 44-46 [19,1-12]; 46-47 [5,31-32]. [NTA 37, 411]

**SELL, Jesse**

1979    Simon Peter's "Confession" and *The Acts of Peter and the Twelve Apostles*. [16,13-19] — *NT* 21 (1979) 344-356. [NTA 24, 679]

1980    Johannine Tradition in Logion 61 of the Gospel of Thomas. [11,27/Jn/Th] — *PerspRelSt* 7/1 (1980) 24-37. [NTA 24, 1063]

**SELLEW, Philip Harl**

1986    *Early Collections of Jesus' Words. The Development of Dominical Discourses*. Diss. Harvard Divinity School, Cambridge, MA, 1986, 296 p. — *DissAbstr* 47 (1986-87) 3453; *SBT* 15 (1987) 268.

1987a    The Last Supper Discourse in Luke 22:21-38. — *Forum* 3/3 (1987) 70-95. Esp. 83-88 [Q 22,28-30]. [NTA 32, 664]

1987b    Reconstruction of Q 12:33-59. — *SBL 1987 Seminar Papers*, 617-668.

1988    Beelzebul in Mark 3. Dialogue, Story, or Sayings Cluster? — *Forum* 4/3 (1988) 93-108. Esp. 98-102: "Literary analysis of the Beelzebul Pericope". [NTA 33, 1150]

1990    Oral and Written Sources in Mark 4.1-34. — *NTS* 36 (1990) 234-267. Esp. 246-249 [13,31-32]. [NTA 34, 1154]

1993    Tracking the Tradition. On the Current State of Tradition-historical Research. — *Forum* 9 (1993) 217-235. [NTA 41, 821]

**SELLIN, Gerhard**

1974a    Gleichnisstrukturen. Zur Auseinandersetzung zwischen D.O. Via, Jr. "Parable and Example Story: A Literary-structuralist Approach" (LingBibl 25/26. 1973, 21-30) und J.D. Crossan, "Structuralist Analysis and the Parables of Jesus" (LingBibl 29/30. 1973, 41-51). — *LingBib* 31 (1974) 89-115. Esp. 97-102. [NTA 19, 81]

1974b    Lukas als Gleichniserzähler: die Erzählung vom barmherzigen Samariter (Lk 10,25-37). — *ZNW* 65 (1974) 166-189. Esp. 185-189 [18,23-35; 20,1-16; 21,28-32; 22,1-14; 25,1-13.14-30]. [NTA 19, 580]; 66 (1975) 19-60. Esp. 20-23 [22,34-40]. [NTA 20, 478]

1978    Komposition, Quellen und Funktion des lukanischen Reiseberichtes (Lk. ix 51–xix 28). — *NT* 20 (1978) 100-135. Esp. 126-132: "Q-Stoff". [NTA 23, 136]

**SELONG, Gabriel**

1971    *The Cleansing of the Temple in Jn 2,13-22. With a Reconsideration of the Dependence of the Fourth Gospel upon the Synoptics*. Diss. Leuven, 3 vols., 1971, VI-194, VI-127 and VII-276 p. Esp. I, 1-66 [survey]; II, 1-24 [Jn 2,13-22/synoptics].

1972    → Van Segbroeck 1972a

**SELVIDGE, Marla Jean**

1984    Violence in Matthew: A Seminal Investigative Essay. — *Proceedings EGLBS* 4 (1984) 209-221.

1985    Violence, Woman, and the Future of the Matthean Community: A Redactional Critical Essay. — *USQR* 39 (1984-85) 213-223. [NTA 29, 514]

**SENDRA, José**

1983    *La identificación de Jesucristo con el pobre en el Evangelio de Mateo I* (Evangelizare, 16). Salamanca: Ceme, 1983, 190 p.

**SENIOR, Donald P.**

1972a  The Fate of the Betrayer. A Redactional Study of Matthew XXVII,3-10. — *ETL* 48 (1972) 372-426. Esp. 374-381: "The setting of the pericope within the passion account"; 381-398: "The formula quotation (XXVII,9-10)"; 398-420: "The narrative context (XXVII,3-8)"; 420-426: "The relation of quotation and context, and the redactional unity of Mt. XXVII,3-10". [NTA 18, 113] → 1975b, 343-397

1972b  The Passion Narrative in the Gospel of Matthew. — DIDIER, M. (ed.), *L'Évangile selon Matthieu*, 1972, 343-357. Esp. 343-349: "A state of the question"; 349-356: "The introduction to the passion (*Mt.*, XXVI,1-16).

1973  *Matthew: A Gospel for the Church* (Herald Biblical Booklets). Chicago, IL: Franciscan Herald, 1973, 78 p. [NTA 18, p. 383]

1974a  *The Gospel of St. Matthew* (Read & Pray, 1). Chicago, IL: Franciscan Herald, 1974, 96 p.

1974b  A Case Study in Matthean Creativity. Matthew 27:3-10. — *BR* 19 (1974) 23-36. [NTA 19, 958]

1975a  *Jesus. A Gospel Portrait.* Cincinnati, OH: Pflaum Standard, 1975, 181 p.; New York – Mahwah, NJ: Paulist, rev. ed., 1992, III-161 p.

1975b  *The Passion Narrative According to Matthew. A Redactional Study* (BETL, 39). Gembloux: Duculot, 1975, 433 p. Esp. 9-27 [26,1-5]; 28-40 [26,6-13]; 41-50 [26,14-16]; 51-65 [26,17-19]; 66-75 [26,20-25]; 76-88 [26,26-30]; 89-99 [26,31-35]; 100-119 [26,36-46]; 120-156 [26,47-56]; 157-191 [26,57-68]; 192-209 [26,69-75]; 210-218 [27,1-2]; 219-262 [27,11-26]; 263-271 [27,27-31]; 272-291 [27,322-44]; 292-334 [27,45-56]; 343-397 (→ 1972a). [NTA 20, p. 113] — Diss. Leuven, 1972 (F. Neirynck).

    F.H. BORSCH, *Interpr* 31 (1977) 73-76; R.E. BROWN, *CBQ* 38 (1976) 259-260; L. DEROUSSEAUX, *MSR* 39 (1982) 98; R.T. FRANCE, *JEvTS* 19 (1976) 137-138; A.S. GEYSER, *ETR* 51 (1976) 527; K. GRAYSTON, *ExpT* 87 (1975-76) 261; M. HUBAUT, *RTL* 8 (1977) 75-80; D.D. HUTTON, *JBL* 96 (1977) 308-309; J. KAHMANN, *TijdTheol* 16 (1976) 326; X. LÉON-DUFOUR, *RSR* 64 (1976) 432-433; J. MURPHY-O'CONNOR, *RB* 83 (1976) 309-311; L. SABOURIN, *BTB* 6 (1976) 106-108; G. SELLIN, *TLZ* 102 (1977) 437-439; W.G. THOMPSON, *TS* 38 (1977) 156-157.

1976a  The Death of Jesus and the Resurrection of the Holy Ones (Mt 27:51-53). — *CBQ* 38 (1976) 312-329. Esp. 312-314: "The general significance of the 'signs'"; 314-321: "The origins of Matthew's special material"; 321-325: "Matthean composition of the death scene"; 325-329: "Matthew's interpretation of the death of Jesus". [NTA 21, 88] → 1976c; → Aguirre Monasterio 1980

1976b  The Ministry of Continuity. Matthew's Gospel and the Interpretation of History. — *BiTod* 82 (1976) 670-676. [NTA 20, 769]

1976c  Escatologia e soteriologia nella passione secondo Matteo. Il significato di Mt 27,51-53. — *La sapienza della croce oggi. Atti del Congresso internazionale, Roma, 13-18 ottobre, 1975.* I: *La sapienza della croce nella rivelazione e nell'ecumenismo*, Torino-Leumann: Elle Di Ci, 1976, 95-105. → 1976a; → Aguirre Monasterio 1980

1977  *Invitation to Matthew. A Commentary on the Gospel of Matthew with Complete Text from The Jerusalem Bible* (Image Books). Garden City, NY: Doubleday & Co., 1977, 277 p. [NTA 22, p. 332]

    P.F. ELLIS, *CBQ* 41 (1979) 175-176.

1979  The Gospel of Matthew and the Ministry of Social Justice. — *Spirituality Today* (Chicago, IL) 31 (1979) 14-25. [NTA 23, 811]

1981  The Gospel of Matthew. — *BiTod* 19 (1981) 7-15. Esp. 7-8 [sources]; 9-10 [structure]; 10-13 [message]. [NTA 25, 457]

1983a  *What Are They Saying About Matthew?* New York – Ramsey, NJ: Paulist, 1983, V-85 p. [NTA 28, p. 87]; revised and expanded ed., New York – Mahwah: Paulist, 1996, III-136 p. Esp. 7-20.107-109: "The setting for Matthew's gospel"; 21-37.109-113: "The sources and structure of the gospel"; 38-50.113-114: "Matthew's view of salvation history"; 51-61.114-116: "Matthew's use of the Old Testament"; 62-73.116-118: "Matthew's attitude to the law"; 74-87.118-121: "Matthew's christology"; 88-104.121-123: "Matthew's view of discipleship and church". [NTA 40, p. 527]

    *ExpT* 95 (1983-84) 191; D.E. GARLAND, *Interpr* 40 (1986) 98-99; H. HUMPHREY, *BTB* 14 (1984) 157-158; H. WANSBROUGH, *CleR* 69 (1984) 63.

    S. GRASSO, *RivBib* 45 (1997) 380; F. NEIRYNCK, *ETL* 72 (1996) 444-445.

1983b  The Foundations for Mission in the New Testament. — ID. – STUHLMUELLER, C., *The Biblical Foundations for Mission*, Maryknoll, NY: Orbis; London: SCM, 1983, ²1984, 139-312. Esp. 141-160: "Jesus and the Church's mission"; 233-254: "The mission theology of Matthew". Trans. Italian 1985.

1985  *The Passion of Jesus in the Gospel of Matthew* (The Passion Series, 1). Wilmington, DE: Glazier, 1985, 200 p. Esp. 17-45: "Preparation for the passion"; 47-161: "The passion of Jesus" [26–27]; 163-184: "The passion of Jesus: Matthew's message". [NTA 30, p. 101]

    K.A. BARTA, *BTB* 17 (1987) 40; D.R. BAUER, *Interpr* 41 (1987) 96.98; F.W. BURNETT, *CBQ* 48 (1986) 573-574; B.R. DOYLE, *AusBR* 36 (1988) 72; F.J. MATERA, *JBL* 106 (1987) 543-544; M.G. REDDISH, *RExp* 83 (1986) 457-458; J.M. REESE, *TS* 47 (1986) 552-553.

    *La passione di Gesù nel Vangelo di Matteo.* Milano: Àncora, 1990.

1986  The New Testament and Peacemaking. Some Problem Passages. [10,34] — *Faith and Mission* (Wake Forest, NC) 4/1 (1986) 71-77. [NTA 31, 835]

1987a  Matthew 18:21-35. — *Interpr* 41 (1987) 403-407.

1987b  Matthew's Special Material in the Passion Story. Implications for the Evangelist's Redactional Technique and Theological Perspective. — *ETL* 63 (1987) 272-294. Esp. 277-290: "Matthew's special material in the passion story" [27,3-10.24-25.51-53]; 290-293: "Implications of the special Matthean interpretation". [NTA 33, 127] → Aguirre Monasterio 1980

1989a  The Gospel of Matthew and Our Jewish Heritage. — *BiTod* 27 (1989) 325-331. Esp. 326-327 [date]; 327-331 [Judaism]. [NTA 34, 605]

1989b  The Jesus of Matthew. Compassionate Teacher, Faithful Son. — *Church* (New York) 5/4 (1989) 10-13. [NTA 34, 606]

1990a  Listening to the Voices. — *BiTod* 28 (1990) 358-363. Esp. 359-361 [26,6-13]; 361-363 [15,21-28]. [NTA 35, 613]

1990b  The Miracles of Jesus. — BROWN, R.E., et al. (eds.), *The New Jerome Biblical Commentary*, 1990, 1369-1373. Esp. 1372.

    *I miracoli di Gesù.* — BROWN, R.E., et al., *Nuovo grande commentario biblico*, 1997, 1800-1805. Esp. 1804.

1990c  & PERKINS, P., Reading Guide: The Gospels and Acts. — ID. (ed.), *The Catholic Study Bible. The New American Bible: Including the Revised New Testament*, New York – Oxford: Oxford University Press, 1990, RG 386-469; 2-65. Esp. 388-405

1992a  The Death of Jesus and the Birth of a New World. Matthew's Theology of History in the Passion Narrative. — *CurrTMiss* 19 (1992) 416-423. [NTA 37, 737]

1992b  Matthew 2:1-12. — *Interpretation* 46 (1992) 395-398.

1992c  Matthew's Account of the Burial of Jesus. Mt 27,57-61. — VAN SEGBROECK, F., et al. (eds.), *The Four Gospels 1992*. FS F. Neirynck, 1992, II, 1433-1448. Esp. 1434-1435: "Resurrection and discipleship"; 1435-1437: "Interlocking motifs of passion and resurrection"; 1437-1442: "Symmetrical schema: an appraisal"; 1442-1446: "Matthew's rendition of the burial account (27,57-61)"; 1446-1448: "The burial narrative and its place in the 'tomb sequence' of Mt 27,57-28,15". → Giblin 1975b, J.P. Heil 1991a, 1991c

1994  Revisiting Matthew's Special Material in the Passion Narrative. A Dialogue with Raymond Brown. — *ETL* 70 (1994) 417-424. Esp. 419-424 [27,51-53]. [NTA 39, 1461] → R.E. Brown 1994a

1995  The Death of Jesus and the Meaning of Discipleship. — CARROLL, J.T. – GREEN, J.B. (eds.), *The Death of Jesus*, 1995, 234-255.

1997 The Lure of the Formula Quotations: Re-assessing Matthew's Use of the Old Testament with the Passion Narrative as Test Case. — TUCKETT, C.M. (ed.), *The Scriptures in the Gospels*, 1997, 89-115. Esp. 90-103: "The lure of the formula quotations"; 103-108: "Situating the formula quotations in the overall context of Matthew's gospel and its use of the Old Testament"; 108-114: "The use of the Old Testament in the passion narrative".

**SERER, Vicente**

1974 Sicología de las bienventuranzas. — *Revista Javeriana* (Bogotá) 82 (1974) 260-267.

**SERIKOFF, Nikolaus I.**

1988 "... und deine Gewalt komme ...". Die arabische Übersetzung des Vaterunsers in al-Ya'qubi's Geschichte und die byzantinisch-arabische konfessionelle Polemik. — *Jahrbuch für Österreichischen Byzantinistik* (Wien) 38 (1988) 235-246.

**SERRA, Aristide**

1977 *Contributi dell'antica letteratura giudaica per l'esegesi di Giovanni 2,1-12 e 19,25-27* (Scripta Pont. Fac. Theol. "Marianum", NS 3). Roma: Herder, 1977, 490 p. Esp. 110-115 [17,1]; 116-121.126-131 [17,1-9].

1985 Dimensioni ecclesiali della figura di Maria nell'esegesi biblica odierna. — *Maria e la Chiesa oggi. Atti del 5° Simposio Mariologico Internazionale (Roma, ottobre 1984)*, Roma: Marianum; Bologna: Dehoniane, 1985, 275-277; = ID., *E c'era la Madre di Gesù (Gv 2,1). Saggi di esegesi biblico-mariana (1978-1988)*, Milano: CENS; Roma: Marianum, 1989, 368-370.

1987 "Entrati nella casa, videro il bambino con Maria sua madre" (Mt 2,11a). — *Servitium* (Bologna) 21 (1987) 361-370.

1991 "Quanto il Signore ha detto, noi lo faremo". Nuove ricerche sugli echi di Es 19,8 e 24,3.7 come formula di alleanza. — CALABUIG, I.M. (ed.), *Virgo, liber Verbi. Miscellanea di studi in onore di P. G.M. Besutti*, Roma: Marianum, 1991, 51-89. Esp. 69-70 [23,3]; = ID., *Nato da donna... (Gal 4,4). Richerche bibliche su Maria di Nazaret (1989-1992)*, Milano: CENS; Roma: Marianum, 1992, 97-140. Esp. 116-117.

1992* & VALENTINI, A. (eds.), *I Vangeli dell'infanzia. XXXI Settimana Biblica Nazionale, Roma 10-14.XI.1990 — Ricerche storico-bibliche* (Bologna) 4/1-2 (1992), 141 and 168 p. I: → Bottino, G. Danieli, da Spinetoli, Estrada Barbier, Panimolle, Rigato 1992a-b; → Leonardi 1990, Testa 1990, Tremolada 1990

**SESBOÜE, Bernard**

1963 Sommeil et réveil. [24,42-44; 25,1-13] — *AssSeign* I/3 (1963) 39-53. Esp. 44-49.

1974 Ministères et structure de l'Église. Réflexion théologique à partir du Nouveau Testament. — DELORME, J. (ed.), *Le ministère et les ministères*, 1974, 347-417. Esp. 389-393.

**SETZER, Claudia J.**

1994 *Jewish Responses to Early Christians. History and Polemics, 30-150 C.E.* Minneapolis, MN: Fortress, 1994, VIII-254 p. Esp. 26-43: "The synoptic gospels" [10,14.17-25; 23,34; 27,62-66; 28,11-15].

**SEVENICH-BAX, Elisabeth**

1993 *Israels Konfrontation mit den letzten Boten der Weisheit. Form, Funktion und Interdependenz der Weisheitselemente in der Logienquelle* (Münsteraner Theologische Abhandlungen, 21). Altenberge: Oros, 1993, XIV-491 p. Esp. 28-30 [3,7-10/Q 3,7-9]; 30-40 [3,11-12/Q 3,16-17]; 45-67 [4,1-11/Q 4,1-13]; 68-103 [5,3-12/Q 6,20-23]; 104-127 [5,39-48/Q 6,27-36]; 127-139 [7,1-5/Q 6,37-42]; 141-151 [7,15-20/Q 6,43-45]; 151-154 [7,21/Q 6,46]; 155-160 [7,24-27/Q 6,47-49]; 160-192 [8,5-13/Q 7,1-10]; 195-202 [11,2-6/Q 7,18-23]; 202-215 [11,7-15/Q 7,24-30]; 215-225 [11,16-

19/Q 7,31-35]; 241-370: "Formkritik: Analysen zur Struktur des Textes Lk 3-7 par." [Q 3,7-9.16-17; 7,18-35]; 371-461: "Analysen zu Struktur und Bedeutung der Rede am Berg und ihres Kontextes" [Q 6,20-49]. [NTA 40, p. 348] — Diss. Münster, 1991-92 (K. Löning).

M. EBNER, *BZ* 38 (1994) 278-281; V. FUSCO, *RivBib* 42 (1994) 224-226; J.S. KLOPPENBORG, *CBQ* 56 (1994) 609-611; H. VON LIPS, *TRev* 90 (1994) 289-291; C.M. TUCKETT, *JTS* 46 (1995) 255-257; R. URO, *JBL* 114 (1995) 514-516.

### SEVENSTER, Jan Nicolaas

1952 *Leven en dood in de evangeliën* (Verkenning en Verklaring, 1). Amsterdam: Uitgeversmaatschappij Holland, 1952, 147 p. Esp. 134-138 [10,28].

1975 *The Roots of Pagan Anti-Semitism in the Ancient World* (SupplNT, 41). Leiden: Brill, 1975, 235 p. Esp. 206-208 [23,15].

### SEVRIN, Jean-Marie

1977 L'Évangile selon Thomas. Paroles de Jésus et révélation gnostique. — *RTL* 8 (1977) 265-292. Esp. 277-280: "Les sources de la matière synoptique de Thomas"; 288-290: "Principes d'une comparaison aux synoptiques". [NTA 22, 655]

1989* (ed.), *The New Testament in Early Christianity. La réception des écrits néotestamentaires dans le christianisme primitif* (BETL, 86). Leuven: University Press / Peeters, 1989, XV-406 p. → B. Aland, Baarda, Beatrice, Boismard, Dehandschutter, Delobel, Tuckett, Verheyden

1989 Un groupement de trois paraboles contre les richesses dans l'Évangile selon Thomas. EvTh 63, 64, 65. — DELORME, J. (ed.), *Les paraboles évangéliques*, 1989, 425-439. Esp. 429-432 [22,1-10/Th 64]; 433-438 [21,33-46/Th 65].

### SEYNAEVE, Jacques

1965 L'Évangile de S. Matthieu. Évangile ecclésiastique. — *RClerAfr* 20 (1965) 162-172. The Gospel according to Matthew. An Ecclesiastical Gospel. — *AfEcclRev* 8 (1966) 23-32. [NTA 10, 898]

1968 "La justice nouvelle" (*Matthieu*, V,17-20). — *Message et Mission. Recueil commémoratif du X^e anniversaire de la Faculté de Théologie de l'Université Lovanium de Kinshasa* (Publications de l'Université Lovanium de Kinshasa, 23), Leuven–Paris: Nauwelaerts, 1968, 53-75.

1969 Perspectives universalistes dans les évangiles de Matthieu et de Luc. [28,16-20] — *RClerAfr* 24 (1969) 162-179.

### SGHERRI, Giuseppe

1980 Eclissi di sole alla passione? Una nota sull'impulsività origeniana e sulla cronologia di due opere. — CROUZEL, H. - QUACQUARELLI, A. (eds.), *Origeniana Secunda*, 1980, 357-362. Esp. 358-362 [27,45].

### SHANER, Donald W.

1969 *A Christian View of Divorce according to the Teachings of the New Testament*. Leiden: Brill, 1969, XI-115 p. Esp. 43-50: "The exception clauses"; 50-57: "Q and the Logia of Jesus"; 67-80: "Criticism and syntheses of Biblical studies".

### SHANKS, Hershel

1963 Is the Title "Rabbi" Anachronistic in the Gospels? — *JQR* 53 (1962-63) 337-345.

### SHARMA, Arvind

1973 Matthew 16:13-16 – An Exegetical Study. — *Jeevadhara* 3 (1973) 187-194. [NTA 18, 111]

### SHAW, Alan

1955 Faith in the Healing Miracles of the Synoptic Gospels. — *Theology* 58 (1955) 291-297. Esp. 294-297.

**SHAW, R.H.**

1965 A Conjecture on the Signs of the End. [24,3.15-16.20.29] — *ATR* 47 (1965) 96-102. [NTA 9, 940]

**SHEA, John J.**

1986 Christian Faith and the Temptations of Christ. — *ChSt* 25 (1986) 65-78. Esp. 68-72 [4,1-11].

**SHEARER, Thomas**

1957 The Concept of 'Faith' in the Synoptic Gospels. — *ExpT* 69 (1957-58) 3-6. [NTA 2, 277]

**SHEERIN, Daniel**

1976 St. John the Baptist in the Lower World. — *VigChr* 30 (1976) 1-22. Esp. 7-16 [11,3].

**SHELTON, James B.**

1991 *Mighty in Word and Deed. The Role of the Holy Spirit in Luke–Acts.* Peabody, MA: Hendrickson, 1991, 196 p.
*"Filled with the Holy Spirit". A Redactional Motif in Luke's Gospel.* Diss. Univ. of Stirling, 1982, VI-510 p. Esp. 8-10 [spirit]; 26-28 [John the baptist]; 40-43 [14,1-2]; 75-78 [3,1-6]; 90-93.113-118 [3,7-12]; 94-98 [Q 3,7-10.16-17]; 153-155 [11,13]; 173-298 [Lk 4,14-30(Q)]; 323-366 [Q 11,14-23.29-32; 12,10-12]; 367-377 [Q 10,21-24]; 377-388 [Q 11,2-4].

**SHEPHERD, Massey H., Jr.**

1956 The Epistle of James and the Gospel of Matthew. — *JBL* 75 (1956) 40-51. Esp. 41-47 [parallels]; 47-50 [relationship]; = ALAND, K., et al., *The Authorship and Integrity of the New Testament* (Theological Collections, 4), London: SPCK, 1965, 98-112. Esp. 100-107; 107-112.

1961 Are Both the Synoptics and John Correct about the Date of Jesus' Death? — *JBL* 80 (1961) 123-132. Esp. 129-130. [NTA 6, 94] → Jaubert 1957

**SHEPHERD, Tom**

1991 Intercalation in Mark and the Synoptic Problem. — *SBL 1991 Seminar Papers*, 687-697. Esp. 691-693; 693-694 [9,18-26/Mk 5,21-43].

**SHEPPARD, John Bunyan**

1965 *A Study of the Parables Common to the Synoptic Gospels and the Coptic Gospel of Thomas.* Diss. Emory Univ., 1965, 455 p. — *DissAbstr* 26 (1965-66) 2360.

**SHERIDAN, J. Mark**

1973 Disciples and Discipleship in Matthew and Luke. — *BTB* 3 (1973) 235-255. Esp. 243-252: "Matthew's picture of the disciples". [NTA 18, 845]

1998 *Rufus of Shotep. Homilies on the Gospels of Matthew and Luke. Introduction, Text, Translation, Commentary.* Roma: C.I.M., 1998, 360 p. Esp 1-125 [text]; 127-164 [translation]; 280-296: "Specific interpretations of Matthew's gospel". — Diss. Catholic University of America, Washington, DC, 1990 (D. Johnson).

**SHERRIFF, J.M.**

1980 Matthew 25:1-13. A Summary of Matthaean Eschatology? — LIVINGSTONE, E.A. (ed.), *Studia Biblica 1978*, II, 1980, 301-305.

**SHERWIN-WHITE, A.N.**

1963 *Roman Society and the Roman Law in the New Testament.* The Sarum Lectures, 1960-61). New York – London: Oxford University Press, 1963, XII-204 p.

**SHERWOOD, Stephen K.**

1993 Jesus' True Relatives. [12,46-50] — *EphMar* 43 (1993) 91-99. [NTA 38, 162]

**SHINN, Roger L.**

1962 *The Sermon on the Mount*. Philadelphia, PA: The United Church Press, 1962, 112 p.

**SHIRAH, T.Q.**

1983 *The Teachings of the New Testament Concerning Marriage Dissolution and Subsequent Relationships*. Diss. New Orleans Baptist Theol. Sem., 1983, 251 p. — *DissAbstr* 44 (1983-84) 1111.

**SHIROCK, Robert**

1992 Whose Exorcists Are They? The Referents of οἱ υἱοὶ ὑμῶν at Matthew 12.27 / Luke 11.19. — *JSNT* 46 (1992) 41-51. [NTA 37, 145]

**SHISHA-HALEVY, Ariel**

1983 "Middle Egyptian" Gleanings: Grammatical Notes on the "Middle Egyptian" Text of Matthew. — *Chronique d'Égypte* (Bruxelles) 58 (1983) 311-329. [NTA 29, 513r] → H.-M. Schenke 1981

**SHOGREN, Gary S.**

1992 Forgiveness (NT). — *ABD* 2 (1992) 835-838. Esp. 836-837.

**SHOONER, H.-V.**

1956 La *Lectura in Matthaeum* de S. Thomas (Deux fragments inédits et la *Reportatio* de Pierre d'Andria). — *Angelicum* 33 (1956) 121-142. Esp. 138-142 [edition].

**SHR, Yichou**

1992 *Three Dimensions of Community in the Gospel of Matthew: Righteousness, Compassion, and Worship*. Diss. Southern Baptist Theol. Sem., Louisville, KY, 1992, 240 p. (W.E. Ward). — *DissAbstr* 53 (1992-93) 1549.

**SHRIVER, Donald W.**

1967 The Prayer That Spans the World. An Exposition: Social Ethics and the Lord's Prayer. — *Interpr* 21 (1967) 274-288. [NTA 12, 152]

1980 *The Social Ethics of the Lord's Prayer*. Madras: CLS, 1980, VI-75 p.

**SHULER, Philip Lester**

1980 The Griesbach Hypothesis and Gospel Genre. — *PerkJourn* 33/4 (1980) 41-49. [NTA 25, 65]

1982 *A Genre for the Gospels. The Biographical Character of Matthew*. Philadelphia, PA: Fortress, 1982, X-131 p. Esp. 1-23.110-113: "The problem under consideration"; 24-57.114-118: "A genre for the gospels"; 58-87.118-20: "Genre examples"; 88-106.120-123: "The relationship of Matthew to biography". [NTA 27, p. 99] — Diss. McMaster Univ., Hamilton, Ont., 1975 (E.P. Sanders).

   D.L. BARR, *SecCent* 3 (1983) 189-190; J.A. DARR, *JRel* 65 (1985) 273-274; G. GREENFIELD, *SWJT* 26/1 (1983-84) 110; R.H. GUNDRY, *The Reformed Journal* (Grand Rapids, MI) 33/6 (1983) 28.30; C.R. HOLLADAY, *JBL* 103 (1984) 474-475; S.E. PORTER, *JEvTS* 26 (1983) 480-482; S.M. PRAEDER, *CBQ* 45 (1983) 708-709; J.W. THOMPSON, *RestQ* 27 (1984) 237-238.

1983 Genre Criticism and the Synoptic Problem. — FARMER, W.R. (ed.), *New Synoptic Studies*, 1983, 467-480. Esp. 475-478 [genre].

1987 The Genre of the Gospels and the Two Gospel Hypothesis. — SANDERS, E.P. (ed.), *Jesus, the Gospels, and the Church*. FS W.R. Farmer, 1987, 69-88. Esp. 74-77.

1990a The Genre(s) of the Gospels. — DUNGAN, D.L. (ed.), *The Interrelations of the Gospels*, 1990, 459-483. Esp. 468-471 [biography]. → Stuhlmacher 1990

1990b Philo's Moses and Matthew's Jesus: A Comparative Study in Ancient Literature. — *The Studia Philonica Annual* (Brown Judaic Studies, 226; Atlanta, GA) 2 (1990) 86-103. Esp. 97-102.

1990c → W.R. Farmer 1990b

1992a Luke 1–2. — *SBL 1992 Seminar Papers*, 82-97. Esp. 83-85 [1,1]; 86-91 [1,18-25]; 92-94 [1,18–2,23].

1992b → W.R. Farmer 1992a/93/94/95

**SIBER, Peter**

1979 Eingeladen zu Entlastetem Leben. Die Arbeiter im Weinberg (Mattäus 2,1-15). — STEINER, A. – WEYMANN, V. (eds.), *Gleichnisse Jesu*, 1979, 169-189.

**SICARI, Antonio Adeonato**

1971 "Ioseph iustus" (Matteo 1,19): La storia dell'interpretazicne e le nuove prospettive. — *EstJos* 25 = *CahJos* 19 (1971) 62-83. Esp. 63-71 [history of interpretation]; 71-82 [1,18-25/OT]. [NTA 16, 850]

1980 La liberazione e le Beatitudini. L'annuncio della fortezza cristiana. — *Communio* (Madrid) 2 (1980) 5-26.

1986 En el principio era la bienaventuranza de la pobreza. — *Ccmmunio* (Madrid) 8/5 (1986) 462-469.
"Au commencement" était la Béatitude de la pauvreté. — *Communio* (Paris) 11/5 (1986) 8-17.

1991a La consolazione degli afflitti. Interpretazione cristologica della seconda beatitudine. — *Communio* (Milano) 119 (1991) 22-28.

1991b The Hunger and Thirst of Christ. [5,6] — *Communio* (Notre Dame, IN) 18 (1991) 590-602. [NTA 36, 1261]

**SICKENBERGER, Joseph**

1933R Drei angebliche Hinweise auf die Matthäuspriorität. [1953] — LANGE, J. (ed.), *Das Matthäus-Evangelium*, 1980, 65-72. Esp. 66-69 [13,8.23/Mk]; 69-70 [22,36/Mk]; 70-72 [19,18/Mk].

**SICRE DÍAZ, José Luis**

1977 El uso del Salmo 118 en la cristología neotestamentaria. — *EstE* 52 (1977) 73-90. Esp. 80-82 [21,42]; 85 [21,9]; 88-89. [NTA 21, 888]
Psalm 118 and New Testament Christology. — *TDig* 28 (1978) 140-144

1991 Temas selectos de San Mateo. I. La Infancia de Jesús. II. Tríptico introductorio. III. El Sermón del monte I. — *Proyección* (Granada) 38 (1991) 3-18, 101-110, 263-274.

1992 El Sermón del monte II. La actitud cristiana ante la ley. III. La actitud ante las obras de piedad. IV. La actitud ante el dinero y el próximo. — *Proyección* 39 (1992) 3-10, 95-102, 193-204.

1994 Jesús poderoso en obras (Mt 8–9). I. El problema de los milagros. II. Comentario. — *Proyección* 41 (1994) 3-17, 259-275.

**SIDEBOTTOM, E. Malcolm**

1956 'Reward' in Matthew v.46, etc. — *ExpT* 67 (1955-56) 219-220.

1976 The So-called Divine Passive in the Gospel Tradition. — *ExpT* 87 (1975-76) 200-204. Esp. 200-201. [NTA 20, 765]

**SIDER, John W.**

1981 The Meaning of *Parabole* in the Usage of the Synoptic Evangelists. — *Bib* 62 (1981) 453-470. Esp. 462-464 [12,1-8]; 468 [13,34-35]. [NTA 26, 457]

1984 Interpreting the Hid Treasure. [13,44] — *Christian Scholar's Review* (Grand Rapids, MI) 13 (1984) 360-372. [NTA 29, 530] → P.S. Hawkins 1983

1985 Proportional Analogy in the Gospel Parables. — *NTS* 31 (1985) 1-23. Esp. 1-8: "Proportion"; 8-12: "Equation"; 12-16: "Ellipsis"; 16-21: "Extension". [NTA 29, 922]

1995 *Interpreting the Parables. A Hermeneutical Guide to Their Meaning.* Grand Rapids, MI: Zondervan, 1995, 283 p.

**SIDER, Ronald J.**

1980 Christ and Power. [5,39] — *International Review of Mission* (Genève) 69 (1980) 8-20. [NTA 24, 982]

**SIDERA, Jaume**

1993 L'us des evangelis en l'Apologia de Justí. — RAURELL, F., et al. (eds.), *Tradició i traducció.* FS G. Camps, 1993, 347-353.

**SIEBEN, Hermann Josef**

1983 *Exegesis Patrum. Saggio bibliografico sull'esegesi biblica dei Patri della Chiesa* (Sussidi Patristici, 2). Roma: Istituto Patristico Augustinianum, 1983, 150 p. Esp. 50-69; 128.

1991 *Kirchenväterhomilien zum Neuen Testament. Ein Repertorium der Textausgaben und Übersetzungen. Mit einem Anhang der Kirchenväterkommentare* (Instrumenta Patristica, 22). Steenbrugge: St. Pietersabdij; Den Haag: Nijhoff, 1991, 202 p. Esp. 15-56: "Repertorium der Textausgaben und Übersetzungen" [Mt]; 185-186 [ComMt]; 202.

**SIEBER, John Harold**

1966 *A Redactional Analysis of the Synoptic Gospels with Regard to the Question of the Sources of the Gospel according to Thomas.* Diss. Claremont Graduate School, 1966, VII-274 p. (J.M. Robinson). Esp. 21-24 [13,53-58/Th 31]; 25-39 [5,3-12; Q 6,20-23/Th 54.68-69]; 40-48 [5,13-16; Q 11,33/Th 32.33b]; 49-55 [6,1-18/Th 62b]; 56-61 [6,19-21; Q 12,33-34/Th 76b]; 62 [6,22-23; Q 11,34-36/Th 24]; 63-69 [6,25-34; Q 12,22-31/Th 36]; 70-75 [7,3-5; Q 6,41-42/Th 26]; 76-80 [7,6/Th 93]; 81-84 [7,7-11; Q 11,9-13/Th 92.94]; 85-91 [7,16; 12,34-35; Q 6,44-45/Th 45]; 92-95 [8,18-22; Q 9,57-60/Th 86]; 96-105 [9,14-17/Th 47.104]; 106-112 [10,26-27; Q 12,2-3/Th 5.6.33a]; 113-118 [10,34-36; Q 12,51-53/Th 10.16]; 119-126 [10,37-39; Q 14,26-27/Th 55.101]; 127-133 [11,7-11; Q 7,24-28/Th 46.78]; 134-136 [11,25-27; Q 10,21-22/Th 61]; 137-140 [11,28-30/Th 90]; 141-144 [12,29; Q 11,21/Th 35]; 145-149 [12,31-32; Q 12,10/Th 44]; 150-154 [12,46-50/Th 99]; 155-162 [13,3-9/Th 9]; 163-166 [13,12; 26,29; Q 19,26/Th 41]; 167-170 [13,24-30/Th 57]; 171-180 [13,31-33; Q 13,18-21/Th 20.96]; 181-186 [13,44-46; Th 76a.109]; 187-190 [13,47-50/Th 8]; 191-196 [15,1-20; Q 6,39/Th 14c.34.40]; 197 [16,13-20/Th 13a]; 198-200 [18,1/Th 12a]; 201-204 [17,20; 21,21; Q 17,6/Th 48.106]; 205-207 [8,12-14; Q 15,4-7/Th 107]; 208-210 [9,37-38; 10,16; Q 10,2.7-8/Th 14b.39b.73]; 227-230 [24,37-40; Q 17,26-35/Th 61a]; 236-240 [21,33-41/Th 65.66]; 241-243 [22,11-14; Q 14,16-24/Th 64]; 244-248 [22,15-22/Th 100]; 249 [22,34-40/Th 25]; 250-254 [23,13.25; Q 11,39.52/Th 39a.89]; 255-259 [24,43-44; Q 12,39-40/Th 21b.103].

1990 The Gospel of Thomas and the New Testament. — GOEHRING, J.E., et al. (eds.), *Gospel Origins.* FS J.M. Robinson, 1990, 64-73.

**SIEG, Franciszek**

1995 Syn Człowieczy-Masjasz-Syn Bozy i Szymon Piotr (Mt 16:13-20). [The Son of Man, the Messiah, the Son of God and Simon Peter (Mt 16,13-20)] — *Bobolanum* (Warszawa) 6 (1995) 27-48. [NTA 40, 175]

**SIEGMAN, Edward F.**

1956 The Stone Hewn from the Mountain (Daniel 2). — *CBQ* 18 (1956) 364-379. Esp. 375-376 [Ps 117(118),22-23/Mt 21,42].

1961 Teaching in Parables (Mk 4,10-12; Lk 8,9-10; Mt 13,10-15). — *CBQ* 23 (1961) 161-181. Esp. 170 [13/Mk]; 172-177 [13,10-15/Mk 4,10-12]. [NTA 6, 138]

1968 St. John's Use of the Synoptic Material. — *CBQ* 30 (1968) 182-198. Esp. 182-186: "History of the problem"; 186-194: "Analysis and comparison" [8,5-13]. [NTA 13, 233]

**SIEMENS, Peter**

1994 *Carl Friedrich Keil (1807-1888). Leben und Werk* (TVG: Monographien und Studienbücher). Gießen: Brunnen, 1994, X-355 p. Esp. 214-217: "Das Matthäusevangelium".

**SIEVERS, Joseph**

1981 "Where Two or Three...": The Rabbinic Concept of *Shekhinah* and Matthew 18,20. — FINKEL, A. – FRIZZELL, L. (eds.), *Standing before God*. FS J.M. Oesterreicher, 1981, 171-182. Esp. 175-176: "The context of Matt 18,20"; 176-179: "Analysis of Matthew 18,20"; = *SIDIC* 17/1 (1984) 4-10. [NTA 32, 1115]
Là où deux ou trois ... Le concept rabbinique de Shekhina et Matthieu 18,20. — *SIDIC* 17/1 (1984) 4-11. "Dove due o tre...". Il concetto rabbinico di "Shekhinah" e Matteo 18 20. — *Nuova Umanità* (Roma) 4/20 (1982) 56-71.

**SIGAL, Phillip**

1981 Aspects of an Inquiry into Dual Covenant Theology. — *HorizonsBT* 3 (1981) 181-209. Esp. 194-197, 200-201 [28,20].

1982 Matthean Priority in the Light of Mark 7. [15,1-20] — *Proceedings EGLBS* 2 (1982) 76-95.

1983a Another Note to 1 Corinthians 10.16. [26,27] — *NTS* 29 (1983) 134-139. [NTA 27, 646]

1983b Aspects of Mark Pointing to Matthean Priority. — FARMER, W.R. (ed.), *New Synoptic Studies*, 1983, 185-208. Esp. 190-194 [13,1-23/Mk]; 195-205 [15,1-20/Mk].

1983c Further Thoughts on Matthean Priority. — *Proceedings EGLBS* 3 (1983) 122-135. Esp. 124-125 [15,1]; 125-129 [12,1-14].

1984 Early Christian and Rabbinic Liturgical Affinities: Exploring Liturgical Acculturation. — *NTS* 30 (1984) 63-90. Esp. 73-75 [6,9-13]. [NTA 28, 1239]

1986 *The Halakhah of Jesus of Nazareth according to the Gospel of Matthew.* New York: University Press of America, 1986, XI-269 p. Esp. 1-27.160-173: "Introduction" [5,17-20; 22,41-46]; 83-118.212-226: "The Matthean Jesus and the halakhah of divorce"; 119-153.227-246: "The Matthean Jesus and the Sabbath halakhah". [NTA 30, p. 357] — Diss. Theol. Sem., Pittsburgh, PA, 1979 (D.R.A. Hare). → H. Falk 1990, Swidler 1989
  J.M. CASCIARO RAMIREZ, *ScriptTheol* 20 (1988) 343-344; R.H. FULLER, *RelStR* 13 (1987) 262; A.J. SALDARINI, *JQR* 79 (1988-89) 88-89; G.S. SLOYAN, *Judaism* 37 (1988) 122-124; B.T. VIVIANO, *CBQ* 49 (1987) 518-519.

**SIJPESTEIJN, Pieter J.**

1984 Matthäus 1,19-20 auf einem Ostrakon. — *ZPapEp* 55 (1984) 145.

**SIKER, Jeffrey Stephen**

1990 *Disinheriting the Jews: The Use of Abraham in Early Christian Controversy with Judaism from Paul Through Justin Martyr.* Louisville, KY: Westminster/Knox, 1990, 497 p. — *DissAbstr* 50 (1989-90) 2099.

**SILBERMAN, Lou H.**

1979 Whence *Siglum* Q? A Conjecture. — *JBL* 98 (1979) 287-288. [NTA 24, 73] → Neirynck 1979c, J.J. Schmitt 1981

1983 Schoolboys and Storytellers: Some Comments on Aphorisms and *Chriae*. — *Semeia* 29 (1983) 109-115. Esp. 113-114 [18,1-5]. → J.D. Crossan 1983c

**SILUVAI, Ignaci**

1981 *Prohibition from or Preparation for the Mission to "Panta ta Ethne"? An Exegetico-theological Study of Mt 10:5b-6.* Diss. Pont. Univ. Greg., Roma, 1981, XVIII-437 p. (J. Caba).

**SILVA, Moisés**

1977 Ned B. Stonehouse and Redaction Criticism. Part I: The Witness of the Synoptic Evangelists to Christ. — *WestTJ* 40 (1977) 77-88. [NTA 22, 751] → Stonehouse 1944

1978 New Lexical Semitisms? — *ZNW* 69 (1978) 253-257. Esp. 255 [13,35]; 256 [13,53; 19,1; 28,19]. [NTA 23, 772]

1990 The Language and Style of the Gospels. — SKILTON, J.H. (ed.), *The Gospels Today*, 1990, 27-37.

**SILVA, Sergio**

1989 Los milagros de Jesús, ¿sólo signos literarios? — *Revista Católica* (Santiago de Chile) 89 (1989) 3-16, 185-189.

**SILVA COSTOYA, Rafael**

1964 & NIETO, T., Estudio critico-literario e interpretación de la parábola de las bodas y de la gran cena (Mt 22,2-14 y Lc 14,16-24). — *Compostellanum* (Santiago de Compostela) 9 (1964) 349-382.

1965a El relato de la transfiguración. Problemas de crítica literaria y motivos teológicos en Mc 9,2-10; Mt 17,1-9; Lc 9,28-37. — *Compostellanum* 10 (1965) 5-26.

1965b Las tentaciones de Jesús (Mt 4,1-11; Mc 1,12-13, Lc 4,1-13). — *Ibid.*, 483-513.

1965c La parábola de los dos hijos (Mt 21,28-32). — *CuBíb* 22 (1965) 98-105.

1967 ¿Cómo murió Judas, el traidor? [27,3-10] — *CuBíb* 23 (1967) 35-40. [NTA 12, 167]

1968 Dos casos de exégesis evangélica de dificil solución (Mt. 8,5-13; Lc. 7,1-10; Jo. 4,46-54 y Mt. 27,3-10; Act. 1,16-20). — *Compostellanum* 13 (1968) 89-107.

1970a La parábola de los renteros homicidas. Estudio crítico(-literario) e interpretación de Mt 21,33-46; Mc 12,1-12; Lc 20,9-19. — *Compostellanum* 15 (1970) 319-355.

1970b La parábola de los viñadores (Estudio crítico-literario e interpretaciones). [21,33-46] — SANTIAGO-OTERO, H. (ed.), *Miscelanea M. Cuervo López*, Burgos: Aldecoa, 1970, 53-81.

**SILVESTRE, Hubert**

1982 Le "plus grand miracle" de Jésus. [21,12-16] — *AnBoll* 100 (1982) 1-15.

1983 La prière des époux selon Rupert de Liège. [6,5-9] — *Studi Medievali* (Spoleto) 24 (1983) 725-728.

**SILVOLA, Kalevi**

1984 *Lapset ja Jeesus. Traditio- ja redaktiohistoriallinen tutkimus synoptisten evankeliumien lapsiperikoopeista* (Suomen eksegeettisen seuran julkaisuja, 41). Helsinki: SESJ, 1984, 188 p. Esp. 48-50 [19,13-15]; 108-113 [18,1-5]; 133-137 [18,6-7]; 137-146 [18,10]; 149-162 [21,14-16].

**SIM, David C.**

1990 The Man Without the Wedding Garment (Matthew 22:11-13). — *HeythJ* 31 (1990) 165-178. [NTA 34, 1141]

1992 Matthew 22.13a and 1 Enoch 10.4a. A Case of Literary Dependence? — *JSNT* 47 (1992) 3-19. Esp. 4-6: "The Greek recensions of 1 Enoch 10.4a and the text of Matthew 22.13a"; 6-13: "The authorship of Matthew 22.13a"; 13-18: "A new interpretation of Matthew 22.11-13". [NTA 37, 736]

1993a The "Confession" of the Soldiers in Matthew 27:54. — *HeythJ* 34 (1993) 401-424. Esp. 402-415 [redaction criticism]; 415-418 [literary criticism]; 418-422: "An alternative reading". [NTA 38, 777]

1993b The Meaning of παλιγγενεσία in Matthew 19.28. — *JSNT* 50 (1993) 3-12. Esp. 3-7 [19,28]; 7-11 [5,18; 24,35]. [NTA 38, 773]

1994 What about the Wives and Children of the Disciples?: The Cost of Discipleship from Another Perspective. — *HeythJ* 35 (1994) 373-390. [NTA 39, 760]

1995 The Gospel of Matthew and the Gentiles. — *JSNT* 57 (1995) 19-48. Esp. 21-25: "The gentiles in Matthew's story"; 25-30: "Anti-gentile statements"; 30-35: "Gentile persecution"; 35-39: "Matthean community and the gentiles"; 39-44: "Gentile mission". [NTA 40, 156]

1996    *Apocalyptic Eschatology in the Gospel of Matthew* (SNTS MS, 88). Cambridge: University Press, 1996, XVII-282 p. Esp. 75-92: "Dualism and determinism in Matthew"; 93-109: "Eschatological woes and the coming of the Son of Man in Matthew"; 110-128: "The judgement in Matthew"; 129-147: "The fate of the wicked and the fate of the righteous in Matthew"; 148-174: "The imminence of the end in Matthew"; 181-221: "The social setting of the Matthean community"; 222-242: "The function of apocalyptic eschatology in the gospel of Matthew". — Diss London, 1992 (G.N. Stanton).

**SIMMONS, Billy E.**

1992    Preaching Ideas from the Sermon on the Mount. — *Theological Educator* (New Orleans) 46 (1992) 125-132. [NTA 37, 716]

**SIMOENS, Yves**

1974    & POUSSET, É., L'ivraie (Matthieu 13,24-30). — *VieChrét* 171 (1974) 13-15. L'ivraie (Matthieu 13,36-43). — *VieChrét* 172 (1974) 13-16.

1985    Une lecture du Discours sur la montagne pour éclairer la conscience chrétienne. — *LumVit* 40 (1985) 415-432.
The Sermon on the Mount. Light for the Christian Conscience. — *LumVt* 41 (1986) 127-143. [NTA 31, 112]

**SIMON, Martha Lucía**

1979    "Bienaventurados los pobres de espíritu" (Mt 5,3). Base y fundamento de la pobreza evangélica. — *BibFe* 5 (1979) 148-162. [NTA 24, 84]

**SIMONETTI, Manlio**

1962    Due note sull'angelologia Origeniana I. Mt 18,10 nell'interpretazione di Origene. — *Rivista di cultura classica e medioevale* (Roma) 4 (1962) 165-179.

1964    Note sul commento a Matteo di Ilario di Poitiers. — *VetChr* 1 (1964) 35-64.

1970    Note sull'*Opus imperfectum in Matthaeum*. — *A Giuseppe Ermini* (Studi Medievali, 3/10,1), Spoleto: Centro Italiano di Studi sull'Alto Medioevo, 1970, 117-200. Esp. 120-141: "La Sacra Scrittura"; 141-173: "L'uomo"; 173-194: "Il popolo di dio"; 194-200: "Cenni trinitari e cristologici".
E. BOULARAND, *BullLitEccl* 75 (1974) 72-73; V.C. DE CLERCQ, *VigChr* 26 (1972) 75-76.

1971    Per una retta valutazione dell'*Opus imperfectum in Matthaeum*. — *VetChr* 8 (1971) 87-97.

1975    Su due passi dell'*Opus imperfectum in Matthaeum* pubblicati di recente. — *Augustinianum* 15 (1975) 423-428. → Étaix 1974a

1976    Matteo 7,17-18 (= Luca 6,43) dagli gnostici ad Agostino. — *Augustinianum* 16 (1976) 271-290. Esp. 271-282 [gnosis]; 282-290 [Augustine].

1979    Su una recente edizione del *Commento a Matteo* di Ilario di Poitiers. — *Augustinianum* 19 (1979) 527-530. → Doignon 1978

1980    Praecursor ad inferos. Una nota sull'interpretazione patristica di Matteo 11,3. — *Augustinianum* 20 (1980) 367-382.

1985    Origene e lo scriba di *Matteo* 13,52. — *VetChr* 22 (1985) 181-196.

1992    Origene e i mercanti nel Tempio. — DUPLEIX, A. (ed.), *Recherches et Tradition: Mélanges patristiques offerts à H. Crouzel* (Théologie historique, 88), Paris: Beauchesne, 1992, 271-284.

**SIMONIS, Walter**

1985    *Jesus von Nazareth. Seine Botschaft vom Reich Gottes und der Glaube der Urgemeinde. Historisch-kritische Erhellung der Ursprünge des Christentums.* Düsseldorf: Patmos, 1985, 282 p. Esp. 70-79 [19,28/Q 22,28-30]; 79-83 [20,20-34/Mk 10,35-41]; 146-163: "Menschensohnworte in der Logienquelle" [Q 7,34; 9,58; 11,29-31; 12,8-9.10.40; 17,26-30; Mt 10,23]; 185-190: "Zur Christologie des Matthäusevangeliums"; 215-219 [Q 13,20-21/Mk 4,30-32]; 222-223 [11,12/Q 16,16]; 225-

228 [12,28/Q 11,20]; 230-234 [11,19/Q 7,34]; 244-247 [12,11/Q 14,5; Mk 3,1-6]; 249-253 [5,21-48/Q 16,18; 6,27.29].

**SIMONSEN, Hejne**

1973 Synet på loven i Mattaeusevangeliet. — *DanskTeolTids* 36 (1973) 174-194. [NTA 18, 846] Die Auffassung vom Gesetz im Mattäusevangelium. — *SNTU* 2 (1977) 44-67. Esp. 46-48 [23,1-36]; 49-53 [5,17-20]; 53-56 [15,1-20]; 57-59 [9,13; 12,5-7]; 59-60 [12,9-14]; 61-63 [19,1-12].

**SIMPSON, R.T.**

1966 The Major Agreements of Matthew and Luke against Mark. — *NTS* 12 (1965-66) 273-284. Esp. 276-279 [3,1-6.11-17]; 279-280 [22,35-40]; 280-284 [12,24-29]. [NTA 11, 184]; = BELLINZONI, A.J., Jr., et al. (eds.), *The Two-Source Hypothesis*, 1985, 381-395. Esp. 385-389; 389-391; 391-395. → N. Turner 1969

**SIMPSON, Robert L.**

1965 *The Interpretation of Prayer in the Early Church* (The Library of History and Doctrine). Philadelphia, PA: Westminster, 1965, 189 p. Esp. 41-73: "The Lord's Prayer as scripture to be interpreted"; 74-92: "A new form of prayer"; 93-114: "The Lord's Prayer as example".

**SINISCALCO, Paolo**

1971 *Mito e storia della salvezza. Ricerche sulle più antiche interpretazione di alcune parabole evangeliche* (Filologia classica e glottologia, 5). Torino: Facolta di Lettere e Filosofia, 1971, 242 p.

1991 *Intra in gaudium Domini tui* – Note su una citazione di Matteo (25,21 e 23) nelle *Confessiones* di Agostino: esperienza mistica e beatitudine celeste. — JAIN, E. – MARGREITER, R. (eds.), *Probleme philosophischer Mystik. Festschrift für Karl Albert zum siebzigsten Geburtstag*, Sankt Augustin: Academia, 1991, 187-196.

**SINT, Josef A.**

1964 Die Eschatologie des Täufers, die Täufergruppen und die Polemik der Evangelien. — SCHUBERT, K. (ed.), *Vom Messias zum Christus*, 1964, 55-163. Esp. 57-83: "Johannes der Täufer"; 107-108; 112-115; 116-121 [11,7-19].

**SIOTIS, Markos A.**

1984a *The Interpretation of the Sermon on the Mount in the First Nine Centuries* [Greek]. Athens, 1984, 120 p.
E.D. THEODOROU, Θεολογία (Athens) 55 (1984) 541-542.

1984b Interpretation of the Sermon on the Mount from the Early Middle Ages to the Early 18th Century. [Greek] — PHEIDAS, J. - GIANNOPOULOS, A. (eds.), *Panepistēmion Athēnôn, Epistimoniki epetiris theol. (FS Andreias I. Phytrakis)* 26 (1984) 3-42.

1984c The Interpretation of the Sermon on the Mount during the 18th and 19th Centuries. [Greek] — Θεολογία (Athens) 55 (1984) 81-112, 609-627.

1986a *The Interpretation of the Sermon on the Mount through the Ages* [Greek]. Athens, 1986, 575 p.
P. SIMOTAS, Θεολογία 58 (1987) 168-173.

1986b The Forefathers of Jesus Christ according to the Flesh. [Greek] [1,1-17] — Θεολογία 57 (1986) 127-154, 273-299.

1987 Joseph Betrothed to Mary, the Father of Jesus Christ according to the Law. [Greek] [1,18-25] — Θεολογία 58 (1987) 712-747.

**SIRKS, G.J.**

1957 Auctor – compositor. [18,12-14] — *NTT* 12 (1957-58) 81-91. [NTA 2, 519]

**SISTI, Adalberto**

1967 L'Ospitalità nella prassi e nell'insegnamento della Bibbia. — *SBF/LA* 17 (1967) 303-334. Esp. 314-320. [NTA 12, 1048]

1968 L'albero genealogico di Gesù. [1,1-17] — *ParVi* 13 (1968) 271-280.

**SIX, Jean-François**

1984 *Les béatitudes aujourd'hui.* Paris: Seuil, 1984, 241 p.
*Las bienaventuranzas hoy.* Madrid: Paulinas, 1985, 232 p.
*Le beatitudini oggi.* Bologna: Dehoniane, 1986.

**SJÖBERG, Erik**

1951 Das Licht in dir. Zur Deutung von Matth. 6,22f Par. — *StudTheol* 5 (1951) 89-105.
Ljuset i dig. Till tolkningen av Matt. 6:22f. par. — *SEÅ* 17 (1952) 31-46.

1955 *Der verborgene Menschensohn in den Evangelien* (Acta Regiae Societatis Humaniorum Litterarum Lundensis, 53). Lund: Gleerup, 1955, X-290 p. Esp. 132-142: "Das Messiasgeheimnis in den Evangelien: Matthäus"; 175-190: "Die Logia-Überlieferung" [Q 7,1-10.18-23.27-28.31-35; 10,21-22.23-24; 11,14-20.31-32; 13,34-35]; 192-197: "Das Sondergut Matthäus"; 230-233 [11,25-27/Q 10,21-22].

**SKALITZKY, Rachel**

1971 Annianus of Celada: His Text of Chrysostom's "Homilies in Matthew". — *Aevum* 45 (1974) 208-233. Esp. 221-233 [Hom. 17].

**SKARSAUNE, Oskar**

1987 *The Proof from Prophecy. A Study in Justin Martyr's Proof-Text Tradition: Text-Type, Provenance, Theological Profile* (SupplNT, 56). Leiden: Brill, 1987, XIV-505 p. Esp. 32-34 [1,23]; 58-59 [11,5]; 60-61 [12,18-21]; 74-76 [21,5]; 88-90 [25,31]; 100-103; 119-121 [2,6.18].

**SKEAT, Theodore Cressy**

1991 & MCGING, B.C., Notes on Chester Beatty Biblical Papyrus I (Gospel and Acts). [P⁴⁵]
— *Hermathena* (Dublin) 150 (1991) 21-25.

**SKIBBE, Eugene M.**

1968 Pentateuchal Themes in the Sermon on the Mount. — *LuthQ* 20 (1968) 44-51. [NTA 12, 866]

**SKILTON, John H.**

1990* (ed.), *The Gospels Today. A Guide to Some Recent Developments* (The New Testament Student, 6). Philadelphia, PA: Skilton, 1990, X-178 p. → Mare, M.J. Robertson, M. Silva

**SKRZYPCZAK, Otto**

1975 As tentações de Jesus e a consciência de sua missão. — *RevistCuBíb* 12 (1975) 5-22. [NTA 20, 411]

**SLADEK, Paulus F.**

1969 "Liebet eure Feinde..." (Mt 5,44). — REISS, K. - SCHÜTZ, H. (eds.), *Kirche, Recht und Land. Festschrift Weihbischof Adolf Kindermann*, Taunus: Königstein, 1969, 30-48.

**SLÁMA, V.**

1955 Podobenství č církvi ć o círckvi a "svètu"? (Mt 13,24-30; 36-43). — *Theologická příloha - Křest'anské revue* (Praha) 1 (1955) 9-12.

**SLATER, Tommy B.**

1980 Notes on Matthew's Structure. — *JBL* 99 (1980) 436. [NTA 25, 458] → Kingsbury 1975a

**SLINGERLAND, H. Dixon**

1979 The Transjordanian Origin of St. Matthew's Gospel. — *JSNT* 3 (1979) 18-28. [NTA 23, 812]

**SLORT, D.**

1968 *De wederkomst van Christus naar de Evangeliën van Mattheüs, Markus en Lukas.* Franeker: Wever, 1968, 166 p. Esp. 11-15 [5,3-10]; 105-127 [24/Mk 13]; 128-155 [24,42-44.45-51; 25,1-13.14-30].

**SLOYAN, Gerard S.**

1958 The Gospel according to St. Matthew. — *Worship* 32 (1958) 342-351. [NTA 3, 68]; = RYAN, M.R. (ed.), *Contemporary New Testament Studies*, 1965, 239-246.

1961 "Primitive" and "Pauline" Concepts of the Eucharist. — *CBQ* 23 (1961) 1-13. Esp. 6-9: "Analysis of the fourfold account of institution" [26,29]. [NTA 5, 831]

1973 *Jesus on Trial. The Development of the Passion Narratives and Their Historical and Ecumenical Implications.* Philadelphia, PA: Fortress, 1973, XIX-156 p. Esp. 74-88: "The history of the tradition of the trial in Matthew".

1979a Conceived by the Holy Ghost, Born of the Virgin Mary. — *Interpr* 33 (1979) 81-84. [NTA 23, 815r] → R.E. Brown 1977

1979b Recent Literature on the Trial Narratives of the Four Gospels. — RYAN, T.J. (ed.), *Critical History and Biblical Faith. New Testament Perspectives*, Villanova, PA: CTS, 1979, 136-176.

1992 Preaching Matthew. — *Church* (New York) 8/4 (1992) 51-54. [NTA 37, 709]

**SMALBRUGGE, Matthias**

1989 L'analogie réexaminée. — *RHPR* 69 (1989) 121-134. Esp. 123-130 [Augustine: 3,13-17].

**SMALLEY, Beryl**

1958 John Baconthorpe's Postill on St. Matthew. — *Medieval and Renaissance Studies* (London) 4 (1958) 91-145; = ID., *Studies in Medieval Thought and Learning: From Abelard to Wyclif* (History Series, 6), London: Hambledon, 1981, 289-343.

1978 Some Gospel Commentaries of the Early Twelfth Century. — *RTAM* 45 (1978) 147-180. Esp. 166-176 [Anselm of Laon]; = ID., *The Gospels*, 1985, 1-35. Esp. 20-30.

1979a The Gospels in the Paris Schools in the Late Twelfth and Early Thirteenth Centuries. Peter the Chanter, Hugh of St. Cher, Alexander of Hales, John of La Rochelle. — *Franciscan Studies* 39 (1979) 230-254; 40 (1980) 298-369; = ID., *The Gospels*, 1985, 99-196. Esp. 144-145, 151-159 [Alexander of Hales]; 172-173 [John of La Rochelle].

1979b Peter Comestor on the Gospels and His Sources. — *RTAM* 46 (1979) 84-129. Esp. 95-105 [Anselm of Laon]; = ID., *The Gospels*, 1985, 37-83. Esp. 48-58.

1985 *The Gospels in the Schools c. 1100 – c. 1280.* London – Ronceverte, West-Virginia: Hambledon, 1985, IX-286 p. → 1978, 1979a-b

**SMALLEY, Stephen S.**

1964 The Delay of the Parousia. — *JBL* 83 (1964) 41-54. Esp. 46-47 [10,23]. [NTA 8, 871]

1974 The Sign in John xxi. — *NTS* 20 (1973-74) 275-288. Esp. 276-277 [Jn/Mt]. [NTA 19, 165]

1977 Redaction Criticism. — MARSHALL, I.H. (ed.), *New Testament Interpretation*, 1977, 181-195. Esp. 185-186 [16,16; 17,1-9].

1978 *John: Evangelist and Interpreter.* Exeter: Paternoster, 1978, 285 p. Esp. 13-30.

**SMEREKA, Wladyslaw**

1973 Konfrontacja egzegezy Ewangelii dzieciństwa Chrystusa z próbami odmitologizowania Ewangelii. [Confrontation of the birth narratives of Christ with attempts of demythologization] — *Kronika Diecezjic Włocławskiej* (Włocławek) 56 (1973) 121-130.

### SMIGA, George M.

1992   *Pain and Polemic. Anti-Judaism in the Gospels* (Stimulus Books). New York –
Mahwah, NJ: Paulist, 1992, VII-210 p. Esp. 52-96: "The gospel of Matthew: an abrogating polemic
with violence" [5,17-20; 11,25-30; 21,33-46; 23, 1-36; 27,24-25].

### SMIT, Joop

1978   *Jezus, hoeksteen of struikelblok? Wat zijn verhaal ons te zeggen heeft.* Hilversum: Gooi
en Sticht, 1978, 192 p. Esp. 12-31 [1–2]; 110-113 [20,1-16]; 114-117 [21,28-32]; 118-121 [21,33-46];
122-125 [22,1-14]; 126-129 [25,14-30]; 130-133 [25,31-46]; 136-140 [14,13-21]; 141-144 [14,22-33]; 172-
174 [5,1-12]; 175-178 [5,13-16]; 179-181 [18,15-20].

1981   *Speelruimte. Een structurele lezing van het evangelie.* Hilversum: Gooi en Sticht, 1981,
139 p. Esp. 63-72 [20,1-16].

### SMITH, B.T.D.

1933[R]  *The Gospel according to St Matthew* [1933] (The Cambridge Bible for Schools and
Colleges). Cambridge: University Press, 1950, XLI-184 p.

### SMITH, Charles William Frederick

1954   Dr Parker's Synoptic Theory. — *ATR* 36 (1954) 210-213. → P. Parker 1953

1962   Lord's Prayer. — *IDB* 3 (1962) 154-158.

1963   The Mixed State of the Church in Matthew's Gospel. — *JBL* 82 (1963) 149-168. Esp.
150-153 [13,24-30.36-43]; 153-156 [13,47-50]; 156-158 [22,11-14]; 158 [25,1-13]; 158-160 [25,31-46].
[NTA 8, 119]

### SMITH, David Whitten

1970   *Wisdom Christology in the Synoptic Gospels.* Roma, 1970, 150 p. Esp. 15-78 [Q]; 85-101
[Mt]. — Diss. Pont. Univ. S. Thomae de Urbe.

1989   Inspired Authors and Saintly Interpreters in Conflict: The New Testament on War and
Peace. — TAMBASCO, A.J. (ed.), *Blessed Are the Peacemakers. Biblical Perspectives
on Peace and Its Social Foundations*, New York – Mahwah, NJ: Paulist, 1989, 154-
184. Esp. 157-165 [5,38-48].

### SMITH, Dennis E.

1989   The Historical Jesus at Table. — *SBL 1989 Seminar Papers*, 466-486. Esp. 477-480 [11,16-
19].

1994   Table Fellowship and the Historical Jesus. — BORMANN, L., et al. (eds.), *Religious
Propaganda and Missionary Competition.* FS D. Georgi. 1994, 135-162. Esp. 148-152:
"Jesus contrasted with John the baptist" [Q 7].

### SMITH, Don T.

1989   The Matthean Exception Clauses in the Light of Matthew s Theology and Community.
— *SBT* 17 (1989) 55-82. Esp. 56-59: "The sources and nature of Matthew's divorce sayings"; 59-63:
"The issue of Matthean redaction and its implications" 63-65: "The Matthean exception clauses"; 66-74:
"Recent interpretations of Matthew's exception clauses"; 74-79: "Reconstructing the *Sitz im Leben* of
Matthew's community".

### SMITH, Dwight Moody

1963   John 12,12ff. and the Question of John's Use of the Synoptics. — *JBL* 82 (1963) 58-64.
Esp. 60-62 [21,9.15]. [NTA 7, 839]; = ID., *Johannine Christianity*, 1984, 97-105. Esp. 99-101.
→ Freed 1961, 1965 (66-68), Neirynck 1992b (26-28)

1969   & SPIVEY, R.A., *Anatomy of the New Testament: A Guide to Its Structure and
Meaning.* New York: Macmillan, 1969, XVIII-510 p.; [2]1974, XVIII-539 p.; [3]1982, XIX-
539 p.; [4]1989, XXIV-500 p.

1972 The Use of the Old Testament in the New. — EFIRD, J.M. (ed.), *The Use of the Old Testament in the New*. FS W.F. Stinespring, 1972, 3-65. Esp. 43-49: "Matthew".

1977 The Presentation of Jesus in the Fourth Gospel. — *Interpr* 31 (1977) 367-378. Esp. 369 [8,5-13]. [NTA 22, 144]; = ID., *Johannine Christianity*, 1984, 175-198. Esp. 177.

1980 John and the Synoptics: Some Dimensions of the Problem. — *NTS* 26 (1979-80) 425-444. Esp. 438-441. [NTA 25, 135]; = ID., *Johannine Christianity*, 1984, 145-172. Esp. 163-167.

1982 John and the Synoptics. — *Bib* 63 (1982) 102-113. Esp. 104-105; 108. [NTA 26, 897r] → de Solages 1979a, Neirynck 1979a
John and the Synoptics: de Solages and Neirynck. — ID., *Johannine Christianity*, 1984, 128-144. Esp. 131-132.134.

1984 *Johannine Christianity. Essays on Its Setting, Sources, and Theology*. Columbia, SC: Univ. of South Carolina, 1984, XIX-233 p. → 1963, 1977, 1980, 1982

1987 John, the Synoptics, and the Canonical Approach to Exegesis. — HAWTHORNE, G.F. - BETZ, O. (eds.), *Tradition and Interpretation*. FS E.E. Ellis, 1987, 166-180. Esp. 170-174: "The canonical balance of Matthew and John".

1990 John and the Synoptics in Light of the Problem of Faith and History. — CARROLL, J.T., et al. (eds.), *Faith and History*. FS P.W. Meyer, 1990, 74-89. Esp. 81-83.

1992a *John among the Gospels. The Relationship in Twentieth-Century Research*. Minneapolis, MN: Augsburg/Fortress, 1992, XIII-210 p. Esp. 124-125 [26,52/Jn]; 156-157 [28,9-10/Jn]; 160-163 [4,46-54; 8,5-13/Jn]. → Dauer 1984, Neirynck 1984b, 1992b (61-62)

1992b John and the Synoptics and the Question of Gospel Genre. — VAN SEGBROECK, F., et al. (eds.), *The Four Gospels 1992*. FS F. Neirynck, 1992, III, 1783-1797. Esp. 1784-1786.

**SMITH, Graham**

1970 The Matthaean 'Additions' to the Lord's Prayer. — *ExpT* 82 (1970-71) 54-55. [NTA 15, 498]

**SMITH, J. Carrington**

1984 Pilate's Wife? [27,19] — *Antichthon* (Melbourne) 18 (1984) 102-107.

**SMITH, Jill**

1976 Figurative Language in Matthew's Gospel. [3,8; 7,6; 10,6; 20,22; 23,24; 26,41] — *BTrans* 27 (1976) 230-233.

**SMITH, Mahlon H.**

1988 No Place for a Son of Man. — *Forum* 4/4 (1988) 83-107. Esp. 83-86.89-91.101-104 [8,20]. [NTA 33, 1131]

1990 Kinship is Relative. Mark 3:31-35 and Parallels. — *Forum* 6 (1990) 80-94. Esp. 81-83: "Synoptic puzzle". [NTA 36, 743]

1991 To Judge the Son of Man. The Synoptic Sayings. — *Forum* 7 (1991) 207-242. Esp. 220-222; 228-239 [Q]. [NTA 38, 737]

**SMITH, Morton**

1951 *Tannaitic Parallels to the Gospels* (JBL MS, 6). Philadelphia, PA: SBL 1951, XII-215 p. Esp. 74-114: "Parallels of literary form" [5-7; 10,5-42; 23,2-39; 24-25]; 135-141: "Complete parallels" [5-7]; 185-198: "The parallelism of Matthew and Luke compared with that of the Mishnah and Tosefta". → Neusner 1993b

1952 Mt. 5:43: "Hate thine enemy". — *HTR* 45 (1952) 71-73.

1978 *Jesus the Magician*. London: Gollancz, 1978, 222 p. Esp. 21-44: "What the outsiders said – Evidence in the gospels"; 153-157 [Pharisees].

**SMITH, M.A.**

1968    The Influence of the Liturgies on the New Testament Text of the Last Supper Narratives. — *Studia Evangelica* 5 (1968) 207-218.

**SMITH, Robert Harry**

1980    Were the Early Christians Middle-Class? A Sociological Analysis of the New Testament. — *CurrTMiss* 7 (1980) 260-276. Esp. 265-271. [NTA 25, 661]

1983    *Easter Gospels. The Resurrection of Jesus according to the Four Evangelists*. Minneapolis, MN: Augsburg, 1983, 254 p. Esp. 55-91 [27,62–28,20].

1984    Celebrating Easter in the Matthean Mode. — *CurrTMiss* 11 (1984) 79-82. [NTA 28, 923]

1989    *Matthew* (Augsburg Commentary on the New Testament). Minneapolis, MN: Augsburg, 1989, 351 p. Esp. 11-23: "Introduction"; 29-341: "Commentary". [NTA 33, p. 391]
        J. BOHNEN, *Neotestamentica* 24 (1990) 386-389; S. BYRSKOG, *SverskTeolKvart* 67 (1991) 53-54; F.W. DANKER, *CurrTMiss* 18 (1991) 139-140; G. GREENFIELD, *SWJT* 32 (1989-90) 51; J.-M. ROUSÉE, *RB* 96 (1989) 637.

1990    Matthew 27:25: The Hardest Verse in Matthew's Gospel. — *CurrTMiss* 17 (1990) 421-428. [NTA 35, 636]

1992a   Interpreting Matthew Today. — *CurrTMiss* 19 (1992) 424-432. [NTA 37, 710]

1992b   Matthew's Message for Insiders. Charisma and Commandment in a First-Century Community. — *Interpr* 46 (1992) 229-239. Esp. 231-232 [7,15-27]; 234 [Sermon on the Mount]; 235 [1,21]; 235-237 [28,16-20]; 237-38 [Pharisees]. [NTA 37, 126]

1993    Matthew 28:16-20, Anticlimax or Key to the Gospel? — *SBL 1993 Seminar Papers*, 589-603. Esp. 589-596: "Three readings"; 596-602: "The GC and the plot of Matthew's gospel".

**SMITH, Robert Houston**

1960    *The Episode of Peter's Confession in Tradition and Gospel* [16,13-20]. Diss. Yale Univ., New Haven, CA, 1960, 342 p. — *DissAbstr* 40 (1979-80) 5477.

**SMITH, Taylor C.**

1976    An Exegesis of Matthew 25:31-46. — *Foundations* (Rochester, NY) 19 (1976) 206-210.

**SMITH, Terence V.**

1985    *Petrine Controversies in Early Christianity. Attitudes towards Peter in Christian Writings of the First Two Centuries* (WUNT, II/15). Tübingen: Mohr, 1985, X-249 p. Esp. 156-160: "Gospel of Matthew"; 201-203; 207. — Diss. London, 1981 (G.N. Stanton).

**SMITMANS, Adolf**

1970    *Maria im Neuen Testament*. Stuttgart: Katholisches Bibelwerk, 1970, 57 p.

1972    & BAUR, A., *Das Gebet des Herrn in der Katechese*.
        *Het Onze Vader in de prediking* (Van exegese tot verkondiging, 5). Boxtel: Katholieke Bijbelstichting, 1972, 118 p. Esp. 7-30: "Exegetisch onderzoek"

1973    Das Gleichnis vom Dieb. — FELD, H. – NOLTE, J. (eds.), *Wort Gottes in der Zeit*. FS K.H. Schelkle, 1973, 43-68. Esp. 45-55: "Rückfrage nach dem Anfang"; 55-68: "Die Geschichte".

**SMITS, Crispinus**

1952    *Oudtestamentische citaten in het Nieuwe Testament*. I. *Synoptische Evangeliën* (Collectanea Franciscana Neerlandica, 8/1). 's Hertogenbosch: Malmberg, 1952, 160 p. Esp. 57-109: "Jezus en het Oude Testament"; 110-156: "De evangelisten en bijbelse citaten".

**SMIT SIBINGA, Joost**

1959    "Zalig de armen van geest". [5,3] — *VoxTheol* 30 (1959-60) 5-15.

1966    Ignatius and Matthew. — *NT* 8 (1966) 263-283. Esp. 267 [3,7]; 267-268 [4,8]; 268-270 [10,42]; 270-272 [7,16-21; 12,33-35]; 272-273 [21,33]; 273-275 [23,27]; 275 [26,7]; 275-277 [3,15]; 277 [8,17]; 277-278 [10,16]; 278-279 [15,13]; 279 [19,12]; 279-280 [23,8]. [NTA 11, 691]

1972    Eine literarische Technik im Matthäusevangelium. — DIDIER, M. (ed.), *L'Évangile selon Matthieu*, 1972, 99-105.

1975    The Structure of the Apocalyptic Discourse, Matthew 24 and 25. — *StudTheol* 29 (1975) 71-79. [NTA 20, 90]

1981    Matthew 14:22-33 - Text and Composition. — EPP, E.J. — FEE, G.D. (eds.), *New Testament Textual Criticism*. FS B.M. Metzger, 1981, 15-33.

1994    Exploring the Composition of Matth. 5–7. The Sermon on the Mount and some of Its "Structures". — *FilolNT* 7 (1994) 175-195. Esp. 175-179.186-195 [structure]; 179-184 [commandments]; 185-186 [God as Father]. [NTA 40, 161]

**SMITT, J.W.**

1975    *Opdat vervuld zou worden. Exegetische monographieën over de vervullingsverbanden in het evangelie naar Mattheüs, bevattende de vervullingscitaten, die worden ingeleid met de vervullingsformules* hopoos plèroothèi, hina plèroothèi *en* tote eplèroothè. Groningen: De Vuurbaak, I, 1975, 201 p.; II, 1977, 211 p. Esp. I, 21-43: "De methode van behandeling van de vervullingsverbanden met de daarin voorkomende vervullingscitaten en inleidende vervullingsformules in het evangelie naar Mattheüs"; 44-78 [1,20-23]; 79-107 [2,14-15]; 108-141 [2,23]; 142-165 [4,13-16]; 166-194 [8,16-17]; II, 13-46 [2,17-18]; 47-75 [2,16-21]; 76-110 [13,34-35]; 111-147 [21,4-5]; 148-179 [22,56]; 180-209 [27,6-10]. [NTA 24, p. 194]

**SMULDERS, Pieter**

1983    Hilarius van Poitiers als exegeet van Mattheüs. Bij de kritische uitgave. — *Bijdragen* 44 (1983) 59-82 (English summary, 82). → Doignon 1978

1987    En marge de l'*In Matthaeum* de S. Hilaire de Poitiers. Principes et méthodes herméneutiques. — MARAVAL, P., et al., *Lectures anciennes de la Bible* [FS André Benoît] (Cahiers de Biblia patristica, 1), Strasbourg: Centre d'analyse et de documentation patristiques, 1987, 217-251.

1995    *Hilary of Poitiers' Preface to His* Opus Historicum. *Translation and Commentary* (Supplements to Vigiliae Christianae, 29). Leiden: Brill, 1995, XI-169 p. Esp. 115-118: "Note on In Mt. 10,12".

**SMYTH, Kevin**

1961    The Guard on the Tomb. [27,65] — *HeythJ* 2 (1961) 157-159. [NTA 6, 462]

1975    Matthew 28: Resurrection as Theophany. — *IrTQ* 42 (1975) 259-271. [NTA 20, 446]

1979    Le principe structurel de l'Évangile de Matthieu. — *FoiVie* 78 = *Cahiers bibliques* 18 (1979) 77-91. Esp. 78-82 [1-2]; 82-85 [11,25-30]; 85-88 [16,16-18]; 88-91 [28,18-20]. [NTA 24, 408]
        The Structural Principle of Matthew's Gospel. — *IBS* 4 (1982) 207-220. Esp. 207-211; 211-214; 214-217; 217-220. [NTA 27, 908]

**SMYTH-FLORENTIN, Françoise**

1973    Jésus, le Fils du Père, vainqueur de Satan. Mt 4,1-11; Mc 1,12-15; Lc 4,1-13. — *AssSeign* II/14 (1973) 56-75. [NTA 17, 936]

**SNAPE, H.C.**

1966    The Synoptic Problem Reopened. — *The Modern Churchman* (Oxford) 9 (1966) 184-191. [NTA 11, 182r] → W.R. Farmer 1964a

**SNELL, A.**

1971    Josef Kürzinger on Papias. [J. KÜRZINGER, *TGeg* 10 (1967) 157-164] — *Colloquium* 4 (1971) 105-109. [NTA 16, 139]

**SNIJDERS, Thomas**

1959 "Jezus, zachtmoedig en nederig van hart" (Mt 11,29 = "anaw"). — *Getuigenis* 3 (1959) 282-289.

**SNODGRASS, Klyne R.**

1972 "Western Non-Interpolations". — *JBL* 91 (1972) 369-379. Esp. 370, 376-377 [6,15.25; 9,34; 13,33; 21,44; 23,26; 27,49]. [NTA 17, 426]

1974 The Parable of the Wicked Husbandmen: Is the Gospel of Thomas Version the Original? — *NTS* 21 (1974-75) 142-144. [NTA 19, 562]

1980 Streams of Tradition Emerging from Isaiah 40:1-5 and their Adaptation in the New Testament. — *JSNT* 8 (1980) 24-45. Esp. 33-36 [3,3/Mk 1,3]. [NTA 25, 93]; = EVANS, C.A. – PORTER, S.E. (eds.), *New Testament Backgrounds. A Sheffield Reader* (The Biblical Seminar, 43), Sheffield: JSOT, 1997, 149-168. Esp. 159-162.

1983 *The Parable of the Wicked Tenants. An Inquiry into Parable Interpretation* (WUNT, 27). Tübingen: Mohr, 1983, X-140 p. Esp. 31-40: "The cultural setting of the parable"; 41-71: "An analysis of the parabe and its development"; 72-110: "The origin and meaning of the parable".

1988 Matthew and the Law. — *SBL 1988 Seminar Papers*, 536-554. Esp. 540-545 [law]; 545-549 [5,17-20]; 549-551: "Did Jesus abrogate the law?"; 551-552: "The antitheses"; 552-553 [8,22]; 553 [23,2-3.23; 24,20]; = BAUER, D.R. – POWELL, M.A. (eds.), *Treasures New and Old*, 1996, 99-127. Esp. 106-111; 111-118; 118-124; 124-125; 125-126; 126.

1989 The Gospel of Thomas: A Secondary Gospel. — *SecCent* 7 (1989-90) 19-38. Esp. 22-23 [Q/Th]; 31-37 [6,20/Th 76b; 9,14-17/Th 104; 10,27/Th 33a; 10,34-35/Th 10.16; 10,37-38/Th 55; 13,57/Th 31; 23,13/Th 39a]. [NTA 34, 1499]

1991 A Response to Hans Dieter Betz on the Sermon on the Mount. — *BR* 36 (1991) 88-94. → H.D. Betz 1991b

1992a Matthew's Understanding of the Law. — *Interpr* 46 (1992) 368-378. Esp. 371-373 [5,17-20]; 374-375 [5,21-48]; 375 [15,1-20]; 375-376 [23,2-3.23; 24,20]. [NTA 37, 711]

1992b Parables. — *DJG*, 1992, 591-601.

**SNOEK, Cornelis Jacobus**

1952 *De idee der gehoorzaamheid in het Nieuwe Testament*. Nijmegen–Utrecht: Dekker & van de Vegt, 1952, XII-72 p. Esp. 1-30: "De gehoorzaamheid bij de Synoptici" [4,18-22; 5,17-48; 18,14; 19,16-30]. — Diss. Angelicum, Roma, 1951 (F. Ceuppens).

**SNOWDEN, R.F.**

1968 *The Lord's Prayer* (The Living Word). London: Epworth, 1968, 62 p.

**SNOY, Thierry**

1972 Une nouvelle lecture de l'Évangile selon Matthieu. — *Bit VieChrét* 107 (1972) 39-43. [NTA 17, 508r] → Radermakers 1972

1977 → Neirynck 1977a

1979 → Neirynck 1979a

**SNYDER, Graydon F.**

1976 The *Tobspruch* in the New Testament. — *NTS* 23 (1976-77) 117-120. Esp. 119 [5,29-30; 18,6-9]. [NTA 21, 329]

**SNYMAN, A.H.**

1977 Analysis of Mt 3:1–4:22. — *Neotestamentica* 11 (1977) 19-31 (addendum, 4-7).

**SOARDS, Marion L.**

1987 A Literary Analysis of the Origin and Purpose of Luke's Account of the Mockery of Jesus. — *BZ* 31 (1987) 110-116. Esp. 113-115 [26,39.42.50-52 54.68.75]. [NTA 32, 1124]

1991    Oral Tradition before, in and outside the Canonical Passion Narratives. — WANSBROUGH, H. (ed.), *Jesus and the Oral Gospel Tradition*, 1991, 334-350. Esp. 336-345: "Oral tradition in the PNs".

**SOARES, P.**

1952    *De usu textus Mt 11,20-24 apud exegetas posttridentinos usque ad annum 1663*. Diss. Pont. Univ. Greg., Roma, 1951-52.

**SOARES-PRABHU, George M.**

1968    & LIVIO, J.B., La fuite en Égypte et les Évangiles de l'Enfance. — *BibTS* 106 (1968) 2-5.

1971    Matthew 4:14-16. A Key to the Origin of the Formula Quotations of Matthew. — *IndianJT* 20 (1971) 70-91. [NTA 17, 116]

1975    Jesus in the Gospel of Matthew. — *Bible Bhashyam* 1 (1975) 37-54. [NTA 20, 82]

1976    *The Formula Quotations in the Infancy Narrative of Matthew. An Enquiry into the Tradition History of Mt 1-2* (AnBib, 63). Roma: Biblical Institute Press, 1976, XV-346 p. Esp. 1-44: "Background and method"; 45-106: "The origin of the formula quotations"; 107-161: "The context of the formula quotations"; 162-191: "The infancy narrative and the formula quotations"; 192-293: "The formula quotations of the infancy narrative"; 294-300: "The tradition-history of Mt 1-2". [NTA 21, p. 90] — Diss. Lyon, 1969 (X. Léon-Dufour).
     R.E. BROWN, *JBL* 96 (1977) 601-603; J. COPPENS, *ETL* 52 (1976) 489*-490*; T. FORNBERG, *SEÅ* 47 (1982) 228-229; K.H. GUNDRY, *Bib* 58 (1977) 591-594; X. JACQUES, *NRT* 100 (1978) 269-270; M.P. JOHN, *IndianJT* 28 (1979) 53-54; X. LÉON-DUFOUR, *RSR* 64 (1976) 429-430; J.P. MEIER, *CBQ* 39 (1977) 292-294; J. MURPHY-O'CONNOR, *RB* 84 (1977) 292-297; G. SCHILLE, *TLZ* 104 (1979) 188-189.

1980    The Dharma of Jesus. An Interpretation of the Sermon on the Mount. — *Bible Bhashyam* 6 (1980) 358-381. [NTA 26, 90]

1983    The Synoptic Love-Commandment: The Dimensions of Love in the Teaching of Jesus. — *Jeevadhara* 13 (1983) 85-103. Esp. 87-91 [22,34-40]. [NTA 28, 84]

1986    "As We Forgive". Interhuman Forgiveness in the Teaching of Jesus. — *Concilium* (London) 184 (1986) 57-66. [NTA 31, 838]
     "Comme nous pardonnons". Le pardon interhumain dans l'enseignement de Jésus. — *Concilium* (Paris) 204 (1986) 73-84. Esp. 74-76.
     "Wie auch wir vergeben": zwischenmenschliche Vergebung in der Lehre Jesu. — *IZT/Concilium* (Mainz) 22 (1986) 120-126. Esp. 120-121.

1990a    Signs Not Wonders: Understanding the Miracles of Jesus as Jesus Understood Them. — *Way* 30 (1990) 307-317. [NTA 35, 585]

1990b    Speaking to "Abba": Prayer as Petition and Thanksgiving in the Teaching of Jesus. [6,9-13; 11,25-26] — *Concilium* (London) 229 (1990) 31-43.
     Parler à "Abba". La prière de demande et d'action de grâces dans l'enseignement de Jésus. — *Concilium* (Paris) 229 (1990) 49-62.

1992    Jesus in Egypt. A Reflection on Mt 2:13-15.19-21 in the Light of the Old Testament. — *EstBíb* 50 (1992) 225-249. Esp. 231-233: "The infancy narrative of Matthew"; 234-240: "The flight into and return from Egypt"; 240-249: "Place names in the story".

1994a    The Church as Mission. A Reflection on Mt. 5:13-16. — *Jeevadhara* 24 (1994) 271-281. [NTA 39, 1446]

1994b    Two Mission Commands. An Interpretation of Matthew 28:16-20 in the Light of a Buddhist Text. — *BibInt* 2 (1994) 264-282. Esp. 274-282. [NTA 39, 1462]; = SUGIRTHARAJAH, R.S. (ed.), *Voices from the Margin. Interpreting the Bible in the Third World*, Maryknoll: Orbis, [1991], ²1995, 319-338.

**SODEN, Hans VON**

1941[R] Die synoptische Frage und der geschichtliche Jesus. [194:] — ID., *Urchristentum und Geschichte. Gesammelte Aufsätze und Vorträge*. 1. *Grundsätzliches und Neutestamentliches*, Tübingen: Mohr, 1951, 159-213. Esp. 169-172 [Q]; 173-175 [Sondergut].

**SÖDING, Thomas**

1985 *Glaube bei Markus. Glaube an das Evangelium, Gebetsglaube und Wunderglaube im Kontext der markinischen Basileiatheologie und Christologie* (Stuttgarter Biblische Beiträge, 12). Stuttgart: Katholisches Bibelwerk, 1985, [2]1987, XIV-634 p. Esp. 567-576: "Zur Besonderheit des matthäischen Glaubensverständnisses gegenüber der markinischen Glaubenskonzeption". — Diss. Münster, 1984 (W. Thüsing).

1992 Die Tempelaktion Jesu. Redaktionskritik – Überlieferungsgeschichte – historische Rückfrage (Mk 11,15-19; Mt 21,12-17; Lk 19,45-48; Joh 2,13-22). — *TTZ* 101 (1992) 36-64. Esp. 41-43. [NTA 36, 1307]

1995 *Mehr als ein Buch. Die Bibel begreifen*. Freiburg: Herder. 1995, [2]1996, 448 p. Esp. 189-201 [5,38-48].

**SÖLL, Georg**

1960 Die Anfänge mariologischer Tradition. Beitrag zur Geschichte der Marienlehre. — BETZ, J. – FRIES, H. (eds.), *Kirche und Überlieferung. [Joseph Rupert Geiselmann zum 70. Geburtstag am 27. Februar 1960]*, Freiburg: Herder, 1960, 35-51. Esp. 40-41 [1,23]. Les débuts de la tradition mariologique. – BETZ, J. – FRIES, H. (eds.), *Église et tradition*, Le Puy–Lyon: Mappus, 1963, 47-63. Esp. 52-53.

**SOLÁ, Francisco de Paula**

1974 Mt 1-2 y las relaciones que establecen entre San José y el misterio de Cristo. — *EstJos* 28 (1974) 33-52.

1978 Los dos primeros capítulos de San Mateo y la Iglesia. — *EstJos* 32 (1978) 3-13. Esp. 4-7 [structure].

**SOLLAMO, Raija**

1983 Semitic Interference in Words Meaning "Before" in the New Testament. An Examination in the Prepositional Usage of *enantion, enanti, cpenanti, katenanti, enōpion, katenōpion, emprosthen, pro prosōpou*, and *kata prosōpon* in the New Testament. — KIILUNEN, J., et al. (eds.), *Glaube und Gerechtigkeit*. FS R. Gyllenberg, 1983, 181-200. Esp. 185 [ἀπέναντι]; 187 [κατέναντι]; 191-195 [ἔμπροσθεν].

**SOLTERO, Carlos**

1967 Pilatus, Jesus et Barabbas. — *VD* 45 (1967) 326-330. [NTA 13, 117] → Bajšić 1967

**SONG, Choan-Seng**

1993 *Jesus and the Reign of God*. Minneapolis, MN: Fortress, 1993, XVI-304 p.

1994 *Jesus in the Power of the Spirit*. Minneapolis, MN: Fortress, 1994, XIV-335 p. Esp. 214-218 [beatitudes]; 264-266 [28,16-20].

**SONGER, Harold S.**

1962a *A Study of the Background of the Concepts of Parable in the Synoptic Gospels*. Diss. Southern Baptist Theol. Sem., Louisville, KY, 1962.

1962b Jesus' Use of Parables: Matthew 13. — *RExp* 59 (1962) 492-500. [NTA 7, 510]

1992 The Sermon on the Mount and Its Jewish Foreground. — *RExp* 89 (1992) 165-177. [NTA 37, 717]

**SONITRAM, José Maria**

1950 Comentario a los versículos 18, 19, 20 y 21 del capitulo 1. de San Mateo y deducciones sobre el primer dolor y gozo de San José. — *EstJos* 3 (1949) 224-236; 4 (1950) 7-43.

**SORANI, Giuseppe**

1987 "Avete udito ... ma io vi dico". — *Studi Ecumenici* (Verona) 5 (1987) 221-235 (English summary, 236).

**SORGER, Karlheinz**

1986 Die Parabel vom gütigen Herrn des Weinbergs (Mt 20,1-16). — *KatBlät* 111 (1986) 190-192.

**SORIA, Fernando**

1974 San José en Mt. 1–2 según los comentarios de Santo Tomás. — *EstJos* 28 (1974) 177-197.

**SOTTOCORNOLA, Franco**

1957 Tradition and the Doubt of St. Joseph concerning Mary's Virginity. — *Marianum* 19 (1957) 127-141. [NTA 2, 287]

**SOUBIGOU, Louis**

1967 A narração da Epifania segundo São Mateus. — *RevistCuBíb* 4 (1967) 104-110; 5 (1968) 8-14. [NTA 14, 135/472]

**SOUČEK, Josef B.**

1957 The Good Shepherd and His Flock. — *Ecumenical Review* (Genève) 9 (1956-57) 143-153. Esp. 146-147 [shepherd]. [NTA 1, 447]

1962 Bratr a blisní. [Brother and neighbour: Mt 5,43-48 par] — *Theologická příloha - Křest'anské revue* 29 (1962) 129-134.

1963 Sûl zeme a sveta. Přispevek k exegesi Mt 5,13-16. — *Theologická příloha - Křest'anské revue* (Praha) 30 (1963) 1-7.
     Le sel de la terre et la lumière du monde. — *CommViat* 6 (1963) 5-12. [NTA 8, 128]
     Salz der Erde und Licht der Welt. Zur Exegese von Matth. 5,13-16. — *TZ* 19 (1963) 169-179. [NTA 8, 574];
     = POKORNÝ, P. — SOUČEK, J.B., *Bibelauslegung*, 1997, 289-299.

**SOULEN, Richard N.**

1969 Marriage and Divorce. A Problem in New Testament Interpretation. — *Interpr* 23 (1969) 439-450. Esp. 442, 444-446, 448. [NTA 14, 680]
     *SelT* 9 (1970) 249-257.

1976 *Handbook of Biblical Criticism*. Atlanta, GA: Knox, 1976, 191 p. Esp. 137-138: "Q"; ²1981. Esp. 157-159.

**SPAANS-MOOLENAAR, A.**

1990 De bergrede: wie is er aan het woord?. — VAN DEN BRINK, G., et al. (eds.), *Verkenningen in de evangeliën*, 1990, 115-128.

**SPADAFORA, Francesco**

1950 *Gesù e la fine di Gerusalemme* [24] (Quaderni esegetici). Rovigo: Istituto Padano di Arti Grafiche, 1950, XXII-136 p.

1951 Le tentazioni di Gesù. — *PalCl* 30 (1951) 337-346.

1958 Montevergine: Il Santuario. L'anthemis è il "giglio dei campi" di cui parla l'évangelo. [6,25-34] — *PalCl* 37 (1958) 1277-1279. [NTA 3, 584]

1961a Le due genealogie di Gesù. — ROSSI, G. (ed.), *Cento problemi biblici*, 1961, 305-307.

1961b Sulla stella dei Magi. Mt 2,1-12. — *PalCl* 40 (1961) 946-949; = ID., *Attualità Bibliche*, 1964, 348-356.

1961c La seconda beatitudine nel testo e contesto evangelico. [5,4] — *Tabor* (Roma) 30 (1961) 101-109.

La terza beatitudine. [5,5] — *Ibid.*, 197-206.
La quarta beatitudine. [5,6] — *Ibid.*, 293-300.
La beatitudine dei misericordiosi. [5,7] — *Ibid.*, 428-436.

1962 Beati i pacificatori perché saranno chiamati figli di Dio. [5,9] — *Tabor* 31 (1962) 5-12.
Beati i perseguitati per la giustizia. [5,10] — *Ibid.*, 101-106.

1964a *Attualità Bibliche*. Roma: Città Nuova, 1964. → 1961b, 1964b-c

1964b I quattro Vangeli. — *Ibid.*, 95-104.

1964c Amore nei Vangeli sinottici. — *Ibid*, 137-159.

1967 & CANNATA, P., Matteo, Evangelista, apostolo, santo. — *Bibl. Sanct. Lateran.* 9 (1967) 110-145.

1968 Il 'criticismo' ovvero il 'feticcio della critica biblica'. [13,1-23; 16,13-19; 19,1-9] — *PalCl* 47 (1968) 1225-1239. [NTA 13, 475]; 48 (1969) 24-44. [NTA 14, 17]

1971 La prima predizione della Passione e la promessa del Primato. Appunti per l'esegesi di Mt. 16,13–17,20. — GIAVARINI, F. (ed.), *Studi e ricerche*, Rovigo: Istituto Padano di Arte Grafiche, 1971, 203-215.

1980 L'Evangelo dell'infanzia. — *PalCl* 59 (1980) 1076-1088, 1137-1150. [NTA 25, 464]; = *Renovatio* 16 (1981) 46-71.

1982 Raymond E. Brown, "La nascita del Messia". — *Lateranum* 48 (1982) 138-154. → R.E. Brown 1977/81

1986 Data di composizione degli Evangeli. — *Divinitas* 30 (1986) 78-84. [NTA 30, 999] → Carmignac 1984, J.A.T. Robinson 1976, Tresmontant 1983

### SPAEMANN, Heinrich

1969 "Selig die Armen im Geiste, denn ihrer ist das Himmelreich". — MÜSSLE, M. (ed.), *Der "politische" Jesus*, 1969, 18-30.

### SPAGNOLINI, Pietro

1972 Il discorso missionario (Mt 9,36–11,1). — *ParVi* 17 (1972) 203-217.

### SPAIN, Peter L.

1968 Church Discipline in Matthew's Gospel. — *BiTod* 36 (1958) 2528-2531.

### SPARKS, Hedley Frederick Davis

1950 St. Matthew's References to Jeremiah. [2,17; 16,14; 27,9] — *JTS* 1 (1950) 155-156. → Sutcliffe 1952a

1952a *The Formation of the New Testament*. London: SCM, 1952, 172 p. Esp. 104-109 [Mk/Mt].

1952b St. John's Knowledge of Matthew. The Evidence of John 13,16 and 15,20. — *JTS* 3 (1952) 58-61. → Gardner-Smith 1953, Neirynck 1992b (21-26)

1955 The Doctrine of the Divine Fatherhood in the Gospels. — NINEHAM, D.E. (ed.), *Studies in the Gospels*. FS R.H. Lightfoot, 1955, 241-262. Esp. 246-248 [Q]; 251-255 [Mt].

1964 *A Synopsis of the Gospels. Part I: The Synoptic Gospels with the Johannine Parallels*. London: Black; Philadelphia, PA: Fortress, 1964, XXV-248 p.; [2]1970, 274 p. Part II: *The Gospel according to St John with the Synoptic Parallels*. 1974, XIII-96 p.

### SPARKS, Irving Alan

1969 A New Uncial Fragment of St. Matthew. — *JBL* 88 (1969) 201-202. [Lect. 852: 1,23-25; 2,1-2]. [NTA 13, 859] → Junack 1970

### SPARKS, Timothy M.

1977 Cajetan on Saint Joseph. — *EstJos* 31 = *CahJos* 25 (1977) 255-282. Esp. 264-269, 273-278.

**SPECHT, Walter Frederick**

1955 *The Saturday and Sunday Lessons from Matthew in the Greek Gospel Lectionary*. Diss. Univ. of Chicago, Chicago, IL, 1955.

**SPEIGL, Jakob**

1975 Das Hauptgebot der Liebe in den pelagischen Schriften. — MAYER, C.P. – ECKERMANN, W. (eds.), *Scientia Augustiniana. Studien über Augustinus, den Augustinismus und den Augustinerorden. Festschrift Adolar Zumkeller OSA zum 60. Geburtstag*, Würzburg: Augustinus-Verlag, 1975, 137-154. Esp. 143-151: "Die goldene Regel" [7,12].

**SPENDEL, Gunter**

1967 Die "Goldene Regel" als Rechtsprinzip. — ESSER, J. — THIEME, H. (eds.), *Festschrift für Fritz von Hippel zum 70. Geburtstag*, Tübingen: Mohr, 1967, 431-516.

**SPERANSKY, M.K.**

1965 Saint Matthew, Apostle and Evangelist. Historical and Exegetical Essay. [Serbo-croatian] — *Bogoslowskie Trudy* 3 (1965) 5-33.

**SPERBER, Daniel**

1969 The Centurion as a Tax-Collector. — *Latomus* (Bruxelles) 28 (1969) 186-188.

**SPERL, Stefan**

1994 The Literary Form of Prayer. Qur'ān Sura One, the Lord's Prayer, and a Babylonian Prayer to the Moon God. — *Bulletin of the School of Oriental and African Studies* (London) 57 (1994) 213-227.

**SPEYER, Wolfgang**

1976 Genealogie. — *RAC* 9 (1976) 1145-1268. Esp. 1213-1243.

1977 Die leibliche Abstammung Jesu im Urteil der Schriftsteller der alten Kirche. — *Helmántica* (Salamanca) 28 (1977) 523-539; = ID., *Frühes Christentum im antiken Strahlungsfeld. Ausgewählte Aufsätze* (WUNT, 50), Tübingen: Mohr, 1989, 202-219.

**SPICQ, Ceslas**

1954 Die Liebe als Gestaltungsprinzip der Moral in den synoptischen Evangelien. — *FZPT* 1 (1954) 394-410.

1958 *Agapè dans le Nouveau Testament. Analyse des textes*, I (Études bibliques). Paris: Gabalda, 1958, 334 p. Esp. 11-80: "La charité dans l'Évangile de saint Matthieu"; 156-174: "La charité dans les Évangiles synoptiques".
*Agape in the New Testament*. Vol. I: *Agape in the Synoptic Gospels*, trans. M.A. McNamara & M.H. Richter. St. Louis, MO – London: B. Herder Book Co., 1963, XIV-153 p. [= 1958, 5-174]. Esp. 3-56; 127-143.
*Agape en el Nuevo Testamento. Análisis de textos*. Madrid: Cares, 1977, 3 vols., 1136 p.

1959 Une allusion au Docteur de Justice dans Matthieu, XXIII,10? — *RB* 66 (1959) 387-396. [NTA 4, 656]

1961 *Dieu et l'homme selon le Nouveau Testament* (LD, 29). Paris: Cerf, 1961. Esp. 54-61 [18,23-35].

1964 "Joseph, son mari, étant juste..." (*Mt.* I,19). — *RB* 71 (1964) 206-214. [NTA 9, 520] → D. Hill 1965

1978a *Notes de lexicographie néo-testamentaire* (Orbis Biblicus et Orientalis, 22/1-2). Freiburg/Schw: Éd. universitaires; Göttingen: Vandenhoeck & Ruprecht, 1978, I, 1-524 p.; II, 525-980 p.; III. *Supplément* (Orbis Biblicus et Orientalis, 22/3), 1982, 698 p.
F. NEIRYNCK, *ETL* 60 (1984) 156-157.
*Lexique théologique du Nouveau Testament. Réédition en un volume des Notes de lexicographie néo-*

*testamentaire*. Paris: Cerf, 1991, 1668 p.
*Note di lessicografia neotestamentaria*, ed. F.L. Viero (Suppl. Grande Lessico del N.T., 4/1). Brescia: Paideia, 1988, 946 p.
*Theological Lexicon of the New Testament*, trans. and ed. J.D. Ernest. Peabody, MA: Hendrickson, 1994, I, LXIV-492; II, XI-603 and III, X-691 p.

1978b Le vocabulaire de l'esclavage dans le Nouveau Testament. — *RB* 85 (1978) 201-226.
Esp. 204-214 [δοῦλος]; 216-218 [κοράσιον]; 220-224 [παῖς]. [NTA 23. 773]

1984 L'amour de charité se refroidira (*Mt.* XXIV,12). — LUCCHESI, E. – SAFFREY, H.D. (eds.), *Mémorial André-Jean Festugière. Antiquité païenne et chrétienne* (Cahiers d'Orientalisme, 10), Genève: Cramer, 1984, 113-117.

1991 → 1978a

**SPIES, Otto**
1975 Die Arbeiter im Weinberg (Mt 20,1-15) in islamischer Überlieferung. — *ZNW* 66 (1975) 279-283. [NTA 20, 780]

**SPIJKERMAN, Augustus**
1956 Coins Mentioned in the New Testament. — *SBF/LA* 6 (1955-56) 279-298. Esp. 285-295.

**SPINELLI, Mario**
1982 (ed.), *Le beatitudini nel commento dei Padri latini* (Letture cristiane delle origini, 8). Roma: Paoline, 1982, 272 p.
C. BURINI, *Benedictina* 30 (1983) 273-275.

**SPIVEY, Robert A.** → D.M. Smith 1969

**SPLETT, Jochen**
1987 (ed.), *Das hymelreich ist gleich einem verporgenen schatz in einem acker...: die hochdeutschen Übersetzungen von Matthäus 13,44-52 in mittelalterlichen Handschriften* (Litterae: Göttinger Beiträge zur Textgeschichte, 108). Göttingen: Kummerle, 1987, 57-220 p.

1991 Die Zuordnung zu Übersetzungszweigen. Dargestellt anhand der hochdeutschen Übersetzungen von Mt 13,44-52 in mittelalterlichen Handschriften. — REINITZER, H. – HENKEL, N. (eds.), *Deutsche Bibelübersetzungen des Mittelalters* (Vestigia Bibliae. Jahrbuch des Deutschen Bibel-Archivs Hamburg, 9-10 [1987-88]), Bern: Lang, 1991, 35-58.

**SPÖRRI, Gottlob**
1969 *... warum hast du gezweifelt? Zum Christusbild der ersten drei Evangelien.* Zürich: Zwingli, 1969, 157 p.

**SPONG, J.S.**
1992 *Born of a Woman. A Bishop Rethinks the Birth of Jesus.* San Francisco, CA: HarperCollins, 1992, XX-245 p.

**SPOTTORNO, María Victoria**
1982 The Relative Pronoun in the New Testament. Some Critical Remarks. — *NTS* 28 (1982) 132-141. Esp. 132-135: "General problems"; 138-139 [ὅσος]. [NTA 26, 809]

1986 El carácter expansivo del Códice de Beza. — MUÑOZ LEÓN, D. (ed.), *Salvación en la palabra. Targum – Derash – Berith. En memoria del profesor Alejandro Díez Macho*, Madrid: Cristiandad, 1986, 689-698. Esp. 691; 692 [10,23]; 693-395 [20,28].

**SPROULE, John A.**
1980 The Problem of the Mustard Seed. — *GraceTJ* 1 (1980) 37-42. [NTA 25, 76]

**SQUILLACI, D.**

1957 Il discorso escatologico. [24-25] — *PalCl* 36 (1957) 1016-1021; 37 (1958) 25-29, 72-77. [NTA 2, 532]

1959a Parabola delle nozze del figlio del re (Mt. 22,1-14). — *PalCl* 38 (1959) 972-976. [NTA 4, 389]

1959b La riprovazione del popolo ebraico. [22,14] — *Ibid.*, 1043-1049. [NTA 4, 390]

1960 I Magi. — *PalCl* 39 (1960) 16-20. [NTA 4, 642]

1962 Il mistero di Betlem nel profeta Michea (5,2-5a). [2,6] — *PalCl* 41 (1962) 763-766. [NTA 7, 124]

1963 Matrimonio di San Giuseppe. [1,16] — *PalCl* 42 (1963) 659-666. [NTA 8, 122]

1964 L'inno dell'Eucaristia. [26,30] — *PalCl* 43 (1964) 287-292. [NTA 8, 955]

1965 L'apparizione di Gesù sopra un monte della Galilea. Missione degli Apostoli. Matt. 28,16-20. — *PalCl* 44 (1965) 641-645. [NTA 10, 131]

**STAAB, Karl**

1951 *Das Evangelium nach Matthäus* (Echter-Bibel. Neues Testament, 1). Würzburg: Echter, 1951, 164 p.; [2]1963, 167 p. Esp. 7-16 [introduction]; 17-164 [commentary]. → Schnackenburg 1985a M.-É. BOISMARD, *RB* 62 (1955) 458-459; P.I. BRATSIOTIS, Θεολογία 23 (1952) 624-625; J. KÜRZINGER, *Klerusblatt* 31 (1951) 260; J.F. MCCONNELL, *CBQ* 15 (1953) 252-256; K.H. SCHELKLE, *BK* 6 (1951) 125; *TQ* 132 (1952) 236-237; SPICQ, *RSPT* 37 (1953) 146-147; K. STAAB, *MüTZ* 5 (1954) 73-75 (→ Vögtle); A. VÖGTLE, *MüTZ* 4 (1953) 364-367.

**STAATS, Reinhart**

1969 Die törichten Jungfrauen von Mt 25 in gnostischer und antignostischer Literatur. — ELTESTER, W. (ed.), *Christentum und Gnosis* (BZNW, 37), Berlin: Töpelmann, 1969, 98-115.

**STACHOWIAK, Lech Remigius**

1957 *Chrestotes. Ihre biblisch-theologische Entwicklung und Eigenart* (Studia Friburgensia, NF 17). Freiburg/Schw: Universitätsverlag, 1957, XIX-137 p. Esp. 46-56 [11,28-30]. — Diss. Freiburg/Schw, 1956 (C. Spicq).

1976 Osiem błogosławieństw na tle pojęć etycznych mieszkańców Palestyny w epoce Chrystusa (Die Seligpreisungen im Lichte der sittlichen Ideale der Palästina-Bewohner zur Zeit Jesu). — *RoczTK* 23/1 (1976) 49-59. [NTA 22, 84]

**STADTLAND-NEUMANN, Hiltrud**

1966a *Evangelische Radikalismen in der Sicht Calvins. Sein Verständnis der Bergpredigt und der Aussendungsrede (Matth. 10)* (Beiträge zur Geschichte und Lehre der Reformierten Kirche, 24). Göttingen: Vandenhoeck & Ruprecht, 1966, 156 p. Esp. 15-54: "Calvins Auslegung der Bergpredigt und der Aussendungsrede"; 55-148: "Gründe für die Erweichung radikaler Aussagen bei Calvin". — Diss. Göttingen, 1963 (O. Weber).

1966b & VOGELBUSCH, G. (eds.), *Johannes Calvins Auslegung der Evangelien-Harmonie* (Johannes Calvins Auslegung der Heiligen Schrift, 12-13). Neukirchen–Vluyn: Neukirchener, I, 1966, 460 p.; II, 1974, 452 p.

**STAEHELIN, Johann**

1954 *Das Matthäus-Evangelium. Text und Deutung.* Bern: Hötzendorfer, 1954, 176 p. *BK* 10 (1955) 25; P.C., *Angelicum* 32 (1955) 180.

**STÄHLIN, Gustav**

1956 "On the Third Day". The Easter Traditions of the Primitive Church. — *Interpr* 10 (1956) 282-299. Esp. 290. [NTA 1, 448]

1962   Zum Gebrauch von Beteuerungsformeln im Neuen Testament. — *NT* 5 (1962) 115-143.
Esp. 116-121.139-140 [5,34-37]; 124-126 [26,63-64]. [NTA 7, 455]

1974   Von der Seelsorge im Neuen Testament. — *TBeitr* 5 (1974) 101-123. [NTA 19, 303]
Matthäus als Seelsorger. — *TGeg* 18 (1975) 20-28.

**STÄHLIN, Rudolf**

1956   Die Schlüssel des Himmelreiches. [16,17-19] — *Evangelisch-Lutherische Kirchliche Zeitschrift* 10 (1956) 69-76.

**STÄHLIN, Wilhelm**

1954   Die politische Bedeutung der Seligpreisungen. — *Neues Abendland* (München) 9 (1954) 579-586.

**STÄPS, Detlef**

1983   Das Täuferwort vom Reinigen der Tenne. [3,12] — *ErbAu*ᶠ 59 (1983) 204-210.

**STAGG, Frank**

1962   The Christology of Matthew. — *RExp* 59 (1962) 457-468. [NTA 7, 499]

1969   & TURLINGTON, H., et al., *General Articles, Matthew, Mark* (The Broadman Bible Commentary, 8). Nashville: Broadman, 1969, 402 p. (Mt: Stagg).
W. KLASSEN, *JBL* 89 (1970) 108-110.

1972   Salvation in Synoptic Tradition. — *RExp* 69 (1972) 355-357. [NTA 17, 895]

1978   & STAGG, Evelyn, *Woman in the World of Jesus*. Philadelphia, PA: Westminster; Edinburgh: St. Andrew, 1978, 292 p. Esp. 101-160: "Jesus and woman"; 215-219: "The gospel of Matthew".

1981   Reassessing the Gospels. — *RExp* 78 (1981) 187-203. Esp 193-195. [NTA 26, 49]

**STAHL, Janine**

1984   À propos du Sermon sur la montagne. — *VSp* 138 (1984) 17-27.

**STALDER, Kurt**

1983   Überlegungen zur Interpretation der Bergpredigt. — LUZ, U. – WEDER, H. (eds.), *Die Mitte des Neuen Testaments*. FS E. Schweizer, 1983, 272-290. Esp. 273-278: "Gebot und Gesetz"; 278-290: "Die Verwendung soziologischer Methoden".

**STAM, Cor**

1950   *De Hemelvaart des Heren in de Godsopenbaring van het Nieuwe Testament*. Kampen: Kok, 1950, 112 p. Esp. 11-14 [28,18-20].

1951   Het slot van het evangelie volgens Mattheus. — *Arcana Revelata. Een bundel nieuw-testamentische studiën aangeboden aan Prof. Dr. F.W. Grosheide ter gelegenheid van zijn zeventigste verjaardag*, Kampen: Kok, 1951, 127-133.

**STANDAERT, Benoît**

1976   'L'Évangile de Vérité': critique et lecture. — *NTS* 22 (1975-76) 243-275. Esp. 251-252 [28,18-20]. [NTA 21, 303]

1989   Crying 'Abba' and saying 'Our Father'. An Intertextual Approach of the Dominical Prayer. — DRAISMA, S. (ed.), *Intertextuality in Biblical Writings*. FS B. van Iersel, 1989, 141-158. Esp. 144-148: "The 'Our Father' in Matthew and in Luke"; 149-151 [Mk 14,36; 11,25/Mt].

1992   L'évangile selon Matthieu. Composition et genre littéraire. — VAN SEGBROECK, F., et al. (eds.), *The Four Gospels 1992*. FS F. Neirynck, 1992, II, 1223-1250. Esp. 1225-1238: "Matthieu lecteur de Marc"; 1238-1249: "Éléments compositionnels spécifiques de Matthieu".

1994   "Misericordia voglio" (Mt 9,13 e 12,7). — *ParSpirV* 29 (1994) 109-119.

1995 *In de school van Matteüs. Commentaar bij de zondagslezingen van de A-cyclus.* Brussel: LICAP, 1995, 224 p.

**STANDER, H.F.**
1987 On Translating Matthew 6:12 (and Luke 11:4). — *NduitseGT* 28 (1987) 241-242.

**STANFIELD, V.L.**
1962 Preaching Values in the Gospel of Matthew. — *RExp* 59 (1962) 512-517. [NTA 7, 500]

**STANLEY, David Michael**
1954a Études matthéennes: La confession de Pierre à Césarée. [16,16] — *ScEccl* 6 (1954) 51-61.

1954b Études matthéennes: L'entrée messianique à Jérusalem. [21,9-10] — *Ibid.*, 93-106.

1954c The Theme of the Servant of Yahweh in Primitive Christian Soteriology, and Its Transposition by St. Paul. — *CBQ* 16 (1954) 385-425. Esp. 398-401: "The servant theology of Greek Matthew".
Paul and the Christian Concept of the Servant of God. — ID., *The Apostolic Church*, 1965, 448-455. Esp. 323-325.

1955a et al., Panel Discussion on the Methods of Teaching Scripture. — *CBQ* 17 (1955) 35-53. Esp. 44-49: "Teaching Matthew's gospel"; 49-50: "Discussion on teaching St. Matthew".

1955b *Didachē* as a Constitutive Element of the Gospel-Form. — *Ibid.*, 336-348 (216-228). Esp. 337-339; 341-342.
Didachē as a Constitutive Element of the Written Gospel. — ID., *The Apostolic Church*, 1965, 199-213, 429-432. Esp. 200-202; 204-205.

1955c Kingdom to Church. — *TS* 16 (1955) 1-29. Esp. 22-29: "The structural development of apostolic christianity in the New Testament"; = ID., *The Apostolic Church*, 1965, 5-37, 395-400. Esp. 29-37.

1956a Baptism in the New Testament. — *Scripture* 8 (1956) 44-57. Esp. 45-46, 51. [NTA 1, 144]; = WORDEN, T. (ed.), *Sacraments in Scripture. A Symposium*, London–Dublin: Chapman, 1966, 45-62. Esp. 46-47, 51.

1956b The Conception of Salvation in the Synoptic Gospels. — *CBQ* 18 (1956) 345-363. Esp. 354-360: "St. Matthew's view of the Christian plan of salvation" [1,21; 4,14-16; 10,23; 12,39-40; 15,24; 16,27-28; 19,28; 23,37-39; 28,18]. [NTA 1, 186]
Salvation in the Synoptic Gospels. — ID., *The Apostolic Church*, 1965, 214-237, 433-436. Esp. 225-233.
Christ as Savior in the Synoptic Gospels. — O'DONOVAN, L.J. (ed.), *Word and Mystery. Biblical Essays on the Person and Mission of Christ*, New York: Newman, 1968, 47-67. Esp. 57-63.

1957 The New Testament Doctrine of Baptism. An Essay in Biblical Theology. — *TS* 18 (1957) 169-215. Esp. 197-198 [3,13-17]. [NTA 2, 142]; = ID., *The Apostolic Church*, 1965, 140-194, 421-428. Esp. 167-169.

1958 Balaam's Ass, or a Problem in New Testament Hermeneutics. — *CBQ* 20 (1958) 50-56. Esp. 52 [8,6; 14,33]. [NTA 2, 493]

1959a The Conception of Our Gospels as Salvation-History. — *TS* 20 (1959) 561-589. [NTA 5, 650]
*TDig* 9 (1961) 23-25.
The Gospels as Salvation History. — HEANEY, J.J. (ed.), *Faith, Reason, and the Gospels. A Selection of Modern Thought on Faith and the Gospels*, Westminster, MD: Newman, 1961, 253-275; = CALLAHAN, D.J. – OBERMAN, H.A. – O'HANLON, D.J. (eds.), *Christianity Divided: Protestant and Roman Catholic Theological Issues*, New York: Sheed & Ward, 1961, 111-145 (slightly revised); = ID., *The Apostolic Church*, 1965, 238-277, 437-440.

1959b Liturgical Influences on the Formation of the Four Gospels. — *CBQ* 21 (1959) 24-38. Esp. 28-29 [28,18-20]. [NTA 3, 567]
Liturgical Influences on the Formation of the Gospels. — ID., *The Apostolic Church*, 1965, 119-139, 419-420. Esp. 125-126.

1960    *The Gospel of St. Matthew* (The New Testament Reading Guide, 4). Collegeville, MN: Liturgical Press, 1960, 97 p. [NTA 6, p. 262]; [2]1963, 129 p. [NTA 8, p. 490]
*Evangelio de S. Mateo* (Conoce la Biblia, NT 4). Santander: Sal Terrae, 1965, 152 p.
*Evangelho de Mateus*. São Paulo: Paulinas, 1975.

1961    Pauline Allusions to the Sayings of Jesus. — *CBQ* 23 (1961) 26-39. Esp. 28-34: "Doctrinal parallels to Logia of Jesus" [15,24; 22,34-40; 24,43-44]; 34-38: "Pauline allusions to Jesus' parables" [13,33; 19,30-20,16; 21,33-43; 25,1-13]. [NTA 5, 780]; = ID., *The Apostolic Church*, 1965, 352-370, 456-457. Esp. 356-363; 363-370.

1963    Reflections on the Church in the New Testament. — *CBQ* 25 (1963) 387-400. Esp. 398: "The church in Matthew's gospel". [NTA 8, 295]

1964a   The Concept of Salvation-History in the New Testament. [1-2] — *BiTod* 11 (1964) 686-693. [NTA 8, 872]; = RYAN, M.R. (ed.), *Contemporary New Testament Studies*, 1965, 93-98.

1964b   The New Testament Basis for the Concept of Collegiality. — *TS* 25 (1964) 197-216. Esp. 203-204 [10,5-42]; 213-214 [16,16-19]. [NTA 9, 300]
        *TDig* 13 (1965) 222-227.

1965    *The Apostolic Church in the New Testament*. Westminster MD: Newman, 1965, XIV-472 p.; [3]1967. → 1954c, 1955b-c, 1956b, 1957, 1959a-b, 1961

1967    Authority in the Church: A New Testament Reality. — *CBQ* 29 (1967) 555-573. Esp. 563.567.570-572. [NTA 12, 702]

1980    *Jesus in Gethsemane*. New York – Ramsey, NJ: Paulist, 1980, 282 p. Esp. 155-187 [26,36-46].

**STANO, Gaetano M.**

1952    Pater Noster. — *Enciclopedia Cattolica* (Vaticano) 9 (1952) 943-946.

1971    La distruzione di Gerusalemme dell'anno 70 e l'esegesi di Dan 9,24-27 (cf. Mt 24,15; Mc 13,14). — *La distruzione di Gerusalemme del 70 nei suoi riflessi storico-letterari*. *Atti del V Convegno Biblico Francescano. Roma, 22-27 settembre 1969* (Collectio Assisiensis, 8), Assisi: Studio teologico "Porziuncola", 1971, 79-110.

**STANTON, Graham N.**

1973    On the Christology of Q. — LINDARS, B. - SMALLEY, S.S. (eds.), *Christ and Spirit in the New Testament. In Honour of Charles Francis Digby Moule*, Cambridge: University Press, 1973, 27-42. Esp. 29-31 [11,2-6]; 31-32 [3,11-12]; 34 [5,3; 12 28]; 34-35 [4,1-11]; 35-37 [11,25-27]; 37 [23,34-36]; 37-38 [23,37-39]; 38 [11,28-30].

1974    *Jesus of Nazareth in New Testament Preaching* (SNTS MS, 27). Cambridge: University Press, 1974, XI-207 p. Esp. 129-136: "The gospel of Thomas and Jesus of Nazareth"; 137-171: "Jesus in the Gospel Traditions". [11,2-6.19]. — Diss. Cambridge, 1969 (C.F.D. Moule).

1975    Form Criticism Revisited. — HOOKER, M.D. - HICKLING C. (eds.), *What about the New Testament?* FS C. Evans, 1975, 13-27. Esp. 17 [Q].

1977    5 Ezra and Matthaean Christianity in the Second Century. — *JTS* 28 (1977) 67-83. Esp. 68-73; 73-79: "5 Ezra and Matthew's gospel"; 79-83. [NTA 21, 980]; = ID., *A Gospel for a New People*, 1992, 256-277 (additional note, 277). Esp. 258-263; 264-272; 272-277.

1982    Salvation Proclaimed. X. Matthew 11,28-30: Comfortable Words? — *ExpT* 94 (1982-83) 3-9. [NTA 27, 100]
        Matthew 11.28-30: Comfortable Words? — ID., *A Gospel for a New People*, 1992, 364-377 (additional note, 377).

1983*   (ed.), *The Interpretation of Matthew* (Issues in Religion and Theology, 3). Philadelphia, PA: Fortress; London: SPCK, 1983, XI-164 p. [NTA 28, p. 87]; (Studies in New Testament Interpretation), Edinburgh: Clark, 1995, XIV-219 p. [NTA 40, p. 349] → G.

Bornkamm 1970, Dahl 1955, von Dobschütz 1928, Luz 1971, O. Michel 1950, Schweizer 1974d, Stanton 1983a-b, Stendahl 1960, Strecker 1966; → Kingsbury 1987a/95

L. ALEXANDER, *JJS* 36 (1985) 242-243; K.A. BARTA, *BTB* 16 (1986) 41; D.A. CARSON, *Themelios* 9/3 (1983-84) 28-29; L. DEVILLERS, *RThom* 87 (1987) 311-312; F. LANGLAMET, *RB* 91 (1984) 621-622; I.H. MARSHALL, *EvQ* 57 (1985) 182-183; F.J. MATERA, *Interpr* 39 (1985) 314.316; F. MONTAGNINI, *BibOr* 27 (1985) 252; M. PAMMENT, *NBlackfr* 65 (1984) 193-194; F. VOUGA, *ETR* 59 (1984) 414-415. F. NEIRYNCK, *ETL* 72 (1996) 445-446.

1983a  Introduction: Matthew's Gospel. A New Storm Centre. — *Ibid.*, 1-18.
Introduction: Matthew's Gospel in Recent Scholarship (1994). — *Ibid.*, ²1995, 1-26 (expanded). Esp. 17-20: "Matthew and contemporary Judaism"; 20-21: "Matthew's use of the OT"; 22-23: "Matthew and the law"; 23-25: "Social-scientific approaches".

1983b  Select Bibliography. — *Ibid.*, 156-161; ²1995, 199-210 (expanded).

1983c  Matthew as a Creative Interpreter of the Sayings of Jesus. — STUHLMACHER, P. (ed.), *Das Evangelium und die Evangelien*, 1983, 273-287. Esp. 274-278 [9,13; 10,5-6; 12,7; 15,24; 21,41.43; 24,10-12.26; 26,52-54/Mk]; 278-283 [5,13-16; 6,9-13; 7,12.15-20.21; 10,1-42; 18,10.14; 23,28-34/Q]; 283-286 [Sg Mt 11,28-30; 25,31-46]; = STUHLMACHER, P. (ed.), *The Gospel and the Gospels*, 1991, 257-272. Esp. 259-262; 263-267; 267-270; = ID., *A Gospel for a New People*, 1992, 326-345. Esp. 328-333; 333-339; 340-345.

1984  The Gospel of Matthew and Judaism. — *BJRL* 66 (1983-84) 264-284. Esp. 267 [5,11-12]; 267-268 [5,20]; 268 [8,11-12]; 268-269 [21,43]; 269-270 [22,1-10]; 270-271 [23,34]; 278-279 [24,10-12]; 279-281 [25,31-46]. [NTA 29, 81]; = ID., *A Gospel for a New People*, 1992, 146-168. Esp. 148-154: "Matthew's anti-Jewish polemic"; 154-157: "The function of the anti-Jewish polemic"; 157-168: "A proposed setting for Matthew's gospel".

1985a  Aspects of Early Christian-Jewish Polemic and Apologetic. — *NTS* 31 (1985) 377-392. Esp. 380-381 [27,63]; 383-384 [5,17]; 386-389 [23,39]. [NTA 30, 465]; = ID., *A Gospel for a New People*, 1992, 232-255. Esp. 238-240; 244-246; 249-250.

1985b  On the Origin and Purpose of Matthew's Gospel. Matthean Scholarship from 1945 to 1980. — *ANRW* II.25.3 (1985) 1889-1951. Esp. 1890-1895: "Recent Matthean scholarship"; 1895-1906: "Matthew as evangelist"; 1906-1921: "Matthew as polemicist or apologist"; 1921-1941: "Matthew as theologian"; 1941-1943: "The origin of Matthew's gospel"; 1945-1951: "Select bibliography". → 1992c, 1992f

1987  The Origin and Purpose of Matthew's Sermon on the Mount. — HAWTHORNE, G.F. – BETZ, O. (eds.), *Tradition and Interpretation*. FS E.E. Ellis, 1987, 181-192. Esp. 182-187: "A pre-Matthean epitome of the teaching of Jesus?"; 187-190: "The SM as an integral part of Matthew's gospel". → H.D. Betz 1985a
The Origin and Purpose of the Sermon on the Mount. — ID., *A Gospel for a New People*, 1992, 307-325. Esp. 310-318; 318-325.

1988  Matthew. — CARSON, D.A. — WILLIAMSON, H.G.M. (eds.), *It is Written: Scripture Citing Scripture. Essays in Honour of Barnabas Lindars*, Cambridge: University Press, 1988, 205-219. Esp. 207-210: "Recent research"; 210-213: "Was the LXX Matthew's Bible?"; 214-217: "Matthew's formula quotations".
Matthew's Use of the Old Testament. — ID., *A Gospel for a New People*, 1992, 346-363. Esp. 349-353; 353-358; 358-363.

1989a  *The Gospels and Jesus* (Oxford Bible Series). Oxford: University Press, 1989, ²1990, X-296 p. Esp. 59-80: "Matthew's gospel. The way of righteousness".

1989b  'Pray that your flight may not be in winter or on a sabbath' (Matthew 24.20). — *JSNT* 37 (1989) 17-30. Esp. 21-24: "Your flight"; 24-26: "On a sabbath". [NTA 34, 635]; = ID., *A Gospel for a New People*, 1992, 192-206. Esp. 198-203; 203-206. → K.-C. Wong 1991

1990a  Matthew, Gospel of. — *DBI*, 1990, 432-435.

1990b  Sermon on the Mount. — *Ibid.*, 625-628.

1992a  *A Gospel for a New People. Studies in Matthew.* Edinburgh: Clark, 1992, XIV-424 p.
[NTA 37, p. 285]; Louisville, KY: Westminster/Knox, 1993. [NTA 38, p. 467] → 1977, 1982,
1983c, 1984, 1985a, 1987, 1988, 1989b, 1992b-h.j

 T. ANGERT-QUILTER, *Pacifica* 7 (1994) 95-97; R. ASCOUGH, *TorontoJT* 10 (1994) 129-131; E.
CUVILLIER, *ETR* 68 (1993) 576-577; H.B. GREEN, *NT* 37 (1995) 95-97; D.A. HAGNER, *JSNT* 51 (1993)
125; D. HILL, *ExpT* 104 (1992-93) 122; N.N. HINGLE, *EvQ* 65 (1993) 358-360; J.D. KINGSBURY, *JTS*
44 (1993) 647-652; F. LANGLAMET, *RB* 100 (1993) 132-133; R.K. MCIVER, *BibInt* 3 (1995) 78-79; J.
MUDDIMAN, *Theology* 96 (1993) 322-323; M.A. POWELL, *CBQ* 56 (1994) 154-155; D. ROURÉ, *EstBíb*
53 (1995) 411-413; E.A. RUSSELL, *IBS* 14 (1992) 200-202.

1992b  Introduction. Conclusions. — *Ibid.*, 1-19; 378-383.

1992c  Redaction Criticism: The End of an Era? — *Ibid.*, 23-53. Esp. 24-28: "The dawn of an era";
28-41: "Source criticism"; 41-45: "Matthew's theology"; 45-53: "Matthew's communities". → 1985, 1895-
1899

1992d  Literary Criticism: Ancient and Modern. — *Ibid.*, 54-84. Esp. 59-71: "Genre"; 71-76: "The
first audience"; 77-84: "Rhetorical strategies".

1992e  Matthew's Gospel and the Damascus Document in Sociological Perspective. — *Ibid.*,
85-107. Esp. 89-98: "Sectarian communities" [Mt: 93-94; 94-98]; 98-104: "Social conflict theory"; 104-
107: "Legitimation".

1992f  Synagogue and Church. — *Ibid.*, 113-145. Esp. 114-118: "The traditional view"; 118-124: "An
internal dispute within Judaism?"; 124-131: "In the wake of the parting of the ways"; 131-142: "For gentiles
not in dispute with Judaism?"; 142-145: "Matthew and the birkath ha-m nim". → 1985 (1910-1921)

1992g  Christology and the Parting of the Ways. — *Ibid.*, 169-191. Esp. 171-180: "Jesus is a
magician and a deceiver" [9,34; 10,25; 12,24.27]; 180-185: "Hostility to Jesus the Son of David" [2,3; 9,27-
28; 21,15]; 185-191: "An early form of the 'two parousias' schema".
 Matthew's Christology and the Parting of the Ways. — DUNN, J.D.G. (ed.), *Jews and Christians*, 1992,
99-116. Esp. 101-108; 108-112; 112-114. → Birdsall 1992

1992h  Once More: Matthew 25.31-46. — *Ibid.*, 207-231. Esp. 212-214: "Who is gathered for
judgement?"; 214-218: "Who are 'the least of these my brothers'?"; 218-221: "Who are the needy?"; 221-
230: "An apocalyptic discourse"; 230-231: "Note on the history of interpretation".

1992i  Q. — *DJG*, 1992, 644-650.

1992j  Sermon on the Mount/Plain. — *Ibid.*, 735-744. Esp. 736-737: "The sermon on the plain in
Luke"; 737-744: "The Sermon on the Mount in Matthew".
 Interpreting the Sermon on the Mount. — ID., *A Gospel for a New People*, 1992, 285-
306. Esp. 286-289: "The sermon in Q and in Luke"; 289-297: "History of interpretation"; 297-06: "The
structure of the sermon".

1992k  The Communities of Matthew. — *Interpr* 46 (1992) 379-391. Esp. 382-384 [Jewish
leaders/church]; 385-376 [Gentiles]. [NTA 37, 712]

1992l  Matthew: βίβλος, εὐαγγέλιον, or βίος? — VAN SEGBROECK, F., et al. (eds.), *The
Four Gospels 1992*. FS F. Neirynck, 1992, II, 1187-1201. Esp. 1189-1190 [1,1]; 1190-1195:
"Matthew, the first to refer to his writing as εὐαγγέλιον?"; 1196-1201: "Matthew's gospel as a βίος".

1993  The Two Parousias of Christ: Justin Martyr and Matthew. — DE BOER, M.C. (ed.),
*From Jesus to John*. FS M. de Jonge, 1993, 183-195. Esp. 190-195.

1994a  Early Objections to the Resurrection of Jesus. — BARTON, S.C. - STANTON, G.N.
(eds.), *Resurrection*. FS L. Houlden, 1994, 79-94. Esp. 85-86 [28,11-15/Justin].

1994b  Jesus of Nazareth: A Magician and a False Prophet Who Deceived God's People? —
GREEN, J.B. - TURNER, M.M.B. (eds.), *Jesus of Nazareth*. FS I.H. Marshall, 1994,
164-180. Esp. 178-180 [Mk/Q 11,14-23].

1994c  Revisiting Matthew's Communities. — *SBL 1994 Seminar Papers*, 9-23. Esp. 10-13:
"Genre and geography"; 13-18: "External affairs"; 18-23: "Internal affairs".

1995*  → 1983*

1995a  *Gospel Truth? New Light on Jesus and the Gospels*. London: HarperCollins; Valley Forge, PA: TPI, 1995, VIII-215 p. Esp. 11-19: "First-century fragments of Matthew's gospel?" [P⁶⁴]; 63-76: "Q: a lost 'gospel'?"; 96-110: "One gospel and four gospellers".

1995b  A Gospel among the Scrolls? — *BibReview* 11/6 (1995) 36-42. [NTA 40, 719] → Thiede 1995c

1995c  Matthew's Gospel. A Survey of Some Recent Commentaries. — *BTrans* 46 (1995) 131-140. [Davies-Allison, Luz, Hagner, Kingsbury, Davies, Garland, Patte, Morris, Gundry, Carson, Harrington]. [NTA 39, 1443]
Trans. Greek in *DeltBM* 24 (1995) 18-31. [NTA 40, 808]

**STAPLES, Peter**

1959  The Kingdom of God Has Come. [26,45-46] — *ExpT* 71 (1959-60) 87-88. [NTA 4, 658] → W.R. Hutton 1952

**STARCKY, Jean**

1971  La quatrième demande du Pater. — *HTR* 64 (1971) 401-409. [NTA 16, 153]

**STARK, Rodney**

1991  Antioch as the Social Situation for Matthew's Gospel. — BALCH, D.L. (ed.), *Social History of the Matthean Community*, 1991, 189-210. → Gundry 1991

**STASSEN, Glen H.**

1992  Grace and Deliverance in the Sermon on the Mount. — *RExp* 89 (1992) 229-244. [NTA 37, 718]

**STATHER HUNT, B.P.W.**

1951  *Primitive Gospel Sources*. London: Clarke; New York: Philosophical Library, 1951, XV-344 p. Esp. 85-102: "Gospel sources" [Mk/Q; Mt 3,13-17; 12,1-8; 16,17-19]; 148-164 [OT]; 165-166 [11,3]; 182-193 [Papias].

**STAUDINGER, Ferdinand**

1968  Die neutestamentlichen Wunder in der Verkündigung. — *ErbAuf* 44 (1968) 355-366. Esp. 359.361-632 [8,23-27]. [NTA 13, 807]

**STAUDINGER, Josef**

1957  *Die Bergpredigt*. Wien: Herder, 1957, 360 p. [NTA 3, p. 212]
BK 12 (1957) 93; M.-É. BOISMARD, RB 65 (1958) 302; B. BRINKMANN, *Scholastik* 33 (1958) 300-301; C.P. CEROKE, *CBQ* 20 (1958) 270-271; J.L. D'ARAGON, *ScEccl* 10 (1958) 537-539; J. DUPONT, *LumièreV* 35 (1957) 32; C. GANCHO, *EstBíb* 17 (1958) 334-335; B. GERHARDSSON, *SEÅ* 25 (1960) 159-160; R. KUGELMAN, *TS* 19 (1958) 256-258; J. LEAL, *EstE* 33 (1959) 245-246; É. MASSAUX, *ETL* 33 (1957) 747-748; J. MICHL, *MüTZ* 11 (1960) 77-78; L.F. RIVERA, *RevistBíb* 20 (1958) 169-170; J. SALGUERO, *Ang* 36 (1959) 102; K.H. SCHELKLE, *TQ* 137 (1957) 483-484; J. SCHNEIDER, *TLZ* 83 (1958) 419-421; J. SINT, *ZKT* 80 (1958) 345; C. SPICQ, *FZPT* 6 (1959) 55; A. STÖGER, *TPQ* 105 (1957) 341-342; A. VIARD, *RSPT* 43 (1959) 304; J.J. VINCENT, *TZ* 14 (1958) 223-224; M. ZERWICK, *VD* 35 (1957) 248-250.

**STAUFFER, Ethelbert**

1941ᴿ  *New Testament Theology*, trans. J. Marsh [German 1941, ⁵1948]. London: SCM, 1955, ²1963, 373 p.

1955  Antike Jesustradition und Jesuspolemik im mittelalterlichen Orient. — *ZNW* 46 (1955) 1-30. Esp. 5.25.30 [11,27]; 15-16 [11,5]; 18-19 [11,6-7]; 24 [11,11.24]; 25-26 [11,29].

1956  Messias oder Menschensohn? — *NT* 1 (1956) 81-102. Esp. 89-90 [Χριστός]. [NTA 1, 137]

1958  Von jedem unnützen Wort? [12,36] — DELLING, G. (ed.), *Gott und die Götter*. FS E. Fascher, 1958, 94-102.

1959  *Die Botschaft Jesu damals und heute* (Dalp-Taschenbücher, 333). Bern–München: Francke, 1959, 215 p. Esp. 55-60 [7,12]; 61-67 [25,31-46]; 92-94 [20,1-16]; 119-146 [5,43-44].

1969 Jeschu ben Mirjam. Kontroversgeschichtliche Anmerkungen zu Mk 6:3. — ELLIS, E.E. – WILCOX, M. (eds.), *Neotestamentica et Semitica*. FS M. Black, 1969, 119-128. Esp. 124-125 [1,18-25].

1982 Jesus, Geschichte und Verkündigung. — *ANRW* II.25.1 (1982) 3-130.

**STECK, Karl Gerhard**
1955 Über Matthäus 11,25-30. — *EvT* 15 (1955) 343-349.

**STECK, Odil Hannes**
1967 *Israel und das gewaltsame Geschick der Propheten. Untersuchungen zur Überlieferung des deuteronomistischen Geschichtsbildes im Alten Testament, Spätjudentum und Urchristentum* (WMANT, 23). Neukirchen-Vluyn: Neukirchener, 1967, 380 p. Esp. 20-26 [5,11-12]; 26-33 [23,29-36]; 33-40 [23,35]; 45-50 [23,37-39]; 99-105; 257-260 [Q 6,22-23]; 280-289: "Die Verwendung der Vorstellung im frühen palästinensischen Urchristentum" [Q 6,22-23; 11,48-51]; 289-316: "Die Verwendung der Vorstellung im vormatthäisch-palästinensischen Judenchristentums und im Matthäusevangelium" [21,28–22,14; 23,29–24,2]. — Diss. Heidelberg, 1965 (G. Bornkamm). → Hoffmann 1992b

1978 *Welt und Umwelt* (Biblische Konfrontationen. Kohlhammer Taschenbücher, 1006). Stuttgart: Kohlhammer, 1978, 235 p. Esp. 177-180 [6,25-34].

**STEEGE, H.**
1970 *Das Vaterunser in unserer Zeit. Versuch einer Deutung* (Evangelische Zeitstimmen, 54). Hamburg: Reich, 1970, 46 p.

**STEFANI, Piero**
1991 Gesù perfezionatore della Legge e dei Profeti. [5,17-20] — *Credere oggi* 11 (1991) 29-41.

**STEFANOVIC, Zdravko**
1992 "One Greater than the Temple". The Sermon on the Mount in the Early Palestinian Liturgical Setting. — *AsiaJT* 6 (1992) 108-116. [NTA 37, 137]; = *AsiaJT* 9 (1995) 341-351. [NTA 40, 819]

**STEGEMANN, Hartmut**
1969 Κύριος ὁ θεός *und* Κύριος Ἰησοῦ. *Aufnahmen und Ausbreitung der religiösen Gebrauchen von* κύριος *und seine Verwendung im Neuen Testament*. Diss. Bonn, 1969, v-433 p.

1971 "Die des Uria". Zur Bedeutung der Frauennamen in der Genealogie von Matthäus 1,1-17. — JEREMIAS, G., et al. (eds.), *Tradition und Glaube*. FS K.G. Kuhn, 1971, 246-276. Esp. 252-266 [OT]; 266-276 [1,1-17].

1993 *Die Essener, Qumran, Johannes der Täufer und Jesus. Ein Sachbuch*. Freiburg: Herder, 1993, 381 p.
*The Library of Qumran. On the Essenes, Qumran, John the Baptist, and Jesus*. Grand Rapids, MI: Eerdmans; Leiden: Brill, 1998, IX-289 p. Esp. 211-227 [John the Baptist]; 228-257 [Jesus].

**STEGEMANN, Wolfgang**
1978 → L. Schottroff 1978a

1979a Wanderradikalismus im Urchristentum? Historische und theologische Auseinandersetzung mit einer interessanten These. — SCHOTTROFF, W. – STEGEMANN, W. (eds.), *Der Gott der kleinen Leute*, II, 1979, 94-120. Esp. 111-115: "Kritische Interpretation der von Theißen verwerteten Texte aus der sogenannten 'Logienquelle'". → Theissen 1973
Vagabond Radicalism in Early Christianity? A Historical and Theological Dimension of a Thesis Proposed by Gerd Theissen. — SCHOTTROFF, W. – STEGEMANN, W. (eds.), *God of the Lowly*, 1984, 148-168.

1979b  → L. Schottroff 1979a

1980   Lasset die Kinder zu mir kommen. Sozialgeschichtliche Aspekte des Kinder-
       evangeliums. — SCHOTTROFF, W. - STEGEMANN, W. (eds.), *Traditionen der Be-
       freiung. Sozialgeschichtliche Bibelauslegungen*. Band 1: *Methodische Zugänge*, Mün-
       chen: Kaiser; Gelnhausen: Burckhardthaus-Laetare, 1980, 114-144. Esp. 135-137 [18,1-5].

1981a  *Das Evangelium und die Armen: Über den Ursprung der Theologie der Armen im Neuen
       Testament* (Kaiser Traktate, 62). München: Kaiser, 1981, 61 p.
       *The Gospel and the Poor*, trans. D. Elliott. Philadelphia, PA: Fortress, 1984, 78 p.

1981b  Plädoyer für die Aktualisierung der Bergpredigt. — *Zur Rettung des Feuers.
       Solidaritätsschrift für Kuno Füssel*, Münster: Christen für den Sozialismus, 1981, 22-30.

1985   Die Versuchung Jesu im Matthäusevangelium. Mt 4,1-11. — *EvT* 45 (1985) 29-44.
       [NTA 29, 928]

1991   *Zwischen Synagoge und Obrigkeit. Zur historischen Situation der lukanischen Christen*
       (FRLANT, 152). Göttingen: Vandenhoeck & Ruprecht, 1991, 304 p. Esp. 41-42.46-48.59-
       61 [10,19-20.26-33/Q 12,2-12]; 113-114 [5,11-12/Q 6,22-23]; 137-139 [synagogues]; 254-255 [24,9]. —
       Diss. Heidelberg, 1983.

       **STEGMÜLLER, Friedrich**

1950   (ed.), *Repertorium Biblicum Medii Aevi*. Madrid: Consejo Superior de Investigaciones
       Científicas, 11 vols., 1950-1980. Esp. I, 1950, 280-284: "Prologi librorum Novi Testamenti" [Mt];
       VIII, 1976, 225; IV, 1977, 521-523 [Glossa ordinaria].

       **STEGNER, William Richard**

1967   Wilderness and Testing in the Scrolls and in Matthew 4:1-11. — *BR* 12 (1967) 18-27.
       [NTA 12, 864]

1976   Lucan Priority in the Feeding of the Five Thousand. — *BR* 21 (1976) 19-28. Esp. 19-22:
       "Agreements of Matthew and Luke against Mark" [14,13-21]. [NTA 22, 423]

1982   The Priority of Luke: An Exposition of Robert Lindsey's Solution to the Synoptic
       Problem. — *BR* 27 (1982) 26-38. [NTA 27, 89] → Lindsey

1988   Narrative Christology in Early Jewish Christianity. — *SBL 1988 Seminar Papers*, 249-
       262. Esp. 252-253 [4,1-11].

1989a  *Narrative Theology in Early Christianity*. Louisville, KY: Westminster, 1989, 156 p.

1989b  Early Jewish Christianity. A Lost Chapter? — *Asbury Theological Journal* (Wilmore,
       KY) 44 (1989) 17-29.

1990   The Temptation Narrative: A Study in the Use of Scripture by Early Jewish Christians.
       — *BR* 35 (1990) 5-17. [NTA 35, 621]

1995   Breaking Away: The Conflict with Formative Judaism. — *BR* 40 (1995) 7-36. Esp. 10-13
       [23,8-10]; 17-18 [17,1-9]; 18-21 [18,20]; 21-26 [forgiveness]; 27-29 [27,63]; 30-33 [persecution]; 33-36
       [polemics]. [NTA 41, 192]

       **STEHLY, Ralph**

1977   Bouddhisme et Nouveau Testament. À propos de la marche de Pierre sur l'eau
       (Matthieu 14.28s). — *RHPR* 57 (1977) 433-437. [NTA 22, 768]

       **STEIGER, Lothar**

1986   Die Predigt und ihr Kommentar. Zum Beispiel Mt 26,1-13. — *BTZ* 3 (1986) 172-187.
       Esp. 177-178.

       **STEIN, Robert H.**

1969   What is Redaktionsgeschichte? — *JBL* 88 (1969) 45-56. Esp. 52-53, 55-56. [NTA 13, 847]

1971   The Proper Methodology for Ascertaining a Markan Redaction History. — *NT* 13
       (1971) 181-198. Esp. 186-188: "The Markan modification of the material". [NTA 16, 169]

1976 Is the Transfiguration (Mark 9:2-8) a Misplaced Resurrection-Account? — *JBL* 95 (1976) 79-96. Esp. 95: "The witness of Matthew and Luke". [NTA 20, 801]

1978 *The Method and Message of Jesus' Teachings*. Philadelphia, PA: Westminster, 1978, XIV-188 p.; [2]1994. Esp. 1-6: "Jesus the teacher"; 7-33: "The form of Jesus' teaching"; 34-59: "The parables of Jesus"; 60-79: "The kingdom of God"; 80-87: "The fatherhood of God"; 88-111: "The ethics of the kingdom"; 112-148: "Christology".

1979 "Is it lawful for a man to divorce his wife?". [19,9] — *JEvTS* 22 (1979) 115-121. [NTA 24, 113]

1980 The "Criteria" for Authenticity. — FRANCE, R.T. - WENHAM, D. (eds.), *Studies of History and Tradition*, 1980, 225-263. Esp. 229-232 [M/Q]; 235 [23,23-24]; 238-239 [18,12-14]; 245-248.

1981a *An Introduction to the Parables of Jesus*. Philadelphia, PA: Westminster, 1981, 180 p.

1981b "Authentic" or "Authorative"? What Is the Difference? [19,9] — *JEvTS* 24 (1981) 127-130. [NTA 26, 442]

1985 *Difficult Sayings in the Gospels. Jesus' Use of Overstatement and Hyperbole*. Grand Rapids, MI: Baker, 1985, 103 p. Esp. 19-32: "Exaggeration in the teachings of Jesus" [5,23-24.29-30.33-37; 6,5-6.7-13; 7,3-5; 14–15; 18,15-17; 26,52]; 33-88: "Recognizing exaggeration in the teachings of Jesus".

1987 *The Synoptic Problem. An Introduction*. Grand Rapids, MI: Baker, 1987; Nottingham: InterVarsity, 1988, 292 p. Esp. 89-112: "The existence of Q"; 113-128: "The Matthew-Luke agreements against Mark"; 129-138: "The 'solution' of the synoptic problem"; [2]1995. → D.A. Black 1988b

1989 Luke 14:26 and the Question of Authenticity. — *Forum* 5/2 (1989) 187-192. [NTA 34, 175]

1991 *Gospels and Tradition: Studies on Redaction Criticism of the Synoptic Gospels*. Grand Rapids, MI: Baker, 1991, 204 p.
    F. NEIRYNCK, *ETL* 68 (1992) 434-435.

1992a Divorce. — *DJG*, 1992, 192-199. Esp. 194, 197.

1992b Synoptic Problem. — *Ibid.*, 784-792.

1992c The Matthew-Luke Agreements against Mark: Insight from John. — *CBQ* 54 (1992) 482-502. Esp. 483-485 [current explanations]; 485-493: "The existence of overlapping traditions as witnessed to by John"; 494-500: "The Matthew-Luke agreements against Mark, and the oral tradition" [3,11.16; 14,13.19-20; 16,16; 26,34.52.74; 27,21.60]. [NTA 37, 694]

**STEINER, Anton**

1979* & WEYMANN, V. (eds.), *Gleichnisse Jesu* (Bibelarbeit in der Gemeinde. Themen und Materialien, 3). Basel: Reinhardt; Zürich-Köln: Benziger, 1979, 224 p. → Pfister, Siber, A. Steiner

1979 Eingeladen zum Entdecken. Der Schatz im Acker (Mattäus 13,44). — *Ibid.*, 63-75.

**STEINER, Luke**

1984 The Magi and the Star. — *BiTod* 22 (1984) 373-375.

**STEINER, M.**

1962 *La tentation de Jésus dans l'interprétation patristique de saint Justin à Origène* (Études bibliques). Paris: Gabalda, 1962, 232 p. Esp. 11-22 [Justin]; 22-34 [Ps-Clement]; 34-43 [Theodotus]; 44-80 [Irenaeus]; 81-97 [Tertullian]; 98-106 [Clement of Alexandria]; 107-192 [Origen].
    T. CHARY, *RevSR* 37 (1963) 208-209; J. COPPENS, *ETL* 38 (1962) 562-564; A. DE HALLEUX, *Muséon* 77 (1964) 504-505; J. SMIT SIBINGA, *VigChr* 18 (1964) 239-240.

**STEINHAUSER, Michael G.**

1974 Neuer Wein braucht neue Schläuche. Zur Exegese von Mk 2,21f par. — MERKLEIN,

H. – LANGE, J. (eds.), *Biblische Randbemerkungen*. FS R. Schnackenburg, 1974, 113-123. Esp. 114-117 [9,16-17].

1976    The Patch of Unshrunk Cloth (Mt 9,16). — *ExpT* 87 (1975-76) 312-313. [NTA 21, 80]

1981    *Doppelbildworte in den synoptischen Evangelien. Eine form- und traditionskritische Studie* (FzB, 44). Würzburg: Echter, 1981, 467 p. Esp. 42-53 [9,16-17]; 69-79 [7,7-11/Q 11,9-13]; 79-96 [7,16/Q 6,44]; 96-121 [8,20/Q 9,58]; 130-147 [12,25-26/Q 11,17-18]; 148-157 [7,13-14/Q 13,24]; 158-179 [11,16-19/Q 7,31-35]; 184-197 [10,24-25/Q 6,40]; 197-214 [24,40-41/Q 17,34-35]; 215-235 [6,26-30/Q 12,24-28]; 236-249 [6,19-20/Q 12,33]; 250-258 [16,2-3/Q 12,54-56]; 259-280 [7,6]; 280-297 [10,16]; 298-312 [24,27-28/Q 17,24.37]; 313-325 [12,33-35/Q 6,43-45]; 328-351 [5,13-16]; 352-383 [5,15/Q 11,33]. — Diss. Würzburg, 1977 (R. Schnackenburg).

1982    The Beatitudes and Eschatology: Announcing the Kingdom. — *LivLight* 19 (1982) 121-129. [NTA 28, 135]

1989    Putting One's Hand to the Plow. The Authenticity of Q 9:61-62. — *Forum* 5/2 (1989) 151-158. [NTA 34, 167]

1990a   The Sayings Gospel Q. Introduction. — KLOPPENBORG, J.S., et al., *Q – Thomas Reader*, 1990, 3-27. Esp. 5-6: "Date and provenance"; 6-13: "The 'discovery' of Q"; 13-22: "Literary genre of Q"; 23-25: "Reconstruction of Q".

1990b   The Saying on Anxieties. Matt 6:25-34 and Luke 12:22-32. — *Forum* 6 (1990) 67-79. Esp. 67-72: "A clustering of concerns"; 72-78: "Remarks and recommendations". [NTA 36, 720]

1990c   The Sayings of Jesus in Mark 4:21-22, 24b-25. — *Ibid.*, 197-217. [NTA 38, 182]

1992    The Violence of Occupation: Matthew 5:40-41 and Q. — *TorontoJT* 8 (1992) 28-37. [NTA 37, 141]

**STEINMETZ, David C.**

1980    Matthew 25:14-30. — *Interpr* 34 (1980) 172-176.

**STEINMETZ, Franz-Josef**

1968    "Dein Reich komme!" Zur zweiten Bitte des Vaterunsers. [6,10] — *GL* 41 (1968) 414-428. [NTA 13, 864]

1977    Gedanken zum Dreikönigstag. Reflexionen über die Huldigung der Magier in Mt 2. — *GL* 50 (1977) 401-408.

1993    "Unkraut unter dem Weizen" (Mt 13,24-30). Ein aktuelles, aber nichtssagendes Gleichnis? — *GL* 66 (1993) 1-9. [NTA 37, 1265]

**STEINMÜLLER, John E.**

1943[R]  *A Companion to Scripture Studies*. Volume III: *Special Introduction to the New Testament* [1943]. New York: Wagner, 1969, VII-376 p. Esp. 37-64 [Mt]; 106-124 [synoptic problem].

1975    The Infancy Gospels. — *HomPastR* 76/3 (1975) 25-28. [NTA 20, 430]

**STEIN-SCHNEIDER, H.**

1985    À la recherche du Judas historique. Une enquête exégétique à la lumière des textes de l'Ancien Testament et des *Logia*. — *ETR* 60 (1985) 403-424.

**STEINSEIFER, Bernd**

1971    Der Ort der Erscheinungen des Auferstandenen. Zur Frage alter galiläischer Oster-traditionen. — *ZNW* 62 (1971) 232-265. Esp. 242-243 [28,16-20]; 246-251 [28,16]. [NTA 16, 826] → Lorenzen 1973

**STELLA, Pietro**

1967    Il Vangelo di Matteo tradotto e annotato de Antonio Martini. Derivazioni e fortune. — *Sal* 29 (1967) 326-367.

**STEMBERGER, Günter**

1991 *Pharisäer, Sadduzäer, Essener* (SBS, 144). Stuttgart: Katholisches Bibelwerk, 1991, 144 p. Esp. 26 [Q]; 27-30 [Mt].
*Jewish Contemporaries of Jesus: Pharisees, Sadducees, Essenes*, trans. A.W. Mahnke. Minneapolis, MN: Fortress, 1995, IX-161 p.

**STENDAHL, Krister**

1953 The Called and the Chosen. An Essay on Election. [22,11-14] — FRIDRICHSEN, A., et al. (eds.), *The Root of the Vine*, 1953, 63-80.

1954 *The School of St. Matthew and Its Use of the Old Testament* (Acta Seminarii Neotestamentici Upsaliensis, 20). Lund: Gleerup; København: Munksgaard, 1954, 249 p.; ²1967; Philadelphia, PA: Fortress, ²1968, XV-249 p. Esp. 9-35: "The school"; 37-217: "The quotations from the Old Testament". [NTA 13, p. 274] — Diss. Uppsala, 1954 (H. Riesenfeld). → E.E. Ellis 1955

P. AHSMANN, *Bijdragen* 18 (1957) 302-304; M.-É. BOISMARD, *RB* 62 (1955) 454-455; B. BRINKMANN, *Scholastik* 33 (1958) 299-300; J. CAMBIER, *RHE* 53 (1958) 841-844; F.V. FILSON, *JBL* 74 (1955) 54-55; E. HAAPA, *TAik* 59 (1954) 211-215; P. KATZ, *Gnomon* (München) 29 (1957) 230-232; X. LÉON-DUFOUR, *RSR* 46 (1958) 250-253; T.W. MANSON, *NTS* 1 (1954-55) 155-157; É. MASSAUX, *ETL* 50 (1954) 480-483; P. MENOUD, *ETR* 32 (1957) 220-221; B.M. METZGER, *PrincSemB* 49/3 (1956) 50-51; P.S. MINEAR, *The Review of Religion* (New York) 19 (1954-55) 211-212; H.A. MUSURILLO, *TS* 15 (1954) 644-646; P. PRIGENT, *RHPR* 38 (1958) 291-293; M. RISSI, *TZ* 13 (1957) 68-69; H.H. ROWLEY, *ExpT* 66 (1954-55) 380; K.H. SCHELKLE, *TQ* 135 (1955) 77-78; J. SCHMID, *TRev* 52 (1956) 53-54; G. SEVENSTER, *VigChr* 11 (1957) 113-114; H.F.D. SPARKS, *JTS* 7 (1956) 103-105; R.T. STAMM, *Interpr* 9 (1955) 354-355; H.M. TEEPLE, *JRel* 36 (1956) 58-59; G. VERMÈS, *Cahiers sioniens* (Paris) 9 (1955) 120-123; A. VIARD, *RSPT* 39 (1955) 276; P. VIELHAUER, *TLZ* 81 (1956) 39-42; M. ZERWICK, *Bib* 36 (1955) 527-529.

J.A. FITZMYER, *JBL* 89 (1970) 250; M. LÀCONI, *RivBib* 20 (1972) 332-334; B.M. METZGER, *PrincSemB* 52/2 (1989) 89-90; P.D. MILLER, Jr, *Interpr* 23 (1969) 347-348.

1958 Prayer and Forgiveness. — *SEÅ* 22-23 (1957-58) 75-86. Esp. 75-77 [6,14-15]; 77-79 [18,10-14]; 80-83 [18,23-35]. [NTA 3, 583]
Prayer and Forgiveness: The Lord's Prayer. — ID., *Meanings*, 1984, 115-125. Esp. 116-117; 117-118; 118-121.

1959 Kirche II. Im Urchristentum. — *RGG* 3 (³1959) 1297-1303. Esp. 1302-1303 [16,17-19].
The Church in Early Christianity. — ID., *Meanings*, 1984, 163-172. Esp. 171-172.

1960 Quis et Unde? An Analysis of Matthew 1–2. — ELTESTER, W. (ed.), *Judentum, Urchristentum, Kirche*. FS J. Jeremias, 1960, 94-105. [NTA 5, 707]; = STANTON, G., *The Interpretation of Matthew*, 1983, 56-66; ²1995, 69-80.
Quis et unde? Eine Analyse von Mt 1–2. — LANGE, J. (ed.), *Das Matthäus-Evangelium*, 1980, 296-311. Quis et unde? Who and Whence? Matthew's Christmas Gospel. — ID., *Meanings*, 1984, 71-83.

1962 Matthew. — BLACK, M. - ROWLEY, H.H. (eds.), *Peake's Commentary on the Bible*, London: Nelson, 1962, 769-798. → Jurgens 1983

1963 Messianic License. The Sermon on the Mount. — PEACHEY, P. (ed.), *Biblical Realism Confronts the Nation*, Nyack, NY: Fellowship of Reconciliation, 1963, 139-152; = ID., *Meanings*, 1984, 85-97.

1978 The Sermon on the Mount and Third Nephi in the Book of Mormon. — MADSEN, T.G. (ed.), *Reflections on Mormonism. Judaeo-Christian Parallels*, Provo, UT: Brigham Young, 1978, 139-154; = ID., *Meanings*, 1984, 99-113.

1980 The Lord's Prayer. — *International Review of Mission* (Genève) 69 (1980) 265-351.
El Padrenuestro. — *Actualidad Pastoral* (Buenos Aires) 13 (1980) 203-206.

1984 *Meanings. The Bible as Document and as Guide*. Philadelphia, PA: Fortress, 1984, XI-244 p. → 1958, 1959, 1960, 1963, 1978

**STENGER, Werner**
→ Schnider 1970, 1971, 1979, 1981a

1978    & SCHNIDER, F., Überlegungen zur Transformation biblischer Texte am Beispiel des
        Gleichnisses von den Talenten (Mt 25,14-30; Lk 19,11-27). — *Religionspädagogische*
        *Beiträge* 1 (1978) 71-103; = ID., *Strukturale Beobachtungen*, 1990, 154-180. Esp. 159-
        165; 166-168.

1984    Zur Rekonstruktion eines Jesusworts anhand der synoptischen Ehescheidungslogien (Mt
        5,32; 19,9; Lk 16,18; Mk 10,11f). — *Kairos* 26 (1984) 194-205. Esp. 194-199 [5,32]. [NTA
        30, 112]; = ID., *Strukturale Beobachtungen*, 1990, 104-118. Esp. 104-112.

1986    Die Seligpreisung der Geschmähten (Mt 5,11-12; Lk 6,22-23). — *Kairos* 28 (1986) 33-
        60. Esp. 34-35: "Struktur von Mt 5,3-12"; 35-36: "Struktur von Lk 6,20-26"; 36-40: "Überlieferungs- und
        Redaktionskritik"; 40-54: "Die abschließende Seligpreisung". [NTA 31, 1071]; = ID., *Strukturale*
        *Beobachtungen*, 1990, 119-153. Esp. 120-122; 122-124; 124-128; 128-149.

1987    *Biblische Methodenlehre* (Leitfaden Theologie, 18). Düsseldorf: Patmos, 1987, 277 p.
        Esp. 88-102 [9,9-13]; 114-123 [12,1-8]; 124-145 [8,18-27]; 146-170 [8,5-13]; 219-232 [1,1-25]; 233-253
        [5,3-12].
        *Metodologia biblica*, trans. E. Gatti (Giornale di teologia, 205). Brescia: Queriniana, 1991, 350 p. Esp. 103-
        121; 135-147; 169-176; 177-192; 268-285; 286-312.
        *Introduction to New Testament Exegesis*, trans. D.W. Stott. Grand Rapids, MI: Eerdmans, 1993, XIV-183 p.
        Esp. 61-72; 73-80; 94-98; 99-108; 133-143; 144-157.
        Trans. Spanish 1990.

1988    *"Gebt dem Kaiser, was des Kaisers ist...!"*. *Eine sozialgeschichtliche Untersuchung zur*
        *Besteuerung Palästinas in neutestamentlicher Zeit* (BBB, 68). Frankfurt/M: Athenäum,
        1988, 281 p. Esp. 179-184 [17,24-27].

1990    *Strukturale Beobachtungen zum Neuen Testament* (New Testament Tools and Studies,
        12). Leiden: Brill, 1990, VII-320 p. → 1978, 1984, 1986; → Schnider 1979, 1981a

1991    Zur Semantik und Pragmatik von *hypokrisis* im Matthäusevangelium. —
        GÜTTGEMANNS, E. (ed.), *Das Phänomen der "Simulation"*. *Beiträge zu einem*
        *semiotischen Kolloquium* (Forum Theologiae Linguisticae, 17), Bonn: Linguistica
        Biblica, 1991, 71-85. Esp. 75-84.

**STEPHENSON, Alan M.G.** → C.F.D. Moule 1955a

**STERLING, Gregory E.**

1993    Jesus as Exorcist: An Analysis of Matthew 17:14-20; Mark 9:14-29; Luke 9:37-43a.
        — *CBQ* 55 (1993) 467-493. [NTA 38, 768]

**STERN, David**

1989    Jesus' Parables from the Perspective of Rabbinic Literature: The Example of the
        Wicked Husbandmen. — THOMA, C. - WYSCHOGROD, M. (eds.), *Parable and Story*,
        1989, 42-80. → Boadt 1989, Milavec 1989

**STERN, Jay B.**

1966    Jesus' Citation of Dt 6,5 and Lv 19,18 in the Light of Jewish Tradition. [22,34-40] —
        *CBQ* 28 (1966) 312-316. [NTA 11, 704]

**STEUDLER, Andreas**

1990    Das Gleichnis vom Unkraut unter dem Weizen: Mt 13,24-30. — *Internationale*
        *kirchliche Zeitschrift* (Bern) 80 (1990) 154-155.

**STEUERNAGEL, Carl**

1953    Die ursprüngliche Zweckbestimmung des Vaterunsers. — *Wissenschaftliche Zeitschrift*
        *der Karl-Marx-Universität Leipzig* 3 (1953) 123-126, 217-220.

**STEVENS, Gerald L.**

1992  Understanding the Sermon on the Mount. Its Rabbinic and New Testament Context. — *Theological Educator* (New Orleans) 46 (1992) 83-95. [NTA 37, 719]

**STEVENS, R. David**

1985  Conflict and the Sermon on the Mount. — *Furrow* 36 (1985) 535-542. [NTA 30, 569]

**STEVENSON, Kenneth**

1990  Lord's Prayer. — *DBI*, 1990, 409-410.

**STEWART-SYKES, Alistair**

1995  Matthew's "Miracle Chapters": From Composition to Narrative, and Back Again. — *ScriptB* 25 (1995) 55-65. [NTA 40, 826]

**STEYN, Gert J.**

1990  Intertextual Similarities between Septuagint Pretexts and Luke's Gospel. — *Neotestamentica* 24 (1990) 229-246. Esp. 235-238 [OT/Q 4,1-13 (Lk)]. [NTA 36, 198]

**STIASSNY, Joseph**

1964  Jésus accomplit la promesse. Essai d'interprétation de Matthieu 5,17-19. — *BibVieChrét* 59 (1964) 30-37. [NTA 9, 905]

**STILLER, Wolfgang**

1952  "Vater Unser". Biblische Erwägungen. — *TGl* 42 (1952) 49-52.

1954  "Geheiligt werde dein Name" — *TGl* 44 (1954) 64-66.

**STINE, Philip C.** → B.M. Newman 1988

**STIRN, Marcel**

1979  *Pour une "sémeiotique" de l'annonce. Essai d'élaboration d'un problème linguistique à partir de Matthieu 19–23.* Leuven: Nauwelaerts, 1979, 371 p. [NTA 26, p. 201]

**STOCK, Augustine**

1978  Matthean Divorce Texts. — *BTB* 8 (1978) 24-33. Esp. 24-25 [5,31-32; Q 16,18]; 25-26 [19,3-9]. [NTA 22, 393]

1987  Is Matthew's Presentation of Peter Ironic? — *BTB* 17 (1987) 64-69. [NTA 31, 1079]

1994  *The Method and Message of Matthew.* Collegeville, MN: Liturgical Press, 1994, IV-443 p. [NTA 38, p. 467]
      D.C. ALLISON, *CRBR* 8 (1995) 301-303; E.L. BODE, *BTB* 25 (1995) 93-94.

**STOCK, Hans**

1959  *Studien zur Auslegung der synoptischen Evangelien im Unterricht.* Gütersloh: Bertelsmann, 1959; Gütersloh: Mohn, ⁴1967, 254 p. Esp. 179-183 [18,1-5]; 208-210 [8,23-27].

**STOCK, Klemens**

1986  *Jesus – Künder der Seligkeit. Betrachtungen zum Matthäus-Evangelium.* Innsbruck: Tyrolia, 1986, 158 p.
      W. BEILNER, *BLtg* 60 (1987) 109; M. HASITSCHKA, *ZKT* 109 (1987) 210.
      *Gesù annuncia la beatitudine. Il messaggio di Matteo*, trans. D. Ronchitelli (Bibbia e preghiera, 4). Roma: Apostolato della Preghiera, 1989, 151 p.
      D. SCAIOLA, *CC* 143/1 (1992) 306.
      Korean trans., 1988.

1988  *Discorso della montagna Mt 5-7. Le beatitudini.* Roma: Pont. Ist. Bibl., 1988, IV-134 p.

1989  Der Weg der Freude. Die acht Seligpreisungen. — *GL* 62 (1989) 360-373, 433-446. [NTA 34, 617/618]

1991a   *Il racconto della passione di Gesù nei vangelo sinottici*. Roma: Pont. Ist. Bibl., 1991, 2 vols.

1991b   I figli sono liberi (Mt 17,26; Lc 15,11-32). — *ParSpirV* 23 (1991) 145-161. Esp. 145-149 [17,24-27]; 150-157: "Dio e gli esseri umani in Matteo".

1993   La beatitudine degli operatori di pace e dei miti. [5,5.9] — LIBERTI, V. (ed.), *La pace secondo la Bibbia* (Studio biblico Aquilano, 12), L'Aquila, 1993, 97-120.

**STOCKMEIER, Peter**

1970   Das Petrusamt in der frühen Kirche. — DENZLER, G., et al., *Zum Thema Petrusamt*, 1970, 61-79. Esp. 70-75: "Die Berufung auf Mt 16,18-19".

1988   Gregors der Grossen Homilie zu Mt 10,5-10 in der römischen Kirche S. Stefano Rotondo. — ALTMANN, L. - RAMISCH, H. (eds.), *Kirchen am Lebensweg. Festgabe zum 60. Geburtstag - 20. Bischofsjubiläum für Seine Eminenz Friedrich Kardinal Wetter, Erzbischoff von München und Freising*, München: Schnell & Steinen, 1988, 377-384.

**STOCKTON, Ian**

1983   Children, Church and Kingdom. — *ScotJT* 36 (1983) 87-97. Esp. 92-94 [18,1-5]. [NTA 27, 1114]

**STOEBE, Hans Joachim**

1992   Überlegungen zur sechsten Bitte des Vaterunsers. — *TZ* 48 (1992) 89-99.

**STÖGER, Alois**

1952   *"Ich aber sage euch". Die Bergpredigt nach Matthäus lebendig gemacht*. München: Pfeiffer, 1952, 138 p.
        P. NOBER, *Bib* 35 (1954) 242-243; K.H. SCHELKLE, *TQ* 134 (1954) 126-127.

1953   *Ich bin gekommen. Das Christusbild aus Matthäus 8-12*. München: Pfeiffer, 1953, 156 p.

1967   *Das Evangelium nach Matthäus. II: 13-28* (Kleiner Kommentar, 1). Stuttgart: Katholisches Bibelwerk, 1967, 44 p.

1980   Fragen zur revidierten Einheitsübersetzung (II). [5,32; 6,12; 8,24; 19,9] — *BLtg* 53 (1980) 100-103. [NTA 25, 41]

1982a   *Die Bergpredigt. Eine Botschaft von Hoffnung und Frieden*. Klosterneuburg: Österreichisches Katholisches Bibelwerk, 1982, 125 p. [NTA 27, p. 214]

1982b   Fragen zur Einheitsübersetzung. [6,13] — *BLtg* 55 (1982) 229. [NTA 27, 919]

1984   Die Predigt der Bergpredigt. Gedanken zur Erneuerung der Homilie. — *TPQ* 132 (1984) 40-52. [NTA 29, 93]

**STÖLLGER, Winfried**

1994   Johannes Chrysostomos bei der Predigtarbeit. Bemerkungen zu Hom. 2 in Matth. [1] — MÜHLENBERG, E. - VAN OORT, J. (eds.), *Predigt in der Alten Kirche*, Kampen: Kok Pharos, 1994, 82-114.

**STOEVESANDT, Hinrich**

1988   Das Wort vom Kreuz. Theologische Überlegungen zu Matthäus 16,13-28. — *Glaube und Lernen* (Göttingen) 3 (1988) 22-33.

**STOLDT, Hans-Herbert**

1977   *Geschichte und Kritik der Markushypothese*. Göttingen: Vandenhoeck & Ruprecht, 1977, 241 p.; (TVG Monographien und Studienbücher, 324). Gießen-Basel: Brunnen, ²1986, 269 p. Esp. 28-124: "Kritische Analyse der Entstehung der Markushypothese"; 125-205: "Kritische Analyse der Beweise für die Richtigkeit der Markushypothese". → W.R. Farmer 1978b, 1980b, Lentzen-Deis 1980, Tuckett 1979, I.M. Zeitlin 1988

M.-É. BOISMARD, *RB* 85 (1978) 630-631; H. CONZELMANN, *TR* 43 (1978) 321; A. FUCHS, *SNTU* 9 (1984) 229-231; 11 (1986) 218-220; H.C. KEE, *JBL* 98 (1979) 140-143; W.H. KELBER, *CBQ* 41 (1979) 499-501; O. LINTON, *TLZ* 106 (1981) 95-98; F. NEIRYNCK, *ETL* 62 (1986) 427-428; R. TREVIJANO ETCHEVERRÍA, *Salmanticensis* 26 (1979) 309-311.
Critical Analysis of the Evidence for the Validity of the Marcan Hypothesis. [1977, 125-144] — *SBL 1978 Seminar Papers*, II, 145-158.
*History and Criticism of the Marcan Hypothesis*, trans. D.L. Niewyk. Macon, GA: Mercer University Press; Edinburgh: Clark, 1980, XVIII-302 p. Esp. 25-131; 133-224.
   J.B. ORCHARD, *HeythJ* 23 (1982) 321-322; C.S. RODD, *ExpT* 93 (1981-82) 163-164; É. TROCMÉ, *RHPR* 63 (1983) 341; C.M. TUCKETT, *JTS* 34 (1983) 251-257.

1980 Reflections on Legitimacy and Limits of Theological Criticism. — *PerkJourn* 33/3 (1980) 49-54. [NTA 25, 66] → W.R. Farmer 1980b

1992 *Aenigma fundamentale evangeliorum* (EHS, XXIII/416). Frankfurt/M – Bern – New York: Lang, 1992, 297 p.

### STOLL, Brigitta

1988 *De Virtute in virtutem. Zur Auslegungs- und Wirkungsgeschichte der Bergpredigt in Kommentaren, Predigten und hagiographischer Literatur von der Merowingerzeit bis um 1200* (Beiträge zur Geschichte der biblischen Exegese, 30). Tübingen: Mohr, 1988, XVIII-351 p. Esp. 38-67: "Der Verstehenshorizont mittelalterlicher Bergpredigtauslegung"; 68-135 [5,13-16]; 136-251 [5,3-12]; 252-301 [5,21-48]. — Diss. Bern, 1986 (A. Schindler – P. Stotz).
   H.D. BETZ, *CRBR* 4 (1991) 237-239; A. HÄRDELIN, *SEÅ* 55 (1990) 173-176; J.-M. ROUSÉE, *RB* 96 (1989) 317; F. RUELLO, *RSR* 80 (1992) 249-252; R. SPRANDEL, *Göttingische gelehrte Anzeigen* 241 (1989) 258-264; P.T. STELLA, *Sal* 55 (1993) 185; B.T. VIVIANO, *RB* 98 (1991) 629-632.

1991 Drei karolingische Matthäuskommentare (Claudius von Turin, Hrabanus Maurus, Ps. Beda) und ihre Quellen zur Bergpredigt. — *Mittellateinisches Jahrbuch* (Ratingen) 26 (1991) 36-55.

### STOLL, C.-D.

1983 *Ehe und Ehescheidung. Die Weisungen Jesu* (Theologie und Dienst, 36). Gießen–Basel: Brunnen, 1983, 62 p. [NTA 28, p. 206]

### STOLLE, Volker

1991 Das Gebet der Gemeinde Jesu Christi nach dem Neuen Testament. — *KerDog* 37 (1991) 307-331. Esp. 324-325 [Lord's prayer]. [NTA 36, 958]

### STONEHOUSE, Ned Bernard

1944R *The Witness of Matthew and Mark to Christ* [1944]. London: Tyndale; Grand Rapids, MI: Eerdmans, 1958, XVI-269 p. Esp. 119-154: "The structure of the earlier chapters of Matthew"; 155-187: "The resurrection narrative in Matthew"; 188-225: "The authority of the Old Testament and the authority of Christ"; 226-258: "The Son of Man and the coming of the kingdom". → M. Silva 1977
   *ExpT* 71 (1959-60) 173; E.E. ELLIS, *RExp* 56 (1959) 205-206; R. SEGUINEAU, *LumièreV* 48 (1960) 30.
*The Witness of the Synoptic Gospels to Christ*. One volume combining *The Witness of Matthew and Mark to Christ* and *The Witness of Luke to Christ* [1951] (Twin Brooks Series). Grand Rapids, MI: Baker, 1979, XXII-269 and 184 p.
   P.L. BREMER, *CalvTJ* 15 (1980) 312.

1963 *Origins of the Synoptic Gospels. Some Basic Questions*. Grand Rapids, MI: Eerdmans, 1963, XIII-201 p.; London: Tyndale, 1964, IX-198 p.; (Twin Brooks Series), Grand Rapids, MI: Baker, 1979, XVII-201 p. Esp. 19-47: "The self-witness of Matthew"; 48-77: "The question of order and interdependence" [Mk/Mt]; 78-92: "The factor of language" [Mt aram.]; 93-112 [19,16-22/Mk 10,17-22].

### STORCH, Rainer

1970 "Was soll diese Verschwendung?". Bemerkungen zur Auslegungsgeschichte von Mk 14,4f. — LOHSE, E., et al. (eds.), *Der Ruf Jesu*. FS J. Jeremias, 1970, 247-258. Esp. 249-250 [26,8-9]; 251-253 [Jerome]; 253-254 [Origen].

**STORNIOLO, Ivo**

1983 A mística da comunidade em Mateus 18. — *Vida Pastoral* (São Paulo) 24 (1983) 2-8.

1990 *Las tentaciones de Jesús* [4,1-11]. Buenos Aires: Paulinas, 1990, 64 p.
M. EGAN, *RevistBíb* 53 (1991) 124-126.

1991 *Como ler o evangelho de Mateus: o caminho da justicia.* São Paulo: Paulinas, 1991, 212 p.

**STOTT, John R.W.**

1968 The Great Commission. [28,16-20] — *ChrTod* 12 (1968) 723-725; 778-782; 826-829. Esp. 778-782 [28,16-20]. [NTA 13, 241]

1971 The Biblical Teaching on Divorce. — *Churchman* (London) 85 (1971) 165-174. [NTA 16, 1014]

1978 *Christian Counter-Culture. The Message of the Sermon on the Mount* (The Bible Speaks Today). Leicester – Downers Grove, IL: Inter-Varsity, 1978, 222 p. [NTA 23, p. 99]; [2]1992, 238 p.
F.F. BRUCE, *EvQ* 50 (1978) 189-190; A.G. PATZIA, *JEvTS* 23 (1980) 145.
*La contracultura cristiana. El mensaje del Sermón del monte.* Downers Grove, IL: Certeza, 1984, 268 p.

**STOUTENBURG, Dennis C.**

1993 "Out of My Sight!", "Get Behind Me!", or "Follow After Me!": There Is No Choice in God's Kingdom". [16,23-24] — *JEvTS* 36 (1993) 173-178. [NTA 38, 767]

**STRACHAN, R.H.**

1951 The Gospel in the New Testament. — BUTTRICK, G.A. (ed.), *The Interpreter's Bible,* VII, 1951, 3-31. Esp. 11-12; 14-15.

**STRACK, Hermann L.** → Billerbeck 1922, 1928

**STRAMARE, Tarcisio**

1965a Le beatitudini e la critica letteraria. — *RivBib* 13 (1965) 31-40. [NTA 10, 113]

1965b Beati i poveri. — *Ibid.*, 179-186. [NTA 10, 508]

1971a Causa fornicationis. Verso una soluzione del problema? — *PalCl* 50 (1971) 1028-1032. [NTA 16, 534]

1971b Matteo divorzista? — *Divinitas* 15 (1971) 213-235. Esp. 214-216 [5,32; 19,9]. [NTA 16, 150]; = *Tabor* 25 (1971) 105-115, 177-185. → Bartina 1973

1971c I sogni di S. Giuseppe. — *EstJos* 25 = *CahJos* 19 (1971) 104-122. Esp. 110-114: "Struttura di Mt 1-2"; 114-117: "Storicità". [NTA 16, 847]

1972 *Figlio di Giuseppe di Nazareth. Problemi dell'Infanzia di Gesù.* Rovigo: Istituto Padano di Arti Grafiche, 1972, 113 p. Esp. 21-33 [literary analysis]; 35-49 [1,1-17]; 50-56 [dreams]; 57-71 [Joseph]; 72-103 [1,18-25].
J.A. CARRASCO, *EstJos* 27 (1973) 104; G. DANIELI, *Divinitas* 17 (1973) 420; G.G. GAMBA, *Sal* 35 (1973) 559; R. GAUTHIER, *CahJos* 22 (1974) 266-267; D. LOMBARDI, *PalCl* 52 (1973) 1412.
Son of Joseph from Nazareth. Problems concerning Jesus' Infancy. — *CahJos* 26 (1978) 31-71 (partial trans.). [NTA 23, 88]

1973 Giuseppe, "uomo giusto", in Mt. 1,18-25. — *RivBib* 21 (1973) 287-300. [NTA 19, 526]

1975 Clausole di Matteo e indissolubilità del matrimonio. [5,32; 19,9] — *BibOr* 17 (1975) 65-74. [NTA 20, 775]

1976 Il problema delle "Citazioni di Adempimento" in Matteo. — *BibOr* 18 (1976) 213-226; = *EstJos* 31 (1977) = *CahJos* 26 (1977) 107-117. [NTA 23, 85]

1978 Profezie dell'Antico Testamento e loro interpretazione in Mt 1-2. — *EstJos* 32 (1978) 165-179.

1983 *San Giuseppe nella Sacra Scrittura nella teologia e nel culto* (Movimento Giuseppino, 1). Roma: Marietti, 1983, 436 p. [NTA 30, p. 102]

1984 Giuseppe da Nazaret. — *Rivista di vita spirituale* (Roma) 38 (1984) 49-51.

1985 Significato della genealogia di Gesù in S. Matteo. — *BibOr* 27 (1985) 205-214. [NTA 30, 1042]
Per un riesame della genealogia di Matteo. — *BibOr* 28 (1986) 3-13. [NTA 31, 109]; = *EstJos* 41 (1987) = *CahJos* 35 (1987) 33-58.

1986 *Matteo divorzista? Studio su* Mt. *5,32 e 19,9* (Studi biblici. 76). Brescia: Paideia, 1986, 96 p. [NTA 31, p. 369] → Marucci 1990b
J.A. CARRASCO, *EstJos* 42 (1988) 268-269; V. FUSCO, *CC* 138/4 (1987) 403-404; M.G., *Divinitas* 31 (1987) 335-336; A. GARCÍA MORENO 19 (1987) 464-466.

1989 L'annunciazione a Giuseppe in Mt. 1,18-25: Analisi letteraria e significato teologico. — *BibOr* 31 (1989) 3-14, 199-217. Esp. 5-14: "Analisi letteraria"; 199-217: "Significato teologico". [NTA 34, 114/1131]; = *EstJos* 45 = *CahJos* 39 (1991) 55-76. [NTA 36, 1256]

1993 I Vangeli dell'Infanzia e della vita nascosta di Gesù e il mistero in essi contenuto. — *BibOr* 35 (1993) 201-216.

1994 Sarà chiamato Nazareno. Era stato detto dai Profeti. — *BibOr* 36 (1994) 231-249. Esp. 234-237 [2,22-23]; 237-239 [2,23/OT]; 239-241 [structure]; 241-248 [Nazareth]. [NTA 40, 159]

1995a Dall'Egitto ho chiamato mio figlio. Un mistero della vita di Cristo. — *BibOr* 37 (1995) 194-213. Esp. 194-195 [2,13-23]; 196-199 [historicity]; 199-202 [reception]; 202-210 [2,15/OT]; 210-213 [salvation]. [NTA 41, 200]

1995b Il "Supplément au Dictionnaire de la Bible" e le clausole di Matteo sul divorzio. — *Divinitas* 39 (1995) 269-273. [NTA 40, 820] → Dumais 1993

**STRANDENÆS, Thor**
1987 *Principles of Chinese Bible Translation as Expressed in Five Selected Versions of the New Testament and Exemplified by Mt 5:1-12 and Col 1* (ConBibNT, 19). Uppsala: Almqvist & Wiksell, 1987, 166 p. — Diss. Uppsala, 1987 (L. Hartman).
P. ELLINGWORTH, *JTS* 40 (1989) 220-222; B. PRICE, *ExpT* 99 (1987-88) 313-314; W. PROMPER, *TRev* 84 (1988) 500-501; F. SMYTH, *ETR* 63 (1988) 449; J.M. VAN MINNEN, *NTT* 43 (1989) 249-250.

**STRANGE, Marcian**
1962a King Herod the Great in a Representative Role. — *BiTod* 3 (1962) 188-193. [NTA 7, 502]
1962b Temptations. [4,1-11] — *Worship* 36 (1962) 227-234. [NTA 6, 764]

**STRATTON, Charles**
1954 Pressure for the Kingdom. An Exposition. [11,12] — *Interpr* 8 (1954) 414-421.

**STRAUSS, L.**
1980 *Prophetic Mysteries Revealed. The Prophetic Significance of the Parables of Matthew 13 and the Letters of Revelation 2–3*. Neptune, NJ: Loizeaux, 1980, 255 p. [NTA 25, p. 90]

**STRAW, Carole E.**
1983 Augustine as Pastoral Theologian: The Exegesis of the Parables of the Field and Threshing Floor. [3,12; 13,24-30.36-43] — *Augustinian Studies* (Villanova, PA) 14 (1983) 129-151.

1989 Cyprian and Mt 5:45: The Evolution of Christian Patronage. — *Studia Patristica* 18/3 (1989) 329-339.

**STRAWSON, William**
1959 *Jesus and the Future Life. A Study in the Synoptic Gospels* (The Fernley-Hartley

Lecture, 1959). London: Epworth, 1959; ²1970; Philadelphia, PA: Westminster, 1960, XII-250 p. Esp. 40-55: "Heavenly father" [12,50; 20,23; 26,29]; 57-64: "Kingdom of heaven" [12,28; 19,24; 21,31.43]; 102-105: "Death" [4,16; 8,22; 10,8]; 118-136: "Judgment" [18,23-35; 20,1-16; 22,1-14; 24,45-51; 25,1-13.14-30.31-46]; 137-143: "Hades" [11,23; 16,18]; 143-146: "Gehenna"; 163-174: "Kingdom" [5,21-30; 7,21-27; 21,43; 26,29; Q 22,28-30]; 180-189: "Eternal life" [7,13-14].

STRECKER, Georg

1958 *Das Judentum in den Pseudoklementinen* (TU, 70). Berlin: Akademie, 1958, X-296 p. Esp. 117-136: "Die Schriftzitate der Pseudoklementinen"; (TU, 70A), ²1981, XIII-326 p. Esp. 117-136, 272-274. — Diss. Bonn, 1954-55 (W. Schneemelcher - P. Vielhauer). → Kline 1975b

1962 *Der Weg der Gerechtigkeit. Untersuchung zur Theologie des Matthäus* (FRLANT, 82). Göttingen: Vandenhoeck & Ruprecht, 1962, 267 p. [NTA 7, p. 392]; ²1966, 283 p. [NTA 12, p. 309]; ³1971, 310 p. Esp. 15-49: "Zeitgeschichtlicher Hintergrund"; 49-85: "Die Reflexionszitate"; 86-122: "Das historische Motiv"; 123-184: "Das eschatologische Motiv"; 191-206: "Die Jünger Jesu"; 207-226: "Die Gemeinde"; 226-236: "Der einzelne"; 236-242: "Das Ziel der Heilsgeschichte"; 243-256: "Nachtrag zur zweiten Auflage"; 257-278: "Nachtrag zur dritten Auflage" [reviews of W.D. Davies 1964; R. Walker 1967; W. Grundmann 1968]. [NTA 16, p. 373]. — Diss. Bonn, 1958-59 (P. Vielhauer). → Dermience 1985, Fannon 1965, Kingsbury 1966, Rohde 1965
M.-É. BOISMARD, *RB* 71 (1964) 448-449; B. BRINKMANN, *Scholastik* 39 (1964) 617-619; E. FASCHER, *TLZ* 92 (1967) 760-762; E. GOETCHIUS, *ATR* 46 (1964) 236; H.B. GREEN, *JTS* 15 (1964) 361-365; A. ISAKSSON, *SEÅ* 27 (1962) 146-148; K.H. SCHELKLE, *TQ* 143 (1963) 358; E. SCHWEIZER, *EvT* 23 (1963) 612-613; B. VAWTER, *CBQ* 26 (1964) 283-284; R.M. WILSON, *ZRelGeist* 17 (1965) 370-372.

1966 Das Geschichtsverständnis des Matthäus. — *EvT* 26 (1966) 57-74. Esp. 61-66 [history]; 66-71 [ethics]; 71-74 [ecclesiology]. [NTA 11, 190]; = ID., *Eschaton und Historie*, 1979, 90-107. Esp. 94-99; 99-104; 104-107; = LANGE, J. (ed.), *Das Matthäus-Evangelium*, 1980, 326-349. Esp. 330-334; 335-338; 339-341.
*SelT* 9 (1970) 41-49.
The Concept of History in Matthew. — *JAAR* 25 (1967) 219-230 (partial transl.). [NTA 12, 550]
The Concept of History in Matthew. — STANTON, G. (ed.), *The Interpretation of Matthew*, 1983, 67-84; ²1995, 81-100.
La conception de l'histoire chez Matthieu. — MARGUERAT, D. - ZUMSTEIN, J. (eds.), *La mémoire et le temps*. FS P. Bonnard, 1991, 93-111. Esp. 98-103; 103-108; 108-111.

1971 Die Makarismen der Bergpredigt. — *NTS* 17 (1970-71) 255-275. Esp. 255-260 [Q 6,20-23]; 260-271 [5,3-12]; 271-274 [Mt theology]. [NTA 16, 147]; = ID., *Eschaton und Historie*, 1979, 108-131. Esp. 108-114; 114-127; 127-130.
Les macarismes du discours sur la montagne. — DIDIER, M. (ed.), *L'Évangile selon Matthieu*, 1972, 185-208. Esp. 185-192; 192-205; 205-208.

1975* (ed.), *Jesus Christus in Historie und Theologie. Neutestamentliche Festschrift für Hans Conzelmann zum 60. Geburtstag*. Tübingen: Mohr, 1975, VIII-589 p. → J. Becker, H.D. Betz, Burchard, Dupont, E.E. Ellis, R.H. Fuller, Grässer, F. Lang, Linnemann, Lohse, Luz, G. Schneider, L. Schottroff, S. Schulz, Strecker, Suggs, Thyen

1975 Das Evangelium Jesu Christi. — *Ibid.*, 503-548. Esp. 513-515 [11,5]; 540-541 [εὐαγγέλιον]; = ID., *Eschaton und Historie*, 1979, 183-228. Esp. 193-195; 220-221.

1978a Die Antithesen der Bergpredigt (Mt 5,21-48 par). — *ZNW* 69 (1978) 36-72. Esp. 38-47: "Tradition und Redaktion"; 47-69: "Interpretation im einzelnen" [47-51: 5,21-26; 51-52: 5,27-30; 52-56: 5,31-32; 56-63: 5,33-37; 63-65: 5,38-42; 65-69: 5,43-48]. [NTA 23, 821]

1978b Eine Evangelienharmonie bei Justin und Pseudoklemens? — *NTS* 24 (1977-78) 297-316. Esp. 300 [4,10; 22,37-38]; 301 [8,11]; 302 [6,8.32; 7,15-16; 24,5]; 304 [23,13]; 305 [10,28]; 306 [6,39-41]; 307 [18,3]; 308 [5,37]; 309 [7,12]; 309-310 [5,44]; 310-312 [11,27]; 312-313 [5,45]; 313-314 [25,30.41]. [NTA 22, 726] → Kline 1975b

1979a *Eschaton und Historie. Aufsätze*. Göttingen: Vandenhoeck & Ruprecht, 1979, 399 p. → 1966, 1971, 1975, 1979b

1979b Redaktionsgeschichte als Aufgabe der Synoptikerexegese. — *Ibid.*, 9-32. Esp. 31.

1981 Compliance – Love of One's Enemy – The Golden Rule. [7,12] — *AusBR* 29 (1981) 38-46. [NTA 26, 468]

1982 Vaterunser und Glaube. — HAHN, F. - KLEIN, H. (eds.), *Glaube im Neuen Testament. Studien zu Ehren von Hermann Binder anläßlich seines 70. Geburtstags* (Biblisch-Theologische Studien, 7), Neukirchen-Vluyn: Neukirchener, 1982, 11-28.

1983a & SCHNELLE, U., *Einführung in die neutestamentliche Exegese* (Uni-Taschenbücher, 1253). Göttingen: Vandenhoeck & Ruprecht, 1983, 156 p. Esp. 52-57: "Die Logienquelle"; 61-63 [3,1-12]; 113-117 [21,33-46]; [2]1985 ("durchgesehen und ergänzt"), 158 p.; [3]1988, 167 p. → A. Fuchs 1983

1983b Neues Testament (NT). — ID. (ed.), *Theologie im 20. Jahrhundert. Stand und Aufgaben* (Uni-Taschenbücher, 1238), Tübingen: Mohr, 1983, 61-145. Esp. 113-114 [redaction criticism]; 97-108 [form criticism].

1984 *Die Bergpredigt. Ein exegetischer Kommentar.* Göttingen: Vandenhoeck & Ruprecht, 1984, 194 p. [NTA 29, p. 93]; [2]1985. → Hengel 1987
E. BEST, *ExpT* 97 (1985-86) 330-331; F. FORESTI, *Teresianum* 36 (1985) 229-231; H. FRANKEMÖLLE, *TRev* 81 (1985) 196-198; G. GEIGER, *BLtg* 57 (1984) 274; L. GROLLENBERG, *TijdTheol* 25 (1985) 194; R.A. GUELICH, *TLZ* 111 (1986) 194-196; H.-W. KUHN, *EvKom* 19 (1986) 182.
*The Sermon on the Mount. An Exegetical Commentary*, trans. O.C. Dean, Jr. Nashville, TN: Abingdon, 1988, 223 p. [NTA 33, p. 113]
D.R. BAUER, *JBL* 109 (1990) 347-349; R.F. COLLINS, *LouvSt* 14 (1989) 69-70; M.D. GOULDER, *Theology* 92 (1989) 328-329; P.J. HARTIN, *Neotestamentica* 24 (1990) 379-381; C.S. RODD, *ExpT* 101 (1989-90) 186; A. RODRÍGUEZ CARMONA, *EstE* 65 (1990) 480-481; R. WEBB, *JSNT* 36 (1989) 125.

1987a Gottes- und Menschenliebe in Neuen Testament. — HAWTHORNE, G.F. - BETZ, O. (eds.), *Tradition and Interpretation.* FS E.E. Ellis, 1987, 53-67. Esp. 56-60.

1987b Judenchristliche Evangelien. — HENNECKE, E. - SCHNEEMELCHER, W. (eds.), *Neutestamentliche Apokryphen*, I, [5]1987, 114-147. → Vielhauer 1959

1989a Apokalyptik des Urchristentums. Einleitung. — SCHNEEMELCHER, W. (ed.), *Neutestamentliche Apokryphen*, II, [5]1989, 516-547. Esp. 527-529 [24/Mk]. → Vielhauer 1964

1989b Neues Testament. — ID. - MAIER, J., *Neues Testament - Antikes Judentum* (Urban Taschenbücher, 422; Grundkurs Theologie, 2), Stuttgart: Kohlhammer, 1989, 9-136.

1990 Das Gesetz in der Bergpredigt – die Bergpredigt als Gesetz. — VEIJOLA, T. (ed.), *The Law in the Bible and in Its Environment* (Publications of the Finnish Exegetical Society, 51), Helsinki: Finnish Exegetical Society; Göttingen: Vandenhoeck & Ruprecht, 1990, 109-125.

1991 Walter Bauers Wörterbuch zum Neuen Testament in neuer Auflage. — *TLZ* 116 (1991) 81-92. [NTA 35, 1067r] → K. Aland [Bauer-Aland 1988]

1992a *Literaturgeschichte des Neuen Testaments* (Uni-Taschenbücher, 1682). Göttingen: Vandenhoeck & Ruprecht, 1992, 300 p. Esp. 123-148: "Die Form des Evangeliums"; 148-155: "Die Zwei-Quellen-Theorie und ihre Modifikationen"; 161-170: "Die Spruchquelle Q in den Evangelien"; 170-205: "Traditionen in den synoptischen Evangelien".

1992b Schriftlichkeit oder Mündlichkeit der synoptischen Tradition? Anmerkungen zur formgeschichtlichen Problematik. — VAN SEGBROECK, F., et al. (eds.), *The Four Gospels 1992.* FS F. Neirynck, 1992, I, 159-172. Esp. 161-162 [redaction crit.]; 167-168 [Q: tradition crit.].

1993* (ed.), *Minor Agreements. Symposium Göttingen 1991* (Göttinger theologische Arbeiten, 50). Göttingen: Vandenhoeck & Ruprecht, 1993, 245 p. [NTA 40, p. 527] → W.R. Farmer, A. Fuchs 1990b, Goulder, Luz, Neirynck 1991f, Schenk, Tuckett; → Neirynck 1991g
F. NEIRYNCK, *ETL* 69 (1993) 428-429; G.J. STEYN, *Neotestamentica* 29 (1995) 135-138.

1995a  *Theologie des Neuen Testaments. Bearbeitet, ergänzt und herausgegeben von Friedrich Wilhelm Horn.* Berlin – New York: de Gruyter, 1995, XV-741 p. Esp. 328-336: "Weisungen des Menschensohnes – Die Logiensammlung"; 384-412: "Der Weg der Gerechtigkeit – Der Evangelist Matthäus".

1995b  Das Kreuz Christi im Neuen Testament – ein Kriterium für die Authentizität der Verkündigung und die Praxis der Kirche? — HORN, F.W. (ed.), *Bilanz und Perspektiven gegenwärtiger Auslegung des Neuen Testaments. Symposion zum 65. Geburtstag von Georg Strecker* (BZNW, 75), Berlin: de Gruyter, 1995, 248-278. Esp. 265-268.

**STREEFKERK, N.**

1965  Waardig en onwaardig. [22,1-14] — *Homiletica en Biblica* (Den Haag) 24 (1965) 272-275. [NTA 10, 914]

**STREETER, Burnett Hillman**

1924R  *The Four Gospels. A Study of Origins* [1924]. London: Macmillan, reprint [7]1951, XXX-624 p. Esp. 150-199: "The synoptic problem: the fundamental solution"; 223-270: "A four document hypothesis"; 271-292: "The reconstruction of Q"; 293-332: "The minor agreements of Matthew and Luke"; 585-589: "The text of Origen on Matthew"; 500-527: "The origin of Matthew". → Meynell 1963
The Priority of Mark. [1924, 157-169.195-197] — BELLINZONI, A.J., Jr., et al. (eds.), *The Two-Source Hypothesis*, 1985, 23-36.
The Document Q. [1924, 182-186] — *Ibid.*, 221-225.

**STRELAN, Rick E.**

1989  The Gospel in the Sermon on the Mount. — *LuthTJ* 23 (1989) 19-26. [NTA 33, 1119]

**STRICKERT, Frederick Markus**

1988  *The Pronouncement Sayings in the Gospel of Thomas and the Synoptics.* Diss. Graduate College of the Univ. of Iowa, 1988, 362 p. (G.W.E. Nickelsburg). Esp. 62-88 [13,31-32; Q 13,18-19/Th 20]; 89-120 [18,1-5; 19,13-15/Th 22]; 121-139 [6,1-18; 7,12; 10,26; Q 6,31; Q 12,2/Th 6a-c]; 202-214 [16,2-3; Q 12,54-56/Th 91]; 236-266 [22,15-22/Th 100]; 267-291 [7,21; 12,46-50/Th 99]; 292-325 [9,14-15/Th 104]. — *DissAbstr* 49 (1988-89) 3394.

**STRITZKY, Maria-Barbara von**

1989  *Studien zur Überlieferung und Interpretation des Vaterunsers in der frühchristlichen Literatur* (Münsterische Beiträge zur Theologie, 57). Münster: Aschendorff, 1989, VIII-208 p. Esp. 7-49: "Die Rezeption der Gebetsunterweisung Jesu in der christlichen Literatur des 1. und 2. Jahrhunderts"; 50-69: "Der älteste lateinische Vaterunserkommentar: Tertullian, *De oratione*"; 70-180: "Der älteste griechische Vaterunserkommentar: Origenes, περὶ εὐχῆς". [NTA 34, p. 115] — Diss. Münster, 1987-88 (W. Cramer).
G. DE DURAND, *RSPT* 73 (1989) 465-466; X. JACQUES, *Études classiques* 59 (1991) 282-283; M. KUNZLER, *TGl* 79 (1989) 628; L. LIES, *ZKT* 115 (1993) 201-202; E. MÜHLENBERG, *TLZ* 114 (1989) 830-831; W. RORDORF, *JTS* 41 (1990) 339; L.P. SCHRENK, *TS* 52 (1991) 178; B. SESBOÜÉ, *RSR* 80 (1992) 154-155; H.J. SIEBEN, *TheolPhil* 64 (1989) 589-590; J. VAN WINDEN, *VigChr* 43 (1989) 305-306.

**STROBEL, August**

1958  Zum Verständnis von Mt xxv 1-13. — *NT* 2 (1957-58) 199-227. [NTA 4, 83]

1961  *Untersuchungen zum eschatologischen Verzögerungsproblem auf Grund der spätjüdisch-urchristlichen Geschichte von Habakuk 2,2 ff.* (SupplNT, 2). Leiden: Brill, 1961, XXXI-305 p. Esp. 207-215 [24,43-44]; 215-222 [24,45-51]; 233-254 [25,1-13]; 265-277 [11,3]; 278-280 [10,22]. — Diss. Erlangen, 1960 (E. Stauffer).

1963  Textgeschichtliches zum Thomas-Logion 86 (Mt 8,20 / Luk 9,58). — *VigChr* 17 (1963) 211-224. [NTA 8, 1169]

1968  *Erkenntnis und Bekenntnis der Sünde in neutestamentlicher Zeit* (Arbeiten zur Theologie, I/37). Stuttgart: Calwer, 1968, 78 p. Esp. 43-45.

1970 Der Berg der Offenbarung (Mt 28,16; Apg 1,12). Erwägungen zu einem urchristlichen Erwartungstopos. — BÖCHER, O. — HAACKER, K. (eds.`, Verborum Veritas. FS G. Stählin, 1970, 133-146. Esp. 134-141.

1978 Macht und Gewalt in der Botschaft des Neuen Testaments. — GREIFENSTEIN, H. (ed.), Macht und Gewalt. Leitlinien lutherischer Theologie zur politischen Ethik heute (Zur Sache, 14), Hamburg: Lutherisches Verlagshaus, 1978, 71-112. Esp. 94-98: "Das Zeugnis des Matthäus".

1984 Die Bergpredigt als ethische Weisung heute. Vier Thesen für Nachfolger Jesu Christi in einer modernen Welt. — TBeitr 15 (1984) 3-16. [NTA 28, 913] → Burkhardt 1984

1985 Der Stern von Bethlehem. Ein Licht unserer Zeit? [2,1-12]. Fürth/Bay: Flacius, 1985, 79 p. [NTA 30, p. 358] → H.-H. Voigt 1989

1987 Weltenjahr, große Konjunktion und Messiasstern. Ein themageschichtlicher Überblick. — ANRW II.20.2 (1987) 988-1187. Esp. 1083-1087: "Zum Verständnis des Mt-Berichtes" [2,1-12]; 1099-1100: "Zur Thema- und Wirkungsgeschichte im 2. und 3. Jahrhundert n. Chr."; 122-128: "Geburtsstern und Erlösererwartung in der orientalischen Legende".

**STROHM, Theodor**

1984 Arbeit und Arbeitslosigkeit in der Verkündigung Jesu. Das Gleichnis von den Arbeitern im Weinberg (Mt 20,1-16). — Theologia Practica 19 (1984) 132-137.

**STROKER, William D.**

1988 Extracanonical Parables and the Historical Jesus. — Semeia 44 (1988) 95-120. Esp. 98-100: "The relation of Thomas to the synoptic tradition"; 104-106 [13,47-50/Th 8]; 106-109 [13,44/Th 109]. [NTA 33, 1000]

**STROLZ, Walter**

1974 Moderne Vaterunser-Interpretation. — BROCKE, M., et al. (eds.), Das Vaterunser, 1974, 13-27.
The Fatherhood of God in Modern Interpretations. — BROCKE, M. – PETUCHOWSKI, J.J. (eds.), The Lord's Prayer, 1978, 191-203.

1977 Die Freiheit und die Macht des Bösen. Die Aktualität der Versuchungsgeschichte Jesu. — Orientierung 41 (1977) 124-127.

**STRONG, David Kenneth**

1990 The Contribution of Structural Semantics to Theological Contextualization. A Case Study on "Righteousness". Diss. Fuller Theol. Sem., Pasadena, CA, 1990, 459 p. (P.G. Hiebert). — DissAbstr 51 (1990-91) 2062.

**STROTHMANN, Werner**

1971 Das Wolfenbütteler Tetraevangelium syriacum. Lesarten und Lesungen (Göttinger Orientforschungen. I. Syriaca, 2). Wiesbaden: Harrassowitz, 1971, 105 p. Esp. 16-24: "Matthäus-Evangelium".

1994 Die Syrische Übersetzung der Bibel. — ELSAS, C., et al. (eds.), Tradition und Translation. FS C. Colpe, 1994, 344-355. Esp. 347-348 [8,1?; 20,7.22.23; 24,31; 28,18].

**STROTMANN, Angelika**

1995 Weisheitschristologie ohne Antijudaismus? Gedanken zu einem bisher vernachlässigten Aspekt in der Diskussion um die Weisheitschristologie im Neuen Testament. — SCHOTTROFF, L. – WACKER, M.-T. (eds.), Von der Wurzel getragen. Christlich-feministische Exegese in Auseinandersetzung mit Antijudaismus (Biblical Interpretation Series, 17), Leiden: Brill, 1995, 153-175. Esp. 161-172 [Q 11,49-51].

**STROUD, William J.**

1990 New Testament Quotations in the Nag Hammadi Gospel of Philip. — *SBL 1990 Seminar Papers*, 68-81. Esp. 70-71 [3,10/GPh log. 123]; 73-74 [3,15/GPh log. 89]; 74 [6,6/Gph log. 69]; 75 [6,9/GPh log. 17]; 76-77 [27,46/GPh log. 72].

**STROUMSA, Gedaliahu Guy**

1993 Le radicalisme religieux du premier christianisme: contexte et implications. — PATLAGEAN, É. — LE BOULLUEC, A. (eds.), *Les retours aux Écritures. Fondamentalismes présents et passés* (Bibliothèque de l'École des Hautes Études. Section des sciences religieuses, 99), Leuven: Peeters, 1993, 357-381. Esp. 361-366 [5,43-48; 10,34].

**STRUNK, Reiner**

1983 Der Gegner wird zum Gegenüber. Neue Literatur zur Bergpredigt. — *EvKom* 16 (1983) 268-270. [NTA 28, 89]

1986 In der Nachfolge des königlichen Menschen: Die Gemeinde des Vertrauens. [14,22-33] — *ZDialTheol* 2 (1986) 204-218.

1988 *Das Gebet Jesu. Betrachtungen und Geschichten zum Vaterunser.* Stuttgart: Quell, 1988, 239 p.
  K. HOLLMANN, *TGl* 70 (1989) 95.

**STRUS, Andrea**

1972 *Mc.* 9,33-37. Problema dell'autenticità e dell'interpretazione. [18,5] — *RivBib* 20 suppl. (1972) 589-619. Esp. 593-600 [18,1-5/Mk 9,33-37]. [NTA 19, 112]

1977 Funkcja obrazu w przekazie biblijnym: obraz winnicy w Iz 5,1-7 i w Ewangelii (Fonction de l'image dans le message biblique: l'image de la vigne en Is 5,1-7 et dans les Évangiles). — *StudTheolVars* 15/2 (1977) 25-54. Esp. 42-50. [NTA 22, 414]

1983 "Géraséniens" dans la tradition synoptique: jalon topographique ou omen onomastique? — COLLADO, V. – ZURRO, E. (eds.), *El misterio de la palabra. Homenaje de sus alumnos al profesor D. Luis Alonso Schökel al cumplir veinticinco años de magisterio en el Instituto Bíblico Pontificio*, Madrid: Cristiandad, 1983, 283-301.

1985 La parole sul calice e la remissione dei peccati in Mt 26,28. — SALVESTRINI, F. (ed.), *La sapienza della croce oggi. Atti del II Congresso internazionale, Roma, 6-9 febbraio 1984.* II: *Salvezza cristiana e culture odierne*, Torino-Leumann: Elle Di Ci, 1985, 357-370.

**STUBBLEFIELD, John Michael**

1990 Matthew 6:5-15. — *RExp* 87 (1990) 303-307.

**[Studi]**

1967* *Studi sull'Oriente e la Bibbia offerti al P. Giovanni Rinaldi nel 60° compleanno da allievi, colleghi, amici.* Genova: Studio e Vita, 1967, 390 p. → G. Bolognesi, Dupont, Gamba

**[Studia Biblica]**

1959* *Studia Biblica et Orientalia. II. Novum Testamentum* (AnBib, 11). Roma: Pontifical Biblical Institute, 1959, 416 p. → Descamps, Dupont, Feuillet, George, Kürzinger, Kuss, Léon-Dufour, Meinertz, Mussner, Rigaux

**[Studies]**

1970* *Studies in John. Presented to Professor Dr. J.N. Sevenster on the Occasion of his Seventieth Birthday* (SupplNT, 24). Leiden: Brill, 1970, 220 p. → Hanhart, Kilpatrick, Lindijer

**STUHLMACHER, Peter**

1965  *Gerechtigkeit Gottes bei Paulus* (FRLANT, 87). Göttinger: Vandenhoeck & Ruprecht, 1965, 276 p. Esp. 188-191: "Das Matthäusevangelium"; 246-248 [18,23-35; 20,1-16]. — Diss. Tübingen, 1962 (E. Käsemann).

1968  *Das paulinische Evangelium. I. Vorgeschichte* (FRLANT, 95). Göttingen: Vandenhoeck & Ruprecht, 1968, 313 p. Esp. 218-225 [11,2-6]; 254-256 [28,16-20]. — Diss. Tübingen, 1966 (E. Käsemann).

1976  Achtzehn Thesen zur paulinischen Kreuzestheologie. — FRIEDRICH, J. – PÖHLMANN, W. – STUHLMACHER, P. (eds.), *Rechtfertigung. Festschrift für Ernst Käsemann zum 70. Geburtstag*, Tübingen: Mohr; Göttingen: Vandenhoeck & Ruprecht, 1976, 509-525. Esp. 523-524 [10,38]; = ID., *Versöhnung, Gesetz und Gerechtigkeit*, 1981, 192-208. Esp. 206-207.

1980  Existenzstellvertretung für die Vielen: Mk 10,45 (Mt 20,28). — ALBERTZ, R., et al. (eds.), *Werden und Wirken des Alten Testaments. Festschrift für Claus Westermann zum 70. Geburtstag*, Göttingen: Vandenhoeck & Ruprecht; Neukirchen-Vluyn: Neukirchener, 1980, 412-427; = ID., *Versöhnung, Gesetz und Gerechtigkeit*, 1981, 27-42.

1981a  *Versöhnung, Gesetz und Gerechtigkeit. Aufsätze zur biblischen Theologie*. Göttingen: Vandenhoeck & Ruprecht, 1981, 320 p. → 1976, 1980, 1981b
Trans. English 1986.

1981b  Die neue Gerechtigkeit in der Jesusverkündigung. — *Ibid.*, 43-65. Esp. 50-52 [18,23-35; 25,31-46]; 52-55 [11,2-6].

1982  Jesu vollkommenes Gesetz der Freiheit. Zum Verständnis der Bergpredigt. — *ZTK* 79 (1982) 283-322. Esp. 285-293: "Was ist die Bergpredigt und welches ist ihr Thema?"; 294-307: "Wie ist die Bergpredigt ausgelegt worden?"; 308-322: "Wie ist die Bergpredigt heute zu verstehen?" [5,3.27-52; 5,38-48; 6,9-13]. [NTA 27, 97]

1983*  (ed.), *Das Evangelium und die Evangelien. Vorträge vom Tübinger Symposium 1982* (WUNT, 28). Tübingen: Mohr, 1983, VIII-455 p. → O. Betz, E.E. Ellis, Feldmeier, Gerhardsson, Guelich, Hofius, P. Lampe, Polag, Stanton, Stuhlmacher
*The Gospel and the Gospels*, trans. J. Vriend. Grand Rapids, MI: Eerdmans, 1991, XXVIII-412 p.

1983  Zum Thema: Das Evangelium und die Evangelien. — *Ibid.*, 1-26. Esp. 21
The Theme: The Gospel and the Gospels. — ID., *The Gospel and the Gospels*, 1991, 1-25. Esp. 20-21.

1989  Die Stellung Jesu und des Paulus zu Jerusalem. Versuch einer Erinnerung. — *ZTK* 86 (1989) 140-156. Esp. 142-146. [NTA 33, 1379]

1990  The Genre(s) of the Gospels: Response to P.L. Shuler. — DUNGAN, D.L. (ed.), *The Interrelations of the Gospels*, 1990, 484-494 ("Nachtrag" by Shuler, 495-496). Esp. 487. → Shuler 1990a

1992  *Biblische Theologie des Neuen Testaments. Band 1: Grundlegung. Von Jesus zu Paulus*. Göttingen: Vandenhoeck & Ruprecht, 1992, XI-419 p.; ²1997. Esp. 57-66 [John the Baptist]; 70-75 [kingdom]; 75-84 [literary genres]; 84-107 [God]; 107-125 [Son of Man]; 125-143 [passion predictions]; 143-156 [passion narrative]; 186-188 [Son of God].

1993  Der messianische Gottesknecht. — *JbBT* 8 (1993) 131-154. Esp. 132-133.141-143 [11,2-6]. → Hofius 1993

**STUHLMANN, Rainer**

1983  *Das eschatologische Maß im Neuen Testament* (FRLANT, 132). Göttingen: Vandenhoeck & Ruprecht, 1983, 265 p. Esp. 15-16 [6,27]; 53-60 [24,22/Mk]; 72-73 [4,17; 8,29]; 89-90 [13,24-30]; 103-105 [23,32]; 107-108 [5,17]; 189-192 [13,47-48; 22,10]

**STUIBER, Alfred**

1973  Ein griechischer Textzeuge für das *Opus Imperfectum in Matthaeum*. — *VigChr* 27 (1973) 146-147. → Bouhot 1970, Coleman-Norton 1950

**STUPPERICH, Robert**

1963   (ed.), *Melanchthon's Werke in Auswahl*, IV. Gütersloh: Mohn, 1963, 464 p. Esp. 133-208: "Annotationes in Evangelium Matthaei iam recens in gratiam studiosorum editae" [1523]

**STURCH, Richard L.**

1983   The Replacement of 'Son of Man' by a Pronoun. [16,21] — *ExpT* 94 (1982-83) 333. [NTA 28, 160]

**STURZ, Harry A.**

1963   The Sermon on the Mount and Its Applications to the Present Age. — *Grace Journal* (Winona Lake, IN) 4/3 (1963) 3-15.

1984   *The Byzantine Text-Type and New Testament Textual Criticism*. Nashville, TN – New York: Nelson, 1984, 305 p. Esp. 145.160.191.201.211-217. — Diss. Grace Theol. Sem., Winona Lake, IN, 1967.

**STUTTS, David Hugh**

1989   *A Textual History of the Gospel of Matthew as Found in the Papyri, Uncials, and Principal Third and Fourth Century Fathers*. Diss. New Orleans Baptist Theol. Sem., 1989, 122 p. (C.L. Winbery). Esp. 9-26: "A survey of the history of classification methodology"; 27-37: "A proposed method for classifying fragmentary manuscripts"; 38-85: "Collations of the subject papyri"; 86-108: "Results of the study". — *DissAbstr* 51 (1990-91) 896.

**STYLER, G.M.**

1962   The Priority of Mark. — MOULE, C.F.D., *The Birth of the New Testament*, 1962, 223-232; ³1982, 285-316; = BELLINZONI, A.J., Jr., et al. (eds.), *The Two-Source Hypothesis*, 1985, 63-75. → Butler 1951/85

1964   Stages in Christology in the Synoptic Gospels. — *NTS* 10 (1963-64) 398-409. Esp. 404-406: "Tendencies of the evangelists, illustrated from Matthew". [NTA 9, 131]

1984   Argumentum e silentio. — BAMMEL, E. - MOULE, C.F.D. (eds.), *Jesus and the Politics of His Day*, 1984, 101-107. → Brandon 1967

1993   Synoptic Problem. — METZGER, B.M. - COOGAN, M.D. (eds.), *The Oxford Companion to the Bible*, 1993, 724-727.

**SUBILIA, Vittorio**

1954   *Gesù nella più antica tradizione cristiana* (Collana della Facoltà Valdese di Teologia). Torre Pellice: Claudiana, 1954, 266 p. Esp. 21-33 [John the Baptist]; 35-39 [1,1-17]; 45-48 [4,1-11]; 84-87 [25,31-46].

1978   *"Tu sei Pietro". L'enigma del fondamento biblico del papato* [16,17-19] (Facoltà Valdese di Teologia. Brevi studi, 2). Torino: Claudiana, 1978, 77 p. → Gherardini 1979
        A. ÁLVAREZ-SUÁREZ, *EphCarm* 31 (1980) 297-298; P. BENOIT, *RB* 87 (1980) 460-461; A. FAVALE, *Sal* 42 (1980) 673; R. WEIJENBORG, *Ant* 55 (1980) 522-523.

**SUEN CHIEN-GH'IEN, F.**

1974   A Commentary on the "Our Father" (Mt 6,9-13). [Chinese] — *ColcTFu* 5/20 (1974) 133-154.

**SUESS, Gloria E.M.**

1994   "Lilies of the field". [6,28] — *Jerusalem Perspective* 46-47 (1994) 18-23. [NTA 39, 1451]

1995   Beating the (Thorny) Bushes. [7,16] — *Jerusalem Perspective* 48 (1995) 16-21.

**SUGGIT, John**

1988   Comrade Judas: Matthew 26:50. — *JTSouthAfr* 63 (1988) 56-58. [NTA 33, 618]

**SUGGS, M. Jack**

1956 The Eusebian Text of Matthew. — *NT* 1 (1956) 233-245. [NTA 2, 288] — Diss. Duke Univ., Durham, NC, 1954.

1957 Eusebius and the Gospel Text. — *HTR* 50 (1957) 307-310. [NTA 2, 500] → Wallace-Hadrill 1956

1970 *Wisdom, Christology, and Law in Matthew's Gospel.* Cambridge, MA: Harvard University Press, 1970, V-132 p. Esp. 5-29: "Traces of a wisdom speculation in Q"; 31-61: "Jesus Christ, the Wisdom of God"; 63-97: "Jesus Christ, God's Wisdom and God's son"; 99-127: "Wisdom and law in the gospel of Matthew". [NTA 15, p. 122] → M.D. Johnson 1974
   W.J. BROGAN, *TS* 32 (1971) 304-306; M.D. GOULDER, *JTS* 22 (1971) 568-569; R.H. GUNDRY, *Interpr* 27 (1973) 369; R. HAMERTON-KELLY, *JAAR* 39 (1971) 528-530; B. MACK, *JBL* 90 (1971) 353-355; C. MATEOS, *EstAgust* 6 (1971) 280-281; G. STRECKER, *TLZ* 98 (1973) 519-522; L. SWEETMAN, *CalvTJ* 6 (1971) 228-234; W.G. THOMPSON, *CBQ* 33 (1971) 145-146.

1972 The Christian Two Ways Tradition: Its Antiquity, Form, and Function. — AUNE, D.E. (ed.), *Studies in New Testament.* FS A.P. Wikgren, 1972, 60-74. Esp. 63 [7,13-14].

1975 The Antitheses as Redactional Products. — STRECKER, G. (ed.), *Jesus Christus in Historie und Theologie.* FS H. Conzelmann, 1975, 433-444; = SCHOTTROFF, L., et al., *Essays on the Love Commandment,* 1978, 93-107.

1976 Gospel, Genre. — *IDBS,* 1976, 370-372.

1985 Matthew 16:13-20. — *Interpr* 39 (1985) 291-295.

**SUGIRTHARAJAH, Rasiah S.**

1990 Wisdom, Q, and a Proposal for a Christology. — *ExpT* 102 (1990-91) 42-46. [NTA 35, 817]

**SUH JOONG-SUK**

1989 Community in the Gospel of Matthew. [Korean] — *Sinhak Sasang* (Seoul) 67 (1989) 901-926.

**SUHL, Alfred**

1968a *Die Wunder Jesu. Ereignis und Überlieferung.* Gütersloh: Mohn, [1968], 54 p. Esp. 7-23 [9,18-26]; 27-31 [classification]; 32-33 [11,2-6.20-24]; 38-42 [12,22-24]; 46-47 [8,14-15]; = ID. (ed.), *Der Wunderbegriff im Neuen Testament,* 1980, 464-509 (with "Nachtrag"). Esp. 464-480; 483-487; 487-488; 493-497; 500-501.

1968b Der Davidssohn im Matthäus-Evangelium. — *ZNW* 59 (1968) 57-81. Esp. 60-61 [Pharisees]; 61 [22,41-46]; 62-68 [1,18-25]; 65 [15,21-28]; 68-69 [1,23]; 69-70 [21,1-9]; 70-72 [12,23-24]; 71-73 [9,32-34]; 73-75 [20,29-34]; 73-75 [9,27-31]; 76 [17,15]; 77-78 [ὄχλος/λαός]. [NTA 13, 152]

1969 Wer ist Jesus von Nazareth? Geboren aus der Jungfrau Maria! — DEMMER, H., et al., *Streit um Jesus,* 1969, 26-37.

1980* (ed.), *Der Wunderbegriff im Neuen Testament* (Wege der Forschung, 295). Darmstadt: Wissenschaftliche Buchgesellschaft, 1980, VI-524 p. → H.D. Betz 1968, Delling 1955, Hengel 1959, Suhl 1968a, 1980

1980 Einleitung. — *Ibid.,* 1-38.

1992 Die Funktion des Schwertstreichs bei der Gefangennahme Jesu. Beobachtungen zur Komposition und Theologie der synoptischen Evangelien. Mk 14,43-52; Mt 26,47-56; Lk 22,47-53. — VAN SEGBROECK, F., et al. (eds.), *The Four Gospels 1992.* FS F. Neirynck, 1992, I, 295-323. Esp. 307-315 [26,47-56].

**SULLIVAN, Clayton**

1988 *Rethinking Realized Eschatology.* Grand Rapids, MI: Mercer; Leuven: Peeters, 1988, VIII-152 p. Esp. 15-36: "A critique of Dodd's utilization of the Two-Document hypothesis"; 37-64: "A comparison of the use of *Basileia* in the writings of Dodd and in the synoptic gospels"; 65-99: "The kingdom version of realized eschatology" [11,2-6.12-13; 12,28.41-42; 13,16-17.24-30.36-43.47-50]; 119-126: "A Listing of all references to kingdom".

**SULLIVAN, Desmond**

1992 New Insights into Matthew 27:24-25. — *NBlackfr* 73 (1992) 453-457. [NTA 37, 739]

**SULLIVAN, Thomas P.**

1993 *On the Temptation of Jesus*. Diss. Harvard Univ., 1993, 138 p. (G. Matthews). — *DissAbstr* 54 (1993-94) 3777.

**SUMMERS, Ray**

1962a Plan of Matthew. — *SWJT* 5 (1962) 7-16.

1962b Matthew 24–25. An Exposition. — *RExp* 59 (1962) 501-511. [NTA 7, 513]

**SUNG, Chong-Hyon**

1993 *Vergebung der Sünden. Jesu Praxis der Sündenvergebung nach den Synoptikern und ihre Voraussetzungen im Alten Testament und frühen Judentum* (WUNT, II/57). Tübingen: Mohr, 1993, XIV-339 p. Esp. 240-242 [11,19]; 251-266 [6,9-13]; 266-268 [18,23-35]; 268-269 [5,44]; 270-275 [12,31-33/Mk]. — Diss. Tübingen, 1984 (P. Stuhlmacher).

**SURIANO, Thomas M.**

1975 "Who then is this?" ... Jesus Masters the Sea. — *BiTod* 79 (1975) 449-456. Esp. 453-454 [8,23-27]. [NTA 20, 459]

**SUSSARELLU, Bernardus**

1952 Le Beatitudini, esegesi delle beatitudini. — *PalCl* 31 (1952) 344-350, 481-486, 913-917; 32 (1953) 102-105, 193-203.

**SUTCLIFFE, Edmund F.**

1952a Matthew 27,9. — *JTS* 3 (1952) 227-228. → Saydon 1953, H.F.D. Sparks 1950

1952b 'Not to resist evil'. Matt V,39. — *Scripture* 5 (1952) 33-35.
    *TDig* 1 (1953) 163.

1952c 'Not to swear at all'. Matthew V,34. — *Ibid.*, 68-69.

1953a Dr Cadoux [The Life of Jesus, 1948] on the Virgin Birth. [1,16] — *Scripture* 6 (1953) 42-45.

1953b "Et tu aliquando conversus," St. Luke 22,32. — *CBQ* 15 (1953) 305-310. Esp. 308-309 [18,3].

1954 Effect as Purpose: A Study in Hebrew Thought Patterns. — *Bib* 35 (1954) 320-327. Esp. 323-325 [ἵνα].

1961 Many Are Called But Few Are Chosen. [20,16; 22,14] — *IrTQ* 28 (1961) 126-131. [NTA 6, 129]

1962a St. Peter's Double Confession in Mt 16:16-19. — *HeythJ* 3 (1962) 31-41. Esp. 32-35; 36-41. [NTA 6, 776]; = RYAN, M.R. (ed.), *Contemporary New Testament Studies*, 1965, 260-269. Esp. 261-264; 264-269. → 1962b

1962b St Peter's Double Confession. An Additional Note. — *Ibid.*, 275-276. [NTA 7, 512] → 1962a

**SWAELES, Romain**

1960a L'arrière-fond scripturaire de Matt. xxi.43 et son lien avec Matt. xxi.44. — *NTS* 6 (1959-60) 310-313. [NTA 5, 399]

1960b L'orientation ecclésiastique de la parabole du festin nuptial en Mt., XXII,1-14. — *ETL* 36 (1960) 655-684. Esp. 657-663: "Examen de la cohérence interne de Mt., XXII,1-14"; 663-671: "Comparaison de Matthieu et Luc. Leurs traits communs"; 671-673: "La parabole du festin et Jésus"; 673-684: "L'orientation ecclésiastique de la parabole". [NTA 6, 131]

1963 La parabole du festin nuptial. [22,1-14] — *AssSeign* I/74 (1963) 33-49.

1966 La parabole des vignerons homicides. [21,33-46] — *AssSeign* I/29 (1966) 36-51.

**SWAIN, Lionel**

1972 Preaching from the Lectionary in 1972. The Gospel according to St Matthew. — *CleR* 57 (1972) 432-438. [NTA 17, 112]

1993 *Reading the Easter Gospels* [28] (Good News Studies, 35). Collegeville, MN: Liturgical Press, 1993, V-131 p.

**SWALLOW, F.R.**

1959 The Keys of God's Household. — *Scripture* 11 (1959) 118-123. [NTA 4, 654]

**SWANSON, James A.** → Kohlenberger 1995

**SWANSON, Reuben J.**

1956 *The Gospel Text of Clement of Alexandria.* Diss. Yale Univ., New Haven, CT, 1956.

1958 Diminutives in the Greek New Testament. — *JBL* 77 (1958) 134-151. Esp. 137-140 [list]; 140-151 [analysis]. [NTA 3, 44]

1968 Notes on the Critical Apparatus in Aland's *Synopsis Quattuor Evangeliorum.* — *HTR* 61 (1968) 39-50. Esp. 41 [cod. Sin.]; 43-44.47-50 [Clement of Alexandria].

1975 *The Horizontal Line Synopsis of the Gospels.* Dillsboro, NC: Western North Carolina Press, 1975, XX-597 p.; rev. ed., Pasadena, CA: W. Carey Library, 1984, XV-528 p. → Léon-Dufour 1972c

1982 *The Horizontal Line Synopsis of the Gospels. Greek Edition.* I: *The Gospel of Matthew.* Dillsboro, NC: Western North Carolina Press, 1982, XXI-448 p.
 D.L. DUNGAN, *Bib* 66 (1985) 426-427; G.D. FEE, *JBL* 103 (1984) 471-472; V.C. PFITZNER, *LuthTJ* 17 (1983) 37-38; C.S. RODD, *ExpT* 94 (1982-83) 222.

1995 *New Testament Greek Manuscripts. Variant Readings Arranged in Horizontal Lines against Codex Vaticanus. Matthew.* Sheffield: JSOT; Pasadena, CA: W. Carey International Univ. Press, 1995, XX-304 p. [NTA 40, p. 527]
 B. EHRMAN, *JBL* 116 (1997) 159-160.

**SWANSON, Theodore N.**

1989 The Ministry of Jesus as Pictured in the Gospel of Matthew. A Bible Study. — *BangalTF* 21/3 (1989) 65-75. [NTA 34, 1126]

**SWART, G.J.**

1993 Twee aardbewings of een? Die assosiasie van literêre motiewe in die eksegese van Matteus 27:51-54 & 28:2-4. [Two earthquakes or one? The association of literary motifs in the exegesis of Mt 27,51-54 and 28,2-4]. — *HervTS* 49 (1993) 255-265. [NTA 38, 776]

**SWARTLEY, Willard M.**

1992* *The Love of Enemy and Nonretaliation in the New Testament* (Studies in Peace and Scripture). Louisville, KY: Westminster/Knox, 1992, XV-336 p. → R.A. Horsley 1986, 1992c, Klassen, L. Schottroff 1984b, D.J. Weaver, Wink 1988/91

1994 *Israel's Scripture Traditions and the Synoptic Gospels. Story Shaping Story.* Peabody, MA: Hendrickson, 1994, XV-367 p. Esp. 61-73 [Exodus and Sinai traditions in Mt 4–15]; 116-126 [Conquest traditions in Mt 16–20]; 170-185 [Temple traditions in Mt 21–25]; 215-232 [Kingship traditions in Mt 26–28].

**SWARTZ, Steve**

1993 The Holy Spirit: Person and Power. The Greek Article and *Pneuma.* — *BTrans* 44 (1993) 124-138. Esp. 136 [12,28]. [NTA 37, 1162]

**SWEET, J.P.M.**

1976    Miracle and Faith: The Miracles of Jesus. — *EpworthR* 3 (1976) 81-91. [NTA 21, 34]

1984    The Zealots and Jesus. — BAMMEL, E. – MOULE, C.F.D. (eds.), *Jesus and the Politics of His Day*, 1984, 1-9. → Brandon 1951, 1967

**SWEETLAND, Dennis M.**

1984    Discipleship and Persecution: A Study of Luke 12,1-12. [10,19-20.26-33; 12,32] — *Bib* 65 (1984) 61-80. [NTA 28, 964]

**SWETE, Henry Barclay**

1910ᴿ   *The Holy Spirit in the New Testament* [1910]. Grand Rapids, MI: Baker, 1964, X-417 p. Esp. 29-32 [1,18-25]; 38-49 [3,13-17]; 50-62 [4,1-11]; 113-128: "The synoptic teaching of our Lord".

**SWETNAM, James**

1971    "Hallowed be Thy name". [6,9] — *Bib* 52 (1971) 556-563. [NTA 16, 855r] → Carmignac 1969

1985    No Sign of Jonah. — *Bib* 66 (1985) 126-130. Esp. 126-128 [12,39; 16,4]; 128-130 [26,63-64]. [NTA 29, 958] → 1987

1987    Some Signs of Jonah. — *Bib* 68 (1987) 74-79. [NTA 32, 123] → 1985

**SWIDLER, Leonard**

1979    *Biblical Affirmations of Woman*. Philadelphia, PA: Westminster, 1979, 382 p. Esp. 235-254: "The gospel according to Matthew".

1989    & CHERNICK, M. – LEVINE, A.-J., The Halakhah of Jesus according to Matthew. — *JEcuSt* 26 (1989) 530-535. [NTA 35, 129r] → H. Falk 1990, Sigal 1986

**SWIHART, Stephen D.**

1981    (ed.), *Logos International Bible Commentary. The Gospels of Matthew, Mark and Luke. With Text from the New International Version Bible*. Plainfield, NJ: Logos International, 1981, XXXIII-591 p. [NTA 27, p. 214]

**SYKES, Marjorie H.**

1962    And do not bring us to the Test. [6,13] — *ExpT* 73 (1961-62) 189-190. [NTA 7, 130] → M.B. Walker 1962

**SYREENI, Kari**

1987    *The Making of the Sermon on the Mount. A procedural analysis of Matthew's redactoral activity*. Part I: *Methodology & Compositional Analysis* (Annales Academiae Scientiarum Fennicae. Dissertationes Humanarum Litterarum, 44). Helsinki: Suomalainen Tiedeakatemia, 1987, VII-245 p. Esp. 75-131: "The Sermon on the Mount in Matthew's overall literary plan"; 132-167: "The compositional basis of the Sermon on the Mount"; 168-226: "Matthew's literary plan for the Sermon on the Mount". [NTA 33, p. 113]
J.M. COURT, *ExpT* 100 (1988-89) 66-67; L.R. DONELSON, *JBL* 108 (1989) 524-526; D. ELLUL, *ETR* 66 (1991) 287-288; H. GIESEN, *SNTU* 16 (1991) 212-213; L.J. WHITE, *BTB* 18 (1988) 119-120.

1990a   Between Heaven and Earth: On the Structure of Matthew's Symbolic Universe. — *JSNT* 40 (1990) 3-13. [NTA 35, 1122]

1990b   Matthew, Luke, and the Law. A Study in Hermeneutical Exegesis. — VEIJOLA, T. (ed.), *The Law in the Bible and in Its Environment* (Publications of the Finnish Exegetical Society, 51), Helsinki: Finnish Exegetical Society; Göttingen: Vandenhoeck & Ruprecht, 1990, 126-155. Esp. 133-138: "Matthew's and Luke's different ideological dynamics"; 138-151: "The law in Matthew's and Luke's symbolic words".

1994    Separation and Identity: Aspects of the Symbolic World of Matt 6.1-18. — *NTS* 40 (1994) 522-541. Esp. 523-527: "The text world of Matt 6.2-6,16-18"; 527-531: "The social setting of the cultic section"; 537-541: "Tradition- and redaction-historical conclusions". [NTA 39, 801]

**SYS, Jacques**

1995 La question du commencement dans l'énonciation du "Notre Père". — *Graphè* (Lille) 4 (1995) 105-124.

**SYX, Raoul**

1992 Jesus and the Unclean Spirit. The Literary Relation between Mark and Q in the Beelzebul Controversy (Mark 3:20-30 par). — *LouvSt* 17 (1992) 166-180. Esp. 167-170 [9,32-33; 12,22-23]; 170-171 [9,34; 12,24]; 171-173 [12,25-26]; 173-174 [12,26]; 174-176 [12,27-28.30; Q 11,19-20.23]; 176-177 [12,29; Q 11,21-22]; 177-178 [12,31-32; Q 12,10]. [NTA 36, 1297]

1994 *Gebruikte Marcus de Q-bron? Een onderzoek van de Beelzebulcontroverse (Mc 3,20-30 en par.).* Diss. Leuven, 1994, XLIX-291, XV-292-477 p. (J. Lambrecht). Esp. 9-44: "De interpretatiemoeilijkheden"; 45-140: "Een historische terugblik"; 141-373: "Analyse van de Beelzebulcontroverse".

**SZABÓ, Andor**

1960 Anfänge einer judenchristlichen Theologie bei Matthäus. — *Judaica* 16 (1960) 193-206. Esp. 193-197.201-203 [23,33-39]; 197-198 [25,31-46]; 199-201 [15,21-28].

1961 "Stecke dein Schwert an seinen Ort" (Mt. 26,52). — *Reformatus Egyhaz* 24 (1961) 351-354.

**SZCZUREK, Tadeusz**

1975 Znaczenie struktur literackich dla hermeneutyki na przykładzie zwiastowań Mt 1,18-25; Łk 1,26-38 oraz cudu w Kanie J 2,1-11 (Quid significant structurae litterariae pro hermeneutica in exemplis Mt 1,18-25; Lc 1,26-38; Jo 2,1-11?). — *RuBi* 28 (1975) 226-228.

**SZLAGA, Jan**

1979 Perykopa o magach w strukturze Mt 1-2 (Die Magierperikope in der Struktur von Mt 1-2). — *StudTheolVars* 17/1 (1979) 71-77. [NTA 24, 415]

1995 Historyczna prawda genealogii Jezusa Chrysusa według św. Mateusza. [The historical truth of Jesus Christ's genealogy according to St. Matthew] — *Analecta Cracoviensia* (Krakow) 27 (1995) 303-313. [NTA 41, 197]

**SZÖRÉNYI, A.**

1967 The Birth of Jesus in Contemporary Exegesis. [Hungarian] — *Teologia* (Budapest) 1 (1967) 87-91.

**SZWARC, Urszula**

1987 The Meaning of Is 6,10 in the Synoptics. [Polish] — *RoczTK* 34/1 (1987) 39-46. [NTA 36, 1275]

**SZYMANEK, Edward**

1978 Jezus Chrystus w Ewangeliach Dziecięctwa. [Jesus Christ in the birth narratives] — *Katecheta* (Poznań) 22 (1978) 252-255.

1983 Mesjasz i Syn Boży w Ewangelii Mateusza. [Messiah and Son of God in the gospel of Matthew] — *Msza Święta* 39 (1983) 218-219.

# T

**TABACHOWITZ, David**

1956    *Die Septuaginta und das Neue Testament. Stilstudien*. Lund: Gleerup, 1956, 135 p. Esp. 28-29.93-95 [3,9]; 35-37 [23,26]; 84-85 [27,25]; 110-112 [6,26-27]; 113-115 [17,17]; 116-117 [6,29].

1963    Mt 16,22 "Ἴλεώς σοι. — *Eranos* (Stockholm) 61 (1963) 25-28.

**TABACZYNSKI, L.**

1950    Textus promissionis Primatus (Mt 16,18ss) in luce problematicae thomisticae et morphocriticae. — *Ateneum Kaplanskie* (Wroclaw) 52 (1950) 266-275.

**TÁBET, Miguel Angel**

1988    La distinzione dei peccati secondo la loro gravità nell'insegnamento di Gesù. — *Annales theologici* 2 (1988) 3-34. Esp. 7-9 [23,23]; 9-11 [5,21-22]; 11-12 [7,3-5]; 13-15 [23,29-34]; 15-18 [25,41-46]; 18-19 [10,14-15]; 19-20 [18,6-7]; 21-22 [18,8-9]; 22-24 [25,24-30]; 24-25 [12,30-32].

**TABOR, James D.**

1992a    & WISE, M.O., 4Q521 "On Resurrection" and the Synoptic Gospel Tradition: A Preliminary Study. — *Journal for the Study of the Pseudepigrapha* (Sheffield) 10 (1992) 149-162. Esp. 158-162 [Q 7,22]; = CHARLESWORTH, J.H. (ed.), *Qumran Questions* (The Biblical Seminar, 36), Sheffield: JSOT, 1995, 151-163. Esp. 159-163. → Fitzmyer 1995, É. Puech 1992, 1993, 1994

1992b    → Wise 1992

**TAGAWA, Kenzo**

1967    People and Community in the Gospel of Matthew. [Japanese] — *Seisho-gaku ronshū* (Tokyo) 5 (1967) 116-132.

        People and Community in the Gospel of Matthew. — *NTS* 16 (1969-70) 149-162. [NTA 14, 847]

**TAHENY, Theodore T.**

1960    *The History of the Exegesis of Matthew 16:18-19 in Commentaries of the Early Middle Ages*. Diss. Woodstock College, 1960, 1969 p.

**TAKÁCS, Gyula**

1995    Die existentiale Interpretation der Gleichnisse Jesu. — *Folia Theologica* (Budapest) 6 (1995) 111-147. [NTA 40, 801]

**TALAMO-ATENOLFI, G.**

1957    I testi della leggenda di S. Matteo. — *Archivi* 24 (1957) 85-97.

**TALAVERO TOVAR, Severino**

1976    *Pasión y resurreción en el IV Evangelio. Interpretación de un cristiano de primera hora* (Biblioteca Salmanticensis, 17. Estudios, 15). Salamanca: Universidad Pontificia, 1976, 277 p. Esp. 45-83: "Juan 18-20 y los sinopticos".

**TALBERT, Charles H.**

1970    The Redaction Critical Quest for Luke the Theologian. — BUTTRICK, D.G. (ed.), *Jesus and Man's Hope*. I, 1970, 171-222. Ep. 172-174 [Q 19,12-27]; 178-180 [Q 17,22-37]; 188-189 [Q 12,39-46]. [NTA 15, 178]

1971    & McKNIGHT, E.V., Can the Griesbach Hypothesis Be Falsified? — *SBL 1971 Seminar Papers*, I, 49-109. Esp. 50-58 [28,1-8]; 58-71 [16,13-23]; 71-77 [12,1-8]; 78-82 [3,13-17]; 83-88 [5,39-

47]; 88-93 [12,38-42]; 93-99 [24,37-39]; = *JBL* 91 (1972) 338-368. Esp. 339-344 [28,1-8]; 344-352 [16,13-23]; 352-357 [12,1-8]; 357-360 [5,39-47]; 361-364 [12,38-42]; 364-367 [24,37-39]. [NTA 17, 500] → G.W. Buchanan 1971, Cope 1973

1975 The Concept of Immortals in Mediterranean Antiquity. — *JBL* 94 (1975) 419-436. Esp. 435-436. [NTA 20, 634]

1977 *What Is a Gospel? The Genre of the Canonical Gospels.* Philadelphia, PA: Fortress, 1977; Macon, GA: Mercer University Press, 1985, XI-147 p. Esp. 40-41 [Mt]; 122-124 [Q]. → Aune 1981

1979 The Gospel and the Gospels. — *Interpr* 33 (1979) 351-362. Esp. 353.355 [Q]. [NTA 24, 384]

1992 Biography, Ancient. — *ABD* 1 (1992) 745-749.

**TALBERT, Ernest William** → Kellogg 1960

**TALBOT, James F.**

1958 Baptism with the Spirit and Fire. [3,11-12] — *The Theologian* 14/2 (1958) 133-138.

**TAN, Kim Huat**

1997 *The Zion Traditions and the Aims of Jesus* (SNTS MS, 91). Cambridge: University Press, 1997, XIV-276 p. Esp. 81-99: "The attraction of Jerusalem: the city of the great king" [5,34-35]; 100-128: "'To gather Jerusalem' (Q 13.34-35)". — Diss. London, 1993 (G.N. Stanton).

**TAN GIOK LIE**

1995 Analysis of Jesus' Teaching Episode within the Framework of the Seven Components of Teaching: Conflict over the Tradition of Ceremonial Defilement (Matt 15:1-20; Mark 7:1-23). — *Stulos Theological Journal* (Bandung) 3 (1995) 83-94. [NTA 41, 211]

**TANKERSLEY, Julian Bruce**

1977 *The Significance of the Moses and Elijah Motifs in the Synoptic Gospels.* Diss. Southwestern Baptist Theol. Sem., Fort Worth, TX, 1977.

**TANNEHILL, Robert C.**

1970 The "Focal Instance" as a Form of New Testament Speech: A Study of Matthew 5:39b-42. — *JRel* 50 (1970) 372-385. [NTA 15, 495]

1975 *The Sword of His Mouth* (SBL *Semeia* Supplements, 1). Missoula, MT: Scholars; Philadelphia, PA: Fortress, 1975, X-224 p. Esp. 46-49 [6,19-20; 7,7-8]; 50-51 [7,24-27]; 60-67 [6,25-33/Q 12,22-31]; 67-77 [5,39-42]; 78-88 [6,1-6.16-18]; 107-114 [7,1-12/Q 6,37-38]; 114-118 [7,3-5/Q 6,41-42]; 118-122 [24,37-39/Th 17,26-30]; 122-128 [11,21-24/Q 10,13-15]; 128-134 [16,2-3/Q 12,54-56]; 134-140 [19,12]; 140-147 [10,34-36/Q 12,49-53]; 157-165 [8,19-22/Q 9 57-62].

1980 Tension in Synoptic Sayings and Stories. — *Interpr* 34 (1980) 138-150. Esp. 141-144. [NTA 24, 776]

1981 Varieties of Synoptic Pronouncement Stories. — *Semeia* 20 (1981) 101-119. Esp. 102-105: "Correction stories" [12,38-42; 16,1-4]; 105-106: "Commendation stories" [13,51-52; 16,13-20]; 107-111: "Objection stories"; 111-114: "Quest stories"; 114-116: "Inquiry stories". [NTA 26, 81]

1984 Types and Functions of Apophthegms in the Synoptic Gospels. — *ANRW* II.25.2 (1984) 1792-1829. [3,13-15; 8,5-13.19-22; 11,2-6.20-24; 12,38-42; 16,1-4.17-19; 17,24-27; 18,1-4.21-22; 19,3-12.23-26; 21,14-16.18-22]

1988 Aphorism and Narrative: A Response to John Dominic Crossan. [Q 11,2-4.9-13] — *Semeia* 43 (1988) 141-144. → J.D. Crossan 1988b

**TAPP, Roland W.** → Bowman 1957a

**TARADACH, Madeleine**

1989 Mt 21,5: une lecture midrashique de Za 9,9. — *RevistCatTeol* 14 (1989) 155-162. Esp. 156-158 [21,5].

**TARAZI, Nicolae**

1973   Jesus Christ and the Law of Moses. The Relation between Christianity and Judaism after Mt 5. [Roumanian] — *Ortodoxia* (Bucuresti) 25 (1973) 621-628.

**TARCHNIŠVILI, Michel**

1942ᴿ   Zwei georgische Lektionarfragmente aus dem 5. und 8. Jahrhundert. [1942] — *Muséon* 73 (1960) 261-196. Esp. 286-287 [28,7-20]; 292-293 [24,29-35]. → Outtier 1972

**TAROCCHI, Stefano**

1992   "Beati i miti..."? (*Mt* 5,5). Appunti in margine alla versione in lingua corrente della beatitudine della mitezza. — *Vivens Homo* (Firenze) 3 (1992) 83-99.

**TASHJIAN, Jirair S.**

1987   *The Social Setting of the Mission Charge in Q*. Diss. Claremont Graduate School, 1987, XI-236 p. (J.M. Robinson). Esp. 73-129: "Literary history of the mission charge"; 130-168: "The social setting of Q in Palestine"; 184-216: "A sociological analysis of the mission charge in Q". — *DissAbstr* 48 (1987-88) 2899; *SBT* 16 (1988) 258-259.

1988   The Social Setting of the Q Mission: Three Dissertations. — *SBL 1988 Seminar Papers*, 636-644. Esp. 636-342 [Tashjian 1987]; 642 [Uro 1987]; 643-644 [Vaage 1987].

**TASKER, R.V.G.**

1961   *The Gospel according to St. Matthew. An Introduction and Commentary* (The Tyndale New Testament Commentaries). London: SCM; Grand Rapids, MI: Eerdmans, 1961, 285 p.; repr. 1963, 1966. Esp. 11-26: "Introduction"; 31-277: "Commentary"; 1971, 288 p.
W. BARCLAY, *ExpT* 73 (1961-62) 369; W. BROWNING, *Theology* 65 (1962) 288-289; P. COUTURE, *CBQ* 24 (1962) 460-461; M. GERAGHTY, *RevistBib* 30 (1968) 187-188; H.B. GREEN, *JTS* 14 (1963) 139-140; I.H. MARSHALL, *EvQ* 34 (1962) 108-110; R.P. MARTIN, *ChrTod* 6 (1961-62) 447-448; D.W.B. ROBINSON, *RTR* 21 (1962) 91-92; R. SUMMERS, *RExp* 59 (1962) 395-396; S.D. TOUSSAINT, *BS* 120 (1963) 175-176.

1962   *The Nature and Purpose of the Gospels*. Richmond, VA: Knox, 1962, 112 p.

1964   (ed.), *The Greek New Testament Being the Text Translated in The New English Bible 1961. Edited with Introduction, Textual Notes, and Appendix*. Oxford–Cambridge: University Press, 1964, XIII-445 p. Esp. 3-53.

**TASSIN, Claude**

1988   La mission selon Matthieu: Deux contextes pour lire Mt 28,16-20. — *Spiritus* (Paris) 29 (1988) 366-385. Esp. 367-377: "Mt 28,16-20 et le contexte des traditions juives"; 378-384: "Mt 28,16-20 et le contexte de l'évangile de Matthieu". [NTA 33, 620]

1990   Matthieu "targumiste"? L'exemple de Mt 12,18 (= Is 42,1). — *EstBíb* 48 (1990) 199-214. Esp. 205-213. [NTA 35, 627]

1991   *L'évangile de Matthieu. Commentaire pastoral* (Commentaires). Paris: Centurion, 1991, 304 p.
B.T. VIVIANO, *RB* 101 (1994) 457.

**TATE, W. Randolph**

1991   *Biblical Interpretation. An Integral Approach*. Peabody, MA: Hendrickson, 1991, XXI-226 p. Esp. 111-115: "The gospel of Matthew: a model".

**TATUM, Scott L.**

1972   Great Prayers of the Bible. [6,9-13] — *SWJT* 14 (1972) 29-42.

**TATUM, Walter Barnes Jr.**

1966   *The Matthaean Infancy Stories. Their Form, Structure, and Relation to the Theology of the First Evangelist*. Diss. Duke Univ., Durham, NC, 1966, 221 p. — *DissAbstr* 27 (1966-67) 3928.

1976 Matthew 2.23 – Wordplay and Misleading Translations. — *BTrans* 27 (1976) 135-138. [NTA 20, 772]

1977 "The Origin of Jesus Messiah" (Matt 1:1,18a): Matthew's Use of the Infancy Traditions. — *JBL* 96 (1977) 523-535. Esp. 524-526 [1,1.18]; 526-529 [1,1-17]; 529-533 [1,18-4,16]. [NTA 22, 758]

1994 *John the Baptist and Jesus. A Report of the Jesus Seminar.* Sonoma, CA: Polebridge, 1994, X-182 p. Esp. 35-42: "Sayings Gospel Q"; 43-53: "Gospel of Matthew".

**TAUSSIG, Hal**

1988 The Lord's Prayer. — *Forum* 4/4 (1988) 25-41. Esp. 26-30: "The prayer as a unit"; 30-38: "The individual lines of the prayer"; 39-40: "The origins of the Lord's prayer". [NTA 33, 1127]

**TAVARES, Antonio Augusto**

1972 *Da Mariologia à cristologia. Estudo de Mt 1,25 na tradição patrística e nas perspectivas da exegese actual.* Lisboa: Universidade católica portuguesa, 1972, 231 p. [NTA 20, p. 114] — Diss. Pont. Univ. S. Thoma, Roma, 1970. → Alonso 1973
J.A. CARRASCO, *EstJos* 27 (1973) 105-107; J. CARREIRA DAS NEVES, *Didaskalia* 2 (1972) 426-430; R. LAURENTIN, *RSPT* 58 (1974) 69-70; E. LLAMAS, *Salmanticensis* 20 (1973) 689; E. PERETTO, *Marianum* 35 (1973) 272-274.

1974 Imposição do nome de Jesus e seu conteudo teológico. — *EstJos* 28 (1974) 3-14. Esp. 6-8 [1,18-25].

1976 A Concepção virginal em Mt. 1 e o seu significado. — *EstJos* 30 (1976) 3-18.

1979 As narrativas da infância em Mt e Lc perante a crítica histórica. — *EstJos* 33 (1979) 11-25. Esp. 12-14 [Mt/Lk]; 14-16 [literary genre]; 16-19 [purpose]; 20-23 [1,23]. Infancy Narratives and Historical Criticism. — *TDig* 28 (1980) 53-54.

**TAX, Petrus W.**

1980 Althochdeutsche Übersetzung und lateinischer Kommentar. Die Monsee-Wiener Matthäusfragmente und die *Commentaria in Mattheum* des Hieronymus. — *Sprachwissenschaft* (Heidelberg) 5 (1980) 343-380.

1991 Remigius of Auxerre's Psalm Commentary and the Matthew Commentary Attributed to Him. Questions of Authenticity. — IOGNA-PRAT, D., et al. (eds.), *L'école carolingienne d'Auxerre de Murethach à Remi 830-908. Entretiens d'Auxerre 1989*, Paris: Beauchesne, 1991, 413-424.

**TAYLOR, Anthony Basil**

1989 *The Master-Servant Type Scene in the Parables of Jesus.* Diss. Fordham Univ., Bronx, NY, 1989, 376 p. (C.H. Giblin). — *DissAbstr* 50 (1989-90) 1706.

**TAYLOR, Brian**

1958 The Prayer of St. Chrysostom: A Liturgical Note. [18,19-20] — *ATR* 40 (1958) 22-26. → Ratcliff 1960

**TAYLOR, D.B.**

1981 Jesus – of Nazareth? [2,23; 26,71] — *ExpT* 92 (1980-81) 336-337. [NTA 26, 63] → Allan 1983

**TAYLOR, Justin**

1987 *As It Was Written. An Introduction to the Bible.* New York – Mahwah, NJ: Paulist, 1987, 164 p.

1989 "The love of many will grow cold": Matt 24:9-13 and the Neronian Persecution. — *RB* 96 (1989) 352-357. [NTA 34, 634]

1991 The Coming of Elijah, Mt 17,10-13 and Mk 9,11-13. The Development of the Texts. — *RB* 98 (1991) 107-109. Esp. 107-109: "The texts"; 109-115: "The Matthean tradition". [NTA 35, 1139]

**TAYLOR, Nicholas H.**

1997    Interpretation of Scripture as an Indicator of Socio-Historical Context. The Case of the Eschatological Discourses in Mark and Q. — TUCKETT, C.M. (ed.), *The Scriptures in the Gospels*, 1997, 459-467.

**TAYLOR, Richard J.**

1970    Divorce in Matthew 5:32; 19:9. Theological Research and Pastoral Care. — *CleR* 55 (1970) 792-800. [NTA 15, 494]

**TAYLOR, Vincent**

1933[R]   *The Formation of the Gospel Tradition* [1933]. London: Macmillan, repr. 1953, XII-217 p. Esp. 88-118: "Sayings and parables" [5,17-48; 10,39-40; Q 6,27-36]; 152-153; 181-185 [Q].

1946[R]   The "Son of Man" Sayings Relating to the Parousia. [1946] — ID., *New Testament Essays*, 1970, 119-126. Esp. 119-122; 124-125 [10,23].

1951    The Life and Ministry of Jesus. — BUTTRICK, G.A. (ed.), *The Interpreter's Bible*, VII, 1951, 114-144.

1953a   *The Names of Jesus*. London: Macmillan; New York: St. Martin's, 1953, IX-179 p.

1953b   The Order of Q. — *JTS* 4 (1953) 27-31; = ID., *New Testament Essays*, 1970, 90-94. → 1959

1954    *The Life and Ministry of Jesus*. London: Macmillan; New York: St Martin's Press, 1954, XI-236 p.; [2]1967, 240 p.
        The Mission of the Twelve. [1954, 106-111] — MCARTHUR, H.K. (ed.), *In Search of the Historical Jesus*, 1969, 194-198.

1958    *The Person of Christ in New Testament Teaching*. London: Macmillan; New York: St Martin's Press, 1958; repr. 1966, X-321 p. Esp. 13-17 [Christ].
        *La personne du Christ dans le Nouveau Testament*, trans. J. Winandy (LD, 57). Paris: Cerf, 1969, 306 p. Esp. 23-27.

1959    The Original Order of Q. — HIGGINS, A.J.B. (ed.), *New Testament Essays*. FS T.W. Manson, 1959, 246-269. Esp. 249-254: "The Sermon on the Mount"; 254-257: "The mission charge"; 257-258: "The discourse teaching in parables"; 258-260: "The discourse on discipleship"; 260-263: "The eschatological discourse"; 264-266: "The rest of Matthew"; = ID., *New Testament Essays*, 1970, 95-118. Esp. 98-104; 104-107; 107-108; 108-111; 111-114; 114-117; = BELLINZONI, A.J., Jr., et al. (eds.), *The Two-Source Hypothesis*, 1985, 295-317. → 1953b

1961    *The Text of the New Testament. A Short Introduction*. London: Macmillan, 1961, XI-113 p. Esp. 32-34 [Syriac, Coptic]; 78-82: "Notes on select readings" [1,16; 16,2-3; 24,39; 27,16-17].

1970    *New Testament Essays*. London: Epworth, 1970, VII-146 p. → 1946, 1953b, 1959

**TAYLOR-WINGENDER, P.**

1988    Kids of the Kingdom (A Study of Matthew 18:1-5 and its Context). — *Direction* (Fresno, CA) 17/2 (1988) 18-25. [NTA 33, 614]

**TEBBE, Walter**

1952    Die zweite Seligpreisung (Matth. 5,4). Ein Beitrag zum Gedenken an Adolf Schlatter. — *EvT* 12 (1952-53) 121-128.

**TEEPLE, Howard M.**

1957    *The Mosaic Eschatological Prophet* (JBL MS, 10). Philadelphia, PA: SBL, 1957, XIII-122 p. Esp. 74-83: "Jesus as the prophet like Moses–Matt.". — Diss. Univ. of Chicago, IL, 1955 (R. Marcus – A. Wikgren).

1965    The Origin of the Son of Man Christology. — *JBL* 84 (1965) 213-250. Esp. 226, 235-237, 249.

1973 The Greek Article with Personal Names in the Synoptic Gospels. — *NTS* 19 (1972-73) 302-317. Esp. 304-311. [NTA 18, 96]

**TELFORD, William R.**

1980 *The Barren Temple and the Withered Tree. A Redaction-critical Analysis of the Cursing of the Fig-Tree Pericope in Mark's Gospel and Its Relation to the Cleansing of the Temple Tradition* (JSNT SS, 1). Sheffield: JSOT, 1980, XVI-319 p. Esp. 69-94: "The fig-tree pericope in Matthew's gospel"; 95-127: "'Whoever says to this mountain': the mountain-moving saying". — Diss. Cambridge, 1976 (E. Bammel).

1992 The Pre-Markan Tradition in Recent Research (1980-1990). — VAN SEGBROECK, F., et al. (eds.), *The Four Gospels 1992*. FS F. Neirynck, 1992, II, 693-723. Esp. 698-699 [Mk/Mt]; 701 [Mk/Q].

**TELLAN, Sergio**

1992 *La correzione fraterna nella Chiesa di Matteo: Mt 18,15-20*. Diss. Pont. Univ. Greg., Roma, 1992, 307 p. (E. Rasco); Exc. 1996, 95 p. Esp. 28-68: "La correzione fraterna: Mt 18,15-17" (= 1992, chapt. 2); 69-94: "Sitz im Leben della Chiesa di Matteo" (= 1992, chapt. 4).

1994 La Chiesa di Matteo e la correzione fraterna. Analisi di Mt 18,15-17. — *Laur* 35 (1994) 91-137. Esp. 97-103 [discipleship]; 104-108 [Church]; 108-118 [text; Qumran]; 118-137: "Analisi del testo". [NTA 39, 156]

**TEMPLE, Patrick J.**

1955 The Rejection at Nazareth. [13,53-58] — *CBQ* 17 (1955) 349-362 (229-242).

**TEMPLE, Sydney**

1960 The Two Traditions of the Last Supper, Betrayal, and Arrest. — *NTS* 7 (1960-61) 77-85. Esp. 78, 84 [26,50]. [NTA 5, 374]

**TEMPLETON, David**

1989 The Lord's Prayer as Eucharist in Daily Life. — *IBS* 11 (1989) 133-140. [NTA 34, 118]

**TENA, Rafael**

1971 El inicio de la sección de los panes en la fuente común a Mt. y Mc. — *Libro Anual 1971-1972*, ed. Instituto Superior de Estudios Eclesiásticos, México, 1971, 41-48.

**TENA GARRIGA, Pedro**

1958 *La palabra Ekklesia. Estudio histórico-teológico* (Colectanea San Paciano. Serie teológica, 6). Barcelona: Casulleras, 1958, 314 p. Esp. 61-72; 73-91: "La promesa de Jesús: Mt. 16/18"; 107-109 [18,17].

**TENA MONTERO, Pere**

1989 Les benaurances en l'"Ordo Lectionum Missae". [5,3-12] — *RevistCatTeol* 14 (1989) 467-477 (English summary, 497).

1991 Los relatos sinópticos de la tentación de Jesús. Redacción y teología. — *EstBíb* 49 (1991) 289-309. Esp. 299-305: "El relato de Mateo". [NTA 37, 167]

**TEN KATE, R.**

1978 Geef ons heden ons "dagelijks" brood. — *NTT* 32 (1978) 125-139. [NTA 23, 99]

**TENNEY, Merrill C.**

1954 *The New Testament. An Historical and Analytical Survey*. London: Inter-Varsity, 1954; Grand Rapids, MI: Eerdmans, 1955; *New Testament Survey*, 1961, XX-484 p. Trans. Portuguese 1960; Japanese 1962.

**TERNANT, Paul**

1963 "Repentez-vous et convertissez-vous". — *AssSeign* I/21 (1963) 50-79. Esp. 66-70.

1967 La Mission, fruit de la compassion du Maître et de la prière des disciples. [9,35-38] — *AssSeign* I/98 (1967) 25-41.

1970 L'envoi des Douze aux brebis perdues. Mt 9,36-10,8. — *AssSeign* II/42 (1970) 18-32.

**TER SCHEGGET, Gijsbertus Hendricus**
1986 Christologie und Jesusbild an Hand der Versuchungsgeschichte Jesu. — *ZDialTheol* 2 (1986) 7-9.

**TERZOLI, Ricardo**
1972 Didachè e S. Scrittura. Un esame letterario. — *ScuolC* 100 (1972) 437-457. Esp. 443 [5,5]; 447-454: "Dipendenze evangeliche?" [6,9-13; 24,4-5].

**TESTA, Emanuele**
1965 Nous avons vu son étoile en orient (Matt. 2,2). — *Terre Sainte* (Jerusalem) 1 (1965) 5-12.

1968a Un ostrakon sull'elogio funebre e *Mt.* 11,16ss. e paralleli. — *RivBib* 16 (1968) 539-546. [NTA 14, 487]

1968b Le comunità orientali dei primi secoli e il primato di Pietro. — *Ibid.*, 547-555. [NTA 14, 488]

1979 I "Discorsi di missione" di Gesù. — *SBF/LA* 29 (1979) 7-41. Esp. 16-29 [9,35-10,42]; 31-33 [28,16-20]. [NTA 25, 75]

**TESTA, Giuseppe**
1972 Studio di Mc 6,6b-13 secondo il metodo della storia della tradizione. — *DivThom* 75 (1972) 177-191. Esp. 178-180 [4,23; 9,35/Mk]; 185-187 [Q 10,1-12/Mk]. [NTA 17, 534]

1990 XXXI Settimana Biblica Nazionale dell'ABI (10-14 settembre 1990) (I Vangeli dell'Infanzia). — *DivThom* 93 (1990) 132-144. [NTA 37, 128]; = *RivBib* 39 (1991) 100-107. → Serra 1992*

**[Testimonium Christi]**
1985* *Testimonium Christi. Scritti in onore di Jacques Dupont.* Brescia: Paideia, 1985, LXIII-494 p. → de Lorenzi, Festorazzi, Marcheselli, Montagnini, Panimolle

**TEVEL, Johannes Marius**
1992 The Labourers in the Vineyard: The Exegesis of Matthew 20,1-7 in the Early Church. — *VigChr* 46 (1992) 356-380. [NTA 37, 732]

**TEVIS, Dennis Gordon**
1983 *An Analysis of Words and Phrases Characteristic of the Gospel of Matthew.* Diss. Southern Methodist Univ., Dallas, TX, 1983, VII-317 p. (W.R. Farmer). Esp. 20-84: "Words and phrases characteristic of the gospel which occur in passages which function redactionally"; 85-137: "Words... which occur in the same immediate context"; 138-196: "Words... which are fairly well distributed and occur in different kinds of material"; 197-247: "Words... which are fairly well distributed and occur in one kind of material"; 248-263: "Words... which are not well distributed"; 264-285: "Other words and phrases characteristic of the gospel"; 286-304: "A comparison with Hawkins' findings".

**THEBAU, D.H.**
1972 On Separating Sheep from Goats. [25,31-46] — *ChrTod* 16 (1972) 1040-1041. [NTA 17, 129]

**THEISOHN, Johannes**
1975 *Der auserwählte Richter. Untersuchungen zum traditionsgeschichtlichem Ort der Menschensohngestalt der Bilderreden des Äthiopischen Henoch* (SUNT, 12). Göttingen: Vandenhoeck & Ruprecht, 1975, XIV-308 p. Esp. 149-201.251-266: "Der Einfluß der MS-Tradition der BR auf die synoptische MS-Überlieferung" [19,28; 25,31]. — Diss. Mainz, 1973 (F. Hahn). → Bultmann 1931

**THEISSEN, Gerd**

1973   Wanderradikalismus. Literatursoziologische Aspekte der Überlieferung von Worten Jesu im Urchristentum. — *ZTK* 70 (1973) 245-271. Esp. 258-263 [mission]. [NTA 18, 813]; = ID., *Studien zur Soziologie*, 1979, 79-105. Esp. 92-97. → W. Stegemann 1979a
Itinerant Radicalism. The Tradition of Jesus Sayings from the Perspective of the Sociology of Literature. — WIRE, A. (ed.), *The Bible and Liberation. A Radical Religion Reader*, II, Berkeley, CA: Graduate Theological Union, 1976, 84-93.
   *SelT* 14 (1975) 69-76.

1974   *Urchristliche Wundergeschichten. Ein Beitrag zur formgeschichtlichen Erforschung der synoptischen Evangelien* (Studien zum Neuen Testament, 8). Gütersloh: Mohn, 1974, 319 p. Esp. 221-224: "Die biographischen Evangelienkompositionen des Matthäus und Lukas". — Diss. Bonn, 1972 (P. Vielhauer).
*The Miracle Stories of the Early Christian Tradition*, trans. F. McDonagh. Edinburgh: Clark; Philadelphia, PA: Fortress, 1983, x-322 p. Esp. 221-225.
   H. BOERS, *Semeia* 11 (1978) 1-48; P.J. ACHTEMEIER, *ibid.*, 49-63; H.D. BETZ, *ibid.*, 69-81; A.C. WIRE, *ibid.*, 83-113.

1975   Legitimation und Lebensunterhalt: Ein Beitrag zur Soziologie urchristlicher Missionare. — *NTS* 21 (1974-75) 192-221. Esp. 193-200: "Die Wanderchariesmatiker". [NTA 19, 1154]; = ID., *Studien zur Soziologie*, 1979, 201-230. Esp. 202-209.

1977   *Soziologie der Jesusbewegung. Ein Beitrag zur Entstehungsgeschichte des Urchristentums* (Theologische Existenz heute, NF 194). München: Kaiser, 1977; ²1978, 111 p.
*The First Followers of Jesus. A Sociological Analysis of the Earliest Christianity*. London: SCM, 1978, IX-131 p.
*Sociology of Early Palestinian Christianity*, trans. J. Bowden. Philadelphia, PA: Fortress, 1978, IX-131 p.
*Le christianisme de Jésus. Ses origines sociales en Palestine*, trans. B. Lauret (Relais Desclée, 6). Paris: Desclée, 1978, 166 p.
*Sociología del movimiento de Jesús. El nacimiento del cristianismo primitivo*. Santander: Sal Terrae, 1979, 111 p.
*Gesù e il suo movimento. Analisi sociologica della comunità cristiana primitiva*. Torino: Claudiana, 1979.
Trans. Danish 1979.

1979a   *Studien zur Soziologie des Urchristentums* (WUNT, 19). Tübingen: Mohr, 1979, VI-317 p.; ²1983, VI-364 p.; ³1989, X-395 p. → 1973, 1975, 1979b
*Social Reality and the Early Christians. Theology, Ethics, and the World of the New Testament*, trans. M. Kohl. Minneapolis, MN: Fortress, 1992; Edinburgh: Clark, 1993, X-303 p.
*Histoire sociale du christianisme primitif: Jésus – Paul – Jean*, trans. I. Taillet & A.-L. Fink (Le monde de la Bible, 33). Genève: Labor et Fides, 1996, 297 p.

1979b   Gewaltverzicht und Feindesliebe (Mt 5,38-48 / Lk 6,27-38) und deren sozialgeschichtlicher Hintergrund. — *Ibid.*, 160-197. Esp. 161-174: "Die Motivation zu Feindesliebe und Gewaltverzicht"; 174-197: "Der soziale Ort von Feindesliebe und Gewaltverzicht" [Mt: 176-180; Q: 183-191].

1985a   "Meer" und "See" in den Evangelien. Ein Beitrag zur Lokalkoloritforschung. — *SNTU* 10 (1985) 5-25. Esp. 17-25. [NTA 30, 533]; cf. ID., *Lokalkolorit*, 1989, 119-131, 246-270.

1985b   Das "schwankende Rohr" in Mt. 11,7 und die Gründungsmünzen von Tiberias. Ein Beitrag zur Lokalkoloritforschung in den synoptischen Evangelien. — *ZDPV* 101 (1985) 43-55. [NTA 30, 1050]; = ID., *Lokalkolorit*, 1989, 26-44.

1989   *Lokalkolorit und Zeitgeschichte in den Evangelien. Ein Beitrag zur Geschichte der synoptischen Tradition* (NTOA, 8). Freiburg/Schw: Universitätsverlag; Göttingen: Vandenhoeck & Ruprecht, 1989, X-333 p. Esp. 25-61: "Die Anfänge der Wortüberlieferung in Palästina" [Q 7,24-28; 10,13-15; 11,31-32.47-48; 13,28-29; 22,28-30]; 62-131: "Grenzüberschreitungen in der Erzählüberlieferung"; 212-245: "Die Logienquelle – palästinazentrierte Perspektiven in der Mitte des 1. Jahrhunderts"; 246-303: "Die Evangelien und ihre Entstehungssituation". → 1985a-b
*The Gospels in Context: Social and Political History in the Synoptic Tradition*, trans. L.M. Maloney.

Minneapolis, MN: Fortress, 1991; Edinburgh: Clark, 1992, xvi-320 p. Esp. 25-29; 60-122; 203-234; 235-289. → R.A. Horsley 1992d

1992 Gruppenmessianismus. Überlegungen zum Ursprung der Kirche im Jüngerkreis Jesu. — *JbBT* 7 (1992) 101-123. Esp. 110-123: "Messianische und theokratische Vorstellungen in der Jesusbewegung".

1995 Jünger als Gewalttäter (Mt 11,12f.; Lk 16,16). Der Stürmerspruch als Selbststigmatisierung einer Minorität. — *StudTheol* 49 (1995) 183-200; = HELLHOLM, D. – MOXNES, H. – SEIM, T.K. (eds.), *Mighty Minorities? Minorities in Early Christianity – Positions and Strategies. Essays in Honour of Jacob Jervell on His 70th Birthday 21 May 1995*, Oslo: Scandinavian University Press, 1995, 183-200.

**THEOBALD, Christoph**

1995 La règle d'or chez Paul Ricœur. Une interrogation théologique. [7,12] — *RSR* 83 (1995) 43-59. [NTA 40, 169] → Ricœur 1990, Thomasset 1996

**THEOBALD, Michael**

1978 Der Primat der Synchronie vor der Diachronie als Grundaxiom der Literarkritik. Methodische Erwägungen an Hand von Mk 2,13-17 / Mt 9,9-13. — *BZ* 22 (1978) 161-186. Esp. 165-172 [9,9-13]; 177-179 [Mk/Mt]. [NTA 23, 457]

1995 Jesu Wort von der Ehescheidung. Gesetz oder Evangelium? — *TQ* 175 (1995) 109-124. Esp. 114-116 [5,32; 19,9]; 117 [Q 16,18]. [NTA 40, 1119]

1992 Die Arbeiter im Weinberg (Mt 20,1-16). Wahrnehmung sozialer Wirklichkeit und Rede von Gott. — MIETH, D. (ed.), *Christliche Sozialethik im Anspruch der Zukunft. Tübinger Beiträge zur katholischen Soziallehre* (Studien zur theologischen Ethik, 4), Freiburg/Schw: Universitätsverlag; Freiburg–Wien: Herder, 1992, 107-127. Esp. 110-115: "Zur Struktur und ursprünglichen Gestalt des Gleichnisses"; 116-120: "Beobachtungen zur im Gleichnis gespiegelten Arbeitswelt"; 120-125: "Zur Aussageintention des Gleichnisses".

**THÉRIAULT, Jean-Yves**

1982 La Règle de Trois. Une lecture sémiotique de *Mt* 1-2. — *SE* 34 (1982) 57-78. Esp. 57-86 [2,1-12]; 66-78 [1-2]. [NTA 26, 838]

1987 Le maître maîtrisé! [15,21-28] — CHENÉ, A., et al., *De Jésus et des femmes. Lectures sémiotiques* (Recherches, NS 14), Montréal: Bellarmin; Paris: Cerf, 1987, 19-34.

**THERON, Daniel J.**

1957 *Evidence of Tradition. Selected Source Material for the Study of the History of the Early Church. Introduction and Canon of the New Testament*. London: Bowes & Bowes, 1957, xiv-135 p. Esp. 26-29 [Papias]; 32-33 [Origen]; 52-53 [Jerome]; 64-67 [Papias, Pantaemus, Jerome].

**THEUNIS, Guy**

1970 *Le récit de la multiplication des pains (Marc 6,30-44) et les accords mineurs de Matthieu 14,13-21 et de Luc 9,10-17. Contribution à la théorie des deux sources*. Diss. Louvain-la-Neuve, 1970, xviii-255 p. (J. Giblet). Esp. 2-71: "Accords mineurs de Mt-Lc et le récit de la multiplication des pains"; 72-162: "'Accords' négatifs"; 163-230: "'Accords' positifs".

**THEUNISSEN, Michael**

1976 Ὁ αἰτῶν λαμβάνει. Der Gebetsglaube Jesu und die Zeitlichkeit des Christseins. — CASPEN, B., et al., *Jesus: Ort der Erfahrung Gottes [FS B. Welte]*, Freiburg: Herder, 1976, 13-68. Esp. 26-32, 50-53.

**THIEDE, Carsten Peter**

1986 *Simon Peter. From Galilee to Rome*. Exeter: Paternoster, 1986, 272 p. Esp. 15-97: "Peter in the gospels".

1990 Papyrus Bodmer L. Das neutestamentliche Papyrusfragment p⁷³ = Mt 25,43 / 26,2-3.
— *Museum Helveticum* (Basel) 47 (1990) 35-40.
Papyrus Bodmer L: The New Testament Papyrus Fragment p⁷³. First Edition. — ID., *Rekindling the Word*, 1995, 151-157.

1995a *Rekindling the Word. In Search of Gospel Truth.* Leominster: Gracewing; Valley Forge, PA: Trinity Press International; Alexandria, NSW: Dwyer, 1995, XII-204 p. → 1990, 1995b-d

1995b The Origin of the Gospels and the Magdalen Papyrus. [P⁶⁴] — *Ibid.*, 1-19. → 1996b

1995c Papyrus Magdalen Greek 17 (Gregory-Aland p⁶⁴): A Reappraisal. — *ZPapEp* 105 (1995) 13-20; = ID., *Rekindling the Word*, 1995, 20-32; = *TyndB* 46 (1995) 29-42.
[NTA 40, 68] → Grelot 1995c-d, Head 1995a, D.C. Parker 1995, Pickering 1995b, É. Puech 1995, Stanton 1995b, Wachtel 1995

1995d Radiocarbon Dating and Papyrus p⁶⁴ at Oxford. — ID. – MASUCH, G. (eds.), *Wissenschaftstheorie und Wissenschaftspraxis. Reichweiten und Zukunftsperspektiven interdisziplinärer Forschung*, Paderborn: Bonifatius, 1995; = ID., *Rekindling the Word*, 1995, 33-36.

1995e → Comfort 1995

1996a & D'ANCONA, M., *Eyewitness to Jesus. Amazing New Manuscript Evidence about the Origin of the Gospels.* New York – London: Doubleday, 1996, XIII-206 p.

1996b *Jésus selon Matthieu. La nouvelle datation du papyrus Magdalen d'Oxford et l'origine des Évangiles. Examen et discussion des dernières objections scientifiques.* Paris: de Guibert, 1996, 119 p. → 1995b

**THIELICKE, Helmut**

1953 *Das Gebet das die Welt umspannt: Reden über das Vaterunser.* Stuttgart: Quell, 1953, 175 p.
*Our Heavenly Father: Sermons on the Lord's Prayer*, trans. J.B. Doberstein. Grand Rapids, MI: Baker, 1974, 157 p.

1956 *Das Leben kann noch einmal beginnen. Ein Gang durch die Bergpredigt.* Stuttgart: Quell, 1956, 247 p.; ⁴1958; ⁷1968; 1980. → Vrolijks 1968
*Het leven kan opnieuw beginnen. Het appel van de Bergrede.* Wageningen Zomers & Keunings, 1961, 215 p.
*Life Can Begin Again. Sermons on the Sermon on the Mount*, trans. J.W. Doberstein. Philadelphia, PA: Fortress, 1963, XV-215 p.
*Il Discorso della montagna.* Torino-Leumann: Elle Di Ci, 1972, 207 p.

1957 *Das Bilderbuch Gottes. Reden über die Gleichnisse Jesu.* Stuttgart: Quell, 1957; repr. 1964, 250 p. Esp. 68-81 [13,31-33]; 81-97 [13,24-30.36-43]; 124-138 [21,33-46]; 138-152 [20,1-16]; 180-192 [18,23-35]; 209-220 [13,44-46]; 220-235 [25,1-13]; 236-250 [22,1-14].

**THIEMANN, Ronald F.**

1977 Matthew's Christology. A Resource for Systematic Theology. — *CurrTMiss* 4 (1977) 350-362. [NTA 22, 391]

1988 The Unnamed Woman at Bethany. — *TTod* 44 (1987-88) 179-188. Esp. 179-184 [disciples]. [NTA 32, 130]

**THIEME, Karl**

1963 Matthäus und die Juden. Ja und Nein zu einem exegetischen Meisterwerk. — *Freiburger Rundbrief* 15 (1963) 55-56.

**THIENEMANN, T.A.**

1955 Comment on an Interpretation by Prof. Cadbury. [6,22-23] — *Gordon Review* (Boston) 1 (1955) 19-22. → Cadbury 1954

**THIERING, Barbara E.**

1979 Are the "Violent Men" False Teachers? [11,12] — *NT* 21 (1979) 293-297. [NTA 24, 422]

**THIMMES, Pamela L.**

1989    *Convention and Invention. Studies in the Biblical Sea-Storm Type Scene.* Diss. Vanderbilt Univ., Nashville, TN, 1989 (M. Tolbert).

1990    The Biblical Sea-Storm Type-Scene: A Proposal. — *Proceedings EGLBS* 10 (1990) 107-122.

1992    *Studies in the Biblical Sea-Storm Type-Scene. Convention and Invention.* San Francisco, CA: Mellen, 1992, XI-229 p. [8,23-27; 14,22-23]. — Diss. Vanderbilt Univ., Nashville, TN, 1989 (M. Tolbert).

**THOM, Johan Carl**

1994    'Don't Walk on the Highways': The Pythagorian *Akousmata* and Early Christian Literature. — *JBL* 113 (1994) 93-112. [NTA 39, 486]

**THOMA, Clemens**

1970    *Kirche aus Juden und Heiden. Biblische Informationen über das Verhältnis der Kirche zum Judentum* (Konfrontationen, 8). Freiburg: Herder, 1970, 200 p. Esp. 70-73 [27,24-25]; 86-87 [23,35].

1989*   & WYSCHOGROD, M. (eds.), *Parable and Story in Judaism and Christianity* (Studies in Judaism and Christianity). New York – Mahwah, NJ: Paulist, 1989, VI-258 p. → Boadt, Flusser, Milavec, D. Stern

**THOMAS, Carolyn**

1988    El pesebre de Navidad: un desafío para los discípulos. — *Mensaje* (Santiago de Chile) 37 (1988) 529-534.
        The Nativity Scene. — *BiTod* 28 (1990) 26-33. Esp. 31-33 [1,18-25]. [NTA 34, 608]

**THOMAS, Jean**

1969    "Selig die Sanftmütigen, denn sie werden das Land besitzen". — MÜSSLE, M. (ed.), *Der "politische" Jesus*, 1969, 41-51.

**THOMAS, John Christopher**

1993    The Kingdom of God in the Gospel according to Matthew. — *NTS* 39 (1993) 136-146. Esp. 138-139.142-143 [12,28]; 139-140.145 [21,31.43]; 144-145 [19,24]. [NTA 37, 1244]

**THOMAS, Joseph**

1982    Tout est grâce. Lecture de Matthieu 19,1-12. — *Christus* 29 (1982) 338-344. [NTA 27, 104]

1984    Être chrétien. Lecture de Matthieu 11,25-30. — *Christus* 31 (1984) 457-462. [NTA 29, 527]

**THOMAS, Kenneth J.**

1976    Liturgical Citations in the Synoptics. — *NTS* 22 (1975-76) 205-214. Esp. 207-209 [9,18-19]; 209-212 [22,37]. [NTA 20, 766]

1977    Torah Citations in the Synoptics. — *NTS* 24 (1977-78) 85-96. Esp. 86-88 [19,4-5]; 87-88 [22,37]; 89-90 [5,21.27]; 91-92 [19,7]; 92 [22,24]; 93-95 [4,7.10-11; 5,31.33.38.43]. [NTA 22, 388]

**THOMAS, Page A.** → Longstaff 1988

**THOMAS, Robert L.**

1976    An Investigation of the Agreements between Matthew and Luke against Mark. — *JEvTS* 19 (1976) 103-112. Esp. 104-108: "The agreements"; 108-111: "Implications". [NTA 21, 367]

1982    The Rich Young Man in Matthew. — *GraceTJ* 3 (1982) 235-260. Esp. 236-246: "The two-source theory and Mt/Lk agreements against Mk"; 246-251: "Present trends"; 251-259: "Matthew's special emphases". [NTA 27, 521]

**THOMASSET, Alain**

1996    *Paul Ricœur, une poétique de la morale. Aux fondements d'une éthique herméneutique et narrative dans une perspective chrétienne* (BETL, 124). Leuven: University Press / Peeters, 1996, XVI-706 p. Esp. 520-533: "Le commandement nouveau et la Règle d'Or"; 533-545: "La Règle d'Or chez Matthieu"; 546-552: "La Règle d'Or chez Luc"; 552-563: "Une vision protestante?". — Diss. Louvain-la-Neuve, 1995 (J. Verstraeten). → Ricœur 1990, C. Theobald 1995

**THOMPSON, G.H.P.**

1959    Thy will be done in earth, as it is in heaven (Matthew vi,11). A Suggested Re-interpretation. — *ExpT* 70 (1958-59) 379-381. [NTA 4, 387]

1960    Called – Proved – Obedient: A Study in the Baptism and Temptation Narratives of Matthew and Luke. — *JTS* 11 (1960) 1-12. [NTA 5, 388]

**THOMPSON, J. David**

1993    *A Critical Concordance to the Gospel of Matthew* (Computer Bible, 39). Wooster, OH: Biblical Research Associates, 1993, IX-979 p.

**THOMPSON, Marianne Meye**

1982    The Structure of Matthew: A Survey of Recent Trends. — *SBT* 12 (1982) 195-238. Esp. 197-224: "The narrative-discourse pattern"; 224-233: "The three-fold division of Matthew"; 233-238: "Programmatic questions".

**THOMPSON, Mark C.**

1981    Matthew 15:21-28. — *Interpr* 35 (1981) 279-284.

**THOMPSON, Mary R.**

1995    *Mary of Magdala. Apostle and Leader.* New York – Mahwah, NJ: Paulist, 1995, v-145 p. Esp. 39-45 "Matthew".

**THOMPSON, P.J.**

1959    The Infancy Gospels of St. Matthew and St. Luke Compared. — *Studia Evangelica* 1 (1959) 217-222.

**THOMPSON, Ronald G.**

1981    *Imminent Judgment of Israel in Matthew: A Key to the Occasion and Purpose of the First Gospel.* Diss. New Orleans, 1981.

**THOMPSON, Thomas L.**

1969    A Catholic View on Divorce. — *JEcuSt* 6 (1969) 53-67. [NTA 15, 147]

**THOMPSON, William G.**

1969    Sermo ecclesiasticus (Mt 17,22–18,35) reconsideratus. — *VD* 47 (1969) 225-231. [NTA 15, 506] → 1970

1970    *Matthew's Advice to a Divided Community. Mt. 17,22–18,35* (AnBib, 44). Roma: Biblical Institute Press, 1970, XVI-297 p. Esp. 13-25: "Context in the gospel of Matthew"; 27-49 [17,22-23]; 50-68 [17,24-27]; 69-84 [18,1-4]; 85-93 [8,1-17]; 93-99 [17 22–18,20]; 100-120 [18,5-9]; 120-147 [Mt/Mk 9,33-50; Lk 9,46-50]; 152-174 [18,10-14]; 175-202 [18,15-20]; 203-237 [18,21-35]; 238-252: "Structural pattern"; 258-264: "The Matthean community". [NTA 15, ɔ. 242] — Diss. Pont. Inst. Bibl., Roma, 1969 (I. de la Potterie). → 1969

         E. BEST, *ScotJT* 25 (1972) 246-247; L. COPE, *JBL* 90 (1971) 494-496; H. FRANKEMÖLLE, *TRev* 68 (1972) 192-194; I. GOMÁ CIVIT, *EstBíb* 41 (1972) 351-353; K. GRAYSTON, *ExpT* 82 (1970-71) 279; R.H. GUNDRY, *Interpr* 26 (1972) 99-100; J.D. KINGSBURY, *Bib* 53 (1972) 152-156; J. MURPHY-O'CONNOR, *RB* 81 (1974) 142-144; B. RINALDI, *RivBib* 23 (1975) 223; J. ROLOFF, *TLZ* 97 (1972) 356-358; H. WANSBROUGH, *CleR* 57 (1972) 475-476; W.P. WINK, *CBQ* 34 (1972) 122-124.

1971    Reflections on the Composition of Mt 8:1–9:34. — *CBQ* 33 (1971) 365-388. Esp. 368-370 [8,1-17]; 371-378 [8,18–9,17]; 379-385 [9,18-31]; 385-387 [9,32-34]. [NTA 16, 155]

1974  An Historical Perspective in the Gospel of Matthew. — *JBL* 93 (1974) 243-262. Esp.
244-256 [24,4-14]; 250-256 [10,17-22]; 256-259 [24,36-25,46]; 259-260 [28,16-20]; 260-262 [17,22-18,35].
[NTA 19, 97]

1976  → LaVerdiere 1976

1981  Matthew's Portrait of Jesus' Disciples. — *BiTod* 19 (1981) 16-24. [NTA 25, 459]
Chinese. — *ColcTFu* 54 (1982) 527-536.

1989  *Matthew's Story: Good News for Uncertain Times*. New York – Mahwah, NJ: Paulist,
1989, IX-165 p. Esp. 1-54: "Describing Matthew's story"; 55-145: "Studying Matthew's story". [NTA
34, p. 114]
        R.B. VINSON, *PerspRelSt* 18 (1991) 185.

**THOMSON, Robert W.**
1967  (ed.), *Athanasiana Syriaca*, II (CSCO, 272-273). Leuven: CSCO, 1967, VII-57 and 49
p. Esp. 1-15 and 1-14: "Homily on Matthew XII 32 (Epistola ad Serapionem IV § 8-23)" [text and
translation].

**THORLEY, John**
1988  Subjunctive Aktionsart in New Testament Greek: A Reassessment. — *NT* 30 (1988)
193-211. Esp. 204-205. [NTA 33, 66]

1989  Aktionsart in New Testament Greek: Infinitive and Imperative. — *NT* 31 (1989) 290-
315. Esp. 296-297.301-302 [infinitive]; 307-310 [imperative]. [NTA 34, 1064] → K.L. McKay 1985

**THORNTON, Thomas Perry**
1954  Luther and the Translation of *Liber generationis* (Matt., 1,1). — *Neophilologus*
(Groningen) 38 (1954) 254-259.

**THORNTON, Thimothy C.G.**
1993  Jerome and the "Hebrew Gospel according to Matthew". — *Studia Patristica* 28 (1993)
118-122.

**THRALL, Margaret E.**
1962  *Greek Particles in the New Testament. Linguistic and Exegetical Studies* (New Testament Tools and Studies, 3). Leiden: Brill, 1962, VIII-107 p. Esp. 67-70 [26,39]; 70-78 [26,64].
— Diss. Cambridge, 1959-60 (C.F.D. Moule).

**THROCKMORTON, Burton H., Jr.**
1959  A Reply to Professor Metzger. [1,16] — *JBL* 78 (1959) 162-163. → B.M. Metzger 1958a

1967  *Gospel Parallels. A Synopsis of the First Three Gospels* [RSV]. London – Camden, NJ,
1967; Nashville, TN – New York: Nelson, [4]1979, XXVI-191 p. → 1992; → N.M. Flanagan
1978, Huck 1936

1977  Mark and Roger of Hoveden. — *CBQ* 39 (1977) 103-106. [NTA 21, 713] → Longstaff 1975a,
1979

1992  (ed.), *Gospel Parallels. A Comparison of the Synoptic Gospels. With Alternative
Readings from the Manuscripts and Noncanonical Parallels*. Nashville, TN: Nelson,
[5]1992, XL-212 p. → 1967

**THÜNGEN, L.**
1974  Evangelium nach Matthäus 5,13-16; 5,22-25 (Vier literarische Papyri aus der Kölner
Sammlung, 4). — *ZPapEp* 14 (1974) 37-40.

**THÜSING, Wilhelm**
1967  Erhöhungsvorstellung und Parusieerwartung in der ältesten nachösterlichen Christologie.
— *BZ* 11 (1967) 95-108, 205-222. [NTA 11, 1012; 12, 534]; 12 (1968) 54-80, 223-240. Esp.
60-63: "Die Bedeutung der Logienquelle für die Frage nach der 'Transformation'"; 64-73: "Nachösterliche

'Transformation' des vorösterlichen Glaubens an die *Exusia* Jesu"; 224-225. [NTA 12, 854; 13, 137]
*Erhöhungsvorstellung und Parusieerwartung in der ältesten nachösterlichen Christologie* (SBS, 42). Stuttgart: Katholisches Bibelwerk, 1970, 116 p. Esp. 55-59; 60-74.

1969 Aufgabe der Kirche und Dienst in der Kirche. — *BibLeb* 10 (1969) 65-80. Esp. 66-69 [28,18-20]. [NTA 14, 300]

1973 Dienstfunktion und Vollmacht kirchlicher Ämter nach dem Neuen Testament. — *BibLeb* 14 (1973) 77-88. Esp. 81-82 [23,8-11]. [NTA 19, 265]
The New Testament on Church Offices. — *TDig* 22 (1974) 121-124.

1976 Strukturen des Christlichen beim Jesus der Geschichte. Zur Frage eines neutestamentlich-christologischen Ansatzpunktes der These vom anonymen Christentum. — KLINGER, E. (ed.), *Christentum innerhalb und außerhalb der Kirche* (QDisp, 73), Freiburg: Herder, 1976, 100-121. Esp. 112-115 [25,31-46]; = ID., *Studien*, 1995, 295-316. Esp. 307-310.

1977 Die Bitten des johanneischen Jesus in dem Gebet Joh 17 und die Intentionen Jesu von Nazaret. — SCHNACKENBURG, R., et al. (eds.), *Die Kirche des Anfangs*. FS H. Schürmann, 1977, 307-337. Esp. 313-319 [6,9/Jn 17,1]; = ID., *Studien*, 1995, 265-294. Esp. 272-277.

1995 *Studien zur neutestamentlichen Theologie*, ed. T. Söding (WUNT, 82). Tübingen: Mohr, 1995, VIII-327 p. → 1976, 1977

**THUNDY, Zacharias P.**
1989 Intertextuality, Buddhism, and the Infancy Gospels. — NEUSNER, J., et al. (eds.), *Religious Writings and Religious Systems. Systemic Analysis of Holy Books in Christianity, Islam, Buddhism, Greco-Roman Religions, Ancient Israel, and Judaism*. I: *Islam, Buddhism, Greco-Roman Religions, Ancient Israel, and Judaism* (Brown Studies in Religion, 1), Atlanta, GA: Scholars, 1989, 17-73.

**THURNEYSEN, Eduard**
1936[R] *Die Bergpredigt* [1936]. (Theologische Existenz Heute, NF 105), München: Kaiser, [5]1963, 44 p. [NTA 9, p. 276]
*Le Sermon sur la montagne*, trans. E. Marion. Genève: Labor et Fides, 1958, 72 p.
   A. SBAFFI, *Protestantesimo* 14 (1959) 183-186.
*The Sermon on the Mount*, trans. W.C. & J.M. Robinson (Chime Paperbacks). Richmond, VA: Knox, 1964, 82 p. [NTA 9, p. 141]; London: SPCK, 1965, 78 p.
   W. ELLIS, *AusBR* 12 (1965) 69; E.S.P. HEAVENOR, *ScotJT* 20 (1967) 254-255.

**THURSTON, Bonnie Bowman**
1987 Matthew 5:43-48. — *Interpr* 41 (1987) 170-173.

1989 *Wait Here and Watch: A Eucharistic Commentary on the Passion according to St. Matthew*. St. Louis, MO: CBP, 1989, 96 p. [NTA 34, p. 115]

**THYEN, Hartwig**
1970 *Studien zur Sündenvergebung im Neuen Testament und seinen alttestamentlichen und jüdischen Voraussetzungen* (FRLANT, 96). Göttingen: Vandenhoeck & Ruprecht, 1970, 281 p. Esp. 218-236 [16,13-28]; 236-343 [18,18]. — Diss. Heidelberg, 1966 (E. Dinkler).

1975 Der irdische Jesus und die Kirche. — STRECKER, G. (ed.), *Jesus Christus in Historie und Theologie*. FS H. Conzelmann, 1975, 127-141. Esp. 127-130 [16,17-19].

1992 Johannes und die Synoptiker. Auf der Suche nach einem neuen Paradigma zur Beschreibung ihrer Beziehungen anhand von Beobachtungen an Passions- und Ostererzählungen. — DENAUX, A. (ed.), *John and the Synoptics*, 1992, 81-107. Esp. 105-107 [28,9-10/Jn 20,14-18].

**THYSMAN, Raymond**

1974 *Communauté et directives éthiques. La catéchèse de Matthieu. Théologie morale du Nouveau Testament. Essai de synthèse* (Recherches et synthèses. Section d'exégèse, 1). Gembloux: Duculot, 1974, 110 p. Esp. 11-33: "L'Église de Jésus, seigneur et juge"; 35-47: "Une justice plus abondante"; 49-64: "Directives pastorales destinées à toute la communauté"; 65-90: "Directives pour la conduite des 'pasteurs'". [NTA 18, p. 388]

J. COPPENS, *ETL* 51 (1975) 162-163; É. COTHENET, *EVie* 85 (1975) 415; C.T. DAVIES, *JBL* 95 (1976) 137-138; A.L. DESCAMPS, *RTL* 6 (1975) 360; G. FRITZ, *ZKT* 98 (1976) 215; M. GILBERT, *NRT* 96 (1974) 819-820; M.D. GOULDER, *JTS* 26 (1975) 252; K. GRAYSTON, *ExpT* 85 (1973-74) 311; J.C. INGELAERE, *RHPR* 54 (1974) 423-424; A. MODA, *Studia Patavina* 23 (1976) 179-180; J. MURPHY-O'CONNOR, *RB* 83 (1976) 308-309; B. NOACK, *TLZ* 100 (1975) 767-768; W. PESCH, *TRev* 71 (1975) 191-192; J.A. SHERLOCK, *CBQ* 37 (1975) 155-156; J. WINANDY, *VSp* 129 (1975) 433.

**TIEDE, David Lenz**

1984 Let Your Light Shine: The Sermon on the Mount in Epiphany. — *WWorld* 4 (1984) 87-95.

**TIGAY, Jeffrey H.**

1979 On the Term Phylacteries (Matt 23:5). — *HTR* 72 (1979) 45-53. [NTA 25, 80]

**TIGCHELER, Jo**

1983 *De Bergrede. Matteüs 5-7* (Verklaring van een Bijbelgedeelte). Kampen: Kok, [1983], 140 p.

P. BEENTJES, *Streven* 51 (1983-84) 848-849; F. VAN SEGBROECK, *Ons Geestelijk Leven* 61 (1984) 334.

1987 *Gemeenschappen in het Nieuwe Testament.* Kampen: Kok, 1987, 137 p. Esp. 85-97 [25,31-46].

**TILDEN, Elwyn E., Jr.**

1953 The Study of Jesus' Interpretive Methods. — *Interpr* 7 (1953) 45-61. Esp. 52-56: "Jesus and the law" [15,1-20; 19,1-12; 22,34-40]; 56-60: "Jesus and historical narratives" [11,2-6.20-24; 15,7-9; 21,33-46; 22,23-33]; 60-61: "Jesus and scriptures".

**TILL, Walter C.**

1952 Coptic Biblical Fragments in the John Rylands Library. — *BJRL* 34 (1951-52) 432-458. Esp. 446-447 [27,63-64].

1960a *Die koptischen Ostraka der Papyrussammlung der Österreichischen Nationalbibliothek: Texte, Übersetzungen, Indices* (Österreichische Akademie der Wissenschaften. Philosophisch-historische Klasse. Denkschriften, 78/1). Wien: Akademie, 1960, X-114 p. Esp. 2 [15,25-28].

1960b Coptic Biblical Texts Published after Vaschalde's List. — *BJRL* 42 (1959-60) 220-240. Esp. 229-230, 237, 239-240.

**TILLARD, Jean-Marie R.**

1962 L'Eucharistie, purification de l'Église pérégrinante. — *NRT* 84 (1962) 449-474, 579-597. Esp. 450-454: "Le texte de Mt 26,28". [NTA 7, 609]

1965 La prière des chrétiens. — *LumièreV* 75 (1965) 39-84. [NTA 10, 908]

1978 Le propos de pauvreté et l'exigence évangélique. — *NRT* 100 (1978) 207-232, 359-372. Esp. 207-216 [19,16-30]; 220-222 [5,3]. [NTA 22, 778]

**TILLEY, W. Clyde**

1992a *The Surpassing Righteousness. Evangelism and Ethics in the Sermon on the Mount.* Greenville, SC: Smyth & Helwys, 1992, X-170 p. [NTA 37, p. 443]

1992b Matthew 7:13-27. — *RExp* 89 (1992) 271-278.

**TILLY, Michael**

1994 *Johannes der Täufer und die Biographie der Propheten. Die synoptische Täuferüberlieferung und das jüdische Prophetenbild zur Zeit des Täufers* (BWANT, 137). Stuttgart: Kohlhammer, 1994, 293 p. Esp. 69-104: "Johannes der Täufer in der Logienquelle Q". — Diss. Mainz, 1993 (O. Böcher).

**TIMMER, John**

1970 *Julius Wellhausen and the Synoptic Gospels. A Study in Tradition Growth.* Rotterdam: Bronder, 1970, 127 p. Esp. 43-48: "Mark versus Q"; 48-51: "Mark versus Matthew's and Luke's Sondergut". — Diss. Amsterdam, 1970 (R. Schippers).

**TISERA, Guido**

1993 *Universalism according to the Gospel of Matthew* (EHS, XXIII/482). Frankfurt/M: Lang, 1993, XIV-388 p. Esp. 21-48 [1,1.3a.5ab.6b]; 49-75 [2,1-12]; 79-100 [4,12-16]; 101-129 [8,5-13]; 131-158 [10,5-6.18.23b]; 159-185 [12,15-21]; 187-211 [15,21-28]; 215-237 [21,33-46]; 241-263 [24,9.10-12.14]; 265-282 [25,31-46]; 285-316 [28,16-20]; 317-333: "Universalism in the gospel of Matthew". — Diss. Pont. Univ. Greg., Roma, 1992 (K. Stock).
    R.A. EDWARDS, *CBQ* 57 (1995) 832-833; J. KUHL, *Verbum SVD* 35 (1994) 215-218.

**TISON, J.-M.**

1976 Le mystère pascal dans l'évangile de S. Matthieu (Mt. 27,62–28,20). — *Telema* (Kinshasa, Congo) 2 (1976) 14-20. [NTA 21, 89]

**TOBIN, William J.**

1967 La primauté de Pierre selon les évangiles. — *LumVit* 22 (1967) 629-673. Esp. 640-658 [16,16-19].
    The Petrine Primacy Evidence of the Gospels. — *LumVit* 23 (1968) 27-70. [NTA 13, 168]

**TÖDT, Heinz Eduard**

1959 *Der Menschensohn in der synoptischen Überlieferung.* Gütersloh: Mohn, 1959, 331 p.; [2]1963; [4]1978. Esp. 29-104: "Die Sprüche vom kommenden Menschensohn in den synoptischen Evangelien" [44-62: Q; 62-88: Mt]; 105-130: "Die Sprüche vom Erdenwerken des Menschensohnes" [106-117: Q; 125-126: Mt]; 131-203: "Die Worte vom Leiden und Auferstehen des Menschensohnes" [138-140.170-172.181-182: Mt]; 204-257: "Das Verhältnis der drei Spruchgruppen vom Menschensohn zueinander"; 258-264: "Zum Fehlen des Präexistenzgedankens und Erhöhungsmotivs in den synoptischen Menschensohnsprüchen" [289-316: → Vielhauer 1957] — Diss. Heidelberg, 1957 (G. Bornkamm). → Coppens 1961, Hoffmann 1992b, van Cangh 1970, Vielhauer 1963, 1965d
    *The Son of Man in the Synoptic Tradition*, trans. D.M. Barton (The New Testament Library). Philadelphia, PA: Westminster, London: SCM; 1965, 366 p. Esp. 32-112 [47-67: Q; 67-94: Mt]; 113-140 [114-125: Q; 135: Mt]; 141-221 [149-151.184-186.195-196: Mt]; 222-283; 284-292; 348-351. → A.J.B. Higgins 1964

**TÖKÉS, István**

1971 Observations on a New Translation of Mt 5–6. [Hungarian] — *Református Szemle* (Kolozsvár) 64 (1971) 275-280.

**TOEWS, John E.**

1981 The Synoptic Problem and the Genre Question. — *Direction* (Fresno, CA) 10/2 (1981) 11-18. [NTA 25, 843]

**TOLAR, William B.**

1992 The Sermon on the Mount from an Exegetical Perspective. — *SWJT* 35 (1992) 4-12. [NTA 37, 138]

**TOLBERT, Mary Ann**

1975 *Good News from Matthew.* Volume 1. Nashville, TN: Broadman, 1975, 128 p. [NTA 20, p. 367]

1979 *Perspectives on the Parables: An Approach to Multiple Interpretations.* Philadelphia, PA: Fortress, 1979, 141 p.

**TOLEDO, Ramiro G.**

1963 Jesús y el sábado. — *CuBíb* 20 (1963) 5-32. Esp. 14-18 [12,1-8]; 18-22 [12,9-14]. [NTA 8, 110]

**TOMSON, P.J.**

1997 The Core of Jesus' Evangel. Εὐαγγελίσασθαι πτωχοῖς (Isa 61). — TUCKETT, C.M. (ed.), *The Scriptures in the Gospels*, 1997, 647-658. Esp. 650-651.

**TONIOLO, Ermanno**

1995 Mt 1,18-25. Testimonianze patristiche. — *Theotokos* 3/1 (1995) 39-87.

**TOOLEY, Wilfred**

1964 The Shepherd and Sheep Image in the Teaching of Jesus. — *NT* 7 (1964-65) 15-25. Esp. 15-16 [9,36]; 16-19 [26,31]; 20 [7,15]; 20-21 [10,6.16; 15,24]; 22 [25,31-46; Q 12,32]; 22-23 [18,12-14]. [NTA 9, 883]

**TOPEL, L. John**

1981 The Lukan Version of the Lord's Sermon. — *BTB* 11 (1981) 48-53. [NTA 25, 894]

1984 The Christian Ethics of the Lukan Sermon. — DALY, R.J., et al. (eds.), *Christian Biblical Ethics*, 1984, 179-199.

**TORIBIO CUADRADO, José Fernando**

1993 "*El viniente*". *Estudio exegético y teológico del verbo* ἔρχεσθαι *en la literatura joánica*. Marcilla: Centro filosófico-teológico, 1993, 566 p. Esp. 177-183.202-203 [24,30/Rev 1,7]. — Diss. Pont. Univ. Greg., Roma, 1992 (U. Vanni).

1994 "Evangelio", obra abierta. — *Mayéutica* 20 (1994) 9-78. [NTA 39, 95]

**TORJESEN, Karen Jo**

1986 *Hermeneutical Procedure and Theological Method in Origen's Exegesis* (Patristische Texte und Studien, 28). Berlin – New York: de Gruyter, 1986, XI-183 p. Esp. 64-65; 66-69.105-107 [13,36].

**TORRANCE, David W.**

1972 & TORRANCE, Thomas F. (eds.), *A Harmony of the Gospels*. 1. *Matthew*, trans. A.W. Morrison (Calvin's Commentaries, 1). Edinburgh: St. Andrew's; Grand Rapids, MI: Eerdmans, 1972, XIV-326 p.

J. ATKINSON, *JTS* 25 (1974) 213; J.G. GIBBS, *CBQ* 36 (1974) 253-254; I.H. MARSHALL, *ExpT* 84 (1972-73) 312; J.N. TYLENDA, *TS* 34 (1973) 757.

**TOSATO, Angelo**

1975 Il battesimo di Gesù e alcuni passi trascurati dello Pseudo-Filone. — *Bib* 56 (1975) 405-409. Esp. 408-409 [10,16]. [NTA 20, 792]

1976a *Il matrimonio nel Giudaismo antico e nel Nuovo Testamento*. Roma: Città Nuova, 1976, 118 p. Esp. 49-80.

1976b Il battesimo di Gesù e le Odi di Salomone. — *BibOr* 18 (1976) 261-269. [NTA 23, 728]

1979 Joseph, Being a Just Man (Matt 1:19). — *CBQ* 41 (1979) 547-551. [NTA 24, 417]

1987 Cristianesimo e capitalismo: il problema esegetico di alcuni passi evangelici. — *RivBib* 35 (1987) 465-476. [NTA 32, 858]

1993 Su di una norma matrimoniale 4QD. — *Bib* 74 (1993) 401-410. Esp. 410 [5,32; 19,9]. [NTA 38, 1101]

**TOSATTO, Giuseppe**

1968 Esegesi dei vangeli sinottici. III: La passione. — CANFORA, G., et al. (eds.), *Il Messaggio della Salvezza*, IV, 1968, 443-793.

1979 → Martini 1979b

**TOSAUS ABADÍA, José Pedro**

1988    Algunas publicaciones recientes sobre san Pedro. — *EstBíb* 46 (1988) 375-398. Esp. 378-379. [NTA 33, 1381]

**TOUILLEUX, Paul**

1968    *L'Église dans les Écritures. Préparation et naissance* (Théologie, pastorale et spiritualité. Recherches et synthèses, 20). Paris: Lethielleux, 1968, 176 p. Esp. 96-100 [date]; 103-106: "Le salut dans les Logia"; 107-112: "Le salut dans la triple tradition".

**TOURN, Giorgio**

1973a   & CORSANI, B. – CUMINETTI, M., *Evangelo secondo Matteo* (Gli Oscar di Mondadori). Milano: Mondadori, 1973, 334 p. → Cuminetti, Tourn
        G. RAVASI, *RivClerIt* 55 (1974) 797-799.

1973b   Introduzione a Matteo. — *Ibid.*, 49-96.

**TOURNAY, Raymond J.**

1995    Que signifie la sixième demande du Notre-Père? — *RTL* 26 (1995) 299-306. [NTA 40, 824]

**TOURÓN DEL PIE, Eliseo**

1995    Comer con Jesús. (Su significación escatológica y eucarística). — *RevistEspTeol* 55 (1995) 285-329, 429-486. Esp. 311-316 [8,11-12]; 316-320 [5,6]; 320-329 [6,11]; 429-430 [25,21]; 436-443 [22,1-14]; 454-455 [10,5-16].

**TOUS, Lorenzo**

1983    ¡Felices, los que sufren! [5,4] — *BibFe* 9 (1983) 150-158.

**TOUSSAINT, Stanley D.**

1957    *The Argument of Matthew*. Diss. Theol. Sem., Dallas, TX, 1957, 169 p.

1964    The Introductory and Concluding Parables of Matthew Thirteen. — *BS* 121 (1964) 351-355. [NTA 9, 533]

1980    *Behold the King. A Study of Matthew*. Portland, OR: Multnomah, 1980, 399 p. Esp. 11-32: "Introduction"; 33-320: "Commentary". [NTA 25, p. 306]
        J.A. MARTIN, *BS* 139 (1982) 73-74.

1986    The Kingdom and Matthew's Gospel. — ID. – DYER, C.H. (eds.), *Essays in Honor of J. Dwight Pentecost*, Chicago, IL: Moody, 1986, n.p.

**TOWNSEND, John T.**

1961    Matthew xxiii.9. — *JTS* 12 (1961) 56-59. [NTA 6, 132]

**TRAGAN, Pius-Ramon**

1977    *La parabole du "Pasteur" et ses explications: Jean 10,1-18. La genèse, les milieux littéraires*. Lille: Université de Lille III, 1977, 370 and 280 p. Esp. 184-187 [26,31/Mk]; 239-248 [20,24-28/Mk]. — Diss. Strasbourg, 1976.

1991    Il battesimo cristiano secondo Mt 28,16-20. — ID. (ed.), *Alle origini del battesimo cristiano. Radici del battesimo e suo significato nelle comunità apostoliche. Atti dell'VIII convegno di teologia sacramentaria. Roma, 9-11 marzo 1989* (Studia Anselmiana, 106), Roma: Pont. Ateneo S. Anselmo, 1991 243-282. Esp. 245-251 [genre]; 251-259 [tradition and redaction]; 260-273 [28,19b]; 273-282 [3,13-17].

**TRAINOR, Michael**

1991    The Begetting of Wisdom: The Teacher and the Disciples in Matthew's Community. — *Pacifica* 4 (1991) 148-164. Esp. 151-153 [Jesus as teacher]; 156-158 [Jesus as rabbi]; 159-161 [discipleship]. [NTA 36, 134] → P.A. Foulkes 1994

**Tràm-Mgoc-Thao, Joseph**

1971 *La Cène du Seigneur. Essai d'étude biblico-théologique sur la tradition Mc 14,22-25; Mt 26,25-29*. Diss. Lyon, 1970-71, 201 p.

**[Translation]**

1984 The Translation of Matthew 20.4-5: An Exchange of Views between a Translator and his Consultants. — *BTrans* 35 (1984) 437-441. [NTA 29, 532]

**Trapè, Agostino**

1964 La "Sedes Patri" in S. Agostino. [16,16-18] — *Miscellanea A. Piolanti II* (Lateranum, NS 30), Roma: Pont. Athenaei Lateranensis, 1964, 57-75.

**Trautman, D.W.**

1966 *The Eunuch Logion of Mt 19,12. Historical and Exegetical Dimensions as Related to Celibacy*. Diss. Pont. Univ. S. Thomae, Roma, 1966, XII-131 p.

**Trautmann, Maria**

1980 *Zeichenhafte Handlungen Jesu. Ein Beitrag zur Frage nach dem geschichtlichen Jesus* (FzB, 37). Würzburg: Echter, 1980, VIII-586 p. Esp. 78-131 [21,12-13]; 132-166 [9,9-13]; 167-233 [10,1-4]; 234-257 [9,1-8]; 258-277 [12,28/Q 11,20]; 278-318 [12,9-14]; 319-346 [21,18-22]; 347-378 [21,1-10]. — Diss. Würzburg, 1979 (R. Schnackenburg).

**Travis, Stephen H.**

1977 Form Criticism. — MARSHALL, I.H. (ed.), *New Testament Interpretation*, 1977, 153-164.

1981 → Neil 1981

1992 Judgment. — *DJG*, 1992, 408-411. Esp. 410-411.

**Treat, James**

1994 The Canaanite Problem. — *Daughters of Sarah* (Chicago, IL) 20/2 (1994) 20-24. [NTA 38, 1370]

**Trebolle Barrera, Julio**

1992 El relato de la huida y regreso de Egipto (Mt 2,13-15a.19-21). Estructura y composición literaria. — *EstBíb* 50 (1992) 251-260.

1995 The Qumran Texts and the New Testament. — GARCÍA MARTÍNEZ, F. - TREBOLLE BARRERA, J., *The People of the Dead Sea Scrolls. Their Writings, Beliefs and Practices*, Leiden: Brill, 1995, 203-220. Esp. 212-213: "The gospel of Matthew and the Qumran texts".

**Treese, Robert Luther**

1958 *The Eschatology of the Compiler of the Gospel according to Saint Matthew*. Diss. Boston Univ. Graduate School, 1958, 310 p. — *DissAbstr* 19 (1959) 1844-1845.

**Trémel, Yves-Bernard**

1955 Béatitudes et morale évangélique. — *LumièreV* 21 (1955) 83-102. Esp. 88-90, 93-97.

1964 L'agonie du Christ. [26,36-46] — *LumièreV* 68 (1964) 79-104. [NTA 8, 328]

1974 Des récits apocalyptiques: baptême et transfiguration. — *LumièreV* 119 (1974) 70-83. Esp. 75-76 [17,1-9]. [NTA 19, 974]

**Tremolada, Pierantonio**

1990 XXXI Settimana Biblica Nazionale dell'ABI. I Vangeli dell'Infanzia. — *ScuolC* 118 (1990) 479-485. → Serra 1992*

**TRESMONTANT, Claude**

1983    *Le Christ hébreu. La langue et l'âge des Évangiles.* Paris: OEIL, 1983, 320 p. Esp. 41-
92: "L'évangile de Matthieu"; 139-216: "Le problème synoptique". → Grelot 1984a; → Rasco 1986, Rossé
1988, P. Sacchi 1986, Spadafora 1986
*The Hebrew Christ. Language in the Age of the Gospels*, trans. K.H. Whitehead. Chicago, IL: Franciscan,
1989, xv-323 p.

1986    *Évangile de Matthieu. Traduction et notes.* Paris: OEIL, 1986, 507 p. Esp. 247-505:
"Notes". [NTA 31, p. 369]; [2]1996 ("nouvelle édition, revue et corrigée").
L. WALTER, *EVie* 97 (1987) 14-16.

**TRETTEL, Giulio**

1984    (trans.), *Cromazio di Aquileia. Commento al Vangelo di Matteo.* I: *Trattati 1-37.* II:
*Trattati 38-59.* Roma: Città Nuova, 1984, 328 and 264 p.
A. BONATO, *Humanitas* 40 (1985) 937-938; M. DIEGO SÁNCHEZ, *Teresianum* 36 (1985) 531-533; 37
(1986) 509; A. FERRUA, *CC* 136/2 (1985) 306.

**TREU, Kurt**

1966    *Die griechischen Handschriften des Neuen Testaments in der UdSSR. Eine systematische
Auswertung der Texthandschriften in Leningrad, Moskou, Kiev, Odessa, Tbilisi und
Ezevan* (TU, 91). Berlin: Akademie, 1966, XIV-392 p. → G.H.R. Horsley 1982

**TREU, Ursula**

1959    "Otterngezücht". Ein patristischer Beitrag zur Quellenkunde des Physiologus. [3,7] —
*ZNW* 50 (1959) 113-122. [NTA 4, 74]

**TREVETT, Christine**

1984    Approaching Matthew from the Second Century: The Under-Used Ignatian
Correspondence. — *JSNT* 20 (1984) 59-67. [NTA 29, 416]

1984    Anomaly and Consistency. Josep Rius-Camps on Ignatius and Matthew. [*RevistCatTeol* 2
(1977) 31-149, 285-371] — *VigChr* 38 (1984) 165-171. [NTA 29, 812]

**TREVIJANO, Pedro**

1994    Pecado, conversión y perdón en el Nuevo Testamento. — *ScriptVict* 41 (1994) 127-170.
Esp. 132-139 [conversion]; 142-145 [16,19; 18,18].

**TREVIJANO ETCHEVERRÍA, Ramón**

1968    La escatología del evangelio de San Mateo. — *Burgense* 9 (1968) 9-23. [NTA 13, 869]

1970    El trasfondo apocalíptico de Mc. 1,24.25; 5,7.8 y par. — *Burgense* 11 (1970) 117-133.
Esp. 121-122 [8,28-29]. [NTA 15, 160]

1971    La tradición sobre el Bautista en Mc. 1,4-5 y par. — *Burgense* 12 (1971) 9-39. Esp. 20-
23: "Tradición de Mateo" [3,1-6]; 28-30 [Gospel of the Ebionites]. [NTA 16, 170]

1974    La multiplicación de los panes (Mc. 6,30-46; 8,1-10 y par.). — *Burgense* 15 (1974)
435-465. Esp. 444-448 [14,13-23]; 461-463 [15,32-39]. [NTA 19, 555]

1976    Discurso escatológico y relato apocalíptico en *Didakhe* 16. — *Burgense* 17 (1976) 365-
393. Esp. 375-383: "Relaciones con otros textos" [24]. [NTA 21, 621]

1977    Matrimonio y divorcio en Mc 10,2-12 y par. — *Burgense* 18 (1977) 113-151. Esp. 127-
132 [19,3-12]; 133-141 [5,32; 19,9]; 141-148: "Historia de la tradición". [NTA 22, 106]

1978    La misión de la iglesia primitiva y los mandatos del Señor en los Evangelios. —
*Salmanticensis* 25 (1978) 5-36. Esp. 9-11 [28,18-20]; 21-22 [15,21-28]; 22-24 [10,5-6]. [NTA 23,
242]

1981    La escatología del Evangelio de Tomás (logion 3). — *Salmanticensis* 28 (1981) 415-
441. Esp. 418-431: "La polemica sobre el Reino". [NTA 26, 1167]

1984    Las prácticas de piedad en el Evangelio de Tomás (logion 6, 14, 27 y 104). —
        *Salmanticensis* 31 (1984) 295-319. Esp. 295-300 [6,16-18; 7,12/Th 6]; 300-306 [10,11-14; 12,36-37;
        15,11/Th 14]. [NTA 28, 1217]

1992    El anciano preguntará al niño (Evangelio de Tomás Log. 4). — *EstBíb* 50 (1992) 521-
        535. Esp. 522-523.

1994    La obra de Papías y sus noticias sobre Mc y Mt. — *Salmanticensis* 41 (1994) 181-212.
        Esp. 206-210. [NTA 39, 617]

1995    *Orígenes del cristianismo. El trasfondo judío del cristianismo primitivo* (Plenitudo
        Temporis, 31). Salamanca: Universidad Pontificia, 1995, 475 p. Esp. 187-190 [5,17-20;
        12,1-8].

### TRICOT, André

1939[R]  ROBERT, A. – TRICOT, A. (eds.), *Initiation Biblique. Introduction à l'étude des saintes
        écritures* [1939]. Paris: Desclée, ²1951, ³1954, XXVI-1082 p. → Huby; → Feuillet 1959a
        Genres littéraires du Nouveau Testament. — *Ibid.*, 314-356. Esp. 316-324: "Les synoptiques".
        La question synoptique. — *Ibid.*, 356-374.

        *Guide to the Bible. An Introduction to the Study of Holy Scripture*, trans. E.P. Arbez & M.R.P. McGuire.
        Paris–Tournai: Desclée, 2 vols., 1955; ²1960 (revised and enlarged) [= French, ³1954], XXVI-812 p.
        The Literary Genre of the New Testament. — *Ibid.*, 1960, I, 514-563.
        The Synoptic Question. — *Ibid.*, 1960, I, 563-580.

### TRILLING, Wolfgang

1959a   *Das wahre Israel. Studien zur Theologie des Matthäus-Evangeliums* (ErfTS, 7). Leipzig:
        St. Benno, 1959, XX-210 p. Esp. 6-36; 37-47; 48-56; 57-77; 78-84; 85-100; 101-118; 119-137; 138-
        159; 160-188; 189-201. [NTA 6, p. 143]; (SANT, 10), München: Kösel, ³1964, 247 p. ("umge-
        arbeitet"). Esp. 21-51: "Der Inhalt des Manifests 28,18-20"; 55-65: "Das Winzergleichnis: 21,33-45"; 66-
        74: "Der Prozess vor Pilatus: 27,15-26"; 75-96: "Gericht über Israel"; 99-105: "Die Sendung zu Israel:
        10,5b-6; 15,24"; 106-123: "Die 'Gemeindeordnung' Kapitel 18"; 124-142: "Zum Kirchenbild I. Kirche aus
        Juden und Heiden"; 143-163: "Zum Kirchenbild II. Der theologische Ort der Ekklesia"; 167-186: "Die
        Gesetzesfrage nach 5,17-20"; 187-211: "Die Erfüllung des Willens Gottes"; 212-224: "Folgerungen und
        Ausblick"; ⁴1975, 250 p. — Diss. München, 1958 (J. Schmid). → Dermience 1985, Fannon 1965,
        Hummel 1963/66, Rohde 1965
            *Bib* 42 (1961) 111-112; G. BARTH, *TLZ* 86 (1961) 756-759; B. BRINKMANN, *Scholastik* 37 (1962) 257-
            260; P. GAECHTER, *ZKT* 83 (1961) 485-486; J. GNILKA, *BZ* 6 (1962) 139-140; V. HASLER, *TZ* 17
            (1961) 136-138; X. LÉON-DUFOUR, *RSR* 50 (1962) 94-98; F. MUSSNER, *TTZ* 70 (1961) 319-320; J.
            REUMANN, *JBL* 79 (1960) 376-379; K.H. SCHELKLE, *TQ* 140 (1960) 332-333; B. SCHWANK, *ErbAuf* 37
            (1961) 163-164; K. THIEME, *Freiburger Rundbrief* 14 (1962) 73-74; G. THILS, *ETL* 35 (1960) 548; P.
            WINTER, *ATR* 43 (1961) 231.
            J.B. BAUER, *Wort und Wahrheit* (München) 20 (1964-65) 644; B. BRINKMANN, *Scholastik* 40 (1965) 617-
            618; N. BROX, *Kairos* 8 (1966) 149-150; L. CILLERUELO, *Archivo Agustiniano* (Madrid) 59 (1965) 89-
            90; J.S. CROATTO, *Stromata* (San Míguel, Arg.) 21 (1965) 621-622; J. DUPONT, *RHE* 60 (1965) 532;
            A.C. FRANCHETTI, *DivThom* 88 (1967) 217-220; P. GRECH, *Augustinianum* 7 (1967) 374; A. KERRIGAN,
            *Ant* 43 (1968) 121-122; E.M. KRENTZ, *ConcTM* 41 (1970) 118-119; B. PEARSON, *VigChr* 21 (1967) 60-
            63; J. RADERMAKERS, *NRT* 86 (1964) 787-788; E. RASCO, *Greg* 46 (1965) 131-133; O.S., *RevistBíb* 29
            (1967) 245-246; A. SAND, *MüTZ* 18 (1967) 245-246; R. SILVA, *Compostellanum* 10 (1965) 849-850;
            *EstBíb* 25 (1966) 96-97; S. STAHR, *TPQ* 116 (1968) 278-279; F.J. STEINMETZ, *GL* 42 (1969) 66-67; J.
            SUDBRACK, *GL* 38 (1965) 393; W.G. THOMPSON, *VD* 42 (1964) 97-98; P. WINTER, *ATR* 47 (1965) 307-
            308; J. ZALOTAY, *CBQ* 27 (1965) 184-185.
            *El verdadero Israel. Estudio de la teología de Mateo* (Actualidad Bíblica, 36). Madrid: Fax, 1974, 370 p.
            F. DÍEZ, *BibFe* 1 (1975) 149.
            *Il vero Israele. Studi sulla teologia del vangelo di Matteo*, trans. E. Gatti (Εὐαγγελιον, 1). Casale
            Monferrato: Piemme, 1992, 319 p.
            G. ANZIANI, *Protestantesimo* 50 (1995) 249-250.

1959b   Die Täufertradition bei Matthäus. — *BZ* 3 (1959) 271-289. Esp. 272-275 [14,3-12]; 275-279
        [11,2-11.16-19]; 279-282 [17,10-13; 11,14-15]; 282-287 [3,2.7; 4,17; 21,32]. [NTA 4, 382]; = *TJb*,

1960, 51-67. Esp. 51-54; 54-58; 58-60; 61-65; = LANGE, J. (ed.), *Das Matthäus-Evangelium*, 1980, 273-295. Esp. 273-276; 276-282; 282-287; 287-289; = ID., *Studien zur Jesus-überlieferung*, 1988, 45-65. Esp. 45-48; 48-53; 53-57; 57-63.

1960a   *Hausordnung Gottes. Eine Auslegung von Matthäus 18.* Leipzig: St. Benno, 1960, 246 p.; (Die Welt der Bibel, 10), Düsseldorf: Patmos, 1960, 99 p. Esp. 19-65: "Auslegung des Textes"; 66-99: "Systematische Zusammenfassung. Das theologische Fundament des christlichen Gemeindelebens".

> BK 16 (1961) 30; M.-É. BOISMARD, *RB* 68 (1961) 447; H. KÜNG. *TQ* 141 (1961) 250; W.E. LYNCH, *CBQ* 23 (1961) 390-391; B. SCHWANK, *ErbAuf* 37 (1961) 164; M. ZERWICK, *VD* 39 (1961) 222.

1960b   Zur Überlieferungsgeschichte des Gleichnisses vom Hochzeitsmahl Mt 22,1-14. — *BZ* 4 (1960) 251-265. Esp. 251-253 [unity]; 253-255 [purpose]; 255-260 [22,11-14]; 260-262 [22,1-10]. [NTA 5, 400]; = BAUER, J.B. (ed.), *Evangelienforschung*, 1968, 221-240. Esp. 222-224; 225-227; 227-233; 233-235. → Schweizer 1989b

1962a   *Das Evangelium nach Matthäus* (Geistliche Schriftlesung, 1/1-2). Leipzig: St. Benno; Düsseldorf: Patmos, 1962/65, 290 and 358 p. [NTA 10, p. 423]

> M.-É. BOISMARD, *RB* 71 (1964) 448; H. JELLOUSCHEK, *ZKT* 89 (1967) 230; H. WULF, *GL* 39 (1966) 309-310.

> *Commento al vangelo di Matteo*, trans. B. da Malè (Commenti spirituali del Nuovo Testamento, 1-2). Roma: Città Nuova, 1964/68, 256 and 333 p.; ²1980; ⁵1983.

> *O evangelho segundo Mateus, Comentado*, trans. E. Binder (NT, Com. ε Mensagem, I/1). Petrópolis: Vozes, 1966, 315 p.

> G. BARAÚNA, *REB* 27 (1967) 221-222.

> *The Gospel according to St. Matthew*, trans. K. Smyth (New Testament for Spiritual Reading, 2). London: Burns & Oats; New York: Herder & Herder, 1969, XVI-240 p.

> P. BEASLEY-MURRAY, *ScotJT* 24 (1971) 362-363; B. HEATHER, *AustralasCR* 47 (1970) 170-171; J. PRIDMORE, *ScriptB* 1 (1969) 89-91; H.&J. THOMPSON, *Theology* 73 (1970) 41-43; R.H. ZUEFELD, *The South East Asia Journal of Theology* (Singapore) 11 (1970) 120.

> *El evangelio según san Mateo*, trans. J.M. Querol (El Nuevo Testamento y su mensaje). Barcelona: Herder, 1970, 2 vols., 288 and 356 p.; ³1980.

> I. ARIAS, *NatGrac* 28 (1971) 415-416; J.M. CABALLERO CUESTA, *EstBíb* 31 (1972) 226-227; M. DE BURGOS NUÑEZ, *Communio* (Sevilla) 4 (1971) 134-135; J. HUERGC, *CiTom* 97 (1970) 475; G. PÉREZ, *Salmanticensis* 20 (1973) 356; J. VÍLCHEZ, *EstE* 47 (1972) 289.

> *L'évangile selon Matthieu. I: La préhistoire du Messie. L'activité du Messie en Galilée. Les actions du Messie. II: La doctrine sur les disciples. Foi et incroyance. Le royaume de Dieu en paraboles. Le mystère du Messie. Le discours sur la fraternité. III: Activité du Messie en Judée*, trans. C. de Nys (Parole et Prière). Paris-Tournai: Desclée, 1971, 226, 234 and 218 p.

> A. BEAUDUIN, *FoiTemps* 2 (1972) 334-335; X. JACQUES, *NRT* 94 (1972) 1097; M.-É. LAUZIÈRE, *RThom* 73 (1973) 482; J. ZUMSTEIN, *RTP* 23 (1973) 201.

1962b   Das Matthäusevangelium - heute. — *BibLeb* 3 (1962) 42-51; = *TJb*, 1964, 62-70.

1962c   Wirken und Botschaft des Täufers. — *BK* 17 (1962) 102-105. [NTA 7, 443] → 1969c

1963   Der Einzug in Jerusalem. Mt 21,1-17. — BLINZLER, J., et al. (eds.), *Neutestamentliche Aufsätze*. FS J. Schmid, 1963, 303-309; = ID., *Studien zur Jesusüberlieferung*, 1988, 67-75.

1965a   Das Kirchenverständnis nach Matthäus (Mt 28,18-20). — *TJb*, 1965, 41-50; = ID., *Vielfalt und Einheit*, 1968, 125-139.
> Les traits essentiels de l'Église du Christ. — *AssSeign* I/53 (1964) 20-32

1965b   Weisung und Anspruch (Mt 22,34-46). — *Am Tisch des Wortes* (Stuttgart) 5 (1965) 26-37.

1965c   Der Passionsbericht nach Matthäus. — *Am Tisch des Wortes* 9 (1965) 33-44.

1966a   *Fragen zur Geschichtlichkeit Jesu.* Düsseldorf: Patmos, 1966; (Patmos Paperbacks), ²1967, 184 p.; Leipzig: St. Benno, ³1969, 186 p. Esp. 71-82 [infancy narrative]; 82-96 [law]; 96-106 [miracles]; 116-118 [10,23].

*Jésus devant l'histoire*, trans. J. Schmitt (Lire la Bible, 15). Paris: Cerf, 1968, 254 p.
*De historiciteit van Jesus*, trans. H. van der Burght. Bilthoven: Nelissen; Antwerpen: Patmos, 1969, 184 p.
*Jesús y los problemas de su historicidad*, trans. C. Ruiz Garrido. Barcelona: Herder, 1975, 224 p.

1966b   Das leere Grab bei Matthäus (Mt 28,1-7). — *Am Tisch des Wortes* 16 (1966) 46-55; =
        ID., *Vielfalt und Einheit*, 1968, 112-124.

1966c   Die Passion Jesu in der Darstellung der synoptischen Evangelien. — *LebZeug* 21/1
        (1966) 28-46. Esp. 39-46: "Matthäus: Messias und Kirche"; = ID., *Vielfalt und Einheit*, 1968,
        83-111. Esp. 100-111.

1968    *Vielfalt und Einheit im Neuen Testament. Zur Exegese und Verkündigung des Neuen*
        *Testaments* (Unterweisen und Verkünden, 3). Einsiedeln: Benziger, 1968, 157 p. →
        1965a, 1966b-c

1969a   *Christusverkündigung in den synoptischen Evangelien. Beispiele gattungsgemäßer Aus-*
        *legung*. Leipzig: St. Benno, 1969; (Biblische Handbibliothek, 4), München: Kösel,
        1969, 243 p. Esp. 13-39 [1,18-25]; 64-85 [5,3-12]; 86-107 [5,20-22]; 165-190 [21,33-46]; 212-243 [28,1-
        8].
        *L'annuncio di Cristo nei vangeli sinottici*. Roma: Herder; Brescia: Morcelliana, 1970.
        *L'annonce du Christ dans les évangiles synoptiques*, trans. G. Bret & A. Chazelle (LD, 69). Paris: Cerf,
        1971, 244 p. Esp. 11-36; 61-82; 83-104; 165-190; 211-242.
        *O anúncio de Cristo nos evangelhos sinóticos*. São Paulo: Paulinas, 1976, 223 p.

1969b   Matthäus, das kirchliche Evangelium. Überlieferungsgeschichte und Theologie. —
        SCHREINER, J. - DAUTZENBERG, G. (eds.), *Gestalt und Anspruch*, 1969, 186-199. Esp.
        186-188: "Matthäus erweitert die Markusordnung"; 188-192: "Matthäus ist eine Neubearbeitung des
        Markusevangeliums"; 192-197: "Die Kirche ist das wahre Israel"; 197-199: "Jüngerschaft zwischen Gesetz
        und Gericht"; = ID., *Studien zur Jesusüberlieferung*, 1988, 93-108. Esp. 93-95; 95-99; 100-
        106; 106-107.

1969c   Jean le Baptiste. Mt 3,1-12. — *AssSeign* II/6 (1969) 19-25. → 1962c

1969d   "De toutes les nations, faites des disciples". Mt 28,16-20. — *AssSeign* II/28 (1969) 24-
        37; = GANTOY, R. (ed.), *La Bonne Nouvelle de la Résurrection* (Lire la Bible, 66),
        Paris: Cerf, 1981; ²1984, 124-137.
        "Andate e ammaestrate tutte le nazioni" (Mt 28,16-20). — GANTOY, R. (ed.), *La buona novella della*
        *risurrezione*, trans. E. De Rosa (Letture Bibliche), Roma: Borla, 1985, 153-170.

1969e   Confession sans crainte. Mt 10,26-33. — *AssSeign* II/43 (1969) 19-24.

1969f   Disponibilité pour suivre le Christ. Mt 10,37-42. — *AssSeign* II/44 (1969) 15-20.

1970a   Amt und Amtsverständnis bei Matthäus. — DESCAMPS, A.L. - DE HALLEUX, A. (eds.),
        *Mélanges bibliques*. FS B. Rigaux, 1970, 29-44. Esp. 30-34: "Lehrer"; 34-39: "Propheten"; 40-
        41: "Apostel"; 42-44: "Petrus"; = *TJb*, 1972, 160-173. Esp. 160-164; 164-169; 169-171; 171-173;
        = KERTELGE, K. (ed.), *Das kirchliche Amt*, 1977, 524-542. Esp. 525-530; 530-536; 537-539;
        539-542; = ID., *Studien zur Jesusüberlieferung*, 1988, 77-92. Esp. 78-82; 82-88; 88-90; 90-92.

1970b   Ist die katholische Primatslehre schriftgemäß? [16,17-19; 18,18] — DENZLER, G., et al.,
        *Zum Thema Petrusamt*, 1970, 51-60. Esp. 55-59: "Exemplarische Erläuterung von Mt 16,17-19 und
        Mt 18,18". → 1971

1971    Zum Petrusamt im Neuen Testament. Traditionsgeschichtliche Überlegungen anhand
        von Matthäus, 1 Petrus und Johannes. — *TQ* 151 (1971) 110-133. Esp. 114-119: "Die
        Petrustradition im Matthäusevangelium". [NTA 16, 143]; = *TVers* 4 (1972) 27-46. Esp. 30-33; =
        ID., *Studien zur Jesusüberlieferung*, 1988, 111-139. Esp. 116-122. → 1970b

1973    "Jesus, der Urheber und Vollender des Glaubens" (Hebr 12,2). Exegetische Thesen.
        — KNOCH, O., et al. (eds.), *Das Evangelium auf dem Weg zum Menschen*. FS H.
        Kahlefeld, 1973, 3-23. Esp. 10 [5,43-48]; 11 [6,25-34]; 13-18 [Kingdom]; 20 [8,22].

1974    Les vignerons homicides. Mt 21,33-43. — *AssSeign* II/58 (1974) 16-23. [NTA 19, 540]

1977a   Zur Entstehung des Zwölferkreises. Eine geschichtskritische Überlegung. — SCHNACKENBURG, R., et al. (eds.), *Die Kirche des Anfangs*. FS H. Schürmann, 1977, 201-222. Esp. 213-219 [Q 22,28-30]; = ID., *Studien zur Jesusüberlieferung*, 1988, 185-208. Esp. 199-205.

1977b   "Implizite Ekklesiologie". Ein Vorschlag zum Thema "Jesus und die Kirche". — ERNST, W., et al. (eds.), *Dienst der Vermittlung*, 1977, 149-164. Esp. 157-160 [16,17-19]; = ID., *Studien zur Jesusüberlieferung*, 1988, 165-183. Esp. 174-178.

1977c   Die Wahrheit von Jesus-Worten in der Interpretation neutestamentlicher Autoren. — *KerDog* 23 (1977) 93-112. Esp. 96-97; 102-103 [10,40-42]; = ID., *Studien zur Jesusüberlieferung*, 1988, 141-164. Esp. 145-146; 152-154.

1978   *Die Botschaft Jesu. Exegetische Orientierungen.* Freiburg: Herder, 1978, 122 p. Esp. 19-56: "Die Botschaft Jesu"; 57-72: "Implizite Ekklesiologie"; 73-95: "Die Wahrheit von Jesusworten in der Interpretation neutestamentlicher Autoren" (84-87: Mt).
*L'annuncio di Gesù. Orientamenti esegetici* (Studi biblici, 74). Brescia: Paideia, 1986, 135 p.

1984   Zum Thema: Ehe und Ehescheidung im Neuen Testament. — *TGl* 74 (1984) 390-406. Esp. 397-402 [Q 16,18]. [NTA 29, 1134]; = *TVers* 16 (1986) 73-84. Esp. 76-77.

1988   *Studien zur Jesusüberlieferung* (Stuttgarter Biblische Aufsatzbände, 1). Stuttgart: Katholisches Bibelwerk, 1988, 368 p. → 1959b, 1963, 1969b, 1970a, 1971, 1977a-c

**TRIMAILLE, Michel**

1990   Citations d'accomplissement et architecture de l'Évangile selon S. Matthieu. — *EstBíb* 48 (1990) 47-79. Esp. 47-51: "Coup d'oeil rétrospectif sur les critères retenus"; 51-74: "Les citations d'accomplissement comme éléments d'architecture" [8,17; 12,17-21; 12,22–16,20]; 74-78: "Le phénomène littéraire de 'tuilage'". [NTA 35, 617]

1993   Le Christ, Sagesse de Dieu et maître de sagesse dans le Nouveau Testament. — LEBRUN, R. (ed.), *Sagesses de l'Orient ancien et chrétien. La voie de vie et la conduite spirituelle chez les peuples et dans les littératures de l'Orient chrétien. Conférences I.R.O.C. 1991-1992* (Sciences théologiques & religieuses, 2), Paris: Beauchesne, 1993, 193-218.

1995   Jésus et la sagesse dans la "Quelle". — TRUBLET, J. (ed.), *La sagesse biblique. De l'Ancien au Nouveau Testament. Actes du XV^e Congrès de l'ACFEB (Paris, 1993)* (LD, 160), Paris: Cerf, 1995, 279-319. Esp. 280-296: "Jésus, maître de sagesse en Q" [Q 11,9-13; 12,22-31]; 293-311: "Jésus et la σοφία divine" [Q 7,31-35; 11,47-51; 13,34-35]; 312-318: "Les conséquences christologiques".

**TRITES, Allison A.**

1977   *The New Testament Concept of Witness* (SNTS MS, 31). Cambridge: University Press, 1977, X-294 p. Esp. 175-198: "The idea of witness in the synoptic gospels".

1979   The Transfiguration of Jesus: The Gospel in Microcosm. [17,1-8] — *EvQ* 51 (1979) 67-79. [NTA 23, 850]

1992a   The Blessings and Warnings of the Kingdom (*Matthew 5:3-12; 7:13-27*). — *RExp* 89 (1992) 179-196. [NTA 37, 722]

1992b   Witness. — *DJG*, 1992, 877-880. Esp. 877-878.

**TROADEC, Henri G.**

1963   *L'évangile selon saint Matthieu.* Tours: Mame, 1963, VII-251 p. [NTA 8, p. 293]
P. BENOIT, *RB* 71 (1964) 447-448; C. LESQUIVIT, *CBQ* 25 (1963) 522; J. PONTHOT, *RevDiocTournai* 18 (1963) 512.
*Evangelho segundo S. Mateus*, trans. A. Lemos. Lisboa: Sampedro, 1968, 242 p.

1965   *Les thèmes majeurs de l'Évangile selon saint Matthieu.* Paris: Équipes Notre-Dame, 1965, 80 p.

1969 La vocation de l'homme riche. — *VSp* 120 (1969) 138-148. Esp. 144-146 [19,16-22]. [NTA 13, 886]

**TROCMÉ, André**

1961 *Jésus et la révolution nonviolente.* Genève: Labor et Fides, 1961, 205 p. Esp. 157-178; 190-200.
*Gesù e la rivoluzione. Il messaggio rivoluzionario dell'Evangelo*, trans. D.S. Bianchi. Torino: Gribaudi, 1968, 256 p.
*Jesus Cristo e a Revolução Não-Violenta*, trans. J.A. de Andrade. Petrópolis: Vozes, 1973, 244 p.

**TROCMÉ, Étienne**

1966 Lecture du Sermon sur la montagne. — *Christianisme social* (Paris) 74 (1966) 325-338.

1968 L'expulsion des marchands du Temple. — *NTS* 15 (1968-69) 1-22. Esp. 7 [21,12-17]. [NTA 13, 868]

1972 *Jésus de Nazareth vu par les témoins de sa vie* (Bibliothèque théologique). Neuchâtel: Delachaux & Niestlé, 1972, 152 p. Esp. 38-39 [sayings]; 94-110 [parables]; 111-124 [miracles].
*Jesus as Seen by His Contemporaries*, trans. R.A. Wilson. Philadelphia, PA: Westminster, 1973, x-134 p.
*Jesús de Nazaret visto por los testigos de su vida*, trans. S. González de Carrea. Barcelona: Herder, 1974, 192 p.
*Gesù di Nazaret visto dai testimoni della sua vita* (Biblioteca di cultura religiosa, 24). Brescia: Paideia, 1975.

1983 *The Passion as Liturgy. A Study in the Origin of the Passion Narratives in the Four Gospels.* London: SCM, 1983, IX-116 p. Esp. 20-26: "The passion narrative in Matthew".

1991a Les Juifs d'après le Nouveau Testament. — *FoiVie* 90/6 (1991) 3-22. Esp. 14-18. [NTA 36, 961]

1991b Matthieu 5,17-48: écouter la voix de Dieu en relisant la Loi de Moïse. — *Les racines juives de la foi chrétienne, sept études bibliques*, Strasbourg: Église Réformée d'Alsace et de Lorraine, 1991, 1-6.

**TROISFONTAINES, Claude**

1969* (ed.), *Au service de la Parole de Dieu. Mélanges offerts à Monseigneur André-Marie Charue, Évêque de Namur.* Gembloux: Duculot, 1969, XX-546 p. → Cerfaux, Didier, Dupont

**TROLL, Christian W.**

1977 Sayyid Ahmad Khan on Mt 5,17-20. — *Islamochristiana* (Roma) 3 (1977) 99-105.

**TROMP, Nico** → Lukken 1983

**TROMPF, Garry W.**

1972 The First Resurrection Appearance and the Ending of Mark's Gospel. — *NTS* 18 (1971-72) 308-330. Esp. 316-322 [28,9-10]. [NTA 17, 153]

**TRONINA, Antoni**

1990 Jeszcze raz o inieniu Maria(m) (More on the Name of Maria[m]). — *RuBi* 43 (1990) 127-130.

**TRUBLET, Jacques**

1978 Une loi pour être heureux. Étude de quelques textes du Deutéronome et de Matthieu. — *Christus* 25 (1978) 474-481. Esp. 478-481. [NTA 23, 428]

**TRUDINGER, L. Paul**

1971 A Much Misunderstood Commandment. [5,34] — *BiTod* 56 (1971) 501-504.

1975 The Word on the Generation Gap. Reflections on a Gospel Metaphor. [9,16-17] — *BTB* 5 (1975) 311-315. [NTA 20, 458]

1989 The "Our Father" in Matthew as Apocalyptic Eschatology. — *DownR* 107 (1989) 49-54. [NTA 33, 1128]

**TRUHLAR, Karel V.**

1968a The Earthly Cast of the Beatitudes. — *Concilium* (New York) 39 (1968) 33-43. [NTA 13, 862]
L'aspect terrestre des Béatitudes. — *Concilium* (Paris) 39 (1968) 31-40

1968b The Beatitudes and the Kingdom. — *Concilium* (London) 4/9 (1968) 18-23.

**TRUMBOWER, Jeffrey A.**

1994 The Role of Malachi in the Career of John the Baptist. — EVANS, C.A. - STEGNER, W.R. (eds.), *The Gospels and the Scriptures of Israel*, 1994, 28-41. Esp. 33-40: "The case of John the Baptist".

**TRUMMER, Peter**

1977 Die Bedeutung Jerusalems für die ntl Chronologie. — BAUER, J.B. - MARBÖCK, J. (eds.), *Memoria Jerusalem. Freundesgabe Franz Sauer zum 70. Geburtstag*, Graz: Akad. Druck- und Verlagsanstalt, 1977, 129-142. Esp. 130-131 [22,1-14].

1982 Warum gewaltlose selig sind. Exegetische Hinweise zum Verständnis von Mt 5,5. — ID. (ed.), *Gedanken des Friedens* (Grazer theologische Studien, 7), Graz: Institut für Ökumenische Theologie und Patrologie an der Universität Graz, 1982, 203-236.

1987a Der "sanfte" Jesus und der zornige Gott. Zum Wechselverhältnis von Jesus- und Gottesbild. — BROX, N., et al. (eds.), *Anfänge der Theologie. FS J.B. Bauer*, 1987, 117-137.
Die Sanftmut Jesu und der Zorn Gottes. Exegetische und hermeneutische Beobachtungen zum Jesus- und Gottesbild. — ID., *Aufsätze*, 1987, 39-79. Esp. 43-49 [ἐπιτιμάω]; 57-59 [ὀργή].

1987b *Aufsätze zum Neuen Testament* (Grazer theologische Studien, 12). Graz: Institut für ökumenische Theologie und Patrologie, 1987, 224 p. → 1987a.c

1987c Was heisst "Armut um des Evangeliums willen?" — *Ibid*, 7-37. Esp. 9-19.

1991 *Die blutende Frau. Wunderheilung im Neuen Testament*. Freiburg: Herder, 1991, 184 p. Esp. 87-89 [9,20-22].

**TRUNK, Dieter**

1994 *Der messianische Heiler. Eine redaktions- und religionsgeschichtliche Studie zu den Exorzismen im Matthäusevangelium* (Herders Biblische Studien - Herder's Biblical Studies, 3). Freiburg: Herder, 1994, XIII-457 p. Esp. 40-93: "Die Belzebulrede: die Exorzismen Jesu im Streit der Interpretationen (Mt 12,22-37)"; 94-102: "Ein dämonologisches Gleichnis: die Rückkehr des unreinen Geistes und das Schicksal 'dieser Generation' (Mt 12,43-45)"; 103-182: "Die Exorzismen Jesu in den Einzelüberlieferungen" [8,28-34; 15,21-28; 17,14-20]; 183-200: ' Die Exorzismen in den Summarien und im Aussendungsbericht" [4,23-25; 8,16-17; 9,35-11,1; 12,15-21] 201-212: "Die Auslassungen des Matthäus gegenüber Markus"; 213-235: "Der 'Sitz im Leben' der Wunder- und Exorzismusüberlieferung des Matthäus". [NTA 39, p. 513] — Diss. Würzburg, 1993-94 (H.-J. Klauck).
J. BECKER, *TLZ* 120 (1995) 1003-1005; S. GRASSO, *RivBib* 45 (1997) 233-238; S.P. SAUNDERS, *JBL* 116 (1997) 143-145.

**TSUJI, Manabu**

1997 *Glaube zwischen Vollkommenheit und Verweltlichung* (WUNT, II/93). Tübingen: Mohr, 1997, XI-244 p. Esp. 118-132: "Jesusüberlieferung im Jakobusbrief". — Diss. Bern, 1995 (S. Vollenweider).

**TSUNODA, Shinsaburo**

1974 Matthew the Harmonist. Considerations on the Narrative of the Mission of the Apostles Mt 10. [Japanese] — *Seisho-gaku ronshū* (Tokyo) 10 (1974) 114-131.

1977 Itinerant Radicalism and the Gospel of Matthew. [Japanese] — *Seisho-gaku ronshū* 12 (1977) 124-156.

1979 The People and the Disciples in Mt 13. Towards an Understanding of the Mysteries of the Kingdom in Matthew. [Japanese] — *Nihondaigaku Hōgakubu 90 Shunen Kinen Ronbunshu*, 1979, 499-534.

1981 The Christian Scribe in Matthew. [Japanese] — *Ōmonronsō (Nihondaigaku Hōgakubu)* 11 (1981) 1-29.

1984 The Function of the Epilogue in Chapter 28 of Matthew. [Japanese] — *Ōmonronsō* 14 (1984) 1-30.

1986a The Problem of Antijudaism in Matthew. [Japanese] — *Ōmonronsō* 20 (1986) 1-22.

1986b Righteousness in Matthew. [Japanese] — *Ōmonronsō* 21 (1986) 23-36.

**TUCK, Russell C.**

1966 The Lord Who Said Go: Some Reflections on Matthew 28:16-20. — *ANQ* 7 (1966) 85-92. [NTA 11, 715]

**TUCKETT, Christopher M.**

1979 The Griesbach Hypothesis in the 19th Century. — *JSNT* 3 (1979) 29-60. [NTA 23, 803] → Stoldt 1977

1980 The Argument from Order and the Synoptic Problem. — *TZ* 36 (1980) 338-354. [NTA 27, 498]

1982a Luke 4,16-30, Isaiah and Q. — DELOBEL, J. (ed.), *Logia*, 1982, 343-354. → 1996, 209-237 (226-237); → Delobel 1973, Schürmann 1964

1982b The Present Son of Man. — *JSNT* 14 (1982) 58-81. Esp. 67-70 [Q 6,22; Q 7,34; Q 9,58; Q 12,10]. [NTA 26, 860]

1982c Synoptic Tradition in Some Nag Hammadi and Related Texts. — *VigChr* 36 (1982) 173-190. Esp. 173-178 [Gospel of Philip]; 178-182 [Gospel of Mary]; 182-184 [Thomas the Contender]. [NTA 27, 828]; → cf. 1986, 35-42; 72-81; 83-87

1983a *The Revival of the Griesbach Hypothesis. An Analysis and Appraisal* (SNTS MS, 44). Cambridge: University Press, 1983, VIII-255 p. Esp. 9-93.192-206: "General phenomena" [duplicate expressions in Mk; historic present; order of the material; conflation; patristic evidence; minor agreements; Mark-Q overlaps]; 95-185.207-226: "Some particular texts. A. Selected Markan passages" [Mk 3,1-6; 7,1-23; 11,15-19; 12,13-17.28-34.38-40]; "B. The double tradition" [Q 17,22-37; wisdom motifs]. — Diss. Lancaster, 1979 (D.R. Catchpole). → McNicol 1987, W.O. Walker Jr. 1987c

1983b The Beatitudes: A Source-Critical Study. With a Reply by M.D. Goulder. — *NT* 25 (1983) 193-216 (207-216: M.D. Goulder). [NTA 28, 90]

1983c 1 Corinthians and Q. — *JBL* 102 (1983) 607-619. Esp. 612 [10,10]; 613 [5,32]; 613-614 [17,20]; 615 [10,37-38]; 616 [13,16-17]; 617 [11,19]; 617-618 [12,32]. [NTA 28, 1044]

1984* (ed.), *Synoptic Studies. The Ampleforth Conferences of 1982 and 1983* (JSNT SS, 7). Sheffield: JSOT, 1984, XII-231 p. → P.S. Alexander, Downing, Dungan, W.R. Farmer 1984a-b, Goulder 1984a-b, H.B. Green 1984a-b, Kilpatrick, Meredith, Tuckett

1984a Arguments from Order: Definition and Evaluation. — *Ibid.*, 197-219.

1984b Paul and the Synoptic Mission Discourse? — *ETL* 60 (1984) 376-381. [NTA 29, 1029] → Allison 1982, 1985b

1984c On the Relationship between Matthew and Luke. — *NTS* 30 (1984) 130-142. Esp. 131 [4,13; 13,54]; 131-132 [4,13-22]; 132-133 [9,2]; 133-134 [10,2-4]; 134-135 [11,10]; 135-136 [10,1]; 136 [17,5]; 136-137 [26,67-68]; 137-138 [26,75]; 138 [27,1]; 138-139 [27,59-60]; 139-140 [28,1]. [NTA 28, 906] → Goulder 1978b

1984d Synoptic Tradition in the Gospel of Truth and the Testimony of Truth. — *JTS* 35 (1984) 131-145. Esp. 132-140 [Gospel of Truth]; 141-144 [Testimonium of Truth]. [NTA 28, 1245]; → cf. 1986, 57-68; 139-145.

1986 *Nag Hammadi and the Gospel Tradition. Synoptic Tradition in the Nag Hammadi Library*. Edinburgh: Clark, 1986, XI-194 p. → 1982c, 1984d

1987 *Reading the New Testament. Methods of Interpretation*. London: SPCK; Philadelphia, PA: Fortress, 1987, V-200 p. Esp. 117-120 [redaction criticism]; 64-65.90-93 [12,11-12]; 79-83 [source criticism]; 175-179 [literary criticism].

1988a Q, the Law and Judaism. — LINDARS, B. (ed.), *Law and Religion. Essays on the Place of the Law in Israel and Early Christianity by Members of the Ehrhardt Seminar of Manchester University*, Cambridge: Clarke, 1988, 90-101.

1988b Thomas and the Synoptics. — *NT* 30 (1988) 132-157. Esp. 141 [5,6/Th 69]; 142 [23,13/Th 39a]; 143-144 [15,11/Th 14]; 146-147 [10,34-35/Th 16]; 148 [10,37-38/Th 55]; 148-153 [13,31-32/Th 20]. [NTA 33, 500] → 1991

1989a A Cynic Q? — *Bib* 70 (1989) 349-376. Esp. 351-355: "Definition"; 355-356: "Date"; 356-358: "Provenance"; 359-364: "Genre of Q"; 364-375: "Contents". [NTA 34, 596] → 1996, 355-391 (368-390); → Downing 1988b

1989b Q, Prayer, and the Kingdom. [Q 11,9-13] — *JTS* 40 (1989) 367-376. [NTA 34, 168] → 1996, 139-163 (149-155); → Catchpole 1983a, 1989

1989c Synoptic Tradition in the Didache. — SEVRIN, J.-M. (ed.), *The New Testament in Early Christianity*, 1989, 197-230. Esp. 200-208.212-214 [24,10-12.13.24.30-31.42/Did 16]; 209 [12,31-32/Did 11,7]; 210 [10,10/Did 13,1]; 210-211 [7,15; 22,38-39/Did 1,2]; 214-230 [5,39-48/Did 1,3-2,1]; = DRAPER, J.A., *The Didache in Modern Research*, 1996, 92-129. Esp. 95-104; 108-110; 104-105; 105-106; 106-107; 110-128.

1990a Response to the Two-Gospel Hypothesis. I. The Position Paper. II. The Eschatological Discourse. — DUNGAN, D.L. (ed.), *The Interrelations of the Gospels*, 1990, 47-62, 63-76. Esp. 47-53 [external evidence]; 54-56 [argument of order]; 59-61 [Q]; 73-75 [10,17-22/Mk 13,9-13]; 75-76 [24,42; 25,13-15/Mk 13,33-37]. → McNicol 1990a

1990b Synoptic Tradition in 1 Thessalonians? — COLLINS, R F. (ed.), *The Thessalonian Correspondence* (BETL, 87), Leuven: University Press / Peeters, 1990, 160-182. Esp. 163-164 [Q 10,16 (Lk)/1Thess 4,8]; 165-167 [23,29-39/1 Thess 2,14-16]; 168-176 [24,36-39.43-51/1 Thess 5,1-11]; 176-180 [24,30-31.40-41; 25,1-13/1 Thess 4,15-17].

1991 Q and Thomas. Evidence of a Primitive "Wisdom Gospel"? A Response to H. Koester. — *ETL* 67 (1991) 346-360. Esp. 350-351 [Q 6,22/Th 68]; 351-352 [Q 6,34/Th 95]; 352-353 [Q 16,13/Th 47]; 353 [Q 11,39-40/Th 89]; 354 [Q 11,52/Th 39]; 355 [Q 12,10/Th 44]; 356-357 [Q 12,49.51-53/Th 10, 16]. [NTA 36, 1247] → 1988b; → Koester 1990a

1992a On the Stratification of Q. A Response. — *Semeia* 55 (1992) 213-222. → Vaage 1992b

1992b Q (Gospel Source). — *ABD* 5 (1992) 567-572.

1992c Synoptic Problem. — *ABD* 6 (1992) 263-271.

1992d The Temptation Narrative in Q. — VAN SEGBROECK, F., et al. (eds.), *The Four Gospels 1992*. FS F. Neirynck, 1992, I, 479-507. Esp. 481-483 [Q 4,1-13 part of Q]; 483-485 [OT/Q 4,1-13]; 485-486 [form]; 487-489 [law]; 489-492 [Messiah]; 493-494 [wisdom]; 494-498 [Q 4,3-4]; 498-501 [Q 4,5-8]; 501-506 [Q 4,9-12].

1993a Les logia et le judaïsme. — *FoiVie* 92/5 = *Cahiers bibliques* 32 (1993) 67-88. Esp. 68-72 [Q 11,49-51]; 72-74 [Q 13,34-35]; 74-76 [Q 7,31-35]; 76 [Q 6,22-23]; 77 [Q 9,58]; 78-79 [Q 10,13-15]. [NTA 38, 739]

1993b Mark and Q. — FOCANT, C. (ed.), *The Synoptic Gospels*, 1993, 149-175. Esp. 158-162 [Q 11,29-30]; 162-168 [Q 7,27]; 168-172 [Q 3,16]; 172-174 [Q 13,18-19].

1993c The Minor Agreements and Textual Criticism. — STRECKER, G. (ed.), *Minor Agreements*, 1993, 119-142. Esp. 121-125 [minor agreements: 8,2]; 125-127: "Textual criticism"; 127-132: "Textual criticism and the synoptic problem"; 132-141: "Two examples" [26,67-68.75]. → Goulder 1993b, Wheeler 1985

1993d The Son of Man in Q. — DE BOER, M.C. (ed.), *From Jesus to John*. FS M. de Jonge, 1993, 196-215. Esp. 204-208 [Q 6,22]; 208 [Q 9,58]; 208-211 [Q 12,8-9.10]; 211-212 [Q 12,40]; 212-215 [Q 17,23-24.26-30]. → 1996, 239-282 (244-253)

1995a The Existence of Q. — PIPER, R.A. (ed.), *The Gospel Behind the Gospels*, 1995, 19-47. Esp. 24-27 [trad. arg.]; 28-31: "The Griesbach hypothesis"; 31-45: "M.D. Goulder". → 1996, 1-39 (1-30)

1995b Das Thomasevangelium und die synoptischen Evangelien. — *BTZ* 12 (1995) 186-200. Esp. 188-189 [Q/Th]; 194-197 [5,3-12/Th]; 198 [15,11/Th]; 198-199 [23,13/Th]. [NTA 40, 1899]

1996 *Q and the History of Early Christianity. Studies on Q.* Edinburgh: Clark; Peabody, MA: Hendrickson, 1996, XV-492 p. Esp. 1-39: "Introduction: the existence of Q" (→ 1995); 41-82: "Redaction criticism in Q"; 83-106: "The nature of Q"; 107-137: "John the Baptist in Q" [Q 3,7-9.16-17; 7,18-35; 16,16]; 139-163: "Eschatology in Q" [Q 6,47-49; 11,2-4.9-13.49-51; 12,22-31.39-46.57-59; 13,18-21.24-25; 14,16-24; 17,23-37] (→ 1989b); 165-207: "Wisdom, prophets and 'this generation'" [Q 6,22-23; 7,31-35; 9,58; 10,2-16; 11,31-32.47-51; 13,34-35]; 209-237: "Q's christology" [Q 4,16-30(Lk); 6,20-21; 7,22] (→ 1982a); 239-282: "The Son of Man in Q" [Q 6,22; 7,34; 9,58; 10,21-22; 11,30; 12,8-9.10.40; 17,23-24.26-30] (→ 1993d); 283-323: "Polemic and persecution" [polemic: Q 3,7-9.16-17; 7,1-10.31-35; 10,2-16; 11,14-32; 12,8-10.51-53; 13,24-30; 14,16-24; 17,22-37; persecution: Q 6,22-23.27-35; 11,47-51; 12,4-5.11-12; 13,34-35; 14,27]; 325-354: "Wisdom in Q"; 355-391: "Discipleship in Q" (→ 1989a); 393-424: "The gentile mission and the law" [mission: Q 7,1-10; 10,8; 12,30; law: Q 7,22-23; 9,60; 10,25-28 (Lk); 11,39-41.42; 14,5; 16,16-18]; 425-450: "Q and Israel" [Q 4,16-30(Lk); 6,27-36]. [NTA 41, p. 153]

A. FUCHS, Zum Umfang von Q. Anfragen an eine neue Arbeit zur Logienquelle. – *SNTU* 21 (1996) 188-210.

D.R. CATCHPOLE, *JTS* 48 (1997) 191-194; F. NEIRYNCK, *ETL* 73 (1997) 173-177.

1997* (ed.), *The Scriptures in the Gospels* (BETL, 131). Leuven: University Press / Peeters, 1997, XXIV-721 p. → Brodie, G. Geiger, S.L. Graham, Hasitschka, Lybaek, Neirynck, Niebuhr, Schröter, Senior, N.H. Taylor, Tomson, Tuckett, Weren

1997 Scripture and Q. — *Ibid.*, 3-26. Esp. 8-13 [strata in Q]; 13-15 [OT]; 15-20 [Q/Is 53]; 20-26 [Q/Is 61].

**TUILIER, André**

1995 La *Didachè* et le problème synoptique. — JEFFORD, C.N. (ed.), *The* Didache *in* Context, 1995, 110-130.

**TUM, D.**

1984 Egzegeza przypowieści o zagubionej owcy (Lk 15,4-7; Mt 18,12-14) u Ireneusza i gnostykow. [The exegesis of the parable about the lost sheep in Irenaeus and in gnostic literature] — *Studia Antiquitatis Christiana* (Warszawa) 7 (1984) 173-201.

**TUM, Janusz**

1986 "Szukajcie najpierw królestwa Bożego i jego sprawiedliwości, a to wszystko będzie wam dodane". Analiza Mt 6,19-7,12 ("Euch aber muss es zuerst um sein Reich und um seine Gerechtigkeit gehen; dann wird euch alles andere dazugegeben". Die Analyse des Textes Mt 6,19-7,12). — *StudTheolVars* 24/1 (1986) 61-98. [NTA 31, 119]

**TUÑÍ, José**

1972 La tipología Israel-Jesús en Mt. 1-2. — *EstE* 47 (1972) 361-376. Esp. 362-371 [typology]; 371-375 [Son of God]. [NTA 18, 99]

**TUPPER, E. Frank**

1991 The Bethlehem Massacre – Christology against Providence? — *RExp* 88 (1991) 399-418. Esp. 403-412: "The scenes in Matthew's nativity – an interpretation". [NTA 37, 713]

**TURIOT, Cécile**

1984 Pierre dans le Nouveau Testament. — *SémBib* 36 (1984) 1-14. Esp. 8-9 [14,22-33]. [NTA 30, 360]

1985 Sémiotique et lisibilité du texte évangélique. — *RSR* 73 (1985) 161-175. Esp. 162-163 [27,57–28,15]; 163-168 [26,6-13.14-16.47-50; 27,3-10; 28,1-15]. [NTA 30, 128]

**TURLINGTON, Darla Dee**

1988 *Views of the Spirit of God in Mark and "Q": A Tradition-Historical Study*. Diss. Columbia Univ., 1988, 308 p. — *DissAbstr* 49 (1988-89) 1495; *SBT* 17 (1989) 99-100.

**TURLINGTON, H.E.**

1956 Jesus and the Law. — *RExp* 53 (1956) 34-45.

**TURNER, David L.**

1989 The Structure and Sequence of Matthew 24:1-41: Interaction with Evangelical Treatments. — *GraceTJ* 10 (1989) 3-27. [NTA 34, 131]

1992 Whom Does God Approve? The Context, Structure, Purpose, and Exegesis of Matthew's Beatitudes. — *Criswell Theological Review* (Dallas, TX) 6 (1992) 29-42. [NTA 37, 1253]

**TURNER, H.E.W.**

1956 The Virgin Birth. — *ExpT* 68 (1956-57) 12-17. Esp. 15 [1,23]. [NTA 1, 206]

1963 *Historicity and the Gospels. A Sketch of Historical Method and Its Application to the Gospels*. London: Mowbray, 1963, IX-108 p.

1966 Expounding the Parables. VI. The Parable of the Sheep and the Goats (Matthew 25,31-46). — *ExpT* 77 (1965-66) 243-246. [NTA 11, 219]

**TURNER, Max M.B.**

1991 The Spirit and the Power of Jesus' Miracles in the Lucan Conception. — *NT* 33 (1991) 124-152. Esp. 127-128.143-146 [12,28.31-32]. [NTA 35, 1170]

1992 Holy Spirit. — *DJG*, 1992, 341-351. Esp. 343-347.

**TURNER, Nigel**

1957 The New-Born King. Matthew ii.2. — *ExpT* 68 (1956-57) 122. [NTA 1, 392]

1959 The Minor Verbal Agreements of Mt. and Lk. against Mk. — *Studia Evangelica* 1 (1959) 223-234.

1960 Philology in New Testament Studies. — *ExpT* 71 (1959-60) 104-107. Esp. 107 [6,11]. [NTA 4, 610]

1963 *Syntax* (A Grammar of New Testament Greek, by J.H. Moulton, Vol. III). Edinburgh: Clark, 1963, XXII-417 p.

1965 *Grammatical Insights into the New Testament*. Edinburgh: Clark, 1965, VIII-198 p. Esp. 29-32: "Grammar in the great sermon"; 24-27 [2]; 58-59 [8,12]; 59-60 [11,12]; 60-61 [19,3]; 68 [16,7]; 69-71 [26,50]; 72-75 [26,64]; 80-82 [16,19].

1969 Q in Recent Thought. — *ExpT* 80 (1968-69) 324-328. [NTA 14, 127] → Farrer 1955, R.T. Simpson 1966

1976 *Style* (A Grammar of New Testament Greek, by J.H. Moulton, Vol. IV). Edinburgh: Clark, 1976; ²1986, X-174 p. Esp. 31-44: "The style of Matthew".

**TURRADO Y TURRADO, Lorenzo**

1952 ¿Se demuestra la existencia del "sensus plenior" por las citas que el Nuevo Testamento hace del Antiguo?. — *La enciclica Humani generis* (XII Semana Biblica Española), Madrid: Consejo Superior de Investigaciones Científicas, 1952, 331-378. Esp. 336-342.

1960 El bautismo "in Spiritu sancto et igni". [3,11] — *EstE* 34 (1960) 807-817. [NTA 6, 449]; = *Miscelanea Biblica Andres Fernandez*, 1960, 503-513.

**TUTTLE, Gary A.**

1977 The Sermon on the Mount: Its Wisdom Affinities and Their Relation to Its Structure. — *JEvTS* 20 (1977) 213-230. [NTA 22, 392]

**TWELFTREE, Graham H.**

1980 → J.D.G. Dunn 1980b

1986 Εἰ δὲ ... ἐγὼ ἐκβάλλω τὰ δαιμόνια... — WENHAM, D. - BLOMBERG, C. (eds.), *The Miracles of Jesus*, 1986, 361-400. Esp. 387-390 [11,2-6]; 387-388 [12,28]; 390-391 [13,24-30].

1992a Demon, Devil, Satan. — *DJG*, 1992, 163-172. Esp. 169.

1992b Scribes. — *Ibid.*, 732-736. Esp. 734.

1992c Temptation of Jesus. — *Ibid.*, 821-827.

1993 *Jesus the Exorcist. A Contribution to the Study of the Historical Jesus* (WUNT, II/54). Tübingen: Mohr, 1993, IX-281 p. Esp. 98-113 [12,22-30]; 114-117 [4,1-11]; 118-121 [11,2-6]; 122-127 [10,1-15]. — Diss. Nottingham, 1991 (J.D.G. Dunn).

**TWOMEY, Vincent**

1982 *Apostolikos Thronos. The Primacy of Rome as Reflected in the Church History of Eusebius and the Historico-Apologetic Writings of Saint Athanasius the Great* (Münsterische Beiträge zur Theologie, 49). Münster: Aschendorff, 1982, IX-623 p. Esp. 221-229: "Mt 16,18 in the writings of Eusebius"; 270-291: "St. Peter and his confession of faith (Mt 16,16-18)" [Athanasius]; 537-552 [Athanasius, *Historia arianorum*]. — Diss. Regensburg, 1978 (J. Ratzinger).

**TYSON, Joseph B.**

1973 *A Study of Early Christianity*. New York - London: Macmillan, 1973, XV-447 p. Esp. 199-204. → 1984

1976 Sequential Parallelism in the Synoptic Gospels. — *NTS* 22 (1975-76) 276-308. Esp. 280.285-286.299-302; 281-282 [Mt/Mk]; 284-285 [Mt/Lk]; 291-298 [synoptic problem]. [NTA 21, 68] → W.O. Walker 1976

1978a & LONGSTAFF, T.R.W., *Synoptic Abstract* (The Computer Bible, 15). Wooster, OH: Biblical Research Associates, 1978, X-193 p. Esp. 17-55: "Verbal agreements in Matthew"; 109-112: "Pericope list for Matthew"; 125-129.139-143.153-157: "Summary pericope lists"; 169: "Analytical table"; 177-185: "Sequential parallelism".

1978b Literary Criticism and the Gospels: The Seminar. — WALKER, W.O., Jr. (ed.), *The Relationships among the Gospels*, 1978, 323-341. Esp. 324-331: "On sequence and dependence: the Griesbach hypothesis". → W.R. Farmer 1978a, Frye 1978

1978c Source Criticism of the Gospel of Luke. — TALBERT, C.H. (ed.), *Perspectives on Luke-Acts*, Edinburgh: Clark, 1978, 24-39.

1984 *The New Testament and Early Christianity*. New York - London: Macmillan, 1984, XV-458 p. Esp. 162-170. → 1973

1985 The Two-Source Hypothesis: A Critical Appraisal. — BELLINZONI, A.J., Jr., et al. (eds.), *The Two-Source Hypothesis*, 1985, 437-452. Esp. 439-444: "The problem of order"; 444-452: "The problem of composition".

1992 Torah and Prophets in Luke-Acts: Temporary or Permanent? — *SBL 1992 Seminar Papers*, 539-548. Esp. 539-541 [Q 16,16].

# U

**UCHIDA, Kazuhiko**

1981 *The Study of the Synoptic Problem in the Twentieth Century: A Critical Assessment.* Diss. Aberdeen, 1981, XIII-538 p. (I.H. Marshall). Esp. 179-293: "The relationship between Matthew and Luke" [Q; alternatives to Q]; 294-410: "Matthean priority" |Augustinian hypothesis; Griesbach; proto-Mt: Hunt; Parker; Vaganay]; 437-491: "Independence of the three gospels"; 506-511 [Lk/Mt].

**UKPONG, Justin S.**

1995a The Problem of the Gentile Mission in Matthew's Gospel. — *Vidyajyoti* 59 (1995) 437-448. [NTA 40, 809]

1995b Tribute to Caesar, Mark 12:13-17 (Matt 22:15-22; Luke 20:20-26). — *Bible Bhashyam* 21 (1995) 147-166. [NTA 40, 1485]

**ULEYN, Arnold**

1957 La doctrine morale de saint Jean Chrysostome dans le Commentaire sur saint Matthieu et ses affinités avec la diatribe. — *RevUnivOtt* 27 (1957) 5*-25*, 99*-140*.
*De zedeleer van Johannes Chrysostomos in zijn Mattheüscommentaar: hellenistische en kristelijke faktoren.* Diss. Leuven, 1956, XX-172 p. (A. Janssen).

**ULONSKA, Herbert**

1987 Glück den Unglücklichen. Zu den Makarismen des Neuen Testaments. — *EvErz* 39 (1987) 530-547. Esp. 534-542. [NTA 32, 859]

1995 *Streiten mit Jesus. Konfliktgeschichten in den Evangelien* (Biblisch-theologische Schwerpunkte, 11). Göttingen: Vandenhoeck & Ruprecht, 1995, 208 p. Esp. 18-25 [10,34-36]; 26-34 [11,2-6]; 35-47 [12,22-32]; 53-63 [12,1-8]; 63-71 [12,9-14]; 35-92 [9,14-17]; 92-101 [15,1-20]; 101-115 [22,34-40]; 116-121 [11,18-19]; 121-130 [9,9-13]; 140-149 [19,13-15]; 153-162 [9,1-8]; 162-171 [21,23-27].

**UMMEL, M.** → Baecher 1994

**UPRICHARD, R.E.H.**

1981 The Baptism of Jesus. — *IBS* 3 (1981) 187-202. [NTA 26, 493]

**UPTON, J.A.**

1982 The Potter's Field and the Death of Judas. — *Concordia Journal* (St. Louis, MO) 8 (1982) 213-219. [NTA 27, 523]

**URBAN, P. Linwood**

1986 *A Short History of Christian Thought.* New York – Oxford: Univerity Press, 1986; rev. and expanded ed., 1995, XVIII-461 p. Esp. 26-28 [Jesus in Q]; 31-34 [Jesus in Mt]; 212-228 [historical Jesus].

**URBANEK, Ferdinand**

1992 "Vater im Himmel" – das alte Vaterunser in sprachlicher Neuauflage. — *LingBib* 66 (1992) 39-54. [NTA 36, 1264]

**URBANELLI, Ortensio** → da Spinetoli

**URBÁN FERNANDEZ, Angel Custodio**

1977a & MATEOS, J. - ALEPUZ, M., *Estudios de Nuevo Testamento.* II: *Cuestiones de gramatica y lexico* (Institución San Jeronimo. Estudios y monografías, 2). Madrid: Cristiandad; Valencia: Institución S. Jeronimo, 1977, 150 p. → 1977b, Mateos 1977b-c

1977b  El doble aspecto estático-dinámico de la preposición ἐν en el NT. — *Ibid.*, 17-62. Esp.
19-22 [3,3]; 34-35 [21,9]; 54-56 [6,4.6.18]; 58 [10,27].

**URBANIAK, Katarzyna**
1984   & DOMASZEWICZ, L., Saidzka wersja Ewangelii Dziecięctwa (Wstęp, przekład z języka
koptyjskiego i komentarz). (La version saïdique de l'Évangile de l'enfance
[introduction, traduction de la langue copte et commentaire]) — *StudTheolVars* 22/2
(1984) 215-224. [NTA 30, 924]

**URICCHIO, Francesco**
1982   Francesco legge Matteo. Rilievi sull'uso di alcuni testi del primo Vangelo negli scritti
del santo. — *MiscFranc* 82 (1982) 326-416.

**URO, Risto**
1987   *Sheep Among the Wolves. A Study on the Mission Instructions of Q* (Annales Academiae
Scientiarum Fennicae. Dissertationes Humanarum Litterarum, 47). Helsinki: Suomalainen Tiedeakatemia, 1987, VIII-271 p. Esp. 25-116: "The redactions of the mission instructions";
117-244: "The settings of the mission instructions". — Diss. Helsinki, 1987 (H. Räisänen). → Sanz Valdivieso
1990, Tashjian 1988
       D.R. CATCHPOLE, *JTS* 40 (1989) 185-187; H. FLEDDERMANN, *CBQ* 51 (1989) 757-759; A. FUCHS,
       *SNTU* 14 (1989) 241-244; G. HAUFE, *TLZ* 114 (1989) 890; J.S. KLOPPENBORG, *JBL* 108 (1989) 337-
       339; R. PESCH, *TRev* 86 (1990) 374; C.M. TUCKETT, *JSNT* 35 (1989) 121.

1990a  *Neither Here Nor There. Lk 17:20-21 and Related Sayings in Thomas, Mark and Q*
(Occasional Papers, 20). Claremont, CA: The Institute for Antiquity and Christianity,
1990.

1990b  Prophetic Writing or Wisdom Collection? New Questions in Q Research. [Finnish] —
*TAik* 95 (1990) 121-125.

1993   "Secondary Orality" in the Gospel of Thomas? Logion 14 as a Test Case. — *Forum* 9
(1993) 305-329. Esp. 316-324: "Logion 14 and its synoptic parallels" [15,11; Q 10,8-9]. [NTA 41, 1400]

1995   John the Baptist and the Jesus Movement: What Does Q Tell Us? — PIPER, R.A. (ed.),
*The Gospel Behind the Gospels*, 1995, 231-257. Esp. 232-233: "The consensus"; 234-239: "The
text of Q 3"; 239-243: "The function of John's preaching in Q"; 243-247: "The collection of Q 3: prehistory
and relation to Mark"; 247-252: "The saying on two baptisms"; 252-255: "John the baptist and the Q
people".

**URREY, T.C.**
1962   The Background of Matthew. — *SWJT* 5 (1962) 7-16 of 17-28.

**UTH, D.F.**
1991   *An Eschatological Interpretation of the Synoptic Miracles in the Mission and Message
of Jesus.* Diss. Southwestern Baptist Theol. Sem., Fort Worth, TX, 1991, 252 p. —
*DissAbstr* 52 (1991-92) 1374-1375.

# V

**VAAGE, Leif Eric**

1984 Q 4. — *SBL 1984 Seminar Papers*, 347-373.

1987 *Q: The Ethos and Ethics of an Itinerant Intelligence*. Diss. Graduate School, Claremont, CA, 1987, XIX-596 p. (J.M. Robinson). Esp. 1-71: "The history of scholarship"; 72-300: "The 'mission' instructions" [Q 10,2-16]; 301-357: "Greco-Roman cynicism and the persons whom Q represents"; 402-430: "'Love your enemies'"; 431-492: "The kingdom of God in Q"; 500-530: "Q and early christian prophecy"; 531-551: "The reconstruction of Q"; 552-571: "Matt 11:8/Luke 7:25"; 572-581: "'Love your enemies' in Matthew and Luke". — *DissAbstr* 48 (1987-88) 152-153. → Tashjian 1988

1988 The Woes in Q (and Matthew and Luke): Deciphering the Rhetoric of Criticism. — *SBL 1988 Seminar Papers*, 582-607. Esp. 584-602 [Q 11,39-41.42.44.46.47-48.52.49-51]; 602-604 [23,1-39].

1989a Composite Texts and Oral Myths: The Case of the "Sermon" (6:20b-49). — *SBL 1989 Seminar Papers*, 424-439.
Composite Texts and Oral Mythology. The Case of the "Sermon" in Q (6:20-49). — KLOPPENBORG, J.S. (ed.), *Conflict and Invention*, 1995, 75-97. Esp. 77-80: "Documentary evidence"; 80-86: "Composition analysis"; 86-90: "Independent integrity or integral independence?"; 90-92: "Perhaps an 'oral' composition?" (revised).

1989b Q¹ and the Historical Jesus. Some Peculiar Sayings (7:33-34; 9:57-58,59-60; 14:26-27). — *Forum* 5/2 (1989) 159-176. Esp. 163-166 [Q 7,33-34]; 166-171 [Q 9,57-60]; 171-173 [Q 14,26-27]. [NTA 34, 165]

1992a Monarchy, Community, Anarchy: The Kingdom of God in Paul and Q. — *TorontoJT* 8 (1992) 52-69. Esp. 60-67: "The kingdom of God in Q" [Q 6,20  10,9; 11,2.20; 12,31; 13,18-21]. [NTA 37, 282]

1992b The Son of Man Sayings in Q: Stratigraphical Location and Significance. — *Semeia* 55 (1992) 103-129. Esp. 107-109 [Q 6,22-23]; 109-113 [Q 7,33-34]; 114-115 [Q 9,57-58]; 115-117 [Q 11,30]; 117-118 [Q 12,8-9.10]; 118-120 [Q 12,39-40]; 120-121 [Q 17,23-24.26-28]. [NTA 36, 1248] → Tuckett 1992a

1992c → Kloppenborg 1992a

1994 *Galilean Upstarts. Jesus' First Followers According to Q*. Valley Forge, PA: Trinity Press International, 1994, XV-239 p. Esp. 1-15: "Social identity, historiography, Q, and cynicism"; 16-39 [Q 10,3-6.9-11.16]; 40-54 [Q 6,27-35]; 55-65 [Q 6,20; 10,9; 11,2.20; 12,31; 13,18-19.20-21]; 66-86 [Q 11,39-48.52]; 87-102 [Q 7,24-26.28.33-34; 9,57-60; 14,26-27]; 103-106: "A cynic Q"; 107-120: "The formative stratum of Q" [Q 7,24-26.28.33-34; 10,2.7; 11,14-52; 13,18-21]; 121-136: "The text of Q: some critical problems" [Q 6,27-35; 10,7-8; 10,16; 11,39-41.42.43]; 137-192: "Notes". [NTA 39, p. 147] → Kloppenborg 1987a
H.A. BREHM, *SWJT* 38 (1995) 54; A. DENAUX, *JBL* 115 (1996) 136-138; W. KLASSEN, *RB* 102 (1995) 425-428.

1995a More Than a Prophet, and Demon-Possessed. Q and the "Historical" John. — KLOPPENBORG, J.S. (ed.), *Conflict and Invention*, 1995, 181-202. Esp. 186-188 [Q 3,7-9.16-17]; 189-193 [Q 7,18-35].

1995b Q and Cynicism: On Comparison and Social Identity. — PIPER, R.A. (ed.), *The Gospel Behind the Gospels*, 1995, 199-229. Esp. 200-206: "A Cynic Q?"; 206-227: "A Cynic Q!" [Q 6,20-21.27-35; 10,2-16; 11,2-4.14-20.39-52; 12,22-31; 13,18-21].

**VACCARI, Alberto**

1952 La parabole du festin de noces. Notes d'exégèse (*Matthieu*, XXII,1-14). — *RSR* 39 (1951-52) 138-145.

1955a  La clausola sul divorzio in Matteo 5,32; 19,9. — *RivBib* 3 (1955) 97-119.
A cláusula sobre o divórcio en Mt 5,32 et 19,9. — *RevistCuBíb* 1 (1956) 1-16.

1955b  De matrimonio et divortio apud Matthaeum. — *Bib* 36 (1955) 149-151. → Leeming 1956,
Vawter 1954

1955c  'Ενταφιάζειν, ἐνταφιασμός in N.T. [26,12] — *Bib* 36 (1955) 559-561.

1956  Il divorzio nei vangeli. — *CC* 107/2 (1956) 350-359, 475-484. Esp. 351-355 [19,3-9]; 357-
359.475-484 [5,31-32; 19,9].
Divorce in the Gospels. — *TDig* 5 (1957) 31-33.
O divórcio nos evangelhos. — *RevistCuBíb* 7 (1963) 60-79. [NTA 9, 919]

1962  Indissolubilità del matrimonio nella Bibbia. — *CC* 113/2 (1962) 259-262. [NTA 7, 128]
→ Alberti 1962

1963  Gesù alla svolta della sua predicazione in Galilea. — *Divinitas* 7 (1963) 223-235. Esp.
226-231 [12,40]. [NTA 8, 943]

**VADAKUMPADAN, Sebastian**

1976  *The Parousia Discourse Mt 24–25: Tradition and Redaction*. Diss. Pont. Inst. Biblicum,
Roma, 1976, VII-342, XXVI-100 p. (L. Sabourin).

1980  The Eschatological Perspective in the Gospel of Matthew. — *Bible Bhashyam* 6 (1980)
213-228. [NTA 25, 460]

1982  Eschatology of the New Testament (Synoptic Gospels). — *Bible Bhashyam* 8 (1982)
138-148. [NTA 27, 902]

**VAGANAY, Léon**

1951  L'absence du Sermon sur la montagne chez Marc. Essai de critique littéraire. — *RB* 58
(1951) 5-46. Esp. 6-12: "L'introduction historique au Sermon sur la montagne chez les trois Synoptiques";
24-32: "La disparition des heurts du texte de Mc. chez Mt.-Lc.". → Vielhauer 1955

1952  La question synoptique. — *ETL* 28 (1952) 238-256. Esp. 242-247: "L'évangile araméen de
l'apôtre Matthieu et sa traduction grecque (M, Mg)"; 247-251: "Seconde source synoptique complémentaire
du Matthieu araméen (S) et traduite en grec (Sg)"; 253-254: "L'évangile grec canonique de Matthieu (Mt.)".

1953  Le schématisme du discours communautaire à la lumière de la critique des sources. —
*RB* 60 (1953) 203-244. Esp. 205-212 [18,1]; 215 [23,11]; 216-218 [18,2-3]; 218-220 [18,5]; 223-225
[10,42]; 225-228 [18,10.14]; 228-231 [18,6]; 231-234 [18,8]; 235-237 [18,9]; 238-241 [5,13]; = ID., *Le
problème synoptique*, 1954, 361-404 (Excursus IV). Esp. 363-370; 373-374; 375-377; 377-379;
382-384; 384-387; 387-390; 390-393; 395-397; 397-401.

1954a  *Le problème synoptique. Une hypothèse de travail* (Bibliothèque de théologie, III/1).
Paris–Tournai: Desclée, 1954, XXIII-474 p. Esp. 34-41: "La tradition orale (O)"; 42-50: "Essais
évangéliques écrits (E)"; 51-100: "Matthieu araméen (M) traduit en grec (Mg)"; 101-151: "Seconde source
synoptique supplémentaire du Matthieu araméen (S.Sg)"; 196-244: "Matthieu grec canonique (Mt.); 281-301:
"Rapports entre Mt. et Lc."; 315-328: "Principales difficultés de la critique littéraire synoptique"; 329-343:
"Témoignages indirects de l'ancienne littérature chrétienne sur Mg et Sg"; 344-360: "Les traits rédactionnels
de Marc dans la première péricope synoptique"; 361-404: "Le schématisme du discours communautaire" [=
1953]; 405-425: "Les accords négatifs de Mt.-Lc. contre Mc. dans l'épisode de l'enfant épileptique"; 426-
442: "L'étude d'un doublet dans la parabole de la lampe" [5,15/Q 11,33]. → E.P. Blair 1959, Botte 1954,
Butler 1955a-b, Cerfaux 1954b, Leal 1956, Levie 1954, 1955, Maio 1959, Mariani 1960, McCool 1956,
Perrot 1959, Ponthot 1958, Sabbe 1954a, J. Schmid 1961, Vielhauer 1955, Weijers 1956
*CC* 107/1 (1956) 210-211; M.T. BARTON, *CleR* 40 (1955) 481-482; M.-É. BOISMARD, *RB* 61 (1954)
453-454; *LumièreV* 19 (1955) 120-121; B. BRINKMANN, *Scholastik* 30 (1955) 257-260; L.G. DA
FONSECA, *Bib* 37 (1956) 384-390; P.E. DAVIES, *JBL* 75 (1956) 66-68; J. DELORME, *AmiCler* 66 (1956)
349-360; S. DEL PÁRAMO, *SalTer* 45 (1957) 53-54; X. DUCROS, *BullLitEccl* 57 (1956) 31-35; H.
DUESBERG, *RBén* 65 (1955) 145; A.M. FARRER, *JTS* 7 (1956) 105-107; P. GAECHTER, *ZKT* 77 (1955)
361-362; A. GELIN, *AmiCler* 64 (1954) 373-375; J. GIBLET, *CollMech* 41 (1956) 409-411; S. GRZYBEK,
*RuBi* 11 (1958) 72-76; J. HÉRING, *RHPR* 35 (1955) 244-245; A. JONES, *Scripture* 7 (1955) 59-61; X.
LÉON-DUFOUR, *RSR* 42 (1954) 557-572; B. MARIANI, *Ant* 31 (1956) 116-118; J.L. MCKENZIE, *TS* 15

(1954) 639-644; C. PERROT, *Cahiers sioniens* (Paris) 9 (1955) 127-132; F. PUZO, *Greg* 37 (1956) 298-300; K.H. SCHELKLE, *TQ* 134 (1954) 479-480; J. SCHMID, *TRev* 52 (1956) 56-62; C. SPICQ, *FZPT* 2 (1955) 227; D.M. STANLEY, *CBQ* 17 (1955) 647-655; L. TURRADO, *Salmanticensis* 2 (1955) 193-195; A. VIARD, *RSPT* 39 (1955) 276-278; M.R. WEIJERS, *VSp* 92 (1955) 320-323; C.S.C. WILLIAMS, *Theology* 57 (1954) 430-431.

1954b Matthieu (évangile selon saint). — *DBS* 5/27 (1954) 940-956.

1955a Autour de la question synoptique. — *ETL* 31 (1955) 343-356. Esp. 344-347: "L'évangile araméen de l'apôtre Matthieu"; 350-351 [18,10.14]; 352-356: "Les cinq ivrets du premier évangile". [NTA 1, 44] → Levie 1954, 1955

1955b Existe-t-il chez Marc quelques traces du Sermon sur la montagne? — *NTS* 1 (1954-55) 192-200.

### VALAVANOLICKAL, Kuriakose A.

1996 *The Use of the Gospel Parables in the Writings of Aphrahat and Ephrem* (Studies in Religion and History of Early Christianity, 2). Frankfurt/M: Lang, 1996, XVII-380 p. Esp. 31-38 [7,24-27]; 39-40 [11,16-19]; 40-42 [12,43-45]; 43-58 [13,3-8]; 59-72 [13,24-30]; 72-77 [13,31-32]; 77-88 [13,33]; 88-104 [13,44-50]; 104-113 [18,12-14]; 113-118 [18,23-35]; 118-131 [20,1-16]; 132-133 [21,28-32]; 133-148 [21,33-44]; 148-168 [22,1-14]; 169-170 [24,32-33]; 170-171 [24,43-44]; 172-177 [24,45-51]; 177-198 [25,1-13]; 198-218 [25,14-30]; 218-235 [25,31-46]. — Diss. Oxford, 1995 (S.P. Brock).

### VALENCEJA, J.J.

1973 Los evangelios de la infancia ¿descripción histórica o expresión de fe? — *SalT* 61 (1973) 943-947.

### VALENTIN, Patrick

1971 Les comparutions de Jésus devant le Sanhédrin. — *RSR* 59 (1971) 230-236. [26,57/Jn]. [NTA 16, 123]

### VALENTINI, A.

1977 La Madre di Gesù nel Vangelo dell'infanzia di Matteo. — *Riparazione Mariana* (Rovigo) 62 (1977) 47-53.

### VALGIGLIO, Ernesto

1985 *Le antiche versioni latine del Nuovo Testamento. Fedeltà e aspetti grammaticali* (Associazione di studi tardoantichi). Napoli: d'Auria, 1985, 337 p. Esp. 17-23 [Afra: 5,10.35; 6,19.20.27; 7,2; 10,5; 12,17; 14,9.12; 15,18.22; 19,5]; 43 [Itala: 27,31]; 51-53 [Vulgata: 24,41; 25,30.46; 27,27.65]; 87 [Afra-Vulgata: 20,19]; 101-106 [Itala-Vulgata: 6,13; 9,9.23; 10,12; 12,25; 13,4.36; 18,9; 19,22.26.28; 24,9]; 121-126.161-162 [Afra-Itala-Vulgata: 2,4; 8,26; 6,1.12; 13,32; 15,22.23; 19,27; 20,18; 24,26.38]; 193-195 [no parr.: 9,32; 10,9; 16,5]; 203-204 [special case: 1,20]; 219-318: "Grammatica".

### VALLA, H.J.

1962 San Mateo veintitrés, veintitrés. [23,23] — *Didascalia* 16 (1962) 65-70. [NTA 7, 143]

### VALLAURI, Emiliano

1972 Lo stato religioso secondo il N.T. Per una teologia biblica dei tre voti. — *Laur* 13 (1972) 265-293. Esp. 274-279 [19,16-22]; 286-287.

1973 L'esegesi moderna di fronte alla verginità di Maria. — *Laur* 14 (1973) 445-480. Esp. 447-454: "Matteo e la concezione verginale di Gesù". [NTA 18, 850] A exegese moderna diante da virgindade de Maria. — *REB* 34 (1974) 375-399. [NTA 19, 527]

1976 Le clausole matteane sul divorzio. Tendenze esegetiche recenti. — *Laur* 17 (1976) 82-112. Esp. 84-88: "Le soluzioni classiche"; 88-93: "L'ipotesi rabbinica"; 94-99: "Le ipotesi rinnovate". [NTA 21, 77]

1978 Natus in Bethlehem. — *Laur* 19 (1978) 413-441. Esp. 420 [1,13]; 429-435 [Son of David]. [NTA 23, 424]
*TDig* 28 (1980) 39-42.

1980 I miracoli di Gesù nel Vangelo. — *Laur* 21 (1980) 70-93. Esp. 79-80; 88-90; 92. [NTA 25, 47]

1985 ...Alzati gli occhi... (Lc. 6,20; Giov. 6,5). — *BibOr* 27 (1985) 163-169. [NTA 30, 628]

1994 Una controversia: il digiuno e lo sposa (Mc 2,18-22; Mt 9,14-17; Lc 5,33-39). — LÀCONI, M. (ed.), *Vangeli sinottici*, 1994, 227-242. Esp. 230-232, 241.

1995 La moglie di Pilato. [27,19] — VOLPI, I. (ed.), *In Spiritu e veritate. Miscellanea di studi offerti al P. Anselmo Mattioli in occasione del suo 81° anno di età*, Roma: Conferenza italiana ministri provinciali cappuccini, 1995, 157-188.

### VAN AARDE, Andries Gideon

1980 "Betekenis" en "gebruik" in die makarisme-reeks (Matt. 5:3-10). ["Meaning" and "use" of the macarisms (Mt 5,3-10)] — *HervTS* 36 (1980) 1-28. → 1982b

1982a Matthew's Portrayal of the Disciples and the Structure of Matthew 13:53–17:27. — *Neotestamentica* 16 (1982) 21-34 (addendum, 1-17).

1982b 'n Onderzoek na die Nuwe-Testamentiese makarisme en makarismereeks as *Gattung*. [An examination of the genre of macarism] — *HervTS* 38 (1982) 36-52. → 1980

1983 *God met ons – die teologiese perspektief van die Matteusevangelie* [God-With-Us. The Dominant Perspective of Matthew's Theology]. Diss. Pretoria, 1983 (G.M.M. Pelser – W.L. Vorster). — *DissAbstr* 45 (1984-85) 1446-1447; *SBT* 14 (1986) 86-87. → 1994a
   J.H. BARKHUIZEN, *HervTS* 40 (1984) 145-147.

1984 Verlede en hede op die gebied van die Matteusnavorsing: 'n oorsig van die verskillende interpretasiemodelle (Past and present in Matthean research: A review of the various interpretation models). — *Scriptura* 11 (1984) 1-49. [NTA 29, 515]

1985 Vertellersperspektief en die "temporele" funksie van die Ou Testament in die Matteusevangelie. [The perspective of the narrator and the "temporal" function of the Old Testament in the gospel of Matthew] — *HervTS* 41 (1985) 272-289.

1986a Plot as Mediated through Point of View. Mt 22:1-14 – A Case Study. — PETZER, J.H. — HARTIN, P.J. (eds.), *A South African Perspective on the New Testament*. FS B.M. Metzger, 1986, 62-75. → 1994a

1986b Die wonderbaarlike vermeerdering van brood (Matt 14:13-21 en par): Historiese kritiek in perspektief. [The miraculous feeding of bread. Historical criticism in perspective] — *HervTS* 42 (1986) 229-256. Esp. 238-248 [tradition- and form-criticism]; 248-254 [redaction criticism]. → 1994a

1986c Die *Wirkungsgeschichte* van Matteus 28:16-20 in die volkskerklike apostolaat. [The reception of Mt 28,16-20] — *HervTS* 42 (1986) 77-93.

1987 Immanuel as die geïnkarneerde tora: Funksionele Jesusbenaminge in die Matteusevangelie as vertelling (Emmanuel as the Torah Incarnate: The names of Jesus in Matthew's story). — *HervTS* 43 (1987) 242-277. [NTA 34, 112]

1989a Ἡγέρθη ἀπὸ τῶν νεκρῶν (Mt 28:7): A Textual Evidence on the Separation of Judaism and Christianity. — *Neotestamentica* 23 (1989) 219-233. Esp. 220-222.230 [28,7]; 225-227 [27,64]; 227-229 [27,52-53]. [NTA 34, 1144]; = ID., *God-With-Us*, 1994, 248-260.

1989b Resonance and Reception. Interpreting Mt 17:24-27 in Context. — *Scriptura* 29 (1989) 1-12. [NTA 34, 128]

1992 The *Evangelium Infantium*, the Abandonment of Children, and the Infancy Narrative in Matthew 1 and 2 from a Social Scientific Perspective. — *SBL 1992 Seminar Papers*, 435-453. Esp. 445-446: "The Matthean infancy narrative"; 446-448: "Remarks about Jesus in Matthew's story". → 1994a

1993   A Silver Coin in the Mouth of a Fish (Matthew 17:24-27) - A Miracle of Nature, Ecology, Economy and the Politics of Holiness. — *Neotestamentica* 27 (1993) 1-25. Esp. 14-20: "Matthew 17:24-27 in context". [NTA 38, 768] → 1994a

1994a   *God-With-Us. The Dominant Perspective in Matthew's Story and Other Essays* (HervTS, Supplementum 5). Pretoria: Nederduitsch Hervormde Kerk van Afrika, 1994, XVIII-326 p. [NTA 39, p. 148] → 1983, 1986a-b, 1989a, 1992, 1993

     M.E. DEAN, *JBL* 115 (1996) 143-145; S.A. HUNT, *JSNT* 59 (1995) 114; I.H. JONES, *ExpT* 106 (1994-95) 211-212.

1994b   → Nel 1994

1995a   The "Third Quest" for the Historical Jesus - Where Should It Begin: With Jesus' Relationship to the Baptiser, or with the Nativity Traditions? — *Neotestamentica* 29 (1995) 325-356. Esp. 341-344; 346-348. [NTA 41, 161]

1995b   → Nel 1995

**VAN AMERSFOORT, Jacobus**

1984a   *Het Evangelie van Thomas en de Pseudo-Clementinen.* Utrecht: Rijksuniversiteit, 1984, 319 p. Esp. 69-82 [13,3-9/Th 9]; 88-92 [13,11/Th 62]; 98-100 [5,3/Th 54]; 106-112 [5,11/Th 69a], 114-121 [5,15/Th 33b]; 124-128 [10,34/Th 16a]; 134-137 [10,35/Th 16b]; 144-151 [12,31/Th 44]; 152-165 [22,1-14/Th 64]; 171-176 [23,13/Th 39]; 180-185 [5,14/Th 32]; 187-193 [7,6/Th 93]; 196-200 [13,45-46/Th 76a]; 203-207 [15,13/Th 40]. — Diss. Utrecht, 1984 (G. Quispel).

1984b   Some Influences of the Diatessaron of Tatian on the Gospel Text of Hilary of Poitiers. [5,45; 9,16; 10,35] — *Studia Patristica* 15 (1984) 200-205.

**VAN BANNING, Jozef**

1982a   The Critical Edition of the *Opus Imperfectum in Matthaeum*, an Arian Source. — *Studia Patristica* 17 (1982) 382-387.

1982b   Saint Thomas et l'*Opus Imperfectum in Matthaeum.* — *Atti dell'VIII Congresso tomistico internazionale 8* (Studi tomistici, 17), Roma: Pont. Acad. di S. Tomasso, 1982, 73-85.

1988   *Opus imperfectum in Matthaeum, Praefatio* (CCL, 87B). Turnhout: Brepols, 1988, CCCLXVII p. — Diss. Oxford, 1982-83 (B. Smalley).

     J. DOIGNON, *RHPR* 70 (1990) 355; Y.-M. DUVAL, *RSR* 80 (1992) 274; R. GRYSON, *RHE* 86 (1991) 347-348.

1989   The Edition of the Arian *Opus Imperfectum in Matthaeum.* Review and Prospects. — *Studia Patristica* 20 (1989) 70-75.

1990   Il Padre Nostro nell'*Opus Imperfectum in Matthaeum.* — *Greg* 71 (1990) 293-313 (French summary, 313).

1993   *"Buchstabe und Geist". Zur Rezeption der Exegese des* Opus Imperfectum in Matthaeum *im Mittelalter, Studien über Claudius von Turin, Hrabanus Maurus, Paschasius Radbertus, die "Glossa Ordinaria", Hugo von St. Cher, Meister Eckhart und Guido Terreni von Perpignan.* Diss. Innsbruck, 1993 (J.B. Bauer).

1995a   & MALI, F., Opus imperfectum in Matthaeum. — *TRE* 25 (1995) 304-307.

1995b   Systematische Überlegungen zur allegorischen Schriftauslegung. — *ZKT* 117 (1995) 265-295, 416-446. Esp. 432-440 [Opus impf. in Mt]. [NTA 40, 710]

**VAN BAVEL, Tarsicius**

1959   *Inferas-inducas.* À propos de Mtth. 6,13 dans les œuvres de saint Augustin. — *RBén* 69 (1959) 348-351.

**VAN BEECK, Frans Jozef**

1994   The Quest of the Historical Jesus. Origins, Achievements, and the Specter of

Diminishing Returns. — CARLSON, J. - LUDWIG, R.A. (eds.), *Jesus and Faith*, 1994, 83-99. Esp. 89-91 [Q].

**VAN BELLE, Gilbert**
→ Neirynck 1977a, 1979a

1988 *Johannine Bibliography 1966-1985. A Cumulative Bibliography on the Fourth Gospel* (BETL, 82). Leuven: University Press / Peeters; (COBRA, 1), Brussel: Koninklijke Academie voor Wetenschappen, Letteren en Schone Kunsten van België, 1988, XVII-563 p. Esp. 143: "The gospel of Matthew".

**VANBERGEN, Piet**
1960a L'évangile du dimanche de la Septuagésime. [20,1-16] — *LumièreV* 47 (1960) 1-10.

1960b La parabole des invités qui se dérobent. — *LumièreV* 49 (1960) 1-9. Esp. 1-5 [22,1-14]; 5-8 [Q 14,16-24]. [NTA 5, 722]

1960c L'impôt dû à César. [22,15-22] — *LumièreV* 50 (1960) 12-18. [NTA 5, 724]

**VAN BOHEMEN, Nicolaas**
1957 L'institution des Douze. Contribution à l'étude des relations entre l'évangile de Matthieu et celui de Marc. — HEUSCHEN, J. (ed.), *La formation des évangiles*, 1957, 116-151. Esp. 118-122: "Vocation et mission des apôtres dans l'évangile selon Matthieu"; 123-128 [4,25-5,1; 10,1-8/Mk 3,7-8.13-19]; 128-140: "La question de la dépendance littéraire et de la priorité". *De prioriteit van Mattheus in de episodes van de roeping en de zending der twaalf.* Diss. Leuven, 1949 (L. Cerfaux). — F. NEIRYNCK, *ETL* 71 (1995) 524-526.

1961 Gegevens over Maria in het Mattheüs-evangelie. Toegelicht vanuit hun christologische context. — *De Mariapassages uit het Matthaüsevangelie* (Verslagboek der achttiende Mariale Dagen), Tongerlo: Norbertijnerabdij, 1961, 71-92; = *De Standaard van Maria* 38 (1962) 137-146, 203-211.

**VAN BOXEL, Piet W.**
1984 Het rabbijnse schoolgesprek in de bergrede. — *Schrift* 93 (1984) 99-104.

1988a Man's Behaviour and God's Justice in Early Jewish Tradition. Some Observations. — VAN DEN BROEK, R. - BAARDA, T. - MANSFELD, J. (eds.), *Knowledge of God in the Graeco-Roman World* (Études préliminaires aux religions orientales dans l'Empire romaine, 112), Leiden: Brill, 1988, 143-159. Esp. 157-159 [5,43-48].

1988b "You have heard that it was said". — *Bijdragen* 49 (1988) 362-377. Esp. 373-375: "The tradition in Matthew". [NTA 33, 601]

1994 Huilen over Jeruzalem. Jeremia en de Klaagliederen in het Nieuwe Testament en de rabbijnse traditie. — *Ter Herkenning* (Breda) 22 (1994) 2-15. Esp. 3-5 [Jeremiah].

1995 Isaiah 29:13 in the New Testament and Early Rabbinic Judaism. [15,1-9] — VAN DER HORST, P.W. (ed.), *Aspects of Religious Contact and Conflict in the Ancient World* (Utrechtse Theologische Reeks, 31), Utrecht: Faculteit der Godgeleerdheid, 1995, 81-90.

**VAN BRUGGEN, Jakob**
1978 The Year of the Death of Herod the Great (Τελευτήσαντος δὲ τοῦ Ἡρῴδου..., Mt ii 19). — BAARDA, T. - KLIJN, A.F.J. - VAN UNNIK, W.C. (eds.), *Miscellanea Neotestamentica* (SupplNT, 48), Leiden: Brill, 1978, II, 1-15.

1979 *Abba, Vader!* Tekst en toonhoogte van het Onze Vader. — TRIMP, C. (ed.), *De biddende Kerk*, Groningen: De Vuurbaak, 1979, 9-42. → 1982; → Bandstra 1981, 1982

1982 The Lord's Prayer and Textual Criticism. — *CalvTJ* 17 (1982) 78-87. [NTA 26, 842] → 1979; → Bandstra 1981, 1982

1990 *Matteüs. Het evangelie voor Israël* (Commentaar op het Nieuwe Testament. Derde serie: Afdeling Evangeliën). Kampen: Kok, 1990, 510 p. Esp. 9-23 [introduction]; 24-478 [commentary].

> P. BEENTJES, *Streven* 59 (1991-92) 175-176; G. DE RU, *KerkT* 42 (1991) 257-258; H. WELZEN, *NTT* 46 (1992) 236-237.

**VAN CAMP, Jean**

1951 La primauté de saint Pierre dans le contexte évangélique. — *NRT* 73 (1951) 405-408.

**VAN CANGH, Jean-Marie**

1970 Le Fils de l'homme dans la tradition synoptique. — *RTL* 1 (1970) 411-419. [NTA 15, 835] → Tödt 1959

1973 Fondement évangélique de la vie religieuse. — *NRT* 95 (1973) 635-647. Esp. 639-641 [19,10-12]. [NTA 19, 307]

> Evangelische grondslag voor het religieuze leven. — *Tijdschrift voor Geestelijk Leven* 29 (1973) 81-99. Esp. 87-89.

1975a *La multiplication des pains et l'Eucharistie* (LD, 86). Paris: Cerf, 1975, 197 p. Esp. 143-148 [14,13-21; 15,29-30]. — Diss. Louvain-la-Neuve, 1974 (J. Giblet).

1975b La Bible de Matthieu: les citations d'accomplissement. — *RTL* 6 (1975) 205-211. [NTA 20, 83]

1980 & VAN ESBROECK, M., La primauté de Pierre (Mt 16,16-19) et son contexte judaïque. — *RTL* 11 (1980) 310-324. Esp. 314-317; 320-324: "L'interprétation de Mt 16,17-19"; 310-311 [17,1]. [NTA 25, 428]

1982 "Par l'esprit de Dieu – par le doigt de Dieu". Mt 12,28 par. Lc 11,20. — DELOBEL, J. (ed.), *Logia*, 1982, 337-342.

1993 Évolution du motif de la foi dans les miracles synoptiques, johanniques et apocryphes. — FOCANT, C. (ed.), *The Synoptic Gospels*, 1993, 566-578. Esp. 566-571: "Foi et miracle synoptique" [9,22; 17,20].

**VAN DAALEN, David H.**

1993 Sermon on the Mount. — METZGER, B.M. – COOGAN, M.D. (eds.), *The Oxford Companion to the Bible*, 1993, 687-689.

**VANDENBERGHE, Bruno H.**

1961 (trans.), *Joannes Chrysostomus. Homélies sur saint Matthieu: l'Évangile de l'enfance*. Namur: Éd. du soleil levant, 1961, 185 p.

**VAN DEN BRANDEN, Albert**

1992 Mt. 19,1-12 dans une perspective historique. — *BibOr* 34 (1992) 65-82. [NTA 37, 731]

**VAN DEN BRINK, Gijsbert**

1989 → Bette 1989

1990* et al. (eds.), *Verkenningen in de evangeliën* (Theologische Verkenningen. Bijbel en exegese, 5). Kampen: Kok; Hilversum: Evangelische Omroep, 1990, 192 p. → M.J. Paul, Spaans-Moolenaar, G. van den Brink 1990a-b, van der Maas

1990a De datering van het evangelie naar Matteüs. — *Ibid.*, 53-59.

1990b Redacteur of evangelist? De literaire onafhankelijkheid van de synoptische evangeliën. — *Ibid.*, 77-85.

1995 *Van koinè tot canon. De overlevering van het Griekse Nieuwe Testament*. Zoetermeer: Boekencentrum, 1995, 135 p. Esp. 127-128 [22,35 textcritical].

**VAN DEN BRINK, Herman**

1995 *Bijbels Recht. Oefeningen in Exegese*. Kampen: Kok, 1995, 368 p. Esp. 113-119 [5,31-32]; 309-315 [2,13-15].

**VAN DEN BRINK, J.**

1988   *De Bergrede.* Gorinchem: Kracht van Omhoog, 1988, 301 p.

**VAN DEN BROEK, Roelof**

1974   A Latin Diatessaron in the 'Vita Beate Virginis Marie et Salvatoris Rhythmica'. — *NTS* 21 (1974-75) 109-132. Esp. 112-113 [1,19]; 113-115 [2,9.11]; 119-120 [27,3]; 126-127 [3,16]; 130-132. [NTA 19, 478] → Birdsall 1976

**VAN DEN BUSSCHE, Henri**

1959   Het Onze Vader. — *CollBrugGand* 5 (1959) 289-335, 467-495. [NTA 4, 650]
       *Het Onze Vader.* Gent: "Die Grael", 1959, 78 p.; (Kernen en Facetten, 2), Tielt – Den Haag: Lannoo, ²1963, 96 p.
       *Le "Notre Père"* (Les Études religieuses, 747). Bruxelles: La Pensée Catholique; Paris: Office général du livre, 1960, 108 p.
       *Understanding the Lord's Prayer*, trans. C. Schaldenbrand. New York: Sheed & Ward, 1963, 144 p.; (Stagbooks), London: Sheed & Ward, 1964.
       *Das Vaterunser*, trans. S. Loersch. Mainz: Matthias-Grünewald, 1963, 127 p.
       *El Padrenuesto*, trans. O. García de la Fuente. Bilbao: Desclée De Brouwer, 1963, 154 p.

1960   Donne-nous aujourd'hui notre pain quotidien. [6,11] — *BibVieChrét* 32 (1960) 42-46. [NTA 4, 652]

**VAN DEN ENDE, Anton**

1972   La Loi et les Prophètes. Mt 22,34-40. — *AssSeign* II/61 (1972) 18-27. [NTA 17, 521]

1981   Jezus: koning en mensenzoon. Notities vanuit het evangelie volgens Matteüs. — *Schrift* 73 (1981) 21-29.

**VAN DEN EYNDE, Damien**

1959   Autour des "Enarrationes in Evangelium S. Matthaei" attribuées à Geoffroi Babion. — *RTAM* 26 (1959) 50-84.

**VAN DER HOEVEN, A.**

1951   *De karakteristiek van de vier Evangeliën* (Bibliotheek van boeken bij de Bijbel). Baarn: Bosch en Keuning, 1951, 192 p. Esp. 74-92: "Mattheus, de architect onder de evangelisten"; 93-112: "Mattheus, de brugbouwer van het Oude naar het Nieuwe Testament".

**VAN DER HORST, Pieter Willem**

1973   Macrobius and the New Testament. A Contribution to the Corpus Hellenisticum. — *NT* 15 (1973) 220-232. Esp. 221-223. [NTA 18, 1097]; = ID. – MUSSIES, G., *Studies*, 1990, 36-48. Esp. 37-39.

1974   Musonius Rufus and the New Testament. A Contribution to the Corpus Hellenisticum. — *NT* 16 (1974) 306-315. Esp. 307. [NTA 19, 1149]; = ID. – MUSSIES, G., *Studies*, 1990, 13-22. Esp. 14.

1975   Hierocles the Stoic and the New Testament. A Contribution to the Corpus Hellenisticum. — *NT* 17 (1975) 156-160. Esp. 157. [NTA 20, 330]; = ID. – MUSSIES, G., *Studies*, 1990, 23-27. Esp. 24.

1978   Pseudo-Phocylides and the New Testament. — *ZNW* 69 (1978) 187-202. Esp. 195.202. [NTA 23, 1051]; = ID., *Essays on the Jewish World of Early Christianity* (NTOA, 14), Freiburg/Schw: Universitätsverlag; Göttingen: Vandenhoeck & Ruprecht, 1990, 19-34. Esp. 27-35.

1980   *Aelius Aristides and the New Testament* (Studia ad Corpus Hellenisticum Novi Testamenti, 6). Leiden: Brill, 1980, IX-115 p. Esp. 9-17.

1981   Cornutus and the New Testament. A Contribution to the Corpus Hellenisticum. — *NT* 23 (1981) 165-172. Esp. 167-168. [NTA 25, 1133]; = ID. – MUSSIES, G., *Studies*, 1990, 5-12. Esp. 7-8.

1983   Chariton and the New Testament. A Contribution to the Corpus Hellenisticum. — *NT* 25 (1983) 348-355. Esp. 349-350. [NTA 28, 804]; = ID. - MUSSIES, G., *Studies*, 1990, 28-35. Esp. 29-30.

1986   Once More: The Translation of οἱ δέ in Matthew 28.17. — *JSNT* 27 (1986) 27-30. [NTA 31, 127]; = ID. - MUSSIES, G., *Studies*, 1990, 96-99. → Grayston 1984, K.L. McKay 1985b, Neirynck 1987a

1990   & MUSSIES, G., *Studies on the Hellenistic Background of the New Testament* (Utrechtse Theologische Reeks, 10). Utrecht: Faculteit Godgeleerdheid, 1990, 242 p. → 1973, 1974, 1975, 1981, 1982, 1986, Mussies 1986, 1988a-b

1993   A Note on the Judas Curse in Early Christian Inscriptions. — *OCP* 59 (1993) 211-215. Esp. 211-212 [27,5]. [NTA 38, 596]; = ID., *Hellenism - Judaism - Christianity. Essays on Their Interaction* (Contributions to Biblical Exegesis and Theology, 8), Kampen: Kok Pharos, 1994, 146-150. Esp. 146-147. → 1994

1994   Het lot van Judas in vroegchristelijke grafinscripties. [27,3-10] — *KerkT* 45 (1994) 138-142. → 1993

**VAN DER KWAAK, Hans**

1966   Die Klage über Jerusalem (Matth. xxiii 37-39). — *NT* 8 (1966) 156-170. [NTA 11, 706]

1969   *Het proces van Jezus. Een vergelijkend onderzoek van de beschrijvingen der evangelisten* (Van Gorcum's Theologische Bibliotheek, 42). Assen: Van Gorcum, 1969, 298 p. Esp. 97-126: "Matteüs" [27,24-25].

**VAN DER LOOS, H.**

1965   *The Miracles of Jesus* (SupplNT, 9). Leiden: Brill, 1965, XV-749 p. Esp. 339-589: "Healing miracles" [8,1-4.5-13.14-15.28-34; 9,1-8.18-26.27-35; 12,9-14.22-25; 15,21-28; 17,14-21; 20,29-34]; 590-706: "Nature miracles" [8,23-27; 14,13-21.22-33; 15,29-39; 17,24-27; 21,18-22].

**VAN DER MAAS, S.P.**

1990   De strekking van het evangelie naar Matteüs. — VAN DEN BRINK, G., et al. (eds.), *Verkenningen in de evangeliën*, 1990, 9-15.

**VAN DER MERWE, M.A.V.**

1977   The Form and Message of Mt 2, Based on a Structural Analysis. — *Neotestamentica* 11 (1977) 10-15 (addendum, 3).

**VAN DER MINDE, Hans-Jürgen**

1995   Die Überquerung des Jordan oder die Rettung vor den Wassern: Jos. 3,1-17 und Mt. 14,22-33. — *IKZ/Communio* (Rodenkirchen) 85 (1995) 34-51. [NTA 40, 172]

**VAN DER PLOEG, Johannes**

1989   *In beeld en gelijkenis. Een verklaring van de beelden en gelijkenissen der vier evangeliën.* Venlo: van Spijk, 1989, 168 p. Esp. 21-90: "Mattheüs".
*Jésus nous parle. Les paraboles et les allégories des quatre évangiles.* Paris: Gabalda, 1994, 242 p.

**VAN DER VAART SMIT, H.W.**

1961   *Geboren zu Bethlehem: Weihnachten, wie es wirklich war.* Düsseldorf: Patmos, 1961, 184 p.; [2]1962; [3]1963. Esp. 37-84; 103-143; 161-175.
*Born in Bethlehem.* Baltimore, MD: Helicon, 1962, 148 p.
*Geboren te Bethlehem. Kerstmis zoals het werkelijk was.* Roermond–Maaseik: Romen, 1964, 215 p. Esp. 36-90; 115-167; 188-205.; & FERRARI D'OCCHIEPPO, K., Helmond: Helmond; Brugge: Orion, [2]1979, 167 p. Esp. 29-65; 82-128; 142-153.
*Né à Bethléem: l'histoire authentique de la nativité.* Mulhouse: Salvator, 1965, 188 p.

VAN DER VLIET, J.
1990  Spirit and Prophecy in the Epistola Iacobi Apocrypha (NHC I,2). — *VigChr* 44 (1990) 25-53. Esp. 37-43 [ComMt x,21-22].

VAN DER VOORT, A.J.
1952  The Originality of St Matthew. — *Scripture* 5 (1952) 72-76. → Butler 1951

VANDERVORST, Joseph
1953  Note sur Matthieu (II, 22, 23). — DíAZ, R.M. (ed.), *Miscellanea Biblica B. Ubach*, 1953, 329-331.

VAN DER WALT, Tjaart
1962  *Die Koninkryk van God – naby! Eksegetiese verkennings van die toekomsperspektief van Jesus Christus volgens die getuienis van die sinoptiese evangelies*. Kampen: Kok, 1962, VIII-332 p. Esp. 32-56 [kingdom]; 56-87 [Son of Man]; 90-106 [passion predictions]; 106-121 [parousia]; 133-149 [24/Mk 13]; 151-157 [24,42–25,46]; 164-167 [Q 17,22-37]; 181-193 [σημεῖον]; 193-198 [ἔγγυς, ἐγγίζω]; 198-204 [αἰών]; 212-239 [fulfilment]; 244-249 [24,36/Mk 13,32]; 276-286 [24,34/Mk 13,30]; 286-300 [10,23]; 301-302 [23,36.39]. — Diss. Kampen, 1962 (H.N. Ridderbos).

VAN DER WATT, J.G.
1991  → K. Aland [Bauer-Aland]

VANDER WERFF, Lyle
1975  Biblical Perspectives on Marriage, Divorce and Remarriage. — *BangalTF* 7/1 (1975) 1-16. Esp. 6-10 [5,32; 19,3-10].

VAN DE SANDT, Huub W.M.
1976  An Explanation of Rom. 8,4a. — *Bijdragen* 37 (1976) 361-378. Esp. 370-371.376 [5,17]. [NTA 21, 489]

VAN DEUN, Peter
1991  (ed.), *Maximi Confessoris Opuscula exegetica duo* (CC SG, 23). Turnhout: Brepols; Leuven: University Press, 1991, CLXXII-135 p. Esp. LXXVIII-CLXXII and 25-73: "Expositio orationis dominicae".
1993  (trans.), *Verklaring van het Onze Vader*, trans. P. Van Deun (Kerkvaderteksten met Commentaar, 10). Bonheiden: Abdij Betlehem, 1993, 75 p.
1994  Les extraits de Maxime le Confesseur contenus dans les chaînes sur l'évangile de Matthieu. — SCHOORS, A. - VAN DEUN, P. (eds.), *Philohistôr. Miscellanea in honorem Caroli Laga septuagenarii* (Orientalia Lovaniensia Analecta, 60), Leuven: Peeters, 1994, 295-328.

VAN DODEWAARD, Johannes A.E.
1954  Jésus s'est-il servi Lui-même du mot "évangile"? — *Bib* 35 (1954) 160-173. Esp. 160-161.171.
1955  La force évocatrice de la citation mise en lumière en prenant pour base l'Évangile de S. Matthieu. — *Bib* 36 (1955) 482-491. Esp. 487-488 [Son of God]; 488-491 [Moses-Jesus].
1957  De synoptische evangeliën. — VAN DEN BORN, A. (ed.), *De wereld van de Bijbel. Inleiding tot het lezen van de heilige Schrift*, Utrecht–Antwerpen: Spectrum, ²1957, ³1964, 750-779.

VANDONE, L.M.
1964  Responsabilità giudaica. [27,25] — *PalCl* 43 (1964) 1276-1281. [NTA 9, 935] → Caprile 1960

VAN ELDEREN, Bastiaan
1974  The Purpose of the Parables according to Matthew 13:10-17. — LONGENECKER, R.N. - TENNEY, M.C. (eds.), *New Dimensions*, 1974, 180-190.

1989 The Significance of the Structure of Matthew 1. — VARDAMAN, J. - YAMAUCHI, E.M. (eds.), *Chronos, Kairos, Christos*. FS J. Finegan, 1989, 3-14. Esp. 7 [1,1]; 9-12 [1,18-25].

1994 Early Christianity in Transjordan. — *TyndB* 45 (1994) 97-117. Esp. 99-100; 112-114 [Gospel of the Ebionites]. [NTA 39, 618]

**VAN ENGELEN, G.C.** → J. Denaux 1969

**VAN ESBROECK, Michel** → van Cangh 1980

**VAN EXEM, Albert**
1991 The Gospel to the Sarna Tribal. — *Bible Bhashyam* 17 (1991) 242-260.

**VAN GANSEWINKEL, Albert**
1986 Ehescheidung und Wiederheirat in neutestamentlicher und moraltheologischer Sicht. — *TGl* 76 (1986) 193-211. Esp. 193-196 [19,9]. [NTA 31, 372]

**VAN GOUDOEVER, J.**
1966 The Place of Israel in Luke's Gospel. — *NT* 8 (1966) 111-123. Esp. 114-115 [Q 11,52]; 115-116 [Q 13,28-29]; 116-117 [21,33-46/Lk 20,9-19]; 118-119 [Q 14,16-2<]; 120-121 [Q 19,12-27]; 121 [21,28-32/Lk 15,11-32]; 122 [9,17/Lk 5,39]; 123 [Q 6,48]. [NTA 11, 731]

**VAN HAELST, Joseph**
1976 *Catalogue des papyrus littéraires juifs et chrétiens* (Série "Papyrologie", 1). Paris: Publ. de la Sorbonne, 1976, XI-424 p. Esp. 123-141 [nos. 331-385].

**VAN HARTINGSVELD, L.**
1977 *Het huwelijk in het Nieuwe Testament*. 's Gravenhage: Boekencentrum, 1977, 176 p. Esp. 73-75 [14,3-4]; 83-85 [5,27-30]; 88-92 [5,31-32; 19,3-10]; 104-107 [22,23-33]; 118-121 [19,12].

**VAN HELMOND, Frank**
1987 'Zijn bloed kome over ons'. René Girard en de structurele lezing van bijbelteksten. — BELLEMAKERS, S. - BOSCH, A. - RADEMAKERS, J. (eds.), *Van horen en verstaan. Verklaring en gebruik van de Schrift. Opgedragen aan Fius Drijvers*, Hilversum: Gooi & Sticht, 1987, 48-60. Esp. 56-59 [27,25].

**VAN HENTEN, Jan Willem**
1991 Christenen binnen en buiten het jodendom. — BAARDA, T., et al. (eds.), *Jodendom en vroeg christendom*, 1991, 137-161. Esp. 142-143, 150-154.

**VANHOYE, Albert**
1967 Structure et théologie des récits de la Passion dans les évangiles synoptiques. — *NRT* 89 (1967) 135-163. Esp. 138; 140-141; 143; 144-145; 146; 147-148; 158-159. [NTA 12, 141] → 1970b
*Structure and Theology of the Accounts of the Passion in the Synoptic Gospels*, trans. C.H. Giblin (The Bible Today Supplementary Studies, No. 1). Collegeville, MN: Liturgical Fress, 1967, 37 p.
*TDig* 16 (1968) 4-7; *SelT* 9 (1970) 107-118.
Struktur und Theologie der Passionsberichte in den synoptischen Evangelien. — LIMBECK, M. (ed.), *Redaktion und Theologie des Passionsberichtes*, 1981, 226-261. Esp. 230; 232-233; 235; 237-238; 241-242; 254-256.
Les récits de la passion dans les évangiles synoptiques. — *AssSeign* II/19 (1972) 38-67; = ID., et al., *La Passion selon les quatre Évangiles* (Lire la Bible, 55), Paris: Cerf, 1981, 11-63. Esp. 22-24; 29-31; 36-38; 51-57.
I racconti della Passione nei Vangeli sinottici. — ID., et al., *La Passione secondo i quatro Vangeli* (Universale theologica, 5), Brescia: Queriniana, 1983, 15-53.

1970a *De narrationibus Passionis Christi in evangeliis synopticis*. Roma: Pont. Inst. Bib., 1969-70, 131 p. Esp. 50-57 [26,47-56]; 70-100 [26,57-27,10]; 107-112 [27,11-26]; 124-125 [27,27-56].

1970b Le diverse prospettive dei quattro racconti evangelici della Passione. — *CC* 121/1 (1970) 463-475. [NTA 15, 74] → 1967

Las diversas perspectivas de los cuatro relatos evangélicos de la Pasión. — *Criterio* (Buenos Aires) 43-44 (1971) 147-153.

1974 Une nouvelle théorie synoptique. — *Bib* 55 (1974) 554-560. Esp. 558-559 [4,24; 23,37; 26,55-56; 28,11]. [NTA 19, 889r] → Boismard 1972

1980 *Prêtres anciens, prêtre nouveau selon le Nouveau Testament* (Parole de Dieu, 20). Paris: Seuil, 1980, 373 p. Esp. 21-30: "Les grands prêtres dans les évangiles".

1992 L'intérêt de Luc pour la prophétie en Lc 1,76; 4,16-30 et 22,60-65. — VAN SEGBROECK, F., et al. (eds.), *The Four Gospels 1992*. FS F. Neirynck, 1992, II, 1529-1548. Esp. 1544-1546 [26,75 minor agr.]; 1547-1548 [26,68 minor agr.].

**VAN IERSEL, Bastiaan M.F.**

1961 *'Der Sohn' in den synoptischen Jesusworten. Christusbezeichnung der Gemeinde oder Selbstbezeichnung Jesu?* (SupplNT, 3). Leiden: Brill, 1961, XXIII-194 p.; [2]1964, XIII-202 p. ("Nachtrag", 185-191). Esp. 117-123 [24,36/Mk]; 124-145 [21,33-41/Mk]; 146-161.175-179 [11,27/Q]; 165-171 [4,1-11]; 171-173 [22,41-46]; 153-155 [13,54-56].

1962a *De Bijbel over mensen in bekoring* (De Bijbel over..., 17). Roermond–Maaseik: Romen, 1962, 87 p. Esp. 42-67 [4,1-11].

1962b Fils de David et Fils de Dieu. — MASSAUX, É. (ed.), *La venue du Messie*, 1962, 113-132. Esp. 115-123.127-129 [Son of David]; 123-124 [1-2].

1962c Tradition und Redaktion in Joh. i 19-36. — *NT* 5 (1962) 245-267. Esp. 259-265. [NTA 7, 831]

1963 Les lignes fondamentales de notre vie chrétienne. [22,34-46] — *AssSeign* I/71 (1963) 27-44.

1964 Die wunderbare Speisung und das Abendmahl in der synoptischen Tradition (Mk vi 35-44 par., viii 1-20 par.). — *NT* 7 (1964-65) 167-194. Esp. 169-173 [Mt/Mk]; 192-193 [14,15-21]; 193-194 [15,32-39]. [NTA 10, 136]

1967 La vocation de Lévi (Mc., II,13-17, Mt., IX,9-13, Lc., V,27-32). Traditions et rédactions. — DE LA POTTERIE, I. (ed.), *De Jésus aux Évangiles*. FS J. Coppens, 1967, 212-232. Esp. 213-215 [Mt/Mk]; 226-228. (IT, 1971, 265-289).

1968a Jezus, duivel en demonen. Notities bij Matteüs 4.1-11 en Markus 5.1-20. — ID., et al., *Engelen en duivels* (Annalen van het Thijmgenootschap, 55/3), Hilversum: Brand, 1968, 5-22. Esp. 6-10 [4,1-11].
Gesù, diavolo e demoni. Note su Mt 4,1-11 e Mc 5,1-20. — ID., et al. (eds.), *Angeli e diavoli*, trans. A. Bonora (Giornale di Teologia, 60), Brescia: Queriniana, 1972, 15-35.

1968b Jezus' verrijzenis in het Nieuwe Testament. Informatie of interpretatie? — *VoxTheol* 38 (1968) 131-143. Esp. 137.140-141 [28,1-10].
Jezus' verrijzenis. Informatie of interpretatie? — *Concilium* (Hilversum) 6/10 (1970) 53-65.
The Resurrection of Jesus – Information or Interpretation? — *Concilium* (London) 60 (1970) 54-67. [NTA 15, 826]
La résurrection de Jésus: information ou interprétation? — *Concilium* (Paris) 60 (1970) 51-62.

1978 & LINMANS, A.J.M., The Storm on the Lake. Mk iv 35-41 and Mt viii 18-27 in the Light of Form Criticism, "Redaktionsgeschichte" and Structural Analysis. — BAARDA, T. - KLIJN, A.F.J. - VAN UNNIK, W.C. (eds.), *Miscellanea Neotestamentica* (SupplNT, 48), Leiden: Brill, 1978, II, 17-48. Esp. 24-28: "Mt viii 18-27 as an elaboration upon Mk iv 35-41 ('redaktionsgeschichtlich')"; 39-43: "Structural analysis of Mt viii 18-27".

1981 Who according to the New Testament has the Say in the Church? — *Concilium* (London) 148 (1981) 11-17. Esp. 12-13. [NTA 26, 665]
À qui le Nouveau Testament accorde-t-il la parole décisive? — *Concilium* (Paris) 168 (1981) 27-35. Esp. 28-29 [ἐκκλησία].
Wer hat nach dem Neuen Testament das entscheidende Wort in der Kirche? — *IZT/Concilium* (Mainz) 17 (1981) 620-625. Esp. 620-621.

1982 "Zoon van God" in het Nieuwe Testament. — *Concilium* (Hilversum) 18/3 (1982) 44-56. Esp. 51.
"Son of God" in the New Testament. — *Concilium* (New York) 153 (1982) 37-48. Esp. 43. [NTA 26, 1036]
"Fils de Dieu" dans le Nouveau Testament. — *Concilium* (Paris) 173 (1982) 67-83. Esp. 76-77.
"Sohn Gottes" im Neuen Testament. — *IZT/Concilium* (Mainz) 18 (1982) 182-193. Esp. 188.

1985 Matteüs 16,18: Simôn, Petros, petra, prôtos. Reflectie op woordspelingen rond Simon, de steenrots. — *TijdTheol* 25 (1985) 402-409 (English summary, 409). Esp. 404-408. [NTA 30, 1059]

1989 *Intertekstualiteit in soorten. Een voorstel tot enkele nieuwe classificaties verhelderd aan Mt 1-2 en Lc 1-2 en experimenteel toegepast op Mc 1,1-13.* Nijmegen: Katholieke Universiteit Nijmegen, 1989, 20 p.

**VAN LEEUWEN, Willem Silvester**

1952 Mattheus. — VOR DER HAKE, J.A. (ed.), *Commentaar op de Heilige Schrift*, Amsterdam: Paris, 1952, 850-899.

**VAN LOPIK, T.**

1995 Once Again: Floating Words, Their Significance for Textual Criticism. — *NTS* 41 (1995) 286-291. Esp. 286-289 [26,39]. [NTA 39, 1347]

**VANN, Gerald**

1957 & MEAGHER, P.K., *Stones or Bread. A Study of Christ's Temptations* (Fontana Books, III/6). London: Collins, 1957, 126 p.
& MEAGHER, P.K., *The Temptations of Christ.* New York: Sheed & Ward, 1958, 127 p.

**VANNI, Ugo**

1974 La passione come rivelazione di condanna e di salvezza in Matteo 26,64 e 27,54. — *EuntDoc* 27 (1974) 65-91. [NTA 20, 94]

1991 L'Apocalisse e il Vangelo di Luca. — O'COLLINS, G. - MARCONI, G. (eds.), *Luca-Atti*, 1991, 17-37.
The Apocalypse and the Gospel of Luke. — O'COLLINS, G. - MARCONI, G. (eds.), *Luke and Acts*, 1993, 9-25. Esp. 12-14 [Q 12,8/Rev].

1993 Il "Padre nostro". I. — *CC* 144/3 (1993) 345-358. Esp. 348-355 [Mt]. [NTA 38, 761]

**VAN OGTROP, Hein Jan**

1994 Jezus volgens de Schriften: Gedachten over Tora-getrouwe verkondiging. — AKERBOOM, D., et al. (eds.), *Broeder Jehosjoea.* FS B. Hemelsoet, 1994, 117-128. Esp. 120-121.

**VAN OTTERLOO, Roger**

1988 Towards an Understanding of 'Lo' and 'Behold'. Functions of ἰδού and ἴδε in the Greek New Testament. — *OPTAT* 2 (1988) 34-64. [NTA 33, 1061]

**VAN PARIJS, Michel J.**

1971 Exégèse et théologie dans les livres contre Eunome de Grégoire de Nysse: Textes scripturaires controversés et élaboration théologique. — HARL, M. (ed.), *Écriture et culture philosophique dans la pensée de Grégoire de Nysse. Actes du Colloque de Chèvetogne (22-26 septembre 1969)*, Leiden: Brill, 1971, 169-196. Esp. 186-192 [28,19].

1977 Unification de l'homme dans le Nom. Exégèse de Mt. 18,19-20. — *Irénikon* 50 (1977) 345-358, 521-532. Esp. 347-351 [Syriac fathers]; 351-353 [Clement of Alexandria]; 353-355 [Origen]; 355-356 [Athanasius]; 356-358 [Basil of Caesarea]; 521-532 [4-6th cent.].

**VAN PRAAG, H.**

1972 *Sleutelwoorden van de Bijbel in het licht van het Onze Vader.* 's-Gravenhage: Boekencentrum, 1972, ²1973, 71 p.

**VAN REETH, Jan M.F.**

1992 Le prophète musulman en tant que Nâsir Allâh et ses antécédents: le "Nazôraios" évangélique et le Livre des Jubilés. — *OrLovPer* 23 (1992) 251-274. [NTA 38, 751]

**VAN RENSBURG, S.P.J.J.**

1965 Die onvergeeflijke sonde. [12,32] — *HervTS* 21 (1965) 1-16.

1967 Sanctification according to the New Testament. — *Neotestamentica* 1 (1967) 73-87. [NTA 18, 311]

**VAN RIJEN, Alois**

1969 "Als ge volmaakt wilt..." (Mt 19,21). — *Ons Geestelijk Leven* 46 (1969) 75-91. Esp. 76-81 [perfection]; 81-85 [wealth]; 85-89 [19,21].

**VAN ROYEN, P.D.**

1953 *Jezus en Johannes de Doper. Een historisch onderzoek op grond van de synoptische evangeliën, naar hun onderlinge verhouding sedert de arrestatie van de laatste.* Leiden: Luctor et emergo, 1953, 119 p.

**VAN SEGBROECK, Frans**

→ Neirynck 1974a, 1977a, 1979a, 1982c.e, 1983a, 1984a, 1986a, 1992a

1964 *De formulecitaten in the Mattheüsevangelie. Bijdrage tot de christologie van Mt. 4–13.* Diss. Leuven, 1964, XXXVII-401 p. (F. Neirynck). Esp. 80-159 [πληρόω]; 160-394 [formula quotations: 1-2; 4,15-16; 8,17; 12,18-21; 13,35; 21,5; 27,9-10]. → 1972b

1965 Le scandale de l'incroyance. La signification de Mt., XIII,35. — *ETL* 41 (1965) 344-372. Esp. 345-352 [13,10-15]; 352-360 [13,34-35]; 360-372 [13,35]. [NTA 10, 910]

1968 Jésus rejeté par sa patrie (Mt 13,54-58). — *Bib* 49 (1968) 167-198. Esp. 171-191: "Analyse du récit" [13,54a.54b-57a.57b.58]; 191-195: "La place du récit dans la trame évangélique". [NTA 13, 166]

1970 De parabelrede van Matteus (Mt 13). — *Ons Geestelijk Leven* 47 (1970) 216-225.

1972a & SELONG, G., *Bibliografie: Evangeliecommentaren. Bibliography: Gospel Commentaries* (Studiorum Novi Testamenti Auxilia, 9). Leuven: Seminarium Neotestamenticum Lovaniense, 1972, 45 p. Esp. 2-13: "Matteüs".

1972b Les citations d'accomplissement dans l'Évangile selon saint Matthieu d'après trois ouvrages récents. — DIDIER, M. (ed.), *L'Évangile selon Matthieu*, 1972, 107-130. Esp. 108-115 [Gundry 1967a]; 115-120 [McConnell 1969]; 120-128 [Rothfuchs 1969]. → 1964

1972c Zonen, wijnbouwers, bruiloftsgasten (Mt 21,28–22,14). — *Ons Geestelijk Leven* 49 (1972) 303-312.

1980 Het evangelie volgens Matteüs. — ID., et al., *De Bijbel verkennen*. II: *Het Nieuwe Testament*, Leuven: Vlaamse Bijbelstichting – Acco, 1980, 96-101.

1984 Het Oude Testament in het evangelie van Matteüs. — *Sacerdos* 51 (1983-84) 481-490.

1989 *The Gospel of Luke. A Cumulative Bibliography 1973-1988* (BETL, 88). Leuven: University Press / Peeters; (COBRA, 2), Brussel: Koninklijke Academie voor Wetenschappen, Letteren en Schone Kunsten van België, 1989, 243 p. Esp. 219: "Luke and Matthew. The Q-document".

1992* & TUCKETT, C.M. – VAN BELLE, G. – VERHEYDEN, J. (eds.), *The Four Gospels 1992. Festschrift Frans Neirynck* (BETL, 100). Leuven: University Press / Peeters, 3 vols., 1992, XVIII-690; X-691-1720 and IX-1721-2668 p. → B. Aland, D.C. Allison, Baarda, Boismard, Borgen, Boring, Breytenbach, Broer, Carlston, Carrez, Catchpole, Chilton, R.F. Collins, Dehandschutter, H.J. de Jonge, Dormeyer, J.D.G. Dunn, R.A. Edwards, J.K. Elliott, W.R. Farmer, Fitzmyer, Fleddermann, Freed, T.A. Friedrichsen, Gerhardsson, Gundry, D.J. Harrington, Hoffmann, Hooker, A.D. Jacobson, Kloppenborg, D.-A. Koch, Légasse, Lindars, März, R. Pesch, J.M. Robinson, Ruckstuhl, Sabbe, Schlosser, Schmithals, Schnackenburg, G. Schneider, Schürmann, Schweizer, Senior, D.M. Smith, Standaert, Stanton, Strecker, Suhl, Telford, Tuckett, Vanhoye, N. Walter, Zeller

**VAN SELMS, Adrianus**

1970 De sleutelmacht. Een exegese van Matth. 16:19. — *KerkT* 21 (1970) 247-260.

**VAN STEMPVOORT, Pieter Albertus**

1954 "Gods Zoon" of "Een Zoon Gods" in Matth. 27,54? — *NTT* 9 (1954-55) 79-89.

**VAN STOCKUM, T.C.**

1964 Idiota cum euangelista Matthaeo luctans. [20,1-16] — *NTT* 19 (1964-65) 15-21. [NTA 9, 920]

**VAN SWIGCHEM, Douwe**

1952 Geschiedenis van de exegese van Luc. 10:22 (Matth. 11,27) in de laatste decennia. — *GTT* 52 (1952) 97-108.

**VAN TILBORG, Sjef**

1969 Ongehuwd omwille van het Rijk der hemelen? Een uitleg van Mt 19,3-12. — *Ons Geestelijk Leven* 46 (1969) 30-36.

1970 Mattheüs 19,3-12 en het onontbindbare huwelijk. — VAN EUPEN, T.A.G. (ed.), *(On)ontbindbaarheid van het huwelijk* (Annalen van het Thijmgenootschap, 58/1), Hilversum: Brand, 1970, 23-34. → Neirynck 1972c

1972a *The Jewish Leaders in Matthew*. Leiden: Brill, 1972, X-199 p. Esp. 8-26: "Ὑποκρίται" [6,1-6.16-18; 7,5; 15,1-9; 22,18; 23,5-7.13-33; 24,51]; 27-45: "Πονηροί" [5,45; 7,11; 9,4; 12,33-35.38-42.43-45; 13,19.38.49; 16,1-4; 22,10.18]; 46-72: "Φονεῖς" [21,28-22,14; 23,29-39]; 73-98: "The passion narrative" [12,9-14; 16,21; 20,17-19; 26,1-5.57-68; 27,1-2.3-10.11-14.15-26.38-44]; 99-141: "Οἱ μαθηταὶ Ἰησοῦ" [5,20; 8,18-22; 9,9-13.14-17; 12,1-8; 13,52; 15,10-20; 16,5-12; 17,10-13; 19,3-12; 23,2-3.8-12.16-24.34-36; 27,62-66; 28,11-15]; 142-165: "Οἱ ὄχλοι" [2,1-12; 5,1-2; 7,28-29; 9,1-8.32-34; 12,22-24.46-50; 13,34-36; 14,13-21; 15,32-39; 21,10-17; 22,23-33.41-46; 23,1; 27,20]. [NTA 17, p. 248] — Diss. Nijmegen, 1972 (B. van Iersel).

J. COPPENS, *ETL* 48 (1972) 686-687; R.H. GUNDRY, *JBL* 92 (1973) 138-140; L. SABOURIN, *Bib* 55 (1974) 137-140; N. WALTER, *TLZ* 98 (1973) 906-908.

1972b A Form-Criticism of the Lord's Prayer. — *NT* 14 (1972) 94-105. [NTA 17, 118]; = TOLLERS, V.L. – MAIER, J.R. (eds.), *The Bible in Its Literary Milieu. Contemporary Essays*, Grand Rapids, MI: Eerdmans, 1979, 334-343.

1972c Volgens Matteüs. — *Getuigenis* 16 (1971-72) 227-236.

1974 Exegetische notities bij de belangrijkste huwelijkstekste1 uit het Nieuwe Testament. — ID., et al., *Alternatief Kerkelijk Huwelijksrecht* (Annalen van het Thijmgenootschap, 62/4), Baarn: Ambo, 1974, 9-23. Esp. 14-18 [19,1-12].
Exegetische Bemerkungen zu den wichtigsten Ehetexten aus dem Neuen Testament. — HUIZING, P.J.M. (ed.), *Für eine neue kirchliche Eheordnung. Ein Alternativentwurf*, Düsseldorf: Patmos, 1975, 9-25.

1978 Als mens te midden van het geweld. Een uitleg van Mattheus 26,36-56. — *Ons Geestelijk Leven* 55 (1978) 132-139.

1979 Over de ideologie rond de Petrustekst in Mattheus. [16,16-19] — *Ons Geestelijk Leven* 56 (1979) 4-15.

1981 Jezus in het krachtenspel van de wetsuitleg. (Over Mattheus 5,17-48). — *Ons Geestelijk Leven* 58 (1981) 282-294.

1985a Een politieke lezing van de Bergrede. — *Ons Geestelijk Leven* 62 (1985) 170-178.

1985b Een vertaling van de parabel van de dagloners in de wijngaard. Een verantwoording. — *Schrift* 102 (1985) 220-223.

1986a *The Sermon on the Mount as an Ideological Intervention. A Reconstruction of Meaning*. Assen/Maastricht, NL – Wolfeboro, NH: van Gorcum, 1986, VII-376 p. Esp. 13-45: "Suffering of the people and its restoration. Mt 5,3-16"; 47-79: "The laws for the people. Mt 5,17-48"; 81-

130: "The practices of justice. Mt 6,1-18"; 131-162: "The problem of the rich and their solution. Mt 6,19-34"; 163-196: "The laws for the people: mutual relations. Mt 7,1-12"; 197-233: "Not words but deeds. Mt 7,13-27". [NTA 33, p. 114]
    J.M. CASCIARO RAMIREZ, *ScriptTheol* 21 (1989) 352; A. CHESTER, *ExpT* 99 (1987-88) 184; P. FARLA, *NTT* 44 (1990) 160-161; N.J. MCELENEY, *CBQ* 51 (1989) 168-169; C.M. TUCKETT, *JSNT* 31 (1987) 125.

1986b  De betekenis van het Mattëusevangelie na de shoah van de joden. — *Schrift* 108 (1986) 213-217.

1988  Language, Meaning, Sense and Reference: Matthew's Passion Narrative and Psalm 22. — *HervTS* 44 (1988) 883-908.

1989  Matthew 27.3-10: an Intertextual Reading. — DRAISMA, S. (ed.), *Intertextuality in Biblical Writings*. FS B. van Iersel, 1989, 159-174. Esp. 159-168: "The allusions, translations and quotes from the Zech text"; 168-174: "The allusions, translations and quotes from the Jer-text".

VAN 'T RIET, Peter → W.J. Barnard 1986

VAN UNNIK, Willem Cornelis

1930[R]  Jesu Verhöhnung vor dem Synedrium (Mc XIV 65 par.). [1930] — ID., *Sparsa Collecta*, I, 1973, 3-5.

1957  L'usage de σῴζειν "sauver" et des dérivés dans les évangiles synoptiques. — HEUSCHEN, J. (ed.), *La formation des évangiles*, 1957, 178-194. Esp. 180-181 [9,20-21]; 181-182 [16,25]; 182-183 [19,25]; 183-184 [27,39-40]; 185-186 [9,18]; 186-187 [24,13]; 187 [8,25; 14,36; 24,22]; = ID., *Sparsa Collecta*, I, 1973, 16-34. Esp. 19; 20-21; 21-23; 24; 25; 26-27.

1959  *Dominus vobiscum*: The Background of a Liturgical Formula. — HIGGINS, A.J.B. (ed.), *New Testament Essays*. FS T.W. Manson, 1959, 270-305. Esp. 287-288 [1,23; 18,20]; = ID., *Sparsa Collecta*. III: *Patristica – Gnostica – Liturgica* (SupplNT, 31), Leiden: Brill, 1983, 362-391. Esp. 376-377.

1966  Die Motivierung der Feindesliebe in Lukas vi 32-35. — *NT* 8 (1966) 284-300. Esp. 297-299. [NTA 11, 736]; = ID., *Sparsa Collecta*, I, 1973, 111-126. Esp. 122-124.

1973  *Sparsa Collecta. The Collected Essays*. Part One: *Evangelia. Paulina. Acta* (SupplNT, 29). Leiden: Brill, 1973, X-409 p. → 1930, 1957, 1966

1974  The Death of Judas in Saint Matthew's Gospel. — *ATR* SS 3 (1974) 44-57. [NTA 19, 99]

1977  Vertaling versus Woordenboek bij Marcus 8,33 - Matthaeus 16,23. — VAN IERSEL, B.M.F. - DE JONGE, M. - NELIS, J. (eds.), *Van taal tot taal. Opstellen over het vertalen van de Schriften aangeboden aan prof. dr. W.K. Grossouw bij diens afscheid van de Nijmeegse Universiteit* (Annalen van het Thijmgenootschap, 65/3), Baarn: Ambo, 1977, 51-61.

VAN WERINGH, Johannes Jacobus

1965  *Heliand and Diatessaron*. Assen: van Gorcum/Prakke, 1965, XI-140 p. Esp. 57-66 [1,19-20.25]; 73-77 [2,9.13-14.19-20]; 79-84 [3,16-17]; 84-89 [4.5-6.9]; 90-95 [5,15.43; 6,13.15]; 95-97 [12,35]; 97-103 [13,4.28.48]; 105-106 [14,22]; 106-108 [16,18.21]; 109-111 [17,2]; 112-113 [20,32]; 114-115 [22,21]; 116-121 [26,3-4.41.58.69]; 124-127 [27,27]. — Diss. Utrecht, 1965 (G. Quispel).

VAN ZYL, Hermias C.

1982a  'n Moontlike verklaring vir Matteus 7:6. [A possible explanation of Mt 7,6] — *TheolEvang* 15 (1982) 67-82. [NTA 27, 517]

1982b  Structural Analysis of Matthew 18. — *Neotestamentica* 16 (1982) 35-55 (addendum, 18-21).

1987  *Matteus 18:15-20: 'n Diachroniese en sinchroniese ondersoek met besondere verwysing na kerklike dissipline* [Mt 18,15-20: A diachronic and synchronic investigation with special reference to church discipline]. Diss. Pretoria, 1987 (A.B. du Toit). — *DissAbstr* 48 (1987-88) 2910-2911.

1988 Matteus 18:15-20: 'n Diachroniese en sinchroniese ondersoek met besondere verwysing na kerklike dissipline. — *Skrif en Kerk* (Pretoria) 9 (1988) 75-92. [NTA 34, 630]

**VAN ZYL, H.J.**

1990 Ironie as taalhandeling in Matteus 5:17-48. — *NduitseGT* 31 (1990) 23-34.

1991 *Die Bergrede as littérature engagée* [The Sermon on the Mount as "littérature engagée"]. Diss. Stellenbosch, 1991.

**VARA, J.**

1986 Dos conjeturas textuales sobre Mateo 25,21.23 y Mateo 26,32/17,22 y par. — *Salmanticensis* 33 (1986) 81-86. [NTA 31, 125]

**VARDAMAN, Jerry**

1989* & YAMAUCHI, E.M. (eds.), *Chronos, Kairos, Christos. Nativity and Chronological Studies Presented to Jack Finegan*. Winona Lake, IN: Eisenbrauns, 1989, XXIII-240 p.
→ Ferrari d'Occhieppo, Kokkinos, P.L. Maier, Van Elderen, E.M. Yamauchi

**VARGAS-MACHUCA, Antonio**

1969a El paralítico perdonado, en la redacción de Mateo (Mt 9,1-8). — *EstE* 44 (1969) 15-43. Esp. 16-24 [pre-synoptic tradition]; 24-29 [redaction]; 29-32 [structure]. 32-33 [genre]; 34-37 [interpretation]; 37-43 [context]. [NTA 14, 142]
*SelT* 9 (1970) 79-82.

1969b (Καὶ) ἰδού en el estilo narrativo de Mateo. — *Bib* 50 (1969) 233-244. Esp. 234-241 [καὶ ἰδού]; 241-242 [gen. abs. + ἰδού]. [NTA 14, 133] → Neirynck 1974b

1975 Los casos de "divorcio" admitidos por S. Mateo (5,32 y 19,9). Consecuencias para la teología actual. — *EstE* 50 (1975) 5-54. Esp. 6-20: "Historia de la tradición"; 20-48: "Las clausulas exceptivas de Mateo: interpretación". [NTA 20, 85]

1981 Divorcio e indisolubilidad del matrimonio en la Sagrada Escritura. — *EstBíb* 39 (1981) 19-61. Esp. 28-33 [5,32; 19,9]; 35-37 [19,3-12/Mk]; 41-57 [5,32; 19,9]. [NTA 26, 1072]

1993 La llamada fuento Q de los evangelios sinopticos. Teoria de las dos fuentes. Modernas precisiones. Origen, composición y redacción de la fuente Q. Su función en el cristianismo primitivo. — PIÑERO, A. (ed.), *Fuentes del cristianismo*, 1993, 63-94. Esp. 63-78: "La fuente Q y la teoria de las dos fuentes"; 78-94: "Origen, composición y redacción".

**VARONE, C.M.**

1975 → Rouiller 1975

1976 Le père, selon S. Matthieu. — *Les Échos de Saint-Maurice* 72 (1976) 44-54.

**VASSE, Denis** → Beauchamp 1991

**VASSILIADIS, Petros**

1975a The Function of John the Baptist in Q and Mark. — *Θεολογία* (Athens) 46 (1975) 405-413. [NTA 20, 767]

1975b Prolegomena to a Discussion on the Relationship between Mark and the Q Document. — *DeltBM* 3 (1975) 31-46. [NTA 20, 422]

1977 *The Q-Document Hypothesis. A Critical Examination of Today's Literary and Theological Problems Concerning the Q-Document*. Athens: Privately published, 1977, 167 p. Esp. 33-85: "The problem of the existence of the Q-document" (→ 1980); 86-118: "Nature, extent and genesis of the Q-document" (→ 1978); 119-149: "Considerations of the theological characteristics of the Q-document". [NTA 22, p. 95] — Diss. Athens, 1977.
O. LINTON, *TLZ* 105 (1980) 745-747; F. NEIRYNCK, *ETL* 55 (1979) 410-411.

1978 The Nature and Extent of the Q-Document. — *NT* 20 (1978) 49-73. Esp. 50-60: "The nature of the Q-document" [written or oral; original language; sources]; 60-71: "The reconstruction of the Q-document". [NTA 23, 81] → 1977, 86-110

1980 Did Q Exist? (A Critical Examination of the Arguments against the Existence of the Q-Document since the Time of Streeter). — Ἐκκλησία καὶ Θεολογία 1 (1980) 287-328. → 1977, 33-85

1982 The Original Order of Q. Some Residual Cases. — DELOBEL, J. (ed.), *Logia*, 1982, 379-387.

**VATTIONI, Francesco**
1960 Porte o portieri dell'inferno in Mt. 16,18b? — *RivBib* 8 (1960) 251-255. [NTA 5, 719]
1962a Nonne hic est fabri filius (Mt 13,55)? — *Studi Sociali* 2 (1962) 1-19.
1962b Il divorzio nella Bibbia. — *Ibid.*, 235-260.
1962c Le beatitudini nella S. Scrittura. — *Ibid.*, 469-491
1963 Beati i poveri ... Guai a voi ricchi (Mt 5,3; Lc 6,20-24). — *Studi Sociali* 3 (1963) 467-499.
1965a Mammona iniquitatis. [Italian] — *Augustinianum* 5 (1965) 379-386. Esp. 383-384 [6,24].
1965b Et tetigit fimbriam vestimenti eius (Mt. 9,20). [Italian] — *Ibid.*, 533-538.
1966 *Beatitudini, Povertà, Ricchezza* (Ricerche Bibliche). Milano: Àncora, 1966, 455 p. Esp. 367-407 [13,55].

**VAUGHT, Carl G.**
1986 *The Sermon on the Mount. A Theological Interpretation.* Albany, NY: State University of New York Press, 1986, XIV-217 p. [NTA 31, p. 238]
C. BERNAS, *TS* 49 (1988) 200; D.J. FALK, *Themelios* 15 (1989-90) 20-21; E. MCMAHON, *CRBR* 2 (1989) 253-255; W.M. TILLMANN, *SWJT* 31/2 (1988-89) 54.

**VAWTER, Bruce**
1954 The Divorce Clauses in Mt 5,32 and 19,9. — *CBQ* 16 (1954) 155-167. Esp. 156-165: "The current interpretations of Mt 5,32 and 19,9"; 165-167: "The context of Mt 5,32 and 19,9". → Leeming 1956, Vaccari 1955b
1967 *The Four Gospels. An Introduction.* Garden City, NY: Doubleday; Dublin–Sydney: M.H. Gill, 1967, 429 p. Esp. 25-27 [author]; 58-70 [birth/infancy narratives]; 118-144 [Sermon on the Mount]; 145-149.152-162 [parables]; 333-345.359-410 [passion narrative]; Garden City, NY: Image Books, ²1969, 316 and 320 p.
*Introducción a los Cuatro Evangelios*, trans. J.M. Gondra ("Palabra Inspirada", 9). Santander: Sal Terrae, 1970, 560 p.
1977 Divorce and the New Testament. — *CBQ* 39 (1977) 528-542. Esp. 529-531 [5,32]; 531-536 [19,3-12]. [NTA 22, 394]; = ID., *The Path of Wisdom. Biblical Investigations* (Background Books, 3), Wilmington, DE: Glazier, 1986, 238-256. Esp. 239-242; 242-248.

**VEERKAMP, Ton**
1981 Nicht Widerstreben und nicht Zurückweichen. [5,38-42] — *TK* 11 (1981) 10-22.
1985 Das mystifizierte Abendmahl – der mystifizierte Messias. Ein Vergleich von Abendmahltexten in den messianischen Schriften und was aus ihnen wurde. — *TK* 25 (1985) 16-42. Esp. 30-33 [26,26-29].
1993a Die Enterbung Israels. Das Gleichnis der mörderischen Bauern in Mt 21,34-43 und die Konzequenzen für die Deutung des Sendungsauftrages, Mt 28,16-20. — *TK* 59 (1993) 25-40. Esp. 25-29: "Der Kontext"; 29-30: "Der Text"; 30-37: "Erklärung des Gleichnisses".
1993b Das Ende der christlichen Mission. — *TK* 60 (1993) 3-30. Esp. 4-24: "Die Auslegung"; 24-29: "Dominanz und Mission".

**VELLANICKAL, Matthew**
1977 *The Divine Sonship of Christians in the Johannine Writings* (AnBib, 72). Roma: Biblical

Institute Press, 1977, XL-400 p. Esp. 53-68: "The divine sonship of Christians in the synoptic gospels" [5,9.43-48; 11,25-27; 12,48-50; 17,25-27]. — Diss. Pont. Inst. Bibl., Roma, 1970 (I. de la Potterie).

1983    Jesus the Poor and His Gospel to the Poor. — *Bible Bhashyam* 9 (1983) 53-64. [NTA 28, 76]

1984a   The Christian Righteousness (Mt 6:1-18). — *Bible Bhashyam* 10 (1984) 106-121. [NTA 29, 521]

1984b   Christian Experience in the Four Gospels. — *Ibid.*, 175-185. Esp. 178-179. [NTA 29, 890]

1985    The Filial Faith of Jesus: Jesus' Experience as Son of God. — *Bible Bhashyam* 11 (1985) 113-129. Esp. 120-123 [11,27]; 124-126 [Q 22,29-30]. [NTA 30, 1019]

**VENCOVSKÝ, Jan**

1971    Der gadarenische Exorzismus. Mt 8,28-34 und Parallelen. — *ComViat* 14 (1971) 13-29. [NTA 16, 156]

**VENEMA, Harm**

1965    *Uitverkiezen en uitverkiezing in het Nieuwe Testament.* Kampen: Kok, 1965, 180 p. Esp. 78-81 [ἐκλεκτός]. — Diss. Kampen, 1965.

**VENETZ, Hermann-Josef**

1976    Kindheitsgeschichten für Erwachsene. Zur Bedeutung der neueren Exegese für die Verkündigung. — *Diakonia* 7 (1976) 390-402.

1980    Bittet den Herrn der Ernte. Überlegungen zu Lk 10,2 / Mt 9,37. — *Diakonia* 11 (1980) 148-161. Esp. 155-161 [9,37]. [NTA 25, 118]

1981a   *So fing es mit der Kirche an. Ein Blick in das Neue Testament.* Zürich: Benziger, 1981, 282 p.; [3]1982. Esp. 189-210: "Mattäus – ein Mann der Kirche".
*C'est ainsi que l'Église a commencé: regard sur le Nouveau Testament* (Théologies). Paris: Cerf, 1986, 182 p.

1981b   Theologische Grundstrukturen in der Verkündigung Jesu? Ein Vergleich von Mk 10,17-22; Lk 10,25-37 und Mt 5,21-48. — CASETTI, P. - KEEL, O. - SCHENKER, A. (eds.), *Mélanges Dominique Barthélemy. Études bibliques offertes à l'occasion de son 60ᵉ anniversaire* (Orbis Biblicus et Orientalis, 38), Freiburg/Schw: Éd. universitaires; Göttingen: Vandenhoeck & Ruprecht, 1981, 613-650. Esp. 636-639.

1982    (ed.), *Provokation der Freiheit. Bergpredigt heute.* Freiburg/Schw: Imba, 1982, 70 p.
*Il Discorso della montagna (Mt 5-7) una provocazione per la coscienza moderna.* Roma: Città Nuova, 1986, 166 p.
A. ROLLA, *Asprenas* 38 (1991) 539-540; G. STEMBERGER, *BLtg* 57 (1984) 274-275.

1987    *Die Bergpredigt. Biblische Anstösse.* Düsseldorf: Patmos; Freiburg: Kanisius, 1987, 128 p.
M. HELSPER, *BK* 43 (1988) 88.
*Il discorso della montagna,* trans. E. Gatti (Universale teologica, 27). Brescia: Queriniana, 1990, 147 p.

1988    Die Ehe unter dem Anspruch der Bergpredigt. Neue Kommentare zum Matthäus-evangelium. — *Orientierung* 52 (1988) 229-233. [NTA 33, 602]

**VENIAMIN, C.**

1992    *The Transfiguration of Christ in Greek Patristic Literature from Irenaeus of Lyons to Gregory of Palamas* [17,1-9]. Diss. Oxford, 1992.

**VERA ARRECHEA, Miguel**

1981    "Los eunucos del evangelio". [19,12] — *CuBíb* 38 (1981) 61-62. → García del Moral 1981

**VERBRAKEN, Pierre-Patrick**

1959    Les sermons CCXV et LVI de saint Augustin *De symbolo* et *De oratione dominica.* — *RBén* 69 (1959) 5-40. Esp. 26-40.

1966 Le sermon CXII de saint Augustin sur les invités au festin. — *RBén* 76 (1966) 41-58.

1967 Les Évangiles commentés par les Pères latins. Répertoire de traductions françaises. — *BibVieChrét* 74 (1967) 63-89. Esp. 65-72. [NTA 12, 96]

1975 Le sermon LXXII de saint Augustin sur l'arbre et son fruit. [12,33] — *Forma futuri. Studi in onore del Cardinale Michele Pellegrino*, Torino: Bottega d'Erasmo, 1975, 796-805. Esp. 800-805 [edition].

1976 *Études critiques sur les sermons authentiques de saint Augustin* (Instrumenta Patristica, 12). Den Haag: Nijhoff; Steenbrugge: St. Pietersabdij, 1976, 267 p. Esp. 65-76: "Fichier signalétique" [Mt].

1981 Le sermon LI de saint Augustin sur les généalogies du Christ selon Matthieu et selon Luc. — *RBén* 91 (1981) 20-45.

1982 Le sermon LIV de saint Augstin *De placendo et non placendo hominibus*. — *AnBoll* 100 (1982) 263-269.

1984 Le sermon LXXXVIII de saint Augustin sur la guérison des deux aveugles de Jéricho. [20,29-34] — *RBén* 94 (1984) 71-101.

1994 Le sermon 53 de saint Augustin sur les Béatitudes selon saint Matthieu. — *RBén* 104 (1994) 19-33.

**VERGARA TIXERA, José**

1961 Significado literal de las treinta y seis parábolas recogidas en los Evangelios. — *Didascalia* 15 (1961) 144-155. [NTA 6, 444]

**VERHEIJEN, Luc M.J.**

1971 The Straw, the Beam, the Tusculan Disputations and the Rule of Saint Augustine. On a Surprising Augustinian Exegesis. [7,3-5] — *Augustinian Studies* (Villanova, PA) 2 (1971) 17-36.

**VERHEUL, Ambroos**

1986 Le "Notre Père" et l'Eucharistie. — *Questions Liturgiques* (Leuven) 67 (1986) 159-179. Esp. 159-170: "L'oraison dominicale chez les Pères de l'Église".

**VERHEY, Allen**

1984 *The Great Reversal. Ethics and the New Testament*. Grand Rapids, MI: Eerdmans, 1984, X-246 p. Esp. 6-33: "The ethic of Jesus"; 37-51: "The forms of tradition"; 53-60: "Q"; 82-92: "Matthew: a surpassing righteousness".

**VERHEYDEN, Jozef**
→ Neirynck 1988a, 1992a

1988a *De vlucht van de christenen naar Pella. Onderzoek van het getuigenis van Eusebius en Epiphanius* (Verhandelingen van de Koninklijke Academie voor Wetenschappen, Letteren en Schone Kunsten van België, 127). Brussel: Paleis der Academiën, 1988, 285 p. Esp. 37-38, 191-193, 199-200 [5,13]; 236-237 [24]. — Diss. Leuven, 1987 (F. Neirynck)

1988b De kindsheidverhalen in Matteüs: preludium en programma. [1-2] — WEREN, W., et al., *Geboorteverhalen van Jezus*, 1988, 61-74.

1989a L'Ascension d'Isaïe et l'évangile de Matthieu. Examen de AI 3,13-18. — SEVRIN, J.-M. (ed.), *The New Testament in Early Christianity*, 1989, 247-274. Esp. 254-270 [1,19; 27,51-23; 28/AscIs 3,13-18]. → Norelli 1994a

1989b The Source(s) of Luke 21. — NEIRYNCK, F. (ed.), *L'Évangile de Luc*, 1989, 491-516. Esp. 514-516: "Lukan dependence on Matthew?".

1992 P. Gardner-Smith and "the Turn of the Tide". — DENAUX, A. (ed.), *John and the Synoptics*, 1992, 423-452. Esp. 432-434 [10,24-25/Jn 13,16; 15,20].

1994 Some Observations on the Gospel Text of Eusebius of Caesarea Illustrated from His Commentary on Isaiah. — SCHOORS, A. - VAN DEUN, P. (eds.), *Philohistôr*. *Miscellanea in honorem Caroli Laga septuagenarii* (Orientalia Lovaniensia Analecta, 60), Leuven: Peeters, 1994, 35-70. Esp. 48-56 [1,23]; 56-68 [4,17]; 68-70 [28,19].

1996 Mark and Q. — *ETL* 72 (1996) 408-417. [NTA 41, 1586] → Fleddermann 1995, Neirynck 1995h

**VÉRICHEL, Maurice**

1965 *L'Évangile commenté par les Pères* (Église d'hier et d'aujourd'hui). Paris: Ouvrières, 1965, 366 p.
*Il Vangelo commentato dai Padri*. Torino: Gribaudi, 1967, 424 p.

**VERMES, Geza**

1967 → M. Black 1946

1973 *Jesus the Jew. A Historian's Reading of the Gospels*. London: Collins, 1973; New York: Macmillan, 1974; Philadelphia, PA: Fortress, 1981, 286 p. Esp. 177-186 [Son of Man]; 213-222 [virgin birth].
*Jesús, el judío. Los evangelios leídos por un historiador*. Barcelona: Muchnik, 1977, 306 p.
*Jésus le juif. Les documents évangéliques à l'épreuve d'un historien* (Jésus et Jésus-Christ, 4). Paris: Desclée, 1978, 298 p.
*Gesù l'ebreo*. Roma: Borla, 1983, VI-263 p.
*Jesus der Jude. Ein Historiker liest die Evangelien*, trans. A. Samely. Neukirchen: Neukirchener, 1993, XII-282 p.

1993 *The Religion of Jesus the Jew*. Minneapolis, MN: Fortress; London: SCM, 1993, X-244 p. Esp. 11-45 [law]; 46-75 [authority]; 76-118 [proverbs and parables]; 119-151 [kingdom].

**VERNOTTE, P.**

1960 À propos d'une interprétation de Mt 5,3. — *BBudé* 4 (1960) 100-104. → Casanova 1960, Delebecque 1959

**VERSEPUT, Donald J.**

1986 *The Rejection of the Humble Messianic King. A Study of the Composition of Matthew 11-12* (EHS, XXIII/291). Frankfurt/M–Bern: Lang, 1986, II-480 p. Esp. 9-54.310-330: "The Matthean gospel"; 55-131.330-364: "The rejection of salvation" [11,1-6.7-15.16-19.20-24]; 132-206.364-396: "God's mercy in Jesus" [11,25-30; 12,1-14.15-21]; 207-279.396-431: "Israel's rejection revisited" [12,22-37.38-45]; 280-294.432-443: "The true messianic community" [12,46-47.48.49-50]; 295-305: "Conclusion" [11,12]. [NTA 31, p. 238]
  F. VOUGA, *ETR* 62 (1987) 435.

1987 The Role and Meaning of the 'Son of God' Title in Matthew's Gospel. — *NTS* 33 (1987) 532-556. Esp. 533-537: "The Davidic Messiah"; 537-548: "The Son of God". [NTA 32, 578]

1992 The Faith of the Reader and the Narrative of Matthew 13.53-16.20. — *JSNT* 46 (1992) 3-24. Esp. 6-13 [structure]; 13-22 [exegesis]. [NTA 37, 146]

1994 Jesus' Pilgrimage to Jerusalem and Encounter in the Temple: A Geographical Motif in Matthew's Gospel. — *NT* 36 (1994) 105-121. Esp. 107-117: "Matthew's version of Jesus pilgrimage" [16,21; 17,22-27; 19,1; 21-23]; 117-120: "Function of the Jerusalem journey motif within the broader context". [NTA 39, 154]

1995 The Davidic Messiah and Matthew's Jewish Christianity. — *SBL 1995 Seminar Papers*, 103-116.

**VERSTEEG, Jan P.**

1977 De oudtestamentische citaten in het Nieuwe Testament, met name in het evangelie naar Mattheüs. — *In die Skriflig* 11/42 (1977) 10-24. → 1982

1980a *Evangelie in viervoud. Een karakteristiek van de vier evangeliën* (Bijbel en Gemeente, 16). Kampen: Kok, 1980, 137 p. Esp. 13-37: "Het evangelie naar Mattheüs: het evangelie van de Messias van Israël".

1980b  *Oog voor elkaar. Het gebruik van het woord "elkaar" in het Nieuwe Testament met betrekking tot de onderlinge verhoudingen binnen de gemeente.* Kampen: Kok, 1980, 112 p. Esp. 7-8 [ἀλλήλους].

1982  Old Testament Citations in the Gospel according to Matthew. — SKILTON, J.H. — LADLEY, C.A. (eds.), *The New Testament Student and His Field* (The New Student, 5), Phillipsburg, NJ: Presbyterian and Reformed Publ. Co., 1982, 98-113. Esp. 102-105 [2,23]; 107-113 [fulfilment quotations]. → 1977

**VERVENNE, Marc** → A. Denaux 1986

**VERWEIJS, P.G.**

1960  *Evangelium und neues Gesetz in der älteste Christenheit bis auf Marcion* (Studia theologica rheno-traiectina, 5). Utrecht: Kemink, 1960, 382 p. Esp. 13-39: "Jesus und das Gesetz".

**VERWEYEN, Hansjürgen**

1981  Die Ostererscheinungen in fundamentaltheologischer Sicht. — *ZKT* 103 (1981) 426-445. Esp. 441-442 [28,1-10].

**VETETO, Stephen George**

1993  *A Linguistic Analysis of Selected Sayings of Jesus as Representative of an Independent Source of the Gospels.* Diss. Mid-America Baptist Theol. Sem., 1993, 232 p. — *DissAbstr* 54 (1993-94) 4476.

**VIA, Dan Otto, Jr.**

1956  *The Doctrine of the Church in the Gospel of Matthew.* Diss. Duke Univ., Durham, NC, 1956.

1958a  Christ and his Church in Mt 16,17ss. — *RExp* 55 (1958) 22-39.

1958b  The Church as the Body of Christ in the Gospel of Matthew. — *ScotJT* 11 (1958) 271-286. Esp. 275-286. [NTA 3, 354]

1965  Matthew on the Understandability of the Parables. [13,11] — *JBL* 84 (1965) 430-432. [NTA 10, 516]

1967  *The Parables. Their Literary and Existential Dimension.* Philadelphia, PA: Fortress, 1967, XII-217 p.; ²1974. Esp. 2-25: "Parable and allegory"; 110-144: "The tragic parables" [18,23-35; 21,33-46; 22,1-14; 25,1-13.14-30]; 145-176: "The comic parables" [20,1-16]; 177-205: "The parables, the gospels, and the historical Jesus".
*Die Gleichnisse Jesu. Ihre literarische und existentiale Dimension*, trans. E. Güttgemanns (BEvT, 57). München: Kaiser, 1970, 217 p. Esp. 15-34; 109-137; 138-177; 178-201 [E. Güttgemanns, "Nachwort", 201-212]. → Klauck 1972

1971  The Relationship of Form to Content in the Parables: The Wedding Feast. — *Interpr* 25 (1971) 171-184. Esp. 176-180 [22,1-10]. [NTA 16, 160]
Die Wechselbeziehung von Form und Inhalt in den Gleichnissen: Das hochzeitliche Mahl. — HARNISCH, W. (ed.), *Die neutestamentliche Gleichnisforschung*, 1982, 59-75. Esp. 65-71.

1978  Narrative World and Ethical Response: The Marvelous and Righteousness in Matthew 1-2. — *Semeia* 12 (1978) 123-149. Esp. 131-135 [1-2]; 136-145 [righteousness]. [NTA 23, 425]

1980  Structure, Christology, and Ethics in Matthew. — SPENCER, R.A. (ed.), *Orientation by Disorientation. Studies in Literary Criticism and Biblical Literary Criticism. Presented in Honor of William A. Beardslee* (Pittsburgh Theological MS, 35), Pittsburgh, PA: Pickwick, 1980, 199-215. Esp. 199-201: "Structure as the organization of thematic content"; 201-210: "Structure as the organization of narrative process".

1987  Ethical Responsibility and Human Wholeness in Matthew 25:31-46. — *HTR* 80 (1987) 79-100. Esp. 80-82 [genre]; 83-90 [context]; 90-94 [interpretation]. [NTA 31, 1083]

1988 The Gospel of Matthew: Hypocrisy as Self-Deception. — *SBL 1988 Seminar Papers*, 508-516. Esp. 508-511 [7,15-20]; 512-513 [6,1-18]; 513-514 [13,11]; 515-516 [18,23-35].

1990 *Self-Deception and Wholeness in Paul and Matthew*. Minneapolis, MN: Fortress, 1990, VIII-173 p. Esp. 77-98: "Self-deception in Matthew" [1,18-25; 5,17-20; 7,15-20; 12,34-35]; 99-132: "The recovery of wholeness in Matthew" [5,3-10; 13,18-23; 16,5-12; 18,21-35]. [NTA 35, p. 261] → Gundry 1982/94, Kea 1991

    J.L. BAILEY, *Interpr* 47 (1993) 82-83; S. BROWN, *TorontoJT* 7 (1991) 287-288; N. CLARK, *ExpT* 102 (1990-91) 346-347; L. FLOOR, *Neotestamentica* 25 (1991) 437-438; M.A. GETTY, *CBQ* 54 (1992) 806-807; X. JACQUES, *NRT* 113 (1991) 761-763; G. SELLIN, *TLZ* 117 (1992) 435-437; L. STEFFEN, *CRBR* 5 (1992) 250-253.

1994 Matthew's Dark Light and the Human Condition. [6,22-23] — MALBON, E.S. – McKNIGHT, E.V., *The New Literary Criticism and the New Testament* (JSNT SS, 109), Sheffield: JSOT, 1994, 348-366.

### VICENT CERNUDA, Antonio

1974a El paralelismo de γεννῶ y τίκτω en Lc 1-2. — *Bib* 55 (1974) 260-264. Esp. 262-263 [1,20; 2,2]. [NTA 19, 574]

1974b La dialéctica γεννῶ-τίκτω en Mt 1-2. — *Ibid.*, 408-417. [NTA 19, 942]

1988 El domicilio de José y la fama de María. — *EstBíb* 46 (1988) 5-25. Esp. 8-12: "La virtual manifestación del domicilio de José en Mateo". [NTA 33, 579]

1990 La condena inopinada de Jesús. I. Pesquisa sobre la identidad de Barrabás. — *EstBíb* 48 (1990) 375-422. Esp. 400, 402-403, 412 [27,16]. [NTA 36, 139]

### VIDAL GARCÍA, Marciano

1967a *La figura ético-religiosa del misionero cristiano en la Instrucción Misionera de Mt. 9,35–11,1*. Diss. Pont. Univ. Lateranensis. Academia Alfonsiana, Roma, 1967, 2 vols., XLII-353 and 355 p. (A. Humbert). Esp. I, 1-29: "Aproximacion literario-tematica a la instrucción misionera de Mateo"; 30-91 [9,35-38]; 92-131 [10,1-5a]; 132-143 [10,5b-42]; 144-253 [10,5b-16]; 254-299 [10,17-33]; 300-330 [10,34-39]; 331-351 [10,40-42].

1967b La actividad misionera de Jesús, vista a la luz del sumario de Mt 9,35. — *Pentecostés* 5 (1967) 151-172.

1968a El comportamiento del apóstol durante la misión según las consignas de Mt 10,1-16. — *Pentecostés* 6 (1968) 3-63.

1968b Apostolado y persecución. Un tema de parénesis cristiana aplicado al apóstol (Mt 10,17-33). — *Ibid.*, 309-341.

1971 Seguimiento de Cristo y evangelización. Variación sobre un tema de moral neotestamentaria (Mt. 10,34-39). — *Salmanticensis* 18 (1971) 289-312. Esp. 290-293: "Modo de presentarse el tema de seguimiento"; 293-298 [10,34-38]; 298-312 [10,37-39]. [NTA 17, 122]

1972 La "Recompensa" como motivación del comportamiento moral cristiano. Estudio exegético-teológico de *Mt.* 10,40-42. — *Salmanticensis* 19 (1972) 261-278. [NTA 18, 109]

### VIDAL MANZANARES, Cesar

1993 *El primer Evangelio: el documenta Q* (Documento, 325). Barcelona: Planeta, 1993.

### VIDIGAL, José R.

1972a Querigma e batismo de Jesus. — *RevistCuBíb* 9 (1972) 36-51. [NTA 18, 435]

1972b O Sermão da montanha: Uma nova lei. — *Atualização* (Belo Horizonte) 3 (1972) 34-42.

### VIELHAUER, Philip

1939[R] Oikodome. Das Bild vom Bau in der christlichen Literatur vom Neuen Testament bis Clemens Alexandrinus. [1939] — ID., *Oikodome. Aufsätze zum Neuen Testament*, II, ed. G. Klein (Theologische Bücherei, 65), München: Kaiser, 1979, 1-168. Esp. 53-71: "Evangelien und Apostelgeschichte" [7,24-27; 16,17-19; 26,61; 27,40].

1955    Zum synoptischen Problem. Ein Bericht über die Theorien Léon Vaganays. — *TLZ* 80 (1955) 647-652. → Vaganay 1951, 1954a

1957    Gottesreich und Menschensohn in der Verkündigung Jesu. — SCHNEEMELCHER, W. (ed.), *Festschrift für Günther Dehn zum 75. Geburtstag am 18. April 1957 dargebracht von der Evangelisch-Theologischen Fakultät der Rheinischen Friedrich Wilhelms-Universität zu Bonn*, Neukirchen: Verlag der Buchhandlung des Erziehungsvereins, 1957, 51-79. Esp. 52-55 [Q]; 56-57 [Q 17,22-30]; 58 [10,23]; 61 [19,28]; 66 [Q 12,39-40; 17,26-30]; 66-68 [Q 17,23-24]; 68-71 [Q 6,22; 12,8-9]; = ID., *Aufsätze zum Neuen Testament*, 1965, 55-91. Esp. 56-59; 61-62; 63; 67; 73-74; 75-76; 76-79. → Tödt 1959

1959    Judenchristliche Evangelien. — HENNECKE, E. – SCHNEEMELCHER, W. (eds.), *Neutestamentliche Apokryphen*, I, ³1959, 75-108 (ET, 117-165). → Strecker 1987b

1963    Jesus und der Menschensohn. Zur Diskussion mit Heinz Eduard Tödt und Eduard Schweizer. — *ZTK* 60 (1963) 133-177. Esp. 141-147 [Q 12,8-9]; 147-148 [Q 12,39-40]; 148-150 [Q 17,23-24]; 150-152.165-166 [Q 11,30]; 161-163 [Q 9,58]; 163-165 [Q 7,34]. [NTA 8, 920]; = ID., *Aufsätze zum Neuen Testament*, 1965, 92-140. Esp. 101-107; 107-108; 108-110; 110-112.127-128; 123-125; 125-127. → Schweizer 1959b/60, Tödt 1959

1964    Apokalyptik des Urchristentums. Einleitung. — HENNECKE, E. – SCHNEEMELCHER, W. (eds.), *Neutestamentliche Apokryphen*, II, ³1964, 428-454. Esp. 436-437. (ET, 608-642). → Strecker 1989a

1965a   Ein Weg zur neutestamentlichen Christologie? Prüfung der Thesen Ferdinand Hahns. — *EvT* 25 (1965) 24-72. [NTA 9, 1145r]; = ID., *Aufsätze zum Neuen Testament*, 1965, 141-198. → F. Hahn 1963a

1965b   *Aufsätze zum Neuen Testament* (Theologische Bücherei, 31). München: Kaiser, 1965, 282 p. → 1957, 1963, 1965a.c

1965c   Tracht und Speise Johannes des Täufers. [3,4] — *Ibid.*, 47-54.

1965d   Zur Frage der christologischen Hoheitstitel. — *TLZ* 90 (1965) 569-588. [NTA 10, 762r] → F. Hahn 1963a, Tödt 1959

1966    Einleitung in das Neue Testament. — *TR* 31 (1966) 97-155, 193-231. [NTA 11, 10/536]; 42 (1977) 175-210. [NTA 22, 308]

1971    → Bultmann 1931/58

1975    *Geschichte der urchristlichen Literatur. Einleitung in das Neue Testament, die Apokryphen und die Apostolischen Väter* (de Gruyter Lehrbuch). Berlin – New York: de Gruyter, 1975, XIX-813 p. Esp. 268-280: "Die Zwei-Quellen-Theorie" (Q: 270-272.275-276); 311-329: "Die Spruchquelle"; 355-366: "Das Matthäusevangelium".
        *Historia de la literatura cristiana primitiva. Introducción al Nuevo Testamento, los Apócrifos y los Padres Apostólicos*, trans. M. Olasagasti, et al. (Biblioteca de estudios bíblicos, 72). Salamanca: Sígueme, 1991, 865 p.

**VIGEN, Larry A.**

1985    *"To Think the Things of God". A Discoursive Reading of Matthew 16:13–18:35*. Diss. Vanderbilt Univ., Nashville, TN, 1985, 429 p. (D. Patte). — *DissAbstr* 47 (1986-87) 554-A; *SBT* 15 (1987) 115-116.

**VIGNE, Daniel**

1992    *Christ au Jourdain. Le Baptême de Jésus dans la tradition judéo-chrétienne* (Études bibliques, NS 16). Paris: Gabalda, 1992, 362 p. — Diss. Inst. Pont. Oriental., Roma, 1980 (T. Špidlík).

**VIJVER, Enrique**

1987    El uso de la Biblia en cuestiones éticas. El caso del divorcio. — *CuadTeol* 8 (1987) 17-33. Esp. 23-25 [5,31-32; 19,1-9]. [NTA 32, 861]

**VILAR HUESO, Vicente**

1992   Notas marginales de san Juan de Ribera a Mt 1–2. — *EstBíb* 50 (1992) 305-316.

**VÍLCHEZ, José**

1983   Presencia y experiencia del Espiritu. — *MiscCom* 78-79 (1983) 293-299. Esp. 293-295.

**VILLAR, Evaristo**

1983   ¡Felices, los pobres de espíritu! [5,3] — *BibFe* 9 (1983) 126-136.

**VILLEGAS, Beltrán**

1987   Peter, Philip and James of Alphaeus. [10,2-4] — *NTS* 33 (1987) 292-294. [NTA 31, 1005]

1989   La madre de Jesús en el Evangelio de Tomás (Logg. 55, 99, 101 y 105). — *RevistCatTeol* 14 (1989) 257-266 (English summary, 266). Esp. 257-261 [10,37-38; 16,24-25/Th 55, 101]; 264-266 [12,46-50/Th 99].

1990   *Introducción crítica a los evangelios sinópticos* (Colleción Fe y Teología, 18). Santiago: Publicaciones teológicas del Seminario Pontificio Mayor de Santiago de Chile, 1990, 135 p.

**VINAY, Valdo**

1971   La parabola dei talenti e l'etica di G. Calvino. [25,14-30] — *Protestantesimo* 26 (1971) 79-87.

**VINCENT, John J.**

1959   The Parables of Jesus as Self-Revelation. — *Studia Evangelica* 1 (1959) 79-99. Esp. 88 [21,28-32]; 89 [18,12-14]; 90 [11,16-19]; 93-94 [24,45-51]; 94 [10,24-25]; 94-95 [20,1-15]; 97 [24,43-44]; 97-98 [25,1-13].

1968   *Secular Christ. A Contemporary Interpretation of Jesus.* Nashville, TN – New York: Abingdon, 1968, 240 p. Esp. 108-125 [parables]; 126-142 [discipleship].

**VINCENT, Louis-Hugues**

1952   Le lithostrotos évangélique. [27,19] — *RB* 59 (1952) 513-530.

**VINE, Victor E.**

1991   Luke 14:15-24 and Anti-Semitism. [22,1-10] — *ExpT* 102 (1990-91) 262-263. [NTA 36, 208]

**VINSON, Richard Bolling**

1982   A Study of Matthean Doublets with Marcan Parallels. — *SBT* 12 (1982) 239-259. Esp. 240-242 [5,29-30/18,8-9]; 242-245 [5,32/19,9]; 245 [10,22/24,9]; 245-247 [10,38/16,24]; 247-250 [10,39/16,25]; 250-251 [12,39/16,4]; 251-253 [13,12/25,29]; 253-254 [17,20/21,21]; 254-255 [19,30/20,16]; 255-257 [20,26-27/23,11]; 257-258 [24,42/25,13].

1984   *The Significance of the Minor Agreements as an Argument against the Two-Document Hypothesis.* Diss. Duke Univ., Durham, NC, 1984, VI-438 p. (D.M. Smith). Esp. 11-373: "A list of the minor agreements". — *DissAbstr* 45 (1984-85) 2553. → T.A. Friedrichsen 1989b

1991   A Comparative Study of the Use of *Enthymemes* in the Synoptic Gospels. — WATSON, D.F. (ed.), *Persuasive Artistry.* FS G.A. Kennedy, 1991, 119-141. Esp. 121-122.124-126.128-129.133-137.

**VIRGULIN, Stefano**

1984   Il lamento di Gesù su Gerusalemme (Mt 23,37-39; Lc 13,34-35). — PROVERA, L. (ed.), *Gesù Apostolo e Sommo Sacerdote.* FS T. Ballarini, 1984, 73-82.

**VISCHER, Wilhelm**

1985   Les combattants du libérateur. Hosanna au plus haut des cieux!? [21,9]; Simon Baryona [16,17]; Youdas Iskarioth. [26,14] — ID., *L'Écriture et la parole. Là où le péché abonde, la grâce surabonde* (Essais bibliques, 12), Genève: Labor et fides, 1985, 165-182.

**VISONÀ, Giuseppe**

1990 *Citazioni patristiche e critica testuale neotestamentaria. Il caso di Lc 12,49* (AnBib, 125). Roma: Pont. Istituto Biblico, 1990, VII-79 p. Esp. 33-50: "Per un'interpretazione di Lc 12,49-50".

**VISOTZKY, Burton L.**

1987 Overturning the Lamp. — *JJS* 38 (1987) 72-80. Esp. 79-80 [5,15]. [NTA 32, 382]; = ID., *Fathers of the World. Essays in Rabbinic and Patristic Literatures* (WUNT, 80), Tübingen: Mohr, 1995, 75-84. Esp. 82-83.

**VISSER, H.B.**

1952 Het slot van de procedure volgens Matth. 18. [18,17] — *GTT* 52 (1952) 148-152.

**VITESTAM, Gösta**

1993 Zu Einflussen des Paternosters in der islamischen Tradition. — *Orientalia Suecana* (Uppsala) 41-42 (1992-93) 299-306.

**VITTMANN, Günther**

1981 Überlegungen zu Matthäus 1,18. — *BibNot* 16 (1981) 39-41.

**VITTONATTO, Giuseppe**

1955 La risurrezione dei morti in Mt 27,52-53. — *RivBib* 3 (1955) 193-219; = *Sapienza* (Roma) 9 (1956) 131-150. Esp. 132-146: "Sentenze"; 146-149: "Esame del testo". [NTA 1, 42]

**VIVIANO, Benedict T.**

1978 *Study as Worship. Aboth and the New Testament* (Studies in Judaism in Late Antiquity, 26). Leiden: Brill, 1978, XI-227 p. Esp. 158-195: "The synoptic gospels and the rabbinic ideal of Torah-study as a form of worship" [5,17-20; 10,24-25.40-42; 11,25-30; 15,1-20; 23,8-10].

1979 Where Was the Gospel according to St. Matthew Written? — *CBQ* 41 (1979) 533-546. Esp. 533-540 [place]; 540-546 [Greek patristics]. [NTA 24, 409]

1983 Matthew, Master of Ecumenical Healing. — *CurrTMiss* 10 (1983) 325-332. Esp. 330-332 [5,17-20; 16,18-19; 28,16-20]. [NTA 28, 483]

1989 The Pharisees in Matthew 23. — *BiTod* 27 (1989) 338-344. [NTA 34, 633]

1990a The Gospel according to Matthew. — BROWN, R.E., et al. (eds.), *The New Jerome Biblical Commentary*, 1990, 630-674.
Il vangelo secondo Matteo. — BROWN, R.E., et al., *Nuovo grande commentario biblico*, 1997, 821-879.

1990b The Genres of Matthew 1-2: Light from I Timothy 1:4. — *RB* 97 (1990) 31-53. Esp. 31-43; 44-50 [1-2/1 Tim 1,4]; 50-53. [NTA 34, 1129]

1990c Rabbouni and Mark 9:5. — *Ibid.*, 207-218. Esp. 209-211 [Rabbi in Mt]. [NTA 35, 651]

1990d Social World and Community Leadership: The Case of Matthew 23.1-12.34. — *JSNT* 39 (1990) 3-21. [NTA 35, 146]

1992 Beatitudes Found among Dead Sea Scrolls. [4Q525] — *BibArchRev* 18/6 (1992) 53-55, 66. [NTA 37, 1019] → 1993; → É. Puech 1991

1993 Eight Beatitudes at Qumran and in Matthew? A New Publication from Cave Four. [4Q525] — *SEÅ* 58 (1993) 71-84. [NTA 38, 1711] → 1992; → É. Puech 1991

**VLEDDER, Evert Jan**

1994 The Social Stratification of the Matthean Community. — *Neotestamentica* 28 (1994) 511-522. [NTA 40, 157] → 1997/94
The Social Location of the Matthean Community. — *HervTS* 51 (1995) 388-408. [NTA 40, 810]

1997 *Conflict in the Miracle Stories: A Socio-Exegetical Study of Matthew 8 and 9* (JSNT SS, 152). Sheffield: JSOT, 1997, 276 p. Esp. 15-56: "Conflict in the miracle stories inadequately

explained"; 57-116: "Conflict theory"; 117-167: "The social location of the Matthean community"; 168-242: "Exegesis of Matthew 8 and 9 in the light of conflict theory". — Diss. Pretoria, 1994 (A.G. van Aarde). →
1994; → Joubert 1995

**VOEGELIN, Eric**

1971   The Gospel and Culture. — MILLER, D.G. - HADIDIAN, D.Y. (eds.), *Jesus and Man's Hope*. II, 1971, 59-101. Esp. 88-101 [11,25-30; 16,13-23].

**VÖGTLE, Anton**

1953   Der Spruch vom Jonaszeichen. [12,39-40; Q 11,31-32] — SCHMID, J. — VÖGTLE, A. (eds.), *Synoptische Studien*. FS A. Wikenhauser, 1953, 230-277; = ID., *Das Evangelium und die Evangelien*, 1971, 103-136.

1954   Der Petrus der Verheissung und der Erfüllung. Zum Petrusbuch von Oscar Cullmann. — *MüTZ* 5 (1954) 1-47; München: Zink, 1954, 47 p. → Cullmann 1952

1957   Messiasbekenntnis und Petrusverheißung. Zur Komposition Mt 16,13-23 Par. — *BZ* 1 (1957) 252-272. Esp. 254-265: "Der Skopus des Messiasbekenntnisses bei Mk und Mt"; 265-266: "Folgerung und Problemstellung"; 266-272: "Angebliche Gründe für die Geschichtlichkeit der Mt-Komposition". [NTA 2, 533]; 2 (1958) 85-103. Esp. 85-89: "Der angeblich sekundäre Charakter der Mk-Fassung"; 89-101: "Der sekundäre Charakter der Komposition Mt 16,13-20". [NTA 3, 76]; = ID., *Das Evangelium und die Evangelien*, 1971, 137-170. Esp. 139-148; 148-149; 149-155; 155-158; 158-168.

1959a   Ekklesiologische Auftragsworte des Auferstandenen. — COPPENS, J., et al. (eds.), *Sacra Pagina*, 1959, II, 280-294. Esp. 284-287.289-293 [16,13-19; 18,18; 28,18-20]; = ID., *Das Evangelium und die Evangelien*, 1971, 243-252. Esp. 244-248; 250-252.

1959b   Jesus und die Kirche. — ROESLE, M. - CULLMANN, O. (eds.), *Begegnung der Christen*. FS O. Karrer, 1959, 54-81. Esp. 58-69.78-81 [16,18-19]; 69-71 [10,23]; = *TJb*, 1964, 121-144.

1961   "Josias zeugte den Jechonias und seine Brüder" (Mt 1,11). — GROSS, H. - MUSSNER, F. (eds.), *Lex tua veritas. Festschrift für Hubert Junker zur Vollendung des siebzigsten Lebensjahres am 8. August 1961*, Trier: Paulinus, 1961, 307-313.

1964a   Das christologische und ekklesiologische Anliegen von Mt. 28,18-20. — *Studia Evangelica* 2 (1964) 266-294. Esp. 269-277 [28,18-20/Dan 7,13-14]; 277-286 [ἐξουσία]; 286-294 [13,36-43]; = ID., *Das Evangelium und die Evangelien*, 1971, 253-272. Esp. 255-260; 260-266; 266-272.

1964b   Exegetische Erwägungen über das Wissen und Selbstbewußtsein Jesu. — METZ, J.B., et al. (eds.), *Gott in Welt*. FS K. Rahner, 1964, I, 608-667. Esp. 609-620 [synoptic tradition: 8,11-12; 10,23; 11,27; 16,28; 24,34]; 622 [12,39; 16,18; Q 12,8-9]; 634 [3,14-15]; 647-651 [10,23]; 653-654 [11,27]; = ID., *Das Evangelium und die Evangelien*, 1971, 296-344. Esp. 296-306; 307-308; 317; 328-332; 333-334.
Exegetische overdenkingen over de kennis en het zelfbewustzijn van Jezus. — *God en wereld*, 1965, IV, 37-97; 158-167. Esp. 39-51; 53-54; 64; 77-81; 84-87.
Réflexions exégétiques sur la psychologie de Jésus. — *Le message de Jésus*, 1969, 41-113. Esp. 42-56: "Données de la tradition synoptique"; 58-59; 72-73; 89-93; 96-98.

1964c   Die Genealogie Mt 1,2-16 und die matthäische Kindheitsgeschichte. — *BZ* 8 (1964) 45-58, 239-262. Esp. 45-54 [historicity of 1-2]; 54-58: "Zur Eigenart der matthäischen KG"; 270-247: "Struktur und Thematik von Mt 1"; 247-248: "Der Haupteinschnitt der matthäischen KG"; 248-258: "Struktur und Thematik von Mt 2". [NTA 8, 936; 9, 519]; 9 (1965) 32-49. Esp. 32-38: "Der Zahlenschematismus"; 38-41: "Zusätzliche Angaben"; 41-46: "Die Verifizierung der Zahlenverhältnisse"; 46-48: "Die Unterbrechung des Schemas in 1,16"; 48-49: "Der Verfasser der Genealogie Mt 1". [NTA 10, 111]; = ID., *Das Evangelium und die Evangelien*, 1971, 57-102. Esp. 57-64; 65-68; 68-73; 74-75; 75-84; 87-92; 92-95; 95-99; 99-102; 102.

1965   Das Schicksahl des Messiaskindes. Zur Auslegung und Theologie von Mt 2. — *BibLeb*
       6 (1965) 246-279. Esp. 249-262 [historical Jesus]; 267-272 [Haggada]. [NTA 10, 900]; = *TJb*, 1968,
       126-159. Esp. 128-141; 146-151.
       *SelT* 9 (1970) 95-106.

1966   *Das Neue Testament und die neuere katholische Exegese.* I: *Grundlegende Fragen zur*
       *Entstehung und Eigenart des NT* (Aktuelle Schriften zur Religionspädagogik). Freiburg:
       Herder, 1966, 179 p. Esp. 59-63; 69-95: "Die Evangelien".

1967   Mt 1,25 und die "Virginitas B.M. Virginis post partum". — *De Beata Virgine Maria*
       *in Evangeliis Synopticis* (Maria in Sacra Scriptura. Acta congressus mariologici-mariani
       in Republica Dominicana anno 1965 celebrati, IV/4), Roma: Pont. Acad. Mariana Int.,
       1967, 433-443; = *TQ* 147 (1967) 28-39. [NTA 12, 147]

1970   *Das Neue Testament und die Zukunft des Kosmos.* Düsseldorf: Patmos, 1970, 259 p.
       Esp. 101-102.104-107 [5,18]; 151-166: "Zwei Wendungen matthäischer Eschatologie" [συντελεία;
       παλιγγενεσία].

1971a  *Messias und Gottessohn. Herkunft und Sinn der matthäischen Geburts- und*
       *Kindheitsgeschichte* (Theologische Perspektiven). Düsseldorf: Patmos, 1971, 88 p. Esp.
       15-31 [sources]; 32-60 [2/Moses]; 61-64 [pre-Mt form]; 65-80: "Zur matthäischen Interpretation der
       Erzählung Mt 2"; 81-88: "Entstehung und Aussageintention". [NTA 16, p. 374]
       L. BOFF, *REB* 32 (1972) 497-498; J. DE JESÚS MARÍA, *EstJos* 27 (1973) 267; G. GOZZELINO, *Sal* 35
       (1973) 365-366; X. JACQUES, *NRT* 94 (1972) 1098; J. MURPHY-O'CONNOR, *RB* 80 (1973) 282-285; E.
       NELLESSEN, *TRev* 68 (1972) 370-371; E. PERETTO, *Marianum* 38 (1976) 324-325; W. PESCH, *TTZ* 82
       (1973) 189-190; B. PIEPIÓRKA, *ZKT* 95 (1973) 218; J. ROLOFF, *TLZ* 98 (1973) 292-293; J.M. TISON,
       *Bijdragen* 34 (1972) 214-215.
       *Messia e figlio di Dio. Origine e significato del racconto della nascita e dell'infanzia in Matteo*, trans.
       Benedettine di Civitella (Studi biblici, 35). Brescia: Paideia, 1976, 110 p.

1971b  *Das Evangelium und die Evangelien. Beiträge zur Evangelienforschung* (Kommentare
       und Beiträge zum Alten und Neuen Testament). Düsseldorf: Patmos, 1971, 360 p. →
       1953, 1957, 1959a, 1964a-c, 1971c-d

1971c  Die Einladung zum großen Gastmahl und zum königlichen Hochzeitsmahl. Ein Para-
       digma für den Wandel des geschichtlichen Verständnishorizonts. — *Ibid.*, 171-218. Esp.
       172-190: "Rekonstruktion der ältesten greifbaren Fassung"; 191-196: "Der Skopos des Gleichnisses im Munde
       Jesu"; 196-215: "Die Verwendung und Neuerzählung des Mahlgleichnisses in der nachösterlichen
       Verkündigung".

1971d  Wunder und Wort in urkirchlicher Glaubenswerbung (Mt 11,2-6 / Lk 7,18-23). —
       *Ibid.*, 219-242. Esp. 219-222: "Die Q-Fassung des Apophthegmas"; 222-236: "Ursprünglicher Bericht
       oder urchristliche Bildung?"; 236-241: "Die Herkunft des Apophthegmas".

1972a  Die matthäische Kindheitsgeschichte. — DIDIER, M. (ed.), *L'Évangile selon Matthieu*,
       1972, 153-183. Esp. 153-156: "Herkunft und Intention von Kap 1"; 156-165: "Liegt Mt., II eine
       vormatthäische Erzählungseinheit zugrunde?"; 165-169: "Voraussetzungen und Aussageintention der
       vormatthäischen Erzählung Mt., II"; 169-181: "Zur matthäischen Interpretation der Erzählung Mt., II"; 182-
       183: "Zur Entstehung des matthäischen 'Prologs'".

1972b  Die sogenannte Taufperikope Mk 1,9-11. Zur Problematik der Herkunft und des ur-
       sprünglichen Sinns. — *EKK NT Vorarbeiten*, 4, 1972, 105-139. Esp. 106-111: "Die älteste
       greifbare Fassung der Taufperikope"; 131-139: "Ein möglicher Sitz der Taufperikope im Leben der
       Urkirche".
       Herkunft und ursprünglicher Sinn der Taufperikope Mk 1,9-11. — ID., *Offenbarungsgeschehen und*
       *Wirkungsgeschichte*, 1985, 70-100 ("Nachtrag", 100-108). Esp. 70-75; 93-100.

1973   Zum Problem der Herkunft von "Mt 16,17-19". — HOFFMANN, P., et al. (eds.),
       *Orientierung an Jesus.* FS J. Schmid, 1973, 372-393. Esp. 373-377: "Die durch V. 17
       aufgegebene Problematik"; 377-383: "Möglichkeit und Grenzen der Protophanieerzählunghypothese"; 384-
       391: "Protophanieerzählung und Matthäus-Redaktion".
       Das Problem der Herkunft von "Mt 16,17-19". — ID., *Offenbarungsgeschehen und Wirkungsgeschichte*,
       1985, 109-127 ("Nachtrag", 127-140). Esp. 110-113; 113-118; 119-125.

1974a    "Theo-logie" und "Eschato-logie" in der Verkündigung Jesu? — GNILKA, J. (ed.), *Neues Testament und Kirche*. FS R. Schnackenburg, 1974, 371-398. Esp. 381-383 [6,26-32]; 386-388; = ID., *Offenbarungsgeschehen und Wirkungsgeschichte*, 1985, 11-33. Esp. 19-21; 23-24.

1974b    Das Vaterunser – ein Gebet für Juden und Christen? — BROCKE, M., et al. (eds.), *Das Vaterunser*, 1974, 165-195. The Lord's Prayer: A Prayer for Jews and Christians. — BROCKE, M. - PETUCHOWSKI, J.J. (eds.), *The Lord's Prayer*, 1978, 93-117.

1975     Der "eschatologische" Bezug der Wir-Bitten des Vaterunser. — ELLIS, E.E. - GRÄSSER, E. (eds.), *Jesus und Paulus*. *Festschrift für Werner Georg Kümmel zum 70. Geburtstag*, Göttingen: Vandenhoeck & Ruprecht, 1975, 344-362. Esp. 344-346 [6,10]; 346-358 [6,11-13]; 358-362 [eschatology]; = ID., *Offenbarungsgeschehen und Wirkungsgeschichte*, 1985, 34-48 ("Nachtrag", 49). Esp. 34-37; 37-45; 45-48.

1976     Todesankündigungen und Todesverständnis Jesu. — KERTELGE, K. (ed.), *Der Tod Jesu*, 1976, 51-113. Esp. 80-88 [Q 12,49-50].

1982     Bezeugt die Logienquelle die authentische Redeweise Jesu vom "Menschensohn"? — DELOBEL, J. (ed.), *Logia*, 1982, 77-99. Esp. 77-90 [Polag]; 91-96 [Hoffmann]; 96-98 [Schürmann]; = ID., *Offenbarungsgeschehen und Wirkungsgeschichte*, 1985, 50-69. Esp. 50-62; 62-67; 67-69.

1983     *Was ist Frieden? Orientierungshilfen aus dem Neuen Testament*. Freiburg: Herder, 1983, 165 p. Esp. 71-74 [5,21-26]; 81-82 [26,51-54]; 90-96 [5,38-42]; 109-140: "'Bergpredigt' und weltliches Regieren".

1985     *Offenbarungsgeschehen und Wirkungsgeschichte*. *Neutestamentliche Beiträge*. Freiburg: Herder, 1985, 328 p. → 1972b, 1973, 1974a, 1975, 1982

1989a    Eine überholte "Menschensohn"-Hypothese? — ALAND, K. - MEURER, S. (eds.), *Wissenschaft und Kirche*. *Festschrift für Eduard Lohse* (Texte und Arbeiten zur Bibel, 4), Bielefeld: Luther, 1989, 70-95. Esp. 73-76 [Q 12,8-9]; 78-83.89-92 [Q 11,30].

1989b    Ein "unablässiger Stachel" (Mt 5,39b-42 par Lk 6,29-30). — MERKLEIN, H. (ed.), *Neues Testament und Ethik*. FS R. Schnackenburg, 1989, 53-70. Esp. 53-63 [Q 6,29-30]; 63-67 [community]; 67-70 [ethics].

1994     *Die "Gretchenfrage" des Menschensohnproblems. Bilanz und Perspektive* (QDisp, 152). Freiburg: Herder, 1994, 182 p. Esp. 9-13: "Die Schlüsselrolle von Lk 12,8f par in der Menschensohnfrage"; 14-21: "Eine Beurteilung des Doppelspruchs in Verbindung mit der Hypothese der erst nachösterlichen Herkunft des Menschensohntitels"; 22-81: "Der Ich / der Menschensohn-Spruch im Rahmen von Authentizitätshypothesen"; 98-101.118-119.147-148 [Q 12,8-9]; 138-139 [Q 17,26-28]; 140 [Q 17,23-24]; 148-159.162-163 [Q 11,29-30]; 159-162 [12,39-40; 24,29-30]. [NTA 40, p. 529]

**VÖLKEL, Martin**

1973     Anmerkungen zur lukanischen Fassung der Täuferanfrage Luk 7,18-23. — DIETRICH, W., et al. (eds.), *Festgabe für K.H. Rengstorf*, 1973, 166-173.

1978     "Freund der Zöllner und Sünder". — *ZNW* 69 (1978) 1-10. Esp. 2-4 [11,19]. [NTA 23, 804]

**VÖLKL, Richard**

1961     *Christ und Welt nach dem Neuen Testament*. Würzburg: Echter, 1961, 515 p. Esp. 15-154: "Die Lehre Jesu nach der synoptischen Überlieferung". — Diss. München, 1959 (R. Egenter).

**VOELTZEL, René**

1973     *L'enfant et son éducation dans la Bible* (Le point théologique, 6). Paris: Beauchesne, 1973, 124 p. Esp. 62-69: "Les Évangiles de l'enfance"; 70-86 "L'enfant de Jésus".

**VOELZ, James W.**

1984 The Language of the New Testament. — *ANRW* II.25.2 (1984) 893-977. Esp. 951-952 [participle]; 960-963 [semitisms].

**VÖÖBUS, Arthur**

1950 The Oldest Extant Traces of the Syriac Peshitta. — *Muséon* 63 (1950) 191-204.

1951a *Die Spuren eines älteren äthiopischen Evangelientextes im Lichte der literarischen Monumente* (Papers of the Estonian Theological Society in Exile, 2). Stockholm: Estonian Theological Society in Exile, 1951, 40 p. Esp. 23-29.

1951b *Studies in the History of the Gospel Text in Syriac* (CSCO, 128). Leuven: Durbecq, 1951, XXV-219 p. Esp. 91-92; 96; 111; 114-116; 137; 148-149; 154-155; 160-165; 179-181; 183-184 [Rabbula]; 187-197 [Graeco-syro translation literature]; 197-200 [Philoxenos].

1952 Die Evangelienzitate in der Einleitung der persischen Märtyrerakten. — *Bib* 33 (1952) 222-234. Esp. 224 [3,17; 18,7]; 225-230 [2,18; 6,24; 10,19-20; 16,18; 23,37].

1953a *Zur Geschichte des altgeorgischen Evangelientextes* (Papers of the Estonian Theological Society in Exile, 4). Stockholm: Estonian Theological Society in Exile, 1953, 40 p. Esp. 11, 14-15, 22-23, 29.

1953b *Neue Materialien zur Geschichte der Vetus Syra in den Evangelienhandschriften. Ein vorläufiger Bericht über die Neuen Funde* (Papers of the Estonian Theological Society in Exile, 5). Stockholm: Estonian Theological Society in Exile, 1953, 20 p. Esp. 14-18 [5,17-24; 11,28; 18,4-28; 25,34].

1954 *Early Versions of the New Testament. Manuscript Studies* (Papers of the Estonian Theological Society in Exile, 6). Stockholm: Estonian Theological Society in Exile, 1954, XVII-412 p. Esp. 16-21 [Diatessaron: 1,24; 2,15.23; 7,25.27; 10,39; 16,21; 17,20; 19,5]; 48-50 [Old Latin: 3,15; 20,33]; 79 [Old Syriac: 9,18; 18,17; 23,5]; 130 [Palest. Syriac: 3,4; 27,16]; 156-158.166-167 [Armenian: 5,18; 7,3-12; 23,31-40; 28,18]; 192-195 [Georgian: 2,6; 11,28; 14,1; 21,12]; 235 [Bohairic: 24,36; 27,49]; 257-261 [Ethiopic: 1,8; 2,13; 3,16; 4,8-9; 10,28; 25,34]; 282-284 [Arabic: 1,24; 2,13-15; 7,25]; 372-373; 384-385; 396-403 [plates].

1973 Découverte du commentaire de Mōšē bar Kēphā sur l'Évangile de Matthieu. — *RB* 80 (1973) 359-362. [NTA 19, 90]

1987 *Studies in the History of the Gospel Text in Syriac. New Contributions to the Sources Elucidating the History of the Traditions.* II (CSCO, 496). Leuven: Peeters, 1987, XXVI-256 p. Esp. 38 [12,29-46]; 44-45 [24,23-30]; 49-51; 56-57 [26]; 61-62; 64 [13]; 78-79; 82-83 [21,16-44; 27,9-17; 27,54-28,2]; 85-89 [8,1-26; 11,1-29]; 90-92; 94 [5,1-24]; 96-97 [10,8-27; 16,4-28]; 98-99; 113-133 [lectionaries]; 147-150 [6,10.12]; 150-153 [5,17-26]; 153-154 [10,28-33]; 157-158 [10,16-31]; 164-180 [18].

**VOGEL, R.A.**

1989 *Against Your Brother. Conflict Themes and the Rhetoric of the Gospel according to Matthew.* Diss. Univ. of Oregon, 1989.

**VOGELS, Heinrich Josef**

1922R *Novum Testamentum Graece et Latine* [1922; ³1949]. Freiburg: Herder, ⁴1955, 2 vols., XIII-478 and VIII-479-794 p. Esp. I, 1-105: "Κατὰ Ματθαῖον".

1923R *Handbuch der Textkritik des Neuen Testaments* [1923]. Bonn: Hanstein, 1955, VIII-236 p. Esp. 152-220: "Die Methode der Textkritik".

1951 Mk 14,25 und Parallelen. — ADLER, N. (ed.), *Vom Wort des Lebens*. FS M. Meinertz, 1951, 93-104. Esp. 94-95.97-99 [26,29].

1952 Codex VII der Cathedralbibliothek von Verona (b²). [1,18-9,9] — FISCHER, B. - FIALA, V.E. (eds.), *Colligere fragmenta: Festschrift Alban Dold zum 70. Geburtstag am 7.7.1952* (Texte und Arbeiten, I/2), Beuron: Beuroner Kunstverlag, 1952, 1-12.

1953 *Evangelium Colbertinum. Codex lat. 254 der Bibliothèque Nationale zu Paris. I. Text* (BBB, 4). Bonn: Hanstein, 1953, 166 p. Esp. 7-51 [edition]; II. *Untersuchungen* (BBB, 5), 1953, 182 p. Esp. 24-31; 35-65 [variant readings].

1955 Der Bibeltext in drei pseudoambrosianischen Predigten. — *ZNW* 46 (1955) 60-68. Esp. 63-64.

**VOGELS, Heinz-Jürgen**

1976 *Christi Abstieg ins Totenreich und das Läuterungsgericht an den Toten. Eine bibeltheologisch-dogmatische Untersuchung zum Glaubensartikel "descendit ad inferos"* (Freiburger theologische Studien, 102). Freiburg: Herder. 1976, 270 p. Esp. 49-50 [27,52-53]; 60-73 [5,25-26]. — Diss. Mainz, 1974.

**VOGELS, Walter**

1974 La proclamation de l'alliance universelle en Mt 28,18-20. — *ZMiss* 58 (1974) 258-272. Esp. 258-262: "Historicité"; 262-264: "Structure et genre littéraire"; 254-269: "L'analyse".

1990 Performers and Receivers of the Kingdom. A Semiotic Analysis of Matthew 11,2-15. — *SE* 42 (1990) 325-336. Esp. 326-329: "Narrative analysis"; 329-333: "Discursive analysis"; 333-335: "The semiotic square". [NTA 36, 151]

1995 Justice et gratuité. Analyse sémiotique de Matthieu 20,1-16. — *Revue de l'Institut Catholique de l'Afrique de l'Ouest* (Abidjan) 10 (1995) 61-71.

**VOGLER, Werner**

1971 Rabbinische Voraussetzungen und Parallelen der urkirchlichen Tradition. — *BibLeb* 12 (1971) 105-118. Esp. 107-108 [23,2]; 110-112 [rabbi]. [NTA 16, 396]

1982 Gib uns, was wir heute zum Leben brauchen. Zur Auslegung der vierten Bitte des Vaterunsers. — SEIDEL, H. - BIERITZ, K.-H. (eds.), *Das lebendige Wort. Beiträge zur kirchlichen Verkündigung. Festgabe für Gottfried Voigt zum 65. Geburtstag*, Berlin: Evangelische Verlagsanstalt, 1982, 52-63.

1983 *Judas Iskarioth. Untersuchungen zu Tradition und Redaktion von Texten des Neuen Testaments und außerkanonischer Schriften* (Theologische Arbeiten, 42). Berlin: Evangelische Verlagsanstalt, 1983, 224 p. Esp. 57-74: "Tradition und Redaktion bei Matthäus". — Diss. Greifswald, 1978 (G. Haufe).

1986 Die "Naherwartung" Jesu. — *TVers* 16 (1986) 57-71.

**VOGT, Ernst**

1953a Ὀψὲ σαββάτων. [28,1] — *Bib* 34 (1953) 120. → 1960

1953b "Quod dictum est per Ieremiam prophetam" (Mt 27,9). — *Ibid.*, 265.

1954 Ὁ ἄρτος ὁ ἐπιούσιος = ὁ ἄρτος ὁ τῆς ἐπιούσης. [6 11] — *Bib* 35 (1954) 136-137, 274.

1960 "Vespere sabbati, illucescente in primam sabbati". [28,1] — *Bib* 41 (1960) 191-193. → 1953a; → Grintz 1960

**VOGT, Hermann Josef**

1972 (ed.), *Martin Bucer & Thomas Cranmer, Annotationes in octo priora capita Evangelii secundum Matthaeum (Croydon 1549)*. Frankfurt: Athenäum, 1972, 177 p.
F.F. BRUCE, *Erasmus* 25 (1973) 521-523.

1980a Falsche Ergänzungen oder Korrekturen im Mattäus-Kommentar des Origenes. — *TQ* 160 (1980) 207-212.

1980b Wie Origenes in seinem Matthäuskommentar Fragen offen läßt. — CROUZEL, H. - QUACQUARELLI, A. (eds.), *Origeniana Secunda*, 1980, 191-198.

1983 (trans.), *Origenes. Der Kommentar zum Evangelium nach Mattäus. Eingeleitet, übersetzt und mit Anmerkungen versehen*, I (Bibliothek der Griechischen Literatur, 18). Stuttgart: Hiersemann, 1983, IX-344 p. Esp. 1-59: "Einleitung"; 61-303: "Übersetzung" [Books 10-13]; II (BGL, 30), 1990, X-371 p. Esp. 1-31: "Einleitung"; 33-324: "Übersetzung" [Books 14-17]; III. *Die Commentariorum Series* (BGL, 38), 1993, XI-417 p. Esp. 1-22: "Einleitung"; 23-374: "Übersetzung".

H. CROUZEL, *BullLitEccl* 85 (1984) 142-144; A. DE HALLEUX, *RHE* 79 (1984) 841; R. GÖGLER, *Jahrbuch für Antike und Christentum* (Münster) 30 (1987) 209-213; P. HÜNERMANN, *TQ* 166 (1986) 59-61; P. MARAVAL, *RHPR* 64 (1984) 154-155; O. NORDERVAL, *NorskTeolTids* 86 (1985) 244-245; A. ORBE, *Greg* 66 (1985) 768-769; J.C.M. VAN WINDEN, *VigChr* 38 (1984) 99.

H. CROUZEL, *BullLitEccl* 92 (1991) 124-125; L. LIES, *TRev* 88 (1992) 94-95; P. MARAVAL, *RHPR* 72 (1992) 375; M. PARMENTIER, *Bijdragen* 53 (1992) 438.

P. MARAVAL, *RHPR* 75 (1995) 347; C.C. MARCHESELLI, *Asprenas* 42 (1995) 599-601; J.C.M. VAN WINDEN, *VigChr* 48 (1994) 389-390.

1993 Bemerkungen zur lateinischen Übersetzung des Mattäus-Kommentares von Origenes. — GRYSON, R. (ed.), *Philologia Sacra*. FS J. Frede – W. Thiele, 1993, 378-396.

**VOICU, Sever J.**

1978 *In operarios undecimae horae*: una omelia pseudocrisostomica arianeggiante. [20,1-16] — *Augustinianum* 18 (1978) 341-360. Esp. 353-356 [edition].

**VOIGT, Hans-Heinrich**

1989 Astronomie, Astrologie, Theologie. [2,1-12] — *TR* 54 (1989) 422-426. [NTA 34, 610r] → Strobel 1985

**VOIGT, Simão**

1971 Solução para um texto difícil do Sermão da montanha (Mt 5,22). — ID. - VIER, F. (eds.), *Atualidades Bíblicas. Miscelânea em memória de Frei João José Pedreira de Castro, o.f.m.*, Petrópolis: Vozes, 1971, 447-486. Esp. 448-456.477-486 [5,22]; 465-466 [18,34]; 466 [22,7].

**VOKES, F.E.**

1970 The Lord's Prayer in the First Three Centuries. — *Studia Patristica* 10 (1970) 253-260.

1993 Life and Order in an Early Church: the Didache. — *ANRW* II.27.1 (1993) 209-233. Esp. 218-221: "The Didache and Scripture".

**VOLCKAERT, Julius**

1953 The Temptations of Christ. [4,1-11] — *The Clergy Monthly* (Ranchi, India) 17 (1953) 15-21.

**VOLLEBREGT, G.N.**

1961 *De Bijbel over het huwelijk* (De Bijbel over..., 12). Roermond–Maaseik: Romen, 1961, 111 p. Esp. 79-90 [5,31-32; 19,1-12].

**VOLLENWEIDER, Samuel**

1989 *Freiheit als neue Schöpfung. Eine Untersuchung zur Eleutheria bei Paulus und in seiner Umwelt* (FRLANT, 147). Göttingen: Vandenhoeck & Ruprecht, 1989, 451 p. Esp. 171-177 [17,24-27].

1993 Christus als Weisheit. Gedanken zu einer bedeutsamen Weichenstellung in der frühchristlichen Theologiegeschichte. — *EvT* 53 (1993) 290-310. Esp. 295-298 [wisdom christology: Q]. [NTA 38, 985]

**VOLTURNO, D.**

1956 *The Four Gospels' Text of Eusebius*. Diss. Union School of Theol., Boston, 1956, 487 p. — *DissAbstr* 16 (1955-56) 1517.

**VONA, Costantino**

1957a La *Margarita pretiosa* nella interpretazione di alcuni scrittori ecclesiastici. [7,6; 13,45-46] — *Divinitas* 1 (1957) 118-160.

1957b L'apparizione di Cristo risorto alla Madre negli antichi scrittori cristiani. — *Ibid.*, 479-527.

1959 La quarta petitio dell'*Oratio dominica* nell'interpretazione di antichi scrittori cristiani. — RAPISARDA, E. (ed.), *Convivium Dominicum*, 1959, 215-255.

**VONCK, Pol**

1981a *Parables: Stories for Retelling* (Spearhead, 66). Eldoret. Kenya: Amecea, 1981, 86 p. Esp. 9-20: "Marcan parables used by Matthew and Luke"; 21-36: "Parables from the sayings source 'Q' behind Matthew and Luke"; 37-52: "Parables peculiar to Matthew". *Understanding 42 Gospel Parables*, 1981, ²1989, XII-128 p.

1981b The Parables, Stories for Retelling. — *Spearhead* (Kenya) 66 (1981) 4-86.

**VORGRIMLER, Herbert**

1963a Das "Binden und Lösen" in der Exegese nach dem Tridentinum bis zu Beginn des 20. Jahrhunderts. [16,19; 18,18] — *ZKT* 85 (1963) 460-477. Esp. 462-469: "Das 'Binden und Lösen' in der dogmatischen Exegese"; 469-475: "Das 'Binden und Lösen' in der philologischen Exegese". [NTA 8, 947]

1963b Matthieu, 16,18s et le sacrement de pénitence. — *L'homme devant Dieu. Mélanges Henri de Lubac. Exégèse et patristique* (Théologie, 56), Paris: Aubier, 1963, 51-61.

1980 *Hoffnung auf Vollendung. Aufriss der Eschatologie* (QDisp, 90). Freiburg: Herder, 1980, 176 p. Esp. 59-63: "Zur Eschatologie bei Q und den Synoptikern".

**VORSTER, Willem S.**

1971 Matt. 12:38 vv. en die historisiteit van die gegevens in Jona. [Mt 12,38ff and the historicity of the data in Jonah] — *TheolEvang* 4 (1971) 223-235.

1977 The Structure of Matthew 13. — *Neotestamentica* 11 (1977) 130-138 (addendum, 34-39).

1979 *Αἰσχύνομαι en stamverwante woorde in die Nuwe Testament* [Αἰσχύνομαι and cognate words in the New Testament]. Pretoria: Universiteit van Suid-Afrika, 1979, 299 p. Esp. 145-147.155-157.168-172.198-200 [10,32-33]; 148-152.169-170.196-197 [16,24-28]; 153-155 [10,26-33].

1980 Die tekssoort evangelie en verwysing. [Reference and the Gospel *Gattung*]. — *TheolEvang* 13 (1980) 27-48. [NTA 26, 51]

1985 Gelijkenisse in konteks. Matteus 13 en die gelijkenisse van Jesus. [Parables in context. Mt 13 and the parables of Jesus] — *HervTS* 41 (1985) 148-163.

1986 The Annunciation of the Birth of Jesus in the Protevangelium of James. — PETZER, J.H. - HARTIN, P.J. (eds.), *A South African Perspective on the New Testament*. FS B.M. Metzger, 1986, 33-53. Esp. 42-52: "'Canonical' and 'apocryphal': the New Testament and PJ xi:2-3".

1990 Stoics and Early Christians on Blessedness. — BALCH, D.L. - FERGUSON, E. - MEEKS, W.A. (eds.), *Greeks, Romans, and Christians. Essays in Honor of Abraham J. Malherbe*, Minneapolis, MN: Fortress, 1990, 38-51. Esp. 44-49.

1991 A Reader-Response Approach to Matthew 24:3-28. — *HervTS* 47 (1991) 1099-1108. [NTA 36, 1280]

**VOS, Howard F.**

1979 *Matthew* (A Study Guide Commentary). Grand Rapids MI: Zondervan, 1979, 190 p. [NTA 24, p. 90]

**Vos, Louis Arthur**

1965  *The Synoptic Traditions in the Apocalypse.* Kampen: Kok, 1965, X-245 p. Esp. 60-71 [24,30/Rev 1,7]; 71-75 [13,9/Rev 2,7]; 75-85 [24,42-43/Rev 3,2-3]; 85-94 [10,32/Rev 3,5]; 100-104 [19,28/Rev 3,21]; 104-109 [26,52/Rev 13,10]; 113-117 [10,34/Rev 6,4]; 130-136 [7,15/Rev 13,11.13]; 136-144 [8,19/Rev 14,4]; 144-152 [13,24-30; 24,29-31/Rev 14,14-19]; 152-157 [24,14/Rev 14,6]; 162-163 [23,35/Rev 18,24]; 163-174 [22,1-14/Rev 19,7-9]; 174-178 [16,27/Rev 22,12]; 178-181 [26,18/Rev 1,3]; 181-192 [24/Rev 6]. — Diss. Amsterdam, 1965 (R. Schippers).

**Vouga, François**

1978  → Mottu 1978

1983  La seconde passion de Jérémie. — *Lumière V* 165 (1983) 71-82. Esp. 73-74 [16,14]; 74-75 [27,9]; 76 [2,17]; 78-79 [11,28-30]; 79-80 [7,15-23]; 80-81 [23,37-39]. [NTA 28, 909]

1987a  Jesus als Erzähler. Überlegungen zu den Gleichnissen. — *WDienst* 19 (1987) 63-86. Esp. 65-75. [NTA 32, 575]

1987b  Les sources de la composition matthéenne. — *Lumière V* 183 (1987) 21-39. Esp. 23-31: "La source des logia"; 31-39: "Les traditions propres à Matthieu". [NTA 32, 587]

1988  *Jésus et la Loi selon la tradition synoptique* (Le monde de la Bible). Genève: Labor et Fides, 1988, 331 p. Esp. 44-48 [12,1-8]; 59-63 [12,9-14]; 82-88 [15,1-20]; 101-110 [19,1-9]; 121-127 [19,16-30]; 146-149 [22,34-40]; 179-183; 189-301: "Les antithèses matthéennes" [5,17-48]. — Diss. Genève, 1985 (F. Bovon).

**Vrancken, Isabel**

1986  Las fuentes de los evangelios y la exégesis del mañana. El trabajo de un perito solitario: Juan Carmignac. — *Revista Católica* (Santiago de Chile) 86 (1986) 179-189. → Carmignac 1984

**Vrolijks, Gelasius**

1968  *De Dei patientia. Synthesis doctrinae H. Thielicke de Sermone montano comparatioque cum catholicorum doctrina de eodem argumento* (Studia Antoniana, 22). Roma: Pont. Athenaeum Antonianum, 1968, LI-298 p. — Diss. Pont. Athenaeum Antonianum, Roma, 1966 (Z. Franz). → Thielicke 1956

**Vugdelija, Marijan**

1987  Najveći medu rodenima od žene (Mt 11,11-13; usp. Lk 7,28; 16,16). — *Bogoslovska Smotra* (Zagreb) 57 (1987) 15-30 (Italian, 31).

**[Vulgata]**

1969  → R. Weber 1969

1979  *Nova Vulgata Bibliorum Sacrorum Editio.* Città del Vaticano: Ed. Vaticana, 1979, XIII-2155 p.; ²1986. Esp. 1779-1824. → K. Aland [NT Graece et Latine, 1984]

# W

**WACHOB, Wesley Hiram**

1993   *"The Rich in Faith" and "the Poor in Spirit": The Socio-Rhetorical Function of a Saying of Jesus in the Epistle of James* [5,3/James 2,5]. Diss. Emory Univ., Atlanta, GA, 1993, 509 p. (V.K. Robbins). — *DissAbstr* 54 (1993-94) 3074-75.

**WACHTEL, Klaus**

1995   P⁶⁴/⁶⁷: Fragmente des Matthäusevangeliums aus dem 1. Jahrhundert? — *ZPapEp* 107 (1995) 73-80. → Thiede 1995c

**WAELKENS, Robert**

1977   L'analyse structurale des paraboles. Deux essais: Luc 15,1-32 et Matthieu 13,44-46. — *RTL* 8 (1977) 160-178. Esp. 170-176 [13,44-46]. [NTA 22, 124]

**WAETJEN, Herman Charles**

1958   *The Transformation of Judaism according to St. Matthew. An Examination of the Theology of the First Gospel.* Diss. Tübingen, 1958, 233 p. (O. Michel) — *TLZ* 84 (1959) 145-146.

1976a  *The Origin and Destiny of Humanness. An Interpretation of the Gospel according to Matthew.* Corte Madera, CA: Omega Books, 1976, 267 p. [NTA 21, p. 202]; ²1976.
    D. GARLAND, *RExp* 75 (1978) 124-125; D.J. HARRINGTON, *CBQ* 39 (1977) 300-301; B.J. HUBBARD, *JBL* 97 (1978) 139-140; E. KRENTZ, *CurrTMiss* 8 (1981) 245-246.

1976b  The Genealogy as the Key to the Gospel according to Matthew. — *JBL* 95 (1976) 205-230. [NTA 21, 72]

**WAGNER, Günter**

1974   *An Exegetical Bibliography on the Gospel of Matthew. Part I: Chapters 1-12. Part II: Chapters 13-28* (New Testament Exegetical Bibliographical Aids, 4a-b). Rüschlikon: Baptist Theological Seminary, 1974, 232 and 238 cards. [NTA 21, p. 321] → 1983

1983   *An Exegetical Bibliography of the New Testament. Matthew and Mark.* Macon, GA: Mercer University Press, 1983, XV-667 p. Esp. 1-394: "Matthew". → 1974
    E.J. EPP, *JBL* 104 (1985) 146-148; A. FUCHS, *SNTU* 12 (1987) 184; J.D. KINGSBURY, *Interpr* 39 (1985) 200-202.

**WAGNER, Guy**

1991   La filiation davidique de Jésus chez Paul, Marc et Matthieu. — *ETR* 66 (1991) 419-422. Esp. 420-421. [NTA 36, 374]

**WAGNER, Josef**

1988   *Auferstehung und Leben. Joh 11,1-12,19 als Spiegel johanneischer Redaktions- und Theologiegeschichte* (BibUnt, 19). Regensburg: Pustet, 1988, 501 p. Esp. 384-393 [21,1-11/Jn 12,12-13]. — Diss. Frankfurt/M, 1987 (J. Hainz – J. Beutler).

**WAIBEL, Maria**

1979   Die Auseinandersetzung mit der Fasten- und Sabbatpraxis Jesu in urchristlichen Gemeinden. — DAUTZENBERG, G., et al. (eds.), *Zur Geschichte des Urchristentums.* FS R. Schnackenburg, 1979, 63-96. Esp. 72-75 [6,16-18; 11,16-19]; 94-95 [12,1-8].

**WAINWRIGHT, Arthur W.**

1957   The Confession "Jesus is God" in the New Testament. — *ScotJT* 10 (1957) 274-299. Esp. 287-288 [1,23].

1962    *The Trinity in the New Testament.* London: SPCK, 1962, VII-278 p. Esp. 41-50 [God as father]; 117-121 [judgement]; 137-138 [11,16-19]; 138-141 [11,25-30]; 207-209 [12,31]; 211 [12,28]; 237-241.251-252 [28,19].
        *La Trinidad en el Nuevo Testamento,* trans. S. Castro (Koinonia, 2). Salamanca: Secretariado Trinitario, 1976, 326 p.

1965    *A Guide to the New Testament.* London: Epworth, 1965, 288 p.

1982    *Beyond Biblical Criticism. Encountering Jesus in Scripture.* Atlanta, GA: Knox; London: SPCK, 1982, IX-154 p. Esp. 21-28: "The first three Gospels and the Acts of the apostles".

**WAINWRIGHT, Elaine Mary**

1988    God Wills to Invite All to the Banquet. Matthew 22:1-10. — *International Review of Mission* (Genève) 77 (1988) 185-193. [NTA 32, 1118]

1991    *Towards a Feminist Critical Reading of the Gospel according to Matthew* (BZNW, 60). Berlin: de Gruyter, 1991, XXIII-410 p. Esp. 61-69 [1,1-17]; 69-76 [1,18-25]; 80-83 [4,17-10,42]; 83-87 [8,14-15]; 87-92 [9,18-26]; 96-102 [11,1-16,20]; 102-116 [15,21-28]; 118-121 [16,21-20,34]; 124-126 [26,6-13]; 140-143 [27,55-56.61]; 143-146 [28,1-10]; 156-171 [1,1-17]; 171-175 [1,18-25]; 178-191 [8,14-15]; 191-214 [9,18-26]; 217-252 [15,21-28]; 253-257 [20,20-22]; 257-283 [26,6-13]; 293-300 [27,55-56.61]; 300-314 [28,1-10]; 325-352 [women in Mt]. [NTA 36, p. 428] — Diss. University of Queensland, Brisbane, 1990 (M. Lattke).
        M. FRANZMANN, *Colloquium* 25 (1993) 44-46; H.-J. KLAUCK, *BK* 50 (1995) 242-243; D.A. LEE, *Pacifica* 6 (1993) 102-104; A.-J. LEVINE, *CRBR* 6 (1993) 573-575; B.E. REID, *CBQ* 55 (1993) 620-622; L. SCHOTTROFF, *TLZ* 118 (1993) 322-324; B.T. VIVIANO, *RB* 101 (1994) 455-456; A. WIESNER, *JSNT* 48 (1992) 121.

1994    The Gospel of Matthew. — FIORENZA, E.S. (ed.), *Searching the Scriptures.* II: *A Feminist Commentary,* New York: Crossroad, 1994; London: SCM, 1995, 635-377. Esp. 641-644 [1-2]; 647-649 [8,14-15]; 649-650 [9,18-26]; 650-654.668-673 [15,21-28]; 659-664 [26,6-13]; 664 [27,56-61]; 664-667 [28,1-10].

**WAINWRIGHT, G.**

1973    Mt. XXII,11-13: une controverse primitive sur l'admission à la Sainte Cène. — *Studia Evangelica* 6 (1973) 595-598.

**WALDRON, Thomas**

1982    For yours is the Kingdom... – The Beatitudes. — *Furrow* 33 (1982) 263-271.

**WALF, Knut**

1982    Richtet nicht. — HOCHGREBE, V. (ed.), *Provokation Bergpredigt,* 1982, 105-115.

**WALKER, Arthur L.**

1956    *An Inquiry into the Inherent Universality of the Teaching of Jesus in the Gospel of Matthew.* Diss. New Orleans Baptist Theol. Sem., New Orleans, LA, 1956.

**WALKER, M.B.**

1962    Lead us not into temptation. [6,13] — *ExpT* 73 (1961-62) 287. [NTA 7, 131] → Sykes 1962

**WALKER, Norman**

1960    "After three days". [27,63] — *NT* 4 (1960) 261-262. [NTA 6, 782]

1963a   The Alleged Matthaean Errata. — *NTS* 9 (1962-63) 391-394. Esp. 391-392 [1,1-17.23]; 392-393 [2,23]; 393 [2,13-15; 12,40]; 393-394 [21,12]; 394 [8,28; 20,30; 21,1-6]. [NTA 8, 120]

1963b   Pauses in the Passion Story and Their Significance for Chronology. [27,17; 28,1] — *NT* 6 (1963) 16-19. [NTA 8, 953] → 1963c; → Jaubert 1957

1963c   Yet Another Look at the Passion Chronology. — *Ibid.,* 286-289. [NTA 9, 161] → 1963b

1966    Patristic Evidence and the Priority of Matthew. — *Studia Patristica* 7 (1966) 571-575. [NTA 11, 692]

**WALKER, Rolf**

1961 Der König kommt in seine Stadt. Zur Auslegung von Mt 21,1-11. — *Deutsches Pfarrerblatt* (Essen) 61 (1961) 135-141.

1967 *Die Heilsgeschichte im ersten Evangelium* (FRLANT, 91). Göttingen: Vandenhoeck & Ruprecht, 1967, 161 p. Esp. 11-74: "Israel im Matthäusevangelium"; 75-113: "Die Heiden im Matthäusevangelium"; 114-149: "Die Heilsgeschichte im Matthäusevangelium". [NTA 12, p. 397] — Diss. Tübingen, 1966-67. → Dermience 1985
L.A. BUSHINSKI, *CBQ* 30 (1968) 642-643; J.H. ELLIOTT, *LuthRundschau* 19 (1969) 112-113; D.R.A. HARE, *JBL* 89 (1970) 371-372; L. HARTMAN, *SEÅ* 36 (1971) 179-180; J.D. KINGSBURY, *TZ* 27 (1971) 432-433; J. MURPHY-O'CONNOR, *RB* 76 (1969) 597-601; P. OCHOA, *Estudio Agustiniana* (Valladolíd) 3 (1968) 396; R. PESCH, *Freiburger Rundbrief* 20 (1968) 118-119; J. RADERMAKERS, *NRT* 94 (1972) 813-814; H. RÄISÄNEN, *TAik* 73 (1978) 183-184; K.H. SCHELKLE, *TQ* 148 (1968) 224; R. SCHNACKENBURG, *BZ* 14 (1970) 288-290; J.N. SEVENSTER, *NTT* 22 (1967-68) 451-452; G. STRECKER, *TLZ* 94 (1969) 435-437; W. TRILLING, *TRev* 65 (1969) 294-298; R. WALKER, *TLZ* 93 (1968) 312.

**WALKER, William O., Jr.**

1968 The Kingdom of the Son of Man and the Kingdom of the Father in Matthew. An Exercise in *Redaktionsgeschichte*. [13,36-43] — *CBQ* 30 (1968) 573-579. [NTA 13, 560]

1976 Joseph B. Tyson's Proposal for the Consultation on the Relationships of the Gospels. A Response. — *SBL 1976 Seminar Papers*, 287-290. → Tyson 1976

1977 A Method for Identifying Redactional Passages in Matthew on Functional and Linguistic Grounds. — *CBQ* 39 (1977) 76-93. Esp. 79-88: "A method for identifying redactional passages"; 88-91: "Distinguishing final redaction from earlier redaction". [NTA 21, 717]

1978* (ed.), *The Relationships among the Gospels. An Interdisciplinary Dialogue* (Trinity University Monograph Series in Religion, 5). San Antonio, TX: Trinity University Press, 1978, XII-359 p. → W.R. Farmer, Frye, R.H. Fuller, G.A. Kennedy, Lord, Meeks, Tyson

1978 Jesus and the Tax Collectors. — *JBL* 97 (1978) 221-238. Esp. 224-226 [5,46-47]; 225-226 [18,15-17]; 226-229 [21,31-32]; 226-227.230-231 [11,18-19]; 231-234 [9,9-13]; 234-236 [10,3]. [NTA 23, 68]

1982a The Lord's Prayer in Matthew and in John. — *NTS* 28 (1982) 237-256. [NTA 26, 843] → Hooker 1992

1982b The Son of Man Question and the Synoptic Problem. — *Ibid.*, 374-388. [NTA 27, 90] → 1983b

1983a The Son of Man: Some Recent Developments. — *CBQ* 45 (1983) 584-607. Esp. 589-595; 597-598 [22,44]; 599 [26,64]; 600 [24,30]. [NTA 28, 680] → 1983b

1983b The Son of Man Question and the Synoptic Problem. — FARMER, W.R. (ed.), *New Synoptic Studies*, 1983, 261-301. → 1982b + 1983a

1987a "Nazareth": A Clue to Synoptic Relationships? — SANDERS, E.P. (ed.), *Jesus, the Gospels, and the Church*. FS W.R. Farmer, 1987, 105-118. Esp. 107-118 [4,13].

1987b Order in the Synoptic Gospels: A Critique. — *SecCent* 6 (1987-88) 83-97. [NTA 34, 99r] → J. Dewey 1987, R.H. Fuller 1987, Longstaff 1977, 1987

1987c The State of the Synoptic Question: Some Reflections on the Work of Tuckett and McNicol. — *PerkJourn* 40/2 (1987) 32. → McNicol 1987 Tuckett 1983a

**WALL, J.** → E. Penner 1989

**WALL, Robert W.**

1983 Introduction: New Testament Ethics. — *HorizonsBT* 5.2 (1983) 49-94. Esp. 56-59.64-67; = ID. - LEMCIO, E.E., *The New Testament as Canon*, 1992, 300-334. Esp. 307-309.314-316.

1985 The Eschatologies of the Peace Movement. — *BTB* 15 (1985) 3-11. Esp. 4-7: "Matthew's eschatology and the christian hawks". [NTA 29, 1138]

1987 Law and Gospel, Church and Canon. — *Journal of the Wesleyan Theological Society* 22 (1987) 38-70; = ID. – LEMCIO, E.E., *The New Testament as Canon*, 1992, 208-249. Esp. 221-223: "Matthew's gospel and the law"; 228-231; 241-243.

1992a & LEMCIO, E.E., *The New Testament as Canon. A Reader in Canonical Criticism* (JSNT SS, 76). Sheffield: JSOT, 1992, 376 p. → 1983, 1987, 1992b, Lemcio 1981, 1986, 1988

1992b Father and Son in the Synoptics and John: A Canonical Reading. — *Ibid.*, 78-108. Esp. 88-91 [Son of God].

1992c Divorce. — *ABD* 2 (1992) 217-219. Esp. 218.

**WALLACE, David H.**
1962 An Exegesis of Matthew 16:13-20. — *Foundations* (Rochester, NY) 5 (1962) 217-225.

1963 The Mystery of the Incarnation. — *ChrTod* 8 (1963) 219-221. [NTA 8, 569]

**WALLACE, Daniel Bernard**
1984 The Relation of Adjective to Noun in Anarthrous Constructions in the New Testament. — *NT* 26 (1984) 128-167. Esp. 150-160: "The phenomenon in the New Testament". [NTA 29, 36]

**WALLACE, Ronald S.**
1960 *The Gospel Miracles. Studies in Matthew, Mark, and Luke*. Edinburgh–London: Oliver and Boyd; Grand Rapids, MI: Eerdmans, 1960, XIII-161 p. Esp. 41-48 [8,5-13]; 106-113 [15,21-28]; 132-138 [17,24-27].

**WALLACE-HADRILL, David S.**
1950 Analysis of Some Quotations from the First Gospel in Eusebius' *Demonstratio Evangelica*. [1,23; 2,6; 4,6.7.15-16; 5,38.43; 8,4; 12,17-21; 13,14; 21,9.13; 22,44; 24,15; 26,15.38; 27,35.43.46] — *JTS* 1 (1950) 168-175.

1951 A Suggested Exegesis of Matthew iii.9,10 (= Luke iii.8,9). — *ExpT* 62 (1950-51) 349.

1956 Eusebius and the Gospel Text of Caesarea. — *HTR* 49 (1956) 105-114. Esp. 105-106. → Suggs 1957

**WALLER, Elizabeth**
1979 The Parable of the Leaven: A Sectarian Teaching and the Inclusion of Women. — *USQR* 35 (1979-80) 99-109. [NTA 24, 795]

1981 The Parable of the Ten Virgins. Matt 25:1-13. — *Proceedings EGLBS* 1 (1981) 85-109. → J. Jeremias 1965c/68

**WALLIS, Ian G.**
1995 *The Faith of Jesus in Early Christian Traditions* (SNTS MS, 84). Cambridge: University Press, 1995, XIX-281 p. Esp. 24-64: "Jesus' faith in the synoptic gospels" [14,28-31; 17,14-21; 21,12-13.21-22]. — Diss. Sheffield, 1991 (L. Alexander).

**WALLS, Andrew F.**
1967 Papias and Oral Tradition. — *VigChr* 21 (1967) 137-140. [NTA 12, 716]

**WALTER, Eugen**
1940R *Glaube, Hoffnung und Liebe im Neuen Testament* [1940]. Freiburg: Herder, ³1953, VII-210 p.
*Geloof, hoop en liefde in het Nieuwe Testament*, trans. T. Verschure. Bussum: Brand, 1953, X-217 p.

1973 "Deinen Tod, O Herr, verkünden wir". Kann der Tod Jesu noch als heilsentscheidend verkündet werden? — KNOCH, O., et al. (eds.), *Das Evangelium auf dem Weg zum Menschen*. FS H. Kahlefeld, 1973, 119-139. Esp. 124-127: "Gibt es nicht ein noch älteres Gegenzeugnis (Q)?"; 132-134: "Gibt es ein Erlösungsverständnis, in dem der Tod Jesu (noch) keine Rolle spielt?".

**WALTER, Nikolaus**

1966 Tempelzerstörung und synoptische Apokalypse. — *ZNW* 57 (1966) 38-49. Esp. 45-48 [24,15]. [NTA 11, 246]

1968 Die Bearbeitung der Seligpreisungen durch Matthäus. — *Studia Evangelica* 4 (1968) 246-258. Esp. 247-250 [Q]; 250-253 [form criticism]; 254-258 [Mt redaction].

1973 Eine vormatthäische Schilderung der Auferstehung Jesu. [Anhang: Zur Literarkritik und zur traditionsgeschichtliche Bedeutung des Petrus-Evangeliums]. — *NTS* 19 (1972-73) 415-429. Esp. 415-419 [28,2-4]; 420-425 [27,62-66; 28,2-4.11-15]; 426-429 [Gospel of Peter]. [NTA 18, 480]; = ID., *Praeparatio Evangelica*, 1997, 12-27. Esp. 12-16; 17-22; 23-26.

1978 Das Markus-Evangelium und Rom. Das kanonische Markus-Evangelium als überarbeitete Fassung des ursprünglichen Textes. — *Helikon* 18-19 (1978-79) 22-40; = ID., *Praeparatio Evangelica*, 1997, 78-92 ("Nachtrag", 92-94). Esp. 87, 91-92 [3,7-12].

1981 Zum Kirchenverständnis des Matthäus. — *TVers* 12 (1981) 25-45. Esp. 26-33: "Gemeinde als strukturierte Gemeinschaft" [18; 23,8-12]; 33-41: "Ekklesiologische Motive bei Matthäus" [16,17-19]; = ID., *Praeparatio Evangelica*, 1997, 118-143 ("Nachtrag", 143). Esp. 119-127; 127-139.

1985 Paulus und die urchristliche Jesustradition. — *NTS* 31 (1985) 498-522. Esp. 500-503 [survey]; 507-508 [24,42-51/1 Thess 5]. [NTA 30, 704] → Allison 1982, Neirynck 1986f Paul and the Early Christian Jesus-Tradition. — WEDDERBURN, A.J.M. (ed.), *Paul and Jesus. Collected Essays* (JSNT SS, 37), Sheffield: JSOT, 1989, 51-80. Esp. 54-56; 66-57.

1991 Die Botschaft vom Jüngsten Gericht im Neuen Testament. — ID. - WENZ, G. - BAYER, O., *Eschatologie und Jüngstes Gericht* (Bekenntnis. Fuldaer Hefte, 32), Hannover: Lutherisches Verlagshaus, 1991, 10-48; = ID., *Praeparatio Evangelica*, 1997, 311-340. Esp. 320-321: "Gerichtssprüche in Q"; 322-324 [25,31-46]; 335-336.

1992 Mk 1,1-8 und die "Agreements" von Mt 3 und Lk 3. Stand die Predigt Johannes des Täufers in Q? — VAN SEGBROECK, F., et al. (eds.), *The Four Gospels 1992*. FS F. Neirynck, 1992, I, 457-478. Esp. 463-470 [Q/Mk]. → Neirynck 1996b

1995 Zur theologischen Problematik des christologischen "Schriftbeweises" im Neuen Testament. — *NTS* 41 (1995) 338-357. Esp. 346-353. [NTA 40, 390]

1997a *Praeparatio Evangelica. Studien zur Umwelt, Exegese und Hermeneutik des Neuen Testaments*, eds. W. Kraus - F. Wilk (WUNT, 98). Tübingen: Mohr, 1997, x-442 p. → 1973, 1978, 1981, 1991, 1997b

1997b "Nicht Frieden, sondern das Schwert"? Mt 10,34 (Lk 12,51) im Kontext der Verkündigung Jesu. — *Festgabe des Kollegiums des Katechetischen Oberseminars Naumburg für Bischof D. Dr. Werner Krusche zu seinem 65. Geburtstag*, 51-72 [not published]; = ID., *Praeparatio Evangelica*, 1997, 169-185 ("Nachtrag", 185-186). Esp. 176-179 [5,21-26]; 179-180 [5,9]; 180-184 [10,34].

**WALVOORD, John F.**

1968 Will Israel Build a Temple in Jerusalem? — *BS* 125 (1968) 99-106. Esp. 103-104 [24,15].

1971 Christ's Olivet Discourse on the End of the Age. [24–25] — *BS* 128 (1971) 109-116; 206-214; 316-326; 129 (1972) 20-32; 99-105; 206-210; 307-315. [NTA 16, 162/163/542]; [NTA 16, 866; 17, 127/128/522]

1974 *Matthew: Thy Kingdom Come*. Chicago, IL: Moody, 1974, 259 p. [NTA 21, p. 202] G.E. LADD, *WestTJ* 38 (1975-76) 251-253; D. MOODY, *RExp* 73 (1976) 81-82; S.D. TOUSSAINT, *BS* 132 (1975) 270.

1975 Posttribulationism Today. — *BS* 132 (1975) 16-24, 114-122, 208-215, 304-315. [NTA 19, 1094; 20, 287/627]; 133 (1976) 11-18, 108-118, 202-212, 299-311; 134 (1977) 3-14, 107-113, 203-214, 299-313. Esp. 202-205 [13]; 205-210 [24]; 207-208 [25,31-46]. [NTA 21, 563/923; 22, 246/582]

1982    Interpreting Prophecy Today. — *BS* 139 (1982) 3-11, 111-128, 205-215, 302-311. Esp.
        208-214 [kingdom]. [NTA 27, 332; 28, 322]

1985    Is a Posttributional Rapture Revealed in Matthew 24? — *GraceTJ* 6 (1985) 257-266.
        [NTA 30, 581]

**WAMBACQ, Benjamin Nestor**

1982    Matthieu 5,31-32. Possibilité de divorce ou obligation de rompre une union illégitime.
        — *NRT* 104 (1982) 34-49. Esp. 35-37: *"Mt 5,31-32:* adultère ou divorce?"; 37-42: "Le logion sur
        l'adultère dans la tradition des évangiles"; 42-49: "Le logion dans l'Église de s. Matthieu". [NTA 26, 841]

**WANAMAKER, Charles A.**

1980    Mark 11:25 and the Gospel of Matthew. — LIVINGSTONE, E.A. (ed.), *Studia Biblica
        1978*, II, 1980, 329-337.

**WANG CHING-HUNG, R.**

1979    Holy Spirit in Mark and Matthew. [Chinese] — *ColcTFu* 11 (1979) 11-22.

**WANKE, Joachim**

1980    "Kommentarworte". Älteste Kommentierungen von Herrenworten. — *BZ* 24 (1980)
        208-233. Esp. 213-214 [10,24-25]; 214-215 [12,34-35]; 215-216 [11,11]; 216 [11,18-19]; 216-217 [8,19-
        20]; 218 [11,27]; 218-220 [12,28]; 220-221 [12,41-42]; 221-222 [6,22-23]; 222-223 [10,27]; 223-224 [12,32];
        224-226 [10,39]. [NTA 25, 451]

1981    *"Bezugs- und Kommentarworte" in den synoptischen Evangelien. Beobachtungen zur
        Interpretationsgeschichte der Herrenworte in der vorevangelischen Überlieferung*
        (ErfTSt, 44). Leipzig: St. Benno, 1981, XIV-117 p. Esp. 21-81: "'Bezugs- und Kommentarworte'
        in der Redequelle (Q)" [Q 6,39-40.43-45; 7,24-28.31-35; 9,57-60; 10,21-22; 11,19-20.29-32.33.34-36; 12,2-
        3.8-9.10; 14,27; 17,33]; 88-92 [Q 11,14-23/Mk]; 92-95 [Q 11,33/Mk]; 95-96 [Q 12,2/Mk]; 96-99 [Q
        14,27/Mk].

**WANSBROUGH, Henry**

1969    St. Matthew. — FULLER, R.C. – JOHNSTON, L. – KEARNS, C. (eds.), *A New Catholic
        Commentary on Holy Scripture*, London: Nelson, 1969, 902-953.
        St. Matthew. — *Scripture Discussion Commentary*, 7, London: Sheed & Ward, 1971,
        137-245.

1970    Event and Interpretation. VI. The Childhood of Jesus. — *CleR* 55 (1970) 112-119. [NTA
        14, 852]

1971a   Theological Trends: The Resurrection. — *Way* 11 (1971) 324-330. [NTA 15, 513]; 12
        (1972) 58-67. Esp. 60-61. [NTA 16, 829]

1971b   → Freyne 1971

1973    *The Resurrection* (Scripture for Meditation, 8). Slough-London: St. Paul, 1973, 109 p.

1978    *Risen from the Dead*. Middlegreen: St. Paul, 1978, 106 p. Esp. 53-59.

1982a   Blessed are the Peacemakers. — *Way* 22 (1982) 10-17. [NTA 26, 840]

1982b   Poverty in the Gospel Tradition. — *ProcIrBibAss* 6 (1982) 47-57. [NTA 27, 499]

1987    The Judgment of Christ in the Gospel of Matthew. — *Priests & People* (London) 1
        (1987) 234, 239-241, 244. [NTA 32, 110]

1991*   (ed.), *Jesus and the Oral Gospel Tradition* (JSNT SS, 64). Sheffield: JSOT, 1991, 469
        p. → Aune, J.D.G. Dunn, E.E. Ellis, Gerhardsson, Riesner, Rordorf, Soards

**WARD, A. Marcus**

1961    *The Gospel according to St. Matthew* (Epworth Preacher's Commentaries). London:
        Epworth, 1961, XI-162 p. [NTA 6, p. 143]
        A.W. WAINWRIGHT, *ExpT* 72 (1960-61) 314.

1970 Uncomfortable Words. IV. Unprofitable Servants. — *ExpT* 81 (1969-70) 200-203. Esp.
200 [25,30]; 201-202 [17,20; 18,6-7.15.21-22]. [NTA 15, 185]

**WARD, Keith**

1989 *The Rule of Love. Reflections on the Sermon on the Mount*. London: Darton, Longman
& Todd, 1989, 134 p.
G. ABBÀ, *Sal* 52 (1990) 174-175.

**WARD, Maisie**

1956 *The Authenticity of the Gospels* (Canterbury Books). New York: Sheed and Ward,
1956, 96 p. Esp. 38-48: "St. Matthew".

**WARD, M.R.**

1973 Once Married Always Married? A Biblical Review and Synthesis. — *Churchman*
(London) 87 (1973) 190-197. [NTA 18, 1055]

**WARD, Roy Bowen**

1972 Abraham Traditions in Early Christianity. — KRAFT, R.A. (ed.), *1972 Proceedings
IOCSC Pseudepigrapha* (SBL Septuagint and Cognate Studies, 2), Philadelphia, PA:
SBL, 1972, 165-179. Esp. 168-170; = NICKELSBURG, G.W.E. (ed.), *Studies on the
Testament of Abraham* (SBL Septuagint and Cognate Studies, 6), Missoula, MT:
Scholars, 1976, 173-184. Esp. 176-177.

**WARE, Bruce A.**

1981 Is the Church in View in Matthew 24–25? — *BS* 138 (1981) 158-172. [NTA 25, 864] →
Gundry 1967a

**WARNACH, Viktor**

1951 *Agape. Die Liebe als Grundmotiv der neutestamentlichen Theologie*. Düsseldorf:
Patmos, 1951, 756 p. Esp. 88-103: "Die Synoptiker".

**WARREN, William F.**

1992 Focuses on Spirituality in the Sermon on the Mount. — *Theological Educator* (New
Orleans) 46 (1992) 115-123. [NTA 37, 728]

**WARSHAW, T.S.** → Juel 1978

**WAST, Hugo**

1951 La ultima palabra del evangelio de San Mateo. [28,16-20] — *RevistBíb* 13 (1951) 125.

**WATERS, Mark**

1993 Matthew 11:16-19. — *RExp* 90 (1993) 565-567.

**WATSON, Alan**

1995 *The Trial of Jesus*. Athens, GA: Univ. of Georgia Press, 1995, XIII-219 p. Esp. 53-65:
"Matthew and Luke"; 66-76: "Mark: Matthew and Luke".

**WATSON, Duane F.**

1991* (ed.), *Persuasive Artistry. Studies in New Testament Rhetoric in Honor of George A.
Kennedy* (JSNT SS, 50). Sheffield: JSOT, 1991, 390 p. → Grams, Robbins, Vinson

1992 People, Crowd. — *DJG*, 1992, 605-609. Esp. 607-608.

1994 & HAUSER, A.J., *Rhetorical Criticism of the Bible. A Comprehensive Bibliography with
Notes on History and Method* (Biblical Interpretation Series, 4). Leiden: Brill, 1994,
XX-206 p. Esp. 167-168.

**WATSON, Francis**

1993 Liberating the Reader: A Theological-Exegetical Study of the Parable of the Sheep and the Goats (Matt. 25.31-46). — ID. (ed.), *The Open Text: New Directions for Biblical Studies?*, London: SCM, 1993, 57-84.

1994 "He is not here": Towards a Theology of the Empty Tomb. — BARTON, S.C. – STANTON, G.N. (eds.), *Resurrection*. FS L. Houlden, 1994, 95-107. Esp. 102-106 [28,1-10].

**WATSON, John H.**

1964 Critical Note on Dr. J.K.S. Reid's "Our Life in Christ". [22,39] — *ExpT* 75 (1963-64) 349-350. [NTA 9, 93] → Cripps 1964
Reply: J.K.S. REID, ibid., 350. [NTA 9, 94]

**WATSON, J.K.**

1979 La naissance du dieu chrétien et la nova de l'an –5. — *CahRenan* 27 (1979) 2-8. [NTA 23, 818]

**WATSON, Nigel M.**

1985 Willi Marxsen's Approach to Christology. — *ExpT* 97 (1985-86) 36-42. Esp. 40-42 [Q: christology]. [NTA 30, 1257] → Marxsen 1960/69

**WATT, J.W.**

1978 (ed.), *Philoxenus of Mabbug. Fragments of the Commentary on Matthew and Luke* (CSCO, 392-393). Leuven: CSCO, 1978, 20*-97 and 14*-87 p. Esp. 3-37 [text] and 2-32 [translation]. — Diss. St. Andrews, 1976 (M. Black). → de Halleux 1980

**WATT, W. Montgomery**

1972 The Camel and the Needle's Eye. [19,24] — *Ex Orbe Religionum. Studia Geo Widengren* (Studies in the History of Religions. Supplements to *Numen*, 22), Leiden: Brill, 1972, II, 155-158.

**WATTIAUX, Henri**

1993 La théologie morale entre l'Écriture et la raison. Réflexions sur un livre récent. — *RTL* 24 (1993) 493-498. → Frahier 1992

**WATTY, William W.**

1982 Jesus and the Temple — Cleansing or Cursing? — *ExpT* 93 (1981-82) 235-239. Esp. 235-237 [21,12-17]. [NTA 27, 105]

**WEAD, David W.**

1970 *The Literary Devices in John's Gospel* (Theologische Dissertationen, 4). Basel: Reinhardt, 1970, VIII-130 p. Esp. 81-82: "Similarities between metaphors in John and Matthew" [5,13-15]. — Diss. Basel, 1968 (B. Reicke).

**WEATHERBY, Harold L.**

1987 Homily on the Transfiguration of Our Lord Jesus Christ by Saint John of Damascus. — *Greek Orthodox Theological Review* (Brookline, MA) 32 (1987) 1-29.

**WEATHERLY, Jon A.**

1992 Anti-Semitism. — *DJG*, 1992, 13-17. Esp. 14-16.

**WEAVER, Dorothy Jean**

1990 *Matthew's Missionary Discourse. A Literary Critical Analysis* (JSNT SS, 38). Sheffield: JSOT, 1990, 250 p. Esp. 13-29.155-165: "Interpretive approaches to Matthew 9.35–11.1. From historical criticism to literary criticism"; 31-70.166-181: "Analysis of Matthew 1.1–9.34. The implied reader's 'pre-information'"; 71-126.181-213: "Literary critical analysis of Matthew 9.35–11.1"; 127-153.213-221: "Analysis of Matthew 11.2–28.20. 'To see the end'". [NTA 35, p. 108] — Diss. Union Theol. Sem., Richmond, VA, 1987 (J.D. Kingsbury).
J.C. ANDERSON, *JBL* 111 (1992) 146-148; G. BISSOLI, *SBF/LA* 42 (1992) 416-418; D. ELLUL, *ETR* 66 (1991) 288-289; J.C. FENTON, *JTS* 42 (1991) 192-193; C.J.A. HICKLING, *JTS* 42 (1991) 189-191; C.

KÄHLER, *TLZ* 116 (1991) 432-433; E. KRENTZ, *CurrTMiss* 19 (1992) 61-62; J. MATEOS, *FilolNT* 7 (1994) 82-83; G.A. PHILLIPS, *CBQ* 54 (1992) 184-186; G. STANTON, *ExpT* 102 (1990-91) 21-22; A. TERIAN, *Interpr* 45 (1991) 422.424.

1992a  Matthew 28:1-10. — *Interpr* 46 (1992) 398-402.

1992b  Power and Powerlessness: Matthew's Use of Irony in the Portrayal of Political Leaders. — *SBL 1992 Seminar Papers*, 454-466. Esp. 456-466: "Matthew's portrayals of political leaders"; = BAUER, D.R. – POWELL, M.A. (eds.), *Treasures New and Old*, 1996, 179-196. 182-195.

1992c  Transforming Nonresistance: From *Lex Talionis* to "do not resist the evil one". — SWARTLEY, W.M. (ed.), *The Love of Enemy*, 1992, 32-71. Esp. 37-47: "Matthew 5:38-42 in canonical context"; 47-58: "Matthew 5:38-42 in Matthean context: the response of Jesus".

**WEAVER, Walter Parker**

1968  *A History of the Tradition of Matthew 11:25-30 (Luke 10:21-22)*. Diss. Drew Univ., Madison, NJ, 1968, 450 p. — *DissAbstr* 29 (1968-69) 1596.

**WEBB, Robert L.**

1991a  *John the Baptizer. A Socio-Historical Study* (JSNT SS, 62). Sheffield: JSOT, 1991, 446 p. Esp. 47-51 [Q]; 55-60 [Mt]; 168-173 [3,1-6/Mk/Q]; 173-178 [3,7-10/Q]; 179.262-278.289-300 [3,11-12/Mk/Q]; 278-282 [11,2-6/Q].

1991b  The Activity of John the Baptist's Expected Figure at the Threshing Floor (Matthew 3.12 = Luke 3.17). — *JSNT* 43 (1991) 103-111. [NTA 36, 707]

1994  John the Baptist and His Relationship to Jesus. — CHILTON, B. – EVANS, C.A. (eds.), *Studying the Historical Jesus*, 1994, 179-229.

**WEBER, Beat**

1992  Schulden erstatten – Schulden erlassen. Zum matthäischen Gebrauch einiger juristischer und monetärer Begriffe. — *ZNW* 83 (1992) 253-256. [NTA 37, 1245]

1993  Alltagswelt und Gottesreich. Überlegungen zum Verstehenshintergrund des Gleichnisses vom "Schalksknecht" (Matthäus 18,23-24). — *BZ* 37 (1993) 161-182. Esp. 164-181: "Überlegungen zur Verortung der Charaktere und Motive des Gleichnisses". [NTA 38, 772]

1994  Vergeltung oder Vergebung!? Matthäus 18,21-35 auf dem Hintergrund des "Erlassjahres". — *TZ* 50 (1994) 124-151. Esp. 132-145: "Das 'Erlassjahr' und Mt 18,21-35"; 145-148: "Konturen einer Erlass- und Jobeljahrtheologie im Mtevangelium". [NTA 39, 157]

**WEBER, Hans-Ruedi**

1971  *The Invitation. Matthew in Mission.* Cincinnati: Board of Missions The United Methodist Church, 1971.
*L'invitation au festin. Matthieu et la mission*, trans. É. de Peyer (Collection missionnaire, 9). Genève: Labor et Fides; Paris: Librairie protestante, 1972, VIII-145 p. [NTA 18, p. 247]
J.A. CARRASCO, *EstJos* 28 (1974) 263-264; P. POKORNÝ, *ComViat* 15 (1972) 191-192.
*De uitnodiging. Matteüs missionair.* Amsterdam: Nederlands Bijbelgenootschap; Boxtel: Katholieke Bijbelstichting, 1972, 152 p.
*Was ich euch ins Ohr sage, das predigt von den Dächern: Mission im Matthäus-Evangelium* (Kühne-Sachbuch). Kassel: Kühne, 1975, 120 + 8 p.

1975  *Kreuz. Überlieferung und Deutung der Kreuzigung Jesu im neutestamentlichen Kulturraum* (Bibliothek Themen der Theologie, Ergänzungsband). Stuttgart–Berlin: Kreuz, 1975, 239 p. Esp. 174-185: "Die Kreuzigung nach Matthäus".
*The Cross, Tradition and Interpretation*, trans. E. Jessett. Grand Rapids, MI: Eerdmans, 1979, 162 p.

1979  *Jesus and the Children. Biblical Resources for Study and Preaching.* Atlanta, GA: Knox; Genève: World Council of Churches, 1979, X-96 p. Esp. 1-13 [11,16-18/Q 7,31-35]; 22-33 [18,3/Mk 10,15]; 34-51 [18,1-5/Mk 9,33-37].

*Jezus en de kinderen. Bijbelse bronnen voor prediking en bijbelstudie.* Kampen: Kok, 1979, 116 p.
*Jésus et les enfants*, trans. N. Lasserre (Foi chrétienne). Paris: Centurion, 1980, 151 p. Esp. 13-31; 47-64; 65-92.
*Jesús y los niños.* Lima: Celadec, 1980, 130 p.
*Gesù e i bambini. Sussidi biblici per lo studio e la predicazione* (Alla scoperta della Bibbia, 11). Roma: Paoline, 1981, 135 p.
*Jesus e as crianças. Subsídios bíblicos para estudo e pregação*, trans. A. Höhn (Estudos bíblico-teológicos NT, 9). São Leopoldo: Sinodal, 1986, 96 p.

**WEBER, Helmut**

1960 *Die Neuheit des Gebotes der Nächstenliebe im Neuen Testament.* Diss. Pont. Univ. Greg., Roma, 1960 (J. Fuchs). Esp. 10-24: "Die neuen Liebesforderungen Jesu nach der synoptischen Tradition" [5,17-20.21-26.38-42.43-48; 7,12; 22,39-40].

**WEBER, Jean-Julien**

1951 *La Vierge Marie dans le Nouveau Testament. Étude exégétique et apologétique.* Colmar: Alsatia, 1951, 132 p.
*Die Jungfrau Maria im Neuen Testament.* Colmar: Alsatia, 1951, 170 p.

1961 Notes exégétiques sur le texte "Tu es Petrus". — *Bulletin ecclésiastique du diocèse de Strasbourg* 80 (1961) 541-560; = *AmiCler* 72 (1962) 113-121. [NTA 6, 778]
*SelT* 1/4 (1962) 5-12.

1967 Permanence des promesses faites à Pierre. [16,13-20] — *AssSeign* I/84 (1967) 27-46.

**WEBER, Kathleen**

1994 *The Events of the End of the Age in Matthew.* Diss. Catholic University of America, Washington, DC, 1994, 363 p. (J.P. Meier). — *DissAbstr* 55 (1994-95) 299-300.

1995 Is There a Qumran Parallel to *Matthew* 24,51 // *Luke* 12,46? — *RQum* 16 (1995) 657-663. [NTA 40, 1469]

**WEBER, Robert**

1969 (ed.), *Biblia Sacra iuxta Vulgatam versionem.* I. *Genesis-Psalmi.* II. *Proverbia-Apocalypsis. Appendix.* Stuttgart: Würtembergische Bibelanstalt, 1969, [2]1975, 2 vols., XXXI-1980 p. Esp. 1527-1574. → K. Aland [NT Graece et Latine, 1969]

1979 → Vulgata 1979

**WECHSLER, Magnus**

1954 The Key to the Present. [3,8] — *HibbJourn* 52 (1953-54) 186-187.

**WEDER, Hans**

1978 *Die Gleichnisse Jesu als Metaphern. Traditions- und redaktionsgeschichtliche Analysen und Interpretationen* (FRLANT, 120). Göttingen: Vandenhoeck & Ruprecht, 1978, [3]1984, [4]1990, 312 p. Esp. 120-128 [13,24-30.36-43]; 128-138 [13,31-32]; 138-142 [13,44-46]; 142-147 [13,47-50]; 160-161 [21,33-46]; 168-177 [18,12-14]; 177-193 [22,1-20]; 193-210 [25,14-30]; 210-218 [18,23-35]; 218-230 [20,1-16]; 230-238 [21,28-32]; 239-249 [25,1-13]. — Diss. Zürich, 1978 (E. Schweizer).
*Metafore del Regno. Le parabole di Gesù: ricostruzione e interpretazione*, trans. G. Garra (Biblioteca di cultura religiosa, 60). Brescia: Paideia, 1991, 389 p.

1985a *Die "Rede der Reden". Eine Auslegung der Bergpredigt heute.* Zürich: Theologischer Verlag, 1985, 253 p.; [2]1987. [NTA 30, p. 358]; [3]1994. → Hengel 1987, H. Riniker 1987
U. ECKERT, *Protestantesimo* 44 (1989) 131-132; S. VOLLENWEIDER, *KirchRefSchweiz* 141 (1985) 394-396.

1985b Die "Rede der Reden". Beobachtungen zum Verständnis der Bergpredigt Jesu. — *EvT* 45 (1985) 45-60. Esp. 47-51 [5,21-48]; 51-55 [6,1-34]; 55-60 [5,3-12]. [NTA 29, 929]

1986a *Neutestamentliche Hermeneutik* (Zürcher Grundrisse zur Bibel). Zürich: Theologischer Verlag, 1986, [2]1989, 452 p. Esp. 219-221 [18,23-35; 20,1-16]; 298-304 [antitheses].

1986b Zur Hermeneutik des Lehrens. Neutestamentliche Überlegungen zum Verhältnis von Hermeneutik und Didaktik. — *EvErz* 38 (1986) 117-128. Esp. 126-128 [5,21-48]; = ID., *Einblicke*, 1992, 95-108. Esp. 105-108.

1989 Einblick ins Menschliche. Anthropologische Entdeckungen in der Bergpredigt. — FRANKEMÖLLE, H. – KERTELGE, K. (eds.), *Vom Urchristentum zu Jesus*. FS J. Gnilka, 1989, 172-193. Esp. 175-178 [5,4.7]; 179-180 [7,7-11]; 180-183 [6,2-4]; 183-184 [7,12]; 184-187 [5,25-26.33-37]; 188-190 [Son of God]; 190-192 [6,25-34]; = ID., *Einblicke*, 1992, 263-285. Esp. 266-269; 270-271; 271-274; 274-275; 275-279; 279-281; 282-284.

1990 "But I say to you..." Concerning the Foundations of Jesus' Interpretation of the Law in the "Sermon on the Mount". — JENNINGS, T.W. (ed.), *Text and Logos*. FS H.W. Boers, 1990, 211-228.
"Ich aber sage euch". Zur Begründung der Gesetzesauslegung Jesu in der Bergpredigt. — ID., *Einblicke*, 1992, 201-217

1991 Die Suche nach den Söhnen und Töchtern des Friedens Auslegung der Botenrede der Logienquelle (Mt 10 par Lk 10). — *Die Zeichen der Zeit* (Berlin) 44 (1991) 54-59. [NTA 36, 149]

1992 *Einblicke ins Evangelium. Exegetische Beiträge zur neutestamentlichen Hermeneutik. Gesammelte Aufsätze aus den Jahren 1980-1991*. Göttingen: Vandenhoeck & Ruprecht, 1992, 493 p. → 1986b, 1989, 1990

1993 *Gegenwart und Gottesherrschaft. Überlegungen zum Zeitverständnis bei Jesus und im frühen Christentum* (Biblisch-theologische Studien, 20). Neukirchen-Vluyn: Neukirchener, 1993, 95 p. Esp. 26-34 [12,28/Q 11,20]; 41-42 [Q 10,9]; 49-50 [5,25-26].

**WEGENAST, Klaus**

1968a Das Ährenausraufen am Sabbat (Mk 2,23-28; vgl. Mt 12,1-8; Lk 6,1-5). — STOCK, H. – WEGENAST, K. – WIBBING, S., *Streitgespräche* (Handbücherei für den Religionsunterricht, 5), Gütersloh: Mohn, 1968, ²1969, 27-51. Esp. 30-31.

1968b Rein und Unrein. Mk 7,1-23; Mt 15,1-20. — *Ibid.*, 52-84. Esp. 56-58.

**WEGNER, Reinhard**

1982 (ed.), *Die Datierung der Evangelien. Durchgeführt vom Institut für wissenschaftstheoretische Grundlagenforschung*. Paderborn: Deutsches Institut für Bildung und Wissen, 1982, 344 p. → J. Ernst 1982, J.A.T. Robinson 1976
F. NEIRYNCK, *ETL* 59 (1983) 369-370.

**WEGNER, Uwe**

1985 *Der Hauptmann von Kafarnaum (Mt 7,28a; 8,5-10.13 par Lk 7,1-10). Ein Beitrag zur Q-Forschung* (WUNT, II/14). Tübingen: Mohr, 1985, XI-522 p. Esp. 18-74: "Mt 8,5-10.13 / Lk 7,1-10 im Vergleich mit Jo 4,46-54"; 75-90: "Textkritische Bemerkungen"; 91-276: "Wortstatistische und stilkritische Untersuchung"; 277-334: "Die rekonstruierte Erzählung als Bestandteil der Q-Quelle"; 335-370: "Formgeschichtliche Analyse der HP [Hauptmannsperikope]"; 371-402: "Einzelanalyse und theologische Bewertung der HP"; 403-428: "Die HP und die Frage nach der Historizität". [NTA 30, p. 103]. — Diss. Tübingen, 1982-83 (M. Hengel).
A. DERMIENCE, *RTL* 19 (1988) 497-499; A. FUCHS, *SNTU* 10 (1985) 214-218; H. GIESEN, *TGeg* 29 (1986) 253; J.S. KLOPPENBORG, *CBQ* 49 (1987) 163-164; P.-G. MÜLLER, *BK* 42 (1987) 87-88; G. MUSSIES, *NTT* 44 (1990) 65-67; F. NEUGEBAUER, *TLZ* 112 (1937) 510-512; K. STOCK, *ZKT* 108 (1986) 188; P.W. VAN DER HORST, *KerkT* 37 (1986) 270-272.

1986 Justiça para os desempregados. Reflexões sobre Mt 20,1-15. — *Estudos Biblicos* (Petrópolis) 11 (1986) 92-109.
Justicia para los desempleados. Reflexiones sobre Mt 20,1-15. — *Christus* (México) 52 (1987) 83-92.

1988 Mateus 6,1-4. — *Proclamar libertaçao* (São Paulo) 14 (1988) 332-345.

**WEHR, Lothar**

1996　*Petrus und Paulus – Kontrahenten und Partner. Die beiden Apostel im Spiegel des Neuen Testaments, der apostolischen Väter und früher Zeugnisse ihrer Verehrung* (NTAbh, NF 30). Münster: Aschendorff, 1996, VIII-416 p. Esp. 251-289: "Das Matthäusevangelium"; 350-354. — Diss. München, 1995 (J. Gnilka).

**WEIJERS, M.-R.**

1956　Où en est le problème synoptique? À propos de publications récentes. — *RThom* 56 (1956) 111-138. → Levie 1954, Vaganay 1954a

**WEINERT, Francis D.**

1982　Luke, the Temple and Jesus' Saying about Jerusalem's Abandoned House (Luke 13:34-35). — *CBQ* 44 (1982) 68-76. Esp. 71-72 [23,37-39]. [NTA 26, 891]

**WEINFELD, Moshe**

1990　The Charge of Hypocrisy in Matthew 23 and in Jewish Sources. — *Immanuel* 24-25 (1990) 52-58.

**WEINREB, Friedrich**

1972　*Die jüdischen Wurzeln des Matthäus Evangeliums* (Lebendige Bausteine, 13). Zürich: Origo, 1972, 216 p. [NTA 18, p. 247]
　　　　P. BEENTJES, *Streven* 27 (1973) 414-415; J. MURPHY-O'CONNOR, *RB* 83 (1976) 302; A. PAUL, *RSR* 62 (1974) 412; R. PESCH, *Freiburger Rundbrief* 24 (1972) 80.
　　　　*De Joodse wortels van het Mattheüsevangelie*, trans. Academie voor de Hebreeuwse Bijbel en de Hebreeuwse Taal. Sint-Baafs-Vijve: Oranje/De Eenhoorn, 1983, 228 p. Esp. 85-226: "Enkele opmerkingen bij het evangelie van Mattheüs".

**WEINRICH, William Carl**

1981　*Spirit and Martyrdom. A Study of the Work of the Holy Spirit in Contexts of Persecution and Martyrdom in the New Testament and Early Christian Literature*. Washington, DC: University Press of America, 1981, XIV-320 p. Esp. 17-25: "Synoptic gospels" [10,17-20.32-33]. — Diss. Basel, 1977 (B. Reicke).

1984*　(ed.), *The New Testament Age. Essays in Honor of Bo Reicke*. Macon, GA: Mercer University Press, 1984, 2 vols., XIII-286 and XIII-287-579 p. → Aalen, W.R. Farmer, Gerhardsson 1978, Grässer, Lövestam, Marshall

**WEISE, Manfred**

1958　Mt 5,21f. – ein Zeugnis sakraler Rechtsprechung in der Urgemeinde. — *ZNW* 49 (1958) 116-123. [NTA 3, 71]

**WEISER, Alfons**

1971　*Die Knechtsgleichnisse der synoptischen Evangelien* (SANT, 29). München: Kösel, 1971, 312 p. Esp. 49-57 [21,33-41/Mk]; 58-71 [22,1-10./Q]; 75-104 [18,23-35]; 178-225 [24,45-51/Q]; 226-272 [25,14-30/Q]. — Diss. Würzburg, 1970 (R. Schnackenburg). → W.J. Harrington 1972b, Klauck 1972

1988　"Die Gabe, Krankheiten zu heilen". Jesus und die Kranken. — *BK* 43 (1988) 2-7. [NTA 33, 1075]; = ID., *Studien zu Christsein und Kirche* (Stuttgarter biblische Aufsatzbände, 9), Stuttgart: Katholisches Bibelwerk, 1990.

1993　*Theologie des Neuen Testaments. II: Die Theologie der Evangelien* (Kohlhammer Studienbücher Theologie, 8). Stuttgart: Kohlhammer, 1993, 237 p. Esp. 21-43: "Die Theologie der Redenquelle" [John the Baptist; christology; ethics]; 79-116: "Die Theologie des Matthäusevangeliums" [structure; OT; church; christology].

**WEISS, Hans-Friedrich**

1983　*Kerygma und Geschichte. Erwägungen zur Frage nach Jesus im Rahmen der Theologie des Neuen Testaments*. Berlin: Evangelische Verlagsanstalt, 1983, 144 p. Esp. 38-39; 54-55 [28,16-20].

**WEISS, Herold**

1990 The Sabbath in the Synoptic Gospels. — *JSNT* 38 (1990) 13-27. Esp. 17 [24,20]; 18-20 [12,1-8.9-14]. [NTA 35, 123]; = EVANS, C.A. – PORTER, S.E. (eds.), *New Testament Backgrounds. A Sheffield Reader* (The Biblical Seminar. 43), Sheffield: JSOT, 1997, 109-123. Esp. 114; 114-116.

**WEISS, Johannes**

1892[R] *Die Predigt Jesu vom Reiche Gottes* [1892, [2]1900], ed. F. Hahn. Göttingen: Vandenhoeck & Ruprecht, [3]1964, XV-251 p. Esp. 40-41 [13,36-43]; 44-45 [βχσιλεία]; 65-69; 69-73 [ἐγγίζω]; 75-76 [6,33]; 77-78 [13,44-46]; 80-82 [11,11]; 88-91 [12,28]; 128-131.179-187 [5,3-12]; 145-154 [δικαιοσύνη]; 159-175.201-210 [Son of Man]; 187-192 [6,33]; 192-197 [Q 16,16].
*Jesus' Proclamation of the Kingdom of God* [1892], trans. and ed. R.H. Hiers & D.L. Holland (Lives of Jesus Series). Philadelphia, PA: Fortress, 1971, XII-148 p.; Chico, CA: Scholars, 1985, VII-148 p.
*La predicazione di Gesù sul Regno di Dio* (Classici neotestamentarie, 2). Napoli: D'Auria, 1993, 249 p.

**WEISS, Wolfgang**

1989 *"Eine neue Lehre in Vollmacht". Die Streit- und Schulgespräche des Markus-Evangeliums* (BZNW, 52). Berlin: de Gruyter, 1989, XI-409 p. Esp. 102-103 [Q 7,31-35/Mk]; 168-169 [Q 11,14-23]; 170 [Q 7,1-10]; 196-197 [Q 16,18/Mk]. — Diss. Mainz, 1986 (E. Brandenburger).

**WEIZSÄCKER, Carl Friedrich** → Lapide 1980

**WELBORN, Laurence L.**

1995 The Dangerous Double Affirmation: Character and Truth in 2 Cor 1,17. — *ZNW* 86 (1995) 34-52. Esp. 40-43 [5,33-37]. [NTA 40, 328]

**WELCH, John W.**

1981 Chiasmus in the New Testament. — ID. (ed.), *Chiasmus in Antiquity. Structures, Analyses, Exegesis*, Hildesheim: Gerstenberg, 1981, 211-249.

**WELLHAUSEN, Julius**

1905[R] *Einleitung in die drei ersten Evangelien* [1905; [2]1911]. — Repr. *Evangelienkommentare*, ed. M. Hengel. Berlin – New York: de Gruyter, 1987, 1-176 ["Vorwort" by M. Hengel, V-XII]. Esp. 49-57: "Markus bei Matthäus und Lukas"; 57-64: "Nicht aus Markus Stammendes bei Matthäus und Lukas"; 64-79: "Markus verglichen mit Q".

1914[R] *Das Evangelium Matthaei* [[2]1914]. — *Ibid.*, 177-320.

**WELLS, G.A.**

1971 *The Jesus of the Early Christians. A Study in Christian Origins*. London: Pemberton, 1971, 362 p. Esp. 11-39 [Virgin birth].

**WELLS, Louise**

1998 *The Greek Language of Healing from Homer to New Testament Times* (BZNW, 83). Berlin – New York: de Gruyter, 1998, XVIII-489 p. Esp. 156-159; 364-368 [Matthew]. — Diss. Univ. of Tasmania, 1993.

**WENDLAND, Heinz-Dietrich**

1970 *Ethik des Neuen Testaments. Eine Einführung* (Grundrisse zum Neuen Testament. NTD Ergänzungsreihe, 4). Göttingen: Vandenhoeck & Ruprecht, 1970, [2]1975, 134 p. Esp. 13-16: "Das Liebesgebot" [5,43-48]; 16-22: "Der Sinn der Bergpredigt"; 42-45. → Schrage 1982a
*Éthique du Nouveau Testament. Introduction aux problèmes*, trans. E. de Peyer. Genève: Labor et Fides; Paris: Librairie protestante, 1972, 163 p.
*Etica do Novo Testamento*. São Leopoldo: Sinodal, 1974, 160 p.; [2]1981.
*Etica del Nuovo Testamento*, trans. G. Casanova (Nuovo Testamento. Supplementi, 4). Brescia: Paideia, 1975, 222 p. Esp. 27-33; 33-43.

**WENDLING, Hermann**

1984    *Jesus in Getsemani. Exegetische Untersuchung zu Mk 14,32-42; Mt 26,36-46; Lk 22,39-46.* Diss. Frankfurt/M, 1984.

**WENGER, E.L.**

1951a   Let the dead bury their dead. [8,21] — *ExpT* 62 (1950-51) 255.

1951b   Our bread for the morrow. [6,11] — *Ibid.*, 285.

**WENGST, Klaus**

1986a   *Pax Romana. Anspruch und Wirklichkeit. Erfahrungen und Wahrnehmungen des Friedens bei Jesus und im Urchristentum.* München: Kaiser, 1986, 292 p. Esp. 80-82.87-88 [10,34-35]; 83-85 [5,3-6]; 88-90 [5,39-40]; 207-210.

1986b   Anmerkungen zur Barthschen Auslegung der Versuchungsgeschichte aus heutiger exegetischer Perspektive. — *ZDialTheol* 2 (1986) 21-38.

1991    *Ostern – Ein wirkliches Gleichnis, eine wahre Geschichte. Zum neutestamentlichen Zeugnis von der Auferweckung Jesu* (Kaiser Taschenbücher, 97). München: Kaiser, 1991.

1994    Wie aus Böcken Ziegen werden (Mt 25,32f). Zur Entstehung und Verbreitung einer Forschungslegende oder: Wissenschaft als "stille Post" — *EvT* 54 (1994) 491-500. [NTA 39, 1460]

**WENHAM, David**

1972    The Synoptic Problem Revisited: Some New Suggestions about the Composition of Mark 4:1-34. — *TyndB* 23 (1972) 3-38. Esp. 17-38: "Mark 4:1-34 – some new suggestions". [NTA 17, 942] — Diss. Manchester, 1970.

1973    The Resurrection Narratives in Matthew's Gospel. — *TyndB* 24 (1973) 21-54. Esp. 21-25: "The historical problems of Matthew 28"; 25-41: "Matthew 28 examined and compared with the other gospels"; 41-53: "The historical problems reviewed". [NTA 19, 547]

1974    The Interpretation of the Parable of the Sower. [13,1-23] — *NTS* 20 (1973-74) 299-319. Esp. 300-304 [Mk/Mt]; 305-309.315-318 [pre-Mk/Mt]. [NTA 19, 107]

1977    Source Criticism. — MARSHALL, I.H. (ed.), *New Testament Interpretation*, 1977, 139-152. Esp. 141-142; 150-152 [12,1-8].

1979a   Jesus and the Law: An Exegesis on Matthew 5:17-20. — *Themelios* 4/3 (1979) 92-96. [NTA 24, 86] → Banks 1974

1979b   The Structure of Matthew xiii. — *NTS* 25 (1978-79) 516-522. [NTA 24, 424]

1980    A Note on Matthew 24:10-12. — *TyndB* 31 (1980) 155-162. [NTA 25, 865]

1981    Paul and the Synoptic Apocalypse. — FRANCE, R.T. - WENHAM, D. (eds.), *Studies of History and Tradition*, 1981, 345-375. Esp. 347-353 [24–25/1 Thess 5]; 361-362 [23,29-38/1 Thess 2,14-16].

1982a   'This generation will not pass...'. A Study of Jesus' Future Expectation in Mark 13. — ROWDON, H.H. (ed.), *Christ the Lord*. FS D. Guthrie, 1982, 127-150. Esp. 144-150 [proto-Mt].

1982b   A Note on Mark 9:33-42 / Matt. 18:1-6 / Luke 9:46-50. — *JSNT* 14 (1982) 113-118. [NTA 26, 866]

1983    Guelich on the Sermon on the Mount: A Critical Review. — *TrinJ* NS 4/2 (1983) 92-108. [NTA 29, 89r] → Guelich 1982

1984    *The Rediscovery of Jesus' Eschatological Discourse* (Gospel Perspectives, 4). Sheffield: JSOT, 1984, XI-406 p. Esp. 51-100: "A pre-synoptic parable collection (Mt 24:42–25:30, Mk 13:33-37, Lk 12:35-48)"; 101-134: "The pre-synoptic conclusion to the eschatological discourse"; 135-174: "Luke 17:22-37: an extract from the eschatological discourse"; 175-218: "The desolating sacrilege and the pre-synoptic tradition (Mt 24:15-22, Mk 13:14-20, Lk 21:20-24)"; 219-252: "The sayings about appearing before the authorities and the mission discourse: Mt 10:17-20, Mk 13:9-11, Lk 12:11,12, Lk 21:12-15"; 253-285: "The pre-synoptic eschatological discourse and the warning of coming sufferings: Mt 24:9-1, Mk 13:9-13, Lk 21:12-15"; 287-334: "Other parts of the eschatological discourse" [Mt 24,1-3.4-8.29-31.32-36]; 335-353: "The context of the discourse".

X. ALEGRE, *ActBibl* 25 (1988) 76-77; R. BAUCKHAM, *ExpT* 96 (1984-85) 345-346; F.W. BURNETT, *CBQ* 48 (1986) 351-353; J.D.G. DUNN, *JTS* 38 (1987) 163-166; T.J. GEDDERT, *EvQ* 58 (1986) 364-367; J. LIEU, *HeythJ* 28 (1987) 203-204; J.R. MICHAELS, *JBL* 106 (1987) 132-134; F. NEIRYNCK, *ETL* 61 (1985) 192-193; R. RIESNER, *TZ* 46 (1990) 82-83; G. STANTON, *Themelios* 11 (1985-86) 99; N. WALTER, *TLZ* 114 (1989) 113-115.

1985*  (ed.), *The Jesus Tradition Outside the Gospels* (Gospel Perspectives, 5). Sheffield: JSOT, 1985, 419 p. → Bauckham, Blomberg, Chilton, Davids, J.A. Draper, Hagner, G. Maier, P. Richardson, D. Wenham, D.F. Wright

1985  Paul's Use of the Jesus Tradition: Three Samples. — *Ibid.*, 7-37. Esp. 7-9 [19,6.9/1 Cor 7,10-11]; 10-15 [5,32; 19,6.9]; 15-17 [5,43-48/Rom 12,14]; 17-24 [5,38-48/Rom 12,17-20]; 25-28 [16,17-19/Gal 1]. → Neirynck 1996c

1986*  & BLOMBERG, C. (eds.), *The Miracles of Jesus* (Gospel Perspectives, 6). Sheffield: JSOT, 1986, 457 p. → Bauckham, Blomberg, M.J. Harris, Twelftree, D.F. Wright, E.M. Yamauchi

1986  2 Corinthians 1:17,18: Echo of a Dominical Logion. — *NT* 28 (1986) 271-279. Esp. 271-272 [5,37/James 5,12; 2 Cor 1,17-18]. [NTA 31, 274]

1989  *The Parables of Jesus: Pictures of Revolution* (The Jesus Library). London–Sydney: Hodder & Stoughton, 1989, 256 p.

1993  Unity and Diversity in the New Testament. — LADD, G.E., *Theology of the New Testament*, 1993, 684-719. Esp. 693-694; 704-707. → Ladd 1974a/93

1994  The Story of Jesus Known to Paul. — GREEN, J.B. - TURNER, M.B.B. (eds.), *Jesus of Nazareth*. FS I.H. Marshall, 1994, 297-311 [Paul/Mt 1-2; 3,13-17; 4,1-11; 10,5-16; 16,17-19].

1995  *Paul. Follower of Jesus or Founder of Christianity?* Grand Rapids, MI: Eerdmans, 1995, XVI-452 p. Esp. 73-78 [5,20]; 81-83 [17,20]; 86-90 [13,1-23]; 92-97 [15]; 113-115.129-136 [11,25-27]; 144-147 [26,26-30]; 154-162 [16,24-28]; 195-199 [10,5-15]; 200-205 [16,16-20]; 210-213 [18,15-20]; 219-222 [5,17-20]; 251-253 [5,38-48]; 263-265 [18,1-9]; 268-271 [20,24-28]; 271-274 [5,33-35]; 274-275 [5,29-30]; 276-280 [26,36-46]; 309-311 [25,1-13]; 320-326 [23,29-39]; 331-333 [24,31]; 357-363 [17,1-9].

## WENHAM, Gordon J.

1984a  Gospel Definitions of Adultery and Women's Rights. [5,28.32] — *ExpT* 95 (1983-84) 330-332. [NTA 29, 728]

1984b  Matthew and Divorce: An Old Crux Revisited. — *JSNT* 22 (1984) 95-107. Esp. 95-101 [19,9]; 101-106 [5,32]. [NTA 29, 531]

1984c  → Heth 1984a

1986  The Syntax of Matthew 19.9. — *JSNT* 28 (1986) 17-23. [NTA 31, 590]

## WENHAM, John William

1972  *Christ and the Bible*. London: Tyndale, 1972, 206 p. Esp. 11-42: "Jesus' view of the Old Testament"; 43-61: "The authority of Jesus as a teacher"; 62-83: "Objections to the claims of Jesus"; 84-108: "The New Testament writers and the Old Testament"; 109-123: "Jesus and the New Testament"; Grand Rapids, MI: Baker, ³1994, 222 p.

1978  Gospel Origins. — *TrinJ* 7 (1978) 112-134. [NTA 24, 50] → Moo 1981

1981a  "Gospel Origins": A Rejoinder. — *TrinJ* NS 2 (1981) 37-39. → Moo 1981

1981b  Synoptic Independence and the Origin of Luke's Travel Narrative. — *NTS* 27 (1980-81) 507-515. Esp. 507-512. [NTA 26, 142] → Prete 1986b

1981c  When Were the Saints Raised? A Note on the Punctuation of Matthew xxvii.51-3. — *JTS* 32 (1981) 150-152. [NTA 25, 868]

1982 Why do you ask me about the good? A Study of the Relation between Text and Source Criticism. [19,16-17] — *NTS* 28 (1982) 116-125. Esp. 116-118: "The interrelation of text and source criticism"; 118-120: "Did the secondary text originate with Matthew?"; 120-122: "Harmonisation as a force in textual change"; 122-124: "Harmonisation or restoration?". [NTA 26, 846]

1984 *Easter Enigma. Do the Resurrection Stories Contradict One Another?* (A Latimer Monograph). Exeter: Paternoster, 1984, 162 p. Esp. 43-45; Grand Rapids, MI: Baker, [2]1993.

1991 *Redating Matthew, Mark and Luke. A Fresh Assault on the Synoptic Problem*. London - Sydney: Hodder & Stoughton, 1991; Downers Grove, IL: InterVarsity, 1992, XVIII-319 p. Esp. 40-87: "Building a synoptic theory: 2. The relation of Luke to Matthew"; 88-115: "Building a synoptic theory: 3. The relation of Matthew to Mark"; 116-135: "Ancient testimony to Matthew's gospel"; 201-202; 213-216 [1,2-17]; 238-243 [date]. [NTA 36, p. 271, 429]

> J.K. ELLIOTT, *NT* 34 (1992) 200-201; P. FITZGERALD-LOMBARD, *Tablet* 246 (1992) 750; M. GOULDER, *Theology* 95 (1992) 53-54; I.H. MARSHALL, *The European Journal of Theology* 1 (1992) 185-186; R.K. MCIVER, *AndrUnS* 31 (1993) 165-167; F. NEIRYNCK, *ETL* 69 (1993) 173-174; H. WANSBROUGH, *NBlackfr* 72 (1991) 502-503; R. WATTS, *Themelios* 19/1 (1993-94) 25.

**WENKER, W.**

1964 Alcance de Mt 20,1-16 en labios de Jesús. — *RevistBíb* 26 (1964) 140-145. [NTA 9, 540]

**WENNEMER, Karl**

1966 Die Segnungen des menschlichen Lebens und der menschlichen Arbeit durch Christus (Mt 13,53-58). — *Am Tisch des Wortes* (Stuttgart) 10 (1966) 30-45.

**WENSCHKEWITZ, Hans**

1959 Die Einheitlichkeit der synoptischen erzählenden Perikopen und ihre Bedeutung für die Verkündigung der Kirche. — HOFFMANN, G. - RENGSTORF, K.H. (eds.), *Stat crux dum volvitur orbis. Eine Festschrift für Landesbischof D. Hans Lilje Abt zu Loccum zum sechzigsten Geburtstag am 20. August 1959*, Berlin: Lutherisches Verlagshaus, 1959, 31-47. Esp. 44-46 [9,1-8; 15,21-28].

**WENTHE, Dean O.**

1974 The Historical-Critical Interpretation of the Baptism of Jesus from the Perspective of Traditional Lutheran Exegesis. — *Springfielder* 37 (1974) 230-240. [NTA 19, 103]

1976 The Parable of the Ten Bridesmaids (Matthew 25:1-13). — *Springfielder* 40 (1976) 9-16. [NTA 20, 782]

**WENTLING, Judith L.**

1982 A Comparison of the Elijah Motifs in the Gospels of Matthew and Mark. — *Proceedings EGLBS* 2 (1982) 104-122. Esp. 113-119.

**WEREN, Wilhelmus Johannes Cornelis**

1978 De onbarmhartige dienaar. Een parabel als toegang tot de visie van Matteüs op vergeven. — *Schrift* 55 (1978) 16-22.

1979 *De broeders van de Mensenzoon. Mt 25,31-46 als toegang tot de eschatologie van Matteüs*. Amsterdam: Bolland, 1979, XVI-265 p. Esp. 5-24.196-198: "De literaire structuur van de eschatologische rede van Matteüs"; 25-73.199-210: "Traditie en redactie in Mt 25,31-46"; 74-115.211-221: "Redactionele elementen in Mt 25,31-46"; 116-176.222-234: "Mt 25,31-46 en eschatologische teksten elders in Mt"; 177-194.235-238: "De eschatologie van Matteüs". [NTA 25, p. 203] — Diss. Nijmegen, 1979 (B.M.F. van Iersel).

> H. BIEZENO, *TijdTheol* 19 (1979) 409-410; H. BOERS, *JBL* 100 (1981) 650-651; J. COPPENS, *ETL* 56 (1980) 445-446; R. DEVLEESCHOUWER, *Collationes* 10 (1980) 477-478; R. HOET, *Bijdragen* 41 (1980) 311-312; J. KAHMANN, *TijdTheol* 20 (1980) 432; J.W. ROGERSON, *JTS* 33 (1982) 245-247; E.J. THEUNISSEN, *CBQ* 43 (1981) 487-488.

1982 Het bestaansrecht van de zwakste. De samenhang tussen Mt 5,3-12 en Mt 25,31-46. — *Ons Geestelijk Leven* 59 (1982) 28-36.

1984 Israël en de kerk. Het substitutiedenken en de lijnen var Jes. 5,1-7 naar Mt. 21,33-44 (Israel and the Church. The idea of substitution and the paths from Is. 5,1-7 to Mt. 21,33-44). — *TijdTheol* 24 (1984) 355-373 (English summary, 373). Esp. 358-364: "Een synchronische analyse"; 364-371: "Lijnen van Jes. 5,1-7 naar Mt. 21,33-44" [NTA 29, 939]
   *Israël en de kerk. Lijnen van Jesaja 5,1-7 naar Matteüs 21,33-44* [Inaugurale rede Theologische Faculteit Tilburg 4 oktober 1984]. Tilburg, 1984, 33 p.; = ID., *Intertextualiteit en bijbel*, Kampen: Kok, 1993, 35-64.

1986a Bergrede en halacha. — ID. – POULSEN, N. (eds.), *Bij de put van Jakob. Exegetische opstellen* [FS M. Rijkhoff] (Theologische Faculteit Tilburg – Studies, 5), Tilburg: University Press, 1986, 46-71. Esp. 54-65: "Overeenkomsten tussen Mt 5,17-48 en de halacha"; 65-68: "Verschillen tussen Mt 5,17-48 en de halacha".

1986b Mt 25,31-46: een analyse. — *Schrift* 105 (1986) 114-120.

1986c Mt 8,5-13: een kapstok voor het substitutiedenken? — *Schrift* 108 (1986) 224-228.

1988* et al., *Geboorteverhalen van Jezus: feit en fictie.* Boxtel: Katholieke Bijbelstichting; Brugge: Tabor, 1988, 180 p. → den Heyer, Verheyden, Weren

1988 Vanuit de stal terug naar Lucas en Matteüs. — *Ibid.*, 7-30. Esp. 24-29.

1991 → Noorda 1991

1994a *Matteüs* (Belichting van het Bijbelboek). 's-Hertogenbosch: Katholieke Bijbelstichting; Brugge: Tabor, 1994, 255 p. [NTA 39, p. 330]
   J.S. Vos, *GTT* 95 (1995) 199.

1994b Broederschap en barmhartigheid in Mattheus. Een tekstsemantische studie. — AKERBOOM, D., et al. (eds.), *Broeder Jehosjoea.* FS B. Hemelsoet, 1994, 249-265. Esp. 249-252 [ἀδελφός]; 253-254 [σπλαγχνίζομαι]; 254-260 [9,13; 12.7/Hos 6,6]; 260-261 [23,23]; 261-262 [5,7].

1997 Jesus' Entry into Jerusalem. Mt 21,1-17 in the Light of the Hebrew Bible and the Septuagint. — TUCKETT, C.M. (ed.), *The Scriptures in the Gospels*, 1997, 117-141. Esp. 118-121: "The textual form of the citations in Mt 21,1-17"; 124-133 [21,5]; 133-135 [21,9.15]; 135-137 [21,13]; 137-138 [21,16].

**WERNBERG-MØLLER, P.**

1956 A Semitic Idiom in Matt. v.22. — *NTS* 3 (1956-57) 71-73. [NTA 2, 50]

**WEST, H. Philip, Jr.**

1967 A Primitive Version of Luke in the Composition of Matthew. — *NTS* 14 (1967-68) 75-95. Esp. 76-79 [Q]; 79-88 [omissions]; 80-83 [women]; 83-85 [lawless people]; 86-87 [wealth]; 88-93 [conflation]. [NTA 12, 547]

**WESTERHOLM, Stephen**

1978 *Jesus and Scribal Authority* (ConBibNT, 10). Lund: Gleerup, 1978, 178 p. Esp. 57-59 [23,23]; 71-85 [15,1-20/Mk]; 85-90 [23,25-26/Q]; 96-100 [12,1-8/Mk]; 100-102 [12,9-14]; 106-108 [5,33-37]; 108-112 [23,16-22]; 117-120 [5,31-32; 19,9]. — Diss. Lund, 1977 (B. Gerhardsson).

1991 Law and Christian Ethics. — RICHARDSON, P. – WESTERHOLM, S. (eds.), *Law in Religious Communities in the Roman Period. The Debate over Torah and Nomos in Post-Biblical Judaism and Early Christianity* (Studies in Christianity and Judaism, 4), Waterloo, Ont.: Laurier, 1991, 75-91. Esp. 83-85: "The messianic Torah in Matthew" → W.D. Davies 1963

1992a Clean and Unclean. — *DJG*, 1992, 125-132. Esp. 130.

1992b Pharisees. — *Ibid.*, 609-614. Esp. 613-614.

1992c Sabbath. — *Ibid.*, 716-719. Esp. 718.

1992d The Law in the Sermon on the Mount: Matt 5:17-48. — *Criswell Theological Review* (Dallas, TX) 6 (1992) 43-56. [NTA 37, 1256]

**WESTERINK, Hendrik Jan**

1951 De *Malkoeth Sjamaim* bij Mattheus. — *Arcana Revelata. Een bundel Nieuw-Testamentische Studiën aangeboden aan Prof. Dr. F.W. Grosheide ter gelegenheid van zijn zeventigste verjaardag*, Kampen: Kok, 1951, 149-162.

**WESTERMANN, Claus**

1968 *Der Segen in der Bibel und im Handeln der Kirche*. München: Kaiser, 1968, 118 p. Esp. 82-84 [19,13-15]; 90-95 [10,12-13]. → Schenk 1967
*Blessing in the Bible and the Life of the Church*, trans. K. Crim (Overtures to Biblical Theology). Philadelphia, PA: Fortress, 1978, XVI-126 p. Esp. 83-85.93-98.

1984 *Vergleiche und Gleichnisse im Alten und Neuen Testament* (Calwer theologische Monographien, 14). Stuttgart: Calwer, 1984, 144 p. Esp. 123-130: "Zur Gliederung der Gleichnisse"; 130-134: "Beobachtungen zu den Vergleichen in der synoptischen Evangelien".
*The Parables of Jesus in the Light of the Old Testament*, ed. and trans. F.W. Golka & A.H.B. Logan. Minneapolis, MN: Fortress; Edinburgh: Clark, 1990, VII-211 p.

1994 & GLOEGE, G. (eds.), *Einführung in die Bibel*. Stuttgart: Kreuz, 1994, VIII-566 p.

**WETZEL, Richard**

1978 *Das vierundzwanstigste Kapitel des Evangelisten Matthäus in der Auslegung durch die griechischen Väter Origenes und Chrysostomus*. Diss. Tübingen, 1978, 214 and 279 p. (K. Schelkle).

**WHEELER, C.B.** → Gabel 1986

**WHEELER, Frank**

1985 *Textual Criticism and the Synoptic Problem: A Textual Commentary on the Minor Agreements of Matthew and Luke against Mark*. Diss. Baylor Univ., Waco, TX, 1985, XIII-473 p. Esp. 1-53: "Textual criticism and the synoptic problem past and present"; 54-85: "The rise and development of textual corruption as an explanation for the minor agreements of Matthew and Luke against Mark"; 86-305: "A textual commentary on the minor agreements of Matthew and Luke against Mark" [8,2.3; 9,17.20; 12,2.4; 13,10.11; 14,21; 17,2.5.17; 19,24.29; 21,1.23.24.44; 22,27.35-36; 26,64.68.73.75; 27,54.58.59-60; 28,1.3]; 306-394: "Analysis and synthesis". — *DissAbstr* 47 (1986-87) 555; *SBT* 15 (1987) 113-114. → Neirynck 1987a, Tuckett 1993c

**WHEELER, Sandra Ely**

1995 *Wealth as Peril and Obligation. The New Testament on Possessions*. Grand Rapids, MI: Eerdmans, 1995, XVIII-158 p. Esp. 108-112. — Diss. Yale University, 1992 (R.B. Hays – G. Outka).

**WHELAN, Caroline F.**

1993 Suicide in the Ancient World: A Re-examination of Matthew 27:3-10. — *LavalTP* 49 (1993) 505-522. Esp. 505-512, 521-522. [NTA 38, 775]

**WHITE, John L.**

1991 Jesus as Actant. — *BR* 36 (1991) 19-29. [NTA 36, 1217]

**WHITE, Leland J.**

1985 Peacemakers in Matthew's World. [5,9] — *BiTod* 23 (1985) 29-34. [NTA 29, 518]

1986 Grid and Group in Matthew's Community: The Righteousness/Honor Code in the Sermon on the Mount. — *Semeia* 35 (1986) 61-90. Esp. 69-80: "Matthew 5–7"; 80-85: "Interpreting the code"; 85-86: "Symbolic meaning and historical reality". [NTA 31, 113]

**WHITE, L. Michael**

1987 Scaling the Strongman's "Court" (Luke 11:21). — *Forum* 3/3 (1987) 3-28. Esp. 5-6.17-18 [Q 11,14-23]; 14-15 [Q 7,1-10]. [NTA 32, 654]

1991 Crisis Management and Boundary Maintenance: The Social Location of the Matthean Community. — BALCH, D.L. (ed.), *Social History of the Matthean Community*, 1991, 211-247. Esp. 213-217: "Locating the Matthean community"; 221-228: "Marking the boundaries of the Matthean community"; 238-242: "Matthew's social location: a suggestion".

**WHITE, Reginald E.O.**

1960 *The Biblical Doctrine of Initiation.* London: Hodder & Stoughton, 1960, 392 p. Esp. 73-89: "Johannine baptism"; 90-109: "The baptism of Jesus"; 338-345: "The reliability of Matt. XXVIII 16f".

1979a *Biblical Ethics.* Atlanta, GA: Knox, 1979, 254 p. Esp. 215-219.

1979b *Matthew Lays it on the Line!* Edinburgh: Saint Andrew Press, 1979, VIII-164 p. [NTA 24, p. 90]
*The Mind of Matthew.* Philadelphia, PA: Westminster, 1980, VIII-164 p. [NTA 24, p. 305]
A. BEHERA, *IndianJT* 31 (1982) 56-57.

**WHITELEY, D.E.H.**

1968 The Doctrine of Salvation in the Synoptic Gospels. — *Studia Evangelica* 4 (1968) 116-130. Esp. 120 [12,18]; 120-121 [20,28]; 126-130.

**WHITTERS, M.**

1996 The Beatitudes: Glimpses of Heaven for Those Stuck on Earth. — *Emmanuel* 102 (1996) 223-229. [NTA 41, 203]

**WIARDA, Timothy**

1994 Simon, Jesus of Nazareth, Son of Jonah, Son of John: Realistic Detail in the Gospels and Acts. — *NTS* 40 (1994) 196-209. Esp. 203-205 [Ναζωραῖος]. [NTA 38, 1312]

**WIBBING, Siegfried**

1959 *Die Tugend- und Lasterkataloge im Neuen Testament und ihre Traditionsgeschichte unter besonderer Berücksichtigung der Qumran-Texte* (BZNW, 25). Berlin, 1959, XVI-127 p. Esp. 82.87.92-84 [15,19].

1966a Die Taufe Jesu (Markus 1,9-11; vgl. Matthäus 3,13-17; Lukas 3,21-22). — DIGNATH, W. - WIBBING, S., *Taufe - Versuchung - Verklärung* (Handbücherei für den Religionsunterricht, 3), Gütersloh: Mohn, 1966, 12-32. Esp. 12-13.

1966b Die Darstellung der Versuchung Jesu (Matthäus 4,1-11; vgl. Markus 1,12-13; Lukas 4,1-13). — *Ibid.*, 33-55. Esp. 34-47.

1968 Das Zöllnergastmahl (Mk 2,13-17; vgl. Mt 9,9-13; Lk 5,27-32). — STOCK, H. - WEGENAST, K. - WIBBING, S., *Streitgespräche* (Handbücherei für den Religionsunterricht, 5), Gütersloh: Mohn, 1968, ²1969, 84-107. Esp. 85-92.

**WIBERG, Bertil**

1958 Forhærdelsestanken i evangelierne. [The idea of obduracy in the gospels] [13,13-15] — *DanskTeolTids* 21 (1958) 16-32. [NTA 3, 55]

**WICKERT, Ulrich**

1971 *Sacramentum Unitatis. Ein Beitrag zum Verständnis der Kirche bei Cyprian* (BZNW, 41). Berlin: de Gruyter, 1971, XI-164 p. Esp. 45-48.56-62.92-94.109-113 [16,18-19].

**WICKHAM FERRIER, Pablo**

1984 *El Sermón del monte.* Madrid: Literatura Bíblica, 1984, 75 p.

**WICKINGS, H.F.**

1977 The Nativity Stories and Docetism. — *NTS* 23 (1976-77) 457-460. [NTA 22, 80]

WIDART, J.M.

1964  L'unité de la Mort et de la Résurrection de Jésus chez S. Matthieu. — *RClerAfr* 19 (1964) 37-47.

WIEBE, Ben

1991  Messianic Ethics. Response to the Kingdom of God. — *Interpr* 45 (1991) 29-42. [NTA 35, 596]

1992  *Messianic Ethics. Jesus' Proclamation of the Kingdom of God and the Church in Response.* Waterloo, Ont. – Scottdale, PA: Herald, 1992, 224 p.

WIEBE, Phillip H.

1989  Jesus' Divorce Exception. [19,9] — *JEvTS* 32 (1989) 327-333. [NTA 34, 631]

WIEFEL, Wolfgang

1969  Vätersprüche und Herrenworte. Ein Beitrag zur Frage der Bewahrung mündlicher Traditionssätze. — *NT* 11 (1969) 105-120. Esp. 115-120. [NTA 14, 128]

1981  Erwägungen zum Thema Jesuanismus im Urchristentum. — *TVers* 12 (1981) 11-24. Esp. 14-20 [Q; historical Jesus].

1998  *Das Evangelium nach Matthäus* (Theologischer Handkommentar zum Neuen Testament, 1). Leipzig: Evangelische Verlagsanstalt, 1998, XXIV-497 p. Esp. 14-22: "Die Arbeit am Matthäusevangelium in den letzten Jahrzehnten".

WIÉNER, Claude

1966  La nouvelle traduction française de la prière du Seigneur. Signification pastorale et œcuménique. — *La Maison-Dieu* (Paris) 85 (1966) 140-152. [NTA 11, 204]

WIESER, Friedrich Emmanuel

1987  *Die Abrahamvorstellungen im Neuen Testament* (EHS, XXIII/317). Bern–Frankfurt/M: Lang, 1987, X-209 p. — Diss. Zürich, 1986 (E. Schweizer).

WIESER, Thomas

1985  Community – Its Unity, Diversity and Universality. — *Semeia* 33 (1985) 83-95. Esp. 84-85 [9,9-13]. [NTA 30, 797]

WIJNGAARDS, John N.M.

1967  The Episode of the Magi and Christian Kerygma. — *IndianJT* 16 (1967) 30-41.

1975  Do Jesus' Words on Divorce (Lk. 16:18) Admit of No Exception? — *Jeevadhara* 5 (1975) 399-411. Esp. 406-408 [5,32; 19,9]. [NTA 20, 812]

1983  Let him take up his cross... [16,27] — *Vidyajyoti* 47 (1983) 106-117. [NTA 28, 516]

1987  Leadership that Fosters Growth. — *Vidyajyoti* 51 (1987) 319-324. [NTA 32, 579]

WIKENHAUSER, Alfred

1953  *Einleitung in das Neue Testament.* Freiburg: Herder, 1953, XV-420 p. Esp. 126-145: "Das Matthäus-Evangelium"; 162-182: "Die synoptische Frage"; [2]1956, XV-441 p.; [3]1958; [4]1961 (ed. A. Vögtle); [5]1963, XV-466 p. Esp. 126-145; 162-182; 414-417: "Ergänzungen". → J. Schmid 1973
*New Testament Introduction*, trans. J. Cunningham. New York: Herder & Herder; Edinburgh: Nelson, 1958 [= German [2]1956], XIX-580 p. Esp. 173-199; 221-253.
*Introduzione al Nuovo Testamento*, trans. F. Montagnini (Biblioteca di Studi Biblici, 1). Brescia: Paideia, 1963 [= German [4]1961], [2]1966, XV-507 p. Esp. 158-180; 200-225.

WIKGREN, Allen

1953  Additional Armenian New Testament Manuscripts in the Kurdian Collection. — *JBL* 72 (1953) 115-126. Esp. 116, 118, 122, 126.

1966  → K. Aland [GNT 1966]

**WILCKEN, J.**

1963 A Commentary on Mt 21,8s. — *Kerygma* (Pymble, Australia) 2 (1963) 103-110.

**WILCKENS, Ulrich**

1963 Die Perikope vom leeren Grabe Jesu in der nachmarkinischen Traditionsgeschichte. — *Festschrift für Friedrich Smend zum 70. Geburtstag dargebracht von Freunden und Schülern*, Berlin: Merseburger, 1963, 30-41. Esp. 31-33 [28,1-10].

1970a *Auferstehung. Das biblische Auferstehungszeugnis historisch untersucht und erklärt* (Themen der Theologie, 4). Stuttgart–Berlin: Kreuz, 1970, 173 p. Esp. 64-66; 69-71 [28,16-20].
*Risurrezione*, trans. A. Rizzi. Brescia: Queriniana, 1976, 187 p.
*Resurrection. Biblical Testimony to the Resurrection: An Historical Examination and Explanation*, trans. A.M. Stewart. Atlanta, GA: Knox, 1978, VI-134 p.
*La resurrección de Jesús. Estudio histórico-crítico del testimonio bíblico* (Biblioteca de estudios bíblicos, 37). Salamanca: Sígueme, 1981, 158 p.

1970b *Das Neue Testament übersetzt und kommentiert.* Hamburg: Furche; Köln–Zürich: Benziger; Zürich: Zwingli, 1970, 928 p. Esp. 13-125. → R. Pesch 1980b

1975 Gottes geringste Brüder – zu Mt 25,31-46. — ELLIS, E.E. – GRÄSSER, E. (eds.), *Jesus und Paulus. Festschrift für Werner Georg Kümmel zum 70. Geburtstag*, Göttingen: Vandenhoeck & Ruprecht, 1975, 363-383. Esp. 365-367 [ἔθνη, ἀδελφός, ἐλάχιστος]; 367-372 [Mt red.]; 372-382 [source].

1982 Jesus' Preaching of the Kingdom of God. — MARCHESELLI, C.C. (ed.), *Parola e Spirito*. FS S. Cipriani, 1982, I, 599-609.

**WILCOX, Max**

1975 Peter and the Rock: A Fresh Look at Matthew xvi.17-19. — *NTS* 22 (1975-76) 73-88. [NTA 20, 442]

1984 Semitisms in the New Testament. — *ANRW* II.25.2 (1984) 978-1029. Esp. 1002-1003 [15,5]; 1004-1007 [27,46].

1988 Text Form. — CARSON, D.A. – WILLIAMSON, H.G.M. (eds.), *It is Written: Scripture Citing Scripture. Essays in Honour of Barnabas Linders, SSF*, Cambridge: University Press, 1988, 193-204. Esp. 199-201 [21,5]; 201-202 [24,30]; 202-203 [27,43].

**WILD, Edith**

1975 *Histoire de l'exégèse de la péricope de Gethsémani (Mt 26,36-46; Mc 14,32-42; Lc 22,39-46).* Diss. Strasbourg, 1975 (P. Prigent).

**WILD, Robert A.**

1985 The Encounter between Pharisaic and Christian Judaism: Some Early Gospel Evidence. — *NT* 27 (1985) 105-124. Esp. 112-114: "The synoptic gospels and Pharisaism"; 114-117: "Texts from the Q source" [23,23.25-26]. [NTA 29, 924]

**WILDER, Amos Niven**

1939R *Eschatology and Ethics in the Teaching of Jesus* [1939]. Rev. ed., New York: Harper & Brothers, 1950, 223 p.; Westport, CT: Greenwood, 1978. Esp. 73-85 [repentance: 3,2; 4,17; 11,12]; 86-115 [judgment: 10,33.38-39; 24,42-44; 25,31-46].

1951 The Sermon on the Mount. — BUTTRICK, G.A. (ed.), *The Interpreter's Bible*, VII, 1951, 155-164.

1959 Eschatological Imagery and Earthly Circumstance. — *NTS* 5 (1958-59) 229-245. Esp. 238. [NTA 4, 326]

1968 The Church and Israel in the Light of Election. — *Studia Evangelica* 4 (1968) 347-357. Esp. 350-354.

**WILES, James W.**

1992 *A Reconstruction and Evaluation of the Matthean Text of John Chrysostom.* Diss. Southwestern Baptist Theol. Sem., Fort Worth, TX, 1992, 285 p. (M. Roark). — *DissAbstr* 53 (1992-93) 4361.

1995 *A Scripture Index to the Works of St. Augustine in English Translations.* Lanham, MD – New York – London: Univ. Press of America, 1995, XX-223 p. Esp. 79-103: "Matthew".

**WILFONG, Terry G.**

1992 Greek and Coptic Texts from the Oriental Institute Museum Exhibition "Another Egypt". — *Bulletin of the American Society of Papyrologists* (New York) 29 (1992) 85-95. Esp. 89 [10,2-4].

**WILHELMS, Eino**

1980 *Die Tempelsteuerperikope Matthäus 17,24-27 in der Exegese der griechischen Väter der Alten Kirche* (Schriften der Finnischen Exegetischen Gesellschaft, 34). Helsinki: Finnish Exegetical Society, 1980, XV-204 p. Esp. 7-78.122-171: "Beschreibung der Auslegungen der Väter"; 79-86: "Zusammenhang und Situation der Perikope"; 87-103: "Detaillierte Auslegung der Perikope"; 104-107: "Praktische Lehren aus der Perikope im Verständnis der Väter"; 108-121: "Beobachtungen zur Verknüpfung der Perikope mit der Lehrentwicklung und dem Lehren der Alten Kirche". — Diss. Helsinki, 1980.

**WILKEN, Robert L.**

1972 The Interpretation of the Baptism of Jesus in the Later Fathers. — *Studia Patristica* 11 (1972) 268-277.

1975* (ed.), *Aspects of Wisdom in Judaism and Early Christianity* (University of Notre Dame Center for the Study of Judaism and Christianity, 1). Notre Dame, IN – London: University of Notre Dame Press, 1975, XXII-218 p. → J.M. Robinson, Schoedel, Wilken

1975 Wisdom and Philosophy in Early Christianity. — *Ibid.*, 143-168. Esp. 154-158 [Sentences of Sextus].

**WILKENS, Wilhelm**

1964 Die Redaktion des Gleichniskapitels Mark. 4 durch Matth. — *TZ* 20 (1964) 305-327. Esp. 307-314 [13,10-15]; 314 [13,18-23]; 314-319 [13,24-30]; 319-320 [13,31-33]; 320-324 [13,36-52]. [NTA 11, 211]

1966 Zur Frage der literarischen Beziehung zwischen Matthäus und Lukas. — *NT* 8 (1966) 48-57. Esp. 49-50 [3,7-10]; 50-51 [3,11-12]; 51 [7,3-5]; 51-52 [9,37-38]; 52-53 [6,25-33]; 53-54 [8,11-12; 20,16]; 54 [8,5-13]; 55 [24,43-51]. [NTA 11, 185]

1982 Die Versuchung Jesu nach Matthäus. — *NTS* 28 (1982) 479-489. [NTA 27, 509]

1985 Die Komposition des Matthäus-Evangeliums. — *NTS* 31 (1985) 24-38. Esp. 25-27 [4,23-25; 9,35-38]; 27-30 [11,25-16,12]; 30-33 [16,12-21,46]; 33-34 [22,28]; 35 [1,1-4,22]. [NTA 29, 925]

1994 Die Täuferüberlieferung des Matthäus und ihre Verarbeitung durch Lukas. — *NTS* 40 (1994) 542-557. Esp. 542-547.549-553 [11,2-19]; 547-548 [5,32]; 554-556 [3,7-12]; 556-557 [11,20-24]. [NTA 39, 857]

**WILKES, Carl Gene**

1985 *The Synoptic Tradition in 1 Peter: An Investigation into Its Forms and Development.* Diss. Southwestern Baptist Theol. Sem., Fort Worth, TX, 1985. — *DissAbstr* 46 (1985-86) 2345.

**WILKIN, Robert Nicholas**

1985 *Repentance as Condition for Salvation in the New Testament.* Diss. Theol. Sem., Dallas, TX, 1985, 270 p. (Z. Hodges). — *DissAbstr* 46 (1985-86) 2727.

**WILKINS, Michael J.**

1988　*The Concept of Disciple in Matthew's Gospel: As Reflected in the Use of the Term* Μαθητής *(SupplNT, 59).* Leiden: Brill, 1988, XI-261 p. Esp. 126-172: "Matthew's use of the term μαθητής"; 173-215: "Matthew's theological understanding of Simon Peter". [NTA 33, p. 255] — Diss. Fuller Theol. Sem., Pasadena, CA, 1986 (R.P. Martin).

*Discipleship in the Ancient World and Matthew's Gospel.* Grand Rapids, MI: Baker, ²1995, XIII-292 p.
　　B.R. DOYLE, *RB* 98 (1991) 624-626; L.E. FRIZZELL, *BTB* 19 ˙1989) 158; R.H. GUNDRY, *JBL* 109 (1990) 534-535; M.A. POWELL, *CBQ* 52 (1990) 769-771; J.-M. ROUSÉE, *RB* 96 (1989) 317; G. STANTON, *JTS* 41 (1990) 179-180.

1991　"Named and Unnamed Disciples in Matthew: A Literary-Theological Study". — *SBL 1991 Seminar Papers*, 418-439. Esp. 420-424: "Features of the Matthean disciples"; 424-432: "The circle of disciples"; 432-436: "Insights from Joseph [of Arimathea] (Matt 27:25ff.)"; 436-438: "Named and unnamed disciples"; 438-439: "Tension in the Matthean disciples".

1992a　*Following the Master. Discipleship in the Steps of Jesus.* Grand Rapids, MI: Zondervan, 1992, XIV-400 p. Esp. 174-193: "Matthew: example with a commission".

1992b　Disciples. — *DJG*, 1992, 176-182.

1992c　Discipleship. — *Ibid.*, 182-189. Esp. 182-183.

**WILKINSON, John**

1964　Apologetic Aspects of the Virgin Birth of Jesus Christ — *ScotJT* 17 (1964) 159-181. Esp. 168, 174-175. [NTA 9, 144]

1967　The Case of the Epileptic Boy. [17,14-21] — *ExpT* 79 (1967-68) 39-42. [NTA 12, 558]

1974　The Mission Charge to the Twelve and Modern Medical Missions. — *ScotJT* 27 (1974) 313-328. Esp. 314-317 [10,5-15]. [NTA 19, 533]

1980　*Health and Healing. Studies in New Testament Principles and Practice.* London–Edinburgh: Handsel, 1980, IX-195 p. Esp. 28-29 [4,24]; 61-69 [17,14-21]; 161-163 [10,5-14].

**WILKINSON, T.L.**

1968　The Role of Elijah in the New Testament. — *Vox Reformata* (Geelong, Victoria) 10 (1968) 1-10. [NTA 13, 76]

**WILLAERT, Benjamin**

1954　*De drie grote synoptische lijdensvoorzeggingen.* Diss. Leuven, 1954, 252 p. (L. Cerfaux). Esp. 48-49; 65-144 [passion predictions and proto-Mt]. → 1956a

1956a　La connexion littéraire entre la première prédiction de la passion et la confession de Pierre chez les Synoptiques. — *ETL* 32 (1956) 24-45. Esp. 28-40: "Comparaison détaillée de Matthieu et de Marc"; 40-44 [16,17-19]. [NTA 1, 35] → 1954

1956b　"Tu es Petrus", Mt. XVI,17-19. — *CollBrugGand* 2 (1956) 452-465. [NTA 1, 393]

1960　Jezus, de lijdende dienaar Gods. — *CollBrugGand* 6 (1960) 163-185. [NTA 5, 528]
　　Jesus as the "Suffering Servant". — *TDig* 10 (1962) 25-30; = RYAN, M.R. (ed.), *Contemporary New Testament Studies*, 1965, 270-276.

1969　Jezus, de Zoon Gods. — *CollBrugGand* 15 (1969) 3-16. [NTA 14, 460]

**WILLAM, Franz Michel**

1961　*Die Welt: vom Vaterunser aus gesehen.* Freiburg: Herder, 1961, 144 p.
　　*Le Pater, prière moderne*, trans. R. Virrion. Tournai: Casterman; Mulhouse: Salvator, 1963, 136 p.

**WILLARD, Conrad R.**

1956　*The Sermon on the Mount in the Writing of the Ante-Nicene Fathers from New Testament Times to Origen.* Diss. Midwestern Baptist Theol. Sem., Kansas City, KS, 1956.

**WILLE, W.**

1968 *Studien zum Matthäuskommentar des Hilarius von Poitiers*. Diss. Hamburg, 1968.

**WILLERT, Niels**

1989 *Pilatusbilledet i den antike jødedom og kristendom* [The figure of Pilate in early Judaism and Christianity] (Bibel og historie, 11). Aarhus: Universitetsforlag, 1989, 409 p. Esp. 245-258: "Mattaeus".

1991 Kristologien i Mattæus' passionsfortælling. Litterære og sociologiske aspekter. [Christology in the Matthean passion story. Literary and sociological aspects] — *DanskTeolTids* 54 (1991) 241-260. Esp. 243-246 [Son of David]; 246-249 [Son of God]; 249-253 [26-28]. [NTA 37, 1274]

**WILLETT, F.**

1964 *St. Matthew and his Gospel*. Valatie, NY: Holy Cross Press, 1964, XII-169 p.

**WILLIAMS, Allen**

1992 *The Relation of Narrative Time to the Plot of Matthew's Gospel*. Diss. New Orleans Baptist Theol. Sem., 1992, 195 p. (G. Stevens). — *DissAbstr* 53 (1992-93) 2415. → Matera 1987b

**WILLIAMS, C.S.C.**

1951 *Alterations to the Text of the Synoptic Gospels and Acts*. Oxford: Blackwell, 1951, XIV-93 p. Esp. 22-23 [3,15; 17,26]; 25-28 [1,16]; 31-33 [27,16-17]; 33-36 [28,19]; 84-85 [Eznik].

1953 → M'Neile 1927

1962 The Synoptic Problem. — BLACK, M. – ROWLEY, H.H. (eds.), *Peake's Commentary on the Bible*, London: Nelson, 1962, 748-755.

**WILLIAMS, D.J.**

1992 Judas. — *DJG*, 1992, 406-408. Esp. 406.

**WILLIAMS, Jacqueline A.**

1984 The Gospel of Truth: Witness to Second Century Exegetical Traditions. — *SBL 1984 Seminar Papers*, 1-10. Esp. 2-7 [18,12-13/Gospel of Truth 31-32].

1988 *Biblical Interpretation in the Gnostic Gospel of Truth from Nag Hammadi* (SBL DS, 79). Atlanta, GA: Scholars, 1988, VII-220 p. Esp. 100-102.205-207 [5,8]; 119-123 [18,12-13]; 123-126 [12,11]; 128-130 [11,28]; 132-134 [6,19]; 136-138 [7,16.20]; 148-150 [7,7]; 154-156 [10,29].

**WILLIAMS, James G.**

1965 A Note on the 'Unforgivable Sin' Logion. [12,31-32] — *NTS* 12 (1965-66) 75-77. [NTA 10, 531]

1981 *Those Who Ponder Proverbs. Aphoristic Thinking and Biblical Literature* (Bible and Literature Series, 2). Sheffield: Almond Press; Winona Lake, IN: Eisenbrauns, 1981, 128 p.

1986 The Sermon on the Mount as a Christian Basis of Altruism. — *Humboldt Journal of Social Relations* (Arcata, CA) 13 (1986) 89-112. [NTA 32, 117]

1988 Parable and Chreia: From Q to Narrative Gospel. — *Semeia* 43 (1988) 85-114. Esp. 87-103: "Parable and Chreia in Q"; 103-109: "The literary form of Q" (→ Kloppenborg 1987a); 109-111: "Theological implications". [NTA 33, 588] → Buss 1988, A.Y. Collins 1988

1989 Neither Here Nor There. Between Wisdom and Apocalyptic in Jesus' Kingdom Sayings. — *Forum* 5/2 (1989) 7-30. Esp. 9-17 [11,12]; 17-24: "The Q kingdom sayings". [NTA 34, 102] → Seeley 1991

1990 Paraenesis, Excess, and Ethics: Matthew's Rhetoric in the Sermon on the Mount. — *Semeia* 50 (1990) 163-187. Esp. 165-167 [genre]; 167-173 [setting; paraenesis]; 173-182 [5]. [NTA 35, 623] → Robbins 1990

1992 *The Bible, Violence, and the Sacred. Liberation from the Myth of Sanctioned Violence.* Valley Forge, PA: Trinity Press International, 1992, XVI-288 p. Esp. 194-199.

1995 Das Matthäusevangelium. Girards Hermeneutik in der praktischen Anwendung. — NIEWIADOMSKI, J. – PALAVER, W. (eds.), *Vom Fluch und Segen der Sündenböcke. Raymund Schwager zum 60. Geburtstag* (Beiträge zur mimetischen Theorie, 1), Wien: Kulturverlag, 1995, 119-140. Esp. 125-134 [anti-Judaism].

**WILLIAMS, Rowan**

1982 *Resurrection. Interpreting the Easter Gospel.* London: Darton, Longman & Todd, 1982, 129 p.
*Interpreting the Easter Gospel.* New York: Pilgrim, 1985, XIII-129 p.

**WILLIAMS, Samuel F., Jr.**

1992 Matthew 5:43-48. — *RExp* 89 (1992) 389-395.

**WILLIAMS, W.H.**

1973 The Transfiguration – A New Approach? — *Studia Evangelica* 6 (1973) 635-650. Esp. 643-645 [11,25-27; 16,16].

**WILLIAMSON, Lamar**

1984a Jesus of the Gospels and the Christian Vision of Shalom. — *HorizonsBT* 6/2 (1984) 49-66. Esp. 50-58 [10,34; 26,52]; 61-62 [peace]. [NTA 30, 1001]

1984b Matthew 4:1-11. — *Interpr* 38 (1984) 51-55.

**WILLIS, Geoffrey G.**

1964 The Lord's Prayer in Irish Gospel Manuscripts. — *Studia Evangelica* 3 (1964) 282-288. Esp. 282-285 [Mt]; 285-287 [Lk].

1966 Patristic Biblical Citations. The Importance of a Good Critical Text, Illustrated from St. Augustine. [23,29-36] — *Studia Patristica* 7 (1966) 576-579. [NTA 11, 596]

1975 Lead us not into temptation. — *DownR* 93 (1975) 281-288. [NTA 20, 436]

**WILLIS, John T.**

1973 "Man does not live by bread alone" (Dt 8:3; Mt 4:4). — *RestQ* 16 (1973) 141-149.

1978 The Meaning of Isaiah 7:14 and Its Application in Matthew 1:23. — *RestQ* 21 (1978) 1-18. Esp. 14-17. [NTA 22, 759]

**WILLIS, Steve**

1993 Matthew's Birth Stories. Prophecy and the Magi. [2,23] — *ExpT* 105 (1993-94) 43-45. [NTA 38, 748]

**WILLIS, Wendell**

1987* (ed.), *The Kingdom of God in 20th-Century Interpretation.* Peabody, MA: Hendrickson, 1987, XII-208 p. → Elmore, Epp, R. Farmer, Hiers, Michaels

**WILSON, A.N.**

1992 *Jesus.* New York – London: Norton, 1992, XVIII-269 p. Esp. 78-81 [infancy narratives]; 136-140 [ethics]; 210-214.223-228 [passion narrative].

**WILSON, Craig Robert**

1990 *The Synoptic Problem: A Case Study in the Control of Knowledge.* Diss. Columbia Teachers' College, New York, 1990, 466 p. (D. Sloar). — *DissAbstr* 51 (1990-91) 2419.

**WILSON, George Todd**

1971   *Entering the Kingdom on the Theology of Matthew.* Diss. Southern Baptist Theol. Sem., 1971, 315 p. — *DissAbstr* 32 (1971) 2795.

1978   Conditions for Entering the Kingdom according to St. Matthew. — *PerspRelSt* 5 (1978) 40-51. [NTA 23, 86]

**WILSON, Robert McLachlan**

1957a   Did Jesus Speak Greek? — *ExpT* 68 (1956-57) 121-122. [NTA 1, 388] → Argyle 1955, H.M. Draper 1956

1957b   The New Testament in the Gnostic Gospel of Mary. — *NTS* 3 (1956-57) 236-243. Esp. 242-243. [NTA 2, 144]

1959a   The Coptic 'Gospel of Thomas'. — *NTS* 5 (1958-59) 273-276. Esp. 276 [Q]. [NTA 4, 533]

1959b   Farrer and Streeter on the Minor Agreements of Matthew and Luke against Mark. — *Studia Evangelica* 1 (1959) 254-257. → Farrer 1954

1960a   *Studies in the Gospel of Thomas.* London: Mowbray, 1960, VII-160 p. Esp. 45-88: "Thomas and our four gospels"; 89-116: "Parables and other sayings"; 117-132: "The Jewish-Christian element"; 133-141: "Thomas and the text of the gospels".

1960b   "Thomas" and the Growth of the Gospels. — *HTR* 53 (1960) 231-250. [NTA 5, 544]

1960c   Thomas and the Synoptic Gospels. — *ExpT* 72 (1960-61) 36-39. [NTA 5, 848] → McArthur 1960b

1963   The New Testament in the Nag Hammadi Gospel of Philip. — *NTS* 9 (1962-63) 291-294. Esp. 293-294 [3,15; 9,15]. [NTA 8, 342]

1968   *Gnosis and the New Testament.* Oxford: Blackwell, 1968, VIII-149 p. Esp. 72-81.

**WILSON, Stephen G.**

1973   *The Gentiles and the Gentile Mission in Luke–Acts* (SNTS MS, 23). Cambridge: University Press, 1973, XI-295 p. Esp. 1-28: "Jesus and the gentiles" [10,5-6; 15,24], 31-34 [Q 7,1-10; 11,33; 13,28; 14,16-24]; 63-66 [Q 16,16]. — Diss. Durham, 1969 (C.K. Barrett).

1983   *Luke and the Law* (SNTS MS, 50). Cambridge: University Press, 1983, VII-142 p. Esp. 43-51 [Q 16,16-18 (Lk)].

1995   *Related Strangers. Jews and Christians 70-170 C.E.* Minneapolis, MN: Fortress, 1995, XVI-416 p. Esp. 46-56: "Matthew: the shadow of Yavneh".

**WILSON, William Riley**

1970   *The Execution of Jesus. A Judicial, Literary and Historical Investigation.* New York: Scribner, 1970, X-243 p. Esp. 41-51: "The trial in Mark and Matthew". — Diss. Duke Univ., Durham, NC, 1960 (K.W. Clark).

**WIMMER, Joseph F.**

1982   *Fasting in the New Testament. A Study in Biblical Theology* (Theological Inquiries). New York – Ramsey, NJ – Toronto, Ont.: Paulist, 1982, VI-141 p. — Diss. Pont. Univ. Greg., Roma, 1979 (E. Malatesta).

**WINANDY, Jacques**

1964   La Cantique des Cantiques et le Nouveau Testament. — *RB* 71 (1964) 161-190. Esp. 164-173 [13,52/Ct 7,14; 21,33-34/Ct 8,11]. [NTA 9, 478]

1966   La scène du Jugement Dernier (*Mt.*, 25,31-46). — *ScEccl* 18 (1966) 169-186. Esp. 171-178: "La personne du juge"; 178-180: "Les nations jugées"; 180-186: "Les petits, frères de Jésus". [NTA 11, 220]

1968   Le logion de l'ignorance (*Mc.* XIII,32; *Mt.* XXIV,36). — *RB* 75 (1968) 63-79. [NTA 13, 205]

1971 *Autour de la naissance de Jésus. Accomplissement et prophétie* (Lire la Bible, 26). Paris: Cerf, 1971, 119 p. Esp. 15-32 [genealogy]. [NTA 15, p. 360]
R.E. BROWN, *CBQ* 33 (1971) 469-471; L.F. RIVERA, *RevistBíb* 36 (1974) 78-79.

**WINBERY, Carlton L.**

1992 Tradition and Grace in the Sermon on the Mount. — *Theological Educator* (New Orleans) 46 (1992) 105-114. [NTA 37, 726]

**WINDISCH, Hans**

1937[R] *The Meaning of the Sermon on the Mount* [German, ₋937], trans. S.M. Gilmour. Philadelphia, PA: Westminster, 1950; New York: Macmillan, 1951, 224 p.
P.E. DAVIES, *JRel* 31 (1951) 296-297; F.V. FILSON, *Interpr* 5 (1951) 353-355; F.C. GRANT, *Crozer Quarterly* (Chester, PA) 28 (1951) 163; K.W. KIM, *JBR* 20 (1952) 50-51; E.W. SAUNDERS, *JBL* 70 (1951) 246-249; W. SCHWEITZER, *The Ecumenical Review* (Genève) 4 (1951-52) 108; C. SPICQ, *RSPT* 37 (1953) 153.

**WINGER, J. Michael**

1994 When Did the Women Visit the Tomb? Sources for Some Temporal Clauses in the Synoptic Gospels. [28,1] — *NTS* 40 (1994) 284-288. [NTA 38, 1376]

**WINGREN, Gustaf**

1978 Tre motforestillinger. [Three revolutionary views] [9,1-8; 10,23] — *NorskTeolTids* 79 (1978) 203-214. → Hognestad 1978b

1979 Behovet av en klar definition. Metodiska synpunkter på H[ognestad]'s doktors-avhandling. [The need for a distinct definition. Methodological views on Hognestad's doctoral dissertation] — *NorskTeolTids* 80 (1979) 114-123. → Hognestad 1978b

**WINK, Walter**

1968 *John the Baptist in the Gospel Tradition* (SNTS MS, 7). Cambridge: University Press, 1968, XII-132 p. Esp. 18-26: "John the Baptist in Q"; 27-41: "John the Baptist in the gospel of Matthew" [11,12-13.14-15; 14,3-12; 17,10-13]. → Payot 1970

1983 Matthew 4:1-11. — *Interpr* 37 (1983) 392-397.

1986 The Third Way. Reclaiming Jesus' Nonviolent Alternative. [5,39-41] — *Sojourners* (Washington, DC) 15 (1986) 28-33. [NTA 31, 584]

1988 Neither Passivity nor Violence: Jesus' Third Way. — *SBL 1988 Seminar Papers*, 210-224. Esp. 211 [5,38-42]; 211-212 [Q 6,29-30]; 212-220: "Interpreting the core sayings"; 220-224: "The introductory setting (Matt 5:38-39ab)". → 1992, 1993
Neither Passivity nor Violence. Jesus' Third Way (Matt 5:38-42//Luke 6:29-30). — *Forum* 7 (1991) 5-28. Esp. 6; 7; 7-18; 18-24 (slightly revised). [NTA 38, 157]; = SWARTLEY, W.M. (ed.), *The Love of Enemy*, 1992, 102-125. Esp. 103; 104; 104-112; 113-117 (slightly revised); 133-136: "Counterresponse to Richard Horsley". → R.A. Horsley 1992c

1989 Jesus' Reply to John. Matt 11:2-6 // Luke 7:18-23. — *Forum* 5/1 (1989) 121-128. [NTA 34, 123]

1991 Jesus and the Domination System. — *SBL 1991 Seminar Papers*, 265-286. Esp. 269-271 [domination]; 271-273 [equality]; 273-275 [family]; 275-277 [law]; 277-278 [purity]; 278-279 [non violence]; 279-284 [women and children].

1992 Beyond Just War and Pacifism: Jesus' Nonviolent Way. [5,38-42] — *RExp* 89 (1992) 197-214. [NTA 37, 727] → 1988, 1993

1993 Jesus and the Nonviolent Struggle of Our Time. [5,39-42] — *LouvSt* 18 (1993) 3-20. [NTA 37, 1258] → 1988, 1992; → Lambrecht 1994b

**WINKELMANN, Michael**

1977 *Biblische Wunder. Kritik, Chance, Deutung* (Pfeiffer-Werkbücher, 140). München: Pfeiffer, 1977, 178 p. Esp. 125-132 [26,51-54]; 133-138 [9,1-8]; 139-146 [8,28-34].

**WINKLE, Ross E.**

1986    The Jeremiah Model for Jesus in the Temple. [21,11; 23,29-24,2] — *AndrUnS* 24 (1986) 155-172. [NTA 31, 580]

**WINKLER, Gabriele**

1983    Ein bedeutsamer Zusammenhang zwischen der Erkenntnis und Ruhe in Mt 11,27-29 und dem Ruhen des Geistes auf Jesus am Jordan. Eine Analyse zur Geist-Christologie in syrischen und armenischen Quellen. — *Muséon* 96 (1983) 267-326. Esp. 273-292.304-325 [11,27-29]; 294-296 [13,32]. [NTA 28, 918]

1994    Die Licht-Erscheinung bei der Taufe Jesu und der Ursprung des Epiphaniefestes. — *Oriens Christianus* (Wiesbaden) 78 (1994) 177-223. Esp. 190-197 [3,17]; 203-206 [3,16]; 212-214 [11,27].

**WINKLHOFER, Alois**

1953    Corpora sanctorum (Mt. 27,51ff). [H. Zeller, *ZKT* 71 (1949)] — *TQ* 133 (1953) 30-67, 210-217. Esp. 39-67: "Der Text"; 210-217: "Die Deutung des Textes in den ersten fünf Jahrhunderten".

**WINN, Albert Curry**

1975    Worship as a Healing Experience. An Exposition of Matthew 17:1-9. — *Interpr* 29 (1975) 68-72.

**WINTER, Bruce W.**

1991    The Messiah as the Tutor: The Meaning of καθηγητής in Matthew 23:10. — *TyndB* 42 (1991) 152-157. [NTA 36, 156]

**WINTER, Ernst Karl**

1953    Das Evangelium der jerusalemitischen Mutterkirche. Aufgaben der Matthäus-Forschung. — *Judaica* 9 (1953) 1-33.

1954    Der historische Christus "secundum Proto-Matthaeum". — *Judaica* 10 (1954) 193-230.

**WINTER, Paul**

1954a   Jewish Folklore in the Matthaean Birth Story. — *HibbJourn* 53 (1954-55) 34-42.

1954b   The Treatment of His Sources by the Third Evangelist in Luke XXI–XXIV. — *StudTheol* 8 (1954) 138-172. Esp. 144-145 [24,26-29.40-41.43-51]; 164-165 [26,63-65].

1956    Matthew xi 27 and Luke x 22 from the First to the Fifth Century. Reflections on the Development of the Text. — *NT* 1 (1956) 112-148, 199. Esp. 112-125: "The evidence considered"; 127-146: "The six main problems". [NTA 1, 36]

1958    Genesis 1,27 and Jesus' Saying on Divorce. — *ZAW* 70 (1958) 260-261.

1961    *On the Trial of Jesus* (Studia Judaica. Forschungen zur Wissenschaft des Judentums, 1). Berlin – New York: de Gruyter, 1961, x-216 p.; ²1974, XXIII-225 p. (rev. and ed. by T.A. Burkill and G. Vermes).
        *El proceso a Jesús*. Barcelona: Muchnik, 1983, 295 p.

**WINTERBAUER, Wolfgang**

1985    Ist Jesus auf dem See gewandelt? Überlegungen zu Mt 14,23-33 aus tiefenpsychologischer Sicht. — *Schönberger Hefte* (Frankfurt/M) 15/3 (1985) 2-11.

**WINTON, Alan P.**

1990    *The Proverbs of Jesus. Issues of History and Rhetoric* (JSNT SS, 35). Sheffield: JSOT, 1990, 236 p. Esp. 13-29: "Aspects of Wisdom in the synoptic gospels"; 31-57: "Classifying and analyzing proverbial sayings"; 59-98: "Issues in the modern interpretation of synoptic proverbial wisdom" [Bultmann, Beardslee, Crossan, Perrin]; 99-125: "Problems of historical reconstruction: wisdom, eschatology and the kingdom of God"; 127-140: "The functions/rhetoric of the proverbial saying in the synoptic literature"; 141-167: "Wisdom of the kingdom: the significance of proverbial wisdom". — Diss. Sheffield, 1987 (B. Chilton – D. Hill).

**WIRE, Antoinette Clark**

1971 L'accueil des petits. Une étude de la théologie de Matthieu. — *Reconnaissance à Suzanne de Diétrich*, 1971, 94-108. Esp. 94-95; 95-100; 100-108 [10; 18; 25].

1991 Gender Roles in a Scribal Community. — BALCH, D.L. (ed.), *Social History of the Matthean Community*, 1991, 87-121. Esp. 98-108: "Matthew as a scribal community"; 113-120: "Matthew's gospel as cultural communication". → Perkins 1991

1995 The God of Jesus in the Gospel Sayings Source. — SEGOVIA, F.F. – TOLBERT, M.A. (eds.), *Reading from This Place*. I: *Social Location and Biblical Interpretation in the United States*, Minneapolis, MN: Fortress, 1995, 277-303.

**WISCHMEYER, Oda**

1986 Das Gebot der nächstenliebe bei Paulus. Eine traditionsgeschichtliche Untersuchung. — *BZ* 30 (1986) 161-187. Esp. 170-180: "Dekalog und Nächstenliebe bei den Synoptikern" [5,21.27.43; 15,4; 19,19]. [NTA 31, 727]

1994 Matthäus 6,25-34 par. Die Spruchreihe vom Sorgen. — *ZNW* 85 (1994) 1-22. Esp. 4-10 [Q 12,22-31]; 10-14: "Motivgeschichte"; 14-16: "Sozialgeschichte" [NTA 39, 147]

**WISE, Michael O.**

1992a & TABOR, J.D., The Messiah at Qumran. — *BibArchRev* 18/6 (1992) 60-63, 65. [NTA 37, 1021]

1992b → Tabor 1992

**WISSE, Frederik**

1989 The Nature and Purpose of Redactional Changes in Early Christian Texts: The Canonical Gospels. — PETERSEN, W.L. (ed.), *Gospel Traditions*, 1989, 39-53. Esp. 42-43; 48-49: "Minor interpolations"; 51 [27,9].

**WISSELINK, Willem Franciscus**

1989 *Assimilation as a Criterion for the Establishment of the Text. A Comparative Study on the Basis of Passages from Matthew, Mark and Luke*. Kampen: Kok, 1989, 249 p. Esp. 66-68.108-161 [9,1-8]. — Diss. Kampen, 1989 (J. van Bruggen).

**WITHERINGTON, Ben**

1984 *Women in the Ministry of Jesus. A Study of Jesus' Attitudes to Women and Their Roles as Reflected in His Earthly Life* (SNTS MS, 51). Cambridge: University Press, 1984, XI-221 p. Esp. 18-25 [5,27-32]; 28-32 [19,10-12]; 32-35 [22,23-33]; 40-41 [13,33]; 41-44 [25,1-13]; 44-45 [12,42]; 45-46 [24,40-41]; 46-47 [23,37-39]; 63-66 [15,21-28]; 66-68 [8,14-15]; 88-92 [12,46-50]; 110-114 [26,6-13]; 117-123 [27,55-56]. — Diss. Durham, 1981 (C.K. Barrett).

1985 Matthew 5.32 and 19.9 – Exception or Exceptional Situation? — *NTS* 31 (1985) 571-576. [NTA 30, 570]

1988a *Women in the Earliest Churches* (SNTS MS, 58). Cambridge: Univ. Press, 1988, XIII-300 p. Esp. 166-174: "Matthew".

1988 Jesus and the Baptist – Two of a Kind? — *SBL 1988 Seminar Papers*, 225-244. Esp. 229-232 [3,7-12]; 233-235 [11,2-6]; 235-236 [11,7-11]; 237-238 [11,12-13]; 239-242 [11,16-19].

1990a *The Christology of Jesus*. Minneapolis, MN: Fortress, 1990, X-310 p. Esp. 33-143: "Christology and the relationships of Jesus" [3; 8,20.21-22; 10,6.34; 11,2-19; 15,24; 19,28]; 145-177: "Christology and the deeds of Jesus"; 179-262: "Christology and the words of Jesus" [6,10; 8,20; 11,25-27; 12,28; 24,36].

1990b *Women and the Genesis of Christianity*. Cambridge, MA: University Press, 1990, XV-273 p. Esp. 36-40 [5,27-30]; 40-45 [5,31-32; 19,3-9]; 45-48 [19,10-12]; 56-61 [12,42; 13,33; 23,37-39; 24,40-42; 25,1-13]; 74-76 [15,21-28]; 76-78 [8,14-15]; 80-84 [9,18-26]; 90-95 [Mary]; 107-110 [26,6-13]; 112-117 [27,55-56]; 229-232 [Mt].

1992a  *Jesus, Paul and the End of the World. A Comparative Study in New Testament Eschatology.* Downers Grove, IL: InterVarsity, 1992, 306 p.

1992b  Birth of Jesus. — *DJG*, 1992, 60-74.

1992c  John the Baptist. — *Ibid.*, 383-391. Esp. 389-390.

1992d  Lord. — *Ibid.*, 484-492. Esp. 490.

1994  *Jesus the Sage. The Pilgrimage of Wisdom.* Edinburgh: Clark, 1994, XI-436 p. Esp. 123-141: "A cynic Jesus?"; 175-179 [10,24-25]; 179-181 [10,40]; 181-183 [5,4]; 190-192 [13,33]; 197-200 [20,1-15]; 205-207 [11,28-30]; 211-247: "Wisdom's legacy: from Q to James"; 336-341 [Jn/Mt]; 341-368: "Matthew: a word to the wise".

1995  *The Jesus Quest. The Third Search for the Jew of Nazareth.* Downers Grove, IL: InterVarsity, 1995, 304 p. Esp. 46-53.112-113 [Q].

**WITHERSPOON, Loy H.**

1962  *The Gospel Text of Cyril of Alexandria.* Diss. Boston Univ., 1962, 2 vols., VIII-408 and 409-805 p. Esp. 58-177: "The gospel text of Cyril"; 515-579: "Collation of Cyril's text with the *textus receptus*"; 756-765 [Western text].

**WITHERUP, Ronald David**

1985  *The Cross of Jesus. A Literary-critical Study of Matthew 27.* Diss. Union Theol. Sem., Richmond, VA, 1985, 409 p. — *DissAbstr* 47 (1986-87) 1363; *SBT* 15 (1987) 117.

1987  The Death of Jesus and the Raising of the Saints: Matthew 27:51-54 in Context. — *SBL 1987 Seminar Papers*, 574-585. Esp. 575-578: "The structure of Matthew 27"; 578-583: "An exposition of Matt 27:51-54"; 584-585: "Matthew 27:51-54 and Matthew's understanding of salvation history".

1994  *Conversion in the New Testament* (Zacchaeus Studies: New Testament). Collegeville, MN: Liturgical Press, 1994, IX-126 p.

**WITT, Rex E.**

1972  The Flight to Egypt. — *Studia Patristica* 11 (1972) 92-98.

**WITTMANN, Dieter**

1984  *Die Auslegung der Friedensweisungen der Bergpredigt in der Predigt der Evangelischen Kirche im 20. Jahrhundert* (EHS, XXIII/224). Frankfurt/M–Bern: Lang, 1984, 101 p. Esp. 17-20: "Exegetische Orientierung zu Mt 5,9 und 5,38-48"; 21-79: "Die Auslegung der Friedensweisungen der Bergrede in Predigten".

**WŁODARCZYK, Stanisław**

1990  Przyjscie Jezusa na świat znakiem nadejścia pełni czasów. [The birth of Jesus as a sign of the on-coming of the fullness of time]. — CHMIEL, J. - MATRAS, T. (eds.), *Studium scripturae anima theologiae. Prace ofiarowane Ksiedzu Profesorowi Stanisławowi Grzybkowi*, Kraków: Polskie Towarzystwo teologiezne, 1990, 340-347.

**WOGAMAN, J. Philip**

1993  Homiletical Resources from the Gospel of Matthew: Faith and Discipleship. — *QuartRev* 13 (1993) 93-111. [NTA 38, 149]

**WOJCIECHOWSKI, Michal**

1988  Mt 2,20: Herod and Antipater? A Supplementary Clue to Dating the Birth of Jesus. — *BibNot* 44 (1988) 61-62. [NTA 33, 597]

**WOJCIK, Jan**

1974  The Two Kingdoms in Matthew's Gospel. — GROS LOUIS, K.R.R. - ACKERMAN, J.S. - WARSHOW, T.S. (eds.), *Literary Interpretations of Biblical Narratives*, I, Nashville, TN - New York: Abingdon, 1974, 283-295.

**WOLBERT, Werner**

1982 Bergpredigt und Gewaltlosigkeit. — *TheolPhil* 57 (1982) 498-525. Esp. 523-525: "Die 5. Antithese und die Polemik". [NTA 27, 515]; = *TJb*, 1984, 210-232. Esp. 230-232.

1984 Die Liebe zum Nächsten, zum Feind und zum Sünder. — *TGl* 74 (1984) 262-282. Esp. 266-271 [5,43-47]. [NTA 29, 520]

1986 Die Goldene Regel und das ius talionis. — *TTZ* 95 (1986) 169-181. [NTA 31, 840]

1988 "Wer seinem Bruder ohne Grund zürnt". Zu einer Lesart der 1. Antithese. — *TGl* 78 (1988) 160-170. Esp. 166-170 [5,22]. [NTA 33, 117]

**WOLF, Carl Umhau**

1958 The Gospel to the Essenes. — *BR* 3 (1958) 28-43. Esp. 31-33 [OT]; 32-34 [eschatology]; 34-36 [vocabulary]; 36-38 [Messiah]; 38-43 [differences]. [NTA 3, 575]

1966 The Continuing Temptation of Christ in the Church. Searching and Preaching on Matthew 4:1-11. — *Interpr* 20 (1966) 288-301.

**WOLF, Erik**

1964 Gottesrecht und Nächstenrecht. Rechtstheologische Exegese des Gleichnisses von den Arbeitern im Weinberg (Mt 20,1-6). — METZ, J.B., et al. (eds.), *Gott in Welt.* FS K. Rahner, 1964, II, 640-662.
Het recht van God en het recht van de naaste. Rechtstheologische exegese van de parabel van de arbeiders in de wijngaard (Mt. 20,1-16). — *God en Wereld*, 1965, I, 51-75.

**WOLF, Herbert M.**

1972 A Solution to the Immanuel Prophecy in Isaiah 7:14–8:22. — *JBL* 91 (1972) 449-456. Esp. 455-456 [1,23].

**WOLFF, Christian**

1976 *Jeremia im Frühjudentum und Urchristentum* (TU, 118). Berlin: Akademie, 1976, XXIII-264 p. Esp. 26-29 [16,14]; 131-134 [26,28]; 157-166 [2,17; 27,9-10]. — Diss. Greifswald, 1971 (T. Holtz).

1988 Niedrigkeit und Verzicht in Wort und Weg Jesu und in der apostolischen Existenz des Paulus. — *NTS* 34 (1988) 183-196. Esp. 186-188 [19,12]; 188-189 [23,11]. [NTA 32, 1082]

**WOLFF, H.U.** → G. Bornkamm 1971a/80

**WOLNIEWICZ, Marian**

1957 Bezżenstwo dla Królestwa Bożego (De caelibatu pro regno Dei observando [Matth. 19:10-12]). — *RuBi* 10 (1957) 23-34. [NTA 2, 289]

1978 Św. Józef w Evangelii (Der Heilige Joseph in die Evangelien). — *Ateneum Kaplanskie* (Wroclaw) 90 (1978) 18-31. Esp. 22-29.

**WOLTER, Michael**

1988 Die anonymen Schriften des Neuen Testaments. Annäherungsversuch an ein literarisches Phänomen. — *ZNW* 79 (1988) 1-16. Esp. 12-13. [NTA 33, 15]

1995 "Was heisset nu Gottes reich?". — *ZNW* 86 (1995) 5-19. Esp. 12-15.17-18. [NTA 40, 453]

**WOLTHUIS, Thomas Ray**

1987 *Experiencing the Kingdom: Reading the Gospel of Matthew.* Diss. Duke Univ., Durham, NC, 1987, 374 p. (D.O. Via). — *DissAbstr* 49 (1988-89) 1483; *SBT* 17 (1989) 97-98.

**WONG, Erik Kun-Chun**

1991 The Matthean Understanding of the Sabbath: A Response to G.N. Stanton. — *JSNT* 44 (1991) 3-18. Esp. 4-8 [12,1-14]; 8-11 [10,17-23]; 11-14 [24,15-22] [NTA 36, 1281] → Stanton 1989b

1992 *Interkulturelle Theologie und multikulturelle Gemeinde im Matthäusevangelium. Zum Verhältnis von Juden- und Heidenchristen im ersten Evangelium* (NTOA, 22).

Freiburg/Schw: Universitätsverlag; Göttingen: Vandenhoeck & Ruprecht, 1992, VIII-223 p. Esp. 36-86: "Thora" [5,17-20; 7,12; 12,1-8; 15,1-20; 22,37-40; 23,23]; 87-124: "Mission" [7,27; 8–9; 10,5-6; 15,24; 28,16-20]; 125-183: "Gericht" [3,7-12; 7,21; 8,11-12; 13,24-30.36-43; 19,28; 21,28-32.33-46; 22,1-14; 24–25; 24,31; 25,31-32.40.44; 27,25]. [NTA 37, p. 286] — Diss. Heidelberg, 1991 (G. Theißen).

> I. Broer, *TLZ* 118 (1993) 931-933; E. Cuvillier, *ETR* 68 (1993) 582-584; D.J. Graham, *CRBR* 7 (1994) 278-280; P.W. van der Horst, *NTT* 49 (1995) 163-164.

1994 Matthew as Servant and Advocate of Unity. — *AsiaJT* 8 (1994) 143-154. Esp. 143-144.148 [mission]; 144-145.149-150 [law]; 145-146.150-153 [judgment]. [NTA 39, 135]

### Wong-Kwan, Teresa

1986 Peter the Rock. [Chinese] — *Theology Annual* (Hong Kong) 9-10 (1985-86) 199-206.

### Wood, Herbert Geoffrey

1953 The Priority of Mark. — *ExpT* 65 (1953-54) 17-19; = Bellinzoni, A.J., Jr., et al. (eds.), *The Two-Source Hypothesis*, 1985, 77-84. → Butler 1951

### Wood, James

1963 *The Sermon on the Mount and Its Application.* London: Bles, 1963, 128 p.

> P.W. Petty, *ChrTod* 7 (1963) 899-900; M. Ward, *ExpT* 74 (1962-63) 332.

1967 *Wisdom Literature. An Introduction.* London: Duckworth, 1967, XII-169 p. Esp. 110-124.

### Woodhouse, John

1984 Jesus and Jonah. [12,38-42; 16,1-4] — *RTR* 43/2 (1984) 33-41. [NTA 29, 529]

### Wootton, R.W.F.

1970 Treatment of Controversial Passages in Recent Roman Catholic Translations and Commentaries. — *BTrans* 21 (1970) 65-71. Esp. 67-69 [1,25; 5,32; 19,9]. [NTA 15, 36]

### Worden, Ronald Dean

1973 *A Philological Analysis of Luke 6,20b-49 and Parallels.* Diss. Theological Sem., Princeton, NJ, 1973, IX-599 p. — *DissAbstr* 34 (1973-74) 3539.

1975 Redaction Criticism of Q: A Survey. — *JBL* 94 (1975) 532-546. Esp. 534-538: "Early redaction-critical treatments of Q or the Q-material"; 538-546: "Deliberate redaction-critical 'methodology'". [NTA 20, 424]

1983 The Q Sermon on the Mount/Plain: Variants and Reconstruction. — *SBL 1983 Seminar Papers*, 455-471.

### Woschitz, Karl Matthäus

1975 Reflexionen zum Zeitverständnis in der Spruchquelle "Q". — *ZKT* 97 (1975) 72-79. [NTA 20, 425]

1985 Erzählter Glaube. Die Geschichte vom starken Glauben als Geschichte Gottes mit Juden und Heiden (Mt 15,21-28 par). — *ZKT* 107 (1985) 319-332. Esp. 320-322: "Analyse und Komposition von Mt 15,21-28"; 322-327: "Das Motiv vom starken Glauben"; 327-330: "Das Motiv der Geschichte Gottes mit Juden und Heiden"; 330-332: "Der theologische Ort". [NTA 30, 575]

### Wouters, Armin

1992 *"... wer den Willen meines Vaters tut". Eine Untersuchung zum Verständnis vom Handeln im Matthäusevangelium* (BibUnt, 23). Regensburg: Pustet, 1992, 458 p. Esp. 13-45: "Die Aufforderung zum Handeln als Problem im Matthäusevangelium"; 47-149: "Die Bedeutung der Zukunft für das menschliche Handeln" [5,20; 7,21; 18,3; 19,23-24; 21,31-32; 25,31-46]; 161-296: "Die Jünger und die Forderung Gottes"; 297-414: "Die Gemeinde im Spannungsfeld von Vergangenheit und Zukunft". [NTA 37, p. 124] — Diss. München, 1990 (F. Laub).

> J. Becker, *TLZ* 118 (1993) 324-326; J. Gutiérrez, *CiudDios* 207 (1994) 517-518; D.J. Harrington, *CBQ* 55 (1993) 402-404; S. Légasse, *BullLitEccl* 93 (1992) 403-404; J. Pelaez, *FilolNT* 6 (1993) 238;

F.F. Ramos, *Salmanticensis* 41 (1994) 336-337; S. Sabugal, *Revista Augustiniana* (Madrid) 379-380; D.J. Weaver, *JBL* 114 (1995) 145-147; W. Weren, *TijdTheol* 33 (1993) 293.

**Wrege, Hans-Theo**

1968 *Die Überlieferungsgeschichte der Bergpredigt* (WUNT, 9). Tübingen: Mohr, 1968, VIII-207 p. Esp. 5-34: "Die Seligpreisungen" [5,3-16]; 35-135: "Die Antithesen" [5,17-7,14]; 136-155: "Der Schluß der Bergpredigt" [7,15-27]; 156-180 [12,32/Q 12,10]. [NTA 12, p. 398] — Diss. Göttingen, 1963-64 (J. Jeremias).

C.E. Carlston, *JAAR* 38 (1970) 104-106; E. Constantini, *ArchTeolGran* 31 (1968) 412-413; B. Corsani, *Protestantesimo* 25 (1970) 109-110; J. Dupont, *RivStoLR* 4 (1968) 558-560; G.G. Gamba, *Sal* 31 (1969) 704-705; M.D. Goulder, *JTS* 20 (1969) 599-602; P. Hoffmann, *TRev* 68 (1972) 115-117; A.F.J. Klijn, *NTT* 23 (1968) 129-130; E. Krentz, *ConcTM* 44 (1973) 390-391; D. Lührmann, *TLZ* 95 (1970) 199-200; H.K. McArthur, *JBL* 88 (1969) 91-92; B. Reicke, *TZ* 25 (1969) 222-223; A. Salas, *CiudDios* 182 (1969) 93.

1970 Jesusgeschichte und Jüngergeschick nach Joh 12,20-33 und Hebr 5,7-10. — Lohse, E., et al. (eds.), *Der Ruf Jesu*. FS J. Jeremias, 1970, 259-288. Esp. 262-267 [10,24-25].

1978 *Die Gestalt des Evangeliums. Aufbau und Struktur der Synoptiker sowie der Apostelgeschichte* (BET, 11). Frankfurt/M: Lang, 1978, 312 p. Esp. 123-160: "Das Geistwort, die Logien und der strukturelle Aufbau des mt sowie des lk Doppelwerkes". — Diss. Kiel, 1976 (G. Friedrich – J. Becker).

1982 Zur Rolle des Geisteswortes in frühchristlichen Traditionen (Lc 12,10 parr.). — Delobel, J. (ed.), *Logia*, 1982, 373-377.

1991 *Das Sondergut des Matthäus-Evangeliums* (Zürcher Werkkommentare zur Bibel). Zürich: Theologischer Verlag, 1991, 143 p. [NTA 36, p. 117]
W. Berflo, *TijdTheol* 32 (1992) 311-312.

**Wrembek, Christoph**

1991 Das Gleichnis vom königlichen Hochzeitsmahl und vom Mann ohne hochzeitliches Gewand. Eine geistliche-theologische Erwägung zu Mt 22,1-14. — *GL* 64 (1991) 17-40. [NTA 35, 1144]

**Wright, Addison G.**

1966 The Literary Genre Midrash. — *CBQ* 28 (1966) 105-138; 417-457. Esp. 454-456: "Are the infancy narratives Midrash?". [NTA 11, 73/568]

1967 *The Literary Genre Midrash*. New York: Alba House, 1967, 164 p. Esp. 140-141 [1-2].

**Wright, Alexandra**

1989 The Sermon on the Mount: A Jewish View. — *NBlackf* 70 (1989) 182-189. [NTA 33, 1120]

**Wright, Benjamin G. III**

1986 A Previously Unnoticed Greek Variant of Matt 16:14 – "Some say John the Baptist...". — *JBL* 105 (1986) 694-697. [NTA 31, 1078]

**Wright, David F.**

1985 Apocryphal Gospels: The 'Unknown Gospel' (Pap. Egerton 2) and the *Gospel of Peter*. — Wenham, D. (ed.), *The Jesus Tradition Outside the Gospels*, 1985, 207-232. Esp. 210-221 [Pap. Egerton 2].

1986 Apologetic and Apocalyptic: The Miraculous in the *Gospel of Peter*. — Wenham, D. – Blomberg, C. (eds.), *The Miracles of Jesus*, 1986, 401-418. Esp. 403-404 [27,46/GP 5,19]; 407-408 [27,51/GP 5,20]; 408-409 [27,51-53/GP 6,21]; 410-411 [28,2-3/GP 9,35-37]; 411-413 [27,51-53/GP 10,38-42]; 413 [28,2/GP 11,44].

**Wright, Leon E.**

1952 *Alterations of the Words of Jesus as Quoted in the Literature of the Second Century*.

Cambridge, MA: Harvard University Press, 1952, X-153 p. Esp. 1-71: "Patristic quotation"; 75-90: "Agrapha"; 91-102: "Jewish-Christian gospels"; 103-107.119-127: "Oxyrhynchus sayings".

**WRIGHT, Nicholas Thomas**

1988    → Neill 1964/88

1992    *Christian Origins and the Question of God*. Vol. I: *New Testament and the People of God*. London: SPCK; Minneapolis, MN: Fortress, 1992, XIX-535 p. Esp. 384-390: "The scribe and the plot: Matthew's story"; 435-443: "Stories but no story? Q and *Thomas*"; Vol. II: *Jesus and the Victory of God*, 1994, 400 p.

**WUELLNER, Wilhelm H.**

1967    *The Meaning of "Fishers of Men"* (The New Testament Library). Philadelphia, PA: Westminster, 1967, 256 p. Esp. 194-196.214-216.225-226.232-233.

1984    & LESLIE, R.C., *The Surprising Gospel. Intriguing Psychological Insights from the New Testament*. Nashville, TN: Abingdon, 1984, 174 p. Esp. 13-21 [1,18-25]; 47-53 [9,1-8].

**WÜNSCH, Dietrich**

1983    *Evangelienharmonien im Reformationszeitalter. Ein Beitrag zur Geschichte der Leben-Jesu-Darstellungen* (Arbeiten zur Kirchengeschichte, 52). Berlin – New York: de Gruyter, 1983, IX-282 p. Esp. 11-20: "Die wichtigsten Vorläufer der Evangelienharmonien des 16. Jahrhunderts"; 21-83: "Evangelienharmonien des 16. Jahrhunderts vor Osiander"; 84-179: "Die Evangelien-harmonie Osianders"; 180-208: "Osiandrische Evangelienharmonien"; 209-230: "Cornelius Jansen d.Ä."; 231-256: "Weitere nachosiandrische Harmonien". — Diss. Erlangen–Nürnberg, 1980 (G. Müller).

**WULF, Friedrich**

1958    Ist die Bergpredigt für Christen in der Welt realisierbar? — *GL* 31 (1958) 184-197. [NTA 3, 579]

**WURZINGER, Anton**

1961    Israel. Die Kirche. Zum Kirchenbild bei Matthäus. — *BLtg* 35 (1961-62) 322-330.

1967    Die eschatologischen Reden Jesu. — SINT, J. (ed.), *Bibel und zeitgemässer Glaube*. II: *Neues Testament*, Klosterneuburg: Buch- und Kunstverlag, 1967, 37-67. Esp. 56-58 [24,37-25,46].

# Y

**YAGI, Seiichi**

1967 Sin and Its Negation in Matthew and Luke. [Japanese] — *Seisho-gaku ronshū* (Tokyo) 4 (1967) 90-106.

**YAMASAKI, Gary**

1995 *John the Baptist in the Gospel of Matthew: A Narrative-Critical Analysis.* Diss. Union Theol. Sem., Virginia, GA, 1995, 147 p. — *DissAbstr* 56 (1995-96) 3166.

**YAMAUCHI, E. Makoto**

1966 The "Daily Bread" Motif in Antiquity. — *WestTJ* 28 (1966) 145-156. [NTA 11, 205]

1971 *The Easter Texts of the New Testament: Their Tradition, Redaction and Theology - With Particular Reference to the Synoptic Gospels and I Corinthians 15.* Diss. Edinburgh, 1971-72. Esp. 131-162.

1986a Logia. — BROMILEY, G.W., et al. (eds.), *The International Standard Bible Encyclopedia,* III, Grand Rapids, MI: Eerdmans, 1986, 152-154.

1986b Magic or Miracle? Diseases, Demons and Exorcisms. — WENHAM, D. - BLOMBERG, C. (eds.), *The Miracles of Jesus,* 1986, 89-183. Esp. 124-142.
Magia o miracolo? Malattie, demoni ed esorcismi. — *Studi di Teologia dell' Istituto Biblico Evangelico* (Roma) 11 (1988) 53-144.

1989 The Episode of the Magi. — VARDAMAN, J. - YAMAUCHI, E.M. (eds.), *Chronos, Kairos, Christos.* FS J. Finegan, 1989, 15-39. Esp. 18-23: "Was Matthew's account also legendary?".

**YAMAUCHI, Ichiro**

1983 Jesus as Teacher Reconsidered. — LUZ, U. - WEDER, H. (eds.), *Die Mitte des Neuen Testaments.* FS E. Schweizer, 1983, 412-426. Esp. 414-416 [διδάσκαλος]; 417-419 [authority]; 419-421 [discipleship].

1986 An Interpretation of Mt 23,8-12. [Japanese] — *Shinyakugaku Kenkyū (New Testament Studies)* 14 (1986) 41-55.

**YANG, Seung Ai**

1983 The Beatitudes. [Korean] — *Sinhak Jonmang* (Kwangju) 62 (1983) 34-43; 63 (1983) 90-101; 64 (1984) 23-39.

1990 Historical Investigation on the Temptation of Jesus according to Matthew 4:1-11 and Luke 4:1-13. [Korean] — *Sinhak Jonmang* 91 (1990).

1992 *The Original Intention of the Longer Version of the Temptation Story of Jesus (Matt 4:11; Luke 4:1-13) as a Jewish Story of God's Testing of the Righteous Man Jesus.* Diss. Chicago, IL, 1992 (H.D. Betz).

**YANG, Yong-Eui**

1997 *Jesus and the Sabbath in Matthew's Gospel* (JSNT, SS 139). Sheffield: JSOT, 1997, 352 p. Esp. 100-138: "Preliminary considerations" [5,17-20.21-48]; 139-229: "Texts, co-texts and contexts" [12,1-14]; 230-241 [24,20]; 242-274: "Comparative studies"; 275-298: 'Its significance and influence in the Early Church". — Diss. Oxford, 1995 (R.T. France).

**YARNOLD, Edward**

1968 Τέλειος in St. Matthew's Gospel. — *Studia Evangelica* 4 (1968) 269-273.

**YATES, J.E.**

1963    *The Spirit and the Kingdom*. London: SPCK, 1963, XVI-268 p. Esp. 6-9; 22-29: "The Q form of the promise and its application" [Q 3,16-17]; 85-90 [Mk/Q 11,14-23]; 90-94 [Q 11,20; 12,10]; 94-95 [10,25]; 180-188: "Matthew: the spirit as agent"; 244-247 [πνεῦμα].

1964    Luke's Pneumatology and Lk. 11,20. — *Studia Evangelica* 2 (1964) 295-299.

**YATES, Roy**

1977    Jesus and the Demonic in the Synoptic Gospels. — *IrTQ* 44 (1977) 39-57. [NTA 21, 714]

**YEOMANS, William**

1993    *The Gospel of Matthew. A Spiritual Commentary*. Dublin: Dominican Publications, 1993, 207 p. [NTA 38, p. 126]

**YOON, Victor Seung-Ku**

1986    *Did the Evangelist Luke Use the Canonical Gospel of Matthew?* Diss. Graduate Theol. Union, Berkeley, CA, 1986, VI-187 p. (W.R. Herzog II). — *DissAbstr* 47 (1986-87) 220; SBT 15 (1987) 119. → T.A. Friedrichsen 1991

**YORK, John O.**

1991    *The Last Shall Be First. The Rhetoric of Reversal in Luke* (JSNT SS, 46). Sheffield: JSOT, 1991, 209 p. Esp. 80-87 [Q 17,33(Lk)]; 87-92 [Q 13,30(Lk)].

**YOUNG, Brad H.**

1984    *The Jewish Background to the Lord's Prayer*. Austin, TX: Center for Judaic-Christian Studies, 1984, VII-46 p.

1989    *Jesus and His Jewish Parables. Rediscovering the Roots of Jesus' Teaching* (Theological Inquiries: Studies in Contemporary Biblical and Theological Problems). New York – Mahwah, NJ: Paulist, 1989, V-365 p. Esp. 129-163: "The parables and the gospels: the synoptic problem"; 164-188: "The parables and their context: reapplication and interpretation in the parallels" [22,1-14; 25,14-30]; 189-235: "The parables of the kingdom of heaven" [13,31-33.44-46]; 236-281: "Jesus, the Jewish sages and their parables" [7,15-20; 20,1-16]; 282-316 [21,33-46].

1995    *Jesus the Jewish Theologian*. Peabody, MA: Hendrickson, 1995, XXXVI-308 p. Esp. 27-34 [4,1-11]; 51-55 [11,12-13]; 85-89 [5,9]; 130-135 [20,1-16]; 168-169 [5,43].

**YOUNG, Franklin W.** → H.C. Kee 1957

**YSEBAERT, Joseph**

1962    *Greek Baptismal Terminology. Its Origins and Early Development* (Graecitas Christianorum primaeva, 1). Nijmegen: Dekker & van de Vegt, 1962, XVIII-435 p. Esp. 40-63 [βαπτίζειν; βάπτισμα]; 130-131 [παλιγγενεσία]; 254-259 [ἄπτομαι].

1994    *Die Amtsterminologie im Neuen Testament und in der Alten Kirche. Eine lexiko-graphische Untersuchung*. Breda: Eureia, 1994, VIII-238 p. Esp. 6-7 [οἱ δώδεκα]; 32-33 [23,8-10].
        J. VERHEYDEN, *ETL* 71 (1995) 234-237.

**YUBERO GALINDO, Dionisio**

1966    *La formación de los Evangelios*. Madrid: Paulinas, 1966, 299 p.

# Z

**ŻABIŃSKI, Zbigniew**

1973   Trzydzieści srebrników (Les trente pièces d'argent). — *CollTheol* 43/2 (1973) 65-75.

**ZAGER, Werner**

1996   *Gottesherrschaft und Endgericht in der Verkündigung Jesu. Eine Untersuchung zur markinischen Jesusüberlieferung einschließlich der Q-Parallelen* (BZNW, 82). Berlin: de Gruyter, 1996, XIII-420 p. Esp. 114-136: "Unmittelbare geschichtliche Zusammenhänge der Endgerichtsverkündigung Jesu" [21,28-33; Q 3,16-17; 7,28; 16,16]; 169-229: "Logien (Weisheitsworte)" [Q 6,38; 12,12; 17,1-2.33; 19,26; Q^Mt 5,29-30; Mt 6,14-15]; 231-303: "Prophetische und apokalyptische Worte" [20,16; Q 10,10-11; 11,43; 12,8-9.10]. — Diss. Bochum, 1995 (H. Balz).

**ZAHN, Peter**

1973   Hrabanus Maurus: *Super Mattheum*. Zu einem neuen Fragmentfund in der Stadtbibliothek Nürnberg. [23,13.15-23] — *Bibliotheksforum Bayern* (München) 1 (1973) 120-125.

**ZAHN, Theodor**

1922^R   *Das Evangelium des Matthäus* [1922]. Wuppertal: Brockhaus, ⁴1984, VI-730 p. [NTA 29, p. 329]
  A. FUCHS, *SNTU* 11 (1986) 229-230.

**ZAKOWITCH, Yair**

1975   Rahab als Mutter des Boas in der Jesus-Genealogie (Matth. i 5). — *NT* 17 (1975) 1-5. [NTA 19, 944]

**ZALĘSKI, Jan**

1977   Elementy egzegezy patrystycznej we współczesnych interpretacjach tekstu Mt 5,32 czy 19,9 (Elemente der patristischen Exegese in der gegenwärtigen Auslegung von Mt 5,32 bzw. 19,9). — *CollTheol* 47/1 (1977) 43-63. [NTA 22, 87]

**ZANDEE, Jan**

1981   "The Teachings of Silvanus" (NHC VII,4) and Jewish Christianity. — VAN DEN BROEK, R. – VERMASEREN, M.J. (eds.), *Studies in Gnosticism and Hellenistic Religions Presented to Gilles Quispel on the Occasion of his 65th Birthday* (Études préliminaires aux religions orientales dans l'empire romain, 91), Leiden: Brill, 1981, 498-584. Esp. 512-513 [6,20]; 580-581 [23,25-26].

**ZANI, Lorenzo**

1972   Influsso del genere letterario midrashico su Mt 2,1-12. — *Studia Patavina* 19 (1972) 257-320. [NTA 17, 904]
  *"Abbiamo visto la sua stella"*. *Studio su Mt 2,1-12*. Exc. diss. Univ. Greg., Roma. Padova, 1972, 85 p.

**ZAPHIRIS, Gérassime**

1970a   *Le texte de l'Évangile selon saint Matthieu d'après les citations de Clément d'Alexandrie comparées aux citations des Pères et des théologiens grecs du II^e au XV^e sciècle*. Gembloux: Duculot, 1970, VIII-1127 p. Esp. 73-160: "Relevé des citations et des réminiscences de Mt. dans l'œuvre littéraire de Clément d'Alexandrie"; 161-918: "Les 'lectures' clémentines de Mt. et les diverses formes du texte néo-testamentaire dans l'Église ancienne". [NTA 18, p. 24] — Diss. Strasbourg, 1964.
  M.-É. BOISMARD, *RB* 80 (1973) 612-613; F.W. DANKER, *CBQ* 35 (1973) 129-130; J. DUPLACY, *Bib* 54 (1973) 106-109; I. GOMÁ, *EstBíb* 32 (1973) 315-317; X. JACQUES, *NRT* 94 (1972) 1095-1096; J.D.

KARAVIDÓPOULOS, *DeltBM* 2 (1971) 80-82; M. KÜNZI, *TZ* 30 (1974) 177-178; M. MARIN, *VetChr* 12 (1975) 223-224; J.É. MÉNARD, *RevSR* 46 (1972) 78-81; B.M. METZGER, *JTS* 24 (1973) 225-228.

1970b Le texte du Discours sur la montagne en Mt. v,1-VII,29 dans les écrits de Clément d'Alexandrie. — Θεολογία (Athens) 41 (1970) 425-440, 557-566; 42 (1971) 686-705; 43 (1972) 341-349, 792-806; 44 (1973) 702-718; 45 (1974) 150-171; 46 (1975) 662-671, 901-916.

1978 *The Pre-Evangelical Texts. The Witness of the Fathers Concerning the Original Form of the Evangelical Tradition and the Value of the Patristic Biblical Quotations* [Greek]. Athens: Privately published, 1978, 468 p. Esp. 141-369 [28,19 and the witness of Eusebius of Caesarea]; 370-391 [English summary]. [NTA 27, p. 100]
    M.-É. BOISMARD, *RB* 90 (1983) 459-460; G. DELLING, *TLZ* 107 (1982) 740-741; P. PRIGENT, *RHPR* 64 (1984) 187-188.

**ZARRELLA, Pietro**

1969 Il battesimo di Gesù nei Sinottici (Mc. 1,9-14; Mt. 3,13-17; Lc. 3,21-22). — *ScuolC* 97 (1969) 3-29. Esp. 14-21: "La testimonianza di Matteo". [NTA 14, 156]

1970a "Les Béatitudes". Un'opera fondamentale. — *Laur* 11 (1970) 459-467. → Dupont 1954

1970b L'entrata di Gesù in Gerusalemme nella redazione di Matteo (21,1-17). — *ScuolC* 98 (1970) 89-112. Esp. 92-106: "L'entrata nella città di Gerusalemme"; 106-111: "L'entrata nel tempio"; = *La distruzione di Gerusalemme del 70 nei suoi riflessi storico-letterari. Atti del V Convegno Biblico Francescano. Roma, 22-27 settembre 1969* (Collectio Assisiensis, 8), Assisi: Studio teologico "Porziuncola", 1971, 111-133. Esp. 114-127; 127-132.

1973 *La risurrezione di Gesù. Storia e messaggio* (Questioni aperte). Assisi: Cittadella, 1973, 145 p.

**ZBIK, F.**

1958 A lei antiga e o quinto mandamento no comentário divino (Mt 5,17-26). — *RevistCuBíb* 2 (1958) 82-93.

1961 O sexto mandamento no Comentário Divino (Mt 5,27-30). — *RevistCuBíb* 5 (1961) 463-472.

**ZECHNER, A.**

1978 *Einblick in die Werkstatt der Evangelisten. Strukturanalyse der vier kanonischen Evangelien.* Schwanberg, Austria: Privately published, 1978, 82 p.

**ZEDDA, Silverio**

1964 *I vangeli e la critica oggi. Dal Cristo della fede al Gesù della storia. I. I Vangeli* ("Verba Vitae", 11). Treviso: Trevigiana, 1964, 208 p.; ⁴1973. Esp. 13-30 [form criticism]; 64-72 [redaction criticism]; 135-143 [patristic evidence]; 152-155 [sources].
    *Los Evangelios y la crítica, hoy. Del Cristo de la fe al Jesús de la historia*, trans. A. Arbia (Orientaciones Bíblicas, 17). Buenos Aires: Paulinas, 1967, 224 p.

**ZEDDE, Italo**

1994 Il racconto della passione nei vangeli sinottici. — LÀCONI, M. (ed.), *Vangeli sinottici*, 1994, 361-379. Esp. 366-372, 374-375.

**ZEGG, A.**

1969 (ed.), *Aurelius Augustinus. De Sermone Domini in monte libri duo.* Diss. Graz, 1969, XIX-215 p.

**ZEHNDORFER, Peter**

1961 *Die Versuchung Jesu und die Versuchung Israels.* Diss. Wien, 1961, XX-162 p.

**ZEHRER, Franz**

1959 *Einführung in die synoptischen Evangelien.* Klosterneuburg: Bibelapostolat, 1959, XXVIII-189 p. Esp. 15-48: "Das Matthäusevangelium"; 133-176: 'Zur synoptischen Frage".

1961 Die synoptische Frage – heute. — *BLtg* 35 (1961-62) 82-95.

1962 *Synoptischer Kommentar zu den drei ersten Evangelien. I. Kindheitsgeschichte und Anfang des öffentlichen Wirkens Jesu (Mt 1,1-4,25; Mk 1,1-39; Lk 1,1-5,11); II: Jesu Wirken in Galiläa (Mt 5,1-13,58; Mk 1,40-6,13; Lk 5.12-9,6); III: Jesu Reise nach Jerusalem (Mt 14,1-20,34; Mk 6,14-10,52; Lk 9,7-19,27).* Klosterneuburg: Buch- und Kunstverlag, I, 1962, IX-198 p.; II, 1963, VI-396 p.; III, 1964, VI-421 p.

1964 Urchristentum und Ehescheidung. Gedanken zur Auslegung der "Unzuchtsklausel" bei Mt 5,31 und 19,9. — *TPQ* 112 (1964) 190-200.

1966 *Die Botschaft der Parabeln. I: Über Gott. II: Über das Reich Gottes. III: Über die Endzeit.* Klosterneuburg: Buch- und Kunstverlag, 1966, 132, 135 and 144 p.
*De boodschap der gelijkenissen. I: Over God. II: Over het Rijk Gods; III: Over de eindtijd,* trans. J. Moebs (Van exegese tot verkondiging, 18-20). Boxtel: Katholieke Bijbelstich.ing; Brugge: Emmaüs, 1974, 105 p. Esp. II, 19-21 [13,44-46]; 26-31 [13,31-33]; 32-46 [13,24-30.36-43 47-50]; 47-62 [13,3-9.18-23]; 63-77 [22,1-14]; 78-83 [21,28-32]; 84-100 [21,33-44]; 101-105 [11,16-19]; I.I, 51-59 [25,1-13]; 60-63 [24,45-51]; 64-79 [25,14-30]; 80-86 [7,13-14.21-23].

1969a *Die Botschaft der Kindheitsgeschichte nach Matthäus und Lukas* (Bibelinformation, 3). Klosterneuburg: Buch- und Kunstverlag, 1969, 126 p.

1969b *Grundzüge der matthäischen und lukanischen Theologie* (Bibelinformation, 1). Klosterneuburg: Buch- und Kunstverlag, 1969, 56 p.

1974 Jesus, der Menschensohn. — *BLtg* 47 (1974) 165-176. [NTA 19, 737]

1975 Jesus, der Sohn Gottes. — *BLtg* 48 (1975) 70-81. Esp. 74-79. [NTA 20, 253]

1977 Gedanken zum Jerusalem-Motiv im Lukasevangelium. — BAUER, J.B. – MARBÖCK, J. (eds.), *Memoria Jerusalem. Freundesgabe Franz Sauer zum 70. Geburtstag,* Graz: Akad. Druck- und Verlagsanstalt, 1977, 117-127. Esp. 121-122 [Q 16,16]; 123 [Q 4,1-13].

1980 *Die Auferstehung Jesu nach den vier Evangelien. Die Osterevangelien und ihre hauptsächlichen Probleme.* Beiheft: *Text der Osterevangelien.* Wien: Mayer, 1980, 277 p.

**ZEILINGER, Franz**

1981 Die Erfüllung der ganzen Gerechtigkeit. Theologische Elemente des Matthäusevangeliums. — *TPQ* 129 (1981) 3-15. Esp. 9-12 [16,13-19]. [NTA 25, 847]

1989 Redaktion in Mt 13,24-30. — KERTELGE, K., et al. (eds ), *Christus bezeugen. FS W. Trilling,* 1989, 102-109. Esp. 102-105: "Die literarische Gesta t des Gleichnisses"; 106-108: "Das Gleichnis in der Gleichnisrede des Mt"; 108-109: "Das Gleichnis im Evangelium des Mt".

**ZEITLIN, Irving M.**

1988 *Jesus and the Judaism of His Time.* Cambridge: Polity Press, 1988, IX-204 p. Esp. 52-56: "Is Matthew untrustworthy where the law is concerned?"; 85-98: "Who was the first evangelist?" (→ Stoldt 1977); 109-112 [5,3-10; 6,9-13/rabbinism].

**ZEITLIN, Solomon**

1969 Prolegomenon. — FRIEDLANDER, G., *Jewish Sources cf the Sermon on the Mount* [1911], 1969, XI-XXXV; = ID., *Studies in the Early History of Judaism.* III: *Judaism and Christianity,* New York: Ktav, 1975, 374-400.

**ZELLER, Dieter**

1971 Das Logion Mt 8,11f / Lk 13,28f und das Motiv der 'Völkerwallfahrt". — *BZ* 15 (1971) 222-237; 16 (1972) 84-93. Esp. 222-224: "Der ursprüng iche Text"; 225-236: "Die Tradition vom Zug der Völker"; 84-89: "Mt 8,11f im Licht der Motivgeschichte'; 89-93: "Folgerungen für den Ort des Spruches". [NTA 16, 535/858] → Grimm 1972

1975 Der Zusammenhang der Eschatologie in der Logienquelle. — FIEDLER, P. - ZELLER, D. (eds.), *Gegenwart und kommendes Reich*. FS A. Vögtle, 1975, 67-77. Esp. 67-69: "Überlegungen zur Methode"; 69-76: "Die eschatologischen Beziehungsfelder".

1976 Zu einer jüdischen Vorlage von Mt 13,52. — *BZ* 20 (1976) 223-226. [NTA 21, 380]

1977a *Die weisheitlichen Mahnsprüche bei den Synoptikern* (FzB, 17). Würzburg: Echter, 1977, ²1983, 224 p. Esp. 54-143: "Der synoptische Bestand an weisheitlichen Mahnsprüchen" [5,23-25.25-26.34-37.39-42.44-47.48;6,2-6.7-8.16-18.19-21.25-33.34;7,1-5.6.7-11.12.13-14;10,16.28-31;18,21-22; 23,8-10.11]; 147-184: "Die weisheitlichen Mahnsprüche in der Verkündigung Jesu"; 184-199: "Tendenzen der Überlieferung im Vorfeld der Synoptiker". — Diss. Freiburg, 1976 (A. Vögtle).
W.A. BEARDSLEE, *JBL* 98 (1979) 441-442; J. BEUTLER, *TheolPhil* 53 (1978) 572-574; R.H. FULLER, *TLZ* 104 (1979) 582; R.L. JESKE, *CBQ* 41 (1979) 357-359; I.H. MARSHALL, *JTS* 29 (1978) 534-535; R. PESCH, *TRev* 75 (1979) 107-108.

1977b Die Bildlogik des Gleichnisses Mt 11,16f. / Lk 7,31f. — *ZNW* 68 (1977) 252-257. [NTA 22, 767]

1977c Prophetisches Wissen um die Zukunft in synoptischen Jesusworten. — *TheolPhil* 52 (1977) 258-271. Esp. 263-269 [Q: kingdom]. [NTA 21, 697]

1980 Die Versuchungen Jesu in der Logienquelle. — *TTZ* 89 (1980) 61-73. Esp. 61-62: "Literatur- und überlieferungskritische Vorfragen"; 62-64: "Formkritische und strukturelle Einordnung"; 64-71: "Der Sinn der Erzählung"; 71-72: "Redaktionskritische Betrachtung". [NTA 24, 784]

1981a Die Ankündigung der Geburt - Wandlungen einer Gattung. — PESCH, R. (ed.), *Zur Theologie der Kindheitsgeschichten*, 1981, 27-48. Esp. 40-41.44-46 [1,18-25].

1981b God as Father in the Proclamation and in the Prayer of Jesus. — FINKEL, A. - FRIZZELL, L. (eds.), *Standing before God*. FS J.M. Oesterreicher, 1981, 117-129. Esp. 119-122: "God as father in the sapiential admonitions of Jesus"; 123 [11,25-27].

1982 Redaktionsprozesse und wechselnder "Sitz im Leben" beim Q-Material. — DELOBEL, J. (ed.), *Logia*, 1982, 395-409. Esp. 399-402: "Redaktionsstufen in Q"; 402-407: "Fallstudien" [Q 7,18-23.24-28.31-35; Q 10,2-16.21-22; Q 11,14-15].
Redactional Processes and Changing Settings in the Q-Material. — KLOPPENBORG, J.S. (ed.), *The Shape of Q*, 1994, 116-130. Esp. 120-123; 123-128.

1984 *Kommentar zur Logienquelle* (Stuttgarter Kleiner Kommentar. Neues Testament, 21). Stuttgart: Katholisches Bibelwerk, 1984, 109 p. Esp. 11-16: "Einleitung"; 17-91: "Kommentar". [NTA 29, p. 329]; ²1986; ³1993. → Sanz Valdivieso 1990
A. FUCHS, *SNTU* 12 (1987) 228-229; J.S. KLOPPENBORG, *CBQ* 48 (1986) 353-354; F. NEIRYNCK, *ETL* 62 (1986) 428.

1985 Entrückung zur Ankunft als Menschensohn (Lk 13,34f.; 11,29f.). — GANTOY, R. (ed.), *À cause de l'Évangile*. FS J. Dupont, 1985, 513-530. Esp. 513-519 [Q 13,34-35]; 519-527 [Q 11,29.30]; 527-530: "Das Geschick Jesu in der Logienquelle".

1988 Jesus als vollmächtiger Lehrer (Mt 5-7) und der hellenistische Gesetzgeber. — SCHENKE, L. (ed.), *Studien zum Matthäusevangelium*. FS W. Pesch, 1988, 299-317. Esp. 301-305: "Jesus - ein neuer Gesetzgeber?"; 305-315: "Die Vollmacht Jesu im Vergleich mit hellenistische Anschauungen".

1992a Geburtsankündigung und Geburtsverkündigung. Formgeschichtliche Untersuchung im Blick auf Mt 1f, Lk 1f. — BERGER, K., et al., *Studien und Texte zur Formgeschichte* (TANZ, 7), Tübingen: Francke, 1992, 59-134. Esp. 59-66: "Die formkritische Bestimmung der Kindheitsgeschichten"; 67-68.100-103 [1,18-25]; 104-105.131-134 [2,1-12].

1992b Kindheitsgeschichte Jesu. — GÖRG, M. - LANG, B. (eds.), *Neues Bibel-Lexikon*, II/8, Zürich: Benziger, 1992, 476-479.

1992c Eine weisheitliche Grundschrift in der Logienquelle? — VAN SEGBROECK, F., et al. (eds.), *The Four Gospels 1992*. FS F. Neirynck, 1992, I, 389-401. Esp. 390-392: "Literar- und formkritische Schwachstellen"; 392-400: "Zum Vergleich mit weisheitlichen Spruchsammlungen der Antike".

**ZENTENO, Arnaldo**

1980 Mateo 25 en la experiencia CCB latinoamericana. — *Christus* (México) 45 (1980) 38-45.

**ZEOLI, Angelo**

1952 Il discorso escatologico di Gesù. Soluzioni vecchie e nuove. — *Humanitas* 7 (1952) 101-112, 226-232.

**ZERBE, Gordon M.**

1993 *Non-Retaliation in Early Jewish and New Testament Texts. Ethical Themes in Social Contexts* (Journal for the Study of the Pseudepigrapha, SS 13). Sheffield: JSOT, 1993, 307 p. Esp. 176-210: "Non-retaliatory ethics in the gospel tradition: Matthew 5.38-48 and Luke 6.27-36". — Diss. Princeton Theol. Sem., Princeton, NJ, 1990 (J. Charlesworth).

**ZERVOS, George T.**

1994 Dating the *Protevangelium of James*: The Justin Martyr Connection. — *SBL 1994 Seminar Papers*, 415-434. Esp. 420-421 [1,20]; 427 [1,23]; 430-432 [1,18-25].

**ZERWICK, Maximilian**

1953 *Analysis philologica Novi Testamenti graeci* (Scripta Pontificii Instituti Biblici, 107). Roma: Pont. Inst. Bibl., 1953, [2]1960, [3]1966, xv-608 p.
& GROSVENOR, M., *A Grammatical Analysis of the Greek New Testament*. 2 vols. I: *Gospels – Acts*. Roma: Biblical Institute Press, 1974, I-XXXVI, 1-456, 1*-15* p. Esp. 1-99; rev ed. in one vol., 1981; [4]1993, XXXVI-778-15* p.

1955 Progressus in "Quaestione synoptica"? — *VD* 33 (1955) 18-23. → P. Parker 1953

1960 De matrimonio et divortio in Evangelio. — *VD* 38 (1960) 193-212. Esp. 196-200 [5,32; 19,9]. [NTA 5, 395] → Dupont 1959a

1968 Das Vaterunser. — *Christlich-pädagogische Blätter* (Wien) 81 (1968) 139-141, 323-325.

**ZIENER, Georg**

1969 Die synoptische Frage. — SCHREINER, J. – DAUTZENBERG, G. (eds.), *Gestalt und Anspruch*, 1969, 173-185. Esp. 179-182: "Die Verwendung von Mk bei Mt".

**ZIESLER, John A.**

1972 The Vow of Abstinence. A Note on Mark 14:25 and Parallels. [26,29] — *Colloquium* 5 (1972) 12-14. [NTA 17, 953] → 1973b

1973a The Removal of the Bridegroom: A Note on Mark ii.18-22 and Parallels. — *NTS* 19 (1972-73) 190-194. Esp. 191-193 [9,14-15]. [NTA 17, 939]

1973b The Vow of Abstinence Again. [26,29] — *Colloquium* 6 (1973) 49-50. [NTA 18, 883] → 1972

1979 Luke and the Pharisees. — *NTS* 25 (1978-79) 146-157. Esp. 148-154. [NTA 23, 482]

1984 Matthew and the Presence of Jesus. [1,23; 8,23-27; 14,22-33. 18,20; 28,20] — *EpworthR* 11 (1984) 55-63, 90-97. [NTA 28, 910; 29, 82]

1985 Which is the Best Commentary? I. The Gospel according to St Matthew. — *ExpT* 97 (1985-86) 67-71. [NTA 30, 560] → Albright–Mann 1971, Barclay 1976, Beare 1981, Fenton 1963, Filson 1960, H.B. Green 1975, Gundry 1982, D. Hill 1972, Kingsbury 1977a, Meier 1980a, Schweizer 1973a

**ZILLIAENS, H.** → Barns 1960

**ZIMMERLI, Walther**

1978 Die Seligpreisungen der Bergpredigt und das Alte Testament. — BAMMEL, E. – BARRETT, C.K. – DAVIES, W.D. (eds.), *Donum gentilicium. New Testament Studies in Honour of David Daube*, Oxford: Clarendon, 1978, 8-26. Esp. 15-25 [5,3-10].

**ZIMMERMANN, Alfred F.**

1984    *Die urchristlichen Lehrer. Studien zum Tradentenkreis der διδάσκαλοι im frühen Urchristentum* (WUNT, II/12). Tübingen: Mohr, 1984, ²1988, XI-258 p. Esp. 144-193: "Von den διδάσκαλοι der vormatthäischen Tradition zu den γραμματεῖς der matthäischen Gemeinde" [10,24-25; 23,8-10]. — Diss. Bern, 1981-82 (C. Maurer).

**ZIMMERMANN, Frank**

1979    *The Aramaic Origin of the Four Gospels.* New York: Ktav, 1979, XIV-244 p. Esp. 33-82: "The evidence from Matthew"; 170-171 [3,16]; 174-176 [17,5]; 176 [5,32]; 184-186 [6,11].

**ZIMMERMANN, Heinrich**

1961    Die Botschaft der Gleichnisse Jesu. — *BibLeb* 2 (1961) 92-105; 171-174; 254-261. Esp. 101-105 [20,1-16].

1962    Μὴ ἐπὶ πορνείᾳ. (Mt 19,9) – ein literarisches Problem. Zur Komposition von Mt 19,3-12. — *Catholica* 16 (1962) 293-299. [NTA 7, 789]

1963    Christus nachfolgen. Eine Studie zu den Nachfolge-Worten der synoptischen Evangelien. — *TGl* 53 (1963) 241-255. Esp. 250-251 [Q 9,57-61; 14,26-27]; 251-253 [8,19-22]. [NTA 8, 568]

1967a   *Neutestamentliche Methodenlehre. Darstellung der historisch-kritischen Methode.* Stuttgart: Katholisches Bibelwerk, 1967, 281 p. Esp. 83-89: "Die literarkritische Methode"; 92-98 [9,9-13/Mk]; 105-115 [19,3-12/Mk]; 116-122 [8,18-22; Q 9,57-62]; 123-127 [13,31-33/Mk]; 128-176: "Formgeschichte"; 184-185 [Q/Mk 4,21-25]; 214-230: "Die redaktionsgeschichtliche Methode"; 231-236 [19,3-12]; ³1970, 282 p.; ⁴1974; ⁵1976; ⁶1978, 291 p. Esp. 89-95; 98-108; 111-121; 122-128; 129-133; 134-182; 190-192; 220-241; 242-247; ⁷1982, 330 p. (ed. K. Kliesch). Esp. 77-84; 89-94; 101-112; 113-120; 120-124; 125-178; 185-187; 215-238; 238-250.
        *Los métodos histórico-críticos en el Nuevo Testamento*, trans. G. Bravo (Biblioteca de autores cristianos, 295). Madrid: Católica, 1969, XVI-305 p.
        *Metodologia del Nuovo Testamento. Esposizione del metodo storico-critico*, trans. V. Leonardi & G.F. Forza. Torino: Marietti, 1971, 255 p.
        *Nytestamentlig metodelære. En framstilling av den historisk-kritiske metode*, trans. D. Mysen. Oslo: Universitetsforlaget, 1974, 175 p.
        Trans. French 1968.

1967b   Gattungen, Formen und Formeln im Neuen Testament. — *LebZeug* 22/1 (1967) 43-76. Esp. 43-45 [gospel: genre]; 50-56 [sayings]; 56-62 [stories].

1969    Der methodische Zugang zur Ur-Überlieferung vom Reden und Handeln Jesu. — *BK* 24 (1969) 42-48. Esp. 44-45 [22,1-14]. [NTA 14, 129]; = *Katholische Gedanke* 25 (1969) 120-123. [NTA 14, 844]

1970    Das Gleichnis vom barmherzigen Samariter: Lk 10,25-37. — BORNKAMM, G. - RAHNER, K. (eds.), *Die Zeit Jesu.* FS H. Schlier, 1970, 58-69. Esp. 60-62 [Lk 10,25-28/Q].

1971    Formen und Gattungen im Neuen Testament. — SCHREINER, J. (ed.), *Einführung in die Methoden der biblischen Exegese*, Würzburg: Echter, 1971, 232-260. Esp. 232-246 [sayings and narrative material].

1973    *Jesus Christus. Geschichte und Verkündigung.* Stuttgart: Katholisches Bibelwerk, 1973, ²1975, 319 p. Esp. 110-121 [22,1-14].
        *Gesù Cristo. Storia e annuncio*, trans. M. Sampaolo (Collectanea Biblica, 313). Torino: Marietti, 1976, 224 p.

1976    Die innere Struktur der Kirche und das Petrusamt nach Mt 18. — *Catholica* 30 (1976) 168-183. [NTA 21, 383]; = BRANDENBURG, A. - URBAN, H.J. (eds.), *Petrus und Papst. Evangelium, Einheit der Kirche, Papstdienst. Beiträge und Notizen*, Münster: Aschendorff, 1977, 4-19.

**ZINCONE, Sergio**

1989  Essere simili a Dio: l'esegesi crisostomiana di Mt 5:45. — *Studia Patristica* 18/1 (1989) 353-358.

**ZINGG, Paul**

1974  *Das Wachsen der Kirche. Beiträge zur Frage der lukanischen Redaktion und Theologie* (Orbis Biblicus et Orientalis, 3). Freiburg/Schw: Universitätsverlag; Göttingen: Vandenhoeck & Ruprecht, 1974, 345 p. Esp. 100-109 [Q 13,18-21].

**ZINK, Jörg**

1982  Sorget nicht. — HOCHGREBE, V. (ed.), *Provokation Bergpredigt*, 1982, 91-104.

**ZINNIKER, Franz**

1972  *Probleme der sogenannten Kindheitsgeschichte bei Matthäus.* Freiburg/Schw: Paulus, 1972, 194 p. Esp. 18-29: "Ist Mattäus 1,18–2,23 eine literarische E nheit?"; 30-95: "Die Erfüllungszitate im Mattäusevangelium"; 96-105: "Ist Mt 1,18-25 ein christologischer Midrasch?"; 111-129: "Der besondere Charakter von Mt 2,1-12"; 130-142: "Die Engelerscheinungen in der mattäischer Vorgeschichte"; 143-153: "Die Herkunft der Josefüberlieferungen in Mt 1 und 2 und ihr historischer Gestalt". [NTA 17, p. 249]
V. BENASSI, *Marianum* 38 (1976) 200-201; T. EGIDO, *EstJos* 30 (1976) 477-478; F. LENTZEN-DEIS, *TheolPhil* 47 (1972) 569-570; U. LUZ, *TZ* 30 (1974) 111-112; B. PIEPIÓRKA, *ZKT* 95 (1973) 218-219; J. RIEDL, *TRev* 68 (1972) 454-455; B. SPÖRLEIN, *TGeg* 16 (1973) 55-56; F. STAUDINGER, *TPQ* 121 (1973) 383-384; H. WANSBROUGH, *CleR* 58 (1973) 647-648.

**ZMIJEWSKI, Josef**

1972  *Die Eschatologiereden des Lukas-Evangeliums. Eine traditions- und redaktionsgeschichtliche Untersuchung zu Lk 21,5-36 und Lk 17,20-37* (BBB, 40). Bonn: Hanstein, 1972, XXXII-591 p. Esp. 326-540: "Die Eschatologierede Lk 17,20-37". — Diss. Bonn, 1971 (H. Zimmermann).

1980*  & NELLESSEN, E. (eds.), *Begegnung mit dem Wort. Festschrift für Heinrich Zimmermann* (BBB, 53). Bonn: Hanstein, 1980, 424 p. → J.B. Bauer, Laufen, Légasse, Schelkle, Schnackenburg, Zmijewski

1980  Der Glaube und seine Macht. Eine traditionsgeschichtliche Untersuchung zu Mt 17,20; 21,21; Mk 11,23; Lk 17,6. — *Ibid.*, 81-103. Esp. 82-83 [Q 17,6]; 84 [21,21]; 85-86 [17,20]; 86-89: "Die Rekonstruktion der Q-Fassung"; 93-96: "Die Urform des Logions"; 96-101: "Die weitere Überlieferung des Logions"; = ID., *Das Neue Testament*, 1986. 265-292. Esp. 267-268; 268-269; 270-271; 271-275; 280-284; 284-289.

1982  Überlegungen zum Verhältnis von Theologie und christlicher Glaubenspraxis anhand des Neuen Testaments. — *TGl* 72 (1982) 40-78. Esp. 47-49: "Die Spruchquelle Q"; 54-62: "Die Bergpredigt Mt 5-7". [NTA 26, 1074]; = ID., *Das Neue Testament*, 1986, 223-264. Esp. 230-232; 236-244.

1984  Neutestamentliche Weisungen für Ehe und Familie. — *SNTU* 9 (1984) 31-78. Esp. 46-49 [5,27-28]; 49-55 [Q 16,18]; 60-62 [5,32]; 63-69 [19,3-12]. [NTA 30, 1310]; = ID., *Das Neue Testament*, 1986, 325-378. Esp. 341-344; 344-350; 355-357; 358-364.

1986  *Das Neue Testament – Quelle christlicher Theologie und Glaubenspraxis. Aufsätze zum Neuen Testament und seiner Auslegung.* Stuttgart: Katholisches Bibelwerk, 1986, 390 p. → 1980, 1982, 1984

1989  *Die Mutter des Messias. Maria in der Christusverkündigung des Neuen Testaments. Eine exegetische Studie.* Kevelaer: Butzon & Bercker, 1989, 186 p. Esp. 49-75: "Maria im Matthäusevangelium" [1,2-17.18-25; 2,1-23; 12,46-50; 13,54-58].
Maria im Neuen Testament. — *ANRW* II.26.1 (1992) 596-716. Esp. 621-642.

1990  Zu unserer Belehrung geschrieben. Das Alte Testament und die urkirchliche Christusverkündigung. — ID. (ed.), *Die alttestamentliche Botschaft als Wegweisung.*

*Festschrift für Heinz Reinelt*, Stuttgart: Katholisches Bibelwerk, 1990, 405-447. Esp. 424-432: "Die Darstellung im Matthäusevangelium".

1993   Markinischer "Prolog" und Täufertradition. Eine Untersuchung zu Mk 1,1-8. — *SNTU* 18 (1993) 41-62. Esp. 49-54 [3,11-12/Mk 1,7-8]. [NTA 39, 172]

**ZODHIATES, Spiros**

1966   *The Pursuit of Happiness. An Exposition of the Beatitudes of Christ in Matthew 5:1-11 and Luke 6:20-26, Based upon the Original Greek Text.* Grand Rapids, MI: Eerdmans, 1966, X-671 p.

**ZOLLI, Eugenio**

1958   Nazarenus Vocabitur. [2,23] — *ZNW* 49 (1958) 135-136. [NTA 3, 70]

1964   *La confessione e il dramma di Pietro* [14,33; 16,13-20]. Roma: Figlie della Chiesa, 1964, III-193 p.

1983   Nuova sintesi delle note esegetiche. — *RivBib* 31 (1983) 71-92. Esp. 89-90 [8,22]; 91 [7,6]; 91-92 [2,23].

**ZONEWSKI, Ilija K.**

1967   The Patristic Exegesis of Mt 16,18: "You are Peter". [Bulgarian] — *Duchovna Kultura* (Sofia) 47/7-8 (1967) 7-12.

**ZORN, R.O.**

1980   The Significance of Jesus' Self-Designation "The Son of Man". — *Vox Reformata* (Geelong, Australia) 34 (1980) 1-21. [NTA 25, 247]

**ZOVKIĆ, Mato**

1972   The Preaching of Jesus in Capernaum (Mt 4,17). [Serbo-Croatian] — *Bogoslovska Smotra* (Zagreb) 42 (1972) 177-191.

**ZUCKER, David J.**

1990   Jesus and Jeremiah in the Matthean Tradition. — *JEcuSt* 27 (1990) 288-305. [NTA 36, 135]

**ZUCKSCHWERDT, Ernst**

1975   Nazōraîos in Matth. 2,23. — *TZ* 31 (1975) 65-77. [NTA 20, 84]

**ZUIDEMA, Willem H.**

1976   De arbeiders in de wijngaard. [20,1-16] — *Ter Herkenning* (Breda) 4 (1976) 79-81. → Flesseman-van Leer 1976

**ZUMKELLER, Adolar**

1961   Wiedergefundene exegetische Werke Hermanns von Schildesche. — *Augustinianum* 1 (1961) 236-272, 452-503. Esp. 452-483: "Expositio dominicae orationis".

**ZUMSTEIN, Jean**

1971   *La relation du maître et du disciple dans le bas-judaïsme palestinien et dans l'évangile selon Matthieu.* Mém. Inst. de Sc. Bibl. de l'Univ. de Lausanne, 1971, 113-295.

1972   Matthieu 28:16-20. — *RTP* 22 (1972) 14-33. Esp. 15-22: "Analyse littéraire"; 22-30: "Exégèse"; 30-33: "Thématisation théologique". [NTA 17, 130]; = ID., *Miettes exégétiques*, 1991, 91-112. Esp. 92-99; 99-108; 108-110.

1977   *La condition du croyant dans l'évangile selon Matthieu* (Orbis Biblicus et Orientalis, 16). Freiburg/Schw: Éd. universitaires; Göttingen: Vandenhoeck & Ruprecht, 1977, 467 p. Esp. 22-46: "Les disciples de Jésus"; 47-83: "Les ennemis de Jésus"; 86-106: "Le Ressuscité et le Jésus terrestre (Mt 28,16-20)"; 107-129: "Le didascale eschatologique (Mt 5,17-20)"; 130-152: "Le Révélateur (Mt 11,25-30)"; 154-170: "Les responsables de la communauté matthéenne" [13,51-52; 23,8-12];

171-200: "Les divisions de la communauté matthéenne" [7,15-23; 13,36-43; 24,9-14]; 202-232: "Le croyant et le Jésus terrestre" [4,18-22; 8,18-22; 9,9; 10,37-39; 13,10-17]; 233-255: "Le croyant et le présent de la foi" [8,23-27; 14,22-33]; 256-281: "Le croyant face à l'avenir" [24,37-44.45-51; 25,1-13]; 284-308: "Le point de départ de l'éthique (Mt 5,3-10)"; 309-326: "Le thème de l'éthique (Mt 5,43-48)"; 327-350: "L'enjeu de l'éthique (Mt 25,31-46)"; 352-385: "Le rassemblement de l'Église" [8,11-12; 21,33-46; 22,1-14]; 386-421: "L'amour du frère (Mt 18)"; 422-453: "L'Église et le monde" [5,13-16; 10,7-8.17-25; 17,14-20]. [NTA 22, p. 95]. — Diss. Lausanne, 1974 (P. Bonnard). → Dermience 1985, Ingelaere 1981, Marguerat 1979a
M. BOUTTIER, ETR 54 (1979) 317-319; J. COPPENS, ETL 54 (1978) 368-369; J. DUPONT, RivStoLR 16 (1980) 100-102; A. FUCHS, SNTU 6-7 (1981-82) 261-264; K. GRAYSTON, ExpT 90 (1978-79) 21; D.R.A. HARE, JBL 101 (1982) 150-151; X. LÉON-DUFOUR, RSR 66 (1973) 131-134; U. LUZ, TLZ 105 (1980) 194-196; A. MODA, Nicolaus (Bari) 16 (1989) 263-265; F. MONTAGNINI, RivBib 26 (1978) 93-95; D. MUÑOZ LEÓN, EstBíb 36 (1977) 131-132; W. PESCH, TRev 75 (1979) 284; X. PIKAZA, EstTrin 13 (1979) 231-232; L. SABOURIN, SE 30 (1978) 197-198; A. SALAS, CiudDios 192 (1979) 92-93; D. SENIOR, CBQ 41 (1979) 506-508.

1978   Conception de l'Église et communication de la foi dans les évangiles synoptiques. — VON ALLMEN, J.J. (ed.), Communion et communication. Structures d'unité et modèles de communication, Genève: Labor et fides, 1978, 43-56; = ID., Miettes exégétiques, 1991, 369-383. Esp. 374-378 [5,17-20; 10,5-40; 11,25-30; 28,16-20].

1979   Matthieu, l'avocat du Jésus terrestre. Brève esquisse de théologie matthéenne. — FoiVie 78/3 = Cahiers bibliques 18 (1979) 34-52. Esp. 34-40: "Le contexte historique"; 40-45: "La christologie"; 45-51: "L'ecclésiologie". [NTA 24, 411]; = ID., Miettes exégétiques, 1991, 113-130. Esp. 113-118; 118-123; 123-129.

1980   Antioche sur l'Oronte et l'évangile selon Matthieu. — SNTU 5 (1980) 122-138. Esp. 131-138. [NTA 28, 484]; = ID., Miettes exégétiques, 1991, 151-167. Esp. 161-167.

1981   Loi et Évangile dans le témoignage de Matthieu. — PINCKAERS, S. – RUMPF, L. (eds.), Loi et évangile. Héritages confessionnels et interpellations contemporaines. Actes du 3e cycle d'éthique des Universités de Suisse romande 1979-80 (Le champ éthique, 5), Genève: Labor et Fides, 1981, 33-51 (P. Bonnard: Six remarques sur l'exposé de Jean Zumstein, 52-53); = ID., Miettes exégétiques, 1991, 131-150. Esp. 133-137: "Inscription littéraire et historique du thème chez Matthieu"; 137-142: "La compréhension de la Loi chez Matthieu"; 143-146: "Le problème de l'indicatif et son rapport à l'impératif chez Matthieu"; 146-150: "Paul et Matthieu".

1982   Matthieu à la croisée des traditions syro-palestiniennes. — FoiVie 81/4 = Cahiers bibliques 21 (1982) 3-11. Esp. 4-8: "Les traditions se référant au message de Jésus"; 8-11: "Les traditions kérygmatiques". [NTA 27, 506]

1983   L'image de Jérusalem dans les Évangiles synoptiques et dans les Actes des Apôtres. — BRUSCHWEILER, F. (ed.), La ville dans le Proche-Orient ancien. Actes du Colloque de Cartigny 1979 (Les Cahiers du CEPOA, 1), Leuven: Peeters, 1983, 257-267; = ID., Miettes exégétiques, 1991, 169-182. Esp. 173-174 [Q 13,34-35]; 175-177 [Mt].

1985   Pluralité et autorité des écrits néotestamentaires. — LumièreV 171 (1985) 19-32. Esp. 26-29: "Le trajectoire matthéen". [NTA 30, 14]; = ID., Miettes exégétiques, 1991, 385-397. Esp. 391-394.
SelT 25 (1986) 49-56.

1986   Matthieu le théologien (Cahiers Évangile, 58). Paris: Cerf, 1986, 68 p. Esp. 7-25: "Une narration enracinée dans l'histoire"; 26-45: "Le Christ enseignant selon Matthieu" [5,17-20.21-48; 28,16-20]; 46-60: "L'Église selon Matthieu".
É. COTHENET, EVie 97 (1987) 531-532.
Mateo el teólogo, trans. N. Darrical (Cuadernos Bíblicos, 58). Estella: Verbo Divino, 1987, 62 p.
F. BRÄNDLE, EstJos 44 (1990) 287-288; R. DE SIVATTE, ActBibl 25 (1988) 224.

1987   Proximité et rupture avec le judaïsme rabbinique. — LumièreV 183 (1987) 5-19. Esp. 6-12: "Le genre littéraire"; 12-17: "Le retour de la Torah". [NTA 32, 588]

1991a  Miettes exégétiques (Le monde de la Bible, 25). Genève: Labor et fides, 1991, 421 p. → 1972, 1978, 1979, 1980, 1981, 1983, 1985, 1991b

1991b Violence et non-violence dans le Nouveau Testament. — *Ibid.*, 355-368. Esp. 357-360 [5,21-48].

**ZUNTZ, Günther**

1945[R] The "Centurion" of Capernaum and His Authority (Matt. viii.5-13). [1945] — ID., *Opuscula Selecta. Classica, hellenistica, christiana,* Manchester: University Press, 1972, 181-188.

1951 Reconstruction of one Leaf of the Chester Beatty Papyrus of the Gospels and Acts (P45) (Matth. 25,41-26,39). — *Chronique d'Égypte* (Bruxelles) 26 (1951) 191-211.

1991 Papiana. — *ZNW* 82 (1991) 242-263. Esp. 247 [20,23]; 262-263 [Papias]. [NTA 36, 1098]

**ZUURMOND, Rochus**

1983 De ethiek van de bergrede. — *Amsterdamse Cahiers* 4 (1983) 83-96 (Engl., 137-138). Esp. 88-91 [5,17-48]; 91-93 [6,1-18]; 93 [6,25-34].

1989 *Novum Testamentum Aethiopice: The Synoptic Gospels. General Introduction - Edition of the Gospel of Mark* (Äthiopische Forschungen, 27). Wiesbaden–Stuttgart: Steiner, 1989, XV-406 p. Esp. 68-72: "The alternative text in Matthew"; 171-219: "Samples of text in synoptic columns with commentary" [1,18-20; 5,17-24; 27,55-58].

1995 The Ethiopic Version of the New Testament. — EHRMAN, B.D. - HOLMES, M.W. (eds.), *The Text of the New Testament in Contemporary Research. Essays on the Status Quaestionis. A Volume in Honor of Bruce M. Metzger* (Studies & Documents, 46), Grand Rapids, MI: Eerdmans, 1995, 142-156. Esp. 151-153 [21,28-31].

**ZWICK, Reinhold**

1992 Die Gleichniserzählung als Szenario. Dargestellt am Beispiel der "Arbeiter im Wein-berg" (Mt 20,1-15). — *BibNot* 64 (1992) 53-92. Esp. 53-56: "Aufmerksamkeit für den Erzählcharakter der Gleichnisse"; 56-65: "Aporien des Dramen-Modells"; 65-85: "Die räumlich-szenische Anlage des Gleichnisses von den Arbeitern im Weinberg"; 85-89: "Folgerungen". [NTA 37, 1268]

**ZYWICA, Zdzisław**

1993 *"Wolność synów" w Mateuszowych Logiach Jezusa (Mt 17,24-27 i 22,15-22 par.)* ["La liberté des fils" dans les paroles de Jésus chez Matthieu]. Diss. Warszawa, 1993, 259 p. (R. Bartnicki).

# BIBLIOTHECA EPHEMERIDUM THEOLOGICARUM LOVANIENSIUM

## SERIES I

\* = Out of print

29. M. DIDIER (ed.), *L'évangile selon Matthieu. Rédaction et théologie*, 1972. 432 p. FB 1000.
*30. J. KEMPENEERS, *Le Cardinal van Roey en son temps*, 1971.

## SERIES II

31. F. NEIRYNCK, *Duality in Mark. Contributions to the Study of the Markan Redaction*, 1972. Revised edition with Supplementary Notes, 1988. 252 p. FB 1200.
32. F. NEIRYNCK (ed.), *L'évangile de Luc. Problèmes littéraires et théologiques*, 1973. *L'évangile de Luc – The Gospel of Luke*. Revised and enlarged edition, 1989. X-590 p. FB 2200.
33. C. BREKELMANS (ed.), *Questions disputées d'Ancien Testament. Méthode et théologie*, 1974. *Continuing Questions in Old Testament Method and Theology*. Revised and enlarged edition by M. VERVENNE, 1989. 245 p. FB 1200.
34. M. SABBE (ed.), *L'évangile selon Marc. Tradition et rédaction*, 1974. Nouvelle édition augmentée, 1988. 601 p. FB 2400.
35. B. WILLAERT (ed.), *Philosophie de la religion – Godsdienstfilosofie. Miscellanea Albert Dondeyne*, 1974. Nouvelle édition, 1987. 458 p. FB 1600.
36. G. PHILIPS, *L'union personnelle avec le Dieu vivant. Essai sur l'origine et le sens de la grâce créée*, 1974. Édition révisée, 1989. 299 p. FB 1000.
37. F. NEIRYNCK, in collaboration with T. HANSEN and F. VAN SEGBROECK, *The Minor Agreements of Matthew and Luke against Mark with a Cumulative List*, 1974. 330 p. FB 900.
38. J. COPPENS, *Le messianisme et sa relève prophétique. Les anticipations vétérotestamentaires. Leur accomplissement en Jésus*, 1974. Édition révisée, 1989. XIII-265 p. FB 1000.
39. D. SENIOR, *The Passion Narrative according to Matthew. A Redactional Study*, 1975. New impression, 1982. 440 p. FB 1000.
40. J. DUPONT (ed.), *Jésus aux origines de la christologie*, 1975. Nouvelle édition augmentée, 1989. 458 p. FB 1500.
41. J. COPPENS (ed.), *La notion biblique de Dieu*, 1976. Réimpression, 1985. 519 p. FB 1600.
42. J. LINDEMANS & H. DEMEESTER (ed.), *Liber Amicorum Monseigneur W. Onclin*, 1976. XXII-396 p. FB 1000.
43. R.E. HOECKMAN (ed.), *Pluralisme et œcuménisme en recherches théologiques. Mélanges offerts au R.P. Dockx, O.P.*, 1976. 316 p. FB 1000.
44. M. DE JONGE (ed.), *L'évangile de Jean. Sources, rédaction, théologie*, 1977. Réimpression, 1987. 416 p. FB 1500.
45. E.J.M. VAN EIJL (ed.), *Facultas S. Theologiae Lovaniensis 1432-1797. Bijdragen tot haar geschiedenis. Contributions to its History. Contributions à son histoire*, 1977. 570 p. FB 1700.
46. M. DELCOR (ed.), *Qumrân. Sa piété, sa théologie et son milieu*, 1978. 432 p. FB 1700.
47. M. CAUDRON (ed.), *Faith and Society. Foi et société. Geloof en maatschappij. Acta Congressus Internationalis Theologici Lovaniensis 1976*, 1978. 304 p. FB 1150.

48. J. KREMER (ed.), *Les Actes des Apôtres. Traditions rédaction, théologie,* 1979. 590 p. FB 1700.

49. F. NEIRYNCK, avec la collaboration de J. DELOBEL, T. SNOY, G. VAN BELLE, F. VAN SEGBROECK, *Jean et les Synoptiques. Examen critique de l'exégèse de M.-É. Boismard,* 1979. XII-428 p. FB 1000.

50. J. COPPENS, *La relève apocalyptique du messianisme royal. I. La royauté – Le règne – Le royaume de Dieu. Cadre de la relève apocalyptique,* 1979. 325 p. FB 1000.

51. M. GILBERT (ed.), *La Sagesse de l'Ancien Testament,* 1979. Nouvelle édition mise à jour, 1990. 455 p. FB 1500.

52. B. DEHANDSCHUTTER, *Martyrium Polycarpi. Een literair-kritische studie,* 1979. 296 p. FB 1000.

53. J. LAMBRECHT (ed.), *L'Apocalypse johannique et l'Apocalyptique dans le Nouveau Testament,* 1980. 458 p. FB 1400.

54. P.-M. BOGAERT (ed.), *Le livre de Jérémie. Le prophète et son milieu. Les oracles et leur transmission,* 1981. *Nouvelle édition mise à jour,* 1997. 448 p. FB 1800.

55. J. COPPENS, *La relève apocalyptique du messianisme royal. III. Le Fils de l'homme néotestamentaire.* Édition posthume par F. NEIRYNCK, 1981. XIV-192 p. FB 800.

56. J. VAN BAVEL & M. SCHRAMA (ed.), *Jansénius et le Jansénisme dans les Pays-Bas. Mélanges Lucien Ceyssens,* 1982. 247 p. FB 1000.

57. J.H. WALGRAVE, *Selected Writings – Thematische geschriften. Thomas Aquinas, J.H. Newman, Theologia Fundamentalis.* Edited by G. DE SCHRIJVER & J.J. KELLY, 1982. XLIII-425 p. FB 1000.

58. F. NEIRYNCK & F. VAN SEGBROECK, avec la collaboration de E. MANNING, *Ephemerides Theologicae Lovanienses 1924-1981. Tables générales. (Bibliotheca Ephemeridum Theologicarum Lovaniensium 1947-1981),* 1982. 400 p. FB 1600.

59. J. DELOBEL (ed.), *Logia. Les paroles de Jésus – The Sayings of Jesus. Mémorial Joseph Coppens,* 1982. 647 p. FB 2000.

60. F. NEIRYNCK, *Evangelica. Gospel Studies – Études d'évangile. Collected Essays.* Edited by F. VAN SEGBROECK, 1982. XIX-1036 p. FB 2000.

61. J. COPPENS, *La relève apocalyptique du messianisme royal. II. Le Fils d'homme vétéro- et intertestamentaire.* Édition posthume par J. LUST, 1983. XVII-272 p. FB 1000.

62. J.J. KELLY, *Baron Friedrich von Hügel's Philosophy of Religion,* 1983. 232 p. FB 1500.

63. G. DE SCHRIJVER, *Le merveilleux accord de l'homme et de Dieu. Étude de l'analogie de l'être chez Hans Urs von Balthasar,* 1983. 344 p. FB 1500.

64. J. GROOTAERS & J.A. SELLING, *The 1980 Synod of Bishops: «On the Role of the Family». An Exposition of the Event and an Analysis of its Texts.* Preface by Prof. emeritus L. JANSSENS, 1983. 375 p. FB 1500.

65. F. NEIRYNCK & F. VAN SEGBROECK, *New Testament Vocabulary. A Companion Volume to the Concordance,* 1984. XVI-494 p. FB 2000.

66. R.F. COLLINS, *Studies on the First Letter to the Thessalonians,* 1984. XI-415 p. FB 1500.

67. A. PLUMMER, *Conversations with Dr. Döllinger 1870-1890.* Edited with Introduction and Notes by R. BOUDENS, with the collaboration of L. KENIS, 1985. LIV-360 p. FB 1800.

68. N. Lohfink (ed.), *Das Deuteronomium. Entstehung, Gestalt und Botschaft / Deuteronomy: Origin, Form and Message*, 1985. xi-382 p. FB 2000.

69. P.F. Fransen, *Hermeneutics of the Councils and Other Studies*. Collected by H.E. Mertens & F. De Graeve, 1985. 543 p. FB 1800.

70. J. Dupont, *Études sur les Évangiles synoptiques*. Présentées par F. Neirynck, 1985. 2 tomes, xxi-ix-1210 p. FB 2800.

71. *Recueil Lucien Cerfaux*, t. III, 1962. Nouvelle édition revue et complétée, 1985. lxxx-458 p. FB 1600.

72. J. Grootaers, *Primauté et collégialité. Le dossier de Gérard Philips sur la Nota Explicativa Praevia (Lumen gentium, Chap. III)*. Présenté avec introduction historique, annotations et annexes. Préface de G. Thils, 1986. 222 p. FB 1000.

73. A. Vanhoye (ed.), *L'apôtre Paul. Personnalité, style et conception du ministère*, 1986. xiii-470 p. FB 2600.

74. J. Lust (ed.), *Ezekiel and His Book. Textual and Literary Criticism and their Interrelation*, 1986. x-387 p. FB 2700.

75. É. Massaux, *Influence de l'Évangile de saint Matthieu sur la littérature chrétienne avant saint Irénée*. Réimpression anastatique présentée par F. Neirynck. *Supplément: Bibliographie 1950-1985*, par B. Dehand-schutter, 1986. xxvii-850 p. FB 2500.

76. L. Ceyssens & J.A.G. Tans, *Autour de l'Unigenitus. Recherches sur la genèse de la Constitution*, 1987. xxvi-845 p. FB 2500.

77. A. Descamps, *Jésus et l'Église. Études d'exégèse et de théologie*. Préface de Mgr A. Houssiau, 1987. xlv-641 p. FB 2500.

78. J. Duplacy, *Études de critique textuelle du Nouveau Testament*. Présentées par J. Delobel, 1987. xxvii-431 p. FB 1800.

79. E.J.M. van Eijl (ed.), *L'image de C. Jansénius jusqu'à la fin du XVIIIᵉ siècle*, 1987. 258 p. FB 1250.

80. E. Brito, *La Création selon Schelling. Universum*, 1987. xxxv-646 p. FB 2980.

81. J. Vermeylen (ed.), *The Book of Isaiah – Le livre d'Isaïe. Les oracles et leurs relectures. Unité et complexité de l'ouvrage*, 1989. x-472 p. FB 2700.

82. G. Van Belle, *Johannine Bibliography 1966-1985. A Cumulative Bibliography on the Fourth Gospel*, 1988. xvii-563 p. FB 2700.

83. J.A. Selling (ed.), *Personalist Morals. Essays in Honor of Professor Louis Janssens*, 1988. viii-344 p. FB 1200.

84. M.-É. Boismard, *Moïse ou Jésus. Essai de christologie johannique*, 1988. xvi-241 p. FB 1000.

84A. M.-É. Boismard, *Moses or Jesus: An Essay in Johannine Christology*. Translated by B.T. Viviano, 1993, xvi-144 p. FB 1000.

85. J.A. Dick, *The Malines Conversations Revisited*, 1989. 278 p. FB 1500.

86. J.-M. Sevrin (ed.), *The New Testament in Early Christianity – La réception des écrits néotestamentaires dans le christianisme primitif*, 1989. xvi-406 p. FB 2500.

87. R.F. Collins (ed.), *The Thessalonian Correspondence*, 1990. xv-546 p. FB 3000.

88. F. Van Segbroeck, *The Gospel of Luke. A Cumulative Bibliography 1973-1988*, 1989. 241 p. FB 1200.

89. G. THILS, *Primauté et infaillibilité du Pontife Romain à Vatican I et autres études d'ecclésiologie*, 1989. XI-422 p. FB 1850.
90. A. VERGOTE, *Explorations de l'espace théologique. Études de théologie et de philosophie de la religion*, 1990. XVI-709 p. FB 2000.
91. J.C. DE MOOR, *The Rise of Yahwism: The Roots of Israelite Monotheism*, 1990. *Revised and Enlarged Edition*, 1997. XV-445 p. FB 1400.
92. B. BRUNING, M. LAMBERIGTS & J. VAN HOUTEM (eds.), *Collectanea Augustiniana. Mélanges T.J. van Bavel*, 1990. 2 tomes, XXXVIII-VIII-1074 p. FB 3000.
93. A. DE HALLEUX, *Patrologie et œcuménisme. Recueil d'études*, 1990. XVI-887 p. FB 3000.
94. C. BREKELMANS & J. LUST (eds.), *Pentateuchal and Deuteronomistic Studies: Papers Read at the XIIIth IOSOT Congress Leuven 1989*, 1990. 307 p. FB 1500.
95. D.L. DUNGAN (ed.), *The Interrelations of the Gospels. A Symposium Led by M.-É. Boismard – W.R. Farmer – F. Neirynck, Jerusalem 1984*, 1990. XXXI-672 p. FB 3000.
96. G.D. KILPATRICK, *The Principles and Practice of New Testament Textual Criticism. Collected Essays*. Edited by J.K. ELLIOTT, 1990. XXXVIII-489 p. FB 3000.
97. G. ALBERIGO (ed.), *Christian Unity. The Council of Ferrara-Florence: 1438/39 – 1989*, 1991. X-681 p. FB 3000.
98. M. SABBE, *Studia Neotestamentica. Collected Essays*, 1991. XVI-573 p. FB 2000.
99. F. NEIRYNCK, *Evangelica II: 1982-1991. Collected Essays*. Edited by F. VAN SEGBROECK, 1991. XIX-874 p. FB 2800.
100. F. VAN SEGBROECK, C.M. TUCKETT, G. VAN BELLE & J. VERHEYDEN (eds.), *The Four Gospels 1992. Festschrift Frans Neirynck*, 1992. 3 volumes, XVII-X-X-2668 p. FB 5000.

SERIES III

101. A. DENAUX (ed.), *John and the Synoptics*, 1992. XXII-696 p. FB 3000.
102. F. NEIRYNCK, J. VERHEYDEN, F. VAN SEGBROECK G. VAN OYEN & R. CORSTJENS, *The Gospel of Mark. A Cumulative Bibliography: 1950-1990*, 1992. XII-717 p. FB 2700.
103. M. SIMON, *Un catéchisme universel pour l'Église catholique. Du Concile de Trente à nos jours*, 1992. XIV-461 p. FB 2200.
104. L. CEYSSENS, *Le sort de la bulle Unigenitus. Recueil d'études offert à Lucien Ceyssens à l'occasion de son 90ᵉ anniversaire*. Présenté par M. LAMBERIGTS, 1992. XXVI-641 p. FB 2000.
105. R.J. DALY (ed.), *Origeniana Quinta. Papers of the 5th International Origen Congress, Boston College, 14-18 August 1989*, 1992. XVII-635 p. FB 2700.
106. A.S. VAN DER WOUDE (ed.), *The Book of Daniel in the Light of New Findings*, 1993. XVIII-574 p. FB 3000.
107. J. FAMERÉE, *L'ecclésiologie d'Yves Congar avant Vatican II: Histoire et Église. Analyse et reprise critique*, 1992. 497 p. FB 2600.

108. C. BEGG, *Josephus' Account of the Early Divided Monarchy (AJ 8, 212-420). Rewriting the Bible*, 1993. IX-377 p. FB 2400.
109. J. BULCKENS & H. LOMBAERTS (eds.), *L'enseignement de la religion catholique à l'école secondaire. Enjeux pour la nouvelle Europe*, 1993. XII-264 p. FB 1250.
110. C. FOCANT (ed.), *The Synoptic Gospels. Source Criticism and the New Literary Criticism*, 1993. XXXIX-670 p. FB 3000.
111. M. LAMBERIGTS (ed.), avec la collaboration de L. KENIS, *L'augustinisme à l'ancienne Faculté de théologie de Louvain*, 1994. VII-455 p. FB 2400.
112. R. BIERINGER & J. LAMBRECHT, *Studies on 2 Corinthians*, 1994. XX-632 p. FB 3000.
113. E. BRITO, *La pneumatologie de Schleiermacher*, 1994. XII-649 p. FB 3000.
114. W.A.M. BEUKEN (ed.), *The Book of Job*, 1994. X-462 p. FB 2400.
115. J. LAMBRECHT, *Pauline Studies: Collected Essays*, 1994. XIV-465 p. FB 2500.
116. G. VAN BELLE, *The Signs Source in the Fourth Gospel: Historical Survey and Critical Evaluation of the Semeia Hypothesis*, 1994. XIV-503 p. FB 2500.
117. M. LAMBERIGTS & P. VAN DEUN (eds.), *Martyrium in Multidisciplinary Perspective. Memorial L. Reekmans*, 1995. X-435 p. FB 3000.
118. G. DORIVAL & A. LE BOULLUEC (eds.), *Origeniana Sexta. Origène et la Bible/Origen and the Bible. Actes du Colloquium Origenianum Sextum, Chantilly, 30 août – 3 septembre 1993*, 1995. XII-865 p. FB 3900.
119. É. GAZIAUX, *Morale de la foi et morale autonome. Confrontation entre P. Delhaye et J. Fuchs*, 1995. XXII-545 p. FB 2700.
120. T.A. SALZMAN, *Deontology and Teleology: An Investigation of the Normative Debate in Roman Catholic Moral Theology*, 1995. XVII-555 p. FB 2700.
121. G.R. EVANS & M. GOURGUES (eds.), *Communion et Réunion. Mélanges Jean-Marie Roger Tillard*, 1995. XI-431 p. FB 2400.
122. H.T. FLEDDERMANN, *Mark and Q: A Study of the Overlap Texts*. With an *Assessment* by F. NEIRYNCK, 1995. XI-307 p. FB 1800.
123. R. BOUDENS, *Two Cardinals: John Henry Newman, Désiré-Joseph Mercier*. Edited by L. GEVERS with the collaboration of B. DOYLE, 1995. 362 p. FB 1800.
124. A. THOMASSET, *Paul Ricœur. Une poétique de la morale. Aux fondements d'une éthique herméneutique et narrative dans une perspective chrétienne*, 1996. XVI-706 p. FB 3000.
125. R. BIERINGER (ed.), *The Corinthian Correspondence*, 1996. XXVII-793 p. FB 2400.
126. M. VERVENNE (ed.), *Studies in the Book of Exodus: Redaction – Reception – Interpretation*, 1996. XI-660 p. FB 2400.
127. A. VANNESTE, *Nature et grâce dans la théologie occidentale. Dialogue avec H. de Lubac*, 1996. 312 p. FB 1800.
128. A. CURTIS & T. RÖMER (eds.), *The Book of Jeremiah and its Reception – Le livre de Jérémie et sa réception*, 1997. 332 p. FB 2400.
129. E. LANNE, *Tradition et Communion des Églises. Recueil d'études*, 1997. XXV-703 p. FB 3000.

130. A. DENAUX & J.A. DICK (eds.), *From Malines to ARCIC. The Malines Conversations Commemorated*, 1997. IX-317 p. FB 1800.
131. C.M. TUCKETT (ed.), *The Scriptures in the Gospels*, 1997. XXIV-721 p. FB 2400.
132. J. VAN RUITEN & M. VERVENNE (eds.), *Studies in the Book of Isaiah. Festschrift Willem A.M. Beuken*, 1997. XX-540 p. FB 3000.
133. M. VERVENNE & J. LUST (eds.), *Deuteronomy and Deuteronomic Literature. Festschrift C.H.W. Brekelmans*, 1997. XI-637 p. FB 3000.
135. G. DE SCHRIJVER, *Liberation Theologies on Shifting Grounds. A Clash of Socio-Economic and Cultural Paradigms*, 1998. XI-453 p. FB 2100.
136. A. SCHOORS, *Qohelet in the Context of Wisdom*, 1998 XI-528 p. FB 2400.
137. W.A. BIENERT, U. KÜHNEWEG, *Origeniana Septima. Origenes in den Auseinandersetzungen des 4 Jahrhunderts*. 1998. XXVI-762 p. FB forthcoming.
138. E. GAZIAUX, *L'autonomie en morale: au croisement de la philosophie et de la théologie*, 1998, forthcoming.

ORIENTALISTE, KLEIN DALENSTRAAT 42, B-3020 HERENT